Department of Economic and Social Affairs
Département des affaires économiques et sociales

2009–2010
Demographic Yearbook
Annuaire démographique

Sixty-first issue/Soixante et unième édition

United Nations/Nations Unies
New York, 2011

The Department of Economic and Social Affairs of the United Nations Secretariat is a vital interface between global policies in the economic, social and environmental spheres and national action. The Department works in three main interlinked areas: (i) it compiles, generates and analyses a wide range of economic, social and environmental data and information on which States Members of the United Nations draw to review common problems and to take stock of policy options; (ii) it facilitates the negotiations of Member States in many intergovernmental bodies on joint courses of action to address ongoing or emerging global challenges; and (iii) it advises interested Governments on the ways and means of translating policy frameworks developed in United Nations conferences and summits into programmes at the country level and, through technical assistance, helps build national capacities.

Le Département des affaires économiques et sociales du Secrétariat de l'Organisation des Nations Unies sert de relais entre les orientations arrêtées au niveau international dans les domaines économiques, sociaux et environnementaux et les politiques exécutées à l'échelon national. Il intervient dans trois grands domaines liés les uns aux autres : i) il compile, produit et analyse une vaste gamme de données et d'éléments d'information sur des questions économiques, sociales et environnementales dont les États Membres de l'Organisation se servent pour examiner des problèmes communs et évaluer les options qui s'offrent à eux; ii) il facilite les négociations entre les États Membres dans de nombreux organes intergouvernementaux sur les orientations à suivre de façon collective afin de faire face aux problèmes mondiaux existants ou en voie d'apparition; iii) il conseille les gouvernements intéressés sur la façon de transposer les orientations politiques arrêtées à l'occasion des conférences et sommets des Nations Unies en programmes exécutables au niveau national et aide à renforcer les capacités nationales au moyen de programmes d'assistance technique.

NOTE

Symbols of United Nations documents are composed of capital letters combined with figures. Mention of such a symbol indicates reference to a United Nations document.

The designations employed and the presentation of material in this publication do not imply the expression of any opinion whatsoever on the part of the Secretariat of the United Nations concerning the legal status of any country, territory, city or area, or of its authorities, or concerning the delimitation of its frontiers or boundaries.

Where the designation "country or area" appears in the headings of tables, it covers countries, territories, or areas.

NOTE

Les cotes des documents de l'Organisation des Nations Unies se composent de lettres majuscules et de chiffres. La simple mention d'une cote dans un texte signifie qu'il s'agit d'un document de l'Organisation.

Les appellations employées dans cette publication et la présentation des données qui y figurent n'impliquent de la part du Secrétariat de l'Organisation des Nations Unies aucune prise de position quant au statut juridique des pays, territoires, villes ou zones, ou de leurs autorités, ni quant au tracé de leurs frontières ou limites.

L'appellation "pays ou zone" figurant dans les titres des rubriques des tableaux désigne des pays, des territoires, ou des zones.

ST/ESA/STAT/SER.R/40

UNITED NATIONS PUBLICATION
Sales number: B.12.XIII.1 H

PUBLICATION DES NATIONS UNIES
Numéro de vente: B.12.XIII.1 H

ISBN 978-92-1-051104-9
ISSN 0082-8041

Topics of the Demographic Yearbook series: 1948 - 2010

Sujets des diverses éditions de l'Annuaire démographique : 1948 - 2010

Year Année	Sales No. - Numéro de vente	Issue - Edition	Special topic - Sujet spécial
1948	49.XIII.1	First-Première	General demography-Démographie générale
1949-50	51.XIII.1	Second-Deuxième	Natality statistics-Statistiques de la natalité
1951	52.XIII.1	Third-Trosième	Mortality statistics-Statistiques de la mortalité
1952	53.XIII.1	Fourth-Quatrième	Population distribution-Répartition de la population
1953	54.XIII.1	Fifth-Cinquième	General demography-Démographie générale
1954	55.XIII.1	Sixth-Sixième	Natality statistics -Statistiques de la natalité
1955	56.XIII.1	Seventh-Septième	Population censuses-Recensement de population
1956	57.XIII.1	Eighth-Huitième	Ethnic and economic characteristics of population-Caractéristiques ethniques et économiques de la population
1957	58.XIII.1	Ninth-Neuvième	Mortality statistics- Statistiques de la mortalité
1958	59.XIII.1	Tenth-Dixième	Marriage and divorce statistics- Statistiques de la nuptialitè et de la divortialité
1959	60.XIII.1	Eleventh-Onzième	Natality statistics- Statistiques de la natalité
1960	61.XIII.1	Twelfth-Douzième	Population trends- l' évolution de la population
1961	62.XIII.1	Thirteenth-Treizième	Mortallty Statistics- Statisliques de la mortalité
1962	63.XIII.1	Fourteenth-Quatorzième	Population census statistics I- Statistiques des recensements de population I
1963	64.XIII.1	Fifteenth-Quinzième	Population census statistics II- Statistiques des recensements de population II
1964	65.XIII.1	Sixteenth-Seizième	Population census statistics III- Statistiques des recensements de population III
1965	66.XIII.1	Seventeenth-Dix-septième	Natality statistics- Statistiques de la natalité
1966	67.XIII.1	Eighteenth-Dix-huitième	Mortality statistics I- Statistiques de la mortalité I
1967	E/F.68.XIII.1	Nineteenth-Dix-neuvième	Mortality statistics II - Statistiques de la mortalité II
1968	E/F.69.XIII.1	Twentieth-Vingtième	Marriage and divorce statistics-Statistiques de la nuptialité et de la divortialité
1969	E/F.70.XIII.1	Twenty-first-Vingt et unième	Natality statistics-Statistiques de la natalité
1970	E/F.71.XIII.1	Twenty-second-Vingt-deuxième	Population trends-l' évolution de la population
1971	E/F.72.XIII.1	Twenty-third-Vingt-troisième	Population census statistics I- Statistiques de recensements de population I
1972	E/F.73.XIII.1	Twenty-fourth-Vingt-quatrième	Population census statistics II- Statistiques des recensements de population II
1973	E/F.74.XIII.1	Twenty-fifth-Vingt-cinquième	Population census statistics III- Statistiques des recensements de population III
1974	E/F.75.XIII.1	Twenty-sixth-Vingt-sixième	Mortality statistics - Statistiques de la mortalité
1975	E/F.76.XIII.1	Twenty-seventh-Vingt-septième	Natality statistics- Statistiques de la natalité
1976	E/F.77.XIII.1	Twenty-eighth-Vingt-huitième	Marriage and divorce statistics- Statistiques de la nuptialité et de la divortialité
1977	E/F.78.XIII.1	Twenty-ninth-Vingt-neuvième	International Migration Statistics- internationales
1978	E/F.79.XIII.1	Thirtieth-Trentième	General tables- Tableaux de caractère général
1978	E/F.79.XIII.8	Special issue-Edition spéciale	Historical supplement-Supplément rétrospectif
1979	E/F.80.XIII.1	Thirty-first-Trente et unième	Population census statistics-Statistiques des recensements de population
1980	E/F.81.XIII.1	Thirty-second-Trente-deuxième	Mortality statistics- Statistiques de la mortalité
1981	E/F.82.XIII.1	Thirty-third-Trente-troisième	Natality statistics-Statistiques de la natalité

Topics of the Demographic Yearbook series: 1948 - 2010

Sujets des diverses éditions de l'Annuaire démographique : 1948 - 2010

Year Année	Sales No. - Numéro de vente	Issue - Edition	Special topic - Sujet spécial
1982	E/F.83.XIII.1	Thirty-fourth- Trente-quatrième	Marriage and divorce statistics- Statistiques de la nuptialité et de la divortialité
1983	E/F.84.XIII.1	Thirty fifth- Trente-cinquième	Population census statistics I- Statistiques des recensements de population I
1984	E/F.85.XIII.1	Thirty-sixth- Trente-sixième	Population census statistics II- Statistiques des recensements de population II
1985	E/F.86.XIII.1	Thirty-seventh- Trente-septième	Mortality statistics- Statistiques de la mortalité
1986	E/F.87.XIII.1	Thirty-eighth- Trente-huitième	Natality statistics- Statistiques de la natalité
1987	E/F.88.XIII.1	Thirty-ninth- Trente-neuvième	Household composition- Les éléments du ménage
1988	E/F.89.XIII.1	Fortieth- Quarantième	Population census statistics- Statistiques des recensements de population
1989	E/F.90.XIII.1	Forty-first- Quarante-et-unième	International Migration Statistics- Statistiques des migration internationales
1990	E/F.91.XIII.1	Forty-second- Quarante-deuxième	Marriage and divorce statistics- Statistiques de la nuptialité et de la divortialité
1991	E/F.92.XIII.1	Forty-third- Quarante-troisième	General tables- Tableaux de caractère général
1991	E/F.92.XIII.9	Special Issue	Population Ageing and the Situation of Elderly Persons Vieillissement de la population et situation des personnes âgées
1992	E/F.94.XIII.1	Forty-fourth- Quarante-quatrième	Fertility and mortality statistics- Statistiques de la fecondité et de la mortalité
1993	E/F.95.XIII.1	Forty-fifth- Quarante-cinquième	Population census statistics I- Statistiques des recensements de population I
1994	E/F.96.XIII.1	Forty-sixth- Quarante-sixième	Population census statistics II- Statistiques des recensements de population II
1995	E/F.97.XIII.1	Forty-seventh- Quarante-septième	Household composition-Les éléments du ménage
1996	E/F.98.XIII.1	Forty-eighth- Quarante-huitième	Mortality statistics- Statistiques de la mortalité
1997	E/F.99.XIII.1	Forty-ninth- Quarante-neuvième	General tables- Tableaux de caractère général
1997	E/F.99.XIII.12	Special issue- Edition spéciale (CD)	Historical supplement- Supplément rétrospectif
1998	E/F.00.XIII.1	Fiftieth- Cinquantième	General tables- Tableaux de caractère général
1999	E/F.01.XIII.1	Fifty-first- Cinquante-et-unième	General tables- Tableaux de caractère général
1999	E/F.02.XIII.6	Special issue- Edition spéciale (CD)	Natality Statistics- Statistiques de la natalité
2000	E/F.02.XIII.1	Fifty-second- Cinquante-deuxième	General tables- Tableaux de caractère général
2001	E/F.03.XIII.1	Fifty-third- Cinquante- troisième	General tables- Tableaux de caractère général
2002	E/F.05.XIII.1	Fifty-fourth- Cinquante-quatrième	General tables- Tableaux de caractère général
2003	E/F.06.XIII.1	Fifty-fifth- Cinquante-cinquième	General tables- Tableaux de caractère général
2004	E/F.07.XIII.1	Fifty-sixth- Cinquante-sixième	General tables- Tableaux de caractère général
2005	E/F.08.XIII.1	Fifty-seventh- Cinquante-septième	General tables- Tableaux de caractère général
2006	E/F.09.XIII.1	Fifty-eighth- Cinquante-huitième	General tables- Tableaux de caractère général

Topics of the Demographic Yearbook series: 1948 - 2010

Sujets des diverses éditions de l'Annuaire démographique : 1948 - 2010

Year Année	Sales No. - Numéro de vente	Issue - Edition	Special topic - Sujet spécial
2007	E/F.10.XIII.1	Fifty-ninth- Cinquante-neuvième	General tables- Tableaux de caractère général
2008	E/F.11.XIII.1	Sixtieth- Soixantième	General tables- Tableaux de caractère général
2009 - 2010	B.12.XIII.1 H	Sixty-first Soixante-et-unième	General tables- Tableaux de caractère général

CONTENTS - TABLE DES MATIERES

EXPLANATIONS OF SYMBOLS

Category not applicable ....

Data not available ....

Magnitude zero or less than half of unit employed .... -

Provisional .... *

Data tabulated by year of registration rather than occurrence .... +

Based on less than specified minimum .... ◆

Relatively reliable data .... Roman type

Data of lesser reliability .... *Italics*

EXPLICATION DES SIGNES

Sans objet ....

Données non disponibles ....

Néant ou chiffre inférieur à la moitié de l'unité employée .... -

Données provisoires .... *

Donnée exploitées selon l'année de l'enregistrement et non l'année de l'événement +

Rapport fondé sur un nombre inférieur à celui spécifié .... ◆

Données relativement sûres .... Caractères romains

Données dont l'exactitude est moindre .... *Italiques*

INTRODUCTION

The *Demographic Yearbook* is an international compendium of national demographic statistics provided by national statistical authorities to the Statistics Division of the United Nations Department of Economic and Social Affairs. The *Demographic Yearbook* is part of the set of coordinated and interrelated publications issued by the United Nations and its specialized agencies, designed to supply statistical data for such users as demographers, economists, public-health workers and sociologists. Through the co-operation of national statistical services, available official demographic statistics are compiled in the *Demographic Yearbook* for more than 230 countries or areas throughout the world.

The *Demographic Yearbook 2009-2010* is the sixty-first in a series published by the United Nations since 1948. It contains tables including a world summary of selected demographic statistics, statistics on the size, distribution and trends in national populations, fertility, foetal mortality, infant and maternal mortality, general mortality, nuptiality and divorce. Data are shown by urban/rural residence, as available. In addition, the volume provides Technical Notes, a synoptic table, a historical index and a listing of the issues of the *Demographic Yearbook* published to date. This issue of *Demographic Yearbook* contains data as available including reference years 2009 and 2010. In population and vital statistics tables presenting time series, the available data of reference years 2009 and 2010 are presented. In the detailed population and vital statistics tables, presenting the latest available data, in addition to the usual tables with the latest reference year 2009, additional tables with the available 2010 data are presented.

The Technical Notes on the Statistical Tables are provided to assist the reader in using the tables. Table A, the synoptic table, provides an overview of the completeness of data coverage of the current *Demographic Yearbook*. The cumulative historical index is a guide on content and coverage of all sixty-one issues, and indicates, for each of the topics that have been published, the issues in which they are presented and the years covered. A list of the *Demographic Yearbook* issues, with their corresponding sales numbers and the special topics featured in each issue are shown on pages iii and iv.

Until the 48th issue (1996), each issue consisted of two parts, the general tables and special topic tables, published in the same volume[1]. Beginning with the 49th issue (1997), the special topic tables were being disseminated in digital format as supplements to the regular issues. Two CD-ROMs have been issued: the *Demographic Yearbook Historical Supplement*, which presents a wide panorama of basic demographic statistics for the period 1948 to 1997, and the *Demographic Yearbook*: *Natality Statistics*, which contains a series of detailed tables dedicated to natality and covering the period from 1980 to 1998. In addition, three volumes of *Demographic Yearbook* Special Census Topics are published on-line at http://unstats.un.org/unsd/demographic/products/dyb/dybcens.htm. These volumes cover the topics of basic population characteristics, educational and ethnocultural characteristics and international migration characteristics. Current *Demographic Yearbook* census topics datasets for reference years 1995 to present are presented at http://unstats.un.org/unsd/demographic/products/dyb/dybcensusdata.htm. These datasets cover basic population characteristics, educational, household, ethnocultural and economic characteristics, and also foreign-born and foreign population.

Population statistics are not available for all countries or areas, for a variety of reasons. In an effort to provide estimates of mid-year population and of selected vital statistics for all countries and areas, two annexes are presented. Annex I presents United Nations population estimates for the period 2001-2010 and Annex II presents the medium variant estimates of crude birth and death rates, infant mortality and total fertility rates, as well as life expectancy at birth over the period 2005-2010. These data were produced by the United Nations Population Division and are published in the *World Population Prospects - The 2010 Revision*[2].

Demographic statistics shown in this issue of the *Demographic Yearbook* are available online at the *Demographic Yearbook* website http://unstats.un.org/unsd/demographic/products/dyb/dyb2009-2010.htm. Information about the Statistics Division's data collection and dissemination programme is also available on the same website. Additional information can be made available by contacting the Statistics Division of the United Nations Secretariat at demostat@un.org.

TECHNICAL NOTES ON THE STATISTICAL TABLES

1. GENERAL REMARKS

1.1 Arrangement of Technical Notes

These Technical Notes are designed to provide the reader with relevant information related to the statistical tables. Information pertaining to the *Demographic Yearbook* in general is presented in the sections dealing with geographical aspects, population and vital statistics. In addition, preceding each table are notes describing the variables, remarks on the reliability and limitation of the data, countries and areas covered, and information on the presentation of earlier data. When appropriate, details on computation of rates, ratios or percentages are presented.

1.2 Arrangement of tables

The numbering of tables from one issue of *Demographic Yearbook* to the next is preserved to the extent possible. However, since for some of the tables the numbering may not correspond exactly to those in previous issues, the reader is advised to use the historical index that appears at the end of this book to find the reference to data in earlier issues.

1.3 Source of data

The statistics presented in the *Demographic Yearbook* are national data provided by official statistical authorities unless otherwise indicated. The primary source of data for the *Demographic Yearbook* is a set of questionnaires sent annually by the United Nations Statistics Division to over 230 national statistical services. Data reported on these questionnaires are supplemented, to the extent possible, with data taken from official national publications, official websites and through correspondence with national statistical services. In the interest of comparability, rates, ratios and percentages have been calculated by the Statistics Division of the United Nations, except for the life table functions, the total fertility rate, and also crude birth rate and crude death rate for some countries or areas as appropriately noted. The methods used by the Statistics Division to calculate these rates and ratios are described in the Technical Notes for each table. The population figures used for these computations are those pertaining to the corresponding years published in this or previous issues of the *Demographic Yearbook*.

In cases when data in this issue of the *Demographic Yearbook* differ from those published in earlier issues or related publications, statistics in this issue may be assumed to reflect revisions to the data received by June 2011.

2. GEOGRAPHICAL ASPECTS

2.1 Coverage

Data are shown for all individual countries or areas that provided information. Table 3 is the most comprehensive in geographical coverage, presenting data on population and surface area for all countries or areas with a population of at least 50 persons. Not all of these countries or areas appear in subsequent tables. In many cases the data required for a particular table are not available. In general, the more detailed the data required for a table, the fewer the number of countries or areas that can provide them.

In addition, rates and ratios are presented only for countries or areas reporting at least a minimum number of relevant events. The minimums are stated in the Technical Notes to individual tables.

Except for summary data shown for the world and by major areas and regions in tables 1 and 2 and data shown for capital cities and cities with a population of 100 000 or more in table 8, all data are presented at the national level. The number of countries shown in each table is provided in table A, the synoptic table.

2.2 Territorial composition

To the extent possible, all data, including time series data, relate to the territory within 2010 boundaries. Exceptions are footnoted in individual tables. Relevant clarifications are specified below.

Data relating to **Denmark** exclude Faeroe Islands and Greenland, which are shown separately.

Data relating to **Finland** include Åland Islands, unless otherwise indicated by a footnote.

Data relating to **France** exclude Overseas Departments, namely, French Guiana, Guadeloupe, Martinique and Réunion, which are shown separately, unless otherwise indicated by a footnote.

Data relating to **Norway** exclude Svalbard and Jan Mayen Island shown separately, if available.

Data relating to **Sudan** include South Sudan. The Republic of South Sudan formally seceded from Sudan on 9 July 2011. However this issue of the *Demographic Yearbook* contains data for the reference years up to 2010.

Data relating to **United Kingdom of Great Britain and Northern Ireland** exclude Guernsey, Isle of Man and Jersey which are shown separately.

Data relating to **Western Sahara** comprise the Northern Region (former Saguia el Hamra) and Southern Region (former Rio de Oro).

2.3 Nomenclature

Because of space limitations, the country or area names listed in the tables are generally the commonly employed short titles currently in use[3] in the United Nations, the full titles being used only when a short form is not available. The latest version of the *Standard Country or Area Codes for Statistics Use* can be accessed at http://unstats.un.org/unsd/methods/m49/m49alpha.htm.

2.3.1 Order of presentation

Countries or areas are listed in English alphabetical order within the following continents: Africa, North America, South America, Asia, Europe and Oceania.

The designations and presentation of the material in this publication were adopted solely for the purpose of providing a convenient geographical basis for the accompanying statistical series. The same qualification applies to all notes and explanations concerning the geographical units for which data are presented.

2.4 Surface area data

Surface area data, shown in tables 1 and 3, represent the total surface area, comprising land area and inland waters (assumed to consist of major rivers and lakes) and excluding only Polar Regions and uninhabited islands. The surface area given is the most recent estimate available. They are presented in square kilometres, a conversion factor of 2.589988 having been applied to surface areas originally reported in square miles.

2.4.1 Comparability over time

Comparability over time in surface area estimates for any given country or area may be affected by changes in the surface area estimation procedures, increases in actual land surface by reclamation, boundary changes, changes in the concept of "land surface area" used or a change in the unit of measurement used. In most cases it was possible to ascertain the reason for a revision; otherwise, the latest figures have generally been accepted as correct and substituted for those previously on file.

2.4.2 International comparability

Lack of international comparability between surface area estimates arises primarily from differences in definition. In particular, there is considerable variation in the treatment of coastal bays, inlets and gulfs, rivers and lakes. International comparability is also impaired by the variation in methods employed to estimate surface area. These range from surveys based on modern scientific methods to conjectures based on diverse types of information. Some estimates are recent while others may not be. Since neither the exact method of determining the surface area nor the precise definition of its composition and time reference is known for all countries or areas, the estimates in table 3 should not be considered strictly comparable from one country or area to another.

3. POPULATION

Population statistics, that is, those pertaining to the size, geographical distribution and demographic characteristics of the population, are presented in a number of tables of the *Demographic Yearbook*.

Summary estimates of the mid-year population of the world, major areas and regions for selected years and of its age and sex distribution in 2010 are set forth in tables 1 and 2, respectively.

Data for countries or areas include population census figures, estimates based on results of sample surveys (in the absence of a census), postcensal or intercensal estimates and those derived from continuous population registers. In the present issue of the *Demographic Yearbook* , the latest available census figure of the total population of each country or area and mid-year estimates for 2005 and 2010 are presented in table 3. Mid-year estimates of total population for ten years (2001-2010) are shown in table 5 and mid-year estimates of urban and total population by sex for ten years (2001-2010) are shown in table 6. The latest available data on population by age, sex and urban/rural residence are given in table 7. The latest available figures on the population of capital cities and of cities or urban agglomerations of 100 000 or more inhabitants are presented in table 8.

The statistics on total population, population by age, sex and urban/rural distribution are used for the calculation of rates in the *Demographic Yearbook* . Vital rates by age, sex and residence (urban/rural) were calculated using data presented in table 7 in this issue or the corresponding tables of previous issues of the *Demographic Yearbook*.

3.1 Sources of variation of data

The comparability of data is affected by several factors, including (1) the definition of total population; (2) the definition used to classify the population into its urban/rural components; (3) the accuracy of age reporting; (4) the extent of over-enumeration or under-enumeration in the most recent census or other source of benchmark population statistics; and (5) the quality of population estimates. These five factors will be discussed in some detail in sections 3.1.1 to 3.2.2 below. Other relevant problems are discussed in the technical notes to the individual tables. Readers interested in more detail, relating in particular to the basic concepts of population size, distribution and characteristics as elaborated by the United Nations, should consult the *Principles and Recommendations for Population and Housing Censuses, Revision 2*[4].

3.1.1 Total population

The most important impediment to comparability of total populations is the difference between the concept of a *de facto* and *de jure* population. A *de facto* population includes all persons physically present in the country or area at the reference date. The *de jure* population, by contrast, includes all usual residents of the given country or area, whether or not they were physically present in the area at the reference date. By definition, therefore, a *de facto* total and a *de jure* total are not entirely comparable.

Comparability of even two *de facto* or *de jure* totals is often affected by the fact that strict conformity to either of these concepts is rare. For example, some so-called *de facto* counts do not include foreign military, naval and diplomatic personnel present in the country or area on official duty, and their accompanying family and household members; some do not include foreign visitors in transit through the country or area or transients on ships in harbours. On the other hand, they may include such persons as merchant seamen and fishermen who are temporarily out of the country or area working at their trade.

The *de jure* population figure presents even greater variations in comparability, in part because it depends in the first place on the concept of "usual residence", which varies from one country or area to another and is difficult to apply consistently in a census or survey enumeration. For example, non-national civilians temporarily in a country or area as short-term workers may officially be considered residents after a stay of a specified period of time or they may be considered as non-residents throughout the duration of their stay; at the same time, these individuals may be officially considered as residents or non-residents of the country or area from which they came, depending on the duration and/or purpose of their absence. Furthermore, regardless of the official treatment, individual respondents may apply their own interpretation of residence in responding to the inquiry. In addition, there may be considerable differences in the accuracy with which countries or areas are informed about the number of their residents temporarily out of the country or area.

As far as possible, the population statistics presented in the tables of the *Demographic Yearbook* refer to the *de facto* population. Those reported to have been based on the *de jure* concept are identified as such. Figures not otherwise qualified may, therefore, be assumed to have been reported by countries or areas as being based on a *de facto* definition of the population. In an effort to overcome, to the extent possible, the effect of the lack of strict conformity to either the *de facto* or the *de jure* concept given above, significant exceptions with respect to inclusions and exclusions of specific population groups, are footnoted when they are known.

It should be remembered, however, that the necessary detailed information has not been available in many cases. It cannot, therefore, be assumed that figures not thus qualified reflect strict *de facto* or *de jure* definitions.

A possible source of variation within the statistics of a single country or area may arise from the fact that some countries or areas collect information on both the *de facto* and the *de jure* population in, for example, a census, but prepare detailed tabulations for only the *de jure* population. Hence, even though the total population shown in table 3 is de facto, the figures shown in the tables presenting various characteristics of the population, for example, urban/rural distribution, age and sex distribution, may be on the *de jure* concept.

3.1.2 Urban/rural classification

International comparability of urban/rural distributions is seriously impaired by the wide variation among national definitions of the concept of "urban". The definitions used by individual countries or areas and their implications are shown at the end of technical notes for table 6.

3.1.3 Age distribution

The classification of population by age is a core element of most analyses, estimation and projection of population statistics. Unfortunately, age data are subject to a number of sources of error and non-comparability. Accordingly, the reliability of age data should be of concern to users of these statistics.

3.1.3.1 Collection and compilation of age data

Age is the estimated or calculated interval of time between the date of birth and the date of the census or survey, expressed in completed solar years[5]. There are two methods of collecting information on age. The first is to obtain the date of birth for each member of the population in a census or survey and then to calculate the completed age of the individual by subtracting the date of birth from the date of enumeration[6]. The second method is to record the individual's completed age at the time of the census or survey, that is to say, age at last birthday.

The recommended method is to calculate age at last birthday by subtracting the exact date of birth from the date of the census. Some practices, however, do not use this method but instead calculate the difference between the year of birth and the year of the census. Classifications of this type are footnoted whenever possible. They can be identified to a certain extent by a smaller than expected population under one year of age. However, an irregular number of births from one year to the next or age selective omission of infants may also obscure the expected population under one year of age.

3.1.3.2 Errors in age data

Errors in age data may be due to a variety of causes, including ignorance of the correct age; reporting years of age in terms of a calendar concept other than completed solar years since birth[7]; carelessness in reporting and recording age; a general tendency to state age in figures ending in certain digits (such as zero, two, five and eight); a tendency to exaggerate length of life at advanced ages; a subconscious aversion to certain numbers; and wilful misrepresentations.

These reasons for errors in reported age data are common to most investigations of age and to most countries or areas, and they may significantly impair comparability of the data.

As a result of the above-mentioned difficulties, the age-sex distribution of population in many countries or areas shows irregularities which may be summarized as follows: (1) a deficiency in the number of infants and young children; (2) a concentration at ages ending with zero and five (that is, 5, 10, 15, 20, ...); (3) heaping at even ages (for example, 10, 12, 14, ...) relative to odd ages (for example, 11, 13, 15, ...); (4) unexpectedly large differences between the frequency of males and females at certain ages; and (5) unaccountably large differences between the frequencies in adjacent age groups. Comparing of identical age-sex cohorts from successive censuses, as well as studying the age-sex composition of each census, may reveal these and other inconsistencies, some of which in varying degree are characteristic of even the most modern censuses.

3.1.3.3 Evaluation of accuracy

The publication of population statistics by single years of age in the *Demographic Yearbook 1955* made it possible to apply a simple, yet highly sensitive, index known as Whipple's Index, or the Index of Concentration[8], the interpretation of which is relatively free from consideration of factors not connected with the accuracy of age reporting. More refined methods for the measurement of accuracy of distributions by single year of age have been devised, but this particular index was selected for presentation in the *Demographic Yearbook* for its simplicity and the wide use it has already found in other sources.

Whipple's Index is obtained by summing the age returns between 23 and 62 years inclusive and finding what percentage is borne by the sum of the returns of years ending with 5 and 0 to one-fifth of the total sum. The results would vary between a minimum of 0, if no returns were recorded ending with 0 or 5, and a maximum of 500, if no returns were recorded ending with any digits other than 0 or 5. If there is no age heaping at ages ending 0 or 5, the Whipple's index is 100.[9]

The index is applicable to all age distributions for which single years are given at least to the age of 62, with the following exceptions: (1) where the data presented are the result of graduation, no irregularity is scored by Whipple's Index, even though the graduated data may still be affected by inaccuracies of a different type; and (2) where statistics on age have been derived by reference to the year of birth, and tendencies to round off the birth year would result in an excessive number of ages ending in odd numbers, the frequency of age reporting with terminal digits 5 and 0 is not an adequate measure of their accuracy.

Most recently, the index has been computed for all the single-year age distributions from censuses held between 1985 and 2003, with the exception of those excluded on the criteria set forth above. Such data are published in the special issue of the *Demographic Yearbook* special topic on population censuses, Volume 1, which is available online at http://unstats.un.org/unsd/demographic/products/dyb/dybcens.htm.

Although Whipple's Index measures only the effects of preferences for ages ending in 5 and 0, it can be assumed that such digit preference is usually connected with other sources of inaccuracy in age statements and the index can be accepted as a fair measure of the general reliability of the age distribution.

3.2 Methods used to indicate quality of published statistics

To the extent possible, efforts have been made to give the reader an indication of reliability of the statistics published in the *Demographic Yearbook*. This has been approached in several ways. Any information regarding a possible under-enumeration or over-enumeration, coming from a postcensal survey, for example, has been noted in the footnotes to table 3. Any deviation from full national coverage, as explained in section 2.1 under Geographical Aspects, has also been noted. In addition, national statistical offices have been asked to evaluate the estimates of total population they submit to the Statistics Division of the United Nations.

3.2.1 Treatment of time series of population estimates

When a series of mid-year population estimates are presented, the same indication of quality is shown for the entire series as was determined for the latest estimate. The quality is indicated by the type face employed.

No attempt has been made to split the series even though it is evident that in cases where the data are now considered reliable, in earlier years, many may have been considerably less reliable than the current classification implies. Thus it will be evident that this method overstates the probable reliability of the time series in many cases. It may also understate the reliability of estimates for years immediately preceding or following a census enumeration.

3.2.2 Treatment of estimated distributions by age and other demographic characteristics

Estimates of the age-sex distribution of population may be constructed by two major methods: (1) by applying the specific components of population change to each age-sex group of the population as enumerated at the time of the census, and (2) by distributing the total estimated for a postcensal year proportionately according to the age-sex structure at the time of the census. Estimates constructed by the latter method are not published in the *Demographic Yearbook*.

Estimated age-sex distributions are categorized as "reliable" or otherwise, according to the method of construction established for the latest estimate of total mid-year population. Hence, the quality designation of the total figure, as indicated by the code, is considered to apply also to the whole distribution by age and sex, and the data are set in *italic* or roman type, as appropriate, on this basis alone. Further evaluation of detailed age structure data has not been undertaken to date.

4. VITAL STATISTICS

For purposes of the *Demographic Yearbook*, vital statistics have been defined as statistics of live birth, death, foetal death, marriage and divorce.

This volume of the *Demographic Yearbook* presents tables on fertility, nuptiality and divorce as well as tables on mortality referring to foetal mortality, infant and maternal mortality and general mortality.

4.1 Sources of variation of data

Most of the vital statistics data published in this *Demographic Yearbook* come from national civil registration systems. The completeness and the accuracy of the data that these systems produce vary from one country or area to another.

The provision for a national civil registration system is not universal, and in some cases, the registration system covers only certain vital events. For example, in some countries or areas only births and deaths are registered. There are also differences in the effectiveness with which national laws pertaining to civil registration operate in the various countries or areas. The manner in which the law is implemented and the degree to which the public complies with the legislation determine the reliability of vital statistics obtained from the civil registers.

It should be noted that some statistics on marriage and divorce are obtained from sources other than civil registers. For example, in some countries or areas, the only source for data on marriages is church registers. Divorce statistics, on the other hand, are obtained from court records and/or civil registers

according to national practice. The actual compilation of these statistics may be the responsibility of the civil registrar, the national statistical office or other government offices.

Other factors affecting international comparability of vital statistics are much the same as those that must be considered in evaluating the variations in other population statistics. Differences in statistical definitions of vital events, differences in geographical and ethnic coverage of the data and diverse tabulation procedures may also influence comparability.

In addition to vital statistics from civil registers, some vital statistics published in the *Demographic Yearbook* are official estimates. These estimates are frequently from population censuses and sample surveys. As such, their comparability may be affected by the national completeness of reporting in population censuses and household surveys, whether a *de facto* or *de jure* based census, non-sampling and sampling errors and other sources of bias.

Readers interested in more detailed information on standards for vital statistics should consult the *Principles and Recommendations for a Vital Statistics System Revision 2*[10]; *Handbook on Civil Registration and Vital Statistics Systems: Preparation of a Legal Framework*[11]; *Handbook on Civil Registration and Vital Statistics Systems: Management, Operation and Maintenance*[12]; *Handbook on Civil Registration and Vital Statistics Systems: Developing Information, Education and Communication*[13]; *Handbook on Civil Registration and Vital Statistics Systems: Policies and Protocols for the Release and Archiving of Individual Records*[14]; and *Handbook on Civil Registration and Vital Statistics Systems: Computerization*[15]. The *Handbook on the Collection of Fertility and Mortality Data*[16] provides information in collection and evaluation of data on fertility and mortality collected in population censuses and household surveys. These publications are also available on the website at http://unstats.un.org/unsd/demographic/standmeth/handbooks/default.htm.

4.1.1 Statistical definition of events

An important source of variation lies in the statistical definition of each vital event. The *Demographic Yearbook* attempts to collect data on vital events, using the standard definitions put forth in paragraph 57 of *Principles and Recommendations for a Vital Statistics System Revision 2*[10]. These are as follows:

LIVE BIRTH is the complete expulsion or extraction from its mother of a product of conception, irrespective of the duration of pregnancy, which after such separation breathes or shows any other evidence of life such as beating of the heart, pulsation of the umbilical cord, or definite movement of voluntary muscles, whether or not the umbilical cord has been cut or the placenta is attached; each product of such a birth is considered live-born regardless of gestational age.

DEATH is the permanent disappearance of all evidence of life at any time after live birth has taken place (postnatal cessation of vital functions without capability of resuscitation). This definition therefore excludes foetal deaths.

FOETAL DEATH is death prior to the complete expulsion or extraction from its mother of a product of conception, irrespective of the duration of pregnancy; the death is indicated by the fact that after such separation the foetus does not breathe or show any other evidence of life, such as beating of the heart, pulsation of the umbilical cord, or definite movement of voluntary muscles. Late foetal deaths are those of twenty-eight or more completed weeks of gestation. These are synonymous with the events reported under the pre-1950 term stillbirth[17].

MARRIAGE is an act, ceremony or process by which the legal relationship of husband and wife is constituted. The legality of the union may be established by civil, religious or other means as recognized by the laws of each country or area.

DIVORCE is a final legal dissolution of a marriage, that is, that separation of husband and wife which confers on the parties the right to remarriage under civil, religious and/or other provisions, according to the laws of each country.

In addition to these internationally recommended definitions, the *Demographic Yearbook* collects and presents data on abortions, defined as:

ABORTION is defined, with reference to the woman, as any interruption of pregnancy before 28 weeks of gestation with a dead foetus. There are two major categories of abortion: spontaneous and induced. Induced abortions are those initiated by deliberate action undertaken with the intention of terminating pregnancy; all other abortions are considered spontaneous.

4.1.2 Problems relating to standard definitions

A basic problem affecting international comparability of vital statistics is deviations from the standard definitions of vital events. An example of this can be seen in the cases of live births and foetal deaths[18]. In some countries or areas, an infant must survive for at least 24 hours, to be inscribed in the live-birth register. Infants who die before the expiration of the 24-hour period are classified as late foetal deaths and, barring special tabulation procedures, they would not be counted either as live births or as deaths. Similarly, in several other countries or areas, those infants who are born alive but die before registration of their birth, are also considered late foetal deaths.

Unless special tabulation procedures are adopted in such cases, the live-birth and death statistics will both be deficient by the number of these infants, while the incidence of late foetal deaths will be increased by the same amount. Hence the infant mortality rate is underestimated. Although both components (infant deaths and live births) are deficient by the same absolute amount, the deficiency is proportionately greater in relation to the infant deaths, causing greater errors in the infant mortality rate than in the birth rate.

Moreover, the practice exaggerates the late foetal death ratios. Some countries or areas make provision for correcting this deficiency (at least in the total frequencies) at the tabulation stage. Data for which the correction has not been made are indicated by a footnote whenever possible.

. The definitions used for marriage and divorce also present problems for international comparability. Unlike birth and death, which are biological events, marriage and divorce are defined only in terms of law and custom and as such are less amenable to universally applicable statistical definitions. They have therefore been defined for statistical purposes in general terms referring to the laws of individual countries or areas. Laws pertaining to marriage and particularly to divorce, vary from one country or area to another. With respect to marriage, the most widespread requirement relates to the minimum age at which persons may marry but frequently other requirements are specified.

When known the minimum legal age of men and women at which marriage can occur with or without parental consent is presented in table 23-1. Laws and regulations relating to the dissolution of marriage by divorce range from total prohibition, through a wide range of grounds upon which divorces may be granted, to the granting of divorce in response to a simple statement of desire or intention by husbands.

4.1.3 Fragmentary geographical or ethnic coverage

Ideally, vital statistics for any given country or area should cover the entire geographical area and include all ethnic groups. Fragmentary coverage is, however, not uncommon. In some countries or areas, registration is compulsory for only a small part of the population, limited to certain ethnic groups, for example. In other places there is no national provision for compulsory registration, but only municipal or state ordinances that do not cover the entire geographical area. Still others have developed a registration area that comprises only a part of the country or area, the remainder being excluded because of inaccessibility or for economic and cultural considerations that make regular registration practically impossible.

4.1.4 Tabulation procedures

4.1.4.1 By place of occurrence

Vital statistics presented at the national level relate to the de facto, that is, the present-in-area population. Thus, unless otherwise noted, vital statistics for a given country or area cover all the events that occur within its present boundaries and among all segments of the population therein. They may be presumed to include events among nomadic tribes and indigenous peoples, and among nationals and foreigners. When known, deviations from the *de facto* concept are footnoted.

Urban/rural differentials in vital rates for some countries may vary considerably depending on whether the relevant vital events were tabulated on the basis of place of occurrence or place of usual residence. For example, if a substantial number of women residing in rural areas near major urban centres travel to hospitals or maternity homes located in a city to give birth, urban fertility and neo-natal and infant mortality rates will usually be higher (and the corresponding rural rates will usually be lower) if the events are tabulated on the basis of place of occurrence rather than on the basis of place of usual residence. A similar process will affect general mortality differentials if substantial numbers of persons residing in rural areas use urban health facilities when seriously ill.

4.1.4.2 By date of occurrence versus by date of registration

To the extent possible, the vital statistics presented in the *Demographic Yearbook* refer to events that occurred during the specified year, rather than to those that were registered during that period. However, a considerable number of countries or areas tabulate their vital statistics not by date of occurrence, but by date of registration. Because such statistics can be misleading, the countries or areas known to tabulate vital statistics by date of registration are identified in the tables by a plus sign "+". Since information on the method of tabulating vital statistics is not available for all countries and areas, tabulation by date of registration may be more prevalent than the symbols on the vital statistics tables would indicate.

Because quality of data is inextricably related to the timeliness of registration, this must always be considered in conjunction with the quality code description in section 4.2.1 below. If registration of births is complete and timely (code "C"), the ill effects of tabulating by date of registration, are, for all practical purposes, nullified. Similarly, with respect to death statistics, the effect of tabulating events by date of registration may be minimized in many countries or areas in which the sanitary code requires that a death must be registered before a burial permit can be issued, and this regulation tends to make registration prompt. With respect to foetal death, registration is usually done right away or not at all. Therefore, if registration is prompt, the difference between statistics tabulated by date of occurrence and those tabulated by date of registration may be negligible. In many cases, the length of the statutory time period allowed for registering various vital events plays an important part in determining the effects of tabulation by date of registration on comparability of data.

With respect to marriage and divorce, the practice of tabulating data by date of registration does not generally pose serious problems. In many countries or areas marriage is a civil legal contract which, to establish its legality, must be celebrated before a civil officer. It follows that for these countries or areas registration would tend to be almost automatic at the time of, or immediately following, the marriage ceremony. Because the registration of a divorce in many countries or areas is the responsibility solely of the court or the authority which granted it, and since the registration record in such cases is part of the records of the court proceedings, it follows that divorces are likely to be registered soon after the decree is granted.

On the other hand, if registration is not prompt, vital statistics by date of registration will not produce internationally comparable data. Under the best circumstances, statistics by date of registration will include primarily events that occurred in the immediately preceding year; in countries or areas with less developed systems, tabulations will include some events that occurred many years in the past. Examination of available information reveals that delays of many years are not uncommon for birth registration, though the majority is recorded between two to four years after birth.

As long as registration is not prompt, statistics by date of registration will not be internationally comparable either among themselves or with statistics by date of occurrence.

It should also be mentioned that lack of international comparability is not the only limitation introduced by date-of-registration tabulation. Even within the same country or area, comparability over time may be lost by the practice of counting registrations rather than occurrences. If the number of events registered from year to year fluctuates because of *ad hoc* incentives to stimulate registration, or to the sudden need, for example, for proof of (unregistered) birth or death to meet certain requirements, vital statistics tabulated by date of registration are not useful in measuring and analyzing demographic levels and trends. All they can give is an indication of the fluctuations in the need for a birth, death or marriage certificate and the work-load of the registrars. Therefore, statistics tabulated by date of registration may be of very limited use for either national or international studies.

4.2   Methods used to indicate quality of published vital statistics

The quality of vital statistics can be assessed in terms of a number of factors. Most fundamental is the completeness of the civil registration system on which these statistics are based. In some cases, the incompleteness of the data obtained from civil registration systems is revealed when these events are used to compute rates.   However, this technique applies only where the data are markedly deficient, where they are tabulated by date of occurrence and where the population base is correctly estimated. Tabulation by date of registration will often produce rates which appear correct, simply because the numerator is artificially inflated by the inclusion of delayed registration and, conversely, rates may be of credible magnitude because the population at risk has been underestimated. Moreover, it should be remembered that knowledge of what is credible in regard to levels of fertility, mortality and nuptiality is extremely scant for many parts of the world, and borderline cases, which are the most difficult to appraise, are frequent.

4.2.1   Quality code for vital statistics from registers.

In the *Demographic Yearbook* annual "Questionnaire on Vital Statistics" national statistical offices are asked to provide their own estimates of the completeness of the births, deaths, late foetal deaths, marriages and divorces recorded in their civil registers.

On the basis of information from the questionnaires, from direct correspondence and from relevant official publications, it has been possible to classify current national statistics from civil registers of birth, death, infant death, late foetal death, marriage and divorce into three broad quality categories, as follows:

C: Data estimated to be virtually complete, that is, representing at least 90 per cent of the events occurring each year.

U: Data estimated to be incomplete, that is representing less than 90 per cent of the events occurring each year.

|: Data not derived from civil registration systems but considered reliable, such as estimates derived from projections, other estimation techniques or population and housing censuses.

...: Data for which no specific information is available regarding completeness.

These quality codes appear in the first column of the tables which show total frequencies and crude rates (or ratios) over a period of years for all tables on live births, late foetal deaths, infant deaths, deaths, marriages, and divorces.   Reliability of maternal mortality statistics is provided by the World Health Organisation.

The classification of countries and areas in terms of these quality codes may not be uniform. Nevertheless, it was felt that national statistical offices were in the best position to judge the quality of their data. It was considered that even the very broad categories that could be established on the basis of the available information would provide useful indicators of the quality of the vital statistics presented in this *Demographic Yearbook*.

In the past, the bases of the national estimates of completeness were usually not available. In connection with the *Demographic Yearbook 1977*, countries were asked, for the first time, to provide some indication of the basis of their completeness estimates. They were requested to indicate whether the completeness estimates reported for registered live births, deaths, and infant deaths were prepared on the basis of demographic analysis, dual record checks or some other specified method. Relatively few countries or areas have responded to this question; therefore, no attempt has been made to revise the system of quality codes used in connection with the vital statistics data presented in the *Demographic Yearbook*. It is hoped that, in the future, more countries will be able to provide this information so that the system of quality codes used in connection with the vital statistics data presented in the *Demographic Yearbook* may be revised.

Among the countries or areas indicating that the registration of live births was estimated to be 90 per cent or more complete (and hence classified as "C" or "+C" in table 9), the following countries or areas provided information on the method used to evaluate the completeness estimate:

(a) Demographic analysis -- Argentina, Austria, Bulgaria, Chile, China - Hong Kong SAR, Croatia, Estonia, Italy, Latvia, Lithuania, Malta, Mauritius, Republic of Korea, Republic of Moldova, Romania, Seychelles and Sweden.

(b) Dual record check -- Austria, Cuba, Estonia, Hungary, Israel, Italy, Norway, Qatar, Republic of Korea, Romania and Switzerland.

(c) Other specified methods -- Aruba, Austria, Denmark, France, Guatemala, Ireland, Kyrgyzstan, Liechtenstein, Luxembourg, Netherlands Antilles, Occupied Palestinian Territory, Panama, Poland, Puerto Rico, Singapore, Slovenia, Spain and Sweden.

Among the countries or areas indicating that the registration of late foetal-deaths was estimated to be 90 per cent or more complete (and hence classified as "C" or "+C" in table 12), the following countries or areas provided information on the method used to evaluate the completeness estimate:

(a) Demographic analysis -- Argentina, Austria, Bulgaria, Croatia, Estonia, Italy, Latvia, Lithuania, Malta, Mauritius, Romania and Sweden.

(b) Dual record check -- Austria, Cuba, Estonia, Hungary, Israel, Italy, Lithuania, Norway, Qatar, Romania and Switzerland.

(c) Other specified methods -- Austria, Denmark, Luxembourg, Poland, Puerto Rico, Slovenia, Spain and Sweden.

Among the countries or areas indicating that the registration of infant deaths was estimated to be 90 per cent or more complete (and hence classified as "C" or "+C" in table 15), the following countries or areas provided information on the method used to evaluate the completeness estimate:

(a) Demographic analysis -- Argentina, Austria, Bulgaria, Chile, China - Hong Kong SAR, Croatia, Estonia, Israel, Italy, Latvia, Lithuania, Malta, Mauritius, Republic of Korea, Republic of Moldova, Romania, Seychelles and Sweden.

(b) Dual record check -- Austria, Cuba, Cyprus, Estonia, Hungary, Ireland, Israel, Italy, Lithuania, Norway, Qatar, Republic of Korea, Romania and Switzerland.

(c) Other specified methods -- Austria, Cayman Islands, Denmark, Kyrgyzstan, Liechtenstein, Luxembourg, Netherlands Antilles, Poland, Puerto Rico, Singapore, Slovenia, Spain and Sweden.

Among the countries or areas indicating that the registration of deaths was estimated to be 90 per cent or more complete (and hence classified as "C" or "+C" in table 18), the following countries or areas provided information on the method used to evaluate the completeness estimate:

(a) Demographic analysis -- Argentina, Austria, Bulgaria, Chile, China - Hong Kong SAR, Croatia, Estonia, Israel, Italy, Latvia, Lithuania, Malta, Mauritius, Republic of Korea, Republic of Moldova, Romania, Seychelles and Sweden.

(b) Dual record check -- Austria, Cuba, Cyprus, Estonia, Hungary, Israel, Italy, Lithuania, Mexico, Norway, Qatar, Republic of Korea, Romania and Switzerland.

(c) Other specified methods -- Aruba, Austria, Denmark, France, Kyrgyzstan, Liechtenstein, Luxembourg, Netherlands Antilles, Poland, Puerto Rico, Singapore, Slovenia, Spain and Sweden.

Among the countries or areas indicating that the registration of marriages was estimated to be 90 per cent or more complete (and hence classified as "C" or "+C" in table 22), the following countries or areas provided information on the method used to evaluate the completeness estimate:

(a) Demographic analysis -- Argentina, Austria, Bulgaria, Chile, China - Hong Kong SAR, Croatia, Estonia, Italy, Latvia, Lithuania, Malta, Mauritius, Mexico, Occupied Palestinian Territory, Republic of Korea, Republic of Moldova, Romania, Seychelles and Sweden.

(b) Dual record check -- Cuba, Estonia, Hungary, Israel, Italy, Mexico, Norway, Qatar, Republic of Korea, Romania and Switzerland.

(c) Other specified methods -- Aruba, Austria, Australia, Cyprus, Denmark, Dominican Republic, France, Liechtenstein, Luxembourg, Mexico, Netherlands Antilles, Poland, Puerto Rico, Slovenia, Spain, Sweden and Tajikistan.

Among the countries or areas indicating that the registration of divorces was estimated to be 90 per cent or more complete (and hence classified as "C" or "+C" in table 24), the following countries or areas provided information on the method used to evaluate the completeness estimate:

(a) Demographic analysis -- Austria, Bulgaria, Croatia, Estonia, Italy, Latvia, Lithuania, Mexico, Occupied Palestinian Territory, Republic of Korea, Republic of Moldova, Romania, Seychelles and Sweden.

(b) Dual record check -- Cuba, Estonia, Hungary, Israel, Italy, Mexico, Norway, Qatar, Republic of Korea, Romania and Switzerland.

(c) Other specified methods -- Aruba, Austria, Cyprus, Denmark, Dominican Republic, Liechtenstein, Luxembourg, Mauritius, Mexico, Netherlands Antilles, Poland, Puerto Rico, Slovenia, Sweden and Tajikistan.

4.2.2 Treatment of vital statistics from registers

On the basis of the quality code described above, the vital statistics shown in all tables of the *Demographic Yearbook* are treated as either reliable or unreliable. Data coded "C" are considered reliable and appear in roman type. Data coded "U" or "..." are considered unreliable and appear in *italics*. Although the quality code itself appears only in certain tables, the indication of reliability (that is, the use of *italics* to indicate unreliable data) is shown in all tables presenting vital statistics data.

In general, the quality code for deaths shown in table 18 is used to determine whether data on deaths in other tables appear in roman or *italic* type. However, for some of the maternal deaths data shown in *italics* in table 17, the known quality code differs from that ascribed on the basis of the completeness of registration of the total number of deaths. In cases where the quality code in table 18 does not correspond with the quality level implied by the typeface used in table 17, relevant information regarding the completeness of maternal mortality is given in a footnote.

It should be noted that the indications of reliability used for infant mortality rates, maternal mortality ratios and late foetal death ratios (all of which are calculated using the number of live births in the denominator) are determined on the basis of the quality codes for infant deaths, deaths and late foetal deaths respectively. To evaluate these rates and ratios more precisely, one would have to take into account the quality of the live-birth data used in the denominator of these rates and ratios. The quality codes for live births are shown in table 9 and described more fully in the text of the technical notes for that table.

4.2.3 Treatment of time series of vital statistics from registers

The quality of a time series of vital statistics is more difficult to determine than the quality of data for a single year. Since a time series of vital statistics is usually generated only by a system of continuous civil registration, it was assumed that the quality of the entire series was the same as that for the latest year's data obtained from the civil register. The entire series is treated as described in section 4.2.2 above. That is, if the quality code for the latest registered data is "C", the frequencies and rates for earlier years are also considered reliable and appear in roman type. Conversely, if the latest registered data are coded as "U" or "..." then data for earlier years are considered unreliable and appear in *italics*. It is recognized that this method is not entirely satisfactory because it is known that data from earlier years in many of the series were considerably less reliable than the current code implies. Efforts are being made to gradually move away from this method and code the registered data of each year or range of years separately. Please see for example the technical notes of table 17 in this issue "Maternal deaths and maternal mortality ratios: 1999-2008".

4.2.4 Treatment of estimated vital statistics

In addition to data from vital registration systems, estimated frequencies and rates of the events, usually *ad hoc* official estimates that have been derived either from the results of a sample survey or by demographic analyses, also appear in the *Demographic Yearbook*. Estimated frequencies and rates have been included in the tables because it is assumed that they provide information that is more accurate than that from existing civil registration systems. By implication, they are assumed to be reliable and as such they are set in roman type. Estimated frequencies and rates continue to be treated in this manner even when they are interspersed in a time series with data from civil registers.

In tables showing the quality code, the code applies only to data from civil registers. If a series of data for a country or area contains both data from a civil register and estimated data, the code applies only to the registered data; if only estimated data are shown, the symbol "|" is shown.

4.3 Cause of death

World Health Organization (WHO) Member States are bound by the International Nomenclature Regulations to provide the Organization with cause of death data coded in accordance with the current revision of the International Statistical Classification of Diseases and Related Health Problems (ICD) as adopted from time to time by the World Health Assembly[19]. The data are collected by the WHO[20] using the ICD. In order to promote international comparability of cause of death statistics, the World Health Organization organizes and conducts an international conference for the revision of the ICD on a regular basis in order to ensure that the Classification is kept current with the most recent clinical and statistical concepts. The data are now usually submitted to WHO at the full four-character level of detail provided by the ICD and are stored in the WHO Mortality Database at the level of detail as provided by the country. For earlier versions, however, the data are only available according to the ICD's list of 150 causes. Data from the WHO Mortality Database are available in electronic format at http://www3.who.int/whosis/menu.cfm.

Although revisions provide an up-to-date version of the ICD, such revisions create several problems related to the comparability of cause of death statistics. The first is the lack of comparability over time that inevitably accompanies the use of a new classification. The second problem affects comparability between countries and areas because they may adopt a new classification at different times. The more refined the classification becomes the greater is the need for expert clinical diagnosis of cause of death. In many countries or areas, few of the deaths occur in the presence of an attendant, who is medically trained, i.e., most deaths are certified by a lay attendant. Because the ICD contains many diagnoses that cannot be identified by a non-medical person, the ICD is not always accurately or precisely used, which affects international comparability particularly between countries and areas where the level of medical services differ widely.

The chapters of the tenth revision[21], the latest revision of the ICD, consist of an alphanumeric coding scheme of one letter followed by three numbers at the four-character level. Chapter one contains infectious and parasitic diseases, chapter two refers to all neoplasms, chapter three to disorders of the immune mechanism including diseases of the blood and blood-forming organs; and chapter four to endocrine, nutritional and metabolic diseases. The remaining chapters group diseases according to the anatomical site affected, except for chapters that refer to mental disorders; complications of pregnancy, childbirth and the puerperium; congenital malformations; and conditions originating in the perinatal period. Finally, an entire chapter is devoted to symptoms, signs, and abnormal findings.

4.3.1 Maternal mortality

According to the tenth revision of the ICD, "Maternal death" is defined as the death of a woman while pregnant or within 42 days of termination of pregnancy, irrespective of the duration and the site of the pregnancy, from any cause related to or aggravated by the pregnancy or its management but not from accidental or incidental causes.

"Maternal deaths" should be subdivided into direct and indirect obstetric deaths. Direct obstetric deaths are those resulting from obstetric complications of the pregnant state (pregnancy, labour and puerperium), from interventions, omissions, incorrect treatment, or from a chain of events resulting from any of the above. Indirect obstetric deaths are those resulting from previous existing disease or disease that developed during pregnancy and which was not due to direct obstetric causes, but which was aggravated by physiologic effects of pregnancy.

While the denominator for the maternal mortality ratio theoretically should be the number of pregnant women, it is impossible to determine the number of pregnant women. A further recommendation by the tenth revision is therefore that maternal mortality ratios be expressed per 100,000 live births or per 100,000 total births (live births and foetal deaths)[22]. The maternal mortality ratio calculated here is expressed per 100,000 live births. Although live births do not represent an unbiased estimate of pregnant women, this figure is more reliable than other estimates, in particular, live births are more accurately registered than live births plus foetal deaths.

---

[1] There are two exceptions – the 1978 and 1991 issues, which were disseminated in separate volumes from the respective regular issues.

[2] *United Nations, Department of Economic and Social Affairs, Population Division (2011). World Population Prospects: The 2010 Revision, DVD Edition – Extended Dataset (United Nations publication, Sales No. E.11.XIII.7).* Highlights and selected output are available by following links at www.unpopulation.org.

[3] ST/ESA/STAT/SER.M/49/Rev.4/WWW ; http://unstats.un.org/unsd/methods/m49/m49.htm; see also Standard Country or Area Codes for Statistical Use, Sales No. M.98.XVII.9, United Nations, New York, 1999.

[4] Sales No. E.07.XVII.8, United Nations, New York, 2007. The publication is available online at : http://unstats.un.org/unsd/demographic/standmeth/principles/Series_M67Rev2en.pdf

[5] Ibid, para. 2.135.

[6] Alternatively, if a population register is used, completed ages are calculated by subtracting the date of birth of individuals listed in the register from a reference date to which the age data pertain.

[7] A source of non-comparability may result from differences in the method of reckoning age, for example, the Western versus the Eastern or, as it is usually known, the English versus the Chinese system. By the latter, a child is considered one year old at birth and advances an additional year at each Chinese New Year. The effect of this system is most obvious at the beginning of the age span, where the frequencies in the under-one-year category are markedly understated. The effect on higher age groups is not so apparent. Distributions constructed on this basis are often adjusted before publication, but the possibility of such aberrations should not be excluded when census data by age are compared.

[8] United States, Bureau of the Census, Thirteenth Census, Vol. I (Washington, D.C., U.S. Government Printing Office, 1913; Reprint: New York, N.Y., Norman Ross Pub., 1999), pp. 291-292.

[9] Sales No. E.83.XIII.2, United Nations, New York, 1983.

[10] Sales No. E.01.XVII.10, United Nations, New York, 2001.

[11] Sales No. E.98.XVII.7, United Nations, New York, 1998.

[12] Sales No. E.98.XVII.11, United Nations, New York, 1998.

[13] Sales No. E.98.XVII.4, United Nations, New York, 1998.

[14] Sales No. E.98.XVII.6, United Nations, New York, 1998.

[15] Sales No. E.98.XVII.10, United Nations, New York, 1998.

[16] Sales No. E.03.XVII.11, United Nations, New York, 2004.

[17] For more detailed discussion on this issue, refer to *Principles and Recommendations for a Vital Statistics System Revision 2,* Sales No. E. 01.XVII.10, United Nations, New York, 2001, para 57.

[18] For more information on historical and legal background on the use of differing definitions of live births and foetal deaths, comparisons of definitions used as of 1 January 1950, and evaluation of the effects of these differences on the calculation of various rates, see *Handbook of Vital Statistics Systems and Methods Volume 2, Review of National Practices,* Sales No. E.84.XVII.11, United Nations, New York, 1985, Chapter IV.

[19] The World Health Assembly is the annual meeting of the Member States of the World Health Organization and its highest governing body.

[20] The data on maternal mortality as one cause of death, and on all deaths by cause and sex are from the World Health Organization, and are available at http://www3.who.int/whosis/menu.cfm.

[21] *International Statistical Classification of Diseases and Related Health Problems,* Tenth Revision, Volume 2, World Health Organization, Geneva, 1992.

[22] *Ibid,* pp. 129-136

INTRODUCTION

L'*Annuaire démographique* est un recueil de statistiques démographiques internationales qui est établi par la Division de statistique du Département des affaires économiques et sociales de l'Organisation des Nations Unies. Il fait partie d'un ensemble de publications complémentaires publiées par l'Organisation des Nations Unies et les institutions spécialisées, qui ont pour objet de fournir des statistiques aux démographes, aux économistes, aux spécialistes de la santé publique et aux sociologues. Grâce à la coopération des services nationaux de statistique, il a été possible de faire figurer dans la présente édition de *l'Annuaire démographique* les statistiques officielles disponibles pour plus de 230 pays ou zones du monde entier.

L'Annuaire démographique 2009-2010 est la soixante-et-unième édition d'une série que publie l'ONU depuis 1948. Le présent volume comprend un aperçu mondial des statistiques démographiques de base et des tableaux qui regroupent des statistiques sur la dimension, la répartition et les tendances de la population, la natalité, la mortalité fœtale, la mortalité infantile et la mortalité liée à la maternité, la mortalité générale, la nuptialité et la divortialité. Des données classées selon le lieu de résidence (zone urbaine ou rurale) sont présentées dans un grand nombre de tableaux. En outre, *l'Annuaire démographique* contient des notes techniques, un tableau synoptique, un index historique et une liste des éditions de *l'Annuaire démographique* publiées jusqu'à présent. Cette édition de l'Annuaire démographique contient les données disponibles couvrant les années de référence 2009 et 2010. Dans les tableaux des statistiques de la population et de l'état civil où figurent des séries chronologiques, sont présentées les données disponibles pour les années de référence 2009 et 2010. Dans les tableaux statistiques détaillés de population et d'état civil qui contiennent les dernières données disponibles pendant 2000-2009, des tableaux supplémentaires sont mis à disposition pour les données disponibles de l'année de référence 2010.

Les notes techniques sur les tableaux statistiques sont destinées à aider le lecteur. Le tableau A, qui correspond au tableau synoptique, donne un aperçu de l''exhaustivité des données publiées dans la présente édition de *l'Annuaire démographique*. Un index cumulatif donne des renseignements sur les matières traitées dans chacune des 61 éditions et sur les années sur lesquelles portent les données. Les numéros de vente des éditions antérieures et une liste des sujets spéciaux traités dans les différentes éditions sont indiqués aux pages iii et iv.

Jusqu'à la 48ème édition (1996), chaque édition se composait de deux parties : les tableaux de caractère général et ceux sur des sujets spéciaux[1]. À partir de 49ème édition (1997), les tableaux sur les sujets spéciaux ont été publiés dans un format numérique en tant que suppléments à l'*Annuaire démographique*. Deux CD-ROM ont été produits : l'*Annuaire démographique : Supplément historique*, qui présente un grand nombre de statistiques démographiques pour la période allant de 1948 à 1997, et l'*Annuaire démographique : Statistiques de la natalité*, qui contient des tableaux détaillés sur la natalité pour la période allant de 1980 à 1998. En plus, trois volumes concernant *l'Annuaire démographique* consacrés à des thèmes de recensement spéciaux sont publiés en ligne à l'adresse suivante : http://unstats.un.org/unsd/demographic/products/dyb/dybcens.htm. Les sujets des statistiques de ces volumes sont : Caractéristiques essentielles de la population, caractéristiques de l'enseignement et des origines ethniques et culturelles, et les caractéristiques des migrations internationales. Les actuelles bases de données sur les thèmes du recensement de l'Annuaire démographique pour les années de référence entre 1995 et aujourd'hui sont mises à disposition sur http://unstats.un.org/unsd/demographic/products/dyb/dybcensusdata.htm. Ces bases de données comprennent des données sur la population selon les principales caractéristiques démographiques, scolaires, ethnoculturelles et économiques, les caractéristiques des ménages ainsi que des données sur les étrangers dans le pays ou les personnes nées à l'étranger.

Les statistiques sur la population ne sont pas disponibles pour tous les pays et zones pour plusieurs raisons. Deux annexes sont présentées afin d'offrir des estimations sur la population en milieu d'année et un aperçu des statistiques de l'état civil pour chaque pays ou zone. La première porte sur des estimations concernant la population pour la période 2001-2010. La seconde présente les estimations des variantes moyennes concernant les taux bruts de natalité et de mortalité, la mortalité infantile, les indicateurs synthétiques de fécondité et l'espérance de vie à la naissance pour la période 2005-2010. Ces données ont été établies par la Division de la population de l'ONU et publiées dans *World Population Prospects - The 2010 Revision*[2].

Les statistiques démographiques figurant dans la présente édition de l'*Annuaire démographique* sont disponibles en ligne sur les pages Web consacrées à *l'Annuaire démographique* :

http://unstats.un.org/unsd/demographic/products/dyb/dyb2009-2010.htm. On trouvera également des renseignements sur le programme de collecte et de diffusion des données de la Division de statistique sur le même site. Il est possible de se procurer d'autres données en contactant la Division de statistique de l'Organisation des Nations Unies à l'adresse suivante : demostat@un.org.

NOTES TECHNIQUES SUR LES TABLEAUX STATISTIQUES

1. REMARQUES D'ORDRE GÉNÉRAL

1.1 Notes techniques

Les notes techniques ont pour but de donner au lecteur des informations pertinentes en lien avec les tableaux statistiques. Les renseignements qui concernent l'*Annuaire démographique* en général sont présentés dans des sections portant sur diverses considérations géographiques, sur la population et sur les statistiques de natalité et de mortalité. Les tableaux sont ensuite commentés séparément et l'on trouvera pour chacun une description des variables et des observations sur la fiabilité et les lacunes des données ainsi que sur les pays et zones visés et sur les données publiées antérieurement. Des détails sont également donnés, le cas échéant, sur le mode de calcul des taux, quotients et pourcentages.

1.2 Tableaux

Dans la mesure du possible, la numérotation des tableaux dans les éditions successives de l'*Annuaire démographique* est préservée. Comme la numérotation des tableaux ne correspond pas exactement à celle des éditions précédentes, il est recommandé de se reporter à l'index qui figure à la fin du présent ouvrage pour trouver les données publiées dans les précédentes éditions.

1.3 Origine des données

Sauf indication contraire, les statistiques présentées dans l'*Annuaire démographique* sont des données nationales fournies par les organismes de statistique officiels. Elles sont recueillies essentiellement au moyen de questionnaires qui sont envoyés tous les ans à plus de 230 services nationaux de statistique et autres services gouvernementaux compétents. Les données communiquées en réponse à ces questionnaires sont complétées, dans toute la mesure possible, par des données tirées de publications nationales officielles et des sites web d'organismes officiels et des renseignements communiqués par les services nationaux de statistique à la demande de l'ONU. Pour que les données soient comparables, les taux, rapports et pourcentages ont été calculés par la Division de statistique de l'ONU, à l'exception des paramètres des tables de mortalité et des indicateurs synthétiques de fécondité ainsi que des taux bruts de natalité et de mortalité pour certains pays et zones, qui ont été dûment signalés en note. Les méthodes suivies par la Division pour le calcul des taux et rapports sont décrites dans les notes techniques relatives à chaque tableau. Les chiffres de population utilisés pour ces calculs sont ceux qui figurent dans la présente édition de l'*Annuaire démographique* ou qui ont paru dans des éditions antérieures.

Chaque fois que l'on constatera des différences entre les données du présent volume et celles des éditions antérieures de l'*Annuaire démographique*, ou de certaines publications apparentées, on pourra en conclure que les statistiques publiées cette année sont des chiffres révisés communiqués à la Division de statistique avant juin 2011.

2. CONSIDÉRATIONS GÉOGRAPHIQUES

2.1 Portée

Des données sont présentées sur tous les pays ou zones qui en ont communiquées. Le tableau 3, le plus complet, contient des données sur la population et la superficie de chaque pays ou zone ayant une population d'au moins 50 habitants. Ces pays ou zones ne figurent pas tous dans les tableaux qui suivent. Dans bien des cas, les données requises pour un tableau particulier n'étaient pas disponibles. En général, les pays ou zones qui peuvent fournir des données sont d'autant moins nombreux que les données demandées sont plus détaillées.

De plus les taux et rapports ne sont présentés que pour les pays ou zones ayant communiqué des chiffres correspondant à un nombre minimal de faits considérés. Les minimums sont indiqués dans les notes techniques relatives à chacun des tableaux.

À l'exception des données récapitulatives présentées dans les tableaux 1 et 2 pour l'ensemble du monde et les grandes zones et régions et des données relatives aux capitales et aux villes de 100 000 habitants ou plus dans le tableau 8, toutes les données se rapportent aux pays. Le nombre de pays sur lequel porte chacun des tableaux est indiqué dans le tableau A.

2.2 Composition territoriale

Autant que possible, toutes les données, y compris les séries chronologiques, se rapportent au territoire de 2010. Les exceptions à cette règle sont signalées en note à la fin des tableaux. Des clarifications importantes sont présentées ci-dessous.

Les données relatives au Danemark ne comprennent pas les Iles Féroé et le Gröenland, qui font l'objet de rubriques distinctes.

Les données relatives à la Finlande comprennent les Îles d'Åland, sauf indication contraire en note de bas de page.

Les données relatives à la France ne comprennent pas les départements d'outre mer, c'est- à -dire la Guyane française, Guadeloupe, la Martinique et La Réunion, qui font l'objet de rubriques distinctes, sauf indication contraire en note de bas de page.

Les données relatives à la Norvège ne comprennent pas Svalbard et Jan Mayen qui font l'objet de rubriques distinctes, si disponible.

Les données relatives au Soudan comprennent le Soudan du Sud. La République du Sud-Soudan a officiellement fait sécession du Soudan, le 9 Juillet 2011. Cependant cette édition de *l'Annuaire démographique* contient les données des années de référence antérieures à 2010.

Les données relatives au Royaume-Uni de Grande-Bretagne et d'Irlande du Nord ne comprennent pas la Guernesey, l'île de Man et Jersey, qui font l'objet de rubriques distinctes.

Les données relatives au Sahara Occidental comprennent la région septentrionale (ancien Saguia-el-Hamra) et la région méridionale (ancien Rio de Oro).

2.3 Nomenclature

En règle générale, pour gagner de la place, on a jugé commode de désigner dans les tableaux les pays ou zones par les noms abrégés couramment utilisés par l'Organisation des Nations Unies[3], les désignations complètes n'étant utilisées que lorsqu'il n'existait pas de forme abrégée. La liste des désignations des pays ou zones est disponible à l'adresse suivante : http://unstats.un.org/unsd/methods/m49/m49alphaf.htm.

2.3.1 Ordre de présentation

Les pays ou zones sont classés dans l'ordre alphabétique anglais et regroupés par continent comme ci-après : Afrique, Amérique du Nord, Amérique du Sud, Asie, Europe et Océanie.

Les appellations employées dans la présente édition et la présentation des données qui y figurent n'ont d'autre objet que de donner un cadre géographique commode aux séries statistiques. La même observation vaut pour toutes les notes et précisions concernant les unités géographiques pour lesquelles des données sont présentées.

2.4 Superficie

Les données relatives à la superficie qui figurent dans les tableaux 1 et 3 représentent la superficie totale, c'est-à-dire qu'elles englobent les terres émergées et les eaux intérieures (qui sont censées comprendre les principaux lacs et cours d'eau) mais excluent les régions polaires et les îles inhabitées. Les données relatives à la superficie correspondent aux chiffres estimatifs les plus récents. Les superficies sont toutes exprimées en kilomètres carrés ; les chiffres qui avaient été communiqués en miles carrés ont été convertis au moyen d'un coefficient de 2,589988.

2.4.1 Comparabilité dans le temps

La révision des estimations antérieures de la superficie, des augmentations effectives de la superficie terrestre due par exemple à des travaux d'assèchement, à des rectifications de frontières, à des changements d'interprétation du concept de « terres émergées » ou à l'utilisation de nouvelles unités de mesure peut avoir des incidences sur la comparabilité dans le temps des estimations relatives à la superficie d'un pays ou d'une zone donnés. Dans la plupart des cas, il a été possible de déterminer la raison de ces révisions; toutefois, même lorsque la raison n'était pas connue, on a remplacé les anciens chiffres par les nouveaux et on a généralement admis que ce sont ces derniers qui sont exacts.

2.4.2 Comparabilité internationale

Le manque de comparabilité internationale entre les données relatives à la superficie est dû principalement à des différences de définition. En particulier, la définition des golfes, baies et criques, lacs et cours d'eau varie sensiblement d'un pays à l'autre. La diversité des méthodes employées pour estimer les superficies nuit elle aussi à la comparabilité internationale. Certaines données proviennent de levés effectués selon des méthodes scientifiques modernes ; d'autres ne représentent que des conjectures reposant sur diverses catégories de renseignements. Certains chiffres sont récents, d'autres pas. Étant donné que ni la méthode de calcul de la superficie ni la composition du territoire et la date à laquelle se rapportent les données ne sont connues avec précision pour tous les pays ou zones, les estimations figurant dans le tableau 3 ne doivent pas être considérées comme rigoureusement comparables d'un pays ou d'une zone à une autre.

3. POPULATION

Les statistiques de la population, c'est-à-dire celles qui se rapportent à la dimension, à la répartition géographique et aux caractéristiques démographiques de la population, sont présentées dans un certain nombre de tableaux de *l'Annuaire démographique*.

Les tableaux 1 et 2 présentent respectivement des estimations récapitulatives de milieu d'année de la population du monde, des grandes zones et régions, pour certaines années présélectionnées, ainsi que de sa répartition selon l'âge et le sexe pour l'année 2010.

Les données concernant les pays ou les zones représentent les résultats de recensements de population, des estimations fondées sur les résultats d'enquêtes par sondage (s'il n'y a pas eu recensement), des estimations postcensitaires ou intercensitaires, ou des estimations établies à partir de données provenant des registres permanents de population. Dans la présente édition, le tableau 3 indique pour chaque pays ou zone le chiffre le plus récent de la population totale issu du dernier recensement et des estimations établies au milieu de l'année 2005 et de l'année 2010. Le tableau 5 contient des estimations de la population totale au milieu de chaque année pendant 10 ans (2001-2010), et le tableau 6 des estimations de la population urbaine et de la population totale, par sexe, au milieu de chaque année pendant 10 ans (2001-2010). Les dernières données disponibles sur la répartition de la population selon l'âge, le sexe et le lieu de résidence (zone urbaine ou rurale) sont présentées dans le tableau 7. Les derniers chiffres disponibles sur la population des capitales et des villes de 100 000 habitants ou plus sont regroupés dans le tableau 8.

On a utilisé pour le calcul des taux les statistiques de la population totale et de la population répartie selon l'âge, le sexe et le lieu de résidence (zone urbaine ou rurale). Les taux démographiques selon l'âge, le sexe et la résidence (urbaine/rurale) ont été calculés à partir des données présentées dans le tableau 7 de la présente édition ou dans les tableaux correspondants d'éditions précédentes de *l'Annuaire démographique*.

3.1 Sources de variation des données

Plusieurs facteurs influent sur la comparabilité des données : 1) la définition de la population totale ; 2) les définitions utilisées pour faire la distinction entre population urbaine et population rurale ; 3) les difficultés liées aux déclarations d'âge ; 4) l'étendue du sur-dénombrement ou du sous-dénombrement dans le recensement le plus récent ou dans une autre source de statistiques de référence sur la population ; 5) la qualité des estimations relatives à la population. Ces cinq facteurs sont analysés en détail aux sections 3.1.1 à 3.2.2 ci-après. D'autres questions seront traitées dans les notes techniques relatives à chaque tableau. Pour plus de précisions concernant, notamment, les notions fondamentales de dimension, de répartition et de caractéristiques de la population qui ont été élaborées par l'Organisation des Nations Unies, le lecteur est invité à se reporter aux *Principes et recommandations concernant les recensements de la population et de l'habitat. Révision 2*[4].

3.1.1 Population totale

Le principal obstacle à la comparabilité des données relatives à la population totale est la différence qui existe entre population de fait et population de droit. La population de fait comprend toutes les personnes présentes dans le pays ou la zone à la date de référence, tandis que la population de droit comprend toutes celles qui résident habituellement dans le pays ou la zone, qu'elles y aient été ou non présentes à la date de référence. Par définition, la population totale de fait et la population totale de droit ne sont donc pas rigoureusement comparables entre elles.

Même lorsque l'on veut comparer deux totaux qui se rapportent à des populations de fait ou deux totaux qui se rapportent à des populations de droit, on risque souvent de faire des erreurs pour cette raison qu'il est rare que l'une et l'autre notions soient appliquées strictement. Pour citer quelques exemples, certains chiffres qui sont censés porter sur la population de fait ne tiennent pas compte du personnel militaire, naval et diplomatique étranger en fonction dans le pays ou la zone, ni des membres de leurs familles et de leurs ménages; d'autres ne comprennent pas les visiteurs étrangers de passage dans le pays ou la zone ni les personnes à bord de navires ancrés dans des ports. En revanche, il arrive que l'on compte des personnes, inscrits maritimes et marins pêcheurs par exemple, qui, en raison de leur activité professionnelle, se trouvent hors du pays ou de la zone de recensement.

Les risques de disparités sont encore plus grands quand il s'agit de comparer des populations de droit, car les comparaisons dépendent au premier chef de la définition que l'on donne à l'expression « lieu de résidence habituel », qui varie d'un pays ou d'une zone à l'autre et qu'il est, de toute façon, difficile d'appliquer uniformément pour le dénombrement lors d'un recensement ou d'une enquête. Par exemple, les civils étrangers qui se trouvent temporairement dans un pays ou une zone comme travailleurs à court terme peuvent officiellement être considérés comme résidents après un séjour d'une durée déterminée, mais ils peuvent aussi être considérés comme non-résidents pendant toute la durée de leur séjour ; ailleurs, ces mêmes personnes peuvent être considérées officiellement comme résidents ou comme non-résidents du pays ou de la zone d'où elles viennent, selon la durée et, éventuellement, la raison de leur absence. Qui plus est, quel que soit son statut officiel, chacun des recensés peut, au moment de l'enquête, interpréter à sa façon la notion de résidence. De plus, les autorités nationales ou les entités responsables des zones ne savent pas toutes avec la même précision combien de leurs résidents se trouvent temporairement à l'étranger.

Les chiffres de population présentés dans les tableaux de l'*Annuaire démographique* représentent, autant qu'il a été possible, la population de fait. Sauf indication contraire, on peut supposer que les chiffres présentés ont été communiqués par les pays ou les zones comme se rapportant à la population de fait. Les chiffres qui ont été communiqués comme se rapportant à la population de droit sont indiqués comme tels. Lorsque l'on savait que les données avaient été recueillies selon une définition de la population de fait ou de la population de droit qui s'écartait sensiblement de celle exposée plus haut, on l'a signalé en note, de manière à compenser dans toute la mesure possible les conséquences des divergences.

Il ne faut pas oublier néanmoins que l'on ne disposait pas toujours de renseignements détaillés à ce sujet. On ne peut donc partir du principe que les chiffres qui ne sont pas accompagnés d'une note signalant une divergence correspondent exactement aux définitions de la population de fait ou de la population de droit.

Il peut y avoir hétérogénéité dans les statistiques d'un même pays ou d'une même zone dans le cas des pays ou zones qui ne font une exploitation statistique détaillée des données que pour la population de droit alors qu'ils recueillent des données sur la population de droit et sur la population de fait à l'occasion

À moins que des méthodes spéciales n'aient été adoptées pour l'exploitation de ces données, les statistiques des naissances vivantes et des décès ne tiendront pas compte de ces cas, qui viendront en revanche accroître d'autant le nombre des morts fœtales tardives. Le taux de mortalité infantile sera donc sous-estimé. Bien que les éléments constitutifs du taux (décès d'enfants de moins d'un an et naissances vivantes) accusent exactement la même insuffisance en valeur absolue, les lacunes sont proportionnellement plus fortes pour les décès de moins d'un an, ce qui cause des erreurs plus importantes dans les taux de mortalité infantile.

De plus, cette pratique augmente les rapports de mortinatalité. Quelques pays ou zones effectuent les ajustements nécessaires pour corriger cette anomalie (du moins dans les fréquences totales) au moment de l'établissement des tableaux. Si aucun ajustement n'a été effectué, cela est indiqué dans les notes chaque fois que possible.

Les définitions du mariage et du divorce posent aussi un problème du point de vue de la comparabilité internationale. Contrairement à la naissance et au décès, qui sont des faits biologiques, le mariage et le divorce sont uniquement déterminés par la législation et la coutume et, de ce fait, il est moins facile d'en donner une définition statistique qui ait une application universelle. À des fins statistiques, ces notions ont donc été définies de manière générale par référence à la législation de chaque pays ou zone. La législation relative au mariage et plus particulièrement au divorce varie d'un pays ou d'une zone à l'autre. En ce qui concerne le mariage, l'âge de nubilité est la condition la plus fréquemment requise mais il arrive souvent que d'autres conditions soient exigées.

Lorsqu'il est connu, l'âge minimum auquel le mariage peut avoir lieu avec le consentement des parents (et dans certains cas sans le consentement des parents) est indiqué au tableau 23-1. Les lois et règlements relatifs à la dissolution du mariage par le divorce vont de l'interdiction absolue, en passant par diverses conditions requises pour l'obtention du divorce, jusqu'à la simple déclaration, par l'époux, de son désir ou de son intention de divorcer.

4.1.3 Portée géographique ou ethnique restreinte

En principe, les statistiques de l'état civil devraient s'étendre à l'ensemble du pays ou de la zone auxquels elles se rapportent et englober tous les groupes ethniques. En fait, il n'est pas rare que les données soient fragmentaires. Dans certains pays ou zones, l'enregistrement n'est obligatoire que pour une petite partie de la population, par exemple pour certains groupes ethniques. Dans d'autres, il n'existe pas de disposition qui prescrive l'enregistrement obligatoire sur le plan national, mais seulement des règlements ou décrets des municipalités ou des États, qui ne s'appliquent pas à l'ensemble du territoire. Il en est encore autrement dans d'autres pays ou zones où les autorités ont institué une zone d'enregistrement comprenant seulement une partie du territoire, le reste étant exclu en raison des difficultés d'accès ou parce qu'il est pratiquement impossible, pour des raisons d'ordre économique ou culturel, d'y procéder à un enregistrement régulier.

4.1.4 Exploitation des données

4.1.4.1 Selon le lieu de l'événement

Les statistiques de l'état civil qui sont présentées pour l'ensemble du territoire national se rapportent à la population de fait ou population présente. En conséquence, sauf indication contraire, les statistiques de l'état civil relatives à une zone ou à un pays donné portent sur tous les faits survenus dans l'ensemble de la population, à l'intérieur des frontières actuelles de la zone ou du pays considéré. On peut donc estimer qu'elles englobent les faits d'état civil survenus dans les tribus nomades et parmi les populations autochtones ainsi que parmi les ressortissants du pays et les étrangers. Des notes signalent les exceptions lorsque celles-ci sont connues.

Pour certains pays, les écarts entre les taux démographiques pour les zones urbaines et pour les zones rurales peuvent varier notablement selon que les faits d'état civil ont été exploités sur la base du lieu de l'événement ou du lieu de résidence habituel. Par exemple, si un nombre appréciable de femmes résidant dans des zones rurales proches de grands centres urbains accouchent dans les hôpitaux ou maternités d'une ville, les taux de fécondité ainsi que les taux de mortalité néo-natale et infantile seront généralement plus élevés dans les zones urbaines (et par conséquent plus faibles dans les zones rurales) si les faits sont exploités en se fondant sur le lieu de l'événement et non sur le lieu de résidence habituel. Le phénomène

sera le même dans le cas de la mortalité générale si un bon nombre de personnes résidant dans des zones rurales font appel aux services de santé des villes lorsqu'elles sont gravement malades.

4.1.4.2 Selon la date de l'événement ou la date de l'enregistrement

Autant que possible, les statistiques de l'état civil figurant dans *l'Annuaire démographique* se rapportent aux faits survenus pendant l'année considérée et non aux faits enregistrés au cours de ladite année. Bon nombre de pays ou zones, toutefois, exploitent leurs statistiques de l'état civil selon la date de l'enregistrement et non selon la date de l'événement. Comme ces statistiques risquent d'induire en erreur, les pays ou zones dont on sait qu'ils établissent leurs statistiques d'après la date de l'enregistrement sont signalés dans les tableaux par un signe plus "+". On ne dispose toutefois pas pour tous les pays ou zones de renseignements complets sur la méthode d'exploitation des statistiques de l'état civil et les données sont peut-être exploitées selon la date de l'enregistrement plus souvent que ne le laisserait supposer l'emploi des signes.

Étant donné que la qualité des données est inextricablement liée aux retards dans l'enregistrement, il faudra toujours considérer en même temps le code de qualité qui est décrit à la section 4.2.1 ci-après. Évidemment, si l'enregistrement des naissances est complet et effectué en temps voulu (code "C"), les effets perturbateurs de la méthode consistant à exploiter les données selon la date de l'enregistrement seront pratiquement annulés. De même, s'agissant des statistiques des décès, les effets pourront bien souvent être réduits au minimum dans les pays ou zones où le code sanitaire subordonne la délivrance du permis d'inhumer à l'enregistrement du décès, ce qui tend à hâter l'enregistrement. Quant aux morts fœtales, elles sont généralement déclarées immédiatement ou ne sont pas déclarées du tout. En conséquence, si l'enregistrement se fait dans un délai très court, la différence entre les statistiques établies selon la date de l'événement et celles qui sont établies selon la date de l'enregistrement peut être négligeable. Dans bien des cas, la durée des délais légaux accordés pour l'enregistrement des faits d'état civil est un facteur dont dépend dans une large mesure l'incidence sur la comparabilité de l'exploitation des données selon la date de l'enregistrement.

En ce qui concerne le mariage et le divorce, la pratique consistant à exploiter les statistiques selon la date de l'enregistrement ne pose généralement pas de graves problèmes. Le mariage étant, dans de nombreux pays ou zones, un contrat juridique civil qui, pour être légal, doit être conclu devant un officier de l'état civil, il s'ensuit que dans ces pays ou zones l'enregistrement a lieu presque systématiquement au moment de la cérémonie ou immédiatement après. De même, dans de nombreux pays ou zones, le tribunal ou l'autorité qui a prononcé le divorce est seul habilité à enregistrer cet acte, et comme l'acte d'enregistrement figure alors sur les registres du tribunal l'enregistrement suit généralement de peu le jugement.

En revanche, si l'enregistrement n'a lieu qu'avec un certain retard, les statistiques de l'état civil établies selon la date de l'enregistrement ne sont pas comparables sur le plan international. Au mieux, les statistiques par date de l'enregistrement prendront surtout en considération des faits survenus au cours de l'année précédente ; dans les pays ou zones où le système d'enregistrement n'est pas très développé, il y entrera des faits datant de plusieurs années. Il ressort des documents dont on dispose que des retards de plusieurs années dans l'enregistrement des naissances ne sont pas rares, encore que, dans la majorité des cas, les retards ne dépassent pas deux à quatre ans.

Tant que l'enregistrement se fera avec retard, les statistiques fondées sur la date d'enregistrement ne seront comparables sur le plan international ni entre elles ni avec les statistiques établies selon la date de fait d'état civil.

Il convient également de noter que l'exploitation des données selon la date de l'enregistrement ne nuit pas seulement à la comparabilité internationale des statistiques. Même à l'intérieur d'un pays ou d'une zone, le procédé qui consiste à compter les enregistrements et non les faits peut compromettre la comparabilité des chiffres sur une longue période. Si le nombre des faits d'état civil enregistrés varie d'une année à l'autre (par suite de l'application de mesures visant tout particulièrement à encourager l'enregistrement ou parce qu'il est subitement devenu nécessaire de produire le certificat d'une naissance ou d'un décès non enregistré pour l'accomplissement de certaines formalités), les statistiques de l'état civil établies d'après la date de l'enregistrement ne permettent pas de quantifier ni d'analyser l'état et l'évolution de la population. Tout au plus peuvent-elles révéler l'évolution des conditions d'exigibilité du certificat de naissance, de décès ou de mariage et les fluctuations du volume de travail des bureaux d'état civil. Les statistiques établies selon la date de l'enregistrement peuvent donc ne présenter qu'une utilité très réduite pour des études nationales ou internationales.

4.2 Méthodes utilisées pour indiquer la qualité des statistiques de l'état civil qui sont publiées

La qualité des statistiques de l'état civil peut être évaluée en se fondant sur plusieurs facteurs. Le facteur essentiel est la complétude du système d'enregistrement des faits d'état civil d'après lequel ces statistiques sont établies. Dans certains cas, on constate que les données tirées de l'enregistrement ne sont pas complètes lorsque l'on les utilise pour le calcul des taux. Toutefois, cette observation est valable uniquement lorsque les statistiques présentent des lacunes évidentes, qu'elles sont exploitées d'après la date de l'événement et que l'estimation du chiffre de population pris pour base est exacte. L'exploitation des données d'après la date de l'enregistrement donne souvent des taux qui paraissent exacts, tout simplement parce que le numérateur est artificiellement gonflé par suite de l'inclusion d'enregistrements tardifs ; inversement, il arrive que des taux paraissent vraisemblables parce que l'on a sous-évalué la population étudiée. Il ne faut pas non plus oublier que les renseignements dont on dispose sur les taux de fécondité, de mortalité et de nuptialité considérés comme normaux sont extrêmement sommaires dans un grand nombre de régions du monde et que les cas limites, qui sont les plus difficiles à évaluer, sont fréquents.

4.2.1 Codage qualitatif des statistiques provenant des registres de l'état civil

Dans le questionnaire relatif au mouvement de la population qui leur est envoyé chaque année dans le cadre de l'établissement de l'*Annuaire démographique*, les services nationaux de statistique sont invités à donner leur propre évaluation du degré de complétude des données sur les naissances, les décès, les décès d'enfants de moins d'un an, les morts fœtales tardives, les mariages et les divorces figurant dans leurs registres d'état civil.

D'après les renseignements directement communiqués par les gouvernements ou extraits des questionnaires ou de publications officielles pertinentes, il a été possible de classer les statistiques de l'enregistrement des faits d'état civil (naissances, décès, décès d'enfants de moins d'un an, morts fœtales tardives, mariages et divorces) en trois grandes catégories, selon leur qualité :

C : Données jugées pratiquement complètes, c'est-à-dire représentant au moins 90 p. 100 des faits d'état civil survenant chaque année.

U : Données jugées incomplètes, c'est-à-dire représentant moins de 90 p. 100 des faits survenant chaque année.

| : Données ne provenant pas des systèmes nationaux d'enregistrement des faits d'état civil mais jugées fiables, telles que les estimations dérivées des projections, d'autres techniques d'estimation ou recensements de population ou du logement.

... : Données dont le degré de complétude ne fait pas l'objet de renseignements précis.

Ces codes de qualité figurent dans la première colonne des tableaux qui présentent, pour un nombre d'années déterminé les chiffres absolus et les taux (ou rapports) bruts concernant les naissances vivantes, les morts fœtales tardives, les décès d'enfants de moins d'un an, les décès, les mariages et les divorces. Les niveaux de fiabilité des statistiques de mortalité maternelle sont transmis par l'Organisation mondiale de la santé.

La classification des pays ou zones selon ces codes de qualité peut ne pas être uniforme. On a estimé néanmoins que les services nationaux de statistique étaient les mieux placés pour juger de la qualité de leurs données. On a pensé que les catégories que l'on pouvait distinguer sur la base des renseignements disponibles, bien que très larges, permettaient cependant de se faire une idée de la qualité des statistiques de l'état civil publiées dans l'*Annuaire démographique*.

Par le passé, les bases sur lesquelles les pays évaluaient l'exhaustivité de leurs données n'étaient généralement pas connues. À l'occasion de l'établissement de l'*Annuaire démographique 1977*, les pays ont été invités, pour la première fois, à donner des indications à ce sujet. On leur a demandé de préciser si leurs estimations du degré d'exhaustivité des données d'enregistrement des naissances vivantes, des décès et de la mortalité infantile reposaient sur une analyse démographique, un double contrôle des registres ou d'autres méthodes qu'ils devaient spécifier. Relativement peu de pays ou zones ont jusqu'à présent répondu à cette nouvelle question ; on n'a donc pas cherché à réviser le système de codage qualitatif utilisé pour les statistiques de l'état civil présentées dans l'*Annuaire démographique*. Il faut espérer qu'à l'avenir davantage

de pays puissent fournir ces renseignements afin que le système de codage qualitatif utilisé dans le cadre des statistiques d'état civil de l'Annuaire démographique soit révisé.

Sur les pays ou zones qui ont estimé à 90 p. 100 ou plus le degré d'exhaustivité de leur enregistrement des naissances vivantes (classé "C" ou "+C" dans le tableau 9), les pays ou zones suivants ont communiqué des renseignements concernant les bases sur lesquelles leur estimation reposait :

a) Analyse démographique : Argentine, Autriche, Bulgarie, Chili, Chine - Hong Kong RAS, Croatie, Estonie, Italie, Lettonie, Lituanie, Malte, Maurice, République de Corée, République de Moldova, Roumanie, Seychelles et Suède.

b) Double contrôle des registres : Autriche, Cuba, Estonie, Hongrie, Israël, Italie, Norvège, Qatar, République de Corée, Roumanie et Suisse.

c) Autre méthode : Antilles néerlandaises, Aruba, Autriche, Danemark, Espagne, France, Guatemala, Irlande, Kirghizstan, Liechtenstein, Luxembourg, Panama, Pologne, Porto Rico, Singapour, Slovénie, Suède et Territoire palestinien occupé.

Sur les pays ou zones qui ont estimé à 90 p. 100 ou plus le degré d'exhaustivité de leur enregistrement des morts fœtales tardives (classé "C" ou "+C" dans le tableau 12), les pays ou zones suivants ont communiqué des renseignements concernant les bases sur lesquelles leur estimation reposait :

a) Analyse démographique : Argentine, Autriche, Bulgarie, Croatie, Estonie, Italie, Lettonie, Lituanie, Malte, Maurice, Roumanie et Suède.

b) Double contrôle des registres : Autriche, Cuba, Estonie, Hongrie, Israël, Italie, Lituanie, Norvège, Qatar, Roumanie et Suisse.

c) Autre méthode : Autriche, Danemark, Espagne, Luxembourg, Pologne, Porto Rico, Slovénie et Suède.

Sur les pays ou zones qui ont estimé à 90 p. 100 ou plus le degré d'exhaustivité de leur enregistrement des décès à moins d'un an (classé "C" ou "+C" dans le tableau 15), les pays ou zones suivants ont donné des indications touchant la base de cette estimation :

a) Analyse démographique : Argentine, Autriche, Bulgarie, Chili, Chine - Hong Kong RAS, Croatie, Estonie, Israël, Italie, Lettonie, Lituanie, Malte, Maurice, République de Corée, République de Moldova, Roumanie, Seychelles et Suède.

b) Double contrôle des registres : Autriche, Cuba, Chypre, Estonie, Hongrie, Irlande, Israël, Italie, Lituanie, Norvège, Qatar, République de Corée, Roumanie et Suisse.

c) Autre méthode : Antilles néerlandaises, Autriche, Danemark, Espagne, Îles Caïmanes, Kirghizstan, Liechtenstein, Luxembourg, Pologne, Porto Rico, Singapour, Slovénie et Suède.

Sur les pays ou zones qui ont estimé à 90 p. 100 ou plus le degré d'exhaustivité de leur enregistrement des décès (classé "C" ou "+C" dans le tableau 18), les pays ou zones suivants ont donné des indications touchant la base de cette estimation :

a) Analyse démographique : Argentine, Autriche, Bulgarie, Chili, Chine - Hong Kong RAS, Croatie, Estonie, Israël, Italie, Lettonie, Lituanie, Malte, Maurice, Mexique, République de Corée, République de Moldova, Roumanie, Seychelles et Suède.

b) Double contrôle des registres : Autriche, Cuba, Chypre, Estonie, Hongrie, Israël, Italie, Lituanie, Mexique, Norvège, Qatar, République de Corée, Roumanie et Suisse.

c) Autre méthode : Antilles néerlandaises, Aruba, Autriche, Danemark, Espagne, France, Kirghizstan, Liechtenstein, Luxembourg, Pologne, Porto Rico, Singapour, Slovénie et Suède.

Sur les pays ou zones qui ont estimé à 90 p. 100 ou plus le degré d'exhaustivité de leur enregistrement des mariages (classé "C" ou "+C" dans le tableau 22), les pays ou zones suivants ont communiqué des renseignements concernant les bases sur lesquelles leur estimation reposait :

a) Analyse démographique : Argentine, Autriche, Bulgarie, Chili, Chine - Hong Kong RAS, Croatie, Estonie, Italie, Lettonie, Lituanie, Malte, Maurice, Mexique, République de Corée, République de Moldova, Roumanie, Seychelles, Suède et Territoire palestinien occupé.

b) Double contrôle des registres : Cuba, Estonie, Hongrie, Israël, Italia, Mexique, Norvège, Qatar, République de Corée, Roumanie et Suisse.

c) Autre méthode : Antilles néerlandaises, Aruba, Australie, Autriche, Chypre, Danemark, Espagne, France, Liechtenstein, Luxembourg, Mexique, Pologne, Porto Rico, République dominicaine, Slovénie, Suède et Tadjikistan.

Sur les pays ou zones qui ont estimé à 90 p. 100 ou plus le degré d'exhaustivité de leur enregistrement des divorces (classé "C" ou "+C" dans le tableau 24), les pays ou zones suivants ont communiqué des renseignements concernant les bases sur lesquelles leur estimation reposait :

a) Analyse démographique : Autriche, Bulgarie, Croatie, Estonie, Italie, Lettonie, Lituanie, Mexique, République de Corée, République de Moldova, Roumanie, Seychelles, Suède et Territoire palestinien occupé.

b) Double contrôle des registres : Cuba, Estonie, Hongrie, Israël, Italie, Mexique, Norvège, Qatar, République de Corée, Roumanie et Suisse.

c) Autre méthode : Antilles néerlandaises, Aruba, Autriche, Chypre, Danemark, Liechtenstein, Luxembourg, Maurice, Mexique, Pologne, Porto Rico, République dominicaine, Slovénie, Suède et Tadjikistan.

4.2.2 Traitement des statistiques tirées des registres d'état civil

Dans tous les tableaux de l'*Annuaire démographique*, on a indiqué le degré de fiabilité des statistiques de l'état civil en se fondant sur le codage qualitatif décrit ci-dessus. Les statistiques codées "C", jugées sûres, sont imprimées en caractères romains. Celles qui sont codées "U" ou "...", jugées douteuses, sont reproduites en *italique*. Bien que le codage qualitatif proprement dit n'apparaisse que dans certains tableaux, l'indication du degré de fiabilité (c'est-à-dire l'emploi des caractères italiques pour désigner les données douteuses) se retrouve dans tous les tableaux présentant des statistiques de l'état civil.

En général, le code de qualité pour les décès utilisé au tableau 18 sert à déterminer si, dans les autres tableaux, les données relatives aux décès apparaissent en caractères romains ou en italique. Toutefois, le code associé à certaines données sur les décès liés à la maternité dans le tableau 17 diffère de celui employé dans le tableau 18 lorsque l'on sait que le degré d'exhaustivité des données diffère grandement de celui du nombre total des décès. Dans les cas où le code de qualité du tableau 18 ne correspond pas aux caractères utilisés dans le tableau 17, les renseignements concernant l'exhaustivité des statistiques des décès selon la cause sont indiqués en note à la fin du tableau.

Il convient de noter que, pour les taux de mortalité infantile, les taux de mortalité maternelle et les rapports de morts fœtales tardives (calculées en utilisant au dénominateur le nombre de naissances vivantes), les indications relatives à la fiabilité sont déterminées sur la base des codes de qualité utilisés pour les décès d'enfants de moins d'un an, les décès totaux et les morts fœtales tardives, respectivement. Pour évaluer ces taux et rapports de façon plus précise, il faudrait tenir compte de la qualité des données relatives aux naissances vivantes, utilisées au dénominateur dans leur calcul. Les codes de qualité pour les naissances vivantes figurent au tableau 9 et sont décrits plus en détail dans les notes techniques se rapportant à ce tableau.

4.2.3 Traitement des séries chronologiques de statistiques tirées des registres d'état civil

Il est plus difficile de déterminer la qualité des séries chronologiques de statistiques de l'état civil que celle des données pour une seule année. Étant donné qu'une série chronologique de statistiques de l'état civil ne peut généralement avoir pour source qu'un système permanent d'enregistrement des faits d'état civil, on a arbitrairement supposé que le degré d'exactitude de la série tout entière était le même que celui de la dernière tranche annuelle de données tirées du registre d'état civil. La série tout entière est traitée de la manière décrite à la section 4.2.2 ci-dessus : lorsque le code de qualité relatif aux données d'enregistrement les plus récentes est "C", les fréquences et les taux relatifs aux années antérieures sont

eux aussi considérés comme sûrs et figurent en caractères romains. Inversement, si les données d'enregistrement les plus récentes sont codées "U" ou "...", les données des années antérieures sont jugées douteuses et figurent en italique. Cette méthode n'est certes pas entièrement satisfaisante, car les données des premières années de la série sont souvent beaucoup moins sûres que le code actuel ne le laisse supposer. On s'efforce d'abandonner progressivement cette méthode et de coder les données enregistrées pour chaque année séparément. Voir par exemple les notes techniques du tableau 17 dans la présente parution «Décès maternels et taux de mortalité maternelle : 1999-2008».

4.2.4 Traitement des estimations fondées sur les statistiques de l'état civil

En plus des données provenant des systèmes d'enregistrement des faits d'état civil, *l'Annuaire démographique* contient aussi des estimations relatives aux fréquences et aux taux. Il s'agit d'estimations officielles, généralement calculées à partir des résultats d'un sondage ou par analyse démographique. Si des estimations concernant les fréquences et les taux figurent dans les tableaux, c'est parce que l'on considère qu'elles fournissent des renseignements plus exacts que les systèmes existants d'enregistrement des faits d'état civil. En conséquence, elles sont également jugées sûres et sont donc imprimées en caractères romains, même si elles sont entrecoupées dans une série chronologique de données tirées des registres d'état civil.

Dans les tableaux qui indiquent le code de qualité, ce code ne s'applique qu'aux données tirées des registres d'état civil. Si une série pour un pays ou une zone comprend à la fois des données tirées d'un registre d'état civil et des données estimatives, le code ne s'applique qu'aux données d'enregistrement. Si seules des données estimatives apparaissent, le symbole "|" est utilisé.

4.3 Causes de décès

Les États membres de l'Organisation mondiale de la santé (OMS) sont tenus de communiquer à celle-ci les données sur les causes de décès codifiées selon la révision en vigueur de la Classification internationale des maladies et des problèmes de santé connexes (CIM) adoptée par l'Assemblé mondiale de la santé[19]. Les données sont collectées par l'OMS[20] sur la base de la CIM. Pour assurer la comparabilité internationale des statistiques des causes de décès, l'OMS organise régulièrement des conférences internationales de révision de la Classification internationale des maladies afin de suivre, au fur et à mesure, les progrès les plus récents de la médecine clinique et de la statistique. Les données sont généralement envoyées à l'OMS selon la classification à 4 caractères prévue par la CIM et sont archivées dans la base de données sur la mortalité de l'OMS telles qu'elles ont été présentées par le pays. Pour les versions antérieures, par contre, les données sont disponibles seulement selon la liste A de 150 causes de la CIM. Les données de l'OMS sont disponibles sur le site Internet suivant : http://www3.who.int/whosis/menu.cfm.

Les révisions de la CIM permettent certes de disposer d'une version actualisée, mais elles posent plusieurs problèmes de comparabilité des statistiques des causes de décès. Le premier tient au manque de comparabilité dans le temps, qui accompagne inévitablement la mise en oeuvre d'une classification nouvelle. Le deuxième est celui de la comparabilité entre pays ou zones, car les différents pays peuvent adopter la nouvelle classification à des époques différentes. Établir la cause des décès exige des compétences de plus en plus poussées à mesure que la classification devient plus précise. Or, dans beaucoup de pays ou zones, il est rare que les décès se produisent en présence d'un témoin possédant une formation médicale et le certificat de décès est le plus souvent établi par quelqu'un qui n'est pas qualifié sur le plan médical. Étant donné que la CIM répertorie de nombreux diagnostics qu'il est impossible d'établir si l'on n'a pas de formation en médecine, la CIM n'est pas toujours exactement ou précisément utilisée ce qui affecte la comparabilité internationale, notamment entre pays ou zones où la qualité des services médicaux est très disparate.

La dixième révision[21] est la dernière qu'ait connue la CIM. Les chapitres de la dixième révision se fondent sur un système de codification alphanumérique à une lettre suivie de trois chiffres pour les catégories à quatre caractères. Le chapitre 1 concerne les maladies infectieuses et parasitaires et le chapitre 2 l'ensemble des néoplasmes. Le chapitre 3 a trait aux troubles du système immunitaire, aux maladies du sang et aux organes hématopoïétiques. Le chapitre 4 porte sur les maladies du système endocrinien, de la nutrition et du métabolisme. Les autres chapitres groupent les maladies selon leur site anatomique, à l'exception de ceux qui concernent les affections mentales, les complications de la grossesse, de l'accouchement et des suites de couches, les malformations congénitales et les affections de la période périnatale. Enfin, un chapitre entier est consacré aux symptômes, manifestations et résultats anormaux.

4.3.1 Mortalité liée à la maternité

D'après la dixième révision de la CIM, la « mortalité liée à la maternité » est définie comme le décès d'une femme survenu au cours de la grossesse ou dans un délai de 42 jours après sa terminaison, quelle qu'en soit la durée et la localisation, pour une cause quelconque déterminée ou aggravée par la grossesse ou les soins qu'elle a motivés, mais ni accidentelle ni fortuite.

Les décès liés à la maternité se répartissent en deux groupes :

1) Décès par cause obstétricale directe qui résultent de complications obstétricales (grossesse, travail et suites de couches), d'interventions, d'omissions, d'un traitement incorrect ou d'un enchaînement d'événements de l'un quelconque des facteurs ci-dessus ;
2) Décès par cause obstétricale indirecte qui résultent d'une maladie préexistante ou d'une affection apparue au cours de la grossesse, sans qu'elle soit due à des causes obstétricales directes, mais qui a été aggravée par les effets physiologiques de la grossesse.

Il est recommandé dans la dixième révision d'exprimer les taux de mortalité maternelles sur la base de 100 000 naissances vivantes ou 100 000 naissances totales (naissances vivantes et morts fœtales)[22]. En théorie, le nombre de femmes enceintes aurait dû être pris comme dénominateur, mais étant donné qu'il est impossible de le déterminer, le taux de mortalité maternelle est ici calculé par 100 000 naissances vivantes. Bien que les naissances vivantes ne permettent pas d'évaluer sans distorsion le nombre des femmes enceintes, leur nombre est plus fiable que d'autres estimations car le nombre des naissances vivantes est plus exactement enregistré que celui des naissances vivantes et des morts fœtales.

---

[1] Les éditions de 1978 et de 1991 font exception à la règle, puisque les tableaux sur des sujets spéciaux ont été publiés séparément.

[2] *Organisation des Nations Unies, Département des affaires économiques et sociales, Division de la population (2011). Perspectives de la population mondiale : La révision de 2010, Edition DVD - ensemble de données étendues (publication des Nations Unies, numéro de vente E.11.XIII.7).* On peut consulter des extraits et certaines données sur le site www.unpopulation.org.

[3] ST/ESA/STAT/SER.M/49/Rev.4/WWW ; http://unstats.un.org/unsd/methods/m49/m49frnch.htm; voir également *Code standard des pays et des zones à usage statistique*, numéro de vente : M.98.XVII.9, Nations Unies, New York, 1999.

[4] Numéro de vente : F.07.XVII.8, Nations Unies, New York, 2007. Avant d'être publiée, cette publication est disponible en ligne à l'adresse suivante : http://unstats.un.org/unsd/demographic/standmeth/principles/Series_M67Rev2en.pdf

[5] Ibid., par. 2.135.

[6] Lorsque l'on utilise un registre de la population, on peut également calculer l'âge en années révolues en soustrayant la date de naissance de chaque personne inscrite sur le registre de la date de référence à laquelle se rapportent les données sur l'âge.

[7] L'emploi de méthodes différentes de calcul de l'âge, par exemple la méthode occidentale et la méthode orientale, ou, comme on les désigne plus communément, la méthode anglaise et la méthode chinoise, représente une cause de non-comparabilité. Selon la méthode chinoise, on considère que l'enfant est âgé d'un an à sa naissance et qu'il avance d'un an à chaque nouvelle année chinoise. Les répercussions de cette méthode sont particulièrement apparentes dans les données pour le premier âge : les données concernant les enfants de moins d'un an sont nettement inférieures à la réalité. Les effets sur les chiffres relatifs aux groupes d'âge suivants sont moins visibles. Les séries ainsi établies sont souvent ajustées avant d'être publiées, mais il ne faut pas exclure la possibilité d'aberrations de ce genre lorsque l'on compare des données censitaires sur l'âge.

[8] United States Bureau of the Census, Thirteenth Census, vol. I (Washington, D.C., U.S. Government Printing Office, 1913; Reprint: New York, N.Y., Norman Ross Pub., 1999), p. 291 et 292.

[9] Numéro de vente : F.83.XIII.2, publication des Nations Unies, New York, 1984.

[10] Numéro de vente : F.01.XVII.10, publication des Nations Unies, New York, 2003.

[11] Numéro de vente : F. 98.XVII.7, publication des Nations Unies, New York, 1998.

[12] Numéro de vente : F.98.XVII.11, publication des Nations Unies, New York, 1998.

[13] Numéro de vente : F.98.XVII.4, publication des Nations Unies, New York, 1998.

[14] Numéro de vente : F.98.XVII.6, publication des Nations Unies, New York, 1998.

[15] Numéro de vente : F.98.XVII.10, publication des Nations Unies, New York, 1998.

[16] Numéro de vente : F.03.XVII.11, United Nations, New York, 2004.

[17] Pour plus de précisions, voir *Principes et recommandations pour un système de statistiques de l'état civil, deuxième révision*, numéro de vente : F.01.XVII.10, publication des Nations Unies, New York, 2001, par. 57.

[18] Pour plus de précisions au sujet des considérations historiques et juridiques auxquelles se rattachent les différentes définitions correspondant aux naissances vivantes et aux morts fœtales, pour une comparaison des définitions utilisées depuis le 1er janvier 1950 et pour une évaluation des effets de ces différences de définition sur le calcul de divers taux, voir le *Manuel de statistique de l'état civil, Volume II, Étude des pratiques nationales*, numéro de vente : F.84.XVII.11, publication des Nations Unies, New York, 1985, chap. IV.

[19] Les États membres de l'Organisation mondiale de la santé se réunissent annuellement dans le cadre de l'Assemblée mondiale de la santé, qui est l'organe directeur de l'Organisation.

[20] Les données relatives à la mortalité maternelle (en tant que cause de décès) et aux décès ventilés par cause et par sexe proviennent de l'Organisation mondiale de la santé et peuvent être consultées sur le site : http://www3.who.int/whosis/menu.cfm.

[21] Organisation mondiale de la santé, *Classification statistique internationale des maladies et problèmes de santé connexes*, dixième révision, vol. 2, Genève, 1992.

[22] Ibid., pp. 129-136.

33

Table A. Demographic Yearbook 2009 - 2010 synoptic table: Availability of data by country/area, table and sex, where applicable

Tableau A. Tableau synoptique de l'Annuaire démographique 2009 - 2010 : Disponibilité des données par pays ou zone, tableau et le sexe, si disponible

Continent and country or area / Continent et pays ou zone	Table totals	Summary - Apercu 3 Total	3 M/F	4	5	Population 6 Total¹	6 M/F	7 Total	7 M/F	8 Total	8 M/F	9	Fertility - Natalité 10 Total	10 M/F	11	Foetal mortality - Mortalité foetale 12	13	14
Total number of countries or areas - Total des pays ou zones	..	236	218	185	220	226	223	216	214	215	152	176	150	123	86	93	62	50

AFRICA - AFRIQUE

Continent and country or area	Table totals	3 Total	3 M/F	4	5	6 Total¹	6 M/F	7 Total	7 M/F	8 Total	8 M/F	9	10 Total	10 M/F	11	12	13	14
Algeria - Algérie	14	•	•	•	•	•	•	•	•	•	...	•	...	...	...	...	...	...
Angola	4	•	•	...	•	•	•	•	•	•	...	...	...	...	...	...	...	...
Benin - Bénin	11	•	•	...	•	•	•	•	•	•	•	...	...	...	...	...	...	...
Botswana	19	•	•	•	•	•	•	•	•	•	•	•	•	•	...	...	...	...
Burkina Faso	14	•	•	•	•	•	•	•	•	•	•	...	...	...	...	...	...	...
Burundi	9	•	•	•	•	•	•	•	•	•	•	...	...	...	...	...	...	...
Cameroon - Cameroun	8	•	•	•	•	•	•	•	•	•	...	...	...	...	...	...	...	...
Cape Verde - Cap-Vert	12	•	•	•	•	•	•	•	•	•	•	...	•	...	...	...	...	...
Central African Republic - République centrafricaine	5	•	•	•	•	•	•	•	...	...	...	...	...	...	...	...	...	...
Chad - Tchad	4	•	•	•	...	•	•	•	...	...	...	...	...	...	...	...	...	...
Comoros - Comores	3	•	...	...	•	•	•	•	...	...	...	...	...	...	...	...	...	...
Congo	3	•	...	...	•	•	•	•	...	...	...	...	...	...	...	...	...	...
Côte d'Ivoire	6	•	•	...	•	•	•	•	...	...	...	...	...	...	...	...	...	...
Democratic Republic of the Congo - République démocratique du Congo	2	•	•	...	•	•	...	...	...	...	...	...	...	...	...	...	...	...
Djibouti	4	•	•	...	•	•	•	•	...	...	...	...	...	...	...	...	...	...
Egypt - Égypte	27	•	•	•	•	•	•	•	•	•	•	•	•	•	•	•	•	•
Equatorial Guinea - Guinée équatoriale	4	•	•	...	•	•	•	...	...	...	...	...	...	...	...	...	...	...
Eritrea - Érythrée	3	•	•	...	•	•	•	•	...	...	...	...	...	...	...	...	...	...
Ethiopia - Éthiopie	13	•	•	•	•	•	•	•	•	•	•	...	...	...	...	...	...	...
Gabon	6	•	...	•	•	•	•	•	...	...	...	...	...	...	...	...	...	...
Gambia - Gambie	7	•	•	•	•	•	•	•	...	...	...	...	...	...	...	...	...	...
Ghana	13	•	•	•	•	•	•	•	•	•	•	...	...	...	...	...	...	...
Guinea - Guinée	8	•	•	•	•	•	•	•	•	...	...	...	...	...	...	...	...	...
Guinea-Bissau - Guinée-Bissau	8	•	•	...	•	•	•	•	•	•	...	...	...	...	...	...	...	...
Kenya	18	•	•	•	•	•	•	•	•	•	•	•	•	•	...	...	...	...
Lesotho	8	•	•	...	•	•	•	•	•	...	...	...	...	...	...	...	...	...
Liberia - Libéria	10	•	•	•	...	•	•	•	•	...	...	...	•	•	...	...	...	...
Libya - Libye	12	•	•	•	•	•	•	•	•	...	...	•	•	•	...	...	...	...
Madagascar	7	•	•	•	•	•	•	•	...	...	...	...	...	...	...	...	...	...
Malawi	13	•	•	•	•	•	•	•	•	•	•	...	...	...	...	...	...	...
Mali	5	•	•	•	•	...	...	...	...	...	...	...	...	...	...	...	...	...
Mauritania - Mauritanie	9	•	•	•	•	•	•	•	•	...	...	...	...	...	...	...	...	...
Mauritius - Maurice	27	•	•	•	•	•	•	•	•	•	•	•	•	•	•	•	•	•
Mayotte	6	•	•	•	•	•	•	...	...	...	...	...	...	...	...	...	...	...
Morocco - Maroc	16	•	•	•	•	•	•	•	•	•	•	•	•	•	...	...	...	...
Mozambique	8	•	•	•	•	•	•	•	•	...	...	...	...	...	...	...	...	...
Namibia - Namibie	16	•	•	•	•	•	•	•	•	•	•	•	•	•	...	...	...	...
Niger	12	•	•	•	•	•	•	•	•	•	•	...	...	...	...	...	...	...
Nigeria - Nigéria	11	•	•	•	•	•	•	•	•	•	...	...	...	...	...	...	...	...
Réunion	27	•	•	•	•	•	•	•	•	•	•	•	•	•	•	•	•	•
Rwanda	13	•	•	•	•	•	•	•	•	•	•	...	•	•	...	...	...	...
Saint Helena ex. dep. - Sainte-Hélène sans dép.	22	•	•	•	•	•	•	•	•	•	•	•	•	•	...	...	...	...
Saint Helena: Ascension - Sainte-Hélène: Ascension	7	•	•	•	•	•	•	...	...	...	...	...	...	...	...	...	...	...
Saint Helena: Tristan da Cunha - Sainte-Hélène: Tristan da Cunha	5	•	•	...	•	•	...	...	...	...	...	...	...	...	...	...	...	...
Sao Tome and Principe - Sao Tomé-et-Principe	10	•	•	...	•	•	•	•	•	...	•	...	...	...	...	...	...	...
Senegal - Sénégal	13	•	•	•	•	•	•	•	•	•	•	...	•	•	...	...	...	...
Seychelles	25	•	•	•	•	•	•	•	•	•	•	•	•	•	•	•	•	•
Sierra Leone	14	•	•	•	•	•	•	•	•	•	•	...	...	...	...	...	...	...
Somalia - Somalie	7	•	•	...	•	•	•	•	...	...	...	...	...	...	...	...	...	...
South Africa - Afrique du Sud	26	•	•	•	•	•	•	•	•	•	•	•	•	•	•	•	...	...
Sudan - Soudan	9	•	•	...	•	•	•	•	•	...	...	...	...	...	...	...	...	...
Swaziland	15	•	•	•	•	•	•	•	•	•	•	...	•	•	...	...	...	...
Togo	4	•	•	...	...	•	...	...	•	...	...	...	...	...	...	...	...	...
Tunisia - Tunisie	17	•	•	•	•	•	•	•	•	•	•	...	•	•	...	•	...	...
Uganda - Ouganda	9	•	•	...	•	•	•	•	•	•	...	...	...	...	...	...	...	...

Table A. Demographic Yearbook 2009 - 2010 synoptic table: Availability of data by country/area, table and sex, where applicable
Tableau A. Tableau synoptique de l'Annuaire démographique 2009 - 2010 : Disponibilité des données par pays ou zone, tableau et le sexe, si disponible

General topic and table number - Sujet général et numéro de tableau

Continent and country or area / Continent et pays ou zone	Infant and maternal mortality - Mortalité infantile et mortalité liée à la maternité				General mortality - Mortalité générale					Nuptiality and divorces - Nuptialité et divortialité			
	15	16 Total	16 M/F	17	18	19 Total	19 M/F	20	21	22	23	24	25
Total number of countries or areas - Total des pays ou zones	138	110	107	110	170	154	150	63	174	135	111	112	81

AFRICA - AFRIQUE

Continent and country or area	15	16 Total	16 M/F	17	18	19 Total	19 M/F	20	21	22	23	24	25
Algeria - Algérie	...	...	...	...	•	...	...	•	...	...	...	...	...
Angola	...	...	...	...	...	...	...	...	...	...	...	...	...
Benin - Bénin	...	...	...	...	...	...	...	•	...	...	...	...	...
Botswana	•	...	...	...	•	•	•	...	•	•	...	...	...
Burkina Faso	•	...	...	...	•	...	...	•	...	...	...	...	...
Burundi	...	...	...	...	...	...	...	...	...	...	...	...	...
Cameroon - Cameroun	...	...	...	...	...	...	...	...	...	...	...	...	...
Cape Verde - Cap-Vert	...	...	...	...	•	...	...	...	...	...	...	...	...
Central African Republic - République centrafricaine	...	...	...	...	...	...	...	...	...	...	...	...	...
Chad - Tchad	...	...	...	...	...	...	...	...	...	...	...	...	...
Comoros - Comores	...	...	...	...	...	...	...	...	...	...	...	...	...
Congo	...	...	...	...	...	...	...	...	...	...	...	...	...
Côte d'Ivoire	...	...	...	...	...	...	...	•	...	...	...	...	...
Democratic Republic of the Congo - République démocratique du Congo	...	...	...	...	...	...	...	•	...	...	...	...	...
Djibouti	...	...	...	...	...	...	...	•	...	...	...	...	...
Egypt - Égypte	•	•	•	•	•	•	•	•	•	•	•	•	•
Equatorial Guinea - Guinée équatoriale	...	...	...	...	...	...	...	...	...	...	...	...	...
Eritrea - Érythrée	...	...	...	...	...	...	...	...	...	...	...	...	...
Ethiopia - Éthiopie	...	...	...	...	•	...	...	...	...	...	...	...	...
Gabon	...	...	...	...	...	...	...	...	...	...	...	...	...
Gambia - Gambie	...	...	...	...	...	...	...	...	...	...	...	...	...
Ghana	•	...	...	...	...	...	...	•	...	...	...	...	...
Guinea - Guinée	...	...	...	...	...	...	...	•	...	...	...	...	...
Guinea-Bissau - Guinée-Bissau	...	...	...	...	...	...	...	•	...	...	...	...	...
Kenya	•	...	...	...	•	•	•	...	•	...	...	...	...
Lesotho	...	...	...	...	...	...	...	•	...	...	...	...	...
Liberia - Libéria	...	...	...	...	...	...	...	...	...	...	...	...	...
Libya - Libye	...	...	...	...	•	•	...	...	•	...	...	...	...
Madagascar	...	...	...	...	...	...	...	•	...	...	...	...	...
Malawi	...	...	...	...	•	...	...	...	...	...	...	...	...
Mali	...	...	...	...	...	...	...	...	...	...	...	...	...
Mauritania - Mauritanie	...	...	...	...	...	...	...	•	...	...	...	...	...
Mauritius - Maurice	•	•	•	•	•	•	•	...	•	•	•	•	•
Mayotte	...	...	...	...	...	...	...	...	...	...	...	...	...
Morocco - Maroc	...	•	•	...	•	...	...	•	...	...	...	...	...
Mozambique	...	...	...	...	...	...	...	...	...	...	...	...	...
Namibia - Namibie	...	...	...	...	•	•	•	...	•	...	...	...	...
Niger	...	...	...	...	•	...	...	...	...	...	...	...	...
Nigeria - Nigéria	...	...	...	...	...	...	...	...	...	...	...	...	...
Réunion	•	•	•	...	•	•	•	...	•	•	•	•	...
Rwanda	...	...	...	...	•	...	...	...	•	...	...	...	...
Saint Helena ex. dep. - Sainte-Hélène sans dép.	•	•	•	...	•	•	•	...	•	•	...	...	...
Saint Helena: Ascension - Sainte-Hélène: Ascension	...	...	...	...	...	...	...	...	...	...	...	...	...
Saint Helena: Tristan da Cunha - Sainte-Hélène: Tristan da Cunha	...	...	...	...	...	...	...	...	...	...	...	...	...
Sao Tome and Principe - Sao Tomé-et-Principe	...	...	...	...	...	...	...	•	...	...	...	...	...
Senegal - Sénégal	•	...	...	...	•	...	...	...	...	...	...	...	...
Seychelles	•	•	•	...	•	...	...	...	•	...	...	...	...
Sierra Leone	•	...	...	...	•	...	...	•	...	...	...	...	...
Somalia - Somalie	...	...	...	...	...	...	...	...	...	...	...	...	...
South Africa - Afrique du Sud	•	...	...	...	•	•	•	...	•	•	•	•	•
Sudan - Soudan	...	...	...	...	•	•	•	...	•	...	...	...	...
Swaziland	...	...	...	...	•	•	•	...	•	...	...	...	...
Togo	...	...	...	...	...	...	...	...	...	...	...	...	...
Tunisia - Tunisie	...	...	...	...	•	...	...	...	•	•	•	•	...
Uganda - Ouganda	...	...	...	...	...	...	...	...	...	...	...	...	...

Table A. Demographic Yearbook 2009 - 2010 synoptic table: Availability of data by country/area, table and sex, where applicable
Tableau A. Tableau synoptique de l'Annuaire démographique 2009 - 2010 : Disponibilité des données par pays ou zone, tableau et le sexe, si disponible (continued - suite)

Continent and country or area / Continent et pays ou zone	Table totals	Summary - Apercu 3 Total	3 M/F	4	5	Population 6 Total¹	6 M/F	7 Total	7 M/F	8 Total	8 M/F	9	Fertility - Natalité 10 Total	10 M/F	11	Foetal mortality - Mortalité foetale 12	13	14
AFRICA - AFRIQUE																		
United Republic of Tanzania - République Unie de Tanzanie	7	•	•	...	•	•	•	•	•	...	...	...	...	...	...	...	...	...
Western Sahara - Sahara occidental	3	•	•	...	•	•	•	...	...	...	...	...	...	...	...	...	...	...
Zambia - Zambie	12	•	•	•	•	•	•	•	•	•	...	...	...	...	...	...	...	...
Zimbabwe	13	•	•	...	•	•	•	•	•	•	•	...	...	...	...	...	...	...
AMERICA, NORTH - AMÉRIQUE DU NORD																		
Anguilla	21	•	•	•	•	•	•	•	•	•	•	•	•	•	...	...	•	...
Antigua and Barbuda - Antigua-et-Barbuda	17	•	•	•	•	•	•	•	•	•	•	•	...	...	...	...	•	...
Aruba	25	•	•	•	•	•	•	•	•	•	•	•	•	•	•	...	...	...
Bahamas	25	•	...	•	•	•	•	•	•	•	•	•	•	•	•	•	•	...
Barbados - Barbade	21	•	•	•	•	•	•	•	•	•	•	•	•	...	...	...	•	...
Belize	14	•	•	...	•	•	•	•	•	•	•	...	...	...	...	...	...	...
Bermuda - Bermudes	26	•	•	•	•	•	•	•	•	•	•	•	•	•	•	...	...	...
British Virgin Islands - Îles Vierges britanniques	10	•	•	...	•	•	•	•	...	...	•	...	...	...	...	...	...	...
Canada	29	•	•	•	•	•	•	•	•	•	•	•	•	•	•	•	•	...
Cayman Islands - Îles Caïmanes	21	•	•	•	•	•	•	•	•	...	•	•	•	•	...	...	...	...
Costa Rica	29	•	•	•	•	•	•	•	•	•	•	•	•	•	•	•	•	...
Cuba	29	•	•	•	•	•	•	•	•	•	•	•	•	•	•	•	•	...
Dominica - Dominique	20	•	•	•	•	•	•	•	•	...	•	•	•	•	...	...	...	...
Dominican Republic - République dominicaine	24	•	•	•	•	•	•	•	•	•	•	•	•	•	•	...	...	...
El Salvador	27	•	•	•	•	•	•	•	•	•	•	•	•	•	•	•	...	...
Greenland - Groenland	24	•	•	•	•	•	•	•	•	•	•	•	•	•	•	...	...	...
Grenada - Grenade	12	•	•	...	•	•	•	•	...	•	•	•	•	...	...	...	...	...
Guadeloupe	24	•	•	•	•	•	•	•	•	•	•	•	•	•	•	...	...	...
Guatemala	26	•	•	•	•	•	•	•	•	•	•	•	•	•	•	...	...	...
Haiti - Haïti	12	•	•	...	•	•	•	•	•	•	•	...	...	...	...	...	...	...
Honduras	13	•	•	•	•	•	•	•	•	•	•	...	...	...	...	...	...	...
Jamaica - Jamaïque	23	•	•	•	•	•	•	•	•	•	•	•	•	•	...	...	...	...
Martinique	27	•	•	•	•	•	•	•	•	•	•	•	•	•	•	•	•	...
Mexico - Mexique	29	•	•	•	•	•	•	•	•	•	•	...	•	•	•	•	•	...
Montserrat	11	•	•	•	•	•	•	•	•	•	•	•	•	...	...	...	...	...
Netherlands Antilles - Antilles néerlandaises	22	•	•	•	•	•	•	•	•	•	•	•	•	•	...	...	...	...
Nicaragua	22	•	•	•	•	•	•	•	•	•	•	•	•	•	•	...	...	...
Panama	28	•	•	•	•	•	•	•	•	•	•	•	•	•	•	...	...	...
Puerto Rico - Porto Rico	27	•	...	•	•	•	•	•	•	•	•	•	•	•	•	•	...	...
Saint Kitts and Nevis - Saint-Kitts-et-Nevis	12	•	•	...	•	•	•	•	•	...	...	•	•	...	...	...	...	...
Saint Lucia - Sainte-Lucie	18	•	•	•	•	•	•	•	•	...	•	•	•	•	...	...	...	...
Saint Pierre and Miquelon - Saint Pierre-et-Miquelon	9	•	•	...	...	•	•	•	•	•	...	...	...	...	...	...	...	...
Saint Vincent and the Grenadines - Saint-Vincent-et-les Grenadines	24	•	•	•	•	•	•	•	•	•	•	•	•	•	•	...	...	...
Trinidad and Tobago - Trinité-et-Tobago	24	•	•	•	•	•	•	•	•	•	...	•	•	•	...	...	...	...
Turks and Caicos Islands - Îles Turques et Caïques	26	•	•	•	•	•	•	•	•	•	•	•	•	•	...	•	•	•
United States of America - États-Unis d'Amérique	22	•	...	•	•	•	•	•	•	•	•	•	•	•	•	•	...	...
United States Virgin Islands - Îles Vierges américaines	16	•	•	•	•	•	•	•	•	•	•	...	...	...	...	...	...	...
AMERICA, SOUTH - AMÉRIQUE DU SUD																		
Argentina - Argentine	22	•	•	•	•	•	•	•	•	•	•	•	•	•	...	...	•	...
Bolivia (Plurinational State of) - Bolivie (État plurinational de)	14	•	•	•	•	•	•	•	•	•	•	•	...	...	...	...	...	...
Brazil - Brésil	27	•	•	•	•	•	•	•	•	•	•	•	•	•	•	...	...	...
Chile - Chili	29	•	•	•	•	•	•	•	•	•	•	•	•	•	•	•	•	...
Colombia - Colombie	23	•	•	•	•	•	•	•	•	•	•	•	•	•	...	...	...	...
Ecuador - Équateur	24	•	...	•	•	•	•	•	•	•	•	•	•	•	...	...	...	...

General topic and table number - Sujet général et numéro de tableau

Continent and country or area / Continent et pays ou zone	Infant and maternal mortality - Mortalité infantile et mortalité liée à la maternité				General mortality - Mortalité générale					Nuptiality and divorces - Nuptialité et divortialité			
	15	16 Total	16 M/F	17	18	19 Total	19 M/F	20	21	22	23	24	25

AFRICA - AFRIQUE

United Republic of Tanzania - République Unie de Tanzanie	...	...	...	...	...	...	...	...	...	...	...	...	...
Western Sahara - Sahara occidental	...	...	...	...	...	...	...	...	...	...	...	...	...
Zambia - Zambie	...	...	...	...	•	...	...	...	...	...	...	...	...
Zimbabwe	...	...	...	...	•	•	•	•	...	...	...	...	...

AMERICA, NORTH - AMÉRIQUE DU NORD

Anguilla	•	...	...	•	•	•	•	...	•	•	•	•	...
Antigua and Barbuda - Antigua-et-Barbuda	•	...	...	•	•	•	•	...	•	•	•	•	...
Aruba	•	•	•	•	•	•	...	...	•	•	•	•	•
Bahamas	•	•	•	•	•	•	•	...	•	•	•	•	...
Barbados - Barbade	•	•	•	•	•	•	•	...	•	•	•	•	...
Belize	•	•	•	•	•	•	•	...	•	•	•	•	...
Bermuda - Bermudes	•	•	•	•	•	•	•	...	•	•	•	•	•
British Virgin Islands - Îles Vierges britanniques	...	...	...	•	•	•	...	...	•	•	•	•	...
Canada	•	•	•	•	•	•	•	•	•	•	•	•	•
Cayman Islands - Îles Caïmanes	•	•	•	•	•	•	...	...	•	•	•	•	...
Costa Rica	•	•	•	•	•	•	•	...	•	•	•	•	•
Cuba	•	•	•	•	•	•	•	...	•	•	•	•	•
Dominica - Dominique	•	...	...	•	•	•	•	...	•	•	•	•	...
Dominican Republic - République dominicaine	•	...	...	•	•	•	•	...	•	•	•	•	...
El Salvador	•	...	...	•	•	•	...	...	•	•	•	•	...
Greenland - Groenland	•	•	•	...	•	•	•	...	•	•	•	•	...
Grenada - Grenade	•	...	...	•	...	•	•	...	...	•	•	•	...
Guadeloupe	...	...	...	•	•	•	•	...	•	•	•	•	...
Guatemala	•	•	•	•	•	•	•	...	•	•	•	•	...
Haiti - Haïti	...	...	...	...	•	•	...	...	...	•	•	•	...
Honduras	•	...	...	•	•	...	...	...	...	•	•	•	...
Jamaica - Jamaïque	•	...	...	•	•	•	•	...	•	•	•	•	•
Martinique	•	•	•	•	•	•	•	...	•	•	•	•	...
Mexico - Mexique	•	•	•	•	•	•	•	...	•	•	•	•	•
Montserrat	•	•	•	•	•	•	•	...	•	•	•	•	...
Netherlands Antilles - Antilles néerlandaises	•	•	•	•	•	•	•	...	•	•	•	•	...
Nicaragua	•	•	•	•	•	•	•	...	•	•	•	•	...
Panama	•	•	•	•	•	•	•	...	•	•	•	•	•
Puerto Rico - Porto Rico	•	•	•	•	•	•	•	...	•	•	•	•	•
Saint Kitts and Nevis - Saint-Kitts-et-Nevis	...	...	...	•	•	•	•	...	•	•	•	•	...
Saint Lucia - Sainte-Lucie	...	...	...	•	•	•	•	...	•	•	•	•	•
Saint Pierre and Miquelon - Saint Pierre-et-Miquelon	...	...	...	•	...	...	...	...	•	•	•	•	...
Saint Vincent and the Grenadines - Saint-Vincent-et-les Grenadines	•	•	•	•	•	•	•	...	•	•	•	•	...
Trinidad and Tobago - Trinité-et-Tobago	...	•	•	•	•	•	•	...	•	•	•	•	...
Turks and Caicos Islands - Îles Turques et Caïques	•	...	...	•	•	•	•	...	•	•	•	•	...
United States of America - États-Unis d'Amérique	•	•	•	•	•	•	•	•	•	•	...	...	•
United States Virgin Islands - Îles Vierges américaines	•	...	...	•	•	•	•	...	•	•	•	•	...

AMERICA, SOUTH - AMÉRIQUE DU SUD

Argentina - Argentine	•	•	•	•	•	•	•	•	•	...	...	•	•
Bolivia (Plurinational State of) - Bolivie (État plurinational de)	...	...	...	•	...	...	...	...	•	...	...	•	...
Brazil - Brésil	•	•	•	•	•	•	•	...	•	•	•	•	•
Chile - Chili	•	•	•	•	•	•	•	...	•	•	•	•	•
Colombia - Colombie	•	•	•	•	•	•	•	...	•	•	•	•	...
Ecuador - Équateur	•	•	•	•	•	•	•	...	•	•	•	•	•

Table A. Demographic Yearbook 2009 - 2010 synoptic table: Availability of data by country/area, table and sex, where applicable

Tableau A. Tableau synoptique de l'Annuaire démographique 2009 - 2010 : Disponibilité des données par pays ou zone, tableau et le sexe, si disponible (continued - suite)

General topic and table number - Sujet général et numéro de tableau

Continent and country or area / Continent et pays ou zone	Table totals	Summary - Apercu 3 Total	M/F	4	5	Population 6 Total[1]	M/F	7 Total	M/F	8 Total	M/F	9	Fertility - Natalité 10 Total	M/F	11	Foetal mortality - Mortalité foetale 12	13	14
AMERICA, SOUTH - AMÉRIQUE DU SUD																		
Falkland Islands (Malvinas) - Îles Falkland (Malvinas)	10	•	•	•	...	•	•	•	•	•	•	•	...	...	•	...	...	...
French Guiana - Guyane française	27	•	•	•	•	•	•	•	•	•	•	•	•	•	•	•	•	...
Guyana	14	•	•	•	•	•	•	•	•	•	•	•	...	...	•	•	...	...
Paraguay	23	•	•	•	•	•	•	•	•	•	•	•	•	•	•	•	•	...
Peru - Pérou	23	•	•	•	•	•	•	•	•	•	•	•	•	•	•	•	•	...
Suriname	23	•	•	•	•	•	•	•	•	•	•	•	•	•	•	•	•	...
Uruguay	26	•	•	•	•	•	•	•	•	•	•	•	•	•	•	•	...	...
Venezuela (Bolivarian Republic of) - Venezuela (République bolivarienne du)	26	•	•	•	•	•	•	•	•	•	•	...	•	•	•	•	...	...
ASIA - ASIE																		
Afghanistan	11	•	•	•	•	•	•	•	•	•	•	•	...	...	...	...	...	...
Armenia - Arménie	30	•	•	•	•	•	•	•	•	•	•	•	•	•	•	•	•	•
Azerbaijan - Azerbaïdjan	29	•	...	•	•	•	•	•	•	•	•	•	•	•	•	•	•	•
Bahrain - Bahreïn	28	•	•	•	•	•	•	•	•	•	•	•	•	•	•	•	•	...
Bangladesh	14	•	•	•	•	•	•	•	•	•	•	...	...	...	•	•	•	...
Bhutan - Bhoutan	14	•	•	...	•	•	•	•	•	•	•	•	...	...	•	•	•	...
Brunei Darussalam - Brunéi Darussalam	24	•	•	•	•	•	•	•	•	•	•	•	•	•	•	•	•	•
Cambodia - Cambodge	11	•	•	•	•	•	•	•	•	•	•	•	...	...	•	•	...	...
China - Chine[2]	15	•	•	•	•	•	•	•	•	•	•	•	•	•	•	•	•	•
China, Hong Kong SAR - Chine, Hong Kong RAS	28	•	...	•	•	•	•	•	•	•	•	•	•	•	•	•	•	•
China, Macao SAR - Chine, Macao RAS	27	•	•	•	•	•	•	•	•	•	•	•	•	•	•	•	•	•
Cyprus - Chypre	25	•	•	•	•	•	•	•	•	•	•	...	•	•	•	•	•	...
Democratic People's Republic of Korea - République populaire démocratique de Corée	18	•	•	•	•	•	•	•	•	•	•	•	•	•	•	•	...	...
Georgia - Géorgie	27	•	•	•	•	•	•	•	•	•	•	•	•	•	•	•	•	•
India - Inde[3]	14	•	•	•	•	•	•	•	•	•	•	•	•	•	•	•	•	...
Indonesia - Indonésie	13	•	•	•	•	•	•	•	•	•	•	...	...	...	•	•	•	...
Iran (Islamic Republic of) - Iran (République islamique d')	14	•	•	•	•	•	•	•	•	•	•	...	...	•	...	•	•	...
Iraq	14	•	•	•	...	•	•	•	•	•	•	•	•	•	...	...	•	...
Israel - Israël[4]	30	•	•	•	•	•	•	•	•	•	•	•	•	•	•	•	•	•
Japan - Japon	30	•	•	•	•	•	•	•	•	•	•	•	•	•	•	•	•	•
Jordan - Jordanie	16	•	•	•	•	•	•	•	•	•	•	•	•	...	...	...	•	...
Kazakhstan	28	•	•	•	•	•	•	•	•	•	•	•	•	•	•	•	•	...
Kuwait - Koweït	26	•	•	•	•	•	•	•	•	•	•	•	•	•	•	•	...	...
Kyrgyzstan - Kirghizstan	30	•	•	•	•	•	•	•	•	•	•	•	•	•	•	•	•	•
Lao People's Democratic Republic - République démocratique populaire lao	9	•	•	...	•	•	•	•	•	•	•	...	...	...	...	•	...	...
Lebanon - Liban	13	•	•	•	...	•	•	•	•	•	•	•	...	...	...	•	...	...
Malaysia - Malaisie	21	•	•	•	•	•	•	•	•	•	•	...	•	•	•	•	•	...
Maldives	24	•	•	•	•	•	•	•	•	•	•	•	•	•	•	•	•	...
Mongolia - Mongolie	23	•	•	•	•	•	•	•	•	•	•	•	•	•	...	•	•	...
Myanmar	14	•	•	•	•	•	•	•	•	•	•	...	•	•	...	...	...	...
Nepal - Népal	13	•	•	•	•	•	•	•	•	•	•	...	•	•	...	...	...	...
Occupied Palestinian Territory - Territoire palestinien occupé	21	•	•	•	•	•	•	•	•	•	•	•	•	•	•	•	•	...
Oman	23	•	...	•	•	•	•	•	•	•	•	•	•	•	•	•	•	...
Pakistan[5]	20	•	•	•	•	•	•	•	•	•	•	•	•	•	•	•	•	...
Philippines	21	•	•	•	•	•	•	•	•	•	•	•	•	•	•	•	•	...
Qatar	28	•	•	•	•	•	•	•	•	•	•	•	•	•	•	•	•	•
Republic of Korea - République de Corée	28	•	•	•	•	•	•	•	•	•	•	•	•	•	•	•	•	•
Saudi Arabia - Arabie saoudite	19	•	•	•	•	•	•	•	•	•	•	•	•	•	•	•	•	...
Singapore - Singapour	28	•	...	•	•	•	•	•	•	•	•	•	•	•	•	•	•	•
Sri Lanka	19	•	•	•	•	•	•	•	•	•	•	•	•	•	•	•	•	...
Syrian Arab Republic - République arabe syrienne	14	•	•	•	•	•	•	•	•	•	•	•	•	•	...	...	...	...
Tajikistan - Tadjikistan	26	•	•	•	•	•	•	•	•	•	•	•	•	•	...	•	•	•
Thailand - Thaïlande	21	•	•	•	•	•	•	•	•	•	•	•	•	•	•	...	...	...
Timor-Leste	9	•	•	...	•	•	•	•	•	•	•	•	...	...	...	...	...	...

Table A. Demographic Yearbook 2009 - 2010 synoptic table: Availability of data by country/area, table and sex, where applicable
Tableau A. Tableau synoptique de l'Annuaire démographique 2009 - 2010 : Disponibilité des données par pays ou zone, tableau et le sexe, si disponible (continued - suite)

Continent and country or area / Continent et pays ou zone	Infant and maternal mortality - Mortalité infantile et mortalité liée à la maternité				General mortality - Mortalité générale					Nuptiality and divorces - Nuptialité et divortialité			
	15	16 Total	16 M/F	17	18	19 Total	19 M/F	20	21	22	23	24	25
AMERICA, SOUTH - AMÉRIQUE DU SUD													
Falkland Islands (Malvinas) - Îles Falkland (Malvinas)	...	...	...	...	•	...	...	...	...	...	...	...	...
French Guiana - Guyane française	•	•	•	•	•	•	•	•	...	•	•	...	•
Guyana	•	•	...	...	•	•	•	•	...	•	•	...	•
Paraguay	•	•	•	•	•	•	•	•	...	•	•	...	•
Peru - Pérou	•	•	•	•	•	•	•	•	...	•	•	...	•
Suriname	•	•	•	•	•	•	•	•	...	•	•	...	•
Uruguay	•	•	•	•	•	•	•	•	...	•	•	...	•
Venezuela (Bolivarian Republic of) - Venezuela (République bolivarienne du)	•	•	•	•	•	...	•	•	•	•	•	•	•
ASIA - ASIE													
Afghanistan	...	...	...	...	...	...	...	•	...	...	...	...	•
Armenia - Arménie	•	•	•	•	•	•	•	•	•	•	•	•	•
Azerbaijan - Azerbaïdjan	•	•	•	•	•	•	•	•	•	•	•	•	•
Bahrain - Bahreïn	•	•	•	•	•	•	•	...	•	•	•	•	•
Bangladesh	•	...	...	...	•	...	...	•	...	•	•	...	•
Bhutan - Bhoutan	...	...	...	...	•	...	...	•	...	...	...	...	•
Brunei Darussalam - Brunéi Darussalam	•	...	...	•	•	•	•	...	•	•	•	•	•
Cambodia - Cambodge	...	...	...	...	•	...	...	•	...	...	...	...	•
China - Chine[2]	...	...	...	...	•	...	...	•	...	...	...	...	...
China, Hong Kong SAR - Chine, Hong Kong RAS	•	•	•	•	•	•	•	•	•	•	•	•	•
China, Macao SAR - Chine, Macao RAS	•	•	•	•	•	•	•	•	•	•	•	•	•
Cyprus - Chypre	•	•	•	•	•	•	•	•	•	•	•	•	•
Democratic People's Republic of Korea - République populaire démocratique de Corée	•	...	...	...	•	•	•	•	•	•	•	•	•
Georgia - Géorgie	•	•	•	•	•	•	•	•	•	•	•	•	•
India - Inde[3]	•	...	...	...	•	...	...	•	...	•	•	...	•
Indonesia - Indonésie	...	...	...	...	...	...	...	...	...	•	•	...	•
Iran (Islamic Republic of) - Iran (République islamique d')	...	...	...	...	•	...	...	•	...	•	...	...	•
Iraq	•	...	...	...	•	...	...	•	...	•	•	...	•
Israel - Israël[4]	•	•	•	•	•	•	•	•	•	•	•	•	•
Japan - Japon	•	•	•	•	•	•	•	•	•	•	•	•	•
Jordan - Jordanie	...	...	...	...	•	...	...	•	...	•	•	...	•
Kazakhstan	•	•	•	•	•	•	•	•	•	•	•	•	•
Kuwait - Koweït	•	•	•	•	•	•	•	•	•	•	•	•	•
Kyrgyzstan - Kirghizstan	•	•	•	•	•	•	•	•	•	•	•	•	•
Lao People's Democratic Republic - République démocratique populaire lao	...	...	...	...	...	...	...	...	...	...	...	...	...
Lebanon - Liban	•	...	...	...	•	...	...	...	...	•	•	...	...
Malaysia - Malaisie	•	•	•	•	•	•	•	...	•	•	•	•	•
Maldives	•	•	•	17	•	•	•	...	•	•	•	•	•
Mongolia - Mongolie	•	...	...	•	•	•	•	...	•	•	•	•	•
Myanmar	•	...	...	...	•	...	...	•	...	...	...	...	•
Nepal - Népal	•	...	...	...	•	...	...	...	...	...	...	...	...
Occupied Palestinian Territory - Territoire palestinien occupé	•	•	•	...	•	•	•	•	•	•	•	•	•
Oman	•	•	•	...	•	•	•	•	•	•	...	...	•
Pakistan[5]	•	•	•	...	•	•	•	•	...	•	•	...	•
Philippines	•	...	...	...	•	...	...	...	...	•	•	...	•
Qatar	•	...	...	...	•	...	...	...	...	•	•	...	•
Republic of Korea - République de Corée	•	•	•	•	•	•	•	•	•	•	•	•	•
Saudi Arabia - Arabie saoudite	•	...	...	...	•	...	...	...	...	•	•	...	•
Singapore - Singapour	•	•	•	•	•	•	•	•	•	•	•	•	•
Sri Lanka	•	...	...	...	•	...	...	•	...	•	...	...	•
Syrian Arab Republic - République arabe syrienne	•	...	...	...	•	...	...	•	...	•	•	...	•
Tajikistan - Tadjikistan	•	•	•	•	•	•	•	•	•	•	•	•	•
Thailand - Thaïlande	•	•	•	•	•	•	•	•	...	•	•	...	•
Timor-Leste	...	...	...	...	...	...	...	...	...	...	...	...	...

Table A. Demographic Yearbook 2009 - 2010 synoptic table: Availability of data by country/area, table and sex, where applicable

Tableau A. Tableau synoptique de l'Annuaire démographique 2009 - 2010 : Disponibilité des données par pays ou zone, tableau et le sexe, si disponible (continued - suite)

General topic and table number - Sujet général et numéro de tableau

Continent and country or area / Continent et pays ou zone	Table totals	Summary - Aperçu 3 Total	M/F	4	5	Population 6 Total[1]	M/F	7 Total	M/F	8 Total	M/F	9	Fertility - Natalité 10 Total	M/F	11	Foetal mortality - Mortalité foetale 12	13	14
ASIA - ASIE																		
Turkey - Turquie	17	•	•	•	•	•	•	•	•	•	•	...	•	...	...	...	...	...
Turkmenistan - Turkménistan	8	•	•	•	•	•	•	•	•	•	•	...	•	...	...	...	...	...
United Arab Emirates - Émirats arabes unis	20	•	•	•	•	•	•	•	•	•	•	...	•	...	...	...	...	...
Uzbekistan - Ouzbékistan	16	•	•	...	•	•	•	•	•	•	•	...	•	...	...	...	...	...
Viet Nam	15	•	•	•	•	•	•	•	•	•	•	...	•	...	...	...	...	...
Yemen - Yémen	12	•	•	•	•	•	•	•	•	•	•	...	•	...	...	...	...	...
EUROPE																		
Åland Islands - Îles d'Åland	25	•	•	•	•	•	•	•	•	•	•	•	•	•	•	•	•	•
Albania - Albanie	25	•	•	•	•	•	•	•	•	•	•	•	•	•	•	•	•	•
Andorra - Andorre	21	•	•	•	•	•	•	•	•	•	•	•	•	•	•	•	•	•
Austria - Autriche	28	•	•	•	•	•	•	•	•	•	•	•	•	•	•	•	•	•
Belarus - Bélarus	30	•	•	•	•	•	•	•	•	•	•	•	•	•	•	•	•	•
Belgium - Belgique	28	•	•	•	•	•	•	•	•	•	•	•	...	...	•	•	•	•
Bosnia and Herzegovina - Bosnie-Herzégovine	25	•	•	•	•	•	•	•	•	•	•	•	•	•	...	...	•	•
Bulgaria - Bulgarie	30	•	•	•	•	•	•	•	•	•	•	•	•	•	•	•	•	•
Croatia - Croatie	28	•	•	•	•	•	•	•	•	•	•	•	•	•	•	•	•	•
Czech Republic - République tchèque	30	•	•	•	•	•	•	•	•	•	•	•	•	•	•	•	•	•
Denmark - Danemark	30	•	•	•	•	•	•	•	•	•	•	•	•	•	•	•	•	•
Estonia - Estonie	30	•	•	•	•	•	•	•	•	•	•	•	•	•	•	•	•	•
Faeroe Islands - Îles Féroé	22	•	•	•	•	•	•	•	•	•	•	•	•	•	•	...	...	•
Finland - Finlande	30	•	•	•	•	•	•	•	•	•	•	•	•	•	•	•	•	•
France	30	•	•	•	•	•	•	•	•	•	•	•	•	•	•	•	•	•
Germany - Allemagne	30	•	•	•	•	•	•	•	•	•	•	•	•	•	•	•	•	•
Gibraltar	18	•	•	•	•	•	•	•	•	•	•	...	•	•	...	•	•	...
Greece - Grèce	30	•	•	•	•	•	•	•	•	•	•	•	•	•	•	•	•	•
Guernsey - Guernesey	16	•	•	•	•	•	•	•	•	•	•	•	•	•	•	•	•	•
Holy See - Saint-Siège	6	•	...	...	•	•	•	•	•	•	•	...	...	...	...	...	...	...
Hungary - Hongrie	30	•	•	•	•	•	•	•	•	•	•	•	•	•	•	•	•	•
Iceland - Islande	30	•	•	•	•	•	•	•	•	•	•	•	•	•	•	•	•	•
Ireland - Irlande	27	•	•	•	•	•	•	•	•	•	•	•	•	•	•	•	•	•
Isle of Man - Île de Man	17	•	...	•	•	•	•	•	•	•	•	...	•	•	...	•	•	•
Italy - Italie	30	•	•	•	•	•	•	•	•	•	•	•	•	•	•	•	•	•
Jersey	15	•	•	•	•	•	•	•	•	•	•	•	•	•	•	•	•	•
Latvia - Lettonie	30	•	•	•	•	•	•	•	•	•	•	•	•	•	•	•	•	•
Liechtenstein	21	•	•	•	•	•	•	•	•	•	•	•	•	•	•	•	•	•
Lithuania - Lituanie	30	•	•	•	•	•	•	•	•	•	•	•	•	•	•	•	•	•
Luxembourg	27	•	•	•	•	•	•	•	•	•	•	...	•	•	•	•	•	•
Malta - Malte	25	•	•	•	•	•	•	•	•	•	•	•	•	•	•	•	•	•
Monaco	11	•	•	•	...	•	•	•	•	•	•	•	•	•	...	•	•	...
Montenegro - Monténégro	27	•	•	•	•	•	•	•	•	•	•	•	...	...	•	•	•	•
Netherlands - Pays-Bas	27	•	•	•	•	•	•	•	•	•	•	•	•	•	•	...	...	•
Norway - Norvège	30	•	•	•	•	•	•	•	•	•	•	•	•	•	•	•	•	•
Poland - Pologne	30	•	•	•	•	•	•	•	•	•	•	•	•	•	•	•	•	•
Portugal	29	•	•	•	•	•	•	•	•	•	•	•	•	•	•	•	•	...
Republic of Moldova - République de Moldova	29	•	•	•	•	•	•	•	•	•	•	•	•	•	•	...	•	•
Romania - Roumanie	30	•	•	•	•	•	•	•	•	•	•	•	•	•	•	•	•	•
Russian Federation - Fédération de Russie	28	•	•	•	•	•	•	•	•	•	•	•	•	•	...	•	•	•
San Marino - Saint-Marin	25	•	•	•	•	•	•	•	•	•	•	•	•	•	•	•	•	•
Serbia - Serbie	30	•	•	•	•	•	•	•	•	•	•	•	•	•	•	•	•	•
Slovakia - Slovaquie	30	•	•	•	•	•	•	•	•	•	•	•	•	•	•	•	•	•
Slovenia - Slovénie	30	•	•	•	•	•	•	•	•	•	•	•	•	•	•	•	•	•
Spain - Espagne	30	•	•	•	•	•	•	•	•	•	•	•	•	•	•	•	•	•
Svalbard and Jan Mayen Islands - Îles Svalbard et Jan Mayen	3	•	...	...	•	•	...	...	•	...	•	...	...	...	...	...	...	...
Sweden - Suède	30	•	•	•	•	•	•	•	•	•	•	•	•	•	•	•	•	•
Switzerland - Suisse	30	•	•	•	•	•	•	•	•	•	•	•	•	•	•	•	•	•
TFYR of Macedonia - L'ex-R. y. de Macédoine	28	•	•	•	•	•	•	•	•	•	•	•	•	•	•	•	...	...

Table A. Demographic Yearbook 2009 - 2010 synoptic table: Availability of data by country/area, table and sex, where applicable

Tableau A. Tableau synoptique de l'Annuaire démographique 2009 - 2010 : Disponibilité des données par pays ou zone, tableau et le sexe, si disponible (continued - suite)

Continent and country or area / Continent et pays ou zone	15	16 Total	16 M/F	17	18	19 Total	19 M/F	20	21	22	23	24	25
ASIA - ASIE													
Turkey - Turquie	•	...	...	...	•	...	...	•	•	•	•	•	•
Turkmenistan - Turkménistan	...	...	...	...	•	...	...	...	...	...	...	...	...
United Arab Emirates - Émirats arabes unis	•	...	...	...	•	...	...	•	•	•	...	...	•
Uzbekistan - Ouzbékistan	...	•	•	•	•	...	...	•	•	•	•	...	...
Viet Nam	•	...	...	...	•	...	...	•	...	...	...	...	...
Yemen - Yémen	...	...	...	...	•	...	...	•	...	...	...	...	...
EUROPE													
Åland Islands - Îles d'Åland	•	...	...	•	•	...	•	•	•	•	•	•	•
Albania - Albanie	•	...	...	•	•	...	•	•	•	•	•	•	...
Andorra - Andorre	•	...	...	...	•	...	•	•	•	•	•	•	•
Austria - Autriche	•	•	•	•	•	•	•	•	•	•	•	•	•
Belarus - Bélarus	•	•	•	•	•	•	•	•	•	•	•	•	•
Belgium - Belgique	•	•	•	•	•	•	•	•	•	•	•	•	•
Bosnia and Herzegovina - Bosnie-Herzégovine	•	...	...	...	•	...	•	•	...	•	•	•	•
Bulgaria - Bulgarie	•	•	•	•	•	•	•	•	•	•	•	•	•
Croatia - Croatie	•	•	•	•	•	•	•	•	•	•	•	•	•
Czech Republic - République tchèque	•	•	•	•	•	•	•	•	•	•	•	•	•
Denmark - Danemark	•	•	•	•	•	•	•	•	•	•	•	•	•
Estonia - Estonie	•	•	•	•	•	•	•	•	•	•	•	•	•
Faeroe Islands - Îles Féroé	...	...	...	...	•	•	•	•	•	•	•	...	...
Finland - Finlande	•	•	•	•	•	•	•	•	•	•	•	•	•
France	•	•	•	•	•	•	•	•	•	•	•	•	•
Germany - Allemagne	•	•	•	•	•	•	•	•	•	•	•	•	•
Gibraltar	•	•	•	...	•	•	•	•	•	•	•	•	•
Greece - Grèce	•	•	•	•	•	•	•	•	•	•	•	•	•
Guernsey - Guernesey	...	...	...	...	•	...	...	•	...	...	...	...	...
Holy See - Saint-Siège	...	...	...	...	...	...	...	...	...	...	...	...	...
Hungary - Hongrie	•	•	•	•	•	•	•	•	•	•	•	•	•
Iceland - Islande	•	•	•	•	•	•	•	•	•	•	•	•	•
Ireland - Irlande	•	•	•	•	•	•	•	•	•	•	•	•	•
Isle of Man - Île de Man	...	•	•	•	•	...	...	•	•	•	•	•	•
Italy - Italie	•	•	•	•	•	•	•	•	•	•	•	•	•
Jersey	•	...	...	...	•	...	...	•	...	...	...	...	...
Latvia - Lettonie	•	•	•	•	•	•	•	•	•	•	•	•	•
Liechtenstein	•	•	•	•	•	•	•	•	•	•	•	•	•
Lithuania - Lituanie	•	•	•	•	•	•	•	•	•	•	•	•	•
Luxembourg	•	•	•	•	•	•	•	•	•	•	•	•	•
Malta - Malte	•	•	•	•	•	•	•	•	...	•	•	•	•
Monaco	...	...	...	...	•	...	...	...	...	...	...	...	...
Montenegro - Monténégro	•	•	•	...	•	•	•	•	•	•	•	•	•
Netherlands - Pays-Bas	•	•	•	•	•	•	•	•	•	•	•	•	•
Norway - Norvège	•	•	•	•	•	•	•	•	•	•	•	•	•
Poland - Pologne	•	•	•	•	•	•	•	•	•	•	•	•	•
Portugal	•	•	•	•	•	•	•	•	•	•	•	•	•
Republic of Moldova - République de Moldova	•	•	•	•	•	•	•	•	•	•	•	•	•
Romania - Roumanie	•	•	•	•	•	•	•	•	•	•	•	•	•
Russian Federation - Fédération de Russie	•	•	•	•	•	•	•	•	•	•	•	•	...
San Marino - Saint-Marin	•	•	•	•	•	•	•	•	•	•	•	...	...
Serbia - Serbie	•	•	•	•	•	•	•	•	•	•	•	•	•
Slovakia - Slovaquie	•	•	•	•	•	•	•	•	•	•	•	•	•
Slovenia - Slovénie	•	•	•	•	•	•	•	•	•	•	•	•	•
Spain - Espagne	•	•	•	•	•	•	•	•	•	•	•	•	•
Svalbard and Jan Mayen Islands - Îles Svalbard et Jan Mayen	...	...	...	...	...	...	...	...	...	...	...	...	...
Sweden - Suède	•	•	•	•	•	•	•	•	•	•	•	•	•
Switzerland - Suisse	•	•	•	•	•	•	•	•	•	•	•	•	•
TFYR of Macedonia - L'ex-R. y. de Macédoine	•	•	•	•	•	•	•	•	•	•	•	•	•

Table A. Demographic Yearbook 2009 - 2010 synoptic table: Availability of data by country/area, table and sex, where applicable

Tableau A. Tableau synoptique de l'Annuaire démographique 2009 - 2010 : Disponibilité des données par pays ou zone, tableau et le sexe, si disponible (continued - suite)

Continent and country or area / Continent et pays ou zone	Table totals	Summary - Aperçu 3 Total	3 M/F	4	5	Population 6 Total[1]	6 M/F	7 Total	7 M/F	8 Total	8 M/F	9	Fertility - Natalité 10 Total	10 M/F	11	Foetal mortality - Mortalité foetale 12	13	14
EUROPE																		
Ukraine	29	•	•	•	•	•	•	•	•	•	•	•	•	...	•	•	•	•
United Kingdom of Great Britain and Northern Ireland - Royaume-Uni de Grande-Bretagne et d'Irlande du Nord	29	•	•	•	•	•	•	•	•	•	•	•	•	•	•	•	•	•
OCEANIA - OCÉANIE																		
American Samoa - Samoas américaines	16	•	•	•	•	•	...	•	•	•	•	•	•	...	...	...	•	...
Australia - Australie	28	•	•	•	•	•	•	•	•	•	•	•	•	...	...	...	•	...
Cook Islands - Îles Cook	14	•	•	•	•	•	•	•	•	...	•	•	•	...	•	...	...	...
Fiji - Fidji	19	•	•	•	•	•	•	•	•	...	•	•	•	...	•	•	...	...
French Polynesia - Polynésie française	14	•	...	•	•	•	•	•	•	•	•	•	•	...	...	•	...	...
Guam	20	•	•	•	•	•	•	•	•	•	•	•	•	...	•	...	...	...
Kiribati	9	•	•	...	...	•	•	•	•	...	•	•	•	...	...	...	...	...
Marshall Islands - Îles Marshall	16	•	•	•	•	•	•	•	•	•	•	•	•	...	•	...	...	...
Micronesia (Federated States of) - Micronésie (États fédérés de)	13	•	•	•	•	•	•	•	•	...	•	•	•	...	...	...	...	...
Nauru	13	•	•	•	•	•	•	•	•	...	•	•	•	...	...	...	...	...
New Caledonia - Nouvelle-Calédonie	23	•	•	•	•	•	•	•	•	•	•	•	•	...	•	...	...	...
New Zealand - Nouvelle-Zélande	30	•	•	•	•	•	•	•	•	•	•	•	•	•	•	•	•	•
Niue - Nioué	17	•	•	•	•	•	•	•	•	...	•	•	•	...	•	...	...	...
Norfolk Island - Île Norfolk	12	•	•	•	•	•	•	•	•	...	•	•	•	...	...	...	...	...
Northern Mariana Islands - Îles Mariannes septentrionales	18	•	•	•	•	•	•	•	•	...	•	•	•	...	•	...	...	...
Palau - Palaos	19	•	•	•	•	•	•	•	•	...	•	•	•	•	•	...	...	...
Papua New Guinea - Papouasie-Nouvelle-Guinée	10	•	•	...	•	•	•	•	•	•	...	•	•	...	...	...	...	...
Pitcairn	13	•	...	•	•	•	•	•	•	•	...	•	•	...	...	...	...	...
Samoa	16	•	•	•	•	•	•	•	•	•	...	•	•	...	•	...	...	...
Solomon Islands - Îles Salomon	9	•	•	...	•	•	•	•	•	•	...	•	•	...	...	...	...	...
Tokelau - Tokélaou	6	•	•	...	...	•	•	•	•	...	•	•	•	...	...	...	...	...
Tonga	17	•	•	•	•	•	•	•	•	•	•	•	•	...	•	...	...	...
Tuvalu	16	•	•	•	•	•	•	•	•	•	•	•	•	...	•	...	...	...
Vanuatu	9	•	•	...	•	•	•	•	•	•	...	•	•	...	...	...	...	...
Wallis and Futuna Islands - Îles Wallis et Futuna	14	•	•	•	...	•	•	...	...	•	•	•	•	...	...	...	...	...

Table A. Demographic Yearbook 2009 - 2010 synoptic table: Availability of data by country/area, table and sex, where applicable
Tableau A. Tableau synoptique de l'Annuaire démographique 2009 - 2010 : Disponibilité des données par pays ou zone, tableau et le sexe, si disponible (continued - suite)

Continent and country or area / Continent et pays ou zone	General topic and table number - Sujet général et numéro de tableau												
	Infant and maternal mortality - Mortalité infantile et mortalité liée à la maternité				General mortality - Mortalité générale					Nuptiality and divorces - Nuptialité et divortialité			
	15	16 Total	16 M/F	17	18	19 Total	19 M/F	20	21	22	23	24	25
EUROPE													
Ukraine	•	•	•	•	•	•	•	•	•	•	•	•	•
United Kingdom of Great Britain and Northern Ireland - Royaume-Uni de Grande-Bretagne et d'Irlande du Nord	•	•	•	•	•	•	•	•	•	•	...	•	•
OCEANIA - OCÉANIE													
American Samoa - Samoas américaines	•	...	...	...	•	•	•	•	•	•	•	•	...
Australia - Australie	•	•	•	•	•	•	•	•	•	•	•	•	•
Cook Islands - Îles Cook	•	...	...	...	•	•	•	•	•	•	•	•	...
Fiji - Fidji	...	•	...	...	•	•	•	•	•	•	...	...	...
French Polynesia - Polynésie française	...	•	...	...	•	•	•	•	•	•	...	•	...
Guam	•	...	...	...	•	•	•	•	•	•	...	•	...
Kiribati	...	...	...	...	•	...	...	...	•	...	...	...	...
Marshall Islands - Îles Marshall	...	...	...	...	•	•	•	•	•	•	...	...	...
Micronesia (Federated States of) - Micronésie (États fédérés de)	...	...	...	...	...	...	...	...	...	...	...	...	...
Nauru	...	...	...	...	...	...	...	•	...	...	...	...	...
New Caledonia - Nouvelle-Calédonie	•	...	...	...	•	•	•	•	•	•	•	•	...
New Zealand - Nouvelle-Zélande	•	•	•	•	•	•	•	•	•	•	•	•	•
Niue - Nioué	...	...	...	...	•	•	•	•	•	•	...	...	...
Norfolk Island - Île Norfolk	...	...	...	...	•	...	...	•	...	...	...	...	...
Northern Mariana Islands - Îles Mariannes septentrionales	•	...	...	...	•	...	...	•	•	•	•	•	...
Palau - Palaos	•	...	...	...	•	...	...	•	...	...	...	...	...
Papua New Guinea - Papouasie-Nouvelle-Guinée	•	...	...	...	•	...	...	•	...	...	...	...	...
Pitcairn	•	...	...	...	•	...	...	•	...	...	...	...	...
Samoa	...	...	...	...	•	...	...	•	•	•	•	•	...
Solomon Islands - Îles Salomon	...	...	...	...	•	...	...	•	...	...	...	...	...
Tokelau - Tokélaou	...	...	...	...	•	...	...	•	...	...	...	...	...
Tonga	...	...	...	...	•	...	...	•	•	•	•	•	...
Tuvalu	...	...	...	...	•	...	...	•	•	•	•	...	...
Vanuatu	...	...	...	...	•	...	...	•	...	...	...	...	...
Wallis and Futuna Islands - Îles Wallis et Futuna	...	...	...	...	•	•	•	•	•	•	•	...	...

FOOTNOTES - NOTES

* Data presented in the table. - Les données présentées dans le tableau.

... Data not available. - Données non disponibles.

1 Including countries with data on total population only and without data on urban population. The number of countries with data on urban population for both sexes and also by sex presented in this issue of the Demographic Yearbook is 143 and 131 respectively. - Y compris les pays avec des données sur la population totale mais pas sur la population urbaine. Le nombre de pays disposant de données sur la population urbaine pour les deux sexes et aussi par sexe présentées dans cette édition de l'Annuaire démographique est de 143 et 131 respectivement.

2 For statistical purposes, the data for China do not include those for the Hong Kong Special Administrative Region (Hong Kong SAR), Macao special Administrative Region (Macao SAR) and Taiwan province of China. - Pour la présentation des statistiques, les données pour Chine ne comprennent pas la Région Administrative Spéciale de Hong Kong (Hong Kong RAS), la Région Administrative Spéciale de Macao (Macao RAS) et Taïwan province de Chine.

3 Including data for the Indian-held part of Jammu and Kashmir, the final status of which has not yet been determined. - Y compris les données pour la partie du Jammu et du Cachemire occupée par l'Inde dont le statut définitif n'a pas encore été déterminé.

4 Including data for East Jerusalem and Israeli residents in certain other territories under occupation by Israeli military forces since June 1967. - Y compris les données pour Jérusalem-Est et les résidents israéliens dans certains autres territoires occupés depuis 1967 par les forces armées israéliennes.

5 Excluding data for the Pakistan-held part of Jammu and Kashmir, the final status of which has not yet been determined. - Non compris les données concernant la partie du Jammu et Cachemire occupée par le Pakistan dont le statut définitif n'a pas été déterminé.

Table 1

Table 1 presents for the world, major areas and regions estimates of the order of magnitude of population size, rates of population increase, crude birth and death rates, surface area as well as population density.

Description of variables: Estimates of world population by major areas and by regions are presented for 1950, 1960, 1970, 1980, 1990, 2000 and 2010. Average annual percentage rates of population growth, crude birth and crude death rates are shown for the period from 2005 to 2010. Surface area in square kilometers and population density estimates relate to 2010.

All population estimates and rates presented in this table were prepared by the Population Division of the United Nations, and have been published in the *2010 Revision of World Population Prospects*[1].

The scheme of regionalization used for these estimates is described below. Although some continental totals are given, and all can be derived, the basic scheme presents six major areas that are so drawn as to obtain greater homogeneity in sizes of population, types of demographic circumstances and accuracy of demographic statistics. Five of the major areas are subdivided into a total of 20 regions, which are arranged within the major areas; these regions together with Northern America, which is not subdivided, make a total of 21 regions.

The major areas of Northern America and Latin America are distinguished, rather than the conventional continents of North America and South America, because population trends in the middle American mainland and the Caribbean region more closely resemble those of South America than those of America north of Mexico. Data for the traditional continents of North and South America can be obtained by adding Central America and Caribbean region to Northern America and deducting from Latin America. Latin America, as defined here, has somewhat wider limits than it would be if defined only to include the Spanish-speaking, French-speaking and Portuguese-speaking countries.

The average annual percentage rates of population growth are calculated by the Population Division, United Nations Department of Economic and Social Affairs, using an exponential rate of increase.

Crude birth and crude death rates are expressed in terms of the average annual number of births and deaths, respectively, per 1 000 mid-year population. These rates are estimated.

Surface area totals are estimated by Population Division, United Nations Department of Economic and Social Affairs.

Computation: Density, calculated by the Statistics Division of the United Nations Department of Social and Economic Affairs, is the number of persons in the 2010 total population per square kilometer of total surface area.

Reliability of data: With the exception of surface area, all data are set in *italic* type to indicate their conjectural quality.

Limitations: The estimated orders of magnitude of population and surface area are subject to all the basic limitations set forth in connection with table 3, and to the same qualifications set forth for population and surface area statistics in sections 3 and 2.4 of the Technical Notes, respectively.

Likewise, rates of population increase and density index are affected by the limitations of the original figures. However, it may be noted that, in compiling data for regional and major areas totals, errors in the components may tend to compensate each other and the resulting aggregates may be more reliable than the quality of the individual components would imply.

Because of their estimated character, many of the birth and death rates shown should also be considered only as orders of magnitude, and not as measures of the true level of natality or mortality.

In interpreting the population densities, one should consider that some of the regions include large segments of land that are uninhabitable or barely habitable, and density values calculated as described make no allowance for this, nor for differences in patterns of land settlement.

Composition of macro geographical regions and sub-regions

AFRICA

Eastern Africa
Burundi
Comoros
Djibouti
Eritrea
Ethiopia
Kenya
Madagascar
Malawi
Mauritius
Mayotte
Mozambique
Réunion
Rwanda
Seychelles
Somalia
Uganda
United Republic of Tanzania
Zambia
Zimbabwe

Middle Africa
Angola
Cameroon
Central African Republic
Chad
Congo
Democratic Republic of the
  Congo
Equatorial Guinea
Gabon
Sao Tome and Principe

Northern Africa
Algeria
Egypt
Libyan Arab Jamahiriya
Morocco
Sudan
Tunisia
Western Sahara

Southern Africa
Botswana
Lesotho
Namibia
South Africa
Swaziland

Western Africa
Benin
Burkina Faso
Cape Verde
Côte d'Ivoire
Gambia
Ghana

Guinea
Guinea-Bissau
Liberia
Mali
Mauritania
Niger
Nigeria
Saint Helena
Senegal
Sierra Leone
Togo

ASIA

Eastern Asia
China
China, Hong Kong SAR
China, Macao SAR
Democratic People's
  Republic of Korea
Japan
Mongolia
Republic of Korea

South-central Asia
Afghanistan
Bangladesh
Bhutan
India
Iran (Islamic Republic of)
Kazakhstan
Kyrgyzstan
Maldives
Nepal
Pakistan
Sri Lanka
Tajikistan
Turkmenistan
Uzbekistan

South-eastern Asia
Brunei Darussalam
Cambodia
Indonesia
Lao People's Democratic
  Republic
Malaysia
Myanmar
Philippines
Singapore
Thailand
Timor Leste
Viet Nam

Western Asia
Armenia
Azerbaijan
Bahrain

Cyprus
Georgia
Iraq
Israel
Jordan
Kuwait
Lebanon
Occupied Palestinian Territory
Oman
Qatar
Saudi Arabia
Syrian Arab Republic
Turkey
United Arab Emirates
Yemen

EUROPE

Eastern Europe
Belarus
Bulgaria
Czech Republic
Hungary
Poland
Republic of Moldova
Romania
Russian Federation
Slovakia
Ukraine

Northern Europe
Åland Islands
Denmark
Estonia
Faeroe Islands
Finland
Guernsey
Iceland
Ireland
Isle of Man
Jersey
Latvia
Lithuania
Norway
Sweden
United Kingdom of Great Britain
  and Northern Ireland

Southern Europe
Albania
Andorra
Bosnia and Herzegovina
Croatia
Gibraltar
Greece
Holy See
Italy

Malta
Montenegro
Portugal
San Marino
Serbia
Slovenia
Spain
TFYR of Macedonia

Western Europe
Austria
Belgium
France
Germany
Liechtenstein
Luxembourg
Monaco
Netherlands
Switzerland

LATIN AMERICA and the CARIBBEAN

Caribbean
Anguilla
Antigua and Barbuda
Aruba
Bahamas
Barbados
British Virgin Islands
Cayman Islands
Cuba
Dominica
Dominican Republic
Grenada
Guadaloupe
Haiti
Jamaica
Martinique
Montserrat

Netherlands Antilles
Puerto Rico
Saint Kitts and Nevis
Saint Lucia
Saint Vincent and the
  Grenadines
Trinidad and Tobago
Turks and Caicos Islands
United States Virgin
  Islands

Central America
Belize
Costa Rica
El Salvador
Guatemala
Honduras
Mexico
Nicaragua
Panama

South America
Argentina
Bolivia (Plurinational State of)
Brazil
Chile
Colombia
Ecuador
Falkland Islands (Malvinas)
French Guiana
Guyana
Paraguay
Peru
Suriname
Uruguay
Venezuela (Bolivarian Republic of)

NORTHERN AMERICA

Bermuda

Canada
Greenland
Saint Pierre and Miquelon
United States of America

OCEANIA

Australia and New Zealand
Australia
New Zealand
Norfolk Island

Melanesia
Fiji
New Caledonia
Papua New Guinea
Solomon Islands
Vanuatu

Micronesia
Guam
Kiribati
Marshall Islands
Micronesia (Federated States of)
Nauru
Northern Mariana Islands
Palau

Polynesia
American Samoa
Cook Islands
French Polynesia
Niue
Pitcairn
Samoa
Tokelau
Tonga
Tuvalu
Wallis and Futuna Islands

---

[1] United Nations, Department of Economic and Social Affairs, Population Division (2011). World Population Prospects: The 2010 Revision, DVD Edition – Extended Dataset (United Nations publication, Sales No. E.11.XIII.7).

Tableau 1

Le tableau 1 présente, pour l'ensemble du monde et les grandes zones et régions, des estimations concernant l'ordre de grandeur de la population, les taux d'accroissement démographique, les taux bruts de natalité et de mortalité, la superficie et la densité de peuplement.

Description des variables : des estimations de la population mondiale par grandes zones et régions sont présentées pour 1950, 1960, 1970, 1980, 1990 et 2000 ainsi que pour 2010. Les taux annuels moyens d'accroissement de la population et les taux bruts de natalité et de mortalité portent sur la période allant de 2005 à 2010. Les indications concernant la superficie exprimée en kilomètres carrés et les estimations de la densité de population se rapportent à 2010.

Toutes les estimations de population et les taux de natalité, taux de mortalité et taux annuels d'accroissement de la population qui sont présentés dans le tableau 1 ont été établis par la Division de la population des Nations Unies, et ont été publiés dans la Perspectives de la population mondiale : La révision de 2010[1].

Bien que l'on ait donné certains totaux pour les continents (tous les autres pouvant être calculés), on a réparti le monde en huit grandes zones qui ont été découpées de manière à obtenir une plus grande homogénéité du point de vue des dimensions de population, des types de situations démographiques et de l'exactitude des statistiques démographiques.

Cinq de ces huit grandes zones ont été subdivisées en 20 régions. Avec l'Amérique septentrionale, qui n'est pas subdivisée, on arrive à un total de 21 régions.

Au lieu de faire la distinction classique entre l'Amérique du Nord et l'Amérique du Sud, on a choisi d'opérer une comparaison entre l'Amérique septentrionale et l'Amérique latine, parce que les tendances démographiques dans la partie continentale de l'Amérique centrale et dans la région des Caraïbes se rapprochent davantage de celles de l'Amérique du Sud que de celles de l'Amérique au nord du Mexique. On obtient les données pour les continents traditionnels de l'Amérique du Nord et de l'Amérique du Sud en extrayant les données concernant l'Amérique centrale et les Caraïbes de celles relatives à l'Amérique latine et en les regroupant avec celles relatives à l'Amérique septentrionale. L'Amérique latine ainsi définie a par conséquent des limites plus larges que celles des pays ou zones de langues espagnole, portugaise et française qui constituent l'Amérique latine au sens le plus strict du terme.

La Division de la population a calculé les taux annuels moyens d'accroissement de la population en appliquant un taux d'accroissement exponentiel.

Les taux bruts de natalité et de mortalité représentent respectivement le nombre annuel moyen de naissances et de décès par millier d'habitants en milieu d'année. Ces taux sont estimatifs.

La superficie totale a été estimée par la Division de la population du Département des affaires économiques et sociales.

Calculs : la densité, calculée par la Division de statistique du Département des affaires économiques et sociales, est égale au rapport entre l'effectif total de la population en 2010 et la superficie totale exprimée en kilomètres carrés.

Fiabilité des données : á l'exception des données concernant la superficie, toutes les données sont reproduites en *italique* pour en faire ressortir le caractère conjectural.

Insuffisance des données : les estimations concernant l'ordre de grandeur de la population et la superficie reposent en partie sur les données du tableau 3 ; elles appellent donc toutes les réserves fondamentales formulées à propos de ce tableau, et celles qui ont été respectivement formulées aux sections 3 et 2.4 des Notes techniques en ce qui concerne les statistiques relatives à la population et à la superficie.

Les taux d'accroissement et les indices de densité de la population se ressentent eux aussi des insuffisances inhérentes aux données de base. Toutefois, il est à noter que, lorsque l'on additionne des données par territoire pour obtenir des totaux régionaux et par grandes zones, les erreurs qu'elles comportent arrivent parfois à s'équilibrer, de sorte que les agrégats obtenus peuvent être un peu plus exacts que chacun des éléments dont on est parti.

Vu leur caractère estimatif, nombre des taux de natalité et de mortalité du tableau 1 doivent être considérés uniquement comme des ordres de grandeur et ne sont pas censés mesurer exactement le niveau de la natalité ou de la mortalité.

Parce que les totaux des superficies ont été obtenus en additionnant les chiffres pour chaque pays ou zones, qui apparaissent dans le tableau 3, ils ne comprennent pas les lieux où la population est inférieure à 50 personnes, tels que les régions polaires inhabitées.

Pour interpréter les valeurs de la densité de population, on se souviendra qu'il existe dans certaines des régions de vastes étendues de terres inhabitables ou à peine habitables et que les chiffres calculés selon la méthode indiquée ne tiennent compte ni de ce fait ni des différences de dispersion de la population selon le mode d'habitat.

Composition des grandes zones et régions

AFRIQUE

Afrique orientale
Burundi
Comores
Djibouti
Érythrée
Éthiopie
Kenya
Madagascar
Malawi
Maurice
Mayotte
Mozambique
Ouganda
République-Unie de Tanzanie
Réunion
Rwanda
Seychelles
Somalie
Zambie
Zimbabwe

Afrique centrale
Angola
Cameroun
Congo
Gabon
Guinée équatoriale
République centrafricaine
République démocratique du Congo
Sao Tomé-et-Principe
Tchad

Afrique septentrionale
Algérie
Égypte
Jamahiriya arabe libyenne
Maroc
Sahara occidental
Soudan
Tunisie

Afrique australe
Afrique du Sud
Botswana
Lesotho
Namibie
Swaziland

Afrique occidentale
Bénin
Burkina Faso
Cap-Vert
Côte d'Ivoire
Gambie
Ghana
Guinée
Guinée-Bissau
Libéria
Mali
Mauritanie
Niger
Nigéria
Sainte-Hélène
Sénégal
Sierra Leone
Togo

AMÉRIQUE LATINE ET CARAÏBES

Caraïbes
Anguilla
Antigua-et-Barbuda
Antilles néerlandaises
Aruba
Bahamas
Barbade
Cuba
Dominique
Grenade
Guadeloupe
Haïti
Îles Caïmanes
Îles Turques et Caïques
Îles Vierges américaines

Îles Vierges britanniques
Jamaïque
Martinique
Montserrat
Porto Rico
République dominicaine
Saint-Kitts-et-Nevis
Sainte-Lucie
Saint-Vincent-et-les Grenadines
Trinité-et-Tobago

Amérique centrale
Belize
Costa Rica
El Salvador
Guatemala
Honduras
Mexique
Nicaragua
Panama

Amérique du Sud
Argentine
Bolivie (État plurinational de)
Brésil
Chili
Colombie
Équateur
Guyana
Guyane française
Îles Falkland (Malvinas)
Paraguay
Pérou
Suriname
Uruguay
Venezuela (République bolivarienne du)

AMÉRIQUE SEPTENTRIONALE

Bermudes
Canada
États-Unis d'Amérique

Groenland
Saint-Pierre-et-Miquelon

ASIE

Asie orientale
Chine
Chine, Région administrative
spéciale de Hong Kong
Chine, Région administrative
spéciale de Macao
Japon
Mongolie
République de Corée
République populaire démocratique
de Corée

Asie centrale et Asie du Sud
Afghanistan
Bangladesh
Bhoutan
Inde
Iran (République Islamique d')
Kazakhstan
Kirghizistan
Maldives
Népal
Ouzbékistan
Pakistan
Sri Lanka
Tadjikistan
Turkménistan

Asie du Sud-Est
Brunéi Darussalam
Cambodge
Indonésie
Malaisie
Myanmar
Philippines
République démocratique populaire
lao
Singapour
Thaïlande
Timor-Leste
Viet Nam

Asie occidentale
Arabie saoudite
Arménie
Azerbaïdjan
Bahreïn
Chypre
Émirats arabes unis
Géorgie

Iraq
Israël
Jordanie
Koweït
Liban
Oman
Qatar
République arabe syrienne
Territoire palestinien occupé
Turquie
Yémen

EUROPE

Europe orientale
Bélarus
Bulgarie
Fédération de Russie
Hongrie
Pologne
République de Moldova
République tchèque
Roumanie
Slovaquie
Ukraine

Europe septentrionale
Danemark
Estonie
Finlande
Guernesey
Île de Man
Îles d'Åland
Îles Féroé
Îles Svalbard et Jan Mayen
Irlande
Islande
Jersey
Lettonie
Lituanie
Norvège
Royaume-Uni de Grande-
Bretagne et d'Irlande du
Nord
Suède

Europe méridionale
Albanie
Andorre
Bosnie-Herzégovine
Croatie
Espagne
Gibraltar
Grèce
Italie

L'ex-R. y. de Macédoine
Malte
Monténégro
Portugal
Saint-Marin
Saint-Siège
Serbie
Slovénie

Europe occidentale
Allemagne
Autriche
Belgique
France
Liechtenstein
Luxembourg
Monaco
Pays-Bas
Suisse

OCÉANIE

Australie et Nouvelle-Zélande
Australie
Île Norfolk
Nouvelle-Zélande

Mélanésie
Fidji
Îles Salomon
Nouvelle-Calédonie
Papouasie-Nouvelle-Guinée
Vanuatu

Micronésie
Guam
Îles Mariannes septentrionales
Îles Marshall
Kiribati
Micronésie (États fédérés de)
Nauru
Palaos

Polynésie
Îles Cook
Îles Wallis et Futuna
Nioué
Pitcairn
Polynésie française
Samoa
Samoa américaines
Tokélaou
Tonga
Tuvalu

NOTE

[1] *Organisation des Nations Unies, Département des affaires économiques et sociales, Division de la population (2011). Perspectives de la population mondiale : La révision de 2010, Edition DVD - ensemble de données étendues (publication des Nations Unies, numéro de vente E.11.XIII.7).*

1. Population, rate of increase, birth and death rates, surface area and density for the world, major areas and regions: selected years
Population, taux d'accroissement, taux de natalité et taux de mortalité, superficie et densité pour l'ensemble du monde, les régions macro géographiques et les composantes géographiques : diverses années

Major areas and regions Régions macro géographiques et composantes	Mid-year population estimates - Estimations de population au milieu de l'année (millions)							Annual rate of increase - Taux d'accroissement annuel (%)	Crude birth rate - Taux bruts de natalité	Crude death rate - Taux bruts de mortalité	Surface area (km2) - Superficie (km2) (000s)	Density - Densité[1]
	1950	1960	1970	1980	1990	2000	2010	2005-2010			2010	
WORLD TOTAL - ENSEMBLE DU MONDE	2 532.2	3 038.4	3 696.2	4 453.0	5 306.4	6 122.8	6 895.9	1.2	20	8	136 127	51
AFRICA - AFRIQUE	229.9	286.7	368.1	482.8	635.3	811.1	1 022.2	2.3	36	12	30 312	34
Eastern Africa - Afrique orientale	64.8	81.9	107.6	143.6	192.8	251.6	324.0	2.5	38	12	6 361	51
Middle Africa - Afrique centrale	26.1	32.0	40.7	53.4	71.7	96.2	126.7	2.7	43	16	6 613	19
Northern Africa - Afrique septentrionale	53.0	67.5	86.9	113.1	146.2	176.2	209.5	1.7	24	6	8 525	25
Southern Africa - Afrique méridionale	15.6	19.7	25.5	33.0	42.1	51.4	57.8	1.0	23	15	2 675	22
Western Africa - Afrique occidentale	70.5	85.6	107.4	139.8	182.5	235.7	304.3	2.6	40	14	6 138	50
LATIN AMERICA AND CARIBBEAN - AMÉRIQUE LATIN ET CARAÏBES	167.4	220.1	286.4	362.3	443.0	521.4	590.1	1.2	19	6	20 546	29
Caribbean - Caraïbes	17.1	20.7	25.3	29.7	34.2	38.4	41.6	0.7	19	7	234	178
Central America - Amérique centrale	37.9	51.7	69.6	91.8	113.2	135.6	155.9	1.4	22	5	2 480	63
South America - Amérique méridionale................	112.4	147.7	191.5	240.9	295.6	347.4	392.6	1.1	18	6	17 832	22
NORTHERN AMERICA - AMÉRIQUE SEPTENTRIONALE[2]	171.6	204.3	231.3	254.5	281.2	313.3	344.5	0.9	14	8	21 776	16
ASIA - ASIE[3]	1 403.4	1 707.7	2 135.0	2 637.6	3 199.5	3 719.0	4 164.3	1.1	19	7	31 880	131
Eastern Asia - Asie orientale	672.4	801.5	984.1	1 178.6	1 359.1	1 495.3	1 574.0	0.5	12	7	11 763	134
South Central Asia - Asie centrale méridionale......	507.1	620.0	778.8	986.0	1 246.4	1 515.6	1 764.9	1.4	24	8	10 791	164
South Eastern Asia - Asie méridionale orientale	172.9	219.3	285.2	359.0	445.4	523.8	593.4	1.2	19	7	4 495	132
Western Asia - Asie occidentale[3]	51.0	66.8	86.9	114.0	148.6	184.4	232.0	2.4	24	5	4 831	48
EUROPE[3]	547.3	603.9	655.9	692.9	720.5	726.8	738.2	0.2	11	11	23 049	32
Eastern Europe - Europe orientale......................	220.1	252.8	276.2	294.9	310.5	304.2	294.8	-0.2	11	14	18 814	16
Northern Europe - Europe septentrionale	78.0	81.9	87.4	89.9	92.1	94.3	99.2	0.6	12	10	1 810	55
Southern Europe - Europe méridionale..................	108.3	117.4	126.8	137.7	142.4	145.1	155.2	0.6	10	10	1 317	118
Western Europe - Europe occidentale...................	140.8	151.8	165.5	170.4	175.4	183.1	189.1	0.3	10	9	1 108	171
OCEANIA - OCÉANIA[2]......................................	12.7	15.8	19.5	23.0	27.0	31.1	36.6	1.7	18	7	8 564	4
Australia and New Zealand - Australie et Nouvelle Zélande	10.1	12.7	15.5	17.9	20.5	23.0	26.6	1.6	14	7	8 012	3
Melanesia - Melanésie	2.2	2.6	3.3	4.3	5.5	7.0	8.7	2.2	30	8	541	16
Micronesia	0.1	0.2	0.2	0.3	0.4	0.5	0.5	0.6	21	5	3	179
Polynesia - Polynésie...	0.2	0.3	0.4	0.5	0.5	0.6	0.7	0.8	22	5	8	84

FOOTNOTES - NOTES

[1] Population per square kilometre of surface area. Figures are estimates of population divided by surface area and are not to be considered as either reflecting density in the urban sense or as indicating the supporting power of a territory's land and resources. - Habitants par kilomètre carré. Il s'agit simplement du quotient calculé en divisant la population par la superficie et n'est par considéré comme indiquant la densité au sens urbain du terme ni l'effectif de population que les terres et les ressources du territoire sont capables de nourrir.

[2] Hawaii, a state of the United States of America, is included in Northern America rather than in Oceania. - Hawaii, un Etat des Etats-Unis d'Amérique, est compris en Amérique septentrionale plutôt qu'en Océanie.

[3] The European part of Turkey is included in Western Asia rather than Europe. - La partie européenne de la Turquie est comprise en Asie Occidentale plutôt qu'en Europe.

Table 2

Table 2 presents estimates of population and the percentage distribution by age and sex as well as the sex ratio for all ages; data are presented for the world, the six major areas and the 20 regions for 2010.

Description of variables: All population estimates presented in this table are prepared by the Population Division of the United Nations Department of Economic and Social Affairs. These estimates were published (using more detailed age groups) in the *2010 Revision of World Population Prospects*[1].

The scheme of regionalization used for these estimates is discussed in detail in the technical notes for table 1. Age groups presented in this table are: under 15 years, 15-64 years and 65 years and over. Sex ratio refers to the number of males per 100 females of all ages.

The percentage distributions and the sex ratios that appear in this table were calculated by the Statistics Division of the United Nations Department of Economic and Social Affairs using the Population Division estimates.

Reliability of data: All data are set in *italic* type to indicate their conjectural quality.

Limitations: The data presented in this table are from the same series of estimates, prepared by the Population Division, presented in table 1. The estimated orders of magnitude of population are subject to all the basic limitations set forth for population statistics in section 3 of the Technical Notes. In brief, because they are estimates, these distributions by broad age groups and sex should be considered only as orders of magnitude. However, in compiling data for regional and macro region totals, errors in the components tend to compensate each other and the resulting aggregates may be somewhat more reliable than the quality of the individual components would imply.

In addition, data in this table are limited by factors affecting data by age. These factors are described in the technical notes for table 7. Because the age groups presented in this table are so broad, these problems are minimized.

NOTES

[1] *United Nations, Department of Economic and Social Affairs, Population Division (2011). World Population Prospects: The 2010 Revision, DVD Edition – Extended Dataset (United Nations publication, Sales No. E.11.XIII.7).*

Tableau 2

Le tableau 2 présente, pour l'ensemble du monde, les six grandes zones et les 20 régions, des estimations concernant la population en 2010 ainsi que sa répartition en pourcentage selon l'âge et le sexe, et le rapport de masculinité pour tous les âges.

Description des variables : toutes les données figurant dans le tableau 2 ont été établies par la Division de la population des Nations Unies, et ont été publiés dans la Perspectives de la population mondiale : La révision de 2010[1].

La classification géographique utilisée pour établir ces estimations est exposée en détail dans les notes techniques relatives au tableau 1. Les groupes d'âge présentés dans ce tableau sont définis comme suit : moins de 15 ans, de 15 à 64 ans et 65 ans et plus. Le rapport de masculinité correspond au nombre d'individus de sexe masculin pour 100 individus de sexe féminin sans considération d'âge.

Les pourcentages et les rapports de masculinité qui sont présentés dans le tableau 2 ont été calculés par la Division de statistique de l'ONU à partir des estimations établies par la Division de la population.

Fiabilité des données : toutes les données figurant dans ce tableau sont reproduites en *italique* pour en faire ressortir le caractère conjectural.

Insuffisance des données : les données de ce tableau appartiennent à la même série d'estimations, établie par la Division de la population, que celles qui figurent au tableau 1. Les estimations concernant l'ordre de grandeur de la population appellent donc toutes les réserves fondamentales qui ont été formulées à la section 3 des Notes techniques à propos des statistiques relatives à la population. Sans entrer dans le détail, il convient de préciser que les données relatives à la répartition par grand groupe d'âge et par sexe doivent être considérées uniquement comme des ordres de grandeur en raison de leur caractère estimatif. Toutefois, il est à noter que, lorsque l'on additionne des données par territoire pour obtenir des totaux régionaux et par grandes zones, les erreurs qu'elles comportent arrivent parfois à s'équilibrer, de sorte que les agrégats obtenus peuvent être un peu plus exacts que chacun des éléments dont on est parti.

En outre, les donnés figurant dans le tableau 2 comportent certaines imprécisions en raison des facteurs influant sur les données par âge (voir à ce propos les notes techniques relatives au tableau 7). Ces imprécisions sont cependant atténuées du fait de l'étendue des groupes d'âge présentés dans le tableau 2.

NOTE

[1] *Organisation des Nations Unies, Département des affaires économiques et sociales, Division de la population (2011). Perspectives de la population mondiale : La révision de 2010, Edition DVD - ensemble de données étendues (publication des Nations Unies, numéro de vente E.11.XIII.7).*

2. Estimates of population and its percentage distribution, by age and sex and sex ratio for all ages for the world, major areas and regions: 2010

Estimations de la population et pourcentage de répartition selon l'âge et le sexe et rapport de masculinité pour l'ensemble du monde, les grandes régions et les régions géographiques : 2010

Major areas and regions / Grandes régions et régions	Population (millions)												Sex ratio - Rapport de masculinité[1]
	Both sexes - Les deux sexes				Male - Masculin				Female - Féminin				
	All ages - Tous âges	-15	15-64	65+	All ages - Tous âges	-15	15-64	65+	All ages - Tous âges	-15	15-64	65+	
WORLD TOTAL - ENSEMBLE DU MONDE													
Number - Nombre	6 896	1 847	4 525	524	3 478	955	2 291	231	3 418	891	2 234	293	
Percent - Pourcentage	100.0	26.8	65.6	7.6	100.0	27.5	65.9	6.7	100.0	26.1	65.4	8.6	101.7
AFRICA - AFRIQUE													
Number - Nombre	1 022	412	575	36	511	208	287	16	511	203	288	20	
Percent - Pourcentage	100.0	40.3	56.2	3.5	100.0	40.8	56.1	3.2	100.0	39.8	56.3	3.9	100.0
Eastern Africa - Afrique orientale													
Number - Nombre	324	140	174	10	161	71	86	5	163	70	88	6	
Percent - Pourcentage	100.0	43.3	53.6	3.1	100.0	43.8	53.4	2.8	100.0	42.8	53.8	3.4	98.9
Middle Africa - Afrique centrale													
Number - Nombre	127	57	66	4	63	28	33	2	64	28	33	2	
Percent - Pourcentage	100.0	44.8	52.3	2.9	100.0	45.2	52.2	2.6	100.0	44.4	52.4	3.2	99.0
Northern Africa - Afrique septentrionale													
Number - Nombre	209	66	133	10	105	34	67	5	104	32	67	5	
Percent - Pourcentage	100.0	31.6	63.6	4.8	100.0	32.2	63.5	4.3	100.0	31.0	63.8	5.3	100.5
Southern Africa - Afrique méridionale													
Number - Nombre	58	18	37	3	29	9	19	1	29	9	19	2	
Percent - Pourcentage	100.0	30.9	64.6	4.5	100.0	31.4	65.1	3.6	100.0	30.5	64.0	5.5	98.1
Western Africa - Afrique occidentale													
Number - Nombre	304	131	164	10	153	67	82	4	151	64	82	5	
Percent - Pourcentage	100.0	43.0	53.8	3.2	100.0	43.4	53.6	2.9	100.0	42.5	54.1	3.4	101.6
LATIN AMERICA AND CARIBBEAN - AMÉRIQUE LATIN ET CARAÏBES													
Number - Nombre	590	164	385	41	291	84	190	18	299	81	195	23	
Percent - Pourcentage	100.0	27.9	65.2	6.9	100.0	28.8	65.1	6.1	100.0	27.0	65.4	7.6	97.6
Caribbean - Caraïbes													
Number - Nombre	42	11	27	4	21	6	13	2	21	5	14	2	
Percent - Pourcentage	100.0	26.6	65.0	8.4	100.0	27.3	65.0	7.7	100.0	25.8	65.0	9.1	98.6
Central America - Amérique centrale													
Number - Nombre	156	48	98	9	77	24	48	4	79	24	50	5	
Percent - Pourcentage	100.0	30.8	63.2	6.0	100.0	31.8	62.6	5.6	100.0	29.8	63.7	6.5	97.2
South America - Amérique méridionale													
Number - Nombre	393	105	259	28	194	54	128	12	199	52	131	16	
Percent - Pourcentage	100.0	26.8	66.1	7.1	100.0	27.7	66.1	6.2	100.0	26.0	66.1	7.9	97.6
NORTHERN AMERICA - AMÉRIQUE SEPTENTRIONALE[2]													
Number - Nombre	345	68	231	45	170	35	116	19	174	33	115	26	
Percent - Pourcentage	100.0	19.7	67.1	13.2	100.0	20.4	68.2	11.4	100.0	19.0	66.1	14.9	97.5
ASIA - ASIE[3]													
Number - Nombre	4 164	1 080	2 805	279	2 131	565	1 437	129	2 033	514	1 368	150	
Percent - Pourcentage	100.0	25.9	67.4	6.7	100.0	26.5	67.4	6.0	100.0	25.3	67.3	7.4	104.8
Eastern Asia - Asie orientale													
Number - Nombre	1 574	297	1 128	150	811	161	581	69	763	136	547	81	
Percent - Pourcentage	100.0	18.8	71.6	9.5	100.0	19.9	71.6	8.5	100.0	17.8	71.7	10.6	106.2
South Central Asia - Asie centrale méridionale													
Number - Nombre	1 765	548	1 132	85	905	284	581	40	859	264	551	45	
Percent - Pourcentage	100.0	31.1	64.1	4.8	100.0	31.4	64.2	4.5	100.0	30.7	64.1	5.2	105.3
South Eastern Asia - Asie méridionale orientale													
Number - Nombre	593	162	398	33	295	83	198	14	298	79	200	19	
Percent - Pourcentage	100.0	27.3	67.1	5.6	100.0	28.0	67.1	4.9	100.0	26.6	67.1	6.3	99.0
Western Asia - Asie occidentale													
Number - Nombre	232	73	148	11	120	38	78	5	112	36	70	6	
Percent - Pourcentage	100.0	31.5	63.7	4.7	100.0	31.3	64.7	4.0	100.0	31.8	62.7	5.5	107.1
EUROPE[3]													
Number - Nombre	738	114	505	119	356	59	250	47	382	55	255	72	
Percent - Pourcentage	100.0	15.4	68.4	16.2	100.0	16.5	70.2	13.3	100.0	14.5	66.6	18.8	93.0
Eastern Europe - Europe orientale													
Number - Nombre	295	44	210	41	138	22	102	14	157	21	108	27	
Percent - Pourcentage	100.0	14.8	71.4	13.8	100.0	16.2	73.8	10.0	100.0	13.6	69.3	17.1	88.3
Northern Europe - Europe septentrionale													
Number - Nombre	99	17	66	16	49	9	33	7	50	8	33	9	
Percent - Pourcentage	100.0	17.3	66.2	16.5	100.0	18.1	67.5	14.5	100.0	16.6	65.0	18.4	96.6
Southern Europe - Europe méridionale													
Number - Nombre	155	23	104	28	76	12	52	12	79	11	52	16	
Percent - Pourcentage	100.0	15.0	67.1	18.0	100.0	15.7	68.8	15.5	100.0	14.2	65.4	20.4	96.4

2. Estimates of population and its percentage distribution, by age and sex and sex ratio for all ages for the world, major areas and regions: 2010
Estimations de la population et pourcentage de répartition selon l'âge et le sexe et rapport de masculinité pour l'ensemble du monde, les grandes régions et les régions géographiques : 2010 (continued - suite)

Major areas and regions	Population (millions)												Sex ratio -
Grandes régions et régions	Both sexes - Les deux sexes				Male - Masculin				Female - Féminin				Rapport de masculinité[1]
	All ages - Tous âges	-15	15-64	65+	All ages - Tous âges	-15	15-64	65+	All ages - Tous âges	-15	15-64	65+	
Western Europe - Europe occidentale													
Number - Nombre	189	30	125	35	93	15	63	15	97	15	62	20	
Percent - Pourcentage	100.0	15.8	65.9	18.3	100.0	16.5	67.6	15.8	100.0	15.1	64.3	20.6	95.9
OCEANIA - OCÉANIA[2]													
Number - Nombre	36.59	8.80	23.89	3.91	18.31	4.53	12.00	1.78	18.28	4.27	11.89	2.12	
Percent - Pourcentage	100.0	24.0	65.3	10.7	100.0	24.7	65.5	9.7	100.0	23.3	65.0	11.6	100.2
Australia and New Zealand - Australie et Nouvelle Zélande													
Number - Nombre	26.64	5.12	17.95	3.56	13.24	2.63	8.98	1.63	13.40	2.50	8.97	1.93	
Percent - Pourcentage	100.0	19.2	67.4	13.4	100.0	19.9	67.8	12.3	100.0	18.6	67.0	14.4	98.8
Melanesia - Melanésie													
Number - Nombre	8.75	3.30	5.17	0.28	4.46	1.71	2.63	0.12	4.28	1.59	2.54	0.15	
Percent - Pourcentage	100.0	37.7	59.1	3.2	100.0	38.3	59.0	2.8	100.0	37.1	59.3	3.6	104.2
Micronesia													
Number - Nombre	0.54	0.16	0.35	0.03	0.27	0.08	0.17	0.01	0.27	0.08	0.17	0.01	
Percent - Pourcentage	100.0	30.6	64.4	5.0	100.0	31.3	64.3	4.5	100.0	30.0	64.6	5.4	101.6
Polynesia - Polynésie													
Number - Nombre	0.67	0.21	0.42	0.04	0.34	0.11	0.21	0.02	0.33	0.10	0.20	0.02	
Percent - Pourcentage	100.0	31.7	62.4	5.9	100.0	32.1	62.6	5.3	100.0	31.4	62.2	6.4	104.2

FOOTNOTES - NOTES

[1] Males per 100 females of all ages - Hommes pour 100 femmes de tous âges
[2] Hawaii, a state of the United States of America, is included in Northern America rather than in Oceania. - Hawaii, un Etat des Etats-Unis d'Amérique, est compris en Amérique septentrionale plutôt qu'en Océanie.
[3] The European part of Turkey is included in Western Asia rather than Europe. - La partie européenne de la Turquie est comprise en Asie Occidentale plutôt qu'en Europe.

Table 3

Table 3 presents for each country or area of the world the total, male and female population enumerated at the latest population census, estimates of the mid-year total population for 2005 and 2010, the average annual exponential rate of population increase (or decrease) for the period 2005 to 2010, the surface area and the population density for 2010.

Description of variables: The total, male and female population is the population enumerated at the most recent census for which data are available. The date of this census is given. Population census data are usually the results of a nation-wide gathering of individual information through full field enumeration. Alternatively other approaches for generating reliable statistics on population and housing can be used by countries, such as the use of population registers. Data that are the result of such an alternative approach are also coded as census and are footnoted accordingly. Also, the results of sample surveys, essentially national in character, may be presented showing the appropriate code. However, results of surveys referring to less than 50 percent of the total territory or population are not included.

Mid-year population estimates refer to the population on 1 July. Otherwise, a footnote is appended. Mid-year estimates of the total population are those provided by national statistical offices.

Surface area, expressed in square kilometres, refers to the total surface area, comprising land area and inland waters (assumed to consist of major rivers and lakes) and excluding polar regions as well as uninhabited islands. Exceptions to this are noted. Surface areas, originally reported in square miles by the country or area, have been converted to square kilometres using a conversion factor of 2.589988.

Computation: The annual rate of population increase is the average annual exponential rate of population growth between 2005 and 2010, computed by the Statistics Division of the United Nations Department of Economic and Social Affairs using the unrounded mid-year estimates of 2005 and 2010. This rate is expressed as percentage.

Density is the number of persons in the 2010 total population per square kilometre of total surface area.

Reliability of data: Reliable mid-year population estimates are those that are based on a complete census (or a sample survey) and have been adjusted by a continuous population register or on the basis of the calculated balance of births, deaths and migration. Mid-year estimates of this type are considered reliable and appear in roman type. Mid-year estimates not calculated on this basis are considered less reliable and are shown in italics.

Census data and sample survey results are considered reliable and, therefore, appear in roman type.

Rates of population increase that were calculated using population estimates considered less reliable, as described above, are set in italics rather than roman type.

All surface area data are assumed to be reliable and therefore appear in roman type.

Population density data, however, are considered reliable or less reliable on the basis of the reliability of the 2010 population estimates used as the numerator.

Limitations: Statistics on the total population enumerated at the time of the census, estimates of the mid-year total population and surface area data are subject to the same qualifications as have been set forth for population and surface area statistics in sections 3 and 2.4 of the Technical Notes, respectively.

Regarding the limitations of census data, it should be noted that although census data are considered reliable, and therefore appear in roman type, the actual quality of census data varies widely from one country or area to another. When known, an estimate of the extent of over-enumeration or under-enumeration is given in footnotes.

Rates of population increase are subject to all the qualifications of the population estimates mentioned above. In some cases, they simply reflect the rate calculated or assumed in constructing the estimates themselves when adequate measures of natural increase and net migration were not available. Despite their shortcomings, these rates provide a useful index for studying population change and can be also useful in evaluating the accuracy of vital and migration statistics.

Population density data as shown in this table give only an indication of actual population density as they do not take account of the dispersion or concentration of population within countries or areas nor the proportion of habitable land. They should not be interpreted as reflecting density in the urban sense or as indicating the supporting power of a territory's land and resources.

Tableau 3

Le tableau 3 indique pour chaque pays ou zone du monde la population totale selon le sexe d'après les derniers recensements effectués, les estimations concernant la population totale au milieu de l'année 2005 et de l'année 2010, le taux moyen d'accroissement annuel exponentiel positif ou négatif de la population pour la période allant de 2005 à 2010, ainsi que la superficie et la densité de population en 2010.

Description des variables : la population masculine et féminine totale est, la population enregistrée lors du recensement le plus récent sur lequel·on dispose de données. La date de ce recensement est indiquée. Les données des recensements de la population sont habituellement le résultat d'un collecte à l'échelle nationale des données individuelles obtenues au moyen d'un dénombrement complet. Les pays peuvent recourir à d'autres moyens pour établir des statistiques fiables sur la population et le logement, tels que des registres de la population. Les données obtenues par ce moyen sont présentées comme celles d'un recensement et sont annotées en conséquence. Par ailleurs, les résultats des enquêtes par sondage, réalisées habituellement à l'échelle nationale, peuvent être présentés à l'aide du code correspondant. En revanche, les résultats des enquêtes portant sur moins de 50 % du territoire total ou de la population ne sont pas indiqués.

Les estimations de la population en milieu d'année sont celles de la population au 1er juillet. Lorsque la date est différente, cela est signalé par une note. Les estimations de la population totale en milieu d'année sont celles qui ont été communiquées par les services nationaux de statistique.

La superficie - exprimée en kilomètres carrés - représente la superficie totale, c'est-à-dire qu'elle englobe les terres émergées et les eaux intérieures (qui sont censées comprendre les principaux lacs et cours d'eau) mais exclut les régions polaires et certaines îles inhabitées. Les exceptions à cette règle sont signalées en note. Les superficies initialement exprimées en miles carrés par les pays ou les zones ont été transformées en kilomètres carrés au moyen d'un coefficient de conversion de 2,589988.

Calculs : le taux d'accroissement annuel est le taux exponentiel annuel moyen de variation (en pourcentage) de la population entre 2005 et 2010, calculé par la Division de statistique du Département des affaires économiques et sociales (Secrétariat de l'Organisation des Nations Unies) à partir des estimations en milieu d'année non arrondies pour les années 2005 et 2010.

La densité est égale au rapport de l'effectif total de la population en 2010 à la superficie totale, exprimée en kilomètres carrés.

Fiabilité des données : les estimations en milieu d'année qui sont considérées sûres sont fondées sur un recensement complet (ou sur une enquête par sondage) et ont été ajustées en fonction des données provenant d'un registre permanent de population ou en fonction de la balance établie par le calcul des naissances, des décès et des migrations. Les estimations de ce type sont considérées comme sûres et apparaissent en caractères romains. Les estimations en milieu d'année dont le calcul n'a pas été effectué sur cette base sont considérées comme moins sûres et apparaissent en italique.

Les données de recensements ou les résultats d'enquêtes par sondage sont considérés comme sûrs et apparaissent par conséquent en caractères romains.

Les taux d'accroissement de la population, calculés à partir d'estimations jugées moins sûres d'après les normes décrites ci-dessus, sont indiqués en italique plutôt qu'en caractères romains.

Toutes les données de superficie sont présumées sûres et apparaissent par conséquent en caractères romains. En revanche, les données relatives à la densité de la population sont considérées plus ou moins sûres en fonction de la fiabilité des estimations de la population en 2010 ayant servi de numérateur.

Insuffisance des données : les statistiques portant sur la population totale dénombrée lors d'un recensement, les estimations de la population totale en milieu d'année et les données de superficie appellent les mêmes réserves que celles formulées aux sections 3 et 2.4 des Notes techniques à propos des statistiques relatives à la population et à la superficie.

S'agissant de l'insuffisance des données obtenues par recensement, il convient d'indiquer que, bien que ces données soient considérées comme sûres et apparaissent par conséquent en caractères romains, leur qualité réelle varie considérablement d'un pays ou d'une région à l'autre. Lorsque l'on possédait les

renseignements voulus, on a donné une estimation du degré de sur-dénombrement ou de sous-dénombrement.

Les taux d'accroissement appellent toutes les réserves formulées plus haut à propos des estimations concernant la population. Dans certains cas, ils représentent seulement le taux calculé ou que l'on a pris pour base pour établir les estimations elles-mêmes lorsque l'on ne disposait pas de mesures appropriées de l'accroissement naturel et des migrations nettes. Malgré leurs imperfections, ces taux fournissent des indications intéressantes pour l'étude du mouvement de la population et, utilisés avec les précautions nécessaires, ils peuvent également servir à évaluer l'exactitude des statistiques de l'état civil et des migrations.

Les données relatives à la densité de population figurant dans le tableau 3 n'ont qu'une valeur indicative en ce qui concerne la densité de population effective, car elles ne tiennent compte ni de la dispersion ou de la concentration de la population à l'intérieur des pays ou zones, ni de la proportion du territoire qui est habitable. Il ne faut donc y voir d'indication ni de la densité au sens urbain du terme ni du nombre d'habitants qui pourraient vivre sur les terres et avec les ressources naturelles du territoire considéré.

3. Population by sex, annual rate of population increase, surface area and density
Population selon le sexe, taux d'accroissement annuel de la population, superficie et densité

Continent, country or area and census date Continent, pays ou zone et date du recensement	Census type[a]	Population at the latest available census Population d'après le dernier recensement disponible (in units — en unités)			Estimate type[a]	Mid-year estimates Estimations au milieu de l'année (in thousands — en milliers)		Annual rate of increase Taux d'accrois sement annuel 2005-10	Surface area Superficie (km²) 2010	Density Densité 2010[b]
		Both sexes Les deux sexes	Male Masculin	Female Feminin		2005	2010			
AFRICA - AFRIQUE										
Algeria - Algérie										
16 IV 2008	DJ	*34 452 759	*17 428 500	*17 024 259	DJ	32 906	*35 978	1.8	2 381 741	15
Angola										
15 XII 1970	DF	5 646 166	2 943 974	2 702 192		...	...	...	1 246 700	...
Benin - Bénin										
11 II 2002	DJ	6 769 914	3 284 119	3 485 795	DF	*7 447[1]	*8 779[1]	3.3	114 763	76
Botswana										
17 VIII 2001	DF	1 680 863	813 625	867 238	DJ	1 708	1 823	1.3	582 000	3
Burkina Faso										
9 XII 2006	DJ	14 196 259	6 842 560	7 353 699	DJ	13 374	15 731[1]	3.2	272 967	58
Burundi										
16 VIII 2008	DF	7 877 728	3 838 045	4 039 683		...	...	...	27 834	...
Cameroon - Cameroun										
11 XI 2005	DF	17 052 134	8 408 495	8 643 639	DJ	...	*19 406[1]	...	475 650	41
Cape Verde - Cap-Vert										
16 VI 2010	DJ	*491 575	*243 315	*248 260	DF	475	518	1.7	4 033	128
Central African Republic - République centrafricaine										
8 XII 2003	DF	3 151 072	1 569 446	1 581 626		...	...	...	622 984	...
Chad - Tchad										
8 IV 1993	DF	6 158 992	2 950 415	3 208 577		...	...	...	1 284 000	...
Comoros - Comores										
1 IX 2003	DF	575 660[2]	...	...		...	...	...	2 235	...
Congo										
28 IV 2007	DF	*3 697 487	...	...	DF	3 488[1]	...	...	342 000	...
Côte d'Ivoire										
21 XI 1998	DF	15 366 672	7 844 621	7 522 050	DF	*19 097[1]	...	...	322 463	...
Democratic Republic of the Congo - République démocratique du Congo										
1 VII 1984	DF	29 916 800	14 543 800	15 373 000		...	...	...	2 344 858	...
Djibouti										
29 V 2009	DF	*818 159	...	...		...	...	...	23 200	...
Egypt - Égypte										
21 XI 2006	DF	72 798 031	37 219 056	35 578 975	DF	70 653	*78 728	2.2	1 002 000	79
Equatorial Guinea - Guinée équatoriale										
1 II 2002	DF	1 014 999	501 387	513 612		...	...	...	28 051	...
Eritrea - Érythrée										
9 V 1984	DF	2 748 304	1 374 452	1 373 852		...	...	...	117 600	...
Ethiopia - Éthiopie										
29 V 2007	DF	73 750 932	37 217 130	36 533 802	DF	73 044[3]	...	...	1 104 300	...
Gabon										
1 XII 2003	DF	*1 269 000	...	...	DF	1 313[4]	...	...	267 668	...
Gambia - Gambie										
15 IV 2003	DF	*1 364 507	*676 726	*687 781	DF	1 436	...	...	11 295	...
Ghana										
26 IX 2010	DF	*24 223 431	*11 801 661	*12 421 770	DF	21 367	...	...	238 533	...
Guinea - Guinée										
1 XII 1996	DF	7 156 406	3 497 979	3 658 427	DF	...	10 537[1]	...	245 857	43
Guinea-Bissau - Guinée-Bissau										
15 III 2009	DF	1 520 830	737 634	783 196	DF	1 326[1]	...	...	36 125	...
Kenya										
24 VIII 2009	DF	*38 610 097	*19 192 458	*19 417 639	DF	35 267[5]	*40 400[5]	2.7	581 313	69
Lesotho										
13 IV 2006	DF	1 741 406	818 379	923 027	DF	...	1 892[1]	...	30 355	62
Liberia - Libéria										
21 III 2008	DF	3 476 608	1 739 945	1 736 663		...	...	...	111 369	...
Libya - Libye										
15 IV 2006	DF	*5 657 692[6]	*2 934 452[6]	*2 723 240[6]		...	...	...	1 759 540	...
Madagascar										
1 VIII 1993	DF	12 238 914	6 088 116	6 150 798	DF	17 730	...	...	587 041	...

Population selon le sexe, taux d'accroissement annuel de la population, superficie et densité (continued - suite)

Continent, country or area and census date / Continent, pays ou zone et date du recensement	Census type[a]	Population at the latest available census / Population d'après le dernier recensement disponible (in units — en unités)			Estimate type[a]	Mid-year estimates Estimations au milieu de l'année (in thousands — en milliers)		Annual rate of increase Taux d' accrois sement annuel 2005-10	Surface area Superficie (km²) 2010	Density Densité 2010[b]
		Both sexes Les deux sexes	Male Masculin	Female Feminin		2005	2010			
AFRICA - AFRIQUE										
Malawi										
8 VI 2008	DF	13 077 160	6 358 933	6 718 227	DF	12 341[1]	...	...	118 484	...
Mali										
1 IV 2009	DJ	*14 517 176	*7 202 744	*7 314 432	DF	11 732[7]	...	...	1 240 192	...
Mauritania - Mauritanie										
1 XI 2000	DF	2 508 159	1 241 712	1 266 447	DF	2 906[1]	...	...	1 030 700	...
Mauritius - Maurice[8]										
2 VII 2000	DJ	1 178 848	583 756	595 092	DJ	1 243	1 281[9]	0.6	1 969	651
Mayotte										
31 VII 2007	DJ	186 387	91 405	94 982		...	...			
Morocco - Maroc										
1 IX 2004	DF	29 680 069	14 640 662	15 039 407	DF	30 172[10]	31 851[10]	1.1	446 550	71
Mozambique										
1 VIII 2007	DF	20 252 223	9 746 690	10 505 533	DF	19 420[1]	21 854[1]	2.4	801 590	27
Namibia - Namibie										
27 VIII 2001	DF	1 830 330	887 721[11]	942 572[11]	DF	1 957[1]	2 143[1]	1.8	824 268	3
Niger										
20 V 2001	DJ	11 060 291	5 516 588	5 543 703	DJ	12 628[1]	15 204[1]	3.7	1 267 000	12
Nigeria - Nigéria										
21 III 2006	DF	140 431 790	71 345 488	69 086 302	DF	133 767[1]	...		923 768	...
Réunion										
1 I 2006	DJ	781 962	379 176	402 786	DJ	777			2 513	...
Rwanda										
16 VIII 2002	DJ	8 128 553	3 879 448	4 249 105	DF	...	10 413	...	26 338	395
Saint Helena ex. dep. - Sainte-Hélène sans dép.										
10 II 2008	DF	*4 255	*2 166	*2 089	DF	...	4	...	122	35
Saint Helena: Ascension - Sainte-Hélène: Ascension										
8 III 1998	DJ	712	458	254		...	...		88	...
Saint Helena: Tristan da Cunha - Sainte-Hélène: Tristan da Cunha										
31 XII 1988	DF	296	139	157		...	...	...	98	...
Sao Tome and Principe - Sao Tomé-et-Principe										
25 VIII 2001	DF	136 554	67 422	69 132	DF	149	*164	1.9	964	170
Senegal - Sénégal										
8 XII 2002	DF	9 555 346	4 672 015	4 883 331	DJ	10 901[12]	12 509[12]	2.8	196 712[13]	64
Seychelles										
26 VIII 2002	DJ	81 755[14]	40 751[14]	41 004[14]	DF	83	87	0.9	452	192
Sierra Leone										
4 XII 2004	DF	4 976 871	2 420 218	2 556 653	DF	5 095	5 747	2.4	72 300	79
Somalia - Somalie										
15 II 1987	DF	7 114 431	3 741 664	3 372 767		...	...	...	637 657	...
South Africa - Afrique du Sud										
10 X 2001	DF	44 819 778	21 434 041	23 385 737	DF	47 335[15]	49 991[15]	1.1	1 221 037	41
Sudan - Soudan										
21 IV 2008	DF	*39 154 490	*20 073 977	*19 080 513	DF	35 397	...	...	2 505 813	...
Swaziland										
11 III 2007	DF	844 223	405 868	438 355	DF	1 126			17 364	...
Togo										
22 XI 1981	DF	2 719 567	1 325 641	1 393 926	DF	5 212			56 785	...
Tunisia - Tunisie										
28 IV 2004	DF	9 910 872	4 965 435	4 945 437	DF	10 029	10 549	1.0	163 610	64
Uganda - Ouganda										
12 IX 2002	DF	24 442 084	11 929 803	12 512 281	DF	26 741	...	...	241 550	...
United Republic of Tanzania - République Unie de Tanzanie										
24 VIII 2002	DF	*34 443 603	*16 829 861	*17 613 742	DF	37 379	...	...	945 087	...

3. Population by sex, annual rate of population increase, surface area and density
Population selon le sexe, taux d'accroissement annuel de la population, superficie et densité (continued - suite)

Continent, country or area and census date — Continent, pays ou zone et date du recensement	Census type[a]	Population at the latest available census — Population d'après le dernier recensement disponible (in units — en unités)			Estimate type[a]	Mid-year estimates — Estimations au milieu de l'année (in thousands — en milliers)		Annual rate of increase — Taux d' accrois sement annuel 2005-10	Surface area Superficie (km²) 2010	Density Densité 2010[b]
		Both sexes Les deux sexes	Male Masculin	Female Feminin		2005	2010			
AFRICA - AFRIQUE										
Western Sahara - Sahara occidental[16]										
31 XII 1970 .... DF	DF	76 425	43 981	32 444		...	...	...	266 000	...
Zambia - Zambie										
16 X 2010 .... DF	DF	*13 046 508	*6 394 455	*6 652 053	DF	11 441[1]	...	...	752 612	...
Zimbabwe										
17 VIII 2002 .... DF	DF	11 631 657	5 634 180	5 997 477	DF	11 830[17]	...	...	390 757	...
AMERICA, NORTH - AMÉRIQUE DU NORD										
Anguilla										
9 V 2001 .... DF	DF	11 430[18]	5 628[18]	5 802[18]	DF	14	...	...	91	...
Antigua and Barbuda - Antigua-et-Barbuda										
28 V 2001 .... DF	DF	76 886	36 107	40 779	DF	83	...	...	442	...
Aruba										
14 X 2000 .... DJ	DJ	90 506	43 434	47 072	DJ	101	108	1.3	180	598
Bahamas										
3 V 2010 .... DF	DF	353 658	...	...	DF	325[1]	347[1]	1.3	13 943	25
Barbados - Barbade										
1 V 2000 .... DF	DF	250 010	119 926	130 084	DF	273	276[19]	0.2	430	643
Belize										
12 V 2000 .... DF	DF	240 204	121 278	118 926	DF	292	...	...	22 966	...
Bermuda - Bermudes										
20 V 2000 .... DJ	DJ	62 059[20]	29 802[20]	32 257[20]	DJ	64	65	0.3	53	1 218
British Virgin Islands - Îles Vierges britanniques										
21 V 2001 .... DF	DF	20 647	10 627	10 020		...	...	...	151	...
Canada										
16 V 2006 .... DJ	DJ	31 612 895[21]	15 475 970[21]	16 136 930[21]	DJ	32 245[22]	*34 109[23]	1.1	9 984 670	3
Cayman Islands - Îles Caïmanes										
10 X 2010 .... DJ	DJ	*54 397[24]	*26 899[24]	*27 498[24]	DJ	48	*55	2.5	264	208
Costa Rica										
26 VI 2000 .... DJ	DJ	3 810 179	1 902 614	1 907 565	DJ	4 266	4 562[25]	1.3	51 100	89
Cuba										
7 IX 2002 .... DJ	DJ	11 177 743	5 597 233	5 580 510	DJ	11 243	11 242	0.0	109 886[26]	102
Dominica - Dominique										
12 V 2001 .... DF	DF	69 625[24]	35 073[24]	34 552[24]	DF	71	...	...	751	...
Dominican Republic - République dominicaine										
1 XII 2010 .... DJ	DJ	*9 378 819[27]	*4 707 921[27]	*4 670 898[27]	DF	9 226[1]	9 884[1]	1.4	48 671	203
El Salvador										
12 V 2007 .... DJ	DJ	5 744 113	2 719 371	3 024 742	DF	6 049[28]	6 183[28]	0.4	21 041[29]	294
Greenland - Groenland										
1 I 2008 .... DJ	DJ	56 462[30]	29 885[30]	26 577[30]	DJ	57[30]	57[30]	-0.1	2 166 086	0
Grenada - Grenade										
25 V 2001 .... DF	DF	102 632	50 481	52 151		...	...	...	344	...
Guadeloupe										
1 I 2006 .... DJ	DJ	400 736[31]	188 720[31]	212 016[31]	DJ	446	404[32]	-1.9	1 705	237
Guatemala										
24 XI 2002 .... DJ	DJ	11 237 196	5 496 839	5 740 357	DF	12 701[33]	14 362[33]	2.5	108 889	132
Haiti - Haïti										
11 I 2003 .... DJ	DJ	8 373 750	4 039 272	4 334 478	DJ	9 292[34]	10 085[34]	1.6	27 750	363
Honduras										
28 VII 2001 .... DF	DF	6 071 200	3 000 530	3 070 670	DF	7 197[35]	8 046[35]	2.2	112 492	72
Jamaica - Jamaïque										
10 IX 2001 .... DJ	DJ	2 607 632[36]	1 283 548[36]	1 324 084[36]	DJ	2 650	*2 702	0.4	10 991	246
Martinique										
1 I 2006 .... DJ	DJ	397 732	185 604	212 128	DJ	396[7]	400[7]	0.2	1 128	354

Population selon le sexe, taux d'accroissement annuel de la population, superficie et densité (continued - suite)

Continent, country or area and census date / Continent, pays ou zone et date du recensement	Census type[a]	Population at the latest available census / Population d'après le dernier recensement disponible (in units — en unités)			Estimate type[a]	Mid-year estimates Estimations au milieu de l'année (in thousands — en milliers)		Annual rate of increase Taux d' accrois sement annuel 2005-10	Surface area Superficie (km²) 2010	Density Densité 2010[b]
		Both sexes Les deux sexes	Male Masculin	Female Feminin		2005	2010			
AMERICA, NORTH - AMÉRIQUE DU NORD										
Mexico - Mexique										
12 VI 2010 .... DF	DF	112 336 538[37]	54 855 231[37]	57 481 307[37]	DJ	*103 947*[1]	...	...	1 964 375	...
Montserrat										
12 V 2001 .... DF	DF	4 491	2 418	2 073	DF	5	...	...	102	...
Netherlands Antilles - Antilles néerlandaises										
29 I 2001 .... DJ	DJ	175 653	82 521	93 132	DJ	*184*[7]	*198*[38]	1.5	800	247
Nicaragua										
4 VI 2005 .... DJ	DJ	5 142 098	2 534 491	2 607 607	DJ	*5 450*	*5 816*	1.3	130 373	45
Panama										
16 V 2010 .... DF	DF	3 405 813	1 712 584	1 693 229	DF	*3 228*[39]	*3 504*[39]	1.6	75 417	46
Puerto Rico - Porto Rico										
1 IV 2010 .... DJ	DJ	*3 725 789	...	...	DJ	*3 912*[40]	*3 979*[40]	0.3	8 870	449
Saint Kitts and Nevis - Saint-Kitts-et-Nevis										
14 V 2001 .... DF	DF	45 841	22 784	23 057	DF	*39	...	...	261	...
Saint Lucia - Sainte-Lucie										
10 V 2010 .... DF	DF	*173 720	...	...	DF	164	...	...	539[41]	...
Saint Pierre and Miquelon - Saint-Pierre-et-Miquelon										
19 I 2006 .... DF	DF	6 125	3 034	3 091		...	...	...	242	...
Saint Vincent and the Grenadines - Saint-Vincent-et-les Grenadines										
14 V 2001 .... DF	DF	109 022[24]	55 456[24]	53 566[24]	DF	104	...	...	389	...
Trinidad and Tobago - Trinité-et-Tobago										
15 V 2000 .... DF	DF	1 262 366[42]	633 051[42]	629 315[42]	DF	*1 294*[42]	*1 318*[42]	0.4	5 130	257
Turks and Caicos Islands - Îles Turques et Caïques										
10 IX 2001 .... DF	DF	19 886	9 897	9 989	DJ	*31*	*40*	5.5	948[43]	43
United States of America - États-Unis d'Amérique										
1 IV 2010 .... DJ	DJ	*308 745 538	...	...	DJ	295 753[44]	*309 051[44]	0.9	9 629 091	32
United States Virgin Islands - Îles Vierges américaines										
1 IV 2000 .... DJ	DJ	108 612[40]	51 864[40]	56 748[40]	DJ	110[40]	*110[40]	0.1	347	317
AMERICA, SOUTH - AMÉRIQUE DU SUD										
Argentina - Argentine										
27 X 2010 .... DF	DF	40 117 096	19 523 766	20 593 330	DF	*38 592*	*40 519*[45]	1.0	2 780 400	15
Bolivia (Plurinational State of) - Bolivie (État plurinational de)										
5 IX 2001 .... DF	DF	8 274 325	4 123 850	4 150 475	DF	*9 427*	*10 426*	2.0	1 098 581	9
Brazil - Brésil										
1 VIII 2010 .... DJ	DJ	*190 755 799[46]	*93 406 990[46]	*97 348 809[46]	DF	*183 383*[46]	*193 253*[46]	1.0	8 514 877	23
Chile - Chili										
24 IV 2002 .... DF	DF	15 116 435	7 447 695	7 668 740	DF	*16 267*	*17 094*	1.0	756 102	23
Colombia - Colombie										
22 V 2005 .... DF	DF	41 468 384	20 336 117	21 132 267	DF	*42 889*[47]	*45 508*[47]	1.2	1 141 748	40
Ecuador - Équateur										
28 XI 2010 .... DF	DF	*14 306 876	...	...	DF	*13 215*[48]	*14 205*[48]	1.4	256 369	55
Falkland Islands (Malvinas) - Îles Falkland (Malvinas)[49]										
8 X 2006 .... DF	DF	2 955[50]	1 569[50]	1 386[50]		...	...	...	12 173	...
French Guiana - Guyane française										
1 I 2006 .... DJ	DJ	205 954	101 930	104 023	DJ	*199*[7]	*232*[7]	3.1	83 534	3

3. Population by sex, annual rate of population increase, surface area and density
Population selon le sexe, taux d'accroissement annuel de la population, superficie et densité (continued - suite)

Continent, country or area and census date / Continent, pays ou zone et date du recensement	Census type[a]	Population at the latest available census / Population d'après le dernier recensement disponible (in units — en unités)			Estimate type[a]	Mid-year estimates / Estimations au milieu de l'année (in thousands — en milliers)		Annual rate of increase Taux d'accrois sement annuel 2005-10	Surface area Superficie (km²) 2010	Density Densité 2010[b]
		Both sexes Les deux sexes	Male Masculin	Female Feminin		2005	2010			
AMERICA, SOUTH - AMÉRIQUE DU SUD										
Guyana										
15 IX 2002	DF	751 223	376 034	375 189	DF	758	*778	0.5	214 969	4
Paraguay										
28 VIII 2002	DF	5 163 198	2 603 242	2 559 956	DF	*5 899*[17]	*6 451*[17]	*1.8*	406 752	16
Peru - Pérou										
21 X 2007	DF	27 412 157	13 622 640	13 789 517	DF	*27 811*	*29 462*	*1.2*	1 285 216	*23*
Suriname										
2 VIII 2004	DJ	492 829[51]	247 846[52]	244 618[52]	DJ	499	...	...	163 820	...
Uruguay										
1 VI 2004	DF	3 241 003[53]	1 565 533[53]	1 675 470[53]	DF	*3 306*[1]	*3 357*[1]	0.3	176 215	19
Venezuela (Bolivarian Republic of) - Venezuela (République bolivarienne du)										
30 X 2001	DF	23 054 210[54]	11 402 869[54]	11 651 341[54]	DF	26 577	28 834	1.6	912 050	32
ASIA - ASIE										
Afghanistan										
23 VI 1979	DF	13 051 358[55]	6 712 377[55]	6 338 981[55]	DF	*22 098*[56]	*24 486*[57]	2.1	652 864	*38*
Armenia - Arménie										
10 X 2001	DF	3 002 594[58]	1 407 220[58]	1 595 374[58]	DJ	3 218	3 256	0.2	29 743	109
Azerbaijan - Azerbaïdjan										
13 IV 2009	DJ	*8 922 300	...	...	DF	8 500[59]	9 047	1.2	86 600	104
Bahrain - Bahreïn										
7 IV 2001	DJ	650 604	373 649	276 955	DF	*889*	...	...	758	...
Bangladesh										
22 I 2001	DF	124 355 263[60]	64 091 508[60]	60 263 755[60]	DF	*138 600*	...	...	143 998	...
Bhutan - Bhoutan										
30 V 2005	DF	634 982	333 595	301 387	DF	...	696[61]	...	38 394	*18*
Brunei Darussalam - Brunéi Darussalam										
21 VIII 2001	DF	*332 844	*168 974	*163 870	DF	*370*	...	...	5 765	...
Cambodia - Cambodge										
3 III 2008	DF	13 395 682[62]	6 516 054[62]	6 879 628[62]	DF	*13 661*[63]	14 303[64]	0.9	181 035	79
China - Chine										
1 XI 2000	DJ	1 242 612 226[65]	640 275 969[65]	602 336 257[65]	DF	*1 307 560*[66]	...	...	9 596 961	...
China, Hong Kong SAR - Chine, Hong Kong RAS										
14 VII 2006	DF	6 752 674	...	...	DJ	6 813	7 068	0.7	1 104	6 402
China, Macao SAR - Chine, Macao RAS										
19 VIII 2006	DJ	502 113	245 167	256 946	DJ	473	545	2.8	30	18 153
Cyprus - Chypre										
1 X 2001	DJ	689 565[67]	338 497[67]	351 068[67]	DJ	*758*[68]	*804*[68]	*1.2*	9 251	87
Democratic People's Republic of Korea - République populaire démocratique de Corée										
1 X 2008	DJ	24 052 231	11 721 838	12 330 393		...	...	...	120 538	...
Georgia - Géorgie										
17 I 2002	DF	4 355 673	2 049 786	2 305 887	DF	4 361	...	...	69 700	...
India - Inde										
9 II 2011	DF	*1 210 193 422[69]	*623 724 248[70]	*586 469 174[69]	DF	*1 101 318*[71]	*1 182 105*[71]	1.4	3 287 263	*360*
Indonesia - Indonésie										
1 V 2010	DJ	237 641 326	119 630 913	118 010 413	DJ	*220 926*[72]	...	...	1 910 931	...
Iran (Islamic Republic of) - Iran (République islamique d')										
28 X 2006	DJ	70 495 782	35 866 362	34 629 420	DJ	*69 390*[73]	*74 340*[73]	1.4	1 628 750[74]	*46*
Iraq										
16 X 1997	DF	19 184 543[75]	9 536 570[75]	9 647 973[75]	DF	*27 963*	...	...	435 244	...

3. Population by sex, annual rate of population increase, surface area and density
Population selon le sexe, taux d'accroissement annuel de la population, superficie et densité (continued - suite)

Continent, country or area and census date / Continent, pays ou zone et date du recensement	Census type[a]	Population at the latest available census / Population d'après le dernier recensement disponible (in units — en unités)			Estimate type[a]	Mid-year estimates Estimations au milieu de l'année (in thousands — en milliers)		Annual rate of increase Taux d'accrois sement annuel 2005-10	Surface area Superficie (km²) 2010	Density Densité 2010[b]
		Both sexes Les deux sexes	Male Masculin	Female Feminin		2005	2010			

ASIA - ASIE

Israel - Israël										
27 XII 2008 .... DF		7 412 180[76]	3 663 910[76]	3 748 270[76]	DJ	6 930[77]	*7 625[77]	1.9	22 072	345
Japan - Japon										
1 X 2005 .... DJ		127 767 994[78]	62 348 977[78]	65 419 017[78]	DJ	127 773[78]	127 450[78]	-0.1	377 930[79]	337
Jordan - Jordanie										
1 X 2004 .... DF		5 103 639[80]	2 626 287[80]	2 477 352[80]	DF	5 473[81]	6 113[81]	2.2	89 342	68
Kazakhstan										
26 II 1999 .... DJ		14 955 106	7 202 954	7 752 152	DF	15 147	...	...	2 724 900	...
Kuwait - Koweït										
20 IV 2005 .... DF		*2 213 403	*1 310 067	*903 336	DF	2 245	...	...	17 818	...
Kyrgyzstan - Kirghizstan										
24 III 2009 .... DF		*5 107 700	*2 489 200	*2 618 500	DF	5 007[82]	5 193	0.7	199 951	26
Lao People's Democratic Republic - République démocratique populaire lao										
1 III 2005 .... DJ		5 621 982	2 800 551	2 821 431	DF	5 679[83]	*6 310[83]	2.1	236 800	27
Lebanon - Liban										
3 III 2007 .... SDF		3 759 134[84]	1 857 659[84]	1 901 475[84]		...	...	...	10 452	...
Malaysia - Malaisie										
5 VII 2000 .... DJ		23 274 690[85]	11 853 432[85]	11 421 258[85]	DJ	26 477[86]	28 250[86]	1.3	330 803	85
Maldives										
21 III 2006 .... DF		298 968	151 459	147 509	DF	294	320	1.7	300	1 066
Mongolia - Mongolie										
5 I 2000 .... DF		2 373 493	1 177 981	1 195 512	DF	2 548	...	...	1 564 100	...
Myanmar										
31 III 1983 .... DF		35 307 913	17 518 255	17 789 658	DF	55 396	...	...	676 578	...
Nepal - Népal										
22 VI 2001 .... DJ		23 151 423[87]	11 563 921[87]	11 587 502[87]	DJ	25 343	...	...	147 181	...
Occupied Palestinian Territory - Territoire palestinien occupé										
1 XII 2007 .... DF		*3 761 646[88]	*1 908 432[88]	*1 853 214[88]	DF	3 508	4 048	2.9	6 020	672
Oman										
12 XII 2010 .... DF		*2 694 094[89]	...	...	DF	2 509	...	...	309 500	...
Pakistan										
2 III 1998 .... DF		130 579 571[90]	67 840 137[90]	62 739 434[90]	DJ	144 367[91]	...	...	796 095	...
Philippines										
1 VIII 2007 .... DJ		*88 574 614	...	...	DJ	85 261[92]	*94 013[92]	2.0	300 000	313
Qatar										
21 IV 2010 .... DF		1 699 435	1 284 739	414 696	DF	906	1 714	12.8	11 607	148
Republic of Korea - République de Corée										
1 XI 2005 .... DJ		47 278 951[93]	23 623 954[93]	23 654 997[93]	DJ	48 138	48 875	0.3	99 897	489
Saudi Arabia - Arabie saoudite										
15 IX 2004 .... DF		22 678 262	12 557 240	10 121 022	DF	23 119	...	...	2 149 690	...
Singapore - Singapour										
30 VI 2010 .... DF		5 076 700	...	...	DF	4 266	5 077	3.5	712	7 130
Sri Lanka										
17 VII 2001 .... DF		16 929 689[94]	8 425 607[94]	8 504 082[94]	DF	19 644	*20 653	1.0	65 610	315
Syrian Arab Republic - République arabe syrienne										
22 IX 2004 .... DF		*17 921 000[95]	*9 161 000[95]	*8 760 000[95]	DF	18 138[95]	...	...	185 180	...
Tajikistan - Tadjikistan										
20 I 2000 .... DF		6 127 493	3 069 100	3 058 393	DF	6 850	...	...	143 100	...
Thailand - Thaïlande										
1 IV 2000 .... DJ		60 916 441[96]	30 015 233[96]	30 901 208[96]	DJ	64 839[1]	67 312[1]	0.7	513 120	131
Timor-Leste										
11 VII 2010 .... DF		*1 066 582	*541 147	*525 435		...	...	...	14 919	...
Turkey - Turquie										
31 XII 2008 .... DJ		71 517 100[97]	35 901 154[97]	35 615 946[97]	DJ	68 582[97]	72 698[97]	1.2	783 562	93
Turkmenistan - Turkménistan										
10 I 1995 .... DF		4 483 251	2 225 331	2 257 920		...	...	...	488 100	...

3. Population by sex, annual rate of population increase, surface area and density
Population selon le sexe, taux d'accroissement annuel de la population, superficie et densité (continued - suite)

Continent, country or area and census date / Continent, pays ou zone et date du recensement	Census type[a]	Population at the latest available census / Population d'après le dernier recensement disponible (in units — en unités)			Estimate type[a]	Mid-year estimates / Estimations au milieu de l'année (in thousands — en milliers)		Annual rate of increase / Taux d'accrois sement annuel 2005-10	Surface area / Superficie (km²) 2010	Density / Densité 2010[b]
		Both sexes / Les deux sexes	Male / Masculin	Female / Feminin		2005	2010			
ASIA - ASIE										
United Arab Emirates - Émirats arabes unis										
5 XII 2005	DF	4 106 427	2 806 141	1 300 286	DF	*4 041*	...	...	83 600	...
Uzbekistan - Ouzbékistan										
12 I 1989	DJ	19 810 077	9 784 156	10 025 921		...	...	...	447 400	...
Viet Nam										
1 IV 2009	DJ	85 846 997	42 413 143	43 433 854	DF	*82 394*[98]	*86 928	1.1	349 340	249
Yemen - Yémen										
16 XII 2004	DF	19 685 161	10 036 953	9 648 208	DF	*20 283*[19]	*23 154*[1]	2.6	527 968	44
EUROPE										
Åland Islands - Îles d'Åland										
31 XII 2000	DJ	25 776[30]	12 700[30]	13 076[30]	DJ	27[30]	28[30]	0.9	1 580	18
Albania - Albanie										
1 IV 2001	DF	3 069 275	1 530 443	1 538 832	DF	3 142	...	...	28 748	...
Andorra - Andorre										
31 XII 2000	DJ	65 844[30]	34 268[30]	31 576[30]	DJ	79[30]	85[30]	1.5	468	181
Austria - Autriche										
15 V 2001	DJ	8 032 926	3 889 189	4 143 737	DJ	8 225	8 390	0.4	83 871	100
Belarus - Bélarus										
16 II 1999	DJ	10 045 237	4 717 621	5 327 616	...	9 775	9 491		207 600	46
Belgium - Belgique										
1 X 2001	DJ	10 296 350	5 035 446	5 260 904	DJ	10 473	*10 879	0.8	30 528	356
Bosnia and Herzegovina - Bosnie-Herzégovine										
31 III 1991	DJ	4 377 033	2 183 795	2 193 238	DF	3 843	*3 844	0.0	51 209	75
Bulgaria - Bulgarie										
1 III 2001	DJ	7 928 901	3 862 465	4 066 436	DJ	7 740	7 534	-0.5	110 879	68
Croatia - Croatie										
31 III 2001	DJ	4 437 460	2 135 900	2 301 560	DJ	4 442	4 426[7]	-0.1	56 594	78
Czech Republic - République tchèque										
1 III 2001	DJ	10 230 060	4 982 071	5 247 989	DJ	10 234	10 520	0.6	78 865	133
Denmark - Danemark[99]										
1 I 2001	DJ	5 349 212[30]	2 644 319[30]	2 704 893[30]	DJ	5 416[30]	5 545[30]	0.5	43 094	129
Estonia - Estonie										
31 III 2000	DJ	1 370 052	631 851	738 201	DJ	1 346	1 340	-0.1	45 227	30
Faeroe Islands - Îles Féroé										
1 I 2008	DJ	48 433[30]	25 174[30]	23 259[30]	DJ	48	...	...	1 393	...
Finland - Finlande										
31 XII 2000	DJ	5 181 115[30]	2 529 341[30]	2 651 774[30]	DJ	5 246[30]	5 335[100]	0.3	336 861[101]	16
France										
1 I 2006	DJ	61 399 541[102]	29 714 539[102]	31 685 002[102]	DJ	61 181[102]	*62 968[102]	0.6	551 500	114
Germany - Allemagne										
28 III 2004	SDJ	82 491 000[103]	40 330 000[103]	42 161 000[103]	DJ	82 464	*81 776	-0.2	357 114	229
Gibraltar										
12 XI 2001	DF	27 495[104]	13 644[104]	13 851[104]	DF	29[105]	...	...	6	...
Greece - Grèce										
18 III 2001	DF	10 964 020[106]	5 427 682[106]	5 536 338[106]	DF	11 104[107]	...	...	131 957	...
Guernsey - Guernesey										
29 IV 2001	DJ	59 807	29 138	30 669	DF	...	62[108]	...	78	800
Holy See - Saint-Siège[109]										
26 II 2010	DJ	*460	...	...		...	...	...	0[110]	...
Hungary - Hongrie										
1 II 2001	DF	10 198 315	4 850 650	5 347 665	DJ	10 087	*10 000	-0.2	93 027	107
Iceland - Islande										
1 VII 2000	DJ	281 154[30]	140 718[30]	140 436[30]	DJ	296[30]	318[30]	1.4	103 000	3
Ireland - Irlande										
23 IV 2006	DF	4 239 848	2 121 171	2 118 677	DF	4 131[111]	*4 474	1.6	70 273	64
Isle of Man - Île de Man										
23 IV 2006	DF	76 657	...	...	DJ	79[112]	...	...	572	...

Population selon le sexe, taux d'accroissement annuel de la population, superficie et densité (continued - suite)

Continent, country or area and census date Continent, pays ou zone et date du recensement	Census type[a]	Population at the latest available census Population d'après le dernier recensement disponible (in units — en unités)			Estimate type[a]	Mid-year estimates Estimations au milieu de l'année (in thousands — en milliers)		Annual rate of increase Taux d'accrois sement annuel 2005-10	Surface area Superficie (km²) 2010	Density Densité 2010[b]
		Both sexes Les deux sexes	Male Masculin	Female Feminin		2005	2010			
EUROPE										
Italy - Italie										
21 X 2001 .... DF		57 110 144	27 617 335	29 492 809	DJ	58 607	*60 483	0.6	301 336	201
Jersey										
11 III 2001 .... DJ		87 186	42 484	44 702	DF	88	...	...	116	...
Latvia - Lettonie										
31 III 2000 .... DJ		2 377 383	1 094 964	1 282 419	DJ	2 301	2 239	-0.5	64 559	35
Liechtenstein										
5 XII 2000 .... DF		33 307	16 420	16 887	DJ	35	*36	0.7	160	225
Lithuania - Lituanie										
6 IV 2001 .... DJ		3 483 972	1 629 148	1 854 824	DJ	3 414	3 287	-0.8	65 300	50
Luxembourg										
15 II 2001 .... DJ		439 539	216 541	222 998	DJ	465	507	1.7	2 586	196
Malta - Malte										
27 XI 2005 .... DJ		404 962	200 819	204 143	DJ	404[113]	*416[113]	0.6	316	1 316
Monaco										
9 VI 2008 .... DJ		31 109	15 076[114]	15 914[114]		...	...	...	2	...
Montenegro - Monténégro										
31 X 2003 .... DJ		620 145	305 225	314 920	DJ	623	*633[7]	0.3	13 812	46
Netherlands - Pays-Bas										
1 I 2002 .... DJ		16 105 285[115]	7 971 967[115]	8 133 318[115]	DJ	16 320	*16 615	0.4	37 354	445
Norway - Norvège[116]										
3 XI 2001 .... DJ		4 520 947[117]	2 240 281[117]	2 280 666[117]	DJ	4 623[118]	4 889[118]	1.1	323 782	15
Poland - Pologne										
20 V 2002 .... DJ		38 230 080[119]	18 516 403[119]	19 713 677[119]	DJ	38 161[119]	38 184[119]	0.0	312 679	122
Portugal										
12 III 2001 .... DF		10 356 117	5 000 141	5 355 976	DJ	10 549	*10 637	0.2	92 207	115
Republic of Moldova - République de Moldova										
5 X 2004 .... DF		3 386 673[120]	1 629 689[120]	1 756 984[120]	DJ	3 595[120]	3 562[120]	-0.2	33 846	105
Romania - Roumanie										
18 III 2002 .... DJ		21 680 974	10 568 741	11 112 233	DJ	21 624	*21 438	-0.2	238 391	90
Russian Federation - Fédération de Russie										
9 X 2002 .... DJ		145 166 731	67 605 133	77 561 598	DJ	143 114	*142 938	0.0	17 098 242	8
San Marino - Saint-Marin										
1 VII 2000 .... DF		26 941[30]	13 185[30]	13 756[30]	DF	31[30]	33[30]	1.4	61	544
Serbia - Serbie										
31 III 2002 .... DJ		7 498 001[121]	3 645 930[121]	3 852 071[121]	DJ	7 441[121]	*7 428[121]	0.0	88 361	84
Slovakia - Slovaquie										
25 V 2001 .... DF		5 193 376	2 502 721	2 690 655	DJ	5 387	5 430	0.2	49 037	111
Slovenia - Slovénie										
31 III 2002 .... DF		1 987 971[118]	971 203[118]	1 016 768[118]	DJ	2 001	2 049	0.5	20 273	101
Spain - Espagne										
1 XI 2001 .... DF		40 847 371[122]	20 012 882[122]	20 834 489[122]	DJ	43 398	46 071	1.2	505 992	91
Svalbard and Jan Mayen Islands - Îles Svalbard et Jan Mayen										
1 XI 1960 .... DF		3 431[123]	2 545[123]	886[123]	DF	2[124]	...	...	62 422	...
Sweden - Suède										
31 XII 2003 .... DJ		8 975 670[30]	4 446 656[30]	4 529 014[30]	DJ	9 030[30]	9 378[30]	0.8	450 295	21
Switzerland - Suisse										
5 XII 2000 .... DF		7 288 010	3 567 567	3 720 443	DJ	7 437	*7 826	1.0	41 285	190
TFYR of Macedonia - L'ex-R. y. de Macédoine										
31 X 2002 .... DJ		2 022 547	1 015 377	1 007 170	DF	2 037	2 053[7]	0.2	25 713	80
Ukraine										
5 XII 2001 .... DF		48 240 902	22 316 317	25 924 585	DF	47 105	45 963[7]	-0.5	603 500	76
United Kingdom of Great Britain and Northern Ireland - Royaume-Uni de Grande-Bretagne et d'Irlande du Nord[125]										
29 IV 2001 .... DF		58 789 187[126]	28 579 867[126]	30 209 320[126]	DF	60 238	*62 222	0.6	242 900	256

3. Population by sex, annual rate of population increase, surface area and density
Population selon le sexe, taux d'accroissement annuel de la population, superficie et densité (continued - suite)

Continent, country or area and census date / Continent, pays ou zone et date du recensement	Census type[a]	Population at the latest available census Population d'après le dernier recensement disponible (in units — en unités)			Estimate type[a]	Mid-year estimates Estimations au milieu de l'année (in thousands — en milliers)		Annual rate of increase Taux d' accrois sement annuel 2005-10	Surface area Superficie (km²) 2010	Density Densité 2010[b]
		Both sexes Les deux sexes	Male Masculin	Female Feminin		2005	2010			
OCEANIA - OCÉANIE										
American Samoa - Samoas américaines										
1 IV 2000 .... DJ	DJ	57 291[40]	29 264[40]	28 027[40]	DJ	66[40]	...	...	199	...
Australia - Australie										
8 VIII 2006 .... DF	DF	20 061 646	9 896 500	10 165 146	DJ	20 395[127]	*22 342[127]	1.8	7 692 024	3
Cook Islands - Îles Cook[128]										
1 XII 2006 .... DF	DF	*19 569	*9 932	*9 637	DF	22	*23	1.4	236	98
Fiji - Fidji										
16 IX 2007 .... DF	DF	837 271	427 176	410 095	DF	825	...	...	18 272	...
French Polynesia - Polynésie française										
20 VIII 2007 .... DJ	DJ	*259 596	...	...	DF	253	...	...	4 000	...
Guam										
1 IV 2000 .... DJ	DJ	154 805[40]	79 181[40]	75 624[40]	DJ	*169[40]	*181[40]	1.4	549	329
Kiribati										
7 XII 2005 .... DF	DF	92 533	45 612	46 921		...	...	...	726[129]	...
Marshall Islands - Îles Marshall										
1 VI 1999 .... DF	DF	50 848	26 034	24 814	DF	...	54[1]	...	181	300
Micronesia (Federated States of) - Micronésie (États fédérés de)										
1 IV 2000 .... DJ	DJ	107 008	54 191	52 817	DJ	108[1]	108[1]	0.0	702	154
Nauru										
23 IX 2002 .... DF	DF	10 065	5 136	4 929		...	...	...	21	...
New Caledonia - Nouvelle-Calédonie										
31 VIII 2004 .... DF	DF	230 789	116 485	114 304	DF	234	...	...	18 575	...
New Zealand - Nouvelle-Zélande										
7 III 2006 .... DF	DF	4 143 282[130]	2 021 277[130]	2 122 005[130]	DJ	4 134[131]	4 368[132]	1.1	270 467	16
Niue - Nioué										
9 IX 2006 .... DF	DF	1 625	802	823	DJ	2	1	-3.1	260	6
Norfolk Island - Île Norfolk										
8 VIII 2006 .... DF	DF	2 523	1 218	1 305	DF	2	...	...	36	...
Northern Mariana Islands - Îles Mariannes septentrionales										
1 IV 2000 .... DF	DF	69 221	31 984	37 237	DF	71	48	-7.6	457	106
Palau - Palaos										
1 IV 2005 .... DJ	DJ	19 907	10 699	9 208		...	...	...	459	...
Papua New Guinea - Papouasie-Nouvelle-Guinée										
9 VII 2000 .... DF	DF	5 190 786	2 691 744	2 499 042		...	...	...	462 840	...
Pitcairn										
31 XII 1991 .... DF	DF	66	...	...		...	...	...	5	...
Samoa										
5 XI 2006 .... DF	DF	180 741	93 677	87 064	DF	183	184	0.1	2 842	65
Solomon Islands - Îles Salomon										
21 XI 1999 .... DF	DF	409 042	211 381	197 661	DF	471[1]	542[1]	2.8	28 896	19
Tokelau - Tokélaou										
19 X 2006 .... DF	DF	1 151	583	568		...	...	...	12	...
Tonga										
30 XI 2006 .... DJ	DJ	101 991	51 772	50 219	DF	102[133]	...	...	747	...
Tuvalu										
1 XI 2002 .... DF	DF	9 561	4 729	4 832	DF	10	...	...	26	...
Vanuatu										
16 XI 1999 .... DJ	DJ	186 678	95 682	90 996		...	...	...	12 189	...
Wallis and Futuna Islands - Îles Wallis et Futuna										
21 VII 2008 .... DF	DF	13 445	6 669	6 776		...	...	...	142	...

67

FOOTNOTES - NOTES

Italics: estimates which are less reliable. - Italiques : estimations moins sûres.

* Provisional. - Données provisoires.

a 'Code' indicates the source of data, as follows:
DF - De facto
DJ - De jure
SDF - Sample survey, de facto
SDJ - Sample survey, de jure

Le 'Code' indique la source des données, comme suit :
DF - Population de fait
DJ - Population de droit
SDF - Enquête par sondage, population de fait
SDJ - Enquête par sondage, Population de droit

b Population per square kilometre of surface area. Figures are estimates of population divided by surface area and are not to be considered either as reflecting density in the urban sense or as indicating the supporting power of a territory's land and resources. - Nombre d'habitants au kilomètre carré. Il s'agit simplement d'éstimations de la population divisé par celui de la superficie: il ne faut pas y voir d'indication de la densité au sens urbain du terme ni de l'effectif de population que les terres et les ressources du territoire sont capables de nourrir.

1 Data refer to national projections. - Les données se réfèrent aux projections nationales.

2 Excluding Mayotte. - Non compris Mayotte.

3 Projections based on the 1994 population census. - Projections fondées sur le recensement de la population de 1994.

4 Based on the results of the Gabonese Survey for the Evaluation and Tracking of Poverty. - Sur base des résultats de l'enquête gabonaise sur l'évaluation et le suivi de la pauvreté.

5 Post-censal estimates based on 1999 Population Census. - Les estimations post-censitaire fondées sur le recensement de la population de 1999.

6 As reported by the country. Reasons for discrepancy with other tables not ascertained. - Données comme déclarées par le pays. On ne sait pas comment s'explique la divergence entre ces chiffres et les chiffres correspondants indiqués ailleurs.

7 Data refer to 1 January. - Données se raportent au 1 janvier.

8 Excludes the islands of St. Brandon and Agalega. - Non compris les îles St. Brandon et Agalega.

9 Based on 2000 Population Census data and adjusted for underenumeration of young children. - D'après le recensement de la population de 2000, ajusté en raison du sous-enregistrement des jeunes enfants.

10 Based on the results of the 2004 Population Census. - D'après des résultats du recensement de la population de 2004.

11 The number of males and/or females excludes persons whose sex is not stated (18 urban, 19 rural). - Il n'est pas tenu compte dans le nombre d'hommes et de femmes des personnes dont le sexe n'est pas indiqué (18 en zone urbaine et 19 en zone rurale).

12 Data are based on projections from 2002 Census. Data refer to 31 December. - Données fondées sur des projections tirées du recensement de 2002. Données se raportent au 31 décembre.

13 Surface area is based on 2002 population and housing census. - La superficie est fondée sur les données provenant du recensement de la population et du logement de 2002.

14 Data have not been adjusted for underenumeration, estimated at 2.4 per cent. - Les données n'ont pas été ajustées pour compenser les lacunes du dénombrement, estimées à 2,4 p. 100.

15 Mid-year estimates have been adjusted for underenumeration at latest census. - Les estimations au millieu de l'année tiennent compte d'un ajustement destiné à compenser les lacunes du dénombrement lors du dernier recensement.

16 Comprising the Northern Region (former Saguia el Hamra) and Southern Region (former Rio de Oro). - Comprend la région septentrionale (ancien Saguia-el-Hamra) et la région méridionale (ancien Rio de Oro).

17 Data are based on projections from 2002 Census. - Données fondées sur des projections tirées du recensement de 2002.

18 Excluding persons who were not contacted at the time of the census. - La population non comprend pas les personnes qui n'ont pas été contactées à l'heure du recensement.

19 Data refer to 31 December. - Données se raportent au 31 décembre.

20 Excluding the institutional population. - Non compris la population dans les institutions.

21 Because of rounding, totals are not in all cases the sum of the parts. - Les chiffres étant arrondis, les totaux ne correspondent pas toujours rigoureusement à la somme des chiffres partiels.

22 Final intercensal estimates. Estimates adjusted for census net undercoverage (including adjustment for incompletely enumerated Indian reserves). - Estimations inter-censitaires definitives. Ajusté pour la sous-estimation du recensement (y compris les réservations en Inde incomplètement énumérées).

23 Estimates adjusted for census net undercoverage (including adjustment for incompletely enumerated Indian reserves). Preliminary postcensal estimates. - Ajusté pour la sous-estimation du recensement (y compris les réservations en Inde incomplètement énumérées). Estimations post censitaires préliminaires.

24 Excluding residents of institutions. - À l'exclusion de personnes en établissements de soins.

25 Based on 2010 National Household Survey. - Basée sur l'Enquête nationale des ménages de 2010.

26 Internal waters include adjacent cays. - Les eaux intérieures comprennent les cayes adjacentes.

27 Population in households only. - Population dans les ménages seulement.

28 Estimates based on 2007 Population Census. - Estimations fondées sur le recensement de la population de 2007.

29 The total surface is 21040.79 square kilometers, without taking into account the last ruling of The Hague. - La superficie totale est égale à 21040.79 km2, sans tenir compte de la dernière décision de la Haye.

30 Population statistics are compiled from registers. - Les statistiques de la population sont compilées à partir des registres.

31 Excluding data for Saint Barthélémy and Saint Martin. - Non compris les données pour Saint Barthélémy et Saint Martin.

32 Excluding data for Saint Barthélémy and Saint Martin. Data refer to 1 January. - Non compris les données pour Saint Barthélémy et Saint Martin. Données se raportent au 1 janvier.

33 Projections based on 2002 population census. - Projections fondées sur le recensement de la population de 2002.

34 Projections produced by l'Institut Haïtien de Statistique et d'Informatique (IHSI) and the Latin American and Caribbean Demographic Centre (CELADE) - Population Division of ECLAC. - Les données sont projections produits par l'Institut Haïtien de Statistique et d'Informatique (IHSI) et le centre démographique de l'Amérique latine et les Caraïbes - Division de la population de la CEPALC.

35 Data are based on projections of the 2001 Population and Housing Census data. - Les données sont basées sur les projections du recensement de 2001 de la population et de l'habitat.

36 Total represents population in private dwellings, the non-institutional population and persons found on the streets between the hours of 5am and 7am on September 26, 2001; the figures represent the census counts adjusted for under-coverage. - Le total représente la population vivant dans des logements privés et les personnes trouvées dans la rue entre 5 et 7 heures du matin le 26 septembre 2001, mais ne tient pas compte des personnes vivant dans des établissements; les chiffres sont ceux du recensement corrigés pour tenir compte du sous-dénombrement.

37 Including an estimation of 1 334 585 persons corresponding to 448 195 housing units without information of the occupants. - Y compris une estimation de 1 334 585 personnes correspondant aux 448 195 unités d'habitation sans information sur les occupants.

38 Includes estimates for St. Eustatius. Data refer to 1 January. - Y compris les estimations pour St. Eustatius. Données se raportent au 1 janvier.

39 Data refer to projections based on the 2000 population census. - Les données se réfèrent aux projections basées sur le recensement de la population de 2000.

40 Including armed forces stationed in the area. - Y compris les militaires en garnison sur le territoire.

41 Refers to habitable area. Excludes St. Lucia's Forest Reserve. - S'applique à la zone habitable. Exclut la réserve forestière de Sainte-Lucie.

42 Based on the results of the 2000 population census. - Basé sur les résultats du rececement de la population de 2000.

43 Including low water level for all islands (area to shoreline). - Incluent le niveau de basses eaux pour toutes les îles.

44 Excluding armed forces overseas and civilian citizens absent from country for an extended period of time. - Non compris les militaires à l'étranger, et les civils hors du pays pendant une période prolongée.

45 Data based on 2010 Population Census. - Données fondées sur le recensement de population de 2010.

46 Data include persons in remote areas, military personnel outside the country, merchant seamen at sea, civilian seasonal workers outside the country, and other civilians outside the country, and exclude nomads, foreign military, civilian aliens temporarily in the country, transients on ships and Indian jungle population. - Y compris les personnes vivant dans des régions éloignées, le personel militaire en

dehors du pays, les marins marchands, les ouvriers saisonniers en dehors du pays, et autres civils en dehors du pays, et non compris les nomades, les militaires étrangers, les étrangers civils temporairement dans le pays, les transiteurs sur des bateaux et les Indiens de la jungle.

[47] Data based on the Population Census of 2005. - Données fondées sur le recensement de la population de 2005.

[48] Data refer to national projections. Excluding nomadic Indian tribes. - Les données se réfèrent aux projections nationales. Non compris les tribus d'Indiens nomades.

[49] A dispute exists between the governments of Argentina and the United Kingdom of Great Britain and Northern Ireland concerning sovereignty over the Falkland Islands (Malvinas). - La souveraineté sur les îles Falkland (Malvinas) fait l'objet d'un différend entre le Gouvernement argentin et le Gouvernement du Royaume-Uni de Grande-Bretagne et d'Irlande du Nord.

[50] Include 477 persons present in the Falkland Islands in connection with the military garrison, but exclude all military personnel and their families. - Comprend 477 personnes installées dans les îles Falkland du fait de la présence d'une garnison militaire, mais exclut tous les membres du personnel militaire et leurs familles.

[51] The previous census was conducted only 16 months earlier (on 31 Mar 2003) but it was repeated because all of its data were destroyed in a fire before they could be fully processed, analyzed, and reported. - Le recensement précédent a eu lieu seulement 16 mois auparavant (le 31 mars 2003), mais a dû être refait parce que toutes les données ont été détruites dans un incendie avant que l'on n'ait pu les traiter et les analyser.

[52] The previous census was conducted only 16 months earlier (on 31 Mar 2003) but it was repeated because all of its data were destroyed in a fire before they could be fully processed, analyzed, and reported. Figures for male and female population do not add up to the figure for total population, because they exclude 365 persons of unknown sex. - Le recensement précédent a eu lieu seulement 16 mois auparavant (le 31 mars 2003), mais a dû être refait parce que toutes les données ont été détruites dans un incendie avant que l'on n'ait pu les traiter et les analyser. Les chiffres relatifs à la population masculine et féminine ne correspondent pas au chiffre de la population totale, parce que l'on en a exclu 365 personnes de sexe inconnu.

[53] Data refer to resident population in Uruguay according to Census Phase 1, carried out between the months of June and July 2004. - Les données se rapportent à la population résidente en Uruguay d'après la phase 1 du recensement, qui a eu lieu entre juin et juillet 2004.

[54] Excluding Indian jungle population. - Non compris les Indiens de la jungle.

[55] Excluding nomad population. - Non compris les nomades.

[56] Data refer to the settled population based on the 1979 Population Census and the latest household prelisting. The refugees of Afghanistan in Iran, Pakistan, and an estimated 1.5 million nomads, are not included. - Les données se rapportent à la population stationnaire sur la base du recensement de 1979 et du recensement préliminaire des logements le plus récent. Sont exclus les réfugiés d'Afghanistan en Iran et au Pakistan et les nomades estimés à 1,5 million.

[57] Data refer to the settled population based on the 1979 Population Census and the latest household prelisting. The refugees of Afghanistan in Iran, Pakistan, and an estimated 1.5 million nomads, are not included. The adjusted total population of the country is 26 million (13.3 million males and 12.7 million females). - Les données se rapportent à la population stationnaire sur la base du recensement de 1979 et du recensement préliminaire des logements le plus récent. Sont exclus les réfugiés d'Afghanistan en Iran et au Pakistan et les nomades estimés à 1,5 million. La population totale ajustée du pays comprend 26 millions de personnes (13.3 millions d'homes et 12.7 millions de femmes).

[58] The methodology used for calculating the number of the de facto and de jure population in the 2001 census data differs as follows from the methodology used in previous censuses: the duration that defines a person as being ' temporary present ' or 'temporary absent' is now 'under one year'. The previously applied definition was for '6 months'. - La méthode utilisée pour dénombrer la population de fait et la population de droit dans le contexte du recensement de 2001 diffère de celle qui a été appliquée lors des recensements antérieurs en ce que la durée considérée pour définir la ' présence temporaire 'ou' l'absence temporaire' était dorénavant fixée à 'moins d'un an' alors qu'elle était de '6 mois' auparavant.

[59] Intercensal estimates. - Estimations inter-censitaires.

[60] Data have not been adjusted for underenumeration, estimated at 4.96 per cent. - Les données n'ont pas été ajustées pour compenser les lacunes du dénombrement, estimées à 4,96 p.100.

[61] Data refer to projections based on the 2005 population census. - Les données se réfèrent aux projections basées sur le recensement de la population de 2005.

[62] Excluding foreign diplomatic personnel and their dependants. - Non compris le personnel diplomatique étranger et les membres de leur famille les accompagnant.

[63] Excluding foreign diplomatic personnel and their dependants. Based on 1998 census results. - Non compris le personnel diplomatique étranger et les

membres de leur famille les accompagnant. A partir des résultats de recensement de l'année 1998.

[64] Data refer to national projections based on 2008 census. Excluding foreign diplomatic personnel and their dependants. - Les données se réfèrent aux projections nationales basées sur le recensement de la population de 2008. Non compris le personnel diplomatique étranger et les membres de leur famille les accompagnant.

[65] For statistical purposes, the data for China do not include those for the Hong Kong Special Administrative Region (Hong Kong SAR), Macao Special Administrative Region (Macao SAR) and Taiwan province of China. Data refer to the civilian population of 31 provinces, municipalities and autonomous regions. - Pour la présentation des statistiques, les données pour la Chine ne comprennent pas la Région Administrative Spéciale de Hong Kong (Hong Kong RAS), la Région Administrative Spéciale de Macao (Macao RAS) et Taïwan province de Chine. Pour la population civile seulement de 31 provinces, municipalités et régions autonomes.

[66] Data have been estimated on the basis of the annual National Sample Survey on Population Changes. For statistical purposes, the data for China do not include those for the Hong Kong Special Administrative Region (Hong Kong SAR), Macao Special Administrative Region (Macao SAR) and Taiwan province of China. - Les données ont été estimées sur la base de l'enquête annuelle "National Sample Survey on Population Changes". Pour la présentation des statistiques, les données pour la Chine ne comprennent pas la Région Administrative Spéciale de Hong Kong (Hong Kong RAS), la Région Administrative Spéciale de Macao (Macao RAS) et Taïwan province de Chine.

[67] Data refer to government controlled areas. Including all persons irrespective of citizenship, who at the time of the census resided in the country or intended to reside for a period of at least one year. It does not distinguish between those present or absent at the time of census. - Les données se rapportent aux zones contrôlées par le Gouvernement. Les chiffres comprennent toute la population, quelle que soit la nationalité, qui à l'époque de recensement avait résidé dans le pays, ou avait l'intention de résider, pendant une période d'au moins un an. Il n'y a pas de distinction entre les personnes présentes ou absentes au moment du recensement.

[68] Data refer to government controlled areas. - Les données se rapportent aux zones contrôlées par le Gouvernement.

[69] Including data for the Indian-held part of Jammu and Kashmir, the final status of which has not yet been determined. - Y compris les données pour la partie du Jammu et du Cachemire occupée par l'Inde dont le statut définitif n'a pas encore été déterminé.

[70] Including data for the Indian-held part of Jammu and Kashmir, the final status of which has not yet been determined. Including unknown sex. - Y compris les données pour la partie du Jammu et du Cachemire occupée par l'Inde dont le statut définitif n'a pas encore été déterminé. Y compris le sexe inconnu.

[71] Data refer to national projections. Including data for the Indian-held part of Jammu and Kashmir, the final status of which has not yet been determined. - Les données se réfèrent aux projections nationales. Y compris les données pour la partie du Jammu et du Cachemire occupée par l'Inde dont le statut définitif n'a pas encore été déterminé.

[72] Final intercensal estimates. - Estimations inter-censitaires definitives.

[73] Data refer to the Iranian Year which begins on 21 March and ends on 20 March of the following year. - Les données concernent l'année iranienne, qui commence le 21 mars et se termine le 20 mars de l'année suivante.

[74] Land area only. - La superficie des terres seulement.

[75] Excluding the population in three autonomous provinces in the north of the country. - La population des trois provinces autonomes dans le nord du pays est exclue.

[76] Data are rounded for confidentiality reasons. - Chiffres arrondis pour des raisons de confidentialité.

[77] Including data for East Jerusalem and Israeli residents in certain other territories under occupation by Israeli military forces since June 1967. - Y compris les données pour Jérusalem-Est et les résidents israéliens dans certains autres territoires occupés depuis 1967 par les forces armées israéliennes.

[78] Excluding diplomatic personnel outside the country and foreign military and civilian personnel and their dependants stationed in the area. - Non compris le personnel diplomatique hors du pays ni les militaires et agents civils étrangers en poste sur le territoire et les membres de leur famille les accompagnant.

[79] Data refer to 1 October 2007. - Les données se réfèrent au 1er octobre 2007.

[80] Excluding data for Jordanian territory under occupation since June 1967 by Israeli military forces. Including registered Palestinian refugees and Jordanians abroad. - Non compris les données pour le territoire jordanien occupé depuis juin 1967 par les forces armées israéliennes. Y compris les réfugiés palestiniens enregistrés et les Jordaniens à l'étranger.

[81] Data refer to 31 December. Excluding data for Jordanian territory under occupation since June 1967 by Israeli military forces. Excluding foreigners, including registered Palestinian refugees. - Données se raportent au 31

décembre. Non compris les données pour le territoire jordanien occupé depuis juin 1967 par les forces armées israéliennes. Non compris les étrangers, mais y compris les réfugiés de Palestine enregistrés.

[82] Data are calculated from results of Population and Housing Census of 2009. - Les données sont calculées à partir des résultats de recensement de la population et de l'habitat de 2009.

[83] Based on the results of the 2005 Population and Housing Census. - Données fondées sur les résultats du recensement de la population et de l'habitat de 2005.

[84] Based on the results of a household survey. - D'après les résultats d'une enquête des ménages.

[85] Data have been adjusted for underenumeration. Excluding Malaysian citizens and permanent residents who were away or intended to be away from the country for more than six months. Excluding Malaysian military, naval and diplomatic personnel and their families outside the country, and tourists, businessman who intended to be in Malaysia for less than six months. - Les données ont été ajustées pour compenser les lacunes du dénombrement. Non compris les citoyens malaisiens et les résidents permanents qui étaient ou qui ont prévu d'être hors du pays pour six mois ou plus. Non compris le personnel militaire Malaisien, le personnel naval ou diplomatique et leurs familles hors du pays, et les touristes et les hommes d'affaires qui avaient l'intention de rester en Malaisie moins de six mois.

[86] Data refer to 30 June. Data refer to projections based on the 2000 population census. - Données se raportent au 30 juin. Les données se réfèrent aux projections basées sur le recensement de la population de 2000.

[87] Data including estimated population from household listing from Village Development Committees and Wards which could not be enumerated at the time of census. - Les données incluent la population estimée par les listes des ménages des comités de développement des villages et des circonscriptions qui n'ont pas pu être énumérée au moment du recensement.

[88] Data have been adjusted for underenumeration, estimated at 2.70 per cent. - Les données ont été ajustées pour compenser les lacunes du dénombrement, estimées à 2,70 p. 100.

[89] 72.4 % are Omani and the rest are Expatriates. - Le pourcentage d'Omanais atteint 72,4 %; le pourcentage restant correspond à des personnes expatriées.

[90] Excluding data for the Pakistan-held part of Jammu and Kashmir, the final status of which has not yet been determined. - Non compris les données concernant la partie du Jammu et Cachemire occupée par le Pakistan dont le statut définitif n'a pas été déterminé.

[91] Excluding data for the Pakistan-held part of Jammu and Kashmir, the final status of which has not yet been determined. Based on the results of the Pakistan Demographic Survey (PDS 2005). These estimates do not reflect completely accurately the actual population and vital events of the country. - Non compris les données concernant la partie du Jammu et Cachemire occupée par le Pakistan dont le statut définitif n'a pas été déterminé. D'après les résultats de l'enquête démographique effectuée par le Pakistan en 2005. Ces estimations ne dénotent pas d'une manière complètement ponctuelle la population actuelle et les statistiques de l'état civil du pays.

[92] Data are based on projections of the 2000 Population and Housing Census data. - Les données sont basées sur les projections du recensement de 2000 de la population et de l'habitat.

[93] Excluding usual residents not in country at time of census. - À l'exclusion des résidents habituels qui ne sont pas dans le pays au moment du recensement.

[94] The Population and Housing Census 2001 did not cover the whole area of the country due to the security problems; data refer to the 18 districts for which the census was completed only (in three districts it was not possible to conduct the census at all and four districts it was partially conducted). - Le recensement de la population et du logement de 2001 n'a pas été réalisé sur la superficie totale du pays à cause de problèmes de sécurité; les données ne concernent que les 18 districts entièrement recensés (3 districts n'ont pas été recensés du tout, et 4 ont été recensés en partie).

[95] Including Palestinian refugees. - Y compris les réfugiés de Palestine.

[96] All persons falling within the scope of the census were enumerated on a de jure basis, except students who were enumerated on a de facto basis. - Toutes les personnes englobées dans le recensement ont été dénombrées comme population de droit, à l'exception des étudiants qui ont été dénombrés comme population de fait.

[97] Data based on Address Based Population Registration System. - Les données sont basées sur le registre national de la population basé sur l'adresse.

[98] Data are adjusted according to the results of 1999 and 2009 censuses. - Les données ont été ajustées à partir des résultats des recensements de la population de 1999 et 2009.

[99] Excluding Faeroe Islands and Greenland shown separately, if available. - Non compris les Iles Féroé et le Groenland, qui font l'objet de rubriques distinctes, si disponible.

[100] Excluding Åland Islands. Population statistics are compiled from registers. - Non compris les Îles d'Åland. Les statistiques de la population sont compilées à partir des registres.

[101] Excluding Åland Islands. - Non compris les Îles d'Åland.

[102] Excluding diplomatic personnel outside the country and including members of alien armed forces not living in military camps and foreign diplomatic personnel not living in embassies or consulates. - Non compris le personnel diplomatique hors du pays et y compris les militaires étrangers ne vivant pas dans des camps militaires et le personnel diplomatique étranger ne vivant pas dans les ambassades ou les consulats.

[103] Data of the microcensus - a 1% household sample survey - refer to a single reference week in spring (usually last week in April). Excluding homeless persons. Excluding foreign military personnel and foreign diplomatic and consular personnel and their family members in the country. - Les données du microrecensement (enquête sur les ménages, réalisée sur un échantillon de 1 %) concernent une seule semaine de référence au printemps (habituellement la dernière semaine d'avril). Non compris les personnes sans domicile fixe. Non compris le personnel militaire étranger, le personnel diplomatique et consulaire étranger et les membres de leur famille se trouvant dans le pays.

[104] Excluding families of military personnel, visitors and transients. - Non compris les familles des militaires, ni les visiteurs et transients.

[105] Excluding military personnel, visitors and transients. - Non compris les militaires, ni les visiteurs et transients.

[106] Including armed forces stationed outside the country and alien armed forces in the area. - Y compris les militaires nationaux hors du pays et les militaires étrangers en garnison sur le territoire.

[107] Excluding armed forces stationed outside the country, but including alien armed forces stationed in the area. - Non compris les militaires en garnison hors du pays, mais y compris les militaires étrangers en garnison sur le territoire.

[108] Data refer to 31 March. - Données se raportent au 31 mars.

[109] Data refer to the Vatican City State. - Les données se rapportent à l'Etat de la Cité du Vatican.

[110] Surface area is 0.44 Km2. - Superficie: 0,44 Km2.

[111] Data refer to 15 April. - Données se raportent au 15 avril.

[112] Data refer to 30 April. - Données se raportent au 30 avril.

[113] Including civilian nationals temporarily outside the country. - Y compris les civils nationaux temporairement hors du pays.

[114] Figures for male and female population do not add up to the figure for total population, because they exclude 119 persons of unknown sex. - Les chiffres relatifs à la population masculine et féminine ne correspondent pas au chiffre de la population totale, parce que l'on en a exclu 119 personnes de sexe inconnu.

[115] Census results based on compilation of continuous accounting and sample surveys. - Le résultat du recensement, d'après les résultats des dénombrements et enquêtes par sondage continue.

[116] Excluding Svalbard and Jan Mayen Islands shown separately, if available. - Non compris Svalbard et Jan Mayen qui font l'objet de rubriques distinctes, si disponible.

[117] Population statistics are compiled from registers. Including residents temporarily outside the country. - Les statistiques de la population sont compilées à partir des registres. Y compris les résidents se trouvant temporairement hors du pays.

[118] Including residents temporarily outside the country. - Y compris les résidents se trouvant temporairement hors du pays.

[119] Excluding civilian aliens within country, but including civilian nationals temporarily outside country. - Non compris les civils étrangers dans le pays, mais y compris les civils nationaux temporairement hors du pays.

[120] Excluding Transnistria and the municipality of Bender. - Les données ne tiennent pas compte de l'information sur la Transnistria et la municipalité de Bender.

[121] Excluding data for Kosovo and Metohia. - Sans les données pour le Kosovo et Metohie.

[122] Excluding transients visitors. - Non compris les visiteurs en transit.

[123] Inhabited only during the winter season. Census data are for total population while estimates refer to Norwegian population only. Included also in the de jure population of Norway. - N'est habitée que pendant la saison d'hiver. Les données de recensement se rapportent à la population totale, mais les estimations ne concernent que la population norvégienne, comprise également dans la population de droit de la Norvège.

[124] Data refer to 1 January. Data refer to Svalbard only. - Données se raportent au 1 janvier. Données ne concernant que le Svalbard.

[125] Excluding Channel Islands (Guernsey and Jersey) and Isle of Man, shown separately, if available. - Non compris les îles Anglo-Normandes (Guernesey et Jersey) et l'île de Man, qui font l'objet de rubriques distinctes, si disponible.

[126] Counts for the 2001 Census are taken from 'Key Statistics table 1 for the Urban/Rural classification: England and Wales' available on CD based on the usually resident population. - Les chiffres du recensement de 2001 proviennent du tableau intitulé « Key Statistics table 1 for the Urban/Rural classification:

England and Wales » disponible sur CD-ROM et sont fondés sur la notion de résidence habituelle.

[127] Intercensal estimates. Data are based on 2009 Australian Standard Geographical Classification boundaries. - Estimations inter-censitaires. Les données réfèrent au découpage de la nomenclature géographique normalisée d'Australie de 2009.

[128] Excluding Niue, shown separately, which is part of Cook Islands, but because of remoteness is administered separately. - Non compris Nioué, qui fait l'objet d'une rubrique distincte et qui fait partie des îles Cook, mais qui, en raison de son éloignement, est administrée séparément.

[129] Land area only. Excluding 84 square km of uninhabited islands. - La superficie des terres seulement. Exclut des îles inhabitées d'une superficie de 84 kilomètres carrés.

[130] This data has been randomly rounded to protect confidentiality. Individual figures may not add up to totals, and values for the same data may vary in different tables. - Ces données ont été arrondies de façon aléatoire afin d'en préserver la confidentialité. La somme de certains chiffres peut ne pas correspondre aux totaux indiqués et les valeurs des mêmes données peuvent varier d'un tableau à un autre.

[131] Excluding diplomatic personnel and armed forces stationed outside country; also excluding alien armed forces within the country. - Non compris le personnel diplomatique et les militaires hors du pays; non compris également les militaires étrangers en garnison dans le pays.

[132] Based on the census, updated for residents missed or counted more than once by the census (net census undercount); residents temporarily overseas on census night, and births, deaths and net migration between the census night and the date of the estimate. - D'après le recensement, mise à jour pour les résidents omis ou dénombrés plus d'une fois par le recensement (sous-dénombrement net); résidents temporairement à l'étranger la nuit du recensement, et naissances, décès et migration nette entre la nuit du recensement et la date de l'estimation.

[133] Based on the results of the 1996 population census. Data refer to national projections. - À partir des résultats du recensement de la population de 1996. Les données se réfèrent aux projections nationales.

Table 4

Table 4 presents, for each country or area of the world, basic vital statistics for the period 2006 - 2010: live births, crude birth rate, deaths, crude death rate, rate of natural increase, infant deaths, infant death rate, life expectancy at birth by sex and total fertility rate.

Description of variables: The vital events and rates shown in this table are defined as follows[1]:

Live birth is the complete expulsion or extraction from its mother of a product of conception, irrespective of the duration of pregnancy, which after such separation breathes or shows any other evidence of life such as beating of the heart, pulsation of the umbilical cord, of definite movement of voluntary muscles, whether or not the umbilical cord has been cut or the placenta is attached. Each product of such a birth is considered live-born regardless of gestational age.

Death is the permanent disappearance of all evidence of life at any time after live birth has taken place (post-natal cessation of vital functions without capability of resuscitation).

Infant deaths are deaths of live-born infants under one year of age.

Life expectancy at birth is defined as the average number of years of life for males and females if they continued to be subject to the same mortality experienced in the year(s) to which these life expectancies refer.

The total fertility rate is the average number of children that would be born alive to a hypothetical cohort of women if, throughout their reproductive years, the age-specific fertility rates remained unchanged. The standard method of calculating the total fertility rate is the sum of the age-specific fertility rates.

Crude birth rates and crude death rates presented in this table are calculated using the number of live births and the number of deaths obtained from civil registers. These civil registration data are used only if they are considered reliable (estimated completeness of 90 per cent or more).

Similarly, infant mortality rates presented in this table are calculated using the number of live births and the number of infant deaths obtained from civil registers. If, however, the registration of births or infant deaths for any given country or area is estimated to be less than 90 per cent complete, the rates are not calculated.

For some countries, the data and rates presented in this table are based on vital statistics data sourced from censuses or demographic surveys.

Rate computation: The crude birth and death rates are the annual number of each of these vital events per 1 000 mid-year population.

Infant mortality rate is the annual number of deaths of infants under one year of age per 1 000 live births in the same year.

Rates of natural increase are the difference between the crude birth rate and the crude death rate. It should be noted that the rates of natural increase presented here may differ from the population growth rates presented in table 3 as rates of natural increase do not take net international migration into account while the population growth rates do.

Rates that appear in this table have been calculated by the Statistics Division of the United Nations Department of Economic and Social Affairs, unless otherwise noted. Exceptions include official estimated rates for Bangladesh and India, which were based on sample registration systems in these countries.

Rates calculated by the Statistics Division of the United Nations presented in this table have been limited to those countries or areas having a minimum number of 30 events (for life births and deaths) or 100 events (for infant deaths) in a given year.

Reliability of data: Rates calculated on the basis of registered vital statistics which are considered unreliable (estimated to be less than 90 per cent complete) are not calculated. Estimated rates, prepared by individual countries or areas, are presented whenever applicable.

The designation of vital statistics as being either reliable or unreliable is discussed in general in section 4.2 of the Technical Notes. The technical notes for tables 9, 15 and 18 provide specific information on reliability of statistics on live births, infant deaths and deaths, respectively.

The values shown for life expectancy in this table come from official life tables. It is assumed that, if necessary, the basic data (population and deaths classified by age and sex) have been adjusted for deficiencies before their use in constructing the life tables.

Limitations: Statistics on births, deaths and infant deaths are subject to the same qualifications as have been set forth for vital statistics, in general, in section 4 of the Technical Notes and in the technical notes for individual tables presenting detailed data on these events (table 9, live births; table 15, infant deaths; table 18, deaths).

In assessing comparability it is important to take into account the reliability of the data used to calculate the rates, as discussed above.

The problem of obtaining precise correspondence between numerator (births and deaths) and denominator (population for crude birth and death rates) as regards the inclusion or exclusion of armed forces, refugees, displaced persons and other special groups is particularly difficult where vital rates are concerned. This is the case for Japan, where births and deaths refer to Japanese nationals only while the population include foreigners except foreign military and civilian personnel and their dependants stationed in the area.

It should also be noted that crude rates are particularly affected by the age-sex structure of the population. Infant mortality rates, and to a much lesser extent crude birth rates and crude death rates, are affected by the variation in the definition of a live birth and tabulation procedures.

NOTES

[1] *Principles and Recommendations for a Vital Statistics System, Revision 2,* United Nations publication, Sales No. E.01.XVII.10, United Nations, New York, 2001.

Tableau 4

Le tableau 4 présente, pour chaque pays ou zone du monde, des statistiques de base de l'état civil pour les années 2006 – 2010 : les naissances vivantes, le taux brut de natalité, les décès, le taux brut de mortalité et le taux d'accroissement naturel de la population, les décès d'enfants de moins d'un an et le taux de mortalité infantile, l'espérance de vie à la naissance par sexe et l'indice synthétique de fécondité.

Description des variables : les faits d'état civil utilisés aux fins du calcul des taux présentés dans le tableau 4 sont définis comme suit[1] :

La naissance vivante est l'expulsion ou l'extraction complète du corps de la mère, indépendamment de la duré de la gestation, d'un produit de la conception qui après cette séparation, respire ou manifeste tout autre signe de vie, tel que battement de cœur, pulsation du cordon ombilical ou contraction effective d'un muscle soumis à l'action de la volonté, que le cordon ombilical ait été coupé ou non et que le placenta soit ou non demeuré attaché ; tout produit d'une telle naissance est considéré comme « enfant né vivant ».

Le décès est la disparition permanente de tout signe de vie à un moment quelconque postérieur à la naissance vivante (cessation des fonctions vitales après la naissance sans possibilité de réanimation).

Il convient de préciser que les chiffres relatifs aux décès d'enfants de moins d'un an se rapportent aux naissances vivantes.

L'espérance de vie à la naissance est le nombre moyen d'années que vivraient les individus de sexe masculin et de sexe féminin s'ils continuaient d'être soumis aux mêmes conditions de mortalité que celles qui existaient pendant les années auxquelles se rapportent les valeurs indiquées.

L'indice synthétique de fécondité représente le nombre moyen d'enfants que mettrait au monde une cohorte hypothétique de femmes qui seraient soumises, tout au long de leur vie, aux mêmes conditions de fécondité par âge que celles auxquelles sont soumises les femmes, dans chaque groupe d'âge, au cours d'une année ou d'une période donnée. La méthode standard pour calculer l'indice synthétique de fécondité consiste à additionner les taux de fécondité par âge simple.

Les taux bruts de natalité et de mortalité ont été établis sur la base du nombre de naissances vivantes et du nombre de décès inscrits sur les registres de l'état civil. Ces données n'ont été utilisées que lorsqu'elles étaient considérées comme sûres (degré estimatif de complétude égal ou supérieur à 90 p. 100).

De même, les taux de mortalité infantile présentés dans le tableau 4 ont été établis à partir du nombre de naissances vivantes et du nombre de décès d'enfants de moins d'un an inscrits sur les registres de l'état civil. Toutefois, lorsque les données relatives aux naissances ou aux décès d'enfants de moins d'un an pour un pays ou zone quelconque n'étaient pas considérées complètes à 90 p. 100 au moins, les indices n'ont pas été calculés.

Pour quelques pays, les données et les taux présentés dans ce tableau ont été extraites des recensements de la population ou des enquêtes démographiques.

Calcul des taux : les taux bruts de natalité et de mortalité, représentent le nombre annuel de chacun de ces faits d'état civil pour 1 000 habitants au milieu de l'année considérée.

Les taux de mortalité infantile correspondent au nombre annuel de décès d'enfants de moins d'un an pour 1 000 naissances vivantes survenues pendant la même année.

Le taux d'accroissement naturel est égal à la différence entre le taux brut de natalité et le taux brut de mortalité. Il y a lieu de noter que les taux d'accroissement naturel indiqués dans le tableau 4 peuvent différer des taux d'accroissement de la population figurant dans le tableau 3, les taux d'accroissement naturel ne tenant pas compte des taux nets de migration internationale, alors que ceux-ci sont inclus dans les taux d'accroissement de la population.

Sauf indication contraire, les taux figurant dans le tableau 4 ont été calculés par la Division de statistique du Département des affaires économiques et sociales (Secrétariat de l'Organisation des Nations Unies). Les exceptions comprennent le Bangladesh et l'Inde, pour lesquels les taux estimatifs officiels ont été fournis sur la base d'un système d'enregistrement par échantillonnage.

Les taux calculés par la Division de statistique de l'ONU qui sont présentés dans le tableau 4 se rapportent aux seuls pays ou zones où l'on a enregistré au moins 30 événements (pour les naissances vivantes et les décès) ou 100 événements (pour les décès d'enfants de moins d'un an) au cours d'une année donnée.

Fiabilité des données : les taux n'ont pas été calculés lorsque les statistiques de l'état civil issues de systèmes d'enregistrement d'état civil étaient jugées douteuses (degré estimatif de complétude inférieur à 90 p.100) et des taux estimatifs, calculés par les pays ou zones, ont été présentés lorsqu'ils étaient disponibles.

On trouve à la section 4.2 des Notes techniques des explications générales concernant la façon dont les statistiques de l'état civil ont été classées selon leur degré de fiabilité. Les notes techniques relatives aux tableaux 9, 15 et 18 ont trait respectivement à la fiabilité des statistiques des naissances vivantes, des décès d'enfants de moins d'un an et des décès.

Les valeurs relatives à l'espérance de vie figurant dans le tableau 4 proviennent de tables officielles de mortalité. On présume que les données de base (population t décès par sexe et âge) ont été rectifiées d'éventuelles insuffisances avant d'être utilisées pour construire les tables de mortalité.

Insuffisance des données : les statistiques des naissances, décès et décès d'enfants de moins d'un an appellent toutes les réserves qui ont été formulées à propos des statistiques de l'état civil en général à la section 4 des Notes techniques et dans les notes techniques relatives aux différents tableaux présentant des données détaillées sur ces événements [tableau 9 (naissances vivantes), tableau 15 (décès d'enfants de moins d'un an) et tableau 18 (décès)].

Pour évaluer la comparabilité des divers taux, il importe de tenir compte de la fiabilité des données utilisées pour calculer ces taux, comme il a été indiqué précédemment.

Le calcul des taux est particulièrement affecté par la difficulté à obtenir une correspondance parfaite entre le numérateur (naissances et décès) et le dénominateur (population, pour les taux bruts de natalité et de mortalité) en raison de l'inclusion ou non dans la population des forces armées, des réfugiés, des personnes déplacées ou d'autres groupes sociaux. C'est le cas pour le Japon, où les naissances et les décès se réfèrent aux seuls nationaux japonais tandis que la population inclus les étrangers, à l'exception toutefois des militaires étrangers ainsi que des personnels civils et leurs familles stationnés sur le territoire.

Il y a lieu de noter que la structure par âge et par sexe de la population influe de façon particulière sur les taux bruts. Le manque d'uniformité dans la définition des naissances vivantes et dans les procédures de mise en tableaux a une incidence sur les taux de mortalité infantile et, à un moindre degré, sur les taux bruts de natalité et les taux bruts de mortalité.

NOTE

[1] *Principes et recommandations pour un système de statistiques de l'état civil, deuxième révision,* numéro de vente : F.01.XVII.10, publication des Nations Unies, New York, 2001.

Aperçu des statistiques de l'état civil et de l'espérance de vie à la naissance : 2006 - 2010

Continent, country or area and year / Continent, pays ou zone et année	Live births Naissances vivantes			Deaths Décès			Rate of natural increase Taux d'accrois-sement naturel	Infant deaths Décès d'enfants de moins d'un an			Life expectancy at birth Espérance de vie à la naissance		Total fertility rate L'indice synthétique de fécondité
	Code[a]	Number Nombre	Crude birth rate Taux brut de natalité	Code[a]	Number Nombre	Crude death rate Taux brut de mortalité		Code[a]	Number Nombre	Rate (per 1000 births) Taux (par 1000 naiss-ances)	Male[b] Masculin[b]	Female[b] Féminin[b]	
AFRICA - AFRIQUE													
Algeria - Algérie[1]													
2006	C	739 000[2]	22.1	U	144 000[2]	...	...		...	...	74.7	76.8	...
2007	C	783 000[2]	23.0	U	149 000[2]	...	...		...	...	74.7	76.8	...
2008	C	817 000[2]	23.6	U	153 000[2]	...	...		...	...	74.9	76.6	...
2009	C	849 000[2]	24.1	U	159 000[2]	...	...		...	...	...	...	...
2010	C	888 000[2]	24.7	U	157 000[2]	...	...		...	...	...	...	...
Benin - Bénin													
2006		...	...		...	...	...		...	...	...	...	5.700
Botswana													
2006	+U	44 709[3]	...	+U	11 509[3]	...	...	+U	1 152[3]	...	54.0[4]	66.0[4]	3.200
2007		...	...	+U	11 075[3]	...	...	+U	658[3]	...			2.900
Burkina Faso													
2006	I	620 784[5]	44.3	I	116 199[6]	8.3	36.0	I	16 259[6]	26.2	55.8[7]	57.5[7]	6.200
2007	I	663 100[8]	46.5	I	176 700[8]	12.4	34.1		...	...	...	...	...
2008	I	679 200[8]	46.1	I	174 800[8]	11.9	34.2		...	...	...	...	...
Cape Verde - Cap-Vert													
2006	C	11 925	24.7	C	2 822	5.8	18.8		...	...	...	...	...
2007	C	12 335	25.1	C	2 846	5.8	19.3		...	...	...	...	...
2008	C	12 697	25.4	C	2 873	5.7	19.7		...	...	...	...	...
2009	C	13 044	25.6	C	2 897	5.7	19.9		...	...	...	...	...
2010	C	13 415	25.9	C	2 917	5.6	20.3		...	...	...	...	...
Egypt - Égypte													
2006	C	1 853 746	25.7	C	451 863	6.3	19.5	C	35 952	19.4			3.000
2007	C	1 949 569	26.5	C	450 596	6.1	20.4	C	34 612	17.8			3.000
2008	C	2 050 704	27.3	C	461 934	6.1	21.1	C	32 174	15.7			3.000
2009	C	2 217 409	28.8	C	476 592	6.2	22.6	C	25 760	11.6			...
2010		...	...		...	...	...		...	...	68.2	70.9	...
Ethiopia - Éthiopie[9]													
2007	I	2 218 457	30.1	I	839 038	11.4	18.7		...	...	...	...	...
Ghana													
2006	+U	620 688[10]	...		...	...	...	+U	52 316	...	...	...	...
2007	+U	767 109[10]	...		...	...	...	+U	52 014	...	...	...	...
2008	+U	553 119[11]	...		...	...	...	+U	52 038	...	...	...	4.000
Guinea-Bissau - Guinée-Bissau													
2006		...	...		...	...	...		...	...	43.4	46.2	6.800
Kenya													
2006	U	538 951	...	U	208 452	...	...	U	35 786	...	...	...	...
2007	U	464 283	...	U	170 167	...	...	U	35 154	...	...	...	...
2008	U	660 383	...	U	219 477	...	...	U	46 565	...	...	...	...
2009	U	691 312	...	U	181 220	...	...	U	40 190	...	...	...	...
Liberia - Libéria[12]													
2008	I	63 171	18.2		...	...	...		...	...	...	...	...
Malawi													
2006	U	614 410[8]	...	U	207 641[8]	...	...		...	...	...	...	...
2007	U	626 181[8]	...	U	206 527[8]	...	...		...	...	45.7[8]	48.3[8]	...
2008	I	516 629[13]	37.9	I	135 865[13]	10.0	27.9		...	...	...	...	...
Mauritius - Maurice[14]													
2006	+C	17 604	14.1	+C	9 162	7.3	6.7	+C	249	14.1	69.1	75.9	1.700
2007	+C	17 034	13.5	+C	8 498	6.7	6.8	+C	261	15.3	...	...	1.662
2008	+C	16 372	12.9	+C	9 004	7.1	5.8	+C	236	14.4	III69.2	76.1	1.582
2009	+C	15 344	12.0	+C	9 224	7.2	4.8	+C	205	13.4	III69.4	76.6	1.502
2010	+C	15 005	11.7	+C	9 131	7.1	4.6	+C	187	12.5	...	...	...
Morocco - Maroc													
2007		...	...	U	105 222	...	...		...	...	...	...	...
Namibia - Namibie													
2006		...	...	I	28 879[8]	14.5	...		...	...	...	...	3.600
2007		...	...	I	28 673[8]	14.1	...		...	...	...	...	...

Continent, country or area and year / Continent, pays ou zone et année	Live births / Naissances vivantes			Deaths / Décès			Rate of natural increase / Taux d'accrois-sement naturel	Infant deaths / Décès d'enfants de moins d'un an			Life expectancy at birth / Espérance de vie à la naissance		Total fertility rate / L'indice synthétique de fécondité
	Code[a]	Number Nombre	Crude birth rate Taux brut de natalité	Code[a]	Number Nombre	Crude death rate Taux brut de mortalité		Code[a]	Number Nombre	Rate (per 1000 births) Taux (par 1000 naiss-ances)	Male[b] Masculin[b]	Female[b] Féminin[b]	
AFRICA - AFRIQUE													
Niger													
2006	...	100 613	...	...	4 256[15]	...	...	...	...	...	...	...	...
2007	...	118 423	...	...	6 337[15]	...	...	...	...	...	...	...	...
Nigeria - Nigéria													
2007	...	1 807 025	...		...	...	...		...	...	...	...	...
Réunion													
2006	C	14 495[2]	18.4	C	4 323[2]	5.5	12.9	C	96[2]	6.6	73.2	80.9	2.440
2007	C	14 808[2]	18.7	C	4 045[2]	5.1	13.6	C	91[2]	6.1	...	...	...
Rwanda													
2007	U	404 792	...	U	141 015	...	...			...	48.5	52.3	5.500
2008	U	417 171	...	U	142 339	...	...			...	49.0	52.8	5.460
2009	U	429 065	...	U	143 538	...	...			...	49.4	53.3	5.420
Saint Helena ex. dep. - Sainte-Hélène sans dép.													
2006	C	35	...	C	52	...	...	C	-	...	...	...	...
2007	C	42	10.6	C	59	14.9	-4.3	C	-	...	X70.8	77.3	...
2008	C	36	9.0	C	44	11.1	-2.0	C	-	...	X71.1	77.6	...
2009	C	35	8.5	C	41	9.9	-1.5	C	-	...	X72.5	79.2	...
2010	C	34	8.0	C	53	12.5	-4.5	C	-	...	...	...	...
Senegal - Sénégal													
2006	I	466 678[16]	41.6	I	133 659[16]	11.9	29.7	I	31 321[16]	67.1	...	...	5.080[8]
2007	I	477 431[16]	41.4	I	135 172[16]	11.7	29.7	I	31 576[16]	66.1	...	...	5.020[8]
2008	I	488 754[16]	41.3	I	136 839[16]	11.6	29.7	I	31 889[16]	65.2	...	...	4.970[8]
2009	I	498 714[16]	41.0	I	138 182[16]	11.4	29.6	I	32 094[16]	64.4	...	...	4.910[8]
2010	I	509 230[16]	40.7	I	139 651[16]	11.2	29.5	I	32 314[16]	63.5	...	...	4.860[8]
Seychelles													
2006	+C	1 467	17.3	+C	664	7.8	9.5	+C	14	...	68.3	77.1	2.200
2007	+C	1 499	17.6	+C	630	7.4	10.2	+C	16	...	68.9	77.7	2.200
2008	+C	1 546	17.8	+C	662	7.6	10.2	+C	20	...	68.4	78.0	2.300
2009	+C	1 580	18.1	+C	684	7.8	10.3	+C	17	...	...	...	2.380
2010	+C	1 504	17.4	+C	664	7.7	9.7	+C	21	...	...	...	2.340
Sierra Leone													
2008	...	115 736	...	...	...	...	...	...	2 914	...	...	...	...
2009	...	101 868	...	...	...	...	...	...	3 238	...	...	...	...
South Africa - Afrique du Sud													
2006	U	1 053 863	...	U	612 778	...	...	...	48 265	...	51.4	55.5	2.550
2007	U	1 027 386	...	U	603 094	...	...	...	46 708	...	52.2	56.1	2.480
2008	U	1 033 403	...	U	592 073	...	...	...	45 316	...	53.3	57.2	2.410
2009	U	937 531	...	U	613 900	...	...		...	...	53.5	57.2	2.380
Swaziland													
2007	I	33 084[9]	39.2	I	18 367[9]	21.8	17.4		...	...	42.2[17]	43.1[17]	...
Tunisia - Tunisie													
2006	C	173 390	17.1	U	57 000	...	...		...	...	71.9	76.0	2.030
2007	C	177 503	17.4	U	56 741	...	...		...	...	72.3	76.2	2.040
2008	C	182 990	17.7	U	60 000	...	...		...	...	...	...	...
Zambia - Zambie[8]													
2006	U	509 766	...	U	152 549	...	...		...	...	...	...	...
AMERICA, NORTH - AMÉRIQUE DU NORD													
Anguilla													
2006	+C	183	12.8	+C	58	4.1	8.8	+C*	1	...	...	...	2.000
2007	+C	148	9.9	+C	70	4.7	5.2	+C	-	...	...	...	...
2008	+C	108	6.9	+C	52	3.3	3.6	+C	-	...	...	...	...

Continent, country or area and year / Continent, pays ou zone et année	Live births / Naissances vivantes			Deaths / Décès			Rate of natural increase / Taux d'accrois-sement naturel	Infant deaths / Décès d'enfants de moins d'un an			Life expectancy at birth / Espérance de vie à la naissance		Total fertility rate / L'indice synthétique de fécondité
	Code[a]	Number / Nombre	Crude birth rate / Taux brut de natalité	Code[a]	Number / Nombre	Crude death rate / Taux brut de mortalité		Code[a]	Number / Nombre	Rate (per 1000 births) / Taux (par 1000 naiss-ances)	Male[b] / Masculin[b]	Female[b] / Féminin[b]	
AMERICA, NORTH - AMÉRIQUE DU NORD													
Antigua and Barbuda - Antigua-et-Barbuda													
2006	+C	1 199	14.2	+C	479	5.7	8.5	+C	8	...	...	...	...
2007	+C	1 240	14.4	+C	504	5.9	8.6	+C	27	...	...	...	...
Aruba													
2006	C	1 227	11.9	C	537	5.2	6.7	+U	8	...	...	...	1.713
2007	C	1 239	11.9	C	521	5.0	6.9	+U	4	...	...	...	1.739
2008	C	1 218	11.6	C	523	5.0	6.6		...	...	...	...	...
2009	C	1 213	11.3	C	623	5.8	5.5		...	...	...	...	...
2010	C	1 141	10.6	C	610	5.7	4.9		...	...	...	...	...
Bahamas													
2006	U	5 296	...	C	1 730	5.3	...	C	79	...	...	...	1.925
2007	U	5 854	...	C	1 798	5.4	...	C	69	...	...	...	2.140
2008	U	5 124[18]	...	C	1 863	5.5	...		...	...	...	...	1.995
2009	U	5 027[18]	...		...	...	...		...	...	...	...	2.025
Barbados - Barbade													
2006	+C	3 414	12.5	+C	2 317	8.5	4.0	+C	59	17.3	...	...	...
2007	+C	3 537	12.9	+C	2 213	8.1	4.8	+C	31	8.8	...	...	...
Bermuda - Bermudes													
2006	C	798[19]	12.5	C	461[19]	7.2	5.3	C	3	...	...	...	1.757
2007	C	859[19]	13.4	C	468[19]	7.3	6.1	C	4	...	...	...	1.762
2008	C	821[19]	12.8	C	443[19]	6.9	5.9	C	4	...	76.8	82.1	1.765
2009	C	819[19]	12.7	C	471[19]	7.3	5.4	C	1	...			1.820
2010		...	...		...	...	...		...	...	76.9	82.3	1.760
Canada													
2006	C	354 617[20]	10.9	C	228 079[20]	7.0	3.9	C	1 771[20]	5.0	...	...	1.586
2007	C	367 864[20]	11.2	C	235 217[20]	7.1	4.0	C	1 881[20]	5.1	III78.3	83.0	1.659
2008	C	377 886[20]	11.3	C	240 961[20]	7.2	4.1	C	...	...	...	...	1.681
Cayman Islands - Îles Caïmanes													
2006	C	710[21]	13.7	C	182	3.5	10.2	C	8	...	76.3[22]	83.8[22]	...
2007	C	744[21]	13.8	C	160	3.0	10.8	C	5	...	...	...	1.600
2008	C	793[21]	14.2	C	166	3.0	11.2		...	...	...	...	...
2009	C	824[21]	15.6	C	152[23]	2.9	12.7	C	3	...	...	...	...
2010	C	821[21]	15.0	C	152[23]	2.8	12.2	C	2	...	...	...	...
Costa Rica													
2006	C	71 291	16.4	C	16 766	3.9	12.5	C	692	9.7	...	...	1.900
2007	C	73 144	16.5	C	17 070	3.8	12.6	C	735	10.0	76.8	81.7	2.000
2008	C	75 187	16.6	C	18 021	4.0	12.6	C	673	9.0	...	...	1.900
2009	C	75 000	16.2	C	18 560	4.0	12.2	C	663	8.8	76.8	81.8	1.974
2010	C*	70 922	15.5	C*	19 077	4.2	11.4	C*	671	9.5	76.8	81.8	1.810
Cuba													
2006	C	111 323	9.9	C	80 831	7.2	2.7	C	589	5.3	...	...	1.393
2007	C	112 472	10.0	C	81 927	7.3	2.7	C	592	5.3	III76.0	80.0	1.432
2008	C	122 569	10.9	C	86 423	7.7	3.2	C	579	4.7	...	...	1.590
2009	C	130 036	11.6	C*	86 943	7.7	3.8	C	626	4.8	...	...	1.704
Dominica - Dominique													
2006	+C	1 058	14.9	+C	536	7.5	7.4	+C	13	...	...	...	...
2008		...	...		...	...	...		...	...	73.8	78.2	...
Dominican Republic - République dominicaine													
2006	U	133 331	...	U	31 301	...	...	U	159	...	...	...	2.734
2007	U	129 211	...	U	32 620	...	...	U	64	...	...	...	2.702[8]
2008	U	130 875	...	U	32 494	...	...	U	96	...	...	...	2.670[8]
2009	U	117 634	...	U	31 580	...	...	U	73	...	69.3	75.7	2.632[8]
2010		...	...		...	...	...		...	...	VI69.2[8]	75.5[8]	2.594[8]

4. Vital statistics summary and life expectancy at birth: 2006 - 2010
Aperçu des statistiques de l'état civil et de l'espérance de vie à la naissance : 2006 - 2010 (continued - suite)

Continent, country or area and year / Continent, pays ou zone et année	Code[a]	Live births - Naissances vivantes Number Nombre	Crude birth rate Taux brut de natalité	Code[a]	Deaths - Décès Number Nombre	Crude death rate Taux brut de mortalité	Rate of natural increase Taux d'accroissement naturel	Code[a]	Infant deaths - Décès d'enfants de moins d'un an Number Nombre	Rate (per 1000 births) Taux (par 1000 naissances)	Life expectancy at birth Male[b] Masculin[b]	Female[b] Féminin[b]	Total fertility rate L'indice synthétique de fécondité
AMERICA, NORTH - AMÉRIQUE DU NORD													
El Salvador													
2006	C	107 111[24]	17.6	C	31 453[25]	5.2	12.5	C	1 013[26]	9.5	...	...	...
2007	C	106 471[24]	17.5	C	31 349[25]	5.1	12.3	C	981[26]	9.2	...	...	...
2008	C	112 049[24]	18.3	C	31 594[25]	5.2	13.1	C	947[26]	8.5	...	...	...
Greenland - Groenland													
2006	C	842	14.8	C	440	7.7	7.1	C	14	...	V65.7	71.0	2.222
2007	C	853	15.1	C	452	8.0	7.1	C	9	...	V66.3	71.3	2.278
2008	C	834	14.8	C	428	7.6	7.2	C	8	...	V66.6	71.6	2.217
2009	C	895	15.9	C	437	7.8	8.1	C	4	...	...	...	...
2010	C	868	15.4	C	504	8.9	6.4	C	6	...	...	...	...
Guadeloupe[2]													
2006	C	7 193	15.7	C	2 902	6.3	9.4		...	...	...	...	...
2007	C	6 862	17.1	C	2 769	6.9	10.2		...	...	...	...	...
Guatemala													
2006	C	368 399	28.3	C	69 756	5.4	22.9	C	9 042	24.5	...	...	3.570
2007	C	366 128	27.4	C	70 030	5.2	22.2		...	...	...	...	...
2008	C	369 769	27.0	C	70 233	5.1	21.9		...	...	...	...	...
Honduras													
2006	+U	222 512	...	+U	35 682			+U	6 400				
Jamaica - Jamaïque													
2006	C	46 277[27]	17.4	U	16 317[28]	...	...		...		69.7	75.2	2.220
2007	C	45 590[27]	17.0	U	17 048[28]	...	...		...		...	...	2.220
2008	C	44 838	16.7	U	17 000	...	...		...		...	...	...
2009	C	44 006	16.3	U	17 553	...	...		...		...	...	...
Martinique													
2006	C	5 370[2]	13.5	C	2 663[2]	6.7	6.8	C	44	8.2	...	...	2.030
2007	C	5 317[2]	13.4	C	2 830[2]	7.1	6.3	C	47	8.8	76.5	82.9	...
Mexico - Mexique													
2006	+U	2 151 204[29]	...	+C	493 296[30]	4.7	...	+U	30 890[30]	...	...	...	2.167
2007	+U*	2 185 888[29]	...	+C	513 122[30]	4.9	...	+U	30 412[30]	...	72.6	77.4	2.134
2008		...	...	+C	538 288[30]	5.0	...	+U	29 519[30]	...	72.8	77.5	2.104
2009		...	...	+C*	563 516[30]	5.2	...	+U	28 983[30]	...	...	...	...
Montserrat													
2006	+C	49	10.5	+C	47	10.1	0.4		...	...	...	...	...
2007	+C	43	8.9	+C	44	9.1	-0.2		...	...	...	...	...
2008	+C	72	14.8	+C	45	9.2	5.5		...	...	...	...	...
Netherlands Antilles - Antilles néerlandaises													
2006	C	2 611[30]	13.8	C	1 327[30]	7.0	6.8	C	40	15.3	...	...	1.987
2007	C	2 558[30]	13.2	C	1 339[30]	6.9	6.3	C	33	12.9	V72.0	79.3	1.887
2008	C	2 765[30]	14.0	C	1 453[30]	7.4	6.7		...	...	...	...	...
2009	C	2 661[30]	13.3	C	1 342[30]	6.7	6.6		...	...	...	...	...
Nicaragua													
2006	+U	123 886	...	+U	16 595	...	...	+U	1 925	...	...	...	2.690
2007	+U	128 171	...	+U	17 288	...	...	+U	1 955	...	...	...	...
2008	+U	125 028	...	+U	18 079	...	...	+U	1 932	...	...	...	...
2010		...	...		...	...	...		...	...	VI63.4	68.9	...
Panama													
2006	C	65 764	20.0	U	14 358	...	...	U	971	...	...	...	2.400
2007	C	67 364	20.2	U	14 775	...	...	U	992	...	...	...	2.500
2008	C	68 759	20.3	U	15 115	...	...	U	877	...	...	...	2.500
2009	C	68 364	19.8	U	15 498	...	...	U	837	...	...	...	2.500
2010		...	...		...	...	...		...	...	73.4[31]	78.7[31]	...
Puerto Rico - Porto Rico													
2006	C	48 744	12.4	C	28 589	7.3	5.1	C	442	9.1	III74.1	81.5	1.696
2007	C	46 744	11.9	C	29 276	7.4	4.4	C	387	8.3	...	...	1.644
2008	C	45 675	11.6	C	29 100	7.4	4.2	C	400	8.8	...	...	...

Continent, country or area and year / Continent, pays ou zone et année	Live births / Naissances vivantes			Deaths / Décès			Rate of natural increase / Taux d'accrois-sement naturel	Infant deaths / Décès d'enfants de moins d'un an			Life expectancy at birth / Espérance de vie à la naissance		Total fertility rate / L'indice synthétique de fécondité
	Code[a]	Number Nombre	Crude birth rate Taux brut de natalité	Code[a]	Number Nombre	Crude death rate Taux brut de mortalité		Code[a]	Number Nombre	Rate (per 1000 births) Taux (par 1000 naissances)	Male[b] Masculin[b]	Female[b] Féminin[b]	
AMERICA, NORTH - AMÉRIQUE DU NORD													
Saint Vincent and the Grenadines - Saint-Vincent-et-les Grenadines													
2006	+C	1 796	17.7	+C	777	7.7	10.0	+C	50	27.8	...	...	2.200
2007	+C	1 822	18.2	+C	779	7.8	10.4	+C	34	18.7	...	...	...
2008	+C	1 901	19.2	+C	848	8.6	10.6	+C	34	17.9	...	...	...
2009	+C	1 905		+C	765			+C	32	16.8	...	...	...
Trinidad and Tobago - Trinité-et-Tobago													
2006	C	18 090	13.9		...				...				
Turks and Caicos Islands - Îles Turques et Caïques													
2006	C	409[32]	12.3	C	73[25]	2.2	10.1	C	4	...	...	...	...
2007	C	455[32]	13.1	C	116[25]	3.3	9.7	C	2	...	...	...	...
2008	C	453[32]	12.4	C	65[25]	1.8	10.6	C	3	...	...	...	...
United States of America - États-Unis d'Amérique													
2006	C	4 265 555	14.3	C	2 426 264	8.1	6.2	C	28 527	6.7	75.1	80.2	2.100
2007	C	4 316 233	14.3	C	2 423 712	8.0	6.3	C	29 138	6.8	75.4	80.4	2.122
2008	C	4 247 694	14.0	C*	2 473 018	8.1	5.8	C*	28 039	6.6	...	...	2.085
United States Virgin Islands - Îles Vierges américaines													
2006	C	1 763	16.1	C	629	5.7	10.3	C	8	...	...	...	...
2007	C	1 771	16.1	C	727	6.6	9.5	C	12	...	...	...	...
AMERICA, SOUTH - AMÉRIQUE DU SUD													
Argentina - Argentine													
2006	+C	696 451	17.9	C	292 313	7.5	10.4	C	8 986	12.9	...	...	2.304
2007	C	700 792	17.8	C	315 852	8.0	9.8	C	9 300	13.3	...	...	2.288
2008	C	746 066	18.8	C	301 801	7.6	11.2	C	9 326	12.5	...	...	2.409
2009	C	745 336	18.6	C	304 525	7.6	11.0	C	9 013	12.1	...	...	2.380
2010		...			...				...		V72.5	80.0	...
Bolivia (Plurinational State of) - Bolivie (État plurinational de)													
2006	U	135 069	...	U*	25 954[18]	...			...		...	...	...
2007	U*	96 856	...	U*	21 846[18]	...			...		...	...	...
Brazil - Brésil													
2006	U	2 798 964[31]	...	U	1 023 545[31]	...	...	U	37 677[31]	...	...	...	1.992
2007	U	2 750 667[31]	...	U	1 032 450[31]	...	...	U	35 159[33]	...	68.8[31]	76.4[31]	1.925
2008	U	2 789 820[31]	...	U	1 060 365[31]	...	...	U	34 375[31]	...	69.1[31]	76.7[31]	1.863
2009	U	2 764 642[34]	...	U	1 079 228[31]	...	...	U	33 713[31]	...	69.7[31]	77.3[31]	1.806
2010		...			...				...		...	...	1.755
Chile - Chili													
2006	C	231 383	14.1	C	85 639	5.2	8.9	C	1 839	7.9	...	...	1.910
2007	C	240 569	14.5	C	93 000	5.6	8.9	C	2 009	8.4	...	...	1.880
2008	C	246 581	14.7	C	90 168	5.4	9.3	C	1 948	7.9	...	...	1.918
2009		...			...				...		75.4	80.9	...
2010		...			...				...		VI75.5	81.5	...
Colombia - Colombie													
2006	U	714 450	...	U	192 814			U	11 049	...	VI69.4	75.5	...
2007	U	709 253	...	U	193 936			U	10 867	...	VI69.6	75.7	...
2008	U	715 453	...	U	196 943	...	...	U	10 560	...	...	...	...

4. Vital statistics summary and life expectancy at birth: 2006 - 2010
Aperçu des statistiques de l'état civil et de l'espérance de vie à la naissance : 2006 - 2010 (continued - suite)

Continent, country or area and year / Continent, pays ou zone et année	Live births / Naissances vivantes			Deaths / Décès			Rate of natural increase / Taux d'accroissement naturel	Infant deaths / Décès d'enfants de moins d'un an			Life expectancy at birth / Espérance de vie à la naissance		Total fertility rate / L'indice synthétique de fécondité
	Code[a]	Number / Nombre	Crude birth rate / Taux brut de natalité	Code[a]	Number / Nombre	Crude death rate / Taux brut de mortalité		Code[a]	Number / Nombre	Rate (per 1000 births) / Taux (par 1000 naissances)	Male[b] / Masculin[b]	Female[b] / Féminin[b]	
AMERICA, SOUTH - AMÉRIQUE DU SUD													
Colombia - Colombie													
2009	U*	686 045	...	U*	193 580	...	...	U*	9 250	...	...	...	...
2010		...	...		...	...	...		...	...	VI70.7[35]	77.5[35]	...
Ecuador - Équateur													
2006	+U	278 591	...	U	57 940[36]	...	...	U	3 715[36]	...	...	...	2.580[8]
2007	+U	283 984	...	U	58 016[36]	...	...	U	3 529[36]	...	...	...	2.580[8]
2008	+U	291 055	...	U	60 023[36]	...	...	U	3 380[36]	...	...	...	2.580[8]
2009	+U	215 906[37]	...	U	59 714[36]	...	...	U	3 279[36]	...	...	...	2.580[8]
2010		...	...		...	...	...		...	...	VI72.1[38]	78.0[38]	...
Falkland Islands (Malvinas) - Îles Falkland (Malvinas)													
2006	+C	27	...	+C	20	...	...		...	...	...	...	...
French Guiana - Guyane française													
2006	C	6 276[2]	31.1	C	711[2]	3.5	27.6	C	79	12.6	74.4	81.0	3.810
2007	C	6 386[2]	29.9	C	690[2]	3.2	26.7	C	77	12.1	75.1	80.8	...
Guyana													
2006		...	...	+C	5 031	6.6	...		...	...	...	...	...
2007		...	...	+C	5 066	6.6	...		...	...	...	...	...
Paraguay													
2006	+U	101 994	...	+U	22 749	...	...	+U	1 824	...	...	...	...
2007	+U	95 788	...	+U	23 025	...	...	+U	1 599	...	...	...	...
2008	+U	99 674	...	+U	24 417	...	...	+U	1 674	...	...	...	...
2010		...	...		...	...	...		...	...	VI69.7	73.9	...
Peru - Pérou													
2006	+U	324 922[39]	...	+U	82 620[40]	...	...	+U	5 837[41]	...	...	...	2.660
2007	+U	324 480[39]	...	+U	87 495[40]	...	...	+U	5 516[41]	...	...	...	2.620
2008	+U	457 033[42]	...	+U*	91 295[40]	...	...	+U	5 581[41]	...	...	...	2.580
2009	+U	457 108[42]	...		...	...	...		...	...	...	...	2.530
2010		...	...		...	...	...		...	...	...	...	2.490
Suriname													
2006	C	9 311[43]	18.5	C	3 247[44]	6.4	12.0	C	129[44]	13.9	68.0	73.7	2.292
2007	C	9 769[43]	19.2	C	3 374[44]	6.6	12.5	C	134[44]	13.7	...	...	2.387
Uruguay													
2006	C	47 231	14.2	C	31 056	9.4	4.9	C*	497	10.5	72.1	79.5	2.030
2007	C	47 372	14.3	C	33 706	10.1	4.1	C	573	12.1	72.3	79.6	2.019
2008	C	47 484	14.2	C	31 363	9.4	4.8	C	504	10.6	72.4	79.7	2.008
2009	C*	47 152	14.1	C*	32 179	9.6	4.5		...	...	...	...	...
Venezuela (Bolivarian Republic of) - Venezuela (République bolivarienne du)													
2006	C	646 225	23.9	C	115 348	4.3	19.6	C	6 804	10.5	...	...	2.618[45]
2007	C	615 371	22.4	C	118 594	4.3	18.1	C	6 340	10.3	70.7	76.6	2.583[45]
2008	C	581 480	20.8	C	124 062	4.4	16.4		...	...	...	...	2.550[45]
ASIA - ASIE													
Afghanistan[46]													
2009		...	...		...	...	...		...	...	...	...	6.300
Armenia - Arménie													
2006	C	37 639	11.7	C	27 202[47]	8.4	3.2	C	523[47]	13.9	...	...	1.348
2007	C	40 105	12.4	C	26 830[47]	8.3	4.1	C	433[47]	10.8	II70.2	76.6	1.417
2008	C	41 185	12.7	C	27 412[47]	8.5	4.3	C	442[47]	10.7	...	...	1.444
2009	C	44 413	13.7	C	27 560[47]	8.5	5.2	C	454[47]	10.2	...	...	1.551
2010	C	44 825	13.8	C	27 921[47]	8.6	5.2	C	512[47]	11.4	...	...	...

Continent, country or area and year / Continent, pays ou zone et année	Live births / Naissances vivantes			Code[a]	Deaths / Décès		Rate of natural increase / Taux d'accrois-sement naturel	Code[a]	Infant deaths / Décès d'enfants de moins d'un an		Life expectancy at birth / Espérance de vie à la naissance		Total fertility rate / L'indice synthétique de fécondité
	Code[a]	Number / Nombre	Crude birth rate / Taux brut de natalité		Number / Nombre	Crude death rate / Taux brut de mortalité			Number / Nombre	Rate (per 1000 births) / Taux (par 1000 naiss-ances)	Male[b] / Masculin[b]	Female[b] / Féminin[b]	
ASIA - ASIE													
Azerbaijan - Azerbaïdjan													
2006	+C	148 946[47]	17.3	+C	52 248[47]	6.1	11.2	+C	1 882[47]	12.6	69.6	75.1	...
2007	+C	151 963[47]	17.4	+C	53 655[47]	6.2	11.3	+C	1 756[47]	11.6	69.7	75.1	2.329
2008	+C	152 086[47]	17.2	+C	52 710[47]	6.0	11.2	+C	1 715[47]	11.3	69.9	75.4	2.251
2009	+C	152 139[47]	17.0	+C	52 514[47]	5.9	11.1	+C	1 731[47]	11.4	71.0	76.1	2.260
2010	+C	165 643[47]	18.3	+C	53 580[47]	5.9	12.4	+C	1 843[47]	11.1	...	...	...
Bahrain - Bahreïn													
2006	C	15 053	15.7	C	2 317	2.4	13.3	C	115	7.6	...	...	2.000
2007	C	16 062	15.5	C	2 270	2.2	13.3	C	133	8.3	...	...	1.960
2008	C	17 022	15.4	C	2 390	2.2	13.2	C	127	7.5	...	...	...
2009	C	17 841	15.1	C	2 387	2.0	13.1	C	128	7.2	...	...	...
Bangladesh													
2006	I	...	20.6[48]	I	...	5.6[48]	...	I	...	45.0[48]	65.2	68.2	2.410
2007	I	...	20.9[48]	I	...	6.2[48]	...	I	...	43.0[48]	65.4	67.9	2.390
Brunei Darussalam - Brunéi Darussalam													
2006	+C	6 526	17.0	+C	1 095	2.9	14.2	+C	43	6.6	75.9	77.5	1.800
2007	+C	6 314	16.2	+C	1 174	3.0	13.2	+C	48	7.6	75.2	77.8	1.700
2008	+C	6 424	16.1	+C	1 091	2.7	13.4	+C	45	7.0	76.6	79.8	1.700
Cambodia - Cambodge													
2008		...	...		...	...	...		...	...	...	...	3.300
China - Chine[49]													
2006	I	15 840 000	12.1	I	8 920 000	6.8	5.3		...	...	...	...	...
2007	I	15 940 000	12.1	I	9 130 000	6.9	5.2		...	...	...	...	...
2008	I	16 080 000	12.1	I	9 350 000	7.0	5.1		...	...	...	...	...
2009	I	16 150 000	12.1	I	9 430 000	7.1	5.0		...	...	...	...	...
China, Hong Kong SAR - Chine, Hong Kong RAS													
2006	C	65 626	9.6	C	37 457	5.5	4.1	C	118	1.8	79.4	85.5	0.984[50]
2007	C	70 875	10.2	C	39 476	5.7	4.5	C	125	1.8	...	...	1.024[50]
2008	C	78 822	11.3	C	41 796	6.0	5.3	C	145	1.8	79.3	85.5	1.056[50]
2009	C	82 095	11.7	C	41 175	5.9	5.8	C	136	1.7	79.7	85.9	1.042[50]
China, Macao SAR - Chine, Macao RAS													
2006	C	4 058	8.1	C	1 566	3.1	5.0	C	11	...	...	...	0.954
2007	C	4 537	8.6	C	1 545	2.9	5.7	C	11	...	...	...	0.993
2008	C	4 717	8.5	C	1 756	3.2	5.4	C	15	...	...	...	0.960
2009	C	4 764	8.8	C	1 664	3.1	5.7	C	10	...	[IV]79.4	85.2	0.994
2010	C*	5 114	9.4	C*	1 768	3.2	6.1		...	...	...	...	...
Cyprus - Chypre[51]													
2006	C	8 731	11.3	C	5 127	6.7	4.7	C	27	...	...	...	1.437
2007	C	8 575	10.9	C	5 391	6.9	4.1	C	32	3.7	[II]78.3	81.9	1.390
2008	C	9 205	11.6	C	5 194	6.5	5.1	C	32	3.5	...	...	1.460
2009	C	9 608	12.0	C	5 182	6.5	5.5	C	32	3.3	...	...	1.510
2010	C*	9 989	12.4	C*	5 392	6.7	5.7		...	...	...	...	...
Democratic People's Republic of Korea - République populaire démocratique de Corée													
2008	I	345 630[52]	14.4	I	216 616[52]	9.0	5.4	I	6 686[52]	19.3	65.6	72.7	2.000
Georgia - Géorgie													
2006	C	47 795	10.9	C	42 255[47]	9.6	1.3	C	753[47]	15.8	69.8	78.5	1.400
2007	C	49 287	11.2	C	41 178[47]	9.4	1.8	C	656[47]	13.3	70.5	79.4	1.450
2008	C	56 565	12.9	C	43 011[47]	9.8	3.1	C	959[47]	17.0	69.3	79.0	1.670
2010	C	62 585	...	C	47 864[47]	...	...	C	701[47]	11.2	...	...	...
India - Inde[53]													
2006	I	...	23.5[54]	I	...	7.5[54]	...	I	...	57.0[54]	[V]62.6	64.2	2.785
2007	I	...	23.1[54]	I	...	7.4[54]	...	I	...	55.0[54]	...	...	2.683
2008	I	...	22.8[54]	I	...	7.4[54]	...	I	...	53.0[54]	...	...	2.600

Continent, country or area and year / Continent, pays ou zone et année	Live births / Naissances vivantes			Deaths / Décès			Rate of natural increase / Taux d'accroissement naturel	Infant deaths / Décès d'enfants de moins d'un an			Life expectancy at birth / Espérance de vie à la naissance		Total fertility rate / L'indice synthétique de fécondité
	Code[a]	Number Nombre	Crude birth rate Taux brut de natalité	Code[a]	Number Nombre	Crude death rate Taux brut de mortalité		Code[a]	Number Nombre	Rate (per 1000 births) Taux (par 1000 naissances)	Male[b] Masculin[b]	Female[b] Féminin[b]	
ASIA - ASIE													
Indonesia - Indonésie													
2006		...	...		...	...	...		...	...	...	...	2.190
2007		...	...		...	...	...		...	...	...	...	2.173
2008		...	...		...	...	...		...	...	...	...	2.163
2009		...	...		...	...	...		...	...	...	...	2.154
2010		...	...		...	...	...		...	...	...	...	2.144
Iran (Islamic Republic of) - Iran (République islamique d')													
2006	+C	1 253 506[55]	17.8	+U	408 566[55]	...	...		...	...	71.1	73.1	1.780
2007	+C	1 286 716[55]	18.1	+U	412 735[55]	...	...		...	...	...	...	...
2008	+C	1 300 166[55]	18.0	+U	417 798[55]	...	...		...	...	...	...	...
Iraq													
2006	U*	902 934	...	U*	211 757	...	...	U*	48 078	...	...	...	...
Israel - Israël[56]													
2006	C	148 170	21.0	C	38 776[57]	5.5	15.5	C	598[57]	4.0	v78.0	82.0	2.879
2007	C	151 679	21.1	C	40 081[57]	5.6	15.5	C	592[57]	3.9	78.8	82.5	2.905
2008	C	156 923	21.5	C	39 484[57]	5.4	16.1	C	602[57]	3.8	79.1	83.0	2.962
2009	C	161 042	21.5	C	38 781[57]	5.2	16.3	C	619[57]	3.8	79.7	83.5	2.962
2010	C*	165 950	21.8	C*	39 361[57]	5.2	16.6		...	...	...	...	...
Japan - Japon[58]													
2006	C	1 092 674	8.7	C	1 084 450	8.6	0.1	C	2 864	2.6	79.0	85.8	1.317
2007	C	1 089 818	8.6	C	1 108 334	8.8	-0.1	C	2 828	2.6	79.2	86.0	1.337
2008	C	1 091 156	8.7	C	1 142 407	9.1	-0.4	C	2 798	2.6	79.3	86.1	1.367
2009	C	1 070 035	8.4	C	1 141 865	9.0	-0.6	C	2 556	2.4	79.6	86.4	1.368
Jordan - Jordanie[59]													
2006	C	162 972	29.1	U	20 397	...	...		...	...	70.8	72.5	3.700
2007	C	185 011	32.3	U	20 924	...	...		...	...	71.6	74.4	3.600
2008	C	181 328	31.0	U	19 403	...	...		...	...	...	...	...
Kazakhstan													
2006	C	301 756[47]	19.7	C	157 210[47]	10.3	9.4	C	4 154[47]	13.8	60.7	72.2	2.350
2007	C	321 963[47]	20.8	C	158 297[47]	10.2	10.6	C	4 646[47]	14.4	60.7	72.6	2.490
2008	C	356 575[47]	22.7	C	152 706[47]	9.7	13.0	C	7 322[47]	20.5	61.9	72.4	2.680
2009	C*	357 552[47]	22.5	C*	142 780[47]	9.0	13.5		...	...	...	...	...
Kuwait - Koweït													
2006	C	52 759	22.7	C	5 247	2.3	20.4	C	456	8.6	...	...	...
2007	C	53 587	22.2	C	5 293	2.2	20.0	C	449	8.4	...	...	...
2008	C	54 571	21.9	C	5 701	2.3	19.6	C	494	9.1	...	...	...
Kyrgyzstan - Kirghizstan													
2006	C	120 737	24.0	C	38 566	7.7	16.3	C	3 526	29.2	63.5	72.1	2.735
2007	C	123 251	24.4	C	38 180	7.6	16.8	C	3 771	30.6	63.7	72.3	2.750
2008	C	127 332	25.1	C	37 710	7.4	17.7	C	3 453	27.1	64.5	72.6	2.808
2009	C	135 494	26.4	C	35 898	7.0	19.4	C	3 393	25.0	65.2	73.2	2.876
Lebanon - Liban													
2006	C	72 790	...	C	18 787	...	...		...	...	...	...	...
2007	C	80 896	21.5	C	21 092	5.6	15.9		...	...	...	...	...
2008	C	84 823	...	C	21 048	...	...		...	...	...	...	...
2009	C	90 388	...	C	22 260	...	...		...	...	...	...	...
2010	C	95 218	...	C	25 500	...	...		...	...	...	...	...
Malaysia - Malaisie													
2006	C	465 112	17.3	C	115 084	4.3	13.0	C	2 877	6.2	71.5	76.2	2.295
2007	C	472 048	17.4	C	118 167	4.3	13.0	C	2 926	6.2	...	...	2.300
2008	C	487 346	17.7	C	124 857	4.5	13.2	C	3 045	6.2	...	...	2.326
2009	C*	481 669	17.3	C*	128 962	4.6	12.6	C*	3 367	7.0	...	...	2.261*
Maldives													
2006	C	5 829	19.5	C	1 084	3.6	15.9	C	92	15.8	...	...	2.100
2007	C	6 569	21.5	C	1 119	3.7	17.9	C	66	10.0	...	...	...
2008	C	6 989	22.6	C	1 083	3.5	19.1	C	76	10.9	...	...	...
2009	C	7 423	23.6	C	1 163	3.7	19.9	C	81	10.9	72.5	74.2	...

Continent, country or area and year / Continent, pays ou zone et année	Code[a]	Live births / Naissances vivantes Number / Nombre	Crude birth rate Taux brut de natalité	Code[a]	Deaths / Décès Number / Nombre	Crude death rate Taux brut de mortalité	Rate of natural increase Taux d'accroissement naturel	Code[a]	Infant deaths / Décès d'enfants de moins d'un an Number / Nombre	Rate (per 1000 births) Taux (par 1000 naissances)	Life expectancy at birth / Espérance de vie à la naissance Male[b] / Masculin[b]	Female[b] / Féminin[b]	Total fertility rate L'indice synthétique de fécondité
ASIA - ASIE													
Mongolia - Mongolie													
2006	C	49 092	19.0	C	16 682	6.5	12.6	C	937	19.1	X62.6	69.4	2.067
2007	C	56 636	21.7	C	16 259	6.2	15.4	C	994	17.6	X63.1	70.2	2.341
2008	C	63 768	24.0	C	15 413	5.8	18.2	C	1 240	19.4	X63.7	71.0	2.595
2009	C	68 762	25.1	C	16 911	6.2	19.0	C	1 386	20.2	64.3	71.8	...
2010	C	65 889	...	C	17 276	...	...	C	1 275	19.4	...	...	...
Myanmar													
2006	+U	857 306	...	+U	247 527	...	...	+U	39 714	...	...	...	2.090[60]
2007	+U	945 859	...	+U	266 206	...	...	+U	43 077	...	64.0[60]	69.0[60]	2.060[60]
2008	+U	890 034	...	+U	483 373	...	...	+U	26 265	...	64.3[60]	68.3[60]	2.047[60]
Nepal - Népal													
2006		...			...				...		62.9	63.7	3.100
2008		...			...				...		63.6	64.5	...
Occupied Palestinian Territory - Territoire palestinien occupé													
2006	C	114 959[61]	31.8	U	9 938	...	...	U	906	...	...	...	...
2007	C	115 371[61]	31.0	U	9 887	...	...	U	794	...	70.0	72.6	4.600
2008		...			...				...		70.2	72.9	...
Oman													
2006	U	49 944[62]	...	U	5 484	...	...	U	499	...	73.2	75.4	2.660
2007	U	53 498[62]	...	U	6 769[62]	...	...	U	524[62]	...	...	...	2.590
2008	U	58 280[62]	...	U	7 298[62]	...	...	U	534[62]	...	72.2	75.7	2.610
2009	U	64 735[62]	...	U	7 098[62]	...	...	U	676[62]	...	...	...	3.300
Pakistan[63]													
2006	I	3 802 928	24.3	I	1 022 625	6.5	17.7	I	289 596	76.2	...	...	3.700
2007	I	3 830 973	24.0	I	1 019 533	6.4	17.6	I	288 192	75.2	63.6	67.6	3.700
Philippines													
2006	C	1 663 029	19.1		...	...	...		...	...	...	...	...
2007	C	1 749 878	19.7		...	...	...		...	...	...	...	...
Qatar													
2006	C	14 120	13.5	C	1 750	1.7	11.9	C	114	8.1	76.7	76.7	2.483
2007	C	15 681	12.9	C	1 776	1.5	11.4	C	117	7.5	81.0	79.2	2.453
2008	C	17 210	11.9	C	1 942	1.3	10.5	C	132	7.7	77.9	78.1	2.428
2009	C	18 351	11.2	C	2 008	1.2	10.0	C	130	7.1	...	...	2.430
2010	C	18 576	10.8	C	1 920	1.1	9.7		...	...	...	...	...
Republic of Korea - République de Corée													
2006	C	448 153[64]	9.2	C	242 266[65]	5.0	4.2	C	1 707[65]	3.8	75.7	82.4	1.123[65]
2007	C	493 189[64]	10.0	C	244 874[65]	5.0	5.1	C	1 703[65]	3.5	76.1	82.7	1.250[65]
2008	C	465 892[64]	9.4	C	246 113[65]	5.0	4.4	C	1 580[65]	3.4	76.5	83.3	1.192[65]
2009	C	444 849[64]	9.0	C	246 942[65]	5.0	4.0	C	1 415[65]	3.2	77.0	83.8	1.149[65]
Saudi Arabia - Arabie saoudite													
2006	...	589 223[66]	...	...	93 752[66]	...	...	...	10 954[66]	...	...	...	3.220
2007	...	595 099[67]	...	...	95 166[67]	...	...	...	10 782[67]	...	...	...	...
2008	...	598 126[67]	...	...	96 641[67]	...	...	...	10 576[67]	...	...	...	...
Singapore - Singapour													
2006	C	38 317	8.7	+C	16 393	3.7	5.0	+C	117	3.1	77.8[30]	82.6[30]	1.280[68]
2007	C	39 490	8.6	+C	17 140	3.7	4.9	+C	94	2.4	78.1[30]	82.9[30]	1.290[68]
2008	C	39 826	8.2	+C	17 222	3.6	4.7	+C	104	2.6	78.4[30]	83.3[30]	1.280[68]
2009	C	39 570	7.9	+C	17 101	3.4	4.5	+C	102	2.6	78.9[30]	83.7[30]	1.220[68]
2010		...			...				...		79.3[30]	84.1[30]	...
Sri Lanka													
2006	+C	373 538	18.8	+C	117 467	5.9	12.9	+C	3 752	10.0	...	...	2.308
2007	+C	386 573	19.3	+C	118 998	5.9	13.4	+C	3 298	8.5	...	...	2.362
2008	+C*	379 912	18.8	+C*	118 279	5.9	12.9		...	...	...	...	...
2009	+C*	376 843	18.4	+C*	120 085	5.9	12.6		...	...	...	...	...
2010	+C*	364 565	17.7	+C*	128 603	6.2	11.4		...	...	...	...	...

4. Vital statistics summary and life expectancy at birth: 2006 - 2010
Aperçu des statistiques de l'état civil et de l'espérance de vie à la naissance : 2006 - 2010 (continued - suite)

Continent, country or area and year / Continent, pays ou zone et année	Live births / Naissances vivantes Code[a]	Number / Nombre	Crude birth rate Taux brut de natalité	Deaths / Décès Code[a]	Number / Nombre	Crude death rate Taux brut de mortalité	Rate of natural increase Taux d'accrois-sement naturel	Infant deaths / Décès d'enfants de moins d'un an Code[a]	Number / Nombre	Rate (per 1000 births) Taux (par 1000 naiss-ances)	Life expectancy at birth Espérance de vie à la naissance Male[b] Masculin[b]	Female[b] Féminin[b]	Total fertility rate L'indice synthétique de fécondité
ASIA - ASIE													
Syrian Arab Republic - République arabe syrienne[69]													
2006	+U	656 599	...	+U	72 534	...	...	...	...	...	...	...	...
2007	+U	727 439	...	+U	76 064	...	...	...	...	...	...	...	...
2009	+U*	670 793	...	+U	76 650	...	...	...	...	...	...	...	...
Tajikistan - Tadjikistan													
2006	U	186 463[70]	...	U	29 366[47]	...	...	U	2 160[47]	...	...	...	3.266
2007	U	200 010[70]	...	U	30 332[47]	...	...	U	2 166[47]	...	...	...	...
2008	U	203 332[70]	...	U	30 743[47]	...	...	U	2 480[47]	...	69.7	74.8	...
2009		...	...		...	...	...		...	...	70.5	75.3	...
Thailand - Thaïlande													
2006	+U	793 623	...	+U	391 126	...	...	+U	5 855	...	II69.9	77.6	...
2007	+U	797 588	...	+U	393 255	...	...	+U	5 781	...	...	...	...
2008	+U	784 256	...	+U	397 327	...	...	+U	5 721	...	...	...	...
2009	+U	765 047	...	+U	393 916	...	...	+U	5 416	...	...	...	...
Turkey - Turquie													
2006	I	1 277 000[71]	18.4[71]	I	440 000[71]	6.3[71]	12.1	I	22 348[71]	17.5[71]	69.1[72]	74.0[72]	2.180
2007	I	1 275 000[71]	18.1[71]	I	447 000[71]	6.4[71]	11.8	I	21 293[71]	16.7[71]	...	...	2.150
2008	I	1 272 000[71]	17.9[71]	I	454 000[71]	6.4[71]	11.5	I	20 352[71]	16.0[71]	71.4[71]	75.8[71]	2.140
2009	I	1 270 000[71]	17.7[71]	I	461 000[71]	6.4[71]	11.3	I	19 431[71]	15.3[71]	71.5[71]	76.1[71]	2.120
2010	I	1 279 000[71]	17.6[71]	I	459 000[71]	6.3[71]	11.3	I	16 883[71]	13.2[71]			
United Arab Emirates - Émirats arabes unis													
2006	...	62 969[66]	...	...	6 563[66]	...	...	...	455[66]	...	76.7	78.8	...
2007	...	67 689[67]	...	...	...	...	...	...	528[67]	...	...	...	...
Viet Nam													
2006	C	1 243 463	14.9	C	334 432	4.0	10.9	C	19 895	16.0	...	...	2.090
2007	C	1 326 464	15.7	C	382 624	4.5	11.2	C	21 223	16.0	...	...	2.070
2008		...	...		...	...	...		...	...	70.6	76.0	2.080
2009		...	...		...	...	...		...	...	70.2	75.6	2.030
2010		...	...		...	...	...		...	...	...	...	2.000
Yemen - Yémen													
2006	U	298 437	...	U	21 456	...	...	...	...	...	...	...	...
2007	U	256 288	...	U	24 449	...	...	...	...	...	...	...	...
EUROPE													
Åland Islands - Îles d'Åland													
2006	C	295	11.0	C	257	9.6	1.4	C	-	...	...	...	1.867
2007	C	286	10.6	C	249	9.2	1.4	C	-	...	79.4	85.1	1.847
2008	C	294	10.8	C	250	9.2	1.6	C	1	...	...	...	1.881
2009	C	267	9.7	C	247	9.0	0.7	C	-	...	...	...	1.682
2010	C	286	10.3	C	233	8.4	1.9	C	...	...	...	...	...
Albania - Albanie													
2006	C	34 229	10.9	C	16 935	5.4	5.5	C	253	7.4	...	...	1.400
2007	C	33 163	10.5	C	14 528	4.6	5.9	C	205	6.2	...	...	...
2008	C	36 251	11.4	C	16 143	5.1	6.3	C	217	6.0	...	...	...
Andorra - Andorre													
2006	C	843	10.5	C	260	3.2	7.3	C	3	...	...	...	1.226
2007	C	826	10.0	C	230	2.8	7.2	C	1	...	...	...	1.170
2008	C	875	10.4	C	237	2.8	7.6	C	3	...	...	...	1.263
2009	C	838	9.8	C	272	3.2	6.6	C	1	...	...	...	1.232
2010	C	828	9.8	C	239	2.8	7.0	C	-	...	...	...	...
Austria - Autriche													
2006	C	77 914	9.4	C	74 295	9.0	0.4	C	281	3.6	77.1	82.6	1.405
2007	C	76 250	9.2	C	74 625	9.0	0.2	C	280	3.7	77.3	82.8	1.379
2008	C	77 752	9.3	C	75 083	9.0	0.3	C	287	3.7	77.6	83.0	1.414

1. Vital statistics summary and life expectancy at birth: 2006 - 2010
Aperçu des statistiques de l'état civil et de l'espérance de vie à la naissance : 2006 - 2010 (continued - suite)

Continent, country or area and year / Continent, pays ou zone et année	Code[a]	Live births / Naissances vivantes Number Nombre	Crude birth rate Taux brut de natalité	Code[a]	Deaths / Décès Number Nombre	Crude death rate Taux brut de mortalité	Rate of natural increase Taux d'accrois-sement naturel	Code[a]	Infant deaths / Décès d'enfants de moins d'un an Number Nombre	Rate (per 1000 births) Taux (par 1000 naiss-ances)	Life expectancy at birth / Espérance de vie à la naissance Male[b] Masculin[b]	Female[b] Féminin[b]	Total fertility rate L'indice synthétique de fécondité
EUROPE													
Austria - Autriche													
2009	C	76 344	9.1	C	77 381[73]	9.3	-0.1	C	289	3.8	77.4	82.9	1.392
2010	C	78 742	9.4	C	77 199[73]	9.2	0.2	C	307	3.9	...	...	...
Belarus - Bélarus													
2006	C	96 721	9.9	C	138 426	14.2	-4.3	C	587	6.1	63.6	75.5	1.287
2007	C	103 626	10.7	C	132 993	13.7	-3.0	C	534	5.2	64.5	76.2	1.373
2008	C	107 876	11.1	C	133 879	13.8	-2.7	C	483	4.5	64.7	76.5	1.424
2009	C	109 263	11.3	C	135 097	14.0	-2.7	C	511	4.7	64.7	76.4	1.442
2010	C	108 050	11.4	C	137 132	14.4	-3.1	C	429	4.0			
Belgium - Belgique													
2006	C	121 382[74]	11.5	C	101 587[74]	9.6	1.9	C	489[74]	4.0	77.0	82.7	...
2007	C	120 663[74]	11.4	C	100 658[74]	9.5	1.9	C	487[74]	4.0	...	...	1.805
2008	C	128 049[74]	12.0	C	104 587[74]	9.8	2.2	C	478[74]	3.7	...	...	...
2009	C	127 297[74]	11.8	C	104 509[74]	9.7	2.1	C	439[74]	3.4	...	...	...
2010	C*	127 000[74]	11.7	C*	104 500[74]	9.6	2.1	C*	440[74]	3.5	...	...	...
Bosnia and Herzegovina - Bosnie-Herzégovine													
2006	C	34 033	8.9	C	33 221	8.6	0.2	C	255	7.5	...	...	1.176
2007	C	33 835	8.8	C	35 044	9.1	-0.3	C	231	6.8	...	...	1.174
2008	C	34 176	8.9	C	34 026	8.9	0.0	C	235	6.9	...	...	...
2009	C	34 550	9.0	C	34 904	9.1	-0.1	C	224	6.5	...	...	1.303
2010	C*	33 779	8.8	C*	34 633	9.0	-0.2	C*	200	5.9	...	...	...
Bulgaria - Bulgarie													
2006	C	73 978	9.6	C	113 438	14.7	-5.1	C	720	9.7	III69.1	76.3	1.377
2007	C	75 349	9.8	C	113 004	14.8	-4.9	C	690	9.2	III69.2	76.3	1.416
2008	C	77 712	10.2	C	110 523	14.5	-4.3	C	668	8.6	III69.5	76.6	1.478
2009	C	80 956	10.7	C	108 068	14.2	-3.6	C	729	9.0	III69.9	77.1	1.565
2010	C	75 513	10.0	C	110 165	14.6	-4.6	C	708	9.4	...	...	...
Croatia - Croatie													
2006	C	41 446	9.3	C	50 378	11.3	-2.0	C	215	5.2	...	...	1.381
2007	C	41 910	9.4	C	52 367	11.8	-2.4	C	234	5.6	...	...	1.401
2008	C	43 753	9.9	C	52 151	11.8	-1.9	C	195	4.5	...	...	1.472
2009	C	44 577	10.1	C	52 414	11.8	-1.8	C	235	5.3	...	...	1.497
2010		...	...	C	52 096	11.8	...	C	...	...	...	...	...
Czech Republic - République tchèque													
2006	C	105 831	10.3	C	104 441	10.2	0.1	C	352	3.3	73.4	79.7	1.328
2007	C	114 632	11.1	C	104 636	10.1	1.0	C	360	3.1	73.7	79.9	1.438
2008	C	119 570	11.5	C	104 948	10.1	1.4	C	338	2.8	74.0	80.1	1.497
2009	C	118 348	11.3	C	107 421	10.2	1.0	C	341	2.9	74.2	80.1	1.492
2010	C	117 153	11.1	C	106 844	10.2	1.0	C	313	2.7	...	...	...
Denmark - Danemark[75]													
2006	C	64 933	11.9	C	55 477	10.2	1.7	C	252	3.9	II75.9	80.4	1.850
2007	C	64 095	11.7	C	55 604	10.2	1.6	C	256	4.0	II75.9	80.5	1.846
2008	C	65 038	11.8	C	54 591	9.9	1.9	C	262	4.0	II76.3	80.7	1.892
2009	C	62 818	11.4	C	54 872	9.9	1.4	C	193	3.1	II76.5	80.8	1.842
2010	C	63 411	11.4	C	54 368	9.8	1.6	C	216	3.4	...	...	...
Estonia - Estonie													
2006	C	14 877	11.1	C	17 316	12.9	-1.8	C	66	4.4	67.4	78.5	1.545
2007	C	15 775	11.8	C	17 409	13.0	-1.2	C	79	5.0	67.2	78.8	1.638
2008	C	16 028	12.0	C	16 675	12.4	-0.5	C	80	5.0	68.6	79.2	1.661
2009	C	15 763	11.8	C	16 081	12.0	-0.2	C	57	3.6	...	...	1.630
2010	C	15 825	11.8	C	15 790	11.8	0.0	C	53	3.3	...	...	...
Faeroe Islands - Îles Féroé													
2006	C	662	13.7	C	416	8.6	5.1	C	3	...	...	...	2.480
2007	C	674	13.9	C	383	7.9	6.0	C	4	...	...	...	2.533
2008		...	...	C	378	7.8	...		...	...	76.8	82.3	...
Finland - Finlande													
2006	C	58 840[76]	11.2	C	48 065[77]	9.1	2.0	C	167[77]	2.8	75.8	82.8	1.837
2007	C	58 729[76]	11.1	C	49 077[77]	9.3	1.8	C	161[77]	2.7	75.8	82.9	1.829

4. Vital statistics summary and life expectancy at birth: 2006 - 2010
Aperçu des statistiques de l'état civil et de l'espérance de vie à la naissance : 2006 - 2010 (continued - suite)

Continent, country or area and year / Continent, pays ou zone et année	Live births Naissances vivantes			Deaths Décès			Rate of natural increase Taux d'accrois-sement naturel	Infant deaths Décès d'enfants de moins d'un an			Life expectancy at birth Espérance de vie à la naissance		Total fertility rate L'indice synthétique de fécondité
	Code[a]	Number Nombre	Crude birth rate Taux brut de natalité	Code[a]	Number Nombre	Crude death rate Taux brut de mortalité		Code[a]	Number Nombre	Rate (per 1000 births) Taux (par 1000 naiss-ances)	Male[b] Masculin[b]	Female[b] Féminin[b]	
EUROPE													
Finland - Finlande													
2008	C	59 530[76]	11.2	C	49 094[77]	9.2	2.0	C	157[77]	2.6	76.3	83.0	1.846
2009	C	60 163[78]	11.3	C	49 636[79]	9.3	2.0	C	158[80]	2.6	76.5	83.1	1.864
2010	C	60 694[78]	11.4	C	50 654[79]	9.5	1.9	C	140[80]	2.3	...	...	...
France													
2006	C	796 896[81]	12.9	C	516 416[81]	8.4	4.6	C	2 906[81]	3.6	77.2[82]	84.2[82]	1.983
2007	C	785 985[81]	12.7	C	521 016[81]	8.4	4.3	C	2 822[81]	3.6	...	...	1.956
2008	C	796 044[81]	12.8	C	532 131[81]	8.5	4.2	C	2 856[81]	3.6	III77.4	84.3	1.998
2009	C	793 420[81]	12.7	C	538 116[81]	8.6	4.1	C	2 903[81]	3.7	...	...	...
2010	C*	797 000[81]	12.7	C*	535 000[81]	8.5	4.2		...	...	...	...	...
Germany - Allemagne													
2006	C	672 724	8.2	C	821 627	10.0	-1.8	C	2 579	3.8	III76.6	82.1	1.331
2007	C	684 862	8.3	C	827 155	10.1	-1.7	C	2 656	3.9	III76.9	82.3	1.370
2008	C	682 514	8.3	C	844 439	10.3	-2.0	C	2 414	3.5	...	...	1.376
2009	C	665 126	8.1	C	854 544	10.4	-2.3	C	2 334	3.5	...	...	...
2010	C*	681 000	8.3	C*	862 000	10.5	-2.2	C*	2 400	3.5	...	...	...
Gibraltar													
2006	+C	373	12.9	+C	230[83]	8.0	5.0	+C	1	...	...	...	...
2007	+C	400[84]	13.7	+C	202[83]	6.9	6.8	+C	1	...	...	...	...
2008	+C	400[84]	13.7	+C	227[83]	7.8	5.9		...	...	...	...	...
Greece - Grèce													
2006	C	112 042	10.0	C	105 476	9.5	0.6	C	415	3.7	77.1	82.0	1.410
2007	C	111 926	10.0	C	109 895	9.8	0.2	C	397	3.5	77.0	82.0	1.417
2008	C	118 302	10.5	C	107 979	9.6	0.9	C	314	2.7	77.5	82.5	1.506
2009	C	117 933	10.5	C	108 316	9.6	0.9	C	371	3.1	77.7	82.8	1.522
2010	C*	109 982	...	C*	106 000	...	...		...	...	...	...	...
Guernsey - Guernesey													
2006	C	598	9.8	C	498	8.2	1.6		...	...	...	...	...
2007	C	645	10.5	C	513	8.4	2.2		...	...	...	...	...
2008	C	631	10.2	C	476	7.7	2.5		...	...	...	...	...
2009	C	675	10.8	C	543	8.7	2.1		...	...	...	...	...
Hungary - Hongrie													
2006	C	99 871	9.9	C	131 603	13.1	-3.2	C	571	5.7	69.0	77.4	1.350
2007	C	97 613	9.7	C	132 938	13.2	-3.5	C	577	5.9	69.2	77.3	1.323
2008	C	99 149	9.9	C	130 027	13.0	-3.1	C	553	5.6	69.8	77.8	1.352
2009	C	96 442	9.6	C	130 414	13.0	-3.4	C	495	5.1	70.1	77.9	1.327
2010	C*	90 335	9.0	C*	130 450	13.0	-4.0	C*	480	5.3	...	...	...
Iceland - Islande													
2006	C	4 415	14.5	C	1 903	6.3	8.3	C	6	...	II79.4	83.0	2.074
2007	C	4 560	14.6	C	1 943	6.2	8.4	C	9	...	II79.4	82.9	2.102
2008	C	4 835	15.1	C	1 987	6.2	8.9	C	12	...	II79.6	81.3	2.140
2009	C	5 027	15.7	C	2 002	6.3	9.5	C	9	...	...	...	2.221
2010	C	4 907	15.4	C	2 017	6.3	9.1	C	11	...	...	...	...
Ireland - Irlande													
2006	+C	64 237	15.2	+C	27 479	6.5	8.7	+C	238	3.7	...	...	1.905
2007	+C	70 620	16.3	+C	28 050	6.5	9.8	+C	221	3.1	...	...	2.030
2008	+C	75 065	17.0	+C	28 192	6.4	10.6	+C	284	3.8	...	...	2.100
2009	+C	74 278	16.7	+C	28 898	6.5	10.2	+C*	240	3.2	...	...	2.000
2010	+C*	73 940	16.5	+C*	27 906	6.2	10.3		...	...	...	...	...
Isle of Man - Île de Man													
2006	+C	905	11.3	+C	768	9.6	1.7		...	...	...	...	...
2007	+C	919	11.4	+C	789	9.8	1.6		...	...	...	...	...
Italy - Italie													
2006	C	560 010	9.5	C	558 614	9.5	0.0	C	2 031	3.6	78.4	84.0	1.352
2007	C	563 933	9.5	C	572 881	9.6	-0.2	C	1 959	3.5	78.7	84.0	1.374
2008	+C	576 659	9.6	C	578 192	9.7	0.0	C	1 896	3.3	...	...	1.414
2009	+C	568 857	9.5	C	591 663	9.8	-0.4	C*	2 110	3.7	...	...	1.411
2010	+C*	561 980	9.3	C*	587 488	9.7	-0.4	C*	1 891	3.4	...	...	...

4. Vital statistics summary and life expectancy at birth: 2006 - 2010
Aperçu des statistiques de l'état civil et de l'espérance de vie à la naissance : 2006 - 2010 (continued - suite)

Continent, country or area and year / Continent, pays ou zone et année	Live births / Naissances vivantes			Deaths / Décès			Rate of natural increase / Taux d'accroissement naturel	Infant deaths / Décès d'enfants de moins d'un an			Life expectancy at birth / Espérance de vie à la naissance		Total fertility rate / L'indice synthétique de fécondité
	Code[a]	Number / Nombre	Crude birth rate / Taux brut de natalité	Code[a]	Number / Nombre	Crude death rate / Taux brut de mortalité		Code[a]	Number / Nombre	Rate (per 1000 births) / Taux (par 1000 naissances)	Male[b] / Masculin[b]	Female[b] / Féminin[b]	
EUROPE													
Jersey													
2006	+C	962[29]	10.8	+C	758	8.5	2.3		...	...	...	...	1.553
2007	+C	1 031[29]	11.4	+C	708	7.9	3.6		...	...	...	...	1.679
2008	+C	973[29]	...	+C	743				...	...	...	...	...
Latvia - Lettonie													
2006	C	22 264	9.7	C	33 098	14.5	-4.7	C	170	7.6	65.9	76.8	1.353
2007	C	23 273	10.2	C	33 042	14.5	-4.3	C	203	8.7	65.8	76.5	1.412
2008	C	23 948	10.6	C	31 006	13.7	-3.1	C	161	6.7	67.2	77.9	1.453
2009	C	21 677	9.6	C	29 897	13.3	-3.6	C	168	7.8	68.3	78.1	1.319
2010	C	19 219	8.6	C	30 040	13.4	-4.8	C	110	5.7			
Liechtenstein													
2006	C	361	10.3	C	220	6.3	4.0	C	2	...	...	...	1.400
2007	C	351	9.9	C	227	6.4	3.5	C	-	...	...	...	1.400
2008	C	350	9.9	C	205	5.8	4.1	C	-	...	...	...	1.400
2009	C*	406	11.3	C*	229	6.4	4.9	C	1	...	...	...	1.728
2010	C*	329	9.1	C*	238	6.6	2.5	C*	1	...	...	...	...
Lithuania - Lituanie													
2006	C	31 265	9.2	C	44 813	13.2	-4.0	C	213	6.8	65.3	77.1	1.306
2007	C	32 346	9.6	C	45 624	13.5	-3.9	C	190	5.9	64.9	77.2	1.353
2008	C	35 065	10.4	C	43 832	13.1	-2.6	C	172	4.9	66.3	77.6	1.470
2009	C	36 682	11.0	C	42 032	12.6	-1.6	C	181	4.9	67.5	78.6	1.546
2010	C	35 626	10.8	C	42 120	12.8	-2.0	C	153	4.3			
Luxembourg													
2006	C	5 514	11.7	C	3 766	8.0	3.7	C	14	...	...	...	1.644
2007	C	5 477	11.4	C	3 866	8.1	3.4	C	10	...	III77.6	82.7	1.607
2008	C	5 596	11.5	C	3 595	7.4	4.1	C	10	...	...	...	1.605
2009	C	5 638	11.3	C	3 655	7.3	4.0	C	14	...	...	...	1.586
2010	C	5 874	11.6	C	3 760	7.4	4.2	C	20	...	...	...	...
Malta - Malte													
2006	C	3 885	9.6	C	3 216	7.9	1.6	C	14	...	76.8	81.2	1.410
2007	C	3 871	9.5	C	3 111	7.6	1.9	C	25	...	77.2	81.7	1.370
2008	C	4 126	10.0	C	3 243	7.9	2.1	C	34	8.2	76.7	82.3	1.430
2009	C	4 143	10.0	C	3 221	7.8	2.2	C	22	...	77.7	82.2	1.440
2010	C	3 999	9.6	C	3 010	7.2	2.4	C	22	...	...	...	...
Monaco[85]													
2006	C	880	...	C	535	...	...		...	...	...	...	...
Montenegro - Monténégro													
2006	C	7 531	12.1	C	5 968	9.6	2.5	C	83	11.0	...	...	1.640
2007	C	7 834	12.5	C	5 979	9.5	3.0	C	58	7.4	...	...	1.690
2008	C	8 258	13.1	C	5 708	9.1	4.1	C	62	7.5	...	...	1.772
2009	C	8 642	13.7	C	5 862	9.3	4.4	C	49	5.7	...	...	...
2010	C	7 415	11.7	C	5 628	8.9	2.8	C	...	...	...	...	...
Netherlands - Pays-Bas													
2006	C	185 057[86]	11.3	C	135 372[86]	8.3	3.0	C	820[86]	4.4	77.4	81.7	1.720
2007	C	181 336[86]	11.1	C	133 022[86]	8.1	2.9	C	736[86]	4.1	78.0	82.3	1.718
2008	C	184 634[86]	11.2	C	135 136[86]	8.2	3.0	C	698[86]	3.8	78.3	82.3	1.775
2009	C	184 915[86]	11.2	C	134 235[86]	8.1	3.1	C	711[86]	3.8	78.5	82.7	1.790
2010	C*	183 866[86]	11.1	C	136 058[86]	8.2	2.9	C	695[86]	3.8	...	...	...
Norway - Norvège[87]													
2006	C	58 545	12.6	C	41 253[88]	8.9	3.7	C	185[88]	3.2	78.1	82.7	1.904
2007	C	58 459	12.4	C	41 954[88]	8.9	3.5	C	180[88]	3.1	78.2	82.7	1.900
2008	C	60 497	12.7	C	41 712[88]	8.7	3.9	C	163[88]	2.7	78.3	83.0	1.960
2009	C	61 807	12.8	C	41 449[88]	8.6	4.2	C	192[88]	3.1	78.6	83.1	1.980
2010	C	61 442	12.6	C	41 499[88]	8.5	4.1	C	171[88]	2.8	...	...	...
Poland - Pologne													
2006	C	374 244	9.8	C	369 686	9.7	0.1	C	2 238	6.0	70.4	79.0	1.267
2007	C	387 873	10.2	C	377 226	9.9	0.3	C	2 322	6.0	71.0	79.7	1.306
2008	C	414 499	10.9	C	379 399	10.0	0.9	C	2 338	5.6	...	...	1.390
2009	C	417 589	10.9	C	384 940	10.1	0.9	C	2 327	5.6	71.5	80.1	1.398
2010	C	413 300	10.8	C	378 478	9.9	0.9	C	2 057	5.0	...	...	...

4. Vital statistics summary and life expectancy at birth: 2006 - 2010
Aperçu des statistiques de l'état civil et de l'espérance de vie à la naissance : 2006 - 2010 (continued - suite)

Continent, country or area and year / Continent, pays ou zone et année	Live births Naissances vivantes			Deaths Décès			Rate of natural increase Taux d'accrois-sement naturel	Infant deaths Décès d'enfants de moins d'un an			Life expectancy at birth Espérance de vie à la naissance		Total fertility rate L'indice synthétique de fécondité
	Co-de[a]	Number Nombre	Crude birth rate Taux brut de natalité	Co-de[a]	Number Nombre	Crude death rate Taux brut de mortalité		Co-de[a]	Number Nombre	Rate (per 1000 births) Taux (par 1000 naiss-ances)	Male[b] Masculin[b]	Female[b] Féminin[b]	
EUROPE													
Portugal													
2006	C	105 449[29]	10.0	C	101 990[30]	9.6	0.3	C	349[30]	3.3	II75.2	81.8	1.362
2007	C	102 492[29]	9.7	C	103 512[30]	9.8	-0.1	C	353[30]	3.4	III75.2	81.6	1.335
2008	C	104 594[29]	9.8	C	104 280[30]	9.8	0.0	C	340[30]	3.3	III75.5	81.7	1.374
2009	C	99 491[29]	9.4	C	104 434[30]	9.8	-0.5	C	362[30]	3.6	III75.8	81.8	1.323
2010	C*	101 320[29]	9.5	C*	105 869[30]	10.0	-0.4	C*	243[30]	2.4	...	...	...
Republic of Moldova - République de Moldova													
2006	C	37 587[89]	10.5	C	43 137[89]	12.0	-1.5	C	442[89]	11.8	64.6	72.2	1.229
2007	C	37 973[89]	10.6	C	43 050[89]	12.0	-1.4	C	428[89]	11.3	65.0	72.6	1.256
2008	C	39 018[90]	10.9	C	41 948[90]	11.7	-0.8	C	473[90]	12.1	...	...	1.277
2009	C	40 803[90]	11.4	C	42 139[90]	11.8	-0.4	C	492[90]	12.1	65.3	73.4	1.326
2010	C	40 474[90]	11.4	C	43 631[90]	12.2	-0.9	C	476[90]	11.8	...	...	...
Romania - Roumanie													
2006	C	219 483	10.2	C	258 094	12.0	-1.8	C	3 052	13.9	III68.7	75.8	1.313
2007	C	214 728	10.0	C	251 965	11.7	-1.7	C	2 574	12.0	III69.2	76.1	1.293
2008	C	221 900	10.3	C	253 202	11.8	-1.5	C	2 434	11.0	III69.5	76.7	1.350
2009	C	222 388	10.4	C	257 213	12.0	-1.6	C	2 250	10.1	III69.7	77.1	1.371
2010	C	212 199	9.9	C	259 723	12.1	-2.2	C	2 078	9.8	...	...	...
Russian Federation - Fédération de Russie													
2006	C	1 479 637[47]	10.4	C	2 166 703[47]	15.2	-4.8	C	15 079[47]	10.2	60.4	73.2	1.296
2007	C	1 610 122[47]	11.3	C	2 080 445[47]	14.6	-3.3	C	14 858[47]	9.2	61.4	73.9	1.406
2008	C	1 713 947[47]	12.1	C	2 075 954[47]	14.6	-2.6	C	14 436[47]	8.4	61.8	74.2	1.494
2009	C	1 761 687[47]	12.4	C	2 010 543[47]	14.2	-1.8	C	14 271[47]	8.1	62.8	74.7	1.537
2010	C	1 788 948[47]	12.5	C	2 028 516[47]	14.2	-1.7	C	13 405[47]	7.5	...	...	...
San Marino - Saint-Marin													
2006	+C	302	9.6	+C	225	7.2	2.5	+C	-	...	...	...	...
2007	+C	292	9.2	+C	225	7.1	2.1	+C	-	...	...	...	...
2008	+C	349	10.7	+C	190	5.8	4.9		...	...	...	...	...
2009	+C	306	9.3	+C	233	7.1	2.2		...	...	...	...	...
Serbia - Serbie													
2006	+C	70 997[91]	9.6	+C	102 884[91]	13.9	-4.3	+C	525[91]	7.4	70.6	75.9	1.432
2007	+C	68 102[91]	9.2	+C	102 805[91]	13.9	-4.7	+C	484[91]	7.1	70.7	76.2	1.379
2008	+C	69 083[91]	9.4	+C	102 711[91]	14.0	-4.6	+C	460[91]	6.7	71.1	76.3	1.406
2009	+C	70 299[91]	9.6	+C	104 000[91]	14.2	-4.6	+C	492[91]	7.0	71.1	76.4	1.437
2010	+C	68 304[91]	9.2	+C	103 211[91]	13.9	-4.7	+C	460[91]	6.7	...	...	...
Slovakia - Slovaquie													
2006	C	53 904	10.0	C	53 301	9.9	0.1	C	355	6.6	70.4	78.2	1.239
2007	C	54 424	10.1	C	53 856	10.0	0.1	C	334	6.1	70.5	78.1	1.251
2008	C	57 360	10.6	C	53 164	9.8	0.8	C	336	5.9	70.9	78.7	1.320
2009	C	61 217	11.3	C	52 913	9.8	1.5	C	346	5.7	71.3	78.7	1.411
2010	C	60 410	11.1	C	53 445	9.8	1.3	C	344	5.7	...	...	...
Slovenia - Slovénie													
2006	C	18 932	9.4	C	18 180	9.1	0.4	C	64	3.4	II74.8	81.9	1.314
2007	C	19 823	9.8	C	18 584	9.2	0.6	C	55	2.8	II75.0	82.3	1.380
2008	C	21 817	10.8	C	18 308	9.1	1.7	C	52	2.4	75.8	82.3	1.528
2009	C	21 856	10.7	C	18 750	9.2	1.5	C	52	2.4	...	...	1.534
2010	C*	21 687	10.6	C*	18 567	9.1	1.5	C*	54	2.5	...	...	...
Spain - Espagne													
2006	C	482 957	11.0	C	371 478	8.4	2.5	C	1 704	3.5	...	...	1.373
2007	C	492 527	11.0	C	385 361	8.6	2.4	C	1 704	3.5	...	...	1.400
2008	C	519 779	11.4	C	386 324	8.5	2.9	C	1 741	3.3	78.9	85.0	1.461
2009	C	494 997	10.8	C	384 933	8.4	2.4	C	1 609	3.3	78.5	84.6	1.393
2010	C*	479 999	10.4	C*	379 270	8.2	2.2	C*	1 534	3.2	...	...	...
Sweden - Suède													
2006	C	105 913	11.7	C	91 177	10.0	1.6	C	297	2.8	78.7	82.9	1.853
2007	C	107 421	11.7	C	91 729	10.0	1.7	C	268	2.5	78.9	83.0	1.879
2008	C	109 301	11.9	C	91 449	9.9	1.9	C	272	2.5	79.1	83.2	1.907

Aperçu des statistiques de l'état civil et de l'espérance de vie à la naissance : 2006 - 2010 (continued - suite)

Continent, country or area and year / Continent, pays ou zone et année	Code[a]	Live births - Naissances vivantes Number Nombre	Crude birth rate Taux brut de natalité	Code[a]	Deaths - Décès Number Nombre	Crude death rate Taux brut de mortalité	Rate of natural increase Taux d'accroissement naturel	Code[a]	Infant deaths - Décès d'enfants de moins d'un an Number Nombre	Rate (per 1000 births) Taux (par 1000 naissances)	Life expectancy at birth - Espérance de vie à la naissance Male[b] Masculin[b]	Female[b] Féminin[b]	Total fertility rate L'indice synthétique de fécondité
EUROPE													
Sweden - Suède													
2009	C	111 801	12.0	C	90 080	9.7	2.3	C	278	2.5	79.4	83.4	1.935
2010	C	115 641	12.3	C	90 487	9.6	2.7	C	294	2.5	...	...	...
Switzerland - Suisse													
2006	C	73 371	9.8	C	60 283	8.1	1.7	C	325	4.4	[II]78.9	83.9	1.437
2007	C	74 494	9.9	C	61 089	8.1	1.8	C	293	3.9	79.2	84.1	1.460
2008	C	76 691	10.0	C	61 233	8.0	2.0	C	308	4.0	[II]79.5	84.2	1.480
2009	C	78 286	10.1	C	62 476	8.1	2.0	C	337	4.3	[II]79.7	84.3	1.497
2010	C*	80 000	10.2	C*	62 500	8.0	2.2		...	...	...	...	...
TFYR of Macedonia - L'ex-R. y. de Macédoine													
2006	C	22 585	11.1	C	18 630	9.1	1.9	C	260	11.5	71.7	75.9	1.460
2007	C	22 688	11.1	C	19 594	9.6	1.5	C	234	10.3	71.9	76.1	1.458
2008	C	22 945	11.2	C	18 982	9.3	1.9	C	223	9.7	72.1	76.3	1.471
2009	C	23 684	11.5	C	19 060	9.3	2.3	C	278	11.7	...	...	1.520
2010	C*	24 296	11.8	C*	19 114	9.3	2.5	C*	186	7.7	...	...	...
Ukraine													
2006	C	460 368[92]	9.8	C	758 092[93]	16.2	-6.4	C	4 433[93]	9.6	[II]62.4	74.1	1.254[94]
2007	C	472 657[92]	10.2	C	762 877[93]	16.4	-6.2	C	5 188[93]	11.0	[II]62.5	74.2	1.300
2008	C	510 589[92]	11.0	C	754 460[93]	16.3	-5.3	C	5 049[93]	9.9	[II]62.5	74.3	1.390
2009	C*	512 526[92]	11.1	C*	706 740[93]	15.3	-4.2	C	4 801[93]	9.4	...	...	...
2010	C	497 689[92]	10.8	C	698 235[93]	15.2	-4.4	C	4 546[93]	9.1	...	...	...
United Kingdom of Great Britain and Northern Ireland - Royaume-Uni de Grande-Bretagne et d'Irlande du Nord[95]													
2006	C	748 563[96]	12.4	C	572 224	9.4	2.9	C	3 737	5.0	...	...	1.840
2007	C	772 245[96]	12.7	C	574 687	9.4	3.2	C	3 740	4.8	[III]77.3	81.5	1.900
2008	C	794 383[96]	12.9	C	579 697	9.4	3.5	C*	3 663	4.6	[III]77.4	81.6	1.958
2009	C	790 204[96]	12.8	C	559 617	9.1	3.7	C*	3 677	4.7	...	...	...
2010	C*	778 823[96]	12.5	C*	561 666	9.0	3.5		...	...	...	...	...
OCEANIA - OCÉANIE													
American Samoa - Samoas américaines													
2006	C	1 442	21.6	C	267	4.0	17.6	C	17	...	68.5	76.2	...
Australia - Australie													
2006	+C	265 949	12.8	+C	133 739	6.5	6.4	+C	1 262	4.7	...	...	1.817
2007	+C	285 213	13.5	+C	137 854	6.5	7.0	+C	1 203	4.2	[III]79.0	83.7	1.920
2008	+C	296 621	13.8	+C	143 946	6.7	7.1	+C	1 226	4.1	[III]79.2	83.7	1.956
2009	+C	295 738	13.5	+C	140 760	6.4	7.1	+C	1 261	4.3	[III]79.3	83.9	1.901
Cook Islands - Îles Cook[97]													
2006	+C	278	11.7	+C	85	3.6	8.1	+C	3	...	...	...	...
2007	+C	289	13.8	+C	87	4.1	9.6	+C	4	...	...	...	...
2008	+C	261	11.8	+C	59	2.7	9.1	+C	1	...	...	...	...
2009	+C*	255	11.1	+C*	74	3.2	7.9	+C*	2	...	...	...	...
Fiji - Fidji													
2006	+C	18 394	22.2	+C	...	...	...		...	...	...	...	...
2007	+C	19 298	23.1	+C	...	...	...		...	...	63.8	67.8	...
2008	+C	18 944	...	+C	...	...	...		...	...	...	...	...
2009	+C	18 854	21.4	+C	...	...	...		...	...	...	...	...
French Polynesia - Polynésie française													
2006	C	4 592	17.9	C	1 152	4.5	13.4	C	31	6.8	73.0	76.9	...
2007	C	4 434	17.1	C	1 215	4.7	12.4	C	30	6.8	...	...	...
2008	C	4 628	17.6	C	1 178	4.5	13.1	C	23	...	73.0	78.2	...

4. Vital statistics summary and life expectancy at birth: 2006 - 2010
Aperçu des statistiques de l'état civil et de l'espérance de vie à la naissance : 2006 - 2010 (continued - suite)

Continent, country or area and year / Continent, pays ou zone et année	Live births Naissances vivantes			Deaths Décès			Rate of natural increase Taux d'accrois-sement naturel	Infant deaths Décès d'enfants de moins d'un an			Life expectancy at birth Espérance de vie à la naissance		Total fertility rate L'indice synthétique de fécondité
	Code[a]	Number Nombre	Crude birth rate Taux brut de natalité	Code[a]	Number Nombre	Crude death rate Taux brut de mortalité		Code[a]	Number Nombre	Rate (per 1000 births) Taux (par 1000 naiss-ances)	Male[b] Masculin[b]	Female[b] Féminin[b]	
OCEANIA - OCÉANIE													
Guam													
2006	C	3 414[98]	20.0	C	682[98]	4.0	16.0	C	46[98]	13.5	75.5	81.8	...
2007	C	3 493[98]	20.1	C	786[98]	4.5	15.6	C	36[98]	10.3	75.7	82.0	...
2008	C	3 466[98]	19.7	C	775[98]	4.4	15.3	C*	31[98]	8.9	75.9	82.2	...
2009	C	3 423[98]	19.2	C	850[98]	4.8	14.4	...	...	...	...	...	...
Marshall Islands - Îles Marshall													
2006	+U	1 576[99]	...	+U	318	...	...						
Micronesia (Federated States of) - Micronésie (États fédérés de)													
2006	+U	2 148			...	...	...		...	...	...	...	...
Nauru													
2006	C	120									55.2	57.1	
New Caledonia - Nouvelle-Calédonie													
2006	C	4 224	17.7	C	1 113	4.7	13.0		...	...	72.9	80.2	2.290
2007	C	4 093	16.9	C	1 207	5.0	11.9	C	25	...	71.8	80.3	2.200
2008	C	4 015	16.6	C	1 173	4.8	11.7		...	...			
2009	C*	4 090	16.7	C*	1 235	5.0	11.6		...	...			
New Zealand - Nouvelle-Zélande													
2006	+C	59 193	14.1	+C	28 245[30]	6.7	7.4	+C	300[30]	5.1	III77.9	81.9	2.007
2007	+C	64 044	15.1	+C	28 522[30]	6.7	8.4	+C	317[30]	4.9	III78.0	82.2	2.172
2008	+C	64 343	15.1	+C	29 188[30]	6.8	8.2	+C	322[30]	5.0	III78.2	82.2	2.183
2009	+C	62 543	14.5	+C	28 964[30]	6.7	7.8	+C	308[30]	4.9	III78.4	82.4	2.116
Niue - Nioué													
2006	C	35[100]	20.8	C	19[101]	...	...		...	...	67.0	76.0	...
2007	C	28[100]	...	C	9[101]	...	...		...	...	...	...	...
2008	C	20[100]	...	C	13[101]	...	...		...	...	...	...	...
2009	C	31[100]	20.0	C	12	...	...		...	...	...	...	...
Norfolk Island - Île Norfolk[102]													
2006	+C	22	...	+C	13	...	...		...	...	...	...	...
2007	+C	22	...	+C	11	...	...		...	...	...	...	...
2008	+C	22	...	+C	20	...	...		...	...	...	...	...
Northern Mariana Islands - Îles Mariannes septentrionales													
2006	U	1 422[103]	...	U	174[103]	...	...	U	9[103]	...	...	...	2.400
2007	U	1 384[103]	...	U	138[103]	...	...	U	6[103]	...	...	...	2.400
2008	U	1 260[103]	...	U	176[103]	...	...	U	4[103]	...	...	...	2.300
2009	...	...	...	...	...	...	...	...	...	...	74.5	79.9	2.200
2010	...	...	...	...	...	...	...	...	...	...	...	...	2.200
Palau - Palaos													
2006	C	259	12.0	C	144	6.6	5.3	C	2	...	...	...	...
Pitcairn													
2007	C	1	...	C	1	...	...	C	-	...	...	...	...
2008	C	1	...		...	...	...		...	...	...	...	...
Samoa													
2006	C	3 171	17.1	U*	541	...	...		...	...	71.5	74.2	...
2007	C	2 528	13.9	U*	482	...	...		...	...	...	...	...
2008	C	2 371	13.0	U*	409	...	...		...	...	...	...	...
2009	C	1 602	8.7	U*	561	...	...		...	...	...	...	...
Tonga													
2006	+C	2 945	28.6	I	709[104]	6.9	21.7		...	...	67.3	73.0	4.100
2007		...	...		...	...	...		...	...	...	...	3.700
Tuvalu													
2006	U	217	...	U	45	...	...		...	...	...	...	...
2007	U	214	...	U	47	...	...		...	...	...	...	...

Continent, country or area and year Continent, pays ou zone et année	Live births Naissances vivantes				Deaths Décès			Rate of natural increase Taux d'accrois-sement naturel	Infant deaths Décès d'enfants de moins d'un an			Life expectancy at birth Espérance de vie à la naissance		Total fertility rate L'indice synthétique de fécondité
	Co-de[a]	Number Nombre	Crude birth rate Taux brut de natalité	Co-de[a]	Number Nombre	Crude death rate Taux brut de mortalité			Co-de[a]	Number Nombre	Rate (per 1000 births) Taux (par 1000 naiss-ances)	Male[b] Masculin[b]	Female[b] Féminin[b]	
OCEANIA - OCÉANIE														
Wallis and Futuna Islands - Îles Wallis et Futuna														
2006	C	220	...	C	77	...	...			...	...	...	...	...
2007	C	215	...	C	...	...	...			...	...	...	...	...
2008	C	185	13.8	C	90	6.7	7.1			...	...	...	...	...

FOOTNOTES - NOTES

Italics: data from civil registers which are incomplete or of unknown completeness. - Italiques : données incomplètes ou dont le degré d'exactitude n'est pas connu, provenant des registres de l'état civil.

* Provisional. - Données provisoires.

[a] 'Code' indicates the source of data, as follows:
C - Civil registration, estimated over 90% complete
U - Civil registration, estimated less than 90% complete
| - Other source, estimated reliable
+ - Data tabulated by date of registration rather than occurence
... - Information not available

Le 'Code' indique la source des données, comme suit :
C - Registres de l'état civil considérés complets à 90 p. 100 au moins
U - Registres de l'état civil qui ne sont pas considérés complets à 90 p. 100 au moins
| - Autre source, considérée fiable
+ - Données exploitées selon la date de l'enregistrement et non la date de l'événement
... - Information non disponible

[b] A Roman number in front of the data for males specifies the range of the reference period of life expectancy for males and females presented on the row. For example, a reference year of 2005 and a range of V years means that the reference period for the life expectancy is 2001 - 2005. The absence of a Roman number means the reference period is one year and the reference period therefore coincides with the reference year. - Un chiffre romain devant la donnée relative aux hommes indique l'étendue de la période de référence concernant l'espérance de vie des hommes et des femmes présentée dans la ligne. Par exemple, une année de référence 2005 et une étendue de V signifie que la période de référence pour l'espérance de vie est 2001-2005. L'absence de chiffre romain signifie que la période de référence est d'un an et donc coïncide avec l'année de référence.

[1] Data refer to Algerian population only. - Les données ne concernent que la population algérienne.
[2] Excluding live-born infants who died before their birth was registered. - Non compris les enfants nés vivants décédés avant l'enregistrement de leur naissance.
[3] Data from Health Statistics Reports since 1998, due to incompleteness of civil registration. - Données provenant des Health Statistics Reports (rapports sur les statistiques sanitaires) depuis 1998, en raison des lacunes de l'état civil.
[4] Based on the results of the Botswana Demographic Survey. - Données extraites de l'enquête démographique effectuée par le Botswana.
[5] Data refer to the twelve months preceding the census in December. Data refer to births to women aged 15-49. - Les données se rapportent aux douze mois précédant le recensement de décembre. Les données concernent les enfants nés de femmes âgées de 15 à 49 ans.
[6] Data refer to the twelve months preceding the census in December. - Les données se rapportent aux douze mois précédant le recensement de décembre.

[7] Based on the results of the 2006 Population and Housing Census. - Données fondées sur les résultats du recensement de la population et de l'habitat de 2006.
[8] Data refer to national projections. - Les données se réfèrent aux projections nationales.
[9] Data refer to the twelve months preceding the census in May. - Les données se rapportent aux douze mois précédant le recensement de mai.
[10] Coverage of live births is below 60%. - La couverture des naissances vivantes est inférieure à 60 %.
[11] Coverage of live births is below 60%. Excluding data for November and December. - La couverture des naissances vivantes est inférieure à 60 %. Ne comprend pas les données pour novembre et décembre.
[12] Data refer to the twelve months preceding the census in March. - Les données se rapportent aux douze mois précédant le recensement de mars.
[13] Data refer to the twelve months preceding the census in June. - Les données se rapportent aux douze mois précédant le recensement de juin.
[14] Excludes the islands of St. Brandon and Agalega. - Non compris les îles St. Brandon et Agalega.
[15] Based on hospital records. - D'après les registres de hôpitaux.
[16] Based on estimates and projections from 'Agence Nationale de la Statistique et de la Démographie'. - Données fondées sur des estimations et des projections provenant de l'Agence Nationale de la Statistique et de la Démographie.
[17] Based on population census of the same year. - Sur la base du recensement de population de la même année.
[18] Data refer to registered events only. - Les données ne concernent que les événements enregistrés.
[19] Excluding non-residents and foreign service personnel and their dependants. - À l'exclusion des non-résidents et du personnel diplomatique et de leurs charges de famille.
[20] Including Canadian residents temporarily in the United States, but excluding United States residents temporarily in Canada. - Y compris les résidents canadiens se trouvant temporairement aux Etats-Unis, mais ne comprenant pas les résidents des Etats-Unis se trouvant temporairement au Canada.
[21] Resident births outside the islands are excluded. - Non compris les naissances de résidents hors des îles.
[22] Data are based on a small number of deaths. - Les données sont basées sur un nombre limité de décès.
[23] Excluding deaths of nationals who were residing and died abroad but were buried in the Cayman Islands. - Exception faite des nationaux qui résidaient à l'étranger au moment de leur décès, mais qui ont été inhumés dans les Îles Caïmanes.
[24] Excluding children born in the country of non-resident mothers. - Exceptés les enfants nés dans le pays des mères non-résidentes.
[25] Excluding deaths occurring abroad. - Exception faite des personnes décédées à l'étranger.
[26] Excluding infant deaths to mothers living abroad. - Exception faite des décès d'enfants en bas âge survenus lorsque la mère résidait à l'étranger.
[27] Data have been adjusted for underenumeration. - Les données ont été ajustées pour compenser les lacunes du dénombrement.
[28] Data have been adjusted for undercoverage of infant deaths and sudden and violent deaths. - Ajusté pour la sous-estimation de la mortalité infantile, du nombre de morts soudaines et de morts violentes.

29 Data refer to births to resident mothers. - Ces données concernent les enfants nés de mères résidentes.

30 Data refer to resident population only. - Pour la population résidante seulement.

31 Excluding Indian jungle population. - Non compris les Indiens de la jungle.

32 Excluding births of nationals outside the country. - Non compris les naissances de nationaux hors du pays.

33 Excluding Indian jungle population. Data as reported by national statistical authorities; they may differ from data presented in other tables. - Non compris les Indiens de la jungle. Les données comme elles ont été déclarées par l'institut national de la statistique; elles peuvent être différentes de celles présentées dans d'autres tableaux.

34 Excluding Indian jungle population. Including births abroad and births of unknown residence. - Non compris les Indiens de la jungle. Y compris les naissances survenues à l'étranger et les naissances d'enfants dont la résidence n'était pas connue.

35 Data refer to projections based on the 2005 population census. - Les données se réfèrent aux projections basées sur le recensement de la population de 2005.

36 Excluding nomadic Indian tribes. - Non compris les tribus d'Indiens nomades.

37 Excluding events registered late. - Non compris les enregistrements tardifs.

38 Excluding nomadic Indian tribes. Data refer to national projections. - Non compris les tribus d'Indiens nomades. Les données se réfèrent aux projections nationales.

39 Source: Ministry of health reports. - Source: Rapports du Ministère de Santé.

40 Source: Ministry of health reports. Data refer to registered events only. - Source: Rapports du Ministère de Santé. Les données ne concernent que les événements enregistrés.

41 Source: Ministry of health reports. Completeness of coverage estimated at 40 per cent. - Source: Rapports du Ministère de Santé. Degré de complétude évalué à 40 pour cent.

42 Based on National Registers of identification and civil status. - Chiffres fondés sur les registres nationaux d'identification et d'état civil.

43 Including births to non-resident mothers. - Y compris les naissances de femmes non résidentes.

44 Including non-residents. - Y compris les non-résidents.

45 Indicators based on projected or estimated fertility from 2001 Population Census. - Les indicateurs sont fondés sur la fécondité projetée ou estimée à partir du recensement de population de 2001.

46 Estimated rate. - Taux estimatif.

47 Excluding infants born alive of less than 28 weeks' gestation, of less than 1 000 grams in weight and 35 centimeters in length, who die within seven days of birth. - Non compris les enfants nés vivants après moins de 28 semaines de gestations, pesant moins de 1 000 grammes, mesurant moins de 35 centimètres et décédés dans les sept jours qui ont suivi leur naissance.

48 Rates were obtained by the Sample Vital Registration System of Bangladesh. - Taux obtenus au moyen du Sample Vital Registration System du Bangladesh.

49 For statistical purposes, the data for China do not include those for the Hong Kong Special Administrative Region (Hong Kong SAR), Macao Special Administrative Region (Macao SAR) and Taiwan province of China. Data have been estimated on the basis of the annual National Sample Survey on Population Changes. - Pour la présentation des statistiques, les données pour la Chine ne comprennent pas la Région Administrative Spéciale de Hong Kong (Hong Kong RAS), la Région Administrative Spéciale de Macao (Macao RAS) et Taïwan province de Chine. Les données ont été estimées sur la base de l'enquête annuelle "National Sample Survey on Population Changes".

50 The fertility rates have been compiled using a population denominator which has excluded female foreign domestic helpers. - Les taux de fécondité ont été compilés pour une population (en dénominateur) ne comprenant pas les domestiques étrangères.

51 Data refer to government controlled areas. - Les données se rapportent aux zones contrôlées par le Gouvernement.

52 Data refer to the twelve months preceding the census in October. - Les données font référence aux 12 mois qui ont précédé le recensement en octobre.

53 Including data for the Indian-held part of Jammu and Kashmir, the final status of which has not yet been determined. - Y compris les données pour la partie du Jammu et du Cachemire occupée par l'Inde dont le statut définitif n'a pas encore été déterminé.

54 Rates were obtained by the Sample Registration System of India, which is a large demographic survey. - Les taux ont été obtenus par le Système de l'enregistrement par échantillon de l'Inde qui est une large enquête démographique.

55 Data refer to the Iranian Year which begins on 21 March and ends on 20 March of the following year. - Les données concernent l'année iranienne, qui commence le 21 mars et se termine le 20 mars de l'année suivante.

56 Including data for East Jerusalem and Israeli residents in certain other territories under occupation by Israeli military forces since June 1967. - Y compris les données pour Jérusalem-Est et les résidents israéliens dans certains autres territoires occupés depuis 1967 par les forces armées israéliennes.

57 Including deaths abroad of Israeli residents who were out of the country for less than a year. - Y compris les décès à l'étranger de résidents israéliens qui ont quitté le pays depuis moins d'un an.

58 Data refer to Japanese nationals in Japan only. - Les données se raportent aux nationaux japonais au Japon seulement.

59 Excluding data for Jordanian territory under occupation since June 1967 by Israeli military forces. Excluding foreigners, including registered Palestinian refugees. - Non compris les données pour le territoire jordanien occupé depuis juin 1967 par les forces armées israéliennes. Non compris les étrangers, mais y compris les réfugiés de Palestine enregistrés.

60 Data refer to urban areas only. - Données ne concernant que les zones urbaines.

61 Source: Palestinian Central Bureau of Statistics 2010, Population Register, Updated Version 30/3/2010. - Source : Bureau central de statistiques de la Palestine, 2010, Registre de la population, version mise à jour le 30 mars 2010.

62 Data from Births and Deaths Notification System (Ministry of Health institutions and all other health care providers). - Les données proviennent du système de notification des naissances et des décès (établissements du Ministère de la santé et tous autres prestataires de soins de santé).

63 Excluding data for the Pakistan-held part of Jammu and Kashmir, the final status of which has not yet been determined. Based on the results of the Pakistan Demographic Survey. - Non compris les données concernant la partie du Jammu et Cachemire occupée par le Pakistan dont le statut définitif n'a pas été déterminé. Données extraites de l'enquête démographique effectuée par le Pakistan.

64 Data refer to residence of child. Excluding alien armed forces, civilian aliens employed by armed forces, and foreign diplomatic personnel and their dependants. - Les données correspondent à la résidence de l'enfant. Non compris les militaires étrangers, les civils étrangers employés par les forces armées ni le personnel diplomatique étranger et les membres de leur famille les accompagnant.

65 Excluding alien armed forces, civilian aliens employed by armed forces, and foreign diplomatic personnel and their dependants. - Non compris les militaires étrangers, les civils étrangers employés par les forces armées ni le personnel diplomatique étranger et les membres de leur famille les accompagnant.

66 The registration of births and deaths is conducted by the Ministry of Health. An estimate of completeness is not provided. - L'enregistrement des naissances et des décès est mené par le Ministère de la Santé. Le degré estimatif de complétude n'est pas fourni.

67 The registration of births and deaths is conducted by the Ministry of Health. An estimate of completeness is not provided. As published by the United Nations Economic and Social Commission for Western Asia. - L'enregistrement des naissances et des décès est mené par le Ministère de la Santé. Le degré estimatif de complétude n'est pas fourni. Publié par la Commission économique et sociale des Nations Unies pour l'Asie occidentale.

68 Data refer to resident total fertility rate. - Les données se rapportent aux indices synthétique de fécondité de la population résidante.

69 Excluding live-born infants who died before their birth was registered. Excluding nomad population and Palestinian refugees. - Non compris les enfants nés vivants décédés avant l'enregistrement de leur naissance. Non compris la population nomade et les réfugiés de Palestine.

70 Data have been adjusted for under-registration. Excluding infants born alive of less than 28 weeks' gestation, of less than 1 000 grams in weight and 35 centimeters in length, who die within seven days of birth. - Y compris un ajustement pour sous-enregistrement. Non compris les enfants nés vivants après moins de 28 semaines de gestations, pesant moins de 1 000 grammes, mesurant moins de 35 centimètres et décédés dans les sept jours qui ont suivi leur naissance.

71 Data based on Address Based Population Registration System. - Les données sont basées sur le registre national de la population basé sur l'adresse.

72 Based on the results of the Population Demographic Survey. - D'après les résultats de l'enquête démographique de la population.

73 Including deaths of nationals abroad. - Y compris les décès des nationaux survenus à l'étranger.

74 Including armed forces stationed outside the country, but excluding alien armed forces stationed in the area. - Y compris les militaires nationaux hors du pays, mais non compris les militaires étrangers en garnison sur le territoire.

75 Excluding Faeroe Islands and Greenland shown separately, if available. - Non compris les Iles Féroé et le Groenland, qui font l'objet de rubriques distinctes, si disponible.

76 Including resident births abroad. - Y compris les naissances de résidents à l'étranger.

77 Including nationals temporarily outside the country. - Y compris les nationaux se trouvant temporairement hors du pays.

78 Including resident births abroad. Excluding Åland Islands. - Y compris les naissances de résidents à l'étranger. Non compris les Îles d'Åland.

79 Excluding Åland Islands. Including nationals temporarily outside the country. - Non compris les Îles d'Åland. Y compris les nationaux se trouvant temporairement hors du pays.

80 Excluding Åland Islands. - Non compris les Îles d'Åland.

81 Including armed forces stationed outside the country. - Y compris les militaires nationaux hors du pays.

82 Provisional. Data include Overseas Departments. - Données provisoires. Y compris les données des départements d'outre-mer.

83 Excluding armed forces. - Non compris les militaires en garnison.

84 Including live births by military personnel and their dependants. - Y compris les naissances vivantes parmi les membres du personnel militaire et leurs personnes à charge.

85 Including residents outside the country. - Y compris les résidents hors du pays.

86 Including residents outside the country if listed in a Netherlands population register. - Y compris les résidents hors du pays, s'ils sont inscrits sur un registre de population néerlandais.

87 Excluding Svalbard and Jan Mayen Islands shown separately, if available. - Non compris Svalbard et Jan Mayen qui font l'objet de rubriques distinctes, si disponible.

88 Including residents temporarily outside the country. - Y compris les résidents se trouvant temporairement hors du pays.

89 Excluding infants born alive of less than 28 weeks' gestation, of less than 1 000 grams in weight and 35 centimeters in length, who die within seven days of birth. Excluding Transnistria and the municipality of Bender. - Non compris les enfants nés vivants après moins de 28 semaines de gestations, pesant moins de 1 000 grammes, mesurant moins de 35 centimètres et décédés dans les sept jours qui ont suivi leur naissance. Les données ne tiennent pas compte de l'information sur la Transnistria et la municipalité de Bender.

90 Excluding Transnistria and the municipality of Bender. - Les données ne tiennent pas compte de l'information sur la Transnistria et la municipalité de Bender.

91 Excluding data for Kosovo and Metohia. - Sans les données pour le Kosovo et Metohie.

92 Data refer to births with weight 500g and more (if weight is unknown - with length 25 centimeters and more, or with gestation during 22 weeks or more). - Données concernant les nouveau-nés de 500 grammes ou plus (si le poids est inconnu – de 25 centimètres de long ou plus, ou après une grossesse de 22 semaines ou plus).

93 Data includes deaths resulting from births with weight 500g and more (if weight is unknown - with length 25 centimeters and more, or with gestation during 22 weeks or more). - Y compris les décès de nouveau-nés de 500 grammes ou plus (si le poids est inconnu – de 25 centimètres de long ou plus, ou après une grossesse de 22 semaines ou plus).

94 Data based on fertility for range of two years shown under the year ending. - Données fournies sur la base de la fécondité pour une période de deux années consécutives ; les données qui apparaissent sont celles de l'année finale de cette période.

95 Excluding Channel Islands (Guernsey and Jersey) and Isle of Man, shown separately, if available. - Non compris les îles Anglo-Normandes (Guernesey et Jersey) et l'île de Man, qui font l'objet de rubriques distinctes, si disponible.

96 Data tabulated by date of occurrence for England and Wales, and by date of registration for Northern Ireland and Scotland. - Données exploitées selon la date de l'événement pour l'Angleterre et le pays de Galles, et selon la date de l'enregistrement pour l'Irlande du Nord et l'Ecosse.

97 Excluding Niue, shown separately, which is part of Cook Islands, but because of remoteness is administered separately. - Non compris Nioué, qui fait l'objet d'une rubrique distincte et qui fait partie des îles Cook, mais qui, en raison de son éloignement, est administrée séparément.

98 Including United States military personnel, their dependants and contract employees. - Y compris les militaires des Etats-Unis, les membres de leur famille les accompagnant et les agents contractuels des Etats-Unis.

99 Excluding United States military personnel, their dependants and contract employees. - Non compris les militaires des Etats-Unis, les membres de leur famille les accompagnant et les agents contractuels des Etats-Unis.

100 Includes children born in New Zealand to women resident in Niue who chose to travel to New Zealand to give birth. - Y compris les enfants nés en Nouvelle-Zélande de femmes résidant à Nioué qui ont choisi de se rendre en Nouvelle-Zélande pour accoucher.

101 Includes deaths occurred in New Zealand but buried in Niue and deaths occurred in Niue but buried elsewhere. - Y compris les personnes décédées en Nouvelle-Zélande qui sont enterrées à Nioué et les personnes décédées à Nioué qui sont enterrées ailleurs.

102 Data cover the period from 1 July previous year to 30 June present year. - Pour la période allant du 1er juillet de l'année précédente au 30 juin de l'année en cours.

103 Source: Commonwealth Health Center - Vital Statistics Office - Source : Centre de Santé du Commonwealth - Bureau des statistiques d'État civil

104 Estimate based on results of the population census. - Estimation fondeé sur les résultats du recensement de la population.

Table 5

Table 5 presents national estimates of mid-year population for all available years between 2001 and 2010.

Description of variables: Mid-year estimates of the total population are those provided by national statistical offices. They refer to the *de facto* or *de jure* population on 1 July of the reference year. Exceptions to this are footnoted accordingly. The data are presented in thousands, rounded by the Statistics Division.

For certain countries or areas, there is a discrepancy between the mid-year population estimates shown in this table and those shown in subsequent tables for the same year. Usually this discrepancy arises because the estimates for a given year are revised and the more detailed tabulations are not.

For some countries or areas the figures presented in this table and the figures used to calculate rates in subsequent tables are not the same, as these countries have provided a reference population for vital events that is different than the total population.

Unless otherwise indicated, all estimates relate to the population within present geographical boundaries. Major exceptions to this principle are explained in footnotes.

Reliability of data: Reliable mid-year population estimates are those that are based on a complete census (or on a sample survey) and have been adjusted on a basis of a continuous population register or on the balance of births, deaths and migration. Reliable mid-year estimates appear in roman type. Mid-year estimates that are not calculated on this basis are considered less reliable and are shown in *italics*.

Limitations: Statistics on estimates of the mid-year total population are subject to the same qualifications as have been set forth for population statistics in general in section 3 of the Technical Notes.

International comparability of mid-year population estimates is also affected by the fact that some of these estimates refer to the *de jure*, and not the *de facto*, population. These are indicated in the column titled "Code". The difference between the *de facto* and the *de jure* population is discussed in section 3.1.1 of the Technical Notes.

Earlier data: Estimates of mid-year population have been shown in previous issues of the *Demographic Yearbook*. Information on the years and specific topics covered is presented in the Historical Index.

Tableau 5

Le tableau 5 présente des estimations nationales de la population en milieu d'année pour le plus grand nombre possible d'années entre 2001 et 2010.

Description des variables : les estimations de la population totale en milieu d'année sont celles qui ont été communiquées par les services nationaux de statistique. Elles correspondent à la population de fait ou se réfèrent à la population de droit, au 1er juillet de l'année de référence. Lorsque la date est différente, cela est signalé par une note. Sauf indication contraire, tous les chiffres sont exprimés en milliers. Les données ont été arrondies par la Division de statistique de l'ONU.

Pour certains pays ou territoires, il existe une différence entre les estimations de la population en milieu d'année et celles présentées dans les tableaux suivants pour la même année. Généralement, les différences apparaissent parce que les estimations de l'année ont été révisées mais que les autres tabulations ne l'ont pas été.

Pour certains pays ou territoires, les données présentées dans ce tableau sont différentes des données utilisées pour calculer les taux dans les tableaux suivants, parce que ces pays ont fourni une population de référence pour les événements démographiques différente de la population totale.

Sauf indication contraire, toutes les estimations se rapportent à la population présente sur le territoire actuel des pays ou zones considérés. Les principales exceptions à cette règle sont expliquées en note.

Fiabilité des données : les estimations de la population en milieu d'année sont considérées sûres quand elles sont fondées sur un recensement complet (ou sur une enquête par sondage) et ont été ajustées en fonction des données provenant d'un registre permanent de population ou en fonction des naissances, décès et mouvements migratoires qui ont eu lieu pendant la période. Les estimations considérées comme sûres apparaissent en caractères romains. Les estimations dont le calcul n'a pas été effectué sur cette base sont considérées comme moins sûres et apparaissent en italique.

Insuffisance des données : les statistiques concernant les estimations de la population totale en milieu d'année appellent toutes les réserves qui ont été formulées à la section 3 des Notes techniques à propos des statistiques de la population en général.

Le fait que certaines des estimations concernant la population en milieu d'année se réfèrent à la population de droit et non à la population de fait influe sur la comparabilité internationale. Ces cas ont été signalés dans la colonne « Code ». La différence entre la population de fait et la population de droit est expliquée à la section 3.1.1 des Notes techniques.

Données publiées antérieurement : des estimations de la population en milieu d'année ont été publiées dans des éditions antérieures de l'*Annuaire démographique*. Pour plus de précisions concernant les années et les sujets pour lesquels des données ont été publiées, se reporter à l'index.

Continent and country or area / Continent et pays ou zone	Code[a]	Population estimates (in thousands) - Estimations (en milliers)									
		2001	2002	2003	2004	2005	2006	2007	2008	2009	2010
AFRICA - AFRIQUE											
Algeria - Algérie	DJ	30 872	31 332	31 848	32 364	32 906	33 481	34 096	*34 591[1]	*35 268	*35 978
Benin - Bénin	DF	*6 417	...	*6 983[2]	*7 209[2]	*7 447[2]	*7 700[2]	*7 959[2]	*8 225[2]	*8 498[2]	*8 779[2]
Botswana	DJ	1 622	1 650	1 673	1 693	1 708	1 720	1 736	1 755	1 776	1 823
Burkina Faso	DJ	11 817	12 185	12 567	12 963	13 374	14 017	14 252[2]	14 731[2]	15 225[2]	15 731[2]
Burundi	DF	6 847	7 032	7 211	7 384	...	...	...	...	...	...
Cameroon - Cameroun[2]	DF	15 731	16 170	16 626	17 000	...	...	...	...	...	...
	DJ	...	...	...	...	...	...	*18 675	...	...	*19 406
Cape Verde - Cap-Vert	DF	445	453	461	468	475	483	491	500	509	518
Central African Republic - République centrafricaine	DF	...	...	3 151	...	...	...	...	...	...	...
Chad - Tchad[2]	DF	8 322	...	...	...	...	...	...	...	...	...
Congo[2]	DF	3 047	3 142	3 241	3 344	3 488	3 589	3 616	3 752	...	...
Côte d'Ivoire[2]	DF	*16 928	*17 461	*18 001	*18 546	*19 097	*19 658	*20 228	*20 807	*21 395	...
Djibouti	DF				632						...
Egypt - Égypte	DF	65 298	66 628	67 965	69 304	70 653	72 009	73 644	75 229	76 925	*78 728
Ethiopia - Éthiopie[3]	DF	65 374	67 220	69 127	71 066	73 044	75 067	77 127	79 221	...	...
Gabon	DF	*1 237	*1 268	*1 300	...	1 313[4]	...	...	...	...	...
Gambia - Gambie	DF	1 420	...	...	...	1 436	1 510	...	...	...	...
Ghana	DF	19 397	19 883	20 371	20 859	21 367	21 876	22 388	22 901	23 417	...
Guinea - Guinée	DF	...	...	...	9 214	...	...	...	10 183[2]	10 218[2]	10 537[2]
Guinea-Bissau - Guinée-Bissau[2]	DF	1 211	1 238	1 267	1 296	1 326	1 357	1 389	...	...	...
Kenya[5]	DF	31 121	32 118	33 142	34 191	35 267	36 433	37 184	*38 300	...	*40 400
Lesotho[2]	DF	...	...	...	...	...	1 878	1 880	1 884	1 887	1 892
Libya - Libye[6]	DF	5 300	5 484	...	...	...	...	...	...	...	...
Madagascar	DF	15 529	15 981	16 441	17 206	17 730	17 865	18 359	18 865	...	...
Malawi[2]	DF	10 816	11 175	11 549	11 938	12 341	12 758	13 188	13 630	...	...
Mali[7]	DF	10 525	10 813	11 111	11 419	11 732	12 051	12 378	*12 706	...	...
Mauritania - Mauritanie[2]	DF	2 724	2 635	2 702	2 823	2 906	2 990	3 075	3 162	...	...
Mauritius - Maurice[8]	DJ	1 200	1 210	1 223	1 233	1 243	1 253	1 260	1 269	1 275[9]	1 281[9]
Morocco - Maroc	DF	29 170	29 631	30 088	29 840[10]	30 172[10]	30 506[10]	30 841[10]	31 177[10]	31 514[10]	31 851[10]
Mozambique[2]	DF	17 653	18 078	18 514	18 962	19 420	19 889	20 367	20 854	21 350	21 854
Namibia - Namibie[2]	DF	1 830	1 860	1 891	1 923	1 957	1 992	2 028	2 065	2 104	2 143
Niger[2]	DJ	11 090	11 456	11 834	12 225	12 628	13 045	13 716	14 198	14 693	15 204
Nigeria - Nigéria	DF	118 801[2]	122 444[2]	126 153[2]	129 175[2]	133 767[2]	*140 004[11]	...	...	...	...
Réunion	DJ	735	746	756	767	777	786	*791[7]	*806[7]	*817[7]	...
Rwanda	DF	...	...	...	...	...	...	9 557	9 832	10 117	10 413
Saint Helena ex. dep. - Sainte-Hélène sans dép.	DF	...	...	...	...	...	...	4	4[12]	4	4
Saint Helena: Ascension - Sainte-Hélène: Ascension	DJ	...	...	...	...	...	...	...	1		
Saint Helena: Tristan da Cunha - Sainte-Hélène: Tristan da Cunha[13]	DF	...	...	...	...	...	...	0[14]	0[15]	0[16]	...
Sao Tome and Principe - Sao Tomé-et-Principe	DF	...	140	143	146	149	152	155	158	*160	*164
Senegal - Sénégal	DJ	9 667	9 858[17]	10 317[17]	10 605[17]	10 901[17]	11 206[17]	11 519[17]	11 841[17]	12 171[17]	12 509[17]
Seychelles	DF	81	84	83	82	83	85	85	87	87	87
Sierra Leone	DF	5 054	5 167	5 280	...	5 095	5 217	5 343	5 474	5 608	5 747
South Africa - Afrique du Sud[18]	DF	44 929	45 587	46 206	46 787	47 335	47 837	48 287	48 687	49 321	49 991
Sudan - Soudan	DF	31 627	32 468	33 334	34 512	35 397	36 297	*37 239	*38 193	...	...
Swaziland	DF	1 030	1 056	1 081	1 105	1 126	1 146	...	...	...	...
Togo	DF	4 740	4 854	4 970	5 090	5 212	5 337	5 465	5 596	5 731	...
Tunisia - Tunisie	DF	9 674	9 749	9 840	9 932	10 029	10 128	10 225	10 329	10 435	10 549
Uganda - Ouganda	DF	22 787	24 067	25 089	25 896	26 741	27 629	28 581	29 593	30 661	...
United Republic of Tanzania - République Unie de Tanzanie	DF	...	...	...	36 308	37 379	38 251	39 446	40 600	41 900	...
Zambia - Zambie[2]	DF	10 089	10 409	10 744	11 090	11 441	11 799	12 161	12 526	12 897	...
Zimbabwe	DF	12 960	...	11 640[19]	11 730[19]	11 830[19]	11 930[19]	12 040[19]	12 150[19]	12 260[19]	...
AMERICA, NORTH - AMÉRIQUE DU NORD											
Anguilla	DF	12	12	12	13	14	14	15	16	16	...
Antigua and Barbuda - Antigua-et-Barbuda	DF	...	78	80	81	83	84	86	...	...	...

Estimations de la population au milieu de l'année : 2001 - 2010 (continued - suite)

Continent and country or area / Continent et pays ou zone	Code[a]	2001	2002	2003	2004	2005	2006	2007	2008	2009	2010
AMERICA, NORTH - AMÉRIQUE DU NORD											
Aruba	DJ	92	93	95	98	101	103	104	105	107	108
Bahamas[2]	DF	308	312	317	321	325	330	334	338	342	347
Barbados - Barbade	DF	270	271	272	272	273	273	274	275	...	276[20]
Belize	DF	257	265	274	283	292	301	311	322	333	...
Bermuda - Bermudes	DJ	62	63	63	63	64	64	64	64	64	65
British Virgin Islands - Îles Vierges britanniques	DF	21	21	21	22	...	...	...	...	...	...
Canada[21]	DJ	31 019[22]	31 354[22]	31 640[22]	31 941[22]	32 245[22]	32 576[23]	32 930[23]	33 316[24]	33 720[24]	*34 109[25]
Cayman Islands - Îles Caïmanes	DJ	41	43	44	44	48	52	54	56	53	*55
Costa Rica	DJ	3 907	3 998	4 089	4 179	4 266	4 354	4 443	4 533[26]	4 620[26]	4 562[27]
Cuba	DJ	11 157	11 184	11 215	11 236	11 243	11 241	11 238	11 236	11 239	11 242
Dominica - Dominique	DF	71	70	70	70	71	71	71	72	...	...
Dominican Republic - République dominicaine[2]	DF	8 688	8 823	8 958	9 093	9 226	9 360	9 493	9 625	9 756	9 884
El Salvador	DF	6 397	6 518	6 638	6 757	6 049[28]	6 074[28]	6 099[28]	6 125[28]	6 153[28]	6 183[28]
Greenland - Groenland[29]	DJ	56	57	57	57	57	57	57	56	56	57
Grenada - Grenade	DF	101	...	...	...	...	...	107	109	...	...
Guadeloupe	DJ	432	437	439	445	446	458	401[30]	402[30]	403[30]	404[30]
Guatemala	DF	11 678[18]	11 987[18]	12 084[18]	12 390[18]	12 701[31]	13 019[31]	13 345[31]	13 678[31]	14 017[31]	14 362[31]
Haiti - Haïti[32]	DJ	8 720	8 861	9 001	9 145	9 292	9 445	9 602	9 762	9 923	10 085
Honduras[33]	DF	6 530	6 695	6 861	7 028	7 197	7 367	7 537	7 707	7 877	8 046
Jamaica - Jamaïque	DJ	2 604	2 615	2 626	2 638	2 650	2 663	2 676	2 687	2 696	*2 702
Martinique[7]	DJ	387	389	392	394	396	398	398	398	399	400
Mexico - Mexique	DJ	99 716	100 909	102 000	103 002	103 947[2]	104 874[2]	105 791[2]	106 683[2]	107 551[2]	...
Montserrat	DF	5	5	4	5	5	5	5	5	...	...
Netherlands Antilles - Antilles néerlandaises[7]	DJ	176	173	177	179	184	189	194	197[34]	200[35]	198[35]
Nicaragua	DJ	5 174	5 245	5 313	5 381	5 450	5 523	5 596	5 669	5 742	5 816
Panama[36]	DF	3 004	3 060	3 116	3 172	3 228	3 284	3 340	3 395	3 450	3 504
Puerto Rico - Porto Rico[37]	DJ	3 840	3 859	3 879	3 895	3 912	3 928	3 942	3 954	3 967	3 979
Saint Kitts and Nevis - Saint-Kitts-et-Nevis	DF	*46	...	...	...	*39	...	...	...	...	...
Saint Lucia - Sainte-Lucie	DF	158	159	161	162	164	166	168	...	...	...
Saint Vincent and the Grenadines - Saint-Vincent-et-les Grenadines	DF	...	108	105	105	104	101	100	99	...	...
Trinidad and Tobago - Trinité-et-Tobago[38]	DF	1 267	1 276	1 282	1 291	1 294	1 298	1 303	1 309	1 310	1 318
Turks and Caicos Islands - Îles Turques et Caïques	DJ	20	21	25	27	31	33	35	*37	38	40
United States of America - États-Unis d'Amérique[39]	DJ	285 082	287 804	290 326	293 046	295 753	298 593	301 580	304 375	307 007	*309 051
United States Virgin Islands - Îles Vierges américaines[37]	DJ	109	109	109	109	110	110	110	110	*110	*110
AMERICA, SOUTH - AMÉRIQUE DU SUD											
Argentina - Argentine	DF	37 156	37 516	37 870	38 226	38 592	38 971	39 356	39 746	40 134	40 519[40]
Bolivia (Plurinational State of) - Bolivie (État plurinational de)	DF	8 624	8 824	9 025	9 227	9 427	9 627	9 828	10 028	10 227	10 426
Brazil - Brésil[41]	DF	173 808	176 304	178 741	181 106	183 383	185 564	187 642	189 613	191 481	193 253
Chile - Chili	DF	15 572	15 746	15 919	16 093	16 267	16 433	16 598	16 763	16 929	17 094
Colombia - Colombie	DF	40 806[42]	41 327[42]	41 847[42]	42 368[42]	42 889[43]	43 405[43]	43 926[43]	44 450[43]	44 978[43]	45 508[43]
Ecuador - Équateur[44]	DF	12 480	12 661	12 843	13 027	13 215	13 408	13 605	13 805	14 005	14 205
French Guiana - Guyane française	DJ	170	175	181	193[7]	199[7]	*202[7]	*214[7]	219[7]	226[7]	232[7]
Guyana	DF	744	748	753	756	758	761	763	766	*770	*778
Paraguay[19]	DF	5 456	5 567	5 677	5 788	5 899	6 009	6 120	6 230	6 341	*6 451
Peru - Pérou	DF	26 367	26 739	27 103	27 460	27 811	28 151	28 482	28 807	29 132	29 462
Suriname	DJ	470	476	483	487	499	504	510	517	...	...
Uruguay[2]	DF	3 308	3 309	3 304	3 302	3 306	3 314	3 324	3 334	3 345	*3 357

5. Estimates of mid-year population: 2001 - 2010
Estimations de la population au milieu de l'année : 2001 - 2010 (continued - suite)

Continent and country or area / Continent et pays ou zone	Code[a]	Population estimates (in thousands) - Estimations (en milliers)									
		2001	2002	2003	2004	2005	2006	2007	2008	2009	2010
AMERICA, SOUTH - AMÉRIQUE DU SUD											
Venezuela (Bolivarian Republic of) - Venezuela (République bolivarienne du)	DF	24 766[45]	25 220[45]	25 674	26 127	26 577	27 031	27 483	27 935	28 384	28 834
ASIA - ASIE											
Afghanistan	DF	22 080	20 298[46]	20 691[46]	21 678[46]	22 098[46]	22 576[47]	23 039[46]	23 511[46]	23 994[48]	24 486[49]
Armenia - Arménie	DJ	3 214	3 212	3 211	3 214	3 218	3 221	3 227	3 234	3 244	3 256
Azerbaijan - Azerbaïdjan	DF	8 153[42]	8 230[42]	8 309[42]	8 398[42]	8 500[42]	8 610[42]	8 723[42]	8 838[42]	8 947[42]	9 047
Bahrain - Bahreïn	DF	661	711	765	824	889	960	1 039	1 107	1 178	...
Bangladesh	DF	131 000	132 900	134 800	136 700	138 600	140 600	142 600	*144 500	*146 600	...
Bhutan - Bhoutan	DF	591	602	613	624	...	647[50]	659[50]	671[50]	683[50]	696[50]
Brunei Darussalam - Brunéi Darussalam	DF	333	344	350	360	370	383	390	398	406	...
Cambodia - Cambodge[51]	DF	12 922[52]	13 164[52]	13 415[52]	13 091[52]	*13 661[52]	...	...	13 868[53]	14 085[53]	14 303[53]
China - Chine[54]	DF	1 276 270	1 284 530	1 292 270	1 299 880	1 307 560	1 314 480	1 321 290	1 328 020	1 334 740	...
China, Hong Kong SAR - Chine, Hong Kong RAS	DJ	6 714	6 744	6 731	6 784	6 813	6 857	6 926	6 978	7 004	7 068
China, Macao SAR - Chine, Macao RAS	DJ	434	438	444	455	473	499	526	552	544	545
Cyprus - Chypre[55]	DJ	701	710	721	737	758	771	785	*793	*800	*804
Democratic People's Republic of Korea - République populaire démocratique de Corée	DF	23 149	23 313	23 464	23 612	...	...	...	...	...	...
Georgia - Géorgie	DF	4 386	4 357	4 329	4 318	4 361	4 398	4 388	4 384	4 411	...
India - Inde[56]	DF	1 034 931[57]	1 051 258[2]	1 068 065[2]	1 084 757[2]	1 101 318[2]	1 117 734[2]	1 134 023[2]	1 150 196[2]	*1 166 000[2]	*1 182 105[2]
Indonesia - Indonésie[22]	DJ	208 198	211 310	214 468	217 673	220 926	224 228	227 579	230 980	234 432	...
Iran (Islamic Republic of) - Iran (République islamique d')[58]	DJ	65 301	66 300	67 315	68 345	69 390	70 603	71 279	72 182	73 202	74 340
Iraq	DF	24 813	25 565	26 340	27 139	27 963	28 810	29 682	31 895	32 105	...
Israel - Israël[59]	DJ	6 439	6 570	6 690	6 809	6 930	7 054	7 180	7 309	7 486	*7 625
Japan - Japon[60]	DJ	127 149	127 445	127 718	127 761	127 773	127 756	127 772	127 704	127 558	127 450
Jordan - Jordanie[61]	DF	4 978	5 098	5 230	5 350	5 473	5 600	5 723	5 850	5 980	6 113
Kazakhstan	DF	14 858	14 859	14 909	15 013	15 147	15 308	15 484	15 674	*15 900	...
Kuwait - Koweït	DF	1 953	2 022	2 093	2 167	2 245	2 328	2 411	2 496	2 583	...
Kyrgyzstan - Kirghizstan	DF	4 902[62]	4 919[62]	4 944[62]	4 977[62]	5 007[62]	5 034[62]	5 056[62]	5 078[62]	5 128	5 193
Lao People's Democratic Republic - République démocratique populaire lao	DF	5 377[63]	5 526[63]	5 679[63]	5 836[63]	5 679[64]	*5 747[64]	5 874[64]	*6 000[64]	*6 128[64]	*6 310[64]
Malaysia - Malaisie[65]	DJ	24 123	24 727	25 320	25 905	26 477	26 832	27 186	27 540	27 895	28 250
Maldives	DF	276	281	285	289	294	299	305	310	315	320
Mongolia - Mongolie	DF	2 425	2 459	2 490	2 519	2 548	2 579	2 615	2 659	2 670[20]	...
Myanmar	DF	51 138	52 171	53 224	54 299	55 396	56 515	57 504	58 377	...	...
Nepal - Népal	DJ	...	23 701	24 250	24 797	25 343	25 887	26 427	26 967	27 504	...
Occupied Palestinian Territory - Territoire palestinien occupé	DF	3 138	3 225	3 315	3 407	3 508	3 612	3 719	3 826	3 935	4 048
Oman	DF	2 478	2 538	...	2 416	2 509	2 577	2 743	2 867	3 174	...
Pakistan[66]	DF	...	145 280	...	151 090	...	...	...	162 370	165 150	...
	DJ	133 652[67]	...	138 979[68]	...	144 367[69]	147 100	149 860[70]	...	...	...
Philippines[71]	DJ	78 568	80 217	81 878	83 559	85 261	86 973	88 706	90 457	*92 150	*94 013
Qatar	DF	643	676	714	798	906	1 043	1 218	1 448	1 639	1 714
Republic of Korea - République de Corée	DJ	47 357	47 622	47 859	48 039	48 138	48 297	48 456	48 607	48 747	48 875
Saudi Arabia - Arabie saoudite	DF	20 979	21 495	22 023	22 564	23 119	23 679	*24 243	*24 807	...	...
Singapore - Singapour	DF	4 138	4 176	4 115	4 167	4 266	4 401	4 589	4 839	4 988	5 077
Sri Lanka	DF	18 732	19 007	19 252	19 435	19 644	19 858	20 039	20 216	*20 450	*20 653
Syrian Arab Republic - République arabe syrienne[72]	DF	16 720	17 130	17 550	17 829	18 138	18 717	19 172	19 644	20 125	...
Tajikistan - Tadjikistan	DF	6 313	6 441	6 573	6 710	6 850	6 992	7 140	7 295	...	...
Thailand - Thaïlande[2]	DJ	62 914	63 482	64 019	64 177	64 839	65 306	66 042	66 480	66 903	67 312
Timor-Leste	DF	...	...	...	...	...	...	...	...	*1 115	...
Turkey - Turquie[73]	DJ	65 135	66 009	66 873	67 734	68 582	69 421	70 256	71 079	71 897	72 698
Turkmenistan - Turkménistan	DF	4 974	5 052	5 124	...	...	...	...	...	...	...

Estimations de la population au milieu de l'année : 2001 - 2010 (continued - suite)

Continent and country or area / Continent et pays ou zone	Code[a]	Population estimates (in thousands) - Estimations (en milliers)									
		2001	2002	2003	2004	2005	2006	2007	2008	2009	2010
ASIA - ASIE											
United Arab Emirates - Émirats arabes unis	DF	3 167	3 349	3 551	3 761	4 041	4 229	4 488	4 765	...	...
Uzbekistan - Ouzbékistan	DF	24 964	25 272	25 568	...	...	...	...	...	...	...
Viet Nam	DF	78 621[74]	79 539[74]	80 468[74]	81 438[74]	82 394[74]	83 313[74]	84 221[74]	85 122[74]	86 025	*86 928
Yemen - Yémen	DF	17 993[20]	18 540[20]	19 104[20]	...	20 283[20]	20 901[20]	21 539[20]	22 198[20]	...	23 154[2]
EUROPE											
Åland Islands - Îles d'Åland[29]	DJ	26	26	26	26	27	27	27	27	28	28
Albania - Albanie	DF	3 074	3 093	3 111	3 127	3 142	3 151	3 161	*3 182	3 194	...
Andorra - Andorre[29]	DJ	66	66	70	75	79	80	82	84	85	85
Austria - Autriche	DJ	8 042	8 082	8 118	8 169	8 225	8 268	8 301	8 337	8 365	8 390
Belarus - Bélarus	DF	9 971	9 925	9 874	9 825	9 775	9 733	9 702			
	DJ	...	...	...	...	...	...	...	9 681	9 665	9 491
Belgium - Belgique	DJ	10 287	10 333	10 372	10 417	10 473	10 542	10 623	10 710	10 796	*10 879
Bosnia and Herzegovina - Bosnie-Herzégovine	DF	3 798	3 828	3 832	3 843	3 843	3 843	3 843	3 842	3 843	*3 844
Bulgaria - Bulgarie	DJ	7 913	7 869	7 824	7 781	7 740	7 699	7 660	7 623	7 585	7 534
Croatia - Croatie	DJ	4 440	4 440	4 440	4 439	4 442	4 440	4 436	4 435	4 429	4 426[7]
Czech Republic - République tchèque	DJ	10 224	10 201	10 202	10 207	10 234	10 267	10 323	10 430	10 491	10 520
Denmark - Danemark[75]	DJ	5 359	5 374	5 387	5 401	5 416	5 435	5 457	5 489	5 519	5 545
Estonia - Estonie	DJ	1 364	1 359	1 354	1 349	1 346	1 344	1 342	1 341	1 340	1 340
Faeroe Islands - Îles Féroé	DJ	47	47	48	48	48	48	48	49	...	...
Finland - Finlande[29]	DJ	5 188	5 201	5 213	5 228	5 246	5 266	5 289	5 313	5 311[76]	5 335[76]
France[77]	DJ	59 476	59 894	60 304	60 734	61 181	61 597	*61 963	*62 300	*62 621	*62 968
Germany - Allemagne	DJ	82 340	82 482	82 520	82 501	82 464	82 366	82 263	82 110	81 902	*81 776
Gibraltar[78]	DF	...	29	29	29	29	29	29	29	29	...
Greece - Grèce[79]	DF	10 950	10 988	11 024	11 062	11 104	11 149	11 193	11 237	11 283	...
Guernsey - Guernesey	DF	...	...	...	60	...	61[80]	61[80]	62[80]	62[80]	62[80]
Holy See - Saint-Siège[81]	DJ	...	...	...	...	...	...	...	...	0	...
Hungary - Hongrie	DJ	10 188	10 159	10 130	10 107	10 087	10 071	10 056	10 038	10 023	*10 000
Iceland - Islande[29]	DJ	285	288	289	293	296	304	311	319	319	318
Ireland - Irlande	DF	3 847[82]	...	3 979[82]	4 044[82]	4 131[82]	4 235[82]	*4 339[82]	*4 422[82]	4 459	*4 474
Isle of Man - Île de Man[83]	DJ	...	77	77	78	79	80	81	82	82	...
Italy - Italie	DJ	56 977	57 157	57 605	58 175	58 607	58 941	59 375	59 832	60 193	*60 483
Jersey	DF	87	88	88	88	88	89	90	...	...	...
Latvia - Lettonie	DJ	2 355	2 339	2 325	2 313	2 301	2 288	2 276	2 266	2 255	2 239
Liechtenstein	DJ	33	34	34	34	35	35	35	35	36	*36
Lithuania - Lituanie	DJ	3 481	3 469	3 454	3 436	3 414	3 394	3 376	3 358	3 339	3 287
Luxembourg	DJ	442	446	452	458	465	473	480	489	498	507
Malta - Malte[84]	DJ	385	387	399	401	404	406	409	412	413	*416
Montenegro - Monténégro	DF	658	...	...	...	...	...	...	...	...	...
	DJ	...	618	620	622	623	624	626	629	632	*633[7]
Netherlands - Pays-Bas	DJ	16 046	16 149	16 225	16 282	16 320	16 346	16 382	16 446	16 530	*16 615
Norway - Norvège[85]	DJ	4 514	4 538	4 565	4 592	4 623	4 661	4 709	4 768	4 829	4 889
Poland - Pologne[86]	DJ	38 251	38 232	38 195	38 180	38 161	38 132	38 116	38 116	38 153	38 184
Portugal	DJ	10 293	10 368	10 441	10 502	10 549	10 584	10 608	10 622	10 632	*10 637
Republic of Moldova - République de Moldova[87]	DJ	3 631	3 623	3 613	3 604	3 595	3 585	3 577	3 570	3 566	3 562
Romania - Roumanie	DJ	22 408	21 795	21 734	21 673	21 624	21 584	21 538	21 504	21 470	*21 438
Russian Federation - Fédération de Russie	DJ	145 976	145 306	144 566	143 821	143 114	142 487	142 115	141 956	141 909	*142 938
San Marino - Saint-Marin[29]	DF	28	28	29	29	31	31	32	33	33	33
Serbia - Serbie[88]	DJ	7 503	7 500	7 481	7 463	7 441	7 412	7 382	7 350	7 321	*7 428
Slovakia - Slovaquie	DJ	5 380	5 379	5 379	5 383	5 387	5 391	5 398	5 407	5 418	5 430
Slovenia - Slovénie	DJ	1 992	1 996	1 997	1 997	2 001	2 009	2 019	2 023	2 042	2 049
Spain - Espagne	DJ	40 721	41 314	42 005	42 692	43 398	44 068	44 874	45 593	45 929	46 071
Svalbard and Jan Mayen Islands - Îles Svalbard et Jan Mayen[89]	DF	2	3	2	2	2	...	...	2	...	...
Sweden - Suède[29]	DJ	8 896	8 925	8 958	8 994	9 030	9 081	9 148	9 220	9 299	9 378
Switzerland - Suisse	DJ	7 227	7 285	7 339	7 390	7 437	7 484	7 551	7 648	7 744	*7 826
TFYR of Macedonia - L'ex-R. y. de Macédoine	DF	2 035	2 031	2 027	2 033	2 037	2 040	2 044	2 047	2 051	2 053[7]
Ukraine	DF	48 690	48 230	47 813	47 452	47 105	46 788	46 509	46 258	46 053	45 963[7]

5. Estimates of mid-year population: 2001 - 2010
Estimations de la population au milieu de l'année : 2001 - 2010 (continued - suite)

Continent and country or area / Continent et pays ou zone	Code[a]	Population estimates (in thousands) - Estimations (en milliers)									
		2001	2002	2003	2004	2005	2006	2007	2008	2009	2010
EUROPE											
United Kingdom of Great Britain and Northern Ireland - Royaume-Uni de Grande-Bretagne et d'Irlande du Nord[90]	DF	59 113[91]	59 323[91]	59 557	59 846	60 238	60 587	60 975	61 394	*61 811	*62 222
OCEANIA - OCÉANIE											
American Samoa - Samoas américaines[37]	DJ	59	61	63	64	66	67	...	...		
Australia - Australie[92]	DJ	19 413	19 651	19 895	20 127	20 395	20 698	21 072	21 499	*21 955	*22 342
Cook Islands - Îles Cook[93]	DF	18	18	18	20	22	24	21	22	*23	*23
Fiji - Fidji	DF	810	811	816	822	825	830	834	...	882	...
French Polynesia - Polynésie française	DF	239	243	247	250	253	256	259	262	264[7]	...
Guam[37]	DJ	158	161	167	166	*169	*171	*173	*176	*178	*181
Marshall Islands - Îles Marshall[2]	DF	55	...	...	55	...	52	53	53	54	54
Micronesia (Federated States of) - Micronésie (États fédérés de)[2]	DJ	107	107	108	108	108	108	108	108	108	108
Nauru	DF	12	...	...	...	...	...	...	...	...	...
New Caledonia - Nouvelle-Calédonie	DF	217	221	226	230	234	238	242	242	246	
New Zealand - Nouvelle-Zélande	DJ	3 881[94]	3 949[94]	4 027[94]	4 088[94]	4 134[94]	4 185[94]	4 228[94]	4 269[94]	4 316[94]	4 368[95]
Niue - Nioué	DJ	...	2	2	2	2	2	2	...	2	1
Norfolk Island - Île Norfolk	DF	...	...	3	3	2	2	...	...	...	...
Northern Mariana Islands - Îles Mariannes septentrionales	DF	72	74	77	79	71	61	59	55	51	48
Palau - Palaos	DF	20	20	20	21	...	22	21	21	...	...
Papua New Guinea - Papouasie-Nouvelle-Guinée	DF	...	5 462	...	...	...	...	...	...	...	...
Pitcairn[20]	DF	...	...	...	...	...	...	0[96]	0[97]	...	...
Samoa	DF	...	178	180	182	183	185	182	182	183	184
Solomon Islands - Îles Salomon[2]	DF	426	437	448	460	471	483	495	507	518	542
Tonga[98]	DF	101	101	101	102	102	103	103	...	...	...
Tuvalu	DF	9	9	9	10	10	11	11	...	...	...
Vanuatu[2]	DF	...	...	...	216	...	221	...	...	...	...

FOOTNOTES - NOTES

Italics: estimates which are less reliable. - Italiques : estimations moins sûres.

* Provisional. - Données provisoires.

[a] 'Code' indicates source of data, as follows: - Le 'Code' indique la source des données, comme suit :
DF: Population de facto - Population de fait
DJ : Population de jure - Population de droit

[1] Based on the 2008 Population and Housing Census. - Basée sur le recensement de la population et de l'habitat de 2008.
[2] Data refer to national projections. - Les données se réfèrent aux projections nationales.
[3] Projections based on the 1994 population census. - Projections fondées sur le recensement de la population de 1994.
[4] Based on the results of the Gabonese Survey for the Evaluation and Tracking of Poverty. - Sur base des résultats de l'enquête gabonaise sur l'évaluation et le suivi de la pauvreté.
[5] Post-censal estimates based on 1999 Population Census. - Les estimations post-censitaire fondées sur le recensement de la population de 1999.
[6] Data refer to Libyan nationals only. - Les données se raportent aux nationaux libyens seulement.
[7] Data refer to 1 January. - Données se raportent au 1 janvier.

[8] Excludes the islands of St. Brandon and Agalega. - Non compris les îles St. Brandon et Agalega.
[9] Based on 2000 Population Census data and adjusted for underenumeration of young children. - D'après le recensement de la population de 2000, ajusté en raison du sous-enregistrement des jeunes enfants.
[10] Based on the results of the 2004 Population Census. - D'après des résultats du recensement de la population de 2004.
[11] Based on the results of the 2006 Population Census. - D'après des résultats du recensement de la population de 2006.
[12] Data based on 2008 Population Census. - Données fondées sur le recensement de population de 2008.
[13] Data refer to 31 December. Based on the results of a population count. - Données se raportent au 31 décembre. D'après les résultats d'un comptage de la population.
[14] The population figure is 264 persons. - La population est égale à 264 personnes.
[15] The population figure is 263 persons. - La population est égale à 263 personnes.
[16] The population figure is 262 persons. - La population est égale à 262 personnes.
[17] Data refer to 31 December. Data are based on projections from 2002 Census. - Données se raportent au 31 décembre. Données fondées sur des projections tirées du recensement de 2002.
[18] Mid-year estimates have been adjusted for underenumeration at latest census. - Les estimations au millieu de l'année tiennent compte d'un ajustement

destiné à compenser les lacunes du dénombrement lors du dernier recensement.

[19] Data are based on projections from 2002 Census. - Données fondées sur des projections tirées du recensement de 2002.

[20] Data refer to 31 December. - Données se raportent au 31 décembre.

[21] Estimates adjusted for census net undercoverage (including adjustment for incompletely enumerated Indian reserves). - Ajusté pour la sous-estimation du recensement (y compris les réservations en Inde incomplètement énumérées).

[22] Final intercensal estimates. - Estimations inter-censitaires definitives.

[23] Final postcensal estimates. - Estimations postcensitaires definitives.

[24] Updated postcensal estimates. - Estimations post censitaires mises à jour.

[25] Preliminary postcensal estimates. - Estimations post censitaires préliminaires.

[26] Result of Household Multiple Purpose Survey. - Les chiffres résultent d'enquêtes sur les ménages polyvalentes.

[27] Based on 2010 National Household Survey. - Basée sur l'Enquête nationale des ménages de 2010.

[28] Estimates based on 2007 Population Census. - Estimations fondées sur le recensement de la population de 2007.

[29] Population statistics are compiled from registers. - Les statistiques de la population sont compilées à partir des registres.

[30] Data refer to 1 January. Excluding data for Saint Barthélémy and Saint Martin. - Données se raportent au 1 janvier. Non compris les données pour Saint Barthélémy et Saint Martin.

[31] Projections based on 2002 population census. - Projections fondées sur le recensement de la population de 2002.

[32] Projections produced by l'Institut Haïtien de Statistique et d'Informatique (IHSI) and the Latin American and Caribbean Demographic Centre (CELADE) - Population Division of ECLAC. - Les données sont projections produits par l'Institut Haïtien de Statistique et d'Informatique (IHSI) et le centre démographique de l'Amérique latine et les Caraïbes - Division de la population de la CEPALC.

[33] Data are based on projections of the 2001 Population and Housing Census data. - Les données sont basées sur les projections du recensement de 2001 de la population et de l'habitat.

[34] Includes the estimates for Saba and St. Eustatius. - Y compris les estimations pour Saba et St. Eustatius.

[35] Includes estimates for St. Eustatius. - Y compris les estimations pour St. Eustatius.

[36] Data refer to projections based on the 2000 population census. - Les données se réfèrent aux projections basées sur le recensement de la population de 2000.

[37] Including armed forces stationed in the area. - Y compris les militaires en garnison sur le territoire.

[38] Based on the results of the 2000 population census. - Basé sur les résultats du recencement de la population de 2000.

[39] Excluding armed forces overseas and civilian citizens absent from country for an extended period of time. - Non compris les militaires à l'étranger, et les civils hors du pays pendant une période prolongée.

[40] Data based on 2010 Population Census. - Données fondées sur le recensement de population de 2010.

[41] Data include persons in remote areas, military personnel outside the country, merchant seamen at sea, civilian seasonal workers outside the country, and other civilians outside the country, and exclude nomads, foreign military, civilian aliens temporarily in the country, transients on ships and Indian jungle population. - Y compris les personnes vivant dans des régions éloignées, le personel militaire en dehors du pays, les marins marchands, les ouvriers saisonniers en dehors du pays, et autres civils en dehors du pays, et non compris les nomades, les militaires étrangers, les étrangers civils temporairement dans le pays, les transiteurs sur des bateaux et les Indiens de la jungle.

[42] Intercensal estimates. - Estimations inter-censitaires.

[43] Data based on the Population Census of 2005. - Données fondées sur le recensement de la population de 2005.

[44] Excluding nomadic Indian tribes. Data refer to national projections. - Non compris les tribus d'Indiens nomades. Les données se réfèrent aux projections nationales.

[45] Excluding Indian jungle population. - Non compris les Indiens de la jungle.

[46] Data refer to the settled population based on the 1979 Population Census and the latest household prelisting. The refugees of Afghanistan in Iran, Pakistan, and an estimated 1.5 million nomads, are not included. - Les données se rapportent à la population stationnaire sur la base du recensement de 1979 et du recensement préliminaire des logements le plus récent. Sont exclus les réfugiés d'Afghanistan en Iran et au Pakistan et les nomades estimés à 1,5 million.

[47] Data refer to the settled population based on the 1979 Population Census and the latest household prelisting. The refugees of Afghanistan in Iran, Pakistan, and an estimated 1.5 million nomads, are not included. The so adjusted total population of the country for 2006 is 24.1 million (12.3 million males and 11.8 million females). - Les données se rapportent à la population stationnaire sur la base du recensement de 1979 et du recensement préliminaire des logements le plus récent. Sont exclus les réfugiés d'Afghanistan en Iran et au Pakistan et les nomades estimés à 1,5 million. La population totale du pays ainsi ajustée pour 2006 comprend 24,1 millions de personnes (12,3 millions d'hommes et 11,8 millions de femmes).

[48] The adjusted total population of the country is 25.5 million. Data refer to the settled population based on the 1979 Population Census and the latest household prelisting. The refugees of Afghanistan in Iran, Pakistan, and an estimated 1.5 million nomads, are not included. - La population totale ajustée du pays comprend 25,5 millions de personnes. Les données se rapportent à la population stationnaire sur la base du recensement de 1979 et du recensement préliminaire des logements le plus récent. Sont exclus les réfugiés d'Afghanistan en Iran et au Pakistan et les nomades estimés à 1,5 million.

[49] The adjusted total population of the country is 26 million (13.3 million males and 12.7 million females). Data refer to the settled population based on the 1979 Population Census and the latest household prelisting. The refugees of Afghanistan in Iran, Pakistan, and an estimated 1.5 million nomads, are not included. - La population totale ajustée du pays comprend 26 millions de personnes (13.3 millions d'homes et 12.7 millions de femmes). Les données se rapportent à la population stationnaire sur la base du recensement de 1979 et du recensement préliminaire des logements le plus récent. Sont exclus les réfugiés d'Afghanistan en Iran et au Pakistan et les nomades estimés à 1,5 million.

[50] Data refer to projections based on the 2005 population census. - Les données se réfèrent aux projections basées sur le recensement de la population de 2005.

[51] Excluding foreign diplomatic personnel and their dependants. - Non compris le personnel diplomatique étranger et les membres de leur famille les accompagnant.

[52] Based on 1998 census results. - A partir des résultats de recensement de l'année 1998.

[53] Data refer to national projections based on 2008 census. - Les données se réfèrent aux projections nationales basées sur le recensement de la population de 2008.

[54] For statistical purposes, the data for China do not include those for the Hong Kong Special Administrative Region (Hong Kong SAR), Macao Special Administrative Region (Macao SAR) and Taiwan province of China. Data have been estimated on the basis of the annual National Sample Survey on Population Changes. - Pour la présentation des statistiques, les données pour la Chine ne comprennent pas la Région Administrative Spéciale de Hong Kong (Hong Kong RAS), la Région Administrative Spéciale de Macao (Macao RAS) et Taïwan province de Chine. Les données ont été estimées sur la base de l'enquête annuelle "National Sample Survey on Population Changes".

[55] Data refer to government controlled areas. - Les données se rapportent aux zones contrôlées par le Gouvernement.

[56] Including data for the Indian-held part of Jammu and Kashmir, the final status of which has not yet been determined. - Y compris les données pour la partie du Jammu et du Cachemire occupée par l'Inde dont le statut définitif n'a pas encore été déterminé.

[57] Excluding estimated population for Mao Maram, Paomata and Purul sub-divisions of Senapati district of Manipur. - Non compris la population estimée de Mao Maram, Paomata et les subdivisions Purul du district Senapati de Manipur.

[58] Data refer to the Iranian Year which begins on 21 March and ends on 20 March of the following year. - Les données concernent l'année iranienne, qui commence le 21 mars et se termine le 20 mars de l'année suivante.

[59] Including data for East Jerusalem and Israeli residents in certain other territories under occupation by Israeli military forces since June 1967. - Y compris les données pour Jérusalem-Est et les résidents israéliens dans certains autres territoires occupés depuis 1967 par les forces armées israéliennes.

[60] Excluding diplomatic personnel outside the country and foreign military and civilian personnel and their dependants stationed in the area. - Non compris le personnel diplomatique hors du pays ni les militaires et agents civils étrangers en poste sur le territoire et les membres de leur famille les accompagnant.

[61] Data refer to 31 December. Excluding data for Jordanian territory under occupation since June 1967 by Israeli military forces. Excluding foreigners, including registered Palestinian refugees. - Données se raportent au 31 décembre. Non compris les données pour le territoire jordanien occupé depuis juin 1967 par les forces armées israéliennes. Non compris les étrangers, mais y compris les réfugiés de Palestine enregistrés.

[62] Data are calculated from results of Population and Housing Census of 2009. - Les données sont calculées à partir des résultats de recensement de la population et de l'habitat de 2009.

[63] Population estimates for 2000 to 2004 are based on the age-sex distribution of 1995 population census and growth rate at year 2000. - Pour les années 2000 à 2004, on a pris pour base la répartition par âge et sexe du recensement de population de 1995 et le taux de croissance de 2000.

64 Based on the results of the 2005 Population and Housing Census. - Données fondées sur les résultats du recensement de la population et de l'habitat de 2005.

65 Data refer to 30 June. Data refer to projections based on the 2000 population census. - Données se raportent au 30 juin. Les données se réfèrent aux projections basées sur le recensement de la population de 2000.

66 Excluding data for the Pakistan-held part of Jammu and Kashmir, the final status of which has not yet been determined. - Non compris les données concernant la partie du Jammu et Cachemire occupée par le Pakistan dont le statut définitif n'a pas été déterminé.

67 Based on the results of the Population Demographic Survey. These estimates do not reflect completely accurately the actual population and vital events of the country. - D'après les résultats de l'Enquête démographique par sondage. Ces estimations ne dénotent pas d'une manière complètement ponctuelle la population actuelle et les statistiques de l'état civil du pays.

68 Based on the results of the Pakistan Demographic Survey (PDS 2003). These estimates do not reflect completely accurately the actual population and vital events of the country. - D'après les résultats de l'enquête démographique effectuée par le Pakistan en 2003. Ces estimations ne dénotent pas d'une manière complètement ponctuelle la population actuelle et les statistiques de l'état civil du pays.

69 Based on the results of the Pakistan Demographic Survey (PDS 2005). These estimates do not reflect completely accurately the actual population and vital events of the country. - D'après les résultats de l'enquête démographique effectuée par le Pakistan en 2005. Ces estimations ne dénotent pas d'une manière complètement ponctuelle la population actuelle et les statistiques de l'état civil du pays.

70 Based on the results of the Pakistan Demographic Survey (PDS 2007). - D'après les résultats de l'enquête démographique effectuée par le Pakistan en 2007.

71 Data are based on projections of the 2000 Population and Housing Census data. - Les données sont basées sur les projections du recensement de 2000 de la population et de l'habitat.

72 Including Palestinian refugees. - Y compris les réfugiés de Palestine.

73 Data based on Address Based Population Registration System. - Les données sont basées sur le registre national de la population basé sur l'adresse.

74 Data are adjusted according to the results of 1999 and 2009 censuses. - Les données ont été ajustées à partir des résultats des recensements de la population de 1999 et 2009.

75 Excluding Faeroe Islands and Greenland shown separately, if available. Population statistics are compiled from registers. - Non compris les Iles Féroé et le Groenland, qui font l'objet de rubriques distinctes, si disponible. Les statistiques de la population sont compilées à partir des registres.

76 Excluding Åland Islands. - Non compris les Îles d'Åland.

77 Excluding diplomatic personnel outside the country and including members of alien armed forces not living in military camps and foreign diplomatic personnel not living in embassies or consulates. - Non compris le personnel diplomatique hors du pays et y compris les militaires étrangers ne vivant pas dans des camps militaires et le personnel diplomatique étranger ne vivant pas dans les ambassades ou les consulats.

78 Excluding military personnel, visitors and transients. - Non compris les militaires, ni les visiteurs et transients.

79 Excluding armed forces stationed outside the country, but including alien armed forces stationed in the area. - Non compris les militaires en garnison hors du pays, mais y compris les militaires étrangers en garnison sur le territoire.

80 Data refer to 31 March. - Données se raportent au 31 mars.

81 Data refer to the Vatican City State. Population statistics are compiled from registers. The population figure for 2009 is 466 persons. - Les données se rapportent à l'État de la Cité du Vatican. Les statistiques de la population sont compilées à partir des registres. La population pour 2009 est égale à 466 personnes.

82 Data refer to 15 April. - Données se raportent au 15 avril.

83 Data refer to 30 April. - Donriées se raportent au 30 avril.

84 Including civilian nationals temporarily outside the country. - Y compris les civils nationaux temporairement hors du pays.

85 Including residents temporarily outside the country. Excluding Svalbard and Jan Mayen Islands shown separately, if available. - Y compris les résidents se trouvant temporairement hors du pays. Non compris Svalbard et Jan Mayen qui font l'objet de rubriques distinctes, si disponible.

86 Excluding civilian aliens within country, but including civilian nationals temporarily outside country. - Non compris les civils étrangers dans le pays, mais y compris les civils nationaux temporairement hors du pays.

87 Excluding Transnistria and the municipality of Bender. - Les données ne tiennent pas compte de l'information sur la Transnistria et la municipalité de Bender.

88 Excluding data for Kosovo and Metohia. - Sans les données pour le Kosovo et Metohie.

89 Data refer to 1 January. Data refer to Svalbard only. - Données se raportent au 1 janvier. Données ne concernant que le Svalbard.

90 Excluding Channel Islands (Guernsey and Jersey) and Isle of Man, shown separately, if available. - Non compris les îles Anglo-Normandes (Guernesey et Jersey) et l'île de Man, qui font l'objet de rubriques distinctes, si disponible.

91 Population estimates for 1994 to 2002 were revised in light of the local studies. - Les estimations de la population pour les années 1994 à 2002 ont été révisées en fonction d'études locales.

92 Intercensal estimates. Data are based on 2009 Australian Standard Geographical Classification boundaries. - Estimations inter-censitaires. Les données réfèrent au découpage de la nomenclature normalisée d'Australie de 2009.

93 Excluding Niue, shown separately, which is part of Cook Islands, but because of remoteness is administered separately. - Non compris Nioué, qui fait l'objet d'une rubrique distincte et qui fait partie des îles Cook, mais qui, en raison de son éloignement, est administrée séparément.

94 Excluding diplomatic personnel and armed forces stationed outside country; also excluding alien armed forces within the country. - Non compris le personnel diplomatique et les militaires hors du pays; non compris également les militaires étrangers en garnison dans le pays.

95 Based on the census, updated for residents missed or counted more than once by the census (net census undercount); residents temporarily overseas on census night, and births, deaths and net migration between the census night and the date of the estimate. - D'après le recensement, mise à jour pour les résidents omis ou dénombrés plus d'une fois par le recensement (sous-dénombrement net); résidents temporairement à l'étranger la nuit du recensement, et naissances, décès et migration nette entre la nuit du recensement et la date de l'estimation.

96 The population figure is 64 persons. - La population est égale à 64 personnes.

97 The population figure is 58 persons. - La population est égale à 58 personnes.

98 Data refer to national projections. Based on the results of the 1996 population census. - Les données se réfèrent aux projections nationales. À partir des résultats du recensement de la population de 1996.

Table 6

Table 6 presents total population by sex for as many years as possible between 2001 and 2010, as well as urban population as available.

Description of variables: Data are from nation-wide population censuses or are estimates, some of which are based on sample surveys of population carried out among all segments of the population. This characteristic of the data is indicated in the column "Code". The codes used are explained at the end of the table.

Urban is defined according to the national census definition. The definition for each country is set forth at the end of the technical notes to this table.

Percentage computation: Percentages urban are the number of persons residing in an area defined as "urban" per 100 total population. They are calculated by the United Nations Statistics Division. In very few cases the data for total population have been revised but the data for the urban and rural population have not been. These data are footnoted accordingly. In these cases, particular caution should be used in interpreting the figures for percentage urban.

Reliability of data: Estimates that are believed to be less reliable are set in *italics* rather than in roman type. Classification in terms of reliability is based on the method of construction of the total population estimate discussed in the technical notes for table 3.

Limitations: Statistics on urban population by sex are subject to the same qualifications as have been set forth for population statistics in general, as discussed in section 3 of the Technical Notes.

The basic limitations imposed by variations in the definition of the total population and in the degree of under-enumeration are perhaps more important in relation to urban/rural than to any other distributions. The classification by urban and rural is affected by variations in defining usual residence for purposes of sub-national tabulations. Likewise, the geographical differentials in the degree of under-enumeration in censuses affect the comparability of these categories throughout the table. The distinction between *de facto* and *de jure* population is also very important with respect to urban/rural distributions. The difference between the *de facto* and the *de jure* population is discussed at length in section 3.1.1 of the Technical Notes.

A most important and specific limitation, however, lies in the national differences in the definition of urban. Because the distinction between urban and rural areas is made in so many different ways, the definitions have been included at the end of this table. The definitions are necessarily brief and, where the classification of urban involves administrative civil divisions, they are often given in the terminology of the particular country or area. As a result of variations in terminology, it may appear that differences between countries or areas are greater than they actually are. On the other hand, similar or identical terms (for example, town, village, district) as used in different countries or areas may have quite different meanings.

It will be seen from an examination of the definitions that they fall roughly into three major types: (1) classification of localities as urban based on size; (2) classification of administrative centres of minor civil divisions as urban and the remainder of the division as rural; and (3) classification of minor civil divisions on a set of criteria, which may include type of local government, number of inhabitants or proportion of population engaged in agriculture.

The designation of areas as urban or rural is so closely bound to historical, political, cultural, and administrative considerations that the process of developing uniform definitions and procedures moves very slowly. Not only do the definitions differ from one country or area to the other, but, they may also no longer reflect the original intention for distinguishing urban from rural. The criteria once established on the basis of administrative subdivisions (as most of these are) become fixed and resistant to change. For this reason, comparisons of time-series data may be severely affected because the definitions used become outdated. Special care must be taken in comparing data from censuses with those from sample surveys because the definitions of urban used may differ.

Despite their shortcomings, however, statistics on urban and rural population are useful in describing the diversity of population distribution within a country or area.

The definition of urban/rural areas is based on both qualitative and quantitative criteria that may include any combination of the following: size of population, population density, distance between built-up areas, predominant type of economic activity, conformity to legal or administrative status and urban characteristics such as specific services and facilities[1]. Although statistics classified by urban/rural areas are widely available, no international standard definition appears to be possible at this time since the meaning differs from one country or area to another. The urban/rural classification of population used here is reported according to the national definition.

Earlier data: Urban and total population by sex have been shown in previous issues of the Demographic Yearbook. For information on specific years covered, readers should consult the Historical Index.

DEFINITION OF "URBAN"

AFRICA

Algeria: The urban/rural delimitation is performed after the census operation based on the classification of built-up areas. Groupings of 100 or more constructions, distant less than 200 metres from one another are considered urban.

Botswana: Agglomeration of 5 000 or more inhabitants where 75 per cent of the economic activity is non-agricultural.

Burundi: Commune of Bujumbura.

Burkina Faso: All administrative centres of provinces (total of 45) plus 4 medium-sized towns are considered as urban areas.

Comoros: Every locality or administrative centre of an island, region or prefecture that has the following facilities: asphalted roads, electricity, a medical centre, telephone services, etc.

Egypt: Governorates of Cairo, Alexandria, Port Said, Ismailia, Suez, frontier governorates and capitals of other governorates, as well as district capitals (Markaz). The definition of urban areas for the November 2006 census is "SHIAKHA", a part of a district.

Equatorial Guinea: District centres and localities with 300 dwellings and/or 1 500 inhabitants or more.

Ethiopia: Localities of 2 000 or more inhabitants.

Kenya: Areas having a population of 2 000 or more inhabitants that have transport systems, build-up areas, industrial/manufacturing structures and other developed structures.

Lesotho: All administrative headquarters and settlements of rapid growth.

Liberia: Localities of 2 000 or more inhabitants.

Malawi: All townships and town planning areas and all district centres.

Mauritius: Towns with proclaimed legal limits.

Namibia: Proclaimed urban areas for which cadastral data is available and other unplanned squatter areas.

Niger: Capital city, capitals of the departments and districts.

Rwanda: All administrative areas recognized as urban by the law. These are all administrative centres of provinces, and the cities of Kigali, Nyanza, Ruhango and Rwamagana.

Senegal: Agglomerations of 10 000 or more inhabitants.

South Africa: Places with some form of local authority.

Sudan: Localities of administrative and/or commercial importance or with population of 5 000 or more inhabitants.

Swaziland: Localities proclaimed as urban.

Tunisia: Population living in communes.

Uganda: Gazettes, cities, municipalities and towns.

United Republic of Tanzania: 16 gazetted townships.

Zambia: Localities of 5 000 or more inhabitants, the majority of whom all depend on non-agricultural activities.

AMERICA, NORTH

Canada: Places of 1 000 or more inhabitants, having a population density of 400 or more per square kilometre.

Costa Rica: Administrative centres of cantons.

Cuba: Towns that fulfil a political or administrative function, or that have a population of 2 000 or more and definite urban characteristics.

Dominican Republic: Administrative centres of municipalities and municipal districts, some of which include suburban zones of rural character.

El Salvador: Administrative centres of municipalities.

Greenland: Localities of 200 or more inhabitants.

Guatemala: Municipality of Guatemala Department and officially recognized centres of other departments and municipalities.

Haiti: Administrative centres of communes.

Honduras: Localities of 2 000 or more inhabitants, having essentially urban characteristics.

Jamaica: Localities of 2 000 or more inhabitants, having urban characteristics.

Mexico: Localities of 2 500 or more inhabitants.

Nicaragua: Administrative centres of municipalities and localities of 1 000 or more inhabitants or with more than 150 dwellings, with streets, electric light, water service, school and health centre.

Panama: Localities of 1 500 or more inhabitants having essentially urban characteristics. Beginning 1970, localities of 1 500 or more inhabitants with such urban characteristics as streets, water supply systems, sewerage systems and electric light.

Puerto Rico: Agglomerations of 2 500 or more inhabitants, generally having population densities of 1 000 persons per square mile or more. Two types of urban areas: urbanized areas of 50 000 or more inhabitants and urban clusters of at least 2 500 and less than 50 000 inhabitants.

United States of America: Agglomerations of 2 500 or more inhabitants, generally having population densities of 1 000 persons per square mile or more. Two types of urban areas: urbanized areas of 50 000 or more inhabitants and urban clusters of at least 2 500 and less than 50 000 inhabitants.

United States Virgin Islands: Agglomerations of 2 500 or more inhabitants, generally having population densities of 1 000 persons per square mile or more. Two types of urban areas: urbanized areas of 50 000 or more inhabitants and urban clusters of at least 2 500 and less than 50 000 inhabitants. (As of Census 2000, no urbanized areas are identified in the United States Virgin Islands.)

AMERICA, SOUTH

Argentina: Populated centres with 2 000 or more inhabitants.

Bolivia: Localities of 2 000 or more inhabitants.

Brazil: Urban and suburban zones of administrative centres of municipalities and districts.

Chile: Areas of concentrated housing units with more than 2 000 inhabitants, or between 1 001 and 2 000 inhabitants having 50 per cent or more of its economically active population doing secondary or tertiary activities. As an exception, centres of tourism and recreation with more than 250 housing units that do not satisfy the population requirement are nevertheless considered urban.

Colombia: Administrative centres of municipalities.

Ecuador: Capitals of provinces and cantons.

Falkland Islands (Malvinas): Town of Stanley.

Paraguay: Cities, towns and administrative centres of departments and districts.

Peru: Populated centres with 100 or more dwellings.

Suriname: The districts of Paramaribo and Wanica.

Uruguay: Cities.

Venezuela (Bolivarian Republic of): Centres with a population of 1 000 or more inhabitants.

ASIA

Armenia: Cities and urban-type localities, officially designated as such, usually according to the criteria of number of inhabitants and predominance of agricultural, or number of non-agricultural workers and their families.

Azerbaijan: Cities and urban-type localities, officially designated as such, usually according to the criteria of number of inhabitants and predominance of agricultural, or number of non-agricultural workers and their families.

Bahrain: Communes or villages of 2 500 or more inhabitants.

Cambodia: Areas at the commune level satisfying the following three conditions: (1) Population Density exceeding 200 per square Km, (2) Percentage of male employed in agriculture below 50 per cent, (3) Total population of the commune exceeds 2 000 inhabitants.

China: Cities only refer to the cities proper of those designated by the State Council. In the case of cities with district establishment, the city proper refers to the whole administrative area of the district if its population density is 1 500 people per kilometre or higher; or the seat of the district government and other areas of streets under the administration of the district if the population density is less than 1 500 people per kilometre. In the case of cities without district establishment, the city proper refers to the seat of the city government and other areas of streets under the administration of the city. For the city district with the population density below 1 500 people per kilometre and the city without district establishment, if the urban construction of the district or city government seat has extended to some part of the neighboring designated town(s) or township(s), the city proper does include the whole administrative area of the town(s) or township(s).

Cyprus: Urban areas are those defined by local town plans.

Georgia: Cities and urban-type localities, officially designated as such, usually according to the criteria of number of inhabitants and predominance of agricultural, or number of non-agricultural workers and their families.

India: Towns (places with municipal corporation, municipal area committee, town committee, notified area committee or cantonment board); also, all places having 5 000 or more inhabitants, a density of not less than 1 000 persons per square mile or 400 per square kilometre, pronounced urban characteristics and at least three fourths of the adult male population employed in pursuits other than agriculture.

Indonesia: Area which satisfies certain criteria in terms of population density, percentage of agricultural households, and a number of urban facilities such as roads, formal education facilities, public health services, etc.

Iran (Islamic Republic of): Every district with a municipality.

Israel: Localities with 2 000 or more residents.

Japan: City (shi) having 50 000 or more inhabitants with 60 per cent or more of the houses located in the main built-up areas and 60 per cent or more of the population (including their dependants) engaged in manufacturing, trade or other urban type of business.

Jordan: Localities of 5 000 or more inhabitants.

Kazakhstan: Cities and urban-type localities, officially designated as such, usually according to the criteria of number of inhabitants and predominance of agricultural, or number of non-agricultural workers and their families.

Kyrgyzstan: Cities and urban-type localities, officially designated as such, usually according to the criteria of number of inhabitants and predominance of agricultural, or number of non-agricultural workers and their families.

Lao People's Democratic Republic: Areas or villages that satisfy at least three of the following five conditions: located in metropolitan areas of district or province, there is access to road in dry and rainy seasons, about 70 per cent or 2/3 of the population has access to piped water, about 70 per cent or 2/3 of the population has access to public electricity, there is a market operating every day.

Occupied Palestinian Territory: Localities with 10 000 or more residents. In addition, it refers to all localities whose populations vary from 4 000 to 9 999 persons provided they have, at least, four of the following elements: public electricity network, public water network, post office, health center with a full time physician and a school offering a general secondary education certificate.

Malaysia: Gazetted areas with population of 10 000 and more.

Maldives: Malé, the capital.

Mongolia: Capital and district centres.

Pakistan: Places with municipal corporation, town committee or cantonment.

Philippines: Cities and municipalities and their central districts with a population density of at least 500 persons per square km. Urban areas are considered other districts regardless of population size that have streets, at least six establishments (commercial, manufacturing, recreational and/or personal services), and at least three public structures such as town hall, church, public park, school, hospital, library, etc.

Republic of Korea: For estimates: Places with 50 000 or more inhabitants. For census: the figures are composed in the basis of the minor administrative divisions such as Dongs (mostly urban areas) and Eups or Myeons (rural areas).

Sri Lanka: Urban sector comprises of all municipal and urban council areas.

Syrian Arab Republic: Cities, Mohafaza centres and Mantika centres, and communities with 20 000 or more inhabitants.

Tajikistan: Cities and urban-type localities, officially designated as such, usually according to the criteria of number of inhabitants and predominance of agricultural, or number of non-agricultural workers and their families.

Thailand: Municipal areas.

Turkey: Province and district centres.

Turkmenistan: Cities and urban-type localities, officially designated as such, usually according to the criteria of number of inhabitants and predominance of agricultural, or number of non-agricultural workers and their families.

Uzbekistan: Cities and urban-type localities, officially designated as such, usually according to the criteria of number of inhabitants and predominance of agricultural, or number of non-agricultural workers and their families.

Viet Nam: Urban areas include inside urban districts of cities, urban quarters and towns. All other local administrative units (communes) belong to rural areas.

EUROPE

Albania: Towns and other industrial centres of more than 400 inhabitants.

Austria: Urban areas are localities with 2 000 or more inhabitants. The delineation of localities goes back to 1991.

Belarus: Cities and urban-type localities, officially designated as such, usually according to the criteria of number of inhabitants and predominance of agricultural, or number of non-agricultural workers and their families.

Bulgaria: All towns and cities according to the Territorial and Administrative-Territorial Division of the country.

Czech Republic: Localities with 2 000 or more inhabitants.

Estonia: Cities and urban-type localities, officially designated as such, usually according to the criteria of number of inhabitants and predominance of agricultural, or number of non-agricultural workers and their families.

Finland: Urban communes.

France: Communes containing an agglomeration of more than 2 000 inhabitants living in contiguous houses or with not more than 200 metres between houses, also communes of which the major portion of the population is part of a multi-communal agglomeration of this nature.

Greece: Urban is considered every municipal or communal department of which the largest locality has 2 000 inhabitants and over.

Hungary: Budapest and all legally designated towns.

Iceland: Localities of 200 or more inhabitants.

Ireland: Cities and towns including suburbs of 1 500 or more inhabitants.

Latvia: Cities and urban-type localities, officially designated as such, usually according to the criteria of number of inhabitants and predominance of agricultural, or number of non-agricultural workers and their families.

Lithuania: Urban population refers to persons who live in cities and towns, i.e., the population areas with closely built permanent dwellings and with the resident population of more than 3 000 of which 2/3 of employees work in industry,

social infrastructure and business. In a number of towns the population may be less than 3 000 since these areas had already the states of "town" before the law was enforced (July 1994)

Malta: Areas with population density of 150 persons or more per square km.

Netherlands: Urban: Municipalities with a population of 2 000 and more inhabitants. Semi-urban: Municipalities with a population of less than 2 000 but with not more than 20 per cent of their economically active male population engaged in agriculture, and specific residential municipalities of commuters.

Norway: Localities of 200 or more inhabitants.

Poland: Towns and settlements of urban type, e.g. workers' settlements, fishermen's settlements, health resorts.

Portugal: Agglomeration of 10 000 or more inhabitants.

Republic of Moldova: Cities and urban-type localities, officially designated as such, usually according to the criteria of number of inhabitants and predominance of agricultural, or number of non-agricultural workers and their families.

Romania: Cities, municipalities and other towns.

Russian Federation: Cities and urban-type localities, officially designated as such, usually according to the criteria of number of inhabitants and predominance of agricultural, or number of non-agricultural workers and their families.

Slovakia: 138 cities with 5 000 inhabitants or more.

Slovenia: Settlements of 3 000 or more inhabitants, settlements that serve as seats of municipalities with at least 1 400 inhabitants, and sub-urban areas that are being gradually integrated with an urban settlement of 5 000 or more inhabitants.

Spain: Localities of 2 000 or more inhabitants.

Switzerland: Communes of 10 000 or more inhabitants, including suburbs.

Ukraine: Cities and urban-type localities, officially designated as such, usually according to the criteria of number of inhabitants and predominance of agricultural, or number of non-agricultural workers and their families.

United Kingdom of Great Britain and Northern Ireland: Settlements where the population is 10 000 or above.

OCEANIA

Australia: An urban centre is generally defined as a population cluster of 1 000 or more people.

American Samoa: Agglomerations of 2 500 or more inhabitants, generally having population densities of 1 000 persons per square mile or more. Two types of urban areas: urbanized areas of 50 000 or more inhabitants and urban clusters of at least 2 500 and less than 50 000 inhabitants. (As of Census 2000, no urbanized areas are identified in American Samoa.)

Guam: Agglomerations of 2 500 or more inhabitants, generally having population densities of 1 000 persons per square mile or more, referred to as "urban clusters".

New Caledonia: Nouméa and communes of Païta, Nouvel Dumbéa and Mont-Dore.

New Zealand: All cities, plus boroughs, town districts, townships and country towns with a population of 1 000 or more usual residents.

Northern Mariana Islands: Agglomerations of 2 500 or more inhabitants, generally having population densities of 1 000 persons per square mile or more. Two types of urban areas: urbanized areas of 50 000 or more inhabitants and urban clusters of at least 2 500 and less than 50 000 inhabitants.

Vanuatu: Luganville centre and Vila urban.

NOTES

[1] For further information, see *Social and Demographic Statistics: Classifications of Size and Type of Locality and Urban/Rural Areas.* E/CN.3/551, United Nations, New York, 1980.

Tableau 6

Le tableau 6 présente des données sur la population totale selon le sexe pour le plus grand nombre possible d'années entre 2001 et 2010, ainsi que la population urbaine si disponible.

Description des variables : les données proviennent de recensements de la population ou sont des estimations fondées, dans certains cas, sur des enquêtes par sondage portant sur toute la population. Le code qui figure dans la colonne « Code » du tableau indique comment les données ont été obtenues. Les codes utilisés sont expliqués à la fin du tableau.

Le sens donné au terme « urbain » est conforme aux définitions utilisées dans les recensements nationaux. La définition pour chaque pays figure à la fin des présentes notes technique.

Calcul des pourcentages : les pourcentages de la population urbaine sont calculés par la Division de statistique de l'Organisation des Nations Unies et représentent le nombre de personnes qui vivent dans des régions considérées comme urbaines pour 100 personnes de la population totale. Dans de très rares cas, les données pour la population totale ont été révisées mais les données pour la population urbaine et la population rurale ne l'ont pas été. Ces données sont indiquées en note. Dans ces cas, les proportions de population urbaine ou rurale sont à interpréter avec précaution.

Fiabilité des données : les estimations considérées comme moins sûres sont indiquées en italique plutôt qu'en caractères romains. Le classement du point de vue de la fiabilité est fondé sur la méthode utilisée pour établir l'estimation de la population totale qui figure au tableau 3 (voir les explications dans les notes techniques relatives à ce même tableau).

Insuffisance des données : les statistiques de la population urbaine selon le sexe appellent toutes les réserves qui ont été formulées à la section 3 des Notes techniques à propos des statistiques de la population en général.

Les limitations fondamentales imposées par les variations de la définition de la population totale et par les lacunes du recensement se font peut-être sentir davantage dans la répartition de la population en population urbaine et population rurale que dans sa répartition suivant toute autre caractéristique. De fait, des différences dans la définition du lieu de résidence habituel utilisée pour l'exploitation des données à l'échelon sous-national influent sur la classification en population urbaine et en population rurale. De même, les différences de degré de sous-dénombrement suivant la zone, à l'occasion des recensements, ont une incidence sur la comparabilité de ces deux catégories dans l'ensemble du tableau. La distinction entre population de fait et population de droit est également très importante du point de vue de la répartition de la population en population urbaine et en population rurale. Cette distinction est expliquée en détail à la section 3.1.1 des Notes techniques.

Toutefois, la difficulté la plus importante tient aux différences de définition du terme « urbain » selon le pays. Les distinctions faites entre « zone urbaine » et « zone rurale » varient tellement que les définitions utilisées ont été reproduites à la fin des notes techniques du tableau 6. Les définitions sont forcément brèves et, lorsque le classement en « zone urbaine » repose sur des divisions administratives, on a souvent désigné celles-ci par le nom qu'elles portent dans la zone ou le pays considéré. Par suite des variations dans la terminologie, les différences entre pays ou zones peuvent sembler plus grandes qu'elles ne le sont réellement. Il se peut aussi que des termes similaires ou identiques, tels que ville, village ou district, aient des significations très différentes selon les pays ou zones.

On constatera, en examinant les définitions adoptées par les différents pays ou zones, qu'elles peuvent être ramenées à trois types principaux : 1) les localités dépassant certaines dimensions sont classées parmi les zones urbaines ; 2) les centres administratifs de petites circonscriptions administratives sont classées parmi les zones urbaines, le reste de la circonscription étant considéré comme zone rurale ; 3) les petites divisions administratives sont classées parmi les zones urbaines selon un critère déterminé, qui peut être soit le type d'administration locale, soit le nombre d'habitants, soit le pourcentage de la population exerçant une activité agricole.

La distinction entre régions urbaines et régions rurales est si étroitement liée à des considérations d'ordre historique, politique, culturel et administratif que l'on ne peut progresser que très lentement vers des définitions et des méthodes uniformes. Non seulement les définitions sont différentes d'une zone ou d'un pays à un autre, mais on n'y retrouve parfois même plus l'intention originale de distinguer les régions rurales des régions urbaines. Lorsque la classification est fondée, en particulier, sur le critère des circonscriptions

administratives (comme la plupart le sont), elle a tendance à devenir rigide avec le temps et à décourager toute modification. Pour cette raison, la comparaison des données appartenant à des séries chronologiques risque d'être gravement faussée du fait que les définitions employées sont désormais périmées. Il faut être particulièrement prudent lorsque l'on compare des données issues de recensements avec des données provenant d'enquêtes par sondage, car il se peut que les définitions du terme « urbain » auxquelles ces données se réfèrent respectivement soient différentes.

Malgré leurs insuffisances, les statistiques sur la population urbaine et rurale permettent de mettre en évidence la diversité de la répartition de la population au sein d'un pays ou d'une zone.

La distinction entre « zone urbaine » et « zone rurale » repose sur une série de critères qualitatifs aussi bien que quantitatifs, notamment l'effectif de la population, la densité de peuplement, la distance entre îlots d'habitations, le type prédominant d'activité économique, le statut juridique ou administratif, et les caractéristiques d'une agglomération urbaine, c'est-à-dire l'existence de services publics et d'équipements collectifs[1]. Bien que les statistiques différenciant les zones urbaines des zones rurales soient très répandues, il ne paraît pas possible pour le moment d'adopter une classification internationale type de ces zones, vu la diversité des interprétations nationales. La classification de la population en population urbaine et population rurale retenue ici est celle qui correspond aux définitions nationales.

Données publiées antérieurement : des statistiques concernant la population urbaine et la population totale selon le sexe ont été publiées dans des éditions antérieures de l'*Annuaire démographique*. Pour plus de précisions concernant les années pour lesquelles ces données ont été publiées, se reporter à l'index historique.

DÉFINITIONS DU TERME « URBAIN »

AFRIQUE

Algérie : La délimitation des zones urbaines et rurales se font après l'opération du recensement sur la base de la classification des agglomérations. Regroupement de 100 constructions ou plus distantes l'une à l'autre de moins de 200m ont été considérées comme zones urbaines.

Afrique du Sud : Zones dotées d'une administration locale.

Botswana : Agglomération de 5 000 habitants ou plus dont 75 p. 100 de l'activité économique n'est pas de type agricole.

Burkina Faso : Tous les chefs-lieux de province (45 au total) plus 4 villes moyennes ont été considérées comme zones urbaines.

Burundi : Commune de Bujumbura.

Comores : Toute localité ou chef-lieu d'une île, région/préfecture disposant des infrastructures suivantes : route bitumée, électricité, centre hospitalier, téléphone, etc.

Égypte : Chefs-lieux des gouvernorats du Caire, d'Alexandrie, de Port Saïd, d'Ismaïlia, de Suez ; chefs-lieux des gouvernorats frontaliers, autres chefs-lieux de gouvernorat et chefs-lieux de district (Markaz). La définition des zones urbaines pour le recensement de novembre 2006 est celle de « SHIAKHA », une partie d'un district.

Éthiopie : Localités de 2 000 habitants ou plus.

Guinée équatoriale : Chefs-lieux de district et localités comprenant 300 habitations et/ou 1 500 habitants ou plus.

Kenya : Zone ayant une population de 2 000 habitants ou plus qui dispose de réseaux de transport, comporte des zones bâties, des structures industrielles ou manufacturières et d'autres équipements modernes.

Lesotho : Tous les chefs-lieux administratifs et établissements urbains en forte croissance.

Libéria : Localités de 2 000 habitants ou plus.

Malawi : Toutes les villes et zones urbanisées et tous les chefs-lieux de district.

Maurice : Villes ayant des limites officiellement définies.

Namibie : Zones urbaines déclarées pour lesquelles il existe des données cadastrales et autres zones d'habitat non planifié.

Niger: Ville capital, villes capitales de départements ou de districts.

Ouganda : «Gazettes», villes, municipalités et bourgs.

République-Unie de Tanzanie : 16 townships érigées en communes.

Rwanda : Toutes les zones administratives reconnues comme urbaines par la loi. Il s'agit de tous les chefs-lieux des provinces, de la ville de Kigali ainsi que des villes de Nyanza, Ruhango et Rwamagana.

Sénégal : Agglomérations de 10 000 habitants ou plus.

Soudan : Centres administratifs et/ou commerciaux ou localités ayant une population de 5 000 habitants ou plus.

Swaziland : Localités déclarées urbaines.

Tunisie : Population vivant dans les communes.

Zambie : Localités de 5 000 habitants ou plus dont l'activité économique prédominante n'est pas de type agricole.

AMÉRIQUE DU NORD

Canada : Agglomérations de 1 000 habitants ou plus ayant une densité de population d'au moins 400 habitants au kilomètre carré.

Costa Rica : Chefs-lieux de canton.

Cuba : Villes ayant une fonction politique ou administrative, ou une population supérieure à 2 000 habitants et présentant des traits urbains.

El Salvador : Chefs-lieux de municipios.

États-Unis d'Amérique : Agglomérations de 2 500 habitants ou plus ayant généralement une densité de population d'au moins 1 000 habitants au mile carré. Deux types de zones urbaines : zones urbanisées de 50 000 habitants ou plus et groupements urbains comptant au moins 2 500 habitants mais moins de 50 000.

Groenland : Localités d'au moins 200 habitants.

Guatemala : Municipio du département de Guatemala et centres administratifs officiels d'autres départements et municipios.

Haïti : Chefs-lieux de communes.

Honduras : Localités d'au moins 2 000 habitants ayant des caractéristiques essentiellement urbaines.

Îles Vierges américaines : Agglomérations de 2 500 habitants ou plus ayant généralement une densité de population d'au moins 1 000 habitants au mile carré. Deux types de zones urbaines : zones urbanisées de 50 000 habitants ou plus et groupements urbains comptant au moins 2 500 habitants mais moins de 50 000. (D'après les résultats du recensement de 2 000, les Îles Vierges américaines ne comptent aucune zone urbanisée.)

Jamaïque : Localités de 2 000 habitants ou plus présentant des traits urbains.

Mexique : Localités d'au moins 2 500 habitants.

Nicaragua : Centres administratifs des municipalités et localités d'au moins 1 000 habitants ou d'au moins 150 logements, possédant des rues, un éclairage électrique, un réseau de distribution d'eau, une école et un dispensaire.

Panama : Localités d'au moins 1 500 habitants ayant des caractéristiques essentiellement urbaines. À partir de 1970, localités de 1 500 habitants ou plus présentant des caractéristiques urbaines, telles que rues, éclairage électrique, systèmes d'approvisionnement en eau et réseaux d'égouts.

Porto Rico : Agglomérations de 2 500 habitants ou plus ayant généralement une densité de population d'au moins 1 000 habitants au mile carré. Deux types de zones urbaines : zones urbanisées de 50 000 habitants ou plus et groupements urbains comptant au moins 2 500 habitants mais moins de 50 000.

République dominicaine : Chefs-lieux de municipios et districts municipaux, dont certains comprennent des zones suburbaines ayant des caractéristiques rurales.

AMÉRIQUE DU SUD

Argentine : Centres comptant au moins 2 000 habitants.

Bolivie : Localités de 2 000 habitants ou plus.

Brésil : Zones urbaines et suburbaines des chefs lieux de municipalités et de districts.

Chili : Zones d'habitat concentré comptant 2 000 habitants ou plus, ou comptant entre 1 001 et 2 000 habitants dont 50 pour cent au moins de la population active a une activité secondaire ou tertiaire. Par dérogation, les centres qui ont une fonction touristique ou récréative et plus de 250 unités de logement mais n'atteignent pas le critère de population sont néanmoins considérés comme zones urbaines.

Colombie : Centre administratif d'une municipalité.
Équateur : Capitales des provinces et chefs-lieux de canton.
Îles Falkland (Malvinas) : Ville de Stanley.
Paraguay : Grandes villes, villes et chefs-lieux des départements et des districts.
Pérou : Centres de peuplement comptant plus de 100 logements.
Suriname : Les districts de Paramaribo et de Wanica.
Uruguay : Villes.
Venezuela (République bolivarienne du) : Centres de 1 000 habitants ou plus.

ASIE

Arménie : Grandes villes et localités de type urbain, officiellement désignées comme telles, généralement sur la base du nombre d'habitants et de la prédominance des travailleurs agricoles ou non agricoles avec leur famille.

Azerbaïdjan : Grandes villes et localités de type urbain, officiellement désignées comme telles, généralement sur la base du nombre d'habitants et de la prédominance des travailleurs agricoles ou non agricoles avec leur famille.

Bahreïn : Communes ou villages comptant au moins 2 500 habitants.

Cambodge : Zones au niveau de la commune répondant aux trois conditions suivantes: 1) Densité démographique supérieure à 200 habitants au km carré, 2) pourcentage d'hommes travaillant dans l'agriculture inférieur à 50 pour cent, 3) population totale de la commune supérieure à 2 000 habitants.

Chine : Villes désignées comme telles par le Conseil d'État. Dans le cas de villes ayant rang de district, la ville s'entend comme l'ensemble de la zone administrative qui relève du district si sa densité est d'au moins 1 500 habitants au kilomètre carré ou comme le siège des autorités du district et les rues qui relèvent du district si sa densité est inférieure à 1 500 habitants au kilomètre carré. Dans le cas des villes qui n'ont pas rang de district, la ville s'entend comme le siège des autorités de la commune et les rues qui relèvent des autorités de la commune. Dans le cas des villes ayant rang de district qui comptent moins de 1 500 habitants au kilomètre carré et des villes n'ayant pas rang de district, si l'urbanisation du siège du district ou du siège des autorités de la commune a empiété sur une partie de la ou des localités voisines, la ville inclut alors l'ensemble de la zone administrative desdites localités.

Chypre : Zones désignées comme urbaines dans les plans d'urbanisme locaux.

Géorgie : Grandes villes et localités de type urbain, officiellement désignées comme telles, généralement sur la base du nombre d'habitants et de la prédominance des travailleurs agricoles ou non agricoles avec leur famille.

Inde : Villes [localités dotées d'une charte municipale, d'un comité de zone municipale, d'un comité de zone déclarée urbaine ou d'un comité de zone de regroupement (cantonnement)] ; également toutes les localités qui ont une population de 5 000 habitants au moins, une densité de population d'au moins 1 000 habitants au mile carré ou 400 au kilomètre carré, des caractéristiques urbaines prononcées et où les trois quarts au moins des adultes de sexe masculin ont une occupation non agricole.

Indonésie : Zones qui répondent à certains critères de densité démographique et de pourcentage des ménages agricoles et possèdent un certain nombre d'équipements urbains tels que routes, écoles, services de santé publique, etc.

Iran (République islamique d') : Tous les districts comptant une municipalité.

Israël : Tous les lieux comptant au moins 2 000 résidents.

Japon : Villes (shi), comptant au moins 50 000 habitants, où 60 p. 100 au moins des logements sont situés dans les principales zones bâties, et dont 60 p. 100 au moins de population (y compris les personnes à charge) exercent un métier dans l'industrie, le commerce et d'autres branches d'activités essentiellement urbaines.

Jordanie : Localités comptant 5 000 habitants ou plus.

Kazakhstan : Grandes villes et localités de type urbain, officiellement désignées comme telles, généralement sur la base du nombre d'habitants et de la prédominance des travailleurs agricoles ou non agricoles avec leur famille.

Kirghizistan : Grandes villes et localités de type urbain, officiellement désignées comme telles, généralement sur la base du nombre d'habitants et de la prédominance des travailleurs agricoles ou non agricoles avec leur famille.

Malaisie : Zones déclarées « zones urbaines » et comptant au moins 10 000 habitants.

Maldives : Malé (capitale).

Mongolie : Capitale et chefs-lieux de district.

Ouzbékistan : Grandes villes et localités de type urbain, officiellement désignées comme telles, généralement sur la base du nombre d'habitants et de la prédominance des travailleurs agricoles ou non agricoles avec leur famille.

Pakistan : Localités dotées d'une charte municipale ou d'un comité municipal et regroupements (cantonments).

Philippines : Villes et municipalités et leurs quartiers centraux dont la densité démographique est d'au moins 500 habitants au km carré. Sont considérés comme zones urbaines les autres quartiers quelle que soit leur population qui sont équipés de routes et possèdent au moins six établissements (commerce, industrie manufacturière, équipements récréatifs ou services aux personnes), et au moins trois équipements publics tels que hôtel de ville, église, parc public, école, hôpital, bibliothèque, etc.

République arabe syrienne : Villes, chefs-lieux de district (Mohafaza) et chefs-lieux de sous district (Mantika), et communes d'au moins 20 000 habitants.

République de Corée : Pour les estimations : localités de 50 000 habitants ou plus. Pour recensements, les données sont établies sont la base des divisions administratives mineures comme les Dongs (principalement en zone urbaines) et des Eups ou Myeons (en zones rurales).

République démocratique populaire lao : Zones ou villages répondant à au moins trois des cinq conditions suivantes: situés dans l'aire métropolitaine du district ou de la province, accessibles par la route en toute saison, quelque 70 pour cent ou deux tiers de la population ayant accès à de l'eau distribuée par canalisation, quelque 70 pour cent ou deux tiers de la population ayant accès au réseau d'électricité et existence d'un marché ouvert tous les jours.

Sri Lanka : Secteur urbain composé de toutes les zones municipales et zones dotées d'un conseil urbain.

Tadjikistan : Grandes villes et localités de type urbain, officiellement désignées comme telles, généralement sur la base du nombre d'habitants et de la prédominance des travailleurs agricoles ou non agricoles avec leur famille.

Territoire palestinien occupé : Localités de 10 000 habitants ou plus. En plus, toutes les localités de 4 000 à 9 999 habitants ayant au moins quatre des services suivants : réseau d'électricité public, approvisionnement en eau public, bureau de poste, céntre medico-social ayant un médecin qui travaille à plein temps ou école offrant un enseignement secondaire général.

Thaïlande : Zones municipales.

Turkménistan : Grandes villes et localités de type urbain, officiellement désignées comme telles, généralement sur la base du nombre d'habitants et de la prédominance des travailleurs agricoles ou non agricoles avec leur famille.

Turquie : Chefs-lieux des provinces et des districts.

Viet Nam : Zones urbaines comprises à l'intérieur des districts urbains des villes ainsi que des quartiers urbains et des localités. Toutes les autres unités administratives locales (communes) sont considérées comme zones rurales.

EUROPE

Albanie : Villes et autres centres industriels de plus de 400 habitants.

Autriche :.Les zones urbaines sont les localités comptant 2 000 habitants ou plus. Leur délimitation remonte à 1991.

Bélarus : Grandes villes et localités de type urbain, officiellement désignées comme telles, généralement sur la base du nombre d'habitants et de la prédominance des travailleurs agricoles ou non agricoles avec leur famille.

Bulgarie : Toutes les zones considérées comme villes et bourgs selon la Division territoriale et administrative du pays.

Espagne : Localités de 2 000 habitants et plus.

Estonie : Grandes villes et localités de type urbain, officiellement désignées comme telles, généralement sur la base du nombre d'habitants et de la prédominance des travailleurs agricoles ou non agricoles avec leur famille.

Fédération de Russie : Grandes villes et localités de type urbain, officiellement désignées comme telles, généralement sur la base du nombre d'habitants et de la prédominance des travailleurs agricoles ou non agricoles avec leur famille.

Finlande : Communes urbaines.

France : Communes comprenant une agglomération de plus de 2 000 habitants vivant dans des habitations contiguës ou qui ne sont pas distantes les unes des autres de plus de 200 mètres et communes où la majeure partie de la population vit dans une agglomération regroupant plusieurs communes de cette nature.

Grèce : Est considérée comme zone urbaine toute municipalité ou commune dont la plus grande localité compte 2 000 habitants ou plus.

Hongrie : Budapest et toutes les autres localités reconnues officiellement comme urbaines.

Irlande : Localités, y compris leur banlieues, comptant 1 500 habitants ou plus.

Islande : Localités de 200 habitants ou plus.

Lettonie : Grandes villes et localités de type urbain, officiellement désignées comme telles, généralement sur la base du nombre d'habitants et de la prédominance des travailleurs agricoles ou non agricoles avec leur famille.

Lituanie : Par population urbaine, on entend les personnes qui vivent dans des villes ou des localités, à savoir les zones habitées comportant des logements permanents proches les uns des autres et dont la population est d'au moins 3 000 habitants, les deux tiers desquels étant employés dans le secteur industriel, l'infrastructure sociale ou le commerce. Un certain nombre de villes peuvent compter moins de 3 000 habitants dans la mesure où elles avaient acquis le statut de ville avant l'entrée en vigueur de la nouvelle loi en juillet 1994.

Malte : Zones ayant une densité démographique supérieure ou égale à 150 habitants au kilomètre carré.

Norvège : Localités de 200 habitants ou plus.

Pays Bas : Zones urbaines : municipalités comptant au moins 2 000 habitants. Zones semi-urbaines : municipalités comptant moins de 2 000 habitants, mais où 20 p. 100 au maximum de la population active de sexe masculin pratiquent l'agriculture, et certaines municipalités de caractère résidentiel dont les habitants travaillent ailleurs.

Pologne : Villes et zones de type urbain, par exemple groupements de travailleurs ou de pêcheurs et stations climatiques.

Portugal : Agglomérations d'au moins 10 000 habitants.

République de Moldova : Grandes villes et localités de type urbain, officiellement désignées comme telles, généralement sur la base du nombre d'habitants et de la prédominance des travailleurs agricoles ou non agricoles avec leur famille.

République tchèque : Localités d'au moins 2 000 habitants.

Roumanie : Grandes villes, municipalités et autres villes.

Royaume-Uni de Grande-Bretagne et d'Irlande du Nord : Agglomérations de population de 10 000 habitants ou plus.

Slovaquie : 138 localités comptant 5 000 habitants ou plus.

Slovénie : Établissements de 3 000 habitants ou plus, chefs-lieux de municipalités comptant au moins 1 400 habitants, et quartiers suburbains qui s'intègrent progressivement dans une ville de 5 000 habitants ou plus.

Suisse : Communes de 10 000 habitants ou plus, et leurs banlieues.

Ukraine : Grandes villes et localités de type urbain, officiellement désignées comme telles, généralement sur la base du nombre d'habitants et de la prédominance des travailleurs agricoles ou non agricoles avec leur famille.

OCÉANIE

Australie : Un regroupement de population de 1 000 personnes ou plus est généralement considéré comme un centre urbain.

Guam : Agglomérations de 2 500 habitants ou plus ayant généralement une densité de population d'au moins 1 000 habitants au mile carré et considérées comme étant des groupements urbains.

Îles Mariannes septentrionales : Agglomérations de 2 500 habitants ou plus ayant généralement une densité de population d'au moins 1 000 habitants au mile carré. Deux types de zones urbaines : zones urbanisées de 50 000 habitants ou plus et groupements urbains comptant au moins 2 500 habitants mais moins de 50 000.

Nouvelle-Calédonie : Nouméa et communes de Païta, Dumbéa et Mont-Dore.

Nouvelle-Zélande : Toutes les villes et les quartiers, districts et bourgs ayant 1 000 habitants permanents ou plus.

Samoa américaines : Agglomérations de 2 500 habitants ou plus ayant généralement une densité de population d'au moins 1 000 habitants au mile carré. Deux types de zones urbaines : zones urbanisées de 50 000 habitants ou plus et groupements urbains comptant au moins 2 500 habitants mais moins de 50 000. (D'après les résultats du recensement de 2000, les Samoa américaines ne comptent aucune zone urbanisée.)

Vanuatu : Centre de Luganville et Port-Vila.

_____

NOTES

[1] Pour plus de précisions, voir *Social and Demographic Statistics: Classifications of Size and Type of Locality and Urban/Rural Areas*, E/CN.3/551, publication des Nations Unies, New York, 1980.

Continent, country or area, and date / Continent, pays ou zone et date	Code[a]	Both sexes - Les deux sexes Total	Urban - Urbaine Number Nombre	Urban - Urbaine Percent P.100	Male - Masculin Total	Urban - Urbaine Number Nombre	Urban - Urbaine Percent P.100	Female - Féminin Total	Urban - Urbaine Number Nombre	Urban - Urbaine Percent P.100
AFRICA - AFRIQUE										
Algeria - Algérie										
1 VII 2001	ESDJ	30 871 734	...	...	15 598 261	...	...	15 273 473	...	...
1 VII 2002	ESDJ	31 332 033	...	...	15 830 343	...	...	15 501 690	...	...
1 VII 2003	ESDJ	31 847 995	...	...	16 090 568	...	...	15 757 427	...	...
16 IV 2008*	CDJC	34 452 759	...	...	17 428 500	...	...	17 024 259	...	...
Benin - Bénin										
1 VII 2001*	ESDF	6 416 692	...	...	3 136 516	...	...	3 280 176	...	...
11 II 2002	CDJC	6 769 914	2 630 133	38.9	3 284 119	1 280 418	39.0	3 485 795	1 349 715	38.7
1 VII 2003*[1]	ESDF	6 982 711	2 740 221	39.2	3 392 055	1 335 810	39.4	3 590 656	1 404 411	39.1
1 VII 2004*[1]	ESDF	7 208 552	2 863 952	39.7	3 506 558	1 397 974	39.9	3 701 994	1 465 978	39.6
1 VII 2005*[1]	ESDF	7 447 454	3 002 229	40.3	3 627 613	1 467 342	40.4	3 819 841	1 534 887	40.2
1 VII 2006*[1]	ESDF	7 699 697	3 156 172	41.0	3 755 408	1 544 515	41.1	3 944 289	1 611 657	40.9
1 VII 2007*[1]	ESDF	7 958 813	3 324 220	41.8	3 886 596	1 628 650	41.9	4 072 217	1 695 570	41.6
1 VII 2008*[1]	ESDF	8 224 642	3 499 506	42.5	4 021 094	1 716 411	42.7	4 203 548	1 783 095	42.4
1 VII 2009*[1]	ESDF	8 497 827	3 682 496	43.3	4 159 291	1 808 057	43.5	4 338 536	1 874 439	43.2
1 VII 2010*[1]	ESDF	8 778 648	3 873 462	44.1	4 301 224	1 903 683	44.3	4 477 424	1 969 779	44.0
Botswana										
1 VII 2001	ESDJ	1 622 129	...	...	780 547	...	...	841 582	...	...
17 VIII 2001	CDFC	1 680 863	910 480[2]	54.2	813 625	428 856[2]	52.7	867 238	481 624[2]	55.5
1 VII 2002	ESDJ	1 649 659	375 461	22.8	795 938	...	...	853 721	...	...
1 VII 2003	ESDJ	1 673 184	384 940	23.0	809 278	...	...	863 906	...	...
1 VII 2004	ESDJ	1 692 731	393 528	23.2	820 577	191 287	23.3	872 155	202 241	23.2
1 VII 2005	ESDJ	1 708 327	...	...	829 850	...	...	878 477	...	...
1 VII 2006	ESDJ	1 719 996	...	...	837 114	...	...	882 882	...	...
1 VIII 2006	SSDJ	1 773 240	1 000 443[2]	56.4	851 670	473 136[2]	55.6	921 570	527 307[2]	57.2
1 VII 2007	ESDJ	1 736 396	...	...	847 539	...	...	888 857	...	...
1 VII 2008	ESDJ	1 755 246	...	...	859 167	...	...	896 079	...	...
1 VII 2009	ESDJ	1 776 494	...	...	871 964	...	...	904 530	...	...
1 VII 2010	ESDJ	1 822 859	439 098	24.1	895 007	215 739	24.1	927 852	223 359	24.1
Burkina Faso										
1 VII 2001	ESDJ	11 816 668	1 848 126[3]	15.6	5 700 266	936 565[3]	16.4	6 116 402	911 561[3]	14.9
1 VII 2002	ESDJ	12 184 859	1 902 225[3]	15.6	5 878 933	964 067[3]	16.4	6 305 926	938 158[3]	14.9
1 VII 2003	ESDJ	12 566 683	1 958 013[3]	15.6	6 064 260	992 431[3]	16.4	6 502 423	965 582[3]	14.8
1 VII 2004	ESDJ	12 962 750	2 015 546[3]	15.5	6 256 552	1 021 683[3]	16.3	6 706 198	993 863[3]	14.8
1 VII 2005	ESDJ	13 373 670	2 074 879[3]	15.5	6 456 103	1 051 853[3]	16.3	6 917 567	1 023 026[3]	14.8
1 VII 2006	ESDJ	14 017 262	3 181 967	22.7	6 768 739	1 588 895	23.5	7 248 523	1 593 072	22.0
9 XII 2006	CDJC	14 196 259	3 230 504	22.8	6 842 560	1 609 349	23.5	7 353 699	1 621 155	22.0
1 VII 2007[1]	ESDJ	14 252 012	3 322 360	23.3	6 880 824	1 629 956	23.7	7 371 188	1 692 404	23.0
1 VII 2008[1]	ESDJ	14 731 167	3 520 744[3]	23.9	7 110 097	1 699 313[3]	23.9	7 621 070	1 821 431[3]	23.9
1 VII 2009[1]	ESDJ	15 224 780	...	...	7 346 835	...	...	7 877 945	...	...
1 VII 2010[1]	ESDJ	15 730 977	...	...	7 590 133	...	...	8 140 844	...	...
Burundi										
1 VII 2001	ESDF	6 847 007	...	...	3 336 727	...	...	3 510 280	...	...
1 VII 2002	ESDF	7 032 178	...	...	3 428 453	...	...	3 603 725	...	...
1 VII 2003	ESDF	7 211 356	...	...	3 515 469	...	...	3 695 887	...	...
1 VII 2004	ESDF	7 384 423	...	...	3 599 838	...	...	3 784 585	...	...
16 VIII 2008	CDFC	7 877 728	799 802	10.2	3 838 045	432 442	11.3	4 039 683	367 360	9.1
Cameroon - Cameroun										
1 VII 2001[1]	ESDF	15 731 000	8 023 000	51.0		...			...	
1 VII 2002[1]	ESDF	16 170 000	8 392 000	51.9		...			...	
1 VII 2003[1]	ESDF	16 626 000	8 779 000	52.8		...			...	
1 VII 2004[1]	ESDF	17 000 000	9 086 000	53.4		...			...	
11 XI 2005	CDFC	17 052 134	...	...	8 408 495			8 643 639		
1 VII 2007[1]	ESDJ	18 674 600	...	...	9 218 700			9 455 900		
1 VII 2010*[1]	ESDJ	19 406 100	10 091 172	52.0	9 599 224	5 029 993	52.4	9 806 876	5 061 179	51.6
Cape Verde - Cap-Vert										
1 VII 2001	ESDF	444 921	248 557	55.9	215 352	...	...	229 569	...	...
1 VII 2002	ESDF	452 835	256 172	56.6	219 177	...	...	233 658	...	...
1 VII 2003	ESDF	460 601	263 791	57.3	222 911	...	...	237 690	...	...
1 VII 2004	ESDF	468 164	271 415	58.0	226 560	...	...	241 604	...	...
1 VII 2005	ESDF	475 465	278 947	58.7	230 063	...	...	245 402	...	...
1 VII 2006	ESDF	483 090	286 687	59.3	233 729	...	...	249 361	...	...
1 VII 2007	ESDF	491 419	295 046	60.0	237 842	...	...	253 577	...	...
1 VII 2008	ESDF	499 796	303 512	60.7	241 914	...	...	257 882	...	...
1 VII 2009	ESDF	508 633	310 958	61.1	246 219	...	...	262 414	...	...

Continent, country or area, and date / Continent, pays ou zone et date	Code[a]	Both sexes - Les deux sexes			Male - Masculin			Female - Féminin		
			Urban - Urbaine			Urban - Urbaine			Urban - Urbaine	
		Total	Number Nombre	Percent P.100	Total	Number Nombre	Percent P.100	Total	Number Nombre	Percent P.100
AFRICA - AFRIQUE										
Cape Verde - Cap-Vert										
16 VI 2010*	CDJC	491 575	...	...	243 315	...	...	248 260	...	...
1 VII 2010	ESDF	517 831	320 111	61.8	250 710	...	...	267 121	...	...
Central African Republic - République centrafricaine										
8 XII 2003	CDFC	3 151 072	1 194 851	37.9	1 569 446	598 880	38.2	1 581 626	595 969	37.7
Comoros - Comores										
1 IX 2003	CDFC	575 660[4]	160 865	27.9	...			...		
Côte d'Ivoire[1]										
1 VII 2001*	ESDF	16 928 324	...	...	8 640 645			8 287 679		
1 VII 2002*	ESDF	17 461 446	...	...	8 911 589			8 549 847		
1 VII 2003*	ESDF	18 000 876	...	...	9 185 371			8 815 505		
1 VII 2004*	ESDF	18 545 968	...	...	9 461 594			9 084 374		
1 VII 2005*	ESDF	19 096 988	...	...	9 740 427			9 356 561		
1 VII 2006*	ESDF	19 657 738	...	...	10 023 964			9 633 774		
1 VII 2007*	ESDF	20 227 876	...	...	10 312 061			9 915 815		
1 VII 2008*	ESDF	20 807 216			10 604 596			10 202 620		
1 VII 2009*	ESDF	21 395 198			10 901 322			10 493 876		
Egypt - Égypte										
1 VII 2001	ESDF	65 298 293	28 168 172	43.1	33 378 636	...	...	31 919 657	...	...
1 VII 2002	ESDF	66 627 610	28 553 755	42.9	34 052 407	...	...	32 575 203	...	...
1 VII 2003	ESDF	67 965 096	29 130 214	42.9	34 720 973	...	...	33 244 123	...	...
1 VII 2004	ESDF	69 303 902	29 652 904	42.8	35 379 626	...	...	33 924 276	...	...
1 VII 2005	ESDF	70 653 326	30 187 331	42.7	36 037 030	...	...	34 616 296	...	...
1 VII 2006	ESDF	72 008 900	30 699 375	42.6	36 725 501	...	...	35 283 399	...	...
21 XI 2006	CDFC	72 798 031	31 370 925	43.1	37 219 056	16 013 864	43.0	35 578 975	15 357 061	43.2
1 VII 2007	ESDF	73 643 587	31 719 927	43.1	37 643 353	16 186 484	43.0	36 000 234	15 533 443	43.1
1 VII 2008	ESDF	75 229 020	32 352 857	43.0	38 459 709	16 514 069	42.9	36 769 311	15 838 788	43.1
1 VII 2009	ESDF	76 925 139	33 082 770	43.0	39 327 098	16 887 176	42.9	37 598 041	16 195 594	43.1
1 VII 2010*	ESDF	78 728 329	33 833 191	43.0	40 250 440	17 270 570	42.9	38 477 889	16 562 621	43.0
Equatorial Guinea - Guinée équatoriale										
1 II 2002	CDFC	1 014 999	...	...	501 387	...	...	513 612	...	...
Ethiopia - Éthiopie										
1 VII 2001[5]	ESDF	65 374 320	9 883 138	15.1	32 815 082	4 938 725	15.1	32 559 238	4 944 413	15.2
1 VII 2002[5]	ESDF	67 220 000	10 307 000	15.3	33 707 000	5 134 000	15.2	33 513 000	5 173 000	15.4
1 VII 2003[5]	ESDF	69 127 000	10 745 000	15.5	34 653 000	5 347 000	15.4	34 474 000	5 398 000	15.7
1 VII 2004[5]	ESDF	71 066 000	11 199 000	15.8	35 618 000	5 568 000	15.6	35 448 000	5 631 000	15.9
1 VII 2005[5]	ESDF	73 043 510	11 674 521	16.0	36 604 591	5 802 931	15.9	36 438 919	5 871 590	16.1
1 VII 2006[5]	ESDF	75 067 000	12 172 000	16.2	37 615 000	6 050 000	16.1	37 452 000	6 122 000	16.3
29 V 2007	CDFC	73 750 932	11 862 821	16.1	37 217 130	5 895 916	15.8	36 533 802	5 966 905	16.3
1 VII 2008[5]	ESDF	79 221 000	13 225 000	16.7	39 691 000	6 575 000	16.6	39 530 000	6 650 000	16.8
Gabon[6]										
1 VII 2005	ESDF	1 312 500	...	...	645 700	...	...	666 700	...	...
Gambia - Gambie										
15 IV 2003*	CDFC	1 364 507	...	...	676 726	...	...	687 781	...	...
Ghana										
1 VII 2001	ESDF	19 397 482	...	...	9 599 088	...	...	9 798 394	...	...
1 VII 2002	ESDF	19 883 276	...	...	9 840 849	...	...	10 042 427	...	...
1 VII 2003	ESDF	20 370 643	...	...	10 083 283	...	...	10 287 360	...	...
1 VII 2004	ESDF	20 859 482	...	...	10 326 358	...	...	10 533 124	...	...
1 VII 2005	ESDF	21 367 006	...	...	10 579 368	...	...	10 787 638	...	...
1 VII 2006	ESDF	21 876 031	...	...	10 833 033	...	...	11 042 998	...	...
1 VII 2007	ESDF	22 387 911	...	...	11 088 060	...	...	11 299 851	...	...
1 VII 2008	ESDF	22 900 927	...	...	11 343 581	...	...	11 557 346	...	...
1 VII 2009	ESDF	23 416 518	10 243 312	43.7	11 600 326	5 006 198	43.2	11 816 192	5 237 114	44.3
26 IX 2010*	CDFC	24 223 431	...	...	11 801 661	...	...	12 421 770	...	...
Guinea - Guinée[1]										
1 VII 2008	ESDF	10 182 926	2 851 219	28.0	...	...	...	...	...	...
1 VII 2009	ESDF	10 217 591	...	...	5 038 823	...	...	5 178 768	...	...

Continent, country or area, and date / Continent, pays ou zone et date	Code[a]	Both sexes - Les deux sexes			Male - Masculin			Female - Féminin		
		Total	Urban - Urbaine		Total	Urban - Urbaine		Total	Urban - Urbaine	
			Number Nombre	Percent P.100		Number Nombre	Percent P.100		Number Nombre	Percent P.100
AFRICA - AFRIQUE										
Guinea-Bissau - Guinée-Bissau										
15 III 2009	CDFC	1 520 830	...	...	737 634	...	...	783 196	...	...
Kenya										
1 VII 2001[7]	ESDF	31 120 677	5 421 964	17.4	15 341 600	3 209 419	20.9	15 779 077	2 212 546	14.0
1 VII 2002[7]	ESDF	32 117 987	5 613 669	17.5	15 850 411	3 325 186	21.0	16 267 576	2 288 483	14.1
1 VII 2003[7]	ESDF	33 141 617	5 809 612	17.5	16 372 798	3 443 644	21.0	16 768 819	2 365 968	14.1
1 VII 2004[7]	ESDF	34 191 382	6 009 718	17.6	16 908 648	3 564 746	21.1	17 282 734	2 444 972	14.1
1 VII 2005[7]	ESDF	35 267 222	6 213 505	17.6	17 457 906	3 688 113	21.1	17 809 316	2 525 392	14.2
1 VII 2006[7]	ESDF	36 432 866	...	...	18 052 944	...	...	18 379 922	...	...
1 VII 2007[7]	ESDF	37 183 923	...	...	18 440 822	...	...	18 743 102	...	...
24 VIII 2009*	CDFC	38 610 097	12 487 375	32.3	19 192 458	6 278 811	32.7	19 417 639	6 208 564	32.0
Lesotho										
1 VII 2001	SSDJ	2 157 537	288 895	13.4	1 065 484	131 861	12.4	1 092 053	157 034	14.4
13 IV 2006	CDFC	1 741 406	403 104	23.1	818 379	181 351	22.2	923 027	221 753	24.0
Liberia - Libéria										
21 III 2008	CDFC	3 476 608	1 633 719	47.0	1 739 945	802 092	46.1	1 736 663	831 627	47.9
Libya - Libye										
1 VII 2001[8]	ESDF	5 299 943	...	...	2 682 254	...	...	2 617 689	...	...
1 VII 2002[8]	ESDF	5 484 426	...	...	2 773 333	...	...	2 711 093	...	...
15 IV 2006*[9]	CDFC	5 657 692	...	...	2 934 452	...	...	2 723 240	...	...
Madagascar										
1 VII 2001	ESDF	15 529 000	4 122 000	26.5	...	...	...	...	...	...
1 VII 2002	ESDF	15 981 000	4 327 000	27.1	...	...	...	...	...	...
1 VII 2003	ESDF	16 441 000	4 544 000	27.6	...	...	...	...	...	...
1 VII 2004	ESDF	17 206 280	4 232 745	24.6	...	...	...	...	...	...
Malawi										
1 VII 2001[1]	ESDF	10 816 294	1 300 093	12.0	5 307 972	675 613	12.7	5 508 322	624 480	11.3
1 VII 2002[1]	ESDF	11 174 648	1 375 794	12.3	5 486 254	713 513	13.0	5 688 394	662 281	11.6
1 VII 2003[1]	ESDF	11 548 841	1 453 771	12.6	5 672 569	752 544	13.3	5 876 272	701 227	11.9
1 VII 2004[1]	ESDF	11 937 934	1 533 930	12.8	5 866 462	792 661	13.5	6 071 472	741 269	12.2
1 VII 2005[1]	ESDF	12 341 170	1 616 169[10]	13.1	6 067 563	833 812[10]	13.7	6 273 607	782 357[10]	12.5
1 VII 2006[1]	ESDF	12 757 883	1 700 379	13.3	6 275 533	875 943	14.0	6 482 350	824 436	12.7
1 VII 2007[1]	ESDF	13 187 632	1 786 434	13.5	6 490 146	918 991	14.2	6 697 486	867 443	13.0
8 VI 2008	CDFC	13 077 160	2 003 309	15.3	6 358 933	1 014 477	16.0	6 718 227	988 832	14.7
1 VII 2008[1]	ESDF	13 630 164	1 874 199[10]	13.8	6 711 263	962 887[10]	14.3	6 918 901	911 312[10]	13.2
Mali										
1 I 2001	ESDF	10 524 600	3 018 079	28.7	5 209 227	1 511 556	29.0	5 315 375	1 506 523	28.3
1 I 2002	ESDF	10 813 478	3 176 399	29.4	5 352 318	1 590 701	29.7	5 461 160	1 585 697	29.0
1 I 2003	ESDF	11 111 219	3 344 066	30.1	5 499 912	1 674 538	30.4	5 611 305	1 669 528	29.8
1 I 2004	ESDF	11 419 483	3 522 033	30.8	5 652 867	1 763 554	31.2	5 766 615	1 758 478	30.5
1 I 2005	ESDF	11 732 416	3 707 315	31.6	5 808 166	1 856 224	32.0	5 924 252	1 851 091	31.2
1 I 2006	ESDF	12 051 021	3 900 404	32.4	5 966 339	1 952 802	32.7	6 084 681	1 947 601	32.0
1 I 2007	ESDF	12 377 542	4 102 223	33.1	6 128 544	2 053 767	33.5	6 248 999	2 048 456	32.8
1 IV 2009*	CDJC	14 517 176	...	...	7 202 744	...	...	7 314 432	...	...
Mauritania - Mauritanie[1]										
1 VII 2005	ESDF	2 905 727	...	...	1 450 418	...	...	1 455 309	...	...
1 VII 2008	ESDF	3 162 338	...	...	1 584 913	...	...	1 577 425	...	...
Mauritius - Maurice[11]										
1 VII 2001	ESDJ	1 199 881	510 822	42.6	594 490	251 721	42.3	605 391	259 101	42.8
1 VII 2002	ESDJ	1 210 203	513 761	42.5	599 165	252 848	42.2	611 038	260 913	42.7
1 VII 2003	ESDJ	1 222 811	518 368	42.4	605 084	255 077	42.2	617 727	263 291	42.6
1 VII 2004	ESDJ	1 233 386	521 588	42.3	610 108	256 542	42.0	623 278	265 046	42.5
1 VII 2005	ESDJ	1 243 253	524 318	42.2	614 786	257 785	41.9	628 467	266 533	42.4
1 VII 2006	ESDJ	1 252 698	527 138	42.1	619 243	259 028	41.8	633 455	268 110	42.3
1 VII 2007	ESDJ	1 260 403	528 961	42.0	622 926	259 800	41.7	637 477	269 161	42.2
1 VII 2008	ESDJ	1 268 565	531 097	41.9	626 556	260 675	41.6	642 009	270 422	42.1
1 VII 2009[12]	ESDJ	1 275 032	532 591	41.8	629 157	261 041	41.5	645 875	271 550	42.0
1 VII 2010[12]	ESDJ	1 280 924	...	...	631 692	...	...	649 232	...	...
Mayotte										
30 VII 2002	CDJC	160 301	...	...	80 281	...	...	80 020	...	...
31 VII 2007	CDJC	186 387	...	...	91 405	...	...	94 982	...	...
Morocco - Maroc										
1 VII 2001	ESDF	29 170 000	16 307 000	55.9	14 512 000	8 000 000	55.1	14 658 000	8 307 000	56.7
1 VII 2002	ESDF	29 631 000	16 772 000	56.6	14 742 000	8 217 000	55.7	14 889 000	8 555 000	57.5

Continent, country or area, and date / Continent, pays ou zone et date	Code[a]	Both sexes - Les deux sexes			Male - Masculin			Female - Féminin		
		Total	Urban - Urbaine Number Nombre	Urban - Urbaine Percent P.100	Total	Urban - Urbaine Number Nombre	Urban - Urbaine Percent P.100	Total	Urban - Urbaine Number Nombre	Urban - Urbaine Percent P.100
AFRICA - AFRIQUE										
Morocco - Maroc										
1 VII 2003	ESDF	30 088 000	17 244 000	57.3	14 972 000	8 438 000	56.4	15 116 000	8 806 000	58.3
1 VII 2004[13]	ESDF	29 840 000	16 433 000	55.1	14 820 000	8 126 000	54.8	15 020 000	8 307 000	55.3
1 IX 2004	CDFC	29 680 069	16 339 561	55.1	14 640 662	8 022 273	54.8	15 039 407	8 317 288	55.3
1 VII 2005[13]	ESDF	30 172 000	16 755 000	55.5	14 961 000	8 273 000	55.3	15 211 000	8 482 000	55.8
1 VII 2006[13]	ESDF	30 506 000	17 079 000	56.0	15 103 000	8 422 000	55.8	15 403 000	8 657 000	56.2
1 VII 2007[13]	ESDF	30 841 000	17 404 000	56.4	15 246 000	8 572 000	56.2	15 595 000	8 832 000	56.6
1 VII 2008[13]	ESDF	31 177 000	17 730 000	56.9	15 391 000	8 722 000	56.7	15 786 000	9 008 000	57.1
1 VII 2009[13]	ESDF	31 514 000	18 059 000	57.3	15 539 000	8 873 000	57.1	15 975 000	9 186 000	57.5
1 VII 2010[13]	ESDF	31 851 000	18 389 000	57.7	15 684 000	9 025 000	57.5	16 167 000	9 364 000	57.9
Mozambique										
1 VII 2001[1]	ESDF	17 653 239	...	...	8 486 603	...	...	9 166 636	...	...
1 VII 2002[1]	ESDF	18 077 570	...	...	8 698 020	...	...	9 379 550	...	...
1 VII 2003[1]	ESDF	18 513 826	...	...	8 915 639	...	...	9 598 187	...	...
1 VII 2004[1]	ESDF	18 961 503	5 828 150	30.7	9 139 205	2 909 903	31.8	9 822 298	2 918 247	29.7
1 VII 2005[1]	ESDF	19 420 036	6 022 319	31.0	9 368 425	3 009 531	32.1	10 051 611	3 012 788	30.0
1 VII 2006[1]	ESDF	19 888 701	...	...	9 603 031	...	...	10 285 670	...	...
1 VII 2007[1]	ESDF	20 366 795	...	...	9 842 760	...	...	10 524 035	...	...
1 VIII 2007	CDFC	20 252 223	6 151 974	30.4	9 746 690	3 021 756	31.0	10 505 533	3 130 218	29.8
1 VII 2008[1]	ESDF	20 854 057	...	...	10 087 479	...	...	10 766 578	...	...
1 VII 2009[1]	ESDF	21 350 008	...	...	10 336 944	...	...	11 013 064	...	...
1 VII 2010[1]	ESDF	21 854 387	...	...	10 591 020	...	...	11 263 367	...	...
Namibia - Namibie										
1 VII 2001[1]	ESDF	1 830 290	...	...	887 721	...	...	942 569	...	...
27 VIII 2001	CDFC	1 830 330	603 612	33.0	887 721[14]	300 358[14]	33.8	942 572[14]	303 236[14]	32.2
1 VII 2002[1]	ESDF	1 860 145	...	...	903 107	...	...	957 038	...	...
1 VII 2003[1]	ESDF	1 891 098	...	...	919 031	...	...	972 067	...	...
1 VII 2004[1]	ESDF	1 923 346	...	...	935 590	...	...	987 756	...	...
1 VII 2005[1]	ESDF	1 956 900	...	...	952 788	...	...	1 004 112	...	...
1 VII 2006[1]	ESDF	1 991 747	...	...	970 617	...	...	1 021 130	...	...
1 VII 2007[1]	ESDF	2 027 871	...	...	989 067	...	...	1 038 804	...	...
1 VII 2008[1]	ESDF	2 065 226	...	...	1 008 115	...	...	1 057 111	...	...
1 VII 2009[1]	ESDF	2 103 761	...	...	1 027 736	...	...	1 076 025	...	...
1 VII 2010[1]	ESDF	2 143 410	...	...	1 047 900	...	...	1 095 510	...	...
Niger										
20 V 2001	CDJC	11 060 291	1 798 501	16.3	5 516 588	899 764	16.3	5 543 703	898 737	16.2
1 VII 2001[1]	ESDJ	11 090 256	1 804 243	16.3	5 531 534	902 637	16.3	5 558 722	901 606	16.2
1 VII 2002[1]	ESDJ	11 456 235	1 863 783	16.3	5 714 075	932 424	16.3	5 742 160	931 359	16.2
1 VII 2003[1]	ESDJ	11 834 290	1 925 288	16.3	5 902 639	963 194	16.3	5 931 651	962 094	16.2
1 VII 2004[1]	ESDJ	12 224 822	1 988 822	16.3	6 097 426	994 979	16.3	6 127 396	993 843	16.2
1 VII 2005[1]	ESDJ	12 628 241	2 054 453	16.3	6 298 641	1 027 814	16.3	6 329 600	1 026 640	16.2
1 VII 2006[1]	ESDJ	13 044 973	2 184 605	16.7	6 506 496	1 092 927	16.8	6 538 477	1 091 678	16.7
1 VII 2007[1]	ESDJ	13 716 233	2 556 499	18.6	6 851 314	1 280 155	18.7	6 864 919	1 276 344	18.6
1 VII 2008[1]	ESDJ	14 197 601	2 728 541	19.2	7 091 818	1 366 304	19.3	7 105 783	1 362 237	19.2
1 VII 2009[1]	ESDJ	14 693 112	2 911 006	19.8	7 339 392	1 458 250	19.9	7 353 720	1 452 756	19.8
1 VII 2010[1]	ESDJ	15 203 822	3 104 574	20.4	7 594 565	1 555 187	20.5	7 609 257	1 549 387	20.4
Nigeria - Nigéria										
1 VII 2001[1]	ESDF	118 800 696	...	...	59 538 640	...	...	59 262 056	...	...
1 VII 2002[1]	ESDF	122 443 748	...	...	61 369 212	...	...	61 074 536	...	...
1 VII 2003[1]	ESDF	126 152 844	...	...	63 241 808	...	...	62 911 036	...	...
1 VII 2004[1]	ESDF	129 175 000	...	...	64 459 000	...	...	64 716 000	...	...
1 VII 2005[1]	ESDF	133 767 000	...	...	67 111 000	...	...	66 656 000	...	...
21 III 2006	CDFC	140 431 790	...	...	71 345 488	...	...	69 086 302	...	...
Réunion										
1 VII 2001	ESDJ	734 609	...	...	359 576	...	...	375 033	...	...
1 VII 2002	ESDJ	745 524	...	...	364 178	...	...	381 346	...	...
1 VII 2003	ESDJ	756 235	...	...	368 715	...	...	387 521	...	...
1 VII 2004	ESDJ	767 269	...	...	373 532	...	...	393 737	...	...
1 VII 2005	ESDJ	777 435	...	...	377 593	...	...	399 842	...	...
1 I 2006	CDJC	781 962	...	...	379 176	...	...	402 786	...	...
1 VII 2006	ESDJ	786 231	...	...	381 030	...	...	405 202	...	...
1 I 2007*	ESDJ	790 500	...	...	382 883	...	...	407 617	...	...
1 I 2008*	ESDJ	805 500	...	...	390 645	...	...	414 855	...	...

Continent, country or area, and date / Continent, pays ou zone et date	Code[a]	Both sexes - Les deux sexes			Male - Masculin			Female - Féminin		
		Total	Urban - Urbaine		Total	Urban - Urbaine		Total	Urban - Urbaine	
			Number Nombre	Percent P.100		Number Nombre	Percent P.100		Number Nombre	Percent P.100
AFRICA - AFRIQUE										
Rwanda										
16 VIII 2002	CDJC	8 128 553	1 372 604	16.9	3 879 448	727 172	18.7	4 249 105	645 432	15.2
1 VII 2007	ESDF	9 556 669	...	...	4 597 277	...	...	4 959 393	...	...
1 VII 2008	ESDF	9 831 501	...	...	4 736 104	...	...	5 095 397	...	...
1 VII 2009	ESDF	10 117 029	...	...	4 880 233	...	...	5 236 796	...	...
1 VII 2010	ESDF	10 412 820	...	...	5 029 450	...	...	5 383 371	...	...
Saint Helena ex. dep. - Sainte-Hélène sans dép.										
10 II 2008*	CDFC	4 255	...	...	2 166	...	...	2 089	...	...
1 VII 2008[15]	ESDF	3 981	...	...	2 022	...	...	1 959	...	...
Saint Helena: Ascension - Sainte-Hélène: Ascension										
1 VII 2008	ESDJ	702	...	...	397	...	...	305	...	...
Saint Helena: Tristan da Cunha - Sainte-Hélène: Tristan da Cunha[16]										
31 XII 2009	ESDF	262[17]	...	...	123	...	...	139	...	...
Sao Tome and Principe - Sao Tomé-et-Principe										
25 VIII 2001	CDFC	136 554	73 907	54.1	67 422	35 679	52.9	69 132	38 228	55.3
1 VII 2002	ESDF	140 365	...	...	69 515	...	...	70 850	...	...
1 VII 2003	ESDF	143 186	...	...	70 821	...	...	72 365	...	...
1 VII 2004	ESDF	146 056	...	...	72 153	...	...	73 903	...	...
1 VII 2005	ESDF	148 968	...	...	73 506	...	...	75 462	...	...
1 VII 2006	ESDF	151 912	...	...	74 876	...	...	77 036	...	...
1 VII 2007	ESDF	154 875	...	...	76 256	...	...	78 619	...	...
1 VII 2008	ESDF	157 847	...	...	77 641	...	...	80 206	...	...
Senegal - Sénégal										
1 VII 2001	ESDJ	9 666 715	...	...	4 740 557	...	...	4 926 158	...	...
8 XII 2002	CDFC	9 555 346	3 938 299[3]	41.2	4 672 015	1 939 894[3]	41.5	4 883 331	1 998 405[3]	40.9
31 XII 2003[18]	ESDJ	9 858 482	4 008 965	40.7	4 852 764	1 987 500	41.0	5 005 718	2 021 465	40.4
31 XII 2003[18]	ESDJ	10 317 339	4 195 560	40.7	5 078 633	2 080 007	41.0	5 238 706	2 115 553	40.4
31 XII 2004[18]	ESDJ	10 604 970	4 312 525	40.7	5 220 217	2 137 994	41.0	5 384 753	2 174 531	40.4
31 XII 2005[18]	ESDJ	10 901 006	4 432 909	40.7	5 365 938	2 197 676	41.0	5 535 068	2 235 233	40.4
31 XII 2006[18]	ESDJ	11 205 774	4 556 843	40.7	5 515 959	2 259 118	41.0	5 689 815	2 297 725	40.4
31 XII 2007[18]	ESDJ	11 519 242	4 684 315	40.7	5 670 261	2 322 314	41.0	5 848 981	2 362 001	40.4
31 XII 2008[18]	ESDJ	11 841 137	4 815 214	40.7	5 828 711	2 387 209	41.0	6 012 426	2 428 005	40.4
31 XII 2009[18]	ESDJ	12 171 264	4 949 461	40.7	5 991 214	2 453 764	41.0	6 180 050	2 495 697	40.4
31 XII 2010[18]	ESDJ	12 509 434	5 086 978	40.7	6 157 675	2 521 940	41.0	6 351 759	2 565 038	40.4
Seychelles										
1 VII 2001	ESDF	81 202	...	...	39 973	...	...	41 229	...	...
1 VII 2002	ESDF	83 723	...	...	41 990	...	...	41 733	...	...
26 VIII 2002[19]	CDJC	81 755	...	...	40 751	...	...	41 004	...	...
1 VII 2003	ESDF	82 781	...	...	40 859	...	...	41 922	...	...
1 VII 2004	ESDF	82 475	...	...	40 652	...	...	41 823	...	...
1 VII 2005	ESDF	82 852	...	...	41 233	...	...	41 619	...	...
1 VII 2006	ESDF	84 600	...	...	42 875	...	...	41 725	...	...
1 VII 2007	ESDF	85 032	...	...	43 160	...	...	41 872	...	...
1 VII 2008	ESDF	86 956	...	...	44 999	...	...	41 957	...	...
1 VII 2009	ESDF	87 298	...	...	45 022	...	...	42 276	...	...
1 VII 2010	ESDF	86 525	...	...	44 253	...	...	42 272	...	...
Sierra Leone										
1 VII 2001	ESDF	5 054 476	1 818 044	36.0	...	...	...	...	...	...
1 VII 2002	ESDF	5 166 508	1 864 177	36.1	...	...	...	...	...	...
1 VII 2003	ESDF	5 280 406	1 910 779	36.2	...	...	...	...	...	...
4 XII 2004	CDFC	4 976 871	...	...	2 420 218	...	...	2 556 653	...	...
1 VII 2005	ESDF	5 094 500	1 934 235	38.0	2 468 832	955 441	38.7	2 625 668	978 794	37.3
1 VII 2006	ESDF	5 216 890	1 999 707	38.3	2 528 430	987 782	39.1	2 688 460	1 011 925	37.6
1 VII 2007*	ESDF	5 343 200	2 069 160	38.7	2 589 965	1 022 089	39.5	2 753 235	1 047 071	38.0
1 VII 2008	ESDF	5 473 530	2 142 918	39.2	2 653 490	1 058 523	39.9	2 820 040	1 084 395	38.5
1 VII 2009	ESDF	5 607 930	2 221 331	39.6	2 719 034	1 097 256	40.4	2 888 896	1 124 075	38.9
1 VII 2010	ESDF	5 746 800	2 304 955	40.1	2 786 797	1 138 563	40.9	2 960 003	1 166 392	39.4

Continent, country or area, and date / Continent, pays ou zone et date	Code[a]	Both sexes - Les deux sexes			Male - Masculin			Female - Féminin		
		Total	Urban - Urbaine		Total	Urban - Urbaine		Total	Urban - Urbaine	
			Number Nombre	Percent P.100		Number Nombre	Percent P.100		Number Nombre	Percent P.100
AFRICA - AFRIQUE										
Somalia - Somalie[20]										
1 VII 2002	SSDF	6 799 079	2 310 817	34.0	3 499 523	1 168 410	33.4	3 299 556	1 142 407	34.6
South Africa - Afrique du Sud										
1 VII 2001[21]	ESDF	44 928 796	23 501 443[3]	52.3	21 537 608	11 439 101[3]	53.1	23 391 188	12 062 342[3]	51.6
10 X 2001	CDFC	44 819 778	...	...	21 434 041	...	...	23 385 737	...	...
1 VII 2002[21]	ESDF	45 587 115	23 888 278[3]	52.4	21 863 840	11 612 775[3]	53.1	23 723 275	12 275 503[3]	51.7
1 VII 2003[21]	ESDF	46 205 956	...	...	22 171 021	...	...	24 034 935	...	...
1 VII 2004[21]	ESDF	46 787 089	...	...	22 461 706	...	...	24 325 383	...	...
1 VII 2005[21]	ESDF	47 335 091	...	...	22 738 921	...	...	24 596 170	...	...
1 VII 2006[21]	ESDF	47 837 137	...	...	22 996 401	...	...	24 840 736	...	...
1 VII 2007[21]	ESDF	48 287 320	...	...	23 231 447	...	...	25 055 873	...	...
1 VII 2008[21]	ESDF	48 687 000	...	...	23 444 800	...	...	25 242 200	...	...
1 VII 2009[21]	ESDF	49 320 500	...	...	23 868 700	...	...	25 451 800	...	...
1 VII 2010[21]	ESDF	49 991 300	...	...	24 329 000	...	...	25 662 300	...	...
Sudan - Soudan										
1 VII 2001	ESDF	31 626 526	...	...	16 014 575	...	...	15 611 951	...	...
1 VII 2002	ESDF	32 468 401	...	...	16 440 837	...	...	16 027 564	...	...
1 VII 2003	ESDF	33 333 648	...	...	16 793 306	...	...	16 540 342	...	...
1 VII 2004	ESDF	34 512 000	...	...	17 390 000	...	...	17 122 000	...	...
21 IV 2008*	CDFC	39 154 490	...	...	20 073 977	...	...	19 080 513	...	...
Swaziland										
11 III 2007	CDFC	844 223	186 890	22.1	405 868	93 918	23.1	438 355	92 972	21.2
Tunisia - Tunisie										
1 VII 2002	ESDF	9 748 900	...	...	4 907 100	...	...	4 841 800	...	...
1 VII 2003	ESDF	9 839 800	...	...	4 933 600	...	...	4 906 200	...	...
28 IV 2004	CDFC	9 910 872	6 429 500[22]	64.9	4 965 435	...	...	4 945 437	...	...
1 VII 2004	ESDF	9 932 400	...	...	4 976 200	...	...	4 956 200	...	...
1 VII 2005	ESDF	10 029 000	...	...	5 020 000	...	...	5 009 000	...	...
1 VII 2006	ESDF	10 127 900	...	...	5 062 100	...	...	5 065 800	...	...
1 VII 2007	ESDF	10 225 100	...	...	5 105 100	...	...	5 120 000	...	...
1 VII 2008	ESDF	10 328 900	...	...	5 156 300	...	...	5 172 600	...	...
Uganda - Ouganda										
1 VII 2001	ESDF	22 787 000	3 789 000	16.6	11 306 000	1 824 000	16.1	11 481 000	1 965 000	17.1
1 VII 2002	ESDF	24 067 187	2 953 381	12.3	11 747 193	1 427 448	12.2	12 319 994	1 525 933	12.4
12 IX 2002	CDFC	24 442 084	2 999 387	12.3	11 929 803	1 449 684	12.2	12 512 281	1 549 703	12.4
1 VII 2003	ESDF	25 089 400	3 708 800	14.8	12 146 100	1 775 300	14.6	12 943 300	1 933 500	14.9
1 VII 2004	ESDF	25 895 700	3 829 000	14.8	12 532 100	1 830 600	14.6	13 363 600	1 998 400	15.0
1 VII 2005	ESDF	26 741 300	3 953 200	14.8	12 944 800	1 889 800	14.6	13 796 500	2 063 400	15.0
1 VII 2006	ESDF	27 629 300	4 084 700	14.8	13 386 100	1 953 300	14.6	14 243 200	2 131 400	15.0
1 VII 2007	ESDF	28 581 300	4 223 800	14.8	13 866 700	2 022 200	14.6	14 714 600	2 201 600	15.0
1 VII 2008	ESDF	29 592 600	4 372 000	14.8	14 383 200	2 095 700	14.6	15 209 400	2 276 300	15.0
1 VII 2009	ESDF	30 661 300	4 524 900	14.8	14 933 900	2 171 400	14.5	15 727 400	2 353 500	15.0
United Republic of Tanzania - République Unie de Tanzanie										
24 VIII 2002*	CDFC	34 443 603	...	...	16 829 861	...	...	17 613 742	...	...
Zambia - Zambie										
16 X 2010*	CDFC	13 046 508	5 068 234	38.8	6 394 455	...	...	6 652 053	...	...
Zimbabwe										
17 VIII 2002	CDFC	11 631 657	4 029 707	34.6	5 634 180	1 988 176	35.3	5 997 477	2 041 531	34.0
1 VII 2003[18]	ESDF	11 640 000	4 032 597	34.6	5 638 152	1 989 577	35.3	6 001 848	2 043 019	34.0
1 VII 2004[18]	ESDF	11 730 000	4 063 777	34.6	5 681 745	2 004 961	35.3	6 048 255	2 058 816	34.0
1 VII 2005[18]	ESDF	11 830 000	4 098 422	34.6	5 730 183	2 022 053	35.3	6 099 817	2 076 367	34.0
1 VII 2006[18]	ESDF	11 930 000	4 133 066	34.6	5 778 621	2 039 146	35.3	6 151 379	2 093 919	34.0
1 VII 2007[18]	ESDF	12 040 000	4 171 175	34.6	5 831 902	2 057 948	35.3	6 208 098	2 113 226	34.0
1 VII 2008[18]	ESDF	12 150 000	3 495 205	28.8	5 885 184	1 691 434	28.7	6 264 816	1 803 752	28.8
1 VII 2009[18]	ESDF	12 260 000	3 526 849	28.8	5 938 465	1 706 747	28.7	6 321 535	1 820 083	28.8

6. Total and urban population by sex: 2001 - 2010
Population totale et population urbaine selon le sexe : 2001 - 2010 (continued - suite)

Continent, country or area, and date / Continent, pays ou zone et date	Code[a]	Both sexes - Les deux sexes			Male - Masculin			Female - Féminin		
		Total	Urban - Urbaine		Total	Urban - Urbaine		Total	Urban - Urbaine	
			Number Nombre	Percent P.100		Number Nombre	Percent P.100		Number Nombre	Percent P.100

AMERICA, NORTH - AMÉRIQUE DU NORD

Anguilla										
9 V 2001[23]	CDFC	11 430	...	...	5 628	...	...	5 802	...	...
1 VII 2001	ESDF	11 561	...	...	5 701	...	...	5 860	...	...
Antigua and Barbuda - Antigua-et-Barbuda										
28 V 2001	CDFC	76 886	...	...	36 107	...	...	40 779	...	...
1 VII 2002	ESDF	78 320	...	...	36 780	...	...	41 540	...	...
1 VII 2003	ESDF	79 781	...	...	37 467	...	...	42 314	...	...
1 VII 2004	ESDF	81 270	...	...	38 166	...	...	43 104	...	...
1 VII 2005	ESDF	82 786	...	...	38 878	...	...	43 908	...	...
1 VII 2006	ESDF	84 330	...	...	39 603	...	...	44 727	...	...
1 VII 2007	ESDF	85 903	...	...	40 342	...	...	45 561	...	...
Aruba										
1 VII 2001	ESDJ	91 870	...	...	44 042	...	...	47 828	...	...
1 VII 2002	ESDJ	93 310	...	...	44 651	...	...	48 659	...	...
1 VII 2003	ESDJ	95 076	...	...	45 461	...	...	49 615	...	...
1 VII 2004	ESDJ	97 658	...	...	46 657	...	...	51 001	...	...
1 VII 2005	ESDJ	100 644	...	...	48 038	...	...	52 606	...	...
1 VII 2006	ESDJ	102 833	...	...	49 063	...	...	53 770	...	...
1 VII 2007	ESDJ	104 005	...	...	49 614	...	...	54 391	...	...
1 VII 2008	ESDJ	105 287	...	...	50 304	...	...	54 983	...	...
1 VII 2009	ESDJ	106 925	...	...	51 227[24]	...	...	55 697[24]	...	...
1 VII 2010	ESDJ	107 553	...	...	51 547	...	...	56 006	...	...
Bahamas[1]										
1 VII 2001	ESDF	307 800	...	...	149 600	...	...	158 200	...	...
1 VII 2002	ESDF	312 100	...	...	151 700	...	...	160 400	...	...
1 VII 2003	ESDF	316 900	...	...	154 100	...	...	162 800	...	...
1 VII 2004	ESDF	320 800	...	...	155 900	...	...	164 900	...	...
1 VII 2005	ESDF	325 200	...	...	158 000	...	...	167 200	...	...
1 VII 2006	ESDF	329 500	...	...	160 100	...	...	169 400	...	...
1 VII 2007	ESDF	334 000	...	...	162 300	...	...	171 700	...	...
1 VII 2008	ESDF	338 300	...	...	164 800	...	...	173 500	...	...
1 VII 2009	ESDF	342 400	...	...	166 800	...	...	175 600	...	...
1 VII 2010	ESDF	346 900	...	...	169 200	...	...	177 700	...	...
Barbados - Barbade										
1 VII 2001	ESDF	269 874	...	...	129 871	...	...	140 003	...	...
1 VII 2002	ESDF	270 750	...	...	130 390	...	...	140 360	...	...
1 VII 2003	ESDF	271 646	...	...	130 887	...	...	140 759	...	...
1 VII 2004	ESDF	272 436	...	...	131 418	...	...	141 018	...	...
1 VII 2005	ESDF	273 018	...	...	131 721	...	...	141 297	...	...
1 VII 2006	ESDF	273 428	...	...	131 916	...	...	141 512	...	...
1 VII 2007	ESDF	274 197	...	...	132 413	...	...	141 784	...	...
1 VII 2008	ESDF	274 937	...	...	132 839	...	...	142 098	...	...
Belize										
1 VII 2001	ESDF	257 310	125 830	48.9	129 890	62 160	47.9	127 420	63 370	49.7
1 VII 2002	ESDF	265 200	130 500	49.2	133 900	64 400	48.1	131 300	66 100	50.3
1 VII 2003	ESDF	273 700	135 600	49.5	138 300	67 000	48.4	135 400	68 600	50.7
1 VII 2004	ESDF	282 600	141 000	49.9	142 700	69 500	48.7	139 900	71 500	51.1
1 VII 2005	ESDF	291 800	146 600	50.2	147 400	72 200	49.0	144 400	74 400	51.5
1 VII 2006	ESDF	301 386	152 583	50.6	149 676	73 495	49.1	151 710	79 089	52.1
1 VII 2008	ESDF	322 100	...	...	160 900	...	...	161 200	...	...
1 VII 2009	ESDF	333 200	...	...	166 500	...	...	166 700	...	...
Bermuda - Bermudes										
1 VII 2001	ESDJ	62 455	...	...	29 969	...	...	32 486	...	...
1 VII 2002	ESDJ	62 754	...	...	30 092	...	...	32 662	...	...
1 VII 2003	ESDJ	63 042	...	...	30 205	...	...	32 837	...	...
1 VII 2004	ESDJ	63 320	...	...	30 323	...	...	32 997	...	...
1 VII 2005	ESDJ	63 571	...	...	30 424	...	...	33 147	...	...
1 VII 2006	ESDJ	63 797	...	...	30 504	...	...	33 293	...	...
1 VII 2007	ESDJ	64 009	...	...	30 577	...	...	33 432	...	...
1 VII 2008	ESDJ	64 209	...	...	30 644	...	...	33 565	...	...
1 VII 2009	ESDJ	64 395	...	...	30 704	...	...	33 691	...	...
1 VII 2010	ESDJ	64 566	...	...	30 755	...	...	33 811	...	...

Continent, country or area, and date / Continent, pays ou zone et date	Code[a]	Both sexes - Les deux sexes Total	Urban - Urbaine Number Nombre	Urban - Urbaine Percent P.100	Male - Masculin Total	Urban - Urbaine Number Nombre	Urban - Urbaine Percent P.100	Female - Féminin Total	Urban - Urbaine Number Nombre	Urban - Urbaine Percent P.100
AMERICA, NORTH - AMÉRIQUE DU NORD										
British Virgin Islands - Îles Vierges britanniques										
21 V 2001	CDFC	20 647	...	...	10 627	...	...	10 020	...	...
Canada										
15 V 2001[25]	CDJC	30 007 095	23 908 105	79.7	14 706 850	11 594 915	78.8	15 300 245	12 313 190	80.5
1 VII 2001[26]	ESDJ	31 019 020	...	...	15 365 609	...	...	15 653 411	...	...
1 VII 2002[26]	ESDJ	31 353 656	...	...	15 533 158	...	...	15 820 498	...	...
1 VII 2003[26]	ESDJ	31 639 670	...	...	15 675 460	...	...	15 964 210	...	...
1 VII 2004[26]	ESDJ	31 940 676	...	...	15 825 754	...	...	16 114 922	...	...
1 VII 2005[26]	ESDJ	32 245 209	...	...	15 979 800	...	...	16 265 409	...	...
16 V 2006[22]	CDJC	31 612 895	25 350 585	80.2	15 475 970	12 289 025	79.4	16 136 930	13 061 560	80.9
1 VII 2006[27]	ESDJ	32 576 074	...	...	16 147 873	...	...	16 428 201	...	...
1 VII 2007[27]	ESDJ	32 929 733	...	...	16 324 732	...	...	16 605 001	...	...
1 VII 2008[28]	ESDJ	33 315 976	...	...	16 519 001	...	...	16 796 975	...	...
1 VII 2009[28]	ESDJ	33 720 184	...	...	16 723 138	...	...	16 997 046	...	...
1 VII 2010*[29]	ESDJ	34 108 752	...	...	16 917 282	...	...	17 191 470	...	...
Cayman Islands - Îles Caïmanes										
1 IV 2007	SSDJ	54 100	...	...	27 281[3]	...	...	26 011[3]	...	...
31 XII 2009	ESDJ	52 830	...	...	26 255	...	...	26 575	...	...
10 X 2010*[30]	CDJC	54 397	...	...	26 899	...	...	27 498	...	...
Costa Rica										
1 VII 2001	ESDJ	3 906 742	2 305 723	59.0	1 935 168	1 119 394	57.8	1 971 574	1 186 329	60.2
1 VII 2002	ESDJ	3 997 883	2 359 158	59.0	1 983 715	1 147 227	57.8	2 014 168	1 211 931	60.2
1 VII 2003	ESDJ	4 088 773	2 412 542	59.0	2 017 467	1 167 617	57.9	2 071 306	1 244 925	60.1
1 VII 2004	ESDJ	4 178 755	2 465 255	59.0	2 062 468	1 191 560	57.8	2 116 287	1 273 695	60.2
1 VII 2005	ESDJ	4 266 185	2 516 602	59.0	2 116 648	1 231 912	58.2	2 149 537	1 284 690	59.8
1 VII 2006	ESDJ	4 353 843	2 567 797	59.0	2 146 610	1 243 202	57.9	2 207 233	1 324 595	60.0
1 VII 2007	ESDJ	4 443 100	2 619 591	59.0	2 195 652	1 273 998	58.0	2 247 448	1 345 593	59.9
1 VII 2008[31]	ESDJ	4 533 162	2 671 667	58.9	2 246 474	1 299 940	57.9	2 286 688	1 371 727	60.0
1 VII 2009[31]	ESDJ	4 620 482	2 722 273	58.9	2 291 886	1 325 468	57.8	2 328 596	1 396 805	60.0
1 VII 2010[32]	ESDJ	4 562 087	2 811 556	61.6	2 233 452	1 344 652	60.2	2 328 635	1 466 904	63.0
Cuba										
1 VII 2001	ESDJ	11 157 364	8 467 052	75.9	5 586 835	4 163 395	74.5	5 570 529	4 303 657	77.3
1 VII 2002	ESDJ	11 184 457	8 483 688	75.9	5 601 052	4 172 285	74.5	5 583 405	4 311 403	77.2
7 IX 2002	CDJC	11 177 743	8 479 329	75.9	5 597 233	4 169 722	74.5	5 580 510	4 309 607	77.2
1 VII 2003	ESDJ	11 215 229	8 501 628	75.8	5 616 275	4 181 234	74.4	5 598 954	4 320 394	77.2
1 VII 2004	ESDJ	11 235 687	8 503 738	75.7	5 626 690	4 183 047	74.3	5 608 997	4 320 691	77.0
1 VII 2005	ESDJ	11 242 519	8 497 885	75.6	5 629 843	4 180 296	74.3	5 612 676	4 317 589	76.9
1 VII 2006	ESDJ	11 241 439	8 490 165	75.5	5 629 233	4 176 609	74.2	5 612 206	4 313 556	76.9
1 VII 2007	ESDJ	11 237 916	8 478 510	75.4	5 627 694	4 171 388	74.1	5 610 222	4 307 122	76.8
1 VII 2008	ESDJ	11 236 444	8 468 168	75.4	5 627 687	4 167 421	74.1	5 608 757	4 300 747	76.7
1 VII 2009	ESDJ	11 239 363	8 469 528	75.4	5 629 345	4 169 181	74.1	5 610 018	4 300 347	76.7
1 VII 2010	ESDJ	11 241 894	8 469 602	75.3	5 629 874	4 169 518	74.1	5 612 020	4 300 084	76.6
Dominica - Dominique										
12 V 2001[30]	CDFC	69 625	...	...	35 073	...	...	34 552	...	...
1 VII 2001	ESDF	70 922	...	...	35 241	...	...	35 681	...	...
1 VII 2002	ESDF	70 382	...	...	35 472	...	...	34 910	...	...
1 VII 2003	ESDF	70 352	...	...	35 442	...	...	34 910	...	...
1 VII 2004	ESDF	70 417	...	...	35 645	...	...	34 772	...	...
1 VII 2005	ESDF	70 665	...	...	35 991	...	...	34 675	...	...
1 VII 2006	ESDF	71 008	...	...	36 169	...	...	34 839	...	...
Dominican Republic - République dominicaine										
1 VII 2001[1]	ESDF	8 688 212	5 213 922	60.0	4 353 126	2 581 512	59.3	4 335 086	2 632 410	60.7
1 VII 2002[1]	ESDF	8 823 188	5 361 984	60.8	4 418 914	2 655 257	60.1	4 404 274	2 706 727	61.5
18 X 2002	CDJC	8 562 541	5 446 704	63.6	4 265 215	2 648 064	62.1	4 297 326	2 798 640	65.1
1 VII 2003[1]	ESDF	8 958 206	5 512 122	61.5	4 484 683	2 730 026	60.9	4 473 523	2 782 096	62.2
1 VII 2004[1]	ESDF	9 092 778	5 664 035	62.3	4 550 204	2 805 678	61.7	4 542 574	2 858 357	62.9
1 VII 2005[1]	ESDF	9 226 449	5 817 419	63.1	4 615 274	2 882 076	62.4	4 611 175	2 935 343	63.7
1 VII 2006[1]	ESDF	9 359 706	5 965 957	63.7	4 680 145	2 955 948	63.2	4 679 561	3 010 009	64.3
1 VII 2007[1]	ESDF	9 492 876	6 116 273	64.4	4 744 960	3 030 711	63.9	4 747 916	3 085 562	65.0

Continent, country or area, and date / Continent, pays ou zone et date	Code[a]	Both sexes - Les deux sexes			Male - Masculin			Female - Femelle		
		Total	Urban - Urbaine		Total	Urban - Urbaine		Total	Urban - Urbaine	
			Number Nombre	Percent P.100		Number Nombre	Percent P.100		Number Nombre	Percent P.100
AMERICA, NORTH - AMÉRIQUE DU NORD										
Dominican Republic - République dominicaine										
1 VII 2008[1]	ESDF	9 625 207	6 267 880	65.1	4 809 337	3 106 114	64.6	4 815 870	3 161 766	65.7
1 VII 2009[1]	ESDF	9 755 954	6 420 260	65.8	4 872 903	3 181 903	65.3	4 883 051	3 238 357	66.3
1 VII 2010[1]	ESDF	9 884 371	6 572 893	66.5	4 935 282	3 257 817	66.0	4 949 089	3 315 076	67.0
1 XII 2010*[33]	CDJC	9 378 819			4 707 921	...	...	4 670 898	...	...
El Salvador										
1 VII 2001	ESDF	6 396 890	3 754 903	58.7	3 141 208	1 804 804	57.5	3 255 682	1 950 099	59.9
1 VII 2002	ESDF	6 517 798	3 843 878	59.0	3 201 720	1 848 194	57.7	3 316 078	1 995 684	60.2
1 VII 2003	ESDF	6 638 168	3 932 569	59.2	3 261 938	1 891 429	58.0	3 376 230	2 041 140	60.5
1 VII 2004	ESDF	6 757 408	4 020 878	59.5	3 321 564	1 934 445	58.2	3 435 844	2 086 433	60.7
1 VII 2005[34]	ESDF	6 049 412	3 646 537	60.3	2 874 929	1 701 356	59.2	3 174 483	1 945 181	61.3
1 VII 2006[34]	ESDF	6 073 859	3 706 525	61.0	2 881 162	1 726 983	59.9	3 192 697	1 979 542	62.0
12 V 2007	CDJC	5 744 113	3 598 836	62.7	2 719 371	1 676 313	61.6	3 024 742	1 922 523	63.6
1 VII 2007[34]	ESDF	6 098 714	3 766 800	61.8	2 887 804	1 752 851	60.7	3 210 910	2 013 949	62.7
1 VII 2008[34]	ESDF	6 124 705	3 828 004	62.5	2 895 210	1 779 210	61.5	3 229 495	2 048 794	63.4
1 VII 2009[34]	ESDF	6 152 558	3 890 523	63.2	2 903 737	1 806 310	62.2	3 248 821	2 084 213	64.2
1 VII 2010[34]	ESDF	6 183 002	...	...	2 913 743	...	...	3 269 259	...	...
Greenland - Groenland[35]										
1 VII 2001	ESDJ	56 394	46 125	81.8	30 102	24 454	81.2	26 292	21 671	82.4
1 VII 2002	ESDJ	56 609	46 462	82.1	30 215	24 626	81.5	26 394	21 836	82.7
1 VII 2003	ESDJ	56 766	46 746	82.3	30 292	24 771	81.8	26 474	21 975	83.0
1 VII 2004	ESDJ	56 912	46 989	82.6	30 327	24 860	82.0	26 585	22 129	83.2
1 VII 2005	ESDJ	56 935	47 080	82.7	30 251	24 837	82.1	26 685	22 243	83.4
1 VII 2006	ESDJ	56 775	47 037	82.8	30 094	24 763	82.3	26 681	22 274	83.5
1 VII 2007	ESDJ	56 555	47 056	83.2	29 945	24 746	82.6	26 610	22 310	83.8
1 I 2008	CDJC	56 462	...	...	29 885	...	...	26 577	...	...
1 VII 2008	ESDJ	56 328	47 103	83.6	29 847	24 790	83.1	26 481	22 313	84.3
1 VII 2009	ESDJ	56 323	47 230	83.9	29 873	24 865	83.2	26 451	22 366	84.6
1 VII 2010	ESDJ	56 534	47 646	84.3	29 939	25 045	83.7	26 595	22 601	85.0
Grenada - Grenade										
25 V 2001	CDFC	102 632	...	...	50 481	...	...	52 151	...	...
Guadeloupe										
1 VII 2001	ESDJ	432 453	...	...	207 453	...	...	225 000	...	...
1 I 2002[36]	ESDJ	393 024	...	...	186 827	...	...	206 197	...	...
1 I 2003[36]	ESDJ	394 881	...	...	187 151	...	...	207 730	...	...
1 I 2004[36]	ESDJ	396 992	...	...	187 603	...	...	209 389	...	...
1 I 2005[36]	ESDJ	399 178	...	...	188 158	...	...	211 020	...	...
1 I 2006[36]	CDJC	400 736	...	...	188 720	...	...	212 016	...	...
1 I 2007[36]	ESDJ	400 584	...	...	188 325	...	...	212 259	...	...
1 I 2008[36]	ESDJ	401 784	...	...	188 385	...	...	213 399	...	...
1 I 2009[36]	ESDJ	403 257	...	...	188 317	...	...	214 940	...	...
Guatemala										
1 VII 2001[21]	ESDF	11 678 411	...	...	5 888 426	...	...	5 789 985	...	...
24 XI 2002	CDJC	11 237 196	...	...	5 496 839	...	...	5 740 357	...	...
1 VII 2008[37]	ESDF	13 677 815	...	...	6 673 533	...	...	7 004 282	...	...
1 VII 2009[37]	ESDF	14 017 057	...	...	6 836 849	...	...	7 180 208	...	...
1 VII 2010[37]	ESDF	14 361 666	...	...	7 003 337	...	...	7 358 328	...	...
Haiti - Haïti										
1 VII 2001[38]	ESDJ	8 719 732	...	...	4 312 285	...	...	4 407 447	...	...
1 VII 2002[38]	ESDJ	8 860 677	...	...	4 382 223	...	...	4 478 454	...	...
11 I 2003	CDJC	8 373 750	...	...	4 039 272	...	...	4 334 478	...	...
1 VII 2003[38]	ESDJ	9 001 471	...	...	4 452 024	...	...	4 549 447	...	...
1 VII 2004[38]	ESDJ	9 144 533	...	...	4 523 032	...	...	4 621 501	...	...
1 VII 2005[38]	ESDJ	9 292 282	...	...	4 596 593	...	...	4 695 689	...	...
1 VII 2006[38]	ESDJ	9 445 410	...	...	4 673 089	...	...	4 772 321	...	...
1 VII 2007[38]	ESDJ	9 602 304	...	...	4 751 622	...	...	4 850 682	...	...
1 VII 2008[38]	ESDJ	9 761 927	...	...	4 831 621	...	...	4 930 306	...	...
1 VII 2009[38]	ESDJ	9 923 243	...	...	4 912 515	...	...	5 010 728	...	...
1 VII 2010[38]	ESDJ	10 085 214	4 817 666	47.8	4 993 731	2 321 608	46.5	5 091 483	2 496 059	49.0
Honduras										
1 VII 2001[39]	ESDF	6 530 331	3 022 150	46.3	3 228 483	1 439 896	44.6	3 301 848	1 582 254	47.9
28 VII 2001	CDFC	6 071 200	...	...	3 000 530	...	...	3 070 670	...	...

Continent, country or area, and date / Continent, pays ou zone et date	Code[a]	Both sexes - Les deux sexes			Male - Masculin			Female - Féminin		
		Total	Urban - Urbaine		Total	Urban - Urbaine		Total	Urban - Urbaine	
			Number Nombre	Percent P.100		Number Nombre	Percent P.100		Number Nombre	Percent P.100
AMERICA, NORTH - AMÉRIQUE DU NORD										
Honduras										
1 VII 2002[39] ....ESDF		6 694 761	3 140 880	46.9	3 308 253	1 497 291	45.3	3 386 508	1 643 589	48.5
1 VII 2003[39] ....ESDF		6 860 842	3 260 934	47.5	3 388 874	1 555 369	45.9	3 471 968	1 705 565	49.1
1 VII 2004[39] ....ESDF		7 028 389	3 382 254	48.1	3 470 259	1 614 104	46.5	3 558 130	1 768 150	49.7
1 VII 2005[39] ....ESDF		7 197 303	3 504 730	48.7	3 552 360	1 673 434	47.1	3 644 943	1 831 296	50.2
1 VII 2006[39] ....ESDF		7 367 021	3 628 228	49.2	3 634 900	1 733 290	47.7	3 732 121	1 894 938	50.8
1 VII 2007[39] ....ESDF		7 536 952	3 752 579	49.8	3 717 577	1 793 588	48.2	3 819 375	1 958 991	51.3
1 VII 2008[39] ....ESDF		7 706 907	...	...	3 800 300	...	...	3 906 607	...	...
1 VII 2009[39] ....ESDF		7 876 662	...	...	3 882 957	...	...	3 993 705	...	...
1 VII 2010[39] ....ESDF		8 045 990	...	...	3 965 430	...	...	4 080 560	...	...
Jamaica - Jamaïque										
1 VII 2001 ....ESDJ		2 604 098	1 353 511	52.0	1 281 752	645 517	50.4	1 322 346	707 993	53.5
10 IX 2001[40] ....CDJC		2 607 632	1 355 347	52.0	1 283 548	646 422	50.4	1 324 084	708 925	53.5
1 VII 2002 ....ESDJ		2 615 248	1 359 292	52.0	1 287 663	648 494	50.4	1 327 585	710 798	53.5
1 VII 2003 ....ESDJ		2 625 708	1 364 719	52.0	1 293 121	651 243	50.4	1 332 587	713 476	53.5
1 VII 2004 ....ESDJ		2 638 074	1 371 144	52.0	1 299 406	654 407	50.4	1 338 668	716 736	53.5
1 VII 2005 ....ESDJ		2 650 402	1 377 546	52.0	1 305 639	657 546	50.4	1 344 763	720 000	53.5
1 VII 2006 ....ESDJ		2 663 106	1 384 145	52.0	1 312 025	660 763	50.4	1 351 081	723 383	53.5
1 VII 2007 ....ESDJ		2 675 831	1 390 754	52.0	1 318 444	663 995	50.4	1 357 387	726 759	53.5
1 VII 2008 ....ESDJ		2 687 241	1 396 470[41]	52.0	1 324 277[22]	666 761[41]	50.3	1 362 964[22]	729 709[41]	53.5
1 VII 2009 ....ESDJ		2 695 583	...	...	1 328 124[22]	...	...	1 367 460[22]	...	...
1 VII 2010* ....ESDJ		2 702 300	...	...	1 324 100[22]	...	...	1 378 200[22]	...	...
Martinique										
1 I 2001 ....ESDJ		386 542	...	...	182 334	...	...	204 208	...	...
1 I 2002 ....ESDJ		389 302	...	...	183 149	...	...	206 153	...	...
1 I 2003 ....ESDJ		391 676	...	...	183 735	...	...	207 941	...	...
1 I 2004 ....ESDJ		393 852	...	...	184 303	...	...	209 549	...	...
1 I 2005 ....ESDJ		395 982	...	...	184 841	...	...	211 141	...	...
1 I 2006 ....CDJC		397 732	355 189	89.3	185 604	165 012	88.9	212 128	190 177	89.7
1 I 2007 ....ESDJ		397 730	...	...	184 970	...	...	212 760	...	...
1 I 2008 ....ESDJ		397 693	...	...	184 404	...	...	213 289	...	...
1 I 2009 ....ESDJ		398 733	...	...	184 148	...	...	214 585	...	...
Mexico - Mexique										
1 VII 2001 ....ESDJ		99 715 527	74 840 402	75.1	49 312 382	...	...	50 403 145	...	...
1 VII 2002 ....ESDJ		100 909 374	76 108 582	75.4	49 862 638	...	...	51 046 736	...	...
1 VII 2003 ....ESDJ		101 999 555	77 303 384	75.8	50 361 179	...	...	51 638 376	...	...
1 VII 2004 ....ESDJ		103 001 867	78 436 582	76.2	50 814 580	...	...	52 187 287	...	...
1 VII 2005[1] ....ESDJ		103 946 866	79 467 885	76.5	51 238 427	...	...	52 708 439	...	...
17 X 2005 ....CDJC		103 263 388	78 986 852	76.5	50 249 955	38 300 417	76.2	53 013 433	40 686 435	76.7
1 VII 2006[1] ....ESDJ		104 874 282	80 373 543	76.6	51 654 642	...	...	53 219 640	...	...
1 VII 2007[1] ....ESDJ		105 790 725	81 288 078	76.8	52 066 743	...	...	53 723 982	...	...
1 VII 2008[1] ....ESDJ		106 682 518	82 179 785	77.0	52 466 262	...	...	54 216 256	...	...
1 VII 2009[1] ....ESDJ		107 550 697	83 088 985	77.3	52 853 788	...	...	54 696 909	...	...
12 VI 2010[42] ....CDFC		112 336 538	86 287 410	76.8	54 855 231	41 946 540	76.5	57 481 307	44 340 870	77.1
Montserrat										
12 V 2001 ....CDFC		4 491	...	...	2 418	...	...	2 073	...	...
Netherlands Antilles - Antilles néerlandaises										
1 I 2001 ....ESDJ		175 704	...	...	82 610	...	...	93 094	...	...
29 I 2001 ....CDJC		175 653	...	...	82 521	...	...	93 132	...	...
1 I 2002 ....ESDJ		172 586	...	...	80 884	...	...	91 702	...	...
1 I 2003 ....ESDJ		176 635	...	...	82 752	...	...	93 883	...	...
1 I 2004 ....ESDJ		178 719	...	...	83 303	...	...	95 416	...	...
1 I 2005 ....ESDJ		183 536	...	...	85 504	...	...	98 032	...	...
1 I 2006 ....ESDJ		188 923	...	...	87 896	...	...	101 027	...	...
1 I 2007 ....ESDJ		193 552	...	...	90 139	...	...	103 413	...	...
1 I 2008[43] ....ESDJ		197 172	...	...	91 863	...	...	105 309	...	...
1 I 2009[44] ....ESDJ		199 999	...	...	93 395	...	...	106 604	...	...
1 I 2010[44] ....ESDJ		197 621	...	...	92 321	...	...	105 300	...	...
Nicaragua										
1 VII 2001 ....ESDJ		5 173 927	...	...	2 575 135	...	...	2 598 792	...	...
1 VII 2002 ....ESDJ		5 244 694	...	...	2 609 277	...	...	2 635 418	...	...
1 VII 2003 ....ESDJ		5 312 750	...	...	2 641 869	...	...	2 670 881	...	...
1 VII 2004 ....ESDJ		5 380 510	...	...	2 674 138	...	...	2 706 372	...	...

Continent, country or area, and date / Continent, pays ou zone et date	Code[a]	Both sexes - Les deux sexes			Male - Masculin			Female - Féminin		
		Total	Urban - Urbaine		Total	Urban - Urbaine		Total	Urban - Urbaine	
			Number Nombre	Percent P.100		Number Nombre	Percent P.100		Number Nombre	Percent P.100

AMERICA, NORTH - AMÉRIQUE DU NORD

Nicaragua

4 VI 2005 .... CDJC		5 142 098	2 875 550	55.9	2 534 491	1 368 622	54.0	2 607 607	1 506 928	57.8
1 VII 2005 .... ESDJ		5 450 387	3 047 740	55.9	2 707 309	1 462 218	54.0	2 743 078	1 585 522	57.8
1 VII 2006 .... ESDJ		5 522 606	3 099 918	56.1	2 741 414	1 488 694	54.3	2 781 192	1 611 224	57.9
1 VII 2007 .... ESDJ		5 595 541	3 152 807	56.3	2 775 638	1 515 432	54.6	2 819 903	1 637 375	58.1
1 VII 2008 .... ESDJ		5 668 866	3 206 205	56.6	2 809 918	1 542 386	54.9	2 858 948	1 663 819	58.2
1 VII 2009 .... ESDJ		5 742 316	3 259 955	56.8	2 844 244	1 569 555	55.2	2 898 072	1 690 400	58.3

Panama

1 VII 2001[45] .... ESDF		3 003 954	1 877 542	62.5	1 516 602	922 991	60.9	1 487 352	954 551	64.2
1 VII 2002[45] .... ESDF		3 060 090	1 921 017	62.8	1 544 727	945 273	61.2	1 515 363	975 744	64.4
1 VII 2003[45] .... ESDF		3 116 277	1 964 517	63.0	1 572 850	967 537	61.5	1 543 427	996 980	64.6
1 VII 2004[45] .... ESDF		3 172 360	2 007 892	63.3	1 600 879	989 709	61.8	1 571 481	1 018 183	64.8
1 VII 2005[45] .... ESDF		3 228 186	2 020 965	62.6	1 628 720	1 011 700	62.1	1 599 466	1 009 265	63.1
1 VII 2006[45] .... ESDF		3 283 959	2 093 871	63.8	1 656 469	1 033 634	62.4	1 627 490	1 060 237	65.1
1 VII 2007[45] .... ESDF		3 339 781	2 136 637	64.0	1 684 189	1 055 455	62.7	1 655 592	1 081 182	65.3
1 VII 2008[45] .... ESDF		3 395 346	2 179 118	64.2	1 711 735	1 077 090	62.9	1 683 611	1 102 028	65.5
1 VII 2009[45] .... ESDF		3 450 349	2 221 211	64.4	1 738 965	1 098 484	63.2	1 711 384	1 122 727	65.6
16 V 2010 .... CDFC		3 405 813	...	...	1 712 584	...	...	1 693 229	...	...
1 VII 2010[45] .... ESDF		3 504 483	2 262 765	64.6	1 765 734	1 119 546	63.4	1 738 749	1 143 219	65.7

Puerto Rico - Porto Rico[46]

1 VII 2001 .... ESDJ		3 839 810	...	...	1 847 559	...	...	1 992 251	...	...
1 VII 2002 .... ESDJ		3 858 806	...	...	1 855 781	...	...	2 003 025	...	...
1 VII 2003 .... ESDJ		3 878 532	...	...	1 865 170	...	...	2 013 362	...	...
1 VII 2004 .... ESDJ		3 894 855	...	...	1 871 657	...	...	2 023 198	...	...
1 VII 2005 .... ESDJ		3 912 054	...	...	1 879 236	...	...	2 032 818	...	...
1 VII 2006 .... ESDJ		3 927 776	...	...	1 886 031	...	...	2 041 745	...	...
1 VII 2007 .... ESDJ		3 942 375	...	...	1 892 503	...	...	2 049 872	...	...
1 VII 2008 .... ESDJ		3 954 037	...	...	1 897 396	...	...	2 056 641	...	...
1 VII 2009 .... ESDJ		3 967 288	...	...	1 903 370	...	...	2 063 918	...	...
1 VII 2010 .... ESDJ		3 978 702	...	...	1 908 360	...	...	2 070 342	...	...

Saint Kitts and Nevis - Saint-Kitts-et-Nevis

14 V 2001 .... CDFC		45 841	...	...	22 784	...	...	23 057	...	...
1 VII 2001* .... ESDF		46 111	...	...	22 919	...	...	23 192	...	...

Saint Lucia - Sainte-Lucie

22 V 2001 .... CDFC		157 164	43 316	27.6	76 741	20 711	27.0	80 423	22 605	28.1
1 VII 2002 .... ESDF		159 133	...	...	77 868	...	...	81 265	...	...
1 VII 2003 .... ESDF		160 673	...	...	78 618	...	...	82 055	...	...
1 VII 2004 .... ESDF		162 434	...	...	79 407	...	...	83 027	...	...
1 VII 2005 .... ESDF		164 330	...	...	80 440	...	...	83 890	...	...
1 VII 2006 .... ESDF		166 387	...	...	81 558	...	...	84 829	...	...
1 VII 2007 .... ESDF		168 338	...	...	82 426	...	...	85 912	...	...
10 V 2010* .... CDJC		166 526	...	...	82 926	...	...	83 600	...	...

Saint Pierre and Miquelon - Saint Pierre-et-Miquelon

19 I 2006 .... CDFC		6 125	...	...	3 034	...	...	3 091	...	...

Saint Vincent and the Grenadines - Saint-Vincent-et-les Grenadines

14 V 2001[30] .... CDFC		109 022	49 590	45.5	55 456	24 809	44.7	53 566	24 781	46.3
1 VII 2002 .... ESDF		107 854	48 535	45.0	54 434	...	...	53 420	...	...
1 VII 2003 .... ESDF		105 158	42 063	40.0	53 073	...	...	52 085	...	...
1 VII 2004 .... ESDF		104 555	41 822	40.0	52 769	...	...	51 786	...	...
1 VII 2005 .... ESDF		103 751	...	...	52 363	...	...	51 388	...	...
1 VII 2006 .... ESDF		101 402	...	...	51 178	...	...	50 224	...	...
1 VII 2007 .... ESDF		100 130	...	...	50 536	...	...	49 594	...	...
1 VII 2008 .... ESDF		99 086	...	...	50 009	...	...	49 077	...	...

Continent, country or area, and date / Continent, pays ou zone et date	Code[a]	Both sexes - Les deux sexes			Male - Masculin			Female - Féminin		
		Total	Urban - Urbaine		Total	Urban - Urbaine		Total	Urban - Urbaine	
			Number Nombre	Percent P.100		Number Nombre	Percent P.100		Number Nombre	Percent P.100
AMERICA, NORTH - AMÉRIQUE DU NORD										
Trinidad and Tobago - Trinité-et-Tobago[47]										
1 VII 2001 .... ESDF		1 266 797	...	...	635 299	...	...	631 498	...	...
1 VII 2002 .... ESDF		1 275 705	...	...	639 766	...	...	635 939	...	...
1 VII 2003 .... ESDF		1 282 447	...	...	642 037	...	...	640 410	...	...
1 VII 2004 .... ESDF		1 290 646	...	...	647 259	...	...	643 387	...	...
1 VII 2005 .... ESDF		1 294 494	...	...	649 189	...	...	645 305	...	...
1 VII 2006 .... ESDF		1 297 944	...	...	650 919	...	...	647 025	...	...
1 VII 2007 .... ESDF		1 303 188	...	...	653 549	...	...	649 639	...	...
1 VII 2008 .... ESDF		1 308 587	...	...	656 257	...	...	652 330	...	...
1 VII 2010 .... ESDF		1 317 714	...	...	656 892	...	...	660 822	...	...
Turks and Caicos Islands - Îles Turques et Caïques										
10 IX 2001 .... CDFC		19 886	...	...	9 897	...	...	9 989	...	...
1 VII 2002 .... ESDJ		20 900	...	...	10 402	...	...	10 498	...	...
1 VII 2003 .... ESDJ		25 143	...	...	12 513	...	...	12 630	...	...
1 VII 2004 .... ESDJ		27 496	...	...	13 684	...	...	13 812	...	...
1 VII 2005 .... ESDJ		30 602	...	...	15 230	...	...	15 372	...	...
1 VII 2006 .... ESDJ		33 202	...	...	16 524	...	...	16 678	...	...
1 VII 2007 .... ESDJ		34 862	...	...	18 023	...	...	16 839	...	...
United States of America - États-Unis d'Amérique[48]										
1 VII 2001 .... ESDJ		285 081 556	...	...	139 998 551	...	...	145 083 005	...	...
1 VII 2002 .... ESDJ		287 803 914	...	...	141 413 818	...	...	146 390 096	...	...
1 VII 2003 .... ESDJ		290 326 418	...	...	142 676 927	...	...	147 649 491	...	...
1 VII 2004 .... ESDJ		293 045 739	...	...	144 137 674	...	...	148 908 065	...	...
1 VII 2005 .... ESDJ		295 753 151	...	...	145 560 767	...	...	150 192 384	...	...
1 VII 2006 .... ESDJ		298 593 212	...	...	147 060 702	...	...	151 532 510	...	...
1 VII 2007 .... ESDJ		301 579 895	...	...	148 612 102	...	...	152 967 793	...	...
1 VII 2008 .... ESDJ		304 374 846	...	...	150 074 226	...	...	154 300 620	...	...
1 VII 2009 .... ESDJ		307 006 550	...	...	151 449 490	...	...	155 557 060	...	...
United States Virgin Islands - Îles Vierges américaines[46]										
1 VII 2001 .... ESDJ		108 749	...	...	51 920	...	...	56 829	...	...
1 VII 2002 .... ESDJ		108 923	...	...	51 893	...	...	57 030	...	...
1 VII 2003 .... ESDJ		109 148	...	...	51 954	...	...	57 194	...	...
1 VII 2004 .... ESDJ		109 354	...	...	52 007	...	...	57 347	...	...
1 VII 2005 .... ESDJ		109 600	...	...	52 081	...	...	57 519	...	...
1 VII 2006 .... ESDJ		109 764	...	...	52 113	...	...	57 651	...	...
1 VII 2007 .... ESDJ		109 821	...	...	52 089	...	...	57 732	...	...
1 VII 2008 .... ESDJ		109 840	...	...	52 045	...	...	57 795	...	...
AMERICA, SOUTH - AMÉRIQUE DU SUD										
Argentina - Argentine										
1 VII 2001 .... ESDF		37 156 195	33 312 347	89.7	18 201 249	16 161 696	88.8	18 954 946	17 150 651	90.5
18 XI 2001 .... CDFC		36 260 130	32 431 950	89.4	17 659 072	15 629 299	88.5	18 601 058	16 802 651	90.3
1 VII 2002 .... ESDF		37 515 632	33 709 927	89.9	18 374 920	16 361 823	89.0	19 140 712	17 348 104	90.6
1 VII 2003 .... ESDF		37 869 730	34 101 536	90.0	18 546 570	16 559 682	89.3	19 323 160	17 541 854	90.8
1 VII 2004 .... ESDF		38 226 051	34 493 965	90.2	18 719 869	16 758 540	89.5	19 506 182	17 735 425	90.9
1 VII 2005 .... ESDF		38 592 150	34 894 057	90.4	18 898 472	16 961 698	89.8	19 693 678	17 932 359	91.1
1 VII 2006 .... ESDF		38 970 611	35 304 205	90.6	19 083 828	17 170 659	90.0	19 886 783	18 133 546	91.2
1 VII 2007 .... ESDF		39 356 383	35 719 891	90.8	19 273 494	17 383 239	90.2	20 082 889	18 336 652	91.3
1 VII 2008 .... ESDF		39 745 613	36 137 648	90.9	19 465 305	17 597 280	90.4	20 280 308	18 540 368	91.4
1 VII 2009 .... ESDF		40 134 425	36 553 965	91.1	19 657 086	17 810 843	90.6	20 477 339	18 743 122	91.5
1 VII 2010[49] .... ESDF		40 518 951	36 965 313	91.2	19 846 671	18 023 080	90.8	20 672 280	18 942 233	91.6
27 X 2010 .... CDFC		40 117 096	...	...	19 523 766	...	...	20 593 330	...	...

Continent, country or area, and date Continent, pays ou zone et date	Code[a]	Both sexes - Les deux sexes			Male - Masculin			Female - Féminin		
		Total	Urban - Urbaine		Total	Urban - Urbaine		Total	Urban - Urbaine	
			Number Nombre	Percent P.100		Number Nombre	Percent P.100		Number Nombre	Percent P.100
AMERICA, SOUTH - AMÉRIQUE DU SUD										
Bolivia (Plurinational State of) - Bolivie (État plurinational de)										
1 VII 2001 .... ESDF		8 624 268	5 373 504	62.3	4 293 345	2 615 967	60.9	4 330 924	2 757 537	63.7
5 IX 2001 .... CDFC		8 274 325	5 165 230	62.4	4 123 850	2 517 106	61.0	4 150 475	2 648 124	63.8
1 VII 2002 .... ESDF		8 823 743	5 541 707	62.8	4 393 968	2 697 501	61.4	4 429 776	2 844 206	64.2
1 VII 2003 .... ESDF		9 024 922	5 712 138	63.3	4 495 426	2 780 137	61.8	4 529 495	2 932 001	64.7
1 VII 2004 .... ESDF		9 226 511	5 883 724	63.8	4 597 081	2 863 378	62.3	4 629 430	3 020 347	65.2
1 VII 2005 .... ESDF		9 427 219	6 055 392	64.2	4 698 293	2 946 725	62.7	4 728 926	3 108 667	65.7
1 VII 2006 .... ESDF		9 627 269	6 227 367	64.7	4 799 178	3 030 290	63.1	4 828 091	3 197 077	66.2
1 VII 2007 .... ESDF		9 827 522	6 400 366	65.1	4 900 162	3 114 403	63.6	4 927 360	3 285 963	66.7
1 VII 2008 .... ESDF		10 027 643	6 574 048	65.6	5 001 071	3 198 900	64.0	5 026 572	3 375 148	67.1
1 VII 2009 .... ESDF		10 227 299	6 748 075	66.0	5 101 733	3 283 616	64.4	5 125 566	3 464 459	67.6
Brazil - Brésil[50]										
1 VII 2001 .... ESDF		173 808 010	...	...	85 562 804	...	...	88 245 206	...	...
1 VII 2002 .... ESDF		176 303 919	...	...	86 758 217	...	...	89 545 702	...	...
1 VII 2003 .... ESDF		178 741 412	...	...	87 923 721	...	...	90 817 691	...	...
1 VII 2004 .... ESDF		181 105 601	...	...	89 051 847	...	...	92 053 754	...	...
1 VII 2005 .... ESDF		183 383 216	...	...	90 135 967	...	...	93 247 249	...	...
1 VII 2006 .... ESDF		185 564 212	...	...	91 171 295	...	...	94 392 917	...	...
1 VII 2007 .... ESDF		187 641 714	...	...	92 154 636	...	...	95 487 078	...	...
1 VII 2008 .... ESDF		189 612 814	...	...	93 084 588	...	...	96 528 226	...	...
1 VII 2009 .... ESDF		191 480 630	...	...	93 962 767	...	...	97 517 863	...	...
1 VII 2010 .... ESDF		193 252 604	...	...	94 792 952	...	...	98 459 652	...	...
1 VIII 2010* .... CDJC		190 755 799	160 925 792	84.4	93 406 990	77 710 174	83.2	97 348 809	83 215 618	85.5
Chile - Chili										
1 VII 2001 .... ESDF		15 571 679	13 494 230	86.7	7 706 752	6 598 130	85.6	7 864 927	6 896 100	87.7
24 IV 2002 .... CDFC		15 116 435	13 090 113	86.6	7 447 695	6 366 311	85.5	7 668 740	6 723 802	87.7
1 VII 2002 .... ESDF		15 745 583	13 651 558	86.7	7 793 208	6 676 157	85.7	7 952 375	6 975 401	87.7
1 VII 2003 .... ESDF		15 919 479	13 808 880	86.7	7 879 658	6 754 181	85.7	8 039 821	7 054 699	87.7
1 VII 2004 .... ESDF		16 093 378	13 966 203	86.8	7 966 110	6 832 205	85.8	8 127 268	7 133 998	87.8
1 VII 2005 .... ESDF		16 267 278	14 123 527	86.8	8 052 564	6 910 230	85.8	8 214 714	7 213 297	87.8
1 VII 2006 .... ESDF		16 432 674	14 272 454	86.9	8 134 314	6 983 850	85.9	8 298 360	7 288 604	87.8
1 VII 2007 .... ESDF		16 598 074	14 421 386	86.9	8 216 068	7 057 476	85.9	8 382 006	7 363 910	87.9
1 VII 2008 .... ESDF		16 763 470	14 570 311	86.9	8 297 819	7 131 097	85.9	8 465 651	7 439 214	87.9
1 VII 2009 .... ESDF		16 928 873	14 719 246	86.9	8 379 571	7 204 720	86.0	8 549 302	7 514 526	87.9
1 VII 2010 .... ESDF		17 094 275	14 868 172	87.0	8 461 327	7 278 342	86.0	8 632 948	7 589 830	87.9
Colombia - Colombie										
1 VII 2001[51] .... ESDF		40 806 313	29 850 360	73.2	20 137 593	14 366 713	71.3	20 668 720	15 483 647	74.9
1 VII 2002[51] .... ESDF		41 327 459	30 367 636	73.5	20 395 870	14 618 104	71.7	20 931 589	15 749 532	75.2
1 VII 2003[51] .... ESDF		41 847 421	30 877 972	73.8	20 653 652	14 865 986	72.0	21 193 769	16 011 986	75.6
1 VII 2004[51] .... ESDF		42 367 528	31 385 112	74.1	20 911 536	15 112 115	72.3	21 455 992	16 272 997	75.8
22 V 2005 .... CDFC		41 468 384	31 510 379	76.0	20 336 117	15 086 536	74.2	21 132 267	16 423 843	77.7
1 VII 2005[52] .... ESDF		42 888 592	31 889 311	74.4	21 169 835	15 356 281	72.5	21 718 757	16 533 030	76.1
1 VII 2006[52] .... ESDF		43 405 387	32 386 600	74.6	21 425 328	15 599 203	72.8	21 980 059	16 787 397	76.4
1 VII 2007[52] .... ESDF		43 926 034	32 888 654	74.9	21 682 836	15 844 867	73.1	22 243 198	17 043 787	76.6
1 VII 2008[52] .... ESDF		44 450 260	33 396 133	75.1	21 942 197	16 093 111	73.3	22 508 063	17 303 022	76.9
1 VII 2009[52] .... ESDF		44 977 758	33 892 207	75.4	22 203 234	16 335 925	73.6	22 774 524	17 556 282	77.1
1 VII 2010[52] .... ESDF		45 508 205	34 387 230	75.6	22 465 760	16 578 297	73.8	23 042 445	17 808 933	77.3
Ecuador - Équateur[53]										
1 VII 2001[1] .... ESDF		12 479 924	7 633 850	61.2	6 265 558	3 778 158	60.3	6 214 366	3 855 692	62.0
25 XI 2001 .... CDFC		12 156 608	7 431 355	61.1	6 018 353	3 625 962	60.2	6 138 255	3 805 393	62.0
1 VII 2002[1] .... ESDF		12 660 728	7 817 018	61.7	6 354 906	3 870 667	60.9	6 305 821	3 946 351	62.6
1 VII 2003[1] .... ESDF		12 842 578	8 001 231	62.3	6 444 656	3 963 574	61.5	6 397 920	4 037 657	63.1
1 VII 2004[1] .... ESDF		13 026 891	8 187 908	62.9	6 535 564	4 057 642	62.1	6 491 327	4 130 266	63.6
1 VII 2005[1] .... ESDF		13 215 089	8 378 469	63.4	6 628 368	4 153 605	62.7	6 586 721	4 224 864	64.1
1 VII 2006[1] .... ESDF		13 408 270	8 580 090	64.0	6 723 629	4 254 974	63.3	6 684 641	4 325 116	64.7
1 VII 2007[1] .... ESDF		13 605 486	8 785 745	64.6	6 820 842	4 358 292	63.9	6 784 644	4 427 453	65.3
1 VII 2008[1] .... ESDF		13 805 092	8 993 796	65.1	6 919 185	4 462 739	64.5	6 885 907	4 531 057	65.8
1 VII 2009[1] .... ESDF		14 005 449	9 202 590	65.7	7 017 839	4 567 499	65.1	6 987 610	4 635 091	66.3
1 VII 2010[1] .... ESDF		14 204 900	9 410 481	66.2	7 115 983	4 671 748	65.7	7 088 917	4 738 733	66.8

Continent, country or area, and date / Continent, pays ou zone et date	Code[a]	Both sexes - Les deux sexes			Male - Masculin			Female - Féminin		
		Total	Urban - Urbaine		Total	Urban - Urbaine		Total	Urban - Urbaine	
			Number Nombre	Percent P.100		Number Nombre	Percent P.100		Number Nombre	Percent P.100
AMERICA, SOUTH - AMÉRIQUE DU SUD										
Falkland Islands (Malvinas) - Îles Falkland (Malvinas)[54]										
8 IV 2001	CDFC	2 913	...	...	1 598	...	...	1 315	...	...
8 X 2006[55]	CDFC	2 955	...	...	1 569	...	...	1 386	...	...
French Guiana - Guyane française										
1 VII 2001	ESDJ	169 667	...	...	84 782	...	...	84 885	...	...
1 VII 2002	ESDJ	175 426	...	...	87 387	...	...	88 039	...	...
1 I 2003	ESDJ	184 792	...	...	92 273	...	...	92 519	...	...
1 I 2004	ESDJ	193 167	...	...	96 300	...	...	96 867	...	...
1 I 2005	ESDJ	199 206	...	...	99 223	...	...	99 983	...	...
1 I 2006	CDJC	205 954	167 454	81.3	101 930	81 888	80.3	104 023	85 565	82.3
1 I 2007*	ESDJ	213 500	...	...	105 549	...	...	107 951	...	...
1 I 2008	ESDJ	219 266	...	...	108 662	...	...	110 604	...	...
1 I 2009	ESDJ	225 751	...	...	111 764	...	...	113 987	...	...
Guyana										
1 VII 2001	ESDF	743 600	...	...	366 372	...	...	377 228	...	...
1 VII 2002	ESDF	747 712	...	...	371 351	...	...	376 361	...	...
15 IX 2002	CDFC	751 223	...	...	376 034	...	...	375 189	...	...
1 VII 2003	ESDF	753 196	...	...	377 019	...	...	376 177	...	...
1 VII 2004	ESDF	755 685	...	...	378 265	...	...	377 420	...	...
1 VII 2005	ESDF	758 183	...	...	379 515	...	...	378 668	...	...
1 VII 2006	ESDF	760 689	...	...	380 770	...	...	379 919	...	...
1 VII 2007	ESDF	763 203	...	...	382 028	...	...	381 175	...	...
1 VII 2008	ESDF	766 183	...	...	383 522	...	...	382 661	...	...
Paraguay										
1 VII 2001[18]	ESDF	5 456 418	3 020 281	55.4	2 761 141	1 473 081	53.4	2 695 278	1 547 200	57.4
1 VII 2002[18]	ESDF	5 566 852	3 101 412	55.7	2 816 687	1 513 168	53.7	2 750 164	1 588 244	57.8
28 VIII 2002	CDFC	5 163 198	2 928 437	56.7	2 603 242	1 422 339	54.6	2 559 956	1 506 098	58.8
1 VII 2003[18]	ESDF	5 677 448	3 183 160	56.1	2 872 186	1 553 561	54.1	2 805 262	1 629 599	58.1
1 VII 2004[18]	ESDF	5 788 088	3 265 346	56.4	2 927 657	1 594 161	54.5	2 860 430	1 671 185	58.4
1 VII 2005[18]	ESDF	5 898 651	3 347 793	56.8	2 983 123	1 634 869	54.8	2 915 528	1 712 924	58.8
1 VII 2006[18]	ESDF	6 009 143	3 430 619	57.1	3 038 590	1 675 752	55.1	2 970 553	1 754 868	59.1
1 VII 2007[18]	ESDF	6 119 642	3 513 944	57.4	3 094 044	1 716 874	55.5	3 025 598	1 797 070	59.4
1 VII 2008[18]	ESDF	6 230 143	3 597 588	57.7	3 149 475	1 758 138	55.8	3 080 668	1 839 450	59.7
1 VII 2009[18]	ESDF	6 340 641	...	...	3 681 376	...	...	2 659 265	...	...
Peru - Pérou										
1 VII 2001	ESDF	26 366 533	18 112 915	68.7	13 230 410	8 972 168	67.8	13 136 123	9 140 747	69.6
1 VII 2002	ESDF	26 739 379	18 534 702	69.3	13 416 024	9 179 165	68.4	13 323 355	9 355 537	70.2
1 VII 2003	ESDF	27 103 457	18 953 109	69.9	13 597 121	9 384 413	69.0	13 506 336	9 568 696	70.8
1 VII 2004	ESDF	27 460 073	19 368 782	70.5	13 774 414	9 588 293	69.6	13 685 659	9 780 489	71.5
1 VII 2005	ESDF	27 810 540	19 782 408	71.1	13 948 639	9 791 272	70.2	13 861 901	9 991 136	72.1
18 VII 2005*[56]	CDFC	26 152 265	...	...	13 061 026	...	...	13 091 239	...	...
1 VII 2006	ESDF	28 151 443	20 191 318	71.7	14 118 112	9 991 965	70.8	14 033 331	10 199 353	72.7
1 VII 2007	ESDF	28 481 901	20 594 600	72.3	14 282 346	10 189 918	71.3	14 199 555	10 404 682	73.3
21 X 2007	CDFC	27 412 157	20 810 288	75.9	13 622 640	10 226 205	75.1	13 789 517	10 584 083	76.8
1 VII 2008	ESDF	28 807 034	20 995 699	72.9	14 443 858	10 386 799	71.9	14 363 176	10 608 900	73.9
1 VII 2009	ESDF	29 132 013	21 398 222	73.5	14 605 206	10 584 348	72.5	14 526 807	10 813 874	74.4
1 VII 2010	ESDF	29 461 933	21 805 837	74.0	14 768 901	10 784 345	73.0	14 693 032	11 021 492	75.0
Suriname										
1 VII 2001	ESDJ	470 064	...	...	236 276	...	...	233 788	...	...
1 VII 2002	ESDJ	476 374	...	...	239 447	...	...	236 927	...	...
31 III 2003*	CDJC	481 146[57]	...	...	241 837	...	...	239 292	...	...
1 VII 2003	ESDJ	482 769	...	...	242 662	...	...	240 107	...	...
2 VIII 2004[58]	CDJC	492 829	328 932	66.7	247 846[59]	164 297[59]	66.3	244 618[59]	164 370[59]	67.2
1 VII 2005	ESDJ	498 543	...	...	251 101	...	...	247 442	...	...
1 VII 2006	ESDJ	504 257	...	...	254 147	...	...	250 110	...	...
1 VII 2007	ESDJ	509 970	...	...	257 181	...	...	252 789	...	...
1 VII 2008	ESDJ	517 052	...	...	260 898	...	...	256 154	...	...
Uruguay										
1 VII 2001[1]	ESDF	3 308 356	3 071 727	92.8	1 601 593	1 466 408	91.6	1 706 763	1 605 319	94.1
1 VII 2002[1]	ESDF	3 308 527	3 077 804	93.0	1 600 814	1 469 148	91.8	1 707 713	1 608 656	94.2
1 VII 2003[1]	ESDF	3 303 540	3 078 812	93.2	1 597 362	1 469 246	92.0	1 706 177	1 609 565	94.3

Continent, country or area, and date / Continent, pays ou zone et date	Code[a]	Both sexes - Les deux sexes			Male - Masculin			Female - Féminin		
		Total	Urban - Urbaine		Total	Urban - Urbaine		Total	Urban - Urbaine	
			Number Nombre	Percent P.100		Number Nombre	Percent P.100		Number Nombre	Percent P.100
AMERICA, SOUTH - AMÉRIQUE DU SUD										
Uruguay										
1 VI 2004[60] ....CDFC		3 241 003	2 974 714	91.8	1 565 533	1 415 362	90.4	1 675 470	1 559 352	93.1
1 VII 2004[1] ....ESDF		3 301 732	3 083 096	93.4	1 595 635	1 471 098	92.2	1 706 097	1 611 998	94.5
1 VII 2005[1] ....ESDF		3 305 723	3 089 988	93.5	1 597 040	1 474 638	92.3	1 708 683	1 615 350	94.5
1 VII 2006[1] ....ESDF		3 314 466	3 101 685	93.6	1 601 024	1 480 779	92.5	1 713 442	1 620 906	94.6
1 VII 2007[1] ....ESDF		3 323 906	3 114 125	93.7	1 605 466	1 487 391	92.6	1 718 440	1 626 734	94.7
1 VII 2008[1] ....ESDF		3 334 052	3 127 318	93.8	1 610 356	1 494 470	92.8	1 723 696	1 632 848	94.7
1 VII 2009[1] ....ESDF		3 344 938	3 141 299	93.9	1 615 709	1 502 032	93.0	1 729 229	1 639 267	94.8
Venezuela (Bolivarian Republic of) - Venezuela (République bolivarienne du)										
1 VII 2001[61] ....ESDF		24 765 581	21 754 766	87.8	12 454 204	10 820 038	86.9	12 311 377	10 934 728	88.8
30 X 2001[61] ....CDFC		23 054 210	...	...	11 402 869			11 651 341		
1 VII 2002[61] ....ESDF		25 219 910	22 163 339	87.9	12 678 275	11 021 146	86.9	12 541 635	11 142 193	88.8
1 VII 2003 ....ESDF		25 673 550	22 570 794	87.9	12 901 999	11 221 668	87.0	12 771 551	11 349 126	88.9
1 VII 2004 ....ESDF		26 127 351	22 977 915	87.9	13 125 804	11 421 991	87.0	13 001 547	11 555 924	88.9
1 VII 2005 ....ESDF		26 577 423	23 381 277	88.0	13 347 732	11 620 413	87.1	13 229 691	11 760 864	88.9
1 VII 2006 ....ESDF		27 030 656	23 786 937	88.0	13 570 418	11 819 341	87.1	13 460 238	11 967 596	88.9
1 VII 2007 ....ESDF		27 483 208	24 191 525	88.0	13 792 761	12 017 754	87.1	13 690 447	12 173 771	88.9
1 VII 2008 ....ESDF		27 934 783	24 594 784	88.0	14 014 614	12 215 477	87.2	13 920 169	12 379 307	88.9
1 VII 2009 ....ESDF		28 384 132	...	...	14 235 351	...	...	14 148 781	...	...
1 VII 2010 ....ESDF		28 833 845	25 396 369	88.1	14 456 287	12 608 398	87.2	14 377 558	12 787 971	88.9
ASIA - ASIE										
Afghanistan										
1 VII 2002[62] ....ESDF		20 297 800	4 463 000	22.0	10 453 500	2 332 600	22.3	9 844 300	2 130 400	21.6
1 VII 2003[62] ....ESDF		20 691 400	...	...	10 657 000	...	...	10 034 400	...	...
1 VII 2004[62] ....ESDF		21 677 700	...	...	11 086 400	...	...	10 591 300	...	...
1 VII 2005[62] ....ESDF		22 097 900	...	...	11 301 300	...	...	10 796 600	...	...
1 VII 2006[63] ....ESDF		22 575 900	4 862 100	21.5	11 545 800	2 503 100	21.7	11 030 100	2 359 000	21.4
1 VII 2007[62] ....ESDF		23 038 900	...	...	11 783 600	...	...	11 255 300	...	...
1 VII 2008[62] ....ESDF		23 511 400	...	...	12 025 700	...	...	11 485 700	...	...
1 VII 2009[62] ....ESDF		23 993 500[64]	5 507 300	23.0	12 272 900	2 835 900	23.1	11 720 600	2 671 400	22.8
1 VII 2010[62] ....ESDF		24 485 600[65]	5 690 300	23.2	12 524 700[65]	2 929 900	23.4	11 960 900[65]	2 760 400	23.1
Armenia - Arménie										
1 VII 2001 ....ESDJ		3 214 095	2 070 947	64.4	1 542 728	977 820	63.4	1 671 367	1 093 127	65.4
10 X 2001[66] ....CDFC		3 002 594	1 945 514	64.8	1 407 220	898 977	63.9	1 595 374	1 046 537	65.6
1 VII 2002 ....ESDJ		3 211 593	2 063 913	64.3	1 542 974	974 775	63.2	1 668 619	1 089 138	65.3
1 VII 2003 ....ESDJ		3 211 267	2 061 952	64.2	1 545 168	975 356	63.1	1 666 099	1 086 596	65.2
1 VII 2004 ....ESDJ		3 214 030	2 061 984	64.2	1 548 713	976 728	63.1	1 665 317	1 085 256	65.2
1 VII 2005 ....ESDJ		3 217 535	2 062 472	64.1	1 552 382	978 396	63.0	1 665 153	1 084 076	65.1
1 VII 2006 ....ESDJ		3 221 094	2 064 268	64.1	1 555 755	980 272	63.0	1 665 339	1 083 996	65.1
1 VII 2007 ....ESDJ		3 226 520	2 067 650	64.1	1 559 978	982 632	63.0	1 666 542	1 085 018	65.1
1 VII 2008 ....ESDJ		3 234 031	2 071 942	64.1	1 565 411	985 913	63.0	1 668 620	1 086 029	65.1
1 VII 2009 ....ESDJ		3 243 729	2 077 181	64.0	1 572 046	989 609	63.0	1 671 683	1 087 572	65.1
1 VII 2010 ....ESDJ		3 256 066	...	...	1 579 705	...	...	1 676 361	...	...
Azerbaijan - Azerbaïdjan										
1 VII 2001[51] ....ESDF		8 152 800	4 193 500	51.4	3 983 000	2 038 900	51.2	4 169 800	2 154 600	51.7
1 VII 2002[51] ....ESDF		8 230 200	4 246 700	51.6	4 021 800	2 083 500	51.8	4 208 400	2 163 200	51.4
1 VII 2003[51] ....ESDF		8 309 100	4 338 700	52.2	4 061 200	2 128 500	52.4	4 247 900	2 210 200	52.0
1 VII 2004[51] ....ESDF		8 398 200	4 440 600	52.9	4 106 100	2 160 000	52.6	4 292 100	2 280 600	53.1
1 VII 2005[51] ....ESDF		8 500 200	4 521 700	53.2	4 157 500	2 200 000	52.9	4 342 700	2 321 700	53.5
1 VII 2006[51] ....ESDF		8 609 500	4 601 200	53.4	4 212 600	2 239 100	53.2	4 396 900	2 362 100	53.7
1 VII 2007[51] ....ESDF		8 722 900	4 685 100	53.7	4 270 000	2 280 600	53.4	4 452 900	2 404 500	54.0
1 VII 2008[51] ....ESDF		8 838 400	4 776 000	54.0	4 328 600	2 325 200	53.7	4 509 800	2 450 800	54.3
1 VII 2009[51] ....ESDF		8 947 200	4 842 500	54.1	4 385 900	2 358 900	53.8	4 561 300	2 483 600	54.4
1 VII 2010 ....ESDF		9 047 400	4 894 600	54.1	4 442 300	2 383 700	53.7	4 605 100	2 510 900	54.5
Bahrain - Bahreïn										
7 IV 2001 ....CDJC		650 604	571 385[67]	87.8	373 649	328 817[67]	88.0	276 955	242 568[67]	87.6
1 VII 2001 ....ESDF		661 317	...	...	386 712	...	...	274 605	...	...

Continent, country or area, and date / Continent, pays ou zone et date	Code[a]	Both sexes - Les deux sexes			Male - Masculin			Female - Féminin		
		Total	Urban - Urbaine		Total	Urban - Urbaine		Total	Urban - Urbaine	
			Number Nombre	Percent P.100		Number Nombre	Percent P.100		Number Nombre	Percent P.100
ASIA - ASIE										
Bahrain - Bahreïn										
1 VII 2002	ESDF	710 554	...	...	418 196	...	...	292 358	...	...
1 VII 2003	ESDF	764 519	...	...	452 900	...	...	311 619	...	...
1 VII 2004	ESDF	823 744	...	...	491 195	...	...	332 549	...	...
1 VII 2005	ESDF	888 824	...	...	533 501	...	...	355 323	...	...
1 VII 2006	ESDF	960 425	...	...	580 285	...	...	380 141	...	...
1 VII 2007	ESDF	1 039 297	...	...	632 074	...	...	407 223	...	...
1 VII 2008	ESDF	1 106 509	...	...	677 999	...	...	428 510	...	...
1 VII 2009	ESDF	1 178 415	...	...	731 997	...	...	446 418	...	...
Bangladesh										
22 I 2001[68]	CDFC	124 355 263	29 255 627	23.5	64 091 508	15 709 427	24.5	60 263 755	13 546 200	22.5
1 VII 2002	ESDF	132 900 000	30 600 000	23.0	68 200 000	...	...	64 700 000	...	...
1 VII 2003	ESDF	134 800 000	31 300 000	23.2	69 100 000	...	...	65 700 000	...	...
1 VII 2004	ESDF	136 700 000	32 400 000	23.7	70 100 000	...	...	66 600 000	...	...
1 VII 2005	ESDF	138 600 000	33 600 000	24.2	71 000 000	...	...	67 600 000	...	...
1 VII 2006	ESDF	140 600 000	34 600 000	24.6	72 000 000	...	...	68 600 000	...	...
1 VII 2007	ESDF	142 600 000	35 700 000	25.0	73 100 000	...	...	69 500 000	...	...
1 VII 2008*	ESDF	144 500 000	36 700 000	25.4	74 000 000	...	...	70 500 000	...	...
Bhutan - Bhoutan										
1 VII 2001	ESDF	590 543	...	...	352 935[3]	...	...	346 014[3]	...	...
1 VII 2002	ESDF	601 582	...	...	361 759[3]	...	...	354 665[3]	...	...
1 VII 2003	ESDF	612 515	...	...	370 805[3]	...	...	363 535[3]	...	...
1 VII 2004	ESDF	623 647	...	...	380 090[3]	...	...	372 610[3]	...	...
30 V 2005	CDFC	634 982	196 111	30.9	333 595	105 559	31.6	301 387	90 552	30.0
1 VII 2006[69]	ESDF	646 851	204 691	31.6	339 403	109 920	32.4	307 448	94 771	30.8
1 VII 2007[69]	ESDF	658 888	213 571	32.4	345 298	114 593	33.2	313 590	98 978	31.6
1 VII 2008[69]	ESDF	671 083	222 753	33.2	351 269	119 342	34.0	319 814	103 411	32.3
1 VII 2009[69]	ESDF	683 407	232 232	34.0	357 305	124 246	34.8	326 102	107 986	33.1
1 VII 2010[69]	ESDF	695 823	242 001	34.8	363 384	129 298	35.6	332 439	112 703	33.9
Brunei Darussalam - Brunéi Darussalam										
1 VII 2001	ESDF	332 800	...	...	168 900	...	...	163 900	...	...
21 VIII 2001*	CDFC	332 844	238 699	71.7	168 974	120 046	71.0	163 870	118 653	72.4
1 VII 2002	ESDF	344 200	...	...	180 600	...	...	163 600	...	...
1 VII 2003	ESDF	349 600	...	...	182 500	...	...	167 100	...	...
1 VII 2004	ESDF	359 700	...	...	189 400	...	...	170 300	...	...
1 VII 2005	ESDF	370 100	...	...	195 300	...	...	174 800	...	...
1 VII 2006	ESDF	383 000	...	...	203 300	...	...	179 700	...	...
1 VII 2007	ESDF	390 000	...	...	206 900	...	...	183 100	...	...
1 VII 2008	ESDF	398 000	...	...	211 000	...	...	187 000	...	...
1 VII 2009	ESDF	406 200	...	...	215 000	...	...	191 200	...	...
Cambodia - Cambodge[70]										
1 I 2002	ESDF	13 040 668	...	...	6 313 131	...	...	6 727 537	...	...
1 I 2003	ESDF	13 287 053	...	...	6 437 037	...	...	6 850 016	...	...
1 VII 2004[71]	SSDF	12 824 170	1 920 752	15.0	6 197 128	932 126	15.0	6 627 042	988 626	14.9
3 III 2008	CDFC	13 395 682	2 614 027	19.5	6 516 054	1 255 570	19.3	6 879 628	1 358 457	19.7
1 VII 2008[72]	ESDF	13 868 227	2 707 240	19.5	6 745 592	1 299 799	19.3	7 122 635	1 407 441	19.8
1 VII 2009[72]	ESDF	14 085 324	2 814 943	20.0	6 859 756	1 351 939	19.7	7 225 568	1 463 004	20.2
1 VII 2010[72]	ESDF	14 302 779	2 926 810	20.5	6 973 994	1 406 183	20.2	7 328 785	1 520 627	20.7
China - Chine[73]										
1 VII 2001	ESDF	1 276 270 000	480 640 000[74]	37.7	656 720 000	...	...	619 550 000	...	...
1 VII 2002	ESDF	1 284 530 000	502 120 000[74]	39.1	661 150 000	...	...	623 380 000	...	...
1 VII 2003	ESDF	1 292 270 000	523 760 000[74]	40.5	665 560 000	...	...	626 710 000	...	...
1 VII 2004	ESDF	1 299 880 000	542 830 000[74]	41.8	669 760 000	...	...	630 120 000	...	...
1 VII 2005	ESDF	1 307 560 000	562 120 000[74]	43.0	673 750 000	...	...	633 810 000	...	...
1 VII 2006	ESDF	1 314 480 000	577 060 000[74]	43.9	677 280 000	...	...	637 200 000	...	...
1 VII 2007	ESDF	1 321 290 000	593 790 000[74]	44.9	680 480 000	...	...	640 810 000	...	...
1 VII 2008	ESDF	1 328 020 000	606 670 000[74]	45.7	683 570 000	...	...	644 450 000	...	...
1 VII 2009	ESDF	1 334 740 000	621 860 000[74]	46.6	686 520 000	...	...	648 220 000	...	...
China, Hong Kong SAR - Chine, Hong Kong RAS										
14 III 2001[75]	CDJC	6 708 389	...	...	3 285 344	...	...	3 423 045	...	...
1 VII 2001	ESDJ	6 714 300	...	...	3 282 000	...	...	3 432 300	...	...
1 VII 2002	ESDJ	6 744 100	...	...	3 279 600	...	...	3 464 500	...	...

Continent, country or area, and date / Continent, pays ou zone et date	Code[a]	Both sexes - Les deux sexes			Male - Masculin			Female - Féminin		
		Total	Urban - Urbaine		Total	Urban - Urbaine		Total	Urban - Urbaine	
			Number Nombre	Percent P.100		Number Nombre	Percent P.100		Number Nombre	Percent P.100
ASIA - ASIE										
China, Hong Kong SAR - Chine, Hong Kong RAS										
1 VII 2003	ESDJ	6 730 800	...	...	3 259 100	...	...	3 471 700	...	...
1 VII 2004	ESDJ	6 783 500	...	...	3 266 800	...	...	3 516 700	...	...
1 VII 2005	ESDJ	6 813 200	...	...	3 264 000	...	...	3 549 200	...	...
1 VII 2006	ESDJ	6 857 100	...	...	3 270 100	...	...	3 587 000	...	...
14 VII 2006	CDJC	6 864 346	...	...	3 272 956	...	...	3 591 390	...	...
1 VII 2007	ESDJ	6 925 900	...	...	3 287 400	...	...	3 638 500	...	...
1 VII 2008	ESDJ	6 977 700	...	...	3 297 500	...	...	3 680 200	...	...
1 VII 2009	ESDJ	7 003 700	...	...	3 296 200	...	...	3 707 500	...	...
1 VII 2010	ESDJ	7 067 800	...	...	3 310 500	...	...	3 757 300	...	...
China, Macao SAR - Chine, Macao RAS										
1 VII 2001	ESDJ	433 903	...	...	208 235	...	...	225 668	...	...
23 VIII 2001	CDJC	435 235	...	...	208 865	...	...	226 370	...	...
1 VII 2002	ESDJ	438 408	...	...	210 218	...	...	228 190	...	...
1 VII 2003	ESDJ	443 600	...	...	212 866	...	...	230 734	...	...
1 VII 2004	ESDJ	454 661	...	...	218 122	...	...	236 539	...	...
1 VII 2005	ESDJ	473 457	...	...	227 600	...	...	245 857	...	...
1 VII 2006	ESDJ	498 852	...	...	243 009	...	...	255 843	...	...
19 VIII 2006	CDJC	502 113	...	...	245 167	...	...	256 946	...	...
1 VII 2007	ESDJ	525 800	...	...	259 100	...	...	266 700	...	...
1 VII 2008	ESDJ	551 800	...	...	273 500	...	...	278 400	...	...
1 VII 2009	ESDJ	544 100	...	...	265 200	...	...	279 000	...	...
1 VII 2010	ESDJ	544 600	...	...	260 400	...	...	284 300	...	...
Cyprus - Chypre[76]										
1 VII 2001	ESDJ	701 300	...	...	344 300	...	...	357 000	...	...
1 X 2001[77]	CDJC	689 565	474 450	68.8	338 497	231 128	68.3	351 068	243 322	69.3
1 VII 2002	ESDJ	709 600	...	...	347 900	...	...	361 700	...	...
1 VII 2003	ESDJ	720 600	...	...	353 700	...	...	366 900	...	...
1 VII 2004	ESDJ	737 100	...	...	363 000	...	...	374 100	...	...
1 VII 2005	ESDJ	758 000	...	...	373 600	...	...	384 400	...	...
1 VII 2006	ESDJ	770 900	...	...	380 100	...	...	390 800	...	...
1 VII 2007	ESDJ	785 300	...	...	386 700	...	...	398 600	...	...
1 VII 2008*	ESDJ	793 000	...	...	391 800	...	...	401 200	...	...
1 VII 2009*	ESDJ	800 011	...	...	396 527	...	...	403 485	...	...
1 VII 2010*	ESDJ	803 791	...	...	399 455	...	...	404 337	...	...
Democratic People's Republic of Korea - République populaire démocratique de Corée										
1 X 2008	CDJC	24 052 231	...	...	11 721 838	...	...	12 330 393	...	...
Georgia - Géorgie										
1 VII 2001	ESDF	4 385 800	2 283 200	52.1	2 068 400	...	...	2 317 400	...	...
17 I 2002	CDFC	4 355 673	2 282 250	52.4	2 049 786	1 045 888	51.0	2 305 887	1 236 362	53.6
1 VII 2002	ESDF	4 357 100	2 275 800	52.2	2 054 200	...	...	2 302 900	...	...
1 VII 2003	ESDF	4 328 900	2 259 700	52.2	2 039 300	...	...	2 289 600	...	...
1 VII 2004	ESDF	4 318 300	2 255 000	52.2	2 034 400	...	...	2 283 900	...	...
1 VII 2005	ESDF	4 361 400	2 284 000	52.4	2 060 300	...	...	2 301 100	...	...
1 VII 2006	ESDF	4 398 000	2 309 700	52.5	2 081 700	...	...	2 316 300	...	...
1 VII 2007	ESDF	4 388 400	2 306 400	52.6	2 079 000	...	...	2 309 400	...	...
1 VII 2008	ESDF	4 383 800	2 306 500	52.6	2 079 600	...	...	2 304 200	...	...
1 VII 2009	ESDF	4 410 915	...	...	2 094 854	...	...	2 316 061	...	...
India - Inde[78]										
1 III 2001[79]	CDFC	1 028 610 328	286 119 689	27.8	532 156 772	150 554 098	28.3	496 453 556	135 565 591	27.3
1 VII 2001[80]	ESDF	1 034 930 863	288 732 422	27.9	535 244 661	151 922 010	28.4	499 686 202	136 810 412	27.4
1 VII 2002[1]	ESDF	1 051 258 250	295 388 359	28.1	543 896 774	155 423 847	28.6	507 361 477	139 964 511	27.6
1 VII 2003[1]	ESDF	1 068 065 117	302 416 034	28.3	552 616 508	159 117 861	28.8	515 448 609	143 298 173	27.8
1 VII 2004[1]	ESDF	1 084 756 558	309 506 730	28.5	561 281 181	162 846 812	29.0	523 475 376	146 659 918	28.0
1 VII 2005[1]	ESDF	1 101 317 709	316 648 000	28.8	569 882 367	166 604 533	29.2	531 435 342	150 043 467	28.2
1 VII 2006[1]	ESDF	1 117 733 826	323 827 490	29.0	578 411 677	170 384 885	29.5	539 322 149	153 442 605	28.5
1 VII 2007[1]	ESDF	1 134 023 232	331 060 644	29.2	586 879 523	174 195 527	29.7	547 143 709	156 865 117	28.7
1 VII 2008[1]	ESDF	1 150 196 000	338 356 000	29.4	595 291 000	178 041 000	29.9	554 905 000	160 315 000	28.9

Continent, country or area, and date / Continent, pays ou zone et date	Code[a]	Both sexes - Les deux sexes Total	Urban - Urbaine Number Nombre	Urban - Urbaine Percent P.100	Male - Masculin Total	Urban - Urbaine Number Nombre	Urban - Urbaine Percent P.100	Female - Féminin Total	Urban - Urbaine Number Nombre	Urban - Urbaine Percent P.100
ASIA - ASIE										
Indonesia - Indonésie										
1 VII 2001[81] ....ESDJ		208 198 132	...	...	104 406 240	...	...	103 791 892	...	...
1 VII 2002[81] ....ESDJ		211 309 622	...	...	105 966 575	...	...	105 343 047	...	...
1 VII 2003[81] ....ESDJ		214 467 613	...	...	107 550 230	...	...	106 917 383	...	...
1 VII 2004[81] ....ESDJ		217 672 800	...	...	109 157 552	...	...	108 515 248	...	...
1 VII 2005[81] ....ESDJ		220 925 888	...	...	110 788 896	...	...	110 136 992	...	...
31 X 2005[82] ....SSDF		213 375 287	92 005 069	43.1	107 274 528	46 055 993	42.9	106 100 759	45 949 076	43.3
1 VII 2006[81] ....ESDJ		224 227 593	...	...	112 444 620	...	...	111 782 973	...	...
1 VII 2007[81] ....ESDJ		227 578 641	...	...	114 125 088	...	...	113 453 553	...	...
1 VII 2008[81] ....ESDJ		230 979 770	...	...	115 830 670	...	...	115 149 100	...	...
1 VII 2009[81] ....ESDJ		234 431 729	...	...	117 561 743	...	...	116 869 986	...	...
1 V 2010 ....CDJC		237 641 326	...	...	119 630 913	...	...	118 010 413	...	...
Iran (Islamic Republic of) - Iran (République islamique d')										
1 VII 2001[83] ....ESDJ		65 301 308	42 587 465	65.2	33 201 477	21 715 641	65.4	32 099 830	20 871 824	65.0
1 VII 2002[83] ....ESDJ		66 300 418	43 709 980	65.9	33 713 360	22 281 715	66.1	32 587 058	21 428 265	65.8
1 VII 2003[83] ....ESDJ		67 314 814	44 834 988	66.6	34 233 497	22 849 043	66.7	33 081 317	21 985 945	66.5
1 VII 2004[83] ....ESDJ		68 344 730	45 966 432	67.3	34 761 738	23 419 649	67.4	33 582 992	22 546 783	67.1
1 VII 2005[83] ....ESDJ		69 390 405	47 095 882	67.9	35 298 812	23 989 204	68.0	34 091 593	23 106 678	67.8
28 X 2006 ....CDJC		70 495 782	48 259 964[84]	68.5	35 866 362	24 576 442[84]	68.5	34 629 420	23 683 522[84]	68.4
1 VII 2007[83] ....ESDJ		71 278 952	48 874 656	68.6	36 247 296	24 891 876	68.7	35 031 392	23 982 780	68.5
1 VII 2008[83] ....ESDJ		72 181 632	49 576 146	68.7	36 691 780	25 253 132	68.8	35 489 488	24 323 014	68.5
1 VII 2009[83] ....ESDJ		73 202 096	50 365 184	68.8	37 198 776	25 660 500	69.0	36 003 320	24 704 684	68.6
1 VII 2010[83] ....ESDJ		74 339 576	51 242 546	68.9	37 767 220	26 114 342	69.1	36 572 356	25 128 204	68.7
Iraq										
1 VII 2001 ....ESDF		24 813 000	...	...	12 424 000	...	...	12 389 000	...	...
1 VII 2002 ....ESDF		25 565 000	...	...	12 814 000	...	...	12 751 000	...	...
1 VII 2003 ....ESDF		26 340 000	...	...	13 216 000	...	...	13 124 000	...	...
1 VII 2004 ....ESDF		27 139 000	...	...	13 629 000	...	...	13 510 000	...	...
1 VII 2005 ....ESDF		27 963 000	...	...	14 055 000	...	...	13 908 000	...	...
1 VII 2006 ....ESDF		28 810 441	19 226 476	66.7	14 493 207	9 698 293	66.9	14 317 234	9 528 183	66.6
1 VII 2007 ....ESDF		29 682 081	19 752 833	66.5	14 943 516	9 970 074	66.7	14 738 565	9 782 759	66.4
1 VII 2008 ....ESDF		31 895 000	...	...	16 058 000	...	...	15 837 000	...	...
1 VII 2009 ....ESDF		32 105 000	...	...	15 942 000	...	...	16 163 000	...	...
Israel - Israël										
1 VII 2001[85] ....ESDJ		6 439 000	5 900 700	91.6	3 176 600	2 900 200	91.3	3 262 500	3 000 500	92.0
1 VII 2002[85] ....ESDJ		6 569 900	6 017 300	91.6	3 241 700	2 958 200	91.3	3 328 200	3 059 100	91.9
1 VII 2003[85] ....ESDJ		6 689 700	6 122 400	91.5	3 301 800	3 010 900	91.2	3 387 900	3 111 600	91.8
1 VII 2004[85] ....ESDJ		6 809 000	6 226 900	91.5	3 362 000	3 063 600	91.1	3 447 000	3 163 300	91.8
1 VII 2005[85] ....ESDJ		6 930 128	6 359 940	91.8	3 423 132	3 131 229	91.5	3 506 996	3 228 711	92.1
1 VII 2006[85] ....ESDJ		7 053 707	6 475 600[86]	91.8	3 485 501	3 189 511[86]	91.5	3 568 206	3 286 089[86]	92.1
1 VII 2007[85] ....ESDJ		7 180 115	6 589 632[86]	91.8	3 549 216	3 247 280[86]	91.5	3 630 899	3 342 352[86]	92.1
1 VII 2008[85] ....ESDJ		7 308 795	6 701 217[86]	91.7	3 614 125	3 303 732[86]	91.4	3 694 671	3 397 485[86]	92.0
27 XII 2008[87] ....CDFC		7 412 180	6 799 340[22]	91.7	3 663 910	3 350 610[22]	91.4	3 748 270	3 448 730[22]	92.0
1 VII 2009[85] ....ESDJ		7 485 565	6 865 023	91.7	3 701 384	3 384 556	91.4	3 784 181	3 480 467	92.0
Japan - Japon[88]										
1 VII 2001 ....ESDJ		127 149 000	...	...	62 178 000	...	...	64 971 000	...	...
1 VII 2002 ....ESDJ		127 445 000	...	...	62 278 000	...	...	65 167 000	...	...
1 VII 2003 ....ESDJ		127 718 000	...	...	62 370 000	...	...	65 348 000	...	...
1 VII 2004 ....ESDJ		127 761 000	...	...	62 355 000	...	...	65 406 000	...	...
1 VII 2005 ....ESDJ		127 773 000	...	...	62 332 000	...	...	65 441 000	...	...
1 X 2005 ....CDJC		127 767 994	110 264 324	86.3	62 348 977	53 886 000	86.4	65 419 017	56 378 324	86.2
1 VII 2006 ....ESDJ		127 756 000	...	...	62 314 000	...	...	65 442 000	...	...
1 VII 2007 ....ESDJ		127 772 000	...	...	62 301 000	...	...	65 471 000	...	...
1 VII 2008 ....ESDJ		127 704 000	...	...	62 252 000	...	...	65 452 000	...	...
1 VII 2009 ....ESDJ		127 558 000	...	...	62 140 000	...	...	65 418 000	...	...
1 VII 2010 ....ESDJ		127 450 000	...	...	62 059 000[22]	...	...	65 392 000[22]	...	...
Jordan - Jordanie										
31 XII 2001[89] ....ESDF		4 978 000	4 112 600	82.6	2 563 700	...	...	2 414 300	...	...
31 XII 2002[89] ....ESDF		5 098 000	4 211 700	82.6	2 625 500	...	...	2 472 500	...	...
31 XII 2003[89] ....ESDF		5 230 000	4 320 600	82.6	2 693 500	...	...	2 536 500	...	...
1 X 2004[90] ....CDFC		5 103 639	3 997 383	78.3	2 626 287	2 055 431	78.3	2 477 352	1 941 952	78.4
31 XII 2004[89] ....ESDF		5 350 000	4 419 000	82.6	2 757 700	...	...	2 592 300	...	...

6. Total and urban population by sex: 2001 - 2010
Population totale et population urbaine selon le sexe : 2001 - 2010 (continued - suite)

Continent, country or area, and date / Continent, pays ou zone et date	Code[a]	Both sexes - Les deux sexes			Male - Masculin			Female - Féminin		
		Total	Urban - Urbaine		Total	Urban - Urbaine		Total	Urban - Urbaine	
			Number Nombre	Percent P.100		Number Nombre	Percent P.100		Number Nombre	Percent P.100
ASIA - ASIE										
Jordan - Jordanie										
31 XII 2005[89] .... ESDF		5 473 000	4 520 600	82.6	2 821 100	...	...	2 651 900	...	...
31 XII 2006[89] .... ESDF		5 600 000	4 625 600	82.6	2 886 600	...	...	2 713 400	...	...
31 XII 2007[89] .... ESDF		5 723 000	4 727 100	82.6	2 950 000	...	...	2 773 000	...	...
31 XII 2008[89] .... ESDF		5 850 000	4 832 100	82.6	3 015 000	...	...	2 835 000	...	...
31 XII 2009[89] .... ESDF		5 980 000	4 939 400	82.6	3 082 000	...	...	2 898 000	...	...
31 XII 2010[89] .... ESDF		6 113 000	5 049 300	82.6	3 151 000	...	...	2 962 000	...	...
Kazakhstan										
1 VII 2001 .... ESDF		14 858 335	8 421 366	56.7	7 156 582	3 942 353	55.1	7 701 753	4 479 013	58.2
1 VII 2002 .... ESDF		14 858 948	8 443 242	56.8	7 156 816	3 952 649	55.2	7 702 132	4 490 593	58.3
1 VII 2003 .... ESDF		14 909 018	8 487 697	56.9	7 179 583	3 971 520	55.3	7 729 435	4 516 177	58.4
1 VII 2004 .... ESDF		15 012 195	8 566 447	57.1	7 227 960	4 005 199	55.4	7 785 025	4 561 248	58.6
1 VII 2005 .... ESDF		15 147 029	8 655 586	57.1	7 290 852	4 044 092	55.5	7 856 177	4 611 494	58.7
1 VII 2006 .... ESDF		15 308 084	8 764 884	57.3	7 367 032	4 094 572	55.6	7 941 052	4 670 312	58.8
1 VII 2007 .... ESDF		15 484 192	8 195 389	52.9	7 450 418	3 815 422	51.2	8 033 774	4 379 967	54.5
1 VII 2008 .... ESDF		15 673 999	8 330 521	53.1	7 541 052	3 877 299	51.4	8 132 947	4 453 222	54.8
Kuwait - Koweït										
1 VII 2001 .... ESDF		1 952 870	...	...	1 145 609	...	...	807 261	...	...
1 VII 2002 .... ESDF		2 021 895	...	...	1 188 384	...	...	833 511	...	...
1 VII 2003 .... ESDF		2 093 396	...	...	1 232 781	...	...	860 615	...	...
1 VII 2004 .... ESDF		2 167 467	...	...	1 278 865	...	...	888 602	...	...
20 IV 2005* .... CDFC		2 213 403	...	...	1 310 067	...	...	903 336	...	...
1 VII 2005 .... ESDF		2 244 995	...	...	1 326 871	...	...	918 124	...	...
1 VII 2006 .... ESDF		2 328 116	...	...	1 378 341	...	...	949 775	...	...
1 VII 2007 .... ESDF		2 410 829	...	...	1 430 584	...	...	980 245	...	...
1 VII 2008 .... ESDF		2 495 851	...	...	1 484 422	...	...	1 011 429	...	...
1 VII 2009 .... ESDF		2 583 020	...	...	1 539 825	...	...	1 043 195	...	...
Kyrgyzstan - Kirghizstan										
1 VII 2001[91] .... ESDF		4 902 123	1 735 661	35.4	2 411 124	824 877	34.2	2 490 999	910 784	36.6
1 VII 2002[91] .... ESDF		4 919 460	1 740 805	35.4	2 416 831	825 612	34.2	2 502 629	915 193	36.6
1 VII 2003[91] .... ESDF		4 943 770	1 749 780	35.4	2 426 226	827 820	34.1	2 517 544	921 960	36.6
1 VII 2004[91] .... ESDF		4 976 881	1 773 667	35.6	2 439 845	836 840	34.3	2 537 036	936 827	36.9
1 VII 2005[91] .... ESDF		5 006 514	1 788 181	35.7	2 450 975	841 960	34.4	2 555 539	946 221	37.0
1 VII 2006[91] .... ESDF		5 033 953	1 790 295	35.6	2 460 578	841 414	34.2	2 573 375	948 881	36.9
1 VII 2007[91] .... ESDF		5 055 671	1 791 267	35.4	2 467 458	839 913	34.0	2 588 213	951 354	36.8
1 VII 2008[91] .... ESDF		5 077 722	1 794 620	35.3	2 475 331	839 873	33.9	2 602 391	954 747	36.7
24 III 2009* .... CDFC		5 107 700	...	...	2 489 200	...	...	2 618 500	...	...
1 VII 2009 .... ESDF		5 128 124	1 809 738	35.3	2 499 977	846 861	33.9	2 628 147	962 877	36.6
1 VII 2010 .... ESDF		5 192 806	1 828 955	35.2	2 532 547	856 262	33.8	2 660 259	972 693	36.6
Lao People's Democratic Republic - République démocratique populaire lao										
1 VII 2001[92] .... ESDF		5 377 000	...	...	2 657 000	...	...	2 720 000	...	...
1 VII 2002[92] .... ESDF		5 526 000	...	...	2 731 000	...	...	2 795 000	...	...
1 VII 2003[92] .... ESDF		5 679 000	...	...	2 807 000	...	...	2 872 000	...	...
1 VII 2004[92] .... ESDF		5 836 000	...	...	2 884 000	...	...	2 952 000	...	...
1 III 2005 .... CDJC		5 621 982	1 522 137[93]	27.1	2 800 551	763 043[93]	27.2	2 821 431	759 094[93]	26.9
1 VII 2005[94] .... ESDF		5 679 000	...	...	2 806 400	...	...	2 872 600	...	...
1 VII 2006[94] .... ESDF		5 747 000	...	...	2 864 000	...	...	2 883 000	...	...
1 VII 2007[94] .... ESDF		5 874 000	...	...	2 929 000	...	...	2 945 000	...	...
Lebanon - Liban[95]										
3 III 2004 .... SSDF		3 755 034	...	...	1 868 322	...	...	1 886 712	...	...
3 III 2007 .... SSDF		3 759 134	...	...	1 857 659	...	...	1 901 475	...	...
Malaysia - Malaisie[45]										
30 VI 2001 .... ESDJ		24 123 379	15 004 042	62.2	12 289 869	7 604 460	61.9	11 833 510	7 399 582	62.5
30 VI 2002 .... ESDJ		24 727 104	15 414 805	62.3	12 602 771	7 808 313	62.0	12 124 333	7 606 492	62.7
30 VI 2003 .... ESDJ		25 319 973	15 819 940	62.5	12 910 003	8 009 149	62.0	12 409 970	7 810 791	62.9
30 VI 2004 .... ESDJ		25 905 123	16 221 004	62.6	13 213 239	8 207 887	62.1	12 691 884	8 013 117	63.1
30 VI 2005 .... ESDJ		26 476 911	16 614 260	62.7	13 509 499	8 402 603	62.2	12 967 412	8 211 657	63.3
30 VI 2006 .... ESDJ		26 831 519	16 877 763	62.9	13 683 823	8 531 892	62.4	13 147 696	8 345 871	63.5
30 VI 2007 .... ESDJ		27 185 976	17 138 690	63.0	13 857 972	8 659 763	62.5	13 328 004	8 478 927	63.6
30 VI 2008 .... ESDJ		27 540 499	17 397 521	63.2	14 031 976	8 786 472	62.6	13 508 523	8 611 049	63.7
30 VI 2009 .... ESDJ		27 895 332	17 654 460	63.3	14 205 949	8 912 131	62.7	13 689 383	8 742 329	63.9
30 VI 2010 .... ESDJ		28 250 458	17 909 524	63.4	14 379 886	9 036 777	62.8	13 870 572	8 872 747	64.0

Continent, country or area, and date / Continent, pays ou zone et date	Code[a]	Both sexes - Les deux sexes			Male - Masculin			Female - Féminin		
		Total	Urban - Urbaine		Total	Urban - Urbaine		Total	Urban - Urbaine	
			Number Nombre	Percent P.100		Number Nombre	Percent P.100		Number Nombre	Percent P.100
ASIA - ASIE										
Maldives										
1 VII 2001	ESDF	275 975	75 680	27.4	140 100	...	...	135 875	...	...
1 VII 2002	ESDF	280 549	76 934	27.4	142 357	...	...	138 192	...	...
1 VII 2003	ESDF	285 066	78 173	27.4	144 599	...	...	140 467	...	...
1 VII 2004	ESDF	289 480	79 383	27.4	146 799	...	...	142 681	...	...
1 VII 2005	ESDF	293 746	...	...	148 929	...	...	144 817	...	...
21 III 2006	CDFC	298 968	103 693	34.7	151 459	51 992	34.3	147 509	51 701	35.0
1 VII 2006	ESDF	298 968	...	...	151 459	...	...	147 509	...	...
1 VII 2007	ESDF	304 869	...	...	154 391	...	...	150 478	...	...
1 VII 2008	ESDF	309 575	...	...	156 714	...	...	152 861	...	...
1 VII 2009	ESDF	314 542	...	...	159 159	...	...	155 383	...	...
1 VII 2010	ESDF	319 738	...	...	161 708	...	...	158 030	...	...
Mongolia - Mongolie										
1 VII 2001	ESDF	2 425 017	1 387 045	57.2	1 202 132	677 838	56.4	1 222 885	709 207	58.0
1 VII 2002	ESDF	2 458 963	1 409 034	57.3	1 218 894	688 417	56.5	1 240 069	720 617	58.1
1 VII 2003	ESDF	2 489 702	1 442 589	57.9	1 235 164	705 367	57.1	1 254 538	737 222	58.8
1 VII 2004	ESDF	2 518 573	1 481 205	58.8	1 249 487	723 856	57.9	1 269 086	757 349	59.7
1 VII 2005	ESDF	2 547 751	1 520 763	59.7	1 263 962	741 689	58.7	1 283 789	779 074	60.7
1 VII 2006	ESDF	2 578 587	1 561 417	60.6	1 268 249	756 004	59.6	1 310 338	805 413	61.5
1 VII 2007	ESDF	2 614 981	1 590 253	60.8	1 274 852	764 608	60.0	1 340 128	825 645	61.6
1 VII 2008	ESDF	2 659 347	1 630 116	61.3	1 297 153	784 189	60.5	1 362 194	845 927	62.1
31 XII 2009	ESDF	2 670 241	1 677 833	62.8	1 304 216	807 887	61.9	1 366 025	869 946	63.7
Myanmar										
1 VII 2001	ESDF	51 138 000	...	...	25 421 000	...	...	25 717 000	...	...
1 VII 2002	ESDF	52 171 000	...	...	25 941 000	...	...	26 230 000	...	...
1 VII 2003	ESDF	53 224 000	...	...	26 467 000	...	...	26 757 000	...	...
1 VII 2004	ESDF	54 299 000	...	...	27 000 000	...	...	27 299 000	...	...
1 VII 2005	ESDF	55 396 000	...	...	27 540 000	...	...	27 856 000	...	...
1 VII 2006	ESDF	56 515 000	...	...	28 097 000	...	...	28 418 000	...	...
1 VII 2007	ESDF	57 504 000	...	...	28 586 000	...	...	28 918 000	...	...
1 VII 2008	ESDF	58 377 000	...	...	29 026 000	...	...	29 351 000	...	...
Nepal - Népal										
22 VI 2001[96]	CDJC	23 151 423	3 227 879	13.9	11 563 921	1 664 362	14.4	11 587 502	1 563 517	13.5
1 VII 2002	ESDJ	23 701 451	...	...	11 845 495	...	...	11 855 956	...	...
1 VII 2003	ESDJ	24 249 996	...	...	12 126 262	...	...	12 123 734	...	...
1 VII 2004	ESDJ	24 797 059	...	...	12 406 222	...	...	12 390 837	...	...
1 VII 2005	ESDJ	25 342 638	...	...	12 685 375	...	...	12 657 263	...	...
1 VII 2006	ESDJ	25 886 736	...	...	12 963 722	...	...	12 923 014	...	...
1 VII 2007	ESDJ	26 427 399	...	...	13 240 233	...	...	13 187 166	...	...
1 VII 2008	ESDJ	26 966 581	...	...	13 515 938	...	...	13 450 643	...	...
1 VII 2009	ESDJ	27 504 280	...	...	13 790 836	...	...	13 713 444	...	...
Occupied Palestinian Territory - Territoire palestinien occupé										
1 VII 2001	ESDF	3 138 471	2 244 007[97]	71.5	1 592 892	...	...	1 545 579	...	...
1 VII 2002	ESDF	3 225 214	2 306 028[97]	71.5	1 636 917	...	...	1 588 297	...	...
1 VII 2003	ESDF	3 314 509	2 369 874[97]	71.5	1 682 238	...	...	1 632 271	...	...
1 VII 2004	ESDF	3 407 417	2 436 303[97]	71.5	1 729 392	...	...	1 678 025	...	...
1 VII 2005	ESDF	3 508 126	2 508 310[97]	71.5	1 780 506	...	...	1 727 620	...	...
1 VII 2006	ESDF	3 611 998	2 582 579[97]	71.5	1 833 225	...	...	1 778 773	...	...
1 VII 2007	ESDF	3 719 189	3 086 102[97]	83.0	1 887 628	...	...	1 831 561	...	...
1 XII 2007*[98]	CDFC	3 761 646	...	...	1 908 432	...	...	1 853 214	...	...
1 VII 2008	ESDF	3 825 512	3 175 546[97]	83.0	1 941 742	...	...	1 883 770	...	...
1 VII 2009	ESDF	3 935 249	3 267 977[97]	83.0	1 997 625	...	...	1 937 624	...	...
1 VII 2010	ESDF	4 048 403	3 363 385[97]	83.1	2 055 211	...	...	1 993 192	...	...
Oman										
1 VII 2001	ESDF	2 477 687	1 775 764	71.7	1 446 294	1 057 073	73.1	1 031 393	718 691	69.7
1 VII 2002	ESDF	2 537 742	1 818 805	71.7	1 481 349	1 082 695	73.1	1 056 393	736 111	69.7
7 XII 2003	CDFC	2 340 815[99]	1 673 480	71.5	1 313 239	950 471	72.4	1 027 576	723 009	70.4
1 VII 2004	ESDF	2 415 576	1 732 701	71.7	1 360 891	988 163	72.6	1 054 685	744 538	70.6
1 VII 2005	ESDF	2 508 837	1 804 995	71.9	1 458 845	1 063 202	72.9	1 049 992	741 793	70.6
1 VII 2006	ESDF	2 577 062	1 857 263	72.1	1 498 143	1 093 546	73.0	1 078 919	763 717	70.8
1 VII 2007	ESDF	2 743 499	1 984 158	72.3	1 622 119	1 188 537	73.3	1 121 380	795 621	71.0
1 VII 2008	ESDF	2 867 428	2 077 862	72.5	1 687 414	1 238 527	73.4	1 180 014	839 335	71.1
1 VII 2009	ESDF	3 173 917	2 314 865	72.9	1 971 115	1 457 197	73.9	1 202 802	857 668	71.3

135

Continent, country or area, and date / Continent, pays ou zone et date	Code[a]	Both sexes - Les deux sexes			Male - Masculin			Female - Féminin		
		Total	Urban - Urbaine		Total	Urban - Urbaine		Total	Urban - Urbaine	
			Number Nombre	Percent P.100		Number Nombre	Percent P.100		Number Nombre	Percent P.100
ASIA - ASIE										
Pakistan[100]										
1 VII 2001[101] .... ESDJ		133 652 121	47 739 853[102]	35.7	68 769 178	24 707 762[102]	35.9	64 882 943	23 032 091[102]	35.5
1 VII 2002 .... ESDF		145 280 000	48 020 000	33.1	75 390 000	...	...	69 900 000	...	...
1 VII 2003[103] .... ESDJ		138 979 270	49 640 104	35.7	71 741 403	25 819 279	36.0	67 237 867	23 820 825	35.4
1 VII 2004 .... ESDF		151 090 000	50 800 000	33.6	78 410 000	...	...	72 690 000	...	...
1 VII 2005[104] .... ESDJ		144 367 293	51 408 193	35.6	74 247 400	26 556 848	35.8	70 119 893	24 851 345	35.4
1 VII 2006 .... ESDJ		147 099 534	...	...	75 582 494	...	...	71 517 040	...	...
1 VII 2007[105] .... ESDJ		149 860 388	52 807 585	35.2	76 857 737	27 178 203	35.4	73 002 651	25 629 382	35.1
1 VII 2008 .... ESDF		162 370 000	57 320 000	35.3	84 270 000	...	...	78 110 000	...	...
Philippines[106]										
1 VII 2001 .... ESDJ		78 568 100	...	...	39 554 100	...	...	39 014 000	...	...
1 VII 2002 .... ESDJ		80 217 200	...	...	40 373 300	...	...	39 843 900	...	...
1 VII 2003 .... ESDJ		81 877 700	...	...	41 200 600	...	...	40 677 100	...	...
1 VII 2004 .... ESDJ		83 558 700	...	...	42 037 200	...	...	41 521 500	...	...
1 VII 2005 .... ESDJ		85 261 000	...	...	42 887 300	...	...	42 373 700	...	...
1 VII 2006 .... ESDJ		86 972 500	...	...	43 742 100	...	...	43 230 400	...	...
1 VII 2007 .... ESDJ		88 706 300	...	...	44 608 300	...	...	44 098 000	...	...
1 VII 2008 .... ESDJ		90 457 200	...	...	45 483 100	...	...	44 974 100	...	...
Qatar										
1 VII 2001 .... ESDF		643 365	...	...	427 321	...	...	216 044	...	...
1 VII 2002 .... ESDF		676 497	...	...	450 349	...	...	226 148	...	...
1 VII 2003 .... ESDF		713 858	...	...	476 508	...	...	237 350	...	...
16 III 2004 .... CDFC		744 029	...	...	496 382	...	...	247 647	...	...
1 VII 2004 .... ESDF		798 060	...	...	546 116	...	...	251 944	...	...
1 VII 2005 .... ESDF		906 117	...	...	637 070	...	...	269 047	...	...
1 VII 2006 .... ESDF		1 042 951	...	...	754 302	...	...	288 649	...	...
1 VII 2007 .... ESDF		1 218 252	...	...	905 751	...	...	312 501	...	...
1 VII 2008 .... ESDF		1 448 484	...	...	1 111 179	...	...	337 305	...	...
1 VII 2009 .... ESDF		1 638 644	...	...	1 265 155	...	...	373 489	...	...
21 IV 2010 .... CDFC		1 699 435	...	...	1 284 739	...	...	414 696	...	...
1 VII 2010 .... ESDF		1 714 195	...	...	1 290 869	...	...	423 326	...	...
Republic of Korea - République de Corée										
1 VII 2001 .... ESDJ		47 357 362	...	...	23 843 136	...	...	23 514 226	...	...
1 VII 2002 .... ESDJ		47 622 179	...	...	23 970 035	...	...	23 652 144	...	...
1 VII 2003 .... ESDJ		47 859 311	...	...	24 089 703	...	...	23 769 608	...	...
1 VII 2004 .... ESDJ		48 039 415	...	...	24 165 488	...	...	23 873 927	...	...
1 VII 2005 .... ESDJ		48 138 077	...	...	24 190 906	...	...	23 947 171	...	...
1 XI 2005[93] .... CDJC		47 278 951	38 514 753	81.5	23 623 954	19 258 840	81.5	23 654 997	19 255 913	81.4
1 VII 2006 .... ESDJ		48 297 184	...	...	24 267 609	...	...	24 029 575	...	...
1 VII 2007 .... ESDJ		48 456 369	...	...	24 344 276	...	...	24 112 093	...	...
1 VII 2008 .... ESDJ		48 606 787	...	...	24 415 883	...	...	24 190 904	...	...
1 VII 2009 .... ESDJ		48 746 693	...	...	24 481 480	...	...	24 265 213	...	...
1 VII 2010 .... ESDJ		48 874 539	...	...	24 540 316	...	...	24 334 223	...	...
Saudi Arabia - Arabie saoudite										
1 VII 2001 .... ESDF		20 979 424	...	...	11 648 157	...	...	9 331 268	...	...
1 VII 2002 .... ESDF		21 494 814	...	...	11 924 224	...	...	9 570 590	...	...
1 VII 2003 .... ESDF		22 022 864	...	...	12 206 825	...	...	9 816 039	...	...
1 VII 2004 .... ESDF		22 563 886	...	...	12 493 910	...	...	10 069 976	...	...
15 IX 2004 .... CDFC		22 678 262	...	...	12 557 240	...	...	10 121 022	...	...
1 VII 2005 .... ESDF		23 118 994	...	...	12 791 330	...	...	10 327 664	...	...
1 VII 2006 .... ESDF		23 678 849	...	...	13 090 840	...	...	10 588 009	...	...
Singapore - Singapour										
1 VII 2001 .... ESDJ		3 325 900	...	...	1 658 600	...	...	1 667 300	...	...
1 VII 2002 .... ESDJ		3 382 900	...	...	1 684 300	...	...	1 698 600	...	...
1 VII 2003 .... ESDJ		3 366 900	...	...	1 673 400	...	...	1 693 500	...	...
1 VII 2004 .... ESDJ		3 413 300	...	...	1 695 000[22]	...	...	1 718 200[22]	...	...
1 VII 2005 .... ESDJ		3 467 814	...	...	1 721 139	...	...	1 746 675	...	...
1 VII 2006 .... ESDJ		3 525 900	...	...	1 748 200	...	...	1 777 700	...	...
1 VII 2007 .... ESDJ		3 583 100	...	...	1 775 500	...	...	1 807 600	...	...
1 VII 2008 .... ESDJ		3 642 700	...	...	1 803 000	...	...	1 839 700	...	...
1 VII 2009 .... ESDJ		3 733 800	...	...	1 844 700	...	...	1 889 100	...	...
1 VII 2010 .... ESDJ		3 771 721	...	...	1 861 133	...	...	1 910 588	...	...

Continent, country or area, and date Continent, pays ou zone et date	Code[a]	Both sexes - Les deux sexes Total	Urban - Urbaine Number Nombre	Urban - Urbaine Percent P.100	Male - Masculin Total	Urban - Urbaine Number Nombre	Urban - Urbaine Percent P.100	Female - Féminin Total	Urban - Urbaine Number Nombre	Urban - Urbaine Percent P.100
ASIA - ASIE										
Sri Lanka										
1 VII 2001	ESDF	18 732 000	...	...	9 267 000	...	...	9 465 000	...	...
17 VII 2001[107]	CDFC	16 929 689	2 467 301	14.6	8 425 607	1 252 173	14.9	8 504 082	1 215 128	14.3
1 VII 2002	ESDF	19 007 000	...	...	9 392 000	...	...	9 615 000	...	...
1 VII 2003	ESDF	19 252 000	...	...	9 510 000	...	...	9 742 000	...	...
1 VII 2004	ESDF	19 435 000	...	...	9 678 000	...	...	9 757 000	...	...
1 VII 2005	ESDF	19 644 000	...	...	9 782 000	...	...	9 862 000	...	...
1 VII 2006	ESDF	19 858 000	...	...	9 889 000	...	...	9 969 000	...	...
1 VII 2007	ESDF	20 039 000	...	...	9 956 000	...	...	10 083 000	...	...
1 VII 2008	ESDF	20 216 000	...	...	9 980 000	...	...	10 236 000	...	...
1 VII 2009*	ESDF	20 450 000	...	...	10 148 000	...	...	10 302 000	...	...
1 VII 2010*	ESDF	20 653 000	...	...	10 249 000	...	...	10 404 000	...	...
Syrian Arab Republic - République arabe syrienne[108]										
1 VII 2001	ESDF	16 720 000	8 376 000	50.1	8 552 000	4 319 000	50.5	8 168 000	4 057 000	49.7
1 VII 2002	ESDF	17 130 000	8 599 000	50.2	8 763 000	4 439 000	50.7	8 367 000	4 160 000	49.7
1 VII 2003	ESDF	17 550 000	8 806 000	50.2	8 979 000	4 541 000	50.6	8 571 000	4 265 000	49.8
1 VII 2004	ESDF	17 829 000	9 539 000	53.5	9 150 000	4 916 000	53.7	8 679 000	4 623 000	53.3
22 IX 2004*	CDFC	17 921 000	...	...	9 161 000	...	...	8 760 000	...	...
1 VII 2005	ESDF	18 138 000	9 705 000	53.5	9 268 000	4 977 000	53.7	8 870 000	4 728 000	53.3
1 VII 2006	ESDF	18 717 000	10 013 000	53.5	9 563 000	5 139 000	53.7	9 154 000	4 874 000	53.2
1 VII 2007	ESDF	19 172 000	10 257 000	53.5	9 798 000	5 265 000	53.7	9 374 000	4 992 000	53.3
1 VII 2008	ESDF	19 644 000	10 511 000	53.5	10 042 000	5 394 000	53.7	9 602 000	5 117 000	53.3
Tajikistan - Tadjikistan										
1 VII 2001	ESDF	6 312 756	1 675 211	26.5	3 163 111	834 679	26.4	3 149 645	840 532	26.7
1 VII 2002	ESDF	6 441 009	1 705 240	26.5	3 228 657	850 897	26.4	3 212 352	854 343	26.6
1 VII 2003	ESDF	6 573 224	1 738 838	26.5	3 296 211	868 890	26.4	3 277 013	869 948	26.5
1 VII 2004	ESDF	6 710 161	1 774 799	26.4	3 365 832	888 087	26.4	3 344 329	886 712	26.5
1 VII 2005	ESDF	6 850 324	1 808 339	26.4	3 436 922	906 229	26.4	3 413 402	902 110	26.4
1 VII 2006	ESDF	6 992 066	1 841 258	26.3	3 508 345	923 963	26.3	3 483 721	917 295	26.3
1 VII 2007	ESDF	7 139 772	1 877 203	26.3	3 581 930	943 032	26.3	3 557 842	934 171	26.3
1 VII 2008	ESDF	7 294 747	1 918 996	26.3	3 659 238	965 220	26.4	3 635 510	953 776	26.2
Thailand - Thaïlande[1]										
1 VII 2001	ESDJ	62 914 000	...	...	31 348 000	...	...	31 566 000	...	...
1 VII 2002	ESDJ	63 482 287	20 731 494	32.7	31 623 509	10 072 055	31.8	31 858 778	10 659 439	33.5
1 VII 2003	ESDJ	64 018 857	20 990 626	32.8	31 883 154	10 188 273	32.0	32 135 703	10 802 353	33.6
1 VII 2004	ESDJ	64 177 484	19 300 414	30.1	31 574 765	9 261 252	29.3	32 602 719	10 039 162	30.8
1 VII 2005	ESDJ	64 838 628	19 538 420	30.1	31 848 905	9 360 642	29.4	32 989 723	10 177 778	30.9
1 VII 2006	ESDJ	65 305 736	19 792 296	30.3	32 060 034	9 474 510	29.6	33 245 702	10 317 786	31.0
1 VII 2007	ESDJ	66 041 512	20 117 497	30.5	32 467 223	9 733 251	30.0	33 574 289	10 384 246	30.9
1 VII 2008	ESDJ	66 480 004	20 471 816	30.8	32 671 831	9 802 741	30.0	33 808 173	10 669 075	31.6
1 VII 2009	ESDJ	66 903 277	21 133 663	31.6	32 872 931	10 112 852	30.8	34 030 346	11 020 811	32.4
1 VII 2010	ESDJ	67 311 917	23 096 811	34.3	33 067 359	11 070 161	33.5	34 244 558	12 026 650	35.1
Timor-Leste										
11 VII 2004	CDFC	923 198	...	...	469 919	...	...	453 279	...	...
11 VII 2010*	CDFC	1 066 582	315 140	29.5	541 147	164 780	30.5	525 435	150 360	28.6
Turkey - Turquie[109]										
1 VII 2001	ESDJ	65 135 000	...	...	32 597 000	...	...	32 538 000	...	...
1 VII 2002	ESDJ	66 009 000	...	...	33 043 000	...	...	32 966 000	...	...
1 VII 2003	ESDJ	66 873 000	...	...	33 495 000	...	...	33 378 000	...	...
1 VII 2004	ESDJ	67 734 000	...	...	33 937 000	...	...	33 797 000	...	...
1 VII 2005	ESDJ	68 582 000	...	...	34 370 000	...	...	34 212 000	...	...
1 VII 2006	ESDJ	69 421 000	...	...	34 798 000	...	...	34 623 000	...	...
1 VII 2007	ESDJ	70 256 000	...	...	35 220 000	...	...	35 036 000	...	...
1 VII 2008	ESDJ	71 079 000	...	...	35 630 000	...	...	35 449 000	...	...
31 XII 2008	CDJC	71 517 100	...	...	35 901 154	...	...	35 615 946	...	...
1 VII 2009	ESDJ	71 897 000	...	...	36 042 000	...	...	35 855 000	...	...
1 VII 2010	ESDJ	72 698 000	...	...	36 443 000	...	...	36 255 000	...	...

6. Total and urban population by sex: 2001 - 2010
Population totale et population urbaine selon le sexe : 2001 - 2010 (continued - suite)

Continent, country or area, and date / Continent, pays ou zone et date	Code[a]	Both sexes - Les deux sexes			Male - Masculin			Female - Féminin		
		Total	Urban - Urbaine Number Nombre	Percent P.100	Total	Urban - Urbaine Number Nombre	Percent P.100	Total	Urban - Urbaine Number Nombre	Percent P.100
ASIA - ASIE										
Turkmenistan - Turkménistan										
1 VII 2003 .... ESDF	ESDF	5 123 940	...	...	2 571 866[22]	...	...	2 552 073[22]	...	...
United Arab Emirates - Émirats arabes unis										
5 XII 2005 .... CDFC	CDFC	4 106 427	3 384 839	82.4	2 806 141	...	...	1 300 286	...	...
1 VII 2006 .... ESDF	ESDF	4 229 000	...	...	2 895 000	...	...	1 334 000	...	...
1 VII 2007 .... ESDF	ESDF	4 488 000	...	...	3 084 000	...	...	1 404 000	...	...
1 VII 2008 .... ESDF	ESDF	4 765 000	...	...	3 286 000	...	...	1 479 000	...	...
Uzbekistan - Ouzbékistan										
1 VII 2001 .... ESDF	ESDF	24 964 433	9 256 101	37.1	12 442 510	4 573 055	36.8	12 521 923	4 683 046	37.4
Viet Nam										
1 VII 2001[110] .... ESDF	ESDF	78 620 977	19 299 193	24.5	38 656 617	...	...	39 964 360	...	...
1 VII 2002[110] .... ESDF	ESDF	79 538 689	19 873 334	25.0	39 112 677	...	...	40 426 012	...	...
1 VII 2003[110] .... ESDF	ESDF	80 468 422	20 725 128	25.8	39 535 505	...	...	40 932 917	...	...
1 VII 2004[110] .... ESDF	ESDF	81 437 728	21 601 403	26.5	40 042 598	...	...	41 395 130	...	...
1 VII 2005[110] .... ESDF	ESDF	82 393 519	22 332 173	27.1	40 522 211	...	...	41 871 308	...	...
1 VII 2006[110] .... ESDF	ESDF	83 312 993	23 046 110	27.7	40 999 887	...	...	42 313 106	...	...
1 VII 2007[110] .... ESDF	ESDF	84 221 105	23 746 705	28.2	41 448 572	...	...	42 772 533	...	...
1 VII 2008[110] .... ESDF	ESDF	85 122 271	24 673 681	29.0	41 957 844	...	...	43 164 427	...	...
1 IV 2009 .... CDJC	CDJC	85 846 997	25 436 896	29.6	42 413 143	12 349 995	29.1	43 433 854	13 086 901	30.1
1 VII 2009 .... ESDF	ESDF	86 024 979	25 584 740	29.7	42 523 416	...	...	43 501 563	...	...
1 VII 2010* .... ESDF	ESDF	86 927 697	26 224 390	30.2	42 990 650	...	...	43 937 047	...	...
Yemen - Yémen										
16 XII 2004 .... CDFC	CDFC	19 685 161	5 637 756	28.6	10 036 953	3 012 256	30.0	9 648 208	2 625 500	27.2
31 XII 2005 .... ESDF	ESDF	20 282 944	5 849 749	28.8	...	...	...	...	...	...
31 XII 2006 .... ESDF	ESDF	20 900 532	6 070 613	29.0	...	...	...	...	...	...
31 XII 2007 .... ESDF	ESDF	21 538 995	6 256 462	29.0	...	...	...	...	...	...
EUROPE										
Åland Islands - Îles d'Åland[35]										
1 VII 2001 .... ESDJ	ESDJ	25 892	10 549	40.7	12 750	4 967	39.0	13 142	5 582	42.5
1 VII 2002 .... ESDJ	ESDJ	26 133	10 621	40.6	12 866	5 004	38.9	13 267	5 617	42.3
1 VII 2003 .... ESDJ	ESDJ	26 302	10 629	40.4	12 945	5 011	38.7	13 358	5 619	42.1
1 VII 2004 .... ESDJ	ESDJ	26 439	10 669	40.4	13 030	5 036	38.7	13 409	5 633	42.0
1 VII 2005 .... ESDJ	ESDJ	26 648	10 746	40.3	13 174	5 087	38.6	13 475	5 660	42.0
1 VII 2006 .... ESDJ	ESDJ	26 845	10 802	40.2	13 299	5 123	38.5	13 546	5 680	41.9
1 VII 2007 .... ESDJ	ESDJ	27 038	10 863	40.2	13 407	5 151	38.4	13 631	5 712	41.9
1 VII 2008 .... ESDJ	ESDJ	27 305	10 954	40.1	13 552	5 189	38.3	13 753	5 765	41.9
1 VII 2009 .... ESDJ	ESDJ	27 595	11 064	40.1	13 724	5 264	38.4	13 871	5 800	41.8
1 VII 2010 .... ESDJ	ESDJ	27 871	11 157	40.0	13 880	5 327	38.4	13 991	5 830	41.7
Albania - Albanie										
1 IV 2001 .... CDFC	CDFC	3 069 275	1 294 196	42.2	1 530 443	639 082	41.8	1 538 832	655 114	42.6
1 VII 2001 .... ESDF	ESDF	3 073 733	1 312 963	42.7	1 532 598	648 278	42.3	1 541 135	664 685	43.1
1 VII 2002 .... ESDF	ESDF	3 093 465	1 347 871	43.6	1 542 211	625 060	40.5	1 551 254	722 811	46.6
1 VII 2003 .... ESDF	ESDF	3 111 163	1 375 367	44.2	1 550 728	636 985	41.1	1 560 435	738 382	47.3
1 VII 2004 .... ESDF	ESDF	3 127 263	1 406 443	45.0	1 558 376	661 335	42.4	1 568 887	745 108	47.5
1 VII 2005 .... ESDF	ESDF	3 142 065	1 468 522	46.7	1 565 316	671 848	42.9	1 576 749	796 864	50.5
1 VII 2006 .... ESDF	ESDF	3 150 886	1 528 877	48.5	1 580 446	711 123	45.0	1 570 440	817 754	52.1
1 VII 2007 .... ESDF	ESDF	3 161 337	...	...	1 587 496	...	...	1 573 841	...	...
1 VII 2009 .... ESDF	ESDF	3 194 417	...	...	1 599 047	...	...	1 595 370	...	...
Andorra - Andorre[35]										
1 VII 2001 .... ESDJ	ESDJ	66 089	...	...	34 344	...	...	31 746	...	...
1 VII 2002 .... ESDJ	ESDJ	66 094	...	...	34 244	...	...	31 850	...	...
1 VII 2003 .... ESDJ	ESDJ	69 840	...	...	36 258	...	...	33 582	...	...
1 VII 2004 .... ESDJ	ESDJ	74 885	...	...	38 990	...	...	35 895	...	...
1 VII 2005 .... ESDJ	ESDJ	78 607	...	...	41 097	...	...	37 510	...	...
1 VII 2006 .... ESDJ	ESDJ	80 104	...	...	41 876	...	...	38 228	...	...
1 VII 2007 .... ESDJ	ESDJ	82 392	...	...	43 100	...	...	39 292	...	...
1 VII 2008 .... ESDJ	ESDJ	83 884	...	...	43 911	...	...	39 973	...	...

Continent, country or area, and date / Continent, pays ou zone et date	Code[a]	Both sexes - Les deux sexes			Male - Masculin			Female - Féminin		
		Total	Urban - Urbaine		Total	Urban - Urbaine		Total	Urban - Urbaine	
			Number Nombre	Percent P.100		Number Nombre	Percent P.100		Number Nombre	Percent P.100
EUROPE										
Andorra - Andorre[35]										
1 VII 2009	ESDJ	85 116	...	...	44 444	...	...	40 672	...	...
1 VII 2010	ESDJ	84 549	...	...	43 992	...	...	40 557	...	...
Austria - Autriche										
15 V 2001	CDJC	8 032 926	5 368 693	66.8	3 889 189	2 564 828	65.9	4 143 737	2 803 865	67.7
1 VII 2001	ESDJ	8 042 293	...	...	3 893 920	...	...	4 148 373	...	...
1 VII 2002	ESDJ	8 082 121	...	...	3 918 940	...	...	4 163 181	...	...
1 VII 2003	ESDJ	8 118 245	...	...	3 940 285	...	...	4 177 960	...	...
1 VII 2004	ESDJ	8 169 441	...	...	3 967 701	...	...	4 201 740	...	...
1 VII 2005	ESDJ	8 225 278	...	...	3 998 952	...	...	4 226 326	...	...
1 VII 2006	ESDJ	8 267 948	...	...	4 022 516	...	...	4 245 432	...	...
1 VII 2007	ESDJ	8 300 954	...	...	4 040 089	...	...	4 260 865	...	...
1 VII 2008	ESDJ	8 336 549	...	...	4 058 635	...	...	4 277 914	...	...
1 VII 2009	ESDJ	8 365 275	...	...	4 073 570	...	...	4 291 705	...	...
1 VII 2010	ESDJ	8 389 771	...	...	4 087 215	...	...	4 302 556	...	...
Belarus - Bélarus										
1 VII 2001	ESDF	9 970 688	7 022 386	70.4	4 677 096	3 298 787	70.5	5 293 592	3 723 599	70.3
1 VII 2002	ESDF	9 924 766	7 034 721	70.9	4 652 109	3 299 920	70.9	5 272 657	3 734 801	70.8
1 VII 2003	ESDF	9 873 826	7 040 950	71.3	4 623 963	3 297 535	71.3	5 249 863	3 743 415	71.3
1 VII 2004	ESDF	9 824 568	7 050 685	71.8	4 596 633	3 296 800	71.7	5 227 935	3 753 885	71.8
1 VII 2005	ESDF	9 775 307	7 057 463	72.2	4 569 189	3 294 851	72.1	5 206 118	3 762 612	72.3
1 VII 2006	ESDF	9 732 501	7 066 903	72.6	4 545 164	3 294 559	72.5	5 187 337	3 772 344	72.7
1 VII 2007	ESDF	9 702 116	7 091 407	73.1	4 528 222	3 302 285	72.9	5 173 894	3 789 122	73.2
1 VII 2008	ESDJ	9 680 841	7 128 283	73.6	4 516 517	3 316 447	73.4	5 164 324	3 811 836	73.8
1 VII 2009	ESDJ	9 665 120	7 173 482	74.2	4 508 125	3 334 319	74.0	5 156 995	3 839 163	74.4
1 VII 2010	ESDJ	9 490 583	...	...	4 413 225	...	...	5 077 358	...	...
Belgium - Belgique										
1 VII 2001	ESDJ	10 286 570	10 138 703	98.6	5 030 154	4 956 176	98.5	5 256 416	5 182 527	98.6
1 X 2001	CDJC	10 296 350	10 148 260	98.6	5 035 446	4 961 374	98.5	5 260 904	5 186 886	98.6
1 VII 2002	ESDJ	10 332 785	10 184 150	98.6	5 054 587	4 980 148	98.5	5 278 198	5 204 003	98.6
1 VII 2003	ESDJ	10 372 469	10 223 221	98.6	5 075 268	5 000 466	98.5	5 297 201	5 222 755	98.6
1 VII 2004	ESDJ	10 417 122	10 267 298	98.6	5 097 709	5 022 559	98.5	5 319 413	5 244 739	98.6
1 VII 2005	ESDJ	10 472 842	10 322 099	98.6	5 125 387	5 049 822	98.5	5 347 455	5 272 277	98.6
1 VII 2006	ESDJ	10 541 893	10 389 801	98.6	5 159 947	5 083 829	98.5	5 381 946	5 305 972	98.6
1 VII 2007	ESDJ	10 622 604	10 469 341	98.6	5 201 670	5 125 007	98.5	5 420 934	5 344 334	98.6
1 VII 2008	ESDJ	10 709 973	...	...	5 246 480	...	...	5 463 493	...	...
1 VII 2009	ESDJ	10 796 493	...	...	5 290 436	...	...	5 506 057	...	...
1 VII 2010*	ESDJ	10 879 155	...	...	5 331 071	...	...	5 548 084	...	...
Bosnia and Herzegovina - Bosnie-Herzégovine										
1 VII 2001	ESDF	3 797 937	...	...	1 860 989	...	...	1 936 948	...	...
1 VII 2002	ESDF	3 828 397	...	...	1 875 915	...	...	1 952 482	...	...
1 VII 2003	ESDF	3 832 301	...	...	1 877 827	...	...	1 954 474	...	...
1 VII 2004	ESDF	3 842 527	...	...	1 882 838	...	...	1 959 689	...	...
1 VII 2005	ESDF	3 842 537	...	...	1 882 843	...	...	1 959 694	...	...
1 VII 2006	ESDF	3 842 762	...	...	1 882 953	...	...	1 959 809	...	...
1 VII 2007	ESDF	3 842 562	...	...	1 877 309	...	...	1 965 253	...	...
1 VII 2008	ESDF	3 842 265	...	...	1 877 165	...	...	1 965 100	...	...
1 VII 2009	ESDF	3 842 566	...	...	1 877 312	...	...	1 965 254	...	...
1 VII 2010*	ESDF	3 843 611	...	...	1 877 701	...	...	1 965 910	...	...
Bulgaria - Bulgarie										
1 III 2001	CDJC	7 928 901	5 474 534	69.0	3 862 465	2 651 312	68.6	4 066 436	2 823 222	69.4
1 VII 2001	ESDJ	7 913 301	5 477 604	69.2	3 853 710	2 652 367	68.8	4 059 591	2 825 237	69.6
1 VII 2002	ESDJ	7 868 900	5 467 777	69.5	3 828 882	2 644 285	69.1	4 040 018	2 823 492	69.9
1 VII 2003	ESDJ	7 823 557	5 459 344	69.8	3 803 501	2 636 908	69.3	4 020 056	2 822 436	70.2
1 VII 2004	ESDJ	7 781 161	5 440 536	69.9	3 779 224	2 624 031	69.4	4 001 937	2 816 505	70.4
1 VII 2005	ESDJ	7 739 900	5 424 661	70.1	3 755 469	2 613 346	69.6	3 984 431	2 811 315	70.6
1 VII 2006	ESDJ	7 699 020	5 428 388	70.5	3 732 130	2 613 030	70.0	3 966 890	2 815 358	71.0
1 VII 2007	ESDJ	7 659 764	5 414 260	70.7	3 710 315	2 604 175	70.2	3 949 449	2 810 085	71.2
1 VII 2008	ESDJ	7 623 395	5 405 147	70.9	3 690 485	2 597 929	70.4	3 932 910	2 807 218	71.4
1 VII 2009	ESDJ	7 585 131	5 408 330	71.3	3 670 296	2 598 442	70.8	3 914 835	2 809 888	71.8
1 VII 2010	ESDJ	7 534 289	...	...	3 644 560	...	...	3 889 729	...	...
Croatia - Croatie										
31 III 2001	CDJC	4 437 460	2 471 328	55.7	2 135 900	1 171 950	54.9	2 301 560	1 299 378	56.5
1 VII 2001	ESDJ	4 439 635	...	...	2 137 014	...	...	2 302 621	...	...
1 VII 2002	ESDJ	4 440 385	...	...	2 136 831	...	...	2 303 554	...	...

Continent, country or area, and date / Continent, pays ou zone et date	Code[a]	Both sexes - Les deux sexes			Male - Masculin			Female - Féminin		
		Total	Urban - Urbaine		Total	Urban - Urbaine		Total	Urban - Urbaine	
			Number Nombre	Percent P.100		Number Nombre	Percent P.100		Number Nombre	Percent P.100
EUROPE										
Croatia - Croatie										
1 VII 2003	ESDJ	4 440 290	...	...	2 137 037	...	...	2 303 253	...	...
1 VII 2004	ESDJ	4 439 353	...	...	2 136 887	...	...	2 302 466	...	...
1 VII 2005	ESDJ	4 441 989	...	...	2 138 663	...	...	2 303 326	...	...
1 VII 2006	ESDJ	4 440 022	...	...	2 138 934	...	...	2 301 088	...	...
1 VII 2007	ESDJ	4 435 982	...	...	2 137 984	...	...	2 297 998	...	...
1 VII 2008	ESDJ	4 434 508	...	...	2 138 022	...	...	2 296 486	...	...
1 VII 2009	ESDJ	4 429 078	...	...	2 136 231	...	...	2 292 847	...	...
1 I 2010	ESDJ	4 425 747	...	...	2 135 169	...	...	2 290 578	...	...
Czech Republic - République tchèque										
1 III 2001	CDJC	10 230 060	7 564 200	73.9	4 982 071	3 657 775	73.4	5 247 989	3 906 425	74.4
1 VII 2001	ESDJ	10 224 192	7 559 732	73.9	4 978 951	3 655 116	73.4	5 245 241	3 904 616	74.4
1 VII 2002	ESDJ	10 200 774	7 536 154	73.9	4 964 598	3 640 572	73.3	5 236 176	3 895 582	74.4
1 VII 2003	ESDJ	10 201 651	7 533 782	73.8	4 968 189	3 640 805	73.3	5 233 462	3 892 977	74.4
1 VII 2004	ESDJ	10 206 923	7 526 698	73.7	4 971 730	3 637 603	73.2	5 235 193	3 889 095	74.3
1 VII 2005	ESDJ	10 234 092	7 552 515	73.8	4 991 439	3 655 100	73.2	5 242 653	3 897 415	74.3
1 VII 2006	ESDJ	10 266 646	7 566 774	73.7	5 013 040	3 666 038	73.1	5 253 606	3 900 736	74.2
1 VII 2007	ESDJ	10 322 689	7 607 487	73.7	5 048 101	3 691 647	73.1	5 274 588	3 915 840	74.2
1 VII 2008	ESDJ	10 429 692	7 697 774	73.8	5 113 332	3 746 004	73.3	5 316 360	3 951 770	74.3
1 VII 2009	ESDJ	10 491 492	7 731 056	73.7	5 150 509	3 767 819	73.2	5 340 983	3 963 237	74.2
1 VII 2010	ESDJ	10 519 792	...	...	5 162 998	...	...	5 356 794	...	...
Denmark - Danemark[111]										
1 I.2001	CDJC	5 349 212	...	...	2 644 319	...	...	2 704 893	...	...
1 VII 2001	ESDJ	5 358 783	...	...	2 649 233	...	...	2 709 551	...	...
1 VII 2002	ESDJ	5 374 255	...	...	2 657 341	...	...	2 716 914	...	...
1 VII 2003	ESDJ	5 387 174	...	...	2 664 526	...	...	2 722 648	...	...
1 VII 2004	ESDJ	5 401 177	...	...	2 671 907	...	...	2 729 270	...	...
1 VII 2005	ESDJ	5 415 978	...	...	2 679 857	...	...	2 736 121	...	...
1 VII 2006	ESDJ	5 434 567	...	...	2 690 179	...	...	2 744 388	...	...
1 VII 2007	ESDJ	5 457 415	...	...	2 702 894	...	...	2 754 521	...	...
1 VII 2008	ESDJ	5 489 022	...	...	2 720 016	...	...	2 769 006	...	...
1 VII 2009	ESDJ	5 519 441	...	...	2 735 983	...	...	2 783 458	...	...
1 VII 2010	ESDJ	5 545 039	...	...	2 748 439	...	...	2 796 600	...	...
Estonia - Estonie										
1 VII 2001	ESDJ	1 364 101	943 944	69.2	629 020	424 985	67.6	735 081	518 959	70.6
1 VII 2002	ESDJ	1 358 644	940 465	69.2	626 276	423 224	67.6	732 368	517 241	70.6
1 VII 2003	ESDJ	1 353 557	937 201	69.2	623 705	421 604	67.6	729 852	515 597	70.6
1 VII 2004	ESDJ	1 349 290	934 665	69.3	621 525	420 309	67.6	727 765	514 356	70.7
1 VII 2005	ESDJ	1 346 097	932 985	69.3	619 949	419 513	67.7	726 148	513 472	70.7
1 VII 2006	ESDJ	1 343 547	931 855	69.4	618 772	419 103	67.7	724 775	512 752	70.7
1 VII 2007	ESDJ	1 341 672	931 163	69.4	617 828	418 873	67.8	723 844	512 290	70.8
1 VII 2008	ESDJ	1 340 675	930 866	69.4	617 354	418 863	67.8	723 321	512 003	70.8
1 VII 2009	ESDJ	1 340 271	930 774	69.4	617 311	419 001	67.9	722 960	511 773	70.8
1 VII 2010	ESDJ	1 340 161	...	...	617 540	...	...	722 621	...	...
Faeroe Islands - Îles Féroé										
1 VII 2001	ESDJ	46 553	...	...	24 116	...	...	22 437	...	...
1 VII 2002	ESDJ	47 315	...	...	24 534	...	...	22 781	...	...
1 VII 2003	ESDJ	47 923	...	...	24 873	...	...	23 051	...	...
1 VII 2004	ESDJ	48 258	...	...	25 070	...	...	23 188	...	...
1 VII 2005	ESDJ	48 260	...	...	25 074	...	...	23 187	...	...
1 VII 2006	ESDJ	48 373	17 537	36.3	25 127	8 828	35.1	23 246	8 709	37.5
1 VII 2007	ESDJ	48 424	17 469	36.1	25 160	8 815	35.0	23 264	8 654	37.2
1 I 2008[35]	CDJC	48 433	...	...	25 174	...	...	23 259	...	...
1 VII 2008	ESDJ	48 618	17 624	36.2	25 263	8 920	35.3	23 355	8 704	37.3
Finland - Finlande[35]										
1 VII 2001	ESDJ	5 188 008	3 442 406	66.4	2 533 469	1 657 185	65.4	2 654 539	1 785 222	67.3
1 VII 2002	ESDJ	5 200 598	3 464 084	66.6	2 541 257	1 668 942	65.7	2 659 342	1 795 142	67.5
1 VII 2003	ESDJ	5 213 014	3 482 747	66.8	2 548 905	1 679 310	65.9	2 664 109	1 803 437	67.7
1 VII 2004	ESDJ	5 228 172	3 501 888	67.0	2 557 485	1 689 778	66.1	2 670 687	1 812 110	67.9
1 VII 2005	ESDJ	5 246 096	3 522 669	67.1	2 567 214	1 700 985	66.3	2 678 882	1 821 684	68.0
1 VII 2006	ESDJ	5 266 268	3 545 913	67.3	2 578 046	1 713 341	66.5	2 688 222	1 832 572	68.2
1 VII 2007	ESDJ	5 288 720	3 571 129	67.5	2 590 265	1 726 895	66.7	2 698 455	1 844 234	68.3
1 VII 2008	ESDJ	5 313 399	3 601 321	67.8	2 604 220	1 743 503	66.9	2 709 179	1 857 819	68.6

Continent, country or area, and date / Continent, pays ou zone et date	Code[a]	Both sexes - Les deux sexes			Male - Masculin			Female - Féminin		
		Total	Urban - Urbaine		Total	Urban - Urbaine		Total	Urban - Urbaine	
			Number Nombre	Percent P.100		Number Nombre	Percent P.100		Number Nombre	Percent P.100
EUROPE										
Finland - Finlande[35]										
1 VII 2009[112]	ESDJ	5 311 276	3 619 503	68.1	2 604 636	1 754 275	67.4	2 706 640	1 865 228	68.9
1 VII 2010[112]	ESDJ	5 335 481	...	...	2 617 862	...	...	2 717 620	...	...
France[113]										
1 VII 2001	ESDJ	59 476 236	...	...	28 845 731	...	...	30 630 505	...	...
1 VII 2002	ESDJ	59 893 870	...	...	29 034 958	...	...	30 858 912	...	...
1 VII 2003	ESDJ	60 303 631	...	...	29 221 986	...	...	31 081 645	...	...
1 VII 2004	ESDJ	60 734 343	...	...	29 416 938	...	...	31 317 405	...	...
1 VII 2005	ESDJ	61 181 499	...	...	29 616 894	...	...	31 564 605	...	...
1 I 2006	CDJC	61 399 541			29 714 539			31 685 002		
1 VII 2006	ESDJ	61 597 486	...	...	29 815 995	...	...	31 781 491	...	...
1 VII 2007*	ESDJ	61 962 723	...	...	30 000 172	...	...	31 962 551	...	...
1 VII 2008*	ESDJ	62 299 664	...	...	30 167 729	...	...	32 131 935	...	...
1 VII 2009*	ESDJ	62 621 205	...	...	30 324 030	...	...	32 297 175	...	...
1 VII 2010*	ESDJ	62 967 680	...	...	30 502 902	...	...	32 464 778	...	...
Germany - Allemagne										
1 VII 2001	ESDJ	82 339 777	...	...	40 214 370	...	...	42 125 407	...	...
1 VII 2002	ESDJ	82 482 309	...	...	40 310 430	...	...	42 171 879	...	...
1 VII 2003	ESDJ	82 520 176	...	...	40 349 200	...	...	42 170 976	...	...
28 III 2004[114]	SSDJ	82 491 000	...	...	40 330 000	...	...	42 161 000	...	...
1 VII 2004	ESDJ	82 501 274	...	...	40 350 091	...	...	42 151 183	...	...
1 VII 2005	ESDJ	82 464 344	...	...	40 348 986	...	...	42 115 358	...	...
1 VII 2006	ESDJ	82 365 810	...	...	40 317 807	...	...	42 048 003	...	...
1 VII 2007	ESDJ	82 262 643	...	...	40 287 823	...	...	41 974 820	...	...
1 VII 2008	ESDJ	82 110 097	...	...	40 229 288	...	...	41 880 809	...	...
1 VII 2009	ESDJ	81 902 307	...	...	40 143 945	...	...	41 758 362	...	...
1 VII 2010*	ESDJ	81 775 575	...	...	40 108 104	...	...	41 667 471	...	...
Gibraltar										
12 XI 2001[115]	CDFC	27 495	...	...	13 644	...	...	13 851	...	...
1 VII 2002[116]	ESDF	28 520	...	...	14 300	...	...	14 220	...	...
1 VII 2003[116]	ESDF	28 605	...	...	14 384	...	...	14 221	...	...
1 VII 2004[116]	ESDF	28 759	...	...	14 426	...	...	14 333	...	...
1 VII 2005[116]	ESDF	28 779	...	...	14 408	...	...	14 371	...	...
1 VII 2006[116]	ESDF	28 875	...	...	14 435	...	...	14 440	...	...
1 VII 2007[116]	ESDF	29 257	...	...	14 655	...	...	14 602	...	...
1 VII 2008[116]	ESDF	29 286	...	...	14 725	...	...	14 561	...	...
1 VII 2009[116]	ESDF	29 431	...	...	14 820	...	...	14 611	...	...
Greece - Grèce										
18 III 2001[117]	CDFC	10 964 020	7 980 414	72.8	5 427 682	3 892 266	71.7	5 536 338	4 088 148	73.8
1 VII 2001[118]	ESDF	10 949 953	...	...	5 421 043	...	...	5 528 910	...	...
1 VII 2002[118]	ESDF	10 987 559	...	...	5 439 332	...	...	5 548 227	...	...
1 VII 2003[118]	ESDF	11 023 532	...	...	5 456 496	...	...	5 567 036	...	...
1 VII 2004[118]	ESDF	11 061 735	...	...	5 475 529	...	...	5 586 206	...	...
1 VII 2005[118]	ESDF	11 103 929	...	...	5 497 372	...	...	5 606 557	...	...
1 VII 2006[118]	ESDF	11 148 533	...	...	5 520 164	...	...	5 628 369	...	...
1 VII 2007[118]	ESDF	11 192 849	...	...	5 543 018	...	...	5 649 831	...	...
1 VII 2008[118]	ESDF	11 237 068	...	...	5 565 281	...	...	5 671 787	...	...
1 VII 2009[118]	ESDF	11 282 751	...	...	5 587 096	...	...	5 695 655	...	...
Guernsey - Guernesey										
29 IV 2001	CDJC	59 807			29 138			30 669		
1 VII 2004	ESDF	60 382	...	...	29 841	...	...	30 541	...	...
31 III 2006	ESDF	61 029	...	...	30 034	...	...	30 995	...	...
31 III 2007	ESDF	61 175	...	...	30 022	...	...	31 153	...	...
31 III 2008	ESDF	61 726	...	...	30 405	...	...	31 321	...	...
31 III 2009	ESDF	62 274	...	...	30 777	...	...	31 497	...	...
31 III 2010	ESDF	62 431	...	...	30 695	...	...	31 736	...	...
Holy See - Saint-Siège[119]										
1 VII 2009	ESDJ	466[120]	...	...	320	...	...	146	...	...
Hungary - Hongrie										
1 II 2001	CDFC	10 198 315	6 572 880	64.5	4 850 650	3 091 857	63.7	5 347 665	3 481 023	65.1
1 VII 2001	ESDJ	10 187 576	6 544 089[121]	64.2	4 843 996	3 073 458[121]	63.4	5 343 580	3 470 631[121]	64.9
1 VII 2002	ESDJ	10 158 608	6 607 159[121]	65.0	4 827 718	3 101 463[121]	64.2	5 330 890	3 505 696[121]	65.8
1 VII 2003	ESDJ	10 129 552	6 568 539[121]	64.8	4 811 285	3 079 592[121]	64.0	5 318 268	3 488 947[121]	65.6
1 VII 2004	ESDJ	10 107 146	6 571 923[121]	65.0	4 798 614	3 078 582[121]	64.2	5 308 532	3 493 342[121]	65.8
1 VII 2005	ESDJ	10 087 065	6 670 187	66.1	4 788 847	3 125 833	65.3	5 298 218	3 544 354	66.9

Continent, country or area, and date / Continent, pays ou zone et date	Code[a]	Both sexes - Les deux sexes			Male - Masculin			Female - Féminin		
		Total	Urban - Urbaine		Total	Urban - Urbaine		Total	Urban - Urbaine	
			Number Nombre	Percent P.100		Number Nombre	Percent P.100		Number Nombre	Percent P.100
EUROPE										
Hungary - Hongrie										
1 VII 2006	ESDJ	10 071 370	6 749 388	67.0	4 781 829	3 163 716	66.2	5 289 541	3 585 673	67.8
1 VII 2007	ESDJ	10 055 780	6 737 792	67.0	4 774 320	3 156 954	66.1	5 281 460	3 580 839	67.8
1 VII 2008	ESDJ	10 038 188	6 810 173	67.8	4 766 306	3 191 030	66.9	5 271 882	3 619 143	68.6
1 VII 2009	ESDJ	10 022 650	6 861 432	68.5	4 759 975	3 215 749	67.6	5 262 675	3 645 683	69.3
1 VII 2010*	ESDJ	10 000 162	...	...	4 749 950	...	...	5 250 212	...	...
Iceland - Islande[35]										
1 VII 2001	ESDJ	285 054	263 409	92.4	142 660	131 217	92.0	142 308	132 192	92.9
1 VII 2002	ESDJ	287 559	266 010	92.5	143 860	132 371	92.0	143 699	133 639	93.0
1 VII 2003	ESDJ	289 272	267 957	92.6	144 713	133 340	92.1	144 559	134 617	93.1
1 VII 2004	ESDJ	292 587	270 931	92.6	146 697	134 827	91.9	145 890	136 104	93.3
1 VII 2005	ESDJ	295 864	275 017	93.0	148 449	137 003	92.3	147 415	138 014	93.6
1 VII 2006	ESDJ	304 334	281 961	92.6	154 287	141 673	91.8	150 047	140 288	93.5
1 VII 2007	ESDJ	311 396	289 119	92.8	158 866	146 168	92.0	152 530	142 951	93.7
1 VII 2008	ESDJ	319 355	298 024	93.3	163 176	151 378	92.8	156 179	146 646	93.9
1 VII 2009	ESDJ	319 246	298 890	93.6	161 548	150 604	93.2	157 698	148 286	94.0
1 VII 2010	ESDJ	318 041	...	...	159 971	...	...	158 070	...	...
Ireland - Irlande										
15 IV 2001	ESDF	3 847 198	...	...	1 913 128	...	...	1 934 070	...	...
28 IV 2002	CDFC	3 917 203	2 334 300	59.6	1 946 164	1 133 500	58.2	1 971 039	1 200 800	60.9
15 IV 2003	ESDF	3 978 862	...	...	1 977 208	...	...	2 001 654	...	...
15 IV 2004	ESDF	4 043 763	...	...	2 011 159	...	...	2 032 604	...	...
15 IV 2005	ESDF	4 130 722	...	...	2 058 952	...	...	2 071 770	...	...
15 IV 2006	ESDF	4 234 872	...	...	2 116 062	...	...	2 118 810	...	...
23 IV 2006*	CDFC	4 239 848	2 574 313	60.7	2 121 171	1 267 960	59.8	2 118 677	1 306 353	61.7
15 IV 2007*	ESDF	4 339 000	...	...	2 171 100	...	...	2 167 900	...	...
15 IV 2008*	ESDF	4 422 100	...	...	2 206 300	...	...	2 215 800	...	...
1 VII 2009	ESDF	4 458 942	...	...	2 215 646	...	...	2 243 297	...	...
1 VII 2010*	ESDF	4 474 015	...	...	2 216 253	...	...	2 257 762	...	...
Isle of Man - Île de Man										
29 IV 2001	CDJC	76 315	...	...	37 372	...	...	38 943	...	...
30 IV 2002	ESDJ	77 156	...	...	37 827	...	...	39 330	...	...
30 IV 2003	ESDJ	77 464	...	...	38 019	...	...	39 444	...	...
30 IV 2004	ESDJ	77 581	...	...	38 111	...	...	39 470	...	...
30 IV 2005	ESDJ	78 800	...	...	38 775	...	...	40 025	...	...
23 IV 2006	CDJC	80 058	...	...	39 523	...	...	40 535	...	...
30 IV 2006	ESDJ	80 058	...	...	39 523	...	...	40 535	...	...
30 IV 2007	ESDJ	80 885	...	...	39 995	...	...	40 889	...	...
30 IV 2008	ESDJ	81 722	...	...	40 472	...	...	41 250	...	...
30 IV 2009	ESDJ	82 371	...	...	40 849	...	...	41 522	...	...
Italy - Italie										
1 VII 2001	ESDJ	56 977 217	...	...	27 581 784	...	...	29 395 433	...	...
21 X 2001	CDFC	57 110 144	...	...	27 617 335	...	...	29 492 809	...	...
1 VII 2002	ESDJ	57 157 406	...	...	27 676 733	...	...	29 480 674	...	...
1 VII 2003	ESDJ	57 604 658	...	...	27 917 416	...	...	29 687 242	...	...
1 VII 2004	ESDJ	58 175 310	...	...	28 222 706	...	...	29 952 604	...	...
1 VII 2005	ESDJ	58 607 043	...	...	28 451 846	...	...	30 155 197	...	...
1 VII 2006	ESDJ	58 941 499	...	...	28 622 665	...	...	30 318 835	...	...
1 VII 2007	ESDJ	59 375 289	...	...	28 834 094	...	...	30 541 195	...	...
1 VII 2008	ESDJ	59 832 179	...	...	29 051 085	...	...	30 781 094	...	...
1 VII 2009	ESDJ	60 192 698	...	...	29 219 913	...	...	30 972 785	...	...
1 VII 2010*	ESDJ	60 483 419	...	...	29 350 360	...	...	31 133 059	...	...
Jersey										
11 III 2001	CDJC	87 186	...	...	42 484	...	...	44 702	...	...
Latvia - Lettonie										
1 VII 2001	ESDJ	2 355 011	1 599 272	67.9	1 084 484	720 359	66.4	1 270 527	878 913	69.2
1 VII 2002	ESDJ	2 338 624	1 586 220	67.8	1 076 587	713 616	66.3	1 262 037	872 604	69.1
1 VII 2003	ESDJ	2 325 342	1 576 965	67.8	1 070 697	709 024	66.2	1 254 645	867 941	69.2
1 VII 2004	ESDJ	2 312 819	1 570 406	67.9	1 065 627	706 082	66.3	1 247 192	864 324	69.3
1 VII 2005	ESDJ	2 300 512	1 563 372	68.0	1 060 101	702 490	66.3	1 240 411	860 882	69.4
1 VII 2006	ESDJ	2 287 948	1 554 766	68.0	1 054 159	697 812	66.2	1 233 789	856 954	69.5
1 VII 2007	ESDJ	2 276 100	1 545 560	67.9	1 048 969	693 369	66.1	1 227 131	852 191	69.4
1 VII 2008	ESDJ	2 266 094	1 536 826	67.8	1 045 012	689 602	66.0	1 221 082	847 224	69.4
1 VII 2009	ESDJ	2 254 834	1 526 930	67.7	1 040 286	685 170	65.9	1 214 549	841 760	69.3
1 VII 2010	ESDJ	2 239 008	...	...	1 033 421	...	...	1 205 587	...	...

6. Total and urban population by sex: 2001 - 2010
Population totale et population urbaine selon le sexe : 2001 - 2010 (continued - suite)

Continent, country or area, and date / Continent, pays ou zone et date	Code[a]	Both sexes - Les deux sexes			Male - Masculin			Female - Féminin		
		Total	Urban - Urbaine		Total	Urban - Urbaine		Total	Urban - Urbaine	
			Number Nombre	Percent P.100		Number Nombre	Percent P.100		Number Nombre	Percent P.100
EUROPE										
Liechtenstein										
1 VII 2001	ESDJ	33 104	...	...	16 195	...	...	16 909	...	...
1 VII 2002	ESDJ	33 678	...	...	16 514	...	...	17 164	...	...
1 VII 2003	ESDJ	34 022	...	...	16 725	...	...	17 297	...	...
1 VII 2004	ESDJ	34 477	...	...	16 974	...	...	17 503	...	...
1 VII 2005	ESDJ	34 734	...	...	17 100	...	...	17 634	...	...
1 VII 2006	ESDJ	35 010	...	...	17 256	...	...	17 754	...	...
1 VII 2007	ESDJ	35 322	...	...	17 426	...	...	17 896	...	...
1 VII 2008	ESDJ	35 446	...	...	17 508	...	...	17 938	...	...
1 VII 2009	ESDJ	35 789	...	...	17 716	...	...	18 073	...	...
1 VII 2010*	ESDJ	36 023	...	...	17 829	...	...	18 194	...	...
Lithuania - Lituanie										
6 IV 2001	CDJC	3 483 972	2 332 098	66.9	1 629 148	1 071 986	65.8	1 854 824	1 260 112	67.9
1 VII 2001	ESDJ	3 481 292	2 330 184	66.9	1 627 704	1 070 901	65.8	1 853 588	1 259 283	67.9
1 VII 2002	ESDJ	3 469 070	2 321 713	66.9	1 620 891	1 065 912	65.8	1 848 179	1 255 801	67.9
1 VII 2003	ESDJ	3 454 205	2 307 326	66.8	1 612 996	1 058 108	65.6	1 841 209	1 249 218	67.8
1 VII 2004	ESDJ	3 435 591	2 289 399	66.6	1 603 421	1 048 397	65.4	1 832 170	1 241 002	67.7
1 VII 2005	ESDJ	3 414 304	2 275 118	66.6	1 592 402	1 040 296	65.3	1 821 902	1 234 822	67.8
1 VII 2006	ESDJ	3 394 082	2 264 535	66.7	1 581 807	1 034 128	65.4	1 812 275	1 230 407	67.9
1 VII 2007	ESDJ	3 375 618	2 255 508	66.8	1 571 979	1 028 619	65.4	1 803 639	1 226 889	68.0
1 VII 2008	ESDJ	3 358 114	2 245 653	66.9	1 563 120	1 022 903	65.4	1 794 994	1 222 750	68.1
1 VII 2009	ESDJ	3 339 455	2 235 033	66.9	1 553 499	1 016 639	65.4	1 785 956	1 218 394	68.2
1 VII 2010	ESDJ	3 286 820	...	...	1 527 510	...	...	1 759 311	...	...
Luxembourg										
15 II 2001	CDJC	439 539	...	...	216 541	...	...	222 998	...	...
1 VII 2001	ESDJ	441 525	...	...	217 562	...	...	223 963	...	...
1 VII 2002	ESDJ	446 175	...	...	219 916	...	...	226 259	...	...
1 VII 2003	ESDJ	451 631	...	...	222 859	...	...	228 772	...	...
1 VII 2004	ESDJ	458 095	...	...	226 432	...	...	231 663	...	...
1 VII 2005	ESDJ	465 158	...	...	230 128	...	...	235 030	...	...
1 VII 2006	ESDJ	472 637	...	...	233 946	...	...	238 691	...	...
1 VII 2007	ESDJ	479 993	...	...	237 700	...	...	242 294	...	...
1 VII 2008	ESDJ	488 650	...	...	242 221	...	...	246 429	...	...
1 VII 2009	ESDJ	497 782	...	...	247 120	...	...	250 662	...	...
1 VII 2010	ESDJ	506 953	...	...	252 013	...	...	254 941	...	...
Malta - Malte										
31 XII 2001[122]	ESDJ	394 641	...	...	195 363	...	...	199 278	...	...
31 XII 2002[122]	ESDJ	397 296	...	...	196 836	...	...	200 460	...	...
1 VII 2003[122]	ESDJ	398 582	...	...	197 468	...	...	201 114	...	...
1 VII 2004[122]	ESDJ	401 306	...	...	198 860	...	...	202 446	...	...
1 VII 2005[122]	ESDJ	403 509	...	...	200 104	...	...	203 405	...	...
27 XI 2005	CDJC	404 962	404 544	99.9	200 819	200 611	99.9	204 143	203 933	99.9
1 VII 2006[122]	ESDJ	406 453	...	...	201 747	...	...	204 706	...	...
1 VII 2007[122]	ESDJ	409 092	...	...	203 381	...	...	205 711	...	...
1 VII 2008[122]	ESDJ	412 001	...	...	205 015	...	...	206 986	...	...
1 VII 2009[122]	ESDJ	413 290	...	...	205 646	...	...	207 644	...	...
1 VII 2010*[122]	ESDJ	415 990	...	...	206 949	...	...	209 041	...	...
Monaco										
9 VI 2008	CDJC	31 109	...	...	15 076[123]	...	...	15 914[123]	...	...
Montenegro - Monténégro										
1 VII 2001	ESDF	658 223	...	...	327 538	...	...	330 685	...	...
1 VII 2002	ESDJ	617 511	...	...	304 814	...	...	312 697	...	...
1 VII 2003	ESDJ	620 279	385 205	62.1	305 745	187 299	61.3	314 534	197 906	62.9
31 X 2003	CDJC	620 145	383 808	61.9	305 225	186 437	61.1	314 920	197 371	62.7
1 VII 2004	ESDJ	622 118	387 501	62.3	306 428	188 266	61.4	315 690	199 235	63.1
1 VII 2005	ESDJ	623 277	389 678	62.5	306 839	189 222	61.7	316 439	200 456	63.3
1 VII 2006	ESDJ	624 241	391 884	62.8	307 271	190 286	61.9	316 970	201 598	63.6
1 VII 2007	ESDJ	626 104	394 653	63.0	308 267	191 692	62.2	317 836	202 961	63.9
1 VII 2008	ESDJ	628 804	397 747	63.3	309 787	193 393	62.4	319 018	204 354	64.1
1 VII 2009	ESDJ	631 536	400 928	63.5	311 258	195 088	62.7	320 278	205 840	64.3
Netherlands - Pays-Bas										
1 VII 2001	ESDJ	16 046 180	10 371 945	64.6	7 940 911	5 098 272	64.2	8 105 269	5 273 673	65.1
1 I 2002[124]	CDJC	16 105 285	10 447 684	64.9	7 971 967	5 137 422	64.4	8 133 318	5 310 262	65.3
1 VII 2002	ESDJ	16 148 929	10 482 679	64.9	7 993 719	5 155 143	64.5	8 155 210	5 327 536	65.3

Continent, country or area, and date / Continent, pays ou zone et date	Code[a]	Both sexes - Les deux sexes			Male - Masculin			Female - Féminin		
		Total	Urban - Urbaine		Total	Urban - Urbaine		Total	Urban - Urbaine	
			Number Nombre	Percent P.100		Number Nombre	Percent P.100		Number Nombre	Percent P.100

EUROPE

Netherlands - Pays-Bas

1 VII 2003 .... ESDJ		16 225 302	10 556 424	65.1	8 030 693	5 191 871	64.7	8 194 610	5 364 553	65.5
1 VII 2004 .... ESDJ		16 281 779	10 687 028	65.6	8 055 947	5 255 716	65.2	8 225 833	5 431 312	66.0
1 VII 2005 .... ESDJ		16 319 868	10 764 171	66.0	8 071 693	5 292 532	65.6	8 248 175	5 471 640	66.3
1 VII 2006 .... ESDJ		16 346 101	10 803 902	66.1	8 082 961	5 311 812	65.7	8 263 141	5 492 090	66.5
1 VII 2007 .... ESDJ		16 381 696	10 825 307	66.1	8 100 294	5 322 596	65.7	8 281 402	5 502 712	66.4
1 VII 2008 .... ESDJ		16 445 593	10 877 858	66.1	8 134 235	5 350 572	65.8	8 311 359	5 527 286	66.5
1 VII 2009 .... ESDJ		16 530 388	10 938 780	66.2	8 179 936	5 383 776	65.8	8 350 452	5 555 004	66.5
1 VII 2010* .... ESDJ		16 614 984	...	...	8 223 283	...	...	8 391 701	...	...

Norway - Norvège[125]

1 VII 2001 .... ESDJ		4 513 751	...	...	2 236 618	...	...	2 277 134	...	...
3 XI 2001[35] .... CDJC		4 520 947	3 458 699	76.5	2 240 281	1 694 153	75.6	2 280 666	1 764 546	77.4
1 VII 2002 .... ESDJ		4 538 159	...	...	2 249 021	...	...	2 289 139	...	...
1 VII 2003 .... ESDJ		4 564 855	...	...	2 262 578	...	...	2 302 277	...	...
1 VII 2004 .... ESDJ		4 591 910	...	...	2 276 560	...	...	2 315 351	...	...
1 VII 2005 .... ESDJ		4 623 291	...	...	2 293 026	...	...	2 330 266	...	...
1 VII 2006 .... ESDJ		4 660 677	...	...	2 313 885	...	...	2 346 792	...	...
1 VII 2007 .... ESDJ		4 709 153	...	...	2 342 739	...	...	2 366 414	...	...
1 VII 2008 .... ESDJ		4 768 212	...	...	2 377 372	...	...	2 390 840	...	...
1 VII 2009 .... ESDJ		4 828 726	...	...	2 410 903	...	...	2 417 823	...	...
1 VII 2010 .... ESDJ		4 889 252	...	...	2 443 801	...	...	2 445 452	...	...

Poland - Pologne[126]

1 VII 2001 .... ESDJ		38 250 790	23 656 606	61.8	18 532 945	11 261 781	60.8	19 717 845	12 394 825	62.9
20 V 2002 .... CDJC		38 230 080	23 610 365	61.8	18 516 403	11 234 165	60.7	19 713 677	12 376 200	62.8
1 VII 2002 .... ESDJ		38 232 301	23 607 932	61.7	18 517 179	11 232 736	60.7	19 715 122	12 375 196	62.8
1 VII 2003 .... ESDJ		38 195 177	23 543 325	61.6	18 492 950	11 195 269	60.5	19 702 227	12 348 056	62.7
1 VII 2004 .... ESDJ		38 180 249	23 490 202	61.5	18 478 368	11 162 807	60.4	19 701 881	12 327 395	62.6
1 VII 2005 .... ESDJ		38 161 313	23 450 597	61.5	18 460 730	11 135 706	60.3	19 700 583	12 314 891	62.5
1 VII 2006 .... ESDJ		38 132 277	23 400 565	61.4	18 436 101	11 103 869	60.2	19 696 176	12 296 696	62.4
1 VII 2007 .... ESDJ		38 115 967	23 350 920	61.3	18 417 074	11 070 886	60.1	19 698 893	12 280 034	62.3
1 VII 2008 .... ESDJ		38 115 909	23 305 018	61.1	18 408 405	11 041 359	60.0	19 707 504	12 263 659	62.2
1 VII 2009 .... ESDJ		38 153 389	23 293 906	61.1	18 423 343	11 032 562	59.9	19 730 046	12 261 344	62.1
1 VII 2010 .... ESDJ		38 183 683	...	...	18 436 558	...	...	19 747 126	...	...

Portugal

12 III 2001 .... CDFC		10 356 117	3 905 633	37.7	5 000 141	1 849 824	37.0	5 355 976	2 055 809	38.4
1 VII 2001 .... ESDJ		10 292 999	...	...	4 969 817	...	...	5 323 183	...	...
1 VII 2002 .... ESDJ		10 368 403	...	...	5 009 592	...	...	5 358 811	...	...
1 VII 2003 .... ESDJ		10 441 075	...	...	5 048 278	...	...	5 392 798	...	...
1 VII 2004 .... ESDJ		10 501 970	...	...	5 080 324	...	...	5 421 647	...	...
1 VII 2005 .... ESDJ		10 549 424	...	...	5 105 041	...	...	5 444 383	...	...
1 VII 2006 .... ESDJ		10 584 344	...	...	5 122 840	...	...	5 461 504	...	...
1 VII 2007 .... ESDJ		10 608 335	...	...	5 134 372	...	...	5 473 963	...	...
1 VII 2008 .... ESDJ		10 622 413	...	...	5 140 687	...	...	5 481 726	...	...
1 VII 2009 .... ESDJ		10 632 482	...	...	5 145 385	...	...	5 487 097	...	...
1 VII 2010* .... ESDJ		10 637 346	...	...	5 147 423	...	...	5 489 923	...	...

Republic of Moldova - République de Moldova[127]

1 VII 2001 .... ESDJ		3 631 462	1 485 810	40.9	1 739 081	717 661	41.3	1 892 381	768 149	40.6
1 VII 2002 .... ESDJ		3 623 062	1 484 676	41.0	1 735 430	716 822	41.3	1 887 632	767 854	40.7
1 VII 2003 .... ESDJ		3 612 874	1 481 035	41.0	1 730 861	714 970	41.3	1 882 013	766 065	40.7
1 VII 2004 .... ESDJ		3 603 940	1 476 980	41.0	1 726 630	712 971	41.3	1 877 310	764 009	40.7
5 X 2004 .... CDFC		3 386 673	1 308 069	38.6	1 629 689	613 221	37.6	1 756 984	694 848	39.5
1 VII 2005 .... ESDJ		3 595 187	1 472 929	41.0	1 722 105	710 796	41.3	1 873 082	762 133	40.7
1 VII 2006 .... ESDJ		3 585 209	1 481 398	41.3	1 720 139	706 649	41.1	1 865 070	774 749	41.5
1 VII 2007 .... ESDJ		3 576 910	1 477 062	41.3	1 719 246	694 308	40.4	1 857 664	782 754	42.1
1 VII 2008 .... ESDJ		3 570 108	1 475 609	41.3	1 716 195	693 550	40.4	1 853 913	782 059	42.2
1 VII 2009 .... ESDJ		3 565 604	1 476 390	41.4	1 714 209	694 134	40.5	1 851 395	782 257	42.3
1 VII 2010 .... ESDJ		3 562 063	...	...	1 712 797	...	...	1 849 266	...	...

Romania - Roumanie

1 VII 2001 .... ESDJ		22 408 393	12 243 748	54.6	10 949 490	5 903 537	53.9	11 458 903	6 340 211	55.3
18 III 2002 .... CDJC		21 680 974	11 435 080	52.7	10 568 741	5 493 397	52.0	11 112 233	5 941 683	53.5
1 VII 2002 .... ESDJ		21 794 793	11 608 735	53.3	10 642 538	5 579 042	52.4	11 152 255	6 029 693	54.1
1 VII 2003 .... ESDJ		21 733 556	11 600 157	53.4	10 606 245	5 566 401	52.5	11 127 311	6 033 756	54.2
1 VII 2004 .... ESDJ		21 673 328	11 895 598	54.9	10 571 606	5 704 297	54.0	11 101 722	6 191 301	55.8
1 VII 2005 .... ESDJ		21 623 849	11 879 897	54.9	10 543 518	5 692 516	54.0	11 080 331	6 187 381	55.8

Continent, country or area, and date / Continent, pays ou zone et date	Code[a]	Both sexes - Les deux sexes			Male - Masculin			Female - Féminin		
		Total	Urban - Urbaine		Total	Urban - Urbaine		Total	Urban - Urbaine	
			Number Nombre	Percent P.100		Number Nombre	Percent P.100		Number Nombre	Percent P.100
EUROPE										
Romania - Roumanie										
1 VII 2006	ESDJ	21 584 365	11 913 938	55.2	10 521 189	5 704 872	54.2	11 063 176	6 209 066	56.1
1 VII 2007	ESDJ	21 537 563	11 877 659	55.1	10 496 720	5 683 983	54.2	11 040 843	6 193 676	56.1
1 VII 2008	ESDJ	21 504 442	11 835 328	55.0	10 477 611	5 658 512	54.0	11 026 831	6 176 816	56.0
1 VII 2009*	ESDJ	21 469 959	11 823 516	55.1	10 457 219	5 649 707	54.0	11 012 740	6 173 809	56.1
1 VII 2010*	ESDJ	21 438 001	...	...	10 437 306	...	...	11 000 695	...	...
Russian Federation - Fédération de Russie										
1 VII 2001	ESDJ	145 976 482	106 898 541	73.2	68 130 474	49 504 491	72.7	77 846 008	57 394 050	73.7
1 VII 2002	ESDJ	145 306 497	106 523 307	73.3	67 706 316	49 224 967	72.7	77 600 181	57 298 340	73.8
9 X 2002	CDJC	145 166 731	106 429 049	73.3	67 605 133	49 149 510	72.7	77 561 598	57 279 539	73.9
1 VII 2003	ESDJ	144 565 934	106 069 837	73.4	67 257 276	48 917 406	72.7	77 308 658	57 152 431	73.9
1 VII 2004	ESDJ	143 821 215	105 268 883	73.2	66 813 322	48 452 954	72.5	77 007 893	56 815 929	73.8
1 VII 2005	ESDJ	143 113 876	104 412 086	73.0	66 383 146	47 962 554	72.3	76 730 730	56 449 532	73.6
1 VII 2006	ESDJ	142 487 259	103 941 621	72.9	66 006 266	47 667 046	72.2	76 480 993	56 274 575	73.6
1 VII 2007	ESDJ	142 114 903	103 775 726	73.0	65 783 031	47 538 667	72.3	76 331 872	56 237 059	73.7
1 VII 2008	ESDJ	141 956 409	103 731 731	73.1	65 879 355	47 481 775	72.3	76 277 054	56 249 956	73.7
1 VII 2009*	ESDJ	141 909 244	103 697 871	73.1	65 640 507	47 439 543	72.3	76 268 737	56 258 328	73.8
San Marino - Saint-Marin[35]										
1 VII 2001	ESDF	27 634	...	...	13 548	...	...	14 086	...	...
1 VII 2002	ESDF	28 486	...	...	13 946	...	...	14 540	...	...
1 VII 2003	ESDF	28 992	...	...	14 207	...	...	14 785	...	...
1 VII 2004	ESDF	29 421	...	...	14 422	...	...	14 999	...	...
1 VII 2005	ESDF	30 913	...	...	15 058	...	...	15 855	...	...
1 VII 2006	ESDF	31 359	...	...	15 309	...	...	16 050	...	...
1 VII 2007	ESDJ	30 580	...	...	15 023	...	...	15 557	...	...
1 VII 2008	ESDF	32 578	...	...	15 879	...	...	16 699	...	...
1 VII 2009	ESDF	32 969	...	...	16 052	...	...	16 917	...	...
1 VII 2010	ESDF	33 163	...	...	16 124	...	...	17 039	...	...
Serbia - Serbie[128]										
1 VII 2001	ESDJ	7 503 433	4 206 307	56.1	3 648 533	2 012 848	55.2	3 854 900	2 193 459	56.9
31 III 2002	CDJC	7 498 001	...	...	3 645 930	...	...	3 852 071	...	...
1 VII 2002	ESDJ	7 500 031	4 241 006	56.5	3 647 190	2 027 187	55.6	3 852 841	2 213 819	57.5
1 VII 2003	ESDJ	7 480 591	4 239 980	56.7	3 637 789	2 026 423	55.7	3 842 802	2 213 557	57.6
1 VII 2004	ESDJ	7 463 157	4 249 544	56.9	3 629 194	2 030 310	55.9	3 833 963	2 219 234	57.9
1 VII 2005	ESDJ	7 440 769	4 257 880	57.2	3 618 040	2 033 179	56.2	3 822 729	2 224 701	58.2
1 VII 2006	ESDJ	7 411 569	4 263 386	57.5	3 603 698	2 034 616	56.5	3 807 871	2 228 770	58.5
1 VII 2007	ESDJ	7 381 579	4 270 400	57.9	3 588 957	2 037 012	56.8	3 792 622	2 233 388	58.9
1 VII 2008	ESDJ	7 350 222	4 275 245	58.2	3 573 814	2 038 642	57.0	3 776 408	2 236 603	59.2
1 VII 2009	ESDJ	7 320 807	4 279 035	58.5	3 560 048	2 039 934	57.3	3 760 759	2 239 101	59.5
Slovakia - Slovaquie										
25 V 2001	CDFC	5 193 376	2 908 701	56.0	2 502 721	1 387 821	55.5	2 690 655	1 520 880	56.5
1 VII 2001	ESDJ	5 379 780	3 017 527	56.1	2 612 684	1 451 387	55.6	2 767 096	1 566 140	56.6
1 VII 2002	ESDJ	5 378 809	3 011 737	56.0	2 611 452	1 447 959	55.4	2 767 357	1 563 778	56.5
1 VII 2003	ESDJ	5 378 950	3 001 619	55.8	2 610 872	1 442 117	55.2	2 768 078	1 559 502	56.3
1 VII 2004	ESDJ	5 382 574	2 994 284	55.6	2 612 313	1 438 019	55.0	2 770 261	1 556 265	56.2
1 VII 2005	ESDJ	5 387 285	2 989 291	55.5	2 614 912	1 435 469	54.9	2 772 373	1 553 822	56.0
1 VII 2006	ESDJ	5 391 184	2 989 769	55.5	2 616 924	1 435 472	54.9	2 774 260	1 554 297	56.0
1 VII 2007	ESDJ	5 397 766	2 985 680	55.3	2 621 095	1 433 808	54.7	2 776 671	1 551 872	55.9
1 VII 2008	ESDJ	5 406 972	2 980 828	55.1	2 626 895	1 432 161	54.5	2 780 077	1 548 667	55.7
1 VII 2009	ESDJ	5 418 374	2 978 004	55.0	2 633 428	1 430 928	54.3	2 784 946	1 547 076	55.6
1 VII 2010	ESDJ	5 430 099	...	...	2 639 589	...	...	2 790 510	...	...
Slovenia - Slovénie										
1 VII 2001	ESDJ	1 992 035	...	...	973 711	...	...	1 018 324	...	...
31 III 2002[129]	CDFC	1 987 971	1 009 404	50.8	971 203	485 670	50.0	1 016 768	523 734	51.5
1 VII 2002	ESDJ	1 995 718	975 163[130]	48.9	976 111[130]	462 513[130]	47.4	1 019 607[130]	512 650[130]	50.3
1 VII 2003	ESDJ	1 996 773	971 513[130]	48.7	977 436[130]	460 811[130]	47.1	1 019 337[130]	510 702[130]	50.1
1 VII 2004	ESDJ	1 997 004	968 989[130]	48.5	977 092[130]	459 504[130]	47.0	1 019 912[130]	509 485[130]	50.0
1 VII 2005	ESDJ	2 001 114	965 538[130]	48.3	980 070[130]	457 869[130]	46.7	1 021 044[130]	507 669[130]	49.7
1 VII 2006	ESDJ	2 008 516	962 740[130]	47.9	985 876[130]	456 764[130]	46.3	1 022 640[130]	505 976[130]	49.5
1 VII 2007	ESDJ	2 019 406	1 006 767	49.9	995 125	490 610	49.3	1 024 281	516 157	50.4
1 VII 2008	ESDJ	2 022 629	1 012 477	50.1	996 969	491 605	49.3	1 025 660	520 872	50.8
1 VII 2009	ESDJ	2 042 335	1 024 087	50.1	1 011 767	500 253	49.4	1 030 568	523 834	50.8
1 VII 2010	ESDJ	2 048 583	...	...	1 014 335	...	...	1 034 248	...	...

6. Total and urban population by sex: 2001 - 2010
Population totale et population urbaine selon le sexe : 2001 - 2010 (continued - suite)

Continent, country or area, and date / Continent, pays ou zone et date	Code[a]	Both sexes - Les deux sexes			Male - Masculin			Female - Féminin		
		Total	Urban - Urbaine Number Nombre	Urban - Urbaine Percent P.100	Total	Urban - Urbaine Number Nombre	Urban - Urbaine Percent P.100	Total	Urban - Urbaine Number Nombre	Urban - Urbaine Percent P.100
EUROPE										
Spain - Espagne										
1 VII 2001 ....ESDJ		40 721 447	...	...	19 956 780[3]	...	...	20 764 667[3]	...	...
1 XI 2001[131]...............CDFC		40 847 371	26 944 564	66.0	20 012 882	13 034 120	65.1	20 834 489	13 910 444	66.8
1 VII 2002 ....ESDJ		41 314 019	...	...	20 266 005	...	...	21 048 014	...	...
1 VII 2003 ....ESDJ		42 004 575	...	...	20 626 192	...	...	21 378 383	...	...
1 VII 2004 ....ESDJ		42 691 751	...	...	20 987 670	...	...	21 704 081	...	...
1 VII 2005 ....ESDJ		43 398 190	...	...	21 367 297	...	...	22 030 893	...	...
1 VII 2006 ....ESDJ		44 068 244	...	...	21 725 232	...	...	22 343 012	...	...
1 VII 2007 ....ESDJ		44 873 567	...	...	22 155 286	...	...	22 718 281	...	...
1 VII 2008 ....ESDJ		45 593 385	...	...	22 512 354	...	...	23 081 031	...	...
1 VII 2009 ....ESDJ		45 929 476	...	...	22 670 863	...	...	23 258 614	...	...
1 VII 2010 ....ESDJ		46 070 971	...	...	22 698 642	...	...	23 372 329	...	...
Sweden - Suède[35]										
1 VII 2001 ....ESDJ		8 895 960	...	...	4 400 599	...	...	4 495 361	...	...
1 VII 2002 ....ESDJ		8 924 958	...	...	4 417 776	...	...	4 507 182	...	...
1 VII 2003 ....ESDJ		8 958 229	...	...	4 436 882	...	...	4 521 348	...	...
31 XII 2003 ....CDJC		8 975 670	...	...	4 446 656	...	...	4 529 014	...	...
1 VII 2004 ....ESDJ		8 993 531	...	...	4 456 484	...	...	4 537 048	...	...
1 VII 2005 ....ESDJ		9 029 572	...	...	4 476 431	...	...	4 553 142	...	...
1 VII 2006 ....ESDJ		9 080 505	...	...	4 505 037	...	...	4 575 468	...	...
1 VII 2007 ....ESDJ		9 148 092	...	...	4 543 722	...	...	4 604 370	...	...
1 VII 2008 ....ESDJ		9 219 637	...	...	4 583 816	...	...	4 635 822	...	...
1 VII 2009 ....ESDJ		9 298 515	...	...	4 626 362	...	...	4 672 153	...	...
1 VII 2010 ....ESDJ		9 378 126	...	...	4 669 629	...	...	4 708 497	...	...
Switzerland - Suisse										
1 VII 2001 ....ESDJ		7 226 647	5 282 037	73.1	3 529 342	2 560 447	72.5	3 697 305	2 721 590	73.6
1 VII 2002 ....ESDJ		7 284 754	5 331 445	73.2	3 559 690	2 586 466	72.7	3 725 064	2 744 979	73.7
1 VII 2003 ....ESDJ		7 339 002	5 375 076	73.2	3 588 285	2 609 517	72.7	3 750 717	2 765 559	73.7
1 VII 2004 ....ESDJ		7 389 626	5 414 867	73.3	3 615 118	2 630 590	72.8	3 774 508	2 784 277	73.8
1 VII 2005 ....ESDJ		7 437 116	5 452 361	73.3	3 640 600	2 650 983	72.8	3 796 516	2 801 378	73.8
1 VII 2006 ....ESDJ		7 483 935	5 489 614	73.4	3 665 931	2 671 318	72.9	3 818 004	2 818 296	73.8
1 VII 2007 ....ESDJ		7 551 117	5 543 848	73.4	3 703 187	2 701 296	72.9	3 847 930	2 842 552	73.9
1 VII 2008 ....ESDJ		7 647 676	5 622 042	73.5	3 756 845	2 744 671	73.1	3 890 831	2 877 371	74.0
1 VII 2009 ....ESDJ		7 743 832	5 699 003	73.6	3 808 621	2 786 186	73.2	3 935 211	2 912 817	74.0
1 VII 2010* ....ESDJ		7 826 153	...	...	3 853 083	...	...	3 973 070	...	...
TFYR of Macedonia - L'ex-R. y. de Macédoine										
1 VII 2001 ....ESDF		2 034 882	...	...	1 017 927	...	...	1 016 955	...	...
1 VII 2002 ....ESDF		2 031 153	...	...	1 019 616	...	...	1 019 035	...	...
31 X 2002 ....CDJC		2 022 547	...	...	1 015 377	...	...	1 007 170	...	...
1 VII 2003 ....ESDF		2 026 773	...	...	1 017 274	...	...	1 009 499	...	...
1 VII 2004 ....ESDF		2 032 544	...	...	1 019 903	...	...	1 012 641	...	...
1 VII 2005 ....ESDF		2 036 855	...	...	1 021 772	...	...	1 015 083	...	...
1 VII 2006 ....ESDF		2 040 228	...	...	1 023 069	...	...	1 017 159	...	...
1 VII 2007 ....ESDF		2 043 559	...	...	1 024 489	...	...	1 019 070	...	...
1 VII 2008 ....ESDF		2 046 898	...	...	1 026 022	...	...	1 020 876	...	...
1 VII 2009 ....ESDF		2 050 671	...	...	1 027 810	...	...	1 022 861	...	...
1 VII 2010* ....ESDF		2 055 003	...	...	1 029 848	...	...	1 025 156	...	...
Ukraine										
1 VII 2001 ....ESDF		48 690 151	32 763 036	67.3	...	...	...	...	...	...
5 XII 2001 ....CDFC		48 240 902	32 290 729	66.9	22 316 317	14 903 592	66.8	25 924 585	17 387 137	67.1
1 VII 2002 ....ESDF		48 230 283	32 451 361	67.3	22 329 926	14 988 910	67.1	25 900 357	17 462 452	67.4
1 XI 2003 ....ESDF		47 812 949	32 237 409	67.4	22 125 646	14 870 398	67.2	25 687 303	17 367 011	67.6
1 VII 2004 ....ESDF		47 451 626	32 077 893	67.6	21 946 375	14 778 929	67.3	25 505 251	17 298 965	67.8
1 VII 2005 ....ESDF		47 105 171	31 943 515	67.8	21 770 304	14 698 072	67.5	25 334 867	17 245 443	68.1
1 VII 2006 ....ESDF		46 787 786	31 827 539	68.0	21 610 648	14 628 495	67.7	25 177 138	17 199 044	68.3
1 VII 2007 ....ESDF		46 509 355	31 723 062	68.2	21 472 153	14 567 851	67.8	25 037 202	17 155 212	68.5
1 VII 2008 ....ESDF		46 258 189	31 627 980	68.4	21 347 279	14 512 344	68.0	24 910 910	17 115 637	68.7
1 VII 2009 ....ESDF		46 053 307	31 556 002	68.5	...	...	...	...	...	...
1 I 2010 ....ESDF		45 962 900	31 524 800	68.6	...	...	...	...	...	...

6. Total and urban population by sex: 2001 - 2010
Population totale et population urbaine selon le sexe : 2001 - 2010 (continued - suite)

Continent, country or area, and date / Continent, pays ou zone et date	Code[a]	Both sexes - Les deux sexes			Male - Masculin			Female - Féminin		
		Total	Urban - Urbaine		Total	Urban - Urbaine		Total	Urban - Urbaine	
			Number Nombre	Percent P.100		Number Nombre	Percent P.100		Number Nombre	Percent P.100
EUROPE										
United Kingdom of Great Britain and Northern Ireland - Royaume-Uni de Grande-Bretagne et d'Irlande du Nord[132]										
29 IV 2001[133]	CDFC	58 789 187	47 007 427	80.0	28 579 867	22 769 606	79.7	30 209 320	24 237 821	80.2
1 VII 2001[134]	ESDF	59 113 497	...	...	28 832 420	...	...	30 281 077	...	...
1 VII 2002[134]	ESDF	59 323 498	...	...	28 964 375	...	...	30 359 123	...	...
1 VII 2003	ESDF	59 557 337	...	...	29 108 774	...	...	30 448 563	...	...
1 VII 2004	ESDF	59 845 842	...	...	29 277 960	...	...	30 567 882	...	...
1 VII 2005	ESDF	60 238 383	...	...	29 497 036	...	...	30 741 347	...	...
1 VII 2006	ESDF	60 587 349	...	...	29 693 967	...	...	30 893 382	...	...
1 VII 2007	ESDF	60 975 355	...	...	29 916 107	...	...	31 059 248	...	...
1 VII 2008	ESDF	61 393 521	...	...	30 149 903	...	...	31 243 618	...	...
1 VII 2010*	ESDF	62 221 879	...	...	30 608 261	...	...	31 613 618	...	...
OCEANIA - OCÉANIE										
Australia - Australie										
1 VII 2001[135]	ESDJ	19 413 240	15 741 902	81.1	9 630 652	7 762 855	80.6	9 782 588	7 979 047	81.6
7 VIII 2001	CDFC	18 972 350	16 528 021	87.1	9 365 941	8 090 031	86.4	9 606 409	8 437 990	87.8
1 VII 2002[135]	ESDJ	19 651 438	15 958 923	81.2	9 753 065	7 874 721	80.7	9 898 373	8 084 202	81.7
1 VII 2003[135]	ESDJ	19 895 435	16 183 448	81.3	9 874 412	7 987 391	80.9	10 021 023	8 196 057	81.8
1 VII 2004[135]	ESDJ	20 127 363	16 395 358	81.5	9 992 728	8 096 009	81.0	10 134 635	8 299 349	81.9
1 VII 2005[135]	ESDJ	20 394 791	16 626 325	81.5	10 128 064	8 213 288	81.1	10 266 727	8 413 037	81.9
1 VII 2006[135]	ESDJ	20 697 880	16 890 471	81.6	10 282 433	8 348 198	81.2	10 415 447	8 542 273	82.0
8 VIII 2006	CDFC	20 061 646	...	...	9 896 500	...	...	10 165 146	...	...
1 VII 2007[135]	ESDJ	21 072 452	17 219 832	81.7	10 475 527	8 518 406	81.3	10 596 925	8 701 426	82.1
1 VII 2008[135]	ESDJ	21 498 540	17 589 251	81.8	10 696 123	8 709 531	81.4	10 802 417	8 879 720	82.2
1 VII 2009*[135]	ESDJ	21 955 256	17 984 840	81.9	10 931 694	8 913 643	81.5	11 023 562	9 071 197	82.3
1 VII 2010*[135]	ESDJ	22 342 398	...	...	11 124 254	...	...	11 218 144	...	...
Cook Islands - Îles Cook[136]										
1 XII 2001	CDFC	18 027	...	...	9 303	...	...	8 724	...	...
1 XII 2006*	CDFC	19 569	...	...	9 932	...	...	9 637	...	...
Fiji - Fidji										
1 VII 2004	ESDF	822 370	408 032	49.6	...	...	...	...	...	...
16 IX 2007	CDFC	837 271	424 846	50.7	427 176	212 454	49.7	410 095	212 392	51.8
French Polynesia - Polynésie française										
1 I 2009	ESDF	264 000	...	...	135 200	...	...	128 800	...	...
Guam[46]										
1 VII 2001	ESDJ	158 330	147 411	93.1	...	...	...	...	...	...
1 VII 2002	ESDJ	161 057	149 950	93.1	...	...	...	...	...	...
1 VII 2003	ESDJ	166 593	152 311	91.4	...	...	...	...	...	...
1 VII 2004	ESDJ	166 090	154 636	93.1	...	...	...	...	...	...
Kiribati										
7 XII 2005	CDFC	92 533	40 311	43.6	45 612	19 435	42.6	46 921	20 876	44.5
Marshall Islands - Îles Marshall[1]										
1 VII 2001	ESDF	54 584	...	...	27 960	...	...	26 624	...	...
1 VII 2004	ESDF	55 366	...	...	28 232	...	...	27 134	...	...
1 VII 2006	ESDF	52 163	...	...	26 746	...	...	25 417	...	...
1 VII 2007	ESDF	52 701	...	...	27 022	...	...	25 679	...	...
1 VII 2008	ESDF	53 236	...	...	27 297	...	...	25 939	...	...
1 VII 2009	ESDF	53 763	...	...	27 567	...	...	26 196	...	...
1 VII 2010	ESDF	54 305	...	...	27 843	...	...	26 462	...	...
Micronesia (Federated States of) - Micronésie (États fédérés de)[1]										
1 VII 2001	ESDJ	107 262	...	...	54 258	...	...	53 004	...	...
1 VII 2002	ESDJ	107 472	...	...	54 315	...	...	53 157	...	...
1 VII 2003	ESDJ	107 644	...	...	54 361	...	...	53 283	...	...
1 VII 2004	ESDJ	107 785	...	...	54 396	...	...	53 389	...	...

6. Total and urban population by sex: 2001 - 2010
Population totale et population urbaine selon le sexe : 2001 - 2010 (continued - suite)

Continent, country or area, and date / Continent, pays ou zone et date	Codea	Both sexes - Les deux sexes			Male - Masculin			Female - Féminin		
		Total	Urban - Urbaine		Total	Urban - Urbaine		Total	Urban - Urbaine	
			Number Nombre	Percent P.100		Number Nombre	Percent P.100		Number Nombre	Percent P.100
OCEANIA - OCÉANIE										
Micronesia (Federated States of) - Micronésie (États fédérés de)[1]										
1 VII 2005	ESDJ	107 885	...	...	54 419	...	...	53 466	...	...
1 VII 2006	ESDJ	107 965	...	...	54 411	...	...	53 554	...	...
1 VII 2007	ESDJ	108 031	...	...	54 403	...	...	53 628	...	...
1 VII 2008	ESDJ	108 026	...	...	54 350	...	...	53 676	...	...
1 VII 2009	ESDJ	107 973	...	...	54 275	...	...	53 698	...	...
1 VII 2010	ESDJ	107 839	...	...	54 158	...	...	53 681	...	...
Nauru										
23 IX 2002	CDFC	10 065	...	...	5 136	...	...	4 929	...	...
New Caledonia - Nouvelle-Calédonie										
1 I 2001	ESDF	215 260	...	...	109 580	...	...	105 680	...	...
1 I 2002	ESDF	219 387	...	...	111 465	...	...	107 922	...	...
1 I 2003	ESDF	223 592	...	...	113 320	...	...	110 272	...	...
1 VII 2004	ESDF	230 068	133 815	58.2	112 716	...	...	109 242	...	...
31 VIII 2004	CDFC	230 789	...	...	116 485	...	...	114 304	...	...
1 I 2005	ESDF	232 258	...	...	117 221	...	...	115 037	...	...
1 I 2006	ESDF	236 528	...	...	119 415	...	...	117 113	...	...
1 VII 2007	ESDF	242 400	...	...	122 261	...	...	120 139	...	...
1 VII 2008	ESDF	242 400	...	...	122 261	...	...	120 139	...	...
New Zealand - Nouvelle-Zélande										
6 III 2001[137]	CDFC	3 820 749	...	...	1 863 306	...	...	1 957 443	...	...
1 VII 2001[138]	ESDJ	3 880 500	3 331 400	85.8	1 903 200	...	...	1 977 300	...	...
1 VII 2002[138]	ESDJ	3 948 500	3 393 200[22]	85.9	1 936 500[22]	1 649 500[22]	85.2	2 012 000[22]	1 743 700[22]	86.7
1 VII 2003[138]	ESDJ	4 027 200	3 464 600[22]	86.0	1 975 600[22]	1 685 300[22]	85.3	2 051 700[22]	1 779 300[22]	86.7
1 VII 2004[138]	ESDJ	4 087 500	3 518 800[22]	86.1	2 003 800[22]	1 710 800[22]	85.4	2 083 800[22]	1 808 000[22]	86.8
1 VII 2005[138]	ESDJ	4 133 900	3 559 400[22]	86.1	2 025 200[22]	1 729 600[22]	85.4	2 108 700[22]	1 829 800[22]	86.8
7 III 2006[137]	CDFC	4 143 282	...	...	2 021 277	...	...	2 122 005	...	...
1 VII 2006[138]	ESDJ	4 184 600	3 603 600[22]	86.1	2 048 300[22]	1 749 800[22]	85.5	2 136 200[22]	1 853 800[22]	86.8
1 VII 2007[138]	ESDJ	4 228 300	3 642 600[22]	86.1	2 070 800[22]	1 770 000[22]	85.5	2 157 600[22]	1 872 600[22]	86.8
1 VII 2008[138]	ESDJ	4 268 900	3 676 900[139]	86.1	2 092 200[22]	1 788 300[139]	85.5	2 176 700[22]	1 888 600[139]	86.8
1 VII 2009[138]	ESDJ	4 315 800	3 717 100[139]	86.1	2 117 500[22]	1 810 200[139]	85.5	2 198 300[22]	1 906 800[139]	86.7
1 VII 2010[140]	ESDJ	4 367 800	3 761 700[141]	86.1	2 144 600	1 833 700[141]	85.5	2 223 200	1 928 000[141]	86.7
Niue - Nioué										
7 IX 2001	CDFC	1 788	...	...	897	...	...	891	...	...
1 VII 2004	ESDJ	1 761	...	...	866	...	...	895	...	...
1 VII 2005	ESDJ	1 746	...	...	849	...	...	896	...	...
1 VII 2006	ESDJ	1 679	...	...	815	...	...	864	...	...
9 IX 2006	CDFC	1 625	...	...	802	...	...	823	...	...
1 VII 2010	ESDJ	1 496	...	...	754	...	...	740	...	...
Norfolk Island - Île Norfolk										
7 VIII 2001	CDFC	2 037	...	...	1 017	...	...	1 020	...	...
8 VIII 2006	CDFC	2 523	...	...	1 218	...	...	1 305	...	...
Northern Mariana Islands - Îles Mariannes septentrionales										
1 VII 2001	ESDF	72 079	...	...	32 750	...	...	39 329	...	...
1 VII 2002	ESDF	74 372	...	...	33 368	...	...	41 004	...	...
1 VII 2003	ESDF	76 617	...	...	33 952	...	...	42 665	...	...
1 VII 2004	ESDF	78 889	...	...	34 550	...	...	44 339	...	...
1 VII 2005	ESDF	70 636	...	...	32 093	...	...	38 543	...	...
1 VII 2006	ESDF	60 662	...	...	29 071	...	...	31 591	...	...
1 VII 2007	ESDF	58 629	...	...	28 124	...	...	30 505	...	...
1 VII 2008	ESDF	55 244	...	...	26 524	...	...	28 720	...	...
1 VII 2009	ESDF	51 484	...	...	24 738	...	...	26 746	...	...
1 VII 2010	ESDF	48 317	...	...	23 231	...	...	25 086	...	...
Palau - Palaos										
1 VII 2001	ESDF	19 626	...	...	10 415	...	...	9 211	...	...
1 VII 2002	ESDF	19 976	...	...	10 590	...	...	9 386	...	...
1 IV 2005	CDJC	19 907	15 399	77.4	10 699	...	...	9 208	...	...

6. Total and urban population by sex: 2001 - 2010
Population totale et population urbaine selon le sexe : 2001 - 2010 (continued - suite)

Continent, country or area, and date / Continent, pays ou zone et date	Code[a]	Both sexes - Les deux sexes			Male - Masculin			Female - Féminin		
		Total	Urban - Urbaine		Total	Urban - Urbaine		Total	Urban - Urbaine	
			Number Nombre	Percent P.100		Number Nombre	Percent P.100		Number Nombre	Percent P.100
OCEANIA - OCÉANIE										
Papua New Guinea - Papouasie-Nouvelle-Guinée										
1 VII 2002 .... ESDF	ESDF	5 461 940	...	...	2 826 212	...	...	2 635 722	...	...
Pitcairn										
31 XII 2007 .... ESDF	ESDF	64[142]	...	...	37	...	...	27	...	...
31 XII 2008 .... ESDF	ESDF	58[143]	...	...	30	...	...	28	...	...
Samoa										
5 XI 2001 .... CDFC	CDFC	176 710	38 836	22.0	92 050	19 837	21.6	84 660	18 999	22.4
1 VII 2002 .... ESDF	ESDF	178 329	39 192	22.0	92 893	20 019	21.6	85 436	19 173	22.4
1 VII 2003 .... ESDF	ESDF	179 962	39 551	22.0	93 744	20 202	21.6	86 218	19 349	22.4
1 VII 2004 .... ESDF	ESDF	181 611	39 913	22.0	94 603	20 387	21.6	87 008	19 526	22.4
1 VII 2005 .... ESDF	ESDF	183 275	40 279	22.0	95 470	20 574	21.6	87 805	19 705	22.4
1 VII 2006 .... ESDF	ESDF	184 955	40 648	22.0	96 345	20 763	21.6	88 610	19 885	22.4
5 XI 2006 .... CDFC	CDFC	180 741	37 708	20.9	93 677	19 120	20.4	87 064	18 588	21.3
1 VII 2007 .... ESDF	ESDF	181 588	37 878	20.9	94 101	19 206	20.4	87 458	18 672	21.3
1 VII 2008 .... ESDF	ESDF	182 379	38 050	20.9	94 526	19 293	20.4	87 853	18 756	21.3
1 VII 2009 .... ESDF	ESDF	183 204	38 222	20.9	94 953	19 381	20.4	88 250	18 841	21.3
1 VII 2010 .... ESDF	ESDF	184 032	38 395	20.9	95 383	19 468	20.4	88 649	18 926	21.3
Solomon Islands - Îles Salomon[1]										
1 VII 2003 .... ESDF	ESDF	448 286	...	...	231 267	...	...	217 019	...	...
1 VII 2004 .... ESDF	ESDF	460 110	...	...	237 626	...	...	222 484	...	...
1 VII 2005 .... ESDF	ESDF	471 266	...	...	242 927	...	...	228 339	...	...
1 VII 2006 .... ESDF	ESDF	483 083	...	...	248 944	...	...	234 139	...	...
1 VII 2007 .... ESDF	ESDF	495 026	...	...	255 063	...	...	239 963	...	...
1 VII 2008 .... ESDF	ESDF	506 992	...	...	261 214	...	...	245 778	...	...
1 VII 2009 .... ESDF	ESDF	518 321	...	...	267 704	...	...	250 617	...	...
Tokelau - Tokélaou										
11 X 2001 .... CDFC	CDFC	1 537	...	...	761	...	...	776	...	...
19 X 2006 .... CDFC	CDFC	1 151	...	...	583	...	...	568	...	...
Tonga										
1 VII 2001[144] .... ESDF	ESDF	100 673	...	...	51 272	...	...	49 400	...	...
1 VII 2002[144] .... ESDF	ESDF	101 002	...	...	51 473	...	...	49 528	...	...
1 VII 2003[144] .... ESDF	ESDF	101 405	...	...	51 710	...	...	49 694	...	...
1 VII 2004[144] .... ESDF	ESDF	101 866	...	...	51 975	...	...	49 890	...	...
1 VII 2005[144] .... ESDF	ESDF	102 371	...	...	52 261	...	...	50 109	...	...
1 VII 2006[144] .... ESDF	ESDF	102 907	...	...	52 561	...	...	50 346	...	...
30 XI 2006 .... CDJC	CDJC	101 991	23 658	23.2	51 772	11 860	22.9	50 219	11 798	23.5
1 VII 2007[144] .... ESDF	ESDF	103 289	...	...	52 771	...	...	50 518	...	...
Tuvalu										
1 XI 2002 .... CDFC	CDFC	9 561	4 492	47.0	4 729	2 281	48.2	4 832	2 211	45.8
Vanuatu[1]										
1 VII 2004 .... ESDF	ESDF	215 541	...	...	110 441[145]	...	...	105 399[145]	...	...
1 VII 2006 .... ESDF	ESDF	221 417	...	...	113 034	...	...	108 383	...	...
Wallis and Futuna Islands - Îles Wallis et Futuna										
22 VII 2003 .... CDFC	CDFC	14 944	...	...	7 494	...	...	7 450	...	...
21 VII 2008 .... CDFC	CDFC	13 445	...	...	6 669	...	...	6 776	...	...

FOOTNOTES - NOTES

Italics: estimates which are less reliable. - Italiques : estimations moins sûres.

* Provisional. - Données provisoires.

[a] 'Code' indicates the source of data, as follows:
CDFC - Census, de facto, complete tabulation
CDFS - Census, de facto, sample tabulation
CDJC - Census, de jure, complete tabulation
CDJS - Census, de jure, sample tabulation
SSDF - Sample survey, de facto
SSDJ - Sample survey, de jure

ESDF - Estimates, de facto
ESDJ - Estimates, de jure

Le 'Code' indique la source des données, comme suit :
CDFC - Recensement, population de fait, tabulation complète
CDFS - Recensement, population de fait, tabulation par sondage
CDJC - Recensement, population de droit, tabulation complète
CDJS - Recensement, population de droit, tabulation par sondage
SSDF - Enquête par sondage, population de fait
SSDJ - Enquête par sondage, population de droit
ESDF - Estimations, population de fait
ESDJ - Estimations, population de droit

[1] Data refer to national projections. - Les données se réfèrent aux projections nationales.

[2] Series not strictly comparable due to differences of definitions of "urban". - Les séries ne sont pas strictement comparables en raison de différences existant dans la définition des "regions urbaines".

[3] Unrevised data. - Les données n'ont pas été révisées.

[4] Excluding Mayotte. - Non compris Mayotte.

[5] Projections based on the 1994 population census. - Projections fondées sur le recensement de la population de 1994.

[6] Based on the results of the Gabonese Survey for the Evaluation and Tracking of Poverty. - Sur base des résultats de l'enquête gabonaise sur l'évaluation et le suivi de la pauvreté.

[7] Post-censal estimates based on 1999 Population Census. - Les estimations post-censitaire fondées sur le recensement de la population de 1999.

[8] Data refer to Libyan nationals only. - Les données se raportent aux nationaux libyens seulement.

[9] As reported by the country. Reasons for discrepancy with other tables not ascertained. - Données comme déclarées par le pays. On ne sait pas comment s'explique la divergence entre ces chiffres et les chiffres correspondants indiqués ailleurs.

[10] Reason for discrepancy between these figures and corresponding figures shown elsewhere not ascertained. - On ne sait pas comment s'explique la divergence entre ces chiffres et les chiffres correspondants indiqués ailleurs.

[11] Excludes the islands of St. Brandon and Agalega. - Non compris les îles St. Brandon et Agalega.

[12] Based on 2000 Population Census data and adjusted for underenumeration of young children. - D'après le recensement de la population de 2000, ajusté en raison du sous-enregistrement des jeunes enfants.

[13] Based on the results of the 2004 Population Census. - D'après des résultats du recensement de la population de 2004.

[14] The number of males and/or females excludes persons whose sex is not stated (18 urban, 19 rural). - Il n'est pas tenu compte dans le nombre d'hommes et de femmes des personnes dont le sexe n'est pas indiqué (18 en zone urbaine et 19 en zone rurale).

[15] Data based on 2008 Population Census. - Données fondées sur le recensement de population de 2008.

[16] Based on the results of a population count. - D'après les résultats d'un comptage de la population.

[17] The population figure is 262 persons. - La population est égale à 262 personnes.

[18] Data are based on projections from 2002 Census. - Données fondées sur des projections tirées du recensement de 2002.

[19] Data have not been adjusted for underenumeration, estimated at 2.4 per cent. - Les données n'ont pas été ajustées pour compenser les lacunes du dénombrement, estimées à 2,4 p. 100.

[20] Based on the results of a Socio Economic Survey. - Basé sur les résultats d'une enquête Socio-Economique.

[21] Mid-year estimates have been adjusted for underenumeration at latest census. - Les estimations au milieu de l'année tiennent compte d'un ajustement destiné à compenser les lacunes du dénombrement lors du dernier recensement.

[22] Because of rounding, totals are not in all cases the sum of the parts. - Les chiffres étant arrondis, les totaux ne correspondent pas toujours rigoureusement à la somme des chiffres partiels.

[23] Excluding persons who were not contacted at the time of the census. - La population non comprend pas les personnes qui n'ont pas été contactées à l'heure du recensement.

[24] Male and female population don't add up to total due to rounding. - La somme des populations d'hommes et des femmes diffère de la population totale au raison des arrondis.

[25] Data have not been adjusted for underenumeration. - Les données n'ont pas été ajustées pour compenser les lacunes du dénombrement.

[26] Final intercensal estimates. Estimates adjusted for census net undercoverage (including adjustment for incompletely enumerated Indian reserves). - Estimations inter-censitaires definitives. Ajusté pour la sous-estimation du recensement (y compris les réservations en Inde incomplètement énumérées).

[27] Estimates adjusted for census net undercoverage (including adjustment for incompletely enumerated Indian reserves). Final postcensal estimates. - Ajusté pour la sous-estimation du recensement (y compris les réservations en Inde incomplètement énumérées). Estimations postcensitaires definitives.

[28] Updated postcensal estimates. Estimates adjusted for census net undercoverage (including adjustment for incompletely enumerated Indian reserves). - Estimations post censitaires mises à jour. Ajusté pour la sous-estimation du recensement (y compris les réservations en Inde incomplètement énumérées).

[29] Estimates adjusted for census net undercoverage (including adjustment for incompletely enumerated Indian reserves). Preliminary postcensal estimates. - Ajusté pour la sous-estimation du recensement (y compris les réservations en Inde incomplètement énumérées). Estimations post censitaires préliminaires.

[30] Excluding residents of institutions. - À l'exclusion de personnes en établissements de soins.

[31] Result of Household Multiple Purpose Survey. - Les chiffres résultent d'enquêtes sur les ménages polyvalentes.

[32] Based on 2010 National Household Survey. - Basée sur l'Enquête nationale des ménages de 2010.

[33] Population in households only. - Population dans les ménages seulement.

[34] Estimates based on 2007 Population Census. - Estimations fondées sur le recensement de la population de 2007.

[35] Population statistics are compiled from registers. - Les statistiques de la population sont compilées à partir des registres.

[36] Excluding data for Saint Barthélémy and Saint Martin. - Non compris les données pour Saint Barthélémy et Saint Martin.

[37] Projections based on 2002 population census. - Projections fondées sur le recensement de la population de 2002.

[38] Projections produced by l'Institut Haïtien de Statistique et d'Informatique (IHSI) and the Latin American and Caribbean Demographic Centre (CELADE) - Population Division of ECLAC. - Les données sont projections produits par l'Institut Haïtien de Statistique et d'Informatique (IHSI) et le centre démographique de l'Amérique latine et les Caraïbes - Division de la population de la CEPALC.

[39] Data are based on projections of the 2001 Population and Housing Census data. - Les données sont basées sur les projections du recensement de 2001 de la population et de l'habitat.

[40] Total represents population in private dwellings, the non-institutional population and persons found on the streets between the hours of 5am and 7am on September 26, 2001; the figures represent the census counts adjusted for under-coverage. - Le total représente la population vivant dans des logements privés et les personnes trouvées dans la rue entre 5 et 7 heures du matin le 26 septembre 2001, mais ne tient pas compte des personnes vivant dans des établissements; les chiffres sont ceux du recensement corrigés pour tenir compte du sous-dénombrement.

[41] Urban and rural distribution derived from census count, held constant and applied to current estimates. Because of rounding, totals are not in all cases the sum of the parts. - La répartition urbain/rural se réfère aux chiffres du recensement, maintenus constants et appliqués aux estimations actuelles. Les chiffres étant arrondis, les totaux ne correspondent pas toujours rigoureusement à la somme des chiffres partiels.

[42] Including an estimation of 1 334 585 persons corresponding to 448 195 housing units without information of the occupants. - Y compris une estimation de 1 334 585 personnes correspondant aux 448 195 unités d'habitation sans information sur les occupants.

[43] Includes the estimates for Saba and St. Eustatius. - Y compris les estimations pour Saba et St. Eustatius.

[44] Includes estimates for St. Eustatius. - Y compris les estimations pour St. Eustatius.

[45] Data refer to projections based on the 2000 population census. - Les données se réfèrent aux projections basées sur le recensement de la population de 2000.

[46] Including armed forces stationed in the area. - Y compris les militaires en garnison sur le territoire.

[47] Based on the results of the 2000 population census. - Basé sur les résultats du recensement de la population de 2000.

[48] Excluding armed forces overseas and civilian citizens absent from country for an extended period of time. - Non compris les militaires à l'étranger, et les civils hors du pays pendant une période prolongée.

[49] Data based on 2010 Population Census. - Données fondées sur le recensement de population de 2010.

[50] Data include persons in remote areas, military personnel outside the country, merchant seamen at sea, civilian seasonal workers outside the country, and other civilians outside the country, and exclude nomads, foreign military, civilian aliens temporarily in the country, transients on ships and Indian jungle population. - Y compris les personnes vivant dans des régions éloignées, le personnel militaire en dehors du pays, les marins marchands, les ouvriers saisonniers en dehors du pays, et autres civils en dehors du pays, et non compris les nomades, les militaires étrangers, les étrangers civils temporairement dans le pays, les transiteurs sur des bateaux et les Indiens de la jungle.

[51] Intercensal estimates. - Estimations inter-censitaires.

[52] Data based on the Population Census of 2005. - Données fondées sur le recensement de la population de 2005.

[53] Excluding nomadic Indian tribes. - Non compris les tribus d'Indiens nomades.

54 A dispute exists between the governments of Argentina and the United Kingdom of Great Britain and Northern Ireland concerning sovereignty over the Falkland Islands (Malvinas). - La souveraineté sur les îles Falkland (Malvinas) fait l'objet d'un différend entre le Gouvernement argentin et le Gouvernement du Royaume-Uni de Grande-Bretagne et d'Irlande du Nord.

55 Include 477 persons present in the Falkland Islands in connection with the military garrison, but exclude all military personnel and their families. - Comprend 477 personnes installées dans les îles Falkland du fait de la présence d'une garnison militaire, mais exclut tous les membres du personnel militaire et leurs familles.

56 The population for the year 2005 corresponds to the population actually enumerated in the census conducted between 18 July and 20 August 2005. The total (adjusted) population is 27 219 264 inhabitants. - La population pour 2005 correspond à la population effectivement dénombrée lors du recensement réalisé entre le 18 juillet et le 20 août 2005. La population totale (après ajustement) compte 27 219 264 habitants.

57 Including 17 diplomats. - La population totale indiquée comprend 17 diplomates.

58 The previous census was conducted only 16 months earlier (on 31 Mar 2003) but it was repeated because all of its data were destroyed in a fire before they could be fully processed, analyzed, and reported. - Le recensement précédent a eu lieu seulement 16 mois auparavant (le 31 mars 2003), mais a dû être refait parce que toutes les données ont été détruites dans un incendie avant que l'on n'ait pu les traiter et les analyser.

59 Figures for male and female population do not add up to the figure for total population, because they exclude 365 persons of unknown sex. - Les chiffres relatifs à la population masculine et féminine ne correspondent pas au chiffre de la population totale, parce que l'on en a exclu 365 personnes de sexe inconnu.

60 Data refer to resident population in Uruguay according to Census Phase 1, carried out between the months of June and July 2004. - Les données se rapportent à la population résidente en Uruguay d'après la phase 1 du recensement, qui a eu lieu entre juin et juillet 2004.

61 Excluding Indian jungle population. - Non compris les Indiens de la jungle.

62 Data refer to the settled population based on the 1979 Population Census and the latest household prelisting. The refugees of Afghanistan in Iran, Pakistan, and an estimated 1.5 million nomads, are not included. - Les données se rapportent à la population stationnaire sur la base du recensement de 1979 et du recensement préliminaire des logements le plus récent. Sont exclus les réfugiés d'Afghanistan en Iran et au Pakistan et les nomades estimés à 1,5 million.

63 Data refer to the settled population based on the 1979 Population Census and the latest household prelisting. The refugees of Afghanistan in Iran, Pakistan, and an estimated 1.5 million nomads, are not included. The so adjusted total population of the country for 2006 is 24.1 million (12.3 million males and 11.8 million females). - Les données se rapportent à la population stationnaire sur la base du recensement de 1979 et du recensement préliminaire des logements le plus récent. Sont exclus les réfugiés d'Afghanistan en Iran et au Pakistan et les nomades estimés à 1,5 million. La population totale du pays ainsi ajustée pour 2006 comprend 24,1 millions de personnes (12,3 millions d'hommes et 11,8 millions de femmes).

64 The adjusted total population of the country is 25.5 million. - La population totale ajustée du pays comprend 25,5 millions de personnes.

65 The adjusted total population of the country is 26 million (13.3 million males and 12.7 million females). - La population totale ajustée du pays comprend 26 millions de personnes (13.3 millions d'homes et 12.7 millions de femmes).

66 The methodology used for calculating the number of the de facto and de jure population in the 2001 census data differs as follows from the methodology used in previous censuses: the duration that defines a person as being ' temporary present ' or 'temporary absent' is now 'under one year'. The previously applied definition was for '6 months'. - La méthode utilisée pour dénombrer la population de fait et la population de droit dans le contexte du recensement de 2001 diffère de celle qui a été appliquée lors des recensements antérieurs en ce que la durée considérée pour définir la ' présence temporaire 'ou' l'absence temporaire' était dorénavant fixée à 'moins d'un an' alors qu'elle était de '6 mois' auparavant.

67 Excluding usual residents not in country at time of census (Total 4053, Male 2238, Female 1815). - À l'exclusion des résidents habituels qui n'étaient pas dans le pays au moment du recensement (au total 4 053 personnes dont 2 238 hommes et 1 815 femmes).

68 Data have not been adjusted for underenumeration, estimated at 4.96 per cent. - Les données n'ont pas été ajustées pour compenser les lacunes du dénombrement, estimées à 4,96 p.100.

69 Data refer to projections based on the 2005 population census. - Les données se réfèrent aux projections basées sur le recensement de la population de 2005.

70 Excluding foreign diplomatic personnel and their dependants. - Non compris le personnel diplomatique étranger et les membres de leur famille les accompagnant.

71 Based on the results of the Cambodia Intercensal Population Survey. Data exclude institutional, homeless households and transient population. - Les données ne comprennent pas la population des institutions, les ménages sans abri et la population de passage.

72 Data refer to national projections based on 2008 census. - Les données se réfèrent aux projections nationales basées sur le recensement de la population de 2008.

73 Data have been estimated on the basis of the annual National Sample Survey on Population Changes. For statistical purposes, the data for China do not include those for the Hong Kong Special Administrative Region (Hong Kong SAR), Macao Special Administrative Region (Macao SAR) and Taiwan province of China. - Les données ont été estimées sur la base de l'enquête annuelle "National Sample Survey on Population Changes". Pour la présentation des statistiques, les données pour la Chine ne comprennent pas la Région Administrative Spéciale de Hong Kong (Hong Kong RAS), la Région Administrative Spéciale de Macao (Macao RAS) et Taïwan province de Chine.

74 The military personnel are classified as urban population. - Le personnel militaire est classé dans la population urbaine.

75 Data refer to Hong Kong resident population at the census moment, which covers usual residents and mobile residents. Usual residents refer to two categories of people: (1) Hong Kong permanent residents who had stayed in Hong Kong for at least three months during the six months before or for at least three months during the six months after the census moment, regardless of whether they were in Hong Kong or not at the census moment; and (2) Hong Kong non-permanent residents who were in Hong Kong at the census moment. Mobile Residents, they are Hong Kong permanent residents who had stayed in Hong Kong for at least one month but less than three months during the six months before or for at least one month but less than three months during the six months after the census moment, regardless of whether they were in Hong Kong or not at the census moment. - Les données se rapportent à la population résidente à Hong Kong au moment du recensement. Cette population est composée des résidants habituels et des résidants mobiles. La population résidente est partagée en deux catégories: (1) les résidents permanents qui ont habité à Hong Kong au moins trois mois pendant les six mois précédents ou les six mois suivants le recensement; (2) les habitants non-permanents de Hong Kong qui étaient à Hong Kong au moment du recensement. La population mobile se rapporte aux résidents permanents de Hong Kong qui ont habité à Hong Kong pendant les six mois après le recensement pour une période comprise entre un mois et trois mois, indépendamment du fait qu'ils étaient à Hong Kong au moment du recensement au pays.

76 Data refer to government controlled areas. - Les données se rapportent aux zones contrôlées par le Gouvernement.

77 Including all persons irrespective of citizenship, who at the time of the census resided in the country or intended to reside for a period of at least one year. It does not distinguish between those present or absent at the time of census. - Les chiffres comprennent toute la population, quelle que soit la nationalité, qui à l'époque de recensement avait résidé dans le pays, ou avait l'intention de résider, pendant une période d'au moins un an. Il n'y a pas de distinction entre les personnes présentes ou absentes au moment du recensement.

78 Including data for the Indian-held part of Jammu and Kashmir, the final status of which has not yet been determined. - Y compris les données pour la partie du Jammu et du Cachemire occupée par l'Inde dont le statut définitif n'a pas encore été déterminé.

79 Excluding Mao-Maram, Paomata and Purul sub-divisions of Senapati district of Manipur. The population of Manipur including the estimated population of the three sub-divisions of Senapati district is 2,291,125 (Males 1,161,173 and females 1,129,952). - Non compris les subdivisions Mao-Maram Paomata et Purul du district de Senapati dans l'État du Manipur. Cet État compte 2 291 125 habitants (1 161 173 hommes et 1 129 952 femmes), y compris la population estimative des trois subdivisions du district de Senapati.

80 Excluding estimated population for Mao Maram, Paomata and Purul sub-divisions of Senapati district of Manipur. - Non compris la population estimée de Mao Maram, Paomata et les subdivisions Purul du district Senapati de Manipur.

81 Final intercensal estimates. - Estimations inter-censitaires definitives.

82 Excluding Province Nanggroe Aceh Darussalam, Regency Nias & Nias Selatan, Regency Boven Digul & Teluk Wondama. Data refer to the "Intercensal Population Survey". - En excluant les provinces de Nanggroe Aceh Darussalam, Regency Nias & Nias Selatan, Regency Boven Digul & Teluk Wondama. Les données concernent l'enquête intercensitaire sur la population.

83 Data refer to the Iranian Year which begins on 21 March and ends on 20 March of the following year. - Les données concernent l'année iranienne, qui commence le 21 mars et se termine le 20 mars de l'année suivante.

84 Differences between the total country figures and sum of urban and rural areas are due to the inclusion of unsettled population numbering 104 717 (53 065 males and females 51 652). - Les différences entre les chiffres pour l'ensemble du pays et la somme des zones urbaines et rurales s'expliquent par l'inclusion de

la population non sédentaire, dont l'effectif est de 104 717 (53 065 de sexe masculin et 51 652 de sexe féminin).

85 Including data for East Jerusalem and Israeli residents in certain other territories under occupation by Israeli military forces since June 1967. - Y compris les données pour Jérusalem-Est et les résidents israéliens dans certains autres territoires occupés depuis 1967 par les forces armées israéliennes.

86 Excluding residents who had been registered in the Israeli localities (the Jewish localities) in the Gaza Area and northern Samaria, which were evacuated in August 2005, but did not notify the Ministry of Interior of their new address. These residents are included in total. - Hors résidents enregistrés dans les localités d'Israel (localités juives) de la Bande de Gaza (verfify) et du nord de la Samarie, qui ont été évacués en Août 2005, mais qui n'ont pas notifié leur nouvelle adresse au ministère de l'intérieur. Ces résidents sont inclus dans le total.

87 Data are rounded for confidentiality reasons. - Chiffres arrondis pour des raisons de confidentialité.

88 Excluding diplomatic personnel outside the country and foreign military and civilian personnel and their dependants stationed in the area. - Non compris le personnel diplomatique hors du pays ni les militaires et agents civils étrangers en poste sur le territoire et les membres de leur famille les accompagnant.

89 Excluding data for Jordanian territory under occupation since June 1967 by Israeli military forces. Excluding foreigners, including registered Palestinian refugees. - Non compris les données pour le territoire jordanien occupé depuis juin 1967 par les forces armées israéliennes. Non compris les étrangers, mais y compris les réfugiés de Palestine enregistrés.

90 Excluding data for Jordanian territory under occupation since June 1967 by Israeli military forces. Including registered Palestinian refugees and Jordanians abroad. - Non compris les données pour le territoire jordanien occupé depuis juin 1967 par les forces armées israéliennes. Y compris les réfugiés palestiniens enregistrés et les Jordaniens à l'étranger.

91 Data are calculated from results of Population and Housing Census of 2009. - Les données sont calculées à partir des résultats de recensement de la population et de l'habitat de 2009.

92 Population estimates for 2000 to 2004 are based on the age-sex distribution of 1995 population census and growth rate at year 2000. - Pour les années 2000 à 2004, on a pris pour base la répartition par âge et sexe du recensement de population de 1995 et le taux de croissance de 2000.

93 Excluding usual residents not in country at time of census. - À l'exclusion des résidents habituels qui ne sont pas dans le pays au moment du recensement.

94 Based on the results of the 2005 Population and Housing Census. - Données fondées sur les résultats du recensement de la population et de l'habitat de 2005.

95 Based on the results of a household survey. - D'après les résultats d'une enquête des ménages.

96 Data including estimated population from household listing from Village Development Committees and Wards which could not be enumerated at the time of census. - Les données incluent la population estimée par les listes des ménages des comités de développement des villages et des circonscriptions qui n'ont pas pu être énumérée au moment du recensement.

97 Data for urban include population in refugee camps. - Les données pour la population urbaine comprennent la population dans les camps réfugiés.

98 Data have been adjusted for underenumeration, estimated at 2.70 per cent. - Les données ont été ajustées pour compenser les lacunes du dénombrement, estimées à 2,70 p. 100.

99 76% are Omani and the rest are Expatriates. - Le pourcentage d'Omanais atteint 76 %; le pourcentage restant correspond à des personnes expatriées.

100 Excluding data for the Pakistan-held part of Jammu and Kashmir, the final status of which has not yet been determined. - Non compris les données concernant la partie du Jammu et Cachemire occupée par le Pakistan dont le statut définitif n'a pas été déterminé.

101 Based on the results of the Population Demographic Survey. These estimates do not reflect completely accurately the actual population and vital events of the country. - D'après les résultats de l'enquête démographique par sondage. Ces estimations ne dénotent pas d'une manière complètement ponctuelle la population actuelle et les statistiques de l'état civil du pays.

102 Urban population is estimated by applying urban census growth rate of 3.5178 per cent during intercensal period. - La population urbaine est estimée sur la base de taux d'accroissement annuel de 3.5178 pour cent obtenus, pour la période entre deux recensements générales de la population, par un recensement urbain.

103 Based on the results of the Pakistan Demographic Survey (PDS 2003). These estimates do not reflect completely accurately the actual population and vital events of the country. - D'après les résultats de l'enquête démographique effectuée par le Pakistan en 2003. Ces estimations ne dénotent pas d'une manière complètement ponctuelle la population actuelle et les statistiques de l'état civil du pays.

104 Based on the results of the Pakistan Demographic Survey (PDS 2005). These estimates do not reflect completely accurately the actual population and vital events of the country. - D'après les résultats de l'enquête démographique effectuée par le Pakistan en 2005. Ces estimations ne dénotent pas d'une manière complètement ponctuelle la population actuelle et les statistiques de l'état civil du pays.

105 Based on the results of the Pakistan Demographic Survey (PDS 2007). - D'après les résultats de l'enquête démographique effectuée par le Pakistan en 2007.

106 Data are based on projections of the 2000 Population and Housing Census data. - Les données sont basées sur les projections du recensement de 2000 de la population et de l'habitat.

107 The Population and Housing Census 2001 did not cover the whole area of the country due to the security problems; data refer to the 18 districts for which the census was completed only (in three districts it was not possible to conduct the census at all and in four districts it was partially conducted). - Le recensement de la population et du logement de 2001 n'a pas été réalisé sur la superficie totale du pays à cause de problèmes de sécurité; les données ne concernent que les 18 districts entièrement recensés (3 districts n'ont pas été recensés du tout, et 4 ont été recensés en partie).

108 Including Palestinian refugees. - Y compris les réfugiés de Palestine.

109 Data based on Address Based Population Registration System. - Les données sont basées sur le registre national de la population basé sur l'adresse.

110 Data are adjusted according to the results of 1999 and 2009 censuses. - Les données ont été ajustées à partir des résultats des recensements de la population de 1999 et 2009.

111 Population statistics are compiled from registers. Excluding Faeroe Islands and Greenland shown separately, if available. - Les statistiques de la population sont compilées à partir des registres. Non compris les Iles Féroé et le Groenland, qui font l'objet de rubriques distinctes, si disponible.

112 Excluding Åland Islands. - Non compris les Îles d'Åland.

113 Excluding diplomatic personnel outside the country and including members of alien armed forces not living in military camps and foreign diplomatic personnel not living in embassies or consulates. - Non compris le personnel diplomatique hors du pays et y compris les militaires étrangers ne vivant pas dans des camps militaires et le personnel diplomatique étranger ne vivant pas dans les ambassades ou les consulats.

114 Data of the microcensus - a 1% household sample survey - refer to a single reference week in spring (usually last week in April). Excluding homeless persons. Excluding foreign military personnel and foreign diplomatic and consular personnel and their family members in the country. - Les données du microrecensement (enquête sur les ménages, réalisée sur un échantillon de 1 %) concernent une seule semaine de référence au printemps (habituellement la dernière semaine d'avril). Non compris les personnes sans domicile fixe. Non compris le personnel militaire étranger, le personnel diplomatique et consulaire étranger et les membres de leur famille se trouvant dans le pays.

115 Excluding families of military personnel, visitors and transients. - Non compris les familles des militaires, ni les visiteurs et transients.

116 Excluding military personnel, visitors and transients. - Non compris les militaires, ni les visiteurs et transients.

117 Including armed forces stationed outside the country and alien armed forces in the area. - Y compris les militaires nationaux hors du pays et les militaires étrangers en garnison sur le territoire.

118 Excluding armed forces stationed outside the country, but including alien armed forces stationed in the area. - Non compris les militaires en garnison hors du pays, mais y compris les militaires étrangers en garnison sur le territoire.

119 Data refer to the Vatican City State. Population statistics are compiled from registers. - Les données se rapportent à l'Etat de la Cité du Vatican. Les statistiques de la population sont compilées à partir des registres.

120 The population figure for 2009 is 466 persons. - La population pour 2009 est égale à 466 personnes.

121 The regional grouping (urban/rural) was made from 1990 to 2000 according to the administrative division of 1 January 2000 and from 2001 according to the administrative division of 1 January 2004. - Pour les années 1990 à 2000, le découpage régional (zone urbaine/rurale) correspond au découpage administratif en vigueur au 1er janvier 2000; à partir de 2001, il correspond à celui en vigueur au 1er janvier 2004.

122 Including civilian nationals temporarily outside the country. - Y compris les civils nationaux temporairement hors du pays.

123 Figures for male and female population do not add up to the figure for total population, because they exclude 119 persons of unknown sex. - Les chiffres relatifs à la population masculine et féminine ne correspondent pas au chiffre de la population totale, parce que l'on en a exclu 119 personnes de sexe inconnu.

124 Census results based on compilation of continuous accounting and sample surveys. - Les résultat du recensement, d'après les résultats des dénombrements et enquêtes par sondage continue.

[125] Including residents temporarily outside the country. Excluding Svalbard and Jan Mayen Islands shown separately, if available. - Y compris les résidents se trouvant temporairement hors du pays. Non compris Svalbard et Jan Mayen qui font l'objet de rubriques distinctes, si disponible.

[126] Excluding civilian aliens within country, but including civilian nationals temporarily outside country. - Non compris les civils étrangers dans le pays, mais y compris les civils nationaux temporairement hors du pays.

[127] Excluding Transnistria and the municipality of Bender. - Les données ne tiennent pas compte de l'information sur la Transnistria et la municipalité de Bender.

[128] Excluding data for Kosovo and Metohia. - Sans les données pour le Kosovo et Metohie.

[129] Including residents temporarily outside the country. - Y compris les résidents se trouvant temporairement hors du pays.

[130] Excluding citizens temporarily residing abroad, the sum by urban and rural does not add up to the total. - Les nationaux se trouvant provisoirement à l'étranger ne sont pas pris en compte. La somme des chiffres disponibles pour les zones urbaines et rurales ne correspond donc pas au total.

[131] Excluding transients visitors. - Non compris les visiteurs en transit.

[132] Excluding Channel Islands (Guernsey and Jersey) and Isle of Man, shown separately, if available. - Non compris les îles Anglo-Normandes (Guernesey et Jersey) et l'île de Man, qui font l'objet de rubriques distinctes, si disponible.

[133] Counts for the 2001 Census are taken from 'Key Statistics table 1 for the Urban/Rural classification: England and Wales' available on CD based on the usually resident population. - Les chiffres du recensement de 2001 proviennent du tableau intitulé « Key Statistics table 1 for the Urban/Rural classification: England and Wales » disponible sur CD-ROM et sont fondés sur la notion de résidence habituelle.

[134] Population estimates for 1994 to 2002 were revised in light of the local studies. - Les estimations de la population pour les années 1994 à 2002 ont été révisées en fonction d'études locales.

[135] Intercensal estimates. Data are based on 2009 Australian Standard Geographical Classification boundaries. - Estimations inter-censitaires. Les données réfèrent au découpage de la nomenclature géographique normalisée d'Australie de 2009.

[136] Excluding Niue, shown separately, which is part of Cook Islands, but because of remoteness is administered separately. - Non compris Nioué, qui fait l'objet d'une rubrique distincte et qui fait partie des îles Cook, mais qui, en raison de son éloignement, est administrée séparément.

[137] This data has been randomly rounded to protect confidentiality. Individual figures may not add up to totals, and values for the same data may vary in different tables. - Ces données ont été arrondies de façon aléatoire afin d'en préserver la confidentialité. La somme de certains chiffres peut ne pas correspondre aux totaux indiqués et les valeurs des mêmes données peuvent varier d'un tableau à un autre.

[138] Excluding diplomatic personnel and armed forces stationed outside country; also excluding alien armed forces within the country. - Non compris le personnel diplomatique et les militaires hors du pays; non compris également les militaires étrangers en garnison dans le pays.

[139] Because of rounding, totals are not in all cases the sum of the parts. Population estimates by urban/rural residence exclude inland waters and oceanic areas. - Les chiffres étant arrondis, les totaux ne correspondent pas toujours rigoureusement à la somme des chiffres partiels. Les estimations de la population par lieu de résidence urbaine ou rurale excluent les eaux intérieures et les zones océaniques.

[140] Based on the census, updated for residents missed or counted more than once by the census (net census undercount); residents temporarily overseas on census night, and births, deaths and net migration between the census night and the date of the estimate. - D'après le recensement, mise à jour pour les résidents omis ou dénombrés plus d'une fois par le recensement (sous-dénombrement net); résidents temporairement à l'étranger la nuit du recensement, et naissances, décès et migration nette entre la nuit du recensement et la date de l'estimation.

[141] Population estimates by urban/rural residence exclude inland waters and oceanic areas. - Les estimations de la population par lieu de résidence urbaine ou rurale excluent les eaux intérieures et les zones océaniques.

[142] The population figure is 64 persons. - La population est égale à 64 personnes.

[143] The population figure is 58 persons. - La population est égale à 58 personnes.

[144] Based on the results of the 1996 population census. Data refer to national projections. - À partir des résultats du recensement de la population de 1996. Les données se réfèrent aux projections nationales.

[145] Figures for male and female do not add up to the total, reason for discrepancy not ascertained. - La some des données pour la population masculine et pour la population féminine n'est pas égale au total, les raisons de cette différence ne sont pas expliquées.

Tables 7 and 7a

Table 7 presents population by age, sex and urban/rural residence for the latest available year between 2000 and 2009. Table 7a presents the available data for year 2010.

Description of variables: Data in this table are either population census figures or estimates, some of which are based on sample surveys. The source of data is indicated by the 'code' explained at the end of the table.

The reference date of the census or estimate appears in the left-most column of the table. In general, the estimates refer to mid-year (1 July).

Age is defined as age at last birthday, that is, the difference between the date of birth and the reference date of the age distribution expressed in completed solar years. The age classification used in this table is the following: under 1 year, 1-4 years, 5-year groups through 95-99 years, and 100 years or over.

Statistics are presented for one year, the most recent available. However, if more complete disaggregation is available for an earlier year, both are displayed.

The urban/rural classification of population is that provided by each country or area; it is presumed to be based on the national census definitions of urban population that have been set forth at the end of the technical notes to table 6.

Estimates of population by age and sex presented in this table have been limited to countries or areas for which estimates have been based on the results of a sample survey or have been constructed by the component method from the results of a population census or sample survey.

Reliability of data: Estimates which are believed to be less reliable are set in *italics* rather than in roman type. No attempt has been made to take account of age-reporting accuracy, the evaluation of which has been described in section 3.1.3 of the Technical Notes.

Limitations: Statistics on population by age and sex are subject to the same qualifications as have been set forth for population statistics in general and age distributions in particular, as discussed in sections 3 and 3.1.3, respectively, of the Technical Notes.

Comparability of population data classified by age and sex is limited by variations in the definition of total population, discussed in detail in section 3 of the Technical Notes, and by the accuracy of the original enumeration. Both factors are more important in relation to certain age groups than to others. For example, under-enumeration is known to be more prevalent among infants and young children than among older persons. Similarly, the exclusion from the total population of certain groups that tend to be of selected ages (such as the armed forces) can markedly affect the age structure and its comparability with that for other countries or areas. Consideration should be given to the implications of these basic limitations in using the data.

In addition to these general qualifications are the special problems of comparability that arise in relation to age statistics in particular. Age distributions of population are known to suffer from certain deficiencies that have their origin in irregularities in age reporting. Although some of the irregularities tend to be obscured or eliminated when data are tabulated in five-year age groups rather than by single years, precision still continues to be affected, though the degree of distortion is not always readily seen.

Another factor limiting comparability is the age classification employed by the various countries or areas. Age may be based on the year of birth rather than the age at last birthday, in other words, calculated using the day, month and year of birth. Distributions based only on the year of birth are footnoted when known.

The absence of data in the unknown age group does not necessarily indicate completely accurate reporting and tabulation of the age item. The unknowns may have been eliminated by assigning ages to them before tabulation, or by proportionately distributing the unknown category across the age groups after tabulation.

As noted in connection with table 5, intercensal estimates of total population are usually revised to accord with the results of a census of population if inexplicable discontinuities appear to exist. Postcensal age-sex distributions, however, are less likely to be revised in this way. When it is known that a total population estimate for a given year has been revised and the corresponding age distribution has not been, the age distribution is shown as provisional. Distributions of this type should be used with caution when studying trends over a period of years, though their utility for studying age structure for the specified year is probably unimpaired.

The comparability of data by urban/rural residence is affected by the national definitions of urban and rural used in tabulating these data. When known, the definitions of urban used in national population censuses are presented at the end of the technical notes for table 6. As discussed in detail in the technical notes for table 6, these definitions vary considerably from one country or area to another.

Earlier data: Population by age, sex and urban/rural residence has been shown in previous issues of the *Demographic Yearbook*. For more information on specific topics, and years for which data are reported, readers should consult the Historical Index. In addition, population data by single years of age, sex and urban/rural residence, for censuses conducted since 1995, are shown in the *Demographic Yearbook* webpage http://unstats.un.org/unsd/demographic/products/dyb/dybcensusdata.htm.

Tableaux 7 et 7a

Le tableau 7 présente les données les plus récentes disponibles pour la période 2000 -2009 sur la population selon l'âge, le sexe et le lieu de résidence (zone urbaine ou rurale). Le tableau 7a présente les données disponibles pour l'année 2010.

Description des variables : les données de ce tableau proviennent de recensements de la population ou correspondent à des estimations, fondées dans certains cas, sur des enquêtes par sondage. Le 'code' indique comment les données ont été obtenues. Les codes utilisés sont expliqués à la fin du tableau.

La date du recensement ou de l'estimation figure dans la colonne de gauche du tableau. En général, les estimations se rapportent au milieu de l'année (1er juillet).

L'âge désigne l'âge au dernier anniversaire, c'est-à-dire la différence entre la date de naissance et la date de référence de la répartition par âge exprimée en années solaires révolues. La classification par âge utilisée dans ce tableau est la suivante : moins d'un an, 1 à 4 ans, groupes quinquennaux jusqu'à 95-99 ans et 100 ans ou plus.

Les statistiques portent sur une année, qui correspond à celle pour laquelle on dispose des statistiques les plus récentes. Toutefois, si l'on dispose de répartitions plus complètes pour des années antérieures, les statistiques sont alors présentées pour les deux années.

La classification par zones urbaines et rurales de la population est celle qui est communiquée par chaque pays ou zone ; on part du principe qu'elle repose sur les définitions de la population urbaine utilisées pour les recensements de la population nationaux telles qu'elles sont reproduites à la fin des notes techniques du tableau 6.

Les estimations de la population selon l'âge et le sexe qui figurent dans ce tableau ne concernent que les pays ou zones pour lesquels les estimations sont fondées sur les résultats d'une enquête par sondage ou ont été établies par la méthode des composantes à partir des résultats d'un recensement de la population ou d'une enquête par sondage.

Fiabilité des données : les estimations considérées comme moins sûres sont indiquées en italique plutôt qu'en caractères romains. On n'a pas tenu compte des inexactitudes dans les déclarations d'âge, dont la méthode d'évaluation est exposée à la section 3.1.3 des Notes techniques.

Insuffisance des données : les statistiques de la population selon l'âge et le sexe appellent les mêmes réserves que celles qui ont été formulées aux sections 3 et 3.1.3 des Notes techniques à propos des statistiques de la population en général et des répartitions par âge en particulier.

La comparabilité des statistiques de la population selon l'âge et le sexe pâtit du manque d'uniformité dans la définition de la population totale (voir la section 3 des Notes techniques) et des lacunes des dénombrements. L'influence de ces deux facteurs varie selon les groupes d'âge. Ainsi, le dénombrement des enfants de moins d'un an et des jeunes enfants comporte souvent plus de lacunes que celui des personnes plus âgées. De même, le fait que certains groupes de personnes appartenant souvent à des groupes d'âge déterminés, par exemple les militaires, ne soient pas pris en compte dans la population totale peut influer sensiblement sur la structure par âge et sur la comparabilité des données avec celles d'autres pays ou zones. Il conviendra de tenir compte de ces facteurs fondamentaux lorsque l'on utilisera les données du tableau.

Outre ces difficultés d'ordre général, la comparabilité pose des problèmes particuliers lorsqu'il s'agit des données par âge. On sait que les répartitions de la population selon l'âge présentent certaines imperfections dues à l'inexactitude des déclarations d'âge. Certaines de ces anomalies ont tendance à s'estomper ou à disparaître lorsque l'on classe les données par groupes d'âge quinquennaux et non par années d'âge, mais une certaine imprécision subsiste, même s'il n'est pas toujours facile de voir à quel point il y a distorsion.

Le degré de comparabilité dépend également de la classification par âge employée dans les divers pays ou zones. L'âge retenu peut être défini par date exacte (jour, mois et année) de naissance ou par celle du dernier anniversaire. Lorsqu'elles étaient connues, les répartitions établies seulement d'après l'année de la naissance ont été signalées en note à la fin du tableau.

Si aucun nombre ne figure dans la rangée réservée aux âges inconnus, cela ne signifie pas nécessairement que les déclarations d'âge et l'exploitation des données par âge aient été tout à fait exactes. C'est souvent une indication que l'on a attribué un âge aux personnes d'âge inconnu avant l'exploitation des données ou qu'elles ont été réparties proportionnellement entre les différents groupes après cette opération.

Comme on l'a indiqué à propos du tableau 5, les estimations intercensitaires de la population totale sont d'ordinaire rectifiées d'après les résultats des recensements de population si l'on constate des discontinuités inexplicables. Les données postcensitaires concernant la répartition de la population par âge et par sexe ont toutefois moins de chance d'être rectifiées de cette manière. Lorsque l'on savait qu'une estimation de la population totale pour une année donnée avait été rectifiée sans qu'il en soit de même pour la répartition par âge correspondante, cette dernière a été indiquée comme ayant un caractère provisoire. Les répartitions de ce type doivent être utilisées avec prudence lorsque l'on étudie les tendances sur un certain nombre d'années, quoique leur utilité pour l'étude de la structure par âge de la population pour l'année visée reste probablement entière.

La comparabilité des données selon le lieu de résidence (zone urbaine ou rurale) peut être limitée par les définitions nationales des termes « urbain » et « rural » utilisées pour la mise en tableaux de ces données. Les définitions du terme « urbain » utilisées pour les recensements nationaux de population ont été présentées à la fin des notes techniques du tableau 6 lorsqu'elles étaient connues. Comme on l'a précisé dans les notes techniques relatives au tableau 6, ces définitions varient considérablement d'un pays ou d'une zone à l'autre.

Données publiées antérieurement : des statistiques concernant la population selon l'âge, le sexe et le lieu de résidence (zone urbaine ou rurale) ont été présentées dans des éditions antérieures de l'*Annuaire démographique*. Pour plus de précisions concernant les années et les sujets pour lesquels des données ont été publiées, se reporter à l'index historique. En plus, des statistiques disponibles concernant la « Population selon chaque année d'âge, le sexe et la résidence urbaine/rurale », pour les recensements depuis 1995, ont été présentées dans la page internet suivante de l'*Annuaire démographique* http://unstats.un.org/unsd/demographic/products/dyb/dybcensusdata.htm.

Continent, country or area, date, code and age (in years) / Continent, pays ou zone, date, code et âge (en annèes)	Total			Urban - Urbaine			Rural - Rurale		
	Both sexes Les deux sexes	Male Masculin	Female Féminin	Both sexes Les deux sexes	Male Masculin	Female Féminin	Both sexes Les deux sexes	Male Masculin	Female Féminin

AFRICA - AFRIQUE

Algeria - Algérie[1]
16 IV 2008* (CDJC)

Total	34 080 030	17 232 747	16 847 283	...	...	...	...	...	...
0 - 4	3 404 918	1 750 097	1 654 821	...	...	...	...	...	...
5 - 9	2 888 376	1 475 674	1 412 702	...	...	...	...	...	...
10 - 14	3 258 774	1 662 260	1 596 513	...	...	...	...	...	...
15 - 19	3 635 170	1 847 311	1 787 859	...	...	...	...	...	...
20 - 24	3 763 506	1 895 704	1 867 802	...	...	...	...	...	...
25 - 29	3 422 377	1 730 409	1 691 968	...	...	...	...	...	...
30 - 34	2 740 995	1 379 085	1 361 910	...	...	...	...	...	...
35 - 39	2 342 778	1 167 249	1 175 529	...	...	...	...	...	...
40 - 44	2 018 327	1 007 683	1 010 644	...	...	...	...	...	...
45 - 49	1 629 435	817 004	812 432	...	...	...	...	...	...
50 - 54	1 346 695	682 357	664 337	...	...	...	...	...	...
55 - 59	1 062 579	547 181	515 398	...	...	...	...	...	...
60 - 64	711 482	354 694	356 788	...	...	...	...	...	...
65 - 69	631 303	314 958	316 345	...	...	...	...	...	...
70 - 74	504 926	248 672	256 254	...	...	...	...	...	...
75 - 79	363 843	181 478	182 364	...	...	...	...	...	...
80 - 84	187 130	93 472	93 657	...	...	...	...	...	...
85 +	132 445	62 141	70 304	...	...	...	...	...	...
Unknown - Inconnu	34 973	15 317	19 657	...	...	...	...	...	...

Benin - Bénin
11 II 2002 (CDJC)

Total	6 769 914	3 284 119	3 485 795	2 630 133	1 280 418	1 349 715	4 139 781	2 003 701	2 136 080
0	235 342	118 243	117 099	82 945	41 797	41 148	152 397	76 446	75 951
1 - 4	939 907	475 297	464 610	309 993	157 189	152 804	629 914	318 108	311 806
5 - 9	1 155 377	589 653	565 724	380 207	188 422	191 785	775 170	401 231	373 939
10 - 14	838 749	438 376	400 373	332 753	162 989	169 764	505 996	275 387	230 609
15 - 19	653 251	321 984	331 267	294 811	144 462	150 349	358 440	177 522	180 918
20 - 24	563 947	243 515	320 432	262 496	123 275	139 221	301 451	120 240	181 211
25 - 29	532 056	228 090	303 966	232 948	107 420	125 528	299 108	120 670	178 438
30 - 34	414 166	192 429	221 737	180 416	88 668	91 748	233 750	103 761	129 989
35 - 39	340 632	157 551	183 081	143 773	69 970	73 803	196 859	87 581	109 278
40 - 44	264 488	125 792	138 696	109 427	54 554	54 873	155 061	71 238	83 823
45 - 49	196 056	94 805	101 251	81 020	40 280	40 740	115 036	54 525	60 511
50 - 54	167 901	81 461	86 440	63 992	31 615	32 377	103 909	49 846	54 063
55 - 59	93 493	46 214	47 279	36 952	18 405	18 547	56 541	27 809	28 732
60 - 64	116 796	53 543	63 253	38 629	17 488	21 141	78 167	36 055	42 112
65 - 69	63 847	28 630	35 217	22 857	10 048	12 809	40 990	18 582	22 408
70 - 74	71 231	32 523	38 708	22 048	9 550	12 498	49 183	22 973	26 210
75 - 79	32 158	14 609	17 549	10 617	4 473	6 144	21 541	10 136	11 405
80 - 84	41 705	18 397	23 308	11 461	4 501	6 960	30 244	13 896	16 348
85 - 89	13 113	6 037	7 076	3 860	1 497	2 363	9 253	4 540	4 713
90 - 94	12 256	5 945	6 311	3 413	1 457	1 956	8 843	4 488	4 355
95 +	23 098	10 753	12 345	5 317	2 201	3 116	17 781	8 552	9 229
Unknown - Inconnu	345	272	73	198	157	41	147	115	32

Botswana
1 VIII 2006 (SSDJ)

Total	1 773 240	851 670	921 570	1 000 443	473 136	527 307	772 797	378 534	394 263
0	48 555	23 864	24 691	25 317	12 680	12 637	23 238	11 184	12 054
1 - 4	163 917	83 700	80 217	80 681	40 540	40 141	83 236	43 160	40 076
5 - 9	199 685	102 650	97 035	100 949	51 227	49 722	98 736	51 423	47 313
10 - 14	214 874	106 643	108 231	112 297	54 176	58 121	102 577	52 467	50 110
15 - 19	183 429	91 806	91 623	109 115	51 830	57 285	74 314	39 976	34 338
20 - 24	196 191	92 134	104 057	124 532	57 134	67 398	71 659	35 000	36 659
25 - 29	169 260	80 087	89 173	113 205	52 679	60 526	56.055	27 408	28 647
30 - 34	131 406	65 142	66 264	85 466	41 546	43 920	45 940	23 596	22 344
35 - 39	95 739	44 147	51 592	62 301	28 348	33 953	33 438	15 799	17 639
40 - 44	82 595	37 525	45 070	48 769	23 197	25 572	33 826	14 328	19 498
45 - 49	69 451	31 320	38 131	40 748	18 431	22 317	28 703	12 889	15 814
50 - 54	55 815	24 853	30 962	28 916	13 436	15 480	26 899	11 417	15 482
55 - 59	39 871	18 041	21 830	18 329	8 895	9 434	21 542	9 146	12 396
60 - 64	30 679	12 980	17 699	13 763	5 742	8 021	16 916	7 238	9 678
65 - 69	26 929	11 783	15 146	10 998	4 490	6 508	15 931	7 293	8 638

Continent, country or area, date, code and age (in years) / Continent, pays ou zone, date, code et âge (en années)	Total			Urban - Urbaine			Rural - Rurale		
	Both sexes Les deux sexes	Male Masculin	Female Féminin	Both sexes Les deux sexes	Male Masculin	Female Féminin	Both sexes Les deux sexes	Male Masculin	Female Féminin
AFRICA - AFRIQUE									
Botswana									
1 VIII 2006 (SSDJ)									
70 +	64 520	24 818	39 702	24 895	8 695	16 200	39 625	16 123	23 502
Unknown - Inconnu	324	177	147	162	90	72	162	87	75
Burkina Faso									
9 XII 2006 (CDJC)									
Total	14 017 262	6 768 739	7 248 523	3 181 967	1 588 895	1 593 072	10 835 295	5 179 844	5 655 451
0	466 516	235 090	231 426	87 021	44 072	42 949	379 495	191 018	188 477
1 - 4	1 970 397	995 520	974 877	333 623	169 737	163 886	1 636 774	825 783	810 991
5 - 9	2 315 710	1 176 473	1 139 237	401 898	200 004	201 894	1 913 812	976 469	937 343
10 - 14	1 746 588	900 103	846 485	369 532	178 639	190 893	1 377 056	721 464	655 592
15 - 19	1 475 285	710 323	764 962	411 383	192 566	218 817	1 063 902	517 757	546 145
20 - 24	1 185 378	530 425	654 953	366 029	178 980	187 049	819 349	351 445	467 904
25 - 29	1 009 285	448 431	560 854	296 420	150 350	146 070	712 865	298 081	414 784
30 - 34	794 820	363 408	431 412	228 658	122 850	105 808	566 162	240 558	325 604
35 - 39	656 824	298 236	358 588	172 705	92 889	79 816	484 119	205 347	278 772
40 - 44	549 287	250 143	299 144	136 961	71 800	65 161	412 326	178 343	233 983
45 - 49	427 739	195 016	232 723	99 671	52 052	47 619	328 068	142 964	185 104
50 - 54	358 810	166 281	192 529	78 866	41 122	37 744	279 944	125 159	154 785
55 - 59	273 563	132 254	141 309	56 234	29 228	27 006	217 329	103 026	114 303
60 - 64	238 962	111 176	127 786	45 740	21 983	23 757	193 222	89 193	104 029
65 - 69	163 609	80 542	83 067	29 765	14 189	15 576	133 844	66 353	67 491
70 - 74	136 282	63 727	72 555	23 129	10 103	13 026	113 153	53 624	59 529
75 - 79	77 113	37 186	39 927	12 366	5 449	6 917	64 747	31 737	33 010
80 - 84	50 317	21 791	28 526	8 171	2 957	5 214	42 146	18 834	23 312
85 - 89	21 694	9 645	12 049	3 512	1 230	2 282	18 182	8 415	9 767
90 - 94	11 529	4 480	7 049	1 898	619	1 279	9 631	3 861	5 770
95 +	13 067	4 727	8 340	1 956	467	1 489	11 111	4 260	6 851
Unknown - Inconnu	74 487	33 762	40 725	16 429	7 609	8 820	58 058	26 153	31 905
1 VII 2009 (ESDJ)[2]									
Total	*15 224 780*	*7 346 835*	*7 877 945*	...	...	...	...	...	...
0	*652 074*	*332 861*	*319 213*	...	...	...	...	...	...
1 - 4	*2 262 278*	*1 166 932*	*1 095 346*	...	...	...	...	...	...
5 - 9	*2 416 407*	*1 236 776*	*1 179 631*	...	...	...	...	...	...
10 - 14	*1 973 815*	*988 126*	*985 689*	...	...	...	...	...	...
15 - 19	*1 577 324*	*774 081*	*803 243*	...	...	...	...	...	...
20 - 24	*1 309 638*	*579 080*	*730 558*	...	...	...	...	...	...
25 - 29	*1 045 616*	*455 063*	*590 553*	...	...	...	...	...	...
30 - 34	*878 095*	*389 101*	*488 994*	...	...	...	...	...	...
35 - 39	*679 903*	*308 106*	*371 797*	...	...	...	...	...	...
40 - 44	*589 777*	*263 840*	*325 937*	...	...	...	...	...	...
45 - 49	*453 094*	*206 387*	*246 707*	...	...	...	...	...	...
50 - 54	*382 895*	*172 330*	*210 565*	...	...	...	...	...	...
55 - 59	*280 518*	*133 841*	*146 677*	...	...	...	...	...	...
60 - 64	*254 972*	*118 221*	*136 751*	...	...	...	...	...	...
65 - 69	*167 320*	*81 902*	*85 418*	...	...	...	...	...	...
70 - 74	*138 614*	*64 975*	*73 639*	...	...	...	...	...	...
75 - 79	*75 664*	*37 101*	*38 563*	...	...	...	...	...	...
80 +	*86 776*	*38 112*	*48 664*	...	...	...	...	...	...
Burundi									
16 VIII 2008 (CDJC)									
Total	8 053 574	3 964 906	4 088 668	811 866	442 596	369 270	7 241 708	3 522 310	3 719 398
0 - 4	1 424 016	701 119	722 897	121 181	60 098	61 083	1 302 835	641 021	661 814
5 - 9	1 133 011	554 819	578 192	93 103	46 020	47 083	1 039 908	508 799	531 109
10 - 14	992 125	479 874	512 251	81 559	39 261	42 298	910 566	440 613	469 953
15 - 19	967 635	462 251	505 384	102 274	51 816	50 458	865 361	410 435	454 926
20 - 24	771 686	364 574	407 112	95 104	52 641	42 463	676 582	311 933	364 649
25 - 29	607 541	304 842	302 699	87 743	52 567	35 176	519 798	252 275	267 523
30 - 34	414 453	209 982	204 471	61 717	38 063	23 654	352 736	171 919	180 817
35 - 39	371 931	186 018	185 913	45 180	27 712	17 468	326 751	158 306	168 445
40 - 44	303 720	153 694	150 026	32 626	20 899	11 727	271 094	132 795	138 299
45 - 49	280 890	146 870	134 020	25 095	15 625	9 470	255 795	131 245	124 550
50 - 54	228 246	116 798	111 448	17 525	10 673	6 852	210 721	106 125	104 596
55 - 59	141 758	76 723	65 035	10 835	6 528	4 307	130 923	70 195	60 728
60 - 64	107 403	52 602	54 801	7 274	3 910	3 364	100 129	48 692	51 437

Continent, country or area, date, code and age (in years) Continent, pays ou zone, date, code et âge (en années)	Total			Urban - Urbaine			Rural - Rurale		
	Both sexes Les deux sexes	Male Masculin	Female Féminin	Both sexes Les deux sexes	Male Masculin	Female Féminin	Both sexes Les deux sexes	Male Masculin	Female Féminin
AFRICA - AFRIQUE									
Burundi									
16 VIII 2008 (CDJC)									
65 - 69	67 434	34 477	32 957	4 369	2 260	2 109	63 065	32 217	30 848
70 - 74	63 458	28 759	34 699	3 656	1 646	2 010	59 802	27 113	32 689
75 - 79	35 140	18 344	16 796	2 120	973	1 147	33 020	17 371	15 649
80 - 84	28 212	12 675	15 537	1 403	556	847	26 809	12 119	14 690
85 - 89	11 836	6 328	5 508	639	298	341	11 197	6 030	5 167
90 - 94	8 545	4 074	4 471	417	156	261	8 128	3 918	4 210
95 +	7 300	3 585	3 715	493	295	198	6 807	3 290	3 517
Unknown - Inconnu	87 234	46 498	40 736	17 553	10 599	6 954	69 681	35 899	33 782
Cape Verde - Cap-Vert									
1 VII 2003 (ESDF)									
Total	460 968	223 254	237 715	257 412	125 652	131 759	203 556	97 600	105 956
0 - 4	58 940	30 004	28 936	30 116	15 352	14 765	28 823	14 652	14 171
5 - 9	61 218	30 867	30 351	30 927	15 643	15 284	30 291	15 224	15 067
10 - 14	64 803	32 445	32 358	34 166	16 918	17 248	30 636	15 526	15 110
15 - 19	57 898	28 923	28 975	33 909	16 551	17 358	23 990	12 372	11 618
20 - 24	42 677	21 383	21 294	26 883	13 427	13 456	15 794	7 956	7 838
25 - 29	31 691	15 870	15 821	20 027	9 970	10 057	11 664	5 901	5 763
30 - 34	27 198	13 321	13 877	16 627	8 322	8 306	10 570	4 999	5 571
35 - 39	26 745	12 770	13 975	16 748	8 330	8 419	9 996	4 440	5 556
40 - 44	22 729	10 461	12 268	13 844	6 826	7 018	8 886	3 635	5 251
45 - 49	16 084	6 733	9 351	9 359	4 438	4 921	6 726	2 296	4 430
50 - 54	9 378	3 674	5 704	5 496	2 386	3 110	3 882	1 288	2 594
55 - 59	5 466	2 224	3 242	2 921	1 271	1 651	2 545	953	1 592
60 - 64	7 569	2 919	4 650	3 580	1 404	2 176	3 989	1 515	2 474
65 - 69	9 285	3 660	5 625	4 224	1 629	2 595	5 062	2 032	3 030
70 - 74	7 654	3 244	4 410	3 316	1 270	2 046	4 338	1 974	2 364
75 - 79	5 041	2 183	2 858	2 264	853	1 410	2 778	1 330	1 448
80 +	6 593	2 573	4 020	3 005	1 064	1 941	3 589	1 510	2 079
1 VII 2009 (ESDF)									
Total	508 633	246 219	262 414	...	...	...	...	...	...
0	12 823	6 456	6 367	...	...	...	...	...	...
1 - 4	47 666	23 908	23 758	...	...	...	...	...	...
5 - 9	58 602	29 360	29 242	...	...	...	...	...	...
10 - 14	57 684	29 043	28 641	...	...	...	...	...	...
15 - 19	63 189	31 560	31 629	...	...	...	...	...	...
20 - 24	58 423	28 977	29 446	...	...	...	...	...	...
25 - 29	43 089	21 237	21 852	...	...	...	...	...	...
30 - 34	31 981	15 734	16 247	...	...	...	...	...	...
35 - 39	26 249	12 619	13 630	...	...	...	...	...	...
40 - 44	26 303	12 436	13 867	...	...	...	...	...	...
45 - 49	23 118	10 735	12 383	...	...	...	...	...	...
50 - 54	16 784	7 277	9 507	...	...	...	...	...	...
55 - 59	10 540	4 149	6 391	...	...	...	...	...	...
60 - 64	5 443	2 260	3 183	...	...	...	...	...	...
65 - 69	6 350	2 491	3 859	...	...	...	...	...	...
70 - 74	8 241	3 167	5 074	...	...	...	...	...	...
75 - 79	6 085	2 449	3 636	...	...	...	...	...	...
80 +	6 063	2 361	3 702	...	...	...	...	...	...
Congo									
1 VII 2004 (ESDF)									
Total	3 231 326	...	...	...	...	...	...	...	...
0 - 4	544 478	...	...	...	...	...	...	...	...
5 - 9	484 376	...	...	...	...	...	...	...	...
10 - 14	414 902	...	...	...	...	...	...	...	...
15 - 19	357 708	...	...	...	...	...	...	...	...
20 - 24	291 466	...	...	...	...	...	...	...	...
25 - 29	231 040	...	...	...	...	...	...	...	...
30 - 34	171 583	...	...	...	...	...	...	...	...
35 - 39	142 178	...	...	...	...	...	...	...	...
40 - 44	130 546	...	...	...	...	...	...	...	...
45 - 49	116 005	...	...	...	...	...	...	...	...
50 - 54	95 970	...	...	...	...	...	...	...	...
55 - 59	80 783	...	...	...	...	...	...	...	...

7. Population by age, sex and urban/rural residence: latest available year, 2000 - 2009
Population selon l'âge, le sexe et la résidence, urbaine/rurale : dernière année disponible, 2000 - 2009 (continued - suite)

Continent, country or area, date, code and age (in years) / Continent, pays ou zone, date, code et âge (en années)	Total			Urban - Urbaine			Rural - Rurale		
	Both sexes Les deux sexes	Male Masculin	Female Féminin	Both sexes Les deux sexes	Male Masculin	Female Féminin	Both sexes Les deux sexes	Male Masculin	Female Féminin
AFRICA - AFRIQUE									
Congo									
1 VII 2004 (ESDF)									
60 - 64	66 565	...	...	...	...	...	...	...	...
65 - 69	48 793	...	...	...	...	...	...	...	...
70 +	54 933	...	...	...	...	...	...	...	...
Egypt - Égypte									
1 VII 2009 (ESDF)									
Total	76 822 251	39 276 611	37 545 640	33 005 492	16 848 228	16 157 264	43 816 759	22 428 383	21 388 376
0 - 4	8 151 146	4 178 272	3 972 874	3 075 040	1 574 238	1 500 802	5 076 106	2 604 034	2 472 072
5 - 9	8 071 205	4 161 585	3 909 620	3 146 406	1 617 292	1 529 114	4 924 799	2 544 293	2 380 506
10 - 14	8 149 845	4 224 711	3 925 134	3 118 634	1 609 486	1 509 148	5 031 211	2 615 225	2 415 986
15 - 19	9 014 322	4 623 062	4 391 260	3 668 857	1 866 998	1 801 859	5 345 465	2 756 064	2 589 401
20 - 24	8 307 334	4 252 709	4 054 625	3 650 615	1 837 269	1 813 346	4 656 719	2 415 440	2 241 279
25 - 29	6 743 445	3 329 427	3 414 018	2 977 620	1 457 099	1 520 521	3 765 825	1 872 328	1 893 497
30 - 34	4 993 388	2 551 162	2 442 226	2 281 137	1 156 309	1 124 828	2 712 251	1 394 853	1 317 398
35 - 39	4 912 987	2 438 402	2 474 585	2 189 244	1 097 435	1 091 809	2 723 743	1 340 967	1 382 776
40 - 44	4 316 568	2 182 906	2 133 662	2 040 827	1 024 677	1 016 150	2 275 741	1 158 229	1 117 512
45 - 49	3 875 325	1 980 511	1 894 814	1 835 813	936 365	899 448	2 039 512	1 044 146	995 366
50 - 54	3 227 840	1 627 478	1 600 362	1 630 843	828 800	802 043	1 596 997	798 678	798 319
55 - 59	2 388 905	1 280 419	1 108 486	1 161 947	623 816	538 131	1 226 958	656 603	570 355
60 - 64	1 797 751	947 793	849 958	936 863	511 920	424 943	860 888	435 873	425 015
65 - 69	1 258 976	676 007	582 969	569 710	323 583	246 127	689 266	352 424	336 842
70 - 74	833 007	424 372	408 635	387 975	206 278	181 697	445 032	218 094	226 938
75 +	780 207	397 795	382 412	333 961	176 663	157 298	446 246	221 132	225 114
Ethiopia - Éthiopie[3]									
1 VII 2008 (ESDF)									
Total	79 221 000	39 691 000	39 530 000	13 225 000	6 575 000	6 650 000	65 996 000	33 116 000	32 880 000
0 - 4	12 634 128	6 381 651	6 252 477	1 608 103	837 115	770 988	11 027 607	5 545 365	5 482 242
5 - 9	11 375 406	5 742 553	5 632 853	1 572 449	796 842	775 606	9 804 015	4 946 304	4 857 711
10 - 14	9 860 705	4 983 414	4 877 291	1 510 467	746 491	763 976	8 350 671	4 237 207	4 113 464
15 - 19	8 178 673	4 146 348	4 032 325	1 390 318	679 466	710 851	6 788 253	3 466 879	3 321 374
20 - 24	7 442 221	3 777 710	3 664 510	1 433 539	700 859	732 680	6 008 054	3 076 545	2 931 509
25 - 29	6 446 813	3 269 384	3 177 429	1 326 898	654 980	671 918	5 119 126	2 613 980	2 505 146
30 - 34	5 337 998	2 677 364	2 660 634	1 100 820	556 544	544 276	4 236 510	2 120 406	2 116 104
35 - 39	4 293 830	2 112 022	2 181 807	871 216	440 672	430 544	3 422 119	1 671 022	1 751 097
40 - 44	3 447 552	1 663 907	1 783 644	658 160	328 837	329 322	2 789 134	1 334 886	1 454 248
45 - 49	2 727 580	1 292 456	1 435 124	491 450	241 120	250 330	2 236 012	1 051 240	1 184 772
50 - 54	2 194 347	1 045 893	1 148 454	378 827	183 526	195 301	1 815 478	862 329	953 149
55 - 59	1 740 176	844 895	895 281	291 867	142 040	149 828	1 448 305	702 849	745 456
60 - 64	1 322 620	649 306	673 314	220 967	103 852	117 115	1 101 659	545 471	556 189
65 - 69	951 626	471 805	479 820	159 064	72 250	86 814	792 569	399 578	392 991
70 - 74	639 657	318 537	321 119	106 400	46 747	59 653	533 265	271 814	261 451
75 +	627 670	313 753	313 917	104 457	43 659	60 798	523 224	270 126	253 098
Ghana									
1 VII 2009 (ESDF)									
Total	23 416 518	11 586 103	11 830 415	10 245 018	5 006 981	5 238 037	13 171 500	6 579 123	6 592 377
0	650 363	324 453	325 909	242 735	121 396	121 339	407 628	203 057	204 571
1 - 4	2 778 673	1 383 948	1 394 726	1 037 209	514 137	523 072	1 741 464	869 811	871 653
5 - 9	3 436 199	1 721 875	1 714 324	1 304 336	640 893	663 443	2 131 862	1 080 981	1 050 881
10 - 14	2 801 026	1 425 305	1 375 721	1 193 080	571 070	622 010	1 607 946	854 235	753 711
15 - 19	2 332 421	1 190 090	1 142 332	1 136 764	546 630	590 134	1 195 658	643 460	552 198
20 - 24	1 982 100	944 793	1 037 307	1 036 154	504 186	531 968	945 946	440 607	505 339
25 - 29	1 841 541	861 145	980 395	926 030	444 398	481 631	915 511	416 747	498 764
30 - 34	1 494 244	701 352	792 892	721 725	346 495	375 230	772 519	354 857	417 662
35 - 39	1 275 032	607 777	667 255	601 306	287 146	314 160	673 726	320 631	353 095
40 - 44	1 098 178	548 864	549 314	500 121	249 698	250 423	598 057	299 166	298 891
45 - 49	891 930	467 183	424 747	394 824	206 921	187 903	497 106	260 263	236 844
50 - 54	703 742	346 628	357 114	297 210	148 714	148 496	406 532	197 914	208 618
55 - 59	440 596	226 392	214 204	191 858	99 806	92 052	248 738	126 586	122 151
60 - 64	453 608	219 587	234 021	176 672	87 169	89 503	276 936	132 418	144 518
65 - 69	320 328	159 836	160 491	128 532	63 731	64 800	191 796	96 105	95 691
70 - 74	278 786	131 882	146 904	103 834	47 698	56 135	174 952	84 184	90 768
75 - 79	179 325	91 957	87 368	69 376	34 293	35 084	109 949	57 664	52 285
80 - 84	174 394	82 885	91 509	64 966	30 046	34 920	109 428	52 839	56 588
85 - 89	133 176	72 129	61 047	57 206	31 238	25 968	75 970	40 891	35 079

Continent, country or area, date, code and age (in years) / Continent, pays ou zone, date, code et âge (en années)	Total			Urban - Urbaine			Rural - Rurale		
	Both sexes Les deux sexes	Male Masculin	Female Féminin	Both sexes Les deux sexes	Male Masculin	Female Féminin	Both sexes Les deux sexes	Male Masculin	Female Féminin
AFRICA - AFRIQUE									
Ghana									
1 VII 2009 (ESDF)									
90 - 94	70 876	34 988	35 887	27 522	13 247	14 275	43 354	21 741	21 612
95 +	79 981	43 034	36 947	33 558	18 069	15 490	46 423	24 965	21 458
Guinea - Guinée[2]									
1 VII 2009 (ESDF)									
Total	10 217 591	5 038 823	5 178 768	...	...	...	...	...	...
0 - 4	1 708 508	866 996	841 512	...	...	...	...	...	...
5 - 9	1 355 253	686 211	669 042	...	...	...	...	...	...
10 - 14	1 155 226	581 127	574 099	...	...	...	...	...	...
15 - 19	1 225 991	621 661	604 330	...	...	...	...	...	...
20 - 24	996 391	517 007	479 384	...	...	...	...	...	...
25 - 29	668 191	344 997	323 194	...	...	...	...	...	...
30 - 34	565 801	260 720	305 081	...	...	...	...	...	...
35 - 39	494 352	216 535	277 817	...	...	...	...	...	...
40 - 44	478 364	204 559	273 805	...	...	...	...	...	...
45 - 49	366 578	163 816	202 762	...	...	...	...	...	...
50 - 54	315 033	147 915	167 118	...	...	...	...	...	...
55 - 59	240 705	118 129	122 576	...	...	...	...	...	...
60 - 64	182 506	87 782	94 724	...	...	...	...	...	...
65 - 69	139 166	66 929	72 237	...	...	...	...	...	...
70 - 74	111 293	54 579	56 714	...	...	...	...	...	...
75 +	214 233	99 860	114 373	...	...	...	...	...	...
Kenya									
24 VIII 2009* (CDFC)									
Total	38 610 097	19 192 458	19 417 639	12 487 375	6 278 811	6 208 564	26 122 722	12 913 647	13 209 075
0 - 4	5 939 306	3 000 439	2 938 867	1 739 251	875 830	863 421	4 200 055	2 124 609	2 075 446
5 - 9	5 597 716	2 832 669	2 765 047	1 484 285	742 473	741 812	4 113 431	2 090 196	2 023 235
10 - 14	5 034 855	2 565 313	2 469 542	1 312 671	650 438	662 233	3 722 184	1 914 875	1 807 309
15 - 19	4 169 543	2 123 653	2 045 890	1 244 054	587 384	656 670	2 925 489	1 536 269	1 389 220
20 - 24	3 775 103	1 754 105	2 020 998	1 572 026	708 458	863 568	2 203 077	1 045 647	1 157 430
25 - 29	3 201 226	1 529 116	1 672 110	1 442 798	715 957	726 841	1 758 428	813 159	945 269
30 - 34	2 519 506	1 257 035	1 262 471	1 056 483	568 615	487 868	1 463 023	688 420	774 603
35 - 39	2 008 632	1 004 361	1 004 271	785 390	431 054	354 336	1 223 242	573 307	649 935
40 - 44	1 476 169	743 594	732 575	533 174	297 202	235 972	942 995	446 392	496 603
45 - 49	1 272 745	635 276	637 469	422 941	235 467	187 474	849 804	399 809	449 995
50 - 54	956 206	478 346	477 860	286 074	159 814	126 260	670 132	318 532	351 600
55 - 59	711 953	359 466	352 487	187 793	103 563	84 230	524 160	255 903	268 257
60 - 64	593 778	295 197	298 581	139 271	73 800	65 471	454 507	221 397	233 110
65 - 69	390 763	183 151	207 612	83 728	41 299	42 429	307 035	141 852	165 183
70 - 74	339 301	160 301	179 000	68 868	32 691	36 177	270 433	127 610	142 823
75 - 79	218 508	99 833	118 675	42 247	19 276	22 971	176 261	80 557	95 704
80 +	383 701	159 125	224 576	77 003	30 335	46 668	306 698	128 790	177 908
Unknown - Inconnu	21 086	11 478	9 608	9 318	5 155	4 163	11 768	6 323	5 445
Lesotho									
13 IV 2006 (CDJC)									
Total	1 862 860	904 392	958 468	421 105	194 097	227 008	1 441 755	710 295	731 460
0 - 4	201 995	101 397	100 598	39 245	19 604	19 641	162 750	81 793	80 957
5 - 9	211 947	106 695	105 252	40 208	20 051	20 157	171 739	86 644	85 095
10 - 14	220 938	110 778	110 160	42 546	20 751	21 795	178 392	90 027	88 365
15 - 19	229 389	114 800	114 589	48 783	21 971	26 812	180 606	92 829	87 777
20 - 24	207 062	101 385	105 677	52 026	21 394	30 632	155 036	79 991	75 045
25 - 29	164 867	82 202	82 665	49 796	21 948	27 848	115 071	60 254	54 817
30 - 34	119 530	60 107	59 423	36 708	17 327	19 381	82 822	42 780	40 042
35 - 39	93 490	45 645	47 845	28 605	13 639	14 966	64 885	32 006	32 879
40 - 44	83 299	39 596	43 703	22 742	10 805	11 937	60 557	28 791	31 766
45 - 49	72 621	34 102	38 519	17 782	8 461	9 321	54 839	25 641	29 198
50 - 54	63 084	28 723	34 361	13 153	6 037	7 116	49 931	22 686	27 245
55 - 59	50 148	23 225	26 923	9 367	4 266	5 101	40 781	18 959	21 822
60 - 64	37 699	16 724	20 975	6 325	2 851	3 474	31 374	13 873	17 501
65 - 69	32 028	13 369	18 659	4 794	1 977	2 817	27 234	11 392	15 842
70 - 74	35 609	13 380	22 229	4 158	1 569	2 589	31 451	11 811	19 640
75 - 79	18 141	6 327	11 814	2 281	742	1 539	15 860	5 585	10 275
80 - 84	10 498	3 251	7 247	1 336	380	956	9 162	2 871	6 291
85 +	10 515	2 686	7 829	1 250	324	926	9 265	2 362	6 903

7. Population by age, sex and urban/rural residence: latest available year, 2000 - 2009
Population selon l'âge, le sexe et la résidence, urbaine/rurale : dernière année disponible, 2000 - 2009 (continued - suite)

Continent, country or area, date, code and age (in years) / Continent, pays ou zone, date, code et âge (en années)	Total			Urban - Urbaine			Rural - Rurale		
	Both sexes Les deux sexes	Male Masculin	Female Féminin	Both sexes Les deux sexes	Male Masculin	Female Féminin	Both sexes Les deux sexes	Male Masculin	Female Féminin

AFRICA - AFRIQUE

Liberia - Libéria
21 III 2008 (CDFC)

Total	3 476 608	1 739 945	1 736 663	...	...	...	...	...	...
0 - 4	534 475	270 564	263 911	...	...	...	...	...	...
5 - 9	501 931	251 411	250 520	...	...	...	...	...	...
10 - 14	421 666	214 859	206 807	...	...	...	...	...	...
15 - 19	375 695	189 407	186 288	...	...	...	...	...	...
20 - 24	342 930	161 951	180 979	...	...	...	...	...	...
25 - 29	291 858	141 006	150 852	...	...	...	...	...	...
30 - 34	219 632	107 326	112 306	...	...	...	...	...	...
35 - 39	203 536	99 136	104 400	...	...	...	...	...	...
40 - 44	155 737	81 670	74 067	...	...	...	...	...	...
45 - 49	118 807	63 827	54 980	...	...	...	...	...	...
50 - 54	82 940	44 870	38 070	...	...	...	...	...	...
55 - 59	56 460	30 975	25 485	...	...	...	...	...	...
60 - 64	52 830	25 473	27 357	...	...	...	...	...	...
65 - 69	39 807	19 250	20 557	...	...	...	...	...	...
70 - 74	25 746	12 343	13 403	...	...	...	...	...	...
75 - 79	22 913	11 580	11 333	...	...	...	...	...	...
80 - 84	12 007	5 408	6 599	...	...	...	...	...	...
85 +	17 638	8 889	8 749	...	...	...	...	...	...

Libya - Libye[4]
15 IV 2006* (CDFC)

Total	5 298 152	2 687 513	2 610 639	4 670 858	2 372 379	2 298 479	627 294	315 134	312 160
0	117 479	60 167	57 312	103 670	53 129	50 541	13 809	7 038	6 771
1 - 4	457 866	234 512	223 354	403 509	206 639	196 870	54 357	27 873	26 484
5 - 9	527 595	269 079	258 516	465 506	237 468	228 038	62 089	31 611	30 478
10 - 14	542 893	277 270	265 623	476 896	243 693	233 203	65 997	33 577	32 420
15 - 19	573 026	290 568	282 458	501 444	254 266	247 178	71 582	36 302	35 280
20 - 24	573 287	289 663	283 624	502 229	253 539	248 690	71 058	36 124	34 934
25 - 29	566 458	287 101	279 357	497 522	252 364	245 158	68 936	34 737	34 199
30 - 34	492 828	248 875	243 953	434 821	220 019	214 802	58 007	28 856	29 151
35 - 39	390 800	195 328	195 472	347 316	174 078	173 238	43 484	21 250	22 234
40 - 44	281 849	140 872	140 977	251 876	126 302	125 574	29 973	14 570	15 403
45 - 49	199 142	100 653	98 489	178 471	90 336	88 135	20 671	10 317	10 354
50 - 54	132 619	64 677	67 942	119 463	58 576	60 887	13 156	6 101	7 055
55 - 59	122 277	61 439	60 838	109 004	55 174	53 830	13 273	6 265	7 008
60 - 64	95 127	51 295	43 832	84 339	45 822	38 517	10 788	5 473	5 315
65 - 69	80 018	42 724	37 294	70 241	37 786	32 455	9 777	4 938	4 839
70 - 74	57 851	30 325	27 526	50 282	26 511	23 771	7 569	3 814	3 755
75 - 79	45 675	23 125	22 550	39 337	19 978	19 359	6 338	3 147	3 191
80 - 84	24 576	12 158	12 418	20 930	10 332	10 598	3 646	1 826	1 820
85 +	16 786	7 682	9 104	14 002	6 367	7 635	2 784	1 315	1 469

Malawi
8 VI 2008 (CDFC)

Total	13 077 160	6 358 933	6 718 227	2 003 309	1 014 477	988 832	11 073 851	5 344 456	5 729 395
0	503 385	247 809	255 576	67 264	33 375	33 889	436 121	214 434	221 687
1 - 4	1 866 626	922 138	944 488	248 703	122 976	125 727	1 617 923	799 162	818 761
5 - 9	1 968 299	972 307	995 992	261 838	127 930	133 908	1 706 461	844 377	862 084
10 - 14	1 670 391	826 076	844 315	232 203	110 545	121 658	1 438 188	715 531	722 657
15 - 19	1 276 692	625 664	651 028	218 307	105 746	112 561	1 058 385	519 918	538 467
20 - 24	1 240 329	554 799	685 530	248 790	117 648	131 142	991 539	437 151	554 388
25 - 29	1 102 976	530 103	572 873	236 512	122 761	113 751	866 464	407 342	459 122
30 - 34	827 547	417 599	409 948	162 061	91 637	70 424	665 486	325 962	339 524
35 - 39	623 330	323 643	299 687	105 572	61 564	44 008	517 758	262 079	255 679
40 - 44	441 231	218 546	222 685	67 267	37 061	30 206	373 964	181 485	192 479
45 - 49	343 190	167 285	175 905	47 706	25 811	21 895	295 484	141 474	154 010
50 - 54	269 634	126 778	142 856	33 849	18 400	15 449	235 785	108 378	127 407
55 - 59	258 214	122 616	135 598	26 253	14 525	11 728	231 961	108 091	123 870
60 - 64	184 679	87 008	97 671	16 622	9 256	7 366	168 057	77 752	90 305
65 - 69	153 829	72 038	81 791	11 298	6 217	5 081	142 531	65 821	76 710
70 - 74	106 020	46 481	59 539	6 992	3 573	3 419	99 028	42 908	56 120
75 - 79	106 769	46 003	60 766	5 629	2 769	2 860	101 140	43 234	57 906
80 - 84	55 970	21 945	34 025	2 926	1 262	1 664	53 044	20 683	32 361
85 - 89	40 784	16 680	24 104	1 895	818	1 077	38 889	15 862	23 027

Continent, country or area, date, code and age (in years) / Continent, pays ou zone, date, code et âge (en annèes)	Total			Urban - Urbaine			Rural - Rurale		
	Both sexes Les deux sexes	Male Masculin	Female Féminin	Both sexes Les deux sexes	Male Masculin	Female Féminin	Both sexes Les deux sexes	Male Masculin	Female Féminin
AFRICA - AFRIQUE									
Malawi									
8 VI 2008 (CDFC)									
90 - 94	18 739	6 967	11 772	780	323	457	17 959	6 644	11 315
95 +	18 526	6 448	12 078	842	280	562	17 684	6 168	11 516
Mauritania - Mauritanie[2]									
1 VII 2008 (ESDF)									
Total	3 162 338	1 584 913	1 577 425	...	...	...	...	...	...
0 - 4	496 558	254 321	242 237	...	...	...	...	...	...
5 - 9	448 960	229 645	219 315	...	...	...	...	...	...
10 - 14	393 487	202 894	190 593	...	...	...	...	...	...
15 - 19	333 383	172 148	161 235	...	...	...	...	...	...
20 - 24	285 570	144 066	141 504	...	...	...	...	...	...
25 - 29	245 422	118 395	127 027	...	...	...	...	...	...
30 - 34	199 769	94 074	105 695	...	...	...	...	...	...
35 - 39	171 863	81 343	90 520	...	...	...	...	...	...
40 - 44	143 266	68 718	74 548	...	...	...	...	...	...
45 - 49	118 988	58 231	60 757	...	...	...	...	...	...
50 - 54	97 069	48 647	48 422	...	...	...	...	...	...
55 - 59	79 682	38 989	40 693	...	...	...	...	...	...
60 - 64	46 800	23 369	23 431	...	...	...	...	...	...
65 - 69	36 406	18 405	18 001	...	...	...	...	...	...
70 - 74	30 625	15 132	15 493	...	...	...	...	...	...
75 +	34 490	16 536	17 954	...	...	...	...	...	...
Mauritius - Maurice[5]									
2 VII 2000 (CDJC)									
Total	1 178 848	583 756	595 092	503 045	247 844	255 201	675 803	335 912	339 891
0	18 915	9 574	9 341	7 127	3 608	3 519	11 788	5 966	5 822
1 - 4	75 388	38 066	37 322	29 620	14 938	14 682	45 768	23 128	22 640
5 - 9	105 189	53 037	52 152	42 660	21 428	21 232	62 529	31 609	30 920
10 - 14	97 740	49 428	48 312	41 020	20 818	20 202	56 720	28 610	28 110
15 - 19	102 088	51 671	50 417	41 369	20 985	20 384	60 719	30 686	30 033
20 - 24	110 892	55 108	55 784	44 167	21 778	22 389	66 725	33 330	33 395
25 - 29	93 797	46 749	47 048	36 979	18 021	18 958	56 818	28 728	28 090
30 - 34	99 515	49 964	49 551	40 103	19 977	20 126	59 412	29 987	29 425
35 - 39	101 946	51 621	50 325	44 743	22 491	22 252	57 203	29 130	28 073
40 - 44	90 406	45 798	44 608	40 283	20 482	19 801	50 123	25 316	24 807
45 - 49	77 931	39 133	38 798	35 122	17 793	17 329	42 809	21 340	21 469
50 - 54	56 939	27 790	29 149	25 928	12 558	13 370	31 011	15 232	15 779
55 - 59	40 491	19 228	21 263	19 033	9 016	10 017	21 458	10 212	11 246
60 - 64	33 097	15 301	17 796	16 474	7 711	8 763	16 623	7 590	9 033
65 - 69	25 768	11 758	14 010	13 159	6 067	7 092	12 609	5 691	6 918
70 - 74	21 694	9 491	12 203	11 050	4 886	6 164	10 644	4 605	6 039
75 - 79	14 910	6 047	8 863	7 697	3 128	4 569	7 213	2 919	4 294
80 - 84	7 132	2 584	4 548	3 713	1 372	2 341	3 419	1 212	2 207
85 - 89	3 498	1 049	2 449	1 916	564	1 352	1 582	485	1 097
90 - 94	1 104	272	832	637	163	474	467	109	358
95 +	289	42	247	173	31	142	116	11	105
Unknown - Inconnu	119	45	74	72	29	43	47	16	31
1 VII 2009 (ESDJ)[6]									
Total	1 275 032	629 157	645 875	...	...	...	...	...	...
0	15 697	7 873	7 824	...	...	...	...	...	...
1 - 4	69 974	35 637	34 337	...	...	...	...	...	...
5 - 9	97 442	49 593	47 849	...	...	...	...	...	...
10 - 14	99 685	50 381	49 304	...	...	...	...	...	...
15 - 19	108 727	55 121	53 606	...	...	...	...	...	...
20 - 24	94 489	47 738	46 751	...	...	...	...	...	...
25 - 29	106 742	53 776	52 966	...	...	...	...	...	...
30 - 34	105 780	52 192	53 588	...	...	...	...	...	...
35 - 39	91 785	45 582	46 203	...	...	...	...	...	...
40 - 44	98 374	48 939	49 435	...	...	...	...	...	...
45 - 49	96 860	48 409	48 451	...	...	...	...	...	...
50 - 54	82 706	40 967	41 739	...	...	...	...	...	...
55 - 59	70 675	34 490	36 185	...	...	...	...	...	...
60 - 64	46 841	21 743	25 098	...	...	...	...	...	...
65 - 69	31 336	14 065	17 271	...	...	...	...	...	...

Continent, country or area, date, code and age (in years) / Continent, pays ou zone, date, code et âge (en années)	Total			Urban - Urbaine			Rural - Rurale		
	Both sexes Les deux sexes	Male Masculin	Female Féminin	Both sexes Les deux sexes	Male Masculin	Female Féminin	Both sexes Les deux sexes	Male Masculin	Female Féminin
AFRICA - AFRIQUE									
Mauritius - Maurice[5]									
1 VII 2009 (ESDJ)[6]									
70 - 74	24 099	10 148	13 951	...	...	...	...	...	...
75 - 79	16 025	6 432	9 593	...	...	...	...	...	...
80 - 84	11 112	4 039	7 073	...	...	...	...	...	...
85 +	6 683	2 032	4 651	...	...	...	...	...	...
Mayotte									
31 VII 2007 (CDJC)									
Total	186 387	91 405	94 982	...	...	...	...	...	...
0	6 424	3 255	3 169	...	...	...	...	...	...
1 - 4	25 429	12 948	12 481	...	...	...	...	...	...
5 - 9	27 239	13 739	13 500	...	...	...	...	...	...
10 - 14	23 403	11 483	11 920	...	...	...	...	...	...
15 - 19	18 724	9 144	9 580	...	...	...	...	...	...
20 - 24	13 660	5 789	7 871	...	...	...	...	...	...
25 - 29	14 987	6 262	8 725	...	...	...	...	...	...
30 - 34	14 376	6 651	7 725	...	...	...	...	...	...
35 - 39	12 390	6 468	5 922	...	...	...	...	...	...
40 - 44	8 375	4 385	3 990	...	...	...	...	...	...
45 - 49	6 133	3 261	2 872	...	...	...	...	...	...
50 - 54	4 763	2 508	2 255	...	...	...	...	...	...
55 - 59	3 566	1 948	1 618	...	...	...	...	...	...
60 - 64	2 522	1 329	1 193	...	...	...	...	...	...
65 - 69	1 621	833	788	...	...	...	...	...	...
70 - 74	1 266	671	595	...	...	...	...	...	...
75 - 79	689	348	341	...	...	...	...	...	...
80 - 84	459	234	225	...	...	...	...	...	...
85 - 89	199	89	110	...	...	...	...	...	...
90 - 94	101	35	66	...	...	...	...	...	...
95 +	61	25	36	...	...	...	...	...	...
Morocco - Maroc									
1 VII 2007* (ESDF)									
Total	30 841 000	15 246 000	15 595 000	17 404 000	8 572 000	8 832 000	13 437 000	6 674 000	6 763 000
0 - 4	2 876 000	1 469 000	1 407 000	1 480 000	754 000	726 000	1 397 000	715 000	681 000
5 - 9	2 961 000	1 507 000	1 453 000	1 514 000	768 000	746 000	1 447 000	739 000	708 000
10 - 14	3 154 000	1 605 000	1 550 000	1 609 000	813 000	795 000	1 545 000	791 000	754 000
15 - 19	3 238 000	1 634 000	1 605 000	1 689 000	846 000	843 000	1 549 000	788 000	761 000
20 - 24	3 053 000	1 504 000	1 549 000	1 693 000	836 000	857 000	1 361 000	669 000	692 000
25 - 29	2 741 000	1 323 000	1 417 000	1 611 000	781 000	830 000	1 130 000	543 000	588 000
30 - 34	2 328 000	1 114 000	1 214 000	1 410 000	670 000	740 000	918 000	444 000	474 000
35 - 39	2 045 000	974 000	1 072 000	1 283 000	608 000	675 000	763 000	366 000	397 000
40 - 44	1 872 000	892 000	980 000	1 195 000	566 000	628 000	677 000	326 000	351 000
45 - 49	1 734 000	854 000	879 000	1 101 000	545 000	557 000	632 000	310 000	323 000
50 - 54	1 370 000	703 000	667 000	865 000	451 000	414 000	505 000	252 000	253 000
55 - 59	1 009 000	508 000	501 000	609 000	314 000	295 000	400 000	193 000	206 000
60 - 64	700 000	328 000	372 000	400 000	187 000	213 000	299 000	141 000	159 000
65 - 69	638 000	294 000	344 000	352 000	159 000	193 000	286 000	135 000	151 000
70 - 74	466 000	225 000	241 000	259 000	121 000	138 000	207 000	104 000	103 000
75 +	656 000	311 000	344 000	334 000	152 000	182 000	322 000	159 000	162 000
Mozambique									
1 VIII 2007 (CDFC)									
Total	20 252 223	9 746 690	10 505 533	6 151 974	3 021 756	3 130 218	14 100 249	6 724 934	7 375 315
0 - 4	3 881 454	1 917 794	1 963 660	975 719	484 625	491 094	2 905 735	1 433 169	1 472 566
5 - 9	3 202 546	1 587 302	1 615 244	854 269	419 428	434 841	2 348 277	1 167 874	1 180 403
10 - 14	2 406 607	1 222 668	1 183 939	771 954	380 380	391 574	1 634 653	842 288	792 365
15 - 19	1 917 052	925 729	991 323	707 479	353 094	354 385	1 209 573	572 635	636 938
20 - 24	1 760 939	774 413	986 526	673 354	319 552	353 802	1 087 585	454 861	632 724
25 - 29	1 549 019	707 603	841 416	534 662	261 595	273 067	1 014 357	446 008	568 349
30 - 34	1 251 554	583 689	667 865	396 532	191 636	204 896	855 022	392 053	462 969
35 - 39	1 037 587	481 396	556 191	314 888	151 166	163 722	722 699	330 230	392 469
40 - 44	755 605	366 518	389 087	247 154	125 016	122 138	508 451	241 502	266 949
45 - 49	649 896	321 236	328 660	201 248	105 420	95 828	448 648	215 816	232 832
50 - 54	514 520	231 232	283 288	150 346	75 258	75 088	364 174	155 974	208 200
55 - 59	402 668	194 011	208 657	106 176	54 038	52 138	296 492	139 973	156 519
60 - 64	299 703	140 146	159 557	75 555	36 842	38 713	224 148	103 304	120 844

Continent, country or area, date, code and age (in years) / Continent, pays ou zone, date, code et âge (en années)	Total			Urban - Urbaine			Rural - Rurale		
	Both sexes Les deux sexes	Male Masculin	Female Féminin	Both sexes Les deux sexes	Male Masculin	Female Féminin	Both sexes Les deux sexes	Male Masculin	Female Féminin
AFRICA - AFRIQUE									
Mozambique									
1 VIII 2007 (CDFC)									
65 - 69	241 634	113 840	127 794	55 906	26 286	29 620	185 728	87 554	98 174
70 - 74	153 617	72 288	81 329	37 666	16 950	20 716	115 951	55 338	60 613
75 - 79	116 460	55 448	61 012	26 084	11 270	14 814	90 376	44 178	46 198
80 - 84	50 695	22 417	28 278	11 090	4 394	6 696	39 605	18 023	21 582
85 - 89	36 024	16 576	19 448	7 222	2 698	4 524	28 802	13 878	14 924
90 - 94	10 686	4 803	5 883	1 896	664	1 232	8 790	4 139	4 651
95 +	13 957	7 581	6 376	2 774	1 444	1 330	11 183	6 137	5 046
Namibia - Namibie									
27 VIII 2001 (CDFC)									
Total	1 830 330	887 721	942 572	603 612	300 358[7]	303 236[7]	1 226 718	587 363[7]	639 336[7]
0	46 852	23 281	23 571	15 281	7 579	7 702	31 571	15 702	15 869
1 - 4	194 377	96 763	97 614	52 204	25 915	26 288	142 174	70 848	71 326
5 - 9	246 964	121 785	125 179	59 123	28 683	30 440	187 841	93 102	94 739
10 - 14	230 287	113 081	117 206	55 162	25 564	29 598	175 125	87 517	87 608
15 - 19	202 298	99 307	102 991	55 865	25 383	30 482	146 433	73 924	72 509
20 - 24	174 484	86 382	88 102	70 592	34 483	36 109	103 892	51 899	51 993
25 - 29	150 783	74 304	76 479	73 635	37 316	36 319	77 148	36 988	40 160
30 - 34	118 529	57 125	61 404	58 312	29 851	28 461	60 217	27 274	32 943
35 - 39	96 416	45 083	51 333	46 071	23 521	22 550	50 345	21 562	28 783
40 - 44	74 050	34 170	39 880	33 152	16 966	16 186	40 898	17 204	23 694
45 - 49	57 749	26 942	30 807	23 576	12 615	10 961	34 173	14 327	19 846
50 - 54	47 779	21 999	25 780	16 798	9 193	7 605	30 981	12 806	18 175
55 - 59	35 209	16 600	18 609	10 890	5 893	4 997	24 319	10 707	13 612
60 - 64	34 378	15 569	18 809	8 512	4 192	4 320	25 866	11 377	14 489
65 - 69	25 262	11 399	13 863	5 458	2 596	2 862	19 804	8 803	11 001
70 - 74	22 052	9 313	12 739	3 707	1 619	2 088	18 345	7 694	10 651
75 - 79	16 007	6 382	9 625	2 531	1 068	1 463	13 476	5 314	8 162
80 - 84	13 818	5 359	8 459	1 753	680	1 073	12 065	4 679	7 386
85 - 89	5 407	2 033	3 374	973	341	632	4 434	1 692	2 742
90 - 94	2 555	927	1 628	376	152	224	2 179	775	1 404
95 +	2 712	897	1 815	262	111	151	2 450	786	1 664
Unknown - Inconnu	32 325	19 020	13 305	9 362	6 637	2 725	22 963	12 383	10 580
1 VII 2009 (ESDF)[2]									
Total	2 103 761	1 027 736	1 076 025	...	...	...	...	...	...
0	61 973	30 983	30 990	...	...	...	...	...	...
1 - 4	218 907	109 298	109 609	...	...	...	...	...	...
5 - 9	234 680	117 447	117 233	...	...	...	...	...	...
10 - 14	243 605	121 345	122 260	...	...	...	...	...	...
15 - 19	240 570	118 986	121 584	...	...	...	...	...	...
20 - 24	216 190	106 543	109 647	...	...	...	...	...	...
25 - 29	185 753	91 819	93 934	...	...	...	...	...	...
30 - 34	159 765	79 375	80 390	...	...	...	...	...	...
35 - 39	132 567	65 052	67 515	...	...	...	...	...	...
40 - 44	103 615	49 345	54 271	...	...	...	...	...	...
45 - 49	82 101	37 963	44 137	...	...	...	...	...	...
50 - 54	61 305	28 147	33 158	...	...	...	...	...	...
55 - 59	47 576	21 756	25 820	...	...	...	...	...	...
60 - 64	35 662	16 126	19 536	...	...	...	...	...	...
65 +	79 492	33 552	45 940	...	...	...	...	...	...
Niger[2]									
1 VII 2008 (ESDJ)									
Total	14 197 601	7 088 858	7 108 743	2 728 541	1 366 304	1 362 237	11 469 060	5 722 554	5 746 506
0 - 4	2 772 294	1 398 479	1 373 815	415 380	206 784	208 597	2 356 913	1 191 695	1 165 219
5 - 9	2 371 488	1 215 095	1 156 392	423 476	213 989	209 486	1 948 012	1 001 106	946 906
10 - 14	1 943 445	992 731	950 714	431 778	219 501	212 278	1 511 667	773 230	738 437
15 - 19	1 423 793	709 730	714 063	335 882	169 492	166 390	1 087 912	540 238	547 673
20 - 24	1 065 568	516 559	549 009	219 299	110 883	108 415	846 269	405 675	440 594
25 - 29	897 791	424 031	473 760	179 185	88 607	90 578	718 606	335 424	383 182
30 - 34	775 516	362 941	412 575	157 712	75 184	82 528	617 805	287 757	330 047
35 - 39	685 244	332 962	352 282	138 488	68 225	70 263	546 756	264 737	282 019
40 - 44	592 064	296 644	295 420	116 797	60 420	56 377	475 267	236 224	239 042
45 - 49	454 577	230 338	224 239	88 522	45 663	42 859	366 055	184 674	181 380
50 - 54	345 072	175 779	169 293	66 726	32 219	34 507	278 345	143 560	134 786

Continent, country or area, date, code and age (in years) / Continent, pays ou zone, date, code et âge (en années)	Total			Urban - Urbaine			Rural - Rurale		
	Both sexes Les deux sexes	Male Masculin	Female Féminin	Both sexes Les deux sexes	Male Masculin	Female Féminin	Both sexes Les deux sexes	Male Masculin	Female Féminin
AFRICA - AFRIQUE									
Niger[2]									
1 VII 2008 (ESDJ)									
55 - 59	283 989	140 750	143 240	54 282	25 466	28 815	229 708	115 283	114 424
60 - 64	222 706	107 899	114 807	41 492	21 912	19 581	181 213	85 987	95 226
65 - 69	139 748	69 004	70 745	24 598	13 189	11 409	115 151	55 815	59 336
70 - 74	83 512	42 509	41 003	13 466	6 517	6 949	70 046	35 992	34 054
75 - 79	56 491	29 140	27 350	8 220	2 655	5 565	48 271	26 485	21 786
80 +	84 303	44 268	40 035	13 238	5 598	7 640	71 066	38 671	32 395
Nigeria - Nigéria									
21 III 2006 (CDFC)									
Total	140 431 790	71 345 488	69 086 302	...	...	...	...	...	...
0 - 4	22 594 967	11 569 218	11 025 749	...	...	...	...	...	...
5 - 9	20 005 380	10 388 611	9 616 769	...	...	...	...	...	...
10 - 14	16 135 950	8 504 319	7 631 631	...	...	...	...	...	...
15 - 19	14 899 419	7 536 532	7 362 887	...	...	...	...	...	...
20 - 24	13 435 079	6 237 549	7 197 530	...	...	...	...	...	...
25 - 29	12 211 426	5 534 458	6 676 968	...	...	...	...	...	...
30 - 34	9 467 538	4 505 186	4 962 352	...	...	...	...	...	...
35 - 39	7 331 755	3 661 133	3 670 622	...	...	...	...	...	...
40 - 44	6 456 470	3 395 489	3 060 981	...	...	...	...	...	...
45 - 49	4 591 293	2 561 526	2 029 767	...	...	...	...	...	...
50 - 54	4 249 219	2 363 937	1 885 282	...	...	...	...	...	...
55 - 59	2 066 247	1 189 770	876 477	...	...	...	...	...	...
60 - 64	2 450 286	1 363 219	1 087 067	...	...	...	...	...	...
65 - 69	1 151 048	628 436	522 612	...	...	...	...	...	...
70 - 74	1 330 597	765 988	564 609	...	...	...	...	...	...
75 - 79	579 838	327 416	252 422	...	...	...	...	...	...
80 - 84	760 053	408 680	351 373	...	...	...	...	...	...
85 +	715 225	404 021	311 204	...	...	...	...	...	...
Réunion									
1 I 2008* (ESDJ)									
Total	805 500	390 645	414 855	...	...	...	...	...	...
0 - 4	68 037	35 331	32 706	...	...	...	...	...	...
5 - 9	70 954	36 469	34 485	...	...	...	...	...	...
10 - 14	70 366	35 533	34 833	...	...	...	...	...	...
15 - 19	72 323	36 925	35 398	...	...	...	...	...	...
20 - 24	56 206	27 885	28 321	...	...	...	...	...	...
25 - 29	50 071	23 013	27 058	...	...	...	...	...	...
30 - 34	55 690	25 550	30 140	...	...	...	...	...	...
35 - 39	62 722	29 335	33 387	...	...	...	...	...	...
40 - 44	67 744	32 708	35 036	...	...	...	...	...	...
45 - 49	55 872	27 051	28 821	...	...	...	...	...	...
50 - 54	47 368	22 944	24 424	...	...	...	...	...	...
55 - 59	36 754	18 120	18 634	...	...	...	...	...	...
60 - 64	27 639	13 461	14 178	...	...	...	...	...	...
65 - 69	21 758	10 026	11 732	...	...	...	...	...	...
70 - 74	17 302	7 406	9 896	...	...	...	...	...	...
75 - 79	11 277	4 567	6 710	...	...	...	...	...	...
80 - 84	7 877	2 837	5 040	...	...	...	...	...	...
85 - 89	3 642	1 065	2 577	...	...	...	...	...	...
90 - 94	1 430	336	1 094	...	...	...	...	...	...
95 +	468	83	385	...	...	...	...	...	...
Rwanda									
16 VIII 2002 (CDJC)									
Total	8 128 553	3 879 448	4 249 105	1 372 604	727 172	645 432	6 755 949	3 152 276	3 603 673
0	325 221	161 653	163 568	46 968	23 496	23 472	278 253	138 157	140 096
1 - 4	995 010	493 437	501 573	147 083	73 621	73 462	847 927	419 816	428 111
5 - 9	1 141 039	563 351	577 688	157 009	77 648	79 361	984 030	485 703	498 327
10 - 14	1 095 225	536 876	558 349	149 787	71 947	77 840	945 438	464 929	480 509
15 - 19	1 078 839	526 563	552 276	184 874	89 576	95 298	893 965	436 987	456 978
20 - 24	810 681	382 561	428 120	177 151	98 145	79 006	633 530	284 416	349 114
25 - 29	555 509	253 180	302 329	130 102	74 049	56 053	425 407	179 131	246 276
30 - 34	448 439	208 742	239 697	100 840	59 871	40 969	347 599	148 871	198 728
35 - 39	382 636	177 816	204 820	76 430	46 117	30 313	306 206	131 699	174 507
40 - 44	363 067	168 934	194 133	63 795	38 834	24 961	299 272	130 100	169 172

7. Population by age, sex and urban/rural residence: latest available year, 2000 - 2009
Population selon l'âge, le sexe et la résidence, urbaine/rurale : dernière année disponible, 2000 - 2009 (continued - suite)

Continent, country or area, date, code and age (in years) / Continent, pays ou zone, date, code et âge (en années)	Total			Urban - Urbaine			Rural - Rurale		
	Both sexes Les deux sexes	Male Masculin	Female Féminin	Both sexes Les deux sexes	Male Masculin	Female Féminin	Both sexes Les deux sexes	Male Masculin	Female Féminin
AFRICA - AFRIQUE									
Rwanda									
16 VIII 2002 (CDJC)									
45 - 49	268 262	122 615	145 647	43 450	26 007	17 443	224 812	96 608	128 204
50 - 54	193 382	86 925	106 457	30 845	17 673	13 172	162 537	69 252	93 285
55 - 59	123 868	50 480	73 388	18 782	9 561	9 221	105 086	40 919	64 167
60 - 64	111 809	45 221	66 588	15 483	7 293	8 190	96 326	37 928	58 398
65 - 69	84 928	35 178	49 750	11 333	5 166	6 167	73 595	30 012	43 583
70 - 74	71 020	30 970	40 050	8 790	4 025	4 765	62 230	26 945	35 285
75 - 79	37 989	16 255	21 734	4 451	1 923	2 528	33 538	14 332	19 206
80 - 84	26 788	12 081	14 707	3 295	1 378	1 917	23 493	10 703	12 790
85 +	14 841	6 610	8 231	2 136	842	1 294	12 705	5 768	6 937
1 VII 2009 (ESDF)									
Total	10 117 029	4 880 233	5 236 796	...	...	...	...	...	...
0 - 4	1 758 971	886 830	872 141	...	...	...	...	...	...
5 - 9	1 334 590	664 761	669 829	...	...	...	...	...	...
10 - 14	1 181 384	584 285	597 099	...	...	...	...	...	...
15 - 19	1 099 485	539 823	559 662	...	...	...	...	...	...
20 - 24	1 098 223	536 057	562 167	...	...	...	...	...	...
25 - 29	920 973	439 505	481 469	...	...	...	...	...	...
30 - 34	630 817	289 091	341 726	...	...	...	...	...	...
35 - 39	468 179	214 650	253 529	...	...	...	...	...	...
40 - 44	390 153	181 054	209 099	...	...	...	...	...	...
45 - 49	359 474	166 078	193 396	...	...	...	...	...	...
50 - 54	292 458	133 259	159 200	...	...	...	...	...	...
55 - 59	204 513	91 408	113 105	...	...	...	...	...	...
60 - 64	129 939	54 379	75 560	...	...	...	...	...	...
65 - 69	94 540	36 922	57 618	...	...	...	...	...	...
70 - 74	70 520	27 952	42 568	...	...	...	...	...	...
75 - 79	47 006	19 332	27 675	...	...	...	...	...	...
80 +	35 804	14 849	20 955	...	...	...	...	...	...
Saint Helena ex. dep. - Sainte-Hélène sans dép.[8]									
1 VII 2008 (ESDF)									
Total	3 981	2 022	1 959	...	...	...	...	...	...
0	30	17	13	...	...	...	...	...	...
1 - 4	136	67	69	...	...	...	...	...	...
5 - 9	198	109	89	...	...	...	...	...	...
10 - 14	236	124	112	...	...	...	...	...	...
15 - 19	285	149	136	...	...	...	...	...	...
20 - 24	155	79	76	...	...	...	...	...	...
25 - 29	162	73	89	...	...	...	...	...	...
30 - 34	185	83	102	...	...	...	...	...	...
35 - 39	281	131	150	...	...	...	...	...	...
40 - 44	322	168	154	...	...	...	...	...	...
45 - 49	342	169	173	...	...	...	...	...	...
50 - 54	288	157	131	...	...	...	...	...	...
55 - 59	326	172	154	...	...	...	...	...	...
60 - 64	331	197	134	...	...	...	...	...	...
65 - 69	242	130	112	...	...	...	...	...	...
70 - 74	183	105	78	...	...	...	...	...	...
75 - 79	128	54	74	...	...	...	...	...	...
80 - 84	83	26	57	...	...	...	...	...	...
85 - 89	45	9	36	...	...	...	...	...	...
90 - 94	18	2	16	...	...	...	...	...	...
95 +	4	-	4	...	...	...	...	...	...
Unknown - Inconnu	1	1	-	...	...	...	...	...	...
Saint Helena: Ascension - Sainte-Hélène: Ascension									
1 VII 2008 (ESDJ)									
Total	702	397	305	...	...	...	...	...	...
0 - 4	32	16	16	...	...	...	...	...	...
5 - 9	19	9	10	...	...	...	...	...	...
10 - 14	41	20	21	...	...	...	...	...	...
15 - 19	30	19	11	...	...	...	...	...	...
20 - 24	63	29	34	...	...	...	...	...	...

Continent, country or area, date, code and age (in years) / Continent, pays ou zone, date, code et âge (en années)	Total			Urban - Urbaine			Rural - Rurale		
	Both sexes Les deux sexes	Male Masculin	Female Féminin	Both sexes Les deux sexes	Male Masculin	Female Féminin	Both sexes Les deux sexes	Male Masculin	Female Féminin
AFRICA - AFRIQUE									
Saint Helena: Ascension - Sainte-Hélène: Ascension									
1 VII 2008 (ESDJ)									
25 - 29	73	42	31	...	...	...	...	...	...
30 - 34	76	41	35	...	...	...	...	...	...
35 - 39	92	58	34	...	...	...	...	...	...
40 - 44	85	42	43	...	...	...	...	...	...
45 - 49	65	36	29	...	...	...	...	...	...
50 - 54	51	32	19	...	...	...	...	...	...
55 - 59	43	29	14	...	...	...	...	...	...
60 - 64	21	15	6	...	...	...	...	...	...
65 - 69	10	9	1	...	...	...	...	...	...
70 - 74	-	-	-	...	...	...	...	...	...
75 - 79	-	-	-	...	...	...	...	...	...
80 +	1	-	1	...	...	...	...	...	...
Sao Tome and Principe - Sao Tomé-et-Principe									
25 VIII 2001 (CDFC)									
Total	136 554	67 422	69 132	73 907	35 679	38 228	62 647	31 743	30 904
0	4 588	2 299	2 289	2 433	1 221	1 212	2 155	1 078	1 077
1 - 4	16 111	8 149	7 962	8 440	4 325	4 115	7 671	3 824	3 847
5 - 9	18 794	9 587	9 207	9 780	4 972	4 808	9 014	4 615	4 399
10 - 14	18 468	9 416	9 052	9 829	4 883	4 946	8 639	4 533	4 106
15 - 19	17 311	8 663	8 648	9 762	4 701	5 061	7 549	3 962	3 587
20 - 24	13 981	6 870	7 111	7 926	3 783	4 143	6 055	3 087	2 968
25 - 29	9 703	4 795	4 908	5 333	2 564	2 769	4 370	2 231	2 139
30 - 34	7 684	3 700	3 984	4 235	1 960	2 275	3 449	1 740	1 709
35 - 39	6 567	3 050	3 517	3 639	1 632	2 007	2 928	1 418	1 510
40 - 44	5 367	2 465	2 902	3 066	1 413	1 653	2 301	1 052	1 249
45 - 49	3 984	1 864	2 120	2 261	1 026	1 235	1 723	838	885
50 - 54	3 020	1 408	1 612	1 659	758	901	1 361	650	711
55 - 59	2 397	1 119	1 278	1 247	559	688	1 150	560	590
60 - 64	2 710	1 301	1 409	1 288	568	720	1 422	733	689
65 - 69	2 108	1 043	1 065	1 014	482	532	1 094	561	533
70 - 74	1 648	780	868	829	366	463	819	414	405
75 - 79	1 124	513	611	593	251	342	531	262	269
80 - 84	616	262	354	349	140	209	267	122	145
85 +	373	138	235	224	75	149	149	63	86
Senegal - Sénégal									
8 XII 2002 (CDJC)									
Total	9 858 482	4 852 764	5 005 718	4 008 965	1 987 500[9]	2 021 465[9]	5 849 517	2 865 264[9]	2 984 253[9]
0 - 4	1 444 705	728 605	716 100	489 392	247 143[9]	242 249[9]	955 313	481 462[9]	473 851[9]
5 - 9	1 471 439	743 683	727 756	478 152	239 554[9]	238 598[9]	993 287	504 129[9]	489 158[9]
10 - 14	1 305 201	661 917	643 284	507 280	252 118[9]	255 162[9]	797 921	409 799[9]	388 122[9]
15 - 19	1 168 873	562 066	606 807	524 780	252 419[9]	272 361[9]	644 093	309 647[9]	334 446[9]
20 - 24	924 554	451 791	472 763	449 134	221 872[9]	227 262[9]	475 420	229 919[9]	245 501[9]
25 - 29	746 678	355 694	390 984	347 141	173 223[9]	173 918[9]	399 537	182 471[9]	217 066[9]
30 - 34	607 574	284 309	323 265	278 165	137 414[9]	140 751[9]	329 409	146 895[9]	182 514[9]
35 - 39	477 099	221 619	255 480	218 170	105 376[9]	112 794[9]	258 929	116 243[9]	142 686[9]
40 - 44	419 507	199 620	219 887	186 580	93 290[9]	93 290[9]	232 927	106 330[9]	126 597[9]
45 - 49	310 824	155 332	155 492	146 234	74 287[9]	71 947[9]	164 590	81 045[9]	83 545[9]
50 - 54	278 770	136 828	141 942	118 187	60 039[9]	58 148[9]	160 583	76 789[9]	83 794[9]
55 - 59	171 540	87 092	84 448	73 151	36 795[9]	36 356[9]	98 389	50 297[9]	48 092[9]
60 - 64	180 204	86 658	93 546	65 808	32 180[9]	33 628[9]	114 396	54 478[9]	59 918[9]
65 - 69	113 005	59 427	53 578	44 177	21 956[9]	22 221[9]	68 828	37 471[9]	31 357[9]
70 - 74	112 110	54 083	58 027	38 870	18 658[9]	20 212[9]	73 240	35 425[9]	37 815[9]
75 - 79	57 681	31 472	26 209	21 011	10 737[9]	10 274[9]	36 670	20 735[9]	15 935[9]
80 - 84	38 128	18 811	19 317	12 394	5 949[9]	6 445[9]	25 734	12 862[9]	12 872[9]
85 - 89	12 851	6 729	6 122	4 447	2 152[9]	2 295[9]	8 404	4 577[9]	3 827[9]
90 - 94	7 402	3 257	4 145	2 402	980[9]	1 422[9]	5 000	2 277[9]	2 723[9]
95 +	10 337	3 771	6 566	3 490	1 169[9]	2 321[9]	6 847	2 602[9]	4 245[9]

7. Population by age, sex and urban/rural residence: latest available year, 2000 - 2009
Population selon l'âge, le sexe et la résidence, urbaine/rurale : dernière année disponible, 2000 - 2009 (continued - suite)

Continent, country or area, date, code and age (in years) / Continent, pays ou zone, date, code et âge (en années)	Total			Urban - Urbaine			Rural - Rurale		
	Both sexes Les deux sexes	Male Masculin	Female Féminin	Both sexes Les deux sexes	Male Masculin	Female Féminin	Both sexes Les deux sexes	Male Masculin	Female Féminin
Seychelles									
1 VII 2008 (ESDF)									
Total	86 956	44 999	41 957	...	...	...	...	...	...
0	1 459	689	770	...	...	...	...	...	...
1 - 4	6 072	3 062	3 010	...	...	...	...	...	...
5 - 9	5 897	2 970	2 927	...	...	...	...	...	...
10 - 14	6 324	3 332	2 992	...	...	...	...	...	...
15 - 19	7 041	3 719	3 322	...	...	...	...	...	...
20 - 24	8 677	4 943	3 734	...	...	...	...	...	...
25 - 29	6 886	4 095	2 791	...	...	...	...	...	...
30 - 34	8 072	4 360	3 712	...	...	...	...	...	...
35 - 39	7 016	3 748	3 268	...	...	...	...	...	...
40 - 44	6 185	3 028	3 157	...	...	...	...	...	...
45 - 49	6 572	3 433	3 139	...	...	...	...	...	...
50 - 54	4 215	2 221	1 994	...	...	...	...	...	...
55 - 59	3 285	1 667	1 618	...	...	...	...	...	...
60 - 64	2 399	1 153	1 246	...	...	...	...	...	...
65 - 69	2 010	873	1 137	...	...	...	...	...	...
70 - 74	1 965	760	1 205	...	...	...	...	...	...
75 - 79	1 400	532	868	...	...	...	...	...	...
80 +	1 481	414	1 067	...	...	...	...	...	...
Sierra Leone									
1 VII 2009 (ESDF)									
Total	5 607 930	2 719 034	2 888 896	2 221 331	1 097 256	1 124 075	3 386 599	1 621 778	1 764 821
0 - 4	858 109	427 894	430 215	287 059	142 212	144 847	571 050	285 682	285 368
5 - 9	836 644	414 466	422 178	295 868	140 357	155 511	540 776	274 109	266 667
10 - 14	645 884	330 018	315 866	292 098	143 017	149 081	353 786	187 001	166 785
15 - 19	621 856	301 158	320 698	277 163	136 428	140 735	344 693	164 730	179 963
20 - 24	475 333	215 950	259 383	232 834	115 282	117 552	242 499	100 668	141 831
25 - 29	468 941	204 560	264 381	204 440	98 773	105 667	264 501	105 787	158 714
30 - 34	347 978	156 757	191 221	143 993	70 648	73 345	203 985	86 109	117 876
35 - 39	333 288	156 414	176 874	128 618	63 705	64 913	204 670	92 709	111 961
40 - 44	242 042	120 265	121 777	93 588	49 759	43 829	148 454	70 506	77 948
45 - 49	196 923	105 354	91 569	73 760	40 315	33 445	123 163	65 039	58 124
50 - 54	145 662	75 382	70 280	53 139	29 455	23 684	92 523	45 927	46 596
55 - 59	94 488	50 091	44 397	36 117	20 389	15 728	58 371	29 702	28 669
60 - 64	97 170	43 851	53 319	29 931	14 374	15 557	67 239	29 477	37 762
65 - 69	69 538	33 277	36 261	23 537	11 006	12 531	46 001	22 271	23 730
70 - 74	60 472	27 578	32 894	18 254	7 968	10 286	42 218	19 610	22 608
75 - 79	40 780	21 093	19 687	12 409	6 125	6 284	28 371	14 968	13 403
80 +	72 822	34 926	37 896	18 523	7 443	11 080	54 299	27 483	26 816
Somalia - Somalie									
1 VII 2002 (SSDF)									
Total	6 799 079	3 499 523	3 299 556	2 310 817	1 168 410	1 142 407	4 488 262	2 331 113	2 157 149
0 - 4	1 235 105	634 959	600 146	408 646	206 987	201 659	826 459	427 972	398 487
5 - 9	1 049 189	544 431	504 758	352 471	179 293	173 178	696 718	365 138	331 580
10 - 14	870 180	455 323	414 857	297 807	151 845	145 962	572 373	303 478	268 895
15 - 19	725 723	373 328	352 395	250 718	125 641	125 077	475 005	247 687	227 318
20 - 24	581 690	280 786	300 904	202 030	95 671	106 359	379 660	185 115	194 545
25 - 29	491 651	231 254	260 397	170 250	78 983	91 267	321 401	152 271	169 130
30 - 34	428 269	198 101	230 168	146 024	67 081	78 943	282 245	131 020	151 225
35 - 39	366 113	175 050	191 063	123 698	58 860	64 838	242 415	116 190	126 225
40 - 44	311 989	164 941	147 048	104 080	54 778	49 302	207 909	110 163	97 746
45 - 49	248 939	139 351	109 588	82 971	46 198	36 773	165 968	93 153	72 815
50 - 54	174 517	105 972	68 545	58 869	35 355	23 514	115 648	70 617	45 031
55 - 59	124 841	79 206	45 635	42 868	26 625	16 243	81 973	52 581	29 392
60 - 64	80 530	51 293	29 237	28 988	17 492	11 496	51 542	33 801	17 741
65 - 69	51 554	32 843	18 711	19 396	11 603	7 793	32 158	21 240	10 918
70 - 74	28 997	17 795	11 202	11 675	6 878	4 797	17 322	10 917	6 405
75 - 79	12 860	6 152	6 708	5 828	3 320	2 508	7 032	2 832	4 200
80 +	16 932	8 738	8 194	4 498	1 800	2 698	12 434	6 938	5 496
South Africa - Afrique du Sud									
10 X 2001 (CDFC)									
Total	44 819 776	21 434 040	23 385 736	25 635 464	12 490 170	13 145 294	19 184 312	8 943 870	10 240 442
0	908 406	453 924	454 482	477 424	238 714	238 710	430 982	215 210	215 772

Continent, country or area, date, code and age (in years) / Continent, pays ou zone, date, code et âge (en années)	Total			Urban - Urbaine			Rural - Rurale		
	Both sexes Les deux sexes	Male Masculin	Female Féminin	Both sexes Les deux sexes	Male Masculin	Female Féminin	Both sexes Les deux sexes	Male Masculin	Female Féminin
AFRICA - AFRIQUE									
South Africa - Afrique du Sud									
10 X 2001 (CDFC)									
1 - 4	3 541 410	1 769 807	1 771 603	1 741 531	870 233	871 298	1 799 879	899 574	900 305
5 - 9	4 853 555	2 425 804	2 427 751	2 265 590	1 130 066	1 135 524	2 587 965	1 295 738	1 292 227
10 - 14	5 061 918	2 518 957	2 542 961	2 375 400	1 175 785	1 199 615	2 686 518	1 343 172	1 343 346
15 - 19	4 981 721	2 453 079	2 528 642	2 534 495	1 239 696	1 294 799	2 447 226	1 213 383	1 233 843
20 - 24	4 294 523	2 099 293	2 195 230	2 615 557	1 301 922	1 313 635	1 678 966	797 371	881 595
25 - 29	3 934 938	1 899 124	2 035 814	2 605 568	1 303 270	1 302 298	1 329 370	595 854	733 516
30 - 34	3 340 900	1 594 488	1 746 412	2 265 059	1 123 790	1 141 269	1 075 841	470 698	605 143
35 - 39	3 071 771	1 441 507	1 630 264	2 068 848	1 012 850	1 055 998	1 002 923	428 657	574 266
40 - 44	2 619 465	1 233 632	1 385 833	1 755 016	859 091	895 925	864 449	374 541	489 908
45 - 49	2 087 380	967 604	1 119 776	1 365 672	657 042	708 630	721 708	310 562	411 146
50 - 54	1 638 021	769 500	868 521	1 045 729	508 585	537 144	592 292	260 915	331 377
55 - 59	1 205 266	552 323	652 943	754 415	355 500	398 915	450 851	196 823	254 028
60 - 64	1 065 294	444 510	620 784	607 009	266 153	340 856	458 285	178 357	279 928
65 - 69	787 926	304 763	483 163	428 899	176 632	252 267	359 027	128 131	230 896
70 - 74	631 470	232 548	398 922	317 444	125 758	191 686	314 026	106 790	207 236
75 - 79	367 538	136 437	231 101	199 460	75 715	123 745	168 078	60 722	107 356
80 - 84	270 945	90 835	180 110	132 959	46 317	86 642	137 986	44 518	93 468
85 - 89	94 222	28 842	65 380	50 606	15 082	35 524	43 616	13 760	29 856
90 - 94	41 714	11 308	30 406	20 262	5 605	14 657	21 452	5 703	15 749
95 - 99	15 436	4 200	11 236	6 300	1 764	4 536	9 136	2 436	6 700
100 +	5 957	1 555	4 402	2 221	600	1 621	3 736	955	2 781
1 VII 2009 (ESDF)[10]									
Total	49 320 500	23 868 700	25 451 800	...	...	...	...	...	...
0 - 4	5 068 900	2 551 200	2 517 700	...	...	...	...	...	...
5 - 9	5 184 600	2 608 300	2 576 300	...	...	...	...	...	...
10 - 14	5 247 200	2 640 100	2 607 100	...	...	...	...	...	...
15 - 19	5 214 300	2 620 100	2 594 200	...	...	...	...	...	...
20 - 24	4 920 900	2 449 400	2 471 500	...	...	...	...	...	...
25 - 29	4 423 500	2 126 100	2 297 400	...	...	...	...	...	...
30 - 34	3 888 300	1 865 000	2 023 300	...	...	...	...	...	...
35 - 39	3 282 300	1 550 900	1 731 400	...	...	...	...	...	...
40 - 44	2 443 200	1 150 700	1 292 500	...	...	...	...	...	...
45 - 49	2 260 000	1 052 500	1 207 500	...	...	...	...	...	...
50 - 54	2 038 700	943 300	1 095 400	...	...	...	...	...	...
55 - 59	1 645 100	754 500	890 600	...	...	...	...	...	...
60 - 64	1 299 100	575 300	723 800	...	...	...	...	...	...
65 - 69	961 800	419 200	542 600	...	...	...	...	...	...
70 - 74	674 700	277 900	396 800	...	...	...	...	...	...
75 - 79	426 600	165 400	261 200	...	...	...	...	...	...
80 +	341 300	118 800	222 500	...	...	...	...	...	...
Sudan - Soudan									
21 IV 2008* (CDFC)									
Total	39 154 490	20 073 977	19 080 513	...	...	...	...	...	...
0 - 4	5 845 991	3 005 746	2 840 245	...	...	...	...	...	...
5 - 9	5 801 776	3 023 603	2 778 173	...	...	...	...	...	...
10 - 14	5 036 037	2 689 626	2 346 411	...	...	...	...	...	...
15 - 19	4 176 355	2 151 401	2 024 954	...	...	...	...	...	...
20 - 24	3 537 012	1 740 076	1 796 936	...	...	...	...	...	...
25 - 29	3 114 966	1 466 418	1 648 548	...	...	...	...	...	...
30 - 34	2 503 963	1 207 987	1 295 976	...	...	...	...	...	...
35 - 39	2 314 365	1 134 069	1 180 296	...	...	...	...	...	...
40 - 44	1 773 831	905 533	868 298	...	...	...	...	...	...
45 - 49	1 303 680	689 233	614 447	...	...	...	...	...	...
50 - 54	1 094 706	581 191	513 515	...	...	...	...	...	...
55 - 59	635 801	350 041	285 760	...	...	...	...	...	...
60 - 64	691 103	380 847	310 256	...	...	...	...	...	...
65 - 69	396 288	227 674	168 614	...	...	...	...	...	...
70 - 74	415 695	229 753	185 942	...	...	...	...	...	...
75 - 79	193 068	112 065	81 003	...	...	...	...	...	...
80 - 84	178 990	97 556	81 434	...	...	...	...	...	...
85 - 89	65 235	38 504	26 731	...	...	...	...	...	...
90 - 94	41 546	23 528	18 018	...	...	...	...	...	...
95 +	34 082	19 126	14 956	...	...	...	...	...	...

Continent, country or area, date, code and age (in years) / Continent, pays ou zone, date, code et âge (en années)	Total			Urban - Urbaine			Rural - Rurale		
	Both sexes Les deux sexes	Male Masculin	Female Féminin	Both sexes Les deux sexes	Male Masculin	Female Féminin	Both sexes Les deux sexes	Male Masculin	Female Féminin
AFRICA - AFRIQUE									
Swaziland									
11 III 2007 (CDFC)									
Total	844 223	405 868	438 355	186 890	93 918	92 972	657 333	311 950	345 383
0 - 4	109 726	54 848	54 878	18 594	9 097	9 497	91 132	45 751	45 381
5 - 9	111 992	56 184	55 808	15 614	7 682	7 932	96 378	48 502	47 876
10 - 14	111 497	54 874	56 623	15 110	7 046	8 064	96 387	47 828	48 559
15 - 19	100 665	50 251	50 414	17 449	8 044	9 405	83 216	42 207	41 009
20 - 24	87 814	42 768	45 046	25 977	12 332	13 645	61 837	30 436	31 401
25 - 29	70 336	33 775	36 561	26 377	13 353	13 024	43 959	20 422	23 537
30 - 34	52 306	25 575	26 731	19 295	10 543	8 752	33 011	15 032	17 979
35 - 39	43 741	20 725	23 016	14 599	8 123	6 476	29 142	12 602	16 540
40 - 44	34 004	14 817	19 187	10 180	5 364	4 816	23 824	9 453	14 371
45 - 49	29 227	12 788	16 439	7 802	4 172	3 630	21 425	8 616	12 809
50 - 54	22 862	10 418	12 444	5 536	3 007	2 529	17 326	7 411	9 915
55 - 59	18 070	8 337	9 733	3 866	2 138	1 728	14 204	6 199	8 005
60 - 64	16 718	6 706	10 012	2 358	1 107	1 251	14 360	5 599	8 761
65 - 69	13 262	5 521	7 741	1 544	732	812	11 718	4 789	6 929
70 - 74	8 164	3 206	4 958	915	423	492	7 249	2 783	4 466
75 - 79	6 239	2 323	3 916	559	218	341	5 680	2 105	3 575
80 +	6 420	2 138	4 282	507	177	330	5 913	1 961	3 952
Unknown - Inconnu	1 180	614	566	608	360	248	572	254	318
Tunisia - Tunisie									
1 VII 2008 (ESDF)									
Total	10 328 900	5 156 300	5 172 600	...	...	...	...	...	...
0 - 4	832 300	425 600	406 800	...	...	...	...	...	...
5 - 9	806 900	416 500	390 400	...	...	...	...	...	...
10 - 14	867 000	444 700	422 300	...	...	...	...	...	...
15 - 19	1 011 800	518 800	493 000	...	...	...	...	...	...
20 - 24	1 053 600	531 600	522 000	...	...	...	...	...	...
25 - 29	964 100	476 500	487 600	...	...	...	...	...	...
30 - 34	828 500	397 700	430 800	...	...	...	...	...	...
35 - 39	714 000	343 700	370 400	...	...	...	...	...	...
40 - 44	702 000	338 400	363 600	...	...	...	...	...	...
45 - 49	623 300	311 200	312 000	...	...	...	...	...	...
50 - 54	531 300	265 800	265 500	...	...	...	...	...	...
55 - 59	395 000	195 000	200 000	...	...	...	...	...	...
60 - 64	278 900	132 800	146 100	...	...	...	...	...	...
65 - 69	236 900	116 000	121 000	...	...	...	...	...	...
70 - 74	214 800	105 000	109 800	...	...	...	...	...	...
75 - 79	147 400	74 700	72 700	...	...	...	...	...	...
80 +	121 100	62 500	58 600	...	...	...	...	...	...
Uganda - Ouganda									
12 IX 2002 (CDFC)									
Total	24 442 084	11 929 803	12 512 281	2 999 387	1 449 684	1 549 703	21 442 697	10 480 119	10 962 578
0	1 007 407	505 006	502 401	104 439	52 481	51 958	902 968	452 525	450 443
1 - 4	3 537 016	1 767 120	1 769 896	347 233	172 444	174 789	3 189 783	1 594 676	1 595 107
5 - 9	4 001 052	1 998 157	2 002 895	399 119	193 271	205 848	3 601 933	1 804 886	1 797 047
10 - 14	3 509 151	1 757 111	1 752 040	391 236	180 572	210 664	3 117 915	1 576 539	1 541 376
15 - 19	2 708 143	1 324 222	1 383 921	407 299	180 461	226 838	2 300 844	1 143 761	1 157 083
20 - 24	2 175 580	981 994	1 193 586	392 217	180 869	211 348	1 783 363	801 125	982 238
25 - 29	1 778 541	831 129	947 412	308 026	152 765	155 261	1 470 515	678 364	792 151
30 - 34	1 420 073	708 138	711 935	215 168	116 304	98 864	1 204 905	591 834	613 071
35 - 39	1 020 968	492 372	528 596	138 208	72 826	65 382	882 760	419 546	463 214
40 - 44	828 317	400 433	427 884	96 870	50 662	46 208	731 447	349 771	381 676
45 - 49	542 862	257 694	285 168	58 821	30 676	28 145	484 041	227 018	257 023
50 - 54	486 060	223 345	262 715	44 728	22 839	21 889	441 332	200 506	240 826
55 - 59	325 875	149 792	176 083	25 198	12 690	12 508	300 677	137 102	163 575
60 - 64	363 765	173 325	190 440	24 371	11 139	13 232	339 394	162 186	177 208
65 - 69	226 029	115 081	110 948	14 175	6 657	7 518	211 854	108 424	103 430
70 - 74	217 160	102 858	114 302	12 538	5 157	7 381	204 622	97 701	106 921
75 - 79	105 318	54 213	51 105	6 582	2 824	3 758	98 736	51 389	47 347
80 - 84	112 785	52 143	60 642	7 542	2 926	4 616	105 243	49 217	56 026
85 - 89	31 184	15 009	16 175	2 146	821	1 325	29 038	14 188	14 850
90 - 94	27 871	13 036	14 835	2 126	786	1 340	25 745	12 250	13 495
95 +	16 927	7 625	9 302	1 345	514	831	15 582	7 111	8 471

Continent, country or area, date, code and age (in years) Continent, pays ou zone, date, code et âge (en années)	Total			Urban - Urbaine			Rural - Rurale		
	Both sexes Les deux sexes	Male Masculin	Female Féminin	Both sexes Les deux sexes	Male Masculin	Female Féminin	Both sexes Les deux sexes	Male Masculin	Female Féminin
AFRICA - AFRIQUE									
Uganda - Ouganda									
1 VII 2009 (ESDF)									
Total	30 661 500	14 934 000	15 727 500	...	...	...	...	...	...
0 - 4	6 586 800	3 273 600	3 313 200	...	...	...	...	...	...
5 - 9	4 846 500	2 413 400	2 433 100	...	...	...	...	...	...
10 - 14	3 949 700	1 954 000	1 995 700	...	...	...	...	...	...
15 - 19	3 354 500	1 643 400	1 711 100	...	...	...	...	...	...
20 - 24	2 760 800	1 342 200	1 418 600	...	...	...	...	...	...
25 - 29	2 235 300	1 078 600	1 156 700	...	...	...	...	...	...
30 - 34	1 777 800	852 000	925 800	...	...	...	...	...	...
35 - 39	1 400 200	664 600	735 600	...	...	...	...	...	...
40 - 44	1 092 800	512 200	580 600	...	...	...	...	...	...
45 - 49	840 700	388 700	452 000	...	...	...	...	...	...
50 - 54	630 100	287 600	342 500	...	...	...	...	...	...
55 - 59	455 700	205 200	250 500	...	...	...	...	...	...
60 - 64	313 900	138 900	175 000	...	...	...	...	...	...
65 - 69	201 900	87 500	114 400	...	...	...	...	...	...
70 - 74	118 300	50 500	67 800	...	...	...	...	...	...
75 - 79	60 900	26 000	34 900	...	...	...	...	...	...
80 +	35 600	15 600	20 000	...	...	...	...	...	...
United Republic of Tanzania - République Unie de Tanzanie									
24 VIII 2002* (CDFC)									
Total	34 443 603	16 829 861	17 613 742	...	...	...	...	...	...
0 - 4	5 664 907	2 830 545	2 834 362	...	...	...	...	...	...
5 - 9	5 130 448	2 573 993	2 556 455	...	...	...	...	...	...
10 - 14	4 443 257	2 233 401	2 209 856	...	...	...	...	...	...
15 - 19	3 595 735	1 761 329	1 834 406	...	...	...	...	...	...
20 - 24	3 148 513	1 402 077	1 746 436	...	...	...	...	...	...
25 - 29	2 801 965	1 309 661	1 492 304	...	...	...	...	...	...
30 - 34	2 229 046	1 087 599	1 141 447	...	...	...	...	...	...
35 - 39	1 669 873	824 338	845 535	...	...	...	...	...	...
40 - 44	1 348 508	669 549	678 959	...	...	...	...	...	...
45 - 49	984 823	478 522	506 301	...	...	...	...	...	...
50 - 54	883 820	428 501	455 319	...	...	...	...	...	...
55 - 59	590 667	290 117	300 550	...	...	...	...	...	...
60 - 64	604 956	287 502	317 454	...	...	...	...	...	...
65 - 69	439 671	213 635	226 036	...	...	...	...	...	...
70 - 74	377 852	180 246	197 606	...	...	...	...	...	...
75 - 79	221 354	113 205	108 149	...	...	...	...	...	...
80 +	308 208	145 641	162 567	...	...	...	...	...	...
Zambia - Zambie									
25 X 2000 (CDFC)									
Total	9 337 425	4 594 290	4 743 135	3 347 069	1 662 739	1 684 330	5 990 356	2 931 551	3 058 805
0	339 228	168 841	170 387	101 775	50 699	51 076	237 453	118 142	119 311
1 - 4	1 317 492	656 948	660 544	420 759	209 814	210 945	896 733	447 134	449 599
5 - 9	1 461 082	729 181	731 901	500 572	247 117	253 455	960 510	482 064	478 446
10 - 14	1 205 646	601 279	604 367	428 831	206 305	222 526	776 815	394 974	381 841
15 - 19	1 069 996	513 320	556 676	415 197	195 518	219 679	654 799	317 802	336 997
20 - 24	908 672	416 083	492 589	376 695	174 331	202 364	531 977	241 752	290 225
25 - 29	741 148	361 901	379 247	308 436	155 070	153 366	432 712	206 831	225 881
30 - 34	557 873	282 439	275 434	225 707	119 524	106 183	332 166	162 915	169 251
35 - 39	429 987	211 356	218 631	169 148	87 763	81 385	260 839	123 593	137 246
40 - 44	325 776	161 179	164 597	125 995	66 050	59 945	199 781	95 129	104 652
45 - 49	245 320	122 486	122 834	91 507	50 128	41 379	153 813	72 358	81 455
50 - 54	203 612	97 850	105 762	65 547	37 513	28 034	138 065	60 337	77 728
55 - 59	144 838	71 905	72 933	39 418	22 860	16 558	105 420	49 045	56 375
60 - 64	131 475	62 678	68 797	29 438	15 308	14 130	102 037	47 370	54 667
65 - 69	100 493	52 499	47 994	20 294	10 642	9 652	80 199	41 857	38 342
70 - 74	68 935	37 066	31 869	12 763	6 634	6 129	56 172	30 432	25 740
75 - 79	40 649	23 301	17 348	7 217	3 793	3 424	33 432	19 508	13 924
80 - 84	24 242	13 311	10 931	4 418	2 206	2 212	19 824	11 105	8 719
85 +	20 961	10 667	10 294	3 352	1 464	1 888	17 609	9 203	8 406

Continent, country or area, date, code and age (in years) / Continent, pays ou zone, date, code et âge (en annèes)	Total			Urban - Urbaine			Rural - Rurale		
	Both sexes Les deux sexes	Male Masculin	Female Féminin	Both sexes Les deux sexes	Male Masculin	Female Féminin	Both sexes Les deux sexes	Male Masculin	Female Féminin
AFRICA - AFRIQUE									
Zimbabwe									
17 VIII 2002 (CDFC)									
Total	11 631 657	5 634 180	5 997 477	4 029 707	1 988 176	2 041 531	7 601 950	3 646 004	3 955 946
0	340 331	170 054	170 277	117 756	59 103	58 653	222 575	110 951	111 624
1 - 4	1 335 738	668 008	667 730	422 397	210 186	212 211	913 341	457 822	455 519
5 - 9	1 533 700	764 453	769 247	424 731	207 986	216 745	1 108 969	556 467	552 502
10 - 14	1 512 244	754 587	757 657	381 331	180 444	200 887	1 130 913	574 143	556 770
15 - 19	1 503 576	736 686	766 890	511 394	217 513	293 881	992 182	519 173	473 009
20 - 24	1 222 907	564 034	658 873	566 584	260 105	306 479	656 323	303 929	352 394
25 - 29	987 777	473 984	513 793	474 294	242 497	231 797	513 483	231 487	281 996
30 - 34	730 127	369 836	360 291	345 675	191 527	154 148	384 452	178 309	206 143
35 - 39	504 489	235 692	268 797	222 381	116 670	105 711	282 108	119 022	163 086
40 - 44	434 429	194 702	239 727	168 100	87 760	80 340	266 329	106 942	159 387
45 - 49	356 605	165 437	191 168	128 388	70 668	57 720	228 217	94 769	133 448
50 - 54	301 258	128 029	173 229	87 458	48 199	39 259	213 800	79 830	133 970
55 - 59	210 915	98 417	112 498	55 467	31 214	24 253	155 448	67 203	88 245
60 - 64	193 867	94 447	99 420	42 546	23 384	19 162	151 321	71 063	80 258
65 - 69	132 152	64 301	67 851	26 735	14 234	12 501	105 417	50 067	55 350
70 - 74	122 775	60 311	62 464	20 371	10 602	9 769	102 404	49 709	52 695
75 +	164 261	71 950	92 311	23 687	10 598	13 089	140 574	61 352	79 222
75 - 79	64 470	29 997	34 473	...	...	...	...	...	...
80 - 84	59 045	26 764	32 281	...	...	...	...	...	...
85 - 89	19 084	7 727	11 357	...	...	...	...	...	...
90 - 94	9 188	3 752	5 436	...	...	...	...	...	...
95 +	12 474	3 710	8 764	...	...	...	...	...	...
Unknown - Inconnu	44 506	19 252	25 254	10 412	5 486	4 926	34 094	13 766	20 328
1 VII 2009 (ESDF)									
Total	13 667 894	6 642 551	7 025 344	...	...	...	...	...	...
0	358 716	179 238	179 477	...	...	...	...	...	...
1 - 4	1 407 894	704 085	703 809	...	...	...	...	...	...
5 - 9	1 616 550	805 739	810 811	...	...	...	...	...	...
10 - 14	1 593 935	795 340	798 595	...	...	...	...	...	...
15 - 19	1 584 799	776 472	808 327	...	...	...	...	...	...
20 - 24	1 288 969	594 496	694 473	...	...	...	...	...	...
25 - 29	1 041 137	499 582	541 554	...	...	...	...	...	...
30 - 34	769 568	389 810	379 758	...	...	...	...	...	...
35 - 39	531 742	248 421	283 321	...	...	...	...	...	...
40 - 44	457 897	205 217	252 680	...	...	...	...	...	...
45 - 49	375 869	174 372	201 497	...	...	...	...	...	...
50 - 54	317 532	134 943	182 589	...	...	...	...	...	...
55 - 59	222 309	103 732	118 577	...	...	...	...	...	...
60 - 64	204 340	99 548	104 792	...	...	...	...	...	...
65 - 69	139 291	67 774	71 517	...	...	...	...	...	...
70 - 74	129 407	63 568	65 839	...	...	...	...	...	...
75 +	173 135	75 836	97 299	...	...	...	...	...	...
Unknown - Inconnu	46 910	20 292	26 619	...	...	...	...	...	...
AMERICA, NORTH - AMÉRIQUE DU NORD									
Anguilla[11]									
9 V 2001 (CDFC)									
Total	11 430	5 628	5 802	...	...	...	...	...	...
0	252	131	121	...	...	...	...	...	...
1 - 4	821	394	427	...	...	...	...	...	...
5 - 9	993	502	491	...	...	...	...	...	...
10 - 14	1 136	563	573	...	...	...	...	...	...
15 - 19	966	477	489	...	...	...	...	...	...
20 - 24	788	375	413	...	...	...	...	...	...
25 - 29	873	440	433	...	...	...	...	...	...
30 - 34	999	494	505	...	...	...	...	...	...
35 - 39	1 040	507	533	...	...	...	...	...	...
40 - 44	881	429	452	...	...	...	...	...	...
45 - 49	714	364	350	...	...	...	...	...	...

Continent, country or area, date, code and age (in years) / Continent, pays ou zone, date, code et âge (en années)	Total			Urban - Urbaine			Rural - Rurale		
	Both sexes Les deux sexes	Male Masculin	Female Féminin	Both sexes Les deux sexes	Male Masculin	Female Féminin	Both sexes Les deux sexes	Male Masculin	Female Féminin
AMERICA, NORTH - AMÉRIQUE DU NORD									
Anguilla[11]									
9 V 2001 (CDFC)									
50 - 54	468	236	232	...	...	...	...	...	...
55 - 59	323	166	157	...	...	...	...	...	...
60 - 64	304	144	160	...	...	...	...	...	...
65 - 69	288	159	129	...	...	...	...	...	...
70 - 74	211	82	129	...	...	...	...	...	...
75 - 79	155	65	90	...	...	...	...	...	...
80 - 84	102	52	50	...	...	...	...	...	...
85 - 89	79	31	48	...	...	...	...	...	...
90 - 94	30	15	15	...	...	...	...	...	...
95 +	7	2	5	...	...	...	...	...	...
Antigua and Barbuda - Antigua-et-Barbuda									
1 VII 2005 (ESDF)									
Total	82 786	38 878	43 908	...	...	...	...	...	...
0	1 537	765	772	...	...	...	...	...	...
1 - 4	6 269	3 230	3 039	...	...	...	...	...	...
5 - 9	7 954	3 966	3 988	...	...	...	...	...	...
10 - 14	7 635	3 699	3 937	...	...	...	...	...	...
15 - 19	6 812	3 230	3 582	...	...	...	...	...	...
20 - 24	6 527	3 119	3 408	...	...	...	...	...	...
25 - 29	6 889	3 169	3 719	...	...	...	...	...	...
30 - 34	7 518	3 344	4 174	...	...	...	...	...	...
35 - 39	7 199	3 251	3 948	...	...	...	...	...	...
40 - 44	5 977	2 697	3 280	...	...	...	...	...	...
45 - 49	4 658	2 176	2 482	...	...	...	...	...	...
50 - 54	3 518	1 659	1 859	...	...	...	...	...	...
55 - 59	2 573	1 162	1 411	...	...	...	...	...	...
60 - 64	2 028	929	1 099	...	...	...	...	...	...
65 - 69	1 700	778	922	...	...	...	...	...	...
70 - 74	1 442	633	809	...	...	...	...	...	...
75 - 79	1 100	507	593	...	...	...	...	...	...
80 - 84	783	332	451	...	...	...	...	...	...
85 - 89	437	160	278	...	...	...	...	...	...
90 - 94	197	65	132	...	...	...	...	...	...
95 +	32	9	23	...	...	...	...	...	...
Aruba[12]									
1 VII 2009 (ESDJ)									
Total	106 925	51 227	55 699	...	...	...	...	...	...
0 - 4	6 324	3 242	3 083	...	...	...	...	...	...
5 - 9	6 878	3 508	3 370	...	...	...	...	...	...
10 - 14	7 716	3 907	3 809	...	...	...	...	...	...
15 - 19	7 527	3 808	3 719	...	...	...	...	...	...
20 - 24	6 218	3 137	3 082	...	...	...	...	...	...
25 - 29	6 393	3 108	3 285	...	...	...	...	...	...
30 - 34	7 276	3 407	3 870	...	...	...	...	...	...
35 - 39	8 696	4 144	4 553	...	...	...	...	...	...
40 - 44	9 301	4 417	4 884	...	...	...	...	...	...
45 - 49	10 014	4 762	5 252	...	...	...	...	...	...
50 - 54	8 566	3 962	4 603	...	...	...	...	...	...
55 - 59	6 772	3 194	3 578	...	...	...	...	...	...
60 - 64	5 034	2 327	2 708	...	...	...	...	...	...
65 - 69	3 667	1 693	1 974	...	...	...	...	...	...
70 - 74	2 860	1 202	1 658	...	...	...	...	...	...
75 - 79	1 903	771	1 133	...	...	...	...	...	...
80 - 84	998	382	616	...	...	...	...	...	...
85 - 89	482	182	300	...	...	...	...	...	...
90 - 94	203	52	151	...	...	...	...	...	...
95 +	98	24	74	...	...	...	...	...	...
Bahamas[2]									
1 VII 2009 (ESDF)									
Total	342 400	166 800	175 600	...	...	...	...	...	...
0 - 4	29 200	15 200	14 000	...	...	...	...	...	...

Continent, country or area, date, code and age (in years) / Continent, pays ou zone, date, code et âge (en années)	Total			Urban - Urbaine			Rural - Rurale		
	Both sexes Les deux sexes	Male Masculin	Female Féminin	Both sexes Les deux sexes	Male Masculin	Female Féminin	Both sexes Les deux sexes	Male Masculin	Female Féminin
AMERICA, NORTH - AMÉRIQUE DU NORD									
Bahamas[2]									
1 VII 2009 (ESDF)									
5 - 9	28 300	14 400	13 900	...	...	...	...	...	...
10 - 14	29 900	14 900	15 000	...	...	...	...	...	...
15 - 19	30 800	15 300	15 500	...	...	...	...	...	...
20 - 24	27 300	13 300	14 000	...	...	...	...	...	...
25 - 29	25 700	12 800	12 900	...	...	...	...	...	...
30 - 34	25 800	12 600	13 200	...	...	...	...	...	...
35 - 39	28 000	13 500	14 500	...	...	...	...	...	...
40 - 44	26 800	12 800	14 000	...	...	...	...	...	...
45 - 49	25 500	12 300	13 200	...	...	...	...	...	...
50 - 54	19 800	9 500	10 300	...	...	...	...	...	...
55 - 59	14 300	6 800	7 500	...	...	...	...	...	...
60 - 64	10 500	4 900	5 600	...	...	...	...	...	...
65 - 69	8 400	3 800	4 600	...	...	...	...	...	...
70 - 74	5 900	2 600	3 300	...	...	...	...	...	...
75 - 79	3 500	1 400	2 100	...	...	...	...	...	...
80 - 84	1 564	438	1 126	...	...	...	...	...	...
85 - 89	763	184	579	...	...	...	...	...	...
90 +	373	78	295	...	...	...	...	...	...
Barbados - Barbade									
1 V 2000 (CDFC)									
Total	250 010	119 926	130 084	...	...	...	...	...	...
0 - 4	17 239	8 763	8 476	...	...	...	...	...	...
5 - 9	18 749	9 479	9 270	...	...	...	...	...	...
10 - 14	18 613	9 425	9 188	...	...	...	...	...	...
15 - 19	18 636	9 434	9 202	...	...	...	...	...	...
20 - 24	17 804	8 913	8 891	...	...	...	...	...	...
25 - 29	19 738	9 758	9 980	...	...	...	...	...	...
30 - 34	19 588	9 574	10 014	...	...	...	...	...	...
35 - 39	21 257	10 155	11 102	...	...	...	...	...	...
40 - 44	20 055	9 544	10 511	...	...	...	...	...	...
45 - 49	16 774	8 007	8 767	...	...	...	...	...	...
50 - 54	13 638	6 563	7 075	...	...	...	...	...	...
55 - 59	9 583	4 376	5 207	...	...	...	...	...	...
60 - 64	8 925	3 969	4 956	...	...	...	...	...	...
65 - 69	8 319	3 648	4 671	...	...	...	...	...	...
70 - 74	7 649	3 208	4 441	...	...	...	...	...	...
75 - 79	5 670	2 310	3 360	...	...	...	...	...	...
80 +	7 773	2 800	4 973	...	...	...	...	...	...
Belize									
1 VII 2006 (ESDF)[13]									
Total	301 298	149 598	151 700	151 994	73 576	78 418	149 394	76 101	73 293
0 - 4	36 761	18 145	18 616	17 720	8 446	9 274	19 808	10 070	9 738
5 - 9	40 974	20 850	20 124	19 294	9 792	9 502	21 574	11 011	10 563
10 - 14	40 474	20 611	19 862	19 185	9 790	9 395	21 185	10 775	10 410
15 - 19	33 960	17 192	16 769	16 629	8 785	7 844	17 246	8 369	8 877
20 - 24	24 423	11 939	12 484	12 728	5 973	6 755	11 631	5 939	5 692
25 - 29	20 990	9 733	11 256	11 262	5 018	6 244	9 673	4 693	4 980
30 - 34	20 405	9 522	10 883	11 277	5 183	6 094	9 075	4 318	4 757
35 - 39	18 464	8 747	9 718	9 745	4 294	5 451	8 672	4 433	4 239
40 - 44	15 793	7 735	8 058	8 174	3 931	4 243	7 579	3 787	3 792
45 - 49	12 378	6 295	6 065	6 555	3 305	3 250	5 791	2 976	2 815
50 - 54	9 686	4 983	4 703	5 176	2 385	2 791	4 485	2 586	1 899
55 - 59	6 637	3 363	3 264	3 385	1 636	1 749	3 235	1 720	1 515
60 - 64	5 692	2 913	2 778	2 838	1 376	1 462	2 839	1 531	1 308
65 - 69	4 877	2 547	2 330	2 584	1 201	1 383	2 281	1 341	940
70 - 74	3 867	2 073	1 794	2 203	999	1 204	1 654	1 069	585
75 - 79	2 708	1 374	1 330	1 511	716	795	1 191	656	535
80 - 84	1 578	782	798	794	327	467	784	453	331
85 +	1 629	794	835	934	419	515	691	374	317
1 VII 2009 (ESDF)									
Total	333 200	166 500	166 700	...	...	...	...	...	...
0 - 4	35 400	18 000	17 400	...	...	...	...	...	...

Continent, country or area, date, code and age (in years) / Continent, pays ou zone, date, code et âge (en années)	Total			Urban - Urbaine			Rural - Rurale		
	Both sexes Les deux sexes	Male Masculin	Female Féminin	Both sexes Les deux sexes	Male Masculin	Female Féminin	Both sexes Les deux sexes	Male Masculin	Female Féminin
AMERICA, NORTH - AMÉRIQUE DU NORD									
Belize									
1 VII 2009 (ESDF)									
5 - 9	43 500	21 900	21 600	...	...	...	...	...	...
10 - 14	43 800	22 700	21 100	...	...	...	...	...	...
15 - 19	38 700	19 700	19 000	...	...	...	...	...	...
20 - 24	27 100	13 600	13 500	...	...	...	...	...	...
25 - 29	22 700	10 500	12 200	...	...	...	...	...	...
30 - 34	21 500	9 900	11 600	...	...	...	...	...	...
35 - 39	20 600	9 700	10 900	...	...	...	...	...	...
40 - 44	19 000	9 200	9 800	...	...	...	...	...	...
45 - 49	16 200	8 200	8 000	...	...	...	...	...	...
50 - 54	12 000	6 000	6 000	...	...	...	...	...	...
55 - 59	8 900	4 700	4 200	...	...	...	...	...	...
60 - 64	6 800	3 600	3 200	...	...	...	...	...	...
65 - 69	5 500	3 000	2 500	...	...	...	...	...	...
70 - 74	4 300	2 200	2 100	...	...	...	...	...	...
75 - 79	3 300	1 700	1 600	...	...	...	...	...	...
80 - 84	2 000	1 000	1 000	...	...	...	...	...	...
85 +	1 900	900	1 000	...	...	...	...	...	...
Bermuda - Bermudes									
1 VII 2009 (ESDJ)									
Total	64 395	30 704	33 691	...	...	...	...	...	...
0	771	391	380	...	...	...	...	...	...
1 - 4	2 979	1 517	1 462	...	...	...	...	...	...
5 - 9	3 761	1 933	1 828	...	...	...	...	...	...
10 - 14	3 768	1 902	1 866	...	...	...	...	...	...
15 - 19	3 716	1 847	1 869	...	...	...	...	...	...
20 - 24	3 549	1 697	1 852	...	...	...	...	...	...
25 - 29	4 217	1 990	2 227	...	...	...	...	...	...
30 - 34	4 374	2 046	2 328	...	...	...	...	...	...
35 - 39	4 893	2 380	2 513	...	...	...	...	...	...
40 - 44	5 274	2 621	2 653	...	...	...	...	...	...
45 - 49	5 938	2 939	2 999	...	...	...	...	...	...
50 - 54	5 168	2 397	2 771	...	...	...	...	...	...
55 - 59	4 278	2 065	2 213	...	...	...	...	...	...
60 - 64	3 594	1 679	1 915	...	...	...	...	...	...
65 - 69	2 624	1 174	1 450	...	...	...	...	...	...
70 - 74	2 035	861	1 174	...	...	...	...	...	...
75 - 79	1 638	663	975	...	...	...	...	...	...
80 - 84	1 069	388	681	...	...	...	...	...	...
85 +	749	214	535	...	...	...	...	...	...
British Virgin Islands - Îles Vierges britanniques									
21 V 2001 (CDFC)									
Total	20 647	10 627	10 020	...	...	...	...	...	...
0 - 4	1 787	913	874	...	...	...	...	...	...
5 - 9	1 865	946	919	...	...	...	...	...	...
10 - 14	1 768	880	888	...	...	...	...	...	...
15 - 19	1 529	778	751	...	...	...	...	...	...
20 - 24	1 465	752	713	...	...	...	...	...	...
25 - 29	1 483	756	727	...	...	...	...	...	...
30 - 34	1 826	913	913	...	...	...	...	...	...
35 - 39	2 085	1 091	994	...	...	...	...	...	...
40 - 44	1 910	991	919	...	...	...	...	...	...
45 - 49	1 501	777	724	...	...	...	...	...	...
50 - 54	1 128	614	514	...	...	...	...	...	...
55 - 59	774	421	353	...	...	...	...	...	...
60 - 64	523	267	256	...	...	...	...	...	...
65 - 69	337	177	160	...	...	...	...	...	...
70 - 74	282	145	137	...	...	...	...	...	...
75 - 79	204	113	91	...	...	...	...	...	...
80 +	180	93	87	...	...	...	...	...	...

Continent, country or area, date, code and age (in years) / Continent, pays ou zone, date, code et âge (en années)	Total			Urban - Urbaine			Rural - Rurale		
	Both sexes Les deux sexes	Male Masculin	Female Féminin	Both sexes Les deux sexes	Male Masculin	Female Féminin	Both sexes Les deux sexes	Male Masculin	Female Féminin
AMERICA, NORTH - AMÉRIQUE DU NORD									
Canada									
16 V 2006 (CDJC)[12]									
Total	31 612 895	15 475 970	16 136 925	25 350 585	12 289 025	13 061 560	6 262 315	3 186 950	3 075 365
0 - 4	1 690 540	864 600	825 940	1 365 015	697 760	667 255	325 520	166 840	158 680
5 - 9	1 809 375	926 860	882 515	1 430 755	732 775	697 980	378 620	194 080	184 540
10 - 14	2 079 925	1 065 860	1 014 060	1 623 165	830 685	792 480	456 760	235 180	221 580
15 - 19	2 140 490	1 095 285	1 045 210	1 680 870	855 915	824 960	459 620	239 370	220 250
20 - 24	2 080 385	1 047 950	1 032 440	1 756 075	877 305	878 775	324 310	170 645	153 660
25 - 29	1 985 580	975 945	1 009 635	1 701 100	833 530	867 575	284 480	142 420	142 060
30 - 34	2 020 230	987 715	1 032 510	1 690 870	824 815	866 050	329 360	162 900	166 460
35 - 39	2 208 270	1 083 495	1 124 780	1 810 135	886 375	923 760	398 140	197 125	201 015
40 - 44	2 610 455	1 285 535	1 324 920	2 088 760	1 024 215	1 064 540	521 705	261 320	260 380
45 - 49	2 620 600	1 290 130	1 330 470	2 067 000	1 009 375	1 057 620	553 600	280 755	272 850
50 - 54	2 357 300	1 158 970	1 198 335	1 833 675	891 450	942 230	523 625	267 525	256 100
55 - 59	2 084 620	1 026 390	1 058 230	1 601 975	777 985	823 990	482 650	248 405	234 240
60 - 64	1 589 870	780 135	809 730	1 205 570	579 700	625 870	384 295	200 430	183 860
65 - 69	1 234 575	593 810	640 770	949 745	443 420	506 330	284 835	150 390	134 440
70 - 74	1 053 785	493 465	560 325	834 670	378 835	455 840	219 110	114 630	104 485
75 - 79	879 575	386 485	493 090	718 780	305 230	413 550	160 800	81 255	79 545
80 - 84	646 705	251 420	395 285	544 780	204 705	340 075	101 920	46 710	55 210
85 - 89	342 685	114 585	228 100	292 910	95 160	197 750	49 770	19 425	30 345
90 - 94	139 105	38 455	100 650	120 735	32 340	88 400	18 370	6 115	12 255
95 - 99	34 185	8 080	26 110	29 890	6 790	23 105	4 300	1 290	3 010
100 +	4 635	805	3 825	4 110	685	3 430	525	125	400
1 VII 2009 (ESDJ)[14]									
Total	33 720 184	16 723 138	16 997 046	...	...	...	...	...	...
0	377 107	193 401	183 706	...	...	...	...	...	...
1 - 4	1 460 976	750 217	710 759	...	...	...	...	...	...
5 - 9	1 798 679	925 404	873 275	...	...	...	...	...	...
10 - 14	1 973 339	1 011 189	962 150	...	...	...	...	...	...
15 - 19	2 250 985	1 152 775	1 098 210	...	...	...	...	...	...
20 - 24	2 320 726	1 192 210	1 128 516	...	...	...	...	...	...
25 - 29	2 346 491	1 185 017	1 161 474	...	...	...	...	...	...
30 - 34	2 258 625	1 130 184	1 128 441	...	...	...	...	...	...
35 - 39	2 299 544	1 158 771	1 140 773	...	...	...	...	...	...
40 - 44	2 481 778	1 250 190	1 231 588	...	...	...	...	...	...
45 - 49	2 788 323	1 401 985	1 386 338	...	...	...	...	...	...
50 - 54	2 574 048	1 282 315	1 291 733	...	...	...	...	...	...
55 - 59	2 216 080	1 092 743	1 123 337	...	...	...	...	...	...
60 - 64	1 887 459	926 027	961 432	...	...	...	...	...	...
65 - 69	1 406 551	681 567	724 984	...	...	...	...	...	...
70 - 74	1 079 982	506 768	573 214	...	...	...	...	...	...
75 - 79	907 976	408 994	498 982	...	...	...	...	...	...
80 - 84	676 169	275 423	400 746	...	...	...	...	...	...
85 - 89	412 449	143 610	268 839	...	...	...	...	...	...
90 - 94	154 854	43 655	111 199	...	...	...	...	...	...
95 - 99	42 097	9 513	32 584	...	...	...	...	...	...
100 +	5 946	1 180	4 766	...	...	...	...	...	...
Cayman Islands - Îles Caïmanes									
31 XII 2009 (ESDJ)									
Total	52 830	26 255	26 575	...	...	...	...	...	...
0 - 4	3 930	2 030	1 900	...	...	...	...	...	...
5 - 9	2 960	1 615	1 345	...	...	...	...	...	...
10 - 14	3 050	1 670	1 380	...	...	...	...	...	...
15 - 19	2 800	1 365	1 435	...	...	...	...	...	...
20 - 24	2 425	1 180	1 245	...	...	...	...	...	...
25 - 29	4 845	2 095	2 750	...	...	...	...	...	...
30 - 34	5 620	2 775	2 845	...	...	...	...	...	...
35 - 39	6 010	2 970	3 040	...	...	...	...	...	...
40 - 44	5 225	2 735	2 490	...	...	...	...	...	...
45 - 49	5 310	2 720	2 590	...	...	...	...	...	...
50 - 54	3 320	1 575	1 745	...	...	...	...	...	...
55 - 59	3 090	1 420	1 670	...	...	...	...	...	...

7. Population by age, sex and urban/rural residence: latest available year, 2000 - 2009
Population selon l'âge, le sexe et la résidence, urbaine/rurale : dernière année disponible, 2000 - 2009 (continued - suite)

Continent, country or area, date, code and age (in years) / Continent, pays ou zone, date, code et âge (en années)	Total			Urban - Urbaine			Rural - Rurale		
	Both sexes Les deux sexes	Male Masculin	Female Féminin	Both sexes Les deux sexes	Male Masculin	Female Féminin	Both sexes Les deux sexes	Male Masculin	Female Féminin
AMERICA, NORTH - AMÉRIQUE DU NORD									
Cayman Islands - Îles Caïmanes									
31 XII 2009 (ESDJ)									
60 - 64	1 425	820	605	...	...	...	...	...	...
65 +	2 820	1 285	1 535	...	...	...	...	...	...
Costa Rica[15]									
1 VII 2009 (ESDJ)									
Total	4 620 482	2 291 886	2 328 596	2 722 273	1 325 468	1 396 805	1 898 209	966 418	931 791
0 - 4	339 497	180 857	158 640	176 549	94 063	82 486	162 948	86 794	76 154
5 - 9	360 073	186 330	173 743	195 734	101 067	94 667	164 339	85 263	79 076
10 - 14	423 306	221 337	201 969	223 523	116 799	106 724	199 783	104 538	95 245
15 - 19	469 195	244 551	224 644	259 277	133 132	126 145	209 918	111 419	98 499
20 - 24	462 317	238 724	223 593	283 200	147 152	136 048	179 117	91 572	87 545
25 - 29	391 394	195 616	195 778	242 060	121 249	120 811	149 334	74 367	74 967
30 - 39	619 623	291 521	328 102	352 092	164 847	187 245	267 531	126 674	140 857
40 - 49	620 165	294 361	325 804	377 015	172 914	204 101	243 150	121 447	121 703
50 - 59	461 585	213 794	247 791	301 442	135 574	165 868	160 143	78 220	81 923
60 - 69	242 885	119 936	122 949	154 467	70 498	83 969	88 418	49 438	38 980
70 +	227 010	103 187	123 823	155 318	67 612	87 706	71 692	35 575	36 117
Unknown - Inconnu	3 432	1 672	1 760	1 596	561	1 035	1 836	1 111	725
Cuba[16]									
1 VII 2009 (ESDJ)									
Total	11 239 363	5 629 345	5 610 018	8 469 528	4 169 181	4 300 347	2 769 835	1 460 163	1 309 671
0 - 4	588 927	303 975	284 952	441 138	227 802	213 335	147 789	76 173	71 616
5 - 9	682 162	351 046	331 116	495 329	254 922	240 407	186 833	96 124	90 708
10 - 14	702 235	361 333	340 901	512 803	263 580	249 223	189 431	97 753	91 678
15 - 19	802 182	412 160	390 022	589 662	301 455	288 207	212 520	110 705	101 815
20 - 24	814 267	420 041	394 226	607 387	310 835	296 552	206 880	109 206	97 674
25 - 29	677 520	351 005	326 515	503 678	259 172	244 506	173 841	91 832	82 009
30 - 34	767 866	394 409	373 457	564 418	289 195	275 223	203 448	105 214	98 234
35 - 39	1 030 481	522 197	508 284	765 488	384 572	380 916	264 992	137 625	127 367
40 - 44	1 068 730	532 443	536 286	812 642	398 392	414 249	256 088	134 051	122 037
45 - 49	915 262	452 841	462 420	713 015	346 348	366 667	202 246	106 493	95 753
50 - 54	641 575	313 006	328 568	495 011	235 563	259 448	146 564	77 443	69 120
55 - 59	618 405	302 141	316 264	483 105	229 780	253 325	135 300	72 361	62 939
60 - 64	542 989	261 165	281 824	424 220	198 314	225 906	118 768	62 850	55 918
65 - 69	460 143	223 518	236 624	356 195	166 350	189 845	103 948	57 168	46 779
70 - 74	344 221	165 931	178 290	264 534	121 171	143 363	79 687	44 760	34 927
75 - 79	247 651	115 557	132 094	188 840	82 115	106 724	58 811	33 441	25 370
80 - 84	171 125	76 941	94 184	130 447	53 747	76 700	40 678	23 194	17 484
85 +	163 618	69 631	93 987	121 612	45 865	75 747	42 006	23 766	18 240
Dominica - Dominique									
31 XII 2006 (ESDF)									
Total	71 180	36 238	34 942	...	...	...	...	...	...
0 - 4	6 317	3 250	3 067	...	...	...	...	...	...
5 - 9	7 554	3 951	3 603	...	...	...	...	...	...
10 - 14	7 105	3 558	3 547	...	...	...	...	...	...
15 - 19	6 818	3 452	3 366	...	...	...	...	...	...
20 - 24	4 578	2 438	2 140	...	...	...	...	...	...
25 - 29	5 121	2 601	2 520	...	...	...	...	...	...
30 - 34	5 663	2 886	2 777	...	...	...	...	...	...
35 - 39	5 296	2 841	2 455	...	...	...	...	...	...
40 - 44	4 476	2 417	2 059	...	...	...	...	...	...
45 - 49	3 561	1 947	1 614	...	...	...	...	...	...
50 - 54	2 820	1 467	1 353	...	...	...	...	...	...
55 - 59	2 391	1 209	1 182	...	...	...	...	...	...
60 - 64	2 255	1 022	1 233	...	...	...	...	...	...
65 - 69	2 324	1 091	1 233	...	...	...	...	...	...
70 - 74	1 844	871	973	...	...	...	...	...	...
75 - 79	1 332	596	736	...	...	...	...	...	...
80 - 84	901	354	547	...	...	...	...	...	...
85 +	825	288	537	...	...	...	...	...	...

7. Population by age, sex and urban/rural residence: latest available year, 2000 - 2009
Population selon l'âge, le sexe et la résidence, urbaine/rurale : dernière année disponible, 2000 - 2009 (continued - suite)

Continent, country or area, date, code and age (in years) / Continent, pays ou zone, date, code et âge (en années)	Total			Urban - Urbaine			Rural - Rurale		
	Both sexes Les deux sexes	Male Masculin	Female Féminin	Both sexes Les deux sexes	Male Masculin	Female Féminin	Both sexes Les deux sexes	Male Masculin	Female Féminin
AMERICA, NORTH - AMÉRIQUE DU NORD									
Dominican Republic - République dominicaine[2]									
1 VII 2009 (ESDF)									
Total	9 755 954	4 872 903	4 883 051	6 420 260	3 181 903	3 238 357	3 335 694	1 691 000	1 644 694
0 - 4	1 065 734	543 457	522 277	684 266	353 389	330 877	381 468	190 068	191 400
5 - 9	1 040 879	529 868	511 011	656 905	337 414	319 491	383 974	192 454	191 520
10 - 14	997 704	506 318	491 386	637 440	322 723	314 717	360 264	183 595	176 669
15 - 19	974 151	491 877	482 274	643 394	321 307	322 087	330 757	170 570	160 187
20 - 24	894 505	446 498	448 007	607 887	300 644	307 243	286 618	145 854	140 764
25 - 29	807 584	398 802	408 782	554 186	272 680	281 506	253 398	126 122	127 276
30 - 34	706 573	346 151	360 422	481 523	234 890	246 633	225 050	111 261	113 789
35 - 39	634 821	311 393	323 428	432 053	210 477	221 576	202 768	100 916	101 852
40 - 44	568 087	280 482	287 605	381 617	186 406	195 211	186 470	94 076	92 394
45 - 49	500 309	248 191	252 118	334 480	163 502	170 978	165 829	84 689	81 140
50 - 54	418 776	208 309	210 467	274 500	134 363	140 137	144 276	73 946	70 330
55 - 59	328 555	163 212	165 343	212 815	103 680	109 135	115 740	59 532	56 208
60 - 64	246 856	121 905	124 951	156 596	74 820	81 776	90 260	47 085	43 175
65 - 69	190 448	93 521	96 927	120 262	56 975	63 287	70 186	36 546	33 640
70 - 74	156 908	76 262	80 646	98 117	45 383	52 734	58 791	30 879	27 912
75 - 79	110 694	53 245	57 449	70 041	31 583	38 458	40 653	21 662	18 991
80 +	113 370	53 412	59 958	74 178	31 667	42 511	39 192	21 745	17 447
El Salvador									
12 V 2007 (CDJC)									
Total	5 744 113	2 719 371	3 024 742	3 598 836	1 676 313	1 922 523	2 145 277	1 043 058	1 102 219
0 - 4	555 893	283 272	272 621	324 299	165 397	158 902	231 594	117 875	113 719
5 - 9	684 727	349 150	335 577	390 873	199 184	191 689	293 854	149 966	143 888
10 - 14	706 347	359 523	346 824	404 755	205 222	199 533	301 592	154 301	147 291
15 - 19	600 565	298 384	302 181	355 376	174 488	180 888	245 189	123 896	121 293
20 - 24	486 542	228 001	258 541	309 107	143 779	165 328	177 435	84 222	93 213
25 - 29	457 890	206 963	250 927	306 456	138 320	168 136	151 434	68 643	82 791
30 - 34	402 249	178 400	223 849	274 037	121 278	152 759	128 212	57 122	71 090
35 - 39	353 147	156 514	196 633	242 566	106 882	135 684	110 581	49 632	60 949
40 - 44	303 631	132 218	171 413	209 958	90 559	119 399	93 673	41 659	52 014
45 - 49	252 122	109 957	142 165	170 464	73 027	97 437	81 658	36 930	44 728
50 - 54	215 734	95 275	120 459	143 882	62 014	81 868	71 852	33 261	38 591
55 - 59	183 075	81 718	101 357	119 193	51 574	67 619	63 882	30 144	33 738
60 - 64	151 864	68 207	83 657	97 101	41 821	55 280	54 763	26 386	28 377
65 - 69	125 157	55 781	69 376	79 690	33 492	46 198	45 467	22 289	23 178
70 - 74	97 457	43 449	54 008	62 075	25 726	36 349	35 382	17 723	17 659
75 - 79	75 984	33 658	42 326	48 760	20 096	28 664	27 224	13 562	13 662
80 - 84	46 870	20 401	26 469	30 578	12 261	18 317	16 292	8 140	8 152
85 +	44 859	18 500	26 359	29 666	11 193	18 473	15 193	7 307	7 886
1 VII 2009 (ESDF)[17]									
Total	6 152 558	2 903 737	3 248 821	...	...	...	...	...	...
0 - 4	608 413	310 918	297 495	...	...	...	...	...	...
5 - 9	636 013	325 062	310 951	...	...	...	...	...	...
10 - 14	741 852	378 460	363 392	...	...	...	...	...	...
15 - 19	687 518	343 438	344 079	...	...	...	...	...	...
20 - 24	553 272	260 316	292 956	...	...	...	...	...	...
25 - 29	457 768	203 480	254 288	...	...	...	...	...	...
30 - 34	413 256	180 505	232 751	...	...	...	...	...	...
35 - 39	382 815	167 718	215 097	...	...	...	...	...	...
40 - 44	333 997	145 973	188 024	...	...	...	...	...	...
45 - 49	283 927	123 650	160 277	...	...	...	...	...	...
50 - 54	240 648	105 747	134 901	...	...	...	...	...	...
55 - 59	206 650	91 328	115 322	...	...	...	...	...	...
60 - 64	173 431	76 794	96 637	...	...	...	...	...	...
65 - 69	143 670	64 142	79 528	...	...	...	...	...	...
70 - 74	115 281	51 097	64 184	...	...	...	...	...	...
75 - 79	82 906	36 461	46 445	...	...	...	...	...	...
80 +	91 141	38 647	52 494	...	...	...	...	...	...

Continent, country or area, date, code and age (in years) / Continent, pays ou zone, date, code et âge (en années)	Total			Urban - Urbaine			Rural - Rurale		
	Both sexes Les deux sexes	Male Masculin	Female Féminin	Both sexes Les deux sexes	Male Masculin	Female Féminin	Both sexes Les deux sexes	Male Masculin	Female Féminin
AMERICA, NORTH - AMÉRIQUE DU NORD									
Greenland - Groenland[18]									
1 VII 2009 (ESDJ)									
Total	56 323	29 873	26 451	47 230	24 865	22 366	9 093	5 008	4 085
0	845	446	399	...	...	...	...	...	...
1 - 4	3 274	1 672	1 602	2 702	1 373	1 329	572	299	273
5 - 9	4 198	2 119	2 079	3 433	1 732	1 701	765	387	379
10 - 14	4 601	2 334	2 268	3 757	1 930	1 827	845	404	441
15 - 19	4 586	2 315	2 272	3 807	1 920	1 887	780	395	385
20 - 24	4 318	2 193	2 125	3 671	1 839	1 832	647	355	293
25 - 29	3 874	2 022	1 853	3 282	1 687	1 595	592	335	258
30 - 34	3 328	1 777	1 552	2 819	1 482	1 337	509	295	215
35 - 39	3 535	1 958	1 578	2 989	1 660	1 329	547	298	249
40 - 44	5 481	2 956	2 525	4 638	2 478	2 161	843	478	365
45 - 49	5 191	2 803	2 388	4 430	2 345	2 086	761	458	303
50 - 54	4 069	2 330	1 740	3 420	1 935	1 486	649	395	254
55 - 59	3 006	1 725	1 281	2 518	1 424	1 094	488	302	187
60 - 64	2 257	1 365	893	1 933	1 157	776	325	208	117
65 - 69	1 713	941	773	1 423	776	647	290	165	126
70 - 74	1 001	508	493	822	414	408	179	94	85
75 - 79	659	280	379	565	238	327	94	43	52
80 - 84	292	106	186	254	91	164	38	16	23
85 - 89	76	25	52	63	19	45	13	6	7
90 - 94	20	3	18	19	3	17	1	-	1
95 +	4	1	3	4	1	3	-	-	-
Grenada - Grenade									
1 VII 2000 (ESDF)									
Total	101 308	50 200	51 108	...	...	...	...	...	...
0 - 4	10 412	5 292	5 120	...	...	...	...	...	...
5 - 9	11 547	5 798	5 749	...	...	...	...	...	...
10 - 14	13 546	6 837	6 709	...	...	...	...	...	...
15 - 19	11 911	6 077	5 834	...	...	...	...	...	...
20 - 24	9 267	4 686	4 581	...	...	...	...	...	...
25 - 29	7 290	3 883	3 407	...	...	...	...	...	...
30 - 34	5 977	2 999	2 978	...	...	...	...	...	...
35 - 39	6 537	3 294	3 243	...	...	...	...	...	...
40 - 44	5 364	2 628	2 736	...	...	...	...	...	...
45 - 49	3 780	1 955	1 825	...	...	...	...	...	...
50 - 54	2 904	1 371	1 533	...	...	...	...	...	...
55 - 59	2 472	1 160	1 312	...	...	...	...	...	...
60 - 64	2 383	1 078	1 305	...	...	...	...	...	...
65 - 69	2 356	1 010	1 346	...	...	...	...	...	...
70 +	5 562	2 132	3 430	...	...	...	...	...	...
Guadeloupe[19]									
1 I 2009 (ESDJ)									
Total	403 257	188 317	214 940	...	...	...	...	...	...
0 - 4	27 697	14 312	13 385	...	...	...	...	...	...
5 - 9	30 395	15 592	14 803	...	...	...	...	...	...
10 - 14	32 249	16 753	15 496	...	...	...	...	...	...
15 - 19	31 621	16 108	15 513	...	...	...	...	...	...
20 - 24	21 363	10 810	10 553	...	...	...	...	...	...
25 - 29	19 150	8 333	10 817	...	...	...	...	...	...
30 - 34	23 254	9 572	13 682	...	...	...	...	...	...
35 - 39	30 217	12 947	17 270	...	...	...	...	...	...
40 - 44	32 328	14 251	18 077	...	...	...	...	...	...
45 - 49	32 077	14 944	17 133	...	...	...	...	...	...
50 - 54	26 328	12 154	14 174	...	...	...	...	...	...
55 - 59	23 786	10 877	12 909	...	...	...	...	...	...
60 - 64	20 404	9 528	10 876	...	...	...	...	...	...
65 - 69	15 336	6 820	8 516	...	...	...	...	...	...
70 - 74	12 840	5 811	7 029	...	...	...	...	...	...
75 - 79	9 664	3 997	5 667	...	...	...	...	...	...
80 - 84	7 383	2 969	4 414	...	...	...	...	...	...
85 - 89	4 408	1 656	2 752	...	...	...	...	...	...

Continent, country or area, date, code and age (in years) / Continent, pays ou zone, date, code et âge (en années)	Total			Urban - Urbaine			Rural - Rurale		
	Both sexes Les deux sexes	Male Masculin	Female Féminin	Both sexes Les deux sexes	Male Masculin	Female Féminin	Both sexes Les deux sexes	Male Masculin	Female Féminin
AMERICA, NORTH - AMÉRIQUE DU NORD									
Guadeloupe[19]									
1 I 2009 (ESDJ)									
90 - 94	1 955	617	1 338	...	...	...	...	...	...
95 +	802	266	536	...	...	...	...	...	...
Guatemala									
1 VII 2005 (ESDF)									
Total	12 699 780[20]	6 197 399	6 502 381	6 345 918	3 059 570	3 286 348	6 353 862	3 137 829	3 216 033
0 - 4	2 036 312	1 035 549	1 000 763	866 844	447 724	419 120	1 169 468	587 825	581 643
5 - 9	1 823 642	921 924	901 718	790 225	405 750	384 475	1 033 417	516 174	517 243
10 - 14	1 624 119	815 791	808 328	755 292	378 704	376 587	868 827	437 087	431 741
15 - 19	1 379 574	685 359	694 215	715 501	351 554	363 947	664 073	333 805	330 268
20 - 24	1 180 264	571 385	608 879	636 046	306 874	329 172	544 218	264 511	279 707
25 - 29	952 695	446 309	506 386	523 699	243 461	280 237	428 996	202 848	226 149
30 - 34	753 145	340 378	412 767	416 357	184 973	231 384	336 788	155 405	181 383
35 - 39	600 160	270 907	329 253	326 576	144 824	181 752	273 584	126 083	147 501
40 - 44	492 747	225 243	267 504	270 162	120 913	149 248	222 585	104 330	118 256
45 - 49	409 688	191 635	218 053	221 123	100 439	120 685	188 565	91 196	97 368
50 - 54	367 062	175 311	191 751	201 790	92 775	109 014	165 272	82 536	82 737
55 - 59	310 913	149 593	161 320	171 480	79 044	92 436	139 433	70 549	68 884
60 - 64	233 643	113 686	119 957	128 803	58 925	69 878	104 840	54 761	50 079
65 - 69	192 992	94 128	98 864	111 865	51 579	60 285	81 127	42 549	38 579
70 - 74	156 267	74 463	81 804	93 750	42 080	51 669	62 517	32 383	30 135
75 - 79	107 429	50 340	57 089	66 759	29 241	37 519	40 670	21 099	19 570
80 +	79 128	35 398	43 730	49 648	20 709	28 939	29 480	14 689	14 791
Haiti - Haïti[21]									
1 VII 2009 (ESDJ)									
Total	9 923 243	4 912 515	5 010 728	...	...	...	...	...	...
0 - 4	1 257 220	641 323	615 897	...	...	...	...	...	...
5 - 9	1 191 597	606 522	585 076	...	...	...	...	...	...
10 - 14	1 151 880	585 088	566 791	...	...	...	...	...	...
15 - 19	1 084 883	547 441	537 442	...	...	...	...	...	...
20 - 24	1 010 426	504 019	506 407	...	...	...	...	...	...
25 - 29	889 173	438 068	451 105	...	...	...	...	...	...
30 - 34	671 707	324 475	347 232	...	...	...	...	...	...
35 - 39	534 885	255 016	279 869	...	...	...	...	...	...
40 - 44	480 384	231 606	248 779	...	...	...	...	...	...
45 - 49	411 831	198 890	212 941	...	...	...	...	...	...
50 - 54	334 252	162 201	172 051	...	...	...	...	...	...
55 - 59	273 665	130 339	143 326	...	...	...	...	...	...
60 - 64	202 889	94 252	108 637	...	...	...	...	...	...
65 - 69	173 339	80 595	92 744	...	...	...	...	...	...
70 - 74	126 020	56 614	69 405	...	...	...	...	...	...
75 - 79	78 000	34 334	43 666	...	...	...	...	...	...
80 +	51 092	21 730	29 362	...	...	...	...	...	...
Honduras[22]									
1 VII 2007 (ESDF)									
Total	7 536 952	3 717 577	3 819 375	3 752 579	1 793 588	1 958 991	3 784 373	1 923 989	1 860 384
0 - 4	1 063 247	541 070	522 177	478 059	243 771	234 288	585 188	297 299	287 889
5 - 9	1 009 399	511 733	497 666	432 422	221 023	211 399	576 977	290 710	286 267
10 - 14	920 850	464 403	456 447	414 394	208 459	205 935	506 456	255 944	250 512
15 - 19	802 793	402 792	400 001	398 138	192 053	206 085	404 655	210 739	193 916
20 - 24	710 751	353 317	357 434	390 899	179 723	211 176	319 852	173 594	146 258
25 - 29	626 413	308 283	318 130	352 025	165 114	186 911	274 388	143 169	131 219
30 - 34	522 679	255 818	266 861	286 860	136 186	150 674	235 819	119 632	116 187
35 - 39	425 045	205 171	219 874	235 598	109 749	125 849	189 447	95 422	94 025
40 - 44	334 632	157 492	177 140	184 004	84 081	99 923	150 628	73 411	77 217
45 - 49	276 277	128 813	147 464	149 861	67 682	82 179	126 416	61 131	65 285
50 - 54	227 421	105 428	121 993	118 577	52 986	65 591	108 844	52 442	56 402
55 - 59	180 676	83 643	97 033	92 810	40 714	52 096	87 866	42 929	44 937
60 - 64	137 652	63 863	73 789	67 361	29 245	38 116	70 291	34 618	35 673
65 - 69	107 540	49 404	58 136	52 443	22 197	30 246	55 097	27 207	27 890
70 - 74	82 118	37 134	44 984	41 131	17 107	24 024	40 987	20 027	20 960
75 - 79	54 593	24 368	30 225	28 183	11 568	16 615	26 410	12 800	13 610
80 +	54 866	24 845	30 021	29 814	11 930	17 884	25 052	12 915	12 137

Continent, country or area, date, code and age (in years) / Continent, pays ou zone, date, code et âge (en annèes)	Total			Urban - Urbaine			Rural - Rurale		
	Both sexes Les deux sexes	Male Masculin	Female Féminin	Both sexes Les deux sexes	Male Masculin	Female Féminin	Both sexes Les deux sexes	Male Masculin	Female Féminin
AMERICA, NORTH - AMÉRIQUE DU NORD									
Honduras[22]									
1 VII 2009 (ESDF)									
Total	7 876 662	3 882 957	3 993 705	...	...	...	...	...	...
0 - 4	1 075 674	547 358	528 316	...	...	...	...	...	...
5 - 9	1 027 477	521 762	505 715	...	...	...	...	...	...
10 - 14	956 965	483 279	473 686	...	...	...	...	...	...
15 - 19	844 670	423 933	420 737	...	...	...	...	...	...
20 - 24	733 986	364 969	369 017	...	...	...	...	...	...
25 - 29	652 082	320 599	331 483	...	...	...	...	...	...
30 - 34	559 944	273 682	286 262	...	...	...	...	...	...
35 - 39	458 038	222 042	235 996	...	...	...	...	...	...
40 - 44	365 205	173 051	192 154	...	...	...	...	...	...
45 - 49	292 212	135 752	156 460	...	...	...	...	...	...
50 - 54	243 565	112 654	130 911	...	...	...	...	...	...
55 - 59	195 638	89 985	105 653	...	...	...	...	...	...
60 - 64	150 400	69 192	81 208	...	...	...	...	...	...
65 - 69	113 954	52 184	61 770	...	...	...	...	...	...
70 - 74	87 455	39 358	48 097	...	...	...	...	...	...
75 - 79	59 546	26 341	33 205	...	...	...	...	...	...
80 +	59 851	26 816	33 035	...	...	...	...	...	...
Jamaica - Jamaïque[12]									
1 VII 2008 (ESDJ)									
Total	2 687 241	1 324 277	1 362 964	1 400 045[23]	667 050[23]	732 995[23]	1 287 196[23]	657 227[23]	629 969[23]
0	44 297	22 468	21 829	22 196[23]	11 351[23]	10 845[23]	22 101[23]	11 117[23]	10 984[23]
1 - 4	181 099	92 187	88 912	91 926[23]	46 791[23]	45 135[23]	89 173[23]	45 396[23]	43 777[23]
5 - 9	251 187	127 655	123 532	123 448[23]	62 326[23]	61 122[23]	127 739[23]	65 329[23]	62 410[23]
10 - 14	277 844	143 534	134 310	136 577[23]	70 150[23]	66 427[23]	141 267[23]	73 384[23]	67 883[23]
15 - 19	249 369	127 495	121 874	127 634[23]	63 829[23]	63 805[23]	121 735[23]	63 666[23]	58 069[23]
20 - 24	208 353	101 013	107 340	115 717[23]	54 318[23]	61 399[23]	92 636[23]	46 695[23]	45 941[23]
25 - 29	215 094	102 110	112 984	121 404[23]	55 338[23]	66 065[23]	93 690[23]	46 772[23]	46 919[23]
30 - 34	220 090	104 166	115 924	123 412[23]	56 019[23]	67 393[23]	96 678[23]	48 147[23]	48 531[23]
35 - 39	224 563	106 101	118 462	124 820[23]	56 218[23]	68 601[23]	99 743[23]	49 883[23]	49 861[23]
40 - 44	190 733	94 542	96 191	103 696[23]	48 612[23]	55 084[23]	87 037[23]	45 930[23]	41 107[23]
45 - 49	131 943	65 412	66 531	72 029[23]	33 813[23]	38 216[23]	59 914[23]	31 599[23]	28 315[23]
50 - 54	114 111	59 675	54 436	60 494[23]	29 973[23]	30 521[23]	53 617[23]	29 702[23]	23 915[23]
55 - 59	84 706	44 394	40 312	42 647[23]	21 207[23]	21 441[23]	42 059[23]	23 187[23]	18 871[23]
60 - 64	68 305	33 356	34 949	33 038[23]	15 293[23]	17 745[23]	35 267[23]	18 063[23]	17 204[23]
65 - 69	64 678	31 159	33 519	30 110[23]	13 714[23]	16 396[23]	34 568[23]	17 445[23]	17 123[23]
70 - 74	58 668	27 832	30 836	26 697[23]	11 959[23]	14 738[23]	31 971[23]	15 873[23]	16 098[23]
75 - 79	44 935	19 592	25 343	19 830[23]	7 912[23]	11 918[23]	25 105[23]	11 680[23]	13 425[23]
80 - 84	28 688	11 395	17 293	12 227[23]	4 465[23]	7 762[23]	16 461[23]	6 930[23]	9 532[23]
85 - 89	17 762	6 637	11 125	7 535[23]	2 460[23]	5 075[23]	10 227[23]	4 177[23]	6 050[23]
90 - 94	7 204	2 454	4 750	3 094[23]	908[23]	2 186[23]	4 110[23]	1 546[23]	2 564[23]
95 +	3 612	1 100	2 512	1 515[23]	393[23]	1 122[23]	2 097[23]	707[23]	1 390[23]
1 VII 2009 (ESDJ)									
Total	2 695 583	1 328 124	1 367 460	...	...	...	...	...	...
0 - 4	223 127	113 345	109 783	...	...	...	...	...	...
5 - 9	244 571	124 326	120 245	...	...	...	...	...	...
10 - 14	277 121	143 578	133 543	...	...	...	...	...	...
15 - 19	249 106	127 502	121 604	...	...	...	...	...	...
20 - 24	207 744	100 666	107 078	...	...	...	...	...	...
25 - 29	215 461	102 256	113 205	...	...	...	...	...	...
30 - 34	222 419	105 207	117 212	...	...	...	...	...	...
35 - 39	228 388	107 383	121 005	...	...	...	...	...	...
40 - 44	195 061	96 825	98 236	...	...	...	...	...	...
45 - 49	134 038	66 542	67 496	...	...	...	...	...	...
50 - 54	116 077	60 895	55 182	...	...	...	...	...	...
55 - 59	85 663	45 054	40 609	...	...	...	...	...	...
60 - 64	68 445	33 442	35 003	...	...	...	...	...	...
65 - 69	65 096	31 362	33 734	...	...	...	...	...	...
70 - 74	59 369	28 154	31 216	...	...	...	...	...	...
75 +	103 901	41 589	62 312	...	...	...	...	...	...

Continent, country or area, date, code and age (in years) / Continent, pays ou zone, date, code et âge (en années)	Total			Urban - Urbaine			Rural - Rurale		
	Both sexes Les deux sexes	Male Masculin	Female Féminin	Both sexes Les deux sexes	Male Masculin	Female Féminin	Both sexes Les deux sexes	Male Masculin	Female Féminin
AMERICA, NORTH - AMÉRIQUE DU NORD									
Martinique									
1 I 2009 (ESDJ)									
Total	398 733	184 148	214 585	...	...	...	...	...	...
0 - 4	24 281	12 346	11 935	...	...	...	...	...	...
5 - 9	27 135	13 431	13 704	...	...	...	...	...	...
10 - 14	28 174	14 087	14 087	...	...	...	...	...	...
15 - 19	30 874	15 300	15 574	...	...	...	...	...	...
20 - 24	23 399	11 736	11 663	...	...	...	...	...	...
25 - 29	18 490	8 332	10 158	...	...	...	...	...	...
30 - 34	21 043	8 795	12 248	...	...	...	...	...	...
35 - 39	28 609	12 313	16 296	...	...	...	...	...	...
40 - 44	33 091	14 450	18 641	...	...	...	...	...	...
45 - 49	32 750	14 998	17 752	...	...	...	...	...	...
50 - 54	27 786	12 941	14 845	...	...	...	...	...	...
55 - 59	24 113	11 031	13 082	...	...	...	...	...	...
60 - 64	20 667	9 634	11 033	...	...	...	...	...	...
65 - 69	16 289	7 531	8 758	...	...	...	...	...	...
70 - 74	14 977	6 733	8 244	...	...	...	...	...	...
75 - 79	11 005	4 757	6 248	...	...	...	...	...	...
80 - 84	8 314	3 255	5 059	...	...	...	...	...	...
85 - 89	4 715	1 685	3 030	...	...	...	...	...	...
90 - 94	2 147	604	1 543	...	...	...	...	...	...
95 +	874	189	685	...	...	...	...	...	...
Mexico - Mexique									
17 X 2005 (CDJC)									
Total	103 263 388	50 249 955	53 013 433	78 986 852	38 300 417	40 686 435	24 276 536	11 949 538	12 326 998
0	1 866 929	953 071	913 858	1 375 346	701 965	673 381	491 583	251 106	240 477
1 - 4	8 319 314	4 222 842	4 096 472	6 099 968	3 098 431	3 001 537	2 219 346	1 124 411	1 094 935
5 - 9	10 511 738	5 339 127	5 172 611	7 612 581	3 868 547	3 744 034	2 899 157	1 470 580	1 428 577
10 - 14	10 952 123	5 545 910	5 406 213	7 809 172	3 950 685	3 858 487	3 142 951	1 595 225	1 547 726
15 - 19	10 109 021	4 995 906	5 113 115	7 519 867	3 724 606	3 795 261	2 589 154	1 271 300	1 317 854
20 - 24	8 964 629	4 253 440	4 711 189	7 051 808	3 376 247	3 675 561	1 912 821	877 193	1 035 628
25 - 29	8 103 358	3 805 724	4 297 634	6 430 726	3 033 228	3 397 498	1 672 632	772 496	900 136
30 - 34	7 933 951	3 745 974	4 187 977	6 362 249	3 001 742	3 360 507	1 571 702	744 232	827 470
35 - 39	7 112 526	3 371 372	3 741 154	5 690 767	2 688 582	3 002 185	1 421 759	682 790	738 969
40 - 44	6 017 268	2 871 549	3 145 719	4 827 524	2 293 754	2 533 770	1 189 744	577 795	611 949
45 - 49	5 015 255	2 388 149	2 627 106	3 986 038	1 885 334	2 100 704	1 029 217	502 815	526 402
50 - 54	4 090 650	1 959 720	2 130 930	3 227 317	1 530 942	1 696 375	863 333	428 778	434 555
55 - 59	3 117 071	1 497 981	1 619 090	2 392 022	1 135 166	1 256 856	725 049	362 815	362 234
60 - 64	2 622 476	1 243 788	1 378 688	1 935 880	900 574	1 035 306	686 596	343 214	343 382
65 - 69	1 958 069	922 592	1 035 477	1 428 290	654 658	773 632	529 779	267 934	261 845
70 - 74	1 496 691	703 277	793 414	1 082 372	489 557	592 815	414 319	213 720	200 599
75 - 79	1 048 315	490 840	557 475	747 992	334 692	413 300	300 323	156 148	144 175
80 - 84	657 011	296 351	360 660	468 965	201 082	267 883	188 046	95 269	92 777
85 - 89	345 154	150 617	194 537	244 298	100 594	143 704	100 856	50 023	50 833
90 - 94	132 325	54 391	77 934	93 124	35 731	57 393	39 201	18 660	20 541
95 - 99	61 145	24 439	36 706	40 465	14 930	25 535	20 680	9 509	11 171
100 +	17 649	6 696	10 953	10 007	3 491	6 516	7 642	3 205	4 437
Unknown - Inconnu	2 810 720	1 406 199	1 404 521	2 550 074	1 275 879	1 274 195	260 646	130 320	130 326
1 VII 2009 (ESDJ)[2]									
Total	107 550 697	52 853 788	54 696 909	...	...	...	...	...	...
0	1 912 061	977 520	934 541	...	...	...	...	...	...
1 - 4	7 666 518	3 915 791	3 750 727	...	...	...	...	...	...
5 - 9	10 516 386	5 374 135	5 142 251	...	...	...	...	...	...
10 - 14	10 811 348	5 494 769	5 316 579	...	...	...	...	...	...
15 - 19	10 476 241	5 258 308	5 217 933	...	...	...	...	...	...
20 - 24	9 739 057	4 806 019	4 933 038	...	...	...	...	...	...
25 - 29	9 005 870	4 361 376	4 644 494	...	...	...	...	...	...
30 - 34	8 511 267	4 103 896	4 407 371	...	...	...	...	...	...
35 - 39	7 998 010	3 871 608	4 126 402	...	...	...	...	...	...
40 - 44	7 117 771	3 455 284	3 662 487	...	...	...	...	...	...
45 - 49	6 065 202	2 938 418	3 126 784	...	...	...	...	...	...
50 - 54	4 883 209	2 349 818	2 533 391	...	...	...	...	...	...
55 - 59	3 754 820	1 789 172	1 965 648	...	...	...	...	...	...

Continent, country or area, date, code and age (in years) — Continent, pays ou zone, date, code et âge (en années)	Total			Urban - Urbaine			Rural - Rurale		
	Both sexes Les deux sexes	Male Masculin	Female Féminin	Both sexes Les deux sexes	Male Masculin	Female Féminin	Both sexes Les deux sexes	Male Masculin	Female Féminin
AMERICA, NORTH - AMÉRIQUE DU NORD									
Mexico - Mexique									
1 VII 2009 (ESDJ)[2]									
60 - 64	2 899 036	1 365 580	1 533 456	...	...	...	...	...	...
65 - 69	2 210 896	1 026 665	1 184 231	...	...	...	...	...	...
70 - 74	1 616 270	737 286	878 984	...	...	...	...	...	...
75 - 79	1 102 767	491 703	611 064	...	...	...	...	...	...
80 - 84	682 552	295 770	386 782	...	...	...	...	...	...
85 - 89	367 894	154 541	213 353	...	...	...	...	...	...
90 - 94	151 889	61 909	89 980	...	...	...	...	...	...
95 +	61 633	24 220	37 413	...	...	...	...	...	...
Montserrat									
12 V 2001 (CDFC)									
Total	4 491	2 418	2 073	...	...	...	...	...	...
0 - 4	311	153	158	...	...	...	...	...	...
5 - 9	277	153	124	...	...	...	...	...	...
10 - 14	281	148	133	...	...	...	...	...	...
15 - 19	273	149	124	...	...	...	...	...	...
20 - 24	206	113	93	...	...	...	...	...	...
25 - 29	319	169	150	...	...	...	...	...	...
30 - 34	346	176	170	...	...	...	...	...	...
35 - 39	382	211	171	...	...	...	...	...	...
40 - 44	325	171	154	...	...	...	...	...	...
45 - 49	335	196	139	...	...	...	...	...	...
50 - 54	282	170	112	...	...	...	...	...	...
55 - 59	239	136	103	...	...	...	...	...	...
60 - 64	203	108	95	...	...	...	...	...	...
65 - 69	148	76	72	...	...	...	...	...	...
70 - 74	169	94	75	...	...	...	...	...	...
75 - 79	139	72	67	...	...	...	...	...	...
80 - 84	107	47	60	...	...	...	...	...	...
85 - 89	67	32	35	...	...	...	...	...	...
90 - 94	38	14	24	...	...	...	...	...	...
95 +	21	9	12	...	...	...	...	...	...
Unknown - Inconnu	23	21	2	...	...	...	...	...	...
Netherlands Antilles - Antilles néerlandaises[24]									
1 I 2009 (ESDJ)									
Total	199 999	93 395	106 604	...	...	...	...	...	...
0 - 4	13 652	7 018	6 634	...	...	...	...	...	...
5 - 9	14 810	7 473	7 337	...	...	...	...	...	...
10 - 14	15 136	7 622	7 514	...	...	...	...	...	...
15 - 19	14 851	7 402	7 449	...	...	...	...	...	...
20 - 24	10 939	5 330	5 609	...	...	...	...	...	...
25 - 29	11 429	5 215	6 214	...	...	...	...	...	...
30 - 34	13 030	6 044	6 986	...	...	...	...	...	...
35 - 39	15 957	7 395	8 562	...	...	...	...	...	...
40 - 44	17 106	7 736	9 370	...	...	...	...	...	...
45 - 49	17 196	7 806	9 390	...	...	...	...	...	...
50 - 54	14 533	6 535	7 998	...	...	...	...	...	...
55 - 59	12 159	5 426	6 733	...	...	...	...	...	...
60 - 64	9 464	4 292	5 172	...	...	...	...	...	...
65 - 69	6 730	2 961	3 769	...	...	...	...	...	...
70 - 74	5 335	2 319	3 016	...	...	...	...	...	...
75 - 79	3 633	1 456	2 177	...	...	...	...	...	...
80 - 84	2 200	819	1 381	...	...	...	...	...	...
85 +	1 839	546	1 293	...	...	...	...	...	...
Nicaragua									
1 VII 2009 (ESDJ)									
Total	5 742 316[12]	2 844 244	2 898 072	3 259 955	1 569 555	1 690 400	2 482 361	1 274 689	1 207 672
0 - 4	680 125[12]	347 205	332 920	335 635	172 875	162 760	344 490	174 330	170 160
5 - 9	660 096[12]	336 817	323 279	332 694	169 358	163 336	327 402	167 459	159 943
10 - 14	677 756[12]	344 831	332 925	359 316	180 457	178 859	318 440	164 374	154 066
15 - 19	660 608[12]	331 536	329 072	363 427	178 690	184 737	297 181	152 846	144 335
20 - 24	576 923[12]	286 484	290 439	332 187	160 315	171 872	244 736	126 169	118 567

Continent, country or area, date, code and age (in years) / Continent, pays ou zone, date, code et âge (en années)	Total			Urban - Urbaine			Rural - Rurale		
	Both sexes Les deux sexes	Male Masculin	Female Féminin	Both sexes Les deux sexes	Male Masculin	Female Féminin	Both sexes Les deux sexes	Male Masculin	Female Féminin
AMERICA, NORTH - AMÉRIQUE DU NORD									
Nicaragua									
1 VII 2009 (ESDJ)									
25 - 29	511 402[12]	250 672	260 730	306 186	145 137	161 049	205 216	105 535	99 681
30 - 34	412 087[12]	197 120	214 967	251 145	115 523	135 622	160 942	81 597	79 345
35 - 39	337 317[12]	162 472	174 845	208 505	96 540	111 965	128 812	65 932	62 880
40 - 44	279 795[12]	136 223	143 572	177 594	83 709	93 885	102 201	52 514	49 687
45 - 49	239 942[12]	115 914	124 028	154 027	71 955	82 072	85 915	43 959	41 956
50 - 54	206 088[12]	98 355	107 733	130 198	59 417	70 781	75 890	38 938	36 952
55 - 59	154 329[12]	74 173	80 156	95 879	43 653	52 226	58 450	30 520	27 930
60 - 64	93 681[12]	45 221	48 460	57 189	25 734	31 455	36 492	19 487	17 005
65 - 69	89 351[12]	43 121	46 230	54 102	24 079	30 023	35 249	19 042	16 207
70 - 74	67 861[12]	32 418	35 443	41 515	18 145	23 370	26 346	14 273	12 073
75 - 79	48 205[12]	22 249	25 956	30 640	12 935	17 705	17 565	9 314	8 251
80 +	46 750[12]	19 433	27 317	29 716	11 033	18 683	17 034	8 400	8 634
Panama[25]									
1 VII 2009 (ESDF)									
Total	3 450 349	1 738 965	1 711 384	2 221 211	1 098 484	1 122 727	1 229 138	640 481	588 657
0 - 4	350 531	179 010	171 521	207 391	106 037	101 354	143 140	72 973	70 167
0	70 700	36 122	34 578	...	...	...	...	...	...
1 - 4	279 831	142 888	136 943	...	...	...	...	...	...
5 - 9	339 697	173 432	166 265	201 809	103 100	98 709	137 888	70 332	67 556
10 - 14	325 520	166 183	159 337	187 349	95 553	91 796	138 171	70 630	67 541
15 - 19	305 562	155 782	149 780	183 511	93 107	90 404	122 051	62 675	59 376
20 - 24	295 474	150 191	145 283	191 318	95 968	95 350	104 156	54 223	49 933
25 - 29	274 347	138 978	135 369	190 234	93 996	96 238	84 113	44 982	39 131
30 - 34	262 621	132 424	130 197	187 337	93 004	94 333	75 284	39 420	35 864
35 - 39	257 058	129 033	128 025	179 076	89 013	90 063	77 982	40 020	37 962
40 - 44	231 288	115 918	115 370	160 790	79 201	81 589	70 498	36 717	33 781
45 - 49	195 349	97 280	98 069	136 050	65 825	70 225	59 299	31 455	27 844
50 - 54	159 614	79 019	80 595	109 657	52 368	57 289	49 957	26 651	23 306
55 - 59	129 188	64 043	65 145	86 479	41 035	45 444	42 709	23 008	19 701
60 - 64	103 017	51 342	51 675	65 715	30 998	34 717	37 302	20 344	16 958
65 - 69	80 593	39 761	40 832	49 058	22 713	26 345	31 535	17 048	14 487
70 - 74	58 431	28 463	29 968	34 195	15 280	18 915	24 236	13 183	11 053
75 - 79	41 913	19 962	21 951	24 957	10 735	14 222	16 956	9 227	7 729
80 +	40 146	18 144	22 002	26 285	10 551	15 734	13 861	7 593	6 268
Puerto Rico - Porto Rico[26]									
1 VII 2009 (ESDJ)									
Total	3 967 288	1 903 370	2 063 918	...	...	...	...	...	...
0 - 4	233 691	119 429	114 262	...	...	...	...	...	...
5 - 9	260 426	132 854	127 572	...	...	...	...	...	...
10 - 14	291 798	149 570	142 228	...	...	...	...	...	...
15 - 19	297 392	151 364	146 028	...	...	...	...	...	...
20 - 24	275 340	138 058	137 282	...	...	...	...	...	...
25 - 29	281 421	139 300	142 121	...	...	...	...	...	...
30 - 34	275 122	133 915	141 207	...	...	...	...	...	...
35 - 39	265 055	128 841	136 214	...	...	...	...	...	...
40 - 44	262 641	125 277	137 364	...	...	...	...	...	...
45 - 49	263 933	123 363	140 570	...	...	...	...	...	...
50 - 54	249 827	115 029	134 798	...	...	...	...	...	...
55 - 59	230 532	105 104	125 428	...	...	...	...	...	...
60 - 64	220 707	100 330	120 377	...	...	...	...	...	...
65 - 69	175 199	78 840	96 359	...	...	...	...	...	...
70 - 74	139 546	62 586	76 960	...	...	...	...	...	...
75 - 79	102 144	43 910	58 234	...	...	...	...	...	...
80 - 84	72 482	29 408	43 074	...	...	...	...	...	...
85 - 89	43 691	16 835	26 856	...	...	...	...	...	...
90 - 94	19 081	6 939	12 142	...	...	...	...	...	...
95 - 99	6 179	2 085	4 094	...	...	...	...	...	...
100 +	1 081	333	748	...	...	...	...	...	...

Continent, country or area, date, code and age (in years) / Continent, pays ou zone, date, code et âge (en années)	Total			Urban - Urbaine			Rural - Rurale		
	Both sexes Les deux sexes	Male Masculin	Female Féminin	Both sexes Les deux sexes	Male Masculin	Female Féminin	Both sexes Les deux sexes	Male Masculin	Female Féminin
AMERICA, NORTH - AMÉRIQUE DU NORD									
Saint Kitts and Nevis - Saint-Kitts-et-Nevis									
1 VII 2000 (ESDF)									
Total	40 410	20 400	20 010	...	...	...	...	...	...
0 - 4	4 250	2 130	2 120	...	...	...	...	...	...
5 - 9	4 100	2 140	1 960	...	...	...	...	...	...
10 - 14	4 040	2 120	1 920	...	...	...	...	...	...
15 - 19	3 870	2 000	1 870	...	...	...	...	...	...
20 - 24	3 620	1 880	1 740	...	...	...	...	...	...
25 - 29	3 240	1 640	1 600	...	...	...	...	...	...
30 - 34	3 100	1 550	1 550	...	...	...	...	...	...
35 - 39	2 910	1 430	1 480	...	...	...	...	...	...
40 - 44	2 520	1 270	1 250	...	...	...	...	...	...
45 - 49	1 880	900	980	...	...	...	...	...	...
50 - 54	1 390	710	680	...	...	...	...	...	...
55 - 59	1 100	560	540	...	...	...	...	...	...
60 - 64	820	400	420	...	...	...	...	...	...
65 - 69	840	410	430	...	...	...	...	...	...
70 - 74	810	380	430	...	...	...	...	...	...
75 - 79	700	330	370	...	...	...	...	...	...
80 - 84	470	240	230	...	...	...	...	...	...
85 +	750	310	440	...	...	...	...	...	...
Saint Lucia - Sainte-Lucie									
22 V 2001 (CDFC)									
Total	157 164	76 741	80 423	42 310	20 208	22 102	111 559	54 897	56 662
0	973	458	515	238	120	118	735	338	397
1 - 4	12 958	6 485	6 473	3 203	1 627	1 576	9 755	4 858	4 897
5 - 9	16 382	8 260	8 122	3 906	1 963	1 943	12 476	6 297	6 179
10 - 14	16 605	8 323	8 282	4 023	2 005	2 018	12 582	6 318	6 264
15 - 19	16 348	8 051	8 297	4 296	2 116	2 180	12 052	5 935	6 117
20 - 24	13 369	6 635	6 734	3 886	1 947	1 939	9 483	4 688	4 795
25 - 29	12 572	6 112	6 460	3 592	1 788	1 804	8 980	4 324	4 656
30 - 34	11 419	5 652	5 767	2 822	1 481	1 341	8 597	4 171	4 426
35 - 39	11 167	5 397	5 770	3 238	1 576	1 662	7 929	3 821	4 108
40 - 44	9 041	4 410	4 631	2 531	1 193	1 338	6 510	3 217	3 293
45 - 49	6 811	3 401	3 410	2 109	995	1 114	4 702	2 406	2 296
50 - 54	5 830	2 926	2 904	1 958	1 000	958	3 872	1 926	1 946
55 - 59	4 479	2 103	2 376	1 353	599	754	3 126	1 504	1 622
60 - 64	3 856	1 788	2 068	1 030	416	614	2 826	1 372	1 454
65 - 69	3 573	1 661	1 912	1 043	440	603	2 530	1 221	1 309
70 - 74	2 776	1 326	1 450	909	399	510	1 867	927	940
75 - 79	2 217	991	1 226	684	283	401	1 533	708	825
80 - 84	1 570	647	923	483	176	307	1 087	471	616
85 - 89	897	352	545	272	81	191	625	271	354
90 - 94	323	128	195	120	39	81	203	89	114
95 +	143	53	90	54	18	36	89	35	54
1 VII 2007 (ESDF)									
Total	168 338	82 426	85 912	...	...	...	...	...	...
0 - 4	14 625	7 389	7 236	...	...	...	...	...	...
5 - 9	14 012	6 932	7 080	...	...	...	...	...	...
10 - 14	16 891	8 509	8 382	...	...	...	...	...	...
15 - 19	17 592	8 790	8 802	...	...	...	...	...	...
20 - 24	16 793	8 225	8 568	...	...	...	...	...	...
25 - 29	14 136	6 953	7 183	...	...	...	...	...	...
30 - 34	12 914	6 229	6 685	...	...	...	...	...	...
35 - 39	11 807	5 700	6 107	...	...	...	...	...	...
40 - 44	11 511	5 557	5 954	...	...	...	...	...	...
45 - 49	9 705	4 720	4 985	...	...	...	...	...	...
50 - 54	7 159	3 609	3 550	...	...	...	...	...	...
55 - 59	5 444	2 683	2 761	...	...	...	...	...	...
60 - 64	4 295	1 977	2 318	...	...	...	...	...	...
65 - 69	3 571	1 643	1 928	...	...	...	...	...	...
70 - 74	3 109	1 439	1 670	...	...	...	...	...	...

Continent, country or area, date, code and age (in years) / Continent, pays ou zone, date, code et âge (en années)	Total			Urban - Urbaine			Rural - Rurale		
	Both sexes Les deux sexes	Male Masculin	Female Féminin	Both sexes Les deux sexes	Male Masculin	Female Féminin	Both sexes Les deux sexes	Male Masculin	Female Féminin
AMERICA, NORTH - AMÉRIQUE DU NORD									
Saint Lucia - Sainte-Lucie									
1 VII 2007 (ESDF)									
75 - 79	2 143	970	1 173	...	...	...	...	...	...
80 +	2 631	1 101	1 530	...	...	...	...	...	...
Saint Pierre and Miquelon - Saint Pierre-et-Miquelon									
19 I 2006 (CDFC)									
Total	6 125	3 034	3 091	...	...	...	...	...	...
0 - 4	289	143	146	...	...	...	...	...	...
5 - 9	417	211	206	...	...	...	...	...	...
10 - 14	461	237	224	...	...	...	...	...	...
15 - 19	366	188	178	...	...	...	...	...	...
20 - 24	258	136	122	...	...	...	...	...	...
25 - 29	333	166	167	...	...	...	...	...	...
30 - 34	431	202	229	...	...	...	...	...	...
35 - 39	568	294	274	...	...	...	...	...	...
40 - 44	575	293	282	...	...	...	...	...	...
45 - 49	471	246	225	...	...	...	...	...	...
50 - 54	435	238	197	...	...	...	...	...	...
55 - 59	432	231	201	...	...	...	...	...	...
60 - 64	280	143	137	...	...	...	...	...	...
65 - 69	243	115	128	...	...	...	...	...	...
70 - 74	208	83	125	...	...	...	...	...	...
75 - 79	128	42	86	...	...	...	...	...	...
80 - 84	114	35	79	...	...	...	...	...	...
85 - 89	75	19	56	...	...	...	...	...	...
90 - 94	30	12	18	...	...	...	...	...	...
95 +	11	-	11	...	...	...	...	...	...
Saint Vincent and the Grenadines - Saint-Vincent-et-les Grenadines[12]									
1 VII 2008 (ESDF)									
Total	99 086	50 009	49 077	...	...	...	...	...	...
0 - 4	9 302	4 782	4 520	...	...	...	...	...	...
5 - 9	10 684	5 352	5 332	...	...	...	...	...	...
10 - 14	10 391	5 269	5 122	...	...	...	...	...	...
15 - 19	10 531	5 293	5 238	...	...	...	...	...	...
20 - 24	9 060	4 639	4 420	...	...	...	...	...	...
25 - 29	7 941	4 057	3 884	...	...	...	...	...	...
30 - 34	7 155	3 747	3 408	...	...	...	...	...	...
35 - 39	7 525	3 911	3 614	...	...	...	...	...	...
40 - 44	6 243	3 214	3 029	...	...	...	...	...	...
45 - 49	4 410	2 252	2 158	...	...	...	...	...	...
50 - 54	3 481	1 807	1 674	...	...	...	...	...	...
55 - 59	2 595	1 299	1 296	...	...	...	...	...	...
60 - 64	2 550	1 222	1 328	...	...	...	...	...	...
65 - 69	2 379	1 143	1 236	...	...	...	...	...	...
70 - 74	1 819	831	989	...	...	...	...	...	...
75 - 79	1 412	591	821	...	...	...	...	...	...
80 - 84	879	359	520	...	...	...	...	...	...
85 +	729	241	488	...	...	...	...	...	...
Trinidad and Tobago - Trinité-et-Tobago[27]									
1 VII 2009 (ESDF)									
Total	1 310 106	...	...	...	...	...	...	...	...
0 - 14	332 036	...	...	...	...	...	...	...	...
15 - 19	143 714	...	...	...	...	...	...	...	...
20 - 24	116 215	...	...	...	...	...	...	...	...
25 - 29	100 258	...	...	...	...	...	...	...	...
30 - 34	95 680	...	...	...	...	...	...	...	...
35 - 39	106 452	...	...	...	...	...	...	...	...
40 - 44	93 789	...	...	...	...	...	...	...	...
45 - 49	77 652	...	...	...	...	...	...	...	...

Continent, country or area, date, code and age (in years) / Continent, pays ou zone, date, code et âge (en années)	Total			Urban - Urbaine			Rural - Rurale		
	Both sexes Les deux sexes	Male Masculin	Female Féminin	Both sexes Les deux sexes	Male Masculin	Female Féminin	Both sexes Les deux sexes	Male Masculin	Female Féminin
AMERICA, NORTH - AMÉRIQUE DU NORD									
Trinidad and Tobago - Trinité-et-Tobago[27]									
1 VII 2009 (ESDF)									
50 - 54	64 794	...	...	...	...	...	...	...	...
55 - 59	48 256	...	...	...	...	...	...	...	...
60 - 64	38 512	...	...	...	...	...	...	...	...
65 +	92 748	...	...	...	...	...	...	...	...
Turks and Caicos Islands - Îles Turques et Caïques									
10 IX 2001 (CDFC)									
Total	19 886	9 897	9 989	...	...	...	...	...	...
0	775	258	517	...	...	...	...	...	...
1 - 4	1 550	795	754	...	...	...	...	...	...
5 - 9	1 731	850	882	...	...	...	...	...	...
10 - 14	1 637	833	804	...	...	...	...	...	...
15 - 19	1 288	636	652	...	...	...	...	...	...
20 - 24	1 376	634	741	...	...	...	...	...	...
25 - 29	2 024	1 001	1 023	...	...	...	...	...	...
30 - 34	2 317	1 177	1 139	...	...	...	...	...	...
35 - 39	2 070	1 073	998	...	...	...	...	...	...
40 - 44	1 590	827	763	...	...	...	...	...	...
45 - 49	1 167	610	557	...	...	...	...	...	...
50 - 54	809	440	370	...	...	...	...	...	...
55 - 59	507	283	224	...	...	...	...	...	...
60 - 64	288	145	143	...	...	...	...	...	...
65 - 69	240	114	125	...	...	...	...	...	...
70 - 74	198	75	123	...	...	...	...	...	...
75 - 79	129	53	76	...	...	...	...	...	...
80 - 84	110	55	55	...	...	...	...	...	...
85 - 89	58	33	25	...	...	...	...	...	...
90 - 94	19	2	17	...	...	...	...	...	...
95 +	4	3	2	...	...	...	...	...	...
United States of America - États-Unis d'Amérique[28]									
1 IV 2000 (CDJC)									
Total	281 421 906	138 053 563	143 368 343	222 360 539	108 375 797	113 984 742	59 061 367	29 677 766	29 383 601
0	3 805 648	1 949 017	1 856 631	3 108 179	1 591 301	1 516 878	697 469	357 716	339 753
1 - 4	15 370 150	7 861 716	7 508 434	12 426 799	6 352 829	6 073 970	2 943 351	1 508 887	1 434 464
5 - 9	20 549 505	10 523 277	10 026 228	16 303 052	8 338 164	7 964 888	4 246 453	2 185 113	2 061 340
10 - 14	20 528 072	10 520 197	10 007 875	15 865 132	8 114 898	7 750 234	4 662 940	2 405 299	2 257 641
15 - 19	20 219 890	10 391 004	9 828 886	15 862 692	8 092 790	7 769 902	4 357 198	2 298 214	2 058 984
20 - 24	18 964 001	9 687 814	9 276 187	16 062 564	8 150 162	7 912 402	2 901 437	1 537 652	1 363 785
25 - 29	19 381 336	9 798 760	9 582 576	16 247 338	8 210 254	8 037 084	3 133 998	1 588 506	1 545 492
30 - 34	20 510 388	10 321 769	10 188 619	16 761 355	8 449 017	8 312 338	3 749 033	1 872 752	1 876 281
35 - 39	22 706 664	11 318 696	11 387 968	17 967 717	8 957 072	9 010 645	4 738 947	2 361 624	2 377 323
40 - 44	22 441 863	11 129 102	11 312 761	17 434 999	8 608 239	8 826 760	5 006 864	2 520 863	2 486 001
45 - 49	20 092 404	9 889 506	10 202 898	15 431 618	7 528 331	7 903 287	4 660 786	2 361 175	2 299 611
50 - 54	17 585 548	8 607 724	8 977 824	13 395 145	6 480 878	6 914 267	4 190 403	2 126 846	2 063 557
55 - 59	13 469 237	6 508 729	6 960 508	10 060 185	4 791 948	5 268 237	3 409 052	1 716 781	1 692 271
60 - 64	10 805 447	5 136 627	5 668 820	8 026 903	3 738 462	4 288 441	2 778 544	1 398 165	1 380 379
65 - 69	9 533 545	4 400 362	5 133 183	7 180 256	3 236 555	3 943 701	2 353 289	1 163 807	1 189 482
70 - 74	8 857 441	3 902 912	4 954 529	6 865 515	2 943 669	3 921 846	1 991 926	959 243	1 032 683
75 - 79	7 415 813	3 044 456	4 371 357	5 901 375	2 367 269	3 534 106	1 514 438	677 187	837 251
80 - 84	4 945 367	1 834 897	3 110 470	3 982 799	1 445 556	2 537 243	962 568	389 341	573 227
85 - 89	2 789 818	876 501	1 913 317	2 274 316	695 943	1 578 373	515 502	180 558	334 944
90 - 94	1 112 531	282 325	830 206	920 357	227 019	693 338	192 174	55 306	136 868
95 - 99	286 784	58 115	228 669	239 942	47 265	192 677	46 842	10 850	35 992
100 +	50 454	10 057	40 397	42 301	8 176	34 125	8 153	1 881	6 272
1 VII 2009 (ESDJ)									
Total	307 006 550	151 449 490	155 557 060	...	...	...	...	...	...
0	4 261 494	2 178 512	2 082 982	...	...	...	...	...	...
1 - 4	17 038 162	8 708 496	8 329 666	...	...	...	...	...	...
5 - 9	20 609 634	10 535 900	10 073 734	...	...	...	...	...	...
10 - 14	19 973 564	10 222 522	9 751 042	...	...	...	...	...	...

Continent, country or area, date, code and age (in years) / Continent, pays ou zone, date, code et âge (en années)	Total			Urban - Urbaine			Rural - Rurale		
	Both sexes Les deux sexes	Male Masculin	Female Féminin	Both sexes Les deux sexes	Male Masculin	Female Féminin	Both sexes Les deux sexes	Male Masculin	Female Féminin
AMERICA, NORTH - AMÉRIQUE DU NORD									
United States of America - États-Unis d'Amérique[28] 1 VII 2009 (ESDJ)									
15 - 19	21 537 837	11 051 289	10 486 548	...	...	...	...	...	...
20 - 24	21 539 559	11 093 552	10 446 007	...	...	...	...	...	...
25 - 29	21 677 719	11 115 560	10 562 159	...	...	...	...	...	...
30 - 34	19 888 603	10 107 974	9 780 629	...	...	...	...	...	...
35 - 39	20 538 351	10 353 016	10 185 335	...	...	...	...	...	...
40 - 44	20 991 605	10 504 139	10 487 466	...	...	...	...	...	...
45 - 49	22 831 092	11 295 524	11 535 568	...	...	...	...	...	...
50 - 54	21 761 391	10 677 847	11 083 544	...	...	...	...	...	...
55 - 59	18 975 026	9 204 666	9 770 360	...	...	...	...	...	...
60 - 64	15 811 923	7 576 933	8 234 990	...	...	...	...	...	...
65 - 69	11 784 320	5 511 164	6 273 156	...	...	...	...	...	...
70 - 74	9 007 747	4 082 226	4 925 521	...	...	...	...	...	...
75 - 79	7 325 528	3 149 236	4 176 292	...	...	...	...	...	...
80 - 84	5 822 334	2 298 260	3 524 074	...	...	...	...	...	...
85 - 89	3 662 397	1 266 899	2 395 498	...	...	...	...	...	...
90 - 94	1 502 263	424 882	1 077 381	...	...	...	...	...	...
95 - 99	401 977	82 135	319 842	...	...	...	...	...	...
100 +	64 024	8 758	55 266	...	...	...	...	...	...
United States Virgin Islands - Îles Vierges américaines[26] 1 VII 2008 (ESDJ)									
Total	109 840	52 045	57 795	...	...	...	...	...	...
0 - 4	7 352	3 781	3 571	...	...	...	...	...	...
5 - 9	7 487	3 859	3 628	...	...	...	...	...	...
10 - 14	8 249	4 058	4 191	...	...	...	...	...	...
15 - 19	8 358	4 114	4 244	...	...	...	...	...	...
20 - 24	6 741	3 075	3 666	...	...	...	...	...	...
25 - 29	5 703	2 600	3 103	...	...	...	...	...	...
30 - 34	5 866	2 595	3 271	...	...	...	...	...	...
35 - 39	7 316	3 265	4 051	...	...	...	...	...	...
40 - 44	7 873	3 728	4 145	...	...	...	...	...	...
45 - 49	8 200	3 907	4 293	...	...	...	...	...	...
50 - 54	7 712	3 609	4 103	...	...	...	...	...	...
55 - 59	7 381	3 469	3 912	...	...	...	...	...	...
60 - 64	7 555	3 673	3 882	...	...	...	...	...	...
65 - 69	5 368	2 607	2 761	...	...	...	...	...	...
70 - 74	3 775	1 713	2 062	...	...	...	...	...	...
75 - 79	2 414	1 066	1 348	...	...	...	...	...	...
80 +	2 490	926	1 564	...	...	...	...	...	...
AMERICA, SOUTH - AMÉRIQUE DU SUD									
Argentina - Argentine 1 VII 2009 (ESDF)									
Total	40 134 425	19 657 086	20 477 339	36 553 965	17 810 843	18 743 122	3 580 460	1 846 243	1 734 217
0 - 4	3 403 145	1 731 906	1 671 239	3 004 102	1 536 198	1 467 904	399 043	195 708	203 335
5 - 9	3 330 005	1 693 267	1 636 738	2 936 518	1 499 905	1 436 613	393 487	193 362	200 125
10 - 14	3 428 408	1 742 200	1 686 208	3 056 869	1 558 594	1 498 275	371 539	183 606	187 933
15 - 19	3 440 578	1 746 747	1 693 831	3 115 423	1 578 132	1 537 291	325 155	168 615	156 540
20 - 24	3 324 013	1 683 868	1 640 145	3 049 349	1 540 757	1 508 592	274 664	143 111	131 553
25 - 29	3 218 927	1 621 994	1 596 933	2 974 786	1 496 242	1 478 544	244 141	125 752	118 389
30 - 34	3 178 957	1 592 477	1 586 480	2 935 061	1 466 794	1 468 267	243 896	125 683	118 213
35 - 39	2 633 229	1 314 010	1 319 219	2 427 445	1 204 718	1 222 727	205 784	109 292	96 492
40 - 44	2 337 919	1 160 710	1 177 209	2 149 738	1 058 229	1 091 509	188 181	102 481	85 700
45 - 49	2 203 867	1 079 970	1 123 897	2 024 587	982 497	1 042 090	179 280	97 473	81 807
50 - 54	2 050 513	982 902	1 067 611	1 881 789	891 806	989 983	168 724	91 096	77 628
55 - 59	1 872 711	892 548	980 163	1 718 693	807 360	911 333	154 018	85 188	68 830
60 - 64	1 590 473	743 658	846 815	1 457 832	670 548	787 284	132 641	73 110	59 531
65 - 69	1 302 162	590 001	712 161	1 200 290	534 873	665 417	101 872	55 128	46 744

Continent, country or area, date, code and age (in years) / Continent, pays ou zone, date, code et âge (en années)	Total			Urban - Urbaine			Rural - Rurale		
	Both sexes Les deux sexes	Male Masculin	Female Féminin	Both sexes Les deux sexes	Male Masculin	Female Féminin	Both sexes Les deux sexes	Male Masculin	Female Féminin
AMERICA, SOUTH - AMÉRIQUE DU SUD									
Argentina - Argentine									
1 VII 2009 (ESDF)									
70 - 74	1 059 580	451 135	608 445	981 404	410 450	570 954	78 176	40 685	37 491
75 - 79	838 996	328 715	510 281	781 209	299 415	481 794	57 787	29 300	28 487
80 +	920 942	300 978	619 964	858 870	274 325	584 545	62 072	26 653	35 419
Bolivia (Plurinational State of) - Bolivie (État plurinational de)									
1 VII 2009 (ESDF)									
Total	10 227 299	5 101 733	5 125 566	6 748 075	3 283 616	3 464 459	3 479 224	1 818 118	1 661 106
0 - 4	1 300 028	662 908	637 120	805 250	407 537	397 713	494 778	255 371	239 407
5 - 9	1 246 963	635 511	611 452	780 085	392 565	387 520	466 878	242 946	223 932
10 - 14	1 161 669	591 928	569 742	755 554	376 224	379 330	406 115	215 703	190 412
15 - 19	1 089 169	553 645	535 524	767 015	377 488	389 527	322 154	176 157	145 998
20 - 24	945 438	478 021	467 418	686 900	339 263	347 636	258 539	138 757	119 781
25 - 29	824 039	413 804	410 235	586 874	286 594	300 279	237 165	127 210	109 956
30 - 34	724 219	360 533	363 686	508 071	244 738	263 333	216 149	115 796	100 353
35 - 39	635 807	313 829	321 978	434 542	207 023	227 519	201 264	106 806	94 458
40 - 44	516 697	253 484	263 213	349 321	165 762	183 559	167 376	87 722	79 654
45 - 49	429 396	208 765	220 631	278 792	131 250	147 542	150 604	77 515	73 089
50 - 54	361 500	173 823	187 677	228 306	106 119	122 187	133 194	67 704	65 490
55 - 59	294 286	139 345	154 941	176 751	80 749	96 002	117 535	58 597	58 938
60 - 64	235 691	110 601	125 091	135 288	60 434	74 854	100 403	50 167	50 236
65 - 69	177 237	81 857	95 379	98 472	43 452	55 020	78 765	38 405	40 360
70 - 74	134 587	60 381	74 206	73 989	31 617	42 372	60 598	28 764	31 834
75 - 79	88 187	38 187	50 000	49 223	20 098	29 125	38 964	18 089	20 875
80 +	62 385	25 111	37 274	33 644	12 703	20 940	28 742	12 408	16 334
Brazil - Brésil[29]									
1 VIII 2000 (CDJC)									
Total	169 799 170	83 576 015	86 223 155	137 953 959	66 882 993	71 070 966	31 845 211	16 693 022	15 152 189
0	3 213 310	1 635 916	1 577 394	2 518 464	1 282 941	1 235 523	694 846	352 975	341 871
1 - 4	13 162 418	6 691 010	6 471 408	10 242 356	5 207 423	5 034 933	2 920 062	1 483 587	1 436 475
5 - 9	16 542 327	8 402 353	8 139 974	12 821 519	6 500 814	6 320 705	3 720 808	1 901 539	1 819 269
10 - 14	17 348 067	8 777 639	8 570 428	13 530 190	6 803 898	6 726 292	3 817 877	1 973 741	1 844 136
15 - 19	17 939 815	9 019 130	8 920 685	14 403 539	7 132 822	7 270 717	3 536 276	1 886 308	1 649 968
20 - 24	16 141 515	8 048 218	8 093 297	13 352 132	6 549 365	6 802 767	2 789 383	1 498 853	1 290 530
25 - 29	13 849 665	6 814 328	7 035 337	11 570 969	5 606 425	5 964 544	2 278 696	1 207 903	1 070 793
30 - 34	13 028 944	6 363 983	6 664 961	10 918 396	5 248 443	5 669 953	2 110 548	1 115 540	995 008
35 - 39	12 261 529	5 955 875	6 305 654	10 326 271	4 929 130	5 397 141	1 935 258	1 026 745	908 513
40 - 44	10 546 694	5 116 439	5 430 255	8 913 019	4 249 804	4 663 215	1 633 675	866 635	767 040
45 - 49	8 721 541	4 216 418	4 505 123	7 309 621	3 472 375	3 837 246	1 411 920	744 043	667 877
50 - 54	7 062 601	3 415 678	3 646 923	5 833 659	2 764 708	3 068 951	1 228 942	650 970	577 972
55 - 59	5 444 715	2 585 244	2 859 471	4 387 995	2 032 135	2 355 860	1 056 720	553 109	503 611
60 - 64	4 600 929	2 153 209	2 447 720	3 712 213	1 676 323	2 035 890	888 716	476 886	411 830
65 - 69	3 581 106	1 639 325	1 941 781	2 916 899	1 284 812	1 632 087	664 207	354 513	309 694
70 - 74	2 742 302	1 229 329	1 512 973	2 249 617	966 115	1 283 502	492 685	263 214	229 471
75 - 79	1 779 587	780 571	999 016	1 456 665	610 767	845 898	322 922	169 804	153 118
80 - 84	1 036 034	428 501	607 533	841 798	331 002	510 796	194 236	97 499	96 737
85 - 89	534 871	208 088	326 783	436 121	160 379	275 742	98 750	47 709	51 041
90 - 94	180 426	65 117	115 309	147 784	50 531	97 253	32 642	14 586	18 056
95 - 99	56 198	19 221	36 977	45 682	14 899	30 783	10 516	4 322	6 194
100 +	24 576	10 423	14 153	19 050	7 882	11 168	5 526	2 541	2 985
1 VII 2009 (ESDF)									
Total	191 480 630	93 962 767	97 517 863	...	...	...	...	...	...
0	3 000 227	1 524 778	1 475 449	...	...	...	...	...	...
1 - 4	12 794 419	6 494 794	6 299 625	...	...	...	...	...	...
5 - 9	17 258 602	8 755 259	8 503 343	...	...	...	...	...	...
10 - 14	16 805 583	8 516 879	8 288 704	...	...	...	...	...	...
15 - 19	16 481 929	8 325 113	8 156 816	...	...	...	...	...	...
20 - 24	17 490 822	8 787 610	8 703 212	...	...	...	...	...	...
25 - 29	17 356 378	8 665 318	8 691 060	...	...	...	...	...	...
30 - 34	15 200 349	7 548 748	7 651 601	...	...	...	...	...	...
35 - 39	13 822 402	6 816 129	7 006 273	...	...	...	...	...	...
40 - 44	13 182 196	6 388 662	6 793 534	...	...	...	...	...	...

Continent, country or area, date, code and age (in years) / Continent, pays ou zone, date, code et âge (en années)	Total			Urban - Urbaine			Rural - Rurale		
	Both sexes Les deux sexes	Male Masculin	Female Féminin	Both sexes Les deux sexes	Male Masculin	Female Féminin	Both sexes Les deux sexes	Male Masculin	Female Féminin
AMERICA, SOUTH - AMÉRIQUE DU SUD									
Brazil - Brésil[29]									
1 VII 2009 (ESDF)									
45 - 49	12 049 293	5 714 413	6 334 880	...	...	...	...	...	...
50 - 54	9 769 342	4 594 571	5 174 771	...	...	...	...	...	...
55 - 59	7 653 346	3 561 155	4 092 191	...	...	...	...	...	...
60 - 64	5 841 863	2 696 319	3 145 544	...	...	...	...	...	...
65 - 69	4 465 584	2 015 020	2 450 564	...	...	...	...	...	...
70 - 74	3 470 174	1 542 151	1 928 023	...	...	...	...	...	...
75 - 79	2 303 523	977 694	1 325 829	...	...	...	...	...	...
80 +	2 534 598	1 038 154	1 496 444	...	...	...	...	...	...
Chile - Chili									
1 VII 2009 (ESDF)									
Total	16 928 873	8 379 571	8 549 302	14 719 246	7 204 720	7 514 526	2 209 627	1 174 851	1 034 776
0 - 4	1 246 153	634 688	611 465	1 089 805	554 814	534 991	156 348	79 874	76 474
5 - 9	1 255 622	639 236	616 386	1 100 181	559 524	540 657	155 441	79 712	75 729
10 - 14	1 360 847	692 423	668 424	1 179 244	599 151	580 093	181 603	93 272	88 331
15 - 19	1 483 285	754 005	729 280	1 279 846	648 409	631 437	203 439	105 596	97 843
20 - 24	1 434 300	727 419	706 881	1 242 025	625 060	616 965	192 275	102 359	89 916
25 - 29	1 290 814	652 331	638 483	1 134 794	565 866	568 928	156 020	86 465	69 555
30 - 34	1 183 619	594 839	588 780	1 046 980	520 935	526 045	136 639	73 904	62 735
35 - 39	1 236 753	618 253	618 500	1 086 277	538 139	548 138	150 476	80 114	70 362
40 - 44	1 237 907	615 994	621 913	1 076 534	529 597	546 937	161 373	86 397	74 976
45 - 49	1 217 407	602 792	614 615	1 056 531	514 406	542 125	160 876	88 386	72 490
50 - 54	1 029 693	506 436	523 257	896 782	432 329	464 453	132 911	74 107	58 804
55 - 59	808 286	392 769	415 517	703 313	334 530	368 783	104 973	58 239	46 734
60 - 64	652 743	310 845	341 898	563 786	262 325	301 461	88 957	48 520	40 437
65 - 69	518 000	239 492	278 508	442 114	198 861	243 253	75 886	40 631	35 255
70 - 74	381 112	168 801	212 311	320 293	136 693	183 600	60 819	32 108	28 711
75 - 79	287 389	119 035	168 354	241 549	95 648	145 901	45 840	23 387	22 453
80 +	304 943	110 213	194 730	259 192	88 433	170 759	45 751	21 780	23 971
Colombia - Colombie[30]									
1 VII 2009 (ESDF)									
Total	44 977 758	22 203 234	22 774 524	33 892 207	16 335 925	17 556 282	11 085 551	5 867 309	5 218 242
0 - 4	4 278 254	2 187 804	2 090 450	3 021 312	1 543 476	1 477 836	1 256 942	644 328	612 614
0	858 137	439 101	419 036	...	...	...	...	...	...
1 - 4	3 420 117	1 748 703	1 671 414	...	...	...	...	...	...
5 - 9	4 340 519	2 215 465	2 125 054	3 051 310	1 553 361	1 497 949	1 289 209	662 104	627 105
10 - 14	4 455 131	2 275 960	2 179 171	3 185 062	1 618 067	1 566 995	1 270 069	657 893	612 176
15 - 19	4 371 386	2 242 855	2 128 531	3 201 986	1 620 796	1 581 190	1 169 400	622 059	547 341
20 - 24	3 985 316	2 019 154	1 966 162	3 017 851	1 490 918	1 526 933	967 465	528 236	439 229
25 - 29	3 559 510	1 745 369	1 814 141	2 780 823	1 326 716	1 454 107	778 687	418 653	360 034
30 - 34	3 206 353	1 561 944	1 644 409	2 503 466	1 187 688	1 315 778	702 887	374 256	328 631
35 - 39	2 914 277	1 404 701	1 509 576	2 272 690	1 064 787	1 207 903	641 587	339 914	301 673
40 - 44	2 934 877	1 405 073	1 529 804	2 316 860	1 075 194	1 241 666	618 017	329 879	288 138
45 - 49	2 679 727	1 282 596	1 397 131	2 144 285	993 458	1 150 827	535 442	289 138	246 304
50 - 54	2 201 856	1 048 157	1 153 699	1 750 250	802 713	947 537	451 606	245 444	206 162
55 - 59	1 743 921	833 360	910 561	1 372 491	629 714	742 777	371 430	203 646	167 784
60 - 64	1 351 396	643 662	707 734	1 040 693	473 710	566 983	310 703	169 952	140 751
65 - 69	1 012 589	476 181	536 408	766 251	342 012	424 239	246 338	134 169	112 169
70 - 74	813 575	370 530	443 045	608 256	260 404	347 852	205 319	110 126	95 193
75 - 79	553 659	246 381	307 278	422 019	177 925	244 094	131 640	68 456	63 184
80 +	575 412	244 042	331 370	436 602	174 986	261 616	138 810	69 056	69 754
Ecuador - Équateur[31]									
1 VII 2009 (ESDF)									
Total	14 005 449	7 017 839	6 987 610	9 202 590	4 567 499	4 635 091	4 802 859	2 450 340	2 352 519
0 - 4	1 431 904	731 055	700 849	876 696	453 757	422 939	555 208	277 298	277 910
5 - 9	1 439 908	734 095	705 813	876 590	449 672	426 918	563 318	284 423	278 895
10 - 14	1 433 856	730 541	703 315	894 140	453 299	440 841	539 716	277 242	262 474
15 - 19	1 365 207	693 723	671 484	902 842	448 669	454 173	462 365	245 054	217 311
20 - 24	1 289 140	652 081	637 059	897 500	445 656	451 844	391 640	206 425	185 215
25 - 29	1 171 812	589 249	582 563	843 414	418 951	424 463	328 398	170 298	158 100
30 - 34	1 046 039	523 296	522 743	755 779	375 782	379 997	290 260	147 514	142 746
35 - 39	933 724	465 327	468 397	654 487	325 243	329 244	279 237	140 084	139 153
40 - 44	828 714	411 558	417 156	563 832	278 721	285 111	264 882	132 837	132 045

7. Population by age, sex and urban/rural residence: latest available year, 2000 - 2009
Population selon l'âge, le sexe et la résidence, urbaine/rurale : dernière année disponible, 2000 - 2009 (continued - suite)

Continent, country or area, date, code and age (in years) / Continent, pays ou zone, date, code et âge (en années)	Total			Urban - Urbaine			Rural - Rurale		
	Both sexes Les deux sexes	Male Masculin	Female Féminin	Both sexes Les deux sexes	Male Masculin	Female Féminin	Both sexes Les deux sexes	Male Masculin	Female Féminin
AMERICA, SOUTH - AMÉRIQUE DU SUD									
Ecuador - Équateur[31]									
1 VII 2009 (ESDF)									
45 - 49	713 368	353 306	360 062	463 586	227 821	235 765	249 782	125 485	124 297
50 - 54	609 201	300 377	308 824	388 346	189 001	199 345	220 855	111 376	109 479
55 - 59	506 872	248 614	258 258	321 332	153 885	167 447	185 540	94 729	90 811
60 - 64	370 066	180 411	189 655	230 807	109 007	121 800	139 259	71 404	67 855
65 - 69	295 531	142 059	153 472	183 319	84 949	98 370	112 212	57 110	55 102
70 - 74	232 861	109 964	122 897	143 107	64 655	78 452	89 754	45 309	44 445
75 - 79	170 927	79 060	91 867	104 903	46 095	58 808	66 024	32 965	33 059
80 +	166 319	73 123	93 196	101 910	42 336	59 574	64 409	30 787	33 622
Falkland Islands (Malvinas) - Îles Falkland (Malvinas)[32]									
8 X 2006 (CDFC)									
Total	2 955	1 569	1 386	...	...	...	...	...	...
0 - 4	156	79	77	...	...	...	...	...	...
5 - 9	161	75	86	...	...	...	...	...	...
10 - 14	154	71	83	...	...	...	...	...	...
15 - 19	155	90	65	...	...	...	...	...	...
20 - 24	207	89	118	...	...	...	...	...	...
25 - 29	232	126	106	...	...	...	...	...	...
30 - 34	266	131	135	...	...	...	...	...	...
35 - 39	291	165	126	...	...	...	...	...	...
40 - 44	261	156	105	...	...	...	...	...	...
45 - 49	249	128	121	...	...	...	...	...	...
50 - 54	215	123	92	...	...	...	...	...	...
55 - 59	194	113	81	...	...	...	...	...	...
60 - 64	148	87	61	...	...	...	...	...	...
65 - 69	98	57	41	...	...	...	...	...	...
70 - 74	68	36	32	...	...	...	...	...	...
75 - 79	48	18	30	...	...	...	...	...	...
80 +	52	25	27	...	...	...	...	...	...
French Guiana - Guyane française									
1 I 2009 (ESDJ)									
Total	225 751	111 764	113 987	...	...	...	...	...	...
0 - 4	28 534	14 544	13 990	...	...	...	...	...	...
5 - 9	27 082	13 719	13 363	...	...	...	...	...	...
10 - 14	23 705	12 081	11 624	...	...	...	...	...	...
15 - 19	20 978	10 410	10 568	...	...	...	...	...	...
20 - 24	15 962	7 573	8 389	...	...	...	...	...	...
25 - 29	16 410	7 555	8 855	...	...	...	...	...	...
30 - 34	16 627	7 958	8 669	...	...	...	...	...	...
35 - 39	16 868	8 118	8 750	...	...	...	...	...	...
40 - 44	14 977	7 444	7 533	...	...	...	...	...	...
45 - 49	12 770	6 450	6 320	...	...	...	...	...	...
50 - 54	10 073	5 198	4 875	...	...	...	...	...	...
55 - 59	7 736	3 850	3 886	...	...	...	...	...	...
60 - 64	5 092	2 799	2 293	...	...	...	...	...	...
65 - 69	3 231	1 542	1 689	...	...	...	...	...	...
70 - 74	2 194	1 083	1 111	...	...	...	...	...	...
75 - 79	1 571	681	890	...	...	...	...	...	...
80 - 84	1 092	416	676	...	...	...	...	...	...
85 - 89	568	219	349	...	...	...	...	...	...
90 - 94	206	89	117	...	...	...	...	...	...
95 +	75	35	40	...	...	...	...	...	...
Guyana									
15 IX 2002 (CDFC)									
Total	751 223	376 034	375 189	213 705	103 127	110 578	537 518	272 907	264 611
0 - 4	88 996	45 291	43 705	22 436	11 372	11 064	66 560	33 919	32 642
5 - 9	96 671	49 119	47 552	25 254	12 909	12 345	71 416	36 210	35 206
10 - 14	81 497	41 218	40 279	22 393	11 215	11 178	59 104	30 002	29 101
15 - 19	66 922	33 496	33 426	19 559	9 737	9 822	47 363	23 759	23 604
20 - 24	64 409	31 908	32 501	19 443	9 301	10 142	44 966	22 608	22 359
25 - 29	61 086	30 232	30 854	18 068	8 439	9 629	43 017	21 792	21 225

Continent, country or area, date, code and age (in years) / Continent, pays ou zone, date, code et âge (en années)	Total			Urban - Urbaine			Rural - Rurale		
	Both sexes Les deux sexes	Male Masculin	Female Féminin	Both sexes Les deux sexes	Male Masculin	Female Féminin	Both sexes Les deux sexes	Male Masculin	Female Féminin
AMERICA, SOUTH - AMÉRIQUE DU SUD									
Guyana									
15 IX 2002 (CDFC)									
30 - 34	57 942	29 088	28 854	16 403	7 687	8 717	41 538	21 401	20 137
35 - 39	52 735	26 441	26 295	14 716	6 779	7 937	38 020	19 662	18 358
40 - 44	46 488	23 338	23 150	13 203	6 194	7 009	33 285	17 144	16 141
45 - 49	35 810	17 952	17 859	10 609	4 910	5 699	25 202	13 042	12 160
50 - 54	28 149	14 207	13 942	8 459	4 008	4 450	19 690	10 198	9 492
55 - 59	18 129	8 980	9 149	5 539	2 628	2 911	12 590	6 352	6 238
60 - 64	15 005	7 191	7 813	4 540	2 081	2 459	10 465	5 110	5 354
65 - 69	11 741	5 575	6 167	3 671	1 649	2 021	8 071	3 925	4 145
70 - 74	8 543	3 965	4 578	2 784	1 212	1 571	5 759	2 753	3 006
75 +	11 746	5 217	6 529	3 977	1 640	2 337	7 769	3 577	4 192
Unknown - Inconnu	5 354	2 818	2 536	2 699	1 394	1 305	2 655	1 424	1 231
Paraguay[33]									
1 VII 2008 (ESDF)									
Total	6 230 143	3 149 475	3 080 668	3 597 588	1 758 138	1 839 450	2 632 555	1 391 337	1 241 218
0	148 736	75 881	72 855	...	...	...	...	...	...
1 - 4	586 306	298 652	287 655	319 965	162 577	157 388	266 342	136 075	130 267
5 - 9	717 813	365 319	352 495	391 720	198 122	193 598	326 093	167 196	158 897
10 - 14	695 085	353 531	341 554	372 499	186 968	185 531	322 586	166 563	156 023
15 - 19	664 150	337 205	326 945	356 119	176 802	179 317	308 030	160 402	147 628
20 - 24	615 570	311 726	303 843	343 986	165 459	178 527	271 584	146 268	125 316
25 - 29	526 498	266 188	260 310	324 202	151 981	172 221	202 297	114 207	88 089
30 - 34	413 975	208 623	205 352	274 380	130 593	143 787	139 595	78 030	61 565
35 - 39	353 019	177 236	175 782	229 002	110 770	118 232	124 017	66 466	57 551
40 - 44	324 734	163 671	161 063	203 193	99 103	104 090	121 541	64 568	56 973
45 - 49	286 361	145 212	141 149	174 596	85 410	89 186	111 765	59 802	51 963
50 - 54	246 231	125 645	120 586	148 133	72 624	75 508	98 098	53 021	45 077
55 - 59	199 004	101 836	97 169	117 695	57 920	59 774	81 310	43 915	37 395
60 - 64	147 779	74 741	73 038	86 035	41 621	44 414	61 744	33 120	28 625
65 - 69	111 922	55 483	56 439	64 462	30 273	34 189	47 461	25 211	22 250
70 - 74	81 557	39 265	42 292	46 340	20 701	25 639	35 217	18 564	16 652
75 - 79	56 865	26 066	30 798	32 768	13 820	18 948	24 096	12 246	11 850
80 +	54 537	23 194	31 343	31 740	12 191	19 548	22 798	11 003	11 795
1 VII 2009 (ESDF)									
Total	6 340 641	3 681 376	2 659 265	...	...	...	...	...	...
0 - 4	736 654	403 029	333 625	...	...	...	...	...	...
5 - 9	721 196	397 235	323 961	...	...	...	...	...	...
10 - 14	699 394	379 152	320 242	...	...	...	...	...	...
15 - 19	669 988	362 753	307 235	...	...	...	...	...	...
20 - 24	624 204	345 955	278 249	...	...	...	...	...	...
25 - 29	546 966	332 339	214 627	...	...	...	...	...	...
30 - 34	430 039	286 922	143 117	...	...	...	...	...	...
35 - 39	357 765	235 140	122 625	...	...	...	...	...	...
40 - 44	330 724	209 282	121 442	...	...	...	...	...	...
45 - 49	292 963	179 954	113 009	...	...	...	...	...	...
50 - 54	252 447	152 699	99 748	...	...	...	...	...	...
55 - 59	208 366	124 241	84 125	...	...	...	...	...	...
60 - 64	154 465	90 237	64 228	...	...	...	...	...	...
65 - 69	115 328	67 083	48 245	...	...	...	...	...	...
70 - 74	85 801	48 888	36 913	...	...	...	...	...	...
75 - 79	57 285	33 161	24 124	...	...	...	...	...	...
80 +	57 056	33 306	23 750	...	...	...	...	...	...
Peru - Pérou[10]									
1 VII 2009 (ESDF)									
Total	29 132 013	14 605 206	14 526 807	21 398 222	10 584 348	10 813 874	7 733 791	4 020 858	3 712 933
0 - 4	2 967 888	1 514 040	1 453 848	1 962 968	1 005 330	957 638	1 004 920	508 710	496 210
5 - 9	2 942 053	1 497 458	1 444 595	2 002 642	1 017 683	984 959	939 411	479 775	459 636
10 - 14	2 932 455	1 489 231	1 443 224	2 052 554	1 034 653	1 017 901	879 901	454 578	425 323
15 - 19	2 888 186	1 464 979	1 423 207	2 100 416	1 050 350	1 050 066	787 770	414 629	373 141
20 - 24	2 709 309	1 369 745	1 339 564	2 023 168	1 004 394	1 018 774	686 141	365 351	320 790
25 - 29	2 469 456	1 245 620	1 223 836	1 902 066	938 966	963 100	567 390	306 654	260 736
30 - 34	2 295 521	1 155 768	1 139 753	1 770 244	870 517	899 727	525 277	285 251	240 026
35 - 39	2 003 054	1 005 264	997 790	1 534 695	753 611	781 084	468 359	251 653	216 706

7. Population by age, sex and urban/rural residence: latest available year, 2000 - 2009
Population selon l'âge, le sexe et la résidence, urbaine/rurale : dernière année disponible, 2000 - 2009 (continued - suite)

Continent, country or area, date, code and age (in years) / Continent, pays ou zone, date, code et âge (en années)	Total			Urban - Urbaine			Rural - Rurale		
	Both sexes Les deux sexes	Male Masculin	Female Féminin	Both sexes Les deux sexes	Male Masculin	Female Féminin	Both sexes Les deux sexes	Male Masculin	Female Féminin
AMERICA, SOUTH - AMÉRIQUE DU SUD									
Peru - Pérou[10]									
1 VII 2009 (ESDF)									
40 - 44	1 750 526	875 166	875 360	1 359 676	667 306	692 370	390 850	207 860	182 990
45 - 49	1 502 509	747 380	755 129	1 172 017	573 345	598 672	330 492	174 035	156 457
50 - 54	1 224 457	605 116	619 341	947 639	460 869	486 770	276 818	144 247	132 571
55 - 59	995 013	488 585	506 428	761 201	368 950	392 251	233 812	119 635	114 177
60 - 64	777 880	378 402	399 478	578 372	279 151	299 221	199 508	99 251	100 257
65 - 69	607 168	290 513	316 655	445 553	211 760	233 793	161 615	78 753	82 862
70 - 74	468 211	218 184	250 027	341 079	157 589	183 490	127 132	60 595	66 537
75 - 79	324 125	145 379	178 746	237 141	104 607	132 534	86 984	40 772	46 212
80 +	274 202	114 376	159 826	206 791	85 267	121 524	67 411	29 109	38 302
Suriname									
2 VIII 2004 (CDJC)[34]									
Total	492 829	248 046	244 783	328 932[35]	164 444[35]	164 488[35]	163 897[35]	83 602[35]	80 295[35]
0 - 4	51 837	26 252	25 585	31 603[35]	16 152[35]	15 451[35]	20 234[35]	10 100[35]	10 134[35]
5 - 9	49 409	25 200	24 209	30 886[35]	15 639[35]	15 247[35]	18 523[35]	9 561[35]	8 962[35]
10 - 14	45 143	22 889	22 254	28 942[35]	14 536[35]	14 406[35]	16 201[35]	8 353[35]	7 848[35]
15 - 19	46 508	23 465	23 043	31 775[35]	16 181[35]	15 594[35]	14 733[35]	7 284[35]	7 449[35]
20 - 24	43 843	22 437	21 406	30 989[35]	16 056[35]	14 933[35]	12 854[35]	6 381[35]	6 473[35]
25 - 29	37 901	19 006	18 895	25 895[35]	12 853[35]	13 042[35]	12 006[35]	6 153[35]	5 853[35]
30 - 34	38 994	19 828	19 166	26 462[35]	13 226[35]	13 236[35]	12 532[35]	6 602[35]	5 930[35]
35 - 39	37 279	19 179	18 100	25 388[35]	12 845[35]	12 543[35]	11 891[35]	6 334[35]	5 557[35]
40 - 44	33 985	17 657	16 328	23 386[35]	11 870[35]	11 516[35]	10 599[35]	5 787[35]	4 812[35]
45 - 49	25 635	12 643	12 992	17 893[35]	8 565[35]	9 328[35]	7 742[35]	4 078[35]	3 664[35]
50 - 54	20 420	9 933	10 487	14 421[35]	6 955[35]	7 466[35]	5 999[35]	2 978[35]	3 021[35]
55 - 59	14 982	6 955	8 027	10 487[35]	4 806[35]	5 681[35]	4 495[35]	2 149[35]	2 346[35]
60 - 64	13 259	6 200	7 059	9 309[35]	4 428[35]	4 881[35]	3 950[35]	1 772[35]	2 178[35]
65 - 69	10 602	5 148	5 454	7 101[35]	3 521[35]	3 580[35]	3 501[35]	1 627[35]	1 874[35]
70 - 74	8 659	4 103	4 556	5 745[35]	2 708[35]	3 037[35]	2 914[35]	1 395[35]	1 519[35]
75 - 79	5 152	2 419	2 733	3 410[35]	1 576[35]	1 834[35]	1 742[35]	843[35]	899[35]
80 - 84	2 853	1 235	1 618	1 905[35]	779[35]	1 126[35]	948[35]	456[35]	492[35]
85 - 89	1 075	392	677	770[35]	274[35]	496[35]	299[35]	118[35]	181[35]
90 - 94	490	196	294	371[35]	157[35]	214[35]	119[35]	39[35]	80[35]
95 +	129	34	95	94[35]	24[35]	70[35]	35[35]	10[35]	25[35]
Unknown - Inconnu	4 704	2 885	1 819	2 100[35]	1 293[35]	807[35]	2 604[35]	1 592[35]	1 012[35]
1 VII 2007 (ESDJ)[36]									
Total	509 970	257 181	252 789	...	...	...	...	...	...
0	9 769	4 889	4 880	...	...	...	...	...	...
1 - 4	40 951	21 022	19 929	...	...	...	...	...	...
5 - 9	50 987	26 030	24 957	...	...	...	...	...	...
10 - 14	48 453	24 646	23 807	...	...	...	...	...	...
15 - 19	46 014	23 357	22 657	...	...	...	...	...	...
20 - 24	43 838	22 293	21 545	...	...	...	...	...	...
25 - 29	41 642	21 239	20 403	...	...	...	...	...	...
30 - 34	39 555	20 225	19 330	...	...	...	...	...	...
35 - 39	37 120	18 995	18 125	...	...	...	...	...	...
40 - 44	33 306	16 963	16 343	...	...	...	...	...	...
45 - 49	29 097	14 715	14 382	...	...	...	...	...	...
50 - 54	24 032	11 983	12 049	...	...	...	...	...	...
55 - 59	18 996	9 274	9 722	...	...	...	...	...	...
60 - 64	15 053	7 236	7 817	...	...	...	...	...	...
65 - 69	11 475	5 426	6 049	...	...	...	...	...	...
70 - 74	8 529	3 976	4 553	...	...	...	...	...	...
75 - 79	5 922	2 727	3 195	...	...	...	...	...	...
80 +	5 231	2 185	3 046	...	...	...	...	...	...
Uruguay[2]									
1 VII 2009 (ESDF)									
Total	3 344 938	1 615 709	1 729 229	3 141 299	1 502 032	1 639 267	203 639	113 677	89 962
0 - 4	240 534	123 221	117 313	227 399	116 486	110 913	13 135	6 735	6 400
5 - 9	250 805	127 979	122 826	236 471	120 538	115 933	14 334	7 441	6 893
10 - 14	273 250	139 565	133 685	257 405	131 259	126 146	15 845	8 306	7 539
15 - 19	266 678	136 149	130 529	251 586	127 980	123 606	15 092	8 169	6 923
20 - 24	256 634	130 254	126 380	242 820	122 504	120 316	13 814	7 750	6 064

Continent, country or area, date, code and age (in years) / Continent, pays ou zone, date, code et âge (en années)	Total			Urban - Urbaine			Rural - Rurale		
	Both sexes Les deux sexes	Male Masculin	Female Féminin	Both sexes Les deux sexes	Male Masculin	Female Féminin	Both sexes Les deux sexes	Male Masculin	Female Féminin
AMERICA, SOUTH - AMÉRIQUE DU SUD									
Uruguay[2]									
1 VII 2009 (ESDF)									
25 - 29	238 332	119 047	119 285	225 093	111 586	113 507	13 239	7 461	5 778
30 - 34	238 826	117 716	121 110	224 985	110 038	114 947	13 841	7 678	6 163
35 - 39	216 332	106 518	109 814	202 819	98 840	103 979	13 513	7 678	5 835
40 - 44	201 813	97 943	103 870	188 522	90 416	98 106	13 291	7 527	5 764
45 - 49	207 867	100 976	106 891	194 261	93 056	101 205	13 606	7 920	5 686
50 - 54	187 270	90 391	96 879	174 755	83 058	91 697	12 515	7 333	5 182
55 - 59	170 542	80 678	89 864	158 337	73 463	84 874	12 205	7 215	4 990
60 - 64	142 396	65 936	76 460	131 760	59 601	72 159	10 636	6 335	4 301
65 - 69	130 655	58 308	72 347	121 259	52 667	68 592	9 396	5 641	3 755
70 - 74	108 578	45 381	63 197	101 079	41 028	60 051	7 499	4 353	3 146
75 - 79	98 029	37 934	60 095	92 322	34 707	57 615	5 707	3 227	2 480
80 - 84	64 336	22 846	41 490	61 019	21 096	39 923	3 317	1 750	1 567
85 - 89	35 231	10 902	24 329	33 492	10 090	23 402	1 739	812	927
90 - 94	12 732	3 166	9 566	12 067	2 904	9 163	665	262	403
95 +	4 098	799	3 299	3 848	715	3 133	250	84	166
Venezuela (Bolivarian Republic of) - Venezuela (République bolivarienne du)									
1 VII 2008 (ESDF)									
Total	27 932 992	14 013 639	13 919 353	24 594 784	12 215 477	12 379 307	3 338 208	1 798 162	1 540 046
0 - 4	2 883 461	1 474 487	1 408 974	2 435 476	1 250 174	1 185 302	447 985	224 313	223 672
0	588 893	301 346	287 547	...	...	...	...	...	...
1 - 4	2 294 568	1 173 141	1 121 427	...	...	...	...	...	...
5 - 9	2 791 412	1 425 904	1 365 508	2 388 133	1 222 777	1 165 356	403 279	203 127	200 152
10 - 14	2 730 731	1 393 790	1 336 941	2 375 391	1 210 077	1 165 314	355 340	183 713	171 627
15 - 19	2 702 883	1 376 149	1 326 734	2 377 547	1 198 747	1 178 800	325 336	177 402	147 934
20 - 24	2 589 846	1 310 811	1 279 035	2 296 517	1 147 867	1 148 650	293 329	162 944	130 385
25 - 29	2 354 453	1 183 680	1 170 773	2 093 830	1 039 155	1 054 675	260 623	144 525	116 098
30 - 34	2 092 251	1 046 851	1 045 400	1 876 877	927 908	948 969	215 374	118 943	96 431
35 - 39	1 866 955	931 096	935 859	1 681 131	827 797	853 334	185 824	103 299	82 525
40 - 44	1 747 941	869 656	878 285	1 578 640	775 355	803 285	169 301	94 301	75 000
45 - 49	1 536 484	762 633	773 851	1 386 492	679 275	707 217	149 992	83 358	66 634
50 - 54	1 272 255	629 692	642 563	1 140 702	556 139	584 563	131 553	73 553	58 000
55 - 59	1 049 616	517 597	532 019	933 182	450 978	482 204	116 434	66 619	49 815
60 - 64	801 359	391 758	409 601	705 041	335 837	369 204	96 318	55 921	40 397
65 - 69	573 084	274 409	298 675	500 856	232 926	267 930	72 228	41 483	30 745
70 - 74	411 910	191 616	220 294	360 424	162 910	197 514	51 486	28 706	22 780
75 +	528 351	233 510	294 841	464 545	197 555	266 990	63 806	35 955	27 851
1 VII 2009 (ESDF)									
Total	28 384 132	14 235 351	14 148 781	...	...	...	...	...	...
0 - 4	2 896 873	1 481 404	1 415 469	...	...	...	...	...	...
5 - 9	2 807 202	1 434 150	1 373 052	...	...	...	...	...	...
10 - 14	2 735 101	1 396 135	1 338 966	...	...	...	...	...	...
15 - 19	2 704 816	1 377 369	1 327 447	...	...	...	...	...	...
20 - 24	2 632 829	1 332 871	1 299 958	...	...	...	...	...	...
25 - 29	2 395 943	1 204 475	1 191 468	...	...	...	...	...	...
30 - 34	2 150 350	1 075 705	1 074 645	...	...	...	...	...	...
35 - 39	1 882 745	938 670	944 075	...	...	...	...	...	...
40 - 44	1 773 092	881 751	891 341	...	...	...	...	...	...
45 - 49	1 591 309	789 486	801 823	...	...	...	...	...	...
50 - 54	1 306 936	646 314	660 622	...	...	...	...	...	...
55 - 59	1 089 678	536 670	553 008	...	...	...	...	...	...
60 - 64	842 425	411 979	430 446	...	...	...	...	...	...
65 - 69	600 411	287 772	312 639	...	...	...	...	...	...
70 - 74	424 439	197 396	227 043	...	...	...	...	...	...
75 - 79	306 564	138 319	168 245	...	...	...	...	...	...
80 +	243 419	104 885	138 534	...	...	...	...	...	...

Continent, country or area, date, code and age (in years) / Continent, pays ou zone, date, code et âge (en années)	Total			Urban - Urbaine			Rural - Rurale		
	Both sexes Les deux sexes	Male Masculin	Female Féminin	Both sexes Les deux sexes	Male Masculin	Female Féminin	Both sexes Les deux sexes	Male Masculin	Female Féminin
ASIA - ASIE									
Afghanistan									
1 VII 2009 (ESDF)									
Total	23 993 500[37]	12 272 900	11 720 600	5 507 300	2 835 900	2 671 400	18 486 200	9 437 000	9 049 200
0 - 4	4 686 322	2 279 522	2 406 800	1 036 546	515 727	520 819	3 649 776	1 763 795	1 885 981
5 - 9	3 595 134	1 826 187	1 768 947	842 238	429 210	413 028	2 752 896	1 396 977	1 355 919
10 - 14	2 780 876	1 463 377	1 317 499	683 601	353 300	330 301	2 097 275	1 110 077	987 198
15 - 19	2 272 452	1 200 504	1 071 948	564 393	288 821	275 572	1 708 059	911 683	796 376
20 - 24	1 946 419	997 097	949 322	468 023	233 544	234 479	1 478 396	763 553	714 843
25 - 29	1 607 394	793 883	813 511	376 197	186 867	189 330	1 231 197	607 016	624 181
30 - 34	1 340 031	638 139	701 892	306 367	153 649	152 718	1 033 664	484 490	549 174
35 - 39	1 177 068	562 577	614 491	258 524	131 991	126 533	918 544	430 586	487 958
40 - 44	1 016 514	513 972	502 542	219 571	115 335	104 236	796 943	398 637	398 306
45 - 49	881 492	466 243	415 249	185 748	100 766	84 982	695 744	365 477	330 267
50 - 54	743 931	409 832	334 099	154 097	86 021	68 076	589 834	323 811	266 023
55 - 59	598 951	339 431	259 520	124 089	71 235	52 854	474 862	268 196	206 666
60 - 64	462 216	265 189	197 027	97 276	56 816	40 460	364 940	208 373	156 567
65 +	884 700	516 947	367 753	190 630	112 618	78 012	694 070	404 329	289 741
Armenia - Arménie									
1 VII 2009 (ESDJ)									
Total	3 243 729	1 572 046	1 671 683	2 077 181	989 609	1 087 572	1 166 548	582 437	584 111
0	42 420	22 644	19 776	...	...	...	...	...	...
1 - 4	152 339	81 458	70 881	96 502	51 182	45 320	55 837	30 276	25 561
5 - 9	181 266	97 146	84 120	111 392	59 029	52 363	69 874	38 117	31 757
10 - 14	222 426	116 748	105 678	130 233	68 205	62 028	92 193	48 543	43 650
15 - 19	299 035	152 683	146 352	175 951	89 661	86 290	123 084	63 022	60 062
20 - 24	316 536	160 108	156 428	194 490	97 520	96 970	122 046	62 588	59 458
25 - 29	287 102	144 320	142 782	188 936	93 345	95 591	98 166	50 975	47 191
30 - 34	235 186	115 690	119 496	158 263	77 282	80 981	76 923	38 408	38 515
35 - 39	200 762	96 713	104 049	131 670	62 623	69 047	69 092	34 090	35 002
40 - 44	208 604	98 835	109 769	128 297	58 549	69 748	80 307	40 286	40 021
45 - 49	264 045	125 019	139 026	167 929	75 977	91 952	96 116	49 042	47 074
50 - 54	232 553	109 024	123 529	158 802	71 868	86 934	73 751	37 156	36 595
55 - 59	169 498	77 108	92 390	123 436	55 048	68 388	46 062	22 060	24 002
60 - 64	99 462	43 526	55 936	73 679	32 057	41 622	25 783	11 469	14 314
65 - 69	93 500	39 220	54 280	64 183	27 034	37 149	29 317	12 186	17 131
70 - 74	109 239	44 443	64 796	69 413	28 182	41 231	39 826	16 261	23 565
75 - 79	76 522	30 545	45 977	45 386	17 834	27 552	31 136	12 711	18 425
80 - 84	43 219	14 309	28 910	25 465	8 217	17 248	17 754	6 092	11 662
85 +	10 015	2 507	7 508	6 195	1 643	4 552	3 820	864	2 956
Azerbaijan - Azerbaïdjan[38]									
1 VII 2009 (ESDF)									
Total	8 947 200	4 385 900	4 561 300	4 842 500	2 358 900	2 483 600	4 104 700	2 027 000	2 077 700
0	152 100	82 000	70 100	74 300	40 000	34 300	77 800	41 900	35 900
1 - 4	588 200	313 900	274 300	290 200	154 500	135 700	298 000	159 400	138 600
5 - 9	575 300	306 600	268 700	277 600	149 400	128 200	297 700	157 200	140 500
10 - 14	685 400	356 000	329 400	327 500	172 000	155 500	357 900	184 000	173 900
15 - 19	920 900	469 100	451 800	479 200	245 100	234 100	441 700	224 000	217 700
20 - 24	920 300	466 400	453 900	503 600	256 400	247 200	416 700	210 000	206 700
25 - 29	778 800	389 500	389 300	432 700	216 400	216 300	346 100	173 100	173 000
30 - 34	658 100	315 700	342 400	359 100	170 000	189 100	299 000	145 700	153 300
35 - 39	627 600	293 300	334 300	331 300	149 100	182 200	296 300	144 200	152 100
40 - 44	676 400	314 800	361 600	365 600	165 100	200 500	310 800	149 700	161 100
45 - 49	696 600	328 300	368 300	405 400	189 200	216 200	291 200	139 100	152 100
50 - 54	539 500	256 800	282 700	329 400	156 700	172 700	210 100	100 100	110 000
55 - 59	339 100	159 600	179 500	218 200	103 200	115 000	120 900	56 400	64 500
60 - 64	193 300	88 500	104 800	126 300	58 400	67 900	67 000	30 100	36 900
65 - 69	165 800	72 100	93 700	98 200	43 100	55 100	67 600	29 000	38 600
70 - 74	210 100	87 400	122 700	111 100	46 200	64 900	99 000	41 200	57 800
75 - 79	126 100	52 200	73 900	63 300	25 600	37 700	62 800	26 600	36 200
80 - 84	60 000	23 000	37 000	32 100	12 100	20 000	27 900	10 900	17 000
85 - 89	22 300	7 200	15 100	12 100	4 200	7 900	10 200	3 000	7 200
90 - 94	6 600	2 200	4 400	3 200	1 100	2 100	3 400	1 100	2 300
95 - 99	3 500	900	2 600	1 400	800	600	2 100	100	2 000
100 +	1 200	500	700	700	300	400	500	200	300

Continent, country or area, date, code and age (in years) / Continent, pays ou zone, date, code et âge (en années)	Total			Urban - Urbaine			Rural - Rurale		
	Both sexes Les deux sexes	Male Masculin	Female Féminin	Both sexes Les deux sexes	Male Masculin	Female Féminin	Both sexes Les deux sexes	Male Masculin	Female Féminin
ASIA - ASIE									
Bahrain - Bahreïn									
1 VII 2008 (ESDF)									
Total	1 106 509	677 999	428 510	...	...	...	...	...	...
0 - 4	79 706	39 996	39 710	...	...	...	...	...	...
5 - 9	75 820	38 488	37 332	...	...	...	...	...	...
10 - 14	67 862	35 143	32 719	...	...	...	...	...	...
15 - 19	65 611	34 102	31 510	...	...	...	...	...	...
20 - 24	104 334	61 234	43 100	...	...	...	...	...	...
25 - 29	155 596	105 066	50 530	...	...	...	...	...	...
30 - 34	141 269	95 222	46 047	...	...	...	...	...	...
35 - 39	120 108	81 098	39 010	...	...	...	...	...	...
40 - 44	96 978	63 266	33 711	...	...	...	...	...	...
45 - 49	76 440	49 193	27 247	...	...	...	...	...	...
50 - 54	53 048	35 203	17 845	...	...	...	...	...	...
55 - 59	29 695	19 376	10 319	...	...	...	...	...	...
60 - 64	13 795	7 913	5 882	...	...	...	...	...	...
65 - 69	9 732	4 935	4 797	...	...	...	...	...	...
70 - 74	6 528	3 141	3 386	...	...	...	...	...	...
75 - 79	4 303	2 017	2 286	...	...	...	...	...	...
80 +	5 686	2 606	3 080	...	...	...	...	...	...
Bangladesh[39]									
22 I 2001 (CDFC)									
Total	124 355 263	64 091 508	60 263 755	29 255 627	15 709 427	13 546 200	95 099 636	48 382 081	46 717 555
0 - 4	16 001 528	8 326 691	7 674 837	3 090 964	1 622 067	1 468 897	12 910 564	6 704 624	6 205 940
5 - 9	16 696 365	8 749 515	7 946 850	3 221 434	1 686 786	1 534 648	13 474 931	7 062 729	6 412 202
10 - 14	15 872 379	8 389 435	7 482 944	3 651 545	1 899 037	1 752 508	12 220 834	6 490 398	5 730 436
15 - 19	12 076 480	6 331 903	5 744 577	3 255 933	1 707 687	1 548 246	8 820 547	4 624 216	4 196 331
20 - 24	11 135 355	4 917 880	6 217 475	3 257 239	1 605 900	1 651 339	7 878 116	3 311 980	4 566 136
25 - 29	10 982 014	4 958 325	6 023 689	3 010 348	1 519 160	1 491 188	7 971 666	3 439 165	4 532 501
30 - 34	8 641 719	4 341 974	4 299 745	2 315 401	1 275 073	1 040 328	6 326 318	3 066 901	3 259 417
35 - 39	7 890 542	4 234 653	3 655 889	2 002 224	1 155 657	846 567	5 888 318	3 078 996	2 809 322
40 - 44	6 261 028	3 443 385	2 817 643	1 550 923	936 686	614 237	4 710 105	2 506 699	2 203 406
45 - 49	4 675 742	2 617 908	2 057 834	1 105 816	674 848	430 968	3 569 926	1 943 060	1 626 866
50 - 54	4 005 072	2 189 469	1 815 603	881 895	530 695	351 200	3 123 177	1 658 774	1 464 403
55 - 59	2 387 825	1 322 502	1 065 323	485 615	292 161	193 454	1 902 210	1 030 341	871 869
60 - 64	2 849 107	1 546 041	1 303 066	543 767	310 178	233 589	2 305 340	1 235 863	1 069 477
65 - 69	1 461 406	817 904	643 502	272 516	156 491	116 025	1 188 890	661 413	527 477
70 +	3 418 701	1 903 923	1 514 778	610 007	337 001	273 006	2 808 694	1 566 922	1 241 772
Bhutan - Bhoutan[40]									
1 VII 2009 (ESDF)									
Total	683 407	357 305	326 102	232 232	124 246	107 986	451 174	233 059	218 116
0 - 4	81 871	41 255	40 616	24 770	12 402	12 368	57 101	28 853	28 248
5 - 9	63 264	31 862	31 402	21 234	10 616	10 618	42 030	21 246	20 784
10 - 14	69 200	35 093	34 107	25 096	12 635	12 462	44 104	22 459	21 645
15 - 19	72 142	36 887	35 255	27 486	14 067	13 419	44 656	22 820	21 836
20 - 24	68 926	35 959	32 967	27 987	14 798	13 189	40 940	21 161	19 778
25 - 29	63 746	34 247	29 499	26 057	14 311	11 746	37 689	19 936	17 753
30 - 34	55 530	30 170	25 360	22 188	12 531	9 657	33 342	17 639	15 703
35 - 39	45 564	25 003	20 561	17 207	9 950	7 256	28 357	15 053	13 305
40 - 44	37 954	20 756	17 198	12 449	7 335	5 115	25 504	13 421	12 083
45 - 49	30 498	16 414	14 084	8 836	5 194	3 642	21 662	11 220	10 442
50 - 54	25 116	13 428	11 688	6 148	3 618	2 529	18 968	9 810	9 159
55 - 59	20 387	10 832	9 555	4 354	2 531	1 824	16 033	8 301	7 731
60 - 64	16 335	8 597	7 738	3 030	1 671	1 358	13 305	6 926	6 380
65 - 69	12 639	6 571	6 068	2 123	1 108	1 015	10 516	5 463	5 053
70 - 74	9 189	4 718	4 471	1 427	687	740	7 762	4 031	3 731
75 - 79	6 029	3 045	2 984	948	406	541	5 081	2 639	2 443
80 +	5 017	2 468	2 549	892	386	506	4 125	2 082	2 043
Brunei Darussalam - Brunéi Darussalam									
21 VIII 2001* (CDFC)									
Total	332 844	168 974	163 870	238 699	120 046	118 653	94 145	48 928	45 217
0 - 14	100 912	52 304	48 608	72 076	37 396	34 680	28 836	14 908	13 928
15 - 19	27 963	14 014	13 949	20 019	10 085	9 934	7 944	3 929	4 015
20 - 24	32 604	15 390	17 214	23 592	10 885	12 707	9 012	4 505	4 507

Continent, country or area, date, code and age (in years) Continent, pays ou zone, date, code et âge (en années)	Total			Urban - Urbaine			Rural - Rurale		
	Both sexes Les deux sexes	Male Masculin	Female Féminin	Both sexes Les deux sexes	Male Masculin	Female Féminin	Both sexes Les deux sexes	Male Masculin	Female Féminin
ASIA - ASIE									
Brunei Darussalam - Brunéi Darussalam									
21 VIII 2001* (CDFC)									
25 - 29	35 773	17 884	17 889	25 856	12 573	13 283	9 917	5 311	4 606
30 - 34	34 375	16 878	17 497	24 973	11 931	13 042	9 402	4 947	4 455
35 - 39	28 764	14 581	14 183	21 112	10 461	10 651	7 652	4 120	3 532
40 - 44	24 198	12 984	11 214	17 808	9 544	8 264	6 390	3 440	2 950
45 - 49	17 149	9 150	7 999	12 402	6 637	5 765	4 747	2 513	2 234
50 - 54	10 687	5 542	5 145	7 609	4 013	3 596	3 078	1 529	1 549
55 - 59	6 140	3 249	2 891	4 153	2 197	1 956	1 987	1 052	935
60 - 64	4 962	2 432	2 530	3 217	1 544	1 673	1 745	888	857
65 - 69	3 757	1 768	1 989	2 366	1 102	1 264	1 391	666	725
70 - 74	2 441	1 263	1 178	1 530	758	772	911	505	406
75 - 79	1 582	793	789	1 027	492	535	555	301	254
80 - 84	844	423	421	548	264	284	296	159	137
85 - 89	397	188	209	252	98	154	145	90	55
90 - 94	197	86	111	111	47	64	86	39	47
95 - 99	66	33	33	33	14	19	33	19	14
100 +	33	12	21	15	5	10	18	7	11
1 VII 2009 (ESDF)									
Total	406 200	215 000	191 200	...	...	...	...	...	...
0 - 4	34 700	18 600	16 100	...	...	...	...	...	...
5 - 9	36 000	19 400	16 600	...	...	...	...	...	...
10 - 14	35 400	19 200	16 200	...	...	...	...	...	...
15 - 19	35 000	18 600	16 400	...	...	...	...	...	...
20 - 24	42 900	21 700	21 200	...	...	...	...	...	...
25 - 29	45 700	24 000	21 700	...	...	...	...	...	...
30 - 34	41 100	21 600	19 500	...	...	...	...	...	...
35 - 39	34 300	18 100	16 200	...	...	...	...	...	...
40 - 44	28 700	16 100	12 600	...	...	...	...	...	...
45 - 49	22 700	12 500	10 200	...	...	...	...	...	...
50 - 54	17 100	9 000	8 100	...	...	...	...	...	...
55 - 59	11 800	6 100	5 700	...	...	...	...	...	...
60 - 64	7 000	3 400	3 600	...	...	...	...	...	...
65 - 69	5 100	2 500	2 600	...	...	...	...	...	...
70 - 74	3 800	1 800	2 000	...	...	...	...	...	...
75 - 79	2 600	1 300	1 300	...	...	...	...	...	...
80 - 84	1 300	600	700	...	...	...	...	...	...
85 +	1 000	500	500	...	...	...	...	...	...
Cambodia - Cambodge[41]									
3 III 2008 (CDFC)									
Total	13 395 682	6 516 054	6 879 628	2 614 027	1 255 570	1 358 457	10 781 655	5 260 484	5 521 171
0 - 4	1 372 615	703 058	669 557	206 551	105 929	100 622	1 166 064	597 129	568 935
5 - 9	1 470 672	752 336	718 336	208 541	106 752	101 789	1 262 131	645 584	616 547
10 - 14	1 670 505	859 412	811 093	249 259	127 075	122 184	1 421 246	732 337	688 909
15 - 19	1 619 290	834 416	784 874	342 335	161 301	181 034	1 276 955	673 115	603 840
20 - 24	1 369 202	669 343	699 859	370 621	173 769	196 852	998 581	495 574	503 007
25 - 29	1 233 361	605 706	627 655	314 864	152 581	162 283	918 497	453 125	465 372
30 - 34	693 235	335 046	358 189	146 363	71 963	74 400	546 872	263 083	283 789
35 - 39	844 948	408 295	436 653	174 291	86 532	87 759	670 657	321 763	348 894
40 - 44	737 451	344 275	393 176	145 549	72 185	73 364	591 902	272 090	319 812
45 - 49	653 650	299 005	354 645	129 703	61 938	67 765	523 947	237 067	286 880
50 - 54	490 726	195 911	294 815	103 822	44 434	59 388	386 904	151 477	235 427
55 - 59	391 116	162 328	228 788	77 859	33 758	44 101	313 257	128 570	184 687
60 - 64	277 611	116 731	160 880	51 236	21 725	29 511	226 375	95 006	131 369
65 - 69	216 839	90 521	126 318	35 697	14 589	21 108	181 142	75 932	105 210
70 - 74	158 945	63 938	95 007	25 621	9 843	15 778	133 324	54 095	79 229
75 - 79	107 886	42 710	65 176	16 738	6 111	10 627	91 148	36 599	54 549
80 - 84	54 604	20 930	33 674	9 110	3 131	5 979	45 494	17 799	27 695
85 - 89	23 994	8 882	15 112	4 082	1 349	2 733	19 912	7 533	12 379
90 - 94	6 240	2 213	4 027	1 268	450	818	4 972	1 763	3 209
95 +	2 792	998	1 794	517	155	362	2 275	843	1 432

Continent, country or area, date, code and age (in years) / Continent, pays ou zone, date, code et âge (en années)	Total			Urban - Urbaine			Rural - Rurale		
	Both sexes Les deux sexes	Male Masculin	Female Féminin	Both sexes Les deux sexes	Male Masculin	Female Féminin	Both sexes Les deux sexes	Male Masculin	Female Féminin
ASIA - ASIE									
China - Chine[42]									
1 XI 2000 (CDJC)									
Total	1242612226	640 275 969	602 336 257	458 770 983	235 264 707	223 506 276	783 841 243	405 011 262	378 829 981
0	13 793 799	7 460 206	6 333 593	4 449 020	2 376 585	2 072 435	9 344 779	5 083 621	4 261 158
1 - 4	55 184 575	30 188 488	24 996 087	17 669 697	9 525 854	8 143 843	37 514 878	20 662 634	16 852 244
5 - 9	90 152 587	48 303 208	41 849 379	26 588 363	14 180 433	12 407 930	63 564 224	34 122 775	29 441 449
10 - 14	125 396 633	65 344 739	60 051 894	35 802 884	18 701 307	17 101 577	89 593 749	46 643 432	42 950 317
15 - 19	103 031 165	52 878 170	50 152 995	42 231 585	21 086 911	21 144 674	60 799 580	31 791 259	29 008 321
20 - 24	94 573 174	47 937 766	46 635 408	41 021 887	20 651 361	20 370 526	53 551 287	27 286 405	26 264 882
25 - 29	117 602 265	60 230 758	57 371 507	48 788 516	24 820 721	23 967 795	68 813 749	35 410 037	33 403 712
30 - 34	127 314 298	65 360 456	61 953 842	49 723 640	25 760 568	23 963 072	77 590 658	39 599 888	37 990 770
35 - 39	109 147 295	56 141 391	53 005 904	44 518 164	23 269 889	21 248 275	64 629 131	32 871 502	31 757 629
40 - 44	81 242 945	42 243 187	38 999 758	33 518 610	17 499 183	16 019 427	47 724 335	24 744 004	22 980 331
45 - 49	85 521 045	43 939 603	41 581 442	31 708 706	16 245 324	15 463 382	53 812 339	27 694 279	26 118 060
50 - 54	63 304 200	32 804 125	30 500 075	22 335 748	11 462 314	10 873 434	40 968 452	21 341 811	19 626 641
55 - 59	46 370 375	24 061 506	22 308 869	16 004 389	8 077 159	7 927 230	30 365 986	15 984 347	14 381 639
60 - 64	41 703 848	21 674 478	20 029 370	14 944 552	7 519 377	7 425 175	26 759 296	14 155 101	12 604 195
65 - 69	34 780 460	17 549 348	17 231 112	12 174 470	6 128 605	6 045 865	22 605 990	11 420 743	11 185 247
70 - 74	25 574 149	12 436 154	13 137 995	8 479 487	4 216 193	4 263 294	17 094 662	8 219 961	8 874 701
75 - 79	15 928 330	7 175 811	8 752 519	5 000 134	2 291 543	2 708 591	10 928 196	4 884 268	6 043 928
80 - 84	7 989 158	3 203 868	4 785 290	2 472 016	1 004 359	1 467 657	5 517 142	2 199 509	3 317 633
85 - 89	3 030 698	1 056 941	1 973 757	994 079	347 550	646 529	2 036 619	709 391	1 327 228
90 - 94	783 594	229 758	553 836	276 586	80 189	196 397	507 008	149 569	357 439
95 - 99	169 756	51 373	118 383	62 255	17 827	44 428	107 501	33 546	73 955
100 +	17 877	4 635	13 242	6 195	1 455	4 740	11 682	3 180	8 502
China, Hong Kong SAR - Chine, Hong Kong RAS									
1 VII 2009 (ESDJ)									
Total	7 003 700	3 296 200	3 707 500	...	...	...	...	...	...
0	46 600	24 100	22 500	...	...	...	...	...	...
1 - 4	182 600	95 500	87 100	...	...	...	...	...	...
5 - 9	265 300	137 700	127 600	...	...	...	...	...	...
10 - 14	378 900	194 100	184 800	...	...	...	...	...	...
15 - 19	435 300	223 900	211 400	...	...	...	...	...	...
20 - 24	458 500	219 600	238 900	...	...	...	...	...	...
25 - 29	536 700	231 000	305 700	...	...	...	...	...	...
30 - 34	539 700	225 900	313 800	...	...	...	...	...	...
35 - 39	574 800	240 700	334 100	...	...	...	...	...	...
40 - 44	599 800	264 200	335 600	...	...	...	...	...	...
45 - 49	673 200	317 600	355 600	...	...	...	...	...	...
50 - 54	609 200	301 500	307 700	...	...	...	...	...	...
55 - 59	476 200	237 300	238 900	...	...	...	...	...	...
60 - 64	333 400	169 200	164 200	...	...	...	...	...	...
65 - 69	222 100	117 100	105 000	...	...	...	...	...	...
70 - 74	232 800	114 500	118 300	...	...	...	...	...	...
75 - 79	199 200	95 000	104 200	...	...	...	...	...	...
80 - 84	128 000	52 300	75 700	...	...	...	...	...	...
85 +	111 400	35 000	76 400	...	...	...	...	...	...
China, Macao SAR - Chine, Macao RAS[12]									
1 VII 2009 (ESDJ)									
Total	544 100	265 200	279 000	...	...	...	...	...	...
0 - 4	20 300	10 600	9 700	...	...	...	...	...	...
5 - 9	18 800	9 800	9 100	...	...	...	...	...	...
10 - 14	30 200	15 700	14 500	...	...	...	...	...	...
15 - 19	40 600	20 800	19 800	...	...	...	...	...	...
20 - 24	51 600	25 300	26 300	...	...	...	...	...	...
25 - 29	44 100	20 500	23 600	...	...	...	...	...	...
30 - 34	41 600	19 700	21 900	...	...	...	...	...	...
35 - 39	47 700	21 600	26 100	...	...	...	...	...	...
40 - 44	48 000	21 000	27 100	...	...	...	...	...	...
45 - 49	55 700	26 800	29 000	...	...	...	...	...	...
50 - 54	50 000	26 300	23 700	...	...	...	...	...	...
55 - 59	33 200	17 300	15 900	...	...	...	...	...	...
60 - 64	21 700	11 700	10 000	...	...	...	...	...	...

Continent, country or area, date, code and age (in years) / Continent, pays ou zone, date, code et âge (en années)	Total			Urban - Urbaine			Rural - Rurale		
	Both sexes Les deux sexes	Male Masculin	Female Féminin	Both sexes Les deux sexes	Male Masculin	Female Féminin	Both sexes Les deux sexes	Male Masculin	Female Féminin
ASIA - ASIE									
China, Macao SAR - Chine, Macao RAS[12]									
1 VII 2009 (ESDJ)									
65 - 69	11 300	6 000	5 400	...	...	...	...	...	...
70 - 74	9 300	4 400	4 900	...	...	...	...	...	...
75 - 79	8 600	3 700	4 900	...	...	...	...	...	...
80 - 84	6 400	2 500	3 800	...	...	...	...	...	...
85 +	5 000	1 500	3 500	...	...	...	...	...	...
Cyprus - Chypre[43]									
1 X 2001 (CDJC)									
Total	689 565	338 497	351 068	474 450	231 128	243 322	215 115	107 369	107 746
0	8 024	4 068	3 956	5 443	2 765	2 678	2 581	1 303	1 278
1 - 4	34 558	17 625	16 933	23 296	11 821	11 475	11 262	5 804	5 458
5 - 9	51 718	26 502	25 216	34 111	17 402	16 709	17 607	9 100	8 507
10 - 14	53 178	27 396	25 782	35 772	18 332	17 440	17 406	9 064	8 342
15 - 19	54 603	28 132	26 471	36 725	18 872	17 853	17 878	9 260	8 618
20 - 24	51 803	26 208	25 595	36 231	18 178	18 053	15 572	8 030	7 542
25 - 29	48 272	23 096	25 176	35 248	16 654	18 594	13 024	6 442	6 582
30 - 34	48 233	22 682	25 551	34 899	16 196	18 703	13 334	6 486	6 848
35 - 39	51 561	24 813	26 748	36 645	17 304	19 341	14 916	7 509	7 407
40 - 44	52 289	25 602	26 687	37 070	17 786	19 284	15 219	7 816	7 403
45 - 49	45 580	22 705	22 875	32 005	15 647	16 358	13 575	7 058	6 517
50 - 54	42 587	21 027	21 560	30 186	14 803	15 383	12 401	6 224	6 177
55 - 59	34 554	16 930	17 624	24 216	11 883	12 333	10 338	5 047	5 291
60 - 64	30 747	14 968	15 779	20 763	10 239	10 524	9 984	4 729	5 255
65 - 69	25 445	11 905	13 540	16 669	7 943	8 726	8 776	3 962	4 814
70 - 74	20 965	9 375	11 590	13 157	5 885	7 272	7 808	3 490	4 318
75 - 79	15 974	7 073	8 901	9 899	4 338	5 561	6 075	2 735	3 340
80 - 84	9 802	4 232	5 570	6 010	2 522	3 488	3 792	1 710	2 082
85 - 89	5 861	2 423	3 438	3 523	1 368	2 155	2 338	1 055	1 283
90 - 94	1 975	825	1 150	1 269	532	737	706	293	413
95 - 99	411	148	263	252	89	163	159	59	100
100 +	40	14	26	25	8	17	15	6	9
Unknown - Inconnu	1 385	748	637	1 036	561	475	349	187	162
1 VII 2008* (ESDJ)									
Total	792 993	391 789	401 204	...	...	...	...	...	...
0	9 126	4 696	4 430	...	...	...	...	...	...
1 - 4	34 298	17 701	16 597	...	...	...	...	...	...
5 - 9	42 215	21 543	20 672	...	...	...	...	...	...
10 - 14	50 061	25 641	24 420	...	...	...	...	...	...
15 - 19	56 502	28 682	27 820	...	...	...	...	...	...
20 - 24	63 743	31 084	32 659	...	...	...	...	...	...
25 - 29	69 257	34 398	34 859	...	...	...	...	...	...
30 - 34	60 010	30 095	29 915	...	...	...	...	...	...
35 - 39	55 812	28 189	27 623	...	...	...	...	...	...
40 - 44	54 477	26 925	27 552	...	...	...	...	...	...
45 - 49	56 559	28 588	27 971	...	...	...	...	...	...
50 - 54	52 314	25 825	26 489	...	...	...	...	...	...
55 - 59	47 296	23 337	23 959	...	...	...	...	...	...
60 - 64	40 318	19 385	20 933	...	...	...	...	...	...
65 - 69	33 055	15 854	17 201	...	...	...	...	...	...
70 - 74	26 062	12 193	13 869	...	...	...	...	...	...
75 - 79	19 192	8 434	10 758	...	...	...	...	...	...
80 - 84	12 593	5 267	7 326	...	...	...	...	...	...
85 - 89	6 436	2 603	3 833	...	...	...	...	...	...
90 - 94	2 528	949	1 579	...	...	...	...	...	...
95 - 99	946	322	624	...	...	...	...	...	...
100 +	193	78	115	...	...	...	...	...	...
Democratic People's Republic of Korea - République populaire démocratique de Corée									
1 X 2008 (CDJC)									
Total	24 052 231	11 721 838	12 330 393	...	...	...	...	...	...
0 - 4	1 710 039	872 173	837 866	...	...	...	...	...	...

Continent, country or area, date, code and age (in years) / Continent, pays ou zone, date, code et âge (en années)	Total			Urban - Urbaine			Rural - Rurale		
	Both sexes Les deux sexes	Male Masculin	Female Féminin	Both sexes Les deux sexes	Male Masculin	Female Féminin	Both sexes Les deux sexes	Male Masculin	Female Féminin
ASIA - ASIE									
Democratic People's Republic of Korea - République populaire démocratique de Corée									
1 X 2008 (CDJC)									
5 - 9	1 846 785	943 048	903 737	...	...	...	...	...	...
10 - 14	2 021 350	1 035 282	986 068	...	...	...	...	...	...
15 - 19	2 052 342	1 050 113	1 002 229	...	...	...	...	...	...
20 - 24	1 841 400	941 017	900 383	...	...	...	...	...	...
25 - 29	1 737 185	887 573	849 612	...	...	...	...	...	...
30 - 34	1 680 272	853 276	826 996	...	...	...	...	...	...
35 - 39	2 214 929	1 118 391	1 096 538	...	...	...	...	...	...
40 - 44	2 015 514	1 005 140	1 010 374	...	...	...	...	...	...
45 - 49	1 559 527	766 054	793 473	...	...	...	...	...	...
50 - 54	1 315 101	637 737	677 364	...	...	...	...	...	...
55 - 59	902 876	423 625	479 251	...	...	...	...	...	...
60 - 64	1 058 263	476 727	581 536	...	...	...	...	...	...
65 - 69	913 304	379 456	533 848	...	...	...	...	...	...
70 - 74	662 627	228 286	434 341	...	...	...	...	...	...
75 - 79	335 467	79 231	256 236	...	...	...	...	...	...
80 - 84	132 149	18 884	113 265	...	...	...	...	...	...
85 - 89	42 760	4 930	37 830	...	...	...	...	...	...
90 - 94	8 634	809	7 825	...	...	...	...	...	...
95 - 99	1 643	86	1 557	...	...	...	...	...	...
100 +	64	-	64	...	...	...	...	...	...
Georgia - Géorgie									
17 I 2002 (CDJC)									
Total	4 371 535	2 061 753	2 309 782	2 284 796	1 048 593	1 236 203	2 086 739	1 013 160	1 073 579
0 - 4	243 568	127 779	115 789	119 175	61 851	57 324	124 393	65 928	58 465
5 - 9	302 308	155 264	147 044	150 564	77 300	73 264	151 744	77 964	73 780
10 - 14	370 068	187 678	182 390	191 865	96 531	95 334	178 203	91 147	87 056
15 - 19	357 145	179 794	177 351	190 150	95 987	94 163	166 995	83 807	83 188
20 - 24	327 471	162 569	164 902	177 627	86 406	91 221	149 844	76 163	73 681
25 - 29	311 176	151 745	159 431	168 296	78 706	89 590	142 880	73 039	69 841
30 - 34	300 627	144 684	155 943	161 487	73 315	88 172	139 140	71 369	67 771
35 - 39	323 458	152 004	171 454	175 874	77 752	98 122	147 584	74 252	73 332
40 - 44	335 467	157 732	177 735	187 574	84 237	103 337	147 893	73 495	74 398
45 - 49	287 627	134 084	153 543	162 159	72 744	89 415	125 468	61 340	64 128
50 - 54	247 379	114 595	132 784	141 002	63 824	77 178	106 377	50 771	55 606
55 - 59	148 879	66 968	81 911	80 951	35 495	45 456	67 928	31 473	36 455
60 - 64	257 825	111 150	146 675	128 088	53 245	74 843	129 737	57 905	71 832
65 - 69	202 359	87 403	114 956	91 740	37 663	54 077	110 619	49 740	60 879
70 - 74	175 880	72 530	103 350	77 423	29 568	47 855	98 457	42 962	55 495
75 - 79	104 771	36 238	68 533	47 593	15 106	32 487	57 178	21 132	36 046
80 - 84	43 731	11 563	32 168	19 338	4 890	14 448	24 393	6 673	17 720
85 - 89	20 057	4 841	15 216	8 573	2 092	6 481	11 484	2 749	8 735
90 - 94	6 884	1 523	5 361	2 428	553	1 875	4 456	970	3 486
95 - 99	1 883	300	1 583	484	90	394	1 399	210	1 189
100 +	650	73	577	127	22	105	523	51	472
Unknown - Inconnu	2 322	1 236	1 086	2 278	1 216	1 062	44	20	24
1 VII 2008 (ESDF)									
Total	4 383 800	2 079 600	2 304 200	...	...	...	...	...	...
0 - 4	239 800	127 500	112 300	...	...	...	...	...	...
5 - 9	232 200	122 400	109 800	...	...	...	...	...	...
10 - 14	280 200	145 500	134 700	...	...	...	...	...	...
15 - 19	360 900	183 200	177 700	...	...	...	...	...	...
20 - 24	360 300	182 200	178 100	...	...	...	...	...	...
25 - 29	332 200	166 200	166 000	...	...	...	...	...	...
30 - 34	310 800	152 600	158 200	...	...	...	...	...	...
35 - 39	299 700	144 400	155 300	...	...	...	...	...	...
40 - 44	302 200	142 200	160 000	...	...	...	...	...	...
45 - 49	334 700	155 300	179 400	...	...	...	...	...	...
50 - 54	286 300	131 600	154 700	...	...	...	...	...	...
55 - 59	248 800	112 600	136 200	...	...	...	...	...	...
60 - 64	158 900	70 900	88 000	...	...	...	...	...	...

7. Population by age, sex and urban/rural residence: latest available year, 2000 - 2009
Population selon l'âge, le sexe et la résidence, urbaine/rurale : dernière année disponible, 2000 - 2009 (continued - suite)

Continent, country or area, date, code and age (in years) Continent, pays ou zone, date, code et âge (en années)	Total			Urban - Urbaine			Rural - Rurale		
	Both sexes Les deux sexes	Male Masculin	Female Féminin	Both sexes Les deux sexes	Male Masculin	Female Féminin	Both sexes Les deux sexes	Male Masculin	Female Féminin
ASIA - ASIE									
Georgia - Géorgie									
1 VII 2008 (ESDF)									
65 - 69	195 800	80 100	115 700	...	...	...	...	...	...
70 - 74	185 800	75 400	110 400	...	...	...	...	...	...
75 - 79	133 200	51 200	82 000	...	...	...	...	...	...
80 - 84	82 900	27 900	55 000	...	...	...	...	...	...
85 +	39 100	8 400	30 700	...	...	...	...	...	...
India - Inde[44]									
1 III 2001 (CDFC)									
Total	1028610328	532 156 772	496 453 556	286 119 689	150 554 098	135 565 591	742 490 639	381 602 674	360 887 965
0 - 4	110 447 164	57 119 612	53 327 552	25 338 754	13 262 414	12 076 340	85 108 410	43 857 198	41 251 212
5 - 9	128 316 790	66 734 833	61 581 957	29 860 545	15 640 135	14 220 410	98 456 245	51 094 698	47 361 547
10 - 14	124 846 858	65 632 877	59 213 981	32 464 536	17 030 132	15 434 404	92 382 322	48 602 745	43 779 577
15 - 19	100 215 890	53 939 991	46 275 899	30 154 067	16 191 573	13 962 494	70 061 823	37 748 418	32 313 405
20 - 24	89 764 132	46 321 150	43 442 982	28 365 228	15 193 668	13 171 560	61 398 904	31 127 482	30 271 422
25 - 29	83 422 393	41 557 546	41 864 847	25 737 253	13 180 373	12 556 880	57 685 140	28 377 173	29 307 967
30 - 34	74 274 044	37 361 916	36 912 128	22 445 165	11 673 137	10 772 028	51 828 879	25 688 779	26 140 100
35 - 39	70 574 085	36 038 727	34 535 358	21 615 541	11 157 103	10 458 438	48 958 544	24 881 624	24 076 920
40 - 44	55 738 297	29 878 715	25 859 582	17 173 126	9 458 276	7 714 850	38 565 171	20 420 439	18 144 732
45 - 49	47 408 976	24 867 886	22 541 090	14 453 974	7 844 213	6 609 761	32 955 002	17 023 673	15 931 329
50 - 54	36 587 559	19 851 608	16 735 951	10 809 961	6 038 917	4 771 044	25 777 598	13 812 691	11 964 907
55 - 59	27 653 347	13 583 022	14 070 325	7 682 278	4 010 268	3 672 010	19 971 069	9 572 754	10 398 315
60 - 64	27 516 779	13 586 347	13 930 432	6 864 810	3 439 621	3 425 189	20 651 969	10 146 726	10 505 243
65 - 69	19 806 955	9 472 103	10 334 852	4 990 199	2 401 397	2 588 802	14 816 756	7 070 706	7 746 050
70 - 74	14 708 644	7 527 688	7 180 956	3 579 168	1 780 696	1 798 472	11 129 476	5 746 992	5 382 484
75 - 79	6 551 225	3 263 209	3 288 016	1 721 085	851 088	869 997	4 830 140	2 412 121	2 418 019
80 +	8 038 718	3 918 980	4 119 738	2 022 345	935 920	1 086 425	6 016 373	2 983 060	3 033 313
Unknown - Inconnu	2 738 472	1 500 562	1 237 910	841 654	465 167	376 487	1 896 818	1 035 395	861 423
Indonesia - Indonésie									
31 X 2005 (SSDF)[45]									
Total	213 375 287	107 274 528	106 100 759	92 005 069	46 055 993	45 949 076	121 370 218	61 218 535	60 151 683
0 - 4	19 095 151	9 732 578	9 362 573	8 117 666	4 129 250	3 988 416	10 977 485	5 603 328	5 374 157
5 - 9	21 563 945	11 089 478	10 474 467	8 573 265	4 417 551	4 155 714	12 990 680	6 671 927	6 318 753
10 - 14	21 306 096	10 956 648	10 349 448	8 472 639	4 343 105	4 129 534	12 833 457	6 613 543	6 219 914
15 - 19	19 796 921	10 103 778	9 693 143	8 585 104	4 254 987	4 330 117	11 211 817	5 848 791	5 363 026
20 - 24	19 445 179	9 533 960	9 911 219	9 594 049	4 647 995	4 946 054	9 851 130	4 885 965	4 965 165
25 - 29	18 680 093	9 078 324	9 601 769	8 955 039	4 392 942	4 562 097	9 725 054	4 685 382	5 039 672
30 - 34	17 420 029	8 543 620	8 876 409	7 945 419	3 905 345	4 040 074	9 474 610	4 638 275	4 836 335
35 - 39	16 454 100	8 186 060	8 268 040	7 267 101	3 642 139	3 624 962	9 186 999	4 543 921	4 643 078
40 - 44	14 489 902	7 273 553	7 216 349	6 311 684	3 162 768	3 148 916	8 178 218	4 110 785	4 067 433
45 - 49	12 382 818	6 303 669	6 079 149	5 294 629	2 706 752	2 587 877	7 088 189	3 596 917	3 491 272
50 - 54	9 941 064	5 175 796	4 765 268	4 154 253	2 167 922	1 986 331	5 786 811	3 007 874	2 778 937
55 - 59	7 262 179	3 755 532	3 506 647	2 830 595	1 440 270	1 390 325	4 431 584	2 315 262	2 116 322
60 - 64	5 611 827	2 748 283	2 863 544	2 193 103	1 079 057	1 114 046	3 418 724	1 669 226	1 749 498
65 - 69	4 112 165	1 957 037	2 155 128	1 565 522	750 321	815 201	2 546 643	1 206 716	1 339 927
70 - 74	2 989 927	1 448 024	1 541 903	1 101 672	519 815	581 857	1 888 255	928 209	960 046
75 - 79	1 573 741	786 789	786 952	604 849	297 376	307 473	968 892	489 413	479 479
80 - 84	797 616	392 368	405 248	283 683	136 765	146 918	513 933	255 603	258 330
85 - 89	287 470	135 751	151 719	97 793	36 302	61 491	189 677	99 449	90 228
90 - 94	104 195	48 039	56 156	40 139	18 078	22 061	64 056	29 961	34 095
95 +	60 869	25 241	35 628	16 865	7 253	9 612	44 004	17 988	26 016
1 VII 2009* (ESDJ)									
Total	231 369 500	115 817 900	115 551 600	...	...	...	...	...	...
0 - 4	21 374 000	10 920 900	10 453 100	...	...	...	...	...	...
5 - 9	20 381 500	10 399 500	9 982 000	...	...	...	...	...	...
10 - 14	20 618 200	10 489 700	10 128 500	...	...	...	...	...	...
15 - 19	21 195 700	10 783 500	10 412 200	...	...	...	...	...	...
20 - 24	21 121 200	10 681 200	10 440 000	...	...	...	...	...	...
25 - 29	20 627 100	10 244 000	10 383 100	...	...	...	...	...	...
30 - 34	19 698 200	9 576 600	10 121 600	...	...	...	...	...	...
35 - 39	18 066 600	8 830 100	9 236 500	...	...	...	...	...	...
40 - 44	16 179 100	8 034 600	8 144 500	...	...	...	...	...	...
45 - 49	14 041 900	7 050 800	6 991 100	...	...	...	...	...	...
50 - 54	11 435 500	5 849 800	5 585 700	...	...	...	...	...	...
55 - 59	8 645 100	4 453 600	4 191 500	...	...	...	...	...	...

Continent, country or area, date, code and age (in years) / Continent, pays ou zone, date, code et âge (en années)	Total			Urban - Urbaine			Rural - Rurale		
	Both sexes Les deux sexes	Male Masculin	Female Féminin	Both sexes Les deux sexes	Male Masculin	Female Féminin	Both sexes Les deux sexes	Male Masculin	Female Féminin
ASIA - ASIE									
Indonesia - Indonésie									
1 VII 2009* (ESDJ)									
60 - 64	6 138 500	3 071 900	3 066 600	...	...	...	...	...	...
65 - 69	4 501 100	2 146 800	2 354 300	...	...	...	...	...	...
70 - 74	3 523 300	1 629 100	1 894 200	...	...	...	...	...	...
75 +	3 822 500	1 655 800	2 166 700	...	...	...	...	...	...
Iran (Islamic Republic of) - Iran (République islamique d')[46]									
28 X 2006 (CDJC)									
Total	70 495 782	35 866 362	34 629 420	48 259 964	24 576 442	23 683 522	22 131 101	11 236 855	10 894 246
0 - 4	5 463 978	2 801 568	2 662 410	3 565 916	1 829 001	1 736 915	1 887 392	967 079	920 313
5 - 9	5 509 057	2 820 524	2 688 533	3 598 374	1 842 333	1 756 041	1 899 692	972 653	927 039
10 - 14	6 708 594	3 441 245	3 267 349	4 277 679	2 191 218	2 086 461	2 418 523	1 243 833	1 174 690
15 - 19	8 726 761	4 442 901	4 283 860	5 776 097	2 935 673	2 840 424	2 936 385	1 499 970	1 436 415
20 - 24	9 011 422	4 511 851	4 499 571	6 259 429	3 100 943	3 158 486	2 739 796	1 404 789	1 335 007
25 - 29	7 224 952	3 660 167	3 564 785	5 077 373	2 562 557	2 514 816	2 137 610	1 092 578	1 045 032
30 - 34	5 553 531	2 837 969	2 715 562	3 928 775	2 010 887	1 917 888	1 618 164	823 809	794 355
35 - 39	4 921 124	2 511 545	2 409 579	3 593 610	1 844 232	1 749 378	1 322 078	664 694	657 384
40 - 44	4 089 158	2 081 679	2 007 479	3 033 650	1 557 353	1 476 297	1 050 975	522 251	528 724
45 - 49	3 522 761	1 792 481	1 730 280	2 573 962	1 325 730	1 248 232	944 457	464 636	479 821
50 - 54	2 755 420	1 386 063	1 369 357	1 979 657	1 023 518	956 139	771 985	360 739	411 246
55 - 59	1 887 981	923 536	964 445	1 315 505	665 561	649 944	569 871	256 680	313 191
60 - 64	1 464 452	726 449	738 003	979 809	497 943	481 866	482 256	227 163	255 093
65 - 69	1 197 550	622 470	575 080	775 173	405 012	370 161	420 834	216 509	204 325
70 - 74	1 119 318	598 231	521 087	692 753	363 249	329 504	425 040	233 970	191 070
75 - 79	694 122	372 570	321 552	426 926	220 338	206 588	266 407	151 703	114 704
80 - 84	445 060	236 980	208 080	279 444	142 408	137 036	165 176	94 298	70 878
85 - 89	127 660	63 992	63 668	82 379	39 265	43 114	45 155	24 656	20 499
90 - 94	39 378	18 792	20 586	24 393	11 007	13 386	14 919	7 742	7 177
95 - 99	16 652	7 754	8 898	9 802	4 284	5 518	6 822	3 453	3 369
100 +	16 851	7 595	9 256	9 258	3 930	5 328	7 564	3 650	3 914
Iraq									
1 VII 2007 (ESDF)									
Total	29 682 081	14 943 516	14 738 565	19 752 833	9 970 074	9 782 759	9 929 248	4 973 442	4 955 806
0 - 4	4 970 829	2 548 402	2 422 427	3 093 542	1 585 669	1 507 873	1 877 287	962 733	914 554
5 - 9	4 222 028	2 166 818	2 055 210	2 665 680	1 367 692	1 297 988	1 556 348	799 126	757 222
10 - 14	3 605 956	1 833 813	1 772 143	2 313 228	1 174 857	1 138 371	1 292 728	658 956	633 772
15 - 19	3 206 547	1 631 272	1 575 275	2 097 711	1 067 009	1 030 702	1 108 836	564 263	544 573
20 - 24	2 745 916	1 394 941	1 350 975	1 836 580	933 972	902 608	909 336	460 969	448 367
25 - 29	2 342 651	1 184 126	1 158 525	1 595 244	808 530	786 714	747 407	375 596	371 811
30 - 34	1 969 141	987 662	981 479	1 367 432	689 466	677 966	601 709	298 196	303 513
35 - 39	1 623 309	806 089	817 220	1 147 326	574 647	572 679	475 983	231 442	244 541
40 - 44	1 280 968	624 348	656 620	925 668	457 710	467 958	355 300	166 638	188 662
45 - 49	1 024 602	494 742	529 860	748 849	368 114	380 735	275 753	126 628	149 125
50 - 54	790 298	378 954	411 344	581 704	284 864	296 840	208 594	94 090	114 504
55 - 59	611 439	292 240	319 199	451 250	220 282	230 968	160 189	71 958	88 231
60 - 64	453 767	218 171	235 596	333 655	163 325	170 330	120 112	54 846	65 266
65 - 69	325 970	154 180	171 790	238 913	114 733	124 180	87 057	39 447	47 610
70 - 74	214 454	98 274	116 180	156 363	72 358	84 005	58 091	25 916	32 175
75 - 79	133 345	58 821	74 524	94 738	41 841	52 897	38 607	16 980	21 627
80 +	160 861	70 663	90 198	104 950	45 005	59 945	55 911	25 658	30 253
Israel - Israël[47]									
1 VII 2009 (ESDJ)									
Total	7 485 565	3 701 384	3 784 181	6 865 023	3 384 556	3 480 467	620 542	316 828	303 714
0	157 666	80 603	77 063	143 758	73 500	70 257	13 909	7 103	6 806
1 - 4	596 064	305 810	290 255	542 791	278 614	264 177	53 273	27 196	26 077
5 - 9	700 579	358 966	341 613	637 625	326 709	310 916	62 954	32 257	30 698
10 - 14	632 523	324 104	308 419	575 724	294 672	281 052	56 799	29 432	27 368
15 - 19	593 914	304 115	289 799	537 484	273 624	263 860	56 430	30 491	25 939
20 - 24	577 003	293 064	283 939	528 538	267 136	261 402	48 465	25 927	22 538
25 - 29	565 875	284 450	281 425	523 031	262 200	260 831	42 844	22 250	20 594
30 - 34	547 172	272 833	274 339	502 442	250 732	251 709	44 731	22 101	22 630
35 - 39	500 939	248 830	252 109	455 013	226 266	228 747	45 926	22 564	23 362
40 - 44	423 713	209 934	213 779	386 967	191 187	195 779	36 746	18 746	18 000

7. Population by age, sex and urban/rural residence: latest available year, 2000 - 2009
Population selon l'âge, le sexe et la résidence, urbaine/rurale : dernière année disponible, 2000 - 2009 (continued - suite)

Continent, country or area, date, code and age (in years) / Continent, pays ou zone, date, code et âge (en années)	Total			Urban - Urbaine			Rural - Rurale		
	Both sexes Les deux sexes	Male Masculin	Female Féminin	Both sexes Les deux sexes	Male Masculin	Female Féminin	Both sexes Les deux sexes	Male Masculin	Female Féminin
ASIA - ASIE									
Israel - Israël[47]									
1 VII 2009 (ESDJ)									
45 - 49	396 933	193 848	203 085	364 691	177 448	187 243	32 243	16 401	15 842
50 - 54	381 822	184 353	197 469	351 700	168 871	182 829	30 123	15 483	14 640
55 - 59	369 008	177 083	191 925	340 789	162 520	178 268	28 219	14 562	13 657
60 - 64	308 243	146 608	161 635	286 833	135 702	151 131	21 410	10 906	10 504
65 - 69	193 676	90 007	103 669	180 235	83 208	97 027	13 441	6 799	6 642
70 - 74	190 629	85 410	105 219	179 459	79 880	99 579	11 170	5 529	5 641
75 - 79	145 200	62 139	83 061	136 542	58 317	78 225	8 658	3 822	4 837
80 - 84	110 643	43 370	67 273	103 974	40 634	63 340	6 669	2 736	3 933
85 - 89	64 608	24 930	39 678	60 333	23 211	37 122	4 276	1 719	2 556
90 - 94	20 452	7 605	12 847	18 900	7 024	11 876	1 552	581	971
95 - 99	7 300	2 654	4 646	6 699	2 464	4 236	600	190	410
100 +	1 603	670	933	1 499	637	862	104	33	71
Japan - Japon[48]									
1 X 2005 (CDJC)									
Total	127 767 994	62 348 977	65 419 017	110 264 324	53 886 000	56 378 324	17 503 670	8 462 977	9 040 693
0 - 4	5 578 087	2 854 502	2 723 585	4 852 006	2 482 703	2 369 303	726 081	371 799	354 282
5 - 9	5 928 495	3 036 503	2 891 992	5 109 001	2 616 615	2 492 386	819 494	419 888	399 606
10 - 14	6 014 652	3 080 678	2 933 974	5 127 976	2 626 071	2 501 905	886 676	454 607	432 069
15 - 19	6 568 380	3 373 430	3 194 950	5 651 131	2 902 583	2 748 548	917 249	470 847	446 402
20 - 24	7 350 598	3 754 822	3 595 776	6 502 213	3 325 698	3 176 515	848 385	429 124	419 261
25 - 29	8 280 049	4 198 551	4 081 498	7 321 003	3 708 770	3 612 233	959 046	489 781	469 265
30 - 34	9 754 857	4 933 265	4 821 592	8 660 059	4 375 975	4 284 084	1 094 798	557 290	537 508
35 - 39	8 735 781	4 402 787	4 332 994	7 742 640	3 907 842	3 834 798	993 141	494 945	498 196
40 - 44	8 080 596	4 065 470	4 015 126	7 062 486	3 557 472	3 505 014	1 018 110	507 998	510 112
45 - 49	7 725 861	3 867 500	3 858 361	6 616 303	3 310 680	3 305 623	1 109 558	556 820	552 738
50 - 54	8 796 499	4 383 240	4 413 259	7 480 089	3 718 540	3 761 549	1 316 410	664 700	651 710
55 - 59	10 255 164	5 077 369	5 177 795	8 818 349	4 353 419	4 464 930	1 436 815	723 950	712 865
60 - 64	8 544 629	4 154 529	4 390 100	7 385 888	3 589 046	3 796 842	1 158 741	565 483	593 258
65 - 69	7 432 610	3 545 006	3 887 604	6 353 609	3 033 231	3 320 378	1 079 001	511 775	567 226
70 - 74	6 637 497	3 039 743	3 597 754	5 584 991	2 560 738	3 024 253	1 052 506	479 005	573 501
75 - 79	5 262 801	2 256 317	3 006 484	4 347 080	1 866 530	2 480 550	915 721	389 787	525 934
80 - 84	3 412 393	1 222 635	2 189 758	2 791 585	1 002 599	1 788 986	620 808	220 036	400 772
85 - 89	1 849 260	555 126	1 294 134	1 508 536	453 182	1 055 354	340 724	101 944	238 780
90 - 94	840 870	210 586	630 284	685 165	172 256	512 909	155 705	38 330	117 375
95 - 99	211 221	41 426	169 795	171 626	33 755	137 871	39 595	7 671	31 924
100 +	25 353	3 760	21 593	20 442	3 037	17 405	4 911	723	4 188
Unknown - Inconnu	482 341	291 732	190 609	472 146	285 258	186 888	10 195	6 474	3 721
1 VII 2009 (ESDJ)[12]									
Total	127 558 000	62 140 000	65 418 000	...	...	...	...	...	...
0 - 4	5 386 000	2 761 000	2 625 000	...	...	...	...	...	...
5 - 9	5 717 000	2 931 000	2 786 000	...	...	...	...	...	...
10 - 14	5 971 000	3 058 000	2 912 000	...	...	...	...	...	...
15 - 19	6 093 000	3 119 000	2 974 000	...	...	...	...	...	...
20 - 24	6 994 000	3 590 000	3 404 000	...	...	...	...	...	...
25 - 29	7 534 000	3 846 000	3 688 000	...	...	...	...	...	...
30 - 34	8 700 000	4 414 000	4 286 000	...	...	...	...	...	...
35 - 39	9 662 000	4 886 000	4 776 000	...	...	...	...	...	...
40 - 44	8 544 000	4 301 000	4 243 000	...	...	...	...	...	...
45 - 49	7 779 000	3 905 000	3 874 000	...	...	...	...	...	...
50 - 54	7 774 000	3 878 000	3 896 000	...	...	...	...	...	...
55 - 59	9 299 000	4 598 000	4 701 000	...	...	...	...	...	...
60 - 64	9 260 000	4 527 000	4 733 000	...	...	...	...	...	...
65 - 69	8 334 000	3 982 000	4 352 000	...	...	...	...	...	...
70 - 74	6 905 000	3 194 000	3 711 000	...	...	...	...	...	...
75 - 79	5 783 000	2 513 000	3 270 000	...	...	...	...	...	...
80 - 84	4 202 000	1 638 000	2 564 000	...	...	...	...	...	...
85 +	3 622 000	999 000	2 622 000	...	...	...	...	...	...
Jordan - Jordanie									
1 X 2004 (CDFC)[49]									
Total	5 103 639	2 626 287	2 477 352	3 997 383	2 055 431	1 941 952	1 106 256	570 856	535 400
0	122 757	62 643	60 114	94 974	48 529	46 445	27 783	14 114	13 669
1 - 4	527 574	270 573	257 001	408 893	209 140	199 753	118 681	61 433	57 248
5 - 9	642 871	329 133	313 738	495 583	253 774	241 809	147 288	75 359	71 929

Continent, country or area, date, code and age (in years) / Continent, pays ou zone, date, code et âge (en annèes)	Total			Urban - Urbaine			Rural - Rurale		
	Both sexes Les deux sexes	Male Masculin	Female Féminin	Both sexes Les deux sexes	Male Masculin	Female Féminin	Both sexes Les deux sexes	Male Masculin	Female Féminin
ASIA - ASIE									
Jordan - Jordanie									
1 X 2004 (CDFC)[49]									
10 - 14	610 129	313 083	297 046	469 321	240 723	228 598	140 808	72 360	68 448
15 - 19	559 838	287 693	272 145	431 275	221 213	210 062	128 563	66 480	62 083
20 - 24	540 193	279 600	260 593	421 400	217 092	204 308	118 793	62 508	56 285
25 - 29	456 261	239 774	216 487	355 950	186 570	169 380	100 311	53 204	47 107
30 - 34	399 169	207 178	191 991	316 235	164 238	151 997	82 934	42 940	39 994
35 - 39	323 426	167 737	155 689	259 736	134 829	124 907	63 690	32 908	30 782
40 - 44	241 400	123 945	117 455	196 923	101 442	95 481	44 477	22 503	21 974
45 - 49	170 456	87 098	83 358	138 372	70 890	67 482	32 084	16 208	15 876
50 - 54	128 240	64 607	63 633	102 179	51 210	50 969	26 061	13 397	12 664
55 - 59	113 721	55 765	57 956	92 893	45 618	47 275	20 828	10 147	10 681
60 - 64	98 787	52 084	46 703	80 269	42 634	37 635	18 518	9 450	9 068
65 - 69	71 823	37 095	34 728	57 484	29 956	27 528	14 339	7 139	7 200
70 - 74	46 820	23 467	23 353	36 958	18 503	18 455	9 862	4 964	4 898
75 - 79	24 268	12 651	11 617	19 160	9 923	9 237	5 108	2 728	2 380
80 +	22 060	10 137	11 923	16 376	7 369	9 007	5 684	2 768	2 916
80 - 84	13 585	6 144	7 441	...	...	...	...	...	...
85 - 89	5 032	2 444	2 588	...	...	...	...	...	...
90 - 94	2 316	1 012	1 304	...	...	...	...	...	...
95 +	1 127	537	590	...	...	...	...	...	...
Unknown - Inconnu	3 846	2 024	1 822	3 402	1 778	1 624	444	246	198
31 XII 2009 (ESDF)[50]									
Total	5 980 000	3 082 000	2 898 000	...	...	...	...	...	...
0	143 924	73 661	70 263	...	...	...	...	...	...
1 - 4	618 546	317 759	300 787	...	...	...	...	...	...
5 - 9	754 080	386 480	367 600	...	...	...	...	...	...
10 - 14	715 210	367 990	347 220	...	...	...	...	...	...
15 - 19	656 600	337 790	318 810	...	...	...	...	...	...
20 - 24	633 280	328 230	305 050	...	...	...	...	...	...
25 - 29	535 210	281 690	253 520	...	...	...	...	...	...
30 - 34	468 230	243 480	224 750	...	...	...	...	...	...
35 - 39	379 130	197 250	181 880	...	...	...	...	...	...
40 - 44	282 850	145 470	137 380	...	...	...	...	...	...
45 - 49	199 730	102 320	97 410	...	...	...	...	...	...
50 - 54	150 100	75 820	74 280	...	...	...	...	...	...
55 - 59	133 350	65 340	68 010	...	...	...	...	...	...
60 - 64	116 010	61 020	54 990	...	...	...	...	...	...
65 - 69	84 360	43 430	40 930	...	...	...	...	...	...
70 - 74	54 990	27 660	27 330	...	...	...	...	...	...
75 - 79	28 500	14 820	13 680	...	...	...	...	...	...
80 - 84	15 950	7 200	8 750	...	...	...	...	...	...
85 - 89	5 910	2 770	3 140	...	...	...	...	...	...
90 - 94	2 720	1 190	1 530	...	...	...	...	...	...
95 +	1 320	630	690	...	...	...	...	...	...
Kazakhstan									
1 VII 2008 (ESDF)									
Total	15 674 000	7 541 053	8 132 947	8 331 030	3 877 559	4 453 471	7 342 970	3 663 494	3 679 476
0	334 121	171 415	162 706	182 521	93 735	88 786	151 600	77 680	73 920
1 - 4	1 123 822	576 735	547 087	598 929	307 667	291 262	524 893	269 068	255 825
5 - 9	1 102 548	564 701	537 847	524 034	268 924	255 110	578 514	295 777	282 737
10 - 14	1 209 513	617 314	592 199	522 195	266 983	255 212	687 318	350 331	336 987
15 - 19	1 486 438	755 608	730 830	695 164	350 949	344 215	791 274	404 659	386 615
20 - 24	1 550 478	784 675	765 803	800 736	396 991	403 745	749 742	387 684	362 058
25 - 29	1 295 879	651 820	644 059	741 385	357 306	384 079	554 494	294 514	259 980
30 - 34	1 176 482	580 262	596 220	654 261	305 967	348 294	522 221	274 295	247 926
35 - 39	1 092 697	533 348	559 349	613 063	284 686	328 377	479 634	248 662	230 972
40 - 44	1 044 896	501 603	543 293	581 382	267 483	313 899	463 514	234 120	229 394
45 - 49	1 095 437	515 147	580 290	616 824	279 070	337 754	478 613	236 077	242 536
50 - 54	887 374	404 797	482 577	502 890	220 181	282 709	384 484	184 616	199 868
55 - 59	700 438	306 307	394 131	403 592	169 371	234 221	296 846	136 936	159 910
60 - 64	382 873	160 524	222 349	220 385	87 967	132 418	162 488	72 557	89 931
65 - 69	440 247	168 503	271 744	241 208	86 342	154 866	199 039	82 161	116 878
70 - 74	353 774	131 480	222 294	200 160	69 161	130 999	153 614	62 319	91 295
75 - 79	208 952	68 446	140 506	121 852	37 430	84 422	87 100	31 016	56 084

Continent, country or area, date, code and age (in years) / Continent, pays ou zone, date, code et âge (en années)	Total			Urban - Urbaine			Rural - Rurale		
	Both sexes Les deux sexes	Male Masculin	Female Féminin	Both sexes Les deux sexes	Male Masculin	Female Féminin	Both sexes Les deux sexes	Male Masculin	Female Féminin
ASIA - ASIE									
Kazakhstan									
1 VII 2008 (ESDF)									
80 - 84	134 530	36 112	98 418	79 726	20 091	59 635	54 804	16 021	38 783
85 - 89	39 793	9 112	30 681	23 445	5 414	18 031	16 348	3 698	12 650
90 - 94	10 304	2 091	8 213	5 713	1 262	4 451	4 591	829	3 762
95 - 99	2 678	731	1 947	1 271	417	854	1 407	314	1 093
100 +	726	322	404	294	162	132	432	160	272
Kuwait - Koweït									
1 VII 2009 (ESDF)									
Total	2 583 020	1 539 825	1 043 195	...	...	...	...	...	...
0	51 213	26 580	24 634	...	...	...	...	...	...
1 - 4	200 165	103 249	96 916	...	...	...	...	...	...
5 - 9	226 855	117 055	109 800	...	...	...	...	...	...
10 - 14	195 106	101 616	93 490	...	...	...	...	...	...
15 - 19	176 296	91 852	84 444	...	...	...	...	...	...
20 - 24	231 623	132 478	99 145	...	...	...	...	...	...
25 - 29	328 863	208 543	120 320	...	...	...	...	...	...
30 - 34	313 230	202 310	110 920	...	...	...	...	...	...
35 - 39	275 906	181 271	94 635	...	...	...	...	...	...
40 - 44	206 372	134 490	71 882	...	...	...	...	...	...
45 - 49	150 009	99 783	50 226	...	...	...	...	...	...
50 - 54	95 739	63 161	32 578	...	...	...	...	...	...
55 - 59	56 755	35 898	20 857	...	...	...	...	...	...
60 - 64	32 491	18 991	13 500	...	...	...	...	...	...
65 - 69	19 865	11 039	8 826	...	...	...	...	...	...
70 - 74	11 647	6 122	5 525	...	...	...	...	...	...
75 - 79	6 166	3 114	3 052	...	...	...	...	...	...
80 +	4 718	2 273	2 445	...	...	...	...	...	...
Kyrgyzstan - Kirghizstan[51]									
1 VII 2009 (ESDJ)									
Total	5 383 277	2 656 660	2 726 617	1 835 028	866 718	968 310	3 548 249	1 789 942	1 758 307
0	124 773	63 983	60 790	...	...	...	...	...	...
1 - 4	458 370	233 440	224 930	135 984	68 906	67 078	322 386	164 534	157 852
5 - 9	502 718	256 174	246 544	143 634	72 891	70 743	359 084	183 283	175 801
10 - 14	539 762	274 902	264 860	152 554	77 267	75 287	387 208	197 635	189 573
15 - 19	601 862	304 302	297 560	203 672	99 440	104 232	398 190	204 862	193 328
20 - 24	588 049	294 299	293 750	227 536	107 460	120 076	360 513	186 839	173 674
25 - 29	454 745	229 893	224 852	161 824	78 551	83 273	292 921	151 342	141 579
30 - 34	379 944	190 075	189 869	135 002	64 390	70 612	244 942	125 685	119 257
35 - 39	346 849	171 282	175 567	126 126	57 929	68 197	220 723	113 353	107 370
40 - 44	320 476	156 712	163 764	117 019	54 150	62 869	203 457	102 562	100 895
45 - 49	308 996	148 834	160 162	111 651	51 247	60 404	197 345	97 587	99 758
50 - 54	241 293	113 570	127 723	88 117	39 147	48 970	153 176	74 423	78 753
55 - 59	167 570	76 702	90 868	62 902	27 054	35 848	104 668	49 648	55 020
60 - 64	96 735	42 423	54 312	39 477	16 068	23 409	57 258	26 355	30 903
65 - 69	71 246	31 146	40 100	26 435	10 360	16 075	44 811	20 786	24 025
70 - 74	79 489	32 479	47 010	29 656	11 046	18 610	49 833	21 433	28 400
75 - 79	51 613	19 956	31 657	16 832	5 665	11 167	34 781	14 291	20 490
80 - 84	33 707	12 468	21 239	11 683	3 512	8 171	22 024	8 956	13 068
85 - 89	11 171	3 252	7 919	3 834	970	2 864	7 337	2 282	5 055
90 - 94	2 637	594	2 043	914	194	720	1 723	400	1 323
95 - 99	808	125	683	182	27	155	626	98	528
100 +	464	49	415	72	10	62	392	39	353
Lao People's Democratic Republic - République démocratique populaire lao									
1 III 2005 (CDJC)									
Total	5 621 982	2 800 551	2 821 431	1 522 137[52]	763 043[52]	759 094[52]	4 093 248[52]	2 033 289[52]	2 059 959[52]
0 - 4	700 915	351 559	349 356	135 758[52]	68 543[52]	67 215[52]	565 003[52]	282 939[52]	282 064[52]
5 - 9	749 208	379 137	370 071	155 490[52]	78 713[52]	76 777[52]	593 565[52]	300 341[52]	293 224[52]
10 - 14	767 156	391 785	375 371	188 311[52]	95 769[52]	92 542[52]	578 719[52]	295 944[52]	282 775[52]
15 - 19	647 269	323 729	323 540	202 877[52]	101 383[52]	101 494[52]	443 763[52]	221 962[52]	221 801[52]
20 - 24	515 297	253 926	261 371	180 777[52]	91 079[52]	89 698[52]	332 618[52]	161 532[52]	171 086[52]
25 - 29	429 609	211 279	218 330	132 858[52]	66 079[52]	66 779[52]	295 521[52]	144 368[52]	151 153[52]
30 - 34	359 995	176 515	183 480	110 035[52]	53 414[52]	56 621[52]	249 181[52]	122 647[52]	126 534[52]

Continent, country or area, date, code and age (in years) / Continent, pays ou zone, date, code et âge (en annèes)	Total			Urban - Urbaine			Rural - Rurale		
	Both sexes Les deux sexes	Male Masculin	Female Féminin	Both sexes Les deux sexes	Male Masculin	Female Féminin	Both sexes Les deux sexes	Male Masculin	Female Féminin
ASIA - ASIE									
Lao People's Democratic Republic - République démocratique populaire lao									
1 III 2005 (CDJC)									
35 - 39	329 777	164 415	165 362	99 816[52]	49 495[52]	50 321[52]	229 447[52]	114 592[52]	114 855[52]
40 - 44	265 867	132 335	133 532	80 714[52]	40 532[52]	40 182[52]	184 777[52]	91 575[52]	93 202[52]
45 - 49	227 167	113 869	113 298	65 746[52]	34 044[52]	31 702[52]	161 139[52]	79 640[52]	81 499[52]
50 - 54	177 980	86 770	91 210	47 891[52]	24 815[52]	23 076[52]	129 913[52]	61 854[52]	68 059[52]
55 - 59	128 331	62 691	65 640	34 546[52]	17 693[52]	16 853[52]	93 669[52]	44 925[52]	48 744[52]
60 - 64	105 014	50 006	55 008	26 734[52]	13 110[52]	13 624[52]	78 226[52]	36 864[52]	41 362[52]
65 - 69	79 540	38 289	41 251	21 869[52]	10 664[52]	11 205[52]	57 637[52]	27 609[52]	30 028[52]
70 - 74	59 579	27 652	31 927	16 214[52]	7 614[52]	8 600[52]	43 343[52]	20 020[52]	23 323[52]
75 - 79	37 172	17 964	19 208	10 859[52]	5 142[52]	5 717[52]	26 293[52]	12 813[52]	13 480[52]
80 - 84	22 582	10 402	12 180	6 248[52]	2 842[52]	3 406[52]	16 320[52]	7 553[52]	8 767[52]
85 - 89	10 328	4 631	5 697	3 070[52]	1 256[52]	1 814[52]	7 254[52]	3 371[52]	3 883[52]
90 - 94	4 745	1 964	2 781	1 216[52]	479[52]	737[52]	3 526[52]	1 484[52]	2 042[52]
95 - 99	2 375	982	1 393	665[52]	252[52]	413[52]	1 710[52]	730[52]	980[52]
100 +	1 416	480	936	252[52]	76[52]	176[52]	1 164[52]	404[52]	760[52]
Unknown - Inconnu	660	171	489	191[52]	49[52]	142[52]	460[52]	122[52]	338[52]
1 VII 2007 (ESDF)[53]									
Total	5 874 000	2 929 000	2 945 000	...	...	...	...	...	...
0 - 4	776 000	391 500	384 300	...	...	...	...	...	...
5 - 9	730 000	368 100	361 600	...	...	...	...	...	...
10 - 14	768 000	391 700	376 500	...	...	...	...	...	...
15 - 19	697 000	351 900	344 700	...	...	...	...	...	...
20 - 24	552 000	273 000	279 000	...	...	...	...	...	...
25 - 29	450 000	221 100	228 700	...	...	...	...	...	...
30 - 34	373 000	182 900	190 400	...	...	...	...	...	...
35 - 39	336 000	166 100	169 500	...	...	...	...	...	...
40 - 44	288 000	143 300	144 600	...	...	...	...	...	...
45 - 49	238 000	118 900	119 000	...	...	...	...	...	...
50 - 54	194 000	95 600	98 800	...	...	...	...	...	...
55 - 59	141 000	68 500	72 700	...	...	...	...	...	...
60 - 64	108 000	51 300	56 200	...	...	...	...	...	...
65 - 69	83 000	39 500	43 600	...	...	...	...	...	...
70 - 74	61 000	28 000	32 300	...	...	...	...	...	...
75 +	80 000	36 800	43 200	...	...	...	...	...	...
Lebanon - Liban[54]									
3 III 2007 (SSDF)									
Total	3 759 134	1 857 659	1 901 475	...	...	...	...	...	...
0 - 4	261 021	136 514	124 507	...	...	...	...	...	...
5 - 9	312 902	160 577	152 325	...	...	...	...	...	...
10 - 14	354 049	183 613	170 436	...	...	...	...	...	...
15 - 19	363 626	195 984	167 642	...	...	...	...	...	...
20 - 24	367 778	191 471	176 307	...	...	...	...	...	...
25 - 29	305 933	148 321	157 612	...	...	...	...	...	...
30 - 34	276 775	132 105	144 670	...	...	...	...	...	...
35 - 39	249 550	111 833	137 717	...	...	...	...	...	...
40 - 44	233 003	102 405	130 598	...	...	...	...	...	...
45 - 49	208 752	95 595	113 157	...	...	...	...	...	...
50 - 54	179 899	84 091	95 808	...	...	...	...	...	...
55 - 59	143 376	66 993	76 383	...	...	...	...	...	...
60 - 64	140 030	65 701	74 329	...	...	...	...	...	...
65 - 69	122 014	59 900	62 114	...	...	...	...	...	...
70 - 74	105 259	53 267	51 992	...	...	...	...	...	...
75 - 79	71 315	38 353	32 962	...	...	...	...	...	...
80 - 84	45 481	21 083	24 398	...	...	...	...	...	...
85 +	18 371	9 853	8 518	...	...	...	...	...	...
Malaysia - Malaisie[25]									
30 VI 2009 (ESDJ)									
Total	27 895 332	14 205 949	13 689 383	17 654 460	8 912 131	8 742 329	10 240 872	5 293 818	4 947 054
0	491 601	251 774	239 827	305 302	156 390	148 912	186 299	95 384	90 915
1 - 4	1 933 916	990 166	943 750	1 218 109	623 556	594 553	715 807	366 610	349 197
5 - 9	2 601 457	1 331 448	1 270 009	1 636 207	837 071	799 136	965 250	494 377	470 873

Continent, country or area, date, code and age (in years) / Continent, pays ou zone, date, code et âge (en années)	Total			Urban - Urbaine			Rural - Rurale		
	Both sexes Les deux sexes	Male Masculin	Female Féminin	Both sexes Les deux sexes	Male Masculin	Female Féminin	Both sexes Les deux sexes	Male Masculin	Female Féminin
ASIA - ASIE									
Malaysia - Malaisie[25]									
30 VI 2009 (ESDJ)									
10 - 14	2 697 211	1 390 485	1 306 726	1 654 315	853 061	801 254	1 042 896	537 424	505 472
15 - 19	2 637 123	1 356 309	1 280 814	1 543 400	794 411	748 989	1 093 723	561 898	531 825
20 - 24	2 524 265	1 281 791	1 242 474	1 454 424	735 656	718 768	1 069 841	546 135	523 706
25 - 29	2 381 477	1 201 253	1 180 224	1 469 118	727 117	742 001	912 359	474 136	438 223
30 - 34	2 256 593	1 142 806	1 113 787	1 551 093	756 246	794 847	705 500	386 560	318 940
35 - 39	2 106 395	1 071 023	1 035 372	1 459 722	719 121	740 601	646 673	351 902	294 771
40 - 44	1 954 109	1 001 231	952 878	1 322 666	665 215	657 451	631 443	336 016	295 427
45 - 49	1 721 023	885 029	835 994	1 160 556	592 801	567 755	560 467	292 228	268 239
50 - 54	1 427 759	734 389	693 370	947 975	488 292	459 683	479 784	246 097	233 687
55 - 59	1 116 483	573 794	542 689	718 379	371 363	347 016	398 104	202 431	195 673
60 - 64	764 437	392 971	371 466	473 840	245 823	228 017	290 597	147 148	143 449
65 - 69	511 025	254 449	256 576	303 236	152 207	151 029	207 789	102 242	105 547
70 - 74	355 502	167 182	188 320	204 071	96 102	107 969	151 431	71 080	80 351
75 - 79	216 789	97 729	119 060	122 767	54 646	68 121	94 022	43 083	50 939
80 - 84	119 636	52 472	67 164	65 971	27 826	38 145	53 665	24 646	29 019
85 - 89	48 957	20 331	28 626	26 921	10 490	16 431	22 036	9 841	12 195
90 +	29 574	9 317	20 257	16 388	4 737	11 651	13 186	4 580	8 606
Maldives									
21 III 2006 (CDFC)[55]									
Total	298 968	151 459	147 509	103 693	51 992	51 701	195 275	99 467	95 808
0	5 462	2 777	2 685	1 601	832	769	3 861	1 945	1 916
1 - 4	20 709	10 585	10 124	5 743	2 912	2 831	14 966	7 673	7 293
5 - 9	29 867	15 352	14 515	7 538	3 829	3 709	22 329	11 523	10 806
10 - 14	36 999	19 111	17 888	10 082	5 171	4 911	26 917	13 940	12 977
15 - 19	39 904	20 155	19 749	15 656	7 457	8 199	24 248	12 698	11 550
20 - 24	34 809	16 933	17 876	15 535	7 401	8 134	19 274	9 532	9 742
25 - 29	24 581	11 915	12 666	10 176	5 054	5 122	14 405	6 861	7 544
30 - 34	20 635	10 022	10 613	8 137	4 089	4 048	12 498	5 933	6 565
35 - 39	18 174	8 780	9 394	6 616	3 381	3 235	11 558	5 399	6 159
40 - 44	15 871	7 828	8 043	5 529	2 731	2 798	10 342	5 097	5 245
45 - 49	13 569	6 872	6 697	4 394	2 207	2 187	9 175	4 665	4 510
50 - 54	7 936	4 147	3 789	2 601	1 415	1 186	5 335	2 732	2 603
55 - 59	5 859	3 046	2 813	1 863	987	876	3 996	2 059	1 937
60 - 64	5 566	2 852	2 714	1 520	752	768	4 046	2 100	1 946
65 - 69	5 678	3 014	2 664	1 265	619	646	4 413	2 395	2 018
70 - 74	4 186	2 333	1 853	765	363	402	3 421	1 970	1 451
75 - 79	2 377	1 444	933	409	217	192	1 968	1 227	741
80 - 84	1 064	617	447	204	92	112	860	525	335
85 - 89	396	241	155	94	48	46	302	193	109
90 - 94	159	89	70	34	14	20	125	75	50
95 +	84	52	32	19	8	11	65	44	21
Unknown - Inconnu	5 083	3 294	1 789	3 912	2 413	1 499	1 171	881	290
1 VII 2009 (ESDF)									
Total	314 542	159 159	155 383	...	...	...	...	...	...
0 - 4	28 508	14 547	13 961	...	...	...	...	...	...
5 - 9	27 393	14 069	13 324	...	...	...	...	...	...
10 - 14	33 445	17 343	16 102	...	...	...	...	...	...
15 - 19	39 817	20 541	19 276	...	...	...	...	...	...
20 - 24	39 633	19 819	19 814	...	...	...	...	...	...
25 - 29	31 311	15 224	16 087	...	...	...	...	...	...
30 - 34	22 752	11 105	11 647	...	...	...	...	...	...
35 - 39	19 972	9 728	10 244	...	...	...	...	...	...
40 - 44	17 526	8 558	8 968	...	...	...	...	...	...
45 - 49	15 377	7 703	7 674	...	...	...	...	...	...
50 - 54	11 499	5 913	5 586	...	...	...	...	...	...
55 - 59	6 640	3 488	3 152	...	...	...	...	...	...
60 - 64	5 507	2 829	2 678	...	...	...	...	...	...
65 - 69	5 425	2 790	2 635	...	...	...	...	...	...
70 - 74	4 895	2 630	2 265	...	...	...	...	...	...
75 - 79	2 730	1 579	1 151	...	...	...	...	...	...
80 +	2 112	1 293	819	...	...	...	...	...	...

Continent, country or area, date, code and age (in years) Continent, pays ou zone, date, code et âge (en années)	Total			Urban - Urbaine			Rural - Rurale		
	Both sexes Les deux sexes	Male Masculin	Female Féminin	Both sexes Les deux sexes	Male Masculin	Female Féminin	Both sexes Les deux sexes	Male Masculin	Female Féminin
ASIA - ASIE									
Mongolia - Mongolie									
5 I 2000 (CDFC)									
Total	2 373 493	1 177 981	1 195 512	1 344 516	657 081	687 435	1 028 977	520 900	508 077
0	49 804	25 356	24 448	23 778	12 119	11 659	26 026	13 237	12 789
1 - 4	196 219	99 126	97 093	91 687	46 096	45 591	104 532	53 030	51 502
5 - 9	285 664	144 315	141 349	150 401	75 700	74 701	135 263	68 615	66 648
10 - 14	317 434	159 294	158 140	179 974	89 670	90 304	137 460	69 624	67 836
15 - 19	263 358	133 327	130 031	154 244	75 040	79 204	109 114	58 287	50 827
20 - 24	235 751	118 023	117 728	135 694	66 010	69 684	100 057	52 013	48 044
25 - 29	216 652	107 962	108 690	125 644	61 274	64 370	91 008	46 688	44 320
30 - 34	187 872	92 473	95 399	113 537	54 332	59 205	74 335	38 141	36 194
35 - 39	172 606	84 846	87 760	108 347	52 275	56 072	64 259	32 571	31 688
40 - 44	127 220	62 619	64 601	79 563	38 840	40 723	47 657	23 779	23 878
45 - 49	82 888	40 562	42 326	50 873	25 089	25 784	32 015	15 473	16 542
50 - 54	57 835	27 707	30 128	35 016	17 094	17 922	22 819	10 613	12 206
55 - 59	55 895	27 379	28 516	30 397	15 011	15 386	25 498	12 368	13 130
60 - 64	42 292	20 778	21 514	21 889	10 658	11 231	20 403	10 120	10 283
65 - 69	35 415	15 982	19 433	18 480	8 145	10 335	16 935	7 837	9 098
70 - 74	20 239	8 766	11 473	10 946	4 579	6 367	9 293	4 187	5 106
75 - 79	14 843	5 832	9 011	7 963	3 197	4 766	6 880	2 635	4 245
80 - 84	7 036	2 329	4 707	3 777	1 281	2 496	3 259	1 048	2 211
85 - 89	3 376	991	2 385	1 746	519	1 227	1 630	472	1 158
90 - 94	869	257	612	441	125	316	428	132	296
95 - 99	196	53	143	104	24	80	92	29	63
100 +	29	4	25	15	3	12	14	1	13
31 XII 2009 (ESDF)									
Total	2 670 241	1 304 216	1 366 025	...	...	...	...	...	...
0 - 4	253 456	128 764	124 692	...	...	...	...	...	...
5 - 9	234 910	119 003	115 907	...	...	...	...	...	...
10 - 14	256 000	129 781	126 219	...	...	...	...	...	...
15 - 19	290 187	145 287	144 900	...	...	...	...	...	...
20 - 24	286 692	139 457	147 235	...	...	...	...	...	...
25 - 29	242 126	117 278	124 848	...	...	...	...	...	...
30 - 34	222 934	108 235	114 699	...	...	...	...	...	...
35 - 39	200 753	96 821	103 932	...	...	...	...	...	...
40 - 44	178 913	85 555	93 358	...	...	...	...	...	...
45 - 49	157 318	74 893	82 425	...	...	...	...	...	...
50 - 54	113 303	53 918	59 385	...	...	...	...	...	...
55 - 59	73 674	34 701	38 973	...	...	...	...	...	...
60 - 64	50 714	23 309	27 405	...	...	...	...	...	...
65 - 69	43 883	20 430	23 453	...	...	...	...	...	...
70 +	65 378	26 784	38 594	...	...	...	...	...	...
Myanmar									
1 VII 2004 (ESDF)									
Total	54 299 000	27 000 000	27 299 000	...	...	...	...	...	...
0 - 4	6 407 000	3 235 000	3 172 000	...	...	...	...	...	...
5 - 9	5 933 000	2 974 000	2 959 000	...	...	...	...	...	...
10 - 14	5 382 000	2 715 000	2 667 000	...	...	...	...	...	...
15 - 19	4 824 000	2 512 000	2 312 000	...	...	...	...	...	...
20 - 24	4 748 000	2 429 000	2 319 000	...	...	...	...	...	...
25 - 29	4 490 000	2 265 000	2 225 000	...	...	...	...	...	...
30 - 34	4 135 000	2 059 000	2 076 000	...	...	...	...	...	...
35 - 39	3 760 000	1 845 000	1 915 000	...	...	...	...	...	...
40 - 44	3 287 000	1 604 000	1 683 000	...	...	...	...	...	...
45 - 49	2 759 000	1 340 000	1 419 000	...	...	...	...	...	...
50 - 54	2 293 000	1 107 000	1 186 000	...	...	...	...	...	...
55 - 59	1 818 000	872 000	946 000	...	...	...	...	...	...
60 - 64	1 478 000	698 000	780 000	...	...	...	...	...	...
65 +	2 985 000	1 345 000	1 640 000	...	...	...	...	...	...
Nepal - Népal									
1 VII 2006 (ESDJ)									
Total	25 886 736	12 963 722	12 923 014	4 322 996	2 232 313	2 090 683	21 563 740	10 731 409	10 832 331
0 - 4	3 568 600	1 832 732	1 735 868	482 534	251 880	230 654	3 086 066	1 580 852	1 505 214
5 - 9	3 112 108	1 603 608	1 508 500	418 722	218 749	199 973	2 693 386	1 384 859	1 308 527
10 - 14	3 017 657	1 535 618	1 482 039	458 911	233 315	225 596	2 558 746	1 302 303	1 256 443

7. Population by age, sex and urban/rural residence: latest available year, 2000 - 2009
Population selon l'âge, le sexe et la résidence, urbaine/rurale : dernière année disponible, 2000 - 2009 (continued - suite)

Continent, country or area, date, code and age (in years) / Continent, pays ou zone, date, code et âge (en annèes)	Total			Urban - Urbaine			Rural - Rurale		
	Both sexes Les deux sexes	Male Masculin	Female Féminin	Both sexes Les deux sexes	Male Masculin	Female Féminin	Both sexes Les deux sexes	Male Masculin	Female Féminin
ASIA - ASIE									
Nepal - Népal									
1 VII 2006 (ESDJ)									
15 - 19	2 869 366	1 452 401	1 416 965	517 173	274 346	242 827	2 352 193	1 178 055	1 174 138
20 - 24	2 457 240	1 205 933	1 251 307	506 464	265 809	240 655	1 950 776	940 124	1 010 652
25 - 29	2 091 314	1 001 466	1 089 848	423 370	213 550	209 820	1 667 944	787 916	880 028
30 - 34	1 777 559	846 995	930 564	352 648	178 640	174 008	1 424 911	668 355	756 556
35 - 39	1 513 800	735 895	777 905	286 249	145 132	141 117	1 227 551	590 763	636 788
40 - 44	1 274 854	630 870	643 984	226 520	120 105	106 415	1 048 334	510 765	537 569
45 - 49	1 058 220	528 209	530 011	176 213	92 653	83 560	882 007	435 556	446 451
50 - 54	866 006	436 625	429 381	137 925	71 822	66 103	728 081	364 803	363 278
55 - 59	697 708	355 765	341 943	106 612	55 686	50 926	591 096	300 079	291 017
60 - 64	551 122	280 939	270 183	76 723	38 696	38 027	474 399	242 243	232 156
65 - 69	417 278	210 038	207 240	59 808	28 731	31 077	357 470	181 307	176 163
70 - 74	290 840	145 150	145 690	41 164	19 121	22 043	249 676	126 029	123 647
75 +	323 064	161 478	161 586	51 959	24 078	27 881	271 105	137 400	133 705
Occupied Palestinian Territory - Territoire palestinien occupé									
1 VII 2009 (ESDF)									
Total	3 935 249	1 997 625	1 937 624	...	...	...	...	...	...
0	124 256	63 248	61 008	...	...	...	...	...	...
1 - 4	456 498	233 112	223 386	...	...	...	...	...	...
5 - 9	545 084	278 535	266 549	...	...	...	...	...	...
10 - 14	521 806	266 433	255 373	...	...	...	...	...	...
15 - 19	471 865	240 808	231 057	...	...	...	...	...	...
20 - 24	375 206	191 703	183 503	...	...	...	...	...	...
25 - 29	296 880	151 815	145 065	...	...	...	...	...	...
30 - 34	251 461	127 746	123 715	...	...	...	...	...	...
35 - 39	211 956	107 324	104 632	...	...	...	...	...	...
40 - 44	178 872	92 127	86 745	...	...	...	...	...	...
45 - 49	146 659	76 359	70 300	...	...	...	...	...	...
50 - 54	105 714	54 437	51 277	...	...	...	...	...	...
55 - 59	74 526	37 385	37 141	...	...	...	...	...	...
60 - 64	55 656	26 015	29 641	...	...	...	...	...	...
65 - 69	41 591	17 998	23 593	...	...	...	...	...	...
70 - 74	31 181	13 011	18 170	...	...	...	...	...	...
75 - 79	23 342	9 831	13 511	...	...	...	...	...	...
80 +	22 696	9 738	12 958	...	...	...	...	...	...
Oman									
1 VII 2009 (ESDF)									
Total	3 173 917	1 971 115	1 202 802	2 314 865	1 457 197	857 668	859 049	513 917	345 132
0 - 4	272 144	139 614	132 530	184 595	94 803	89 792	87 549	44 811	42 738
5 - 9	245 026	124 776	120 250	162 307	82 954	79 353	82 718	41 821	40 897
10 - 14	254 610	129 964	124 646	168 924	86 326	82 598	85 685	43 638	42 047
15 - 19	284 826	145 215	139 611	194 123	99 854	94 269	90 703	45 361	45 342
20 - 24	387 448	238 483	148 965	285 594	176 341	109 253	101 854	62 142	39 712
25 - 29	475 403	327 686	147 717	362 531	249 782	112 749	112 871	77 904	34 967
30 - 34	367 536	247 107	120 429	288 055	192 969	95 086	79 481	54 138	25 343
35 - 39	272 100	192 483	79 617	212 145	150 865	61 280	59 955	41 618	18 337
40 - 44	207 202	149 090	58 112	161 282	117 670	43 612	45 920	31 420	14 500
45 - 49	145 430	103 908	41 522	111 077	81 065	30 012	34 353	22 843	11 510
50 - 54	113 587	83 057	30 530	84 975	63 752	21 223	28 612	19 305	9 307
55 - 59	59 890	40 488	19 402	42 674	29 489	13 185	17 216	10 999	6 217
60 - 64	39 730	23 538	16 192	26 050	15 494	10 556	13 680	8 044	5 636
65 - 69	20 811	11 811	9 000	13 363	7 537	5 826	7 448	4 274	3 174
70 - 74	14 933	7 721	7 212	9 224	4 703	4 521	5 709	3 018	2 691
75 - 79	6 817	3 303	3 514	4 201	1 981	2 220	2 616	1 322	1 294
80 +	6 424	2 871	3 553	3 745	1 612	2 133	2 679	1 259	1 420
Pakistan[56]									
1 VII 2007 (ESDJ)									
Total	149 860 388	76 857 737	73 002 651	52 807 585	27 178 203	25 629 382	97 052 803	49 679 534	47 373 269
0 - 4	19 540 467	9 783 859	9 756 608	5 761 626	2 854 601	2 907 026	13 778 841	6 929 259	6 849 582
5 - 9	22 554 631	11 710 324	10 844 307	6 759 356	3 414 295	3 345 061	15 795 276	8 296 029	7 499 246
10 - 14	20 255 889	10 636 015	9 619 874	6 854 564	3 572 029	3 282 536	13 401 325	7 063 987	6 337 339
15 - 19	17 275 679	9 063 876	8 211 804	6 630 532	3 454 683	3 175 849	10 645 147	5 609 193	5 035 954

Continent, country or area, date, code and age (in years) / Continent, pays ou zone, date, code et âge (en années)	Total			Urban - Urbaine			Rural - Rurale		
	Both sexes Les deux sexes	Male Masculin	Female Féminin	Both sexes Les deux sexes	Male Masculin	Female Féminin	Both sexes Les deux sexes	Male Masculin	Female Féminin
ASIA - ASIE									
Pakistan[56]									
1 VII 2007 (ESDJ)									
20 - 24	13 558 584	6 824 723	6 733 861	5 604 996	2 913 936	2 691 060	7 953 588	3 910 786	4 042 801
25 - 29	10 833 092	5 268 436	5 564 656	4 174 036	2 128 117	2 045 919	6 659 055	3 140 318	3 518 737
30 - 34	8 432 325	3 957 414	4 474 911	3 112 553	1 539 219	1 573 334	5 319 772	2 418 195	2 901 576
35 - 39	8 352 417	4 132 910	4 219 507	3 081 885	1 522 176	1 559 709	5 270 532	2 610 734	2 659 798
40 - 44	6 777 652	3 496 263	3 281 389	2 564 848	1 348 144	1 216 704	4 212 804	2 148 119	2 064 685
45 - 49	6 276 492	3 277 150	2 999 342	2 458 241	1 271 498	1 186 743	3 818 252	2 005 652	1 812 599
50 - 54	4 586 117	2 429 295	2 156 822	1 772 219	967 032	805 188	2 813 897	1 462 263	1 351 634
55 - 59	3 544 175	1 864 568	1 679 608	1 325 845	693 075	632 770	2 218 330	1 171 493	1 046 838
60 - 64	2 933 669	1 637 251	1 296 418	1 003 276	574 578	428 698	1 930 393	1 062 673	867 720
65 - 69	2 038 506	1 106 476	932 030	713 604	371 079	342 526	1 324 901	735 397	589 504
70 - 74	1 464 156	857 310	606 846	499 821	282 013	217 808	964 335	575 297	389 039
75 - 79	654 088	358 255	295 833	244 044	125 467	118 577	410 044	232 788	177 256
80 - 84	428 280	250 734	177 547	129 604	84 073	45 531	298 676	166 661	132 015
85 +	354 168	202 880	151 288	116 534	62 189	54 345	237 634	140 691	96 943
Philippines[57]									
1 VII 2008 (ESDJ)									
Total	90 457 200	45 483 100	44 974 100	...	...	...	...	...	...
0 - 4	10 755 400	5 494 900	5 260 500	...	...	...	...	...	...
5 - 9	10 106 800	5 161 400	4 945 400	...	...	...	...	...	...
10 - 14	9 803 300	5 012 300	4 791 000	...	...	...	...	...	...
15 - 19	9 353 700	4 759 900	4 593 800	...	...	...	...	...	...
20 - 24	8 487 300	4 270 800	4 216 500	...	...	...	...	...	...
25 - 29	7 567 300	3 765 700	3 801 600	...	...	...	...	...	...
30 - 34	6 572 800	3 279 400	3 293 400	...	...	...	...	...	...
35 - 39	5 834 800	2 932 100	2 902 700	...	...	...	...	...	...
40 - 44	5 189 400	2 622 200	2 567 200	...	...	...	...	...	...
45 - 49	4 460 600	2 254 900	2 205 700	...	...	...	...	...	...
50 - 54	3 627 700	1 827 100	1 800 600	...	...	...	...	...	...
55 - 59	2 827 900	1 406 600	1 421 300	...	...	...	...	...	...
60 - 64	2 040 300	992 700	1 047 600	...	...	...	...	...	...
65 - 69	1 530 500	717 800	812 700	...	...	...	...	...	...
70 - 74	1 074 900	482 300	592 600	...	...	...	...	...	...
75 - 79	652 100	278 500	373 600	...	...	...	...	...	...
80 +	572 400	224 500	347 900	...	...	...	...	...	...
Qatar									
1 VII 2009 (ESDF)									
Total	1 638 644	1 265 155	373 489	...	...	...	...	...	...
0	17 651	9 000	8 651	...	...	...	...	...	...
1 - 4	66 959	34 541	32 418	...	...	...	...	...	...
5 - 9	75 542	39 053	36 489	...	...	...	...	...	...
10 - 14	63 619	32 894	30 725	...	...	...	...	...	...
15 - 19	62 174	36 558	25 616	...	...	...	...	...	...
20 - 24	228 412	193 513	34 899	...	...	...	...	...	...
25 - 29	309 450	259 945	49 505	...	...	...	...	...	...
30 - 34	244 248	199 362	44 886	...	...	...	...	...	...
35 - 39	198 388	163 049	35 339	...	...	...	...	...	...
40 - 44	145 130	118 394	26 736	...	...	...	...	...	...
45 - 49	98 937	79 522	19 415	...	...	...	...	...	...
50 - 54	65 288	53 047	12 241	...	...	...	...	...	...
55 - 59	32 861	26 047	6 814	...	...	...	...	...	...
60 - 64	14 277	10 551	3 726	...	...	...	...	...	...
65 - 69	6 535	4 231	2 304	...	...	...	...	...	...
70 - 74	3 962	2 374	1 588	...	...	...	...	...	...
75 - 79	2 414	1 444	970	...	...	...	...	...	...
80 +	2 797	1 630	1 167	...	...	...	...	...	...
Republic of Korea - République de Corée									
1 XI 2005 (CDJC)[58]									
Total	47 041 434	23 465 650	23 575 784	38 337 699	19 145 912	19 191 787	8 703 735	4 319 738	4 383 997
0	413 805	213 786	200 019	343 865	177 539	166 326	69 940	36 247	33 693
1 - 4	1 968 545	1 023 515	945 030	1 624 142	844 076	780 066	344 403	179 439	164 964
5 - 9	3 168 887	1 654 228	1 514 659	2 624 437	1 370 557	1 253 880	544 450	283 671	260 779
10 - 14	3 434 891	1 816 318	1 618 573	2 898 270	1 533 726	1 364 544	536 621	282 592	254 029

Continent, country or area, date, code and age (in years) Continent, pays ou zone, date, code et âge (en années)	Total			Urban - Urbaine			Rural - Rurale		
	Both sexes Les deux sexes	Male Masculin	Female Féminin	Both sexes Les deux sexes	Male Masculin	Female Féminin	Both sexes Les deux sexes	Male Masculin	Female Féminin
ASIA - ASIE									
Republic of Korea -									
République de Corée									
1 XI 2005 (CDJC)[58]									
15 - 19	3 100 523	1 626 378	1 474 145	2 629 214	1 378 088	1 251 126	471 309	248 290	223 019
20 - 24	3 662 123	1 915 902	1 746 221	3 147 034	1 611 993	1 535 041	515 089	303 909	211 180
25 - 29	3 671 847	1 858 332	1 813 515	3 174 220	1 589 865	1 584 355	497 627	268 467	229 160
30 - 34	4 096 282	2 059 913	2 036 369	3 485 192	1 739 536	1 745 656	611 090	320 377	290 713
35 - 39	4 112 785	2 065 668	2 047 117	3 474 836	1 726 349	1 748 487	637 949	339 319	298 630
40 - 44	4 123 041	2 082 427	2 040 614	3 479 360	1 738 972	1 740 388	643 681	343 455	300 226
45 - 49	3 900 899	1 961 859	1 939 040	3 252 059	1 626 493	1 625 566	648 840	335 366	313 474
50 - 54	2 855 297	1 426 597	1 428 700	2 314 379	1 157 586	1 156 793	540 918	269 011	271 907
55 - 59	2 278 438	1 126 997	1 151 441	1 773 373	882 089	891 284	505 065	244 908	260 157
60 - 64	1 888 853	897 384	991 469	1 370 485	665 921	704 564	518 368	231 463	286 905
65 - 69	1 680 067	755 949	924 118	1 106 537	508 208	598 329	573 530	247 741	325 789
70 - 74	1 252 734	514 241	738 493	773 269	319 475	453 794	479 465	194 766	284 699
75 - 79	766 870	270 632	496 238	466 206	161 741	304 465	300 664	108 891	191 773
80 - 84	432 259	136 705	295 554	261 192	79 567	181 625	171 067	57 138	113 929
85 +	233 288	58 819	174 469	139 629	34 131	105 498	93 659	24 688	68 971
1 VII 2009 (ESDJ)									
Total	48 746 693	24 481 480	24 265 213	...	...	...	...	...	...
0	443 017	229 620	213 397	...	...	...	...	...	...
1 - 4	1 773 902	919 680	854 222	...	...	...	...	...	...
5 - 9	2 691 271	1 403 384	1 287 887	...	...	...	...	...	...
10 - 14	3 272 176	1 721 323	1 550 853	...	...	...	...	...	...
15 - 19	3 350 366	1 781 088	1 569 278	...	...	...	...	...	...
20 - 24	3 145 632	1 647 301	1 498 331	...	...	...	...	...	...
25 - 29	3 869 568	1 995 603	1 873 965	...	...	...	...	...	...
30 - 34	3 828 324	1 975 428	1 852 896	...	...	...	...	...	...
35 - 39	4 356 322	2 234 979	2 121 343	...	...	...	...	...	...
40 - 44	4 132 628	2 108 390	2 024 238	...	...	...	...	...	...
45 - 49	4 238 746	2 144 231	2 094 515	...	...	...	...	...	...
50 - 54	3 733 465	1 882 442	1 851 023	...	...	...	...	...	...
55 - 59	2 617 987	1 302 116	1 315 871	...	...	...	...	...	...
60 - 64	2 100 579	1 023 109	1 077 470	...	...	...	...	...	...
65 - 69	1 819 626	833 140	986 486	...	...	...	...	...	...
70 - 74	1 485 732	636 512	849 220	...	...	...	...	...	...
75 - 79	1 000 155	376 918	623 237	...	...	...	...	...	...
80 - 84	541 966	175 102	366 864	...	...	...	...	...	...
85 - 89	255 268	71 582	183 686	...	...	...	...	...	...
90 - 94	70 874	16 529	54 345	...	...	...	...	...	...
95 +	19 089	3 003	16 086	...	...	...	...	...	...
Saudi Arabia - Arabie									
saoudite									
1 VII 2006 (ESDF)									
Total	23 678 849	13 090 839	10 588 009	...	...	...	...	...	...
0 - 4	2 754 108	1 399 669	1 354 439	...	...	...	...	...	...
5 - 9	2 595 789	1 310 112	1 285 677	...	...	...	...	...	...
10 - 14	2 430 136	1 215 671	1 214 465	...	...	...	...	...	...
15 - 19	2 206 139	1 093 786	1 112 353	...	...	...	...	...	...
20 - 24	2 095 772	1 081 896	1 013 876	...	...	...	...	...	...
25 - 29	2 316 893	1 329 970	986 922	...	...	...	...	...	...
30 - 34	2 336 313	1 402 957	933 355	...	...	...	...	...	...
35 - 39	1 992 635	1 237 652	754 983	...	...	...	...	...	...
40 - 44	1 532 030	988 595	543 437	...	...	...	...	...	...
45 - 49	1 119 319	716 867	402 452	...	...	...	...	...	...
50 - 54	779 419	483 487	295 933	...	...	...	...	...	...
55 - 59	513 520	300 719	212 801	...	...	...	...	...	...
60 - 64	348 682	189 197	159 485	...	...	...	...	...	...
65 - 69	244 232	126 042	118 189	...	...	...	...	...	...
70 - 74	170 480	86 502	83 979	...	...	...	...	...	...
75 - 79	112 027	57 538	54 489	...	...	...	...	...	...
80 +	131 354	70 180	61 174	...	...	...	...	...	...

Continent, country or area, date, code and age (in years) — Continent, pays ou zone, date, code et âge (en années)	Total			Urban - Urbaine			Rural - Rurale		
	Both sexes Les deux sexes	Male Masculin	Female Féminin	Both sexes Les deux sexes	Male Masculin	Female Féminin	Both sexes Les deux sexes	Male Masculin	Female Féminin
ASIA - ASIE									
Singapore - Singapour[59]									
1 VII 2009 (ESDJ)									
Total	3 733 800	1 844 700	1 889 100	...	...	...	...	...	...
0 - 4	197 800	100 700	97 100	...	...	...	...	...	...
5 - 9	221 400	113 700	107 700	...	...	...	...	...	...
10 - 14	248 600	127 500	121 100	...	...	...	...	...	...
15 - 19	262 800	133 500	129 300	...	...	...	...	...	...
20 - 24	241 700	120 900	120 800	...	...	...	...	...	...
25 - 29	274 300	132 000	142 300	...	...	...	...	...	...
30 - 34	297 300	142 700	154 600	...	...	...	...	...	...
35 - 39	317 300	155 100	162 200	...	...	...	...	...	...
40 - 44	313 000	155 800	157 200	...	...	...	...	...	...
45 - 49	322 500	162 900	159 600	...	...	...	...	...	...
50 - 54	297 400	149 600	147 800	...	...	...	...	...	...
55 - 59	239 900	120 400	119 500	...	...	...	...	...	...
60 - 64	169 700	83 700	86 000	...	...	...	...	...	...
65 - 69	116 300	55 400	60 900	...	...	...	...	...	...
70 - 74	87 500	40 400	47 100	...	...	...	...	...	...
75 - 79	61 400	26 700	34 700	...	...	...	...	...	...
80 - 84	37 100	14 500	22 600	...	...	...	...	...	...
85 +	27 800	9 200	18 600	...	...	...	...	...	...
Sri Lanka									
17 VII 2001 (CDFC)[60]									
Total	16 929 689	8 425 607	8 504 082	2 467 301	1 252 173	1 215 128	14 462 388[61]	7 173 434[61]	7 288 954[61]
0 - 4	1 439 761	733 775	705 986	190 571	97 476	93 095	1 249 190[61]	636 299[61]	612 891[61]
5 - 9	1 483 591	754 518	729 073	187 979	96 025	91 954	1 295 612[61]	658 493[61]	637 119[61]
10 - 14	1 525 674	777 519	748 155	191 194	97 360	93 834	1 334 480[61]	680 159[61]	654 321[61]
15 - 19	1 646 827	834 695	812 132	235 729	120 467	115 262	1 411 098[61]	714 228[61]	696 870[61]
20 - 24	1 591 126	798 288	792 838	274 372	143 696	130 676	1 316 754[61]	654 592[61]	662 162[61]
25 - 29	1 340 562	660 586	679 976	223 920	115 973	107 947	1 116 642[61]	544 613[61]	572 029[61]
30 - 34	1 290 121	636 734	653 387	200 909	104 230	96 679	1 089 212[61]	532 504[61]	556 708[61]
35 - 39	1 258 112	622 957	635 155	187 868	95 408	92 460	1 070 244[61]	527 549[61]	542 695[61]
40 - 44	1 170 941	583 894	587 047	170 722	86 768	83 954	1 000 219[61]	497 126[61]	503 093[61]
45 - 49	1 030 560	509 247	521 313	147 346	74 582	72 764	883 214[61]	434 665[61]	448 549[61]
50 - 54	917 139	452 311	464 828	135 177	68 548	66 629	781 962[61]	383 763[61]	398 199[61]
55 - 59	671 403	324 223	347 180	99 601	49 225	50 376	571 802[61]	274 998[61]	296 804[61]
60 - 64	496 177	241 081	255 096	72 657	35 246	37 411	423 520[61]	205 835[61]	217 685[61]
65 - 69	404 749	188 007	216 742	56 403	26 252	30 151	348 346[61]	161 755[61]	186 591[61]
70 - 74	303 473	142 030	161 443	42 974	19 404	23 570	260 499[61]	122 626[61]	137 873[61]
75 - 79	193 171	89 023	104 148	27 286	11 953	15 333	165 885[61]	77 070[61]	88 815[61]
80 - 84	105 036	48 757	56 279	14 558	6 264	8 294	90 478[61]	42 493[61]	47 985[61]
85 - 89	42 962	19 839	23 123	5 758	2 357	3 401	37 204[61]	17 482[61]	19 722[61]
90 - 94	13 096	5 870	7 226	1 708	708	1 000	11 388[61]	5 162[61]	6 226[61]
95 - 99	3 904	1 684	2 220	413	163	250	3 491[61]	1 521[61]	1 970[61]
100 +	1 304	569	735	156	68	88	1 148[61]	501[61]	647[61]
1 VII 2009 (ESDF)									
Total	20 450 000	10 148 000	10 302 000	...	...	...	...	...	...
0 - 4	1 738 000	883 000	855 000	...	...	...	...	...	...
5 - 9	1 799 000	913 000	886 000	...	...	...	...	...	...
10 - 14	1 841 000	934 000	907 000	...	...	...	...	...	...
15 - 19	1 984 000	1 005 000	979 000	...	...	...	...	...	...
20 - 24	1 922 000	964 000	958 000	...	...	...	...	...	...
25 - 29	1 616 000	792 000	824 000	...	...	...	...	...	...
30 - 34	1 564 000	771 000	793 000	...	...	...	...	...	...
35 - 39	1 524 000	751 000	773 000	...	...	...	...	...	...
40 - 44	1 411 000	700 000	711 000	...	...	...	...	...	...
45 - 49	1 237 000	609 000	628 000	...	...	...	...	...	...
50 - 54	1 115 000	548 000	567 000	...	...	...	...	...	...
55 - 59	808 000	386 000	422 000	...	...	...	...	...	...
60 - 64	603 000	294 000	309 000	...	...	...	...	...	...
65 - 69	480 000	223 000	257 000	...	...	...	...	...	...
70 - 74	368 000	172 000	196 000	...	...	...	...	...	...
75 - 79	236 000	112 000	124 000	...	...	...	...	...	...
80 +	204 000	91 000	113 000	...	...	...	...	...	...

Continent, country or area, date, code and age (in years) Continent, pays ou zone, date, code et âge (en annèes)	Total			Urban - Urbaine			Rural - Rurale		
	Both sexes Les deux sexes	Male Masculin	Female Féminin	Both sexes Les deux sexes	Male Masculin	Female Féminin	Both sexes Les deux sexes	Male Masculin	Female Féminin
ASIA - ASIE									
Syrian Arab Republic - République arabe syrienne[62]									
1 VII 2008 (ESDF)									
Total	19 644 000	10 042 000	9 602 000	10 511 000	5 394 000	5 117 000	9 133 000	4 648 000	4 485 000
0 - 4	2 621 000	1 358 000	1 263 000	1 319 000	685 000	634 000	1 302 000	673 000	629 000
5 - 9	2 538 000	1 311 000	1 227 000	1 298 000	674 000	624 000	1 240 000	637 000	603 000
10 - 14	2 280 000	1 185 000	1 095 000	1 178 000	615 000	563 000	1 102 000	570 000	532 000
15 - 19	2 205 000	1 132 000	1 073 000	1 143 000	589 000	554 000	1 062 000	543 000	519 000
20 - 24	1 908 000	989 000	919 000	1 038 000	535 000	503 000	870 000	454 000	416 000
25 - 29	1 531 000	739 000	792 000	830 000	405 000	425 000	701 000	334 000	367 000
30 - 34	1 251 000	602 000	649 000	699 000	338 000	361 000	552 000	264 000	288 000
35 - 39	1 175 000	574 000	601 000	650 000	315 000	335 000	525 000	259 000	266 000
40 - 44	1 028 000	509 000	519 000	600 000	300 000	300 000	428 000	209 000	219 000
45 - 49	817 000	409 000	408 000	470 000	241 000	229 000	347 000	168 000	179 000
50 - 54	690 000	353 000	337 000	399 000	207 000	192 000	291 000	146 000	145 000
55 - 59	479 000	248 000	231 000	267 000	140 000	127 000	212 000	108 000	104 000
60 - 64	409 000	220 000	189 000	236 000	129 000	107 000	173 000	91 000	82 000
65 +	712 000	413 000	299 000	384 000	221 000	163 000	328 000	192 000	136 000
Tajikistan - Tadjikistan									
1 VII 2007 (ESDF)									
Total	7 139 772	3 581 930	3 557 842	1 877 204	943 033	934 171	5 262 569	2 638 898	2 623 671
0	188 189	96 091	92 099	46 726	23 872	22 854	141 463	72 219	69 244
1 - 4	689 639	354 266	335 374	168 404	86 479	81 925	521 236	267 787	253 449
5 - 9	840 191	429 027	411 164	204 862	104 716	100 146	635 330	324 311	311 019
10 - 14	863 247	438 139	425 108	207 261	105 568	101 693	655 986	332 571	323 415
15 - 19	871 357	442 027	429 330	219 572	113 498	106 074	651 786	328 530	323 256
20 - 24	756 501	381 333	375 168	194 162	100 629	93 533	562 340	280 705	281 635
25 - 29	577 281	289 722	287 560	157 434	84 699	72 735	419 847	205 023	214 825
30 - 34	472 119	231 988	240 131	127 880	61 163	66 717	344 239	170 825	173 414
35 - 39	425 623	208 788	216 836	125 807	60 035	65 772	299 817	148 753	151 064
40 - 44	382 070	187 288	194 782	113 910	55 130	58 780	268 160	132 159	136 002
45 - 49	335 257	165 549	169 708	100 613	49 300	51 313	234 644	116 250	118 395
50 - 54	220 261	108 337	111 924	65 694	31 757	33 938	154 567	76 581	77 986
55 - 59	147 153	72 245	74 908	44 974	21 694	23 280	102 179	50 551	51 628
60 - 64	72 617	38 180	34 437	20 588	10 146	10 442	52 029	28 034	23 995
65 - 69	97 971	49 594	48 377	27 621	13 359	14 262	70 351	36 236	34 115
70 - 74	81 237	38 325	42 912	20 958	9 550	11 408	60 280	28 775	31 505
75 - 79	65 484	31 396	34 088	16 474	7 195	9 279	49 010	24 201	24 809
80 - 84	34 924	15 116	19 808	9 369	3 371	5 998	25 555	11 745	13 810
85 - 89	13 015	3 697	9 318	3 282	673	2 609	9 733	3 024	6 709
90 - 94	3 456	542	2 915	1 002	96	906	2 454	446	2 009
95 - 99	1 475	238	1 237	468	79	390	1 007	159	848
100 +	710	46	665	149	28	121	561	18	544
Thailand - Thaïlande[2]									
1 VII 2009 (ESDJ)									
Total	66 903 277	32 872 931	34 030 346	21 133 663	10 112 852	11 020 811	45 769 614	22 760 079	23 009 535
0 - 4	4 416 902	2 252 694	2 164 208	1 420 082	715 146	704 936	2 996 820	1 537 548	1 459 272
5 - 9	4 761 074	2 429 993	2 331 081	1 506 769	757 874	748 895	3 254 305	1 672 119	1 582 186
10 - 14	4 874 106	2 500 606	2 373 500	1 367 004	689 998	677 006	3 507 102	1 810 608	1 696 494
15 - 19	5 264 720	2 691 217	2 573 503	1 473 955	736 717	737 238	3 790 765	1 954 500	1 836 265
20 - 24	5 233 855	2 669 626	2 564 229	1 495 142	737 033	758 109	3 738 713	1 932 593	1 806 120
25 - 29	5 324 786	2 694 688	2 630 098	1 700 009	825 817	874 192	3 624 777	1 868 871	1 755 906
30 - 34	5 389 022	2 689 197	2 699 825	1 931 718	925 985	1 005 733	3 457 304	1 763 212	1 694 092
35 - 39	5 541 382	2 688 952	2 852 430	1 909 207	902 558	1 006 649	3 632 175	1 786 394	1 845 781
40 - 44	5 519 273	2 661 432	2 857 841	1 838 405	865 000	973 405	3 680 868	1 796 432	1 884 436
45 - 49	5 116 727	2 474 763	2 641 964	1 669 580	787 202	882 378	3 447 147	1 687 561	1 759 586
50 - 54	4 409 384	2 119 688	2 289 696	1 423 122	667 983	755 139	2 986 262	1 451 705	1 534 557
55 - 59	3 370 400	1 603 696	1 766 704	1 066 587	495 971	570 616	2 303 813	1 107 725	1 196 088
60 - 64	2 502 685	1 174 987	1 327 698	773 352	355 434	417 918	1 729 333	819 553	909 780
65 - 69	1 939 835	883 720	1 056 115	581 060	258 829	322 231	1 358 775	624 891	733 884
70 - 74	1 517 964	662 435	855 529	462 755	197 575	265 180	1 055 209	464 860	590 349
75 - 79	955 729	391 854	563 875	279 933	110 915	169 018	675 796	280 939	394 857
80 +	765 433	283 383	482 050	234 983	82 815	152 168	530 450	200 568	329 882

7. Population by age, sex and urban/rural residence: latest available year, 2000 - 2009
Population selon l'âge, le sexe et la résidence, urbaine/rurale : dernière année disponible, 2000 - 2009 (continued - suite)

Continent, country or area, date, code and age (in years) Continent, pays ou zone, date, code et âge (en années)	Total			Urban - Urbaine			Rural - Rurale		
	Both sexes Les deux sexes	Male Masculin	Female Féminin	Both sexes Les deux sexes	Male Masculin	Female Féminin	Both sexes Les deux sexes	Male Masculin	Female Féminin
ASIA - ASIE									
Timor-Leste									
11 VII 2004 (CDFC)									
Total	923 198	469 919	453 279	...	...	...	...	...	...
0 - 4	150 744	77 720	73 024	...	...	...	...	...	...
5 - 9	129 420	66 661	62 759	...	...	...	...	...	...
10 - 14	118 647	61 422	57 225	...	...	...	...	...	...
15 - 19	95 274	47 953	47 321	...	...	...	...	...	...
20 - 24	75 701	37 640	38 061	...	...	...	...	...	...
25 - 29	57 138	28 366	28 772	...	...	...	...	...	...
30 - 34	62 410	32 227	30 183	...	...	...	...	...	...
35 - 39	48 800	24 894	23 906	...	...	...	...	...	...
40 - 44	45 946	22 513	23 433	...	...	...	...	...	...
45 - 49	34 320	16 917	17 403	...	...	...	...	...	...
50 - 54	32 933	16 651	16 282	...	...	...	...	...	...
55 - 59	19 205	9 910	9 295	...	...	...	...	...	...
60 - 64	20 516	10 613	9 903	...	...	...	...	...	...
65 - 69	11 746	5 952	5 794	...	...	...	...	...	...
70 - 74	9 686	4 922	4 764	...	...	...	...	...	...
75 +	10 712	5 558	5 154	...	...	...	...	...	...
Turkey - Turquie									
22 X 2000 (CDFC)									
Total	67 803 927	34 346 735	33 457 192	44 006 184	22 427 541	21 578 643	23 797 743	11 919 194	11 878 549
0	1 244 675	640 760	603 915	782 345	402 411	379 934	462 330	238 349	223 981
1 - 4	5 340 147	2 755 930	2 584 217	3 305 206	1 705 097	1 600 109	2 034 941	1 050 833	984 108
5 - 9	6 756 617	3 485 746	3 270 871	4 239 165	2 186 542	2 052 623	2 517 452	1 299 204	1 218 248
10 - 14	6 878 656	3 570 657	3 307 999	4 390 788	2 300 008	2 090 780	2 487 868	1 270 649	1 217 219
15 - 19	7 209 475	3 691 218	3 518 257	4 739 997	2 485 379	2 254 618	2 469 478	1 205 839	1 263 639
20 - 24	6 690 146	3 426 714	3 263 432	4 616 661	2 412 164	2 204 497	2 073 485	1 014 550	1 058 935
25 - 29	5 895 255	2 976 430	2 918 825	4 043 769	2 043 050	2 000 719	1 851 486	933 380	918 106
30 - 34	5 009 655	2 552 370	2 457 285	3 438 719	1 744 869	1 693 850	1 570 936	807 501	763 435
35 - 39	4 854 387	2 453 579	2 400 808	3 324 204	1 671 775	1 652 429	1 530 183	781 804	748 379
40 - 44	4 068 756	2 083 531	1 985 225	2 781 018	1 424 035	1 356 983	1 287 738	659 496	628 242
45 - 49	3 368 769	1 710 757	1 658 012	2 251 794	1 153 831	1 097 963	1 116 975	556 926	560 049
50 - 54	2 717 349	1 356 391	1 360 958	1 724 908	874 696	850 212	992 441	481 695	510 746
55 - 59	2 058 422	1 016 254	1 042 168	1 225 898	612 517	613 381	832 524	403 737	428 787
60 - 64	1 829 288	864 299	964 989	1 030 173	484 919	545 254	799 115	379 380	419 735
65 - 69	1 645 517	794 881	850 636	883 835	417 191	466 644	761 682	377 690	383 992
70 - 74	1 172 643	517 870	654 773	635 249	270 030	365 219	537 394	247 840	289 554
75 - 79	577 597	254 443	323 154	321 179	135 075	186 104	256 418	119 368	137 050
80 - 84	246 692	98 797	147 895	137 630	52 964	84 666	109 062	45 833	63 229
85 - 89	138 361	55 298	83 063	77 087	28 707	48 380	61 274	26 591	34 683
90 - 94	52 426	18 616	33 810	28 975	9 770	19 205	23 451	8 846	14 605
95 - 99	19 504	7 402	12 102	10 919	4 100	6 819	8 585	3 302	5 283
100 +	6 209	2 256	3 953	3 183	1 118	2 065	3 026	1 138	1 888
Unknown - Inconnu	23 381	12 536	10 845	13 482	7 293	6 189	9 899	5 243	4 656
1 VII 2009 (ESDJ)[63]									
Total	71 897 000	36 042 000	35 855 000	...	...	...	...	...	...
0	1 249 000	638 000	611 000	...	...	...	...	...	...
1 - 4	5 008 000	2 556 000	2 452 000	...	...	...	...	...	...
5 - 9	6 281 000	3 201 000	3 080 000	...	...	...	...	...	...
10 - 14	6 413 000	3 288 000	3 125 000	...	...	...	...	...	...
15 - 19	6 187 000	3 173 000	3 014 000	...	...	...	...	...	...
20 - 24	6 206 000	3 163 000	3 043 000	...	...	...	...	...	...
25 - 29	6 461 000	3 272 000	3 189 000	...	...	...	...	...	...
30 - 34	5 902 000	2 987 000	2 915 000	...	...	...	...	...	...
35 - 39	5 345 000	2 687 000	2 658 000	...	...	...	...	...	...
40 - 44	4 762 000	2 407 000	2 355 000	...	...	...	...	...	...
45 - 49	4 304 000	2 164 000	2 140 000	...	...	...	...	...	...
50 - 54	3 697 000	1 850 000	1 847 000	...	...	...	...	...	...
55 - 59	2 932 000	1 453 000	1 479 000	...	...	...	...	...	...
60 - 64	2 220 000	1 053 000	1 167 000	...	...	...	...	...	...
65 - 69	1 710 000	784 000	926 000	...	...	...	...	...	...
70 - 74	1 262 000	572 000	690 000	...	...	...	...	...	...
75 +	1 958 000	794 000	1 164 000	...	...	...	...	...	...

Continent, country or area, date, code and age (in years) / Continent, pays ou zone, date, code et âge (en années)	Total			Urban - Urbaine			Rural - Rurale		
	Both sexes Les deux sexes	Male Masculin	Female Féminin	Both sexes Les deux sexes	Male Masculin	Female Féminin	Both sexes Les deux sexes	Male Masculin	Female Féminin
ASIA - ASIE									
Turkmenistan - Turkménistan[12]									
1 VII 2003 (ESDF)									
Total	5 123 940	2 571 866	2 552 073	...	...	...	...	...	...
0 - 4	571 355	277 748	293 607	...	...	...	...	...	...
5 - 9	613 767	300 841	312 925	...	...	...	...	...	...
10 - 14	645 136	316 247	328 889	...	...	...	...	...	...
15 - 19	579 113	284 926	294 186	...	...	...	...	...	...
20 - 24	479 053	235 762	243 291	...	...	...	...	...	...
25 - 29	423 109	210 578	212 531	...	...	...	...	...	...
30 - 34	380 948	194 438	186 510	...	...	...	...	...	...
35 - 39	341 403	173 922	167 481	...	...	...	...	...	...
40 - 44	316 309	161 800	154 509	...	...	...	...	...	...
45 - 49	233 504	120 701	112 803	...	...	...	...	...	...
50 - 54	161 151	84 220	76 931	...	...	...	...	...	...
55 - 59	85 927	44 454	41 472	...	...	...	...	...	...
60 - 64	92 992	49 068	43 924	...	...	...	...	...	...
65 - 69	76 006	41 263	34 743	...	...	...	...	...	...
70 - 74	61 177	34 393	26 784	...	...	...	...	...	...
75 +	62 987	41 503	21 484	...	...	...	...	...	...
United Arab Emirates - Émirats arabes unis									
5 XII 2005 (CDFC)									
Total	4 106 427	2 806 141	1 300 286	3 384 839[64]	2 328 906[64]	1 055 933[64]	721 588[64]	477 235[64]	244 353[64]
0 - 4	282 139	145 601	136 538	224 169[64]	115 800[64]	108 369[64]	57 970[64]	29 801[64]	28 169[64]
5 - 9	269 382	139 929	129 453	213 815[64]	111 645[64]	102 170[64]	55 567[64]	28 284[64]	27 283[64]
10 - 14	249 057	130 778	118 279	192 350[64]	101 461[64]	90 889[64]	56 707[64]	29 317[64]	27 390[64]
15 - 19	232 226	121 388	110 838	173 192[64]	91 065[64]	82 127[64]	59 034[64]	30 323[64]	28 711[64]
20 - 24	433 566	272 036	161 530	349 079[64]	222 387[64]	126 692[64]	84 487[64]	49 649[64]	34 838[64]
25 - 29	661 794	483 657	178 137	558 690[64]	410 228[64]	148 462[64]	103 104[64]	73 429[64]	29 675[64]
30 - 34	640 361	489 879	150 482	548 499[64]	417 909[64]	130 590[64]	91 862[64]	71 970[64]	19 892[64]
35 - 39	500 606	386 762	113 844	427 468[64]	329 059[64]	98 409[64]	73 138[64]	57 703[64]	15 435[64]
40 - 44	341 261	262 718	78 543	288 792[64]	220 959[64]	67 833[64]	52 469[64]	41 759[64]	10 710[64]
45 - 49	225 770	174 459	51 311	188 732[64]	145 298[64]	43 434[64]	37 038[64]	29 161[64]	7 877[64]
50 - 54	138 878	107 339	31 539	116 519[64]	89 983[64]	26 536[64]	22 359[64]	17 356[64]	5 003[64]
55 - 59	67 107	51 303	15 804	55 810[64]	42 788[64]	13 022[64]	11 297[64]	8 515[64]	2 782[64]
60 - 64	27 347	18 820	8 527	22 157[64]	15 510[64]	6 647[64]	5 190[64]	3 310[64]	1 880[64]
65 - 69	14 457	9 172	5 285	10 515[64]	6 623[64]	3 892[64]	3 942[64]	2 549[64]	1 393[64]
70 - 74	9 404	5 391	4 013	6 421[64]	3 659[64]	2 762[64]	2 983[64]	1 732[64]	1 251[64]
75 +[64]	...	...	...	8 631	4 532	4 099	4 441	2 377	2 064
75 - 79	4 277	2 440	1 837	...	...	...	...	...	...
80 - 84	2 976	1 537	1 439	...	...	...	...	...	...
85 +	2 415	1 250	1 165	...	...	...	...	...	...
Unknown - Inconnu	3 404	1 682	1 722	...	...	...	...	...	...
1 VII 2008 (ESDF)									
Total	4 765 000	3 286 000	1 479 000	...	...	...	...	...	...
0 - 4	321 310	166 467	154 843	...	...	...	...	...	...
5 - 9	306 464	159 877	146 587	...	...	...	...	...	...
10 - 14	281 979	148 621	133 358	...	...	...	...	...	...
15 - 19	261 871	137 446	124 425	...	...	...	...	...	...
20 - 24	501 760	318 395	183 365	...	...	...	...	...	...
25 - 29	777 186	573 214	203 972	...	...	...	...	...	...
30 - 34	754 289	581 283	173 006	...	...	...	...	...	...
35 - 39	588 505	457 828	130 677	...	...	...	...	...	...
40 - 44	399 102	309 126	89 976	...	...	...	...	...	...
45 - 49	262 363	203 876	58 487	...	...	...	...	...	...
50 - 54	160 817	124 996	35 821	...	...	...	...	...	...
55 - 59	77 204	59 374	17 830	...	...	...	...	...	...
60 - 64	31 067	21 550	9 517	...	...	...	...	...	...
65 - 69	16 147	10 290	5 857	...	...	...	...	...	...
70 - 74	10 417	5 992	4 425	...	...	...	...	...	...
75 - 79	4 762	2 731	2 031	...	...	...	...	...	...
80 - 84	9 757	4 934	4 823	...	...	...	...	...	...

Continent, country or area, date, code and age (in years) / Continent, pays ou zone, date, code et âge (en années)	Total			Urban - Urbaine			Rural - Rurale		
	Both sexes Les deux sexes	Male Masculin	Female Féminin	Both sexes Les deux sexes	Male Masculin	Female Féminin	Both sexes Les deux sexes	Male Masculin	Female Féminin
ASIA - ASIE									
Uzbekistan - Ouzbékistan									
1 VII 2001 (ESDF)									
Total	24 964 433	12 442 510	12 521 923	9 256 101	4 573 055	4 683 046	15 708 332	7 869 455	7 838 877
0	513 043	263 408	249 635	158 893	81 393	77 500	354 150	182 015	172 135
1 - 4	2 219 863	1 138 212	1 081 651	693 448	355 999	337 449	1 526 415	782 213	744 202
5 - 9	3 237 989	1 653 776	1 584 213	1 015 989	519 360	496 629	2 222 000	1 134 416	1 087 584
10 - 14	3 203 022	1 627 673	1 575 349	1 049 577	533 870	515 707	2 153 445	1 093 803	1 059 642
15 - 19	2 821 926	1 422 296	1 399 630	984 385	497 725	486 660	1 837 541	924 571	912 970
20 - 24	2 296 834	1 157 998	1 138 836	841 326	425 348	415 978	1 455 508	732 650	722 858
25 - 29	2 030 200	1 023 174	1 007 026	788 176	397 184	390 992	1 242 024	625 990	616 034
30 - 34	1 749 557	861 368	888 189	726 099	372 846	353 253	1 023 458	488 522	534 936
35 - 39	1 672 397	816 665	855 732	660 932	323 492	337 440	1 011 465	493 173	518 292
40 - 44	1 479 057	728 780	750 277	612 755	297 460	315 295	866 302	431 320	434 982
45 - 49	1 034 628	506 734	527 894	464 375	223 425	240 950	570 253	283 309	286 944
50 - 54	696 648	337 634	359 014	340 008	161 069	178 939	356 640	176 565	180 075
55 - 59	394 997	197 700	197 297	185 073	88 314	96 759	209 924	109 386	100 538
60 - 64	553 697	265 428	288 269	254 409	115 715	138 694	299 288	149 713	149 575
65 - 69	399 550	185 653	213 897	171 869	75 277	96 592	227 681	110 376	117 305
70 - 74	325 230	143 466	181 764	146 702	57 100	89 602	178 528	86 366	92 162
75 - 79	185 449	67 568	117 881	87 515	27 439	60 076	97 934	40 129	57 805
80 - 84	78 794	23 459	55 335	39 138	10 729	28 409	39 656	12 730	26 926
85 - 89	41 343	10 761	30 582	20 793	4 904	15 889	20 550	5 857	14 693
90 - 94	19 195	6 220	12 975	9 150	2 774	6 376	10 045	3 446	6 599
95 - 99	10 114	4 171	5 943	4 954	1 461	3 493	5 160	2 710	2 450
100 +	900	366	534	535	171	364	365	195	170
1 VII 2003 (ESDF)[12]									
Total	25 567 663	12 809 713	12 757 950	...	...	...	...	...	...
0 - 4	2 584 779	1 257 871	1 326 908	...	...	...	...	...	...
5 - 9	3 057 832	1 492 224	1 565 608	...	...	...	...	...	...
10 - 14	3 247 432	1 593 319	1 654 113	...	...	...	...	...	...
15 - 19	3 036 011	1 502 977	1 533 033	...	...	...	...	...	...
20 - 24	2 440 283	1 210 643	1 229 640	...	...	...	...	...	...
25 - 29	2 077 200	1 032 960	1 044 240	...	...	...	...	...	...
30 - 34	1 852 315	929 765	922 550	...	...	...	...	...	...
35 - 39	1 654 410	848 383	806 026	...	...	...	...	...	...
40 - 44	1 586 930	807 669	779 261	...	...	...	...	...	...
45 - 49	1 170 247	595 727	574 520	...	...	...	...	...	...
50 - 54	821 154	423 337	397 817	...	...	...	...	...	...
55 - 59	426 436	218 173	208 263	...	...	...	...	...	...
60 - 64	499 732	256 051	243 680	...	...	...	...	...	...
65 - 69	416 696	220 394	196 302	...	...	...	...	...	...
70 - 74	324 533	182 720	141 812	...	...	...	...	...	...
75 +	371 669	237 497	134 172	...	...	...	...	...	...
Viet Nam									
1 IV 2009 (CDJC)									
Total	85 846 997	42 413 143	43 433 854	25 436 896	12 349 995	13 086 901	60 410 101	30 063 148	30 346 953
0 - 4	7 034 144	3 662 889	3 371 255	1 949 105	1 019 547	929 558	5 085 039	2 643 342	2 441 697
5 - 9	6 710 737	3 458 159	3 252 578	1 757 679	910 339	847 340	4 953 058	2 547 820	2 405 238
10 - 14	7 248 378	3 725 369	3 523 009	1 761 650	904 731	856 919	5 486 728	2 820 638	2 666 090
15 - 17	5 236 771	2 681 653	2 555 118	1 311 350	662 369	648 981	3 925 421	2 019 284	1 906 137
18 - 19	3 727 131	1 896 261	1 830 870	1 188 578	562 169	626 409	2 538 553	1 334 092	1 204 461
20 - 24	8 432 867	4 253 618	4 179 249	2 759 456	1 305 436	1 454 020	5 673 411	2 948 182	2 725 229
25 - 29	7 790 003	3 904 730	3 885 273	2 519 920	1 205 518	1 314 402	5 270 083	2 699 212	2 570 871
30 - 34	6 868 158	3 462 905	3 405 253	2 164 824	1 062 838	1 101 986	4 703 334	2 400 067	2 303 267
35 - 39	6 531 607	3 298 266	3 233 341	2 059 356	1 027 075	1 032 281	4 472 251	2 271 191	2 201 060
40 - 44	5 966 856	2 967 934	2 998 922	1 818 188	896 290	921 898	4 148 668	2 071 644	2 077 024
45 - 49	5 450 928	2 642 466	2 808 462	1 728 008	840 047	887 961	3 722 920	1 802 419	1 920 501
50 - 54	4 412 051	2 082 098	2 329 953	1 435 970	683 749	752 221	2 976 081	1 398 349	1 577 732
55 - 59	2 984 619	1 364 319	1 620 300	931 382	421 296	510 086	2 053 237	943 023	1 110 214
60 - 64	1 937 948	861 897	1 076 051	590 161	259 193	330 968	1 347 787	602 704	745 083
65 - 69	1 554 678	653 287	901 391	453 756	195 857	257 899	1 100 922	457 430	643 492
70 - 74	1 412 538	568 312	844 226	378 105	155 224	222 881	1 034 433	413 088	621 345
75 - 79	1 198 893	480 088	718 805	306 226	125 948	180 278	892 667	354 140	538 527
80 - 84	725 985	264 997	460 988	182 550	69 573	112 977	543 435	195 424	348 011
85 +	622 705	183 895	438 810	140 632	42 796	97 836	482 073	141 099	340 974

Continent, country or area, date, code and age (in years) / Continent, pays ou zone, date, code et âge (en années)	Total			Urban - Urbaine			Rural - Rurale		
	Both sexes Les deux sexes	Male Masculin	Female Féminin	Both sexes Les deux sexes	Male Masculin	Female Féminin	Both sexes Les deux sexes	Male Masculin	Female Féminin
ASIA - ASIE									
Yemen - Yémen									
31 XII 2007 (ESDF)									
Total	21 538 995	10 551 463	10 987 532	...	...	...	...	...	...
0 - 4	3 214 848	1 571 365	1 643 483	...	...	...	...	...	...
5 - 9	3 342 236	1 626 640	1 715 596	...	...	...	...	...	...
10 - 14	3 138 981	1 482 165	1 656 816	...	...	...	...	...	...
15 - 19	2 709 342	1 324 632	1 384 710	...	...	...	...	...	...
20 - 24	2 069 808	1 012 321	1 057 487	...	...	...	...	...	...
25 - 29	1 609 588	810 850	798 738	...	...	...	...	...	...
30 - 34	1 058 035	524 368	533 667	...	...	...	...	...	...
35 - 39	993 236	521 941	471 295	...	...	...	...	...	...
40 - 44	796 335	407 965	388 370	...	...	...	...	...	...
45 - 49	639 759	329 288	310 471	...	...	...	...	...	...
50 - 54	545 804	266 941	278 863	...	...	...	...	...	...
55 - 59	314 541	150 219	164 322	...	...	...	...	...	...
60 - 64	355 195	168 650	186 545	...	...	...	...	...	...
65 - 69	200 326	94 621	105 705	...	...	...	...	...	...
70 - 74	239 210	114 259	124 951	...	...	...	...	...	...
75 - 79	102 931	47 167	55 764	...	...	...	...	...	...
80 - 84	109 209	52 740	56 469	...	...	...	...	...	...
85 +	86 202	39 951	46 251	...	...	...	...	...	...
Unknown - Inconnu	13 409	5 380	8 029	...	...	...	...	...	...
EUROPE									
Åland Islands - Îles d'Åland[18]									
1 VII 2009 (ESDJ)									
Total	27 595	13 724	13 871	11 064	5 264	5 800	16 531	8 460	8 071
0	279	157	122	100	57	43	178	99	78
1 - 4	1 203	624	579	407	201	206	796	423	374
5 - 9	1 472	777	695	501	263	238	971	514	457
10 - 14	1 677	851	827	613	301	312	1 065	550	515
15 - 19	1 741	899	842	673	342	332	1 068	558	510
20 - 24	1 312	703	609	655	329	327	657	374	283
25 - 29	1 571	808	763	820	417	403	751	391	360
30 - 34	1 665	858	807	741	380	361	924	478	447
35 - 39	1 770	893	877	674	326	349	1 096	568	528
40 - 44	2 091	1 026	1 066	790	382	408	1 302	644	658
45 - 49	1 912	959	953	718	337	382	1 194	623	571
50 - 54	1 914	916	998	737	332	406	1 177	584	593
55 - 59	2 074	998	1 077	846	382	464	1 229	616	613
60 - 64	2 063	1 050	1 014	844	409	436	1 219	641	578
65 - 69	1 452	777	676	556	275	282	896	502	394
70 - 74	1 113	533	580	443	195	248	671	339	332
75 - 79	859	399	460	338	153	186	521	247	274
80 - 84	738	302	436	296	111	186	442	192	250
85 - 89	459	147	313	208	60	148	251	87	165
90 - 94	173	43	131	80	15	65	94	28	66
95 - 99	60	11	49	26	3	23	34	8	27
100 +	4	1	3	2	-	2	2	1	2
Albania - Albanie									
1 IV 2001 (CDFC)									
Total	3 069 275	1 530 443	1 538 832	1 294 196	639 082	655 114	1 775 079	891 361	883 718
0 - 4	269 926	139 824	130 102	100 619	52 602	48 017	169 307	87 222	82 085
5 - 9	303 663	155 666	147 997	115 444	59 272	56 172	188 219	96 394	91 825
10 - 14	325 249	165 890	159 359	125 308	63 750	61 558	199 941	102 140	97 801
15 - 19	295 286	144 896	150 390	112 595	55 410	57 185	182 691	89 486	93 205
20 - 24	232 112	111 143	120 969	88 121	40 944	47 177	143 991	70 199	73 792
25 - 29	213 009	101 942	111 067	85 480	38 559	46 921	127 529	63 383	64 146
30 - 34	216 246	104 542	111 704	94 083	44 107	49 976	122 163	60 435	61 728
35 - 39	219 223	108 516	110 707	100 021	48 673	51 348	119 202	59 843	59 359
40 - 44	215 112	108 701	106 411	103 459	52 247	51 212	111 653	56 454	55 199
45 - 49	171 093	87 753	83 340	87 390	44 183	43 207	83 703	43 570	40 133
50 - 54	143 589	73 856	69 733	70 300	36 228	34 072	73 289	37 628	35 661

Continent, country or area, date, code and age (in years) / Continent, pays ou zone, date, code et âge (en années)	Total			Urban - Urbaine			Rural - Rurale		
	Both sexes Les deux sexes	Male Masculin	Female Féminin	Both sexes Les deux sexes	Male Masculin	Female Féminin	Both sexes Les deux sexes	Male Masculin	Female Féminin
EUROPE									
Albania - Albanie									
1 IV 2001 (CDFC)									
55 - 59	120 135	61 754	58 381	54 391	27 534	26 857	65 744	34 220	31 524
60 - 64	113 269	57 859	55 410	52 369	26 514	25 855	60 900	31 345	29 555
65 - 69	87 606	45 222	42 384	41 052	20 801	20 251	46 554	24 421	22 133
70 - 74	65 459	31 835	33 624	30 584	14 696	15 888	34 875	17 139	17 736
75 - 79	39 159	16 723	22 436	18 285	8 018	10 267	20 874	8 705	12 169
80 - 84	24 224	9 637	14 587	9 479	3 895	5 584	14 745	5 742	9 003
85 - 89	9 514	3 191	6 323	3 413	1 126	2 287	6 101	2 065	4 036
90 - 94	3 831	1 032	2 799	1 228	329	899	2 603	703	1 900
95 - 99	1 048	302	746	435	137	298	613	165	448
100 +	522	159	363	140	57	83	382	102	280
1 VII 2007 (ESDF)									
Total	3 161 337	1 587 496	1 573 841	...	...	...	...	...	...
0 - 4	235 302	123 046	112 256	...	...	...	...	...	...
5 - 9	253 793	132 777	121 016	...	...	...	...	...	...
10 - 14	286 308	147 958	138 350	...	...	...	...	...	...
15 - 19	313 936	161 708	152 228	...	...	...	...	...	...
20 - 24	295 727	147 905	147 822	...	...	...	...	...	...
25 - 29	235 258	113 683	121 575	...	...	...	...	...	...
30 - 34	206 086	98 976	107 110	...	...	...	...	...	...
35 - 39	209 124	101 371	107 753	...	...	...	...	...	...
40 - 44	206 518	102 083	104 435	...	...	...	...	...	...
45 - 49	211 488	107 301	104 187	...	...	...	...	...	...
50 - 54	173 514	88 893	84 621	...	...	...	...	...	...
55 - 59	141 043	72 321	68 722	...	...	...	...	...	...
60 - 64	109 574	56 104	53 470	...	...	...	...	...	...
65 - 69	105 484	52 256	53 228	...	...	...	...	...	...
70 - 74	80 010	40 034	39 976	...	...	...	...	...	...
75 - 79	53 319	24 567	28 752	...	...	...	...	...	...
80 - 84	27 870	10 696	17 174	...	...	...	...	...	...
85 - 89	13 478	4 789	8 689	...	...	...	...	...	...
90 - 94	3 013	907	2 106	...	...	...	...	...	...
95 +	492	121	371	...	...	...	...	...	...
Andorra - Andorre[18]									
1 VII 2009 (ESDJ)									
Total	85 116	44 444	40 672	...	...	...	...	...	...
0	278	139	139	...	...	...	...	...	...
1 - 4	3 118	1 647	1 471	...	...	...	...	...	...
5 - 9	4 314	2 250	2 064	...	...	...	...	...	...
10 - 14	4 217	2 201	2 016	...	...	...	...	...	...
15 - 19	3 938	2 081	1 857	...	...	...	...	...	...
20 - 24	4 407	2 267	2 140	...	...	...	...	...	...
25 - 29	6 453	3 240	3 213	...	...	...	...	...	...
30 - 34	8 184	4 235	3 949	...	...	...	...	...	...
35 - 39	8 333	4 328	4 005	...	...	...	...	...	...
40 - 44	8 097	4 239	3 858	...	...	...	...	...	...
45 - 49	7 502	3 993	3 509	...	...	...	...	...	...
50 - 54	6 221	3 365	2 856	...	...	...	...	...	...
55 - 59	4 965	2 745	2 220	...	...	...	...	...	...
60 - 64	4 093	2 251	1 842	...	...	...	...	...	...
65 - 69	3 132	1 638	1 494	...	...	...	...	...	...
70 - 74	2 241	1 155	1 086	...	...	...	...	...	...
75 - 79	2 012	999	1 013	...	...	...	...	...	...
80 - 84	1 628	773	855	...	...	...	...	...	...
85 - 89	1 074	476	598	...	...	...	...	...	...
90 - 94	473	219	254	...	...	...	...	...	...
95 - 99	232	102	130	...	...	...	...	...	...
100 +	204	101	103	...	...	...	...	...	...
Austria - Autriche									
15 V 2001 (CDJC)									
Total	8 032 926	3 889 189	4 143 737	5 368 693	2 564 828	2 803 865	2 664 233	1 324 361	1 339 872
0	77 060	39 641	37 419	50 942	26 172	24 770	26 118	13 469	12 649
1 - 4	332 964	170 439	162 525	215 492	110 553	104 939	117 472	59 886	57 586
5 - 9	469 735	240 593	229 142	296 471	151 887	144 584	173 264	88 706	84 558

7. Population by age, sex and urban/rural residence: latest available year, 2000 - 2009
Population selon l'âge, le sexe et la résidence, urbaine/rurale : dernière année disponible, 2000 - 2009 (continued - suite)

Continent, country or area, date, code and age (in years) / Continent, pays ou zone, date, code et âge (en années)	Total			Urban - Urbaine			Rural - Rurale		
	Both sexes Les deux sexes	Male Masculin	Female Féminin	Both sexes Les deux sexes	Male Masculin	Female Féminin	Both sexes Les deux sexes	Male Masculin	Female Féminin
EUROPE									
Austria - Autriche									
15 V 2001 (CDJC)									
10 - 14	473 723	242 791	230 932	294 674	151 245	143 429	179 049	91 546	87 503
15 - 19	483 957	247 452	236 505	300 985	153 733	147 252	182 972	93 719	89 253
20 - 24	472 777	240 171	232 606	309 267	154 636	154 631	163 510	85 535	77 975
25 - 29	539 031	268 179	270 852	364 619	178 639	185 980	174 412	89 540	84 872
30 - 34	668 281	337 121	331 160	456 030	227 926	228 104	212 251	109 195	103 056
35 - 39	704 872	358 748	346 124	473 632	239 432	234 200	231 240	119 316	111 924
40 - 44	625 783	316 280	309 503	416 601	207 478	209 123	209 182	108 802	100 380
45 - 49	525 207	261 903	263 304	352 245	172 161	180 084	172 962	89 742	83 220
50 - 54	514 535	255 906	258 629	356 937	174 415	182 522	157 598	81 491	76 107
55 - 59	452 265	220 827	231 438	326 907	157 892	169 015	125 358	62 935	62 423
60 - 64	451 057	217 191	233 866	305 628	145 952	159 676	145 429	71 239	74 190
65 - 69	332 596	152 844	179 752	215 372	97 381	117 991	117 224	55 463	61 761
70 - 74	327 321	140 193	187 128	217 723	90 939	126 784	109 598	49 254	60 344
75 - 79	290 140	97 886	192 254	202 551	66 803	135 748	87 589	31 083	56 506
80 - 84	151 242	45 800	105 442	108 554	32 170	76 384	42 688	13 630	29 058
85 - 89	96 166	25 556	70 610	70 458	18 358	52 100	25 708	7 198	18 510
90 - 94	37 255	8 413	28 842	28 193	6 138	22 055	9 062	2 275	6 787
95 +	6 959	1 255	5 704	5 412	918	4 494	1 547	337	1 210
1 VII 2009 (ESDJ)									
Total	8 365 275	4 073 570	4 291 705	...	...	...	...	...	...
0	76 475	39 298	37 177	...	...	...	...	...	...
1 - 4	318 216	162 820	155 397	...	...	...	...	...	...
5 - 9	407 061	208 954	198 107	...	...	...	...	...	...
10 - 14	451 478	231 144	220 335	...	...	...	...	...	...
15 - 19	501 802	257 228	244 574	...	...	...	...	...	...
20 - 24	520 970	263 354	257 616	...	...	...	...	...	...
25 - 29	554 119	278 150	275 969	...	...	...	...	...	...
30 - 34	532 763	266 775	265 988	...	...	...	...	...	...
35 - 39	615 466	306 252	309 214	...	...	...	...	...	...
40 - 44	711 164	359 633	351 532	...	...	...	...	...	...
45 - 49	689 804	348 325	341 479	...	...	...	...	...	...
50 - 54	582 274	289 299	292 976	...	...	...	...	...	...
55 - 59	491 610	240 973	250 638	...	...	...	...	...	...
60 - 64	448 672	216 483	232 189	...	...	...	...	...	...
65 - 69	472 884	222 446	250 439	...	...	...	...	...	...
70 - 74	322 758	146 183	176 575	...	...	...	...	...	...
75 - 79	272 333	113 690	158 643	...	...	...	...	...	...
80 - 84	217 485	76 769	140 716	...	...	...	...	...	...
85 - 89	134 181	36 072	98 109	...	...	...	...	...	...
90 - 94	32 195	7 449	24 746	...	...	...	...	...	...
95 - 99	10 588	2 123	8 465	...	...	...	...	...	...
100 +	982	155	827	...	...	...	...	...	...
Belarus - Bélarus									
1 VII 2009 (ESDJ)									
Total	9 665 120	4 508 125	5 156 995	7 173 482	3 334 319	3 839 163	2 491 638	1 173 806	1 317 832
0	108 175	55 723	52 452	82 252	42 420	39 832	25 923	13 303	12 620
1 - 4	386 976	198 881	188 095	291 034	149 800	141 234	95 942	49 081	46 861
5 - 9	448 695	230 760	217 935	335 785	172 735	163 050	112 910	58 025	54 885
10 - 14	472 112	242 723	229 389	334 076	171 896	162 180	138 036	70 827	67 209
15 - 19	642 330	329 240	313 090	493 187	248 987	244 200	149 143	80 253	68 890
20 - 24	823 884	420 279	403 605	650 769	326 279	324 490	173 115	94 000	79 115
25 - 29	791 916	403 246	388 670	651 978	328 473	323 505	139 938	74 773	65 165
30 - 34	700 485	351 550	348 935	561 136	279 558	281 578	139 349	71 992	67 357
35 - 39	674 016	331 507	342 509	516 203	249 798	266 405	157 813	81 709	76 104
40 - 44	676 185	328 179	348 006	504 973	237 837	267 136	171 212	90 342	80 870
45 - 49	791 886	379 349	412 537	598 465	275 908	322 557	193 421	103 441	89 980
50 - 54	755 789	351 179	404 610	576 141	257 476	318 665	179 648	93 703	85 945
55 - 59	612 371	273 509	338 862	470 906	203 184	267 722	141 465	70 325	71 140
60 - 64	426 346	180 785	245 561	319 296	133 424	185 872	107 050	47 361	59 689
65 - 69	355 131	133 762	221 369	234 286	89 215	145 071	120 845	44 547	76 298
70 - 74	405 643	138 403	267 240	244 481	84 478	160 003	161 162	53 925	107 237
75 - 79	294 938	89 181	205 757	150 061	44 884	105 177	144 877	44 297	100 580

Continent, country or area, date, code and age (in years) Continent, pays ou zone, date, code et âge (en annèes)	Total			Urban - Urbaine			Rural - Rurale		
	Both sexes Les deux sexes	Male Masculin	Female Féminin	Both sexes Les deux sexes	Male Masculin	Female Féminin	Both sexes Les deux sexes	Male Masculin	Female Féminin
EUROPE									
Belarus - Bélarus									
1 VII 2009 (ESDJ)									
80 - 84	202 990	51 603	151 387	104 901	27 652	77 249	98 089	23 951	74 138
85 +	95 252	18 266	76 986	53 552	10 315	43 237	41 700	7 951	33 749
Belgium - Belgique									
1 VII 2007 (ESDJ)									
Total	10 622 604	5 201 670	5 420 934	10 469 341	5 125 007	5 344 334	153 263	76 663	76 600
0	122 066	62 586	59 480	120 389	61 712	58 677	1 677	874	803
1 - 4	474 044	242 475	231 569	466 767	238 729	228 038	7 277	3 746	3 531
5 - 9	589 949	301 270	288 679	580 511	296 562	283 949	9 438	4 708	4 730
10 - 14	612 220	312 689	299 531	602 307	307 552	294 755	9 913	5 137	4 776
15 - 19	647 604	330 619	316 985	637 307	325 326	311 981	10 297	5 293	5 004
20 - 24	637 565	320 082	317 483	628 503	315 496	313 007	9 062	4 586	4 476
25 - 29	682 339	341 911	340 428	673 926	337 622	336 304	8 413	4 289	4 124
30 - 34	687 465	346 878	340 587	678 252	342 213	336 039	9 213	4 665	4 548
35 - 39	761 622	385 601	376 021	750 602	380 013	370 589	11 020	5 588	5 432
40 - 44	814 230	412 721	401 509	802 238	406 505	395 733	11 992	6 216	5 776
45 - 49	797 886	401 667	396 219	786 486	395 703	390 783	11 400	5 964	5 436
50 - 54	733 119	367 244	365 875	723 048	361 956	361 092	10 071	5 288	4 783
55 - 59	673 925	336 546	337 379	664 705	331 743	332 962	9 220	4 803	4 417
60 - 64	574 166	281 842	292 324	566 368	277 892	288 476	7 798	3 950	3 848
65 - 69	465 964	220 871	245 093	459 164	217 553	241 611	6 800	3 318	3 482
70 - 74	451 455	204 190	247 265	444 877	201 093	243 784	6 578	3 097	3 481
75 - 79	404 242	168 276	235 966	398 354	165 744	232 610	5 888	2 532	3 356
80 - 84	290 317	106 856	183 461	285 965	105 101	180 864	4 352	1 755	2 597
85 - 89	142 260	44 177	98 083	140 262	43 527	96 735	1 998	650	1 348
90 - 94	46 706	10 941	35 765	46 019	10 767	35 252	687	174	513
95 - 99	12 113	2 082	10 031	11 960	2 055	9 905	153	27	126
100 +	1 347	146	1 201	1 331	143	1 188	16	3	13
1 I 2008 (ESDJ)									
Total	10 666 866	5 224 309	5 442 557	...	...	...	...	...	...
0	121 006	61 863	59 143	...	...	...	...	...	...
1 - 4	479 722	245 309	234 413	...	...	...	...	...	...
5 - 9	590 108	301 395	288 713	...	...	...	...	...	...
10 - 14	609 619	311 519	298 100	...	...	...	...	...	...
15 - 19	652 315	332 870	319 445	...	...	...	...	...	...
20 - 24	640 516	321 424	319 092	...	...	...	...	...	...
25 - 29	686 192	343 935	342 257	...	...	...	...	...	...
30 - 34	686 601	346 326	340 275	...	...	...	...	...	...
35 - 39	761 910	385 287	376 623	...	...	...	...	...	...
40 - 44	811 766	411 776	399 990	...	...	...	...	...	...
45 - 49	802 015	404 072	397 943	...	...	...	...	...	...
50 - 54	739 278	370 283	368 995	...	...	...	...	...	...
55 - 59	676 975	337 939	339 036	...	...	...	...	...	...
60 - 64	589 117	289 377	299 740	...	...	...	...	...	...
65 - 69	461 720	219 042	242 678	...	...	...	...	...	...
70 - 74	450 437	204 647	245 790	...	...	...	...	...	...
75 - 79	406 356	169 513	236 843	...	...	...	...	...	...
80 - 84	292 033	107 782	184 251	...	...	...	...	...	...
85 - 89	150 443	47 078	103 365	...	...	...	...	...	...
90 - 94	44 768	10 570	34 198	...	...	...	...	...	...
95 - 99	12 588	2 158	10 430	...	...	...	...	...	...
100 +	1 381	144	1 237	...	...	...	...	...	...
Bosnia and Herzegovina - Bosnie-Herzégovine									
1 VII 2009 (ESDF)									
Total	3 842 566	1 877 312	1 965 254	...	...	...	...	...	...
0	33 309	17 121	16 188	...	...	...	...	...	...
1 - 4	133 238	68 484	64 754	...	...	...	...	...	...
5 - 9	229 575	117 313	112 262	...	...	...	...	...	...
10 - 14	274 740	139 842	134 898	...	...	...	...	...	...
15 - 19	279 328	146 368	132 960	...	...	...	...	...	...
20 - 24	284 952	144 755	140 197	...	...	...	...	...	...
25 - 29	268 234	131 971	136 263	...	...	...	...	...	...
30 - 34	240 950	120 957	119 993	...	...	...	...	...	...

Continent, country or area, date, code and age (in years) / Continent, pays ou zone, date, code et âge (en années)	Total			Urban - Urbaine			Rural - Rurale		
	Both sexes Les deux sexes	Male Masculin	Female Féminin	Both sexes Les deux sexes	Male Masculin	Female Féminin	Both sexes Les deux sexes	Male Masculin	Female Féminin
EUROPE									
Bosnia and Herzegovina - Bosnie-Herzégovine									
1 VII 2009 (ESDF)									
35 - 39	246 686	121 616	125 070	...	...	...	...	...	...
40 - 44	283 845	141 922	141 923	...	...	...	...	...	...
45 - 49	306 913	150 388	156 525	...	...	...	...	...	...
50 - 54	266 536	135 667	130 869	...	...	...	...	...	...
55 - 59	231 561	105 129	126 432	...	...	...	...	...	...
60 - 64	182 761	86 080	96 681	...	...	...	...	...	...
65 - 69	202 245	89 999	112 246	...	...	...	...	...	...
70 - 74	184 362	82 410	101 952	...	...	...	...	...	...
75 - 79	120 347	50 546	69 801	...	...	...	...	...	...
80 - 84	47 925	19 602	28 323	...	...	...	...	...	...
85 +	25 059	7 142	17 917	...	...	...	...	...	...
Bulgaria - Bulgarie									
1 VII 2009 (ESDJ)									
Total	7 585 131	3 670 296	3 914 835	5 408 330	2 598 442	2 809 888	2 176 801	1 071 854	1 104 947
0	75 233	38 533	36 700	56 677	29 044	27 633	18 556	9 489	9 067
1 - 4	290 081	149 177	140 904	216 108	111 060	105 048	73 973	38 117	35 856
5 - 9	336 193	172 949	163 244	241 726	124 425	117 301	94 467	48 524	45 943
10 - 14	322 391	165 317	157 074	226 973	116 355	110 618	95 418	48 962	46 456
15 - 19	430 969	221 204	209 765	308 818	157 605	151 213	122 151	63 599	58 552
20 - 24	520 064	266 324	253 740	399 333	202 337	196 996	120 731	63 987	56 744
25 - 29	542 777	278 811	263 966	424 423	214 922	209 501	118 354	63 889	54 465
30 - 34	581 398	297 129	284 269	450 886	228 116	222 770	130 512	69 013	61 499
35 - 39	553 728	281 240	272 488	420 225	209 896	210 329	133 503	71 344	62 159
40 - 44	513 717	258 311	255 406	383 579	188 882	194 697	130 138	69 429	60 709
45 - 49	523 587	260 175	263 412	389 865	188 803	201 062	133 722	71 372	62 350
50 - 54	532 447	258 798	273 649	394 352	186 850	207 502	138 095	71 948	66 147
55 - 59	536 915	254 082	282 833	389 239	180 815	208 424	147 676	73 267	74 409
60 - 64	500 763	228 684	272 079	340 408	154 118	186 290	160 355	74 566	85 789
65 - 69	391 764	171 279	220 485	237 857	103 935	133 922	153 907	67 344	86 563
70 - 74	350 101	145 893	204 208	199 587	80 989	118 598	150 514	64 904	85 610
75 - 79	298 833	119 212	179 621	167 483	63 779	103 704	131 350	55 433	75 917
80 - 84	186 739	69 538	117 201	105 962	38 220	67 742	80 777	31 318	49 459
85 - 89	80 300	27 916	52 384	45 287	15 217	30 070	35 013	12 699	22 314
90 - 94	13 757	4 613	9 144	7 741	2 502	5 239	6 016	2 111	3 905
95 - 99	2 987	974	2 013	1 615	502	1 113	1 372	472	900
100 +	387	137	250	186	70	116	201	67	134
Croatia - Croatie									
31 III 2001 (CDJC)									
Total	4 437 460	2 135 900	2 301 560	2 471 328	1 171 950	1 299 378	1 966 132	963 950	1 002 182
0	42 942	22 097	20 845	23 438	12 112	11 326	19 504	9 985	9 519
1 - 4	194 580	99 621	94 959	104 707	53 579	51 128	89 873	46 042	43 831
5 - 9	248 528	127 274	121 254	134 027	68 669	65 358	114 501	58 605	55 896
10 - 14	268 584	137 175	131 409	144 935	74 118	70 817	123 649	63 057	60 592
15 - 19	298 606	152 676	145 930	165 511	84 240	81 271	133 095	68 436	64 659
20 - 24	305 631	155 739	149 892	176 487	88 565	87 922	129 144	67 174	61 970
25 - 29	294 497	148 666	145 831	171 776	84 620	87 156	122 721	64 046	58 675
30 - 34	295 431	147 920	147 511	169 076	82 749	86 327	126 355	65 171	61 184
35 - 39	317 273	158 506	158 767	177 369	85 563	91 806	139 904	72 943	66 961
40 - 44	333 403	166 499	166 904	189 206	89 569	99 637	144 197	76 930	67 267
45 - 49	333 576	168 290	165 286	195 040	93 697	101 343	138 536	74 593	63 943
50 - 54	299 773	148 224	151 549	178 220	84 433	93 787	121 553	63 791	57 762
55 - 59	229 775	108 673	121 102	134 170	61 988	72 182	95 605	46 685	48 920
60 - 64	262 016	120 667	141 349	142 207	65 853	76 354	119 809	54 814	64 995
65 - 69	252 947	110 459	142 488	131 008	58 413	72 595	121 939	52 046	69 893
70 - 74	203 885	81 884	122 001	102 578	41 358	61 220	101 307	40 526	60 781
75 - 79	137 201	44 149	93 052	69 924	22 818	47 106	67 277	21 331	45 946
80 - 84	56 954	17 040	39 914	29 302	8 963	20 339	27 652	8 077	19 575
85 - 89	30 833	8 682	22 151	16 108	4 575	11 533	14 725	4 107	10 618
90 - 94	10 265	2 571	7 694	5 386	1 310	4 076	4 879	1 261	3 618
95 - 99	1 371	302	1 069	753	153	600	618	149	469
100 +	84	21	63	54	16	38	30	5	25
Unknown - Inconnu	19 305	8 765	10 540	10 046	4 589	5 457	9 259	4 176	5 083

Continent, country or area, date, code and age (in years) / Continent, pays ou zone, date, code et âge (en années)	Total			Urban - Urbaine			Rural - Rurale		
	Both sexes Les deux sexes	Male Masculin	Female Féminin	Both sexes Les deux sexes	Male Masculin	Female Féminin	Both sexes Les deux sexes	Male Masculin	Female Féminin
EUROPE									
Croatia - Croatie									
1 VII 2009 (ESDJ)									
Total	4 429 078	2 136 231	2 292 847	...	...	...	...	...	...
0	43 420	22 239	21 181	...	...	...	...	...	...
1 - 4	168 687	86 719	81 968	...	...	...	...	...	...
5 - 9	211 034	108 324	102 710	...	...	...	...	...	...
10 - 14	252 127	128 882	123 245	...	...	...	...	...	...
15 - 19	257 453	131 840	125 613	...	...	...	...	...	...
20 - 24	285 849	145 635	140 214	...	...	...	...	...	...
25 - 29	313 382	159 831	153 551	...	...	...	...	...	...
30 - 34	306 408	155 046	151 362	...	...	...	...	...	...
35 - 39	293 233	147 632	145 601	...	...	...	...	...	...
40 - 44	310 153	154 620	155 533	...	...	...	...	...	...
45 - 49	321 528	159 635	161 893	...	...	...	...	...	...
50 - 54	332 610	164 179	168 431	...	...	...	...	...	...
55 - 59	310 658	152 670	157 988	...	...	...	...	...	...
60 - 64	240 194	112 696	127 498	...	...	...	...	...	...
65 - 69	224 033	99 180	124 853	...	...	...	...	...	...
70 - 74	213 822	88 756	125 066	...	...	...	...	...	...
75 - 79	173 095	64 618	108 477	...	...	...	...	...	...
80 - 84	99 072	31 702	67 370	...	...	...	...	...	...
85 +	53 127	13 338	39 789	...	...	...	...	...	...
Unknown - Inconnu	19 193	8 689	10 504	...	...	...	...	...	...
Czech Republic - République tchèque[65]									
1 VII 2009 (ESDJ)									
Total	10 487 178	5 146 787	5 340 391	7 724 605	3 763 104	3 961 501	2 762 573	1 383 683	1 378 890
0	119 262	60 969	58 293	87 492	44 737	42 755	31 769	16 232	15 537
1 - 4	434 607	222 942	211 665	316 101	162 220	153 881	118 507	60 722	57 785
5 - 9	465 712	239 580	226 133	334 672	172 206	162 466	131 041	67 374	63 667
10 - 14	467 608	239 989	227 620	331 034	169 503	161 531	136 574	70 486	66 089
15 - 19	626 620	321 282	305 338	450 799	230 516	220 284	175 821	90 766	85 055
20 - 24	704 121	363 523	340 598	522 637	269 913	252 724	181 484	93 610	87 874
25 - 29	771 767	399 506	372 262	577 100	298 622	278 478	194 668	100 884	93 784
30 - 34	935 004	480 197	454 808	692 558	354 688	337 870	242 447	125 509	116 938
35 - 39	820 090	422 273	397 817	602 092	307 469	294 623	217 999	114 804	103 195
40 - 44	704 429	361 529	342 900	521 234	264 162	257 072	183 195	97 367	85 828
45 - 49	667 218	339 343	327 876	493 387	248 109	245 278	173 831	91 234	82 598
50 - 54	715 852	356 462	359 390	525 516	257 516	268 000	190 336	98 947	91 390
55 - 59	763 069	371 445	391 625	563 114	269 825	293 289	199 955	101 620	98 336
60 - 64	714 304	337 578	376 726	530 081	246 093	283 988	184 223	91 485	92 738
65 - 69	521 633	235 993	285 640	392 374	175 497	216 877	129 259	60 496	68 763
70 - 74	365 535	154 250	211 285	271 719	114 067	157 652	93 816	40 183	53 633
75 - 79	322 894	124 834	198 060	239 243	92 213	147 030	83 652	32 621	51 031
80 - 84	226 089	76 290	149 799	167 992	56 884	111 108	58 097	19 406	38 691
85 - 89	113 875	32 298	81 577	85 555	24 264	61 292	28 320	8 035	20 285
90 - 94	20 482	4 999	15 483	15 143	3 641	11 502	5 339	1 358	3 981
95 - 99	6 339	1 354	4 985	4 373	869	3 504	1 966	485	1 481
100 +	674	156	518	394	93	301	280	63	217
Denmark - Danemark[66]									
1 VII 2009 (ESDJ)									
Total	5 519 441	2 735 983	2 783 458	...	...	...	...	...	...
0	64 696	33 373	31 323	...	...	...	...	...	...
1 - 4	261 955	134 091	127 864	...	...	...	...	...	...
5 - 9	329 869	168 773	161 096	...	...	...	...	...	...
10 - 14	348 119	178 486	169 633	...	...	...	...	...	...
15 - 19	345 863	177 269	168 594	...	...	...	...	...	...
20 - 24	319 156	162 874	156 282	...	...	...	...	...	...
25 - 29	312 082	156 529	155 553	...	...	...	...	...	...
30 - 34	357 933	179 434	178 499	...	...	...	...	...	...
35 - 39	386 503	194 738	191 765	...	...	...	...	...	...
40 - 44	420 042	213 412	206 630	...	...	...	...	...	...
45 - 49	394 023	199 511	194 512	...	...	...	...	...	...
50 - 54	363 425	182 917	180 508	...	...	...	...	...	...
55 - 59	350 511	175 035	175 476	...	...	...	...	...	...

Continent, country or area, date, code and age (in years) / Continent, pays ou zone, date, code et âge (en années)	Total			Urban - Urbaine			Rural - Rurale		
	Both sexes Les deux sexes	Male Masculin	Female Féminin	Both sexes Les deux sexes	Male Masculin	Female Féminin	Both sexes Les deux sexes	Male Masculin	Female Féminin

EUROPE

Denmark - Danemark[66]
1 VII 2009 (ESDJ)

60 - 64	376 280	187 389	188 891	...	...	...	...	...	...
65 - 69	289 525	141 450	148 075	...	...	...	...	...	...
70 - 74	214 093	100 549	113 544	...	...	...	...	...	...
75 - 79	158 429	70 022	88 407	...	...	...	...	...	...
80 - 84	118 124	47 141	70 983	...	...	...	...	...	...
85 - 89	72 948	24 145	48 803	...	...	...	...	...	...
90 - 94	27 904	7 292	20 612	...	...	...	...	...	...
95 - 99	7 115	1 430	5 685	...	...	...	...	...	...
100 +	846	123	723	...	...	...	...	...	...

Estonia - Estonie
1 VII 2009 (ESDJ)

Total	1 340 271	617 311	722 960	930 774	419 001	511 773	409 497	198 310	211 187
0	15 834	8 104	7 730	10 874	5 565	5 309	4 960	2 539	2 421
1 - 4	59 665	30 860	28 805	42 130	21 837	20 293	17 535	9 023	8 512
5 - 9	64 181	32 938	31 243	44 048	22 637	21 411	20 133	10 301	9 832
10 - 14	61 889	31 776	30 113	40 115	20 541	19 574	21 774	11 235	10 539
15 - 19	85 535	43 903	41 632	53 930	27 644	26 286	31 605	16 259	15 346
20 - 24	106 656	54 369	52 287	70 184	35 805	34 379	36 472	18 564	17 908
25 - 29	100 930	51 113	49 817	71 341	35 194	36 147	29 589	15 919	13 670
30 - 34	92 876	46 633	46 243	70 182	34 105	36 077	22 694	12 528	10 166
35 - 39	92 996	45 958	47 038	67 470	32 673	34 797	25 526	13 285	12 241
40 - 44	86 778	41 833	44 945	60 226	28 446	31 780	26 552	13 387	13 165
45 - 49	94 211	44 441	49 770	65 221	29 659	35 562	28 990	14 782	14 208
50 - 54	92 760	42 372	50 388	65 329	28 583	36 746	27 431	13 789	13 642
55 - 59	85 745	37 672	48 073	61 291	25 738	35 553	24 454	11 934	12 520
60 - 64	70 980	29 785	41 195	49 727	20 010	29 717	21 253	9 775	11 478
65 - 69	64 709	25 272	39 437	44 296	16 526	27 770	20 413	8 746	11 667
70 - 74	62 624	22 187	40 437	44 021	15 118	28 903	18 603	7 069	11 534
75 - 79	48 332	15 317	33 015	33 521	10 294	23 227	14 811	5 023	9 788
80 - 84	33 318	8 702	24 616	23 533	6 059	17 474	9 785	2 643	7 142
85 - 89	14 581	2 999	11 582	9 813	1 963	7 850	4 768	1 036	3 732
90 - 94	3 957	735	3 222	2 549	432	2 117	1 408	303	1 105
95 - 99	1 316	236	1 080	748	121	627	568	115	453
100 +	258	45	213	116	18	98	142	27	115
Unknown - Inconnu	140	61	79	109	33	76	31	28	3

Faeroe Islands - Îles Féroé
1 VII 2008 (ESDJ)

Total	48 618	25 263	23 355	17 624	8 920	8 704	30 994	16 343	14 651
0	679	331	348	246	122	124	433	209	224
1 - 4	2 805	1 424	1 381	1 014	501	513	1 791	923	868
5 - 9	3 555	1 862	1 693	1 334	695	639	2 221	1 167	1 054
10 - 14	3 656	1 872	1 784	1 388	699	689	2 268	1 173	1 095
15 - 19	3 971	2 055	1 916	1 470	769	701	2 501	1 286	1 215
20 - 24	2 976	1 669	1 307	1 009	549	460	1 967	1 120	847
25 - 29	2 542	1 400	1 142	881	465	416	1 661	935	726
30 - 34	2 994	1 639	1 355	1 093	589	504	1 901	1 050	851
35 - 39	3 205	1 689	1 516	1 172	578	594	2 033	1 111	922
40 - 44	3 594	1 936	1 658	1 510	792	718	2 084	1 144	940
45 - 49	3 278	1 702	1 576	1 258	657	601	2 020	1 045	975
50 - 54	3 033	1 572	1 461	1 140	559	581	1 893	1 013	880
55 - 59	2 973	1 553	1 420	1 091	548	543	1 882	1 005	877
60 - 64	2 535	1 383	1 152	856	448	408	1 679	935	744
65 - 69	2 053	1 076	977	686	337	349	1 367	739	628
70 - 74	1 522	782	740	485	236	249	1 037	546	491
75 - 79	1 358	635	723	420	186	234	938	449	489
80 - 84	1 003	386	617	298	113	185	705	273	432
85 - 89	590	202	388	163	50	113	427	152	275
90 - 94	246	81	165	93	24	69	153	57	96
95 - 99	45	11	34	16	3	13	29	8	21
100 +	5	3	2	1	-	1	4	3	1

Continent, country or area, date, code and age (in years) Continent, pays ou zone, date, code et âge (en années)	Total			Urban - Urbaine			Rural - Rurale		
	Both sexes Les deux sexes	Male Masculin	Female Féminin	Both sexes Les deux sexes	Male Masculin	Female Féminin	Both sexes Les deux sexes	Male Masculin	Female Féminin
EUROPE									
Finland - Finlande[67]									
1 VII 2009 (ESDJ)									
Total	5 311 276	2 604 636	2 706 640	3 619 503	1 754 275	1 865 228	1 691 773	850 361	841 412
0	59 772	30 487	29 285	42 466	21 612	20 854	17 306	8 875	8 431
1 - 4	235 305	120 234	115 072	162 924	83 225	79 699	72 382	37 009	35 373
5 - 9	285 831	146 266	139 565	190 488	97 519	92 969	95 343	48 747	46 596
10 - 14	304 206	155 105	149 101	199 264	101 447	97 817	104 942	53 658	51 284
15 - 19	332 166	169 373	162 793	223 037	111 919	111 118	109 130	57 454	51 676
20 - 24	323 645	165 536	158 109	251 408	125 183	126 226	72 237	40 353	31 884
25 - 29	340 955	175 061	165 894	266 165	135 626	130 539	74 790	39 435	35 355
30 - 34	334 358	171 695	162 664	251 007	128 824	122 183	83 351	42 871	40 481
35 - 39	309 580	158 357	151 223	221 701	113 463	108 238	87 879	44 894	42 986
40 - 44	361 349	183 462	177 887	251 351	126 518	124 833	109 998	56 944	53 054
45 - 49	376 249	190 016	186 233	253 307	126 276	127 032	122 942	63 740	59 202
50 - 54	377 941	189 073	188 868	247 400	120 870	126 530	130 541	68 203	62 338
55 - 59	389 267	193 363	195 904	252 415	121 190	131 225	136 852	72 173	64 679
60 - 64	384 258	188 503	195 755	251 256	119 523	131 734	133 002	68 980	64 022
65 - 69	255 344	120 762	134 583	164 647	75 706	88 941	90 698	45 056	45 642
70 - 74	220 196	98 921	121 275	136 402	59 384	77 018	83 794	39 537	44 257
75 - 79	179 412	73 563	105 849	109 661	43 260	66 401	69 751	30 303	39 448
80 - 84	135 899	47 877	88 022	81 174	27 344	53 830	54 725	20 533	34 192
85 - 89	74 133	20 384	53 749	44 168	11 614	32 555	29 965	8 770	21 195
90 - 94	25 172	5 522	19 650	15 426	3 158	12 268	9 746	2 364	7 382
95 - 99	5 709	1 004	4 705	3 516	570	2 946	2 193	434	1 760
100 +	537	79	458	326	48	278	211	31	180
France[68]									
1 VII 2009* (ESDJ)									
Total	62 621 205	30 324 030	32 297 175	...	...	...	...	...	...
0	791 731	402 680	389 051	...	...	...	...	...	...
1 - 4	3 085 592	1 576 676	1 508 916	...	...	...	...	...	...
5 - 9	3 832 148	1 962 135	1 870 013	...	...	...	...	...	...
10 - 14	3 758 636	1 926 451	1 832 185	...	...	...	...	...	...
15 - 19	3 843 122	1 962 386	1 880 736	...	...	...	...	...	...
20 - 24	4 005 732	2 019 271	1 986 461	...	...	...	...	...	...
25 - 29	3 955 481	1 967 966	1 987 515	...	...	...	...	...	...
30 - 34	3 836 247	1 911 220	1 925 027	...	...	...	...	...	...
35 - 39	4 356 158	2 166 045	2 190 113	...	...	...	...	...	...
40 - 44	4 358 197	2 155 473	2 202 724	...	...	...	...	...	...
45 - 49	4 335 583	2 129 812	2 205 771	...	...	...	...	...	...
50 - 54	4 163 666	2 027 999	2 135 667	...	...	...	...	...	...
55 - 59	4 108 744	2 000 718	2 108 026	...	...	...	...	...	...
60 - 64	3 685 917	1 791 466	1 894 451	...	...	...	...	...	...
65 - 69	2 536 193	1 205 188	1 331 005	...	...	...	...	...	...
70 - 74	2 421 190	1 086 389	1 334 801	...	...	...	...	...	...
75 - 79	2 254 635	934 496	1 320 139	...	...	...	...	...	...
80 - 84	1 751 652	647 446	1 104 206	...	...	...	...	...	...
85 - 89	1 117 691	355 213	762 478	...	...	...	...	...	...
90 - 94	288 607	71 242	217 365	...	...	...	...	...	...
95 +	127 541	22 999	104 542	...	...	...	...	...	...
Germany - Allemagne									
1 I 2009 (ESDJ)									
Total	82 002 356	40 184 283	41 818 073	...	...	...	...	...	...
0	683 350	350 238	333 112	...	...	...	...	...	...
1 - 4	2 761 822	1 417 517	1 344 305	...	...	...	...	...	...
5 - 9	3 714 997	1 904 962	1 810 035	...	...	...	...	...	...
10 - 14	3 978 937	2 041 802	1 937 135	...	...	...	...	...	...
15 - 19	4 479 630	2 295 761	2 183 869	...	...	...	...	...	...
20 - 24	4 899 839	2 496 201	2 403 638	...	...	...	...	...	...
25 - 29	4 984 192	2 523 056	2 461 136	...	...	...	...	...	...
30 - 34	4 702 670	2 381 693	2 320 977	...	...	...	...	...	...
35 - 39	5 613 543	2 857 095	2 756 448	...	...	...	...	...	...
40 - 44	7 052 899	3 611 539	3 441 360	...	...	...	...	...	...
45 - 49	6 894 046	3 507 476	3 386 570	...	...	...	...	...	...
50 - 54	5 906 471	2 974 555	2 931 916	...	...	...	...	...	...
55 - 59	5 372 216	2 659 741	2 712 475	...	...	...	...	...	...

7. Population by age, sex and urban/rural residence: latest available year, 2000 - 2009
Population selon l'âge, le sexe et la résidence, urbaine/rurale : dernière année disponible, 2000 - 2009 (continued - suite)

Continent, country or area, date, code and age (in years) / Continent, pays ou zone, date, code et âge (en années)	Total			Urban - Urbaine			Rural - Rurale		
	Both sexes Les deux sexes	Male Masculin	Female Féminin	Both sexes Les deux sexes	Male Masculin	Female Féminin	Both sexes Les deux sexes	Male Masculin	Female Féminin
EUROPE									
Germany - Allemagne									
1 I 2009 (ESDJ)									
60 - 64	4 228 731	2 078 987	2 149 744	...	...	...	...	...	...
65 - 69	5 144 557	2 469 600	2 674 957	...	...	...	...	...	...
70 - 74	4 522 256	2 079 806	2 442 450	...	...	...	...	...	...
75 - 79	3 001 088	1 271 267	1 729 821	...	...	...	...	...	...
80 - 84	2 258 736	791 628	1 467 108	...	...	...	...	...	...
85 - 89	1 296 993	345 829	951 164	...	...	...	...	...	...
90 - 94	320 972	73 685	247 287	...	...	...	...	...	...
95 +	184 411	51 845	132 566	...	...	...	...	...	...
Gibraltar[69]									
12 XI 2001 (CDFC)									
Total	27 495	13 644	13 851	...	...	...	...	...	...
0	143	74	69	...	...	...	...	...	...
1 - 4	1 315	693	622	...	...	...	...	...	...
5 - 9	1 773	932	841	...	...	...	...	...	...
10 - 14	1 831	956	875	...	...	...	...	...	...
15 - 19	1 801	917	884	...	...	...	...	...	...
20 - 24	1 764	912	852	...	...	...	...	...	...
25 - 29	1 770	867	903	...	...	...	...	...	...
30 - 34	1 916	959	957	...	...	...	...	...	...
35 - 39	2 044	1 008	1 036	...	...	...	...	...	...
40 - 44	1 995	987	1 008	...	...	...	...	...	...
45 - 49	1 904	988	916	...	...	...	...	...	...
50 - 54	1 944	1 056	888	...	...	...	...	...	...
55 - 59	1 610	844	766	...	...	...	...	...	...
60 - 64	1 379	691	688	...	...	...	...	...	...
65 - 69	1 247	611	636	...	...	...	...	...	...
70 - 74	1 037	477	560	...	...	...	...	...	...
75 - 79	895	329	566	...	...	...	...	...	...
80 - 84	605	186	419	...	...	...	...	...	...
85 - 89	306	100	206	...	...	...	...	...	...
90 - 94	134	25	109	...	...	...	...	...	...
95 +	34	9	25	...	...	...	...	...	...
Unknown - Inconnu	48	23	25	...	...	...	...	...	...
Greece - Grèce									
18 III 2001 (CDJC)[70]									
Total	10 934 097	5 413 426	5 520 671	8 211 646	4 017 999	4 193 647	2 722 451	1 395 427	1 327 024
0	122 023	62 897	59 126	95 783	49 303	46 480	26 240	13 594	12 646
1 - 4	407 376	208 409	198 967	316 327	161 769	154 558	91 049	46 640	44 409
5 - 9	545 105	280 484	264 621	420 066	215 922	204 144	125 039	64 562	60 477
10 - 14	586 395	305 404	280 991	451 379	234 354	217 025	135 016	71 050	63 966
15 - 19	726 174	380 500	345 674	565 715	292 114	273 601	160 459	88 386	72 073
20 - 24	835 463	437 018	398 445	658 208	336 273	321 935	177 255	100 745	76 510
25 - 29	847 427	436 199	411 228	665 663	335 021	330 642	181 764	101 178	80 586
30 - 34	869 932	441 543	428 389	689 002	343 214	345 788	180 930	98 329	82 601
35 - 39	783 413	392 326	391 087	617 411	302 640	314 771	166 002	89 686	76 316
40 - 44	781 943	387 644	394 299	613 859	296 590	317 269	168 084	91 054	77 030
45 - 49	713 975	356 135	357 840	557 890	274 226	283 664	156 085	81 909	74 176
50 - 54	687 349	338 090	349 259	525 975	257 416	268 559	161 374	80 674	80 700
55 - 59	560 215	271 095	289 120	408 147	197 301	210 846	152 068	73 794	78 274
60 - 64	640 074	298 181	341 893	439 491	203 323	236 168	200 583	94 858	105 725
65 - 69	623 245	291 600	331 645	410 331	189 243	221 088	212 914	102 357	110 557
70 - 74	545 018	247 136	297 882	355 411	156 679	198 732	189 607	90 457	99 150
75 - 79	328 918	144 761	184 157	212 662	90 869	121 793	116 256	53 892	62 364
80 - 84	188 193	78 700	109 493	120 099	48 569	71 530	68 094	30 131	37 963
85 - 89	105 194	45 961	59 233	65 805	27 639	38 166	39 389	18 322	21 067
90 - 94	29 500	8 045	21 455	17 966	4 690	13 276	11 534	3 355	8 179
95 - 99	5 467	770	4 697	3 378	486	2 892	2 089	284	1 805
100 +	1 698	528	1 170	1 078	358	720	620	170	450
1 VII 2009 (ESDF)[71]									
Total	11 282 751	5 587 096	5 695 655	...	...	...	...	...	...
0	117 800	60 719	57 081	...	...	...	...	...	...
1 - 4	445 333	230 055	215 278	...	...	...	...	...	...
5 - 9	522 761	269 809	252 952	...	...	...	...	...	...

Continent, country or area, date, code and age (in years) / Continent, pays ou zone, date, code et âge (en années)	Total			Urban - Urbaine			Rural - Rurale		
	Both sexes Les deux sexes	Male Masculin	Female Féminin	Both sexes Les deux sexes	Male Masculin	Female Féminin	Both sexes Les deux sexes	Male Masculin	Female Féminin
EUROPE									
Greece - Grèce									
1 VII 2009 (ESDF)[71]									
10 - 14	532 665	273 616	259 049	...	...	...	...	...	...
15 - 19	573 203	295 918	277 285	...	...	...	...	...	...
20 - 24	634 657	330 095	304 562	...	...	...	...	...	...
25 - 29	793 540	413 801	379 739	...	...	...	...	...	...
30 - 34	866 957	450 040	416 917	...	...	...	...	...	...
35 - 39	878 871	451 175	427 696	...	...	...	...	...	...
40 - 44	873 262	441 216	432 046	...	...	...	...	...	...
45 - 49	802 320	399 535	402 785	...	...	...	...	...	...
50 - 54	766 873	378 459	388 414	...	...	...	...	...	...
55 - 59	694 538	341 498	353 040	...	...	...	...	...	...
60 - 64	657 800	314 768	343 032	...	...	...	...	...	...
65 - 69	539 293	247 805	291 488	...	...	...	...	...	...
70 - 74	573 932	253 809	320 123	...	...	...	...	...	...
75 - 79	502 014	217 473	284 541	...	...	...	...	...	...
80 - 84	325 357	137 224	188 133	...	...	...	...	...	...
85 - 89	141 577	59 887	81 690	...	...	...	...	...	...
90 - 94	31 806	15 563	16 243	...	...	...	...	...	...
95 - 99	5 197	3 270	1 927	...	...	...	...	...	...
100 +	2 995	1 361	1 634	...	...	...	...	...	...
Guernsey - Guernesey									
31 III 2009 (ESDF)									
Total	62 274	30 777	31 497	...	...	...	...	...	...
0 - 4	3 055	1 605	1 450	...	...	...	...	...	...
5 - 9	3 106	1 587	1 519	...	...	...	...	...	...
10 - 14	3 309	1 681	1 628	...	...	...	...	...	...
15 - 19	3 929	2 022	1 907	...	...	...	...	...	...
20 - 24	4 137	2 132	2 005	...	...	...	...	...	...
25 - 29	4 123	2 145	1 978	...	...	...	...	...	...
30 - 34	3 765	1 877	1 888	...	...	...	...	...	...
35 - 39	4 616	2 289	2 327	...	...	...	...	...	...
40 - 44	4 942	2 429	2 513	...	...	...	...	...	...
45 - 49	4 915	2 415	2 500	...	...	...	...	...	...
50 - 54	4 382	2 234	2 148	...	...	...	...	...	...
55 - 59	4 067	2 009	2 058	...	...	...	...	...	...
60 - 64	3 904	1 955	1 949	...	...	...	...	...	...
65 - 69	2 635	1 296	1 339	...	...	...	...	...	...
70 - 74	2 466	1 194	1 272	...	...	...	...	...	...
75 - 79	2 014	892	1 122	...	...	...	...	...	...
80 - 84	1 485	571	914	...	...	...	...	...	...
85 - 89	966	335	631	...	...	...	...	...	...
90 - 94	320	81	239	...	...	...	...	...	...
95 +	138	28	110	...	...	...	...	...	...
Hungary - Hongrie									
1 VII 2009 (ESDJ)									
Total	10 022 650	4 759 975	5 262 675	6 861 432	3 215 749	3 645 683	3 161 218	1 544 226	1 616 992
0	95 941	49 203	46 738	...	...	...	...	...	...
1 - 4	392 475	201 350	191 125	269 028	137 959	131 069	123 447	63 391	60 056
5 - 9	481 590	247 159	234 432	316 842	162 546	154 296	164 749	84 613	80 136
10 - 14	514 727	264 019	250 709	326 752	167 298	159 454	187 975	96 721	91 255
15 - 19	607 543	310 582	296 961	408 505	206 332	202 173	199 038	104 250	94 788
20 - 24	649 110	330 927	318 183	444 723	223 197	221 526	204 388	107 730	96 658
25 - 29	713 347	364 282	349 065	512 708	256 553	256 156	200 639	107 729	92 910
30 - 34	859 338	438 335	421 003	620 917	312 339	308 578	238 421	125 996	112 426
35 - 39	738 992	375 230	363 763	514 525	258 373	256 152	224 468	116 857	107 611
40 - 44	663 908	333 579	330 329	448 473	222 052	226 421	215 435	111 527	103 908
45 - 49	608 401	297 782	310 619	400 465	191 303	209 162	207 936	106 479	101 457
50 - 54	735 958	350 010	385 948	492 452	226 791	265 661	243 507	123 220	120 287
55 - 59	722 975	333 680	389 295	498 548	223 966	274 583	224 427	109 714	114 713
60 - 64	586 468	260 045	326 423	410 392	178 596	231 797	176 076	81 450	94 627
65 - 69	513 223	213 518	299 705	354 948	147 176	207 772	158 276	66 343	91 933
70 - 74	408 785	153 913	254 872	275 936	104 436	171 500	132 849	49 477	83 372
75 - 79	341 007	120 377	220 630	230 221	82 244	147 978	110 786	38 133	72 653
80 - 84	229 987	71 639	158 348	157 702	49 500	108 202	72 285	22 139	50 147

7. Population by age, sex and urban/rural residence: latest available year, 2000 - 2009
Population selon l'âge, le sexe et la résidence, urbaine/rurale : dernière année disponible, 2000 - 2009 (continued - suite)

Continent, country or area, date, code and age (in years) / Continent, pays ou zone, date, code et âge (en années)	Total			Urban - Urbaine			Rural - Rurale		
	Both sexes Les deux sexes	Male Masculin	Female Féminin	Both sexes Les deux sexes	Male Masculin	Female Féminin	Both sexes Les deux sexes	Male Masculin	Female Féminin
EUROPE									
Hungary - Hongrie									
1 VII 2009 (ESDJ)									
85 - 89	121 082	34 000	87 083	84 609	23 744	60 865	36 473	10 256	26 218
90 +	37 798	10 352	27 446	27 835	7 574	20 262	9 963	2 779	7 185
Iceland - Islande[18]									
1 VII 2009 (ESDJ)									
Total	319 246	161 548	157 698	298 669	150 495	148 174	20 577	11 053	9 524
0	4 910	2 493	2 417	4 668	2 362	2 306	242	131	111
1 - 4	18 132	9 346	8 786	17 244	8 873	8 371	888	473	415
5 - 9	21 457	10 880	10 577	20 210	10 230	9 980	1 247	650	597
10 - 14	22 068	11 263	10 805	20 629	10 521	10 108	1 439	742	697
15 - 19	23 899	12 197	11 702	22 107	11 277	10 830	1 792	920	872
20 - 24	23 065	11 794	11 271	21 554	10 974	10 580	1 511	820	691
25 - 29	24 914	12 900	12 014	23 694	12 244	11 450	1 220	656	564
30 - 34	22 760	11 815	10 945	21 677	11 223	10 454	1 083	592	491
35 - 39	22 054	11 480	10 574	20 904	10 875	10 029	1 150	605	545
40 - 44	21 933	11 123	10 810	20 504	10 351	10 153	1 429	772	657
45 - 49	22 510	11 457	11 053	20 913	10 621	10 292	1 597	836	761
50 - 54	21 040	10 745	10 295	19 520	9 897	9 623	1 520	848	672
55 - 59	18 091	9 285	8 806	16 748	8 531	8 217	1 343	754	589
60 - 64	14 851	7 594	7 257	13 709	6 958	6 751	1 142	636	506
65 - 69	10 752	5 258	5 494	9 908	4 799	5 109	844	459	385
70 - 74	8 583	4 130	4 453	7 870	3 731	4 139	713	399	314
75 - 79	7 863	3 633	4 230	7 229	3 281	3 948	634	352	282
80 - 84	5 652	2 438	3 214	5 244	2 211	3 033	408	227	181
85 - 89	3 245	1 262	1 983	3 009	1 138	1 871	236	124	112
90 - 94	1 170	385	785	1 057	338	719	113	47	66
95 - 99	258	63	195	234	54	180	24	9	15
100 +	39	7	32	37	6	31	2	1	1
Ireland - Irlande									
23 IV 2006 (CDFC)									
Total	4 239 848	2 121 171	2 118 677	2 574 313	1 267 960	1 306 353	1 665 535	853 211	812 324
0 - 4	302 252	154 556	147 696	181 695	92 814	88 881	120 557	61 742	58 815
5 - 9	288 325	147 984	140 341	163 881	83 949	79 932	124 444	64 035	60 409
10 - 14	273 872	140 504	133 368	151 383	77 732	73 651	122 489	62 772	59 717
15 - 19	290 257	148 241	142 016	170 608	85 539	85 069	119 649	62 702	56 947
20 - 24	342 475	172 766	169 709	243 712	119 249	124 463	98 763	53 517	45 246
25 - 29	373 078	189 252	183 826	271 375	136 375	135 000	101 703	52 877	48 826
30 - 34	349 361	177 487	171 874	233 263	118 430	114 833	116 098	59 057	57 041
35 - 39	322 105	163 811	158 294	196 599	99 799	96 800	125 506	64 012	61 494
40 - 44	301 329	151 438	149 891	176 046	87 432	88 614	125 283	64 006	61 277
45 - 49	274 745	137 983	136 762	156 884	77 580	79 304	117 861	60 403	57 458
50 - 54	247 068	124 550	122 518	138 311	67 916	70 395	108 757	56 634	52 123
55 - 59	225 328	113 943	111 385	125 161	61 343	63 818	100 167	52 600	47 567
60 - 64	181 727	91 561	90 166	101 440	49 283	52 157	80 287	42 278	38 009
65 - 69	143 396	70 895	72 501	82 540	39 002	43 538	60 856	31 893	28 963
70 - 74	119 152	56 540	62 612	67 900	30 394	37 506	51 252	26 146	25 106
75 - 79	92 466	40 121	52 345	51 858	21 089	30 769	40 608	19 032	21 576
80 - 84	64 884	24 694	40 190	35 537	12 621	22 916	29 347	12 073	17 274
85 - 89	33 302	11 021	22 281	17 954	5 483	12 471	15 348	5 538	9 810
90 - 94	12 045	3 231	8 814	6 629	1 617	5 012	5 416	1 614	3 802
95 - 99	2 392	547	1 845	1 372	292	1 080	1 020	255	765
100 +	289	46	243	165	21	144	124	25	99
1 VII 2009 (ESDF)									
Total	4 458 942	2 215 646	2 243 297	...	...	...	...	...	...
0	73 408	37 676	35 732	...	...	...	...	...	...
1 - 4	271 076	139 061	132 015	...	...	...	...	...	...
5 - 9	308 788	158 015	150 773	...	...	...	...	...	...
10 - 14	289 265	148 235	141 030	...	...	...	...	...	...
15 - 19	277 301	141 177	136 124	...	...	...	...	...	...
20 - 24	297 537	145 012	152 525	...	...	...	...	...	...
25 - 29	405 864	200 260	205 604	...	...	...	...	...	...
30 - 34	373 376	186 487	186 889	...	...	...	...	...	...
35 - 39	347 609	175 055	172 554	...	...	...	...	...	...
40 - 44	313 286	157 746	155 540	...	...	...	...	...	...

Continent, country or area, date, code and age (in years) / Continent, pays ou zone, date, code et âge (en années)	Total			Urban - Urbaine			Rural - Rurale		
	Both sexes Les deux sexes	Male Masculin	Female Féminin	Both sexes Les deux sexes	Male Masculin	Female Féminin	Both sexes Les deux sexes	Male Masculin	Female Féminin
EUROPE									
Ireland - Irlande									
1 VII 2009 (ESDF)									
45 - 49	294 669	147 468	147 201	...	...	...	...	...	...
50 - 54	263 042	132 053	130 989	...	...	...	...	...	...
55 - 59	236 399	118 934	117 466	...	...	...	...	...	...
60 - 64	208 596	104 769	103 828	...	...	...	...	...	...
65 - 69	157 062	77 683	79 379	...	...	...	...	...	...
70 - 74	123 834	59 153	64 681	...	...	...	...	...	...
75 - 79	95 594	43 042	52 552	...	...	...	...	...	...
80 - 84	66 110	26 017	40 093	...	...	...	...	...	...
85 - 89	37 879	12 859	25 020	...	...	...	...	...	...
90 - 94	13 759	3 904	9 855	...	...	...	...	...	...
95 - 99	3 940	921	3 019	...	...	...	...	...	...
100 +	554	123	432	...	...	...	...	...	...
Isle of Man - Île de Man[12]									
30 IV 2009 (ESDJ)									
Total	82 371	40 849	41 522	...	...	...	...	...	...
0 - 4	4 359	2 286	2 074	...	...	...	...	...	...
5 - 9	4 320	2 311	2 009	...	...	...	...	...	...
10 - 14	4 865	2 478	2 388	...	...	...	...	...	...
15 - 19	5 183	2 688	2 494	...	...	...	...	...	...
20 - 24	4 842	2 467	2 374	...	...	...	...	...	...
25 - 29	4 666	2 312	2 355	...	...	...	...	...	...
30 - 34	4 719	2 326	2 392	...	...	...	...	...	...
35 - 39	5 851	2 885	2 966	...	...	...	...	...	...
40 - 44	6 375	3 198	3 177	...	...	...	...	...	...
45 - 49	6 329	3 178	3 150	...	...	...	...	...	...
50 - 54	5 613	2 801	2 812	...	...	...	...	...	...
55 - 59	5 399	2 730	2 669	...	...	...	...	...	...
60 - 64	5 464	2 812	2 652	...	...	...	...	...	...
65 - 69	4 146	2 032	2 114	...	...	...	...	...	...
70 - 74	3 436	1 653	1 784	...	...	...	...	...	...
75 - 79	2 698	1 204	1 494	...	...	...	...	...	...
80 - 84	2 055	805	1 251	...	...	...	...	...	...
85 - 89	1 390	496	894	...	...	...	...	...	...
90 +	661	188	473	...	...	...	...	...	...
Italy - Italie									
1 VII 2009 (ESDJ)									
Total	60 192 698	29 219 913	30 972 785	...	...	...	...	...	...
0	566 225	290 753	275 472	...	...	...	...	...	...
1 - 4	2 274 653	1 169 715	1 104 938	...	...	...	...	...	...
5 - 9	2 820 417	1 449 009	1 371 409	...	...	...	...	...	...
10 - 14	2 792 029	1 437 455	1 354 574	...	...	...	...	...	...
15 - 19	2 973 700	1 530 569	1 443 131	...	...	...	...	...	...
20 - 24	3 117 361	1 590 889	1 526 472	...	...	...	...	...	...
25 - 29	3 529 982	1 779 906	1 750 076	...	...	...	...	...	...
30 - 34	4 282 814	2 159 915	2 122 900	...	...	...	...	...	...
35 - 39	4 818 542	2 424 209	2 394 334	...	...	...	...	...	...
40 - 44	4 963 095	2 487 520	2 475 576	...	...	...	...	...	...
45 - 49	4 569 664	2 267 732	2 301 932	...	...	...	...	...	...
50 - 54	4 005 645	1 968 322	2 037 323	...	...	...	...	...	...
55 - 59	3 702 969	1 804 408	1 898 562	...	...	...	...	...	...
60 - 64	3 629 791	1 754 188	1 875 603	...	...	...	...	...	...
65 - 69	3 205 795	1 512 221	1 693 575	...	...	...	...	...	...
70 - 74	2 999 524	1 363 445	1 636 079	...	...	...	...	...	...
75 - 79	2 515 274	1 063 499	1 451 775	...	...	...	...	...	...
80 - 84	1 868 966	701 418	1 167 548	...	...	...	...	...	...
85 - 89	1 109 504	352 721	756 783	...	...	...	...	...	...
90 - 94	315 718	83 371	232 347	...	...	...	...	...	...
95 - 99	116 681	25 971	90 710	...	...	...	...	...	...
100 +	14 354	2 683	11 671	...	...	...	...	...	...
Jersey									
11 III 2001 (CDJC)									
Total	87 186	42 484	44 702	...	...	...	...	...	...
0	856	417	439	...	...	...	...	...	...

Continent, country or area, date, code and age (in years) / Continent, pays ou zone, date, code et âge (en années)	Total			Urban - Urbaine			Rural - Rurale		
	Both sexes Les deux sexes	Male Masculin	Female Féminin	Both sexes Les deux sexes	Male Masculin	Female Féminin	Both sexes Les deux sexes	Male Masculin	Female Féminin
EUROPE									
Jersey									
11 III 2001 (CDJC)									
1 - 4	3 857	1 986	1 871	...	...	...	...	...	...
5 - 9	5 016	2 616	2 400	...	...	...	...	...	...
10 - 14	5 038	2 569	2 469	...	...	...	...	...	...
15 - 19	4 628	2 356	2 272	...	...	...	...	...	...
20 - 24	5 243	2 488	2 755	...	...	...	...	...	...
25 - 29	6 196	2 988	3 208	...	...	...	...	...	...
30 - 34	7 646	3 761	3 885	...	...	...	...	...	...
35 - 39	7 898	3 921	3 977	...	...	...	...	...	...
40 - 44	7 011	3 467	3 544	...	...	...	...	...	...
45 - 49	6 238	3 073	3 165	...	...	...	...	...	...
50 - 54	6 240	3 132	3 108	...	...	...	...	...	...
55 - 59	4 664	2 319	2 345	...	...	...	...	...	...
60 - 64	4 325	2 148	2 177	...	...	...	...	...	...
65 - 69	3 619	1 790	1 829	...	...	...	...	...	...
70 - 74	3 019	1 373	1 646	...	...	...	...	...	...
75 - 79	2 432	1 051	1 381	...	...	...	...	...	...
80 - 84	1 591	560	1 031	...	...	...	...	...	...
85 - 89	1 101	340	761	...	...	...	...	...	...
90 - 94	444	105	339	...	...	...	...	...	...
95 - 99	109	19	90	...	...	...	...	...	...
100 +	15	5	10	...	...	...	...	...	...
Latvia - Lettonie									
1 VII 2009 (ESDJ)									
Total	2 254 834	1 040 285	1 214 549	1 526 930	685 170	841 760	727 904	355 115	372 789
0	22 607	11 507	11 100	15 633	7 997	7 636	6 974	3 510	3 464
1 - 4	90 541	46 178	44 363	62 649	31 936	30 713	27 892	14 242	13 650
5 - 9	99 534	50 844	48 690	65 306	33 232	32 074	34 228	17 612	16 616
10 - 14	97 051	49 870	47 181	60 199	30 819	29 380	36 852	19 051	17 801
15 - 19	149 997	76 290	73 707	91 746	46 444	45 302	58 251	29 846	28 405
20 - 24	183 897	93 795	90 102	119 975	60 046	59 929	63 922	33 749	30 173
25 - 29	170 394	86 865	83 529	118 407	58 731	59 676	51 987	28 134	23 853
30 - 34	156 510	79 174	77 336	109 934	54 025	55 909	46 576	25 149	21 427
35 - 39	158 919	79 443	79 476	109 197	52 993	56 204	49 722	26 450	23 272
40 - 44	153 459	75 238	78 221	102 984	48 636	54 348	50 475	26 602	23 873
45 - 49	168 324	80 283	88 041	113 836	52 065	61 771	54 488	28 218	26 270
50 - 54	159 334	74 007	85 327	110 097	48 790	61 307	49 237	25 217	24 020
55 - 59	138 083	61 050	77 033	97 048	40 822	56 226	41 035	20 228	20 807
60 - 64	115 653	48 300	67 353	81 639	32 629	49 010	34 014	15 671	18 343
65 - 69	118 520	45 736	72 784	79 783	29 746	50 037	38 737	15 990	22 747
70 - 74	106 531	37 455	69 076	73 634	25 248	48 386	32 897	12 207	20 690
75 - 79	79 334	24 657	54 677	54 339	16 775	37 564	24 995	7 882	17 113
80 - 84	54 955	13 542	41 413	38 995	9 870	29 125	15 960	3 672	12 288
85 - 89	23 230	4 506	18 724	16 020	3 226	12 794	7 210	1 280	5 930
90 - 94	5 938	1 159	4 779	4 083	846	3 237	1 855	313	1 542
95 - 99	1 793	330	1 463	1 258	249	1 009	535	81	454
100 +	230	56	174	168	45	123	62	11	51
Liechtenstein									
1 VII 2009 (ESDJ)									
Total	35 789	17 716	18 073	...	...	...	...	...	...
0	393	210	183	...	...	...	...	...	...
1 - 4	1 457	755	702	...	...	...	...	...	...
5 - 9	1 905	977	928	...	...	...	...	...	...
10 - 14	2 111	1 044	1 067	...	...	...	...	...	...
15 - 19	2 157	1 082	1 075	...	...	...	...	...	...
20 - 24	2 194	1 118	1 076	...	...	...	...	...	...
25 - 29	2 249	1 156	1 093	...	...	...	...	...	...
30 - 34	2 308	1 147	1 161	...	...	...	...	...	...
35 - 39	2 789	1 433	1 356	...	...	...	...	...	...
40 - 44	3 126	1 517	1 609	...	...	...	...	...	...
45 - 49	3 046	1 502	1 544	...	...	...	...	...	...
50 - 54	2 724	1 345	1 379	...	...	...	...	...	...
55 - 59	2 409	1 234	1 175	...	...	...	...	...	...
60 - 64	2 190	1 130	1 060	...	...	...	...	...	...

Continent, country or area, date, code and age (in years) / Continent, pays ou zone, date, code et âge (en années)	Total			Urban - Urbaine			Rural - Rurale		
	Both sexes Les deux sexes	Male Masculin	Female Féminin	Both sexes Les deux sexes	Male Masculin	Female Féminin	Both sexes Les deux sexes	Male Masculin	Female Féminin
EUROPE									
Liechtenstein									
1 VII 2009 (ESDJ)									
65 - 69	1 705	846	859	...	...	...	...	...	...
70 - 74	1 117	525	592	...	...	...	...	...	...
75 - 79	765	318	447	...	...	...	...	...	...
80 - 84	614	219	395	...	...	...	...	...	...
85 - 89	383	116	267	...	...	...	...	...	...
90 - 94	117	35	82	...	...	...	...	...	...
95 - 99	28	7	21	...	...	...	...	...	...
100 +	2	-	2	...	...	...	...	...	...
Lithuania - Lituanie									
1 VII 2009 (ESDJ)									
Total	3 339 455	1 553 499	1 785 956	2 235 033	1 016 639	1 218 394	1 104 422	536 860	567 562
0	35 705	18 319	17 386	24 290	12 501	11 789	11 415	5 818	5 597
1 - 4	125 457	64 076	61 381	82 547	42 233	40 314	42 910	21 843	21 067
5 - 9	155 186	79 779	75 407	97 814	50 175	47 639	57 372	29 604	27 768
10 - 14	185 770	95 329	90 441	118 388	60 702	57 686	67 382	34 627	32 755
15 - 19	247 315	126 232	121 083	155 347	78 899	76 448	91 968	47 333	44 635
20 - 24	270 195	137 593	132 602	174 810	87 754	87 056	95 385	49 839	45 546
25 - 29	239 233	122 511	116 722	169 048	83 077	85 971	70 185	39 434	30 751
30 - 34	218 596	109 666	108 930	161 103	77 808	83 295	57 493	31 858	25 635
35 - 39	237 373	117 120	120 253	169 567	81 900	87 667	67 806	35 220	32 586
40 - 44	244 640	118 973	125 667	167 224	78 918	88 306	77 416	40 055	37 361
45 - 49	263 449	125 649	137 800	181 249	82 837	98 412	82 200	42 812	39 288
50 - 54	229 121	105 478	123 643	158 274	69 513	88 761	70 847	35 965	34 882
55 - 59	192 581	85 279	107 302	132 937	55 888	77 049	59 644	29 391	30 253
60 - 64	159 519	66 373	93 146	107 603	42 671	64 932	51 916	23 702	28 214
65 - 69	158 526	61 659	96 867	102 648	38 848	63 800	55 878	22 811	33 067
70 - 74	142 898	51 206	91 692	89 747	31 395	58 352	53 151	19 811	33 340
75 - 79	115 472	37 717	77 755	69 643	22 832	46 811	45 829	14 885	30 944
80 - 84	76 699	20 889	55 810	46 709	12 846	33 863	29 990	8 043	21 947
85 - 89	32 666	7 541	25 125	19 427	4 400	15 027	13 239	3 141	10 098
90 - 94	6 823	1 589	5 234	4 653	1 007	3 646	2 170	582	1 588
95 - 99	1 768	384	1 384	1 559	311	1 248	209	73	136
100 +	463	137	326	446	124	322	17	13	4
Luxembourg									
1 VII 2009 (ESDJ)									
Total	497 782	247 120	250 662	...	...	...	...	...	...
0	5 617	2 895	2 722	...	...	...	...	...	...
1 - 4	22 965	11 781	11 184	...	...	...	...	...	...
5 - 9	29 764	15 362	14 402	...	...	...	...	...	...
10 - 14	30 506	15 615	14 891	...	...	...	...	...	...
15 - 19	29 471	15 135	14 336	...	...	...	...	...	...
20 - 24	29 498	15 014	14 484	...	...	...	...	...	...
25 - 29	34 297	17 243	17 054	...	...	...	...	...	...
30 - 34	36 973	18 470	18 503	...	...	...	...	...	...
35 - 39	39 554	19 761	19 793	...	...	...	...	...	...
40 - 44	42 221	21 544	20 677	...	...	...	...	...	...
45 - 49	39 551	20 245	19 306	...	...	...	...	...	...
50 - 54	34 435	17 525	16 910	...	...	...	...	...	...
55 - 59	29 186	14 873	14 313	...	...	...	...	...	...
60 - 64	24 275	12 314	11 961	...	...	...	...	...	...
65 - 69	19 516	9 405	10 111	...	...	...	...	...	...
70 - 74	17 155	7 825	9 330	...	...	...	...	...	...
75 - 79	15 016	6 447	8 569	...	...	...	...	...	...
80 - 84	10 614	3 920	6 694	...	...	...	...	...	...
85 - 89	5 384	1 431	3 953	...	...	...	...	...	...
90 - 94	1 518	305	1 213	...	...	...	...	...	...
95 +	266	10	256	...	...	...	...	...	...
Malta - Malte									
27 XI 2005 (CDJC)									
Total	404 962	200 819	204 143	404 544	200 611	203 933	418	208	210
0	3 825	1 947	1 878	3 822	1 946	1 876	3	1	2
1 - 4	15 707	8 027	7 680	15 690	8 014	7 676	17	13	4
5 - 9	23 054	11 837	11 217	23 024	11 820	11 204	30	17	13

Continent, country or area, date, code and age (in years) / Continent, pays ou zone, date, code et âge (en années)	Total			Urban - Urbaine			Rural - Rurale		
	Both sexes Les deux sexes	Male Masculin	Female Féminin	Both sexes Les deux sexes	Male Masculin	Female Féminin	Both sexes Les deux sexes	Male Masculin	Female Féminin
EUROPE									
Malta - Malte									
27 XI 2005 (CDJC)									
10 - 14	26 900	13 828	13 072	26 878	13 817	13 061	22	11	11
15 - 19	28 734	14 781	13 953	28 710	14 769	13 941	24	12	12
20 - 24	29 365	14 980	14 385	29 343	14 962	14 381	22	18	4
25 - 29	29 676	15 346	14 330	29 660	15 337	14 323	16	9	7
30 - 34	27 670	14 192	13 478	27 645	14 181	13 464	25	11	14
35 - 39	24 583	12 514	12 069	24 550	12 496	12 054	33	18	15
40 - 44	27 733	14 144	13 589	27 705	14 130	13 575	28	14	14
45 - 49	30 433	15 233	15 200	30 410	15 225	15 185	23	8	15
50 - 54	28 830	14 411	14 419	28 799	14 394	14 405	31	17	14
55 - 59	31 018	15 423	15 595	30 985	15 410	15 575	33	13	20
60 - 64	21 763	10 538	11 225	21 742	10 532	11 210	21	6	15
65 - 69	17 897	8 368	9 529	17 873	8 357	9 516	24	11	13
70 - 74	14 863	6 366	8 497	14 839	6 358	8 481	24	8	16
75 - 79	10 919	4 429	6 490	10 899	4 419	6 480	20	10	10
80 - 84	7 385	2 899	4 486	7 368	2 891	4 477	17	8	9
85 - 89	3 314	1 190	2 124	3 310	1 188	2 122	4	2	2
90 - 94	1 022	300	722	1 022	300	722	-	-	-
95 - 99	237	59	178	236	58	178	1	1	-
100 +	34	7	27	34	7	27	-	-	-
1 VII 2009 (ESDJ)[72]									
Total	413 290	205 646	207 644	...	...	...	...	...	...
0	4 155	2 154	2 001	...	...	...	...	...	...
1 - 4	16 106	8 326	7 780	...	...	...	...	...	...
5 - 9	20 468	10 354	10 114	...	...	...	...	...	...
10 - 14	24 332	12 570	11 762	...	...	...	...	...	...
15 - 19	27 978	14 339	13 639	...	...	...	...	...	...
20 - 24	29 957	15 675	14 282	...	...	...	...	...	...
25 - 29	31 094	16 068	15 026	...	...	...	...	...	...
30 - 34	30 436	15 811	14 625	...	...	...	...	...	...
35 - 39	26 556	13 619	12 937	...	...	...	...	...	...
40 - 44	24 792	12 527	12 265	...	...	...	...	...	...
45 - 49	29 079	14 750	14 329	...	...	...	...	...	...
50 - 54	30 086	15 152	14 934	...	...	...	...	...	...
55 - 59	28 900	14 380	14 520	...	...	...	...	...	...
60 - 64	29 697	14 526	15 171	...	...	...	...	...	...
65 - 69	17 652	8 286	9 366	...	...	...	...	...	...
70 - 74	16 334	7 356	8 978	...	...	...	...	...	...
75 - 79	12 210	4 877	7 333	...	...	...	...	...	...
80 - 84	7 865	3 009	4 856	...	...	...	...	...	...
85 - 89	4 146	1 454	2 692	...	...	...	...	...	...
90 +	1 447	413	1 034	...	...	...	...	...	...
Monaco									
21 VI 2000 (CDJC)									
Total	32 020	15 544	16 476	...	...	...	...	...	...
0	145	69	76	...	...	...	...	...	...
1 - 4	1 223	644	579	...	...	...	...	...	...
5 - 9	1 462	747	715	...	...	...	...	...	...
10 - 14	1 407	746	661	...	...	...	...	...	...
15 - 19	1 337	706	631	...	...	...	...	...	...
20 - 24	1 297	661	636	...	...	...	...	...	...
25 - 29	1 638	830	808	...	...	...	...	...	...
30 - 34	2 346	1 184	1 162	...	...	...	...	...	...
35 - 39	2 386	1 205	1 181	...	...	...	...	...	...
40 - 44	2 328	1 151	1 177	...	...	...	...	...	...
45 - 49	2 178	1 107	1 071	...	...	...	...	...	...
50 - 54	2 584	1 264	1 320	...	...	...	...	...	...
55 - 59	2 405	1 163	1 242	...	...	...	...	...	...
60 - 64	2 083	1 018	1 065	...	...	...	...	...	...
65 - 69	1 794	854	940	...	...	...	...	...	...
70 - 74	1 704	803	901	...	...	...	...	...	...
75 - 79	1 598	704	894	...	...	...	...	...	...
80 - 84	937	347	590	...	...	...	...	...	...
85 - 89	669	216	453	...	...	...	...	...	...

Continent, country or area, date, code and age (in years) Continent, pays ou zone, date, code et âge (en années)	Total			Urban - Urbaine			Rural - Rurale		
	Both sexes Les deux sexes	Male Masculin	Female Féminin	Both sexes Les deux sexes	Male Masculin	Female Féminin	Both sexes Les deux sexes	Male Masculin	Female Féminin
EUROPE									
Monaco									
21 VI 2000 (CDJC)									
90 - 94	374	96	278	...	...	...	...	...	...
95 - 99	96	20	76	...	...	...	...	...	...
100 +	11	2	9	...	...	...	...	...	...
Unknown - Inconnu	18	7	11	...	...	...	...	...	...
Montenegro - Monténégro									
1 VII 2009 (ESDJ)									
Total	631 536	311 258	320 278	400 928	195 088	205 840	230 608	116 170	114 438
0	8 505	4 479	4 026	6 534	3 445	3 089	1 971	1 034	937
1 - 4	30 803	16 154	14 649	24 821	13 047	11 774	5 982	3 107	2 875
5 - 9	40 305	20 873	19 432	26 596	13 860	12 736	13 709	7 013	6 696
10 - 14	42 486	21 930	20 556	26 551	13 685	12 866	15 935	8 245	7 690
15 - 19	45 222	23 398	21 824	28 409	14 652	13 757	16 813	8 746	8 067
20 - 24	49 371	25 311	24 060	31 618	16 137	15 481	17 753	9 174	8 579
25 - 29	49 370	25 044	24 326	31 816	15 686	16 130	17 554	9 358	8 196
30 - 34	45 159	22 358	22 801	29 266	14 044	15 222	15 893	8 314	7 579
35 - 39	41 857	20 551	21 306	26 746	12 637	14 109	15 111	7 914	7 197
40 - 44	41 395	20 517	20 878	26 487	12 549	13 938	14 908	7 968	6 940
45 - 49	43 747	21 642	22 105	28 354	13 403	14 951	15 393	8 239	7 154
50 - 54	43 648	21 874	21 774	28 495	13 796	14 699	15 153	8 078	7 075
55 - 59	39 941	19 494	20 447	25 989	12 460	13 529	13 952	7 034	6 918
60 - 64	27 981	12 818	15 163	17 298	7 936	9 362	10 683	4 882	5 801
65 - 69	25 521	11 246	14 275	14 050	6 113	7 937	11 471	5 133	6 338
70 - 74	24 994	11 001	13 993	13 384	5 872	7 512	11 610	5 129	6 481
75 - 79	17 011	7 116	9 895	8 422	3 495	4 927	8 589	3 621	4 968
80 - 84	9 512	3 793	5 719	4 306	1 659	2 647	5 206	2 134	3 072
85 - 89	3 639	1 322	2 317	1 451	516	935	2 188	806	1 382
90 - 94	663	230	433	224	70	154	439	160	279
95 - 99	274	89	185	71	14	57	203	75	128
100 +	132	18	114	40	12	28	92	6	86
Netherlands - Pays-Bas									
1 I 2009 (ESDJ)									
Total	16 485 787	8 156 396	8 329 391	10 916 466	5 371 446	5 545 020	5 569 321	2 784 950	2 784 371
0	184 408	94 691	89 717	127 152	65 389	61 763	57 256	29 302	27 954
1 - 4	747 148	381 981	365 167	498 951	255 036	243 915	248 197	126 945	121 252
5 - 9	1 010 634	516 996	493 638	644 775	329 703	315 072	365 859	187 293	178 566
10 - 14	980 868	501 973	478 895	616 332	315 154	301 178	364 536	186 819	177 717
15 - 19	1 010 527	516 252	494 275	657 365	332 463	324 902	353 162	183 789	169 373
20 - 24	996 859	504 317	492 542	724 584	357 822	366 762	272 275	146 495	125 780
25 - 29	991 973	498 376	493 597	738 479	367 278	371 201	253 494	131 098	122 396
30 - 34	1 008 420	504 564	503 856	727 681	364 780	362 901	280 739	139 784	140 955
35 - 39	1 236 609	620 662	615 947	841 000	424 301	416 699	395 609	196 361	199 248
40 - 44	1 295 569	655 721	639 848	850 334	431 481	418 853	445 235	224 240	220 995
45 - 49	1 271 548	641 003	630 545	826 319	415 890	410 429	445 229	225 113	220 116
50 - 54	1 157 680	581 509	576 171	745 514	371 873	373 641	412 166	209 636	202 530
55 - 59	1 081 132	544 195	536 937	688 259	344 011	344 248	392 873	200 184	192 689
60 - 64	1 040 597	522 201	518 396	652 847	325 343	327 504	387 750	196 858	190 892
65 - 69	747 759	368 170	379 589	463 939	225 685	238 254	283 820	142 485	141 335
70 - 74	603 510	283 316	320 194	378 910	175 193	203 717	224 600	108 123	116 477
75 - 79	489 338	210 662	278 676	313 700	132 807	180 893	175 638	77 855	97 783
80 - 84	345 821	129 189	216 632	228 045	83 888	144 157	117 776	45 301	72 475
85 - 89	200 625	61 875	138 750	134 610	40 972	93 638	66 015	20 903	45 112
90 - 94	67 920	15 867	52 053	46 084	10 545	35 539	21 836	5 322	16 514
95 - 99	15 214	2 666	12 548	10 462	1 695	8 767	4 752	971	3 781
100 +	1 628	210	1 418	1 124	137	987	504	73	431
Norway - Norvège[73]									
3 XI 2001 (CDJC)[18]									
Total	4 520 947	2 240 281	2 280 666	3 458 699	1 694 153	1 764 546	1 018 422	522 925	495 497
0	57 205	29 340	27 865	44 798	23 002	21 796	11 828	6 048	5 780
1 - 4	240 268	123 153	117 115	186 738	95 742	90 996	51 255	26 232	25 023
5 - 9	307 650	158 230	149 420	235 620	121 061	114 559	69 433	35 833	33 600
10 - 14	300 609	153 989	146 620	227 068	116 054	111 014	71 100	36 697	34 403
15 - 19	267 596	137 494	130 102	199 238	102 194	97 044	66 278	34 188	32 090
20 - 24	273 126	138 679	134 447	211 551	106 040	105 511	59 030	31 337	27 693

7. Population by age, sex and urban/rural residence: latest available year, 2000 - 2009
Population selon l'âge, le sexe et la résidence, urbaine/rurale : dernière année disponible, 2000 - 2009 (continued - suite)

Continent, country or area, date, code and age (in years) / Continent, pays ou zone, date, code et âge (en années)	Total			Urban - Urbaine			Rural - Rurale		
	Both sexes Les deux sexes	Male Masculin	Female Féminin	Both sexes Les deux sexes	Male Masculin	Female Féminin	Both sexes Les deux sexes	Male Masculin	Female Féminin
EUROPE									
Norway - Norvège[73]									
3 XI 2001 (CDJC)[18]									
25 - 29	316 989	160 678	156 311	255 685	128 167	127 518	57 993	30 759	27 234
30 - 34	351 386	178 688	172 698	280 044	141 397	138 647	67 654	35 193	32 461
35 - 39	338 689	173 595	165 094	265 141	134 740	130 401	70 226	36 890	33 336
40 - 44	319 293	162 807	156 486	246 090	124 014	122 076	70 273	37 050	33 223
45 - 49	309 642	157 276	152 366	236 578	118 274	118 304	70 375	37 421	32 954
50 - 54	301 283	154 010	147 273	227 967	114 779	113 188	70 543	37 669	32 874
55 - 59	269 320	136 414	132 906	203 022	101 540	101 482	63 778	33 413	30 365
60 - 64	190 808	93 953	96 855	140 947	67 923	73 024	47 966	25 008	22 958
65 - 69	163 197	77 766	85 431	119 675	55 351	64 324	41 888	21 553	20 335
70 - 74	161 097	73 389	87 708	118 670	52 350	66 320	40 811	20 243	20 568
75 - 79	151 839	63 682	88 157	111 134	44 980	66 154	38 918	17 898	21 020
80 - 84	113 628	41 784	71 844	83 558	29 286	54 272	28 500	11 877	16 623
85 - 89	60 467	18 752	41 715	44 821	12 816	32 005	14 644	5 617	9 027
90 - 94	22 093	5 668	16 425	16 645	3 797	12 848	4 988	1 744	3 244
95 - 99	4 307	849	3 458	3 333	580	2 753	872	239	633
100 +	455	85	370	376	66	310	69	16	53
1 VII 2009 (ESDJ)									
Total	4 828 726	2 410 903	2 417 823	...	...	...	...	...	...
0	61 369	31 584	29 785	...	...	...	...	...	...
1 - 4	239 826	122 780	117 046	...	...	...	...	...	...
5 - 9	298 705	152 548	146 157	...	...	...	...	...	...
10 - 14	315 072	161 823	153 249	...	...	...	...	...	...
15 - 19	320 623	164 855	155 769	...	...	...	...	...	...
20 - 24	300 125	152 998	147 127	...	...	...	...	...	...
25 - 29	304 844	154 674	150 170	...	...	...	...	...	...
30 - 34	319 000	162 394	156 606	...	...	...	...	...	...
35 - 39	360 573	184 543	176 031	...	...	...	...	...	...
40 - 44	362 926	186 763	176 163	...	...	...	...	...	...
45 - 49	331 553	170 232	161 321	...	...	...	...	...	...
50 - 54	316 779	161 163	155 617	...	...	...	...	...	...
55 - 59	294 170	149 287	144 883	...	...	...	...	...	...
60 - 64	289 422	145 924	143 498	...	...	...	...	...	...
65 - 69	205 015	100 682	104 334	...	...	...	...	...	...
70 - 74	155 170	72 454	82 716	...	...	...	...	...	...
75 - 79	133 731	59 032	74 700	...	...	...	...	...	...
80 - 84	110 063	43 824	66 239	...	...	...	...	...	...
85 - 89	74 607	24 637	49 971	...	...	...	...	...	...
90 - 94	28 348	7 353	20 995	...	...	...	...	...	...
95 - 99	6 171	1 255	4 917	...	...	...	...	...	...
100 +	639	104	535	...	...	...	...	...	...
Poland - Pologne[74]									
1 VII 2009 (ESDJ)									
Total	38 153 389	18 423 343	19 730 046	23 293 906	11 032 562	12 261 344	14 859 483	7 390 781	7 468 702
0	424 772	218 239	206 533	...	...	...	...	...	...
1 - 4	1 505 215	773 426	731 789	873 100	448 877	424 223	632 115	324 549	307 566
5 - 9	1 803 455	925 978	877 477	1 000 350	513 789	486 561	803 105	412 189	390 916
10 - 14	2 082 127	1 066 162	1 015 965	1 111 628	568 937	542 691	970 499	497 225	473 274
15 - 19	2 574 668	1 315 787	1 258 881	1 426 178	725 935	700 243	1 148 490	589 852	558 638
20 - 24	3 017 381	1 535 686	1 481 695	1 788 483	903 304	885 179	1 228 898	632 382	596 516
25 - 29	3 256 947	1 651 240	1 605 707	2 035 594	1 017 259	1 018 335	1 221 353	633 981	587 372
30 - 34	3 007 065	1 522 478	1 484 587	1 926 769	961 334	965 435	1 080 296	561 144	519 152
35 - 39	2 594 210	1 310 939	1 283 271	1 591 355	796 195	795 160	1 002 855	514 744	488 111
40 - 44	2 340 543	1 176 928	1 163 615	1 388 221	682 267	705 954	952 322	494 661	457 661
45 - 49	2 584 159	1 281 698	1 302 461	1 564 493	746 259	818 234	1 019 666	535 439	484 227
50 - 54	3 008 069	1 462 841	1 545 228	1 939 066	902 408	1 036 658	1 069 003	560 433	508 570
55 - 59	2 781 330	1 315 504	1 465 826	1 850 758	842 381	1 008 377	930 572	473 123	457 449
60 - 64	2 027 154	927 335	1 099 819	1 354 530	604 483	750 047	672 624	322 852	349 772
65 - 69	1 395 484	600 842	794 642	905 474	382 542	522 932	490 010	218 300	271 710
70 - 74	1 371 982	549 677	822 305	863 703	339 632	524 071	508 279	210 045	298 234
75 - 79	1 154 256	425 016	729 240	702 223	257 886	444 337	452 033	167 130	284 903
80 - 84	762 308	241 049	521 259	449 191	141 340	307 851	313 117	99 709	213 408
85 +	462 264	122 518	339 746	273 800	69 780	204 020	188 464	52 738	135 726

7. Population by age, sex and urban/rural residence: latest available year, 2000 - 2009
Population selon l'âge, le sexe et la résidence, urbaine/rurale : dernière année disponible, 2000 - 2009 (continued - suite)

Continent, country or area, date, code and age (in years) / Continent, pays ou zone, date, code et âge (en années)	Total			Urban - Urbaine			Rural - Rurale		
	Both sexes Les deux sexes	Male Masculin	Female Féminin	Both sexes Les deux sexes	Male Masculin	Female Féminin	Both sexes Les deux sexes	Male Masculin	Female Féminin
EUROPE									
Portugal									
12 III 2001 (CDFC)									
Total	10 356 117	5 000 141	5 355 976	3 905 633	1 849 824	2 055 809	6 450 484	3 150 317	3 300 167
0	110 914	56 866	54 048	42 149	21 549	20 600	68 765	35 317	33 448
1 - 4	428 577	219 103	209 474	158 581	80 931	77 650	269 996	138 172	131 824
5 - 9	537 521	275 199	262 322	193 243	98 860	94 383	344 278	176 339	167 939
10 - 14	579 590	296 385	283 205	202 848	103 056	99 792	376 742	193 329	183 413
15 - 19	688 686	351 422	337 264	244 896	124 090	120 806	443 790	227 332	216 458
20 - 24	790 901	400 087	390 814	307 397	152 923	154 474	483 504	247 164	236 340
25 - 29	814 661	409 243	405 418	329 363	163 114	166 249	485 298	246 129	239 169
30 - 34	761 457	379 363	382 094	297 265	145 591	151 674	464 192	233 772	230 420
35 - 39	770 781	378 783	391 998	293 262	140 883	152 379	477 519	237 900	239 619
40 - 44	728 518	357 528	370 990	280 138	132 956	147 182	448 380	224 572	223 808
45 - 49	686 134	333 382	352 752	271 720	127 948	143 772	414 414	205 434	208 980
50 - 54	642 516	309 484	333 032	263 825	124 177	139 648	378 691	185 307	193 384
55 - 59	571 452	268 899	302 553	225 998	106 413	119 585	345 454	162 486	182 968
60 - 64	550 916	256 179	294 737	202 966	93 216	109 750	347 950	162 963	184 987
65 - 69	538 165	244 230	293 935	191 521	83 961	107 560	346 644	160 269	186 375
70 - 74	453 962	196 615	257 347	159 991	65 708	94 283	293 971	130 907	163 064
75 - 79	348 066	143 439	204 627	120 388	46 449	73 939	227 678	96 990	130 688
80 - 84	201 706	76 014	125 692	67 685	23 317	44 368	134 021	52 697	81 324
85 - 89	108 419	36 167	72 252	37 237	11 153	26 084	71 182	25 014	46 168
90 - 94	36 063	10 241	25 822	12 553	3 088	9 465	23 510	7 153	16 357
95 - 99	6 523	1 417	5 106	2 389	415	1 974	4 134	1 002	3 132
100 +	589	95	494	218	26	192	371	69	302
1 VII 2009 (ESDJ)									
Total	10 632 482	5 145 385	5 487 097	...	...	...	...	...	...
0	101 703	52 211	49 492	...	...	...	...	...	...
1 - 4	422 673	217 138	205 535	...	...	...	...	...	...
5 - 9	556 471	286 118	270 353	...	...	...	...	...	...
10 - 14	538 958	275 144	263 814	...	...	...	...	...	...
15 - 19	571 028	291 179	279 849	...	...	...	...	...	...
20 - 24	623 220	317 998	305 223	...	...	...	...	...	...
25 - 29	751 648	380 715	370 933	...	...	...	...	...	...
30 - 34	842 116	424 462	417 654	...	...	...	...	...	...
35 - 39	818 060	409 270	408 790	...	...	...	...	...	...
40 - 44	782 433	387 136	395 297	...	...	...	...	...	...
45 - 49	770 843	377 735	393 108	...	...	...	...	...	...
50 - 54	706 397	342 942	363 455	...	...	...	...	...	...
55 - 59	659 014	315 689	343 326	...	...	...	...	...	...
60 - 64	600 241	279 684	320 557	...	...	...	...	...	...
65 - 69	515 656	235 258	280 398	...	...	...	...	...	...
70 - 74	492 363	216 369	275 994	...	...	...	...	...	...
75 - 79	411 286	170 145	241 141	...	...	...	...	...	...
80 - 84	277 237	103 211	174 026	...	...	...	...	.⊥.	...
85 +	191 140	62 984	128 156	...	...	...	...	...	...
Republic of Moldova - République de Moldova[75]									
1 VII 2008 (ESDJ)									
Total	3 570 108	1 716 195	1 853 913	1 475 609	693 550	782 059	2 094 499	1 022 645	1 071 854
0	37 744	19 576	18 168	13 692	7 092	6 600	24 052	12 484	11 568
1 - 4	149 484	76 855	72 629	54 788	28 411	26 377	94 696	48 444	46 252
5 - 9	189 439	97 291	92 148	65 254	33 740	31 514	124 185	63 551	60 634
10 - 14	241 976	123 332	118 644	81 831	41 952	39 879	160 145	81 380	78 765
15 - 19	319 423	162 437	156 986	123 892	62 570	61 322	195 531	99 867	95 664
20 - 24	356 029	180 884	175 145	177 131	85 902	91 229	178 898	94 982	83 916
25 - 29	301 304	152 932	148 372	138 039	67 183	70 856	163 265	85 749	77 516
30 - 34	260 872	130 234	130 638	114 111	55 828	58 283	146 761	74 406	72 355
35 - 39	232 129	114 215	117 914	100 109	47 916	52 193	132 020	66 299	65 721
40 - 44	236 148	113 795	122 353	100 805	46 309	54 496	135 343	67 486	67 857
45 - 49	281 633	133 695	147 938	122 139	55 055	67 084	159 494	78 640	80 854
50 - 54	256 041	119 552	136 489	111 880	49 524	62 356	144 161	70 028	74 133
55 - 59	218 434	99 118	119 316	94 463	41 693	52 770	123 971	57 425	66 546
60 - 64	122 202	53 853	68 349	51 827	23 368	28 459	70 375	30 485	39 890
65 - 69	122 682	50 263	72 419	45 952	19 283	26 669	76 730	30 980	45 750

Continent, country or area, date, code and age (in years) / Continent, pays ou zone, date, code et âge (en années)	Total			Urban - Urbaine			Rural - Rurale		
	Both sexes Les deux sexes	Male Masculin	Female Féminin	Both sexes Les deux sexes	Male Masculin	Female Féminin	Both sexes Les deux sexes	Male Masculin	Female Féminin
EUROPE									
Republic of Moldova - République de Moldova[75]									
1 VII 2008 (ESDJ)									
70 - 74	101 895	39 511	62 384	34 770	13 193	21 577	67 125	26 318	40 807
75 - 79	76 346	27 952	48 394	23 845	8 307	15 538	52 501	19 645	32 856
80 - 84	43 721	13 863	29 858	14 380	4 323	10 057	29 341	9 540	19 801
85 +	22 606	6 837	15 769	6 701	1 901	4 800	15 905	4 936	10 969
1 VII 2009 (ESDJ)									
Total	3 565 604	1 714 209	1 851 395	...	...	...	...	...	...
0	39 267	20 257	19 011	...	...	...	...	...	...
1 - 4	150 242	77 272	72 970	...	...	...	...	...	...
5 - 9	186 260	95 823	90 437	...	...	...	...	...	...
10 - 14	226 691	115 704	110 987	...	...	...	...	...	...
15 - 19	303 946	154 709	149 238	...	...	...	...	...	...
20 - 24	358 539	182 142	176 397	...	...	...	...	...	...
25 - 29	310 896	158 001	152 895	...	...	...	...	...	...
30 - 34	267 116	133 748	133 368	...	...	...	...	...	...
35 - 39	235 998	116 192	119 806	...	...	...	...	...	...
40 - 44	229 714	111 022	118 692	...	...	...	...	...	...
45 - 49	273 188	129 685	143 503	...	...	...	...	...	...
50 - 54	261 847	121 976	139 871	...	...	...	...	...	...
55 - 59	226 471	102 699	123 772	...	...	...	...	...	...
60 - 64	132 268	58 516	73 753	...	...	...	...	...	...
65 - 69	117 548	48 388	69 160	...	...	...	...	...	...
70 - 74	102 670	39 406	63 264	...	...	...	...	...	...
75 - 79	73 928	26 926	47 002	...	...	...	...	...	...
80 - 84	45 136	14 480	30 656	...	...	...	...	...	...
85 - 89	18 984	5 815	13 169	...	...	...	...	...	...
90 - 94	3 662	1 083	2 580	...	...	...	...	...	...
95 - 99	1 033	309	724	...	...	...	...	...	...
100 +	206	62	144	...	...	...	...	...	...
Romania - Roumanie									
1 VII 2009 (ESDJ)									
Total	21 469 959	10 457 219	11 012 740	11 823 516	5 649 707	6 173 809	9 646 443	4 807 512	4 838 931
0	218 346	112 384	105 962	...	...	...	...	...	...
1 - 4	860 731	441 949	418 782	464 135	238 523	225 612	396 596	203 426	193 170
5 - 9	1 060 158	544 930	515 228	506 232	260 142	246 090	553 926	284 788	269 138
10 - 14	1 106 540	566 897	539 643	513 449	262 621	250 828	593 091	304 276	288 815
15 - 19	1 325 569	677 428	648 141	694 579	351 966	342 613	630 990	325 462	305 528
20 - 24	1 722 804	879 022	843 782	1 018 241	510 029	508 212	704 563	368 993	335 570
25 - 29	1 627 924	833 631	794 293	989 214	493 703	495 511	638 710	339 928	298 782
30 - 34	1 775 260	910 647	864 613	1 040 432	520 540	519 892	734 828	390 107	344 721
35 - 39	1 678 096	852 829	825 267	938 473	456 857	481 616	739 623	395 972	343 651
40 - 44	1 611 779	811 426	800 353	961 505	454 579	506 926	650 274	356 847	293 427
45 - 49	1 258 455	623 476	634 979	775 099	358 665	416 434	483 356	264 811	218 545
50 - 54	1 538 167	743 586	794 581	976 956	454 658	522 298	561 211	288 928	272 283
55 - 59	1 411 490	666 790	744 700	849 824	401 576	448 248	561 666	265 214	296 452
60 - 64	1 070 415	492 427	577 988	564 246	260 853	303 393	506 169	231 574	274 595
65 - 69	923 844	403 762	520 082	436 027	190 334	245 693	487 817	213 428	274 389
70 - 74	929 212	383 565	545 647	408 989	167 039	241 950	520 223	216 526	303 697
75 - 79	704 995	279 022	425 973	295 408	113 062	182 346	409 587	165 960	243 627
80 - 84	428 578	159 915	268 663	178 188	64 062	114 126	250 390	95 853	154 537
85 - 89	175 858	59 439	116 419	74 256	23 040	51 216	101 602	36 399	65 203
90 - 94	28 035	9 160	18 875	13 469	4 000	9 469	14 566	5 160	9 406
95 - 99	10 992	4 001	6 991	4 447	1 421	3 026	6 545	2 580	3 965
100 +	2 711	933	1 778	846	286	560	1 865	647	1 218
Russian Federation - Fédération de Russie									
1 VII 2009 (ESDJ)									
Total	141 909 244	65 640 507	76 268 737	103 697 871	47 439 543	56 258 328	38 211 373	18 200 964	20 010 409
0	1 726 366	886 327	840 039	1 205 985	619 385	586 600	520 381	266 942	253 439
1 - 4	6 097 456	3 131 346	2 966 110	4 294 718	2 206 926	2 087 792	1 802 738	924 420	878 318
5 - 9	6 762 068	3 465 124	3 296 944	4 707 889	2 414 926	2 292 963	2 054 179	1 050 198	1 003 981
10 - 14	6 660 639	3 404 713	3 255 926	4 488 403	2 296 116	2 192 287	2 172 236	1 108 597	1 063 639
15 - 19	8 878 301	4 532 695	4 345 606	6 075 136	3 086 080	2 989 056	2 803 165	1 446 615	1 356 550

Continent, country or area, date, code and age (in years) / Continent, pays ou zone, date, code et âge (en années)	Total			Urban - Urbaine			Rural - Rurale		
	Both sexes Les deux sexes	Male Masculin	Female Féminin	Both sexes Les deux sexes	Male Masculin	Female Féminin	Both sexes Les deux sexes	Male Masculin	Female Féminin

EUROPE

Russian Federation - Fédération de Russie
1 VII 2009 (ESDJ)

20 - 24	12 414 342	6 286 998	6 127 344	9 059 757	4 520 877	4 538 880	3 354 585	1 766 121	1 588 464
25 - 29	12 075 172	6 063 963	6 011 209	9 421 977	4 695 171	4 726 806	2 653 195	1 368 792	1 284 403
30 - 34	10 739 393	5 309 763	5 429 630	8 238 403	4 034 478	4 203 925	2 500 990	1 275 285	1 225 705
35 - 39	9 961 143	4 900 872	5 060 271	7 554 848	3 693 503	3 861 345	2 406 295	1 207 369	1 198 926
40 - 44	9 297 130	4 489 162	4 807 968	6 800 638	3 239 863	3 560 775	2 496 492	1 249 299	1 247 193
45 - 49	11 464 822	5 409 117	6 055 705	8 361 907	3 856 921	4 504 986	3 102 915	1 552 196	1 550 719
50 - 54	11 228 912	5 102 410	6 126 502	8 254 144	3 644 714	4 609 430	2 974 768	1 457 696	1 517 072
55 - 59	9 674 034	4 204 733	5 469 301	7 273 971	3 081 111	4 192 860	2 400 063	1 123 622	1 276 441
60 - 64	6 334 906	2 605 098	3 729 808	4 882 882	1 972 347	2 910 535	1 452 024	632 751	819 273
65 - 69	4 980 314	1 826 880	3 153 434	3 608 405	1 312 965	2 295 440	1 371 909	513 915	857 994
70 - 74	5 943 659	2 008 526	3 935 133	4 193 876	1 391 211	2 802 665	1 749 783	617 315	1 132 468
75 - 79	3 740 059	1 117 139	2 622 920	2 539 561	739 131	1 800 430	1 200 498	378 008	822 490
80 - 84	2 725 096	668 636	2 056 460	1 880 323	465 065	1 415 258	844 773	203 571	641 202
85 - 89	896 160	170 120	726 040	637 296	125 002	512 294	258 864	45 118	213 746
90 - 94	229 579	41 667	187 912	161 778	31 793	129 985	67 801	9 874	57 927
95 - 99	57 811	11 518	46 293	41 571	9 086	32 485	16 240	2 432	13 808
100 +	21 882	3 700	18 182	14 403	2 872	11 531	7 479	828	6 651

San Marino - Saint-Marin[18]
1 VII 2004* (ESDF)

Total	29 457	14 442	15 015	...	...	...	...	...	...
0	308	160	149	...	...	...	...	...	...
1 - 4	1 274	678	596	...	...	...	...	...	...
5 - 9	1 508	800	708	...	...	...	...	...	...
10 - 14	1 383	707	676	...	...	...	...	...	...
15 - 19	1 292	672	620	...	...	...	...	...	...
20 - 24	1 519	779	740	...	...	...	...	...	...
25 - 29	2 038	983	1 055	...	...	...	...	...	...
30 - 34	2 559	1 256	1 304	...	...	...	...	...	...
35 - 39	2 863	1 385	1 478	...	...	...	...	...	...
40 - 44	2 617	1 297	1 320	...	...	...	...	...	...
45 - 49	2 067	1 054	1 013	...	...	...	...	...	...
50 - 54	1 876	932	944	...	...	...	...	...	...
55 - 59	1 819	892	927	...	...	...	...	...	...
60 - 64	1 526	751	775	...	...	...	...	...	...
65 - 69	1 383	688	696	...	...	...	...	...	...
70 - 74	1 207	553	655	...	...	...	...	...	...
75 - 79	946	413	533	...	...	...	...	...	...
80 - 84	765	290	475	...	...	...	...	...	...
85 - 89	321	102	219	...	...	...	...	...	...
90 - 94	163	47	116	...	...	...	...	...	...
95 - 99	29	9	20	...	...	...	...	...	...
100 +	2	-	2	...	...	...	...	...	...

Serbia - Serbie[76]
1 VII 2009 (ESDJ)

Total	7 320 807	3 560 048	3 760 759	4 279 035	2 039 934	2 239 101	3 041 772	1 520 114	1 521 658
0	69 274	35 885	33 389	46 086	23 876	22 210	23 188	12 009	11 179
1 - 4	283 293	146 056	137 237	185 087	95 433	89 654	98 206	50 623	47 583
5 - 9	378 026	193 986	184 040	221 013	113 792	107 221	157 013	80 194	76 819
10 - 14	384 412	197 219	187 193	212 821	109 435	103 386	171 591	87 784	83 807
15 - 19	427 700	218 881	208 819	243 158	123 988	119 170	184 542	94 893	89 649
20 - 24	480 717	245 752	234 965	287 026	144 056	142 970	193 691	101 696	91 995
25 - 29	511 603	259 906	251 697	325 374	160 604	164 770	186 229	99 302	86 927
30 - 34	516 217	260 848	255 369	325 871	159 869	166 002	190 346	100 979	89 367
35 - 39	485 083	242 577	242 506	296 024	144 007	152 017	189 059	98 570	90 489
40 - 44	475 799	234 960	240 839	281 134	134 514	146 620	194 665	100 446	94 219
45 - 49	504 906	247 738	257 168	299 472	140 821	158 651	205 434	106 917	98 517
50 - 54	549 201	269 040	280 161	325 656	152 414	173 242	223 545	116 626	106 919
55 - 59	578 927	280 745	298 182	346 063	160 692	185 371	232 864	120 053	112 811
60 - 64	424 831	199 007	225 824	252 596	114 832	137 764	172 235	84 175	88 060
65 - 69	353 702	159 321	194 381	192 368	84 721	107 647	161 334	74 600	86 734
70 - 74	360 758	156 067	204 691	188 688	80 878	107 810	172 070	75 189	96 881
75 - 79	291 779	120 463	171 316	137 987	55 778	82 209	153 792	64 685	89 107

238

7. Population by age, sex and urban/rural residence: latest available year, 2000 - 2009
Population selon l'âge, le sexe et la résidence, urbaine/rurale : dernière année disponible, 2000 - 2009 (continued - suite)

Continent, country or area, date, code and age (in years) / Continent, pays ou zone, date, code et âge (en années)	Total			Urban - Urbaine			Rural - Rurale		
	Both sexes Les deux sexes	Male Masculin	Female Féminin	Both sexes Les deux sexes	Male Masculin	Female Féminin	Both sexes Les deux sexes	Male Masculin	Female Féminin
EUROPE									
Serbia - Serbie[76]									
1 VII 2009 (ESDJ)									
80 - 84	163 491	62 819	100 672	75 433	27 696	47 737	88 058	35 123	52 935
85 - 89	65 735	23 229	42 506	29 947	10 117	19 830	35 788	13 112	22 676
90 - 94	9 744	3 528	6 216	4 473	1 489	2 984	5 271	2 039	3 232
95 - 99	4 327	1 548	2 779	2 118	675	1 443	2 209	873	1 336
100 +	1 282	473	809	640	247	393	642	226	416
Slovakia - Slovaquie									
1 VII 2009 (ESDJ)									
Total	5 418 374	2 633 428	2 784 946	2 978 004	1 430 928	1 547 076	2 440 370	1 202 500	1 237 870
0	59 118	30 346	28 772	31 508	16 138	15 370	27 610	14 208	13 402
1 - 4	217 512	111 550	105 962	113 167	58 185	54 982	104 345	53 365	50 980
5 - 9	261 329	134 005	127 324	129 243	66 121	63 122	132 086	67 884	64 202
10 - 14	295 959	151 618	144 341	143 948	73 661	70 287	152 011	77 957	74 054
15 - 19	374 693	191 656	183 037	195 097	99 571	95 526	179 596	92 085	87 511
20 - 24	424 328	216 358	207 970	235 920	120 031	115 889	188 408	96 327	92 081
25 - 29	456 194	233 285	222 909	261 913	133 616	128 297	194 281	99 669	94 612
30 - 34	470 419	240 198	230 221	269 048	136 636	132 412	201 371	103 562	97 809
35 - 39	403 300	204 732	198 568	222 172	110 757	111 415	181 128	93 975	87 153
40 - 44	364 928	183 528	181 400	201 748	97 480	104 268	163 180	86 048	77 132
45 - 49	380 677	190 145	190 532	218 423	104 491	113 932	162 254	85 654	76 600
50 - 54	399 444	195 707	203 737	235 581	110 999	124 582	163 863	84 708	79 155
55 - 59	373 134	178 293	194 841	220 195	102 593	117 602	152 939	75 700	77 239
60 - 64	276 394	125 338	151 056	158 068	70 761	87 307	118 326	54 577	63 749
65 - 69	212 563	89 722	122 841	114 593	48 213	66 380	97 970	41 509	56 461
70 - 74	164 646	63 718	100 928	85 190	33 421	51 769	79 456	30 297	49 159
75 - 79	136 775	48 488	88 287	69 055	25 123	43 932	67 720	23 365	44 355
80 - 84	89 458	28 216	61 242	44 641	14 588	30 053	44 817	13 628	31 189
85 - 89	44 696	12 808	31 888	22 042	6 589	15 453	22 654	6 219	16 435
90 - 94	8 283	2 336	5 947	4 294	1 230	3 064	3 989	1 106	2 883
95 - 99	3 587	1 039	2 548	1 725	531	1 194	1 862	508	1 354
100 +	937	342	595	433	193	240	504	149	355
Slovenia - Slovénie									
1 VII 2009 (ESDJ)									
Total	2 042 335	1 011 767	1 030 568	1 024 087	500 253	523 834	1 018 248	511 514	506 734
0	22 024	11 303	10 721	10 922	5 574	5 348	11 102	5 729	5 373
1 - 4	78 274	40 120	38 154	37 749	19 314	18 435	40 525	20 806	19 719
5 - 9	90 587	46 681	43 906	41 585	21 494	20 091	49 002	25 187	23 815
10 - 14	94 624	48 729	45 895	42 620	21 862	20 758	52 004	26 867	25 137
15 - 19	107 478	55 358	52 120	49 719	25 492	24 227	57 759	29 866	27 893
20 - 24	133 409	70 145	63 264	70 712	36 709	34 003	62 697	33 436	29 261
25 - 29	151 036	79 751	71 285	76 989	40 869	36 120	74 047	38 882	35 165
30 - 34	156 986	82 541	74 445	79 202	41 654	37 548	77 784	40 887	36 897
35 - 39	147 733	77 326	70 407	72 746	37 856	34 890	74 987	39 470	35 517
40 - 44	155 667	79 605	76 062	76 383	38 635	37 748	79 284	40 970	38 314
45 - 49	155 803	79 706	76 097	78 090	39 192	38 898	77 713	40 514	37 199
50 - 54	156 451	80 115	76 336	79 443	39 662	39 781	77 008	40 453	36 555
55 - 59	148 207	75 691	72 516	76 616	38 139	38 477	71 591	37 552	34 039
60 - 64	107 196	52 396	54 800	55 711	26 228	29 483	51 485	26 168	25 317
65 - 69	100 890	46 725	54 165	51 853	23 052	28 801	49 037	23 673	25 364
70 - 74	85 634	36 953	48 681	44 010	18 940	25 070	41 624	18 013	23 611
75 - 79	72 196	27 159	45 037	37 159	13 812	23 347	35 037	13 347	21 690
80 - 84	47 771	14 448	33 323	25 302	7 707	17 595	22 469	6 741	15 728
85 - 89	23 742	5 684	18 058	13 277	3 260	10 017	10 465	2 424	8 041
90 - 94	4 739	971	3 768	2 840	591	2 249	1 899	380	1 519
95 - 99	1 709	322	1 387	1 038	188	850	671	134	537
100 +	179	38	141	121	23	98	58	15	43
Spain - Espagne									
1 XI 2001 (CDFC)[77]									
Total	40 847 371	20 012 882	20 834 489	26 944 564	13 034 120	13 910 444	13 902 807	6 978 762	6 924 045
0	409 749	209 750	199 999	276 424	141 757	134 667	133 325	67 993	65 332
1 - 4	1 513 336	777 292	736 044	1 012 335	519 929	492 406	501 001	257 363	243 638
5 - 9	1 906 092	978 494	927 598	1 256 738	645 268	611 470	649 354	333 226	316 128
10 - 14	2 103 476	1 080 744	1 022 732	1 377 845	707 465	670 380	725 631	373 279	352 352
15 - 19	2 464 580	1 263 528	1 201 052	1 643 165	838 886	804 279	821 415	424 642	396 773

Continent, country or area, date, code and age (in years) / Continent, pays ou zone, date, code et âge (en années)	Total			Urban - Urbaine			Rural - Rurale		
	Both sexes Les deux sexes	Male Masculin	Female Féminin	Both sexes Les deux sexes	Male Masculin	Female Féminin	Both sexes Les deux sexes	Male Masculin	Female Féminin
EUROPE									
Spain - Espagne									
1 XI 2001 (CDFC)[77]									
20 - 24	3 184 683	1 629 701	1 554 982	2 172 741	1 104 448	1 068 293	1 011 942	525 253	486 689
25 - 29	3 500 248	1 787 805	1 712 443	2 410 151	1 223 621	1 186 530	1 090 097	564 184	525 913
30 - 34	3 378 579	1 716 189	1 662 390	2 271 841	1 144 591	1 127 250	1 106 738	571 598	535 140
35 - 39	3 292 986	1 656 075	1 636 911	2 185 429	1 080 937	1 104 492	1 107 557	575 138	532 419
40 - 44	3 028 209	1 511 048	1 517 161	2 011 645	978 073	1 033 572	1 016 564	532 975	483 589
45 - 49	2 609 708	1 299 753	1 309 955	1 759 522	848 656	910 866	850 186	451 097	399 089
50 - 54	2 433 775	1 202 830	1 230 945	1 654 444	797 312	857 132	779 331	405 518	373 813
55 - 59	2 212 801	1 081 811	1 130 990	1 482 637	712 535	770 102	730 164	369 276	360 888
60 - 64	1 850 633	887 299	963 334	1 200 015	567 593	632 422	650 618	319 706	330 912
65 - 69	2 090 389	974 563	1 115 826	1 292 302	588 091	704 211	798 087	386 472	411 615
70 - 74	1 847 044	825 119	1 021 925	1 128 389	486 735	641 654	718 655	338 384	380 271
75 - 79	1 440 761	598 876	841 885	872 556	347 615	524 941	568 205	251 261	316 944
80 - 84	875 435	319 419	556 016	525 021	182 774	342 247	350 414	136 645	213 769
85 - 89	478 794	151 203	327 591	282 032	85 321	196 711	196 762	65 882	130 880
90 - 94	183 189	51 249	131 940	104 851	27 383	77 468	78 338	23 866	54 472
95 - 99	38 686	9 226	29 460	22 133	4 704	17 429	16 553	4 522	12 031
100 +	4 218	908	3 310	2 348	426	1 922	1 870	482	1 388
1 VII 2009 (ESDJ)									
Total	45 929 476	22 670 863	23 258 614	...	...	...	...	...	...
0	504 126	259 728	244 398	...	...	...	...	...	...
1 - 4	1 935 265	995 330	939 935	...	...	...	...	...	...
5 - 9	2 271 669	1 167 546	1 104 123	...	...	...	...	...	...
10 - 14	2 104 021	1 079 937	1 024 084	...	...	...	...	...	...
15 - 19	2 256 923	1 160 209	1 096 714	...	...	...	...	...	...
20 - 24	2 675 619	1 367 160	1 308 459	...	...	...	...	...	...
25 - 29	3 469 804	1 780 458	1 689 346	...	...	...	...	...	...
30 - 34	4 057 780	2 101 710	1 956 070	...	...	...	...	...	...
35 - 39	3 929 371	2 027 105	1 902 267	...	...	...	...	...	...
40 - 44	3 698 237	1 879 716	1 818 521	...	...	...	...	...	...
45 - 49	3 396 965	1 701 846	1 695 119	...	...	...	...	...	...
50 - 54	2 971 461	1 470 154	1 501 308	...	...	...	...	...	...
55 - 59	2 578 561	1 260 998	1 317 563	...	...	...	...	...	...
60 - 64	2 393 107	1 151 313	1 241 794	...	...	...	...	...	...
65 - 69	1 978 175	934 572	1 043 602	...	...	...	...	...	...
70 - 74	1 811 595	818 789	992 806	...	...	...	...	...	...
75 - 79	1 694 989	724 045	970 944	...	...	...	...	...	...
80 - 84	1 211 280	470 852	740 428	...	...	...	...	...	...
85 - 89	676 172	233 015	443 158	...	...	...	...	...	...
90 - 94	244 379	69 125	175 254	...	...	...	...	...	...
95 - 99	62 787	15 466	47 321	...	...	...	...	...	...
100 +	7 190	1 790	5 399	...	...	...	...	...	...
Sweden - Suède[18]									
1 VII 2009 (ESDJ)									
Total	9 298 515	4 626 362	4 672 153	...	...	...	...	...	...
0	110 892	57 124	53 768	...	...	...	...	...	...
1 - 4	431 710	221 783	209 928	...	...	...	...	...	...
5 - 9	496 335	254 626	241 709	...	...	...	...	...	...
10 - 14	506 986	260 121	246 865	...	...	...	...	...	...
15 - 19	639 971	328 871	311 100	...	...	...	...	...	...
20 - 24	592 894	303 156	289 739	...	...	...	...	...	...
25 - 29	567 324	290 801	276 523	...	...	...	...	...	...
30 - 34	582 653	297 384	285 270	...	...	...	...	...	...
35 - 39	630 605	320 316	310 289	...	...	...	...	...	...
40 - 44	668 655	340 962	327 693	...	...	...	...	...	...
45 - 49	610 673	310 510	300 163	...	...	...	...	...	...
50 - 54	583 603	294 827	288 776	...	...	...	...	...	...
55 - 59	580 630	291 526	289 105	...	...	...	...	...	...
60 - 64	627 657	313 637	314 020	...	...	...	...	...	...
65 - 69	497 789	247 022	250 768	...	...	...	...	...	...
70 - 74	371 843	176 890	194 953	...	...	...	...	...	...
75 - 79	304 548	135 245	169 304	...	...	...	...	...	...
80 - 84	247 407	100 227	147 180	...	...	...	...	...	...
85 - 89	167 366	59 662	107 705	...	...	...	...	...	...

Continent, country or area, date, code and age (in years) / Continent, pays ou zone, date, code et âge (en annèes)	Total			Urban - Urbaine			Rural - Rurale		
	Both sexes Les deux sexes	Male Masculin	Female Féminin	Both sexes Les deux sexes	Male Masculin	Female Féminin	Both sexes Les deux sexes	Male Masculin	Female Féminin
EUROPE									
Sweden - Suède[18]									
1 VII 2009 (ESDJ)									
90 - 94	62 697	18 218	44 479	...	...	...	...	...	...
95 - 99	14 690	3 218	11 472	...	...	...	...	...	...
100 +	1 591	243	1 348	...	...	...	...	...	...
Switzerland - Suisse									
5 XII 2000 (CDFC)									
Total	7 288 010	3 567 567	3 720 443	5 345 452	2 597 686	2 747 766	1 942 558	969 881	972 677
0	69 043	35 556	33 487	49 718	25 600	24 118	19 325	9 956	9 369
1 - 4	318 145	163 182	154 963	224 811	115 241	109 570	93 334	47 941	45 393
5 - 9	427 105	218 782	208 323	294 679	150 897	143 782	132 426	67 885	64 541
10 - 14	430 367	220 319	210 048	292 880	150 001	142 879	137 487	70 318	67 169
15 - 19	420 953	216 059	204 894	294 997	150 359	144 638	125 956	65 700	60 256
20 - 24	431 272	218 823	212 449	327 211	164 058	163 153	104 061	54 765	49 296
25 - 29	488 872	245 247	243 625	375 384	188 057	187 327	113 488	57 190	56 298
30 - 34	591 426	295 449	295 977	443 272	221 948	221 324	148 154	73 501	74 653
35 - 39	629 489	318 448	311 041	463 033	234 257	228 776	166 456	84 191	82 265
40 - 44	565 875	287 213	278 662	412 108	208 336	203 772	153 767	78 877	74 890
45 - 49	504 882	254 135	250 747	371 012	183 788	187 224	133 870	70 347	63 523
50 - 54	496 241	249 326	246 915	369 748	183 045	186 703	126 493	66 281	60 212
55 - 59	444 040	221 861	222 179	335 909	165 939	169 970	108 131	55 922	52 209
60 - 64	351 294	169 582	181 712	264 575	126 760	137 815	86 719	42 822	43 897
65 - 69	314 099	145 343	168 756	232 658	106 534	126 124	81 441	38 809	42 632
70 - 74	274 959	118 558	156 401	202 997	86 220	116 777	71 962	32 338	39 624
75 - 79	231 061	92 068	138 993	169 857	66 500	103 357	61 204	25 568	35 636
80 - 84	152 688	55 862	96 826	111 512	39 912	71 600	41 176	15 950	25 226
85 - 89	97 520	30 025	67 495	72 277	21 673	50 604	25 243	8 352	16 891
90 - 94	39 856	10 047	29 809	30 077	7 332	22 745	9 779	2 715	7 064
95 - 99	8 036	1 571	6 465	6 108	1 146	4 962	1 928	425	1 503
100 +	787	111	676	629	83	546	158	28	130
1 VII 2009 (ESDJ)									
Total	7 743 832	3 808 621	3 935 211	...	...	...	...	...	...
0	77 032	39 740	37 292	...	...	...	...	...	...
1 - 4	302 242	155 403	146 839	...	...	...	...	...	...
5 - 9	381 827	196 675	185 152	...	...	...	...	...	...
10 - 14	419 187	215 625	203 562	...	...	...	...	...	...
15 - 19	455 291	233 781	221 510	...	...	...	...	...	...
20 - 24	467 537	236 449	231 088	...	...	...	...	...	...
25 - 29	502 592	251 511	251 081	...	...	...	...	...	...
30 - 34	522 492	260 782	261 710	...	...	...	...	...	...
35 - 39	575 364	288 445	286 919	...	...	...	...	...	...
40 - 44	646 064	325 701	320 363	...	...	...	...	...	...
45 - 49	625 077	315 930	309 147	...	...	...	...	...	...
50 - 54	542 327	274 420	267 907	...	...	...	...	...	...
55 - 59	479 497	239 399	240 098	...	...	...	...	...	...
60 - 64	455 571	225 201	230 370	...	...	...	...	...	...
65 - 69	374 779	179 795	194 984	...	...	...	...	...	...
70 - 74	298 433	136 532	161 901	...	...	...	...	...	...
75 - 79	251 851	107 188	144 663	...	...	...	...	...	...
80 - 84	189 925	71 758	118 167	...	...	...	...	...	...
85 - 89	117 235	38 649	78 586	...	...	...	...	...	...
90 - 94	43 502	12 072	31 430	...	...	...	...	...	...
95 +	16 007	3 565	12 442	...	...	...	...	...	...
TFYR of Macedonia - L'ex-R. y. de Macédoine									
1 VII 2009 (ESDF)									
Total	2 050 671	1 027 810	1 022 861	...	...	...	...	...	...
0	23 061	11 946	11 115	...	...	...	...	...	...
1 - 4	89 610	46 136	43 474	...	...	...	...	...	...
5 - 9	119 468	61 674	57 794	...	...	...	...	...	...
10 - 14	134 704	69 572	65 132	...	...	...	...	...	...
15 - 19	155 316	79 805	75 511	...	...	...	...	...	...
20 - 24	164 286	84 228	80 058	...	...	...	...	...	...
25 - 29	163 591	84 091	79 500	...	...	...	...	...	...
30 - 34	155 188	79 510	75 678	...	...	...	...	...	...

Continent, country or area, date, code and age (in years) / Continent, pays ou zone, date, code et âge (en années)	Total			Urban - Urbaine			Rural - Rurale		
	Both sexes Les deux sexes	Male Masculin	Female Féminin	Both sexes Les deux sexes	Male Masculin	Female Féminin	Both sexes Les deux sexes	Male Masculin	Female Féminin
EUROPE									
TFYR of Macedonia - L'ex-R. y. de Macédoine									
1 VII 2009 (ESDF)									
35 - 39	147 766	74 884	72 882	...	...	...	...	...	...
40 - 44	149 078	75 603	73 475	...	...	...	...	...	...
45 - 49	145 233	73 663	71 570	...	...	...	...	...	...
50 - 54	140 607	71 440	69 167	...	...	...	...	...	...
55 - 59	126 459	62 317	64 142	...	...	...	...	...	...
60 - 64	98 640	47 035	51 605	...	...	...	...	...	...
65 - 69	81 508	38 196	43 312	...	...	...	...	...	...
70 - 74	69 353	31 337	38 016	...	...	...	...	...	...
75 - 79	49 985	21 573	28 412	...	...	...	...	...	...
80 - 84	24 729	10 247	14 482	...	...	...	...	...	...
85 - 89	9 190	3 587	5 603	...	...	...	...	...	...
90 - 94	1 608	580	1 028	...	...	...	...	...	...
95 +	695	242	453	...	...	...	...	...	...
Unknown - Inconnu	596	144	452	...	...	...	...	...	...
Ukraine									
1 I 2009 (ESDJ)									
Total	45 963 359	21 184 932	24 778 427	31 331 587	14 349 742	16 981 845	14 631 772	6 835 190	7 796 582
0	506 342	261 138	245 204	337 913	174 476	163 437	168 429	86 662	81 767
1 - 4	1 766 133	907 330	858 803	1 179 819	606 742	573 077	586 314	300 588	285 726
5 - 9	1 925 229	989 902	935 327	1 216 803	626 187	590 616	708 426	363 715	344 711
10 - 14	2 278 484	1 166 792	1 111 692	1 390 406	712 356	678 050	888 078	454 436	433 642
15 - 19	3 028 414	1 551 406	1 477 008	2 040 309	1 037 663	1 002 646	988 105	513 743	474 362
20 - 24	3 801 494	1 940 203	1 861 291	2 717 791	1 369 801	1 347 990	1 083 703	570 402	513 301
25 - 29	3 626 587	1 839 257	1 787 330	2 681 364	1 358 485	1 322 879	945 223	480 772	464 451
30 - 34	3 348 620	1 664 605	1 684 015	2 388 514	1 175 086	1 213 428	960 106	489 519	470 587
35 - 39	3 198 823	1 566 857	1 631 966	2 224 994	1 071 760	1 153 234	973 829	495 097	478 732
40 - 44	3 081 504	1 476 471	1 605 033	2 113 242	981 645	1 131 597	968 262	494 826	473 436
45 - 49	3 588 710	1 674 495	1 914 215	2 518 425	1 137 694	1 380 731	1 070 285	536 801	533 484
50 - 54	3 366 046	1 518 806	1 847 240	2 391 573	1 045 116	1 346 457	974 473	473 690	500 783
55 - 59	3 074 616	1 335 537	1 739 079	2 207 107	935 465	1 271 642	867 509	400 072	467 437
60 - 64	2 054 981	842 366	1 212 615	1 440 321	585 933	854 388	614 660	256 433	358 227
65 - 69	2 241 587	845 645	1 395 942	1 436 206	545 206	891 000	805 381	300 439	504 942
70 - 74	2 214 046	797 571	1 416 475	1 389 309	502 856	886 453	824 737	294 715	530 022
75 - 79	1 368 663	439 324	929 339	790 678	259 126	531 552	577 985	180 198	397 787
80 - 84	1 034 820	272 668	762 152	606 041	166 593	439 448	428 779	106 075	322 704
85 - 89	353 870	74 827	279 043	198 306	44 325	153 981	155 564	30 502	125 062
90 - 94	82 705	15 782	66 923	49 168	10 502	38 666	33 537	5 280	28 257
95 - 99	20 260	3 663	16 597	12 271	2 528	9 743	7 989	1 135	6 854
100 +	1 425	287	1 138	1 027	197	830	398	90	308
United Kingdom of Great Britain and Northern Ireland - Royaume-Uni de Grande-Bretagne et d'Irlande du Nord[78]									
29 IV 2001 (CDFC)[79]									
Total	58 789 194	28 579 869	30 209 325	47 007 427	22 769 606	24 237 821	11 781 767	5 810 263	5 971 504
0	660 025	337 154	322 871	545 015	278 159	266 856	115 010	58 995	56 015
1 - 4	2 826 228	1 448 534	1 377 694	2 305 860	1 181 014	1 124 846	520 368	267 520	252 848
5 - 9	3 738 042	1 914 727	1 823 315	3 009 441	1 541 475	1 467 966	728 601	373 252	355 349
10 - 14	3 880 557	1 987 606	1 892 951	3 103 939	1 588 218	1 515 721	776 618	399 388	377 230
15 - 19	3 663 782	1 870 508	1 793 274	2 968 710	1 505 467	1 463 243	695 072	365 041	330 031
20 - 24	3 545 984	1 765 257	1 780 727	3 041 392	1 493 532	1 547 860	504 592	271 725	232 867
25 - 29	3 867 015	1 895 469	1 971 546	3 299 342	1 610 026	1 689 316	567 673	285 443	282 230
30 - 34	4 493 532	2 199 767	2 293 765	3 723 844	1 824 665	1 899 179	769 688	375 102	394 586
35 - 39	4 625 777	2 277 678	2 348 099	3 727 542	1 835 623	1 891 919	898 235	442 055	456 180
40 - 44	4 151 613	2 056 545	2 095 068	3 290 231	1 629 251	1 660 980	861 382	427 294	434 088
45 - 49	3 735 986	1 851 391	1 884 595	2 911 582	1 441 854	1 469 728	824 404	409 537	414 867
50 - 54	4 040 576	2 003 158	2 037 418	3 082 777	1 526 738	1 556 039	957 799	476 420	481 379
55 - 59	3 339 004	1 651 396	1 687 608	2 514 831	1 238 414	1 276 417	824 173	412 982	411 191
60 - 64	2 880 074	1 409 684	1 470 390	2 203 267	1 070 975	1 132 292	676 807	338 709	338 098
65 - 69	2 596 939	1 241 382	1 355 557	2 005 735	948 325	1 057 410	591 204	293 057	298 147
70 - 74	2 339 319	1 059 156	1 280 163	1 821 307	812 938	1 008 369	518 012	246 218	271 794

Continent, country or area, date, code and age (in years) Continent, pays ou zone, date, code et âge (en annèes)	Total			Urban - Urbaine			Rural - Rurale		
	Both sexes Les deux sexes	Male Masculin	Female Féminin	Both sexes Les deux sexes	Male Masculin	Female Féminin	Both sexes Les deux sexes	Male Masculin	Female Féminin
EUROPE									
United Kingdom of Great Britain and Northern Ireland - Royaume-Uni de Grande-Bretagne et d'Irlande du Nord[78]									
29 IV 2001 (CDFC)[79]									
75 - 79	1 967 088	817 738	1 149 350	1 542 567	632 032	910 535	424 521	185 706	238 815
80 - 84	1 313 592	482 707	830 885	1 030 404	373 231	657 173	283 188	109 476	173 712
85 - 89	752 035	226 520	525 515	589 543	174 135	415 408	162 492	52 385	110 107
90 - 94	293 961	68 682	225 279	229 205	52 178	177 027	64 756	16 504	48 252
95 - 99	68 655	12 920	55 735	53 532	9 866	43 666	15 123	3 054	12 069
100 +	9 410	1 890	7 520	7 361	1 490	5 871	2 049	400	1 649
1 VII 2008 (ESDF)									
Total	61 393 521	30 149 903	31 243 618	...	...	...	...	...	...
0	779 011	399 038	379 974	...	...	...	...	...	...
1 - 4	2 913 953	1 492 507	1 421 447	...	...	...	...	...	...
5 - 9	3 403 835	1 740 393	1 663 443	...	...	...	...	...	...
10 - 14	3 657 289	1 872 513	1 784 776	...	...	...	...	...	...
15 - 19	3 988 525	2 050 478	1 938 047	...	...	...	...	...	...
20 - 24	4 217.004	2 159 157	2 057 847	...	...	...	...	...	...
25 - 29	4 071 326	2 061 367	2 009 959	...	...	...	...	...	...
30 - 34	3 846 523	1 928 012	1 918 512	...	...	...	...	...	...
35 - 39	4 433 193	2 195 347	2 237 846	...	...	...	...	...	...
40 - 44	4 705 780	2 331 343	2 374 437	...	...	...	...	...	...
45 - 49	4 353 566	2 144 026	2 209 540	...	...	...	...	...	...
50 - 54	3 810 303	1 883 213	1 927 090	...	...	...	...	...	...
55 - 59	3 653 401	1 797 009	1 856 392	...	...	...	...	...	...
60 - 64	3 621 796	1 770 334	1 851 462	...	...	...	...	...	...
65 - 69	2 762 353	1 327 601	1 434 752	...	...	...	...	...	...
70 - 74	2 400 344	1 123 996	1 276 349	...	...	...	...	...	...
75 - 79	1 983 259	872 094	1 111 166	...	...	...	...	...	...
80 - 84	1 457 605	580 156	877 450	...	...	...	...	...	...
85 - 89	910 335	310 419	599 916	...	...	...	...	...	...
90 +	424 124	110 906	313 218	...	...	...	...	...	...
OCEANIA - OCÉANIE									
American Samoa - Samoas américaines[26]									
1 IV 2000 (CDJC)									
Total	57 291	29 264	28 027	...	...	...	...	...	...
0 - 4	7 820	4 008	3 812	...	...	...	...	...	...
5 - 9	7 788	4 058	3 730	...	...	...	...	...	...
10 - 14	6 604	3 389	3 215	...	...	...	...	...	...
15 - 19	5 223	2 747	2 476	...	...	...	...	...	...
20 - 24	4 476	2 328	2 148	...	...	...	...	...	...
25 - 29	4 356	2 218	2 138	...	...	...	...	...	...
30 - 34	4 351	2 167	2 184	...	...	...	...	...	...
35 - 39	4 059	1 980	2 079	...	...	...	...	...	...
40 - 44	3 302	1 654	1 648	...	...	...	...	...	...
45 - 49	2 660	1 331	1 329	...	...	...	...	...	...
50 - 54	2 073	1 071	1 002	...	...	...	...	...	...
55 - 59	1 474	817	657	...	...	...	...	...	...
60 - 64	1 204	636	568	...	...	...	...	...	...
65 - 69	790	407	383	...	...	...	...	...	...
70 - 74	555	231	324	...	...	...	...	...	...
75 +	556	222	334	...	...	...	...	...	...
Australia - Australie[80]									
1 VII 2009* (ESDJ)									
Total	21 955 256	10 931 694	11 023 562	17 984 840	8 913 643	9 071 197	3 970 416	2 018 051	1 952 365
0	300 292	154 048	146 244	249 007	127 667	121 340	51 285	26 381	24 904
1 - 4	1 125 843	577 998	547 845	923 864	474 379	449 485	201 979	103 619	98 360
5 - 9	1 357 989	696 353	661 636	1 092 538	559 825	532 713	265 451	136 528	128 923
10 - 14	1 405 090	720 836	684 254	1 121 173	574 061	547 112	283 917	146 775	137 142

Continent, country or area, date, code and age (in years) / Continent, pays ou zone, date, code et âge (en années)	Total			Urban - Urbaine			Rural - Rurale		
	Both sexes Les deux sexes	Male Masculin	Female Féminin	Both sexes Les deux sexes	Male Masculin	Female Féminin	Both sexes Les deux sexes	Male Masculin	Female Féminin
OCEANIA - OCÉANIE									
Australia - Australie[80]									
1 VII 2009* (ESDJ)									
15 - 19	1 499 786	772 070	727 716	1 232 590	632 277	600 313	267 196	139 793	127 403
20 - 24	1 612 004	830 048	781 956	1 406 680	721 335	685 345	205 324	108 713	96 611
25 - 29	1 603 435	813 699	789 736	1 392 433	705 451	686 982	211 002	108 248	102 754
30 - 34	1 502 481	751 688	750 793	1 283 279	641 455	641 824	219 202	110 233	108 969
35 - 39	1 617 308	803 190	814 118	1 353 399	671 439	681 960	263 909	131 751	132 158
40 - 44	1 528 738	759 929	768 809	1 258 687	623 946	634 741	270 051	135 983	134 068
45 - 49	1 571 554	778 491	793 063	1 273 376	627 815	645 561	298 178	150 676	147 502
50 - 54	1 440 043	712 887	727 156	1 152 674	565 616	587 058	287 369	147 271	140 098
55 - 59	1 306 014	647 343	658 671	1 033 704	506 853	526 851	272 310	140 490	131 820
60 - 64	1 169 777	584 439	585 338	916 706	453 361	463 345	253 071	131 078	121 993
65 - 69	868 588	430 169	438 419	671 552	328 520	343 032	197 036	101 649	95 387
70 - 74	685 773	330 764	355 009	533 835	252 923	280 912	151 938	77 841	74 097
75 - 79	549 762	254 552	295 210	434 616	198 041	236 575	115 146	56 511	58 635
80 - 84	431 337	183 548	247 789	345 755	144 522	201 233	85 582	39 026	46 556
85 +	379 442	129 642	249 800	308 972	104 157	204 815	70 470	25 485	44 985
85 - 89	258 102	94 838	163 264	...	...	...	...	...	...
90 - 94	92 962	28 008	64 954	...	...	...	...	...	...
95 - 99	24 977	6 078	18 899	...	...	...	...	...	...
100 +	3 401	718	2 683	...	...	...	...	...	...
Cook Islands - Îles Cook[81]									
1 XII 2006* (CDFC)									
Total	19 569	9 932	9 637	...	...	...	...	...	...
0 - 14	5 098	2 649	2 449	...	...	...	...	...	...
15 - 44	8 865	4 405	4 460	...	...	...	...	...	...
45 - 59	3 287	1 689	1 598	...	...	...	...	...	...
60 +	2 319	1 189	1 130	...	...	...	...	...	...
Fiji - Fidji									
16 IX 2007 (CDFC)									
Total	837 271	427 176	410 095	424 846	212 454	212 392	412 425	214 722	197 703
0 - 4	82 718	42 835	39 883	39 209	20 264	18 945	43 509	22 571	20 938
5 - 9	78 019	40 441	37 578	35 981	18 528	17 453	42 038	21 913	20 125
10 - 14	82 384	42 369	40 015	38 916	19 790	19 126	43 468	22 579	20 889
15 - 19	79 518	40 818	38 700	42 458	21 051	21 407	37 060	19 767	17 293
20 - 24	80 352	41 325	39 027	45 837	22 896	22 941	34 515	18 429	16 086
25 - 29	73 487	37 390	36 097	40 669	20 260	20 409	32 818	17 130	15 688
30 - 34	63 535	32 825	30 710	33 612	17 017	16 595	29 923	15 808	14 115
35 - 39	56 552	28 778	27 774	29 288	14 674	14 614	27 264	14 104	13 160
40 - 44	56 274	28 598	27 676	28 147	14 058	14 089	28 127	14 540	13 587
45 - 49	50 322	25 835	24 487	25 556	12 780	12 776	24 766	13 055	11 711
50 - 54	40 009	20 215	19 794	20 581	10 118	10 463	19 428	10 097	9 331
55 - 59	31 161	15 735	15 426	15 667	7 715	7 952	15 494	8 020	7 474
60 - 64	24 120	11 956	12 164	11 655	5 647	6 008	12 465	6 309	6 156
65 - 69	16 808	8 098	8 710	7 597	3 509	4 088	9 211	4 589	4 622
70 - 74	10 110	4 716	5 394	4 360	1 887	2 473	5 750	2 829	2 921
75 +	11 902	5 242	6 660	5 313	2 260	3 053	6 589	2 982	3 607
75 - 79	6 138	2 811	3 327	...	...	...	...	...	...
80 - 84	3 236	1 376	1 860	...	...	...	...	...	...
85 - 89	1 638	702	936	...	...	...	...	...	...
90 - 94	572	212	360	...	...	...	...	...	...
95 +	318	141	177	...	...	...	...	...	...
French Polynesia - Polynésie française									
1 I 2009 (ESDF)									
Total	264 000	135 200	128 800	...	...	...	...	...	...
0 - 4	21 900	11 200	10 700	...	...	...	...	...	...
5 - 9	23 000	11 700	11 200	...	...	...	...	...	...
10 - 14	23 600	12 100	11 400	...	...	...	...	...	...
15 - 19	25 900	13 400	12 500	...	...	...	...	...	...
20 - 24	24 000	12 000	11 900	...	...	...	...	...	...
25 - 29	19 500	9 900	9 600	...	...	...	...	...	...
30 - 34	20 300	10 300	10 000	...	...	...	...	...	...
35 - 39	20 900	10 800	10 100	...	...	...	...	...	...
40 - 44	20 500	10 600	9 900	...	...	...	...	...	...

Continent, country or area, date, code and age (in years) / Continent, pays ou zone, date, code et âge (en années)	Total			Urban - Urbaine			Rural - Rurale		
	Both sexes Les deux sexes	Male Masculin	Female Féminin	Both sexes Les deux sexes	Male Masculin	Female Féminin	Both sexes Les deux sexes	Male Masculin	Female Féminin
OCEANIA - OCÉANIE									
French Polynesia - Polynésie française									
1 I 2009 (ESDF)									
45 - 49	16 700	8 700	8 000	...	...	...	...	...	...
50 - 54	13 900	7 300	6 600	...	...	...	...	...	...
55 - 59	10 500	5 500	5 000	...	...	...	...	...	...
60 - 64	8 000	4 100	3 900	...	...	...	...	...	...
65 - 69	6 200	3 200	3 000	...	...	...	...	...	...
70 - 74	4 300	2 100	2 200	...	...	...	...	...	...
75 - 79	2 700	1 300	1 400	...	...	...	...	...	...
80 - 84	1 400	600	800	...	...	...	...	...	...
85 - 89	500	200	300	...	...	...	...	...	...
90 +	200	100	100	...	...	...	...	...	...
Guam[26]									
1 IV 2000 (CDJC)									
Total	154 805	79 181	75 624	...	...	...	...	...	...
0	3 535	1 862	1 673	...	...	...	...	...	...
1 - 4	13 250	6 945	6 305	...	...	...	...	...	...
5 - 9	16 090	8 270	7 820	...	...	...	...	...	...
10 - 14	14 281	7 232	7 049	...	...	...	...	...	...
15 - 19	12 379	6 273	6 106	...	...	...	...	...	...
20 - 24	11 989	6 140	5 849	...	...	...	...	...	...
25 - 29	12 944	6 584	6 360	...	...	...	...	...	...
30 - 34	12 906	6 727	6 179	...	...	...	...	...	...
35 - 39	12 751	6 692	6 059	...	...	...	...	...	...
40 - 44	10 390	5 344	5 046	...	...	...	...	...	...
45 - 49	9 042	4 608	4 434	...	...	...	...	...	...
50 - 54	7 506	3 813	3 693	...	...	...	...	...	...
55 - 59	4 993	2 548	2 445	...	...	...	...	...	...
60 - 64	4 534	2 190	2 344	...	...	...	...	...	...
65 - 69	3 399	1 628	1 771	...	...	...	...	...	...
70 - 74	2 461	1 287	1 174	...	...	...	...	...	...
75 - 79	1 384	681	703	...	...	...	...	...	...
80 - 84	616	234	382	...	...	...	...	...	...
85 - 89	248	83	165	...	...	...	...	...	...
90 - 94	79	30	49	...	...	...	...	...	...
95 - 99	22	9	13	...	...	...	...	...	...
100 +	6	1	5	...	...	...	...	...	...
Kiribati									
7 XII 2005 (CDFC)									
Total	92 533	45 612	46 921	40 311	19 435	20 876	52 222	26 177	26 045
0 - 4	10 917	5 613	5 304	4 587	2 379	2 208	6 330	3 234	3 096
5 - 9	12 466	6 315	6 151	4 908	2 438	2 470	7 558	3 877	3 681
10 - 14	10 810	5 597	5 213	4 297	2 185	2 112	6 513	3 412	3 101
15 - 19	10 793	5 511	5 282	4 634	2 288	2 346	6 159	3 223	2 936
20 - 24	8 574	4 247	4 327	4 568	2 132	2 436	4 006	2 115	1 891
25 - 29	6 782	3 274	3 508	3 385	1 631	1 754	3 397	1 643	1 754
30 - 34	5 561	2 631	2 930	2 567	1 196	1 371	2 994	1 435	1 559
35 - 39	6 459	3 095	3 364	2 774	1 304	1 470	3 685	1 791	1 894
40 - 44	5 253	2 575	2 678	2 286	1 093	1 193	2 967	1 482	1 485
45 - 49	4 298	2 046	2 252	1 915	905	1 010	2 383	1 141	1 242
50 - 54	3 150	1 479	1 671	1 396	639	757	1 754	840	914
55 - 59	2 450	1 143	1 307	1 038	458	580	1 412	685	727
60 - 64	1 740	802	938	708	309	399	1 032	493	539
65 - 69	1 288	547	741	516	219	297	772	328	444
70 - 74	1 111	428	683	403	150	253	708	278	430
75 +	881	309	572	329	109	220	552	200	352
Marshall Islands - Îles Marshall									
1 VII 2007 (ESDF)									
Total	52 701	27 022	25 679	...	...	...	...	...	...
0 - 4	7 632	3 916	3 716	...	...	...	...	...	...
5 - 9	7 297	3 768	3 529	...	...	...	...	...	...
10 - 14	6 668	3 422	3 246	...	...	...	...	...	...
15 - 19	6 568	3 378	3 189	...	...	...	...	...	...

7, Population by age, sex and urban/rural residence: latest available year, 2000 - 2009
Population selon l'âge, le sexe et la résidence, urbaine/rurale : dernière année disponible, 2000 - 2009 (continued suite)

Continent, country or area, date, code and age (in years) / Continent, pays ou zone, date, code et âge (en annèes)	Total			Urban - Urbaine			Rural - Rurale		
	Both sexes Les deux sexes	Male Masculin	Female Féminin	Both sexes Les deux sexes	Male Masculin	Female Féminin	Both sexes Les deux sexes	Male Masculin	Female Féminin
OCEANIA - OCÉANIE									
Marshall Islands - Îles Marshall									
1 VII 2007 (ESDF)									
20 - 24	6 194	3 215	2 979	...	...	...	...	...	...
25 - 29	3 949	1 999	1 951	...	...	...	...	...	...
30 - 34	2 556	1 282	1 274	...	...	...	...	...	...
35 - 39	2 304	1 174	1 129	...	...	...	...	...	...
40 - 44	2 202	1 130	1 073	...	...	...	...	...	...
45 - 49	2 053	1 018	1 034	...	...	...	...	...	...
50 - 54	1 798	919	878	...	...	...	...	...	...
55 - 59	1 428	784	645	...	...	...	...	...	...
60 - 64	839	438	400	...	...	...	...	...	...
65 - 69	478	242	236	...	...	...	...	...	...
70 - 74	344	159	185	...	...	...	...	...	...
75 +	392	177	216	...	...	...	...	...	...
Micronesia (Federated States of) - Micronésie (États fédérés de)[2]									
1 VII 2009 (ESDJ)									
Total	107 973	54 275	53 698	...	...	...	...	...	...
0 - 4	13 653	6 992	6 661	...	...	...	...	...	...
5 - 9	13 330	6 819	6 511	...	...	...	...	...	...
10 - 14	12 531	6 414	6 117	...	...	...	...	...	...
15 - 19	11 448	5 887	5 561	...	...	...	...	...	...
20 - 24	9 560	4 940	4 620	...	...	...	...	...	...
25 - 29	7 834	3 887	3 947	...	...	...	...	...	...
30 - 34	6 294	3 152	3 142	...	...	...	...	...	...
35 - 39	6 248	2 931	3 317	...	...	...	...	...	...
40 - 44	5 712	2 698	3 014	...	...	...	...	...	...
45 - 49	5 483	2 716	2 767	...	...	...	...	...	...
50 - 54	5 001	2 521	2 480	...	...	...	...	...	...
55 - 59	3 992	2 058	1 934	...	...	...	...	...	...
60 - 64	2 572	1 300	1 272	...	...	...	...	...	...
65 - 69	1 447	654	793	...	...	...	...	...	...
70 - 74	1 348	640	708	...	...	...	...	...	...
75 +	1 520	666	854	...	...	...	...	...	...
Nauru									
23 IX 2002 (CDFC)									
Total	10 065	5 136	4 929	...	...	...	...	...	...
0 - 4	1 266	648	618	...	...	...	...	...	...
5 - 9	1 359	718	641	...	...	...	...	...	...
10 - 14	1 213	640	573	...	...	...	...	...	...
15 - 19	1 010	502	508	...	...	...	...	...	...
20 - 24	961	500	461	...	...	...	...	...	...
25 - 29	786	397	389	...	...	...	...	...	...
30 - 34	728	375	353	...	...	...	...	...	...
35 - 39	743	375	369	...	...	...	...	...	...
40 - 44	622	292	331	...	...	...	...	...	...
45 - 49	492	236	256	...	...	...	...	...	...
50 - 54	337	162	175	...	...	...	...	...	...
55 - 59	183	95	88	...	...	...	...	...	...
60 - 64	126	79	47	...	...	...	...	...	...
65 - 69	58	31	27	...	...	...	...	...	...
70 - 74	37	18	19	...	...	...	...	...	...
75 - 79	19	6	13	...	...	...	...	...	...
80 - 84	9	2	7	...	...	...	...	...	...
85 - 89	5	1	4	...	...	...	...	...	...
90 +	1	-	1	...	...	...	...	...	...
Unknown - Inconnu	110	59	49	...	...	...	...	...	...
New Caledonia - Nouvelle-Calédonie									
1 VII 2008 (ESDF)									
Total	242 400	122 261	120 139	...	...	...	...	...	...
0 - 4	20 428	10 525	9 903	...	...	...	...	...	...
5 - 9	20 149	10 308	9 841	...	...	...	...	...	...

Continent, country or area, date, code and age (in years) / Continent, pays ou zone, date, code et âge (en années)	Total			Urban - Urbaine			Rural - Rurale		
	Both sexes Les deux sexes	Male Masculin	Female Féminin	Both sexes Les deux sexes	Male Masculin	Female Féminin	Both sexes Les deux sexes	Male Masculin	Female Féminin
OCEANIA - OCÉANIE									
New Caledonia - Nouvelle-Calédonie									
1 VII 2008 (ESDF)									
10 - 14	22 357	11 577	10 780	...	...	...	...	...	...
15 - 19	21 782	11 099	10 683	...	...	...	...	...	...
20 - 24	19 851	10 011	9 840	...	...	...	...	...	...
25 - 29	17 210	8 606	8 604	...	...	...	...	...	...
30 - 34	18 578	9 101	9 477	...	...	...	...	...	...
35 - 39	19 424	9 637	9 787	...	...	...	...	...	...
40 - 44	17 715	8 905	8 810	...	...	...	...	...	...
45 - 49	15 191	7 585	7 606	...	...	...	...	...	...
50 - 54	12 392	6 300	6 092	...	...	...	...	...	...
55 - 59	10 854	5 716	5 138	...	...	...	...	...	...
60 - 64	8 938	4 766	4 172	...	...	...	...	...	...
65 - 69	6 662	3 314	3 348	...	...	...	...	...	...
70 - 74	4 546	2 188	2 358	...	...	...	...	...	...
75 - 79	3 092	1 375	1 717	...	...	...	...	...	...
80 +	3 231	1 248	1 983	...	...	...	...	...	...
New Zealand - Nouvelle-Zélande[82]									
1 VII 2009 (ESDJ)									
Total	4 315 800	2 117 500	2 198 300	3 717 100[83]	1 810 200[83]	1 906 800[83]	597 900[83]	306 700[83]	291 200[83]
0 - 4	305 510	156 900	148 610	264 450[83]	135 960[83]	128 500[83]	41 050[83]	20 940[83]	20 100[83]
5 - 9	288 150	147 410	140 740	245 580[83]	125 640[83]	119 940[83]	42 560[83]	21 760[83]	20 800[83]
10 - 14	297 550	152 590	144 960	250 300[83]	128 170[83]	122 130[83]	47 230[83]	24 400[83]	22 820[83]
15 - 19	323 190	165 310	157 880	280 720[83]	142 640[83]	138 080[83]	42 460[83]	22 660[83]	19 800[83]
20 - 24	304 290	154 930	149 360	277 010[83]	139 730[83]	137 280[83]	27 240[83]	15 170[83]	12 070[83]
25 - 29	280 640	138 640	141 990	256 260[83]	126 230[83]	130 020[83]	24 340[83]	12 390[83]	11 960[83]
30 - 34	268 750	128 810	139 930	239 070[83]	114 230[83]	124 840[83]	29 620[83]	14 540[83]	15 080[83]
35 - 39	307 730	146 210	161 510	266 940[83]	126 510[83]	140 430[83]	40 730[83]	19 670[83]	21 070[83]
40 - 44	312 060	149 940	162 120	265 370[83]	127 140[83]	138 230[83]	46 640[83]	22 770[83]	23 870[83]
45 - 49	322 740	156 550	166 190	270 430[83]	130 350[83]	140 080[83]	52 230[83]	26 150[83]	26 080[83]
50 - 54	283 970	139 200	144 770	235 080[83]	114 180[83]	120 900[83]	48 780[83]	24 960[83]	23 820[83]
55 - 59	247 330	121 650	125 690	203 770[83]	99 050[83]	104 720[83]	43 470[83]	22 530[83]	20 940[83]
60 - 64	221 260	108 780	112 480	182 350[83]	88 470[83]	93 880[83]	38 800[83]	20 240[83]	18 560[83]
65 - 69	171 670	83 830	87 840	142 600[83]	68 320[83]	74 280[83]	28 990[83]	15 450[83]	13 540[83]
70 - 74	130 230	62 230	68 000	110 960[83]	51 730[83]	59 230[83]	19 230[83]	10 470[83]	8 760[83]
75 - 79	104 790	48 320	56 470	92 410[83]	41 610[83]	50 810[83]	12 350[83]	6 700[83]	5 650[83]
80 - 84	79 320	33 930	45 390	71 910[83]	30 020[83]	41 900[83]	7 400[83]	3 900[83]	3 490[83]
85 +	66 610	22 260	44 350	61 830[83]	20 240[83]	41 590[83]	4 780[83]	2 030[83]	2 750[83]
Niue - Nioué									
1 VII 2006 (ESDJ)									
Total	1 679	815	864	...	...	...	...	...	...
0 - 4	137	58	79	...	...	...	...	...	...
5 - 9	136	65	71	...	...	...	...	...	...
10 - 14	145	77	68	...	...	...	...	...	...
15 - 19	175	96	79	...	...	...	...	...	...
20 - 24	137	56	81	...	...	...	...	...	...
25 - 29	103	53	50	...	...	...	...	...	...
30 - 34	97	49	48	...	...	...	...	...	...
35 - 39	96	50	46	...	...	...	...	...	...
40 - 44	101	50	51	...	...	...	...	...	...
45 - 49	104	60	44	...	...	...	...	...	...
50 - 54	121	60	61	...	...	...	...	...	...
55 - 59	67	27	40	...	...	...	...	...	...
60 - 64	61	30	31	...	...	...	...	...	...
65 - 69	82	32	50	...	...	...	...	...	...
70 - 74	62	30	32	...	...	...	...	...	...
75 +	55	22	33	...	...	...	...	...	...
Norfolk Island - Île Norfolk									
8 VIII 2006 (CDFC)									
Total	2 523	1 218	1 305	...	...	...	...	...	...
0 - 4	116	60	56	...	...	...	...	...	...
5 - 9	127	67	60	...	...	...	...	...	...

7. Population by age, sex and urban/rural residence: latest available year, 2000 - 2009

Population selon l'âge, le sexe et la résidence, urbaine/rurale : dernière année disponible, 2000 - 2009 (continued - suite)

Continent, country or area, date, code and age (in years) / Continent, pays ou zone, date, code et âge (en années)	Total			Urban - Urbaine			Rural - Rurale		
	Both sexes Les deux sexes	Male Masculin	Female Féminin	Both sexes Les deux sexes	Male Masculin	Female Féminin	Both sexes Les deux sexes	Male Masculin	Female Féminin
OCEANIA - OCÉANIE									
Norfolk Island - Île Norfolk									
8 VIII 2006 (CDFC)									
10 - 14	116	58	58	...	...	...	...	...	...
15 - 19	78	34	44	...	...	...	...	...	...
20 - 24	64	22	42	...	...	...	...	...	...
25 - 29	96	48	48	...	...	...	...	...	...
30 - 34	140	70	70	...	...	...	...	...	...
35 - 39	156	78	78	...	...	...	...	...	...
40 - 44	170	86	84	...	...	...	...	...	...
45 - 49	194	95	99	...	...	...	...	...	...
50 - 54	212	95	117	...	...	...	...	...	...
55 - 59	255	126	129	...	...	...	...	...	...
60 - 64	222	109	113	...	...	...	...	...	...
65 - 69	184	81	103	...	...	...	...	...	...
70 +	377	182	195	...	...	...	...	...	...
Unknown - Inconnu	16	7	9	...	...	...	...	...	...
Northern Mariana Islands - Îles Mariannes septentrionales									
1 VII 2003 (ESDF)[84]									
Total	63 419	27 488	35 931	56 941	24 932	32 009	6 478	2 556	3 922
0 - 4	4 555	2 498	2 057	4 230	2 285	1 945	325	213	112
5 - 9	5 534	2 836	2 698	5 212	2 656	2 556	322	180	142
10 - 14	4 586	2 362	2 224	4 322	2 216	2 106	264	145	119
15 - 19	3 825	1 848	1 977	3 538	1 684	1 854	287	165	122
20 - 24	7 253	1 671	5 582	6 101	1 492	4 609	1 152	179	973
25 - 29	8 449	2 405	6 044	7 055	2 026	5 029	1 394	379	1 015
30 - 34	8 085	2 900	5 185	7 168	2 597	4 571	917	303	614
35 - 39	6 330	3 033	3 297	5 928	2 834	3 094	402	199	203
40 - 44	5 117	2 615	2 502	4 547	2 320	2 227	569	294	275
45 - 49	4 105	2 270	1 835	3 815	2 102	1 713	290	168	122
50 - 54	2 263	1 240	1 023	1 995	1 107	888	268	133	135
55 - 59	1 505	729	776	1 339	623	716	166	106	60
60 - 64	886	616	270	804	564	240	82	52	30
65 - 69	370	246	124	333	209	124	38	38	-
70 - 74	329	95	234	327	93	234	2	2	-
75 +	227	124	103	227	124	103	-	-	-
1 VII 2008* (ESDF)									
Total	86 616	37 078	49 538	...	...	...	...	...	...
0 - 4	6 189	3 217	2 972	...	...	...	...	...	...
5 - 9	4 659	2 476	2 183	...	...	...	...	...	...
10 - 14	5 088	2 649	2 439	...	...	...	...	...	...
15 - 19	6 040	2 630	3 410	...	...	...	...	...	...
20 - 24	8 628	2 342	6 286	...	...	...	...	...	...
25 - 29	12 965	3 441	9 524	...	...	...	...	...	...
30 - 34	12 342	4 485	7 857	...	...	...	...	...	...
35 - 39	10 053	4 429	5 624	...	...	...	...	...	...
40 - 44	6 373	3 294	3 079	...	...	...	...	...	...
45 - 49	4 934	2 823	2 111	...	...	...	...	...	...
50 - 54	3 953	2 238	1 715	...	...	...	...	...	...
55 - 59	2 506	1 468	1 038	...	...	...	...	...	...
60 - 64	1 447	846	601	...	...	...	...	...	...
65 - 69	689	411	278	...	...	...	...	...	...
70 - 74	404	196	208	...	...	...	...	...	...
75 - 79	205	82	123	...	...	...	...	...	...
80 +	141	51	90	...	...	...	...	...	...
Palau - Palaos									
1 IV 2005 (CDJC)									
Total	19 907	10 699	9 208	...	...	...	...	...	...
0 - 4	1 363	685	678	...	...	...	...	...	...
5 - 9	1 521	805	716	...	...	...	...	...	...
10 - 14	1 914	964	950	...	...	...	...	...	...
15 - 19	1 462	715	747	...	...	...	...	...	...
20 - 24	1 266	712	554	...	...	...	...	...	...
25 - 29	1 583	942	641	...	...	...	...	...	...

Continent, country or area, date, code and age (in years) / Continent, pays ou zone, date, code et âge (en années)	Total			Urban - Urbaine			Rural - Rurale		
	Both sexes Les deux sexes	Male Masculin	Female Féminin	Both sexes Les deux sexes	Male Masculin	Female Féminin	Both sexes Les deux sexes	Male Masculin	Female Féminin
OCEANIA - OCÉANIE									
Palau - Palaos									
1 IV 2005 (CDJC)									
30 - 34	1 856	1 072	784	...	...	...	...	...	...
35 - 39	1 965	1 132	833	...	...	...	...	...	...
40 - 44	1 887	1 096	791	...	...	...	...	...	...
45 - 49	1 534	842	692	...	...	...	...	...	...
50 - 54	1 182	624	558	...	...	...	...	...	...
55 - 59	732	393	339	...	...	...	...	...	...
60 - 64	506	254	252	...	...	...	...	...	...
65 - 69	373	170	203	...	...	...	...	...	...
70 - 74	257	119	138	...	...	...	...	...	...
75 - 79	214	71	143	...	...	...	...	...	...
80 - 84	151	56	95	...	...	...	...	...	...
85 +	141	47	94	...	...	...	...	...	...
Papua New Guinea - Papouasie-Nouvelle-Guinée									
9 VII 2000 (CDFC)									
Total	5 190 786	2 691 744	2 499 042	686 301	372 453	313 848	4 504 485	2 319 291	2 185 194
0	125 718	65 539	60 179	16 930	8 991	7 939	108 788	56 548	52 240
1 - 4	600 962	312 237	288 725	71 219	37 178	34 041	529 743	275 059	254 684
5 - 9	727 370	381 339	346 031	86 078	45 216	40 862	641 292	336 123	305 169
10 - 14	620 874	330 965	289 909	75 022	39 374	35 648	545 852	291 591	254 261
15 - 19	554 481	293 277	261 204	78 912	41 679	37 233	475 569	251 598	223 971
20 - 24	474 801	239 863	234 938	79 915	43 166	36 749	394 886	196 697	198 189
25 - 29	448 414	219 680	228 734	70 866	37 802	33 064	377 548	181 878	195 670
30 - 34	384 260	191 662	192 598	57 156	30 983	26 173	327 104	160 679	166 425
35 - 39	330 337	166 656	163 681	48 585	26 512	22 073	281 752	140 144	141 608
40 - 44	252 368	128 910	123 458	36 195	20 956	15 239	216 173	107 954	108 219
45 - 49	198 757	104 867	93 890	25 337	15 595	9 742	173 420	89 272	84 148
50 - 54	151 013	79 899	71 114	16 428	10 414	6 014	134 585	69 485	65 100
55 - 59	108 708	59 308	49 400	9 692	6 131	3 561	99 016	53 177	45 839
60 - 64	89 503	48 530	40 973	6 723	4 247	2 476	82 780	44 283	38 497
65 - 69	57 221	31 351	25 870	3 641	2 141	1 500	53 580	29 210	24 370
70 - 74	35 134	19 657	15 477	1 930	1 105	825	33 204	18 552	14 652
75 - 79	16 864	9 782	7 082	880	498	382	15 984	9 284	6 700
80 - 84	8 669	5 041	3 628	489	295	194	8 180	4 746	3 434
85 - 89	3 315	1 984	1 331	176	99	77	3 139	1 885	1 254
90 +	2 017	1 197	820	127	71	56	1 890	1 126	764
Pitcairn									
31 XII 2008 (ESDF)									
Total	58	30	28	...	...	...	...	...	...
0	1	-	1	...	...	...	...	...	...
1 - 4	2	1	1	...	...	...	...	...	...
5 - 9	4	2	2	...	...	...	...	...	...
10 - 14	2	2	-	...	...	...	...	...	...
15 - 19	1	-	1	...	...	...	...	...	...
20 - 24	2	2	-	...	...	...	...	...	...
25 - 29	1	-	1	...	...	...	...	...	...
30 - 34	3	2	1	...	...	...	...	...	...
35 - 39	4	1	3	...	...	...	...	...	...
40 - 44	3	3	-	...	...	...	...	...	...
45 - 49	8	4	4	...	...	...	...	...	...
50 - 54	7	6	1	...	...	...	...	...	...
55 - 59	6	2	4	...	...	...	...	...	...
60 - 64	2	-	2	...	...	...	...	...	...
65 - 69	3	-	3	...	...	...	...	...	...
70 - 74	3	2	1	...	...	...	...	...	...
75 - 79	1	1	-	...	...	...	...	...	...
80 - 84	3	1	2	...	...	...	...	...	...
85 +	1	-	1	...	...	...	...	...	...
Unknown - Inconnu	1	1	-	...	...	...	...	...	...
Samoa									
5 XI 2006 (CDFC)									
Total	180 741	93 677	87 064	...	...	...	...	...	...
0 - 4	24 737	12 893	11 844	...	...	...	...	...	...

7. Population by age, sex and urban/rural residence: latest available year, 2000 - 2009
Population selon l'âge, le sexe et la résidence, urbaine/rurale : dernière année disponible, 2000 - 2009 (continued - suite)

Continent, country or area, date, code and age (in years) / Continent, pays ou zone, date, code et âge (en années)	Total			Urban - Urbaine			Rural - Rurale		
	Both sexes Les deux sexes	Male Masculin	Female Féminin	Both sexes Les deux sexes	Male Masculin	Female Féminin	Both sexes Les deux sexes	Male Masculin	Female Féminin
OCEANIA - OCÉANIE									
Samoa									
5 XI 2006 (CDFC)									
5 - 9	23 547	12 321	11 226	...	...	...	...	...	...
10 - 14	22 653	11 810	10 843	...	...	...	...	...	...
15 - 19	17 945	9 457	8 488	...	...	...	...	...	...
20 - 24	14 057	7 456	6 601	...	...	...	...	...	...
25 - 29	12 494	6 478	6 016	...	...	...	...	...	...
30 - 34	11 870	6 146	5 724	...	...	...	...	...	...
35 - 39	11 319	6 017	5 302	...	...	...	...	...	...
40 - 44	9 724	5 029	4 695	...	...	...	...	...	...
45 - 49	8 249	4 307	3 942	...	...	...	...	...	...
50 - 54	6 711	3 423	3 288	...	...	...	...	...	...
55 - 59	4 819	2 485	2 334	...	...	...	...	...	...
60 - 64	3 811	1 868	1 943	...	...	...	...	...	...
65 - 69	3 270	1 575	1 695	...	...	...	...	...	...
70 - 74	2 346	1 109	1 237	...	...	...	...	...	...
75 +	3 131	1 256	1 875	...	...	...	...	...	...
Unknown - Inconnu	58	47	11	...	...	...	...	...	...
Solomon Islands - Îles Salomon[2]									
1 VII 2009 (ESDF)									
Total	518 321	267 704	250 617	...	...	...	...	...	...
0 - 4	71 158	37 125	34 033	...	...	...	...	...	...
5 - 9	67 612	35 327	32 285	...	...	...	...	...	...
10 - 14	61 702	32 194	29 508	...	...	...	...	...	...
15 - 19	53 425	27 869	25 556	...	...	...	...	...	...
20 - 24	50 403	26 300	24 103	...	...	...	...	...	...
25 - 29	44 184	22 734	21 450	...	...	...	...	...	...
30 - 34	38 611	19 347	19 264	...	...	...	...	...	...
35 - 39	33 455	16 811	16 644	...	...	...	...	...	...
40 - 44	24 717	12 582	12 135	...	...	...	...	...	...
45 - 49	20 106	10 266	9 840	...	...	...	...	...	...
50 - 54	14 685	7 611	7 074	...	...	...	...	...	...
55 - 59	12 157	6 206	5 951	...	...	...	...	...	...
60 - 64	9 182	4 586	4 596	...	...	...	...	...	...
65 +	16 924	8 746	8 178	...	...	...	...	...	...
Tokelau - Tokélaou									
19 X 2006 (CDFC)									
Total	1 151	583	568	...	...	...	...	...	...
0 - 4	123	63	60	...	...	...	...	...	...
5 - 9	143	66	77	...	...	...	...	...	...
10 - 14	155	86	69	...	...	...	...	...	...
15 - 19	115	69	46	...	...	...	...	...	...
20 - 24	66	31	35	...	...	...	...	...	...
25 - 29	52	30	22	...	...	...	...	...	...
30 - 34	65	29	36	...	...	...	...	...	...
35 - 39	72	36	36	...	...	...	...	...	...
40 - 44	69	34	35	...	...	...	...	...	...
45 - 49	67	31	36	...	...	...	...	...	...
50 - 54	48	26	22	...	...	...	...	...	...
55 - 59	46	21	25	...	...	...	...	...	...
60 - 64	36	22	14	...	...	...	...	...	...
65 - 69	33	12	21	...	...	...	...	...	...
70 - 74	23	10	13	...	...	...	...	...	...
75 +	38	17	21	...	...	...	...	...	...
Tonga									
30 XI 2006 (CDJC)									
Total	101 991	51 772	50 219	23 658	11 860	11 798	78 333	39 912	38 421
0 - 4	13 782	7 174	6 608	3 015	1 514	1 501	10 767	5 660	5 107
5 - 9	12 804	6 745	6 059	2 721	1 447	1 274	10 083	5 298	4 785
10 - 14	12 320	6 412	5 908	2 631	1 357	1 274	9 689	5 055	4 634
15 - 19	10 280	5 383	4 897	2 362	1 196	1 166	7 918	4 187	3 731
20 - 24	9 191	4 648	4 543	2 503	1 276	1 227	6 688	3 372	3 316
25 - 29	7 304	3 639	3 665	1 872	913	959	5 432	2 726	2 706
30 - 34	6 337	3 146	3 191	1 551	787	764	4 786	2 359	2 427

Continent, country or area, date, code and age (in years) / Continent, pays ou zone, date, code et âge (en années)	Total			Urban - Urbaine			Rural - Rurale		
	Both sexes Les deux sexes	Male Masculin	Female Féminin	Both sexes Les deux sexes	Male Masculin	Female Féminin	Both sexes Les deux sexes	Male Masculin	Female Féminin
OCEANIA - OCÉANIE									
Tonga									
30 XI 2006 (CDJC)									
35 - 39	6 229	3 112	3 117	1 448	711	737	4 781	2 401	2 380
40 - 44	5 014	2 578	2 436	1 240	647	593	3 774	1 931	1 843
45 - 49	3 982	1 923	2 059	982	458	524	3 000	1 465	1 535
50 - 54	3 465	1 634	1 831	844	406	438	2 621	1 228	1 393
55 - 59	2 849	1 359	1 490	639	323	316	2 210	1 036	1 174
60 - 64	2 470	1 169	1 301	556	260	296	1 914	909	1 005
65 - 69	2 174	1 092	1 082	466	211	255	1 708	881	827
70 - 74	1 586	777	809	340	152	188	1 246	625	621
75 - 79	1 099	510	589	253	107	146	846	403	443
80 - 84	625	260	365	144	48	96	481	212	269
85 - 89	246	96	150	45	21	24	201	75	126
90 - 94	86	22	64	15	5	10	71	17	54
95 - 99	20	6	14	5	2	3	15	4	11
100 +	6	-	6	-	-	-	6	-	6
Unknown - Inconnu	122	87	35	26	19	7	96	68	28
1 VII 2008 (ESDF)[85]									
Total	103 647	52 972	50 673	...	...	...	...	...	...
0 - 4	11 970	6 164	5 806	...	...	...	...	...	...
5 - 9	11 419	5 910	5 508	...	...	...	...	...	...
10 - 14	11 968	6 212	5 756	...	...	...	...	...	...
15 - 19	11 383	6 060	5 323	...	...	...	...	...	...
20 - 24	10 612	5 573	5 040	...	...	...	...	...	...
25 - 29	8 609	4 406	4 204	...	...	...	...	...	...
30 - 34	5 874	2 955	2 919	...	...	...	...	...	...
35 - 39	5 397	2 718	2 680	...	...	...	...	...	...
40 - 44	5 250	2 661	2 590	...	...	...	...	...	...
45 - 49	4 471	2 186	2 285	...	...	...	...	...	...
50 - 54	3 914	1 867	2 047	...	...	...	...	...	...
55 - 59	3 294	1 556	1 737	...	...	...	...	...	...
60 - 64	2 844	1 355	1 489	...	...	...	...	...	...
65 - 69	2 482	1 243	1 239	...	...	...	...	...	...
70 - 74	1 896	981	915	...	...	...	...	...	...
75 +	2 263	1 127	1 136	...	...	...	...	...	...
Tuvalu									
1 XI 2002 (CDFC)									
Total	9 561	4 729	4 832	...	...	...	...	...	...
0	182	92	90	...	...	...	...	...	...
1 - 4	996	528	468	...	...	...	...	...	...
5 - 9	1 201	612	589	...	...	...	...	...	...
10 - 14	1 079	591	488	...	...	...	...	...	...
15 - 19	826	474	352	...	...	...	...	...	...
20 - 24	682	326	356	...	...	...	...	...	...
25 - 29	523	245	278	...	...	...	...	...	...
30 - 34	545	278	267	...	...	...	...	...	...
35 - 39	684	331	353	...	...	...	...	...	...
40 - 44	697	310	387	...	...	...	...	...	...
45 - 49	580	261	319	...	...	...	...	...	...
50 - 54	467	199	268	...	...	...	...	...	...
55 - 59	276	129	147	...	...	...	...	...	...
60 - 64	280	131	149	...	...	...	...	...	...
65 - 69	207	84	123	...	...	...	...	...	...
70 - 74	167	75	92	...	...	...	...	...	...
75 - 79	101	40	61	...	...	...	...	...	...
80 - 84	56	20	36	...	...	...	...	...	...
85 - 89	10	1	9	...	...	...	...	...	...
90 +	2	2	-	...	...	...	...	...	...
Vanuatu[86]									
1 VII 2004 (ESDF)									
Total	215 541	110 141	105 399	...	...	...	...	...	...
0 - 4	33 815	17 435	16 380	...	...	...	...	...	...
5 - 9	27 846	14 474	13 372	...	...	...	...	...	...
10 - 14	27 125	14 025	13 100	...	...	...	...	...	...
15 - 19	23 437	12 132	11 305	...	...	...	...	...	...

Continent, country or area, date, code and age (in years) Continent, pays ou zone, date, code et âge (en années)	Total			Urban - Urbaine			Rural - Rurale		
	Both sexes Les deux sexes	Male Masculin	Female Féminin	Both sexes Les deux sexes	Male Masculin	Female Féminin	Both sexes Les deux sexes	Male Masculin	Female Féminin
OCEANIA - OCÉANIE									
Vanuatu[86]									
1 VII 2004 (ESDF)									
20 - 24	*18 951*	*9 684*	*9 267*	...	...	...	...	...	...
25 - 29	*16 235*	*8 027*	*8 207*	...	...	...	...	...	...
30 - 34	*14 670*	*7 175*	*7 494*	...	...	...	...	...	...
35 - 39	*12 560*	*6 214*	*6 346*	...	...	...	...	...	...
40 - 44	*10 429*	*5 221*	*5 208*	...	...	...	...	...	...
45 - 49	*8 303*	*4 221*	*4 082*	...	...	...	...	...	...
50 - 54	*6 476*	*3 333*	*3 143*	...	...	...	...	...	...
55 - 59	*5 083*	*2 632*	*2 452*	...	...	...	...	...	...
60 - 64	*3 824*	*1 996*	*1 828*	...	...	...	...	...	...
65 - 69	*2 714*	*1 417*	*1 296*	...	...	...	...	...	...
70 - 74	*1 810*	*957*	*854*	...	...	...	...	...	...
75 +	*2 265*	*1 198*	*1 066*	...	...	...	...	...	...

FOOTNOTES - NOTES

Italics: estimates which are less reliable. - Italiques : estimations moins sûres.

* Provisional. - Données provisoires.

'Code' indicates the source of data, as follows:
CDFC - Census, de facto, complete tabulation
CDFS - Census, de facto, sample tabulation
CDJC - Census, de jure, complete tabulation
CDJS - Census, de jure, sample tabulation
SSDF - Sample survey, de facto
SSDJ - Sample survey, de jure
ESDF - Estimates, de facto
ESDJ - Estimates, de jure

Le 'Code' indique la source des données, comme suit :
CDFC - Recensement, population de fait, tabulation complète
CDFS - Recensement, population de fait, tabulation par sondage
CDJC - Recensement, population de droit, tabulation complète
CDJS - Recensement, population de droit, tabulation par sondage
SSDF - Enquête par sondage, population de fait
SSDJ - Enquête par sondage, population de droit
ESDF - Estimations, population de fait
ESDJ - Estimations, population de droit

[1] Data refer to population in housing units and collective living quarters only. - Correspond aux personnes qui vivent dans des unités d'habitation et dans des logements collectifs seulement.
[2] Data refer to national projections. - Les données se réfèrent aux projections nationales.
[3] Data refer to national projections. Data as reported by national statistical authorities. Figures for urban and rural do not add up to the total. - Les données se réfèrent aux projections nationales. Les données comme elles ont été déclarées par l'institut national de la statistique. La somme des données pour la residence urbaine et rurale n'est pas égale au total.
[4] As reported by the country. Reasons for discrepancy with other tables not ascertained. - Données comme déclarées par le pays. On ne sait pas comment s'explique la divergence entre ces chiffres et les chiffres correspondants indiqués ailleurs.
[5] Excludes the islands of St. Brandon and Agalega. - Non compris les îles St. Brandon et Agalega.
[6] Based on 2000 Population Census data and adjusted for underenumeration of young children. - D'après le recensement de la population de 2000, ajusté en raison du sous-enregistrement des jeunes enfants.
[7] The number of males and/or females excludes persons whose sex is not stated (18 urban, 19 rural). - Il n'est pas tenu compte dans le nombre d'hommes et de femmes des personnes dont le sexe n'est pas indiqué (18 en zone urbaine et 19 en zone rurale).

[8] Data based on 2008 Population Census. - Données fondées sur le recensement de population de 2008.
[9] Data computed by the UN Statistics Division based on the percentage distribution of population by age and sex, as reported in the census report. - Les données ont été calculées par la Division des statistiques des Nations Unies sur la base de la répartition en pourcentage de la population par âge et par sexe, compte tenu des résultats du recensement.
[10] Mid-year estimates have been adjusted for underenumeration at latest census. - Les estimations au milieu de l'année tiennent compte d'un ajustement destiné à compenser les lacunes du dénombrement lors du dernier recensement.
[11] Excluding persons who were not contacted at the time of the census. - La population non comprend pas les personnes qui n'ont pas été contactées à l'heure du recensement.
[12] Because of rounding, totals are not in all cases the sum of the parts. - Les chiffres étant arrondis, les totaux ne correspondent pas toujours rigoureusement à la somme des chiffres partiels.
[13] Data as reported by national statistical authorities. Summation of frequencies gives a different total; reason for discrepancy not ascertained. - Les données comme elles ont été déclarées par l'institut national de la statistique. La somme des fréquences un total différent; on ne sait pas comment s'explique la divergence.
[14] Updated postcensal estimates. Estimates adjusted for census net undercoverage (including adjustment for incompletely enumerated Indian reserves). - Estimations post censitaires mises à jour. Ajusté pour la sous-estimation du recensement (y compris les réservations en Inde incomplètement énumérées).
[15] Result of Household Multiple Purpose Survey. - Les chiffres résultent d'enquêtes sur les ménages polyvalentes.
[16] Data refer to average population; in some cases the sum of the parts is not equal to the total. - Correspond à la population moyenne; dans certains cas, la somme des différentes parties ne correspond pas au total.
[17] Estimates based on 2007 Population Census. - Estimations fondées sur le recensement de la population de 2007.
[18] Population statistics are compiled from registers. - Les statistiques de la population sont compilées à partir des registres.
[19] Excluding data for Saint Barthélémy and Saint Martin. - Non compris les données pour Saint Barthélémy et Saint Martin.
[20] The total in this table is not equal to the 2005 population estimate in table 5 because this dataset of population by age, sex and urban/rural residence has not been revised. - Le total dans ce tableau n'est pas égal à l'estimation de la population pour 2005 dans le tableau 5, parce que cet ensemble de données selon l'âge, le sexe et la résidence, urbaine/rurale n'a pas été révisé.
[21] Projections produced by l'Institut Haïtien de Statistique et d'Informatique (IHSI) and the Latin American and Caribbean Demographic Centre (CELADE) - Population Division of ECLAC. - Les données sont projections produits par l'Institut Haïtien de Statistique et d'Informatique (IHSI) et le centre démographique de l'Amérique latine et les Caraïbes - Division de la population de la CEPALC.

22 Data are based on projections of the 2001 Population and Housing Census data. - Les données sont basées sur les projections du recensement de 2001 de la population et de l'habitat.

23 Urban and rural distribution derived from census count, held constant and applied to current estimates. - La répartition urbain/rural se réfère aux chiffres du recensement, maintenus constants et appliqués aux estimations actuelles.

24 Includes estimates for St. Eustatius. - Y compris les estimations pour St. Eustatius.

25 Data refer to projections based on the 2000 population census. - Les données se réfèrent aux projections basées sur le recensement de la population de 2000.

26 Including armed forces stationed in the area. - Y compris les militaires en garnison sur le territoire.

27 Based on the results of the 2000 population census. - Basé sur les résultats du recensement de la population de 2000.

28 Excluding armed forces overseas and civilian citizens absent from country for an extended period of time. - Non compris les militaires à l'étranger, et les civils hors du pays pendant une période prolongée.

29 Data include persons in remote areas, military personnel outside the country, merchant seamen at sea, civilian seasonal workers outside the country, and other civilians outside the country, and exclude nomads, foreign military, civilian aliens temporarily in the country, transients on ships and Indian jungle population. - Y compris les personnes vivant dans des régions éloignées, le personnel militaire en dehors du pays, les marins marchands, les ouvriers saisonniers en dehors du pays, et autres civils en dehors du pays, et non compris les nomades, les militaires étrangers, les étrangers civils temporairement dans le pays, les transiteurs sur des bateaux et les Indiens de la jungle.

30 Data based on the Population Census of 2005. - Données fondées sur le recensement de la population de 2005.

31 Data refer to national projections. Excluding nomadic Indian tribes. - Les données se réfèrent aux projections nationales. Non compris les tribus d'Indiens nomades.

32 A dispute exists between the governments of Argentina and the United Kingdom of Great Britain and Northern Ireland concerning sovereignty over the Falkland Islands (Malvinas). - La souveraineté sur les îles Falkland (Malvinas) fait l'objet d'un différend entre le Gouvernement argentin et le Gouvernement du Royaume-Uni de Grande-Bretagne et d'Irlande du Nord.

33 Data are based on projections from 2002 Census. - Données fondées sur des projections tirées du recensement de 2002.

34 Totals may not add up because cases with age unknown and/or sex unknown have been prorated. - Les totaux peuvent ne pas tomber juste du fait que l'on a calculé au prorata les cas pour lesquels l'âge ou le sexe n'était pas connu.

35 The districts of Paramaribo and Wanica are considered urban areas, whereas all other districts are considered more or less rural areas. - Les districts de Paramaribo et de Wanica sont considérés comme des zones urbaines, les autres districts étant considérés comme des zones rurales à divers degrés.

36 The unknown age and sex is proportionately distributed over all age groups and both sexes. - La répartition d'âge ou de sexe inconnu est répartie proportionnellement dans tous les groupes d'âge et dans chaque sexe.

37 The adjusted total population of the country is 25.5 million. Data refer to the settled population based on the 1979 Population Census and the latest household prelisting. The refugees of Afghanistan in Iran, Pakistan, and an estimated 1.5 million nomads, are not included. - La population totale ajustée du pays comprend 25,5 millions de personnes. Les données se rapportent à la population stationnaire sur la base du recensement de 1979 et du recensement préliminaire des logements le plus récent. Sont exclus les réfugiés d'Afghanistan en Iran et au Pakistan et les nomades estimés à 1,5 million.

38 Intercensal estimates. Because of rounding, totals are not in all cases the sum of the parts. - Estimations inter-censitaires. Les chiffres étant arrondis, les totaux ne correspondent pas toujours rigoureusement à la somme des chiffres partiels.

39 Data have not been adjusted for underenumeration, estimated at 4.96 per cent. - Les données n'ont pas été ajustées pour compenser les lacunes du dénombrement, estimées à 4,96 p.100.

40 Data refer to projections based on the 2005 population census. - Les données se réfèrent aux projections basées sur le recensement de la population de 2005.

41 Excluding foreign diplomatic personnel and their dependants. - Non compris le personnel diplomatique étranger et les membres de leur famille les accompagnant.

42 For statistical purposes, the data for China do not include those for the Hong Kong Special Administrative Region (Hong Kong SAR), Macao Special Administrative Region (Macao SAR) and Taiwan province of China. - Pour la présentation des statistiques, les données pour la Chine ne comprennent pas la Région Administrative Spéciale de Hong Kong (Hong Kong RAS), la Région Administrative Spéciale de Macao (Macao RAS) et Taïwan province de Chine.

43 Data refer to government controlled areas. - Les données se rapportent aux zones contrôlées par le Gouvernement.

44 Including data for the Indian-held part of Jammu and Kashmir, the final status of which has not yet been determined. Excluding Mao-Maram, Paomata and Purul sub-divisions of Senapati district of Manipur. The population of Manipur including the estimated population of the three sub-divisions of Senapati district is 2,291,125 (Males 1,161,173 and females 1,129,952). - Y compris les données pour la partie du Jammu et du Cachemire occupée par l'Inde dont le statut définitif n'a pas encore été déterminé. Non compris les subdivisions Mao-Maram Paomata et Purul du district de Senapati dans l'État du Manipur. Cet État compte 2 291 125 habitants (1 161 173 hommes et 1 129 952 femmes), y compris la population estimative des trois subdivisions du district de Senapati.

45 Data refer to the "Intercensal Population Survey". Excluding Province Nanggroe Aceh Darussalam, Regency Nias & Nias Selatan, Regency Boven Digul & Teluk Wondama. - Les données concernent l'enquête intercensitaire sur la population. En excluant les provinces de Nanggroe Aceh Darussalam, Regency Nias & Nias Selatan, Regency Boven Digul & Teluk Wondama.

46 Differences between the total country figures and sum of urban and rural areas are due to the inclusion of unsettled population numbering 104 717 (53 065 males and females 51 652). - Les différences entre les chiffres pour l'ensemble du pays et la somme des zones urbaines et rurales s'expliquent par l'inclusion de la population non sédentaire, dont l'effectif est de 104 717 (53 065 de sexe masculin et 51 652 de sexe féminin).

47 Including data for East Jerusalem and Israeli residents in certain other territories under occupation by Israeli military forces since June 1967. - Y compris les données pour Jérusalem-Est et les résidents israéliens dans certains autres territoires occupés depuis 1967 par les forces armées israéliennes.

48 Excluding diplomatic personnel outside the country and foreign military and civilian personnel and their dependants stationed in the area. - Non compris le personnel diplomatique hors du pays ni les militaires et agents civils étrangers en poste sur le territoire et les membres de leur famille les accompagnant.

49 Excluding data for Jordanian territory under occupation since June 1967 by Israeli military forces. Including registered Palestinian refugees and Jordanians abroad. - Non compris les données pour le territoire jordanien occupé depuis juin 1967 par les forces armées israéliennes. Y compris les réfugiés palestiniens enregistrés et les Jordaniens à l'étranger.

50 Excluding data for Jordanian territory under occupation since June 1967 by Israeli military forces. Excluding foreigners, including registered Palestinian refugees. - Non compris les données pour le territoire jordanien occupé depuis juin 1967 par les forces armées israéliennes. Non compris les étrangers, mais y compris les réfugiés de Palestine enregistrés.

51 Data refer to annual average of resident population. - Les données correspondent à la population résidente annuelle moyenne.

52 Excluding usual residents not in country at time of census. - À l'exclusion des résidents habituels qui ne sont pas dans le pays au moment du recensement.

53 Based on the results of the 2005 Population and Housing Census. Because of rounding, totals are not in all cases the sum of the parts. - Données fondées sur les résultats du recensement de la population et de l'habitat de 2005. Les chiffres étant arrondis, les totaux ne correspondent pas toujours rigoureusement à la somme des chiffres partiels.

54 Based on the results of a household survey. - D'après les résultats d'une enquête des ménages.

55 Total Population is taken as de facto and de jure together. - Population totale considérée comme de fait et de droit.

56 Excluding data for the Pakistan-held part of Jammu and Kashmir, the final status of which has not yet been determined. Based on the results of the Pakistan Demographic Survey (PDS 2007). - Non compris les données concernant la partie du Jammu et Cachemire occupée par le Pakistan dont le statut définitif n'a pas été déterminé. D'après les résultats de l'enquête démographique effectuée par le Pakistan en 2007.

57 Data are based on projections of the 2000 Population and Housing Census data. - Les données sont basées sur les projections du recensement de 2000 de la population et de l'habitat.

58 Excluding foreigners. - Non compris étrangers.

59 Data refer to resident population only. - Pour la population résidante seulement.

60 The Population and Housing Census 2001 did not cover the whole area of the country due to the security problems; data refer to the 18 districts for which the census was completed only (in three districts it was not possible to conduct the census at all and in four districts it was partially conducted). Unrevised data. - Le recensement de la population et du logement de 2001 n'a pas été réalisé sur la superficie totale du pays à cause de problèmes de sécurité; les données ne concernent que les 18 districts entièrement recensés (3 districts n'ont pas été recensés du tout, et 4 ont été recensés en partie). Les données n'ont pas été révisées.

61 Data for rural areas include data of estate sectors consist of all plantations which are 20 acres or more in extent and with ten or more resident labourers. - Les données pour les zones rurales comprennent celles pour les domaines, dont l'ensemble des plantations de plus de 10 hectares comptant au moins 10 travailleurs résidents.

62 Including Palestinian refugees. - Y compris les réfugiés de Palestine.

63 Data based on Address Based Population Registration System. - Les données sont basées sur le registre national de la population basé sur l'adresse.

64 As published by the United Nations Economic and Social Commission for Western Asia. - Publié par la Commission économique et sociale des Nations Unies pour l'Asie occidentale.

65 Totals may not match due to rounding. - Les totaux peuvent ne pas correspondre à la somme des chiffres, certains de ces derniers ayant été arrondis.

66 Excluding Faeroe Islands and Greenland shown separately, if available. Population statistics are compiled from registers. - Non compris les Iles Féroé et le Groenland, qui font l'objet de rubriques distinctes, si disponible. Les statistiques de la population sont compilées à partir des registres.

67 Population statistics are compiled from registers. Excluding Åland Islands. - Les statistiques de la population sont compilées à partir des registres. Non compris les Îles d'Åland.

68 Excluding diplomatic personnel outside the country and including members of alien armed forces not living in military camps and foreign diplomatic personnel not living in embassies or consulates. - Non compris le personnel diplomatique hors du pays et y compris les militaires étrangers ne vivant pas dans des camps militaires et le personnel diplomatique étranger ne vivant pas dans les ambassades ou les consulats.

69 Excluding families of military personnel, visitors and transients. - Non compris les familles des militaires, ni les visiteurs et transients.

70 Including armed forces stationed outside the country and alien armed forces in the area. - Y compris les militaires nationaux hors du pays et les militaires étrangers en garnison sur le territoire.

71 Excluding armed forces stationed outside the country, but including alien armed forces stationed in the area. - Non compris les militaires en garnison hors du pays, mais y compris les militaires étrangers en garnison sur le territoire.

72 Including civilian nationals temporarily outside the country. - Y compris les civils nationaux temporairement hors du pays.

73 Including residents temporarily outside the country. Excluding Svalbard and Jan Mayen Islands shown separately, if available. - Y compris les résidents se trouvant temporairement hors du pays. Non compris Svalbard et Jan Mayen qui font l'objet de rubriques distinctes, si disponible.

74 Excluding civilian aliens within country, but including civilian nationals temporarily outside country. - Non compris les civils étrangers dans le pays, mais y compris les civils nationaux temporairement hors du pays.

75 Excluding Transnistria and the municipality of Bender. - Les données ne tiennent pas compte de l'information sur la Transnistria et la municipalité de Bender.

76 Excluding data for Kosovo and Metohia. - Sans les données pour le Kosovo et Metohie.

77 Excluding transients visitors. - Non compris les visiteurs en transit.

78 Excluding Channel Islands (Guernsey and Jersey) and Isle of Man, shown separately, if available. - Non compris les îles Anglo-Normandes (Guernesey et Jersey) et l'île de Man, qui font l'objet de rubriques distinctes, si disponible.

79 Counts for the 2001 Census are taken from 'Key Statistics table 1 for the Urban/Rural classification: England and Wales' available on CD based on the usually resident population. - Les chiffres du recensement de 2001 proviennent du tableau intitulé « Key Statistics table 1 for the Urban/Rural classification: England and Wales » disponible sur CD-ROM et sont fondés sur la notion de résidence habituelle.

80 Intercensal estimates. Data are based on 2009 Australian Standard Geographical Classification boundaries. - Estimations inter-censitaires. Les données réfèrent au découpage de la nomenclature géographique normalisée d'Australie de 2009.

81 Excluding Niue, shown separately, which is part of Cook Islands, but because of remoteness is administered separately. - Non compris Nioué, qui fait l'objet d'une rubrique distincte et qui fait partie des îles Cook, mais qui, en raison de son éloignement, est administrée séparément.

82 Excluding diplomatic personnel and armed forces stationed outside country; also excluding alien armed forces within the country. Because of rounding, totals are not in all cases the sum of the parts. - Non compris le personnel diplomatique et les militaires hors du pays; non compris également les militaires étrangers en garnison dans le pays. Les chiffres étant arrondis, les totaux ne correspondent pas toujours rigoureusement à la somme des chiffres partiels.

83 Population estimates by urban/rural residence exclude inland waters and oceanic areas. - Les estimations de la population par lieu de résidence urbaine ou rurale excluent les eaux intérieures et les zones océaniques.

84 Based on the results of a sample survey. Data refer to the island of Saipan only. - D'après les résultats de l'enquête par sondage. Les données se réfèrent uniquement à l'île de Saipan.

85 Based on the results of the 1996 population census. Data refer to national projections. - À partir des résultats du recensement de la population de 1996. Les données se réfèrent aux projections nationales.

86 Data refer to national projections. Figures for male and female do not add up to the total, reason for discrepancy not ascertained. - Les données se réfèrent aux projections nationales. La some des données pour la population masculine et pour la population féminine n'est pas égale au total, les raisons de cette différence ne sont pas expliquées.

Continent, country or area, date, code and age (in years) / Continent, pays ou zone, date, code et âge (en années)	Total			Urban - Urbaine			Rural - Rurale		
	Both sexes Les deux sexes	Male Masculin	Female Féminin	Both sexes Les deux sexes	Male Masculin	Female Féminin	Both sexes Les deux sexes	Male Masculin	Female Féminin
AFRICA - AFRIQUE									
Benin - Bénin[1]									
1 VII 2010* (ESDF)									
Total	8 778 648	4 301 224	4 477 424	3 873 462	1 903 683	1 969 779	4 905 186	2 397 541	2 507 645
0 - 4	1 592 244	809 196	783 048	607 155	308 406	298 749	985 089	500 790	484 299
0	342 370	174 542	167 828	...	...	...	...	...	...
1 - 4	1 249 874	634 654	615 220	...	...	...	...	...	...
5 - 9	1 266 850	640 586	626 264	476 164	233 530	242 634	790 686	407 056	383 630
10 - 14	1 150 694	580 668	570 026	514 486	243 440	271 046	636 208	337 228	298 980
15 - 19	1 021 008	525 697	495 311	511 929	261 480	250 449	509 079	264 217	244 862
20 - 24	727 897	375 425	352 472	379 419	208 077	171 342	348 478	167 348	181 130
25 - 29	590 308	274 671	315 637	289 248	142 715	146 533	301 060	131 956	169 104
30 - 34	535 984	225 225	310 759	259 269	114 748	144 521	276 715	110 477	166 238
35 - 39	473 448	207 868	265 580	223 060	102 446	120 614	250 388	105 422	144 966
40 - 44	364 848	169 965	194 883	168 996	81 988	87 008	195 852	87 977	107 875
45 - 49	295 943	136 848	159 095	136 930	64 798	72 132	159 013	72 050	86 963
50 - 54	219 467	104 341	115 126	94 385	45 496	48 889	125 082	58 845	66 237
55 - 59	169 463	81 158	88 305	75 352	36 232	39 120	94 111	44 926	49 185
60 - 64	121 383	58 485	62 898	45 810	21 758	24 052	75 573	36 727	38 846
65 - 69	81 462	38 078	43 384	33 071	15 138	17 933	48 391	22 940	25 451
70 - 74	76 182	33 550	42 632	27 092	11 305	15 787	49 090	22 245	26 845
75 - 79	38 849	16 736	22 113	14 690	5 864	8 826	24 159	10 872	13 287
80 +	52 618	22 727	29 891	16 406	6 262	10 144	36 212	16 465	19 747
Cameroon - Cameroun[1]									
1 VII 2010* (ESDJ)									
Total	19 406 100	9 599 224	9 806 876	...	...	...	...	...	...
0 - 4	3 287 234	1 662 298	1 624 936	...	...	...	...	...	...
5 - 9	2 783 459	1 412 467	1 370 992	...	...	...	...	...	...
10 - 14	2 394 671	1 227 470	1 167 201	...	...	...	...	...	...
15 - 19	2 170 035	1 068 509	1 101 526	...	...	...	...	...	...
20 - 24	1 837 289	855 334	981 955	...	...	...	...	...	...
25 - 29	1 525 816	712 550	813 266	...	...	...	...	...	...
30 - 34	1 209 607	588 210	621 397	...	...	...	...	...	...
35 - 39	942 713	460 394	482 319	...	...	...	...	...	...
40 - 44	793 846	388 539	405 307	...	...	...	...	...	...
45 - 49	640 247	323 507	316 740	...	...	...	...	...	...
50 - 54	521 910	261 626	260 284	...	...	...	...	...	...
55 - 59	337 988	178 876	159 112	...	...	...	...	...	...
60 - 64	315 879	155 208	160 671	...	...	...	...	...	...
65 - 69	227 290	110 645	116 645	...	...	...	...	...	...
70 - 74	189 571	88 969	100 602	...	...	...	...	...	...
75 - 79	98 078	47 173	50 905	...	...	...	...	...	...
80 - 84	71 585	31 609	39 976	...	...	...	...	...	...
85 - 89	26 564	12 109	14 455	...	...	...	...	...	...
90 - 94	15 715	6 942	8 773	...	...	...	...	...	...
95 +	16 603	6 789	9 814	...	...	...	...	...	...
Cape Verde - Cap-Vert									
16 VI 2010* (CDJC)									
Total	491 575	243 315	248 260	...	...	...	...	...	...
0 - 4	50 198	25 122	25 076	...	...	...	...	...	...
5 - 9	50 204	25 167	25 037	...	...	...	...	...	...
10 - 14	55 219	27 862	27 357	...	...	...	...	...	...
15 - 19	59 055	29 655	29 400	...	...	...	...	...	...
20 - 24	52 886	27 309	25 577	...	...	...	...	...	...
25 - 29	44 311	23 310	21 001	...	...	...	...	...	...
30 - 34	34 484	18 147	16 337	...	...	...	...	...	...
35 - 39	27 225	14 097	13 128	...	...	...	...	...	...
40 - 44	26 290	12 988	13 302	...	...	...	...	...	...
45 - 49	23 510	11 348	12 162	...	...	...	...	...	...
50 - 54	18 158	8 160	9 998	...	...	...	...	...	...
55 - 59	12 142	4 946	7 196	...	...	...	...	...	...
60 - 64	6 190	2 610	3 580	...	...	...	...	...	...
65 - 69	6 215	2 499	3 716	...	...	...	...	...	...
70 - 74	8 666	3 437	5 229	...	...	...	...	...	...
75 - 79	7 433	2 979	4 454	...	...	...	...	...	...
80 - 84	5 276	2 092	3 184	...	...	...	...	...	...

7a. Population by age, sex and urban/rural residence: 2010
Population selon l'âge, le sexe et la résidence, urbaine/rurale: 2010 (continued suite)

Continent, country or area, date, code and age (in years) / Continent, pays ou zone, date, code et âge (en années)	Total			Urban - Urbaine			Rural - Rurale		
	Both sexes Les deux sexes	Male Masculin	Female Féminin	Both sexes Les deux sexes	Male Masculin	Female Féminin	Both sexes Les deux sexes	Male Masculin	Female Féminin
AFRICA - AFRIQUE									
Cape Verde - Cap-Vert									
16 VI 2010* (CDJC)									
85 - 89	2 185	827	1 358	...	...	...	...	...	...
90 +	1 570	549	1 021	...	...	...	...	...	...
Unknown - Inconnu	358	211	147	...	...	...	...	...	...
Egypt - Égypte									
1 VII 2010* (ESDF)									
Total	78 728 329	40 250 440	38 477 889	33 833 191	17 270 570	16 562 621	44 895 138	22 979 870	21 915 268
0	1 663 617	852 985	810 632	596 492	305 879	290 613	1 067 125	547 106	520 019
1 - 4	6 690 517	3 429 331	3 261 186	2 556 172	1 308 084	1 248 088	4 134 345	2 121 247	2 013 098
5 - 9	8 272 584	4 265 412	4 007 172	3 225 902	1 658 136	1 567 766	5 046 682	2 607 276	2 439 406
10 - 14	8 353 763	4 330 443	4 023 320	3 197 572	1 650 222	1 547 350	5 156 191	2 680 221	2 475 970
15 - 19	9 238 892	4 738 218	4 500 674	3 761 314	1 914 006	1 847 308	5 477 578	2 824 212	2 653 366
20 - 24	8 513 103	4 358 058	4 155 045	3 742 332	1 883 403	1 858 929	4 770 771	2 474 655	2 296 116
25 - 29	6 910 068	3 411 636	3 498 432	3 052 176	1 493 576	1 558 600	3 857 892	1 918 060	1 939 832
30 - 34	5 116 405	2 613 911	2 502 494	2 338 060	1 185 148	1 152 912	2 778 345	1 428 763	1 349 582
35 - 39	5 034 356	2 498 485	2 535 871	2 244 024	1 124 866	1 119 158	2 790 332	1 373 619	1 416 713
40 - 44	4 422 992	2 236 659	2 186 333	2 091 650	1 050 210	1 041 440	2 331 342	1 186 449	1 144 893
45 - 49	3 971 022	2 029 328	1 941 694	1 881 580	959 754	921 826	2 089 442	1 069 574	1 019 868
50 - 54	3 307 397	1 667 511	1 639 886	1 671 273	849 355	821 918	1 636 124	818 156	817 968
55 - 59	2 447 936	1 312 016	1 135 920	1 190 822	639 304	551 518	1 257 114	672 712	584 402
60 - 64	1 842 093	971 087	871 006	960 012	524 548	435 464	882 081	446 539	435 542
65 - 69	1 290 267	692 772	597 495	583 894	331 613	252 281	706 373	361 159	345 214
70 - 74	853 699	434 889	418 810	397 627	211 403	186 224	456 072	223 486	232 586
75 +	799 618	407 699	391 919	342 289	181 063	161 226	457 329	226 636	230 693
Mauritius - Maurice[2]									
1 VII 2010 (ESDJ)									
Total	1 280 924	631 692	649 232	...	...	...	...	...	...
0 - 4	82 127	41 689	40 438	...	...	...	...	...	...
5 - 9	96 353	48 937	47 416	...	...	...	...	...	...
10 - 14	98 251	49 841	48 410	...	...	...	...	...	...
15 - 19	108 580	54 905	53 675	...	...	...	...	...	...
20 - 29	197 952	99 958	97 994	...	...	...	...	...	...
30 - 39	201 663	99 783	101 880	...	...	...	...	...	...
40 - 49	195 641	97 470	98 171	...	...	...	...	...	...
50 - 59	157 394	77 443	79 951	...	...	...	...	...	...
60 - 64	50 089	23 450	26 639	...	...	...	...	...	...
65 +	92 874	38 216	54 658	...	...	...	...	...	...
Rwanda									
1 VII 2010 (ESDF)									
Total	10 412 820	5 029 450	5 383 371	...	...	...	...	...	...
0 - 4	1 818 152	916 676	901 476	...	...	...	...	...	...
5 - 9	1 389 635	694 199	695 436	...	...	...	...	...	...
10 - 14	1 199 057	593 297	605 760	...	...	...	...	...	...
15 - 19	1 104 050	542 911	561 139	...	...	...	...	...	...
20 - 24	1 091 715	532 937	558 779	...	...	...	...	...	...
25 - 29	974 632	468 261	506 372	...	...	...	...	...	...
30 - 34	678 660	313 166	365 495	...	...	...	...	...	...
35 - 39	483 563	220 162	263 401	...	...	...	...	...	...
40 - 44	401 306	186 410	214 896	...	...	...	...	...	...
45 - 49	357 741	165 034	192 708	...	...	...	...	...	...
50 - 54	309 675	141 541	168 134	...	...	...	...	...	...
55 - 59	214 896	96 042	118 855	...	...	...	...	...	...
60 - 64	141 303	60 359	80 944	...	...	...	...	...	...
65 - 69	93 189	36 208	56 981	...	...	...	...	...	...
70 - 74	72 930	28 692	44 238	...	...	...	...	...	...
75 - 79	45 835	18 530	27 305	...	...	...	...	...	...
80 +	36 482	15 028	21 454	...	...	...	...	...	...
Senegal - Sénégal[3]									
31 XII 2010 (ESDJ)									
Total	12 496 300	6 177 251	6 319 049	...	...	...	...	...	...
0 - 4	2 060 535	1 040 234	1 020 301	...	...	...	...	...	...
5 - 9	1 656 892	843 592	813 300	...	...	...	...	...	...
10 - 14	1 486 441	759 199	727 242	...	...	...	...	...	...
15 - 19	1 397 139	707 601	689 538	...	...	...	...	...	...

256

7a. Population by age, sex and urban/rural residence: 2010
Population selon l'âge, le sexe et la résidence, urbaine/rurale: 2010 (continued - suite)

Continent, country or area, date, code and age (in years) / Continent, pays ou zone, date, code et âge (en années)	Total			Urban - Urbaine			Rural - Rurale		
	Both sexes Les deux sexes	Male Masculin	Female Féminin	Both sexes Les deux sexes	Male Masculin	Female Féminin	Both sexes Les deux sexes	Male Masculin	Female Féminin
AFRICA - AFRIQUE									
Senegal - Sénégal[3]									
31 XII 2010 (ESDJ)									
20 - 24	1 228 971	611 192	617 779	...	...	...	...	...	...
25 - 29	1 028 779	498 183	530 596	...	...	...	...	...	...
30 - 34	791 366	382 180	409 186	...	...	...	...	...	...
35 - 39	653 021	307 879	345 142	...	...	...	...	...	...
40 - 44	525 850	242 441	283 409	...	...	...	...	...	...
45 - 49	419 856	191 839	228 017	...	...	...	...	...	...
50 - 54	338 742	163 550	175 192	...	...	...	...	...	...
55 - 59	277 726	135 401	142 325	...	...	...	...	...	...
60 - 64	211 036	95 714	115 322	...	...	...	...	...	...
65 - 69	147 084	68 563	78 521	...	...	...	...	...	...
70 - 74	119 899	57 129	62 770	...	...	...	...	...	...
75 - 79	68 501	31 739	36 762	...	...	...	...	...	...
80 +	84 462	40 815	43 647	...	...	...	...	...	...
Seychelles									
1 VII 2010 (ESDF)									
Total	86 525	44 253	42 272	...	...	...	...	...	...
0	1 489	776	713	...	...	...	...	...	...
1 - 4	5 981	2 972	3 009	...	...	...	...	...	...
5 - 9	6 582	3 277	3 305	...	...	...	...	...	...
10 - 14	5 639	2 930	2 709	...	...	...	...	...	...
15 - 19	7 073	3 812	3 261	...	...	...	...	...	...
20 - 24	7 287	4 010	3 277	...	...	...	...	...	...
25 - 29	7 536	4 370	3 166	...	...	...	...	...	...
30 - 34	6 634	3 667	2 967	...	...	...	...	...	...
35 - 39	8 112	4 362	3 750	...	...	...	...	...	...
40 - 44	5 782	2 776	3 006	...	...	...	...	...	...
45 - 49	6 154	3 015	3 139	...	...	...	...	...	...
50 - 54	5 223	2 705	2 518	...	...	...	...	...	...
55 - 59	3 288	1 661	1 627	...	...	...	...	...	...
60 - 64	2 934	1 372	1 562	...	...	...	...	...	...
65 - 69	1 848	819	1 029	...	...	...	...	...	...
70 - 74	1 964	778	1 186	...	...	...	...	...	...
75 - 79	1 473	525	948	...	...	...	...	...	...
80 +	1 526	426	1 100	...	...	...	...	...	...
Sierra Leone									
1 VII 2010 (ESDF)									
Total	5 746 800	2 786 797	2 960 003	2 304 955	1 138 563	1 166 392	3 441 845	1 648 234	1 793 611
0 - 4	878 231	437 908	440 323	297 865	147 565	150 300	580 366	290 343	290 023
5 - 9	856 605	424 222	432 383	307 007	145 641	161 366	549 598	278 581	271 017
10 - 14	662 651	338 453	324 198	303 094	148 401	154 693	359 557	190 052	169 505
15 - 19	637 914	308 982	328 932	287 597	141 564	146 033	350 317	167 418	182 899
20 - 24	488 054	221 932	266 122	241 599	119 622	121 977	246 455	102 310	144 145
25 - 29	473 952	210 004	263 948	205 137	102 492	102 645	268 815	107 512	161 303
30 - 34	356 727	160 822	195 905	149 414	73 308	76 106	207 313	87 514	119 799
35 - 39	341 470	160 326	181 144	133 461	66 104	67 357	208 009	94 222	113 787
40 - 44	247 978	123 279	124 699	97 102	51 623	45 479	150 876	71 656	79 220
45 - 49	201 708	107 932	93 776	76 536	41 832	34 704	125 172	66 100	59 072
50 - 54	149 167	77 236	71 931	55 139	30 564	24 575	94 028	46 672	47 356
55 - 59	96 801	51 344	45 457	37 477	21 157	16 320	59 324	30 187	29 137
60 - 64	99 394	44 873	54 521	31 058	14 915	16 143	68 336	29 958	38 378
65 - 69	71 174	34 054	37 120	24 423	11 420	13 003	46 751	22 634	24 117
70 - 74	61 847	28 198	33 649	18 941	8 268	10 673	42 906	19 930	22 976
75 - 79	41 728	21 586	20 142	12 876	6 356	6 520	28 852	15 230	13 622
80 +	81 399	35 646	45 753	26 229	7 731	18 498	55 170	27 915	27 255
AMERICA, NORTH - AMÉRIQUE DU NORD									
Aruba[4]									
1 VII 2010 (ESDJ)									
Total	107 553	51 547	56 006	...	...	...	...	...	...
0 - 4	6 160	3 161	2 999	...	...	...	...	...	...

Continent, country or area, date, code and age (in years) / Continent, pays ou zone, date, code et âge (en années)	Total			Urban - Urbaine			Rural - Rurale		
	Both sexes Les deux sexes	Male Masculin	Female Féminin	Both sexes Les deux sexes	Male Masculin	Female Féminin	Both sexes Les deux sexes	Male Masculin	Female Féminin
AMERICA, NORTH - AMÉRIQUE DU NORD									
Aruba[4]									
1 VII 2010 (ESDJ)									
5 - 9	6 697	3 422	3 275	...	...	...	...	...	...
10 - 14	7 609	3 854	3 755	...	...	...	...	...	...
15 - 19	7 584	3 850	3 734	...	...	...	...	...	...
20 - 24	6 266	3 193	3 073	...	...	...	...	...	...
25 - 29	6 337	3 085	3 251	...	...	...	...	...	...
30 - 34	7 270	3 391	3 879	...	...	...	...	...	...
35 - 39	8 420	4 002	4 418	...	...	...	...	...	...
40 - 44	9 198	4 386	4 812	...	...	...	...	...	...
45 - 49	10 064	4 798	5 266	...	...	...	...	...	...
50 - 54	8 897	4 134	4 763	...	...	...	...	...	...
55 - 59	7 074	3 303	3 771	...	...	...	...	...	...
60 - 64	5 317	2 474	2 842	...	...	...	...	...	...
65 - 69	3 814	1 759	2 055	...	...	...	...	...	...
70 - 74	2 951	1 253	1 698	...	...	...	...	...	...
75 - 79	1 998	808	1 190	...	...	...	...	...	...
80 - 84	1 098	413	685	...	...	...	...	...	...
85 - 89	485	180	305	...	...	...	...	...	...
90 - 94	217	59	158	...	...	...	...	...	...
95 +	100	22	78	...	...	...	...	...	...
Bahamas[1]									
1 VII 2010 (ESDF)									
Total	346 900	169 200	177 700	...	...	...	...	...	...
0 - 4	29 300	15 300	14 000	...	...	...	...	...	...
5 - 9	28 700	14 700	14 000	...	...	...	...	...	...
10 - 14	29 000	14 400	14 600	...	...	...	...	...	...
15 - 19	31 100	15 500	15 600	...	...	...	...	...	...
20 - 24	27 800	13 500	14 300	...	...	...	...	...	...
25 - 29	26 000	12 900	13 100	...	...	...	...	...	...
30 - 34	25 500	12 500	13 000	...	...	...	...	...	...
35 - 39	28 100	13 600	14 500	...	...	...	...	...	...
40 - 44	26 900	12 900	14 000	...	...	...	...	...	...
45 - 49	26 200	12 700	13 500	...	...	...	...	...	...
50 - 54	20 900	10 000	10 900	...	...	...	...	...	...
55 - 59	15 300	7 300	8 000	...	...	...	...	...	...
60 - 64	10 900	5 100	5 800	...	...	...	...	...	...
65 - 69	8 600	3 900	4 700	...	...	...	...	...	...
70 - 74	6 100	2 700	3 400	...	...	...	...	...	...
75 - 79	3 700	1 500	2 200	...	...	...	...	...	...
80 +	2 800	700	2 100	...	...	...	...	...	...
Bermuda - Bermudes									
1 VII 2010 (ESDJ)									
Total	64 566	30 755	33 811	...	...	...	...	...	...
0	766	389	377	...	...	...	...	...	...
1 - 4	2 963	1 500	1 463	...	...	...	...	...	...
5 - 9	3 702	1 924	1 778	...	...	...	...	...	...
10 - 14	3 753	1 870	1 883	...	...	...	...	...	...
15 - 19	3 717	1 843	1 874	...	...	...	...	...	...
20 - 24	3 555	1 720	1 835	...	...	...	...	...	...
25 - 29	4 290	2 024	2 266	...	...	...	...	...	...
30 - 34	4 329	2 026	2 303	...	...	...	...	...	...
35 - 39	4 735	2 292	2 443	...	...	...	...	...	...
40 - 44	5 123	2 537	2 586	...	...	...	...	...	...
45 - 49	5 870	2 883	2 987	...	...	...	...	...	...
50 - 54	5 331	2 532	2 799	...	...	...	...	...	...
55 - 59	4 426	2 114	2 312	...	...	...	...	...	...
60 - 64	3 693	1 725	1 968	...	...	...	...	...	...
65 - 69	2 718	1 211	1 507	...	...	...	...	...	...
70 - 74	2 044	875	1 169	...	...	...	...	...	...
75 - 79	1 653	661	992	...	...	...	...	...	...
80 - 84	1 100	396	704	...	...	...	...	...	...
85 +	798	233	565	...	...	...	...	...	...

Continent, country or area, date, code and age (in years) Continent, pays ou zone, date, code et âge (en années)	Total			Urban - Urbaine			Rural - Rurale		
	Both sexes Les deux sexes	Male Masculin	Female Féminin	Both sexes Les deux sexes	Male Masculin	Female Féminin	Both sexes Les deux sexes	Male Masculin	Female Féminin
AMERICA, NORTH - AMÉRIQUE DU NORD									
Canada[5]									
1 VII 2010* (ESDJ)									
Total	34 108 752	16 917 282	17 191 470	...	...	...	...	...	...
0	380 631	195 223	185 408	...	...	...	...	...	...
1 - 4	1 497 529	768 223	729 306	...	...	...	...	...	...
5 - 9	1 803 266	928 386	874 880	...	...	...	...	...	...
10 - 14	1 935 244	992 060	943 184	...	...	...	...	...	...
15 - 19	2 226 819	1 140 059	1 086 760	...	...	...	...	...	...
20 - 24	2 364 868	1 214 756	1 150 112	...	...	...	...	...	...
25 - 29	2 394 544	1 212 138	1 182 406	...	...	...	...	...	...
30 - 34	2 301 397	1 150 687	1 150 710	...	...	...	...	...	...
35 - 39	2 294 682	1 153 074	1 141 608	...	...	...	...	...	...
40 - 44	2 421 020	1 219 633	1 201 387	...	...	...	...	...	...
45 - 49	2 793 377	1 405 280	1 388 097	...	...	...	...	...	...
50 - 54	2 618 766	1 306 535	1 312 231	...	...	...	...	...	...
55 - 59	2 288 313	1 128 182	1 160 131	...	...	...	...	...	...
60 - 64	1 968 695	965 010	1 003 685	...	...	...	...	...	...
65 - 69	1 468 925	712 574	756 351	...	...	...	...	...	...
70 - 74	1 104 550	519 504	585 046	...	...	...	...	...	...
75 - 79	912 367	412 120	500 247	...	...	...	...	...	...
80 - 84	688 152	283 842	404 310	...	...	...	...	...	...
85 - 89	427 471	150 622	276 849	...	...	...	...	...	...
90 - 94	166 042	47 583	118 459	...	...	...	...	...	...
95 - 99	45 564	10 457	35 107	...	...	...	...	...	...
100 +	6 530	1 334	5 196	...	...	...	...	...	...
Costa Rica[6]									
1 VII 2010 (ESDJ)									
Total	4 562 087	2 233 452	2 328 635	2 811 556	1 344 652	1 466 904	1 750 531	888 800	861 731
0 - 4	327 889	172 145	155 744	189 287	100 116	89 171	138 602	72 029	66 573
5 - 9	357 242	183 275	173 967	197 008	99 237	97 771	160 234	84 038	76 196
10 - 14	404 933	206 183	198 750	221 495	112 885	108 610	183 438	93 298	90 140
15 - 19	458 019	225 081	232 938	266 606	125 614	140 992	191 413	99 467	91 946
20 - 24	447 670	228 071	219 599	293 102	147 868	145 234	154 568	80 203	74 365
25 - 29	375 700	188 006	187 694	242 790	123 579	119 211	132 910	64 427	68 483
30 - 39	608 755	286 241	322 514	371 814	173 288	198 526	236 941	112 953	123 988
40 - 49	610 775	288 635	322 140	380 540	175 998	204 542	230 235	112 637	117 598
50 - 59	457 626	219 314	238 312	304 554	139 563	164 991	153 072	79 751	73 321
60 - 69	270 437	129 470	140 967	181 522	81 832	99 690	88 915	47 638	41 277
70 +	241 384	106 169	135 215	162 662	64 556	98 106	78 722	41 613	37 109
Unknown - Inconnu	1 657	862	795	176	116	60	1 481	746	735
Cuba[7]									
1 VII 2010 (ESDJ)									
Total	11 241 894	5 629 874	5 612 020	8 469 602	4 169 518	4 300 084	2 772 292	1 460 356	1 311 936
0 - 4	594 488	306 750	287 738	450 718	232 627	218 091	143 770	74 123	69 647
5 - 9	657 975	338 836	319 138	477 571	246 105	231 466	180 403	92 731	87 672
10 - 14	703 248	362 853	340 395	513 843	264 844	248 998	189 405	98 009	91 396
15 - 19	764 870	391 652	373 218	560 208	285 727	274 481	204 662	105 925	98 737
20 - 24	826 649	426 145	400 504	615 385	314 857	300 528	211 263	111 287	99 976
25 - 29	704 765	365 110	339 655	525 571	270 224	255 347	179 194	94 886	84 308
30 - 34	716 359	369 230	347 129	527 448	271 207	256 241	188 911	98 023	90 888
35 - 39	994 770	505 278	489 491	737 820	372 027	365 793	256 949	133 251	123 698
40 - 44	1 043 550	520 577	522 973	786 310	386 217	400 093	257 240	134 360	122 880
45 - 49	982 495	486 794	495 700	765 845	372 973	392 872	216 649	113 821	102 828
50 - 54	661 269	323 185	338 084	509 831	243 128	266 703	151 437	80 056	71 381
55 - 59	618 166	301 427	316 739	482 157	228 780	253 377	136 008	72 647	63 361
60 - 64	554 001	266 868	287 133	432 828	202 748	230 079	121 173	64 119	57 054
65 - 69	467 150	225 706	241 444	361 962	168 387	193 575	105 187	57 318	47 869
70 - 74	361 457	174 131	187 325	277 833	127 376	150 457	83 623	46 755	36 868
75 - 79	247 587	115 168	132 419	188 244	81 559	106 685	59 343	33 609	25 734
80 - 84	176 050	79 114	96 935	133 667	54 969	78 697	42 383	24 145	18 238
85 +	167 042	71 046	95 996	122 355	45 759	76 596	44 687	25 287	19 400

Continent, country or area, date, code and age (in years) / Continent, pays ou zone, date, code et âge (en années)	Total			Urban - Urbaine			Rural - Rurale		
	Both sexes Les deux sexes	Male Masculin	Female Féminin	Both sexes Les deux sexes	Male Masculin	Female Féminin	Both sexes Les deux sexes	Male Masculin	Female Féminin
AMERICA, NORTH - AMÉRIQUE DU NORD									
Dominican Republic - République dominicaine[1]									
1 VII 2010 (ESDF)									
Total	9 884 371	4 935 282	4 949 089	6 572 893	3 257 817	3 315 076	3 311 478	1 677 465	1 634 013
0 - 4	1 065 821	543 574	522 247	691 739	357 374	334 365	374 082	186 200	187 882
5 - 9	1 046 926	533 013	513 913	668 053	343 277	324 776	378 873	189 736	189 137
10 - 14	998 486	506 690	491 796	644 895	326 629	318 266	353 591	180 061	173 530
15 - 19	979 241	494 717	484 524	653 463	326 714	326 749	325 778	168 003	157 775
20 - 24	902 810	451 176	451 634	619 608	306 990	312 618	283 202	144 186	139 016
25 - 29	820 076	405 406	414 670	568 248	280 045	288 203	251 828	125 361	126 467
30 - 34	717 221	351 524	365 697	493 603	241 017	252 586	223 618	110 507	113 111
35 - 39	643 877	315 683	328 194	442 551	215 609	226 942	201 326	100 074	101 252
40 - 44	577 198	284 612	292 586	391 657	191 179	200 478	185 541	93 433	92 108
45 - 49	511 872	253 501	258 371	345 699	168 814	176 885	166 173	84 687	81 486
50 - 54	433 039	215 051	217 988	286 832	140 263	146 569	146 207	74 788	71 419
55 - 59	342 808	170 072	172 736	224 419	109 270	115 149	118 389	60 802	57 587
60 - 64	257 509	126 928	130 581	165 154	78 831	86 323	92 355	48 097	44 258
65 - 69	194 240	95 169	99 071	124 018	58 676	65 342	70 222	36 493	33 729
70 - 74	160 052	77 569	82 483	101 211	46 731	54 480	58 841	30 838	28 003
75 - 79	114 432	54 854	59 578	73 212	32 940	40 272	41 220	21 914	19 306
80 +	118 763	55 743	63 020	78 531	33 458	45 073	40 232	22 285	17 947
El Salvador[8]									
1 VII 2010 (ESDF)									
Total	6 183 002	2 913 743	3 269 259	...	...	...	...	...	...
0 - 4	606 853	310 111	296 742	...	...	...	...	...	...
5 - 9	614 788	314 297	300 491	...	...	...	...	...	...
10 - 14	730 418	372 464	357 954	...	...	...	...	...	...
15 - 19	697 647	349 342	348 305	...	...	...	...	...	...
20 - 24	566 024	267 265	298 759	...	...	...	...	...	...
25 - 29	463 011	205 743	257 268	...	...	...	...	...	...
30 - 34	414 120	180 189	233 931	...	...	...	...	...	...
35 - 39	386 008	168 528	217 480	...	...	...	...	...	...
40 - 44	339 465	147 990	191 475	...	...	...	...	...	...
45 - 49	289 673	125 671	164 002	...	...	...	...	...	...
50 - 54	244 822	107 104	137 718	...	...	...	...	...	...
55 - 59	210 179	92 551	117 628	...	...	...	...	...	...
60 - 64	176 355	77 782	98 573	...	...	...	...	...	...
65 - 69	145 876	64 990	80 886	...	...	...	...	...	...
70 - 74	117 728	52 093	65 635	...	...	...	...	...	...
75 - 79	85 694	37 627	48 067	...	...	...	...	...	...
80 +	94 341	39 996	54 345	...	...	...	...	...	...
Greenland - Groenland[9]									
1 VII 2010 (ESDJ)									
Total	56 534	29 939	26 595	47 646	25 045	22 601	8 888	4 894	3 994
0	875	457	418	728	378	350	147	79	68
1 - 4	3 271	1 679	1 593	2 711	1 394	1 317	560	285	276
5 - 9	4 160	2 111	2 049	3 418	1 731	1 687	742	380	363
10 - 14	4 454	2 254	2 200	3 657	1 873	1 784	797	381	416
15 - 19	4 563	2 292	2 271	3 803	1 903	1 900	760	390	371
20 - 24	4 461	2 263	2 198	3 799	1 903	1 896	662	360	302
25 - 29	3 997	2 078	1 919	3 413	1 742	1 671	584	337	248
30 - 34	3 465	1 838	1 628	2 961	1 549	1 413	504	289	215
35 - 39	3 324	1 846	1 478	2 836	1 576	1 260	488	270	219
40 - 44	5 091	2 736	2 355	4 314	2 299	2 015	777	437	340
45 - 49	5 324	2 857	2 467	4 551	2 408	2 143	773	449	324
50 - 54	4 267	2 435	1 832	3 613	2 040	1 574	654	396	258
55 - 59	3 133	1 798	1 335	2 642	1 492	1 150	492	306	186
60 - 64	2 256	1 348	908	1 925	1 141	785	331	208	123
65 - 69	1 773	985	788	1 484	818	666	289	167	122
70 - 74	1 032	527	505	855	430	425	177	97	80
75 - 79	654	286	368	560	245	315	94	41	53
80 - 84	329	120	209	286	102	184	44	19	25
85 - 89	86	29	58	72	22	50	15	7	8

Continent, country or area, date, code and age (in years) / Continent, pays ou zone, date, code et âge (en années)	Total			Urban - Urbaine			Rural - Rurale		
	Both sexes Les deux sexes	Male Masculin	Female Féminin	Both sexes Les deux sexes	Male Masculin	Female Féminin	Both sexes Les deux sexes	Male Masculin	Female Féminin
AMERICA, NORTH - AMÉRIQUE DU NORD									
Greenland - Groenland[9]									
1 VII 2010 (ESDJ)									
90 - 94	22	3	20	20	3	18	2	-	2
95 +	3	1	2	3	1	2	-	-	-
Guatemala[10]									
1 VII 2010 (ESDF)									
Total	14 361 666	7 003 337	7 358 328	...	...	...	...	...	...
0 - 4	2 165 745	1 103 521	1 062 224	...	...	...	...	...	...
5 - 9	2 004 670	1 017 180	987 490	...	...	...	...	...	...
10 - 14	1 798 262	906 603	891 659	...	...	...	...	...	...
15 - 19	1 590 147	794 459	795 688	...	...	...	...	...	...
20 - 24	1 322 125	646 911	675 214	...	...	...	...	...	...
25 - 29	1 128 960	538 214	590 746	...	...	...	...	...	...
30 - 34	913 192	418 535	494 657	...	...	...	...	...	...
35 - 39	725 691	323 010	402 681	...	...	...	...	...	...
40 - 44	580 303	258 454	321 849	...	...	...	...	...	...
45 - 49	475 449	215 304	260 145	...	...	...	...	...	...
50 - 54	393 702	182 662	211 040	...	...	...	...	...	...
55 - 59	350 124	165 910	184 214	...	...	...	...	...	...
60 - 64	292 331	139 395	152 936	...	...	...	...	...	...
65 - 69	214 491	103 433	111 058	...	...	...	...	...	...
70 - 74	170 028	81 809	88 219	...	...	...	...	...	...
75 - 79	128 990	60 257	68 733	...	...	...	...	...	...
80 +	107 456	47 678	59 778	...	...	...	...	...	...
Haiti - Haïti[11]									
1 VII 2010 (ESDJ)									
Total	10 085 214	4 993 731	5 091 483	4 817 666	2 321 608	2 496 059	5 267 548	2 672 123	2 595 424
0 - 4	1 263 322	644 550	618 772	532 352	274 597	257 755	730 970	369 953	361 017
5 - 9	1 195 479	608 495	586 984	493 368	249 982	243 386	702 111	358 513	343 598
10 - 14	1 158 478	588 618	569 860	532 573	255 002	277 571	625 905	333 616	292 289
15 - 19	1 092 364	551 467	540 897	583 183	276 258	306 925	509 181	275 209	233 972
20 - 24	1 019 589	509 042	510 547	600 175	296 233	303 943	419 414	212 809	206 604
25 - 29	919 636	454 123	465 513	537 063	267 198	269 865	382 573	186 925	195 648
30 - 34	702 596	340 518	362 078	390 054	189 432	200 622	312 542	151 086	161 456
35 - 39	548 004	261 157	286 847	272 855	128 575	144 280	275 149	132 582	142 567
40 - 44	488 482	235 182	253 300	225 057	106 072	118 985	263 425	129 110	134 315
45 - 49	423 377	204 077	219 300	179 712	81 240	98 472	243 665	122 837	120 828
50 - 54	342 913	166 418	176 495	138 580	61 854	76 726	204 333	104 564	99 769
55 - 59	284 731	136 034	148 697	107 391	46 062	61 329	177 340	89 972	87 368
60 - 64	206 835	95 939	110 896	73 562	29 974	43 588	133 273	65 965	67 308
65 - 69	175 898	81 854	94 044	61 671	24 975	36 696	114 227	56 879	57 348
70 - 74	129 436	58 181	71 255	44 448	17 100	27 347	84 988	41 081	43 908
75 - 79	80 898	35 538	45 360	27 630	10 473	17 158	53 268	25 065	28 202
80 +	53 176	22 538	30 638	17 992	6 581	11 412	35 184	15 957	19 226
Honduras[12]									
1 VII 2010 (ESDF)									
Total	8 045 990	3 965 430	4 080 560	...	...	...	...	...	...
0 - 4	1 079 289	549 179	530 110	...	...	...	...	...	...
5 - 9	1 035 077	525 938	509 139	...	...	...	...	...	...
10 - 14	973 613	492 090	481 523	...	...	...	...	...	...
15 - 19	866 193	434 856	431 337	...	...	...	...	...	...
20 - 24	747 514	371 818	375 696	...	...	...	...	...	...
25 - 29	663 903	326 377	337 526	...	...	...	...	...	...
30 - 34	577 561	282 042	295 519	...	...	...	...	...	...
35 - 39	474 884	230 506	244 378	...	...	...	...	...	...
40 - 44	381 715	181 554	200 161	...	...	...	...	...	...
45 - 49	301 565	140 031	161 534	...	...	...	...	...	...
50 - 54	251 618	116 240	135 378	...	...	...	...	...	...
55 - 59	203 187	93 205	109 982	...	...	...	...	...	...
60 - 64	157 317	72 071	85 246	...	...	...	...	...	...
65 - 69	117 790	53 835	63 955	...	...	...	...	...	...
70 - 74	90 125	40 470	49 655	...	...	...	...	...	...
75 - 79	62 138	27 381	34 757	...	...	...	...	...	...
80 +	62 501	27 837	34 664	...	...	...	...	...	...

Continent, country or area, date, code and age (in years) / Continent, pays ou zone, date, code et âge (en annèes)	Total			Urban - Urbaine			Rural - Rurale		
	Both sexes Les deux sexes	Male Masculin	Female Féminin	Both sexes Les deux sexes	Male Masculin	Female Féminin	Both sexes Les deux sexes	Male Masculin	Female Féminin
AMERICA, NORTH - AMÉRIQUE DU NORD									
Mexico - Mexique[13]									
12 VI 2010 (CDFC)									
Total	112 336 538	54 855 231	57 481 307	86 287 410	41 946 540	44 340 870	26 049 128	12 908 691	13 140 437
0 - 4	10 528 322	5 346 943	5 181 379	7 766 149	3 945 636	3 820 513	2 762 173	1 401 307	1 360 866
5 - 9	11 047 537	5 604 175	5 443 362	8 124 337	4 124 524	3 999 813	2 923 200	1 479 651	1 443 549
10 - 14	10 939 937	5 547 613	5 392 324	7 974 649	4 041 649	3 933 000	2 965 288	1 505 964	1 459 324
15 - 19	11 026 112	5 520 121	5 505 991	8 191 229	4 097 876	4 093 353	2 834 883	1 422 245	1 412 638
20 - 24	9 892 271	4 813 204	5 079 067	7 725 598	3 775 245	3 950 353	2 166 673	1 037 959	1 128 714
25 - 29	8 788 177	4 205 975	4 582 202	6 985 279	3 354 569	3 630 710	1 802 898	851 406	951 492
30 - 34	8 470 798	4 026 031	4 444 767	6 719 047	3 188 789	3 530 258	1 751 751	837 242	914 509
35 - 39	8 292 987	3 964 738	4 328 249	6 642 253	3 160 713	3 481 540	1 650 734	804 025	846 709
40 - 44	7 009 226	3 350 322	3 658 904	5 633 205	2 676 230	2 956 975	1 376 021	674 092	701 929
45 - 49	5 928 730	2 824 364	3 104 366	4 739 911	2 241 753	2 498 158	1 188 819	582 611	606 208
50 - 54	5 064 291	2 402 451	2 661 840	4 051 487	1 904 317	2 147 170	1 012 804	498 134	514 670
55 - 59	3 895 365	1 869 537	2 025 828	3 043 924	1 443 868	1 600 056	851 441	425 669	425 772
60 - 64	3 116 466	1 476 667	1 639 799	2 403 645	1 119 077	1 284 568	712 821	357 590	355 231
65 - 69	2 317 265	1 095 273	1 221 992	1 719 078	794 137	924 941	598 187	301 136	297 051
70 - 74	1 873 934	873 893	1 000 041	1 338 906	603 945	734 961	535 028	269 948	265 080
75 - 79	1 245 483	579 689	665 794	892 237	399 026	493 211	353 246	180 663	172 583
80 - 84	798 936	355 277	443 659	576 855	244 082	332 773	222 081	111 195	110 886
85 - 89	454 164	197 461	256 703	322 844	132 826	190 018	131 320	64 635	66 685
90 - 94	164 924	68 130	96 794	116 950	45 123	71 827	47 974	23 007	24 967
95 - 99	65 732	25 920	39 812	44 084	16 122	27 962	21 648	9 798	11 850
100 +	18 475	7 228	11 247	10 451	3 753	6 698	8 024	3 475	4 549
Unknown - Inconnu	1 397 406	700 219	697 187	1 265 292	633 280	632 012	132 114	66 939	65 175
Netherlands Antilles - Antilles néerlandaises[14]									
1 I 2010 (ESDJ)									
Total	197 621	92 321	105 300	...	...	...	...	...	...
0 - 4	13 628	7 049	6 579	...	...	...	...	...	...
5 - 9	14 528	7 396	7 132	...	...	...	...	...	...
10 - 14	14 364	7 150	7 214	...	...	...	...	...	...
15 - 19	14 722	7 348	7 374	...	...	...	...	...	...
20 - 24	10 976	5 361	5 615	...	...	...	...	...	...
25 - 29	11 062	5 127	5 935	...	...	...	...	...	...
30 - 34	12 398	5 747	6 651	...	...	...	...	...	...
35 - 39	15 204	7 039	8 165	...	...	...	...	...	...
40 - 44	16 398	7 486	8 912	...	...	...	...	...	...
45 - 49	17 010	7 697	9 313	...	...	...	...	...	...
50 - 54	14 817	6 617	8 200	...	...	...	...	...	...
55 - 59	12 347	5 530	6 817	...	...	...	...	...	...
60 - 64	9 857	4 461	5 396	...	...	...	...	...	...
65 - 69	6 871	3 018	3 853	...	...	...	...	...	...
70 - 74	5 453	2 324	3 129	...	...	...	...	...	...
75 - 79	3 820	1 549	2 271	...	...	...	...	...	...
80 - 84	2 311	863	1 448	...	...	...	...	...	...
85 +	1 855	559	1 296	...	...	...	...	...	...
Panama[15]									
1 VII 2010 (ESDF)									
Total	3 504 483	1 765 734	1 738 749	2 262 765	1 119 546	1 143 219	1 241 718	646 188	595 530
0 - 4	351 221	179 371	171 850	208 269	106 475	101 794	142 952	72 896	70 056
5 - 9	341 709	174 456	167 253	205 648	105 111	100 537	136 061	69 345	66 716
10 - 14	329 340	168 137	161 203	190 973	97 407	93 566	138 367	70 730	67 637
15 - 19	307 769	156 928	150 841	183 791	93 422	90 369	123 978	63 506	60 472
20 - 24	298 800	151 900	146 900	193 108	97 226	95 882	105 692	54 674	51 018
25 - 29	277 505	140 612	136 893	191 549	94 536	97 013	85 956	46 076	39 880
30 - 34	263 334	132 845	130 489	189 011	93 774	95 237	74 323	39 071	35 252
35 - 39	259 755	130 366	129 389	182 595	90 863	91 732	77 160	39 503	37 657
40 - 44	236 952	118 777	118 175	165 600	81 805	83 795	71 352	36 972	34 380
45 - 49	201 998	100 644	101 354	141 013	68 336	72 677	60 985	32 308	28 677
50 - 54	165 538	81 908	83 630	113 611	54 248	59 363	51 927	27 660	24 267
55 - 59	134 094	66 304	67 790	90 029	42 678	47 351	44 065	23 626	20 439
60 - 64	106 753	53 121	53 632	68 245	32 196	36 049	38 508	20 925	17 583
65 - 69	84 013	41 413	42 600	51 441	23 860	27 581	32 572	17 553	15 019

Continent, country or area, date, code and age (in years) / Continent, pays ou zone, date, code et âge (en annèes)	Total			Urban - Urbaine			Rural - Rurale		
	Both sexes Les deux sexes	Male Masculin	Female Féminin	Both sexes Les deux sexes	Male Masculin	Female Féminin	Both sexes Les deux sexes	Male Masculin	Female Féminin
AMERICA, NORTH - AMÉRIQUE DU NORD									
Panama[15]									
1 VII 2010 (ESDF)									
70 - 74	60 678	29 519	31 159	35 148	15 728	19 420	25 530	13 791	11 739
75 - 79	43 317	20 618	22 699	25 559	10 990	14 569	17 758	9 628	8 130
80 +	41 707	18 815	22 892	27 175	10 891	16 284	14 532	7 924	6 608
Puerto Rico - Porto Rico[16]									
1 VII 2010 (ESDJ)									
Total	3 978 702	1 908 360	2 070 342	...	...	...	...	...	...
0 - 4	228 431	116 736	111 695	...	...	...	...	...	...
5 - 9	253 291	129 288	124 003	...	...	...	...	...	...
10 - 14	286 458	146 507	139 951	...	...	...	...	...	...
15 - 19	294 436	150 011	144 425	...	...	...	...	...	...
20 - 24	278 123	139 502	138 621	...	...	...	...	...	...
25 - 29	274 976	136 350	138 626	...	...	...	...	...	...
30 - 34	278 779	135 835	142 944	...	...	...	...	...	...
35 - 39	264 929	128 782	136 147	...	...	...	...	...	...
40 - 44	261 657	125 456	136 201	...	...	...	...	...	...
45 - 49	266 277	124 926	141 351	...	...	...	...	...	...
50 - 54	252 997	116 660	136 337	...	...	...	...	...	...
55 - 59	232 869	106 239	126 630	...	...	...	...	...	...
60 - 64	226 344	102 736	123 608	...	...	...	...	...	...
65 - 69	181 934	81 981	99 953	...	...	...	...	...	...
70 - 74	142 848	63 778	79 070	...	...	...	...	...	...
75 - 79	107 538	46 309	61 229	...	...	...	...	...	...
80 - 84	73 312	29 898	43 414	...	...	...	...	...	...
85 - 89	45 475	17 416	28 059	...	...	...	...	...	...
90 - 94	20 177	7 347	12 830	...	...	...	...	...	...
95 - 99	6 641	2 236	4 405	...	...	...	...	...	...
100 +	1 210	367	843	...	...	...	...	...	...
Trinidad and Tobago - Trinité-et-Tobago[17]									
1 VII 2010 (ESDF)									
Total	1 317 714	...	...	...	...	...	...	...	...
0 - 14	333 965	...	...	...	...	...	...	...	...
15 - 19	144 548	...	...	...	...	...	...	...	...
20 - 24	116 890	...	...	...	...	...	...	...	...
25 - 29	100 841	...	...	...	...	...	...	...	...
30 - 34	96 235	...	...	...	...	...	...	...	...
35 - 39	107 070	...	...	...	...	...	...	...	...
40 - 44	94 333	...	...	...	...	...	...	...	...
45 - 49	78 103	...	...	...	...	...	...	...	...
50 - 54	65 170	...	...	...	...	...	...	...	...
55 - 59	48 537	...	...	...	...	...	...	...	...
60 - 64	38 736	...	...	...	...	...	...	...	...
65 +	93 286	...	...	...	...	...	...	...	...
AMERICA, SOUTH - AMÉRIQUE DU SUD									
Argentina - Argentine[18]									
1 VII 2010 (ESDF)									
Total	40 518 951	19 846 671	20 672 280	36 965 313	18 023 080	18 942 233	3 553 638	1 823 591	1 730 047
0 - 4	3 419 673	1 740 485	1 679 188	3 023 554	1 547 261	1 476 293	396 119	193 224	202 895
5 - 9	3 321 992	1 689 364	1 632 628	2 934 173	1 499 800	1 434 373	387 819	189 564	198 255
10 - 14	3 414 646	1 735 344	1 679 302	3 049 461	1 555 902	1 493 559	365 185	179 442	185 743
15 - 19	3 449 559	1 751 386	1 698 173	3 128 485	1 585 792	1 542 693	321 074	165 594	155 480
20 - 24	3 349 723	1 697 550	1 652 173	3 077 724	1 556 632	1 521 092	271 999	140 918	131 081
25 - 29	3 209 903	1 618 705	1 591 198	2 971 029	1 496 405	1 474 624	238 874	122 300	116 574
30 - 34	3 248 807	1 628 149	1 620 658	3 004 180	1 502 866	1 501 314	244 627	125 283	119 344
35 - 39	2 712 018	1 353 587	1 358 431	2 503 937	1 243 679	1 260 258	208 081	109 908	98 173
40 - 44	2 373 257	1 179 076	1 194 181	2 185 597	1 077 307	1 108 290	187 660	101 769	85 891
45 - 49	2 225 891	1 093 940	1 131 951	2 047 919	997 371	1 050 548	177 972	96 569	81 403
50 - 54	2 068 656	991 757	1 076 899	1 901 341	901 803	999 538	167 315	89 954	77 361

Continent, country or area, date, code and age (in years) / Continent, pays ou zone, date, code et âge (en années)	Total			Urban - Urbaine			Rural - Rurale		
	Both sexes Les deux sexes	Male Masculin	Female Féminin	Both sexes Les deux sexes	Male Masculin	Female Féminin	Both sexes Les deux sexes	Male Masculin	Female Féminin
AMERICA, SOUTH - AMÉRIQUE DU SUD									
Argentina - Argentine[18]									
1 VII 2010 (ESDF)									
55 - 59	1 903 397	906 470	996 927	1 749 543	821 749	927 794	153 854	84 721	69 133
60 - 64	1 627 136	760 092	867 044	1 493 723	686 872	806 851	133 413	73 220	60 193
65 - 69	1 329 074	602 756	726 318	1 226 914	547 630	679 284	102 160	55 126	47 034
70 - 74	1 071 331	456 960	614 371	993 712	416 654	577 058	77 619	40 306	37 313
75 - 79	845 028	331 313	513 715	787 929	302 437	485 492	57 099	28 876	28 223
80 +	948 860	309 737	639 123	886 092	282 920	603 172	62 768	26 817	35 951
Bolivia (Plurinational State of) - Bolivie (État plurinational de)									
1 VII 2010 (ESDF)									
Total	10 426 154	5 201 974	5 224 180	...	...	...	...	...	...
0 - 4	1 302 875	664 395	638 480	...	...	...	...	...	...
5 - 9	1 259 095	641 645	617 450	...	...	...	...	...	...
10 - 14	1 172 211	597 320	574 891	...	...	...	...	...	...
15 - 19	1 110 391	564 646	545 745	...	...	...	...	...	...
20 - 24	969 621	490 571	479 050	...	...	...	...	...	...
25 - 29	844 571	424 516	420 055	...	...	...	...	...	...
30 - 34	739 447	368 570	370 877	...	...	...	...	...	...
35 - 39	655 569	323 850	331 719	...	...	...	...	...	...
40 - 44	534 658	262 521	272 137	...	...	...	...	...	...
45 - 49	441 637	214 941	226 696	...	...	...	...	...	...
50 - 54	372 064	179 173	192 891	...	...	...	...	...	...
55 - 59	302 976	143 483	159 493	...	...	...	...	...	...
60 - 64	244 370	114 583	129 787	...	...	...	...	...	...
65 - 69	182 400	84 241	98 159	...	...	...	...	...	...
70 - 74	138 160	61 994	76 166	...	...	...	...	...	...
75 - 79	90 392	39 109	51 283	...	...	...	...	...	...
80 +	65 717	26 416	39 301	...	...	...	...	...	...
Brazil - Brésil[19]									
1 VIII 2010* (CDJC)									
Total	190 755 799	93 406 990	97 348 809	160 925 792	77 710 174	83 215 618	29 830 007	15 696 816	14 133 191
0 - 4	13 796 159	7 016 987	6 779 172	11 301 147	5 745 123	5 556 024	2 495 012	1 271 864	1 223 148
5 - 9	14 969 375	7 624 144	7 345 231	12 135 284	6 169 531	5 965 753	2 834 091	1 454 613	1 379 478
10 - 14	17 166 761	8 725 413	8 441 348	13 956 984	7 062 055	6 894 929	3 209 777	1 663 358	1 546 419
15 - 19	16 990 870	8 558 868	8 432 002	14 038 999	6 998 102	7 040 897	2 951 871	1 560 766	1 391 105
20 - 24	17 245 190	8 630 227	8 614 963	14 706 067	7 276 963	7 429 104	2 539 123	1 353 264	1 185 859
25 - 29	17 104 413	8 460 995	8 643 418	14 772 955	7 225 732	7 547 223	2 331 458	1 235 263	1 096 195
30 - 34	15 744 512	7 717 657	8 026 855	13 611 919	6 586 875	7 025 044	2 132 593	1 130 782	1 001 811
35 - 39	13 888 581	6 766 665	7 121 916	11 975 408	5 750 498	6 224 910	1 913 173	1 016 167	897 006
40 - 44	13 009 367	6 320 570	6 688 797	11 187 428	5 344 981	5 842 447	1 821 939	975 589	846 350
45 - 49	11 833 351	5 692 013	6 141 338	10 181 394	4 806 322	5 375 072	1 651 957	885 691	766 266
50 - 54	10 140 402	4 834 995	5 305 407	8 708 339	4 074 679	4 633 660	1 432 063	760 316	671 747
55 - 59	8 276 219	3 902 344	4 373 875	7 025 474	3 238 531	3 786 943	1 250 745	663 813	586 932
60 - 64	6 509 119	3 041 034	3 468 085	5 474 943	2 479 882	2 995 061	1 034 176	561 152	473 024
65 - 69	4 840 810	2 224 065	2 616 745	4 040 016	1 792 798	2 247 218	800 794	431 267	369 527
70 - 74	3 741 637	1 667 373	2 074 264	3 142 173	1 349 329	1 792 844	599 464	318 044	281 420
75 - 79	2 563 448	1 090 518	1 472 930	2 174 039	889 909	1 284 130	389 409	200 609	188 800
80 - 84	1 666 972	668 623	998 349	1 423 603	546 865	876 738	243 369	121 758	121 611
85 - 89	819 483	310 759	508 724	695 385	251 112	444 273	124 098	59 647	64 451
90 - 94	326 559	114 964	211 595	273 348	90 960	182 388	53 211	24 004	29 207
95 - 99	98 335	31 529	66 806	81 121	24 365	56 756	17 214	7 164	10 050
100 +	24 236	7 247	16 989	19 766	5 562	14 204	4 470	1 685	2 785
Chile - Chili									
1 VII 2010 (ESDF)									
Total	17 094 275	8 461 327	8 632 948	14 868 172	7 278 342	7 589 830	2 226 103	1 182 985	1 043 118
0 - 4	1 248 325	635 810	612 515	1 090 616	555 247	535 369	157 709	80 563	77 146
5 - 9	1 237 497	630 053	607 444	1 087 281	552 946	534 335	150 216	77 107	73 109
10 - 14	1 328 935	676 215	652 720	1 153 204	586 004	567 200	175 731	90 211	85 520
15 - 19	1 488 317	756 626	731 691	1 284 374	651 013	633 361	203 943	105 613	98 330
20 - 24	1 462 346	741 731	720 615	1 262 718	636 363	626 355	199 628	105 368	94 260
25 - 29	1 320 741	667 792	652 949	1 159 420	577 963	581 457	161 321	89 829	71 492
30 - 34	1 169 556	588 124	581 432	1 036 060	515 587	520 473	133 496	72 537	60 959

Continent, country or area, date, code and age (in years) / Continent, pays ou zone, date, code et âge (en années)	Total			Urban - Urbaine			Rural - Rurale		
	Both sexes Les deux sexes	Male Masculin	Female Féminin	Both sexes Les deux sexes	Male Masculin	Female Féminin	Both sexes Les deux sexes	Male Masculin	Female Féminin
AMERICA, SOUTH - AMÉRIQUE DU SUD									
Chile - Chili									
1 VII 2010 (ESDF)									
35 - 39	1 236 191	618 163	618 028	1 088 474	539 511	548 963	147 717	78 652	69 065
40 - 44	1 231 974	613 175	618 799	1 072 331	528 259	544 072	159 643	84 916	74 727
45 - 49	1 249 164	618 588	630 576	1 083 459	527 892	555 567	165 705	90 696	75 009
50 - 54	1 072 667	527 804	544 863	934 287	450 679	483 608	138 380	77 125	61 255
55 - 59	835 126	406 235	428 891	727 572	346 485	381 087	107 554	59 750	47 804
60 - 64	671 677	320 361	351 316	581 243	270 943	310 300	90 434	49 418	41 016
65 - 69	539 279	249 712	289 567	461 661	208 182	253 479	77 618	41 530	36 088
70 - 74	389 319	173 101	216 218	327 449	140 360	187 089	61 870	32 741	29 129
75 - 79	295 148	122 538	172 610	247 645	98 346	149 299	47 503	24 192	23 311
80 +	318 013	115 299	202 714	270 378	92 562	177 816	47 635	22 737	24 898
Colombia - Colombie[20]									
1 VII 2010 (ESDF)									
Total	45 508 205	22 465 760	23 042 445	34 387 230	16 578 297	17 808 933	11 120 975	5 887 463	5 233 512
0 - 4	4 280 363	2 188 958	2 091 405	3 031 089	1 548 758	1 482 331	1 249 274	640 200	609 074
0	859 612	439 836	419 776	...	...	...	...	...	...
1 - 4	3 420 751	1 749 122	1 671 629	...	...	...	...	...	...
5 - 9	4 305 015	2 198 365	2 106 650	3 030 897	1 544 021	1 486 876	1 274 118	654 344	619 774
10 - 14	4 425 547	2 259 161	2 166 386	3 161 771	1 606 272	1 555 499	1 263 776	652 889	610 887
15 - 19	4 394 301	2 254 152	2 140 149	3 214 471	1 630 105	1 584 366	1 179 830	624 047	555 783
20 - 24	4 047 540	2 059 923	1 987 617	3 055 658	1 518 673	1 536 985	991 882	541 250	450 632
25 - 29	3 615 528	1 778 725	1 836 803	2 826 979	1 352 779	1 474 200	788 549	425 946	362 603
30 - 34	3 266 736	1 592 485	1 674 251	2 563 506	1 216 560	1 346 946	703 230	375 925	327 305
35 - 39	2 919 906	1 409 377	1 510 529	2 286 040	1 072 844	1 213 196	633 866	336 533	297 333
40 - 44	2 936 124	1 405 255	1 530 869	2 320 865	1 076 758	1 244 107	615 259	328 497	286 762
45 - 49	2 742 033	1 312 256	1 429 777	2 201 715	1 020 203	1 181 512	540 318	292 053	248 265
50 - 54	2 286 879	1 087 530	1 199 349	1 828 672	838 300	990 372	458 207	249 230	208 977
55 - 59	1 814 786	865 359	949 427	1 439 601	659 348	780 253	375 185	206 011	169 174
60 - 64	1 411 771	671 124	740 647	1 097 462	498 869	598 593	314 309	172 255	142 054
65 - 69	1 045 929	491 943	553 986	799 168	357 194	441 974	246 761	134 749	112 012
70 - 74	832 587	379 420	453 167	627 012	268 790	358 222	205 575	110 630	94 945
75 - 79	589 649	260 950	328 699	449 630	187 837	261 793	140 019	73 113	66 906
80 +	593 511	250 777	342 734	452 694	180 986	271 708	140 817	69 791	71 026
Ecuador - Équateur[21]									
1 VII 2010 (ESDF)									
Total	14 204 900	7 115 983	7 088 917	9 410 481	4 671 748	4 738 733	4 794 419	2 444 235	2 350 184
0 - 4	1 428 944	729 658	699 286	883 421	457 436	425 985	545 523	272 222	273 301
5 - 9	1 436 738	732 520	704 218	882 681	453 015	429 666	554 057	279 505	274 552
10 - 14	1 440 171	733 902	706 269	905 066	459 142	445 924	535 105	274 760	260 345
15 - 19	1 372 730	697 754	674 976	915 778	455 606	460 172	456 952	242 148	214 804
20 - 24	1 302 452	659 047	643 405	912 861	453 753	459 108	389 591	205 294	184 297
25 - 29	1 190 993	598 999	591 994	862 917	428 993	433 924	328 076	170 006	158 070
30 - 34	1 065 219	532 857	532 362	775 112	385 582	389 530	290 107	147 275	142 832
35 - 39	951 023	473 855	477 168	671 519	333 805	337 714	279 504	140 050	139 454
40 - 44	847 633	420 767	426 866	580 741	287 103	293 638	266 892	133 664	133 228
45 - 49	732 108	362 447	369 661	479 767	235 796	243 971	252 341	126 651	125 690
50 - 54	624 515	307 863	316 652	401 338	195 398	205 940	223 177	112 465	110 712
55 - 59	529 600	259 636	269 964	337 355	161 567	175 788	192 245	98 069	94 176
60 - 64	386 367	188 298	198 069	244 485	115 567	128 918	141 882	72 731	69 151
65 - 69	304 808	146 500	158 308	191 085	88 638	102 447	113 723	57 862	55 861
70 - 74	240 246	113 430	126 816	148 912	67 332	81 580	91 334	46 098	45 236
75 - 79	177 156	81 878	95 278	109 659	48 202	61 457	67 497	33 676	33 821
80 +	174 197	76 572	97 625	107 784	44 813	62 971	66 413	31 759	34 654
Peru - Pérou[22]									
1 VII 2010 (ESDF)									
Total	29 461 933	14 768 901	14 693 032	21 805 837	10 784 345	11 021 492	7 656 096	3 984 556	3 671 540
0 - 4	2 958 307	1 509 339	1 448 968	1 974 352	1 011 250	963 102	983 955	498 089	485 866
5 - 9	2 938 148	1 495 997	1 442 151	2 015 280	1 024 502	990 778	922 868	471 495	451 373
10 - 14	2 926 874	1 486 658	1 440 216	2 059 499	1 038 555	1 020 944	867 375	448 103	419 272
15 - 19	2 894 913	1 468 615	1 426 298	2 125 494	1 063 479	1 062 015	769 419	405 136	364 283
20 - 24	2 736 208	1 383 547	1 352 661	2 054 870	1 020 836	1 034 034	681 338	362 711	318 627
25 - 29	2 485 715	1 253 777	1 231 938	1 921 927	949 143	972 784	563 788	304 634	259 154
30 - 34	2 327 388	1 171 945	1 155 443	1 806 638	888 463	918 175	520 750	283 482	237 268

Continent, country or area, date, code and age (in years) / Continent, pays ou zone, date, code et âge (en années)	Total			Urban - Urbaine			Rural - Rurale		
	Both sexes Les deux sexes	Male Masculin	Female Féminin	Both sexes Les deux sexes	Male Masculin	Female Féminin	Both sexes Les deux sexes	Male Masculin	Female Féminin
AMERICA, SOUTH - AMÉRIQUE DU SUD									
Peru - Pérou[22]									
1 VII 2010 (ESDF)									
35 - 39	2 040 580	1 024 331	1 016 249	1 571 782	771 507	800 275	468 798	252 824	215 974
40 - 44	1 784 657	892 531	892 126	1 392 919	683 235	709 684	391 738	209 296	182 442
45 - 49	1 544 094	768 430	775 664	1 213 335	593 710	619 625	330 759	174 720	156 039
50 - 54	1 262 267	623 862	638 405	985 917	479 531	506 386	276 350	144 331	132 019
55 - 59	1 029 294	505 214	524 080	795 445	385 230	410 215	233 849	119 984	113 865
60 - 64	804 729	391 304	413 425	604 506	291 583	312 923	200 223	99 721	100 502
65 - 69	623 443	298 276	325 167	462 144	219 638	242 506	161 299	78 638	82 661
70 - 74	480 926	224 143	256 783	353 833	163 554	190 279	127 093	60 589	66 504
75 - 79	336 472	150 917	185 555	248 583	109 701	138 882	87 889	41 216	46 673
80 +	287 918	120 015	167 903	219 313	90 428	128 885	68 605	29 587	39 018
Venezuela (Bolivarian Republic of) - Venezuela (République bolivarienne du)									
1 VII 2010 (ESDF)									
Total	28 833 845	14 456 287	14 377 558	25 396 369	12 608 398	12 787 971	3 437 476	1 847 889	1 589 587
0 - 4	2 910 131	1 488 261	1 421 870	2 457 882	1 262 072	1 195 810	452 249	226 189	226 060
5 - 9	2 822 855	1 442 324	1 380 531	2 411 710	1 235 540	1 176 170	411 145	206 784	204 361
10 - 14	2 739 346	1 398 415	1 340 931	2 383 900	1 215 039	1 168 861	355 446	183 376	172 070
15 - 19	2 706 612	1 378 512	1 328 100	2 381 106	1 201 454	1 179 652	325 506	177 058	148 448
20 - 24	2 675 644	1 354 831	1 320 813	2 371 287	1 186 528	1 184 759	304 357	168 303	136 054
25 - 29	2 437 246	1 225 178	1 212 068	2 165 872	1 074 648	1 091 224	271 374	150 530	120 844
30 - 34	2 208 300	1 104 475	1 103 825	1 981 640	979 453	1 002 187	226 660	125 022	101 638
35 - 39	1 898 430	946 190	952 240	1 710 203	841 941	868 262	188 227	104 249	83 978
40 - 44	1 798 146	893 795	904 351	1 624 771	797 742	827 029	173 375	96 053	77 322
45 - 49	1 646 079	816 313	829 766	1 485 583	727 957	757 626	160 496	88 356	72 140
50 - 54	1 341 579	662 904	678 675	1 202 974	585 971	617 003	138 605	76 933	61 672
55 - 59	1 129 726	555 736	573 990	1 004 962	484 861	520 101	124 764	70 875	53 889
60 - 64	883 464	432 186	451 278	778 721	371 383	407 338	104 743	60 803	43 940
65 - 69	627 725	301 129	326 596	549 562	256 191	293 371	78 163	44 938	33 225
70 - 74	436 968	203 164	233 804	382 854	173 209	209 645	54 114	29 955	24 159
75 +	571 594	252 874	318 720	503 342	214 409	288 933	68 252	38 465	29 787
ASIA - ASIE									
Armenia - Arménie									
1 I 2010 (ESDJ)									
Total	3 249 482	1 575 826	1 673 656	...	...	...	...	...	...
0	44 034	23 443	20 591	...	...	...	...	...	...
1 - 4	154 165	82 350	71 815	...	...	...	...	...	...
5 - 9	179 952	96 574	83 378	...	...	...	...	...	...
10 - 14	217 566	114 552	103 014	...	...	...	...	...	...
15 - 19	292 190	149 299	142 891	...	...	...	...	...	...
20 - 24	316 076	160 100	155 976	...	...	...	...	...	...
25 - 29	291 871	146 984	144 887	...	...	...	...	...	...
30 - 34	239 741	118 271	121 470	...	...	...	...	...	...
35 - 39	202 065	97 573	104 492	...	...	...	...	...	...
40 - 44	203 446	96 478	106 968	...	...	...	...	...	...
45 - 49	260 284	123 127	137 157	...	...	...	...	...	...
50 - 54	238 531	111 861	126 670	...	...	...	...	...	...
55 - 59	175 176	79 856	95 320	...	...	...	...	...	...
60 - 64	107 399	46 967	60 432	...	...	...	...	...	...
65 - 69	84 591	35 455	49 136	...	...	...	...	...	...
70 - 74	113 222	45 894	67 328	...	...	...	...	...	...
75 - 79	74 150	29 499	44 651	...	...	...	...	...	...
80 - 84	43 861	14 700	29 161	...	...	...	...	...	...
85 +	11 162	2 843	8 319	...	...	...	...	...	...
Azerbaijan - Azerbaïdjan									
1 I 2010 (ESDF)									
Total	8 997 400	4 413 400	4 584 000	...	...	...	...	...	...
0	152 100	82 200	69 900	...	...	...	...	...	...
1 - 4	596 500	318 900	277 600	...	...	...	...	...	...

Continent, country or area, date, code and age (in years) / Continent, pays ou zone, date, code et âge (en années)	Total			Urban - Urbaine			Rural - Rurale		
	Both sexes Les deux sexes	Male Masculin	Female Féminin	Both sexes Les deux sexes	Male Masculin	Female Féminin	Both sexes Les deux sexes	Male Masculin	Female Féminin
ASIA - ASIE									
Azerbaijan - Azerbaïdjan									
1 I 2010 (ESDF)									
5 - 9	582 300	310 700	271 600	...	...	...	...	...	...
10 - 14	657 000	342 200	314 800	...	...	...	...	...	...
15 - 19	911 000	464 600	446 400	...	...	...	...	...	...
20 - 24	928 800	471 100	457 700	...	...	...	...	...	...
25 - 29	795 200	399 000	396 200	...	...	...	...	...	...
30 - 34	666 400	320 800	345 600	...	...	...	...	...	...
35 - 39	624 700	291 800	332 900	...	...	...	...	...	...
40 - 44	671 100	312 200	358 900	...	...	...	...	...	...
45 - 49	700 700	329 700	371 000	...	...	...	...	...	...
50 - 54	559 900	266 300	293 600	...	...	...	...	...	...
55 - 59	355 000	167 300	187 700	...	...	...	...	...	...
60 - 64	206 600	94 600	112 000	...	...	...	...	...	...
65 - 69	154 200	66 900	87 300	...	...	...	...	...	...
70 - 74	209 900	86 800	123 100	...	...	...	...	...	...
75 - 79	130 400	53 500	76 900	...	...	...	...	...	...
80 - 84	59 800	23 400	36 400	...	...	...	...	...	...
85 - 89	24 700	7 900	16 800	...	...	...	...	...	...
90 - 94	6 200	2 100	4 100	...	...	...	...	...	...
95 - 99	3 800	1 000	2 800	...	...	...	...	...	...
100 +	1 100	400	700	...	...	...	...	...	...
Bhutan - Bhoutan[23]									
1 VII 2010 (ESDF)									
Total	695 823	363 384	332 439	242 001	129 298	112 703	453 822	234 086	219 736
0 - 4	86 247	43 489	42 758	26 746	13 395	13 351	59 500	30 094	29 407
5 - 9	62 421	31 415	31 006	21 475	10 725	10 751	40 946	20 690	20 256
10 - 14	68 051	34 470	33 581	25 297	12 716	12 581	42 754	21 754	21 000
15 - 19	72 005	36 730	35 276	28 119	14 352	13 768	43 886	22 378	21 508
20 - 24	69 545	36 072	33 473	28 941	15 210	13 731	40 604	20 862	19 742
25 - 29	64 830	34 684	30 146	27 159	14 851	12 308	37 671	19 833	17 838
30 - 34	57 298	31 059	26 238	23 463	13 218	10 245	33 834	17 841	15 993
35 - 39	47 134	25 834	21 301	18 242	10 534	7 708	28 892	15 300	13 592
40 - 44	39 342	21 559	17 784	13 229	7 806	5 423	26 113	13 753	12 361
45 - 49	31 587	17 038	14 549	9 382	5 524	3 858	22 205	11 513	10 691
50 - 54	25 901	13 852	12 049	6 498	3 825	2 674	19 403	10 028	9 375
55 - 59	20 986	11 151	9 835	4 594	2 669	1 925	16 392	8 482	7 910
60 - 64	16 768	8 823	7 945	3 188	1 758	1 430	13 581	7 066	6 515
65 - 69	12 947	6 725	6 222	2 229	1 162	1 067	10 718	5 563	5 155
70 - 74	9 395	4 817	4 578	1 496	719	777	7 899	4 098	3 801
75 - 79	6 172	3 112	3 060	995	426	569	5 177	2 687	2 491
80 +	5 192	2 554	2 638	946	409	537	4 246	2 145	2 101
Cambodia - Cambodge[24]									
1 VII 2010 (ESDF)									
Total	14 302 779	6 973 994	7 328 785	2 926 810	1 406 183	1 520 627	11 375 969	5 567 811	5 808 158
0	327 301	167 929	159 371	61 675	30 866	30 809	265 625	137 064	128 562
1 - 4	1 180 736	600 921	579 816	196 983	100 801	96 182	983 754	500 119	483 634
5 - 9	1 437 400	734 505	702 895	211 238	108 616	102 622	1 226 162	625 889	600 273
10 - 14	1 652 039	847 378	804 661	238 615	122 907	115 708	1 413 424	724 471	688 953
15 - 19	1 721 753	890 277	831 476	335 868	160 072	175 796	1 385 885	730 205	655 680
20 - 24	1 502 762	750 333	752 429	413 466	191 164	222 302	1 089 296	559 169	530 127
25 - 29	1 356 253	662 000	694 253	390 387	186 440	203 947	965 866	475 560	490 306
30 - 34	895 820	436 760	459 060	220 449	108 240	112 209	675 371	328 520	346 851
35 - 39	779 742	376 959	402 783	166 887	83 154	83 733	612 855	293 805	319 050
40 - 44	816 938	386 938	430 000	169 733	84 649	85 084	647 205	302 289	344 916
45 - 49	704 545	326 501	378 044	142 092	69 440	72 652	562 453	257 061	305 392
50 - 54	563 355	237 905	325 450	119 492	53 311	66 181	443 863	184 594	259 269
55 - 59	431 639	173 359	258 280	91 368	38 926	52 442	340 271	134 433	205 838
60 - 64	318 577	133 743	184 834	62 517	26 799	35 718	256 060	106 944	149 116
65 - 69	231 774	97 040	134 734	41 024	16 925	24 099	190 750	80 115	110 635
70 - 74	171 257	69 745	101 512	28 536	11 182	17 354	142 721	58 563	84 158
75 - 79	115 615	45 471	70 144	19 443	7 026	12 417	96 172	38 445	57 727
80 +	95 273	36 230	59 043	17 037	5 665	11 372	78 236	30 565	47 671

Continent, country or area, date, code and age (in years) / Continent, pays ou zone, date, code et âge (en années)	Total			Urban - Urbaine			Rural - Rurale		
	Both sexes Les deux sexes	Male Masculin	Female Féminin	Both sexes Les deux sexes	Male Masculin	Female Féminin	Both sexes Les deux sexes	Male Masculin	Female Féminin
ASIA - ASIE									
China, Hong Kong SAR - Chine, Hong Kong RAS									
1 VII 2010 (ESDJ)									
Total	7 067 800	3 310 500	3 757 300	...	...	...	...	...	...
0	49 300	25 700	23 600	...	...	...	...	...	...
1 - 4	195 100	102 000	93 100	...	...	...	...	...	...
5 - 9	255 300	132 100	123 200	...	...	...	...	...	...
10 - 14	358 300	183 900	174 400	...	...	...	...	...	...
15 - 19	433 200	222 800	210 400	...	...	...	...	...	...
20 - 24	457 800	221 500	236 300	...	...	...	...	...	...
25 - 29	541 400	231 400	310 000	...	...	...	...	...	...
30 - 34	543 800	223 900	319 900	...	...	...	...	...	...
35 - 39	574 900	240 100	334 800	...	...	...	...	...	...
40 - 44	584 200	252 200	332 000	...	...	...	...	...	...
45 - 49	669 400	309 600	359 800	...	...	...	...	...	...
50 - 54	628 500	310 300	318 200	...	...	...	...	...	...
55 - 59	492 000	244 300	247 700	...	...	...	...	...	...
60 - 64	372 500	188 000	184 500	...	...	...	...	...	...
65 - 69	226 000	118 400	107 600	...	...	...	...	...	...
70 - 74	231 800	115 200	116 600	...	...	...	...	...	...
75 - 79	201 300	95 400	105 900	...	...	...	...	...	...
80 - 84	134 200	56 300	77 900	...	...	...	...	...	...
85 +	118 800	37 400	81 400	...	...	...	...	...	...
China, Macao SAR - Chine, Macao RAS[4]									
1 VII 2010 (ESDJ)									
Total	544 600	260 400	284 300	...	...	...	...	...	...
0 - 4	22 100	11 500	10 600	...	...	...	...	...	...
5 - 9	17 900	9 300	8 600	...	...	...	...	...	...
10 - 14	28 200	14 600	13 600	...	...	...	...	...	...
15 - 19	39 100	20 000	19 100	...	...	...	...	...	...
20 - 24	50 400	25 000	25 400	...	...	...	...	...	...
25 - 29	45 200	20 600	24 600	...	...	...	...	...	...
30 - 34	40 100	18 100	22 000	...	...	...	...	...	...
35 - 39	45 700	19 800	25 800	...	...	...	...	...	...
40 - 44	47 100	19 500	27 600	...	...	...	...	...	...
45 - 49	55 000	25 100	29 900	...	...	...	...	...	...
50 - 54	50 900	25 900	25 000	...	...	...	...	...	...
55 - 59	35 900	18 700	17 200	...	...	...	...	...	...
60 - 64	24 000	12 900	11 200	...	...	...	...	...	...
65 - 69	12 700	6 600	6 100	...	...	...	...	...	...
70 - 74	9 300	4 600	4 700	...	...	...	...	...	...
75 - 79	8 600	3 700	4 900	...	...	...	...	...	...
80 - 84	6 800	2 800	4 000	...	...	...	...	...	...
85 +	5 600	1 700	3 800	...	...	...	...	...	...
Cyprus - Chypre[25]									
1 I 2010 (ESDJ)									
Total	803 147	398 052	405 095	...	...	...	...	...	...
0	9 654	4 936	4 718	...	...	...	...	...	...
1 - 4	35 274	18 334	16 940	...	...	...	...	...	...
5 - 9	42 329	21 749	20 580	...	...	...	...	...	...
10 - 14	48 365	24 756	23 609	...	...	...	...	...	...
15 - 19	56 944	28 896	28 048	...	...	...	...	...	...
20 - 24	62 722	30 831	31 891	...	...	...	...	...	...
25 - 29	70 338	34 581	35 757	...	...	...	...	...	...
30 - 34	61 805	31 161	30 644	...	...	...	...	...	...
35 - 39	56 944	28 870	28 074	...	...	...	...	...	...
40 - 44	53 525	26 751	26 774	...	...	...	...	...	...
45 - 49	55 867	28 510	27 357	...	...	...	...	...	...
50 - 54	54 020	26 926	27 094	...	...	...	...	...	...
55 - 59	48 060	23 706	24 354	...	...	...	...	...	...
60 - 64	42 437	20 451	21 986	...	...	...	...	...	...
65 - 69	34 174	16 349	17 825	...	...	...	...	...	...
70 - 74	27 288	12 860	14 428	...	...	...	...	...	...
75 - 79	19 850	8 832	11 018	...	...	...	...	...	...

Continent, country or area, date, code and age (in years) Continent, pays ou zone, date, code et âge (en années)	Total			Urban - Urbaine			Rural - Rurale		
	Both sexes Les deux sexes	Male Masculin	Female Féminin	Both sexes Les deux sexes	Male Masculin	Female Féminin	Both sexes Les deux sexes	Male Masculin	Female Féminin
ASIA - ASIE									
Cyprus - Chypre[25]									
1 I 2010 (ESDJ)									
80 - 84	13 135	5 522	7 613	...	...	...	...	...	...
85 - 89	6 671	2 704	3 967	...	...	...	...	...	...
90 - 94	2 451	924	1 527	...	...	...	...	...	...
95 - 99	1 097	335	762	...	...	...	...	...	...
100 +	197	68	129	...	...	...	...	...	...
Indonesia - Indonésie									
1 V 2010 (CDJC)									
Total	237 641 326	119 630 913	118 010 413	...	...	...	...	...	...
0	4 397 046	2 259 245	2 137 801	...	...	...	...	...	...
1 - 4	18 275 014	9 399 611	8 875 403	...	...	...	...	...	...
5 - 9	23 247 170	11 970 804	11 276 366	...	...	...	...	...	...
10 - 14	22 677 490	11 659 310	11 018 180	...	...	...	...	...	...
15 - 19	20 871 086	10 610 119	10 260 967	...	...	...	...	...	...
20 - 24	19 878 417	9 881 969	9 996 448	...	...	...	...	...	...
25 - 29	21 300 087	10 626 458	10 673 629	...	...	...	...	...	...
30 - 34	19 822 200	9 945 211	9 876 989	...	...	...	...	...	...
35 - 39	18 497 502	9 333 720	9 163 782	...	...	...	...	...	...
40 - 44	16 518 468	8 319 453	8 199 015	...	...	...	...	...	...
45 - 49	14 035 952	7 030 168	7 005 784	...	...	...	...	...	...
50 - 54	11 556 859	5 863 756	5 693 103	...	...	...	...	...	...
55 - 59	8 445 336	4 398 805	4 046 531	...	...	...	...	...	...
60 - 64	6 056 311	2 926 073	3 130 238	...	...	...	...	...	...
65 - 69	4 692 150	2 224 273	2 467 877	...	...	...	...	...	...
70 - 74	3 455 185	1 530 938	1 924 247	...	...	...	...	...	...
75 - 79	1 977 177	842 096	1 135 081	...	...	...	...	...	...
80 - 84	1 142 908	481 328	661 580	...	...	...	...	...	...
85 - 89	437 815	182 379	255 436	...	...	...	...	...	...
90 - 94	170 856	63 932	106 924	...	...	...	...	...	...
95 +	104 607	36 082	68 525	...	...	...	...	...	...
Unknown - Inconnu	81 690	45 183	36 507	...	...	...	...	...	...
Japan - Japon[26]									
1 VII 2010 (ESDJ)									
Total	127 450 000	62 059 000	65 392 000	...	...	...	...	...	...
0 - 4	5 393 000	2 767 000	2 626 000	...	...	...	...	...	...
5 - 9	5 599 000	2 868 000	2 731 000	...	...	...	...	...	...
10 - 14	5 929 000	3 038 000	2 891 000	...	...	...	...	...	...
15 - 19	6 056 000	3 100 000	2 956 000	...	...	...	...	...	...
20 - 24	6 795 000	3 483 000	3 312 000	...	...	...	...	...	...
25 - 29	7 425 000	3 796 000	3 629 000	...	...	...	...	...	...
30 - 34	8 338 000	4 230 000	4 107 000	...	...	...	...	...	...
35 - 39	9 712 000	4 915 000	4 797 000	...	...	...	...	...	...
40 - 44	8 669 000	4 366 000	4 304 000	...	...	...	...	...	...
45 - 49	7 941 000	3 988 000	3 953 000	...	...	...	...	...	...
50 - 54	7 657 000	3 821 000	3 836 000	...	...	...	...	...	...
55 - 59	8 753 000	4 330 000	4 423 000	...	...	...	...	...	...
60 - 64	9 839 000	4 813 000	5 026 000	...	...	...	...	...	...
65 - 69	8 267 000	3 944 000	4 323 000	...	...	...	...	...	...
70 - 74	6 969 000	3 232 000	3 737 000	...	...	...	...	...	...
75 - 79	5 927 000	2 584 000	3 343 000	...	...	...	...	...	...
80 - 84	4 328 000	1 702 000	2 626 000	...	...	...	...	...	...
85 +	3 853 000	1 082 000	2 771 000	...	...	...	...	...	...
Malaysia - Malaisie[15]									
30 VI 2010 (ESDJ)									
Total	28 250 458	14 379 886	13 870 572	17 909 524	9 036 777	8 872 747	10 340 934	5 343 109	4 997 825
0	495 791	253 932	241 859	306 309	156 912	149 397	189 482	97 020	92 462
1 - 4	1 940 036	993 358	946 678	1 219 481	624 282	595 199	720 555	369 076	351 479
5 - 9	2 516 925	1 288 228	1 228 697	1 589 608	813 263	776 345	927 317	474 965	452 352
10 - 14	2 737 781	1 408 648	1 329 133	1 698 244	873 571	824 673	1 039 537	535 077	504 460
15 - 19	2 658 950	1 369 674	1 289 276	1 571 409	810 078	761 331	1 087 541	559 596	527 945
20 - 24	2 543 624	1 294 098	1 249 526	1 456 093	739 163	716 930	1 087 531	554 935	532 596
25 - 29	2 405 393	1 213 040	1 192 353	1 450 490	721 050	729 440	954 903	491 990	462 913
30 - 34	2 279 421	1 153 307	1 126 114	1 559 254	759 730	799 524	720 167	393 577	326 590
35 - 39	2 128 311	1 080 385	1 047 926	1 482 882	727 958	754 924	645 429	352 427	293 002

Continent, country or area, date, code and age (in years) Continent, pays ou zone, date, code et âge (en années)	Total			Urban - Urbaine			Rural - Rurale		
	Both sexes Les deux sexes	Male Masculin	Female Féminin	Both sexes Les deux sexes	Male Masculin	Female Féminin	Both sexes Les deux sexes	Male Masculin	Female Féminin
ASIA - ASIE									
Malaysia - Malaisie[15]									
30 VI 2010 (ESDJ)									
40 - 44	1 984 344	1 014 882	969 462	1 348 612	675 373	673 239	635 732	339 509	296 223
45 - 49	1 766 833	907 417	859 416	1 196 906	609 681	587 225	569 927	297 736	272 191
50 - 54	1 476 886	758 761	718 125	986 765	507 055	479 710	490 121	251 706	238 415
55 - 59	1 174 851	602 354	572 497	761 704	392 499	369 205	413 147	209 855	203 292
60 - 64	811 468	416 139	395 329	507 654	262 661	244 993	303 814	153 478	150 336
65 - 69	530 687	265 123	265 564	318 052	160 243	157 809	212 635	104 880	107 755
70 - 74	367 803	173 868	193 935	212 677	100 742	111 935	155 126	73 126	82 000
75 - 79	224 288	101 011	123 277	128 097	57 089	71 008	96 191	43 922	52 269
80 - 84	125 275	54 677	70 598	69 788	29 352	40 436	55 487	25 325	30 162
85 - 89	51 286	21 401	29 885	28 384	11 145	17 239	22 902	10 256	12 646
90 +	30 505	9 583	20 922	17 115	4 930	12 185	13 390	4 653	8 737
Maldives									
1 VII 2010 (ESDF)									
Total	319 738	161 708	158 030	...	...	...	...	...	...
0	6 635	3 355	3 280	...	...	...	...	...	...
1 - 4	22 858	11 630	11 228	...	...	...	...	...	...
5 - 9	26 871	13 787	13 084	...	...	...	...	...	...
10 - 14	31 897	16 502	15 395	...	...	...	...	...	...
15 - 19	38 900	20 141	18 759	...	...	...	...	...	...
20 - 24	40 331	20 334	19 997	...	...	...	...	...	...
25 - 29	33 543	16 339	17 204	...	...	...	...	...	...
30 - 34	23 683	11 552	12 131	...	...	...	...	...	...
35 - 39	20 473	9 991	10 482	...	...	...	...	...	...
40 - 44	17 992	8 756	9 236	...	...	...	...	...	...
45 - 49	15 673	7 810	7 863	...	...	...	...	...	...
50 - 54	12 669	6 473	6 196	...	...	...	...	...	...
55 - 59	7 130	3 741	3 389	...	...	...	...	...	...
60 - 64	5 560	2 866	2 694	...	...	...	...	...	...
65 - 69	5 294	2 697	2 597	...	...	...	...	...	...
70 - 74	4 985	2 643	2 342	...	...	...	...	...	...
75 - 79	2 993	1 695	1 298	...	...	...	...	...	...
80 +	2 251	1 396	855	...	...	...	...	...	...
Qatar									
21 IV 2010 (CDFC)									
Total	1 699 435	1 284 739	414 696	...	...	...	...	...	...
0	19 565	10 042	9 523	...	...	...	...	...	...
1 - 4	69 942	35 796	34 146	...	...	...	...	...	...
5 - 9	78 086	40 007	38 079	...	...	...	...	...	...
10 - 14	64 991	33 295	31 696	...	...	...	...	...	...
15 - 19	60 544	33 868	26 676	...	...	...	...	...	...
20 - 24	191 953	153 931	38 022	...	...	...	...	...	...
25 - 29	279 187	219 575	59 612	...	...	...	...	...	...
30 - 34	270 243	216 278	53 965	...	...	...	...	...	...
35 - 39	234 573	194 313	40 260	...	...	...	...	...	...
40 - 44	178 328	148 899	29 429	...	...	...	...	...	...
45 - 49	116 940	95 688	21 252	...	...	...	...	...	...
50 - 54	68 920	54 751	14 169	...	...	...	...	...	...
55 - 59	37 377	29 327	8 050	...	...	...	...	...	...
60 - 64	14 969	10 820	4 149	...	...	...	...	...	...
65 - 69	6 454	4 075	2 379	...	...	...	...	...	...
70 - 74	3 637	2 108	1 529	...	...	...	...	...	...
75 +	3 726	1 966	1 760	...	...	...	...	...	...
Republic of Korea - République de Corée									
1 VII 2010 (ESDJ)									
Total	48 874 539	24 540 316	24 334 223	...	...	...	...	...	...
0	438 169	226 952	211 217	...	...	...	...	...	...
1 - 4	1 763 296	914 174	849 122	...	...	...	...	...	...
5 - 9	2 517 298	1 310 285	1 207 013	...	...	...	...	...	...
10 - 14	3 188 145	1 670 825	1 517 320	...	...	...	...	...	...
15 - 19	3 402 266	1 807 825	1 594 441	...	...	...	...	...	...
20 - 24	3 113 166	1 641 439	1 471 727	...	...	...	...	...	...
25 - 29	3 720 641	1 921 508	1 799 133	...	...	...	...	...	...

Continent, country or area, date, code and age (in years) / Continent, pays ou zone, date, code et âge (en années)	Total			Urban - Urbaine			Rural - Rurale		
	Both sexes Les deux sexes	Male Masculin	Female Féminin	Both sexes Les deux sexes	Male Masculin	Female Féminin	Both sexes Les deux sexes	Male Masculin	Female Féminin
ASIA - ASIE									
Republic of Korea - République de Corée									
1 VII 2010 (ESDJ)									
30 - 34	3 828 448	1 977 245	1 851 203	...	...	...	...	...	...
35 - 39	4 270 214	2 194 306	2 075 908	...	...	...	...	...	...
40 - 44	4 184 430	2 131 520	2 052 910	...	...	...	...	...	...
45 - 49	4 191 988	2 125 488	2 066 500	...	...	...	...	...	...
50 - 54	3 907 712	1 965 669	1 942 043	...	...	...	...	...	...
55 - 59	2 805 204	1 395 331	1 409 873	...	...	...	...	...	...
60 - 64	2 186 709	1 067 753	1 118 956	...	...	...	...	...	...
65 - 69	1 811 334	833 561	977 773	...	...	...	...	...	...
70 - 74	1 526 896	658 563	868 333	...	...	...	...	...	...
75 - 79	1 066 945	410 554	656 391	...	...	...	...	...	...
80 - 84	579 110	188 636	390 474	...	...	...	...	...	...
85 - 89	273 944	76 812	197 132	...	...	...	...	...	...
90 - 94	78 391	18 623	59 768	...	...	...	...	...	...
95 +	20 233	3 247	16 986	...	...	...	...	...	...
Singapore - Singapour[27]									
1 VII 2010 (ESDJ)									
Total	3 771 721	1 861 133	1 910 588	...	...	...	...	...	...
0 - 4	194 432	98 890	95 542	...	...	...	...	...	...
5 - 9	215 675	110 215	105 460	...	...	...	...	...	...
10 - 14	244 302	125 271	119 031	...	...	...	...	...	...
15 - 19	263 750	134 003	129 747	...	...	...	...	...	...
20 - 24	247 190	123 942	123 248	...	...	...	...	...	...
25 - 29	272 639	131 299	141 340	...	...	...	...	...	...
30 - 34	298 687	143 048	155 639	...	...	...	...	...	...
35 - 39	320 024	156 318	163 706	...	...	...	...	...	...
40 - 44	309 441	152 995	156 446	...	...	...	...	...	...
45 - 49	323 459	163 237	160 222	...	...	...	...	...	...
50 - 54	303 044	152 721	150 323	...	...	...	...	...	...
55 - 59	248 696	124 822	123 874	...	...	...	...	...	...
60 - 64	191 995	94 796	97 199	...	...	...	...	...	...
65 - 69	111 511	53 321	58 190	...	...	...	...	...	...
70 - 74	92 618	42 887	49 731	...	...	...	...	...	...
75 - 79	65 178	28 214	36 964	...	...	...	...	...	...
80 - 84	39 839	15 532	24 307	...	...	...	...	...	...
85 - 89	18 481	6 446	12 035	...	...	...	...	...	...
90 - 94	7 644	2 279	5 365	...	...	...	...	...	...
95 - 99	2 392	639	1 753	...	...	...	...	...	...
100 +	724	258	466	...	...	...	...	...	...
Sri Lanka									
1 VII 2010* (ESDF)									
Total	20 653 000	10 249 000	10 404 000	...	...	...	...	...	...
0 - 4	1 755 000	892 000	863 000	...	...	...	...	...	...
5 - 9	1 817 000	922 000	895 000	...	...	...	...	...	...
10 - 14	1 859 000	943 000	916 000	...	...	...	...	...	...
15 - 19	2 003 000	1 015 000	988 000	...	...	...	...	...	...
20 - 24	1 942 000	974 000	968 000	...	...	...	...	...	...
25 - 29	1 631 000	799 000	832 000	...	...	...	...	...	...
30 - 34	1 580 000	779 000	801 000	...	...	...	...	...	...
35 - 39	1 538 000	758 000	780 000	...	...	...	...	...	...
40 - 44	1 425 000	707 000	718 000	...	...	...	...	...	...
45 - 49	1 250 000	615 000	635 000	...	...	...	...	...	...
50 - 54	1 126 000	554 000	572 000	...	...	...	...	...	...
55 - 59	817 000	390 000	427 000	...	...	...	...	...	...
60 - 64	609 000	297 000	312 000	...	...	...	...	...	...
65 - 69	485 000	225 000	260 000	...	...	...	...	...	...
70 - 74	372 000	174 000	198 000	...	...	...	...	...	...
75 +	444 000	205 000	239 000	...	...	...	...	...	...
Thailand - Thaïlande[1]									
1 VII 2010 (ESDJ)									
Total	67 311 917	33 067 359	34 244 558	23 096 811	11 070 161	12 026 650	44 215 106	21 997 198	22 217 908
0 - 4	4 240 182	2 166 497	2 073 685	1 446 040	729 284	716 756	2 794 142	1 437 213	1 356 929
0	777 163	399 143	378 020	...	...	...	...	...	...

Continent, country or area, date, code and age (in years) / Continent, pays ou zone, date, code et âge (en années)	Total			Urban - Urbaine			Rural - Rurale		
	Both sexes Les deux sexes	Male Masculin	Female Féminin	Both sexes Les deux sexes	Male Masculin	Female Féminin	Both sexes Les deux sexes	Male Masculin	Female Féminin
ASIA - ASIE									
Thailand - Thaïlande[1]									
1 VII 2010 (ESDJ)									
1 - 4	3 463 019	1 767 354	1 695 665	...	...	...	...	...	...
5 - 9	4 755 650	2 423 045	2 332 605	1 667 004	837 595	829 409	3 088 646	1 585 450	1 503 196
10 - 14	4 807 951	2 466 554	2 341 397	1 501 630	758 989	742 641	3 306 321	1 707 565	1 598 756
15 - 19	5 229 231	2 673 020	2 556 211	1 611 398	806 632	804 766	3 617 833	1 866 388	1 751 445
20 - 24	5 223 980	2 666 818	2 557 162	1 618 773	801 648	817 125	3 605 207	1 865 170	1 740 037
25 - 29	5 308 616	2 689 331	2 619 285	1 789 214	873 715	915 499	3 519 402	1 815 616	1 703 786
30 - 34	5 359 566	2 687 096	2 672 470	2 043 864	985 299	1 058 565	3 315 702	1 701 797	1 613 905
35 - 39	5 509 563	2 682 393	2 827 170	2 058 381	976 088	1 082 293	3 451 182	1 706 305	1 744 877
40 - 44	5 546 008	2 672 764	2 873 244	2 008 540	945 786	1 062 754	3 537 468	1 726 978	1 810 490
45 - 49	5 202 807	2 514 945	2 687 862	1 846 754	872 144	974 610	3 356 053	1 642 801	1 713 252
50 - 54	4 570 315	2 197 779	2 372 536	1 607 508	756 315	851 193	2 962 807	1 441 464	1 521 343
55 - 59	3 548 083	1 687 548	1 860 535	1 226 937	571 358	655 579	2 321 146	1 116 190	1 204 956
60 - 64	2 621 897	1 231 302	1 390 595	889 447	410 038	479 409	1 732 450	821 264	911 186
65 - 69	1 996 967	910 573	1 086 394	656 276	293 357	362 919	1 340 691	617 216	723 475
70 - 74	1 561 835	681 180	880 655	519 929	222 164	297 765	1 041 906	459 016	582 890
75 - 79	1 025 321	420 478	604 843	334 931	133 875	201 056	690 390	286 603	403 787
80 +	803 945	296 036	507 909	270 185	95 874	174 311	533 760	200 162	333 598
Turkey - Turquie[28]									
1 VII 2010 (ESDJ)									
Total	72 698 000	36 443 000	36 255 000	...	...	...	...	...	...
0	1 249 000	638 000	611 000	...	...	...	...	...	...
1 - 4	5 003 000	2 554 000	2 449 000	...	...	...	...	...	...
5 - 9	6 272 000	3 197 000	3 075 000	...	...	...	...	...	...
10 - 14	6 378 000	3 265 000	3 113 000	...	...	...	...	...	...
15 - 19	6 246 000	3 203 000	3 043 000	...	...	...	...	...	...
20 - 24	6 179 000	3 153 000	3 026 000	...	...	...	...	...	...
25 - 29	6 404 000	3 246 000	3 158 000	...	...	...	...	...	...
30 - 34	6 078 000	3 075 000	3 003 000	...	...	...	...	...	...
35 - 39	5 413 000	2 724 000	2 689 000	...	...	...	...	...	...
40 - 44	4 875 000	2 458 000	2 417 000	...	...	...	...	...	...
45 - 49	4 375 000	2 203 000	2 172 000	...	...	...	...	...	...
50 - 54	3 815 000	1 907 000	1 908 000	...	...	...	...	...	...
55 - 59	3 061 000	1 519 000	1 542 000	...	...	...	...	...	...
60 - 64	2 316 000	1 108 000	1 208 000	...	...	...	...	...	...
65 - 69	1 752 000	801 000	951 000	...	...	...	...	...	...
70 - 74	1 295 000	587 000	708 000	...	...	...	...	...	...
75 +	1 987 000	805 000	1 182 000	...	...	...	...	...	...
EUROPE									
Åland Islands - Îles d'Åland[9]									
1 VII 2010 (ESDJ)									
Total	27 871	13 880	13 991	11 157	5 327	5 830	16 714	8 553	8 161
0	277	152	126	97	57	40	181	95	86
1 - 4	1 210	636	574	412	210	202	798	426	372
5 - 9	1 480	772	708	498	254	244	982	518	465
10 - 14	1 642	854	788	598	300	299	1 044	554	490
15 - 19	1 730	875	855	673	336	338	1 057	540	517
20 - 24	1 388	760	628	677	352	326	711	409	302
25 - 29	1 563	796	767	803	413	390	760	383	377
30 - 34	1 662	856	806	748	379	369	915	478	437
35 - 39	1 794	919	875	692	343	349	1 103	576	527
40 - 44	2 047	1 009	1 038	770	370	400	1 277	639	638
45 - 49	1 955	981	974	740	344	396	1 215	637	578
50 - 54	1 922	919	1 003	721	332	390	1 201	587	614
55 - 59	2 071	997	1 074	850	385	465	1 221	612	609
60 - 64	2 095	1 052	1 044	859	405	455	1 236	647	589
65 - 69	1 563	832	731	598	295	303	965	537	428
70 - 74	1 138	553	585	452	204	248	687	350	337
75 - 79	892	412	480	350	159	192	542	253	289
80 - 84	726	301	425	296	112	184	430	189	241
85 - 89	474	156	318	212	63	149	262	94	169

Continent, country or area, date, code and age (in years) / Continent, pays ou zone, date, code et âge (en années)	Total			Urban - Urbaine			Rural - Rurale		
	Both sexes Les deux sexes	Male Masculin	Female Féminin	Both sexes Les deux sexes	Male Masculin	Female Féminin	Both sexes Les deux sexes	Male Masculin	Female Féminin
EUROPE									
Åland Islands - Îles d'Åland[9]									
1 VII 2010 (ESDJ)									
90 - 94	180	40	140	83	16	67	97	24	73
95 - 99	62	11	51	30	3	27	32	8	24
100 +	6	1	5	1	-	1	5	1	4
Andorra - Andorre[9]									
1 VII 2010 (ESDJ)									
Total	84 614	44 021	40 593	...	...	...	...	...	...
0	273	131	142	...	...	...	...	...	...
1 - 4	3 100	1 578	1 522	...	...	...	...	...	...
5 - 9	4 199	2 197	2 002	...	...	...	...	...	...
10 - 14	4 246	2 212	2 034	...	...	...	...	...	...
15 - 19	3 927	2 097	1 830	...	...	...	...	...	...
20 - 24	4 171	2 139	2 032	...	...	...	...	...	...
25 - 29	5 954	2 961	2 993	...	...	...	...	...	...
30 - 34	7 720	3 951	3 769	...	...	...	...	...	...
35 - 39	8 290	4 291	3 999	...	...	...	...	...	...
40 - 44	7 899	4 126	3 773	...	...	...	...	...	...
45 - 49	7 594	4 030	3 564	...	...	...	...	...	...
50 - 54	6 407	3 444	2 963	...	...	...	...	...	...
55 - 59	5 113	2 780	2 333	...	...	...	...	...	...
60 - 64	4 297	2 371	1 926	...	...	...	...	...	...
65 - 69	3 202	1 712	1 490	...	...	...	...	...	...
70 - 74	2 395	1 218	1 177	...	...	...	...	...	...
75 - 79	2 013	1 035	978	...	...	...	...	...	...
80 - 84	1 734	797	937	...	...	...	...	...	...
85 - 89	1 103	509	594	...	...	...	...	...	...
90 - 94	511	219	292	...	...	...	...	...	...
95 - 99	252	118	134	...	...	...	...	...	...
100 +	214	105	109	...	...	...	...	...	...
Austria - Autriche									
1 I 2010 (ESDJ)									
Total	8 375 290	4 079 093	4 296 197	...	...	...	...	...	...
0	75 711	38 757	36 954	...	...	...	...	...	...
1 - 4	317 142	162 366	154 776	...	...	...	...	...	...
5 - 9	406 779	208 830	197 949	...	...	...	...	...	...
10 - 14	445 238	227 924	217 314	...	...	...	...	...	...
15 - 19	501 244	257 147	244 097	...	...	...	...	...	...
20 - 24	520 986	263 387	257 599	...	...	...	...	...	...
25 - 29	557 088	279 220	277 868	...	...	...	...	...	...
30 - 34	529 346	265 521	263 825	...	...	...	...	...	...
35 - 39	602 957	299 500	303 457	...	...	...	...	...	...
40 - 44	707 342	357 275	350 067	...	...	...	...	...	...
45 - 49	698 207	352 532	345 675	...	...	...	...	...	...
50 - 54	593 235	295 169	298 066	...	...	...	...	...	...
55 - 59	493 170	241 571	251 599	...	...	...	...	...	...
60 - 64	450 924	217 828	233 096	...	...	...	...	...	...
65 - 69	463 946	218 059	245 887	...	...	...	...	...	...
70 - 74	341 865	155 526	186 339	...	...	...	...	...	...
75 - 79	270 200	113 064	157 136	...	...	...	...	...	...
80 - 84	217 259	78 323	138 936	...	...	...	...	...	...
85 - 89	137 530	37 003	100 527	...	...	...	...	...	...
90 - 94	33 368	7 780	25 588	...	...	...	...	...	...
95 - 99	10 713	2 144	8 569	...	...	...	...	...	...
100 +	1 040	167	873	...	...	...	...	...	...
Bulgaria - Bulgarie									
1 I 2010 (ESDJ)									
Total	7 563 710	3 659 311	3 904 399	...	...	...	...	...	...
0	76 585	39 091	37 494	...	...	...	...	...	...
1 - 4	293 490	150 902	142 588	...	...	...	...	...	...
5 - 9	336 730	173 285	163 445	...	...	...	...	...	...
10 - 14	319 395	163 855	155 540	...	...	...	...	...	...
15 - 19	416 428	213 718	202 710	...	...	...	...	...	...
20 - 24	516 606	264 403	252 203	...	...	...	...	...	...
25 - 29	536 952	276 081	260 871	...	...	...	...	...	...

Continent, country or area, date, code and age (in years) Continent, pays ou zone, date, code et âge (en années)	Total			Urban - Urbaine			Rural - Rurale		
	Both sexes Les deux sexes	Male Masculin	Female Féminin	Both sexes Les deux sexes	Male Masculin	Female Féminin	Both sexes Les deux sexes	Male Masculin	Female Féminin
EUROPE									
Bulgaria - Bulgarie									
1 I 2010 (ESDJ)									
30 - 34	577 153	295 404	281 749	...	...	...	...	...	...
35 - 39	555 128	282 046	273 082	...	...	...	...	...	...
40 - 44	518 236	260 808	257 428	...	...	...	...	...	...
45 - 49	521 135	259 088	262 047	...	...	...	...	...	...
50 - 54	529 280	257 396	271 884	...	...	...	...	...	...
55 - 59	530 843	251 375	279 468	...	...	...	...	...	...
60 - 64	509 858	232 764	277 094	...	...	...	...	...	...
65 - 69	393 744	172 098	221 646	...	...	...	...	...	...
70 - 74	342 280	142 362	199 918	...	...	...	...	...	...
75 - 79	302 190	120 122	182 068	...	...	...	...	...	...
80 - 84	186 380	69 565	116 815	...	...	...	...	...	...
85 - 89	82 882	28 772	54 110	...	...	...	...	...	...
90 - 94	14 801	4 994	9 807	...	...	...	...	...	...
95 - 99	3 186	1 028	2 158	...	...	...	...	...	...
100 +	428	154	274	...	...	...	...	...	...
Croatia - Croatie									
1 I 2010 (ESDJ)									
Total	4 425 747	2 135 169	2 290 578	...	...	...	...	...	...
0	44 360	22 767	21 593	...	...	...	...	...	...
1 - 4	169 807	87 270	82 537	...	...	...	...	...	...
5 - 9	208 477	107 088	101 389	...	...	...	...	...	...
10 - 14	250 890	128 389	122 501	...	...	...	...	...	...
15 - 19	256 586	131 141	125 445	...	...	...	...	...	...
20 - 24	281 760	143 747	138 013	...	...	...	...	...	...
25 - 29	312 355	159 248	153 107	...	...	...	...	...	...
30 - 34	307 916	155 926	151 990	...	...	...	...	...	...
35 - 39	293 755	147 942	145 813	...	...	...	...	...	...
40 - 44	307 949	153 578	154 371	...	...	...	...	...	...
45 - 49	319 037	158 324	160 713	...	...	...	...	...	...
50 - 54	329 719	162 467	167 252	...	...	...	...	...	...
55 - 59	313 307	154 134	159 173	...	...	...	...	...	...
60 - 64	249 931	117 680	132 251	...	...	...	...	...	...
65 - 69	216 970	96 013	120 957	...	...	...	...	...	...
70 - 74	214 201	89 125	125 076	...	...	...	...	...	...
75 - 79	173 437	65 031	108 406	...	...	...	...	...	...
80 - 84	101 389	32 840	68 549	...	...	...	...	...	...
85 +	54 711	13 773	40 938	...	...	...	...	...	...
Unknown - Inconnu	19 190	8 686	10 504	...	...	...	...	...	...
Czech Republic - République tchèque									
1 I 2010 (ESDJ)									
Total	10 506 813	5 157 197	5 349 616	7 732 884	3 767 715	3 965 169	2 773 929	1 389 482	1 384 447
0	118 609	60 494	58 115	86 726	44 248	42 478	31 883	16 246	15 637
1 - 4	445 936	228 638	217 298	324 068	166 164	157 904	121 868	62 474	59 394
5 - 9	470 960	242 402	228 558	338 512	174 404	164 108	132 448	67 998	64 450
10 - 14	458 865	235 471	223 394	324 368	166 019	158 349	134 497	69 452	65 045
15 - 19	615 991	315 905	300 086	441 464	225 754	215 710	174 527	90 151	84 376
20 - 24	700 740	361 233	339 507	520 059	268 082	251 977	180 681	93 151	87 530
25 - 29	758 921	393 253	365 668	567 488	294 222	273 266	191 433	99 031	92 402
30 - 34	927 504	476 520	450 984	686 827	352 242	334 585	240 677	124 278	116 399
35 - 39	845 964	435 327	410 637	620 613	316 746	303 867	225 351	118 581	106 770
40 - 44	700 861	359 838	341 023	517 215	262 201	255 014	183 646	97 637	86 009
45 - 49	679 938	345 961	333 977	502 977	252 990	249 987	176 961	92 971	83 990
50 - 54	700 751	349 514	351 237	513 574	252 090	261 484	187 177	97 424	89 753
55 - 59	761 690	370 932	390 758	561 918	269 433	292 485	199 772	101 499	98 273
60 - 64	721 200	341 085	380 115	533 285	247 670	285 615	187 915	93 415	94 500
65 - 69	537 277	243 367	293 910	404 524	180 961	223 563	132 753	62 406	70 347
70 - 74	367 737	155 444	212 293	273 657	115 078	158 579	94 080	40 366	53 714
75 - 79	320 822	124 365	196 457	237 793	91 856	145 937	83 029	32 509	50 520
80 - 84	227 014	77 384	149 630	168 705	57 653	111 052	58 309	19 731	38 578
85 - 89	117 447	33 230	84 217	88 477	25 084	63 393	28 970	8 146	20 824
90 - 94	21 415	5 305	16 110	15 841	3 869	11 972	5 574	1 436	4 138

7a. Population by age, sex and urban/rural residence: 2010
Population selon l'âge, le sexe et la résidence, urbaine/rurale: 2010 (continued - suite)

Continent, country or area, date, code and age (in years) / Continent, pays ou zone, date, code et âge (en années)	Total			Urban - Urbaine			Rural - Rurale		
	Both sexes Les deux sexes	Male Masculin	Female Féminin	Both sexes Les deux sexes	Male Masculin	Female Féminin	Both sexes Les deux sexes	Male Masculin	Female Féminin
EUROPE									
Czech Republic - République tchèque									
1 I 2010 (ESDJ)									
95 - 99	6 441	1 362	5 079	4 370	851	3 519	2 071	511	1 560
100 +	730	167	563	423	98	325	307	69	238
Denmark - Danemark[29]									
1 VII 2010 (ESDJ)									
Total	5 543 819	2 748 185	2 795 634	...	...	...	...	...	...
0	63 569	32 608	30 961	...	...	...	...	...	...
1 - 4	262 465	134 715	127 750	...	...	...	...	...	...
5 - 9	328 581	168 088	160 493	...	...	...	...	...	...
10 - 14	343 314	176 017	167 297	...	...	...	...	...	...
15 - 19	353 069	180 986	172 083	...	...	...	...	...	...
20 - 24	329 802	168 189	161 613	...	...	...	...	...	...
25 - 29	309 632	155 506	154 126	...	...	...	...	...	...
30 - 34	347 870	174 274	173 596	...	...	...	...	...	...
35 - 39	389 141	195 538	193 603	...	...	...	...	...	...
40 - 44	409 070	207 287	201 783	...	...	...	...	...	...
45 - 49	404 521	204 711	199 810	...	...	...	...	...	...
50 - 54	365 305	183 802	181 503	...	...	...	...	...	...
55 - 59	349 290	174 342	174 948	...	...	...	...	...	...
60 - 64	369 012	183 415	185 597	...	...	...	...	...	...
65 - 69	309 047	151 277	157 770	...	...	...	...	...	...
70 - 74	220 491	104 199	116 292	...	...	...	...	...	...
75 - 79	161 422	71 782	89 640	...	...	...	...	...	...
80 - 84	117 410	47 503	69 907	...	...	...	...	...	...
85 - 89	72 998	24 458	48 540	...	...	...	...	...	...
90 - 94	29 589	7 849	21 740	...	...	...	...	...	...
95 - 99	7 312	1 507	5 805	...	...	...	...	...	...
100 +	909	132	777	...	...	...	...	...	...
Estonia - Estonie									
1 I 2010 (ESDJ)									
Total	1 340 127	617 323	722 804	...	...	...	...	...	...
0	15 711	7 991	7 720	...	...	...	...	...	...
1 - 4	60 690	31 402	29 288	...	...	...	...	...	...
5 - 9	65 107	33 424	31 683	...	...	...	...	...	...
10 - 14	61 266	31 481	29 785	...	...	...	...	...	...
15 - 19	81 447	41 748	39 699	...	...	...	...	...	...
20 - 24	106 663	54 479	52 184	...	...	...	...	...	...
25 - 29	102 028	51 585	50 443	...	...	...	...	...	...
30 - 34	93 094	46 883	46 211	...	...	...	...	...	...
35 - 39	92 886	45 927	46 959	...	...	...	...	...	...
40 - 44	86 852	41 901	44 951	...	...	...	...	...	...
45 - 49	93 373	44 085	49 288	...	...	...	...	...	...
50 - 54	92 972	42 575	50 397	...	...	...	...	...	...
55 - 59	85 633	37 621	48 012	...	...	...	...	...	...
60 - 64	73 518	30 875	42 643	...	...	...	...	...	...
65 - 69	62 555	24 491	38 064	...	...	...	...	...	...
70 - 74	63 731	22 567	41 164	...	...	...	...	...	...
75 - 79	47 810	15 141	32 669	...	...	...	...	...	...
80 - 84	33 890	8 961	24 929	...	...	...	...	...	...
85 - 89	15 215	3 105	12 110	...	...	...	...	...	...
90 - 94	3 939	723	3 216	...	...	...	...	...	...
95 - 99	1 317	245	1 072	...	...	...	...	...	...
100 +	296	53	243	...	...	...	...	...	...
Unknown - Inconnu	134	60	74	...	...	...	...	...	...
Finland - Finlande[9]									
1 I 2010 (ESDJ)									
Total	5 351 427	2 625 067	2 726 360	...	...	...	...	...	...
0	60 525	30 862	29 663	...	...	...	...	...	...
1 - 4	237 589	121 335	116 254	...	...	...	...	...	...
5 - 9	287 786	147 367	140 419	...	...	...	...	...	...
10 - 14	302 423	154 256	148 167	...	...	...	...	...	...
15 - 19	334 636	170 583	164 053	...	...	...	...	...	...
20 - 24	324 472	165 988	158 484	...	...	...	...	...	...

Continent, country or area, date, code and age (in years) Continent, pays ou zone, date, code et âge (en années)	Total			Urban - Urbaine			Rural - Rurale		
	Both sexes Les deux sexes	Male Masculin	Female Féminin	Both sexes Les deux sexes	Male Masculin	Female Féminin	Both sexes Les deux sexes	Male Masculin	Female Féminin
EUROPE									
Finland - Finlande[9]									
1 I 2010 (ESDJ)									
25 - 29	344 634	177 022	167 612	...	...	...	...	...	...
30 - 34	337 970	173 572	164 398	...	...	...	...	...	...
35 - 39	310 768	158 921	151 847	...	...	...	...	...	...
40 - 44	358 754	182 143	176 611	...	...	...	...	...	...
45 - 49	378 341	191 110	187 231	...	...	...	...	...	...
50 - 54	378 037	189 311	188 726	...	...	...	...	...	...
55 - 59	388 165	192 402	195 763	...	...	...	...	...	...
60 - 64	396 886	194 857	202 029	...	...	...	...	...	...
65 - 69	258 319	122 578	135 741	...	...	...	...	...	...
70 - 74	225 043	101 250	123 793	...	...	...	...	...	...
75 - 79	179 671	74 193	105 478	...	...	...	...	...	...
80 - 84	138 717	49 230	89 487	...	...	...	...	...	...
85 - 89	76 940	21 357	55 583	...	...	...	...	...	...
90 - 94	25 260	5 618	19 642	...	...	...	...	...	...
95 - 99	5 925	1 030	4 895	...	...	...	...	...	...
100 +	566	82	484	...	...	...	...	...	...
France[30]									
1 I 2010* (ESDJ)									
Total	62 793 432	30 413 779	32 379 653	...	...	...	...	...	...
0	786 272	399 168	387 104	...	...	...	...	...	...
1 - 4	3 098 155	1 582 816	1 515 339	...	...	...	...	...	...
5 - 9	3 841 419	1 966 731	1 874 688	...	...	...	...	...	...
10 - 14	3 783 928	1 940 517	1 843 411	...	...	...	...	...	...
15 - 19	3 815 432	1 949 381	1 866 051	...	...	...	...	...	...
20 - 24	4 008 962	2 022 307	1 986 655	...	...	...	...	...	...
25 - 29	3 956 792	1 967 866	1 988 926	...	...	...	...	...	...
30 - 34	3 821 064	1 902 811	1 918 253	...	...	...	...	...	...
35 - 39	4 340 563	2 158 654	2 181 909	...	...	...	...	...	...
40 - 44	4 345 299	2 151 121	2 194 178	...	...	...	...	...	...
45 - 49	4 353 712	2 140 122	2 213 590	...	...	...	...	...	...
50 - 54	4 174 775	2 033 465	2 141 310	...	...	...	...	...	...
55 - 59	4 098 041	1 993 592	2 104 449	...	...	...	...	...	...
60 - 64	3 802 745	1 847 480	1 955 265	...	...	...	...	...	...
65 - 69	2 553 832	1 215 547	1 338 285	...	...	...	...	...	...
70 - 74	2 410 515	1 085 444	1 325 071	...	...	...	...	...	...
75 - 79	2 258 796	939 070	1 319 726	...	...	...	...	...	...
80 - 84	1 763 445	655 016	1 108 429	...	...	...	...	...	...
85 - 89	1 154 561	366 642	787 919	...	...	...	...	...	...
90 - 94	287 477	71 806	215 671	...	...	...	...	...	...
95 +	137 647	24 223	113 424	...	...	...	...	...	...
Germany - Allemagne									
1 I 2010* (ESDJ)									
Total	81 802 257	40 103 606	41 698 651	...	...	...	...	...	...
0	665 151	341 123	324 028	...	...	...	...	...	...
1 - 4	2 744 457	1 408 329	1 336 128	...	...	...	...	...	...
5 - 9	3 647 727	1 869 921	1 777 806	...	...	...	...	...	...
10 - 14	3 965 299	2 035 044	1 930 255	...	...	...	...	...	...
15 - 19	4 317 072	2 214 032	2 103 040	...	...	...	...	...	...
20 - 24	4 934 457	2 516 653	2 417 804	...	...	...	...	...	...
25 - 29	4 978 420	2 522 868	2 455 552	...	...	...	...	...	...
30 - 34	4 731 257	2 394 924	2 336 333	...	...	...	...	...	...
35 - 39	5 244 072	2 660 706	2 583 366	...	...	...	...	...	...
40 - 44	6 864 580	3 510 685	3 353 895	...	...	...	...	...	...
45 - 49	7 023 310	3 575 913	3 447 397	...	...	...	...	...	...
50 - 54	6 053 207	3 053 638	2 999 569	...	...	...	...	...	...
55 - 59	5 423 912	2 681 496	2 742 416	...	...	...	...	...	...
60 - 64	4 307 594	2 118 460	2 189 134	...	...	...	...	...	...
65 - 69	4 880 509	2 345 401	2 535 108	...	...	...	...	...	...
70 - 74	4 739 924	2 187 216	2 552 708	...	...	...	...	...	...
75 - 79	3 100 616	1 327 478	1 773 138	...	...	...	...	...	...
80 - 84	2 311 895	844 367	1 467 528	...	...	...	...	...	...
85 - 89	1 338 934	360 488	978 446	...	...	...	...	...	...

Continent, country or area, date, code and age (in years) / Continent, pays ou zone, date, code et âge (en années)	Total			Urban - Urbaine			Rural - Rurale		
	Both sexes Les deux sexes	Male Masculin	Female Féminin	Both sexes Les deux sexes	Male Masculin	Female Féminin	Both sexes Les deux sexes	Male Masculin	Female Féminin
EUROPE									
Germany - Allemagne									
1 I 2010* (ESDJ)									
90 - 94	337 187	79 171	258 016	...	...	...	...	...	...
95 +	192 677	55 693	136 984	...	...	...	...	...	...
Greece - Grèce[31]									
1 I 2010 (ESDF)									
Total	11 305 118	5 597 465	5 707 653	...	...	...	...	...	...
0	117 780	60 740	57 040	...	...	...	...	...	...
1 - 4	451 420	233 077	218 343	...	...	...	...	...	...
5 - 9	525 800	271 566	254 234	...	...	...	...	...	...
10 - 14	528 759	271 477	257 282	...	...	...	...	...	...
15 - 19	571 920	294 950	276 970	...	...	...	...	...	...
20 - 24	622 656	323 833	298 823	...	...	...	...	...	...
25 - 29	783 371	408 564	374 807	...	...	...	...	...	...
30 - 34	861 210	447 661	413 549	...	...	...	...	...	...
35 - 39	881 583	452 857	428 726	...	...	...	...	...	...
40 - 44	880 281	445 351	434 930	...	...	...	...	...	...
45 - 49	804 618	400 931	403 687	...	...	...	...	...	...
50 - 54	772 454	381 162	391 292	...	...	...	...	...	...
55 - 59	704 638	346 511	358 127	...	...	...	...	...	...
60 - 64	656 842	314 572	342 270	...	...	...	...	...	...
65 - 69	540 407	248 698	291 709	...	...	...	...	...	...
70 - 74	566 467	250 015	316 452	...	...	...	...	...	...
75 - 79	512 623	221 454	291 169	...	...	...	...	...	...
80 - 84	331 276	140 151	191 125	...	...	...	...	...	...
85 - 89	148 187	61 938	86 249	...	...	...	...	...	...
90 - 94	34 883	17 391	17 492	...	...	...	...	...	...
95 - 99	4 653	2 957	1 696	...	...	...	...	...	...
100 +	3 290	1 609	1 681	...	...	...	...	...	...
Guernsey - Guernesey									
31 III 2010 (ESDF)									
Total	62 431	30 695	31 736	...	...	...	...	...	...
0 - 4	3 180	1 682	1 498	...	...	...	...	...	...
5 - 9	3 031	1 549	1 482	...	...	...	...	...	...
10 - 14	3 302	1 678	1 624	...	...	...	...	...	...
15 - 19	3 726	1 883	1 843	...	...	...	...	...	...
20 - 24	4 167	2 078	2 089	...	...	...	...	...	...
25 - 29	4 082	2 092	1 990	...	...	...	...	...	...
30 - 34	3 803	1 911	1 892	...	...	...	...	...	...
35 - 39	4 404	2 185	2 219	...	...	...	...	...	...
40 - 44	4 999	2 419	2 580	...	...	...	...	...	...
45 - 49	4 989	2 457	2 532	...	...	...	...	...	...
50 - 54	4 476	2 223	2 253	...	...	...	...	...	...
55 - 59	3 977	2 004	1 973	...	...	...	...	...	...
60 - 64	4 069	2 021	2 048	...	...	...	...	...	...
65 - 69	2 706	1 353	1 353	...	...	...	...	...	...
70 - 74	2 506	1 207	1 299	...	...	...	...	...	...
75 - 79	2 032	896	1 136	...	...	...	...	...	...
80 - 84	1 496	594	902	...	...	...	...	...	...
85 - 89	989	347	642	...	...	...	...	...	...
90 - 94	358	90	268	...	...	...	...	...	...
95 +	139	26	113	...	...	...	...	...	...
Hungary - Hongrie									
1 I 2010 (ESDJ)									
Total	10 014 324	4 756 900	5 257 424	...	...	...	...	...	...
0	94 859	48 693	46 166	...	...	...	...	...	...
1 - 4	394 690	202 476	192 214	...	...	...	...	...	...
5 - 9	482 221	247 472	234 749	...	...	...	...	...	...
10 - 14	505 086	259 049	246 037	...	...	...	...	...	...
15 - 19	603 793	308 679	295 114	...	...	...	...	...	...
20 - 24	649 624	331 682	317 942	...	...	...	...	...	...
25 - 29	699 967	357 194	342 773	...	...	...	...	...	...
30 - 34	851 771	435 141	416 630	...	...	...	...	...	...
35 - 39	753 409	382 713	370 696	...	...	...	...	...	...
40 - 44	675 078	339 699	335 379	...	...	...	...	...	...

7a. Population by age, sex and urban/rural residence: 2010
Population selon l'âge, le sexe et la résidence, urbaine/rurale: 2010 (continued - suite)

Continent, country or area, date, code and age (in years) / Continent, pays ou zone, date, code et âge (en années)	Total			Urban - Urbaine			Rural - Rurale		
	Both sexes Les deux sexes	Male Masculin	Female Féminin	Both sexes Les deux sexes	Male Masculin	Female Féminin	Both sexes Les deux sexes	Male Masculin	Female Féminin
EUROPE									
Hungary - Hongrie									
1 I 2010 (ESDJ)									
45 - 49	602 997	295 749	307 248	...	...	...	...	...	...
50 - 54	710 470	337 712	372 758	...	...	...	...	...	...
55 - 59	737 394	340 577	396 817	...	...	...	...	...	...
60 - 64	589 482	261 729	327 753	...	...	...	...	...	...
65 - 69	520 321	216 940	303 381	...	...	...	...	...	...
70 - 74	409 179	154 020	255 159	...	...	...	...	...	...
75 - 79	340 238	119 908	220 330	...	...	...	...	...	...
80 - 84	231 923	72 454	159 469	...	...	...	...	...	...
85 +	161 822	45 013	116 809	...	...	...	...	...	...
Iceland - Islande[9]									
1 I 2010 (ESDJ)									
Total	317 630	159 936	157 694	...	...	...	...	...	...
0	4 978	2 533	2 445	...	...	...	...	...	...
1 - 4	18 272	9 412	8 860	...	...	...	...	...	...
5 - 9	21 400	10 860	10 540	...	...	...	...	...	...
10 - 14	21 844	11 134	10 710	...	...	...	...	...	...
15 - 19	23 799	12 182	11 617	...	...	...	...	...	...
20 - 24	22 994	11 644	11 350	...	...	...	...	...	...
25 - 29	24 105	12 358	11 747	...	...	...	...	...	...
30 - 34	22 456	11 537	10 919	...	...	...	...	...	...
35 - 39	21 707	11 185	10 522	...	...	...	...	...	...
40 - 44	21 413	10 809	10 604	...	...	...	...	...	...
45 - 49	22 171	11 147	11 024	...	...	...	...	...	...
50 - 54	21 098	10 713	10 385	...	...	...	...	...	...
55 - 59	18 202	9 267	8 935	...	...	...	...	...	...
60 - 64	15 122	7 704	7 418	...	...	...	...	...	...
65 - 69	11 075	5 416	5 659	...	...	...	...	...	...
70 - 74	8 578	4 144	4 434	...	...	...	...	...	...
75 - 79	7 833	3 636	4 197	...	...	...	...	...	...
80 - 84	5 821	2 524	3 297	...	...	...	...	...	...
85 - 89	3 300	1 270	2 030	...	...	...	...	...	...
90 - 94	1 169	395	774	...	...	...	...	...	...
95 - 99	250	58	192	...	...	...	...	...	...
100 +	43	8	35	...	...	...	...	...	...
Ireland - Irlande									
1 I 2010 (ESDF)									
Total	4 467 854	2 216 444	2 251 410	...	...	...	...	...	...
0	73 708	37 846	35 862	...	...	...	...	...	...
1 - 4	277 055	142 114	134 941	...	...	...	...	...	...
5 - 9	310 701	159 136	151 565	...	...	...	...	...	...
10 - 14	292 218	149 683	142 535	...	...	...	...	...	...
15 - 19	274 651	139 832	134 819	...	...	...	...	...	...
20 - 24	282 980	137 115	145 865	...	...	...	...	...	...
25 - 29	397 526	194 732	202 794	...	...	...	...	...	...
30 - 34	376 505	187 147	189 358	...	...	...	...	...	...
35 - 39	348 723	174 941	173 782	...	...	...	...	...	...
40 - 44	314 635	158 462	156 173	...	...	...	...	...	...
45 - 49	297 697	148 855	148 842	...	...	...	...	...	...
50 - 54	265 532	133 215	132 317	...	...	...	...	...	...
55 - 59	238 259	119 738	118 521	...	...	...	...	...	...
60 - 64	211 784	106 219	105 565	...	...	...	...	...	...
65 - 69	160 466	79 327	81 139	...	...	...	...	...	...
70 - 74	125 081	59 882	65 199	...	...	...	...	...	...
75 - 79	96 365	43 486	52 879	...	...	...	...	...	...
80 - 84	66 545	26 370	40 175	...	...	...	...	...	...
85 - 89	38 353	13 112	25 241	...	...	...	...	...	...
90 - 94	14 279	4 093	10 186	...	...	...	...	...	...
95 - 99	4 175	1 001	3 174	...	...	...	...	...	...
100 +	616	138	478	...	...	...	...	...	...
Italy - Italie									
1 I 2010 (ESDJ)									
Total	60 340 328	29 287 403	31 052 925	...	...	...	...	...	...
0	562 566	289 084	273 482	...	...	...	...	...	...

Continent, country or area, date, code and age (in years) / Continent, pays ou zone, date, code et âge (en années)	Total			Urban - Urbaine			Rural - Rurale		
	Both sexes Les deux sexes	Male Masculin	Female Féminin	Both sexes Les deux sexes	Male Masculin	Female Féminin	Both sexes Les deux sexes	Male Masculin	Female Féminin
EUROPE									
Italy - Italie									
1 I 2010 (ESDJ)									
1 - 4	2 282 087	1 173 124	1 108 963	...	...	...	...	...	...
5 - 9	2 834 290	1 456 435	1 377 855	...	...	...	...	...	...
10 - 14	2 798 994	1 441 015	1 357 979	...	...	...	...	...	...
15 - 19	2 967 361	1 527 934	1 439 427	...	...	...	...	...	...
20 - 24	3 118 392	1 591 662	1 526 730	...	...	...	...	...	...
25 - 29	3 504 534	1 766 298	1 738 236	...	...	...	...	...	...
30 - 34	4 203 563	2 118 717	2 084 846	...	...	...	...	...	...
35 - 39	4 811 717	2 418 876	2 392 841	...	...	...	...	...	...
40 - 44	4 957 917	2 483 227	2 474 690	...	...	...	...	...	...
45 - 49	4 650 644	2 307 605	2 343 039	...	...	...	...	...	...
50 - 54	4 047 168	1 988 299	2 058 869	...	...	...	...	...	...
55 - 59	3 704 742	1 803 643	1 901 099	...	...	...	...	...	...
60 - 64	3 689 883	1 782 949	1 906 934	...	...	...	...	...	...
65 - 69	3 163 189	1 493 194	1 669 995	...	...	...	...	...	...
70 - 74	3 035 304	1 383 138	1 652 166	...	...	...	...	...	...
75 - 79	2 530 250	1 073 503	1 456 747	...	...	...	...	...	...
80 - 84	1 882 772	710 730	1 172 042	...	...	...	...	...	...
85 - 89	1 147 892	365 864	782 028	...	...	...	...	...	...
90 - 94	312 948	82 881	230 067	...	...	...	...	...	...
95 - 99	119 141	26 387	92 754	...	...	...	...	...	...
100 +	14 974	2 838	12 136	...	...	...	...	...	...
Lithuania - Lituanie									
1 I 2010 (ESDJ)									
Total	3 329 039	1 547 751	1 781 288	...	...	...	...	...	...
0	36 536	18 698	17 838	...	...	...	...	...	...
1 - 4	127 677	65 277	62 400	...	...	...	...	...	...
5 - 9	152 253	78 179	74 074	...	...	...	...	...	...
10 - 14	182 833	93 889	88 944	...	...	...	...	...	...
15 - 19	241 075	123 074	118 001	...	...	...	...	...	...
20 - 24	268 121	136 620	131 501	...	...	...	...	...	...
25 - 29	242 212	123 951	118 261	...	...	...	...	...	...
30 - 34	217 406	109 356	108 050	...	...	...	...	...	...
35 - 39	233 825	115 227	118 598	...	...	...	...	...	...
40 - 44	242 430	117 796	124 634	...	...	...	...	...	...
45 - 49	260 884	124 534	136 350	...	...	...	...	...	...
50 - 54	234 485	107 957	126 528	...	...	...	...	...	...
55 - 59	192 189	85 257	106 932	...	...	...	...	...	...
60 - 64	162 712	67 519	95 193	...	...	...	...	...	...
65 - 69	155 401	60 407	94 994	...	...	...	...	...	...
70 - 74	143 045	51 247	91 798	...	...	...	...	...	...
75 - 79	115 222	37 533	77 689	...	...	...	...	...	...
80 - 84	77 729	21 425	56 304	...	...	...	...	...	...
85 - 89	33 900	7 721	26 179	...	...	...	...	...	...
90 - 94	6 865	1 600	5 265	...	...	...	...	...	...
95 - 99	1 755	361	1 394	...	...	...	...	...	...
100 +	484	123	361	...	...	...	...	...	...
Luxembourg									
1 I 2010 (ESDJ)									
Total	502 066	249 406	252 660	...	...	...	...	...	...
0	5 638	2 916	2 722	...	...	...	...	...	...
1 - 4	23 014	11 791	11 223	...	...	...	...	...	...
5 - 9	29 842	15 433	14 409	...	...	...	...	...	...
10 - 14	30 617	15 701	14 916	...	...	...	...	...	...
15 - 19	29 804	15 266	14 538	...	...	...	...	...	...
20 - 24	29 751	15 105	14 646	...	...	...	...	...	...
25 - 29	34 700	17 485	17 215	...	...	...	...	...	...
30 - 34	37 333	18 722	18 611	...	...	...	...	...	...
35 - 39	39 482	19 670	19 812	...	...	...	...	...	...
40 - 44	42 241	21 523	20 718	...	...	...	...	...	...
45 - 49	40 271	20 628	19 643	...	...	...	...	...	...
50 - 54	34 902	17 812	17 090	...	...	...	...	...	...
55 - 59	29 666	15 089	14 577	...	...	...	...	...	...
60 - 64	24 759	12 550	12 209	...	...	...	...	...	...

Continent, country or area, date, code and age (in years) / Continent, pays ou zone, date, code et âge (en années)	Total			Urban - Urbaine			Rural - Rurale		
	Both sexes Les deux sexes	Male Masculin	Female Féminin	Both sexes Les deux sexes	Male Masculin	Female Féminin	Both sexes Les deux sexes	Male Masculin	Female Féminin
EUROPE									
Luxembourg									
1 I 2010 (ESDJ)									
65 - 69	19 528	9 468	10 060	...	...	...	...	...	...
70 - 74	17 338	7 942	9 396	...	...	...	...	...	...
75 - 79	14 942	6 432	8 510	...	...	...	...	...	...
80 - 84	10 893	4 086	6 807	...	...	...	...	...	...
85 - 89	5 598	1 474	4 124	...	...	...	...	...	...
90 - 94	1 464	301	1 163	...	...	...	...	...	...
95 - 99	245	11	234	...	...	...	...	...	...
100 +	38	1	37	...	...	...	...	...	...
Montenegro - Monténégro									
1 I 2010 (ESDJ)									
Total	632 922	312 044	320 878	...	...	...	...	...	...
0	8 674	4 613	4 061	...	...	...	...	...	...
1 - 4	31 062	16 323	14 739	...	...	...	...	...	...
5 - 9	40 268	20 831	19 437	...	...	...	...	...	...
10 - 14	42 079	21 757	20 322	...	...	...	...	...	...
15 - 19	44 983	23 288	21 695	...	...	...	...	...	...
20 - 24	48 933	25 021	23 912	...	...	...	...	...	...
25 - 29	49 656	25 247	24 409	...	...	...	...	...	...
30 - 34	45 493	22 587	22 906	...	...	...	...	...	...
35 - 39	42 058	20 652	21 406	...	...	...	...	...	...
40 - 44	41 193	20 415	20 778	...	...	...	...	...	...
45 - 49	43 558	21 477	22 081	...	...	...	...	...	...
50 - 54	43 427	21 778	21 649	...	...	...	...	...	...
55 - 59	40 539	19 875	20 664	...	...	...	...	...	...
60 - 64	29 153	13 376	15 777	...	...	...	...	...	...
65 - 69	24 622	10 818	13 804	...	...	...	...	...	...
70 - 74	25 230	11 055	14 175	...	...	...	...	...	...
75 - 79	17 398	7 293	10 105	...	...	...	...	...	...
80 - 84	9 675	3 894	5 781	...	...	...	...	...	...
85 - 89	3 841	1 395	2 446	...	...	...	...	...	...
90 - 94	681	248	433	...	...	...	...	...	...
95 - 99	278	88	190	...	...	...	...	...	...
100 +	121	13	108	...	...	...	...	...	...
Netherlands - Pays-Bas									
1 I 2010 (ESDJ)									
Total	16 574 989	8 203 476	8 371 513	10 961 093	5 396 105	5 564 988	5 613 896	2 807 371	2 806 525
0	184 586	94 400	90 186	127 497	65 075	62 422	57 089	29 325	27 764
1 - 4	740 295	378 974	361 321	496 540	254 091	242 449	243 755	124 883	118 872
5 - 9	1 003 249	512 808	490 441	641 327	327 889	313 438	361 922	184 919	177 003
10 - 14	984 781	504 126	480 655	617 003	315 642	301 361	367 778	188 484	179 294
15 - 19	1 015 423	519 322	496 101	658 646	333 370	325 276	356 777	185 952	170 825
20 - 24	1 012 910	511 916	500 994	735 202	362 627	372 575	277 708	149 289	128 419
25 - 29	999 355	503 012	496 343	743 576	370 328	373 248	255 779	132 684	123 095
30 - 34	999 558	500 713	498 845	724 262	363 138	361 124	275 296	137 575	137 721
35 - 39	1 180 949	591 406	589 543	806 906	406 411	400 495	374 043	184 995	189 048
40 - 44	1 296 780	655 752	641 028	850 332	431 236	419 096	446 448	224 516	221 932
45 - 49	1 288 557	650 126	638 431	836 632	421 742	414 890	451 925	228 384	223 541
50 - 54	1 177 367	591 039	586 328	756 239	377 479	378 760	421 128	213 560	207 568
55 - 59	1 082 844	544 323	538 521	688 540	343 579	344 961	394 304	200 744	193 560
60 - 64	1 070 007	536 910	533 097	670 621	334 183	336 438	399 386	202 727	196 659
65 - 69	775 949	383 052	392 897	478 601	233 464	245 137	297 348	149 588	147 760
70 - 74	618 558	291 874	326 684	386 507	179 737	206 770	232 051	112 137	119 914
75 - 79	495 827	215 467	280 360	314 821	134 632	180 189	181 006	80 835	100 171
80 - 84	351 308	133 496	217 812	229 347	85 854	143 493	121 961	47 642	74 319
85 - 89	208 819	64 937	143 882	139 295	42 720	96 575	69 524	22 217	47 307
90 - 94	69 901	16 653	53 248	47 000	10 881	36 119	22 901	5 772	17 129
95 - 99	16 223	2 926	13 297	10 997	1 866	9 131	5 226	1 060	4 166
100 +	1 743	244	1 499	1 202	161	1 041	541	83	458
Norway - Norvège[32]									
1 I 2010 (ESDJ)									
Total	4 858 199	2 426 752	2 431 447	...	...	...	...	...	...
0	62 064	31 928	30 136	...	...	...	...	...	...
1 - 4	241 864	123 954	117 910	...	...	...	...	...	...

Continent, country or area, date, code and age (in years) / Continent, pays ou zone, date, code et âge (en années)	Total			Urban - Urbaine			Rural - Rurale		
	Both sexes Les deux sexes	Male Masculin	Female Féminin	Both sexes Les deux sexes	Male Masculin	Female Féminin	Both sexes Les deux sexes	Male Masculin	Female Féminin

EUROPE

Norway - Norvège[32]
1 I 2010 (ESDJ)

5 - 9	298 473	152 416	146 057	...	...	...	...	...	...
10 - 14	315 324	161 955	153 369	...	...	...	...	...	...
15 - 19	322 032	165 748	156 284	...	...	...	...	...	...
20 - 24	305 514	155 602	149 912	...	...	...	...	...	...
25 - 29	307 103	155 740	151 363	...	...	...	...	...	...
30 - 34	318 158	162 005	156 153	...	...	...	...	...	...
35 - 39	359 303	183 832	175 471	...	...	...	...	...	...
40 - 44	366 019	188 180	177 839	...	...	...	...	...	...
45 - 49	334 676	171 934	162 742	...	...	...	...	...	...
50 - 54	318 599	162 279	156 320	...	...	...	...	...	...
55 - 59	295 215	149 665	145 550	...	...	...	...	...	...
60 - 64	291 182	146 836	144 346	...	...	...	...	...	...
65 - 69	212 061	104 467	107 594	...	...	...	...	...	...
70 - 74	157 734	73 833	83 901	...	...	...	...	...	...
75 - 79	132 856	58 738	74 118	...	...	...	...	...	...
80 - 84	109 151	43 727	65 424	...	...	...	...	...	...
85 - 89	75 216	25 016	50 200	...	...	...	...	...	...
90 - 94	28 718	7 502	21 216	...	...	...	...	...	...
95 - 99	6 301	1 292	5 009	...	...	...	...	...	...
100 +	636	103	533	...	...	...	...	...	...

Poland - Pologne[33]
1 I 2010 (ESDJ)

Total	38 167 329	18 428 742	19 738 587	...	...	...	...	...	...
0	416 830	214 417	202 413	...	...	...	...	...	...
1 - 4	1 535 970	788 998	746 972	...	...	...	...	...	...
5 - 9	1 790 025	919 512	870 513	...	...	...	...	...	...
10 - 14	2 039 952	1 045 121	994 831	...	...	...	...	...	...
15 - 19	2 529 063	1 292 121	1 236 942	...	...	...	...	...	...
20 - 24	2 957 225	1 505 995	1 451 230	...	...	...	...	...	...
25 - 29	3 277 651	1 662 169	1 615 482	...	...	...	...	...	...
30 - 34	3 034 932	1 536 639	1 498 293	...	...	...	...	...	...
35 - 39	2 638 657	1 333 609	1 305 048	...	...	...	...	...	...
40 - 44	2 332 488	1 173 044	1 159 444	...	...	...	...	...	...
45 - 49	2 529 831	1 255 836	1 273 995	...	...	...	...	...	...
50 - 54	2 994 063	1 457 314	1 536 749	...	...	...	...	...	...
55 - 59	2 807 913	1 328 423	1 479 490	...	...	...	...	...	...
60 - 64	2 121 259	971 114	1 150 145	...	...	...	...	...	...
65 - 69	1 379 123	594 688	784 435	...	...	...	...	...	...
70 - 74	1 370 459	549 236	821 223	...	...	...	...	...	...
75 - 79	1 154 667	425 667	729 000	...	...	...	...	...	...
80 - 84	776 869	247 559	529 310	...	...	...	...	...	...
85 - 89	366 955	100 194	266 761	...	...	...	...	...	...
90 - 94	84 630	20 650	63 980	...	...	...	...	...	...
95 - 99	25 002	5 513	19 489	...	...	...	...	...	...
100 +	3 765	923	2 842	...	...	...	...	...	...

Portugal
1 I 2010 (ESDJ)

Total	10 637 713	5 148 203	5 489 510	...	...	...	...	...	...
0	99 183	50 678	48 505	...	...	...	...	...	...
1 - 4	420 585	216 164	204 421	...	...	...	...	...	...
5 - 9	554 644	285 311	269 333	...	...	...	...	...	...
10 - 14	542 205	276 580	265 625	...	...	...	...	...	...
15 - 19	566 702	289 113	277 589	...	...	...	...	...	...
20 - 24	614 733	313 708	301 025	...	...	...	...	...	...
25 - 29	742 761	376 449	366 312	...	...	...	...	...	...
30 - 34	836 117	421 730	414 387	...	...	...	...	...	...
35 - 39	825 737	413 302	412 435	...	...	...	...	...	...
40 - 44	780 348	386 785	393 563	...	...	...	...	...	...
45 - 49	776 878	380 620	396 258	...	...	...	...	...	...
50 - 54	710 089	344 853	365 236	...	...	...	...	...	...
55 - 59	661 584	316 730	344 854	...	...	...	...	...	...
60 - 64	604 994	282 768	322 226	...	...	...	...	...	...
65 - 69	517 874	235 904	281 970	...	...	...	...	...	...

7a. Population by age, sex and urban/rural residence: 2010
Population selon l'âge, le sexe et la résidence, urbaine/rurale: 2010 (continued - suite)

Continent, country or area, date, code and age (in years) / Continent, pays ou zone, date, code et âge (en années)	Total			Urban - Urbaine			Rural - Rurale		
	Both sexes Les deux sexes	Male Masculin	Female Féminin	Both sexes Les deux sexes	Male Masculin	Female Féminin	Both sexes Les deux sexes	Male Masculin	Female Féminin
EUROPE									
Portugal									
1 I 2010 (ESDJ)									
70 - 74	492 671	216 854	275 817	...	...	...	...	...	...
75 - 79	415 324	171 990	243 334	...	...	...	...	...	...
80 - 84	279 501	103 965	175 536	...	...	...	...	...	...
85 +	195 783	64 699	131 084	...	...	...	...	...	...
Republic of Moldova - République de Moldova[34]									
1 I 2010 (ESDJ)									
Total	3 563 695	1 713 487	1 850 208	1 476 681	694 469	782 212	2 087 014	1 019 018	1 067 996
0	40 118	20 710	19 408	...	...	...	...	...	...
1 - 4	150 479	77 365	73 114	55 046	28 454	26 592	95 433	48 911	46 522
5 - 9	185 434	95 510	89 924	65 706	34 174	31 532	119 728	61 336	58 392
10 - 14	219 465	112 127	107 338	73 842	38 068	35 774	145 623	74 059	71 564
15 - 19	296 521	150 928	145 593	107 544	54 726	52 818	188 977	96 202	92 775
20 - 24	358 005	181 847	176 158	171 031	83 972	87 059	186 974	97 875	89 099
25 - 29	315 855	160 613	155 242	149 348	72 093	77 255	166 507	88 520	77 987
30 - 34	270 624	135 754	134 870	120 151	58 823	61 328	150 473	76 931	73 542
35 - 39	238 750	117 562	121 188	104 074	50 084	53 990	134 676	67 478	67 198
40 - 44	226 562	109 695	116 867	96 212	44 575	51 637	130 350	65 120	65 230
45 - 49	267 820	127 113	140 707	116 796	52 812	63 984	151 024	74 301	76 723
50 - 54	264 730	123 198	141 532	115 371	50 896	64 475	149 359	72 302	77 057
55 - 59	228 954	103 845	125 109	100 088	43 563	56 525	128 866	60 282	68 584
60 - 64	139 577	61 953	77 624	60 359	27 297	33 062	79 218	34 656	44 562
65 - 69	114 976	47 481	67 495	43 306	18 517	24 789	71 670	28 964	42 706
70 - 74	102 431	39 018	63 413	37 282	14 083	23 199	65 149	24 935	40 214
75 - 79	73 385	26 606	46 779	23 192	8 033	15 159	50 193	18 573	31 620
80 - 84	45 414	14 685	30 729	15 087	4 620	10 467	30 327	10 065	20 262
85 - 89	19 565	5 952	13 613	5 938	1 634	4 304	13 627	4 318	9 309
90 - 94	3 648	1 099	2 549	1 238	389	849	2 410	710	1 700
95 - 99	1 141	353	788	363	119	244	778	234	544
100 +	241	73	168	101	19	82	140	54	86
Romania - Roumanie									
1 I 2010 (ESDJ)									
Total	21 462 186	10 451 093	11 011 093	...	...	...	...	...	...
0	220 591	113 384	107 207	...	...	...	...	...	...
1 - 4	865 654	444 848	420 806	...	...	...	...	...	...
5 - 9	1 060 239	544 950	515 289	...	...	...	...	...	...
10 - 14	1 105 634	566 271	539 363	...	...	...	...	...	...
15 - 19	1 263 708	646 396	617 312	...	...	...	...	...	...
20 - 24	1 725 796	880 085	845 711	...	...	...	...	...	...
25 - 29	1 623 966	830 994	792 972	...	...	...	...	...	...
30 - 34	1 769 535	908 512	861 023	...	...	...	...	...	...
35 - 39	1 672 074	850 839	821 235	...	...	...	...	...	...
40 - 44	1 676 364	844 271	832 093	...	...	...	...	...	...
45 - 49	1 237 767	613 462	624 305	...	...	...	...	...	...
50 - 54	1 505 116	728 226	776 890	...	...	...	...	...	...
55 - 59	1 421 332	671 502	749 830	...	...	...	...	...	...
60 - 64	1 108 002	509 384	598 618	...	...	...	...	...	...
65 - 69	905 888	396 275	509 613	...	...	...	...	...	...
70 - 74	930 211	382 994	547 217	...	...	...	...	...	...
75 - 79	709 570	279 752	429 818	...	...	...	...	...	...
80 - 84	434 076	162 052	272 024	...	...	...	...	...	...
85 - 89	177 821	61 253	116 568	...	...	...	...	...	...
90 - 94	33 491	10 587	22 904	...	...	...	...	...	...
95 - 99	12 854	4 259	8 595	...	...	...	...	...	...
100 +	2 497	797	1 700	...	...	...	...	...	...
Russian Federation - Fédération de Russie									
1 I 2010 (ESDJ)									
Total	141 914 509	65 639 380	76 275 129	...	...	...	...	...	...
0	1 750 177	898 734	851 443	...	...	...	...	...	...
1 - 4	6 205 526	3 186 582	3 018 944	...	...	...	...	...	...
5 - 9	6 880 863	3 526 812	3 354 051	...	...	...	...	...	...
10 - 14	6 564 046	3 355 989	3 208 057	...	...	...	...	...	...

282

Continent, country or area, date, code and age (in years) Continent, pays ou zone, date, code et âge (en annèes)	Total			Urban - Urbaine			Rural - Rurale		
	Both sexes Les deux sexes	Male Masculin	Female Féminin	Both sexes Les deux sexes	Male Masculin	Female Féminin	Both sexes Les deux sexes	Male Masculin	Female Féminin
EUROPE									
Russian Federation - Fédération de Russie									
1 I 2010 (ESDJ)									
15 - 19	8 495 662	4 338 040	4 157 622	..:	...	...	...	...	...
20 - 24	12 256 143	6 212 084	6 044 059	...	...	...	...	...	...
25 - 29	12 257 349	6 158 595	6 098 754	...	...	...	...	...	...
30 - 34	10 798 991	5 341 307	5 457 684	...	...	...	...	...	...
35 - 39	10 068 892	4 951 679	5 117 213	...	...	...	...	...	...
40 - 44	9 193 316	4 444 165	4 749 151	...	...	...	...	...	...
45 - 49	11 247 260	5 308 734	5 938 526	...	...	...	...	...	...
50 - 54	11 260 733	5 121 251	6 139 482	...	...	...	...	...	...
55 - 59	9 747 960	4 235 095	5 512 865	...	...	...	...	...	...
60 - 64	6 896 925	2 833 901	4 063 024	...	...	...	...	...	...
65 - 69	4 479 576	1 644 173	2 835 403	...	...	...	...	...	...
70 - 74	6 169 297	2 075 235	4 094 062	...	...	...	...	...	...
75 - 79	3 616 578	1 080 449	2 536 129	...	...	...	..:	...	...
80 - 84	2 763 382	686 972	2 076 410	...	...	...	...	...	...
85 - 89	954 959	181 766	773 193	...	...	...	...	...	...
90 - 94	224 395	41 759	182 636	...	...	...	...	...	...
95 - 99	59 600	12 073	47 527	...	...	...	...	...	...
100 +	22 879	3 985	18 894	...	...	...	...	...	...
Serbia - Serbie[35]									
1 I 2010 (ESDJ)									
Total	7 306 677	3 553 575	3 753 102	...	...	...	...	...	...
0	69 875	36 210	33 665	...	...	...	...	...	...
1 - 4	278 617	143 742	134 875	...	...	...	...	...	...
5 - 9	382 185	196 150	186 035	...	...	...	...	...	...
10 - 14	378 584	194 263	184 321	...	...	...	...	...	...
15 - 19	425 052	217 667	207 385	...	...	...	...	...	...
20 - 24	473 426	242 187	231 239	...	...	...	...	...	...
25 - 29	511 939	259 979	251 960	...	...	...	...	...	...
30 - 34	516 947	261 510	255 437	...	...	...	...	...	...
35 - 39	487 733	244 085	243 648	...	...	...	...	...	...
40 - 44	475 942	235 126	240 816	...	...	...	...	...	...
45 - 49	499 567	245 049	254 518	...	...	...	...	...	...
50 - 54	536 949	262 724	274 225	...	...	...	...	...	...
55 - 59	583 924	283 357	300 567	...	...	...	...	...	...
60 - 64	442 033	207 317	234 716	...	...	...	...	...	...
65 - 69	345 138	155 307	189 831	...	...	...	...	...	...
70 - 74	355 150	153 403	201 747	...	...	...	...	...	...
75 - 79	292 338	120 791	171 547	...	...	...	...	...	...
80 - 84	166 162	64 476	101 686	...	...	...	...	...	...
85 - 89	66 512	23 426	43 086	...	...	...	...	...	...
90 - 94	12 305	4 493	7 812	...	...	...	...	...	...
95 - 99	4 801	1 758	3 043	...	...	...	...	...	...
100 +	1 498	555	943	...	...	...	...	...	...
Slovakia - Slovaquie									
1 I 2010 (ESDJ)									
Total	5 424 925	2 636 938	2 787 987	...	...	...	...	...	...
0	60 981	31 411	29 570	...	...	...	...	...	...
1 - 4	219 195	112 335	106 860	...	...	...	...	...	...
5 - 9	260 113	133 488	126 625	...	...	...	...	...	...
10 - 14	291 031	149 147	141 884	...	...	...	...	...	...
15 - 19	368 186	188 232	179 954	...	...	...	...	...	...
20 - 24	419 859	214 113	205 746	...	...	...	...	...	...
25 - 29	452 967	231 702	221 265	...	...	...	...	...	...
30 - 34	472 925	241 369	231 556	...	...	...	...	...	...
35 - 39	412 647	209 669	202 978	...	...	...	...	...	...
40 - 44	362 460	182 386	180 074	...	...	...	...	...	...
45 - 49	381 530	190 523	191 007	...	...	...	...	...	...
50 - 54	396 528	194 517	202 011	...	...	...	...	...	...
55 - 59	378 598	181 087	197 511	...	...	...	...	...	...
60 - 64	282 771	128 670	154 101	...	...	...	...	...	...
65 - 69	215 606	91 121	124 485	...	...	...	...	...	...
70 - 74	165 683	64 114	101 569	...	...	...	...	...	...

Continent, country or area, date, code and age (in years) / Continent, pays ou zone, date, code et âge (en années)	Total			Urban - Urbaine			Rural - Rurale		
	Both sexes Les deux sexes	Male Masculin	Female Féminin	Both sexes Les deux sexes	Male Masculin	Female Féminin	Both sexes Les deux sexes	Male Masculin	Female Féminin
EUROPE									
Slovakia - Slovaquie									
1 I 2010 (ESDJ)									
75 - 79	136 404	48 428	87 976	...	...	...	...	...	...
80 - 84	89 806	28 322	61 484	...	...	...	...	...	...
85 - 89	45 114	12 810	32 304	...	...	...	...	...	...
90 - 94	8 562	2 366	6 196	...	...	...	...	...	...
95 - 99	3 022	786	2 236	...	...	...	...	...	...
100 +	937	342	595	...	...	...	...	...	...
Slovenia - Slovénie									
1 I 2010 (ESDJ)									
Total	2 046 976	1 014 107	1 032 869	...	...	...	...	...	...
0	21 793	11 280	10 513	...	...	...	...	...	...
1 - 4	80 625	41 386	39 239	...	...	...	...	...	...
5 - 9	90 964	46 802	44 162	...	...	...	...	...	...
10 - 14	93 893	48 340	45 553	...	...	...	...	...	...
15 - 19	105 735	54 376	51 359	...	...	...	...	...	...
20 - 24	132 119	69 356	62 763	...	...	...	...	...	...
25 - 29	149 639	78 708	70 931	...	...	...	...	...	...
30 - 34	157 966	83 189	74 777	...	...	...	...	...	...
35 - 39	148 639	77 763	70 876	...	...	...	...	...	...
40 - 44	154 887	79 426	75 461	...	...	...	...	...	...
45 - 49	156 062	79 697	76 365	...	...	...	...	...	...
50 - 54	155 235	79 546	75 689	...	...	...	...	...	...
55 - 59	149 688	76 299	73 389	...	...	...	...	...	...
60 - 64	111 466	54 632	56 834	...	...	...	...	...	...
65 - 69	99 032	45 999	53 033	...	...	...	...	...	...
70 - 74	86 368	37 556	48 812	...	...	...	...	...	...
75 - 79	72 695	27 388	45 307	...	...	...	...	...	...
80 - 84	48 668	15 077	33 591	...	...	...	...	...	...
85 - 89	24 285	5 828	18 457	...	...	...	...	...	...
90 - 94	5 273	1 114	4 159	...	...	...	...	...	...
95 - 99	1 748	310	1 438	...	...	...	...	...	...
100 +	196	35	161	...	...	...	...	...	...
Spain - Espagne									
1 VII 2010 (ESDJ)									
Total	46 072 831	22 697 679	23 375 152	...	...	...	...	...	...
0	506 028	260 899	245 129	...	...	...	...	...	...
1 - 4	1 971 447	1 014 603	956 844	...	...	...	...	...	...
5 - 9	2 317 883	1 191 506	1 126 377	...	...	...	...	...	...
10 - 14	2 129 035	1 093 506	1 035 529	...	...	...	...	...	...
15 - 19	2 225 067	1 142 596	1 082 471	...	...	...	...	...	...
20 - 24	2 578 740	1 312 862	1 265 878	...	...	...	...	...	...
25 - 29	3 294 758	1 678 195	1 616 563	...	...	...	...	...	...
30 - 34	3 990 363	2 056 066	1 934 297	...	...	...	...	...	...
35 - 39	3 966 549	2 042 336	1 924 213	...	...	...	...	...	...
40 - 44	3 727 260	1 894 045	1 833 215	...	...	...	...	...	...
45 - 49	3 453 642	1 729 371	1 724 271	...	...	...	...	...	...
50 - 54	3 055 151	1 510 261	1 544 890	...	...	...	...	...	...
55 - 59	2 617 280	1 278 925	1 338 355	...	...	...	...	...	...
60 - 64	2 426 218	1 166 603	1 259 615	...	...	...	...	...	...
65 - 69	2 059 052	972 880	1 086 172	...	...	...	...	...	...
70 - 74	1 763 533	798 969	964 564	...	...	...	...	...	...
75 - 79	1 708 817	731 055	977 762	...	...	...	...	...	...
80 - 84	1 244 016	485 169	758 847	...	...	...	...	...	...
85 - 89	706 810	245 371	461 439	...	...	...	...	...	...
90 - 94	257 855	74 311	183 544	...	...	...	...	...	...
95 - 99	65 246	16 058	49 188	...	...	...	...	...	...
100 +	8 081	2 092	5 989	...	...	...	...	...	...
Sweden - Suède[9]									
1 I 2010 (ESDJ)									
Total	9 340 682	4 649 014	4 691 668	...	...	...	...	...	...
0	112 120	57 720	54 400	...	...	...	...	...	...
1 - 4	436 102	224 106	211 996	...	...	...	...	...	...
5 - 9	503 934	258 574	245 360	...	...	...	...	...	...
10 - 14	497 286	255 238	242 048	...	...	...	...	...	...

7a. Population by age, sex and urban/rural residence: 2010
Population selon l'âge, le sexe et la résidence, urbaine/rurale: 2010 (continued - suite)

Continent, country or area, date, code and age (in years) / Continent, pays ou zone, date, code et âge (en années)	Total			Urban - Urbaine			Rural - Rurale		
	Both sexes Les deux sexes	Male Masculin	Female Féminin	Both sexes Les deux sexes	Male Masculin	Female Féminin	Both sexes Les deux sexes	Male Masculin	Female Féminin
EUROPE									
Sweden - Suède[9]									
1 I 2010 (ESDJ)									
15 - 19	638 533	328 011	310 522	...	...	...	...	...	...
20 - 24	605 453	309 505	295 948	...	...	...	...	...	...
25 - 29	571 759	293 280	278 479	...	...	...	...	...	...
30 - 34	580 069	296 143	283 926	...	...	...	...	...	...
35 - 39	634 498	322 241	312 257	...	...	...	...	...	...
40 - 44	663 060	337 930	325 130	...	...	...	...	...	...
45 - 49	621 146	315 776	305 370	...	...	...	...	...	...
50 - 54	585 136	295 746	289 390	...	...	...	...	...	...
55 - 59	575 354	288 996	286 358	...	...	...	...	...	...
60 - 64	625 455	312 140	313 315	...	...	...	...	...	...
65 - 69	513 757	255 340	258 417	...	...	...	...	...	...
70 - 74	378 574	180 700	197 874	...	...	...	...	...	...
75 - 79	304 061	135 418	168 643	...	...	...	...	...	...
80 - 84	246 209	100 039	146 170	...	...	...	...	...	...
85 - 89	168 195	60 035	108 160	...	...	...	...	...	...
90 - 94	63 451	18 563	44 888	...	...	...	...	...	...
95 - 99	14 894	3 263	11 631	...	...	...	...	...	...
100 +	1 636	250	1 386	...	...	...	...	...	...
Switzerland - Suisse									
1 I 2010 (ESDJ)									
Total	7 785 806	3 830 566	3 955 240	...	...	...	...	...	...
0	77 786	40 147	37 639	...	...	...	...	...	...
1 - 4	304 384	156 654	147 730	...	...	...	...	...	...
5 - 9	381 376	196 406	184 970	...	...	...	...	...	...
10 - 14	417 675	214 858	202 817	...	...	...	...	...	...
15 - 19	454 904	233 589	221 315	...	...	...	...	...	...
20 - 24	470 871	237 898	232 973	...	...	...	...	...	...
25 - 29	507 179	254 043	253 136	...	...	...	...	...	...
30 - 34	525 183	261 907	263 276	...	...	...	...	...	...
35 - 39	570 943	286 440	284 503	...	...	...	...	...	...
40 - 44	642 499	323 426	319 073	...	...	...	...	...	...
45 - 49	634 893	321 162	313 731	...	...	...	...	...	...
50 - 54	550 052	278 357	271 695	...	...	...	...	...	...
55 - 59	481 840	240 698	241 142	...	...	...	...	...	...
60 - 64	457 530	226 156	231 374	...	...	...	...	...	...
65 - 69	383 053	184 254	198 799	...	...	...	...	...	...
70 - 74	300 300	137 629	162 671	...	...	...	...	...	...
75 - 79	253 734	108 634	145 100	...	...	...	...	...	...
80 - 84	191 585	72 813	118 772	...	...	...	...	...	...
85 - 89	119 610	39 441	80 169	...	...	...	...	...	...
90 - 94	43 767	12 243	31 524	...	...	...	...	...	...
95 +	16 642	3 811	12 831	...	...	...	...	...	...
TFYR of Macedonia - L'ex-R. y. de Macédoine									
1 I 2010 (ESDF)									
Total	2 052 722	1 028 815	1 023 907	...	...	...	...	...	...
0	23 415	12 185	11 230	...	...	...	...	...	...
1 - 4	89 456	45 986	43 470	...	...	...	...	...	...
5 - 9	118 878	61 408	57 470	...	...	...	...	...	...
10 - 14	131 708	68 114	63 594	...	...	...	...	...	...
15 - 19	154 423	79 274	75 149	...	...	...	...	...	...
20 - 24	163 497	83 878	79 619	...	...	...	...	...	...
25 - 29	164 108	84 251	79 857	...	...	...	...	...	...
30 - 34	155 962	80 101	75 861	...	...	...	...	...	...
35 - 39	147 872	74 874	72 998	...	...	...	...	...	...
40 - 44	148 682	75 405	73 277	...	...	...	...	...	...
45 - 49	145 527	73 785	71 742	...	...	...	...	...	...
50 - 54	140 919	71 558	69 361	...	...	...	...	...	...
55 - 59	128 118	63 337	64 781	...	...	...	...	...	...
60 - 64	101 092	48 135	52 957	...	...	...	...	...	...
65 - 69	81 462	38 111	43 351	...	...	...	...	...	...
70 - 74	69 033	31 218	37 815	...	...	...	...	...	...
75 - 79	51 212	22 162	29 050	...	...	...	...	...	...

Continent, country or area, date, code and age (in years) / Continent, pays ou zone, date, code et âge (en années)	Total			Urban - Urbaine			Rural - Rurale		
	Both sexes Les deux sexes	Male Masculin	Female Féminin	Both sexes Les deux sexes	Male Masculin	Female Féminin	Both sexes Les deux sexes	Male Masculin	Female Féminin
EUROPE									
TFYR of Macedonia - L'ex-R. y. de Macédoine									
1 I 2010 (ESDF)									
80 - 84	24 975	10 363	14 612	...	...	...	...	...	...
85 - 89	9 394	3 675	5 719	...	...	...	...	...	...
90 - 94	1 697	606	1 091	...	...	...	...	...	...
95 +	733	254	479	...	...	...	...	...	...
Unknown - Inconnu	559	135	424	...	...	...	...	...	...
OCEANIA - OCÉANIE									
Australia - Australie[36]									
1 VII 2010* (ESDJ)									
Total	22 342 398	11 124 254	11 218 144	...	...	...	...	...	...
0	301 033	154 426	146 607	...	...	...	...	...	...
1 - 4	1 160 055	595 185	564 870	...	...	...	...	...	...
5 - 9	1 365 747	701 203	664 544	...	...	...	...	...	...
10 - 14	1 403 778	719 763	684 015	...	...	...	...	...	...
15 - 19	1 501 010	770 614	730 396	...	...	...	...	...	...
20 - 24	1 649 659	849 732	799 927	...	...	...	...	...	...
25 - 29	1 665 263	844 968	820 295	...	...	...	...	...	...
30 - 34	1 534 043	768 096	765 947	...	...	...	...	...	...
35 - 39	1 616 051	802 527	813 524	...	...	...	...	...	...
40 - 44	1 552 666	772 142	780 524	...	...	...	...	...	...
45 - 49	1 575 053	781 143	793 910	...	...	...	...	...	...
50 - 54	1 470 376	726 885	743 491	...	...	...	...	...	...
55 - 59	1 326 013	655 993	670 020	...	...	...	...	...	...
60 - 64	1 212 537	604 200	608 337	...	...	...	...	...	...
65 - 69	909 512	450 385	459 127	...	...	...	...	...	...
70 - 74	710 444	343 844	366 600	...	...	...	...	...	...
75 - 79	551 621	256 110	295 511	...	...	...	...	...	...
80 - 84	439 306	188 982	250 324	...	...	...	...	...	...
85 - 89	267 148	99 033	168 115	...	...	...	...	...	...
90 - 94	100 828	31 669	69 159	...	...	...	...	...	...
95 - 99	26 509	6 526	19 983	...	...	...	...	...	...
100 +	3 746	828	2 918	...	...	...	...	...	...
Micronesia (Federated States of) - Micronésie (États fédérés de)[1]									
1 VII 2010 (ESDJ)									
Total	107 839	54 158	53 681	...	...	...	...	...	...
0 - 4	13 651	6 992	6 659	...	...	...	...	...	...
5 - 9	13 203	6 753	6 450	...	...	...	...	...	...
10 - 14	12 489	6 387	6 102	...	...	...	...	...	...
15 - 19	11 478	5 878	5 600	...	...	...	...	...	...
20 - 24	9 345	4 862	4 483	...	...	...	...	...	...
25 - 29	7 667	3 782	3 885	...	...	...	...	...	...
30 - 34	6 198	3 118	3 080	...	...	...	...	...	...
35 - 39	6 198	2 920	3 278	...	...	...	...	...	...
40 - 44	5 712	2 673	3 039	...	...	...	...	...	...
45 - 49	5 478	2 694	2 784	...	...	...	...	...	...
50 - 54	5 073	2 546	2 527	...	...	...	...	...	...
55 - 59	4 183	2 149	2 034	...	...	...	...	...	...
60 - 64	2 801	1 428	1 373	...	...	...	...	...	...
65 - 69	1 551	714	837	...	...	...	...	...	...
70 - 74	1 257	580	677	...	...	...	...	...	...
75 +	1 555	682	873	...	...	...	...	...	...
New Zealand - Nouvelle-Zélande[37]									
1 VII 2010 (ESDJ)									
Total	4 367 770	2 144 600	2 223 180	3 761 650[38]	1 833 650[38]	1 928 000[38]	605 290[38]	310 390[38]	294 870[38]
0 - 4	311 850	160 020	151 830	270 130[38]	138 760[38]	131 370[38]	41 710[38]	21 250[38]	20 460[38]
5 - 9	286 820	146 900	139 920	244 980[38]	125 550[38]	119 430[38]	41 830[38]	21 340[38]	20 480[38]
10 - 14	295 780	151 580	144 210	249 260[38]	127 620[38]	121 640[38]	46 500[38]	23 940[38]	22 550[38]

Continent, country or area, date, code and age (in years) / Continent, pays ou zone, date, code et âge (en années)	Total			Urban - Urbaine			Rural - Rurale		
	Both sexes Les deux sexes	Male Masculin	Female Féminin	Both sexes Les deux sexes	Male Masculin	Female Féminin	Both sexes Les deux sexes	Male Masculin	Female Féminin
OCEANIA - OCÉANIE									
New Zealand - Nouvelle-Zélande[37]									
1 VII 2010 (ESDJ)									
15 - 19	322 390	165 510	156 880	279 690[38]	142 620[38]	137 070[38]	42 690[38]	22 880[38]	19 810[38]
20 - 24	315 220	161 380	153 840	286 190[38]	145 220[38]	140 970[38]	29 010[38]	16 140[38]	12 860[38]
25 - 29	288 410	143 180	145 230	263 600[38]	130 360[38]	133 240[38]	24 760[38]	12 790[38]	11 970[38]
30 - 34	269 330	129 330	139 990	240 420[38]	115 140[38]	125 270[38]	28 850[38]	14 140[38]	14 710[38]
35 - 39	301 290	143 000	158 290	262 040[38]	123 980[38]	138 060[38]	39 200[38]	18 990[38]	20 210[38]
40 - 44	311 730	149 330	162 400	265 980[38]	127 080[38]	138 900[38]	45 700[38]	22 220[38]	23 490[38]
45 - 49	322 670	156 140	166 530	270 620[38]	130 280[38]	140 340[38]	51 980[38]	25 810[38]	26 160[38]
50 - 54	291 480	142 640	148 850	241 510[38]	117 120[38]	124 390[38]	49 870[38]	25 460[38]	24 420[38]
55 - 59	251 340	123 430	127 910	206 830[38]	100 390[38]	106 440[38]	44 400[38]	22 970[38]	21 430[38]
60 - 64	230 310	113 090	117 220	189 170[38]	91 710[38]	97 460[38]	41 040[38]	21 320[38]	19 720[38]
65 - 69	176 220	85 990	90 230	145 760[38]	69 780[38]	75 980[38]	30 370[38]	16 150[38]	14 220[38]
70 - 74	136 950	65 490	71 460	115 860[38]	54 110[38]	61 750[38]	21 060[38]	11 350[38]	9 700[38]
75 - 79	105 180	48 880	56 300	92 150[38]	41 760[38]	50 380[38]	13 010[38]	7 100[38]	5 900[38]
80 - 84	80 710	34 800	45 910	72 670[38]	30 570[38]	42 110[38]	8 020[38]	4 230[38]	3 800[38]
85 +	70 090	23 910	46 180	64 790[38]	21 600[38]	43 200[38]	5 290[38]	2 310[38]	2 980[38]
Niue - Nioué									
1 VII 2010 (ESDJ)									
Total	1 496[39]	754	740	...	...	...	...	...	...
0 - 4	135[39]	69	64	...	...	...	...	...	...
5 - 9	134	58	76	...	...	...	...	...	...
10 - 14	116	60	56	...	...	...	...	...	...
15 - 19	124	79	45	...	...	...	...	...	...
20 - 24	100	50	50	...	...	...	...	...	...
25 - 29	90	38	52	...	...	...	...	...	...
30 - 34	71	39	32	...	...	...	...	...	...
35 - 39	85	45	40	...	...	...	...	...	...
40 - 44	101	55	46	...	...	...	...	...	...
45 - 49	92	42	50	...	...	...	...	...	...
50 - 54	107	58	49	...	...	...	...	...	...
55 - 59	89	42	47	...	...	...	...	...	...
60 - 64	70	34	36	...	...	...	...	...	...
65 - 69	75	37	38	...	...	...	...	...	...
70 - 74	53	23	30	...	...	...	...	...	...
75 +	54	25	29	...	...	...	...	...	...

FOOTNOTES - NOTES

Italics: estimates which are less reliable. - Italiques: estimations moins sûres.

* Provisional. - Données provisoires.

'Code' indicates the source of data, as follows:
CDFC - Census, de facato, complete tabulation
CDFS - Census, de facto, sample tabulation
CDJC - Census, de jure, complete tabulation
CDJS - Census, de jure, sample tabulation
SSDF - Sample survey, de facto
SSDJ - Sample survey, de jure
ESDF - Estimates, de facto
ESDJ - Estimates, de jure

Le 'Code' indique la source des données, comme suit:
CDFC - Recensement, population de fait, tabulation complète
CDFS - Recensement, population de fait, tabulation par sondage
CDJC - Recensement, population de droit, tabulation complète
CDJS - Recensement, population de droit, tabulation par sondage
SSDF - Enquête par sondage, population de fait
SSDJ - Enquête par sondage, population de droit
ESDF - Estimations, population de fait

ESDJ - Estimations, population de droit

[1] Data refer to national projections. - Les données se réfèrent aux projections nationales.

[2] Excludes the islands of St. Brandon and Agalega. Based on 2000 Population Census data and adjusted for underenumeration of young children. - Non compris les îles St. Brandon et Agalega. D'après le recensement de la population de 2000, ajusté en raison du sous-enregistrement des jeunes enfants.

[3] Data are based on projections from 2002 Census. - Données fondées sur des projections tirées du recensement de 2002.

[4] Because of rounding, totals are not in all cases the sum of the parts. - Les chiffres étant arrondis, les totaux ne correspondent pas toujours rigoureusement à la somme des chiffres partiels.

[5] Preliminary postcensal estimates. Estimates adjusted for census net undercoverage (including adjustment for incompletely enumerated Indian reserves). - Estimations post censitaires préliminaires. Ajusté pour la sous-estimation du recensement (y compris les réservations en Inde incomplètement énumérées).

[6] Based on 2010 National Household Survey. - Basée sur l'Enquête nationale des ménages de 2010.

[7] As a result of the adjusting method used to calculate midyear population, the totals are not always equal to the sum of the parts. - Du fait de la méthode d'ajustement utilisée pour calculer la population en milieu d'année, les totaux ne correspondent pas nécessairement à la somme des différents éléments.

[8] Estimates based on 2007 Population Census. - Estimations fondées sur le recensement de la population de 2007.

[9] Population statistics are compiled from registers. - Les statistiques de la population sont compilées à partir des registres.

[10] Projections based on 2002 population census. - Projections fondées sur le recensement de la population de 2002.

[11] Projections produced by l'Institut Haïtien de Statistique et d'Informatique (IHSI) and the Latin American and Caribbean Demographic Centre (CELADE) - Population Division of ECLAC. - Les données sont projections produits par l'Institut Haïtien de Statistique et d'Informatique (IHSI) et le centre démographique de l'Amérique latine et les Caraïbes - Division de la population de la CEPALC.

[12] Data are based on projections of the 2001 Population and Housing Census data. - Les données sont basées sur les projections du recensement de 2001 de la population et de l'habitat.

[13] Including an estimation of 1 334 585 persons corresponding to 448 195 housing units without information of the occupants. - Y compris une estimation de 1 334 585 personnes correspondant aux 448 195 unités d'habitation sans information sur les occupants.

[14] Includes estimates for St. Eustatius. - Y compris les estimations pour St. Eustatius.

[15] Data refer to projections based on the 2000 population census. - Les données se réfèrent aux projections basées sur le recensement de la population de 2000.

[16] Including armed forces stationed in the area. - Y compris les militaires en garnison sur le territoire.

[17] Based on the results of the 2000 population census. - Basé sur les résultats du recensement de la population de 2000.

[18] Data based on 2010 Population Census. - Données fondées sur le recensement de population de 2010.

[19] Data include persons in remote areas, military personnel outside the country, merchant seamen at sea, civilian seasonal workers outside the country, and other civilians outside the country, and exclude nomads, foreign military, civilian aliens temporarily in the country, transients on ships and Indian jungle population. - Y compris les personnes vivant dans des régions éloignées, le personel militaire en dehors du pays, les marins marchands, les ouvriers saisonniers en dehors du pays, et autres civils en dehors du pays, et non compris les nomades, les militaires étrangers, les étrangers civils temporairement dans le pays, les transiteurs sur des bateaux et les Indiens de la jungle.

[20] Data based on the Population Census of 2005. - Données fondées sur le recensement de la population de 2005.

[21] Data refer to national projections. Excluding nomadic Indian tribes. - Les données se réfèrent aux projections nationales. Non compris les tribus d'Indiens nomades.

[22] Based on 2007 Population and Housing Census. - D'après le résultats du recensement de la population et de l'habitat de 2007.

[23] Data refer to national projections without smoothing, and are based on the 2005 population census. - Les données font référence à des projections nationales brutes et sont fondées sur des données provenant du recensement de population de 2005.

[24] Data refer to national projections based on 2008 census. Excluding foreign diplomatic personnel and their dependants. - Les données se réfèrent aux projections nationales basées sur le recensement de la population de 2008. Non compris le personnel diplomatique étranger et les membres de leur famille les accompagnant.

[25] Data refer to government controlled areas. - Les données se rapportent aux zones contrôlées par le Gouvernement.

[26] Because of rounding, totals are not in all cases the sum of the parts. Excluding diplomatic personnel outside the country and foreign military and civilian personnel and their dependants stationed in the area. - Les chiffres étant arrondis, les totaux ne correspondent pas toujours rigoureusement à la somme des chiffres partiels. Non compris le personnel diplomatique hors du pays ni les militaires et agents civils étrangers en poste sur le territoire et les membres de leur famille les accompagnant.

[27] Data refer to resident population only. - Pour la population résidante seulement.

[28] Data based on Address Based Population Registration System. - Les données sont basées sur le registre national de la population basé sur l'adresse.

[29] Population statistics are compiled from registers. Excluding Faeroe Islands and Greenland shown separately, if available. - Les statistiques de la population sont compilées à partir des registres. Non compris les Iles Féroé et le Groenland, qui font l'objet de rubriques distinctes, si disponible.

[30] Excluding diplomatic personnel outside the country and including members of alien armed forces not living in military camps and foreign diplomatic personnel not living in embassies or consulates. - Non compris le personnel diplomatique hors du pays et y compris les militaires étrangers ne vivant pas dans des camps militaires et le personnel diplomatique étranger ne vivant pas dans les ambassades ou les consulats.

[31] Excluding armed forces stationed outside the country, but including alien armed forces stationed in the area. - Non compris les militaires en garnison hors du pays, mais y compris les militaires étrangers en garnison sur le territoire.

[32] Including residents temporarily outside the country. Excluding Svalbard and Jan Mayen Islands shown separately, if available. - Y compris les résidents se trouvant temporairement hors du pays. Non compris Svalbard et Jan Mayen qui font l'objet de rubriques distinctes, si disponible.

[33] Excluding civilian aliens within country, but including civilian nationals temporarily outside country. - Non compris les civils étrangers dans le pays, mais y compris les civils nationaux temporairement hors du pays.

[34] Excluding Transnistria and the municipality of Bender. - Les données ne tiennent pas compte de l'information sur la Transnistria et la municipalité de Bender.

[35] Excluding data for Kosovo and Metohia. - Sans les données pour le Kosovo et Metohie.

[36] Intercensal estimates. Data are based on 2009 Australian Standard Geographical Classification boundaries. - Estimations inter-censitaires. Les données réfèrent au découpage de la nomenclature géographique normalisée d'Australie de 2009.

[37] Based on the census, updated for residents missed or counted more than once by the census (net census undercount); residents temporarily overseas on census night, and births, deaths and net migration between the census night and the date of the estimate. - D'après le recensement, mise à jour pour les résidents omis ou dénombrés plus d'une fois par le recensement (sous-dénombrement net); résidents temporairement à l'étranger la nuit du recensement, et naissances, décès et migration nette entre la nuit du recensement et la date de l'estimation.

[38] Population estimates by urban/rural residence exclude inland waters and oceanic areas. - Les estimations de la population par lieu de résidence urbaine ou rurale excluent les eaux intérieures et les zones océaniques.

[39] Including unknown sex. - Y compris le sexe inconnu.

Tables 8 and 8a

Table 8 presents population of capital cities and cities of 100 000 or more inhabitants for the latest available year between 1990 and 2009. Table 8a presents the available data for year 2010.

Description of variables: Since the way in which cities are delimited differs from one country or area to another, the table not only presents data for the so-called city proper, but also for the urban agglomeration, if available.

City proper is defined as a locality with legally fixed boundaries and an administratively recognized urban status, usually characterized by some form of local government.

Urban agglomeration has been defined as comprising the city or town proper and also the suburban fringe or densely settled territory lying outside of, but adjacent to, the city boundaries.

For some countries or areas, however, the data relate to entire administrative divisions known, for example, as shi or municipalities (municipios) which are composed of a populated centre and adjoining territory, some of which may contain other, often separate urban localities or may be distinctively rural in character. For this group of countries or areas the type of civil division is given in a footnote.

The surface area of the city or urban agglomeration is presented, when available.

City names are presented in the original language of the country or area in which the cities are located. In cases where the original names are not in the Roman alphabet, they have been romanized. Cities are listed in English alphabetical order.

Capital cities are shown in the table regardless of their population size. The names of the capital cities are printed in capital letters. The designation of any specific city as a capital city is as reported by the country or area.

The table also covers cities whose urban agglomeration's population exceeds 100 000; that is, while the urban agglomeration should have a population of 100 000 or more to be included in the table, the city proper may be of a smaller population size.

The reference date of each population figure appears in the left-most column of the table. Estimates based on results of sample surveys and city censuses as well as those derived from other sources are explained by the 'code' also appearing in the left-most column of the table. The codes are explained at the end of the table.

Reliability of data: Specific information is generally not available on the reliability of the estimates of the population of cities or urban agglomerations presented in this table.

In the absence of such quality assessment, data from population censuses, sample surveys and city censuses are considered to be reliable and, therefore, set in Roman type. Other estimates are considered to be reliable if they are based on a complete census (or a sample survey), and have been adjusted by a continuous population register or adjusted on the basis of the calculated balance of births, deaths, and migration.

Limitations: Statistics on the population of capital cities and cities of 100 000 or more inhabitants are subject to the same qualifications as have been set forth for population statistics in general as discussed in section 3 of the Technical Notes.

International comparability of data on city population is limited to a great extent by variations in national concepts and definitions. Although an effort is made to reduce the sources of non-comparability somewhat by presenting the data for both city proper and urban agglomeration, many serious problems of comparability remain.

Data presented in the "city proper" column for some countries represent an urban administrative area legally distinguished from surrounding rural territory, while for other countries these data represent a commune or an equally small administrative unit. In still other countries, the administrative units may be relatively extensive and thereby include considerable territories beyond the urban centre itself.

City data are also especially affected by whether the data refer to *de facto* or *de jure* population, as well as variations among countries in how each of these concepts is applied. With reference to the total population, the difference between the *de facto* and *de jure* population is discussed at length in section 3.1.1 of the Technical Notes.

Data on city populations based on intercensal estimates present additional problems: comparability is impaired by the different methods used in making the estimates and by the loss of precision in applying to selected segments of the population, methods best suited for the whole population. For example, it is far more difficult to apply the component method of estimating population growth to cities than it is to the entire country.

Births and deaths occurring in the cities do not all originate in the population present in or resident of that area. Therefore, the use of natural increase to estimate the probable size of the city population is a potential source of error. Internal migration is another component of population change that cannot be measured with accuracy in many areas. Because of these factors, estimates in this table may be less valuable in general and in particular limited for purposes of international comparison.

City data, even when set in Roman type, are often not as reliable as estimates for the total population of the country or area. Furthermore, because the sources of these data include censuses (national or city), surveys and estimates, the years to which they refer vary widely. In addition, because city boundaries may alter over time, comparisons covering different years should be carried out with caution.

Earlier data: Population of capital cities and cities with a population of 100 000 or more have been shown in previous issues of the *Demographic Yearbook*. For more information on specific topics and years for which data are reported, readers should consult the Historical Index.

Tableaux 8 et 8a

Le tableau 8 présente les données les plus récentes disponibles pour la période 1990 – 2009 sur la population des capitales et des villes de 100 000 habitants ou plus. Le tableau 8a présente les données disponibles pour l'année 2010.

Description des variables : étant donné que les villes ne sont pas délimitées de la même manière dans tous les pays ou zones, on s'est efforcé de donner, dans ce tableau, des chiffres correspondant non seulement aux villes proprement dites, mais aussi, le cas échéant, aux agglomérations urbaines.

On entend par villes proprement dites les localités qui ont des limites juridiquement définies et sont administrativement considérées comme villes, ce qui se caractérise généralement par l'existence d'une autorité locale.

L'agglomération urbaine comprend, par définition, la ville proprement dite ainsi que la proche banlieue, c'est-à-dire la zone fortement peuplée qui est extérieure, mais contiguë aux limites de la ville.

En outre, dans certains pays ou zones, les données se rapportent à des divisions administratives entières, connues par exemple sous le nom de shi ou de municipios, qui comportent une agglomération et le territoire avoisinant, lequel peut englober d'autres agglomérations urbaines tout à fait distinctes ou être à caractère essentiellement rural. Pour ce groupe de pays ou zones, le type de division administrative est indiqué en note.

On trouvera à la fin du tableau la superficie de la ville ou agglomération urbaine chaque fois que possible.

Les noms des villes sont indiqués dans la langue du pays ou zone où ces villes sont situées. Les noms de villes qui ne sont pas à l'origine libellés en caractères latins ont été romanisés. Les villes sont énumérées dans l'ordre alphabétique anglais.

Les capitales figurent dans le tableau quel que soit le chiffre de leur population et leur nom a été imprimé en lettres majuscules. Ne sont indiquées comme capitales que les villes ainsi désignées par le pays ou zone intéressé.

En ce qui concerne les autres villes, le tableau indique celles dont la population est égale ou supérieure à 100 000 habitants. Ce chiffre limite s'applique à l'agglomération urbaine et non à la ville proprement dite, dont la population peut être moindre.

La date à laquelle se réfère le chiffre correspondant, figure dans la colonne de gauche du tableau. Le 'code' aussi figurant dans la colonne de gauche du tableau, permet de savoir si les estimations sont fondées sur les résultats d'enquêtes par sondage ou de recensements municipaux ou sont tirées d'autres sources. Les codes utilisés sont expliqués à la fin du tableau.

Fiabilité des données : on ne possède généralement pas de renseignements précis sur la fiabilité des estimations de la population des villes ou agglomérations urbaines présentées dans ce tableau.

Les données provenant de recensements de la population, d'enquêtes par sondage ou de recensements municipaux sont jugées sûres et figurent par conséquent en caractères romains. D'autres estimations sont considérées comme sûres si elles sont fondées sur un recensement complet (ou une enquête par sondage) et ont été ajustées en fonction des données provenant d'un registre permanent de population ou en fonction de la balance, établie par le calcul des naissances, des décès et des migrations.

Insuffisance des données : les statistiques portant sur la population des capitales et des villes de 100 000 habitants ou plus appellent toutes les réserves qui ont été formulées à la section 3 des Notes techniques à propos des statistiques de la population en général.

La comparabilité internationale des données portant sur la population des villes est compromise dans une large mesure par la diversité des définitions nationales. Bien que l'on se soit efforcé de réduire les facteurs de non-comparabilité en présentant à la fois dans le tableau les données relatives aux villes proprement dites et celles concernant les agglomérations urbaines, de graves problèmes de comparabilité n'en subsistent pas moins.

Pour certains pays, les données figurant dans la colonne intitulée « Ville proprement dite » correspondent à une zone administrative urbaine juridiquement distincte du territoire rural environnant, tandis que pour d'autres pays ces données correspondent à une commune ou petite unité administrative analogue. Pour d'autres encore, les unités administratives en cause peuvent être relativement étendues et englober par conséquent un vaste territoire au-delà du centre urbain lui-même.

L'emploi de données se rapportant tantôt à la population de fait, tantôt à la population de droit, ainsi que les différences de traitement de ces deux notions d'un pays à l'autre influent particulièrement sur les statistiques urbaines. En ce qui concerne la population totale, la différence entre population de fait et population de droit est expliquée en détail à la section 3.1.1 des Notes techniques.

Les statistiques relatives à la population urbaine qui sont fondées sur des estimations intercensitaires posent encore plus de problèmes que les données issues de recensement. Leur comparabilité est compromise par la diversité des méthodes employées pour établir les estimations et par l'imprécision qui résulte de l'application de certaines méthodes à telles ou telles composantes de la population alors qu'elles sont conçues pour être appliquées à l'ensemble de la population. La méthode des composantes, par exemple, est beaucoup plus difficile à appliquer en vue de l'estimation de l'accroissement de la population lorsqu'il s'agit de villes que lorsqu'il s'agit d'un pays tout entier.

Les naissances et décès qui surviennent dans les villes ne correspondent pas tous à la population présente ou résidente. En conséquence, des erreurs peuvent se produire si l'on établit pour les villes des estimations fondées sur l'accroissement naturel de la population. Les migrations intérieures constituent un second élément d'estimation que, dans bien des régions, on ne peut pas toujours mesurer avec exactitude. Pour ces raisons, les estimations présentées dans ce tableau risquent dans l'ensemble d'être peu fiables et leur valeur est particulièrement limitée du point de vue des comparaisons internationales.

Même lorsqu'elles figurent en caractères romains, il arrive souvent que les statistiques urbaines ne soient pas aussi fiables que les estimations concernant la population totale de la zone ou du pays considéré. De surcroît, comme ces statistiques proviennent aussi bien de recensements (nationaux ou municipaux) que d'enquêtes ou d'estimations, les années auxquelles elles se rapportent sont extrêmement variables. Enfin, comme les limites urbaines varient parfois d'une époque à une autre, il y a lieu d'être prudent lorsque l'on compare des données se rapportant à des années différentes.

Données publiées antérieurement : des statistiques concernant la population des capitales et des villes de 100 000 habitants ou plus ont été présentées dans des éditions antérieures de l'*Annuaire démographique*. Pour plus de précisions concernant les années et les sujets pour lesquels des données ont été publiées, se reporter à l'index historique.

8. Population of capital cities and cities of 100 000 or more inhabitants: latest available year, 1990 - 2009
Population des capitales et des villes de 100 000 habitants ou plus : dernière année disponible, 1990 - 2009

Continent, country or area, date, code and city / Continent, pays ou zone, date, code et ville	City proper - Ville proprement dite				Urban agglomeration - Agglomération urbaine			
	Population			Surface area - Superficie (km²)	Population			Surface area - Superficie (km²)
	Both sexes - Les deux sexes	Male - Masculin	Female - Féminin		Both sexes - Les deux sexes	Male - Masculin	Female - Féminin	
AFRICA - AFRIQUE								
Algeria - Algérie								
25 VI 1998 (CDJC)								
ALGIERS (EL DJAZAIR)	1 569 897	...	...	...	...	...	...	...
Annaba	352 523	...	...	...	...	...	...	...
Batna	246 800	...	...	...	...	...	...	...
Béchar	134 523	...	...	...	...	...	...	...
Bejaïa	144 405	...	...	...	...	...	...	...
Beskra	177 060	...	...	...	...	...	...	...
Bordj Bou Arreridj	129 004	...	...	...	...	...	...	...
Bordj el Kiffan	103 690	...	...	...	...	...	...	...
Ech Cheliff (El Asnam)	174 314	...	...	...	...	...	...	...
El Boulaïda (Blida)	229 788	...	...	...	...	...	...	...
El Djelfa	158 679	...	...	...	...	...	...	...
El Eulma	104 758	...	...	...	...	...	...	...
El Wad	105 151	...	...	...	...	...	...	...
Ghardaïa	127 959	...	...	...	...	...	...	...
Ghilizane	104 644	...	...	...	...	...	...	...
Guelma	108 682	...	...	...	...	...	...	...
Jijel	106 306	...	...	...	...	...	...	...
Lemdiyya (Medea)	128 427	...	...	...	...	...	...	...
Mestghanem (Mostaganem)	125 911	...	...	...	...	...	...	...
M'Sila	102 151	...	...	...	...	...	...	...
Qacentina (Constantine)	465 021	...	...	...	...	...	...	...
Saïda	113 533	...	...	...	...	...	...	...
Sidi-bel-Abbès	183 931	...	...	...	...	...	...	...
Skikda	153 531	...	...	...	...	...	...	...
Souq Ahras	114 512	...	...	...	...	...	...	...
Stif (Sétif)	214 842	...	...	...	...	...	...	...
Tbessa	154 335	...	...	...	...	...	...	...
Tihert	148 850	...	...	...	...	...	...	...
Tilimsen (Tlemcen)	156 258	...	...	...	...	...	...	...
Touggourt	114 183	...	...	...	...	...	...	...
Wahran (Oran)	705 335	...	...	...	...	...	...	...
Wargla	139 381	...	...	...	...	...	...	...
Angola								
1 VII 1993 (ESDF)								
Huambo	...	...	...	...	400 000	...	...	...
LUANDA	...	...	...	...	1 822 407	855 676	936 731	...
Benin - Bénin								
1 VII 2000 (ESDF)								
Cotonou	650 660[1]	318 752[1]	331 908[1]	79	...	...	...	...
Parakou	144 627[1]	73 603[1]	71 024[1]	441	...	...	...	...
PORTO-NOVO	232 756[1]	113 737[1]	119 019[1]	50	...	...	...	...
Botswana								
17 VIII 2001 (CDFC)								
Francistown	101 028	50 213	50 815	79	113 315	...	...	...
GABORONE	233 136	116 897	116 239	169	282 150	...	...	...
Burkina Faso								
9 XII 2006 (CDJC)								
Banfora	75 917	38 399	37 518	...	109 824	54 581	55 243	...
Bobo Dioulasso	489 967	244 136	245 831	...	554 042	275 703	278 339	...
Dori	21 078	10 431	10 647	...	106 808	52 992	53 816	...
Fada N'gourma	41 785	21 220	20 565	...	124 577	62 193	62 384	...
Gorom-Gorom	8 882	4 509	4 373	...	106 346	53 129	53 217	...
Kaya	54 365	26 989	27 376	...	117 122	56 209	60 913	...
Koudougou	88 184	42 803	45 381	...	138 209	64 362	73 847	...
OUAGADOUGOU	1 475 223	745 289	729 934	...	1 475 223	745 289	729 934	...
Ouahigouya	73 153	36 370	36 783	...	125 030	61 002	64 028	...
Solenzo	16 850	8 557	8 293	...	121 819	59 892	61 927	...
Tenkodogo	44 491	21 476	23 015	...	124 985	58 003	66 982	...
Burundi								
16 VIII 2008 (CDJC)								
BUJUMBURA	497 169	274 979	222 190	...	...	...	...	...

8. Population of capital cities and cities of 100 000 or more inhabitants: latest available year, 1990 - 2009
Population des capitales et des villes de 100 000 habitants ou plus : dernière année disponible, 1990 - 2009 (continued - suite)

Continent, country or area, date, code and city / Continent, pays ou zone, date, code et ville	City proper - Ville proprement dite				Urban agglomeration - Agglomération urbaine			
	Population			Surface area - Superficie (km²)	Population			Surface area - Superficie (km²)
	Both sexes - Les deux sexes	Male - Masculin	Female - Féminin		Both sexes - Les deux sexes	Male - Masculin	Female - Féminin	
AFRICA - AFRIQUE								
Cameroon - Cameroun								
11 XI 2005 (CDJC)								
Bafoussam	239 287	...	...	...	...	...	...	...
Bamenda	269 530	...	...	...	...	...	...	...
Douala	1 907 479	...	...	...	...	...	...	...
Garoua	235 996	...	...	...	...	...	...	...
Kumba	144 268	...	...	...	...	...	...	...
Maroua	201 371	...	...	...	...	...	...	...
Ngaoundéré	152 698	...	...	...	...	...	...	...
Nkongsamba	104 050	...	...	...	...	...	...	...
YAOUNDE	1 817 524	...	...	...	...	...	...	...
Cape Verde - Cap-Vert								
1 VII 2009 (ESDF)								
PRAIA	...	...	...	...	127 524	62 219	65 305	...
Chad - Tchad								
8 IV 1993 (CDFC)								
N'DJAMENA	530 965							
Comoros - Comores								
15 IX 1991 (CDFC)								
MORONI	30 365	...	...	...	...	...	...	...
Djibouti								
1 VII 1995 (ESDF)								
DJIBOUTI	383 000	...	...	...	...	...	...	...
Egypt - Égypte								
21 XI 2006 (CDFC)								
6th of October City	154 093	85 227	68 866	...	...	...	...	...
Abo Keber	103 175	52 271	50 904	...	...	...	...	...
Akhmim	101 509	52 685	48 824	...	...	...	...	...
Alexandria	4 030 582	2 056 265	1 974 317	...	...	...	...	...
Assyût	389 307	201 023	188 284	...	...	...	...	...
Aswan	266 013	135 522	130 491	...	...	...	...	...
Banha	157 701	78 988	78 713	...	...	...	...	...
Beni-Suef	193 048	95 910	97 138	...	...	...	...	...
Bilbes	137 182	69 794	67 388	...	...	...	...	...
CAIRO	7 771 617	3 949 266	3 822 351	...	...	...	...	...
Damanhûr	244 043	122 816	121 227	...	...	...	...	...
Damietta	206 664	105 445	101 219	...	...	...	...	...
Desok	106 827	53 429	53 398	...	...	...	...	...
El-Aresh	137 944	72 751	65 193	...	...	...	...	...
El-Hwamdia	109 314	55 884	53 430	...	...	...	...	...
El-Khosos	291 242	150 846	140 396	...	...	...	...	...
El-Mahalla El-Kubra	442 958	222 488	220 470	...	...	...	...	...
El-Mataria	100 566	51 882	48 684	...	...	...	...	...
Faiyûm	315 940	160 577	155 363	...	...	...	...	...
Gerga	102 597	52 264	50 333	...	...	...	...	...
Giza	2 572 581	1 310 710	1 261 871	...	...	...	...	...
Ismailia	293 184	146 337	146 847	...	...	...	...	...
Kafr-El-Dwar	114 030	57 895	56 135	...	...	...	...	...
Kaluop	107 303	54 467	52 836	...	...	...	...	...
Kena	201 191	101 279	99 912	...	...	...	...	...
Luxer	202 232	104 598	97 634	...	...	...	...	...
Malawe	139 929	71 519	68 410	...	...	...	...	...
Mansûra	439 348	219 247	220 101	...	...	...	...	...
Matrouh	109 852	57 651	52 201	...	...	...	...	...
Menia	236 043	117 774	118 269	...	...	...	...	...
Met Ghamr	116 593	59 032	57 561	...	...	...	...	...
Port Said	570 603	290 580	280 023	...	...	...	...	...
Ramadan	125 920	68 511	57 409	...	...	...	...	...
Shebin-El-Kom	177 112	88 513	88 599	...	...	...	...	...
Shubra-El-Khema	1 025 569	525 952	499 617	...	...	...	...	...
Sohag	190 132	94 889	95 243	...	...	...	...	...
Suez	512 135	260 887	251 248	...	...	...	...	...
Tanta	422 854	211 368	211 486	...	...	...	...	...
Zagazig	302 840	151 535	151 305	...	...	...	...	...

Continent, country or area, date, code and city Continent, pays ou zone, date, code et ville	City proper - Ville proprement dite				Urban agglomeration - Agglomération urbaine			
	Population			Surface area - Superficie (km²)	Population			Surface area - Superficie (km²)
	Both sexes - Les deux sexes	Male - Masculin	Female - Féminin		Both sexes - Les deux sexes	Male - Masculin	Female - Féminin	
AFRICA - AFRIQUE								
Eritrea - Érythrée								
1 VII 1990 (ESDF)								
ASMARA	358 100	...	...	...	...	...	...	...
Ethiopia - Éthiopie								
1 VII 2002 (ESDF)								
ADDIS ABABA	2 646 000	1 273 000	1 373 000	...	...	...	...	...
Awassa	103 725	52 308	51 417	...	...	...	...	...
Bahir Dar	140 084	72 736	67 348	28	...	...	...	...
Debre Zeit	108 632	53 648	54 984	...	...	...	...	...
Dessie	141 616	72 578	69 038	15	...	...	...	...
Dire Dawa	237 012	118 880	118 132	18	...	...	...	...
Gondar	163 097	82 229	80 868	40	...	...	...	...
Harar	105 000	53 000	52 000	...	...	...	...	...
Jimma	131 708	67 138	64 570	...	...	...	...	...
Mekele	141 433	71 990	69 443	24	...	...	...	...
Nazareth	189 362	94 822	94 540	...	...	...	...	...
Gabon								
31 VII 1993 (CDFC)								
LIBREVILLE	362 386	184 192	178 194	...	418 616	212 383	206 233	...
Gambia - Gambie								
15 IV 1993 (CDFC)								
BANJU	42 326	22 268	20 058	12	...	...	...	...
Ghana								
1 VII 2009 (ESDF)								
ACCRA	...	...	...	...	2 263 785	1 109 255	1 154 530	...
Ashiaman	...	...	...	...	281 283	140 698	140 585	...
Koforidua	...	...	...	...	109 846	52 726	57 120	...
Kumasi	...	...	...	...	1 922 130	964 909	957 221	...
Madina	...	...	...	...	136 415	66 843	69 572	...
Obuasi	...	...	...	...	167 897	82 270	85 627	...
Sekondi	...	...	...	...	151 240	75 166	76 074	...
Takoradi	...	...	...	...	220 718	108 152	112 566	...
Tamale	...	...	...	...	254 669	126 825	127 844	...
Tema	...	...	...	...	172 900	82 992	89 908	...
Guinea - Guinée								
1 XII 1996 (CDFC)								
CONAKRY	1 091 500	...	...	...	...	...	...	...
Kankan	...	...	...	...	261 341	...	...	...
Kindia	...	...	...	...	287 607	...	...	...
Labé	...	...	...	...	249 515	...	...	...
Nzérékoré	...	...	...	...	282 772	...	...	...
Guinea-Bissau - Guinée-Bissau								
1 XII 1991 (CDFC)								
BISSAU	197 600	...	...	...	...	...	...	...
Kenya								
24 VIII 2009* (CDFC)								
Eldoret	144 223	72 733	71 490	151	...	...	...	...
Kisumu	390 164	194 585	195 579	475	...	...	...	...
Mombasa	523 183	268 038	255 145	230	...	...	...	...
NAIROBI	3 138 369	1 605 230	1 533 139	896	...	...	...	...
Nakuru	326 125	164 915	161 210	290	...	...	...	...
Libya - Libye								
1 VII 1990 (ESDF)								
Al Khums	200 000	...	...	...	...	...	...	...
BENGHAZI[2]	800 000	...	...	...	...	...	...	...
Misurata	360 000	...	...	...	...	...	...	...
Sebha	150 000	...	...	...	...	...	...	...
TRIPOLI[2]	1 500 000	...	...	...	...	...	...	...
Zuwarah	280 000	...	...	...	...	...	...	...
Madagascar								
1 VII 2005 (ESDF)								
ANTANANARIVO[3]	1 015 140	495 393	519 747	72	...	...	...	...
Antsirabe	...	...	...	...	180 180	87 691	92 489	...
Fianarantsoa	...	...	...	...	165 220	80 410	84 810	...
Mahajanga	...	...	...	...	152 785	74 359	78 426	...

8. Population of capital cities and cities of 100 000 or more inhabitants: latest available year, 1990 - 2009
Population des capitales et des villes de 100 000 habitants ou plus : dernière année disponible, 1990 - 2009 (continued - suite)

Continent, country or area, date, code and city / Continent, pays ou zone, date, code et ville	City proper - Ville proprement dite				Urban agglomeration - Agglomération urbaine			
	Population			Surface area - Superficie (km²)	Population			Surface area - Superficie (km²)
	Both sexes - Les deux sexes	Male - Masculin	Female - Féminin		Both sexes - Les deux sexes	Male - Masculin	Female - Féminin	
AFRICA - AFRIQUE								
Madagascar								
1 VII 2005 (ESDF)								
Toamasina	...	...	...	...	203 469	99 026	104 443	...
Toliara	...	...	...	...	113 993	55 479	58 514	...
Malawi								
8 VI 2008 (CDFC)								
Blantyre City	661 444	...	...	220	...	...	...	...
LILONGWE	669 021	...	...	328	...	...	...	...
Mauritania - Mauritanie[1]								
1 VII 2008 (ESDF)								
NOUAKCHOTT	846 871	471 243	375 628	...	...	...	...	...
Mauritius - Maurice[4]								
1 VII 2009 (ESDJ)								
Beau Bassin - Rose Hill	110 337	53 675	56 662	20	...	...	...	...
PORT LOUIS	148 928	73 690	75 238	46	...	...	...	...
Vacoas - Phoenix	107 678	52 877	54 801	54	...	...	...	...
Morocco - Maroc								
1 VII 2007 (ESDF)								
Agadir	527 000	...	...	...	...	...	...	...
Béni-Mellal	959 000	...	...	...	...	...	...	...
Casablanca (Dar-el-Beida)	2 995 000	...	...	...	...	...	...	...
El-Jadida	1 132 000	...	...	...	...	...	...	...
Fès	1 026 000	...	...	...	...	...	...	...
Inezgane ait Melloul	462 000	...	...	...	...	...	...	...
Kénitra	1 214 000	...	...	...	...	...	...	...
Khemisset	532 000	...	...	...	...	...	...	...
Khouribga	502 000	...	...	...	...	...	...	...
Laayoune	227 000	...	...	...	...	...	...	...
Larache	479 000	...	...	...	...	...	...	...
Marrakech	1 126 000	...	...	...	...	...	...	...
Meknès	739 000	...	...	...	...	...	...	...
Mohammedia	336 000	...	...	...	...	...	...	...
Nador	740 000	...	...	...	...	...	...	...
Oujda	489 000	...	...	...	...	...	...	...
RABAT	642 000	...	...	...	...	...	...	...
Safi	888 000	...	...	...	...	...	...	...
Salé	879 000	...	...	...	...	...	...	...
Settat	980 000	...	...	...	...	...	...	...
Skhirate-Témara	447 000	...	...	...	...	...	...	...
Tanger	811 000	...	...	...	...	...	...	...
Taza	750 000	...	...	...	...	...	...	...
Tétouan	545 000	...	...	...	...	...	...	...
Mozambique								
1 VIII 1997 (CDFC)								
Beira	397 368	...	...	...	...	...	...	...
Chimoio	171 056	...	...	...	...	...	...	...
MAPUTO	966 837	...	...	...	1 391 499	...	...	...
Matola	424 662	...	...	...	...	...	...	...
Mocuba	124 650	...	...	...	...	...	...	...
Nacala	158 248	...	...	...	...	...	...	...
Nampula	303 346	...	...	...	...	...	...	...
Quelimane	150 116	...	...	...	...	...	...	...
Tete	101 984	...	...	...	...	...	...	...
Namibia - Namibie								
27 VIII 2001 (CDFC)								
WINDHOEK	...	...	...	...	233 529	117 306	116 222	...
Niger								
20 V 2001 (CDJC)								
Maradi	148 017	...	...	...	...	...	...	...
NIAMEY	707 951	358 500	349 451	...	...	...	...	...
Zinder	170 575	...	...	...	...	...	...	...
Nigeria - Nigéria								
26 XI 1991 (CDFC)								
Aba	500 183	...	...	...	...	...	...	...
Abeokuta	352 735	...	...	...	...	...	...	...

8. Population of capital cities and cities of 100 000 or more inhabitants: latest available year, 1990 - 2009
Population des capitales et des villes de 100 000 habitants ou plus : dernière année disponible, 1990 - 2009 (continued - suite)

Continent, country or area, date, code and city / Continent, pays ou zone, date, code et ville	City proper - Ville proprement dite				Urban agglomeration - Agglomération urbaine			
	Population			Surface area - Superficie (km²)	Population			Surface area - Superficie (km²)
	Both sexes - Les deux sexes	Male - Masculin	Female - Féminin		Both sexes - Les deux sexes	Male - Masculin	Female - Féminin	

AFRICA - AFRIQUE

Nigeria - Nigéria
26 XI 1991 (CDFC)

ABUJA	107 069	...	...	...	378 671	...	...	...
Ado-Ekiti	156 122	...	...	...	...	...	...	...
Akure	239 124	...	...	...	...	...	...	...
Awka	104 682	...	...	...	...	...	...	...
Bauchi	206 537	...	...	...	...	...	...	...
Benin City	762 719	...	...	...	...	...	...	...
Bida	111 245	...	...	...	...	...	...	...
Calabar	310 839	...	...	...	...	...	...	...
Damaturu	141 897	...	...	...	...	...	...	...
Ede	142 363	...	...	...	...	...	...	...
Effon-Alaiye	158 977	...	...	...	...	...	...	...
Enugu	407 756	...	...	...	...	...	...	...
Gboko	101 281	...	...	...	...	...	...	...
Gombe	163 604	...	...	...	...	...	...	...
Gusau	132 393	...	...	...	...	...	...	...
Ibadan	1 835 300	...	...	...	...	...	...	...
Ife	186 856	...	...	...	...	...	...	...
Ijebu-Ode	124 313	...	...	...	...	...	...	...
Ikare	103 843	...	...	...	...	...	...	...
Ikire	111 435	...	...	...	...	...	...	...
Ikorodu	184 674	...	...	...	...	...	...	...
Ikot Ekpene	119 402	...	...	...	...	...	...	...
Ilawe-Ekiti	104 049	...	...	...	...	...	...	...
Ilesha	139 445	...	...	...	...	...	...	...
Ilorin	532 089	...	...	...	...	...	...	...
Ise	108 136	...	...	...	...	...	...	...
Iseyin	170 936	...	...	...	...	...	...	...
Iwo	125 645	...	...	...	...	...	...	...
Jimeta	141 724	...	...	...	...	...	...	...
Jos	510 300	...	...	...	...	...	...	...
Kaduna	993 642	...	...	...	...	...	...	...
Kano	2 166 554	...	...	...	...	...	...	...
Katsina	259 315	...	...	...	...	...	...	...
Lagos	5 195 247	...	...	...	...	...	...	...
Maiduguri	618 278	...	...	...	...	...	...	...
Makurdi	151 515	...	...	...	...	...	...	...
Minna	189 191	...	...	...	...	...	...	...
Mubi	128 900	...	...	...	...	...	...	...
Nnewi	121 065	...	...	...	...	...	...	...
Ogbomosho	433 030	...	...	...	...	...	...	...
Okene	312 775	...	...	...	...	...	...	...
Okpogho	105 127	...	...	...	...	...	...	...
Ondo	146 051	...	...	...	...	...	...	...
Onitsha	350 280	...	...	...	...	...	...	...
Oshogbo	250 951	...	...	...	...	...	...	...
Owerri	119 711	...	...	...	...	...	...	...
Owo	157 181	...	...	...	...	...	...	...
Oyo	369 894	...	...	...	...	...	...	...
Port Harcourt	703 421	...	...	...	...	...	...	...
Sagamu	127 513	...	...	...	...	...	...	...
Sango Otta	103 332	...	...	...	...	...	...	...
Sapele	109 576	...	...	...	...	...	...	...
Sokoto	329 639	...	...	...	...	...	...	...
Suleja	105 075	...	...	...	...	...	...	...
Ugep	134 773	...	...	...	...	...	...	...
Umuahia	147 167	...	...	...	...	...	...	...
Warri	363 382	...	...	...	...	...	...	...
Zaria	612 257	...	...	...	...	...	...	...

Réunion
1 I 2006 (CDJC)

SAINT-DENIS	138 314	64 552	73 762	143	...	...	...	...

8. Population of capital cities and cities of 100 000 or more inhabitants: latest available year, 1990 - 2009
Population des capitales et des villes de 100 000 habitants ou plus : dernière année disponible, 1990 - 2009 (continued - suite)

Continent, country or area, date, code and city / Continent, pays ou zone, date, code et ville	City proper - Ville proprement dite				Urban agglomeration - Agglomération urbaine			
	Population			Surface area - Superficie (km²)	Population			Surface area - Superficie (km²)
	Both sexes - Les deux sexes	Male - Masculin	Female - Féminin		Both sexes - Les deux sexes	Male - Masculin	Female - Féminin	
AFRICA - AFRIQUE								
Rwanda								
16 VIII 2002 (CDJC)								
KIGALI	603 049	325 778	277 271	...	...	...	...	...
Saint Helena ex. dep. - Sainte-Hélène sans dép.								
10 II 2008* (CDFC)								
JAMESTOWN	714	354	360	4	...	...	...	...
Sao Tome and Principe - Sao Tomé-et-Principe								
25 VIII 2001 (CDJC)								
SAO TOME	...	...	...	...	49 957	24 003	25 954	...
Senegal - Sénégal								
31 XII 2007 (ESDF)								
DAKAR	1 075 582	...	...	500	...	...	...	...
Diourbel	101 215	...	...	...	...	...	...	...
Guediawaye	293 737	...	...	...	...	...	...	...
Kaolack	185 976	...	...	...	...	...	...	...
Mbour	181 825	...	...	...	...	...	...	...
Pikine	874 062	...	...	...	...	...	...	...
Rufisque	162 055	...	...	...	...	...	...	...
Saint Louis	171 263	...	...	...	...	...	...	...
Thiès	181 825	...	...	...	...	...	...	...
Ziguinchor	158 370	...	...	...	...	...	...	...
Seychelles								
29 VIII 1997 (CDFC)								
VICTORIA	...	...	...	...	24 701	...	...	...
Sierra Leone								
1 VII 2009 (ESDF)								
Bo	226 961	109 600	117 361	...	...	...	...	...
FREETOWN	923 341	466 632	456 709	...	...	...	...	...
Kenema	191 626	94 155	97 471	...	...	...	...	...
Makeni	112 521	54 247	58 274	...	...	...	...	...
Somalia - Somalie								
1 VII 2001 (ESDF)								
MOGADISHU	1 212 000	...	...	...	...	...	...	...
South Africa - Afrique du Sud								
10 X 1996 (CDFC)								
Alexandra	171 284	...	...	...	...	...	...	...
Benoni	366 343	...	...	...	...	...	...	...
Bloemfontein	350 504	...	...	...	...	...	...	...
Boksburg	263 179	...	...	...	...	...	...	...
Botshabelo	177 971	...	...	...	...	...	...	...
CAPE TOWN[5]	987 007	...	...	...	...	...	...	...
Durban	669 242	...	...	...	...	...	...	...
Germiston	164 252	...	...	...	...	...	...	...
Johannesburg	752 349	...	...	...	...	...	...	...
Kathlehong	344 803	...	...	...	...	...	...	...
Kempton Park	344 426	...	...	...	...	...	...	...
Khayelitsa	314 239	...	...	...	...	...	...	...
Kimberley	206 070	...	...	...	...	...	...	...
Mangaung	176 525	...	...	...	...	...	...	...
Pietermaritzburg	405 385	...	...	...	...	...	...	...
Port Elizabeth	775 255	...	...	...	...	...	...	...
PRETORIA[5]	692 348	340 363	351 985	...	...	...	...	...
Roodepoort	279 340	...	...	...	...	...	...	...
Soweto	904 165	...	...	...	...	...	...	...
Springs	163 304	...	...	...	...	...	...	...
Tembisa	237 676	...	...	...	...	...	...	...
Umlazi	339 715	...	...	...	...	...	...	...
Vereeniging	379 638	...	...	...	...	...	...	...
Sudan - Soudan								
15 IV 1993 (CDFC)								
Al-Fasher	141 884	...	...	...	...	...	...	...
Al-Gadarif	191 164	...	...	...	...	...	...	...
Al-Gezira	211 362	...	...	...	...	...	...	...
Al-Obeid	229 425	...	...	...	...	...	...	...
Juba	114 980	...	...	...	...	...	...	...

8. Population of capital cities and cities of 100 000 or more inhabitants: latest available year, 1990 - 2009
Population des capitales et des villes de 100 000 habitants ou plus : dernière année disponible, 1990 - 2009 (continued - suite)

Continent, country or area, date, code and city / Continent, pays ou zone, date, code et ville	City proper - Ville proprement dite				Urban agglomeration - Agglomération urbaine			
	Population			Surface area - Superficie (km²)	Population			Surface area - Superficie (km²)
	Both sexes - Les deux sexes	Male - Masculin	Female - Féminin		Both sexes - Les deux sexes	Male - Masculin	Female - Féminin	
AFRICA - AFRIQUE								
Sudan - Soudan								
15 IV 1993 (CDFC)								
Kassala	234 622	...	...	...	...	...	...	...
KHARTOUM	947 483	...	...	...	2 919 773	...	...	...
Khartoum North	700 887	...	...	...	...	...	...	...
Kosti	173 599	...	...	...	...	...	...	...
Nyala	227 183	...	...	...	...	...	...	...
Omdurman	1 271 403	...	...	...	...	...	...	...
Port Sudan	308 195	...	...	...	...	...	...	...
Togo								
1 VII 1990 (ESDF)								
LOME	450 000	...	...	...	...	...	...	...
Tunisia - Tunisie								
1 VII 1998 (ESDF)								
Bizerte	105 520	...	...	...	...	...	...	...
Gabes	104 950	...	...	...	...	...	...	...
Kairouan	110 280	...	...	...	...	...	...	...
Sfax	248 800	...	...	...	...	...	...	...
TUNIS	702 330	...	...	...	...	...	...	...
Uganda - Ouganda								
1 VII 2009 (ESDF)								
Gulu	...	...	...	...	146 600	72 700	73 900	...
KAMPALA	1 533 600	726 400	807 200	...	...	...	...	...
Kira	...	...	...	...	164 700	77 400	87 300	...
Lira	...	...	...	...	102 200	50 800	51 400	...
Western Sahara - Sahara occidental[6]								
1 VII 1999 (ESDF)								
EL AAIUN	169 000	...	...	...	...	...	...	...
Zambia - Zambie								
1 VII 2000 (ESDF)								
Chingola	164 964	82 643	82 321	1 678	...	...	...	...
Kabwe	170 387	84 041	86 346	1 572	...	...	...	...
Kitwe	362 423	180 865	181 558	777	...	...	...	...
Luanshya	144 009	72 449	71 560	811	...	...	...	...
LUSAKA	1 057 212	528 891	528 321	360	...	...	...	...
Mufulira	137 272	68 253	69 019	1 637	...	...	...	...
Ndola	371 221	185 043	186 178	1 103	...	...	...	...
Zimbabwe								
1 VII 2009 (ESDF)								
Bulawayo	713 532	341 211	372 321	479	...	...	...	...
Chitungwiza	340 724	164 876	175 848	...	...	...	...	...
Gweru	148 488	71 378	77 110	...	...	...	...	...
HARARE	1 513 173	758 856	754 317	872	...	...	...	...
Mutare	179 776	89 654	90 122	...	...	...	...	...
AMERICA, NORTH - AMÉRIQUE DU NORD								
Anguilla								
1 VII 2001 (ESDF)								
THE VALLEY	4 904	...	...	...	...	...	...	...
Antigua and Barbuda - Antigua-et-Barbuda								
28 V 1991 (CDFC)								
ST. JOHN	22 342	...	...	...	...	...	...	...
Aruba								
6 X 1991 (CDJC)								
ORANJESTAD	20 045	9 441	10 604	...	...	...	...	...
Bahamas								
1 VII 2009 (ESDF)								
NASSAU	244 400	119 700	124 700	...	...	...	...	...
Belize								
1 VII 2000 (ESDF)								
BELMOPAN	8 305	4 050	4 255	...	...	...	...	...

8. Population of capital cities and cities of 100 000 or more inhabitants: latest available year, 1990 - 2009
Population des capitales et des villes de 100 000 habitants ou plus : dernière année disponible, 1990 - 2009 (continued - suite)

Continent, country or area, date, code and city / Continent, pays ou zone, date, code et ville	City proper - Ville proprement dite				Urban agglomeration - Agglomération urbaine			
	Population			Surface area - Superficie (km²)	Population			Surface area - Superficie (km²)
	Both sexes - Les deux sexes	Male - Masculin	Female - Féminin		Both sexes - Les deux sexes	Male - Masculin	Female - Féminin	
AMERICA, NORTH - AMÉRIQUE DU NORD								
Bermuda - Bermudes								
20 V 2000 (CDJC)								
HAMILTON	969[7]	508[7]	461[7]	0[8]	...	...	...	...
British Virgin Islands - Îles Vierges britanniques								
1 VII 1992 (ESDF)								
ROAD TOWN	3 500	...	...	...	...	...	...	...
Canada								
1 VII 2009* (ESDJ)								
Abbotsford-Mission	...	...	...	...	173 692[9]	87 152[9]	86 540[9]	626[10]
Barrie	...	...	...	...	190 400[9]	94 682[9]	95 718[9]	897[10]
Brantford	...	...	...	...	137 663[9]	67 718[9]	69 945[9]	1 073[10]
Calgary	...	...	...	...	1 230 248[9]	627 297[9]	602 951[9]	5 107[10]
Edmonton	...	...	...	...	1 155 383[9]	587 065[9]	568 318[9]	9 418[10]
Greater Sudbury / Grand Sudbury	...	...	...	...	165 322[9]	81 586[9]	83 736[9]	3 382[10]
Guelph	...	...	...	...	135 863[9]	67 644[9]	68 219[9]	378[10]
Halifax	...	...	...	...	398 037[9]	193 195[9]	204 842[9]	5 496[10]
Hamilton	...	...	...	...	739 415[9]	364 058[9]	375 357[9]	1 372[10]
Kelowna	...	...	...	...	178 446[9]	87 835[9]	90 611[9]	2 904[10]
Kingston	...	...	...	...	160 723[9]	79 326[9]	81 397[9]	1 907[10]
Kitchener-Cambridge-Waterloo	...	...	...	...	489 054[9]	243 838[9]	245 216[9]	827[10]
London	...	...	...	...	489 274[9]	240 576[9]	248 698[9]	2 665[10]
Moncton	...	...	...	...	133 880[9]	65 595[9]	68 285[9]	2 406[10]
Montréal	...	...	...	...	3 814 738[9]	1 879 347[9]	1 935 391[9]	4 259[10]
Oshawa	...	...	...	...	361 375[9]	178 556[9]	182 819[9]	903[10]
Ottawa - Gatineau	...	...	...	...	1 220 674[11]	599 344[11]	621 330[11]	5 716[10]
Peterborough	...	...	...	...	121 428[9]	59 279[9]	62 149[9]	1 506[10]
Québec	...	...	...	...	746 252[9]	365 325[9]	380 927[9]	3 277[10]
Regina	...	...	...	...	210 006[9]	103 456[9]	106 550[9]	3 408[10]
Saguenay	...	...	...	...	151 715[9]	75 459[9]	76 256[9]	1 754[10]
Saint John	...	...	...	...	126 594[9]	61 287[9]	65 307[9]	3 360[10]
Saskatoon	...	...	...	...	257 298[9]	127 628[9]	129 670[9]	5 207[10]
Sherbrooke	...	...	...	...	194 555[9]	95 082[9]	99 473[9]	1 232[10]
St Catharines-Niagara	...	...	...	...	404 378[9]	197 911[9]	206 467[9]	1 397[10]
St. John's	...	...	...	...	187 596[9]	91 667[9]	95 929[9]	805[10]
Thunder Bay	...	...	...	...	124 816[9]	61 869[9]	62 947[9]	2 550[10]
Toronto	...	...	...	...	5 623 450[9]	2 761 593[9]	2 861 857[9]	5 904[10]
Trois-Rivières	...	...	...	...	145 103[9]	70 850[9]	74 253[9]	880[10]
Vancouver	...	...	...	...	2 328 007[9]	1 151 435[9]	1 176 572[9]	2 877[10]
Victoria	...	...	...	...	352 421[9]	170 609[9]	181 812[9]	695[10]
Windsor	...	...	...	...	331 537[9]	164 842[9]	166 695[9]	1 023[10]
Winnipeg	...	...	...	...	742 408[9]	366 358[9]	376 050[9]	5 303[10]
Cayman Islands - Îles Caïmanes								
1 IV 2007 (SSDJ)								
GEORGE TOWN	28 836	...	...	...	...	...	...	...
Costa Rica								
1 VII 2009 (ESDJ)								
Alajuela	278 859[1]	141 110[1]	137 749[1]	388	...	...	...	...
Alajuelita	119 616[1]	60 508[1]	59 108[1]	21	...	...	...	...
Cartago	153 819[1]	77 016[1]	76 803[1]	288	...	...	...	...
Desamparados	281 499[1]	140 370[1]	141 129[1]	188	...	...	...	...
Goicoechea	130 851[1]	64 713[1]	66 138[1]	32	...	...	...	...
Heredia	130 279[1]	64 723[1]	65 556[1]	283	...	...	...	...
La Unión	103 496[1]	51 650[1]	51 846[1]	45	...	...	...	...
Limón	104 214[1]	53 440[1]	50 774[1]	1 766	...	...	...	...
Pavas	109 207[1]	54 649[1]	54 558[1]	9	...	...	...	...
Perez Zeledon	130 621[1]	65 428[1]	65 193[1]	1 906	...	...	...	...
Pococi	146 818[1]	77 651[1]	69 167[1]	2 403	...	...	...	...
Puntarenas	106 237[1]	55 003[1]	51 234[1]	1 842	...	...	...	...
San Carlos	148 962[1]	76 547[1]	72 415[1]	3 348	...	...	...	...
SAN JOSE	346 298[1]	172 761[1]	173 537[1]	45	...	...	...	...

8. Population of capital cities and cities of 100 000 or more inhabitants: latest available year, 1990 - 2009
Population des capitales et des villes de 100 000 habitants ou plus : dernière année disponible, 1990 - 2009 (continued - suite)

Continent, country or area, date, code and city / Continent, pays ou zone, date, code et ville	City proper - Ville proprement dite				Urban agglomeration - Agglomération urbaine			
	Population			Surface area - Superficie (km²)	Population			Surface area - Superficie (km²)
	Both sexes - Les deux sexes	Male - Masculin	Female - Féminin		Both sexes - Les deux sexes	Male - Masculin	Female - Féminin	
AMERICA, NORTH - AMÉRIQUE DU NORD								
Cuba								
1 VII 2009 (ESDJ)								
Bayamo	147 548	...	...	27[12]	...	...	...	...
Camagüey	306 047	...	...	82[12]	...	...	...	...
Ciego de Avila	110 907	...	...	21[12]	...	...	...	...
Cienfuegos	143 625	...	...	46[12]	...	...	...	...
Guantánamo	208 014	...	...	34[12]	...	...	...	...
Holguín	277 108	...	...	58[12]	...	...	...	...
LA HABANA	2 145 063	...	...	721[12]	...	...	...	...
Las Tunas	152 964	...	...	31[12]	...	...	...	...
Matanzas	132 362	...	...	44[12]	...	...	...	...
Pinar del Río	137 564	...	...	32[12]	...	...	...	...
Santa Clara	206 774	...	...	44[12]	...	...	...	...
Santiago de Cuba	426 760	...	...	70[12]	...	...	...	...
Dominica - Dominique								
12 V 1991 (CDFC)								
ROSEAU	16 243	...	...	...	...	...	...	...
Dominican Republic - République dominicaine								
18 X 2002 (CDJC)								
La Romana	191 303	92 460	98 843	...	202 488	98 113	104 375	263
San Pedro de Macoris	193 713	93 246	100 467	...	217 141	105 070	112 071	146
Santiago de los Caballeros	507 418	244 935	262 483	...	622 101	302 619	319 482	529
SANTO DOMINGO	...	...	...	...	1 234 721	599 785	634 936	91
Santo Domingo East - Santo Domingo Este	...	...	...	...	492 302	233 450	258 852	169
Santo Domingo North - Santo Domingo Norte	...	...	...	...	326 484	162 487	163 997	387
Santo Domingo West - Santo Domingo Oeste	...	...	...	...	415 935	203 848	212 087	56
El Salvador								
12 V 2007 (CDJC)								
Ahuachapan	63 981	29 898	34 083	245	110 511	52 808	57 703	...
Apopa	131 286	61 172	70 114	52	...	...	...	...
Ciudad Delgado	112 161	52 381	59 780	33	120 200	56 297	63 903	...
Ilopango	103 862	47 726	56 136	35	...	...	...	...
Mejicanos	140 751	64 509	76 242	22	...	...	...	...
San Miguel	158 136	71 132	87 004	594	218 410	99 672	118 738	...
SAN SALVADOR	316 090	144 217	171 873	886	...	...	...	...
Santa Ana	204 340	97 115	107 225	400	245 421	117 565	127 856	...
Santa Tecla	108 840	49 315	59 525	112	121 908	55 780	66 128	...
Soyapango	241 403	111 234	130 169	30	...	...	...	...
Greenland - Groenland								
1 I 2009 (ESDJ)								
NUUK (GODTHAB)	15 105	7 982	7 123	...	...	...	...	...
Guadeloupe								
8 III 1999 (CDJC)								
BASSE-TERRE	12 377	5 687	6 690	...	44 747	21 252	23 495	...
Pointe-à-Pitre	...	...	...	...	171 773	...	...	...
Guatemala								
1 VII 2001 (ESDF)								
CUIDAD DE GUATEMALA	1 022 001	491 891	530 110	228	...	...	...	...
Escuintla	114 626	57 893	56 733	332	...	...	...	...
Mixco	452 134	221 928	230 206	99	...	...	...	...
Quetzaltenango	152 223	76 272	75 951	120	...	...	...	...
Villa Nueva	390 329	192 238	198 091	114	...	...	...	...
Haiti - Haïti								
1 VII 1999 (ESDJ)								
Cap-Haitien	113 555	50 064	63 491	10	...	...	...	...
Carrefour	336 222	146 838	189 384	23	...	...	...	...
Delmas	284 079	124 774	159 305	26	...	...	...	...
PORT-AU-PRINCE	990 558	436 170	554 388	21	...	...	...	...
Honduras								
1 VII 2003 (ESDF)								
La Ceiba	137 815	67 691	70 124	...	...	...	...	...
San Pedro Sula	518 736	251 514	267 222	...	...	...	...	...
TEGUCIGALPA	858 437	411 687	446 749	...	...	...	...	...

8. Population of capital cities and cities of 100 000 or more inhabitants: latest available year, 1990 - 2009
Population des capitales et des villes de 100 000 habitants ou plus : dernière année disponible, 1990 - 2009 (continued - suite)

Continent, country or area, date, code and city / Continent, pays ou zone, date, code et ville	City proper - Ville proprement dite				Urban agglomeration - Agglomération urbaine			
	Population			Surface area - Superficie (km²)	Population			Surface area - Superficie (km²)
	Both sexes - Les deux sexes	Male - Masculin	Female - Féminin		Both sexes - Les deux sexes	Male - Masculin	Female - Féminin	
AMERICA, NORTH - AMÉRIQUE DU NORD								
Jamaica - Jamaïque								
10 IX 2001 (CDJC)								
KINGSTON	579 137[13]	272 587[13]	306 550[13]	22	...	...	...	...
Portmore[13]	156 467	72 292	84 175	...	...	...	...	...
Spanish Town[13]	131 510	63 791	67 719		...	...	...	...
Martinique								
1 I 2006 (CDJC)								
FORT-DE-FRANCE	90 347	40 128	50 219	...	133 281	59 945	73 336	...
Mexico - Mexique[1]								
1 VII 2008 (ESDJ)								
Acapulco (de Juárez)	...	...	...	...	631 051	...	...	...
Aguascalientes	...	...	...	...	742 486	...	...	...
Campeche	...	...	...	...	222 886	...	...	...
Cancun	...	...	...	...	581 010	...	...	...
Celaya	...	...	...	...	331 253	...	...	...
Chihuahua	...	...	...	...	798 862	...	...	...
Ciudad Del Carmen	...	...	...	...	169 930	...	...	...
Ciudad Victoria	...	...	...	...	291 116	...	...	...
Coatzacoalcos	...	...	...	...	425 890	...	...	...
Colimas	...	...	...	...	238 135	...	...	...
Cuernavaca	...	...	...	...	742 992	...	...	...
Culiacán Rosales	...	...	...	...	641 709	...	...	...
Durango (Victoria de Durango)	...	...	...	...	491 436	...	...	...
Guadalajara	...	...	...	...	3 942 640	...	...	...
Hermosillo	...	...	...	...	681 668	...	...	...
Irapuato	...	...	...	...	352 097	...	...	...
Juárez	...	...	...	...	1 379 996	...	...	...
La Paz, Distrito Federal	...	...	...	...	198 030	...	...	...
León (de los Aldama)	...	...	...	...	1 332 505	...	...	...
Manzanillo	...	...	...	...	122 769	...	...	...
Matamoros	...	...	...	...	444 067	...	...	...
Mérida	...	...	...	...	914 535	...	...	...
Mexicali	...	...	...	...	711 567	...	...	...
MEXICO, CIUDAD DE	...	...	...	...	18 460 523	...	...	...
Monclova	...	...	...	...	268 895	...	...	...
Monterrey	...	...	...	...	3 542 333	...	...	...
Morelia	...	...	...	...	681 700	...	...	...
Nuevo Laredo	...	...	...	...	367 541	...	...	...
Oaxaca de Juárez	...	...	...	...	516 373	...	...	...
Orizaba	...	...	...	...	486 309	...	...	...
Pachuca (de Soto)	...	...	...	...	339 351	...	...	...
Puebla de Zaragoza	...	...	...	...	1 971 076	...	...	...
Querétaro	...	...	...	...	720 217	...	...	...
Reynosa	...	...	...	...	573 518	...	...	...
Salamanca	...	...	...	...	147 353	...	...	...
Saltillo	...	...	...	...	733 056	...	...	...
San Luis Potosí	...	...	...	...	968 588	...	...	...
Tampico	...	...	...	...	657 156	...	...	...
Tepic	...	...	...	...	314 124	...	...	...
Tijuana	...	...	...	...	1 380 101	...	...	...
Tlaxcala	...	...	...	...	477 371	...	...	...
Toluca (de Lerdo)	...	...	...	...	1 113 076	...	...	...
Torreón	...	...	...	...	912 312	...	...	...
Tuxpan	...	...	...	...	103 408	...	...	...
Tuxtla Gutiérrez	...	...	...	...	524 090	...	...	...
Veracruz	...	...	...	...	658 593	...	...	...
Villahermosa	...	...	...	...	380 072	...	...	...
Zacatecas	...	...	...	...	247 940	...	...	...
Netherlands Antilles - Antilles néerlandaises								
27 I 1992 (CDJC)								
WILLEMSTAD	2 345	...		...	...	...		...
Nicaragua								
1 VII 2009 (ESDJ)								
Chinandega	...	...	...	...	106 635	...	...	...
Leon	...	...	...	...	156 049	...	...	...

8. Population of capital cities and cities of 100 000 or more inhabitants: latest available year, 1990 - 2009
Population des capitales et des villes de 100 000 habitants ou plus : dernière année disponible, 1990 - 2009 (continued - suite)

Continent, country or area, date, code and city / Continent, pays ou zone, date, code et ville	City proper - Ville proprement dite				Urban agglomeration - Agglomération urbaine			
	Population			Surface area - Superficie (km²)	Population			Surface area - Superficie (km²)
	Both sexes - Les deux sexes	Male - Masculin	Female - Féminin		Both sexes - Les deux sexes	Male - Masculin	Female - Féminin	
AMERICA, NORTH - AMÉRIQUE DU NORD								
Nicaragua								
1 VII 2009 (ESDJ)								
MANAGUA	...	...	...	...	*985 143*	...	...	...
Masaya	...	...	...	...	*110 491*	...	...	...
Tipitapa	...	...	...	...	*105 773*	...	...	...
Panama								
1 VII 2009 (ESDF)								
PANAMA DE PANAMA	*464 761*[14]	*221 160*[14]	*243 601*[14]	107	...	...	...	...
San Miguelito	*366 782*[14]	*179 125*[14]	*187 657*[14]	50	...	...	...	...
Puerto Rico - Porto Rico								
1 VII 2007 (ESDJ)								
Arecibo	102 495[15]	49 923[15]	52 572[15]	327	...	...	...	...
Bayamón	220 629[15]	105 446[15]	115 183[15]	115	...	...	...	...
Caguas	142 984[15]	67 000[15]	75 984[15]	152	...	...	...	...
Carolina	187 607[15]	86 860[15]	100 747[15]	118	...	...	...	...
Guaynabo	102 838[15]	48 886[15]	53 952[15]	70	...	...	...	...
Ponce	180 376[15]	87 283[15]	93 093[15]	301	...	...	...	...
SAN JUAN	424 951[15]	195 961[15]	228 990[15]	124	...	...	...	...
Saint Lucia - Sainte-Lucie								
22 V 2001 (CDFC)								
CASTRIES	11 092	5 238	5 854	...	...	...	...	...
Saint Pierre and Miquelon - Saint Pierre-et-Miquelon								
8 III 1999 (CDFC)								
SAINT-PIERRE	5 618	2 781	2 837	...	...	...	...	...
Saint Vincent and the Grenadines - Saint-Vincent-et-les Grenadines								
12 V 1991 (CDFC)								
KINGSTOWN	15 466	...						
Trinidad and Tobago - Trinité-et-Tobago								
1 VII 1996 (ESDF)								
PORT-OF-SPAIN	43 396	20 739	22 657	12	...	...	...	...
Turks and Caicos Islands - Îles Turques et Caïques								
1 VII 2006 (ESDJ)								
GRAND TURK	*5 718*	*2 846*	*2 872*	17	...	...	...	...
United States of America - États-Unis d'Amérique[16]								
1 VII 2009 (ESDJ)								
Abilene (TX)	117 180	...	...	274	...	...	...	...
Akron (OH)	207 209	...	...	161	...	...	...	...
Albuquerque (NM)	529 219	...	...	487	...	...	...	...
Alexandria (VA)	150 006	...	...	39	...	...	...	...
Allentown (PA)	107 815	...	...	45	...	...	...	...
Amarillo (TX)	189 392	...	...	254	...	...	...	...
Anaheim (CA)	337 896	...	...	129	...	...	...	...
Anchorage (AK)	286 174	...	...	4 415	...	...	...	...
Ann Arbor (MI)	112 920	...	...	72	...	...	...	...
Antioch (CA)	101 181	...	...	73	...	...	...	...
Arlington (TX)	380 085	...	...	248	...	...	...	...
Arlington (VA)	217 483	...	...	67	...	...	...	...
Arvada (CO)	108 208	...	...	91	...	...	...	...
Athens (GA)	114 983	...	...	301	...	...	...	...
Atlanta (GA)	540 922	...	...	345	...	...	...	...
Augusta (GA)	194 343	...	...	783	...	...	...	...
Aurora (CO)	323 348	...	...	400	...	...	...	...
Aurora (IL)	172 950	...	...	116	...	...	...	...
Austin (TX)	786 386	...	...	766	...	...	...	...
Bakersfield (CA)	324 463	...	...	335	...	...	...	...
Baltimore (MD)	637 418	...	...	210	...	...	...	...
Baton Rouge (LA)	225 388	...	...	199	...	...	...	...
Beaumont (TX)	110 110	...	...	214	...	...	...	...
Bellevue (WA)	126 626	...	...	82	...	...	...	...
Berkeley (CA)	102 804	...	...	27	...	...	...	...
Billings (MT)	105 845	...	...	112	...	...	...	...
Birmingham (AL)	230 131	...	...	387	...	...	...	...
Boise City (ID)	205 707	...	...	200	...	...	...	...

8. Population of capital cities and cities of 100 000 or more inhabitants: latest available year, 1990 - 2009
Population des capitales et des villes de 100 000 habitants ou plus : dernière année disponible, 1990 - 2009 (continued - suite)

Continent, country or area, date, code and city / Continent, pays ou zone, date, code et ville	City proper - Ville proprement dite				Urban agglomeration - Agglomération urbaine			
	Population			Surface area - Superficie (km²)	Population			Surface area - Superficie (km²)
	Both sexes - Les deux sexes	Male - Masculin	Female - Féminin		Both sexes - Les deux sexes	Male - Masculin	Female - Féminin	

AMERICA, NORTH - AMÉRIQUE DU NORD

United States of America - États-Unis d'Amérique[16]
1 VII 2009 (ESDJ)

Boston (MA)	645 169	...	...	125	...	...	...	...
Boulder (CO)	100 160	...	...	64	...	...	...	...
Bridgeport (CT)	137 298	...	...	41	...	...	...	...
Brownsville (TX)	176 859	...	...	343	...	...	...	...
Buffalo (NY)	270 240	...	...	105	...	...	...	...
Burbank (CA)	103 121	...	...	45	...	...	...	...
Cambridge (MA)	108 771	...	...	17	...	...	...	...
Cape Coral (FL)	154 202	...	...	274	...	...	...	...
Carrollton (TX)	129 209	...	...	94	...	...	...	...
Cary (NC)	136 637	...	...	140	...	...	...	...
Cedar Rapids (IA)	127 764	...	...	184	...	...	...	...
Centennial (CO)	100 557	...	...	73	...	...	...	...
Chandler (AZ)	249 535	...	...	167	...	...	...	...
Charleston (SC)	115 638	...	...	282	...	...	...	...
Charlotte (NC)	704 422	...	...	741	...	...	...	...
Chattanooga (TN)	171 350	...	...	353	...	...	...	...
Chesapeake (VA)	222 455	...	...	883	...	...	...	...
Chicago (IL)	2 851 268	...	...	589	...	...	...	...
Chula Vista (CA)	223 739	...	...	129	...	...	...	...
Cincinnati (OH)	333 012	...	...	202	...	...	...	...
Clarksville (TN)	124 565	...	...	253	...	...	...	...
Clearwater (FL)	106 081	...	...	66	...	...	...	...
Cleveland (OH)	431 369	...	...	201	...	...	...	...
Colorado Springs (CO)	399 827	...	...	504	...	...	...	...
Columbia (MO)	102 324	...	...	162	...	...	...	...
Columbia (SC)	129 333	...	...	342	...	...	...	...
Columbus (GA)	190 414	...	...	560	...	...	...	...
Columbus (OH)	769 332	...	...	561	...	...	...	...
Concord (CA)	122 224	...	...	79	...	...	...	...
Coral Springs (FL)	126 518	...	...	61	...	...	...	...
Corona (CA)	151 027	...	...	100	...	...	...	...
Corpus Christi (TX)	287 439	...	...	416	...	...	...	...
Costa Mesa (CA)	110 419	...	...	41	...	...	...	...
Dallas (TX)	1 299 542	...	...	882	...	...	...	...
Daly City (CA)	102 165	...	...	20	...	...	...	...
Davenport (IA)	101 335	...	...	163	...	...	...	...
Dayton (OH)	153 843	...	...	144	...	...	...	...
Denton (TX)	122 830	...	...	220	...	...	...	...
Denver (CO)	610 345	...	...	397	...	...	...	...
Des Moines (IA)	200 538	...	...	210	...	...	...	...
Detroit (MI)	910 921	...	...	359	...	...	...	...
Downey (CA)	107 117	...	...	32	...	...	...	...
Durham (NC)	229 171	...	...	276	...	...	...	...
El Monte (CA)	121 447	...	...	25	...	...	...	...
El Paso (TX)	620 456	...	...	657	...	...	...	...
Elgin (IL)	107 519	...	...	96	...	...	...	...
Elizabeth (NJ)	125 285	...	...	32	...	...	...	...
Elk Grove (CA)	135 285	...	...	109	...	...	...	...
Erie (PA)	103 571	...	...	49	...	...	...	...
Escondido (CA)	140 170	...	...	96	...	...	...	...
Eugene (OR)	153 272	...	...	113	...	...	...	...
Evansville (IN)	116 584	...	...	114	...	...	...	...
Fairfield (CA)	103 586	...	...	97	...	...	...	...
Fayetteville (NC)	207 288	...	...	378	...	...	...	...
Flint (MI)	111 475	...	...	87	...	...	...	...
Fontana (CA)	188 013	...	...	110	...	...	...	...
Fort Collins (CO)	138 733	...	...	135	...	...	...	...
Fort Lauderdale (FL)	184 892	...	...	90	...	...	...	...
Fort Wayne (IN)	255 890	...	...	287	...	...	...	...
Fort Worth (TX)	727 577	...	...	878	...	...	...	...
Fremont (CA)	205 517	...	...	201	...	...	...	...
Fresno (CA)	479 918	...	...	286	...	...	...	...
Frisco (TX)	102 413	...	...	160	...	...	...	...

8. Population of capital cities and cities of 100 000 or more inhabitants: latest available year, 1990 - 2009
Population des capitales et des villes de 100 000 habitants ou plus : dernière année disponible, 1990 - 2009 (continued - suite)

Continent, country or area, date, code and city / Continent, pays ou zone, date, code et ville	City proper - Ville proprement dite				Urban agglomeration - Agglomération urbaine			
	Population			Surface area - Superficie (km²)	Population			Surface area - Superficie (km²)
	Both sexes - Les deux sexes	Male - Masculin	Female - Féminin		Both sexes - Les deux sexes	Male - Masculin	Female - Féminin	

AMERICA, NORTH - AMÉRIQUE DU NORD

United States of America - États-Unis d'Amérique[16]
1 VII 2009 (ESDJ)

Continent, country or area, date, code and city	Both sexes	Male	Female	Surface area	Both sexes	Male	Female	Surface area
Fullerton (CA)	132 620	...	...	58	...	...	...	...
Gainesville (FL)	116 616	...	...	156	...	...	...	...
Garden Grove (CA)	166 332	...	...	47	...	...	...	...
Garland (TX)	222 013	...	...	148	...	...	...	...
Gilbert (AZ)	222 075	...	...	175	...	...	...	...
Glendale (AZ)	253 209	...	...	154	...	...	...	...
Glendale (CA)	196 882	...	...	79	...	...	...	...
Grand Prairie (TX)	163 351	...	...	187	...	...	...	...
Grand Rapids (MI)	193 710	...	...	115	...	...	...	...
Green Bay (WI)	101 412	...	...	118	...	...	...	...
Greensboro (NC)	254 344	...	...	306	...	...	...	...
Greshan (OR)	102 295	...	...	60	...	...	...	...
Hampton (VA)	144 236	...	...	133	...	...	...	...
Hartford (CT)	124 060	...	...	45	...	...	...	...
Hayward (CA)	144 291	...	...	117	...	...	...	...
Henderson (NV)	256 445	...	...	279	...	...	...	...
Hialeah (FL)	218 896	...	...	55	...	...	...	...
High Point City (NC)	103 368	...	...	139	...	...	...	...
Hollywood (FL)	142 622	...	...	71	...	...	...	...
Honolulu (HI)	374 658	...	...	222	...	...	...	...
Houston (TX)	2 257 926	...	...	1 550	...	...	...	...
Huntington Beach (CA)	193 366	...	...	69	...	...	...	...
Huntsville (AL)	179 652	...	...	536	...	...	...	...
Independence (MO)	121 180	...	...	201	...	...	...	...
Indianapolis (IN)	807 584	...	...	936	...	...	...	...
Inglewood (CA)	112 241	...	...	24	...	...	...	...
Irvine (CA)	209 716	...	...	171	...	...	...	...
Irving (TX)	205 541	...	...	173	...	...	...	...
Jackson (MS)	175 021	...	...	282	...	...	...	...
Jacksonville (FL)	813 518	...	...	1 935	...	...	...	...
Jersey City (NJ)	242 503	...	...	38	...	...	...	...
Joliet (IL)	147 648	...	...	139	...	...	...	...
Kansas City (KS)	143 209	...	...	323	...	...	...	...
Kansas City (MO)	482 299	...	...	814	...	...	...	...
Killeen (TX)	119 512	...	...	137	...	...	...	...
Knoxville (TN)	185 100	...	...	255	...	...	...	...
Lafayette (LA)	114 915	...	...	127	...	...	...	...
Lakewood (CO)	141 937	...	...	111	...	...	...	...
Lancaster (CA)	145 776	...	...	244	...	...	...	...
Lansing (MI)	113 802	...	...	93	...	...	...	...
Laredo (TX)	226 124	...	...	233	...	...	...	...
Las Vegas (NV)	567 641	...	...	350	...	...	...	...
Lewisville (TX)	105 170	...	...	94	...	...	...	...
Lexington-Fayette (KY)	296 545	...	...	735	...	...	...	...
Lincoln (NE)	254 001	...	...	226	...	...	...	...
Little Rock (AR)	191 933	...	...	305	...	...	...	...
Long Beach (CA)	462 604	...	...	131	...	...	...	...
Los Angeles (CA)	3 831 868	...	...	1 214	...	...	...	...
Louisville (KY)	566 503	...	...	843	...	...	...	...
Lowell (MA)	104 390	...	...	35	...	...	...	...
Lubbock (TX)	225 859	...	...	316	...	...	...	...
Madison (WI)	235 419	...	...	198	...	...	...	...
Manchester (NH)	109 279	...	...	86	...	...	...	...
McAllen (TX)	132 225	...	...	125	...	...	...	...
McKinney City (TX)	127 672	...	...	160	...	...	...	...
Memphis (TN)	676 640	...	...	816	...	...	...	...
Mesa (AZ)	467 157	...	...	353	...	...	...	...
Mesquite (TX)	133 509	...	...	119	...	...	...	...
Miami (FL)	433 136	...	...	93	...	...	...	...
Miami Gardens (FL)	109 332	...	...	47	...	...	...	...
Midland City (TX)	108 668	...	...	181	...	...	...	...
Milwaukee (WI)	605 013	...	...	249	...	...	...	...
Minneapolis (MN)	385 378	...	...	142	...	...	...	...

8. Population of capital cities and cities of 100 000 or more inhabitants: latest available year, 1990 - 2009
Population des capitales et des villes de 100 000 habitants ou plus : dernière année disponible, 1990 - 2009 (continued - suite)

Continent, country or area, date, code and city / Continent, pays ou zone, date, code et ville	City proper - Ville proprement dite				Urban agglomeration - Agglomération urbaine			
	Population			Surface area - Superficie (km²)	Population			Surface area - Superficie (km²)
	Both sexes - Les deux sexes	Male - Masculin	Female - Féminin		Both sexes - Les deux sexes	Male - Masculin	Female - Féminin	
AMERICA, NORTH - AMÉRIQUE DU NORD								
United States of America - États-Unis d'Amérique[16]								
1 VII 2009 (ESDJ)								
Miramar (FL)	109 176	...	...	76	...	...	...	...
Mobile (AL)	197 539	...	...	358	...	...	...	...
Modesto (CA)	202 743	...	...	95	...	...	...	...
Montgomery (AL)	202 124	...	...	413	...	...	...	...
Moreno Valley (CA)	191 754	...	...	133	...	...	...	...
Murfreesboro (TN)	105 209	...	...	142	...	...	...	...
Naperville (IL)	143 661	...	...	100	...	...	...	...
Nashville-Davidson (TN)	605 473	...	...	1 230	...	...	...	...
New Haven (CT)	123 330	...	...	48	...	...	...	...
New Orleans (LA)	354 850	...	...	439	...	...	...	...
New York (NY)	8 391 881	...	...	786	...	...	...	...
Newark (NJ)	278 154	...	...	63	...	...	...	...
Newport News (VA)	193 172	...	...	178	...	...	...	...
Norfolk (VA)	233 333	...	...	140	...	...	...	...
Norman (OK)	109 062	...	...	463	...	...	...	...
North Las Vegas (NV)	224 387	...	...	212	...	...	...	...
Norwalk (CA)	102 508	...	...	25	...	...	...	...
Oakland (CA)	409 189	...	...	145	...	...	...	...
Oceanside (CA)	172 901	...	...	106	...	...	...	...
Odessa (TX)	100 810	...	...	97	...	...	...	...
Oklahoma City (OK)	560 333	...	...	1 571	...	...	...	...
Olathe (KS)	121 962	...	...	153	...	...	...	...
Omaha (NE)	454 731	...	...	329	...	...	...	...
Ontario (CA)	171 603	...	...	129	...	...	...	...
Orange (CA)	136 990	...	...	64	...	...	...	...
Orlando (FL)	235 860	...	...	264	...	...	...	...
Overland Park (KS)	174 907	...	...	194	...	...	...	...
Oxnard (CA)	187 535	...	...	70	...	...	...	...
Palm Bay City (FL)	100 999	...	...	170	...	...	...	...
Palmdale (CA)	143 985	...	...	276	...	...	...	...
Pasadena (CA)	143 667	...	...	60	...	...	...	...
Pasadena (TX)	145 789	...	...	113	...	...	...	...
Paterson (NJ)	145 835	...	...	22	...	...	...	...
Pembroke Pines (FL)	146 600	...	...	86	...	...	...	...
Peoria (AZ)	163 226	...	...	460	...	...	...	...
Peoria (IL)	115 520	...	...	124	...	...	...	...
Philadelphia (PA)	1 547 297	...	...	347	...	...	...	...
Phoenix (AZ)	1 593 659	...	...	1 335	...	...	...	...
Pittsburgh (PA)	311 647	...	...	143	...	...	...	...
Plano (TX)	273 613	...	...	185	...	...	...	...
Pomona (CA)	152 367	...	...	59	...	...	...	...
Pompano Beach (FL)	102 609	...	...	62	...	...	...	...
Port St. Lucie (FL)	154 410	...	...	296	...	...	...	...
Portland (OR)	566 143	...	...	346	...	...	...	...
Providence (RI)	171 909	...	...	48	...	...	...	...
Provo (UT)	119 775	...	...	106	...	...	...	...
Pueblo (CO)	104 877	...	...	123	...	...	...	...
Raleigh (NC)	405 612	...	...	368	...	...	...	...
Rancho Cucamonga (CA)	171 809	...	...	103	...	...	...	...
Reno (NV)	219 636	...	...	263	...	...	...	...
Richardson (TX)	103 201	...	...	74	...	...	...	...
Richmond (CA)	103 165	...	...	78	...	...	...	...
Richmond (VA)	204 451	...	...	155	...	...	...	...
Riverside (CA)	297 841	...	...	210	...	...	...	...
Rochester (MN)	103 486	...	...	139	...	...	...	...
Rochester (NY)	207 294	...	...	93	...	...	...	...
Rockford (IL)	157 280	...	...	158	...	...	...	...
Roseville (CA)	115 677	...	...	94	...	...	...	...
Round Rock (TX)	105 424	...	...	88	...	...	...	...
Sacramento (CA)	466 676	...	...	254	...	...	...	...
Salem (OR)	155 469	...	...	124	...	...	...	...
Salinas (CA)	144 278	...	...	50	...	...	...	...
Salt Lake City (UT)	183 102	...	...	288	...	...	...	...

8. Population of capital cities and cities of 100 000 or more inhabitants: latest available year, 1990 - 2009
Population des capitales et des villes de 100 000 habitants ou plus : dernière année disponible, 1990 - 2009 (continued - suite)

Continent, country or area, date, code and city / Continent, pays ou zone, date, code et ville	City proper - Ville proprement dite				Urban agglomeration - Agglomération urbaine			
	Population			Surface area - Superficie (km²)	Population			Surface area - Superficie (km²)
	Both sexes - Les deux sexes	Male - Masculin	Female - Féminin		Both sexes - Les deux sexes	Male - Masculin	Female - Féminin	
AMERICA, NORTH - AMÉRIQUE DU NORD								
United States of America - États-Unis d'Amérique[16]								
1 VII 2009 (ESDJ)								
San Antonio (TX)	1 373 668	...	...	1 315	...	...	...	...
San Bernardino (CA)	198 411	...	...	153	...	...	...	...
San Buenaventura (CA)	104 423	...	...	56	...	...	...	...
San Diego (CA)	1 306 300	...	...	842	...	...	...	...
San Francisco (CA)	815 358	...	...	121	...	...	...	...
San Jose (CA)	964 695	...	...	456	...	...	...	...
Santa Ana (CA)	340 338	...	...	71	...	...	...	...
Santa Clara (CA)	111 997	...	...	48	...	...	...	...
Santa Clarita (CA)	169 174	...	...	139	...	...	...	...
Santa Rosa (CA)	157 468	...	...	107	...	...	...	...
Savannah (GA)	134 699	...	...	266	...	...	...	...
Scottsdale (AZ)	237 844	...	...	476	...	...	...	...
Seattle (WA)	616 627	...	...	217	...	...	...	...
Shreveport (LA)	199 244	...	...	273	...	...	...	...
Simi Valley (CA)	120 921	...	...	107	...	...	...	...
Sioux Falls (SD)	158 008	...	...	188	...	...	...	...
South Bend (IN)	104 215	...	...	107	...	...	...	...
Spokane (WA)	203 268	...	...	153	...	...	...	...
Springfield (IL)	118 033	...	...	154	...	...	...	...
Springfield (MA)	155 580	...	...	83	...	...	...	...
Springfield (MO)	157 630	...	...	211	...	...	...	...
St. Louis (MO)	356 587	...	...	160	...	...	...	...
St. Paul (MN)	281 253	...	...	135	...	...	...	...
St. Petersburg (FL)	244 324	...	...	160	...	...	...	...
Stamford (CT)	121 026	...	...	97	...	...	...	...
Sterling Heights (MI)	127 176	...	...	95	...	...	...	...
Stockton (CA)	287 578	...	...	148	...	...	...	...
Sunnyvale (CA)	133 963	...	...	57	...	...	...	...
Syracuse (NY)	138 560	...	...	65	...	...	...	...
Tacoma (WA)	199 638	...	...	129	...	...	...	...
Tallahassee (FL)	172 574	...	...	259	...	...	...	...
Tampa (FL)	343 890	...	...	294	...	...	...	...
Tempe (AZ)	178 519	...	...	103	...	...	...	...
Thornton (CO)	117 628	...	...	90	...	...	...	...
Thousand Oaks (CA)	123 520	...	...	142	...	...	...	...
Toledo (OH)	316 179	...	...	209	...	...	...	...
Topeka (KS)	124 331	...	...	155	...	...	...	...
Torrance (CA)	140 317	...	...	53	...	...	...	...
Tucson (AZ)	543 910	...	...	587	...	...	...	...
Tulsa (OK)	389 625	...	...	510	...	...	...	...
Vallejo (CA)	114 622	...	...	79	...	...	...	...
Vancouver (WA)	165 742	...	...	120	...	...	...	...
Victorville City (CA)	110 921	...	...	190	...	...	...	...
Virginia Beach (VA)	433 575	...	...	645	...	...	...	...
Visalia (CA)	122 111	...	...	94	...	...	...	...
Waco (TX)	126 222	...	...	231	...	...	...	...
Warren (MI)	133 873	...	...	89	...	...	...	...
WASHINGTON (DC)	599 657	...	...	158	...	...	...	...
Waterbury (CT)	107 143	...	...	74	...	...	...	...
West Covina (CA)	105 464	...	...	42	...	...	...	...
West Jordan (UT)	104 968	...	...	84	...	...	...	...
West Valley City (UT)	125 096	...	...	92	...	...	...	...
Westminster (CO)	109 180	...	...	82	...	...	...	...
Wichita (KS)	372 186	...	...	412	...	...	...	...
Wichita Falls (TX)	101 314	...	...	186	...	...	...	...
Wilmington (NC)	101 350	...	...	128	...	...	...	...
Winston-Salem (NC)	229 828	...	...	343	...	...	...	...
Worcester (MA)	182 882	...	...	97	...	...	...	...
Yonkers (NY)	201 066	...	...	47	...	...	...	...
United States Virgin Islands - Îles Vierges américaines[15]								
1 IV 2000 (CDJC)								
CHARLOTTE AMALIE	11 004	...	...	...	18 914	...	...	...

8. Population of capital cities and cities of 100 000 or more inhabitants: latest available year, 1990 - 2009
Population des capitales et des villes de 100 000 habitants ou plus : dernière année disponible, 1990 - 2009 (continued - suite)

Continent, country or area, date, code and city / Continent, pays ou zone, date, code et ville	City proper - Ville proprement dite				Urban agglomeration - Agglomération urbaine			
	Population			Surface area - Superficie (km²)	Population			Surface area - Superficie (km²)
	Both sexes - Les deux sexes	Male - Masculin	Female - Féminin		Both sexes - Les deux sexes	Male - Masculin	Female - Féminin	

AMERICA, SOUTH - AMÉRIQUE DU SUD

Argentina - Argentine
1 VII 2009 (ESDF)

Bahía Blanca-Cerri	...	...	...	...	307 728	...	...	...
BUENOS AIRES	...	...	...	...	12 948 884	...	...	...
Catamarca	...	...	...	...	201 174	...	...	...
Comodoro Rivadavia-Rada Tilly	...	...	...	...	142 188	...	...	...
Concordia	...	...	...	...	150 435	...	...	...
Córdoba	...	...	...	...	1 393 235	...	...	...
Corrientes	...	...	...	...	352 974	...	...	...
Formosa	...	...	...	...	235 556	...	...	...
La Plata	...	...	...	...	738 271	...	...	...
La Rioja	...	...	...	...	177 944	...	...	...
Mar del Plata-Batán	...	...	...	...	612 777	...	...	...
Mendoza	...	...	...	...	895 008	...	...	...
Neuquén-Plottier	...	...	...	...	261 029	...	...	...
Paraná	...	...	...	...	273 209	...	...	...
Posadas	...	...	...	...	293 819	...	...	...
Rawson-Trelew-Playa Unión	...	...	...	...	127 391	...	...	...
Resistencia	...	...	...	...	384 419	...	...	...
Río Cuarto	...	...	...	...	162 974	...	...	...
Rosario	...	...	...	...	1 253 451	...	...	...
Salta	...	...	...	...	528 426	...	...	...
San Juan	...	...	...	...	462 255	...	...	...
San Luis - El Chorrillo	...	...	...	...	198 619	...	...	...
San Nicolás-Villa Constitución	...	...	...	...	178 761	...	...	...
San Salvador de Jujuy-Palpalá	...	...	...	...	304 360	...	...	...
Santa Fé	...	...	...	...	500 927	...	...	...
Santa Rosa-Toay	...	...	...	...	119 146	...	...	...
Santiago del Estero-La Banda	...	...	...	...	364 901	...	...	...
Tucumán-Tafí Viejo	...	...	...	...	803 492	...	...	...
Ushuaia-Río Grande	...	...	...	...	119 230	...	...	...

Bolivia (Plurinational State of) - Bolivie (État plurinational de)
1 VII 2009 (ESDF)

Cochabamba	611 056	291 324	319 732	...	...	...	...	...
El Alto	921 987	448 691	473 296	...	...	...	...	...
LA PAZ	835 301	397 600	437 701	...	...	...	...	...
Oruro	216 714	104 288	112 426	...	...	...	...	...
Potosí	153 328	73 884	79 444	...	...	...	...	...
Sacaba	148 512	71 677	76 835	...	...	...	...	...
Santa Cruz	1 561 061	759 232	801 829	...	...	...	...	...
SUCRE	274 576	133 092	141 484	...	...	...	...	...
Tarija	188 544	91 305	97 239	...	...	...	...	...
Yacuiba	106 444	52 479	53 965	...	...	...	...	...

Brazil - Brésil[17]
1 VII 2009 (ESDF)

Abaeteluba	139 819	...	...	1 090	...	...	...	...
Açailândia	101 130	...	...	...	...	...	...	...
Aguas Lindas de Goiás	143 179	...	...	...	...	...	...	...
Alagoinhas	137 810	...	...	761	...	...	...	...
Alvorada	213 894	...	...	...	...	...	...	...
Americana	205 229	...	...	...	...	...	...	...
Ananindeua	505 512	...	...	485	...	...	...	...
Anápolis	335 960	...	...	...	...	...	...	...
Angra dos Reis	168 664	...	...	...	...	...	...	...
Aparecida de Goiania	510 770	...	...	...	...	...	...	...
Apucarana	121 290	...	...	556	...	...	...	...
Aracaju	544 039	...	...	151	...	...	...	...
Araçatuba	182 204	...	...	2 668	...	...	...	...
Araguaina	119 637	...	...	...	...	...	...	...
Araguario	111 095	...	...	...	...	...	...	...
Arapiraca	210 521	...	...	...	...	...	...	...
Arapongas	103 025	...	...	...	...	...	...	...
Araraquara	200 666	...	...	...	...	...	...	...
Araras	114 515	...	...	...	...	...	...	...

8. Population of capital cities and cities of 100 000 or more inhabitants: latest available year, 1990 - 2009
Population des capitales et des villes de 100 000 habitants ou plus : dernière année disponible, 1990 - 2009 (continued - suite)

Continent, country or area, date, code and city / Continent, pays ou zone, date, code et ville	City proper - Ville proprement dite				Urban agglomeration - Agglomération urbaine			
	Population			Surface area - Superficie (km²)	Population			Surface area - Superficie (km²)
	Both sexes - Les deux sexes	Male - Masculin	Female - Féminin		Both sexes - Les deux sexes	Male - Masculin	Female - Féminin	

AMERICA, SOUTH - AMÉRIQUE DU SUD

Brazil - Brésil[17]
  1 VII 2009 (ESDF)

Araruama	109 705	...	...	...	...	...	...	...
Araucária	117 964	...	...	...	...	...	...	...
Atibaia	126 757	...	...	...	...	...	...	...
Bagé	115 745	...	...	7 185	...	...	...	...
Balneário Camboriú	102 081	...	...	...	...	...	...	...
Barbacena	128 572	...	...	...	...	...	...	...
Barra do Piraí	103 833	...	...	...	...	...	...	...
Barra Mansa	176 899	...	...	830	...	...	...	...
Barreiras	137 832	...	...	...	...	...	...	...
Barretos	113 618	...	...	...	...	...	...	...
Barueri	270 173	...	...	...	...	...	...	...
Bauru	359 429	...	...	702	...	...	...	...
Belém	1 437 600	...	...	736	...	...	...	...
Belford Roxo	501 544	...	...	...	...	...	...	...
Belo Horizonte	2 452 617	...	...	335	...	...	...	...
Bento Gonçalves	106 999	...	...	...	...	...	...	...
Betim	441 748	...	...	376	...	...	...	...
Birigui	110 911	...	...	...	...	...	...	...
Blumenou	299 416	...	...	509	...	...	...	...
Boa Vista	266 901	...	...	...	...	...	...	...
Botucatu	130 348	...	...	...	...	...	...	...
Bragança	107 060	...	...	...	...	...	...	...
Bragança Paulista	145 894	...	...	770	...	...	...	...
BRASILIA	2 606 885	...	...	5 794	...	...	...	...
Breves	101 094	...	...	...	...	...	...	...
Brusque	102 280	...	...	...	...	...	...	...
Cabo de Santo Agostinho	171 583	...	...	...	...	...	...	...
Cabo Frio	186 004	...	...	...	...	...	...	...
Cachoeirinha	118 089	...	...	...	...	...	...	...
Cachoeiro de Itapemirim	201 259	...	...	892	...	...	...	...
Camacari	234 558	...	...	718	...	...	...	...
Camaragibe	143 210	...	...	...	...	...	...	...
Cametá	117 099	...	...	...	...	...	...	...
Campina Grande	383 764	...	...	970	...	...	...	...
Campinas	1 064 669	...	...	781	...	...	...	...
Campo Grande	755 107	...	...	8 091	...	...	...	...
Campo Largo	112 548	...	...	...	...	...	...	...
Campos dos Goytacazes	434 008	...	...	4 536	...	...	...	...
Canoas	332 056	...	...	...	...	...	...	...
Carapicuíba	392 701	...	...	...	...	...	...	...
Cariacica	365 859	...	...	279	...	...	...	...
Caruaru	298 501	...	...	936	...	...	...	...
Cascavel	296 254	...	...	2 074	...	...	...	...
Castanhal	161 497	...	...	1 003	...	...	...	...
Catanduva	114 812	...	...	...	...	...	...	...
Caucaia	334 364	...	...	1 293	...	...	...	...
Caxias	148 072	...	...	6 724	...	...	...	...
Caxias do Sul	410 166	...	...	1 601	...	...	...	...
Chapecó	174 187	...	...	...	...	...	...	...
Codo	113 937	...	...	4 923	...	...	...	...
Colatina	111 365	...	...	2 094	...	...	...	...
Colombo	247 268	...	...	...	...	...	...	...
Conselheiro Lafaiete	114 579	...	...	...	...	...	...	...
Contagem	625 393	...	...	167	...	...	...	...
Coronel Fabriciano	105 037	...	...	...	...	...	...	...
Cotia	182 045	...	...	...	...	...	...	...
Crato	116 759	...	...	...	...	...	...	...
Criciúma	188 557	...	...	...	...	...	...	...
Cubatao	129 582	...	...	...	...	...	...	...
Cuiabá	550 562	...	...	3 922	...	...	...	...
Curitiba	1 851 215	...	...	427	...	...	...	...
Diadema	397 738	...	...	...	...	...	...	...
Divinópolis	216 099	...	...	716	...	...	...	...

8. Population of capital cities and cities of 100 000 or more inhabitants: latest available year, 1990 - 2009
Population des capitales et des villes de 100 000 habitants ou plus : dernière année disponible, 1990 - 2009 (continued - suite)

Continent, country or area, date, code and city / Continent, pays ou zone, date, code et ville	City proper - Ville proprement dite				Urban agglomeration - Agglomération urbaine			
	Population			Surface area - Superficie (km²)	Population			Surface area - Superficie (km²)
	Both sexes - Les deux sexes	Male - Masculin	Female - Féminin		Both sexes - Les deux sexes	Male - Masculin	Female - Féminin	

AMERICA, SOUTH - AMÉRIQUE DU SUD

Brazil - Brésil[17]
1 VII 2009 (ESDF)

Dourados	189 762	...	...	4 082	...	...	...	...
Duque de Caxias	872 762	...	...	463	...	...	...	...
Embu	248 722	...	...	...	...	...	...	...
Feira de Santana	591 707	...	...	1 344	...	...	...	...
Ferraz de Vasconcelos	179 231	...	...	...	...	...	...	...
Florianópolis	408 161	...	...	440	...	...	...	...
Fortaleza	2 505 552	...	...	336	...	...	...	...
Foz do Iguaçu	325 137	...	...	596	...	...	...	...
Franca	330 938	...	...	...	...	...	...	...
Francisco Morato	157 294	...	...	...	...	...	...	...
Franco da Rocha	131 366	...	...	...	...	...	...	...
Garanhuns	131 313	...	...	456	...	...	...	...
Goiânia	1 281 975	...	...	788	...	...	...	...
Governador Valadares	263 274	...	...	2 447	...	...	...	...
Gravatai	269 446	...	...	...	...	...	...	...
Guarapari	104 534	...	...	...	...	...	...	...
Guarapuava	172 728	...	...	5 365	...	...	...	...
Guaratinguetá	113 357	...	...	...	...	...	...	...
Guarujá	308 058	...	...	...	...	...	...	...
Guarulhos	1 299 283	...	...	...	...	...	...	...
Hortolandia	205 856	...	...	...	...	...	...	...
Ibirité	157 438	...	...	...	...	...	...	...
Igarassu	100 191	...	...	...	...	...	...	...
Ilhéus	219 266	...	...	1 712	...	...	...	...
Imperatriz	236 691	...	...	6 014	...	...	...	...
Indaiatuba	183 803	...	...	...	...	...	...	...
Ipatinga	244 508	...	...	231	...	...	...	...
Itabiraí	110 419	...	...	...	...	...	...	...
Itaboraí	228 996	...	...	569	...	...	...	...
Itabuna	213 656	...	...	...	...	...	...	...
Itaguaí	105 633	...	...	...	...	...	...	...
Itaituba	127 848	...	...	...	...	...	...	...
Itajaí	172 081	...	...	...	...	...	...	...
Itapecerica da Serra	161 983	...	...	...	...	...	...	...
Itapetininga	148 808	...	...	2 035	...	...	...	...
Itapevi	205 881	...	...	...	...	...	...	...
Itapipoca	114 441	...	...	...	...	...	...	...
Itaquaquecetuba	359 253	...	...	...	...	...	...	...
Itu	157 384	...	...	640	...	...	...	...
Jaboatao dos Guarapes	687 688	...	...	...	...	...	...	...
Jacareí	212 824	...	...	...	...	...	...	...
Jandira	112 130	...	...	...	...	...	...	...
Japeri	101 690	...	...	...	...	...	...	...
Jaraguá do Sul	139 017	...	...	...	...	...	...	...
Jaú	135 546	...	...	...	...	...	...	...
Jequié	150 541	...	...	3 113	...	...	...	...
Ji-Paraná	111 010	...	...	...	...	...	...	...
Joao Pessoa	702 235	...	...	...	...	...	...	...
Joinville	497 331	...	...	1 080	...	...	...	...
Juazeiro	243 896	...	...	5 615	...	...	...	...
Juàzeiro do Norte	249 829	...	...	...	...	...	...	...
Juiz de Fora	526 706	...	...	1 424	...	...	...	...
Jundiaí	349 929	...	...	432	...	...	...	...
Lages	167 805	...	...	5 287	...	...	...	...
Lauro de Freitas	156 936	...	...	...	...	...	...	...
Limeira	281 583	...	...	...	...	...	...	...
Linhares	132 664	...	...	4 388	...	...	...	...
Londrina	510 707	...	...	2 129	...	...	...	...
Luziânia	210 064	...	...	4 653	...	...	...	...
Macae	194 413	...	...	...	...	...	...	...
Macapá	366 484	...	...	...	...	...	...	...
Maceió	936 314	...	...	517	...	...	...	...
Magé	244 334	...	...	744	...	...	...	...

8. Population of capital cities and cities of 100 000 or more inhabitants: latest available year, 1990 - 2009
Population des capitales et des villes de 100 000 habitants ou plus : dernière année disponible, 1990 - 2009 (continued - suite)

Continent, country or area, date, code and city / Continent, pays ou zone, date, code et ville	City proper - Ville proprement dite				Urban agglomeration - Agglomération urbaine			
	Population			Surface area - Superficie (km²)	Population			Surface area - Superficie (km²)
	Both sexes - Les deux sexes	Male - Masculin	Female - Féminin		Both sexes - Les deux sexes	Male - Masculin	Female - Féminin	
AMERICA, SOUTH - AMÉRIQUE DU SUD								
Brazil - Brésil[17]								
1 VII 2009 (ESDF)								
Manaus	1 738 641	...	...	11 349	...	...	...	...
Maraba	203 049	...	...	14 320	...	...	...	...
Maracanau	201 693	...	...	...	...	...	...	...
Maranguape	110 523	...	...	...	...	...	...	...
Maricá	123 492	...	...	...	...	...	...	...
Marília	225 938	...	...	1 194	...	...	...	...
Maringá	335 511	...	...	490	...	...	...	...
Marituba	101 158	...	...	...	...	...	...	...
Mauá	417 458	...	...	...	...	...	...	...
Mesquita	190 056	...	...	...	...	...	...	...
Moji das Cruzes	375 268	...	...	749	...	...	...	...
Moji-Guaçu	139 836	...	...	960	...	...	...	...
Montes Claros	363 227	...	...	4 135	...	...	...	...
Mossoró	244 287	...	...	2 108	...	...	...	...
Natal	806 203	...	...	...	...	...	...	...
Nilópolis	159 408	...	...	...	...	...	...	...
Niterói	479 384	...	...	131	...	...	...	...
Nossa Senhora do Socorro	155 334	...	...	...	...	...	...	...
Nova Friburgo	178 653	...	...	930	...	...	...	...
Nova Iguaçu	865 089	...	...	795	...	...	...	...
Nôvo Hamburgo	257 746	...	...	...	...	...	...	...
Olinda	397 268	...	...	...	...	...	...	...
Osasco	718 646	...	...	...	...	...	...	...
Ourinhos	104 542	...	...	...	...	...	...	...
Paço do Lumiar	103 958	...	...	...	...	...	...	...
Palhoça	130 878	...	...	...	...	...	...	...
Palmas	188 645	...	...	...	...	...	...	...
Paranaguá	139 796	...	...	1 015	...	...	...	...
Parauapebas	152 777	...	...	...	...	...	...	...
Parintins	107 250	...	...	...	...	...	...	...
Parnaíba	146 059	...	...	1 053	...	...	...	...
Parnamirim	184 222	...	...	...	...	...	...	...
Passo Fundo	187 507	...	...	1 596	...	...	...	...
Passos	107 619	...	...	...	...	...	...	...
Patos	100 732	...	...	...	...	...	...	...
Patos de Minas	139 841	...	...	3 336	...	...	...	...
Paulista	319 373	...	...	...	...	...	...	...
Paulo Afonso	106 703	...	...	...	...	...	...	...
Pelotas	345 181	...	...	1 924	...	...	...	...
Petrolina	281 851	...	...	6 116	...	...	...	...
Petrópolis	315 119	...	...	771	...	...	...	...
Pindamonhangaba	144 613	...	...	719	...	...	...	...
Pinhais	118 319	...	...	...	...	...	...	...
Piracicaba	368 843	...	...	1 426	...	...	...	...
Poà	112 481	...	...	...	...	...	...	...
Poços de Caldas	151 449	...	...	533	...	...	...	...
Ponta Grossa	314 681	...	...	2 212	...	...	...	...
Porto Alegre	1 436 123	...	...	...	...	...	...	...
Porto Seguro	122 896	...	...	...	...	...	...	...
Porto Velho	382 829	...	...	...	...	...	...	...
Pouso Alegre	127 974	...	...	...	...	...	...	...
Praia Grande	249 551	...	...	...	...	...	...	...
Presidente Prudente	207 725	...	...	554	...	...	...	...
Queimados	139 378	...	...	...	...	...	...	...
Recife	1 561 659	...	...	...	...	...	...	...
Resende	130 035	...	...	...	...	...	...	...
Ribeirao das Neves	349 307	...	...	...	...	...	...	...
Ribeirao Pires	112 011	...	...	...	...	...	...	...
Ribeirao Prêto	563 107	...	...	...	...	...	...	...
Rio Branco	305 954	...	...	...	...	...	...	...
Rio Claro	191 886	...	...	503	...	...	...	...
Rio de Janeiro	6 186 710	...	...	1 256	...	...	...	...
Rio Grande	196 337	...	...	2 825	...	...	...	...

8. Population of capital cities and cities of 100 000 or more inhabitants: latest available year, 1990 - 2009
Population des capitales et des villes de 100 000 habitants ou plus : dernière année disponible, 1990 - 2009 (continued - suite)

Continent, country or area, date, code and city / Continent, pays ou zone, date, code et ville	City proper - Ville proprement dite				Urban agglomeration - Agglomération urbaine			
	Population			Surface area - Superficie (km²)	Population			Surface area - Superficie (km²)
	Both sexes - Les deux sexes	Male - Masculin	Female - Féminin		Both sexes - Les deux sexes	Male - Masculin	Female - Féminin	

AMERICA, SOUTH - AMÉRIQUE DU SUD

Brazil - Brésil[17]

1 VII 2009 (ESDF)

Rio Verde	163 021	...	...	9 136	...	...	...	...
Rondonópolis	181 902	...	...	4 594	...	...	...	...
Sabára	126 195	...	...	...	...	...	...	...
Salto	109 948	...	...	...	...	...	...	...
Salvador	2 998 056	...	...	313	...	...	...	...
Santa Bárbara D'Oeste	189 573	...	...	...	...	...	...	...
Santa Cruz do Sul	122 451	...	...	...	...	...	...	...
Santa Luzia (Minas Gerais)	231 607	...	...	...	...	...	...	...
Santa Maria	268 969	...	...	3 279	...	...	...	...
Santa Rita	126 775	...	...	...	...	...	...	...
Santana de Parnaíba	114 321	...	...	...	...	...	...	...
Santarém	276 665	...	...	...	...	...	...	...
Santo André	673 396	...	...	...	...	...	...	...
Santos	417 098	...	...	725	...	...	...	...
Sao Bernardo do Campo	810 979	...	...	319	...	...	...	...
Sao Caetano do Sul	152 093	...	...	...	...	...	...	...
Sao Carlo	220 463	...	...	1 120	...	...	...	...
Sao Gonçalo	991 382	...	...	...	...	...	...	...
Sao Joao de Meriti	469 827	...	...	...	...	...	...	...
Sao José	201 746	...	...	...	...	...	...	...
Sao José de Ribamar	139 473	...	...	...	...	...	...	...
Sao José do Rio Prêto	419 632	...	...	586	...	...	...	...
Sao José dos Campos	615 871	...	...	1 186	...	...	...	...
Sao José dos Pinhais	279 297	...	...	923	...	...	...	...
Sao Leopoldo	211 663	...	...	...	...	...	...	...
Sao Luís	997 098	...	...	822	...	...	...	...
São Mateus	101 613	...	...	...	...	...	...	...
Sao Paulo	11 037 593	...	...	1 493	...	...	...	...
Sao Vicente	330 795	...	...	...	...	...	...	...
Sapucaia do Sul	126 316	...	...	...	...	...	...	...
Serra	404 688	...	...	549	...	...	...	...
Sertaozinho	110 999	...	...	...	...	...	...	...
Sete Lagoas	225 358	...	...	...	...	...	...	...
Simoes Filho	116 662	...	...	...	...	...	...	...
Sinop	114 051	...	...	...	...	...	...	...
Sobral	182 431	...	...	1 646	...	...	...	...
Sorocaba	584 313	...	...	...	...	...	...	...
Sumaré	241 077	...	...	208	...	...	...	...
Susano	284 356	...	...	...	...	...	...	...
Taboao da Serra	227 343	...	...	...	...	...	...	...
Tatuí	109 017	...	...	...	...	...	...	...
Taubaté	273 426	...	...	...	...	...	...	...
Teixeira de Freitas	125 430	...	...	...	...	...	...	...
Teófilo Otoni	130 517	...	...	...	...	...	...	...
Teresina	802 537	...	...	1 356	...	...	...	...
Teresópolis	162 075	...	...	768	...	...	...	...
Timon	150 635	...	...	1 702	...	...	...	...
Toledo	116 774	...	...	...	...	...	...	...
Trindade	104 979	...	...	...	...	...	...	...
Uberaba	296 261	...	...	4 524	...	...	...	...
Uberlândia	634 345	...	...	4 040	...	...	...	...
Uruguaiana	127 045	...	...	6 763	...	...	...	...
Valinhos	107 481	...	...	...	...	...	...	...
Valparaíso de Goiás	123 444	...	...	...	...	...	...	...
Varginha	121 785	...	...	...	...	...	...	...
Varzea Grande	240 038	...	...	900	...	...	...	...
Varzea Paulista	107 211	...	...	...	...	...	...	...
Vespasiano	101 846	...	...	...	...	...	...	...
Viamao	260 740	...	...	...	...	...	...	...
Vila Velha	413 548	...	...	...	...	...	...	...
Vitória	320 156	...	...	...	...	...	...	...
Vitória da Conquista	318 901	...	...	3 743	...	...	...	...
Vitória de Santo Antao	126 399	...	...	344	...	...	...	...

8. Population of capital cities and cities of 100 000 or more inhabitants: latest available year, 1990 - 2009
Population des capitales et des villes de 100 000 habitants ou plus : dernière année disponible, 1990 - 2009 (continued - suite)

Continent, country or area, date, code and city / Continent, pays ou zone, date, code et ville	City proper - Ville proprement dite				Urban agglomeration - Agglomération urbaine			
	Population			Surface area - Superficie (km²)	Population			Surface area - Superficie (km²)
	Both sexes - Les deux sexes	Male - Masculin	Female - Féminin		Both sexes - Les deux sexes	Male - Masculin	Female - Féminin	

AMERICA, SOUTH - AMÉRIQUE DU SUD								
Brazil - Brésil[17]								
1 VII 2009 (ESDF)								
Volta Redonda	261 403	...	...	...	...	...	...	...
Votorantim	105 193	...	...	...	...	...	...	...
Chile - Chili								
1 VII 2009 (ESDF)								
Antofagasta	360 481	187 369	173 112	44	...	...	...	...
Arica	168 325	80 264	88 061	42	...	...	...	...
Calama	146 305	74 558	71 747	18	...	...	...	...
Chiguallante	115 193	54 063	61 130	34	...	...	...	...
Chillán	159 527	75 793	83 734	33	...	...	...	...
Concepción	221 972	107 346	114 626	56	...	...	...	...
Copiapó	153 348	76 922	76 426	48	...	...	...	...
Coquimbo	185 103	90 949	94 154	42	...	...	...	...
Coronel	101 902	49 622	52 280	25	...	...	...	...
Iquique	181 282	87 595	93 687	22	...	...	...	...
La Serena	187 726	90 963	96 763	66	...	...	...	...
Los Angeles	137 753	66 888	70 865	27	...	...	...	...
Osorno	144 832	70 884	73 948	32	...	...	...	...
Puente Alto	689 499	337 974	351 525	64	...	...	...	...
Puerto Montt	197 113	98 632	98 481	40	...	...	...	...
Punta Arenas	121 338	60 834	60 504	39	...	...	...	...
Quilpué	153 497	74 618	78 879	38	...	...	...	...
Rancagua	233 780	116 047	117 733	50	...	...	...	...
San Bernardo	292 142	143 633	148 509	52	...	...	...	...
SANTIAGO	5 015 680	2 431 015	2 584 665	727	...	...	...	...
Talca	213 619	103 324	110 295	46	...	...	...	...
Talcahuano	143 347	67 652	75 695	51	...	...	...	...
Temuco	260 969	125 559	135 410	46	...	...	...	...
Valdivia	138 827	67 900	70 927	42	...	...	...	...
Valparaíso	257 475	127 899	129 576	47	...	...	...	...
Villa Alemana	123 528	60 246	63 282	31	...	...	...	...
Viña del Mar	291 442	139 762	151 680	87	...	...	...	...
Colombia - Colombie[18]								
1 VII 2009 (ESDF)								
Apartadó	...	...	...	...	148 745	...	...	607
Armenia	...	...	...	...	287 330	...	...	115
Barrancabermeja	...	...	...	...	191 334	...	...	1 274
Barranquilla	...	...	...	...	1 179 027	...	...	166
Bello	...	...	...	...	404 844	...	...	151
BOGOTA, D.C.	...	...	...	...	7 259 597	...	...	1 605
Bucaramanga	...	...	...	...	522 905	...	...	154
Buenaventura	...	...	...	...	355 736	...	...	6 785
Cali	...	...	...	...	2 219 714	...	...	552
Cartagena	...	...	...	...	933 334	...	...	559
Cartago	...	...	...	...	127 756	...	...	260
Chía	...	...	...	...	109 160	...	...	76
Ciénaga	...	...	...	...	102 835	...	...	1 366
Colombia: Jamundí	...	...	...	...	105 510	...	...	603
Colombia: Yumbo	...	...	...	...	101 551	...	...	243
Cúcuta	...	...	...	...	612 116	...	...	1 098
Dosquebradas	...	...	...	...	187 153	...	...	80
Duitama	...	...	...	...	109 914	...	...	229
Envigado	...	...	...	...	192 646	...	...	51
Facatativá	...	...	...	...	117 396	...	...	160
Florencia	...	...	...	...	154 595	...	...	2 292
Floridablanca	...	...	...	...	260 042	...	...	101
Fusagasugá	...	...	...	...	118 955	...	...	206
Girardot	...	...	...	...	101 043	...	...	130
Girón	...	...	...	...	152 608	...	...	681
Gudalajara de Buga	...	...	...	...	116 241	...	...	873
Ibagué	...	...	...	...	521 008	...	...	1 439
Ipiales	...	...	...	...	120 392	...	...	1 707
Itagüi	...	...	...	...	248 950	...	...	17
Lorica	...	...	...	...	113 341	...	...	890

8. Population of capital cities and cities of 100 000 or more inhabitants: latest available year, 1990 - 2009
Population des capitales et des villes de 100 000 habitants ou plus : dernière année disponible, 1990 - 2009 (continued - suite)

Continent, country or area, date, code and city / Continent, pays ou zone, date, code et ville	City proper - Ville proprement dite				Urban agglomeration - Agglomération urbaine			
	Population			Surface area - Superficie (km²)	Population			Surface area - Superficie (km²)
	Both sexes - Les deux sexes	Male - Masculin	Female - Féminin		Both sexes - Les deux sexes	Male - Masculin	Female - Féminin	

AMERICA, SOUTH - AMÉRIQUE DU SUD

Colombia - Colombie[18]
1 VII 2009 (ESDF)

Magangué	...	...	...	...	122 680	...	...	1 102
Maicao	...	...	...	...	138 497	...	...	1 789
Malambo	...	...	...	...	109 279	...	...	108
Manizales	...	...	...	...	386 872	...	...	477
Medellín	...	...	...	...	2 317 336	...	...	387
Montería	...	...	...	...	403 280	...	...	3 043
Neiva	...	...	...	...	327 840	...	...	1 468
Palmira	...	...	...	...	292 510	...	...	1 044
Pasto	...	...	...	...	405 885	...	...	1 131
Pereira	...	...	...	...	454 495	...	...	702
Piedecuesta	...	...	...	...	129 532	...	...	481
Pitalito	...	...	...	...	111 669	...	...	653
Popayán	...	...	...	...	263 707	...	...	464
Quibdo	...	...	...	...	114 220	...	...	3 075
Riohacha	...	...	...	...	203 819	...	...	3 171
Rionegro	...	...	...	...	108 356	...	...	198
San Andres de Tumaco	...	...	...	...	175 093	...	...	3 778
Santa Marta	...	...	...	...	441 123	...	...	2 369
Sincelejo	...	...	...	...	252 522	...	...	292
Soacha	...	...	...	...	445 148	...	...	187
Sogamoso	...	...	...	...	115 933	...	...	214
Soledad	...	...	...	...	520 323	...	...	67
Tuluá	...	...	...	...	196 834	...	...	818
Tunja	...	...	...	...	167 780	...	...	118
Turbo	...	...	...	...	135 967	...	...	3 090
Uribia	...	...	...	...	139 397	...	...	7 904
Valledupar	...	...	...	...	393 553	...	...	4 225
Villavicencio	...	...	...	...	421 074	...	...	1 328
Yopal	...	...	...	...	120 082	...	...	2 532
Zipaquirá	...	...	...	...	110 003	...	...	194

Ecuador - Équateur
1 VII 2009 (ESDF)

Ambato	217 076[1]	...	...	31	...	...	...	...
Babahoyo	115 972[1]	...	...	10	...	...	...	...
Cuenca	388 420[1]	...	...	56	...	...	...	...
Durán	198 144[1]	...	...	40	...	...	...	...
Esmeraldas	122 003[1]	...	...	8	...	...	...	...
Guayaquil	2 253 987[1]	...	...	369	...	...	...	...
Ibarra	151 146[1]	...	...	36	...	...	...	...
Loja	152 018[1]	...	...	25	...	...	...	...
Machala	245 791[1]	...	...	34	...	...	...	...
Manta	207 939[1]	...	...	45	...	...	...	...
Milagro	128 788[1]	...	...	19	...	...	...	...
Portoviejo	247 528[1]	...	...	50	...	...	...	...
Quevedo	142 481[1]	...	...	20	...	...	...	...
QUITO	1 599 361[1]	...	...	181	...	...	...	...
Riobamba	181 962[1]	...	...	29	...	...	...	...
Santo Domingo de los Colorados	228 384[1]	...	...	43	...	...	...	...

Falkland Islands (Malvinas) - Îles Falkland (Malvinas)
8 X 2006 (CDFC)

STANLEY	2 115	...	...		...			

French Guiana - Guyane française
1 I 2006 (CDJC)

CAYENNE	58 004	27 412	30 591	24[19]	75 740	36 484	39 256	70[19]

Guyana
15 IX 2002 (CDFC)

GEORGETOWN	134 497	63 973	70 524	...	...	...	...	...

Paraguay
1 VII 2008 (ESDF)

ASUNCION[20]	518 792	240 940	277 852	117	2 448 710	1 191 827	1 256 883	2 582
Capiatá	209 012	104 112	104 900	82	...	...	...	...

8. Population of capital cities and cities of 100 000 or more inhabitants: latest available year, 1990 - 2009
Population des capitales et des villes de 100 000 habitants ou plus : dernière année disponible, 1990 - 2009 (continued - suite)

Continent, country or area, date, code and city / Continent, pays ou zone, date, code et ville	City proper - Ville proprement dite				Urban agglomeration - Agglomération urbaine			
	Population			Surface area - Superficie (km²)	Population			Surface area - Superficie (km²)
	Both sexes - Les deux sexes	Male - Masculin	Female - Féminin		Both sexes - Les deux sexes	Male - Masculin	Female - Féminin	
AMERICA, SOUTH - AMÉRIQUE DU SUD								
Paraguay								
1 VII 2008 (ESDF)								
Ciudad del Este	279 655	140 381	139 274	149	...	...	...	...
Fernando de la Mora	162 652	77 609	85 042	21	...	...	...	...
Lambaré	171 282	82 375	88 907	27	...	...	...	...
Luque	291 225	143 243	147 982	152	...	...	...	...
San Lorenzo	287 977	139 637	148 339	57	...	...	...	...
Peru - Pérou								
21 X 2007 (CDFC)								
Arequipa	784 651	375 634	409 017	...	...	...	...	...
Ayacucho	151 019	73 526	77 493	...	...	...	...	...
Cajamarca	162 326	78 926	83 400	...	...	...	...	...
Callao	876 877	430 582	446 295	...	...	...	...	...
Chiclayo	524 442	250 081	274 361	...	...	...	...	...
Chimbote	334 568	165 621	168 947	...	...	...	...	...
Chincha Alta	153 598	75 379	78 219	...	...	...	...	...
Cuzco	348 935	168 077	180 858	...	...	...	...	...
Huancayo	323 054	153 868	169 186	...	...	...	...	...
Huánuco	149 210	71 664	77 546	...	...	...	...	...
Huaraz	100 931	49 152	51 779	...	...	...	...	...
Ica	219 856	106 578	113 278	...	...	...	...	...
Iquitos	370 962	182 712	188 250	...	...	...	...	...
Juliaca	216 716	106 685	110 031	...	...	...	...	...
LIMA[21]	8 472 935	4 138 941	4 333 994	...	...	...	...	...
Piura	377 496	181 453	196 043	...	...	...	...	...
Pucallpa	204 772	101 800	102 972	...	...	...	...	...
Puno	120 229	58 965	61 264	...	...	...	...	...
Sullana	181 954	88 223	93 731	...	...	...	...	...
Tacna	242 451	119 055	123 396	...	...	...	...	...
Tarapoto	117 184	58 215	58 969	...	...	...	...	...
Trujillo	682 834	327 729	355 105	...	...	...	...	...
Suriname								
2 VIII 2004 (CDJC)								
PARAMARIBO	...	...	...	...	242 946	120 292	122 405	182
Uruguay								
1 VII 2009 (ESDF)								
MONTEVIDEO	1 338 408[1]	624 746[1]	713 662[1]	530	...	...	...	...
Venezuela (Bolivarian Republic of) - Venezuela (République bolivarienne du)								
1 VII 1998 (ESDF)								
Acarigua-Araure	227 684	...	...	1 065	...	...	...	...
Barcelona	301 595	...	...	463	...	...	...	...
Barcelona-Puerto La Cruz	484 149	...	...	707	...	...	...	...
Barinas	221 558	...	...	848	...	...	...	...
Barquisimeto	810 809	...	...	2 645	...	...	...	...
Cabimas	213 290	...	...	175	...	...	...	...
CARACAS	1 975 294	...	...	433	...	...	...	...
Carúpano	116 107	...	...	203	...	...	...	...
Catia la Mar	117 013	...	...	76	...	...	...	...
Ciudad Bolívar	278 525	...	...	5 851	...	...	...	...
Ciudad Guayana	641 998	...	...	1 612	...	...	...	...
Coro	167 048	...	...	438	...	...	...	...
Cumaná	265 621	...	...	405	...	...	...	...
Guarenas	169 202	...	...	180	...	...	...	...
Los Teques	176 292	...	...	98	...	...	...	...
Maracaibo	1 706 547	...	...	604	...	...	...	...
Maracay	458 761	...	...	169	...	...	...	...
Maturín	262 167	...	...	...	...	...	...	...
Mérida	272 437	...	...	482	...	...	...	...
Puerto Cabello	176 347	...	...	309	...	...	...	...
Punto Fijo	118 126	...	...	31	...	...	...	...
San Cristóbal	272 374	...	...	248	...	...	...	...
San Fernando de Apure	121 949	...	...	...	...	...	...	...
Turmero	203 434	...	...	208	...	...	...	...

Continent, country or area, date, code and city / Continent, pays ou zone, date, code et ville	City proper - Ville proprement dite				Urban agglomeration - Agglomération urbaine			
	Population			Surface area - Superficie (km²)	Population			Surface area - Superficie (km²)
	Both sexes - Les deux sexes	Male - Masculin	Female - Féminin		Both sexes - Les deux sexes	Male - Masculin	Female - Féminin	
AMERICA, SOUTH - AMÉRIQUE DU SUD								
Venezuela (Bolivarian Republic of) - Venezuela (République bolivarienne du)								
1 VII 1998 (ESDF)								
Valencia	1 263 888	...	...	1 212	...	...	...	...
Valera	121 090	...	...	55	...	...	...	...
ASIA - ASIE								
Armenia - Arménie								
1 VII 2009 (ESDJ)								
Gyumri (Leninakan)	146 355	70 468	75 887	50	...	...	...	...
Vanadzoz (Kirovakan)	104 825	50 143	54 682	25	...	...	...	...
YEREVAN	1 116 648	522 409	594 239	227	...	...	...	...
Azerbaijan - Azerbaïdjan								
1 VII 2009 (ESDF)								
BAKU	2 052 322	1 004 789	1 047 533	2 130	...	...	...	...
Ganja	313 791	152 113	161 678	110	...	...	...	...
Sumgayit	310 346	152 640	157 706	80	...	...	...	...
Bahrain - Bahreïn								
1 VII 2006 (ESDF)								
MANAMA	176 909	113 503	63 406	30	...	...	...	...
Bangladesh								
22 I 2001 (CDFC)								
Barisal	...	...	...	...	192 810	103 785	89 025	20
Bogra	...	...	...	...	154 807	82 368	72 439	11
Brahmanbaria	...	...	...	...	129 278	66 890	62 388	18
Chittagong	...	...	...	...	2 023 489	1 127 516	895 973	168
Comilla	...	...	...	...	166 519	88 927	77 592	11
DHAKA	...	...	...	...	5 333 571	3 025 395	2 308 176	154
Dinajpur	...	...	...	...	157 914	82 068	75 846	19
Gazipur	...	...	...	...	122 801	65 522	57 279	49
Jamalpur	...	...	...	...	120 955	62 059	58 896	53
Jessore	...	...	...	...	176 655	94 203	82 452	15
Kadamrasul	...	...	...	...	128 561	66 799	61 762	6
Khulna	...	...	...	...	770 498	412 661	357 837	60
Mymensingh	...	...	...	...	227 204	119 172	108 032	22
Naogaon	...	...	...	...	124 046	65 406	58 640	37
Narayanganj	...	...	...	...	241 393	131 168	110 225	13
Narsingdi	...	...	...	...	124 204	67 575	56 629	9
Nawabganj	...	...	...	...	152 223	75 375	76 848	34
Pabna	...	...	...	...	116 305	60 666	55 639	27
Rajshahi	...	...	...	...	388 811	208 525	180 286	97
Rangpur	...	...	...	...	241 310	124 296	117 014	51
Saidpur	...	...	...	...	112 609	58 289	54 320	34
Sirajganj	...	...	...	...	128 144	66 673	61 471	28
Tangail	...	...	...	...	128 785	66 856	61 929	29
Tongi	...	...	...	...	283 099	156 335	126 764	30
Bhutan - Bhoutan								
30 V 2005 (CDFC)								
THIMPHU	...	...	...	...	79 185	42 465	36 720	...
Brunei Darussalam - Brunéi Darussalam								
21 VIII 2001 (CDFC)								
BANDAR SERI BEGAWAN	27 285	13 639	13 646	100	...	...	...	...
Cambodia - Cambodge								
1 VII 2002 (ESDF)								
Bat Dambang	171 382	82 785	88 597	114	...	...	...	...
PHNOM PENH	703 963	339 763	364 200	21	1 234 444	...	...	...
Seam Reab	140 966	69 052	71 914	292	...	...	...	...
China - Chine								
1 XI 2000 (CDJC)								
Acheng	638 894	327 774	311 120	...	...	...	...	...
Akeshu	561 822	295 811	266 011	...	...	...	...	...
Aletai	178 510	91 207	87 303	...	...	...	...	...
Anda	473 091	243 349	229 742	...	...	...	...	...

8. Population of capital cities and cities of 100 000 or more inhabitants: latest available year, 1990 - 2009
Population des capitales et des villes de 100 000 habitants ou plus : dernière année disponible, 1990 - 2009 (continued - suite)

Continent, country or area, date, code and city / Continent, pays ou zone, date, code et ville	City proper - Ville proprement dite				Urban agglomeration - Agglomération urbaine			
	Population			Surface area - Superficie (km²)	Population			Surface area - Superficie (km²)
	Both sexes - Les deux sexes	Male - Masculin	Female - Féminin		Both sexes - Les deux sexes	Male - Masculin	Female - Féminin	
ASIA - ASIE								
China - Chine								
1 XI 2000 (CDJC)								
Anguo	378 830	189 944	188 886	...	...	...	...	...
Ankang	843 426	443 270	400 156	...	...	...	...	...
Anlu	611 990	314 089	297 901	...	...	...	...	...
Anning	295 173	161 481	133 692	...	...	...	...	...
Anqing	582 751	293 884	288 867	...	...	...	...	...
Anqiu	1 096 782	554 403	542 379	...	...	...	...	...
Anshan	1 556 285	787 838	768 447	...	...	...	...	...
Anshun	767 307	395 894	371 413	...	...	...	...	...
Anyang	768 992	390 120	378 872	...	...	...	...	...
Atushi	200 345	101 867	98 478	...	...	...	...	...
Baicheng	484 979	244 453	240 526	...	...	...	...	...
Baise	340 483	177 310	163 173	...	...	...	...	...
Baishan	335 400	172 109	163 291	...	...	...	...	...
Baiyin	460 982	243 672	217 310	...	...	...	...	...
Baoding	902 496	455 625	446 871	...	...	...	...	...
Baoji	600 377	308 493	291 884	...	...	...	...	...
Baoshan	846 865	430 076	416 789	...	...	...	...	...
Baotou	1 671 181	862 495	808 686	...	...	...	...	...
Bazhong	1 185 862	616 323	569 539	...	...	...	...	...
Bazhou	557 901	285 321	272 580	...	...	...	...	...
Bei'an	442 474	226 743	215 731	...	...	...	...	...
Beihai	558 635	290 544	268 091	...	...	...	...	...
BEIJING (PEKING)	11 509 595	6 020 903	5 488 692	...	...	...	...	...
Beiliu	1 049 035	557 967	491 068	...	...	...	...	...
Beining	527 217	270 153	257 064	...	...	...	...	...
Beipiao	573 836	291 584	282 252	...	...	...	...	...
Bengbu	809 399	413 444	395 955	...	...	...	...	...
Benxi	980 069	495 102	484 967	...	...	...	...	...
Bijie	1 128 230	589 537	538 693	...	...	...	...	...
Binzhou	600 883	299 952	300 931	...	...	...	...	...
Bole	224 869	116 506	108 363	...	...	...	...	...
Botou	550 888	280 209	270 679	...	...	...	...	...
Bozhou	1 351 939	697 126	654 813	...	...	...	...	...
Cangzhou	443 561	223 648	219 913	...	...	...	...	...
Cenxi	731 623	384 212	347 411	...	...	...	...	...
Changchun	3 225 557	1 647 216	1 578 341	...	...	...	...	...
Changde	1 346 739	686 467	660 272	...	...	...	...	...
Changge	646 306	332 022	314 284	...	...	...	...	...
Changji	387 169	202 275	184 894	...	...	...	...	...
Changle	689 815	358 963	330 852	...	...	...	...	...
Changning	795 223	428 332	366 891	...	...	...	...	...
Changsha	2 122 873	1 099 304	1 023 569	...	...	...	...	...
Changshu	1 239 637	598 034	641 603	...	...	...	...	...
Changyi	683 182	340 763	342 419	...	...	...	...	...
Changzhi	648 981	332 246	316 735	...	...	...	...	...
Changzhou	1 081 845	552 850	528 995	...	...	...	...	...
Chaohu	778 864	396 961	381 903	...	...	...	...	...
Chaoyang (Guangdong)	2 470 812	1 256 428	1 214 384	...	...	...	...	...
Chaoyang (Liaoning)	475 038	238 128	236 910	...	...	...	...	...
Chaozhou	363 582	181 260	182 322	...	...	...	...	...
Chengde	437 251	221 221	216 030	...	...	...	...	...
Chengdu	4 333 541	2 258 996	2 074 545	...	...	...	...	...
Chenghai	860 003	428 157	431 846	...	...	...	...	...
Chenzhou	655 014	340 799	314 215	...	...	...	...	...
Chibi	510 926	267 233	243 693	...	...	...	...	...
Chifeng	1 153 723	589 450	564 273	...	...	...	...	...
Chishui	251 780	130 227	121 553	...	...	...	...	...
Chizhou	555 489	280 395	275 094	...	...	...	...	...
Chongqing	9 691 901	5 013 398	4 678 503	...	...	...	...	...
Chongzhou	650 698	330 345	320 353	...	...	...	...	...
Chuxiong	503 682	261 315	242 367	...	...	...	...	...
Chuzhou	493 735	251 117	242 618	...	...	...	...	...
Cixi	1 214 537	615 279	599 258	...	...	...	...	...

Continent, country or area, date, code and city / Continent, pays ou zone, date, code et ville	City proper - Ville proprement dite				Urban agglomeration - Agglomération urbaine			
	Population			Surface area - Superficie (km²)	Population			Surface area - Superficie (km²)
	Both sexes - Les deux sexes	Male - Masculin	Female - Féminin		Both sexes - Les deux sexes	Male - Masculin	Female - Féminin	
ASIA - ASIE								
China - Chine								
1 XI 2000 (CDJC)								
Conghua	517 552	264 150	253 402	...	...	...	...	...
Da'an	430 512	219 682	210 830	...	...	...	...	...
Dafeng	756 766	383 391	373 375	...	...	...	...	...
Dali	521 169	262 564	258 605	...	...	...	...	...
Dalian	3 245 191	1 641 485	1 603 706	...	...	...	...	...
Dandong	780 414	389 277	391 137	...	...	...	...	...
Dangyang	495 946	253 125	242 821	...	...	...	...	...
Danjiangkou	501 126	262 922	238 204	...	...	...	...	...
Danyang	877 232	442 296	434 936	...	...	...	...	...
Danzhou	835 465	442 636	392 829	...	...	...	...	...
Daqing	1 380 051	704 765	675 286	...	...	...	...	...
Dashiqiao	714 670	370 713	343 957	...	...	...	...	...
Datong	1 526 744	785 754	740 990	...	...	...	...	...
Daye	873 859	460 417	413 442	...	...	...	...	...
Dazhou	384 525	192 819	191 706	...	...	...	...	...
Dehui	878 349	448 146	430 203	...	...	...	...	...
Dengfeng	609 085	321 081	288 004	...	...	...	...	...
Dengta	502 149	259 895	242 254	...	...	...	...	...
Dengzhou	1 290 656	677 791	612 865	...	...	...	...	...
Dexing	297 784	155 178	142 606	...	...	...	...	...
Deyang	628 876	324 823	304 053	...	...	...	...	...
Dezhou	552 445	277 994	274 451	...	...	...	...	...
Dingzhou	1 107 903	559 214	548 689	...	...	...	...	...
Dongfang	358 318	188 840	169 478	...	...	...	...	...
Donggang	640 340	324 344	315 996	...	...	...	...	...
Dongguan	6 445 777	3 035 742	3 410 035	...	...	...	...	...
Dongsheng	252 566	129 512	123 054	...	...	...	...	...
Dongtai	1 164 653	583 122	581 531	...	...	...	...	...
Dongxing	108 131	58 939	49 192	...	...	...	...	...
Dongyang	753 094	375 565	377 529	...	...	...	...	...
Dongying	788 844	407 241	381 603	...	...	...	...	...
Dujiangyan	621 980	314 845	307 135	...	...	...	...	...
Dunhua	480 834	247 966	232 868	...	...	...	...	...
Dunhuang	187 578	96 679	90 899	...	...	...	...	...
Duyun	463 426	241 421	222 005	...	...	...	...	...
Emeishan	423 070	217 201	205 869	...	...	...	...	...
Enping	464 898	240 765	224 133	...	...	...	...	...
Enshi	755 725	397 284	358 441	...	...	...	...	...
Ezhou	1 023 285	533 940	489 345	...	...	...	...	...
Fangchenggang	422 514	233 979	188 535	...	...	...	...	...
Feicheng	948 602	476 032	472 570	...	...	...	...	...
Fengcheng (Jiangxi)	1 216 412	644 029	572 383	...	...	...	...	...
Fengcheng (Liaoning)	560 384	288 402	271 982	...	...	...	...	...
Fenghua	471 558	239 252	232 306	...	...	...	...	...
Fengnan	550 872	285 442	265 430	...	...	...	...	...
Fengzhen	264 204	137 562	126 642	...	...	...	...	...
Fenyang	387 046	199 129	187 917	...	...	...	...	...
Foshan	768 656	398 973	369 683	...	...	...	...	...
Fu'an	554 057	296 379	257 678	...	...	...	...	...
Fuding	521 070	276 419	244 651	...	...	...	...	...
Fujin	420 579	215 650	204 929	...	...	...	...	...
Fukang	152 965	80 372	72 593	...	...	...	...	...
Fuqing	1 174 540	597 890	576 650	...	...	...	...	...
Fuquan	292 720	155 972	136 748	...	...	...	...	...
Fushun	1 434 447	722 549	711 898	...	...	...	...	...
Fuxin	627 855	311 912	315 943	...	...	...	...	...
Fuyang (Anhui)	628 633	324 172	304 461	...	...	...	...	...
Fuyang (Zhejiang)	1 719 057	878 560	840 497	...	...	...	...	...
Fuzhou (Fujian)	2 124 435	1 086 638	1 037 797	...	...	...	...	...
Fuzhou (Jiangxi)	1 007 391	533 936	473 455	...	...	...	...	...
Gaizhou	883 811	455 641	428 170	...	...	...	...	...
Ganzhou	494 600	254 272	240 328	...	...	...	...	...
Gaoan	788 329	416 678	371 651	...	...	...	...	...

Continent, country or area, date, code and city / Continent, pays ou zone, date, code et ville	City proper - Ville proprement dite				Urban agglomeration - Agglomération urbaine			
	Population			Surface area - Superficie (km²)	Population			Surface area - Superficie (km²)
	Both sexes - Les deux sexes	Male - Masculin	Female - Féminin		Both sexes - Les deux sexes	Male - Masculin	Female - Féminin	
ASIA - ASIE								
China - Chine								
1 XI 2000 (CDJC)								
Gaobeidian	538 582	268 027	270 555	...	...	...	...	...
Gaocheng	758 269	380 317	377 952	...	...	...	...	...
Gaomi	842 403	420 956	421 447	...	...	...	...	...
Gaoming	301 041	159 746	141 295	...	...	...	...	...
Gaoping	471 671	236 439	235 232	...	...	...	...	...
Gaoyao	625 125	314 474	310 651	...	...	...	...	...
Gaoyou	797 752	392 863	404 889	...	...	...	...	...
Gaozhou	1 219 132	639 497	579 635	...	...	...	...	...
Geermu	135 897	73 572	62 325	...	...	...	...	...
Gejiu	453 311	243 377	209 934	...	...	...	...	...
Genhe	157 337	80 485	76 852	...	...	...	...	...
Gongyi	777 202	395 784	381 418	...	...	...	...	...
Gongzhuling	1 041 735	532 134	509 601	...	...	...	...	...
Guangan	1 093 103	561 454	531 649	...	...	...	...	...
Guanghan	577 298	289 596	287 702	...	...	...	...	...
Guangshui	885 936	458 607	427 329	...	...	...	...	...
Guangyuan	905 057	467 422	437 635	...	...	...	...	...
Guangzhou	8 524 826	4 445 052	4 079 774	...	...	...	...	...
Guigang	1 413 128	731 298	681 830	...	...	...	...	...
Guilin	804 571	414 004	390 567	...	...	...	...	...
Guiping	1 359 035	716 617	642 418	...	...	...	...	...
Guixi	535 517	282 662	252 855	...	...	...	...	...
Guiyang	2 985 105	1 568 544	1 416 561	...	...	...	...	...
Gujiao	205 702	110 105	95 597	...	...	...	...	...
Haerbin	3 481 504	1 759 609	1 721 895	...	...	...	...	...
Haicheng	1 181 130	606 805	574 325	...	...	...	...	...
Haikou	830 192	431 774	398 418	...	...	...	...	...
Hailaer	262 184	132 849	129 335	...	...	...	...	...
Hailin	435 677	222 525	213 152	...	...	...	...	...
Hailun	720 008	368 751	351 257	...	...	...	...	...
Haimen	942 952	431 066	511 886	...	...	...	...	...
Haining	666 080	331 349	334 731	...	...	...	...	...
Haiyang	654 594	329 202	325 392	...	...	...	...	...
Hami	388 714	201 005	187 709	...	...	...	...	...
Hancheng	387 041	201 881	185 160	...	...	...	...	...
Hanchuan	1 057 396	552 093	505 303	...	...	...	...	...
Handan	1 329 734	693 882	635 852	...	...	...	...	...
Hangzhou	2 451 319	1 301 103	1 150 216	...	...	...	...	...
Hanzhong	503 871	258 142	245 729	...	...	...	...	...
Hebi	495 336	260 212	235 124	...	...	...	...	...
Hechi	318 348	167 526	150 822	...	...	...	...	...
Hechuan	1 420 520	732 503	688 017	...	...	...	...	...
Hefei	1 659 075	879 749	779 326	...	...	...	...	...
Hegang	694 640	354 262	340 378	...	...	...	...	...
Heihe	192 764	97 488	95 276	...	...	...	...	...
Hejian	757 581	383 621	373 960	...	...	...	...	...
Hejin	368 572	195 677	172 895	...	...	...	...	...
Helong	215 266	110 051	105 215	...	...	...	...	...
Hengshui	422 761	212 417	210 344	...	...	...	...	...
Hengyang	879 051	450 222	428 829	...	...	...	...	...
Heshan (Guangdong)	405 779	202 461	203 318	...	...	...	...	...
Heshan (Guangxi)	131 249	69 205	62 044	...	...	...	...	...
Hetian	186 127	94 034	92 093	...	...	...	...	...
Heyuan	227 773	115 330	112 443	...	...	...	...	...
Heze	1 280 031	656 790	623 241	...	...	...	...	...
Hezhou	850 023	446 208	403 815	...	...	...	...	...
Honghu	877 775	459 997	417 778	...	...	...	...	...
Hongjiang	485 061	250 434	234 627	...	...	...	...	...
Houma	225 123	113 997	111 126	...	...	...	...	...
Huadian	444 415	228 624	215 791	...	...	...	...	...
Huaian	1 200 679	619 541	581 138	...	...	...	...	...
Huaibei	741 195	382 444	358 751	...	...	...	...	...
Huaihua	346 522	178 221	168 301	...	...	...	...	...

8. Population of capital cities and cities of 100 000 or more inhabitants: latest available year, 1990 - 2009
Population des capitales et des villes de 100 000 habitants ou plus : dernière année disponible, 1990 - 2009 (continued - suite)

Continent, country or area, date, code and city / Continent, pays ou zone, date, code et ville	City proper - Ville proprement dite				Urban agglomeration - Agglomération urbaine			
	Population			Surface area - Superficie (km²)	Population			Surface area - Superficie (km²)
	Both sexes - Les deux sexes	Male - Masculin	Female - Féminin		Both sexes - Les deux sexes	Male - Masculin	Female - Féminin	

ASIA - ASIE

China - Chine
1 XI 2000 (CDJC)

Huainan	1 357 228	701 205	656 023	...	...	...	...	...
Huaiyin	555 052	282 186	272 866	...	...	...	...	...
Huanggang	373 568	194 607	178 961	...	...	...	...	...
Huanghua	483 273	251 128	232 145	...	...	...	...	...
Huangshan	406 200	208 004	198 196	...	...	...	...	...
Huangshi (Hubei)	653 722	334 712	319 010	...	...	...	...	...
Huayin	242 488	125 006	117 482	...	...	...	...	...
Huaying	352 257	183 962	168 295	...	...	...	...	...
Huazhou	1 007 796	529 550	478 246	...	...	...	...	...
Huhehaote	1 406 955	724 328	682 627	...	...	...	...	...
Huixian	776 326	394 763	381 563	...	...	...	...	...
Huiyang	862 822	429 006	433 816	...	...	...	...	...
Huizhou	591 686	292 216	299 470	...	...	...	...	...
Hulin	311 509	160 842	150 667	...	...	...	...	...
Huludao	900 936	456 211	444 725	...	...	...	...	...
Hunchun	211 091	108 873	102 218	...	...	...	...	...
Huozhou	274 955	142 316	132 639	...	...	...	...	...
Huzhou	1 145 414	573 421	571 993	...	...	...	...	...
Jiamusi	859 944	433 369	426 575	...	...	...	...	...
Ji'an (Jiangxi)	473 113	244 476	228 637	...	...	...	...	...
Jian (Jilin)	239 849	124 475	115 374	...	...	...	...	...
Jiande	473 062	242 606	230 456	...	...	...	...	...
Jiangdu	1 053 023	512 151	540 872	...	...	...	...	...
Jiangjin	1 322 890	686 106	636 784	...	...	...	...	...
Jiangmen	536 317	271 693	264 624	...	...	...	...	...
Jiangshan	473 222	241 301	231 921	...	...	...	...	...
Jiangyan	861 321	419 333	441 988	...	...	...	...	...
Jiangyin	1 315 472	665 719	649 753	...	...	...	...	...
Jiangyou	849 761	436 112	413 649	...	...	...	...	...
Jianou	478 651	249 624	229 027	...	...	...	...	...
Jianyang (Fujian)	317 848	167 066	150 782	...	...	...	...	...
Jianyang (Sichuan)	1 412 523	728 353	684 170	...	...	...	...	...
Jiaohe	474 109	243 510	230 599	...	...	...	...	...
Jiaonan	827 771	419 331	408 440	...	...	...	...	...
Jiaozhou	783 478	388 207	395 271	...	...	...	...	...
Jiaozuo	747 299	384 395	362 904	...	...	...	...	...
Jiaxing	881 923	445 646	436 277	...	...	...	...	...
Jiayuguan	159 541	85 959	73 582	...	...	...	...	...
Jieshou	640 878	327 384	313 494	...	...	...	...	...
Jiexiu	372 993	190 675	182 318	...	...	...	...	...
Jieyang	633 570	324 831	308 739	...	...	...	...	...
Jilin	1 953 134	984 762	968 372	...	...	...	...	...
Jimo	1 111 202	553 261	557 941	...	...	...	...	...
Jinan	2 999 934	1 539 067	1 460 867	...	...	...	...	...
Jinchang	204 902	106 725	98 177	...	...	...	...	...
Jincheng	304 221	157 663	146 558	...	...	...	...	...
Jingdezhen	444 720	228 747	215 973	...	...	...	...	...
Jinggangshan	145 769	74 722	71 047	...	...	...	...	...
Jinghong	443 672	229 846	213 826	...	...	...	...	...
Jingjiang	639 665	316 885	322 780	...	...	...	...	...
Jingmen	583 373	300 284	283 089	...	...	...	...	...
Jingzhou	1 177 150	598 951	578 199	...	...	...	...	...
Jinhua	424 859	216 773	208 086	...	...	...	...	...
Jining (Inner Mongolia)	272 448	136 913	135 535	...	...	...	...	...
Jining (Shandong)	1 050 522	530 322	520 200	...	...	...	...	...
Jinjiang	1 479 259	772 066	707 193	...	...	...	...	...
Jinshi	243 242	126 619	116 623	...	...	...	...	...
Jintan	533 350	256 798	276 552	...	...	...	...	...
Jinzhong	534 357	274 957	259 400	...	...	...	...	...
Jinzhou (Hebei)	520 942	265 012	255 930	...	...	...	...	...
Jinzhou (Liaoning)	861 991	430 777	431 214	...	...	...	...	...
Jishou	294 297	151 422	142 875	...	...	...	...	...
Jiujiang	551 329	280 126	271 203	...	...	...	...	...

Continent, country or area, date, code and city / Continent, pays ou zone, date, code et ville	City proper - Ville proprement dite				Urban agglomeration - Agglomération urbaine			
	Population			Surface area - Superficie (km²)	Population			Surface area - Superficie (km²)
	Both sexes - Les deux sexes	Male - Masculin	Female - Féminin		Both sexes - Les deux sexes	Male - Masculin	Female - Féminin	
ASIA - ASIE								
China - Chine								
1 XI 2000 (CDJC)								
Jiuquan	346 258	177 943	168 315	...	...	...	...	...
Jiutai	799 729	411 067	388 662	...	...	...	...	...
Jixi	910 782	467 547	443 235	...	...	...	...	...
Jiyuan	626 478	323 554	302 924	...	...	...	...	...
Jizhou	373 825	187 005	186 820	...	...	...	...	...
Jurong	594 316	302 713	291 603	...	...	...	...	...
Kaifeng	796 171	398 133	398 038	...	...	...	...	...
Kaili	433 236	230 692	202 544	...	...	...	...	...
Kaiping	668 692	326 560	342 132	...	...	...	...	...
Kaiyuan (Liaoning)	529 736	271 422	258 314	...	...	...	...	...
Kaiyuan (Yunnan)	292 039	152 771	139 268	...	...	...	...	...
Kashi (Xinjiang)	340 640	172 136	168 504	...	...	...	...	...
Kelamayi	270 232	143 500	126 732	...	...	...	...	...
Kuerle	381 943	199 344	182 599	...	...	...	...	...
Kuitun	285 299	148 740	136 559	...	...	...	...	...
Kunming	3 035 406	1 615 096	1 420 310	...	...	...	...	...
Kunshan	750 074	377 433	372 641	...	...	...	...	...
Laiwu	1 233 525	626 549	606 976	...	...	...	...	...
Laixi	728 796	366 400	362 396	...	...	...	...	...
Laiyang	897 681	453 293	444 388	...	...	...	...	...
Laizhou	889 361	450 192	439 169	...	...	...	...	...
Langfang	715 388	363 094	352 294	...	...	...	...	...
Langzhong	787 809	400 390	387 419	...	...	...	...	...
Lanxi	607 196	314 090	293 106	...	...	...	...	...
Lanzhou	2 087 759	1 092 661	995 098	...	...	...	...	...
Laohekou	509 468	257 204	252 264	...	...	...	...	...
Lasa	223 001	117 004	105 997	...	...	...	...	...
Lechang	423 444	223 788	199 656	...	...	...	...	...
Leiyang	1 180 235	631 431	548 804	...	...	...	...	...
Leizhou	1 268 298	674 213	594 085	...	...	...	...	...
Leling	615 833	313 642	302 191	...	...	...	...	...
Lengshuijiang	339 701	175 071	164 630	...	...	...	...	...
Leping	729 639	381 937	347 702	...	...	...	...	...
Leqing	1 162 765	605 494	557 271	...	...	...	...	...
Leshan	1 120 158	567 028	553 130	...	...	...	...	...
Lianjiang	1 205 764	642 214	563 550	...	...	...	...	...
Lianyuan	996 893	521 941	474 952	...	...	...	...	...
Lianyungang	687 242	354 350	332 892	...	...	...	...	...
Lianzhou	409 360	212 292	197 068	...	...	...	...	...
Liaocheng	950 319	474 976	475 343	...	...	...	...	...
Liaoyang	728 492	365 833	362 659	...	...	...	...	...
Liaoyuan	462 233	234 701	227 532	...	...	...	...	...
Lichuan	786 984	417 988	368 996	...	...	...	...	...
Liling	934 396	484 127	450 269	...	...	...	...	...
Linan	514 238	261 852	252 386	...	...	...	...	...
Linfen	724 403	367 377	357 026	...	...	...	...	...
Lingbao	722 890	377 872	345 018	...	...	...	...	...
Linghai	647 310	332 906	314 404	...	...	...	...	...
Lingwu	249 890	128 364	121 526	...	...	...	...	...
Lingyuan	620 121	324 554	295 567	...	...	...	...	...
Linhai	948 618	479 625	468 993	...	...	...	...	...
Linhe	510 965	260 835	250 130	...	...	...	...	...
Linjiang	184 901	94 904	89 997	...	...	...	...	...
Linqing	694 247	348 411	345 836	...	...	...	...	...
Linxia	202 498	104 017	98 481	...	...	...	...	...
Linxiang	448 452	235 723	212 729	...	...	...	...	...
Linyi	1 938 510	988 940	949 570	...	...	...	...	...
Linzhou	982 254	501 659	480 595	...	...	...	...	...
Lishi	235 678	121 253	114 425	...	...	...	...	...
Lishui	348 241	178 908	169 333	...	...	...	...	...
Liupanshui	995 055	523 692	471 363	...	...	...	...	...
Liuyang	1 307 572	680 610	626 962	...	...	...	...	...
Liuzhou	1 220 392	634 909	585 483	...	...	...	...	...

8. Population of capital cities and cities of 100 000 or more inhabitants: latest available year, 1990 - 2009
Population des capitales et des villes de 100 000 habitants ou plus : dernière année disponible, 1990 - 2009 (continued - suite)

Continent, country or area, date, code and city / Continent, pays ou zone, date, code et ville	City proper - Ville proprement dite				Urban agglomeration - Agglomération urbaine			
	Population			Surface area - Superficie (km²)	Population			Surface area - Superficie (km²)
	Both sexes - Les deux sexes	Male - Masculin	Female - Féminin		Both sexes - Les deux sexes	Male - Masculin	Female - Féminin	

ASIA - ASIE

China - Chine
1 XI 2000 (CDJC)

Liyang	740 871	375 694	365 177	...	...	...	...	...
Longhai	816 318	415 936	400 382	...	...	...	...	...
Longjing	261 551	132 150	129 401	...	...	...	...	...
Longkou	671 335	337 507	333 828	...	...	...	...	...
Longquan	250 398	131 534	118 864	...	...	...	...	...
Longyan	543 731	298 481	245 250	...	...	...	...	...
Loudi	398 577	205 172	193 405	...	...	...	...	...
Lu'an	1 559 037	807 902	751 135	...	...	...	...	...
Lucheng	213 944	111 293	102 651	...	...	...	...	...
Lufeng	1 164 767	600 959	563 808	...	...	...	...	...
Luoding	866 190	449 131	417 059	...	...	...	...	...
Luohe	304 105	150 273	153 832	...	...	...	...	...
Luoyang	1 491 680	759 425	732 255	...	...	...	...	...
Luquan	397 449	202 340	195 109	...	...	...	...	...
Luxi (Yunnan)	337 406	172 038	165 368	...	...	...	...	...
Luzhou	1 252 884	636 652	616 232	...	...	...	...	...
Ma'anshan	567 576	292 994	274 582	...	...	...	...	...
Macheng	1 129 047	595 391	533 656	...	...	...	...	...
Manzhouli	181 112	92 853	88 259	...	...	...	...	...
Maoming	644 301	335 713	308 588	...	...	...	...	...
Meihekou	617 674	317 226	300 448	...	...	...	...	...
Meishan	799 309	402 889	396 420	...	...	...	...	...
Meizhou	354 302	178 658	175 644	...	...	...	...	...
Mianyang	1 162 962	604 414	558 548	...	...	...	...	...
Mianzhu	515 830	263 098	252 732	...	...	...	...	...
Miluo	658 867	342 113	316 754	...	...	...	...	...
Mingguang	569 585	290 126	279 459	...	...	...	...	...
Miquan	180 952	95 368	85 584	...	...	...	...	...
Mishan	438 277	224 565	213 712	...	...	...	...	...
Mudanjiang	1 014 206	512 000	502 206	...	...	...	...	...
Muling	310 096	158 623	151 473	...	...	...	...	...
Nanan	1 385 276	700 218	685 058	...	...	...	...	...
Nanchang	1 844 253	952 504	891 749	...	...	...	...	...
Nanchong	1 771 920	922 452	849 468	...	...	...	...	...
Nanchuan	631 853	326 307	305 546	...	...	...	...	...
Nangong	467 356	234 978	232 378	...	...	...	...	...
Nanhai	2 133 741	1 111 731	1 022 010	...	...	...	...	...
Nanjing	3 624 234	1 935 931	1 688 303	...	...	...	...	...
Nankang	694 987	338 836	356 151	...	...	...	...	...
Nanning	1 766 701	924 916	841 785	...	...	...	...	...
Nanping	488 818	257 352	231 466	...	...	...	...	...
Nantong	771 386	386 206	385 180	...	...	...	...	...
Nanxiong	372 844	185 330	187 514	...	...	...	...	...
Nanyang	1 584 715	814 822	769 893	...	...	...	...	...
Nehe	672 295	343 873	328 422	...	...	...	...	...
Neijiang	1 391 931	709 053	682 878	...	...	...	...	...
Ningan	437 328	223 201	214 127	...	...	...	...	...
Ningbo	1 567 499	804 850	762 649	...	...	...	...	...
Ningde	400 293	213 131	187 162	...	...	...	...	...
Ningguo	381 842	199 915	181 927	...	...	...	...	...
Panjin	602 541	309 377	293 164	...	...	...	...	...
Panshi	530 470	273 219	257 251	...	...	...	...	...
Panzhihua	690 739	363 585	327 154	...	...	...	...	...
Penglai	500 408	252 726	247 682	...	...	...	...	...
Pengzhou	770 749	389 697	381 052	...	...	...	...	...
Pingdingshan	900 903	470 362	430 541	...	...	...	...	...
Pingdu	1 321 975	670 685	651 290	...	...	...	...	...
Pinghu	507 899	249 848	258 051	...	...	...	...	...
Pingliang	454 996	236 426	218 570	...	...	...	...	...
Pingxiang (Guangxi)	107 046	57 445	49 601	...	...	...	...	...
Pingxiang (Jiangxi)	783 445	402 198	381 247	...	...	...	...	...
Pizhou	1 539 922	791 332	748 590	...	...	...	...	...
Pulandian	757 844	385 636	372 208	...	...	...	...	...

Continent, country or area, date, code and city / Continent, pays ou zone, date, code et ville	City proper - Ville proprement dite				Urban agglomeration - Agglomération urbaine			
	Population			Surface area - Superficie (km²)	Population			Surface area - Superficie (km²)
	Both sexes - Les deux sexes	Male - Masculin	Female - Féminin		Both sexes - Les deux sexes	Male - Masculin	Female - Féminin	
ASIA - ASIE								
China - Chine								
1 XI 2000 (CDJC)								
Puning	1 856 402	954 242	902 160	...	...	...	...	...
Putian	443 926	216 578	227 348	...	...	...	...	...
Puyang	448 290	229 387	218 903	...	...	...	...	...
Qianan	632 704	323 330	309 374	...	...	...	...	...
Qianjiang	992 438	506 290	486 148	...	...	...	...	...
Qidong	1 057 073	495 819	561 254	...	...	...	...	...
Qingdao	2 720 972	1 359 527	1 361 445	...	...	...	...	...
Qingtongxia	248 640	129 121	119 519	...	...	...	...	...
Qingyuan	506 680	258 819	247 861	...	...	...	...	...
Qingzhen	471 305	248 079	223 226	...	...	...	...	...
Qingzhou	894 468	450 090	444 378	...	...	...	...	...
Qinhuangdao	817 487	411 355	406 132	...	...	...	...	...
Qinyang	446 404	224 725	221 679	...	...	...	...	...
Qinzhou	1 035 504	578 428	457 076	...	...	...	...	...
Qionghai	449 845	236 560	213 285	...	...	...	...	...
Qionglai	631 577	321 382	310 195	...	...	...	...	...
Qlongshan	678 149	355 557	322 592	...	...	...	...	...
Qiqihaer	1 540 089	776 191	763 898	...	...	...	...	...
Qitaihe	486 704	254 500	232 204	...	...	...	...	...
Qixia	651 357	331 148	320 209	...	...	...	...	...
Quanzhou	1 192 286	616 826	575 460	...	...	...	...	...
Qufu	625 313	317 685	307 628	...	...	...	...	...
Qujing	648 956	333 756	315 200	...	...	...	...	...
Quzhou	286 271	148 054	138 217	...	...	...	...	...
Renhuai	520 759	270 091	250 668	...	...	...	...	...
Renqiu	768 900	390 649	378 251	...	...	...	...	...
Rizhao	1 148 190	576 050	572 140	...	...	...	...	...
Rongcheng	732 147	368 156	363 991	...	...	...	...	...
Rugao	1 362 533	659 720	702 813	...	...	...	...	...
Ruian	1 207 788	627 593	580 195	...	...	...	...	...
Ruichang	398 844	209 755	189 089	...	...	...	...	...
Ruijin	535 499	280 328	255 171	...	...	...	...	...
Ruili	155 210	80 532	74 678	...	...	...	...	...
Rushan	580 326	291 047	289 279	...	...	...	...	...
Ruzhou	923 245	474 090	449 155	...	...	...	...	...
Sanhe	456 882	229 788	227 094	...	...	...	...	...
Sanmenxia	288 746	149 846	138 900	...	...	...	...	...
Sanming	337 105	178 031	159 074	...	...	...	...	...
Sanshui	440 119	230 835	209 284	...	...	...	...	...
Sanya	482 296	254 293	228 003	...	...	...	...	...
Shahe	474 260	243 171	231 089	...	...	...	...	...
Shanghai	14 348 535	7 414 274	6 934 261	...	...	...	...	...
Shangqiu	1 428 983	729 319	699 664	...	...	...	...	...
Shangrao	327 703	164 698	163 005	...	...	...	...	...
Shangyu	722 523	354 917	367 606	...	...	...	...	...
Shangzhi	582 764	298 966	283 798	...	...	...	...	...
Shangzhou	530 883	279 160	251 723	...	...	...	...	...
Shantou	1 270 112	636 189	633 923	...	...	...	...	...
Shanwei	409 677	211 746	197 931	...	...	...	...	...
Shaoguan	535 979	282 515	253 464	...	...	...	...	...
Shaowu	288 401	151 117	137 284	...	...	...	...	...
Shaoxing	633 118	310 860	322 258	...	...	...	...	...
Shaoyang	607 868	309 563	298 305	...	...	...	...	...
Shengzhou	671 221	345 614	325 607	...	...	...	...	...
Shenyang	5 303 053	2 700 380	2 602 673	...	...	...	...	...
Shenzhen	7 008 831	3 454 392	3 554 439	...	...	...	...	...
Shenzhou	568 558	289 086	279 472	...	...	...	...	...
Shifang	432 579	218 447	214 132	...	...	...	...	...
Shihezi	590 115	305 253	284 862	...	...	...	...	...
Shijiazhuang	1 969 975	1 005 476	964 499	...	...	...	...	...
Shishi	498 786	264 700	234 086	...	...	...	...	...
Shishou	602 649	310 486	292 163	...	...	...	...	...
Shiyan	589 824	309 552	280 272	...	...	...	...	...

8. Population of capital cities and cities of 100 000 or more inhabitants: latest available year, 1990 - 2009
Population des capitales et des villes de 100 000 habitants ou plus : dernière année disponible, 1990 - 2009 (continued - suite)

Continent, country or area, date, code and city / Continent, pays ou zone, date, code et ville	City proper - Ville proprement dite				Urban agglomeration - Agglomération urbaine			
	Population			Surface area - Superficie (km²)	Population			Surface area - Superficie (km²)
	Both sexes - Les deux sexes	Male - Masculin	Female - Féminin		Both sexes - Les deux sexes	Male - Masculin	Female - Féminin	

ASIA - ASIE

China - Chine
1 XI 2000 (CDJC)

Shizuishan	314 296	163 261	151 035	...	...	...	...	...
Shouguang	1 081 991	548 020	533 971	...	...	...	...	...
Shuangcheng	749 182	382 673	366 509	...	...	...	...	...
Shuangliao	404 499	206 071	198 428	...	...	...	...	...
Shuangyashan	487 294	248 542	238 752	...	...	...	...	...
Shulan	660 065	340 293	319 772	...	...	...	...	...
Shunde	1 694 152	893 580	800 572	...	...	...	...	...
Shuozhou	563 896	290 621	273 275	...	...	...	...	...
Sihui	409 804	209 936	199 868	...	...	...	...	...
Simao	230 834	120 071	110 763	...	...	...	...	...
Siping	492 841	247 416	245 425	...	...	...	...	...
Songyuan	538 469	273 101	265 368	...	...	...	...	...
Songzi	859 941	437 980	421 961	...	...	...	...	...
Suihua	800 207	405 382	394 825	...	...	...	...	...
Suining	1 355 388	696 590	658 798	...	...	...	...	...
Suizhou	1 598 752	818 936	779 816	...	...	...	...	...
Suqian	244 651	124 719	119 932	...	...	...	...	...
Suzhou (Anhui)	1 601 181	819 067	782 114	...	...	...	...	...
Suzhou (Jiangsu)	1 344 709	686 919	657 790	...	...	...	...	...
Tacheng	149 210	76 056	73 154	...	...	...	...	...
Tai'an	1 538 211	775 346	762 865	...	...	...	...	...
Taicang	515 063	250 788	264 275	...	...	...	...	...
Taishan	948 716	478 773	469 943	...	...	...	...	...
Taixing	1 235 454	618 158	617 296	...	...	...	...	...
Taiyuan	2 558 382	1 321 216	1 237 166	...	...	...	...	...
Taizhou (Jiangsu)	607 660	303 078	304 582	...	...	...	...	...
Taizhou (Zhejiang)	1 491 963	766 497	725 466	...	...	...	...	...
Tangshan	1 711 311	863 091	848 220	...	...	...	...	...
Taonan	441 096	224 878	216 218	...	...	...	...	...
Tengzhou	1 548 817	811 999	736 818	...	...	...	...	...
Tianchang	590 745	297 550	293 195	...	...	...	...	...
Tianjin	7 499 181	3 825 069	3 674 112	...	...	...	...	...
Tianmen	1 613 739	849 283	764 456	...	...	...	...	...
Tianshui	1 146 986	594 508	552 478	...	...	...	...	...
Tiefa	239 636	121 471	118 165	...	...	...	...	...
Tieli	354 601	181 024	173 577	...	...	...	...	...
Tieling	433 799	217 795	216 004	...	...	...	...	...
Tongcheng	660 772	321 098	339 674	...	...	...	...	...
Tongchuan	404 257	211 294	192 963	...	...	...	...	...
Tonghua	460 148	231 960	228 188	...	...	...	...	...
Tongjiang	164 595	85 426	79 169	...	...	...	...	...
Tongliao	793 913	400 930	392 983	...	...	...	...	...
Tongling	362 477	188 130	174 347	...	...	...	...	...
Tongren	308 583	163 632	144 951	...	...	...	...	...
Tongshi	100 836	53 146	47 690	...	...	...	...	...
Tongxiang	713 399	360 567	352 832	...	...	...	...	...
Tongzhou	1 371 498	652 777	718 721	...	...	...	...	...
Tulufan	251 652	129 183	122 469	...	...	...	...	...
Tumen	132 368	67 067	65 301	...	...	...	...	...
Urumqi	1 753 298	911 328	841 970	...	...	...	...	...
Wafangdian	956 063	489 377	466 686	...	...	...	...	...
Wanning	513 604	272 751	240 853	...	...	...	...	...
Wanyuan	536 685	278 918	257 767	...	...	...	...	...
Weifang	1 380 300	696 720	683 580	...	...	...	...	...
Weihai	609 219	307 867	301 352	...	...	...	...	...
Weihui	464 371	233 151	231 220	...	...	...	...	...
Weinan	888 866	451 028	437 838	...	...	...	...	...
Wenchang	509 271	260 432	248 839	...	...	...	...	...
Wendeng	675 061	335 330	339 731	...	...	...	...	...
Wenling	1 162 783	604 031	558 752	...	...	...	...	...
Wenzhou	1 915 548	1 028 001	887 547	...	...	...	...	...
Wuan	720 196	373 108	347 088	...	...	...	...	...
Wuchang	888 782	454 587	434 195	...	...	...	...	...

Continent, country or area, date, code and city / Continent, pays ou zone, date, code et ville	City proper - Ville proprement dite				Urban agglomeration - Agglomération urbaine			
	Population			Surface area - Superficie (km²)	Population			Surface area - Superficie (km²)
	Both sexes - Les deux sexes	Male - Masculin	Female - Féminin		Both sexes - Les deux sexes	Male - Masculin	Female - Féminin	
ASIA - ASIE								
China - Chine								
1 XI 2000 (CDJC)								
Wuchuan	822 482	429 336	393 146	...	...	...	...	...
Wudalianchi	338 689	176 002	162 687	...	...	...	...	...
Wugang (Henan)	313 089	164 347	148 742	...	...	...	...	...
Wugang (Hunan)	694 847	363 904	330 943	...	...	...	...	...
Wuhai	427 553	223 947	203 606	...	...	...	...	...
Wuhan	8 312 700	4 306 729	4 005 971	...	...	...	...	...
Wuhu	697 197	359 560	337 637	...	...	...	...	...
Wujiang	857 104	426 423	430 681	...	...	...	...	...
Wujin	1 420 204	719 200	701 004	...	...	...	...	...
Wulanhaote	269 162	135 406	133 756	...	...	...	...	...
Wusu	190 359	100 288	90 071	...	...	...	...	...
Wuwei	946 506	488 872	457 634	...	...	...	...	...
Wuxi	1 425 766	732 231	693 535	...	...	...	...	...
Wuxian	1 128 429	557 717	570 712	...	...	...	...	...
Wuxue	719 426	381 959	337 467	...	...	...	...	...
Wuyishan	212 156	112 006	100 150	...	...	...	...	...
Wuzhong	355 442	181 909	173 533	...	...	...	...	...
Wuzhou	381 043	193 424	187 619	...	...	...	...	...
Xiamen	2 053 070	1 061 697	991 373	...	...	...	...	...
Xi'an	4 481 508	2 320 642	2 160 866	...	...	...	...	...
Xiangcheng	1 052 468	546 760	505 708	...	...	...	...	...
Xiangfan	871 388	443 899	427 489	...	...	...	...	...
Xiangtan	707 783	363 619	344 164	...	...	...	...	...
Xiangxiang	807 718	413 489	394 229	...	...	...	...	...
Xianning	567 598	295 836	271 762	...	...	...	...	...
Xiantao	1 474 078	774 487	699 591	...	...	...	...	...
Xianyang	953 860	493 153	460 707	...	...	...	...	...
Xiaogan	883 123	454 917	428 206	...	...	...	...	...
Xiaoshan	1 233 348	613 229	620 119	...	...	...	...	...
Xiaoyi	414 154	215 941	198 213	...	...	...	...	...
Xichang	615 212	318 658	296 554	...	...	...	...	...
Xifeng	317 669	163 228	154 441	...	...	...	...	...
Xilinhaote	173 796	89 527	84 269	...	...	...	...	...
Xingcheng	524 527	269 567	254 960	...	...	...	...	...
Xinghua	1 441 659	745 856	695 803	...	...	...	...	...
Xingning	871 507	436 749	434 758	...	...	...	...	...
Xingping	551 523	284 879	266 644	...	...	...	...	...
Xingtai	536 282	272 661	263 621	...	...	...	...	...
Xingyang	619 840	316 049	303 791	...	...	...	...	...
Xingyi	719 605	375 079	344 526	...	...	...	...	...
Xinhui	932 425	467 557	464 868	...	...	...	...	...
Xining	854 466	440 359	414 107	...	...	...	...	...
Xinji	623 219	314 536	308 683	...	...	...	...	...
Xinle	439 644	220 811	218 833	...	...	...	...	...
Xinmi	779 014	406 291	372 723	...	...	...	...	...
Xinmin	653 719	333 683	320 036	...	...	...	...	...
Xintai	1 344 395	687 569	656 826	...	...	...	...	...
Xinxiang	775 941	394 224	381 717	...	...	...	...	...
Xinyang	1 255 750	644 031	611 719	...	...	...	...	...
Xinyi (Guangdong)	907 978	464 088	443 890	...	...	...	...	...
Xinyi (Jiangsu)	962 656	491 509	471 147	...	...	...	...	...
Xinyu	778 391	408 940	369 451	...	...	...	...	...
Xinzheng	609 173	315 462	293 711	...	...	...	...	...
Xinzhou	496 608	251 708	244 900	...	...	...	...	...
Xishan	1 181 073	599 540	581 533	...	...	...	...	...
Xuancheng	822 707	428 470	394 237	...	...	...	...	...
Xuanwei	1 292 825	691 846	600 979	...	...	...	...	...
Xuchang	373 387	188 476	184 911	...	...	...	...	...
Xuzhou	1 679 626	866 686	812 940	...	...	...	...	...
Ya'an	334 475	171 237	163 238	...	...	...	...	...
Yakeshi	405 806	207 451	198 355	...	...	...	...	...
Yan'an	403 868	209 240	194 628	...	...	...	...	...
Yancheng	683 663	347 576	336 087	...	...	...	...	...

8. Population of capital cities and cities of 100 000 or more inhabitants: latest available year, 1990 - 2009
**Population des capitales et des villes de 100 000 habitants ou plus : dernière année disponible, 1990 - 2009 (continued -
suite)**

Continent, country or area, date, code and city	City proper - Ville proprement dite				Urban agglomeration - Agglomération urbaine			
	Population				Population			
Continent, pays ou zone, date, code et ville	Both sexes - Les deux sexes	Male - Masculin	Female - Féminin	Surface area - Superficie (km²)	Both sexes - Les deux sexes	Male - Masculin	Female - Féminin	Surface area - Superficie (km²)

ASIA - ASIE

China - Chine
1 XI 2000 (CDJC)

Yangchun	840 581	440 930	399 651	...	...	...	...	...
Yangjiang	538 069	276 769	261 300	...	...	...	...	...
Yangquan	655 317	346 209	309 108	...	...	...	...	...
Yangzhong	301 672	150 538	151 134	...	...	...	...	...
Yangzhou	711 993	362 425	349 568	...	...	...	...	...
Yanji	432 339	223 342	208 997	...	...	...	...	...
Yanshi	816 026	414 890	401 136	...	...	...	...	...
Yantai	1 724 404	871 452	852 952	...	...	...	...	...
Yanzhou	598 387	303 581	294 806	...	...	...	...	...
Yibin	809 099	419 397	389 702	...	...	...	...	...
Yichang	712 738	371 510	341 228	...	...	...	...	...
Yicheng	522 835	266 340	256 495	...	...	...	...	...
Yichun (Heilongjiang)	814 016	413 071	400 945	...	...	...	...	...
Yichun (Jiangxi)	920 357	480 945	439 412	...	...	...	...	...
Yidu	385 779	196 716	189 063	...	...	...	...	...
Yima	136 543	73 411	63 132	...	...	...	...	...
Yinchuan	807 487	415 203	392 284	...	...	...	...	...
Yingcheng	650 485	340 907	309 578	...	...	...	...	...
Yingde	810 446	421 964	388 482	...	...	...	...	...
Yingko	698 059	353 751	344 308	...	...	...	...	...
Yingtan	178 406	92 050	86 356	...	...	...	...	...
Yining	357 519	179 862	177 657	...	...	...	...	...
Yiwu	912 670	461 103	451 567	...	...	...	...	...
Yixing	1 164 275	592 095	572 180	...	...	...	...	...
Yiyang	1 228 881	629 842	599 039	...	...	...	...	...
Yizheng	610 356	311 144	299 212	...	...	...	...	...
Yizhou	549 434	288 084	261 350	...	...	...	...	...
Yongan	334 852	180 109	154 743	...	...	...	...	...
Yongcheng	1 264 607	654 047	610 560	...	...	...	...	...
Yongchuan	984 730	507 848	476 882	...	...	...	...	...
Yongji	421 244	214 446	206 798	...	...	...	...	...
Yongkang	557 067	290 946	266 121	...	...	...	...	...
Yongzhou	976 539	508 021	468 518	...	...	...	...	...
Yuanjiang	700 236	363 730	336 506	...	...	...	...	...
Yuanping	471 853	244 751	227 102	...	...	...	...	...
Yucheng	494 301	248 103	246 198	...	...	...	...	...
Yueyang	912 993	471 170	441 823	...	...	...	...	...
Yuhang	817 715	419 877	397 838	...	...	...	...	...
Yulin (Guangxi)	918 229	491 729	426 500	...	...	...	...	...
Yulin (Shaanxi)	451 337	232 951	218 386	...	...	...	...	...
Yumen	188 931	99 832	89 099	...	...	...	...	...
Yuncheng	604 381	304 489	299 892	...	...	...	...	...
Yunfu	261 636	136 789	124 847	...	...	...	...	...
Yushu	1 155 670	592 213	563 457	...	...	...	...	...
Yuxi	409 044	206 139	202 905	...	...	...	...	...
Yuyao	852 719	429 835	422 884	...	...	...	...	...
Yuzhou	1 122 669	587 728	534 941	...	...	...	...	...
Zaoyang	1 054 374	538 588	515 786	...	...	...	...	...
Zaozhuang	1 996 798	1 025 190	971 608	...	...	...	...	...
Zengcheng	899 644	466 540	433 104	...	...	...	...	...
Zhalantun	409 051	211 922	197 129	...	...	...	...	...
Zhangjiagang	957 223	466 771	490 452	...	...	...	...	...
Zhangjiajie	453 723	234 454	219 269	...	...	...	...	...
Zhangjiakou	903 348	455 048	448 300	...	...	...	...	...
Zhangping	264 757	140 779	123 978	...	...	...	...	...
Zhangqiu	977 324	485 925	491 399	...	...	...	...	...
Zhangshu	527 823	273 691	254 132	...	...	...	...	...
Zhangye	486 688	248 469	238 219	...	...	...	...	...
Zhangzhou	567 884	291 597	276 287	...	...	...	...	...
Zhanjiang	1 350 665	707 187	643 478	...	...	...	...	...
Zhaodong	832 657	424 694	407 963	...	...	...	...	...
Zhaoqing	507 834	254 086	253 748	...	...	...	...	...
Zhaotong	727 959	377 931	350 028	...	...	...	...	...

Continent, country or area, date, code and city / Continent, pays ou zone, date, code et ville	City proper - Ville proprement dite				Urban agglomeration - Agglomération urbaine			
	Population			Surface area - Superficie (km²)	Population			Surface area - Superficie (km²)
	Both sexes - Les deux sexes	Male - Masculin	Female - Féminin		Both sexes - Les deux sexes	Male - Masculin	Female - Féminin	
ASIA - ASIE								
China - Chine								
1 XI 2000 (CDJC)								
Zhaoyuan	593 705	297 504	296 201	...	...	...	...	...
Zhengzhou	2 589 387	1 347 037	1 242 350	...	...	...	...	...
Zhenjiang	695 663	364 429	331 234	...	...	...	...	...
Zhijiang	508 835	257 013	251 822	...	...	...	...	...
Zhongshan	2 363 322	1 175 587	1 187 735	...	...	...	...	...
Zhongxiang	1 021 998	516 758	505 240	...	...	...	...	...
Zhoukou	323 738	162 443	161 295	...	...	...	...	...
Zhoushan	715 685	362 426	353 259	...	...	...	...	...
Zhuanghe	835 062	422 677	412 385	...	...	...	...	...
Zhucheng	1 053 695	531 390	522 305	...	...	...	...	...
Zhuhai	833 908	414 067	419 841	...	...	...	...	...
Zhuji	1 070 675	535 820	534 855	...	...	...	...	...
Zhumadian	338 036	170 485	167 551	...	...	...	...	...
Zhuozhou	546 754	275 834	270 920	...	...	...	...	...
Zhuzhou	879 996	454 057	425 939	...	...	...	...	...
Zibo	2 817 479	1 429 838	1 387 641	...	...	...	...	...
Zigong	1 051 384	532 479	518 905	...	...	...	...	...
Zixing	351 581	181 632	169 949	...	...	...	...	...
Ziyang	1 016 034	527 326	488 708	...	...	...	...	...
Zoucheng	1 101 003	571 761	529 242	...	...	...	...	...
Zunhua	683 662	348 121	335 541	...	...	...	...	...
Zunyi	691 694	358 839	332 855	...	...	...	...	...
China, Hong Kong SAR - Chine, Hong Kong RAS								
1 VII 2009 (ESDJ)								
HONG KONG SAR	7 003 700	3 296 200	3 707 500	1 104	...	...	...	...
China, Macao SAR - Chine, Macao RAS								
1 VII 2009 (ESDJ)								
MACAO	544 100	265 200	279 000	29	...	...	...	...
Cyprus - Chypre								
1 I 2006 (ESDJ)								
LEFKOSIA[22]	...	...	...	...	224 500	...	...	...
Lemesos[23]	...	...	...	...	176 900	...	...	...
Democratic People's Republic of Korea - République populaire démocratique de Corée								
1 X 2008 (CDJC)								
Anju	167 646	79 187	88 459	...	...	...	...	...
Chongjin	614 892	292 741	322 151	...	...	...	...	...
Haeju	241 599	116 594	125 005	...	...	...	...	...
Hamhung	614 198	292 058	322 140	...	...	...	...	...
Huichon	136 093	64 547	71 546	...	...	...	...	...
Hyesan	174 015	82 604	91 411	...	...	...	...	...
Jongju	102 659	48 423	54 236	...	...	...	...	...
Kaechon	262 389	124 222	138 167	...	...	...	...	...
Kaesong	192 578	90 653	101 925	...	...	...	...	...
Kanggye	251 971	120 305	131 666	...	...	...	...	...
Kim Chaek	155 284	73 133	82 151	...	...	...	...	...
Kusong	155 181	73 677	81 504	...	...	...	...	...
Nampho	310 864	150 091	160 773	...	...	...	...	...
Phyongsong	236 583	115 817	120 766	...	...	...	...	...
PYONGYANG	2 581 076	1 233 765	1 347 311	...	...	...	...	...
Rason	158 337	74 777	83 560	...	...	...	...	...
Sariwon	271 434	130 181	141 253	...	...	...	...	...
Sinpho	130 951	63 207	67 744	...	...	...	...	...
Sinuiju	334 031	158 139	175 892	...	...	...	...	...
Sunchon	250 738	119 727	131 011	...	...	...	...	...
Tanchon	240 873	113 221	127 652	...	...	...	...	...
Tokchon	210 571	99 655	110 916	...	...	...	...	...
Wonsan	328 467	155 903	172 564	...	...	...	...	...
Georgia - Géorgie								
1 VII 2008 (ESDF)								
Batumi	122 300	...	...	...	...	...	...	...
Kutaisi	188 600	...	...	...	...	...	...	...

8. Population of capital cities and cities of 100 000 or more inhabitants: latest available year, 1990 - 2009
Population des capitales et des villes de 100 000 habitants ou plus : dernière année disponible, 1990 - 2009 (continued - suite)

Continent, country or area, date, code and city / Continent, pays ou zone, date, code et ville	City proper - Ville proprement dite				Urban agglomeration - Agglomération urbaine			
	Population			Surface area - Superficie (km²)	Population			Surface area - Superficie (km²)
	Both sexes - Les deux sexes	Male - Masculin	Female - Féminin		Both sexes - Les deux sexes	Male - Masculin	Female - Féminin	
ASIA - ASIE								
Georgia - Géorgie								
1 VII 2008 (ESDF)								
Rustavi	117 300	...	...	...	...	...	...	...
TBILISI	1 106 700	...	...	...	...	...	...	...
India - Inde[24]								
1 III 2001 (CDFC)								
Abohar	124 339	66 445	57 894	23	...	...	...	...
Achalpur	107 316	55 687	51 629	17	...	...	...	...
Adilabad	109 529	55 641	53 888	16	129 403	65 501	63 902	21
Adityapur	119 233	63 837	55 396	50	...	...	...	...
Adoni	157 305	79 639	77 666	30	162 458	82 345	80 113	...
Agartala	189 998	94 742	95 256	16	...	...	...	...
Agra	1 275 134	690 599	584 535	121	1 331 339	720 707	610 632	141
Ahmedabad	3 520 085	1 867 249	1 652 836	191	4 525 013	2 401 422	2 123 591	438
Ahmednagar	307 615	159 564	148 051	18	347 549	184 765	162 784	30
Aizawl	228 280	115 986	112 294	110	...	...	...	...
Ajmer	485 575	254 164	231 411	218	490 520	256 695	233 825	223
Akola	400 520	206 649	193 871	23	...	...	...	...
Alandur	146 287	74 836	71 451	20	...	...	...	...
Alappuzha	177 029	85 725	91 304	70	282 675	137 244	145 431	84
Aligarh	669 087	356 725	312 362	40	...	...	...	...
Alipurduar	...	...	...	...	114 035	58 503	55 532	26
Allahabad	975 393	539 772	435 621	63	1 042 229	576 122	466 107	86
Alwar	260 593	139 585	121 008	...	266 203	143 699	122 504	58
Ambala	139 279	74 016	65 263	17	168 316	92 977	75 339	38
Ambala Sadar	106 568	55 750	50 818	...	...	...	...	...
Ambarnath	203 804	107 325	96 479	36	...	...	...	...
Ambattur	310 967	160 282	150 685	40	...	...	...	...
Amravati	549 510	284 247	265 263	122	...	...	...	...
Amritsar	966 862	518 388	448 474	136	1 003 917	538 744	465 173	...
Amroha	165 129	86 943	78 186	6	...	...	...	...
Anand	130 685	68 074	62 611	21	218 486	115 295	103 191	60
Anantapur	218 808	110 979	107 829	...	243 143	123 713	119 430	...
Anklesvar	...	...	...	...	112 643	60 249	52 394	...
Arcot	...	...	...	...	126 671	62 787	63 884	19
Arrah	203 380	109 867	93 513	31	...	...	...	...
Asansol	475 439	250 886	224 553	128	1 067 369	564 837	502 532	352
Ashoknagar Kalyangarh	111 607	56 490	55 117	...	...	...	...	...
Aurangabad	873 311	459 295	414 016	139	892 483	469 237	423 246	148
Avadi	229 403	117 991	111 412	65	...	...	...	...
Bahadurgarh	119 846	65 859	53 987	21	131 925	72 873	59 052	30
Baharampur	160 143	81 737	78 406	17	170 322	86 969	83 353	19
Bahraich	168 323	89 581	78 742	13	...	...	...	...
Baidyabati	108 229	56 394	51 835	8	...	...	...	...
Baleshwar	106 082	55 691	50 391	...	156 430	82 106	74 324	42
Ballia	101 465	54 496	46 969	16	...	...	...	...
Bally	260 906	149 603	111 303	12	...	...	...	...
Balurghat	135 737	68 871	66 866	10	143 321	72 764	70 557	12
Banda	134 839	72 632	62 207	16	139 436	75 174	64 262	28
Bangalore	4 301 326	2 242 835	2 058 491	...	5 701 446	2 988 561	2 712 885	540
Bangaon	102 163	52 537	49 626	25	...	...	...	...
Bankura	128 781	66 429	62 352	19	...	...	...	...
Bansberia	104 412	55 389	49 023	9	...	...	...	...
Baranagar	250 768	132 559	118 209	7	...	...	...	...
Barasat	231 521	118 374	113 147	31	...	...	...	...
Barddhaman	285 602	148 562	137 040	23	...	...	...	...
Bareilly	718 395	378 848	339 547	106	748 353	397 304	351 049	125
Baripada	...	...	...	...	100 651	53 606	47 045	38
Barrackpur	144 391	76 299	68 092	11	...	...	...	...
Barshi	104 785	53 848	50 937	36	...	...	...	...
Basirhat	113 159	57 965	55 194	22	...	...	...	...
Basti	107 601	57 053	50 548	19	...	...	...	...
Batala	125 677	66 508	59 169	9	147 872	78 393	69 479	...
Bathinda	217 256	116 946	100 310	110	...	...	...	...
Beawar	123 759	64 417	59 342	18	125 981	65 586	60 395	24

Continent, country or area, date, code and city / Continent, pays ou zone, date, code et ville	City proper - Ville proprement dite				Urban agglomeration - Agglomération urbaine			
	Population			Surface area - Superficie (km²)	Population			Surface area - Superficie (km²)
	Both sexes - Les deux sexes	Male - Masculin	Female - Féminin		Both sexes - Les deux sexes	Male - Masculin	Female - Féminin	
ASIA - ASIE								
India - Inde[24]								
1 III 2001 (CDFC)								
Begusarai	...	...	...	...	107 623	57 541	50 082	12
Belgaum	399 653	204 598	195 055	100	506 480	261 639	244 841	173
Bellary	316 766	162 699	154 067	66	...	...	...	...
Bettiah	116 670	61 753	54 917	8	...	...	...	...
Bhadravati	160 662	81 351	79 311	...	...	...	...	...
Bhadreswar	106 071	58 040	48 031	6	...	...	...	...
Bhagalpur	340 767	182 806	157 961	30	350 133	187 723	162 410	31
Bhalswa Jahangir Pur	152 339	83 802	68 537	7	...	...	...	...
Bharatpur	204 587	110 057	94 530	41	205 235	110 397	94 838	51
Bharuch	148 140	76 506	71 634	18	176 364	91 281	85 083	20
Bhatpara	442 385	243 157	199 228	30	...	...	...	...
Bhavani	...	...	...	...	104 646	52 998	51 648	10
Bhavnagar	511 085	266 838	244 247	90	517 708	270 278	247 430	91
Bheemavaram	137 409	69 473	67 936	26	142 064	71 929	70 135	26
Bhilai Nagar	556 366	291 070	265 296	141	...	...	...	...
Bhilwara	280 128	148 794	131 334	118	...	...	...	...
Bhind	153 752	82 945	70 807	17	...	...	...	...
Bhiwandi	598 741	367 565	231 176	26	621 427	382 184	239 243	28
Bhiwani	169 531	91 697	77 834	28	...	...	...	...
Bhopal	1 437 354	757 408	679 946	285	1 458 416	768 391	690 025	298
Bhubaneswar	648 032	360 739	287 293	135	658 220	366 134	292 086	148
Bhuj	...	...	...	...	136 429	71 056	65 373	...
Bhusawal	172 372	89 208	83 164	13	187 564	97 243	90 321	25
Bid	138 196	71 827	66 369	8	...	...	...	...
Bidar	172 877	89 934	82 943	...	174 257	90 662	83 595	47
Bidhan Nagar	164 221	83 220	81 001	34	...	...	...	...
Bihar	232 071	122 019	110 052	24	...	...	...	...
Bijapur	228 175	117 375	110 800	...	253 891	130 416	123 475	75
Bikaner	529 690	283 067	246 623	166	...	...	...	...
Bilaspur	275 694	143 518	132 176	36	335 293	174 351	160 942	46
Birnagar	...	...	...	...	115 127	59 232	55 895	40
Bokaro Steel City	393 805	213 231	180 574	163	497 780	268 969	228 811	188
Bommanahalli	201 652	108 108	93 544	36	...	...	...	...
Botad	100 194	52 752	47 442	10	...	...	...	...
Brahmapur	307 792	160 354	147 438	80	...	...	...	...
Budaun	148 029	78 141	69 888	4	...	...	...	...
Bulandshahr	176 425	93 531	82 894	12	...	...	...	...
Burhanpur	193 725	99 751	93 974	13	...	...	...	...
Byatarayanapura	181 744	95 508	86 236	45	...	...	...	...
Chakdaha	...	...	...	...	101 320	51 485	49 835	...
Champdani	103 246	57 842	45 404	6	...	...	...	...
Chandan Nagar	162 187	84 181	78 006	22	...	...	...	...
Chandausi	103 749	55 127	48 622	9	...	...	...	...
Chandigarh	808 515	450 122	358 393	79	...	...	...	...
Chandrapur	289 450	151 202	138 248	56	...	...	...	...
Chapra	179 190	95 494	83 696	17	...	...	...	...
Chennai (Madras)	4 343 645	2 219 539	2 124 106	174	6 560 242	3 355 524	3 204 718	702
Cherthala	...	...	...	...	141 558	68 756	72 802	92
Chhatarpur	...	...	...	...	109 078	58 421	50 657	17
Chhindwara	122 247	63 584	58 663	11	153 552	79 889	73 663	22
Chikmagalur	101 251	51 694	49 557	33	...	...	...	...
Chirala	...	...	...	...	166 294	82 954	83 340	48
Chirkunda	...	...	...	...	106 227	56 536	49 691	26
Chitradurga	122 702	62 845	59 857	24	125 170	64 112	61 058	26
Chittoor	152 654	76 879	75 775	33	...	...	...	...
Churu	...	...	...	...	101 874	53 079	48 795	30
Coimbatore	930 882	477 937	452 945	106	1 461 139	748 376	712 763	379
Coonoor	...	...	...	...	101 490	51 208	50 282	44
Cuddalore	158 634	80 012	78 622	28	...	...	...	...
Cuddapah	126 505	63 669	62 836	42	262 506	133 224	129 282	78
Cuttack	534 654	285 838	248 816	149	587 182	314 101	273 081	195
Dallo Pura	132 621	71 362	61 259	2	...	...	...	...
Damoh	112 185	58 962	53 223	16	127 967	67 321	60 646	36

Continent, country or area, date, code and city / Continent, pays ou zone, date, code et ville	City proper - Ville proprement dite				Urban agglomeration - Agglomération urbaine			
	Population			Surface area - Superficie (km²)	Population			Surface area - Superficie (km²)
	Both sexes - Les deux sexes	Male - Masculin	Female - Féminin		Both sexes - Les deux sexes	Male - Masculin	Female - Féminin	
ASIA - ASIE								
India - Inde[24]								
1 III 2001 (CDFC)								
Darbhanga	267 348	142 377	124 971	19	...	...	...	...
Darjiling	107 197	55 963	51 234	11	108 830	56 769	52 061	13
Dasarahalli	264 940	143 909	121 031	23	...	...	...	...
Davangere	364 523	187 987	176 536	...	...	...	...	...
Dehradun	426 674	224 546	202 128	52	530 263	283 064	247 199	103
Dehri	119 057	63 540	55 517	21	...	...	...	...
Delhi	9 879 172	5 412 497	4 466 675	554	12 877 470[25]	7 069 371[25]	5 808 099[25]	889[25]
Delhi Cantonment	124 917	75 827	49 090	43	...	...	...	...
Deoghar	...	...	...	...	112 525	61 442	51 083	22
Deoli	119 468	66 594	52 874	10	...	...	...	...
Deoria	104 227	54 681	49 546	16	...	...	...	...
Dewas	231 672	121 075	110 597	100	...	...	...	...
Dhanbad	199 258	108 512	90 746	23	1 065 327	579 150	486 177	223
Dharmavaram	103 357	52 785	50 572	40	...	...	...	...
Dhule	341 755	177 772	163 983	46	...	...	...	...
Dibrugarh	121 893	65 118	56 775	25	137 661	73 307	64 354	26
Dinapur Nizamat	131 176	69 419	61 757	12	...	...	...	...
Dindigul	196 955	99 124	97 831	14	...	...	...	...
Dohad	...	...	...	...	112 026	57 642	54 384	26
Dumdum	101 296	52 890	48 406	9	...	...	...	...
Durg	232 517	119 315	113 202	66	...	...	...	...
Durgapur	493 405	263 721	229 684	154	...	...	...	...
Durg-Bhilai Nagar	...	...	...	...	927 864	482 304	445 560	341
Eluru	190 062	92 790	97 272	15	215 804	105 476	110 328	...
English Bazar	161 456	82 845	78 611	...	224 415	115 356	109 059	19
Erode	150 541	76 462	74 079	8	389 906	198 842	191 064	132
Etah	107 110	56 763	50 347	13	...	...	...	...
Etawah	210 453	111 749	98 704	9	...	...	...	...
Faizabad	144 705	75 935	68 770	33	208 162	114 330	93 832	63
Faridabad	1 055 938	581 069	474 869	199	...	...	...	...
Farrukhabad-cum-Fategarh	228 333	120 829	107 504	17	242 997	129 643	113 354	21
Fatehpur	152 078	80 011	72 067	57	...	...	...	...
Firozabad	279 102	148 263	130 839	9	432 866	230 802	202 064	12
Gadag-Betgeri	154 982	78 713	76 269	35	...	...	...	...
Gajuwaka	259 180	133 469	125 711	128	...	...	...	...
Gandhidham	151 693	79 379	72 314	30	...	...	...	...
Gandhinagar	195 985	103 876	92 109	57	...	...	...	...
Ganganagar	210 713	115 321	95 392	21	222 858	121 865	100 993	...
Gangapur City	...	...	...	...	105 396	56 009	49 387	12
Gangawati	...	...	...	...	101 392	51 211	50 181	16
Gaya	385 432	204 483	180 949	29	394 945	210 410	184 535	32
Ghatlodiya	106 684	56 219	50 465	4	...	...	...	...
Ghaziabad	968 256	521 026	447 230	145	...	...	...	...
Ghazipur	...	...	...	...	103 298	54 371	48 927	20
Giridih	...	...	...	...	105 634	55 490	50 144	11
Godhra	121 879	63 176	58 703	20	131 172	67 969	63 203	23
Gonda	120 301	66 207	54 094	15	...	...	...	...
Gondiya	120 902	61 418	59 484	18	...	...	...	...
Gorakhpur	622 701	329 807	292 894	141	...	...	...	...
Gudivada	113 054	55 867	57 187	13	...	...	...	...
Gudiyatham	...	...	...	...	100 115	49 794	50 321	14
Gulbarga	422 569	219 409	203 160	...	430 265	223 594	206 671	43
Guna	137 175	72 538	64 637	46	...	...	...	...
Guntakul	117 103	59 211	57 892	41	...	...	...	...
Guntur	514 461	257 775	256 686	46	...	...	...	...
Gurgaon	172 955	92 934	80 021	15	228 820	123 377	105 443	24
Guruvayur	...	...	...	...	138 681	64 554	74 127	57
Guwahati	809 895	440 288	369 607	217	818 809	446 311	372 498	217
Gwalior	827 026	442 343	384 683	167	865 548	465 057	400 491	180
Habra	127 602	65 141	62 461	18	239 209	121 631	117 578	37
Hajipur	119 412	63 838	55 574	20	...	...	...	...
Haldia	170 673	89 893	80 780	69	...	...	...	...
Haldwani-cum-Kathgodam	129 015	68 755	60 260	11	158 896	84 541	74 355	...

8. Population of capital cities and cities of 100 000 or more inhabitants: latest available year, 1990 - 2009
Population des capitales et des villes de 100 000 habitants ou plus : dernière année disponible, 1990 - 2009 (continued - suite)

Continent, country or area, date, code and city / Continent, pays ou zone, date, code et ville	City proper - Ville proprement dite				Urban agglomeration - Agglomération urbaine			
	Population			Surface area - Superficie (km²)	Population			Surface area - Superficie (km²)
	Both sexes - Les deux sexes	Male - Masculin	Female - Féminin		Both sexes - Les deux sexes	Male - Masculin	Female - Féminin	
ASIA - ASIE								
India - Inde[24]								
1 III 2001 (CDFC)								
Halisahar	124 510	67 151	57 359	8	...	...	...	...
Hanumangarh	129 556	69 532	60 024	13	...	...	...	...
Haora (Howrah)	1 007 532	547 068	460 464	52	...	...	...	...
Hapur	211 983	113 175	98 808	14	...	...	...	...
Hardoi	112 486	59 876	52 610	6	...	...	...	...
Hardwar	175 340	94 736	80 604	15	220 767	119 234	101 533	42
Hassan	116 574	59 743	56 831	27	133 262	68 242	65 020	30
Hathras	123 244	65 778	57 466	8	126 355	67 436	58 919	8
Hazaribag	127 269	67 900	59 369	26	135 473	72 288	63 185	27
Hindupur	125 074	64 132	60 942	38	...	...	...	...
Hisar	256 689	140 083	116 606	45	263 186	143 795	119 391	49
Hoshiarpur	149 668	79 454	70 214	35	...	...	...	...
Hospet	164 240	83 767	80 473	28	...	...	...	...
Hubli-Dharwad	786 195	403 085	383 110	213	...	...	...	...
Hugli-Chinsurah	170 206	86 788	83 418	17	...	...	...	...
Hyderabad	3 637 483	1 883 064	1 754 419	173	5 742 036	2 973 472	2 768 564	822
Ichalakaranji	257 610	136 063	121 547	30	285 860	150 977	134 883	38
Imphal	221 492	109 815	111 677	33	250 234	123 859	126 375	37
Indore	1 474 968	774 540	700 428	130	1 516 918	796 673	720 245	165
Itarsi	...	...	...	...	107 831	56 347	51 484	24
Jabalpur	932 484	488 479	444 005	119	1 098 000	580 038	517 962	205
Jagadhri	101 290	55 844	45 446	...	...	...	...	...
Jagdalpur	...	...	...	...	103 123	52 909	50 214	26
Jaipur	2 322 575	1 237 765	1 084 810	485	...	...	...	...
Jalandhar	706 043	379 439	326 604	102	714 077	383 624	330 453	...
Jalgaon	368 618	193 496	175 122	62	...	...	...	...
Jalna	235 795	121 922	113 873	82	...	...	...	...
Jalpaiguri	100 348	50 629	49 719	13	...	...	...	...
Jammu	369 959	198 956	171 003	40	612 163	334 452	277 711	202
Jamnagar	443 518	232 845	210 673	26	556 956	292 168	264 788	...
Jamshedpur	573 096	301 433	271 663	60	1 104 713	581 829	522 884	160
Jamuria	129 484	68 695	60 789	73	...	...	...	...
Jaunpur	160 055	84 203	75 852	25	...	...	...	...
Jetpur Navagadh	104 312	54 768	49 544	36	...	...	...	...
Jhansi	383 644	202 745	180 899	58	460 278	244 169	216 109	84
Jhunjhunun	100 485	52 781	47 704	37	...	...	...	...
Jind	135 855	73 407	62 448	15	...	...	...	...
Jodhpur	851 051	454 075	396 976	79	860 818	459 198	401 620	90
Jorhat	...	...	...	...	137 814	73 213	64 601	69
Junagadh	168 515	86 980	81 535	13	252 108	130 461	121 647	...
Kalthal	117 285	63 098	54 187	44	...	...	...	...
Kakinada	296 329	146 476	149 853	39	376 861	187 064	189 797	58
Kalol	100 008	53 110	46 898	17	112 013	59 539	52 474	30
Kalyan	1 193 512	633 508	560 004	105	...	...	...	...
Kamarhati	314 507	168 555	145 952	11	...	...	...	...
Kamptee	...	...	...	...	136 491	71 270	65 221	37
Kancheepuram	153 140	77 069	76 071	12	188 733	95 068	93 665	40
Kanchrapara	126 191	65 264	60 927	9	...	...	...	...
Kanhangad	65 503	31 627	33 876	40	129 367	62 002	67 365	84
Kannur	...	...	...	...	498 207	237 108	261 099	154
Kanpur	2 551 337	1 374 121	1 177 216	267	2 715 555	1 465 142	1 250 413	301
Kapra	159 002	82 579	76 423	65	...	...	...	...
Karaikkudi	...	...	...	...	125 717	62 479	63 238	43
Karawal Nagar	148 624	80 495	68 129	5	...	...	...	...
Karimnagar	205 653	105 336	100 317	24	218 302	111 875	106 427	...
Karnal	207 640	110 595	97 045	22	221 236	117 875	103 361	24
Karur	...	...	...	...	153 365	77 207	76 158	33
Katihar	175 199	93 617	81 582	25	190 873	102 161	88 712	...
Khammam	159 544	80 574	78 970	...	198 620	100 930	97 690	26
Khandwa	172 242	88 950	83 292	36	...	...	...	...
Khanna	103 099	55 276	47 823	25	...	...	...	...
Kharagpur	188 761	97 721	91 040	91	272 865	140 730	132 135	125
Khardaha	116 470	61 214	55 256	7	...	...	...	...

8. Population of capital cities and cities of 100 000 or more inhabitants: latest available year, 1990 - 2009
Population des capitales et des villes de 100 000 habitants ou plus : dernière année disponible, 1990 - 2009 (continued - suite)

Continent, country or area, date, code and city / Continent, pays ou zone, date, code et ville	City proper - Ville proprement dite				Urban agglomeration - Agglomération urbaine			
	Population			Surface area - Superficie (km²)	Population			Surface area - Superficie (km²)
	Both sexes - Les deux sexes	Male - Masculin	Female - Féminin		Both sexes - Les deux sexes	Male - Masculin	Female - Féminin	
ASIA - ASIE								
India - Inde[24]								
1 III 2001 (CDFC)								
Khargone	...	...	...	...	103 448	53 921	49 527	33
Kirari Suleman Nagar	154 633	85 362	69 271	5	...	...	...	...
Kishangarh	116 222	61 075	55 147	25	...	...	...	...
Koch Bihar	...	...	...	...	103 008	52 275	50 733	17
Kochi	595 575	294 756	300 819	95	1 355 972	670 340	685 632	453
Kolar	113 907	58 060	55 847	18	...	...	...	...
Kolhapur	493 167	255 778	237 389	67	505 541	262 258	243 283	67
Kolkata (Calcutta)	4 572 876	2 500 040	2 072 836	185	13 205 697[26]	7 064 138[26]	6 141 559[26]	1 034[26]
Kollam	361 560	177 677	183 883	41	380 091	186 924	193 167	68
Korba	315 690	164 768	150 922	35	...	...	...	...
Kota	694 316	368 451	325 865	221	703 150	373 094	330 056	226
Kothagudem	...	...	...	...	105 266	52 318	52 948	25
Kottayam	...	...	...	...	172 878	84 960	87 918	64
Kozhikode	436 556	211 888	224 668	84	880 247	429 163	451 084	235
Krishnanagar	139 110	70 576	68 534	16	148 709	75 495	73 214	18
Krishnarajapura	186 210	97 412	88 798	25	...	...	...	...
Kukatpalle	292 289	153 331	138 958	72	...	...	...	...
Kulti	289 903	152 821	137 082	100	...	...	...	...
Kumbakonam	139 954	69 785	70 169	13	160 767	80 188	80 579	15
Kurnool	269 122	136 619	132 503	15	342 973	174 190	168 783	46
Lakhimpur	121 486	65 236	56 250	7	...	...	...	...
Lal Bahadur Nagar	268 689	138 667	130 022	85	...	...	...	...
Lalitpur	111 892	58 993	52 899	...	...	...	...	...
Latur	299 985	156 547	143 438	21	...	...	...	...
Loni	120 945	65 278	55 667	7	...	...	...	...
Lucknow	2 185 927	1 156 151	1 029 776	310	2 245 509	1 189 466	1 056 043	338
Ludhiana	1 398 467	793 142	605 325	159	...	...	...	...
Machilipatnam	179 353	89 100	90 253	27	...	...	...	...
Madanapalle	...	...	...	...	107 449	54 497	52 952	13
Madhyamgram	155 451	79 728	75 723	21	...	...	...	...
Madurai	928 869	469 396	459 473	52	1 203 095	608 531	594 564	141
Mahadevapura	135 794	72 882	62 912	53	...	...	...	...
Mahbubnagar	130 986	67 007	63 979	14	139 662	71 516	68 146	14
Mahesana	...	...	...	...	141 453	74 866	66 587	...
Maheshtala	385 266	202 304	182 962	44	...	...	...	...
Mainpuri	...	...	...	...	104 851	55 462	49 389	17
Malappuram	...	...	...	...	170 409	83 709	86 700	111
Malegaon	409 403	208 864	200 539	13	...	...	...	...
Malerkotla	107 009	56 767	50 242	21	...	...	...	...
Malkajgiri	193 863	98 972	94 891	18	...	...	...	...
Mancherial	...	...	...	...	118 195	60 371	57 824	62
Mandsaur	116 505	60 269	56 236	...	117 555	60 859	56 696	...
Mandya	131 179	66 551	64 628	17	...	...	...	...
Mangalore	399 565	200 630	198 935	118	539 387	269 562	269 825	201
Mango	166 125	87 375	78 750	19	...	...	...	...
Mathura	302 770	162 021	140 749	9	323 315	174 335	148 980	22
Maunath Bhanjan	212 657	109 958	102 699	9	...	...	...	...
Medinipur	149 769	76 503	73 266	15	...	...	...	...
Meerut	1 068 772	568 081	500 691	142	1 161 716	621 481	540 235	178
Mira-Bhayandar	520 388	286 391	233 997	79	...	...	...	...
Mirzapur-cum-Vindhyachal	205 053	109 647	95 406	39	...	...	...	...
Modinagar	113 218	60 468	52 750	16	139 929	74 788	65 141	23
Moga	125 573	66 888	58 685	16	135 279	72 043	63 236	...
Moradabad	641 583	340 314	301 269	89	...	...	...	...
Morena	150 959	82 305	68 654	12	...	...	...	...
Mormugoa	...	...	...	...	104 758	55 954	48 804	40
Morvi	145 719	75 745	69 974	25	178 055	92 639	85 416	...
Motihari	100 683	54 261	46 422	14	108 428	59 148	49 280	16
Mughalsarai	...	...	...	...	116 308	61 579	54 729	29
Mumbai (Bombay)	11 978 450	6 619 966	5 358 484	603	16 434 386	9 021 789	7 412 597	1 133
Munger	188 050	101 264	86 786	18	...	...	...	...
Murwara (Katni)	187 029	97 843	89 186	107	...	...	...	...
Muzaffarnagar	316 729	167 397	149 332	...	331 668	175 283	156 385	12

8. Population of capital cities and cities of 100 000 or more inhabitants: latest available year, 1990 - 2009
Population des capitales et des villes de 100 000 habitants ou plus : dernière année disponible, 1990 - 2009 (continued - suite)

Continent, country or area, date, code and city Continent, pays ou zone, date, code et ville	City proper - Ville proprement dite				Urban agglomeration - Agglomération urbaine			
	Population			Surface area - Superficie (km²)	Population			Surface area - Superficie (km²)
	Both sexes - Les deux sexes	Male - Masculin	Female - Féminin		Both sexes - Les deux sexes	Male - Masculin	Female - Féminin	
ASIA - ASIE								
India - Inde[24]								
1 III 2001 (CDFC)								
Muzaffarpur	305 525	164 000	141 525	26	...	...	...	...
Mysore	755 379	383 480	371 899	89	799 228	406 363	392 865	132
Nabadwip	115 016	58 287	56 729	12	125 341	63 574	61 767	13
Nadiad	192 913	100 322	92 591	28	196 793	102 336	94 457	30
Nagaon	107 667	56 815	50 852	...	123 265	64 895	58 370	16
Nagercoil	208 179	102 907	105 272	24	...	...	...	...
Nagpur	2 052 066	1 059 765	992 301	218	2 129 500	1 102 009	1 027 491	229
Naihati	215 303	113 777	101 526	12	...	...	...	...
Nala Sopara	184 538	98 870	85 668	...	...	...	...	...
Nalgonda	110 286	56 299	53 987	12	111 380	56 848	54 532	51
Nanded	430 733	224 843	205 890	21	...	...	...	...
Nandyal	152 676	77 273	75 403	15	157 120	79 500	77 620	...
Nangloi Jat	150 948	82 687	68 261	7	...	...	...	...
Nashik	1 077 236	575 737	501 499	259	1 152 326	616 088	536 238	322
Navghar-Manikpur	116 723	61 757	54 966	...	...	...	...	...
Navi Mumbai (New Bombay)	704 002	395 705	308 297	133	...	...	...	...
Navsari	134 017	69 794	64 223	...	232 411	122 282	110 129	...
Neemuch	107 663	56 588	51 075	13	112 852	59 320	53 532	13
Nellore	378 428	190 522	187 906	48	404 775	203 823	200 952	...
NEW DELHI[27]	302 363	165 723	136 640	43	...	...	...	...
Neyveli	127 552	65 348	62 204	97	138 035	70 746	67 289	116
Nizamabad	288 722	146 198	142 524	37	...	...	...	...
Noida	305 058	168 958	136 100	90	...	...	...	...
North Barrackpur	123 668	63 796	59 872	9	...	...	...	...
North Dumdum	220 042	113 034	107 008	26	...	...	...	...
Ongole	150 471	76 511	73 960	27	153 829	78 242	75 587	27
Orai	139 318	74 703	64 615	20	...	...	...	...
Ozhukarai	217 707	110 042	107 665	35	...	...	...	...
Palakkad	130 767	64 379	66 388	30	197 369	96 928	100 441	59
Palanpur	110 419	58 055	52 364	20	122 300	64 365	57 935	40
Pali	187 641	99 267	88 374	84	...	...	...	...
Pallavaram	144 623	73 385	71 238	18	...	...	...	...
Palwal	100 722	53 648	47 074	8	...	...	...	...
Panchkula Urban Estate	140 925	75 897	65 028	26	...	...	...	...
Panihati	348 438	180 307	168 131	19	...	...	...	...
Panipat	261 740	143 644	118 096	21	354 148	194 850	159 298	...
Panvel	104 058	54 963	49 095	12	...	...	...	...
Parbhani	259 329	133 959	125 370	58	...	...	...	...
Patan	112 219	59 097	53 122	14	113 749	59 955	53 794	...
Pathankot	157 925	86 520	71 405	22	168 485	92 003	76 482	...
Patiala	303 151	162 573	140 578	65	323 884	173 682	150 202	...
Patna	1 366 444	746 344	620 100	99	1 697 976	922 971	775 005	135
Phagwara	...	...	...	...	102 253	55 335	46 918	...
Phusro	...	...	...	...	174 402	93 700	80 702	84
Pilibhit	124 245	65 853	58 392	10	...	...	...	...
Pimpri Chinchwad	1 012 472	547 050	465 422	171	...	...	...	...
Pollachi	...	...	...	...	128 458	64 657	63 801	29
Pondicherry	220 865	109 389	111 476	20	505 959	253 375	252 584	72
Porbandar	133 051	68 201	64 850	12	197 382	101 824	95 558	...
Proddatur	150 309	75 372	74 937	7	...	...	...	...
Pudukkottai	109 217	54 614	54 603	13	...	...	...	...
Pune	2 538 473	1 321 338	1 217 135	430	3 760 636	1 980 621	1 780 015	669
Puri	157 837	82 269	75 568	17	...	...	...	...
Purnia	171 687	92 826	78 861	45	197 211	106 313	90 898	60
Puruliya	113 806	59 092	54 714	14	...	...	...	...
Quthbullapur	231 108	120 690	110 418	47	...	...	...	...
Rae Bareli	169 333	88 911	80 422	50	...	...	...	...
Raichur	207 421	105 763	101 658	...	...	...	...	...
Raiganj	165 212	87 458	77 754	11	175 047	92 703	82 344	15
Raigarh	111 154	57 650	53 504	18	115 908	60 101	55 807	21
Raipur	605 747	314 584	291 163	56	700 113	364 436	335 677	116
Rajahmundry	315 251	158 454	156 797	52	413 616	207 869	205 747	64
Rajapalayam	122 307	61 221	61 086	10	...	...	...	...

8. Population of capital cities and cities of 100 000 or more inhabitants: latest available year, 1990 - 2009
Population des capitales et des villes de 100 000 habitants ou plus : dernière année disponible, 1990 - 2009 (continued - suite)

Continent, country or area, date, code and city / Continent, pays ou zone, date, code et ville	City proper - Ville proprement dite				Urban agglomeration - Agglomération urbaine			
	Population			Surface area - Superficie (km²)	Population			Surface area - Superficie (km²)
	Both sexes - Les deux sexes	Male - Masculin	Female - Féminin		Both sexes - Les deux sexes	Male - Masculin	Female - Féminin	
ASIA - ASIE								
India - Inde[24]								
1 III 2001 (CDFC)								
Rajarhat Gopalpur	271 811	140 218	131 593	35	...	...	...	...
Rajendranagar	143 240	74 889	68 351	52	...	...	...	...
Rajkot	967 476	506 993	460 483	105	1 003 015	525 898	477 117	163
Rajnandgaon	143 770	72 949	70 821	78	...	...	...	...
Rajpur Sonarpur	336 707	174 140	162 567	55	...	...	...	...
Ramagundam	236 600	120 687	115 913	28	237 686	121 250	116 436	...
Ramgarh	...	...	...	...	110 496	61 591	48 905	50
Rampur	281 494	146 652	134 842	20	...	...	...	...
Ranaghat	...	...	...	...	145 285	73 933	71 352	25
Ranchi	847 093	450 727	396 366	177	863 495	459 462	404 033	182
Raniganj	111 116	59 270	51 846	23	...	...	...	...
Ratlam	222 202	114 370	107 832	39	234 419	120 874	113 545	41
Raurkela	224 987	121 240	103 747	133	484 874	258 731	226 143	157
Raurkela Industrialship	206 693	109 394	97 299	122	...	...	...	...
Rewa	183 274	98 793	84 481	55	...	...	...	...
Rewari	100 684	53 935	46 749	12	...	...	...	...
Rishra	113 305	62 585	50 720	6	...	...	...	...
Robertson Pet	141 424	70 619	70 805	...	157 084	78 578	78 506	...
Rohtak	286 807	154 148	132 659	28	294 577	158 287	136 290	...
Roorkee	...	...	...	...	115 278	64 240	51 038	17
S.A.S. Nagar (Mohali)	123 484	65 642	57 842	24	...	...	...	...
Sagar	232 133	122 385	109 748	36	308 922	162 919	146 003	52
Saharanpur	455 754	241 508	214 246	26	...	...	...	...
Saharasa	125 167	67 718	57 449	21	...	...	...	...
Salem	696 760	353 933	342 827	91	751 438	382 211	369 227	108
Sambalpur	153 643	79 683	73 960	50	226 469	117 745	108 724	90
Sambhal	182 478	97 011	85 467	16	...	...	...	...
Sangli-Miraj-Kupwad	436 781	224 300	212 481	118	447 774	229 958	217 816	121
Santipur	138 235	70 089	68 146	25	...	...	...	...
Sasaram	131 172	69 682	61 490	11	...	...	...	...
Satara	108 048	55 938	52 110	...	...	...	...	...
Satna	225 464	120 277	105 187	...	229 307	122 401	106 906	...
Sawai Madhopur	...	...	...	...	101 997	53 903	48 094	60
Secunderabad	206 102	104 335	101 767	40	...	...	...	...
Serampore	197 857	105 415	92 442	15	...	...	...	...
Serilingampalle	153 364	79 225	74 139	98	...	...	...	...
Shahjahanpur	296 662	160 178	136 484	13	321 885	174 276	147 609	23
Shillong	132 867	66 106	66 761	10	267 662	134 497	133 165	25
Shimla	142 555	81 186	61 369	29	144 975	82 840	62 135	30
Shimoga	274 352	140 224	134 128	...	...	...	...	...
Shivapuri	146 892	78 433	68 459	81	...	...	...	...
Sikar	185 323	96 379	88 944	23	185 925	96 697	89 228	...
Silchar	142 199	72 679	69 520	16	184 105	94 306	89 799	...
Siliguri	472 374	250 645	221 729	42	...	...	...	...
Singrauli	185 190	100 149	85 041	...	...	...	...	...
Sirsa	160 735	85 993	74 742	19	...	...	...	...
Sitapur	151 908	79 767	72 141	26	...	...	...	...
Sivakasi	...	...	...	...	121 358	60 841	60 517	27
Siwan	109 919	58 262	51 657	13	...	...	...	...
Solapur	872 478	444 734	427 744	179	...	...	...	...
Sonipat	214 974	117 020	97 954	28	225 074	122 480	102 594	...
South Dum Dum	392 444	200 298	192 146	14	...	...	...	...
Srikakulam	109 905	54 926	54 979	12	117 320	58 753	58 567	14
Srinagar	898 440	484 627	413 813	184	988 210	537 512	450 698	243
Sultan Pur Majra	164 426	88 729	75 697	3	...	...	...	...
Sultanpur	100 065	53 189	46 876	12	...	...	...	...
Surat	2 433 835	1 372 415	1 061 420	112	2 811 614	1 597 156	1 214 458	237
Surendranagar Dudhrej	156 161	81 377	74 784	39	...	...	...	...
Tadepalligudem	102 622	50 925	51 697	21	...	...	...	...
Tambaram	137 933	70 419	67 514	21	...	...	...	...
Tenali	153 756	77 404	76 352	15	...	...	...	...
Tezpur	...	...	...	...	105 377	59 869	45 508	23
Thane	1 262 551	675 147	587 404	128	...	...	...	...

Continent, country or area, date, code and city / Continent, pays ou zone, date, code et ville	City proper - Ville proprement dite				Urban agglomeration - Agglomération urbaine			
	Population			Surface area - Superficie (km²)	Population			Surface area - Superficie (km²)
	Both sexes - Les deux sexes	Male - Masculin	Female - Féminin		Both sexes - Les deux sexes	Male - Masculin	Female - Féminin	
ASIA - ASIE								
India - Inde[24]								
1 III 2001 (CDFC)								
Thanesar	119 687	65 525	54 162	33	122 319	66 978	55 341	36
Thanjavur	215 314	106 625	108 689	15	...	...	...	...
Thiruvananthapuram	744 983	366 235	378 748	142	889 635	437 407	452 228	178
Thoothukkudi (Tuticorin)	216 054	107 758	108 296	13	243 415	121 428	121 987	140
Thrissur	317 526	154 248	163 278	...	330 122	160 443	169 679	88
Tinsukia	...	...	...	...	108 123	59 561	48 562	26
Tiruchchirappalli	752 066	376 125	375 941	147	866 354	434 321	432 033	196
Tirunelveli	411 831	203 232	208 599	109	433 352	214 133	219 219	135
Tirupati	228 202	118 187	110 015	16	303 521	155 468	148 053	20
Tiruppur	344 543	179 930	164 613	27	550 826	286 862	263 964	147
Tiruvannamalai	130 567	66 125	64 442	14	...	...	...	...
Tiruvottiyur	212 281	108 720	103 561	21	...	...	...	...
Titagarh	124 213	70 705	53 508	3	...	...	...	...
Tonk	135 689	70 255	65 434	61	...	...	...	...
Tumkur	248 929	129 273	119 656	...	...	...	...	...
Udaipur	389 438	205 335	184 103	64	...	...	...	...
Udupi	113 112	55 893	57 219	64	127 124	62 596	64 528	73
Ujjain	430 427	223 998	206 429	...	431 162	224 475	206 687	92
Ulhasnagar	473 731	251 888	221 843	13	...	...	...	...
Uluberia	202 135	105 843	96 292	34	...	...	...	...
Unnao	144 662	76 254	68 408	21	...	...	...	...
Uppal Kalan	117 217	60 857	56 360	20	...	...	...	...
Uttarpara Kotrung	150 363	78 808	71 555	16	...	...	...	...
Vadakara	...	...	...	...	124 083	59 803	64 280	51
Vadodara	1 306 227	684 013	622 214	108	1 491 045	782 251	708 794	214
Valsad	...	...	...	...	145 592	75 216	70 376	...
Vaniyambadi	...	...	...	...	103 950	51 886	52 064	16
Varanasi	1 091 918	582 096	509 822	92	1 203 961	643 043	560 918	111
Vasai	...	...	...	...	174 396	91 030	83 366	...
Vejalpur	113 445	58 878	54 567	7	...	...	...	...
Vellore	177 230	87 977	89 253	12	386 746	193 176	193 570	62
Veraval	141 357	72 148	69 209	38	158 032	80 889	77 143	41
Vidisha	125 453	66 572	58 881	6	...	...	...	...
Vijayawada	851 282	431 243	420 039	60	1 039 518	527 307	512 211	101
Virar	118 928	63 704	55 224	20	...	...	...	...
Visakhapatnam	982 904	501 406	481 498	112	1 345 938	687 985	657 953	326
Vizianagarm	174 651	86 375	88 276	21	195 801	97 032	98 769	30
Wadhwan	...	...	...	...	219 585	114 175	105 410	59
Warangal	530 636	268 954	261 682	68	579 216	293 709	285 507	97
Wardha	111 118	57 499	53 619	8	...	...	...	...
Yamunanagar	189 696	101 782	87 914	16	306 740	166 137	140 603	42
Yavatmal	120 676	61 780	58 896	10	139 835	71 908	67 927	13
Indonesia - Indonésie								
31 X 2005 (SSDF)								
Ambon	204 218[28]	102 464[28]	101 754[28]	359	...	...	...	...
Balikpapan	440 552[28]	223 192[28]	217 360[28]	503	...	...	...	...
Bandar Lampung	790 057[28]	397 214[28]	392 843[28]	193	...	...	...	...
Bandjarmasin	576 413[28]	289 619[28]	286 794[28]	72	...	...	...	...
Bandung	2 288 570[28]	1 150 954[28]	1 137 616[28]	1 670	...	...	...	...
Batam	587 227[28]	277 877[28]	309 350[28]	969	...	...	...	...
Bengkulu	252 768[28]	122 801[28]	129 967[28]	145	...	...	...	...
Binjai	222 299[28]	112 218[28]	110 081[28]	9	...	...	...	...
Bitung	131 999[28]	69 469[28]	62 530[28]	304	...	...	...	...
Blitar	126 776[28]	62 310[28]	64 466[28]	33	...	...	...	...
Bogor	891 467[28]	440 346[28]	451 121[28]	119	...	...	...	...
Cirebon (Tjirebon)	312 771[28]	156 411[28]	156 360[28]	37	...	...	...	...
Denpasar	574 610[28]	288 621[28]	285 989[28]	124	...	...	...	...
Gorontalo	137 461[28]	65 153[28]	72 308[28]	65	...	...	...	...
JAKARTA	8 820 603[28]	4 380 888[28]	4 439 715[28]	740	...	...	...	...
Jambi	409 202[28]	212 043[28]	197 159[28]	205	...	...	...	...
Jayapura	164 220[28]	86 625[28]	77 595[28]	740	...	...	...	...
Kediri	248 640[28]	122 227[28]	126 413[28]	63	...	...	...	...

8. Population of capital cities and cities of 100 000 or more inhabitants: latest available year, 1990 - 2009
Population des capitales et des villes de 100 000 habitants ou plus : dernière année disponible, 1990 - 2009 (continued - suite)

Continent, country or area, date, code and city / Continent, pays ou zone, date, code et ville	City proper - Ville proprement dite				Urban agglomeration - Agglomération urbaine			
	Population			Surface area - Superficie (km²)	Population			Surface area - Superficie (km²)
	Both sexes - Les deux sexes	Male - Masculin	Female - Féminin		Both sexes - Les deux sexes	Male - Masculin	Female - Féminin	
ASIA - ASIE								
Indonesia - Indonésie								
31 X 2005 (SSDF)								
Madiun	171 390[28]	81 758[28]	89 632[28]	34	...	...	...	...
Magelang	124 374[28]	60 761[28]	63 613[28]	18	...	...	...	...
Makasar (Ujung Pandang)	1 168 258[28]	562 358[28]	605 900[28]	199	...	...	...	...
Malang	773 174[28]	386 100[28]	387 074[28]	145	...	...	...	...
Manado	370 139[28]	184 415[28]	185 724[28]	157	...	...	...	...
Mataram	342 896[28]	173 511[28]	169 385[28]	61	...	...	...	...
Medan	2 029 797[28]	984 046[28]	1 045 751[28]	265	...	...	...	...
Mojokerto	111 860[28]	54 738[28]	57 122[28]	16	...	...	...	...
Padang	686 908[28]	336 655[28]	350 253[28]	694	...	...	...	...
Pakalongan	263 921[28]	128 347[28]	135 574[28]	45	...	...	...	...
Pakanbaru	703 956[28]	351 598[28]	352 358[28]	632	...	...	...	...
Palangkaraya	148 139[28]	74 497[28]	73 642[28]	2 400	...	...	...	...
Palembang	1 323 169[28]	651 161[28]	672 008[28]	369	...	...	...	...
Pangkal Pinang	139 385[28]	70 995[28]	68 390[28]	89	...	...	...	...
Pare Pare	101 453[28]	50 153[28]	51 300[28]	99	...	...	...	...
Pasuruan	166 519[28]	84 375[28]	82 144[28]	35	...	...	...	...
Pematang Siantar	229 525[28]	114 684[28]	114 841[28]	80	...	...	...	...
Pontianak	501 843[28]	252 304[28]	249 539[28]	108	...	...	...	...
Probolinggo	168 734[28]	83 946[28]	84 788[28]	57	...	...	...	...
Salatiga	152 913[28]	74 184[28]	78 729[28]	57	...	...	...	...
Samarinda	505 664[28]	262 407[28]	243 257[28]	781	...	...	...	...
Semarang	1 352 869[28]	674 649[28]	678 220[28]	374	...	...	...	...
Sukabumi	280 373[28]	145 910[28]	134 463[28]	48	...	...	...	...
Surabaya	2 611 506[28]	1 270 795[28]	1 340 711[28]	351	...	...	...	...
Surakarta	506 397[28]	251 977[28]	254 420[28]	44	...	...	...	...
Tangerang	1 451 595[28]	740 589[28]	711 006[28]	187	...	...	...	...
Tanjung Balai	133 897[28]	65 893[28]	68 004[28]	68	...	...	...	...
Tebing Tinggi	134 548[28]	65 801[28]	68 747[28]	32	...	...	...	...
Tegal	238 676[28]	119 457[28]	119 219[28]	35	...	...	...	...
Yogyakarta	433 539[28]	216 222[28]	217 317[28]	33	...	...	...	...
Iran (Islamic Republic of) - Iran (République islamique d')								
28 X 2006 (CDJC)								
Abadan	219 772	...	...	...	...	...	...	...
Ahwaz	985 614	...	...	...	...	...	...	...
Amol	199 698	...	...	...	...	...	...	...
Andimeshk	120 177	...	...	...	...	...	...	...
Arak	446 760	...	...	...	...	...	...	...
Ardabil	418 262	...	...	...	...	...	...	...
Babol	201 335	...	...	...	...	...	...	...
Bandar Anzali	110 643	...	...	...	...	...	...	...
Bandar-e-Abbas	379 301	...	...	...	...	...	...	...
Bandar-e-Mahshahr	111 448	...	...	...	...	...	...	...
Behbahan	101 178	...	...	...	...	...	...	...
Birjand	166 138	...	...	...	...	...	...	...
Bojnurd	176 726	...	...	...	...	...	...	...
Borujerd	229 541	...	...	...	...	...	...	...
Bukand	150 703	...	...	...	...	...	...	...
Bushehr	169 966	...	...	...	...	...	...	...
Dezful	235 819	...	...	...	...	...	...	...
Dorud	101 219	...	...	...	...	...	...	...
Esfahan	1 602 110	...	...	...	...	...	...	...
Golestan (Soltanabad)	231 905	...	...	...	...	...	...	...
Gonbad-e-Kavus	129 167	...	...	...	...	...	...	...
Gorgan	274 438	...	...	...	...	...	...	...
Hamadan	479 640	...	...	...	...	...	...	...
Ilam	160 355	...	...	...	...	...	...	...
Iranshahr	100 642	...	...	...	...	...	...	...
Islam Shahr (Qasemabad)	357 389	...	...	...	...	...	...	...
Izeh	104 364	...	...	...	...	...	...	...
Jahrom	105 285	...	...	...	...	...	...	...

8. Population of capital cities and cities of 100 000 or more inhabitants: latest available year, 1990 - 2009
Population des capitales et des villes de 100 000 habitants ou plus : dernière année disponible, 1990 - 2009 (continued - suite)

Continent, country or area, date, code and city	City proper - Ville proprement dite				Urban agglomeration - Agglomération urbaine			
	Population			Surface area - Superficie (km²)	Population			Surface area - Superficie (km²)
Continent, pays ou zone, date, code et ville	Both sexes - Les deux sexes	Male - Masculin	Female - Féminin		Both sexes - Les deux sexes	Male - Masculin	Female - Féminin	
ASIA - ASIE								
Iran (Islamic Republic of) - Iran (République islamique d')								
28 X 2006 (CDJC)								
Karaj	1 386 030	...	...	...	...	...	...	...
Kashan	253 509	...	...	...	...	...	...	...
Kerman	515 114	...	...	...	...	...	...	...
Kermanshah	794 863	...	...	...	...	...	...	...
Khomeini shahr	223 071	...	...	...	...	...	...	...
Khoramabad	333 945	...	...	...	...	...	...	...
Khoramshahr	125 859	...	...	...	...	...	...	...
Khoy	181 465	...	...	...	...	...	...	...
Mahabad	135 780	...	...	...	...	...	...	...
Malard	228 713	...	...	...	...	...	...	...
Malayer	156 289	...	...	...	...	...	...	...
Marand	114 841	...	...	...	...	...	...	...
Maraqeh	149 929	...	...	...	...	...	...	...
Marvadsht	124 350	...	...	...	...	...	...	...
Mashhad	2 427 316	...	...	...	...	...	...	...
Masjed Soleyman	108 682	...	...	...	...	...	...	...
Miandoab	114 153	...	...	...	...	...	...	...
Najafabad	208 647	...	...	...	...	...	...	...
Nasim Shahr	135 846	...	...	...	...	...	...	...
Neyshabur	208 860	...	...	...	...	...	...	...
Orumiyeh	583 255	...	...	...	...	...	...	...
Pakdasht	126 937	...	...	...	...	...	...	...
Qaem shahr	174 768	...	...	...	...	...	...	...
Qarchak	174 006	...	...	...	...	...	...	...
Qazvin	355 338	...	...	...	...	...	...	...
Qods	230 147	...	...	...	...	...	...	...
Qom	964 706	...	...	...	...	...	...	...
Quchan	101 313	...	...	...	...	...	...	...
Rafsanjan	139 219	...	...	...	...	...	...	...
Rasht	557 366	...	...	...	...	...	...	...
Sabzewar	214 582	...	...	...	...	...	...	...
Sanandaj	316 862	...	...	...	...	...	...	...
Saqez	133 331	...	...	...	...	...	...	...
Sari	261 293	...	...	...	...	...	...	...
Saveh	180 548	...	...	...	...	...	...	...
Semnan	126 780	...	...	...	...	...	...	...
Shahinshahr	127 412	...	...	...	...	...	...	...
Shahr-e-Kord	131 612	...	...	...	...	...	...	...
Shahreza	109 601	...	...	...	...	...	...	...
Shahriar	189 421	...	...	...	...	...	...	...
Shahrud	132 379	...	...	...	...	...	...	...
Shiraz	1 227 331	...	...	...	...	...	...	...
Sirjan	170 916	...	...	...	...	...	...	...
Tabriz	1 398 060	...	...	...	...	...	...	...
TEHRAN	7 088 287	...	...	...	...	...	...	...
Torbat-e-heydariyeh	121 300	...	...	...	...	...	...	...
Varamin	208 996	...	...	...	...	...	...	...
Yasooj	100 544	...	...	...	...	...	...	...
Yazd	432 194	...	...	...	...	...	...	...
Zabol	136 956	...	...	...	...	...	...	...
Zahedan	567 449	...	...	...	...	...	...	...
Zanjan	349 713	...	...	...	...	...	...	...
Israel - Israël								
1 VII 2009 (ESDJ)								
Ashdod	205 401	100 437	104 964	47	...	...	...	...
Ashqelon	111 223	54 057	57 165	48	...	...	...	...
Bat Yam	130 162	61 686	68 476	8	...	...	...	...
Be'er Sheva	193 920	94 310	99 610	53	...	...	...	...
Bene Beraq	153 165	77 400	75 765	7	...	...	...	...
Haifa	265 021	126 581	138 440	64	...	...	...	...
Holon	180 552	87 613	92 939	19	...	...	...	...
JERUSALEM[29]	766 701	380 219	386 482	125	...	...	...	...

8. Population of capital cities and cities of 100 000 or more inhabitants: latest available year, 1990 - 2009
Population des capitales et des villes de 100 000 habitants ou plus : dernière année disponible, 1990 - 2009 (continued - suite)

Continent, country or area, date, code and city Continent, pays ou zone, date, code et ville	City proper - Ville proprement dite				Urban agglomeration - Agglomération urbaine			
	Population			Surface area - Superficie (km²)	Population			Surface area - Superficie (km²)
	Both sexes - Les deux sexes	Male - Masculin	Female - Féminin		Both sexes - Les deux sexes	Male - Masculin	Female - Féminin	
ASIA - ASIE								
Israel - Israël								
1 VII 2009 (ESDJ)								
Netanya	181 702	88 032	93 670	29	...	...	...	...
Petah Tiqwa	204 962	100 068	104 894	36	...	...	...	...
Ramat Gan	144 315	68 659	75 656	13	...	...	...	...
Rehovot	111 877	54 716	57 160	23	...	...	...	...
Rishon Leziyyon	227 567	111 652	115 915	59	...	...	...	...
Tel Aviv-Yafo	403 259	196 135	207 124	52	...	...	...	...
Japan - Japon								
1 X 2005 (CDJC)								
Abiko	131 205[30]	64 853[30]	66 352[30]	43	...	...	...	...
Ageo	220 232[30]	110 102[30]	110 130[30]	46	...	...	...	...
Aizuwakamatsu	122 248[30]	58 067[30]	64 181[30]	343	...	...	...	...
Akashi	291 027[30]	141 749[30]	149 278[30]	49	...	...	...	...
Akishima	110 143[30]	55 446[30]	54 697[30]	17	...	...	...	...
Akita	333 109[30]	158 107[30]	175 002[30]	906	...	...	...	...
Amagasaki	462 647[30]	226 084[30]	236 563[30]	50	...	...	...	...
Anjo	170 250[30]	87 022[30]	83 228[30]	86	...	...	...	...
Aomori	311 508[30]	145 965[30]	165 543[30]	825	...	...	...	...
Asahikawa	355 004[30]	165 387[30]	189 617[30]	748	...	...	...	...
Asaka	124 393[30]	65 460[30]	58 933[30]	18	...	...	...	...
Ashikaga	159 756[30]	78 120[30]	81 636[30]	178	...	...	...	...
Atsugi	222 403[30]	116 150[30]	106 253[30]	94	...	...	...	...
Beppu	126 959[30]	57 392[30]	69 567[30]	125	...	...	...	...
Chiba	924 319[30]	462 961[30]	461 358[30]	272	...	...	...	...
Chigasaki	228 420[30]	113 272[30]	115 148[30]	36	...	...	...	...
Chikusei	112 581[30]	55 795[30]	56 786[30]	205	...	...	...	...
Chofu	216 119[30]	109 098[30]	107 021[30]	22	...	...	...	...
Daito	126 504[30]	62 840[30]	63 664[30]	18	...	...	...	...
Ebetsu	125 601[30]	60 807[30]	64 794[30]	188	...	...	...	...
Ebina	123 764[30]	63 089[30]	60 675[30]	26	...	...	...	...
Fuchu	245 623[30]	127 575[30]	118 048[30]	29	...	...	...	...
Fuji	236 474[30]	117 069[30]	119 405[30]	214	...	...	...	...
Fujieda	129 248[30]	62 921[30]	66 327[30]	141	...	...	...	...
Fujimi	104 748[30]	52 491[30]	52 257[30]	20	...	...	...	...
Fujimino	101 960[30]	51 349[30]	50 611[30]	15	...	...	...	...
Fujinomiya	121 779[30]	60 113[30]	61 666[30]	315	...	...	...	...
Fujisawa	396 014[30]	198 365[30]	197 649[30]	70	...	...	...	...
Fukaya	103 529[30]	51 692[30]	51 837[30]	69	...	...	...	...
Fukui	252 220[30]	122 750[30]	129 470[30]	341	...	...	...	...
Fukuoka	1 401 279[30]	673 097[30]	728 182[30]	341	...	...	...	...
Fukushima	290 869[30]	140 013[30]	150 856[30]	746	...	...	...	...
Fukuyama	418 509[30]	201 999[30]	216 510[30]	461	...	...	...	...
Funabashi	569 835[30]	288 667[30]	281 168[30]	86	...	...	...	...
Gifu	399 931[30]	189 633[30]	210 298[30]	195	...	...	...	...
Habikino	118 695[30]	56 447[30]	62 248[30]	26	...	...	...	...
Hachinohe	244 700[30]	117 446[30]	127 254[30]	305	...	...	...	...
Hachioji	560 012[30]	286 154[30]	273 858[30]	186	...	...	...	...
Hadano	168 317[30]	86 664[30]	81 653[30]	104	...	...	...	...
Hakodate	294 264[30]	134 868[30]	159 396[30]	678	...	...	...	...
Hakusan	109 450[30]	53 129[30]	56 321[30]	755	...	...	...	...
Hamamatsu	804 032[30]	399 704[30]	404 328[30]	1 511	...	...	...	...
Handa	115 845[30]	57 626[30]	58 219[30]	47	...	...	...	...
Higashihiroshima	184 430[30]	93 960[30]	90 470[30]	635	...	...	...	...
Higashikurume	115 330[30]	57 123[30]	58 207[30]	13	...	...	...	...
Higashimurayama	144 929[30]	71 635[30]	73 294[30]	17	...	...	...	...
Higashiosaka	513 821[30]	251 708[30]	262 113[30]	62	...	...	...	...
Hikone	109 779[30]	54 136[30]	55 643[30]	98	...	...	...	...
Himeji	482 304[30]	232 553[30]	249 751[30]	276	...	...	...	...
Hino	176 538[30]	90 636[30]	85 902[30]	28	...	...	...	...
Hirakata	404 044[30]	195 236[30]	208 808[30]	65	...	...	...	...
Hiratsuka	258 958[30]	132 156[30]	126 802[30]	68	...	...	...	...

8. Population of capital cities and cities of 100 000 or more inhabitants: latest available year, 1990 - 2009
Population des capitales et des villes de 100 000 habitants ou plus : dernière année disponible, 1990 - 2009 (continued - suite)

Continent, country or area, date, code and city / Continent, pays ou zone, date, code et ville	City proper - Ville proprement dite				Urban agglomeration - Agglomération urbaine			
	Population			Surface area - Superficie (km²)	Population			Surface area - Superficie (km²)
	Both sexes - Les deux sexes	Male - Masculin	Female - Féminin		Both sexes - Les deux sexes	Male - Masculin	Female - Féminin	
ASIA - ASIE								
Japan - Japon								
1 X 2005 (CDJC)								
Hirosaki	173 221[30]	79 299[30]	93 922[30]	274	...	...	...	...
Hiroshima	1 154 391[30]	559 345[30]	595 046[30]	905	...	...	...	...
Hitachi	199 218[30]	99 212[30]	100 006[30]	226	...	...	...	...
Hitachinaka	153 639[30]	77 331[30]	76 308[30]	99	...	...	...	...
Hofu	116 818[30]	56 332[30]	60 486[30]	189	...	...	...	...
Ibaraki	267 961[30]	131 135[30]	136 826[30]	77	...	...	...	...
Ichihara	280 255[30]	143 404[30]	136 851[30]	368	...	...	...	...
Ichikawa	466 608[30]	239 659[30]	226 949[30]	57	...	...	...	...
Ichinomiya	371 687[30]	181 614[30]	190 073[30]	114	...	...	...	...
Ichinoseki	125 818[30]	60 793[30]	65 025[30]	1 133	...	...	...	...
Iga	100 623[30]	48 675[30]	51 948[30]	558	...	...	...	...
Iida	108 624[30]	51 706[30]	56 918[30]	659	...	...	...	...
Ikeda	101 616[30]	49 682[30]	51 934[30]	22	...	...	...	...
Ikoma	113 686[30]	53 937[30]	59 749[30]	53	...	...	...	...
Imabari	173 983[30]	80 745[30]	93 238[30]	420	...	...	...	...
Inazawa	136 965[30]	67 754[30]	69 211[30]	79	...	...	...	...
Iruma	148 576[30]	73 574[30]	75 002[30]	45	...	...	...	...
Isahaya	144 034[30]	68 154[30]	75 880[30]	312	...	...	...	...
Isehara	100 579[30]	51 630[30]	48 949[30]	56	...	...	...	...
Isesaki	202 447[30]	101 019[30]	101 428[30]	139	...	...	...	...
Ishinomaki	167 324[30]	80 553[30]	86 771[30]	556	...	...	...	...
Itami	192 250[30]	94 232[30]	98 018[30]	25	...	...	...	...
Iwaki	354 492[30]	172 169[30]	182 323[30]	1 231	...	...	...	...
Iwakuni	103 507[30]	49 240[30]	54 267[30]	222	...	...	...	...
Iwata	170 899[30]	86 262[30]	84 637[30]	164	...	...	...	...
Izumi (Osaka)	177 856[30]	86 339[30]	91 517[30]	85	...	...	...	...
Izumo	146 307[30]	69 901[30]	76 406[30]	543	...	...	...	...
Joetsu	208 082[30]	100 884[30]	107 198[30]	973	...	...	...	...
Kadoma	131 706[30]	65 229[30]	66 477[30]	12	...	...	...	...
Kagoshima	604 367[30]	281 389[30]	322 978[30]	547	...	...	...	...
Kakamigahara	144 174[30]	70 696[30]	73 478[30]	88	...	...	...	...
Kakegawa	117 857[30]	58 862[30]	58 995[30]	266	...	...	...	...
Kakogawa	267 100[30]	130 694[30]	136 406[30]	139	...	...	...	...
Kamagaya	102 812[30]	50 969[30]	51 843[30]	21	...	...	...	...
Kamakura	171 158[30]	81 443[30]	89 715[30]	40	...	...	...	...
Kanazawa	454 607[30]	220 679[30]	233 928[30]	468	...	...	...	...
Karatsu	128 564[30]	59 962[30]	68 602[30]	425	...	...	...	...
Kariya	142 134[30]	74 800[30]	67 334[30]	50	...	...	...	...
Kashihara	124 728[30]	59 792[30]	64 936[30]	40	...	...	...	...
Kashiwa	380 963[30]	190 138[30]	190 825[30]	115	...	...	...	...
Kasuga	108 402[30]	52 815[30]	55 587[30]	14	...	...	...	...
Kasugai	295 802[30]	147 732[30]	148 070[30]	93	...	...	...	...
Kasukabe	238 506[30]	118 931[30]	119 575[30]	66	...	...	...	...
Kawachinagano	117 239[30]	55 618[30]	61 621[30]	110	...	...	...	...
Kawagoe	333 795[30]	168 943[30]	164 852[30]	109	...	...	...	...
Kawaguchi	480 079[30]	246 310[30]	233 769[30]	56	...	...	...	...
Kawanishi	157 668[30]	74 928[30]	82 740[30]	53	...	...	...	...
Kawasaki	1 327 011[30]	687 080[30]	639 931[30]	143	...	...	...	...
Kiryu	128 037[30]	61 796[30]	66 241[30]	275	...	...	...	...
Kisarazu	122 234[30]	60 947[30]	61 287[30]	139	...	...	...	...
Kishiwada	201 000[30]	96 866[30]	104 134[30]	72	...	...	...	...
Kitakyushu[31]	993 525[30]	466 779[30]	526 746[30]	488	...	...	...	...
Kitami	110 715[30]	53 484[30]	57 231[30]	421	...	...	...	...
Kobe	1 525 393[30]	724 427[30]	800 966[30]	552	...	...	...	...
Kochi	333 484[30]	155 025[30]	178 459[30]	264	...	...	...	...
Kodaira	183 796[30]	91 756[30]	92 040[30]	20	...	...	...	...
Kofu	194 244[30]	95 535[30]	98 709[30]	172	...	...	...	...
Koga	145 265[30]	72 399[30]	72 866[30]	124	...	...	...	...
Koganei	114 112[30]	57 696[30]	56 416[30]	11	...	...	...	...

8. Population of capital cities and cities of 100 000 or more inhabitants: latest available year, 1990 - 2009
Population des capitales et des villes de 100 000 habitants ou plus : dernière année disponible, 1990 - 2009 (continued - suite)

Continent, country or area, date, code and city / Continent, pays ou zone, date, code et ville	City proper - Ville proprement dite				Urban agglomeration - Agglomération urbaine			
	Population			Surface area - Superficie (km²)	Population			Surface area - Superficie (km²)
	Both sexes - Les deux sexes	Male - Masculin	Female - Féminin		Both sexes - Les deux sexes	Male - Masculin	Female - Féminin	

ASIA - ASIE

Japan - Japon
1 X 2005 (CDJC)

Continent, country or area, date, code and city	Both sexes	Male	Female	Surface area (km²)	Both sexes	Male	Female	Surface area (km²)
Kokubunji	117 604[30]	58 889[30]	58 715[30]	11	...	...	...	...
Komaki	147 182[30]	74 526[30]	72 656[30]	63	...	...	...	...
Komatsu	109 084[30]	52 782[30]	56 302[30]	371	...	...	...	...
Konosu	119 594[30]	59 595[30]	59 999[30]	67	...	...	...	...
Koriyama	338 834[30]	167 071[30]	171 763[30]	757	...	...	...	...
Koshigaya	315 792[30]	158 721[30]	157 071[30]	60	...	...	...	...
Kumagaya	191 107[30]	95 743[30]	95 364[30]	137	...	...	...	...
Kumamoto	669 603[30]	316 048[30]	353 555[30]	267	...	...	...	...
Kurashiki	469 377[30]	227 334[30]	242 043[30]	354	...	...	...	...
Kure	251 003[30]	120 435[30]	130 568[30]	353	...	...	...	...
Kurume	306 434[30]	145 210[30]	161 224[30]	230	...	...	...	...
Kusatsu	121 159[30]	63 071[30]	58 088[30]	48	...	...	...	...
Kushiro	181 516[30]	86 007[30]	95 509[30]	222	...	...	...	...
Kuwana	138 963[30]	68 145[30]	70 818[30]	137	...	...	...	...
Kyoto	1 474 811[30]	703 210[30]	771 601[30]	828	...	...	...	...
Machida	405 534[30]	200 197[30]	205 337[30]	72	...	...	...	...
Maebashi	318 584[30]	155 480[30]	163 104[30]	241	...	...	...	...
Marugame	110 085[30]	53 090[30]	56 995[30]	112	...	...	...	...
Matsubara	127 276[30]	61 776[30]	65 500[30]	17	...	...	...	...
Matsudo	472 579[30]	237 562[30]	235 017[30]	61	...	...	...	...
Matsue	196 603[30]	94 638[30]	101 965[30]	530	...	...	...	...
Matsumoto	227 627[30]	112 083[30]	115 544[30]	919	...	...	...	...
Matsusaka	168 973[30]	81 320[30]	87 653[30]	624	...	...	...	...
Matsuyama	514 937[30]	242 463[30]	272 474[30]	429	...	...	...	...
Mihara	104 196[30]	49 729[30]	54 467[30]	471	...	...	...	...
Minoh	127 135[30]	61 286[30]	65 849[30]	48	...	...	...	...
Misato	128 278[30]	65 307[30]	62 971[30]	30	...	...	...	...
Mishima	112 241[30]	55 054[30]	57 187[30]	62	...	...	...	...
Mitaka	177 016[30]	88 579[30]	88 437[30]	17	...	...	...	...
Mito	262 603[30]	127 435[30]	135 168[30]	217	...	...	...	...
Miyakonojo	133 062[30]	62 426[30]	70 636[30]	306	...	...	...	...
Miyazaki	310 123[30]	145 263[30]	164 860[30]	287	...	...	...	...
Moriguchi	147 465[30]	71 972[30]	75 493[30]	13	...	...	...	...
Morioka	287 192[30]	137 262[30]	149 930[30]	489	...	...	...	...
Musashino	137 525[30]	66 628[30]	70 897[30]	11	...	...	...	...
Nagano	378 512[30]	183 065[30]	195 447[30]	731	...	...	...	...
Nagaoka	236 344[30]	115 726[30]	120 618[30]	526	...	...	...	...
Nagareyama	152 641[30]	75 643[30]	76 998[30]	35	...	...	...	...
Nagasaki	442 699[30]	203 292[30]	239 407[30]	339	...	...	...	...
Nagoya	2 215 062[30]	1 099 582[30]	1 115 480[30]	326	...	...	...	...
Naha	312 393[30]	150 463[30]	161 930[30]	39	...	...	...	...
Nara	370 102[30]	174 469[30]	195 633[30]	277	...	...	...	...
Narashino	158 785[30]	80 308[30]	78 477[30]	21	...	...	...	...
Narita	100 717[30]	50 592[30]	50 125[30]	131	...	...	...	...
Nasushiobara	115 032[30]	57 184[30]	57 848[30]	593	...	...	...	...
Neyagawa	241 816[30]	118 593[30]	123 223[30]	25	...	...	...	...
Niigata	785 134[30]	378 725[30]	406 409[30]	650	...	...	...	...
Niihama	123 952[30]	59 190[30]	64 762[30]	234	...	...	...	...
Niiza	153 305[30]	77 310[30]	75 995[30]	23	...	...	...	...
Nishinomiya	465 337[30]	221 205[30]	244 132[30]	99	...	...	...	...
Nishio	104 321[30]	52 584[30]	51 737[30]	76	...	...	...	...
Nishitokyo	189 735[30]	94 046[30]	95 689[30]	16	...	...	...	...
Nobeoka	121 635[30]	56 816[30]	64 819[30]	284	...	...	...	...
Noda	151 240[30]	75 797[30]	75 443[30]	104	...	...	...	...
Numazu	208 005[30]	102 259[30]	105 746[30]	187	...	...	...	...
Obihiro	170 580[30]	81 906[30]	88 674[30]	619	...	...	...	...
Odawara	198 741[30]	97 501[30]	101 240[30]	114	...	...	...	...
Ogaki	151 030[30]	73 398[30]	77 632[30]	80	...	...	...	...
Oita	462 317[30]	221 539[30]	240 778[30]	501	...	...	...	...

Continent, country or area, date, code and city / Continent, pays ou zone, date, code et ville	City proper - Ville proprement dite				Urban agglomeration - Agglomération urbaine			
	Population			Surface area - Superficie (km²)	Population			Surface area - Superficie (km²)
	Both sexes - Les deux sexes	Male - Masculin	Female - Féminin		Both sexes - Les deux sexes	Male - Masculin	Female - Féminin	
ASIA - ASIE								
Japan - Japon								
1 X 2005 (CDJC)								
Okayama	674 746[30]	324 623[30]	350 123[30]	659	...	...	...	...
Okazaki	354 704[30]	179 294[30]	175 410[30]	227	...	...	...	...
Okinawa	126 400[30]	60 896[30]	65 504[30]	49	...	...	...	...
Ome	142 354[30]	71 731[30]	70 623[30]	103	...	...	...	...
Omuta	131 090[30]	59 452[30]	71 638[30]	82	...	...	...	...
Onomichi	114 486[30]	54 018[30]	60 468[30]	212	...	...	...	...
Osaka	2 628 811[30]	1 280 325[30]	1 348 486[30]	222	...	...	...	...
Ota	213 299[30]	107 556[30]	105 743[30]	176	...	...	...	...
Otaru	142 161[30]	64 436[30]	77 725[30]	243	...	...	...	...
Otsu	301 672[30]	146 353[30]	155 319[30]	302	...	...	...	...
Oyama	160 150[30]	80 723[30]	79 427[30]	172	...	...	...	...
Saga	206 967[30]	98 013[30]	108 954[30]	355	...	...	...	...
Sagamihara	628 698[30]	318 986[30]	309 712[30]	90	...	...	...	...
Saijo	113 371[30]	54 144[30]	59 227[30]	509	...	...	...	...
Saitama	1 176 314[30]	590 972[30]	585 342[30]	217	...	...	...	...
Sakai	830 966[30]	400 294[30]	430 672[30]	150	...	...	...	...
Saku	100 462[30]	49 041[30]	51 421[30]	424	...	...	...	...
Sakura	171 246[30]	84 050[30]	87 196[30]	104	...	...	...	...
Sanda	113 572[30]	54 881[30]	58 691[30]	210	...	...	...	...
Sanjo	104 749[30]	50 660[30]	54 089[30]	432	...	...	...	...
Sano	123 926[30]	60 917[30]	63 009[30]	356	...	...	...	...
Sapporo	1 880 863[30]	889 054[30]	991 809[30]	1 121	...	...	...	...
Sasebo	248 041[30]	116 726[30]	131 315[30]	308	...	...	...	...
Satsumasendai	102 370[30]	48 195[30]	54 175[30]	684	...	...	...	...
Sayama	158 074[30]	80 072[30]	78 002[30]	49	...	...	...	...
Sendai	1 025 098[30]	500 597[30]	524 501[30]	784	...	...	...	...
Seto	131 925[30]	65 471[30]	66 454[30]	112	...	...	...	...
Shibata	104 634[30]	50 431[30]	54 203[30]	533	...	...	...	...
Shimonoseki	290 693[30]	134 741[30]	155 952[30]	716	...	...	...	...
Shizuoka	700 886[30]	340 999[30]	359 887[30]	1 374	...	...	...	...
Shunan	152 387[30]	73 058[30]	79 329[30]	656	...	...	...	...
Soka	236 316[30]	120 673[30]	115 643[30]	27	...	...	...	...
Suita	353 885[30]	173 154[30]	180 731[30]	36	...	...	...	...
Suzuka	193 114[30]	96 577[30]	96 537[30]	195	...	...	...	...
Tachikawa	172 566[30]	85 889[30]	86 677[30]	24	...	...	...	...
Tajimi	103 821[30]	50 283[30]	53 538[30]	78	...	...	...	...
Takamatsu	337 902[30]	163 509[30]	174 393[30]	274	...	...	...	...
Takaoka	167 685[30]	80 216[30]	87 469[30]	151	...	...	...	...
Takarazuka	219 862[30]	103 495[30]	116 367[30]	102	...	...	...	...
Takasaki	245 100[30]	120 607[30]	124 493[30]	111	...	...	...	...
Takatsuki	351 826[30]	170 102[30]	181 724[30]	105	...	...	...	...
Tama	145 877[30]	73 140[30]	72 737[30]	21	...	...	...	...
Toda	116 696[30]	61 254[30]	55 442[30]	18	...	...	...	...
Tokai	104 339[30]	54 737[30]	49 602[30]	43	...	...	...	...
Tokorozawa	336 100[30]	169 176[30]	166 924[30]	72	...	...	...	...
Tokushima	267 833[30]	127 241[30]	140 592[30]	191	...	...	...	...
TOKYO[32]	8 489 653[30]	4 210 749[30]	4 278 904[30]	621	12 576 601[30]	6 264 895[30]	6 311 706[30]	2 187
Tomakomai	172 758[30]	83 935[30]	88 823[30]	561	...	...	...	...
Tondabayashi	123 837[30]	58 946[30]	64 891[30]	40	...	...	...	...
Toride	111 327[30]	54 899[30]	56 428[30]	70	...	...	...	...
Tottori	201 740[30]	98 333[30]	103 407[30]	766	...	...	...	...
Toyama	421 239[30]	204 407[30]	216 832[30]	1 242	...	...	...	...
Toyohashi	372 479[30]	186 116[30]	186 363[30]	261	...	...	...	...
Toyokawa	120 967[30]	60 337[30]	60 630[30]	65	...	...	...	...
Toyonaka	386 623[30]	186 440[30]	200 183[30]	36	...	...	...	...
Toyota	412 141[30]	218 286[30]	193 855[30]	918	...	...	...	...
Tsu	165 182[30]	80 544[30]	84 638[30]	102	...	...	...	...
Tsuchiura	135 058[30]	67 254[30]	67 804[30]	82	...	...	...	...
Tsukuba	200 528[30]	103 110[30]	97 418[30]	284	...	...	...	...

8. Population of capital cities and cities of 100 000 or more inhabitants: latest available year, 1990 - 2009
Population des capitales et des villes de 100 000 habitants ou plus : dernière année disponible, 1990 - 2009 (continued - suite)

Continent, country or area, date, code and city / Continent, pays ou zone, date, code et ville	City proper - Ville proprement dite				Urban agglomeration - Agglomération urbaine			
	Population			Surface area - Superficie (km²)	Population			Surface area - Superficie (km²)
	Both sexes - Les deux sexes	Male - Masculin	Female - Féminin		Both sexes - Les deux sexes	Male - Masculin	Female - Féminin	

ASIA - ASIE

Japan - Japon
1 X 2005 (CDJC)

Tsuruoka	142 384[30]	67 676[30]	74 708[30]	1 311	...	...	...	...
Tsuyama	110 569[30]	52 418[30]	58 151[30]	506	...	...	...	...
Ube	178 955[30]	85 444[30]	93 511[30]	288	...	...	...	...
Ueda	123 680[30]	60 383[30]	63 297[30]	177	...	...	...	...
Uji	189 591[30]	92 286[30]	97 305[30]	68	...	...	...	...
Urasoe	106 049[30]	52 128[30]	53 921[30]	19	...	...	...	...
Urayasu	155 290[30]	79 275[30]	76 015[30]	17	...	...	...	...
Uruma	113 535[30]	56 598[30]	56 937[30]	86	...	...	...	...
Utsunomiya	457 673[30]	229 006[30]	228 667[30]	312	...	...	...	...
Wakayama	375 591[30]	176 825[30]	198 766[30]	209	...	...	...	...
Yachiyo	180 729[30]	89 601[30]	91 128[30]	51	...	...	...	...
Yaizu	120 109[30]	58 484[30]	61 625[30]	46	...	...	...	...
Yamagata	256 012[30]	122 903[30]	133 109[30]	381	...	...	...	...
Yamaguchi	191 677[30]	91 263[30]	100 414[30]	730	...	...	...	...
Yamato	221 220[30]	111 802[30]	109 418[30]	27	...	...	...	...
Yao	273 487[30]	132 627[30]	140 860[30]	42	...	...	...	...
Yatsushiro	136 886[30]	63 823[30]	73 063[30]	680	...	...	...	...
Yokkaichi	303 845[30]	149 692[30]	154 153[30]	205	...	...	...	...
Yokohama	3 579 628[30]	1 803 579[30]	1 776 049[30]	437	...	...	...	...
Yokosuka	426 178[30]	214 029[30]	212 149[30]	101	...	...	...	...
Yokote	103 652[30]	48 811[30]	54 841[30]	694	...	...	...	...
Yonago	149 584[30]	71 053[30]	78 531[30]	132	...	...	...	...
Zama	128 174[30]	65 860[30]	62 314[30]	18	...	...	...	...

Jordan - Jordanie
31 XII 2009 (ESDF)

AMMAN	1 228 287	631 725	596 562	...	...	...	...	...
Aqaba	102 177	57 290	44 887	...	...	...	...	...
Irbid	287 401	147 468	139 933	...	...	...	...	...
Russiefa	265 365	137 981	127 384	...	...	...	...	...
Zarqa	460 538	237 883	222 655	...	...	...	...	...

Kazakhstan
1 I 2009 (ESDF)

Aktau	152 227	74 261	77 966	29	154 353	75 319	79 034	...
Aktobe	273 599	126 591	147 008	234	312 942	145 877	167 065	...
Almaty	1 365 105	620 876	744 229	319	...	...	...	...
ASTANA	639 311	311 810	327 501	710	...	...	...	...
Atirau	167 902	79 027	88 875	347	222 516	105 581	116 935	...
Ekibastuz	121 814	56 700	65 114	31	143 933	67 458	76 475	...
Karaganda	465 634	211 149	254 485	50	465 698	211 169	254 529	...
Koktshetau	132 426	60 201	72 225	43	145 676	66 402	79 274	...
Kustanai	212 378	95 648	116 730	21	...	...	...	...
Kyzylorda	169 914	80 921	88 993	236	211 943	102 266	109 677	...
Pavlodar	307 880	139 518	168 362	56	328 100	149 232	178 868	...
Petropavlovsk (Severo- Kazakhstanskaya oblast)	193 268	86 739	106 529	22	194 094	87 176	106 918	...
Rudni	110 900	50 877	60 023	19	124 098	57 285	66 813	...
Semipalatinsk	285 473	128 584	156 889	9	313 503	142 416	171 087	...
Shimkent	566 996	269 600	297 396	36	...	...	...	...
Taldykorgan	116 558	52 183	64 375	39	141 143	64 361	76 782	...
Taraz	347 486	159 035	188 451	13	...	...	...	...
Temirtau	164 969	75 390	89 579	30	174 402	79 954	94 448	...
Uralsk	211 116	94 992	116 124	71	243 544	110 575	132 969	...
Ust-Kamenogorsk	287 308	128 518	158 790	54	298 866	134 162	164 704	...

Kuwait - Koweït
1 VII 2009 (ESDF)

Hawalli	123 635	81 462	42 173	...	...	...	...	...
Jaleeb Al-Shuykh	211 953	174 275	37 678	...	...	...	...	...
Salmiya	171 077	99 404	71 673	...	...	...	...	...
South Kheetan	109 393	100 886	8 507	...	...	...	...	...

8. Population of capital cities and cities of 100 000 or more inhabitants: latest available year, 1990 - 2009
Population des capitales et des villes de 100 000 habitants ou plus : dernière année disponible, 1990 - 2009 (continued - suite)

Continent, country or area, date, code and city / Continent, pays ou zone, date, code et ville	City proper - Ville proprement dite				Urban agglomeration - Agglomération urbaine			
	Population			Surface area - Superficie (km²)	Population			Surface area - Superficie (km²)
	Both sexes - Les deux sexes	Male - Masculin	Female - Féminin		Both sexes - Les deux sexes	Male - Masculin	Female - Féminin	
ASIA - ASIE								
Kyrgyzstan - Kirghizstan								
1 VII 2009 (ESDJ)								
BISHKEK	846 256[33]	392 490[33]	453 766[33]	...	859 795[33]	399 207[33]	460 588[33]	127
Osh	232 685[33]	110 792[33]	121 893[33]	...	257 477[33]	123 557[33]	133 920[33]	182
Lao People's Democratic Republic - République démocratique populaire lao								
1 III 1995 (CDFC)								
VIENTIANE	...	...	...	...	528 100	...	...	...
Lebanon - Liban[34]								
3 III 2007 (SSDF)								
BEIRUT	361 366	166 282	195 084	...	...	...	...	...
Malaysia - Malaisie[35]								
1 VII 2008 (ESDF)								
Alor Setar	148 159	...	...	...	...	...	...	...
Ampang/Ulu Kelang	118 338	...	...	...	...	...	...	...
Bintulu	126 509	...	...	...	...	...	...	...
George Town	192 740	...	...	...	...	...	...	...
Ipoh	478 975	...	...	...	...	...	...	...
Johor Bahru	520 285	...	...	...	...	...	...	...
Kajang dan Sungai Chua	111 382	...	...	...	...	...	...	...
Klang	355 986	...	...	...	...	...	...	...
Kota Bharu	238 371	...	...	...	...	...	...	...
Kota Kinabalu	284 721	...	...	...	...	...	...	...
KUALA LUMPUR	1 575 512	...	...	...	...	...	...	...
Kuala Terengganu	194 777	...	...	...	...	...	...	...
Kuantan	331 781	...	...	...	...	...	...	...
Kuching	201 822	...	...	...	...	...	...	...
Miri	164 905	...	...	...	...	...	...	...
Petaling Jaya	234 900	...	...	...	...	...	...	...
Sandakan	209 056	...	...	...	...	...	...	...
Seleyang Baru	182 652	...	...	...	...	...	...	...
Seremban	277 823	...	...	...	...	...	...	...
Shah Alam	180 585	...	...	...	...	...	...	...
Sibu	188 651	...	...	...	...	...	...	...
Subang Jaya	186 512	...	...	...	...	...	...	...
Sungai Petani	203 457	...	...	...	...	...	...	...
Taiping	197 372	...	...	...	...	...	...	...
Tawau	129 270	...	...	...	...	...	...	...
Maldives								
21 III 2006 (CDFC)								
MALE'	103 693	51 992	51 701	2	...	...	...	...
Mongolia - Mongolie								
31 XII 2009 (ESDF)								
ULAANBAATAR	1 087 096	523 266	563 830	4 700	...	...	...	...
Nepal - Népal								
22 VI 2001 (CDJC)								
Biratnagar	166 674	87 664	79 010	58	...	...	...	...
Birgunj	112 484	60 956	51 528	21	...	...	...	...
KATHMANDU	671 846	360 103	311 743	49	...	...	...	...
Lalitpur	162 991	84 502	78 489	15	...	...	...	...
Pokhara	156 312	79 563	76 749	55	...	...	...	...
Occupied Palestinian Territory - Territoire palestinien occupé								
1 VII 2009 (ESDF)								
Gaza	469 687	...	...	38	...	...	...	...
Hebron	171 653	...	...	49	...	...	...	...
Jabalya	130 280	...	...	...	...	...	...	...
Khan Yunis	149 115	...	...	...	...	...	...	...
Nablus	130 676	...	...	26	...	...	...	...
Rafah	128 150	...	...	...	...	...	...	...
Oman								
7 XII 2003 (CDFC)								
As Seeb	223 449	128 068	95 381	...	...	...	...	...
As Suwayq	101 122	54 997	46 125	...	...	...	...	...
Bawshar	150 420	91 687	58 733	...	...	...	...	...

8. Population of capital cities and cities of 100 000 or more inhabitants: latest available year, 1990 - 2009
Population des capitales et des villes de 100 000 habitants ou plus : dernière année disponible, 1990 - 2009 (continued - suite)

Continent, country or area, date, code and city / Continent, pays ou zone, date, code et ville	City proper - Ville proprement dite				Urban agglomeration - Agglomération urbaine			
	Population			Surface area - Superficie (km²)	Population			Surface area - Superficie (km²)
	Both sexes - Les deux sexes	Male - Masculin	Female - Féminin		Both sexes - Les deux sexes	Male - Masculin	Female - Féminin	

ASIA - ASIE

Oman
7 XII 2003 (CDFC)

MUSCAT	24 893	13 695	11 198	...	...	...	...	...
Mutrah	153 526	96 878	56 648	...	...	...	...	...
Salalah	156 530	92 489	64 041	...	...	...	...	...
Sohar	104 312	57 695	46 617	...	...	...	...	...

Pakistan[36]
2 III 1998 (CDFC)

Abbotabad	106 101	61 698	44 403	...	...	...	...	...
Bahawalnagar	111 313	57 779	53 534	...	...	...	...	...
Bahawalpur	408 395	222 228	186 167	...	...	...	...	...
Burewala	152 097	78 726	73 371	...	...	...	...	...
Chiniot	172 522	90 474	82 048	...	...	...	...	...
Chishtian	102 287	52 427	49 860	...	...	...	...	...
Dadu	102 550	53 508	49 042	...	...	...	...	...
Daska	102 883	52 359	50 524	...	...	...	...	...
Dera Ghazi Khan	190 542	98 738	91 804	...	...	...	...	...
Faisalabad (Lyallpur)	2 008 861	1 053 085	955 776	...	...	...	...	...
Gojra	117 872	60 598	57 274	...	...	...	...	...
Gujranwala	1 132 509	588 512	543 997	...	...	...	...	...
Gujrat	251 792	128 524	123 268	...	...	...	...	...
Hafizabad	133 678	69 231	64 447	...	...	...	...	...
Hyderabad	1 166 894	612 283	554 611	...	...	...	...	...
ISLAMABAD	529 180	290 717	238 463	...	...	...	...	...
Jacobabad	138 780	71 854	66 926	...	...	...	...	...
Jaranwala	106 785	55 619	51 166	...	...	...	...	...
Jhang	293 366	153 123	140 243	...	...	...	...	...
Jhelum	147 392	79 169	68 223	...	...	...	...	...
Kamoke	152 288	78 848	73 440	...	...	...	...	...
Karachi	9 339 023	5 029 900	4 309 123	...	...	...	...	...
Kasur	245 321	129 553	115 768	...	...	...	...	...
Khairpur	105 637	55 358	50 279	...	...	...	...	...
Khanewal	133 986	69 145	64 841	...	...	...	...	...
Khanpur	120 382	62 371	58 011	...	...	...	...	...
Kohat	126 627	71 505	55 122	...	...	...	...	...
Lahore	5 143 495	2 707 220	2 436 275	...	...	...	...	...
Larkana	270 283	140 622	129 661	...	...	...	...	...
Mangora	173 868	91 742	82 126	...	...	...	...	...
Mardan	245 926	129 247	116 679	...	...	...	...	...
Mirpur Khas	189 671	97 940	91 731	...	...	...	...	...
Multan	1 197 384	637 911	559 473	...	...	...	...	...
Muridke	111 951	58 210	53 741	...	...	...	...	...
Muzaffargharh	123 404	66 556	56 848	...	...	...	...	...
Nawabshah	189 244	98 116	91 128	...	...	...	...	...
Okara	201 815	104 245	97 570	...	...	...	...	...
Pakpattan	109 033	56 676	52 357	...	...	...	...	...
Peshawar	982 816	521 901	460 915	...	...	...	...	...
Quetta	565 137	307 759	257 378	...	...	...	...	...
Rahimyar Khan	233 537	121 446	112 091	...	...	...	...	...
Rawalpindi	1 409 768	750 530	659 238	...	...	...	...	...
Sadiqabad	144 391	75 217	69 174	...	...	...	...	...
Sahiwal	208 778	108 992	99 786	...	...	...	...	...
Sargodha	458 440	239 837	218 603	...	...	...	...	...
Shakkarpur	134 883	69 713	65 170	...	...	...	...	...
Sheikhu Pura	280 263	146 739	133 524	...	...	...	...	...
Sialkote	421 502	227 398	194 104	...	...	...	...	...
Sukkur	335 551	175 679	159 872	...	...	...	...	...
Tandoadam	104 907	54 670	50 237	...	...	...	...	...
Wah Cantonment	198 891	104 230	94 661	...	...	...	...	...

Philippines
1 V 2000 (CDJC)

Angeles	267 788	132 972	134 816	60	...	...	...	...
Bacolod	429 076	209 729	219 347	156	...	...	...	...
Bago	141 721	72 777	68 944	402	...	...	...	...
Baguio	252 386	124 208	128 178	58	...	...	...	...

8. Population of capital cities and cities of 100 000 or more inhabitants: latest available year, 1990 - 2009
Population des capitales et des villes de 100 000 habitants ou plus : dernière année disponible, 1990 - 2009 (continued - suite)

Continent, country or area, date, code and city / Continent, pays ou zone, date, code et ville	City proper - Ville proprement dite				Urban agglomeration - Agglomération urbaine			
	Population			Surface area - Superficie (km²)	Population			Surface area - Superficie (km²)
	Both sexes - Les deux sexes	Male - Masculin	Female - Féminin		Both sexes - Les deux sexes	Male - Masculin	Female - Féminin	
ASIA - ASIE								
Philippines								
1 V 2000 (CDJC)								
Basilan	332 828	166 413	166 415	...	...	...	...	...
Batangas	247 588	123 740	123 848	283	...	...	...	...
Butuan	267 279	135 735	131 544	816	...	...	...	...
Cabanatuan	222 859	111 461	111 398	283	...	...	...	...
Cadiz	141 954	72 701	69 253	467	...	...	...	...
Cagayan de Oro	461 877	228 524	233 353	413	...	...	...	...
Calbayog	147 187	75 157	72 030	...	...	...	...	...
Cebu	718 821	351 640	367 181	281	...	...	...	...
Cotabato	163 849	79 853	83 996	144	...	...	...	...
Dagupan	130 328	64 468	65 860	37	...	...	...	...
Davao	1 147 116	573 242	573 874	1 211	...	...	...	...
Digos	125 171	63 107	62 064	...	...	...	...	...
Dumaguete	102 265	49 378	52 887	34	...	...	...	...
General Santos	471 822	207 496	264 326	402	...	...	...	...
Gingoog	102 379	52 302	50 077	...	...	...	...	...
Iligan	285 061	141 641	143 420	673	...	...	...	...
Iloilo	366 391	177 620	188 771	56	...	...	...	...
Kabankalan	149 769	76 479	73 290	697	...	...	...	...
Kalookan (caloocan)	1 177 604	587 890	589 714	56	...	...	...	...
Kidapawan	101 205	51 278	49 927	...	...	...	...	...
Koronadal	133 786	67 493	66 293	...	...	...	...	...
Lapu-Lapu	217 019	106 099	110 920	...	...	...	...	...
Las Piñas	472 780	229 776	243 004	33	...	...	...	...
Legasp	157 010	78 141	78 869	154	...	...	...	...
Lipa	218 447	109 938	108 509	209	...	...	...	...
Lucena City	196 075	97 380	98 695	80	...	...	...	...
Makati	471 379	226 422	244 957	18	...	...	...	...
Malabalay	123 672	63 381	60 291	969	...	...	...	...
Malabon	338 855	168 587	170 268	...	...	...	...	...
Malolos	175 291	86 600	88 691	67	...	...	...	...
Mandaluyong	278 474	135 287	143 187	9	...	...	...	...
Mandaue	259 728	128 501	131 227	12	...	...	...	...
MANILA	1 581 082	770 491	810 591	614	...	...	...	...
Marawi	131 090	63 110	67 980	23	...	...	...	...
Marikina	391 170	191 585	199 585	22	...	...	...	...
Muntinlupa	379 310	187 381	191 929	40	...	...	...	...
Naga	137 810	68 040	69 770	85	...	...	...	...
Navotas	230 403	115 697	114 706	...	...	...	...	...
Olongapo	194 260	95 585	98 675	185	...	...	...	...
Ormoc	154 297	78 612	75 685	...	...	...	...	...
Ozamis	110 420	54 986	55 434	...	...	...	...	...
Pagadian	142 585	71 009	71 576	332	...	...	...	...
Paranaque	449 811	217 828	231 983	47	...	...	...	...
Pasay	354 908	175 041	179 867	14	...	...	...	...
Pasig	505 058	246 047	259 011	49	...	...	...	...
Puerto Princesa	161 912	83 045	78 867	2 381	...	...	...	...
Quezon City	2 173 831	1 064 780	1 109 051	172	...	...	...	...
Roxas	126 352	62 542	63 810	95	...	...	...	...
Sagay City	129 765	65 935	63 830	330	...	...	...	...
San Carlos (Negros Occidental)	118 259	60 073	58 186	452	...	...	...	...
San Carlos (Pangasinan)	154 264	77 652	76 612	...	...	...	...	...
San Fernando City	221 857	111 798	110 059	68	...	...	...	...
San Juan	117 680	54 604	63 076	6	...	...	...	...
San Pablo	207 927	102 685	105 242	...	...	...	...	...
Silay	107 722	54 419	53 303	215	...	...	...	...
Surigao	118 534	59 253	59 281	225	...	...	...	...
Tacloban	178 639	88 490	90 149	...	...	...	...	...
Taguig	467 375	233 712	233 663	...	...	...	...	...
Tagum	179 531	90 004	89 527	...	...	...	...	...
Tarlac	262 481	132 532	129 949	...	...	...	...	...
Toledo	141 174	71 719	69 455	...	...	...	...	...
Tuguegarao	120 645	60 270	60 375	145	...	...	...	...

Continent, country or area, date, code and city / Continent, pays ou zone, date, code et ville	City proper - Ville proprement dite				Urban agglomeration - Agglomération urbaine			
	Population			Surface area - Superficie (km²)	Population			Surface area - Superficie (km²)
	Both sexes - Les deux sexes	Male - Masculin	Female - Féminin		Both sexes - Les deux sexes	Male - Masculin	Female - Féminin	
ASIA - ASIE								
Philippines								
1 V 2000 (CDJC)								
Valenzuela	485 433	244 373	241 060	47	...	...	...	...
Zamboanga	601 794	302 089	299 705	464	...	...	...	...
Qatar								
1 VII 2008 (ESDF)								
Al-Khoor	...	...	...	...	164 324	156 286	8 038	106
Al-Rayyan	...	...	...	...	368 174	250 233	117 941	63
DOHA	...	...	...	...	711 000	542 346	168 654	3 042
Republic of Korea - République de Corée								
1 VII 2009 (ESDJ)								
Busan (Pusan)	3 471 154	1 722 519	1 748 635	766	...	...	...	...
Daegu (Taegu)	2 443 994	1 225 468	1 218 526	884	...	...	...	...
Daejeon (Taejon)	1 505 957	757 580	748 377	540	...	...	...	...
Gwangju (Kwangchu)	1 448 818	722 057	726 761	501	...	...	...	...
Icheon	2 645 189	1 337 273	1 307 916	1 010	...	...	...	...
SEOUL	10 036 377	4 980 234	5 056 143	605	...	...	...	...
Ulsan	1 089 451	564 057	525 394	1 058	...	...	...	...
Saudi Arabia - Arabie saoudite								
15 IX 2004 (CDFC)								
Abha	201 912	113 102	88 810	...	...	...	...	...
Ad-Dammam	744 321	450 494	293 827	...	...	...	...	...
Al-Hawiyah	132 078	69 481	62 597	...	...	...	...	...
Al-Hufuf	287 841	155 924	131 917	...	...	...	...	...
Al-Jubayl	222 544	135 659	86 885	...	...	...	...	...
Al-Kharj	200 958	109 112	91 846	...	...	...	...	...
Al-Khubar	165 799	101 818	63 981	...	...	...	...	...
Al-Madinah	918 889	493 929	424 960	...	...	...	...	...
Al-Mubarraz	285 067	150 449	134 618	...	...	...	...	...
Al-Qurrayyat	100 436	52 869	47 567	...	...	...	...	...
Ar'ar	145 237	77 744	67 493	...	...	...	...	...
Ath-Thuqbah	191 826	117 165	74 661	...	...	...	...	...
At-Ta'if	521 273	274 531	246 742	...	...	...	...	...
Buraydah	378 422	211 317	167 105	...	...	...	...	...
Hafar al-Batin	231 978	122 781	109 197	...	...	...	...	...
Ha'il	267 005	142 015	124 990	...	...	...	...	...
Jiddah	2 801 481	1 619 932	1 181 549	...	...	...	...	...
Jizan	100 694	57 988	42 706	...	...	...	...	...
Khamis Mushayt	372 695	208 397	164 298	...	...	...	...	...
Makkah	1 294 168	704 672	589 496	...	...	...	...	...
Najran (Aba as-Suud)	246 880	133 405	113 475	...	...	...	...	...
RIYADH	4 087 152	2 354 246	1 732 906	...	...	...	...	...
Sekaka	122 686	66 672	56 014	...	...	...	...	...
Tabuk	441 351	241 913	199 438	...	...	...	...	...
Unayzah	128 930	71 841	57 089	...	...	...	...	...
Yanbu al-Bahr	188 430	105 966	82 464	...	...	...	...	...
Singapore - Singapour								
1 VII 2009 (ESDF)								
SINGAPORE	4 987 600	...	...	710	...	...	...	...
Sri Lanka[37]								
17 VII 2001 (CDFC)								
COLOMBO	647 100	346 366	300 734	...	...	...	...	...
Dehiwala-Mount Lavinia	210 546	105 522	105 024	...	...	...	...	...
Kandy	109 343	54 288	55 055	...	...	...	...	...
Moratuwa	177 563	87 313	90 250	...	...	...	...	...
Negombo	121 701	60 947	60 754	...	...	...	...	...
Sri Jayawardanapura Kotte	116 366	59 993	56 373	...	...	...	...	...
Syrian Arab Republic - République arabe syrienne								
1 VII 2008 (ESDF)								
Aleppo	4 450 000	2 292 000	2 158 000	...	...	...	...	...
Al-Hasakeh	1 392 000	701 000	691 000	...	...	...	...	...
Al-Rakka	865 000	456 000	409 000	...	...	...	...	...
Al-sweida	349 000	171 000	178 000	...	...	...	...	...
DAMASCUS	1 680 000	857 000	823 000	...	...	...	...	...
Damasus rural	2 529 000	1 302 000	1 227 000	...	...	...	...	...

Continent, country or area, date, code and city / Continent, pays ou zone, date, code et ville	City proper - Ville proprement dite				Urban agglomeration - Agglomération urbaine			
	Population			Surface area - Superficie (km²)	Population			Surface area - Superficie (km²)
	Both sexes - Les deux sexes	Male - Masculin	Female - Féminin		Both sexes - Les deux sexes	Male - Masculin	Female - Féminin	
ASIA - ASIE								
Syrian Arab Republic - République arabe syrienne								
1 VII 2008 (ESDF)								
Deir El-Zor	1 111 000	563 000	548 000	...	...	...	...	...
Dra'a	930 000	472 000	458 000	...	...	...	...	...
Hama	1 508 000	768 000	740 000	...	...	...	...	...
Homs	1 667 000	852 000	815 000	...	...	...	...	...
Idleb	1 376 000	704 000	672 000	...	...	...	...	...
Lattakia	951 000	480 000	471 000	...	...	...	...	...
Tartous	756 000	383 000	373 000	...	...	...	...	...
Tajikistan - Tadjikistan								
1 VII 2007 (ESDF)								
DUSHANBE	670 168	348 864	321 304	...	...	...	...	...
Khujand	155 316	...	...	...	...	...	...	...
Thailand - Thaïlande								
1 VII 2009 (ESDJ)								
BANGKOK	...	...	...	...	6 866 000[1]	3 198 000[1]	3 668 000[1]	1 569
Buri Ram	...	...	...	...	227 668[1]	111 569[1]	116 099[1]	10 322
Chachoengsao	...	...	...	...	165 974[1]	79 672[1]	86 302[1]	5 351
Chaiyaphum	...	...	...	...	162 689[1]	78 742[1]	83 947[1]	12 778
Chanthaburi	...	...	...	...	175 499[1]	84 979[1]	90 520[1]	6 338
Chon Buri	...	...	...	...	664 876[1]	322 879[1]	341 997[1]	4 363
Chumphon	...	...	...	...	102 239[1]	49 749[1]	52 490[1]	6 009
Kalasin	...	...	...	...	214 147[1]	105 436[1]	108 711[1]	6 947
Kanchanaburi	...	...	...	...	171 468[1]	81 283[1]	90 185[1]	19 483
Khon Kaen	...	...	...	...	416 474[1]	202 623[1]	213 851[1]	10 886
Loei	...	...	...	...	101 410[1]	50 127[1]	51 283[1]	11 425
Lop Buri	...	...	...	...	202 722[1]	103 428[1]	99 294[1]	6 200
Maha Sarakham	...	...	...	...	106 803[1]	51 169[1]	55 634[1]	5 292
Nakhon Pathom	...	...	...	...	230 549[1]	110 859[1]	119 690[1]	2 168
Nakhon Ratchasima	...	...	...	...	608 973[1]	297 215[1]	311 758[1]	20 494
Nakhon Si Thammarat	...	...	...	...	321 331[1]	155 602[1]	165 729[1]	9 943
Narathiwat	...	...	...	...	171 984[1]	84 977[1]	87 007[1]	4 475
Nong Bua Lam Phu	...	...	...	...	110 596[1]	54 582[1]	56 014[1]	3 859
Nong Khai	...	...	...	...	191 001[1]	95 015[1]	95 986[1]	7 322
Nonthaburi	...	...	...	...	565 700[1]	270 353[1]	295 347[1]	662
Pathum Thani	...	...	...	...	333 630[1]	160 690[1]	172 940[1]	1 526
Pattani	...	...	...	...	124 748[1]	62 075[1]	62 673[1]	1 940
Phetchaburi	...	...	...	...	155 182[1]	74 417[1]	80 765[1]	6 225
Phra Nakhon Si Ayutthaya	...	...	...	...	305 957[1]	147 256[1]	158 701[1]	2 557
Phuket	...	...	...	...	203 936[1]	99 241[1]	104 695[1]	543
Prachuap Khiri Khan	...	...	...	...	154 000[1]	74 132[1]	79 868[1]	6 368
Ratchaburi	...	...	...	...	287 264[1]	138 146[1]	149 118[1]	5 197
Rayong	...	...	...	...	250 595[1]	124 538[1]	126 057[1]	3 552
Roi Et	...	...	...	...	159 132[1]	77 902[1]	81 230[1]	8 300
Sakon Nakhon	...	...	...	...	144 476[1]	70 998[1]	73 478[1]	9 606
Samut Prakan	...	...	...	...	730 987[1]	345 572[1]	385 415[1]	1 004
Samut Songkhram	...	...	...	...	216 495[1]	107 201[1]	109 294[1]	872
Saraburi	...	...	...	...	237 775[1]	117 365[1]	120 410[1]	3 576
Si Sa Ket	...	...	...	...	134 659[1]	65 568[1]	69 091[1]	8 840
Songkhla	...	...	...	...	637 543[1]	306 141[1]	331 402[1]	7 394
Suphan Buri	...	...	...	...	153 978[1]	73 412[1]	80 566[1]	5 838
Surat Thani	...	...	...	...	357 051[1]	174 424[1]	182 627[1]	12 891
Trang	...	...	...	...	130 228[1]	62 762[1]	67 466[1]	4 918
Ubon Ratchathani	...	...	...	...	344 849[1]	169 373[1]	175 476[1]	15 745
Udon Thani	...	...	...	...	417 260[1]	205 885[1]	211 375[1]	11 730
Yala	...	...	...	...	112 112[1]	54 573[1]	57 539[1]	4 521
Timor-Leste								
1 VII 2001 (ESDF)								
DILI	56 000	...	...	...	...	...	...	...

8. Population of capital cities and cities of 100 000 or more inhabitants: latest available year, 1990 - 2009
Population des capitales et des villes de 100 000 habitants ou plus : dernière année disponible, 1990 - 2009 (continued - suite)

Continent, country or area, date, code and city / Continent, pays ou zone, date, code et ville	City proper - Ville proprement dite				Urban agglomeration - Agglomération urbaine			
	Population			Surface area - Superficie (km²)	Population			Surface area - Superficie (km²)
	Both sexes - Les deux sexes	Male - Masculin	Female - Féminin		Both sexes - Les deux sexes	Male - Masculin	Female - Féminin	
ASIA - ASIE								
Turkey - Turquie								
1 VII 2007 (ESDF)								
Adana[38]	...	...	...	...	1 251 863	...	...	...
Adiyaman	241 260	...	...	...	...	...	...	...
Afyon	1 488 350	...	...	...	...	...	...	...
Aksaray	157 232	...	...	...	...	...	...	...
Alanya (Antalya)	115 927	...	...	...	...	...	...	...
ANKARA[39]	...	...	...	...	3 953 344	...	...	...
Antalya	763 205	...	...	...	...	...	...	...
Aydin	164 525	...	...	...	...	...	...	...
Balikesir	241 682	...	...	...	...	...	...	...
Bandirma	109 000	...	...	...	...	...	...	...
Batman	321 222	...	...	...	...	...	...	...
Bursa[40]	...	...	...	...	1 597 162	...	...	...
Ceyhan	122 699	...	...	...	...	...	...	...
Corlu	199 714	...	...	...	...	...	...	...
Corum	190 430	...	...	...	...	...	...	...
Denizli	320 460	...	...	...	...	...	...	...
Derince[41]	111 659	...	...	...	...	...	...	...
Diyarbakir	662 954	...	...	...	...	...	...	...
Edirne	125 753	...	...	...	...	...	...	...
Elazig	297 703	...	...	...	...	...	...	...
Erzincan	112 069	...	...	...	...	...	...	...
Erzurum	443 423	...	...	...	...	...	...	...
Eskisehir	512 972	...	...	...	...	...	...	...
Gaziantep[42]	...	...	...	...	1 024 411	...	...	...
Gebze	325 021	...	...	...	...	...	...	...
Hatay	153 581	...	...	...	...	...	...	...
Içel	604 236	...	...	...	...	...	...	...
Inegol	125 507	...	...	...	...	...	...	...
Iskenderun	154 706	...	...	...	...	...	...	...
Isparta	168 872	...	...	...	...	...	...	...
Istanbul[43]	...	...	...	...	10 822 846	...	...	...
Izmir[44]	...	...	...	...	2 583 670	...	...	...
Kahramanmaras	393 583	...	...	...	...	...	...	...
Karaman	124 603	...	...	...	...	...	...	...
Kayseri[45]	...	...	...	...	710 735	...	...	...
Kirikkale	207 613	...	...	...	...	...	...	...
Kiziltepe	157 834	...	...	...	...	...	...	...
Kocaeli	186 951	...	...	...	...	...	...	...
Konya	...	...	...	...	994 883	...	...	...
Kütahya	186 516	...	...	...	...	...	...	...
Malatya	454 249	...	...	...	...	...	...	...
Manavgat (Antalya)	100 588	...	...	...	...	...	...	...
Manisa	250 943	...	...	...	...	...	...	...
Nazilli	119 972	...	...	...	...	...	...	...
Ordu	112 746	...	...	...	...	...	...	...
Osmaniye	209 907	...	...	...	...	...	...	...
Patnos (Agri)	108 507	...	...	...	...	...	...	...
Sakarya	276 713	...	...	...	...	...	...	...
Samsun	393 334	...	...	...	...	...	...	...
Sanliurfa	438 134	...	...	...	...	...	...	...
Siirt	118 567	...	...	...	...	...	...	...
Sivas	258 746	...	...	...	...	...	...	...
Siverek	184 121	...	...	...	...	...	...	...
Tarsus	227 595	...	...	...	...	...	...	...
Tekirdag	119 518	...	...	...	...	...	...	...
Tokat	132 929	...	...	...	...	...	...	...
Trabzon	242 445	...	...	...	...	...	...	...
Turgutlu (Manisa)	105 565	...	...	...	...	...	...	...
Turhal	113 457	...	...	...	...	...	...	...
Usak	156 672	...	...	...	...	...	...	...
Van	381 653	...	...	...	...	...	...	...
Viransehir	182 095	...	...	...	...	...	...	...

8. Population of capital cities and cities of 100 000 or more inhabitants: latest available year, 1990 - 2009
Population des capitales et des villes de 100 000 habitants ou plus : dernière année disponible, 1990 - 2009 (continued - suite)

	City proper - Ville proprement dite				Urban agglomeration - Agglomération urbaine			
	Population			Surface area - Superficie (km²)	Population			Surface area - Superficie (km²)
Continent, country or area, date, code and city Continent, pays ou zone, date, code et ville	Both sexes - Les deux sexes	Male - Masculin	Female - Féminin		Both sexes - Les deux sexes	Male - Masculin	Female - Féminin	
ASIA - ASIE								
Turkmenistan - Turkménistan								
1 VII 1990 (ESDF)								
ASHKHABAD	407 000	...	...	...	...	...	...	...
Tashauz	114 000	...	...	...	...	...	...	...
Türkmenabat (Chardzhou)	164 000	...	...	...	...	...	...	...
United Arab Emirates - Émirats arabes unis								
1 VII 2002 (ESDF)								
ABU DHABI	527 000	359 000	168 000	...	...	...	...	...
Ajman	205 000	122 000	83 000	...	...	...	...	...
Al-Ayn	328 000	215 000	113 000	...	...	...	...	...
Al-Sharjah	488 000	317 000	171 000	...	...	...	...	...
Dubai	1 089 000	759 000	330 000	...	...	...	...	...
Uzbekistan - Ouzbékistan								
1 VII 2001 (ESDF)								
Almalyk	113 114	56 317	56 797	...	...	...	...	...
Andizhan	338 366	165 159	173 207	...	...	...	...	...
Angren	128 757	64 060	64 697	...	...	...	...	...
Banjzak	131 512	68 441	63 071	...	...	...	...	...
Bukhara	237 361	118 613	118 748	...	...	...	...	...
Chirchik	141 742	70 203	71 539	...	...	...	...	...
Fergana	183 037	87 142	95 895	...	...	...	...	...
Karshi	204 690	104 159	100 531	...	...	...	...	...
Kokand	197 450	95 872	101 578	...	...	...	...	...
Margilan	149 646	73 899	75 747	...	...	...	...	...
Namangan	391 297	197 962	193 335	...	...	...	...	...
Navoi	138 082	70 577	67 505	...	...	...	...	...
Nukus	212 012	103 918	108 094	...	...	...	...	...
Samarkand	361 339	178 608	182 731	...	...	...	...	...
TASHKENT	2 137 218	1 043 213	1 094 005	...	...	...	...	...
Termez	116 467	60 031	56 436	...	...	...	...	...
Urgentch	138 609	67 667	70 942	...	...	...	...	...
Viet Nam								
1 VII 1992 (ESDF)								
Buonmathuot	282 095	...	...	...	...	...	...	...
Campha	209 086	...	...	...	...	...	...	...
Cantho	215 587	...	...	...	...	...	...	...
Da Nang	382 674	...	...	...	...	...	...	...
Dalat	106 409	...	...	...	...	...	...	...
Haiphong	783 133	...	...	22	...	...	...	...
HANOI	1 073 760	...	...	46	...	...	...	...
Ho Chi Minh[46]	3 015 743	...	...	140	...	...	...	...
Hon Gai	127 484	...	...	...	...	...	...	...
Hué	219 149	...	...	...	...	...	...	...
Longxuyen	132 681	...	...	...	...	...	...	...
Mytho	108 404	...	...	...	...	...	...	...
Namdinh	171 699	...	...	...	...	...	...	...
Nhatrang	221 331	...	...	...	...	...	...	...
Qui Nhon	163 385	...	...	...	...	...	...	...
Rach Gia	141 132	...	...	...	...	...	...	...
Thai Nguyen	127 643	...	...	...	...	...	...	...
Vinh	112 455	...	...	...	...	...	...	...
Vungtau	145 145	...	...	...	...	...	...	...
Yemen - Yémen								
16 XII 1994 (CDFC)								
Adan	398 294	...	...	...	...	...	...	...
Al-Hudaydah (Hodeidah)	298 452	...	...	...	...	...	...	...
Al-Mukalla	122 359	...	...	...	...	...	...	...
Ibb	103 312	...	...	...	...	...	...	...
SANA'A	954 448	...	...	...	...	...	...	...
Ta'izz	317 571	...	...	...	...	...	...	...

8. Population of capital cities and cities of 100 000 or more inhabitants: latest available year, 1990 - 2009
Population des capitales et des villes de 100 000 habitants ou plus : dernière année disponible, 1990 - 2009 (continued - suite)

Continent, country or area, date, code and city / Continent, pays ou zone, date, code et ville	City proper - Ville proprement dite				Urban agglomeration - Agglomération urbaine			
	Population			Surface area - Superficie (km²)	Population			Surface area - Superficie (km²)
	Both sexes - Les deux sexes	Male - Masculin	Female - Féminin		Both sexes - Les deux sexes	Male - Masculin	Female - Féminin	
EUROPE								
Åland Islands - Îles d'Åland								
1 VII 2009 (ESDJ)								
MARIEHAMN	11 064[47]	5 264[47]	5 800[47]	12	...	...	...	...
Albania - Albanie								
1 VII 2003 (ESDF)								
TIRANA	392 863	194 006	198 857	31	...	...	...	...
Andorra - Andorre[47]								
1 VII 2009 (ESDJ)								
ANDORRA LA VELLA	...	...	...	...	24 779	12 539	12 240	...
Austria - Autriche								
1 I 2009 (ESDJ)								
Graz	253 994[48]	122 042[48]	131 952[48]	128	...	...	...	...
Innsbruck	118 035[48]	56 109[48]	61 926[48]	105	...	...	...	...
Linz	189 122[48]	89 923[48]	99 199[48]	96	...	...	...	...
Salzburg	147 732[48]	69 606[48]	78 126[48]	66	...	...	...	...
WIEN	1 687 271[48]	807 088[48]	880 183[48]	415	...	...	...	...
Belarus - Bélarus								
1 I 2009 (ESDF)								
Baranovichi	168 858	77 746	91 112	50	...	...	...	...
Bobruisk	218 993	102 086	116 907	90	...	...	...	...
Borisov	150 006	70 602	79 404	48	...	...	...	...
Brest	318 043	146 819	171 224	145	...	...	...	...
Gomel	...	...	...	...	498 727	227 179	271 548	128
Grodno	338 244	155 734	182 510	142	...	...	...	...
MINSK	1 829 084	841 447	987 637	307	...	...	...	...
Mogilev	371 982	171 018	200 964	109	...	...	...	...
Mozir	112 165	53 449	58 716	38	...	...	...	...
Novopolotsk	...	...	...	...	107 068	50 839	56 229	48
Orsha	...	...	...	...	138 569	65 837	72 732	39
Pinsk	131 220	61 155	70 065	48	...	...	...	...
Soligorsk	101 395	47 785	53 610	11	...	...	...	...
Vitebsk	...	...	...	...	355 746	158 586	197 160	92
Belgium - Belgique								
1 VII 2007 (ESDJ)								
Antwerpen (Anvers)	469 137	230 622	238 515	205	686 554	336 570	349 984	394
Brugge	117 028	56 613	60 415	138	...	...	...	...
BRUXELLES (BRUSSEL)	147 395	73 923	73 472	33	1 441 201	695 054	746 147	573
Charleroi	201 572	97 554	104 018	102	288 461	139 001	149 460	199
Gent (Gand)	236 197	115 704	120 493	156	267 014	130 705	136 309	207
Liège (Luik)	189 505	92 702	96 803	69	479 484	231 030	248 454	367
Namur	107 796	51 792	56 004	176	...	...	...	...
Schaerbeek	114 766	56 467	58 299	8	...	...	...	...
Bosnia and Herzegovina - Bosnie-Herzégovine								
31 III 1991 (CDJC)								
Banja Luka	195 692	97 110	98 582	1 239	...	...	...	...
Doboj	102 549	51 144	51 405	697	...	...	...	...
Mostar	126 628	62 291	64 337	1 227	...	...	...	...
Prijedor	112 543	56 092	56 451	834	...	...	...	...
SARAJEVO	527 049	257 284	269 765	2 095	...	...	...	...
Tuzla	131 318	64 514	66 804	303	...	...	...	...
Zenica	145 517	72 985	72 532	505	...	...	...	...
Bulgaria - Bulgarie								
1 VII 2009 (ESDJ)								
Bourgas	191 313	91 643	99 670	...	...	...	...	...
Plévène	111 899	53 821	58 078	...	...	...	...	...
Plovdiv	348 033	165 660	182 373	...	...	...	...	...
Roussé	156 734	75 360	81 374	...	...	...	...	...
SOFIA	1 164 201	552 131	612 070	...	...	...	...	...
Stara Zagora	140 583	67 892	72 691	...	...	...	...	...
Varna	319 575	154 848	164 727	...	...	...	...	...
Croatia - Croatie								
31 III 2001 (CDJC)								
Osijek	90 411[49]	41 592[49]	48 819[49]	...	114 616[50]	53 497[50]	61 119[50]	...
Rijeka	143 800[49]	68 382[49]	75 418[49]	...	144 043[50]	68 511[50]	75 532[50]	...

Continent, country or area, date, code and city / Continent, pays ou zone, date, code et ville	City proper - Ville proprement dite				Urban agglomeration - Agglomération urbaine			
	Population			Surface area - Superficie (km²)	Population			Surface area - Superficie (km²)
	Both sexes - Les deux sexes	Male - Masculin	Female - Féminin		Both sexes - Les deux sexes	Male - Masculin	Female - Féminin	
EUROPE								
Croatia - Croatie								
31 III 2001 (CDJC)								
Split	175 140[49]	83 720[49]	91 420[49]	...	188 694[50]	90 484[50]	98 210[50]	...
ZAGREB	691 724[49]	321 507[49]	370 217[49]	...	779 145[50]	363 992[50]	415 153[50]	...
Czech Republic - République tchèque								
31 XII 2009 (ESDJ)								
Brno	371 399	178 429	192 970	230	...	...	...	...
Liberec	101 625	49 035	52 590	106	...	...	...	...
Olomouc	100 362	47 401	52 961	103	...	...	...	...
Ostrava	306 006	148 183	157 823	214	...	...	...	...
Plzen	169 935	82 729	87 206	138	...	...	...	...
PRAHA	1 249 026	608 316	640 710	496	...	...	...	...
Denmark - Danemark[51]								
1 VII 2009 (ESDJ)								
Ålborg	196 096[47]	97 756[47]	98 340[47]	1 144	...	...	...	...
Århus	303 107[47]	148 873[47]	154 234[47]	469	...	...	...	...
Esbjerg	114 806[47]	57 371[47]	57 435[47]	753	...	...	...	...
KOBENHAVN	521 397[47]	257 925[47]	263 472[47]	88	...	...	...	...
Odense	187 884[47]	92 096[47]	95 788[47]	304	...	...	...	...
Vejle	106 281[47]	52 860[47]	53 421[47]	1 066	...	...	...	...
Estonia - Estonie								
1 VII 2009 (ESDJ)								
TALLINN	398 967	180 448	218 519	158	...	...	...	...
Tartu	103 051	46 164	56 887	39	...	...	...	...
Faeroe Islands - Îles Féroé								
1 VII 2008 (ESDJ)								
THORSHAVN	17 624	8 920	8 704	63	1 916	1 025	891	110
Finland - Finlande								
1 VII 2009 (ESDJ)								
Espoo	242 948	119 650	123 298	312	...	...	...	...
HELSINKI	579 991	271 877	308 115	214	...	...	...	...
Jyvaskyla	128 826	62 527	66 299	1 171	...	...	...	...
Lahti	100 467	47 576	52 891	135	...	...	...	...
Oulu	138 097	67 914	70 183	1 410	...	...	...	...
Tampere	210 530	101 506	109 024	525	...	...	...	...
Turku	175 835	82 853	92 982	246	...	...	...	...
Vantaa	196 517	96 159	100 358	238	...	...	...	...
France								
8 III 1999 (CDJC)								
Aix-en-Provence[52]	134 324	62 375	71 949	186	...	...	...	...
Amiens	135 449[52]	63 604[52]	71 845[52]	49[52]	160 767	75 963	84 804	...
Angers	151 322[52]	68 981[52]	82 341[52]	43[52]	226 912	106 007	120 905	...
Besançon	117 691[52]	54 563[52]	63 128[52]	65[52]	134 335	62 807	71 528	...
Bordeaux	215 374[52]	99 340[52]	116 034[52]	49[52]	754 017	357 301	396 716	...
Boulogne-Billancourt[52]	106 316	49 794	56 522	6	...	...	...	...
Brest	149 649[52]	71 731[52]	77 918[52]	50[52]	210 058	101 716	108 342	...
Caen	114 007[52]	52 349[52]	61 658[52]	26[52]	199 381	93 713	105 668	...
Clermont-Ferrand	137 154[52]	63 514[52]	73 640[52]	43[52]	258 542	121 940	136 602	...
Dijon	150 138[52]	69 321[52]	80 817[52]	40[52]	237 203	111 347	125 856	...
Grenoble	153 426[52]	73 153[52]	80 273[52]	18[52]	419 468	203 302	216 166	...
Le Havre	190 924[52]	90 784[52]	100 140[52]	47[52]	248 560	119 056	129 504	...
Le Mans	146 064[52]	68 960[52]	77 104[52]	53[52]	194 757	92 714	102 043	...
Lille[53]	184 647[52]	86 697[52]	97 950[52]	30[52]	1 000 714	479 233	521 481	...
Limoges	133 942[52]	61 787[52]	72 137[52]	77[52]	173 243	80 860	92 383	...
Lyon	445 274[52]	205 824[52]	239 450[52]	48[52]	1 348 422[54]	644 758[54]	703 664[54]	...
Marseille	797 491[52]	376 814[52]	420 677[52]	241[52]	1 349 584[55]	644 374[55]	705 210[55]	...
Metz	123 704[52]	59 657[52]	64 047[52]	42[52]	322 448	156 823	165 625	...
Montpellier	225 511[52]	103 471[52]	122 040[52]	57[52]	288 059	134 005	154 054	...
Mulhouse	110 141[52]	53 875[52]	56 266[52]	22[52]	234 188	114 496	119 692	...
Nancy	103 552[52]	47 705[52]	55 847[52]	15[52]	331 249	157 519	173 730	...
Nantes	270 343[52]	126 401[52]	143 942[52]	65[52]	545 063	259 204	285 859	...
Nice	343 123[52]	157 197[52]	185 926[52]	72[52]	889 265	415 613	473 652	...
Nîmes	133 406[52]	62 426[52]	70 980[52]	162[52]	148 866	70 058	78 808	...

8. Population of capital cities and cities of 100 000 or more inhabitants: latest available year, 1990 - 2009
Population des capitales et des villes de 100 000 habitants ou plus : dernière année disponible, 1990 - 2009 (continued - suite)

Continent, country or area, date, code and city Continent, pays ou zone, date, code et ville	City proper - Ville proprement dite				Urban agglomeration - Agglomération urbaine			
	Population			Surface area - Superficie (km²)	Population			Surface area - Superficie (km²)
	Both sexes - Les deux sexes	Male - Masculin	Female - Féminin		Both sexes - Les deux sexes	Male - Masculin	Female - Féminin	
EUROPE								
France								
8 III 1999 (CDJC)								
Orléans	113 089[52]	53 569[52]	59 520[52]	27[52]	263 252	127 535	135 717	...
PARIS	2 125 851[52]	996 922[52]	1 128 929[52]	105[52]	9 643 880[56]	4 654 352[56]	4 989 528[56]	...
Perpignan	105 096[52]	48 032[52]	57 064[52]	68[52]	162 653	75 837	86 816	...
Reims	187 181[52]	88 814[52]	98 367[52]	47[52]	215 556	102 758	112 798	...
Rennes	206 194[52]	95 268[52]	110 926[52]	50[52]	272 182	127 991	144 191	...
Rouen	106 560[52]	49 520[52]	57 040[52]	21[52]	389 929	185 077	204 852	...
Saint-Denis (La Réunion)[52]	131 649	62 746	68 903	...	...	...	...	...
Saint-Étienne	180 438[52]	84 225[52]	96 213[52]	80[52]	292 166	138 416	153 750	...
Strasbourg[53]	263 941[52]	124 937[52]	139 004[52]	78[52]	427 184	203 815	223 369	...
Toulon	160 712[52]	75 127[52]	85 585[52]	43[52]	519 561	246 945	272 616	...
Toulouse	390 301[52]	184 572[52]	205 729[52]	118[52]	761 107	366 624	394 483	...
Tours	132 677[52]	59 995[52]	72 682[52]	34[52]	297 439	139 891	157 548	...
Villeurbanne[52]	124 152	59 345	64 807	15	...	...	...	...
Germany - Allemagne								
1 VII 1999 (ESDJ)								
Aachen	243 825	121 671	122 154	161	...	...	...	...
Augsburg	254 867	121 846	133 021	147	...	...	...	...
Bergisch Gladbach	106 150	50 723	55 427	83	...	...	...	...
BERLIN	3 386 667	1 644 575	1 742 092	891	...	...	...	...
Bielefeld	321 125	152 701	168 424	258	...	...	...	...
Bochum	392 830	190 433	202 397	145	...	...	...	...
Bonn	301 048	143 416	157 632	141	...	...	...	...
Bottrop	121 097	58 490	62 607	101	...	...	...	...
Braunschweig	246 322	119 350	126 972	192	...	...	...	...
Bremen	540 330	259 439	280 891	327	...	...	...	...
Bremerhaven	122 735	59 991	62 744	78	...	...	...	...
Chemnitz	263 222	125 123	138 099	176	...	...	...	...
Cottbus	110 894	53 712	57 182	150	...	...	...	...
Darmstadt	137 776	67 680	70 096	122	...	...	...	...
Dortmund	590 213	286 880	303 333	280	...	...	...	...
Dresden	476 668	229 565	247 103	237	...	...	...	...
Duisburg	519 793	252 735	267 058	233	...	...	...	...
Düsseldorf	568 855	268 630	300 225	217	...	...	...	...
Erfurt	201 267	96 937	104 330	269	...	...	...	...
Erlangen	100 750	48 939	51 811	77	...	...	...	...
Essen	599 515	286 350	313 165	210	...	...	...	...
Frankfurt am Main	643 821	314 431	329 390	248	...	...	...	...
Freiburg im Breisgau	202 455	96 025	106 430	153	...	...	...	...
Fürth	109 771	52 773	56 998	63	...	...	...	...
Gelsenkirchen	281 979	135 781	146 198	105	...	...	...	...
Gera	114 718	55 211	59 507	152	...	...	...	...
Göttingen	124 775	60 334	64 441	117	...	...	...	...
Hagen	205 201	98 338	106 863	160	...	...	...	...
Halle	254 360	121 314	133 046	135	...	...	...	...
Hamburg	1 704 735	824 686	880 049	755	...	...	...	...
Hamm	181 804	89 307	92 497	226	...	...	...	...
Hannover	514 718	245 017	269 701	204	...	...	...	...
Heidelberg	139 672	65 694	73 978	109	...	...	...	...
Heilbronn	119 526	58 400	61 126	100	...	...	...	...
Herne	175 661	85 577	90 084	51	...	...	...	...
Hildesheim	104 013	48 910	55 103	93	...	...	...	...
Ingolstadt	114 826	56 417	58 409	133	...	...	...	...
Kaiserslautern	100 025	49 247	50 778	140	...	...	...	...
Karlsruhe	277 204	134 775	142 429	173	...	...	...	...
Kassel	196 211	93 058	103 153	107	...	...	...	...
Kiel	233 795	113 274	120 521	117	...	...	...	...
Koblenz	108 003	51 340	56 663	105	...	...	...	...
Köln	962 507	466 543	495 964	405	...	...	...	...
Krefeld	241 769	117 087	124 682	138	...	...	...	...
Leipzig	489 532	235 789	253 743	176	...	...	...	...
Leverkusen	160 841	78 116	82 725	79	...	...	...	...
Lübeck	213 326	101 024	112 302	214	...	...	...	...

Continent, country or area, date, code and city / Continent, pays ou zone, date, code et ville	City proper - Ville proprement dite				Urban agglomeration - Agglomération urbaine			
	Population			Surface area - Superficie (km²)	Population			Surface area - Superficie (km²)
	Both sexes - Les deux sexes	Male - Masculin	Female - Féminin		Both sexes - Les deux sexes	Male - Masculin	Female - Féminin	
EUROPE								
Germany - Allemagne								
1 VII 1999 (ESDJ)								
Ludwigshafen am Rhein	163 771	81 257	82 514	78	...	...	...	...
Magdeburg	235 073	112 839	122 234	193	...	...	...	...
Mainz	183 134	89 093	94 041	98	...	...	...	...
Mannheim	307 730	151 145	156 585	145	...	...	...	...
Moers	106 837	51 824	55 013	68	...	...	...	...
Mönchengladbach	263 697	126 721	136 976	170	...	...	...	...
Mülheim an der Ruhr	173 895	82 677	91 218	91	...	...	...	...
München	1 194 560	571 363	623 197	311	...	...	...	...
Münster (Westf.)	264 670	123 825	140 845	303	...	...	...	...
Neuss	149 702	72 522	77 180	99	...	...	...	...
Nürnberg	486 628	233 415	253 213	186	...	...	...	...
Oberhausen	222 349	107 562	114 787	77	...	...	...	...
Offenbach am Main	116 627	57 539	59 088	45	...	...	...	...
Oldenburg	154 125	73 572	80 553	103	...	...	...	...
Osnabrück	164 539	77 981	86 558	120	...	...	...	...
Paderborn	137 647	67 010	70 637	179	...	...	...	...
Pforzheim	117 227	55 738	61 489	98	...	...	...	...
Potsdam	128 983	62 651	66 332	109	...	...	...	...
Recklinghausen	125 022	60 456	64 566	66	...	...	...	...
Regensburg	125 236	59 600	65 636	81	...	...	...	...
Remscheid	120 125	57 923	62 202	75	...	...	...	...
Reutlingen	110 343	53 564	56 779	87	...	...	...	...
Rostock	203 279	99 627	103 652	181	...	...	...	...
Saarbrücken	183 836	87 875	95 961	167	...	...	...	...
Salzgitter	112 934	54 808	58 126	224	...	...	...	...
Schwerin	102 878	49 428	53 450	130	...	...	...	...
Siegen	109 225	53 585	55 640	115	...	...	...	...
Solingen	165 583	79 712	85 871	89	...	...	...	...
Stuttgart	582 443	284 977	297 466	207	...	...	...	...
Ulm	116 103	56 511	59 592	119	...	...	...	...
Wiesbaden	268 716	129 032	139 684	204	...	...	...	...
Witten	103 384	49 545	53 839	72	...	...	...	...
Wolfsburg	121 954	59 761	62 193	204	...	...	...	...
Wuppertal	368 993	176 350	192 643	168	...	...	...	...
Würzburg	127 350	58 801	68 549	88	...	...	...	...
Zwickau	104 146	49 513	54 633	73	...	...	...	...
Gibraltar								
14 X 1991 (CDFC)								
GIBRALTAR	28 074	...	...	...	...	...	...	...
Greece - Grèce								
18 III 2001 (CDJC)								
ATHINAI	789 166[57]	374 900[57]	414 266[57]	39	...	...	...	...
Calithèa	115 150[57]	54 137[57]	61 013[57]	5	...	...	...	...
Iraclion	135 761[57]	66 956[57]	68 805[57]	52	...	...	...	...
Larissa	131 095[57]	64 000[57]	67 095[57]	88	...	...	...	...
Patrai	168 530[57]	82 981[57]	85 549[57]	57	...	...	...	...
Pésterion	146 743[57]	72 391[57]	74 352[57]	10	...	...	...	...
Pireas[57]	181 933	87 362	94 571	...	...	...	...	...
Thessaloniki[57]	385 406	180 122	205 284	...	...	...	...	...
Guernsey - Guernesey								
29 IV 2001 (CDJC)								
ST. PETER PORT	16 488	...	...	...	...	...	...	...
Holy See - Saint-Siège[58]								
1 VII 2000* (CDFC)								
VATICAN CITY	798[47]	529[47]	269[47]	0[59]	...	...	...	...
Hungary - Hongrie								
1 VII 2009 (ESDJ)								
BUDAPEST	1 716 883	783 738	933 145	525	2 516 218	1 168 815	1 347 404	2 538
Debrecen	206 748	95 540	111 208	462	242 032	112 934	129 098	805
Györ	130 477	61 203	69 274	175	188 398	89 636	98 762	783
Kecskemét	111 831	51 827	60 004	321	144 229	67 691	76 538	840
Miskolc	169 730	78 303	91 427	237	209 548	97 567	111 982	460
Nyiregyhaza	117 715	54 317	63 398	275	134 510	62 491	72 020	405

8. Population of capital cities and cities of 100 000 or more inhabitants: latest available year, 1990 - 2009
Population des capitales et des villes de 100 000 habitants ou plus : dernière année disponible, 1990 - 2009 (continued - suite)

Continent, country or area, date, code and city Continent, pays ou zone, date, code et ville	City proper - Ville proprement dite				Urban agglomeration - Agglomération urbaine			
	Population			Surface area - Superficie (km²)	Population			Surface area - Superficie (km²)
	Both sexes - Les deux sexes	Male - Masculin	Female - Féminin		Both sexes - Les deux sexes	Male - Masculin	Female - Féminin	
EUROPE								
Hungary - Hongrie								
1 VII 2009 (ESDJ)								
Pécs	157 327	72 084	85 244	163	182 082	84 269	97 813	430
Szeged	169 372	77 539	91 833	281	208 006	96 635	111 371	713
Székesfehérvar	102 004	47 646	54 359	171	126 939	60 075	66 864	543
Iceland - Islande								
1 VII 2009 (ESDJ)								
REYKJAVIK	119 021[60]	59 320[60]	59 701[60]	100[60]	201 598[61]	100 896[61]	100 702[61]	...
Ireland - Irlande								
23 IV 2006 (CDFC)								
Cork	119 418	58 449	60 969	40	190 384	93 610	96 774	...
DUBLIN	506 211	248 087	258 124	118	1 045 769	512 031	533 738	...
Isle of Man - Île de Man								
23 IV 2006 (CDJC)								
DOUGLAS	26 218	13 000	13 218	...	...	...	...	...
Italy - Italie								
1 VII 2009 (ESDJ)								
Ancona	102 284	48 717	53 568	123	...	...	...	...
Bari	320 414	153 905	166 509	116	...	...	...	...
Bergamo	117 348	54 886	62 462	40	...	...	...	...
Bologna	376 082	176 130	199 952	141	...	...	...	...
Bolzano	102 527	49 074	53 454	52	...	...	...	...
Brescia	191 231	90 177	101 054	91	...	...	...	...
Cagliari	157 124	72 796	84 329	86	...	...	...	...
Catania	296 030	139 309	156 721	181	...	...	...	...
Ferrara	134 716	62 927	71 789	404	...	...	...	...
Firenze	367 280	171 431	195 849	102	...	...	...	...
Foggia	153 099	73 709	79 390	508	...	...	...	...
Forli	116 879	56 351	60 528	228	...	...	...	...
Genova	610 459	286 790	323 669	244	...	...	...	...
Giugliano in Campania	114 648	56 383	58 265	94	...	...	...	...
Latina	117 881	56 764	61 117	278	...	...	...	...
Livorno	160 919	76 877	84 042	104	...	...	...	...
Messina	243 123	115 720	127 403	211	...	...	...	...
Milano	1 301 600	616 887	684 714	182	...	...	...	...
Modena	182 461	87 397	95 064	183	...	...	...	...
Monza	121 413	58 122	63 291	33	...	...	...	...
Napoli	963 301	457 504	505 797	117	...	...	...	...
Novara	103 983	49 856	54 127	103	...	...	...	...
Padova	212 463	99 857	112 606	93	...	...	...	...
Palermo	657 757	311 835	345 923	159	...	...	...	...
Parma	183 428	87 103	96 325	261	...	...	...	...
Perugia	165 937	79 088	86 850	450	...	...	...	...
Pescara	123 042	57 644	65 399	33	...	...	...	...
Piacenza	102 233	48 772	53 461	118	...	...	...	...
Prato	185 945	90 589	95 356	98	...	...	...	...
Ravenna	156 728	76 266	80 463	653	...	...	...	...
Reggio di Calabria	185 738	89 170	96 568	24	...	...	...	...
Reggio nell'Emilia	166 591	81 202	85 389	232	...	...	...	...
Rimini	140 821	67 699	73 122	134	...	...	...	...
ROMA	2 734 072	1 288 026	1 446 046	1 308	...	...	...	...
Salerno	140 097	64 817	75 280	59	...	...	...	...
Sassari	130 336	62 679	67 658	546	...	...	...	...
Siracusa	123 926	60 607	63 319	204	...	...	...	...
Taranto	193 579	91 878	101 701	210	...	...	...	...
Terni	112 378	53 071	59 308	212	...	...	...	...
Torino	909 182	433 338	475 844	130	...	...	...	...
Trento	114 874	55 013	59 861	158	...	...	...	...
Trieste	205 432	96 166	109 267	84	...	...	...	...
Venezia	270 450	128 104	142 346	416	...	...	...	...
Verona	264 922	126 072	138 850	207	...	...	...	...
Vicenza	115 281	54 909	60 373	81	...	...	...	...
Jersey								
11 III 2001 (CDJC)								
ST. HELIER	28 310	13 669	14 641	9	...	...	...	...

8. Population of capital cities and cities of 100 000 or more inhabitants: latest available year, 1990 - 2009
Population des capitales et des villes de 100 000 habitants ou plus : dernière année disponible, 1990 - 2009 (continued - suite)

Continent, country or area, date, code and city / Continent, pays ou zone, date, code et ville	City proper - Ville proprement dite				Urban agglomeration - Agglomération urbaine			
	Population			Surface area - Superficie (km²)	Population			Surface area - Superficie (km²)
	Both sexes - Les deux sexes	Male - Masculin	Female - Féminin		Both sexes - Les deux sexes	Male - Masculin	Female - Féminin	
EUROPE								
Latvia - Lettonie								
1 VII 2009 (ESDJ)								
Daugavpils	104 390	46 671	57 719	72	...	...	...	...
RIGA	709 715	315 184	394 531	303	...	...	...	...
Liechtenstein								
1 VII 2009 (ESDJ)								
VADUZ	5 172	2 505	2 667	17	...	...	...	...
Lithuania - Lituanie[62]								
1 VII 2009 (ESDJ)								
Kaunas	350 451	156 628	193 823	157	...	...	...	...
Klaipeda	183 092	83 684	99 408	98	...	...	...	...
Panevezhis	112 289	51 098	61 191	50	...	...	...	...
Shauliai	125 834	57 144	68 690	81	...	...	...	...
VILNIUS	547 784	247 716	300 068	394	...	...	...	...
Luxembourg								
1 VII 2009 (ESDJ)								
LUXEMBOURG-VILLE	89 717	...	...	51	...	...	...	...
Malta - Malte								
1 VII 2009 (ESDJ)								
VALLETTA	6 266[63]	3 062[63]	3 204[63]	1	...	...	...	...
Monaco								
1 VII 2000 (ESDJ)								
MONACO	*32 020*	*15 544*	*16 476*	...	...	...	...	...
Montenegro - Monténégro								
1 VII 2009 (ESDJ)								
PODGORICA	180 810	88 381	92 429	1 441	...	...	...	...
Netherlands - Pays-Bas								
1 I 2009 (ESDJ)								
Almere	185 746	92 252	93 494	130	...	...	...	...
Amersfoort	143 212	70 304	72 908	63	171 795	84 343	87 452	122
AMSTERDAM	755 605	371 858	383 747	166	1 039 029	510 094	528 935	337
Apeldoorn	155 332	76 473	78 859	340	155 332	76 473	78 859	340
Arnhem	145 574	72 212	73 362	98	147 089	72 952	74 137	126
Breda	171 916	83 676	88 240	127	171 916	83 676	88 240	127
Dordrecht	118 408	58 179	60 229	79	235 883	115 689	120 194	139
Ede	107 623	52 761	54 862	318	...	...	...	...
Eindhoven	212 269	107 570	104 699	88	325 342	163 659	161 683	199
Emmen	109 441	54 084	55 357	337	...	...	...	...
Enschede	156 071	79 375	76 696	141	156 071	79 375	76 696	141
Geleen-Sittard	...	...	...	...	137 799	67 773	70 026	121
Groningen	184 227	91 022	93 205	78	202 859	99 789	103 070	124
Haarlem	148 191	72 022	76 169	29	195 940	94 476	101 464	94
Haarlemmermeer	142 042	70 691	71 351	179	...	...	...	...
Heerlen-Kerkrade	...	...	...	...	205 677	101 354	104 323	109
Leiden	116 787	56 918	59 869	22	250 154	122 132	128 022	77
Maastricht	118 286	56 767	61 519	57	118 286	56 767	61 519	57
Nijmegen	161 817	77 415	84 402	54	161 817	77 415	84 402	54
Rotterdam	587 134	288 102	299 032	206	989 319	484 936	504 383	329
s-Gravenhage	...	...	...	...	627 228	306 443	320 785	180
s-Hertogenbosch	137 775	67 715	70 060	84	163 063	80 261	82 802	118
The Hague	481 864	237 265	244 599	82	...	...	...	...
Tilburg	203 464	100 960	102 504	117	225 930	112 098	113 832	159
Utrecht	299 891	144 924	154 967	95	434 697	211 315	223 382	167
Zaanstad	144 055	71 055	73 000	74	...	...	...	...
Zoetermeer	120 881	59 242	61 639	35	...	...	...	...
Zwolle	117 703	57 233	60 470	112	117 703	57 233	60 470	112
Norway - Norvège[64]								
1 VII 2009 (ESDJ)								
Bergen	254 326	126 680	127 646	445	...	...	...	...
OSLO	581 168	287 260	293 908	426	...	...	...	...
Stavanger	122 730	61 620	61 110	68	...	...	...	...
Trondheim	169 597	84 738	84 859	322	...	...	...	...

8. Population of capital cities and cities of 100 000 or more inhabitants: latest available year, 1990 - 2009
Population des capitales et des villes de 100 000 habitants ou plus : dernière année disponible, 1990 - 2009 (continued - suite)

Continent, country or area, date, code and city / Continent, pays ou zone, date, code et ville	City proper - Ville proprement dite				Urban agglomeration - Agglomération urbaine			
	Population			Surface area - Superficie (km²)	Population			Surface area - Superficie (km²)
	Both sexes - Les deux sexes	Male - Masculin	Female - Féminin		Both sexes - Les deux sexes	Male - Masculin	Female - Féminin	
EUROPE								
Poland - Pologne[65]								
1 VII 2009 (ESDJ)								
Bialystok	294 399	137 554	156 845	102	...	...	...	...
Bielsko-Biala	175 513	82 765	92 748	125	...	...	...	...
Bydgoszcz	358 029	167 606	190 423	176	...	...	...	...
Bytom	183 251	88 489	94 762	69	...	...	...	...
Chorzów	113 162	53 890	59 272	33	...	...	...	...
Czestochowa	240 027	112 800	127 227	160	...	...	...	...
Dabrowa Górnicza	128 040	61 653	66 387	189	...	...	...	...
Elblag	126 432	60 533	65 899	80	...	...	...	...
Gdansk	455 830	215 782	240 048	262	...	...	...	...
Gdynia	248 889	118 386	130 503	135	...	...	...	...
Gliwice	196 361	94 577	101 784	134	...	...	...	...
Gorzów Wielkopolski	125 149	59 503	65 646	86	...	...	...	...
Kalisz	106 829	49 788	57 041	69	...	...	...	...
Katowice	308 724	145 884	162 840	165	...	...	...	...
Kielce	204 891	96 869	108 022	110	...	...	...	...
Koszalin	107 217	50 921	56 296	83	...	...	...	...
Kraków	754 854	353 047	401 807	327	...	...	...	...
Legnica	104 393	49 431	54 962	56	...	...	...	...
Lódz	744 541	338 355	406 186	293	...	...	...	...
Lublin	350 392	161 154	189 238	147	...	...	...	...
Olsztyn	176 387	81 861	94 526	88	...	...	...	...
Opole	125 992	58 827	67 165	97	...	...	...	...
Plock	126 675	60 251	66 424	88	...	...	...	...
Poznan	556 022	258 953	297 069	262	...	...	...	...
Radom	223 914	106 847	117 067	112	...	...	...	...
Ruda Slaska	143 583	69 862	73 721	78	...	...	...	...
Rybnik	141 387	69 158	72 229	148	...	...	...	...
Rzeszów	172 813	81 620	91 193	98	...	...	...	...
Sosnowiec	220 450	104 517	115 933	91	...	...	...	...
Szczecin	406 427	192 755	213 672	301	...	...	...	...
Tarnów	115 341	54 608	60 733	72	...	...	...	...
Torun	205 934	95 250	110 684	116	...	...	...	...
Tychy	129 527	62 672	66 855	82	...	...	...	...
Walbrzych	121 919	57 414	64 505	85	...	...	...	...
WARSZAWA	1 711 466	786 962	924 504	517	...	...	...	...
Wloclawek	117 785	55 434	62 351	84	...	...	...	...
Wroclaw	632 240	294 949	337 291	293	...	...	...	...
Zabrze	188 122	90 879	97 243	80	...	...	...	...
Zielona Góra	117 557	55 087	62 470	58	...	...	...	...
Portugal								
1 VII 2009 (ESDJ)								
Amadora	171 469	81 708	89 762	24	...	...	...	...
LISBOA	484 723	220 157	264 567	85	...	...	...	...
Porto	213 319	96 260	117 059	41	...	...	...	...
Republic of Moldova - République de Moldova								
1 VII 2008 (ESDJ)								
Balti (Beltsy)	143 204	65 605	77 599	41	148 108	67 941	80 167	78
CHIŞINĂU (KISHINEV)	663 127	308 735	354 392	123	785 344	368 732	416 612	572
Romania - Roumanie								
1 VII 2009 (ESDJ)								
Arad	165 477	77 292	88 185	267	...	...	...	...
Bacau	176 366	84 285	92 081	43	...	...	...	...
Baia Mare	138 722	66 254	72 468	233	...	...	...	...
Botosani	114 506	54 611	59 895	41	...	...	...	...
Braila	211 884	100 878	111 006	33	...	...	...	...
Brasov	278 003	132 230	145 773	267	...	...	...	...
BUCURESTI	1 944 226	908 430	1 035 796	238	...	...	...	...
Buzau	131 905	62 882	69 023	81	...	...	...	...
Cluj-Napoca	306 009	143 280	162 729	180	...	...	...	...
Constanta	302 040	141 980	160 060	127	...	...	...	...
Craiova	298 643	142 350	156 293	81	...	...	...	...
Drobeta Turnu-Severin	106 061	51 116	54 945	55	...	...	...	...
Galati	290 733	140 516	150 217	246	...	...	...	...

8. Population of capital cities and cities of 100 000 or more inhabitants: latest available year, 1990 - 2009
Population des capitales et des villes de 100 000 habitants ou plus : dernière année disponible, 1990 - 2009 (continued - suite)

Continent, country or area, date, code and city / Continent, pays ou zone, date, code et ville	City proper - Ville proprement dite				Urban agglomeration - Agglomération urbaine			
	Population			Surface area - Superficie (km²)	Population			Surface area - Superficie (km²)
	Both sexes - Les deux sexes	Male - Masculin	Female - Féminin		Both sexes - Les deux sexes	Male - Masculin	Female - Féminin	
EUROPE								
Spain - Espagne								
1 I 2008 (ESDJ)								
Oviedo	220 644	103 006	117 638	187	...	...	...	...
Palma de Mallorca	396 570	195 026	201 544	209	...	...	...	...
Palmas de Gran Canaria	381 123	185 770	195 353	101	...	...	...	...
Pamplona	197 275	94 588	102 687	25	...	...	...	...
Parla	108 051	55 581	52 470	25	...	...	...	...
Reus	107 770	53 845	53 925	53	...	...	...	...
Sabadell	203 969	99 947	104 022	38	...	...	...	...
Salamanca	155 740	72 154	83 586	39	...	...	...	...
San Cristóbal de La Laguna	148 375	72 890	75 485	102	...	...	...	...
Santa Coloma de Gramanet	117 336	59 829	57 507	7	...	...	...	...
Santa Cruz de Tenerife	221 956	106 858	115 098	43	...	...	...	...
Santander	182 302	84 747	97 555	35	...	...	...	...
Sevilla	699 759	333 490	366 269	141	...	...	...	...
Spain: Torrevieja	101 381	52 035	49 346	71	...	...	...	...
Tarragona	137 536	68 213	69 323	62	...	...	...	...
Terrassa	206 245	102 875	103 370	70	...	...	...	...
Torrejón de Ardoz	116 455	58 113	58 342	33	...	...	...	...
Valencia	807 200	388 589	418 611	135	...	...	...	...
Valladolid	318 461	152 085	166 376	197	...	...	...	...
Vigo	295 703	140 870	154 833	109	...	...	...	...
Vitoria-Gasteiz	232 477	114 703	117 774	277	...	...	...	...
Zaragoza	666 129	324 017	342 112	973	...	...	...	...
Sweden - Suède								
1 VII 2007 (ESDJ)								
Göteborg	491 630	242 916	248 714	449	...	...	...	...
Helsingborg	124 188	60 672	63 516	346	...	...	...	...
Jönköping	122 952	60 462	62 490	1 485	...	...	...	...
Linköping	139 474	70 239	69 235	1 431	...	...	...	...
Malmö	278 523	135 997	142 526	154	...	...	...	...
Norrköping	126 072	62 323	63 749	1 491	...	...	...	...
Orebro	129 703	63 123	66 581	1 371	...	...	...	...
STOCKHOLM	789 024	384 243	404 781	187	...	...	...	...
Umeå	111 503	55 549	55 955	2 316	...	...	...	...
Uppsala	186 364	91 149	95 215	2 465	...	...	...	...
Västerås	133 324	66 056	67 269	956	...	...	...	...
Switzerland - Suisse								
1 VII 2009 (ESDJ)								
Baden-Brugg	27 790	13 997	13 793	19	114 993	57 371	57 622	124
Bâle	165 489	78 922	86 567	24	496 020	240 076	255 944	481
BERNE	123 154	58 295	64 859	52	349 688	168 207	181 481	481
Fribourg	34 273	16 653	17 620	9	102 114	50 661	51 453	212
Genève	184 538	87 808	96 730	16	517 151	249 637	267 514	457
Lausanne	124 030	58 970	65 060	41	327 562	158 469	169 093	312
Lugano	54 727	25 746	28 981	32	134 174	64 011	70 163	228
Luzern	76 419	36 336	40 083	16	206 453	100 822	105 631	198
Olten-Zofingen	27 411	13 321	14 090	23	108 597	53 863	54 734	183
St. Gallen	72 313	35 050	37 263	39	149 015	72 887	76 128	175
Winterthur	98 774	48 046	50 728	68	135 954	66 526	69 428	151
Zug	25 743	12 971	12 772	22	106 257	53 590	52 667	180
Zürich	366 765	180 143	186 622	88	1 162 024	574 938	587 086	1 086
TFYR of Macedonia - L'ex-R. y. de Macédoine								
1 VII 2009 (ESDF)								
SKOPLJE	529 051	259 383	269 668	...	...	...	...	...
Ukraine								
1 I 2009 (ESDJ)								
Alchevsk	114 212	52 239	61 973	49	...	...	...	...
Belaya Tserkov (Bila Crkva)	204 754	94 474	110 280	34	...	...	...	...
Berdyansk	118 002	52 440	65 562	83	121 179	53 939	67 240	208
Cherkassy	286 166	130 942	155 224	78	286 910	131 326	155 584	88
Chernigov	291 996	134 790	157 206	78	...	...	...	...
Chernovtsy	245 779	112 516	133 263	152	...	...	...	...
Dneprodzerzhinsk	244 532	109 840	134 692	118	251 436	112 957	138 479	138
Dnepropetrovsk	1 007 389	456 965	550 424	387	1 009 699	458 092	551 607	405

Continent, country or area, date, code and city / Continent, pays ou zone, date, code et ville	City proper - Ville proprement dite				Urban agglomeration - Agglomération urbaine			
	Population			Surface area - Superficie (km²)	Population			Surface area - Superficie (km²)
	Both sexes - Les deux sexes	Male - Masculin	Female - Féminin		Both sexes - Les deux sexes	Male - Masculin	Female - Féminin	
EUROPE								
Ukraine								
1 I 2009 (ESDJ)								
Donetsk (Donestskaya oblast)	965 933	427 387	538 546	363	982 122	434 722	547 400	571
Enakievo (Yenakievo)	89 110	39 512	49 598	67	140 150	63 025	77 125	425
Evpatoriya	104 589	46 546	58 043	43	120 400	53 720	66 680	66
Gorlovka	264 082	118 344	145 738	186	284 855	127 731	157 124	422
Ivano-Frankovsk	220 781	104 310	116 471	37	236 778	111 785	124 993	84
Kamyanetsk Podilsky	100 481	47 033	53 448	28	...	...	...	...
Kertch	149 414	67 261	82 153	108	...	...	...	...
Kharkov	1 436 397	657 099	779 298	306	...	...	...	...
Kherson	302 965	135 952	167 013	65	340 069	153 210	186 859	423
Khmelnitsky (Hmilnyk)	257 555	119 376	138 179	86	...	...	...	...
KIEV	2 724 224	1 258 693	1 465 531	836	...	...	...	...
Kirovograd	233 988	105 643	128 345	...	242 046	109 290	132 756	103
Kramatorsk	168 625	75 005	93 620	77	202 545	90 677	111 868	356
Krasny Lutch	85 498	39 419	46 079	58	129 152	59 846	69 306	154
Krementchug	227 547	103 749	123 798	96	...	...	...	...
Kryvy Rig	674 066	304 159	369 907	430	677 416	305 849	371 567	431
Lugansk	434 500	192 385	242 115	257	473 782	210 835	262 947	286
Lutsk	206 202	92 933	113 269	42	...	...	...	...
Lvov	727 852	341 194	386 658	149	754 127	353 650	400 477	171
Lysychansk	107 330	48 487	58 843	76	123 721	55 940	67 781	96
Makeyevka	361 986	163 361	198 625	185	401 326	181 668	219 658	426
Mariupol	468 580	213 380	255 200	150	490 546	223 708	266 838	244
Melitopol	157 910	71 514	86 396	43	...	...	...	...
Mykolaiv (Nikolaevskaya oblast)	499 833	226 167	273 666	260	...	...	...	...
Nikopol	127 653	57 063	70 590	50	...	...	...	...
Odessa	990 964	461 668	529 296	162	...	...	...	...
Pavlograd	112 094	51 667	60 427	59	...	...	...	...
Poltava	294 552	134 994	159 558	104	...	...	...	...
Rivne	245 576	112 508	133 068	58	...	...	...	...
Sevastopol	338 076	153 796	184 280	...	378 106	172 283	205 823	864
Severodonetsk	112 658	50 435	62 223	32	122 952	55 322	67 630	58
Simferopol	331 790	146 074	185 716	...	355 330	156 839	198 491	107
Slavyansk	118 145	51 390	66 755	61	137 561	60 251	77 310	74
Sumy	273 104	123 582	149 522	88	275 965	124 951	151 014	146
Ternopol	215 818	100 454	115 364	59	...	...	...	...
Uzhgorod	114 705	53 555	61 150	32	...	...	...	...
Vinnutsya	365 918	167 523	198 395	69	...	...	...	...
Yevpatoriya	104 589	46 546	58 043	43	120 400	53 720	66 680	66
Zaporozhye	777 717	351 301	426 416	277	780 329	352 474	427 855	278
Zhitomir	270 618	124 999	145 619	61	...	...	...	...
United Kingdom of Great Britain and Northern Ireland - Royaume-Uni de Grande-Bretagne et d'Irlande du Nord[67]								
29 IV 2001 (CDFC)								
Aberdeen	...	...	...	...	212 125	103 818	108 307	...
Aberdeenshire	...	...	...	...	226 871	112 470	114 401	...
Aldershot	...	...	...	...	243 344	121 127	122 217	...
Angus	...	...	...	...	108 400	52 458	55 942	...
Basildon/North Benfleet	...	...	...	...	101 492	48 649	52 843	...
Bedford/Kempston	...	...	...	...	101 928	50 341	51 587	...
Belfast[68]	...	...	...	...	276 459	129 321	147 138	...
Birkenhead	...	...	...	...	319 675	152 133	167 542	...
Blackburn/Darwen	...	...	...	...	136 655	66 834	69 821	...
Blackpool	...	...	...	...	261 088	124 698	136 390	...
Bournemouth	...	...	...	...	383 713	182 875	200 838	...
Brighton/Worthing/Littlehampton	...	...	...	...	461 181	220 275	240 906	...
Bristol	...	...	...	...	551 066	269 689	281 377	...
Burnley/Nelson	...	...	...	...	149 796	72 657	77 139	...
Cambridge	...	...	...	...	131 465	65 343	66 122	...
Cardiff[69]	...	...	...	...	327 706	156 272	171 434	...
Cheltenham/Charlton Kings	...	...	...	...	110 320	53 526	56 794	...
Chesterfield/Staveley	...	...	...	...	100 879	49 204	51 675	...
Colchester	...	...	...	...	104 390	51 652	52 738	...

8. Population of capital cities and cities of 100 000 or more inhabitants: latest available year, 1990 - 2009
Population des capitales et des villes de 100 000 habitants ou plus : dernière année disponible, 1990 - 2009 (continued - suite)

Continent, country or area, date, code and city	City proper - Ville proprement dite				Urban agglomeration - Agglomération urbaine			
	Population			Surface area - Superficie (km²)	Population			Surface area - Superficie (km²)
Continent, pays ou zone, date, code et ville	Both sexes - Les deux sexes	Male - Masculin	Female - Féminin		Both sexes - Les deux sexes	Male - Masculin	Female - Féminin	

EUROPE

United Kingdom of Great Britain and Northern Ireland - Royaume-Uni de Grande-Bretagne et d'Irlande du Nord[67]
29 IV 2001 (CDFC)

Coventry/Bedworth	...	...	...	...	336 452	166 666	169 786	...
Crawley	...	...	...	...	180 177	88 404	91 773	...
Dearne Valley	...	...	...	...	207 726	100 992	106 734	...
Derby	...	...	...	...	236 738	115 644	121 094	...
Doncaster	...	...	...	...	127 851	62 127	65 724	...
Dumfries & Galloway	...	...	...	...	147 765	71 303	76 462	...
Dundee	...	...	...	...	145 663	69 140	76 523	...
East Ayrshire	...	...	...	...	120 235	57 842	62 393	...
East Dunbartonshire	...	...	...	...	108 243	52 014	56 229	...
Eastbourne	...	...	...	...	106 562	49 369	57 193	...
Edinburgh[70]	...	...	...	...	448 624	214 711	233 913	...
Exeter	...	...	...	...	106 772	52 045	54 727	...
Falkirk	...	...	...	...	145 191	70 016	75 175	...
Fife	...	...	...	...	349 429	167 628	181 801	...
Glasgow	...	...	...	...	577 869	272 309	305 560	...
Gloucester	...	...	...	...	136 203	66 669	69 534	...
Grimsby/Cleethorpes	...	...	...	...	138 842	67 360	71 482	...
Hastings/Bexhill	...	...	...	...	126 386	59 247	67 139	...
High Wycombe	...	...	...	...	118 229	57 857	60 372	...
Highland	...	...	...	...	208 914	102 297	106 617	...
Ipswich	...	...	...	...	141 658	69 468	72 190	...
Kingston-upon-Hull	...	...	...	...	301 416	146 926	154 490	...
Leicester	...	...	...	...	441 213	214 060	227 153	...
Lincoln	...	...	...	...	104 221	50 794	53 427	...
Liverpool	...	...	...	...	816 216	389 119	427 097	...
LONDON[71]	...	...	...	...	8 278 251	4 007 297	4 270 954	...
Luton/Dunstable	...	...	...	...	236 318	117 707	118 611	...
Manchester	...	...	...	...	2 244 931	1 090 898	1 154 033	...
Mansfield	...	...	...	...	158 114	76 884	81 230	...
Milton Keynes	...	...	...	...	184 506	91 441	93 065	...
Newport	...	...	...	...	139 298	66 884	72 414	...
North Ayrshire	...	...	...	...	135 817	64 238	71 579	...
North Lanarkshire	...	...	...	...	321 067	153 966	167 101	...
Northampton	...	...	...	...	197 199	96 670	100 529	...
Norwich	...	...	...	...	194 839	94 523	100 316	...
Nottingham	...	...	...	...	666 358	327 851	338 507	...
Nuneaton	...	...	...	...	132 236	64 837	67 399	...
Oxford	...	...	...	...	143 016	70 462	72 554	...
Perth & Kinross	...	...	...	...	134 949	65 172	69 777	...
Peterborough	...	...	...	...	136 292	66 139	70 153	...
Plymouth	...	...	...	...	243 795	119 076	124 719	...
Portsmouth	...	...	...	...	442 252	216 341	225 911	...
Preston	...	...	...	...	264 601	129 665	134 936	...
Reading/Wokingham	...	...	...	...	369 804	185 475	184 329	...
Renfrewshire	...	...	...	...	172 867	82 525	90 342	...
Scottish Borders	...	...	...	...	106 764	51 361	55 403	...
Sheffield	...	...	...	...	640 720	312 619	328 101	...
Slough	...	...	...	...	141 848	70 286	71 562	...
South Ayrshire	...	...	...	...	112 097	53 406	58 691	...
South Lanarkshire	...	...	...	...	302 216	144 206	158 010	...
Southampton	...	...	...	...	304 400	151 534	152 866	...
Southend	...	...	...	...	269 415	129 650	139 765	...
Southport/Formby	...	...	...	...	115 882	54 337	61 545	...
St. Albans/Hatfield	...	...	...	...	114 710	56 585	58 125	...
Sunderland	...	...	...	...	182 974	88 892	94 082	...
Swansea	...	...	...	...	270 506	130 648	139 858	...
Swindon	...	...	...	...	155 432	77 551	77 881	...
Teesside	...	...	...	...	365 323	176 475	188 848	...
Telford	...	...	...	...	138 241	67 770	70 471	...
Thanet	...	...	...	...	119 144	56 266	62 878	...
The Medway Towns	...	...	...	...	231 659	114 069	117 590	...

8. Population of capital cities and cities of 100 000 or more inhabitants: latest available year, 1990 - 2009
Population des capitales et des villes de 100 000 habitants ou plus : dernière année disponible, 1990 - 2009 (continued - suite)

Continent, country or area, date, code and city / Continent, pays ou zone, date, code et ville	City proper - Ville proprement dite				Urban agglomeration - Agglomération urbaine			
	Population			Surface area - Superficie (km²)	Population			Surface area - Superficie (km²)
	Both sexes - Les deux sexes	Male - Masculin	Female - Féminin		Both sexes - Les deux sexes	Male - Masculin	Female - Féminin	
EUROPE								
United Kingdom of Great Britain and Northern Ireland - Royaume-Uni de Grande-Bretagne et d'Irlande du Nord[67]								
29 IV 2001 (CDFC)								
The Potteries	...	...	...	...	362 403	176 467	185 936	...
Torbay	...	...	...	...	110 366	52 551	57 815	...
Tyneside	...	...	...	...	879 996	425 119	454 877	...
Warrington	...	...	...	...	158 195	77 334	80 861	...
West Lothian	...	...	...	...	158 714	76 701	82 013	...
West Midlands	...	...	...	...	2 284 093	1 109 397	1 174 696	...
West Yorkshire	...	...	...	...	1 499 465	724 818	774 647	...
Wigan	...	...	...	...	166 840	81 254	85 586	...
York	...	...	...	...	137 505	66 142	71 363	...
OCEANIA - OCÉANIE								
American Samoa - Samoas américaines[15]								
1 IV 2000 (CDJC)								
PAGO PAGO	4 278	2 086	2 192		...	...	...	...
Australia - Australie[72]								
1 VII 2009* (ESDJ)								
Adelaide	1 187 466	580 355	607 111	1 827	...	...	...	...
Albury-Wodonga	104 609	51 784	52 825	4 400	...	...	...	...
Brisbane	2 004 262	994 339	1 009 923	5 950	...	...	...	...
Cairns	147 118	73 910	73 208	491	...	...	...	...
CANBERRA	351 868	174 833	177 035	808	...	...	...	...
Darwin	124 760	65 733	59 027	3 122	...	...	...	...
Geelong	175 803	86 365	89 438	388	...	...	...	...
Gold Coast-Tweed	577 977	286 472	291 505	1 252	...	...	...	...
Greater Wollongong	288 984	144 188	144 796	1 089	...	...	...	...
Hobart	212 019	103 166	108 853	1 357	...	...	...	...
Launceston	105 445	51 633	53 812	803	...	...	...	...
Melbourne	3 995 537	1 981 585	2 013 952	7 692	...	...	...	...
Newcastle	540 796	267 902	272 894	4 052	...	...	...	...
Perth	1 658 992	833 110	825 882	5 386	...	...	...	...
Sunshine Coast	245 309	119 613	125 696	462	...	...	...	...
Sydney	4 504 469	2 226 913	2 277 556	12 140	...	...	...	...
Toowoomba	128 600	62 927	65 673	554	...	...	...	...
Townsville	168 402	85 056	83 346	455	...	...	...	...
Cook Islands - Îles Cook[73]								
1 XII 2001 (CDFC)								
RAROTONGA	12 188	...	...	...	...	...	...	...
Fiji - Fidji								
25 VIII 1996 (CDFC)								
SUVA	77 366	38 518	38 848	...	167 975	83 910	84 065	...
French Polynesia - Polynésie française								
7 XI 2002 (CDFC)								
PAPEETE	26 181	...	...	...	124 864	...	...	...
Guam								
1 IV 2000 (CDJC)								
AGANA	1 100[15]	672[15]	428[15]	3	...	...	...	...
Kiribati								
7 XI 2000* (CDFC)								
TARAWA	...	...	...	...	36 717	...	...	...
Marshall Islands - Îles Marshall								
1 VI 1999 (CDFC)								
MAJURO	23 676	12 075	11 601	...	...	...	...	...
Micronesia (Federated States of) - Micronésie (États fédérés de)								
1 IV 2000 (CDJC)								
PALIKIR	6 227	...	...	...	...	...	...	...
Nauru								
17 IV 1992 (CDFC)								
YAREN	672	...	...	...	...	...	...	...

8. Population of capital cities and cities of 100 000 or more inhabitants: latest available year, 1990 - 2009
Population des capitales et des villes de 100 000 habitants ou plus : dernière année disponible, 1990 - 2009 (continued - suite)

Continent, country or area, date, code and city / Continent, pays ou zone, date, code et ville	City proper - Ville proprement dite				Urban agglomeration - Agglomération urbaine			
	Population			Surface area - Superficie (km²)	Population			Surface area - Superficie (km²)
	Both sexes - Les deux sexes	Male - Masculin	Female - Féminin		Both sexes - Les deux sexes	Male - Masculin	Female - Féminin	
OCEANIA - OCÉANIE								
New Caledonia - Nouvelle-Calédonie								
16 IV 1996 (CDFC)								
NOUMEA	76 293	38 443	37 850	46	118 823	60 327	58 496	1 643
New Zealand - Nouvelle-Zélande								
1 VII 2009 (ESDJ)								
Auckland	444 100	218 300	225 800	664[74]	1 333 300	653 400	680 000	1 084[74]
Christchurch	372 600	181 500	191 100	608[74]	386 100	188 100	198 000	1 541[74]
Dunedin	115 700	55 600	60 100	255[74]	123 700	59 700	64 000	3 342[74]
Hamilton	140 700	68 100	72 600	98[74]	200 200	97 200	103 000	1 099[74]
Lower Hutt	102 100	50 100	52 000	377[74]	...	...	...	...
Manukau	368 600	180 200	188 400	683[74]	...	...	...	...
Napier-Hastings	...	...	...	...	123 200	59 400	63 800	389[74]
North Shore	225 800	110 900	114 900	129[74]	...	...	...	...
Tauranga	112 600	54 100	58 500	175[74]	118 200	56 900	61 300	184[74]
Waitakere	204 500	100 100	104 500	367[74]	...	...	...	...
WELLINGTON	195 500	95 200	100 300	290[74]	386 000	188 700	197 200	447[74]
Niue - Nioué								
7 IX 2001 (CDFC)								
ALOFI	615							
Norfolk Island - Île Norfolk								
1 VII 1997 (ESDF)								
KINGSTON	*800*	...	...	...	...	...	...	...
Northern Mariana Islands - Îles Mariannes septentrionales								
1 IV 2000 (CDFC)								
GARAPAN	3 588	...	...	...	...	...	...	...
Palau - Palaos								
15 IV 2000 (CDFC)								
KOROR	10 600	...	...	...	...	...	...	...
Papua New Guinea - Papouasie-Nouvelle-Guinée								
9 VII 2000 (CDFC)								
PORT MORESBY	254 158	138 974	115 184	...	...	...	...	...
Pitcairn								
31 XII 1993 (ESDF)								
ADAMSTOWN	53	25	28	0[75]	...	...	...	...
Samoa								
5 XI 2001 (CDFC)								
APIA	38 836	...	...	...	...	...	...	...
Solomon Islands - Îles Salomon								
21 XI 1999 (CDFC)								
HONIARA	49 107	...	...	...	...	...	...	...
Tonga								
1 VII 2000 (ESDF)								
NUKU'ALOFA	*21 538*	*10 625*	*10 913*	...	*30 336*	*15 115*	*15 221*	...
Tuvalu								
1 XI 2002 (CDFC)								
FUNAFUTI	4 492	2 281	2 211	...	...	...	...	...
Vanuatu								
16 XI 1999 (CDJC)								
PORT VILA	29 356	...	...	...	...	...	...	...
Wallis and Futuna Islands - Îles Wallis et Futuna								
3 X 1996 (CDFC)								
META-UTU	1 137							

FOOTNOTES - NOTES

The capital city of each country is shown in capital letters. Figures in italics are estimates of questionable reliability. For definition of city proper and urban agglomeration, method of evaluation and limitations of data see Technical Notes for this table. - Le nom de la capitale de chaque pays est imprimé en majuscules. Les chiffres en italique sont des estimations dont la fiabilité n'est pas assurée. Pour la définition de la ville proprement dite et de l'agglomération urbaine, et pour les méthodes d'évaluation et les insuffisances de données,

voir les notes techniques pour ce tableau.

Italics: estimates which are less reliable. - Italiques : estimations moins sûres.

* Provisional. - Données provisoires.

'Code' indicates the source of data, as follows:
CDFC - Census, de facto, complete tabulation
CDFS - Census, de facto, sample tabulation
CDJC - Census, de jure, complete tabulation

CDJS - Census, de jure, sample tabulation
SSDF - Sample survey, de facto
SSDJ - Sample survey, de jure
ESDF - Estimates, de facto
ESDJ - Estimates, de jure

Le 'Code' indique la source des données, comme suit :
CDFC - Recensement, population de fait, tabulation complète
CDFS - Recensement, population de fait, tabulation par sondage
CDJC - Recensement, population de droit, tabulation complète
CDJS - Recensement, population de droit, tabulation par sondage
SSDF - Enquête par sondage, population de fait
SSDJ - Enquête par sondage, population de droit
ESDF - Estimations, population de fait
ESDJ - Estimations, population de droit

[1] Data refer to national projections. - Les données se réfèrent aux projections nationales.

[2] Dual capitals. - Le pays a deux capitales.

[3] Data refer to the urban commune of Antananarivo. - Pour la commune urbaine de Antananarivo.

[4] Excludes the islands of St. Brandon and Agalega. - Non compris les îles St. Brandon et Agalega.

[5] Pretoria is the administrative capital, Cape Town the legislative capital. - Pretoria est la capital administrative, Le Cap la capitale législative.

[6] Comprising the Northern Region (former Saguia el Hamra) and Southern Region (former Rio de Oro). - Comprend la région septentrionale (ancien Saguia-el-Hamra) et la région méridionale (ancien Rio de Oro).

[7] Excluding the institutional population. - Non compris la population dans les institutions.

[8] Surface area is 0.28 Km2. - Superficie: 0,28 Km2.

[9] Population estimates and components of demographic growth according to Standard Geographical Classification (SGC) 2006. Estimates adjusted for census net undercoverage (including adjustment for incompletely enumerated Indian reserves). Preliminary postcensal estimates. - Les estimations de population et les composantes de la croissance démographique correspondent à la Classification géographique type de 2006. Ajusté pour la sous-estimation du recensement (y compris les réservations en Inde incomplètement énumérées). Estimations post censitaires préliminaires.

[10] Area (Sq.Km) are based on 2006 Census boundaries. - La superficie (kilomètres carrés) est fondée sur les limites du recensement de 2006.

[11] Estimates adjusted for census net undercoverage (including adjustment for incompletely enumerated Indian reserves). Ottawa is the capital city, but the data are reported for the Ottawa-Gatineau urban agglomeration. Population estimates and components of demographic growth according to Standard Geographical Classification (SGC) 2006. Preliminary postcensal estimates. - Ajusté pour la sous-estimation du recensement (y compris les réservations en Inde incomplètement énumérées). Ottawa est la capitale, mais les données se rapportent à l'agglomération urbaine d'Ottawa-Gatineau. Les estimations de population et les composantes de la croissance démographique correspondent à la Classification géographique type de 2006. Estimations post censitaires préliminaires.

[12] Surface area includes interior waters. - La superficie comprend les eaux intérieures.

[13] Total represents population in private dwellings, the non-institutional population and persons found on the streets between the hours of 5am and 7am on September 26, 2001; the figures represent the census counts adjusted for under-coverage. - Le total représente la population vivant dans des logements privés et les personnes trouvées dans la rue entre 5 et 7 heures du matin le 26 septembre 2001, mais ne tient pas compte des personnes vivant dans des établissements; les chiffres sont ceux du recensement corrigés pour tenir compte du sous-dénombrement.

[14] Data refer to projections based on the 2000 population census. - Les données se réfèrent aux projections basées sur le recensement de la population de 2000.

[15] Including armed forces stationed in the area. - Y compris les militaires en garnison sur le territoire.

[16] Excluding armed forces overseas and civilian citizens absent from country for an extended period of time. City refers to a type of incorporated place in 49 states and the District of Columbia, that has an elected government and provides a range of government functions and services. Also included are Honolulu, Hawaii Census Designated Place (CDP), for which the Census Bureau reports data under agreement with the State of Hawaii (instead of the combined city and county of Honolulu), and Arlington, VA CDP (which is coextensive with Arlington County - an entirely urban county that provides the same levels of services and functions as a municipality). - Non compris les militaires à l'étranger, et les civils hors du pays pendant une période prolongée. Par ville, on entend un lieu doté

de la personnalité morale dans 49 États et dans le district de Columbia, qui a un gouvernement élu et fournit tout un ensemble de fonctions et de services publics. Sont également inclus Honolulu, lieu chargé du recensement pour Hawaii, pour lequel le Census Bureau établit les données en accord avec l'État de Hawaii (au lieu de la ville et du comté d'Honolulu), et Arlington, lieu chargé du recensement pour la Virginie, qui est de même étendue que le comté d'Arlington, lequel est un comté entièrement urbain qui offre les mêmes niveaux de services et de fonctions qu'une municipalité.

[17] Data refer to municipalities, which may contain an urban centre as well as rural areas. - Pour municipios qui peuvent comprendre un centre urbain et aussi une zone rurale.

[18] Data based on the Population Census of 2005. - Données fondées sur le recensement de la population de 2005.

[19] Data refer to communes, which may contain an urban centre as well as rural areas. - Commune(s) pouvant comprendre un centre urbain et une zone rurale.

[20] The Metropolitan Area of Asunción is made up of Asunción and the 19 Central Department districts. - La zone métropolitaine d'Asunción est composée d'Asunción et de 19 districts du Département central.

[21] Data refer to the Province of Lima and the Constitutional Province of Callao. - Les données concernent la province de Lima et la province constitutionnelle de Callao.

[22] Lefkosia urban agglomeration is composed of Lefkosia municipality, Agios Dometios, Egkomi, Strovolos, Aglangia, Lakatameia, Anthoupoli, Latsia and Geri. - L'agglomération urbaine de Lefkosia se comprend de la municipalité de Lefkosia et Agios Dometios, Egkomi, Strovolos, Aglangia, Lakatameia, Anthoupoli, Latsia et Geri.

[23] Lemesos urban agglomeration is composed of Lemesos municipality, Mesa Geitonia, Agios Athanasios, Germasogeia, Pano Polemidia, Ypsonas, Kato Polemidia, and parts of Mouttagiaka, Agios Tychon, Parekklisia, Monagrouli, Moni, Pyrgos and Tserkezoi. - L'agglomération urbaine de Lemesos se comprend de la municipalité de Lemesos et Mesa Geitonia, Agios Athanasios, Germasogeia, Pano Polemidia, Ypsonas, Kato Polemidia, et certaines parties des Mouttagiaka, Agios Tychon, Parekklisia, Monagrouli, Moni, Pyrgos et Tserkezoi.

[24] Including data for the Indian-held part of Jammu and Kashmir, the final status of which has not yet been determined. - Y compris les données pour la partie du Jammu et du Cachemire occupée par l'Inde dont le statut définitif n'a pas encore été déterminé.

[25] Data for urban agglomeration include New Delhi. - Les données pour l'agglomération urbaine y compris New Delhi.

[26] Data for urban agglomeration include Bally, Baranagar, Barrackpur, Bhatpara, Calcutta Municipal Corporation, Chandan Nagar, Garden Reach, Houghly-Chinsura, Howrah, Jadarpur, Kamarhati, Naihati, Panihati, Serampore, South Dum Dum, South Suburban, and Titagarh. - Les données pour l'agglomération urbaine y compris Bally, Baranagar, Barrackpur, Bhatpara, Calcutta Municipal Corporation, Chandan Nagar, Garden Reach, Houghly Chinsura, Howrah, Jadarpur, Kamarhati, Naihati, Panihati, Serampopre, South Dum Dum, South Suburban et Titagarh.

[27] Included in urban agglomeration of Delhi. Data refer to the New Delhi Municipal Council. - Comprise dans l'agglomération urbaine de Delhi. Les données se rapportent au New Delhi Municipal Council.

[28] Excluding Province Nanggroe Aceh Darussalam, Regency Nias & Nias Selatan, Regency Boven Digul & Teluk Wondama. Data refer to the "Intercensal Population Survey". - En excluant les provinces de Nanggroe Aceh Darussalam, Regency Nias & Nias Selatan, Regency Boven Digul & Teluk Wondama. Les données concernent l'enquête intercensitaire sur la population.

[29] Designation and data provided by Israel. The position of the United Nations on the question of Jerusalem is contained in General Assembly resolution 181 (II) and subsequent resolutions of the General Assembly and the Security Council concerning this question. Including East Jerusalem. - Appelation de données fournies par Israel. La position des Nations Unies concernant la question de Jérusalem est décrite dans la resolution 181 (II) de l'Assemblée générale et résolutions ultérieures de l'Assemblée générale et du Conseil de sécurité sur cette question. Y compris Jérusalem-Est.

[30] Except for Tokyo, all data refer to shi, a minor division which may include some scattered or rural population as well as an urban centre. Excluding diplomatic personnel outside the country and foreign military and civilian personnel and their dependants stationed in the area. - Sauf pour Tokyo, toutes les données se rapportent à des shi, petites divisions administratives qui peuvent comprendre des peuplements dispersés ou ruraux en plus d'un centre urbain. Non compris le personnel diplomatique hors du pays ni les militaires et agents civils étrangers en poste sur le territoire et les membres de leur famille les accompagnant.

[31] Including Kokura, Moji, Tobata, Wakamatsu and Yahata (Yawata). - Y compris Kokura, Moji, Tobata, Wakamatsu et Yahata (Yawata).

[32] Data for city proper refer to 23 ku (wards) of Tokyo; data for urban agglomeration refer to Tokyo-to (Tokyo prefecture). - Les données concernant la

ville proprement dite se rapportent aux 23 circonscriptions de Tokyo; les chiffres pour l'agglomération urbaine se raportent à Tokyo-to (préfecture de Tokyo).

[33] Data refer to annual average of resident population. - Les données correspondent à la population résidente annuelle moyenne.

[34] Based on the results of a household survey. - D'après les résultats d'une enquête des ménages.

[35] Data refer to projections by Local Authority. - Les données se réfèrent aux projections de la collectivité locale.

[36] Excluding data for the Pakistan-held part of Jammu and Kashmir, the final status of which has not yet been determined, and for Junagardh, Manavadar, Gilgit and Baltistan. - Non compris les données pour la partie de Jammu-Cachemire occupée par le Pakistan dont le status definitif n'a pas encore été déterminé, et le Junagardh, le Manavadar, le Gilgit et le Baltistan.

[37] The Population and Housing Census 2001 did not cover the whole area of the country due to the security problems; data refer to the 18 districts for which the census was completed only (in three districts it was not possible to conduct the census at all and in four districts it was partially conducted). - Le recensement de la population et du logement de 2001 n'a pas été réalisé sur la superficie totale du pays à cause de problèmes de sécurité; les données ne concernent que les 18 districts entièrement recensés (3 districts n'ont pas été recensés du tout, et 4 ont été recensés en partie).

[38] Covering Seyhan and Yuregir districts in Adana. - Y compris la population des districts de Seyhan et de Yuregir.

[39] Covering Altindag, Cankaya, Etimesgut, Golbasi, Kecioren, Mamak, Sincan, and Yenimahalle districts in Ankara. - Y compris la population des districts de Altindag, de Cankaya, de Etimesgut, de Golbasi, de Kecioren, de Mamak, de Sincan, et de Yenimahalle.

[40] Covering Nilufer, Osmangazi and Yildirim districts in Bursa. - Y compris la population des districts de Nilufer, de Osmangazi et de Yildirim.

[41] District centre. - Le centre du district.

[42] Covering Sahinbey and Sehitkamil districts in Gaziantep. - Y compris la population des districts de Sahinbey et de Sehitkamil.

[43] Covering Adalar, Avcilar, Bagcilar, Bahcelievler, Bakirkoy, Bayrampasa, Besiktas, Beykoz, Beyoglu, Eminonu, Esenler, Eyup, Fatih, Gaziosmanpasa, Gungoren, Kadikoy, Kagithane, Kartal, Kucukcekmece, Maltepe, Pendik, Sariyer, Sisli, Sultanbeyli, Tuzla, Umraniye, Uskudar, Zentinburnu districts in Istanbul. - Y compris la population des districts de Adalar, de Avcilar, de Bagcilar, de Bahcelievler, de Bakirkoy, de Bayrampasa, de Besiktas, de Beykoz, de Beyoglu, de Eminonu, de Esenler, de Eyup, de Fatih, de Gaziosmanpasa, de Gungoren, de Kadikoy, de Kagithane, de Kartal, de Kucukcekmece, de Maltepe, de Pendik, de Sariyer, de Sisli, de Sultanbeyli, de Tuzla, de Umraniye, de Uskudar, et de Zentinburnu.

[44] Covering Bolcova, Bornova, Buca, Cigli, Gaziemir, Guzelbahce, Karsiyaka, Konak and Narlidere districts in Izmir. - Y compris la population des districts de Bolcova, de Bornova, de Buca, de Cigli, de Gaziemir, de Guzelbahce, de Karsiyaka, de Konak et de Narlidere.

[45] Covering Kocasinan and Melikgazi districts in Kayseri. - Y compris la population des districts de Kocasinan et de Melikgazi.

[46] Including Cholon. - Y compris Cholon.

[47] Population statistics are compiled from registers. - Les statistiques de la population sont compilées à partir des registres.

[48] City proper refers to commune or municipality. - La ville proprement dite se rapporte à la commune ou à la municipalité

[49] Data for city proper refer to settlements. - Les données pour la ville proprement dite concernent les établissements.

[50] Data for urban agglomeration refer to the city. - Les données pour l'agglomération urbaine concernent la ville.

[51] Excluding Faeroe Islands and Greenland shown separately, if available. - Non compris les Iles Féroé et le Groenland, qui font l'objet de rubriques distinctes, si disponible.

[52] Data for cities proper refer to communes which are centres for urban agglomeration. - Les données concernant les villes proprement dites se rapportent à des communes qui sont des centres d'agglomérations urbaines.

[53] Data refer to French territory of this international agglomeration. - Les données se rapportent aux habitants de cette agglomération internationale qui vivent en territoire francais.

[54] The city of Villeurbanne is part of the urban agglomeration of Lyon. - La ville de Villeurbanne fait partie de l'agglomération urbaine de Lyon.

[55] The city of Aix-en-Provence is part of the urban agglomeration of Marseille. - La ville d'Aix-en-Provence fait partie de l'agglomération urbaine de Marseille.

[56] The city of Boulogne-Billancourt is part of the urban agglomeration of Paris. - La ville de Boulogne-Billancourt fait partie de l'agglomération urbaine de Paris.

[57] Including armed forces stationed outside the country and alien armed forces in the area. - Y compris les militaires nationaux hors du pays et les militaires étrangers en garnison sur le territoire.

[58] Data refer to the Vatican City State. - Les données se rapportent à l'Etat de la Cité du Vatican.

[59] Surface area is 0.44 Km2. - Superficie: 0,44 Km2.

[60] The boundaries of the city are related to the boundaries of the respective commune. - Les limites de la ville correspondent aux limites de la commune respective.

[61] The urban agglomeration of the capital area includes the following communes: Bessastaðahreppur, Garðabær, Hafnarfjörður, Kjósarhreppur, Kópavogur, Mosfellsbær ,Reykjavík, Seltjarnarnes. - L'agglomération urbaine de la capitale comprend les communes suivantes : Bessastaðahreppur, Garðabær, Hafnarfjörður, Kjósarhreppur, Kópavogur, Mosfellsbær ,Reykjavík, Seltjarnarnes.

[62] City refers to densely built-up residential areas with a resident population of more than 3000 persons. - Une ville est définie comme une zone résidentielle agglomérée avec une population permanente de plus de 3000 personnes.

[63] Including civilian nationals temporarily outside the country. - Y compris les civils nationaux temporairement hors du pays.

[64] Excluding Svalbard and Jan Mayen Islands shown separately, if available. - Non compris Svalbard et Jan Mayen qui font l'objet de rubriques distinctes, si disponible.

[65] City is defined as an administratively separated area entitled to civil (municipal) rights. - Une ville est définie comme une zone administrativement distincte dotée de droits municipaux.

[66] Data for urban agglomeration refer to communes which are administrative divisions. - Les données pour l'agglomération urbaine se rapportent aux communes qui sont des divisions administrative.

[67] Excluding Channel Islands (Guernsey and Jersey) and Isle of Man, shown separately, if available. Data refer to urban areas with 100,000+ residents. - Non compris les îles Anglo-Normandes (Guernesey et Jersey) et l'île de Man, qui font l'objet de rubriques distinctes, si disponible. Les données se rapportent aux zones urbaines avec plus de 100 000 résidents.

[68] Capital of Northern Ireland. - Capitale de l'Irlande du Nord.

[69] Capital of Wales for certain purposes. - Considérée à certains égards comme la capitale du pays de Galles.

[70] Capital of Scotland. - Capitale de l'Ecosse.

[71] 'Greater London' conurbation as reconstituted in 1965 and comprising 32 new Greater London Boroughs. - Ensemble urbain du 'Grand Londres', tel qu'il a été reconstitué en 1965, comprenant 32 nouveaux Greater London Boroughs.

[72] It is not possible to distinguish for all regions between 'city proper' and 'urban agglomeration' areas, therefore data has been included under 'city proper'. - Il n'est pas possible de distinguer pour toutes les régions entre 'ville proprement dite' et 'agglomération urbaine', et les données sont donc présentées sous 'ville proprement dite'.

[73] Excluding Niue, shown separately, which is part of Cook Islands, but because of remoteness is administered separately. - Non compris Nioué, qui fait l'objet d'une rubrique distincte et qui fait partie des îles Cook, mais qui, en raison de son éloignement, est administrée séparément.

[74] Excludes inland water and oceanic areas. - Exclut les eaux intérieures et les zones océaniques.

[75] Surface area is 0.24 Km2. - Superficie: 0,24 Km2.

8a. Population of capital cities and cities of 100 000 or more inhabitants: 2010
Population des capitales et des villes de 100 000 habitants ou plus: 2010

Continent, country or area, date, code and city / Continent, pays ou zone, date, code et ville	City proper - Ville proprement dite				Urban agglomeration - Agglomération urbaine			
	Population			Surface area - Superficie (km²)	Population			Surface area - Superficie (km²)
	Both sexes - Les deux sexes	Male - Masculin	Female - Féminin		Both sexes - Les deux sexes	Male - Masculin	Female - Féminin	
AFRICA - AFRIQUE								
Benin - Bénin								
1 VII 2010* (ESDF)								
Cotonou	862 445[1]	426 247[1]	436 198[1]	79	...	...	...	...
Parakou	194 247[1]	98 756[1]	95 490[1]	441	...	...	...	...
PORTO-NOVO	289 880[1]	139 960[1]	149 920[1]	50	...	...	...	...
Cape Verde - Cap-Vert								
1 VII 2010 (ESDF)								
PRAIA	...	...	...	...	131 453	64 191	67 262	
Egypt - Égypte								
1 VII 2010* (ESDF)								
6th of October City	802 306	420 009	382 297	...	...	...	...	...
Alexandria	4 358 439	2 225 558	2 132 881	...	...	...	...	...
Assyût	991 929	508 403	483 526	...	...	...	...	...
Aswan	543 396	277 732	265 664	...	...	...	...	...
Behera	985 850	500 999	484 851	...	...	...	...	...
Beni-Suef	582 396	293 887	288 509	...	...	...	...	...
CAIRO	7 248 671	3 682 152	3 566 519	...	...	...	...	...
Dakahlia	1 503 395	758 471	744 924	...	...	...	...	...
Damietta	462 154	236 522	225 632	...	...	...	...	...
Faiyûm	621 268	318 679	302 589	...	...	...	...	...
Gharbia	1 285 492	645 533	639 959	...	...	...	...	...
Giza	3 122 041	1 592 292	1 529 749	...	...	...	...	...
Helwan	1 295 854	660 776	635 078	...	...	...	...	...
Ismailia	472 655	237 174	235 481	...	...	...	...	...
Kafr-Elsheikh	655 002	327 445	327 557	...	...	...	...	...
Kalyoubia	2 053 859	1 051 232	1 002 627	...	...	...	...	...
Luxer	391 460	200 250	191 210	...	...	...	...	...
Matrouh	258 699	136 995	121 704	...	...	...	...	...
Menia	859 719	434 498	425 221	...	...	...	...	...
Menoufia	724 352	368 333	356 019	...	...	...	...	...
North Sinai	229 462	120 302	109 160	...	...	...	...	...
Port Said	610 468	310 881	299 587	...	...	...	...	...
Qena	534 766	270 422	264 344	...	...	...	...	...
Red Sea	295 993	180 622	115 371	...	...	...	...	...
Sharkia	1 340 060	682 941	657 119	...	...	...	...	...
Sohag	870 362	443 082	427 280	...	...	...	...	...
Suez	556 665	283 571	273 094	...	...	...	...	...
Sierra Leone								
1 VII 2010 (ESDF)								
Bo	231 494	111 731	119 763	...	...	...	...	...
FREETOWN	945 423	479 526	465 897	...	...	...	...	...
Kenema	195 498	95 988	99 510	...	...	...	...	...
Makeni	114 960	55 388	59 572	...	...	...	...	...
AMERICA, NORTH - AMÉRIQUE DU NORD								
Canada								
1 VII 2010* (ESDJ)								
Abbotsford-Mission	...	...	...	...	174 300[2]	87 304[2]	86 996[2]	626[3]
Barrie	...	...	...	...	190 872[2]	95 163[2]	95 709[2]	897[3]
Brampton	...	...	...	...	139 124[2]	68 432[2]	70 692[2]	1 073[3]
Calgary	...	...	...	...	1 242 624[2]	633 047[2]	609 577[2]	5 107[3]
Edmonton	...	...	...	...	1 176 307[2]	597 335[2]	578 972[2]	9 418[3]
Greater Sudbury / Grand Sudbury	...	...	...	...	164 680[2]	81 066[2]	83 614[2]	3 382[3]
Guelph	...	...	...	...	138 158[2]	68 684[2]	69 474[2]	378[3]
Halifax	...	...	...	...	403 188[2]	195 597[2]	207 591[2]	5 496[3]
Hamilton	...	...	...	...	740 238[2]	364 186[2]	376 052[2]	1 372[3]
Kelowna	...	...	...	...	178 854[2]	88 141[2]	90 713[2]	2 904[3]
Kingston	...	...	...	...	162 543[2]	80 279[2]	82 264[2]	1 907[3]
Kitchener-Cambridge-Waterloo	...	...	...	...	492 390[2]	245 541[2]	246 849[2]	827[3]
London	...	...	...	...	492 249[2]	242 027[2]	250 222[2]	2 665[3]
Moncton	...	...	...	...	137 346[2]	67 489[2]	69 857[2]	2 406[3]
Montréal	...	...	...	...	3 859 318[2]	1 902 000[2]	1 957 318[2]	4 259[3]

8a. Population of capital cities and cities of 100 000 or more inhabitants: 2010
Population des capitales et des villes de 100 000 habitants ou plus: 2010 (continued - suite)

Continent, country or area, date, code and city / Continent, pays ou zone, date, code et ville	City proper - Ville proprement dite				Urban agglomeration - Agglomération urbaine			
	Population			Surface area - Superficie (km²)	Population			Surface area - Superficie (km²)
	Both sexes - Les deux sexes	Male - Masculin	Female - Féminin		Both sexes - Les deux sexes	Male - Masculin	Female - Féminin	
AMERICA, NORTH - AMÉRIQUE DU NORD								
Canada								
1 VII 2010* (ESDJ)								
Oshawa	...	...	...	...	364 193[2]	179 822[2]	184 371[2]	903[3]
Ottawa - Gatineau	...	...	...	...	1 239 140[2]	608 662[2]	630 478[2]	5 716[3]
Peterborough	...	...	...	...	121 054[2]	58 807[2]	62 247[2]	1 506[3]
Québec	...	...	...	...	754 358[2]	369 797[2]	384 561[2]	3 277[3]
Regina	...	...	...	...	215 138[2]	106 222[2]	108 916[2]	3 408[3]
Saguenay	...	...	...	...	152 150[2]	75 590[2]	76 560[2]	1 754[3]
Saint John	...	...	...	...	127 973[2]	61 945[2]	66 028[2]	3 360[3]
Saskatoon	...	...	...	...	265 259[2]	132 073[2]	133 186[2]	5 207[3]
Sherbrooke	...	...	...	...	197 299[2]	96 557[2]	100 742[2]	1 232[3]
St Catharines-Niagara	...	...	...	...	404 357[2]	197 712[2]	206 645[2]	1 397[3]
St. John's	...	...	...	...	192 326[2]	94 159[2]	98 167[2]	805[3]
Thunder Bay	...	...	...	...	126 683[2]	62 866[2]	63 817[2]	2 550[3]
Toronto	...	...	...	...	5 741 419[2]	2 818 996[2]	2 922 423[2]	5 904[3]
Trois-Rivières	...	...	...	...	146 516[2]	71 373[2]	75 143[2]	880[3]
Vancouver	...	...	...	...	2 391 252[2]	1 182 263[2]	1 208 989[2]	2 877[3]
Victoria	...	...	...	...	358 054[2]	173 360[2]	184 694[2]	695[3]
Windsor	...	...	...	...	330 856[2]	164 246[2]	166 610[2]	1 023[3]
Winnipeg	...	...	...	...	753 555[2]	372 742[2]	380 813[2]	5 303[3]
Costa Rica								
1 VII 2010 (ESDJ)								
Alajuela	283 166[1]	143 186[1]	139 980[1]	388	...	...	...	...
Alajuelita	125 638[1]	63 573[1]	62 065[1]	21	...	...	...	...
Cartago	155 402[1]	77 798[1]	77 604[1]	288	...	...	...	...
Desamparados	292 883[1]	146 144[1]	146 739[1]	188	...	...	...	...
Goicoechea	131 637[1]	65 187[1]	66 450[1]	32	...	...	...	...
Heredia	132 579[1]	65 962[1]	66 617[1]	283	...	...	...	...
La Unión	105 612[1]	52 692[1]	52 920[1]	45	...	...	...	...
Limón	104 917[1]	53 804[1]	51 113[1]	1 766	...	...	...	...
Pavas	112 077[1]	56 156[1]	55 921[1]	9	...	...	...	...
Perez Zeledon	130 552[1]	65 368[1]	65 184[1]	1 906	...	...	...	...
Pococi	150 633[1]	79 610[1]	71 023[1]	2 403	...	...	...	...
Puntarenas	106 020[1]	54 840[1]	51 180[1]	1 842	...	...	...	...
San Carlos	150 241[1]	77 104[1]	73 137[1]	3 348	...	...	...	...
SAN JOSE	349 152[1]	174 432[1]	174 720[1]	45	...	...	...	...
Cuba								
31 XII 2010 (ESDJ)								
Bayamo	147 639	...	...	27[4]	...	...	...	...
Camagüey	305 701	...	...	82[4]	...	...	...	...
Ciego de Avila	111 086	...	...	21[4]	...	...	...	...
Cienfuegos	143 894	...	...	46[4]	...	...	...	...
Guantánamo	207 973	...	...	34[4]	...	...	...	...
Holguín	277 260	...	...	58[4]	...	...	...	...
LA HABANA	2 141 996	...	...	721[4]	...	...	...	...
Las Tunas	153 129	...	...	31[4]	...	...	...	...
Matanzas	132 678	...	...	44[4]	...	...	...	...
Pinar del Río	137 320	...	...	32[4]	...	...	...	...
Santa Clara	206 379	...	...	44[4]	...	...	...	...
Santiago de Cuba	426 841	...	...	70[4]	...	...	...	...
Dominican Republic - République dominicaine								
1 VII 2010 (ESDF)								
Azua	101 218	51 068	50 150	155	...	...	...	...
Bajos de Haina	141 050	69 769	71 281	40	...	...	...	...
Baní	175 042	87 540	87 502	740	...	...	...	...
Boca Chica	120 135	60 297	59 838	142	...	...	...	...
Bonao	146 992	73 008	73 984	674	...	...	...	...
Higüey	206 632	104 240	102 392	2 026	...	...	...	...
La Romana	150 499	72 368	78 131	263	...	...	...	...
La Vega	270 950	136 229	134 721	641	...	...	...	...
Los Alcarrizos	245 345	123 905	121 440	46	...	...	...	...
Moca	181 487	90 889	90 598	337	...	...	...	...

8a. Population of capital cities and cities of 100 000 or more inhabitants: 2010
Population des capitales et des villes de 100 000 habitants ou plus: 2010 (continued - suite)

Continent, country or area, date, code and city / Continent, pays ou zone, date, code et ville	City proper - Ville proprement dite				Urban agglomeration - Agglomération urbaine			
	Population			Surface area - Superficie (km²)	Population			Surface area - Superficie (km²)
	Both sexes - Les deux sexes	Male - Masculin	Female - Féminin		Both sexes - Les deux sexes	Male - Masculin	Female - Féminin	
AMERICA, NORTH - AMÉRIQUE DU NORD								
Dominican Republic - République dominicaine								
1 VII 2010 (ESDF)								
Puerto Plata	154 973	76 222	78 751	496	...	...	...	...
San Cristóbal	273 421	135 961	137 460	214	...	...	...	...
San Francisco de Macoris	184 907	91 788	93 119	760	...	...	...	...
San Juan de la Maguana	138 101	70 502	67 599	1 722	...	...	...	...
San Pedro de Macoris	230 023	111 696	118 327	146	...	...	...	...
Santiago de los Caballeros	747 576	367 362	380 214	529	...	...	...	...
SANTO DOMINGO	1 111 838	530 838	581 000	91	...	...	...	...
Santo Domingo East - Santo Domingo Este	949 923	460 689	489 234	169	...	...	...	...
Santo Domingo North - Santo Domingo Norte	445 333	225 033	220 300	388	...	...	...	...
Santo Domingo West - Santo Domingo Oeste	343 226	168 007	175 219	54	...	...	...	...
Greenland - Groenland[5]								
1 VII 2010 (ESDJ)								
NUUK (GODTHAB)	15 666	8 230	7 436	...	...	...	...	...
Mexico - Mexique								
12 VI 2010 (CDFC)								
Acapulco (de Juárez)	673 479	324 746	348 733	...	863 431	418 236	445 195	...
Acayucan	83 817	40 242	43 575	...	112 996	54 333	58 663	...
Aguascalientes	722 250	348 722	373 528	...	932 369	453 097	479 272	...
Apizaco	76 492	36 269	40 223	...	499 567	240 285	259 282	...
Campeche	...	...	...	...	259 005	125 561	133 444	...
Cancun	628 306	317 990	310 316	...	677 379	343 303	334 076	...
Celaya	...	...	...	...	468 469	225 024	243 445	...
Chalco de Diaz Covarrubias	168 720	81 192	87 528	...	...	...	...	...
Chetumal	...	...	...	...	151 243	74 273	76 970	...
Chicoloapán de Juárez	172 919	84 285	88 634	...	...	...	...	...
Chihuahua	809 232	394 144	415 088	...	852 533	416 866	435 667	...
Chilpacingo (de los Bravo)	...	...	...	...	241 717	115 443	126 274	...
Chimalhuacan	612 383	301 250	311 133	...	...	...	...	...
Ciudad Acuña	...	...	...	...	136 755	68 350	68 405	...
Ciudad Apodaca	467 157	234 492	232 665	...	...	...	...	...
Ciudad de Villa de Alvárez	117 600	57 124	60 476	...	334 240	163 648	170 592	...
Ciudad Del Carmen	...	...	...	...	169 466	83 802	85 664	...
Ciudad General Escobedo	352 444	177 382	175 062	...	...	...	...	...
Ciudad Juárez	151 893	76 140	75 753	...	...	...	...	...
Ciudad López Mateos	489 160	237 729	251 431	...	...	...	...	...
Ciudad Madero	197 216	94 384	102 832	...	859 419	418 362	441 057	...
Ciudad Obregón	...	...	...	...	298 625	146 788	151 837	...
Ciudad Santa Catarina	268 347	134 044	134 303	...	...	...	...	...
Ciudad Valles	...	...	...	...	167 713	81 226	86 487	...
Ciudad Victoria	...	...	...	...	321 953	157 152	164 801	...
Coatzacoalcos	235 983	112 989	122 994	...	347 257	168 301	178 956	...
Colimas	137 383	66 698	70 685	...	334 240	163 648	170 592	...
Córdoba	140 896	65 279	75 617	...	316 032	148 861	167 171	...
Cuauhtemoc	...	...	...	...	154 639	75 936	78 703	...
Cuautitlan Izcalli	484 573	235 136	249 437	...	...	...	...	...
Cuautla	154 358	73 384	80 974	...	434 147	209 752	224 395	...
Cuernavaca	338 650	159 999	178 651	...	876 083	421 781	454 302	...
Culiacán Rosales	...	...	...	...	675 773	329 608	346 165	...
Delicias	...	...	...	...	137 935	68 013	69 922	...
Durango (Victoria de Durango)	...	...	...	...	518 709	250 073	268 636	...
Ecatepec (de Morelos)	1 655 015	805 890	849 125	...	...	...	...	...
Ensenada	...	...	...	...	466 814	235 130	231 684	...
Fresnillo	...	...	...	...	213 139	104 348	108 791	...
Gómez Palacio	257 352	126 001	131 351	...	1 215 817	596 961	618 856	...
Guadalajara	1 495 182	717 399	777 783	...	4 434 878	2 171 514	2 263 364	...
Guadalupe, Nuevo León	673 616	334 519	339 097	...	4 089 962	2 036 484	2 053 478	...
Guadalupe, Zacatecas	124 623	60 349	64 274	...	298 167	144 140	154 027	...
Guanajuato	...	...	...	...	171 709	82 830	88 879	...
Hermosillo	...	...	...	...	784 342	392 697	391 645	...
Heroica Guaymas	113 082	56 090	56 992	...	203 430	101 736	101 694	...
Heroica Nogales	212 533	106 299	106 234	...	...	...	...	...
Hidalgo del Parral	...	...	...	...	107 061	51 883	55 178	...
Iguala (de la Independencia)	...	...	...	...	140 363	67 611	72 752	...

370

Continent, country or area, date, code and city / Continent, pays ou zone, date, code et ville	City proper - Ville proprement dite				Urban agglomeration - Agglomération urbaine			
	Population			Surface area - Superficie (km²)	Population			Surface area - Superficie (km²)
	Both sexes - Les deux sexes	Male - Masculin	Female - Féminin		Both sexes - Les deux sexes	Male - Masculin	Female - Féminin	
AMERICA, NORTH - AMÉRIQUE DU NORD								
Mexico - Mexique								
12 VI 2010 (CDFC)								
Irapuato	...	...	...	...	529 440	254 784	274 656	...
Ixtapaluca	322 271	156 847	165 424	...	...	...	...	
Jiutepec	162 427	78 012	84 415	...	876 083	421 781	454 302	...
Juárez	1 321 004	659 857	661 147	...	1 332 131	665 691	666 440	...
La Paz, Baja California Sur	...	...	...	...	251 871	126 397	125 474	
La Paz, Distrito Federal	253 845	123 956	129 889	...	...	...	...	
La Piedad	99 576	47 492	52 084	...	249 512	118 043	131 469	...
Lázaro Cárdenas	...	...	...	...	178 817	89 221	89 596	...
León (de los Aldama)	1 238 962	603 633	635 329	...	1 609 504	785 729	823 775	...
Los Mochis	...	...	...	...	256 613	124 228	132 385	...
Manzanillo	...	...	...	...	161 420	81 007	80 413	...
Matamoros	449 815	221 006	228 809	...	489 193	242 234	246 959	...
Mazatlán	...	...	...	...	438 434	216 266	222 168	...
Mérida	777 615	374 542	403 073	...	973 046	472 213	500 833	...
Mexicali	689 775	346 642	343 133	...	936 826	473 203	463 623	...
MEXICO, CIUDAD DE	8 851 080	4 233 783	4 617 297	...	20 116 842	9 729 967	10 386 875	...
Minatitlán	157 840	76 222	81 618	...	356 137	171 979	184 158	...
Monclova	215 271	106 901	108 370	...	317 313	157 907	159 406	...
Monterrey	1 135 512	561 638	573 874	...	4 089 962	2 036 484	2 053 478	...
Morelia	597 511	284 708	312 803	...	807 902	386 945	420 957	...
Moroleón - Uriangato	108 669	51 613	57 056	...	108 669	51 613	57 056	...
Naucalpan de Juárez	792 211	384 234	407 977	...	...	...	...	
Navojoa	157 729	78 242	79 487					
Netzahualcóyotl	1 104 585	532 528	572 057					
Nuevo Laredo	373 725	185 747	187 978	...	384 033	191 001	193 032	...
Oaxaca de Juárez	255 029	118 367	136 662	...	593 658	279 311	314 347	...
Ocotlán	92 967	45 453	47 514	...	141 375	69 174	72 201	...
Orizaba	120 844	55 772	65 072	...	410 508	194 618	215 890	...
Pachuca (de Soto)	256 584	121 719	134 865	...	512 196	244 839	267 357	...
Piedras Negras	150 178	74 655	75 523	...	180 734	90 641	90 093	...
Playa del Carmen	149 923	78 169	71 754		...	...	...	
Poza Rica de Hidalgo	185 242	87 456	97 786	...	513 518	247 486	266 032	...
Puebla de Zaragoza	1 434 062	682 505	751 557	...	2 668 437	1 278 555	1 389 882	...
Puerto Vallarta	203 342	101 712	101 630		379 886	191 576	188 310	...
Querétaro	626 495	301 972	324 523	...	1 097 025	533 253	563 772	...
Reynosa	589 466	293 880	295 586		727 150	363 027	364 123	...
Rioverde - Ciudad Fernández	135 452	65 832	69 620	...	135 452	65 832	69 620	...
Salamanca	...	...	...	...	260 732	126 354	134 378	...
Saltillo	709 671	351 302	358 369	...	823 128	409 208	413 920	...
San Cristobal de las Casas	185 917	88 996	96 921	...	...	...	...	
San Francisco Coacalco	277 959	134 086	143 873	...	...	...	...	
San Francisco del Rincón	113 570	55 026	58 544	...	182 365	88 808	93 557	...
San Juan Bautista Tuxtepec	...	...	...	...	155 766	74 788	80 978	...
San Juan del Río	...	...	...	...	241 699	117 628	124 071	...
San Luis Potosí	722 772	347 676	375 096	...	1 040 443	501 897	538 546	...
San Luis Rio Colorado	...	...	...	...	178 380	90 545	87 835	...
San Martín Texmelucan	141 112	67 505	73 607	...	2 668 437	1 278 555	1 389 882	...
San Nicolas de los Garza	443 273	219 337	223 936	...	...	...	...	
San Pedro Garza Garcia	122 627	57 608	65 019		...	...	...	
Soledad de Graciano Sanchez	255 015	123 480	131 535	...	1 040 443	501 897	538 546	...
Tampico	297 284	142 189	155 095	...	859 419	418 362	441 057	...
Tapachula (de Cordova y Ordoñez)	...	...	...	...	202 672	95 450	107 222	...
Tecomán	112 726	56 804	55 922	...	141 421	71 260	70 161	...
Tehuacán	248 716	117 127	131 589	...	296 899	140 079	156 820	...
Tepic	332 863	160 708	172 155	...	429 351	209 204	220 147	...
Tijuana	1 300 983	653 241	647 742	...	1 751 430	883 277	868 153	...
Tlalnepantla	653 410	316 348	337 062	...	20 116 842	9 729 967	10 386 875	...
Tlaquepaque	575 942	284 064	291 878	...	4 434 878	2 171 514	2 263 364	...
Tlaxcala	89 795	42 529	47 266	...	499 567	240 285	259 282	...
Toluca (de Lerdo)	489 333	232 774	256 559	...	1 846 116	898 202	947 914	...
Tonala	408 759	202 269	206 490	...	4 434 878	2 171 514	2 263 364	...
Torreón	608 836	296 781	312 055	...	1 215 817	596 961	618 856	...
Tula, Tula de Allende	103 919	50 490	53 429	...	205 812	100 413	105 399	...

8a. Population of capital cities and cities of 100 000 or more inhabitants: 2010
Population des capitales et des villes de 100 000 habitants ou plus: 2010 (continued - suite)

Continent, country or area, date, code and city / Continent, pays ou zone, date, code et ville	City proper - Ville proprement dite				Urban agglomeration - Agglomération urbaine			
	Population			Surface area - Superficie (km²)	Population			Surface area - Superficie (km²)
	Both sexes - Les deux sexes	Male - Masculin	Female - Féminin		Both sexes - Les deux sexes	Male - Masculin	Female - Féminin	
AMERICA, NORTH - AMÉRIQUE DU NORD								
Mexico - Mexique								
12 VI 2010 (CDFC)								
Tulancingo, Tulancingo de Bravo	151 584	71 287	80 297	...	239 579	113 118	126 461	...
Tuxpan	...	...	...	...	143 362	69 764	73 598	...
Tuxtla Gutiérrez	537 102	255 879	281 223	...	640 977	307 242	333 735	...
Uruapan	...	...	...	...	315 350	152 442	162 908	...
Veracruz	428 323	201 018	227 305	...	801 295	380 239	421 056	...
Villa Nicolas Romero	281 799	138 181	143 618	...	...	...	...	...
Villahermosa	353 577	169 721	183 856	...	755 425	368 212	387 213	...
Xalapa-Enriquez	424 755	197 560	227 195	...	666 535	314 563	351 972	...
Xico	356 352	175 135	181 217	...	...	...	...	...
Zacatecas	129 011	61 655	67 356	...	298 167	144 140	154 027	...
Zamora de Hidalgo	141 627	67 993	73 634	...	250 113	120 697	129 416	...
Zapopan	1 142 483	557 305	585 178	...	4 434 878	2 171 514	2 263 364	...
Panama[6]								
1 VII 2010 (ESDF)								
PANAMA DE PANAMA	*894 565*	*443 516*	*451 049*	...	...	...	...	...
San Miguelito	*373 703*	*182 468*	*191 236*	...	...	...	...	...
AMERICA, SOUTH - AMÉRIQUE DU SUD								
Argentina - Argentine[7]								
1 VII 2010 (ESDF)								
Bahía Blanca-Cerri	...	...	...	...	310 151	...	...	...
BUENOS AIRES[8]	...	...	...	...	13 047 384	...	...	...
Catamarca	...	...	...	...	204 866	...	...	...
Comodoro Rivadavia-Rada Tilly	...	...	...	...	143 291	...	...	...
Concordia	...	...	...	...	152 271	...	...	...
Córdoba	...	...	...	...	1 405 547	...	...	...
Corrientes	...	...	...	...	358 278	...	...	...
Formosa	...	...	...	...	240 089	...	...	...
La Plata	...	...	...	...	744 886	...	...	...
La Rioja	...	...	...	...	181 938	...	...	...
Mar del Plata-Batán	...	...	...	...	618 112	...	...	...
Mendoza	...	...	...	...	902 127	...	...	...
Neuquén-Plottier	...	...	...	...	265 216	...	...	...
Paraná	...	...	...	...	276 605	...	...	...
Posadas	...	...	...	...	298 450	...	...	...
Rawson-Trelew-Playa Unión	...	...	...	...	128 971	...	...	...
Resistencia	...	...	...	...	389 940	...	...	...
Río Cuarto	...	...	...	...	164 344	...	...	...
Rosario	...	...	...	...	1 261 404	...	...	...
Salta	...	...	...	...	537 107	...	...	...
San Juan	...	...	...	...	468 330	...	...	...
San Luis - El Chorrillo	...	...	...	...	203 162	...	...	...
San Nicolás-Villa Constitución	...	...	...	...	179 757	...	...	...
San Salvador de Jujuy-Palpalá	...	...	...	...	309 034	...	...	...
Santa Fé	...	...	...	...	506 054	...	...	...
Santa Rosa-Toay	...	...	...	...	121 229	...	...	...
Santiago del Estero-La Banda	...	...	...	...	370 561	...	...	...
Tucumán-Tafí Viejo[9]	...	...	...	...	811 804	...	...	...
Ushuaia-Río Grande	...	...	...	...	122 105	...	...	...
Brazil - Brésil[10]								
1 VIII 2010* (CDJC)								
Abaeteluba	82 998	40 943	42 055	...	141 100	71 630	69 470	...
Açailândia	78 237	38 571	39 666	...	104 047	52 115	51 932	...
Aguas Lindas de Goiás	159 138	79 587	79 551	...	159 378	79 726	79 652	...
Alagoinhas	124 042	58 132	65 910	...	141 949	67 212	74 737	...
Almirante Tamandaré	98 892	48 880	50 012	...	103 204	51 136	52 068	...
Alvorada	195 673	95 080	100 593	...	195 673	95 080	100 593	...
Americana	209 654	102 644	107 010	...	210 638	103 174	107 464	...
Ananindeua	470 819	226 022	244 797	...	471 980	226 635	245 345	...
Anápolis	328 755	160 123	168 632	...	334 613	163 256	171 357	...
Angra dos Reis	163 290	81 480	81 810	...	169 511	84 666	84 845	...

8a. Population of capital cities and cities of 100 000 or more inhabitants: 2010
Population des capitales et des villes de 100 000 habitants ou plus: 2010 (continued - suite)

Continent, country or area, date, code and city / Continent, pays ou zone, date, code et ville	City proper - Ville proprement dite				Urban agglomeration - Agglomération urbaine			
	Population			Surface area - Superficie (km²)	Population			Surface area - Superficie (km²)
	Both sexes - Les deux sexes	Male - Masculin	Female - Féminin		Both sexes - Les deux sexes	Male - Masculin	Female - Féminin	
AMERICA, SOUTH - AMÉRIQUE DU SUD								
Brazil - Brésil[10]								
1 VIII 2010* (CDJC)								
Aparecida de Goiania	455 193	224 547	230 646	...	455 657	224 798	230 859	...
Apucarana	114 098	55 067	59 031	...	120 919	58 682	62 237	...
Aracaju	571 149	265 484	305 665	...	571 149	265 484	305 665	...
Araçatuba	178 077	85 466	92 611	...	181 579	87 329	94 250	...
Araguaina	142 925	69 468	73 457	...	150 484	73 587	76 897	...
Araguario	102 583	50 186	52 397	...	109 801	54 160	55 641	...
Arapiraca	181 481	85 682	95 799	...	214 006	101 884	112 122	...
Arapongas	101 851	49 820	52 031	...	104 150	51 039	53 111	...
Araraquara	202 730	97 508	105 222	...	208 662	100 655	108 007	...
Araras	112 444	55 341	57 103	...	118 843	58 688	60 155	...
Araruama	106 486	51 488	54 998	...	112 008	54 283	57 725	...
Araucária	110 205	55 026	55 179	...	119 123	59 606	59 517	...
Atibaia	115 229	56 235	58 994	...	126 603	62 211	64 392	...
Bacabal	77 860	36 406	41 454	...	100 014	47 757	52 257	...
Bagé	97 765	46 097	51 668	...	116 794	55 804	60 990	...
Balneário Camboriú	108 089	51 393	56 696	...	108 089	51 393	56 696	...
Barbacena	115 568	54 566	61 002	...	126 284	60 162	66 122	...
Barra Mansa	176 193	84 894	91 299	...	177 813	85 792	92 021	...
Barreiras	123 741	60 645	63 096	...	137 427	67 913	69 514	...
Barretos	108 686	52 342	56 344	...	112 101	54 169	57 932	...
Barueri	240 749	117 051	123 698	...	240 749	117 051	123 698	...
Bauru	338 184	162 053	176 131	...	343 937	166 649	177 288	...
Belém	1 381 475	652 860	728 615	...	1 393 399	659 008	734 391	...
Belford Roxo	469 332	226 757	242 575	...	469 332	226 757	242 575	...
Belo Horizonte	2 375 151	1 113 513	1 261 638	...	2 375 151	1 113 513	1 261 638	...
Bento Gonçalves	99 069	48 415	50 654	...	107 278	52 645	54 633	...
Betim	375 331	184 910	190 421	...	378 089	186 352	191 737	...
Birigui	105 487	51 249	54 238	...	108 728	53 075	55 653	...
Blumenou	294 773	144 346	150 427	...	309 011	151 542	157 469	...
Boa Vista	277 799	136 877	140 922	...	284 313	140 801	143 512	...
Botucatu	122 678	59 366	63 312	...	127 328	61 761	65 567	...
Bragança	72 621	35 699	36 922	...	113 227	57 291	55 936	...
Bragança Paulista	142 255	69 700	72 555	...	146 744	72 081	74 663	...
BRASILIA	2 482 210	1 180 777	1 301 433	...	2 570 160	1 228 880	1 341 280	...
Brusque	102 025	50 586	51 439	...	105 503	52 400	53 103	...
Cabo de Santo Agostinho	167 783	81 917	85 866	...	185 025	90 859	94 166	...
Cabo Frio	140 486	68 010	72 476	...	186 227	90 831	95 396	...
Cachoeirinha	118 278	57 173	61 105	...	118 278	57 173	61 105	...
Cachoeiro de Itapemirim	173 589	84 201	89 388	...	189 889	92 845	97 044	...
Camacari	231 973	114 874	117 099	...	242 970	120 704	122 266	...
Camaragibe	144 466	69 212	75 254	...	144 466	69 212	75 254	...
Cametá	52 838	26 136	26 702	...	120 896	62 016	58 880	...
Campina Grande	367 209	173 191	194 018	...	385 213	182 205	203 008	...
Campinas	1 061 540	511 483	550 057	...	1 080 113	520 865	559 248	...
Campo Grande	776 242	375 248	400 994	...	786 797	381 333	405 464	...
Campo Largo	94 171	46 303	47 868	...	112 377	55 660	56 717	...
Campos dos Goytacazes	418 725	200 256	218 469	...	463 731	223 259	240 472	...
Canoas	323 827	155 936	167 891	...	323 827	155 936	167 891	...
Caraguatatuba	96 673	47 741	48 932	...	100 840	49 959	50 881	...
Carapicuíba	369 584	179 284	190 300	...	369 584	179 284	190 300	...
Cariacica	337 643	164 374	173 269	...	348 738	169 958	178 780	...
Caruaru	279 589	131 317	148 272	...	314 912	149 153	165 759	...
Cascavel	270 049	130 813	139 236	...	286 205	139 771	146 434	...
Castanhal	153 378	74 176	79 202	...	173 149	84 476	88 673	...
Catanduva	111 914	54 307	57 607	...	112 820	54 776	58 044	...
Caucaia	290 220	141 210	149 010	...	325 441	159 598	165 843	...
Caxias	118 534	55 811	62 723	...	155 129	75 082	80 047	...
Caxias do Sul	419 406	205 081	214 325	...	435 564	213 612	221 952	...
Chapecó	168 113	82 179	85 934	...	183 530	90 626	92 904	...
Codo	81 045	38 207	42 838	...	118 038	57 403	60 635	...
Colatina	98 395	47 235	51 160	...	111 788	54 291	57 497	...
Colombo	203 203	100 016	103 187	...	212 967	105 010	107 957	...
Conselheiro Lafaiete	111 266	53 751	57 515	...	116 512	56 383	60 129	...

Population of capital cities and cities of 100 000 or more inhabitants: 2010
Population des capitales et des villes de 100 000 habitants ou plus: 2010 (continued - suite)

Continent, country or area, date, code and city Continent, pays ou zone, date, code et ville	City proper - Ville proprement dite				Urban agglomeration - Agglomération urbaine			
	Population			Surface area - Superficie (km²)	Population			Surface area - Superficie (km²)
	Both sexes - Les deux sexes	Male - Masculin	Female - Féminin		Both sexes - Les deux sexes	Male - Masculin	Female - Féminin	

AMERICA, SOUTH - AMÉRIQUE DU SUD

Brazil - Brésil[10]
1 VIII 2010* (CDJC)

Contagem	601 400	291 709	309 691	...	603 442	292 798	310 644	...
Coronel Fabriciano	102 395	49 378	53 017	...	103 694	50 035	53 659	...
Corumbá	93 452	46 132	47 320	...	103 703	52 285	51 418	...
Cotia	201 150	98 455	102 695	...	201 150	98 455	102 695	...
Crato	100 916	47 285	53 631	...	121 428	57 616	63 812	...
Criciúma	189 630	93 047	96 583	...	192 308	94 607	97 701	...
Cubatao	118 720	59 229	59 491	...	118 720	59 229	59 491	...
Cuiabá	540 814	263 510	277 304	...	551 098	269 204	281 894	...
Curitiba	1 751 907	835 115	916 792	...	1 751 907	835 115	916 792	...
Diadema	386 089	186 803	199 286	...	386 089	186 803	199 286	...
Divinópolis	207 516	100 880	106 636	...	213 016	103 828	109 188	...
Dourados	181 005	88 555	92 450	...	196 035	96 274	99 761	...
Duque de Caxias	852 138	409 537	442 601	...	855 048	411 074	443 974	...
Embu	240 230	116 728	123 502	...	240 230	116 728	123 502	...
Eunápolis	93 413	45 820	47 593	...	100 196	49 396	50 800	...
Feira de Santana	510 635	241 310	269 325	...	556 642	263 999	292 643	...
Ferraz de Vasconcelos	160 754	78 255	82 499	...	168 306	82 143	86 163	...
Florianópolis	405 286	194 945	210 341	...	421 240	203 047	218 193	...
Formosa	92 023	45 385	46 638	...	100 085	49 959	50 126	...
Fortaleza	2 452 185	1 147 918	1 304 267	...	2 452 185	1 147 918	1 304 267	...
Foz do Iguaçu	253 962	123 104	130 858	...	256 088	124 218	131 870	...
Franca	313 046	152 402	160 644	...	318 640	155 464	163 176	...
Francisco Morato	154 158	76 474	77 684	...	154 472	76 636	77 836	...
Franco da Rocha	121 244	59 594	61 650	...	131 604	67 462	64 142	...
Garanhuns	115 356	53 825	61 531	...	129 408	60 976	68 432	...
Goiânia	1 297 076	618 271	678 805	...	1 302 001	620 857	681 144	...
Governador Valadares	253 300	119 609	133 691	...	263 689	125 237	138 452	...
Gravatai	243 497	118 532	124 965	...	255 660	124 880	130 780	...
Guarapari	100 528	48 985	51 543	...	105 286	51 494	53 792	...
Guarapuava	152 993	74 273	78 720	...	167 328	81 797	85 531	...
Guaratinguetá	106 762	51 197	55 565	...	112 072	53 946	58 126	...
Guarujá	290 696	141 682	149 014	...	290 752	141 711	149 041	...
Guarulhos	1 221 979	595 043	626 936	...	1 221 979	595 043	626 936	...
Hortolandia	192 692	97 439	95 253	...	192 692	97 439	95 253	...
Ibirité	158 590	77 644	80 946	...	158 954	77 839	81 115	...
Igarassu	93 931	45 182	48 749	...	102 021	49 316	52 705	...
Ilhéus	155 281	74 049	81 232	...	184 236	89 440	94 796	...
Imperatriz	234 547	112 566	121 981	...	247 505	119 227	128 278	...
Indaiatuba	199 592	99 101	100 491	...	201 619	100 178	101 441	...
Ipatinga	236 968	114 954	122 014	...	239 468	116 209	123 259	...
Itabiraí	102 316	48 931	53 385	...	109 783	52 733	57 050	...
Itaboraí	215 412	104 850	110 562	...	218 008	106 190	111 818	...
Itabuna	199 643	94 198	105 445	...	204 667	96 936	107 731	...
Itaguaí	104 209	51 783	52 426	...	109 091	54 409	54 682	...
Itajaí	173 452	85 030	88 422	...	183 373	90 111	93 262	...
Itapecerica da Serra	151 349	75 626	75 723	...	152 614	76 270	76 344	...
Itapetininga	131 050	63 919	67 131	...	144 377	72 167	72 210	...
Itapevi	200 769	98 746	102 023	...	200 769	98 746	102 023	...
Itapipoca	66 909	32 477	34 432	...	116 065	58 243	57 822	...
Itaquaquecetuba	321 770	158 542	163 228	...	321 770	158 542	163 228	...
Itatiba	85 666	42 062	43 604	...	101 471	50 147	51 324	...
Itu	144 269	71 002	73 267	...	154 147	76 219	77 928	...
Jaboatao dos Guarapes	630 595	297 903	332 692	...	644 620	304 850	339 770	...
Jacareí	208 297	101 489	106 808	...	211 214	103 092	108 122	...
Jandira	108 344	53 063	55 281	...	108 344	53 063	55 281	...
Jaraguá do Sul	132 800	66 511	66 289	...	143 123	71 801	71 322	...
Jaú	126 943	62 004	64 939	...	131 040	64 214	66 826	...
Jequié	139 426	66 855	72 571	...	151 895	73 612	78 283	...
Ji-Paraná	104 858	51 589	53 269	...	116 610	57 824	58 786	...
Joao Pessoa	720 785	336 409	384 376	...	723 515	337 783	385 732	...
Joinville	497 850	246 707	251 143	...	515 288	255 756	259 532	...
Juazeiro	160 775	77 799	82 976	...	197 965	97 085	100 880	...
Juàzeiro do Norte	240 128	113 409	126 719	...	249 939	118 353	131 586	...

8a. Population of capital cities and cities of 100 000 or more inhabitants: 2010
Population des capitales et des villes de 100 000 habitants ou plus: 2010 (continued - suite)

Continent, country or area, date, code and city / Continent, pays ou zone, date, code et ville	City proper - Ville proprement dite				Urban agglomeration - Agglomération urbaine			
	Population			Surface area - Superficie (km²)	Population			Surface area - Superficie (km²)
	Both sexes - Les deux sexes	Male - Masculin	Female - Féminin		Both sexes - Les deux sexes	Male - Masculin	Female - Féminin	

AMERICA, SOUTH - AMÉRIQUE DU SUD

Brazil - Brésil[10]
1 VIII 2010* (CDJC)

Juiz de Fora	510 378	240 877	269 501	...	516 247	244 024	272 223	...
Jundiaí	354 204	171 931	182 273	...	370 126	180 049	190 077	...
Lages	153 937	74 458	79 479	...	156 727	75 952	80 775	...
Lauro de Freitas	163 449	79 276	84 173	...	163 449	79 276	84 173	...
Limeira	267 785	131 365	136 420	...	276 022	135 628	140 394	...
Linhares	121 567	59 882	61 685	...	141 306	70 415	70 891	...
Londrina	493 520	235 638	257 882	...	506 701	243 059	263 642	...
Luziânia	162 807	80 684	82 123	...	174 531	87 087	87 444	...
Macae	202 859	100 337	102 522	...	206 728	102 432	104 296	...
Macapá	381 214	186 657	194 557	...	398 204	195 613	202 591	...
Maceió	932 129	436 142	495 987	...	932 748	436 492	496 256	...
Magé	215 236	104 479	110 757	...	227 322	110 576	116 746	...
Manaus	1 792 881	874 749	918 132	...	1 802 014	879 742	922 272	...
Maraba	186 270	92 780	93 490	...	233 669	118 196	115 473	...
Maracanau	207 623	101 354	106 269	...	209 057	102 078	106 979	...
Maranguape	86 309	42 194	44 115	...	113 561	56 619	56 942	...
Maricá	125 491	61 647	63 844	...	127 461	62 649	64 812	...
Marília	207 021	99 682	107 339	...	216 745	104 726	112 019	...
Maringá	350 653	168 417	182 236	...	357 077	171 724	185 353	...
Marituba	107 123	53 327	53 796	...	108 246	53 884	54 362	...
Mauá	417 064	204 093	212 971	...	417 064	204 093	212 971	...
Mesquita	168 376	79 790	88 586	...	168 376	79 790	88 586	...
Moji das Cruzes	357 313	173 193	184 120	...	387 779	188 857	198 922	...
Moji-Guaçu	130 295	64 407	65 888	...	137 245	68 094	69 151	...
Montes Claros	344 427	164 985	179 442	...	361 915	174 249	187 666	...
Mossoró	237 241	113 580	123 661	...	259 815	125 747	134 068	...
Muriaé	93 225	44 709	48 516	...	100 765	48 757	52 008	...
Natal	803 739	377 947	425 792	...	803 739	377 947	425 792	...
Nilópolis	157 425	73 674	83 751	...	157 425	73 674	83 751	...
Niterói	487 562	225 838	261 724	...	487 562	225 838	261 724	...
Nossa Senhora do Socorro	155 823	75 707	80 116	...	160 827	78 287	82 540	...
Nova Friburgo	159 372	75 599	83 773	...	182 082	87 254	94 828	...
Nova Iguaçu	787 563	377 336	410 227	...	796 257	381 750	414 507	...
Nôvo Hamburgo	234 798	113 628	121 170	...	238 940	115 766	123 174	...
Olinda	370 332	171 066	199 266	...	377 779	174 724	203 055	...
Osasco	666 740	320 436	346 304	...	666 740	320 436	346 304	...
Ourinhos	100 374	48 586	51 788	...	103 035	49 981	53 054	...
Paço do Lumiar	78 811	37 764	41 047	...	105 121	50 910	54 211	...
Palhoça	135 311	67 385	67 926	...	137 334	68 436	68 898	...
Palmas	221 742	109 092	112 650	...	228 332	112 848	115 484	...
Paranaguá	135 386	66 581	68 805	...	140 469	69 306	71 163	...
Parauapebas	138 690	70 054	68 636	...	153 908	77 893	76 015	...
Parintins	69 890	34 763	35 127	...	102 033	52 304	49 729	...
Parnaíba	137 485	65 418	72 067	...	145 705	69 727	75 978	...
Parnamirim	202 456	96 995	105 461	...	202 456	96 995	105 461	...
Passo Fundo	180 120	85 646	94 474	...	184 826	88 050	96 776	...
Passos	100 842	49 518	51 324	...	106 290	52 568	53 722	...
Patos	97 278	45 995	51 283	...	100 674	47 805	52 869	...
Patos de Minas	127 724	61 949	65 775	...	138 710	67 924	70 786	...
Paulista	300 466	141 630	158 836	...	300 466	141 630	158 836	...
Paulo Afonso	93 404	44 279	49 125	...	108 396	51 970	56 426	...
Pelotas	306 193	142 848	163 345	...	328 275	154 198	174 077	...
Petrolina	219 215	104 751	114 464	...	293 962	143 252	150 710	...
Petrópolis	281 286	133 694	147 592	...	295 917	140 996	154 921	...
Pindamonhangaba	141 708	69 505	72 203	...	146 995	72 288	74 707	...
Pinhais	117 008	56 809	60 199	...	117 008	56 809	60 199	...
Piracicaba	356 743	174 190	182 553	...	364 571	178 345	186 226	...
Poà	104 338	50 443	53 895	...	106 013	51 292	54 721	...
Poços de Caldas	148 722	71 676	77 046	...	152 435	73 680	78 755	...
Ponta Grossa	304 733	147 731	157 002	...	311 611	151 362	160 249	...
Porto Alegre	1 409 351	653 787	755 564	...	1 409 351	653 787	755 564	...
Porto Seguro	104 078	51 512	52 566	...	126 929	63 489	63 440	...
Porto Velho	390 733	193 768	196 965	...	428 527	217 618	210 909	...

8a. Population of capital cities and cities of 100 000 or more inhabitants: 2010
Population des capitales et des villes de 100 000 habitants ou plus: 2010 (continued - suite)

Continent, country or area, date, code and city / Continent, pays ou zone, date, code et ville	City proper - Ville proprement dite				Urban agglomeration - Agglomération urbaine			
	Population			Surface area - Superficie (km²)	Population			Surface area - Superficie (km²)
	Both sexes - Les deux sexes	Male - Masculin	Female - Féminin		Both sexes - Les deux sexes	Male - Masculin	Female - Féminin	

AMERICA, SOUTH - AMÉRIQUE DU SUD

Brazil - Brésil[10]
1 VIII 2010* (CDJC)

Pouso Alegre	119 590	58 566	61 024	...	130 615	64 519	66 096	...
Praia Grande	262 051	125 926	136 125	...	262 051	125 926	136 125	...
Presidente Prudente	203 375	97 102	106 273	...	207 610	99 894	107 716	...
Queimados	137 962	66 585	71 377	...	137 962	66 585	71 377	...
Recife	1 537 704	709 819	827 885	...	1 537 704	709 819	827 885	...
Resende	112 331	54 405	57 926	...	119 769	58 268	61 501	...
Ribeirao das Neves	294 153	145 898	148 255	...	296 317	146 982	149 335	...
Ribeirao Pires	113 068	55 318	57 750	...	113 068	55 318	57 750	...
Ribeirao Prêto	602 966	289 272	313 694	...	604 682	290 171	314 511	...
Rio Branco	308 545	148 437	160 108	...	336 038	163 592	172 446	...
Rio Claro	181 720	88 224	93 496	...	186 253	90 687	95 566	...
Rio das Ostras	99 905	49 219	50 686	...	105 676	52 207	53 469	...
Rio de Janeiro	6 320 446	2 959 817	3 360 629	...	6 320 446	2 959 817	3 360 629	...
Rio Grande	189 429	90 514	98 915	...	197 228	94 983	102 245	...
Rio Verde	163 540	82 870	80 670	...	176 424	90 030	86 394	...
Rondonópolis	188 028	93 785	94 243	...	195 476	98 197	97 279	...
Sabára	123 084	59 080	64 004	...	126 269	60 828	65 441	...
Salto	104 774	51 772	53 002	...	105 516	52 132	53 384	...
Salvador	2 674 923	1 248 513	1 426 410	...	2 675 656	1 248 897	1 426 759	...
Santa Bárbara D'Oeste	178 596	88 488	90 108	...	180 009	89 222	90 787	...
Santa Cruz do Sul	105 190	50 142	55 048	...	118 374	56 943	61 431	...
Santa Luzia (Minas Gerais)	202 378	98 202	104 176	...	202 942	98 485	104 457	...
Santa Maria	248 347	117 104	131 243	...	261 031	123 634	137 397	...
Santa Rita	103 717	49 703	54 014	...	120 310	58 119	62 191	...
Santana	99 111	49 201	49 910	...	101 262	50 414	50 848	...
Santana de Parnaíba	108 813	53 671	55 142	...	108 813	53 671	55 142	...
Santarém	215 790	104 001	111 789	...	294 580	145 533	149 047	...
Santo André	676 407	324 458	351 949	...	676 407	324 458	351 949	...
Santos	419 086	191 754	227 332	...	419 400	191 912	227 488	...
Sao Bernardo do Campo	752 658	363 148	389 510	...	765 463	369 626	395 837	...
Sao Caetano do Sul	149 263	68 853	80 410	...	149 263	68 853	80 410	...
Sao Carlo	213 061	104 241	108 820	...	221 950	108 914	113 036	...
Sao Gonçalo	998 999	474 894	524 105	...	999 728	475 264	524 464	...
Sao Joao de Meriti	458 673	218 104	240 569	...	458 673	218 104	240 569	...
Sao José	207 312	100 118	107 194	...	209 804	101 392	108 412	...
Sao José de Ribamar	37 709	18 392	19 317	...	163 045	78 683	84 362	...
Sao José do Rio Prêto	383 490	182 947	200 543	...	408 258	196 016	212 242	...
Sao José dos Campos	617 106	301 886	315 220	...	629 921	308 624	321 297	...
Sao José dos Pinhais	236 895	116 457	120 438	...	264 210	130 597	133 613	...
Sao Leopoldo	213 238	103 790	109 448	...	214 087	104 242	109 845	...
São Lourenço da Mata	96 777	46 741	50 036	...	102 895	50 016	52 879	...
Sao Luís	958 522	447 007	511 515	...	1 014 837	474 995	539 842	...
São Mateus	84 541	41 171	43 370	...	109 028	53 930	55 098	...
Sao Paulo	11 152 344	5 278 168	5 874 176	...	11 253 503	5 328 632	5 924 871	...
Sao Vicente	331 817	159 303	172 514	...	332 445	159 664	172 781	...
Sapucaia do Sul	130 469	63 500	66 969	...	130 957	63 747	67 210	...
Serra	406 450	199 641	206 809	...	409 267	201 415	207 852	...
Sertaozinho	108 772	54 013	54 759	...	110 074	54 701	55 373	...
Sete Lagoas	208 956	101 263	107 693	...	214 152	103 991	110 161	...
Simoes Filho	105 811	51 624	54 187	...	118 047	58 013	60 034	...
Sinop	93 753	47 139	46 614	...	113 099	57 565	55 534	...
Sobral	166 310	80 213	86 097	...	188 233	91 462	96 771	...
Sorocaba	580 655	283 919	296 736	...	586 625	287 014	299 611	...
Sumaré	238 470	118 381	120 089	...	241 311	119 863	121 448	...
Susano	253 240	123 883	129 357	...	262 480	128 694	133 786	...
Taboao da Serra	244 528	116 895	127 633	...	244 528	116 895	127 633	...
Tatuí	102 256	50 323	51 933	...	107 326	53 034	54 292	...
Taubaté	272 673	133 530	139 143	...	278 686	136 752	141 934	...
Teixeira de Freitas	129 263	63 334	65 929	...	138 341	68 077	70 264	...
Teófilo Otoni	110 076	51 536	58 540	...	134 745	64 466	70 279	...
Teresina	767 557	356 607	410 950	...	814 230	380 612	433 618	...
Teresópolis	146 207	69 442	76 765	...	163 746	78 275	85 471	...
Timon	135 133	65 025	70 108	...	155 460	75 561	79 899	...

8a. Population of capital cities and cities of 100 000 or more inhabitants: 2010
Population des capitales et des villes de 100 000 habitants ou plus: 2010 (continued - suite)

Continent, country or area, date, code and city / Continent, pays ou zone, date, code et ville	City proper - Ville proprement dite				Urban agglomeration - Agglomération urbaine			
	Population			Surface area - Superficie (km²)	Population			Surface area - Superficie (km²)
	Both sexes - Les deux sexes	Male - Masculin	Female - Féminin		Both sexes - Les deux sexes	Male - Masculin	Female - Féminin	
AMERICA, SOUTH - AMÉRIQUE DU SUD								
Brazil - Brésil[10]								
1 VIII 2010* (CDJC)								
Toledo	108 259	52 625	55 634	...	119 313	58 337	60 976	...
Três Lagoas	97 069	47 876	49 193	...	101 791	50 523	51 268	...
Trindade	100 106	49 070	51 036	...	104 488	51 445	53 043	...
Ubá	97 636	48 166	49 470	...	101 519	50 258	51 261	...
Uberaba	289 376	140 640	148 736	...	295 988	144 461	151 527	...
Uberlândia	587 266	285 611	301 655	...	604 013	294 914	309 099	...
Umuarama	93 455	45 045	48 410	...	100 676	48 788	51 888	...
Uruguaiana	117 415	56 486	60 929	...	125 435	61 009	64 426	...
Valinhos	101 626	49 974	51 652	...	106 793	52 676	54 117	...
Valparaíso de Goiás	132 982	64 624	68 358	...	132 982	64 624	68 358	...
Varginha	119 061	57 831	61 230	...	123 081	59 957	63 124	...
Varzea Grande	248 704	123 112	125 592	...	252 596	125 267	127 329	...
Varzea Paulista	107 089	53 415	53 674	...	107 089	53 415	53 674	...
Vespasiano	104 527	51 006	53 521	...	104 527	51 006	53 521	...
Viamao	224 943	109 013	115 930	...	239 384	116 483	122 901	...
Vila Velha	412 575	197 926	214 649	...	414 586	199 146	215 440	...
Vitória	327 801	153 948	173 853	...	327 801	153 948	173 853	...
Vitória da Conquista	274 739	131 262	143 477	...	306 866	147 879	158 987	...
Vitória de Santo Antao	113 429	53 820	59 609	...	129 974	62 409	67 565	...
Volta Redonda	257 686	122 859	134 827	...	257 803	122 919	134 884	...
Votorantim	104 659	51 858	52 801	...	108 809	54 013	54 796	...
Chile - Chili								
1 VII 2010 (ESDF)								
Antofagasta	367 040	190 803	176 238	44	...	...	...	...
Arica	166 493	78 970	87 523	42	...	...	...	...
Calama	146 798	74 748	72 051	18	...	...	...	...
Chiguallante	119 274	55 908	63 366	34	...	...	...	...
Chillán	160 551	76 291	84 260	33	...	...	...	...
Concepción	222 667	107 690	114 978	56	...	...	...	...
Copiapó	156 192	78 354	77 839	48	...	...	...	...
Coquimbo	188 868	92 848	96 020	42	...	...	...	...
Coronel	102 917	50 065	52 852	25	...	...	...	...
Iquique	182 259	87 913	94 347	22	...	...	...	...
La Serena	192 177	93 134	99 043	66	...	...	...	...
Los Angeles	139 487	67 806	71 681	27	...	...	...	...
Osorno	145 766	71 446	74 320	32	...	...	...	...
Puente Alto	712 499	349 241	363 258	64	...	...	...	...
Puerto Montt	201 829	100 994	100 836	40	...	...	...	...
Punta Arenas	121 835	61 068	60 768	39	...	...	...	...
Quilpué	156 590	76 198	80 392	38	...	...	...	...
Rancagua	236 189	117 385	118 805	50	...	...	...	...
San Bernardo	297 964	146 422	151 542	52	...	...	...	...
SANTIAGO	6 045 404	2 936 160	3 109 245	727	...	...	...	...
Talca	215 646	104 474	111 173	46	...	...	...	...
Talcahuano	138 643	64 549	74 094	51	...	...	...	...
Temuco	262 628	126 351	136 277	46	...	...	...	...
Valdivia	139 475	68 302	71 173	42	...	...	...	...
Valparaíso	256 823	127 847	128 976	47	...	...	...	...
Villa Alemana	126 912	61 962	64 950	31	...	...	...	...
Viña del Mar	291 397	139 796	151 601	87	...	...	...	...
Colombia - Colombie[11]								
1 VII 2010 (ESDF)								
Apartadó	...	...	...	...	153 319	77 717	75 602	607[4]
Armenia	...	...	...	...	288 908	139 256	149 652	115[4]
Barrancabermeja	...	...	...	...	191 498	94 219	97 279	1 274[4]
Barranquilla	...	...	...	...	1 186 640	574 499	612 141	166[4]
Bello	...	...	...	...	413 107	199 497	213 610	151[4]
BOGOTA, D.C.	...	...	...	...	7 363 782	3 548 713	3 815 069	1 605[4]
Bucaramanga	...	...	...	...	524 112	250 651	273 461	154[4]
Buenaventura	...	...	...	...	362 625	176 388	186 237	6 785[4]
Cali	...	...	...	...	2 244 639	1 073 479	1 171 160	552[4]
Cartagena	...	...	...	...	944 250	454 841	489 409	559[4]

8a. Population of capital cities and cities of 100 000 or more inhabitants: 2010
Population des capitales et des villes de 100 000 habitants ou plus: 2010 (continued - suite)

Continent, country or area, date, code and city / Continent, pays ou zone, date, code et ville	City proper - Ville proprement dite				Urban agglomeration - Agglomération urbaine			
	Population			Surface area - Superficie (km²)	Population			Surface area - Superficie (km²)
	Both sexes - Les deux sexes	Male - Masculin	Female - Féminin		Both sexes - Les deux sexes	Male - Masculin	Female - Féminin	

AMERICA, SOUTH - AMÉRIQUE DU SUD

Colombia - Colombie[11]
1 VII 2010 (ESDF)

Cartago	...	...	...	...	128 566	61 684	66 882	260[4]
Chía	...	...	...	...	111 998	53 732	58 266	76[4]
Ciénaga	...	...	...	...	103 066	51 332	51 734	1 366[4]
Colombia: Jamundí	...	...	...	...	107 730	52 543	55 187	603[4]
Colombia: Yumbo	...	...	...	...	104 014	52 142	51 872	243[4]
Cúcuta	...	...	...	...	618 310	299 064	319 246	1 098[4]
Dosquebradas	...	...	...	...	189 112	91 034	98 078	80[4]
Duitama	...	...	...	...	110 418	51 927	58 491	229[4]
Envigado	...	...	...	...	197 440	95 106	102 334	51[4]
Facatativá	...	...	...	...	119 849	59 625	60 224	160[4]
Florencia	...	...	...	...	157 450	77 253	80 197	2 292[4]
Floridablanca	...	...	...	...	261 142	123 550	137 592	101[4]
Fusagasugá	...	...	...	...	121 535	59 751	61 784	206[4]
Girardot	...	...	...	...	101 792	48 220	53 572	130[4]
Girón	...	...	...	...	156 995	77 876	79 119	681[4]
Gudalajara de Buga	...	...	...	...	116 105	56 889	59 216	873[4]
Ibagué	...	...	...	...	526 547	255 939	270 608	1 439[4]
Ipiales	...	...	...	...	123 341	60 484	62 857	1 707[4]
Itagüi	...	...	...	...	252 158	122 315	129 843	17[4]
Lorica	...	...	...	...	114 145	57 289	56 856	890[4]
Magangué	...	...	...	...	122 913	62 083	60 830	1 102[4]
Maicao	...	...	...	...	141 917	69 645	72 272	1 789[4]
Malambo	...	...	...	...	111 257	56 303	54 954	108[4]
Manizales	...	...	...	...	388 525	184 821	203 704	477[4]
Medellín	...	...	...	...	2 343 049	1 103 159	1 239 890	387[4]
Montería	...	...	...	...	409 476	198 569	210 907	3 043[4]
Neiva	...	...	...	...	330 487	158 107	172 380	1 468[4]
Palmira	...	...	...	...	294 580	142 819	151 761	1 044[4]
Pasto	...	...	...	...	411 706	197 828	213 878	1 131[4]
Pereira	...	...	...	...	457 103	218 208	238 895	702[4]
Piedecuesta	...	...	...	...	132 680	64 624	68 056	481[4]
Pitalito	...	...	...	...	113 980	56 605	57 375	653[4]
Popayán	...	...	...	...	265 702	128 370	137 332	464[4]
Quibdo	...	...	...	...	114 548	56 705	57 843	3 075[4]
Riohacha	...	...	...	...	213 046	104 555	108 491	3 171[4]
Rionegro	...	...	...	...	110 329	54 832	55 497	198[4]
San Andres de Tumaco	...	...	...	...	179 005	89 911	89 094	3 778[4]
Santa Marta	...	...	...	...	447 857	217 502	230 355	2 369[4]
Sincelejo	...	...	...	...	256 241	125 165	131 076	292[4]
Soacha	...	...	...	...	455 992	224 785	231 207	187[4]
Sogamoso	...	...	...	...	115 564	54 925	60 639	214[4]
Soledad	...	...	...	...	535 417	264 656	270 761	67[4]
Tuluá	...	...	...	...	199 244	95 937	103 307	818[4]
Tunja	...	...	...	...	171 082	81 322	89 760	118[4]
Turbo	...	...	...	...	139 628	70 728	68 900	3 090[4]
Uribia	...	...	...	...	144 990	71 109	73 881	7 904[4]
Valledupar	...	...	...	...	403 414	195 946	207 468	4 225[4]
Villavicencio	...	...	...	...	431 476	209 065	222 411	1 328[4]
Yopal	...	...	...	...	123 361	61 825	61 536	2 532[4]
Zipaquirá	...	...	...	...	112 069	54 951	57 118	194[4]

Ecuador - Équateur
1 VII 2010 (ESDF)

Ambato	224 719[1]	...	...	31	...	...	...	...
Babahoyo	120 627[1]	...	...	10	...	...	...	...
Cuenca	402 068[1]	...	...	56	...	...	...	...
Durán	201 026[1]	...	...	40	...	...	...	...
Esmeraldas	125 034[1]	...	...	8	...	...	...	...
Guayaquil	2 286 772[1]	...	...	369	...	...	...	...
Ibarra	156 102[1]	...	...	36	...	...	...	...

Continent, country or area, date, code and city / Continent, pays ou zone, date, code et ville	City proper - Ville proprement dite				Urban agglomeration - Agglomération urbaine			
	Population			Surface area - Superficie (km²)	Population			Surface area - Superficie (km²)
	Both sexes - Les deux sexes	Male - Masculin	Female - Féminin		Both sexes - Les deux sexes	Male - Masculin	Female - Féminin	
AMERICA, SOUTH - AMÉRIQUE DU SUD								
Ecuador - Équateur								
1 VII 2010 (ESDF)								
Loja	156 848[1]	...	...	25	...	...	...	...
Machala	249 992[1]	...	...	34	...	...	...	...
Manta	210 675[1]	...	...	45	...	...	...	...
Milagro	130 661[1]	...	...	19	...	...	...	...
Portoviejo	256 993[1]	...	...	50	...	...	...	...
Quevedo	144 750[1]	...	...	20	...	...	...	...
QUITO	1 619 791[1]	...	...	181	...	...	...	...
Riobamba	189 470[1]	...	...	29	...	...	...	...
Santa Elena	126 271[1]	...	...	36	...	...	...	...
Santo Domingo de los Colorados	231 302[1]	...	...	43	...	...	...	...
ASIA - ASIE								
Afghanistan								
1 VII 2010 (ESDF)								
Herat	410 700	208 600	202 100	...	...	...	...	...
Jalalabad	194 400	100 100	94 300	...	...	...	...	...
KABUL	3 052 000	1 579 600	1 472 400	...	...	...	...	...
Kandahar (Quandahar)	374 200	192 600	181 600	...	...	...	...	...
Kunduz	135 400	69 600	65 800	...	...	...	...	...
Mazar-e-Sharif	346 500	177 800	168 700	...	...	...	...	...
Cambodia - Cambodge[12]								
1 VII 2010 (ESDF)								
Bat Dambang	1 104 520	547 295	557 225	...	...	...	...	...
PHNOM PENH	1 504 361	707 320	797 042	...	...	...	...	...
Seam Reab	975 497	480 472	495 025	...	...	...	...	...
China, Hong Kong SAR - Chine, Hong Kong RAS								
1 VII 2010 (ESDJ)								
HONG KONG SAR	7 067 800	3 310 500	3 757 300	...	...	...	...	...
China, Macao SAR - Chine, Macao RAS								
1 VII 2010 (ESDJ)								
MACAO	544 600	260 400	284 300	...	...	...	...	...
Indonesia - Indonésie								
1 V 2010 (CDJC)								
Ambon	331 254	165 926	165 328	...	...	...	...	...
Balikpapan	557 579	288 847	268 732	...	...	...	...	...
Banda Aceh	223 446	115 097	108 349	...	...	...	...	...
Bandar Lampung	881 801	445 959	435 842	...	...	...	...	...
Bandjarmasin	625 481	312 740	312 741	...	...	...	...	...
Bandung	2 394 873	1 215 348	1 179 525	...	...	...	...	...
Batam	944 285	484 867	459 418	...	...	...	...	...
Bengkulu	308 544	155 288	153 256	...	...	...	...	...
Binjai	246 154	122 997	123 157	...	...	...	...	...
Bitung	187 652	96 001	91 651	...	...	...	...	...
Blitar	131 968	65 441	66 527	...	...	...	...	...
Bogor	950 334	484 791	465 543	...	...	...	...	...
Cirebon (Tjirebon)	296 389	148 600	147 789	...	...	...	...	...
Denpasar	788 589	403 293	385 296	...	...	...	...	...
Gorontalo	180 127	88 283	91 844	...	...	...	...	...
JAKARTA	9 607 787	4 870 938	4 736 849	...	...	...	...	...
Jambi	531 857	268 102	263 755	...	...	...	...	...
Jayapura	256 705	136 587	120 118	...	...	...	...	...
Kediri	268 507	133 884	134 623	...	...	...	...	...
Madiun	170 964	82 738	88 226	...	...	...	...	...
Magelang	118 227	58 311	59 916	...	...	...	...	...
Makasar (Ujung Pandang)	1 338 663	662 009	676 654	...	...	...	...	...
Malang	820 243	404 553	415 690	...	...	...	...	...
Manado	410 481	206 292	204 189	...	...	...	...	...
Mataram	402 843	199 332	203 511	...	...	...	...	...
Medan	2 097 610	1 036 926	1 060 684	...	...	...	...	...
Mojokerto	120 196	59 127	61 069	...	...	...	...	...

Continent, country or area, date, code and city / Continent, pays ou zone, date, code et ville	City proper - Ville proprement dite				Urban agglomeration - Agglomération urbaine			
	Population			Surface area - Superficie (km²)	Population			Surface area - Superficie (km²)
	Both sexes - Les deux sexes	Male - Masculin	Female - Féminin		Both sexes - Les deux sexes	Male - Masculin	Female - Féminin	
ASIA - ASIE								
Indonesia - Indonésie								
1 V 2010 (CDJC)								
Padang	833 562	415 315	418 247	...	...	...	...	...
Pakalongan	281 434	140 983	140 451	...	...	...	...	...
Pakanbaru	897 767	456 385	441 382	...	...	...	...	...
Palangkaraya	220 962	113 005	107 957	...	...	...	...	...
Palembang	1 455 284	728 296	726 988	...	...	...	...	...
Pangkal Pinang	174 758	89 500	85 258	...	...	...	...	...
Pare Pare	129 262	63 481	65 781	...	...	...	...	...
Pasuruan	186 262	92 370	93 892	...	...	...	...	...
Pematang Siantar	234 698	114 561	120 137	...	...	...	...	...
Pontianak	234 021	118 980	115 041	...	...	...	...	...
Probolinggo	217 062	106 915	110 147	...	...	...	...	...
Salatiga	170 332	83 479	86 853	...	...	...	...	...
Samarinda	727 500	377 283	350 217	...	...	...	...	...
Semarang	1 555 984	764 487	791 497	...	...	...	...	...
Sukabumi	298 681	152 080	146 601	...	...	...	...	...
Surabaya	2 765 487	1 367 841	1 397 646	...	...	...	...	...
Surakarta	499 337	243 296	256 041	...	...	...	...	...
Tangerang	1 798 601	921 043	877 558	...	...	...	...	...
Tanjung Balai	154 445	77 933	76 512	...	...	...	...	...
Tebing Tinggi	145 248	71 892	73 356	...	...	...	...	...
Tegal	239 599	118 872	120 727	...	...	...	...	...
Yogyakarta	388 627	189 137	199 490	...	...	...	...	...
Malaysia - Malaisie[6]								
30 VI 2010 (ESDJ)								
Alor Setar	153 158	...	...	...	...	...	...	...
Ampang/Ulu Kelang	120 283	...	...	...	...	...	...	...
Bintulu	133 357	...	...	...	...	...	...	...
George Town	193 172	...	...	...	...	...	...	...
Ipoh	497 359	...	...	...	...	...	...	...
Johor Bahru	545 175	...	...	...	...	...	...	...
Kajang dan Sungai Chua	116 355	...	...	...	...	...	...	...
Klang	369 816	...	...	...	...	...	...	...
Kota Bharu	243 339	...	...	...	...	...	...	...
Kota Kinabalu	297 342	...	...	...	...	...	...	...
KUALA LUMPUR	1 625 989	...	...	...	...	...	...	...
Kuala Terengganu	200 808	...	...	...	...	...	...	...
Kuantan	345 607	...	...	...	...	...	...	...
Kuching	211 451	...	...	...	...	...	...	...
Miri	171 662	...	...	...	...	...	...	...
Petaling Jaya	242 285	...	...	...	...	...	...	...
Sandakan	218 111	...	...	...	...	...	...	...
Seleyang Baru	186 754	...	...	...	...	...	...	...
Seremban	286 324	...	...	...	...	...	...	...
Shah Alam	187 437	...	...	...	...	...	...	...
Sibu	195 733	...	...	...	...	...	...	...
Subang Jaya	193 920	...	...	...	...	...	...	...
Sungai Petani	213 417	...	...	...	...	...	...	...
Taiping	202 994	...	...	...	...	...	...	...
Tawau	134 376	...	...	...	...	...	...	...
Republic of Korea - République de Corée								
1 VII 2010 (ESDJ)								
Busan (Pusan)	3 445 562	1 708 455	1 737 107	766	...	...	...	...
Daegu (Taegu)	2 431 017	1 218 102	1 212 915	884	...	...	...	...
Daejeon (Taejon)	1 515 084	761 913	753 171	540	...	...	...	...
Gwangju (Kwangchu)	1 450 267	722 389	727 878	501	...	...	...	...
Incheon	2 660 610	1 344 728	1 315 882	1 027	...	...	...	...
SEOUL	10 038 916	4 974 070	5 064 846	605	...	...	...	...
Ulsan	1 093 657	566 165	527 492	1 058	...	...	...	...
Singapore - Singapour								
1 VII 2010 (ESDF)								
SINGAPORE	5 076 700	...	...	712	...	...	...	...

8a. Population of capital cities and cities of 100 000 or more inhabitants: 2010
Population des capitales et des villes de 100 000 habitants ou plus: 2010 (continued - suite)

Continent, country or area, date, code and city / Continent, pays ou zone, date, code et ville	City proper - Ville proprement dite				Urban agglomeration - Agglomération urbaine			
	Population			Surface area - Superficie (km²)	Population			Surface area - Superficie (km²)
	Both sexes - Les deux sexes	Male - Masculin	Female - Féminin		Both sexes - Les deux sexes	Male - Masculin	Female - Féminin	
ASIA - ASIE								
Thailand - Thaïlande								
1 VII 2010 (ESDJ)								
BANGKOK............	...	...	...	...	6 876 000[1]	3 193 000[1]	3 683 000[1]	1 569
Buri Ram	...	...	...	...	356 410[1]	175 800[1]	180 610[1]	10 323
Chachoengsao	...	...	...	...	166 584[1]	80 029[1]	86 555[1]	5 351
Chai Nat	...	...	...	...	111 586[1]	52 940[1]	58 646[1]	2 470
Chaiyaphum	...	...	...	...	163 165[1]	78 897[1]	84 268[1]	12 778
Chanthaburi	...	...	...	...	234 176[1]	114 087[1]	120 089[1]	6 338
Chiang Mai	...	...	...	...	588 433[1]	283 283[1]	305 150[1]	20 107
Chiang Rai............	...	...	...	...	305 803[1]	150 202[1]	155 601[1]	11 678
Chon Buri	...	...	...	...	693 021[1]	336 099[1]	356 922[1]	4 363
Chumphon	...	...	...	...	102 197[1]	49 758[1]	52 439[1]	6 009
Kalasin............	...	...	...	...	299 198[1]	148 161[1]	151 037[1]	6 947
Kamphaeng Phet	...	...	...	...	183 051[1]	88 901[1]	94 150[1]	8 608
Kanchanaburi	...	...	...	...	207 790[1]	98 792[1]	108 998[1]	19 483
Khon Kaen	...	...	...	...	416 354[1]	202 639[1]	213 715[1]	10 886
Lampang	...	...	...	...	275 107[1]	133 748[1]	141 359[1]	12 534
Lamphun	...	...	...	...	190 868[1]	91 994[1]	98 874[1]	4 506
Loei............	...	...	...	...	166 839[1]	83 022[1]	83 817[1]	11 425
Lop Buri	...	...	...	...	203 400[1]	103 564[1]	99 836[1]	6 200
Maha Sarakham	...	...	...	...	126 597[1]	60 304[1]	66 293[1]	5 292
Nakhon Pathom............	...	...	...	...	268 663[1]	129 066[1]	139 597[1]	2 168
Nakhon Ratchasima............	...	...	...	...	706 747[1]	345 249[1]	361 498[1]	20 494
Nakhon Sawan	...	...	...	...	227 546[1]	107 615[1]	119 931[1]	9 598
Nakhon Si Thammarat	...	...	...	...	334 604[1]	162 202[1]	172 402[1]	9 943
Narathiwat	...	...	...	...	173 937[1]	85 938[1]	87 999[1]	4 475
Nong Bua Lam Phu	...	...	...	...	120 769[1]	59 697[1]	61 072[1]	3 859
Nong Khai	...	...	...	...	222 919[1]	111 010[1]	111 909[1]	7 332
Nonthaburi	...	...	...	...	564 534[1]	270 537[1]	293 997[1]	622
Pathum Thani	...	...	...	...	382 373[1]	184 191[1]	198 182[1]	1 526
Pattani	...	...	...	...	125 957[1]	62 676[1]	63 281[1]	1 940
Phatthalung	...	...	...	...	131 102[1]	63 995[1]	67 107[1]	3 425
Phayao	...	...	...	...	239 405[1]	117 464[1]	121 941[1]	6 335
Phetchabun	...	...	...	...	190 241[1]	91 669[1]	98 572[1]	12 668
Phetchaburi	...	...	...	...	161 238[1]	77 372[1]	83 866[1]	6 225
Phitsanulok	...	...	...	...	180 500[1]	86 102[1]	94 398[1]	10 816
Phra Nakhon Si Ayutthaya	...	...	...	...	305 822[1]	147 043[1]	158 779[1]	2 557
Phrae............	...	...	...	...	139 358[1]	67 764[1]	71 594[1]	6 539
Phuket............	...	...	...	...	206 399[1]	100 549[1]	105 850[1]	543
Prachuap Khiri Khan	...	...	...	...	155 819[1]	75 253[1]	80 566[1]	6 368
Ratchaburi	...	...	...	...	299 985[1]	144 559[1]	155 426[1]	5 197
Rayong	...	...	...	...	264 332[1]	131 438[1]	132 894[1]	3 552
Roi Et............	...	...	...	...	254 385[1]	124 947[1]	129 438[1]	8 299
Sakon Nakhon	...	...	...	...	207 942[1]	102 275[1]	105 667[1]	9 606
Samut Prakan	...	...	...	...	733 887[1]	347 759[1]	386 128[1]	1 004
Samut Songkhram	...	...	...	...	267 469[1]	129 370[1]	138 099[1]	872
Saraburi	...	...	...	...	230 783[1]	113 706[1]	117 077[1]	3 577
Si Sa Ket	...	...	...	...	184 383[1]	90 197[1]	94 186[1]	8 840
Songkhla	...	...	...	...	685 047[1]	329 785[1]	355 262[1]	7 394
Sukhothai	...	...	...	...	130 968[1]	61 952[1]	69 016[1]	6 596
Suphan Buri	...	...	...	...	198 751[1]	94 661[1]	104 090[1]	5 358
Surat Thani	...	...	...	...	393 607[1]	192 503[1]	201 104[1]	12 892
Surin	...	...	...	...	100 437[1]	48 044[1]	52 393[1]	8 124
Tak	...	...	...	...	122 358[1]	59 949[1]	62 409[1]	16 407
Trang	...	...	...	...	131 349[1]	63 148[1]	68 201[1]	4 918
Ubon Ratchathani............	...	...	...	...	374 786[1]	183 941[1]	190 845[1]	15 745
Udon Thani............	...	...	...	...	521 032[1]	258 460[1]	262 572[1]	11 730
Uttaradit............	...	...	...	...	167 196[1]	80 607[1]	86 589[1]	7 839
Yala............	...	...	...	...	139 922[1]	67 998[1]	71 924[1]	4 475

Continent, country or area, date, code and city / Continent, pays ou zone, date, code et ville	City proper - Ville proprement dite				Urban agglomeration - Agglomération urbaine			
	Population			Surface area - Superficie (km²)	Population			Surface area - Superficie (km²)
	Both sexes - Les deux sexes	Male - Masculin	Female - Féminin		Both sexes - Les deux sexes	Male - Masculin	Female - Féminin	
ASIA - ASIE								
Timor-Leste								
11 VII 2010* (CDFC)								
DILI	193 563	103 096	90 467	...	...	...	...	...
EUROPE								
Åland Islands - Îles d'Åland								
1 VII 2010 (ESDJ)								
MARIEHAMN	11 157[5]	5 327[5]	5 830[5]	12	...	...	...	...
Andorra - Andorre[5]								
1 VII 2010 (ESDJ)								
ANDORRA LA VELLA	...	...	...	...	23 505	11 750	11 755	...
Austria - Autriche								
1 I 2010 (ESDJ)								
Graz	257 328	123 882	133 446	128	...	...	...	...
Innsbruck	119 249	56 702	62 547	105	...	...	...	...
Linz	189 311	90 053	99 258	96	...	...	...	...
Salzburg	147 571	69 621	77 950	66	...	...	...	...
WIEN	1 698 822	812 867	885 955	415	...	...	...	...
Denmark - Danemark[13]								
1 VII 2010 (ESDJ)								
Ålborg	197 516[5]	98 518[5]	98 998[5]	1 144	...	...	...	...
Århus	306 799[5]	150 778[5]	156 021[5]	469	...	...	...	...
Esbjerg	115 129[5]	57 522[5]	57 607[5]	753	...	...	...	...
KOBENHAVN	531 199[5]	262 947[5]	268 252[5]	88	...	...	...	...
Odense	189 058[5]	92 650[5]	96 408[5]	304	...	...	...	...
Vejle	106 867[5]	53 190[5]	53 677[5]	1 066	...	...	...	...
Netherlands - Pays-Bas								
1 I 2010 (ESDJ)								
Almere	188 160	93 508	94 652	130	...	...	...	...
Amersfoort	144 862	71 085	73 777	63	173 674	85 257	88 417	122
AMSTERDAM	767 457	378 193	389 264	166	1 053 413	517 559	535 854	337
Apeldoorn	155 726	76 754	78 972	340	155 726	76 754	78 972	...
Arnhem	147 018	72 967	74 051	98	148 513	73 715	74 798	126
Breda	173 299	84 447	88 852	127	173 299	84 447	88 852	...
Dordrecht	118 480	58 314	60 166	79	236 285	116 016	120 269	139
Ede	107 756	52 849	54 907	318	...	...	...	...
Eindhoven	213 809	108 496	105 313	88	327 245	164 723	162 522	199
Emmen	109 491	54 128	55 363	337	...	...	...	...
Enschede	157 052	79 838	77 214	141	157 052	79 838	77 214	...
Geleen-Sittard	...	...	...	...	137 495	67 656	69 839	121
Groningen	187 298	92 673	94 625	78	205 814	101 394	104 420	124
Haarlem	149 579	72 743	76 836	29	197 660	95 361	102 299	94
Haarlemmermeer	142 788	70 998	71 790	179	...	...	...	...
Heerlen-Kerkrade	...	...	...	...	204 825	101 032	103 793	109
Leiden	117 123	57 074	60 049	22	251 436	122 764	128 672	77
Maastricht	118 533	56 957	61 576	57	118 533	56 957	61 576	...
Nijmegen	162 963	78 097	84 866	54	162 963	78 097	84 866	...
Rotterdam	593 049	291 628	301 421	206	996 183	488 960	507 223	329
s-Gravenhage	...	...	...	...	633 201	309 492	323 709	180
s-Hertogenbosch	139 607	68 628	70 979	84	165 007	81 224	83 783	118
The Hague	488 553	240 696	247 857	82	...	...	...	...
Tilburg	204 853	101 695	103 158	117	227 614	112 980	114 634	159
Utrecht	307 081	148 549	158 532	95	441 866	214 820	227 046	167
Zaanstad	145 332	71 697	73 635	74	...	...	...	...
Zoetermeer	121 532	59 544	61 988	35	...	...	...	...
Zwolle	119 030	57 936	61 094	112	119 030	57 936	61 094	...
Republic of Moldova - République de Moldova								
1 I 2010 (ESDJ)								
Balti (Beltsy)	143 229	65 674	77 555	41	148 128	68 009	80 119	78
CHIŞINĂU (KISHINEV)	663 200	308 718	354 482	123	785 917	369 176	416 741	572

Continent, country or area, date, code and city / Continent, pays ou zone, date, code et ville	City proper - Ville proprement dite				Urban agglomeration - Agglomération urbaine			
	Population			Surface area - Superficie (km²)	Population			Surface area - Superficie (km²)
	Both sexes - Les deux sexes	Male - Masculin	Female - Féminin		Both sexes - Les deux sexes	Male - Masculin	Female - Féminin	
OCEANIA - OCÉANIE								
New Zealand - Nouvelle-Zélande								
1 VII 2010 (ESDJ)								
Auckland	450 200	221 600	228 600	664[14]	1 354 900	664 300	690 600	1 084[14]
Christchurch	376 700	183 800	192 800	608[14]	390 300	190 500	199 800	1 541[14]
Dunedin	116 600	56 200	60 500	255[14]	124 800	60 300	64 500	3 342[14]
Hamilton	143 100	69 300	73 800	98[14]	203 400	98 900	104 500	1 099[14]
Lower Hutt	102 700	50 400	52 300	377[14]	...	...	...	...
Manukau	375 700	183 600	192 000	683[14]	...	...	...	...
Napier-Hastings	...	...	...	...	124 400	60 000	64 400	389[14]
North Shore	229 000	112 500	116 400	129[14]	...	...	...	...
Tauranga	114 300	55 000	59 300	175[14]	120 000	57 800	62 200	184[14]
Waitakere	208 100	101 800	106 300	367[14]	...	...	...	...
WELLINGTON	197 700*	96 400	101 300	290[14]	389 700	190 800	198 900	447[14]

FOOTNOTES - NOTES

The capital city of each country is shown in capital letters. Figures in italics are estimates of questionnable reliability. For definition of city proper and urban agglomeration, method of evaluation and limitations of data see Technical Notes for this table. - Le nom de la capitale de chaque pays est imprimé en majuscules. Les chiffres en italique sont des estimations dont la fiabilité n'est pas assurée. Pour la définition de la ville proprement dite et de l'agglomération urbaine, et pour les méthodes d'évaluation et les insuffisances de données, voir les notes techniques pour ce tableau.

Italics: estimates which are less reliable. - Italiques: estimations moins sûres.

* Provisional. - Données provisoires.

'Code' indicates the source of data, as follows:
CDFC - Census, de facto, complete tabulation
CDFS - Census, de facto, sample tabulation
CDJC - Census, de jure, complete tabulation
CDJS - Census, de jure, sample tabulation
SSDF - Sample survey, de facto
SSDJ - Sample survey, de jure
ESDF - Estimates, de facto
ESDJ - Estimates, de jure

Le 'Code' indique la source des données, comme suit:
CDFC - Recensement, population de fait, tabulation complète
CDFS - Recensement, population de fait, tabulation par sondage
CDJC - Recensement, population de droit, tabulation complète
CDJS - Recensement, population de droit, tabulation par sondage
SSDF - Enquête par sondage, population de fait
SSDJ - Enquête par sondage, population de droit
ESDF - Données estimatées, population de fait
ESDJ - Données estimatées, population de droit

[1] Data refer to national projections. - Les données se réfèrent aux projections nationales.
[2] Population estimates and components of demographic growth according to Standard Geographical Classification (SGC) 2006. Estimates adjusted for census net undercoverage (including adjustment for incompletely enumerated Indian reserves). Preliminary postcensal estimates. - Les estimations de population et les composantes de la croissance démographique correspondent à la Classification géographique type de 2006. Ajusté pour la sous-estimation du recensement (y compris les réservations en Inde incomplètement énumérées). Estimations post censitaires préliminaires.
[3] Area (Sq.Km) are based on 2006 Census boundaries. - La superficie (kilomètres carrés) est fondée sur les limites du recensement de 2006.
[4] Surface area includes interior waters. - La superficie comprend les eaux intérieures.

[5] Population statistics are compiled from registers. - Les statistiques de la population sont compilées à partir des registres.
[6] Data refer to projections based on the 2000 population census. - Les données se réfèrent aux projections basées sur le recensement de la population de 2000.
[7] Data refer to private households only. - Les données concernent les ménages privés seulement.
[8] The urban agglomeration of Buenos Aires includes the city of Buenos Aires, and the 24 parts of the Buenos Aires province; among them, General San Martín, La Matanza, Lanús, Lomas de Zamora, Morón, Quilmes, San Fernando, San Isidro y Vicente López. - L'agglomération urbaine de Buenos Aires englobe la ville de Buenos Aires et les 24 circonscriptions de la province de Buenos Aires, dont General San Martín, La Matanza, Lanús, Lomas de Zamora, Morón, Quilmes, San Fernando, San Isidro y Vicente López.
[9] The urban agglomeration of Tucumán-Tafí Viejo includes San Miguel de Tucumán. - L'agglomération urbaine de Tucumán-Tafí Viejo englobe San Miguel de Tucumán.
[10] Data include persons in remote areas, military personnel outside the country, merchant seamen at sea, civilian seasonal workers outside the country, and other civilians outside the country, and exclude nomads, foreign military, civilian aliens temporarily in the country, transients on ships and Indian jungle population. - Y compris les personnes vivant dans des régions éloignées, le personnel militaire en dehors du pays, les marins marchands, les ouvriers saisonniers en dehors du pays, et autres civils en dehors du pays, et non compris les nomades, les militaires étrangers, les étrangers civils temporairement dans le pays, les transiteurs sur des bateaux et les Indiens de la jungle.
[11] Data based on the Population Census of 2005. - Données fondées sur le recensement de la population de 2005.
[12] Excluding foreign diplomatic personnel and their dependants. Data refer to national projections based on 2008 census. - Non compris le personnel diplomatique étranger et les membres de leur famille les accompagnant. Les données se réfèrent aux projections nationales basées sur le recensement de la population de 2008.
[13] Excluding Faeroe Islands and Greenland shown separately, if available. - Non compris les Iles Féroé et le Groenland, qui font l'objet de rubriques distinctes, si disponible.
[14] Excludes inland water and oceanic areas. - Exclut les eaux intérieures et les zones océaniques.

Table 9

Table 9 presents live births and crude birth rates by urban/rural residence for as many years as possible between 2006 and 2010.

Description of variables: Live birth is defined as the complete expulsion or extraction from its mother of a product of conception, irrespective of the duration of pregnancy, which after such separation, breathes or shows any other evidence of life such as beating of the heart, pulsation of the umbilical cord, or definite movements of voluntary muscles, whether or not the umbilical cord has been cut or the placenta is attached; each product of such a birth is considered live-born[1].

Statistics on the number of live births are obtained from civil registers unless otherwise noted. For those countries or areas where civil registration statistics on live births are considered reliable the birth rates shown have been calculated on the basis of registered live births.

For certain countries, there is a discrepancy between the total number of live births shown in this table and those shown in subsequent tables for the same year. Usually this discrepancy arises because the total number of live births occurring in a given year is revised but not the remaining tabulations.

Rate computation: Crude birth rates are the annual number of live births per 1 000 mid-year population.

Rates by urban/rural residence are the annual number of live births, in the appropriate urban or rural category, per 1 000 corresponding mid-year population. Rates are calculated only for data considered complete, that is, coded with a "C" and for estimates and live births statistics for the 12 month period prior to the census date, coded with a "|". These rates are calculated by the Statistics Division of the United Nations based on the appropriate reference population (for example: total population, nationals only, etc.) if known and available. If the reference population is not known or unavailable, the total population is used to calculate the rates. Therefore, if the population that is used to calculate the rates is different from the correct reference population, the rates presented might under- or overstate the true situation in a country or area.

Rates presented in this table are limited to those countries or areas having a minimum number of 30 live births in a given year.

Reliability of data: Each country or area has been asked to indicate the estimated completeness of the live births recorded in its civil register. These national assessments are indicated by the quality codes "C" and "U" that appear in the first column of this table.

"C" indicates that the data are estimated to be virtually complete, that is, representing at least 90 per cent of the live births occurring each year, whereas "U" indicates that data are estimated to be incomplete, that is, representing less than 90 per cent of the live births occurring each year. A third code "..." indicates that no information was provided regarding completeness.

Data from civil registers that are reported as incomplete or of unknown completeness (coded "U" or "...") are considered unreliable. They appear in italics in this table and rates are not calculated for these data.

These quality codes apply only to data from civil registers. If data from other sources are presented, the symbol "|" is shown instead of the quality code. For more information about the quality of vital statistics data in general, and the information available on the basis of the completeness estimates in particular, see section 4.2 of the Technical Notes.

Limitations: Statistics on live births are subject to the same qualifications as have been set forth for vital statistics in general and birth statistics in particular as discussed in section 4 of the Technical Notes.

The reliability of data, an indication of which is described above, is an important factor in considering the limitations. In addition, some live births are tabulated by date of registration and not by date of occurrence; these have been indicated by a plus sign "+". Whenever the lag between the date of occurrence and date of registration is prolonged and, therefore, a large proportion of the live birth registrations are delayed, birth statistics for any given year may be seriously affected.

Another factor that limits international comparability is the practice of some countries or areas not to include in live birth statistics infants who were born alive but died before the registration of the birth or within

the first 24 hours of life, thus underestimating the total number of life births. Statistics of this type are footnoted.

In addition, it should be noted that rates are affected also by the quality and limitations of the population estimates that are used in their computation. The problems of under-enumeration or over-enumeration and, to some extent, the differences in definition of total population have been discussed in section 3 of the Technical Notes dealing with population data in general, and specific information pertaining to individual countries or areas is given in the footnotes to table 3.

The rates estimated from the results of sample surveys are subject to possibilities of considerable error as a result of omissions in reporting of births, or as a result of erroneous reporting of births that occurred outside the reference period. However, rates estimated from sample surveys have the advantage of the availability of a built-in and strictly corresponding population base.

It should be emphasized that crude birth rates - like crude death, marriage and divorce rates - may be seriously affected by the age-sex structure of the populations to which they relate. Nevertheless, they do provide a simple measure of the level of and changes in natality.

The urban/rural classification of birth may refer to the residence of mother or the place of delivery, as the national practices vary and is provided by each country or area. In addition, the comparability of data by urban/rural residence is affected by the national definition of urban and rural used in tabulating these data. It is assumed, in the absence of specific information to the contrary, that the definitions of urban and rural used in connection with the national population census were also used in the compilation of the vital statistics for each country or area. However, it cannot be ruled out that, for a given country or area, different definitions of urban and rural are used for the vital statistics data and the population census data respectively. When known, the definitions of urban used in national population census are presented at the end of the technical notes to table 6. As discussed in detail in the technical notes to table 6, these definitions vary considerably from one area or country to another. Urban/rural differentials in vital rates may also be affected by whether the vital events have been tabulated in terms of place of occurrence or place of usual residence. This problem is discussed in more detail in section 4.1.4.1 of the Technical notes.

Earlier data: Live births have been shown in each issue of the *Demographic Yearbook*. Information on the years and specific topics covered is presented in the Historical Index.

NOTES

[1] *Principles and Recommendations for a Vital Statistics System Revision 2*, Sales No. E. 01 XVII.10, United Nations, New York, 2001.

Tableau 9

Le tableau 9 présente des données sur les naissances vivantes et les taux bruts de natalité selon le lieu de résidence (zone urbaine ou rurale) pour le plus grand nombre d'années possible entre 2006 et 2010.

Description des variables : La naissance vivante est l'expulsion ou l'extraction complète du corps de la mère, indépendamment de la durée de gestation, d'un produit de la conception qui, après cette séparation, respire ou manifeste tout autre signe de vie, tel que battement de cœur, pulsation du cordon ombilical ou contraction effective d'un muscle soumis à l'action de la volonté, que le cordon ombilical ait été coupé ou non et que le placenta soit ou non demeuré attaché ; tout produit d'une telle naissance est considéré comme « enfant né vivant »[1].

Sauf indication contraire, les statistiques relatives au nombre de naissances vivantes sont établies sur la base des registres de l'état civil. Pour les pays ou zones où les statistiques obtenues auprès des services de l'état civil sont jugées sûres, les taux de natalité indiqués ont été calculés par la Division de statistique de l'ONU d'après les naissances vivantes enregistrées.

Pour quelques pays il y a une discordance entre le nombre total des décès présenté dans ce tableau et ceux présentés après pour la même année. Habituellement ces différences apparaissent lorsque le nombre total des décès pour une certaine année a été révisé alors que les autres tabulations ne l'ont pas été.

Calcul des taux : Les taux bruts de natalité représentent le nombre annuel de naissances vivantes pour 1 000 habitants au milieu de l'année.

Les taux selon le lieu de résidence (zone urbaine ou rurale) représentent le nombre annuel de naissances vivantes, classées selon la catégorie urbaine ou rurale appropriée pour 1 000 habitants au milieu de l'année. Les taux ont été calculés seulement pour les données considérées complètes, c'est-à-dire celles associées au code « C », ainsi que pour les estimations et les statistiques des naissances vivantes dans la periode des douze mois précédante la date de recensement associées au code « | ». Ces taux sont calculés par la division de statistique des Nations Unies sur la base de la population de référence adéquate (par exemple : population totale, nationaux seulement, etc.) si connue et disponible. Si la population de référence n'est pas connue ou n'est pas disponible, la population totale est utilisée pour calculer les taux. Par conséquent, si la population utilisée pour calculer les taux est différente de la population de référence adéquate, les taux présentés sont susceptibles de sous ou sur estimer la situation réelle d'un pays ou d'un territoire.

Les taux présentés dans ce tableau se rapportent seulement aux pays ou zones où l'on a enregistré un nombre minimal de 30 naissances vivantes au cours d'une année donnée.

Fiabilité des données : Il a été demandé à chaque pays ou zone d'indiquer le degré estimatif de complétude des données sur les naissances vivantes figurant dans ses registres d'état civil. Ces évaluations nationales sont signalées par les codes de qualité "C" et "U" qui apparaissent dans la deuxième colonne du tableau.

La lettre "C" indique que les données sont jugées à peu près complètes, c'est-à-dire qu'elles représentent au moins 90 p. 100 des naissances vivantes survenues chaque année ; la lettre "U" signifie que les données sont jugées incomplètes, c'est-à-dire qu'elles représentent moins de 90 p. 100 des naissances vivantes survenues chaque année. Un troisième code, "...", indique qu'aucun renseignement n'a été communiqué quant à la complétude des données.

Les données provenant des registres de l'état civil qui sont déclarées incomplètes ou dont le degré de complétude n'est pas connu (code "U" ou "...") sont jugées douteuses. Elles apparaissent en italique dans le tableau. Les taux pour ces données ne sont pas calculés.

Les codes de qualité ne s'appliquent qu'aux données provenant des registres de l'état civil. Si l'on présente des données autres que celles de l'état civil, le signe "|" est utilisé à la place du code de qualité. Pour plus de précisions sur la qualité des données reposant sur les statistiques de l'état civil en général et les estimations de complétude en particulier, voir la section 4.2 des Notes techniques.

Insuffisance des données : Les statistiques concernant les naissances vivantes appellent toutes les réserves qui ont été formulées à propos des statistiques de l'état civil en général et des statistiques des naissances en particulier (voir la section 4 des Notes techniques).

La fiabilité des données, au sujet de laquelle des indications ont été fournies plus haut, est un facteur important. Il faut également tenir compte du fait que, dans certains cas, les données relatives aux naissances vivantes sont exploitées selon la date de l'enregistrement et non selon la date de l'événement ; ces cas ont été signalés par le signe '+'. Chaque fois que le décalage entre l'événement et son enregistrement est grand et qu'une forte proportion des naissances vivantes fait l'objet d'un enregistrement tardif, les statistiques des naissances vivantes pour une année donnée peuvent être considérablement faussées.

Un autre facteur qui nuit à la comparabilité internationale est la pratique de certains pays ou zones qui consiste à ne pas inclure dans les statistiques des naissances vivantes les enfants nés vivants mais décédés avant l'enregistrement de leur naissance ou dans les 24 heures qui ont suivi la naissance, pratique qui conduit à sous-estimer le nombre total de naissances vivantes. Lorsque ce facteur a joué, cela a été signalé en note à la fin du tableau.

La qualité et les limitations des estimations concernant la population ont également une incidence sur le calcul des taux. Les problèmes liés au sur-dénombrement ou au sous-dénombrement et, dans une certaine mesure, aux différences dans la définition de la population totale ont été abordés à la section 3 des Notes techniques relative aux données sur la population en général et des précisions sur certains pays ou zones sont données dans les notes se rapportant au tableau 3.

Les taux estimatifs fondés sur les résultats d'enquêtes par sondage comportent des possibilités d'erreurs considérables dues soit à des omissions dans les déclarations, soit au fait que l'on a déclaré à tort des naissances survenues en réalité hors de la période considérée. Toutefois, les taux estimatifs fondés sur les résultats d'enquêtes par sondage présentent un gros avantage : le chiffre de population utilisé comme base est, par définition, rigoureusement correspondant.

Il faut souligner que les taux bruts de natalité, de même que les taux bruts de mortalité, de nuptialité et de divortialité, peuvent varier très sensiblement selon la structure par âge et par sexe de la population à laquelle ils se rapportent. Ils offrent néanmoins un moyen simple de mesurer le niveau et l'évolution de la natalité.

La classification des naissances selon le lieu de résidence (zone urbaine ou rurale) peut se rapporter au lieu de résidence de la mère ou au lieu d'occurrence et correspond à celle indiquée par chaque pays ou zone. En outre, la comparabilité des données selon le lieu de résidence (zone urbaine ou rurale) peut être limitée par les définitions nationales des termes « urbain » et « rural » utilisées pour la mise en tableaux de ces données. En l'absence d'indications contraires, on a supposé que les mêmes définitions avaient servi pour le recensement national de la population et pour l'établissement des statistiques de l'état civil pour chaque pays ou zone. Toutefois, il n'est pas exclu que, pour une zone ou un pays donné, des définitions différentes aient été retenues. Les définitions du terme « urbain » utilisées pour les recensements nationaux de population ont été présentées à la fin des notes techniques du tableau 6 lorsqu'elles étaient connues. Comme on l'a précisé dans les notes techniques relatives au tableau 6, ces définitions varient considérablement d'un pays ou d'une zone à l'autre. La différence entre ces taux pour les zones urbaines et rurales pourra aussi être faussée selon que les faits d'état civil auront été classés d'après le lieu de l'événement ou le lieu de résidence habituel. Ce problème est examiné plus en détail à la section 4.1.4.1 des Notes techniques.

Données publiées antérieurement : Les différentes éditions de l'*Annuaire démographique* contiennent des données sur les naissances vivantes. Pour plus de précisions concernant les années et les sujets pour lesquels des données ont été publiées, se reporter à l'index historique.

NOTES

[1] *Principes et recommandations pour un système de statistique de l'état civil, deuxième révision*, numéro de vente : F.01.XVII.10, publication des Nations Unies, New York, 2003.

9. Live births and crude birth rates, by urban/rural residence: 2006 - 2010
Naissances vivantes et taux bruts de natalité selon la résidence, urbaine/rurale : 2006 - 2010

Continent, country or area, and urban/rural residence / Continent, pays ou zone et résidence, urbaine/rurale	Code[a]	Number - Nombre					Rate - Taux				
		2006	2007	2008	2009	2010	2006	2007	2008	2009	2010
AFRICA - AFRIQUE											
Algeria - Algérie[1]											
Total	C	739 000	783 000	817 000	849 000	888 000	22.1	23.0	23.6	24.1	24.7
Botswana[2]											
Total	+U	44 709	...	...	...	...	...	...	...	...	...
Burkina Faso											
Total	I	620 784[3]	663 100[4]	679 200[4]	...	...	44.3	46.5	46.1	...	...
Urban - Urbaine	I	109 381	...	...	...	...	34.4	...	...	...	...
Rural - Rurale	I	511 403	...	...	...	...	47.2	...	...	...	...
Cape Verde - Cap-Vert											
Total	C	11 925	12 335	12 697	13 044	13 415	24.7	25.1	25.4	25.6	25.9
Egypt - Égypte											
Total	C	1 853 746	1 949 569	2 050 704	2 217 409	...	25.7	26.5	27.3	28.8	...
Urban - Urbaine	C	740 228	763 798	799 571	913 141	...	24.1	24.1	24.7	27.6	...
Rural - Rurale	C	1 113 518	1 185 771	1 251 134	1 304 268	...	27.0	28.3	29.2	29.7	...
Ethiopia - Éthiopie[5]											
Total	I	...	2 218 457	...	...	...	...	30.1	...	...	...
Urban - Urbaine	I	...	240 167	...	...	...	...	20.2	...	...	...
Rural - Rurale	I	...	1 978 290	...	...	...	...	32.0	...	...	...
Ghana[6]											
Total	+U	620 688	767 109	553 119[7]	...	...	...	...	...	...	...
Kenya											
Total	U	538 951	464 283	660 383	691 312	...	...	...	...	...	...
Urban - Urbaine	U	320 874	280 471	436 480	462 476	...	...	...	...	...	...
Rural - Rurale	U	218 077	183 812	223 903	228 836	...	...	...	...	...	...
Liberia - Libéria[8]											
Total	I	...	...	63 171	...	...	...	...	18.2	...	...
Malawi											
Total[4]	U	614 410	626 181	...	...	...	...	...	...	...	...
Total[9]	I	...	...	516 629	...	...	...	...	37.9	...	...
Mauritius - Maurice[10]											
Total	+C	17 604	17 034	16 372	15 344	15 005	14.1	13.5	12.9	12.0	11.7
Urban - Urbaine	+C	6 691	6 467	6 284	5 895	...	12.7	12.2	11.8	11.1	...
Rural - Rurale	+C	10 913	10 567	10 088	9 449	...	15.0	14.4	13.7	12.7	...
Niger											
Total	...	100 613	118 423	...	...	...	...	...	...	...	...
Nigeria - Nigéria											
Total	...	...	1 807 025	...	...	...	...	...	...	...	...
Réunion[11]											
Total	C	14 495	14 808	...	...	...	18.4	18.7	...	...	...
Rwanda											
Total	U	...	404 792	417 171	429 065	...	...	...	...	...	...
Saint Helena ex. dep. - Sainte-Hélène sans dép.											
Total	C	35	42	36	35	34	...	10.6	9.0	8.5	8.0
Senegal - Sénégal[12]											
Total	I	466 678	477 431	488 754	498 714	509 230	41.6	41.4	41.3	41.0	40.7
Urban - Urbaine	I	183 837	188 780	194 084	198 984	204 137	40.3	40.3	40.3	40.2	40.1
Rural - Rurale	I	282 841	288 651	294 670	299 730	305 093	42.5	42.2	41.9	41.5	41.1
Seychelles											
Total	+C	1 467	1 499	1 546	1 580	1 504	17.3	17.6	17.8	18.1	17.4
Sierra Leone											
Total	...	...	...	115 736	101 868	...	...	...	...	...	...
South Africa - Afrique du Sud											
Total	U	1 053 863	1 027 386	1 033 403	937 531	...	...	...	...	...	...
Swaziland[5]											
Total	I	...	33 084	...	...	...	...	39.2	...	...	...
Tunisia - Tunisie											
Total	C	173 390	177 503	182 990	...	...	17.1	17.4	17.7	...	...
Zambia - Zambie[4]											
Total	U	509 766	...	...	...	...	...	...	...	...	...
AMERICA, NORTH - AMÉRIQUE DU NORD											
Anguilla											
Total	+C	183	148	108	...	...	12.8	9.9	6.9	...	...

Continent, country or area, and urban/rural residence / Continent, pays ou zone et résidence, urbaine/rurale	Code[a]	Number - Nombre					Rate - Taux				
		2006	2007	2008	2009	2010	2006	2007	2008	2009	2010
AMERICA, NORTH - AMÉRIQUE DU NORD											
Antigua and Barbuda - Antigua-et-Barbuda											
Total	+C	1 199	1 240	...	...	...	14.2	14.4	...	...	...
Aruba											
Total	C	1 227	1 239	1 218	1 213	1 141	11.9	11.9	11.6	11.3	10.6
Bahamas											
Total	U	5 296	5 854	5 124[13]	5 027[13]	...	...	...	...	...	...
Barbados - Barbade											
Total	+C	3 414	3 537	...	...	...	12.5	12.9	...	...	...
Bermuda - Bermudes[14]											
Total	C	798	859	821	819	...	12.5	13.4	12.8	12.7	...
Canada[15]											
Total	C	354 617	367 864	377 886	...	...	10.9	11.2	11.3	...	...
Cayman Islands - Îles Caïmanes[16]											
Total	C	710	744	793	824	821	13.7	13.8	14.2	15.6	15.0
Costa Rica											
Total	C	71 291	73 144	75 187	75 000	*70 922	16.4	16.5	16.6	16.2	*15.5
Urban - Urbaine	C	29 515	28 883	28 828	28 308	*26 047	11.5	11.0	10.8	10.4	*9.3
Rural - Rurale	C	41 776	44 261	46 359	46 692	*44 875	23.4	24.3	24.9	24.6	*25.6
Cuba											
Total	C	111 323	112 472	122 569	130 036	...	9.9	10.0	10.9	11.6	...
Urban - Urbaine	C	83 389	84 828	93 735	99 754	...	9.8	10.0	11.1	11.8	...
Rural - Rurale	C	27 934	27 644	28 834	30 282	...	10.2	10.0	10.4	10.9	...
Dominica - Dominique											
Total	+C	1 058	...	...	...	...	14.9	...	...	...	...
Dominican Republic - République dominicaine											
Total	U	133 331	129 211	130 875	117 634	...	...	...	...	...	...
Urban - Urbaine[17]	U	98 380	93 731	97 881	98 697	...	...	...	...	...	...
Rural - Rurale[17]	U	27 466	26 198	26 005	18 730	...	...	...	...	...	...
El Salvador[18]											
Total	C	107 111	106 471	112 049	...	...	17.6	17.5	18.3	...	...
Urban - Urbaine	C	70 810	68 439	...	...	...	19.1	18.2	...	...	...
Rural - Rurale	C	36 301	38 032	...	...	...	15.3	16.3	...	...	...
Greenland - Groenland											
Total	C	842	853	834	895	868	14.8	15.1	14.8	15.9	15.4
Urban - Urbaine	C	660	728	677	736	736	14.0	15.5	14.4	15.6	15.4
Rural - Rurale	C	182	125	157	159	132	18.7	13.2	17.0	17.5	14.9
Guadeloupe[11]											
Total	C	7 193	6 862	...	...	...	15.7	17.1	...	...	...
Guatemala											
Total	C	368 399	366 128	369 769	...	...	28.3	27.4	27.0	...	...
Urban - Urbaine	C	158 159	...	...	...	...	...	...	...	...	...
Rural - Rurale	C	210 240	...	...	...	...	...	...	...	...	...
Honduras											
Total	+U	222 512	...	...	...	...	...	...	...	...	...
Urban - Urbaine	+U	99 818	...	...	...	...	...	...	...	...	...
Rural - Rurale	+U	122 694	...	...	...	...	...	...	...	...	...
Jamaica - Jamaïque											
Total	C	46 277[19]	45 590[19]	44 838	44 006	...	17.4	17.0	16.7	16.3	...
Martinique[11]											
Total	C	5 370	5 317	...	...	...	13.5	13.4	...	...	...
Urban - Urbaine	C	4 858	4 822	...	...	...	...	...	...	...	...
Rural - Rurale	C	512	495	...	...	...	...	...	...	...	...
Mexico - Mexique[20]											
Total	+U	2 151 204	*2 185 888	...	...	...	...	...	...	...	...
Urban - Urbaine[17]	+U	1 588 093	*1 609 991	...	...	...	...	...	...	...	...
Rural - Rurale[17]	+U	505 361	*502 582	...	...	...	...	...	...	...	...
Montserrat											
Total	+C	49	43	72	...	...	10.5	8.9	14.8	...	...
Netherlands Antilles - Antilles néerlandaises[21]											
Total	C	2 611	2 558	2 765	2 661	...	13.8	13.2	14.0	13.3	...

Continent, country or area, and urban/rural residence / Continent, pays ou zone et résidence, urbaine/rurale	Code[a]	Number - Nombre					Rate - Taux				
		2006	2007	2008	2009	2010	2006	2007	2008	2009	2010
AMERICA, NORTH - AMÉRIQUE DU NORD											
Nicaragua											
Total	+U	123 886	128 171	125 028	...	...	...	...	...	...	...
Urban - Urbaine	+U	62 438	64 803	65 690	...	...	...	...	...	...	...
Rural - Rurale	+U	61 448	63 368	59 338	...	...	...	...	...	...	...
Panama											
Total	C	65 764	67 364	68 759	68 364	...	20.0	20.2	20.3	19.8	...
Urban - Urbaine	C	40 113	41 146	42 326	42 483	...	19.2	19.3	19.4	19.1	...
Rural - Rurale	C	25 651	26 218	26 433	25 881	...	21.6	21.8	21.7	21.1	...
Puerto Rico - Porto Rico											
Total	C	48 744	46 744	45 675	...	...	12.4	11.9	11.6	...	...
Urban - Urbaine[17]	C	...	...	23 899	...	...	...	...	...	...	...
Rural - Rurale[17]	C	...	...	21 750	...	...	...	...	...	...	...
Saint Vincent and the Grenadines - Saint-Vincent-et-les Grenadines											
Total	+C	1 796	1 822	1 901	1 905	...	17.7	18.2	19.2	...	...
Trinidad and Tobago - Trinité-et-Tobago											
Total	C	18 090	...	...	...	...	13.9	...	...	...	...
Turks and Caicos Islands - Îles Turques et Caïques[22]											
Total	C	409	455	453	...	...	12.3	13.1	12.4	...	...
United States of America - États-Unis d'Amérique											
Total	C	4 265 555	4 316 233	4 247 694	...	...	14.3	14.3	14.0	...	...
United States Virgin Islands - Îles Vierges américaines											
Total	C	1 763	1 771	...	...	...	16.1	16.1	...	...	...
AMERICA, SOUTH - AMÉRIQUE DU SUD											
Argentina - Argentine											
Total	+C	696 451	...	...	...	...	17.9	...	...	...	...
Total	C	...	700 792	746 066	745 336	...	...	17.8	18.8	18.6	...
Bolivia (Plurinational State of) - Bolivie (État plurinational de)											
Total	U	135 069	*96 856	...	...	...	...	...	...	...	...
Brazil - Brésil[23]											
Total	U	2 798 964	2 750 667	2 789 820	2 764 642[24]	...	...	...	...	...	...
Chile - Chili											
Total	C	231 383	240 569	246 581	...	...	14.1	14.5	14.7	...	...
Urban - Urbaine	C	208 709	217 104	226 170	...	...	14.6	15.1	15.5	...	...
Rural - Rurale	C	22 674	23 465	20 411	...	...	10.5	10.8	9.3	...	...
Colombia - Colombie											
Total	U	714 450	709 253	715 453	*686 045	...	...	...	...	...	...
Urban - Urbaine[17]	U	555 009	555 926	558 545	*535 423	...	...	...	...	...	...
Rural - Rurale[17]	U	147 921	141 605	143 892	*137 893	...	...	...	...	...	...
Ecuador - Équateur											
Total	+U	278 591	283 984	291 055	215 906[25]	...	...	...	...	...	...
Urban - Urbaine	+U	226 667	228 013	228 647	171 489[25]	...	...	...	...	...	...
Rural - Rurale	+U	51 924	55 971	62 408	44 417[25]	...	...	...	...	...	...
Falkland Islands (Malvinas) - Îles Falkland (Malvinas)											
Total	+C	27	...	...	...	...	...	...	...	...	...
French Guiana - Guyane française[11]											
Total	C	6 276	6 386	...	...	...	31.1	29.9	...	...	...
Urban - Urbaine	C	4 990	5 003	...	...	...	...	...	...	...	...
Rural - Rurale	C	1 286	1 383	...	...	...	...	...	...	...	...
Paraguay											
Total	+U	101 994	95 788	99 674	...	...	...	...	...	...	...
Urban - Urbaine	+U	68 583	65 713	71 747	...	...	...	...	...	...	...
Rural - Rurale	+U	33 411	30 075	27 927	...	...	...	...	...	...	...

9. Live births and crude birth rates, by urban/rural residence: 2006 - 2010
Naissances vivantes et taux bruts de natalité selon la résidence, urbaine/rurale : 2006 - 2010 (continued - suite)

Continent, country or area, and urban/rural residence — Continent, pays ou zone et résidence, urbaine/rurale	Code[a]	Number - Nombre					Rate - Taux				
		2006	2007	2008	2009	2010	2006	2007	2008	2009	2010
AMERICA, SOUTH - AMÉRIQUE DU SUD											
Peru - Pérou											
Total	+U	324 922[26]	324 480[26]	457 033[27]	457 108[27]	...	...	...	...	...	...
Suriname[28]											
Total	C	9 311	9 769	...	...	...	18.5	19.2	...	...	...
Urban - Urbaine[29]	C	5 726	6 103	...	...	...	...	...	...	...	...
Rural - Rurale[29]	C	3 585	3 666	...	...	...	...	...	...	...	...
Uruguay											
Total	C	47 231	47 372	47 484	*47 152	...	14.2	14.3	14.2	*14.1	...
Venezuela (Bolivarian Republic of) - Venezuela (République bolivarienne du)											
Total	C	646 225	615 371	581 480	...	...	23.9	22.4	20.8	...	...
ASIA - ASIE											
Armenia - Arménie											
Total	C	37 639	40 105	41 185	44 413	44 825	11.7	12.4	12.7	13.7	13.8
Urban - Urbaine	C	23 793	25 519	26 176	28 260	...	11.5	12.3	12.6	13.6	...
Rural - Rurale	C	13 846	14 586	15 009	16 153	...	12.0	12.6	12.9	13.8	...
Azerbaijan - Azerbaïdjan[30]											
Total	+C	148 946	151 963	152 086	152 139	165 643	17.3	17.4	17.2	17.0	18.3
Urban - Urbaine	+C	70 541	73 102	73 923	74 700	...	15.3	15.6	15.5	15.4	...
Rural - Rurale	+C	78 405	78 861	78 163	77 439	...	19.6	19.5	19.2	18.9	...
Bahrain - Bahreïn											
Total	C	15 053	16 062	17 022	17 841	...	15.7	15.5	15.4	15.1	...
Bangladesh[31]											
Total	I	...	...	...	...	...	20.6	20.9	...	...	...
Urban - Urbaine	I	...	...	...	...	...	17.5	17.4	...	...	...
Rural - Rurale	I	...	...	...	...	...	21.7	22.1	...	...	...
Brunei Darussalam - Brunéi Darussalam											
Total	+C	6 526	6 314	6 424	...	...	17.0	16.2	16.1	...	...
China - Chine[32]											
Total	I	15 840 000	15 940 000	16 080 000	16 150 000	...	12.1	12.1	12.1	12.1	...
China, Hong Kong SAR - Chine, Hong Kong RAS											
Total	C	65 626	70 875	78 822	82 095	...	9.6	10.2	11.3	11.7	...
China, Macao SAR - Chine, Macao RAS											
Total	C	4 058	4 537	4 717	4 764	*5 114	8.1	8.6	8.5	8.8	*9.4
Cyprus - Chypre[33]											
Total	C	8 731	8 575	9 205	9 608	*9 989	11.3	10.9	11.6	12.0	*12.4
Urban - Urbaine[17]	C	5 184	5 022	5 467	...	...	...	...	...	...	...
Rural - Rurale[17]	C	2 875	2 827	2 967	...	...	...	...	...	...	...
Democratic People's Republic of Korea - République populaire démocratique de Corée[34]											
Total	I	...	...	345 630	...	...	...	...	14.4	...	...
Urban - Urbaine	I	...	...	200 910	...	...	...	...	...	...	...
Rural - Rurale	I	...	...	144 720	...	...	...	...	...	...	...
Georgia - Géorgie											
Total	C	47 795	49 287	56 565	...	62 585	10.9	11.2	12.9	...	...
Urban - Urbaine	C	33 547	34 301	39 206	...	...	14.5	14.9	17.0	...	...
Rural - Rurale	C	14 248	14 986	17 359	...	...	6.8	7.2	8.4	...	...
India - Inde[35]											
Total	I	...	...	...	...	...	23.5	23.1	22.8	...	...
Urban - Urbaine	I	...	...	...	...	...	18.8	18.6	18.5	...	...
Rural - Rurale	I	...	...	...	...	...	25.2	24.7	24.4	...	...
Iran (Islamic Republic of) - Iran (République islamique d')[36]											
Total	+C	1 253 506	1 286 716	1 300 166	...	...	17.8	18.1	18.0	...	...
Urban - Urbaine	+C	844 813	872 658	895 117	...	...	...	17.9	18.1	...	...
Rural - Rurale	+C	408 693	414 058	405 049	...	...	...	18.5	17.9	...	...

9. Live births and crude birth rates, by urban/rural residence: 2000 - 2010
Naissances vivantes et taux bruts de natalité selon la résidence, urbaine/rurale : 2006 - 2010 (continued - suite)

Continent, country or area, and urban/rural residence — Continent, pays ou zone et résidence, urbaine/rurale	Code[a]	Number - Nombre					Rate - Taux				
		2006	2007	2008	2009	2010	2006	2007	2008	2009	2010
ASIA - ASIE											
Iraq											
Total	U	*902 934	...	...	...	...	...	...	...	...	...
Israel - Israël[37]											
Total	C	148 170	151 679	156 923	161 042	*165 950	21.0	21.1	21.5	21.5	*21.8
Urban - Urbaine	C	133 924[17]	138 143[17]	142 664[17]	146 305	...	20.7	21.0	21.3	21.3	...
Rural - Rurale	C	14 084[17]	13 478[17]	14 239[17]	14 737	...	24.5	22.9	23.5	23.7	...
Japan - Japon[38]											
Total	C	1 092 674	1 089 818	1 091 156	1 070 035	...	8.7	8.6	8.7	8.4	...
Urban - Urbaine[39]	C	984 329	987 851	991 477	973 701	...	...	...	...	...	...
Rural - Rurale[39]	C	108 169	101 807	99 506	96 235	...	...	...	...	...	...
Jordan - Jordanie[40]											
Total	C	162 972	185 011	181 328	...	...	29.1	32.3	31.0	...	...
Kazakhstan[30]											
Total	C	301 756	321 963	356 575	*357 552	...	19.7	20.8	22.7	*22.5	...
Urban - Urbaine	C	175 582	174 343	196 839	...	...	20.0	21.3	23.6	...	...
Rural - Rurale	C	126 174	147 620	159 736	...	...	19.3	20.3	21.8	...	...
Kuwait - Koweït											
Total	C	52 759	53 587	54 571	...	...	22.7	22.2	21.9	...	...
Kyrgyzstan - Kirghizstan											
Total	C	120 737	123 251	127 332	135 494	...	24.0	24.4	25.1	26.4	...
Urban - Urbaine	C	39 414	41 402	43 974	46 924	...	22.0	23.1	24.5	25.9	...
Rural - Rurale	C	81 323	81 849	83 358	88 570	...	25.1	25.1	25.4	26.7	...
Lebanon - Liban											
Total	C	72 790	80 896	84 823	90 388	95 218	...	21.5	...	...	...
Malaysia - Malaisie											
Total	C	465 112	472 048	487 346	*481 669	...	17.3	17.4	17.7	*17.3	...
Urban - Urbaine	C	295 561	300 745	307 793	...	...	17.5	17.5	17.7	...	...
Rural - Rurale	C	169 551	171 303	179 553	...	...	17.0	17.0	17.7	...	...
Maldives											
Total	C	5 829	6 569	6 989	7 423	...	19.5	21.5	22.6	23.6	...
Urban - Urbaine	C	2 707	3 083	3 349	3 685	...	...	...	...	...	...
Rural - Rurale	C	3 122	3 486	3 640	3 738	...	...	...	...	...	...
Mongolia - Mongolie											
Total	C	49 092	56 636	63 768	68 762	65 889	19.0	21.7	24.0	25.1	...
Urban - Urbaine	C	29 717	36 256	40 590	...	...	19.0	22.8	24.9	...	...
Rural - Rurale	C	19 375	20 380	23 178	...	...	19.0	19.9	22.5	...	...
Myanmar											
Total	+U	857 306	945 859	890 034	...	...	...	...	...	...	...
Urban - Urbaine	+U	240 828	248 713	248 600	...	...	...	...	...	...	...
Rural - Rurale	+U	616 478	697 146	641 434	...	...	...	...	...	...	...
Occupied Palestinian Territory - Territoire palestinien occupé[41]											
Total	C	114 959	115 371	...	...	...	31.8	31.0	...	...	...
Oman[42]											
Total	U	49 944	53 498	58 280	64 735	...	...	...	...	...	...
Pakistan[43]											
Total	I	3 802 928	3 830 973	...	...	...	24.3	24.0	...	...	...
Urban - Urbaine	I	1 212 745	1 238 053	...	...	...	22.4	22.2	...	...	...
Rural - Rurale	I	2 590 183	2 592 920	...	...	...	25.2	25.0	...	...	...
Philippines											
Total	C	1 663 029	1 749 878	...	...	...	19.1	19.7	...	...	...
Qatar											
Total	C	14 120	15 681	17 210	18 351	18 576	13.5	12.9	11.9	11.2	10.8
Republic of Korea - République de Corée[44]											
Total	C	448 153	493 189	465 892	444 849	...	9.2	10.0	9.4	9.0	...
Urban - Urbaine[17]	C	370 703	406 636	384 901	366 022	...	9.4	10.2	9.6	9.1	...
Rural - Rurale[17]	C	76 906	86 117	80 728	78 524	...	8.2	9.2	8.7	8.4	...
Saudi Arabia - Arabie saoudite[45]											
Total	...	589 223	595 099[46]	598 126[46]	...	...	...	...	...	...	...
Singapore - Singapour											
Total	C	38 317	39 490	39 826	39 570	...	8.7	8.6	8.2	7.9	...

9. Live births and crude birth rates, by urban/rural residence: 2006 - 2010
Naissances vivantes et taux bruts de natalité selon la résidence, urbaine/rurale : 2006 - 2010 (continued - suite)

Continent, country or area, and urban/rural residence / Continent, pays ou zone et résidence, urbaine/rurale	Code[a]	Number - Nombre					Rate - Taux				
		2006	2007	2008	2009	2010	2006	2007	2008	2009	2010
ASIA - ASIE											
Sri Lanka											
Total	+C	373 538	386 573	*379 912	*376 843	*364 565	18.8	19.3	*18.8	*18.4	*17.7
Urban - Urbaine	+C	252 013	264 960	...	...	...	...	...	...	...	...
Rural - Rurale	+C	121 525	121 613	...	...	...	...	...	...	...	...
Syrian Arab Republic - République arabe syrienne[47]											
Total	+U	656 599	727 439	...	*670 793						
Tajikistan - Tadjikistan[48]											
Total	U	186 463	200 010	203 332	...	...	...	...	...	...	...
Urban - Urbaine	U	44 298	51 384	51 582	...	...	...	...	...	...	...
Rural - Rurale	U	142 165	148 626	151 750	...	...	...	...	...	...	...
Thailand - Thaïlande											
Total	+U	793 623	797 588	784 256	765 047	...	...	...	...	...	...
Turkey - Turquie[49]											
Total	I	1 277 000	1 275 000	1 272 000	1 270 000	1 279 000	18.4	18.1	17.9	17.7	17.6
United Arab Emirates - Émirats arabes unis[45]											
Total	...	62 969	67 689[46]	...	...	...	...	...	...	...	...
Viet Nam											
Total	C	1 243 463	1 326 464	...	...	...	14.9	15.7	...	...	...
Urban - Urbaine	C	320 456	358 119	...	...	...	13.9	15.1	...	...	...
Rural - Rurale	C	923 007	968 345	...	...	...	15.3	16.0	...	...	...
Yemen - Yémen											
Total	U	298 437	256 288	...	...	...	...	...	...	...	...
EUROPE											
Åland Islands - Îles d'Åland											
Total	C	295	286	294	267	286	11.0	10.6	10.8	9.7	10.3
Urban - Urbaine	C	113	109	121	95	...	10.5	10.0	11.0	8.6	...
Rural - Rurale	C	182	177	173	172	...	11.3	10.9	10.6	10.4	...
Albania - Albanie											
Total	C	34 229	33 163	36 251	...	...	10.9	10.5	11.4	...	...
Andorra - Andorre											
Total	C	843	826	875	838	828	10.5	10.0	10.4	9.8	9.8
Austria - Autriche											
Total	C	77 914	76 250	77 752	76 344	78 742	9.4	9.2	9.3	9.1	9.4
Belarus - Bélarus											
Total	C	96 721	103 626	107 876	109 263	108 050	9.9	10.7	11.1	11.3	11.4
Urban - Urbaine	C	71 186	77 137	81 643	82 780	...	10.1	10.9	11.5	11.5	...
Rural - Rurale	C	25 535	26 489	26 233	26 483	...	9.6	10.1	10.3	10.6	...
Belgium - Belgique[50]											
Total	C	121 382	120 663	128 049	127 297	*127 000	11.5	11.4	12.0	11.8	*11.7
Urban - Urbaine	C	119 696	119 040	...	...	...	11.5	11.4	...	...	...
Rural - Rurale	C	1 686	1 623	...	...	...	11.1	10.6	...	...	...
Bosnia and Herzegovina - Bosnie-Herzégovine											
Total	C	34 033	33 835	34 176	34 550	*33 779	8.9	8.8	8.9	9.0	*8.8
Bulgaria - Bulgarie											
Total	C	73 978	75 349	77 712	80 956	75 513	9.6	9.8	10.2	10.7	10.0
Urban - Urbaine	C	55 043	56 257	58 367	60 664	...	10.1	10.4	10.8	11.2	...
Rural - Rurale	C	18 935	19 092	19 345	20 292	...	8.3	8.5	8.7	9.3	...
Croatia - Croatie											
Total	C	41 446	41 910	43 753	44 577	...	9.3	9.4	9.9	10.1	...
Urban - Urbaine	C	23 085	23 302	24 316	24 927	...	...	...	...	...	...
Rural - Rurale	C	18 361	18 608	19 437	19 650	...	...	...	...	...	...
Czech Republic - République tchèque											
Total	C	105 831	114 632	119 570	118 348	117 153	10.3	11.1	11.5	11.3	11.1
Urban - Urbaine	C	78 561	84 759	88 648	87 245	...	10.4	11.1	11.5	11.3	...
Rural - Rurale	C	27 270	29 873	30 922	31 103	...	10.1	11.0	11.3	11.3	...
Denmark - Danemark[51]											
Total	C	64 933	64 095	65 038	62 818	63 411	11.9	11.7	11.8	11.4	11.4

9. Live births and crude birth rates, by urban/rural residence: 2000 - 2010
Naissances vivantes et taux bruts de natalité selon la résidence, urbaine/rurale : 2006 - 2010 (continued - suite)

Continent, country or area, and urban/rural residence / Continent, pays ou zone et résidence, urbaine/rurale	Code[a]	Number - Nombre					Rate - Taux				
		2006	2007	2008	2009	2010	2006	2007	2008	2009	2010
EUROPE											
Estonia - Estonie											
Total	C	14 877	15 775	16 028	15 763	15 825	11.1	11.8	12.0	11.8	11.8
Urban - Urbaine	C	10 554	11 134	11 078	10 807	...	11.3	12.0	11.9	11.6	...
Rural - Rurale	C	4 323	4 641	4 950	4 956	...	10.5	11.3	12.1	12.1	...
Faeroe Islands - Îles Féroé											
Total	C	662	674	...	...	...	13.7	13.9	...	...	...
Urban - Urbaine	C	251	237	...	...	...	14.3	13.6	...	...	...
Rural - Rurale	C	411	437	...	...	...	13.3	14.1	...	...	...
Finland - Finlande[52]											
Total	C	58 840	58 729	59 530	60 163[53]	60 694[53]	11.2	11.1	11.2	11.3	11.4
Urban - Urbaine	C	41 933	41 909	42 534	42 919[53]	...	11.8	11.7	11.8	11.9	...
Rural - Rurale	C	16 907	16 820	16 996	17 244[53]	...	9.8	9.8	9.9	10.2	...
France[54]											
Total	C	796 896	785 985	796 044	793 420	*797 000	12.9	12.7	12.8	12.7	*12.7
Urban - Urbaine[55]	C	596 949	587 384	593 785	593 291	...	...	...	...	...	...
Rural - Rurale[55]	C	198 494	197 161	200 753	198 595	...	...	...	...	...	...
Germany - Allemagne											
Total	C	672 724	684 862	682 514	665 126	*681 000	8.2	8.3	8.3	8.1	*8.3
Gibraltar											
Total	+C	373	400[56]	400[56]	...	...	12.9	13.7	13.7	...	...
Greece - Grèce											
Total	C	112 042	111 926	118 302	117 933	*109 982	10.0	10.0	10.5	10.5	...
Urban - Urbaine	C	77 090	76 513	80 476	80 678	...	...	...	...	...	...
Rural - Rurale	C	34 952	35 413	37 826	37 255	...	...	...	...	...	...
Guernsey - Guernesey											
Total	C	598	645	631	675	...	9.8	10.5	10.2	10.8	...
Hungary - Hongrie											
Total	C	99 871	97 613	99 149	96 442	*90 335	9.9	9.7	9.9	9.6	*9.0
Urban - Urbaine[57]	C	66 223	65 417	66 877	65 684	...	9.8	9.7	9.8	9.6	...
Rural - Rurale[57]	C	32 789	31 525	31 475	29 747	...	9.9	9.5	9.8	9.4	...
Iceland - Islande											
Total	C	4 415	4 560	4 835	5 027	4 907	14.5	14.6	15.1	15.7	15.4
Urban - Urbaine	C	4 204	4 314	4 605	4 793	...	14.9	14.9	15.5	16.0	...
Rural - Rurale	C	211	246	230	234	...	9.4	11.0	10.8	11.5	...
Ireland - Irlande											
Total	+C	64 237	70 620	75 065	74 278	*73 940	15.2	16.3	17.0	16.7	*16.5
Isle of Man - Île de Man											
Total	+C	905	919	...	...	...	11.3	11.4	...	...	...
Italy - Italie											
Total	C	560 010	563 933	...	...	...	9.5	9.5	...	...	...
Total	+C	...	...	576 659	568 857	*561 980	...	...	9.6	9.5	*9.3
Jersey[20]											
Total	+C	962	1 031	973	...	...	10.8	11.4	...	...	...
Latvia - Lettonie											
Total	C	22 264	23 273	23 948	21 677	19 219	9.7	10.2	10.6	9.6	8.6
Urban - Urbaine	C	15 342	16 123	16 574	14 849	...	9.9	10.4	10.8	9.7	...
Rural - Rurale	C	6 922	7 150	7 374	6 828	...	9.4	9.8	10.1	9.4	...
Liechtenstein											
Total	C	361	351	350	*406	*329	10.3	9.9	9.9	*11.3	*9.1
Lithuania - Lituanie											
Total	C	31 265	32 346	35 065	36 682	35 626	9.2	9.6	10.4	11.0	10.8
Urban - Urbaine	C	20 691	21 656	23 824	25 043	...	9.1	9.6	10.6	11.2	...
Rural - Rurale	C	10 574	10 690	11 241	11 639	...	9.4	9.5	10.1	10.5	...
Luxembourg											
Total	C	5 514	5 477	5 596	5 638	5 874	11.7	11.4	11.5	11.3	11.6
Malta - Malte											
Total	C	3 885	3 871	4 126	4 143	3 999	9.6	9.5	10.0	10.0	9.6
Monaco[58]											
Total	C	880	...	...	...	...	...	...	...	...	...
Montenegro - Monténégro											
Total	C	7 531	7 834	8 258	8 642	7 415	12.1	12.5	13.1	13.7	11.7
Urban - Urbaine	C	6 598	6 200	6 431	6 579	...	16.8	15.7	16.2	16.4	...
Rural - Rurale	C	933	1 634	1 827	2 063	...	4.0	7.1	7.9	8.9	...
Netherlands - Pays-Bas[59]											
Total	C	185 057	181 336	184 634	184 915	*183 866	11.3	11.1	11.2	11.2	*11.1
Urban - Urbaine	C	126 775	125 067	127 683	128 524	...	11.7	11.6	11.7	11.7	...
Rural - Rurale	C	58 282	56 269	56 951	56 391	...	10.5	10.1	10.2	10.1	...

Continent, country or area, and urban/rural residence / Continent, pays ou zone et résidence, urbaine/rurale	Code[a]	Number - Nombre					Rate - Taux				
		2006	2007	2008	2009	2010	2006	2007	2008	2009	2010
EUROPE											
Norway - Norvège[60]											
Total	C	58 545	58 459	60 497	61 807	61 442	12.6	12.4	12.7	12.8	12.6
Poland - Pologne											
Total	C	374 244	387 873	414 499	417 589	413 300	9.8	10.2	10.9	10.9	10.8
Urban - Urbaine	C	218 000	225 638	241 288	246 429	...	9.3	9.7	10.4	10.6	...
Rural - Rurale	C	156 244	162 235	173 211	171 160	...	10.6	11.0	11.7	11.5	...
Portugal[20]											
Total	C	105 449	102 492	104 594	99 491	*101 320	10.0	9.7	9.8	9.4	*9.5
Republic of Moldova - République de Moldova[61]											
Total	C	37 587[30]	37 973[30]	39 018	40 803	40 474	10.5	10.6	10.9	11.4	11.4
Urban - Urbaine	C	13 579[30]	13 679[30]	14 288	14 906	...	9.2	9.3	9.7	10.1	...
Rural - Rurale	C	24 008[30]	24 294[30]	24 730	25 897	...	11.4	11.6	11.8	12.4	...
Romania - Roumanie											
Total	C	219 483	214 728	221 900	222 388	212 199	10.2	10.0	10.3	10.4	9.9
Urban - Urbaine	C	119 477	116 367	121 518	121 864	...	10.0	9.8	10.3	10.3	...
Rural - Rurale	C	100 006	98 361	100 382	100 524	...	10.3	10.2	10.4	10.4	...
Russian Federation - Fédération de Russie[30]											
Total	C	1 479 637	1 610 122	1 713 947	1 761 687	1 788 948	10.4	11.3	12.1	12.4	12.5
Urban - Urbaine	C	1 044 540	1 120 741	1 194 820	1 237 615	...	10.0	10.8	11.5	11.9	...
Rural - Rurale	C	435 097	489 381	519 127	524 072	...	11.3	12.8	13.6	13.7	...
San Marino - Saint-Marin											
Total	+C	302	292	349	306	...	9.6	9.2	10.7	9.3	...
Serbia - Serbie[62]											
Total	+C	70 997	68 102	69 083	70 299	68 304	9.6	9.2	9.4	9.6	9.2
Urban - Urbaine	+C	46 401	44 776	45 389	46 896	...	10.9	10.5	10.6	11.0	...
Rural - Rurale	+C	24 596	23 326	23 694	23 403	...	7.8	7.5	7.7	7.7	...
Slovakia - Slovaquie											
Total	C	53 904	54 424	57 360	61 217	60 410	10.0	10.1	10.6	11.3	11.1
Urban - Urbaine	C	28 411	28 970	30 663	32 636	...	9.5	9.7	10.3	11.0	...
Rural - Rurale	C	25 493	25 454	26 697	28 581	...	10.6	10.6	11.0	11.7	...
Slovenia - Slovénie											
Total	C	18 932	19 823	21 817	21 856	*21 687	9.4	9.8	10.8	10.7	*10.6
Urban - Urbaine	C	9 190	9 629	10 612	10 761	...	9.5	9.6	10.5	10.5	...
Rural - Rurale	C	9 742	10 194	11 205	11 095	...	9.8	10.1	11.1	10.9	...
Spain - Espagne											
Total	C	482 957	492 527	519 779	494 997	*479 999	11.0	11.0	11.4	10.8	*10.4
Sweden - Suède											
Total	C	105 913	107 421	109 301	111 801	115 641	11.7	11.7	11.9	12.0	12.3
Switzerland - Suisse											
Total	C	73 371	74 494	76 691	78 286	*80 000	9.8	9.9	10.0	10.1	*10.2
Urban - Urbaine	C	54 480	55 252	57 114	58 542	...	9.9	10.0	10.2	10.3	...
Rural - Rurale	C	18 891	19 242	19 577	19 744	...	9.5	9.6	9.7	9.7	...
TFYR of Macedonia - L'ex-R. y. de Macédoine											
Total	C	22 585	22 688	22 945	23 684	*24 296	11.1	11.1	11.2	11.5	*11.8
Urban - Urbaine	C	12 653	12 761	13 200	13 621	...	...	...	...	...	...
Rural - Rurale	C	9 932	9 927	9 745	10 063	...	...	...	...	...	...
Ukraine[63]											
Total	C	460 368	472 657	510 589	*512 526	497 689	9.8	10.2	11.0	*11.1	10.8
Urban - Urbaine	C	306 635	314 065	340 594	...	...	9.6	9.9	10.8	...	...
Rural - Rurale	C	153 733	158 592	169 995	...	...	10.3	10.7	11.6	...	...
United Kingdom of Great Britain and Northern Ireland - Royaume-Uni de Grande-Bretagne et d'Irlande du Nord[64]											
Total	C	748 563	772 245	794 383	790 204	*778 823	12.4	12.7	12.9	12.8	*12.5
OCEANIA - OCÉANIE											
American Samoa - Samoas américaines											
Total	C	1 442	...	...	...	...	21.6	...	...	...	...

Continent, country or area, and urban/rural residence / Continent, pays ou zone et résidence, urbaine/rurale	Code[a]	Number - Nombre					Rate - Taux				
		2006	2007	2008	2009	2010	2006	2007	2008	2009	2010
OCEANIA - OCÉANIE											
Australia - Australie											
Total	+C	265 949	285 213	296 621	295 738	...	12.8	13.5	13.8	13.5	...
Urban - Urbaine[65]	+C	220 302	236 445	245 991	246 066	...	13.0	13.7	14.0	13.7	...
Rural - Rurale[65]	+C	45 121	48 021	49 833	49 086	...	11.9	12.5	12.7	12.4	...
Cook Islands - Îles Cook[66]											
Total	+C	278	289	261	*255		11.7	13.8	11.8	*11.1	
Fiji - Fidji											
Total	+C	18 394	19 298	18 944	18 854	...	22.2	23.1	...	21.4	...
French Polynesia - Polynésie française											
Total	C	4 592	4 434	4 628	...		17.9	17.1	17.6		
Guam[67]											
Total	C	3 414	3 493	3 466	3 423	...	20.0	20.1	19.7	19.2	...
Marshall Islands - Îles Marshall[68]											
Total	+U	1 576	...	...	...	...	...	...	...	...	...
Micronesia (Federated States of) - Micronésie (États fédérés de)											
Total	+U	2 148	...	...	...	...	...	...	...	...	...
Nauru											
Total	C	120	...	...	...	...	...	...	...	...	...
New Caledonia - Nouvelle-Calédonie											
Total	C	4 224	4 093	4 015	*4 090	...	17.7	16.9	16.6	*16.7	...
Urban - Urbaine	C	...	2 678	...	...	...	...	...	...	...	...
Rural - Rurale	C	...	1 415	...	...	...	...	...	...	...	...
New Zealand - Nouvelle-Zélande											
Total	+C	59 193	64 044	64 343	62 543	...	14.1	15.1	15.1	14.5	...
Urban - Urbaine[17]	+C	51 540	55 822	56 220	54 650	...	14.3	15.3	15.3	14.7	...
Rural - Rurale[17]	+C	7 518	8 065	8 066	7 809	...	13.0	13.8	13.6	13.1	...
Niue - Nioué[69]											
Total	C	35	28	20	31	...	20.8	...	...	20.0	...
Norfolk Island - Île Norfolk[70]											
Total	+C	22	22	22	...	...	...	...	...	...	...
Northern Mariana Islands - Îles Mariannes septentrionales[71]											
Total	U	1 422	1 384	1 260	...	...	...	...	...	...	...
Palau - Palaos											
Total	C	259	...	...	...	...	12.0	...	...	...	...
Pitcairn											
Total	C	...	1	1	...	...	...	...	...	...	...
Samoa											
Total	C	3 171	2 528	2 371	1 602	...	17.1	13.9	13.0	8.7	...
Tonga											
Total	+C	2 945	...	...	...	...	28.6	...	...	...	...
Tuvalu											
Total	U	217	214	...	...	...	...	...	...	...	...
Wallis and Futuna Islands - Îles Wallis et Futuna											
Total	C	220	215	185	...	...	...	...	13.8	...	...

FOOTNOTES - NOTES

Italics: data from civil registers which are incomplete or of unknown completeness. - Italiques : données incomplètes ou dont le degré d'exactitude n'est pas connu, provenant des registres de l'état civil.

* Provisional. - Données provisoires.

[a] 'Code' indicates the source of data, as follows:
C - Civil registration, estimated over 90% complete
U - Civil registration, estimated less than 90% complete
| - Other source, estimated reliable

+ - Data tabulated by date of registration rather than occurence
... - Information not available

Le 'Code' indique la source des données, comme suit :
C - Registres de l'état civil considérés complets à 90 p. 100 au moins
U - Registres de l'état civil qui ne sont pas considérés complets à 90 p. 100 au moins
| - Autre source, considérée pas douteuses
+ - Données exploitées selon la date de l'enregistrement et non la date de l'événement
... - Information pas disponible

[1] Excluding live-born infants who died before their birth was registered. Data refer to Algerian population only. - Non compris les enfants nés vivants décédés avant l'enregistrement de leur naissance. Les données ne concernent que la population algérienne.

[2] Data from Health Statistics Reports since 1998, due to incompleteness of civil registration. - Données provenant des Health Statistics Reports (rapports sur les statistiques sanitaires) depuis 1998, en raison des lacunes de l'état civil.

[3] Data refer to the twelve months preceding the census in December. Data refer to births to women aged 15-49. - Les données se rapportent aux douze mois précédant le recensement de décembre. Les données concernent les enfants nés de femmes âgées de 15 à 49 ans.

[4] Data refer to national projections. - Les données se réfèrent aux projections nationales.

[5] Data refer to the twelve months preceding the census in May. - Les données se rapportent aux douze mois précédant le recensement de mai.

[6] Coverage of live births is below 60%. - La couverture des naissances vivantes est inférieure à 60 %.

[7] Excluding data for November and December. - Ne comprend pas les données pour novembre et décembre.

[8] Data refer to the twelve months preceding the census in March. - Les données se rapportent aux douze mois précédant le recensement de mars.

[9] Data refer to the twelve months preceding the census in June. - Les données se raportent aux douze mois précédant le recensement de juin.

[10] Excludes the islands of St. Brandon and Agalega. - Non compris les îles St. Brandon et Agalega.

[11] Excluding live-born infants who died before their birth was registered. - Non compris les enfants nés vivants décédés avant l'enregistrement de leur naissance.

[12] Based on estimates and projections from 'Agence Nationale de la Statistique et de la Démographie'. - Données fondées sur des estimations et des projections provenant de l'Agence Nationale de la Statistique et de la Démographie.

[13] Data refer to registered events only. - Les données ne concernent que les événements enregistrés.

[14] Excluding non-residents and foreign service personnel and their dependants. - À l'exclusion des non-résidents et du personnel diplomatique et de leurs charges de famille.

[15] Including Canadian residents temporarily in the United States, but excluding United States residents temporarily in Canada. - Y compris les résidents canadiens se trouvant temporairement aux Etats-Unis, mais ne comprenant pas les résidents des Etats-Unis se trouvant temporairement au Canada.

[16] Resident births outside the islands are excluded. - Non compris les naissances de résidents hors des îles.

[17] The total number includes 'Unknown residence', but the categories urban and rural do not. - Le nombre total inclue 'Résidence inconnue ', mais les catégories urbaine et rurale ne l'incluent pas.

[18] Excluding children born in the country of non-resident mothers. - Exceptés les enfants nés dans le pays des mères non-résidentes.

[19] Data have been adjusted for underenumeration. - Les données ont été ajustées pour compenser les lacunes du dénombrement.

[20] Data refer to births to resident mothers. - Ces données concernent les enfants nés de mères résidentes.

[21] Data refer to resident population only. - Pour la population résidante seulement.

[22] Excluding births of nationals outside the country. - Non compris les naissances de nationaux hors du pays.

[23] Excluding Indian jungle population. - Non compris les Indiens de la jungle.

[24] Including births abroad and births of unknown residence. - Y compris les naissances survenues à l'étranger et les naissances d'enfants dont la résidence n'était pas connue.

[25] Excluding events registered late. - Non compris les enregistrements tardifs.

[26] Source: Ministry of health reports. - Source: Rapports du Ministère de Santé.

[27] Based on National Registers of identification and civil status. - Chiffres fondés sur les registres nationaux d'identification et d'état civil.

[28] Including births to non-resident mothers. - Y compris les naissances de femmes non résidentes.

[29] The districts of Paramaribo and Wanica are considered urban areas, whereas all other districts are considered more or less rural areas. - Les districts de Paramaribo et de Wanica sont considérés comme des zones urbaines, les autres districts étant considérés comme des zones rurales à divers degrés.

[30] Excluding infants born alive of less than 28 weeks' gestation, of less than 1 000 grams in weight and 35 centimeters in length, who die within seven days of birth. - Non compris les enfants nés vivants après moins de 28 semaines de gestation, pesant moins de 1 000 grammes, mesurant moins de 35 centimètres et décédés dans les sept jours qui ont suivi leur naissance.

[31] Rates were obtained by the Sample Vital Registration System of Bangladesh. - Taux obtenus au moyen du Sample Vital Registration System du Bangladesh.

[32] Data have been estimated on the basis of the annual National Sample Survey on Population Changes. For statistical purposes, the data for China do not include those for the Hong Kong Special Administrative Region (Hong Kong SAR), Macao Special Administrative Region (Macao SAR) and Taiwan province of China. - Les données ont été estimées sur la base de l'enquête annuelle "National Sample Survey on Population Changes". Pour la présentation des statistiques, les données pour la Chine ne comprennent pas la Région Administrative Spéciale de Hong Kong (Hong Kong RAS), la Région Administrative Spéciale de Macao (Macao RAS) et Taïwan province de Chine.

[33] Data refer to government controlled areas. - Les données se rapportent aux zones contrôlées par le Gouvernement.

[34] Data refer to the twelve months preceding the census in October. - Les données font référence aux 12 mois qui ont précédé le recensement en octobre.

[35] Rates were obtained by the Sample Registration System of India, which is a large demographic survey. Including data for the Indian-held part of Jammu and Kashmir, the final status of which has not yet been determined. - Les taux ont été obtenus par le Système de l'enregistrement par échantillon de l'Inde qui est une large enquête démographique. Y compris les données pour la partie du Jammu et du Cachemire occupée par l'Inde dont le statut définitif n'a pas encore été déterminé.

[36] Data refer to the Iranian Year which begins on 21 March and ends on 20 March of the following year. - Les données concernent l'année iranienne, qui commence le 21 mars et se termine le 20 mars de l'année suivante.

[37] Including data for East Jerusalem and Israeli residents in certain other territories under occupation by Israeli military forces since June 1967. - Y compris les données pour Jérusalem-Est et les résidents israéliens dans certains autres territoires occupés depuis 1967 par les forces armées israéliennes.

[38] Data refer to Japanese nationals in Japan only. - Les données se raportent aux nationaux japonais au Japon seulement.

[39] The total number includes 'Unknown residence', but the categories urban and rural do not. Urban and rural distribution refers to the residence of the child. - Le nombre total inclue 'Résidence inconnue ', mais les catégories urbaine et rurale ne l'incluent pas. La répartition urbain/rural se réfère au domicile de l'enfant.

[40] Excluding data for Jordanian territory under occupation since June 1967 by Israeli military forces. Excluding foreigners, including registered Palestinian refugees. - Non compris les données pour le territoire jordanien occupé depuis juin 1967 par les forces armées israéliennes. Non compris les étrangers, mais y compris les réfugiés de Palestine enregistrés.

[41] Source: Palestinian Central Bureau of Statistics 2010, Population Register, Updated Version 30/3/2010. - Source : Bureau central de statistiques de la Palestine, 2010, Registre de la population, version mise à jour le 30 mars 2010.

[42] Data from Births and Deaths Notification System (Ministry of Health institutions and all other health care providers). - Les données proviennent du système de notification des naissances et des décès (établissements du Ministère de la santé et tous autres prestataires de soins de santé).

[43] Based on the results of the Pakistan Demographic Survey. Excluding data for the Pakistan-held part of Jammu and Kashmir, the final status of which has not yet been determined. - Données extraites de l'enquête démographique effectuée par le Pakistan. Non compris les données concernant la partie du Jammu et Cachemire occupée par le Pakistan dont le statut définitif n'a pas été déterminé.

[44] Excluding alien armed forces, civilian aliens employed by armed forces, and foreign diplomatic personnel and their dependants. Data refer to residence of child. - Non compris les militaires étrangers, les civils étrangers employés par les forces armées ni le personnel diplomatique étranger et les membres de leur famille les accompagnant. Les données correspondent à la résidence de l'enfant.

[45] The registration of births and deaths is conducted by the Ministry of Health. An estimate of completeness is not provided. - L'enregistrement des naissances et des décès est mené par le Ministère de la Santé. Le degré estimatif de complétude n'est pas fourni.

[46] As published by the United Nations Economic and Social Commission for Western Asia. - Publié par la Commission économique et sociale des Nations Unies pour l'Asie occidentale.

[47] Excluding nomad population and Palestinian refugees. Excluding live-born infants who died before their birth was registered. - Non compris la population nomade et les réfugiés de Palestine. Non compris les enfants nés vivants décédés avant l'enregistrement de leur naissance.

[48] Excluding infants born alive of less than 28 weeks' gestation, of less than 1 000 grams in weight and 35 centimeters in length, who die within seven days of birth. Data have been adjusted for under-registration. - Non compris les enfants nés vivants après moins de 28 semaines de gestations, pesant moins de 1 000 grammes, mesurant moins de 35 centimètres et décédés dans les sept jours qui ont suivi leur naissance. Y compris un ajustement pour sous-enregistrement.

[49] Data based on Address Based Population Registration System. - Les données sont basées sur le registre national de la population basé sur l'adresse.

[50] Including armed forces stationed outside the country, but excluding alien armed forces stationed in the area. - Y compris les militaires nationaux hors du pays, mais non compris les militaires étrangers en garnison sur le territoire.
[51] Excluding Faeroe Islands and Greenland shown separately, if available. - Non compris les Iles Féroé et le Groenland, qui font l'objet de rubriques distinctes, si disponible.
[52] Including resident births abroad. - Y compris les naissances de résidents à l'étranger.
[53] Excluding Åland Islands. - Non compris les Îles d'Åland.
[54] Including armed forces stationed outside the country. - Y compris les militaires nationaux hors du pays.
[55] Data for urban and rural, excluding nationals outside the country. - Les données pour la résidence urbaine et rurale , non compris les nationaux hors du pays.
[56] Including live births by military personnel and their dependants. - Y compris les naissances vivantes parmi les membres du personnel militaire et leurs personnes à charge.
[57] Total includes the data of foreigners, persons of unknown residence and homeless, but the categories urban and rural do not. - Total incluant les étrangers, les personnes de résidence inconnue et les sans-abri, ce qui n'est pas le cas pour les catégories urbaines et rurales.
[58] Including residents outside the country. - Y compris les résidents hors du pays.
[59] Including residents outside the country if listed in a Netherlands population register. - Y compris les résidents hors du pays, s'ils sont inscrits sur un registre de population néerlandais.
[60] Excluding Svalbard and Jan Mayen Islands shown separately, if available. - Non compris Svalbard et Jan Mayen qui font l'objet de rubriques distinctes, si disponible.
[61] Excluding Transnistria and the municipality of Bender. - Les données ne tiennent pas compte de l'information sur la Transnistria et la municipalité de Bender.
[62] Excluding data for Kosovo and Metohia. - Sans les données pour le Kosovo et Metohie.
[63] Data refer to births with weight 500g and more (if weight is unknown - with length 25 centimeters and more, or with gestation during 22 weeks or more). - Données concernant les nouveau-nés de 500 grammes ou plus (si le poids est inconnu – de 25 centimètres de long ou plus, ou après une grossesse de 22 semaines ou plus).
[64] Excluding Channel Islands (Guernsey and Jersey) and Isle of Man, shown separately, if available. Data tabulated by date of occurrence for England and Wales, and by date of registration for Northern Ireland and Scotland. - Non compris les îles Anglo-Normandes (Guernesey et Jersey) et l'île de Man, qui font l'objet de rubriques distinctes, si disponible. Données exploitées selon la date de l'événement pour l'Angleterre et le pays de Galles, et selon la date de l'enregistrement pour l'Irlande du Nord et l'Ecosse.
[65] Excluding data where place of usual residence of mother was overseas, undefined, no fixed place of abode, offshore, migratory or unknown. - Les données n'ont pas été prises en compte lorsque le domicile habituel de la mère était à l'étranger ou dans une zone extraterritoriale, était indéfini ou inconnu ou que la mère n'avait pas de domicile fixe ou était une migrante.
[66] Excluding Niue, shown separately, which is part of Cook Islands, but because of remoteness is administered separately. - Non compris Nioué, qui fait l'objet d'une rubrique distincte et qui fait partie des îles Cook, mais qui, en raison de son éloignement, est administrée séparément.
[67] Including United States military personnel, their dependants and contract employees. - Y compris les militaires des Etats-Unis, les membres de leur famille les accompagnant et les agents contractuels des Etats-Unis.
[68] Excluding United States military personnel, their dependants and contract employees. - Non compris les militaires des Etats-Unis, les membres de leur famille les accompagnant et les agents contractuels des Etats-Unis.
[69] Includes children born in New Zealand to women resident in Niue who chose to travel to New Zealand to give birth. - Y compris les enfants nés en Nouvelle-Zélande de femmes résidant à Nioué qui ont choisi de se rendre en Nouvelle-Zélande pour accoucher.
[70] Data cover the period from 1 July previous year to 30 June present year. - Pour la période allant du 1er juillet de l'année précédente au 30 juin de l'année en cours.
[71] Source: Commonwealth Health Center - Vital Statistics Office - Source : Centre de Santé du Commonwealth - Bureau des statistiques d'État civil

Tables 10 and 10a

Table 10 presents live births by age of mother and sex of the child, general fertility rate, and age-specific fertility rates for the latest available year between 2000 and 2009. Table 10a presents the available data for year 2010.

Description of variables: Age is defined as age at last birthday, that is, the difference between the date of birth and the date of the occurrence of the event, expressed in completed solar years. The age classification used in this table is the following: under 15 years, 5-year age groups through 45-49 years, and 50 years and over. A different classification may appear as provided by reporting country or area.

Rate computation: Age-specific fertility rates are the annual number of births to women in each age group per 1 000 female population in the same age group. These rates are calculated by the Statistics Division of the United Nations.

Since relatively few births occur to women below 15 or above 50 years of age, age-specific fertility rates for women under 20 years of age and for those 45 years of age or over are computed on the female population aged 15-19 and 45-49, respectively. Similarly, the rate for women of "All ages" is based on all live births irrespective of age of mother, and is computed on the female population aged 15-49 years. This rate for "All ages" is known as the general fertility rate. The age-specific fertility rates for age groups of women below 15 or 50 and above years of age are not calculated.

Births to mothers of unknown age are distributed proportionately across the age groups, by the Statistics Division of the United Nations, in accordance with the distribution of births by age of mother prior to the calculation of the rates.

The population used in computing the rates is the estimated or enumerated distribution of females by age. First priority was given to the estimated population and second priority to the enumerated population, i.e. to census returns of the year to which the births referred.

Rates presented in this table are limited to those for countries or areas having at least a total of 100 live births in a given year.

Reliability of data: Data from civil registers of live births which are reported as incomplete (less than 90 per cent completeness) or of unknown completeness are considered unreliable and are set in *italics* rather than in roman type. Rates are not computed if the data on live births from civil registers are reported as incomplete (less than 90 per cent completeness) or of unknown completeness. Table 9 and the technical notes for that table provide more detailed information on the completeness of live-birth registration. For more information about the quality of vital statistics data in general, see section 4.2 of the Technical Notes.

Limitations: Statistics on live births by age of mother are subject to the same qualifications as have been set forth for vital statistics in general and birth statistics in particular as discussed in section 4 of the Technical Notes. These include differences in the completeness of registration, the method used to determine age of mother and the quality of the reported information relating to age of mother.

The reliability of the data described above, is an important factor in considering the limitations. In addition, some live births are tabulated by date of registration and not by date of occurrence; these are indicated in the table by a plus sign "+". Whenever the lag between the date of occurrence and date of registration is prolonged and, therefore, a large proportion of the live birth registrations are delayed, birth statistics for any given year may be seriously affected. For example, the age of the mother will almost always refer to the date of registration rather than to the date of birth of the child. Hence, in those countries or areas where registration of births is delayed, possibly for years, statistics on births by age of mother should be used with caution.

Another factor which limits international comparability is the practice of some countries or areas of not including in live birth statistics infants who were born alive but died before the registration of the birth or within the first 24 hours of life, thus underestimating the total number of live births. Statistics of this type are footnoted.

Because these statistics are classified according to age, they are subject to the limitations with respect to accuracy of age reporting similar to those already discussed in connection with section 3.1.3 of the

Technical Notes. The factors influencing the accuracy of reporting may be somewhat dissimilar in vital statistics (because of the differences in the method of taking a census and registering a birth) but, in general, the same errors can be observed. The absence of frequencies in the unknown age group does not necessarily indicate completely accurate reporting and tabulation of the age item. It is often an indication that the unknowns have been eliminated by assigning ages to them before tabulation, or by proportionate distribution after tabulation.

On the other hand, large frequencies in the unknown age category may indicate that a large proportion of the births are born outside of wedlock, the records for which tend to be incomplete so far as characteristics of the parents are concerned.

Another limitation of age reporting may result from calculating age of mother at birth of child (or at time of registration) from year of birth rather than from day, month and year of birth. Information on this factor is given in footnotes when known.

In few countries, data by age refer to deliveries rather than to live births causing under-enumeration in the event of a multiple birth. This practice leads to lack of strict comparability, both among countries or areas relying on this practice and between data shown in this table and table 9.

Rates shown in this table are subject to the same limitations that affect the corresponding statistics on live births. In cases of rates based on births tabulated by date of registration and not by date of occurrence; the effect of including delayed registration on the distribution of births by age of mother may be noted in the age-specific fertility rates for women at older ages. In some cases, high age-specific rates for women aged 45 years and over may reflect age of mother at registration of birth and not fertility at these older ages.

Earlier data: Live births and live-birth rates by age of mother (i.e. age-specific fertility rates), have been shown for the latest available year in each issue of the Yearbook. Information on the years and specific topics covered is presented in the Historical Index.

Tableaux 10 et 10a

Le tableau 10 présente les données les plus récentes disponibles pour la période 2000 -2009 sur les naissances vivantes selon l'âge de la mère et le sexe de l'enfant, le taux de fécondité et les taux de fécondité par âge. Le tableau 10a présente les données disponibles pour l'année 2010.

Description des variables : l'âge désigne l'âge au dernier anniversaire, c'est-à-dire la différence entre la date de naissance et la date de l'événement exprimée en années solaires révolues. La classification par âge utilisée dans ce tableau comprend les catégories suivantes : moins de 15 ans, groupes quinquennaux jusqu'à 45-49 ans, 50 ans et plus, et âge inconnu. Des groupes d'âge différents sont parfois utilisés lorsque les pays ou territoires ont fourni les données dans une autre classification.

Les taux de fécondité par âge représentent le nombre annuel de naissances vivantes intervenues dans un groupe d'âge donné pour 1 000 femmes du groupe d'âge. Ces taux ont été calculés par la Division de statistique de l'ONU.

Étant donné que le nombre de naissances parmi les femmes de moins de 15 ans ou de plus de 50 ans est relativement peu élevé, les taux de fécondité par âge parmi les femmes âgées de moins de 20 ans et celles de 45 ans et plus ont été calculés sur la base des populations féminines âgées de 15 à 19 ans et de 45 à 49 ans, respectivement. De même, le taux pour les femmes de « tous âges » est fondé sur la totalité des naissances vivantes, indépendamment de l'âge de la mère et ce chiffre est rapporté à l'effectif de la population féminine âgée de 15 à 49 ans. Ce taux « tous âges » est le taux global de fécondité ou simplement taux de fécondité. Les taux de fécondité parmi les femmes âgées de moins de 15 ans ou celles de 50 ans et plus n'ont pas été calculés.

Les naissances pour lesquelles l'âge de la mère était inconnu ont été réparties par la Division de statistique de l'ONU, avant le calcul des taux, suivant les proportions observées pour celles où l'âge de la mère était connu.

Les chiffres de population utilisés pour le calcul des taux proviennent de dénombrements ou de répartitions estimatives de la population féminine selon l'âge. On a utilisé de préférence les estimations de la population; à défaut, on s'est contenté des données censitaires se rapportant à l'année des naissances.

Les taux présentés dans ce tableau ne concernent que les pays ou zones où l'on a enregistré un total d'au moins 100 naissances vivantes dans une année donnée.

Fiabilité des données : les données sur les naissances vivantes provenant des registres de l'état civil qui sont déclarées incomplètes (degré de complétude inférieur à 90 p. 100) ou dont le degré de complétude n'est pas connu sont jugées douteuses et apparaissent en italique et non en caractères romains. On a choisi de ne pas faire figurer des taux calculés à partir de données sur les naissances vivantes issues de registres de l'état civil qui sont déclarées incomplètes (degré de complétude inférieur à 90 p. 100) ou dont le degré de complétude n'est pas connu. Le tableau 9 et les notes techniques qui s'y rapportent présentent des renseignements plus détaillés sur le degré de complétude de l'enregistrement des naissances vivantes. Pour plus de précisions sur la qualité des statistiques de l'état civil en général, voir la section 4.2 des Notes techniques.

Insuffisance des données : les statistiques relatives aux naissances vivantes selon l'âge de la mère appellent toutes les réserves qui ont été formulées à propos des statistiques de l'état civil en général et des statistiques de naissances en particulier (voir la section 4 des Notes techniques). Ceci inclut les différences de complétude d'enregistrement des faits d'état civil, de méthode pour déterminer l'âge de la mère et de qualité d'information concernant l'âge de la mère.

La fiabilité des données, au sujet de laquelle des indications ont été données plus haut, est un facteur important. Il faut également tenir compte du fait que, dans certains cas, les données relatives aux naissances vivantes sont exploitées selon la date de l'enregistrement et non la date de l'événement ; ces cas ont été signalés dans le tableau par le signe '+'. Chaque fois que le décalage entre l'événement et son enregistrement est grand et qu'une forte proportion des naissances vivantes fait l'objet d'un enregistrement tardif, les statistiques des naissances vivantes pour une année donnée peuvent être considérablement faussées. Par exemple, l'âge de la mère représente presque toujours son âge à la date de l'enregistrement et non à la date de la naissance de l'enfant. Ainsi, dans les pays ou zones où l'enregistrement des naissances est tardif, le retard atteignant parfois plusieurs années, il faut utiliser avec prudence les statistiques concernant les naissances selon l'âge de la mère.

Un autre facteur qui nuit à la comparabilité internationale est la pratique de certains pays ou zones qui consiste à ne pas inclure dans les statistiques des naissances vivantes les enfants nés vivants mais décédés avant l'enregistrement de leur naissance ou dans les 24 heures qui ont suivi la naissance, pratique qui conduit à sous-estimer le nombre total de naissances vivantes. Quand pareil facteur a joué, cela a été signalé en note à la fin du tableau.

Étant donné que les statistiques du tableau 10 sont classées selon l'âge, elles appellent les mêmes réserves concernant l'exactitude des déclarations d'âge que celles formulées à la section 3.1.3 des Notes techniques. Dans le cas des statistiques de l'état civil, les facteurs qui interviennent à cet égard sont parfois différents, étant donné que le recensement de la population et l'enregistrement des naissances se font par des méthodes différentes, mais, d'une manière générale, les erreurs observées seront les mêmes. Si aucun nombre ne figure dans la rangée réservée aux âges inconnus, cela ne signifie pas nécessairement que les déclarations d'âge et l'exploitation des données par âge ont été tout à fait exactes. C'est souvent une indication que l'on a attribué un âge aux personnes d'âge inconnu avant l'exploitation des données ou qu'elles ont été réparties proportionnellement entre les différents groupes après cette opération.

À l'inverse, lorsque le nombre des personnes d'âge inconnu est important, cela peut signifier que la proportion de naissances parmi les mères célibataires est élevée, étant donné qu'en pareil cas l'acte de naissance ne contient pas tous les renseignements concernant les parents.

Les déclarations par âge peuvent comporter des distorsions, du fait que l'âge de la mère au moment de la naissance d'un enfant (ou de la déclaration de naissance) est donné par année de naissance et non par date exacte (jour, mois et année).

Dans quelques pays, la classification par âges se réfère aux accouchements, et non aux naissances vivantes, ce qui conduit à un sous-dénombrement en cas de naissances gémellaires. Cette pratique nuit à la comparabilité des données, à la fois entre pays ou zones qui recourent à cette méthode et entre les données présentées dans le tableau 10 et celles du tableau 9.

Les taux présentés dans ce tableau sont sujets aux mêmes limitations qui affectent les statistiques correspondantes de naissances vivantes. Dans le cas des taux basés sur des naissances par date d'enregistrement et non par date d'occurrence, l'effet peut être visible sur les taux de fécondité par âge des femmes aux âges plus élevés. Dans certains cas, les taux de fécondité des femmes de plus de 45 ans peuvent refléter l'âge de la mère à l'enregistrement plus que la fécondité à ces âges.

Données publiées antérieurement : les différentes éditions de l'*Annuaire démographique* regroupent les dernières statistiques dont on disposait à l'époque sur les naissances vivantes selon l'âge de la mère et les taux des naissances vivantes selon l'âge de la mère (taux de fécondité par âge). Pour plus de précisions concernant les années pour lesquels des données ont été publiées, se reporter à l'index historique.

10. Live births by age of mother and sex of child, general and age-specific fertility rates: latest available year, 2000 - 2009
Naissances vivantes selon l'âge de la mère et le sexe de l'enfant, taux de fécondité et taux de fécondité par âge : dernière année disponible, 2000 - 2009

Continent, country or area, year, code and age of mother (in years) / Continent, pays ou zone, année, code et âge de la mère (en années)	Number - Nombre			Rate Taux
	Total	Male Masculin	Female Féminin	

AFRICA - AFRIQUE

	Total	Male	Female	Rate
Botswana[1]				
2006 (+U)				
Total	44 709	23 534	21 175	...
15 - 19	5 493	2 916	2 577	...
20 - 24	15 118	7 883	7 235	...
25 - 29	11 383	6 023	5 360	...
30 - 34	7 115	3 760	3 355	...
35 - 39	3 813	1 989	1 824	...
40 - 44	1 556	838	718	...
45 +	231	125	106	...
Egypt - Égypte				
2009 (C)				
Total	2 217 409	1 147 592	1 069 817	106.6
0 - 19	66 153	34 380	31 773	31.2
20 - 24	370 947	191 996	178 951	189.5
25 - 29	342 515	176 804	165 711	207.8
30 - 34	187 627	96 452	91 175	159.2
35 - 39	79 720	41 147	38 573	66.7
40 - 44	20 455	10 481	9 974	19.9
45 +	2 974	1 519	1 455	3.3
Unknown - Inconnu	1 147 018	594 813	552 205	..
Kenya				
2009 (U)				
Total	691 312	354 154	337 158	...
0 - 14	3 877	2 019	1 858	..
15 - 19	89 664	45 562	44 102	...
20 - 24	221 828	113 572	108 256	...
25 - 29	174 571	89 674	84 897	...
30 - 34	103 940	53 395	50 545	...
35 - 39	49 527	25 424	24 103	...
40 - 44	13 231	6 713	6 518	...
45 - 49	2 165	1 097	1 068	...
50 +	823	423	400	..
Unknown - Inconnu	31 686	16 275	15 411	..
Liberia - Libéria[2]				
2008 (|)				
Total	63 171	33 511	29 660	73.1
12 - 14	304	157	147	..
15 - 19	6 973	3 668	3 305	37.4
20 - 24	16 181	8 486	7 695	89.4
25 - 29	14 915	8 017	6 898	98.9
30 - 34	10 277	5 433	4 844	91.5
35 - 39	8 336	4 374	3 962	79.8
40 - 44	3 961	2 138	1 823	53.5
45 - 49	2 224	1 238	986	40.5
Libya - Libye				
2002 (C)				
Total	111 053	57 722	53 331	...
0 - 19	1 196	592	604	...
20 - 24	15 018	7 845	7 173	...
25 - 29	32 713	16 877	15 836	...
30 - 34	33 325	17 384	15 941	...
35 - 39	18 702	9 777	8 925	...
40 - 44	6 422	3 296	3 126	...
45 +	676	364	312	...
Unknown - Inconnu	3 001	1 587	1 414	...
Malawi[3]				
2008 (|)				
Total	516 629	...	...	160.1
15 - 19	70 737	...	...	101.5
20 - 24	169 406	...	...	285.0
25 - 29	130 331	...	...	242.3
30 - 34	79 232	...	...	153.6
35 - 39	43 747	...	...	117.2
40 - 44	15 956	...	...	57.9

AFRICA - AFRIQUE

	Total	Male	Female	Rate
Malawi[3]				
2008 (|)				
45 - 49	5 599	...	...	25.1
Unknown - Inconnu	1 621	...	...	..
Mauritius - Maurice[4]				
2009 (C)				
Total	15 259	7 732	7 527	43.5
0 - 14	38	21	17	...
15 - 19	1 690	834	856	31.9
20 - 24	3 799	1 948	1 851	82.1
25 - 29	4 780	2 416	2 364	91.2
30 - 34	3 219	1 639	1 580	60.7
35 - 39	1 191	584	607	26.1
40 - 44	351	187	164	7.2
45 - 49	23	9	14	♦0.5
50 +	3	2	1	..
Unknown - Inconnu	165	92	73	..
Morocco - Maroc				
2001 (C)				
Total	541 298	277 242	264 056	66.7
0 - 14	1 016	525	491	..
15 - 19	45 049	23 151	21 898	28.3
20 - 24	131 163	67 353	63 810	88.3
25 - 29	136 599	69 989	66 610	102.3
30 - 34	117 851	60 300	57 551	104.4
35 - 39	75 484	38 586	36 898	73.6
40 - 44	27 453	13 958	13 495	32.1
45 - 49	3 974	1 998	1 976	5.9
50 +	1 105	556	549	..
Unknown - Inconnu	1 604	826	778	..
Namibia - Namibie[5]				
2001 (|)				
Total	45 157	22 643	22 514	100.1
12 - 14	74	37	37	..
15 - 19	5 278	2 638	2 640	51.2
20 - 24	11 964	5 997	5 967	135.8
25 - 29	11 056	5 563	5 493	144.6
30 - 34	8 429	4 259	4 170	137.3
35 - 39	5 292	2 636	2 656	103.1
40 - 44	2 383	1 187	1 196	59.8
45 +	681	326	355	22.1
Nigeria - Nigéria				
2007 (...)				
Total	1 807 025	...	...	...
0 - 14	2 528	...	...	...
15 - 19	129 716	...	...	...
20 - 24	471 036	...	...	...
25 - 29	588 454	...	...	...
30 - 34	377 593	...	...	...
35 - 39	172 081	...	...	...
40 - 44	49 519	...	...	...
45 - 49	13 411	...	...	...
50 +	2 687	...	...	...
Réunion[6]				
2007 (C)				
Total	14 808	7 711	7 097	69.2
0 - 14	23	11	12	..
15 - 19	1 517	769	748	44.1
20 - 24	3 348	1 752	1 596	117.2
25 - 29	3 968	2 075	1 893	144.2
30 - 34	3 429	1 779	1 650	116.2
35 - 39	1 931	1 009	922	58.6
40 - 44	572	307	265	16.8
45 +	20	9	11	♦0.7

10. Live births by age of mother and sex of child, general and age-specific fertility rates: latest available year, 2000 - 2009
Naissances vivantes selon l'âge de la mère et le sexe de l'enfant, taux de fécondité et taux de fécondité par âge : dernière année disponible, 2000 - 2009 (continued - suite)

Continent, country or area, year, code and age of mother (in years) / Continent, pays ou zone, année, code et âge de la mère (en années)	Total	Male Masculin	Female Féminin	Rate Taux
AFRICA - AFRIQUE				
Saint Helena ex. dep. - Sainte-Hélène sans dép.				
2000 (C)				
Total	56	32	24	...
15 - 19	7	3	4	...
20 - 24	16	10	6	...
25 - 29	12	5	7	...
30 - 34	13	9	4	...
35 - 39	7	4	3	...
40 - 44	1	1	-	...
Senegal - Sénégal[7]				
2002 (I)				
Total	399 967	...	...	156.4
15 - 19	70 532	...	...	115.6
20 - 24	102 101	...	...	199.1
25 - 29	95 932	...	...	227.0
30 - 34	69 955	...	...	201.7
35 - 39	40 465	...	...	143.1
40 - 44	16 624	...	...	74.5
45 - 49	4 358	...	...	27.5
Seychelles				
2009 (+C)				
Total	1 580	825	755	...
0 - 14	4	3	1	..
15 - 19	244	129	115	...
20 - 24	445	224	221	...
25 - 29	398	200	198	...
30 - 34	274	155	119	...
35 - 39	171	89	82	...
40 - 44	42	24	18	...
45 +	2	1	1	...
South Africa - Afrique du Sud				
2007 (U)[8]				
Total	858 866	432 282	426 584	...
0 - 14	804	381	423	..
15 - 19	93 451	47 102	46 349	...
20 - 24	246 545	124 213	122 332	...
25 - 29	222 601	112 241	110 360	...
30 - 34	165 240	83 254	81 986	...
35 - 39	95 875	47 952	47 923	...
40 - 44	29 099	14 544	14 555	...
45 - 49	4 196	2 093	2 103	...
50 +	659	310	349	...
Unknown - Inconnu	396	192	204	..
2009 (U)				
Total	937 531	...	...	...
15 +	879 707	...	...	...
15 - 19	109 804	...	...	...
20 - 24	246 916	...	...	...
25 - 29	231 135	...	...	...
30 - 34	162 782	...	...	...
35 - 39	93 833	...	...	...
40 - 44	29 583	...	...	...
45 - 49	4 086	...	...	...
50 +	347	...	...	...
Unknown - Inconnu	1 221	...	...	...
Swaziland[9]				
2007 (I)				
Total	33 084	18 905	14 179	152.2
0 - 14	67	33	34	..
15 - 19	3 581	1 775	1 806	71.0
20 - 24	8 303	4 449	3 854	184.4
25 - 29	6 839	3 830	3 009	187.1
30 - 34	5 039	2 969	2 070	188.5
35 - 39	3 839	2 324	1 515	166.8

Continent, country or area, year, code and age of mother (in years) / Continent, pays ou zone, année, code et âge de la mère (en années)	Total	Male Masculin	Female Féminin	Rate Taux
AFRICA - AFRIQUE				
Swaziland[9]				
2007 (I)				
40 - 44	2 008	1 340	668	104.7
45 - 49	1 246	892	354	75.8
50 +	2 155	1 288	867	..
Unknown - Inconnu	7	5	2	..
Tunisia - Tunisie				
2007 (C)				
Total	177 503	...	...	60.1
0 - 14	-	...	...	..
15 - 19	2 555	...	...	6.0
20 - 24	23 334	...	...	52.6
25 - 29	47 786	...	...	117.4
30 - 34	44 906	...	...	126.2
35 - 39	24 726	...	...	79.8
40 - 44	6 964	...	...	22.8
45 +	510	...	...	2.0
Unknown - Inconnu	26 721			
AMERICA, NORTH - AMÉRIQUE DU NORD				
Anguilla				
2006 (+C)				
Total	183	...	...	...
0 - 14	2	...	...	..
15 - 19	26	...	...	...
20 - 24	56	...	...	...
25 - 29	42	...	...	...
30 - 34	26	...	...	...
35 - 39	27	...	...	...
40 +	4	...	...	..
Unknown - Inconnu	-	...	...	...
Aruba				
2007 (C)				
Total	1 239	642	597	43.2
0 - 14	3	2	1	..
15 - 19	149	78	71	41.0
20 - 24	305	157	148	101.2
25 - 29	314	149	165	94.7
30 - 34	280	159	121	71.7
35 - 39	149	79	70	31.6
40 - 44	36	17	19	7.1
45 +	2	1	1	+0.4
50 +	-	-	-	..
Unknown - Inconnu	1	-	1	..
2009 (C)				
Total	1 213	...	...	42.3
0 - 14	2	...	...	..
15 - 19	146	...	...	39.3
20 - 24	284	...	...	92.2
25 - 29	322	...	...	98.0
30 - 34	269	...	...	69.5
35 - 39	158	...	...	34.7
40 - 44	32	...	...	6.6
45 - 49	-	...	...	-
50 +	-	...	...	..
Unknown - Inconnu	-	...	...	..
Bahamas[10]				
2009 (U)				
Total	5 027[11]	2 508	2 517	...
0 - 14	5	2	3	...
15 - 19	527	272	255	...
20 - 24	1 209[11]	599	609	...
25 - 29	1 279[11]	640	638	...

10. Live births by age of mother and sex of child, general and age-specific fertility rates: latest available year, 2000 - 2009
Naissances vivantes selon l'âge de la mère et le sexe de l'enfant, taux de fécondité et taux de fécondité par âge : dernière année disponible, 2000 - 2009 (continued - suite)

Continent, country or area, year, code and age of mother (in years) / Continent, pays ou zone, année, code et âge de la mère (en années)	Total	Male Masculin	Female Féminin	Rate Taux
AMERICA, NORTH - AMÉRIQUE DU NORD				
Bahamas[10]				
2009 (U)				
30 - 34	*1 102*	*555*	*547*	...
35 - 39	*690*	*339*	*351*	...
40 - 44	*197*	*93*	*104*	...
45 - 49	*18*	*8*	*10*	...
50 +	-	-	-	..
Unknown - Inconnu	-	-	-	..
Barbados - Barbade				
2007 (+C)				
Total	3 537	1 850	1 687	...
0 - 14	10	7	3	..
15 - 19	462	226	236	...
20 - 24	894	487	407	...
25 - 29	805	420	385	...
30 - 34	730	387	343	...
35 - 39	463	235	228	...
40 - 44	164	84	80	...
45 - 49	7	3	4	...
Unknown - Inconnu	2	1	1	...
Belize				
2002 (U)				
Total	*7 356*	...	...	...
0 - 14	*22*	...	...	...
15 - 19	*1 237*	...	...	...
20 - 24	*2 233*	...	...	...
25 - 29	*1 712*	...	...	...
30 - 34	*1 106*	...	...	...
35 - 39	*566*	...	...	...
40 - 44	*165*	...	...	...
45 +	*17*	...	...	...
Unknown - Inconnu	*298*	...	...	...
Bermuda - Bermudes[12]				
2009 (C)				
Total	819	427	392	49.8
0 - 14	2	1	1	..
15 - 19	33	19	14	17.7
20 - 24	109	64	45	58.9
25 - 29	186	96	90	83.5
30 - 34	252	128	124	108.2
35 - 39	192	94	98	76.4
40 - 44	39	21	18	14.7
45 - 49	6	4	2	♦2.0
50 +	-	-	-	..
Unknown - Inconnu	-	-	-	..
Canada[13]				
2008 (C)				
Total	377 886	193 755	184 131	45.9
0 - 14	134	73	61	..
15 - 19	15 570	7 969	7 601	14.2
20 - 24	59 060	30 181	28 879	53.1
25 - 29	115 705	59 130	56 575	102.2
30 - 34	118 775	61 112	57 663	107.5
35 - 39	57 316	29 513	27 803	50.1
40 - 44	10 705	5 474	5 231	8.4
45 - 49	559	270	289	0.4
Unknown - Inconnu[14]	62	33	29	..
Cayman Islands - Îles Caïmanes[15]				
2009 (C)				
Total	824	...	...	50.3
0 - 14	1	...	...	..
15 - 19	49	...	...	34.1
20 - 24	130	...	...	104.4
25 - 29	194	...	...	70.5
AMERICA, NORTH - AMÉRIQUE DU NORD				
Cayman Islands - Îles Caïmanes[15]				
2009 (C)				
30 - 34	261	...	...	91.7
35 - 39	144	...	...	47.4
40 - 44	45	...	...	18.1
Costa Rica				
2009 (C)				
Total	75 000	38 277	36 723	57.8
0 - 14	551	275	276	..
15 - 19	14 117	7 208	6 909	63.0
20 - 24	22 837	11 671	11 166	102.4
25 - 29	18 707	9 512	9 195	95.8
30 - 34	11 486	5 819	5 667	...
35 - 39	5 581	2 895	2 686	...
40 - 44	1 424	737	687	...
45 - 49	81	44	37	...
50 +	2	2	-	...
Unknown - Inconnu	214	114	100	..
Cuba				
2009 (C)				
Total	130 036	67 153	62 883	43.5
0 - 14	325	181	144	..
15 - 19	19 687	10 209	9 478	50.5
20 - 24	42 479	21 892	20 587	107.8
25 - 29	31 041	15 997	15 044	95.1
30 - 34	21 108	10 925	10 183	56.5
35 - 39	12 893	6 666	6 227	25.4
40 - 44	2 342	1 206	1 136	4.4
45 - 49	101	43	58	0.2
50 +	44	26	18	..
Unknown - Inconnu	16	8	8	..
Dominica - Dominique				
2006 (+C)				
Total	1 056	505	551	62.4
0 - 14	3	-	3	..
15 - 19	154	80	74	45.8
20 - 24	250	115	135	116.8
25 - 29	197	91	106	78.2
30 - 34	207	99	108	74.5
35 - 39	179	86	93	72.9
40 - 44	59	29	30	28.7
45 - 49	5	3	2	♦3.1
Dominican Republic - République dominicaine				
2009 (U)				
Total	*117 634*	*60 162*	*57 472*	...
0 - 14	*1 135*	*585*	*550*	..
15 - 19	*17 255*	*8 816*	*8 439*	...
20 - 24	*37 285*	*19 049*	*18 236*	...
25 - 29	*32 418*	*16 696*	*15 722*	...
30 - 34	*19 878*	*10 105*	*9 773*	...
35 - 39	*7 796*	*3 989*	*3 807*	...
40 - 44	*1 670*	*839*	*831*	...
45 - 49	*152*	*63*	*89*	...
50 +	*45*	*20*	*25*	...
Unknown - Inconnu	-	-	-	..
El Salvador[16]				
2007 (C)				
Total	106 471	55 742	50 729	68.9
12 - 14	1 067	549	518	..
15 - 19	22 272	11 661	10 611	73.9
20 - 24	30 060	15 770	14 290	116.5
25 - 29	25 793	13 601	12 192	103.0
30 - 34	16 619	8 706	7 913	74.4

Continent, country or area, year, code and age of mother (in years) / Continent, pays ou zone, année, code et âge de la mère (en années)	Number - Nombre			Rate Taux
	Total	Male Masculin	Female Féminin	

Continent, country or area, year, code and age of mother (in years) / Continent, pays ou zone, année, code et âge de la mère (en années)	Total	Male Masculin	Female Féminin	Rate Taux
AMERICA, NORTH - AMÉRIQUE DU NORD				
El Salvador[16]				
2007 (C)				
35 - 39	7 903	4 079	3 824	40.3
40 - 44	2 312	1 147	1 165	13.5
45 - 49	173	90	83	1.2
50 +	22	11	11	..
Unknown - Inconnu	250	128	122	..
Greenland - Groenland				
2009 (C)				
Total	895	474	421	62.6
0 - 14	2	-	2	..
15 - 19	143	79	64	63.0
20 - 24	265	134	131	124.7
25 - 29	256	144	112	138.2
30 - 34	138	67	71	88.9
35 - 39	69	36	33	43.7
40 - 44	22	14	8	♦8.7
45 - 49	-	-	-	..
50 +	-	-	-	..
Unknown - Inconnu	-	-	-	..
Grenada - Grenade				
2000 (+C)				
Total	1 883	...	...	76.5
0 - 14	9	...	...	..
15 - 19	310	...	...	53.1
20 - 24	490	...	...	107.0
25 - 29	452	...	...	132.7
30 - 34	339	...	...	113.8
35 - 39	208	...	...	64.1
40 - 44	73	...	...	26.7
45 +	2	...	...	♦1.1
Guadeloupe				
2003 (C)				
Total	7 047	3 543	3 504	60.4
0 - 14	7	2	5	..
15 - 19	431	215	216	25.5
20 - 24	1 148	588	560	81.3
25 - 29	1 815	912	903	132.3
30 - 34	2 001	1 005	996	108.6
35 - 39	1 280	637	643	64.6
40 - 44	352	177	175	19.3
45 +	13	7	6	♦0.8
Guatemala				
2006 (C)				
Total	368 399	187 190	181 209	...
0 - 14	2 209	1 101	1 108	...
15 - 19	65 284	33 335	31 949	...
20 - 24	107 634	54 736	52 898	...
25 - 29	86 944	44 413	42 531	...
30 - 34	56 080	28 468	27 612	...
35 - 39	32 668	16 478	16 190	...
40 - 44	12 790	6 341	6 449	...
45 - 49	2 280	1 141	1 139	...
50 +	1 009	487	522	..
Unknown - Inconnu	1 501	690	811	..
Jamaica - Jamaïque[17]				
2006 (C)				
Total	42 387	21 671	20 716	...
0 - 14	211	111	100	...
15 - 19	7 809	4 029	3 780	...
20 - 24	11 699	5 972	5 727	...
25 - 29	9 283	4 722	4 561	...
30 - 34	7 339	3 781	3 558	...
35 - 39	4 455	2 280	2 175	...
40 - 44	1 496	732	764	...

Continent, country or area, year, code and age of mother (in years) / Continent, pays ou zone, année, code et âge de la mère (en années)	Total	Male Masculin	Female Féminin	Rate Taux
AMERICA, NORTH - AMÉRIQUE DU NORD				
Jamaica - Jamaïque[17]				
2006 (C)				
45 +	79	35	44	...
Unknown - Inconnu	16	9	7	..
Martinique[6]				
2007 (C)				
Total	5 317	2 676	2 641	51.0
0 - 14	2	1	1	..
15 - 19	305	165	140	19.8
20 - 24	911	447	464	77.6
25 - 29	1 202	617	585	117.2
30 - 34	1 376	678	698	98.2
35 - 39	1 105	560	545	64.1
40 - 44	393	194	199	20.9
45 +	23	14	9	♦1.4
Mexico - Mexique[18]				
2006 (+U)				
Total	2 151 204[19]	1 096 051	1 054 940	...
0 - 14	6 342[19]	3 247	3 093	..
15 - 19	350 838[19]	179 231	171 580	...
20 - 24	641 028[19]	326 983	313 994	...
25 - 29	551 825[19]	281 497	270 274	...
30 - 34	379 499[19]	192 696	186 758	...
35 - 39	167 335[19]	84 784	82 536	...
40 - 44	40 544[19]	20 332	20 206	...
45 - 49	3 827	1 978	1 849	...
50 +	954	464	490	...
Unknown - Inconnu	9 012[19]	4 839	4 160	...
2007* (+U)				
Total	2 185 888	...	...	...
0 - 14	6 807	...	...	..
15 - 19	369 118	...	...	...
20 - 24	648 888	...	...	...
25 - 29	554 769	...	...	...
30 - 34	380 940	...	...	...
35 - 39	172 041	...	...	...
40 - 44	40 179	...	...	...
45 - 49	3 529	...	...	...
50 +	963	...	...	...
Unknown - Inconnu	8 654	...	...	...
Netherlands Antilles - Antilles néerlandaises[20]				
2007 (C)				
Total	2 558	1 289	1 269	48.5
0 - 14	4	1	3	..
15 - 19	220	108	112	31.7
20 - 24	515	237	278	96.0
25 - 29	599	321	278	106.1
30 - 34	591	301	290	83.7
35 - 39	423	218	205	51.3
40 - 44	108	50	58	11.9
45 - 49	5	3	2	♦0.6
50 +	1	-	1	..
Unknown - Inconnu	92	50	42	..
Nicaragua				
2008 (+U)				
Total	125 028	64 802	60 226	...
0 - 14	1 448	706	742	...
15 - 19	32 390	16 748	15 642	...
20 - 24	37 567	19 505	18 062	...
25 - 29	28 795	14 966	13 829	...
30 - 34	15 493	8 104	7 389	...
35 - 39	7 357	3 728	3 629	...
40 - 44	1 796	948	848	...

10. Live births by age of mother and sex of child, general and age-specific fertility rates: latest available year, 2000 - 2009
Naissances vivantes selon l'âge de la mère et le sexe de l'enfant, taux de fécondité et taux de fécondité par âge : dernière année disponible, 2000 - 2009 (continued - suite)

Continent, country or area, year, code and age of mother (in years) / Continent, pays ou zone, année, code et âge de la mère (en années)	Total	Male Masculin	Female Féminin	Rate Taux
AMERICA, NORTH - AMÉRIQUE DU NORD				
Nicaragua				
2008 (+U)				
45 - 49	*170*	*89*	*81*	...
50 +	*12*	*8*	*4*	..
Panama				
2009 (C)				
Total	68 364	35 061	33 303	75.8
0 - 14	612	337	275	..
15 - 19	13 143	6 838	6 305	88.4
20 - 24	19 633	9 965	9 668	136.2
25 - 29	16 148	8 251	7 897	120.2
30 - 34	10 966	5 640	5 326	84.9
35 - 39	5 840	3 038	2 802	46.0
40 - 44	1 385	673	712	12.1
45 - 49	93	47	46	1.0
50 +	13	7	6	..
Unknown - Inconnu	531	265	266	..
Puerto Rico - Porto Rico				
2008 (C)				
Total	45 675	23 443	22 232	46.5
0 - 14	147	72	75	..
15 - 19	7 989	4 036	3 953	54.6
20 - 24	14 580	7 399	7 181	106.0
25 - 29	11 828	6 135	5 693	81.9
30 - 34	7 297	3 785	3 512	52.4
35 - 39	3 124	1 652	1 472	23.0
40 - 44	657	339	318	4.7
45 - 49	35	17	18	0.3
50 +	2	1	1	..
Unknown - Inconnu	16	7	9	..
Saint Kitts and Nevis - Saint-Kitts-et-Nevis				
2001 (+C)				
Total	803	...	...	...
10 - 14	3	...	...	..
15 - 19	164	...	...	...
20 - 24	241	...	...	...
25 - 29	166	...	...	...
30 - 34	148	...	...	...
35 - 39	67	...	...	...
40 +	14	...	...	...
Saint Lucia - Sainte-Lucie				
2002 (C)				
Total	2 529	1 299	1 230	58.2
0 - 14	8	5	3	..
15 - 19	447	223	224	51.4
20 - 24	686	356	330	96.1
25 - 29	569	284	285	83.9
30 - 34	469	238	231	76.4
35 - 39	277	156	121	45.9
40 - 44	71	36	35	14.1
45 - 49	2	1	1	♦0.6
2005* (C)				
Total	2 298	...	...	49.4
0 - 14	7	...	...	..
15 - 19	390	...	...	43.9
20 - 24	639	...	...	79.5
25 - 29	549	...	...	79.0
30 - 34	396	...	...	61.2
35 - 39	245	...	...	40.2
40 - 44	62	...	...	10.9
45 +	10	...	...	♦2.3

Continent, country or area, year, code and age of mother (in years) / Continent, pays ou zone, année, code et âge de la mère (en années)	Total	Male Masculin	Female Féminin	Rate Taux
AMERICA, NORTH - AMÉRIQUE DU NORD				
Saint Vincent and the Grenadines - Saint-Vincent-et-les Grenadines				
2009 (+C)				
Total	1 905	949	956	...
0 - 14	9	3	6	..
15 - 19	365	164	201	...
20 - 24	511	269	242	...
25 - 29	446	226	220	...
30 - 34	332	162	170	...
35 - 39	172	95	77	...
40 - 44	64	28	36	...
45 +	5	2	3	...
Unknown - Inconnu	1	-	1	
Trinidad and Tobago - Trinité-et-Tobago				
2006 (C)				
Total	18 090	9 330	8 760	...
0 - 14	27	7	20	..
15 - 19	2 115	1 114	1 001	...
20 - 24	5 640	2 912	2 728	...
25 - 29	4 938	2 523	2 415	...
30 - 34	3 268	1 710	1 558	...
35 - 39	1 578	805	773	...
40 - 44	462	228	234	...
45 - 49	28	16	12	...
50 +	1	-	1	...
Unknown - Inconnu	33	15	18	...
Turks and Caicos Islands - Îles Turques et Caïques				
2005 (C)				
Total	318	158	160	...
0 - 14	1	-	1	..
15 - 19	28	13	15	...
20 - 24	65	29	36	...
25 - 29	83	40	43	...
30 - 34	76	47	29	...
35 - 39	52	23	29	...
40 - 44	11	5	6	...
45 +	2	1	1	...
United States of America - États-Unis d'Amérique				
2008 (C)				
Total	4 247 694	...	...	57.8
0 - 14	5 764	...	...	..
15 - 19	434 758	...	...	41.5
20 - 24	1 052 184	...	...	103.0
25 - 29	1 195 774	...	...	115.1
30 - 34	956 716	...	...	99.3
35 - 39	488 875	...	...	46.9
40 - 44	105 973	...	...	9.8
45 - 49	7 109	...	...	0.6
50 +	541	...	...	..
United States Virgin Islands - Îles Vierges américaines				
2007 (C)				
Total	1 771	...	...	65.9
0 - 14	2	...	...	..
15 - 19	226	...	...	53.1
20 - 24	550	...	...	146.6
25 - 29	424	...	...	146.1
30 - 34	319	...	...	93.9
35 - 39	196	...	...	48.6
40 +	46	...	...	5.5
Unknown - Inconnu	8	...	...	

10. Live births by age of mother and sex of child, general and age-specific fertility rates: latest available year, 2000 - 2009
Naissances vivantes selon l'âge de la mère et le sexe de l'enfant, taux de fécondité et taux de fécondité par âge . Dernière
année disponible, 2000 - 2009 (continued - suite)

Continent, country or area, year, code and age of mother (in years) / Continent, pays ou zone, année, code et âge de la mère (en années)	Number - Nombre			Rate Taux
	Total	Male Masculin	Female Féminin	
AMERICA, SOUTH - AMÉRIQUE DU SUD				
Argentina - Argentine 2009 (C)				
Total	745 336	...	...	73.5
0 - 14	3 346	...	...	..
15 - 19	113 478	...	...	67.7
20 - 24	182 747	...	...	112.6
25 - 29	178 935	...	...	113.2
30 - 34	155 464	...	...	99.0
35 - 39	81 397	...	...	62.3
40 - 44	20 840	...	...	17.9
45 - 49	1 440	...	...	1.3
50 +	106	...	...	..
Unknown - Inconnu	7 583	...	...	..
Brazil - Brésil[21] 2009 (U)				
Total	2 764 642[19]	1 415 650	1 348 674	...
0 - 14	22 665[19]	11 684	10 980	...
15 - 19	501 547[19]	257 388	244 111	...
20 - 24	780 465[19]	400 262	380 163	...
25 - 29	696 349[19]	355 691	340 622	...
30 - 34	464 391[19]	237 698	226 669	...
35 - 39	220 875[19]	112 953	107 917	...
40 - 44	57 811[19]	29 498	28 311	...
45 - 49	4 106[19]	2 064	2 041	...
50 +	318	160	158	...
Unknown - Inconnu	16 115[19]	8 252	7 702	..
Chile - Chili 2008 (C)				
Total	246 581	125 858	120 723	55.0
0 - 14	1 025	510	515	..
15 - 19	39 902	20 488	19 414	54.9
20 - 24	57 915	29 632	28 283	83.6
25 - 29	58 338	29 849	28 489	93.5
30 - 34	50 391	25 676	24 715	84.5
35 - 39	30 234	15 280	14 954	48.9
40 - 44	8 307	4 192	4 115	13.3
45 - 49	436	218	218	0.7
50 +	-	-	-	..
Unknown - Inconnu	33	13	20	..
Colombia - Colombie 2009* (U)				
Total	686 045	353 465	332 580	...
0 - 14	6 706	3 477	3 229	...
15 - 19	154 272	79 447	74 825	...
20 - 24	198 693	102 496	96 197	...
25 - 29	156 543	80 730	75 813	...
30 - 34	98 792	50 721	48 071	...
35 - 39	51 073	26 426	24 647	...
40 - 44	14 714	7 471	7 243	...
45 - 49	1 155	584	571	...
50 +	121	56	65	..
Unknown - Inconnu	3 976	2 057	1 919	..
Ecuador - Équateur[22] 2009 (+U)				
Total	215 906	110 413	105 493	...
0 - 14	1 358	683	675	..
15 - 19	42 554	21 716	20 838	...
20 - 24	62 732	32 294	30 438	...
25 - 29	49 771	25 380	24 391	...
30 - 34	33 006	16 869	16 137	...
35 - 39	16 832	8 523	8 309	...
40 - 44	5 110	2 607	2 503	...
45 - 49	567	304	263	...
50 +	-	-	-	..
Unknown - Inconnu	3 976	2 037	1 939	..

Continent, country or area, year, code and age of mother (in years) / Continent, pays ou zone, année, code et âge de la mère (en années)	Number - Nombre			Rate Taux
	Total	Male Masculin	Female Féminin	
AMERICA, SOUTH - AMÉRIQUE DU SUD				
French Guiana - Guyane française[6] 2007 (C)				
Total	6 386	3 269	3 117	114.5
0 - 14	23	12	11	..
15 - 19	828	428	400	83.3
20 - 24	1 477	726	751	182.2
25 - 29	1 590	821	769	195.5
30 - 34	1 312	707	605	154.0
35 - 39	844	414	430	102.2
40 - 44	289	152	137	40.9
45 - 49	22	8	14	♦3.8
50 +	1	1	-	..
Paraguay 2008 (+U)				
Total	99 674	51 066	48 608	...
0 - 14	538	269	269	..
15 - 19	20 188	10 404	9 784	...
20 - 24	28 246	14 396	13 850	...
25 - 29	23 863	12 261	11 602	...
30 - 34	14 721	7 480	7 241	...
35 - 39	8 899	4 600	4 299	...
40 - 44	2 819	1 440	1 379	...
45 - 49	250	134	116	...
50 +	2	2	-	..
Unknown - Inconnu	148	80	68	..
Peru - Pérou[23] 2008* (+U)				
Total	359 140	184 244	174 896	...
0 - 14	1 186	583	603	..
15 - 19	50 513	26 002	24 511	...
20 - 24	95 268	49 056	46 212	...
25 - 29	87 959	45 155	42 804	...
30 - 34	69 669	35 443	34 226	...
35 - 39	40 621	20 821	19 800	...
40 - 44	12 767	6 577	6 190	...
45 - 49	1 031	549	482	...
50 +	122	55	67	...
Unknown - Inconnu	4	3	1	..
Suriname[24] 2007 (C)				
Total	9 769	...	...	73.6
0 - 14	65	...	...	..
15 - 19	1 485	...	...	65.5
20 - 24	2 818	...	...	130.8
25 - 29	2 487	...	...	121.9
30 - 34	1 716	...	...	88.8
35 - 39	943	...	...	52.0
40 - 44	243	...	...	14.9
45 +	12	...	...	♦0.8
Unknown - Inconnu	-	...	...	..
Uruguay 2000 (C)				
Total	52 770[25]	27 119	25 641	65.7
0 - 14	207	91	116	..
15 - 19	8 268[25]	4 293	3 974	63.3
20 - 24	13 173[25]	6 729	6 442	106.3
25 - 29	12 404[25]	6 460	5 943	107.0
30 - 34	11 342[25]	5 792	5 547	100.0
35 - 39	5 373[25]	2 765	2 606	48.1
40 - 44	1 340[25]	669	670	12.9
45 +	71	34	37	0.7
Unknown - Inconnu	592	286	306	

10. Live births by age of mother and sex of child, general and age-specific fertility rates: latest available year, 2000 - 2009
Naissances vivantes selon l'âge de la mère et le sexe de l'enfant, taux de fécondité et taux de fécondité par âge : dernière année disponible, 2000 - 2009 (continued - suite)

Continent, country or area, year, code and age of mother (in years) / Continent, pays ou zone, année, code et âge de la mère (en années)	Number - Nombre			Rate Taux
	Total	Male Masculin	Female Féminin	

AMERICA, SOUTH - AMÉRIQUE DU SUD

Uruguay
2007 (C)

Total	47 372	...	...	58.3
0 - 14	213	...	...	..
15 - 19	7 562	...	...	58.8
20 - 24	11 341	...	...	92.2
25 - 29	11 082	...	...	92.2
30 - 34	10 141	...	...	86.5
35 - 39	5 111	...	...	48.3
40 - 44	1 307	...	...	12.5
45 +	91	...	...	0.9
Unknown - Inconnu	524			..

Venezuela (Bolivarian Republic of) - Venezuela (République bolivarienne du)
2007 (C)

Total	615 371	316 636	298 735	84.4
0 - 14	7 402	3 838	3 564	..
15 - 19	133 508	68 666	64 842	101.8
20 - 24	182 051	93 787	88 264	146.3
25 - 29	140 049	72 079	67 970	123.1
30 - 34	87 546	45 200	42 346	87.1
35 - 39	43 865	22 372	21 493	47.8
40 - 44	12 225	6 245	5 980	14.3
45 - 49	1 457	732	725	2.0
50 +	463	208	255	..
Unknown - Inconnu	6 805	3 509	3 296	..

ASIA - ASIE

Armenia - Arménie
2009 (C)

Total	44 413	23 652	20 761	48.4
15 - 19	4 035	2 055	1 980	27.6
20 - 24	19 686	10 292	9 394	125.8
25 - 29	13 628	7 422	6 206	95.4
30 - 34	5 156	2 859	2 297	43.1
35 - 39	1 590	866	724	15.3
40 - 44	287	141	146	2.6
45 - 49	27	14	13	♦0.2
50 +	4	3	1	..
Unknown - Inconnu	-	-	-	..

Azerbaijan - Azerbaïdjan[26]
2009 (+C)

Total	152 139	82 216	69 923	56.3
12 - 14	8	4	4	..
15 - 19	18 693	9 602	9 091	41.4
20 - 24	64 007	33 961	30 046	141.0
25 - 29	42 414	23 333	19 081	108.9
30 - 34	18 056	10 328	7 728	52.7
35 - 39	6 926	3 866	3 060	20.7
40 - 44	1 798	991	807	5.0
45 - 49	226	123	103	0.6
50 +	11	8	3	..
Unknown - Inconnu	-	-	-	..

Bahrain - Bahreïn
2008 (C)

Total	17 022	8 677	8 345	62.8
0 - 14	4	2	2	..
15 - 19	433	214	219	13.7
20 - 24	3 683	1 865	1 818	85.5
25 - 29	5 592	2 864	2 728	110.7
30 - 34	4 367	2 259	2 108	94.8
35 - 39	2 136	1 067	1 069	54.8

ASIA - ASIE

Bahrain - Bahreïn
2008 (C)

40 - 44	735	372	363	21.8
45 - 49	61	30	31	2.2
50 +	11	4	7	..
Unknown - Inconnu	-	-	-	..

Bhutan - Bhoutan[9]
2005 (I)

Total	12 538	6 306	6 232	79.4
15 - 19	1 376	711	665	36.5
20 - 24	4 211	2 156	2 055	138.9
25 - 29	3 677	1 814	1 863	141.6
30 - 34	1 753	880	873	89.4
35 - 39	960	463	497	54.5
40 - 44	434	207	227	31.3
45 - 49	127	75	52	9.9

Brunei Darussalam - Brunéi Darussalam
2008 (+C)

Total	6 424	3 332	3 092	...
0 - 14	4	-	4	..
15 - 19	279	159	120	...
20 - 24	1 206	654	552	...
25 - 29	2 113	1 092	1 021	...
30 - 34	1 697	866	831	...
35 - 39	913	453	460	...
40 - 44	198	99	99	...
45 - 49	12	7	5	...
50 +	-	-	-	...
Unknown - Inconnu	2	2	-	..

Cambodia - Cambodge
2004 (U)

Total	320 594	...	...	...
15 - 19	23 238	...	...	...
20 - 24	106 787	...	...	...
25 - 29	66 573	...	...	...
30 - 34	57 861	...	...	...
35 - 39	43 391	...	...	...
40 - 44	19 386	...	...	...
45 - 49	3 358	...	...	...

China, Hong Kong SAR - Chine, Hong Kong RAS
2009 (C)

Total	82 095[25]	43 965	38 129	39.2
0 - 14	10	7	3	..
15 - 19	749	374	375	3.5
20 - 24	8 627	4 538	4 089	36.1
25 - 29	22 089	11 827	10 262	72.3
30 - 34	28 814	15 412	13 402	91.8
35 - 39	18 518[25]	10 005	8 512	55.4
40 - 44	3 115	1 714	1 401	9.3
45 - 49	134	70	64	0.4
50 +	35	18	17	..
Unknown - Inconnu	4	-	4	..

China, Macao SAR - Chine, Macao RAS
2009 (C)

Total	4 764	2 484	2 280	27.4
0 - 14	1	-	1	..
15 - 19	64	34	30	3.2
20 - 24	874	449	425	33.2
25 - 29	1 626	864	762	68.9
30 - 34	1 286	650	636	58.7
35 - 39	767	406	361	29.4
40 - 44	141	79	62	5.2

Continent, country or area, year, code and age of mother (in years) / Continent, pays ou zone, année, code et âge de la mère (en années)	Number - Nombre			Rate Taux
	Total	Male Masculin	Female Féminin	

ASIA - ASIE

China, Macao SAR - Chine, Macao RAS
2009 (C)

45 - 49	5	2	3	◆0.2
50 +	-	-	-	..

Cyprus - Chypre[27]
2009 (C)

Total	9 608	4 904	4 704	46.0
12 - 14	2	2	-	..
15 - 19	167	78	89	6.0
20 - 24	1 320	668	652	40.4
25 - 29	3 425	1 780	1 645	98.2
30 - 34	3 069	1 556	1 513	102.5
35 - 39	1 330	664	666	48.1
40 - 44	248	131	117	9.0
45 - 49	31	16	15	1.1
50 +	4	1	3	..
Unknown - Inconnu	12	8	4	..

Democratic People's Republic of Korea - République populaire démocratique de Corée[28]
2008 (I)

Total	345 630	176 399	169 231	53.3
15 - 19	633	330	303	0.6
20 - 24	52 214	26 657	25 557	58.0
25 - 29	178 032	90 850	87 182	209.5
30 - 34	90 973	46 224	44 749	110.0
35 - 39	20 275	10 505	9 770	18.5
40 - 44	3 202	1 673	1 529	3.2
45 - 49	301	160	141	0.4

Georgia - Géorgie
2006 (C)

Total	47 795	25 236	22 559	40.3
0 - 14	25	13	12	..
15 - 19	6 608	3 478	3 130	36.6
20 - 24	17 666	9 301	8 365	100.8
25 - 29	12 409	6 487	5 922	76.0
30 - 34	6 831	3 673	3 158	43.3
35 - 39	2 929	1 597	1 332	18.9
40 - 44	791	423	368	4.6
45 - 49	87	49	38	0.5
50 +	34	15	19	..
Unknown - Inconnu	415	200	215	..

Iraq[29]
2000 (U)

Total	471 886	...	...	...
15 - 19	21 367	...	...	...
20 - 24	115 973	...	...	...
25 - 29	149 287	...	...	...
30 - 34	110 981	...	...	...
35 - 39	52 196	...	...	...
40 - 44	16 717	...	...	...
45 +	5 365	...	...	...

Israel - Israël[30]
2009 (C)

Total	161 042	82 398	78 644	89.5
0 - 14	2	2	-	..
15 - 19	3 873	2 003	1 870	13.4
20 - 24	30 529	15 547	14 982	107.7
25 - 29	47 876	24 535	23 341	170.4
30 - 34	47 472	24 343	23 129	173.3
35 - 39	25 053	12 820	12 233	99.5
40 - 44	5 458	2 766	2 692	25.6
45 - 49	453	225	228	2.2

ASIA - ASIE

Israel - Israël[30]
2009 (C)

50 +	86	42	44	..
Unknown - Inconnu	240	115	125	..

Japan - Japon[31]
2009 (C)

Total	1 070 035	548 993	521 042	39.3
0 - 14	67	37	30	..
15 - 19	14 620	7 535	7 085	4.9
20 - 24	116 808	60 195	56 613	34.3
25 - 29	307 765	157 968	149 797	83.5
30 - 34	389 793	199 619	190 174	90.9
35 - 39	209 706	107 541	102 165	43.9
40 - 44	30 566	15 750	14 816	7.2
45 - 49	684	335	349	0.2
50 +	20	11	9	..
Unknown - Inconnu	6	2	4	..

Kazakhstan[26]
2008 (C)

Total	356 575	183 263	173 312	80.7
0 - 14	35	19	16	..
15 - 19	22 689	11 697	10 992	31.1
20 - 24	121 095	62 340	58 755	158.2
25 - 29	103 323	53 053	50 270	160.5
30 - 34	66 732	34 153	32 579	112.0
35 - 39	33 931	17 534	16 397	60.7
40 - 44	8 105	4 125	3 980	14.9
45 - 49	396	203	193	0.7
50 +	17	12	5	..
Unknown - Inconnu	252	127	125	..

Kuwait - Koweït
2008 (C)

Total	54 571	27 913	26 658	89.1
15 - 19	1 154	602	552	14.4
20 - 24	11 481	5 925	5 556	122.2
25 - 29	17 656	9 010	8 646	154.9
30 - 34	13 565	6 960	6 605	129.1
35 - 39	7 263	3 691	3 572	81.0
40 - 44	1 967	992	975	28.9
45 +	244	129	115	5.1
Unknown - Inconnu	1 241	604	637	..

Kyrgyzstan - Kirghizstan
2009 (C)

Total	135 494	69 823	65 671	90.0
0 - 14	3	3	-	..
15 - 19	9 283	4 798	4 485	31.2
20 - 24	50 998	26 298	24 700	173.9
25 - 29	38 131	19 725	18 406	169.8
30 - 34	21 774	11 147	10 627	114.9
35 - 39	11 392	5 860	5 532	65.0
40 - 44	3 259	1 652	1 607	19.9
45 - 49	436	225	211	2.7
50 +	11	5	6	..
Unknown - Inconnu	207	110	97	..

Malaysia - Malaisie
2008 (C)

Total	487 346	252 052	235 294	67.9
0 - 14	188	105	83	..
15 - 19	17 510	9 080	8 430	13.9
20 - 24	85 216	44 235	40 981	69.7
25 - 29	161 468	83 561	77 907	144.4
30 - 34	130 876	67 529	63 347	131.9
35 - 39	69 156	35 797	33 359	74.5
40 - 44	19 674	10 048	9 626	22.6
45 - 49	1 655	847	808	2.2

Continent, country or area, year, code and age of mother (in years) / Continent, pays ou zone, année, code et âge de la mère (en années)	Number - Nombre			Rate Taux
	Total	Male Masculin	Female Féminin	

ASIA - ASIE

Malaysia - Malaisie
2008 (C)
| 50 + | 90 | 44 | 46 | .. |
| Unknown - Inconnu | 1 513 | 806 | 707 | .. |

Maldives
2009 (C)
Total	7 423	3 784	3 639	79.2
0 - 14	1	1	-	..
15 - 19	343	181	162	18.0
20 - 24	2 677	1 360	1 317	136.7
25 - 29	2 281	1 128	1 153	143.5
30 - 34	1 313	676	637	114.1
35 - 39	578	305	273	57.1
40 - 44	133	79	54	15.0
45 - 49	9	5	4	♦1.2
50 +	-	-	-	..
Unknown - Inconnu	88	49	39	..

Mongolia - Mongolie
2008 (C)
Total	63 768	32 527	31 241	79.3
0 - 14	56	34	22	..
15 - 19	2 954	1 496	1 458	19.3
20 - 24	19 998	10 161	9 837	141.4
25 - 29	19 551	9 863	9 688	160.6
30 - 34	12 896	6 682	6 214	114 4
35 - 39	6 577	3 396	3 181	64.3
40 - 44	1 545	800	745	16.6
45 - 49	170	88	82	2.1
50 +	21	7	14	..

Oman[32]
2009 (U)
Total	64 734[11]	32 927	31 744	...
0 - 14	17	6	11	...
15 - 19	1 833	975	858	...
20 - 24	14 545[11]	7 445	7 090	...
25 - 29	21 107[11]	10 645	10 451	...
30 - 34	15 301[11]	7 813	7 472	...
35 - 39	6 972[11]	3 562	3 400	...
40 - 44	2 143[11]	1 077	1 064	...
45 - 49	397[11]	201	195	...
50 +	103	51	52	..
Unknown - Inconnu	2 316[11]	1 152	1 151	..

Pakistan[33]
2005 (|)
Total	3 772 494	1 993 492	1 779 002	110.6
15 - 19	161 490	90 049	71 441	20.3
20 - 24	1 050 830	556 310	494 520	157.6
25 - 29	1 166 365	611 186	555 179	225.5
30 - 34	754 513	395 425	359 088	179.9
35 - 39	425 352	222 186	203 166	106.6
40 - 44	161 914	86 273	75 641	50.1
45 +	52 030	32 063	19 967	18.1

Philippines
2007 (C)
Total	1 749 878	911 309	838 569	...
0 - 14	1 013	530	483	...
15 - 19	172 269	89 718	82 551	...
20 - 24	488 610	255 167	233 443	...
25 - 29	480 350	250 232	230 118	...
30 - 34	330 699	171 920	158 779	...
35 - 39	198 134	103 002	95 132	...
40 - 44	66 814	34 574	32 240	...
45 - 49	7 906	4 058	3 848	...
50 +	579	288	291	...
Unknown - Inconnu	3 504	1 820	1 684	..

Continent, country or area, year, code and age of mother (in years) / Continent, pays ou zone, année, code et âge de la mère (en années)	Number - Nombre			Rate Taux
	Total	Male Masculin	Female Féminin	

ASIA - ASIE

Qatar
2009 (C)
Total	18 351	9 401	8 950	77.6
0 - 14	-	-	-	..
15 - 19	407	226	181	15.9
20 - 24	3 410	1 729	1 681	97.7
25 - 29	5 847	3 022	2 825	118.1
30 - 34	5 007	2 591	2 416	111.6
35 - 39	2 788	1 384	1 404	78.9
40 - 44	783	390	393	29.3
45 - 49	97	51	46	5.0
50 +	11	7	4	..
Unknown - Inconnu	1	1	-	..

Republic of Korea - République de Corée[34]
2009 (C)
Total	444 849	229 351	215 498	34.1
0 - 14	27	22	5	..
15 - 19	2 788	1 494	1 294	1.8
20 - 24	24 911	12 810	12 101	16.7
25 - 29	155 906	80 203	75 703	83.3
30 - 34	192 112	99 013	93 099	103.9
35 - 39	60 694	31 461	29 233	28.7
40 - 44	7 303	3 750	3 553	3.6
45 - 49	330	175	155	0.2
50 +	28	15	13	..
Unknown - Inconnu	750	408	342	..

Saudi Arabia - Arabie saoudite[35]
2005 (...)
Total	582 582	298 396	284 186	...
15 - 19	25 652	13 139	12 513	...
20 - 24	153 901	78 827	75 074	...
25 - 29	194 252	99 495	94 757	...
30 - 34	135 325	69 313	66 012	...
35 - 39	57 941	29 677	28 264	...
40 - 44	14 373	7 362	7 011	...
45 - 49	1 137	583	555	...

Singapore - Singapour
2009 (C)
Total	39 570	20 502	19 068	38.6
0 - 14	10	5	5	..
15 - 19	668	311	357	5.2
20 - 24	3 239	1 672	1 567	26.8
25 - 29	11 335	5 894	5 441	79.7
30 - 34	15 310	7 924	7 386	99.0
35 - 39	7 714	4 025	3 689	47.6
40 - 44	1 241	641	600	7.9
45 - 49	51	28	23	0.3
50 +	2	2	-	..
Unknown - Inconnu	-	-	-	..

Sri Lanka
2006 (+C)
Total	373 538	191 263	182 275	67.9
0 - 14	113	57	56	..
15 - 19	20 040	10 335	9 705	21.2
20 - 24	81 003	41 508	39 495	87.5
25 - 29	121 968	62 480	59 488	151.5
30 - 34	90 483	46 346	44 137	118.4
35 - 39	46 534	23 759	22 775	61.6
40 - 44	12 104	6 149	5 955	17.4
45 - 49	1 275	622	653	2.1
50 +	18	7	11	..

10. Live births by age of mother and sex of child, general and age-specific fertility rates: latest available year, 2000 - 2009
Naissances vivantes selon l'âge de la mère et le sexe de l'enfant, taux de fécondité et taux de fécondité par âge : dernière année disponible, 2000 - 2009 (continued - suite)

Continent, country or area, year, code and age of mother (in years) / Continent, pays ou zone, année, code et âge de la mère (en années)	Total	Male Masculin	Female Féminin	Rate Taux
ASIA - ASIE				
Thailand - Thaïlande				
2009 (+U)				
Total	765 046	394 555	370 491	...
0 - 14	2 908	1 451	1 457	..
15 - 19	119 828	61 702	58 126	...
20 - 24	184 096	95 000	89 096	...
25 - 29	203 386	105 308	98 078	...
30 - 34	156 397	80 544	75 853	...
35 - 39	76 340	39 220	37 120	...
40 - 44	19 036	9 752	9 284	...
45 - 49	1 266	671	595	...
50 +	79	32	47	..
Unknown - Inconnu	1 710	875	835	..
Timor-Leste				
2004 (C)				
Total	39 168	...	...	187.3
15 - 19	1 999	...	...	42.2
20 - 24	9 387	...	...	246.6
25 - 29	9 335	...	...	324.4
30 - 34	9 214	...	...	305.3
35 - 39	5 403	...	...	226.0
40 - 44	2 814	...	...	120.1
45 - 49	787	...	...	45.2
50 +	229	...	...	
United Arab Emirates - Émirats arabes unis[35]				
2003 (...)				
Total	61 165	31 241	29 924	...
15 - 19	2 647	1 415	1 232	...
20 - 24	12 551	6 386	6 165	...
25 - 29	18 710	9 605	9 105	...
30 - 34	14 699	7 484	7 215	...
35 - 39	7 670	3 876	3 794	...
40 - 44	2 796	1 409	1 387	...
45 - 49	620	316	304	...
50 +	101	51	50	..
Unknown - Inconnu	1 371	699	672	..
Uzbekistan - Ouzbékistan[26]				
2000 (C)				
Total	527 580	...	...	82.7
15 - 19	28 179	...	...	21.1
20 - 24	228 743	...	...	205.4
25 - 29	160 082	...	...	161.4
30 - 34	78 316	...	...	89.7
35 - 39	26 866	...	...	31.5
40 - 44	4 979	...	...	7.0
45 - 49	348	...	...	0.7
50 +	67	...	...	
EUROPE				
Åland Islands - Îles d'Åland				
2009 (C)				
Total	267	158	109	45.1
0 - 14	-	...	...	
15 - 19	1	...	...	♦1.2
20 - 24	25	...	...	♦41.1
25 - 29	73	...	...	95.7
30 - 34	99	...	...	122.7
35 - 39	55	...	...	62.7
40 - 44	14	...	...	♦13.1
45 - 49	-	...	...	-
50 +	-	...	...	

Continent, country or area, year, code and age of mother (in years) / Continent, pays ou zone, année, code et âge de la mère (en années)	Total	Male Masculin	Female Féminin	Rate Taux
EUROPE				
Albania - Albanie				
2004 (C)				
Total	43 022	22 859	20 163	51.8
15 - 19	2 249	1 213	1 036	14.5
20 - 24	13 516	7 006	6 510	99.3
25 - 29	14 476	7 669	6 807	127.6
30 - 34	8 491	4 597	3 894	78.8
35 - 39	3 239	1 800	1 439	30.0
40 - 44	736	419	317	6.7
45 - 49	64	38	26	0.7
50 +	12	7	5	..
Unknown - Inconnu	239	110	129	
2007 (C)				
Total	33 163	...	...	39.2
0 - 19	1 705	...	...	11.3
20 - 24	10 330	...	...	70.4
25 - 29	11 053	...	...	91.6
30 - 34	6 504	...	...	61.2
35 - 39	2 683	...	...	25.1
40 - 44	554	...	...	5.3
45 - 49	76	...	...	0.7
50 +	22	...	...	..
Unknown - Inconnu	236	...	...	
Andorra - Andorre				
2009 (C)				
Total	838	397	441	37.2
12 - 14	-	-	-	
15 - 19	9	6	3	♦4.8
20 - 24	74	36	38	34.6
25 - 29	208	94	114	64.7
30 - 34	303	146	157	76.7
35 - 39	205	100	105	51.2
40 - 44	36	14	22	9.3
45 - 49	3	1	2	♦0.9
50 +	-	-	-	
Unknown - Inconnu	-	-	-	..
Austria - Autriche				
2009 (C)				
Total	76 344	39 072	37 272	37.3
12 - 14	14	6	8	..
15 - 19	2 537	1 324	1 213	10.4
20 - 24	12 545	6 390	6 155	48.7
25 - 29	23 683	12 092	11 591	85.8
30 - 34	22 531	11 549	10 982	84.7
35 - 39	12 196	6 230	5 966	39.4
40 - 44	2 723	1 425	1 298	7.7
45 - 49	110	53	57	0.3
50 +	5	3	2	
Belarus - Bélarus				
2006 (C)				
Total	96 721	49 849	46 872	36.6
0 - 14	10	5	5	
15 - 19	8 238	4 234	4 004	21.9
20 - 24	36 120	18 613	17 507	88.9
25 - 29	29 846	15 372	14 474	83.0
30 - 34	15 950	8 229	7 721	46.3
35 - 39	5 488	2 846	2 642	16.1
40 - 44	935	488	447	2.4
45 - 49	47	23	24	0.1
50 +	-	-	-	
Unknown - Inconnu	87	39	48	
2008 (C)				
Total	107 876	...	...	41.6
12 - 14	14	...	...	..
15 - 19	7 399	...	...	22.1
20 - 24	37 635	...	...	91.9

10. Live births by age of mother and sex of child, general and age-specific fertility rates: latest available year, 2000 - 2009
Naissances vivantes selon l'âge de la mère et le sexe de l'enfant, taux de fécondité et taux de fécondité par âge : dernière année disponible, 2000 - 2009 (continued - suite)

Continent, country or area, year, code and age of mother (in years) — Continent, pays ou zone, année, code et âge de la mère (en années)	Total	Male Masculin	Female Féminin	Rate Taux
EUROPE				
Belarus - Bélarus				
2008 (C)				
25 - 29	35 122	...	...	93.2
30 - 34	19 355	...	...	56.0
35 - 39	7 055	...	...	20.7
40 - 44	1 151	...	...	3.2
45 - 49	38	...	...	0.1
Unknown - Inconnu	105	...	...	..
Bosnia and Herzegovina - Bosnie-Herzégovine				
2009 (C)				
Total	34 550	18 001	16 549	36.3
12 - 14	10	5	5	..
15 - 19	1 972	1 018	954	14.9
20 - 24	9 040	4 715	4 325	64.7
25 - 29	12 080	6 284	5 796	89.0
30 - 34	7 925	4 154	3 771	66.3
35 - 39	2 821	1 458	1 363	22.6
40 - 44	544	280	264	3.8
45 - 49	23	14	9	♦0.1
50 +	2	2	-	..
Unknown - Inconnu	133	71	62	..
Bulgaria - Bulgarie				
2009 (C)				
Total	80 956	41 312	39 644	44.9
12 - 14	464	229	235	..
15 - 19	9 787	5 013	4 774	46.7
20 - 24	20 373	10 338	10 035	80.3
25 - 29	24 191	12 418	11 773	91.7
30 - 34	18 428	9 420	9 008	64.8
35 - 39	6 677	3 358	3 319	24.5
40 - 44	970	503	467	3.8
45 - 49	53	29	24	0.2
50 +	-	-	-	..
Unknown - Inconnu	13	4	9	..
Croatia - Croatie				
2009 (C)				
Total	44 577	22 877	21 700	43.1
12 - 14	9	6	3	..
15 - 19	1 630	813	817	13.0
20 - 24	8 538	4 316	4 222	60.9
25 - 29	15 561	8 087	7 474	101.4
30 - 34	12 664	6 434	6 230	83.7
35 - 39	5 128	2 693	2 435	35.2
40 - 44	960	482	478	6.2
45 - 49	49	22	27	0.3
50 +	-	-	-	..
Unknown - Inconnu	38	24	14	..
Czech Republic - République tchèque				
2009 (C)				
Total	118 348	60 368	57 980	46.6
12 - 14	15	6	9	..
15 - 19	3 599	1 795	1 804	11.8
20 - 24	15 949	8 100	7 849	46.8
25 - 29	38 261	19 544	18 717	102.8
30 - 34	44 140	22 585	21 555	97.1
35 - 39	14 397	7 328	7 069	36.2
40 - 44	1 909	973	936	5.6
45 - 49	74	35	39	0.2
50 +	4	2	2	..
Unknown - Inconnu	-	-	-	..
Denmark - Danemark[36]				
2009 (C)				
Total	62 818	32 261	30 557	50.2
13 - 14	2	-	2	..
EUROPE				
Denmark - Danemark[36]				
2009 (C)				
15 - 19	922	470	452	5.5
20 - 24	6 639	3 446	3 193	42.5
25 - 29	19 098	9 922	9 176	122.8
30 - 34	23 267	11 947	11 320	130.3
35 - 39	10 814	5 421	5 393	56.4
40 - 44	1 984	1 009	975	9.6
45 - 49	87	45	42	0.4
50 +	5	1	4	..
Unknown - Inconnu	-	-	-	..
Estonia - Estonie				
2009 (C)				
Total	15 763	8 022	7 741	47.5
12 - 14	3	2	1	..
15 - 19	851	428	423	20.4
20 - 24	3 325	1 681	1 644	63.6
25 - 29	5 193	2 639	2 554	104.2
30 - 34	3 850	1 965	1 885	83.3
35 - 39	2 100	1 067	1 033	44.6
40 - 44	425	231	194	9.5
45 - 49	16	9	7	♦0.3
50 +	-	-	-	..
Unknown - Inconnu	-	-	-	..
Faeroe Islands - Îles Féroé				
2007 (C)				
Total	674	318	356	64.7
15 - 19	20	11	9	♦10.5
20 - 24	104	47	57	83.5
25 - 29	187	93	94	160.9
30 - 34	211	102	109	154.4
35 - 39	129	56	73	83.0
40 - 44	23	9	14	♦13.9
45 +	-	-	-	..
Finland - Finlande[37]				
2009 (C)				
Total	60 430	30 795	29 635	51.9
12 - 14	4	3	1	..
15 - 19	1 387	696	691	8.5
20 - 24	9 422	4 822	4 600	59.6
25 - 29	19 282	9 869	9 413	116.2
30 - 34	19 528	9 911	9 617	120.1
35 - 39	8 589	4 369	4 220	56.8
40 - 44	2 136	1 088	1 048	12.0
45 - 49	79	37	42	0.4
50 +	3	-	3	..
Unknown - Inconnu	-	-	-	..
France[38]				
2008 (C)				
Total	796 044	405 569	390 475	55.2
12 - 14	94	51	43	..
15 - 19	19 609	10 040	9 569	10.2
20 - 24	119 146	61 117	58 029	60.7
25 - 29	264 843	134 936	129 907	134.0
30 - 34	241 970	122 960	119 010	123.5
35 - 39	123 586	62 755	60 831	56.1
40 - 44	25 463	13 039	12 424	11.5
45 - 49	1 254	635	619	0.6
50 +	79	36	43	..
Unknown - Inconnu	-	-	-	..
Germany - Allemagne				
2008 (C)				
Total	682 514	349 862	332 652	35.8
12 - 14	130	58	72	..
15 - 19	21 682	11 179	10 503	9.8

Continent, country or area, year, code and age of mother (in years) / Continent, pays ou zone, année, code et âge de la mère (en années)	Number - Nombre			Rate Taux
	Total	Male Masculin	Female Féminin	

EUROPE

Germany - Allemagne				
2008 (C)				
20 - 24	100 708	51 423	49 285	42.1
25 - 29	202 342	103 960	98 382	82.3
30 - 34	208 617	107 073	101 544	89.9
35 - 39	121 095	61 803	59 292	42.4
40 - 44	26 721	13 749	12 972	7.7
45 - 49	1 040	526	514	0.3
50 +	30	18	12	..
Unknown - Inconnu	149	73	76	..
2009 (C)				
Total	665 126	...	...	35.3
10 - 14	120	...	...	..
15 - 19	19 447	...	...	9.1
20 - 24	95 514	...	...	39.6
25 - 29	196 656	...	...	80.0
30 - 34	208 818	...	...	89.7
35 - 39	115 992	...	...	43.5
40 - 44	27 018	...	...	8.0
45 - 49	1 135	...	...	0.3
50 +	54	...	...	..
Unknown - Inconnu	372	...	...	..
Gibraltar[39]				
2002 (+C)				
Total	375	...	...	...
15 - 19	25	...	...	...
20 - 24	59	...	...	...
25 - 29	120	...	...	...
30 - 34	115	...	...	...
35 - 39	46	...	...	...
40 - 44	10	...	...	...
Greece - Grèce				
2009 (C)				
Total	117 933	60 832	57 101	44.7
12 - 14	93	41	52	..
15 - 19	3 219	1 644	1 575	11.6
20 - 24	14 145	7 332	6 813	46.4
25 - 29	32 819	17 050	15 769	86.4
30 - 34	41 258	21 207	20 051	99.0
35 - 39	21 342	11 012	10 330	49.9
40 - 44	4 468	2 251	2 217	10.3
45 - 49	515	265	250	1.3
50 +	74	30	44	..
Guernsey - Guernesey				
2000 (C)				
Total	644	336	308	...
15 - 19	42	15	27	...
20 - 24	84	49	35	...
25 - 29	192	101	91	...
30 - 34	200	102	98	...
35 - 39	106	60	46	...
40 - 44	20	9	11	...
Hungary - Hongrie				
2009 (C)				
Total	96 442	49 565	46 877	40.4
12 - 14	93	55	38	..
15 - 19	5 784	2 989	2 795	19.5
20 - 24	14 124	7 224	6 900	44.4
25 - 29	28 389	14 592	13 797	81.3
30 - 34	33 581	17 354	16 227	79.8
35 - 39	12 280	6 225	6 055	33.8
40 - 44	2 107	1 083	1 024	6.4
45 - 49	81	40	41	0.3
50 +	3	3	-	..
Unknown - Inconnu	-	-	-	..

EUROPE

Iceland - Islande				
2009 (C)				
Total	5 027	2 561	2 466	64.1
12 - 14	-	-	-	..
15 - 19	170	86	84	14.5
20 - 24	840	455	385	74.5
25 - 29	1 692	839	853	140.9
30 - 34	1 434	735	699	131.0
35 - 39	722	363	359	68.3
40 - 44	160	80	80	14.8
45 - 49	8	2	6	♦0.7
50 +	-	-	-	..
Unknown - Inconnu	1	1	-	..
Ireland - Irlande				
2009 (+C)				
Total	74 278	38 082	36 196	64.2
12 - 14	5	2	3	..
15 - 19	2 218	1 147	1 071	16.3
20 - 24	8 733	4 482	4 251	57.3
25 - 29	17 895	9 138	8 757	87.1
30 - 34	24 895	12 851	12 044	133.3
35 - 39	17 120	8 736	8 384	99.3
40 - 44	3 214	1 632	1 582	20.7
45 - 49	159	69	90	1.1
50 +	6	4	2	..
Unknown - Inconnu	33	21	12	..
Italy - Italie[18]				
2005 (C)				
Total	544 030	280 606	263 424	39.1
0 - 14	3	2	1	..
15 - 19	9 416	4 863	4 553	6.8
20 - 24	50 715	26 262	24 453	32.9
25 - 29	135 713	69 895	65 818	72.2
30 - 34	198 611	102 392	96 219	88.1
35 - 39	117 659	60 755	56 904	50.0
40 - 44	23 874	12 310	11 564	10.4
45 - 49	880	467	413	0.4
50 +	113	59	54	..
Unknown - Inconnu	7 046	3 601	3 445	..
Jersey[18]				
2007 (+C)				
Total	1 031	515	516	...
0 - 14	-	-	-	...
15 - 19	29	14	15	...
20 - 24	114	56	58	...
25 - 29	228	114	114	...
30 - 34	325	170	155	...
35 - 39	273	134	139	...
40 - 44	61	27	34	...
45 - 49	1	-	1	...
50 +	-	-	-	...
Latvia - Lettonie				
2009 (C)				
Total	21 677	11 014	10 663	38.0
12 - 14	1	1	-	..
15 - 19	1 534	788	746	20.8
20 - 24	5 339	2 741	2 598	59.3
25 - 29	6 946	3 488	3 458	83.2
30 - 34	4 741	2 404	2 337	61.3
35 - 39	2 512	1 291	1 221	31.6
40 - 44	564	282	282	7.2
45 - 49	27	12	15	♦0.3
50 +	-	-	-	..
Unknown - Inconnu	13	7	6	..

10. Live births by age of mother and sex of child, general and age-specific fertility rates: latest available year, 2000 - 2009
Naissances vivantes selon l'âge de la mère et le sexe de l'enfant, taux de fécondité et taux de fécondité par âge : dernière année disponible, 2000 - 2009 (continued - suite)

Continent, country or area, year, code and age of mother (in years) / Continent, pays ou zone, année, code et âge de la mère (en années)	Number - Nombre			Rate Taux
	Total	Male Masculin	Female Féminin	

EUROPE

Liechtenstein
2009* (C)
	Total	Male	Female	Rate
Total	406	226	180	45.5
12 - 14	-	-	-	..
15 - 19	3	1	2	♦2.8
20 - 24	36	22	14	33.5
25 - 29	110	64	46	100.6
30 - 34	150	84	66	129.2
35 - 39	85	45	40	62.7
40 - 44	22	10	12	♦13.7
45 - 49	-	-	-	..
50 +	-	-	-	..
Unknown - Inconnu	-	-	-	..

Lithuania - Lituanie
2009 (C)
	Total	Male	Female	Rate
Total	36 682	18 786	17 896	42.5
12 - 14	8	4	4	..
15 - 19	2 041	1 055	986	16.9
20 - 24	8 203	4 106	4 097	61.9
25 - 29	12 982	6 655	6 327	111.2
30 - 34	8 923	4 626	4 297	81.9
35 - 39	3 817	1 995	1 822	31.7
40 - 44	676	330	346	5.4
45 - 49	30	14	16	0.2
50 +	-	-	-	..
Unknown - Inconnu	2	1	1	..

Luxembourg
2009 (C)
	Total	Male	Female	Rate
Total	5 638	2 916	2 722	45.4
12 - 14	-	-	-	..
15 - 19	101	60	41	7.1
20 - 24	626	309	317	43.3
25 - 29	1 525	766	759	89.5
30 - 34	2 038	1 096	942	110.2
35 - 39	1 108	567	541	56.0
40 - 44	223	111	112	10.8
45 - 49	13	5	8	♦0.7
50 +	-	-	-	..
Unknown - Inconnu	4	2	2	..

Malta - Malte
2009 (C)
	Total	Male	Female	Rate
Total	4 143	2 146	1 997	42.7
12 - 14	6	1	5	..
15 - 19	275	161	114	20.2
20 - 24	600	308	292	42.0
25 - 29	1 398	720	678	93.0
30 - 34	1 316	691	625	90.0
35 - 39	472	227	245	36.5
40 - 44	73	36	37	6.0
45 - 49	3	2	1	♦0.2
50 +	-	-	-	..
Unknown - Inconnu	-	-	-	..

Montenegro - Monténégro
2009 (C)
	Total	Male	Female	Rate
Total	8 642	4 597	4 045	54.9
12 - 14	10	6	4	..
15 - 19	486	269	217	22.5
20 - 24	2 064	1 072	992	86.7
25 - 29	2 862	1 527	1 335	119.0
30 - 34	2 018	1 053	965	89.5
35 - 39	914	504	410	43.4
40 - 44	165	101	64	8.0
45 - 49	24	10	14	♦1.1
50 +	3	2	1	..
Unknown - Inconnu	96	53	43	..

EUROPE

Netherlands - Pays-Bas[40]
2009 (C)
	Total	Male	Female	Rate
Total	184 915	94 619	90 296	47.8
12 - 14	-	-	-	..
15 - 19	2 636	1 387	1 249	5.3
20 - 24	18 902	9 724	9 178	38.0
25 - 29	55 302	28 269	27 033	111.7
30 - 34	67 578	34 560	33 018	134.8
35 - 39	34 776	17 832	16 944	57.7
40 - 44	5 523	2 744	2 779	8.6
45 - 49	190	101	89	0.3
50 +	8	2	6	..
Unknown - Inconnu	-	-	-	..

Norway - Norvège[41]
2009 (C)
	Total	Male	Female	Rate
Total	61 807	31 833	29 974	55.0
12 - 14	1	1	-	..
15 - 19	1 480	759	721	9.5
20 - 24	9 032	4 709	4 323	61.4
25 - 29	19 227	9 899	9 328	128.1
30 - 34	19 908	10 239	9 669	127.2
35 - 39	10 254	5 252	5 002	58.3
40 - 44	1 798	921	877	10.2
45 - 49	78	38	40	0.5
50 +	2	1	1	..
Unknown - Inconnu	27	14	13	..

Poland - Pologne
2009 (C)
	Total	Male	Female	Rate
Total	417 589	214 908	202 681	43.6
12 - 14	63	34	29	..
15 - 19	20 451	10 585	9 866	16.2
20 - 24	87 080	45 032	42 048	58.8
25 - 29	154 089	79 158	74 931	96.0
30 - 34	110 485	56 648	53 837	74.4
35 - 39	38 386	19 847	18 539	29.9
40 - 44	6 714	3 438	3 276	5.8
45 - 49	317	165	152	0.2
50 +	4	1	3	..
Unknown - Inconnu	-	-	-	..

Portugal[18]
2009 (C)
	Total	Male	Female	Rate
Total	99 491	50 873	48 618	38.7
12 - 14	63	32	31	..
15 - 19	4 284	2 130	2 154	15.3
20 - 24	13 362	6 878	6 484	43.8
25 - 29	26 977	13 776	13 201	72.7
30 - 34	34 448	17 684	16 764	82.5
35 - 39	17 001	8 687	8 314	41.6
40 - 44	3 174	1 594	1 580	8.0
45 - 49	178	88	90	0.5
50 +	3	3	-	..
Unknown - Inconnu	1	1	-	..

Republic of Moldova - République de Moldova[42]
2009 (C)
	Total	Male	Female	Rate
Total	40 803	21 089	19 714	41.1
0 - 14	10	3	7	..
15 - 19	4 023	2 114	1 909	27.0
20 - 24	15 406	7 948	7 458	87.3
25 - 29	12 228	6 335	5 893	80.0
30 - 34	6 307	3 278	3 029	47.3
35 - 39	2 405	1 190	1 215	20.1
40 - 44	398	211	187	3.4
45 - 49	19	9	10	♦0.1

Continent, country or area, year, code and age of mother (in years) / Continent, pays ou zone, année, code et âge de la mère (en années)	Number - Nombre			Rate Taux
	Total	Male Masculin	Female Féminin	
EUROPE				
Republic of Moldova - République de Moldova[42] 2009 (C)				
50 +	3	-	3	..
Unknown - Inconnu	4	1	3	..
Romania - Roumanie 2009 (C)				
Total	222 388	114 422	107 966	41.1
12 - 14	758	399	359	..
15 - 19	25 456	13 230	12 226	39.3
20 - 24	56 985	29 319	27 666	67.5
25 - 29	65 684	33 890	31 794	82.7
30 - 34	51 371	26 247	25 124	59.4
35 - 39	18 262	9 325	8 937	22.1
40 - 44	3 746	1 950	1 796	4.7
45 - 49	126	62	64	0.2
50 +	-	-	-	..
Unknown - Inconnu	-	-	-	..
Russian Federation - Fédération de Russie[26] 2009 (C)				
Total	1 761 687	905 380	856 307	46.6
12 - 14	385	203	182	..
15 - 19	131 057	67 292	63 765	30.2
20 - 24	552 829	284 790	268 039	90.3
25 - 29	563 014	289 551	273 463	93.7
30 - 34	346 388	177 230	169 158	63.8
35 - 39	140 558	72 221	68 337	27.8
40 - 44	25 025	12 898	12 127	5.2
45 - 49	1 334	638	696	0.2
50 +	87	46	41	..
Unknown - Inconnu	1 010	511	499	..
San Marino - Saint-Marin 2003 (+C)				
Total	300	161	139	40.1
0 - 14	1	-	1	..
15 - 19	4	1	3	♦6.4
20 - 24	17	10	7	♦22.2
25 - 29	72	40	32	66.4
30 - 34	121	66	55	91.5
35 - 39	73	36	37	50.0
40 - 44	11	8	3	♦9.0
45 +	1	-	1	♦1.0
2004 (+C)				
Total	306	...	...	40.7
15 - 19	1	...	...	♦1.6
20 - 24	15	...	...	♦20.3
25 - 29	69	...	...	65.4
30 - 34	134	...	...	102.8
35 - 39	75	...	...	50.7
40 - 44	11	...	...	♦8.3
45 - 49	1	...	...	♦1.0
Serbia - Serbie[43] 2009 (+C)				
Total	70 299	36 450	33 849	41.6
12 - 14	83	41	42	..
15 - 19	4 484	2 332	2 152	21.7
20 - 24	16 261	8 495	7 766	69.8
25 - 29	22 875	11 738	11 137	91.7
30 - 34	17 804	9 315	8 489	70.3
35 - 39	6 988	3 580	3 408	29.1
40 - 44	1 112	565	547	4.7
45 - 49	64	33	31	0.3
50 +	8	5	3	..
Unknown - Inconnu	620	346	274	..

Continent, country or area, year, code and age of mother (in years) / Continent, pays ou zone, année, code et âge de la mère (en années)	Number - Nombre			Rate Taux
	Total	Male Masculin	Female Féminin	
EUROPE				
Slovakia - Slovaquie 2009 (C)				
Total	61 217	31 563	29 654	43.3
12 - 14	31	15	16	..
15 - 19	3 987	2 028	1 959	21.8
20 - 24	11 728	5 964	5 764	56.4
25 - 29	20 372	10 558	9 814	91.4
30 - 34	17 941	9 313	8 628	77.9
35 - 39	6 132	3 157	2 975	30.9
40 - 44	978	505	473	5.4
45 - 49	45	21	24	0.2
50 +	3	2	1	..
Unknown - Inconnu	-	-	-	..
Slovenia - Slovénie 2009 (C)				
Total	21 856	11 309	10 547	45.2
12 - 14	1	-	1	..
15 - 19	283	146	137	5.4
20 - 24	2 656	1 345	1 311	42.0
25 - 29	7 868	4 016	3 852	110.4
30 - 34	7 815	4 110	3 705	105.0
35 - 39	2 786	1 450	1 336	39.6
40 - 44	435	237	198	5.7
45 - 49	12	5	7	♦0.2
50 +	-	-	-	..
Unknown - Inconnu	-	-	-	..
Spain - Espagne 2009* (C)				
Total	494 306	255 776	238 530	43.1
12 - 14	-	-	-	..
15 - 19	13 395	6 904	6 491	12.2
20 - 24	46 530	24 053	22 477	35.6
25 - 29	107 093	55 454	51 639	63.4
30 - 34	188 366	97 721	90 645	96.3
35 - 39	115 915	59 923	55 992	60.9
40 - 44	21 433	10 927	10 506	11.8
45 - 49	1 574	794	780	0.9
50 +	-	-	-	..
Unknown - Inconnu	-	-	-	..
Sweden - Suède 2009 (C)				
Total	111 801	57 564	54 237	53.2
12 - 14	3	1	2	..
15 - 19	1 829	941	888	5.9
20 - 24	14 628	7 531	7 097	50.5
25 - 29	31 871	16 408	15 463	115.3
30 - 34	38 344	19 832	18 512	134.4
35 - 39	20 719	10 613	10 106	66.8
40 - 44	4 182	2 131	2 051	12.8
45 - 49	211	103	108	0.7
50 +	14	4	10	..
Switzerland - Suisse 2009 (C)				
Total	78 286	40 407	37 879	41.6
12 - 14	4	4	-	..
15 - 19	909	484	425	4.1
20 - 24	7 833	4 021	3 812	33.9
25 - 29	20 678	10 710	9 968	82.4
30 - 34	28 384	14 636	13 748	108.5
35 - 39	16 887	8 707	8 180	58.9
40 - 44	3 399	1 737	1 662	10.6
45 - 49	181	100	81	0.6
50 +	11	8	3	..
Unknown - Inconnu	-	-	-	..

10. Live births by age of mother and sex of child, general and age-specific fertility rates: latest available year, 2000 - 2009
Naissances vivantes selon l'âge de la mère et le sexe de l'enfant, taux de fécondité et taux de fécondité par âge : dernière année disponible, 2000 - 2009 (continued - suite)

Continent, country or area, year, code and age of mother (in years) / Continent, pays ou zone, année, code et âge de la mère (en années)	Number - Nombre			Rate
	Total	Male Masculin	Female Féminin	Taux
EUROPE				
TFYR of Macedonia - L'ex-R. y. de Macédoine				
2009 (C)				
Total	23 684	12 340	11 344	44.8
12 - 14	33	14	19	..
15 - 19	1 501	772	729	19.9
20 - 24	6 066	3 161	2 905	75.8
25 - 29	8 506	4 446	4 060	107.0
30 - 34	5 380	2 807	2 573	71.1
35 - 39	1 873	975	898	25.7
40 - 44	299	150	149	4.1
45 - 49	20	12	8	♦0.3
50 +	3	-	3	..
Unknown - Inconnu	3	3	-	..
Ukraine[44]				
2007 (C)				
Total	472 657	...	...	38.6
12 - 14	143	...	...	..
15 - 19	48 425	...	...	29.3
20 - 24	174 577	...	...	92.3
25 - 29	139 976	...	...	82.0
30 - 34	76 252	...	...	45.3
35 - 39	27 174	...	...	17.0
40 - 44	4 871	...	...	2.8
45 - 49	213	...	...	0.1
50 +	17	...	...	..
Unknown - Inconnu	1 009	...	...	..
United Kingdom of Great Britain and Northern Ireland - Royaume-Uni de Grande-Bretagne et d'Irlande du Nord[45]				
2009 (C)				
Total	790 204	405 099	385 105	53.5
0 - 14	195	94	101	..
15 - 19	48 372	24 892	23 480	25.0
20 - 24	151 312	77 660	73 652	73.0
25 - 29	217 460	111 301	106 159	107.3
30 - 34	214 789	110 343	104 446	112.6
35 - 39	128 065	65 482	62 583	57.9
40 - 44	28 244	14 408	13 836	11.9
45 - 49	1 636	850	786	0.7
50 +	111	61	50	..
Unknown - Inconnu	20	8	12	..
OCEANIA - OCÉANIE				
American Samoa - Samoas américaines				
2006 (C)				
Total	1 442	...	...	...
0 - 14	1	...	...	..
15 - 19	110	...	...	...
20 - 24	342	...	...	...
25 - 29	410	...	...	...
30 - 34	303	...	...	...
35 - 39	218	...	...	...
40 - 44	55	...	...	...
45 - 49	3	...	...	...
Australia - Australie				
2009 (+C)				
Total	295 738	152 019	143 719	54.5
0 - 14	98	46	52	..
15 - 19	12 022	6 210	5 812	16.5
OCEANIA - OCÉANIE				
Australia - Australie				
2009 (+C)				
20 - 24	42 067	21 717	20 350	53.8
25 - 29	80 863	41 524	39 339	102.5
30 - 34	93 027	47 832	45 195	124.0
35 - 39	55 937	28 722	27 215	68.8
40 - 44	10 905	5 536	5 369	14.2
45 - 49	531	278	253	0.7
50 +	34	21	13	..
Unknown - Inconnu	254	133	121	..
Fiji - Fidji				
2004 (+C)				
Total	17 189	8 944	8 245	79.4
0 - 14	7	1	6	..
15 - 19	1 194	622	572	29.7
20 - 24	5 684	2 961	2 723	154.7
25 - 29	5 126	2 665	2 461	155.8
30 - 34	3 033	1 526	1 507	100.4
35 - 39	1 592	868	724	57.0
40 - 44	464	254	210	18.2
45 - 49	43	23	20	1.9
50 +	-	-	-	..
Unknown - Inconnu	46	24	22	..
Guam[46]				
2004 (C)				
Total	3 427	1 783	1 644	...
10 - 14	2	1	1	..
15 - 19	352	168	184	...
20 - 24	887	486	401	...
25 - 29	939	483	456	...
30 - 34	738	393	345	...
35 - 39	395	196	199	...
40 - 44	102	50	52	...
45 - 49	10	5	5	...
50 +	-	-	-	..
Unknown - Inconnu	2	1	1	..
Marshall Islands - Îles Marshall[47]				
2006 (+U)				
Total	*1 576*	...	...	...
0 - 14	*2*	...	...	..
15 - 19	*268*	...	...	...
20 - 24	*551*	...	...	...
25 - 29	*431*	...	...	...
30 - 34	*211*	...	...	...
35 - 39	*91*	...	...	...
40 - 44	*19*	...	...	...
45 - 49	*3*	...	...	...
Unknown - Inconnu	-	...	...	..
Micronesia (Federated States of) - Micronésie (États fédérés de)				
2006 (+U)				
Total	*2 148*	...	...	...
10 - 14	*8*	...	...	..
15 - 17	*89*	...	...	...
18 - 19	*155*	...	...	...
20 - 24	*619*	...	...	...
25 - 29	*514*	...	...	...
30 - 34	*379*	...	...	...
35 - 39	*259*	...	...	...
40 - 44	*43*	...	...	...
45 +	*9*	...	...	...
Unknown - Inconnu	*73*	...	...	..

Continent, country or area, year, code and age of mother (in years) / Continent, pays ou zone, année, code et âge de la mère (en années)	Number - Nombre			Rate Taux
	Total	Male Masculin	Female Féminin	

Continent, country or area, year, code and age of mother (in years) / Continent, pays ou zone, année, code et âge de la mère (en années)	Number - Nombre			Rate Taux
	Total	Male Masculin	Female Féminin	

OCEANIA - OCÉANIE

	Total	Male Masculin	Female Féminin	Rate Taux
New Caledonia - Nouvelle-Calédonie				
2007 (C)				
Total	4 093	...	...	64.2
0 - 19	213	...	...	20.0
20 - 24	902	...	...	97.1
25 - 29	1 150	...	...	131.5
30 - 34	1 072	...	...	110.7
35 - 39	611	...	...	63.6
40 - 44	138	...	...	16.2
45 - 49	7	...	...	♦1.0
50 +	-	...	...	..
New Zealand - Nouvelle-Zélande				
2009 (+C)				
Total	62 543	32 112	30 431	58.0
0 - 14	29	16	13	..
15 - 19	4 641	2 378	2 263	29.4
20 - 24	11 504	5 854	5 650	77.0
25 - 29	15 295	7 846	7 449	107.7
30 - 34	17 305	8 874	8 431	123.7
35 - 39	11 312	5 883	5 429	70.0
40 - 44	2 355	1 211	1 144	14.5
45 - 49	100	49	51	0.6
50 +	2	1	1	..
Niue - Nioué[48]				
2009 (C)				
Total	31	...	...	...
0 - 14	-	...	...	...
15 - 19	1	...	...	...
20 - 24	9	...	...	...
25 - 29	12	...	...	...
30 - 34	6	...	...	...
35 - 39	1	...	...	...
40 - 44	1	...	...	...
45 +	1	...	...	...
Northern Mariana Islands - Îles Mariannes septentrionales				
2002 (U)				
Total	1 289	...	...	...
0 - 19	110	...	...	...
20 - 24	298	...	...	...
25 - 29	347	...	...	...
30 - 34	317	...	...	...
35 - 39	182	...	...	...
40 +	35	...	...	...
Unknown - Inconnu	-	...	...	...
Palau - Palaos				
2003 (C)				
Total	312	163	149	...
15 - 19	21	13	8	...
20 - 24	71	34	37	...

OCEANIA - OCÉANIE

	Total	Male Masculin	Female Féminin	Rate Taux
Palau - Palaos				
2003 (C)				
25 - 29	81	40	41	...
30 - 34	63	35	28	...
35 - 39	56	29	27	...
40 - 44	16	11	5	...
45 - 49	4	1	3	...
2005 (C)				
Total	279	...	...	55.3
0 - 14	-	...	...	...
15 - 19	23	...	...	♦30.8
20 - 24	65	...	...	117.3
25 - 29	56	...	...	87.4
30 - 34	73	...	...	93.1
35 - 39	40	...	...	48.0
40 - 44	20	...	...	♦25.3
45 - 49	2	...	...	♦2.9
Tonga				
2003 (+C)				
Total	2 781	...	...	114.1
0 - 14	-	...	...	...
15 - 19	94	...	...	17.5
20 - 24	619	...	...	129.9
25 - 29	787	...	...	230.6
30 - 34	643	...	...	222.6
35 - 39	405	...	...	155.0
40 - 44	110	...	...	48.2
45 - 49	10	...	...	♦4.8
50 +	-	...	...	...
Unknown - Inconnu	113	...	...	...
Tuvalu				
2003 (U)				
Total	239	...	...	...
15 - 19	17	...	...	...
20 - 24	76	...	...	...
25 - 29	53	...	...	...
30 - 34	35	...	...	...
35 - 39	37	...	...	...
40 - 44	20	...	...	...
45 - 49	-	...	...	...
Wallis and Futuna Islands - Îles Wallis et Futuna				
2008 (C)				
Total	185	...	...	...
0 - 14	-	...	...	...
15 - 19	9	...	...	...
20 - 24	38	...	...	...
25 - 29	53	...	...	...
30 - 34	51	...	...	...
35 - 39	29	...	...	...
40 - 44	5	...	...	...
45 +	-	...	...	...
Unknown - Inconnu	-	...	...	...

FOOTNOTES - NOTES

♦ Rates based on 30 or fewer births. - Taux basés sur 30 naissances ou moins.

* Provisional. - Données provisoires.

'Code' indicates the source of data, as follows:
C - Civil registration, estimated over 90% complete
U - Civil registration, estimated less than 90% complete
| - Other source, estimated reliable
+ - Data tabulated by date of registration rather than occurrence

... Information not available

Le 'Code' indique la source des données, comme suit :
C - Registres de l'état civil considérés complets à 90 p. 100 au moins
U - Registres de l'état civil qui ne sont pas considérés complets à 90 p. 100 au moins
| - Autre source, considérée fiable
+ - Données exploitées selon la date de l'enregistrement et non la date de l'événement
... Information non disponible

[1] Data from Health Statistics Reports since 1998, due to incompleteness of civil registration. - Données provenant des Health Statistics Reports (rapports sur les statistiques sanitaires) depuis 1998, en raison des lacunes de l'état civil.

[2] Data refer to the twelve months preceding the census in March. - Les données se rapportent aux douze mois précédant le recensement de mars.

[3] Data refer to the twelve months preceding the census in June. - Les données se rapportent aux douze mois précédant le recensement de juin.

[4] Excludes the islands of St. Brandon and Agalega. - Non compris les îles St. Brandon et Agalega.

[5] Data refer to the twelve months preceding the census in August. - Les données se rapportent aux douze mois précédant le recensement d'août.

[6] Excluding live-born infants who died before their birth was registered. - Non compris les enfants nés vivants décédés avant l'enregistrement de leur naissance.

[7] Data refer to the twelve months preceding the census date. - Les données portent sur les douze mois précédant la date du recensement.

[8] Excluding late registration (after 28/29 February of the following year). - En excluant les enregistrements tardifs (après les 28/29 février de l'année suivante).

[9] Data refer to the twelve months preceding the census in May. - Les données se rapportent aux douze mois précédant le recensement de mai.

[10] Data refer to registered events only. - Les données ne concernent que les événements enregistrés.

[11] Figures for male and female do not add up to the total, since they do not include the category "Unknown". - La somme des chiffres indiqués pour les sexes masculin et féminin n'est pas égale au total parce qu'elle n'inclut pas la catégorie " inconnue ".

[12] Excluding non-residents and foreign service personnel and their dependants. - À l'exclusion des non-résidents et du personnel diplomatique et de leurs charges de famille.

[13] Including Canadian residents temporarily in the United States, but excluding United States residents temporarily in Canada. - Y compris les résidents canadiens se trouvant temporairement aux Etats-Unis, mais ne comprenant pas les résidents des Etats-Unis se trouvant temporairement au Canada.

[14] For confidentiality reasons, live births to mothers aged 50 and over and where information was unavailable on the birth mother of children who were adopted, were included in age of mother not stated. - Pour des raisons de confidentialité, on a classé dans la catégorie « âge de la mère non déclaré » les naissances vivantes concernant des femmes âgées de plus de 50 ans et les enfants adoptés nés de mères sur lesquelles on ne dispose pas d'information.

[16] Resident births outside the islands are excluded. - Non compris les naissances de résidents hors des îles.

[16] Excluding children born in the country of non-resident mothers. - Exceptés les enfants nés dans le pays des mères non-résidentes.

[17] Data have not been adjusted for underenumeration. - Les données n'ont pas été ajustées pour compenser les lacunes du dénombrement.

[18] Data refer to births to resident mothers. - Ces données concernent les enfants nés de mères résidentes.

[19] Data for male and female categories exclude births of unknown sex. - Les données pour le sexe masculin et féminin ne comprennent pas les naissances ou on ignore le sexe.

[20] Data refer to resident population only. - Pour la population résidante seulement.

[21] Excluding Indian jungle population. Including births abroad and births of unknown residence. - Non compris les Indiens de la jungle. Y compris les naissances survenues à l'étranger et les naissances d'enfants dont la résidence n'était pas connue.

[22] Excluding events registered late. - Non compris les enregistrements tardifs.

[23] Source: Ministry of health reports. - Source: Rapports du Ministère de Santé.

[24] Including births to non-resident mothers. - Y compris les naissances de femmes non résidentes.

[25] Including unknown sex. - Y compris le sexe inconnu.

[26] Excluding infants born alive of less than 28 weeks' gestation, of less than 1 000 grams in weight and 35 centimeters in length, who die within seven days of birth. - Non compris les enfants nés vivants après moins de 28 semaines de gestation, pesant moins de 1 000 grammes, mesurant moins de 35 centimètres et décédés dans les sept jours qui ont suivi leur naissance.

[27] Data refer to government controlled areas. - Les données se rapportent aux zones contrôlées par le Gouvernement.

[28] Data refer to the twelve months preceding the census in October. - Les données font référence aux 12 mois qui ont précédé le recensement en octobre.

[29] As published by the United Nations Economic and Social Commission for Western Asia. - Publié par la Commission économique et sociale des Nations Unies pour l'Asie occidentale.

[30] Including data for East Jerusalem and Israeli residents in certain other territories under occupation by Israeli military forces since June 1967. - Y compris les données pour Jérusalem-Est et les résidents israéliens dans certains autres territoires occupés depuis 1967 par les forces armées israéliennes.

[31] Data refer to Japanese nationals in Japan only. - Les données se raportent aux nationaux japonais au Japon seulement.

[32] Data from Births and Deaths Notification System (Ministry of Health institutions and all other health care providers). - Les données proviennent du système de notification des naissances et des décès (établissements du Ministère de la santé et tous autres prestataires de soins de santé).

[33] Based on the results of the Pakistan Demographic Survey. Excluding data for the Pakistan-held part of Jammu and Kashmir, the final status of which has not yet been determined. - Données extraites de l'enquête démographique effectuée par le Pakistan. Non compris les données concernant la partie du Jammu et Cachemire occupée par le Pakistan dont le statut définitif n'a pas été déterminé.

[34] Excluding alien armed forces, civilian aliens employed by armed forces, and foreign diplomatic personnel and their dependants. - Non compris les militaires étrangers, les civils étrangers employés par les forces armées ni le personnel diplomatique étranger et les membres de leur famille les accompagnant.

[35] The registration of births and deaths is conducted by the Ministry of Health. An estimate of completeness is not provided. - L'enregistrement des naissances et des décès est mené par le Ministère de la Santé. Le degré estimatif de complétude n'est pas fourni.

[36] Excluding Faeroe Islands and Greenland shown separately, if available. - Non compris les îles Féroé et le Groenland, qui font l'objet de rubriques distinctes, si disponible.

[37] Including resident births abroad. - Y compris les naissances de résidents à l'étranger.

[38] Including armed forces stationed outside the country. - Y compris les militaires nationaux hors du pays.

[39] Including events registered late. - Y compris les événements enregistrés avec retard.

[40] Including residents outside the country if listed in a Netherlands population register. - Y compris les résidents hors du pays, s'ils sont inscrits sur un registre de population néerlandais.

[41] Excluding Svalbard and Jan Mayen Islands shown separately, if available. - Non compris Svalbard et Jan Mayen qui font l'objet de rubriques distinctes, si disponible.

[42] Excluding Transnistria and the municipality of Bender. - Les données ne tiennent pas compte de l'information sur la Transnistria et la municipalité de Bender.

[43] Excluding data for Kosovo and Metohia. - Sans les données pour le Kosovo et Metohie.

[44] Data refer to births with weight 500g and more (if weight is unknown - with length 25 centimeters and more, or with gestation during 22 weeks or more). - Données concernant les nouveau-nés de 500 grammes ou plus (si le poids est inconnu – de 25 centimètres de long ou plus, ou après une grossesse de 22 semaines ou plus).

[45] Data tabulated by date of occurrence for England and Wales, and by date of registration for Northern Ireland and Scotland. Excluding Channel Islands (Guernsey and Jersey) and Isle of Man, shown separately, if available. - Données exploitées selon la date de l'événement pour l'Angleterre et le pays de Galles, et selon la date de l'enregistrement pour l'Irlande du Nord et l'Ecosse. Non compris les îles Anglo-Normandes (Guernesey et Jersey) et l'île de Man, qui font l'objet de rubriques distinctes, si disponible.

[46] Including United States military personnel, their dependants and contract employees. - Y compris les militaires des Etats-Unis, les membres de leur famille les accompagnant et les agents contractuels des Etats-Unis.

[47] Excluding United States military personnel, their dependants and contract employees. - Non compris les militaires des Etats-Unis, les membres de leur famille les accompagnant et les agents contractuels des Etats-Unis.

[48] Includes children born in New Zealand to women resident in Niue who chose to travel to New Zealand to give birth. - Y compris les enfants nés en Nouvelle-Zélande de femmes résidant à Nioué qui ont choisi de se rendre en Nouvelle-Zélande pour accoucher.

10a. Live births by age of mother and sex of child, general and age-specific fertility rates: 2010
Naissances vivantes selon l'âge de la mère et le sexe de l'enfant, taux de fécondité et taux de fécondité par âge : 2010

Continent, pays ou zone, année, code et âge de la mère (en années)	Total	Male Masculin	Female Féminin	Rate Taux
AFRICA - AFRIQUE				
Seychelles				
2010 (+C)				
Total	1 504	761	743	66.6
0 - 14	4	2	2	..
15 - 19	203	107	96	62.3
20 - 24	398	202	196	121.5
25 - 29	357	177	180	112.8
30 - 34	285	153	132	96.1
35 - 39	193	91	102	51.5
40 - 44	63	28	35	21.0
45 +	1	1	-	◆0.3
AMERICA, NORTH - AMÉRIQUE DU NORD				
Aruba				
2010 (C)				
Total	1 141	...	...	40.1
0 - 14	-	...	...	..
15 - 19	149	...	...	39.9
20 - 24	282	...	...	91.8
25 - 29	280	...	...	86.1
30 - 34	264	...	...	68.1
35 - 39	128	...	...	29.0
40 - 44	37	...	...	7.7
45 - 49	1	...	...	◆0.2
50 +	-	...	...	..
Unknown - Inconnu	-	...	...	..
Costa Rica				
2010* (C)				
Total	70 922	36 382	34 540	55.2
0 - 14	428	234	194	..
15 - 19	12 828	6 598	6 230	55.2
20 - 24	21 353	10 945	10 408	97.5
25 - 29	18 001	9 303	8 698	96.2
30 - 34	11 648	5 907	5 741	...

Continent, pays ou zone, année, code et âge de la mère (en années)	Total	Male Masculin	Female Féminin	Rate Taux
AMERICA, NORTH - AMÉRIQUE DU NORD				
Costa Rica				
2010* (C)				
35 - 39	5 098	2 577	2 521	...
40 - 44	1 265	666	599	...
45 +	95	52	43	...
Unknown - Inconnu	206	100	106	..
Greenland - Groenland				
2010 (C)				
Total	868	451	417	60.6
0 - 14	4	4	-	..
15 - 19	117	69	48	51.5
20 - 24	247	117	130	112.4
25 - 29	263	133	130	137.1
30 - 34	139	74	65	85.4
35 - 39	72	39	33	48.7
40 - 44	26	15	11	◆11.0
45 - 49	-	-	-	..
50 +	-	-	-	..
Unknown - Inconnu	-	-	-	..
EUROPE				
Lithuania - Lituanie				
2010 (C)				
Total	35 626	18 224	17 402	41.6
0 - 14	5	3	2	..
15 - 19	1 639	831	808	13.9
20 - 24	7 080	3 662	3 418	53.9
25 - 29	13 214	6 753	6 461	111.8
30 - 34	9 151	4 620	4 531	84.7
35 - 39	3 763	1 970	1 793	31.7
40 - 44	722	359	363	5.8
45 - 49	40	20	20	0.3
50 +	-	-	-	..
Unknown - Inconnu	12	6	6	..

FOOTNOTES - NOTES

◆ Rates based on 30 or fewer births. - Taux basés sur 30 naissances ou moins.
* Provisional. - Données provisoires.
  'Code' indicates the source of data, as follows:

C - Civil registration, estimated over 90% complete
U - Civil registration, estimated less than 90% complete
| - Other source, estimated reliable
+ - Data tabulated by date of registration rather than occurrence.
... Information not available

Le 'Code' indique la source des données, comme suit:

C - Registres de l'état civil considérés complets à 90 p. 100 au moins.
U - Registres de l'état civil qui ne sont pas considérés complets à 90 p. 100 au moins.
| - Autre source, considérée fiable.
+ - Données exploitées selon la date de l'enregistrement et non la date de l'événement.
... Information non disponible.

Tables 11 and 11a

Table 11 presents live births by age of father and live birth rates by age of father for the latest available year between 2000 and 2009. Table 11a presents the available data for year 2010.

Description of variables: Age is defined as age at last birthday, that is, the difference between the date of birth and the date of the occurrence of the event, expressed in completed solar years. The age classification used in this table is the following: under 20 years, 5-year age groups through 60-64 years, 65 years and over, and age unknown. A different classification may appear as provided by reporting country or area.

Rate computation: Live-birth rates specific to age of father are the annual number of births to a man in each age group per 1 000 male population in the same age group. These rates are calculated by the Statistics Division of the United Nations.

Since relatively few births occur to men below 15 or above 59 years of age, birth rates for men under 20 years of age and for those 55 years of age or over are computed on the male population aged 15-19 and 55-59, respectively. Similarly, the rate for men of "All ages" is based on all live births irrespective of age of father, and is computed on the male population aged 15-59 years.

Births to fathers of unknown age are distributed proportionately across the age groups, by the Statistics Division of the United Nations, in accordance with the distribution of births by age of father prior to the calculation of the rates.

The population used in computing the rates is the estimated or enumerated distribution of males by age. First priority is given to the estimated population and second priority to the enumerated population, i.e. to census returns of the year to which the births refer.

Rates presented in this table are limited to those for countries or areas having at least a total of 100 live births in a given year.

Reliability of data: Data from civil registers of live births which are reported as incomplete (less than 90 per cent completeness) or of unknown completeness are considered unreliable and are set in *italics* rather than in roman type. Rates are not computed if the data on live births from civil registers are reported as incomplete (less than 90 per cent completeness) or of unknown completeness. Table 9 and the technical notes for that table provide more detailed information on the completeness of birth registration. For more information about the quality of vital statistics data in general, see section 4.2 of the Technical Notes.

Limitations: Statistics on live births by age of father are subject to the same qualifications as have been set forth for vital statistics in general and birth statistics in particular as discussed in section 4 of the Technical Notes. These include differences in the completeness of registration, the method used to determine age of father and the quality of the reported information relating to age of father.

The reliability of the data described above, is an important factor in considering the limitations. In addition, some live births are tabulated by date of registration and not by date of occurrence; these are indicated in the table by a plus sign "+". Whenever the lag between the date of occurrence and date of registration is prolonged and, therefore, a large proportion of the live-birth registrations are delayed, birth statistics for any given year may be seriously affected. For example, the age of the father will almost always refer to the date of registration rather than to the date of birth of the child. Hence, in those countries or areas where registration of births is delayed, possibly for years, statistics on births by age of father should be used with caution.

Another factor which limits international comparability is the practice of some countries or areas of not including in live birth statistics infants who were born alive but died before the registration of the birth or within the first 24 hours of life, thus underestimating the total number of live births. Statistics of this type are footnoted.

Because these statistics are classified according to age, they are subject to the limitations with respect to accuracy of age reporting similar to those already discussed in connection with section 3.1.3 of the Technical Notes. The factors influencing the accuracy of reporting may be somewhat dissimilar in vital statistics (because of the differences in the method of taking a census and registering a birth) but, in

general, the same errors can be observed. The absence of frequencies in the unknown age group does not necessarily indicate completely accurate reporting and tabulation of the age item. It is often an indication that the unknowns have been eliminated by assigning ages to them before tabulation, or by proportionate distribution after tabulation.

On the other hand, large frequencies in the unknown age category may indicate that a large proportion of the births are born outside of wedlock, the records for which tend to be incomplete so far as characteristics of the parents are concerned.

Another limitation of age reporting may result from calculating age of father at birth of child (or at time of registration) from year of birth rather than from day, month and year of birth. Information on this factor is given in footnotes when known.

In few countries, data by age refer to deliveries rather than to live births causing under-enumeration in the event of a multiple birth. This practice leads to lack of strict comparability, both among countries or areas relying on this practice and between data shown in this table and table 9.

Rates shown in this table are subject to the same limitations that affect the corresponding statistics on live births. In cases of rates based on births tabulated by date of registration and not by date of occurrence; the effect of including delayed registration on the distribution of births by age of father may be noted in the age-specific fertility rates for men at older ages. In some cases, high age-specific rates for men aged 55 years and over may reflect age of father at registration of birth and not fertility at these older ages.

Earlier data: Live births and live birth rates by age of father have been shown in previous issues of the *Demographic Yearbook*. Information on the specific years is presented in the Historical Index.

Tableaux 11 et 11a

Le tableau 11 présente les données les plus récentes disponibles pour la période 2000 -2009 sur les naissances vivantes selon l'âge du père et les taux des naissances vivantes selon l'âge du père. Le tableau 11a présente les données disponibles pour l'année 2010.

Description des variables : l'âge désigne l'âge au dernier anniversaire, c'est-à-dire la différence entre la date de naissance et la date de l'événement exprimée en années solaires révolues. La classification par âge utilisée dans ce tableau comprend les catégories suivantes : moins de 20 ans, groupes quinquennaux jusqu'à 60-64 ans, 65 ans et plus, et âge inconnu. Des groupes d'âge différents sont parfois utilisés lorsque les pays ou territoires ont fourni les données dans une autre classification.

Les taux de natalité selon l'âge du père représentent le nombre annuel de naissances vivantes intervenues dans un groupe d'âge donné pour 1 000 hommes du groupe d'âge. Ces taux ont été calculés par la Division de statistique de l'ONU.

Étant donné que le nombre de naissances parmi les hommes de moins de 15 ans ou de plus de 59 ans est relativement peu élevé, les taux de natalité parmi les hommes âgées de moins de 20 ans et celles de 55 ans et plus ont été calculés sur la base des populations masculines âgées de 15 à 19 ans et de 55 à 59 ans, respectivement. De même, le taux pour les hommes de « tous âges » est fondé sur la totalité des naissances vivantes, indépendamment de l'âge du père et ce chiffre est rapporté à l'effectif de la population masculine âgée de 15 à 59 ans.

Les naissances pour lesquelles l'âge du père était inconnu ont été réparties par la Division de statistique de l'ONU, avant le calcul des taux, suivant les proportions observées pour celles où l'âge du père était connu.

Les chiffres de population utilisés pour le calcul des taux proviennent de dénombrements ou de répartitions estimatives de la population masculine selon l'âge. On a utilisé de préférence les estimations de la population; à défaut, on s'est contenté des données censitaires se rapportant à l'année des naissances.

Les taux présentés dans ce tableau ne concernent que les pays ou zones où l'on a enregistré un total d'au moins 100 naissances vivantes dans une année donnée.

Fiabilité des données : les données sur les naissances vivantes provenant des registres de l'état civil qui sont déclarées incomplètes (degré de complétude inférieur à 90 p. 100) ou dont le degré de complétude n'est pas connu sont jugées douteuses et apparaissent en italique et non en caractères romains. On a choisi de ne pas faire figurer dans le tableau 11 des taux calculés à partir de données sur les naissances vivantes issues de registres de l'état civil qui sont déclarées incomplètes (degré de complétude inférieur à 90 p. 100) ou dont le degré de complétude n'est pas connu. Le tableau 9 et les notes techniques qui s'y rapportent présentent des renseignements plus détaillés sur le degré de complétude de l'enregistrement des naissances vivantes. Pour plus de précisions sur la qualité des statistiques de l'état civil en général, voir la section 4.2 des Notes techniques.

Insuffisance des données : les statistiques relatives aux naissances vivantes selon l'âge du père appellent toutes les réserves qui ont été formulées à propos des statistiques de l'état civil en général et des statistiques de naissances en particulier (voir la section 4 des Notes techniques). Ceci inclut les différences de complétude d'enregistrement des faits d'état civil, de méthode pour déterminer l'âge du père et de qualité d'information concernant l'âge du père.

La fiabilité des données, au sujet de laquelle des indications ont été données plus haut, est un facteur important. Il faut également tenir compte du fait que, dans certains cas, les données relatives aux naissances vivantes sont exploitées selon la date de l'enregistrement et non la date de l'événement ; ces cas ont été signalés dans le tableau par le signe '+'. Chaque fois que le décalage entre l'événement et son enregistrement est grand et qu'une forte proportion des naissances vivantes fait l'objet d'un enregistrement tardif, les statistiques des naissances vivantes pour une année donnée peuvent être considérablement faussées. Par exemple, l'âge du père représente presque toujours son âge à la date de l'enregistrement et non à la date de la naissance de l'enfant. Ainsi, dans les pays ou zones où l'enregistrement des naissances est tardif, le retard atteignant parfois plusieurs années, il faut utiliser avec prudence les statistiques concernant les naissances selon l'âge du père.

Un autre facteur qui nuit à la comparabilité internationale est la pratique de certains pays ou zones qui consiste à ne pas inclure dans les statistiques des naissances vivantes les enfants nés vivants mais décédés avant l'enregistrement de leur naissance ou dans les 24 heures qui ont suivi la naissance, pratique qui conduit à sous-estimer le nombre total de naissances vivantes. Quand pareil facteur a joué, cela a été signalé en note à la fin du tableau.

Étant donné que les statistiques du tableau 11 sont classées selon l'âge, elles appellent les mêmes réserves concernant l'exactitude des déclarations d'âge que celles formulées à la section 3.1.3 des Notes techniques. Dans le cas des statistiques de l'état civil, les facteurs qui interviennent à cet égard sont parfois différents, étant donné que le recensement de la population et l'enregistrement des naissances se font par des méthodes différentes, mais, d'une manière générale, les erreurs observées seront les mêmes. Si aucun nombre ne figure dans la rangée réservée aux âges inconnus, cela ne signifie pas nécessairement que les déclarations d'âge et l'exploitation des données par âge ont été tout à fait exactes. C'est souvent une indication que l'on a attribué un âge aux personnes d'âge inconnu avant l'exploitation des données ou qu'elles ont été réparties proportionnellement entre les différents groupes après cette opération.

À l'inverse, lorsque le nombre des personnes d'âge inconnu est important, cela peut signifier que la proportion de naissances parmi les parents célibataires est élevée, étant donné qu'en pareil cas l'acte de naissance ne contient pas tous les renseignements concernant les parents.

Les déclarations par âge peuvent comporter des distorsions, du fait que l'âge du père au moment de la naissance d'un enfant (ou de la déclaration de naissance) est donné par année de naissance et non par date exacte (jour, mois et année).

Dans quelques pays, la classification par âges se réfère aux accouchements, et non aux naissances vivantes, ce qui conduit à un sous-dénombrement en cas de naissances gémellaires. Cette pratique nuit à la comparabilité des données, à la fois entre pays ou zones qui recourent à cette méthode et entre les données présentées dans le tableau 11 et celles du tableau 9.

Les taux présentés dans ce tableau, sont sujets aux mêmes limitations qui affectent les statistiques correspondantes de naissances vivantes. Dans le cas des taux basés sur des naissances par date d'enregistrement et non par date d'occurrence, l'effet peut être visible sur les taux de fécondité par âge des hommes aux âges plus élevés. Dans certains cas, les taux de fécondité des hommes de plus de 55 ans peuvent refléter l'âge du père à l'enregistrement plus que la fécondité à ces âges.

Données publiées antérieurement : Les données sur les naissances vivantes selon l'âge du père et les taux des naissances vivantes selon l'âge du père ont été publié antérieurement dans l'*Annuaire démographique*. Pour plus de précisions concernant les années pour lesquels des données ont été publiées, se reporter à l'index historique.

11. Live births and live birth rates by age of father: latest available year, 2000 - 2009
Naissances vivantes et taux de natalité selon l'âge du père : dernière année disponible, 2000 - 2009

Continent, country or area, year, code and age of father (in years) Continent, pays ou zone, année, code et âge du père (en années)	Number - Nombre Both sexes Les deux sexes	Rate Taux	Continent, country or area, year, code and age of father (in years) Continent, pays ou zone, année, code et âge du père (en années)	Number - Nombre Both sexes Les deux sexes	Rate Taux
AFRICA - AFRIQUE			**AMERICA, NORTH - AMÉRIQUE DU NORD**		
Egypt - Égypte			Barbados - Barbade		
2009 (C)			2007 (+C)		
Total	2 217 409	91.4	30 - 34	784	...
0 - 19	3 406	1.5	35 - 39	605	...
20 - 24	99 665	47.6	40 - 44	381	...
25 - 29	307 777	187.7	45 - 49	163	...
30 - 34	316 254	251.7	50 - 54	53	...
35 - 39	195 562	162.9	55 - 59	17	...
40 - 44	102 643	95.5	60 - 64	8	...
45 - 49	44 023	45.1	65 +	3	..
50 - 54	13 068	16.3	Unknown - Inconnu	119	..
55 - 59	5 338	8.5	Canada[4]		
60 +	4 143	..	2008 (C)		
Unknown - Inconnu	1 125 530	..	Total	377 815	35.1
Mauritius - Maurice[1]			0 - 19	4 943	4.5
2009 (C)			20 - 24	30 718	27.6
Total	15 259	35.7	25 - 29	83 760	76.5
0 - 19	258	4.9	30 - 34	116 155	110.0
20 - 24	1 521	33.3	35 - 39	78 848	71.2
25 - 29	3 830	74.5	40 - 44	31 437	25.6
30 - 34	4 508	90.3	45 - 49	9 619	7.3
35 - 39	2 512	57.6	50 - 54	2 501	2.1
40 - 44	1 280	27.4	55 - 59	651	0.6
45 - 49	488	10.5	60 - 64	199	..
50 - 54	126	3.2	65 +	71	..
55 - 59	47	1.4	Unknown - Inconnu	18 984	..
60 - 64	15	..	Costa Rica		
65 +	5	..	2009 (C)		
Unknown - Inconnu	669	..	Total	75 000	50.7
Réunion[2]			0 - 19	1 858	7.6
2007 (C)			20 - 24	10 125	42.4
Total	14 808	61.9	25 - 29	12 170	62.2
0 - 19	352	10.0	30 - 34	10 282	...
20 - 24	2 409	88.2	35 - 39	6 652	...
25 - 29	3 283	139.4	40 - 44	3 469	...
30 - 34	3 693	141.6	45 - 49	1 387	...
35 - 39	2 860	96.2	50 - 54	616	...
40 - 44	1 488	46.6	55 - 59	223	...
45 - 49	491	19.2	60 - 64	128	..
50 - 54	151	6.8	65 +	28 090	..
55 - 59	53	3.0	Cuba		
60 - 64	28	..	2009 (C)		
			Total	130 036	35.1
			0 - 19	3 366	9.3
AMERICA, NORTH - AMÉRIQUE DU NORD			20 - 24	23 235	63.0
			25 - 29	27 469	89.1
Bahamas[3]			30 - 34	24 203	69.9
2009 (U)			35 - 39	20 141	43.9
Total	5 027	...	40 - 44	10 375	22.2
0 - 19	99	...	45 - 49	3 794	9.5
20 - 24	654	...	50 - 54	990	3.6
25 - 29	977	...	55 - 59	355	1.3
30 - 34	1 011	...	60 - 64	165	..
35 - 39	860	...	65 +	91	..
40 - 44	439	...	Unknown - Inconnu	15 852	..
45 - 49	224	...	Dominican Republic - République dominicaine		
50 - 54	88	...	2009 (U)		
55 - 59	25	...	Total	117 634	...
60 - 64	7	..	0 - 19	2 190	...
65 +	5	..	20 - 24	18 681	...
Unknown - Inconnu	638		25 - 29	28 038	...
Barbados - Barbade			30 - 34	24 470	...
2007 (+C)			35 - 39	15 178	...
Total	3 418	...	40 - 44	7 964	...
0 - 19	95	...	45 - 49	3 808	...
20 - 24	564	...	50 - 54	1 816	...
25 - 29	745	...	55 - 59	793	...

Naissances vivantes et taux de natalité selon l'âge du père : dernière année disponible, 2000 - 2009 (continued - suite)

Continent, country or area, year, code and age of father (in years) / Continent, pays ou zone, année, code et âge du père (en années)	Number - Nombre Both sexes Les deux sexes	Rate Taux	Continent, country or area, year, code and age of father (in years) / Continent, pays ou zone, année, code et âge du père (en années)	Number - Nombre Both sexes Les deux sexes	Rate Taux
AMERICA, NORTH - AMÉRIQUE DU NORD			**AMERICA, NORTH - AMÉRIQUE DU NORD**		
Dominican Republic - République dominicaine			Jamaica - Jamaïque[5]		
2009 (U)			2006 (C)		
60 - 64	326	..	35 - 39	3 635	...
65 +	196	..	40 - 44	2 166	...
Unknown - Inconnu	14 174	..	45 - 49	986	...
El Salvador			50 - 54	373	...
2007 (C)			55 - 59	131	..
Total	106 471	71.6	60 - 64	53	..
12 - 14	1 067		65 +	37	..
15 - 19	22 272	74.8	Unknown - Inconnu	20 356	..
20 - 24	30 060	132.2	Martinique[2]		
25 - 29	25 793	124.9	2007 (C)		
30 - 34	16 619	93.4	Total	5 317	47.3
35 - 39	7 903	50.6	0 - 19	98	6.2
40 - 44	2 312	17.5	20 - 24	710	60.7
45 - 49	173	1.6	25 - 29	1 043	119.9
50 +	22	♦0.1	30 - 34	1 173	111.7
Unknown - Inconnu	250	..	35 - 39	1 293	95.6
Greenland - Groenland			40 - 44	702	46.1
2008 (C)			45 - 49	235	16.2
Total	834	...	50 - 54	42	3.5
0 - 19	25	...	55 - 59	16	♦1.5
20 - 24	109	...	60 +	3	..
25 - 29	169	...	Mexico - Mexique[6]		
30 - 34	150	...	2006 (+U)		
35 - 39	112	...	Total	2 151 204	...
40 - 44	91	...	0 - 19	120 550	...
45 - 49	35	...	20 - 24	466 280	...
50 - 54	9	...	25 - 29	526 918	...
55 - 59	1	...	30 - 34	433 030	...
60 +	-		35 - 39	238 858	...
Unknown - Inconnu	133	..	40 - 44	106 166	...
Guadeloupe[2]			45 - 49	42 502	...
2003 (C)			50 +	30 568	...
Total	7 047	55.0	Unknown - Inconnu	186 332	...
0 - 19	112	6.4	Panama		
20 - 24	809	55.5	2009 (C)		
25 - 29	1 303	103.0	Total	68 364	64.3
30 - 34	1 950	125.6	0 - 19	3 152	22.5
35 - 39	1 698	102.0	20 - 24	13 323	98.6
40 - 44	877	53.1	25 - 29	15 342	122.7
45 - 49	211	15.9	30 - 34	12 699	106.6
50 - 54	59	5.1	35 - 39	8 870	76.4
55 - 59	20	♦2.1	40 - 44	4 514	43.3
60 +	8	..	45 - 49	2 019	23.1
Guatemala			50 - 54	860	12.1
2006 (C)			55 - 59	377	6.5
Total	368 399	...	60 - 64	200	..
0 - 19	17 875	...	65 +	126	..
20 - 24	77 239	...	Unknown - Inconnu	6 882	..
25 - 29	84 377	...	Puerto Rico - Porto Rico		
30 - 34	59 956	...	2008 (C)		
35 - 39	38 741	...	Total	45 675	39.5
40 - 44	23 591	...	0 - 19	3 200	21.8
45 - 49	11 709	...	20 - 24	11 615	86.9
50 - 54	4 785	...	25 - 29	12 284	90.2
55 - 59	2 150	...	30 - 34	8 969	70.4
60 - 64	941	..	35 - 39	4 753	38.3
65 +	862	..	40 - 44	2 060	16.9
Unknown - Inconnu	46 173	...	45 - 49	752	6.4
Jamaica - Jamaïque[5]			50 - 54	284	2.6
2006 (C)			55 - 59	142	1.4
Total	42 399	...	60 - 64	63	..
0 - 19	496	...	65 +	27	..
20 - 24	3 756	...	Unknown - Inconnu	1 526	..
25 - 29	5 341	...			
30 - 34	5 069	...			

Continent, country or area, year, code and age of father (in years) / Continent, pays ou zone, année, code et âge du père (en années)	Number - Nombre — Both sexes Les deux sexes	Rate Taux
AMERICA, NORTH - AMÉRIQUE DU NORD		
Trinidad and Tobago - Trinité-et-Tobago		
2006 (C)		
Total	18 090	...
0 - 19	400	...
20 - 24	3 291	...
25 - 29	4 889	...
30 - 34	4 079	...
35 - 39	2 713	...
40 - 44	1 491	...
45 - 49	616	...
50 - 54	248	...
55 - 59	87	...
60 +	45	..
Unknown - Inconnu	231	..
United States of America - États-Unis d'Amérique		
2008 (C)		
Total	4 247 694	44.7
0 - 19	142 862	15.1
20 - 24	615 796	66.0
25 - 29	960 144	102.0
30 - 34	948 291	110.7
35 - 39	616 630	67.8
40 - 44	250 629	27.1
45 - 49	84 963	8.7
50 - 54	24 459	2.7
55 +	10 308	1.3
Unknown - Inconnu	593 612	..
AMERICA, SOUTH - AMÉRIQUE DU SUD		
Chile - Chili		
2008 (C)		
Total	246 581	45.7
0 - 19	15 488	23.2
20 - 24	41 015	64.8
25 - 29	50 505	89.3
30 - 34	49 692	93.0
35 - 39	34 849	63.5
40 - 44	17 241	31.4
45 - 49	6 670	12.8
50 +	3 467	4.5
Unknown - Inconnu	27 654	
Colombia - Colombie		
2009* (U)		
Total	686 045	...
0 - 19	43 460	...
20 - 24	159 519	...
25 - 29	174 324	...
30 - 34	126 783	...
35 - 39	79 977	...
40 - 44	42 532	...
45 - 49	18 530	...
50 - 54	7 882	...
55 - 59	2 645	...
60 - 64	1 077	...
65 +	631	...
Unknown - Inconnu	28 685	...
French Guiana - Guyane française[2]		
2007 (C)		
Total	6 386	104.6
0 - 19	323	32.6
20 - 24	1 263	164.2
25 - 29	1 401	203.5
30 - 34	1 334	175.5
35 - 39	1 043	138.4
40 - 44	622	90.0

Continent, country or area, year, code and age of father (in years) / Continent, pays ou zone, année, code et âge du père (en années)	Number - Nombre — Both sexes Les deux sexes	Rate Taux
AMERICA, SOUTH - AMÉRIQUE DU SUD		
French Guiana - Guyane française[2]		
2007 (C)		
45 - 49	230	38.8
50 - 54	94	19.2
55 - 59	59	16.1
60 - 64	17	..
65 +	-	..
Uruguay		
2004 (C)		
Total	50 052	52.8
0 - 19	805	10.3
20 - 24	4 203	57.8
25 - 29	7 179	100.3
30 - 34	7 629	118.5
35 - 39	5 142	87.4
40 - 44	2 622	43.3
45 - 49	978	17.9
50 - 54	420	8.5
55 - 59	117	2.8
60 - 64	43	..
65 +	32	..
Unknown - Inconnu	20 882	..
Venezuela (Bolivarian Republic of) - Venezuela (République bolivarienne du)		
2007 (C)		
Total	615 371	72.6
0 - 19	37 015	32.7
20 - 24	124 442	117.3
25 - 29	130 575	136.4
30 - 34	96 162	114.7
35 - 39	60 376	79.4
40 - 44	32 010	45.3
45 - 49	14 774	24.4
50 - 54	6 837	13.5
55 - 59	2 888	7.0
60 - 64	977	..
65 +	525	..
Unknown - Inconnu	108 790	..
ASIA - ASIE		
Armenia - Arménie[7]		
2000 (C)		
Total	29 287	25.2
0 - 19	3 774	20.0
20 - 24	13 933	84.7
25 - 29	6 776	46.5
30 - 34	2 894	21.3
35 - 39	1 503	10.1
40 - 44	380	2.6
45 - 49	16	♦0.1
55 - 59	11	♦0.2
Azerbaijan - Azerbaïdjan[8]		
2009 (+C)		
Total	147 137	49.2
0 - 19	721	1.5
20 - 24	25 555	54.8
25 - 29	55 903	143.5
30 - 34	38 020	120.4
35 - 39	17 107	58.3
40 - 44	6 986	22.2
45 - 49	1 995	6.1
50 - 54	540	2.1
55 +	310	1.9

Continent, country or area, year, code and age of father (in years) / Continent, pays ou zone, année, code et âge du père (en années)	Number - Nombre — Both sexes Les deux sexes	Rate Taux
ASIA - ASIE		
Bahrain - Bahreïn		
2007 (C)		
Total	16 062	32.1
0 - 14	-	..
15 - 19	19	♦0.5
20 - 24	930	16.1
25 - 29	3 652	39.9
30 - 34	4 486	52.6
35 - 39	3 447	46.4
40 - 44	2 200	37.8
45 - 49	911	19.5
50 - 54	255	7.8
55 - 59	89	5.0
60 - 64	35	..
65 +	30	..
Unknown - Inconnu	8	..
Brunei Darussalam - Brunéi Darussalam		
2008 (+C)		
Total	6 424	...
0 - 19	23	...
20 - 24	466	...
25 - 29	1 612	...
30 - 34	1 733	...
35 - 39	1 125	...
40 - 44	555	...
45 - 49	212	...
50 - 54	57	...
55 +	23	...
Unknown - Inconnu	618	..
China, Hong Kong SAR - Chine, Hong Kong RAS		
2009 (C)		
Total	82 095	36.3
0 - 19	189	0.9
20 - 24	3 204	15.1
25 - 29	12 545	56.1
30 - 34	23 710	108.5
35 - 39	23 246	99.8
40 - 44	10 329	40.4
45 - 49	4 005	13.0
50 - 54	1 447	5.0
55 - 59	506	2.2
60 - 64	166	..
65 +	101	..
Unknown - Inconnu	2 647	..
China, Macao SAR - Chine, Macao RAS		
2009 (C)		
Total	4 764	23.9
0 - 19	14	♦0.7
20 - 24	425	17.0
25 - 29	1 103	54.5
30 - 34	1 284	66.1
35 - 39	973	45.7
40 - 44	471	22.7
45 - 49	263	9.9
50 - 54	107	4.1
55 - 59	42	2.5
60 - 64	13	..
65 +	5	..
Unknown - Inconnu	64	..
Cyprus - Chypre[9]		
2008 (C)		
Total	9 205	35.8
0 - 19	39	1.4
20 - 24	551	17.9
25 - 29	2 365	69.5
30 - 34	3 002	100.8
35 - 39	1 892	67.8
ASIA - ASIE		
Cyprus - Chypre[9]		
2008 (C)		
40 - 44	820	30.8
45 - 49	298	10.5
50 +	140	2.9
Unknown - Inconnu	98	..
Israel - Israël[10]		
2009 (C)		
Total	161 042	74.3
0 - 19	352	1.2
20 - 24	13 169	47.4
25 - 29	35 759	132.5
30 - 34	50 299	194.4
35 - 39	34 314	145.4
40 - 44	13 691	68.8
45 - 49	3 785	20.6
50 - 54	914	5.2
55 - 59	277	1.6
60 - 64	109	..
65 +	72	..
Unknown - Inconnu	8 301	..
Japan - Japon[11]		
2009 (C)		
Total	1 047 175	28.7
0 - 19	4 801	1.5
20 - 24	74 218	20.7
25 - 29	242 773	63.1
30 - 34	363 613	82.4
35 - 39	251 812	51.5
40 - 44	83 197	19.3
45 - 49	19 696	5.0
50 - 54	4 845	1.2
55 - 59	1 562	0.3
60 - 64	521	..
65 +	132	..
Unknown - Inconnu	5	..
Kazakhstan[12]		
2006 (C)		
Total	301 756	61.4
0 - 19	2 897	4.2
20 - 24	46 772	73.1
25 - 29	82 596	152.2
30 - 34	66 344	134.3
35 - 39	41 180	90.8
40 - 44	17 594	38.6
45 - 49	4 336	10.0
50 - 54	873	2.7
55 - 59	296	1.2
60 - 64	74	..
65 +	74	..
Unknown - Inconnu	38 720	..
Kyrgyzstan - Kirghizstan		
2009 (C)		
Total	135 494	80.4
0 - 19	614	2.3
20 - 24	18 599	72.8
25 - 29	39 991	200.4
30 - 34	29 285	177.5
35 - 39	17 642	118.6
40 - 44	8 158	60.0
45 - 49	2 492	19.3
50 - 54	564	5.7
55 - 59	171	2.6
60 - 64	60	..
65 +	49	..
Unknown - Inconnu	17 869	..

Continent, country or area, year, code and age of father (in years) Continent, pays ou zone, année, code et âge du père (en années)	Number - Nombre Both sexes Les deux sexes	Rate Taux	Continent, country or area, year, code and age of father (in years) Continent, pays ou zone, année, code et âge du père (en années)	Number - Nombre Both sexes Les deux sexes	Rate Taux
ASIA - ASIE			**ASIA - ASIE**		
Malaysia - Malaisie			**Republic of Korea - République de Corée**[14]		
2008 (C)			2009 (C)		
Total	487 346	56.6	50 - 54	961	0.5
0 - 19	1 994	1.6	55 - 59	189	0.1
20 - 24	31 222	26.1	60 - 64	47	..
25 - 29	114 869	105.6	65 +	12	..
30 - 34	135 909	141.5	Unknown - Inconnu	4 142	..
35 - 39	98 002	108.8	**Singapore - Singapour**		
40 - 44	51 441	60.7	2009 (C)		
45 - 49	19 202	25.6	Total	39 570	31.1
50 - 54	5 638	8.9	0 - 19	159	1.2
55 - 59	1 644	3.4	20 - 24	1 113	9.3
60 - 64	488	..	25 - 29	6 092	46.9
65 +	248	..	30 - 34	13 583	96.6
Unknown - Inconnu	26 689	..	35 - 39	11 737	76.8
Oman[13]			40 - 44	4 365	28.4
2009 (U)			45 - 49	1 368	8.5
Total	64 734	...	50 - 54	391	2.7
0 - 19	71	...	55 - 59	123	1.0
20 - 24	4 300	...	60 - 64	38	..
25 - 29	17 262	...	65 +	5	..
30 - 34	17 807	...	Unknown - Inconnu	596	..
35 - 39	11 086	...			
40 - 44	5 820	...	**EUROPE**		
45 - 49	3 180	...			
50 - 54	1 173	...	**Åland Islands - Îles d'Åland**[7]		
55 - 59	556	...	2006 (C)		
60 - 64	318	..	Total	120	15.0
65 +	387	..	0 - 19	-	-
Unknown - Inconnu	2 774	..	20 - 24	4	♦6.0
Philippines			25 - 29	13	♦17.1
2007 (C)			30 - 34	38	43.4
Total	1 749 878	...	35 - 39	36	38.7
0 - 19	36 203	...	40 - 44	23	♦23.0
20 - 24	306 531	...	45 - 49	2	♦2.2
25 - 29	458 949	...	50 - 54	3	♦3.1
30 - 34	372 744	...	55 - 59	1	♦1.0
35 - 39	249 378	...	60 - 64	-	..
40 - 44	128 315	...	65 +	-	..
45 - 49	52 500	...	Unknown - Inconnu	-	..
50 - 54	16 619	...	**Albania - Albanie**		
55 - 59	5 847	...	2004 (C)		
60 - 64	2 079	...	Total	43 022	45.5
65 +	1 716	...	0 - 19	293	1.9
Unknown - Inconnu	118 997	..	20 - 24	2 812	22.3
Qatar			25 - 29	11 631	113.3
2009 (C)			30 - 34	14 648	148.4
Total	18 351	16.2	35 - 39	8 622	85.5
0 - 19	22	♦0.6	40 - 44	3 353	30.6
20 - 24	966	5.0	45 - 49	835	8.5
25 - 29	3 655	14.1	50 - 54	180	2.3
30 - 34	5 248	26.3	55 - 59	68	1.1
35 - 39	4 272	26.2	60 - 64	36	..
40 - 44	2 409	20.4	Unknown - Inconnu	544	..
45 - 49	1 133	14.3	**Austria - Autriche**[7]		
50 +	637	8.1	2009 (C)		
Unknown - Inconnu	9	..	Total	46 356	17.8
Republic of Korea - République de Corée[14]			0 - 19	128	0.5
2009 (C)			20 - 24	2 744	10.4
Total	444 849	26.1	25 - 29	9 598	34.5
0 - 19	459	0.3	30 - 34	14 361	53.8
20 - 24	5 812	3.6	35 - 39	11 511	37.6
25 - 29	77 502	39.2	40 - 44	5 589	15.5
30 - 34	195 345	99.8	45 - 49	1 757	5.0
35 - 39	126 166	57.0	50 - 54	482	1.7
40 - 44	28 816	13.8	55 - 59	117	0.5
45 - 49	5 398	2.5			

Continent, country or area, year, code and age of father (in years) / Continent, pays ou zone, année, code et âge du père (en années)	Number - Nombre — Both sexes Les deux sexes	Rate Taux
EUROPE		
Austria - Autriche[7]		
2009 (C)		
60 - 64	48	..
65 +	21	..
Belarus - Bélarus[7]		
2009 (C)		
Total	87 497	27.5
0 - 19	927	2.7
20 - 24	19 171	45.3
25 - 29	32 241	80.9
30 - 34	20 996	60.3
35 - 39	9 764	29.6
40 - 44	3 174	9.6
45 - 49	930	2.4
50 - 54	222	0.6
55 +	72	0.3
Belgium - Belgique		
2007 (C)		
Total	124 095	38.3
0 - 19	646	2.1
20 - 24	7 487	24.7
25 - 29	30 246	93.5
30 - 34	40 197	122.5
35 - 39	24 371	66.8
40 - 44	9 727	24.9
45 - 49	3 226	8.5
50 - 54	1 024	2.9
55 - 59	356	1.1
60 - 64	94	..
65 +	48	..
Unknown - Inconnu	6 673	..
Bulgaria - Bulgarie		
2009 (C)		
Total	80 956	34.1
0 - 19	1 153	6.4
20 - 24	7 892	36.2
25 - 29	18 363	80.5
30 - 34	21 451	88.2
35 - 39	11 852	51.5
40 - 44	3 873	18.3
45 - 49	1 191	5.6
50 - 54	323	1.5
55 - 59	101	0.5
60 - 64	33	..
65 +	8	..
Unknown - Inconnu	14 716	..
Croatia - Croatie		
2009 (C)		
Total	44 577	32.5
0 - 19	207	1.6
20 - 24	3 788	26.8
25 - 29	11 811	76.1
30 - 34	14 547	96.6
35 - 39	8 443	58.9
40 - 44	3 284	21.9
45 - 49	892	5.8
50 - 54	239	1.5
55 - 59	52	0.4
60 - 64	18	..
65 +	7	..
Unknown - Inconnu	1 289	..
Czech Republic - République tchèque		
2009 (C)		
Total	118 348	34.6
0 - 19	522	1.8
20 - 24	5 924	17.8
25 - 29	24 025	65.8

Continent, country or area, year, code and age of father (in years) / Continent, pays ou zone, année, code et âge du père (en années)	Number - Nombre — Both sexes Les deux sexes	Rate Taux
EUROPE		
Czech Republic - République tchèque		
2009 (C)		
30 - 34	43 608	99.4
35 - 39	22 836	59.2
40 - 44	7 440	22.5
45 - 49	2 489	8.0
50 - 54	884	2.7
55 - 59	316	0.9
60 - 64	103	..
65 +	25	..
Unknown - Inconnu	10 176	..
Denmark - Danemark[15]		
2009 (C)		
Total	62 818	38.3
0 - 19	27	0.3
20 - 24	849	9.0
25 - 29	6 253	69.1
30 - 34	14 117	136.2
35 - 39	9 894	87.9
40 - 44	3 726	30.2
45 - 49	1 047	9.1
50 - 54	234	2.2
55 - 59	103	1.0
60 - 64	35	..
65 +	9	..
Unknown - Inconnu	26 524	..
Estonia - Estonie		
2009 (C)		
Total	15 763	38.6
0 - 19	159	3.9
20 - 24	1 831	36.4
25 - 29	4 132	87.3
30 - 34	4 188	97.0
35 - 39	2 677	62.9
40 - 44	1 088	28.1
45 - 49	363	8.8
50 - 54	115	2.9
55 - 59	30	0.9
60 - 64	6	..
65 +	4	..
Unknown - Inconnu	1 170	..
Finland - Finlande[16]		
2009 (C)		
Total	60 163	37.7
0 - 19	64	0.6
20 - 24	1 889	19.3
25 - 29	8 036	77.6
30 - 34	13 101	128.9
35 - 39	7 783	83.0
40 - 44	3 328	30.7
45 - 49	1 012	9.0
50 - 54	305	2.7
55 - 59	67	0.6
60 - 64	16	..
65 +	4	..
Unknown - Inconnu	24 558	..
France[17]		
2009 (C)		
Total	793 420	43.3
0 - 19	3 852	2.0
20 - 24	54 701	27.1
25 - 29	183 121	93.1
30 - 34	253 449	132.6
35 - 39	182 243	84.1
40 - 44	76 509	35.5
45 - 49	26 336	12.4
50 - 54	8 759	4.3

Continent, country or area, year, code and age of father (in years) / Continent, pays ou zone, année, code et âge du père (en années)	Number - Nombre Both sexes Les deux sexes	Rate Taux	Continent, country or area, year, code and age of father (in years) / Continent, pays ou zone, année, code et âge du père (en années)	Number - Nombre Both sexes Les deux sexes	Rate Taux
EUROPE			**EUROPE**		
France[17]			Ireland - Irlande		
2009 (C)			2006 (+C)		
55 - 59	3 135	1.6	Total	64 237	46.8
60 - 64	1 201	..	0 - 19	714	5.1
65 +	114	..	20 - 24	4 382	26.9
Unknown - Inconnu	-	..	25 - 29	10 351	57.1
Germany - Allemagne			30 - 34	19 695	121.1
2007 (C)			35 - 39	16 702	111.2
Total	684 862	26.9	40 - 44	6 268	45.2
0 - 19	3 217	1.5	45 - 49	1 585	12.4
20 - 24	40 602	18.0	50 - 54	374	3.2
25 - 29	126 408	55.1	55 - 59	119	1.1
30 - 34	184 082	83.5	60 - 64	27	..
35 - 39	167 942	57.7	65 +	6	..
40 - 44	76 017	22.5	Unknown - Inconnu	4 014	..
45 - 49	20 424	6.6	Italy - Italie		
50 - 54	5 485	2.1	2008 (+C)		
55 - 59	1 843	0.8	Total	576 659	32.0
60 - 64	635	..	0 - 19	1 855	1.3
65 +	292	..	20 - 24	17 582	11.9
Unknown - Inconnu	57 915	..	25 - 29	70 376	41.9
Greece - Grèce			30 - 34	169 196	81.8
2009 (C)			35 - 39	169 672	75.2
Total	117 933	33.7	40 - 44	79 531	34.5
0 - 19	234	0.8	45 - 49	21 421	10.5
20 - 24	2 867	9.3	50 - 54	5 121	2.9
25 - 29	16 722	43.3	55 - 59	1 067	0.6
30 - 34	37 981	90.3	60 - 64	-	..
35 - 39	32 007	75.9	65 +	-	..
40 - 44	14 737	35.7	Unknown - Inconnu	40 838	..
45 - 49	4 281	11.5	Latvia - Lettonie		
50 - 54	1 041	2.9	2009 (C)		
55 - 59	230	0.7	Total	21 677	30.7
60 - 64	68	..	0 - 19	198	2.8
65 +	16	..	20 - 24	2 841	32.5
Unknown - Inconnu	7 749	..	25 - 29	5 952	73.6
Hungary - Hongrie			30 - 34	5 451	73.9
2009 (C)			35 - 39	3 401	46.0
Total	96 442	30.8	40 - 44	1 541	22.0
0 - 19	998	3.6	45 - 49	516	6.9
20 - 24	5 644	19.1	50 - 54	202	2.9
25 - 29	17 719	54.4	55 - 59	55	1.0
30 - 34	33 852	86.4	60 - 64	19	..
35 - 39	18 399	54.9	65 +	8	..
40 - 44	6 622	22.2	Unknown - Inconnu	1 493	..
45 - 49	1 919	7.2	Lithuania - Lituanie		
50 - 54	717	2.3	2009 (C)		
55 - 59	245	0.8	Total	36 682	35.0
60 - 64	68	..	0 - 19	333	2.8
65 +	23	..	20 - 24	4 460	34.7
Unknown - Inconnu	10 236	..	25 - 29	10 979	96.0
Iceland - Islande			30 - 34	10 187	99.5
2009 (C)			35 - 39	5 420	49.6
Total	5 027	48.9	40 - 44	1 950	17.6
0 - 19	53	4.4	45 - 49	663	5.7
20 - 24	510	43.8	50 - 54	174	1.8
25 - 29	1 412	110.9	55 - 59	49	0.6
30 - 34	1 493	128.0	60 - 64	15	..
35 - 39	960	84.7	65 +	4	..
40 - 44	376	34.2	Unknown - Inconnu	2 448	..
45 - 49	109	9.6	Luxembourg		
50 - 54	28	♦2.6	2009 (C)		
55 - 59	17	♦1.9	Total	5 638	35.3
60 - 64	2	..	0 - 19	21	♦1.4
65 +	2	..	20 - 24	305	20.9
Unknown - Inconnu	65	..	25 - 29	1 022	60.9
			30 - 34	1 865	103.7

11. Live births and live birth rates by age of father: latest available year, 2000 - 2009
Naissances vivantes et taux de natalité selon l'âge du père : dernière année disponible, 2000 - 2009 (continued - suite)

Continent, country or area, year, code and age of father (in years) / Continent, pays ou zone, année, code et âge du père (en années)	Number - Nombre Both sexes Les deux sexes	Rate Taux
EUROPE		
Luxembourg		
2009 (C)		
35 - 39	1 393	72.4
40 - 44	614	29.3
45 - 49	191	9.7
50 - 54	51	3.0
55 - 59	22	♦1.5
60 - 64	6	..
65 +	-	..
Unknown - Inconnu	148	..
Malta - Malte		
2009 (C)		
Total	4 143	31.3
0 - 19	42	3.2
20 - 24	277	19.2
25 - 29	969	65.7
30 - 34	1 442	99.3
35 - 39	736	58.9
40 - 44	224	19.5
45 - 49	76	5.6
50 - 54	30	2.2
55 - 59	4	♦0.3
60 - 64	2	..
65 +	2	..
Unknown - Inconnu	339	..
Montenegro - Monténégro		
2009 (C)		
Total	8 642	43.2
0 - 19	32	1.5
20 - 24	616	27.3
25 - 29	2 011	90.0
30 - 34	2 268	113.7
35 - 39	1 574	85.9
40 - 44	800	43.7
45 - 49	287	14.9
50 - 54	89	4.6
55 - 59	23	♦1.3
60 - 64	1	..
65 +	6	..
Unknown - Inconnu	935	..
Norway - Norvège[18]		
2009 (C)		
Total	61 807	41.6
0 - 19	411	2.6
20 - 24	4 243	28.9
25 - 29	13 403	90.3
30 - 34	19 095	122.5
35 - 39	14 194	80.1
40 - 44	5 628	31.4
45 - 49	1 614	9.9
50 - 54	515	3.3
55 - 59	155	1.1
60 - 64	52	..
65 +	15	..
Unknown - Inconnu	2 482	..
Poland - Pologne		
2009 (C)		
Total	417 589	33.2
0 - 19	2 873	2.3
20 - 24	45 905	31.2
25 - 29	130 923	82.6
30 - 34	132 091	90.4
35 - 39	59 759	47.5
40 - 44	20 063	17.8
45 - 49	6 474	5.3
50 - 54	1 888	1.3
55 - 59	508	0.4

Continent, country or area, year, code and age of father (in years) / Continent, pays ou zone, année, code et âge du père (en années)	Number - Nombre Both sexes Les deux sexes	Rate Taux
EUROPE		
Poland - Pologne		
2009 (C)		
60 +	211	..
Unknown - Inconnu	16 894	..
Portugal[6]		
2009 (C)		
Total	99 491	30.6
0 - 19	1 319	4.6
20 - 24	8 239	26.3
25 - 29	21 050	56.2
30 - 34	33 818	81.0
35 - 39	21 802	54.1
40 - 44	8 183	21.5
45 - 49	2 381	6.4
50 - 54	746	2.2
55 - 59	268	0.9
60 - 64	65	..
65 +	20	..
Unknown - Inconnu	1 600	..
Republic of Moldova - République de Moldova[19]		
2009 (C)		
Total	40 803	33.7
0 - 19	409	2.9
20 - 24	8 307	50.5
25 - 29	12 912	90.4
30 - 34	8 841	73.2
35 - 39	4 308	41.0
40 - 44	1 524	15.2
45 - 49	400	3.4
50 - 54	114	1.0
55 - 59	37	0.4
60 - 64	9	..
65 +	6	..
Unknown - Inconnu	3 936	..
Romania - Roumanie		
2009 (C)		
Total	222 388	31.8
0 - 19	4 242	6.7
20 - 24	27 414	33.4
25 - 29	58 839	75.5
30 - 34	68 253	80.2
35 - 39	32 299	40.5
40 - 44	12 112	16.0
45 - 49	3 115	5.3
50 - 54	1 136	1.6
55 - 59	310	0.5
60 - 64	95	..
65 +	32	..
Unknown - Inconnu	14 541	..
San Marino - Saint-Marin		
2004 (+C)		
Total	306	33.1
0 - 24	7	♦4.8
25 - 29	46	46.8
30 - 34	116	92.4
35 - 39	85	61.4
40 - 44	37	28.5
45 - 49	14	♦13.3
60 +	1	♦0.5
Serbia - Serbie[20]		
2009 (+C)		
Total	70 299	31.1
0 - 19	451	2.3
20 - 24	5 789	26.8
25 - 29	17 771	77.9
30 - 34	20 960	91.5
35 - 39	11 178	52.5

Continent, country or area, year, code and age of father (in years) / Continent, pays ou zone, année, code et âge du père (en années)	Number - Nombre — Both sexes Les deux sexes	Rate Taux	Continent, country or area, year, code and age of father (in years) / Continent, pays ou zone, année, code et âge du père (en années)	Number - Nombre — Both sexes Les deux sexes	Rate Taux
EUROPE			**EUROPE**		
Serbia - Serbie[20]			Sweden - Suède		
2009 (+C)			2009 (C)		
40 - 44	3 887	18.8	65 +	44	..
45 - 49	1 228	5.6	Unknown - Inconnu	1 703	..
50 - 54	325	1.4	Switzerland - Suisse[7]		
55 - 59	111	0.5	2009 (C)		
60 - 64	26	..	Total	64 266	26.5
65 +	7	..	0 - 19	13	♦0.1
Unknown - Inconnu	8 566	..	20 - 24	1 775	7.5
Slovakia - Slovaquie[7]			25 - 29	10 055	40.0
2009 (C)			30 - 34	20 250	77.7
Total	41 893	22.8	35 - 39	19 321	67.0
0 - 19	244	1.3	40 - 44	9 987	30.7
20 - 24	2 925	13.5	45 - 49	1 772	5.6
25 - 29	11 036	47.3	50 - 54	719	2.6
30 - 34	16 373	68.2	55 - 59	231	1.0
35 - 39	8 020	39.2	60 - 64	92	..
40 - 44	2 430	13.2	65 +	51	..
45 - 49	660	3.5	TFYR of Macedonia - L'ex-R. y. de Macédoine		
50 - 54	143	0.7	2009 (C)		
55 - 59	41	0.2	Total	23 684	34.5
60 - 64	11	..	0 - 19	179	2.4
65 +	10	..	20 - 24	2 496	31.6
Slovenia - Slovénie			25 - 29	7 202	91.3
2009 (C)			30 - 34	7 221	96.8
Total	21 856	32.1	35 - 39	3 506	49.9
0 - 19	62	1.1	40 - 44	1 158	16.3
20 - 24	1 041	15.1	45 - 49	362	5.2
25 - 29	5 353	68.3	50 - 54	65	1.0
30 - 34	8 184	100.9	55 - 59	18	♦0.3
35 - 39	4 630	60.9	60 - 64	5	..
40 - 44	1 605	20.5	65 +	3	..
45 - 49	431	5.5	Unknown - Inconnu	1 469	..
50 - 54	113	1.4	Ukraine[21]		
55 - 59	47	0.6	2008 (C)		
60 - 64	7	..	Total	510 589	34.8
65 +	3	..	0 - 19	6 720	4.6
Unknown - Inconnu	380	..	20 - 24	103 396	60.0
Spain - Espagne			25 - 29	150 517	98.3
2009 (C)			30 - 34	104 640	72.6
Total	494 997	33.6	35 - 39	52 324	38.8
0 - 19	3 444	3.0	40 - 44	18 330	13.6
20 - 24	22 533	16.8	45 - 49	6 084	4.1
25 - 29	71 339	40.9	50 - 54	1 637	1.3
30 - 34	169 731	82.4	55 +	698	0.6
35 - 39	145 680	73.3	Unknown - Inconnu	66 243	..
40 - 44	52 812	28.7	United Kingdom of Great Britain and Northern Ireland - Royaume-Uni de Grande-Bretagne et d'Irlande du Nord[22]		
45 - 49	14 272	8.6	2003 (C)		
50 - 54	3 916	2.7	Total	695 549	38.6
55 - 59	1 117	0.9	0 - 19	13 848	7.5
60 - 64	352	..	20 - 24	70 484	40.7
65 +	85	..	25 - 29	132 039	77.8
Unknown - Inconnu	9 716	..	30 - 34	206 797	101.9
Sweden - Suède			35 - 39	143 461	66.2
2009 (C)			40 - 44	55 851	27.6
Total	111 801	40.2	45 - 49	15 730	8.8
0 - 19	546	1.7	50 - 54	4 661	2.7
20 - 24	6 792	22.8	55 - 59	1 616	0.9
25 - 29	22 887	79.9	60 - 64	465	..
30 - 34	36 698	125.3	65 +	280	..
35 - 39	26 855	85.1	Unknown - Inconnu	50 317	..
40 - 44	11 158	33.2			
45 - 49	3 593	11.8			
50 - 54	1 072	3.7			
55 - 59	339	1.2			
60 - 64	114	..			

11. Live births and live birth rates by age of father: latest available year, 2000 - 2009
Naissances vivantes et taux de natalité selon l'âge du père : dernière année disponible, 2000 - 2009 (continued - suite)

Continent, country or area, year, code and age of father (in years) / Continent, pays ou zone, année, code et âge du père (en années)	Number - Nombre — Both sexes Les deux sexes	Rate Taux
OCEANIA - OCÉANIE		
Australia - Australie		
2009 (+C)		
Total	295 738	43.1
0 - 19	4 337	5.8
20 - 24	24 129	30.1
25 - 29	60 324	76.8
30 - 34	88 546	122.0
35 - 39	68 721	88.6
40 - 44	26 970	36.8
45 - 49	8 877	11.8
50 - 54	2 451	3.6
55 - 59	745	1.2
60 - 64	284	..
65 +	106	..
Unknown - Inconnu[23]	10 248	..
Fiji - Fidji		
2004 (+C)		
Total	17 189	65.6
0 - 19	45	1.3
20 - 24	1 677	52.6
25 - 29	4 265	151.0
30 - 34	3 706	144.1
35 - 39	2 382	99.7
40 - 44	1 242	57.2
45 - 49	403	21.6
50 - 54	106	6.9
55 - 59	44	3.7
60 +	19	..
Unknown - Inconnu	3 300	..
Guam[24]		
2004 (C)		
Total	3 425	...
0 - 19	113	...
20 - 24	511	...
25 - 29	654	...
30 - 34	651	...
35 - 39	412	...
40 - 44	222	...
45 +	107	...
Unknown - Inconnu	757	..

Continent, country or area, year, code and age of father (in years) / Continent, pays ou zone, année, code et âge du père (en années)	Number - Nombre — Both sexes Les deux sexes	Rate Taux
OCEANIA - OCÉANIE		
New Caledonia - Nouvelle-Calédonie		
2007 (C)		
Total	4 093	54.0
0 - 19	27	2.9
20 - 24	354	44.7
25 - 29	741	104.2
30 - 34	993	126.3
35 - 39	761	97.6
40 - 44	348	47.7
45 - 49	121	20.0
50 - 54	35	6.9
55 - 59	17	♦3.6
60 +	5	..
Unknown - Inconnu	691	..
New Zealand - Nouvelle-Zélande		
2009 (+C)		
Total	62 543	48.1
0 - 19	2 251	14.4
20 - 24	7 525	51.4
25 - 29	12 051	92.0
30 - 34	15 865	130.3
35 - 39	13 099	94.8
40 - 44	5 756	40.6
45 - 49	1 828	12.4
50 - 54	524	4.0
55 - 59	152	1.3
60 - 64	42	..
65 +	14	..
Unknown - Inconnu	3 436	..
Palau - Palaos		
2003 (C)		
Total	312	...
0 - 19	6	...
20 - 24	50	...
25 - 29	56	...
30 - 34	76	...
35 - 39	59	...
40 - 44	29	...
45 - 49	17	...
50 - 54	9	...
Unknown - Inconnu	10	...

FOOTNOTES - NOTES

♦ Rates based on 30 or fewer births. - Taux basés sur 30 naissances ou moins.

* Provisional. - Données provisoires.

'Code' indicates the source of data, as follows:
C - Civil registration, estimated over 90% complete
U - Civil registration, estimated less than 90% complete
| - Other source, estimated reliable
+ - Data tabulated by date of registration rather than occurrence
... Information not available

Le 'Code' indique la source des données, comme suit :
C - Registres de l'état civil considérés complets à 90 p. 100 au moins
U - Registres de l'état civil qui ne sont pas considérés complets à 90 p. 100 au moins
| - Autre source, considérée fiable
+ - Données exploitées selon la date de l'enregistrement et non la date de l'événement
... Information non disponible

[1] Excludes the islands of St. Brandon and Agalega. - Non compris les îles St. Brandon et Agalega.

[2] Excluding live-born infants who died before their birth was registered. - Non compris les enfants nés vivants décédés avant l'enregistrement de leur naissance.

[3] Data refer to registered events only. - Les données ne concernent que les événements enregistrés.

[4] Including Canadian residents temporarily in the United States, but excluding United States residents temporarily in Canada. - Y compris les résidents canadiens se trouvant temporairement aux Etats-Unis, mais ne comprenant pas les résidents des Etats-Unis se trouvant temporairement au Canada.

[5] Data have not been adjusted for underenumeration. - Les données n'ont pas été ajustées pour compenser les lacunes du dénombrement.

[6] Data refer to births to resident mothers. - Ces données concernent les enfants nés de mères résidentes.

[7] Data refer to live births in wedlock only. - Les données ne concernent que les naissances vivantes de parents mariés.

[8] Excluding infants born alive of less than 28 weeks' gestation, of less than 1 000 grams in weight and 35 centimeters in length, who die within seven days of birth. Excluding newborns registered by application of mothers. - Non compris les enfants nés vivants après moins de 28 semaines de gestations, pesant moins de 1 000 grammes, mesurant moins de 35 centimètres et décédés dans les sept jours qui ont suivi leur naissance. Exception faite des nouveau-nés qui ont été enregistrés à la demande des mères.

[9] Data refer to government controlled areas. - Les données se rapportent aux zones contrôlées par le Gouvernement.

[10] Including data for East Jerusalem and Israeli residents in certain other territories under occupation by Israeli military forces since June 1967. - Y compris les données pour Jérusalem-Est et les résidents israéliens dans certains autres territoires occupés depuis 1967 par les forces armées israéliennes.

[11] Data refer to Japanese nationals in Japan only. Data refer to live births in wedlock only. - Les données se raportent aux nationaux japonais au Japon seulement. Les données ne concernent que les naissances vivantes de parents mariés.

[12] Excluding infants born alive of less than 28 weeks' gestation, of less than 1 000 grams in weight and 35 centimeters in length, who die within seven days of birth. - Non compris les enfants nés vivants après moins de 28 semaines de gestations, pesant moins de 1 000 grammes, mesurant moins de 35 centimètres et décédés dans les sept jours qui ont suivi leur naissance.

[13] Data from Births and Deaths Notification System (Ministry of Health institutions and all other health care providers). - Les données proviennent du système de notification des naissances et des décès (établissements du Ministère de la santé et tous autres prestataires de soins de santé).

[14] Excluding alien armed forces, civilian aliens employed by armed forces, and foreign diplomatic personnel and their dependants. - Non compris les militaires étrangers, les civils étrangers employés par les forces armées ni le personnel diplomatique étranger et les membres de leur famille les accompagnant.

[15] Excluding Faeroe Islands and Greenland shown separately, if available. - Non compris les Iles Féroé et le Groenland, qui font l'objet de rubriques distinctes, si disponible.

[16] Excluding Åland Islands. - Non compris les Îles d'Åland.

[17] Including armed forces stationed outside the country. - Y compris les militaires nationaux hors du pays.

[18] Excluding Svalbard and Jan Mayen Islands shown separately, if available. - Non compris Svalbard et Jan Mayen qui font l'objet de rubriques distinctes, si disponible.

[19] Excluding Transnistria and the municipality of Bender. - Les données ne tiennent pas compte de l'information sur la Transnistria et la municipalité de Bender.

[20] Excluding data for Kosovo and Metohia. - Sans les données pour le Kosovo et Metohie.

[21] Data refer to births with weight 500g and more (if weight is unknown - with length 25 centimeters and more, or with gestation during 22 weeks or more). - Données concernant les nouveau-nés de 500 grammes ou plus (si le poids est inconnu – de 25 centimètres de long ou plus, ou après une grossesse de 22 semaines ou plus).

[22] Excluding births to non-resident mothers of Northern Ireland. Excluding Channel Islands (Guernsey and Jersey) and Isle of Man, shown separately, if available. Data tabulated by date of occurrence for England and Wales, and by date of registration for Northern Ireland and Scotland. - Les données ne tiennent pas compte des enfants nés de mères non résidentes en Irlande du Nord. Non compris les îles Anglo-Normandes (Guernesey et Jersey) et l'île de Man, qui font l'objet de rubriques distinctes, si disponible. Données exploitées selon la date de l'événement pour l'Angleterre et le pays de Galles, et selon la date de l'enregistrement pour l'Irlande du Nord et l'Ecosse.

[23] Data includes births born in wedlock for which age of father is unknown and births born out of wedlock not acknowledged by the father for which therefore age of father is unknown. - Les données se rapportent aux enfants légitimes pour lesquels l'âge du père n'est pas connu et aux naissances hors mariage non reconnues par le père et pour lesquelles l'âge du père n'est par conséquent pas connu.

[24] Including United States military personnel, their dependants and contract employees. - Y compris les militaires des Etats-Unis, les membres de leur famille les accompagnant et les agents contractuels des Etats-Unis.

11a. Live births and live birth rates by age of father: 2010
Naissances vivantes et taux de natalité selon l'âge du père : 2010

Continent, country or area, year, code and age of father (in years) / Continent, pays ou zone, année, code et âge du père (en années)	Number - Nombre	Rate Taux	Continent, country or area, year, code and age of father (in years) / Continent, pays ou zone, année, code et âge du père (en années)	Number - Nombre	Rate Taux
AMERICA, NORTH - AMÉRIQUE DU NORD			**AMERICA, NORTH - AMÉRIQUE DU NORD**		
Costa Rica			Costa Rica		
2010* (C)			2010* (C)		
Total	70 922	49.4	45 - 49	1 393	...
0 - 19	1 593	10.2	50 - 54	550	...
20 - 24	9 156	57.8	55 - 59	177	...
25 - 29	11 340	86.9	60 - 64	67	...
30 - 34	10 082	...	65 +	5 769	..
35 - 39	5 970	...	Unknown - Inconnu	21 676	..
40 - 44	3 149	...			

FOOTNOTES - NOTES

♦ Rates based on 30 or fewer births. - Taux basés sur 30 naissances ou moins.
* Provisional. - Données provisoires.

'Code' indicates the source of data, as follows:

C - Civil registration, estimated over 90% complete
U - Civil registration, estimated less than 90% complete
| - Other source, estimated reliable
+ - Data tabulated by date of registration rather than occurrence.
... Information not available

Le 'Code' indique la source des données, comme suit:

C - Registres de l'état civil considérés complets à 90 p. 100 au moins.
U - Registres de l'état civil qui ne sont pas considérés complets à 90 p. 100 au moins.
| - Autre source, considérée fiable.
+ - Données exploitées selon la date de l'enregistrement et non la date de l'événement.
... Information non disponible.

Table 12

Table 12 presents late foetal deaths and late foetal-death ratios by urban/rural residence for as many years as possible between 2006 and 2010.

Description of variables: Late foetal deaths are foetal deaths[1] of 28 or more completed weeks of gestation. Foetal deaths of unknown gestational age are included with those 28 or more weeks.

Statistics on the number of late foetal deaths are obtained from civil registers unless otherwise noted.

The urban/rural classification of late foetal deaths is as provided by each country or area; it is presumed to be based on the national census definitions of urban population that have been set forth at the end of the technical notes for table 6.

Ratio computation: Late foetal-death ratios are the annual number of late foetal deaths per 1 000 live births (as shown in table 9) in the same year. The live-birth base was adopted because it is assumed to be more comparable from one country or area to another than the sum of live births and foetal deaths.

Ratios by urban/rural residence are the annual number of late foetal deaths, in the appropriate urban or rural category, per 1 000 corresponding live births (as shown in table 9). These ratios are calculated by the Statistics Division of the United Nations.

Ratios presented in this table are limited to those for countries or areas and urban/rural areas having at least a total of 30 late foetal deaths in a given year.

Reliability of data: Each country or area is asked to indicate the estimated completeness of the late foetal deaths recorded in its civil register. These national assessments are indicated by the quality codes "C", "U" and "..." that appear in the first column of this table.

"C" indicates that the data are estimated to be virtually complete, that is, representing at least 90 per cent of the late foetal deaths occurring each year, while "U" indicates that data are estimated to be incomplete, that is, representing less than 90 per cent of the late foetal deaths occurring each year. The code "..." indicates that no information was provided regarding completeness.

Data from civil registers which are reported as incomplete or of unknown completeness (coded "U" or "...") are considered unreliable. They appear in italics in this table. Ratios are not computed for data so coded.

For more information about the quality of vital statistics data in general, see section 4.2 of the Technical Notes.

Limitations: Statistics on late foetal deaths are subject to the same qualifications as have been set forth for vital statistics in general and foetal-death statistics in particular as discussed in section 4 of the Technical Notes.

The reliability of the data is a very important factor. Of all vital statistics, the registration of foetal deaths is probably the most incomplete.

Variation in the definition of foetal deaths, and in particular late foetal deaths, also limits international comparability. The criterion of 28 or more completed weeks of gestation to distinguish late foetal deaths is not universally used; some countries or areas use different durations of gestation or other criteria such as size of the foetus. In addition, the difficulty of accurately determining gestational age further reduces comparability. However, to promote comparability, late foetal deaths shown in this table are restricted to those of at least 28 or more completed weeks of gestation. Wherever this is not possible, a footnote is provided.

Another factor introducing variation in the definition of late foetal deaths is the practice by some countries or areas of including in late foetal-death statistics infants who were born alive but died before the registration of the birth or within the first 24 hours of life, thus overestimating the total number of late foetal deaths. This has also the effect of inflating the late foetal-death ratios unduly by decreasing the birth denominator and increasing the foetal-death numerator. Statistics of this type are footnoted.

In addition, late foetal-death ratios are subject to the limitations of the data on live births with which they have been calculated. These have been set forth in the technical notes for table 9.

Regarding the computation of the ratios, it must be pointed out that when late foetal deaths and live births are both under registered, the resulting ratios may be of reasonable magnitude. For the countries or areas where live-birth registration is poorest, the late foetal-death ratios may be the largest, effectively masking the completeness of the base data. For this reason, possible variations in birth-registration completeness as well as the reported completeness of late foetal deaths must always be borne in mind in evaluating late foetal-death ratios.

In addition to the indirect effect of live-birth under-registration, late foetal-death ratios may be seriously affected by date-of-registration tabulation of live births. When the annual number of live births registered and reported fluctuates over a wide range due to changes in legislation or to special needs for proof of birth on the part of large segments of the population, then the late foetal-death ratios will also fluctuate, but inversely. Because of these effects, data for countries or areas known to tabulate live births by date of registration should be used with caution.

Finally, it may be noted that the counting of live-born infants as late foetal deaths, because they died before the registration of the birth or within the first 24 hours of life, has the effect of inflating the late foetal-death ratios unduly by decreasing the birth denominator and increasing the foetal-death numerator. This factor should not be overlooked in using data from this table.

The comparability of data by urban/rural residence is affected by the national definitions of urban and rural used in tabulating these data. It is assumed, in the absence of specific information to the contrary, that the definitions of urban and rural used in connection with the national population census were also used in the compilation of the vital statistics for each country or area. However, it cannot be excluded that, for a given country or area, different definitions of urban and rural are used for the vital statistics data and the population census data respectively. When known, the definitions of urban used in national population censuses are presented at the end of the technical notes for table 6. As discussed in detail in the technical notes for table 6, these definitions vary considerably from one country or area to another.

Urban/rural differentials in late foetal death ratios may also be affected by whether the late foetal deaths and live births have been tabulated in terms of place of occurrence or place of usual residence. This problem is discussed in more detail in section 4.1.4.1 of the Introduction.

Earlier data: Late foetal deaths and late foetal-death ratios have been shown in each issue of the Demographic Yearbook beginning with the 1951 issue. A special topic CD on natality published in 2001 presents the data for all available years from 1990 to 1998. For more information on specific topics, and years for which data are reported, readers should consult the Historical Index.

NOTES

[1] For definition, see section 4.1.1 of the Introduction.

Tableau 12

Le tableau 12 présente des données sur les morts fœtales tardives et les rapports de mortinatalité selon le lieu de résidence (zone urbaine ou rurale) pour le plus grand nombre d'années possible entre 2006 et 2010.

Description des variables : Par mort fœtale tardive, on entend le décès d'un fœtus[1] survenu après 28 semaines complètes de gestation au moins. Les morts fœtales pour lesquelles la durée de la période de gestation n'est pas connue sont comprises dans cette catégorie.

Sauf indication contraire, les statistiques du nombre de morts fœtales tardives sont établies sur la base des registres de l'état civil.

La classification des morts fœtales tardives selon le lieu de résidence (zone urbaine ou rurale) est celle qui a été communiquée par chaque pays ou zone ; on part du principe qu'elle repose sur les définitions de la population urbaine utilisées pour les recensements nationaux, telles qu'elles sont reproduites à la fin des notes techniques du tableau 6.

Calcul des rapports : les rapports de mortinatalité représentent le nombre annuel de morts fœtales tardives pour 1 000 naissances vivantes (telles qu'elles sont présentées au tableau 9) survenues pendant la même année. On a pris pour base de calcul les naissances vivantes parce que l'on pense qu'elle sont plus facilement comparables d'un pays ou d'une zone à l'autre que la somme des naissances vivantes et des morts fœtales.

Les rapports selon le lieu de résidence (zone urbaine ou rurale) représentent le nombre annuel de morts fœtales tardives, classées selon la catégorie urbaine ou rurale appropriée pour 1 000 naissances vivantes (telles qu'elles sont présentées au tableau 9) survenues parmi la population correspondante. Ces rapports ont été calculés par la Division de statistique de l'ONU.

Les rapports présentés dans le tableau 12 ne concernent que les pays ou zones où l'on a enregistré un total d'au moins 1 000 morts fœtales tardives pendant une année donnée.

Fiabilité des données : il a été demandé à chaque pays ou zone d'indiquer le degré estimatif de complétude des données sur les morts fœtales tardives figurant dans ses registres d'état civil. Ces évaluations nationales sont signalées par les codes de qualité "C", "U" et "..." qui apparaissent dans la deuxième colonne du tableau.

La lettre "C" indique que les données sont jugées à peu près complètes, c'est-à-dire qu'elles représentent au moins 90 p. 100 des morts fœtales tardives survenues chaque année ; la lettre "U" signifie que les données sont jugées incomplètes, c'est-à-dire qu'elles représentent moins de 90 p.100 des morts fœtales tardives survenues chaque année. Le code "..." indique qu'aucun renseignement n'a été communiqué quant à la complétude des données.

Les données provenant des registres de l'état civil qui sont déclarées incomplètes ou dont le degré de complétude n'est pas connu (code "U" ou "...") sont jugées douteuses. Elles apparaissent en italique dans le tableau ; les rapports, dans ces cas, n'ont pas été calculés.

Pour plus de précisions sur la qualité des données reposant sur les statistiques de l'état civil en général, voir la section 4.2 des Notes techniques.

Insuffisance des données : les statistiques des morts fœtales tardives appellent toutes les réserves qui ont été formulées à propos des statistiques de l'état civil en général et des statistiques concernant les morts fœtales en particulier (voir la section 4 des Notes techniques).

La fiabilité des données est un facteur très important. Les statistiques concernant les morts fœtales sont probablement les moins complètes de toutes les statistiques de l'état civil.

L'hétérogénéité des définitions de la mort fœtale et, en particulier, de la mort fœtale tardive nuit aussi à la comparabilité internationale des données. Le critère des 28 semaines complètes de gestation au moins n'est pas universellement utilisé ; certains pays ou zones retiennent des critères différents pour la durée de la période de gestation ou d'autres critères tels que la taille du fœtus. De surcroît, la comparabilité est rendue malaisée par le fait qu'il est difficile d'établir avec précision l'âge gestationnel. Pour faciliter les

comparaisons, les morts fœtales tardives considérées ici sont exclusivement celles qui sont survenues au terme de 28 semaines de gestation au moins. Les exceptions sont signalées en note.

Un autre facteur d'hétérogénéité dans la définition de la mort fœtale tardive est la pratique de certains pays ou zones qui consiste à inclure dans les statistiques des morts fœtales tardives les enfants nés vivants mais décédés avant l'enregistrement de leur naissance ou dans les 24 heures qui ont suivi la naissance, pratique qui conduit à surestimer le nombre total des morts fœtales tardives. Cela donne aussi des rapports de mortinatalité exagérés parce que le dénominateur (nombre de naissances) se trouve alors diminué et le numérateur (morts fœtales) augmenté. Quand pareil facteur a joué, cela a été signalé en note.

Les rapports de mortinatalité appellent en outre toutes les réserves qui ont été formulées à propos des statistiques des naissances vivantes qui ont servi à leur calcul (voir à ce sujet les notes techniques relatives au tableau 9).

En ce qui concerne le calcul des rapports, il convient de noter que, si l'enregistrement des morts fœtales tardives et celui des naissances vivantes sont loin d'être exhaustifs, les rapports de mortinatalité peuvent être raisonnables. C'est parfois pour les pays ou zones où l'enregistrement des naissances vivantes laisse le plus à désirer que les rapports de mortinatalité sont les plus élevés, ce qui masque le caractère incomplet des données de base. Aussi, pour porter un jugement sur la qualité des rapports de mortinatalité, il ne faut jamais oublier que la complétude de l'enregistrement des naissances comme celle de l'enregistrement des morts fœtales tardives peuvent varier sensiblement.

Hormis les effets indirects des lacunes de l'enregistrement des naissances vivantes, il arrive que les rapports de mortinatalité soient considérablement faussés lorsque l'exploitation des données relatives aux naissances se fait d'après la date de l'enregistrement. Si le nombre des naissances vivantes enregistrées vient à varier notablement d'une année à l'autre par suite de modifications de la législation ou parce que de très nombreuses personnes ont besoin de se procurer une attestation de naissance, les rapports de mortinatalité varient également, mais en sens inverse. Il convient donc d'utiliser avec prudence le données des pays ou zones où les statistiques sont établies d'après la date de l'enregistrement.

Enfin, on notera que l'inclusion parmi les morts fœtales tardives des décès d'enfants nés vivants qui sont décédés avant l'enregistrement de leur naissance ou dans les 24 heures qui ont suivi la naissance conduit à des rapports de mortinatalité exagérés parce que le dénominateur (nombre de naissances) se trouve alors diminué et le numérateur (morts fœtales) augmenté. Il importe de ne pas négliger ce facteur lorsque l'on utilise les données du tableau 12.

La comparabilité des données selon le lieu de résidence (zone urbaine ou rurale) peut être limitée par les définitions nationales des termes « urbain » et « rural » utilisées pour la mise en tableaux de ces données. En l'absence d'indications contraires, on a supposé que les mêmes définitions avaient servi pour le recensement national de la population et pour l'établissement des statistiques de l'état civil pour chaque pays ou zone. Toutefois, il n'est pas exclu que, pour une zone ou un pays donné, des définitions différentes aient été retenues. Les définitions du terme « urbain » utilisées pour les recensements nationaux de population ont été présentées à la fin des notes techniques du tableau 6 lorsqu'elles étaient connues. Comme on l'a précisé dans les notes techniques relatives au tableau 6, ces définitions varient considérablement d'un pays ou d'une zone à l'autre.

La différence entre les rapports de mortinatalité pour les zones urbaines et rurales pourra aussi être faussée selon que les morts fœtales tardives et les naissances vivantes auront été classées d'après le lieu de l'événement ou le lieu de résidence habituel. Ce problème est examiné plus en détail à la section 4.1.4.1 des Notes techniques.

Données publiées antérieurement : les éditions de l'*Annuaire démographique* parues à partir de 1951 contiennent des statistiques concernant les morts fœtales tardives et les rapports de mortinatalité. Un CD-ROM sur la natalité paru en 2001 présente les données pour toutes les années disponibles de 1990 à 1998. Pour plus de précisions concernant les années et les sujets pour lesquels des données ont été publiées, se reporter à l'index.

NOTE

[1] Pour la définition, voir la section 4.1.1 de l'Introduction.

12. Late foetal deaths and late foetal death ratios, by urban/rural residence: 2006 - 2010
Morts foetales tardives et rapports de mortinatalité, selon la résidence, urbaine/rurale : 2006 - 2010

Continent, country or area, and urban/rural residence / Continent, pays ou zone et résidence, urbaine/rurale	Code	Number - Nombre					Ratio - Rapport				
		2006	2007	2008	2009	2010	2006	2007	2008	2009	2010
AFRICA - AFRIQUE											
Egypt - Égypte											
Total	+U	4 557	4 468	4 105	4 039	...	...	...	...	...	...
Urban - Urbaine	+U	3 869	3 895	3 495	3 314	...	...	...	...	...	...
Rural - Rurale	+U	688	573	610	725	...	...	...	...	...	...
Mauritius - Maurice[1]											
Total	+C	147	172	165	138	103	8.4	10.1	10.1	9.0	6.9
Urban - Urbaine	+C	49	59	65	51	...	7.3	9.1	10.3	8.7	...
Rural - Rurale	+C	98	113	100	87	...	9.0	10.7	9.9	9.2	...
Réunion											
Total	C	178	194	...	...	...	12.3	13.1	...	...	...
Seychelles											
Total	+C	7	...	...	...	...	...	...	...	...	...
South Africa - Afrique du Sud											
Total	...	14 375	14 222	14 626	...	...	...	...	...	...	...
Tunisia - Tunisie											
Total	U	1 576	1 580	1 582	...	...	...	...	...	...	...
AMERICA, NORTH - AMÉRIQUE DU NORD											
Bahamas											
Total	C	94	119	...	...	...	17.7	20.3	...	...	...
Bermuda - Bermudes											
Total	C	-	...	...	...	...	...	...	...	...	...
Canada[2]											
Total	C	1 078	1 172	1 170	...	...	3.0	3.2	3.1	...	...
Costa Rica											
Total	C	436	345	400	409	*389	6.1	4.7	5.3	5.5	*5.5
Urban - Urbaine	C	183	143	180	181	*169	6.2	5.0	6.2	6.4	*6.5
Rural - Rurale	C	253	202	220	228	*220	6.1	4.6	4.7	4.9	*4.9
Cuba[3]											
Total	C	1 438	1 395	1 513	1 451	...	12.9	12.4	12.3	11.2	...
El Salvador											
Total	C	378	369	412	...	...	3.5	3.5	3.7	...	...
Urban - Urbaine	C	348	349	...	...	...	4.9	5.1	...	...	...
Rural - Rurale	C	30	20	...	...	...	0.8	...	...	...	...
Greenland - Groenland											
Total	C	8	3	5	...	...	...	...	...	...	...
Guatemala											
Total	C	2 980	...	...	...	...	8.1	...	...	...	...
Martinique											
Total	C	102	98	...	...	...	19.0	18.4	...	...	...
Urban - Urbaine	C	94	87	...	...	...	19.3	18.0	...	...	...
Rural - Rurale	C	8	11	...	...	...	...	...	...	...	...
Mexico - Mexique[4]											
Total	+U	12 812	12 325	11 929	*11 459	...	...	...	...	...	...
Urban - Urbaine[5]	+U	9 584	...	8 822	*8 451	...	...	...	...	...	...
Rural - Rurale[5]	+U	3 098	...	2 911	*2 830	...	...	...	...	...	...
Panama											
Total	U	394	415	449	369	...	...	...	...	...	...
Puerto Rico - Porto Rico											
Total	C	205	483	460	...	...	4.2	10.3	10.1	...	...
Urban - Urbaine[5]	C	...	...	273	...	...	...	...	11.4	...	...
Rural - Rurale[5]	C	...	...	179	...	...	...	...	8.2	...	...
Saint Vincent and the Grenadines - Saint-Vincent-et-les Grenadines											
Total	+C	24	20	...	...	...	...	...	...	...	...
Trinidad and Tobago - Trinité-et-Tobago											
Total	C	233	...	...	...	...	12.9	...	...	...	...
Turks and Caicos Islands - Îles Turques et Caïques											
Total	C	2	7	7	...	...	...	...	...	...	...

Continent, country or area, and urban/rural residence / Continent, pays ou zone et résidence, urbaine/rurale	Co-de	Number - Nombre					Ratio - Rapport				
		2006	2007	2008	2009	2010	2006	2007	2008	2009	2010
AMERICA, SOUTH - AMÉRIQUE DU SUD											
Argentina - Argentine											
Total	C	4 983	4 833	5 167	5 100	...	7.2	6.9	6.9	6.8	...
Brazil - Brésil[6]											
Total	U	25 564	23 648	23 868	23 580	...	...	...	...	...	...
Chile - Chili[7]											
Total	C	2 124	2 165	2 167	...	...	9.2	9.0	8.8	...	...
Urban - Urbaine	C	1 980	2 072	1 951	...	...	9.5	9.5	8.6	...	...
Rural - Rurale	C	144	93	216	...	...	6.4	4.0	10.6	...	...
Colombia - Colombie[8]											
Total	...	11 958	12 675	12 466							
Urban - Urbaine[5]	...	9 067	9 675	9 667	...						
Rural - Rurale[5]	...	2 246	2 259	2 223	...						
Total	U	...	...	...	*11 137	...	...	...	...	...	...
Urban - Urbaine[5]	U	...	...	...	*8 548	...	...	...	...	...	...
Rural - Rurale[5]	U	...	...	...	*2 216	...	...	...	...	...	...
Ecuador - Équateur[9]											
Total	...	1 499	1 424	1 310	1 295	...	...	...	...	...	...
French Guiana - Guyane française											
Total	C	66	83	...	...	...	10.5	13.0	...	...	...
Urban - Urbaine	C	53	69	...	...	...	10.6	13.8	...	...	...
Rural - Rurale	C	13	14	...	...	...					
Paraguay											
Total	+U	760	636	679	...	...	...	...	...	...	...
Urban - Urbaine	+U	601	488	503	...	...	...	...	...	...	...
Rural - Rurale	+U	159	148	176	...	...	...	...	...	...	...
Suriname[10]											
Total	...	221	...	...	...	...	...	...	...	...	...
Venezuela (Bolivarian Republic of) - Venezuela (République bolivarienne du)											
Total	...	2 989	2 889	...	...	...	...	...	...	...	...
ASIA - ASIE											
Armenia - Arménie											
Total	C	662	563	601	802	...	17.6	14.0	14.6	18.1	...
Urban - Urbaine	C	456	342	370	473	...	19.2	13.4	14.1	16.7	...
Rural - Rurale	C	206	221	231	329	...	14.9	15.2	15.4	20.4	...
Azerbaijan - Azerbaïdjan											
Total	+C	603	536	677	672	...	4.0	3.5	4.5	4.4	...
Bahrain - Bahreïn											
Total	...	59	54	17	...	...	...	...	...	...	...
China, Hong Kong SAR - Chine, Hong Kong RAS											
Total	...	152	176	169	158	152	...	...	...	...	...
China, Macao SAR - Chine, Macao RAS											
Total	C	9	8	8	8	...	...	...	...	...	...
Georgia - Géorgie											
Total	C	712	632	660	...	...	14.9	12.8	11.7	...	...
Urban - Urbaine	C	539	459	495	...	...	16.1	13.4	12.6	...	...
Rural - Rurale	C	173	173	165	...	...	12.1	11.5	9.5	...	...
Israel - Israël[11]											
Total	C	566	565	544	...	...	3.8	3.7	3.5	...	...
Urban - Urbaine[5]	C	500	507	494	...	...	3.7	3.7	3.5	...	...
Rural - Rurale[5]	C	62	50	44	...	...	4.4	3.7	3.1	...	...
Japan - Japon[12]											
Total	C	2 367	2 254	2 209	2 222	...	2.2	2.1	2.0	2.1	...
Urban - Urbaine[5]	C	2 137	2 009	1 971	2 030	...	2.2	2.0	2.0	2.1	...
Rural - Rurale[5]	C	227	244	234	191	...	2.1	2.4	2.4	2.0	...
Kazakhstan											
Total	C	1 987	2 112	3 798	...	...	6.6	6.6	10.7	...	...
Urban - Urbaine	C	1 416	1 443	2 509	...	...	8.1	8.3	12.7	...	...
Rural - Rurale	C	571	669	1 289	...	...	4.5	4.5	8.1	...	...

12. Late foetal deaths and late foetal death ratios, by urban/rural residence: 2006 - 2010
Morts foetales tardives et rapports de mortinatalité, selon la résidence, urbaine/rurale : 2006 - 2010 (continued - suite)

Continent, country or area, and urban/rural residence / Continent, pays ou zone et résidence, urbaine/rurale	Co-de	Number - Nombre					Ratio - Rapport				
		2006	2007	2008	2009	2010	2006	2007	2008	2009	2010
ASIA - ASIE											
Kuwait - Koweït											
Total	C	347	374	367	...	...	6.6	7.0	6.7	...	...
Kyrgyzstan - Kirghizstan											
Total	C	1 621	1 730	1 664	1 703	...	13.4	14.0	13.1	12.6	...
Urban - Urbaine	C	1 066	1 172	1 127	1 161	...	27.0	28.3	25.6	24.7	...
Rural - Rurale	C	555	558	537	542	...	6.8	6.8	6.4	6.1	...
Malaysia - Malaisie											
Total	C	2 136	2 106	2 128	*2 176	...	4.6	4.5	4.4	*4.5	...
Urban - Urbaine	C	1 288	1 240	1 262	...	...	4.4	4.1	4.1	...	...
Rural - Rurale	C	848	866	866	...	...	5.0	5.1	4.8	...	...
Maldives[7]											
Total	...	59	58	49	54	...	...	...	...	...	...
Urban - Urbaine	...	27	18	26	23	...	...	...	...	...	...
Rural - Rurale	...	32	40	23	31	...	...	...	...	...	...
Myanmar											
Total	+U	...	...	10 783	...	...	...	...	...	...	...
Urban - Urbaine	+U	1 744	1 718	2 610	...	...	...	...	...	...	...
Rural - Rurale	+U	...	...	8 173	...	...	...	...	...	...	...
Oman[13]											
Total	U	371	447	454	495	...	...	...	...	...	...
Philippines											
Total	...	4 279	...	...	...	...	...	...	...	...	...
Qatar											
Total	C	79	95	133	123	...	5.6	6.1	7.7	6.7	...
Republic of Korea - République de Corée[14]											
Total	C	...	1 173	1 055	980	...	...	2.4	2.3	2.2	...
Singapore - Singapour											
Total	+C	99	90	86	79	...	2.6	2.3	2.2	2.0	...
Tajikistan - Tadjikistan											
Total	U	1 326	1 497	1 578	...	...	...	...	...	...	...
Urban - Urbaine	U	1 134	1 292	1 281	...	...	...	...	...	...	...
Rural - Rurale	U	192	205	297	...	...	...	...	...	...	...
EUROPE											
Åland Islands - Îles d'Åland											
Total	C	-	-	-	-	...	...	...	...	...	...
Urban - Urbaine	C	-	-	-	-	...	...	...	...	...	...
Rural - Rurale	C	-	-	-	-	...	...	...	...	...	...
Andorra - Andorre											
Total	C	1	-	2	3	...	...	...	...	...	...
Austria - Autriche											
Total	C	222	205	184	199	...	2.8	2.7	2.4	2.6	...
Belarus - Bélarus											
Total	C	352	324	318	304	...	3.6	3.1	2.9	2.8	...
Urban - Urbaine	C	250	223	230	223	...	3.5	2.9	2.8	2.7	...
Rural - Rurale	C	102	101	88	81	...	4.0	3.8	3.4	3.1	...
Belgium - Belgique											
Total	C	518	534	...	...	...	4.3	4.4	...	...	...
Urban - Urbaine	C	512	524	...	...	...	4.3	4.4	...	...	...
Rural - Rurale	C	6	10	...	...	...	...	...	...	...	...
Bosnia and Herzegovina - Bosnie-Herzégovine											
Total	C	160	174	171	...	...	4.7	5.1	5.0	...	...
Bulgaria - Bulgarie											
Total	C	517	566	571	616	...	7.0	7.5	7.3	7.6	...
Urban - Urbaine	C	349	378	383	424	...	6.3	6.7	6.6	7.0	...
Rural - Rurale	C	168	188	188	192	...	8.9	9.8	9.7	9.5	...
Croatia - Croatie[15]											
Total	C	182	160	176	177	...	4.4	3.8	4.0	4.0	...
Urban - Urbaine	C	99	89	108	98	...	4.3	3.8	4.4	3.9	...
Rural - Rurale	C	83	71	68	79	...	4.5	3.8	3.5	4.0	...

12. Late foetal deaths and late foetal death ratios, by urban/rural residence: 2006 - 2010
Morts foetales tardives et rapports de mortinatalité, selon la résidence, urbaine/rurale : 2006 - 2010 (continued - suite)

Continent, country or area, and urban/rural residence / Continent, pays ou zone et résidence, urbaine/rurale	Code - Code	Number - Nombre					Ratio - Rapport				
		2006	2007	2008	2009	2010	2006	2007	2008	2009	2010
EUROPE											
Czech Republic - République tchèque[16]											
Total	C	291	309	261	309	...	2.7	2.7	2.2	2.6	...
Urban - Urbaine	C	207	227	187	234	...	2.6	2.7	2.1	2.7	...
Rural - Rurale	C	84	82	74	75	...	3.1	2.7	2.4	2.4	...
Denmark - Danemark[17]											
Total	C	346	331	314	...	...	5.3	5.2	4.8	...	...
Estonia - Estonie[7]											
Total	C	56	65	64	77	...	3.8	4.1	4.0	4.9	...
Urban - Urbaine	C	38	40	38	55	...	3.6	3.6	3.4	5.1	...
Rural - Rurale	C	18	25	26	22	...	...	...	...	...	...
Finland - Finlande[18]											
Total	C	139	148	122	129	...	2.4	2.5	2.0	2.1	...
Urban - Urbaine	C	96	105	83	87	...	2.3	2.5	2.0	2.0	...
Rural - Rurale	C	43	43	39	42	...	2.5	2.6	2.3	2.4	...
France											
Total	C	7 531[19]	7 246[19]	8 356	9 377	...	9.5	9.2	10.5	11.8	...
Urban - Urbaine[20]	C	5 824[19]	5 604[19]	6 317	7 092	...	9.8	9.5	10.6	12.0	...
Rural - Rurale[20]	C	1 643[19]	1 575[19]	1 936	2 190	...	8.3	8.0	9.6	11.0	...
Germany - Allemagne											
Total	C	2 420	2 371	2 412	...	...	3.6	3.5	3.5	...	...
Greece - Grèce[7]											
Total	C	376	434	392	505	...	3.4	3.9	3.3	4.3	...
Urban - Urbaine	C	274	301	246	349	...	3.6	3.9	3.1	4.3	...
Rural - Rurale	C	102	133	146	156	...	2.9	3.8	3.9	4.2	...
Hungary - Hongrie[21]											
Total	C	489	485	431	519	...	4.9	5.0	4.3	5.4	...
Urban - Urbaine[22]	C	271	290	254	313	...	4.1	4.4	3.8	4.8	...
Rural - Rurale[22]	C	211	193	174	202	...	6.4	6.1	5.5	6.8	...
Iceland - Islande											
Total	C	15	7	11	12	...	...	...	...	...	...
Urban - Urbaine	C	14	7	11	11	...	...	...	...	...	...
Rural - Rurale	C	1	-	-	1	...	...	...	...	...	...
Ireland - Irlande											
Total	+C	...	...	198	...	...	...	...	2.6	...	...
Italy - Italie											
Total	C	*1 628	*1 570	*1 549	*1 552	...	*2.9	*2.8	*2.7	*2.7	...
Latvia - Lettonie[23]											
Total	C	154	121	150	130	...	6.9	5.2	6.3	6.0	...
Urban - Urbaine	C	103	83	100	85	...	6.7	5.1	6.0	5.7	...
Rural - Rurale	C	51	38	50	45	...	7.4	5.3	6.8	6.6	...
Lithuania - Lituanie[15]											
Total	C	137	161	164	151	...	4.4	5.0	4.7	4.1	...
Urban - Urbaine	C	79	93	109	90	...	3.8	4.3	4.6	3.6	...
Rural - Rurale	C	58	68	55	61	...	5.5	6.4	4.9	5.2	...
Luxembourg											
Total	C	14	20	21	31	...	...	...	...	5.5	...
Malta - Malte[15]											
Total	C	10	12	29	28	...	...	...	...	...	...
Montenegro - Monténégro[7]											
Total	C	20	22	34	43	...	...	...	4.1	5.0	...
Urban - Urbaine	C	...	...	24	37	...	...	...	...	5.6	...
Rural - Rurale	C	...	...	10	6	...	...	...	...	...	...
Netherlands - Pays-Bas[24]											
Total	C	642	608	608	648	...	3.5	3.4	3.3	3.5	...
Urban - Urbaine	C	456	435	423	453	...	3.6	3.5	3.3	3.5	...
Rural - Rurale	C	186	173	185	195	...	3.2	3.1	3.2	3.5	...
Norway - Norvège[25]											
Total	C	201	241	221	215	...	3.4	4.1	3.7	3.5	...
Poland - Pologne											
Total	C	1 338	1 346	1 422	1 157	...	3.6	3.5	3.4	2.8	...
Urban - Urbaine	C	710	753	767	634	...	3.3	3.3	3.2	2.6	...
Rural - Rurale	C	628	593	655	523	...	4.0	3.7	3.8	3.1	...
Portugal[4]											
Total	C	324	289	265	291	...	3.1	2.8	2.5	2.9	...

12. Late foetal deaths and late foetal death ratios, by urban/rural residence: 2006 - 2010
Morts foetales tardives et rapports de mortinatalité, selon la résidence, urbaine/rurale : 2006 - 2010 (continued - suite)

Continent, country or area, and urban/rural residence / Continent, pays ou zone et résidence, urbaine/rurale	Co-de	Number - Nombre					Ratio - Rapport				
		2006	2007	2008	2009	2010	2006	2007	2008	2009	2010
EUROPE											
Romania - Roumanie											
Total	C	1 143	1 009	993	969	...	5.2	4.7	4.5	4.4	...
Urban - Urbaine	C	538	498	468	474	...	4.5	4.3	3.9	3.9	...
Rural - Rurale	C	605	511	525	495	...	6.0	5.2	5.2	4.9	...
Russian Federation - Fédération de Russie											
Total	C	7 934	8 612	8 594	8 380	...	5.4	5.3	5.0	4.8	...
Urban - Urbaine	C	5 678	6 061	6 112	5 815	...	5.4	5.4	5.1	4.7	...
Rural - Rurale	C	2 256	2 551	2 482	2 565	...	5.2	5.2	4.8	4.9	...
Serbia - Serbie[26]											
Total	+C	365	369	345	366	...	5.1	5.4	5.0	5.2	...
Urban - Urbaine	+C	244	245	240	243	...	5.3	5.5	5.3	5.2	...
Rural - Rurale	+C	121	124	105	123	...	4.9	5.3	4.4	5.3	...
Slovakia - Slovaquie											
Total	C	218	207	226	228	...	4.0	3.8	3.9	3.7	...
Urban - Urbaine	C	98	89	101	99	...	3.4	3.1	3.3	3.0	...
Rural - Rurale	C	120	118	125	129	...	4.7	4.6	4.7	4.5	...
Slovenia - Slovénie											
Total	C	57	69	68	64	...	3.0	3.5	3.1	2.9	...
Spain - Espagne											
Total	C	1 177	1 099	1 134	1 081	...	2.4	2.2	2.2	2.2	...
Sweden - Suède											
Total	C	319	326	396	451	...	3.0	3.0	3.6	4.0	...
Switzerland - Suisse[7]											
Total	C	342	297	341	345	...	4.7	4.0	4.4	4.4	...
Urban - Urbaine	C	249	217	270	255	...	4.6	3.9	4.7	4.4	...
Rural - Rurale	C	93	80	71	90	...	4.9	4.2	3.6	4.6	...
TFYR of Macedonia - L'ex-R. y. de Macédoine											
Total	C	201	215	222	226	...	8.9	9.5	9.7	9.5	...
Urban - Urbaine	C	112	106	117	125	...	8.9	8.3	8.9	9.2	...
Rural - Rurale	C	89	109	105	101	...	9.0	11.0	10.8	10.0	...
Ukraine											
Total	C	2 314	3 070	3 416	...	...	5.0	6.5	6.7	...	...
Urban - Urbaine	C	1 532	2 088	2 304	...	...	5.0	6.6	6.8	...	...
Rural - Rurale	C	782	982	1 112	...	...	5.1	6.2	6.5	...	...
United Kingdom of Great Britain and Northern Ireland - Royaume-Uni de Grande-Bretagne et d'Irlande du Nord[27]											
Total	C	...	...	4 057	...	...	...	...	5.1	...	...
OCEANIA - OCÉANIE											
Australia - Australie[8]											
Total	+C	903	1 205	1 323	...	...	3.4	4.2	4.5	...	...
Guam											
Total	C	36	46	...	...	...	10.5	13.2	...	...	...
New Zealand - Nouvelle-Zélande[4]											
Total	+C	162	226	234	175	...	2.7	3.5	3.6	2.8	...
Urban - Urbaine	+C	139	205	210	159	...	2.7	3.7	3.7	2.9	...
Rural - Rurale	+C	23	20	24	16	...	...	...	...	...	...
Palau - Palaos											
Total	C	6	...	...	...	...	...	...	...	...	...

FOOTNOTES - NOTES

Italics: data from civil registers which are incomplete or of unknown completeness. - Italiques : données incomplètes ou dont le degré d'exactitude n'est pas connu, provenant des registres de l'état civil.

* Provisional. - Données provisoires.

[1] Excludes the islands of St. Brandon and Agalega. - Non compris les îles St. Brandon et Agalega.

[2] Including Canadian residents temporarily in the United States, but excluding United States residents temporarily in Canada. - Y compris les résidents canadiens se trouvant temporairement aux Etats-Unis, mais ne comprenant pas les résidents des Etats-Unis se trouvant temporairement au Canada.

[3] Late foetal death is indicated by the fact that the foetus is at least 500 grams or more in weight. - Les décès foetaux tardifs sont caractérisés par le fait que le foetus pèse au moins 500 grammes.

[4] Data refer to resident population only. - Pour la population résidante seulement.

[5] The total number includes 'Unknown residence', but the categories urban and rural do not. - Le nombre total inclue 'Résidence inconnue ', mais les catégories urbaine et rurale ne l'incluent pas.

[6] Excluding Indian jungle population. - Non compris les Indiens de la jungle.

[7] Data refer to total foetal deaths. - Y compris toutes les morts foetales.

[8] Data include foetal deaths of unknown gestational weeks. - Les données comprennnent les morts foetales où le nombre de semaines de gestation n'est pas connu.

[9] Excluding nomadic Indian tribes. - Non compris les tribus d'Indiens nomades.

[10] Data from the 4 hospitals in Paramaribo and that of the hospital of the Nickerie district. - Données provenant de 4 hôpitaux à Paramaribo et d'un hôpital du district de Nickerie.

[11] Including data for East Jerusalem and Israeli residents in certain other territories under occupation by Israeli military forces since June 1967. - Y compris les données pour Jérusalem-Est et les résidents israéliens dans certains autres territoires occupés depuis 1967 par les forces armées israéliennes.

[12] Data refer to Japanese nationals in Japan only. Data exclude unknown duration of pregnancy. - Les données se raportent aux nationaux japonais au Japon seulement. Exception faite des grossesses dont la durée n'est pas connue.

[13] Data from Births and Deaths Notification System (Ministry of Health institutions and all other health care providers). - Les données proviennent du système de notification des naissances et des décès (établissements du Ministère de la santé et tous autres prestataires de soins de santé).

[14] Excluding alien armed forces, civilian aliens employed by armed forces, and foreign diplomatic personnel and their dependants. - Non compris les militaires étrangers, les civils étrangers employés par les forces armées ni le personnel diplomatique étranger et les membres de leur famille les accompagnant.

[15] Late foetal death is defined as an infant born without any signs of life, weighing at least 500 grams, after duration of pregnancy of at least 22 weeks. - On dit qu'il y a mort intra-utérine tardive lorsqu'un enfant pesant au minimum 500 grammes naît sans donner aucun signe de vie au terme d'une grossesse qui a duré au moins 22 semaines.

[16] Late foetal death is defined as an infant born without any signs of life, weighing at least 1000 grams. - La mortalité fœtale en fin de période de gestation s'entend de nourrissons mort-nés et pesant au moins 1 kilo.

[17] Excluding Faeroe Islands and Greenland shown separately, if available. - Non compris les Iles Féroé et le Groenland, qui font l'objet de rubriques distinctes, si disponible.

[18] Including nationals temporarily outside the country. - Y compris les nationaux se trouvant temporairement hors du pays.

[19] Foetal deaths after at least 180 days (6 calendar months or 26 weeks) of gestation. - Morts foetales survenues après 180 jours (6 mois civils ou 26 semaines) au moins de gestation.

[20] Data for urban and rural, excluding nationals outside the country. - Les données pour la résidence urbaine et rurale , non compris les nationaux hors du pays.

[21] Late foetal death is indicated by the fact that the foetus is at least 24 (it has been 28 weeks until 1996) completed weeks of gestation and does not show any sign of life after the separation from its mother; the foetus has to be 30 cm or more in length or 500 grams or more in weight if its gestational age cannot be determined. - Pour qu'il y ait mort foetale tardive, il faut que le décès d'un foetus survienne après 24 semaines complètes de gestation au moins (28 semaines jusqu'en 1996), que le foetus n'ait pas donné signe de vie après avoir été séparé de la mère, qu'il mesure 30 centimètres au moins ou pèse 500 grammes si la durée de la période de gestation n'est pas connue.

[22] Total includes the data of foreigners, persons of unknown residence and homeless, but the categories urban and rural do not. - Total incluant les étrangers, les personnes de résidence inconnue et les sans-abri, ce qui n'est pas le cas pour les catégories urbaines et rurales.

[23] Data refer to the death of a foetus at least 22 completed weeks of gestation. - Les données concernent le décès d'un fœtus après 22 semaines de gestation au moins.

[24] Including residents outside the country if listed in a Netherlands population register. - Y compris les résidents hors du pays, s'ils sont inscrits sur un registre de population néerlandais.

[25] Excluding Svalbard and Jan Mayen Islands shown separately, if available. - Non compris Svalbard et Jan Mayen qui font l'objet de rubriques distinctes, si disponible.

[26] Excluding data for Kosovo and Metohia. Data refer to total foetal deaths. - Sans les données pour le Kosovo et Metohie. Y compris toutes les morts foetales.

[27] Excluding Channel Islands (Guernsey and Jersey) and Isle of Man, shown separately, if available. - Non compris les îles Anglo-Normandes (Guernesey et Jersey) et l'île de Man, qui font l'objet de rubriques distinctes, si disponible.

Table 13

Table 13 presents legally induced abortions for as many years as available between 2001 and 2010.

Description of variables: There are two major categories of abortion: spontaneous and induced. Induced abortions are those initiated by deliberate action undertaken with the intention of terminating pregnancy; all other abortions are considered spontaneous.

The induction of abortion is subject to governmental regulation in most, if not all, countries or areas. This regulation varies from complete prohibition in some countries or areas to abortion on request, with services provided by governmental health authorities, in others. More generally, governments have attempted to define the conditions under which a pregnancy may lawfully be terminated and have established procedures for authorizing abortion in individual cases.

Information on abortion policies is collected by the United Nations Population Division and published in the World Population Policies[1]. An overview is also published as a wall chart[2].

Reliability of data: Unlike data on live births and foetal deaths, which are generally collected through systems of vital registration, data on abortion are collected from a variety of sources. Because of this, the quality specification on the completeness of civil registers, which is presented for other tables, does not appear here.

Limitations: With regard to the collection of information on abortions, a variety of sources are used, but hospital records are the most common source of information. This implies that most cases that have no contact with hospitals are missed. Data from other sources are probably also incomplete. The data in the present table are limited to legally induced abortions, which, by their nature, might be assumed to be more complete than data on all induced abortions.

Earlier data: Legally induced abortions have been shown previously in all issues of the *Demographic Yearbook* since the 1971 issue. For more information on specific topics and years for which data are reported, readers should consult the Historical Index.

NOTES

[1] World Population Policies 2009 (United Nations Publication, Sales No. E.09.XIII.14), New York 2010. See also: http://www.un.org/esa/population/publications/wpp2009/Publication_index.htm

[2] World Abortion Policies 2011 (United Nations Publication, Sales No. E.11.XIII.4), New York, 2011. See also: http://www.un.org/esa/population/publications/2011abortion/2011wallchart.pdf

Tableau 13

Le tableau 13 présente des données disponible, relatives aux avortements provoqués légalement, entre 2001 et 2010.

Description des variables : l'avortement peut être spontané ou provoqué. L'avortement provoqué est celui qui résulte de manœuvres délibérées, entreprises afin d'interrompre la grossesse ; tous les autres avortements sont considérés comme spontanés.

L'interruption délibérée de la grossesse fait l'objet d'une réglementation officielle dans la plupart des pays ou zones, sinon dans tous. Cette réglementation va de l'interdiction totale à l'autorisation de l'avortement sur demande, pratiqué par des services de santé publique. Le plus souvent, les gouvernements se sont efforcés de définir les circonstances dans lesquelles la grossesse peut être interrompue licitement et de fixer une procédure d'autorisation.

La Division de la population des Nations Unies collecte des informations sur les politiques en matière d'avortement et les publient dans "World Population Policies"[1]. Une vue d'ensemble est également publiée sous forme de poster[2].

Fiabilité des données : à la différence des données sur les naissances vivantes et les morts fœtales, qui proviennent généralement des registres d'état civil, les données sur l'avortement sont tirées de sources diverses. Aussi ne trouve-t-on pas ici une évaluation de la qualité des données semblable à celle qui indique, pour les autres tableaux, le degré d'exhaustivité des données de l'état civil.

Insuffisance des données : en ce qui concerne les renseignements sur l'avortement, un grand nombre de sources sont utilisées, les relevés hospitaliers restant cependant la source la plus commune. Il s'ensuit que la plupart des cas qui ne passent pas par les hôpitaux sont ignorés. Il faut aussi tenir compte du fait que les données provenant d'autres sources sont probablement incomplètes. Les données du tableau 13 se limitent aux avortements provoqués pour raisons légales dont on peut supposer, en raison de leur nature même, que les statistiques sont plus complètes que les données concernant l'ensemble des avortements provoqués.

Données publiées antérieurement : des statistiques concernant les avortements provoqués pour raisons légales sont publiées dans *l'Annuaire démographique* depuis 1971. Pour plus de précisions concernant les années et les sujets pour lesquels des données ont été publiées, se reporter à l'index historique.

NOTES

[1] World Population Policies 2009 (publication des Nations Unies, Numéro de vente E.09.XIII.14), New York 2010. Voir aussi : http://www.un.org/esa/population/publications/wpp2009/Publication_index.htm

[2] World Abortion Policies 2011 (publication des Nations Unies, Numéro de vente E.11.XIII.4), New York, 2011. Voir aussi : http://www.un.org/esa/population/publications/2011abortion/2011wallchart.pdf

Continent and country or area / Continent et pays ou zone	Number - Nombre									
	2001	2002	2003	2004	2005	2006	2007	2008	2009	2010
AFRICA - AFRIQUE										
Réunion	4 339	4 385	4 129	4 155	4 421	4 523	...	...	...	...
Seychelles	461	460	440	435	413	443	446	453	471	...
AMERICA, NORTH - AMÉRIQUE DU NORD										
Anguilla	...	27	24	26	21	...	...	...	...	...
Canada[1]	106 418	105 154	103 768	100 039	96 815	91 310[2]	...	...	...	...
Costa Rica[3]	7 637	8 288	8 446	8 801	8 411	8 367	8 504	8 733	7 848[4]	7 697[4]
Cuba	69 563	70 823	65 628	67 277	62 530	67 903	66 008	74 905	84 724	...
Dominican Republic - République dominicaine	20 187	28 091	24 899	26 438	29 167	...	...	...	...	...
Greenland - Groenland	809	821	869	901	899	867	887	894		...
Martinique	2 502	2 614	2 394	2 426	2 304	2 392	...	...	...	...
Mexico - Mexique[5]	565	589	675	748	729	793	833	764	*867	...
Puerto Rico - Porto Rico[6]	8 802	8 516	7 781	9 215	6 904	5 538[7]	...	...	...	...
Turks and Caicos Islands - Îles Turques et Caïques[8]	...	39	32	43	32	...	...	...	...	...
United States of America - États-Unis d'Amérique[9]	1 291 000	1 269 000	1 250 000	1 222 000	1 206 200	...	...	...	...	...
AMERICA, SOUTH - AMÉRIQUE DU SUD										
Chile - Chili	1 278	1 197	1 404	1 510	1 841	...	...	...	...	...
French Guiana - Guyane française	1 386	1 699	1 783	1 639	1 612	1 661	...	...	...	...
ASIA - ASIE										
Armenia - Arménie	10 419	9 372	10 290	10 487	10 925	11 132	11 501	12 469	13 797	...
Azerbaijan - Azerbaïdjan	18 332	16 606	16 903	19 798	19 577	20 864	22 323	25 247	24 554	...
Bahrain - Bahreïn	1 747	1 749	...	...	...	...	...	...	...	...
China, Hong Kong SAR - Chine, Hong Kong RAS	20 235	18 651	17 420	15 882	14 192	13 510	13 515	13 199	12 028	...
Georgia - Géorgie	15 008	13 908	13 834	17 210	19 681	21 204	20 644	22 062	...	...
Israel - Israël[10]	19 131	19 126	19 671	19 712	19 090	19 452	19 470	19 638	...	...
Japan - Japon	341 588	329 326	319 831	301 673	289 127	276 352	256 672	242 326	223 444	...
Kyrgyzstan - Kirghizstan[11]	23 390	18 995	19 225	19 984	20 035	19 762	21 884	20 800	22 088	...
Mongolia - Mongolie	12 056	9 977	10 472	8 919	9 064	12 594	15 817	...	...	...
Qatar	127	121	131	172	169	...	...	...	...	...
Singapore - Singapour	13 140	12 749	12 272	12 070	11 482	12 032	11 933	12 222	12 318	12 082
Tajikistan - Tadjikistan	19 087	20 007	18 822	20 495	19 418	17 489	18 986	18 481	...	...
EUROPE										
Åland Islands - Îles d'Åland	59	61	70	59	68	53	73	66	68	...
Albania - Albanie	17 125	17 500	12 087	10 517	9 403	9 552	9 030	8 335	...	...
Belarus - Bélarus	101 402	89 895	80 174	71 700	64 655	58 516	46 285	42 197	35 967	...
Belgium - Belgique	14 775	14 791	15 595	16 024	16 696	17 640	18 033	...	...	...
Bulgaria - Bulgarie	51 165	50 824	48 035	47 223	41 795	37 272	37 594	36 593	33 733	...
Croatia - Croatie	6 574	6 191	5 923	5 232	4 563	4 733	4 573	4 497	...	...
Czech Republic - République tchèque	32 528	31 142	29 298	27 574	26 453	25 352	25 414	25 760	24 636	...
Denmark - Danemark[12]	15 314	14 991	15 622	15 231	15 295	15 227	15 690	16 394	16 205	...
Estonia - Estonie[1]	11 653	10 834	10 619	10 074	9 610	9 378	8 883	8 409	7 542	...
Faeroe Islands - Îles Féroé	42	49	37	44	29	41	46	...	...	...
Finland - Finlande	10 738	10 974	10 767	11 162	10 969	10 645	10 533	10 423	10 359[13]	...
France	201 434	205 898	202 591	209 907	205 392	214 360	212 285	...	...	...
Germany - Allemagne	134 964	130 387	128 030	129 650	124 023	119 710	116 871	114 484	...	...
Greece - Grèce	22 223	16 173	15 782	16 135	16 495	...	...	...	...	...
Hungary - Hongrie	56 404	56 075	53 789	52 539	48 689	46 324	43 870	44 089	43 181	...
Iceland - Islande	984	926	951	889	868	904	905	957	971	...
Italy - Italie	132 073	131 039[14]	124 118[14]	137 140[15]	129 272[16]	125 782[17]	125 116[18]	118 891	114 793	...

13. Legally induced abortions: 2001 - 2010
Avortements provoqués légalement : 2001 - 2010 (continued - suite)

Continent and country or area / Continent et pays ou zone	Number - Nombre									
	2001	2002	2003	2004	2005	2006	2007	2008	2009	2010
EUROPE										
Latvia - Lettonie	15 647	14 685	14 508	13 723	12 785	11 825	11 814	10 425	8 881	...
Lithuania - Lituanie	13 677	12 495	11 513	10 644	9 972	9 536	9 596	9 031	8 024	...
Montenegro - Monténégro	...	...	...	...	1 952	...	...	...	...	...
Norway - Norvège[19]	13 887	13 557	13 888	14 071	13 989	14 417	15 165	16 054	...	...
Poland - Pologne[20]	123	159	174	199	225	339	328	506	...	...
Portugal	675	828	563	710	798	1 215	4 325[21]	13 541[21]	17 942[21]	...
Republic of Moldova - République de Moldova	16 028	15 739	17 551	17 965	16 642	15 742	15 843	15 900	14 634	...
Romania - Roumanie	254 855	247 608	224 803	191 038	163 359	150 246	137 226	127 907	116 060	...
Russian Federation - Fédération de Russie	2 014 710	1 944 481	1 864 647	1 797 567	1 732 289	1 582 398	1 479 010	1 385 600	1 292 389	...
Serbia - Serbie[22]	34 255	30 794	29 856	29 650	26 645	25 665	24 273	22 867	...	...
Slovakia - Slovaquie	18 026	17 382	16 222	15 307	14 427	14 243	13 424	13 394	13 240	...
Slovenia - Slovénie	7 799	7 327	6 873	6 403	5 851	5 632	5 176	4 946	4 653	...
Spain - Espagne	69 857	77 125	79 788	84 985	91 664	101 592	112 138	115 812	111 482	...
Sweden - Suède	31 772	33 365	34 473	34 454	34 978	36 045	37 205	38 049	...	...
Switzerland - Suisse	12 418	11 844	10 820	10 959	10 818	10 594	10 035[23]	10 310[23]	10 137[23]	...
Ukraine	369 750	345 967	315 835	289 065	263 590	229 618	210 454	...	...	...
United Kingdom of Great Britain and Northern Ireland - Royaume-Uni de Grande-Bretagne et d'Irlande du Nord[24]	197 913[1]	...	...	...	...	...	...	209 113	...	...
OCEANIA - OCÉANIE										
New Zealand - Nouvelle-Zélande	16 410	17 380	18 511	18 211	17 531	17 934	18 382	17 940	17 550	...

FOOTNOTES - NOTES

* Provisional. - Données provisoires.

[1] Data refer to resident population only. - Pour la population résidante seulement.

[2] Significant undercoverage of medically induced abortions in clinics in 2006 due to non response in some provinces. - Sous-dénombrement notable des interruptions volontaires de grossesse pratiquées dans les centres médicaux en 2006 faute de réponse dans certaines provinces.

[3] Number of abortions the woman had before the birth of the registered child. - Nombre d'avortements de la femme avant la naissance de l'enfant enregistré.

[4] Excluding abortions performed in private hospitals. - Non comprises les interruptions volontaires de grossesse effectuées dans des hôpitaux privés.

[5] Data refer to 'Therapeutic Abortions'. According to the Mexican law, only the induced abortions, prescribed by medical reasons and induced because of pregnancy coming from sexual agression, are considered as legal. Data refer to abortions prescribed by a physician. Refers to residence of the mother. To calculate the total number of abortions, foetal deaths of less than 20 weeks of gestation were considered. - Les données se rapportent aux « interruptions volontaires de grossesse pour des motifs thérapeutiques ». D'après la loi mexicaine, seuls sont considérés légaux les avortements déclenchés pour des raisons médicales ou parce que la grossesse est le résultat d'une agression sexuelle. Les données se réfèrent aux avortements prescrits par un médecin. Correspond à la résidence de la mère. Les morts fœtales survenues à moins de 20 semaines de gestation ont été prises en compte aux fins du calcul du nombre total d'avortements.

[6] Data refer to the fiscal year from 1 July to 30 June. - Les données se réfèrent à l'année budgétaire de 1 juillet à 30 juin.

[7] Excluding abortions performed in a clinic which closed operations without reporting the data. - Non comprises les avortements effectuées dans une clinique qui a fermé sans envoyer les données.

[8] Data refer to abortions performed in hospitals at Grand Turk and Providenciales. - Pour des avortements exécutés dans les hôpitaux dans Grand Turk et Providenciales.

[9] Abortions have been estimated by interpolation. - Les avortements ont été estimés après des interpolations.

[10] Including data for East Jerusalem and Israeli residents in certain other territories under occupation by Israeli military forces since June 1967. Data refer to applications to commissions for termination of pregnancy and not to authorizations. - Y compris les données pour Jérusalem-Est et les résidents israéliens dans certains autres territoires occupés depuis 1967 par les forces armées israéliennes. Les données relatives aux avortements provoqués légalement se rapportent aux demandes d'autorisation et non aux autorisations elles-mêmes.

[11] Based on administrative reporting of the Ministry of Health. - Les données reposent sur les rapports administratifs du Ministère de la santé.

[12] Excluding Faeroe Islands and Greenland shown separately, if available. - Non compris les Iles Féroé et le Groenland, qui font l'objet de rubriques distinctes, si disponible.

[13] Excluding Åland Islands. - Non compris les Îles d'Åland.

[14] Data are incomplete for Campania region. - Les données sont incomplètes pour la région de la Campanie.

[15] Data are incomplete for Sicilia region. - Les données sont incomplètes pour la région de la Sicile.

[16] Data are incomplete for Friuli-Venezia Giulia, Campania, Molise and Sicilia regions. - Les données sont incomplètes pour le Frioul-Vénétie julienne, la Campanie, la Molise et la Sicile.

[17] Data are incomplete for Friuli-Venezia Giulia, Campania and Sicilia regions. - Les données sont incomplètes pour les régions Frioul-Vénétie Julienne, la Campanie et la Sicile.

[18] Data are incomplete for Campania and Sicilia regions. - Les données sont incomplètes pour les régions de la Campanie et de la Sicile.

[19] Excluding Svalbard and Jan Mayen Islands shown separately, if available. - Non compris Svalbard et Jan Mayen qui font l'objet de rubriques distinctes, si disponible.

[20] Based on hospital and polyclinic records. - D'après les registres des hôpitaux et des polycliniques.

[21] From July 2007, includes legally induced abortions up to the first 10 weeks of pregnancy due to the change in abortion related laws and regulations of the country. - Depuis juillet 2007, comprend les interruptions volontaires de grossesse pratiquées jusqu'à la dixième semaine de grossesse, par suite des modifications apportées aux lois régissant les avortements dans le pays.

[22] Excluding data for Kosovo and Metohia. Data refer to institutions included in the Health Institutions Network Plan in the Republic of Serbia. - Sans les données pour le Kosovo et Metohie. Les données se rapportent aux institutions membres du "Health Institutions Network Plan" de la République de Serbie.

[23] Data refer to termination of pregnancy for women who are Switzerland residents. - Les données portent sur les interruptions de grossesse pratiquées sur des femmes qui résident en Suisse.

[24] Excluding Channel Islands (Guernsey and Jersey) and Isle of Man, shown separately, if available. - Non compris les îles Anglo-Normandes (Guernesey et Jersey) et l'île de Man, qui font l'objet de rubriques distinctes, si disponible.

Tables 14 and 14a

Table 14 presents legally induced abortions by age and number of previous live births of women for the latest available year between 2000 and 2009. Table 14a presents the available data for the year 2010.

Description of variables: Age is defined as age at last birthday, that is, the difference between the date of birth and the date of the occurrence of the event, expressed in complete solar years. The age classification used in this table is the following: under 15 years, 5-year age groups through 45-49 years and 50 years and over.

Except where otherwise indicated, eight categories are used in classifying the number of previous live births: 0 through 5, 6 or more live births, and, if required, number of live births unknown.

Information on abortion policies is collected by the United Nations Population Division and published in the World Population Policies[1]. An overview is also published as a wall chart[2].

Reliability of data: Unlike data on live births and foetal deaths, which are generally collected through systems of vital registration, data on abortion are collected from a variety of sources. Because of this, the quality specification on the completeness of civil registers, which is presented for other tables, does not appear here.

Limitations: With regard to the collection of information on abortions, a variety of sources are used, but hospital records are the most common source of information. This implies that most cases that have no contact with hospitals are missed. Data from other sources are probably also incomplete. The data in the present table are limited to legally induced abortions, which, by their nature, might be assumed to be more complete than data on all induced abortions.

In addition, deficiencies in the reporting of age and number of previous live births of the woman, differences in the method used for obtaining the age of the woman, and the proportion of abortions for which age or previous live births of the woman are unknown must all be taken into account in using these data.

Earlier data: Legally induced abortions by age and previous live births of women have been shown previously in most issues of the *Demographic Yearbook* since the 1971 issue. For more information on specific topics and years for which data are reported, readers should consult the Historical Index.

NOTES

[1] World Population Policies 2009 (United Nations Publication, Sales No. E.09.XIII.14), New York 2010. See also: http://www.un.org/esa/population/publications/wpp2009/Publication_index.htm

[2] World Abortion Policies 2011 (United Nations Publication, Sales No. E. 11.XIII.4), New York, 2011. See also: http://www.un.org/esa/population/publications/2011abortion/2011wallchart.pdf

Tableaux 14 et 14a

Le tableau 14 présente les données les plus récentes disponible entre 2000 et 2009 sur les avortements provoqués pour des raisons légales, selon l'âge de la mère et le nombre de naissances vivantes précédentes. Le tableau 14a présente les données disponibles pour l'année 2010.

Description des variables : L'âge considéré est l'âge au dernier anniversaire, c'est-à-dire la différence entre la date de naissance et la date de l'avortement, exprimée en années solaires révolues. La classification par âge utilisée dans le tableau 14 est la suivante : moins de 15 ans, groupes quinquennaux jusqu'à 45-49 ans, 50 ans et plus, et âge inconnu.

Sauf indication contraire, les naissances vivantes antérieures sont classées dans les huit catégories suivantes: 0 à 5 naissances vivantes, 6 naissances vivantes ou plus et, le cas échéant, nombre de naissances vivantes inconnu.

La Division de la population des Nations Unies collecte des informations sur les politiques en matière d'avortement et les publient dans "World Population Policies"[1]. Une vue d'ensemble est également publiée sous forme de poster[2].

Fiabilité des données : à la différence des données sur les naissances vivantes et les morts fœtales, qui proviennent généralement des registres d'état civil, les données sur l'avortement sont tirées de sources diverses. Aussi ne trouve-t-on pas ici une évaluation de la qualité des données semblable à celle qui indique, pour les autres tableaux, le degré d'exhaustivité des données de l'état civil.

Insuffisance des données : en ce qui concerne les renseignements sur l'avortement, un grand nombre de sources sont utilisées, les relevés hospitaliers restant cependant la source la plus commune. Il s'ensuit que la plupart des cas qui ne passent pas par les hôpitaux sont ignorés. Il faut aussi tenir compte du fait que les données provenant d'autres sources sont probablement incomplètes. Les données du tableau 14 se limitent aux avortements provoqués pour raisons légales dont on peut supposer, en raison de leur nature même, que les statistiques sont plus complètes que les données concernant l'ensemble des avortements provoqués.

En outre, on doit tenir compte, lorsque l'on utilise ces données, des erreurs de déclaration de l'âge de la mère et du nombre des naissances vivantes précédentes, de l'hétérogénéité des méthodes de calcul de l'âge de la mère et de la proportion d'avortements pour lesquels l'âge de la mère ou le nombre des naissances vivantes ne sont pas connus.

Données publiées antérieurement : Depuis 1971, la plupart des éditions de l'*Annuaire démographique* contiennent des statistiques concernant les avortements provoqués pour raisons légales, selon l'âge de la mère et le nombre de naissances vivantes antérieures. Pour plus de précisions concernant les années et les sujets pour lesquels des données ont été publiées, se reporter à l'index historique.

NOTES

[1] World Population Policies 2009 (publication des Nations Unies, Numéro de vente E.09.XIII.14), New York 2010. http://www.un.org/esa/population/publications/wpp2009/Publication_index.htm.

[2] World Abortion Policies 2011 (publication des Nations Unies, Numéro de vente E. 11.XIII.4), New York, 2011. Voir aussi : http://www.un.org/esa/population/publications/2011abortion/2011wallchart.pdf

11. Legally induced abortions by age and number of previous live births of women: latest available year, 2000 - 2009
Avortments provoqués légalement selon l'âge de la femme et selon le nombre des naissances vivantes précédentes : dernière année disponible, 2000 - 2009

Continent, country or area, year and age / Continent, pays ou zone, année et âge	Number of previous live births / Nombre des naissances vivantes précédentes								
	Total	0	1	2	3	4	5	6+	Unknown - Inconnu
AMERICA, NORTH - AMÉRIQUE DU NORD									
Canada[1]									
2006									
Total	91 310	...	...	...	...	...	...	...	...
0 - 14	267	...	...	...	...	...	...	...	...
15 - 19	15 217	...	...	...	...	...	...	...	...
20 - 24	28 358	...	...	...	...	...	...	...	...
25 - 29	20 315	...	...	...	...	...	...	...	...
30 - 34	13 615	...	...	...	...	...	...	...	...
35 - 39	9 444	...	...	...	...	...	...	...	...
40 +	3 938	...	...	...	...	...	...	...	...
Unknown - Inconnu	156	...	...	...	...	...	...	...	...
Costa Rica[2]									
2009									
Total	7 848	...	...	...	...	...	...	...	...
10 - 14	68	...	...	...	...	...	...	...	...
15 - 19	1 275	...	...	...	...	...	...	...	...
20 - 44	6 437	...	...	...	...	...	...	...	...
45 +	68	...	...	...	...	...	...	...	...
Cuba									
2009									
Total	84 724	...	...	...	...	...	...	...	...
0 - 14	1 272	...	...	...	...	...	...	...	...
15 - 19	23 653	...	...	...	...	...	...	...	...
20 - 34	48 433	...	...	...	...	...	...	...	...
35 +	11 366	...	...	...	...	...	...	...	...
Mexico - Mexique[3]									
2009*									
Total	867	202	258	162	68	29	10	2	136
0 - 14	5	2	1	-	-	-	-	-	2
15 - 19	119	51	22	5	-	-	-	1	40
20 - 24	212	59	74	33	4	2	-	-	40
25 - 29	188	33	67	36	24	8	-	-	20
30 - 34	154	25	48	38	18	7	2	1	15
35 - 39	96	13	20	33	13	8	1	-	8
40 - 44	24	4	10	2	3	1	4	-	-
45 - 49	4	1	-	1	-	1	1	-	-
50 +	-	-	-	-	-	-	-	-	-
Unknown - Inconnu	65	14	16	14	6	2	2	-	11
Panama[4]									
2000									
Total	11	7	3	-	-	-	-	1	-
15 - 19	2	2	-	-	-	-	-	-	-
20 - 24	4	3	1	-	-	-	-	-	-
25 - 29	2	1	1	-	-	-	-	-	-
30 - 34	2	-	1	-	-	-	-	1	-
35 +	1	1	-	-	-	-	-	-	-
Puerto Rico - Porto Rico[5]									
2006									
Total	5 538	1 991	1 639	1 013	588	229	46	32	-
0 - 14	21	...	...	...	...	...	...	...	...
15 - 19	968	...	...	...	...	...	...	...	...
20 - 24	1 868	...	...	...	...	...	...	...	...
25 - 29	1 413	...	...	...	...	...	...	...	...
30 - 34	767	...	...	...	...	...	...	...	...
35 - 39	351	...	...	...	...	...	...	...	...
40 - 44	129	...	...	...	...	...	...	...	...
45 +	21	...	...	...	...	...	...	...	...
Turks and Caicos Islands - Îles Turques et Caïques[6]									
2005									
Total	32	...	...	...	...	...	...	...	...
15 - 19	4	...	...	...	...	...	...	...	...
20 - 24	7	...	...	...	...	...	...	...	...
25 - 29	9	...	...	...	...	...	...	...	...
30 - 34	6	...	...	...	...	...	...	...	...
35 - 39	4	...	...	...	...	...	...	...	...
40 - 44	1	...	...	...	...	...	...	...	...
45 +	1	...	...	...	...	...	...	...	...

14. Legally induced abortions by age and number of previous live births of women: latest available year, 2000 - 2009
Avortments provoqués légalement selon l'âge de la femme et selon le nombre des naissances vivantes précédentes : dernière année disponible, 2000 - 2009 (continued - suite)

Continent, country or area, year and age Continent, pays ou zone, année et âge	Total	0	1	2	3	4	5	6+	Unknown - Inconnu
ASIA - ASIE									
Armenia - Arménie									
2008									
Total..	12 469	...	...	...	...	...	...	...	...
0 - 14	1	...	...	...	...	...	...	...	...
15 - 19	610	...	...	...	...	...	...	...	...
20 - 24	9 459	...	...	...	...	...	...	...	...
25 + ...	2 399	...	...	...	...	...	...	...	...
Azerbaijan - Azerbaïdjan									
2007									
Total..	22 323	...	...	...	...	...	...	...	...
0 - 14	-	...	...	...	...	...	...	...	...
15 - 19	1 100	...	...	...	...	...	...	...	...
20 - 24	4 944	...	...	...	...	...	...	...	...
25 - 29	6 977	...	...	...	...	...	...	...	...
30 - 34	5 438	...	...	...	...	...	...	...	...
35 + ...	3 864	...	...	...	...	...	...	...	...
China, Hong Kong SAR - Chine, Hong Kong RAS									
2009									
Total..	12 028	6 988	2 314	2 262	382	^82	...	...	-
0 - 14	28	28	-	-	-	^-	...	...	-
15 - 19	1 052	1 013	30	9	-	^-	...	...	-
20 - 24	2 583	2 351	176	50	6	^-	...	...	-
25 - 29	2 565	1 844	463	231	21	^6	...	...	-
30 - 34	2 305	989	633	586	83	^14	...	...	-
35 - 39	2 192	549	660	798	155	^30	...	...	-
40 - 44	1 162	197	314	523	101	^27	...	...	-
45 + ...	141	17	38	65	16	^5	...	...	-
Unknown - Inconnu	-	-	-	-	-	^-	...	...	-
Georgia - Géorgie									
2008									
Total..	22 062	...	...	...	...	...	...	...	...
0 - 14	6	...	...	...	...	...	...	...	...
15 + ...	1 359	...	...	...	...	...	...	...	...
Unknown - Inconnu	20 697	...	...	...	...	...	...	...	...
Israel - Israël[7]									
2008									
Total..	19 638	8 769	2 880	3 701	2 555	1 015	390	328	...
0 - 14	61	59	1	1	-	-	-	-	...
15 - 19	2 728	2 657	59	10	2	-	-	-	...
20 - 24	4 186	3 335	521	251	69	10	-	-	...
25 - 29	3 722	1 679	858	702	310	114	42	17	...
30 - 34	3 966	729	854	1 251	712	251	109	60	...
35 - 39	3 210	240	422	1 055	914	333	127	119	...
40 - 44	1 569	56	145	395	490	278	96	109	...
45 - 49	183	8	17	35	58	28	15	22	...
50 + ...	13	6	3	1	-	1	1	1	...
Japan - Japon									
2009									
Total..	223 444	...	...	...	...	...	...	...	...
0 - 14	390	...	...	...	...	...	...	...	...
15 - 19	20 809	...	...	...	...	...	...	...	...
20 - 24	50 625	...	...	...	...	...	...	...	...
25 - 29	47 962	...	...	...	...	...	...	...	...
30 - 34	45 162	...	...	...	...	...	...	...	...
35 - 39	40 923	...	...	...	...	...	...	...	...
40 - 44	16 255	...	...	...	...	...	...	...	...
45 - 49	1 274	...	...	...	...	...	...	...	...
50 + ...	27	...	...	...	...	...	...	...	...
Unknown - Inconnu	17	...	...	...	...	...	...	...	...
Kyrgyzstan - Kirghizstan[8]									
2008									
Total..	20 800	...	...	...	...	...	...	...	...
0 - 14	1	...	...	...	...	...	...	...	...
15 - 19	1 814	...	...	...	...	...	...	...	...
20 - 24	5 018	...	...	...	...	...	...	...	...
25 - 29	5 462	...	...	...	...	...	...	...	...
30 - 34	4 598	...	...	...	...	...	...	...	...
35 - 39	2 776	...	...	...	...	...	...	...	...

14. Legally induced abortions by age and number of previous live births of women: latest available year, 2000 - 2009
Avortments provoqués légalement selon l'âge de la femme et selon le nombre des naissances vivantes précédentes :
dernière année disponible, 2000 - 2009 (continued - suite)

Continent, country or area, year and age Continent, pays ou zone, année et âge	Number of previous live births Nombre des naissances vivantes précédentes								
	Total	0	1	2	3	4	5	6+	Unknown - Inconnu
ASIA - ASIE									
Kyrgyzstan - Kirghizstan[8]									
2008									
40 - 44	1 019	...	...	...	...	...	...	...	...
45 +	112	...	...	...	...	...	...	...	...
Singapore - Singapour									
2009									
Total	12 318	6 225	2 338	2 399	969	^387	...	...	...
0 - 14	20	20	-	-	-	^-	...	...	...
15 - 19	1 175	1 079	80	13	3	^-	...	...	...
20 - 24	3 118	2 462	395	202	46	^13	...	...	...
25 - 29	3 131	1 718	727	452	160	^74	...	...	...
30 - 34	2 382	645	613	750	274	^100	...	...	...
35 - 39	1 794	242	402	685	327	^138	...	...	...
40 - 44	647	55	112	278	147	^55	...	...	...
45 +	51	4	9	19	12	^7	...	...	...
Tajikistan - Tadjikistan									
2008									
Total	18 481	...	...	...	...	...	...	...	...
0 - 14	6	...	...	...	...	...	...	...	...
15 - 17	49	...	...	...	...	...	...	...	...
18 - 19	1 250	...	...	...	...	...	...	...	...
20 - 34	12 251	...	...	...	...	...	...	...	...
35 +	4 925	...	...	...	...	...	...	...	...
EUROPE									
Åland Islands - Îles d'Åland									
2009									
Total	68	...	...	...	...	...	...	...	...
0 - 14	-	...	...	...	...	...	...	...	...
15 - 19	10	...	...	...	...	...	...	...	...
20 - 24	21	...	...	...	...	...	...	...	...
25 - 29	15	...	...	...	...	...	...	...	...
30 - 34	11	...	...	...	...	...	...	...	...
35 - 39	7	...	...	...	...	...	...	...	...
40 - 44	4	...	...	...	...	...	...	...	...
45 - 49	-	...	...	...	...	...	...	...	...
50 +	-	...	...	...	...	...	...	...	...
Belarus - Bélarus									
2009									
Total	35 967	...	...	...	...	...	...	...	...
0 - 14	41	...	...	...	...	...	...	...	...
15 - 19	3 153	...	...	...	...	...	...	...	...
20 - 24	8 377	...	...	...	...	...	...	...	...
25 - 29	9 505	...	...	...	...	...	...	...	...
30 - 34	7 373	...	...	...	...	...	...	...	...
35 - 39	5 144	...	...	...	...	...	...	...	...
40 - 44	2 106	...	...	...	...	...	...	...	...
45 - 49	268	...	...	...	...	...	...	...	...
50 +	-	...	...	...	...	...	...	...	...
Unknown - Inconnu	-	...	...	...	...	...	...	...	...
Belgium - Belgique									
2003									
Total	15 595	...	...	...	...	...	...	...	...
0 - 14	65	...	...	...	...	...	...	...	...
15 - 19	2 097	...	...	...	...	...	...	...	...
20 - 24	4 032	...	...	...	...	...	...	...	...
25 - 29	3 411	...	...	...	...	...	...	...	...
30 - 34	3 001	...	...	...	...	...	...	...	...
35 - 39	2 107	...	...	...	...	...	...	...	...
40 - 44	810	...	...	...	...	...	...	...	...
45 - 49	67	...	...	...	...	...	...	...	...
50 +	1	...	...	...	...	...	...	...	...
Unknown - Inconnu	4	...	...	...	...	...	...	...	...

14. Legally induced abortions by age and number of previous live births of women: latest available year, 2000 - 2009
Avortments provoqués légalement selon l'âge de la femme et selon le nombre des naissances vivantes précédentes :
dernière année disponible, 2000 - 2009 (continued - suite)

| Continent, country or area, year and age / Continent, pays ou zone, année et âge | Total | Number of previous live births / Nombre des naissances vivantes précédentes | | | | | | | Unknown - Inconnu |
		0	1	2	3	4	5	6+	
EUROPE									
Bulgaria - Bulgarie									
2009									
Total	33 733	...	...	...	...	...	...	...	...
0 - 14	166	...	...	...	...	...	...	...	...
15 - 19	3 248	...	...	...	...	...	...	...	...
20 - 24	7 169	...	...	...	...	...	...	...	...
25 - 29	8 437	...	...	...	...	...	...	...	...
30 - 34	7 982	...	...	...	...	...	...	...	...
35 - 39	5 114	...	...	...	...	...	...	...	...
40 - 44	1 523	...	...	...	...	...	...	...	...
45 - 49	94	...	...	...	...	...	...	...	...
50 +	-	...	...	...	...	...	...	...	...
Unknown - Inconnu	-	...	...	...	...	...	...	...	...
Croatia - Croatie									
2008									
Total	4 497	1 322	894	1 362	589	174	47	50	59
0 - 14	5	5	-	-	-	-	-	-	-
15 - 19	353	297	32	9	-	1	-	-	14
20 - 24	838	523	187	87	25	2	-	2	12
25 - 29	962	299	237	288	81	32	8	5	12
30 - 34	902	110	199	317	187	53	13	14	9
35 - 39	887	46	160	405	195	45	15	16	5
40 - 44	437	24	59	213	82	37	7	11	4
45 - 49	47	3	10	22	8	3	-	1	-
50 +	-	-	-	-	-	-	-	-	-
Unknown - Inconnu	66	15	10	21	11	1	4	1	3
Czech Republic - République tchèque									
2009									
Total	24 636	7 110	6 326	8 244	2 213	514	142	87	-
0 - 14	45	45	-	-	-	-	-	-	-
15 - 19	2 237	1 976	236	24	1	-	-	-	-
20 - 24	4 413	2 570	1 274	472	78	14	5	-	-
25 - 29	4 937	1 523	1 666	1 361	270	93	14	10	-
30 - 34	6 198	746	1 762	2 785	677	155	48	25	-
35 - 39	4 770	207	1 020	2 514	786	171	43	29	-
40 - 44	1 837	37	333	978	363	75	31	20	-
45 - 49	192	6	33	105	38	6	1	3	-
50 +	7	-	2	5	-	-	-	-	-
Unknown - Inconnu	-	-	-	-	-	-	-	-	-
Denmark - Danemark[9]									
2006									
Total	15 053	...	...	...	...	...	...	...	...
15 - 19	2 518	...	...	...	...	...	...	...	...
20 - 24	3 138	...	...	...	...	...	...	...	...
25 - 29	2 861	...	...	...	...	...	...	...	...
30 - 34	2 973	...	...	...	...	...	...	...	...
35 - 39	2 373	...	...	...	...	...	...	...	...
40 - 44	1 107	...	...	...	...	...	...	...	...
45 - 49	83	...	...	...	...	...	...	...	...
50 +	-	...	...	...	...	...	...	...	...
Estonia - Estonie[10]									
2009									
Total	7 542	1 951	2 617	2 132	612	158	46	21	5
0 - 14	11	11	-	-	-	-	-	-	-
15 - 19	864	725	127	12	-	-	-	-	-
20 - 24	1 860	799	825	210	20	4	1	-	1
25 - 29	1 695	304	747	522	95	17	5	3	2
30 - 34	1 387	60	463	622	173	51	13	5	-
35 - 39	1 195	41	316	546	210	51	20	9	2
40 - 44	482	11	124	197	105	35	6	4	-
45 - 49	48	-	15	23	9	-	1	-	-
50 +	-	-	-	-	-	-	-	-	-
Unknown - Inconnu	-	-	-	-	-	-	-	-	-
Faeroe Islands - Îles Féroé									
2005									
Total	29	...	...	...	...	...	...	...	...
0 - 14	-	...	...	...	...	...	...	...	...
15 - 19	6	...	...	...	...	...	...	...	...
20 - 24	2	...	...	...	...	...	...	...	...

Avortments provoqués légalement selon l'âge de la femme et selon le nombre des naissances vivantes précédentes : dernière année disponible, 2000 - 2009 (continued - suite)

Continent, country or area, year and age / Continent, pays ou zone, année et âge	Number of previous live births / Nombre des naissances vivantes précédentes								
	Total	0	1	2	3	4	5	6+	Unknown - Inconnu
EUROPE									
Faeroe Islands - Îles Féroé									
2005									
25 - 29	5	...	...	...	...	...	...	...	...
30 - 34	8	...	...	...	...	...	...	...	...
35 - 39	5	...	...	...	...	...	...	...	...
40 - 44	3	...	...	...	...	...	...	...	...
45 - 49	-	...	...	...	...	...	...	...	...
50 +	-	...	...	...	...	...	...	...	...
Finland - Finlande									
2009									
Total	10 427	5 303	1 963	1 806	824	270	65	37	159
0 - 14	42	42	-	-	-	-	-	-	-
15 - 19	2 059	1 913	85	12	2	-	-	-	47
20 - 24	2 819	1 877	622	218	39	7	-	-	56
25 - 29	2 103	886	503	474	171	31	5	1	32
30 - 34	1 718	369	400	538	272	92	21	12	14
35 - 39	1 091	147	226	374	212	90	24	14	4
40 - 44	535	64	119	169	114	38	15	10	6
45 - 49	59	5	8	21	13	12	-	-	-
50 +	1	-	-	-	1	-	-	-	-
Unknown - Inconnu	-	-	-	-	-	-	-	-	-
France									
2005									
Total	205 392	...	...	...	...	...	...	...	...
15 - 19	29 796	...	...	...	...	...	...	...	...
20 - 24	52 541	...	...	...	...	...	...	...	...
25 - 29	42 735	...	...	...	...	...	...	...	...
30 - 34	38 552	...	...	...	...	...	...	...	...
35 - 39	28 407	...	...	...	...	...	...	...	...
40 - 44	12 234	...	...	...	...	...	...	...	...
45 - 49	1 127	...	...	...	...	...	...	...	...
Germany - Allemagne									
2008									
Total	114 484	46 683	29 961	25 798	8 626	2 322	703	391	-
0 - 14	475	475	-	-	-	-	-	-	-
15 - 19	13 300	12 121	1 084	90	2	-	1	2	-
20 - 24	27 790	17 279	7 382	2 555	469	90	11	4	-
25 - 29	25 938	9 241	8 428	5 977	1 736	423	98	35	-
30 - 34	20 915	4 241	6 091	7 065	2 526	663	224	105	-
35 - 39	17 259	2 256	4 795	6 561	2 556	726	229	136	-
40 - 44	8 102	1 010	2 029	3 232	1 235	380	123	93	-
45 - 49	685	59	146	311	101	38	16	14	-
50 +	20	1	6	7	1	2	1	2	-
Greece - Grèce									
2003									
Total	15 782	...	...	...	...	...	...	...	...
0 - 14	8	...	...	...	...	...	...	...	...
15 - 19	569	...	...	...	...	...	...	...	...
20 - 29	5 934	...	...	...	...	...	...	...	...
30 - 39	7 557	...	...	...	...	...	...	...	...
40 - 49	1 345	...	...	...	...	...	...	...	...
50 +	48	...	...	...	...	...	...	...	...
Unknown - Inconnu	321	...	...	...	...	...	...	...	...
Guernsey - Guernesey									
2000									
Total	89	46	21	11	9	1	1	-	-
0 - 14	1	1	-	-	-	-	-	-	-
15 - 19	12	11	1	-	-	-	-	-	-
20 - 24	30	17	13	-	-	-	-	-	-
25 - 29	18	11	3	3	1	-	-	-	-
30 - 34	15	4	3	4	2	1	1	-	-
35 - 39	10	1	1	4	4	-	-	-	-
40 - 44	3	1	-	-	2	-	-	-	-
45 +	-	-	-	-	-	-	-	-	-
Hungary - Hongrie									
2009									
Total	43 181	11 635	10 331	11 166	6 000	2 350	935	764	-
0 - 14	164	162	2	-	-	-	-	-	-
15 - 19	5 173	3 986	933	210	42	2	-	-	-

14. Legally induced abortions by age and number of previous live births of women: latest available year, 2000 - 2009
Avortments provoqués légalement selon l'âge de la femme et selon le nombre des naissances vivantes précédentes : dernière année disponible, 2000 - 2009 (continued - suite)

Continent, country or area, year and age / Continent, pays ou zone, année et âge	Total	Number of previous live births / Nombre des naissances vivantes précédentes							Unknown - Inconnu
		0	1	2	3	4	5	6+	
EUROPE									
Hungary - Hongrie									
2009									
20 - 24	8 573	3 733	2 391	1 494	724	188	34	9	-
25 - 29	8 939	2 091	2 418	2 206	1 321	580	196	127	-
30 - 34	10 357	1 210	2 605	3 252	1 869	765	347	309	-
35 - 39	7 161	365	1 494	2 774	1 447	577	272	232	-
40 - 44	2 643	81	468	1 145	562	219	83	85	-
45 - 49	168	6	20	84	34	19	3	2	-
50 +	3	1	-	1	1	-	-	-	-
Unknown - Inconnu	-	-	-	-	-	-	-	-	-
Iceland - Islande									
2009									
Total	971	113	251	185	94	22	6	2	298
0 - 14	1	-	-	-	-	-	-	-	1
15 - 19	139	35	9	-	-	-	-	-	95
20 - 24	262	48	78	12	5	-	-	-	119
25 - 29	244	18	102	49	15	2	-	-	58
30 - 34	152	6	37	53	27	10	1	2	16
35 - 39	107	4	19	45	29	4	1	-	5
40 - 44	56	2	5	22	14	5	4	-	4
45 - 49	10	-	1	4	4	1	-	-	-
50 +	-	-	-	-	-	-	-	-	-
Unknown - Inconnu	-	-	-	-	-	-	-	-	-
Italy - Italie									
2003[11]									
Total	124 118	52 804	28 193	30 616	9 001	2 007	464	216	817
0 - 14	255	242	3	1	-	-	-	-	9
15 - 19	9 725	8 722	744	114	13	2	1	-	129
20 - 24	24 074	17 042	4 694	1 757	251	47	4	3	276
25 - 29	28 656	13 633	7 686	5 655	1 212	217	44	11	198
30 - 34	27 794	7 948	7 527	9 078	2 470	502	107	52	110
35 - 39	22 877	3 840	5 299	9 387	3 273	734	180	95	69
40 - 44	9 580	1 147	2 016	4 191	1 604	449	113	46	14
45 - 49	760	76	133	333	149	47	12	9	1
50 +	36	9	9	12	4	1	1	-	-
Unknown - Inconnu	361	145	82	88	25	8	2	-	11
2009									
Total	114 793	...	...	...	...	...	...	...	...
0 - 14	236	...	...	...	...	...	...	...	...
15 - 19	9 603	...	...	...	...	...	...	...	...
20 - 24	20 950	...	...	...	...	...	...	...	...
25 - 29	23 302	...	...	...	...	...	...	...	...
30 - 34	25 699	...	...	...	...	...	...	...	...
35 - 39	22 916	...	...	...	...	...	...	...	...
40 - 44	10 228	...	...	...	...	...	...	...	...
45 - 49	955	...	...	...	...	...	...	...	...
50 +	25	...	...	...	...	...	...	...	...
Unknown - Inconnu	879	...	...	...	...	...	...	...	...
Latvia - Lettonie									
2009									
Total	8 881	...	...	...	...	...	...	...	...
0 - 14	6	...	...	...	...	...	...	...	...
15 - 19	794	...	...	...	...	...	...	...	...
20 - 24	2 046	...	...	...	...	...	...	...	...
25 - 29	2 031	...	...	...	...	...	...	...	...
30 - 34	1 794	...	...	...	...	...	...	...	...
35 - 39	1 483	...	...	...	...	...	...	...	...
40 - 44	642	...	...	...	...	...	...	...	...
45 - 49	83	...	...	...	...	...	...	...	...
50 +	2	...	...	...	...	...	...	...	...
Unknown - Inconnu	-	...	...	...	...	...	...	...	...
Lithuania - Lituanie									
2009									
Total	8 024	...	...	...	...	...	...	...	...
0 - 14	2	...	...	...	...	...	...	...	...
15 - 19	628	...	...	...	...	...	...	...	...
20 - 24	1 657	...	...	...	...	...	...	...	...
25 - 29	1 685	...	...	...	...	...	...	...	...
30 - 34	1 732	...	...	...	...	...	...	...	...

14. Legally induced abortions by age and number of previous live births of women: latest available year, 2000 - 2009
Avortments provoqués légalement selon l'âge de la femme et selon le nombre des naissances vivantes précédentes :
dernière année disponible, 2000 - 2009 (continued - suite)

Continent, country or area, year and age / Continent, pays ou zone, année et âge	Number of previous live births / Nombre des naissances vivantes précédentes								
	Total	0	1	2	3	4	5	6+	Unknown - Inconnu
EUROPE									
Lithuania - Lituanie									
2009									
35 - 39	1 520	...	...	...	...	...	...	...	...
40 - 44	715	...	...	...	...	...	...	...	...
45 - 49	85	...	...	...	...	...	...	...	...
50 +	-	...	...	...	...	...	...	...	...
Unknown - Inconnu	-	...	...	...	...	...	...	...	...
Montenegro - Monténégro									
2005									
Total	1 952	307	283	677	473	139	45	26	2
0 - 14	3	-	2	1	-	-	-	-	-
15 - 16	5	5	-	-	-	-	-	-	-
17 - 19	46	31	7	4	2	1	-	-	1
20 - 29	685	179	155	219	98	21	10	3	-
30 - 39	982	80	108	365	286	91	33	18	1
40 - 49	223	11	11	86	82	26	2	5	-
50 +	4	1	-	1	2	-	-	-	-
Unknown - Inconnu	4	-	-	1	3	-	-	-	-
Norway - Norvège[12]									
2006									
Total	14 132	...	...	...	...	...	...	...	...
0 - 14	37	...	...	...	...	...	...	...	...
15 - 19	2 307	...	...	...	...	...	...	...	...
20 - 24	3 740	...	...	...	...	...	...	...	...
25 - 29	2 904	...	...	...	...	...	...	...	...
30 - 34	2 495	...	...	...	...	...	...	...	...
35 - 39	1 877	...	...	...	...	...	...	...	...
40 - 44	694	...	...	...	...	...	...	...	...
45 - 49	55	...	...	...	...	...	...	...	...
50 +	-	...	...	...	...	...	...	...	...
Unknown - Inconnu	23	...	...	...	...	...	...	...	...
Poland - Pologne[13]									
2008									
Total	506	...	...	...	...	...	...	...	...
15 - 19	42	...	...	...	...	...	...	...	...
20 - 24	119	...	...	...	...	...	...	...	...
25 - 29	115	...	...	...	...	...	...	...	...
30 - 34	130	...	...	...	...	...	...	...	...
35 - 39	100	...	...	...	...	...	...	...	...
Republic of Moldova - République de Moldova									
2008									
Total	15 900	...	...	...	...	...	...	...	...
0 - 14	26	...	...	...	...	...	...	...	...
15 +	1 327	...	...	...	...	...	...	...	...
Unknown - Inconnu	14 547	...	...	...	...	...	...	...	...
Romania - Roumanie									
2009									
Total	116 060	...	...	...	...	...	...	...	...
0 - 14	588	...	...	...	...	...	...	...	...
15 - 19	11 982	...	...	...	...	...	...	...	...
20 - 24	25 442	...	...	...	...	...	...	...	...
25 - 29	25 794	...	...	...	...	...	...	...	...
30 - 34	26 220	...	...	...	...	...	...	...	...
35 - 39	18 468	...	...	...	...	...	...	...	...
40 - 44	7 167	...	...	...	...	...	...	...	...
45 - 49	384	...	...	...	...	...	...	...	...
50 +	15	...	...	...	...	...	...	...	...
Russian Federation - Fédération de Russie									
2009									
Total	1 292 389	...	...	...	...	...	...	...	...
0 - 14	721	...	...	...	...	...	...	...	...
15 - 19	99 634	...	...	...	...	...	...	...	...
20 - 24	324 467	...	...	...	...	...	...	...	...
25 - 29	342 821	...	...	...	...	...	...	...	...
30 - 34	272 883	...	...	...	...	...	...	...	...
35 - 39	179 061	...	...	...	...	...	...	...	...
40 - 44	65 937	...	...	...	...	...	...	...	...
45 - 49	6 667	...	...	...	...	...	...	...	...

14. Legally induced abortions by age and number of previous live births of women: latest available year, 2000 - 2009
Avortments provoqués légalement selon l'âge de la femme et selon le nombre des naissances vivantes précédentes : dernière année disponible, 2000 - 2009 (continued - suite)

Continent, country or area, year and age / Continent, pays ou zone, année et âge	Total	Number of previous live births / Nombre des naissances vivantes précédentes							Unknown - Inconnu
		0	1	2	3	4	5	6+	
EUROPE									
Russian Federation - Fédération de Russie									
2009									
50 +	198	...	...	...	...	...	...	...	...
Unknown - Inconnu	-	...	...	...	...	...	...	...	...
Serbia - Serbie[14]									
2008									
Total	22 867	6 601	4 346	8 509	2 437	663	198	113	-
0 - 14	9	6	1	2	-	-	-	-	-
15 - 19	975	808	124	35	7	1	-	-	-
20 - 24	3 427	1 823	848	570	122	52	9	3	-
25 - 29	5 117	1 510	1 173	1 757	479	141	47	10	-
30 - 34	5 953	1 240	1 114	2 569	719	212	62	37	-
35 - 39	4 929	806	768	2 354	730	170	59	42	-
40 - 44	2 174	363	279	1 072	347	76	17	20	-
45 - 49	266	40	34	146	31	10	4	1	-
50 +	16	5	4	4	2	1	-	-	-
Unknown - Inconnu	1	-	1	-	-	-	-	-	-
Slovakia - Slovaquie									
2009									
Total	13 240	4 155	3 519	3 666	1 188	363	180	169	...
0 - 14	14	14	-	-	-	-	-	-	...
15 - 19	1 106	940	139	24	3	-	-	-	...
20 - 24	2 382	1 344	646	303	64	17	8	-	...
25 - 29	3 005	1 099	974	611	194	72	37	18	...
30 - 34	3 341	521	1 034	1 212	347	113	56	58	...
35 - 39	2 385	170	577	1 033	395	111	47	52	...
40 - 44	915	62	140	434	171	44	28	36	...
45 - 49	89	5	6	49	14	6	4	5	...
50 +	3	-	3	-	-	-	-	-	...
Unknown - Inconnu	-	-	-	-	-	-	-	-	...
Slovenia - Slovénie									
2009									
Total	4 653	1 679	1 070	1 408	401	62	19	10	4
0 - 14	4	4	-	-	-	-	-	-	-
15 - 19	342	319	17	6	-	-	-	-	-
20 - 24	847	639	151	47	6	-	1	-	3
25 - 29	1 058	429	304	270	47	5	3	-	-
30 - 34	1 127	210	309	439	145	14	5	5	-
35 - 39	838	56	203	413	130	27	7	2	-
40 - 44	392	19	79	210	62	15	3	3	1
45 - 49	44	3	7	23	10	1	-	-	-
50 +	1	-	-	-	1	-	-	-	-
Unknown - Inconnu	-	-	-	-	-	-	-	-	-
Spain - Espagne									
2004									
Total	84 985	42 757	19 962	15 023	4 772	1 400	^741	...	330
0 - 14	369	365	1	-	-	-	^-	...	3
15 - 19	11 677	10 415	1 057	145	16	4	^-	...	40
20 - 24	22 461	15 193	5 127	1 680	353	33	^13	...	62
25 - 29	20 309	9 931	5 541	3 457	981	239	^77	...	83
30 - 34	15 212	4 630	4 381	4 186	1 329	424	^195	...	67
35 - 39	10 572	1 777	2 846	3 757	1 373	476	^288	...	55
40 - 44	4 072	414	949	1 665	661	211	^153	...	19
45 - 49	313	32	60	133	59	13	^15	...	1
50 +	-	-	-	-	-	-	^-	...	-
Sweden - Suède[15]									
2008									
Total	38 049	20 447	5 937	7 176	2 945	751	281	137	375
0 - 14	219	212	1	2	1	-	-	-	3
15 - 19	7 338	7 016	202	20	3	1	1	2	93
20 - 24	9 636	7 514	1 470	447	64	10	4	-	127
25 - 29	7 274	3 574	1 678	1 466	371	94	23	10	58
30 - 34	5 902	1 348	1 317	2 080	841	191	55	22	48
35 - 39	5 091	580	879	2 121	1 039	274	125	49	24
40 - 44	2 351	174	361	963	566	160	64	46	17
45 - 49	196	10	23	69	56	21	9	7	1
50 +	4	1	-	-	2	-	-	1	-
Unknown - Inconnu	38	18	6	8	2	-	-	-	4

14. Legally induced abortions by age and number of previous live births of women: latest available year, 2000 - 2009
Avortments provoqués légalement selon l'âge de la femme et selon le nombre des naissances vivantes précédentes :
dernière année disponible, 2000 - 2009 (continued - suite)

Continent, country or area, year and age / Continent, pays ou zone, année et âge	Number of previous live births / Nombre des naissances vivantes précédentes								
	Total	0	1	2	3	4	5	6+	Unknown - Inconnu
EUROPE									
Switzerland - Suisse[16]									
2009									
Total	10 137	2 109	775	772	271	88	...	...	6 122
0 - 14	24	9	-	-	-	-	...	...	15
15 - 19	1 082	469	10	1	-	-	...	...	602
20 - 24	2 316	758	170	37	4	1	...	...	1 346
25 - 29	2 190	452	200	153	29	11	...	...	1 345
30 - 34	2 030	256	195	203	91	27	...	...	1 258
35 - 39	1 554	100	140	223	82	30	...	...	979
40 - 44	806	45	47	135	54	18	...	...	507
45 - 49	97	7	9	15	10	1	...	...	55
50 +	7	3	-	-	1	-	...	...	3
Unknown - Inconnu	31	10	4	5	-	-	...	...	12
Ukraine									
2007									
Total	210 454	...	...	...	...	...	...	...	...
0 - 14	84	...	...	...	...	...	...	...	...
15 - 19	19 693	...	...	...	...	...	...	...	...
20 - 34	155 379	...	...	...	...	...	...	...	...
35 +	35 298	...	...	...	...	...	...	...	...
United Kingdom of Great Britain and Northern Ireland - Royaume-Uni de Grande-Bretagne et d'Irlande du Nord[17]									
2000[10]									
Total	197 366	105 328	37 645	33 532	13 982	4 683	1 414	753	29
0 - 14	1 170	1 165	4	1	-	-	-	-	-
15 - 19	40 225	35 254	4 393	528	40	4	-	-	6
20 - 24	53 590	35 263	11 732	5 183	1 150	222	25	9	6
25 - 29	42 680	20 273	9 640	8 295	3 212	953	231	71	5
30 - 34	31 928	8 925	7 004	9 504	4 339	1 491	455	205	5
35 - 39	20 684	3 562	3 711	7 438	3 771	1 433	485	279	5
40 - 44	6 526	794	1 081	2 375	1 359	542	203	171	1
45 - 49	490	62	66	189	108	36	14	15	-
50 +	25	4	4	9	2	2	1	3	-
Unknown - Inconnu	48	26	10	10	1	-	-	-	1
2008									
Total	209 113	...	...	...	...	...	...	...	...
0 - 14	1 192	...	...	...	...	...	...	...	...
15 - 19	44 974	...	...	...	...	...	...	...	...
20 - 24	60 449	...	...	...	...	...	...	...	...
25 - 29	44 638	...	...	...	...	...	...	...	...
30 - 34	28 638	...	...	...	...	...	...	...	...
35 - 39	20 434	...	...	...	...	...	...	...	...
40 - 44	8 096	...	...	...	...	...	...	...	...
45 - 49	671	...	...	...	...	...	...	...	...
50 +	21	...	...	...	...	...	...	...	...
Unknown - Inconnu	-	...	...	...	...	...	...	...	...
OCEANIA - OCÉANIE									
New Zealand - Nouvelle-Zélande									
2009									
Total	17 550	8 370	3 580	3 235	1 401	602	195	167	-
0 - 14	79	79	-	-	-	-	-	-	-
15 - 19	3 873	3 227	563	74	9	-	-	-	-
20 - 24	5 332	2 964	1 393	723	203	41	4	4	-
25 - 29	3 539	1 343	772	830	380	139	51	24	-
30 - 34	2 311	496	456	713	359	187	50	50	-
35 - 39	1 692	193	291	605	315	175	62	51	-
40 - 44	674	64	101	274	123	52	27	33	-
45 - 49	50	4	4	16	12	8	1	5	-
50 +	-	-	-	-	-	-	-	-	-

FOOTNOTES - NOTES

* Provisional. - Données provisoires.

^ Indicates an open-ended group, for example 4+. - indique un groupe d'âge ouvert, par exemple 4 ou plus.

[1] Data refer to resident population only. Significant undercoverage of medically induced abortions in clinics in 2006 due to non response in some provinces. - Pour la population résidante seulement. Sous-dénombrement notable des interruptions volontaires de grossesse pratiquées dans les centres médicaux en 2006 faute de réponse dans certaines provinces.

[2] Number of abortions the woman had before the birth of the registered child. Excluding abortions performed in private hospitals. - Nombre d'avortements de la femme avant la naissance de l'enfant enregistré. Non comprises les interruptions volontaires de grossesse effectuées dans des hôpitaux privés.

[3] Data refer to 'Therapeutic Abortions'. According to the Mexican law, only the induced abortions, prescribed by medical reasons and induced because of pregnancy coming from sexual agression, are considered as legal. Data refer to abortions prescribed by a physician. Refers to residence of the mother. To calculate the total number of abortions, foetal deaths of less than 20 weeks of gestation were considered. - Les données se rapportent aux « interruptions volontaires de grossesse pour des motifs thérapeutiques ». D'après la loi mexicaine, seuls sont considérés légaux les avortements déclenchés pour des raisons médicales ou parce que la grossesse est le résultat d'une agression sexuelle. Les données se réfèrent aux avortements prescrits par un médecin. Correspond à la résidence de la mère. Les morts fœtales survenues à moins de 20 semaines de gestation ont été prises en compte aux fins du calcul du nombre total d'avortements.

[4] Data refer to abortions granted for medical reasons by the Comision Multidisciplinaria Nacional de Aborto Terapéutico. - Les données se réfèrent aux avortements autorisés pour des raisons médicales par la Comision Multidisciplinaria Nacional de Aborto Terapéutico.

[5] Data refer to the fiscal year from 1 July to 30 June. Excluding abortions performed in a clinic which closed operations without reporting the data. - Les données se réfèrent à l'année budgétaire de 1 juillet à 30 juin. Non comprises les avortements effectuées dans une clinique qui a fermé sans envoyer les données.

[6] Data refer to abortions performed in hospitals at Grand Turk and Providenciales. - Pour des avortements exécutés dans les hôpitaux dans Grand Turk et Providenciales.

[7] Including data for East Jerusalem and Israeli residents in certain other territories under occupation by Israeli military forces since June 1967. Data refer to applications to commissions for termination of pregnancy and not to authorizations. - Y compris les données pour Jérusalem-Est et les résidents israéliens dans certains autres territoires occupés depuis 1967 par les forces armées israéliennes. Les données relatives aux avortements provoqués légalement se rapportent aux demandes d'autorisation et non aux autorisations elles-mêmes.

[8] Based on administrative reporting of the Ministry of Health. - Les données reposent sur les rapports administratifs du Ministère de la santé.

[9] Excluding Faeroe Islands and Greenland shown separately, if available. Unrevised data. - Non compris les Iles Féroé et le Groenland, qui font l'objet de rubriques distinctes, si disponible. Les données n'ont pas été révisées.

[10] Data refer to resident population only. - Pour la population résidante seulement.

[11] Data are incomplete for Campania region. - Les données sont incomplètes pour la région de la Campanie.

[12] Unrevised data. Excluding Svalbard and Jan Mayen Islands shown separately, if available. - Les données n'ont pas été révisées. Non compris Svalbard et Jan Mayen qui font l'objet de rubriques distinctes, si disponible.

[13] Based on hospital and polyclinic records. - D'après les registres des hôpitaux et des polycliniques.

[14] Excluding data for Kosovo and Metohia. Data refer to institutions included in the Health Institutions Network Plan in the Republic of Serbia. - Sans les données pour le Kosovo et Metohie. Les données se rapportent aux institutions membres du "Health Institutions Network Plan" de la République de Serbie.

[15] Data refer to abortions by previous deliveries of mother rather than previous live births of mother. - Avortements selon les accouchements précédents de la mère plutôt que selon les naissances vivantes de la mère.

[16] Data refer to termination of pregnancy for women who are Switzerland residents. - Les données portent sur les interruptions de grossesse pratiquées sur des femmes qui résident en Suisse.

[17] Excluding Channel Islands (Guernsey and Jersey) and Isle of Man, shown separately, if available. - Non compris les îles Anglo-Normandes (Guernesey et Jersey) et l'île de Man, qui font l'objet de rubriques distinctes, si disponible.

14a. Legally induced abortions by age and number of previous live births of women: 2010
Avortments provoqués légalement selon l'âge de la femme et selon le nombre des naissances vivantes précédentes: 2010

Continent, country or area, year and age Continent, pays ou zone, année et âge	Total	Number of previous live births Nombre des naissances vivantes précédentes							
		0	1	2	3	4	5	6+	Unknown - Inconnu

ASIA - ASIE

Singapore - Singapour
  2010

	Total	0	1	2	3	4	5	6+	Unknown - Inconnu
Total	12 082	5 885	2 422	2 442	959	^374	...	...	...
0 - 14	23	22	1	-	-	^-	...	...	...
15 - 19	1 072	982	81	9	-	^-	...	...	...
20 - 24	2 934	2 296	398	181	41	^18	...	...	...
25 - 29	3 101	1 665	732	486	159	^59	...	...	...
30 - 34	2 431	642	657	761	264	^107	...	...	...
35 - 39	1 832	232	417	734	335	^114	...	...	...
40 - 44	624	43	128	247	136	^70	...	...	...
45 +	65	3	8	24	24	^6	...	...	...

FOOTNOTES - NOTES

* Provisional. - Données provisoires.

^ Indicates an open-ended group, for example 4+. - indique un groupe d'âge
  ouvert, par exemple 4 ou plus.

Table 15

Table 15 presents infant deaths and infant mortality rates by urban/rural residence for as many years as possible between 2006 and 2010.

Description of variables: Infant deaths are deaths of live-born infants under one year of age.

Statistics on the number of infant deaths are obtained from civil registers unless otherwise noted. Infant mortality rates are, in most instances, calculated from data on registered infant deaths and registered live births for a country or area where civil registration is considered reliable (that is, with an estimated completeness of 90 per cent or more).

The urban/rural classification of infant deaths is that provided by each reporting country or area; it is presumed to be based on the national census definitions of urban population that have been set forth at the end of the technical notes of table 6.

Rate computation: Infant mortality rates are the annual number of deaths of infants under one year of age per 1 000 live births (as shown in table 9) in the same year.

Rates by urban/rural residence are the annual number of infant deaths, in the appropriate urban or rural category, per 1 000 corresponding live births (as shown in table 9). These rates have been calculated by the Statistics Division of the United Nations.

Rates presented in this table have been limited to those countries or areas having at least a total of 30 infant deaths in a given year and for which the quality code is represented by a "C" or a symbol "|".

Reliability of data: Each country or area has been asked to indicate the estimated completeness of the infant deaths recorded in its civil register. These national assessments are indicated by the quality codes "C", "U" and "|" that appear in the first column of this table.

"C" indicates that the data are estimated to be virtually complete, that is, representing at least 90 per cent of the infant deaths occurring each year, while "U" indicates that data are estimated to be incomplete that is, representing less than 90 per cent of the infant deaths occurring each year. The code "|" indicates that the source of data is not civil registration, but is still considered reliable. The code "..." indicates that no information was provided regarding completeness.

Data from civil registers that are reported as incomplete or of unknown completeness (coded "U" or "...") are considered unreliable. They appear in italics in this table; rates are not computed for data so coded.

Limitations: Statistics on infant deaths are subject to the same qualifications as have been set forth for vital statistics in general and death statistics in particular as discussed in section 4 of the Technical Notes.

The reliability of the data, an indication of which is described above, is an important factor in considering the limitations. In addition, some infant deaths are tabulated by date of registration and not by date of occurrence; these have been indicated by a plus sign "+". Whenever the lag between the date of occurrence and date of registration is prolonged and, therefore, a large proportion of the infant-death registrations are delayed, infant-death statistics for any given year may be seriously affected.

Another factor that limits international comparability is the practice of some countries or areas not to include in infant-death statistics infants who were born alive but died before the registration of the birth or within the first 24 hours of life, thus underestimating the total number of infant deaths. Statistics of this type are footnoted.

The method of reckoning age at death for infants may also introduce non-comparability. If year alone, rather than completed minutes, hours, days and months elapsed since birth, is used to calculate age at time of death, many of the infants who died during the eleventh month of life and some of those who died at younger ages will be classified as having completed one year of age and thus be excluded. The effect would be to underestimate the number of infant deaths. Information on this factor is given in footnotes when known. Reckoning of infant age is further discussed in the technical notes for table 16.

In addition, infant mortality rates are subject to the limitations of the data on live births that have been used as denominators for these rates. These have been set forth in the technical notes for table 9.

Because the two components of the infant mortality rate, infant deaths in the numerator and live births in the denominator, are both obtained from systems of civil registration, the limitations which affect live birth statistics are very similar to those which have been mentioned above in connection with the infant death statistics. It is important to consider the reliability of the data (the completeness of registration) and the method of tabulation (by date of occurrence or by date of registration) of live birth statistics as well as infant death statistics, both of which are used to calculate infant mortality rates. The quality code and use of italics to indicate unreliable data presented in this table refer only to infant deaths. Similarly, the indication of the basis of tabulation (the use of the symbol "+" to indicate data tabulated by date of registration) presented in this table also refers only to infant deaths. Table 9 provides the corresponding information for live births.

If the registration of infant deaths is more complete than the registration of live births, then infant mortality rates would be biased upwards. If, however, the registration of live births is more complete than registration of infant deaths, infant mortality rates would be biased downwards. If both infant deaths and live births are tabulated by registration, it should be noted that deaths tend to be more promptly reported than births.

Infant mortality rates may be seriously affected by the practice of some countries or areas of not considering infants that were born alive but died before the registration of the birth or within the first 24 hours of life as live birth and subsequently infant death. Although this practice results in both the number of infant deaths in the numerator and the number of live births in the denominator being underestimated, its impact is greater on the numerator of the infant mortality rate. As a result this practice causes infant mortality rates to be biased downwards.

Infant mortality rates will also be underestimated if the method of reckoning age at death results in an underestimation of the number of infant deaths. This point has been discussed above.

Because of all these factors care should be taken in comparing infant mortality rates.

With respect to the method of calculating infant mortality rates used in this table, it should be noted that no adjustment was made to take account of the fact that a proportion of the infant deaths that occur during a given year are deaths of infants that were born during the preceding year and hence are not taken from the universe of births used to compute the rates. However, unless the number of live births or infant deaths is changing rapidly, the error involved is insignificant.

The comparability of data by urban/rural residence is affected by the national definitions of urban and rural used in tabulating these data. It is assumed, in the absence of specific information to the contrary, that the definitions of urban and rural used in connection with the national population census were also used in the compilation of the vital statistics for each country or area. However, it cannot be denied that, for some countries or areas, different definitions of urban and rural may be used for the vital statistics data and the population census data respectively. When known, the definitions of urban used in national population censuses are presented at the end of the technical notes for table 6. As discussed in detail in the technical notes for table 6, these definitions vary considerably from one country or area to another.

Urban/rural differentials in infant mortality rates may also be affected by whether the infant deaths and live births have been tabulated in terms of place of occurrence or place of usual residence. This problem is discussed in more detail in section 4.1.4.1 of the Technical Notes.

Earlier data: Infant deaths and infant mortality rates have been shown in previous issues of the *Demographic Yearbook*. For more information on specific topics and years for which data are reported, readers should consult the Historical Index.

Tableau 15

Le tableau 15 présente des données sur les décès d'enfants de moins d'un an et les taux de mortalité infantile selon le lieu de résidence (zone urbaine ou rurale) pour le plus grand nombre d'années possible entre 2006 et 2010.

Description des variables : les chiffres se rapportent aux décès d'enfants de moins d'un an.

Sauf indication contraire, les statistiques concernant le nombre de décès d'enfants de moins d'un an sont établies à partir des registres de l'état civil. Dans la plupart des cas, les taux de mortalité infantile sont calculés à partir des données relatives aux décès enregistrés d'enfants de moins d'un an et aux naissances vivantes enregistrées dans un pays ou une zone lorsque les registres de l'état civil sont jugés fiables (exhaustivité estimée à 90 p. 100 ou plus).

La classification des décès d'enfants de moins d'un an selon le lieu de résidence (zone urbaine ou rurale) est celle qui a été communiquée par chaque pays ou zone ; on part du principe qu'elle repose sur les définitions de la population urbaine utilisées pour les recensements nationaux, telles qu'elles sont reproduites à la fin des notes techniques du tableau 6.

Calcul des taux : Les taux de mortalité infantile représentent le nombre annuel de décès d'enfants de moins d'un an pour 1 000 naissances vivantes (présentées dans le tableau 9) survenues pendant la même année.

Les taux selon le lieu de résidence (zone urbaine ou rurale) représentent le nombre annuel de décès d'enfants de moins d'un an, classés selon la catégorie urbaine ou rurale appropriée pour 1 000 naissances vivantes survenues parmi la population correspondante (présentées dans le tableau 9). Ces taux ont été calculés par la Division de statistique de l'ONU.

Les taux présentés dans ce tableau se rapportent seulement aux pays ou zones où l'on a enregistré au moins un total de 30 décès d'enfants de moins d'un an au cours d'une année donnée et pour lesquels le code de qualité est soit "C" ou "I".

Fiabilité des données : il a été demandé à chaque pays ou zone d'indiquer le degré estimatif de complétude des données sur les décès d'enfants de moins d'un an figurant dans ses registres d'état civil. Ces évaluations nationales sont signalées par les codes de qualité "C", "U" et "I" qui apparaissent dans la deuxième colonne du tableau.

La lettre "C" indique que les données sont jugées à peu près complètes, c'est-à-dire qu'elles représentent au moins 90 p. 100 des décès d'enfants de moins d'un an survenus chaque année ; la lettre "U" signifie que les données sont jugées incomplètes, c'est-à-dire qu'elles représentent moins de 90 p.100 des décès d'enfants de moins d'un an survenus chaque année. Le symbole 'I' indique que la source des données n'est pas un registre de l'état civil, mais est quand même considérée fiable. Le code "..." dénote qu'aucun renseignement n'a été communiqué quant à la complétude des données.

Les données provenant des registres de l'état civil qui sont déclarées incomplètes ou dont le degré de complétude n'est pas connu (code "U" ou "...") sont jugées douteuses. Elles apparaissent en italique dans le tableau ; les taux, dans ces cas là, n'ont pas été calculés.

Insuffisance des données : les statistiques des décès d'enfants de moins d'un an appellent toutes les réserves qui ont été formulées à propos des statistiques de l'état civil en général et des statistiques concernant les décès en particulier (voir la section 4 des notes techniques).

La fiabilité des données, au sujet de laquelle des indications ont été fournies plus haut, est un facteur important. Il faut également tenir compte du fait que, dans certains cas, les données relatives aux décès d'enfants de moins d'un an sont exploitées selon la date de l'enregistrement et non la date de l'événement ; ces cas ont été signalés par le signe "+". Chaque fois que le décalage entre l'événement et son enregistrement est grand et qu'une forte proportion des décès d'enfants de moins d'un an fait l'objet d'un enregistrement tardif, les statistiques des décès d'enfants de moins d'un an pour une année donnée peuvent être considérablement faussées.

Un autre facteur qui nuit à la comparabilité internationale est la pratique de certains pays ou zones qui consiste à ne pas inclure dans les statistiques des décès d'enfants de moins d'un an les enfants nés vivants

mais décédés avant l'enregistrement de leur naissance ou dans les 24 heures qui ont suivi la naissance, pratique qui conduit à sous-estimer le nombre total de décès d'enfants de moins d'un an. Quand pareil facteur a joué, cela a été signalé en note.

Les méthodes appliquées pour calculer l'âge au moment du décès peuvent également nuire à la comparabilité des données. Si l'on utilise à cet effet l'année seulement, et non pas les minutes, heures, jours et mois qui se sont écoulés depuis la naissance, de nombreux enfants décédés au cours du onzième mois qui a suivi leur naissance et certains enfants décédés encore plus jeunes seront classés comme décédés à un an révolu et donc exclus des données. Cette pratique conduit à sous-estimer le nombre de décès d'enfants de moins d'un an. Les renseignements dont on dispose sur ce facteur apparaissent en note à la fin du tableau. La question du calcul de l'âge au moment du décès est examinée plus en détail dans les notes techniques se rapportant au tableau 16.

Les taux de mortalité infantile appellent en outre toutes les réserves qui ont été formulées à propos des statistiques des naissances vivantes qui ont servi à leur calcul (voir à ce sujet les notes techniques relatives au tableau 9).

Les deux composantes du taux de mortalité infantile - décès d'enfants de moins d'un an au numérateur et naissances vivantes au dénominateur - étant obtenues à partir des registres de l'état civil, les statistiques des naissances vivantes appellent des réserves presque identiques à celles qui ont été formulées plus haut à propos des statistiques des décès d'enfants de moins d'un an. Il importe de prendre en considération la fiabilité des données (complétude de l'enregistrement) et le mode d'exploitation (selon la date de l'événement ou selon la date de l'enregistrement) dans le cas des statistiques des naissances vivantes tout comme dans le cas de celles des décès d'enfants de moins d'un an, puisque les unes et les autres servent au calcul des taux de mortalité infantile. Dans le tableau 15, le code de qualité et l'emploi de caractères italiques pour signaler les données moins sûres ne concernent que les décès d'enfants de moins d'un an. L'indication du mode d'exploitation des données (emploi du signe "+" pour signaler les données exploitées selon la date de l'enregistrement) ne porte là aussi que sur les décès d'enfants de moins d'un an. Le tableau 9 contient les renseignements correspondants pour les naissances vivantes.

Si l'enregistrement des décès d'enfants de moins d'un an est plus complet que l'enregistrement des naissances vivantes, les taux de mortalité infantile seront entachés d'une erreur par excès. En revanche, si l'enregistrement des naissances vivantes est plus complet que l'enregistrement des décès d'enfants de moins d'un an, les taux de mortalité infantile seront entachés d'une erreur par défaut. Si les décès d'enfants de moins d'un an et les naissances vivantes sont exploitées selon la date de l'enregistrement, il convient de ne pas perdre de vue que les décès sont, en règle générale, déclarés plus rapidement que les naissances.

Les taux de mortalité infantile peuvent être gravement faussés par la pratique de certains pays ou zones qui consiste à ne pas classer dans les naissances vivantes et ensuite dans les décès d'enfants de moins d'un an les enfants nés vivants mais décédés soit avant l'enregistrement de leur naissance, soit dans les 24 heures qui ont suivi la naissance. Cette pratique conduit à sous-estimer aussi bien le nombre des décès d'enfants de moins d'un an, qui constitue le numérateur, que le nombre des naissances vivantes, qui constitue le dénominateur, mais c'est pour le numérateur du taux de mortalité infantile que la distorsion est la plus marquée. Ce système a pour effet d'introduire une erreur par défaut dans les taux de mortalité infantile.

Les taux de mortalité infantile seront également sous-estimés si la méthode utilisée pour calculer l'âge au moment du décès conduit à sous-estimer le nombre de décès d'enfants de moins d'un an. Cette question a été examinée plus haut.

Tous ces facteurs sont importants et il faut donc en tenir compte lorsque l'on compare les taux de mortalité infantile.

En ce qui concerne la méthode de calcul des taux de mortalité infantile utilisée dans le tableau, il convient de noter qu'il n'a pas été tenu compte du fait qu'une partie des décès survenus pendant une année donnée sont des décès d'enfants nés l'année précédente et ne correspondent donc pas à l'ensemble des naissances utilisé pour le calcul des taux. Toutefois, l'erreur n'est pas grave, à moins que le nombre des naissances vivantes ou des décès d'enfants de moins d'un an ne varie rapidement.

La comparabilité des données selon le lieu de résidence (zone urbaine ou rurale) peut être limitée par les définitions nationales des termes « urbain » et « rural » utilisées pour la mise en tableaux de ces données. En l'absence d'indications contraires, on a supposé que les mêmes définitions avaient servi pour

le recensement national de la population et pour l'établissement des statistiques de l'état civil pour chaque pays ou zone. Toutefois, il n'est pas exclu que, pour une zone ou un pays donné, des définitions différentes aient été retenues. Les définitions du terme « urbain » utilisées pour les recensements nationaux de population ont été présentées à la fin des notes techniques du tableau 6 lorsqu'elles étaient connues. Comme on l'a précisé dans les notes techniques relatives au tableau 6, ces définitions varient considérablement d'un pays ou d'une zone à l'autre.

La différence entre les taux de mortalité infantile pour les zones urbaines et rurales pourra aussi être faussée selon que les décès d'enfants de moins d'un an et les naissances vivantes auront été classés d'après le lieu de l'événement ou le lieu de résidence habituel. Ce problème est examiné plus en détail à la section 4.1.4.1 des Notes techniques.

Données publiées antérieurement : des statistiques concernant les décès d'enfants de moins d'un an et les taux de mortalité infantile ont déjà été présentées dans des éditions antérieures de l'*Annuaire démographique*. Pour plus de précisions concernant les années et les sujets pour lesquels des données ont été publiées, se reporter à l'index historique.

15. Infant deaths and infant mortality rates, by urban/rural residence: 2006 - 2010
Décès d'enfants de moins d'un an et taux de mortalité infantile, selon la résidence, urbaine/rurale : 2006 - 2010

Continent, country or area, and urban/rural residence / Continent, pays ou zone et résidence, urbaine/rurale	Co-de[a]	Number - Nombre					Rate - Taux				
		2006	2007	2008	2009	2010	2006	2007	2008	2009	2010
AFRICA - AFRIQUE											
Botswana[1]											
Total	+U	1 152	658	...	...	...	...	...	...	...	...
Burkina Faso[2]											
Total	I	16 259	...	...	...	...	26.2	...	...	...	...
Urban - Urbaine	I	1 704	...	...	...	...	15.6	...	...	...	...
Rural - Rurale	I	14 555	...	...	...	...	28.5	...	...	...	...
Egypt - Égypte											
Total	C	35 952	34 612	32 174	25 760	...	19.4	17.8	15.7	11.6	...
Urban - Urbaine	C	17 792	17 030	15 916	12 728	...	24.0	22.3	19.9	13.9	...
Rural - Rurale	C	18 160	17 582	16 258	13 032	...	16.3	14.8	13.0	10.0	...
Ghana											
Total	+U	52 316	52 014	52 038	...	...	...	...	...	...	...
Kenya											
Total	U	35 786	35 154	46 565	40 190	...	...	...	...	...	...
Mauritius - Maurice[3]											
Total	+C	249	261	236	205	187	14.1	15.3	14.4	13.4	12.5
Urban - Urbaine	+C	79	106	92	75	...	11.8	16.4	14.6	12.7	...
Rural - Rurale	+C	170	155	144	130	...	15.6	14.7	14.3	13.8	...
Réunion[4]											
Total	C	96	91	...	...	...	6.6	6.1	...	...	...
Saint Helena ex. dep. - Sainte-Hélène sans dép.											
Total	C	-	-	-	-	-	...	...	...	...	...
Senegal - Sénégal[5]											
Total	I	31 321	31 576	31 889	32 094	32 314	67.1	66.1	65.2	64.4	63.5
Seychelles											
Total	+C	14	16	20	17	21	...	...	...	...	...
Sierra Leone											
Total	...	...	...	2 914	3 238	...	...	...	...	...	...
South Africa - Afrique du Sud											
Total	...	48 265	46 708	45 316	...	...	...	...	...	...	...
AMERICA, NORTH - AMÉRIQUE DU NORD											
Anguilla											
Total	+C	*1	-	-	...	...	...	...	...	...	...
Antigua and Barbuda - Antigua-et-Barbuda											
Total	+C	8	27	...	...	...	...	...	...	...	...
Aruba											
Total	+U	8	4	...	...	...	...	...	...	...	...
Bahamas											
Total	C	79	69	...	...	...	14.9	11.8	...	...	...
Barbados - Barbade											
Total	+C	59	31	...	...	...	17.3	8.8	...	...	...
Bermuda - Bermudes											
Total	C	3	4	4	1	...	...	...	...	...	...
Canada[6]											
Total	C	1 771	1 881	...	...	...	5.0	5.1	...	...	...
Cayman Islands - Îles Caïmanes											
Total	C	8	5	...	3	2	...	...	...	...	...
Costa Rica											
Total	C	692	735	673	663	*671	9.7	10.0	9.0	8.8	*9.5
Urban - Urbaine	C	301	326	321	293	*323	10.2	11.3	11.1	10.4	*12.4
Rural - Rurale	C	391	409	352	370	*348	9.4	9.2	7.6	7.9	*7.8
Cuba											
Total	C	589	592	579	626	...	5.3	5.3	4.7	4.8	...
Urban - Urbaine	C	475	401	423	470	...	5.7	4.7	4.5	4.7	...
Rural - Rurale	C	114	191	156	156	...	4.1	6.9	5.4	5.2	...
Dominica - Dominique											
Total	+C	13	...	...	...	...	...	...	...	...	...

15. Infant deaths and infant mortality rates, by urban/rural residence: 2006 - 2010
Décès d'enfants de moins d'un an et taux de mortalité infantile, selon la résidence, urbaine/rurale : 2006 - 2010 (continued - suite)

Continent, country or area, and urban/rural residence Continent, pays ou zone et résidence, urbaine/rurale	Code[a]	Number - Nombre					Rate - Taux				
		2006	2007	2008	2009	2010	2006	2007	2008	2009	2010
AMERICA, NORTH - AMÉRIQUE DU NORD											
Dominican Republic - République dominicaine											
Total	U	159	64	96	73	...	...	...	...	...	...
Urban - Urbaine[7]	U	141	52	81	52	...	...	...	...	...	...
Rural - Rurale[7]	U	16	10	11	15	...	...	...	...	...	...
El Salvador[8]											
Total	C	1 013	981	947	...	...	9.5	9.2	8.5	...	...
Urban - Urbaine	C	822	713	...	...	...	11.6	10.4	...	...	...
Rural - Rurale	C	191	268	...	...	...	5.3	7.0	...	...	...
Greenland - Groenland											
Total	C	14	9	8	4	6	...	...	...	...	...
Urban - Urbaine	C	10	8	5	2	6	...	...	...	...	...
Rural - Rurale	C	4	1	3	2	-	...	...	...	...	...
Guatemala											
Total	C	9 042	...	...	...	...	24.5	...	...	...	...
Urban - Urbaine	C	4 993	...	...	...	...	31.6	...	...	...	...
Rural - Rurale	C	4 049	...	...	...	...	19.3	...	...	...	...
Honduras											
Total	+U	6 400	...	...	...	...	...	...	...	...	...
Urban - Urbaine	+U	2 077	...	...	...	...	...	...	...	...	...
Rural - Rurale	+U	4 323	...	...	...	...	...	...	...	...	...
Martinique											
Total	C	44	47	...	...	...	8.2	8.8	...	...	...
Urban - Urbaine	C	41	43	...	...	...	8.4	8.9	...	...	...
Rural - Rurale	C	3	4	...	...	...	...	...	...	...	...
Mexico - Mexique[9]											
Total	+U	30 890	30 412	29 519	28 983	...	...	...	...	...	...
Urban - Urbaine[7]	+U	23 057	22 656	22 141	22 061	...	...	...	...	...	...
Rural - Rurale[7]	+U	7 263	7 284	6 894	6 453	...	...	...	...	...	...
Netherlands Antilles - Antilles néerlandaises											
Total	C	40	33	...	...	...	15.3	12.9	...	...	...
Nicaragua											
Total	+U	1 925	1 955	1 932	...	...	...	...	...	...	...
Urban - Urbaine	+U	973	1 072	977	...	...	...	...	...	...	...
Rural - Rurale	+U	952	883	955	...	...	...	...	...	...	...
Panama											
Total	U	971	992	877	837	...	...	...	...	...	...
Urban - Urbaine	U	490	500	473	428	...	...	...	...	...	...
Rural - Rurale	U	481	492	404	409	...	...	...	...	...	...
Puerto Rico - Porto Rico											
Total	C	442	387	400	...	...	9.1	8.3	8.8	...	...
Urban - Urbaine[7]	C	...	...	206	...	...	...	...	8.6	...	...
Rural - Rurale[7]	C	...	...	136	...	...	...	...	6.3	...	...
Saint Vincent and the Grenadines - Saint-Vincent-et-les Grenadines											
Total	+C	50	34	34	32	...	27.8	18.7	17.9	16.8	...
Turks and Caicos Islands - Îles Turques et Caïques											
Total	C	4	2	3	...	...	...	...	...	...	...
United States of America - États-Unis d'Amérique											
Total	C	28 527	29 138	*28 039	...	...	6.7	6.8	*6.6	...	...
United States Virgin Islands - Îles Vierges américaines											
Total	C	8	12	...	...	...	...	...	...	...	...
AMERICA, SOUTH - AMÉRIQUE DU SUD											
Argentina - Argentine											
Total	C	8 986	9 300	9 326	9 013	...	12.9	13.3	12.5	12.1	...
Brazil - Brésil[10]											
Total	U	37 677	35 159[11]	34 375	33 713	...	...	...	...	...	...

Continent, country or area, and urban/rural residence / Continent, pays ou zone et résidence, urbaine/rurale	Code[a]	Number - Nombre					Rate - Taux				
		2006	2007	2008	2009	2010	2006	2007	2008	2009	2010
AMERICA, SOUTH - AMÉRIQUE DU SUD											
Chile - Chili											
Total	C	1 839	2 009	1 948	...	...	7.9	8.4	7.9	...	...
Urban - Urbaine	C	1 587	1 792	1 766	...	...	7.6	8.3	7.8	...	...
Rural - Rurale	C	252	217	182	...	...	11.1	9.2	8.9	...	...
Colombia - Colombie											
Total	U	11 049	10 867	10 560	*9 250	...	...	...	...	...	...
Urban - Urbaine[7]	U	7 812	7 833	7 759	*6 576	...	...	...	...	...	...
Rural - Rurale[7]	U	2 703	2 544	2 312	*2 281	...	...	...	...	...	...
Ecuador - Équateur[12]											
Total	U	3 715	3 529	3 380	3 279	...	...	...	...	...	...
Urban - Urbaine	U	2 923	2 883	2 669	2 657	...	...	...	...	...	...
Rural - Rurale	U	792	646	711	622	...	...	...	...	...	...
French Guiana - Guyane française											
Total	C	79	77	...	...	...	12.6	12.1	...	...	...
Urban - Urbaine	C	58	60	...	...	...	11.6	12.0	...	...	...
Rural - Rurale	C	21	17	...	...	...	...	...	...	...	...
Paraguay											
Total	+U	1 824	1 599	1 674	...	...	...	...	...	...	...
Urban - Urbaine	+U	1 321	1 145	1 162	...	...	...	...	...	...	...
Rural - Rurale	+U	503	454	512	...	...	...	...	...	...	...
Peru - Pérou[13]											
Total	+U	5 837	5 516	5 581	...	...	...	...	...	...	...
Suriname[14]											
Total	C	129	134	...	...	...	13.9	13.7	...	...	...
Urban - Urbaine[15]	C	88	97	...	...	...	15.4	15.9	...	...	...
Rural - Rurale[15]	C	41	37	...	...	...	11.4	10.1	...	...	...
Uruguay											
Total	C	*497	573	504	...	...	*10.5	12.1	10.6	...	...
Venezuela (Bolivarian Republic of) - Venezuela (République bolivarienne du)											
Total	C	6 804	6 340	...	...	...	10.5	10.3	...	...	...
ASIA - ASIE											
Armenia - Arménie[16]											
Total	C	523	433	442	454	512	13.9	10.8	10.7	10.2	11.4
Urban - Urbaine	C	389	315	312	269	...	16.3	12.3	11.9	9.5	...
Rural - Rurale	C	134	118	130	185	...	9.7	8.1	8.7	11.5	...
Azerbaijan - Azerbaïdjan[16]											
Total	+C	1 882	1 756	1 715	1 731	1 843	12.6	11.6	11.3	11.4	11.1
Urban - Urbaine	+C	1 082	1 036	1 047	1 094	...	15.3	14.2	14.2	14.6	...
Rural - Rurale	+C	800	720	668	637	...	10.2	9.1	8.5	8.2	...
Bahrain - Bahreïn											
Total	C	115	133	127	128	...	7.6	8.3	7.5	7.2	...
Bangladesh[17]											
Total	I	...	...	...	...	...	45.0	43.0	...	...	...
Urban - Urbaine	I	...	...	...	...	...	38.0	42.0	...	...	...
Rural - Rurale	I	...	...	...	...	...	47.0	43.0	...	...	...
Brunei Darussalam - Brunéi Darussalam											
Total	+C	43	48	45	...	...	6.6	7.6	7.0	...	...
China, Hong Kong SAR - Chine, Hong Kong RAS											
Total	C	118	125	145	136	...	1.8	1.8	1.8	1.7	...
China, Macao SAR - Chine, Macao RAS											
Total	C	11	11	15	10	...	...	...	...	...	...
Cyprus - Chypre[18]											
Total	C	27	32	32	32	...	...	3.7	3.5	3.3	...

15. Infant deaths and infant mortality rates, by urban/rural residence: 2006 - 2010
Décès d'enfants de moins d'un an et taux de mortalité infantile, selon la résidence, urbaine/rurale : 2006 - 2010 (continued - suite)

Continent, country or area, and urban/rural residence — Continent, pays ou zone et résidence, urbaine/rurale	Code[a]	Number - Nombre					Rate - Taux				
		2006	2007	2008	2009	2010	2006	2007	2008	2009	2010
ASIA - ASIE											
Democratic People's Republic of Korea - République populaire démocratique de Corée[19]											
Total	I	...	...	6 686	...	...	...	...	19.3	...	...
Urban - Urbaine	I	...	...	3 540	...	...	...	...	17.6	...	...
Rural - Rurale	I	...	...	3 146	...	...	...	...	21.7	...	...
Georgia - Géorgie[16]											
Total	C	753	656	959	...	701	15.8	13.3	17.0	...	11.2
Urban - Urbaine	C	651	555	724	...	...	19.4	16.2	18.5	...	...
Rural - Rurale	C	102	101	235	...	...	7.2	6.7	13.5	...	...
India - Inde[20]											
Total	I	...	...	...	...	...	57.0	55.0	53.0	...	...
Urban - Urbaine	I	...	...	...	...	...	39.0	37.0	36.0	...	...
Rural - Rurale	I	...	...	...	...	...	62.0	61.0	58.0	...	...
Iraq											
Total	U	*48 078	...	...	...	...	...	...	...	...	...
Israel - Israël[21]											
Total	C	598	592	602	619	...	4.0	3.9	3.8	3.8	...
Urban - Urbaine	C	536	531	537	570	...	4.0	3.8	3.8	3.9	...
Rural - Rurale	C	62	61	65	49	...	4.4	4.5	4.6	3.3	...
Japan - Japon[22]											
Total	C	2 864	2 828	2 798	2 556	...	2.6	2.6	2.6	2.4	...
Urban - Urbaine[7]	C	2 581	2 564	2 526	2 324	...	2.6	2.6	2.5	2.4	...
Rural - Rurale[7]	C	280	259	267	227	...	2.6	2.5	2.7	2.4	...
Kazakhstan[16]											
Total	C	4 154	4 646	7 322	...	...	13.8	14.4	20.5	...	...
Urban - Urbaine	C	2 730	2 765	4 419	...	...	15.5	15.9	22.4	...	...
Rural - Rurale	C	1 424	1 881	2 903	...	...	11.3	12.7	18.2	...	...
Kuwait - Koweït											
Total	C	456	449	494	...	...	8.6	8.4	9.1	...	...
Kyrgyzstan - Kirghizstan											
Total	C	3 526	3 771	3 453	3 393	...	29.2	30.6	27.1	25.0	...
Urban - Urbaine	C	1 802	1 963	1 852	1 893	...	45.7	47.4	42.1	40.3	...
Rural - Rurale	C	1 724	1 808	1 601	1 500	...	21.2	22.1	19.2	16.9	...
Malaysia - Malaisie											
Total	C	2 877	2 926	3 045	*3 367	...	6.2	6.2	6.2	*7.0	...
Urban - Urbaine	C	1 701	1 762	1 841	...	...	5.8	5.9	6.0	...	...
Rural - Rurale	C	1 176	1 164	1 204	...	...	6.9	6.8	6.7	...	...
Maldives											
Total	C	92	66	76	81	...	15.8	10.0	10.9	10.9	...
Urban - Urbaine	C	36	28	39	52	...	13.3	...	11.6	14.1	...
Rural - Rurale	C	56	38	37	29	...	17.9	10.9	10.2	...	...
Mongolia - Mongolie											
Total	C	937	994	1 240	1 386	1 275	19.1	17.6	19.4	20.2	19.4
Urban - Urbaine	C	583	707	...	...	...	19.6	19.5	...	...	...
Rural - Rurale	C	354	287	...	...	...	18.3	14.1	...	...	...
Myanmar											
Total	+U	39 714	43 077	26 265	...	...	...	...	...	...	...
Urban - Urbaine	+U	10 817	10 797	7 004	...	...	...	...	...	...	...
Rural - Rurale	+U	28 897	32 280	19 261	...	...	...	...	...	...	...
Occupied Palestinian Territory - Territoire palestinien occupé											
Total	U	906	794	...	...	...	...	...	...	...	...
Oman											
Total	U	499	524[23]	534[23]	676[23]	...	...	...	...	...	...
Pakistan[24]											
Total	I	289 596	288 192	...	...	...	76.2	75.2	...	...	...
Urban - Urbaine	I	80 576	82 299	...	...	...	66.4	66.5	...	...	...
Rural - Rurale	I	209 022	205 893	...	...	...	80.7	79.4	...	...	...
Qatar											
Total	C	114	117	132	130	...	8.1	7.5	7.7	7.1	...

Continent, country or area, and urban/rural residence / Continent, pays ou zone et résidence, urbaine/rurale	Code[a]	Number - Nombre					Rate - Taux				
		2006	2007	2008	2009	2010	2006	2007	2008	2009	2010
ASIA - ASIE											
Republic of Korea - République de Corée[25]											
Total	C	1 707	1 703	1 580	1 415	...	3.8	3.5	3.4	3.2	...
Urban - Urbaine[7]	C	1 356	1 347	1 282	1 139	...	3.7	3.3	3.3	3.1	...
Rural - Rurale[7]	C	348	352	285	265	...	4.5	4.1	3.5	3.4	...
Saudi Arabia - Arabie saoudite[26]											
Total	...	10 954	10 782[27]	10 576[27]	...	...	...	...	...	...	...
Singapore - Singapour											
Total	+C	117	94	104	102	...	3.1	2.4	2.6	2.6	...
Sri Lanka											
Total	+C	3 752	3 298	...	...	...	10.0	8.5	...	...	...
Urban - Urbaine	+C	3 293	2 833	...	...	...	13.1	10.7	...	...	...
Rural - Rurale	+C	459	465	...	...	...	3.8	3.8	...	...	...
Tajikistan - Tadjikistan[16]											
Total	U	2 160	2 166	2 480	...	...	...	...	...	...	...
Urban - Urbaine	U	994	998	1 123	...	...	...	...	...	...	...
Rural - Rurale	U	1 166	1 168	1 357	...	...	...	...	...	...	...
Thailand - Thaïlande											
Total	+U	5 855	5 781	5 721	5 416	...	...	...	...	...	...
Turkey - Turquie[28]											
Total	I	22 348	21 293	20 352	19 431	16 883	17.5	16.7	16.0	15.3	13.2
United Arab Emirates - Émirats arabes unis[26]											
Total	...	455	528[27]	...	...	...	...	...	...	...	...
Viet Nam											
Total	C	19 895	21 223	...	...	...	16.0	16.0	...	...	...
Urban - Urbaine	C	3 205	3 581	...	...	...	10.0	10.0	...	...	...
Rural - Rurale	C	16 690	17 642	...	...	...	18.1	18.2	...	...	...
EUROPE											
Åland Islands - Îles d'Åland											
Total	C	-	-	1	-	...	...	...	...	...	...
Urban - Urbaine	C	-	-	1	-	...	...	...	...	...	...
Rural - Rurale	C	-	-	-	-	...	...	...	...	...	...
Albania - Albanie											
Total	C	253	205	217	...	...	7.4	6.2	6.0	...	...
Andorra - Andorre											
Total	C	3	1	3	1	-	...	...	...	...	...
Austria - Autriche											
Total	C	281	280	287	289	307	3.6	3.7	3.7	3.8	3.9
Belarus - Bélarus											
Total	C	587	534	483	511	429	6.1	5.2	4.5	4.7	4.0
Urban - Urbaine	C	407	339	317	345	...	5.7	4.4	3.9	4.2	...
Rural - Rurale	C	180	195	166	166	...	7.0	7.4	6.3	6.3	...
Belgium - Belgique[29]											
Total	C	489	487	478	439	*440	4.0	4.0	3.7	3.4	*3.5
Urban - Urbaine	C	482	485	...	...	...	4.0	4.1	...	...	...
Rural - Rurale	C	7	2	...	...	...	...	...	...	...	...
Bosnia and Herzegovina - Bosnie-Herzégovine											
Total	C	255	231	235	224	*200	7.5	6.8	6.9	6.5	*5.9
Bulgaria - Bulgarie											
Total	C	720	690	668	729	708	9.7	9.2	8.6	9.0	9.4
Urban - Urbaine	C	472	447	444	468	...	8.6	7.9	7.6	7.7	...
Rural - Rurale	C	248	243	224	261	...	13.1	12.7	11.6	12.9	...
Croatia - Croatie											
Total	C	215	234	195	235	...	5.2	5.6	4.5	5.3	...
Urban - Urbaine	C	113	136	107	141	...	4.9	5.8	4.4	5.7	...
Rural - Rurale	C	102	98	88	94	...	5.6	5.3	4.5	4.8	...
Czech Republic - République tchèque											
Total	C	352	360	338	341	313	3.3	3.1	2.8	2.9	2.7
Urban - Urbaine	C	268	259	241	254	...	3.4	3.1	2.7	2.9	...
Rural - Rurale	C	84	101	97	87	...	3.1	3.4	3.1	2.8	...

15. Infant deaths and infant mortality rates, by urban/rural residence: 2006 - 2010
Décès d'enfants de moins d'un an et taux de mortalité infantile, selon la résidence, urbaine/rurale : 2006 - 2010 (continued - suite)

Continent, country or area, and urban/rural residence / Continent, pays ou zone et résidence, urbaine/rurale	Co-de[a]	Number - Nombre					Rate - Taux				
		2006	2007	2008	2009	2010	2006	2007	2008	2009	2010
EUROPE											
Denmark - Danemark[30]											
Total	C	252	256	262	193	216	3.9	4.0	4.0	3.1	3.4
Estonia - Estonie											
Total	C	66	79	80	57	53	4.4	5.0	5.0	3.6	3.3
Urban - Urbaine	C	47	56	52	35	...	4.5	5.0	4.7	3.2	...
Rural - Rurale	C	19	23	28	22	...	...	...	...	...	...
Faeroe Islands - Îles Féroé											
Total	C	3	4	...	...	...	...	...	...	...	...
Urban - Urbaine	C	1	2	...	...	...	...	...	...	...	...
Rural - Rurale	C	2	2	...	...	...	...	...	...	...	...
Finland - Finlande											
Total	C	167[31]	161[31]	157[31]	158[32]	140[32]	2.8	2.7	2.6	2.6	2.3
Urban - Urbaine	C	111[31]	108[31]	99[31]	100[32]	...	2.6	2.6	2.3	2.3	...
Rural - Rurale	C	56[31]	53[31]	58[31]	58[32]	...	3.3	3.2	3.4	3.4	...
France[33]											
Total	C	2 906	2 822	2 856	2 903	...	3.6	3.6	3.6	3.7	...
Urban - Urbaine[34]	C	2 271	2 207	2 251	2 242	...	3.8	3.8	3.8	3.8	...
Rural - Rurale[34]	C	618	585	582	636	...	3.1	3.0	2.9	3.2	...
Germany - Allemagne											
Total	C	2 579	2 656	2 414	2 334	*2 400	3.8	3.9	3.5	3.5	*3.5
Gibraltar											
Total	+C	1	1	...	...	...	...	...	...	...	...
Greece - Grèce											
Total	C	415	397	314	371	...	3.7	3.5	2.7	3.1	...
Urban - Urbaine	C	299	293	223	261	...	3.9	3.8	2.8	3.2	...
Rural - Rurale	C	116	104	91	110	...	3.3	2.9	2.4	3.0	...
Hungary - Hongrie											
Total	C	571	577	553	495	*480	5.7	5.9	5.6	5.1	*5.3
Urban - Urbaine[35]	C	349	352	328	301	...	5.3	5.4	4.9	4.6	...
Rural - Rurale[35]	C	215	221	218	187	...	6.6	7.0	6.9	6.3	...
Iceland - Islande											
Total	C	6	9	12	9	11	...	...	...	...	...
Urban - Urbaine	C	6	9	12	8	...	...	...	...	...	...
Rural - Rurale	C	-	-	-	1	...	...	...	...	...	...
Ireland - Irlande											
Total	+C	238	221	284	*240	...	3.7	3.1	3.8	*3.2	...
Italy - Italie											
Total	C	2 031	1 959	1 896	*2 110	*1 891	3.6	3.5	3.3	*3.7	*3.4
Latvia - Lettonie											
Total	C	170	203	161	168	110	7.6	8.7	6.7	7.8	5.7
Urban - Urbaine	C	99	123	90	99	...	6.5	7.6	5.4	6.7	...
Rural - Rurale	C	71	80	71	69	...	10.3	11.2	9.6	10.1	...
Liechtenstein											
Total	C	2	-	-	1	*1	...	...	...	...	...
Lithuania - Lituanie											
Total	C	213	190	172	181	153	6.8	5.9	4.9	4.9	4.3
Urban - Urbaine	C	167	155	130	136	...	8.1	7.2	5.5	5.4	...
Rural - Rurale	C	46	35	42	45	...	4.4	3.3	3.7	3.9	...
Luxembourg											
Total	C	14	10	10	14	20	...	...	...	...	...
Malta - Malte											
Total	C	14	25	34	22	22	...	...	8.2	...	...
Montenegro - Monténégro											
Total	C	83	58	62	49	...	11.0	7.4	7.5	5.7	...
Urban - Urbaine	C	...	...	58	45	...	...	...	9.0	6.8	...
Rural - Rurale	C	...	...	4	4	...	...	...	...	...	...
Netherlands - Pays-Bas[36]											
Total	C	820	736	698	711	695	4.4	4.1	3.8	3.8	3.8
Urban - Urbaine	C	538	530	500	514	...	4.2	4.2	3.9	4.0	...
Rural - Rurale	C	282	206	198	197	...	4.8	3.7	3.5	3.5	...
Norway - Norvège[37]											
Total	C	185	180	163	192	171	3.2	3.1	2.7	3.1	2.8
Poland - Pologne											
Total	C	2 238	2 322	2 338	2 327	2 057	6.0	6.0	5.6	5.6	5.0
Urban - Urbaine	C	1 343	1 371	1 363	1 385	...	6.2	6.1	5.6	5.6	...
Rural - Rurale	C	895	951	975	942	...	5.7	5.9	5.6	5.5	...

15. Infant deaths and infant mortality rates, by urban/rural residence: 2006 - 2010
Décès d'enfants de moins d'un an et taux de mortalité infantile, selon la résidence, urbaine/rurale : 2006 - 2010 (continued - suite)

Continent, country or area, and urban/rural residence / Continent, pays ou zone et résidence, urbaine/rurale	Code[a]	Number - Nombre					Rate - Taux				
		2006	2007	2008	2009	2010	2006	2007	2008	2009	2010
EUROPE											
Portugal[9]											
Total	C	349	353	340	362	*243	3.3	3.4	3.3	3.6	*2.4
Republic of Moldova - République de Moldova[38]											
Total	C	442[16]	428[16]	473	492	476	11.8	11.3	12.1	12.1	11.8
Urban - Urbaine	C	177[16]	141[16]	159	168	...	13.0	10.3	11.1	11.3	...
Rural - Rurale	C	265[16]	287[16]	314	324	...	11.0	11.8	12.7	12.5	...
Romania - Roumanie											
Total	C	3 052	2 574	2 434	2 250	2 078	13.9	12.0	11.0	10.1	9.8
Urban - Urbaine	C	1 341	1 186	1 030	982	...	11.2	10.2	8.5	8.1	...
Rural - Rurale	C	1 711	1 388	1 404	1 268	...	17.1	14.1	14.0	12.6	...
Russian Federation - Fédération de Russie[16]											
Total	C	15 079	14 858	14 436	14 271	13 405	10.2	9.2	8.4	8.1	7.5
Urban - Urbaine	C	9 839	9 497	9 273	9 189	...	9.4	8.5	7.8	7.4	...
Rural - Rurale	C	5 240	5 361	5 163	5 082	...	12.0	11.0	9.9	9.7	...
San Marino - Saint-Marin											
Total	+C	-	-	...	...	...	...	...	...	...	...
Serbia - Serbie[39]											
Total	+C	525	484	460	492	460	7.4	7.1	6.7	7.0	6.7
Urban - Urbaine	+C	352	339	331	346	...	7.6	7.6	7.3	7.4	...
Rural - Rurale	+C	173	145	129	146	...	7.0	6.2	5.4	6.2	...
Slovakia - Slovaquie											
Total	C	355	334	336	346	344	6.6	6.1	5.9	5.7	5.7
Urban - Urbaine	C	153	156	158	159	...	5.4	5.4	5.2	4.9	...
Rural - Rurale	C	202	178	178	187	...	7.9	7.0	6.7	6.5	...
Slovenia - Slovénie											
Total	C	64	55	52	52	*54	3.4	2.8	2.4	2.4	*2.5
Urban - Urbaine	C	37	19	26	21	...	4.0	...	...	...	...
Rural - Rurale	C	27	36	26	31	...	...	3.5	...	2.8	...
Spain - Espagne											
Total	C	1 704	1 704	1 741	1 609	*1 534	3.5	3.5	3.3	3.3	*3.2
Sweden - Suède											
Total	C	297	268	272	278	294	2.8	2.5	2.5	2.5	2.5
Switzerland - Suisse											
Total	C	325	293	308	337	...	4.4	3.9	4.0	4.3	...
Urban - Urbaine	C	255	221	245	258	...	4.7	4.0	4.3	4.4	...
Rural - Rurale	C	70	72	63	79	...	3.7	3.7	3.2	4.0	...
TFYR of Macedonia - L'ex-R. y. de Macédoine											
Total	C	260	234	223	278	*186	11.5	10.3	9.7	11.7	*7.7
Urban - Urbaine	C	144	125	120	150	...	11.4	9.8	9.1	11.0	...
Rural - Rurale	C	116	109	103	128	...	11.7	11.0	10.6	12.7	...
Ukraine[40]											
Total	C	4 433	5 188	5 049	4 801	4 546	9.6	11.0	9.9	9.4	9.1
Urban - Urbaine	C	2 828	3 330	3 220	...	...	9.2	10.6	9.5	...	...
Rural - Rurale	C	1 605	1 858	1 829	...	...	10.4	11.7	10.8	...	...
United Kingdom of Great Britain and Northern Ireland - Royaume-Uni de Grande-Bretagne et d'Irlande du Nord[41]											
Total	C	3 737	3 740	*3 663	*3 677	...	5.0	4.8	*4.6	*4.7	...
OCEANIA - OCÉANIE											
American Samoa - Samoas américaines											
Total	C	17	...	...	...	...	...	...	...	...	...
Australia - Australie											
Total	+C	1 262	1 203	1 226	1 261	...	4.7	4.2	4.1	4.3	...
Urban - Urbaine[42]	+C	980	936	962	982	...	4.4	4.0	3.9	4.0	...
Rural - Rurale[42]	+C	267	235	234	250	...	5.9	4.9	4.7	5.1	...
Cook Islands - Îles Cook[43]											
Total	+C	3	4	1	*2	...	...	...	...	...	...

15. Infant deaths and infant mortality rates, by urban/rural residence: 2006 - 2010
Décès d'enfants de moins d'un an et taux de mortalité infantile, selon la résidence, urbaine/rurale : 2006 - 2010 (continued - suite)

Continent, country or area, and urban/rural residence / Continent, pays ou zone et résidence, urbaine/rurale	Code[a]	Number - Nombre					Rate - Taux				
		2006	2007	2008	2009	2010	2006	2007	2008	2009	2010
OCEANIA - OCÉANIE											
French Polynesia - Polynésie française											
Total	C	31	30	23	...	...	6.8	6.8	...	...	...
Guam[44]											
Total	C	46	36	*31	...	...	13.5	10.3	*8.9	...	...
New Caledonia - Nouvelle-Calédonie											
Total	C	...	25	...	...	...	...	...	...	...	...
New Zealand - Nouvelle-Zélande[9]											
Total	+C	300	317	322	308	...	5.1	4.9	5.0	4.9	...
Urban - Urbaine[7]	+C	251	263	271	273	...	4.9	4.7	4.8	5.0	...
Rural - Rurale[7]	+C	33	34	38	17	...	4.4	4.2	4.7		...
Northern Mariana Islands - Îles Mariannes septentrionales[45]											
Total	U	9	6	4	...	...	...	...	...	...	...
Palau - Palaos											
Total	C	2	...	...	...	...	...	...	...	...	...
Pitcairn											
Total	C	...	-	...	...	...	...	...	...	...	...

FOOTNOTES - NOTES

Italics: data from civil registers which are incomplete or of unknown completeness. - Italiques : données incomplètes ou dont le degré d'exactitude n'est pas connu, provenant des registres de l'état civil.

* Provisional. - Données provisoires.

[a] 'Code' indicates the source of data, as follows:
C - Civil registration, estimated over 90% complete
U - Civil registration, estimated less than 90% complete
| - Other source, estimated reliable
+ - Data tabulated by date of registration rather than occurence
... - Information not available

Le 'Code' indique la source des données, comme suit :
C - Registres de l'état civil considérés complets à 90 p. 100 au moins
U - Registres de l'état civil qui ne sont pas considérés complets à 90 p. 100 au moins
| - Autre source, considérée pas douteuses
+ - Données exploitées selon la date de l'enregistrement et non la date de l'événement
... - Information pas disponible

[1] Data from Health Statistics Reports since 1998, due to incompleteness of civil registration. - Données provenant des Health Statistics Reports (rapports sur les statistiques sanitaires) depuis 1998, en raison des lacunes de l'état civil.
[2] Data refer to the twelve months preceding the census in December. - Les données se rapportent aux douze mois précédant le recensement de décembre.
[3] Excludes the islands of St. Brandon and Agalega. - Non compris les îles St. Brandon et Agalega.
[4] Excluding live-born infants who died before their birth was registered. - Non compris les enfants nés vivants décédés avant l'enregistrement de leur naissance.
[5] Based on estimates and projections from 'Agence Nationale de la Statistique et de la Démographie'. - Données fondées sur des estimations et des projections provenant de l'Agence Nationale de la Statistique et de la Démographie.
[6] Including Canadian residents temporarily in the United States, but excluding United States residents temporarily in Canada. - Y compris les résidents canadiens se trouvant temporairement aux Etats-Unis, mais ne comprenant pas les résidents des Etats-Unis se trouvant temporairement au Canada.
[7] The total number includes 'Unknown residence', but the categories urban and rural do not. - Le nombre total inclue 'Résidence inconnue ', mais les catégories urbaine et rurale ne l'incluent pas.

[8] Excluding infant deaths to mothers living abroad. - Exception faite des décès d'enfants en bas âge survenus lorsque la mère résidait à l'étranger.
[9] Data refer to resident population only. - Pour la population résidante seulement.
[10] Excluding Indian jungle population. - Non compris les Indiens de la jungle.
[11] Data as reported by national statistical authorities; they may differ from data presented in other tables. - Les données comme elles ont été déclarées par l'institut national de la statistique; elles peuvent être différentes de celles présentées dans d'autres tableaux.
[12] Excluding nomadic Indian tribes. - Non compris les tribus d'Indiens nomades.
[13] Source: Ministry of health reports. Completeness of coverage estimated at 40 per cent. - Source: Rapports du Ministère de Santé. Degré de complétude évalué à 40 pour cent.
[14] Including non-residents. - Y compris les non-résidents.
[15] The districts of Paramaribo and Wanica are considered urban areas, whereas all other districts are considered more or less rural areas. - Les districts de Paramaribo et de Wanica sont considérés comme des zones urbaines, les autres districts étant considérés comme des zones rurales à divers degrés.
[16] Excluding infants born alive of less than 28 weeks' gestation, of less than 1 000 grams in weight and 35 centimeters in length, who die within seven days of birth. - Non compris les enfants nés vivants après moins de 28 semaines de gestations, pesant moins de 1 000 grammes, mesurant moins de 35 centimètres et décédés dans les sept jours qui ont suivi leur naissance.
[17] Rates were obtained by the Sample Vital Registration System of Bangladesh. - Taux obtenus au moyen du Sample Vital Registration System du Bangladesh.
[18] Data refer to government controlled areas. - Les données se rapportent aux zones contrôlées par le Gouvernement.
[19] Data refer to the twelve months preceding the census in October. - Les données font référence aux 12 mois qui ont précédé le recensement en octobre.
[20] Rates were obtained by the Sample Registration System of India, which is a large demographic survey. Including data for the Indian-held part of Jammu and Kashmir, the final status of which has not yet been determined. - Les taux ont été obtenus par le Système de l'enregistrement par échantillon de l'Inde qui est une large enquête démographique. Y compris les données pour la partie du Jammu et du Cachemire occupée par l'Inde dont le statut définitif n'a pas encore été déterminé.
[21] Including data for East Jerusalem and Israeli residents in certain other territories under occupation by Israeli military forces since June 1967. Including deaths abroad of Israeli residents who were out of the country for less than a year. - Y compris les données pour Jérusalem-Est et les résidents israéliens dans certains autres territoires occupés depuis 1967 par les forces armées israéliennes. Y compris les décès à l'étranger de résidents israéliens qui ont quitté le pays depuis moins d'un an.

[22] Data refer to Japanese nationals in Japan only. - Les données se raportent aux nationaux japonais au Japon seulement.

[23] Data from Births and Deaths Notification System (Ministry of Health institutions and all other health care providers). - Les données proviennent du système de notification des naissances et des décès (établissements du Ministère de la santé et tous autres prestataires de soins de santé).

[24] Based on the results of the Pakistan Demographic Survey. Excluding data for the Pakistan-held part of Jammu and Kashmir, the final status of which has not yet been determined. - Données extraites de l'enquête démographique effectuée par le Pakistan. Non compris les données concernant la partie du Jammu et Cachemire occupée par le Pakistan dont le statut définitif n'a pas été déterminé.

[25] Excluding alien armed forces, civilian aliens employed by armed forces, and foreign diplomatic personnel and their dependants. - Non compris les militaires étrangers, les civils étrangers employés par les forces armées ni le personnel diplomatique étranger et les membres de leur famille les accompagnant.

[26] The registration of births and deaths is conducted by the Ministry of Health. An estimate of completeness is not provided. - L'enregistrement des naissances et des décès est mené par le Ministère de la Santé. Le degré estimatif de complétude n'est pas fourni.

[27] As published by the United Nations Economic and Social Commission for Western Asia. - Publié par la Commission économique et sociale des Nations Unies pour l'Asie occidentale.

[28] Data based on Address Based Population Registration System. - Les données sont basées sur le registre national de la population basé sur l'adresse.

[29] Including armed forces stationed outside the country, but excluding alien armed forces stationed in the area. - Y compris les militaires nationaux hors du pays, mais non compris les militaires étrangers en garnison sur le territoire.

[30] Excluding Faeroe Islands and Greenland shown separately, if available. - Non compris les Iles Féroé et le Groenland, qui font l'objet de rubriques distinctes, si disponible.

[31] Including nationals temporarily outside the country. - Y compris les nationaux se trouvant temporairement hors du pays.

[32] Excluding Åland Islands. - Non compris les Îles d'Åland.

[33] Including armed forces stationed outside the country. - Y compris les militaires nationaux hors du pays.

[34] Data for urban and rural, excluding nationals outside the country. - Les données pour la résidence urbaine et rurale , non compris les nationaux hors du pays.

[35] Total includes the data of foreigners, persons of unknown residence and homeless, but the categories urban and rural do not. - Total incluant les étrangers, les personnes de résidence inconnue et les sans-abri, ce qui n'est pas le cas pour les catégories urbaines et rurales.

[36] Including residents outside the country if listed in a Netherlands population register. - Y compris les résidents hors du pays, s'ils sont inscrits sur un registre de population néerlandais.

[37] Including residents temporarily outside the country. Excluding Svalbard and Jan Mayen Islands shown separately, if available. - Y compris les résidents se trouvant temporairement hors du pays. Non compris Svalbard et Jan Mayen qui font l'objet de rubriques distinctes, si disponible.

[38] Excluding Transnistria and the municipality of Bender. - Les données ne tiennent pas compte de l'information sur la Transnistria et la municipalité de Bender.

[39] Excluding data for Kosovo and Metohia. - Sans les données pour le Kosovo et Metohie.

[40] Data includes deaths resulting from births with weight 500g and more (if weight is unknown - with length 25 centimeters and more, or with gestation during 22 weeks or more). - Y compris les décès de nouveau-nés de 500 grammes ou plus (si le poids est inconnu – de 25 centimètres de long ou plus, ou après une grossesse de 22 semaines ou plus).

[41] Excluding Channel Islands (Guernsey and Jersey) and Isle of Man, shown separately, if available. - Non compris les îles Anglo-Normandes (Guernesey et Jersey) et l'île de Man, qui font l'objet de rubriques distinctes, si disponible.

[42] Excluding data where place of usual residence was overseas, undefined, no fixed place of abode or offshore or migratory and unknown. - Les données n'ont pas été prises en compte lorsque le domicile habituel était à l'étranger ou dans une zone extraterritoriale, était indéfini ou inconnu ou que la personne n'avait pas de domicile fixe ou était une migrante.

[43] Excluding Niue, shown separately, which is part of Cook Islands, but because of remoteness is administered separately. - Non compris Nioué, qui fait l'objet d'une rubrique distincte et qui fait partie des îles Cook, mais qui, en raison de son éloignement, est administrée séparément.

[44] Including United States military personnel, their dependants and contract employees. - Y compris les militaires des Etats-Unis, les membres de leur famille les accompagnant et les agents contractuels des Etats-Unis.

[45] Source: Commonwealth Health Center - Vital Statistics Office - Source : Centre de Santé du Commonwealth - Bureau des statistiques d'État civil

Table 16 presents infant deaths and infant mortality rates by age and sex for latest available year between 2000 and 2009. Table 16a presents the available data for the year 2010.

Description of variables: Age is defined as hours, days and months of life completed, based on the difference between the hour, day, month and year of birth and the hour, day, month and year of death. The age classification used in this table is as follows: Main categories are "under 1 day", "1-6 days", "7-27 days" and "28 days – 11 months". Additional subcategories are shown within "7-27 days" and "28 days to 11 months" wherever available.

Rate computation: Infant mortality rates by age and sex are the annual number of infant deaths that occurred in a specific age-sex group per 1 000 live births in the corresponding sex group. These rates have been calculated by the Statistics Division of the United Nations. The denominator for all these rates, regardless of age of infant at death, is the total number of live births by sex.

Infant deaths of unknown age are included only in the rate for under one year of age. Infant deaths of unknown sex are included in the rate for the total and, hence, these rates, should agree with the infant mortality rates shown in table 15. Discrepancies are explained in footnotes.

Rates presented in this table have been limited to those for countries or areas having at least a total of 100 deaths in a given year. Moreover, rates specific for individual sub-categories based on 30 or fewer infant deaths are identified by the symbol "♦".

Reliability of data: Data from civil registers of infant deaths which are reported as incomplete (less than 90 percent completeness) or of unknown completeness are considered unreliable and are set in italics rather than in roman type. Rates on these data are not computed. Table 15 and its technical notes provide more detailed information on the completeness of infant death registration. For more information about the quality of vital statistics, and the information available on the basis of the completeness of estimates in particular, see section 4.2 of the Technical Notes.

Limitations: Statistics on infant deaths by age and sex are subject to the same qualifications as have been set forth for vital statistics in general and death statistics in particular as discussed in section 4 of the Technical Notes.

The reliability of the data, an indication of which is described above, is an important factor in considering the limitations. In addition, some infant deaths are tabulated by date of registration and not by date of occurrence; these have been indicated by a plus sign "+". Whenever the lag between the date of occurrence and date of registration is prolonged and, therefore, a large proportion of the infant-death registrations are delayed, infant-death statistics for any given year may be seriously affected.

Another factor that limits international comparability is the practice of some countries or areas of not including in infant-death statistics infants who were born alive but died before the registration of the birth or within the first 24 hours of life, thus underestimating the total number of infant deaths. Statistics of this type are footnoted. In this table in particular, this practice may contribute to the lack of comparability among deaths under one year, under 28 days, under one week and under one day.

Variation in the method of reckoning age at the time of death may also introduce non-comparability. Although it is to some degree a limiting factor throughout the age span, it is an especially important consideration with respect to deaths at ages under one day and under one week (early neonatal deaths) and under 28 days (neonatal deaths). As noted above, the recommended method of reckoning infant age at death is to calculate duration of life in minutes, hours and days, as appropriate. This gives age in completed units of time. In some countries or areas, however, infant age is calculated to the nearest day only, that is, age at death for an infant is the difference between the day, month and year of birth and the day, month and year of death. The result of this procedure is to classify as deaths at age one day, many deaths of infants that occurred before the infants had completed 24 hours of life. The under-one-day class is thus understated while the frequency in the 1-6-day age group is inflated.

A special limitation on comparability of neonatal (under 28 days) deaths is the variation in the classification of infant age used. It is evident from the footnotes that some countries or areas continue to report infant age in calendar, rather than lunar month (4-week or 28-day) periods. This failure to tabulate infant deaths under 4 weeks of age in terms of completed days introduces another source of variation

between countries or areas. Deaths classified as occurring under one month usually connote deaths within any one calendar month; these frequencies are not strictly comparable with those referring to deaths within 4 weeks or 27 completed days.

In addition, infant mortality rates by age and sex are subject to the limitations of the data on live births with which they have been calculated. These have been set forth in the technical notes for table 9. These limitations have also been discussed in the technical notes for table 15.

In addition, it should be noted that infant mortality rates by age are affected by the problems related to the practice of excluding infants who were born alive but died before the registration of the birth or within the first 24 hours of life from both infant-death and live-birth statistics and the problems related to the reckoning of infant age at death. These factors, which have been described above, may affect certain age groups more than others. In so far as the numbers of infant deaths for the various age groups are underestimated or overestimated, the corresponding rates for the various age groups will also be underestimated or overestimated. The youngest age groups are more likely to be underestimated than other age groups; the youngest age group (under one day) is likely to be the most seriously affected.

Earlier data: Infant deaths and infant mortality rates by age and sex have been shown in previous issues of the *Demographic Yearbook*. For information on specific years covered, readers should consult the Historical Index.

Tableaux 16 et 16a

Le tableau 16 présente les données les plus récentes disponible, entre 2000 et 2009, sur les décès d'enfants de moins d'un an et les taux de mortalité infantile selon l'âge et le sexe. Le tableau 16a présente les données disponibles pour l'année 2010.

Description des variables : l'âge est exprimé en heures, jours et mois révolus et est calculé en retranchant la date de la naissance (heure, jour, mois et année) de celle du décès (heure, jour, mois et année). Les tranches d'âge utilisées dans ce tableau se présentent comme suit : les catégories principales sont « moins d'un jour », « 1-6 jours », « 7-27 jours » et « 28 jours à 11 mois ». Des sous-catégories additionnelles pour « 7-27 jours » et « 28 jours à 11 mois » sont présentées lorsque disponibles.

Calcul des taux : les taux de mortalité infantile selon l'âge et le sexe représentent le nombre annuel de décès d'enfants de moins d'un an intervenu dans un groupe d'âge donné parmi la population de sexe masculin ou féminin pour 1 000 naissances vivantes survenues parmi la population du même sexe. Ces taux ont été calculés par la Division de statistique de l'ONU. Le dénominateur de tous ces taux, quel que soit l'âge de l'enfant au moment du décès, est le nombre total de naissances vivantes selon le sexe.

Il n'est tenu compte des décès d'enfants d'âge « inconnu » que pour le calcul du taux relatif à l'ensemble des décès de moins d'un an. Étant donné que les décès d'enfants de sexe inconnu sont compris dans le numérateur des taux concernant le total, les chiffres obtenus devraient concorder avec les taux de mortalité infantile du tableau 15. Les divergences sont expliquées en note.

Les taux présentés dans le tableau 16 ne concernent que les pays ou zones où l'on a enregistré un total d'au moins 100 décès au cours d'une année donnée. Les taux relatifs à des sous-catégories qui sont fondées sur un nombre égal ou inférieur à 30 décès d'enfants âgés de moins d'un an sont signalés par le signe "♦".

Fiabilité des données : les données relatives aux décès d'enfants de moins d'un an provenant de registres de l'état civil qui sont déclarées incomplètes (degré de complétude inférieur à 90 p.100) ou dont le degré de complétude n'est pas connu sont jugées douteuses et apparaissent en italique et non en caractères romains. Les taux à partir de ces données n'ont pas été calculés. Le tableau 15 et les notes techniques se rapportant à ce tableau comportent des renseignements plus détaillés sur le degré de complétude de l'enregistrement des décès d'enfants de moins d'un an. Pour plus de précisions sur la qualité des données reposant sur les statistiques de l'état civil en général et les estimations de complétude en particulier, voir la section 4.2 des Notes techniques.

Insuffisance des données : les statistiques des décès d'enfants de moins d'un an selon l'âge et le sexe appellent toutes les réserves qui ont été formulées à propos des statistiques de l'état civil en général et des statistiques concernant les décès en particulier (voir la section 4 des Notes techniques).

La fiabilité des données, au sujet de laquelle des indications ont été fournies plus haut, est un facteur important. Il faut également tenir compte du fait que, dans certains cas, les données relatives aux décès d'enfants de moins d'un an sont exploitées selon la date de l'enregistrement et non la date de l'événement ; ces cas ont été signalés par le signe "+". Chaque fois que le décalage entre l'événement et son enregistrement est grand et qu'une forte proportion des décès d'enfants de moins d'un an fait l'objet d'un enregistrement tardif, les statistiques des décès d'enfants de moins d'un an pour une année donnée peuvent être considérablement faussées.

Un autre facteur qui nuit à la comparabilité internationale est la pratique de certains pays ou zones qui consiste à ne pas inclure dans les statistiques des décès d'enfants de moins d'un an les enfants nés vivants mais décédés soit avant l'enregistrement de leur naissance, soit dans les 24 heures qui ont suivi la naissance, pratique qui conduit à sous-estimer le nombre total de décès d'enfants de moins d'un an. Quand pareil facteur a joué, cela a été signalé en note. Dans le tableau 16 en particulier, ce système peut limiter la comparabilité des données concernant les décès d'enfants de moins d'un an, de moins de 28 jours, de moins d'une semaine et de moins d'un jour.

Le manque d'uniformité des méthodes suivies pour calculer l'âge au moment du décès nuit également à la comparabilité des données. Ce facteur influe dans une certaine mesure sur les données relatives à la mortalité à tous les âges, mais il a des répercussions particulièrement marquées sur les statistiques des décès de moins d'un jour et de moins d'une semaine (mortalité néo-natale précoce) et de moins de 28 jours (mortalité néo-natale). Comme on l'a dit, l'âge d'un enfant de moins d'un an à son décès est calculé, selon

la méthode recommandée, en évaluant la durée de vie en minutes, heures et jours, selon le cas. L'âge est ainsi exprimé en unités de temps révolues. Toutefois, dans certains pays ou zones, l'âge de ces enfants est ramené au jour le plus proche en retranchant la date de la naissance (jour, mois et année) de celle du décès (jour, mois et année). Il s'ensuit que de nombreux décès survenus dans les vingt-quatre heures qui suivent la naissance sont classés comme décès d'un jour. Dans ces conditions, les données concernant les décès de moins d'un jour sont entachées d'une erreur par défaut et celles qui se rapportent aux décès de 1 à 6 jours d'une erreur par excès.

La comparabilité des données relatives à la mortalité néo-natale (moins de 28 jours) est influencée par un facteur spécial : l'hétérogénéité de la classification par âge utilisée pour les enfants de moins d'un an. Les notes figurant à la fin des tableaux montrent que, dans un certain nombre de pays ou zones, on continue d'utiliser le mois civil au lieu du mois lunaire (4 semaines ou 28 jours).

Lorsque les données relatives aux décès de moins de 4 semaines ne sont pas exploitées sur la base de l'âge en jours révolus, il existe une nouvelle cause de non-comparabilité internationale. Les décès de moins d'un mois sont généralement ceux qui se produisent au cours d'un mois civil ; les taux calculés sur la base de ces données ne sont pas strictement comparables à ceux qui sont établis à partir des données concernant les décès survenus dans les 4 semaines ou 27 jours révolus qui suivent la naissance.

Les taux de mortalité infantile selon l'âge et le sexe appellent en outre toutes les réserves qui ont été formulées à propos des statistiques des naissances vivantes qui ont servi à leur calcul (voir à ce sujet les notes techniques relatives au tableau 9). Ces insuffisances ont également été examinées dans les notes techniques relatives au tableau 15.

Il convient de signaler aussi que les taux de mortalité infantile selon l'âge peuvent être gravement faussés par la pratique qui consiste à ne pas classer dans les naissances vivantes et ensuite dans les décès d'enfants de moins d'un an les enfants nés vivants mais décédés soit avant l'enregistrement de leur naissance, soit dans les 24 heures qui ont suivi la naissance, et par les problèmes que pose le calcul de l'âge de l'enfant au moment du décès. Ces facteurs, qui ont été décrits plus haut, peuvent fausser les statistiques concernant certains groupes d'âge plus que d'autres. Si le nombre des décès d'enfants de moins d'un an pour chaque groupe d'âge est sous-estimé ou surestimé, les taux correspondants pour chacun de ces groupes d'âge seront eux aussi sous-estimés ou surestimés. Les risques de sous-estimation sont plus grands pour les groupes les plus jeunes ; c'est pour le groupe d'âge le plus jeune de tous (moins d'un jour) que les données risquent de comporter les plus grosses erreurs.

Données publiées antérieurement : des statistiques des décès d'enfants de moins d'un an et des taux de mortalité infantile selon l'âge et le sexe ont déjà été présentées dans des éditions antérieures de l'*Annuaire démographique*. Pour plus de précisions concernant les années pour lesquelles ces données ont été publiées, se reporter à l'index historique.

16. Infant deaths and infant mortality rates by age and sex: latest available year, 2000 - 2009
Décès d'enfants de moins d'un an et taux de mortalité infantile selon l'âge et le sexe : dernière année disponible, 2000 - 2009

Continent, country or area, year and age Continent, pays ou zone, année et âge	Number - Nombre			Rate - Taux		
	Both sexes Les deux sexes	Male Masculin	Female Féminin	Both sexes Les deux sexes	Male Masculin	Female Féminin
AFRICA - AFRIQUE						
Egypt - Égypte						
2009 (C)						
Total	25 760	13 899	11 861	11.6	12.1	11.1
1 - 6 days - 1 - 6 jours	7 382	4 330	3 052	3.3	3.8	2.9
7 - 27 days - 7 - 27 jours	5 120	2 879	2 241	2.3	2.5	2.1
7 - 13 days - 7 - 13 jours	2 474	1 381	1 093	1.1	1.2	1.0
14 - 20 days - 14 - 20 jours	1 744	976	768	0.8	0.9	0.7
21 - 27 days - 21 - 27 jours	902	522	380	0.4	0.5	0.4
28 days - 11 months - 28 jours - 11 mois	13 258	6 690	6 568	6.0	5.8	6.1
28 days - less than 2 months - 28 jours - moins de 2 mois	2 787	1 435	1 352	1.3	1.3	1.3
2 months - 2 mois	2 184	1 134	1 050	1.0	1.0	1.0
3 months - 3 mois	1 741	913	828	0.8	0.8	0.8
4 months - 4 mois	1 475	746	729	0.7	0.7	0.7
5 months - 5 mois	1 075	535	540	0.5	0.5	0.5
6 months - 6 mois	1 078	545	533	0.5	0.5	0.5
7 months - 7 mois	759	387	372	0.3	0.3	0.3
8 months - 8 mois	822	331	491	0.4	0.3	0.5
9 months - 9 mois	589	286	303	0.3	0.2	0.3
10 months - 10 mois	435	230	205	0.2	0.2	0.2
11 months - 11 mois	313	148	165	0.1	0.1	0.2
Mauritius - Maurice[1]						
2009 (+C)						
Total	205	114	91	13.4	14.7	12.0
Less than 1 day - Moins de 1 jour	23	16	7	♦1.5	♦2.1	♦0.9
1 - 6 days - 1 - 6 jours	76	43	33	5.0	5.5	4.4
7 - 27 days - 7 - 27 jours	42	22	20	2.7	♦2.8	♦2.6
7 - 13 days - 7 - 13 jours	20	12	8	♦1.3	♦1.5	♦1.1
14 - 20 days - 14 - 20 jours	16	8	8	♦1.0	♦1.0	♦1.1
21 - 27 days - 21 - 27 jours	6	2	4	♦0.4	♦0.3	♦0.5
28 days - 11 months - 28 jours - 11 mois	64	33	31	4.2	4.3	4.1
28 days - less than 2 months - 28 jours - moins de 2 mois	21	11	10	♦1.4	♦1.4	♦1.3
2 months - 2 mois	8	4	4	♦0.5	♦0.5	♦0.5
3 months - 3 mois	7	4	3	♦0.5	♦0.5	♦0.4
4 months - 4 mois	8	3	5	♦0.5	♦0.4	♦0.7
5 months - 5 mois	5	3	2	♦0.3	♦0.4	♦0.3
6 months - 6 mois	3	-	3	♦0.2	-	♦0.4
7 months - 7 mois	5	4	1	♦0.3	♦0.5	♦0.1
8 months - 8 mois	3	2	1	♦0.2	♦0.3	♦0.1
9 months - 9 mois	1	1	-	♦0.1	♦0.1	-
10 months - 10 mois	3	1	2	♦0.2	♦0.1	♦0.3
11 months - 11 mois	-	-	-	-	-	-
Morocco - Maroc						
2001 (U)						
Total	7 379	4 022	3 357	...	...	...
Less than 28 days - Moins de 28 jours	1 638	912	726	...	...	...
28 days - 11 months - 28 jours - 11 mois	5 729	3 103	2 626	...	...	...
28 days - less than 2 months - 28 jours - moins de 2 mois	1 331	733	598	...	...	...
2 months - 2 mois	941	556	385	...	...	...
3 months - 3 mois	753	421	332	...	...	...
4 months - 4 mois	610	320	290	...	...	...
5 months - 5 mois	512	274	238	...	...	...
6 months - 6 mois	405	212	193	...	...	...
7 months - 7 mois	339	174	165	...	...	...
8 months - 8 mois	321	156	165	...	...	...
9 months - 9 mois	234	118	116	...	...	...
10 months - 10 mois	186	94	92	...	...	...
11 months - 11 mois	97	45	52	...	...	...
Unknown - Inconnu	12	7	5	...	...	...
Réunion[2]						
2007 (C)						
Total	91	48	43	...	...	...
Less than 1 day - Moins de 1 jour	24	14	10	...	...	...
1 - 6 days - 1 - 6 jours	20	9	11	...	...	...
7 - 27 days - 7 - 27 jours	18	7	11	...	...	...
7 - 13 days - 7 - 13 jours	7	3	4	...	...	...
14 - 20 days - 14 - 20 jours	9	2	7	...	...	...
21 - 27 days - 21 - 27 jours	7	2	5	...	...	...
28 days - 11 months - 28 jours - 11 mois	30	18	12	...	...	...

Continent, country or area, year and age Continent, pays ou zone, année et âge	Number - Nombre			Rate - Taux		
	Both sexes Les deux sexes	Male Masculin	Female Féminin	Both sexes Les deux sexes	Male Masculin	Female Féminin

AFRICA - AFRIQUE

Saint Helena ex. dep. - Sainte-Hélène sans dép.
2005 (C)

Total	1	1	-	...	...	...
Less than 1 day - Moins de 1 jour	-	-	-	...	...	...
1 - 6 days - 1 - 6 jours	1	1	-	...	...	...
7 - 27 days - 7 - 27 jours	-	-	-	...	...	...
28 days - 11 months - 28 jours - 11 mois	-	-	-	...	...	...

Seychelles
2006 (+C)

Total	14	5	9	...	...	...
Less than 1 day - Moins de 1 jour	5	1	4	...	...	...
1 - 6 days - 1 - 6 jours	2	1	1	...	...	...
7 - 27 days - 7 - 27 jours	2	-	2	...	...	...
7 - 13 days - 7 - 13 jours	1	-	1	...	...	...
14 - 20 days - 14 - 20 jours	-	-	-	...	...	...
21 - 27 days - 21 - 27 jours	1	-	1	...	...	...
28 days - 11 months - 28 jours - 11 mois	5	3	2	...	...	...
28 days - less than 2 months - 28 jours - moins de 2 mois	1	1	-	...	...	...
2 months - 2 mois	-	-	-	...	...	...
3 months - 3 mois	-	-	-	...	...	...
4 months - 4 mois	1	-	1	...	...	...
5 months - 5 mois	2	2	-	...	...	...
6 months - 6 mois	1	-	1	...	...	...
7 months - 7 mois	-	-	-	...	...	...
8 months - 8 mois	-	-	-	...	...	...
9 months - 9 mois	-	-	-	...	...	...
10 months - 10 mois	-	-	-	...	...	...
11 months - 11 mois	-	-	-	...	...	...

South Africa - Afrique du Sud[3]
2006 (...)

Total	47 703	25 178[4]	21 810[4]	...	...	...
Less than 1 day - Moins de 1 jour	2 422	1 387[4]	969[4]	...	...	...
1 - 6 days - 1 - 6 jours	7 217	4 146[4]	2 892[4]	...	...	...
7 - 27 days - 7 - 27 jours	3 640	1 991[4]	1 568[4]	...	...	...
7 - 13 days - 7 - 13 jours	1 613	912[4]	667[4]	...	...	...
14 - 20 days - 14 - 20 jours	1 074	589[4]	460[4]	...	...	...
21 - 27 days - 21 - 27 jours	953	490[4]	441[4]	...	...	...
28 days - 11 months - 28 jours - 11 mois	34 424	17 654	16 381	...	...	...
28 days - less than 2 months - 28 jours - moins de 2 mois	4 770	2 509[4]	2 175[4]	...	...	...
2 months - 2 mois	5 786	2 784[4]	2 934[4]	...	...	...
3 months - 3 mois	5 472	2 783[4]	2 621[4]	...	...	...
4 months - 4 mois	3 711	1 958[4]	1 714[4]	...	...	...
5 months - 5 mois	3 041	1 548[4]	1 465[4]	...	...	...
6 months - 6 mois	2 704	1 393[4]	1 281[4]	...	...	...
7 months - 7 mois	2 258	1 181[4]	1 059[4]	...	...	...
8 months - 8 mois	1 948	1 020[4]	910[4]	...	...	...
9 months - 9 mois	1 811	954[4]	841[4]	...	...	...
10 months - 10 mois	1 544	803[4]	730[4]	...	...	...
11 months - 11 mois	1 379	721[4]	651[4]	...	...	...

AMERICA, NORTH - AMÉRIQUE DU NORD

Aruba
2007 (+U)

Total	4	2	2	...	...	...
Less than 1 day - Moins de 1 jour	-	-	-	...	...	...
1 - 6 days - 1 - 6 jours	2	1	1	...	...	...
7 - 27 days - 7 - 27 jours	1	1	-	...	...	...
7 - 13 days - 7 - 13 jours	1	1	-	...	...	...
14 - 27 days - 14 - 27 jours	-	-	-	...	...	...
28 days - 11 months - 28 jours - 11 mois	1	-	1	...	...	...
28 days - less than 2 months - 28 jours - moins de 2 mois	-	-	-	...	...	...
2 - 9 months - 2 - 9 mois	-	-	-	...	...	...
10 months - 10 mois	1	-	1	...	...	...
11 months - 11 mois	-	-	-	...	...	...

16. Infant deaths and infant mortality rates by age and sex: latest available year, 2000 - 2009
Décès d'enfants de moins d'un an et taux de mortalité infantile selon l'âge et le sexe : dernière année disponible, 2000 -
2009 (continued - suite)

Continent, country or area, year and age / Continent, pays ou zone, année et âge	Number - Nombre			Rate - Taux		
	Both sexes Les deux sexes	Male Masculin	Female Féminin	Both sexes Les deux sexes	Male Masculin	Female Féminin
AMERICA, NORTH - AMÉRIQUE DU NORD						
Bahamas						
2006 (C)						
Total	79	42	37	...	...	...
Less than 1 day - Moins de 1 jour	-	-	-	...	...	...
1 - 6 days - 1 - 6 jours	29	18	11	...	...	...
7 - 27 days - 7 - 27 jours	24	15	9	...	...	...
7 - 13 days - 7 - 13 jours	13	10	3	...	...	...
14 - 20 days - 14 - 20 jours	9	4	5	...	...	...
21 - 27 days - 21 - 27 jours	3	2	1	...	...	...
28 days - 11 months - 28 jours - 11 mois	26	9	17	...	...	...
28 days - less than 2 months - 28 jours - moins de 2 mois	8	3	5	...	...	...
2 months - 2 mois	3	1	2	...	...	...
3 months - 3 mois	4	2	2	...	...	...
4 months - 4 mois	6	1	5	...	...	...
5 months - 5 mois	1	1	-	...	...	...
6 months - 6 mois	-	-	-	...	...	...
7 months - 7 mois	2	-	2	...	...	...
8 months - 8 mois	1	1	-	...	...	...
9 months - 9 mois	-	-	-	...	...	...
10 months - 10 mois	1	-	1	...	...	...
11 months - 11 mois	-	-	-	...	...	...
Barbados - Barbade						
2007 (+C)						
Total	31	18	13	...	...	...
Less than 1 day - Moins de 1 jour	-	1	1	...	...	...
1 - 6 days - 1 - 6 jours	10	8	18	...	...	...
7 - 27 days - 7 - 27 jours	6	4	2	...	...	...
7 - 20 days - 7 - 20 jours	6	4	2	...	...	...
21 - 27 days - 21 - 27 jours	-	-	-	...	...	...
28 days - 11 months - 28 jours - 11 mois	4	2	2	...	...	...
28 days - 2 months - 28 jours - 2 mois	3	2	1	...	...	...
3 - 4 months - 3 - 4 mois	1	-	1	...	...	...
5 - 11 months - 5 - 11 mois	-	-	-	...	...	...
Unknown - Inconnu	2	2	-	...	...	...
Bermuda - Bermudes						
2009 (C)						
Total	1	-	1	...	...	...
Less than 1 day - Moins de 1 jour	-	-	-	...	...	...
1 - 6 days - 1 - 6 jours	-	-	-	...	...	...
7 - 27 days - 7 - 27 jours	-	-	-	...	...	...
7 - 13 days - 7 - 13 jours	-	-	-	...	...	...
14 - 20 days - 14 - 20 jours	-	-	-	...	...	...
21 - 27 days - 21 - 27 jours	-	-	-	...	...	...
28 days - 11 months - 28 jours - 11 mois	-	-	-	...	...	...
28 days - less than 2 months - 28 jours - moins de 2 mois	-	-	-	...	...	...
2 months - 2 mois	-	-	-	...	...	...
3 months - 3 mois	-	-	-	...	...	...
4 months - 4 mois	-	-	-	...	...	...
5 months - 5 mois	-	-	-	...	...	...
6 months - 6 mois	-	-	-	...	...	...
7 months - 7 mois	-	-	-	...	...	...
8 months - 8 mois	-	-	-	...	...	...
9 months - 9 mois	-	-	-	...	...	...
10 months - 10 mois	-	-	-	...	...	...
11 months - 11 mois	-	-	-	...	...	...
Unknown - Inconnu	1	-	1	...	...	...
Canada[5]						
2006 (C)						
Total	1 771	983	788	5.0	5.4	4.6
Less than 1 day - Moins de 1 jour	888	481	407	2.5	2.6	2.4
1 - 6 days - 1 - 6 jours	194	110	84	0.5	0.6	0.5
7 - 27 days - 7 - 27 jours	214	123	91	0.6	0.7	0.5
7 - 13 days - 7 - 13 jours	110	62	48	0.3	0.3	0.3
14 - 20 days - 14 - 20 jours	60	34	26	0.2	0.2	♦0.2
21 - 27 days - 21 - 27 jours	44	27	17	0.1	♦0.1	♦0.1
28 days - 11 months - 28 jours - 11 mois	475	269	206	1.3	1.5	1.2
28 days - less than 2 months - 28 jours - moins de 2 mois	141	80	61	0.4	0.4	0.4
2 months - 2 mois	78	42	36	0.2	0.2	0.2

Continent, country or area, year and age / Continent, pays ou zone, année et âge	Number - Nombre			Rate - Taux		
	Both sexes Les deux sexes	Male Masculin	Female Féminin	Both sexes Les deux sexes	Male Masculin	Female Féminin
AMERICA, NORTH - AMÉRIQUE DU NORD						
Canada[5]						
2006 (C)						
3 months - 3 mois	60	37	23	0.2	0.2	♦0.1
4 months - 4 mois	55	33	22	0.2	0.2	♦0.1
5 months - 5 mois	42	21	21	0.1	♦0.1	♦0.1
6 months - 6 mois	24	16	8	♦0.1	♦0.1	-
7 months - 7 mois	19	9	10	♦0.1	-	♦0.1
8 months - 8 mois	19	14	5	♦0.1	♦0.1	-
9 months - 9 mois	18	8	10	♦0.1	-	♦0.1
10 months - 10 mois	9	4	5	-	-	-
11 months - 11 mois	10	5	5	-	-	-
Cayman Islands - Îles Caïmanes						
2007 (C)						
Total	5	4	1	...	...	...
Less than 1 day - Moins de 1 jour	3	2	1	...	...	...
1 - 6 days - 1 - 6 jours	2	2	-	...	...	...
7 - 27 days - 7 - 27 jours	-	-	-	...	...	...
28 days - 11 months - 28 jours - 11 mois	-	-	-	...	...	...
Costa Rica						
2009 (C)						
Total	663	355	308	8.8	9.3	8.4
Less than 1 day - Moins de 1 jour	191	104	87	2.5	2.7	2.4
1 - 6 days - 1 - 6 jours	180	100	80	2.4	2.6	2.2
7 - 27 days - 7 - 27 jours	112	65	47	1.5	1.7	1.3
7 - 13 days - 7 - 13 jours	63	37	26	0.8	1.0	♦0.7
14 - 20 days - 14 - 20 jours	25	14	11	♦0.3	♦0.4	♦0.3
21 - 27 days - 21 - 27 jours	24	14	10	♦0.3	♦0.4	♦0.3
28 days - 11 months - 28 jours - 11 mois	180	86	94	2.4	2.2	2.6
28 days - less than 2 months - 28 jours - moins de 2 mois	45	25	20	0.6	♦0.7	♦0.5
2 months - 2 mois	23	14	9	♦0.3	♦0.4	♦0.2
3 months - 3 mois	24	13	11	♦0.3	♦0.3	♦0.3
4 months - 4 mois	16	3	13	♦0.2	♦0.1	♦0.4
5 months - 5 mois	12	8	4	♦0.2	♦0.2	♦0.1
6 months - 6 mois	16	8	8	♦0.2	♦0.2	♦0.2
7 months - 7 mois	10	3	7	♦0.1	♦0.1	♦0.2
8 months - 8 mois	8	2	6	♦0.1	♦0.1	♦0.2
9 months - 9 mois	9	3	6	♦0.1	♦0.1	♦0.2
10 months - 10 mois	8	5	3	♦0.1	♦0.1	♦0.1
11 months - 11 mois	9	2	7	♦0.1	♦0.1	♦0.2
Cuba						
2009 (C)						
Total	626	351	275	4.8	5.2	4.4
Less than 1 day - Moins de 1 jour	67	43	24	0.5	0.6	♦0.4
1 - 6 days - 1 - 6 jours	170	106	64	1.3	1.6	1.0
7 - 27 days - 7 - 27 jours	114	70	44	0.9	1.0	0.7
7 - 13 days - 7 - 13 jours	59	38	21	0.5	0.6	♦0.3
14 - 20 days - 14 - 20 jours	34	19	15	0.3	♦0.3	♦0.2
21 - 27 days - 21 - 27 jours	21	13	8	♦0.2	♦0.2	♦0.1
28 days - 11 months - 28 jours - 11 mois	275	132	143	2.1	2.0	2.3
28 days - less than 2 months - 28 jours - moins de 2 mois	77	37	40	0.6	0.6	0.6
2 months - 2 mois	56	27	29	0.4	♦0.4	♦0.5
3 months - 3 mois	43	19	24	0.3	♦0.3	♦0.4
4 months - 4 mois	20	10	10	♦0.2	♦0.1	♦0.2
5 months - 5 mois	17	10	7	♦0.1	♦0.1	♦0.1
6 months - 6 mois	9	4	5	♦0.1	♦0.1	♦0.1
7 months - 7 mois	8	2	6	♦0.1	-	♦0.1
8 months - 8 mois	11	4	7	♦0.1	♦0.1	♦0.1
9 months - 9 mois	10	6	4	♦0.1	♦0.1	♦0.1
10 months - 10 mois	16	9	7	♦0.1	♦0.1	♦0.1
11 months - 11 mois	8	4	4	♦0.1	♦0.1	♦0.1
El Salvador[6]						
2007 (C)						
Total	981	579	402	9.2	10.4	7.9
Less than 1 day - Moins de 1 jour	133	76	57	1.2	1.4	1.1
1 - 6 days - 1 - 6 jours	166	94	72	1.6	1.7	1.4
7 - 27 days - 7 - 27 jours	163	99	64	1.5	1.8	1.3
7 - 13 days - 7 - 13 jours	79	50	29	0.7	0.9	♦0.6
14 - 20 days - 14 - 20 jours	52	33	19	0.5	0.6	♦0.4

16. Infant deaths and infant mortality rates by age and sex: latest available year, 2000 - 2009
Décès d'enfants de moins d'un an et taux de mortalité infantile selon l'âge et le sexe : dernière année disponible, 2000 - 2009 (continued - suite)

Continent, country or area, year and age Continent, pays ou zone, année et âge	Number - Nombre			Rate - Taux		
	Both sexes Les deux sexes	Male Masculin	Female Féminin	Both sexes Les deux sexes	Male Masculin	Female Féminin
AMERICA, NORTH - AMÉRIQUE DU NORD						
El Salvador[6]						
2007 (C)						
21 - 27 days - 21 - 27 jours	32	16	16	0.3	♦0.3	♦0.3
28 days - 11 months - 28 jours - 11 mois..............	519	310	209	4.9	5.6	4.1
28 days - less than 2 months - 28 jours - moins de 2 mois	119	82	37	1.1	1.5	0.7
2 months - 2 mois.................................	69	44	25	0.6	0.8	♦0.5
3 months - 3 mois.................................	64	33	31	0.6	0.6	0.6
4 months - 4 mois.................................	49	29	20	0.5	♦0.5	♦0.4
5 months - 5 mois.................................	41	20	21	0.4	♦0.4	♦0.4
6 months - 6 mois.................................	37	21	16	0.3	♦0.4	♦0.3
7 months - 7 mois.................................	34	22	12	0.3	♦0.4	♦0.2
8 months - 8 mois.................................	34	19	15	0.3	♦0.3	♦0.3
9 months - 9 mois.................................	25	12	13	♦0.2	♦0.2	♦0.3
10 months - 10 mois...............................	29	17	12	♦0.3	♦0.3	♦0.2
11 months - 11 mois...............................	18	11	7	♦0,2	♦0.2	♦0.1
Greenland - Groenland[3]						
2006 (C)						
Total..	13	7	6	...	...	...
Less than 1 day - Moins de 1 jour	8	5	3	...	...	...
1 - 6 days - 1 - 6 jours	-	-	-	...	...	...
7 - 27 days - 7 - 27 jours	-	-	-	...	...	...
28 days - 11 months - 28 jours - 11 mois............	5	2	3	...	...	...
28 days - less than 2 months - 28 jours - moins de 2 mois	5	2	3	...	...	...
2 - 11 months - 2 - 11 mois	-	-	-	...	...	...
Guadeloupe[2]						
2003 (C)						
Total..	56	34	22	...	...	...
Less than 1 day - Moins de 1 jour	13	5	8	...	...	...
1 - 6 days - 1 - 6 jours	8	4	4	...	...	...
7 - 27 days - 7 - 27 jours	19	12	7	...	...	...
7 - 13 days - 7 - 13 jours	5	3	2	...	...	...
14 - 20 days - 14 - 20 jours	10	5	5	...	...	...
21 - 27 days - 21 - 27 jours	4	4	-	...	...	...
28 days - 11 months - 28 jours - 11 mois............	16	13	3	...	...	...
28 days - less than 2 months - 28 jours - moins de 2 mois	7	6	1	...	...	...
2 months - 2 mois.................................	4	2	2	...	...	...
3 months - 3 mois.................................	3	3	-	...	...	...
4 months - 4 mois.................................	1	1	-	...	...	...
5 months - 5 mois.................................	-	-	-	...	...	...
6 months - 6 mois.................................	1	1	-	...	...	...
7 months - 7 mois.................................	-	-	-	...	...	...
8 months - 8 mois.................................	-	-	-	...	...	...
9 months - 9 mois.................................	-	-	-	...	...	...
10 months - 10 mois...............................	-	-	-	...	...	...
11 months - 11 mois...............................	-	-	-	...	...	...
Guatemala						
2006 (C)						
Total..	9 042	5 012	4 030	24.5	26.8	22.2
Less than 1 day - Moins de 1 jour	842	478	364	2.3	2.6	2.0
1 - 6 days - 1 - 6 jours	2 040	1 162	878	5.5	6.2	4.8
7 - 27 days - 7 - 27 jours	1 209	681	528	3.3	3.6	2.9
7 - 13 days - 7 - 13 jours	550	318	232	1.5	1.7	1.3
14 - 20 days - 14 - 20 jours	359	185	174	1.0	1.0	1.0
21 - 27 days - 21 - 27 jours	300	178	122	0.8	1.0	0.7
28 days - 11 months - 28 jours - 11 mois............	4 951	2 691	2 260	13.4	14.4	12.5
28 days - less than 2 months - 28 jours - moins de 2 mois	1 017	564	453	2.8	3.0	2.5
2 months - 2 mois.................................	773	402	371	2.1	2.1	2.0
3 months - 3 mois.................................	527	274	253	1.4	1.5	1.4
4 months - 4 mois.................................	438	248	190	1.2	1.3	1.0
5 months - 5 mois.................................	323	162	161	0.9	0.9	0.9
6 months - 6 mois.................................	367	211	156	1.0	1.1	0.9
7 months - 7 mois.................................	332	171	161	0.9	0.9	0.9
8 months - 8 mois.................................	297	166	131	0.8	0.9	0.7
9 months - 9 mois.................................	296	170	126	0.8	0.9	0.7
10 months - 10 mois...............................	282	152	130	0.8	0.8	0.7
11 months - 11 mois...............................	299	171	128	0.8	0.9	0.7

Continent, country or area, year and age / Continent, pays ou zone, année et âge	Number - Nombre			Rate - Taux		
	Both sexes Les deux sexes	Male Masculin	Female Féminin	Both sexes Les deux sexes	Male Masculin	Female Féminin
AMERICA, NORTH - AMÉRIQUE DU NORD						
Martinique[7]						
2007 (C)						
Total	43	26	17	...	...	...
Less than 1 day - Moins de 1 jour	18	10	8	...	...	...
1 - 6 days - 1 - 6 jours	8	7	1	...	...	...
7 - 27 days - 7 - 27 jours	9	3	6	...	...	...
7 - 13 days - 7 - 13 jours	5	1	4	...	...	...
14 - 20 days - 14 - 20 jours	3	2	1	...	...	...
21 - 27 days - 21 - 27 jours	1	-	1	...	...	...
28 days - 11 months - 28 jours - 11 mois	8	6	2	...	...	...
28 days - less than 2 months - 28 jours - moins de 2 mois	-	-	-	...	...	...
2 months - 2 mois	5	3	2	...	...	...
3 months - 3 mois	-	-	-	...	...	...
4 months - 4 mois	1	1	-	...	...	...
5 months - 5 mois	-	-	-	...	...	...
6 months - 6 mois	-	-	-	...	...	...
7 months - 7 mois	1	1	-	...	...	...
8 months - 8 mois	-	-	-	...	...	...
9 - 11 months - 9 - 11 mois	1	1	-	...	...	...
Mexico - Mexique[8]						
2009 (+U)						
Total	28 983	16 229[4]	12 694[4]	...	...	...
Less than 1 day - Moins de 1 jour	6 048	3 364[4]	2 647[4]	...	...	...
1 - 6 days - 1 - 6 jours	7 124	4 121[4]	2 987[4]	...	...	...
7 - 27 days - 7 - 27 jours	5 397	3 056[4]	2 338[4]	...	...	...
7 - 13 days - 7 - 13 jours	2 914	1 640[4]	1 272[4]	...	...	...
14 - 20 days - 14 - 20 jours	1 469	844[4]	624[4]	...	...	...
21 - 27 days - 21 - 27 jours	1 014	572[4]	442[4]	...	...	...
28 days - 11 months - 28 jours - 11 mois	10 389	5 673	4 712	...	...	...
28 days - less than 2 months - 28 jours - moins de 2 mois	2 992	1 671[4]	1 321[4]	...	...	...
2 months - 2 mois	1 916	1 112[4]	804[4]	...	...	...
3 months - 3 mois	1 346	747[4]	599[4]	...	...	...
4 months - 4 mois	932	510[4]	421[4]	...	...	...
5 months - 5 mois	727	386[4]	340[4]	...	...	...
6 months - 6 mois	630	308[4]	320[4]	...	...	...
7 months - 7 mois	468	239[4]	229[4]	...	...	...
8 months - 8 mois	444	233[4]	211[4]	...	...	...
9 months - 9 mois	333	176[4]	157[4]	...	...	...
10 months - 10 mois	310	145[4]	165[4]	...	...	...
11 months - 11 mois	291	146[4]	145[4]	...	...	...
Netherlands Antilles - Antilles néerlandaises						
2004 (C)						
Total	20	13	7	...	...	...
Less than 1 day - Moins de 1 jour	4	3	1	...	...	...
1 - 6 days - 1 - 6 jours	5	2	3	...	...	...
7 - 27 days - 7 - 27 jours	3	2	1	...	...	...
7 - 13 days - 7 - 13 jours	-	-	-	...	...	...
14 - 20 days - 14 - 20 jours	2	1	1	...	...	...
21 - 27 days - 21 - 27 jours	1	1	-	...	...	...
28 days - 11 months - 28 jours - 11 mois	8	6	2	...	...	...
28 days - less than 2 months - 28 jours - moins de 2 mois	4	3	1	...	...	...
2 months - 2 mois	3	3	-	...	...	...
3 months - 3 mois	-	-	-	...	...	...
4 months - 4 mois	1	-	1	...	...	...
5 - 11 months - 5 - 11 mois	-	-	-	...	...	...
Nicaragua						
2008 (+U)						
Total	1 932	1 123	809	...	...	...
Less than 1 day - Moins de 1 jour	386	219	167	...	...	...
1 - 6 days - 1 - 6 jours	664	418	246	...	...	...
7 - 27 days - 7 - 27 jours	277	151	126	...	...	...
7 - 13 days - 7 - 13 jours	156	89	67	...	...	...
14 - 20 days - 14 - 20 jours	74	41	33	...	...	...
21 - 27 days - 21 - 27 jours	47	21	26	...	...	...
28 days - 11 months - 28 jours - 11 mois	591	326	265	...	...	...
28 days - less than 2 months - 28 jours - moins de 2 mois	169	86	83	...	...	...
2 months - 2 mois	116	74	42	...	...	...

16. Infant deaths and infant mortality rates by age and sex: latest available year, 2000 - 2009

Décès d'enfants de moins d'un an et taux de mortalité infantile selon l'âge et le sexe : dernière année disponible, 2000 - 2009 (continued - suite)

Continent, country or area, year and age / Continent, pays ou zone, année et âge	Number - Nombre			Rate - Taux		
	Both sexes Les deux sexes	Male Masculin	Female Féminin	Both sexes Les deux sexes	Male Masculin	Female Féminin
AMERICA, NORTH - AMÉRIQUE DU NORD						
Nicaragua						
2008 (+U)						
3 months - 3 mois	66	38	28	...	...	...
4 months - 4 mois	49	29	20	...	...	...
5 months - 5 mois	45	22	23	...	...	...
6 months - 6 mois	27	13	14	...	...	...
7 months - 7 mois	36	18	18	...	...	...
8 months - 8 mois	27	17	10	...	...	...
9 months - 9 mois	18	8	10	...	...	...
10 months - 10 mois	21	9	12	...	...	...
11 months - 11 mois	17	12	5	...	...	...
Panama						
2009 (U)						
Total	837	486	351	...	...	...
Less than 1 day - Moins de 1 jour	143	82	61	...	...	...
1 - 6 days - 1 - 6 jours	184	111	73	...	...	...
7 - 27 days - 7 - 27 jours	132	78	54	...	...	...
7 - 13 days - 7 - 13 jours	63	41	22	...	...	...
14 - 20 days - 14 - 20 jours	42	23	19	...	...	...
21 - 27 days - 21 - 27 jours	27	14	13	...	...	...
28 days - 11 months - 28 jours - 11 mois	378	215	163	...	...	...
28 days - less than 2 months - 28 jours - moins de 2 mois	100	51	49	...	...	...
2 months - 2 mois	51	38	13	...	...	...
3 months - 3 mois	47	27	20	...	...	...
4 months - 4 mois	25	10	15	...	...	...
5 months - 5 mois	28	15	13	...	...	...
6 months - 6 mois	25	16	9	...	...	...
7 months - 7 mois	20	9	11	...	...	...
8 months - 8 mois	25	13	12	...	...	...
9 months - 9 mois	17	13	4	...	...	...
10 months - 10 mois	17	7	10	...	...	...
11 months - 11 mois	23	16	7	...	...	...
Puerto Rico - Porto Rico						
2008 (C)						
Total	400	225	175	8.8	9.6	7.9
Less than 1 day - Moins de 1 jour	75	38	37	1.6	1.6	1.7
1 - 6 days - 1 - 6 jours	110	72	38	2.4	3.1	1.7
7 - 27 days - 7 - 27 jours	61	36	25	1.3	1.5	♦1.1
7 - 13 days - 7 - 13 jours	30	19	11	0.7	♦0.8	♦0.5
14 - 20 days - 14 - 20 jours	18	9	9	♦0.4	♦0.4	♦0.4
21 - 27 days - 21 - 27 jours	13	8	5	♦0.3	♦0.3	♦0.2
28 days - 11 months - 28 jours - 11 mois	96	44	52	2.1	1.9	2.3
28 days - less than 2 months - 28 jours - moins de 2 mois	5	3	2	♦0.1	♦0.1	♦0.1
2 - 11 months - 2 - 11 mois	91	41	50	2.0	1.7	2.2
Unknown - Inconnu	58	35	23	1.3	1.5	♦1.0
Saint Lucia - Sainte-Lucie						
2002 (C)						
Total	36	17	19	...	...	...
Less than 1 day - Moins de 1 jour	11	5	6	...	...	...
1 - 6 days - 1 - 6 jours	16	6	10	...	...	...
7 - 27 days - 7 - 27 jours	2	1	1	...	...	...
7 - 20 days - 7 - 20 jours	-	-	-	...	...	...
21 - 27 days - 21 - 27 jours	2	1	1	...	...	...
28 days - 11 months - 28 jours - 11 mois	7	5	2	...	...	...
28 days - less than 2 months - 28 jours - moins de 2 mois	-	-	-	...	...	...
2 months - 2 mois	1	1	-	...	...	...
3 months - 3 mois	1	1	-	...	...	...
4 months - 4 mois	1	1	-	...	...	...
5 months - 5 mois	1	1	-	...	...	...
6 months - 6 mois	-	-	-	...	...	...
7 months - 7 mois	-	-	-	...	...	...
8 months - 8 mois	2	1	1	...	...	...
9 months - 9 mois	-	-	-	...	...	...
10 months - 10 mois	1	-	1	...	...	...
11 months - 11 mois	-	-	-	...	...	...

16. Infant deaths and infant mortality rates by age and sex: latest available year, 2000 - 2009
Décès d'enfants de moins d'un an et taux de mortalité infantile selon l'âge et le sexe : dernière année disponible, 2000 - 2000 (continued - suite)

Continent, country or area, year and age / Continent, pays ou zone, année et âge	Number - Nombre			Rate - Taux		
	Both sexes Les deux sexes	Male Masculin	Female Féminin	Both sexes Les deux sexes	Male Masculin	Female Féminin
AMERICA, NORTH - AMÉRIQUE DU NORD						
Saint Vincent and the Grenadines - Saint-Vincent-et-les Grenadines						
2005 (+C)						
Total	29	17	12	...	...	...
Less than 1 day - Moins de 1 jour	6	3	3	...	...	...
1 - 6 days - 1 - 6 jours	11	6	5	...	...	...
7 - 27 days - 7 - 27 jours	3	2	1	...	...	...
28 days - 11 months - 28 jours - 11 mois	9	6	3	...	...	...
28 days - less than 2 months - 28 jours - moins de 2 mois	-	-	-	...	...	...
2 - 11 months - 2 - 11 mois	9	6	3	...	...	...
Trinidad and Tobago - Trinité-et-Tobago						
2002 (C)						
Total	412	247	165	24.2	28.7	19.7
Less than 1 day - Moins de 1 jour	91	51	40	5.4	5.9	4.8
1 - 6 days - 1 - 6 jours	148	92	56	8.7	10.7	6.7
7 - 27 days - 7 - 27 jours	105	71	34	6.2	8.2	4.1
7 - 13 days - 7 - 13 jours	66	44	22	3.9	5.1	♦2.6
14 - 20 days - 14 - 20 jours	21	16	5	♦1.2	♦1.9	♦0.6
21 - 27 days - 21 - 27 jours	18	11	7	♦1.1	♦1.3	♦0.8
28 days - 11 months - 28 jours - 11 mois	68	33	35	4.0	3.8	4.2
28 days - less than 2 months - 28 jours - moins de 2 mois	25	12	13	♦1.5	♦1.4	♦1.6
2 - 3 months - 2 - 3 mois	4	2	2	♦0.2	♦0.2	♦0.2
4 - 6 months - 4 - 6 mois	18	9	9	♦1.1	♦1.0	♦1.1
7 - 9 months - 7 - 9 mois	11	4	7	♦0.6	♦0.5	♦0.8
10 - 11 months - 10 - 11 mois	10	6	4	♦0.6	♦0.7	♦0.5
United States of America - États-Unis d'Amérique						
2008* (C)						
Total	28 039	15 658	12 381	6.6	...	...
Less than 1 day - Moins de 1 jour	11 126	6 165	4 961	2.6	...	...
1 - 6 days - 1 - 6 jours	3 480	2 018	1 462	0.8	...	...
7 - 27 days - 7 - 27 jours	3 556	1 923	1 633	0.8	...	...
7 - 13 days - 7 - 13 jours	1 650	888	762	0.4	...	...
14 - 20 days - 14 - 20 jours	1 074	595	479	0.3	...	...
21 - 27 days - 21 - 27 jours	832	440	392	0.2	...	...
28 days - 11 months - 28 jours - 11 mois	9 877	5 552	4 325	2.3	...	...
28 days - less than 2 months - 28 jours - moins de 2 mois	2 848	1 545	1 303	0.7	...	...
2 months - 2 mois	1 794	1 030	764	0.4	...	...
3 months - 3 mois	1 365	772	593	0.3	...	...
4 months - 4 mois	1 093	634	459	0.3	...	...
5 months - 5 mois	715	409	306	0.2	...	...
6 months - 6 mois	544	301	243	0.1	...	...
7 months - 7 mois	417	248	169	0.1	...	...
8 months - 8 mois	349	197	152	0.1	...	...
9 months - 9 mois	273	146	127	0.1	...	...
10 months - 10 mois	231	138	93	0.1	...	...
11 months - 11 mois	248	132	116	0.1	...	...
AMERICA, SOUTH - AMÉRIQUE DU SUD						
Argentina - Argentine						
2006 (C)						
Total	8 986	5 063[4]	3 911[4]	12.9	14.1	11.7
Less than 7 days - Moins de 7 jours	4 312	2 465[4]	1 838[4]	6.2	6.8	5.5
7 - 27 days - 7 - 27 jours	1 591	898[4]	691[4]	2.3	2.5	2.1
28 days - 11 months - 28 jours - 11 mois	3 083	1 700[4]	1 382[4]	4.4	4.7	4.1
Brazil - Brésil[9]						
2009 (U)						
Total	33 713	18 954	14 759	...	...	...
Less than 1 day - Moins de 1 jour	7 771	4 373	3 398	...	...	...
1 - 6 days - 1 - 6 jours	9 273	5 379	3 894	...	...	...
7 - 27 days - 7 - 27 jours	5 784	3 202	2 582	...	...	...
7 - 13 days - 7 - 13 jours	3 101	1 710	1 391	...	...	...
14 - 20 days - 14 - 20 jours	1 536	857	679	...	...	...
21 - 27 days - 21 - 27 jours	1 147	635	512	...	...	...
28 days - 11 months - 28 jours - 11 mois	10 885	6 000	4 885	...	...	...
28 days - less than 2 months - 28 jours - moins de 2 mois	3 210	1 799	1 411	...	...	...
2 months - 2 mois	1 810	983	827	...	...	...

Continent, country or area, year and age Continent, pays ou zone, année et âge	Number - Nombre			Rate - Taux		
	Both sexes Les deux sexes	Male Masculin	Female Féminin	Both sexes Les deux sexes	Male Masculin	Female Féminin
AMERICA, SOUTH - AMÉRIQUE DU SUD						
Brazil - Brésil[9]						
2009 (U)						
3 months - 3 mois	1 238	707	531	...	...	...
4 months - 4 mois	1 000	548	452	...	...	...
5 months - 5 mois	765	417	348	...	...	...
6 months - 6 mois	654	354	300	...	...	...
7 months - 7 mois	588	331	257	...	...	...
8 months - 8 mois	487	267	220	...	...	...
9 months - 9 mois	398	215	183	...	...	...
10 months - 10 mois	381	197	184	...	...	...
11 months - 11 mois	354	182	172	...	...	...
Chile - Chili						
2008 (C)						
Total	1 948	1 054	894	7.9	8.4	7.4
Less than 1 day - Moins de 1 jour	755	409	346	3.1	3.2	2.9
1 - 6 days - 1 - 6 jours	367	210	157	1.5	1.7	1.3
7 - 27 days - 7 - 27 jours	247	131	116	1.0	1.0	1.0
7 - 13 days - 7 - 13 jours	134	69	65	0.5	0.5	0.5
14 - 20 days - 14 - 20 jours	62	35	27	0.3	0.3	♦0.2
21 - 27 days - 21 - 27 jours	51	27	24	0.2	♦0.2	♦0.2
28 days - 11 months - 28 jours - 11 mois	579	304	275	2.3	2.4	2.3
28 days - less than 2 months - 28 jours - moins de 2 mois	182	92	90	0.7	0.7	0.7
2 months - 2 mois	115	59	56	0.5	0.5	0.5
3 months - 3 mois	72	34	38	0.3	0.3	0.3
4 months - 4 mois	57	41	16	0.2	0.3	♦0.1
5 months - 5 mois	35	15	20	0.1	♦0.1	♦0.2
6 months - 6 mois	26	11	15	♦0.1	♦0.1	♦0.1
7 months - 7 mois	26	16	10	♦0.1	♦0.1	♦0.1
8 months - 8 mois	21	12	9	♦0.1	♦0.1	♦0.1
9 months - 9 mois	13	9	4	♦0.1	♦0.1	-
10 months - 10 mois	16	7	9	♦0.1	♦0.1	♦0.1
11 months - 11 mois	16	8	8	♦0.1	♦0.1	♦0.1
Colombia - Colombie						
2009* (U)						
Total	9 250	5 182	4 068	...	...	...
Less than 1 day - Moins de 1 jour	1 749	991	758	...	...	...
1 - 6 days - 1 - 6 jours	2 105	1 241	864	...	...	...
7 - 27 days - 7 - 27 jours	1 679	914	765	...	...	...
7 - 13 days - 7 - 13 jours	901	478	423	...	...	...
14 - 20 days - 14 - 20 jours	470	254	216	...	...	...
21 - 27 days - 21 - 27 jours	308	182	126	...	...	...
28 days - 11 months - 28 jours - 11 mois	3 464	1 894	1 570	...	...	...
28 days - less than 2 months - 28 jours - moins de 2 mois	860	484	376	...	...	...
2 months - 2 mois	576	326	250	...	...	...
3 months - 3 mois	423	222	201	...	...	...
4 months - 4 mois	309	153	156	...	...	...
5 months - 5 mois	240	132	108	...	...	...
6 months - 6 mois	232	135	97	...	...	...
7 months - 7 mois	200	104	96	...	...	...
8 months - 8 mois	199	105	94	...	...	...
9 months - 9 mois	153	87	66	...	...	...
10 months - 10 mois	137	80	57	...	...	...
11 months - 11 mois	135	66	69	...	...	...
Unknown - Inconnu	253	142	111	...	...	...
Ecuador - Équateur[10]						
2009 (U)						
Total	3 279	1 792	1 487	...	...	...
Less than 1 day - Moins de 1 jour	643	356	287	...	...	...
1 - 6 days - 1 - 6 jours	720	403	317	...	...	...
7 - 27 days - 7 - 27 jours	526	281	245	...	...	...
7 - 13 days - 7 - 13 jours	252	130	122	...	...	...
14 - 20 days - 14 - 20 jours	153	84	69	...	...	...
21 - 27 days - 21 - 27 jours	121	67	54	...	...	...
28 days - 11 months - 28 jours - 11 mois	1 390	752	638	...	...	...
28 days - less than 2 months - 28 jours - moins de 2 mois	232	123	109	...	...	...
2 months - 2 mois	273	144	129	...	...	...
3 months - 3 mois	170	94	76	...	...	...
4 months - 4 mois	144	85	59	...	...	...

Continent, country or area, year and age / Continent, pays ou zone, année et âge	Number - Nombre			Rate - Taux		
	Both sexes Les deux sexes	Male Masculin	Female Féminin	Both sexes Les deux sexes	Male Masculin	Female Féminin
AMERICA, SOUTH - AMÉRIQUE DU SUD						
Ecuador - Équateur[10]						
2009 (U)						
5 months - 5 mois	123	57	66	...	...	...
6 months - 6 mois	102	52	50	...	...	...
7 months - 7 mois	73	36	37	...	...	...
8 months - 8 mois	85	44	41	...	...	...
9 months - 9 mois	60	38	22	...	...	...
10 months - 10 mois	64	42	22	...	...	...
11 months - 11 mois	64	37	27	...	...	...
French Guiana - Guyane française						
2007 (C)						
Total	73	39	34	...	...	...
Less than 1 day - Moins de 1 jour	18	10	8	...	...	...
1 - 6 days - 1 - 6 jours	15	5	10	...	...	...
7 - 27 days - 7 - 27 jours	17	12	5	...	...	...
7 - 13 days - 7 - 13 jours	9	5	4	...	...	...
14 - 20 days - 14 - 20 jours	3	3	-	...	...	...
21 - 27 days - 21 - 27 jours	5	4	1	...	...	...
28 days - 11 months - 28 jours - 11 mois	23	12	11	...	...	...
28 days - less than 2 months - 28 jours - moins de 2 mois	1	-	1	...	...	...
2 months - 2 mois	7	4	3	...	...	...
3 months - 3 mois	4	1	3	...	...	...
4 months - 4 mois	2	1	1	...	...	...
5 months - 5 mois	2	2	-	...	...	...
6 months - 6 mois	2	1	1	...	...	...
7 months - 7 mois	1	1	-	...	...	...
8 months - 8 mois	1	1	-	...	...	...
9 months - 9 mois	2	1	1	...	...	...
10 months - 10 mois	-	-	-	...	...	...
11 months - 11 mois	1	-	1	...	...	...
Paraguay						
2006 (U)						
Total	549	...	...	...	...	...
Less than 28 days - Moins de 28 jours	270	...	...	...	...	...
28 days - 11 months - 28 jours - 11 mois[11]	279	...	...	...	...	...
Peru - Pérou[12]						
2008 (+U)						
Total	5 581	3 056	2 524	...	...	...
Less than 1 day - Moins de 1 jour	771	443	328	...	...	...
1 - 6 days - 1 - 6 jours	1 334	733	601	...	...	...
7 - 27 days - 7 - 27 jours	878	491	387	...	...	...
7 - 13 days - 7 - 13 jours	454	264	190	...	...	...
14 - 20 days - 14 - 20 jours	233	126	107	...	...	...
21 - 27 days - 21 - 27 jours	191	101	90	...	...	...
28 days - 11 months - 28 jours - 11 mois	2 597	1 389	1 208	...	...	...
28 days - less than 2 months - 28 jours - moins de 2 mois	755	414	341	...	...	...
2 months - 2 mois	480	249	231	...	...	...
3 months - 3 mois	288	158	130	...	...	...
4 months - 4 mois	198	94	104	...	...	...
5 months - 5 mois	168	95	73	...	...	...
6 months - 6 mois	137	69	68	...	...	...
7 months - 7 mois	150	79	71	...	...	...
8 months - 8 mois	115	57	58	...	...	...
9 months - 9 mois	113	61	52	...	...	...
10 months - 10 mois	92	52	40	...	...	...
11 months - 11 mois	101	61	40	...	...	...
Unknown - Inconnu	1	1	-	...	...	...
Uruguay						
2000 (C)						
Total	742	434[4]	304[4]	14.1	16.0	11.9
Less than 1 day - Moins de 1 jour	152	87[4]	61[4]	2.9	3.2	2.4
1 - 6 days - 1 - 6 jours	124	74	50	2.3	2.7	2.0
7 - 27 days - 7 - 27 jours	142	90	52	2.7	3.3	2.0
7 - 13 days - 7 - 13 jours	71	46	25	1.3	1.7	+1.0
14 - 20 days - 14 - 20 jours	42	27	15	0.8	+1.0	+0.6
21 - 27 days - 21 - 27 jours	29	17	12	+0.5	+0.6	+0.5
28 days - 11 months - 28 jours - 11 mois	324	183	141	6.1	6.7	5.5
28 days - less than 2 months - 28 jours - moins de 2 mois	96	62	34	1.8	2.3	1.3

16. Infant deaths and infant mortality rates by age and sex: latest available year, 2000 - 2009
Décès d'enfants de moins d'un an et taux de mortalité infantile selon l'âge et le sexe : dernière année disponible, 2000 - 2009 (continued - suite)

Continent, country or area, year and age Continent, pays ou zone, année et âge	Number - Nombre			Rate - Taux		
	Both sexes Les deux sexes	Male Masculin	Female Féminin	Both sexes Les deux sexes	Male Masculin	Female Féminin
AMERICA, SOUTH - AMÉRIQUE DU SUD						
Uruguay						
2000 (C)						
2 months - 2 mois...	46	23	23	0.9	♦0.8	♦0.9
3 months - 3 mois...	44	25	19	0.8	♦0.9	♦0.7
4 months - 4 mois...	33	19	14	0.6	♦0.7	♦0.5
5 months - 5 mois...	26	15	11	♦0.5	♦0.6	♦0.4
6 months - 6 mois...	18	10	8	♦0.3	♦0.4	♦0.3
7 months - 7 mois...	12	7	5	♦0.2	♦0.3	♦0.2
8 months - 8 mois...	14	7	7	♦0.3	♦0.3	♦0.3
9 months - 9 mois...	17	7	10	♦0.3	♦0.3	♦0.4
10 months - 10 mois...	9	6	3	♦0.2	♦0.2	♦0.1
11 months - 11 mois...	9	2	7	♦0.2	♦0.1	♦0.3
Venezuela (Bolivarian Republic of) - Venezuela (République bolivarienne du)						
2007 (C)						
Total...	6 340	3 715	2 625	10.3	11.7	8.8
Less than 28 days - Moins de 28 jours...............	4 379	2 599	1 780	7.1	8.2	6.0
28 days 11 months - 28 jours - 11 mois.............	1 961	1 116	845	3.2	3.5	2.8
28 days - less than 2 months - 28 jours - moins de 2 mois........	455	258	197	0.7	0.8	0.7
2 months - 2 mois...	325	182	143	0.5	0.6	0.5
3 months - 3 mois...	231	136	95	0.4	0.4	0.3
4 months - 4 mois...	190	119	71	0.3	0.4	0.2
5 months - 5 mois...	157	87	70	0.3	0.3	0.2
6 months - 6 mois...	153	89	64	0.2	0.3	0.2
7 months - 7 mois...	104	57	47	0.2	0.2	0.2
8 months - 8 mois...	122	63	59	0.2	0.2	0.2
9 months - 9 mois...	77	39	38	0.1	0.1	0.1
10 months - 10 mois...	81	50	31	0.1	0.2	0.1
11 months - 11 mois...	66	36	30	0.1	0.1	0.1
ASIA - ASIE						
Armenia - Arménie[13]						
2009 (C)						
Total...	454	258	196	10.2	10.9	9.4
Less than 1 day - Moins de 1 jour......................	82	47	35	1.8	2.0	1.7
1 - 6 days - 1 - 6 jours.....................................	165	93	72	3.7	3.9	3.5
7 - 27 days - 7 - 27 jours..................................	72	37	35	1.6	1.6	1.7
7 - 13 days - 7 - 13 jours.................................	28	16	12	♦0.6	♦0.7	♦0.6
14 - 20 days - 14 - 20 jours..............................	24	12	12	♦0.5	♦0.5	♦0.6
21 - 27 days - 21 - 27 jours..............................	20	9	11	♦0.5	♦0.4	♦0.5
28 days - 11 months - 28 jours - 11 mois.............	135	81	54	3.0	3.4	2.6
28 days - less than 2 months - 28 jours - moins de 2 mois........	37	23	14	0.8	♦1.0	♦0.7
2 months - 2 mois...	24	14	10	♦0.5	♦0.6	♦0.5
3 months - 3 mois...	20	10	10	♦0.5	♦0.4	♦0.5
4 months - 4 mois...	15	12	3	♦0.3	♦0.5	♦0.1
5 months - 5 mois...	13	7	6	♦0.3	♦0.3	♦0.3
6 months - 6 mois...	4	2	2	♦0.1	♦0.1	♦0.1
7 months - 7 mois...	1	1	-	-	-	-
8 months - 8 mois...	4	3	1	♦0.1	♦0.1	-
9 months - 9 mois...	9	6	3	♦0.2	♦0.3	♦0.1
10 months - 10 mois...	6	3	3	♦0.1	♦0.1	♦0.1
11 months - 11 mois...	2	-	2	-	-	♦0.1
Azerbaijan - Azerbaïdjan[13]						
2009 (+C)						
Total...	1 731	950	781	11.4	11.6	11.2
Less than 1 day - Moins de 1 jour......................	297	195	102	2.0	2.4	1.5
1 - 6 days - 1 - 6 jours.....................................	524	323	201	3.4	3.9	2.9
7 - 27 days - 7 - 27 jours..................................	76	49	27	0.5	0.6	♦0.4
7 - 13 days - 7 - 13 jours.................................	32	27	5	0.2	♦0.3	♦0.1
14 - 20 days - 14 - 20 jours..............................	22	11	11	♦0.1	♦0.1	♦0.2
21 - 27 days - 21 - 27 jours..............................	22	11	11	♦0.1	♦0.1	♦0.2
28 days - 11 months - 28 jours - 11 mois.............	834	383	451	5.5	4.7	6.4
28 days - less than 2 months - 28 jours - moins de 2 mois........	68	34	34	0.4	0.4	0.5
2 months - 2 mois...	67	40	27	0.4	0.5	♦0.4
3 months - 3 mois...	75	29	46	0.5	♦0.4	0.7
4 months - 4 mois...	97	48	49	0.6	0.6	0.7

16. Infant deaths and infant mortality rates by age and sex: latest available year, 2000 - 2009
Décès d'enfants de moins d'un an et taux de mortalité infantile selon l'âge et le sexe : dernière année disponible, 2000 - 2009 (continued - suite)

Continent, country or area, year and age — Continent, pays ou zone, année et âge	Number - Nombre			Rate - Taux		
	Both sexes Les deux sexes	Male Masculin	Female Féminin	Both sexes Les deux sexes	Male Masculin	Female Féminin
ASIA - ASIE						
Azerbaijan - Azerbaïdjan[13]						
2009 (+C)						
5 months - 5 mois	111	50	61	0.7	0.6	0.9
6 months - 6 mois	108	50	58	0.7	0.6	0.8
7 months - 7 mois	62	38	24	0.4	0.5	♦0.3
8 months - 8 mois	92	31	61	0.6	0.4	0.9
9 months - 9 mois	72	29	43	0.5	♦0.4	0.6
10 months - 10 mois	40	19	21	0.3	♦0.2	♦0.3
11 months - 11 mois	42	15	27	0.3	♦0.2	♦0.4
Bahrain - Bahreïn						
2008 (C)						
Total	127	69	58	7.5	8.0	7.0
Less than 1 day - Moins de 1 jour	18	11	7	♦1.1	♦1.3	♦0.8
1 - 6 days - 1 - 6 jours	20	7	13	♦1.2	♦0.8	♦1.6
7 - 27 days - 7 - 27 jours	15	8	7	♦0.9	♦0.9	♦0.8
7 - 13 days - 7 - 13 jours	4	3	1	♦0.2	♦0.3	♦0.1
14 - 20 days - 14 - 20 jours	7	4	3	♦0.4	♦0.5	♦0.4
21 - 27 days - 21 - 27 jours	4	1	3	♦0.2	♦0.1	♦0.4
28 days - 11 months - 28 jours - 11 mois	74	43	31	4.3	5.0	3.7
28 days - less than 2 months - 28 jours - moins de 2 mois	28	14	14	♦1.6	♦1.6	♦1.7
2 months - 2 mois	11	9	2	♦0.6	♦1.0	♦0.2
3 months - 3 mois	10	7	3	♦0.6	♦0.8	♦0.4
4 months - 4 mois	5	2	3	♦0.3	♦0.2	♦0.4
5 months - 5 mois	5	3	2	♦0.3	♦0.3	♦0.2
6 months - 6 mois	6	5	1	♦0.4	♦0.6	♦0.1
7 months - 7 mois	1	-	1	♦0.1	-	♦0.1
8 months - 8 mois	4	1	3	♦0.2	♦0.1	♦0.4
9 months - 9 mois	2	1	1	♦0.1	♦0.1	♦0.1
10 months - 10 mois	1	1	-	♦0.1	♦0.1	-
11 months - 11 mois	1	-	1	♦0.1	-	♦0.1
China, Hong Kong SAR - Chine, Hong Kong RAS						
2009 (C)						
Total	136	71	65	1.7	1.6	1.7
Less than 1 day - Moins de 1 jour	16	7	9	♦0.2	♦0.2	♦0.2
1 - 6 days - 1 - 6 jours	50	24	26	0.6	♦0.5	♦0.7
7 - 27 days - 7 - 27 jours	15	8	7	♦0.2	♦0.2	♦0.2
7 - 13 days - 7 - 13 jours	9	6	3	♦0.1	♦0.1	♦0.1
14 - 20 days - 14 - 20 jours	1	-	1	-	-	-
21 - 27 days - 21 - 27 jours	5	2	3	♦0.1	-	♦0.1
28 days - 11 months - 28 jours - 11 mois	55	32	23	0.7	0.7	♦0.6
28 days - less than 2 months - 28 jours - moins de 2 mois	13	4	9	♦0.2	♦0.1	♦0.2
2 months - 2 mois	5	2	3	♦0.1	-	♦0.1
3 months - 3 mois	6	5	1	♦0.1	♦0.1	-
4 months - 4 mois	8	7	1	♦0.1	♦0.2	-
5 months - 5 mois	4	2	2	-	-	♦0.1
6 months - 6 mois	6	2	4	♦0.1	-	♦0.1
7 months - 7 mois	3	2	1	-	-	-
8 months - 8 mois	6	4	2	♦0.1	♦0.1	♦0.1
9 months - 9 mois	2	2	-	-	-	-
10 months - 10 mois	-	-	-	-	-	-
11 months - 11 mois	2	2	-	-	-	-
China, Macao SAR - Chine, Macao RAS						
2009 (C)						
Total	10	6	4	...	...	...
Less than 1 day - Moins de 1 jour	5	2	3	...	...	...
1 - 6 days - 1 - 6 jours	1	1	-	...	...	...
7 - 27 days - 7 - 27 jours	2	1	1	...	...	...
7 - 13 days - 7 - 13 jours	-	-	-	...	...	...
14 - 20 days - 14 - 20 jours	2	1	1	...	...	...
21 - 27 days - 21 - 27 jours	-	-	-	...	...	...
28 days - 11 months - 28 jours - 11 mois	2	2	-	...	...	...
28 days - less than 2 months - 28 jours - moins de 2 mois	-	-	-	...	...	...
2 months - 2 mois	-	-	-	...	...	...
3 months - 3 mois	-	-	-	...	...	...
4 months - 4 mois	1	1	-	...	...	...
5 months - 5 mois	-	-	-	...	...	...
6 - 11 months - 6 - 11 mois	1	1	-	...	...	...

16. Infant deaths and infant mortality rates by age and sex: latest available year, 2000 - 2009
Décès d'enfants de moins d'un an et taux de mortalité infantile selon l'âge et le sexe : dernière année disponible, 2000 - 2009 (continued - suite)

Continent, country or area, year and age / Continent, pays ou zone, année et âge	Number - Nombre			Rate - Taux		
	Both sexes Les deux sexes	Male Masculin	Female Féminin	Both sexes Les deux sexes	Male Masculin	Female Féminin
ASIA - ASIE						
Cyprus - Chypre[14]						
2006 (C)						
Total............	27	16	11	...	...	...
Less than 1 day - Moins de 1 jour	9	5	4	...	...	...
1 - 6 days - 1 - 6 jours	6	4	2	...	...	...
7 - 27 days - 7 - 27 jours	4	3	1	...	...	...
28 days - 11 months - 28 jours - 11 mois...........	7	4	3	...	...	...
28 days - less than 2 months - 28 jours - moins de 2 mois	1	-	1	...	...	...
2 months - 2 mois	3	3	-	...	...	...
3 months - 3 mois	1	1	-	...	...	...
4 months - 4 mois	-	-	-	...	...	...
5 months - 5 mois	-	-	-	...	...	...
6 months - 6 mois	-	-	-	...	...	...
7 months - 7 mois	-	-	-	...	...	...
8 months - 8 mois	1	-	1	...	...	...
9 months - 9 mois	1	-	1	...	...	...
10 months - 10 mois	-	-	-	...	...	...
11 months - 11 mois	-	-	-	...	...	...
Unknown - Inconnu	1	-	1	...	...	...
Georgia - Géorgie[13]						
2008 (C)						
Total............	959	549	410	17.0	17.3	16.5
Less than 1 day - Moins de 1 jour	494	266	228	8.7	8.4	9.2
1 - 6 days - 1 - 6 jours	216	120	96	3.8	3.8	3.9
7 - 27 days - 7 - 27 jours	79	54	25	1.4	1.7	♦1.0
7 - 13 days - 7 - 13 jours	42	28	14	0.7	♦0.9	♦0.6
14 - 20 days - 14 - 20 jours	22	16	6	♦0.4	♦0.5	♦0.2
21 - 27 days - 21 - 27 jours	15	10	5	♦0.3	♦0.3	♦0.2
28 days - 11 months - 28 jours - 11 mois...........	170	109	61	3.0	3.4	2.5
28 days - less than 2 months - 28 jours - moins de 2 mois	39	24	15	0.7	♦0.8	♦0.6
2 months - 2 mois	23	16	7	♦0.4	♦0.5	♦0.3
3 months - 3 mois	20	13	7	♦0.4	♦0.4	♦0.3
4 months - 4 mois	17	11	6	♦0.3	♦0.3	♦0.2
5 months - 5 mois	16	9	7	♦0.3	♦0.3	♦0.3
6 months - 6 mois	10	7	3	♦0.2	♦0.2	♦0.1
7 months - 7 mois	12	8	4	♦0.2	♦0.3	♦0.2
8 months - 8 mois	9	4	5	♦0.2	♦0.1	♦0.2
9 months - 9 mois	10	8	2	♦0.2	♦0.3	♦0.1
10 months - 10 mois	7	5	2	♦0.1	♦0.2	♦0.1
11 months - 11 mois	7	4	3	♦0.1	♦0.1	♦0.1
Israel - Israël[15]						
2009 (C)						
Total............	619	339	280	3.8	4.1	3.6
Less than 1 day - Moins de 1 jour	137	76	61	0.9	0.9	0.8
1 - 6 days - 1 - 6 jours	171	89	82	1.1	1.1	1.0
7 - 27 days - 7 - 27 jours	110	61	49	0.7	0.7	0.6
7 - 13 days - 7 - 13 jours	62	27	35	0.4	♦0.3	0.4
14 - 20 days - 14 - 20 jours	29	18	11	♦0.2	♦0.2	♦0.1
21 - 27 days - 21 - 27 jours	19	16	3	♦0.1	♦0.2	-
28 days - 11 months - 28 jours - 11 mois...........	201	113	88	1.2	1.4	1.1
28 days - less than 2 months - 28 jours - moins de 2 mois	47	31	16	0.3	0.4	♦0.2
2 months - 2 mois	32	15	17	0.2	♦0.2	♦0.2
3 months - 3 mois	22	16	6	♦0.1	♦0.2	♦0.1
4 months - 4 mois	27	14	13	♦0.2	♦0.2	♦0.2
5 months - 5 mois	20	10	10	♦0.1	♦0.1	♦0.1
6 months - 6 mois	9	5	4	♦0.1	♦0.1	♦0.1
7 months - 7 mois	7	3	4	-	-	♦0.1
8 months - 8 mois	12	6	6	♦0.1	♦0.1	♦0.1
9 months - 9 mois	10	6	4	♦0.1	♦0.1	♦0.1
10 months - 10 mois	4	1	3	-	-	-
11 months - 11 mois	11	6	5	♦0.1	♦0.1	♦0.1
Japan - Japon[16]						
2009 (C)						
Total............	2 556	1 441	1 115	2.4	2.6	2.1
Less than 1 day - Moins de 1 jour	583	342	241	0.5	0.6	0.5
1 - 6 days - 1 - 6 jours	291	156	135	0.3	0.3	0.3
7 - 27 days - 7 - 27 jours	380	207	173	0.4	0.4	0.3
7 - 13 days - 7 - 13 jours	166	88	78	0.2	0.2	0.1

Continent, country or area, year and age Continent, pays ou zone, année et âge	Number - Nombre			Rate - Taux		
	Both sexes Les deux sexes	Male Masculin	Female Féminin	Both sexes Les deux sexes	Male Masculin	Female Féminin
ASIA - ASIE						
Japan - Japon[16]						
2009 (C)						
14 - 20 days - 14 - 20 jours	121	70	51	0.1	0.1	0.1
21 - 27 days - 21 - 27 jours	93	49	44	0.1	0.1	0.1
28 days - 11 months - 28 jours - 11 mois	1 302	736	566	1.2	1.3	1.1
28 days - less than 2 months - 28 jours - moins de 2 mois	275	171	104	0.3	0.3	0.2
2 months - 2 mois	175	98	77	0.2	0.2	0.1
3 months - 3 mois	150	81	69	0.1	0.1	0.1
4 months - 4 mois	129	70	59	0.1	0.1	0.1
5 months - 5 mois	136	81	55	0.1	0.1	0.1
6 months - 6 mois	105	48	57	0.1	0.1	0.1
7 months - 7 mois	81	50	31	0.1	0.1	0.1
8 months - 8 mois	77	45	32	0.1	0.1	0.1
9 months - 9 mois	62	36	26	0.1	0.1	-
10 months - 10 mois	58	30	28	0.1	0.1	♦0.1
11 months - 11 mois	54	26	28	0.1	-	♦0.1
Kazakhstan[13]						
2008 (C)						
Total	7 322	4 154	3 168	20.5	22.7	18.3
Less than 1 day - Moins de 1 jour	1 445	789	656	4.1	4.3	3.8
1 - 6 days - 1 - 6 jours	2 944	1 696	1 248	8.3	9.3	7.2
7 - 27 days - 7 - 27 jours	962	536	426	2.7	2.9	2.5
7 - 13 days - 7 - 13 jours	579	321	258	1.6	1.8	1.5
14 - 20 days - 14 - 20 jours	241	135	106	0.7	0.7	0.6
21 - 27 days - 21 - 27 jours	142	80	62	0.4	0.4	0.4
28 days - 11 months - 28 jours - 11 mois	1 969	1 133	836	5.5	6.2	4.8
28 days - less than 2 months - 28 jours - moins de 2 mois	560	338	222	1.6	1.8	1.3
2 months - 2 mois	280	167	113	0.8	0.9	0.7
3 months - 3 mois	237	122	115	0.7	0.7	0.7
4 months - 4 mois	206	111	95	0.6	0.6	0.5
5 months - 5 mois	168	93	75	0.5	0.5	0.4
6 months - 6 mois	131	71	60	0.4	0.4	0.3
7 months - 7 mois	93	60	33	0.3	0.3	0.2
8 months - 8 mois	96	56	40	0.3	0.3	0.2
9 months - 9 mois	97	57	40	0.3	0.3	0.2
10 months - 10 mois	58	32	26	0.2	0.2	♦0.2
11 months - 11 mois	43	26	17	0.1	♦0.1	♦0.1
Unknown - Inconnu	2	-	2	-	-	-
Kuwait - Koweït						
2008 (C)						
Total	494	272	222	9.1	9.7	8.3
Less than 1 day - Moins de 1 jour	111	70	41	2.0	2.5	1.5
1 - 6 days - 1 - 6 jours	98	48	50	1.8	1.7	1.9
7 - 27 days - 7 - 27 jours	102	55	47	1.9	2.0	1.8
7 - 13 days - 7 - 13 jours	56	31	25	1.0	1.1	♦0.9
14 - 20 days - 14 - 20 jours	28	13	15	♦0.5	♦0.5	♦0.6
21 - 27 days - 21 - 27 jours	18	11	7	♦0.3	♦0.4	♦0.3
28 days - 11 months - 28 jours - 11 mois	183	99	84	3.4	3.5	3.2
28 days - less than 2 months - 28 jours - moins de 2 mois	63	31	32	1.2	1.1	1.2
2 months - 2 mois	29	16	13	♦0.5	♦0.6	♦0.5
3 months - 3 mois	29	14	15	♦0.5	♦0.5	♦0.6
4 months - 4 mois	14	10	4	♦0.3	♦0.4	♦0.2
5 months - 5 mois	9	5	4	♦0.2	♦0.2	♦0.2
6 months - 6 mois	12	8	4	♦0.2	♦0.3	♦0.2
7 months - 7 mois	7	3	4	♦0.1	♦0.1	♦0.2
8 months - 8 mois	9	5	4	♦0.2	♦0.2	♦0.2
9 months - 9 mois	3	3	-	♦0.1	♦0.1	-
10 months - 10 mois	5	2	3	♦0.1	♦0.1	♦0.1
11 months - 11 mois	3	2	1	♦0.1	♦0.1	-
Kyrgyzstan - Kirghizstan						
2009 (C)						
Total	3 393	1 933	1 460	25.0	27.7	22.2
Less than 1 day - Moins de 1 jour	1 142	643	499	8.4	9.2	7.6
1 - 6 days - 1 - 6 jours	1 088	619	469	8.0	8.9	7.1
7 - 27 days - 7 - 27 jours	228	129	99	1.7	1.8	1.5
7 - 13 days - 7 - 13 jours	142	82	60	1.0	1.2	0.9
14 - 20 days - 14 - 20 jours	53	30	23	0.4	0.4	♦0.4
21 - 27 days - 21 - 27 jours	33	17	16	0.2	♦0.2	♦0.2

16. Infant deaths and infant mortality rates by age and sex: latest available year, 2000 - 2009
Décès d'enfants de moins d'un an et taux de mortalité infantile selon l'âge et le sexe : dernière année disponible, 2000 - 2009 (continued - suite)

Continent, country or area, year and age / Continent, pays ou zone, année et âge	Number - Nombre			Rate - Taux		
	Both sexes Les deux sexes	Male Masculin	Female Féminin	Both sexes Les deux sexes	Male Masculin	Female Féminin
ASIA - ASIE						
Kyrgyzstan - Kirghizstan						
2009 (C)						
28 days - 11 months - 28 jours - 11 mois..................	935	542	393	6.9	7.8	6.0
28 days - less than 2 months - 28 jours - moins de 2 mois.......	205	127	78	1.5	1.8	1.2
2 months - 2 mois................	148	92	56	1.1	1.3	0.9
3 months - 3 mois................	120	67	53	0.9	1.0	0.8
4 months - 4 mois................	88	57	31	0.6	0.8	0.5
5 months - 5 mois................	93	52	41	0.7	0.7	0.6
6 months - 6 mois................	74	38	36	0.5	0.5	0.5
7 months - 7 mois................	48	34	14	0.4	0.5	♦0.2
8 months - 8 mois................	56	28	28	0.4	♦0.4	♦0.4
9 months - 9 mois................	40	15	25·	0.3	♦0.2	♦0.4
10 months - 10 mois................	33	17	16	0.2	♦0.2	♦0.2
11 months - 11 mois................	30	15	15	0.2	♦0.2	♦0.2
Malaysia - Malaisie						
2004 (C)						
Total.................	3 105	1 784	1 321	6.5	7.2	5.7
Less than 1 day - Moins de 1 jour	443	262	181	0.9	1.1	0.8
1 - 6 days - 1 - 6 jours	834	500	334	1.7	2.0	1.4
7 - 27 days - 7 - 27 jours	492	268	224	1.0	1.1	1.0
28 days - 11 months - 28 jours - 11 mois..................	1 336	754	582	2.8	3.1	2.5
28 days - 2 months - 28 jours - 2 mois..................	568	335	233	1.2	1.4	1.0
3 - 5 months - 3 - 5 mois	393	216	177	0.8	0.9	0.8
6 - 8 months - 6 - 8 mois	220	122	98	0.5	0.5	0.4
9 - 11 months - 9 - 11 mois	155	81	74	0.3	0.3	0.3
Maldives						
2009 (C)						
Total.................	81	42	39	...	...	...
Less than 1 day - Moins de 1 jour	31	13	18	...	...	...
1 - 6 days - 1 - 6 jours	20	12	8	...	...	...
7 - 27 days - 7 - 27 jours	8	4	4	...	...	...
7 - 13 days - 7 - 13 jours	6	3	3	...	...	...
14 - 20 days - 14 - 20 jours	2	1	1	...	...	...
21 - 27 days - 21 - 27 jours	-	-	-	...	...	...
28 days - 11 months - 28 jours - 11 mois..................	22	13	9	...	...	...
28 days - less than 2 months - 28 jours - moins de 2 mois.......	7	6	1	...	...	...
2 months - 2 mois................	4	4	-	...	...	...
3 months - 3 mois................	3	1	2	...	...	...
4 months - 4 mois................	2	-	2	...	...	...
5 months - 5 mois................	1	-	1	...	...	...
6 months - 6 mois................	2	1	1	...	...	...
7 months - 7 mois................	1	-	1	...	...	...
8 months - 8 mois................	1	-	1	...	...	...
9 months - 9 mois................	-	-	-	...	...	...
10 months - 10 mois................	1	1	-	...	...	...
11 months - 11 mois................	-	-	-	...	...	...
Occupied Palestinian Territory - Territoire palestinien occupé						
2007 (U)						
Total.................	794	420	374	...	...	...
Less than 1 day - Moins de 1 jour	42	24	18	...	...	...
1 - 6 days - 1 - 6 jours	183	113	70	...	...	...
7 - 27 days - 7 - 27 jours	156	79	77	...	...	...
7 - 13 days - 7 - 13 jours	79	44	35	...	...	...
14 - 20 days - 14 - 20 jours	47	19	28	...	...	...
21 - 27 days - 21 - 27 jours	30	16	14	...	...	...
28 days - 11 months - 28 jours - 11 mois..................	413	204	209	...	...	...
28 days - less than 2 months - 28 jours - moins de 2 mois.......	111	64	47	...	...	...
2 months - 2 mois................	56	25	31	...	...	...
3 months - 3 mois................	50	28	22	...	...	...
4 months - 4 mois................	32	14	18	...	...	...
5 months - 5 mois................	40	20	20	...	...	...
6 months - 6 mois................	28	17	11	...	...	...
7 months - 7 mois................	19	8	11	...	...	...
8 months - 8 mois................	19	10	9	...	...	...
9 months - 9 mois................	22	8	14	...	...	...
10 months - 10 mois................	21	5	16	...	...	...
11 months - 11 mois................	15	5	10	...	...	...

Continent, country or area, year and age / Continent, pays ou zone, année et âge	Number - Nombre			Rate - Taux		
	Both sexes Les deux sexes	Male Masculin	Female Féminin	Both sexes Les deux sexes	Male Masculin	Female Féminin
ASIA - ASIE						
Oman[17]						
2008 (U)						
Total	534	291	243	...	...	...
Less than 1 day - Moins de 1 jour	83	46	37	...	...	...
1 - 6 days - 1 - 6 jours	85	45	39	...	...	...
7 - 27 days - 7 - 27 jours	65	37	28	...	...	...
7 - 13 days - 7 - 13 jours	33	20	13	...	...	...
14 - 20 days - 14 - 20 jours	18	8	10	...	...	...
21 - 27 days - 21 - 27 jours	14	9	5	...	...	...
28 days - 11 months - 28 jours - 11 mois	98	57	41	...	...	...
28 days - less than 2 months - 28 jours - moins de 2 mois	29	16	13	...	...	...
2 months - 2 mois	12	6	6	...	...	...
3 months - 3 mois	7	6	1	...	...	...
4 months - 4 mois	8	5	3	...	...	...
5 months - 5 mois	11	5	6	...	...	...
6 months - 6 mois	6	4	2	...	...	...
7 months - 7 mois	3	2	1	...	...	...
8 months - 8 mois	6	4	2	...	...	...
9 months - 9 mois	5	3	2	...	...	...
10 months - 10 mois	9	5	4	...	...	...
11 months - 11 mois	2	1	1	...	...	...
Unknown - Inconnu	204	106	99	...	...	...
Pakistan[18]						
2007 (I)						
Total	288 191	167 402	120 789	75.2	83.5	66.2
Less than 1 day - Moins de 1 jour	11 990	8 027	3 963	3.1	4.0	2.2
1 - 6 days - 1 - 6 jours	115 664	74 312	41 352	30.2	37.0	22.7
7 - 27 days - 7 - 27 jours	39 726	23 382	16 344	10.4	11.7	9.0
7 - 13 days - 7 - 13 jours	21 846	13 191	8 655	5.7	6.6	4.7
14 - 20 days - 14 - 20 jours	16 376	9 475	6 901	4.3	4.7	3.8
21 - 27 days - 21 - 27 jours	1 504	716	788	0.4	0.4	0.4
28 days - 11 months - 28 jours - 11 mois	120 811	61 681	59 130	31.5	30.8	32.4
28 days - less than 2 months - 28 jours - moins de 2 mois	23 563	9 553	14 010	6.2	4.8	7.7
2 months - 2 mois	10 666	7 662	3 004	2.8	3.8	1.6
3 months - 3 mois	16 938	9 692	7 246	4.4	4.8	4.0
4 months - 4 mois	10 577	4 135	6 442	2.8	2.1	3.5
5 months - 5 mois	14 148	8 863	5 285	3.7	4.4	2.9
6 months - 6 mois	17 012	6 641	10 371	4.4	3.3	5.7
7 months - 7 mois	8 480	4 209	4 271	2.2	2.1	2.3
8 months - 8 mois	6 221	5 116	1 105	1.6	2.6	0.6
9 months - 9 mois	7 602	3 819	3 783	2.0	1.9	2.1
10 months - 10 mois	3 546	1 291	2 255	0.9	0.6	1.2
11 months - 11 mois	2 058	700	1 358	0.5	0.3	0.7
Philippines						
2005 (C)						
Total	21 674	12 752	8 922	12.8	14.5	11.0
Less than 1 day - Moins de 1 jour	4 117	2 411	1 706	2.4	2.7	2.1
1 - 6 days - 1 - 6 jours	5 709	3 461	2 248	3.4	3.9	2.8
7 - 27 days - 7 - 27 jours	2 656	1 600	1 056	1.6	1.8	1.3
7 - 13 days - 7 - 13 jours	1 434	885	549	0.8	1.0	0.7
14 - 20 days - 14 - 20 jours	726	418	308	0.4	0.5	0.4
21 - 27 days - 21 - 27 jours	496	297	199	0.3	0.3	0.2
28 days - 11 months - 28 jours - 11 mois	9 192	5 280	3 912	5.4	6.0	4.8
28 days - less than 2 months - 28 jours - moins de 2 mois	2 000	1 229	771	1.2	1.4	1.0
2 months - 2 mois	1 286	753	533	0.8	0.9	0.7
3 months - 3 mois	889	522	367	0.5	0.6	0.5
4 months - 4 mois	817	438	379	0.5	0.5	0.5
5 months - 5 mois	725	411	314	0.4	0.5	0.4
6 months - 6 mois	754	401	353	0.4	0.5	0.4
7 months - 7 mois	663	369	294	0.4	0.4	0.4
8 months - 8 mois	614	325	289	0.4	0.4	0.4
9 months - 9 mois	534	321	213	0.3	0.4	0.3
10 months - 10 mois	431	233	198	0.3	0.3	0.2
11 months - 11 mois	479	278	201	0.3	0.3	0.2
Qatar						
2009 (C)						
Total	130	72	58	7.1	7.7	6.5
Less than 1 day - Moins de 1 jour	-	-	-	-	-	-

16. Infant deaths and infant mortality rates by age and sex: latest available year, 2000 - 2009
Décès d'enfants de moins d'un an et taux de mortalité infantile selon l'âge et le sexe : dernière année disponible, 2000 - 2009 (continued - suite)

Continent, country or area, year and age Continent, pays ou zone, année et âge	Number - Nombre			Rate - Taux		
	Both sexes Les deux sexes	Male Masculin	Female Féminin	Both sexes Les deux sexes	Male Masculin	Female Féminin
ASIA - ASIE						
Qatar						
2009 (C)						
1 - 6 days - 1 - 6 jours	64	35	29	3.5	3.7	♦3.2
7 - 27 days - 7 - 27 jours	24	12	12	♦1.3	♦1.3	♦1.3
7 - 13 days - 7 - 13 jours	10	4	6	♦0.5	♦0.4	♦0.7
14 - 20 days - 14 - 20 jours	8	5	3	♦0.4	♦0.5	♦0.3
21 - 27 days - 21 - 27 jours	6	3	3	♦0.3	♦0.3	♦0.3
28 days - 11 months - 28 jours - 11 mois	34	20	14	1.9	♦2.1	♦1.6
28 days - less than 2 months - 28 jours - moins de 2 mois	4	4	-	♦0.2	♦0.4	-
2 months - 2 mois	11	7	4	♦0.6	♦0.7	♦0.4
3 months - 3 mois	7	3	4	♦0.4	♦0.3	♦0.4
4 months - 4 mois	5	3	2	♦0.3	♦0.3	♦0.2
5 months - 5 mois	2	1	1	♦0.1	♦0.1	♦0.1
6 months - 6 mois	2	1	1	♦0.1	♦0.1	♦0.1
7 months - 7 mois	3	1	2	♦0.2	♦0.1	♦0.2
8 months - 8 mois	-	-	-	-	-	-
9 months - 9 mois	-	-	-	-	-	-
10 months - 10 mois	-	-	-	-	-	-
11 months - 11 mois	-	-	-	-	-	-
Republic of Korea - République de Corée[19]						
2009 (C)						
Total	1 415	757	658	3.2	3.3	3.1
Less than 1 day - Moins de 1 jour	203	106	97	0.5	0.5	0.5
1 - 6 days - 1 - 6 jours	320	178	142	0.7	0.8	0.7
7 - 27 days - 7 - 27 jours	248	129	119	0.6	0.6	0.6
7 - 13 days - 7 - 13 jours	100	50	50	0.2	0.2	0.2
14 - 20 days - 14 - 20 jours	83	47	36	0.2	0.2	0.2
21 - 27 days - 21 - 27 jours	65	32	33	0.1	0.1	0.2
28 days - 11 months - 28 jours - 11 mois	644	344	300	1.4	1.5	1.4
28 days - less than 2 months - 28 jours - moins de 2 mois	170	99	71	0.4	0.4	0.3
2 months - 2 mois	109	54	55	0.2	0.2	0.3
3 months - 3 mois	83	47	36	0.2	0.2	0.2
4 months - 4 mois	72	40	32	0.2	0.2	0.1
5 months - 5 mois	56	30	26	0.1	0.1	♦0.1
6 months - 6 mois	38	21	17	0.1	♦0.1	♦0.1
7 months - 7 mois	34	15	19	0.1	♦0.1	♦0.1
8 months - 8 mois	23	11	12	♦0.1	-	♦0.1
9 months - 9 mois	26	11	15	♦0.1	-	♦0.1
10 months - 10 mois	14	6	8	-	-	-
11 months - 11 mois	19	10	9	-	-	-
Singapore - Singapour						
2009 (+C)						
Total	102	58	44	2.6	2.8	2.3
Less than 1 day - Moins de 1 jour	13	10	3	♦0.3	♦0.5	♦0.2
1 - 6 days - 1 - 6 jours	34	13	21	0.9	♦0.6	♦1.1
7 - 27 days - 7 - 27 jours	16	10	6	♦0.4	♦0.5	♦0.3
7 - 13 days - 7 - 13 jours	10	5	5	♦0.3	♦0.2	♦0.3
14 - 20 days - 14 - 20 jours	4	3	1	♦0.1	♦0.1	♦0.1
21 - 27 days - 21 - 27 jours	2	2	-	♦0.1	♦0.1	-
28 days - 11 months - 28 jours - 11 mois	39	25	14	1.0	♦1.2	♦0.7
28 days - less than 2 months - 28 jours - moins de 2 mois	12	10	2	♦0.3	♦0.5	♦0.1
2 months - 2 mois	5	2	3	♦0.1	♦0.1	♦0.2
3 months - 3 mois	6	4	2	♦0.2	♦0.2	♦0.1
4 months - 4 mois	2	2	-	♦0.1	♦0.1	-
5 months - 5 mois	7	4	3	♦0.2	♦0.2	♦0.2
6 months - 6 mois	-	-	-	-	-	-
7 months - 7 mois	2	1	1	♦0.1	-	♦0.1
8 months - 8 mois	-	-	-	-	-	-
9 months - 9 mois	-	-	-	-	-	-
10 months - 10 mois	1	1	-	-	-	-
11 months - 11 mois	4	1	3	♦0.1	-	♦0.2
Tajikistan - Tadjikistan[13]						
2008 (U)						
Total	2 480	1 478	1 002	...	...	...
Less than 1 day - Moins de 1 jour	420	255	165	...	...	...
1 - 6 days - 1 - 6 jours	699	443	256	...	...	...
7 - 27 days - 7 - 27 jours	248	140	108	...	...	...
7 - 13 days - 7 - 13 jours	145	87	58	...	...	...

16. Infant deaths and infant mortality rates by age and sex: latest available year, 2000 - 2009
Décès d'enfants de moins d'un an et taux de mortalité infantile selon l'âge et le sexe : dernière année disponible, 2000 - 2009 (continued - suite)

Continent, country or area, year and age / Continent, pays ou zone, année et âge	Number - Nombre			Rate - Taux		
	Both sexes Les deux sexes	Male Masculin	Female Féminin	Both sexes Les deux sexes	Male Masculin	Female Féminin
ASIA - ASIE						
Tajikistan - Tadjikistan[13]						
2008 (U)						
14 - 20 days - 14 - 20 jours	63	33	30	...	...	...
21 - 27 days - 21 - 27 jours	40	20	20	...	...	...
28 days - 11 months - 28 jours - 11 mois	1 113	640	473	...	...	...
28 days - less than 2 months - 28 jours - moins de 2 mois	180	103	77	...	...	...
2 months - 2 mois	155	92	63	...	...	...
3 months - 3 mois	138	77	61	...	...	...
4 months - 4 mois	111	71	40	...	...	...
5 months - 5 mois	106	56	50	...	...	...
6 months - 6 mois	106	62	44	...	...	...
7 months - 7 mois	75	43	32	...	...	...
8 months - 8 mois	79	49	30	...	...	...
9 months - 9 mois	56	23	33	...	...	...
10 months - 10 mois	56	39	17	...	...	...
11 months - 11 mois	51	25	26	...	...	...
Thailand - Thaïlande						
2009 (+U)						
Total	5 416	3 018	2 398	...	...	...
Less than 1 day - Moins de 1 jour	567	313	254	...	...	...
1 - 6 days - 1 - 6 jours	1 629	947	682	...	...	...
7 - 27 days - 7 - 27 jours	1 034	567	467	...	...	...
7 - 13 days - 7 - 13 jours	532	299	233	...	...	...
14 - 20 days - 14 - 20 jours	285	148	137	...	...	...
21 - 27 days - 21 - 27 jours	217	120	97	...	...	...
28 days - 11 months - 28 jours - 11 mois	2 186	1 191	995	...	...	...
28 days - less than 2 months - 28 jours - moins de 2 mois	576	318	258	...	...	...
2 mois	350	191	159	...	...	...
3 months - 3 mois	289	140	149	...	...	...
4 months - 4 mois	197	106	91	...	...	...
5 months - 5 mois	184	106	78	...	...	...
6 months - 6 mois	131	77	54	...	...	...
7 months - 7 mois	123	60	63	...	...	...
8 months - 8 mois	117	65	52	...	...	...
9 months - 9 mois	86	50	36	...	...	...
10 months - 10 mois	83	51	32	...	...	...
11 months - 11 mois	50	27	23	...	...	...
Uzbekistan - Ouzbékistan[13]						
2000 (C)						
Total	10 091	5 805	4 286	19.1	21.4	16.7
Less than 1 day - Moins de 1 jour	607	355	252	1.2	1.3	1.0
1 - 6 days - 1 - 6 jours	2 179	1 352	827	4.1	5.0	3.2
7 - 27 days - 7 - 27 jours	1 279	731	548	2.4	2.7	2.1
7 - 13 days - 7 - 13 jours	719	421	298	1.4	1.6	1.2
14 - 20 days - 14 - 20 jours	343	192	151	0.7	0.7	0.6
21 - 27 days - 21 - 27 jours	217	118	99	0.4	0.4	0.4
28 days - 11 months - 28 jours - 11 mois	6 026	3 367	2 659	11.4	12.4	10.4
28 days - less than 2 months - 28 jours - moins de 2 mois	976	582	394	1.8	2.1	1.5
2 months - 2 mois	680	363	317	1.3	1.3	1.2
3 months - 3 mois	693	411	282	1.3	1.5	1.1
4 months - 4 mois	691	377	314	1.3	1.4	1.2
5 months - 5 mois	612	324	288	1.2	1.2	1.1
6 months - 6 mois	538	293	245	1.0	1.1	1.0
7 months - 7 mois	486	269	217	0.9	1.0	0.8
8 months - 8 mois	445	259	186	0.8	1.0	0.7
9 months - 9 mois	388	204	184	0.7	0.8	0.7
10 months - 10 mois	274	150	124	0.5	0.6	0.5
11 months - 11 mois	243	135	108	0.5	0.5	0.4
EUROPE						
Albania - Albanie						
2006 (C)						
Total	253	...	...	7.4	...	...
Less than 1 day - Moins de 1 jour	10	...	...	♦0.3	...	...
1 - 6 days - 1 - 6 jours	40	...	...	1.2	...	...
7 - 27 days - 7 - 27 jours	21	...	...	♦0.6	...	...

16. Infant deaths and infant mortality rates by age and sex: latest available year, 2000 - 2009
Décès d'enfants de moins d'un an et taux de mortalité infantile selon l'âge et le sexe : dernière année disponible, 2000 - 2009 (continued - suite)

Continent, country or area, year and age / Continent, pays ou zone, année et âge	Number - Nombre			Rate - Taux		
	Both sexes Les deux sexes	Male Masculin	Female Féminin	Both sexes Les deux sexes	Male Masculin	Female Féminin
EUROPE						
Albania - Albanie						
2006 (C)						
28 days - 11 months - 28 jours - 11 mois	182	...	...	5.3	...	...
28 days - less than 2 months - 28 jours - moins de 2 mois	35	...	...	1.0	...	...
2 - 11 months - 2 - 11 mois	147	...	...	4.3	...	...
Andorra - Andorre						
2009 (C)						
Total	1	-	1	...	...	...
Less than 1 day - Moins de 1 jour	-	-	-	...	...	...
1 - 6 days - 1 - 6 jours	1	-	1	...	...	...
7 - 27 days - 7 - 27 jours	-	-	-	...	...	...
28 days - 11 months - 28 jours - 11 mois	-	-	-	...	...	...
Austria - Autriche						
2009 (C)						
Total	289	158	131	3.8	4.0	3.5
Less than 1 day - Moins de 1 jour	108	62	46	1.4	1.6	1.2
1 - 6 days - 1 - 6 jours	37	17	20	0.5	♦0.4	♦0.5
7 - 27 days - 7 - 27 jours	47	26	21	0.6	♦0.7	♦0.6
7 - 13 days - 7 - 13 jours	21	9	12	♦0.3	♦0.2	♦0.3
14 - 20 days - 14 - 20 jours	17	11	6	♦0.2	♦0.3	♦0.2
21 - 27 days - 21 - 27 jours	9	6	3	♦0.1	♦0.2	♦0.1
28 days - 11 months - 28 jours - 11 mois	97	53	44	1.3	1.4	1.2
28 days - less than 2 months - 28 jours - moins de 2 mois	24	13	11	♦0.3	♦0.3	♦0.3
2 months - 2 mois	16	9	7	♦0.2	♦0.2	♦0.2
3 months - 3 mois	10	6	4	♦0.1	♦0.2	♦0.1
4 months - 4 mois	12	5	7	♦0.2	♦0.1	♦0.2
5 months - 5 mois	8	4	4	♦0.1	♦0.1	♦0.1
6 months - 6 mois	7	6	1	♦0.1	♦0.2	-
7 months - 7 mois	5	3	2	♦0.1	♦0.1	♦0.1
8 months - 8 mois	2	1	1	-	-	-
9 months - 9 mois	6	3	3	♦0.1	♦0.1	♦0.1
10 months - 10 mois	6	3	3	♦0.1	♦0.1	♦0.1
11 months - 11 mois	1	-	1	-	-	-
Belarus - Bélarus						
2009 (C)						
Total	511	301	210	4.7	5.3	4.0
Less than 1 day - Moins de 1 jour	49	25	24	0.4	♦0.4	♦0.5
1 - 6 days - 1 - 6 jours	95	60	35	0.9	1.1	0.7
7 - 27 days - 7 - 27 jours	81	45	36	0.7	0.8	0.7
7 - 13 days - 7 - 13 jours	32	17	15	0.3	♦0.3	♦0.3
14 - 20 days - 14 - 20 jours	25	14	11	♦0.2	♦0.2	♦0.2
21 - 27 days - 21 - 27 jours	24	14	10	♦0.2	♦0.2	♦0.2
28 days - 11 months - 28 jours - 11 mois	286	171	115	2.6	3.0	2.2
28 days - less than 2 months - 28 jours - moins de 2 mois	82	48	34	0.8	0.9	0.6
2 months - 2 mois	49	29	20	0.4	♦0.5	♦0.4
3 months - 3 mois	37	22	15	0.3	♦0.4	♦0.3
4 months - 4 mois	23	15	8	♦0.2	♦0.3	♦0.2
5 months - 5 mois	25	13	12	♦0.2	♦0.2	♦0.2
6 months - 6 mois	16	11	5	♦0.1	♦0.2	♦0.1
7 months - 7 mois	18	14	4	♦0.2	♦0.2	♦0.1
8 months - 8 mois	15	8	7	♦0.1	♦0.1	♦0.1
9 months - 9 mois	12	6	6	♦0.1	♦0.1	♦0.1
10 months - 10 mois	4	2	2	-	-	-
11 months - 11 mois	5	3	2	-	♦0.1	-
Belgium - Belgique						
2007 (C)						
Total[20]	508	297	211	4.2	4.8	3.6
Less than 1 day - Moins de 1 jour	110	62	48	0.9	1.0	0.8
1 - 6 days - 1 - 6 jours	128	79	49	1.1	1.3	0.8
7 - 27 days - 7 - 27 jours	82	47	35	0.7	0.8	0.6
7 - 13 days - 7 - 13 jours	46	25	21	0.4	♦0.4	♦0.4
14 - 20 days - 14 - 20 jours	26	14	12	♦0.2	♦0.2	♦0.2
21 - 27 days - 21 - 27 jours	10	8	2	♦0.1	♦0.1	-
28 days - 11 months - 28 jours - 11 mois	188	109	79	1.6	1.8	1.3
28 days - less than 2 months - 28 jours - moins de 2 mois	50	31	19	0.4	0.5	♦0.3
2 months - 2 mois	34	18	16	0.3	♦0.3	♦0.3
3 months - 3 mois	22	9	13	♦0.2	♦0.1	♦0.2
4 months - 4 mois	14	8	6	♦0.1	♦0.1	♦0.1

16. Infant deaths and infant mortality rates by age and sex: latest available year, 2000 - 2009
Décès d'enfants de moins d'un an et taux de mortalité infantile selon l'âge et le sexe : dernière année disponible, 2000 - 2009 (continued - suite)

Continent, country or area, year and age / Continent, pays ou zone, année et âge	Number - Nombre			Rate - Taux		
	Both sexes Les deux sexes	Male Masculin	Female Féminin	Both sexes Les deux sexes	Male Masculin	Female Féminin
EUROPE						
Belgium - Belgique						
2007 (C)						
5 months - 5 mois	28	21	7	♦0.2	♦0.3	♦0.1
6 months - 6 mois	16	11	5	♦0.1	♦0.2	♦0.1
7 months - 7 mois	5	1	4	-	-	♦0.1
8 months - 8 mois	4	4	-	-	♦0.1	-
9 months - 9 mois	3	1	2	-	-	-
10 months - 10 mois	9	3	6	♦0.1	-	♦0.1
11 months - 11 mois	3	2	1	-	-	-
Bosnia and Herzegovina - Bosnie-Herzégovine						
2009 (C)						
Total	224	116	108	6.5	6.4	6.5
Less than 1 day - Moins de 1 jour	67	31	36	1.9	1.7	2.2
1 - 6 days - 1 - 6 jours	75	40	35	2.2	2.2	2.1
7 - 27 days - 7 - 27 jours	29	19	10	♦0.8	♦1.1	♦0.6
7 - 13 days - 7 - 13 jours	9	8	1	♦0.3	♦0.4	♦0.1
14 - 20 days - 14 - 20 jours	12	7	5	♦0.3	♦0.4	♦0.3
21 - 27 days - 21 - 27 jours	8	4	4	♦0.2	♦0.2	♦0.2
28 days - 11 months - 28 jours - 11 mois	53	26	27	1.5	♦1.4	♦1.6
28 days - less than 2 months - 28 jours - moins de 2 mois	11	5	6	♦0.3	♦0.3	♦0.4
2 months - 2 mois	8	6	2	♦0.2	♦0.3	♦0.1
3 months - 3 mois	8	5	3	♦0.2	♦0.3	♦0.2
4 months - 4 mois	5	2	3	♦0.1	♦0.1	♦0.2
5 months - 5 mois	8	3	5	♦0.2	♦0.2	♦0.3
6 months - 6 mois	4	2	2	♦0.1	♦0.1	♦0.1
7 months - 7 mois	2	1	1	♦0.1	♦0.1	♦0.1
8 months - 8 mois	4	1	3	♦0.1	♦0.1	♦0.2
9 months - 9 mois	1	1	-	-	♦0.1	-
10 months - 10 mois	1	-	1	-	-	♦0.1
11 months - 11 mois	1	-	1	-	-	♦0.1
Bulgaria - Bulgarie						
2009 (C)						
Total	729	422	307	9.0	10.2	7.7
Less than 1 day - Moins de 1 jour	122	80	42	1.5	1.9	1.1
1 - 6 days - 1 - 6 jours	184	112	72	2.3	2.7	1.8
7 - 27 days - 7 - 27 jours	130	68	62	1.6	1.6	1.6
7 - 13 days - 7 - 13 jours	65	32	33	0.8	0.8	0.8
14 - 20 days - 14 - 20 jours	34	19	15	0.4	♦0.5	♦0.4
21 - 27 days - 21 - 27 jours	31	17	14	0.4	♦0.4	♦0.4
28 days - 11 months - 28 jours - 11 mois	293	162	131	3.6	3.9	3.3
28 days - less than 2 months - 28 jours - moins de 2 mois	89	54	35	1.1	1.3	0.9
2 months - 2 mois	44	29	15	0.5	♦0.7	♦0.4
3 months - 3 mois	35	20	15	0.4	♦0.5	♦0.4
4 months - 4 mois	31	10	21	0.4	♦0.2	♦0.5
5 months - 5 mois	27	15	12	♦0.3	♦0.4	♦0.3
6 months - 6 mois	18	6	12	♦0.2	♦0.1	♦0.3
7 months - 7 mois	7	5	2	♦0.1	♦0.1	♦0.1
8 months - 8 mois	13	7	6	♦0.2	♦0.2	♦0.2
9 months - 9 mois	8	5	3	♦0.1	♦0.1	♦0.1
10 months - 10 mois	14	9	5	♦0.2	♦0.2	♦0.1
11 months - 11 mois	7	2	5	♦0.1	-	♦0.1
Croatia - Croatie						
2009 (C)						
Total	235	119	116	5.3	5.2	5.3
Less than 1 day - Moins de 1 jour	86	44	42	1.9	1.9	1.9
1 - 6 days - 1 - 6 jours	56	32	24	1.3	1.4	♦1.1
7 - 27 days - 7 - 27 jours	49	20	29	1.1	♦0.9	♦1.3
7 - 13 days - 7 - 13 jours	30	9	21	0.7	♦0.4	♦1.0
14 - 20 days - 14 - 20 jours	14	8	6	♦0.3	♦0.3	♦0.3
21 - 27 days - 21 - 27 jours	5	3	2	♦0.1	♦0.1	♦0.1
28 days - 11 months - 28 jours - 11 mois	44	23	21	1.0	♦1.0	♦1.0
28 days - less than 2 months - 28 jours - moins de 2 mois	12	7	5	♦0.3	♦0.3	♦0.2
2 months - 2 mois	9	3	6	♦0.2	♦0.1	♦0.3
3 months - 3 mois	8	5	3	♦0.2	♦0.2	♦0.1
4 months - 4 mois	5	2	3	♦0.1	♦0.1	♦0.1
5 months - 5 mois	5	2	3	♦0.1	♦0.1	♦0.1
6 months - 6 mois	1	1	-	-	-	-
7 months - 7 mois	2	1	1	-	-	-

16. Infant deaths and infant mortality rates by age and sex: latest available year, 2000 - 2009
Décès d'enfants de moins d'un an et taux de mortalité infantile selon l'âge et le sexe : dernière année disponible, 2000 - 2009 (continued - suite)

Continent, country or area, year and age / Continent, pays ou zone, année et âge	Number - Nombre			Rate - Taux		
	Both sexes Les deux sexes	Male Masculin	Female Féminin	Both sexes Les deux sexes	Male Masculin	Female Féminin
EUROPE						
Croatia - Croatie						
2009 (C)						
8 months - 8 mois	2	2	-	-	♦0.1	-
9 months - 9 mois	-	-	-	-	-	-
10 months - 10 mois	-	-	-	-	-	-
11 months - 11 mois	-	-	-	-	-	-
Czech Republic - République tchèque						
2009 (C)						
Total	341	185	156	2.9	3.1	2.7
Less than 1 day - Moins de 1 jour	43	25	18	0.4	♦0.4	♦0.3
1 - 6 days - 1 - 6 jours	60	30	30	0.5	0.5	0.5
7 - 27 days - 7 - 27 jours	91	54	37	0.8	0.9	0.6
7 - 13 days - 7 - 13 jours	42	25	17	0.4	♦0.4	♦0.3
14 - 20 days - 14 - 20 jours	30	18	12	0.3	♦0.3	♦0.2
21 - 27 days - 21 - 27 jours	19	11	8	♦0.2	♦0.2	♦0.1
28 days - 11 months - 28 jours - 11 mois	147	76	71	1.2	1.3	1.2
28 days - less than 2 months - 28 jours - moins de 2 mois	57	35	22	0.5	0.6	♦0.4
2 months - 2 mois	23	11	12	♦0.2	♦0.2	♦0.2
3 months - 3 mois	13	5	8	♦0.1	♦0.1	♦0.1
4 months - 4 mois	6	3	3	♦0.1	-	♦0.1
5 months - 5 mois	15	4	11	♦0.1	♦0.1	♦0.2
6 months - 6 mois	10	6	4	♦0.1	♦0.1	♦0.1
7 months - 7 mois	12	7	5	♦0.1	♦0.1	♦0.1
8 months - 8 mois	5	4	1	-	♦0.1	-
9 months - 9 mois	4	-	4	-	-	♦0.1
10 months - 10 mois	1	1	-	-	-	-
11 months - 11 mois	1	-	1	-	-	-
Denmark - Danemark[21]						
2009 (C)						
Total	193	103	90	3.1	3.2	2.9
Less than 1 day - Moins de 1 jour	74	35	39	1.2	1.1	1.3
1 - 6 days - 1 - 6 jours	40	23	17	0.6	♦0.7	♦0.6
7 - 27 days - 7 - 27 jours	30	16	14	0.5	♦0.5	♦0.5
7 - 13 days - 7 - 13 jours	18	9	9	♦0.3	♦0.3	♦0.3
14 - 20 days - 14 - 20 jours	8	5	3	♦0.1	♦0.2	♦0.1
21 - 27 days - 21 - 27 jours	4	2	2	♦0.1	♦0.1	♦0.1
28 days - 11 months - 28 jours - 11 mois	49	29	20	0.8	♦0.9	♦0.7
28 days - less than 2 months - 28 jours - moins de 2 mois	13	8	5	♦0.2	♦0.2	♦0.2
2 months - 2 mois	7	2	5	♦0.1	♦0.1	♦0.2
3 months - 3 mois	4	4	-	♦0.1	♦0.1	-
4 months - 4 mois	6	4	2	♦0.1	♦0.1	♦0.1
5 months - 5 mois	3	3	-	-	♦0.1	-
6 months - 6 mois	6	3	3	♦0.1	♦0.1	♦0.1
7 months - 7 mois	2	-	2	-	-	♦0.1
8 months - 8 mois	1	-	1	-	-	-
9 months - 9 mois	2	1	1	-	-	-
10 months - 10 mois	2	2	-	-	♦0.1	-
11 months - 11 mois	3	2	1	-	♦0.1	-
Estonia - Estonie						
2009 (C)						
Total	57	34	23	...	...	...
Less than 1 day - Moins de 1 jour	10	3	7	...	...	...
1 - 6 days - 1 - 6 jours	12	7	5	...	...	...
7 - 27 days - 7 - 27 jours	17	12	5	...	...	...
7 - 13 days - 7 - 13 jours	8	4	4	...	...	...
14 - 20 days - 14 - 20 jours	1	1	-	...	...	...
21 - 27 days - 21 - 27 jours	3	2	1	...	...	...
28 days - 11 months - 28 jours - 11 mois	23	17	6	...	...	...
28 days - less than 2 months - 28 jours - moins de 2 mois	5	5	-	...	...	...
2 months - 2 mois	1	1	-	...	...	...
3 months - 3 mois	2	1	1	...	...	...
4 months - 4 mois	5	3	2	...	...	...
5 months - 5 mois	2	2	-	...	...	...
6 months - 6 mois	4	3	1	...	...	...
7 months - 7 mois	2	-	2	...	...	...
8 months - 8 mois	1	1	-	...	...	...
9 months - 9 mois	-	-	-	...	...	...

16. Infant deaths and infant mortality rates by age and sex: latest available year, 2000 - 2009
Décès d'enfants de moins d'un an et taux de mortalité infantile selon l'âge et le sexe : dernière année disponible, 2000 - 2009 (continued - suite)

Continent, country or area, year and age Continent, pays ou zone, année et âge	Number - Nombre			Rate - Taux		
	Both sexes Les deux sexes	Male Masculin	Female Féminin	Both sexes Les deux sexes	Male Masculin	Female Féminin
EUROPE						
Estonia - Estonie						
2009 (C)						
10 months - 10 mois	1	1	-	...	...	...
11 months - 11 mois	-	-	-	...	...	...
Finland - Finlande[22]						
2009 (C)						
Total	158	78	80	2.6	2.5	2.7
Less than 1 day - Moins de 1 jour	51	32	19	0.8	1.0	♦0.6
1 - 6 days - 1 - 6 jours	44	20	24	0.7	♦0.7	♦0.8
7 - 27 days - 7 - 27 jours	26	14	12	♦0.4	♦0.5	♦0.4
7 - 13 days - 7 - 13 jours	12	6	6	♦0.2	♦0.2	♦0.2
14 - 20 days - 14 - 20 jours	8	3	5	♦0.1	♦0.1	♦0.2
21 - 27 days - 21 - 27 jours	6	5	1	♦0.1	♦0.2	-
28 days - 11 months - 28 jours - 11 mois	37	12	25	0.6	♦0.4	♦0.8
28 days - less than 2 months - 28 jours - moins de 2 mois	10	4	6	♦0.2	♦0.1	♦0.2
2 months - 2 mois	2	2	-	-	♦0.1	-
3 months - 3 mois	5	-	5	♦0.1	-	♦0.2
4 months - 4 mois	8	2	6	♦0.1	♦0.1	♦0.2
5 months - 5 mois	3	1	2	-	-	♦0.1
6 months - 6 mois	2	-	2	-	-	♦0.1
7 months - 7 mois	2	-	2	-	-	♦0.1
8 months - 8 mois	2	2	-	-	♦0.1	-
9 months - 9 mois	1	-	1	-	-	-
10 months - 10 mois	1	1	-	-	-	-
11 months - 11 mois	1	-	1	-	-	-
France[23]						
2009 (C)						
Total	2 903	1 635	1 268	3.7	4.0	3.3
Less than 1 day - Moins de 1 jour	696	375	321	0.9	0.9	0.8
1 - 6 days - 1 - 6 jours	624	354	270	0.8	0.9	0.7
7 - 27 days - 7 - 27 jours	581	335	246	0.7	0.8	0.6
7 - 13 days - 7 - 13 jours	311	175	136	0.4	0.4	0.4
14 - 20 days - 14 - 20 jours	160	98	62	0.2	0.2	0.2
21 - 27 days - 21 - 27 jours	110	62	48	0.1	0.2	0.1
28 days - 11 months - 28 jours - 11 mois	1 002	571	431	1.3	1.4	1.1
28 days - less than 2 months - 28 jours - moins de 2 mois	286	163	123	0.4	0.4	0.3
2 months - 2 mois	157	89	68	0.2	0.2	0.2
3 months - 3 mois	127	75	52	0.2	0.2	0.1
4 months - 4 mois	96	63	33	0.1	0.2	0.1
5 months - 5 mois	75	45	30	0.1	0.1	0.1
6 months - 6 mois	59	38	21	0.1	0.1	♦0.1
7 months - 7 mois	54	27	27	0.1	♦0.1	♦0.1
8 months - 8 mois	50	22	28	0.1	♦0.1	♦0.1
9 months - 9 mois	39	17	22	-	-	♦0.1
10 months - 10 mois	22	12	10	-	-	-
11 months - 11 mois	37	20	17	-	-	-
Germany - Allemagne						
2007 (C)						
Total	2 656	1 518	1 138	3.9	4.3	3.4
Less than 1 day - Moins de 1 jour	825	453	372	1.2	1.3	1.1
1 - 6 days - 1 - 6 jours	599	371	228	0.9	1.1	0.7
7 - 27 days - 7 - 27 jours	398	213	185	0.6	0.6	0.6
7 - 13 days - 7 - 13 jours	203	111	92	0.3	0.3	0.3
14 - 20 days - 14 - 20 jours	110	60	50	0.2	0.2	0.2
21 - 27 days - 21 - 27 jours	85	42	43	0.1	0.1	0.1
28 days - 11 months - 28 jours - 11 mois	834	481	353	1.2	1.4	1.1
28 days - less than 2 months - 28 jours - moins de 2 mois	203	111	92	0.3.	0.3	0.3
2 months - 2 mois	139	75	64	0.2	0.2	0.2
3 months - 3 mois	106	61	45	0.2	0.2	0.1
4 months - 4 mois	76	40	36	0.1	0.1	0.1
5 months - 5 mois	63	43	20	0.1	0.1	♦0.1
6 months - 6 mois	55	36	19	0.1	0.1	♦0.1
7 months - 7 mois	50	31	19	0.1	0.1	♦0.1
8 months - 8 mois	44	30	14	0.1	0.1	-
9 months - 9 mois	41	23	18	0.1	♦0.1	♦0.1
10 months - 10 mois	31	13	18	-	-	♦0.1
11 months - 11 mois	26	18	8	-	♦0.1	-

16. Infant deaths and infant mortality rates by age and sex: latest available year, 2000 - 2009
Décès d'enfants de moins d'un an et taux de mortalité infantile selon l'âge et le sexe : dernière année disponible, 2000 - 2009 (continued - suite)

Continent, country or area, year and age / Continent, pays ou zone, année et âge	Number - Nombre			Rate - Taux		
	Both sexes Les deux sexes	Male Masculin	Female Féminin	Both sexes Les deux sexes	Male Masculin	Female Féminin
EUROPE						
Gibraltar						
2006 (+C)						
Total	1	1	-	...	...	...
Less than 7 days - Moins de 7 jours	-	-	-	...	...	...
7 - 27 days - 7 - 27 jours	-	-	-	...	...	...
28 days - 11 months - 28 jours - 11 mois	1	1	-	...	...	...
28 days - 2 months - 28 jours - 2 mois	-	-	-	...	...	...
3 months - 3 mois	1	1	-	...	...	...
4 - 11 months - 4 - 11 mois	-	-	-	...	...	...
Greece - Grèce						
2009 (C)						
Total	371	204	167	3.1	3.4	2.9
Less than 1 day - Moins de 1 jour	47	24	23	0.4	♦0.4	♦0.4
1 - 6 days - 1 - 6 jours	99	45	54	0.8	0.7	0.9
7 - 27 days - 7 - 27 jours	92	54	38	0.8	0.9	0.7
7 - 13 days - 7 - 13 jours	55	31	24	0.5	0.5	♦0.4
14 - 20 days - 14 - 20 jours	27	13	14	♦0.2	♦0.2	♦0.2
21 - 27 days - 21 - 27 jours	12	10	2	♦0.1	♦0.2	-
28 days - 11 months - 28 jours - 11 mois	133	81	52	1.1	1.3	0.9
28 days - less than 2 months - 28 jours - moins de 2 mois	45	26	19	0.4	♦0.4	♦0.3
2 months - 2 mois	30	20	10	0.3	♦0.3	♦0.2
3 months - 3 mois	11	7	4	♦0.1	♦0.1	♦0.1
4 months - 4 mois	5	3	2	-	-	-
5 months - 5 mois	8	4	4	♦0.1	♦0.1	♦0.1
6 months - 6 mois	8	5	3	♦0.1	♦0.1	♦0.1
7 months - 7 mois	3	2	1	-	-	-
8 months - 8 mois	5	3	2	-	-	-
9 months - 9 mois	13	8	5	♦0.1	♦0.1	♦0.1
10 months - 10 mois	1	-	1	-	-	-
11 months - 11 mois	4	3	1	-	-	-
Hungary - Hongrie						
2009 (C)						
Total	495	263	232	5.1	5.3	4.9
Less than 1 day - Moins de 1 jour	99	48	51	1.0	1.0	1.1
1 - 6 days - 1 - 6 jours	126	76	50	1.3	1.5	1.1
7 - 27 days - 7 - 27 jours	102	56	46	1.1	1.1	1.0
7 - 13 days - 7 - 13 jours	49	31	18	0.5	0.6	♦0.4
14 - 20 days - 14 - 20 jours	38	20	18	0.4	♦0.4	♦0.4
21 - 27 days - 21 - 27 jours	15	5	10	♦0.2	♦0.1	♦0.2
28 days - 11 months - 28 jours - 11 mois	168	83	85	1.7	1.7	1.8
28 days - less than 2 months - 28 jours - moins de 2 mois	48	24	24	0.5	♦0.5	♦0.5
2 months - 2 mois	32	20	12	0.3	♦0.4	♦0.3
3 months - 3 mois	21	9	12	♦0.2	♦0.2	♦0.3
4 months - 4 mois	26	11	15	♦0.3	♦0.2	♦0.3
5 months - 5 mois	6	3	3	♦0.1	♦0.1	♦0.1
6 months - 6 mois	6	3	3	♦0.1	♦0.1	♦0.1
7 months - 7 mois	11	6	5	♦0.1	♦0.1	♦0.1
8 months - 8 mois	6	2	4	♦0.1	-	♦0.1
9 months - 9 mois	6	2	4	♦0.1	-	♦0.1
10 months - 10 mois	-	-	-	-	-	-
11 months - 11 mois	6	3	3	♦0.1	♦0.1	♦0.1
Iceland - Islande						
2009 (C)						
Total	9	5	4	...	...	...
Less than 1 day - Moins de 1 jour	3	3	-	...	...	...
1 - 6 days - 1 - 6 jours	1	1	-	...	...	...
7 - 27 days - 7 - 27 jours	1	-	1	...	...	...
7 - 13 days - 7 - 13 jours	-	-	-	...	...	...
14 - 20 days - 14 - 20 jours	1	-	1	...	...	...
21 - 27 days - 21 - 27 jours	-	-	-	...	...	...
28 days - 11 months - 28 jours - 11 mois	4	1	3	...	...	...
28 days - less than 2 months - 28 jours - moins de 2 mois	1	-	1	...	...	...
2 months - 2 mois	2	-	2	...	...	...
3 months - 3 mois	1	1	-	...	...	...
4 - 11 months - 4 - 11 mois	-	-	-	...	...	...

Continent, country or area, year and age / Continent, pays ou zone, année et âge	Number - Nombre			Rate - Taux		
	Both sexes Les deux sexes	Male Masculin	Female Féminin	Both sexes Les deux sexes	Male Masculin	Female Féminin
EUROPE						
Ireland - Irlande						
2006* (+C)						
Total	238	136	102	3.7	4.1	3.3
Less than 1 day - Moins de 1 jour	86	48	38	1.3	1.5	1.2
1 - 6 days - 1 - 6 jours	43	23	20	0.7	♦0.7	♦0.6
7 - 27 days - 7 - 27 jours	39	20	19	0.6	♦0.6	♦0.6
7 - 13 days - 7 - 13 jours	20	11	9	♦0.3	♦0.3	♦0.3
14 - 20 days - 14 - 20 jours	12	5	7	♦0.2	♦0.2	♦0.2
21 - 27 days - 21 - 27 jours	7	4	3	♦0.1	♦0.1	♦0.1
28 days - 11 months - 28 jours - 11 mois	69	45	24	1.1	1.4	♦0.8
28 days - less than 2 months - 28 jours - moins de 2 mois	24	17	7	♦0.4	♦0.5	♦0.2
2 months - 2 mois	11	8	3	♦0.2	♦0.2	♦0.1
3 months - 3 mois	5	3	2	♦0.1	♦0.1	♦0.1
4 months - 4 mois	7	3	4	♦0.1	♦0.1	♦0.1
5 months - 5 mois	4	3	1	♦0.1	♦0.1	-
6 months - 6 mois	8	5	3	♦0.1	♦0.2	♦0.1
7 months - 7 mois	2	1	1	-	-	-
8 months - 8 mois	3	2	1	-	♦0.1	-
9 months - 9 mois	2	2	-	-	♦0.1	-
10 months - 10 mois	3	1	2	-	-	♦0.1
11 months - 11 mois	-	-	-	-	-	-
Isle of Man - Île de Man						
2004 (+C)						
Total	2	1	1	...	...	...
Less than 7 days - Moins de 7 jours	-	-	-	...	...	...
7 - 27 days - 7 - 27 jours	1	-	1	...	...	....
7 - 13 days - 7 - 13 jours	1	-	1	...	...	...
14 - 27 days - 14 - 27 jours	-	-	-	...	...	...
28 days - 11 months - 28 jours - 11 mois	1	1	-	...	...	...
28 days - 4 months - 28 jours - 4 mois	-	-	-	...	...	...
5 months - 5 mois	1	1	-	...	...	...
6 - 11 months - 6 - 11 mois	-	-	-	...	...	...
Italy - Italie						
2007 (C)						
Total	1 959	1 070	889	3.5	3.7	3.2
Less than 1 day - Moins de 1 jour	501	265	236	0.9	0.9	0.9
1 - 6 days - 1 - 6 jours	463	264	199	0.8	0.9	0.7
7 - 27 days - 7 - 27 jours	409	231	178	0.7	0.8	0.7
7 - 13 days - 7 - 13 jours	205	110	95	0.4	0.4	0.3
14 - 20 days - 14 - 20 jours	113	64	49	0.2	0.2	0.2
21 - 27 days - 21 - 27 jours	91	57	34	0.2	0.2	0.1
28 days - 11 months - 28 jours - 11 mois	586	310	276	1.0	1.1	1.0
28 days - less than 2 months - 28 jours - moins de 2 mois	220	114	106	0.4	0.4	0.4
2 months - 2 mois	86	45	41	0.2	0.2	0.1
3 months - 3 mois	59	34	25	0.1	0.1	♦0.1
4 months - 4 mois	49	31	18	0.1	0.1	♦0.1
5 months - 5 mois	36	21	15	0.1	♦0.1	♦0.1
6 months - 6 mois	37	17	20	0.1	♦0.1	♦0.1
7 months - 7 mois	28	13	15	-	-	♦0.1
8 months - 8 mois	21	11	10	-	-	-
9 months - 9 mois	22	14	8	-	-	-
10 months - 10 mois	16	7	9	-	-	-
11 months - 11 mois	12	3	9	-	-	-
Latvia - Lettonie						
2009 (C)						
Total	168	88	80	7.8	8.0	7.5
Less than 1 day - Moins de 1 jour	21	8	13	♦1.0	♦0.7	♦1.2
1 - 6 days - 1 - 6 jours	56	35	21	2.6	3.2	♦2.0
7 - 27 days - 7 - 27 jours	32	17	15	1.5	♦1.5	♦1.4
7 - 13 days - 7 - 13 jours	15	10	5	♦0.7	♦0.9	♦0.5
14 - 20 days - 14 - 20 jours	9	5	4	♦0.4	♦0.5	♦0.4
21 - 27 days - 21 - 27 jours	8	2	6	♦0.4	♦0.2	♦0.6
28 days - 11 months - 28 jours - 11 mois	59	28	31	2.7	♦2.5	2.9
28 days - less than 2 months - 28 jours - moins de 2 mois	19	8	11	♦0.9	♦0.7	♦1.0
2 months - 2 mois	9	5	4	♦0.4	♦0.5	♦0.4
3 months - 3 mois	7	4	3	♦0.3	♦0.4	♦0.3
4 months - 4 mois	5	2	3	♦0.2	♦0.2	♦0.3
5 months - 5 mois	6	2	4	♦0.3	♦0.2	♦0.4

Continent, country or area, year and age / Continent, pays ou zone, année et âge	Number - Nombre			Rate - Taux		
	Both sexes Les deux sexes	Male Masculin	Female Féminin	Both sexes Les deux sexes	Male Masculin	Female Féminin
EUROPE						
Latvia - Lettonie						
2009 (C)						
6 months - 6 mois	3	1	2	♦0.1	♦0.1	♦0.2
7 months - 7 mois	4	2	2	♦0.2	♦0.2	♦0.2
8 months - 8 mois	2	1	1	♦0.1	♦0.1	♦0.1
9 months - 9 mois	2	2	-	♦0.1	♦0.2	-
10 months - 10 mois	1	-	1	-	-	♦0.1
11 months - 11 mois	1	1	-	-	♦0.1	-
Lithuania - Lituanie						
2009 (C)						
Total	181	109	72	4.9	5.8	4.0
Less than 1 day - Moins de 1 jour	25	15	10	♦0.7	♦0.8	♦0.6
1 - 6 days - 1 - 6 jours	46	31	15	1.3	1.7	♦0.8
7 - 27 days - 7 - 27 jours	34	20	14	0.9	♦1.1	♦0.8
7 - 13 days - 7 - 13 jours	19	11	8	♦0.5	♦0.6	♦0.4
14 20 days - 14 - 20 jours	6	3	3	♦0.2	♦0.2	♦0.2
21 - 27 days - 21 - 27 jours	9	6	3	♦0.2	♦0.3	♦0.2
28 days - 11 months - 28 jours - 11 mois	76	43	33	2.1	2.3	1.8
28 days - less than 2 months - 28 jours - moins de 2 mois	21	15	6	♦0.6	♦0.8	♦0.3
2 months - 2 mois	14	4	10	♦0.4	♦0.2	♦0.6
3 months - 3 mois	12	7	5	♦0.3	♦0.4	♦0.3
4 months - 4 mois	6	4	2	♦0.2	♦0.2	♦0.1
5 months - 5 mois	5	4	1	♦0.1	♦0.2	♦0.1
6 months - 6 mois	5	3	2	♦0.1	♦0.2	♦0.1
7 months - 7 mois	6	3	3	♦0.2	♦0.2	♦0.2
8 months - 8 mois	3	2	1	♦0.1	♦0.1	♦0.1
9 months - 9 mois	2	1	1	♦0.1	♦0.1	♦0.1
10 months - 10 mois	-	-	-	-	-	-
11 months - 11 mois	2	-	2	♦0.1	-	♦0.1
Luxembourg						
2009 (C)						
Total	14	5	9	...	...	...
Less than 1 day - Moins de 1 jour	1	1	-	...	...	...
1 - 6 days - 1 - 6 jours	4	-	4	...	...	...
7 - 27 days - 7 - 27 jours	3	1	2	...	...	...
7 - 13 days - 7 - 13 jours	1	1	-	...	...	...
14 - 20 days - 14 - 20 jours	1	-	1	...	...	...
21 - 27 days - 21 - 27 jours	1	-	1	...	...	...
28 days - 11 months - 28 jours - 11 mois	6	3	3	...	...	...
28 days - less than 2 months - 28 jours - moins de 2 mois	1	-	1	...	...	...
2 months - 2 mois	1	-	1	...	...	...
3 months - 3 mois	2	1	1	...	...	...
4 months - 4 mois	-	-	-	...	...	...
5 months - 5 mois	1	1	-	...	...	...
6 months - 6 mois	-	-	-	...	...	...
7 months - 7 mois	-	-	-	...	...	...
8 months - 8 mois	-	-	-	...	...	...
9 months - 9 mois	-	-	-	...	...	...
10 months - 10 mois	-	-	-	...	...	...
11 months - 11 mois	1	1	-	...	...	...
Malta - Malte						
2009 (C)						
Total	22	11	11	...	...	...
Less than 1 day - Moins de 1 jour	6	3	3	...	...	...
1 - 6 days - 1 - 6 jours	8	5	3	...	...	...
7 - 27 days - 7 - 27 jours	4	-	4	...	...	...
7 - 13 days - 7 - 13 jours	1	-	1	...	...	...
14 - 20 days - 14 - 20 jours	2	-	2	...	...	...
21 - 27 days - 21 - 27 jours	1	-	1	...	...	...
28 days - 11 months - 28 jours - 11 mois	4	3	1	...	...	...
28 days - less than 2 months - 28 jours - moins de 2 mois	-	-	-	...	...	...
2 months - 2 mois	-	-	-	...	...	...
3 months - 3 mois	2	1	1	...	...	...
4 months - 4 mois	-	-	-	...	...	...
5 months - 5 mois	-	-	-	...	...	...
6 months - 6 mois	2	2	-	...	...	...
7 months - 7 mois	-	-	-	...	...	...
8 months - 8 mois	-	-	-	...	...	...

Continent, country or area, year and age / Continent, pays ou zone, année et âge	Number - Nombre			Rate - Taux		
	Both sexes Les deux sexes	Male Masculin	Female Féminin	Both sexes Les deux sexes	Male Masculin	Female Féminin
EUROPE						
Malta - Malte						
2009 (C)						
9 months - 9 mois	-	-	-	...	...	...
10 months - 10 mois	-	-	-	...	...	...
11 months - 11 mois	-	-	-	...	...	...
Montenegro - Monténégro						
2009 (C)						
Total	49	28	21	...	...	...
Less than 1 day - Moins de 1 jour	7	4	3	...	...	...
1 - 6 days - 1 - 6 jours	20	11	9	...	...	...
7 - 27 days - 7 - 27 jours	7	4	3	...	...	...
7 - 13 days - 7 - 13 jours	2	1	1	...	...	...
14 - 20 days - 14 - 20 jours	3	2	1	...	...	...
21 - 27 days - 21 - 27 jours	2	1	1	...	...	...
28 days - 11 months - 28 jours - 11 mois	15	9	6	...	...	...
28 days - less than 2 months - 28 jours - moins de 2 mois	10	7	3	...	...	...
2 months - 2 mois	1	1	-	...	...	...
3 months - 3 mois	3	1	2	...	...	...
4 months - 4 mois	1	-	1	...	...	...
5 - 11 months - 5 - 11 mois	-	-	-	...	...	...
Netherlands - Pays-Bas[24]						
2008 (C)						
Total	698	378	320	3.8	4.0	3.6
Less than 1 day - Moins de 1 jour	238	126	112	1.3	1.3	1.2
1 - 6 days - 1 - 6 jours	152	82	70	0.8	0.9	0.8
7 - 27 days - 7 - 27 jours	131	71	60	0.7	0.7	0.7
7 - 13 days - 7 - 13 jours	76	43	33	0.4	0.5	0.4
14 - 20 days - 14 - 20 jours	36	18	18	0.2	◊0.2	◊0.2
21 - 27 days - 21 - 27 jours	19	10	9	◊0.1	◊0.1	◊0.1
28 days - 11 months - 28 jours - 11 mois	177	99	78	1.0	1.0	0.9
28 days - less than 2 months - 28 jours - moins de 2 mois	56	34	22	0.3	0.4	◊0.2
2 months - 2 mois	26	16	10	◊0.1	◊0.2	◊0.1
3 months - 3 mois	15	6	9	◊0.1	◊0.1	◊0.1
4 months - 4 mois	24	10	14	◊0.1	◊0.1	◊0.2
5 months - 5 mois	11	6	5	◊0.1	◊0.1	◊0.1
6 months - 6 mois	14	10	4	◊0.1	◊0.1	-
7 months - 7 mois	5	3	2	-	-	-
8 months - 8 mois	5	4	1	-	-	-
9 months - 9 mois	11	5	6	◊0.1	◊0.1	◊0.1
10 months - 10 mois	6	2	4	-	-	-
11 months - 11 mois	4	3	1	-	-	-
Norway - Norvège[25]						
2009 (C)						
Total	192	119	73	3.1	3.7	2.4
Less than 1 day - Moins de 1 jour	40	28	12	0.6	◊0.9	◊0.4
1 - 6 days - 1 - 6 jours	56	40	16	0.9	1.3	◊0.5
7 - 27 days - 7 - 27 jours	30	16	14	0.5	◊0.5	◊0.5
7 - 13 days - 7 - 13 jours	16	9	7	◊0.3	◊0.3	◊0.2
14 - 20 days - 14 - 20 jours	8	4	4	◊0.1	◊0.1	◊0.1
21 - 27 days - 21 - 27 jours	6	3	3	◊0.1	◊0.1	◊0.1
28 days - 11 months - 28 jours - 11 mois	66	35	31	1.1	1.1	1.0
28 days - less than 2 months - 28 jours - moins de 2 mois	20	11	9	◊0.3	◊0.3	◊0.3
2 months - 2 mois	10	4	6	◊0.2	◊0.1	◊0.2
3 months - 3 mois	6	4	2	◊0.1	◊0.1	◊0.1
4 months - 4 mois	6	4	2	◊0.1	◊0.1	◊0.1
5 months - 5 mois	8	4	4	◊0.1	◊0.1	◊0.1
6 months - 6 mois	3	2	1	-	◊0.1	-
7 months - 7 mois	4	2	2	◊0.1	◊0.1	◊0.1
8 months - 8 mois	4	2	2	◊0.1	◊0.1	◊0.1
9 months - 9 mois	3	1	2	-	-	◊0.1
10 months - 10 mois	1	1	-	-	-	-
11 months - 11 mois	1	-	1	-	-	-
Poland - Pologne						
2009 (C)						
Total	2 327	1 298	1 029	5.6	6.0	5.1
Less than 1 day - Moins de 1 jour	821	466	355	2.0	2.2	1.8
1 - 6 days - 1 - 6 jours	445	257	188	1.1	1.2	0.9

Continent, country or area, year and age Continent, pays ou zone, année et âge	Number - Nombre			Rate - Taux		
	Both sexes Les deux sexes	Male Masculin	Female Féminin	Both sexes Les deux sexes	Male Masculin	Female Féminin
EUROPE						
Poland - Pologne						
2009 (C)						
7 - 27 days - 7 - 27 jours	410	224	186	1.0	1.0	0.9
7 - 13 days - 7 - 13 jours	196	108	88	0.5	0.5	0.4
14 - 20 days - 14 - 20 jours	132	66	66	0.3	0.3	0.3
21 - 27 days - 21 - 27 jours	82	50	32	0.2	0.2	0.2
28 days - 11 months - 28 jours - 11 mois	651	351	300	1.6	1.6	1.5
28 days - less than 2 months - 28 jours - moins de 2 mois	187	102	85	0.4	0.5	0.4
2 months - 2 mois	114	59	55	0.3	0.3	0.3
3 months - 3 mois	69	40	29	0.2	0.2	◆0.1
4 months - 4 mois	62	33	29	0.1	0.2	◆0.1
5 months - 5 mois	50	27	23	0.1	◆0.1	◆0.1
6 months - 6 mois	39	20	19	0.1	◆0.1	◆0.1
7 months - 7 mois	30	16	14	0.1	◆0.1	◆0.1
8 months - 8 mois	29	16	13	◆0.1	◆0.1	◆0.1
9 months - 9 mois	28	16	12	◆0.1	◆0.1	◆0.1
10 months - 10 mois	28	12	16	◆0.1	◆0.1	◆0.1
11 months - 11 mois	15	10	5	-	-	-
Portugal[8]						
2009 (C)						
Total	362	210	152	3.6	4.1	3.1
Less than 1 day - Moins de 1 jour	88	53	35	0.9	1.0	0.7
1 - 6 days - 1 - 6 jours	77	48	29	0.8	0.9	◆0.6
7 - 27 days - 7 - 27 jours	80	46	34	0.8	0.9	0.7
7 - 13 days - 7 - 13 jours	38	23	15	0.4	◆0.5	◆0.3
14 - 20 days - 14 - 20 jours	25	14	11	◆0.3	◆0.3	◆0.2
21 - 27 days - 21 - 27 jours	17	9	8	◆0.2	◆0.2	◆0.2
28 days - 11 months - 28 jours - 11 mois	117	63	54	1.2	1.2	1.1
28 days - less than 2 months - 28 jours - moins de 2 mois	33	18	15	0.3	◆0.4	◆0.3
2 months - 2 mois	19	10	9	◆0.2	◆0.2	◆0.2
3 months - 3 mois	9	8	1	◆0.1	◆0.2	-
4 months - 4 mois	15	6	9	◆0.2	◆0.1	◆0.2
5 months - 5 mois	6	1	5	◆0.1	-	◆0.1
6 months - 6 mois	6	3	3	◆0.1	◆0.1	◆0.1
7 months - 7 mois	9	7	2	◆0.1	◆0.1	-
8 months - 8 mois	7	4	3	◆0.1	◆0.1	◆0.1
9 months - 9 mois	2	1	1	-	-	-
10 months - 10 mois	9	5	4	◆0.1	◆0.1	◆0.1
11 months - 11 mois	2	-	2	-	-	-
Republic of Moldova - République de Moldova[26]						
2009 (C)						
Total	492	293	199	12.1	13.9	10.1
Less than 1 day - Moins de 1 jour	93	52	41	2.3	2.5	2.1
1 - 6 days - 1 - 6 jours	155	92	63	3.8	4.4	3.2
7 - 27 days - 7 - 27 jours	71	46	25	1.7	2.2	◆1.3
7 - 13 days - 7 - 13 jours	42	31	11	1.0	1.5	◆0.6
14 - 20 days - 14 - 20 jours	12	7	5	◆0.3	◆0.3	◆0.3
21 - 27 days - 21 - 27 jours	17	8	9	◆0.4	◆0.4	◆0.5
28 days - 11 months - 28 jours - 11 mois	173	103	70	4.2	4.9	3.6
28 days - less than 2 months - 28 jours - moins de 2 mois	53	33	20	1.3	1.6	◆1.0
2 months - 2 mois	29	18	11	◆0.7	◆0.9	◆0.6
3 months - 3 mois	21	14	7	◆0.5	◆0.7	◆0.4
4 months - 4 mois	13	5	8	◆0.3	◆0.2	◆0.4
5 months - 5 mois	12	8	4	◆0.3	◆0.4	◆0.2
6 months - 6 mois	9	3	6	◆0.2	◆0.1	◆0.3
7 months - 7 mois	11	4	7	◆0.3	◆0.2	◆0.4
8 months - 8 mois	7	4	3	◆0.2	◆0.2	◆0.2
9 months - 9 mois	5	4	1	◆0.1	◆0.2	◆0.1
10 months - 10 mois	7	5	2	◆0.2	◆0.2	◆0.1
11 months - 11 mois	6	5	1	◆0.1	◆0.2	◆0.1
Romania - Roumanie						
2009 (C)						
Total	2 250	1 287	963	10.1	11.2	8.9
Less than 1 day - Moins de 1 jour	192	117	75	0.9	1.0	0.7
1 - 6 days - 1 - 6 jours	632	379	253	2.8	3.3	2.3
7 - 27 days - 7 - 27 jours	445	260	185	2.0	2.3	1.7
7 - 13 days - 7 - 13 jours	224	129	95	1.0	1.1	0.9
14 - 20 days - 14 - 20 jours	129	74	55	0.6	0.6	0.5

Continent, country or area, year and age / Continent, pays ou zone, année et âge	Number - Nombre			Rate - Taux		
	Both sexes Les deux sexes	Male Masculin	Female Féminin	Both sexes Les deux sexes	Male Masculin	Female Féminin
EUROPE						
Romania - Roumanie						
2009 (C)						
21 - 27 days - 21 - 27 jours	92	57	35	0.4	0.5	0.3
28 days - 11 months - 28 jours - 11 mois	981	531	450	4.4	4.6	4.2
28 days - less than 2 months - 28 jours - moins de 2 mois	284	149	135	1.3	1.3	1.3
2 months - 2 mois	180	108	72	0.8	0.9	0.7
3 months - 3 mois	147	83	64	0.7	0.7	0.6
4 months - 4 mois	90	46	44	0.4	0.4	0.4
5 months - 5 mois	70	34	36	0.3	0.3	0.3
6 months - 6 mois	60	34	26	0.3	0.3	♦0.2
7 months - 7 mois	41	22	19	0.2	♦0.2	♦0.2
8 months - 8 mois	39	21	18	0.2	♦0.2	♦0.2
9 months - 9 mois	23	11	12	♦0.1	♦0.1	♦0.1
10 months - 10 mois	30	15	15	0.1	♦0.1	♦0.1
11 months - 11 mois	17	8	9	♦0.1	♦0.1	♦0.1
Russian Federation - Fédération de Russie[13]						
2009 (C)						
Total	14 271	8 182	6 089	8.1	9.0	7.1
Less than 1 day - Moins de 1 jour	1 575	858	717	0.9	0.9	0.8
1 - 6 days - 1 - 6 jours	3 881	2 356	1 525	2.2	2.6	1.8
7 - 27 days - 7 - 27 jours	2 613	1 514	1 099	1.5	1.7	1.3
7 - 13 days - 7 - 13 jours	1 319	787	532	0.7	0.9	0.6
14 - 20 days - 14 - 20 jours	733	396	337	0.4	0.4	0.4
21 - 27 days - 21 - 27 jours	561	331	230	0.3	0.4	0.3
28 days - 11 months - 28 jours - 11 mois	6 194	3 450	2 744	3.5	3.8	3.2
28 days - less than 2 months - 28 jours - moins de 2 mois	1 866	1 067	799	1.1	1.2	0.9
2 months - 2 mois	1 094	617	477	0.6	0.7	0.6
3 months - 3 mois	817	444	373	0.5	0.5	0.4
4 months - 4 mois	599	345	254	0.3	0.4	0.3
5 months - 5 mois	473	254	219	0.3	0.3	0.3
6 months - 6 mois	348	180	168	0.2	0.2	0.2
7 months - 7 mois	257	140	117	0.1	0.2	0.1
8 months - 8 mois	241	142	99	0.1	0.2	0.1
9 months - 9 mois	207	107	100	0.1	0.1	0.1
10 months - 10 mois	153	80	73	0.1	0.1	0.1
11 months - 11 mois	139	74	65	0.1	0.1	0.1
Unknown - Inconnu	8	4	4	-	-	-
San Marino - Saint-Marin						
2003 (+C)						
Total	2	1	1	...	...	...
Less than 1 day - Moins de 1 jour	1	-	1	...	...	...
1 - 6 days - 1 - 6 jours	-	-	-	...	...	...
7 - 27 days - 7 - 27 jours	1	1	-	...	...	...
28 days - 11 months - 28 jours - 11 mois	-	-	-	...	...	...
Serbia - Serbie[27]						
2009 (+C)						
Total	492	279	213	7.0	7.7	6.3
Less than 1 day - Moins de 1 jour	143	84	59	2.0	2.3	1.7
1 - 6 days - 1 - 6 jours	122	73	49	1.7	2.0	1.4
7 - 27 days - 7 - 27 jours	80	45	35	1.1	1.2	1.0
7 - 13 days - 7 - 13 jours	33	20	13	0.5	♦0.5	♦0.4
14 - 20 days - 14 - 20 jours	29	15	14	♦0.4	♦0.4	♦0.4
21 - 27 days - 21 - 27 jours	18	10	8	♦0.3	♦0.3	♦0.2
28 days - 11 months - 28 jours - 11 mois	147	77	70	2.1	2.1	2.1
28 days - less than 2 months - 28 jours - moins de 2 mois	50	27	23	0.7	♦0.7	♦0.7
2 months - 2 mois	22	11	11	♦0.3	♦0.3	♦0.3
3 months - 3 mois	18	12	6	♦0.3	♦0.3	♦0.2
4 months - 4 mois	17	7	10	♦0.2	♦0.2	♦0.3
5 months - 5 mois	11	6	5	♦0.2	♦0.2	♦0.1
6 months - 6 mois	9	3	6	♦0.1	♦0.1	♦0.2
7 months - 7 mois	6	5	1	♦0.1	♦0.1	-
8 months - 8 mois	5	2	3	♦0.1	♦0.1	♦0.1
9 months - 9 mois	5	1	4	♦0.1	-	♦0.1
10 months - 10 mois	2	1	1	-	-	-
11 months - 11 mois	2	2	-	-	♦0.1	-

Continent, country or area, year and age / Continent, pays ou zone, année et âge	Number - Nombre			Rate - Taux		
	Both sexes Les deux sexes	Male Masculin	Female Féminin	Both sexes Les deux sexes	Male Masculin	Female Féminin

EUROPE

Slovakia - Slovaquie
2009 (C)

Total	346	209	137	5.7	6.6	4.6
Less than 1 day - Moins de 1 jour	44	23	21	0.7	♦0.7	♦0.7
1 - 6 days - 1 - 6 jours	83	53	30	1.4	1.7	1.0
7 - 27 days - 7 - 27 jours	61	35	26	1.0	1.1	♦0.9
7 - 13 days - 7 - 13 jours	26	15	11	♦0.4	♦0.5	♦0.4
14 - 20 days - 14 - 20 jours	20	9	11	♦0.3	♦0.3	♦0.4
21 - 27 days - 21 - 27 jours	15	11	4	♦0.2	♦0.3	♦0.1
28 days - 11 months - 28 jours - 11 mois	158	98	60	2.6	3.1	2.0
28 days - less than 2 months - 28 jours - moins de 2 mois	48	29	19	0.8	♦0.9	♦0.6
2 months - 2 mois	33	24	9	0.5	♦0.8	♦0.3
3 months - 3 mois	13	8	5	♦0.2	♦0.3	♦0.2
4 months - 4 mois	16	10	6	♦0.3	♦0.3	♦0.2
5 months - 5 mois	9	7	2	♦0.1	♦0.2	♦0.1
6 months - 6 mois	8	5	3	♦0.1	♦0.2	♦0.1
7 months - 7 mois	9	5	4	♦0.1	♦0.2	♦0.1
8 months - 8 mois	6	2	4	♦0.1	♦0.1	♦0.1
9 months - 9 mois	5	2	3	♦0.1	♦0.1	♦0.1
10 months - 10 mois	8	4	4	♦0.1	♦0.1	♦0.1
11 months - 11 mois	3	2	1	-	♦0.1	-

Slovenia - Slovénie
2009 (C)

Total	52	25	27	...	...	...
Less than 1 day - Moins de 1 jour	18	9	9	...	...	...
1 - 6 days - 1 - 6 jours	11	7	4	...	...	...
7 - 27 days - 7 - 27 jours	5	3	2	...	...	...
7 - 13 days - 7 - 13 jours	2	1	1	...	...	...
14 - 20 days - 14 - 20 jours	1	1	-	...	...	...
21 - 27 days - 21 - 27 jours	2	1	1	...	...	...
28 days - 11 months - 28 jours - 11 mois	18	6	12	...	...	...
28 days - less than 2 months - 28 jours - moins de 2 mois	9	2	7	...	...	...
2 months - 2 mois	2	1	1	...	...	...
3 months - 3 mois	-	-	-	...	...	...
4 months - 4 mois	2	1	1	...	...	...
5 months - 5 mois	1	1	-	...	...	...
6 months - 6 mois	2	-	2	...	...	...
7 months - 7 mois	-	-	-	...	...	...
8 months - 8 mois	-	-	-	...	...	...
9 months - 9 mois	-	-	-	...	...	...
10 months - 10 mois	2	1	1	...	...	...
11 months - 11 mois	-	-	-	...	...	...

Spain - Espagne
2009 (C)

Total	1 609	892	717	3.3	3.5	3.0
Less than 1 day - Moins de 1 jour	308	173	135	0.6	0.7	0.6
1 - 6 days - 1 - 6 jours	374	196	178	0.8	0.8	0.7
7 - 27 days - 7 - 27 jours	370	216	154	0.7	0.8	0.6
7 - 13 days - 7 - 13 jours	181	108	73	0.4	0.4	0.3
14 - 20 days - 14 - 20 jours	119	65	54	0.2	0.3	0.2
21 - 27 days - 21 - 27 jours	70	43	27	0.1	0.2	♦0.1
28 days - 11 months - 28 jours - 11 mois	557	307	250	1.1	1.2	1.0
28 days - less than 2 months - 28 jours - moins de 2 mois	162	91	71	0.3	0.4	0.3
2 months - 2 mois	75	46	29	0.2	0.2	♦0.1
3 months - 3 mois	60	34	26	0.1	0.1	♦0.1
4 months - 4 mois	59	32	27	0.1	0.1	♦0.1
5 months - 5 mois	42	25	17	0.1	♦0.1	♦0.1
6 months - 6 mois	27	12	15	♦0.1	-	♦0.1
7 months - 7 mois	40	21	19	0.1	♦0.1	♦0.1
8 months - 8 mois	22	10	12	-	-	♦0.1
9 months - 9 mois	34	15	19	0.1	♦0.1	♦0.1
10 months - 10 mois	15	8	7	-	-	-
11 months - 11 mois	21	13	8	-	♦0.1	-
Unknown - Inconnu	-	1	2	-	-	-

Sweden - Suède
2009 (C)

Total	278	148	130	2.5	2.6	2.4
Less than 1 day - Moins de 1 jour	65	32	33	0.6	0.6	0.6

Continent, country or area, year and age Continent, pays ou zone, année et âge	Number - Nombre			Rate - Taux		
	Both sexes Les deux sexes	Male Masculin	Female Féminin	Both sexes Les deux sexes	Male Masculin	Female Féminin
EUROPE						
Sweden - Suède						
2009 (C)						
1 - 6 days - 1 - 6 jours	68	36	32	0.6	0.6	0.6
7 - 27 days - 7 - 27 jours	47	34	13	0.4	0.6	♦0.2
7 - 13 days - 7 - 13 jours	22	16	6	♦0.2	♦0.3	♦0.1
14 - 20 days - 14 - 20 jours	14	9	5	♦0.1	♦0.2	♦0.1
21 - 27 days - 21 - 27 jours	11	9	2	♦0.1	♦0.2	-
28 days - 11 months - 28 jours - 11 mois	98	46	52	0.9	0.8	1.0
28 days - less than 2 months - 28 jours - moins de 2 mois	38	17	21	0.3	♦0.3	♦0.4
2 months - 2 mois	19	11	8	♦0.2	♦0.2	♦0.1
3 months - 3 mois	7	3	4	♦0.1	♦0.1	♦0.1
4 months - 4 mois	4	2	2	-	-	-
5 months - 5 mois	6	3	3	♦0.1	♦0.1	♦0.1
6 months - 6 mois	4	2	2	-	-	-
7 months - 7 mois	4	3	1	-	♦0.1	-
8 months - 8 mois	5	2	3	-	-	♦0.1
9 months - 9 mois	3	2	1	-	-	-
10 months - 10 mois	2	-	2	-	-	-
11 months - 11 mois	6	1	5	♦0.1	-	♦0.1
Switzerland - Suisse						
2009 (C)						
Total	337	194	143	4.3	4.8	3.8
Less than 1 day - Moins de 1 jour	198	111	87	2.5	2.7	2.3
1 - 6 days - 1 - 6 jours	43	27	16	0.5	♦0.7	♦0.4
7 - 27 days - 7 - 27 jours	36	22	14	0.5	♦0.5	♦0.4
7 - 13 days - 7 - 13 jours	15	11	4	♦0.2	♦0.3	♦0.1
14 - 20 days - 14 - 20 jours	11	5	6	♦0.1	♦0.1	♦0.2
21 - 27 days - 21 - 27 jours	10	6	4	♦0.1	♦0.1	♦0.1
28 days - 11 months - 28 jours - 11 mois	60	34	26	0.8	0.8	♦0.7
28 days - less than 2 months - 28 jours - moins de 2 mois	16	10	6	♦0.2	♦0.2	♦0.2
2 months - 2 mois	5	4	1	♦0.1	♦0.1	-
3 months - 3 mois	11	5	6	♦0.1	♦0.1	♦0.2
4 months - 4 mois	7	4	3	♦0.1	♦0.1	♦0.1
5 months - 5 mois	7	5	2	♦0.1	♦0.1	♦0.1
6 months - 6 mois	2	1	1	-	-	-
7 months - 7 mois	2	2	-	-	-	-
8 months - 8 mois	3	1	2	-	-	♦0.1
9 months - 9 mois	2	1	1	-	-	-
10 months - 10 mois	2	-	2	-	-	♦0.1
11 months - 11 mois	3	1	2	-	-	♦0.1
TFYR of Macedonia - L'ex-R. y. de Macédoine						
2009 (C)						
Total	278	162	116	11.7	13.1	10.2
Less than 1 day - Moins de 1 jour	74	42	32	3.1	3.4	2.8
1 - 6 days - 1 - 6 jours	93	59	34	3.9	4.8	3.0
7 - 27 days - 7 - 27 jours	52	24	28	2.2	♦1.9	♦2.5
7 - 13 days - 7 - 13 jours	31	13	18	1.3	♦1.1	♦1.6
14 - 20 days - 14 - 20 jours	12	7	5	♦0.5	♦0.6	♦0.4
21 - 27 days - 21 - 27 jours	9	4	5	♦0.4	♦0.3	♦0.4
28 days - 11 months - 28 jours - 11 mois	59	37	22	2.5	3.0	♦1.9
28 days - less than 2 months - 28 jours - moins de 2 mois	24	17	7	♦1.0	♦1.4	♦0.6
2 months - 2 mois	9	4	5	♦0.4	♦0.3	♦0.4
3 months - 3 mois	6	5	1	♦0.3	♦0.4	♦0.1
4 months - 4 mois	3	2	1	♦0.1	♦0.2	♦0.1
5 months - 5 mois	2	1	1	♦0.1	♦0.1	♦0.1
6 months - 6 mois	4	3	1	♦0.2	♦0.2	♦0.1
7 months - 7 mois	2	1	1	♦0.1	♦0.1	♦0.1
8 months - 8 mois	3	2	1	♦0.1	♦0.2	♦0.1
9 months - 9 mois	3	1	2	♦0.1	♦0.1	♦0.2
10 months - 10 mois	2	1	1	♦0.1	♦0.1	♦0.1
11 months - 11 mois	1	-	1	-	-	♦0.1
Ukraine[28]						
2008 (C)						
Total	5 049	2 892	2 157	9.9	11.0	8.7
Less than 1 day - Moins de 1 jour	817	466	351	1.6	1.8	1.4
1 - 6 days - 1 - 6 jours	1 508	874	634	3.0	3.3	2.6
7 - 27 days - 7 - 27 jours	860	523	337	1.7	2.0	1.4
7 - 13 days - 7 - 13 jours	415	251	164	0.8	1.0	0.7

16. Infant deaths and infant mortality rates by age and sex: latest available year, 2000 - 2009
Décès d'enfants de moins d'un an et taux de mortalité infantile selon l'âge et le sexe : dernière année disponible, 2000 - 2009 (continued - suite)

Continent, country or area, year and age Continent, pays ou zone, année et âge	Number - Nombre			Rate - Taux		
	Both sexes Les deux sexes	Male Masculin	Female Féminin	Both sexes Les deux sexes	Male Masculin	Female Féminin
EUROPE						
Ukraine[28]						
2008 (C)						
14 - 20 days - 14 - 20 jours	252	163	89	0.5	0.6	0.4
21 - 27 days - 21 - 27 jours	193	109	84	0.4	0.4	0.3
28 days - 11 months - 28 jours - 11 mois	1 864	1 029	835	3.7	3.9	3.4
28 days - less than 2 months - 28 jours - moins de 2 mois	611	343	268	1.2	1.3	1.1
2 months - 2 mois	303	174	129	0.6	0.7	0.5
3 months - 3 mois	232	121	111	0.5	0.5	0.4
4 months - 4 mois	167	91	76	0.3	0.3	0.3
5 months - 5 mois	126	69	57	0.2	0.3	0.2
6 months - 6 mois	99	53	46	0.2	0.2	0.2
7 months - 7 mois	92	55	37	0.2	0.2	0.1
8 months - 8 mois	71	33	38	0.1	0.1	0.2
9 months - 9 mois	70	44	26	0.1	0.2	◆0.1
10 months - 10 mois	44	23	21	0.1	◆0.1	◆0.1
11 months - 11 mois	49	23	26	0.1	◆0.1	◆0.1
United Kingdom of Great Britain and Northern Ireland - **Royaume-Uni de Grande-Bretagne et d'Irlande du Nord[29]**						
2007 (C)						
Total	3 740	2 113	1 627	4.8	...	...
Less than 1 day - Moins de 1 jour	1 113	628	485	1.4	...	...
1 - 6 days - 1 - 6 jours	856	464	392	1.1	...	...
7 - 27 days - 7 - 27 jours	582	324	258	0.8	...	...
7 - 13 days - 7 - 13 jours	273	145	128	0.4	...	...
14 - 20 days - 14 - 20 jours	182	111	71	0.2	...	...
21 - 27 days - 21 - 27 jours	127	68	59	0.2	...	...
28 days - 11 months - 28 jours - 11 mois	1 189	697	492	1.5	...	...
28 days - less than 2 months - 28 jours - moins de 2 mois	378	215	163	0.5	...	...
2 months - 2 mois	173	114	59	0.2	...	...
3 months - 3 mois	140	91	49	0.2	...	...
4 months - 4 mois	110	63	47	0.1	...	...
5 months - 5 mois	98	62	36	0.1	...	...
6 months - 6 mois	65	37	28	0.1	...	...
7 months - 7 mois	67	33	34	0.1	...	...
8 months - 8 mois	46	21	25	0.1	...	...
9 months - 9 mois	46	28	18	0.1	...	...
10 months - 10 mois	34	20	14	-	...	...
11 months - 11 mois	32	13	19	-	...	...
OCEANIA - OCÉANIE						
Australia - Australie						
2009 (+C)						
Total	1 261	728	533	4.3	4.8	3.7
Less than 1 day - Moins de 1 jour	526	301	225	1.8	2.0	1.6
1 - 6 days - 1 - 6 jours	234	127	107	0.8	0.8	0.7
7 - 27 days - 7 - 27 jours	131	82	49	0.4	0.5	0.3
7 - 13 days - 7 - 13 jours	64	42	22	0.2	0.3	◆0.2
14 - 20 days - 14 - 20 jours	48	29	19	0.2	◆0.2	◆0.1
21 - 27 days - 21 - 27 jours	19	11	8	◆0.1	◆0.1	◆0.1
28 days - 11 months - 28 jours - 11 mois	370	218	152	1.3	1.4	1.1
28 days - less than 2 months - 28 jours - moins de 2 mois	110	64	46	0.4	0.4	0.3
2 months - 2 mois	57	32	25	0.2	0.2	◆0.2
3 months - 3 mois	59	38	21	0.2	0.2	◆0.1
4 months - 4 mois	38	26	12	0.1	◆0.2	◆0.1
5 months - 5 mois	21	12	9	◆0.1	◆0.1	◆0.1
6 months - 6 mois	22	12	10	◆0.1	◆0.1	◆0.1
7 months - 7 mois	16	9	7	◆0.1	◆0.1	-
8 months - 8 mois	8	4	4	-	-	-
9 months - 9 mois	18	12	6	◆0.1	◆0.1	-
10 months - 10 mois	12	5	7	-	-	-
11 months - 11 mois	9	4	5	-	-	-
French Polynesia - Polynésie française						
2008 (C)						
Total	23	...	...	...	...	...
Less than 7 days - Moins de 7 jours	14	...	...	...	...	...

16. Infant deaths and infant mortality rates by age and sex: latest available year, 2000 - 2009
Décès d'enfants de moins d'un an et taux de mortalité infantile selon l'âge et le sexe : dernière année disponible, 2000 - 2009 (continued - suite)

Continent, country or area, year and age Continent, pays ou zone, année et âge	Number - Nombre			Rate - Taux		
	Both sexes Les deux sexes	Male Masculin	Female Féminin	Both sexes Les deux sexes	Male Masculin	Female Féminin
OCEANIA - OCÉANIE						
French Polynesia - Polynésie française						
2008 (C)						
7 - 27 days - 7 - 27 jours	-	...	...	...	...	...
28 days - 11 months - 28 jours - 11 mois	9	...	...	...	...	...
New Caledonia - Nouvelle-Calédonie						
2007 (C)						
Total	25	15	10	...	...	...
Less than 1 day - Moins de 1 jour	-	-	-	...	...	...
1 - 6 days - 1 - 6 jours	11	9	2	...	...	...
7 - 27 days - 7 - 27 jours	6	2	4	...	...	...
7 - 13 days - 7 - 13 jours	6	2	4	...	...	...
14 - 20 days - 14 - 20 jours	-	-	-	...	...	...
21 - 27 days - 21 - 27 jours	-	-	-	...	...	...
28 days - 11 months - 28 jours - 11 mois	8	4	4	...	...	...
28 days - less than 2 months - 28 jours - moins de 2 mois	-	-	-	...	...	...
2 months - 2 mois	-	-	-	...	...	...
3 months - 3 mois	-	2	-	...	...	...
4 months - 4 mois	-	-	-	...	...	...
5 months - 5 mois	-	-	-	...	...	...
6 months - 6 mois	2	2	-	...	...	...
7 months - 7 mois	-	-	-	...	...	...
8 months - 8 mois	-	-	-	...	...	...
9 months - 9 mois	-	-	-	...	...	...
10 months - 10 mois	-	-	-	...	...	...
11 months - 11 mois	4	-	4	...	...	...
New Zealand - Nouvelle-Zélande[8]						
2009 (+C)						
Total	308	170	138	4.9	5.3	4.5
Less than 1 day - Moins de 1 jour	78	42	36	1.2	1.3	1.2
1 - 6 days - 1 - 6 jours	55	27	28	0.9	♦0.8	♦0.9
7 - 27 days - 7 - 27 jours	42	24	18	0.7	♦0.7	♦0.6
7 - 13 days - 7 - 13 jours	23	13	10	♦0.4	♦0.4	♦0.3
14 - 20 days - 14 - 20 jours	7	4	3	♦0.1	♦0.1	♦0.1
21 - 27 days - 21 - 27 jours	12	7	5	♦0.2	♦0.2	♦0.2
28 days - 11 months - 28 jours - 11 mois	133	77	56	2.1	2.4	1.8
28 days - less than 2 months - 28 jours - moins de 2 mois	36	20	16	0.6	♦0.6	♦0.5
2 months - 2 mois	21	12	9	♦0.3	♦0.4	♦0.3
3 months - 3 mois	21	14	7	♦0.3	♦0.4	♦0.2
4 months - 4 mois	9	6	3	♦0.1	♦0.2	♦0.1
5 months - 5 mois	13	8	5	♦0.2	♦0.2	♦0.2
6 months - 6 mois	5	4	1	♦0.1	♦0.1	-
7 months - 7 mois	8	5	3	♦0.1	♦0.2	♦0.1
8 months - 8 mois	9	4	5	♦0.1	♦0.1	♦0.2
9 months - 9 mois	5	1	4	♦0.1	-	♦0.1
10 months - 10 mois	4	2	2	♦0.1	♦0.1	♦0.1
11 months - 11 mois	2	1	1	-	-	-

FOOTNOTES - NOTES

Italics: data from civil registers which are incomplete or of unknown completeness. - Italiques : données incomplètes ou dont le degré d'exactitude n'est pas connu, provenant des registres de l'état civil.

♦ Rates based on 30 or fewer infant deaths. - Taux basés sur 30 décès d'enfants ou moins.

¨ Provisional. - Données provisoires.

'Code' indicates the source of data, as follows:
C - Civil registration, estimated over 90% complete
U - Civil registration, estimated less than 90% complete
| - Other source, estimated reliable
+ - Data tabulated by date of registration rather than occurence
... - Information not available

Le 'Code' indique la source des données, comme suit :
C - Registres de l'état civil considérés complèts à 90 p. 100 au moins

U - Registres de l'état civil qui ne sont pas considérés complèts à 90 p. 100 au moins
| - Autre source, considérée pas douteuses
+ - Données exploitées selon la date de l'enregistrement et non la date de l'événement
... - Information pas disponible

[1] Excludes the islands of St. Brandon and Agalega. - Non compris les îles St. Brandon et Agalega.
[2] Excluding live-born infants who died before their birth was registered. - Non compris les enfants nés vivants décédés avant l'enregistrement de leur naissance.
[3] Unrevised data. - Les données n'ont pas été révisées.
[4] Data for male and female categories exclude infant deaths of unknown sex. - Il n'est pas tenu compte dans les données classées par sexe des décès d'enfant de moins d'un an de sexe inconnu.
[5] Including Canadian residents temporarily in the United States, but excluding United States residents temporarily in Canada. - Y compris les résidents canadiens se trouvant temporairement aux Etats-Unis, mais ne comprenant pas les résidents des Etats-Unis se trouvant temporairement au Canada.

⁶ Excluding infant deaths to mothers living abroad. - Exception faite des décès d'enfants en bas âge survenus lorsque la mère résidait à l'étranger.

⁷ Data refer to urban areas only. - Données ne concernant que les zones urbaines.

⁸ Data refer to resident population only. - Pour la population résidante seulement.

⁹ Excluding Indian jungle population. - Non compris les Indiens de la jungle.

¹⁰ Excluding nomadic Indian tribes. - Non compris les tribus d'Indiens nomades.

¹¹ Data refer to infants 30 days - 12 months old. - Les données se réfèrent aux nouveaux-nés âgées de 30 jours à 12 mois.

¹² Source: Ministry of health reports. Completeness of coverage estimated at 40 per cent. - Source: Rapports du Ministère de Santé. Degré de complétude évalué à 40 pour cent.

¹³ Excluding infants born alive of less than 28 weeks' gestation, of less than 1 000 grams in weight and 35 centimeters in length, who die within seven days of birth. - Non compris les enfants nés vivants après moins de 28 semaines de gestations, pesant moins de 1 000 grammes, mesurant moins de 35 centimètres et décédés dans les sept jours qui ont suivi leur naissance.

¹⁴ Data refer to government controlled areas. - Les données se rapportent aux zones contrôlées par le Gouvernement.

¹⁵ Including data for East Jerusalem and Israeli residents in certain other territories under occupation by Israeli military forces since June 1967. Including deaths abroad of Israeli residents who were out of the country for less than a year. - Y compris les données pour Jérusalem-Est et les résidents israéliens dans certains autres territoires occupés depuis 1967 par les forces armées israéliennes. Y compris les décès à l'étranger de résidents israéliens qui ont quitté le pays depuis moins d'un an.

¹⁶ Data refer to Japanese nationals in Japan only. - Les données se raportent aux nationaux japonais au Japon seulement.

¹⁷ Data from Births and Deaths Notification System (Ministry of Health institutions and all other health care providers). - Les données proviennent du système de notification des naissances et des décès (établissements du Ministère de la santé et tous autres prestataires de soins de santé).

¹⁸ Based on the results of the Pakistan Demographic Survey. Excluding data for the Pakistan-held part of Jammu and Kashmir, the final status of which has not yet been determined. - Données extraites de l'enquête démographique effectuée par le Pakistan. Non compris les données concernant la partie du Jammu et Cachemire occupée par le Pakistan dont le statut définitif n'a pas été déterminé.

¹⁹ Excluding alien armed forces, civilian aliens employed by armed forces, and foreign diplomatic personnel and their dependants. - Non compris les militaires étrangers, les civils étrangers employés par les forces armées ni le personnel diplomatique étranger et les membres de leur famille les accompagnant.

²⁰ Total in this table is different from data presented in other tables due to different data source. - Le total figurant dans ce tableau ne correspond pas aux données présentées dans d'autres tableaux parce que les sources de données ne sont pas les mêmes.

²¹ Excluding Faeroe Islands and Greenland shown separately, if available. - Non compris les Iles Féroé et le Groenland, qui font l'objet de rubriques distinctes, si disponible.

²² Excluding Åland Islands. - Non compris les Îles d'Åland.

²³ Including armed forces stationed outside the country. - Y compris les militaires nationaux hors du pays.

²⁴ Including residents outside the country if listed in a Netherlands population register. - Y compris les résidents hors du pays, s'ils sont inscrits sur un registre de population néerlandais.

²⁵ Including residents temporarily outside the country. Excluding Svalbard and Jan Mayen Islands shown separately, if available. - Y compris les résidents se trouvant temporairement hors du pays. Non compris Svalbard et Jan Mayen qui font l'objet de rubriques distinctes, si disponible.

²⁶ Excluding Transnistria and the municipality of Bender. - Les données ne tiennent pas compte de l'information sur la Transnistria et la municipalité de Bender.

²⁷ Excluding data for Kosovo and Metohia. - Sans les données pour le Kosovo et Metohie.

²⁸ Data includes deaths resulting from births with weight 500g and more (if weight is unknown - with length 25 centimeters and more, or with gestation during 22 weeks or more). - Y compris les décès de nouveau-nés de 500 grammes ou plus (si le poids est inconnu – de 25 centimètres de long ou plus, ou après une grossesse de 22 semaines ou plus).

²⁹ Excluding Channel Islands (Guernsey and Jersey) and Isle of Man, shown separately, if available. - Non compris les îles Anglo-Normandes (Guernesey et Jersey) et l'île de Man, qui font l'objet de rubriques distinctes, si disponible.

16a. Infant deaths and infant mortality rates by age and sex: 2010
Décès d'enfants de moins d'un an et taux de mortalité infantile selon l'âge et le sexe : 2010

Continent, country or area, year and age / Continent, pays ou zone, année et âge	Number - Nombre			Rate - Taux		
	Both sexes Les deux sexes	Male Masculin	Female Féminin	Both sexes Les deux sexes	Male Masculin	Female Féminin
AMERICA, NORTH - AMÉRIQUE DU NORD						
Costa Rica						
2010* (C)						
Total	671	387	284	9.5	10.6	8.2
Less than 1 day - Moins de 1 jour	177	104	73	2.5	2.9	2.1
1 - 6 days - 1 - 6 jours	180	107	73	2.5	2.9	2.1
7 - 27 days - 7 - 27 jours	127	71	56	1.8	2.0	1.6
7 - 13 days - 7 - 13 jours	65	41	24	0.9	1.1	♦0.7
14 - 20 days - 14 - 20 jours	40	19	21	0.6	♦0.5	♦0.6
21 - 27 days - 21 - 27 jours	22	11	11	♦0.3	♦0.3	♦0.3
28 days - 11 months - 28 jours - 11 mois	160	93	67	2.3	2.6	1.9
28 days - less than 2 months - 28 jours - moins de 2 mois	26	21	5	♦0.4	♦0.6	♦0.1
2 months - 2 mois	27	12	15	♦0.4	♦0.3	♦0.4
3 months - 3 mois	30	14	16	0.4	♦0.4	♦0.5
4 months - 4 mois	16	10	6	♦0.2	♦0.3	♦0.2
5 months - 5 mois	17	13	4	♦0.2	♦0.4	♦0.1
6 months - 6 mois	15	4	11	♦0.2	♦0.1	♦0.3
7 months - 7 mois	4	2	2	♦0.1	♦0.1	♦0.1
8 months - 8 mois	8	7	1	♦0.1	♦0.2	-
9 months - 9 mois	7	4	3	♦0.1	♦0.1	♦0.1
10 months - 10 mois	4	1	3	♦0.1	-	♦0.1
11 months - 11 mois	6	5	1	♦0.1	♦0.1	-
Unknown - Inconnu	27	12	15	♦0.4	♦0.3	♦0.4

FOOTNOTES - NOTES

Italics: data from civil registers which are incomplete or of unknown completeness. - Italiques: données incomplètes ou dont le degré d'exactitude n'est pas connu, provenant des registres de l'état civil.

♦ Rates based on 30 or fewer infant deaths. — Taux basés sur 30 décès d'enfants ou moins.

* Provisional. - Données provisoires.

'Code' indicates the source of data, as follows:
C - Civil registration, estimated over 90% complete
U - Civil registration, estimated less than 90% complete
| - Other source, estimated reliable
+ - Data tabulated by date of registration rather than occurence.
... - Information not available

Le 'Code' indique la source des données, comme suit:
C - Registres de l'état civil considérés complèts à 90 p. 100 au moins.
U - Registres de l'état civil qui ne sont pas considérés complèts à 90 p. 100 au moins.
| - Autre source, considérée pas douteuses.
+ - Données exploitées selon la date de l'enregistrement et non la date de l'événement.
... - Information pas disponible.

Table 17

Table 17 presents maternal deaths and maternal mortality ratios for as many years available between 1999 and 2008.

Description of variables: Maternal deaths are defined for the purposes of the Demographic Yearbook as those caused by deliveries and complications of pregnancy, childbirth and the puerperium, within 42 days of termination of pregnancy. They are usually defined as deaths coded "38-41" for ICD-9 Basic Tabulation List or as deaths coded "A34", "O00-O95", "O98-O99" for ICD-10, respectively. However, data for ICD-10 shown in this table include deaths due to "O96" and "O97" which refer to deaths from any obstetric cause occurring more than 42 days but less than one year after delivery and death from sequelae of direct obstetric causes occurring one year or more after delivery.

For further information on the definition of maternal mortality from the tenth revisions of the *International Statistical Classification of Diseases and Related Health Problems*[1], see also section 4.3 of the Technical Notes.

Statistics on maternal death presented in this table are provided by the World Health Organisation. They are limited to countries or areas that meet the criterion that cause-of-death statistics are either classified by or convertible to the ninth or tenth revisions mentioned above. Data that are classified by the tenth revision are set in bold in the table.

Ratios computation: Maternal mortality ratios are the annual number of maternal deaths per 100 000 live births (table 9) in the same year. These ratios have been calculated by the Statistics Division of the United Nations. If maternal mortality data are considered incomplete, or if live birth data for the year are not available, no ratio has been calculated. Ratios based on 30 or fewer maternal deaths are identified by the symbol "♦".

Reliability of data: Countries and areas that have incomplete (less than 90 per cent completeness) or of unknown completeness of cause of deaths data coverage are considered to provide unreliable data, which are set in *italics* rather than in roman type. Ratios on these data are not computed. Information on completeness is normally provided by the World Health Organisation. When this is not the case, information on completeness is set to coincide with that of table 18. Similarly, the reliability of data for the completeness of cause of death is provided by the World Health Organisation[2] and it may differ from the reliability of data for the total number of reported deaths. Therefore, there are cases when the quality code in table 18 does not correspond with the typeface used in this table.

Territorial composition as set in Section 2.2 of "Technical Notes on the Statistical Tables", including or excluding certain population of a country refers only to the denominator.

Limitations: Statistics on maternal deaths are subject to the same qualifications that have been set forth for vital statistics in general and death statistics in particular as discussed in section 4 of the Technical Notes. The reliability of the data, an indication of which is described above, is an important factor in considering the limitations. In addition, maternal-death statistics are subject to all the qualifications relating to cause-of-death statistics. These have been set forth in section 4 of the Technical Notes.

Maternal mortality ratios are subject to the limitations of the data on live births with which they have been calculated. These have been set forth in the technical notes for table 9. Specific information pertaining to individual countries or areas is given in the footnotes to table 9.

The calculation of the maternal mortality ratios based on the total number of live births approximates the risk of dying from complications of pregnancy, childbirth or puerperium. Ideally this rate should be based on the number of women exposed to the risk of pregnancy, in other words, the number of women conceiving. Since it is impossible to know how many women have conceived, the total number of live births is used in calculating this rate.

Earlier data: Maternal deaths and maternal mortality rates have been shown in previous issues of the *Demographic Yearbook*. For information on specific years covered, the reader should consult the Index.

It should however be noted that in issues prior to 1975, maternal mortality rates were calculated using the female population rather than live births. Therefore, maternal mortality ratios published since 1975 are not comparable to the earlier maternal death rates.

NOTES

[1] *International Statistical Classification of Diseases and Related Health Problems*, Tenth Revision, Volume 2, World Health Organization, Geneva, 1992.
[2] For more information on specific method used for countries, see "Mathers CD, Bernard C, Iburg KM, Inoue M, Ma Fat D, Shibuya K et al. *Global burden of disease in 2002: data sources, methods and results*. Geneva, World Health Organization, 2003 (GPE Discussion Paper No. 54).

Tableau 17

Le tableau 17 présente des statistiques et des taux de mortalité liée à la maternité pour les années disponibles entre 1999 et 2008.

Description des variables : aux fins de *l'Annuaire démographique*, les décès liés à la maternité sont ceux entraînés par l'accouchement ou les complications de la grossesse, de l'accouchement et des suites de couches dans un délai de 42 jours après la terminaison de la grossesse. Ils sont généralement associés aux codes 38 à 41 dans le cas de la liste de base pour la mise en tableaux de la CIM-9 et aux codes A34, O00 à O95 et O98 et O99 dans le cas de la CIM-10. Les statistiques associées à des codes correspondant à la CIM-10 englobent des décès de type O96 et O97, qui désignent les décès liés à des causes obstétriques se produisant après 42 jours mais moins d'un an après l'accouchement et les décès entraînés par les séquelles de complications obstétriques directes qui se produisent un an ou plus après l'accouchement.

Pour plus de précisions concernant les définitions de la mortalité liée à la maternité dans la dixième révision de la *Classification statistique internationale des maladies et des problèmes de santé connexes*[1], se reporter également à la section 4.3 des Notes techniques.

Les statistiques de mortalité liée à la maternité présentées dans le tableau 17 émanent de l'Organisation mondiale de la santé. Elles ne se rapportent qu'aux pays ou zones qui répondent aux critères selon lesquels les statistiques relatives à la cause des décès sont conformes à la liste de la neuvième ou de la dixième révision de la CIM ou peuvent être aisément comparées aux catégories de cette liste. Les données conformes à la dixième révision sont indiquées en gras dans le tableau.

Calcul des taux : les taux de mortalité maternelle représentent le nombre annuel de décès dus à la maternité pour 100 000 naissances vivantes (données du tableau 9) de la même année. Ces taux ont été calculés par la Division de statistique de l'ONU. Si les données des décès dus à la maternité sont incomplètes ou si les naissances vivantes pour l'année ne sont pas disponibles, les taux ne sont pas calculés. Les taux fondés sur 30 décès liés à la maternité ou moins sont signalés par le signe "♦".

Fiabilité des données : les statistiques relatives aux pays et aux zones pour lesquels la couverture des données concernant les causes de décès est incomplète (mois de 90 pour cent) ou dont le degré de complétude n'est pas connue sont jugés douteuses et apparaissent en *italique* et non en caractères romains. Les taux correspondant ne sont pas calculés. L'information sur la complétude est normalement fournie par l'Organisation Mondiale de la Santé. Si ce n'est pas le cas, l'information sur la complétude est reprise de tableau 18. De même, la fiabilité des données relatives aux causes de décès est fournie par l'Organisation Mondiale de la Santé[2] et peut différer de la fiabilité des données relatives au nombre de décès enregistrés. En conséquence, il peut apparaître de différences entre les codes de fiabilité du tableau 18 et du présent tableau.

La composition territoriale est définie dans la Section 2.2 des "Notes Techniques sur les tableaux statistiques". L'inclusion ou l'exclusion de certaines populations d'un pays ne concerne que le dénominateur.

Insuffisance des données : les statistiques de la mortalité liée à la maternité appellent toutes les réserves qui ont été formulées à propos des statistiques de l'état civil en général et des statistiques relatives à la mortalité en particulier (voir la section 4 des Notes techniques). La fiabilité des données, au sujet de laquelle des indications ont été fournies plus haut, est un facteur important. En outre, les statistiques de la mortalité liée à la maternité appellent les mêmes réserves que celles exposées à la section 4 des Notes techniques en ce qui concerne les statistiques des causes de décès.

Les taux de mortalité maternelle appellent également toutes les réserves formulées à propos des statistiques des naissances vivantes qui ont servi à leur calcul (voir à ce sujet les notes techniques relatives au tableau 9). Des précisions sur certains pays ou zones sont données dans les notes se rapportant au tableau 9.

En prenant le nombre total des naissances vivantes comme base pour le calcul des taux de mortalité maternelle, on obtient une mesure approximative de la probabilité de décès dus aux complications de la grossesse, de l'accouchement et des suites de couches. Idéalement, ces taux devraient être calculés sur la base du nombre de femmes exposées aux risques liés à la grossesse, c'est-à-dire sur la base du nombre de femmes qui conçoivent. Étant donné qu'il est impossible de connaître le nombre de femmes ayant conçu, c'est le nombre total de naissances vivantes que l'on utilise pour calculer ces taux.

Données publiées antérieurement : des statistiques concernant les décès liés à la maternité (nombre de décès et taux) ont déjà été présentées dans des éditions antérieures de l'*Annuaire démographique*. Pour plus de précisions concernant les années pour lesquelles ces données ont été publiées, se reporter à l'index.

Il faut souligner que, avant 1975, les taux de mortalité maternelle étaient calculés sur la base de la population féminine et non sur celle du nombre de naissances vivantes. Ils ne sont donc pas comparables à ceux qui figurent dans les éditions de l'*Annuaire démographique* parues après 1975.

NOTES

[1] *Classification statistique internationale des maladies et des problèmes de santé connexes*, dixième révision, volume 2. Genève, Organisation mondiale de la santé, 1992.

[2] Pour plus d'information sur les méthodes spécifiques utilisées pour les pays, voir "Mathers CD, Bernard C, Iburg KM, Inoue M, Ma Fat D, Shibuya K et al. *Global burden of disease in 2002: data sources, methods and results*. Geneva, World Health Organization, 2003 (GPE Discussion Paper No. 54).

17. Maternal deaths and maternal mortality ratios: 1999 - 2008
Mortalité liée à la maternité, nombre de décès et taux : 1999 - 2008

Continent and country or area / Continent et pays ou zone	Code[a]	1999	2000	2001	2002	2003	2004	2005	2006	2007	2008
AFRICA - AFRIQUE											
Egypt - Égypte											
Number - Nombre	U	...	492	...	...	...	...	...	...	...	449
Mauritius - Maurice											
Number - Nombre	+C	7	3	4	1	4	3	4	3	6	6
Rate - Taux	+C	♦34.5	♦14.8	♦20.3	♦5.0	♦20.7	♦15.6	♦21.3	♦17.0	♦35.2	♦36.6
Réunion											
Number - Nombre	...	...	...	-	3	3	4	4	5	...	...
Seychelles											
Number - Nombre	+C	...	...	-	1	1	-	1	...	...	...
Rate - Taux	+C	...	...	-	♦67.5	♦66.8	-	♦65.1	...	...	...
South Africa - Afrique du Sud											
Number - Nombre	U	693	737	854	794	898	1 158	1 249	1 388	1 762	...
AMERICA, NORTH - AMÉRIQUE DU NORD											
Anguilla											
Number - Nombre	+...	...	-	-	...	-	-	...	...	...	...
Antigua and Barbuda - Antigua-et-Barbuda											
Number - Nombre	+U	...	-	-	-	-	-	-	...	...	...
Aruba											
Number - Nombre	...	-	...	...	...	...	1	...	...	...	...
Bahamas											
Number - Nombre	...	1[1]	2[1]	...	...	...	2[1]	4[2]	...	...	...
Rate - Taux	...	...	...	...	...	...	...	♦72.1	...	...	...
Barbados - Barbade											
Number - Nombre	C	...	1	-	...	...	...	...	...	...	...
Rate - Taux	C	...	♦26.6	-	...	...	...	...	...	...	...
Belize											
Number - Nombre	...	3[1]	5[1]	3[1]	...	...	3[1]	10[2]	...	...	...
Rate - Taux	...	...	...	...	...	...	...	♦119.1	...	...	...
Bermuda - Bermudes											
Number - Nombre	...	-	...	...	...	-	-	1	...	...	
British Virgin Islands - Îles Vierges britanniques											
Number - Nombre	...	-	-	-	-	...	...	...	...	...	
Canada											
Number - Nombre	C	8	11	26	15	23	20	...	...	...	...
Rate - Taux	C	♦2.4	♦3.4	♦7.8	♦4.6	♦6.9	♦5.9	...	...	...	...
Cayman Islands - Îles Caïmanes											
Number - Nombre	...	-	1	...	...	...	-	...	...	...	...
Costa Rica											
Number - Nombre	...	15[3]	28[3]	24[3]	27[3]	24[3]	25[3]	24[3]	24[4]	...	...
Rate - Taux	...	...	...	...	...	...	...	...	♦33.7	...	...
Cuba											
Number - Nombre	C	66	58	57	65	62	56	66	62	42	...
Rate - Taux	C	43.8	40.4	41.1	46.0	45.3	44.0	54.7	55.7	37.3	...
Dominica - Dominique											
Number - Nombre	+C	-	-	1	1	-	-	-	-	...	...
Rate - Taux	+C	-	-	♦82.2	♦92.5	-	-	-	-	...	...
Dominican Republic - République dominicaine											
Number - Nombre	U	69	51	64	...	58	85	...	...	...	...
El Salvador											
Number - Nombre	+U	23	31	28	32	27	22	23	21	...	...
Grenada - Grenade											
Number - Nombre	U	...	...	-	1	...	-	-	...	-	...
Guadeloupe											
Number - Nombre	...	...	3	2	6	4	3	1	2	...	...
Guatemala											
Number - Nombre	U	316	346	278	280	293	296	354	298	...	...
Haiti - Haïti											
Number - Nombre	...	156	...	180	135	124	...	...	...	...	...
Martinique											
Number - Nombre	...	...	2	1	2	2	1	-	1	...	...

Continent and country or area / Continent et pays ou zone	Code[a]	1999	2000	2001	2002	2003	2004	2005	2006	2007	2008
AMERICA, NORTH - AMÉRIQUE DU NORD											
Mexico - Mexique											
Number - Nombre	+C	1 411	1 325	1 268	1 324	1 332	1 266	1 269	1 188	1 122	...
Rate - Taux	+C	62.9	57.6	56.9	59.9	61.5	58.7	59.3	55.2	51.3	
Montserrat											
Number - Nombre	+...	-	1	-	-	-	-	-	-	...	
Nicaragua											
Number - Nombre	+U	138	97	124	114	88	108	93	...	...	
Panama											
Number - Nombre	+U	31	30	37	38	34	23	...	36		
Puerto Rico - Porto Rico											
Number - Nombre	+...	10	14	6	5	8	...	5	...	...	
Saint Kitts and Nevis - Saint-Kitts-et-Nevis											
Number - Nombre	+C	-	-	2	-	2	-	-	1	...	...
Rate - Taux	+C	-	-	♦249.1	...	...	...	...	...	...	...
Saint Lucia - Sainte-Lucie											
Number - Nombre	C	1	3	1	1	...	...	...	...	...	...
Rate - Taux	C	♦33.4	♦103.3	♦35.9	♦38.5	...	...	...	...	...	...
Saint Pierre and Miquelon - Saint-Pierre-et-Miquelon											
Number - Nombre	...							-	-	...	
Saint Vincent and the Grenadines - Saint-Vincent-et-les Grenadines											
Number - Nombre	+C	1	1	-	-	-	1	...	...	...	
Rate - Taux	+C	♦46.1	♦46.5	-	-	-	♦55.4	...	...	...	
Trinidad and Tobago - Trinité-et-Tobago											
Number - Nombre	C	7	10	7	5	...	...	...	...	...	
Rate - Taux	C	♦38.2	♦55.1	♦38.7	♦29.4	...	...	...	...	...	
Turks and Caicos Islands - Îles Turques et Caïques											
Number - Nombre	...	-	-	1	-	1	1	-	...	...	
United States of America - États-Unis d'Amérique											
Number - Nombre	C	406	404	416	379	545	697	760	...	...	...
Rate - Taux	C	10.3	10.0	10.3	9.4	13.3	17.0	18.4	...	...	...
United States Virgin Islands - Îles Vierges américaines											
Number - Nombre	...	-	1	2	-	-	-	-	...	...	
AMERICA, SOUTH - AMÉRIQUE DU SUD											
Argentina - Argentine											
Number - Nombre	+C	287	245	309	356	321	313	290	341	332	...
Rate - Taux	+C	41.8	34.9	45.2	51.2	46.0	42.5	40.7	49.0	47.4	...
Brazil - Brésil											
Number - Nombre	U	1 823	1 648	1 587	1 648	1 597	1 672	1 661	...	...	
Chile - Chili											
Number - Nombre	C	60	49	45	42	33	42	48	...	...	
Rate - Taux	C	23.9	19.7	18.3	17.6	14.1	18.2	20.8	...	...	
Colombia - Colombie											
Number - Nombre	...		676[1]	776[1]	689[1]	577[1]	...	546[1]	504[1]	519[2]	...	
Rate - Taux	...		...	...	...	...	...	...	...	72.6	...	
Ecuador - Équateur											
Number - Nombre	U	209	232	187	149	139	129	143	135	...	
French Guiana - Guyane française											
Number - Nombre	...	...	...	2	2	1	1	1	1	...	
Guyana											
Number - Nombre	U	17	...	17	20	21	19	24	...	...	
Paraguay											
Number - Nombre	+U	103	140	132	163	150	154	135	123	...	
Peru - Pérou											
Number - Nombre	+U	261	263	...	...	...	...	...	...	...	...

Continent and country or area / Continent et pays ou zone	Code[a]	1999	2000	2001	2002	2003	2004	2005	2006	2007	2008
AMERICA, SOUTH - AMÉRIQUE DU SUD											
Suriname											
Number - Nombre	U	4	9	...	...	...	7	4	...	...	...
Uruguay											
Number - Nombre	C	6	9	19	...	...	9	...	...	...	...
Rate - Taux	C	♦11.1	♦17.1	♦36.6	...	...	♦18.0	...	...	...	...
Venezuela (Bolivarian Republic of) - Venezuela (République bolivarienne du)											
Number - Nombre	C	313	327	356	335	321	318	351	...	332	...
Rate - Taux	C	59.3	60.1	67.2	68.0	57.8	49.9	52.7	...	54.0	...
ASIA - ASIE											
Armenia - Arménie											
Number - Nombre	U	12	18	7	3	8	...	...	10	...	...
Azerbaijan - Azerbaïdjan											
Number - Nombre	U	51	44	27	22	21	34	...	...	30	...
Bahrain - Bahreïn											
Number - Nombre	C	3	2	3	...	...	...	...	...	...	...
Rate - Taux	C	♦21.0	♦14.3	♦22.3	...	...	...	...	...	...	...
Brunei Darussalam - Brunéi Darussalam											
Number - Nombre	+C	-	2	...	...	...	...	...	...	...	...
Rate - Taux	+C	-	♦26.7	...	...	...	...	...	...	...	...
China, Hong Kong SAR - Chine, Hong Kong RAS											
Number - Nombre	...	1	3	1	1	2	2	2	1	1	...
Cyprus - Chypre											
Number - Nombre	C	-	-	...	...	...	-	2	1	-	...
Rate - Taux	C	-	-	...	...	...	-	♦24.3	♦11.5	-	...
Georgia - Géorgie											
Number - Nombre	U	9	4	4	...	...	...	...	...	...	...
Israel - Israël											
Number - Nombre	C	9	5	9	6	3	6	4	11	...	...
Rate - Taux	C	♦6.8	♦3.7	♦6.6	♦4.3	♦2.1	♦4.1	♦2.8	♦7.4	...	...
Japan - Japon											
Number - Nombre	C	79	84	79	90	74	56	66	63	39	41
Rate - Taux	C	6.7	7.1	6.7	7.8	6.6	5.0	6.2	5.8	3.6	3.8
Kazakhstan											
Number - Nombre	U	98	94	87	80	67	63	81	100	107	86
Kuwait - Koweït											
Number - Nombre	C	3	2	1	3	...	...	...	...	...	5
Rate - Taux	C	♦7.3	♦4.8	♦2.4	♦6.9	...	...	...	...	...	♦9.2
Kyrgyzstan - Kirghizstan											
Number - Nombre	U	44	44	43	54	52	56	66	67	64	...
Maldives											
Number - Nombre	+U	...	4	3	7	-	2	1	...	...	...
Republic of Korea - République de Corée											
Number - Nombre	C	77	62	70	71	58	59	53	54	...	...
Rate - Taux	C	12.5	9.8	12.6	14.4	11.8	12.5	12.2	12.0	...	...
Singapore - Singapour											
Number - Nombre	+U	2	8	4	4	2	1	4	3	...	...
Tajikistan - Tadjikistan											
Number - Nombre	U	45	36	40	57	36	37	28	...	...	...
Thailand - Thaïlande											
Number - Nombre	+U	93	102	...	114	...	...	...	92	...	...
Uzbekistan - Ouzbékistan											
Number - Nombre	U	80	182	...	143	151	156	145	...	...	...
EUROPE											
Albania - Albanie											
Number - Nombre	U	2	8	2	5	1	1	...	...	...	...

Continent and country or area / Continent et pays ou zone	Code[a]	1999	2000	2001	2002	2003	2004	2005	2006	2007	2008
EUROPE											
Austria - Autriche											
Number - Nombre	C	1	2	5	2	2	3	3	2	3	2
Rate - Taux	C	♦1.3	♦2.6	♦6.6	♦2.6	♦2.6	♦3.8	♦3.8	♦2.6	♦3.9	♦2.6
Belarus - Bélarus											
Number - Nombre	C	19	20	13	17	18	...	...	...	7	...
Rate - Taux	C	♦20.4	♦21.3	♦14.2	♦19.2	♦20.3	...	...	...	♦6.8	...
Belgium - Belgique											
Number - Nombre	C	...	...	...	...	...	1	...	...	...	...
Rate - Taux	C	...	...	...	...	...	♦0.9	...	...	...	...
Bulgaria - Bulgarie											
Number - Nombre	C	16	13	13	11	4	7	8	5	8	5
Rate - Taux	C	♦22.1	♦17.6	♦19.1	♦16.5	♦5.9	♦10.0	♦11.3	♦6.8	♦10.6	♦6.4
Croatia - Croatie											
Number - Nombre	C	5	3	1	4	3	3	3	4	6	3
Rate - Taux	C	♦11.1	♦6.9	♦2.4	♦10.0	♦7.6	♦7.4	♦7.1	♦9.7	♦14.3	♦6.9
Czech Republic - République tchèque											
Number - Nombre	C	6	5	3	3	4	5	3	9	3	7
Rate - Taux	C	♦6.7	♦5.5	♦3.3	♦3.1	♦4.3	♦5.1	♦2.9	♦8.5	♦2.6	♦5.9
Denmark - Danemark											
Number - Nombre	C	4	-	2	...	...	-	-	5	...	...
Rate - Taux	C	♦6.0	-	♦3.1	...	...	-	-	♦7.7	...	...
Estonia - Estonie											
Number - Nombre	C	2	5	1	1	4	4	2	1	-	-
Rate - Taux	C	♦16.1	♦38.3	♦7.9	♦7.7	♦30.7	♦28.6	♦13.9	♦6.7	-	-
Finland - Finlande											
Number - Nombre	C	2	3	3	3	2	7	3	4	1	5
Rate - Taux	C	♦3.5	♦5.3	♦5.3	♦5.4	♦3.5	♦12.1	♦5.2	♦6.8	♦1.7	♦8.4
France											
Number - Nombre	C	55	50	56	67	56	53	41	59	60	...
Rate - Taux	C	7.4	6.5	7.3	8.8	7.4	6.9	5.3	7.4	7.6	...
Germany - Allemagne											
Number - Nombre	C	37	43	27	21	30	37	28	41	...	...
Rate - Taux	C	4.8	5.6	♦3.7	♦2.9	♦4.2	5.2	♦4.1	6.1	...	...
Greece - Grèce											
Number - Nombre	C	6	-	4	1	2	3	-	3	2	-
Rate - Taux	C	♦6.0	-	♦3.9	♦1.0	♦1.9	♦2.8	-	♦2.7	♦1.8	-
Hungary - Hongrie											
Number - Nombre	C	4	10	5	8	7	4	5	8	8	17
Rate - Taux	C	♦4.2	♦10.2	♦5.2	♦8.3	♦7.4	♦4.2	♦5.1	♦8.0	♦8.2	♦17.1
Iceland - Islande											
Number - Nombre	C	-	-	1	-	-	-	-	-	-	-
Rate - Taux	C	-	-	♦24.4	-	-	-	-	-	-	-
Ireland - Irlande											
Number - Nombre	...	1	1	3	5	-	1	2	-	1	2
Rate - Taux	...	♦1.9	♦1.8	♦5.2	♦8.3	-	♦1.6	♦3.3	-	♦1.4	♦2.7
Italy - Italie											
Number - Nombre	C	14	16	11	17	28	...	...	11	13	...
Rate - Taux	C	♦2.6	♦2.9	♦2.1	♦3.2	♦5.1	...	...	♦2.0	♦2.3	...
Latvia - Lettonie											
Number - Nombre	+C	8	5	5	1	3	2	1	2	6	2
Rate - Taux	+C	♦41.2	♦24.7	♦25.4	♦5.0	♦14.3	♦9.8	♦4.7	♦9.0	♦25.8	♦8.4
Lithuania - Lituanie											
Number - Nombre	+C	5	3	4	6	1	5	4	-	2	3
Rate - Taux	+C	♦13.7	♦8.8	♦12.7	♦20.0	♦3.3	♦16.4	♦13.1	-	♦6.2	♦8.6
Luxembourg											
Number - Nombre	+C	-	1	-	-	-	1	1	-	...	...
Rate - Taux	+C	-	♦17.5	-	-	-	♦18.3	♦18.6	-	...	...
Malta - Malte											
Number - Nombre	+C	1	-	2	-	-	-	-	-	-	1
Rate - Taux	+C	♦22.7	-	♦50.5	-	-	-	-	-	-	♦24.2
Netherlands - Pays-Bas											
Number - Nombre	+C	19	18	14	20	8	10	16	15	9	8
Rate - Taux	+C	♦9.5	♦8.7	♦6.9	♦9.9	♦4.0	♦5.2	♦8.5	♦8.1	♦5.0	♦4.3
Norway - Norvège											
Number - Nombre	+C	5	2	3	2	7	-	2	5	4	...
Rate - Taux	+C	♦8.4	♦3.4	♦5.3	♦3.6	♦12.4	-	♦3.5	♦8.5	♦6.8	...

17. Maternal deaths and maternal mortality ratios: 1999 - 2008
Mortalité liée à la maternité, nombre de décès et taux : 1999 - 2008 (continued - suite)

Continent and country or area / Continent et pays ou zone	Code[a]	1999	2000	2001	2002	2003	2004	2005	2006	2007	2008
EUROPE											
Poland - Pologne											
Number - Nombre	C	20	30	13	19	14	17	11	11	11	19
Rate - Taux	C	♦5.2	♦7.9	♦3.5	♦5.4	♦4.0	♦4.8	♦3.0	♦2.9	♦2.8	♦4.6
Portugal											
Number - Nombre	+C	6	3	6	8	8	...	...	...	...	...
Rate - Taux	+C	♦5.2	♦2.5	♦5.3	♦7.0	♦7.1	...	...	...	...	...
Republic of Moldova - République de Moldova											
Number - Nombre	...	11[3]	10[3]	16[3]	11[3]	8[3]	9[3]	8[3]	6[3]	7[3]	17[4]
Rate - Taux	...	...	...	...	...	...	...	...	...	...	♦43.6
Romania - Roumanie											
Number - Nombre	+C	98	75	75	47	65	52	37	34	33	30
Rate - Taux	+C	41.8	32.0	34.0	22.3	30.6	24.0	16.7	15.5	15.4	♦13.5
Russian Federation - Fédération de Russie											
Number - Nombre	+C	537[5]	503[5]	479[5]	469[5]	463[5]	352	370	352	...	...
Rate - Taux	+C	44.2	39.7	36.5	33.6	31.3	23.4	25.4	23.8	...	...
San Marino - Saint-Marin											
Number - Nombre	+U	-	-	...	-	...	...	-	...	...	...
Serbia - Serbie											
Number - Nombre	+U	...	...	...	...	...	2	10	9	-	4
Slovakia - Slovaquie											
Number - Nombre	C	5	1	7	4	2	3	2	...	...	...
Rate - Taux	C	♦8.9	♦1.8	♦13.7	♦7.9	♦3.9	♦5.6	♦3.7	...	...	...
Slovenia - Slovénie											
Number - Nombre	C	2	2	3	-	-	2	1	3	3	2
Rate - Taux	C	♦11.4	♦11.0	♦17.2	-	-	♦11.1	♦5.5	♦15.8	♦15.1	♦9.2
Spain - Espagne											
Number - Nombre	C	14	14	17	14	20	21	18	...	...	...
Rate - Taux	C	♦3.7	♦3.5	♦4.2	♦3.3	♦4.5	♦4.6	♦3.9	...	...	...
Sweden - Suède											
Number - Nombre	C	1	4	3	4	2	2	6	5	2	...
Rate - Taux	C	♦1.1	♦4.4	♦3.3	♦4.2	♦2.0	♦2.0	♦5.9	♦4.7	♦1.9	...
Switzerland - Suisse											
Number - Nombre	C	6	5	1	3	4	4	4	6	1	...
Rate - Taux	C	♦7.7	♦6.4	♦1.4	♦4.1	♦5.6	♦5.5	♦5.5	♦8.2	♦1.3	...
TFYR of Macedonia - L'ex-R. y. de Macédoine											
Number - Nombre	C	2	4	4	3	1	...	...	...	...	...
Rate - Taux	C	♦7.3	♦13.6	♦14.8	♦10.8	♦3.7	...	...	...	...	...
Ukraine											
Number - Nombre	C	98	95	90	85	71	56	75	70	...	...
Rate - Taux	C	25.2	24.7	23.9	21.8	17.4	13.1	17.6	15.2	...	...
United Kingdom of Great Britain and Northern Ireland - Royaume-Uni de Grande-Bretagne et d'Irlande du Nord											
Number - Nombre	+C	37	46	50	40	53	55	51	50	56	...
Rate - Taux	+C	5.3	6.8	7.5	6.0	7.6	7.7	7.1	6.7	7.3	...
OCEANIA - OCÉANIE											
Australia - Australie											
Number - Nombre	C	13	13	12	13	8	12	...	9	...	...
Rate - Taux	C	♦5.2	♦5.2	♦4.9	♦5.2	♦3.2	♦4.7	...	♦3.4	...	...
Fiji - Fidji											
Number - Nombre	+U	-	...	...	...	...	...	...	...	...	...
Kiribati											
Number - Nombre	U	1	-	1	...	...	...	...	...	...	...
New Zealand - Nouvelle-Zélande											
Number - Nombre	+C	4	5	3	8	4	4	6	9	...	...
Rate - Taux	+C	♦7.0	♦8.8	♦5.4	♦14.8	♦7.1	♦6.9	♦10.4	♦15.2	...	...

FOOTNOTES - NOTES

Data in bold refer to maternal deaths based on ICD-10 Classification, otherwise data refer to maternal deaths based on ICD-9 Classification. - Les données en typographie gras se rapportent aux décès maternelles basées sur la classification CIM-10, autrement les données se rapportent aux décès maternelles basées sur la classification CIM-9.

Italics: data from civil registers which are incomplete or of unknown completeness. - Italiques : données incomplètes ou dont le degré d'exactitude n'est pas connu, provenant des registres de l'état civil.

* Provisional. - Données provisoires.

♦ Rates based on 30 or fewer deaths. - Taux basés sur 30 décès ou moins.

a 'Code' indicates the source of data, as follows:
C - Civil registration, estimated over 90% complete
U - Civil registration, estimated less than 90% complete
| - Other source, estimated reliable
+ - Data tabulated by date of registration rather than occurence
... - Information not available

Le 'Code' indique la source des données, comme suit :
C - Registres de l'état civil considérés complèts à 90 p. 100 au moins
U - Registres de l'état civil qui ne sont pas considérés complèts à 90 p. 100 au moins
| - Autre source, considérée pas douteuses
+ - Données exploitées selon la date de l'enregistrement et non la date de l'événement
... - Information pas disponible

1 The code is U. - Le code est U.
2 The code is C. - Le code est C.
3 The code is +U. - Le code est +U.
4 The code is +C. - Le code est +C.
5 For 2003 and before, data on cause of death do not include the Chechnya region. Therefore, rates must be used with caution as they are based on the total population, which is assumed to include all regions. - Pour 2003 et avant, les données sur les causes de décès ne comprennent par la région de Chechnya. Par conséquent, les taux doivent être utilisés avec précaution car ils sont basés sur la population totale, qui est supposée inclure toutes les régions.

Table 18

Table 18 presents deaths and crude death rates by urban/rural residence for as many years as possible between 2006 and 2010.

Description of variables: Death is defined as the permanent disappearance of all evidence of life at any time after live birth has taken place (post-natal cessation of vital functions without capability of resuscitation).

Statistics on the number of deaths are obtained from civil registers unless otherwise noted. For those countries or areas where civil registration statistics on deaths are considered reliable (estimated completeness of 90 per cent or more), the death rates shown have been calculated on the basis of registered deaths.

The urban/rural classification of deaths is that provided by each country or area; it is presumed to be based on the national census definitions of urban population that have been set forth at the end of the technical notes for table 6.

For certain countries, there is a discrepancy between the total number of deaths shown in this table and those shown in subsequent tables for the same year. Usually this discrepancy arises because the total number of deaths occurring in a given year is revised although the remaining tabulations are not.

Rate computation: Crude death rates are the annual number of deaths per 1 000 mid-year population.

Rates by urban/rural residence are the annual number of deaths, in the appropriate urban or rural category, per 1 000 corresponding mid-year population. These rates are calculated by the Statistics Division of the United Nations based on the appropriate reference population (for example: total population, nationals only etc.) if known and available. If the reference population is not known or unavailable the total population is used to calculate the rates. Therefore, if the population that is used to calculate the rates is different from the correct reference population, the rates presented might under- or overstate the true situation in a country or area.

Rates presented in this table are limited to those countries or areas with a minimum number of 30 deaths in a given year.

Reliability of data: Each country or area has been asked to indicate the estimated completeness of the deaths recorded in its civil register. These national assessments are indicated by the quality codes "C", "U" and "|" that appear in the first column of this table. "C" indicates that the data are estimated to be virtually complete, that is, representing at least 90 per cent of the deaths occurring each year, while "U" indicates that data are estimated to be incomplete that is, representing less than 90 per cent of the deaths occurring each year. The code "|" indicates that the source of data is different than civil registration and is explained by a footnote. The code "..." indicates that no information was provided regarding completeness or no assessment has been done in the country.

Data from civil registers that are reported as incomplete or of unknown completeness (code "U" or "...") are considered unreliable. They appear in italics in this table; rates based on these data are not computed.

Limitations: Statistics on deaths are subject to the same qualifications as have been set forth for vital statistics in general and death statistics in particular as discussed in section 4 of the Introduction.

The reliability of the data, an indication of which is described above, is an important factor in considering the limitations. In addition, some deaths are tabulated by date of registration and not by date of occurrence; these have been indicated with a plus sign "+". Whenever the lag between the date of occurrence and date of registration is prolonged and, therefore, a large proportion of the death registrations are delayed, death statistics for any given year may be seriously affected. However, delays in the registration of deaths are less common and shorter than in the registration of live births.

International comparability in mortality statistics may also be affected by the exclusion of deaths of infants who were born alive but died before the registration of the birth or within the first 24 hours of life. Statistics of this type are footnoted.

In addition, it should be noted that rates are affected also by the quality and limitations of the population estimates that are used in their computation. The problems of under-enumeration or over-enumeration and,

to some extent, the differences in definition of total population have been discussed in section 3 of the Introduction dealing with population data in general, and specific information pertaining to individual countries or areas is given in the footnotes to table 3.

Estimated rates based directly on the results of sample surveys are subject to considerable error as a result of omissions in reporting deaths or as a result of erroneous reporting of those that occurred outside the period of reference. However, such rates do have the advantage of having a "built-in" and corresponding base.

It should be emphasized that crude death rates -- like other crude rates, such as of birth, marriage and divorce -- may be seriously affected by the age-sex structure of the populations to which they relate. Nevertheless, they do provide a simple measure of the level and changes in mortality.

The comparability of data by urban/rural residence is affected by the national definitions of urban and rural used in tabulating these data. It is assumed, in the absence of specific information to the contrary, that the definitions of urban and rural used in connection with the national population census were also used in the compilation of the vital statistics for each country or area. However, it cannot be excluded that, for a given country or area, different definitions of urban and rural are used for the vital statistics data and the population census data respectively. When known, the definitions of urban used in national population censuses are presented at the end of the technical notes for table 6. As discussed in detail in the technical notes for table 6, these definitions vary considerably from one country or area to another.

In addition to problems of comparability, vital rates classified by urban/rural residence are also subject to certain types of bias. If, when calculating vital rates, different definitions of urban are used in connection with the vital events and the population data and if this results in a net difference between the numerator and denominator of the rate in the population at risk, then the vital rates would be biased. Urban/rural differentials in vital rates may also be affected by whether the vital events have been tabulated in terms of place of occurrence or place of usual residence. This problem is discussed in more detail in section 4.1.4.1 of the Introduction.

Earlier data: Deaths and crude death rates have been shown in each issue of the Demographic Yearbook. For information on specific years covered, the reader should consult the Index.

Tableau 18

Le tableau 18 présente le nombre des décès et les taux bruts de mortalité selon le lieu de résidence (zone urbaine ou rurale) pour le plus grand nombre d'années possible entre 2006 et 2010.

Description des variables : Le décès est défini comme la disparition permanente de tout signe de vie à un moment quelconque postérieur à la naissance vivante (cessation des fonctions vitales après la naissance sans possibilité de réanimation).

Sauf indication contraire, les statistiques relatives au nombre de décès sont établies sur la base des registres d'état civil. Pour les pays ou zones où les données concernant l'enregistrement des décès par les services de l'état civil sont jugées sûres (complétude estimée à 90 p. 100 ou plus), les taux de mortalité ont été calculés d'après les décès enregistrés.

La répartition des décès entre zones urbaines et zones rurales est celle qui a été communiquée par chaque pays ou zone ; on part du principe qu'elle repose sur les définitions de la population urbaine utilisées pour les recensements nationaux, qui sont reproduites à la fin des notes techniques du tableau 6.

Pour quelques pays il y a une discordance entre le nombre total des décès présenté dans ce tableau et ceux présentés après pour la même année. Habituellement ces différences apparaissent lorsque le nombre total des décès pour une certaine année a été révisé alors que les autres tabulations ne l'ont pas été.

Calcul des taux : Les taux bruts de mortalité représentent le nombre annuel de décès pour 1 000 habitants en milieu d'année.

Les taux selon le lieu de résidence (zone urbaine ou rurale) représentent le nombre annuel de décès, classés selon la catégorie urbaine ou rurale appropriée, pour 1 000 habitants en milieu d'année. Ces taux sont calculés par la division de statistique des Nations Unies sur la base de la population de référence adéquate (par exemple : population totale, nationaux seulement, etc.) si elle est connue et disponible. Si la population de référence n'est pas connue ou n'est pas disponible, la population totale est utilisée pour calculer les taux. Par conséquent, si la population utilisée pour calculer les taux est différente de la population de référence adéquate, les taux présentés sont susceptibles de sous ou sur estimer la situation réelle d'un pays ou d'un territoire.

Les taux présentés dans ce tableau se rapportent seulement aux pays ou zones où l'on a enregistré un nombre minimal de 30 décès au cours d'une année donnée.

Fiabilité des données : Il a été demandé à chaque pays ou zone d'indiquer le degré estimatif de complétude des données sur les décès d'enfants de moins d'un an figurant dans ses registres d'état civil. Ces évaluations nationales sont signalées par les codes de qualité "C", "U" et "I" qui apparaissent dans la deuxième colonne du tableau.

La lettre "C" indique que les données sont jugées à peu près complètes, c'est-à-dire qu'elles représentent au moins 90 p. 100 des décès d'enfants de moins d'un an survenus chaque année ; la lettre "U" signifie que les données sont jugées incomplètes, c'est-à-dire qu'elles représentent moins de 90 p.100 des décès d'enfants de moins d'un an survenus chaque année. Le symbole "I" indique que la source des données n'est pas un registre de l'état civil ; le symbole, dans ce cas, est accompagné par une note explicative. Le code "..." dénote qu'aucun renseignement n'a été communiqué quant à la complétude des données.

Les données provenant des registres de l'état civil qui sont déclarées incomplètes ou dont le degré de complétude n'est pas connu (code "U" ou "...") sont jugées douteuses. Elles apparaissent en italique dans le présent tableau et les taux correspondants n'ont pas été calculés.

Insuffisance des données : Les statistiques relatives à la mortalité appellent les mêmes réserves que celles qui ont été formulées à propos des statistiques de l'état civil en général et des statistiques relatives aux décès en particulier (voir la section 4 des Notes techniques).

La fiabilité des données, au sujet de laquelle des indications ont été fournies plus haut, est un facteur important. Il faut également tenir compte du fait que, dans certains cas, les décès sont classés par date d'enregistrement et non par date d'occurrence ; ces cas ont été signalés par le signe "+". Chaque fois que le décalage entre le décès et son enregistrement est grand et qu'une forte proportion des décès fait l'objet d'un enregistrement tardif, les statistiques relatives aux décès survenus pendant l'année peuvent être considérablement faussées.

En règle générale, toutefois, les décès sont enregistrés beaucoup plus rapidement que les naissances vivantes, et les retards prolongés sont rares.

Un autre facteur qui nuit à la comparabilité internationale est la pratique qui consiste à ne pas inclure dans les statistiques de la mortalité les enfants nés vivants mais décédés avant l'enregistrement de leur naissance ou dans les 24 heures qui ont suivi la naissance. Quand pareil facteur a joué, cela a été signalé en note à la fin du tableau.

Il convient de noter par ailleurs que l'exactitude des taux dépend également de la qualité et des limitations des estimations de la population qui sont utilisées pour leur calcul. Le problème des erreurs par excès ou par défaut commises lors du dénombrement et, dans une certaine mesure, le problème de l'hétérogénéité des définitions de la population totale ont été examinés à la section 3 de l'Introduction, relative à la population en général ; des indications concernant certains pays ou zones sont données en note à la fin du tableau 3.

Les taux estimatifs fondés directement sur les résultats d'enquêtes par sondage comportent des possibilités d'erreurs considérables dues soit à des omissions dans les déclarations des décès, soit au fait que l'on a déclaré à tort des décès survenus en réalité hors de la période considérée. Toutefois, ces taux présentent un avantage : le chiffre de population utilisé comme base est connu par définition et rigoureusement correspondant.

Il faut souligner que les taux bruts de mortalité, de même que les taux bruts de natalité, de nuptialité et de divortialité, peuvent varier très sensiblement selon la composition par âge et par sexe de la population à laquelle ils se rapportent. Ils offrent néanmoins un moyen simple de mesurer le niveau et l'évolution de la mortalité.

La comparabilité des données selon le lieu de résidence (zone urbaine ou rurale) peut être limitée par les définitions nationales des termes « urbain » et « rural » utilisées pour le classement de ces données. En l'absence d'indications contraires, on a supposé que les mêmes définitions avaient servi pour le recensement national de la population et pour l'établissement des statistiques de l'état civil pour chaque pays ou zone. Toutefois, il n'est pas exclu que, pour une zone ou un pays donné, des définitions différentes aient été retenues. Les définitions du terme « urbain » utilisées pour les recensements nationaux de population ont été présentées à la fin du tableau 6 lorsqu'elles étaient connues. Comme on l'a précisé dans les notes techniques relatives au tableau 6, ces définitions varient considérablement d'un pays ou d'une zone à l'autre.

Outre les problèmes de comparabilité, les taux démographiques classés selon le lieu de résidence « urbaine » ou « rurale » sont également sujets à des distorsions particulières. Si l'on utilise des définitions différentes du terme « urbain » pour classer les faits d'état civil et les données relatives à la population lors du calcul des taux et qu'il en résulte une différence nette entre le numérateur et le dénominateur pour le taux de la population exposée au risque, les taux démographiques s'en trouveront faussés. La différence entre ces taux pour les zones urbaines et rurales pourra aussi être faussée selon que les faits d'état civil auront été classés d'après le lieu où ils se sont produits ou d'après le lieu de résidence habituel. Ce problème est examiné plus en détail à la section 4.1.4.1 de l'Introduction.

Données publiées antérieurement : les différentes éditions de l'*Annuaire démographique* contiennent des statistiques des décès et des taux bruts de mortalité. Pour plus de précisions concernant les années pour lesquelles ces données ont été publiées, se reporter à l'index.

18. Deaths and crude death rates, by urban/rural residence: 2006 - 2010
Décès et taux bruts de mortalité, selon la résidence, urbaine/rurale : 2006 - 2010

Continent, country or area, and urban/rural residence / Continent, pays ou zone et résidence, urbaine/rurale	Co-de[a]	Number - Nombre					Rate - Taux				
		2006	2007	2008	2009	2010	2006	2007	2008	2009	2010
AFRICA - AFRIQUE											
Algeria - Algérie[1]											
Total	U	144 000	149 000	153 000	159 000	157 000	...	...	...	...	...
Botswana[2]											
Total	+U	11 509	11 075	...	...	...	...	...	...	...	...
Burkina Faso											
Total	I	116 199[3]	176 700[4]	174 800[4]	...	...	8.3	...	...	...	...
Urban - Urbaine[3]	I	16 411	...	...	...	...	5.2	...	...	...	...
Rural - Rurale[3]	I	99 788	...	...	...	...	9.2	...	...	...	...
Cape Verde - Cap-Vert											
Total	C	2 822	2 846	2 873	2 897	2 917	5.8	5.8	5.7	5.7	5.6
Egypt - Égypte											
Total	C	451 863	450 596	461 934	476 592	...	6.3	6.1	6.1	6.2	...
Urban - Urbaine	C	214 008	212 305	216 023	217 897	...	7.0	6.7	6.7	6.6	...
Rural - Rurale	C	237 855	238 291	245 911	258 695	...	5.8	5.7	5.7	5.9	...
Ethiopia - Éthiopie[5]											
Total	I	...	839 038	...	...	...	...	11.4	...	...	...
Kenya											
Total	U	208 452	170 167	219 477	181 220	...	...	...	...	...	...
Malawi											
Total[4]	U	207 641	206 527	...	...	...	...	...	...	...	...
Total[6]	I	...	...	135 865	...	...	...	...	10.0	...	...
Mauritius - Maurice[7]											
Total	+C	9 162	8 498	9 004	9 224	9 131	7.3	6.7	7.1	7.2	7.1
Urban - Urbaine	+C	4 142	4 036	4 159	4 324	...	7.9	7.6	7.8	8.1	...
Rural - Rurale	+C	5 020	4 462	4 845	4 900	...	6.9	6.1	6.6	6.6	...
Morocco - Maroc											
Total	U	...	105 222	...	...	...	...	...	...	...	...
Namibia - Namibie[4]											
Total	I	28 879	28 673	...	...	...	14.5	14.1	...	...	...
Niger[8]											
Total	...	4 256	6 337	...	...	...	...	...	...	...	...
Réunion[9]											
Total	C	4 323	4 045	...	...	...	5.5	5.1	...	...	...
Rwanda											
Total	U	...	141 015	142 339	143 538	...	...	...	...	...	...
Saint Helena ex. dep. - Sainte-Hélène sans dép.											
Total	C	52	59	44	41	53	...	14.9	11.1	9.9	12.5
Senegal - Sénégal[10]											
Total	I	133 659	135 172	136 839	138 182	139 651	11.9	11.7	11.6	11.4	11.2
Urban - Urbaine	I	49 296	49 858	50 477	50 975	51 518	10.8	10.6	10.5	10.3	10.1
Rural - Rurale	I	84 363	85 314	86 362	87 207	88 133	12.7	12.5	12.3	12.1	11.9
Seychelles											
Total	+C	664	630	662	684	664	7.8	7.4	7.6	7.8	7.7
South Africa - Afrique du Sud											
Total	U	612 778	603 094	592 073	613 900	...	...	...	...	...	...
Swaziland[5]											
Total	I	...	18 367	...	...	...	...	21.8	...	...	...
Tunisia - Tunisie											
Total	U	57 000	56 741	60 000	...	...	...	...	...	...	...
Zambia - Zambie[4]											
Total	U	152 549	...	...	...	...	...	...	...	...	...
AMERICA, NORTH - AMÉRIQUE DU NORD											
Anguilla											
Total	+C	58	70	52	...	...	4.1	4.7	3.3	...	...
Antigua and Barbuda - Antigua-et-Barbuda											
Total	+C	479	504	...	...	...	5.7	5.9	...	...	...
Aruba											
Total	C	537	521	523	623	610	5.2	5.0	5.0	5.8	5.7
Bahamas											
Total	C	1 730	1 798	1 863	...	...	5.3	5.4	5.5	...	...

Continent, country or area, and urban/rural residence / Continent, pays ou zone et résidence, urbaine/rurale	Code[a]	Number - Nombre					Rate - Taux				
		2006	2007	2008	2009	2010	2006	2007	2008	2009	2010

AMERICA, NORTH - AMÉRIQUE DU NORD

Continent, country or area	Code	2006	2007	2008	2009	2010	2006	2007	2008	2009	2010
Barbados - Barbade											
Total	+C	2 317	2 213	...	...	...	8.5	8.1	...	...	...
Bermuda - Bermudes[11]											
Total	C	461	468	443	471	...	7.2	7.3	6.9	7.3	...
Canada[12]											
Total	C	228 079	235 217	240 961	...	...	7.0	7.1	7.2	...	...
Cayman Islands - Îles Caïmanes											
Total	C	182	160	166	152[13]	152[13]	3.5	3.0	3.0	2.9	2.8
Costa Rica											
Total	C	16 766	17 070	18 021	18 560	*19 077	3.9	3.8	4.0	4.0	*4.2
Urban - Urbaine	C	8 786	8 779	9 170	9 561	*9 887	3.4	3.4	3.4	3.5	*3.5
Rural - Rurale	C	7 980	8 291	8 851	8 999	*9 190	4.5	4.5	4.8	4.7	*5.2
Cuba											
Total	C	80 831	81 927	86 423	*86 943	...	7.2	7.3	7.7	*7.7	...
Urban - Urbaine	C	67 002	66 913	71 444	*72 220	...	7.9	7.9	8.4	*8.5	...
Rural - Rurale	C	13 829	15 014	14 979	*14 723	...	5.0	5.4	5.4	*5.3	...
Dominica - Dominique											
Total	+C	536	...	...	...	...	7.5	...	...	...	...
Dominican Republic - République dominicaine											
Total	U	31 301	32 620	32 494	31 580	...	...	...	...	...	...
Urban - Urbaine[14]	U	23 960	25 629	25 384	25 093	...	...	...	...	...	...
Rural - Rurale[14]	U	6 228	5 770	6 045	5 347	...	...	...	...	...	...
El Salvador[15]											
Total	C	31 453	31 349	31 594	...	...	5.2	5.1	5.2	...	...
Urban - Urbaine	C	24 682	23 358	...	...	...	6.7	6.2	...	...	...
Rural - Rurale	C	6 771	7 991	...	...	...	2.9	3.4	...	...	...
Greenland - Groenland											
Total	C	440	452	428	437	504	7.7	8.0	7.6	7.8	8.9
Urban - Urbaine	C	356	374	354	366	415	7.6	7.9	7.5	7.7	8.7
Rural - Rurale	C	84	78	74	71	89	8.6	8.2	8.0	7.8	10.0
Guadeloupe[9]											
Total	C	2 902	2 769	...	...	...	6.3	6.9	...	...	...
Guatemala											
Total	C	69 756	70 030	70 233	...	...	5.4	5.2	5.1	...	...
Urban - Urbaine	C	38 897	...	...	...	...	...	...	...	...	...
Rural - Rurale	C	30 859	...	...	...	...	...	...	...	...	...
Honduras											
Total	+U	35 682	...	...	...	...	...	...	...	...	...
Urban - Urbaine	+U	14 654	...	...	...	...	...	...	...	...	...
Rural - Rurale	+U	21 028	...	...	...	...	...	...	...	...	...
Jamaica - Jamaïque											
Total	U	16 317[16]	17 048[16]	17 000	17 553	...	...	...	...	...	...
Martinique[9]											
Total	C	2 663	2 830	...	...	...	6.7	7.1	...	...	...
Urban - Urbaine	C	2 291	2 482	...	...	...	...	...	...	...	...
Rural - Rurale	C	372	348	...	...	...	...	...	...	...	...
Mexico - Mexique[17]											
Total	+C	493 296	513 122	538 288	*563 516	...	4.7	4.9	5.0	*5.2	...
Urban - Urbaine[14]	+C	370 811	384 724	403 798	*424 362	...	4.6	4.7	4.9	*5.1	...
Rural - Rurale[14]	+C	116 393	121 743	128 004	*131 946	...	4.8	5.0	5.2	*5.4	...
Montserrat											
Total	+C	47	44	45	...	...	10.1	9.1	9.2	...	...
Netherlands Antilles - Antilles néerlandaises[17]											
Total	C	1 327	1 339	1 453	1 342	...	7.0	6.9	7.4	6.7	...
Nicaragua											
Total	+U	16 595	17 288	18 079	...	...	...	...	...	...	...
Urban - Urbaine	+U	11 129	11 456	11 982	...	...	...	...	...	...	...
Rural - Rurale	+U	5 466	5 832	6 097	...	...	...	...	...	...	...
Panama											
Total	U	14 358	14 775	15 115	15 498	...	...	...	...	...	...
Urban - Urbaine	U	9 396	9 768	10 238	9 201	...	...	...	...	...	...
Rural - Rurale	U	4 962	5 007	4 877	6 297	...	...	...	...	...	...

18. Deaths and crude death rates, by urban/rural residence: 2006 - 2010
Décès et taux bruts de mortalité, selon la résidence, urbaine/rurale : 2006 - 2010 (continued - suite)

Continent, country or area, and urban/rural residence / Continent, pays ou zone et résidence, urbaine/rurale	Co-de[a]	Number - Nombre					Rate - Taux				
		2006	2007	2008	2009	2010	2006	2007	2008	2009	2010
AMERICA, NORTH - AMÉRIQUE DU NORD											
Puerto Rico - Porto Rico											
Total	C	28 589	29 276	29 100	...	...	7.3	7.4	7.4	...	...
Urban - Urbaine[14]	C	...	...	15 477	...	...	...	...	...	...	...
Rural - Rurale[14]	C	...	...	13 440	...	...	...	...	...	...	...
Saint Vincent and the Grenadines - Saint-Vincent-et-les Grenadines											
Total	+C	777	779	848	765	...	7.7	7.8	8.6	...	...
Turks and Caicos Islands - Îles Turques et Caïques[15]											
Total	C	73	116	65	...	...	2.2	3.3	1.8	...	...
United States of America - États-Unis d'Amérique											
Total	C	2 426 264	2 423 712	*2 473 018	...	...	8.1	8.0	*8.1	...	...
United States Virgin Islands - Îles Vierges américaines											
Total	C	629	727	...	...	...	5.7	6.6	...	...	...
AMERICA, SOUTH - AMÉRIQUE DU SUD											
Argentina - Argentine											
Total	C	292 313	315 852	301 801	304 525	...	7.5	8.0	7.6	7.6	...
Bolivia (Plurinational State of) - Bolivie (État plurinational de)[18]											
Total	U	*25 954	*21 846	...	...	...	...	...	...	...	...
Brazil - Brésil[19]											
Total	U	1 023 545	1 032 450	1 060 365	1 079 228	...	...	...	...	...	...
Chile - Chili											
Total	C	85 639	93 000	90 168	...	...	5.2	5.6	5.4	...	...
Urban - Urbaine	C	73 406	81 723	78 790	...	...	5.1	5.7	5.4	...	...
Rural - Rurale	C	12 233	11 277	11 378	...	...	5.7	5.2	5.2	...	...
Colombia - Colombie											
Total	U	192 814	193 936	196 943	*193 580	...	...	...	...	...	...
Urban - Urbaine[14]	U	148 690	150 375	153 016	*150 480	...	...	...	...	...	...
Rural - Rurale[14]	U	37 445	36 843	36 715	*35 774	...	...	...	...	...	...
Ecuador - Équateur[20]											
Total	U	57 940	58 016	60 023	59 714	...	...	...	...	...	...
Urban - Urbaine	U	43 038	44 644	44 700	45 419	...	...	...	...	...	...
Rural - Rurale	U	14 902	13 372	15 323	14 295	...	...	...	...	...	...
Falkland Islands (Malvinas) - Îles Falkland (Malvinas)											
Total	+C	20	...	...	...	...	...	...	...	...	...
French Guiana - Guyane française[9]											
Total	C	711	690	...	...	...	3.5	3.2	...	...	...
Urban - Urbaine	C	552	567	...	...	...	...	...	...	...	...
Rural - Rurale	C	159	123	...	...	...	...	...	...	...	...
Guyana											
Total	+C	5 031	5 066	...	...	...	6.6	6.6	...	...	...
Paraguay											
Total	+U	22 749	23 025	24 417	...	...	...	...	...	...	...
Urban - Urbaine	+U	15 958	15 882	16 722	...	...	...	...	...	...	...
Rural - Rurale	+U	6 791	7 143	7 695	...	...	...	...	...	...	...
Peru - Pérou[21]											
Total	+U	82 620	87 495	*91 295	...	...	...	...	...	...	...
Suriname[22]											
Total	C	3 247	3 374	...	...	...	6.4	6.6	...	...	...
Urban - Urbaine[23]	C	2 205	2 334	...	...	...	...	...	...	...	...
Rural - Rurale[23]	C	1 042	1 040	...	...	...	...	...	...	...	...
Uruguay											
Total	C	31 056	33 706	31 363	*32 179	...	9.4	10.1	9.4	*9.6	...

Continent, country or area, and urban/rural residence / Continent, pays ou zone et résidence, urbaine/rurale	Code[a]	Number - Nombre					Rate - Taux				
		2006	2007	2008	2009	2010	2006	2007	2008	2009	2010
AMERICA, SOUTH - AMÉRIQUE DU SUD											
Venezuela (Bolivarian Republic of) - Venezuela (République bolivarienne du)											
Total	C	115 348	118 594	124 062	...	...	4.3	4.3	4.4	...	...
ASIA - ASIE											
Armenia - Arménie[24]											
Total	C	27 202	26 830	27 412	27 560	27 921	8.4	8.3	8.5	8.5	8.6
Urban - Urbaine	C	17 689	17 213	17 451	17 433	...	8.6	8.3	8.4	8.4	...
Rural - Rurale	C	9 513	9 617	9 961	10 127	...	8.2	8.3	8.6	8.7	...
Azerbaijan - Azerbaïdjan[24]											
Total	+C	52 248	53 655	52 710	52 514	53 580	6.1	6.2	6.0	5.9	5.9
Urban - Urbaine	+C	27 581	28 162	27 817	27 690	...	6.0	6.0	5.8	5.7	...
Rural - Rurale	+C	24 667	25 493	24 893	24 824	...	6.2	6.3	6.1	6.0	...
Bahrain - Bahreïn											
Total	C	2 317	2 270	2 390	2 387	...	2.4	2.2	2.2	2.0	...
Bangladesh[25]											
Total	I	...	...	...	...	...	5.6	6.2	...	...	...
Urban - Urbaine	I	...	...	...	...	...	4.4	5.1	...	...	...
Rural - Rurale	I	...	...	...	...	...	6.0	6.6	...	...	...
Brunei Darussalam - Brunéi Darussalam											
Total	+C	1 095	1 174	1 091	...	...	2.9	3.0	2.7	...	...
China - Chine[26]											
Total	I	8 920 000	9 130 000	9 350 000	9 430 000	...	6.8	6.9	7.0	7.1	...
China, Hong Kong SAR - Chine, Hong Kong RAS											
Total	C	37 457	39 476	41 796	41 175	...	5.5	5.7	6.0	5.9	...
China, Macao SAR - Chine, Macao RAS											
Total	C	1 566	1 545	1 756	1 664	*1 768	3.1	2.9	3.2	3.1	*3.2
Cyprus - Chypre[27]											
Total	C	5 127	5 391	5 194	5 182	*5 392	6.7	6.9	6.5	6.5	*6.7
Democratic People's Republic of Korea - République populaire démocratique de Corée[28]											
Total	I	...	...	216 616	...	...	...	...	9.0	...	...
Urban - Urbaine	I	...	...	119 805	...	...	...	...	...	...	...
Rural - Rurale	I	...	...	96 811	...	...	...	...	...	...	...
Georgia - Géorgie[24]											
Total	C	42 255	41 178	43 011	...	47 864	9.6	9.4	9.8	...	...
Urban - Urbaine	C	27 267	26 387	27 321	...	...	11.8	11.4	11.8	...	...
Rural - Rurale	C	14 988	14 791	15 690	...	...	7.2	7.1	7.6	...	...
India - Inde[29]											
Total	I	...	...	...	...	...	7.5	7.4	7.4	...	...
Urban - Urbaine	I	...	...	...	...	...	6.0	6.0	5.9	...	...
Rural - Rurale	I	...	...	...	...	...	8.1	8.0	8.0	...	...
Iran (Islamic Republic of) - Iran (République islamique d')[30]											
Total	+U	408 566	412 735	417 798	...	...	...	...	...	...	...
Urban - Urbaine	+U	257 436	260 855	270 877	...	...	...	...	...	...	...
Rural - Rurale	+U	151 130	151 880	146 921	...	...	...	...	...	...	...
Iraq											
Total	U	*211 757	...	...	...	...	...	...	...	...	...
Israel - Israël[31]											
Total	C	38 776	40 081	39 484	38 781	*39 361	5.5	5.6	5.4	5.2	*5.2
Urban - Urbaine	C	36 473[14]	37 658[14]	37 178	36 571[14]	...	5.6	5.7	5.5	5.3	...
Rural - Rurale	C	2 300[14]	2 417[14]	2 306	2 209[14]	...	4.0	4.1	3.8	3.6	...

Continent, country or area, and urban/rural residence / Continent, pays ou zone et résidence, urbaine/rurale	Code[a]	Number - Nombre					Rate - Taux				
		2006	2007	2008	2009	2010	2006	2007	2008	2009	2010
ASIA - ASIE											
Japan - Japon[32]											
Total	C	1 084 450	1 108 334	1 142 407	1 141 865	...	8.6	8.8	9.1	9.0	...
Urban - Urbaine[14]	C	936 383	964 905	997 547	998 621	...	...	...	...	...	...
Rural - Rurale[14]	C	146 174	141 514	142 989	141 387	...	...	...	...	...	...
Jordan - Jordanie[33]											
Total	U	20 397	20 924	19 403			...	...	...	...	...
Kazakhstan[24]											
Total	C	157 210	158 297	152 706	*142 780	...	10.3	10.2	9.7	*9.0	...
Urban - Urbaine	C	100 526	92 385	88 767	...	...	11.5	11.3	10.7	...	...
Rural - Rurale	C	56 684	65 912	63 939		...	8.7	9.0	8.7	...	...
Kuwait - Koweït											
Total	C	5 247	5 293	5 701			2.3	2.2	2.3		
Kyrgyzstan - Kirghizstan											
Total	C	38 566	38 180	37 710	35 898	...	7.7	7.6	7.4	7.0	...
Urban - Urbaine	C	14 930	14 744	14 096	13 351	...	8.3	8.2	7.9	7.4	...
Rural - Rurale	C	23 636	23 436	23 614	22 547	...	7.3	7.2	7.2	6.8	...
Lebanon - Liban											
Total	C	18 787	21 092	21 048	22 260	25 500	...	5.6	...	...	...
Malaysia - Malaisie											
Total	C	115 084	118 167	124 857	*128 962	...	4.3	4.3	4.5	*4.6	...
Urban - Urbaine	C	67 759	69 809	73 427	...	...	4.0	4.1	4.2	...	...
Rural - Rurale	C	47 325	48 358	51 430	...	...	4.8	4.8	5.1	...	...
Maldives											
Total	C	1 084	1 119	1 083	1 163	...	3.6	3.7	3.5	3.7	...
Urban - Urbaine	C	354	372	390	450	...	...	...	...	...	...
Rural - Rurale	C	730	747	693	713	...	...	...	...	...	...
Mongolia - Mongolie											
Total	C	16 682	16 259	15 413	16 911	17 276	6.5	6.2	5.8	6.2	...
Urban - Urbaine	C	10 811	10 498	9 968	...	...	6.9	6.6	6.1	...	...
Rural - Rurale	C	5 871	5 761	5 445	...	...	5.8	5.6	5.3	...	...
Myanmar											
Total	+U	247 527	266 206	483 373	...	...	...	...	...	...	...
Urban - Urbaine	+U	67 554	71 483	135 114	...	...	...	...	...	...	...
Rural - Rurale	+U	179 973	194 723	348 259	...	...	...	...	...	...	...
Occupied Palestinian Territory - Territoire palestinien occupé											
Total	U	9 938	9 887	...	...	...	...	...	...	...	...
Oman											
Total	U	5 484	6 769[34]	7 298[34]	7 098[34]		...	...	...	...	...
Pakistan[35]											
Total	I	1 022 625	1 019 533	...	...	...	6.5	6.4	...	...	...
Urban - Urbaine	I	300 069	287 516	...	...	...	5.6	5.2	...	...	...
Rural - Rurale	I	722 558	732 017	...	...	...	7.0	7.0	...	...	...
Qatar											
Total	C	1 750	1 776	1 942	2 008	1 920	1.7	1.5	1.3	1.2	1.1
Republic of Korea - République de Corée[36]											
Total	C	242 266	244 874	246 113	246 942	...	5.0	5.0	5.0	5.0	...
Urban - Urbaine[14]	C	159 834	162 982	164 439	166 356	...	4.0	4.1	4.1	4.1	...
Rural - Rurale[14]	C	82 389	81 883	81 664	80 575	...	8.8	8.8	8.8	8.6	...
Saudi Arabia - Arabie saoudite[37]											
Total	...	93 752	95 166[38]	96 641[38]	...	...	...	...	...	...	...
Singapore - Singapour											
Total	+C	16 393	17 140	17 222	17 101		3.7	3.7	3.6	3.4	...
Sri Lanka											
Total	+C	117 467	118 998	*118 279	*120 085	*128 603	5.9	5.9	*5.9	*5.9	*6.2
Urban - Urbaine	+C	52 173	49 499	...	...	...	...	...	...	...	...
Rural - Rurale	+C	65 294	69 499	...	...	...	...	...	...	...	...
Syrian Arab Republic - République arabe syrienne[39]											
Total	+U	72 534	76 064	...	76 650	...	...	...	...	...	...
Tajikistan - Tadjikistan[24]											
Total	U	29 366	30 332	30 743	...	...	...	...	...	...	...
Urban - Urbaine	U	9 308	9 464	9 276	...	...	...	...	...	...	...
Rural - Rurale	U	20 058	20 868	21 467	...	...	...	...	...	...	...

Continent, country or area, and urban/rural residence — Continent, pays ou zone et résidence, urbaine/rurale	Code[a]	Number - Nombre					Rate - Taux				
		2006	2007	2008	2009	2010	2006	2007	2008	2009	2010
ASIA - ASIE											
Thailand - Thaïlande											
Total	+U	*391 126*	*393 255*	*397 327*	*393 916*	...	...	...	...	...	...
Turkey - Turquie[40]											
Total	I	440 000	447 000	454 000	461 000	459 000	6.3	6.4	6.4	6.4	6.3
United Arab Emirates - Émirats arabes unis[37]											
Total	...	*6 563*	...	...	...	...	...	...	...	...	...
Viet Nam											
Total	C	334 432	382 624	...	...	...	4.0	4.5	...	...	...
Urban - Urbaine	C	82 499	93 222	...	...	...	3.6	3.9	...	...	...
Rural - Rurale	C	251 933	289 402	...	...	...	4.2	4.8	...	...	...
Yemen - Yémen											
Total	U	*21 456*	*24 449*	...	...	...	...	...	...	...	...
EUROPE											
Åland Islands - Îles d'Åland											
Total	C	257	249	250	247	233	9.6	9.2	9.2	9.0	8.4
Urban - Urbaine	C	91	108	114	101	...	8.4	9.9	10.4	9.1	...
Rural - Rurale	C	166	141	136	146	...	10.3	8.7	8.3	8.8	...
Albania - Albanie											
Total	C	16 935	14 528	16 143	...	...	5.4	4.6	5.1	...	...
Andorra - Andorre											
Total	C	260	230	237	272	239	3.2	2.8	2.8	3.2	2.8
Austria - Autriche											
Total	C	74 295	74 625	75 083	77 381[41]	77 199[41]	9.0	9.0	9.0	9.3	9.2
Belarus - Bélarus											
Total	C	138 426	132 993	133 879	135 097	137 132	14.2	13.7	13.8	14.0	14.4
Urban - Urbaine	C	75 437	74 017	75 536	76 629	...	10.7	10.4	10.6	10.7	...
Rural - Rurale	C	62 989	58 976	58 343	58 468	...	23.6	22.6	22.9	23.5	...
Belgium - Belgique[42]											
Total	C	101 587	100 658	104 587	104 509	*104 500	9.6	9.5	9.8	9.7	*9.6
Urban - Urbaine	C	100 118	99 118	...	...	...	9.6	9.5	...	...	...
Rural - Rurale	C	1 469	1 540	...	...	...	9.7	10.0	...	...	...
Bosnia and Herzegovina - Bosnie-Herzégovine											
Total	C	33 221	35 044	34 026	34 904	*34 633	8.6	9.1	8.9	9.1	*9.0
Bulgaria - Bulgarie											
Total	C	113 438	113 004	110 523	108 068	110 165	14.7	14.8	14.5	14.2	14.6
Urban - Urbaine	C	66 352	66 486	65 168	64 335	...	12.2	12.3	12.1	11.9	...
Rural - Rurale	C	47 086	46 518	45 355	43 733	...	20.7	20.7	20.4	20.1	...
Croatia - Croatie											
Total	C	50 378	52 367	52 151	52 414	52 096	11.3	11.8	11.8	11.8	11.8
Urban - Urbaine	C	25 144	26 241	26 172	26 275	...	...	...	...	...	...
Rural - Rurale	C	25 234	26 126	25 979	26 139	...	...	...	...	...	...
Czech Republic - République tchèque											
Total	C	104 441	104 636	104 948	107 421	106 844	10.2	10.1	10.1	10.2	10.2
Urban - Urbaine	C	75 900	76 441	76 664	78 590	...	10.0	10.0	10.0	10.2	...
Rural - Rurale	C	28 541	28 195	28 284	28 831	...	10.6	10.4	10.4	10.4	...
Denmark - Danemark[43]											
Total	C	55 477	55 604	54 591	54 872	54 368	10.2	10.2	9.9	9.9	9.8
Estonia - Estonie											
Total	C	17 316	17 409	16 675	16 081	15 790	12.9	13.0	12.4	12.0	11.8
Urban - Urbaine	C	11 500	11 611[14]	11 227[14]	10 805	...	12.3	12.5	12.1	11.6	...
Rural - Rurale	C	5 816	5 797[14]	5 445[14]	5 276	...	14.1	14.1	13.3	12.9	...
Faeroe Islands - Îles Féroé											
Total	C	416	383	378	...	...	8.6	7.9	7.8	...	...
Urban - Urbaine	C	116	101	...	...	...	6.6	5.8	...	...	...
Rural - Rurale	C	300	282	...	...	...	9.7	9.1	...	...	...
Finland - Finlande[44]											
Total	C	48 065	49 077	49 094	49 636[45]	50 654[45]	9.1	9.3	9.2	9.3	9.5
Urban - Urbaine	C	29 028	29 833	29 624	30 346[45]	...	8.2	8.4	8.2	8.4	...
Rural - Rurale	C	19 037	19 244	19 470	19 290[45]	...	11.1	11.2	11.4	11.4	...

18. Deaths and crude death rates, by urban/rural residence: 2006 - 2010
Décès et taux bruts de mortalité, selon la résidence, urbaine/rurale : 2006 - 2010 (continued - suite)

Continent, country or area, and urban/rural residence / Continent, pays ou zone et résidence, urbaine/rurale	Code[a]	Number - Nombre					Rate - Taux				
		2006	2007	2008	2009	2010	2006	2007	2008	2009	2010
EUROPE											
France[46]											
Total	C	516 416	521 016	532 131	538 116	*535 000	8.4	8.4	8.5	8.6	*8.5
Urban - Urbaine[47]	C	366 641	369 654	377 265	381 865	...	...	...	...	...	...
Rural - Rurale[47]	C	148 125	149 552	153 136	154 512	...	...	...	...	...	...
Germany - Allemagne											
Total	C	821 627	827 155	844 439	854 544	*862 000	10.0	10.1	10.3	10.4	*10.5
Gibraltar[48]											
Total	+C	230	202	227	...	...	8.0	6.9	7.8	...	...
Greece - Grèce											
Total	C	105 476	109 895	107 979	108 316	*106 000	9.5	9.8	9.6	9.6	...
Urban - Urbaine	C	57 700	60 764	59 738	60 342	...	...	...	...	...	...
Rural - Rurale	C	47 776	49 131	48 241	47 974	...	...	...	...	...	...
Guernsey - Guernesey											
Total	C	498	513	476	543	...	8.2	8.4	7.7	8.7	...
Hungary - Hongrie											
Total	C	131 603	132 938	130 027	130 414	*130 450	13.1	13.2	13.0	13.0	*13.0
Urban - Urbaine[49]	C	84 656	85 832	84 390	85 507	...	12.5	12.7	12.4	12.5	...
Rural - Rurale[49]	C	46 233	46 475	44 968	44 304	...	13.9	14.0	13.9	14.0	...
Iceland - Islande											
Total	C	1 903	1 943	1 987	2 002	2 017	6.3	6.2	6.2	6.3	6.3
Urban - Urbaine	C	1 750	1 806	1 851	1 861	...	6.2	6.2	6.2	6.2	...
Rural - Rurale	C	153	136	136	141	...	6.8	6.1	6.4	6.9	...
Ireland - Irlande											
Total	+C	27 479	28 050	28 192	28 898	*27 906	6.5	6.5	6.4	6.5	*6.2
Isle of Man - Île de Man											
Total	+C	768	789	...	...	...	9.6	9.8	...	...	...
Italy - Italie											
Total	C	558 614	572 881	578 192	591 663	*587 488	9.5	9.6	9.7	9.8	*9.7
Jersey											
Total	¹C	758	708	743	...	...	8.5	7.9	...	...	...
Latvia - Lettonie											
Total	C	33 098	33 042	31 006	29 897	30 040	14.5	14.5	13.7	13.3	13.4
Urban - Urbaine	C	21 535	21 555	20 323	19 326	...	13.9	13.9	13.2	12.7	...
Rural - Rurale	C	11 563	11 487	10 683	10 571	...	15.8	15.7	14.6	14.5	...
Liechtenstein											
Total	C	220	227	205	*229	*238	6.3	6.4	5.8	*6.4	*6.6
Lithuania - Lituanie											
Total	C	44 813	45 624	43 832	42 032	42 120	13.2	13.5	13.1	12.6	12.8
Urban - Urbaine	C	26 194	26 796	25 863	24 972	...	11.6	11.9	11.5	11.2	...
Rural - Rurale	C	18 619	18 828	17 969	17 060	...	16.5	16.8	16.2	15.4	...
Luxembourg											
Total	C	3 766	3 866	3 595	3 655	3 760	8.0	8.1	7.4	7.3	7.4
Malta - Malte											
Total	C	3 216	3 111	3 243	3 221	3 010	7.9	7.6	7.9	7.8	7.2
Monaco[50]											
Total	C	535	...	...	...	...	...	...	...	...	...
Montenegro - Monténégro											
Total	C	5 968	5 979	5 708	5 862	5 628	9.6	9.5	9.1	9.3	8.9
Urban - Urbaine	C	...	...	3 602	3 809	...	...	...	9.1	9.5	...
Rural - Rurale	C	...	...	2 106	2 053	...	...	...	9.1	8.9	...
Netherlands - Pays-Bas[51]											
Total	C	135 372	133 022	135 136	134 235	136 058	8.3	8.1	8.2	8.1	8.2
Urban - Urbaine	C	90 611	89 272	90 365	89 495	...	8.4	8.2	8.3	8.2	...
Rural - Rurale	C	44 761	43 750	44 771	44 740	...	8.1	7.9	8.0	8.0	...
Norway - Norvège[52]											
Total	C	41 253	41 954	41 712	41 449	41 499	8.9	8.9	8.7	8.6	8.5
Poland - Pologne											
Total	C	369 686	377 226	379 399	384 940	378 478	9.7	9.9	10.0	10.1	9.9
Urban - Urbaine	C	222 219	226 495	228 650	231 772	...	9.5	9.7	9.8	9.9	...
Rural - Rurale	C	147 467	150 731	150 749	153 168	...	10.0	10.2	10.2	10.3	...
Portugal[17]											
Total	C	101 990	103 512	104 280	104 434	*105 869	9.6	9.8	9.8	9.8	*10.0
Republic of Moldova - République de Moldova[53]											
Total	C	43 137[24]	43 050[24]	41 948	42 139	43 631	12.0	12.0	11.7	11.8	12.2
Urban - Urbaine	C	13 764[24]	13 855[24]	13 463	13 296	...	9.3	9.4	9.1	9.0	...
Rural - Rurale	C	29 373[24]	29 195[24]	28 485	28 843	...	14.0	13.9	13.6	13.8	...

Continent, country or area, and urban/rural residence / Continent, pays ou zone et résidence, urbaine/rurale	Code[a]	Number - Nombre					Rate - Taux				
		2006	2007	2008	2009	2010	2006	2007	2008	2009	2010
EUROPE											
Romania - Roumanie											
Total	C	258 094	251 965	253 202	257 213	259 723	12.0	11.7	11.8	12.0	12.1
Urban - Urbaine	C	116 384	114 562	114 352	116 168	...	9.8	9.6	9.7	9.8	...
Rural - Rurale	C	141 710	137 403	138 850	141 045	...	14.7	14.2	14.4	14.6	...
Russian Federation - Fédération de Russie[24]											
Total	C	2 166 703	2 080 445	2 075 954	2 010 543	2 028 516	15.2	14.6	14.6	14.2	14.2
Urban - Urbaine	C	1 501 245	1 445 411	1 443 529	1 397 591	...	14.4	13.9	13.9	13.5	...
Rural - Rurale	C	665 458	635 034	632 425	612 952	...	17.3	16.6	16.5	16.0	...
San Marino - Saint-Marin											
Total	+C	225	225	190	233	...	7.2	7.1	5.8	7.1	...
Serbia - Serbie[54]											
Total	+C	102 884	102 805	102 711	104 000	103 211	13.9	13.9	14.0	14.2	13.9
Urban - Urbaine	+C	53 073	53 469	52 783	54 234	...	12.4	12.5	12.3	12.7	...
Rural - Rurale	+C	49 811	49 336	49 928	49 766	...	15.8	15.9	16.2	16.4	...
Slovakia - Slovaquie											
Total	C	53 301	53 856	53 164	52 913	53 445	9.9	10.0	9.8	9.8	9.8
Urban - Urbaine	C	26 157	26 347	26 189	26 197	...	8.7	8.8	8.8	8.8	...
Rural - Rurale	C	27 144	27 509	26 975	26 716	...	11.3	11.4	11.1	10.9	...
Slovenia - Slovénie											
Total	C	18 180	18 584	18 308	18 750	*18 567	9.1	9.2	9.1	9.2	*9.1
Urban - Urbaine	C	8 571	8 336	9 294	9 666	...	8.9	8.3	9.2	9.4	...
Rural - Rurale	C	9 609	10 248	9 014	9 084	...	9.7	10.1	8.9	8.9	...
Spain - Espagne											
Total	C	371 478	385 361	386 324	384 933	*379 270	8.4	8.6	8.5	8.4	*8.2
Sweden - Suède											
Total	C	91 177	91 729	91 449	90 080	90 487	10.0	10.0	9.9	9.7	9.6
Switzerland - Suisse											
Total	C	60 283	61 089	61 233	62 476	*62 500	8.1	8.1	8.0	8.1	*8.0
Urban - Urbaine	C	44 280	44 576	44 777	45 798	...	8.1	8.0	8.0	8.0	...
Rural - Rurale	C	16 003	16 513	16 456	16 678	...	8.0	8.2	8.1	8.2	...
TFYR of Macedonia - L'ex-R. y. de Macédoine											
Total	C	18 630	19 594	18 982	19 060	*19 114	9.1	9.6	9.3	9.3	*9.3
Urban - Urbaine	C	10 931	11 517	11 099	11 201	...	...	...	...	...	...
Rural - Rurale	C	7 699	8 077	7 883	7 859	...	...	...	...	...	...
Ukraine[55]											
Total	C	758 092	762 877	754 460	*706 740	698 235	16.2	16.4	16.3	*15.3	15.2
Urban - Urbaine	C	461 774	466 253	462 897	...	...	14.5	14.7	14.6	...	...
Rural - Rurale	C	296 318	296 624	291 563	...	...	19.8	20.1	19.9	...	...
United Kingdom of Great Britain and Northern Ireland - Royaume-Uni de Grande-Bretagne et d'Irlande du Nord[56]											
Total	C	572 224	574 687	579 697	559 617	*561 666	9.4	9.4	9.4	9.1	*9.0
OCEANIA - OCÉANIE											
American Samoa - Samoas américaines											
Total	C	267	...	...	...	...	4.0	...	...	...	...
Australia - Australie											
Total	+C	133 739	137 854	143 946	140 760	...	6.5	6.5	6.7	6.4	...
Urban - Urbaine[57]	+C	104 879	108 454	113 279	110 305	...	6.2	6.3	6.4	6.1	...
Rural - Rurale[57]	+C	28 394	28 918	30 183	30 011	...	7.5	7.5	7.7	7.6	...
Cook Islands - Îles Cook[58]											
Total	+C	85	87	59	*74	...	3.6	4.1	2.7	*3.2	...
French Polynesia - Polynésie française											
Total	C	1 152	1 215	1 178	...	...	4.5	4.7	4.5	...	...
Guam[59]											
Total	C	682	786	775	850	...	4.0	4.5	4.4	4.8	...
Marshall Islands - Îles Marshall											
Total	+U	318	...	...	...	...	...	...	...	...	...

18. Deaths and crude death rates, by urban/rural residence: 2006 - 2010
Décès et taux bruts de mortalité, selon la résidence, urbaine/rurale : 2006 - 2010 (continued - suite)

Continent, country or area, and urban/rural residence / Continent, pays ou zone et résidence, urbaine/rurale	Code[a]	Number - Nombre					Rate - Taux				
		2006	2007	2008	2009	2010	2006	2007	2008	2009	2010
OCEANIA - OCÉANIE											
New Caledonia - Nouvelle-Calédonie											
Total	C	1 113	1 207	1 173	*1 235	...	4.7	5.0	4.8	*5.0	...
Urban - Urbaine	C	...	664	...	...	...	...	...	...	...	...
Rural - Rurale	C	...	543	...	...	...	...	...	...	...	...
New Zealand - Nouvelle-Zélande[17]											
Total	+C	28 245	28 522	29 188	28 964	...	6.7	6.7	6.8	6.7	...
Urban - Urbaine[14]	+C	25 398	25 588	26 238	26 036	...	7.0	7.0	7.1	7.0	...
Rural - Rurale[14]	+C	2 711	2 801	2 850	2 867	...	4.7	4.8	4.8	4.8	...
Niue - Nioué											
Total	C	19[60]	9[60]	13[60]	12	...					
Norfolk Island - Île Norfolk[61]											
Total	+C	13	11	20	...						
Northern Mariana Islands - Îles Mariannes septentrionales[62]											
Total	U	174	138	176	...	...	...	...	...	...	...
Palau - Palaos											
Total	C	144	...	...	...	...	6.6	...	...	...	...
Pitcairn											
Total	C	...	1	...							
Samoa											
Total	U	*541	*482	*409	*561	...	...	...	...	...	...
Tonga[63]											
Total	|	709	...	...	...	...	6.9	...	...	...	...
Tuvalu											
Total	U	45	47	...							
Wallis and Futuna Islands - Îles Wallis et Futuna											
Total	C	77	...	90	...	...	...	...	6.7	...	...

FOOTNOTES - NOTES

Italics: data from civil registers which are incomplete or of unknown completeness. - Italiques : données incomplètes ou dont le degré d'exactitude n'est pas connu, provenant des registres de l'état civil.

* Provisional. - Données provisoires.

[a] 'Code' indicates the source of data, as follows:
C - Civil registration, estimated over 90% complete
U - Civil registration, estimated less than 90% complete
| - Other source, estimated reliable
+ - Data tabulated by date of registration rather than occurence
... - Information not available

Le 'Code' indique la source des données, comme suit :
C - Registres de l'état civil considérés complets à 90 p. 100 au moins
U - Registres de l'état civil qui ne sont pas considérés complets à 90 p. 100 au moins
| - Autre source, considérée pas douteuses
+ - Données exploitées selon la date de l'enregistrement et non la date de l'événement
... - Information pas disponible

[1] Excluding live-born infants who died before their birth was registered. Data refer to Algerian population only. - Non compris les enfants nés vivants décédés avant l'enregistrement de leur naissance. Les données ne concernent que la population algérienne.
[2] Data from Health Statistics Reports since 1998, due to incompleteness of civil registration. - Données provenant des Health Statistics Reports (rapports sur les statistiques sanitaires) depuis 1998, en raison des lacunes de l'état civil.
[3] Data refer to the twelve months preceding the census in December. - Les données se rapportent aux douze mois précédant le recensement de décembre.

[4] Data refer to national projections. - Les données se réfèrent aux projections nationales.
[5] Data refer to the twelve months preceding the census in May. - Les données se rapportent aux douze mois précédant le recensement de mai.
[6] Data refer to the twelve months preceding the census in June. - Les données se raportent aux douze mois précédant le recensement de juin.
[7] Excludes the islands of St. Brandon and Agalega. - Non compris les îles St. Brandon et Agalega.
[8] Based on hospital records. - D'après les registres de hôpitaux.
[9] Excluding live-born infants who died before their birth was registered. - Non compris les enfants nés vivants décédés avant l'enregistrement de leur naissance.
[10] Based on estimates and projections from 'Agence Nationale de la Statistique et de la Démographie'. - Données fondées sur des estimations et des projections provenant de l'Agence Nationale de la Statistique et de la Démographie.
[11] Excluding non-residents and foreign service personnel and their dependants. - À l'exclusion des non-résidents et du personnel diplomatique et de leurs charges de famille.
[12] Including Canadian residents temporarily in the United States, but excluding United States residents temporarily in Canada. - Y compris les résidents canadiens se trouvant temporairement aux Etats-Unis, mais ne comprenant pas les résidents des Etats-Unis se trouvant temporairement au Canada.
[13] Excluding deaths of nationals who were residing and died abroad but were buried in the Cayman Islands. - Exception faite des nationaux qui résidaient à l'étranger au moment de leur décès, mais qui ont été inhumés dans les Îles Caïmanes.
[14] The total number includes 'Unknown residence', but the categories urban and rural do not. - Le nombre total inclue 'Résidence inconnue ', mais les catégories urbaine et rurale ne l'incluent pas.
[15] Excluding deaths occurring abroad. - Exception faite des personnes décédées à l'étranger.
[16] Data have been adjusted for undercoverage of infant deaths and sudden and violent deaths. - Ajusté pour le sous-estimation de la mortalité infantile, du nombre de morts soudaines et de morts violentes.

17 Data refer to resident population only. - Pour la population résidante seulement.

18 Data refer to registered events only. - Les données ne concernent que les événements enregistrés.

19 Excluding Indian jungle population. - Non compris les Indiens de la jungle.

20 Excluding nomadic Indian tribes. - Non compris les tribus d'Indiens nomades.

21 Data refer to registered events only. Source: Ministry of health reports. - Les données ne concernent que les événements enregistrés. Source: Rapports du Ministère de Santé.

22 Including non-residents. - Y compris les non-résidents.

23 The districts of Paramaribo and Wanica are considered urban areas, whereas all other districts are considered more or less rural areas. - Les districts de Paramaribo et de Wanica sont considérés comme des zones urbaines, les autres districts étant considérés comme des zones rurales à divers degrés.

24 Excluding infants born alive of less than 28 weeks' gestation, of less than 1 000 grams in weight and 35 centimeters in length, who die within seven days of birth. - Non compris les enfants nés vivants après moins de 28 semaines de gestations, pesant moins de 1 000 grammes, mesurant moins de 35 centimètres et décédés dans les sept jours qui ont suivi leur naissance.

25 Rates were obtained by the Sample Vital Registration System of Bangladesh. - Taux obtenus au moyen du Sample Vital Registration System du Bangladesh.

26 Data have been estimated on the basis of the annual National Sample Survey on Population Changes. For statistical purposes, the data for China do not include those for the Hong Kong Special Administrative Region (Hong Kong SAR), Macao Special Administrative Region (Macao SAR) and Taiwan province of China. - Les données ont été estimées sur la base de l'enquête annuelle "National Sample Survey on Population Changes". Pour la présentation des statistiques, les données pour la Chine ne comprennent pas la Région Administrative Spéciale de Hong Kong (Hong Kong RAS), la Région Administrative Spéciale de Macao (Macao RAS) et Taïwan province de Chine.

27 Data refer to government controlled areas. - Les données se rapportent aux zones contrôlées par le Gouvernement.

28 Data refer to the twelve months preceding the census in October. - Les données font référence aux 12 mois qui ont précédé le recensement en octobre.

29 Rates were obtained by the Sample Registration System of India, which is a large demographic survey. Including data for the Indian-held part of Jammu and Kashmir, the final status of which has not yet been determined. - Les taux ont été obtenus par le Système de l'enregistrement par échantillon de l'Inde qui est une large enquête démographique. Y compris les données pour la partie du Jammu et du Cachemire occupée par l'Inde dont le statut définitif n'a pas encore été déterminé.

30 Data refer to the Iranian Year which begins on 21 March and ends on 20 March of the following year. - Les données concernent l'année iranienne, qui commence le 21 mars et se termine le 20 mars de l'année suivante.

31 Including deaths abroad of Israeli residents who were out of the country for less than a year. Including data for East Jerusalem and Israeli residents in certain other territories under occupation by Israeli military forces since June 1967. - Y compris les décès à l'étranger de résidents israéliens qui ont quitté le pays depuis moins d'un an. Y compris les données pour Jérusalem-Est et les résidents israéliens dans certains autres territoires occupés depuis 1967 par les forces armées israéliennes.

32 Data refer to Japanese nationals in Japan only. - Les données se raportent aux nationaux japonais au Japon seulement.

33 Excluding data for Jordanian territory under occupation since June 1967 by Israeli military forces. Excluding foreigners, including registered Palestinian refugees. - Non compris les données pour le territoire jordanien occupé depuis juin 1967 par les forces armées israéliennes. Non compris les étrangers, mais y compris les réfugiés de Palestine enregistrés.

34 Data from Births and Deaths Notification System (Ministry of Health institutions and all other health care providers). - Les données proviennent du système de notification des naissances et des décès (établissements du Ministère de la santé et tous autres prestataires de soins de santé).

35 Based on the results of the Pakistan Demographic Survey. Excluding data for the Pakistan-held part of Jammu and Kashmir, the final status of which has not yet been determined. - Données extraites de l'enquête démographique effectuée par le Pakistan. Non compris les données concernant la partie du Jammu et Cachemire occupée par le Pakistan dont le statut définitif n'a pas été déterminé.

36 Excluding alien armed forces, civilian aliens employed by armed forces, and foreign diplomatic personnel and their dependants. - Non compris les militaires étrangers, les civils étrangers employés par les forces armées ni le personnel diplomatique étranger et les membres de leur famille les accompagnant.

37 The registration of births and deaths is conducted by the Ministry of Health. An estimate of completeness is not provided. - L'enregistrement des naissances et des décès est mené par le Ministère de la Santé. Le degré estimatif de complétude n'est pas fourni.

38 As published by the United Nations Economic and Social Commission for Western Asia. - Publié par la Commission économique et sociale des Nations Unies pour l'Asie occidentale.

39 Excluding live-born infants who died before their birth was registered. Excluding nomad population and Palestinian refugees. - Non compris les enfants nés vivants décédés avant l'enregistrement de leur naissance. Non compris la population nomade et les réfugiés de Palestine.

40 Data based on Address Based Population Registration System. - Les données sont basées sur le registre national de la population basé sur l'adresse.

41 Including deaths of nationals abroad. - Y compris les décès des nationaux survenus à l'étranger.

42 Including armed forces stationed outside the country, but excluding alien armed forces stationed in the area. - Y compris les militaires nationaux hors du pays, mais non compris les militaires étrangers en garnison sur le territoire.

43 Excluding Faeroe Islands and Greenland shown separately, if available. - Non compris les îles Féroé et le Groenland, qui font l'objet de rubriques distinctes, si disponible.

44 Including nationals temporarily outside the country. - Y compris les nationaux se trouvant temporairement hors du pays.

45 Excluding Åland Islands. - Non compris les Îles d'Åland.

46 Including armed forces stationed outside the country. - Y compris les militaires nationaux hors du pays.

47 Data for urban and rural, excluding nationals outside the country. - Les données pour la résidence urbaine et rurale , non compris les nationaux hors du pays.

48 Excluding armed forces. - Non compris les militaires en garnison.

49 Total includes the data of foreigners, persons of unknown residence and homeless, but the categories urban and rural do not. - Total incluant les étrangers, les personnes de résidence inconnue et les sans-abri, ce qui n'est pas le cas pour les catégories urbaines et rurales.

50 Including residents outside the country. - Y compris les résidents hors du pays.

51 Including residents outside the country if listed in a Netherlands population register. - Y compris les résidents hors du pays, s'ils sont inscrits sur un registre de population néerlandais.

52 Including residents temporarily outside the country. Excluding Svalbard and Jan Mayen Islands shown separately, if available. - Y compris les résidents se trouvant temporairement hors du pays. Non compris Svalbard et Jan Mayen qui font l'objet de rubriques distinctes, si disponible.

53 Excluding Transnistria and the municipality of Bender. - Les données ne tiennent pas compte de l'information sur la Transnistria et la municipalité de Bender.

54 Excluding data for Kosovo and Metohia. - Sans les données pour le Kosovo et Metohie.

55 Data includes deaths resulting from births with weight 500g and more (if weight is unknown - with length 25 centimeters and more, or with gestation during 22 weeks or more). - Y compris les décès de nouveau-nés de 500 grammes ou plus (si le poids est inconnu – de 25 centimètres de long ou plus, ou après une grossesse de 22 semaines ou plus).

56 Excluding Channel Islands (Guernsey and Jersey) and Isle of Man, shown separately, if available. - Non compris les îles Anglo-Normandes (Guernesey et Jersey) et l'île de Man, qui font l'objet de rubriques distinctes, si disponible.

57 Excluding data where place of usual residence was overseas, undefined, no fixed place of abode or offshore or migratory and unknown. - Les données n'ont pas été prises en compte lorsque le domicile habituel était à l'étranger ou dans une zone extraterritoriale, était indéfini ou inconnu ou que la personne n'avait pas de domicile fixe ou était une migrante.

58 Excluding Niue, shown separately, which is part of Cook Islands, but because of remoteness is administered separately. - Non compris Nioué, qui fait l'objet d'une rubrique distincte et qui fait partie des îles Cook, mais qui, en raison de son éloignement, est administrée séparément.

59 Including United States military personnel, their dependants and contract employees. - Y compris les militaires des Etats-Unis, les membres de leur famille les accompagnant et les agents contractuels des Etats-Unis.

60 Includes deaths occurred in New Zealand but buried in Niue and deaths occurred in Niue but buried elsewhere. - Y compris les personnes décédées en Nouvelle-Zélande qui sont enterrées à Nioué et les personnes décédées à Nioué qui sont enterrées ailleurs.

61 Data cover the period from 1 July previous year to 30 June present year. - Pour la période allant du 1er juillet de l'année précédente au 30 juin de l'année en cours.

62 Source: Commonwealth Health Center - Vital Statistics Office - Source : Centre de Santé du Commonwealth - Bureau des statistiques d'État civil

63 Estimate based on results of the population census. - Estimation fondeé sur les résultats du recensement de la population.

Tables 19 and 19a

Table 19 presents deaths by age and sex and age-specific death rates by sex for the latest available year between 2000 and 2009. Table 19a presents the available data for year 2010.

Description of variables: Age is defined as age at last birthday, that is, the difference between the date of birth and the date of the occurrence of the event, expressed in completed solar years. The age classification used in this table is the following: under 1 year, 1-4 years, 5-year age groups through 95-99 years, and 100 years or over.

Rate computation: Age-specific death rates by sex are the annual number of deaths in each age-sex group per 1 000 population in the same age-sex group. These rates are calculated by the Statistics Division of the United Nations.

Deaths at unknown age and the population of unknown age are excluded from age-specific rate calculations but are part of the death rate for all ages combined.

Death rates for infants under one year of age in this table differ from the infant mortality rates shown elsewhere, because the latter are computed per 1 000 live births rather than per 1 000 population.

The population used in computing the rates is the estimated or the enumerated population by age and sex reported to United Nations Statistics Division. First priority is given to an estimate and second priority to census returns of the year to which the deaths refer.

Rates presented in this table have been limited to those for countries or areas having at least a total of 100 deaths in a given year. Moreover, rates specific for individual sub-categories that are based on 30 or fewer deaths are identified by the symbol "♦".

Reliability of data: Data from civil registers of deaths that are reported as incomplete (less than 90 per cent completeness) or of unknown completeness are considered unreliable and are set in italics rather than in roman type. Table 18 and the technical notes for that table provide more detailed information on the completeness of death registration. For more information about the quality of vital statistics data in general and the information available on the basis of the completeness estimates in particular, see section 4.2 of the Introduction.

Rates are not computed if data from civil registers of deaths are reported as incomplete (less than 90 per cent completeness) or of unknown completeness, and therefore deemed unreliable.

Limitations: Statistics on deaths by age and sex are subject to the same qualifications as are set forth for vital statistics in general and death statistics in particular as discussed in section 4 of the Introduction.

The reliability of the data is an important factor in considering the limitations. In addition, some deaths are tabulated by date of registration and not by date of occurrence; these have been indicated by a plus sign "+". Whenever the lag between the date of occurrence and date of registration is prolonged and, therefore, a large proportion of the death registrations are delayed, death statistics for any given year may be seriously affected. However, delays in the registration of deaths are less common and shorter than in the registration of live births.

International comparability in mortality statistics may also be affected by the exclusion of deaths of infants who were born alive but died before the registration of the birth or within the first 24 hours of life. Statistics of this type are footnoted.

Because these statistics are classified according to age, they are subject to the limitations with respect to accuracy of age reporting similar to those already discussed in connection with section 3.1.3 of the Introduction. The factors influencing the accuracy of reporting may be somewhat dissimilar in vital statistics (because of the differences in the method of taking a census and registering a death) but, in general, the same errors can be observed.

The absence of data in the unknown age group does not necessarily indicate completely accurate reporting and tabulation of the age item. It is often an indication that the unknowns have been eliminated by assigning ages to them before tabulation, or by proportionate distribution after tabulation.

International comparability of statistics on deaths by age is also affected by the use of different methods to determine age at death. If age is obtained from an item that simply requests age at death in completed years or is derived from information on year of birth and death rather than from information on complete date (day, month and year) of birth and death, the number of deaths classified in the under-one-year age group will tend to be reduced and the number of deaths in the next age group will tend to be somewhat increased. A similar bias may affect other age groups but its impact is usually negligible. Information on this factor is given in the footnotes when known.

Limitations of rates: Rates shown in this table are subject to the same limitations that affect the corresponding data and are set forth in the technical notes for table 18. These include differences in the completeness of registration, the treatment of infants who were born alive but died before the registration of their birth or within the first 24 hours of life, the method used to determine age at death and the quality of the reported information relating to age at death. In addition, some rates are based on deaths tabulated by date of registration and not by date of occurrence; these have been indicated with a plus sign "+".

The problem of obtaining precise correspondence between deaths (numerator) and population (denominator) as regards the inclusion or exclusion of armed forces, refugees, displaced persons and other special groups is particularly difficult where age-specific death rates are concerned. Even when deaths and population do correspond conceptually, comparability of the rates may be affected by abnormal conditions such as absence from the country or area of large numbers of young men in the military forces or working abroad as temporary workers. Death rates may appear high in the younger ages, simply because a large section of the able-bodied members of the age group, whose death rates under normal conditions might be less than the average for persons of their age, is not included. Therefore, care should be exercised in using these rates for comparative purposes.

Also, in a number of cases the rates shown here for all ages combined differ from crude death rates shown elsewhere, because in this table they are computed on the population for which an appropriate age-sex distribution was available, while the crude death rates shown elsewhere may utilize a different total population. The population by age and sex might refer to a census date within the year rather than to the mid-point, or it might be more or less inclusive as regards ethnic groups, armed forces and so forth. In a few instances, the difference is attributable to the fact that the rates in this table were computed on the mean population whereas the corresponding rates in other tables were computed on an estimate for 1 July.

Earlier data: Age-specific deaths and death rates by sex have been shown for the latest available year in each issue of the Yearbook since the 1955 issue. For information on specific years covered, the reader should consult the Historical Index.

Tableaux 19 et 19a

Le tableau 19 présente les données disponibles les plus récentes, entre 2000 et 2009, sur les décès et les taux de mortalité selon l'âge et le sexe. Le tableau 19a présente les données disponibles pour l'année 2010.

Description des variables : L'âge considéré est l'âge au dernier anniversaire, c'est-à-dire la différence entre la date de naissance et la date du décès, exprimée en années solaires révolues. La classification par âge est la suivante : moins d'un an, 1 à 4 ans, groupes quinquennaux jusqu'à 95-99 ans et 100 ans et plus.

Calcul des taux : les taux de mortalité selon l'âge et le sexe représentent le nombre annuel de décès survenus pour chaque sexe et chaque groupe d'âge pour 1 000 personnes du même groupe. Ces taux ont été calculés par la Division de statistique de l'ONU.

On n'a pas tenu compte des décès à un âge inconnu ni de la population d'âge inconnu, sauf dans les taux de mortalité pour tous les âges combinés.

Il convient de noter que, dans ce tableau, les taux de mortalité des groupes de moins d'un an sont différents des taux de mortalité infantile qui figurent dans d'autres tableaux, ces derniers ayant été établis pour 1 000 naissances vivantes et non pour 1 000 habitants.

Les chiffres de population utilisés pour le calcul des taux proviennent de dénombrements ou de répartitions estimatives de la population selon l'âge et le sexe. On a utilisé de préférence les estimations de la population; à défaut, on s'est contenté des données censitaires se rapportant à l'année des décès.

Les taux présentés dans ce tableau ne se rapportent qu'aux pays ou zones où l'on a enregistré un total d'au moins 100 décès pendant l'année. Les taux relatifs à des sous-catégories, qui sont fondés sur 30 décès ou moins, sont signalés par le signe "♦".

Fiabilité des données : Les données sur les décès issues des registres d'état civil qui sont déclarées incomplètes (degré d'exhaustivité inférieur à 90 p.100) ou dont le degré d'exhaustivité n'est pas connu sont jugées douteuses et apparaissent en italique et non en caractères romains. Le tableau 18 et les notes techniques s'y rapportant présentent des renseignements plus détaillés sur le degré d'exhaustivité de l'enregistrement des décès. Pour plus de précisions sur la qualité des statistiques de l'état civil en général et le degré de complétude en particulier, voir la section 4.2 de l'Introduction.

On a choisi de ne pas faire figurer dans le tableau 19 des taux calculés à partir de données sur les décès issues de registres d'état civil qui sont déclarées incomplètes (degré d'exhaustivité inférieur à 90 p. 100) ou dont le degré d'exhaustivité n'est pas connu.

Insuffisance des données : Les statistiques des décès selon l'âge et le sexe appellent les mêmes réserves que les statistiques de l'état civil en général et les statistiques relatives à la mortalité en particulier (voir la section 4 de l'Introduction).

La fiabilité des données est un facteur important. Il faut également tenir compte du fait que, dans certains cas, les données relatives aux décès sont classées par date d'enregistrement et non par date d'occurrence ; ces cas ont été signalés par le signe "+". Chaque fois que le décalage entre le décès et son enregistrement est grand et qu'une forte proportion des décès fait l'objet d'un enregistrement tardif, les statistiques des décès de l'année peuvent être considérablement faussées. En règle générale, toutefois, les décès sont enregistrés beaucoup plus rapidement que les naissances vivantes, et les retards prolongés sont rares.

Un autre facteur qui nuit à la comparabilité internationale est la pratique de certains pays ou zones qui consiste à ne pas inclure dans les statistiques des décès les enfants nés vivants mais décédés avant l'enregistrement de leur naissance ou dans les 24 heures qui ont suivi la naissance, pratique qui conduit à sous-évaluer le nombre de décès à moins d'un an. Quand pareil facteur a joué, cela a été signalé en note à la fin du tableau.

Étant donné que les statistiques relatives à la mortalité sont classées selon l'âge, elles appellent les mêmes réserves concernant l'exactitude des déclarations d'âge que celles qui ont été formulées à la section 3.1.3 des Introduction. Dans le cas des données d'état civil, les facteurs qui interviennent à cet égard sont

parfois un peu différents, du fait que le recensement et l'enregistrement des décès se font par des méthodes différentes, mais, d'une manière générale, les erreurs observées sont les mêmes.

Si aucun nombre ne figure dans la rangée réservée aux âges inconnus, cela ne signifie pas nécessairement que les déclarations d'âge et le classement par âge sont tout à fait exacts. C'est souvent une indication que l'on a attribué un âge aux personnes d'âge inconnu avant l'exploitation des données ou qu'elles ont été réparties proportionnellement entre les différents groupes après cette opération.

Le manque d'uniformité des méthodes suivies pour obtenir l'âge au moment du décès nuit également à la comparabilité internationale des données. Si l'âge est connu, soit d'après la réponse à une simple question sur l'âge du décès en années révolues, soit d'après l'année de la naissance et l'année du décès, et non d'après des renseignements concernant la date exacte (jour, mois et année) de la naissance et du décès, le nombre de décès classés dans la catégorie « moins d'un an » sera entaché d'une erreur par défaut et le chiffre figurant dans la catégorie suivante d'une erreur par excès.

Les données pour les autres groupes d'âge pourront être entachées d'une distorsion analogue, mais les répercussions seront généralement négligeables. Les imperfections, lorsqu'elles étaient connues, ont été signalées en note à la fin du tableau.

Insuffisance des taux : les taux présentés dans le tableau 19 appellent les mêmes réserves que celles formulées à propos des fréquences correspondantes (voir à ce sujet les notes techniques se rapportant au tableau 18). Leurs imperfections tiennent notamment aux différences d'exhaustivité de l'enregistrement, au classement des enfants nés vivants mais décédés avant l'enregistrement de leur naissance ou dans les 24 heures qui ont suivi la naissance, à la méthode utilisée pour obtenir l'âge au moment du décès, et à la qualité des déclarations concernant l'âge au moment du décès. En outre, dans certains cas, les données relatives aux décès sont classées par date d'enregistrement et non par date de l'événement ; ces cas ont été signalés par le signe "+".

S'agissant des taux de mortalité par âge, il est particulièrement difficile d'établir une correspondance exacte entre les décès (numérateur) et la population (dénominateur) du fait de l'inclusion ou de l'exclusion des militaires, des réfugiés, des personnes déplacées et d'autres groupes spéciaux. Il convient d'ajouter que, même lorsque population et décès correspondent, la comparabilité des taux peut être compromise par des conditions anormales telles que l'absence du pays ou de la zone d'un grand nombre de jeunes gens qui sont sous les drapeaux ou qui travaillent à l'étranger comme travailleurs temporaires. Il arrive ainsi que les taux de mortalité paraissent élevés parmi les groupes les plus jeunes simplement parce que l'on en a exclu un grand nombre d'individus en bonne santé pour lesquels le taux de mortalité pourrait être, dans des conditions normales, inférieur à la moyenne observée pour les personnes du même âge. Par conséquent, il importe d'être prudent quand on les utilise ces taux de mortalité dans des comparaisons.

De même, les taux indiqués pour tous les âges combinés diffèrent dans plusieurs cas des taux bruts de mortalité qui figurent dans d'autres tableaux, parce qu'ils se rapportent à une population pour laquelle on disposait d'une répartition par âge et par sexe appropriée, tandis que les taux bruts de mortalité indiqués ailleurs peuvent avoir été calculés sur la base d'un chiffre de population totale différent. Ainsi, il est possible que les chiffres de population par âge et par sexe proviennent d'un recensement effectué dans le courant de l'année et non au milieu de l'année, et qu'ils se différencient des autres chiffres de population en excluant ou en incluant certains groupes ethniques, les militaires, etc. Quelquefois, la différence tient à ce que les taux du tableau 19 ont été calculés sur la base de la population moyenne, alors que les taux correspondants des autres tableaux reposent sur une estimation au 1er juillet.

Données publiées antérieurement : Les éditions de l'*Annuaire démographique* parues depuis 1955 présentent les statistiques les plus récentes dont on disposait à l'époque sur les décès selon l'âge et le sexe et sur les taux de mortalité selon l'âge et le sexe. Pour plus de précisions concernant les années pour lesquelles ces données ont été publiées, se reporter à l'index historique.

19. Deaths by age and sex, age-specific death rates by sex: latest available year, 2000 - 2009
Décès et taux de mortalité selon l'âge et le sexe : dernière année disponible, 2000 - 2009

Continent, country or area, date, code and age (in years) Continent, pays ou zone, date, code et âge (en années)	Number - Nombre			Rate - Taux		
	Both sexes Les deux sexes	Male Masculin	Female Féminin	Both sexes Les deux sexes	Male Masculin	Female Féminin
AFRICA - AFRIQUE						
Botswana[1]						
2007 (+U)						
Total	11 074	5 971	5 103	...	...	...
0	658	353	305	...	...	...
1 - 4	643	338	305	...	...	...
5 - 14	192	100	92	...	...	...
15 - 24	438	132	306	...	...	...
25 - 34	2 330	1 047	1 283	...	...	...
35 - 44	2 202	1 293	909	...	...	...
45 - 54	1 509	937	572	...	...	...
55 - 64	1 045	659	386	...	...	...
65 +	2 039	1 106	933	...	...	...
Unknown - Inconnu	18	6	12	..	..	..
Egypt - Égypte						
2009 (C)						
Total	476 592	261 127	215 465	6.2	6.6	5.7
0	25 760	13 899	11 861	38.8	40.8	36.7
1 - 4	11 678	6 243	5 435	1.6	1.6	1.5
5 - 9	4 919	2 923	1 996	0.6	0.7	0.5
10 - 14	3 836	2 346	1 490	0.5	0.6	0.4
15 - 19	5 354	3 762	1 592	0.6	0.8	0.4
20 - 24	8 061	5 291	2 770	1.0	1.2	0.7
25 - 29	7 403	4 643	2 760	1.1	1.4	0.8
30 - 34	7 034	4 272	2 762	1.4	1.7	1.1
35 - 39	8 158	4 876	3 282	1.7	2.0	1.3
40 - 44	11 752	7 423	4 329	2.7	3.4	2.0
45 - 49	20 172	13 228	6 944	5.2	6.7	3.7
50 - 54	36 652	21 553	15 099	11.4	13.2	9.4
55 - 59	42 788	26 653	16 135	17.9	20.8	14.6
60 - 64	45 740	26 713	19 027	25.4	28.2	22.4
65 - 69	43 790	24 330	19 460	34.8	36.0	33.4
70 - 74	50 059	26 132	23 927	60.1	61.6	58.6
75 +	124 193	56 126	68 067	159.2	141.1	178.0
75 - 79	48 030	23 623	24 407	...	...	...
80 - 84	39 180	17 799	21 381	...	...	...
85 +	36 983	14 704	22 279	...	...	...
Unknown - Inconnu	19 243	10 714	8 529	..	..	..
Kenya						
2009 (U)						
Total	181 220	98 704	82 516	...	...	...
0[2]	26 273	13 719	12 554	...	...	...
1 - 4	13 917	7 471	6 446	...	...	...
5 - 14	8 653	4 716	3 937	...	...	...
15 - 24	12 163	5 901	6 262	...	...	...
25 - 34	22 165	11 558	10 607	...	...	...
35 - 44	22 122	12 755	9 367	...	...	...
45 - 54	19 159	11 283	7 876	...	...	...
55 - 74	29 446	17 265	12 181	...	...	...
75 +	27 322	14 036	13 286	...	...	...
Libya - Libye						
2002 (U)						
Total	19 362	11 278	8 084	...	...	...
0	2 194	1 190	1 004	...	...	...
1 - 4	891	546	345	...	...	...
5 - 9	267	142	125	...	...	...
10 - 19	670	432	238	...	...	...
20 - 29	1 100	824	276	...	...	...
30 - 39	1 287	820	467	...	...	...
40 - 49	1 118	621	497	...	...	...
50 - 59	1 492	860	632	...	...	...
60 - 69	2 936	1 754	1 182	...	...	...
70 - 79	3 812	2 254	1 558	...	...	...
80 +	3 595	1 835	1 760	...	...	...
Mauritius - Maurice[3]						
2009 (+C)						
Total	9 224	5 226	3 998	7.2	8.3	6.2
0	205	114	91	13.1	14.5	11.6

Continent, country or area, date, code and age (in years) / Continent, pays ou zone, date, code et âge (en années)	Number - Nombre			Rate - Taux		
	Both sexes Les deux sexes	Male Masculin	Female Féminin	Both sexes Les deux sexes	Male Masculin	Female Féminin
AFRICA - AFRIQUE						
Mauritius - Maurice[3]						
2009 (+C)						
1 - 4	42	21	21	0.6	♦0.6	♦0.6
5 - 9	29	20	9	♦0.3	♦0.4	♦0.2
10 - 14	29	17	12	♦0.3	♦0.3	♦0.2
15 - 19	66	47	19	0.6	0.9	♦0.4
20 - 24	73	45	28	0.8	0.9	♦0.6
25 - 29	101	74	27	0.9	1.4	♦0.5
30 - 34	159	111	48	1.5	2.1	0.9
35 - 39	191	134	57	2.1	2.9	1.2
40 - 44	354	252	102	3.6	5.1	2.1
45 - 49	517	372	145	5.3	7.7	3.0
50 - 54	699	493	206	8.5	12.0	4.9
55 - 59	823	558	265	11.6	16.2	7.3
60 - 64	838	493	345	17.9	22.7	13.7
65 - 69	880	522	358	28.1	37.1	20.7
70 - 74	919	514	405	38.1	50.7	29.0
75 - 79	1 018	537	481	63.5	83.5	50.1
80 - 84	1 060	476	584	95.4	117.9	82.6
85 +	1 221	426	795	182.7	209.6	170.9
Morocco - Maroc						
2007 (U)						
Total	105 222	66 522	38 700	...	...	...
0	5 140	2 823	2 317	...	...	...
1 - 4	2 320	1 266	1 054	...	...	...
5 - 9	1 075	591	484	...	...	...
10 - 14	859	533	326	...	...	...
15 - 19	1 575	1 024	551	...	...	...
20 - 24	2 204	1 442	762	...	...	...
25 - 29	2 503	1 570	933	...	...	...
30 - 34	2 705	1 660	1 045	...	...	...
35 - 39	2 948	1 767	1 181	...	...	...
40 - 44	3 400	2 052	1 348	...	...	...
45 - 49	4 547	2 766	1 781	...	...	...
50 - 54	5 616	3 672	1 944	...	...	...
55 - 59	6 132	4 046	2 086	...	...	...
60 - 64	7 193	4 626	2 567	...	...	...
65 - 69	10 331	6 494	3 837	...	...	...
70 - 74	12 441	7 990	4 451	...	...	...
75 - 79	13 183	8 491	4 692	...	...	...
80 +	20 051	13 159	6 892	...	...	...
Unknown - Inconnu	999	550	449	..	..	..
Namibia - Namibie[4]						
2001 (I)						
Total	25 061	12 338[5]	12 137[5]	13.7	13.9	12.9
0 - 4	4 631	2 180[5]	2 343[5]	19.2	18.2	19.3
5 - 9	938	461[5]	447[5]	3.8	3.8	3.6
10 - 14	508	246[5]	256[5]	2.2	2.2	2.2
15 - 19	658	317[5]	330[5]	3.3	3.2	3.2
20 - 24	1 240	492[5]	740[5]	7.1	5.7	8.4
25 - 29	1 791	799[5]	989[5]	11.9	10.8	12.9
30 - 34	2 032	1 029[5]	988[5]	17.1	18.0	16.1
35 - 39	1 845	1 003[5]	837[5]	19.1	22.2	16.3
40 - 44	1 370	753[5]	615[5]	18.5	22.0	15.4
45 - 49	1 099	609[5]	485[5]	19.0	22.6	15.7
50 - 54	866	547[5]	317[5]	18.1	24.9	12.3
55 - 59	699	419[5]	279[5]	19.9	25.2	15.0
60 - 64	761	431[5]	315[5]	22.1	27.7	16.7
65 - 69	576	310[5]	260[5]	22.8	27.2	18.8
70 - 74	729	405[5]	322[5]	33.1	43.5	25.3
75 - 79	571	266[5]	291[5]	35.7	41.7	30.2
80 - 84	539	228[5]	299[5]	39.0	42.5	35.3
85 - 89	361	162[5]	189[5]	66.8	79.7	56.0
90 - 94	246	102[5]	138[5]	96.3	110.0	84.8
95 +	373	131[5]	242[5]	137.5	146.0	133.3
Unknown - Inconnu	3 228	1 448[5]	1 455[5]	..	..	..

Continent, country or area, date, code and age (in years) / Continent, pays ou zone, date, code et âge (en années)	Number - Nombre			Rate - Taux		
	Both sexes Les deux sexes	Male Masculin	Female Féminin	Both sexes Les deux sexes	Male Masculin	Female Féminin
AFRICA - AFRIQUE						
Réunion[6]						
2007 (C)						
Total	4 045	2 247	1 798	5.1	5.9	4.4
0 - 4	114	58	56	1.7	1.7	1.7
0	99	49	50	...	...	...
1 - 4	15	9	6	...	...	...
5 - 9	6	6	-	♦0.1	♦0.2	-
10 - 14	10	7	3	♦0.1	♦0.2	♦0.1
15 - 19	32	25	7	0.5	♦0.7	♦0.2
20 - 24	44	35	9	0.8	1.3	♦0.3
25 - 29	39	27	12	0.8	♦1.1	♦0.4
30 - 34	55	37	18	1.0	1.4	♦0.6
35 - 39	97	68	29	1.5	2.3	♦0.9
40 - 44	158	106	52	2.4	3.3	1.5
45 - 49	211	150	61	4.0	5.9	2.3
50 - 54	236	183	53	5.1	8.2	2.2
55 - 59	266	188	78	7.5	10.7	4.4
60 - 64	287	176	111	10.8	14.1	7.9
65 - 69	375	246	129	17.4	24.8	11.1
70 - 74	427	250	177	25.9	34.7	19.1
75 - 79	448	231	217	39.5	50.3	32.2
80 - 84	496	222	274	65.3	78.9	57.3
85 - 89	393	149	244	106.6	140.6	92.9
90 - 94	233	66	167	166.1	182.8	160.3
95 +	118	17	101	308.9	♦369.6	300.6
95 - 99	96	15	81	...	...	...
100 +	22	2	20	...	...	...
Saint Helena ex. dep. - Sainte-Hélène sans dép.						
2009 (C)						
Total	41	20	21	...	...	...
0	-	-	-	...	...	...
1 - 4	-	-	-	...	...	...
5 - 9	-	-	-	...	...	...
10 - 14	-	-	-	...	...	...
15 - 19	-	-	-	...	...	...
20 - 24	-	-	-	...	...	...
25 - 29	-	-	-	...	...	...
30 - 34	-	-	-	...	...	...
35 - 39	-	-	-	...	...	...
40 - 44	-	-	-	...	...	...
45 - 49	-	-	-	...	...	...
50 - 54	3	1	2	...	...	...
55 - 59	2	2	-	...	...	...
60 - 64	3	2	1	...	...	...
65 - 69	8	6	2	...	...	...
70 - 74	7	4	3	...	...	...
75 - 79	3	1	2	...	...	...
80 - 84	5	1	4	...	...	...
85 - 89	4	1	3	...	...	...
90 - 94	5	2	3	...	...	...
95 - 99	1	-	1	...	...	...
100 +	-	-	-	...	...	...
Seychelles						
2009 (+C)						
Total	684	398	286	...	...	...
0	17	6	11	...	...	...
1 - 4	1	1	-	...	...	...
5 - 9	1	1	-	...	...	...
10 - 14	1	-	1	...	...	...
15 - 19	3	-	3	...	...	...
20 - 24	8	7	1	...	...	...
25 - 29	13	11	2	...	...	...
30 - 34	8	5	3	...	...	...
35 - 39	22	13	9	...	...	...
40 - 44	25	21	4	...	...	...
45 - 49	31	16	15	...	...	...
50 - 54	42	31	11	...	...	...

Continent, country or area, date, code and age (in years) / Continent, pays ou zone, date, code et âge (en années)	Number - Nombre			Rate - Taux		
	Both sexes Les deux sexes	Male Masculin	Female Féminin	Both sexes Les deux sexes	Male Masculin	Female Féminin
AFRICA - AFRIQUE						
Seychelles						
2009 (+C)						
55 - 59	42	31	11	...	...	...
60 - 64	48	39	9	...	...	...
65 - 69	50	32	18	...	...	...
70 - 74	49	31	18	...	...	...
75 - 79	104	67	37	...	...	...
80 - 84	91	43	48	...	...	...
85 +	125	41	84	...	...	...
Unknown - Inconnu	3	2	1	..	...	..
Sierra Leone[7]						
2004 (|)						
Total	99 020	...	...	20.1	...	...
0	16 637	...	...	106.6	...	...
1 - 4	20 362	...	...	34.1	...	...
5 - 9	6 806	...	...	9.2	...	...
10 - 14	3 087	...	...	5.5	...	...
15 - 19	3 679	...	...	6.9	...	...
20 - 24	5 278	...	...	12.7	...	...
25 - 29	3 809	...	...	9.4	...	...
30 - 34	3 707	...	...	11.9	...	...
35 - 39	3 387	...	...	11.3	...	...
40 - 44	3 689	...	...	17.3	...	...
45 - 49	3 045	...	...	17.2	...	...
50 - 54	3 491	...	...	27.2	...	...
55 - 59	2 022	...	...	23.8	...	...
60 - 64	3 885	...	...	44.3	...	...
65 - 69	2 446	...	...	40.0	...	...
70 - 74	3 423	...	...	62.9	...	...
75 - 79	2 390	...	...	65.1	...	...
80 - 84	2 780	...	...	102.6	...	...
85 +	5 097	...	...	142.3	...	...
South Africa - Afrique du Sud						
2008 (U)						
Total	592 073	302 744[5]	288 541[5]	...	...	...
0	45 316	23 838[5]	21 203[5]	...	...	...
1 - 4	15 332	8 147[5]	7 156[5]	...	...	...
5 - 9	4 998	2 709[5]	2 283[5]	...	...	...
10 - 14	4 098	2 216[5]	1 881[5]	...	...	...
15 - 19	8 928	4 817[5]	4 085[5]	...	...	...
20 - 24	23 478	10 624[5]	12 815[5]	...	...	...
25 - 29	41 789	18 349[5]	23 401[5]	...	...	...
30 - 34	53 809	26 647[5]	27 111[5]	...	...	...
35 - 39	53 204	28 927[5]	24 233[5]	...	...	...
40 - 44	46 072	25 939[5]	20 109[5]	...	...	...
45 - 49	42 162	24 671[5]	17 462[5]	...	...	...
50 - 54	38 132	22 609[5]	15 502[5]	...	...	...
55 - 59	36 399	21 500[5]	14 881[5]	...	...	...
60 - 64	31 515	17 664[5]	13 835[5]	...	...	...
65 - 69	33 522	17 979[5]	15 533[5]	...	...	...
70 - 74	29 339	14 095[5]	15 242[5]	...	...	...
75 - 79	29 641	12 513[5]	17 125[5]	...	...	...
80 - 84	22 806	8 985[5]	13 820[5]	...	...	...
85 - 89	17 098	5 955[5]	11 142[5]	...	...	...
90 - 94	13 467	3 947[5]	9 493[5]	...	...	...
Unknown - Inconnu	968	613[5]	229[5]	..	...	...
Swaziland[8]						
2007 (|)						
Total	18 367	8 738	9 629	21.8	21.5	22.0
0 - 4	4 843	2 131	2 712	44.1	38.9	49.4
0	3 613	1 555	2 058	...	...	...
1 - 4	1 230	576	654	...	...	...
5 - 9	408	198	210	3.6	3.5	3.8
10 - 14	302	165	137	2.7	3.0	2.4
15 - 19	431	174	257	4.3	3.5	5.1
20 - 24	1 145	353	792	13.0	8.3	17.6

Continent, country or area, date, code and age (in years) / Continent, pays ou zone, date, code et âge (en années)	Number - Nombre			Rate - Taux		
	Both sexes Les deux sexes	Male Masculin	Female Féminin	Both sexes Les deux sexes	Male Masculin	Female Féminin
AFRICA - AFRIQUE						
Swaziland[8]						
2007 (|)						
25 - 29	1 773	707	1 066	25.2	20.9	29.2
30 - 34	1 792	839	953	34.3	32.8	35.7
35 - 39	1 586	828	758	36.3	40.0	32.9
40 - 44	1 145	652	493	33.7	44.0	25.7
45 - 49	865	502	363	29.6	39.3	22.1
50 - 54	752	453	299	32.9	43.5	24.0
55 - 59	557	364	193	30.8	43.7	19.8
60 - 64	618	342	276	37.0	51.0	27.6
65 - 69	436	238	198	32.9	43.1	25.6
70 - 74	392	214	178	48.0	66.7	35.9
75 - 79	283	158	125	45.4	68.0	31.9
80 +	612	261	351	95.3	122.1	82.0
Unknown - Inconnu	427	159	268	..	..	..
Zimbabwe[9]						
2002 (|)						
Total	200 294	103 741	96 553	17.2	18.4	16.1
0	23 672	12 887	10 785	69.6	75.8	63.3
1 - 4	16 231	8 688	7 543	12.2	13.0	11.3
5 - 9	5 166	2 793	2 373	3.4	3.7	3.1
10 - 14	3 599	1 946	1 653	2.4	2.6	2.2
15 - 19	4 165	1 802	2 363	2.8	2.4	3.1
20 - 24	9 623	3 440	6 183	7.9	6.1	9.4
25 - 29	17 414	6 930	10 484	17.6	14.6	20.4
30 - 34	21 358	10 286	11 072	29.3	27.8	30.7
35 - 39	19 611	10 176	9 435	38.9	43.2	35.1
40 - 44	15 322	8 608	6 714	35.3	44.2	28.0
45 - 49	11 993	6 907	5 086	33.6	41.8	26.6
50 - 54	8 845	5 029	3 816	29.4	39.3	22.0
55 - 59	6 229	3 857	2 372	29.5	39.2	21.1
60 - 64	5 910	3 649	2 261	30.5	38.6	22.7
65 - 69	4 504	2 682	1 822	34.1	41.7	26.9
70 - 74	4 638	2 810	1 828	37.8	46.6	29.3
75 +	11 781	6 066	5 715	71.7	84.3	61.9
Unknown - Inconnu	10 233	5 185	5 048	..	..	..
AMERICA, NORTH - AMÉRIQUE DU NORD						
Anguilla						
2007 (+C)						
Total	70	43	27	...	...	...
0 - 4	1	-	1	...	...	...
5 - 14	-	-	-	...	...	...
15 - 29	5	4	1	...	...	...
30 - 44	9	6	3	...	...	...
45 - 59	10	7	3	...	...	...
60 - 64	1	1	-	...	...	...
65 - 69	1	1	-	...	...	...
70 - 74	8	3	5	...	...	...
75 - 79	10	8	2	...	...	...
80 - 84	5	4	1	...	...	...
85 +	20	9	11	...	...	...
Antigua and Barbuda - Antigua-et-Barbuda[10]						
2002 (+C)						
Total	444	234	210	5.7	6.4	5.1
0	21	14	7	♦14.4	♦19.3	♦9.6
1 - 4	3	2	1	♦0.5	♦0.7	♦0.3
5 - 9	1	-	1	♦0.1	-	♦0.3
10 - 14	2	1	1	♦0.3	♦0.3	♦0.3
15 - 19	2	2	-	♦0.3	♦0.7	-
20 - 24	9	6	3	♦1.5	♦2.0	♦0.9
25 - 29	3	3	-	♦0.5	♦1.0	-
30 - 34	11	8	3	♦1.5	♦2.5	♦0.8
35 - 39	10	8	2	♦1.5	♦2.6	♦0.5
40 - 44	13	5	8	♦2.3	♦2.0	♦2.6

19. Deaths by age and sex, age-specific death rates by sex: latest available year, 2000 - 2009
Décès et taux de mortalité selon l'âge et le sexe : dernière année disponible, 2000 - 2009 (continued - suite)

Continent, country or area, date, code and age (in years) / Continent, pays ou zone, date, code et âge (en années)	Number - Nombre			Rate - Taux		
	Both sexes Les deux sexes	Male Masculin	Female Féminin	Both sexes Les deux sexes	Male Masculin	Female Féminin
AMERICA, NORTH - AMÉRIQUE DU NORD						
Antigua and Barbuda - Antigua-et-Barbuda[10]						
2002 (+C)						
45 - 49	13	6	7	♦2.9	♦2.9	♦3.0
50 - 54	16	7	9	♦4.8	♦4.5	♦5.1
55 - 59	18	9	9	♦7.4	♦8.2	♦6.7
60 - 64	24	15	9	♦12.5	♦17.1	♦8.7
65 - 69	28	17	11	♦17.4	♦23.1	♦12.6
70 - 74	52	27	25	38.1	♦45.1	♦32.6
75 - 79	48	30	18	46.1	♦62.5	♦32.1
80 - 84	64	32	32	86.4	101.9	74.9
85 - 89	54	25	29	130.4	♦165.6	♦110.3
90 - 94	30	10	20	♦161.3	♦163.9	♦160.0
95 +	22	7	15	♦709.7	♦1000.0	♦625.0
Aruba						
2007 (C)						
Total	521	279	242	5.0	5.6	4.4
0	4	2	2	♦3.2	♦3.2	♦3.3
1 - 4	-	-	-	-	-	-
5 - 9	-	-	-	-	-	-
10 - 14	-	-	-	-	-	-
15 - 19	7	6	1	♦1.0	♦1.6	♦0.3
20 - 24	3	2	1	♦0.5	♦0.7	♦0.3
25 - 29	6	3	3	♦1.0	♦1.0	♦0.9
30 - 34	5	3	2	♦0.7	♦0.9	♦0.5
35 - 39	9	4	5	♦1.0	♦1.0	♦1.1
40 - 44	16	11	5	♦1.7	♦2.4	♦1.0
45 - 49	22	13	9	♦2.3	♦2.9	♦1.8
50 - 54	23	14	9	♦3.0	♦3.9	♦2.2
55 - 59	47	28	19	7.8	♦9.9	♦5.9
60 - 64	45	28	17	10.0	♦13.4	♦7.0
65 - 69	55	31	24	16.1	20.0	♦12.8
70 - 74	60	37	23	22.9	34.0	♦15.0
75 - 79	60	39	21	35.5	55.3	♦21.4
80 - 84	62	30	32	74.2	♦89.6	63.8
85 - 89	32	8	24	74.6	♦52.0	♦87.3
90 - 94	44	13	31	228.4	♦255.6	218.6
95 - 99	18	7	11	...	...	...
100 +	3	-	3	♦176.5	-	♦187.5
2009 (C)						
Total	623	...	...	5.8	...	...
0	5	...	...	...	...	...
1 - 49	74	...	...	...	...	...
50 - 59	65	...	...	4.2	...	...
60 - 69	126	...	...	14.5	...	...
70 - 79	167	...	...	35.1	...	...
80 - 89	134	...	...	90.6	...	...
90 +	52	...	...	172.9	...	...
Bahamas						
2007 (C)						
Total	1 798	1 001	797	5.4	6.2	4.6
0	69	33	36	11.7	10.8	12.6
1 - 4	6	3	3	♦0.3	♦0.3	♦0.3
5 - 9	11	7	4	♦0.4	♦0.5	♦0.3
10 - 14	9	6	3	♦0.3	♦0.4	♦0.2
15 - 19	27	23	4	♦0.9	♦1.6	♦0.3
20 - 24	39	26	13	1.5	♦2.0	♦1.0
25 - 29	54	40	14	2.2	3.3	♦1.1
30 - 34	60	40	20	2.2	3.1	♦1.4
35 - 39	109	66	43	4.0	5.0	3.0
40 - 44	105	66	39	3.9	5.2	2.8
45 - 49	130	76	54	5.6	6.8	4.4
50 - 54	138	97	41	7.8	11.4	4.5
55 - 59	116	68	48	9.0	11.1	7.1
60 - 64	125	79	46	12.5	17.2	8.5
65 - 69	159	87	72	20.1	24.2	16.7
70 - 74	150	86	64	27.8	35.8	21.3
75 - 79	144	70	74	43.6	53.8	37.0

Continent, country or area, date, code and age (in years) Continent, pays ou zone, date, code et âge (en années)	Number - Nombre			Rate - Taux		
	Both sexes Les deux sexes	Male Masculin	Female Féminin	Both sexes Les deux sexes	Male Masculin	Female Féminin
AMERICA, NORTH - AMÉRIQUE DU NORD						
Bahamas						
2007 (C)						
80 + ...	345	126	219	127.8	157.5	115.3
80 - 84	122	46	76	...	...	...
85 - 89	114	44	70	...	...	...
90 - 94	72	26	46	...	...	...
95 - 99	32	9	23	...	...	...
100 + ...	5	1	4	...	...	...
Unknown - Inconnu	2	2	-	..	..	..
Barbados - Barbade[11]						
2007 (+C)						
Total...	2 195	1 143	1 052	...	...	...
0	31	18	13	...	...	...
1 - 4	8	5	3	...	...	...
5 - 9	5	3	2	...	...	...
10 - 14	8	6	2	...	...	...
15 - 19	17	13	4	...	...	...
20 - 24	10	4	6	...	...	...
25 - 29	15	14	1	...	...	...
30 - 34	30	16	14	...	...	...
35 - 39	38	23	15	...	...	...
40 - 44	45	26	19	...	...	...
45 - 49	58	28	30	...	...	...
50 - 54	76	46	30	...	...	...
55 - 59	90	54	36	...	...	...
60 - 64	113	63	50	...	...	...
65 - 69	142	83	59	...	...	...
70 - 74	182	105	77	...	...	...
75 - 79	309	160	149	...	...	...
80 - 84	281	152	129	...	...	...
85 - 89	339	139	200	...	...	...
90 - 94	199	59	140	...	...	...
95 + ...	97	30	67	...	...	...
Unknown - Inconnu	102	96	6	..	..	...
Belize						
2000 (U)						
Total...	*1 534*	*895*	*639*	...	...	...
0	*155*	*87*	*68*	...	...	...
1 - 4	*35*	*15*	*20*	...	...	...
5 - 9	*14*	*4*	*10*	...	...	...
10 - 14	*20*	*11*	*9*	...	...	...
15 - 19	*31*	*22*	*9*	...	...	...
20 - 24	*40*	*32*	*8*	...	...	...
25 - 29	*41*	*31*	*10*	...	...	...
30 - 34	*54*	*35*	*19*	...	...	...
35 - 39	*55*	*30*	*25*	...	...	...
40 - 44	*30*	*21*	*9*	...	...	...
45 - 49	*50*	*41*	*9*	...	...	...
50 - 54	*77*	*41*	*36*	...	...	...
55 - 59	*72*	*43*	*29*	...	...	...
60 - 64	*109*	*60*	*49*	...	...	...
65 - 69	*134*	*69*	*65*	...	...	...
70 - 74	*151*	*102*	*49*	...	...	...
75 - 79	*160*	*93*	*67*	...	...	...
80 + ...	*305*	*157*	*148*	...	...	...
Unknown - Inconnu	*1*	*1*	...	..	..	...
2001 (U)						
Total...	*1 261*	...	...	...	...	...
0	*120*	...	...	...	...	...
1 - 4	*32*	...	...	...	...	...
5 - 9	*15*	...	...	...	...	...
10 - 14	*12*	...	...	...	...	...
15 - 19	*35*	...	...	...	...	...
20 - 24	*41*	...	...	...	...	...
25 - 29	*54*	...	...	...	...	...
30 - 34	*51*	...	...	...	...	...
35 - 39	*56*	...	...	...	...	...

19. Deaths by age and sex, age-specific death rates by sex: latest available year, 2000 - 2009
Décès et taux de mortalité selon l'âge et le sexe : dernière année disponible, 2000 - 2009 (continued - suite)

Continent, country or area, date, code and age (in years) / Continent, pays ou zone, date, code et âge (en années)	Number - Nombre			Rate - Taux		
	Both sexes Les deux sexes	Male Masculin	Female Féminin	Both sexes Les deux sexes	Male Masculin	Female Féminin
AMERICA, NORTH - AMÉRIQUE DU NORD						
Belize						
2001 (U)						
40 - 44	53	...	...	...	...	...
45 - 49	62	...	...	...	...	...
50 - 54	53	...	...	...	...	...
55 - 59	57	...	...	...	...	...
60 - 64	68	...	...	...	...	...
65 - 69	98	...	...	...	...	...
70 - 74	122	...	...	...	...	...
75 - 79	87	...	...	...	...	...
80 +	239	...	...	...	...	...
Unknown - Inconnu	6	...	...	...	...	...
Bermuda - Bermudes[12]						
2009 (C)						
Total	471	252	219	7.3	8.2	6.5
0	1	-	1	♦1.3	-	♦2.6
1 - 4	1	1	-	♦0.3	♦0.7	-
5 - 9	-	-	-	-	-	-
10 - 14	-	-	-	-	-	-
15 - 19	-	-	-	-	-	-
20 - 24	2	2	-	♦0.6	♦1.2	-
25 - 29	5	3	2	♦1.2	♦1.5	♦0.9
30 - 34	7	6	1	♦1.6	♦2.9	♦0.4
35 - 39	7	5	2	♦1.4	♦2.1	♦0.8
40 - 44	10	5	5	♦1.9	♦1.9	♦1.9
45 - 49	20	14	6	♦3.4	♦4.8	♦2.0
50 - 54	15	7	8	♦2.9	♦2.9	♦2.9
55 - 59	30	17	13	♦7.0	♦8.2	♦5.9
60 - 64	39	30	9	10.9	♦17.9	♦4.7
65 - 69	39	21	18	14.9	♦17.9	♦12.4
70 - 74	39	26	13	19.2	♦30.2	♦11.1
75 - 79	75	38	37	45.8	57.3	37.9
80 - 84	65	28	37	60.8	♦72.2	54.3
85 +	116	49	67	154.9	229.0	125.2
85 - 89	49	26	23	...	...	...
90 - 94	42	18	24	...	...	...
95 - 99	12	3	9	...	...	...
100 +	13	2	11	...	...	...
Canada[13]						
2007 (C)						
Total	235 217	118 681	116 536	7.1	7.3	7.0
0	1 881	1 043	838	5.3	5.8	4.9
1 - 4	271	155	116	0.2	0.2	0.2
5 - 9	210	102	108	0.1	0.1	0.1
10 - 14	273	161	112	0.1	0.2	0.1
15 - 19	956	670	286	0.4	0.6	0.3
20 - 24	1 291	962	329	0.6	0.8	0.3
25 - 29	1 265	905	360	0.6	0.8	0.3
30 - 34	1 384	927	457	0.6	0.8	0.4
35 - 39	2 068	1 379	689	0.9	1.2	0.6
40 - 44	3 518	2 199	1 319	1.3	1.7	1.0
45 - 49	5 857	3 477	2 380	2.2	2.6	1.8
50 - 54	8 389	5 126	3 263	3.4	4.2	2.6
55 - 59	11 194	6 850	4 344	5.3	6.6	4.1
60 - 64	14 072	8 600	5 472	8.3	10.3	6.3
65 - 69	17 041	10 249	6 792	13.4	16.7	10.3
70 - 74	22 468	13 132	9 336	21.4	26.7	16.8
75 - 79	31 105	17 513	13 592	34.8	43.9	27.4
80 - 84	38 209	18 931	19 278	58.7	73.5	49.0
85 - 89	37 176	15 366	21 810	100.7	122.4	89.5
90 +	36 584	10 930	25 654	196.5	218.9	188.3
90 - 94	25 102	8 224	16 878	...	...	...
95 - 99	9 518	2 371	7 147	...	...	...
100 +	1 964	335	1 629	...	...	...
Unknown - Inconnu	5	4	1	...	...	...

19. Deaths by age and sex, age-specific death rates by sex: latest available year, 2000 - 2009
Décès et taux de mortalité selon l'âge et le sexe : dernière année disponible, 2000 - 2009 (continued - suite)

Continent, country or area, date, code and age (in years) / Continent, pays ou zone, date, code et âge (en années)	Number - Nombre			Rate - Taux		
	Both sexes Les deux sexes	Male Masculin	Female Féminin	Both sexes Les deux sexes	Male Masculin	Female Féminin
AMERICA, NORTH - AMÉRIQUE DU NORD						
Cayman Islands - Îles Caïmanes[14]						
2009 (C)						
Total	152	88	64	2.9	3.4	2.4
0 - 4	6	5	1	♦1.5	♦2.5	♦0.5
0	3	3	-	...	...	...
1 - 4	3	2	1	...	...	...
5 - 9	-	-	-	-	-	-
10 - 14	1	1	-	♦0.3	♦0.6	-
15 - 19	1	1	-	♦0.4	♦0.7	-
20 - 24	3	2	1	♦1.2	♦1.7	♦0.8
25 - 29	3	3	-	♦0.6	♦1.4	-
30 - 34	3	2	1	♦0.5	♦0.7	♦0.4
35 - 39	2	2	-	♦0.3	♦0.7	-
40 - 44	5	3	2	♦1.0	♦1.1	♦0.8
45 - 49	9	4	5	♦1.7	♦1.5	♦1.9
50 - 54	8	6	2	♦2.4	♦3.8	♦1.1
55 - 59	13	10	3	♦4.2	♦7.0	♦1.8
60 - 64	8	5	3	♦5.6	♦6.1	♦5.0
65 - 69	90	44	46	...	...	...
Costa Rica						
2009 (C)						
Total	18 560	10 706	7 854	4.0	4.7	3.4
0 - 4	772	414	358	2.3	2.3	2.3
0	663	355	308	...	...	...
1 - 4	109	59	50	...	...	...
5 - 9	64	39	25	0.2	0.2	♦0.1
10 - 14	97	48	49	0.2	0.2	0.2
15 - 19	270	202	68	0.6	0.8	0.3
20 - 24	429	330	99	0.9	1.4	0.4
25 - 29	452	358	94	1.2	1.8	0.5
30 - 34	404	303	101	...	...	...
35 - 39	464	316	148	...	...	...
40 - 44	619	408	211	...	...	...
45 - 49	793	516	277	...	...	...
50 - 54	905	581	324	...	...	...
55 - 59	1 108	659	449	...	...	...
60 - 64	1 184	744	440	...	...	...
65 - 69	1 428	843	585	...	...	...
70 +	9 551	4 926	4 625	42.1	47.7	37.4
70 - 74	1 716	1 002	714	...	...	...
75 - 79	1 945	1 079	866	...	...	...
80 - 84	2 168	1 137	1 031	...	...	...
85 +	3 722	1 708	2 014	...	...	...
Unknown - Inconnu	20	19	1	..	..	..
Cuba						
2009* (C)						
Total	86 943	46 632	40 311	7.7	8.3	7.2
0	626	351	275	5.0	5.4	4.5
1 - 4	162	106	56	0.3	0.4	0.2
5 - 9	116	57	59	0.2	0.2	0.2
10 - 14	164	102	62	0.2	0.3	0.2
15 - 19	325	225	100	0.4	0.5	0.3
20 - 24	436	286	150	0.5	0.7	0.4
25 - 29	422	301	121	0.6	0.9	0.4
30 - 34	685	458	227	0.9	1.2	0.6
35 - 39	1 224	802	422	1.2	1.5	0.8
40 - 44	1 969	1 207	762	1.8	2.3	1.4
45 - 49	2 787	1 663	1 124	3.0	3.7	2.4
50 - 54	3 188	1 914	1 274	5.0	6.1	3.9
55 - 59	4 843	2 873	1 970	7.8	9.5	6.2
60 - 64	6 362	3 782	2 580	11.7	14.5	9.2
65 - 69	8 172	4 871	3 301	17.8	21.8	14.0
70 - 74	9 220	5 140	4 080	26.8	31.0	22.9
75 - 79	11 208	6 055	5 153	45.3	52.4	39.0
80 - 84	12 120	6 227	5 893	70.8	80.9	62.6
85 +	22 908	10 207	12 701	140.0	146.6	135.1
85 - 89	11 085	5 244	5 841	...	...	...

Continent, country or area, date, code and age (in years) / Continent, pays ou zone, date, code et âge (en années)	Number - Nombre			Rate - Taux		
	Both sexes Les deux sexes	Male Masculin	Female Féminin	Both sexes Les deux sexes	Male Masculin	Female Féminin
AMERICA, NORTH - AMÉRIQUE DU NORD						
Cuba						
2009* (C)						
90 - 94	7 688	3 373	4 315	...	...	...
95 - 99	3 265	1 254	2 011	...	...	...
100 +	870	336	534	...	...	...
Unknown - Inconnu	6	5	1	..	..	...
Dominica - Dominique						
2006 (+C)						
Total	536	285	251	7.5	7.9	7.2
0 - 4	14	12	2	♦2.2	♦3.7	♦0.7
0	13	11	2	...	...	...
1 - 4	1	1	-	...	...	...
5 - 9	1	1	-	♦0.1	♦0.3	-
10 - 14	2	2	-	♦0.3	♦0.6	-
15 - 19	8	7	1	♦1.2	♦2.0	♦0.3
20 - 24	9	6	3	♦2.0	♦2.5	♦1.4
25 - 29	5	3	2	♦1.0	♦1.2	♦0.8
30 - 34	9	5	4	♦1.6	♦1.7	♦1.4
35 - 39	8	6	2	♦1.5	♦2.1	♦0.8
40 - 44	8	5	3	♦1.8	♦2.1	♦1.5
45 - 49	23	7	16	♦6.5	♦3.6	♦9.9
50 - 54	17	9	8	♦6.0	♦6.1	♦5.9
55 - 59	19	11	8	♦7.9	♦9.1	♦6.8
60 - 64	19	13	6	♦8.4	♦12.7	♦4.9
65 - 69	34	16	18	14.6	♦14.7	♦14.6
70 - 74	57	26	31	30.9	♦29.9	31.9
75 - 79	76	39	37	57.1	65.4	50.3
80 - 84	68	38	30	75.5	107.3	♦54.8
85 +	152	73	79	184.2	253.5	147.1
Unknown - Inconnu	7	6	1	..	..	...
Dominican Republic - République dominicaine						
2009 (U)						
Total	31 580	19 348	12 232	...	...	...
0	73	50	23	...	...	...
1 - 4	440	257	183	...	...	...
5 - 9	93	52	41	...	...	...
10 - 14	118	75	43	...	...	...
15 - 19	314	238	76	...	...	...
20 - 24	463	348	115	...	...	...
25 - 29	506	351	155	...	...	...
30 - 34	565	370	195	...	...	...
35 - 39	600	397	203	...	...	...
40 - 44	729	454	275	...	...	...
45 - 49	894	553	341	...	...	...
50 - 54	1 097	676	421	...	...	...
55 - 59	1 193	703	490	...	...	...
60 - 64	1 449	852	597	...	...	...
65 - 69	1 696	1 005	691	...	...	...
70 - 74	2 120	1 263	857	...	...	...
75 - 79	2 519	1 411	1 108	...	...	...
80 - 84	2 151	1 230	921	...	...	...
85 - 89	1 721	926	795	...	...	...
90 - 94	934	527	407	...	...	...
95 - 99	486	240	246	...	...	...
100 +	182	97	85	...	...	...
Unknown - Inconnu	11 237	7 273	3 964	..	..	...
El Salvador[15]						
2007 (C)						
Total	31 349	18 317	13 032	5.5	6.7	4.3
0	981	579	402	9.6	11.2	8.0
1 - 4	286	160	126	0.6	0.7	0.6
5 - 9	179	102	77	0.3	0.3	0.2
10 - 14	287	174	113	0.4	0.5	0.3
15 - 19	922	696	226	1.5	2.3	0.7
20 - 24	1 170	966	204	2.4	4.2	0.8
25 - 29	1 469	1 225	244	3.2	5.9	1.0
30 - 34	1 286	1 036	250	3.2	5.8	1.1

19. Deaths by age and sex, age-specific death rates by sex: latest available year, 2000 - 2009
Décès et taux de mortalité selon l'âge et le sexe : dernière année disponible, 2000 - 2009 (continued - suite)

Continent, country or area, date, code and age (in years) Continent, pays ou zone, date, code et âge (en années)	Number - Nombre			Rate - Taux		
	Both sexes Les deux sexes	Male Masculin	Female Féminin	Both sexes Les deux sexes	Male Masculin	Female Féminin
AMERICA, NORTH - AMÉRIQUE DU NORD						
El Salvador[15]						
2007 (C)						
35 - 39	1 173	864	309	3.3	5.5	1.6
40 - 44	1 164	794	370	3.8	6.0	2.2
45 - 49	1 352	891	461	5.4	8.1	3.2
50 - 54	1 461	912	549	6.8	9.6	4.6
55 - 59	1 748	1 062	686	9.5	13.0	6.8
60 - 64	1 758	1 015	743	11.6	14.9	8.9
65 - 69	2 351	1 284	1 067	18.8	23.0	15.4
70 - 74	2 555	1 342	1 213	26.2	30.9	22.5
75 - 79	3 086	1 543	1 543	40.6	45.8	36.5
80 - 84	3 088	1 484	1 604	65.9	72.7	60.6
85 +	5 033	2 188	2 845	112.2	118.3	107.9
Greenland - Groenland						
2009 (C)						
Total	437	249	188	7.8	8.3	7.1
0	4	1	3	♦4.7	♦2.2	♦7.5
1 - 4	4	3	1	♦1.2	♦1.8	♦0.6
5 - 9	2	2	-	♦0.5	♦0.9	-
10 - 14	6	3	3	♦1.3	♦1.3	♦1.3
15 - 19	12	8	4	♦2.6	♦3.5	♦1.8
20 - 24	7	5	2	♦1.6	♦2.3	♦0.9
25 - 29	12	11	1	♦3.1	♦5.4	♦0.5
30 - 34	8	5	3	♦2.4	♦2.8	♦1.9
35 - 39	5	3	2	♦1.4	♦1.5	♦1.3
40 - 44	9	7	2	♦1.6	♦2.4	♦0.8
45 - 49	26	10	16	♦5.0	♦3.6	♦6.7
50 - 54	28	19	9	♦6.9	♦8.2	♦5.2
55 - 59	50	29	21	16.6	♦16.8	♦16.4
60 - 64	40	23	17	17.7	♦16.9	♦19.0
65 - 69	50	28	22	29.2	♦29.8	♦28.5
70 - 74	55	35	20	55.0	68.9	♦40.6
75 - 79	61	32	29	92.6	114.3	♦76.6
80 - 84	39	16	23	133.6	♦150.9	♦123.7
85 - 89	12	7	5	♦157.9	♦285.7	♦97.1
90 - 94	5	2	3	♦250.0	♦800.0	♦171.4
95 +	2	-	2	♦571.4	-	♦800.0
95 - 99	2	-	2	...	...	...
100 +	-	-	-	...	...	...
Grenada - Grenade						
2000 (+C)						
Total	716	365	351	7.1	7.3	6.9
0 - 4	28	11	17	♦2.7	♦2.1	♦3.3
0	27	10	17	...	...	...
1 - 4	1	1	-	...	...	...
5 - 9	1	1	-	♦0.1	♦0.2	-
10 - 14	4	4	-	♦0.3	♦0.6	-
15 - 19	8	2	6	♦0.7	♦0.3	♦1.0
20 - 24	11	9	2	♦1.2	♦1.9	♦0.4
25 - 29	17	13	4	♦2.3	♦3.3	♦1.2
30 - 34	21	11	10	♦3.5	♦3.7	♦3.4
35 - 39	17	7	10	♦2.6	♦2.1	♦3.1
40 - 44	14	9	5	♦2.6	♦3.4	♦1.8
45 - 49	21	13	8	♦5.6	♦6.6	♦4.4
50 - 54	27	15	12	♦9.3	♦10.9	♦7.8
55 - 59	24	17	7	♦9.7	♦14.7	♦5.3
60 - 64	50	30	20	21.0	♦27.8	♦15.3
65 - 69	61	35	26	25.9	34.7	♦19.3
70 +	412	188	224	74.1	88.2	65.3
70 - 74	81	52	29	...	...	...
75 - 79	96	50	46	...	...	...
80 - 84	69	27	42	...	...	...
85 - 89	84	34	50	...	...	...
90 - 94	52	16	36	...	...	...
95 - 99	24	8	16	...	...	...
100 +	6	1	5	...	...	...

Continent, country or area, date, code and age (in years) Continent, pays ou zone, date, code et âge (en années)	Number - Nombre			Rate - Taux		
	Both sexes Les deux sexes	Male Masculin	Female Féminin	Both sexes Les deux sexes	Male Masculin	Female Féminin
AMERICA, NORTH - AMÉRIQUE DU NORD						
Guadeloupe[6]						
2003 (C)						
Total	2 636	1 405	1 231	6.0	6.7	5.4
0	56	34	22	8.1	9.7	♦6.5
1 - 4	9	5	4	♦0.3	♦0.3	♦0.3
5 - 9	5	4	1	♦0.1	♦0.2	♦0.1
10 - 14	5	3	2	♦0.1	♦0.2	♦0.1
15 - 19	21	18	3	♦0.6	♦1.0	♦0.2
20 - 24	23	19	4	♦0.8	♦1.3	♦0.3
25 - 29	23	17	6	♦0.9	♦1.3	♦0.4
30 - 34	39	31	8	1.1	2.0	♦0.4
35 - 39	60	40	20	1.6	2.4	♦1.0
40 - 44	76	47	29	2.2	2.8	♦1.6
45 - 49	102	71	31	3.5	5.3	2.0
50 - 54	112	87	25	4.5	7.5	♦1.9
55 - 59	128	85	43	6.3	8.7	4.1
60 - 64	177	96	81	10.9	12.7	9.3
65 - 69	213	126	87	14.9	19.1	11.2
70 - 74	257	141	116	22.7	28.5	18.2
75 - 79	316	180	136	34.1	45.4	25.6
80 - 84	356	185	171	53.8	68.2	43.8
85 - 89	329	124	205	96.8	98.9	95.6
90 +	329	92	237	148.6	142.2	151.2
90 - 94	205	65	140	...	...	...
95 - 99	96	19	77	...	...	...
100 +	28	8	20	...	...	...
Guatemala						
2006 (C)						
Total	69 756	40 650	29 106	...	...	...
0	9 042	5 012	4 030	...	...	...
1 - 4	3 567	1 900	1 667	...	...	...
5 - 9	1 016	556	460	...	...	...
10 - 14	922	519	403	...	...	...
15 - 19	2 271	1 597	674	...	...	...
20 - 24	3 053	2 342	711	...	...	...
25 - 29	3 227	2 448	779	...	...	...
30 - 34	2 777	2 054	723	...	...	...
35 - 39	2 721	1 905	816	...	...	...
40 - 44	2 765	1 835	930	...	...	...
45 - 49	2 829	1 803	1 026	...	...	...
50 - 54	3 048	1 846	1 202	...	...	...
55 - 59	3 342	1 857	1 485	...	...	...
60 - 64	3 420	1 870	1 550	...	...	...
65 - 69	3 955	2 124	1 831	...	...	...
70 +	21 532	10 787	10 745	...	...	...
Unknown - Inconnu	269	195	74	..	..	..
Haiti - Haïti[10]						
2003 (U)						
Total	8 011	4 135	3 876	...	...	...
0	724	388	336	...	...	...
1 - 4	501	270	231	...	...	...
5 - 9	161	85	76	...	...	...
10 - 14	135	66	69	...	...	...
15 - 19	216	114	102	...	...	...
20 - 24	324	158	166	...	...	...
25 - 29	371	179	192	...	...	...
30 - 34	442	229	213	...	...	...
35 - 39	392	215	177	...	...	...
40 - 44	434	234	200	...	...	...
45 - 49	363	190	173	...	...	...
50 - 54	346	177	169	...	...	...
55 - 59	316	176	140	...	...	...
60 - 64	397	205	192	...	...	...
65 - 69	378	196	182	...	...	...
70 - 74	460	245	215	...	...	...
75 - 79	416	223	193	...	...	...
80 - 84	417	208	209	...	...	...

Continent, country or area, date, code and age (in years)	Number - Nombre			Rate - Taux		
Continent, pays ou zone, date, code et âge (en années)	Both sexes Les deux sexes	Male Masculin	Female Féminin	Both sexes Les deux sexes	Male Masculin	Female Féminin
AMERICA, NORTH - AMÉRIQUE DU NORD						
Haiti - Haïti[10]						
2003 (U)						
85 - 89	266	110	156	...	...	...
90 - 94	162	57	105	...	...	...
95 +	132	48	84	...	...	...
Unknown - Inconnu	658	362	296	..	..	..
Jamaica - Jamaïque[16]						
2005 (U)						
Total	17 552	9 473	8 079	...	...	...
0	1 007	517	490	...	...	...
1 - 4	197	98	99	...	...	...
5 - 9	75	45	30	...	...	...
10 - 14	73	32	41	...	...	...
15 - 19	248	195	53	...	...	...
20 - 24	505	404	101	...	...	...
25 - 29	550	398	152	...	...	...
30 - 34	555	386	169	...	...	...
35 - 39	568	350	218	...	...	...
40 - 44	597	370	227	...	...	...
45 - 49	597	329	268	...	...	...
50 - 54	636	382	254	...	...	...
55 - 59	670	397	273	...	...	...
60 - 64	981	566	415	...	...	...
65 - 69	1 159	658	501	...	...	...
70 - 74	1 701	974	727	...	...	...
75 +	7 433	3 372	4 061	...	...	...
Martinique[6]						
2007 (C)						
Total	2 830	1 439	1 391	7.1	7.7	6.5
0 - 4	51	31	20	2.0	2.4	♦1.6
0	47	28	19	...	...	...
1 - 4	4	3	1	...	...	...
5 - 9	4	3	1	♦0.1	♦0.2	♦0.1
10 - 14	7	5	2	♦0.2	♦0.3	♦0.1
15 - 19	16	12	4	♦0.5	♦0.8	♦0.3
20 - 24	26	22	4	♦1.1	♦1.9	♦0.3
25 - 29	19	13	6	♦1.0	♦1.5	♦0.6
30 - 34	35	22	13	1.4	♦2.1	♦0.9
35 - 39	36	22	14	1.2	♦1.6	♦0.8
40 - 44	53	31	22	1.6	2.0	♦1.2
45 - 49	64	46	18	2.0	3.2	♦1.1
50 - 54	107	68	39	4.1	5.6	2.8
55 - 59	97	57	40	4.3	5.5	3.2
60 - 64	146	91	55	7.8	10.3	5.5
65 - 69	226	135	91	14.2	18.7	10.4
70 - 74	305	173	132	21.3	27.2	16.6
75 - 79	382	200	182	35.8	44.2	29.6
80 - 84	443	217	226	59.2	76.6	48.6
85 - 89	388	168	220	92.5	122.1	78.1
90 - 94	269	91	178	137.9	159.6	128.9
95 +	156	32	124	212.8	196.3	217.5
Mexico - Mexique[17]						
2009* (+C)						
Total	563 516	315 254[5]	248 020[5]	5.2	6.0	4.5
0	28 983	16 229[5]	12 694[5]	15.2	16.6	13.6
1 - 4	5 963	3 290[5]	2 673[5]	0.8	0.8	0.7
5 - 9	3 140	1 690[5]	1 449[5]	0.3	0.3	0.3
10 - 14	3 769	2 233[5]	1 536[5]	0.3	0.4	0.3
15 - 19	9 409	6 552[5]	2 855[5]	0.9	1.2	0.5
20 - 24	12 661	9 476[5]	3 178[5]	1.3	2.0	0.6
25 - 29	13 783	10 367[5]	3 408[5]	1.5	2.4	0.7
30 - 34	15 484	11 481[5]	3 999[5]	1.8	2.8	0.9
35 - 39	17 942	12 894[5]	5 037[5]	2.2	3.3	1.2
40 - 44	19 866	13 424[5]	6 438[5]	2.8	3.9	1.8
45 - 49	24 529	15 492[5]	9 035[5]	4.0	5.3	2.9
50 - 54	29 999	18 241[5]	11 755[5]	6.1	7.8	4.6

Continent, country or area, date, code and age (in years) Continent, pays ou zone, date, code et âge (en années)	Number - Nombre			Rate - Taux		
	Both sexes Les deux sexes	Male Masculin	Female Féminin	Both sexes Les deux sexes	Male Masculin	Female Féminin
AMERICA, NORTH - AMÉRIQUE DU NORD						
Mexico - Mexique[17]						
2009* (+C)						
55 - 59	34 637	20 060[5]	14 575[5]	9.2	11.2	. 7.4
60 - 64	39 951	22 447[5]	17 502[5]	13.8	16.4	11.4
65 - 69	45 655	25 159[5]	20 490[5]	20.6	24.5	17.3
70 - 74	52 295	28 070[5]	24 220[5]	32.4	38.1	27.6
75 - 79	57 758	29 728[5]	28 025[5]	52.4	60.5	45.9
80 - 84	54 495	26 626[5]	27 863[5]	79.8	90.0	72.0
85 - 89	47 821	22 377[5]	25 443[5]	130.0	144.8	119.3
90 - 94	25 643	10 752[5]	14 889[5]	168.8	173.7	165.5
95 +	17 208	6 672	10 534	279.2	275.5	281.6
95 - 99	13 414	5 268[5]	8 144[5]	...	...	...
100 +	3 794	1 404[5]	2 390[5]	...	...	...
Unknown - Inconnu	2 525	1 994[5]	422[5]	..	..	...
Netherlands Antilles - Antilles néerlandaises[17]						
2006 (C)						
Total	1 327	706	621	7.0	8.0	6.1
0 - 4	41	22	19	3.0	♦3.2	♦2.8
0	40	21	19	...	...	...
1 - 4	1	1	-	...	...	...
5 - 9	3	2	1	♦0.2	♦0.3	♦0.1
10 - 14	1	1	-	♦0.1	♦0.1	-
15 - 19	7	4	3	♦0.5	♦0.6	♦0.4
20 - 24	11	10	1	♦1.1	♦2.0	♦0.2
25 - 29	9	6	3	♦0.8	♦1.2	♦0.5
30 - 34	14	10	4	♦1.0	♦1.6	♦0.6
35 - 39	25	16	9	♦1.6	♦2.3	♦1.1
40 - 44	33	18	15	2.0	♦2.4	♦1.6
45 - 49	61	38	23	3.9	5.5	♦2.7
50 - 54	59	35	24	4.6	6.1	♦3.3
55 - 59	89	51	38	8.3	10.4	6.6
60 - 64	113	72	41	13.9	19.7	9.1
65 - 69	107	69	38	17.4	25.5	11.0
70 - 74	146	86	60	30.2	40.5	22.1
75 - 79	172	87	85	52.8	65.4	44.1
80 - 84	172	88	84	81.3	114.1	62.5
85 +	264	91	173	157.7	178.3	148.6
85 - 89	141	58	83	...	...	...
90 - 94	85	25	60	...	...	...
95 - 99	33	8	25	...	...	...
100 +	5	-	5	...	...	...
Nicaragua						
2008 (+U)						
Total	18 079	10 385	7 694	...	...	...
0	1 932	1 123	809	...	...	...
1 - 4	287	155	132	...	...	...
5 - 9	164	95	69	...	...	...
10 - 14	198	118	80	...	...	...
15 - 19	448	289	159	...	...	...
20 - 24	577	431	146	...	...	...
25 - 29	595	463	132	...	...	...
30 - 34	619	442	177	...	...	...
35 - 39	530	398	132	...	...	...
40 - 44	663	449	214	...	...	...
45 - 49	793	525	268	...	...	...
50 - 54	955	578	377	...	...	...
55 - 59	1 001	548	453	...	...	...
60 - 64	1 120	632	488	...	...	...
65 - 69	1 143	638	505	...	...	...
70 - 74	1 446	763	683	...	...	...
75 - 79	1 529	812	717	...	...	...
80 - 84	1 490	778	712	...	...	...
85 - 89	1 271	588	683	...	...	...
90 - 94	780	328	452	...	...	...
95 +	538	232	306	...	...	...

Continent, country or area, date, code and age (in years) / Continent, pays ou zone, date, code et âge (en années)	Number - Nombre			Rate - Taux		
	Both sexes Les deux sexes	Male Masculin	Female Féminin	Both sexes Les deux sexes	Male Masculin	Female Féminin
AMERICA, NORTH - AMÉRIQUE DU NORD						
Panama						
2009 (U)						
Total	15 498	9 200	6 298	...	...	...
0	837	486	351	...	...	...
1 - 4	330	170	160	...	...	...
5 - 9	100	65	35	...	...	...
10 - 14	113	75	38	...	...	...
15 - 19	292	232	60	...	...	...
20 - 24	449	360	89	...	...	...
25 - 29	436	344	92	...	...	...
30 - 34	413	291	122	...	...	...
35 - 39	464	322	142	...	...	...
40 - 44	516	352	164	...	...	...
45 - 49	575	349	226	...	...	...
50 - 54	681	422	259	...	...	...
55 - 59	738	468	270	...	...	...
60 - 64	927	578	349	...	...	...
65 - 69	1 060	659	401	...	...	...
70 - 74	1 308	780	528	...	...	...
75 - 79	1 495	847	648	...	...	...
80 - 84	1 572	856	716	...	...	...
85 - 89	1 492	749	743	...	...	...
90 - 94	1 054	500	554	...	...	...
95 - 99	449	196	253	...	...	...
100 +	112	34	78	...	...	...
Unknown - Inconnu	85	65	20	..	..	...
Puerto Rico - Porto Rico						
2008 (C)						
Total	29 100	15 906	13 194	7.4	8.4	6.4
0 - 4	442	250	192	1.8	2.0	1.6
0	400	225	175	...	...	...
1 - 4	42	25	17	...	...	...
5 - 9	22	15	7	◆0.1	◆0.1	◆0.1
10 - 14	33	23	10	0.1	◆0.2	◆0.1
15 - 19	201	160	41	0.7	1.1	0.3
20 - 24	345	293	52	1.3	2.1	0.4
25 - 29	429	353	76	1.5	2.5	0.5
30 - 34	389	305	84	1.4	2.3	0.6
35 - 39	466	326	140	1.8	2.5	1.0
40 - 44	635	426	209	2.4	3.4	1.5
45 - 49	902	599	303	3.5	4.9	2.2
50 - 54	1 206	780	426	4.9	6.9	3.2
55 - 59	1 497	967	530	6.5	9.3	4.3
60 - 64	2 151	1 346	805	10.0	13.8	6.9
65 - 69	2 504	1 500	1 004	14.8	19.7	10.8
70 - 74	2 883	1 637	1 246	21.4	27.1	16.7
75 - 79	3 264	1 726	1 538	32.8	40.5	27.1
80 - 84	4 023	1 907	2 116	57.1	66.8	50.5
85 +	7 658	3 250	4 408	115.4	130.2	106.5
85 - 89	3 684	1 704	1 980	...	...	...
90 - 94	2 565	1 009	1 556	...	...	...
95 - 99	1 146	449	697	...	...	...
100 +	263	88	175	...	...	...
Unknown - Inconnu	50	43	7	..	...	..
Saint Kitts and Nevis - Saint-Kitts-et-Nevis						
2001 (+C)						
Total	352	181	171	...	...	...
0	10	3	7	...	...	...
1 - 4	6	1	5	...	...	...
5 - 9	3	3	-	...	...	...
10 - 14	2	1	1	...	...	...
15 - 19	2	1	1	...	...	...
20 - 24	2	1	1	...	...	...
25 - 29	6	4	2	...	...	...
30 - 34	5	3	2	...	...	...
35 - 39	8	6	2	...	...	...
40 - 44	9	6	3	...	...	...

Continent, country or area, date, code and age (in years)	Number - Nombre			Rate - Taux		
Continent, pays ou zone, date, code et âge (en années)	Both sexes Les deux sexes	Male Masculin	Female Féminin	Both sexes Les deux sexes	Male Masculin	Female Féminin
AMERICA, NORTH - AMÉRIQUE DU NORD						
Saint Kitts and Nevis - Saint-Kitts-et-Nevis						
2001 (+C)						
45 - 49	22	16	6	...	...	...
50 - 54	9	4	5	...	...	...
55 - 59	12	8	4	...	...	...
60 - 64	13	9	4	...	...	...
65 - 69	19	9	10	...	...	...
70 - 74	29	17	12	...	...	...
75 - 79	63	31	32	...	...	...
80 - 84	56	25	31	...	...	...
85 +	76	33	43	...	...	...
Saint Lucia - Sainte-Lucie						
2005* (C)						
Total	1 107	625	482	6.7	7.8	5.7
0 - 4	53	30	23	3.9	◆4.4	◆3.3
0	46	28	18	...	...	...
1 - 4	7	2	5	...	...	...
5 - 9	2	1	1	◆0.1	◆0.1	◆0.1
10 - 14	7	4	3	◆0.4	◆0.5	◆0.3
15 - 19	14	12	2	◆0.8	◆1.4	◆0.2
20 - 24	19	15	4	◆1.2	◆1.9	◆0.5
25 - 29	24	18	6	◆1.8	◆2.7	◆0.9
30 - 34	33	21	12	2.6	◆3.5	◆1.9
35 - 39	25	19	6	◆2.1	◆3.3	◆1.0
40 - 44	40	30	10	3.6	◆5.6	◆1.8
45 - 49	38	28	10	4.4	◆6.5	◆2.3
50 - 54	49	25	24	7.6	◆7.6	◆7.5
55 - 59	42	23	19	8.4	◆9.6	◆7.3
60 - 64	82	52	30	20.1	27.5	◆13.7
65 - 69	103	63	40	28.8	37.5	21.1
70 - 74	88	52	36	29.2	36.6	22.6
75 - 79	114	72	42	58.7	79.4	40.5
80 +	361	154	207	127.0	129.4	125.3
80 - 84	154	70	84	...	...	...
85 +	207	84	123	...	...	...
Unknown - Inconnu	13	6	7	..	..	..
Saint Vincent and the Grenadines - Saint-Vincent-et-les Grenadines						
2009 (+C)						
Total	765	395	370	...	...	...
0	32	19	13	...	...	...
1 - 4	4	2	2	...	...	...
5 - 9	2	2	-	...	...	...
10 - 14	7	3	4	...	...	...
15 - 19	8	5	3	...	...	...
20 - 24	13	9	4	...	...	...
25 - 29	21	13	8	...	...	...
30 - 34	18	10	8	...	...	...
35 - 39	17	13	4	...	...	...
40 - 44	27	17	10	...	...	...
45 - 49	36	27	9	...	...	...
50 - 54	26	13	13	...	...	...
55 - 59	24	13	11	...	...	...
60 - 64	35	23	12	...	...	...
65 - 69	56	30	26	...	...	...
70 - 74	69	38	31	...	...	...
75 - 79	102	53	49	...	...	...
80 - 84	106	45	61	...	...	...
85 +	159	58	101	...	...	...
Unknown - Inconnu	3	2	1	..	..	..
Trinidad and Tobago - Trinité-et-Tobago						
2005 (C)						
Total	9 885	5 702	4 183	...	...	...
0	266	149	117	...	...	...
1 - 4	39	23	16	...	...	...
5 - 9	20	13	7	...	...	...
10 - 14	31	14	17	...	...	...

19. Deaths by age and sex, age-specific death rates by sex: latest available year, 2000 - 2009
Décès et taux de mortalité selon l'âge et le sexe : dernière année disponible, 2000 - 2009 (continued - suite)

Continent, country or area, date, code and age (in years) Continent, pays ou zone, date, code et âge (en années)	Number - Nombre			Rate - Taux		
	Both sexes Les deux sexes	Male Masculin	Female Féminin	Both sexes Les deux sexes	Male Masculin	Female Féminin

AMERICA, NORTH - AMÉRIQUE DU NORD

Trinidad and Tobago - Trinité-et-Tobago
2005 (C)

15 - 19	136	94	42	...	...	...
20 - 24	234	185	49	...	...	...
25 - 29	246	182	64	...	...	...
30 - 34	252	170	82	...	...	...
35 - 39	258	161	97	...	...	...
40 - 44	434	284	150	...	...	...
45 - 49	479	306	173	...	...	...
50 - 54	540	345	195	...	...	...
55 - 59	712	452	260	...	...	...
60 - 64	812	482	330	...	...	...
65 - 69	949	568	381	...	...	...
70 - 74	927	515	412	...	...	...
75 - 79	1 057	572	485	...	...	...
80 - 84	1 043	552	491	...	...	...
85 +	1 445	631	814	...	...	...
Unknown - Inconnu	5	4	1	..	..	..

Turks and Caicos Islands - Îles Turques et Caïques[15]
2005 (C)

Total	53	32	21	...	...	...
0	1	1	-	...	...	...
1 - 4	-	-	-	...	...	...
5 - 9	-	-	-	...	...	...
10 - 14	1	1	-	...	...	...
15 - 19	1	1	-	...	...	...
20 - 24	-	-	-	...	...	...
25 - 29	2	2	-	...	...	...
30 - 34	8	5	3	...	...	...
35 - 39	3	2	1	...	...	...
40 - 44	3	1	2	...	...	...
45 - 49	1	1	-	...	...	...
50 - 54	2	-	2	...	...	...
55 - 59	2	2	-	...	...	...
60 - 64	2	2	-	...	...	...
65 - 69	-	-	-	...	...	...
70 - 74	3	3	-	...	...	...
75 - 79	6	1	5	...	...	...
80 - 84	5	3	2	...	...	...
85 +	11	5	6	...	...	...
Unknown - Inconnu	2	2	-	..	..	..

United States of America - États-Unis d'Amérique
2008* (C)

Total	2 473 018	1 226 721	1 246 297	8.1	8.2	8.1
0	28 033	15 651	12 382	6.5	7.1	5.9
1 - 4	4 747	2 703	2 044	0.3	0.3	0.3
5 - 9	2 505	1 395	1 109	0.1	0.1	0.1
10 - 14	3 158	1 889	1 269	0.2	0.2	0.1
15 - 19	12 410	8 956	3 454	0.6	0.8	0.3
20 - 24	19 798	15 074	4 724	0.9	1.4	0.5
25 - 29	20 800	15 012	5 788	1.0	1.4	0.6
30 - 34	21 509	14 650	6 859	1.1	1.5	0.7
35 - 39	29 883	19 113	10 769	1.4	1.8	1.0
40 - 44	46 527	28 604	17 923	2.2	2.7	1.7
45 - 49	77 472	47 366	30 105	3.4	4.2	2.6
50 - 54	109 171	67 731	41 440	5.1	6.4	3.8
55 - 59	134 751	83 456	51 295	7.3	9.3	5.4
60 - 64	161 518	96 143	65 375	10.7	13.3	8.3
65 - 69	183 524	105 460	78 064	16.2	19.9	12.9
70 - 74	218 226	120 052	98 174	24.9	30.3	20.4
75 - 79	287 522	149 275	138 247	39.5	48.2	33.1
80 - 84	366 323	172 756	193 567	63.7	77.1	55.1
85 +	744 976	261 319	483 656	130.2	140.2	125.4
Unknown - Inconnu	166	115	51	..	..	..

Continent, country or area, date, code and age (in years) Continent, pays ou zone, date, code et âge (en années)	Number - Nombre			Rate - Taux		
	Both sexes Les deux sexes	Male Masculin	Female Féminin	Both sexes Les deux sexes	Male Masculin	Female Féminin
AMERICA, NORTH - AMÉRIQUE DU NORD						
United States Virgin Islands - Îles Vierges américaines						
2007 (C)						
Total	727	424	303	6.6	8.1	5.2
0 - 4	14	8	6	♦1.9	♦2.1	♦1.6
0	12	6	6	...	...	...
1 - 4	2	2	-	...	...	...
5 - 9	-	-	-	-	-	-
10 - 14	2	1	1	♦0.2	♦0.2	♦0.2
15 - 19	9	8	1	♦1.1	♦2.0	♦0.2
20 - 24	16	15	1	♦2.3	♦4.7	♦0.3
25 - 29	20	14	6	♦3.7	♦5.7	♦2.1
30 - 34	16	10	6	♦2.6	♦3.7	♦1.8
35 - 39	16	13	3	♦2.2	♦3.9	♦0.7
40 - 44	33	21	12	4.1	♦5.6	♦2.8
45 - 49	26	13	13	♦3.2	♦3.3	♦3.1
50 - 54	50	34	16	6.6	9.6	♦3.9
55 - 59	51	29	22	6.8	♦8.1	♦5.6
60 - 64	79	55	24	10.7	15.3	♦6.3
65 - 69	50	36	14	10.1	14.8	♦5.5
70 - 74	68	43	25	18.8	26.6	♦12.5
75 +	273	120	153	59.0	63.7	55.7
Unknown - Inconnu	4	4	-	...	...	...
AMERICA, SOUTH - AMÉRIQUE DU SUD						
Argentina - Argentine						
2009 (C)						
Total	304 525[18]	159 983	144 060	7.6	8.1	7.0
0	9 026[18]	5 112	3 901	13.1	14.6	11.5
1 - 4	1 483[18]	786	692	0.5	0.6	0.5
5 - 9	863[18]	463	400	0.3	0.3	0.2
10 - 14	1 025[18]	606	409	0.3	0.3	0.2
15 - 19	2 708[18]	1 893	806	0.8	1.1	0.5
20 - 24	3 364[18]	2 482	876	1.0	1.5	0.5
25 - 29	3 494[18]	2 434	1 055	1.1	1.5	0.7
30 - 34	3 742[18]	2 422	1 315	1.2	1.5	0.8
35 - 39	4 276[18]	2 670	1 604	1.6	2.0	1.2
40 - 44	5 399[18]	3 298	2 096	2.3	2.8	1.8
45 - 49	7 832[18]	4 808	3 018	3.6	4.5	2.7
50 - 54	11 995[18]	7 574	4 408	5.8	7.7	4.1
55 - 59	16 833[18]	10 825	5 993	9.0	12.1	6.1
60 - 64	21 783[18]	13 824	7 942	13.7	18.6	9.4
65 - 69	26 128[18]	16 465	9 636	20.1	27.9	13.5
70 - 74	31 093[18]	18 421	12 648	29.3	40.8	20.8
75 - 79	39 177[18]	21 242	17 902	46.7	64.6	35.1
80 +	113 009	43 965	68 944	122.7	146.1	111.2
80 - 84	44 135[18]	20 675	23 420	...	...	...
85 +	68 874[18]	23 290	45 524	...	...	...
Unknown - Inconnu	1 295[18]	693	415	...	...	...
Brazil - Brésil[19]						
2009 (U)						
Total	1 083 399	622 143	461 018	...	...	...
0	33 713	18 954	14 759	...	...	...
1 - 4	6 684	3 662	3 022	...	...	...
5 - 9	4 258	2 484	1 774	...	...	...
10 - 14	5 433	3 316	2 117	...	...	...
15 - 19	17 759	13 976	3 783	...	...	...
20 - 24	27 460	22 292	5 168	...	...	...
25 - 29	28 474	22 114	6 360	...	...	...
30 - 34	28 618	21 047	7 571	...	...	...
35 - 39	31 699	22 113	9 586	...	...	...
40 - 44	40 752	27 214	13 538	...	...	...
45 - 49	51 480	33 380	18 100	...	...	...
50 - 54	63 841	40 647	23 194	...	...	...

Continent, country or area, date, code and age (in years) / Continent, pays ou zone, date, code et âge (en années)	Number - Nombre			Rate - Taux		
	Both sexes Les deux sexes	Male Masculin	Female Féminin	Both sexes Les deux sexes	Male Masculin	Female Féminin
AMERICA, SOUTH - AMÉRIQUE DU SUD						
Brazil - Brésil[19]						
2009 (U)						
55 - 59	72 959	45 809	27 150	...	...	...
60 - 64	80 194	48 791	31 403	...	...	...
65 - 69	92 061	54 209	37 852	...	...	...
70 - 74	107 289	60 261	47 028	...	...	...
75 - 79	114 312	60 332	53 980	...	...	...
80 - 84	112 415	54 047	58 368	...	...	...
85 - 89	84 277	36 506	47 771	...	...	...
90 - 94	50 032	19 016	31 016	...	...	...
95 - 99	20 025	7 013	13 012	...	...	...
100 +	4 884	1 471	3 413	...	...	...
Unknown - Inconnu	4 780	3 489	1 053	..	...	...
Chile - Chili						
2008 (C)						
Total	90 168	48 588	41 580	5.4	5.9	4.9
0	1 948	1 054	894	7.8	8.3	7.3
1 - 4	304	175	129	0.3	0.3	0.3
5 - 9	219	127	92	0.2	0.2	0.1
10 - 14	281	151	130	0.2	0.2	0.2
15 - 19	779	543	236	0.5	0.7	0.3
20 - 24	1 061	826	235	0.8	1.2	0.3
25 - 29	1 066	801	265	0.8	1.3	0.4
30 - 34	1 299	958	341	1.1	1.6	0.6
35 - 39	1 610	1 145	465	1.3	1.9	0.8
40 - 44	2 234	1 530	704	1.8	2.5	1.1
45 - 49	3 109	2 076	1 033	2.6	3.5	1.7
50 - 54	4 011	2 566	1 445	4.1	5.3	2.9
55 - 59	4 899	3 054	1 845	6.3	8.1	4.6
60 - 64	6 581	4 087	2 494	10.4	13.6	7.5
65 - 69	8 060	4 932	3 128	16.2	21.5	11.7
70 - 74	9 309	5 395	3 914	25.0	32.8	18.8
75 - 79	11 945	6 451	5 494	42.7	55.8	33.5
80 +	31 453	12 717	18 736	107.8	121.0	100.3
80 - 84	12 308	5 886	6 422	...	...	...
85 - 89	9 894	4 076	5 818	...	...	...
90 - 94	6 446	2 055	4 391	...	...	...
95 - 99	2 372	611	1 761	...	...	...
100 +	433	89	344	...	...	...
Colombia - Colombie						
2009* (U)						
Total	193 580	111 551[5]	82 007[5]	...	...	...
0	9 250	5 182[5]	4 068[5]	...	...	...
1 - 4	2 015	1 111[5]	904[5]	...	...	...
5 - 9	1 080	619[5]	461[5]	...	...	...
10 - 14	1 350	841[5]	509[5]	...	...	...
15 - 19	4 575	3 554[5]	1 020[5]	...	...	...
20 - 24	6 756	5 534[5]	1 222[5]	...	...	...
25 - 29	7 246	5 991[5]	1 251[5]	...	...	...
30 - 34	6 092	4 754[5]	1 337[5]	...	...	...
35 - 39	5 665	4 111[5]	1 554[5]	...	...	...
40 - 44	6 155	4 088[5]	2 066[5]	...	...	...
45 - 49	7 307	4 550[5]	2 757[5]	...	...	...
50 - 54	8 492	5 029[5]	3 463[5]	...	...	...
55 - 59	10 010	5 933[5]	4 077[5]	...	...	...
60 - 64	11 460	6 671[5]	4 789[5]	...	...	...
65 - 69	14 439	8 211[5]	6 228[5]	...	...	...
70 - 74	18 064	9 776[5]	8 288[5]	...	...	...
75 - 79	21 243	11 195[5]	10 048[5]	...	...	...
80 - 84	21 229	10 596[5]	10 633[5]	...	...	...
85 +	30 279	13 140[5]	17 139[5]	...	...	...
Unknown - Inconnu	873	665[5]	193[5]	...	...	...
Ecuador - Équateur[20]						
2009 (U)						
Total	59 714	33 868	25 846	...	...	...
0	3 279	1 792	1 487	...	...	...

Continent, country or area, date, code and age (in years)	Number - Nombre			Rate - Taux		
Continent, pays ou zone, date, code et âge (en années)	Both sexes Les deux sexes	Male Masculin	Female Féminin	Both sexes Les deux sexes	Male Masculin	Female Féminin

AMERICA, SOUTH - AMÉRIQUE DU SUD

Ecuador - Équateur[20]
2009 (U)

1 - 4	1 187	659	528	...	...	...
5 - 9	620	324	296	...	...	...
10 - 14	595	337	258	...	...	...
15 - 19	1 288	909	379	...	...	...
20 - 24	1 933	1 455	478	...	...	...
25 - 29	2 086	1 585	501	...	...	...
30 - 34	1 858	1 374	484	...	...	...
35 - 39	1 828	1 276	552	...	...	...
40 - 44	1 936	1 278	658	...	...	...
45 - 49	2 307	1 437	870	...	...	...
50 - 54	2 789	1 697	1 092	...	...	...
55 - 59	3 034	1 759	1 275	...	...	...
60 - 64	3 586	2 033	1 553	...	...	...
65 - 69	3 920	2 195	1 725	...	...	...
70 - 74	4 645	2 625	2 020	...	...	...
75 - 79	5 487	3 005	2 482	...	...	...
80 - 84	5 905	3 067	2 838	...	...	...
85 +	11 349	5 011	6 338	...	...	...
Unknown - Inconnu	82	50	32	..	..	..

French Guiana - Guyane française[6]
2007 (C)

Total	690	405	285	3.2	3.8	2.6
0 - 4	95	50	45	3.5	3.6	3.3
0	77	39	38	...	...	...
1 - 4	18	11	7	...	...	...
5 - 9	9	4	5	♦0.3	♦0.3	♦0.4
10 - 14	8	5	3	♦0.3	♦0.4	♦0.3
15 - 19	13	10	3	♦0.7	♦1.0	♦0.3
20 - 24	14	12	2	♦0.9	♦1.6	♦0.2
25 - 29	16	11	5	♦1.1	♦1.6	♦0.6
30 - 34	23	15	8	♦1.4	♦2.0	♦0.9
35 - 39	28	21	7	♦1.8	♦2.8	♦0.8
40 - 44	41	24	17	2.9	♦3.5	♦2.4
45 - 49	48	35	13	4.1	5.9	♦2.3
50 - 54	26	16	10	♦2.7	♦3.3	♦2.1
55 - 59	32	24	8	4.6	♦6.5	♦2.4
60 - 64	33	25	8	7.4	♦10.5	♦3.8
65 - 69	48	24	24	17.0	♦16.5	♦17.5
70 - 74	46	29	17	21.8	♦28.3	♦15.7
75 - 79	62	32	30	46.6	53.9	♦40.8
80 - 84	57	26	31	60.7	♦66.5	56.6
85 - 89	50	27	23	84.0	♦112.0	♦65.0
90 - 94	28	12	16	♦129.0	♦176.5	♦107.4
95 +	13	3	10	♦123.8	♦111.1	♦128.2
95 - 99	10	3	7	...	...	...
100 +	3	-	3	...	...	...

Guyana[10]
2003 (+C)

Total	4 986	2 898	2 088	...	...	...
0	290	157	133	...	...	...
1 - 4	72	40	32	...	...	...
5 - 9	33	21	12	...	...	...
10 - 14	43	24	19	...	...	...
15 - 19	64	39	25	...	...	...
20 - 24	148	97	51	...	...	...
25 - 29	175	120	55	...	...	...
30 - 34	263	169	94	...	...	...
35 - 39	274	188	86	...	...	...
40 - 44	277	195	82	...	...	...
45 - 49	305	197	108	...	...	...
50 - 54	338	207	131	...	...	...
55 - 59	339	212	127	...	...	...
60 - 64	377	228	149	...	...	...
65 - 69	401	226	175	...	...	...
70 - 74	418	214	204	...	...	...

19. Deaths by age and sex, age-specific death rates by sex: latest available year, 2000 - 2009
Décès et taux de mortalité selon l'âge et le sexe : dernière année disponible, 2000 - 2009 (continued - suite)

Continent, country or area, date, code and age (in years) / Continent, pays ou zone, date, code et âge (en années)	Number - Nombre			Rate - Taux		
	Both sexes Les deux sexes	Male Masculin	Female Féminin	Both sexes Les deux sexes	Male Masculin	Female Féminin
AMERICA, SOUTH - AMÉRIQUE DU SUD						
Guyana[10]						
2003 (+C)						
75 - 79	441	224	217	...	...	...
80 - 84	291	145	146	...	...	...
85 - 89	220	97	123	...	...	...
90 - 94	104	39	65	...	...	...
95 - 99	36	12	24	...	...	...
100 +	77	47	30	...	...	...
Paraguay						
2006 (U)						
Total	19 298	10 544[5]	8 709[5]	...	...	...
0	549	318[5]	229[5]	...	...	...
1 - 4	235	123	112	...	...	...
5 - 9	154	89	65	...	...	...
10 - 14	161	93[5]	67[5]	...	...	...
15 - 19	403	275	128	...	...	...
20 - 24	493	380[5]	112[5]	...	...	...
25 - 29	472	336[5]	135[5]	...	...	...
30 - 34	438	292[5]	145[5]	...	...	...
35 - 39	519	328	191	...	...	...
40 - 44	678	403	275	...	...	...
45 - 49	829	489[5]	336[5]	...	...	...
50 - 54	976	583	393	...	...	...
55 - 59	1 190	689[5]	499[5]	...	...	...
60 - 64	1 283	739[5]	542[5]	...	...	...
65 - 69	1 479	821[5]	655[5]	...	...	...
70 - 74	1 737	957[5]	775[5]	...	...	...
75 - 79	2 187	1 188[5]	994[5]	...	...	...
80 - 84	2 040	993[5]	1 040[5]	...	...	...
85 +	3 256	1 330[5]	1 921[5]	...	...	...
Unknown - Inconnu	219	118[5]	95[5]	..	..	..
Peru - Pérou[21]						
2008* (+U)						
Total	91 295	49 015	42 280	...	...	...
0	5 594	3 060	2 534	...	...	...
1 - 4	1 641	909	732	...	...	...
5 - 9	754	431	323	...	...	...
10 - 14	780	441	339	...	...	...
15 - 19	1 480	892	588	...	...	...
20 - 24	1 876	1 200	676	...	...	...
25 - 29	2 091	1 394	697	...	...	...
30 - 34	2 185	1 427	758	...	...	...
35 - 39	2 497	1 531	966	...	...	...
40 - 44	2 947	1 686	1 261	...	...	...
45 - 49	3 427	1 988	1 439	...	...	...
50 - 54	4 049	2 204	1 845	...	...	...
55 - 59	4 474	2 469	2 005	...	...	...
60 - 64	5 462	3 019	2 443	...	...	...
65 - 69	6 481	3 584	2 897	...	...	...
70 - 74	8 345	4 567	3 778	...	...	...
75 - 79	9 825	5 261	4 564	...	...	...
80 - 84	10 046	5 197	4 849	...	...	...
85 - 89	8 896	4 353	4 543	...	...	...
90 - 94	5 294	2 266	3 028	...	...	...
95 - 99	2 356	859	1 497	...	...	...
100 +	643	190	453	...	...	...
Unknown - Inconnu	152	87	65	..	..	..
Suriname[22]						
2007 (C)						
Total	3 374	1 864	1 510	6.6	7.2	6.0
0	134	72	62	13.7	14.7	12.7
1 - 4	42	21	21	1.0	♦1.0	♦1.1
5 - 9	16	9	7	♦0.3	♦0.3	♦0.3
10 - 14	19	10	9	♦0.4	♦0.4	♦0.4
15 - 19	48	26	22	1.0	♦1.1	♦1.0
20 - 24	71	45	26	1.6	2.0	♦1.2

Continent, country or area, date, code and age (in years) / Continent, pays ou zone, date, code et âge (en années)	Number - Nombre			Rate - Taux		
	Both sexes Les deux sexes	Male Masculin	Female Féminin	Both sexes Les deux sexes	Male Masculin	Female Féminin
AMERICA, SOUTH - AMÉRIQUE DU SUD						
Suriname[22]						
2007 (C)						
25 - 29	96	51	45	2.3	2.4	2.2
30 - 34	107	62	45	2.7	3.1	2.3
35 - 39	127	89	38	3.4	4.7	2.1
40 - 44	148	96	52	4.4	5.7	3.2
45 - 49	192	116	76	6.6	7.9	5.3
50 - 54	178	111	67	7.4	9.3	5.6
55 - 59	204	122	82	10.7	13.2	8.4
60 - 64	242	142	100	16.1	19.6	12.8
65 - 69	289	165	124	25.2	30.4	20.5
70 - 74	407	226	181	47.7	56.8	39.8
75 - 79	373	204	169	63.0	74.8	52.9
80 +	681	297	384	130.2	135.9	126.1
80 - 84	333	162	171	...	...	...
85 - 89	200	85	115	...	...	...
90 - 94	103	36	67	...	...	...
95 - 99	36	13	23	...	...	...
100 +	9	1	8	...	...	...
Uruguay						
2002 (C)						
Total	31 628	16 796[5]	14 819[5]	9.6	10.5	8.7
0	708	401[5]	304[5]	14.0	15.4	12.3
1 - 4	104	69	35	0.5	0.6	0.3
5 - 9	63	31	32	0.2	0.2	0.2
10 - 14	67	42	25	0.2	0.3	♦0.2
15 - 19	182	139	43	0.7	1.0	0.3
20 - 24	249	199	50	1.0	1.5	0.4
25 - 29	260	196	64	1.1	1.6	0.5
30 - 34	301	200	101	1.4	1.8	0.9
35 - 39	339	218[5]	120[5]	1.6	2.1	1.1
40 - 44	494	273	221	2.4	2.7	2.1
45 - 49	754	467	287	4.0	5.1	2.9
50 - 54	1 108	724	384	6.5	8.8	4.3
55 - 59	1 501	990	511	9.9	13.8	6.4
60 - 64	2 095	1 422	673	15.0	22.0	9.0
65 - 69	2 842	1 818	1 024	22.0	31.8	14.3
70 - 74	3 938	2 395[5]	1 542[5]	33.3	47.7	22.7
75 +	16 534	7 149[5]	9 381[5]	88.5	105.3	78.9
Unknown - Inconnu	89	63[5]	22[5]	..	..	..
2007 (C)						
Total	33 706	...	...	10.1	...	...
0	572	...	...	11.9	...	...
1 - 4	83	...	...	0.4	...	...
5 - 9	50	...	...	0.2	...	...
10 - 14	76	...	...	0.3	...	...
15 - 19	185	...	...	0.7	...	...
20 - 24	224	...	...	0.9	...	...
25 - 29	267	...	...	1.1	...	...
30 - 34	301	...	...	1.3	...	...
35 - 39	358	...	...	1.7	...	...
40 - 44	454	...	...	2.2	...	...
45 - 49	679	...	...	3.3	...	...
50 - 54	1 080	...	...	5.9	...	...
55 - 59	1 468	...	...	9.0	...	...
60 - 64	2 058	...	...	14.6	...	...
65 - 69	2 689	...	...	21.1	...	...
70 - 74	3 656	...	...	32.6	...	...
75 - 79	4 953	...	...	51.6	...	...
80 - 84	5 324	...	...	86.1	...	...
85 - 89	4 690	...	...	141.7	...	...
90 +	4 122	...	...	255.6	...	...
Venezuela (Bolivarian Republic of) - Venezuela (République bolivarienne du)						
2007 (C)						
Total	118 594	73 756	44 838	4.3	5.3	3.3
0 - 4	7 678	4 456	3 222	2.7	3.0	2.3

Continent, country or area, date, code and age (in years)	Number - Nombre			Rate - Taux		
Continent, pays ou zone, date, code et âge (en années)	Both sexes Les deux sexes	Male Masculin	Female Féminin	Both sexes Les deux sexes	Male Masculin	Female Féminin
AMERICA, SOUTH - AMÉRIQUE DU SUD						
Venezuela (Bolivarian Republic of) - Venezuela (République bolivarienne du)						
2007 (C)						
0	6 340	3 715	2 625	...	...	...
1 - 4	1 338	741	597	...	...	...
5 - 9	740	461	279	0.3	0.3	0.2
10 - 14	940	597	343	0.3	0.4	0.3
15 - 19	4 010	3 393	617	1.5	2.5	0.5
20 - 24	5 900	5 166	734	2.3	4.0	0.6
25 - 29	5 436	4 633	803	2.4	4.0	0.7
30 - 34	4 327	3 403	924	2.1	3.3	0.9
35 - 39	4 074	2 995	1 079	2.2	3.2	1.2
40 - 44	4 495	3 115	1 380	2.6	3.6	1.6
45 - 49	5 391	3 511	1 880	3.6	4.8	2.5
50 - 54	6 398	4 121	2 277	5.2	6.7	3.6
55 - 59	7 386	4 739	2 647	7.3	9.5	5.2
60 - 64	7 726	4 824	2 902	10.2	13.0	7.5
65 - 69	8 761	5 357	3 404	16.1	20.5	12.0
70 - 74	9 915	5 779	4 136	24.8	31.1	19.4
75 - 79	10 992	5 992	5 000	38.0	45.9	31.5
80 +	24 422	11 213	13 209	112.2	120.0	106.2
80 - 84	10 121	5 148	4 973	...	...	...
85 - 89	7 745	3 504	4 241	...	...	...
90 - 94	4 364	1 757	2 607	...	...	...
95 - 99	1 682	608	1 074	...	...	...
100 +	510	196	314	...	...	...
Unknown - Inconnu	3	1	2	..	..	..
ASIA - ASIE						
Armenia - Arménie[23]						
2009 (C)						
Total	27 560	14 253	13 307	8.5	9.1	8.0
0 - 4	528	299	229	2.7	2.9	2.5
0	454	258	196	10.7	11.4	9.9
1 - 4	74	41	33	0.5	0.5	0.5
5 - 9	40	18	22	0.2	♦0.2	♦0.3
10 - 14	40	31	9	0.2	0.3	♦0.1
15 - 19	145	106	39	0.5	0.7	0.3
20 - 24	152	107	45	0.5	0.7	0.3
25 - 29	211	155	56	0.7	1.1	0.4
30 - 34	243	183	60	1.0	1.6	0.5
35 - 39	320	223	97	1.6	2.3	0.9
40 - 44	547	404	143	2.6	4.1	1.3
45 - 49	1 044	728	316	4.0	5.8	2.3
50 - 54	1 431	980	451	6.2	9.0	3.7
55 - 59	1 715	1 142	573	10.1	14.8	6.2
60 - 64	1 539	962	577	15.5	22.1	10.3
65 - 69	2 522	1 477	1 045	27.0	37.7	19.3
70 - 74	4 463	2 419	2 044	40.9	54.4	31.5
75 - 79	5 211	2 484	2 727	68.1	81.3	59.3
80 - 84	4 781	1 854	2 927	110.6	129.6	101.2
85 +	2 628	681	1 947	262.4	271.6	259.3
85 - 89	1 702	454	1 248	...	...	...
90 - 94	637	141	496	...	...	...
95 - 99	212	52	160	...	...	...
100 +	77	34	43	...	...	...
Azerbaijan - Azerbaïdjan[23]						
2009 (+C)						
Total	52 514	27 710	24 804	5.9	6.3	5.4
0 - 4	2 201	1 227	974	3.0	3.1	2.8
0	1 731	950	781	11.4	11.6	11.1
1 - 4	470	277	193	0.8	0.9	0.7
5 - 9	239	133	106	0.4	0.4	0.4
10 - 14	222	135	87	0.3	0.4	0.3
15 - 19	452	305	147	0.5	0.7	0.3

19. Deaths by age and sex, age-specific death rates by sex: latest available year, 2000 - 2009
Décès et taux de mortalité selon l'âge et le sexe : dernière année disponible, 2000 - 2009 (continued - suite)

Continent, country or area, date, code and age (in years)	Number - Nombre			Rate - Taux		
Continent, pays ou zone, date, code et âge (en années)	Both sexes Les deux sexes	Male Masculin	Female Féminin	Both sexes Les deux sexes	Male Masculin	Female Féminin

ASIA - ASIE

Azerbaijan - Azerbaïdjan[23]
2009 (+C)

20 - 24	582	396	186	0.6	0.8	0.4
25 - 29	624	400	224	0.8	1.0	0.6
30 - 34	750	510	240	1.1	1.6	0.7
35 - 39	949	631	318	1.5	2.2	1.0
40 - 44	1 557	1 006	551	2.3	3.2	1.5
45 - 49	2 598	1 748	850	3.7	5.3	2.3
50 - 54	3 360	2 201	1 159	6.2	8.6	4.1
55 - 59	3 434	2 211	1 223	10.1	13.9	6.8
60 - 64	3 090	1 913	1 177	16.0	21.6	11.2
65 - 69	4 449	2 551	1 898	26.8	35.4	20.3
70 - 74	9 028	4 607	4 421	43.0	52.7	36.0
75 - 79	8 572	4 052	4 520	68.0	77.6	61.2
80 - 84	5 958	2 541	3 417	99.3	110.5	92.4
85 - 89	2 626	789	1 837	117.8	109.6	121.7
90 - 94	988	227	761	149.7	103.2	173.0
95 - 99	512	88	424	146.3	97.8	163.1
100 +	323	39	284	269.2	78.0	405.7

Bahrain - Bahreïn
2008 (C)

Total	2 390	1 469	921	2.2	2.2	2.1
0 - 4	160	87	73	2.0	2.2	1.8
0	127	69	58	...	...	...
1 - 4	33	18	15	...	...	...
5 - 9	21	14	7	◆0.3	◆0.4	◆0.2
10 - 14	15	11	4	◆0.2	◆0.3	◆0.1
15 - 19	39	28	11	0.6	◆0.8	◆0.3
20 - 24	68	53	15	0.7	0.9	◆0.3
25 - 29	91	77	14	0.6	0.7	◆0.3
30 - 34	91	69	22	0.6	0.7	◆0.5
35 - 39	72	51	21	0.6	0.6	◆0.5
40 - 44	120	85	35	1.2	1.3	1.0
45 - 49	125	93	32	1.6	1.9	1.2
50 - 54	149	111	38	2.8	3.2	2.1
55 - 59	158	103	55	5.3	5.3	5.3
60 - 64	125	86	39	9.1	10.9	6.6
65 - 69	206	120	86	21.2	24.3	17.9
70 - 74	274	124	150	42.0	39.5	44.3
75 +	676	357	319	67.7	77.2	59.5

Bhutan - Bhoutan[8]
2005 (|)

Total	4 498	2 390	2 108	7.1	7.2	7.0
0	503	270	233	40.8	44.3	37.5
1 - 4	269	143	126	5.4	5.6	5.1
5 - 9	139	85	54	2.0	2.4	1.5
10 - 14	88	46	42	1.1	1.2	1.1
15 - 19	126	65	61	1.7	1.7	1.6
20 - 24	123	65	58	1.7	1.6	1.9
25 - 29	133	74	59	2.3	2.4	2.3
30 - 34	145	79	66	3.4	3.4	3.4
35 - 39	182	107	75	4.7	5.1	4.3
40 - 44	174	95	79	5.8	5.9	5.7
45 - 49	250	129	121	9.0	8.7	9.5
50 - 54	204	113	91	9.3	9.6	8.9
55 - 59	239	126	113	14.6	14.4	14.8
60 - 64	291	145	146	20.0	19.2	20.8
65 - 69	331	163	168	29.1	27.2	31.3
70 - 74	368	188	180	42.1	41.8	42.4
75 +	933	497	436	96.8	102.7	90.8

Brunei Darussalam - Brunéi Darussalam
2008 (+C)

Total	1 091	636	455	...	...	...
0	45	24	21	...	...	...
1 - 4	16	11	5	...	...	...
5 - 9	6	2	4	...	...	...
10 - 14	5	1	4	...	...	...

Continent, country or area, date, code and age (in years) Continent, pays ou zone, date, code et âge (en années)	Number - Nombre			Rate - Taux		
	Both sexes Les deux sexes	Male Masculin	Female Féminin	Both sexes Les deux sexes	Male Masculin	Female Féminin
ASIA - ASIE						
Brunei Darussalam - Brunéi Darussalam						
2008 (+C)						
15 - 19	13	7	6	...	...	...
20 - 24	20	13	7	...	...	...
25 - 29	25	22	3	...	...	...
30 - 34	29	19	10	...	...	...
35 - 39	38	23	15	...	...	...
40 - 44	45	32	13	...	...	...
45 - 49	73	43	30	...	...	...
50 - 54	69	47	22	...	...	...
55 - 59	73	38	35	...	...	...
60 - 64	63	36	27	...	...	...
65 - 69	105	59	46	...	...	...
70 - 74	103	51	52	...	...	...
75 - 79	131	76	55	...	...	...
80 - 84	105	52	53	...	...	...
85 - 89	65	45	20	...	...	...
90 - 94	33	16	17	...	...	...
95 - 99	24	14	10	...	...	...
100 +	5	5	-	...	...	...
China, Hong Kong SAR - Chine, Hong Kong RAS						
2009 (C)						
Total	41 175	22 939[5]	18 228[5]	5.9	7.0	4.9
0	136	71	65	2.9	2.9	2.9
1 - 4	38	20	18	0.2	♦0.2	♦0.2
5 - 9	19	10	9	♦0.1	♦0.1	♦0.1
10 - 14	32	16	16	0.1	♦0.1	♦0.1
15 - 19	79	42	37	0.2	0.2	0.2
20 - 24	148	101	47	0.3	0.5	0.2
25 - 29	200	127	73	0.4	0.5	0.2
30 - 34	287	185	102	0.5	0.8	0.3
35 - 39	394	226	168	0.7	0.9	0.5
40 - 44	562	321	241	0.9	1.2	0.7
45 - 49	1 119	695	424	1.7	2.2	1.2
50 - 54	1 685	1 071	614	2.8	3.6	2.0
55 - 59	2 013	1 365	648	4.2	5.8	2.7
60 - 64	2 134	1 507	627	6.4	8.9	3.8
65 - 69	2 517	1 782	735	11.3	15.2	7.0
70 - 74	4 408	2 965	1 443	18.9	25.9	12.2
75 - 79	6 389	4 021	2 368	32.1	42.3	22.7
80 - 84	7 012	3 852	3 160	54.8	73.7	41.7
85 +	11 973	4 543	7 430	107.5	129.8	97.3
Unknown - Inconnu	30	19[5]	3[5]	..	..	..
China, Macao SAR - Chine, Macao RAS						
2009 (C)						
Total	1 664	923	741	3.1	3.5	2.7
0	10	6	4	♦2.2	♦2.5	♦1.9
1 - 4	3	1	2	♦0.2	♦0.1	♦0.3
5 - 9	1	1	-	♦0.1	♦0.1	-
10 - 14	2	1	1	♦0.1	♦0.1	♦0.1
15 - 19	8	4	4	♦0.2	♦0.2	♦0.2
20 - 24	14	9	5	♦0.3	♦0.4	♦0.2
25 - 29	17	7	10	♦0.4	♦0.3	♦0.4
30 - 34	16	12	4	♦0.4	♦0.6	♦0.2
35 - 39	30	19	11	♦0.6	♦0.9	♦0.4
40 - 44	34	16	18	0.7	♦0.8	♦0.7
45 - 49	74	52	22	1.3	1.9	♦0.8
50 - 54	129	88	41	2.6	3.3	1.7
55 - 59	117	78	39	3.5	4.5	2.5
60 - 64	123	91	32	5.7	7.8	3.2
65 - 69	96	72	24	8.5	12.0	♦4.4
70 - 74	129	87	42	13.9	19.8	8.6
75 - 79	203	111	92	23.6	30.0	18.8
80 - 84	250	119	131	39.1	47.6	34.5
85 +	405	147	258	81.0	98.0	73.7
Unknown - Inconnu	3	2	1	..	..	..

19. Deaths by age and sex, age-specific death rates by sex: latest available year, 2000 - 2009
Décès et taux de mortalité selon l'âge et le sexe : dernière année disponible, 2000 - 2000 (continued - suite)

Continent, country or area, date, code and age (in years) / Continent, pays ou zone, date, code et âge (en années)	Number - Nombre			Rate - Taux		
	Both sexes Les deux sexes	Male Masculin	Female Féminin	Both sexes Les deux sexes	Male Masculin	Female Féminin
ASIA - ASIE						
Cyprus - Chypre[24]						
2009 (C)						
Total	5 182	2 780	2 402	6.5	7.0	6.0
0 - 4	42	27	15	1.0	♦1.2	♦0.7
0	32	22	10	3.5	♦4.6	♦2.3
1 - 4	10	5	5	♦0.3	♦0.3	♦0.3
5 - 9	-	-	-	-	-	-
10 - 14	5	5	-	♦0.1	♦0.2	-
15 - 19	13	10	3	♦0.2	♦0.3	♦0.1
20 - 24	37	32	5	0.6	1.0	♦0.2
25 - 29	46	35	11	0.7	1.0	♦0.3
30 - 34	44	33	11	0.7	1.1	♦0.4
35 - 39	32	17	15	0.6	♦0.6	♦0.5
40 - 44	62	42	20	1.1	1.5	♦0.7
45 - 49	90	56	34	1.6	1.9	1.2
50 - 54	173	108	65	3.3	4.1	2.4
55 - 59	195	147	48	4.1	6.2	2.0
60 - 64	290	193	97	7.2	9.9	4.6
65 - 69	350	233	117	10.5	14.6	6.8
70 - 74	486	310	176	18.6	25.2	12.7
75 - 79	735	373	362	38.1	43.9	33.6
80 - 84	963	435	528	76.1	81.8	71.9
85 - 89	850	395	455	131.4	150.4	118.4
90 - 94	543	235	308	213.9	245.6	194.7
95 - 99	184	77	107	193.3	235.5	171.2
100 +	28	11	17	♦144.3	♦139.2	♦147.8
Unknown - Inconnu	14	6	8	..	..	..
Democratic People's Republic of Korea - République populaire démocratique de Corée[25]						
2008 (I)						
Total	216 616	112 827	103 789	9.0	9.6	8.4
0	6 686	3 593	3 093	19.6	20.6	18.5
1 - 4	2 552	1 372	1 180	1.9	2.0	1.8
5 - 9	1 680	960	720	0.9	1.0	0.8
10 - 14	1 614	869	745	0.8	0.8	0.8
15 - 19	2 426	1 348	1 078	1.2	1.3	1.1
20 - 24	3 171	1 922	1 249	1.7	2.0	1.4
25 - 29	3 528	2 160	1 368	2.0	2.4	1.6
30 - 34	3 907	2 424	1 483	2.3	2.8	1.8
35 - 39	5 792	3 655	2 137	2.6	3.3	1.9
40 - 44	6 312	3 907	2 405	3.1	3.9	2.4
45 - 49	6 468	3 915	2 553	4.1	5.1	3.2
50 - 54	7 630	4 715	2 915	5.8	7.4	4.3
55 - 59	11 295	7 113	4 182	12.5	16.8	8.7
60 - 64	26 360	16 815	9 545	24.9	35.3	16.4
65 - 69	34 068	22 281	11 787	37.3	58.7	22.1
70 - 74	34 093	18 886	15 207	51.5	82.7	35.0
75 - 79	28 690	10 991	17 699	85.5	138.7	69.1
80 +	30 344	5 901	24 443	163.8	238.8	152.3
Georgia - Géorgie[23]						
2008 (C)						
Total	43 011	23 320	19 691	9.8	11.2	8.5
0 - 4	1 044	593	451	4.4	4.7	4.0
0	959	549	410	...	...	...
1 - 4	85	44	41	...	...	...
5 - 9	73	47	26	0.3	0.4	♦0.2
10 - 14	100	61	39	0.4	0.4	0.3
15 - 19	186	123	63	0.5	0.7	0.4
20 - 24	379	276	103	1.1	1.5	0.6
25 - 29	451	356	95	1.4	2.1	0.6
30 - 34	540	412	128	1.7	2.7	0.8
35 - 39	736	566	170	2.5	3.9	1.1
40 - 44	1 106	819	287	3.7	5.8	1.8
45 - 49	1 537	1 147	390	4.6	7.4	2.2
50 - 54	1 878	1 393	485	6.6	10.6	3.1
55 - 59	2 082	1 458	624	8.4	12.9	4.6
60 - 64	1 901	1 263	638	12.0	17.8	7.3

Continent, country or area, date, code and age (in years) Continent, pays ou zone, date, code et âge (en années)	Number - Nombre			Rate - Taux		
	Both sexes Les deux sexes	Male Masculin	Female Féminin	Both sexes Les deux sexes	Male Masculin	Female Féminin
ASIA - ASIE						
Georgia - Géorgie[23]						
2008 (C)						
65 - 69	5 540	3 439	2 101	28.3	42.9	18.2
70 - 74	6 013	3 279	2 734	32.4	43.5	24.8
75 - 79	7 748	3 830	3 918	58.2	74.8	47.8
80 - 84	6 390	2 629	3 761	77.1	94.2	68.4
85 +	5 288	1 615	3 673	135.2	192.3	119.6
85 - 89	3 235	1 021	2 214	...	...	...
90 - 94	1 443	420	1 023	...	...	...
95 - 99	464	141	323	...	...	...
100 +	146	33	113	...	...	...
Unknown - Inconnu	19	14	5	..	..	..
Israel - Israël[26]						
2009 (C)						
Total	38 781	19 250	19 531	5.2	5.2	5.2
0	619	339	280	3.9	4.2	3.6
1 - 4	125	63	62	0.2	0.2	0.2
5 - 9	86	52	34	0.1	0.1	0.1
10 - 14	78	39	39	0.1	0.1	0.1
15 - 19	147	105	42	0.2	0.3	0.1
20 - 24	268	206	62	0.5	0.7	0.2
25 - 29	231	171	60	0.4	0.6	0.2
30 - 34	280	207	73	0.5	0.8	0.3
35 - 39	356	217	139	0.7	0.9	0.6
40 - 44	461	281	180	1.1	1.3	0.8
45 - 49	712	437	275	1.8	2.3	1.4
50 - 54	1 076	685	391	2.8	3.7	2.0
55 - 59	1 723	1 016	707	4.7	5.7	3.7
60 - 64	2 149	1 288	861	7.0	8.8	5.3
65 - 69	2 245	1 355	890	11.6	15.1	8.6
70 - 74	3 713	2 083	1 630	19.5	24.4	15.5
75 - 79	5 077	2 591	2 486	35.0	41.7	29.9
80 - 84	6 671	3 039	3 632	60.3	70.1	54.0
85 - 89	6 884	2 898	3 986	106.6	116.2	100.5
90 - 94	3 702	1 438	2 264	181.0	189.1	176.2
95 - 99	1 845	631	1 214	252.7	237.8	261.3
100 +	333	109	224	207.7	162.7	240.1
Japan - Japon[27]						
2009 (C)						
Total	1 141 865	609 042	532 823	9.0	9.8	8.1
0 - 4	3 460	1 935	1 525	0.6	0.7	0.6
0	2 556	1 441	1 115	...	...	...
1 - 4	904	494	410	...	...	...
5 - 9	534	293	241	0.1	0.1	0.1
10 - 14	487	282	205	0.1	0.1	0.1
15 - 19	1 467	994	473	0.2	0.3	0.2
20 - 24	2 960	2 046	914	0.4	0.6	0.3
25 - 29	3 561	2 368	1 193	0.5	0.6	0.3
30 - 34	4 931	3 256	1 675	0.6	0.7	0.4
35 - 39	7 786	5 061	2 725	0.8	1.0	0.6
40 - 44	10 375	6 817	3 558	1.2	1.6	0.8
45 - 49	14 584	9 621	4 963	1.9	2.5	1.3
50 - 54	22 686	15 316	7 370	2.9	3.9	1.9
55 - 59	41 934	29 123	12 811	4.5	6.3	2.7
60 - 64	61 606	43 254	18 352	6.7	9.6	3.9
65 - 69	82 052	56 771	25 281	9.8	14.3	5.8
70 - 74	109 527	73 054	36 473	15.9	22.9	9.8
75 - 79	159 471	100 771	58 700	27.6	40.1	18.0
80 - 84	201 406	112 983	88 423	47.9	69.0	34.5
85 +	412 407	144 560	267 847	113.9	144.7	102.2
85 - 89	189 913	80 424	109 489	...	...	...
90 - 94	139 746	45 519	94 227	...	...	...
95 - 99	67 799	16 227	51 572	...	...	...
100 +	14 949	2 390	12 559	...	...	...
Unknown - Inconnu	631	537	94	..	..	..

Continent, country or area, date, code and age (in years)	Number - Nombre			Rate - Taux		
Continent, pays ou zone, date, code et âge (en années)	Both sexes Les deux sexes	Male Masculin	Female Féminin	Both sexes Les deux sexes	Male Masculin	Female Féminin
ASIA - ASIE						
Kazakhstan[23]						
2008 (C)						
Total	152 706	85 174	67 532	9.7	11.3	8.3
0	7 322	4 154	3 168	21.9	24.2	19.5
1 - 4	1 066	614	452	0.9	1.1	0.8
5 - 9	477	292	185	0.4	0.5	0.3
10 - 14	500	310	190	0.4	0.5	0.3
15 - 19	1 574	1 055	519	1.1	1.4	0.7
20 - 24	2 971	2 203	768	1.9	2.8	1.0
25 - 29	3 858	2 905	953	3.0	4.5	1.5
30 - 34	4 882	3 722	1 160	4.1	6.4	1.9
35 - 39	5 282	3 928	1 354	4.8	7.4	2.4
40 - 44	6 449	4 711	1 738	6.2	9.4	3.2
45 - 49	9 230	6 696	2 534	8.4	13.0	4.4
50 - 54	10 390	7 374	3 016	11.7	18.2	6.2
55 - 59	11 726	7 738	3 988	16.7	25.3	10.1
60 - 64	9 003	5 653	3 350	23.5	35.2	15.1
65 - 69	15 730	9 038	6 692	35.7	53.6	24.6
70 - 74	17 675	9 321	8 354	50.0	70.9	37.6
75 - 79	16 379	7 276	9 103	78.4	106.3	64.8
80 - 84	15 793	5 141	10 652	117.4	142.4	108.2
85 - 89	7 333	1 783	5 550	184.3	195.7	180.9
90 - 94	3 173	651	2 522	307.9	311.3	307.1
95 - 99	1 084	181	903	404.8	247.6	463.8
100 +	369	52	317	508.3	161.5	784.7
Unknown - Inconnu	440	376	64	..	..	..
Kuwait - Koweït						
2008 (C)						
Total	5 701	3 597	2 104	2.3	2.4	2.1
0 - 4	574	310	264	2.4	2.5	2.2
0	494	272	222	...	...	...
1 - 4	80	38	42	...	...	...
5 - 9	49	35	14	0.2	0.3	♦0.1
10 - 14	54	27	27	0.3	♦0.3	♦0.3
15 - 19	85	65	20	0.5	0.7	♦0.2
20 - 24	156	125	31	0.7	1.0	0.3
25 - 29	231	197	34	0.7	1.0	0.3
30 - 34	214	161	53	0.7	0.8	0.5
35 - 39	292	220	72	1.1	1.3	0.8
40 - 44	295	208	87	1.5	1.6	1.2
45 - 49	371	286	85	2.6	3.0	1.7
50 - 54	421	324	97	4.6	5.3	3.1
55 - 59	384	269	115	7.0	7.8	5.7
60 - 64	367	227	140	11.7	12.4	10.7
65 - 69	481	257	224	25.0	24.1	26.2
70 - 74	494	280	214	43.8	47.3	39.9
75 - 79	371	185	186	62.1	61.4	62.9
80 +	653	312	341	142.8	141.8	143.8
80 - 84	313	143	170	...	...	...
85 +	340	169	171	...	...	...
Unknown - Inconnu	209	109	100	..	..	..
Kyrgyzstan - Kirghizstan						
2009 (C)						
Total	35 898	20 125	15 773	6.7	7.6	5.8
0	3 393	1 933	1 460	27.2	30.2	24.0
1 - 4	530	274	256	1.2	1.2	1.1
5 - 9	164	100	64	0.3	0.4	0.3
10 - 14	183	114	69	0.3	0.4	0.3
15 - 19	358	218	140	0.6	0.7	0.5
20 - 24	634	399	235	1.1	1.4	0.8
25 - 29	755	537	218	1.7	2.3	1.0
30 - 34	1 013	739	274	2.7	3.9	1.4
35 - 39	1 196	862	334	3.4	5.0	1.9
40 - 44	1 517	1 094	423	4.7	7.0	2.6
45 - 49	2 048	1 452	596	6.6	9.8	3.7
50 - 54	2 317	1 621	696	9.6	14.3	5.4
55 - 59	2 407	1 545	862	14.4	20.1	9.5

19. Deaths by age and sex, age-specific death rates by sex: latest available year, 2000 - 2009
Décès et taux de mortalité selon l'âge et le sexe : dernière année disponible, 2000 - 2009 (continued - suite)

Continent, country or area, date, code and age (in years) Continent, pays ou zone, date, code et âge (en années)	Number - Nombre			Rate - Taux		
	Both sexes Les deux sexes	Male Masculin	Female Féminin	Both sexes Les deux sexes	Male Masculin	Female Féminin
ASIA - ASIE						
Kyrgyzstan - Kirghizstan						
2009 (C)						
60 - 64	1 915	1 193	722	19.8	28.1	13.3
65 - 69	2 544	1 526	1 018	35.7	49.0	25.4
70 - 74	3 828	2 072	1 756	48.2	63.8	37.4
75 - 79	4 346	2 077	2 269	84.2	104.1	71.7
80 - 84	3 876	1 654	2 222	115.0	132.7	104.6
85 - 89	1 839	516	1 323	164.6	158.7	167.1
90 - 94	620	128	492	235.1	215.5	240.8
95 - 99	269	48	221	332.9	384.0	323.6
100 +	138	15	123	297.4	♦306.1	296.4
Unknown - Inconnu	8	8	-	..	..	..
Malaysia - Malaisie						
2008 (C)						
Total	124 857	72 205	52 652	4.5	5.1	3.9
0	3 045	1 729	1 316	4.7	5.1	4.1
1 - 4	842	469	373	0.3	0.4	0.3
5 - 9	616	362	254	0.2	0.2	0.2
10 - 14	793	486	307	0.3	0.3	0.2
15 - 19	1 836	1 360	476	0.7	1.0	0.4
20 - 24	2 242	1 703	539	0.9	1.3	0.4
25 - 29	2 345	1 741	604	1.0	1.5	0.5
30 - 34	2 749	2 061	688	1.4	2.0	0.7
35 - 39	3 393	2 461	932	1.8	2.6	1.0
40 - 44	4 434	3 042	1 392	2.5	3.4	1.6
45 - 49	5 935	3 951	1 984	3.8	5.0	2.6
50 - 54	7 920	5 179	2 741	6.0	7.7	4.3
55 - 59	9 668	6 189	3 479	9.5	11.9	7.0
60 - 64	10 984	6 895	4 089	15.7	19.3	11.9
65 - 69	13 076	7 941	5 135	26.1	32.0	20.3
70 - 74	15 875	8 830	7 045	45.9	55.2	37.8
75 - 79	14 530	7 155	7 375	73.9	80.7	68.3
80 - 84	11 725	5 524	6 201	104.4	115.3	96.3
85 - 89	7 930	3 269	4 661	171.8	165.7	176.3
90 - 94	3 363	1 310	2 053	174.0	168.5	177.7
95 +	1 537	548	989	149.7	136.0	158.6
Unknown - Inconnu	19	-	19	..	..	..
Maldives						
2009 (C)						
Total	1 163	675	488	3.7	4.2	3.1
0	81	42	39	12.8	13.1	12.5
1 - 4	10	5	5	♦0.5	♦0.4	♦0.5
5 - 9	8	3	5	♦0.3	♦0.2	♦0.4
10 - 14	16	11	5	♦0.5	♦0.6	♦0.3
15 - 19	12	9	3	♦0.3	♦0.4	♦0.2
20 - 24	18	11	7	♦0.5	♦0.6	♦0.4
25 - 29	19	13	6	♦0.6	♦0.9	♦0.4
30 - 34	15	10	5	♦0.7	♦0.9	♦0.4
35 - 39	8	2	6	♦0.4	♦0.2	♦0.6
40 - 44	24	16	8	♦1.4	♦1.9	♦0.9
45 - 49	31	15	16	2.0	♦1.9	♦2.1
50 - 54	46	24	22	4.0	♦4.1	♦3.9
55 - 59	42	28	14	6.3	♦8.0	♦4.4
60 - 64	44	27	17	8.0	♦9.5	♦6.3
65 - 69	151	86	65	27.8	30.8	24.7
70 - 74	207	121	86	42.3	46.0	38.0
75 - 79	197	106	91	72.2	67.1	79.1
80 +	234	146	88	110.8	112.9	107.4
80 - 84	131	85	46	...	...	...
85 - 89	70	43	27	...	...	...
90 - 94	22	12	10	...	...	...
95 - 99	9	6	3	...	...	...
100 +	2	-	2	...	...	...
Mongolia - Mongolie						
2009 (C)						
Total	16 911	9 845	7 066	6.3	7.5	5.2
0 - 4	1 753	981	772	6.9	7.6	6.2

19. Deaths by age and sex, age-specific death rates by sex: latest available year, 2000 - 2009
Décès et taux de mortalité selon l'âge et le sexe : dernière année disponible, 2000 - 2009 (continued - suite)

Continent, country or area, date, code and age (in years) Continent, pays ou zone, date, code et âge (en annèes)	Number - Nombre			Rate - Taux		
	Both sexes Les deux sexes	Male Masculin	Female Féminin	Both sexes Les deux sexes	Male Masculin	Female Féminin

ASIA - ASIE

Mongolia - Mongolie
  2009 (C)

0 - 1	1 585	894	691	...	...	...
5 - 9	100	63	37	0.4	0.5	0.3
10 - 14	113	73	40	0.4	0.6	0.3
15 - 19	188	116	72	0.6	0.8	0.5
20 - 24	339	233	106	1.2	1.7	0.7
25 - 29	455	315	140	1.9	2.7	1.1
30 - 34	549	376	173	2.5	3.5	1.5
35 - 39	712	487	225	3.5	5.0	2.2
40 - 44	967	684	283	5.4	8.0	3.0
45 - 49	1 289	862	427	8.2	11.5	5.2
50 - 54	1 431	942	489	12.6	17.5	8.2
55 - 59	1 254	808	446	17.0	23.3	11.4
60 - 64	1 176	705	471	23.2	30.2	17.2
65 - 69	1 578	938	640	36.0	45.9	27.3
70 +	5 007	2 262	2 745	76.6	84.5	71.1

Myanmar[28]
  2008 (+U)

Total	135 114	...	...	...	...	...
0	7 004	...	...	...	...	...
1 - 4	2 896	...	...	...	...	...
5 - 9	1 867	...	...	...	...	...
10 - 14	1 306	...	...	...	...	...
15 - 19	1 913	...	...	...	...	...
20 - 24	3 031	...	...	...	...	...
25 - 29	4 734	...	...	...	...	...
30 - 34	6 414	...	...	...	...	...
35 - 39	7 574	...	...	...	...	...
40 - 44	7 771	...	...	...	...	...
45 - 49	8 137	...	...	...	...	...
50 - 54	8 457	...	...	...	...	...
55 - 59	8 626	...	...	...	...	...
60 - 64	8 887	...	...	...	...	...
65 - 69	10 265	...	...	...	...	...
70 - 74	12 667	...	...	...	...	...
75 - 79	12 364	...	...	...	...	...
80 - 84	10 301	...	...	...	...	...
85 +	10 900	...	...	...	...	...

Nepal - Népal[29]
  2001 (|)

Total	106 789	59 544	47 245	4.7	5.2	4.2
0	13 037	6 956	6 081	26.3	27.5	25.1
1 - 4	9 790	5 590	4 200	4.3	4.9	3.8
5 - 9	3 320	1 726	1 594	1.0	1.1	1.0
10 - 14	2 304	1 332	972	0.8	0.9	0.7
15 - 19	2 523	1 293	1 230	1.1	1.1	1.0
20 - 24	2 747	1 449	1 298	1.4	1.5	1.2
25 - 29	2 688	1 429	1 259	1.6	1.7	1.4
30 - 34	2 474	1 303	1 172	1.7	1.8	1.5
35 - 39	2 839	1 594	1 244	2.2	2.4	1.9
40 - 44	2 970	1 828	1 142	2.7	3.4	2.1
45 - 49	3 553	2 027	1 526	3.8	4.3	3.4
50 - 54	4 662	2 771	1 891	6.1	7.1	5.1
55 - 59	6 115	3 612	2 503	10.2	11.3	8.8
60 - 64	8 337	4 710	3 626	16.0	18.0	14.0
65 - 69	8 667	4 764	3 903	22.4	24.3	20.4
70 - 74	9 606	5 512	4 093	35.1	38.9	31.0
75 - 79	8 113	4 657	3 456	48.9	56.6	41.4
80 +	13 042	6 990	6 052	100.6	111.8	90.1

Occupied Palestinian Territory - Territoire palestinien occupé
  2007 (U)

Total	9 887	5 697	4 190	...	...	...
0	794	420	374	...	...	...
1 - 4	299	165	134	...	...	...
5 - 9	143	71	72	...	...	...

19. Deaths by age and sex, age-specific death rates by sex: latest available year, 2000 - 2009
Décès et taux de mortalité selon l'âge et le sexe : dernière année disponible, 2000 - 2009 (continued - suite)

Continent, country or area, date, code and age (in years) / Continent, pays ou zone, date, code et âge (en années)	Number - Nombre			Rate - Taux		
	Both sexes Les deux sexes	Male Masculin	Female Féminin	Both sexes Les deux sexes	Male Masculin	Female Féminin
ASIA - ASIE						
Occupied Palestinian Territory - Territoire palestinien occupé						
2007 (U)						
10 - 14	134	101	33	...	...	...
15 - 19	263	223	40	...	...	...
20 - 24	410	361	49	...	...	...
25 - 29	254	207	47	...	...	...
30 - 34	229	178	51	...	...	...
35 - 39	193	129	64	...	...	...
40 - 44	264	173	91	...	...	...
45 - 49	293	204	89	...	...	...
50 - 54	397	253	144	...	...	...
55 - 59	534	341	193	...	...	...
60 - 64	728	410	318	...	...	...
65 - 69	751	377	374	...	...	...
70 - 74	1 031	534	497	...	...	...
75 - 79	1 069	509	560	...	...	...
80 - 84	937	464	473	...	...	...
85 - 89	617	290	327	...	...	...
90 - 94	317	154	163	...	...	...
95 - 99	117	69	48	...	...	...
100 +	113	64	49	...	...	...
Oman[30]						
2009 (U)						
Total	7 098	4 623[5]	2 466[5]	...	...	...
0	676	397	279	...	...	...
1 - 4	125	74	51	...	...	...
5 - 9	70	42	28	...	...	...
10 - 14	72	45	27	...	...	...
15 - 19	136	106	30	...	...	...
20 - 24	248	211	37	...	...	...
25 - 29	291	239	52	...	...	...
30 - 34	241	189	52	...	...	...
35 - 39	215	175	40	...	...	...
40 - 44	250	192	58	...	...	...
45 - 49	300	237	63	...	...	...
50 - 54	408	307	101	...	...	...
55 - 59	436	291	145	...	...	...
60 - 64	476	294	182	...	...	...
65 - 69	660	403	257	...	...	...
70 - 74	601	382	219	...	...	...
75 - 79	615	393	222	...	...	...
80 - 84	345	207	138	...	...	...
85 - 89	239	141	98	...	...	...
90 - 94	89	41	48	...	...	...
95 - 99	46	23	23	...	...	...
100 +	21	5	16	...	...	...
Unknown - Inconnu	538	229[5]	300[5]	..	..	..
Pakistan[31]						
2007 (I)						
Total	1 019 533	598 820	420 713	6.8	7.8	5.8
0 - 4	365 729	205 840	159 889	18.7	21.0	16.4
5 - 9	33 029	16 652	16 376	1.5	1.4	1.5
10 - 14	20 510	6 871	13 640	1.0	0.6	1.4
15 - 19	27 417	16 500	10 917	1.6	1.8	1.3
20 - 24	20 192	11 195	8 997	1.5	1.6	1.3
25 - 29	23 990	13 101	10 888	2.2	2.5	2.0
30 - 34	11 624	8 007	3 617	1.4	2.0	0.8
35 - 39	24 880	11 482	13 398	3.0	2.8	3.2
40 - 44	30 926	18 802	12 124	4.6	5.4	3.7
45 - 49	27 537	17 884	9 652	4.4	5.5	3.2
50 - 54	43 405	30 870	12 535	9.5	12.7	5.8
55 - 59	51 031	35 120	15 911	14.4	18.8	9.5
60 - 64	68 531	41 470	27 061	23.4	25.3	20.9
65 - 69	58 286	35 664	22 621	28.6	32.2	24.3
70 - 74	82 325	49 296	33 029	56.2	57.5	54.4
75 - 79	37 357	24 072	13 285	57.1	67.2	44.9

Continent, country or area, date, code and age (in years) Continent, pays ou zone, date, code et âge (en années)	Number - Nombre			Rate - Taux		
	Both sexes Les deux sexes	Male Masculin	Female Féminin	Both sexes Les deux sexes	Male Masculin	Female Féminin
ASIA - ASIE						
Pakistan[31]						
2007 (I)						
80 - 84	34 079	21 720	12 359	79.6	86.6	69.6
85 +	58 685	34 274	24 411	165.7	168.9	161.4
Philippines						
2005 (C)						
Total	426 054	250 102	175 952	5.1	5.9	4.2
0 - 4	30 825	17 758	13 067	3.2	3.6	2.8
0	21 674	12 752	8 922	...	...	...
1 - 4	9 151	5 006	4 145	...	...	...
5 - 9	5 230	2 961	2 269	0.6	0.6	0.5
10 - 14	4 790	2 816	1 974	0.5	0.6	0.4
15 - 19	7 102	4 623	2 479	0.8	1.0	0.6
20 - 24	10 120	7 044	3 076	1.3	1.8	0.8
25 - 29	11 862	8 258	3 604	1.7	2.3	1.0
30 - 34	12 669	8 681	3 988	2.0	2.8	1.3
35 - 39	16 153	10 877	5 276	2.9	3.9	1.9
40 - 44	18 717	12 601	6 116	3.9	5.3	2.6
45 - 49	23 528	15 693	7 835	5.9	7.8	3.9
50 - 54	27 815	18 641	9 174	8.5	11.4	5.6
55 - 59	31 534	21 198	10 336	12.1	16.3	7.8
60 - 64	33 221	21 324	11 897	16.8	22.1	11.7
65 - 69	38 251	23 465	14 786	26.0	33.3	19.3
70 - 74	38 815	22 189	16 626	38.0	46.7	30.4
75 - 79	37 864	19 858	18 006	56.3	66.6	48.1
80 +	76 969	31 827	45 142	136.7	136.9	136.5
80 - 84	33 418	15 312	18 106	...	...	...
85 - 89	24 701	9 904	14 797	...	...	...
90 - 94	13 747	4 893	8 854	...	...	...
95 +	5 103	1 718	3 385	...	...	...
Unknown - Inconnu	589	288	301	..	..	..
Qatar						
2009 (C)						
Total	2 008	1 515	493	1.2	1.2	1.3
0	130	72	58	7.4	8.0	6.7
1 - 4	31	15	16	0.5	◆0.4	◆0.5
5 - 9	15	9	6	◆0.2	◆0.2	◆0.2
10 - 14	14	11	3	◆0.2	◆0.3	◆0.1
15 - 19	40	36	4	0.6	1.0	◆0.2
20 - 24	124	118	6	0.5	0.6	◆0.2
25 - 29	154	145	9	0.5	0.6	◆0.2
30 - 34	140	124	16	0.6	0.6	◆0.4
35 - 39	137	124	13	0.7	0.8	◆0.4
40 - 44	142	121	21	1.0	1.0	◆0.8
45 - 49	145	119	26	1.5	1.5	◆1.3
50 - 54	153	129	24	2.3	2.4	◆2.0
55 - 59	141	113	28	4.3	4.3	◆4.1
60 - 64	106	72	34	7.4	6.8	9.1
65 - 69	125	77	48	19.1	18.2	20.8
70 - 74	133	73	60	33.6	30.7	37.8
75 - 79	112	65	47	46.4	45.0	48.5
80 +	166	92	74	59.3	56.4	63.4
80 - 84	72	36	36	...	...	...
85 - 89	48	34	14	...	...	...
90 - 94	27	13	14	...	...	...
95 +	19	9	10	...	...	...
Republic of Korea - République de Corée[32]						
2009 (C)						
Total	246 942	137 736	109 206	5.1	5.6	4.5
0	1 415	757	658	3.2	3.3	3.1
1 - 4	405	203	202	0.2	0.2	0.2
5 - 9	384	247	137	0.1	0.2	0.1
10 - 14	441	265	176	0.1	0.2	0.1
15 - 19	1 073	709	364	0.3	0.4	0.2
20 - 24	1 507	936	571	0.5	0.6	0.4
25 - 29	2 544	1 526	1 018	0.7	0.8	0.5
30 - 34	3 040	1 858	1 182	0.8	0.9	0.6

19. Deaths by age and sex, age-specific death rates by sex: latest available year, 2000 - 2009
Décès et taux de mortalité selon l'âge et le sexe : dernière année disponible, 2000 - 2009 (continued - suite)

Continent, country or area, date, code and age (in years) / Continent, pays ou zone, date, code et âge (en années)	Number - Nombre			Rate - Taux		
	Both sexes Les deux sexes	Male Masculin	Female Féminin	Both sexes Les deux sexes	Male Masculin	Female Féminin
ASIA - ASIE						
Republic of Korea - République de Corée[32]						
2009 (C)						
35 - 39	4 718	3 087	1 631	1.1	1.4	0.8
40 - 44	7 000	4 979	2 021	1.7	2.4	1.0
45 - 49	10 970	8 079	2 891	2.6	3.8	1.4
50 - 54	13 988	10 484	3 504	3.7	5.6	1.9
55 - 59	13 394	9 899	3 495	5.1	7.6	2.7
60 - 64	16 113	11 612	4 501	7.7	11.3	4.2
65 - 69	24 020	16 435	7 585	13.2	19.7	7.7
70 - 74	31 975	19 977	11 998	21.5	31.4	14.1
75 - 79	34 553	17 885	16 668	34.5	47.5	26.7
80 - 84	33 981	14 543	19 438	62.7	83.1	53.0
85 - 89	27 439	9 740	17 699	107.5	136.1	96.4
90 - 94	13 179	3 541	9 638	185.9	214.2	177.3
95 +	4 755	940	3 815	249.1	313.0	237.2
95 - 99	4 040	852	3 188	...	...	...
100 +	715	88	627	...	...	...
Unknown - Inconnu	48	34	14	..	..	..
Saudi Arabia - Arabie saoudite[33]						
2005 (...)						
Total	*92 486*	*54 253*	*38 233*	...	...	...
0 - 4	*12 889*	*6 692*	*6 197*	...	...	...
5 - 9	*977*	*524*	*453*	...	...	...
10 - 14	*977*	*566*	*411*	...	...	...
15 - 19	*1 350*	*791*	*559*	...	...	...
20 - 24	*1 695*	*998*	*697*	...	...	...
25 - 29	*2 248*	*1 371*	*877*	...	...	...
30 - 34	*2 750*	*1 681*	*1 069*	...	...	...
35 - 39	*3 309*	*2 131*	*1 178*	...	...	...
40 - 44	*3 997*	*2 698*	*1 299*	...	...	...
45 - 49	*4 754*	*3 266*	*1 488*	...	...	...
50 - 54	*5 285*	*3 629*	*1 656*	...	...	...
55 - 59	*5 538*	*3 658*	*1 880*	...	...	...
60 - 64	*6 116*	*3 756*	*2 360*	...	...	...
65 - 69	*6 924*	*3 985*	*2 939*	...	...	...
70 - 74	*8 082*	*4 448*	*3 634*	...	...	...
75 - 79	*8 176*	*4 484*	*3 692*	...	...	...
80 +	*17 419*	*9 575*	*7 844*	...	...	...
Singapore - Singapour						
2009 (+C)						
Total	17 101[34]	9 450	7 647	4.6	5.1	4.0
0 - 4	141	77	64	0.7	0.8	0.7
0	102	58	44	...	...	...
1 - 4	39	19	20	...	...	...
5 - 9	24	16	8	♦0.1	♦0.1	♦0.1
10 - 14	41	24	17	0.2	♦0.2	♦0.1
15 - 19	77	53	24	0.3	0.4	♦0.2
20 - 24	148	104	44	0.6	0.9	0.4
25 - 29	176	135	41	0.6	1.0	0.3
30 - 34	195	142	53	0.7	1.0	0.3
35 - 39	249	172	77	0.8	1.1	0.5
40 - 44	357	232	125	1.1	1.5	0.8
45 - 49	589	373	216	1.8	2.3	1.4
50 - 54	966	627	339	3.2	4.2	2.3
55 - 59	1 189	767	422	5.0	6.4	3.5
60 - 64	1 343	881	462	7.9	10.5	5.4
65 - 69	1 580	960	620	13.6	17.3	10.2
70 - 74	2 009	1 230	779	23.0	30.4	16.5
75 - 79	2 358	1 283	1 075	38.4	48.1	31.0
80 - 84	2 221	1 092	1 129	59.9	75.3	50.0
85 +	3 425	1 277	2 148	123.2	138.8	115.5
85 - 89	1 751	732	1 019	...	...	...
90 - 94	1 103	388	715	...	...	...
95 - 99	467	127	340	...	...	...
100 +	104	30	74	...	...	...
Unknown - Inconnu	13[34]	5	4	..	..	..

19. Deaths by age and sex, age-specific death rates by sex: latest available year, 2000 - 2009
Décès et taux de mortalité selon l'âge et le sexe : dernière année disponible, 2000 - 2009 (continued - suite)

Continent, country or area, date, code and age (in years) / Continent, pays ou zone, date, code et âge (en années)	Number - Nombre			Rate - Taux		
	Both sexes Les deux sexes	Male Masculin	Female Féminin	Both sexes Les deux sexes	Male Masculin	Female Féminin
ASIA - ASIE						
Sri Lanka						
2007 (+C)						
Total	118 998	71 207	47 791	5.9	7.2	4.7
0	3 298	1 856	1 442	...	...	...
1 - 4	708	392	316	...	...	...
5 - 9	533	292	241	0.3	0.3	0.3
10 - 14	541	295	246	0.3	0.3	0.3
15 - 19	1 227	780	447	0.6	0.8	0.5
20 - 24	2 174	1 648	526	1.2	1.8	0.6
25 - 29	2 339	1 733	606	1.5	2.3	0.7
30 - 34	2 227	1 687	540	1.5	2.3	0.7
35 - 39	2 760	2 073	687	1.9	2.9	0.9
40 - 44	3 495	2 678	817	2.6	4.0	1.2
45 - 49	5 080	3 771	1 309	4.2	6.4	2.1
50 - 54	6 604	4 702	1 902	6.1	8.8	3.4
55 - 59	8 621	6 041	2 580	10.8	15.7	6.2
60 - 64	9 349	6 122	3 227	15.8	21.3	10.6
65 - 69	11 088	6 868	4 220	22.6	30.3	16.0
70 - 74	13 838	7 909	5 929	38.4	47.1	30.9
75 +	45 114	22 358	22 756	104.7	112.9	97.7
75 - 79	13 781	7 515	6 266	...	...	...
80 - 84	14 391	7 079	7 312	...	...	...
85 - 89	9 803	4 690	5.113	...	...	...
90 - 94	4 822	2 157	2 665	...	...	...
95 - 99	1 768	725	1 043	...	...	...
100 +	549	192	357	...	...	...
Unknown - Inconnu	2	2	-	...	...	...
Tajikistan - Tadjikistan[23]						
2008 (U)						
Total	30 743	17 063	13 680	...	...	...
0	2 480	1 478	1 002	...	...	...
1 - 4	725	414	311	...	...	...
5 - 9	242	139	103	...	...	...
10 - 14	270	183	87	...	...	...
15 - 19	418	279	139	...	...	...
20 - 24	508	302	206	...	...	...
25 - 29	573	345	228	...	...	...
30 - 34	728	467	261	...	...	...
35 - 39	785	480	305	...	...	...
40 - 44	947	623	324	...	...	...
45 - 49	1 313	793	520	...	...	...
50 - 54	1 462	890	572	...	...	...
55 - 59	1 703	1 023	680	...	...	...
60 - 64	1 517	890	627	...	...	...
65 - 69	2 887	1 728	1 159	...	...	...
70 - 74	3 941	2 182	1 759	...	...	...
75 - 79	4 435	2 330	2 105	...	...	...
80 - 84	3 146	1 532	1 614	...	...	...
85 - 89	1 620	630	990	...	...	...
90 - 94	622	239	383	...	...	...
95 - 99	266	77	189	...	...	...
100 +	141	33	108	...	...	...
Unknown - Inconnu	14	6	8	...	...	...
Thailand - Thaïlande						
2009 (+U)						
Total	393 916	222 815	171 101	...	...	...
0	5 416	3 018	2 398	...	...	...
1 - 4	7 476	4 234	3 242	...	...	...
5 - 9	1 686	1 062	624	...	...	...
10 - 14	2 317	1 440	877	...	...	...
15 - 19	5 464	4 212	1 252	...	...	...
20 - 24	6 015	4 639	1 376	...	...	...
25 - 29	8 245	6 118	2 127	...	...	...
30 - 34	11 275	8 106	3 169	...	...	...
35 - 39	14 662	10 454	4 208	...	...	...
40 - 44	18 433	12 874	5 559	...	...	...
45 - 49	21 725	14 774	6 951	...	...	...

19. Deaths by age and sex, age-specific death rates by sex: latest available year, 2000 - 2009
Décès et taux de mortalité selon l'âge et le sexe : dernière année disponible, 2000 - 2009 (continued - suite)

Continent, country or area, date, code and age (in years) Continent, pays ou zone, date, code et âge (en années)	Number - Nombre			Rate - Taux		
	Both sexes Les deux sexes	Male Masculin	Female Féminin	Both sexes Les deux sexes	Male Masculin	Female Féminin
ASIA - ASIE						
Thailand - Thaïlande						
2009 (+U)						
50 - 54	24 878	16 268	8 610	...	...	...
55 - 59	27 786	17 338	10 448	...	...	...
60 - 64	29 567	17 516	12 051	...	...	...
65 - 69	34 223	19 582	14 641	...	...	...
70 +	179 995	84 147	95 848	...	...	...
United Arab Emirates - Émirats arabes unis[33]						
2003 (...)						
Total	6 002	4 305	1 697	...	...	...
0	477	272	205	...	...	...
1 - 4	132	74	58	...	...	...
5 - 9	94	59	35	...	...	...
10 - 14	79	57	22	...	...	...
15 - 19	174	134	40	...	...	...
20 - 24	253	221	32	...	...	...
25 - 29	302	249	53	...	...	...
30 - 34	297	256	41	...	...	...
35 - 39	308	269	39	...	...	...
40 - 44	405	347	58	...	...	...
45 - 49	515	437	78	...	...	...
50 - 54	502	411	91	...	...	...
55 - 59	357	284	73	...	...	...
60 - 64	565	348	217	...	...	...
65 - 69	418	225	193	...	...	...
70 - 74	386	204	182	...	...	...
75 - 79	244	147	97	...	...	...
80 +	378	209	169	...	...	...
Unknown - Inconnu	116	102	14	..	..	
Uzbekistan - Ouzbékistan[23]						
2000 (C)						
Total	135 598	70 794	64 804	5.5	5.8	5.2
0	10 091	5 805	4 286	19.1	21.4	16.6
1 - 4	5 417	2 925	2 492	2.3	2.4	2.2
5 - 9	1 474	886	588	0.4	0.5	0.4
10 - 14	1 436	852	584	0.5	0.5	0.4
15 - 19	2 001	1 289	712	0.7	0.9	0.5
20 - 24	2 849	1 758	1 091	1.3	1.6	1.0
25 - 29	3 427	2 177	1 250	1.7	2.2	1.3
30 - 34	3 660	2 403	1 257	2.1	2.9	1.4
35 - 39	4 181	2 759	1 422	2.5	3.4	1.7
40 - 44	5 086	3 277	1 809	3.6	4.8	2.6
45 - 49	5 290	3 445	1 845	5.4	7.2	3.7
50 - 54	5 765	3 647	2 118	9.4	12.2	6.7
55 - 59	6 104	3 794	2 310	14.2	17.6	10.8
60 - 64	12 287	7 257	5 030	22.3	27.5	17.5
65 - 69	14 077	7 757	6 320	35.9	43.2	29.7
70 - 74	17 094	8 713	8 381	52.7	61.0	46.2
75 - 79	12 547	4 824	7 723	72.9	80.3	68.9
80 - 84	8 807	2 836	5 971	114.2	129.9	108.1
85 - 89	7 198	2 312	4 886	164.0	194.7	152.6
90 - 94	3 782	1 295	2 487	195.5	192.3	197.2
95 +	3 025	783	2 242	316.6	202.4	394.2
95 - 99	1 963	579	1 384	...	...	...
100 +	1 062	204	858	...	...	...
EUROPE						
Åland Islands - Îles d'Åland						
2009 (C)						
Total	247	126	121	9.0	9.2	8.7
0	-	-	-	-	-	-
1 - 4	-	-	-	-	-	-
5 - 9	-	-	-	-	-	-
10 - 14	-	-	-	-	-	-
15 - 19	-	-	-	-	-	-

Continent, country or area, date, code and age (in years)	Number - Nombre			Rate - Taux		
Continent, pays ou zone, date, code et âge (en années)	Both sexes Les deux sexes	Male Masculin	Female Féminin	Both sexes Les deux sexes	Male Masculin	Female Féminin
EUROPE						
Åland Islands - Îles d'Åland						
2009 (C)						
20 - 24	1	1	-	♦0.8	♦1.4	-
25 - 29	2	-	2	♦1.3	-	♦2.6
30 - 34	1	1	-	♦0.6	♦1.2	-
35 - 39	-	-	-	-	-	-
40 - 44	4	2	2	♦1.9	♦1.9	♦1.9
45 - 49	6	4	2	♦3.1	♦4.2	♦2.1
50 - 54	2	2	-	♦1.0	♦2.2	-
55 - 59	13	7	6	♦6.3	♦7.0	♦5.6
60 - 64	12	6	6	♦5.8	♦5.7	♦5.9
65 - 69	17	12	5	♦11.7	♦15.4	♦7.4
70 - 74	21	13	8	♦18.9	♦24.4	♦13.8
75 - 79	25	14	11	♦29.1	♦35.1	♦23.9
80 - 84	43	22	21	58.3	♦72.8	♦48.2
85 - 89	43	27	16	93.7	♦183.7	♦51.1
90 - 94	32	10	22	185.0	♦232.6	♦167.9
95 - 99	23	5	18	♦383.3	♦454.5	♦367.3
100 +	2	-	2	♦500.0	-	♦666.7
Albania - Albanie						
2004 (C)						
Total	17 749	9 950	7 799	5.7	6.4	5.0
0	336	181	155	6.9	7.2	6.6
1 - 4	237	132	105	1.2	1.2	1.1
5 - 9	164	108	56	0.6	0.7	0.4
10 - 14	140	86	54	0.5	0.5	0.4
15 - 19	157	106	51	0.5	0.7	0.3
20 - 24	219	147	72	0.8	1.2	0.5
25 - 29	181	140	41	0.8	1.3	0.4
30 - 34	225	159	66	1.1	1.6	0.6
35 - 39	244	160	84	1.2	1.6	0.8
40 - 44	365	249	116	1.6	2.2	1.0
45 - 49	469	313	156	2.4	3.1	1.6
50 - 54	586	397	189	3.8	5.0	2.5
55 - 59	676	451	225	5.6	7.3	3.8
60 - 64	1 248	820	428	10.4	13.7	7.1
65 - 69	1 720	1 158	562	17.5	22.9	11.7
70 - 74	2 428	1 478	950	33.8	42.5	25.7
75 - 79	2 608	1 462	1 146	56.9	72.9	44.4
80 - 84	2 768	1 256	1 512	100.3	114.3	91.1
85 - 89	1 652	719	933	182.5	212.1	164.8
90 - 94	936	298	638	266.4	305.2	251.4
95 +	390	130	260	781.6	1070.0	688.7
95 - 99	300	103	197	...	...	...
100 +	90	27	63	...	...	...
2007 (C)						
Total	14 528	...	...	4.6	...	...
0 - 4	289	...	...	1.2	...	...
0	205	...	...	...	...	...
1 - 4	84	...	...	...	...	...
5 - 9	87	...	...	0.3	...	...
10 - 14	99	...	...	0.3	...	...
15 - 19	137	...	...	0.4	...	...
20 - 24	159	...	...	0.5	...	...
25 - 29	161	...	...	0.7	...	...
30 - 34	165	...	...	0.8	...	...
35 - 39	198	...	...	0.9	...	...
40 - 44	238	...	...	1.2	...	...
45 - 49	398	...	...	1.9	...	...
50 - 54	539	...	...	3.1	...	...
55 - 59	626	...	...	4.4	...	...
60 - 64	741	...	...	6.8	...	...
65 - 69	1 348	...	...	12.8	...	...
70 - 74	1 884	...	...	23.5	...	...
75 - 79	2 371	...	...	44.5	...	...
80 - 84	2 121	...	...	76.1	...	...

19. Deaths by age and sex, age-specific death rates by sex: latest available year, 2000 - 2009
Décès et taux de mortalité selon l'âge et le sexe : dernière année disponible, 2000 - 2009 (continued - suite)

Continent, country or area, date, code and age (in years) Continent, pays ou zone, date, code et âge (en années)	Number - Nombre			Rate - Taux		
	Both sexes Les deux sexes	Male Masculin	Female Féminin	Both sexes Les deux sexes	Male Masculin	Female Féminin
EUROPE						
Albania - Albanie						
2007 (C)						
85 +	2 954	...	...	173.9	...	...
Unknown - Inconnu	13	...	...	..	..	..
Andorra - Andorre						
2009 (C)						
Total	272	159	113	3.2	3.6	2.8
0 - 4	2	1	1	♦0.6	♦0.6	♦0.6
0	1	-	1	♦3.6	-	♦7.2
1 - 4	1	1	-	♦0.3	♦0.6	-
5 - 9	-	-	-	-	-	-
10 - 14	-	-	-	-	-	-
15 - 19	1	1	-	♦0.3	♦0.5	-
20 - 24	2	1	1	♦0.5	♦0.4	♦0.5
25 - 29	1	1	-	♦0.2	♦0.3	-
30 - 34	2	1	1	♦0.2	♦0.2	♦0.3
35 - 39	4	3	1	♦0.5	♦0.7	♦0.2
40 - 44	6	4	2	♦0.7	♦0.9	♦0.5
45 - 49	16	9	7	♦2.1	♦2.3	♦2.0
50 - 54	9	6	3	♦1.4	♦1.8	♦1.1
55 - 59	15	10	5	♦3.0	♦3.6	♦2.3
60 - 64	14	11	3	♦3.4	♦4.9	♦1.6
65 - 69	10	5	5	♦3.2	♦3.1	♦3.3
70 - 74	25	16	9	♦11.2	♦13.9	♦8.3
75 - 79	34	21	13	16.9	♦21.0	♦12.8
80 - 84	42	29	13	25.8	♦37.5	♦15.2
85 - 89	55	26	29	51.2	♦54.6	♦48.5
90 - 94	19	10	9	♦40.2	♦45.7	♦35.4
95 - 99	12	4	8	♦51.7	♦39.2	♦61.5
100 +	3	-	3	♦14.7	-	♦29.1
Austria - Autriche[35]						
2009 (C)						
Total	77 381	36 630	40 751	9.3	9.0	9.5
0 - 4	355	190	165	0.9	0.9	0.9
0	289	158	131	3.8	4.0	3.5
1 - 4	66	32	34	0.2	0.2	0.2
5 - 9	39	22	17	0.1	♦0.1	♦0.1
10 - 14	58	33	25	0.1	0.1	♦0.1
15 - 19	203	152	51	0.4	0.6	0.2
20 - 24	267	201	66	0.5	0.8	0.3
25 - 29	272	197	75	0.5	0.7	0.3
30 - 34	292	202	90	0.5	0.8	0.3
35 - 39	482	320	162	0.8	1.0	0.5
40 - 44	897	599	298	1.3	1.7	0.8
45 - 49	1 559	1 045	514	2.3	3.0	1.5
50 - 54	2 178	1 415	763	3.7	4.9	2.6
55 - 59	2 873	1 959	914	5.8	8.1	3.6
60 - 64	4 203	2 787	1 416	9.4	12.9	6.1
65 - 69	6 299	4 031	2 268	13.3	18.1	9.1
70 - 74	6 456	3 940	2 516	20.0	27.0	14.2
75 - 79	9 777	5 398	4 379	35.9	47.5	27.6
80 - 84	14 176	6 268	7 908	65.2	81.6	56.2
85 - 89	16 166	5 244	10 922	120.5	145.4	111.3
90 - 94	6 696	1 770	4 926	208.0	237.6	199.1
95 - 99	3 650	783	2 867	344.7	368.8	338.7
100 +	483	74	409	491.9	477.4	494.6
Belarus - Bélarus						
2009 (C)						
Total	135 097	70 565	64 532	14.0	15.6	12.5
0 - 4	653	384	269	1.3	1.5	1.1
0	407	234	173	3.8	4.2	3.3
1 - 4	246	150	96	0.7	0.8	0.5
5 - 9	121	81	40	0.3	0.3	0.2
10 - 14	103	66	37	0.2	0.3	0.2
15 - 19	315	231	84	0.5	0.7	0.3
20 - 24	923	741	182	1.1	1.7	0.4
25 - 29	1 320	1 047	273	1.7	2.6	0.7

Continent, country or area, date, code and age (in years)	Number - Nombre			Rate - Taux		
Continent, pays ou zone, date, code et âge (en années)	Both sexes Les deux sexes	Male Masculin	Female Féminin	Both sexes Les deux sexes	Male Masculin	Female Féminin
EUROPE						
Belarus - Bélarus						
2009 (C)						
30 - 34	1 835	1 399	436	2.6	4.0	1.3
35 - 39	2 494	1 924	570	3.7	5.8	1.7
40 - 44	3 392	2 638	754	5.0	7.9	2.1
45 - 49	5 751	4 425	1 326	7.2	11.5	3.2
50 - 54	7 997	5 944	2 053	10.7	17.1	5.1
55 - 59	9 804	6 963	2 841	16.1	25.5	8.4
60 - 64	10 295	7 260	3 035	25.7	42.9	13.2
65 - 69	10 620	6 698	3 922	28.4	47.6	16.8
70 - 74	17 957	9 885	8 072	44.9	72.3	30.7
75 - 79	20 024	8 919	11 105	66.5	97.4	53.0
80 - 84	21 576	7 341	14 235	107.3	145.5	94.5
85 +	19 838	4 557	15 281	217.7	259.0	207.9
85 - 89	13 316	3 234	10 082	...	...	...
90 - 94	4 390	925	3 465	...	...	...
95 - 99	1 776	345	1 431	...	...	...
100 +	356	53	303	...	...	...
Unknown - Inconnu	79	62	17	..	..	..
Belgium - Belgique[36]						
2007 (C)						
Total	100 658	49 804	50 854	9.5	9.6	9.4
0 - 4	593	349	244	1.0	1.1	0.8
0	487	287	200	4.0	4.6	3.4
1 - 4	106	62	44	0.2	0.3	0.2
5 - 9	53	29	24	0.1	♦0.1	♦0.1
10 - 14	83	47	36	0.1	0.2	0.1
15 - 19	248	172	76	0.4	0.5	0.2
20 - 24	378	288	90	0.6	0.9	0.3
25 - 29	385	279	106	0.6	0.8	0.3
30 - 34	520	360	160	0.8	1.0	0.5
35 - 39	759	479	280	1.0	1.2	0.7
40 - 44	1 238	773	465	1.5	1.9	1.2
45 - 49	2 022	1 238	784	2.5	3.1	2.0
50 - 54	3 104	1 938	1 166	4.2	5.3	3.2
55 - 59	4 179	2 691	1 488	6.2	8.0	4.4
60 - 64	5 283	3 425	1 858	9.2	12.2	6.4
65 - 69	6 392	4 119	2 273	13.7	18.6	9.3
70 - 74	9 880	5 962	3 918	21.9	29.2	15.8
75 - 79	15 164	8 441	6 723	37.5	50.2	28.5
80 - 84	19 367	9 228	10 139	66.7	86.4	55.3
85 - 89	16 682	6 380	10 302	117.3	144.4	105.0
90 - 94	9 861	2 740	7 121	211.1	250.4	199.1
95 - 99	3 791	767	3 024	313.0	368.4	301.5
100 +	676	99	577	501.9	678.1	480.4
Bosnia and Herzegovina - Bosnie-Herzégovine						
2009 (C)						
Total	34 904	17 884	17 020	9.1	9.5	8.7
0 - 4	255	135	120	1.5	1.6	1.5
0	224	116	108	6.7	6.8	6.7
1 - 4	31	19	12	0.2	♦0.3	♦0.2
5 - 9	21	15	6	♦0.1	♦0.1	♦0.1
10 - 14	24	15	9	♦0.1	♦0.1	♦0.1
15 - 19	65	42	23	0.2	0.3	♦0.2
20 - 24	143	105	38	0.5	0.7	0.3
25 - 29	154	112	42	0.6	0.8	0.3
30 - 34	190	127	63	0.8	1.0	0.5
35 - 39	244	171	73	1.0	1.4	0.6
40 - 44	473	316	157	1.7	2.2	1.1
45 - 49	910	590	320	3.0	3.9	2.0
50 - 54	1 492	1 026	466	5.6	7.6	3.6
55 - 59	2 161	1 461	700	9.3	13.9	5.5
60 - 64	2 440	1 599	841	13.4	18.6	8.7
65 - 69	3 787	2 128	1 659	18.7	23.6	14.8
70 - 74	6 145	3 299	2 846	33.3	40.0	27.9
75 - 79	6 876	3 269	3 607	57.1	64.7	51.7
80 - 84	5 643	2 223	3 420	117.7	113.4	120.7

19. Deaths by age and sex, age-specific death rates by sex: latest available year, 2000 - 2009
Décès et taux de mortalité selon l'âge et le sexe : dernière année disponible, 2000 - 2009 (continued - suite)

Continent, country or area, date, code and age (in years) / Continent, pays ou zone, date, code et âge (en annèes)	Number - Nombre			Rate - Taux		
	Both sexes Les deux sexes	Male Masculin	Female Féminin	Both sexes Les deux sexes	Male Masculin	Female Féminin

EUROPE

Bosnia and Herzegovina - Bosnie-Herzégovine
2009 (C)

85 +	3 851	1 231	2 620	153.7	172.4	146.2
85 - 89	2 945	947	1 998	...	...	...
90 - 94	625	197	428	...	...	...
95 - 99	240	70	170	...	...	...
100 +	41	17	24	...	...	...
Unknown - Inconnu	30	20	10	..	..	..

Bulgaria - Bulgarie
2009 (C)

Total	108 068	56 849	51 219	14.2	15.5	13.1
0 - 4	858	483	375	2.3	2.6	2.1
0	729	422	307	9.7	11.0	8.4
1 - 4	129	61	68	0.4	0.4	0.5
5 - 9	84	58	26	0.2	0.3	♦0.2
10 - 14	87	57	30	0.3	0.3	♦0.2
15 - 19	224	155	69	0.5	0.7	0.3
20 - 24	369	282	87	0.7	1.1	0.3
25 - 29	442	312	130	0.8	1.1	0.5
30 - 34	639	441	198	1.1	1.5	0.7
35 - 39	904	630	274	1.6	2.2	1.0
40 - 44	1 381	981	400	2.7	3.8	1.6
45 - 49	2 478	1 735	743	4.7	6.7	2.8
50 - 54	4 112	2 938	1 174	7.7	11.4	4.3
55 - 59	6 251	4 419	1 832	11.6	17.4	6.5
60 - 64	8 561	5 874	2 687	17.1	25.7	9.9
65 - 69	9 708	6 134	3 574	24.8	35.8	16.2
70 - 74	13 445	7 476	5 969	38.4	51.2	29.2
75 - 79	18 656	9 131	9 525	62.4	76.6	53.0
80 - 84	20 473	8 748	11 725	109.6	125.8	100.0
85 - 89	14 501	5 318	9 183	180.6	190.5	175.3
90 - 94	3 675	1 265	2 410	267.1	274.2	263.6
95 - 99	1 112	377	735	372.3	387.1	365.1
100 +	108	35	73	279.1	255.5	292.0

Croatia - Croatie
2009 (C)

Total	52 414	26 019	26 395	11.8	12.2	11.5
0 - 4	271	142	129	1.3	1.3	1.3
0	235	119	116	5.4	5.4	5.5
1 - 4	36	23	13	0.2	♦0.3	♦0.2
5 - 9	25	13	12	♦0.1	♦0.1	♦0.1
10 - 14	45	28	17	0.2	♦0.2	♦0.1
15 - 19	113	77	36	0.4	0.6	0.3
20 - 24	175	145	30	0.6	1.0	♦0.2
25 - 29	175	125	50	0.6	0.8	0.3
30 - 34	204	161	43	0.7	1.0	0.3
35 - 39	320	226	94	1.1	1.5	0.6
40 - 44	595	427	168	1.9	2.8	1.1
45 - 49	1 055	755	300	3.3	4.7	1.9
50 - 54	1 889	1 367	522	5.7	8.3	3.1
55 - 59	2 632	1 913	719	8.5	12.5	4.6
60 - 64	3 085	2 143	942	12.8	19.0	7.4
65 - 69	4 533	2 880	1 653	20.2	29.0	13.2
70 - 74	6 986	4 022	2 964	32.7	45.3	23.7
75 - 79	9 991	4 918	5 073	57.7	76.1	46.8
80 - 84	9 980	3 840	6 140	100.7	121.1	91.1
85 +	10 332	2 831	7 501	194.5	212.3	188.5
85 - 89	7 500	2 137	5 363	...	...	...
90 - 94	1 932	506	1 426	...	...	...
95 - 99	809	169	640	...	...	...
100 +	91	19	72	...	...	...
Unknown - Inconnu	8	6	2	..	..	..

Czech Republic - République tchèque
2009 (C)

Total	107 421	54 080	53 341	10.2	10.5	10.0
0 - 4	417	226	191	0.8	0.8	0.7
0	341	185	156	2.9	3.0	2.7

Continent, country or area, date, code and age (in years) / Continent, pays ou zone, date, code et âge (en années)	Number - Nombre			Rate - Taux		
	Both sexes Les deux sexes	Male Masculin	Female Féminin	Both sexes Les deux sexes	Male Masculin	Female Féminin
EUROPE						
Czech Republic - République tchèque						
2009 (C)						
1 - 4	76	41	35	0.2	0.2	0.2
5 - 9	50	26	24	0.1	♦0.1	♦0.1
10 - 14	72	48	24	0.2	0.2	♦0.1
15 - 19	210	148	62	0.3	0.5	0.2
20 - 24	389	281	108	0.6	0.8	0.3
25 - 29	408	317	91	0.5	0.8	0.2
30 - 34	681	487	194	0.7	1.0	0.4
35 - 39	858	602	256	1.0	1.4	0.6
40 - 44	1 236	855	381	1.8	2.4	1.1
45 - 49	1 972	1 349	623	3.0	4.0	1.9
50 - 54	3 676	2 557	1 119	5.1	7.2	3.1
55 - 59	6 336	4 387	1 949	8.3	11.8	5.0
60 - 64	9 281	6 280	3 001	13.0	18.6	8.0
65 - 69	10 162	6 522	3 640	19.5	27.6	12.7
70 - 74	10 659	6 159	4 500	29.2	39.9	21.3
75 - 79	15 998	7 933	8 065	49.5	63.5	40.7
80 - 84	19 686	8 023	11 663	87.1	105.2	77.9
85 - 89	17 648	5 943	11 705	155.0	184.0	143.5
90 - 94	5 121	1 337	3 784	250.0	267.5	244.4
95 - 99	2 305	548	1 757	363.7	404.7	352.5
100 +	256	52	204	380.1	334.4	393.8
Denmark - Danemark[37]						
2009 (C)						
Total	54 872	26 937	27 935	9.9	9.8	10.0
0 - 4	237	119	118	0.7	0.7	0.7
0	193	103	90	3.0	3.1	2.9
1 - 4	44	16	28	0.2	♦0.1	♦0.2
5 - 9	24	10	14	♦0.1	♦0.1	♦0.1
10 - 14	29	17	12	♦0.1	♦0.1	♦0.1
15 - 19	102	68	34	0.3	0.4	0.2
20 - 24	127	93	34	0.4	0.6	0.2
25 - 29	170	118	52	0.5	0.8	0.3
30 - 34	221	149	72	0.6	0.8	0.4
35 - 39	352	237	115	0.9	1.2	0.6
40 - 44	606	392	214	1.4	1.8	1.0
45 - 49	964	581	383	2.4	2.9	2.0
50 - 54	1 598	995	603	4.4	5.4	3.3
55 - 59	2 440	1 506	934	7.0	8.6	5.3
60 - 64	3 972	2 447	1 525	10.6	13.1	8.1
65 - 69	4 579	2 677	1 902	15.8	18.9	12.8
70 - 74	5 466	3 128	2 338	25.5	31.1	20.6
75 - 79	7 209	3 824	3 385	45.5	54.6	38.3
80 - 84	8 882	4 365	4 517	75.2	92.6	63.6
85 - 89	9 186	3 710	5 476	125.9	153.7	112.2
90 - 94	5 978	1 941	4 037	214.2	266.2	195.9
95 - 99	2 359	504	1 855	331.6	352.4	326.3
100 +	371	56	315	438.5	455.3	435.7
Estonia - Estonie						
2009 (C)						
Total	16 081	7 996	8 085	12.0	13.0	11.2
0 - 4	70	40	30	0.9	1.0	♦0.8
0	57	34	23	3.6	4.2	♦3.0
1 - 4	13	6	7	♦0.2	♦0.2	♦0.2
5 - 9	10	2	8	♦0.2	♦0.1	♦0.3
10 - 14	7	6	1	♦0.1	♦0.2	-
15 - 19	29	22	7	♦0.3	♦0.5	♦0.2
20 - 24	105	76	29	1.0	1.4	♦0.6
25 - 29	163	138	25	1.6	2.7	♦0.5
30 - 34	160	140	20	1.7	3.0	♦0.4
35 - 39	183	130	53	2.0	2.8	1.1
40 - 44	231	169	62	2.7	4.0	1.4
45 - 49	445	323	122	4.7	7.3	2.5
50 - 54	716	531	185	7.7	12.5	3.7
55 - 59	986	714	272	11.5	19.0	5.7
60 - 64	1 111	758	353	15.7	25.4	8.6

Continent, country or area, date, code and age (in years) Continent, pays ou zone, date, code et âge (en annèes)	Number - Nombre			Rate - Taux		
	Both sexes Les deux sexes	Male Masculin	Female Féminin	Both sexes Les deux sexes	Male Masculin	Female Féminin
EUROPE						
Estonia - Estonie						
2009 (C)						
65 - 69	1 411	923	488	21.8	36.5	12.4
70 - 74	2 002	1 151	851	32.0	51.9	21.0
75 - 79	2 415	1 153	1 262	50.0	75.3	38.2
80 - 84	2 702	956	1 746	81.1	109.9	70.9
85 - 89	2 005	511	1 494	137.5	170.4	129.0
90 - 94	904	191	713	228.5	259.9	221.3
95 - 99	369	55	314	280.4	233.1	290.7
100 +	50	2	48	193.8	✦44.4	225.4
Unknown - Inconnu	7	5	2	..	..	..
Faeroe Islands - Îles Féroé						
2008 (C)						
Total	378	201	177	7.8	8.0	7.6
0	2	1	1	✦2.9	✦3.0	✦2.9
1 - 4	1	1	-	✦0.4	✦0.7	-
5 - 9	-	-	-	-	-	-
10 - 14	-	-	-	-	-	-
15 - 19	1	-	1	✦0.3	-	✦0.5
20 - 24	-	-	-	-	-	-
25 - 29	1	1	-	✦0.4	✦0.7	-
30 - 34	2	1	1	✦0.7	✦0.6	✦0.7
35 - 39	2	1	1	✦0.6	✦0.6	✦0.7
40 - 44	2	2	-	✦0.6	✦1.0	-
45 - 49	7	5	2	✦2.1	✦2.9	✦1.3
50 - 54	7	4	3	✦2.3	✦2.5	✦2.1
55 - 59	20	16	4	✦6.7	✦10.3	✦2.8
60 - 64	24	17	7	✦9.5	✦12.3	✦6.1
65 - 69	26	17	9	✦12.7	✦15.8	✦9.2
70 - 74	34	19	15	22.3	✦24.3	✦20.3
75 - 79	46	32	14	33.9	50.4	✦19.4
80 - 84	69	33	36	68.8	85.5	58.3
85 - 89	71	32	39	120.3	158.4	100.5
90 - 94	38	11	27	154.5	✦135.8	✦163.6
95 - 99	19	6	13	✦422.2	✦545.5	✦382.4
100 +	6	2	4	✦1200.0	✦666.7	✦2000.0
Finland - Finlande						
2009 (C)						
Total	49 883	25 150	24 733	9.4	9.7	9.1
0 - 4	184	91	93	0.6	0.6	0.6
0	158	78	80	2.6	2.6	2.7
1 - 4	26	13	13	✦0.1	✦0.1	✦0.1
5 - 9	20	12	8	✦0.1	✦0.1	✦0.1
10 - 14	35	17	18	0.1	✦0.1	✦0.1
15 - 19	146	106	40	0.4	0.6	0.2
20 - 24	212	160	52	0.7	1.0	0.3
25 - 29	244	183	61	0.7	1.0	0.4
30 - 34	309	237	72	0.9	1.4	0.4
35 - 39	346	256	90	1.1	1.6	0.6
40 - 44	629	434	195	1.7	2.4	1.1
45 - 49	1 092	766	326	2.9	4.0	1.8
50 - 54	1 590	1 100	490	4.2	5.8	2.6
55 - 59	2 478	1 677	801	6.4	8.7	4.1
60 - 64	3 604	2 471	1 133	9.4	13.1	5.8
65 - 69	3 541	2 389	1 152	13.9	19.8	8.6
70 - 74	4 593	2 909	1 684	20.9	29.4	13.9
75 - 79	6 334	3 613	2 721	35.3	49.1	25.7
80 - 84	8 655	4 009	4 646	63.7	83.7	52.8
85 - 89	8 618	2 982	5 636	116.3	146.3	104.9
90 - 94	5 090	1 294	3 796	202.2	234.4	193.2
95 - 99	1 896	396	1 500	332.1	394.6	318.8
100 +	267	48	219	497.7	607.6	478.7
France[38]						
2005 (C)						
Total	527 533	270 634	256 899	8.6	9.1	8.1
0	2 775	1 583	1 192	3.7	4.1	3.3
1 - 4	601	332	269	0.2	0.2	0.2

Continent, country or area, date, code and age (in years) / Continent, pays ou zone, date, code et âge (en années)	Number - Nombre			Rate - Taux		
	Both sexes Les deux sexes	Male Masculin	Female Féminin	Both sexes Les deux sexes	Male Masculin	Female Féminin
EUROPE						
France[38]						
2005 (C)						
5 - 9	368	215	153	0.1	0.1	0.1
10 - 14	408	245	163	0.1	0.1	0.1
15 - 19	1 507	1 087	420	0.4	0.5	0.2
20 - 24	2 312	1 751	561	0.6	0.9	0.3
25 - 29	2 251	1 663	588	0.6	0.9	0.3
30 - 34	3 321	2 354	967	0.8	1.1	0.5
35 - 39	4 889	3 259	1 630	1.1	1.5	0.7
40 - 44	7 938	5 270	2 668	1.8	2.4	1.2
45 - 49	13 144	8 877	4 267	3.1	4.3	2.0
50 - 54	18 997	13 092	5 905	4.6	6.4	2.8
55 - 59	25 402	17 800	7 602	6.3	9.0	3.7
60 - 64	23 431	16 139	7 292	8.6	12.2	5.2
65 - 69	32 278	21 745	10 533	12.5	18.1	7.6
70 - 74	49 531	31 666	17 865	19.6	28.5	12.6
75 - 79	70 064	40 332	29 732	32.1	45.6	22.9
80 - 84	96 969	48 064	48 905	57.5	78.7	45.5
85 - 89	64 217	26 104	38 113	100.1	129.2	86.7
90 - 94	72 170	21 985	50 185	188.0	231.8	173.7
95 - 99	29 671	6 365	23 306	306.4	350.1	296.3
100 +	5 289	706	4 583	405.5	327.2	421.1
Germany - Allemagne						
2009 (C)						
Total	854 544	404 969	449 575	10.4	10.1	10.8
0 - 4	2 863	1 652	1 211	0.8	0.9	0.7
0	2 334	1 339	995	3.5	3.9	3.0
1 - 4	529	313	216	0.2	0.2	0.2
5 - 9	318	171	147	0.1	0.1	0.1
10 - 14	404	218	186	0.1	0.1	0.1
15 - 19	1 249	844	405	0.3	0.4	0.2
20 - 24	1 894	1 342	552	0.4	0.5	0.2
25 - 29	2 194	1 565	629	0.4	0.6	0.3
30 - 34	2 585	1 759	826	0.5	0.7	0.4
35 - 39	4 216	2 779	1 437	0.8	1.0	0.5
40 - 44	9 031	5 870	3 161	1.3	1.6	0.9
45 - 49	16 405	10 675	5 730	2.4	3.0	1.7
50 - 54	23 764	15 693	8 071	4.0	5.2	2.7
55 - 59	33 161	21 917	11 244	6.1	8.2	4.1
60 - 64	38 890	25 428	13 462	9.1	12.1	6.2
65 - 69	68 738	44 386	24 352	13.7	18.4	9.3
70 - 74	98 584	61 014	37 570	21.3	28.6	15.0
75 - 79	115 565	64 136	51 429	37.9	49.4	29.4
80 - 84	154 502	68 698	85 804	67.6	84.0	58.5
85 - 89	163 965	51 439	112 526	124.4	145.7	116.6
90 - 94	69 783	16 926	52 857	212.1	221.5	209.2
95 +	46 190	8 342	37 848	245.0	155.1	280.8
95 - 99	40 083	7 519	32 564	...	...	...
100 +	6 107	823	5 284	...	...	...
Unknown - Inconnu	243	115	128	..	..	..
Greece - Grèce						
2009 (C)						
Total	108 316	57 015	51 301	9.6	10.2	9.0
0 - 4	456	252	204	0.8	0.9	0.7
0	371	204	167	3.1	3.4	2.9
1 - 4	85	48	37	0.2	0.2	0.2
5 - 9	59	29	30	0.1	♦0.1	♦0.1
10 - 14	72	45	27	0.1	0.2	♦0.1
15 - 19	218	165	53	0.4	0.6	0.2
20 - 24	449	367	82	0.7	1.1	0.3
25 - 29	606	477	129	0.8	1.2	0.3
30 - 34	713	541	172	0.8	1.2	0.4
35 - 39	758	515	243	0.9	1.1	0.6
40 - 44	1 186	857	329	1.4	1.9	0.8
45 - 49	1 811	1 257	554	2.3	3.1	1.4
50 - 54	2 592	1 786	806	3.4	4.7	2.1
55 - 59	3 627	2 554	1 073	5.2	7.5	3.0

Continent, country or area, date, code and age (in years) / Continent, pays ou zone, date, code et âge (en années)	Number - Nombre			Rate - Taux		
	Both sexes Les deux sexes	Male Masculin	Female Féminin	Both sexes Les deux sexes	Male Masculin	Female Féminin
EUROPE						
Greece - Grèce						
2009 (C)						
60 - 64	5 089	3 578	1 511	7.7	11.4	4.4
65 - 69	6 142	4 054	2 088	11.4	16.4	7.2
70 - 74	11 153	6 902	4 251	19.4	27.2	13.3
75 - 79	17 471	9 802	7 669	34.8	45.1	27.0
80 - 84	22 982	10 912	12 070	70.6	79.5	64.2
85 - 89	17 977	7 470	10 507	127.0	124.7	128.6
90 - 94	10 127	3 796	6 331	318.4	243.9	389.8
95 - 99	4 089	1 418	2 671	786.8	433.6	1386.1
100 +	739	238	501	246.7	174.9	306.6
Guernsey - Guernesey						
2000 (C)						
Total	565	264	301	...	...	...
0	4	3	1	...	...	...
1 - 4	1	-	1	...	...	...
5 - 9	-	-	-	...	...	...
10 - 14	-	-	-	...	...	...
15 - 19	4	3	1	...	...	...
20 - 24	1	-	1	...	...	...
25 - 29	1	1	-	...	...	...
30 - 34	2	1	1	...	...	...
35 - 39	2	2	-	...	...	...
40 - 44	4	4	-	...	...	...
45 - 49	7	5	2	...	...	...
50 - 54	13	9	4	...	...	...
55 - 59	13	7	6	...	...	...
60 - 64	30	15	15	...	...	...
65 - 69	45	29	16	...	...	...
70 - 74	57	27	30	...	...	...
75 - 79	71	38	33	...	...	...
80 - 84	103	55	48	...	...	...
85 - 89	108	45	63	...	...	...
90 - 94	68	14	54	...	...	...
95 - 99	24	3	21	...	...	...
100 +	5	2	3	...	...	...
Unknown - Inconnu	2	1	1	..	..	..
Hungary - Hongrie						
2009 (C)						
Total	130 414	66 324	64 090	13.0	13.9	12.2
0 - 4	579	307	272	1.2	1.2	1.1
0	495	263	232	5.2	5.3	5.0
1 - 4	84	44	40	0.2	0.2	0.2
5 - 9	61	35	26	0.1	0.1	◆0.1
10 - 14	84	48	36	0.2	0.2	0.1
15 - 19	209	139	70	0.3	0.4	0.2
20 - 24	339	261	78	0.5	0.8	0.2
25 - 29	398	305	93	0.6	0.8	0.3
30 - 34	710	511	199	0.8	1.2	0.5
35 - 39	1 100	752	348	1.5	2.0	1.0
40 - 44	1 905	1 332	573	2.9	4.0	1.7
45 - 49	3 506	2 443	1 063	5.8	8.2	3.4
50 - 54	7 270	5 040	2 230	9.9	14.4	5.8
55 - 59	9 727	6 710	3 017	13.5	20.1	7.7
60 - 64	10 782	7 112	3 670	18.4	27.3	11.2
65 - 69	12 669	7 884	4 785	24.7	36.9	16.0
70 - 74	14 496	7 920	6 576	35.5	51.5	25.8
75 - 79	19 033	9 148	9 885	55.8	76.0	44.8
80 - 84	21 144	8 265	12 879	91.9	115.4	81.3
85 - 89	18 086	5 920	12 166	149.4	174.1	139.7
90 +	8 301	2 178	6 123	219.6	210.4	223.1
90 - 94	5 552	1 559	3 993	...	...	...
95 - 99	2 468	572	1 896	...	...	...
100 +	281	47	234	...	...	...
Unknown - Inconnu	15	14	1	..	..	..

Continent, country or area, date, code and age (in years) Continent, pays ou zone, date, code et âge (en années)	Number - Nombre			Rate - Taux		
	Both sexes Les deux sexes	Male Masculin	Female Féminin	Both sexes Les deux sexes	Male Masculin	Female Féminin
EUROPE						
Iceland - Islande						
2009 (C)						
Total	2 002	1 033	969	6.3	6.4	6.1
0 - 4	11	7	4	♦0.5	♦0.6	♦0.4
0	9	5	4	♦1.8	♦2.0	♦1.7
1 - 4	2	2	-	♦0.1	♦0.2	-
5 - 9	1	1	-	-	♦0.1	-
10 - 14	1	1	-	-	♦0.1	-
15 - 19	6	5	1	♦0.3	♦0.4	♦0.1
20 - 24	8	3	5	♦0.3	♦0.3	♦0.4
25 - 29	10	8	2	♦0.4	♦0.6	♦0.2
30 - 34	18	16	2	♦0.8	♦1.4	♦0.2
35 - 39	20	10	10	♦0.9	♦0.9	♦0.9
40 - 44	21	16	5	♦1.0	♦1.4	♦0.5
45 - 49	40	25	15	1.8	♦2.2	♦1.4
50 - 54	61	44	17	2.9	4.1	♦1.7
55 - 59	61	36	25	3.4	3.9	♦2.8
60 - 64	100	67	33	6.7	8.8	4.5
65 - 69	117	73	44	10.9	13.9	8.0
70 - 74	175	93	82	20.4	22.5	18.4
75 - 79	274	147	127	34.8	40.5	30.0
80 - 84	348	188	160	61.6	77.1	49.8
85 - 89	362	159	203	111.6	126.0	102.4
90 - 94	252	91	161	215.4	236.4	205.1
95 - 99	96	39	57	372.1	619.0	292.3
100 +	20	4	16	♦512.8	♦571.4	♦500.0
Ireland - Irlande						
2009 (+C)						
Total	28 898	15 044	13 854	6.5	6.8	6.2
0 - 4	306	177	129	0.9	1.0	0.8
0	240	140	100	3.3	3.7	2.8
1 - 4	66	37	29	0.2	0.3	♦0.2
5 - 9	22	11	11	♦0.1	♦0.1	♦0.1
10 - 14	33	19	14	0.1	♦0.1	♦0.1
15 - 19	130	97	33	0.5	0.7	0.2
20 - 24	204	156	48	0.7	1.1	0.3
25 - 29	285	208	77	0.7	1.0	0.4
30 - 34	304	219	85	0.8	1.2	0.5
35 - 39	396	273	123	1.1	1.6	0.7
40 - 44	438	286	152	1.4	1.8	1.0
45 - 49	651	376	275	2.2	2.5	1.9
50 - 54	878	546	332	3.3	4.1	2.5
55 - 59	1 233	748	485	5.2	6.3	4.1
60 - 64	1 786	1 122	664	8.6	10.7	6.4
65 - 69	2 148	1 401	747	13.7	18.0	9.4
70 - 74	2 861	1 706	1 155	23.1	28.8	17.9
75 - 79	3 903	2 195	1 708	40.8	51.0	32.5
80 - 84	4 972	2 489	2 483	75.2	95.7	61.9
85 - 89	4 700	1 952	2 748	124.1	151.8	109.8
90 - 94	2 596	827	1 769	188.7	211.9	179.5
95 - 99	925	221	704	234.8	240.0	233.2
100 +	127	15	112	229.2	♦122.4	259.6
Isle of Man - Île de Man						
2004 (+C)						
Total	798	390	408	10.3	10.2	10.3
0	2	1	1	♦2.3	♦2.3	♦2.4
1 - 4	-	-	-	-	-	-
5 - 9	-	-	-	-	-	-
10 - 14	1	1	-	♦0.2	♦0.4	-
15 - 19	3	3	-	♦0.6	♦1.3	-
20 - 24	5	4	1	♦1.1	♦1.8	♦0.4
25 - 29	3	3	-	♦0.7	♦1.4	-
30 - 34	3	1	2	♦0.6	♦0.4	♦0.7
35 - 39	6	5	1	♦1.0	♦1.7	♦0.3
40 - 44	7	4	3	♦1.2	♦1.3	♦1.0
45 - 49	11	5	6	♦2.0	♦1.9	♦2.2
50 - 54	17	8	9	♦3.3	♦3.0	♦3.5

19. Deaths by age and sex, age-specific death rates by sex: latest available year, 2000 - 2009
Décès et taux de mortalité selon l'âge et le sexe : dernière année disponible, 2000 - 2009 (continued - suite)

Continent, country or area, date, code and age (in years) / Continent, pays ou zone, date, code et âge (en années)	Number - Nombre			Rate - Taux		
	Both sexes Les deux sexes	Male Masculin	Female Féminin	Both sexes Les deux sexes	Male Masculin	Female Féminin
EUROPE						
Isle of Man - Île de Man						
2004 (+C)						
55 - 59	31	18	13	5.7	♦6.4	♦5.0
60 - 64	33	19	14	7.8	♦9.1	♦6.6
65 - 69	60	45	15	16.4	25.0	♦8.1
70 - 74	82	46	36	27.1	33.4	21.8
75 - 79	118	59	59	46.0	55.6	39.2
80 - 84	169	77	92	80.5	98.2	70.0
85 - 89	111	43	68	112.2	126.5	104.7
90 +	136	48	88	208.7	278.5	183.6
90 - 94	96	36	60	...	...	...
95 +	40	12	28	...	...	...
Italy - Italie						
2008 (C)						
Total	578 192	281 825	296 367	9.7	9.7	9.6
0	1 896	1 054	842	3.4	3.6	3.1
1 - 4	344	191	153	0.2	0.2	0.1
5 - 9	208	115	93	0.1	0.1	0.1
10 - 14	291	187	104	0.1	0.1	0.1
15 - 19	931	680	251	0.3	0.4	0.2
20 - 24	1 186	923	263	0.4	0.6	0.2
25 - 29	1 469	1 123	346	0.4	0.6	0.2
30 - 34	2 198	1 570	628	0.5	0.7	0.3
35 - 39	3 185	2 132	1 053	0.7	0.9	0.4
40 - 44	5 200	3 362	1 838	1.1	1.4	0.7
45 - 49	7 667	4 829	2 838	1.7	2.2	1.3
50 - 54	10 792	6 776	4 016	2.8	3.5	2.0
55 - 59	16 730	10 686	6 044	4.5	5.9	3.2
60 - 64	24 798	16 040	8 758	7.1	9.5	4.8
65 - 69	36 731	23 564	13 167	11.2	15.3	7.6
70 - 74	54 355	33 556	20 799	18.6	25.3	13.0
75 - 79	81 939	46 456	35 483	32.9	44.5	24.6
80 - 84	112 580	54 896	57 684	61.1	80.2	49.8
85 - 89	110 199	43 667	66 532	108.6	136.0	96.0
90 - 94	66 952	20 902	46 050	199.1	235.6	186.0
95 - 99	33 362	8 283	25 079	300.5	334.8	290.7
100 +	5 177	832	4 345	393.4	345.7	404.1
Unknown - Inconnu	2	1	1	..	..	..
Latvia - Lettonie						
2009 (C)						
Total	29 897	14 539	15 358	13.3	14.0	12.6
0 - 4	204	110	94	1.8	1.9	1.7
0	168	88	80	7.4	7.6	7.2
1 - 4	36	22	14	0.4	♦0.5	♦0.3
5 - 9	30	18	12	♦0.3	♦0.4	♦0.2
10 - 14	25	17	8	♦0.3	♦0.3	♦0.2
15 - 19	73	57	16	0.5	0.7	♦0.2
20 - 24	150	112	38	0.8	1.2	0.4
25 - 29	242	202	40	1.4	2.3	0.5
30 - 34	283	223	60	1.8	2.8	0.8
35 - 39	411	297	114	2.6	3.7	1.4
40 - 44	577	418	159	3.8	5.6	2.0
45 - 49	966	673	293	5.7	8.4	3.3
50 - 54	1 373	961	412	8.6	13.0	4.8
55 - 59	1 819	1 277	542	13.2	20.9	7.0
60 - 64	2 203	1 451	752	19.0	30.0	11.2
65 - 69	3 015	1 897	1 118	25.4	41.5	15.4
70 - 74	3 847	2 122	1 725	36.1	56.7	25.0
75 - 79	4 519	2 017	2 502	57.0	81.8	45.8
80 - 84	4 928	1 565	3 363	89.7	115.6	81.2
85 - 89	3 248	716	2 532	139.8	158.9	135.2
90 - 94	1 387	294	1 093	233.6	253.7	228.7
95 - 99	524	94	430	292.2	284.8	293.9
100 +	71	16	55	308.7	♦285.7	316.1
Unknown - Inconnu	2	2	-	..	..	..

Continent, country or area, date, code and age (in years) / Continent, pays ou zone, date, code et âge (en années)	Number - Nombre			Rate - Taux		
	Both sexes Les deux sexes	Male Masculin	Female Féminin	Both sexes Les deux sexes	Male Masculin	Female Féminin
EUROPE						
Liechtenstein						
2009* (C)						
Total	229	115	114	6.4	6.5	6.3
0 - 4	2	-	2	♦1.1	-	♦2.3
0	1	-	1	♦2.5	-	♦5.5
1 - 4	1	-	1	♦0.7	-	♦1.4
5 - 9	-	-	-	-	-	-
10 - 14	-	-	-	-	-	-
15 - 19	1	-	1	♦0.5	-	♦0.9
20 - 24	1	1	-	♦0.5	♦0.9	-
25 - 29	1	1	-	♦0.4	♦0.9	-
30 - 34	3	2	1	♦1.3	♦1.7	♦0.9
35 - 39	-	-	-	-	-	-
40 - 44	2	1	1	♦0.6	♦0.7	♦0.6
45 - 49	5	2	3	♦1.6	♦1.3	♦1.9
50 - 54	11	7	4	♦4.0	♦5.2	♦2.9
55 - 59	10	8	2	♦4.2	♦6.5	♦1.7
60 - 64	18	12	6	♦8.2	♦10.6	♦5.7
65 - 69	20	12	8	♦11.7	♦14.2	♦9.3
70 - 74	15	12	3	♦13.4	♦22.9	♦5.1
75 - 79	31	12	19	40.5	♦37.7	♦42.5
80 - 84	37	21	16	. 60.3	♦95.9	♦40.5
85 - 89	40	14	26	104.4	♦120.7	♦97.4
90 - 94	22	8	14	♦188.0	♦228.6	♦170.7
95 - 99	9	2	7	♦321.4	♦285.7	♦333.3
100 +	1	-	1	♦500.0	...	♦500.0
Lithuania - Lituanie						
2009 (C)						
Total	42 032	21 828	20 204	12.6	14.1	11.3
0 - 4	213	127	86	1.3	1.5	1.1
0	181	109	72	5.1	6.0	4.1
1 - 4	32	18	14	0.3	♦0.3	♦0.2
5 - 9	26	18	8	♦0.2	♦0.2	♦0.1
10 - 14	50	33	17	0.3	0.3	♦0.2
15 - 19	197	157	40	0.8	1.2	0.3
20 - 24	292	238	54	1.1	1.7	0.4
25 - 29	315	262	53	1.3	2.1	0.5
30 - 34	456	361	95	2.1	3.3	0.9
35 - 39	691	539	152	2.9	4.6	1.3
40 - 44	1 010	746	264	4.1	6.3	2.1
45 - 49	1 638	1 223	415	6.2	9.7	3.0
50 - 54	2 030	1 455	575	8.9	13.8	4.7
55 - 59	2 555	1 818	737	13.3	21.3	6.9
60 - 64	3 053	2 090	963	19.1	31.5	10.3
65 - 69	3 969	2 589	1 380	25.0	42.0	14.2
70 - 74	4 737	2 660	2 077	33.1	51.9	22.7
75 - 79	6 130	2 929	3 201	53.1	77.7	41.2
80 - 84	6 780	2 463	4 317	88.4	117.9	77.4
85 - 89	4 976	1 383	3 593	152.3	183.4	143.0
90 - 94	1 897	472	1 425	278.0	297.0	272.3
95 - 99	837	197	640	473.4	513.0	462.4
100 +	180	68	112	388.8	496.4	343.6
Luxembourg						
2009 (C)						
Total	3 655	1 801	1 854	7.3	7.3	7.4
0 - 4	20	10	10	♦0.7	♦0.7	♦0.7
0	14	5	9	♦2.5	♦1.7	♦3.3
1 - 4	6	5	1	♦0.3	♦0.4	♦0.1
5 - 9	3	2	1	♦0.1	♦0.1	♦0.1
10 - 14	3	3	-	♦0.1	♦0.2	-
15 - 19	7	5	2	♦0.2	♦0.3	♦0.1
20 - 24	8	8	-	♦0.3	♦0.5	-
25 - 29	14	10	4	♦0.4	♦0.6	♦0.2
30 - 34	22	12	10	♦0.6	♦0.6	♦0.5
35 - 39	34	27	7	0.9	♦1.4	♦0.4
40 - 44	45	32	13	1.1	1.5	♦0.6
45 - 49	78	48	30	2.0	2.4	♦1.6

19. Deaths by age and sex, age-specific death rates by sex: latest available year, 2000 - 2009
Décès et taux de mortalité selon l'âge et le sexe : dernière année disponible, 2000 - 2009 (continued - suite)

Continent, country or area, date, code and age (in years) Continent, pays ou zone, date, code et âge (en années)	Number - Nombre			Rate - Taux		
	Both sexes Les deux sexes	Male Masculin	Female Féminin	Both sexes Les deux sexes	Male Masculin	Female Féminin
EUROPE						
Luxembourg						
2009 (C)						
50 - 54	152	91	61	4.4	5.2	3.6
55 - 59	158	100	58	5.4	6.7	4.1
60 - 64	214	134	80	8.8	10.9	6.7
65 - 69	244	150	94	12.5	15.9	9.3
70 - 74	355	210	145	20.7	26.8	15.5
75 - 79	536	298	238	35.7	46.2	27.8
80 - 84	694	322	372	65.4	82.1	55.6
85 - 89	618	216	402	114.8	150.9	101.7
90 - 94	277	87	190	182.5	285.2	156.6
95 +	173	36	137	650.4	3600.0	535.2
95 - 99	148	31	117	...	...	...
100 +	25	5	20	...	...	...
Malta - Malte						
2009 (C)						
Total	3 221	1 672	1 549	7.8	8.1	7.5
0 - 4	25	12	13	♦1.2	♦1.1	♦1.3
0	22	11	11	♦5.3	♦5.1	♦5.5
1 - 4	3	1	2	♦0.2	♦0.1	♦0.3
5 - 9	2	1	1	♦0.1	♦0.1	♦0.1
10 - 14	4	2	2	♦0.2	♦0.2	♦0.2
15 - 19	8	6	2	♦0.3	♦0.4	♦0.1
20 - 24	15	11	4	♦0.5	♦0.7	♦0.3
25 - 29	25	15	10	♦0.8	♦0.9	♦0.7
30 - 34	17	12	5	♦0.6	♦0.8	♦0.3
35 - 39	20	16	4	♦0.8	♦1.2	♦0.3
40 - 44	18	12	6	♦0.7	♦1.0	♦0.5
45 - 49	41	23	18	1.4	♦1.6	♦1.3
50 - 54	82	48	34	2.7	3.2	2.3
55 - 59	130	84	46	4.5	5.8	3.2
60 - 64	228	138	90	7.7	9.5	5.9
65 - 69	235	149	86	13.3	18.0	9.2
70 - 74	334	203	131	20.4	27.6	14.6
75 - 79	530	290	240	43.4	59.5	32.7
80 - 84	596	282	314	75.8	93.7	64.7
85 - 89	576	263	313	138.9	180.9	116.3
90 +	335	105	230	231.5	254.2	222.4
90 - 94	249	85	164	...	...	...
95 - 99	75	18	57	...	...	...
100 +	11	2	9	...	...	...
Montenegro - Monténégro						
2009 (C)						
Total	5 862	3 008	2 854	9.3	9.7	8.9
0 - 4	52	31	21	1.3	1.5	♦1.1
0	49	28	21	5.8	♦6.3	♦5.2
1 - 4	3	3	-	♦0.1	♦0.2	-
5 - 9	7	4	3	♦0.2	♦0.2	♦0.2
10 - 14	8	6	2	♦0.2	♦0.3	♦0.1
15 - 19	23	14	9	♦0.5	♦0.6	♦0.4
20 - 24	27	20	7	♦0.5	♦0.8	♦0.3
25 - 29	30	22	8	♦0.6	♦0.9	♦0.3
30 - 34	44	30	14	1.0	♦1.3	♦0.6
35 - 39	49	32	17	1.2	1.6	♦0.8
40 - 44	92	62	30	2.2	3.0	♦1.4
45 - 49	182	111	71	4.2	5.1	3.2
50 - 54	266	173	93	6.1	7.9	4.3
55 - 59	375	237	138	9.4	12.2	6.7
60 - 64	418	255	163	14.9	19.9	10.7
65 - 69	591	349	242	23.2	31.0	17.0
70 - 74	900	503	397	36.0	45.7	28.4
75 - 79	1 033	511	522	60.7	71.8	52.8
80 - 84	1 015	401	614	106.7	105.7	107.4
85 - 89	519	184	335	142.6	139.2	144.6
90 - 94	141	41	100	212.7	178.3	230.9
95 - 99	70	17	53	255.5	♦191.0	286.5
100 +	20	5	15	♦151.5	♦277.8	♦131.6

Continent, country or area, date, code and age (in years) Continent, pays ou zone, date, code et âge (en années)	Number - Nombre			Rate - Taux		
	Both sexes Les deux sexes	Male Masculin	Female Féminin	Both sexes Les deux sexes	Male Masculin	Female Féminin
EUROPE						
Netherlands - Pays-Bas[39]						
2009 (C)						
Total	134 235	65 365	68 870	8.1	8.0	8.2
0 - 4	847	470	377	0.9	1.0	0.8
0	711	394	317	3.9	4.2	3.5
1 - 4	136	76	60	0.2	0.2	0.2
5 - 9	95	53	42	0.1	0.1	0.1
10 - 14	95	54	41	0.1	0.1	0.1
15 - 19	238	150	88	0.2	0.3	0.2
20 - 24	313	221	92	0.3	0.4	0.2
25 - 29	373	243	130	0.4	0.5	0.3
30 - 34	437	271	166	0.4	0.5	0.3
35 - 39	833	482	351	0.7	0.8	0.6
40 - 44	1 483	836	647	1.1	1.3	1.0
45 - 49	2 439	1 346	1 093	1.9	2.1	1.7
50 - 54	3 898	2 153	1 745	3.3	3.7	3.0
55 - 59	5 581	3 310	2 271	5.2	6.1	4.2
60 - 64	8 735	5 331	3 404	8.3	10.1	6.5
65 - 69	9 776	6 092	3 684	12.8	16.2	9.5
70 - 74	13 025	8 028	4 997	21.3	27.9	15.4
75 - 79	18 360	10 486	7 874	37.3	49.2	28.2
80 - 84	23 495	11 441	12 054	67.4	87.1	55.5
85 - 89	24 227	9 301	14 926	118.3	146.7	105.6
90 - 94	14 063	3 968	10 095	204.1	244.0	191.7
95 - 99	5 105	1 023	4 082	324.8	365.9	315.9
100 +	817	106	711	484.7	467.0	487.5
Norway - Norvège[40]						
2009 (C)						
Total	41 449	19 912	21 537	8.6	8.3	8.9
0 - 4	228	138	90	0.8	0.9	0.6
0	192	119	73	3.1	3.8	2.5
1 - 4	36	19	17	0.2	♦0.2	♦0.1
5 - 9	32	18	14	0.1	♦0.1	♦0.1
10 - 14	30	15	15	♦0.1	♦0.1	♦0.1
15 - 19	125	85	40	0.4	0.5	0.3
20 - 24	153	112	41	0.5	0.7	0.3
25 - 29	186	133	53	0.6	0.9	0.4
30 - 34	202	143	59	0.6	0.9	0.4
35 - 39	294	192	102	0.8	1.0	0.6
40 - 44	413	278	135	1.1	1.5	0.8
45 - 49	587	352	235	1.8	2.1	1.5
50 - 54	997	584	413	3.1	3.6	2.7
55 - 59	1 397	891	506	4.7	6.0	3.5
60 - 64	2 245	1 384	861	7.8	9.5	6.0
65 - 69	2 538	1 565	973	12.4	15.5	9.3
70 - 74	3 073	1 823	1 250	19.8	25.2	15.1
75 - 79	4 717	2 673	2 044	35.3	45.3	27.4
80 - 84	7 199	3 573	3 626	65.4	81.5	54.7
85 - 89	8 882	3 603	5 279	119.1	146.2	105.6
90 - 94	5 688	1 790	3 898	200.7	243.4	185.7
95 - 99	2 041	462	1 579	330.7	368.3	321.2
100 +	318	53	265	498.0	509.6	495.8
Unknown - Inconnu	104	45	59	..	..	..
Poland - Pologne						
2009 (C)						
Total	384 940	203 826	181 114	10.1	11.1	9.2
0 - 4	2 656	1 470	1 186	1.4	1.5	1.3
0	2 327	1 298	1 029	5.5	5.9	5.0
1 - 4	329	172	157	0.2	0.2	0.2
5 - 9	259	149	110	0.1	0.2	0.1
10 - 14	365	201	164	0.2	0.2	0.2
15 - 19	1 267	951	316	0.5	0.7	0.3
20 - 24	2 092	1 707	385	0.7	1.1	0.3
25 - 29	2 345	1 868	477	0.7	1.1	0.3
30 - 34	3 124	2 440	684	1.0	1.6	0.5
35 - 39	4 206	3 226	980	1.6	2.5	0.8
40 - 44	6 277	4 726	1 551	2.7	4.0	1.3

Continent, country or area, date, code and age (in years) / Continent, pays ou zone, date, code et âge (en années)	Number - Nombre			Rate - Taux		
	Both sexes Les deux sexes	Male Masculin	Female Féminin	Both sexes Les deux sexes	Male Masculin	Female Féminin
EUROPE						
Poland - Pologne						
2009 (C)						
45 - 49	11 537	8 436	3 101	4.5	6.6	2.4
50 - 54	21 564	15 402	6 162	7.2	10.5	4.0
55 - 59	29 725	20 793	8 932	10.7	15.8	6.1
60 - 64	30 755	20 834	9 921	15.2	22.5	9.0
65 - 69	29 543	19 193	10 350	21.2	31.9	13.0
70 - 74	42 083	24 980	17 103	30.7	45.4	20.8
75 - 79	56 733	28 798	27 935	49.2	67.8	38.3
80 - 84	62 984	25 479	37 505	82.6	105.7	72.0
85 +	77 425	23 173	54 252	167.5	189.1	159.7
85 - 89	49 532	16 119	33 413	...	...	...
90 - 94	18 735	4 995	13 740	...	...	...
95 - 99	8 009	1 829	6 180	...	...	...
100 +	1 149	230	919	...	...	...
Portugal[17]						
2009 (C)						
Total	104 434	53 310	51 124	9.8	10.4	9.3
0 - 4	451	261	190	0.9	1.0	0.7
0	362	210	152	3.6	4.0	3.1
1 - 4	89	51	38	0.2	0.2	0.2
5 - 9	59	33	26	0.1	0.1	♦0.1
10 - 14	69	40	29	0.1	0.1	♦0.1
15 - 19	187	131	56	0.3	0.4	0.2
20 - 24	314	227	87	0.5	0.7	0.3
25 - 29	393	291	102	0.5	0.8	0.3
30 - 34	617	434	183	0.7	1.0	0.4
35 - 39	1 004	679	325	1.2	1.7	0.8
40 - 44	1 487	1 029	458	1.9	2.7	1.2
45 - 49	2 259	1 569	690	2.9	4.2	1.8
50 - 54	3 089	2 131	958	4.4	6.2	2.6
55 - 59	3 750	2 605	1 145	5.7	8.3	3.3
60 - 64	5 095	3 392	1 703	8.5	12.1	5.3
65 - 69	6 585	4 233	2 352	12.8	18.0	8.4
70 - 74	10 371	6 292	4 079	21.1	29.1	14.8
75 - 79	15 536	8 591	6 945	37.8	50.5	28.8
80 - 84	20 175	9 522	10 653	72.8	92.3	61.2
85 +	32 963	11 826	21 137	172.5	187.8	164.9
85 - 89	18 706	7 614	11 092	...	...	...
90 - 94	10 051	3 217	6 834	...	...	...
95 - 99	3 654	908	2 746	...	...	...
100 +	552	87	465	...	...	...
Unknown - Inconnu	30	24	6	..	..	..
Republic of Moldova - République de Moldova[41]						
2009 (C)						
Total	42 139	22 258	19 881	11.8	13.0	10.7
0 - 4	582	344	238	3.1	3.5	2.6
0	492	293	199	12.5	14.5	10.5
1 - 4	90	51	39	0.6	0.7	0.5
5 - 9	63	41	22	0.3	0.4	♦0.2
10 - 14	76	50	26	0.3	0.4	♦0.2
15 - 19	160	105	55	0.5	0.7	0.4
20 - 24	307	234	73	0.9	1.3	0.4
25 - 29	362	280	82	1.2	1.8	0.5
30 - 34	527	410	117	2.0	3.1	0.9
35 - 39	775	586	189	3.3	5.0	1.6
40 - 44	1 194	855	339	5.2	7.7	2.9
45 - 49	2 049	1 448	601	7.5	11.2	4.2
50 - 54	3 106	2 157	949	11.9	17.7	6.8
55 - 59	3 992	2 611	1 381	17.6	25.4	11.2
60 - 64	3 113	1 830	1 283	23.5	31.3	17.4
65 - 69	4 491	2 472	2 019	38.2	51.1	29.2
70 - 74	5 778	2 882	2 896	56.3	73.1	45.8
75 - 79	5 975	2 661	3 314	80.8	98.8	70.5
80 - 84	5 204	1 928	3 276	115.3	133.1	106.9
85 - 89	3 182	1 033	2 149	167.6	177.6	163.2
90 - 94	903	261	642	246.6	241.0	248.8

Continent, country or area, date, code and age (in years) Continent, pays ou zone, date, code et âge (en années)	Number - Nombre			Rate - Taux		
	Both sexes Les deux sexes	Male Masculin	Female Féminin	Both sexes Les deux sexes	Male Masculin	Female Féminin
EUROPE						
Republic of Moldova - République de Moldova[41]						
2009 (C)						
95 - 99	272	64	208	263.3	207.1	287.3
100 +	28	6	22	♦136.3	♦97.6	♦152.8
Romania - Roumanie						
2009 (C)						
Total	257 213	137 550	119 663	12.0	13.2	10.9
0 - 4	2 660	1 517	1 143	2.5	2.7	2.2
0	2 250	1 287	963	10.3	11.5	9.1
1 - 4	410	230	180	0.5	0.5	0.4
5 - 9	266	159	107	0.3	0.3	0.2
10 - 14	301	189	112	0.3	0.3	0.2
15 - 19	721	501	220	0.5	0.7	0.3
20 - 24	1 210	878	332	0.7	1.0	0.4
25 - 29	1 171	886	285	0.7	1.1	0.4
30 - 34	1 841	1 365	476	1.0	1.5	0.6
35 - 39	2 841	2 063	778	1.7	2.4	0.9
40 - 44	4 766	3 446	1 320	3.0	4.2	1.6
45 - 49	6 862	4 926	1 936	5.5	7.9	3.0
50 - 54	13 021	9 355	3 666	8.5	12.6	4.6
55 - 59	17 319	12 065	5 254	12.3	18.1	7.1
60 - 64	18 187	12 208	5 979	17.0	24.8	10.3
65 - 69	22 852	14 207	8 645	24.7	35.2	16.6
70 - 74	35 049	19 580	15 469	37.7	51.0	28.3
75 - 79	42 645	21 017	21 628	60.5	75.3	50.8
80 - 84	43 893	18 816	25 077	102.4	117.7	93.3
85 - 89	29 709	10 514	19 195	168.9	176.9	164.9
90 - 94	8 284	2 669	5 615	295.5	291.4	297.5
95 - 99	3 294	1 080	2 214	299.7	269.9	316.7
100 +	321	109	212	118.4	116.8	119.2
Russian Federation - Fédération de Russie[23]						
2009 (C)						
Total	2 010 543	1 048 314	962 229	14.2	16.0	12.6
0 - 4	17 512	10 053	7 459	2.2	2.5	2.0
0	14 271	8 182	6 089	8.3	9.2	7.2
1 - 4	3 241	1 871	1 370	0.5	0.6	0.5
5 - 9	2 101	1 266	835	0.3	0.4	0.3
10 - 14	2 302	1 408	894	0.3	0.4	0.3
15 - 19	8 667	6 038	2 629	1.0	1.3	0.6
20 - 24	21 596	16 697	4 899	1.7	2.7	0.8
25 - 29	35 549	27 682	7 867	2.9	4.6	1.3
30 - 34	46 364	35 973	10 391	4.3	6.8	1.9
35 - 39	49 526	37 401	12 125	5.0	7.6	2.4
40 - 44	58 905	43 800	15 105	6.3	9.8	3.1
45 - 49	98 560	72 757	25 803	8.6	13.5	4.3
50 - 54	136 129	98 382	37 747	12.1	19.3	6.2
55 - 59	164 109	113 063	51 046	17.0	26.9	9.3
60 - 64	148 857	99 655	49 202	23.5	38.3	13.2
65 - 69	158 594	94 166	64 428	31.8	51.5	20.4
70 - 74	269 854	140 893	128 961	45.4	70.1	32.8
75 - 79	263 382	110 855	152 527	70.4	99.2	58.2
80 - 84	293 610	90 634	202 976	107.7	135.6	98.7
85 - 89	143 471	28 206	115 265	160.1	165.8	158.8
90 - 94	60 904	10 216	50 688	265.3	245.2	269.7
95 - 99	20 544	2 845	17 699	355.4	247.0	382.3
100 +	2 412	276	2 136	110.2	74.6	117.5
Unknown - Inconnu	7 595	6 048	1 547	..	..	..
San Marino - Saint-Marin						
2004 (+C)						
Total	185	94	91	6.3	6.5	6.1
0	1	1	-	♦3.2	♦6.3	-
1 - 14	-	-	-	-	-	-
15 - 19	2	2	-	♦1.5	♦3.0	-
20 - 24	2	2	-	♦1.3	♦2.6	-
25 - 29	-	-	-	-	-	-
30 - 34	1	-	1	♦0.4	-	♦0.8
35 - 39	-	-	-	-	-	-

19. Deaths by age and sex, age-specific death rates by sex: latest available year, 2000 - 2009
Décès et taux de mortalité selon l'âge et le sexe : dernière année disponible, 2000 - 2009 (continued - suite)

Continent, country or area, date, code and age (in years) Continent, pays ou zone, date, code et âge (en années)	Number - Nombre			Rate - Taux		
	Both sexes Les deux sexes	Male Masculin	Female Féminin	Both sexes Les deux sexes	Male Masculin	Female Féminin

EUROPE

San Marino - Saint-Marin
2004 (+C)

40 - 44	3	-	3	♦1.1	-	♦2.3
45 - 49	2	-	2	♦1.0	-	♦2.0
50 - 54	7	5	2	♦3.7	♦5.4	♦2.1
55 - 59	9	6	3	♦4.9	♦6.7	♦3.2
60 - 64	8	6	2	♦5.2	♦8.0	♦2.6
65 - 69	12	7	5	♦8.7	♦10.2	♦7.2
70 - 74	14	9	5	♦11.6	♦16.3	♦7.6
75 - 79	22	13	9	♦23.3	♦31.5	♦16.9
80 - 84	35	16	19	45.8	♦55.3	♦40.0
85 - 89	34	16	18	106.1	♦156.9	♦82.4
90 - 94	27	7	20	♦165.6	♦148.9	♦172.4
95 - 99	5	4	1	♦172.4	♦444.4	♦50.0
100 +	1	-	1	♦666.7	...	♦666.7

Serbia - Serbie[42]
2009 (+C)

Total	104 000	52 377	51 623	14.2	14.7	13.7
0 - 4	562	323	239	1.6	1.8	1.4
0	492	279	213	7.1	7.8	6.4
1 - 4	70	44	26	0.2	0.3	♦0.2
5 - 9	55	31	24	0.1	0.2	♦0.1
10 - 14	77	47	30	0.2	0.2	♦0.2
15 - 19	151	100	51	0.4	0.5	0.2
20 - 24	277	216	61	0.6	0.9	0.3
25 - 29	390	296	94	0.8	1.1	0.4
30 - 34	554	394	160	1.1	1.5	0.6
35 - 39	643	430	213	1.3	1.8	0.9
40 - 44	1 101	728	373	2.3	3.1	1.5
45 - 49	2 110	1 396	714	4.2	5.6	2.8
50 - 54	3 833	2 545	1 288	7.0	9.5	4.6
55 - 59	6 521	4 293	2 228	11.3	15.3	7.5
60 - 64	6 860	4 482	2 378	16.1	22.5	10.5
65 - 69	9 252	5 545	3 707	26.2	34.8	19.1
70 - 74	15 096	8 069	7 027	41.8	51.7	34.3
75 - 79	21 759	10 187	11 572	74.6	84.6	67.5
80 - 84	19 796	7 955	11 841	121.1	126.6	117.6
85 - 89	11 930	4 300	7 630	181.5	185.1	179.5
90 - 94	2 089	722	1 367	214.4	204.6	219.9
95 - 99	789	236	553	182.3	152.5	199.0
100 +	93	31	62	72.5	65.5	76.6
Unknown - Inconnu	62	51	11	..	..	..

Slovakia - Slovaquie
2009 (C)

Total	52 913	27 446	25 467	9.8	10.4	9.1
0 - 4	429	253	176	1.6	1.8	1.3
0	346	209	137	5.9	6.9	4.8
1 - 4	83	44	39	0.4	0.4	0.4
5 - 9	38	24	14	0.1	♦0.2	♦0.1
10 - 14	61	33	28	0.2	0.2	♦0.2
15 - 19	128	87	41	0.3	0.5	0.2
20 - 24	244	202	42	0.6	0.9	0.2
25 - 29	292	223	69	0.6	1.0	0.3
30 - 34	365	269	96	0.8	1.1	0.4
35 - 39	533	392	141	1.3	1.9	0.7
40 - 44	937	678	259	2.6	3.7	1.4
45 - 49	1 535	1 100	435	4.0	5.8	2.3
50 - 54	2 774	1 989	785	6.9	10.2	3.9
55 - 59	3 950	2 782	1 168	10.6	15.6	6.0
60 - 64	4 295	2 934	1 361	15.5	23.4	9.0
65 - 69	4 698	3 006	1 692	22.1	33.5	13.8
70 - 74	5 741	3 173	2 568	34.9	49.8	25.4
75 - 79	7 691	3 651	4 040	56.2	75.3	45.8
80 - 84	8 848	3 450	5 398	98.9	122.3	88.1
85 - 89	7 357	2 348	5 009	164.6	183.3	157.1
90 - 94	2 043	604	1 439	246.6	258.6	242.0

Continent, country or area, date, code and age (in years) Continent, pays ou zone, date, code et âge (en années)	Number - Nombre			Rate - Taux		
	Both sexes Les deux sexes	Male Masculin	Female Féminin	Both sexes Les deux sexes	Male Masculin	Female Féminin
EUROPE						
Slovakia - Slovaquie						
2009 (C)						
95 - 99	863	228	635	240.6	219.4	249.2
100 +	91	20	71	97.1	♦58.5	119.3
Slovenia - Slovénie						
2009 (C)						
Total	18 750	9 293	9 457	9.2	9.2	9.2
0 - 4	64	32	32	0.6	0.6	0.7
0	52	25	27	2.4	♦2.2	♦2.5
1 - 4	12	7	5	♦0.2	♦0.2	♦0.1
5 - 9	12	6	6	♦0.1	♦0.1	♦0.1
10 - 14	6	5	1	♦0.1	♦0.1	..
15 - 19	37	25	12	0.3	♦0.5	♦0.2
20 - 24	75	62	13	0.6	0.9	♦0.2
25 - 29	86	69	17	0.6	0.9	♦0.2
30 - 34	96	82	14	0.6	1.0	♦0.2
35 - 39	134	92	42	0.9	1.2	0.6
40 - 44	248	189	59	1.6	2.4	0.8
45 - 49	426	294	132	2.7	3.7	1.7
50 - 54	708	502	206	4.5	6.3	2.7
55 - 59	1 047	733	314	7.1	9.7	4.3
60 - 64	1 100	771	329	10.3	14.7	6.0
65 - 69	1 570	1 066	504	15.6	22.8	9.3
70 - 74	2 070	1 258	812	24.2	34.0	16.7
75 - 79	2 967	1 534	1 433	41.1	56.5	31.8
80 - 84	3 454	1 334	2 120	72.3	92.3	63.6
85 - 89	2 990	861	2 129	125.9	151.5	117.9
90 - 94	1 020	254	766	215.2	261.6	203.3
95 - 99	576	111	465	337.0	344.7	335.3
100 +	64	13	51	357.5	♦342.1	361.7
Spain - Espagne[43]						
2009* (C)						
Total	381 859	197 646	184 213	8.3	8.7	7.9
0 - 4	2 053	1 146	907	0.8	0.9	0.8
0	1 657	924	733	3.3	3.6	3.0
1 - 4	396	222	174	0.2	0.2	0.2
5 - 9	211	114	97	0.1	0.1	0.1
10 - 14	228	145	83	0.1	0.1	0.1
15 - 19	624	431	193	0.3	0.4	0.2
20 - 24	936	647	289	0.3	0.5	0.2
25 - 29	1 447	1 042	405	0.4	0.6	0.2
30 - 34	2 025	1 441	584	0.5	0.7	0.3
35 - 39	2 971	2 029	942	0.8	1.0	0.5
40 - 44	4 833	3 241	1 592	1.3	1.7	0.9
45 - 49	7 433	5 002	2 431	2.2	2.9	1.4
50 - 54	10 046	6 874	3 172	3.4	4.7	2.1
55 - 59	12 819	9 103	3 716	5.0	7.2	2.8
60 - 64	17 625	12 526	5 099	7.4	10.9	4.1
65 - 69	22 112	15 441	6 671	11.2	16.5	6.4
70 - 74	32 619	21 129	11 490	18.0	25.8	11.6
75 - 79	54 122	32 179	21 943	31.9	44.4	22.6
80 - 84	71 029	35 878	35 151	58.6	76.2	47.5
85 - 89	72 853	30 057	42 796	107.7	129.0	96.6
90 - 94	44 742	14 069	30 673	183.1	203.5	175.0
95 - 99	17 888	4 501	13 387	284.9	291.0	282.9
100 +	3 240	651	2 589	450.7	363.6	479.5
Unknown - Inconnu	3	-	3	..	..	..
Sweden - Suède						
2009 (C)						
Total	90 080	43 692	46 388	9.7	9.4	9.9
0 - 4	364	202	162	0.7	0.7	0.6
0	278	148	130	2.5	2.6	2.4
1 - 4	86	54	32	0.2	0.2	0.2
5 - 9	47	28	19	0.1	♦0.1	♦0.1
10 - 14	57	37	20	0.1	0.1	♦0.1
15 - 19	173	109	64	0.3	0.3	0.2
20 - 24	268	204	64	0.5	0.7	0.2

19. Deaths by age and sex, age-specific death rates by sex: latest available year, 2000 - 2009
Décès et taux de mortalité selon l'âge et le sexe : dernière année disponible, 2000 - 2009 (continued - suite)

Continent, country or area, date, code and age (in years) / Continent, pays ou zone, date, code et âge (en années)	Number - Nombre			Rate - Taux		
	Both sexes Les deux sexes	Male Masculin	Female Féminin	Both sexes Les deux sexes	Male Masculin	Female Féminin
EUROPE						
Sweden - Suède						
2009 (C)						
25 - 29	265	200	65	0.5	0.7	0.2
30 - 34	281	198	83	0.5	0.7	0.3
35 - 39	437	280	157	0.7	0.9	0.5
40 - 44	685	420	265	1.0	1.2	0.8
45 - 49	1 016	609	407	1.7	2.0	1.4
50 - 54	1 718	1 032	686	2.9	3.5	2.4
55 - 59	2 654	1 619	1 035	4.6	5.6	3.6
60 - 64	4 612	2 764	1 848	7.3	8.8	5.9
65 - 69	5 809	3 517	2 292	11.7	14.2	9.1
70 - 74	7 304	4 252	3 052	19.6	24.0	15.7
75 - 79	10 340	5 827	4 513	34.0	43.1	26.7
80 - 84	15 556	7 898	7 658	62.9	78.8	52.0
85 - 89	19 875	8 596	11 279	118.8	144.1	104.7
90 - 94	12 919	4 480	8 439	206.1	245.9	189.7
95 - 99	4 922	1 274	3 648	335.1	396.0	318.0
100 +	778	146	632	489.2	602.1	468.8
Switzerland - Suisse						
2009 (C)						
Total	62 476	30 028	32 448	8.1	7.9	8.2
0 - 4	381	215	166	1.0	1.1	0.9
0	337	194	143	4.4	4.9	3.8
1 - 4	44	21	23	0.1	♦0.1	♦0.2
5 - 9	37	19	18	0.1	♦0.1	♦0.1
10 - 14	42	24	18	0.1	♦0.1	♦0.1
15 - 19	143	102	41	0.3	0.4	0.2
20 - 24	199	152	47	0.4	0.6	0.2
25 - 29	209	152	57	0.4	0.6	0.2
30 - 34	238	160	78	0.5	0.6	0.3
35 - 39	381	265	116	0.7	0.9	0.4
40 - 44	637	422	215	1.0	1.3	0.7
45 - 49	1 044	651	393	1.7	2.1	1.3
50 - 54	1 556	989	567	2.9	3.6	2.1
55 - 59	2 111	1 336	775	4.4	5.6	3.2
60 - 64	3 090	1 962	1 128	6.8	8.7	4.9
65 - 69	3 944	2 443	1 501	10.5	13.6	7.7
70 - 74	5 151	3 080	2 071	17.3	22.6	12.8
75 - 79	7 441	4 172	3 269	29.5	38.9	22.6
80 - 84	10 640	5 209	5 431	56.0	72.6	46.0
85 - 89	12 563	5 080	7 483	107.2	131.4	95.2
90 - 94	8 445	2 634	5 811	194.1	218.2	184.9
95 +	4 224	961	3 263	263.9	269.6	262.3
95 - 99	3 660	881	2 779	...	...	...
100 +	564	80	484	...	...	...
TFYR of Macedonia - L'ex-R. y. de Macédoine						
2009 (C)						
Total	19 060	10 040	9 020	9.3	9.8	8.8
0 - 4	315	183	132	2.8	3.2	2.4
0	278	162	116	12.1	13.6	10.4
1 - 4	37	21	16	0.4	♦0.5	♦0.4
5 - 9	23	17	6	♦0.2	♦0.3	♦0.1
10 - 14	17	10	7	♦0.1	♦0.1	♦0.1
15 - 19	57	41	16	0.4	0.5	♦0.2
20 - 24	73	57	16	0.4	0.7	♦0.2
25 - 29	74	56	18	0.5	0.7	♦0.2
30 - 34	104	73	31	0.7	0.9	0.4
35 - 39	156	92	64	1.1	1.2	0.9
40 - 44	259	167	92	1.7	2.2	1.3
45 - 49	493	327	166	3.4	4.4	2.3
50 - 54	778	535	243	5.5	7.5	3.5
55 - 59	1 210	782	428	9.6	12.5	6.7
60 - 64	1 375	865	510	13.9	18.4	9.9
65 - 69	1 999	1 191	808	24.5	31.2	18.7
70 - 74	2 840	1 527	1 313	40.9	48.7	34.5
75 - 79	3 588	1 736	1 852	71.8	80.5	65.2
80 - 84	3 059	1 291	1 768	123.7	126.0	122.1

Continent, country or area, date, code and age (in years)	Number - Nombre			Rate - Taux		
Continent, pays ou zone, date, code et âge (en années)	Both sexes Les deux sexes	Male Masculin	Female Féminin	Both sexes Les deux sexes	Male Masculin	Female Féminin
EUROPE						
TFYR of Macedonia - L'ex-R. y. de Macédoine						
2009 (C)						
85 - 89	2 025	819	1 206	220.3	228.3	215.2
90 - 94	449	202	247	279.2	348.3	240.3
95 +	166	69	97	238.8	285.1	214.1
95 - 99	143	60	83	...	...	...
100 +	23	9	14	...	...	...
Ukraine[44]						
2008 (C)						
Total	754 460	386 464	367 996	16.3	18.1	14.7
0 - 4	6 024	3 449	2 575	2.8	3.2	2.5
0	5 049	2 892	2 157	10.9	12.2	9.6
1 - 4	975	557	418	0.6	0.6	0.5
5 - 9	592	343	249	0.3	0.3	0.3
10 - 14	657	390	267	0.3	0.3	0.2
15 - 19	2 257	1 599	658	0.7	0.9	0.4
20 - 24	5 540	4 303	1 237	1.4	2.2	0.7
25 - 29	9 141	6 982	2 159	2.6	4.0	1.3
30 - 34	14 244	10 798	3 446	4.3	6.5	2.0
35 - 39	17 594	13 167	4 427	5.6	8.5	2.7
40 - 44	23 305	17 607	5 698	7.2	11.3	3.4
45 - 49	35 055	26 213	8 842	9.6	15.3	4.5
50 - 54	44 030	32 353	11 677	13.4	21.8	6.5
55 - 59	54 728	37 682	17 046	18.2	28.8	10.1
60 - 64	46 105	30 262	15 843	24.8	39.9	14.4
65 - 69	79 536	46 693	32 843	29.1	44.7	19.4
70 - 74	99 069	52 091	46 978	53.2	76.6	39.8
75 - 79	108 148	46 244	61 904	68.6	91.6	57.7
80 - 84	116 460	36 581	79 879	121.2	152.4	110.8
85 - 89	60 009	13 676	46 333	192.7	206.6	188.9
90 - 94	22 703	4 220	18 483	263.3	269.1	262.0
95 - 99	7 837	1 327	6 510	449.2	439.3	451.3
100 +	489	70	419	282.9	268.7	285.4
Unknown - Inconnu	937	414	523	..	..	..
United Kingdom of Great Britain and Northern Ireland - Royaume-Uni de Grande-Bretagne et d'Irlande du Nord[45]						
2009 (C)						
Total	559 617	270 804	288 813	9.1	8.9	9.2
0	3 677	2 067	1 610	4.7	5.1	4.2
1 - 4	549	276	273	0.2	0.2	0.2
5 - 9	320	170	150	0.1	0.1	0.1
10 - 14	404	216	188	0.1	0.1	0.1
15 - 19	1 326	925	401	0.3	0.5	0.2
20 - 24	1 850	1 341	509	0.4	0.6	0.2
25 - 29	2 363	1 659	704	0.6	0.8	0.3
30 - 34	2 810	1 888	922	0.7	1.0	0.5
35 - 39	4 581	3 010	1 571	1.0	1.4	0.7
40 - 44	7 291	4 574	2 717	1.6	2.0	1.1
45 - 49	9 910	5 978	3 932	2.2	2.8	1.8
50 - 54	13 536	8 061	5 475	3.5	4.2	2.8
55 - 59	20 000	12 042	7 958	5.5	6.8	4.3
60 - 64	31 315	18 710	12 605	8.5	10.4	6.7
65 - 69	38 360	22 911	15 449	13.7	17.0	10.6
70 - 74	53 875	31 062	22 813	22.3	27.4	17.7
75 - 79	74 462	40 270	34 192	37.5	45.9	30.8
80 - 84	96 575	47 058	49 517	66.1	80.4	56.5
85 - 89	105 806	43 121	62 685	114.3	136.1	103.0
90 +	90 607	25 465	65 142	212.2	224.2	207.8
90 - 94	59 224	18 626	40 598	...	...	...
95 - 99	26 499	6 146	20 353	...	...	...
100 +	4 884	693	4 191	...	...	...

Continent, country or area, date, code and age (in years) Continent, pays ou zone, date, code et âge (en années)	Number - Nombre			Rate - Taux		
	Both sexes Les deux sexes	Male Masculin	Female Féminin	Both sexes Les deux sexes	Male Masculin	Female Féminin

OCEANIA - OCÉANIE

American Samoa - Samoas américaines
2006 (C)

Total	267	156	111	...	...	...
0	17	9	8	...	...	...
1 - 4	7	3	4	...	...	...
5 - 9	1	1	-	...	...	...
10 - 14	5	2	3	...	...	...
15 - 19	3	-	3	...	...	...
20 - 24	5	4	1	...	...	...
25 - 29	4	3	1	...	...	...
30 - 34	5	5	-	...	...	...
35 - 39	10	6	4	...	...	...
40 - 44	9	4	5	...	...	...
45 - 49	19	10	9	...	...	...
50 - 54	18	11	7	...	...	...
55 - 59	21	13	8	...	...	...
60 - 64	23	15	8	...	...	...
65 - 69	27	18	9	...	...	...
70 - 74	31	22	9	...	...	...
75 - 79	28	19	9	...	...	...
80 - 84	13	6	7	...	...	...
85 +	21	5	16	...	...	...

Australia - Australie[46]
2009 (+C)

Total	140 760	72 320	68 440	6.4	6.6	6.2
0	1 261	728	533	4.2	4.7	3.6
1 - 4	230	131	99	0.2	0.2	0.2
5 - 9	134	78	56	0.1	0.1	0.1
10 - 14	151	84	67	0.1	0.1	0.1
15 - 19	535	378	157	0.4	0.5	0.2
20 - 24	727	529	198	0.5	0.6	0.3
25 - 29	914	644	270	0.6	0.8	0.3
30 - 34	1 027	740	287	0.7	1.0	0.4
35 - 39	1 510	984	526	0.9	1.2	0.6
40 - 44	1 947	1 258	689	1.3	1.7	0.9
45 - 49	3 004	1 802	1 202	1.9	2.3	1.5
50 - 54	4 149	2 515	1 634	2.9	3.5	2.2
55 - 59	5 434	3 347	2 087	4.2	5.2	3.2
60 - 64	7 604	4 796	2 808	6.5	8.2	4.8
65 - 69	9 141	5 714	3 427	10.5	13.3	7.8
70 - 74	12 090	7 398	4 692	17.6	22.4	13.2
75 - 79	16 815	9 845	6 970	30.6	38.7	23.6
80 - 84	24 167	12 624	11 543	56.0	68.8	46.6
85 - 89	25 608	11 225	14 383	99.2	118.4	88.1
90 - 94	16 621	5 660	10 961	178.8	202.1	168.8
95 - 99	6 560	1 638	4 922	262.6	269.5	260.4
100 +	1 120	192	928	329.3	267.4	345.9
Unknown - Inconnu	11	10	3	..	..	..

Fiji - Fidji
2004 (C)

Total	5 628	3 150	2 478	6.8	7.5	6.1
0	316	180	136	18.8	20.6	16.9
1 - 4	83	53	30	1.2	1.5	♦0.9
5 - 9	47	27	20	0.6	♦0.6	♦0.5
10 - 14	51	24	27	0.6	♦0.5	♦0.7
15 - 19	100	61	39	1.2	1.4	1.0
20 - 24	103	58	45	1.4	1.5	1.2
25 - 29	116	71	45	1.7	2.0	1.4
30 - 34	124	64	60	2.0	2.0	2.0
35 - 39	140	89	51	2.4	3.0	1.8
40 - 44	247	138	109	4.7	5.1	4.3
45 - 49	371	232	139	8.1	10.0	6.2
50 - 54	463	267	196	12.3	14.1	10.6
55 - 59	527	321	206	18.0	22.0	13.9
60 - 64	641	366	275	29.5	34.7	24.5
65 - 69	569	323	246	36.1	43.5	29.4
70 - 74	597	311	286	56.4	64.8	49.4

Continent, country or area, date, code and age (in years) / Continent, pays ou zone, date, code et âge (en années)	Number - Nombre			Rate - Taux		
	Both sexes Les deux sexes	Male Masculin	Female Féminin	Both sexes Les deux sexes	Male Masculin	Female Féminin
OCEANIA - OCÉANIE						
Fiji - Fidji						
2004 (C)						
75 +	1 133	565	568	85.3	103.0	72.9
75 - 79	414	219	195	...	...	...
80 - 84	361	191	170	...	...	...
85 - 89	223	97	126	...	...	...
90 - 94	81	40	41	...	...	...
95 +	54	18	36	...	...	...
Guam[47]						
2004 (C)						
Total	691	426	265	...	...	...
0	42	25	17	...	...	...
1 - 4	4	1	3	...	...	...
5 - 9	3	3	-	...	...	...
10 - 14	5	3	2	...	...	...
15 - 19	13	9	4	...	...	...
20 - 24	16	12	4	...	...	...
25 - 29	12	7	5	...	...	...
30 - 34	20	16	4	...	...	...
35 - 39	19	17	2	...	...	...
40 - 44	39	30	9	...	...	...
45 - 49	37	24	13	...	...	...
50 - 54	52	40	12	...	...	...
55 - 59	60	36	24	...	...	...
60 - 64	56	29	27	...	...	...
65 - 69	59	32	27	...	...	...
70 - 74	65	40	25	...	...	...
75 - 79	77	47	30	...	...	...
80 - 84	53	31	22	...	...	...
85 +	59	24	35	...	...	...
Marshall Islands - Îles Marshall						
2006 (+U)						
Total	318	171	147	...	...	...
0	27	17	10	...	...	...
1 - 4	13	7	6	...	...	...
5 - 9	4	3	1	...	...	...
10 - 14	1	1	-	...	...	...
15 - 19	11	7	4	...	...	...
20 - 24	8	4	4	...	...	...
25 - 29	6	5	1	...	...	...
30 - 34	10	4	6	...	...	...
35 - 39	15	10	5	...	...	...
40 - 44	20	10	10	...	...	...
45 - 49	16	11	5	...	...	...
50 - 54	26	11	15	...	...	...
55 - 59	38	26	12	...	...	...
60 - 64	21	9	12	...	...	...
65 +	102	46	56	...	...	...
Micronesia (Federated States of) - Micronésie (États fédérés de)						
2003 (U)						
Total	427	...	...	...	...	...
0	21	...	...	...	...	...
1 - 4	20	...	...	...	...	...
5 - 9	8	...	...	...	...	...
10 - 14	4	...	...	...	...	...
15 - 19	14	...	...	...	...	...
20 - 24	8	...	...	...	...	...
25 - 29	13	...	...	...	...	...
30 - 34	6	...	...	...	...	...
35 - 39	10	...	...	...	...	...
40 - 44	19	...	...	...	...	...
45 - 49	21	...	...	...	...	...
50 - 54	47	...	...	...	...	...
55 - 59	33	...	...	...	...	...
60 - 64	32	...	...	...	...	...

19. Deaths by age and sex, age-specific death rates by sex: latest available year, 2000 - 2009
Décès et taux de mortalité selon l'âge et le sexe : dernière année disponible, 2000 - 2009 (continued - suite)

Continent, country or area, date, code and age (in years) / Continent, pays ou zone, date, code et âge (en années)	Number - Nombre			Rate - Taux		
	Both sexes Les deux sexes	Male Masculin	Female Féminin	Both sexes Les deux sexes	Male Masculin	Female Féminin
OCEANIA - OCÉANIE						
Micronesia (Federated States of) - Micronésie (États fédérés de)						
2003 (U)						
65 - 69	*50*	...	...	...	...	...
70 +	*121*	...	...	...	...	...
Nauru						
2002 (C)						
Total	75	40	35	...	...	...
0	6	5	1	...	...	...
1 - 4	3	-	3	...	...	...
5 - 9	1	1	-	...	...	...
10 - 14	1	1	-	...	...	...
15 - 19	1	-	1	...	...	...
20 - 24	3	3	-	...	...	...
25 - 29	2	-	2	...	...	...
30 - 34	6	4	2	...	...	...
35 - 39	6	2	4	...	...	...
40 - 44	4	3	1	...	...	...
45 - 49	9	6	3	...	...	...
50 - 54	7	5	2	...	...	...
55 - 59	5	4	1	...	...	...
60 - 64	3	3	-	...	...	...
65 - 69	5	1	4	...	...	...
70 - 74	4	1	3	...	...	...
75 +	9	1	8	...	...	...
New Caledonia - Nouvelle-Calédonie						
2007 (C)						
Total	1 207	749	458	5.0	6.2	3.8
0	25	15	10	♦5.9	♦6.9	♦4.9
1 - 4	11	9	2	♦0.7	♦1.1	♦0.3
5 - 9	5	4	1	♦0.2	♦0.3	♦0.1
10 - 14	8	6	2	♦0.4	♦0.5	♦0.2
15 - 19	21	15	6	♦1.0	♦1.4	♦0.6
20 - 24	25	23	2	♦1.3	♦2.4	♦0.2
25 - 29	20	16	4	♦1.2	♦1.9	♦0.5
30 - 34	29	20	9	♦1.5	♦2.1	♦0.9
35 - 39	26	17	9	♦1.4	♦1.8	♦0.9
40 - 44	38	26	12	2.2	♦3.0	♦1.4
45 - 49	64	47	17	4.4	6.5	♦2.3
50 - 54	61	40	21	5.1	6.5	♦3.6
55 - 59	78	59	19	7.3	10.5	♦3.8
60 - 64	97	72	25	11.7	16.4	♦6.4
65 - 69	120	87	33	19.0	27.8	10.3
70 - 74	127	73	54	29.8	35.7	24.3
75 - 79	146	87	59	50.3	69.1	35.9
80 - 84	120	61	59	73.6	90.4	61.8
85 - 89	104	47	57	137.9	165.5	121.3
90 - 94	52	20	32	134.7	♦151.5	126.0
95 +	30	5	25	♦211.3	♦128.2	♦242.7
New Zealand - Nouvelle-Zélande[17]						
2009 (+C)						
Total	28 964	14 480	14 484	6.7	6.8	6.6
0	308	170	138	4.9	5.2	4.5
1 - 4	72	37	35	0.3	0.3	0.3
5 - 9	33	14	19	0.1	♦0.1	♦0.1
10 - 14	54	27	27	0.2	♦0.2	♦0.2
15 - 19	184	130	54	0.6	0.8	0.3
20 - 24	200	153	47	0.7	1.0	0.3
25 - 29	173	108	65	0.6	0.8	0.5
30 - 34	225	162	63	0.8	1.3	0.5
35 - 39	288	172	116	0.9	1.2	0.7
40 - 44	438	254	184	1.4	1.7	1.1
45 - 49	661	370	291	2.0	2.4	1.8
50 - 54	937	529	408	3.3	3.8	2.8
55 - 59	1 114	653	461	4.5	5.4	3.7
60 - 64	1 669	988	681	7.5	9.1	6.1
65 - 69	2 119	1 248	871	12.3	14.9	9.9

Continent, country or area, date, code and age (in years) / Continent, pays ou zone, date, code et âge (en années)	Number - Nombre			Rate - Taux		
	Both sexes Les deux sexes	Male Masculin	Female Féminin	Both sexes Les deux sexes	Male Masculin	Female Féminin
OCEANIA - OCÉANIE						
New Zealand - Nouvelle-Zélande[17]						
2009 (+C)						
70 - 74	2 659	1 535	1 124	20.4	24.7	16.5
75 - 79	3 523	2 053	1 470	33.6	42.5	26.0
80 - 84	4 794	2 442	2 352	60.4	72.0	51.8
85 +	9 513	3 435	6 078	142.8	154.3	137.0
85 - 89	4 963	2 069	2 894	...	...	...
90 - 94	3 150	1 016	2 134	...	...	...
95 - 99	1 179	316	863	...	...	...
100 +	221	34	187	...	...	...
Niue - Nioué						
2009 (C)						
Total	12	6	6	...	...	...
0	-	-	-	...	...	...
1 - 4	-	-	-	...	...	...
5 - 9	-	-	-	...	...	...
10 - 14	-	-	-	...	...	...
15 - 19	-	-	-	...	...	...
20 - 24	-	-	-	...	...	...
25 - 29	-	-	-	...	...	...
30 - 34	-	-	-	...	...	...
35 - 39	-	-	-	...	...	...
40 - 44	-	-	-	...	...	...
45 - 49	-	-	-	...	...	...
50 - 54	-	-	-	...	...	...
55 - 59	2	2	-	...	...	...
60 - 64	-	-	-	...	...	...
65 - 69	-	-	-	...	...	...
70 - 74	1	-	1	...	...	...
75 - 79	1	1	-	...	...	...
80 +	8	3	5	...	...	...
Northern Mariana Islands - Îles Mariannes septentrionales						
2005 (U)						
Total	188	107	81	...	...	...
0	5	1	4	...	...	...
1 - 4	4	3	1	...	...	...
5 - 9	-	-	-	...	...	...
10 - 14	3	2	1	...	...	...
15 - 19	1	-	1	...	...	...
20 - 24	3	2	1	...	...	...
25 - 29	10	3	7	...	...	...
30 - 34	11	9	2	...	...	...
35 - 39	7	4	3	...	...	...
40 - 44	11	6	5	...	...	...
45 - 49	7	6	1	...	...	...
50 - 54	17	13	4	...	...	...
55 - 59	19	11	8	...	...	...
60 - 64	20	9	11	...	...	...
65 - 69	20	14	6	...	...	...
70 - 74	20	11	9	...	...	...
75 - 79	13	6	7	...	...	...
80 - 84	8	5	3	...	...	...
85 - 89	5	1	4	...	...	...
90 - 94	2	-	2	...	...	...
95 - 99	2	1	1	...	...	...
100 +	-	-	-	...	...	...
Palau - Palaos						
2003 (C)						
Total	136	79	57	...	...	...
0	3	1	2	...	...	...
1 - 14	5	4	1	...	...	...
15 - 24	7	4	3	...	...	...
25 - 44	17	12	5	...	...	...
45 - 64	33	29	4	...	...	...
65 +	71	29	42	...	...	...

19. Deaths by age and sex, age-specific death rates by sex: latest available year, 2000 - 2009
Décès et taux de mortalité selon l'âge et le sexe : dernière année disponible, 2000 - 2009 (continued - suite)

Continent, country or area, date, code and age (in years) / Continent, pays ou zone, date, code et âge (en années)	Number - Nombre			Rate - Taux		
	Both sexes Les deux sexes	Male Masculin	Female Féminin	Both sexes Les deux sexes	Male Masculin	Female Féminin
OCEANIA - OCÉANIE						
Palau - Palaos						
2005 (C)						
Total	134	...	...	6.7	...	...
0	5	...	...	♦18.5	...	...
1 - 4	1	...	...	♦0.9	...	...
5 - 9	-	...	...	-	...	...
10 - 14	-	...	...	-	...	...
15 - 19	2	...	...	♦1.4	...	...
20 - 24	1	...	...	♦0.8	...	...
25 - 29	5	...	...	♦3.2	...	...
30 - 34	4	...	...	♦2.2	...	...
35 - 39	6	...	...	♦3.1	...	...
40 - 44	9	...	...	♦4.8	...	...
45 - 49	13	...	...	♦8.5	...	...
50 - 54	14	...	...	♦11.8	...	...
55 - 59	9	...	...	♦12.3	...	...
60 - 64	10	...	...	♦19.8	...	...
65 - 69	8	...	...	♦21.4	...	...
70 - 74	11	...	...	♦42.8	...	...
75 +	36	...	...	71.1	...	...
Pitcairn						
2007 (C)						
Total	1	...	...	...	...	...
0	-	...	...	...	...	...
1 - 4	-	...	...	...	...	...
5 - 9	-	...	...	...	...	...
10 - 14	-	...	...	...	...	...
15 - 19	-	...	...	...	...	...
20 - 24	-	...	...	...	...	...
25 - 29	-	...	...	...	...	...
30 - 34	-	...	...	...	...	...
35 - 39	-	...	...	...	...	...
40 - 44	-	...	...	...	...	...
45 - 49	-	...	...	...	...	...
50 - 54	-	...	...	...	...	...
55 - 59	-	...	...	...	...	...
60 - 64	-	...	...	...	...	...
65 - 69	-	...	...	...	...	...
70 - 74	-	...	...	...	...	...
75 - 79	1	...	...	...	...	...
80 - 84	-	...	...	...	...	...
85 - 89	-	...	...	...	...	...
90 +	-	...	...	...	...	...
Tonga[48]						
2006 (I)						
Total	709	402	307	6.9	7.6	6.1
0 - 4	61	38	24	5.1	6.2	♦4.1
0	53	32	21	...	...	...
1 - 4	8	6	3	...	...	...
5 - 9	10	5	4	♦0.9	♦0.8	♦0.7
10 - 14	7	4	4	♦0.6	♦0.6	♦0.7
15 - 19	12	8	3	♦1.1	♦1.3	♦0.6
20 - 24	11	9	2	♦1.0	♦1.6	♦0.4
25 - 29	7	5	2	♦0.9	♦1.2	♦0.5
30 - 34	12	9	4	♦2.1	♦3.2	♦1.4
35 - 39	12	7	5	♦2.1	♦2.4	♦1.8
40 - 44	19	11	8	♦3.8	♦4.4	♦3.2
45 - 49	29	18	11	♦6.8	♦8.8	♦4.9
50 - 54	29	16	13	♦7.7	♦8.9	♦6.5
55 - 59	37	23	15	11.8	♦15.6	♦9.0
60 - 64	53	33	20	18.5	23.9	♦13.5
65 - 69	49	28	21	20.2	♦22.5	♦17.7
70 - 74	70	38	32	37.5	39.7	35.2
75 +	288	149	139	135.1	141.2	129.2
75 - 79	95	54	41	...	...	...
80 +	193	95	98	...	...	...

Continent, country or area, date, code and age (in years) Continent, pays ou zone, date, code et âge (en années)	Number - Nombre			Rate - Taux		
	Both sexes Les deux sexes	Male Masculin	Female Féminin	Both sexes Les deux sexes	Male Masculin	Female Féminin
OCEANIA - OCÉANIE						
Tuvalu						
2005 (U)						
Total	59	33	26	...	...	...
0	6	5	1	...	...	...
1 - 4	2	1	1	...	...	...
5 - 9	-	-	-	...	...	...
10 - 14	-	-	-	...	...	...
15 - 19	-	-	-	...	...	...
20 - 24	1	1	-	...	...	...
25 - 29	-	-	-	...	...	...
30 - 34	1	1	-	...	...	...
35 - 39	2	2	-	...	...	...
40 - 44	2	2	-	...	...	...
45 - 49	3	3	-	...	...	...
50 - 54	6	3	3	...	...	...
55 - 59	4	3	1	...	...	...
60 - 64	7	2	5	...	...	...
65 - 69	6	2	4	...	...	...
70 - 74	1	-	1	...	...	...
75 - 79	8	4	4	...	...	...
80 - 84	8	3	5	...	...	...
85 - 89	2	1	1	...	...	...
Wallis and Futuna Islands - Îles Wallis et Futuna						
2008 (C)						
Total	90	51	39	...	...	...
0 - 4	1	1	-	...	...	...
5 - 9	-	-	-	...	...	...
10 - 14	1	1	-	...	...	...
15 - 19	2	1	1	...	...	...
20 - 24	4	3	1	...	...	...
25 - 29	4	4	-	...	...	...
30 - 34	3	3	-	...	...	...
35 - 39	2	1	1	...	...	...
40 - 44	-	-	-	...	...	...
45 - 49	2	1	1	...	...	...
50 - 54	2	1	1	...	...	...
55 - 59	4	2	2	...	...	...
60 - 64	5	4	1	...	...	...
65 - 69	12	8	4	...	...	...
70 - 74	15	9	6	...	...	...
75 - 79	13	4	9	...	...	...
80 - 84	11	4	7	...	...	...
85 - 89	5	3	2	...	...	...
90 - 94	4	1	3	...	...	...
95 - 99	-	-	-	...	...	...
100 +	-	-	-	...	...	...
Unknown - Inconnu	-	-	-	...	...	...

FOOTNOTES - NOTES

♦ Rates based on 30 or fewer deaths. - Taux basés sur 30 décès ou moins.

Italics: estimates which are less reliable. - Italiques : estimations moins sûres.

* Provisional. - Données provisoires.

'Code' indicates the source of data, as follows:
C - Civil registration, estimated over 90% complete
U - Civil registration, estimated less than 90% complete
| - Other source, estimated reliable
+ - Data tabulated by date of registration rather than occurence
... - Information not available

Le 'Code' indique la source des données, comme suit :
C - Registres de l'état civil considérés complets à 90 p. 100 au moins
U - Registres de l'état civil qui ne sont pas considérés complets à 90 p. 100 au

moins
| - Autre source, considérée pas douteuses
+ - Données exploitées selon la date de l'enregistrement et non la date de l'événement
... - Information pas disponible

[1] Data from Health Statistics Reports since 1998, due to incompleteness of civil registration. - Données provenant des Health Statistics Reports (rapports sur les statistiques sanitaires) depuis 1998, en raison des lacunes de l'état civil.
[2] Data as reported by national statistical authorities; they may differ from data presented in other tables. - Les données comme elles ont été déclarées par l'institut national de la statistique; elles peuvent être différentes de celles présentées dans d'autres tableaux.
[3] Excludes the islands of St. Brandon and Agalega. - Non compris les îles St. Brandon et Agalega.
[4] Data refer to January-August only. - Le chiffre correspond à la période allant de janvier à août.
[5] Figures for male and female do not add up to the total, since they do not include the category "Unknown". - La somme des chiffres indiqués pour les

sexes masculin et féminin n'est pas égale au total parce qu'elle n'inclut pas la catégorie " inconnue ".

[6] Excluding live-born infants who died before their birth was registered. - Non compris les enfants nés vivants décédés avant l'enregistrement de leur naissance.

[7] Data refer to the twelve months preceding the census date. - Les données portent sur les douze mois précédant la date du recensement.

[8] Data refer to the twelve months preceding the census in May. - Les données se rapportent aux douze mois précédant le recensement de mai.

[9] Data refer to the twelve months preceding the census in August. - Les données se rapportent aux douze mois précédant le recensement d'août.

[10] Source: World Health Organization. - Source : Organisation mondiale de la santé.

[11] Reason for discrepancy between these figures and corresponding figures shown elsewhere not ascertained. - On ne sait pas comment s'explique la divergence entre ces chiffres et les chiffres correspondants indiqués ailleurs.

[12] Excluding non-residents and foreign service personnel and their dependants. - À l'exclusion des non-résidents et du personnel diplomatique et de leurs charges de famille.

[13] Including Canadian residents temporarily in the United States, but excluding United States residents temporarily in Canada. - Y compris les résidents canadiens se trouvant temporairement aux Etats-Unis, mais ne comprenant pas les résidents des Etats-Unis se trouvant temporairement au Canada.

[14] Excluding deaths of nationals who were residing and died abroad but were buried in the Cayman Islands. - Exception faite des nationaux qui résidaient à l'étranger au moment de leur décès, mais qui ont été inhumés dans les Îles Caïmanes.

[15] Excluding deaths occurring abroad. - Exception faite des personnes décédées à l'étranger.

[16] Data have been adjusted for undercoverage of infant deaths and sudden and violent deaths. - Ajusté pour la sous-estimation de la mortalité infantile, du nombre de morts soudaines et de morts violentes.

[17] Data refer to resident population only. - Pour la population résidante seulement.

[18] Including unknown sex. - Y compris le sexe inconnu.

[19] Excluding Indian jungle population. Including deaths of foreigners and deaths of unknown residence. - Non compris les Indiens de la jungle. Y compris les décès d'étrangers et de personnes dont le lieu de résidence est inconnu.

[20] Excluding nomadic Indian tribes. - Non compris les tribus d'Indiens nomades.

[21] Data refer to registered events only. Source: Ministry of health reports. - Les données ne concernent que les événements enregistrés. Source: Rapports du Ministère de Santé.

[22] Including non-residents. - Y compris les non-résidents.

[23] Excluding infants born alive of less than 28 weeks' gestation, of less than 1 000 grams in weight and 35 centimeters in length, who die within seven days of birth. - Non compris les enfants nés vivants après moins de 28 semaines de gestations, pesant moins de 1 000 grammes, mesurant moins de 35 centimètres et décédés dans les sept jours qui ont suivi leur naissance.

[24] Data refer to government controlled areas. - Les données se rapportent aux zones contrôlées par le Gouvernement.

[25] Data refer to the twelve months preceding the census in October. - Les données font référence aux 12 mois qui ont précédé le recensement en octobre.

[26] Including data for East Jerusalem and Israeli residents in certain other territories under occupation by Israeli military forces since June 1967. Including deaths abroad of Israeli residents who were out of the country for less than a year. - Y compris les données pour Jérusalem-Est et les résidents israéliens dans certains autres territoires occupés depuis 1967 par les forces armées israéliennes. Y compris les décès à l'étranger de résidents israéliens qui ont quitté le pays depuis moins d'un an.

[27] Data refer to Japanese nationals in Japan only. - Les données se raportent aux nationaux japonais au Japon seulement.

[28] Data refer to urban areas only. - Données ne concernant que les zones urbaines.

[29] Data refer to the twelve months preceding the census in June. - Les données se rapportent aux douze mois précédant le recensement de juin.

[30] Data from Births and Deaths Notification System (Ministry of Health institutions and all other health care providers). - Les données proviennent du système de notification des naissances et des décès (établissements du Ministère de la santé et tous autres prestataires de soins de santé).

[31] Excluding data for the Pakistan-held part of Jammu and Kashmir, the final status of which has not yet been determined. Based on the results of the Pakistan Demographic Survey. - Non compris les données concernant la partie du Jammu et Cachemire occupée par le Pakistan dont le statut définitif n'a pas été déterminé. Données extraites de l'enquête démographique effectuée par le Pakistan.

[32] Excluding alien armed forces, civilian aliens employed by armed forces, and foreign diplomatic personnel and their dependants. - Non compris les militaires étrangers, les civils étrangers employés par les forces armées ni le personnel diplomatique étranger et les membres de leur famille les accompagnant.

[33] The registration of births and deaths is conducted by the Ministry of Health. An estimate of completeness is not provided. - L'enregistrement des naissances et des décès est mené par le Ministère de la Santé. Le degré estimatif de complétude n'est pas fourni.

[34] Data include four cases of unknown sex. - Les données comprennent quatre cas de sexe inconnu.

[35] Including deaths of nationals abroad. - Y compris les décès des nationaux survenus à l'étranger.

[36] Including armed forces stationed outside the country, but excluding alien armed forces stationed in the area. - Y compris les militaires nationaux hors du pays, mais non compris les militaires étrangers en garnison sur le territoire.

[37] Excluding Faeroe Islands and Greenland shown separately, if available. - Non compris les Iles Féroé et le Groenland, qui font l'objet de rubriques distinctes, si disponible.

[38] Including armed forces stationed outside the country. - Y compris les militaires nationaux hors du pays.

[39] Including residents outside the country if listed in a Netherlands population register. - Y compris les résidents hors du pays, s'ils sont inscrits sur un registre de population néerlandais.

[40] Including residents temporarily outside the country. Excluding Svalbard and Jan Mayen Islands shown separately, if available. - Y compris les résidents se trouvant temporairement hors du pays. Non compris Svalbard et Jan Mayen qui font l'objet de rubriques distinctes, si disponible.

[41] Excluding Transnistria and the municipality of Bender. - Les données ne tiennent pas compte de l'information sur la Transnistria et la municipalité de Bender.

[42] Excluding data for Kosovo and Metohia. - Sans les données pour le Kosovo et Metohie.

[43] Unrevised data. - Les données n'ont pas été révisées.

[44] Data includes deaths resulting from births with weight 500g and more (if weight is unknown - with length 25 centimeters and more, or with gestation during 22 weeks or more). - Y compris les décès de nouveau-nés de 500 grammes ou plus (si le poids est inconnu – de 25 centimètres de long ou plus, ou après une grossesse de 22 semaines ou plus).

[45] Excluding Channel Islands (Guernsey and Jersey) and Isle of Man, shown separately, if available. - Non compris les îles Anglo-Normandes (Guernesey et Jersey) et l'île de Man, qui font l'objet de rubriques distinctes, si disponible.

[46] Data for certain cells suppressed by national statistical office for confidentiality reasons. - Les données pour certaines cases ont été supprimées par le bureau national de statistiques pour des raisons de confidentialité.

[47] Including United States military personnel, their dependants and contract employees. - Y compris les militaires des Etats-Unis, les membres de leur famille les accompagnant et les agents contractuels des Etats-Unis.

[48] Estimate based on results of the population census. - Estimation fondeé sur les résultats du recensement de la population.

19a. Deaths by age and sex, age-specific death rates by sex: 2010
Décès et taux de mortalité selon l'âge et le sexe : 2010

Continent, country or area, date, code and age (in years) / Continent, pays ou zone, date, code et âge (en années)	Number - Nombre			Rate - Taux		
	Both sexes Les deux sexes	Male Masculin	Female Féminin	Both sexes Les deux sexes	Male Masculin	Female Féminin

AFRICA - AFRIQUE

Saint Helena ex. dep. - Sainte-Hélène sans dép.
2010 (C)

Total	53	31	22	...	...	...
0	-	-	-	...	...	...
1 - 4	-	-	-	...	...	...
5 - 9	-	-	-	...	...	...
10 - 14	-	-	-	...	...	...
15 - 19	-	-	-	...	...	...
20 - 24	-	-	-	...	...	...
25 - 29	-	-	-	...	...	...
30 - 34	2	1	1	...	...	...
35 - 39	2	1	1	...	...	...
40 - 44	1	1	-	...	...	...
45 - 49	1	1	-	...	...	...
50 - 54	1	1	-	...	...	...
55 - 59	2	2	-	...	...	...
60 - 64	6	4	2	...	...	...
65 - 69	7	7	-	...	...	...
70 - 74	3	2	1	...	...	...
75 - 79	7	4	3	...	...	...
80 - 84	8	5	3	...	...	...
85 - 89	9	2	7	...	...	...
90 - 94	4	-	4	...	...	...
95 - 99	-	-	-	...	...	...
100 +	-	-	-	...	...	...

AMERICA, NORTH - AMÉRIQUE DU NORD

Aruba
2010 (C)

Total	610	...	...	...	...	...
0	4	...	...	...	...	...
1 - 49	59	...	...	...	...	...
50 - 59	76	...	...	...	...	...
60 - 69	114	...	...	...	...	...
70 - 79	165	...	...	...	...	...
80 - 89	140	...	...	...	...	...
90 +	52	...	...	...	...	...

Costa Rica
2010* (C)

Total	19 077	10 909	8 168	4.2	4.9	3.5
0	671	387	284	...	...	...
1 - 4	121	76	45	...	...	...
5 - 9	67	36	31	0.2	0.2	0.2
10 - 14	92	53	39	0.2	0.3	0.2
15 - 19	248	189	59	0.5	0.8	0.3
20 - 24	380	286	94	0.8	1.3	0.4
25 - 29	382	292	90	1.0	1.6	0.5
30 - 34	422	313	109	...	...	...
35 - 39	449	317	132	...	...	...
40 - 44	562	382	180	...	...	...
45 - 49	713	448	265	...	...	...
50 - 54	945	601	344	...	...	...
55 - 59	1 123	679	444	...	...	...
60 - 64	1 251	761	490	...	...	...
65 - 69	1 453	872	581	...	...	...
70 +	10 187	5 207	4 980	42.2	49.0	36.8
70 - 74	1 741	987	754	...	...	...
75 - 79	2 134	1 187	947	...	...	...
80 - 84	2 322	1 209	1 113	...	...	...
85 - 89	2 011	956	1 055	...	...	...
90 - 94	1 221	559	662	...	...	...
95 - 99	604	255	349	...	...	...
100 +	154	54	100	...	...	...
Unknown - Inconnu	11	10	1	...	...	...

Continent, country or area, date, code and age (in years)	Number - Nombre			Rate - Taux		
Continent, pays ou zone, date, code et âge (en années)	Both sexes Les deux sexes	Male Masculin	Female Féminin	Both sexes Les deux sexes	Male Masculin	Female Féminin

EUROPE

Lithuania - Lituanie
2010 (C)

Total	42 120	21 536	20 584	12.7	13.9	11.6
0	153	85	68	4.2	4.5	3.8
1 - 4	36	20	16	0.3	◆0.3	◆0.3
5 - 9	22	12	10	◆0.1	◆0.2	◆0.1
10 - 14	33	22	11	0.2	◆0.2	◆0.1
15 - 19	146	120	26	0.6	1.0	◆0.2
20 - 24	250	209	41	0.9	1.5	0.3
25 - 29	271	212	59	1.1	1.7	0.5
30 - 34	426	341	85	2.0	3.1	0.8
35 - 39	653	528	125	2.8	4.6	1.1
40 - 44	976	757	219	4.0	6.4	1.8
45 - 49	1 555	1 121	434	6.0	9.0	3.2
50 - 54	2 072	1 505	567	8.8	13.9	4.5
55 - 59	2 581	1 827	754	13.4	21.4	7.1
60 - 64	3 030	2 106	924	18.6	31.2	9.7
65 - 69	3 684	2 400	1 284	23.7	39.7	13.5
70 - 74	4 732	2 718	2 014	33.1	53.0	21.9
75 - 79	5 920	2 796	3 124	51.4	74.5	40.2
80 - 84	6 940	2 524	4 416	89.3	117.8	78.4
85 - 89	5 472	1 448	4 024	161.4	187.5	153.7
90 - 94	2 101	528	1 573	306.0	330.0	298.8
95 - 99	881	186	695	502.0	515.2	498.6
100 +	186	71	115	384.3	577.2	318.6
Unknown - Inconnu	-	-	-	..	..	..

FOOTNOTES - NOTES

◆ Rates based on 30 or fewer deaths. - Taux basés sur 30 décès ou moins.

Italics: estimates which are less reliable. - Italiques : estimations moins sûres.

* Provisional. - Données provisoires.

'Code' indicates the source of data, as follows:
C - Civil registration, estimated over 90% complete
U - Civil registration, estimated less than 90% complete
| - Other source, estimated reliable
+ - Data tabulated by date of registration rather than occurence.
... - Information not available

Le 'Code' indique la source des données, comme suit :
C - Registres de l'état civil considérés complets à 90 p. 100 au moins.
U - Registres de l'état civil qui ne sont pas considérés complets à 90 p. 100 au moins.
| - Autre source, considérée pas douteuses.
+ - Données exploitées selon la date de l'enregistrement et non la date de l'événement.
... - Information pas disponible.

Table 20

Table 20 presents the life tables' probabilities of dying in the five year interval following specified ages ($_5q_x$), for each sex, for the latest available year between 1991 and 2010. The probabilities are multiplied by a thousand, that is, the values presented in the table are $1000*_5q_x$.

Male and female probabilities of dying are shown separately for selected ages beginning at birth and proceeding at every fifth age thereafter up to age 100.

The values presented in the table are derived by the United Nations Statistics Division from the official complete life tables reported by the countries or areas.

Data are shown with one decimal regardless of the number of digits provided in the original computation.

The life table is a statistical device for summarizing the mortality experience of a population, from which the probability of dying, survivorship and expectation of life can be calculated. It is based on the assumption that the theoretical cohort is subject, throughout its existence, to the age-specific mortality rates observed at a particular time. Thus, levels of mortality prevailing at the time a life table is constructed are assumed to remain unchanged into the future until all members of the cohort have died.

Reliability of data: The values shown in this table are derived from official complete life tables. It is assumed that, if necessary, the basic data (population and deaths classified by age and sex) have been adjusted for deficiencies before their use in constructing the complete life tables.

Limitations: The life tables' probabilities of dying are subject to the same qualifications as have been set forth for population statistics in general and death statistics in particular, as discussed in sections 3 and 4, respectively, of the Technical Notes. They must be interpreted strictly using the underlying assumption that surviving cohorts are subjected to the same age-specific mortality rates of the period to which the life table refers.

Earlier data: The life tables' probabilities of dying at specified ages, for each sex, have been shown in previous issues of the *Demographic Yearbook*. For information on specific years covered, the reader should consult the Historical Index.

Tableau 20

Le tableau 20 donne les probabilités de décès dans l'intervalle de cinq ans que suit l'âge spécifié ($_5q_x$), pour chaque sexe, pour la dernière année disponible entre 1991 et 2010. Les probabilités sont multipliées par mille, c'est-à-dire que les valeurs indiquées dans le tableau sont égales à $1000*_5q_x$.

Les probabilités de décès sont indiquées séparément pour les hommes et les femmes pour différents âges, depuis la naissance puis tous les cinq ans jusqu'à 100 ans.

Les chiffres indiqués dans ce tableau ont été calculés par la Division de statistique de l'Organisation des Nations Unies à partir des tables de mortalité complètes communiquées par les pays ou zones.

Les données sont arrondies à la première décimale, indépendamment du nombre de décimales qui figurent dans le calcul initial.

La table de mortalité est un moyen statistique que s'utilise pour donner un aperçu complet de la mortalité d'une population incluant les probabilités de décès et l'espérance de vie à chaque âge. Les tables de mortalité reposent sur l'hypothèse que chaque cohorte théoriquement distinguée connaît, pendant toute son existence, les taux de mortalité par âge observé à un moment donné. Les taux de mortalité correspondant à l'époque à laquelle sont calculées les tables de mortalité sont ainsi censés demeurer inchangées dans l'avenir jusqu'au décès de tous les membres de la cohorte.

Fiabilité des donnés : Les chiffres indiqués dans ce tableau ont été calculés à partir des tables officielles de mortalité complètes. En ce qui concerne les chiffres extraits de tables officielles de mortalité, on part du principe que les données de base (effectif de la population et nombre de décès selon l'âge et le sexe) ont été ajustées, en tant que de besoin, avant de servir à l'établissement de la table de mortalité.

Insuffisance des données : Les probabilités de décès appellent les mêmes réserves que celles qui ont été formulées à propos des statistiques de la population en général et des statistiques de mortalité en particulier (voir les sections 3 et 4 des Notes techniques). Lorsque l'on interprète les données, il ne faut jamais perdre de vue que, par hypothèse, les cohortes de survivants sont soumises, pour chaque âge, aux conditions de mortalité de la période visée par la table de mortalité.

Données publiées antérieurement : Les probabilités de décès pour chaque sexe figuraient déjà dans des éditions antérieures de *l'Annuaire démographique*. Pour plus de précisions concernant les années pour lesquelles ces données ont été publiées, se reporter à l'index historique.

20. Probability of dying in the five year interval following specified age (5qx), by sex, latest available year: 1991 - 2010
Probabilité de décès dans l'intervalle de cinq ans qui suit un âge donné (5qx), par sexe, dernière année disponible .
1991 - 2010

Continent, country or area and date / Continent, pays ou zone et date	0	5	10	15	20	25	30	35	40	45	50	55	60	65	70	75	80	85	90	95	100
AFRICA - AFRIQUE																					
Zimbabwe																					
2001 - 2002																					
Male - Hommes	116.9	18.0	12.8	12.2	30.6	70.9	129.9	193.2	193.5	186.2	175.7	177.3	167.1	186.5	197.2	270.7	297.7	432.4	545.1	...	...
Female - Femmes	100.5	15.2	10.8	15.2	46.7	97.4	141.4	159.8	125.9	122.9	101.0	99.6	100.9	122.5	128.8	161.1	223.5	304.5	438.0	...	...
AMERICA, NORTH - AMÉRIQUE DU NORD																					
Canada																					
2000 - 2002																					
Male - Hommes	6.9	0.5	1.3	3.6	4.2	4.2	4.9	6.0	9.8	14.2	23.1	35.7	58.9	93.6	147.5	232.0	356.1	522.1	699.2	832.4	...
Female - Femmes	5.5	0.4	0.7	1.5	1.7	1.7	2.3	3.6	5.5	8.8	13.9	22.4	35.1	55.7	88.8	145.8	244.8	402.2	576.2	750.4	
Costa Rica																					
2007																					
Male - Hommes	12.6	0.8	1.2	4.2	5.3	6.8	7.9	9.0	10.5	16.8	24.2	35.4	54.0	83.4	126.3	208.9	323.3	458.3	637.6	793.5	*1000
Female - Femmes	10.2	0.6	0.8	1.5	1.9	1.9	3.0	4.3	5.4	8.9	13.2	20.5	33.2	58.2	83.7	147.7	240.8	407.6	563.5	791.3	*1000
Cuba																					
2005 - 2007																					
Male - Hommes	7.5	1.2	1.5	2.7	3.9	4.8	5.8	7.7	11.7	19.1	30.0	45.4	67.1	100.4	153.8	231.5	340.6	482.1	616.8	675.5	*1000
Female - Femmes	6.5	0.7	0.8	1.4	2.0	2.5	3.1	4.5	7.3	12.3	19.4	29.6	45.0	70.9	112.1	174.8	276.2	420.9	573.8	657.2	*1000
Greenland - Groenland																					
1992 - 1996																					
Male - Hommes	25.0	2.5	7.4	24.2	26.7	18.2	19.0	16.5	23.5	33.9	42.0	91.2	134.8	220.9	316.3	444.5	542.1	...	...	...	...
Female - Femmes	14.1	1.6	3.7	10.2	10.2	11.7	8.5	9.7	14.5	30.7	44.3	54.7	125.5	160.1	230.0	395.0	513.4	...	...	...	...
Guadeloupe																					
2002																					
Male - Hommes	8.7	1.1	2.1	4.6	9.3	11.1	10.0	12.7	14.6	24.3	31.1	45.3	68.9	95.0	141.6	219.3	290.6	421.7	994.4	*1000	...
Female - Femmes	6.0	0.3	0.3	1.2	2.9	1.4	4.3	5.8	8.0	8.1	10.9	22.1	39.9	55.5	87.1	112.0	212.4	331.5	984.3	*1000	...
Jamaica - Jamaïque																					
2006																					
Male - Hommes	31.7	2.8	2.5	4.5	6.5	6.5	7.0	9.4	14.5	23.2	37.5	60.5	96.9	153.2	236.8	353.8	502.7	667.6	817.2	921.8	*1000
Female - Femmes	18.0	1.3	1.1	1.7	2.6	3.4	4.3	5.9	8.7	13.9	22.8	38.0	63.2	104.5	169.8	268.2	405.3	574.1	747.0	883.6	*1000
Martinique																					
2007																					
Male - Hommes	11.6	1.0	1.1	4.2	8.8	7.5	8.8	8.5	10.4	13.5	26.7	28.9	42.2	87.6	122.7	202.9	325.3	532.7	663.7	834.4	*1000
Female - Femmes	7.8	0.4	0.7	0.6	2.1	2.9	4.6	4.1	4.8	5.3	11.3	14.8	28.6	45.6	76.8	135.3	216.7	362.2	508.4	810.4	*1000
Mexico - Mexique																					
2005																					
Male - Hommes	21.6	1.7	2.2	4.3	7.4	9.9	12.0	15.1	20.3	28.7	41.3	59.9	86.6	124.3	176.5	246.8	337.7	448.7	574.2	702.2	*1000
Female - Femmes	17.4	1.3	1.2	1.8	2.4	3.1	4.3	6.4	9.9	15.4	23.9	37.2	57.5	88.4	134.4	201.1	293.6	414.1	557.1	705.8	*1000
Netherlands Antilles - Antilles néerlandaises																					
2003 - 2007																					
Male - Hommes	13.7	1.0	1.7	6.5	13.8	10.0	10.5	11.3	13.2	22.9	33.9	50.9	87.5	131.8	193.6	285.0	414.1	545.1	691.6	770.3	*1000
Female - Femmes	10.4	0.7	0.9	2.0	1.5	3.3	3.0	4.8	7.3	12.6	19.4	30.7	45.5	72.9	114.0	184.2	269.4	432.4	615.2	730.8	*1000
United States of America - États-Unis d'Amérique																					
2007																					
Male - Hommes	8.6	0.7	1.0	4.3	7.2	7.0	7.4	9.2	13.7	21.0	31.9	45.3	64.8	95.3	144.8	227.9	345.3	496.8	665.8	819.2	*1000
Female - Femmes	7.1	0.6	0.7	1.8	2.4	2.8	3.6	5.3	8.3	12.8	18.7	26.9	41.0	62.4	98.2	163.9	265.3	409.2	587.2	766.4	*1000
AMERICA, SOUTH - AMÉRIQUE DU SUD																					
Argentina - Argentine																					
1992																					
Male - Hommes	31.7	1.9	2.2	5.0	7.2	7.8	8.8	12.5	19.5	31.9	51.2	78.3	112.2	161.8	237.8	340.0	485.6	...	...	...	...
Female - Femmes	26.1	1.4	1.4	2.4	3.1	4.0	5.2	7.6	11.1	16.3	23.7	34.5	51.0	79.8	132.5	222.1	376.9	...	...	...	...
Brazil - Brésil[1]																					
2009																					
Male - Hommes	31.2	1.9	2.1	8.1	12.9	13.9	15.7	19.3	25.3	34.9	47.3	67.9	93.6	131.7	190.7	266.8	*1000	...	...	...	...
Female - Femmes	22.5	1.3	1.2	2.2	3.0	4.0	5.4	7.7	11.9	17.9	26.4	38.8	57.9	85.5	130.1	197.2	*1000	...	...	...	...

20. Probability of dying in the five year interval following specified age (5qx), by sex, latest available year: 1991 - 2010
Probabilité de décès dans l'intervalle de cinq ans qui suit un âge donné (5qx), par sexe, dernière année disponible : 1991 - 2010 (continued - suite)

Continent, country or area and date / Continent, pays ou zone et date	0	5	10	15	20	25	30	35	40	45	50	55	60	65	70	75	80	85	90	95	100
AMERICA, SOUTH - AMÉRIQUE DU SUD																					
Chile - Chili 2010																					
Male - Hommes	9.2	0.9	1.0	3.3	5.5	6.1	7.2	8.7	11.5	16.9	25.5	38.6	64.2	100.2	147.6	243.2	349.7	537.0	741.0	*1000	...
Female - Femmes	8.1	0.7	0.9	1.5	1.6	2.0	2.7	3.6	5.4	8.4	14.1	22.3	36.0	56.3	88.1	155.1	256.6	446.7	710.9	*1000	...
French Guiana - Guyane française 2007																					
Male - Hommes	16.3	1.5	2.1	4.9	7.7	8.1	10.0	14.0	17.2	29.4	16.0	32.3	52.4	79.5	135.5	261.3	306.7	474.0	733.7	...	...
Female - Femmes	15.1	1.9	1.3	1.4	1.2	3.0	4.6	4.2	11.9	11.0	10.4	11.6	26.7	85.4	77.4	203.8	253.1	321.1	434.3	...	...
Uruguay 2004																					
Male - Hommes	20.0	1.3	1.3	3.5	5.8	6.8	7.2	9.0	12.8	21.2	36.4	62.2	95.4	145.2	204.6	305.7	430.5	610.5	776.7	862.5	*1000
Female - Femmes	15.5	1.0	1.1	1.6	1.9	2.7	3.8	5.2	7.9	12.5	19.4	30.5	41.2	63.4	97.2	177.7	292.9	472.0	654.3	820.5	*1000
ASIA - ASIE																					
Armenia - Arménie 2006 - 2007																					
Male - Hommes	15.3	1.1	1.1	2.9	3.9	4.9	7.3	11.4	20.4	28.6	45.0	68.2	112.2	173.3	246.9	350.8	495.4	691.9	870.7	975.9	...
Female - Femmes	11.9	1.0	0.9	0.9	1.6	1.8	2.7	4.4	7.8	11.3	18.4	29.4	52.7	95.7	158.1	254.3	413.9	670.0	851.3	957.0	...
Azerbaijan - Azerbaïdjan 2009																					
Male - Hommes	15.0	2.2	1.9	3.2	4.3	5.1	8.1	10.7	15.8	26.3	42.5	67.3	105.5	157.4	241.3	370.6	517.8	459.7	412.0	350.2	...
Female - Femmes	13.9	2.0	1.4	1.6	2.1	2.9	3.5	4.7	7.6	11.5	20.7	33.9	56.6	92.6	174.4	299.7	429.2	466.6	593.4	602.8	...
China, Hong Kong SAR - Chine, Hong Kong RAS 2009																					
Male - Hommes	2.3	0.4	0.4	1.0	2.2	2.9	3.9	4.6	6.2	10.7	17.7	28.1	44.2	73.7	121.4	195.8	314.5	469.2	644.8	809.0	*1000
Female - Femmes	2.7	0.4	0.4	0.8	1.0	1.2	1.7	2.5	3.6	6.1	9.8	13.3	19.5	33.9	59.6	109.9	191.3	303.4	455.8	639.5	*1000
China, Macao SAR - Chine, Macao RAS 2002 - 2005																					
Male - Hommes	7.2	0.6	0.4	1.7	3.9	5.4	6.2	7.6	9.0	13.6	17.8	25.8	43.1	72.1	128.9	239.9	369.5	574.4	841.2	991.4	*1000
Female - Femmes	5.2	0.4	0.2	0.9	1.5	1.9	2.3	3.8	4.7	5.9	7.4	10.9	19.3	33.3	70.4	186.2	317.0	485.2	717.3	923.7	*1000
Israel - Israël[2] 2005 - 2009																					
Male - Hommes	5.2	0.7	0.7	2.2	3.7	3.2	3.8	5.2	7.8	12.3	19.7	31.4	49.7	78.8	125.2	199.6	315.0	478.1	668.3	831.7	*1000
Female - Femmes	4.2	0.6	0.5	0.8	1.2	1.2	1.7	2.7	4.4	7.1	11.2	17.8	28.7	47.9	82.9	146.8	259.0	435.9	663.7	872.1	*1000
Japan - Japon 2005																					
Male - Hommes	4.1	0.7	0.6	1.8	3.1	3.4	4.1	5.7	8.5	13.7	21.7	34.4	50.6	75.5	125.3	202.6	321.3	485.7	665.4	815.9	919.2
Female - Femmes	3.4	0.4	0.4	0.9	1.5	1.6	2.1	3.0	4.4	6.8	10.4	15.2	21.1	32.4	55.6	96.6	180.6	321.7	512.0	707.8	867.3
Kazakhstan 2005																					
Male - Hommes	21.2	2.9	3.3	7.8	17.2	27.1	34.1	41.8	55.6	75.9	105.2	141.1	191.0	256.5	329.2	413.6	513.6	662.0	795.9	896.1	...
Female - Femmes	16.8	1.9	1.9	3.3	5.3	7.5	10.5	13.3	17.9	26.0	38.8	58.0	83.8	125.4	194.3	297.4	433.3	608.9	783.7	914.7	...
Kyrgyzstan - Kirghizstan 2009																					
Male - Hommes	31.2	1.9	2.1	3.6	6.8	11.7	19.4	24.9	34.3	47.7	69.6	96.7	133.8	212.2	276.8	408.0	494.8	560.1	720.1	876.1	*1000
Female - Femmes	26.0	1.3	1.3	2.3	4.0	4.9	7.2	9.5	12.9	18.5	27.1	46.7	65.5	115.5	173.0	302.0	418.4	590.4	740.2	806.6	*1000
Qatar 2006																					
Male - Hommes	10.2	0.8	1.8	9.4	8.9	6.5	5.6	6.6	7.1	9.0	16.1	22.1	42.2	88.0	167.5	248.6	376.7	*1000	...	...	...
Female - Femmes	9.0	1.3	0.9	2.2	1.4	2.4	1.2	1.8	3.8	6.7	9.8	22.1	76.0	120.2	253.6	354.1	348.3	*1000	...	...	...
Republic of Korea - République de Corée 2009																					
Male - Hommes	4.6	0.8	0.8	2.0	2.9	3.8	4.7	6.7	11.1	17.6	27.0	37.4	55.2	87.7	143.6	232.4	370.6	531.0	685.9	808.8	*1000
Female - Femmes	4.3	0.5	0.6	1.1	1.9	2.7	3.1	3.7	4.7	6.6	9.3	13.3	20.6	35.2	66.1	128.5	238.0	399.5	581.1	743.2	*1000

Continent, country or area and date / Continent, pays ou zone et date	0	5	10	15	20	25	30	35	40	45	50	55	60	65	70	75	80	85	90	95	100
ASIA - ASIE																					
Singapore - Singapour[3] 2010																					
Male - Hommes	3.1	0.6	0.8	1.4	2.1	2.3	2.7	4.0	6.3	10.9	19.3	29.2	46.9	81.8	130.4	205.6	310.8	459.2	633.4	801.3	*1000
Female - Femmes	2.6	0.4	0.6	0.7	1.0	1.0	1.4	2.3	3.7	6.2	10.4	16.3	25.7	46.8	76.3	133.1	219.6	360.4	540.8	728.1	*1000
EUROPE																					
Austria - Autriche 2009																					
Male - Hommes	4.8	0.5	0.7	2.9	3.8	3.5	3.8	5.2	8.3	15.0	24.4	40.0	63.2	85.8	129.6	212.5	342.9	529.7	722.2	...	...
Female - Femmes	4.4	0.4	0.6	1.0	1.3	1.4	1.7	2.6	4.2	7.5	13.0	18.1	30.4	43.9	70.2	129.0	246.5	437.3	659.4	...	...
Belarus - Bélarus 2009																					
Male - Hommes	7.2	2.2	1.1	4.3	9.0	13.3	20.3	29.2	40.6	58.9	82.0	124.8	176.7	233.2	313.1	382.3	495.6	663.2	849.5	969.8	...
Female - Femmes	5.3	1.1	0.7	1.5	2.3	3.7	6.4	8.4	11.5	16.2	26.3	41.5	61.7	87.8	141.7	248.2	390.4	561.0	737.5	882.8	...
Belgium - Belgique 2006																					
Male - Hommes	4.4	0.6	0.7	2.6	4.6	4.4	5.6	7.1	10.7	17.3	27.2	42.4	65.1	93.3	149.7	248.7	387.2	570.9	751.3	886.0	...
Female - Femmes	3.9	0.5	0.6	1.3	1.1	1.8	2.4	3.8	5.8	10.2	16.3	22.5	33.8	48.2	79.3	149.1	270.8	466.0	663.7	835.2	...
Bulgaria - Bulgarie 2007 - 2009																					
Male - Hommes	11.0	1.7	1.6	3.7	5.4	6.6	7.6	11.0	18.6	33.6	55.8	85.5	119.8	163.3	238.4	333.4	486.0	625.1	790.6	814.3	...
Female - Femmes	9.4	1.1	1.2	1.8	1.9	2.4	3.4	5.3	8.2	13.8	21.8	32.5	47.2	78.0	142.7	245.5	415.2	584.5	759.0	834.8	...
Czech Republic - République tchèque 2009																					
Male - Hommes	3.8	0.5	1.0	2.2	3.8	4.0	5.0	7.3	11.5	19.8	35.1	57.2	90.1	129.6	183.7	274.6	415.4	599.8	794.8	937.5	...
Female - Femmes	3.3	0.5	0.5	1.0	1.6	1.3	2.1	3.1	5.6	9.6	15.3	24.5	39.6	62.0	102.0	184.8	329.5	556.3	812.9	969.0	...
Denmark - Danemark[4] 2008 - 2009																					
Male - Hommes	4.7	0.5	0.4	2.1	3.7	3.5	4.2	6.3	9.4	16.4	27.3	41.3	61.9	94.6	151.1	243.9	379.3	553.6	762.1	864.2	...
Female - Femmes	4.5	0.3	0.4	1.2	1.1	1.6	2.1	3.4	5.3	10.1	17.3	26.7	39.8	64.2	102.8	175.2	280.5	446.0	647.5	829.3	...
Estonia - Estonie 2008																					
Male - Hommes	6.9	1.4	1.4	4.4	9.0	11.0	13.6	15.8	24.3	40.6	65.7	97.1	133.5	180.4	246.1	331.6	437.6	555.7	678.0	790.8	...
Female - Femmes	5.2	0.2	1.1	2.0	2.5	2.5	3.3	4.2	7.2	13.2	21.5	32.1	47.2	64.8	106.7	191.1	316.7	492.7	693.6	863.7	...
Finland - Finlande 2009																					
Male - Hommes	3.0	0.4	0.5	3.1	4.8	5.2	6.8	8.0	11.7	19.9	28.6	42.2	64.0	94.3	137.9	219.0	349.4	535.2	710.2	876.4	...
Female - Femmes	3.2	0.3	0.6	1.2	1.6	1.8	2.2	3.0	5.4	8.7	12.9	20.1	28.6	41.6	67.4	120.0	235.5	423.3	634.2	820.4	...
France 2006 - 2008																					
Male - Hommes	4.9	0.5	0.6	2.3	4.0	4.3	5.0	7.2	11.4	19.2	30.8	42.8	58.5	81.7	122.2	194.3	313.2	486.4	689.3	849.6	...
Female - Femmes	3.9	0.4	0.4	0.9	1.3	1.5	2.1	3.6	5.7	9.4	13.8	18.4	25.5	36.1	58.0	103.0	192.0	353.0	572.5	778.4	...
Germany - Allemagne 2005 - 2007																					
Male - Hommes	5.1	0.6	0.6	2.1	3.1	3.2	3.7	5.3	9.4	16.7	27.3	40.9	61.1	92.1	146.9	234.0	360.4	525.1	719.7	853.6	...
Female - Femmes	4.2	0.4	0.5	1.0	1.1	1.2	1.8	2.8	5.0	9.0	14.1	21.1	30.8	45.5	79.3	143.8	263.8	445.4	670.9	826.6	...
Greece - Grèce 2009																					
Male - Hommes	4.2	0.6	0.9	2.7	5.1	5.6	5.7	5.9	9.6	15.4	23.5	36.6	55.1	79.2	128.1	211.0	339.9	483.0	628.9	780.6	...
Female - Femmes	3.9	0.6	0.5	0.9	1.4	1.7	2.0	2.8	4.1	6.7	10.4	15.4	22.2	36.9	70.6	147.5	299.8	472.0	623.7	777.8	...
Hungary - Hongrie 2009																					
Male - Hommes	6.2	0.7	0.9	2.5	3.6	4.1	5.9	10.1	20.5	40.0	67.6	97.3	129.0	168.6	228.2	320.6	442.3	640.9	868.2	986.5	...
Female - Femmes	5.8	0.5	0.7	1.2	1.2	1.3	2.4	4.5	9.2	17.3	27.1	39.2	54.0	76.9	120.9	206.6	335.9	563.0	840.3	985.8	...
Iceland - Islande 2007 - 2008																					
Male - Hommes	4.0	0.4	0.7	2.0	4.9	2.5	2.7	3.5	6.8	9.0	14.8	23.0	40.5	61.9	126.9	194.1	327.2	529.9	695.4	748.4	...
Female - Femmes	3.5	0.4	0.4	1.2	2.8	1.8	2.1	2.9	5.7	7.8	11.9	20.6	35.5	54.0	104.4	171.2	280.2	464.7	656.4	775.0	...
Ireland - Irlande 2002																					
Male - Hommes	7.8	0.6	0.9	3.5	5.4	5.6	5.4	6.4	9.1	14.0	23.7	39.0	65.6	108.8	177.1	286.9	443.0	615.6	772.1	889.6	...
Female - Femmes	6.1	0.5	0.7	1.4	1.7	1.6	2.1	3.9	5.6	9.0	15.3	23.0	38.0	61.5	106.2	184.5	322.4	495.8	670.3	817.0	...

20. Probability of dying in the five year interval following specified age (5qx), by sex, latest available year: 1991 - 2010
Probabilité de décès dans l'intervalle de cinq ans qui suit un âge donné (5qx), par sexe, dernière année disponible :
1991 - 2010 (continued - suite)

Continent, country or area and date / Continent, pays ou zone et date	0	5	10	15	20	25	30	35	40	45	50	55	60	65	70	75	80	85	90	95	100
EUROPE																					
Italy - Italie																					
2007																					
Male - Hommes	4.5	0.5	0.7	2.3	3.4	3.8	3.8	4.8	7.1	11.1	18.0	30.0	48.2	75.8	124.6	207.6	340.6	504.1	711.1	809.5	...
Female - Femmes	3.7	0.4	0.5	0.9	1.0	1.1	1.5	2.4	4.0	6.3	10.2	15.7	24.5	38.8	64.7	119.5	226.3	388.2	618.9	774.3	...
Latvia - Lettonie																					
2006																					
Male - Hommes	10.5	1.4	1.6	3.0	6.2	11.3	18.6	28.3	40.6	56.3	76.6	104.3	143.2	199.8	282.1	397.7	547.0	712.6	...	...	...
Female - Femmes	12.7	1.3	1.2	1.5	2.2	3.2	4.8	7.3	11.2	17.3	26.7	41.0	63.0	96.1	145.1	215.5	312.2	436.5	...	...	...
Lithuania - Lituanie																					
2009																					
Male - Hommes	7.0	1.1	1.7	5.9	8.6	10.5	16.3	22.7	31.5	46.3	68.6	100.1	148.2	188.0	232.3	323.1	460.1	621.6	793.4	923.2	*1000
Female - Femmes	5.0	0.5	0.9	1.5	2.1	2.2	4.4	6.3	10.2	15.2	22.7	34.2	49.6	68.6	108.8	188.3	329.2	532.1	771.2	905.6	*1000
Luxembourg																					
2005 - 2007																					
Male - Hommes	4.2	0.4	0.5	1.3	4.5	3.5	5.2	6.3	8.6	16.2	25.5	39.7	65.9	94.7	151.9	231.1	361.3	563.3	867.2	*1000	...
Female - Femmes	3.5	0.1	0.5	1.1	1.7	2.6	1.8	3.5	5.4	8.6	14.6	21.7	34.1	52.2	80.3	149.2	258.5	447.8	734.9	*1000	...
Netherlands - Pays-Bas																					
2009																					
Male - Hommes	4.8	0.5	0.6	1.4	2.3	2.4	3.0	4.1	6.6	10.7	18.7	30.3	49.9	79.1	132.1	225.2	363.5	539.8	738.0	...	...
Female - Femmes	4.1	0.4	0.5	0.8	1.0	1.3	1.7	2.9	5.0	8.9	15.0	21.5	32.5	47.8	76.4	136.1	249.6	428.5	644.7	...	...
Norway - Norvège[5]																					
2009																					
Male - Hommes	4.4	0.6	0.5	2.6	3.6	4.4	4.5	5.2	7.5	10.4	18.1	29.5	46.6	76.3	120.5	204.2	340.1	531.2	724.8	857.7	...
Female - Femmes	3.0	0.5	0.5	1.3	1.4	1.8	1.9	2.9	3.8	7.3	13.2	17.5	29.7	46.1	73.4	128.5	242.1	420.1	627.2	820.3	...
Poland - Pologne																					
2009																					
Male - Hommes	6.9	0.7	0.9	3.5	5.6	5.7	7.8	12.3	19.9	32.3	51.1	76.4	107.6	147.0	203.2	291.3	416.5	563.2	714.5	845.1	...
Female - Femmes	5.9	0.6	0.8	1.2	1.3	1.5	2.3	3.8	6.7	11.8	19.6	30.4	44.0	62.2	98.8	176.4	305.4	472.2	655.0	816.7	...
Portugal																					
2007 - 2009																					
Male - Hommes	4.5	0.7	0.8	2.3	3.7	4.1	5.9	8.6	13.7	21.0	31.3	40.1	59.5	88.9	141.2	232.8	398.8	691.4	890.0	977.7	...
Female - Femmes	3.9	0.5	0.8	1.0	1.4	1.5	2.3	3.8	5.7	8.8	12.2	17.7	25.1	41.9	74.2	140.0	281.2	567.5	819.5	957.9	...
Republic of Moldova - République de Moldova																					
1999																					
Male - Hommes	24.6	2.9	2.8	5.3	9.1	14.2	18.8	25.0	38.7	55.6	78.5	113.7	164.8	228.0	303.4	437.2	579.8	795.9	976.7	990.9	...
Female - Femmes	20.9	2.3	1.7	2.3	2.7	4.4	6.4	9.1	14.2	25.5	38.7	60.8	93.9	147.2	220.7	351.6	510.3	713.5	954.5	991.0	...
Romania - Roumanie																					
2007 - 2009																					
Male - Hommes	14.9	1.6	1.8	3.8	4.9	5.2	7.5	12.2	21.9	38.2	61.1	84.8	115.4	160.0	226.9	316.6	453.9	616.6	769.9	887.7	...
Female - Femmes	11.6	1.2	1.1	2.0	1.7	1.9	3.0	4.6	8.6	14.8	22.7	34.9	52.3	80.0	135.8	233.0	386.9	569.9	741.4	873.5	...
Russian Federation - Fédération de Russie																					
2009																					
Male - Hommes	11.4	1.8	2.1	6.4	13.2	22.9	33.5	37.7	47.8	65.2	92.8	127.0	177.5	222.3	302.4	393.2	500.0	575.3	723.9	692.5	*1000
Female - Femmes	8.9	1.3	1.4	3.0	4.0	6.6	9.5	11.9	15.6	21.0	30.4	45.8	65.4	93.3	155.6	251.1	398.9	568.8	761.2	851.0	*1000
Serbia - Serbie																					
2001 - 2003																					
Male - Hommes	13.7	1.2	1.5	3.1	5.0	5.9	6.8	9.8	17.3	31.7	53.4	83.0	115.8	173.6	258.6	378.2	514.5	674.0	800.7	884.7	*1000
Female - Femmes	9.9	0.8	0.8	1.5	1.7	2.2	3.4	5.4	9.3	17.0	26.0	39.6	64.1	107.2	187.2	310.3	479.8	648.8	805.4	867.7	*1000
Slovakia - Slovaquie																					
2009																					
Male - Hommes	8.4	1.0	1.0	2.4	4.4	5.0	5.5	9.6	17.9	28.5	49.9	75.0	112.7	154.9	221.7	321.7	466.4	644.6	822.2	945.4	...
Female - Femmes	6.1	0.6	1.0	1.1	1.0	1.6	2.0	3.6	6.5	11.6	18.8	29.7	44.7	66.6	119.9	207.4	364.2	593.0	835.6	973.9	...
Slovenia - Slovénie																					
2007																					
Male - Hommes	3.7	0.5	0.5	3.0	5.9	5.8	6.1	7.8	12.5	21.3	34.4	52.1	77.3	113.4	175.4	270.7	390.9	556.2	764.3	884.6	...
Female - Femmes	3.9	0.7	1.0	1.4	1.6	1.3	1.7	2.5	4.7	9.2	15.1	21.6	31.2	48.6	86.3	152.0	280.7	460.4	656.7	830.3	...
Spain - Espagne																					
2009																					
Male - Hommes	4.2	0.5	0.7	1.7	2.2	2.8	3.3	4.9	8.5	14.5	23.2	35.4	52.9	79.9	120.9	202.0	324.7	492.9	669.1	783.0	...
Female - Femmes	3.6	0.4	0.4	0.8	1.0	1.1	1.5	2.5	4.3	7.2	10.5	14.0	20.3	31.7	56.1	108.4	216.9	397.9	609.4	779.3	...

20. Probability of dying in the five year interval following specified age (5qx), by sex, latest available year: 1991 - 2010
Probabilité de décès dans l'intervalle de cinq ans qui suit un âge donné (5qx), par sexe, dernière année disponible · 1991 - 2010 (continued - suite)

Continent, country or area and date / Continent, pays ou zone et date	0	5	10	15	20	25	30	35	40	45	50	55	60	65	70	75	80	85	90	95	100
EUROPE																					
Sweden - Suède 2009																					
Male - Hommes	3.5	0.5	0.7	1.6	3.4	3.4	3.3	4.4	6.1	9.8	17.4	27.4	43.1	69.8	115.0	195.4	330.7	526.5	719.9	856.1	...
Female - Femmes	3.0	0.4	0.4	1.0	1.1	1.2	1.4	2.5	4.0	6.8	11.8	17.7	29.0	45.3	76.1	125.2	231.8	416.9	624.8	788.1	...
Switzerland - Suisse 2009																					
Male - Hommes	5.3	0.4	0.5	1.8	3.4	2.9	3.3	4.4	6.4	10.4	17.5	27.9	42.7	66.1	106.9	181.9	309.9	491.2	679.1	740.1	...
Female - Femmes	4.4	0.3	0.4	0.8	1.1	1.1	1.4	2.1	3.4	6.0	10.5	16.5	24.4	37.4	61.7	109.5	206.4	389.2	620.9	739.1	...
TFYR of Macedonia - L'ex-R. y. de Macédoine 2008																					
Male - Hommes	13.2	0.9	0.8	2.3	3.8	4.0	5.0	6.2	11.2	21.3	37.1	61.0	92.4	146.4	227.5	351.3	497.9	711.4	839.2	...	...
Female - Femmes	10.9	0.7	0.5	1.2	1.3	1.6	2.0	4.1	6.0	11.9	20.6	33.3	51.4	94.2	165.5	293.9	477.6	672.1	745.0	...	...
Ukraine 2007 - 2008																					
Male - Hommes	14.8	2.0	1.8	4.8	10.6	18.8	31.3	40.6	56.0	73.6	100.0	129.2	170.8	220.1	290.8	384.1	501.4	617.9	771.2	899.1	...
Female - Femmes	11.6	1.4	1.1	2.1	3.2	5.8	9.8	13.1	16.8	22.0	31.0	46.4	65.4	98.4	161.7	257.2	406.1	579.9	755.4	894.1	...
United Kingdom of Great Britain and Northern Ireland - Royaume-Uni de Grande-Bretagne et d'Irlande du Nord[6] 2006 - 2008																					
Male - Hommes	6.3	0.6	0.7	2.4	3.5	4.1	5.3	6.9	9.4	14.1	22.4	34.4	54.8	86.9	136.5	222.9	353.3	502.9	684.7	836.1	...
Female - Femmes	5.2	0.4	0.5	1.1	1.3	1.7	2.4	3.7	5.8	9.2	14.7	22.1	34.9	55.1	90.9	155.8	265.4	419.9	627.3	801.1	...
OCEANIA - OCÉANIE																					
Australia - Australie 2007 - 2009																					
Male - Hommes	5.8	0.5	0.6	2.3	3.5	4.2	5.1	6.2	8.1	11.9	17.9	26.5	41.8	67.9	109.4	184.8	308.5	475.4	666.6	793.4	...
Female - Femmes	4.7	0.4	0.5	1.1	1.3	1.7	2.2	3.1	4.7	7.4	10.9	16.0	25.2	40.1	66.2	116.6	216.5	378.7	597.9	758.8	...
New Zealand - Nouvelle-Zélande 2005 - 2007																					
Male - Hommes	6.9	0.7	1.0	3.6	5.3	4.9	4.9	6.4	8.8	12.4	19.0	30.0	47.8	76.8	125.4	204.1	324.1	512.1	694.0	841.5	...
Female - Femmes	5.6	0.6	0.7	1.9	1.9	1.6	2.7	3.8	5.9	8.7	13.2	20.5	32.2	51.1	83.5	137.4	238.4	409.6	628.6	813.6	...

FOOTNOTES - NOTES

* Open-ended group (e.g. 80+). - Groupe d'âge ouvert (par exemple, 80 ans et plus).

[1] Excluding Indian jungle population. - Non compris les Indiens de la jungle.

[2] Including data for East Jerusalem and Israeli residents in certain other territories under occupation by Israeli military forces since June 1967. - Y compris les données pour Jérusalem-Est et les résidents israéliens dans certains autres territoires occupés depuis 1967 par les forces armées israéliennes.

[3] Data refer to resident population only. - Pour la population résidante seulement.

[4] Excluding Faeroe Islands and Greenland shown separately, if available. - Non compris les Iles Féroé et le Groenland, qui font l'objet de rubriques distinctes, si disponible.

[5] Excluding Svalbard and Jan Mayen Islands shown separately, if available. - Non compris Svalbard et Jan Mayen qui font l'objet de rubriques distinctes, si disponible.

[6] Excluding Channel Islands (Guernsey and Jersey) and Isle of Man, shown separately, if available. - Non compris les îles Anglo-Normandes (Guernesey et Jersey) et l'île de Man, qui font l'objet de rubriques distinctes, si disponible.

Table 21

Table 21 presents life expectancy at specified ages for each sex for the latest available year between 1991 and 2010.

Description of variables: Life expectancy at age x, e_x is defined as the average number of years of life remaining to persons who have reached age *x* if they continue to be subject to the mortality conditions of the period indicated in the life table.

Male and female life expectancy values are shown separately at selected ages beginning at birth and proceeding at every fifth age thereafter up to age 100.

The table shows life expectancy derived from a complete or abridged life table as reported by the country or area.

Data are shown with one decimal regardless of the number of digits provided in the original computation.

The life table is a statistical device for summarizing the mortality experience of a population, from which the probability of dying, survivorship and expectation of life can be calculated. It is based on the assumption that the theoretical cohort is subject, throughout its existence, to the age-specific mortality rates observed at a particular time. Thus, levels of mortality prevailing at the time a life table is constructed are assumed to remain unchanged into the future until all members of the cohort have died.

Reliability of data: The values shown in this table come from official life tables. It is assumed that, if necessary, the basic data (population and deaths classified by age and sex) have been adjusted for deficiencies before their use in constructing the life tables.

Limitations: Life expectancy values are subject to the same qualifications as have been set forth for population statistics in general and death statistics in particular, as discussed in sections 3 and 4, respectively, of the Technical Notes. They must be interpreted strictly using the underlying assumption that surviving cohorts are subjected to the same age-specific mortality rates of the period to which the life table refers.

Earlier data: Life expectancy values at specified ages for each sex have been shown in previous issues of the *Demographic Yearbook*. For information on specific years covered, the reader should consult the Historical Index.

Tableau 21

Le tableau 21 présente les espérances de vie à des âges déterminés, pour chaque sexe, pour la dernière année disponible entre 1991 et 2010.

Description des variables : L'espérance de vie à l'âge x, e_x, se définit comme le nombre moyen d'années restant à vivre aux hommes et aux femmes qui ont atteint l'âge x, à supposer qu'ils continuent de connaître les mêmes conditions de mortalité observées pendant la période sur laquelle porte la table de mortalité.

Les chiffres sont présentés séparément pour chaque sexe à partir de la naissance et puis tous les cinq ans jusqu'à 100 ans.

Dans le tableau figurent les espérances de vie calculées selon les tables de mortalité complètes ou abrégées communiquées par les pays et les zones.

Les données sont arrondies à la première décimale, indépendamment du nombre de décimales qui figurent dans le calcul initial.

La table de mortalité est un moyen statistique que s'utilise pour donner un aperçu complet de la mortalité d'une population incluant les probabilités de décès et l'espérance de vie à chaque âge. Les tables de mortalité reposent sur l'hypothèse que chaque cohorte théoriquement distinguée connaît, pendant toute son existence, les taux de mortalité par âge observé à un moment donné. Les taux de mortalité correspondant à l'époque à laquelle sont calculées les tables de mortalité sont ainsi censés demeurer inchangées dans l'avenir jusqu'au décès de tous les membres de la cohorte.

Fiabilité des donnés : Les chiffres figurant dans ce tableau proviennent de tables officielles de mortalité. En ce qui concerne les chiffres extraits de tables officielles de mortalité, on part du principe que les données de base (effectif de la population et nombre de décès selon l'âge et le sexe) ont été ajustées, en tant que de besoin, avant de servir à l'établissement de la table de mortalité.

Insuffisance des données : les espérances de vie appellent les mêmes réserves que celles qui ont été formulées à propos des statistiques de la population en général et des statistiques de mortalité en particulier (voir les sections 3 et 4 des Notes techniques). Lorsque l'on interprète les données, il ne faut jamais perdre de vue que, par hypothèse, les cohortes de survivants sont soumises, pour chaque âge, aux conditions de mortalité de la période visée par la table de mortalité.

Données publiées antérieurement : les espérances de vie à des âges déterminés pour chaque sexe figuraient déjà dans des éditions antérieures de l'*Annuaire démographique*. Pour plus de précisions concernant les années pour lesquelles ces données ont été publiées, se reporter à l'index historique.

21. Life expectancy at specified ages for each sex: latest available year, 1991 - 2010
Espérance de vie à un âge donné pour chaque sexe : dernière année disponible, 1991 - 2010

Continent, country or area and date / Continent, pays ou zone et date	0	5	10	15	20	25	30	35	40	45	50	55	60	65	70	75	80	85	90	95	100
AFRICA - AFRIQUE																					
Algeria - Algérie[1]																					
2002																					
Male - Hommes	72.5	70.6	65.8	61.0	56.3	51.6	46.9	42.2	37.6	33.0	28.5	24.1	19.9	16.1	12.4	9.0	5.9	...	...	...	...
Female - Femmes	74.2	72.1	67.3	62.5	57.7	52.9	48.1	43.3	38.6	34.0	29.5	25.1	20.7	16.6	12.8	9.3	6.1	...	...	...	...
2008																					
Male - Hommes	74.9	...	...	...	...	...	...	...	...	...	...	...	...	...	...	...	...	...	...	...	...
Female - Femmes	76.6	...	...	...	...	...	...	...	...	...	...	...	...	...	...	...	...	...	...	...	...
Benin - Bénin[2]																					
2002																					
Male - Hommes	57.2	63.4	59.1	54.7	50.2	45.9	41.8	37.8	33.8	30.0	26.2	22.7	19.4	16.2	13.2	10.6	8.1	5.5	3.8	...	...
Female - Femmes	61.3	65.4	61.2	56.7	52.3	48.1	43.9	39.9	36.0	32.1	28.3	24.6	21.2	18.0	14.2	10.8	7.7	4.8	2.9	...	...
Botswana[3]																					
2006																					
Male - Hommes	54.0	57.6	54.0	49.7	45.6	41.8	37.9	34.0	30.0	26.2	22.4	19.9	15.4	12.3	9.4	7.0	4.8	...	...	...	...
Female - Femmes	66.0	65.7	61.4	56.8	52.3	47.8	43.4	39.1	34.7	30.4	26.2	22.1	18.2	14.5	11.2	8.3	5.8	...	...	...	...
Burkina Faso[4]																					
2006																					
Male - Hommes	55.8	60.0	55.9	51.3	46.9	42.8	38.6	34.5	30.5	26.6	22.8	19.3	16.0	12.9	10.3	8.1	6.2	4.8	...	...	...
Female - Femmes	57.5	61.6	57.6	53.1	48.6	44.4	40.2	36.1	32.0	28.0	24.1	20.3	16.8	13.5	10.7	8.4	6.4	4.9	...	...	...
Côte d'Ivoire[5]																					
1998																					
Male - Hommes	49.2	...	...	...	...	...	...	...	...	...	...	...	...	...	...	...	...	...	...	...	...
Female - Femmes	52.7	...	...	...	...	...	...	...	...	...	...	...	...	...	...	...	...	...	...	...	...
Djibouti																					
1998																					
Male - Hommes	49.0	...	...	...	...	...	...	...	...	...	...	...	...	...	...	...	...	...	...	...	...
Female - Femmes	52.0	...	...	...	...	...	...	...	...	...	...	...	...	...	...	...	...	...	...	...	...
Egypt - Égypte																					
2001																					
Male - Hommes	65.6	64.7	59.9	55.1	50.4	45.6	40.9	36.2	31.6	27.2	22.9	18.9	15.4	12.1	9.2	6.8	5.2	4.0	...	...	...
Female - Femmes	67.4	66.8	62.0	57.2	52.3	47.5	42.7	37.9	33.1	28.4	23.9	19.5	15.5	11.7	8.6	5.7	4.0	2.8	...	...	...
2010																					
Male - Hommes	68.2	...	...	...	...	...	...	...	...	...	...	...	...	...	...	...	...	...	...	...	...
Female - Femmes	70.9	...	...	...	...	...	...	...	...	...	...	...	...	...	...	...	...	...	...	...	...
Ethiopia - Éthiopie																					
1994																					
Male - Hommes	49.8	55.2	51.2	46.8	42.7	38.9	35.0	31.1	27.4	23.7	20.2	16.9	13.8	11.0	8.6	6.5	5.0	...	...	...	...
Female - Femmes	51.8	56.9	53.0	48.8	44.8	40.9	37.1	33.4	29.6	25.9	22.1	18.6	15.2	12.1	9.4	7.1	5.4	...	...	...	...
Ghana																					
2005																					
Male - Hommes	58.3	...	...	...	...	...	...	...	...	...	...	...	...	...	...	...	...	...	...	...	...
Female - Femmes	62.0	...	...	...	...	...	...	...	...	...	...	...	...	...	...	...	...	...	...	...	...
Guinea-Bissau - Guinée-Bissau																					
2006																					
Male - Hommes	43.4	...	...	...	...	...	...	...	...	...	...	...	...	...	...	...	...	...	...	...	...
Female - Femmes	46.2	...	...	...	...	...	...	...	...	...	...	...	...	...	...	...	...	...	...	...	...
Kenya																					
1989 - 1999																					
Male - Hommes	52.9	54.8	51.1	46.6	42.3	38.3	34.5	31.0	27.7	24.4	21.0	17.7	14.5	11.6	8.9	6.7	5.0	3.8	3.1	2.5	...
Female - Femmes	60.4	63.0	59.0	54.3	49.9	45.9	42.2	38.6	34.8	30.9	27.0	23.1	19.3	15.6	12.2	9.2	6.7	4.8	3.6	2.5	...
Lesotho																					
2001																					
Male - Hommes	48.7	...	...	...	...	...	...	...	...	...	...	...	...	...	...	...	...	...	...	...	...
Female - Femmes	56.3	...	...	...	...	...	...	...	...	...	...	...	...	...	...	...	...	...	...	...	...
Madagascar																					
1993																					
Male - Hommes	51.3	56.1	52.7	48.8	44.9	41.0	37.2	33.3	29.6	26.0	22.6	19.2	16.1	13.0	10.3	7.6	4.6	...	...	...	...
Female - Femmes	53.2	58.1	54.6	50.5	46.7	43.0	39.4	35.8	32.3	28.7	25.2	21.6	18.1	14.7	11.9	9.0	5.8	...	...	...	...
Malawi																					
1992 - 1997																					
Male - Hommes	43.5	52.1	49.5	45.7	41.9	38.4	34.8	31.2	27.6	24.0	20.6	17.3	14.1	11.2	8.6	6.3	4.4	...	...	...	...
Female - Femmes	46.8	54.5	52.0	48.2	44.4	40.6	36.9	33.2	29.6	25.9	22.2	18.6	15.1	11.9	9.2	6.8	4.6	...	...	...	...
2007[6]																					
Male - Hommes	45.7	...	...	...	...	...	...	...	...	...	...	...	...	...	...	...	...	...	...	...	...
Female - Femmes	48.3	...	...	...	...	...	...	...	...	...	...	...	...	...	...	...	...	...	...	...	...

21. Life expectancy at specified ages for each sex: latest available year, 1991 - 2010
Espérance de vie à un âge donné pour chaque sexe : dernière année disponible, 1991 - 2010 (continued - suite)

Continent, country or area and date / Continent, pays ou zone et date	Age (in years) - Age (en années)																				
	0	5	10	15	20	25	30	35	40	45	50	55	60	65	70	75	80	85	90	95	100
AFRICA - AFRIQUE																					
Mauritius - Maurice[7]																					
2007 - 2009																					
Male - Hommes	69.4	65.6	60.7	55.7	50.9	46.2	41.5	36.9	32.5	28.2	24.2	20.5	16.9	13.8	11.0	8.5	6.6	4.7	...	...	...
Female - Femmes	76.6	72.6	67.7	62.8	57.9	53.0	48.1	43.3	38.6	34.0	29.4	25.1	21.0	17.3	13.9	10.7	8.0	5.8	...	...	...
Namibia - Namibie																					
2001																					
Male - Hommes	47.6	54.0	50.1	45.8	41.7	38.0	34.2	30.5	26.8	23.2	19.8	16.6	13.5	10.8	8.4	6.4	4.9	...	...	...	...
Female - Femmes	50.2	56.1	52.2	48.1	44.1	40.3	36.6	32.9	29.2	25.5	21.8	18.3	14.9	12.0	9.3	7.0	5.3	...	...	...	...
Réunion																					
2006																					
Male - Hommes	73.2	...	...	...	54.0	...	...	...	35.5	...	...	...	19.0	...	...	9.3	...	...	...	...	...
Female - Femmes	80.9	...	...	...	61.6	...	...	...	42.1	...	...	...	23.9	...	...	12.2	...	...	...	...	...
Rwanda																					
2002																					
Male - Hommes	48.4	58.4	54.4	49.9	45.6	41.6	37.5	33.5	29.4	25.4	21.6	17.9	14.5	11.4	8.6	6.3	4.6	...	...	...	...
Female - Femmes	53.8	63.1	58.8	54.3	49.9	45.7	41.4	37.2	32.9	28.7	24.5	20.4	16.5	12.9	9.8	7.1	5.1	...	...	...	...
2009																					
Male - Hommes	49.4	...	...	...	...	...	...	...	...	...	...	...	...	...	...	...	...	...	...	...	...
Female - Femmes	53.3	...	...	...	...	...	...	...	...	...	...	...	...	...	...	...	...	...	...	...	...
Saint Helena ex. dep. - Sainte-Hélène sans dép.																					
2000 - 2009																					
Male - Hommes	72.5	68.7	64.2	...	54.4	...	44.9	...	35.9	...	27.4	...	19.5	...	12.3	...	6.6	...	...	...	...
Female - Femmes	79.2	74.7	69.7	...	60.0	...	50.9	...	41.5	...	32.0	...	23.5	...	16.0	...	9.7	...	...	...	...
Sao Tome and Principe - Sao Tomé-et-Principe																					
2001																					
Male - Hommes	61.3	63.1	59.2	55.0	50.5	46.1	41.5	37.5	33.5	29.8	25.5	22.2	18.3	15.1	13.1	10.6	8.4	6.5	...	...	...
Female - Femmes	66.5	68.1	64.1	59.8	55.2	50.8	46.1	41.6	37.5	33.0	28.6	25.0	21.1	17.3	14.4	12.0	9.5	8.1	...	...	...
Seychelles																					
2007																					
Male - Hommes	68.9	65.0	60.2	55.3	50.5	45.9	41.6	37.0	32.7	28.7	24.4	20.9	17.1	14.1	11.0	9.0	7.4	...	...	...	...
Female - Femmes	77.7	73.3	68.5	63.5	58.5	53.7	48.9	44.3	39.5	35.3	31.0	26.4	22.2	18.5	15.1	12.1	9.2	...	...	...	...
2008																					
Male - Hommes	68.4	...	...	...	...	...	...	...	...	...	...	...	...	...	...	...	...	...	...	...	...
Female - Femmes	78.0	...	...	...	...	...	...	...	...	...	...	...	...	...	...	...	...	...	...	...	...
Sierra Leone																					
2004																					
Male - Hommes	47.5	...	...	...	...	...	...	...	...	...	...	...	...	...	...	...	...	...	...	...	...
Female - Femmes	49.4	...	...	...	...	...	...	...	...	...	...	...	...	...	...	...	...	...	...	...	...
South Africa - Afrique du Sud																					
2009																					
Male - Hommes	53.5	...	...	...	...	...	...	...	...	...	...	...	...	...	...	...	...	...	...	...	...
Female - Femmes	57.2	...	...	...	...	...	...	...	...	...	...	...	...	...	...	...	...	...	...	...	...
Sudan - Soudan																					
1993																					
Male - Hommes	52.5	...	...	...	...	...	...	...	...	...	...	...	...	...	...	...	...	...	...	...	...
Female - Femmes	55.5	...	...	...	...	...	...	...	...	...	...	...	...	...	...	...	...	...	...	...	...
Swaziland[5]																					
2007																					
Male - Hommes	42.2	...	...	...	...	...	...	...	...	...	...	...	...	...	...	...	...	...	...	...	...
Female - Femmes	43.1	...	...	...	...	...	...	...	...	...	...	...	...	...	...	...	...	...	...	...	...
Tunisia - Tunisie																					
1995																					
Male - Hommes	69.6	67.5	62.7	57.9	53.1	48.4	43.8	39.2	34.6	30.1	25.8	21.6	17.7	14.1	10.8	7.9	5.2	3.5	...	...	...
Female - Femmes	73.1	70.7	65.9	61.0	56.2	51.3	46.5	41.7	37.0	32.4	27.8	23.3	19.1	15.0	11.3	7.8	4.8	2.9	...	...	...
2007																					
Male - Hommes	72.3	...	...	...	...	...	...	...	...	...	...	...	...	...	...	...	...	...	...	...	...
Female - Femmes	76.2	...	...	...	...	...	...	...	...	...	...	...	...	...	...	...	...	...	...	...	...
Zimbabwe																					
2001 - 2002																					
Male - Hommes	45.8	44.2	40.0	35.4	30.9	26.8	23.8	22.1	21.8	21.3	20.4	19.2	17.7	15.7	13.7	11.4	9.5	7.5	6.2	5.2	...
Female - Femmes	50.3	48.6	44.2	39.7	35.3	32.1	30.4	30.1	30.2	29.0	27.6	25.3	22.9	20.2	17.6	14.8	12.2	9.9	8.1	7.3	...

21. Life expectancy at specified ages for each sex: latest available year, 1991 - 2010
Espérance de vie à un âge donné pour chaque sexe : dernière année disponible, 1991 - 2010 (continued - suite)

Continent, country or area and date / Continent, pays ou zone et date	Age (in years) - Age (en années)																				
	0	5	10	15	20	25	30	35	40	45	50	55	60	65	70	75	80	85	90	95	100
AMERICA, NORTH - AMÉRIQUE DU NORD																					
Anguilla																					
2000 - 2002																					
Male - Hommes	76.5	72.1	67.1	62.1	57.3	53.1	48.4	43.7	39.4	34.7	30.2	25.4	21.1	16.5	12.7	10.0	8.0	6.9	...	...	...
Female - Femmes	81.1	76.4	71.4	66.4	61.4	57.1	52.7	47.7	42.7	38.3	33.5	28.7	24.0	19.4	15.3	10.8	8.3	7.6	...	...	...
Aruba																					
2000																					
Male - Hommes	70.0	65.4	60.5	55.6	50.9	46.7	42.3	37.7	33.0	28.5	24.2	20.1	16.3	13.1	10.4	8.1	5.7	3.9	4.0	3.2	...
Female - Femmes	76.0	71.9	67.0	62.0	57.2	52.5	47.7	43.0	38.3	33.6	28.9	24.4	20.5	16.7	13.1	10.4	7.5	5.5	4.7	3.6	...
Bahamas																					
1989 - 1991																					
Male - Hommes	68.3	64.8	60.0	55.1	50.3	45.9	41.5	37.1	33.1	29.1	25.1	21.6	18.2	15.0	12.3	9.8	7.5	5.6	...	...	...
Female - Femmes	75.3	71.5	66.6	61.6	56.8	52.0	47.3	42.8	38.3	33.9	29.7	25.6	21.6	17.9	14.5	11.3	8.8	6.6	...	...	...
1999 - 2001																					
Male - Hommes	69.9	...	...	...	...	...	...	...	...	...	...	...	...	...	...	...	...	...	...	...	...
Female - Femmes	76.4	...	...	...	...	...	...	...	...	...	...	...	...	...	...	...	...	...	...	...	...
Belize																					
1991																					
Male - Hommes	70.0	67.9	63.0	58.2	53.4	48.8	44.5	40.1	35.3	30.8	26.7	22.6	18.9	15.2	12.2	9.4	6.3	...	...	...	...
Female - Femmes	74.1	72.0	67.1	62.3	57.4	52.5	47.7	43.0	38.4	34.4	29.8	25.5	21.5	17.3	13.8	10.3	7.0	...	...	...	...
Bermuda - Bermudes																					
2010																					
Male - Hommes	76.9	72.1	67.1	62.1	57.3	52.3	47.5	42.8	37.9	33.1	28.5	24.1	20.0	16.1	12.7	9.5	7.1	5.2	...	...	...
Female - Femmes	82.3	77.5	72.5	67.5	62.5	57.5	52.6	47.7	42.8	38.1	33.4	28.8	24.3	20.1	16.0	12.3	9.0	6.3	...	...	...
British Virgin Islands - Îles Vierges britanniques																					
2004																					
Male - Hommes	69.9	...	...	...	...	...	...	...	...	...	...	...	...	...	...	...	...	...	...	...	...
Female - Femmes	78.5	...	...	...	...	...	...	...	...	...	...	...	...	...	...	...	...	...	...	...	...
Canada																					
2005 - 2007																					
Male - Hommes	78.3	73.8	68.8	63.9	59.1	54.3	49.5	44.7	40.0	35.3	30.7	26.3	22.1	18.1	14.5	11.2	8.4	6.1	4.4	...	...
Female - Femmes	83.0	78.4	73.4	68.5	63.6	58.7	53.8	48.9	44.0	39.2	34.6	30.0	25.5	21.3	17.3	13.6	10.3	7.4	5.3	...	...
Cayman Islands - Îles Caïmanes[8]																					
2006																					
Male - Hommes	76.3	72.1	67.1	62.1	57.7	53.3	48.9	44.0	39.3	34.5	29.8	25.3	20.8	17.1	13.6	10.2	8.2	6.4	3.3	5.3	2.5
Female - Femmes	83.8	79.8	74.8	69.8	65.1	60.1	55.2	50.2	45.3	40.4	35.7	30.9	26.1	21.9	17.5	13.9	10.4	6.9	7.0	3.1	2.5
Costa Rica																					
2010																					
Male - Hommes	76.8	72.8	67.8	62.9	58.2	53.5	48.8	44.2	39.5	34.9	30.5	26.2	22.0	18.1	14.5	11.2	8.5	6.3	4.5	3.2	11.6
Female - Femmes	81.8	77.6	72.7	67.7	62.8	57.9	53.0	48.2	43.4	38.6	33.9	29.3	24.9	20.6	16.7	13.0	9.8	7.1	5.1	3.5	5.7
Cuba																					
2005 - 2007																					
Male - Hommes	76.0	71.6	66.7	61.8	56.9	52.1	47.4	42.6	37.9	33.4	29.0	24.8	20.8	17.1	13.7	10.8	8.2	6.2	4.7	3.6	1.8
Female - Femmes	80.0	75.5	70.6	65.6	60.7	55.8	51.0	46.1	41.3	36.6	32.0	27.6	23.4	19.3	15.6	12.3	9.3	6.9	5.1	3.7	1.9
Dominica - Dominique																					
2008																					
Male - Hommes	73.8	...	...	...	...	...	...	...	...	...	...	...	...	...	...	...	...	...	...	...	...
Female - Femmes	78.2	...	...	...	...	...	...	...	...	...	...	...	...	...	...	...	...	...	...	...	...
Dominican Republic - République dominicaine[6]																					
2005 - 2010																					
Male - Hommes	69.2	66.8	62.0	57.2	52.6	48.3	44.1	39.9	35.7	31.6	27.6	23.7	20.1	16.8	13.9	11.3	9.3	...	...	...	...
Female - Femmes	75.5	72.6	67.8	62.9	58.1	53.3	48.7	44.2	39.6	35.2	30.9	26.7	22.7	19.0	15.6	12.7	10.3	...	...	...	...
El Salvador[9]																					
2000 - 2005																					
Male - Hommes	67.7	65.3	60.6	55.8	51.2	46.8	42.5	38.4	34.2	30.2	26.2	22.4	18.7	15.2	12.0	9.1	6.8	...	...	...	...
Female - Femmes	73.7	71.1	66.3	61.5	56.8	52.2	47.6	43.1	38.6	34.2	29.9	25.7	21.7	17.9	14.4	11.1	8.4	...	...	...	...
Greenland - Groenland																					
2004 - 2008																					
Male - Hommes	66.6	62.7	57.9	53.1	49.1	45.2	40.9	36.4	32.1	27.8	23.4	19.1	15.3	11.8	8.9	6.9	5.0	3.3	4.2	...	...
Female - Femmes	71.6	67.4	62.5	57.8	53.2	48.5	43.7	39.2	34.5	29.9	25.5	21.3	17.6	13.9	10.8	8.8	6.5	4.8	4.3	...	...

21. Life expectancy at specified ages for each sex: latest available year, 1991 - 2010
Espérance de vie à un âge donné pour chaque sexe : dernière année disponible, 1991 - 2010 (continued - suite)

Continent, country or area and date / Continent, pays ou zone et date	Age (in years) - Age (en années)																				
	0	5	10	15	20	25	30	35	40	45	50	55	60	65	70	75	80	85	90	95	100
AMERICA, NORTH - AMÉRIQUE DU NORD																					
Guadeloupe 2002																					
Male - Hommes	74.6	70.2	65.3	60.5	55.7	51.2	46.8	42.2	37.7	33.2	29.0	24.8	20.9	17.3	13.8	10.6	7.9	5.1	2.0	0.5	...
Female - Femmes	81.5	77.0	72.1	67.1	62.1	57.3	52.4	47.6	42.9	38.2	33.5	28.8	24.4	20.3	16.4	12.7	9.0	5.7	2.3	0.5	...
Guatemala 1995 - 2000																					
Male - Hommes	61.4	60.6	56.0	51.2	46.8	42.7	38.8	34.9	31.2	27.4	23.7	20.1	16.8	13.6	10.7	8.2	6.1	...	...	...	...
Female - Femmes	67.2	66.2	62.6	56.9	52.3	47.7	43.3	38.9	34.6	30.4	26.3	22.3	18.6	15.2	12.0	9.2	6.9	...	...	...	...
Jamaica - Jamaïque 2006																					
Male - Hommes	69.7	67.0	62.2	57.3	52.6	47.9	43.2	38.5	33.8	29.3	24.9	20.8	16.9	13.5	10.4	7.8	5.8	4.1	2.9	2.1	1.5
Female - Femmes	75.2	71.6	66.7	61.7	56.8	52.0	47.1	42.3	37.6	32.9	28.3	23.9	19.7	15.9	12.4	9.4	6.9	5.0	3.5	2.4	1.7
Martinique 2007																					
Male - Hommes	76.5	72.4	67.5	62.6	57.8	53.3	48.7	44.1	39.5	34.9	30.3	26.1	21.8	17.6	14.1	10.7	7.7	5.2	3.7	1.8	...
Female - Femmes	82.9	78.5	73.6	68.6	63.7	58.8	54.0	49.2	44.4	39.6	34.8	30.1	25.6	21.2	17.1	13.4	10.0	7.1	4.6	1.9	...
Mexico - Mexique 2008																					
Male - Hommes	72.8	69.2	64.3	59.4	54.7	50.0	45.5	40.9	36.5	32.1	27.9	23.9	20.2	16.8	13.7	11.0	8.7	6.6	4.9	3.5	2.6
Female - Femmes	77.5	73.8	68.9	63.9	59.0	54.2	49.3	44.5	39.7	35.1	30.6	26.2	22.1	18.3	14.8	11.7	9.0	6.8	4.9	3.5	2.6
Netherlands Antilles - Antilles néerlandaises 2003 - 2007																					
Male - Hommes	72.0	68.0	63.1	58.2	53.6	49.3	44.8	40.2	35.6	31.1	26.7	22.6	18.7	15.2	12.1	9.4	7.2	5.5	4.3	3.9	5.1
Female - Femmes	79.3	75.1	70.2	65.3	60.4	55.5	50.6	45.8	41.0	36.3	31.7	27.3	23.1	19.0	15.3	12.0	9.1	6.5	4.6	3.4	1.6
Nicaragua 2005 - 2010																					
Male - Hommes	63.4	47.9	44.2	40.5	36.5	32.5	28.6	24.9	21.3	17.7	14.6	11.6	9.0	6.5	...	...	...	...	...	...	...
Female - Femmes	68.9	52.1	47.6	43.0	38.5	34.1	29.8	25.7	21.9	18.1	14.9	11.8	9.3	6.9	...	...	...	...	...	...	...
Panama[10] 2010																					
Male - Hommes	73.4	70.3	65.4	60.6	55.9	51.4	46.9	42.4	37.9	33.5	29.1	24.9	20.9	17.0	13.4	10.3	7.6	...	...	...	...
Female - Femmes	78.7	75.2	70.3	65.4	60.5	55.7	50.9	46.1	41.4	36.7	32.1	27.6	23.2	19.1	15.2	11.6	8.5	...	...	...	...
Puerto Rico - Porto Rico 2004 - 2006																					
Male - Hommes	74.1	69.8	64.9	59.9	55.2	50.9	46.5	42.0	37.6	33.3	29.1	25.1	21.3	17.7	14.4	11.3	8.7	6.5	4.8	3.4	2.3
Female - Femmes	81.5	77.2	72.3	67.3	62.4	57.5	52.7	47.9	43.1	38.4	33.8	29.3	24.9	20.8	16.9	13.3	10.1	7.4	5.2	3.7	3.1
Saint Kitts and Nevis - Saint-Kitts-et-Nevis 1998																					
Male - Hommes	68.2	65.0	60.1	55.3	50.5	45.8	41.1	36.5	32.7	28.5	24.3	20.6	16.6	13.3	11.0	9.1	6.6	4.7	3.4	2.2	0.4
Female - Femmes	70.7	67.5	62.5	57.6	52.7	48.0	43.4	38.8	34.4	29.8	25.4	21.3	17.6	14.3	11.3	8.9	6.3	4.6	3.3	2.2	0.4
Saint Lucia - Sainte-Lucie 2005																					
Male - Hommes	69.9	66.4	61.5	56.6	52.0	47.4	43.1	38.6	34.3	30.1	25.9	21.7	17.9	14.7	11.8	9.0	7.2	5.2	...	...	...
Female - Femmes	75.7	72.2	67.3	62.4	57.5	52.6	47.8	43.2	38.4	33.8	29.2	25.0	20.8	17.2	13.8	10.4	7.7	4.8	...	...	...
Saint Vincent and the Grenadines - Saint-Vincent-et-les Grenadines 2001																					
Male - Hommes	66.9	63.9	59.2	54.3	49.6	45.1	40.7	36.5	32.3	28.2	24.1	19.9	16.2	12.8	9.7	7.3	4.3	4.1	...	...	...
Female - Femmes	72.9	69.3	64.5	59.5	54.7	49.8	45.2	40.7	36.1	31.7	27.3	23.0	19.0	14.6	10.8	7.3	4.1	3.6	...	...	...
Trinidad and Tobago - Trinité-et-Tobago 2000																					
Male - Hommes	68.3	65.2	60.3	55.5	50.7	46.1	41.7	37.3	33.1	29.0	24.9	21.2	17.9	14.7	12.0	9.7	7.8	...	...	...	...
Female - Femmes	73.7	70.2	65.3	60.4	55.6	50.9	46.2	41.7	37.1	32.7	28.4	24.4	20.7	17.4	14.4	11.7	9.6	...	...	...	...

Continent, country or area and date / Continent, pays ou zone et date	Age (in years) - Age (en années)																				
	0	5	10	15	20	25	30	35	40	45	50	55	60	65	70	75	80	85	90	95	100
AMERICA, NORTH - AMÉRIQUE DU NORD																					
Turks and Caicos Islands - Îles Turques et Caïques 2001																					
Male - Hommes	79.0	75.3	70.3	65.3	60.3	55.8	50.8	46.0	41.2	37.1	33.0	28.4	24.3	20.8	17.5	12.5	7.5	4.1	...	...	...
Female - Femmes	77.4	72.5	67.5	62.5	57.5	52.9	48.2	43.4	38.6	33.8	29.6	25.0	20.0	17.0	13.2	11.7	10.3	8.8	...	...	...
United States of America - États-Unis d'Amérique 2007																					
Male - Hommes	75.4	71.0	66.1	61.1	56.4	51.8	47.1	42.5	37.8	33.3	29.0	24.9	20.9	17.2	13.7	10.6	7.9	5.8	4.1	2.9	2.1
Female - Femmes	80.4	76.0	71.0	66.1	61.2	56.3	51.5	46.7	41.9	37.2	32.7	28.2	23.9	19.9	16.0	12.5	9.4	6.8	4.8	3.3	2.3
AMERICA, SOUTH - AMÉRIQUE DU SUD																					
Argentina - Argentine 2000 - 2001																					
Male - Hommes	70.0	66.6	61.7	56.8	52.1	47.4	42.8	38.2	33.7	29.3	25.0	21.1	17.4	14.1	11.1	8.6	6.5	4.9	3.7	2.9	...
Female - Femmes	77.5	73.9	69.0	64.1	59.2	54.4	49.5	44.7	40.0	35.4	30.9	26.5	22.3	18.4	14.7	11.3	8.4	6.2	4.6	3.5	...
2006 - 2010																					
Male - Hommes	72.5	...	...	...	...	...	...	...	...	...	...	...	...	...	...	...	...	...	...	...	...
Female - Femmes	80.0	...	...	...	...	...	...	...	...	...	...	...	...	...	...	...	...	...	...	...	...
Bolivia (Plurinational State of) - Bolivie (État plurinational de) 1995 - 2000																					
Male - Hommes	59.8	60.8	56.7	52.2	48.0	43.7	39.5	35.3	31.2	27.1	23.2	19.5	15.9	12.7	9.8	7.5	5.9	...	...	...	...
Female - Femmes	63.2	63.8	59.7	55.2	50.8	46.5	42.1	37.8	33.6	29.4	25.3	21.4	17.6	14.0	10.8	8.3	6.5	...	...	...	...
Brazil - Brésil[10] 2009																					
Male - Hommes	69.4	66.6	61.8	56.9	52.3	48.0	43.6	39.3	35.0	30.8	26.9	23.1	19.5	16.3	13.4	10.9	9.0	...	...	...	...
Female - Femmes	77.0	73.8	68.9	63.9	59.1	54.2	49.5	44.7	40.0	35.5	31.1	26.9	22.8	19.1	15.6	12.6	10.0	...	...	...	...
Chile - Chili 2010																					
Male - Hommes	75.8	71.5	66.6	61.6	56.8	52.1	47.4	42.8	38.1	33.5	29.1	24.8	20.6	16.9	13.5	10.3	7.8	5.7	4.4	5.9	...
Female - Femmes	81.2	76.9	71.9	67.0	62.1	57.2	52.3	47.4	42.6	37.8	33.1	28.6	24.1	19.9	16.0	12.3	9.0	6.2	4.2	3.7	...
Colombia - Colombie[11] 2005 - 2010																					
Male - Hommes	70.7	67.7	62.9	58.0	53.5	49.4	45.2	40.9	36.5	32.2	27.8	23.7	19.7	16.0	12.7	9.8	7.4	...	...	...	...
Female - Femmes	77.5	74.1	69.2	64.3	59.5	54.7	49.9	45.1	40.4	35.7	31.2	26.7	22.5	18.5	14.8	11.5	8.6	...	...	...	...
Ecuador - Équateur[12] 2005 - 2010																					
Male - Hommes	72.1	69.3	64.5	59.7	55.2	50.9	46.6	42.3	38.1	33.8	29.7	25.7	21.7	18.0	14.6	11.3	8.2	...	...	...	...
Female - Femmes	78.0	74.8	69.9	65.1	60.4	55.6	50.9	46.2	41.6	37.0	32.6	28.2	24.1	20.0	16.1	12.5	9.1	...	...	...	...
French Guiana - Guyane française 2007																					
Male - Hommes	75.1	71.3	66.4	61.5	56.8	52.2	47.7	43.1	38.7	34.3	30.3	25.7	21.5	17.5	13.8	10.5	8.2	5.7	3.6	2.1	...
Female - Femmes	80.8	77.0	72.1	67.2	62.3	57.4	52.6	47.8	43.0	38.5	33.9	29.2	24.5	19.9	16.6	12.7	10.2	7.8	5.1	2.2	...
Paraguay 1990 - 1995																					
Male - Hommes	66.3	65.5	60.8	56.0	51.3	46.7	42.1	37.5	32.9	28.5	24.2	20.2	16.5	13.2	10.2	7.7	5.6	...	...	...	...
Female - Femmes	70.8	69.3	64.5	59.7	54.9	50.1	45.4	40.7	36.0	31.5	27.0	22.8	18.7	14.9	11.5	8.5	6.3	...	...	...	...
2005 - 2010																					
Male - Hommes	69.7	...	...	...	...	...	...	...	...	...	...	...	...	...	...	...	...	...	...	...	...
Female - Femmes	73.9	...	...	...	...	...	...	...	...	...	...	...	...	...	...	...	...	...	...	...	...
Peru - Pérou[10] 1995 - 2000																					
Male - Hommes	65.9	65.9	61.4	56.6	52.0	47.4	42.9	38.5	34.1	29.8	25.7	21.7	18.1	14.7	11.7	9.2	7.0	...	...	...	...
Female - Femmes	70.9	70.2	65.6	60.7	55.9	51.2	46.5	41.9	37.3	32.9	28.5	24.3	20.3	16.5	13.3	10.4	7.8	...	...	...	...
2000 - 2005																					
Male - Hommes	69.0	...	...	...	...	...	...	...	...	...	...	...	...	...	...	...	...	...	...	...	...
Female - Femmes	74.3	...	...	...	...	...	...	...	...	...	...	...	...	...	...	...	...	...	...	...	...

Continent, country or area and date / Continent, pays ou zone et date	0	5	10	15	20	25	30	35	40	45	50	55	60	65	70	75	80	85	90	95	100
AMERICA, SOUTH - AMÉRIQUE DU SUD																					
Suriname																					
2006																					
Male - Hommes	68.0	60.4	55.5	50.6	46.0	41.5	37.0	32.8	28.6	24.6	20.7	16.9	13.5	10.5	8.1	7.1	6.5	...	...	...	...
Female - Femmes	73.7	66.0	61.1	56.2	51.5	46.8	42.3	37.7	33.2	28.8	24.5	20.3	16.4	12.9	9.9	8.0	8.5	...	...	...	...
Uruguay																					
2006																					
Male - Hommes	72.1	68.5	63.6	58.7	53.8	49.1	44.4	39.7	35.0	30.5	26.0	21.9	18.1	14.7	11.7	9.0	6.7	4.8	3.4	2.7	...
Female - Femmes	79.5	75.7	70.8	65.8	60.9	56.1	51.2	46.3	41.6	36.8	32.3	27.8	23.6	19.4	15.5	11.9	8.8	6.3	4.4	3.1	...
2008																					
Male - Hommes	72.4	...	...	...	...	...	...	...	...	...	...	...	...	...	...	...	...	...	...	...	...
Female - Femmes	79.7	...	...	...	...	...	...	...	...	...	...	...	...	...	...	...	...	...	...	...	...
Venezuela (Bolivarian Republic of) - Venezuela (République bolivarienne du)																					
1995 - 2000																					
Male - Hommes	68.6	66.6	61.8	56.9	52.3	47.8	43.3	38.8	34.3	29.9	25.6	21.6	17.9	14.5	11.4	8.6	5.9	...	...	...	...
Female - Femmes	74.5	72.1	67.2	62.3	57.5	52.6	47.8	43.1	38.4	33.7	29.2	24.9	20.8	16.9	13.3	9.9	6.9	...	...	...	...
2007																					
Male - Hommes	70.7	...	...	...	...	...	...	...	...	...	...	...	...	...	...	...	...	...	...	...	...
Female - Femmes	76.6	...	...	...	...	...	...	...	...	...	...	...	...	...	...	...	...	...	...	...	...
ASIA - ASIE																					
Afghanistan																					
2002																					
Male - Hommes	43.0	...	...	...	...	...	...	...	...	...	...	...	...	...	...	...	...	...	...	...	...
Female - Femmes	43.0	...	...	...	...	...	...	...	...	...	...	...	...	...	...	...	...	...	...	...	...
Armenia - Arménie																					
2006 - 2007																					
Male - Hommes	70.2	66.3	61.4	56.4	51.6	46.8	42.0	37.3	32.7	28.3	24.1	20.1	16.4	13.1	10.3	7.8	5.7	3.9	2.6	1.6	0.7
Female - Femmes	76.6	72.5	67.6	62.7	57.7	52.8	47.9	43.0	38.2	33.5	28.8	24.3	20.0	15.9	12.4	9.2	6.4	4.1	2.7	1.8	0.7
Azerbaijan - Azerbaïdjan																					
2009																					
Male - Hommes	71.0	67.0	62.2	57.3	52.4	47.7	42.9	38.2	33.6	29.1	24.8	20.8	17.1	13.8	10.9	8.5	7.1	7.3	6.6	4.5	1.0
Female - Femmes	76.1	72.2	67.3	62.4	57.5	52.6	47.8	42.9	38.1	33.4	28.7	24.3	20.0	16.1	12.5	9.5	7.5	6.3	4.8	3.5	0.8
Bahrain - Bahreïn																					
2001																					
Male - Hommes	73.2	69.3	64.4	59.5	54.7	49.9	45.2	40.4	35.6	30.9	26.4	22.0	17.8	14.1	11.3	9.5	...	...	...	...	...
Female - Femmes	76.2	72.0	67.1	62.1	57.2	52.3	47.4	42.5	37.7	32.9	28.2	23.7	19.6	15.9	12.9	10.9	...	...	...	...	...
2005																					
Male - Hommes	73.1	...	...	...	...	...	...	...	...	...	...	...	...	...	...	...	...	...	...	...	...
Female - Femmes	77.3	...	...	...	...	...	...	...	...	...	...	...	...	...	...	...	...	...	...	...	...
Bangladesh																					
1994																					
Male - Hommes	58.7	61.4	57.3	53.0	48.7	44.0	40.1	34.8	30.8	26.0	22.0	18.6	15.1	12.1	9.1	6.4	4.6	...	...	...	...
Female - Femmes	58.3	60.4	56.6	51.4	47.1	42.6	38.4	34.1	30.0	26.3	22.3	18.5	15.0	11.9	8.6	5.9	4.0	...	...	...	...
2007																					
Male - Hommes	65.4	...	...	...	...	...	...	...	...	...	...	...	...	...	...	...	...	...	...	...	...
Female - Femmes	67.9	...	...	...	...	...	...	...	...	...	...	...	...	...	...	...	...	...	...	...	...
Bhutan - Bhoutan																					
2005																					
Male - Hommes	65.7	...	...	...	...	...	...	...	...	...	...	...	...	...	...	...	...	...	...	...	...
Female - Femmes	66.9	...	...	...	...	...	...	...	...	...	...	...	...	...	...	...	...	...	...	...	...
Brunei Darussalam - Brunéi Darussalam																					
2008																					
Male - Hommes	76.6	...	...	...	...	...	...	...	...	...	...	...	...	...	...	...	...	...	...	...	...
Female - Femmes	79.8	...	...	...	...	...	...	...	...	...	...	...	...	...	...	...	...	...	...	...	...
China - Chine[13]																					
2000																					
Male - Hommes	69.6	...	...	...	...	...	...	...	...	...	...	...	...	...	...	...	...	...	...	...	...
Female - Femmes	73.3	...	...	...	...	...	...	...	...	...	...	...	...	...	...	...	...	...	...	...	...

21. Life expectancy at specified ages for each sex: latest available year, 1991 - 2010
Espérance de vie à un âge donné pour chaque sexe : dernière année disponible, 1991 - 2010 (continued - suite)

Continent, country or area and date / Continent, pays ou zone et date	0	5	10	15	20	25	30	35	40	45	50	55	60	65	70	75	80	85	90	95	100
ASIA - ASIE																					
China, Hong Kong SAR - Chine, Hong Kong RAS																					
2009																					
Male - Hommes	79.7	74.9	69.9	64.9	60.0	55.1	50.3	45.5	40.7	35.9	31.3	26.8	22.5	18.4	14.6	11.3	8.4	6.1	4.3	3.0	2.1
Female - Femmes	85.9	81.1	76.2	71.2	66.3	61.3	56.4	51.5	46.6	41.8	37.0	32.3	27.7	23.2	19.0	15.0	11.5	8.6	6.2	4.3	2.9
China, Macao SAR - Chine, Macao RAS																					
2006 - 2009																					
Male - Hommes	79.4	74.7	69.7	64.8	59.8	55.0	50.2	45.5	40.8	36.2	31.6	27.2	23.0	19.1	15.6	12.5	9.8	7.8	...	...	...
Female - Femmes	85.2	80.5	75.6	70.6	65.7	60.8	56.0	51.1	46.2	41.4	36.7	32.1	27.5	23.0	18.9	15.0	11.8	9.3	...	...	...
Cyprus - Chypre[14]																					
2006 - 2007																					
Male - Hommes	78.3	73.6	68.7	63.8	58.9	54.2	49.5	44.7	39.9	35.2	30.5	26.0	21.7	17.6	13.9	10.6	7.8	5.7	...	...	...
Female - Femmes	81.9	77.2	72.3	67.4	62.5	57.5	52.6	47.7	42.8	37.9	33.1	28.4	23.8	19.3	15.0	11.1	7.8	5.3	...	...	...
Democratic People's Republic of Korea - République populaire démocratique de Corée																					
2008																					
Male - Hommes	65.6	...	...	...	...	...	...	...	...	...	...	...	...	...	...	...	...	...	...	...	...
Female - Femmes	72.7	...	...	...	...	...	...	...	...	...	...	...	...	...	...	...	...	...	...	...	...
Georgia - Géorgie																					
2008																					
Male - Hommes	69.3	65.7	60.9	56.0	51.2	46.5	42.0	37.6	33.2	29.1	25.2	21.4	17.7	14.1	11.9	9.2	7.2	5.2	...	...	...
Female - Femmes	79.0	75.5	70.6	65.7	60.8	56.0	51.1	46.3	41.6	36.9	32.3	27.8	23.3	19.1	15.7	12.5	10.2	8.3	...	...	...
India - Inde[15]																					
2002 - 2006																					
Male - Hommes	62.6	63.8	59.3	54.6	49.9	45.4	40.9	36.5	32.2	28.0	24.0	20.2	16.7	13.6	10.9	...	...	...	...	...	...
Female - Femmes	64.2	67.4	62.9	58.2	53.7	49.2	44.8	40.2	35.7	31.3	26.9	22.7	18.9	15.4	12.4	...	...	...	...	...	...
Indonesia - Indonésie																					
1990 - 1995																					
Male - Hommes	61.0	...	...	...	...	...	...	...	...	...	...	...	...	...	...	...	...	...	...	...	...
Female - Femmes	64.5	...	...	...	...	...	...	...	...	...	...	...	...	...	...	...	...	...	...	...	...
Iran (Islamic Republic of) - Iran (République islamique d')																					
1996																					
Male - Hommes	66.1	64.6	59.9	55.1	50.5	46.0	41.4	36.8	32.3	27.9	23.7	19.8	16.2	12.9	10.1	7.7	5.7	4.2	3.1	...	...
Female - Femmes	68.4	66.8	62.1	57.3	52.7	48.0	43.5	39.0	34.5	30.1	25.8	21.7	17.8	14.3	11.1	8.4	6.2	4.5	3.2	...	...
2006																					
Male - Hommes	71.1	...	...	...	...	...	...	...	...	...	...	...	...	...	...	...	...	...	...	...	...
Female - Femmes	73.1	...	...	...	...	...	...	...	...	...	...	...	...	...	...	...	...	...	...	...	...
Iraq																					
1997																					
Male - Hommes	58.0	...	...	...	...	...	...	...	...	...	...	...	...	...	...	...	...	...	...	...	...
Female - Femmes	59.0	...	...	...	...	...	...	...	...	...	...	...	...	...	...	...	...	...	...	...	...
Israel - Israël[16]																					
2005 - 2009																					
Male - Hommes	78.7	74.1	69.1	64.2	59.3	54.5	49.7	44.9	40.1	35.4	30.8	26.4	22.1	18.2	14.5	11.2	8.3	6.0	4.2	3.0	3.1
Female - Femmes	82.5	77.9	72.9	67.9	63.0	58.1	53.1	48.2	43.3	38.5	33.8	29.1	24.6	20.3	16.1	12.4	9.0	6.3	4.1	2.7	2.5
Japan - Japon[17]																					
2009																					
Male - Hommes	79.6	74.9	69.9	64.9	60.0	55.2	50.4	45.6	40.8	36.1	31.5	27.1	22.9	18.9	15.1	11.6	8.7	6.3	4.5	3.2	2.4
Female - Femmes	86.4	81.7	76.7	71.8	66.8	61.9	57.0	52.1	47.3	42.4	37.7	33.0	28.5	24.0	19.6	15.5	11.7	8.4	5.9	4.1	3.0
Jordan - Jordanie[18]																					
2007																					
Male - Hommes	71.6	...	...	...	...	...	...	...	...	...	...	...	...	...	...	...	...	...	...	...	...
Female - Femmes	74.4	...	...	...	...	...	...	...	...	...	...	...	...	...	...	...	...	...	...	...	...
Kazakhstan																					
2008																					
Male - Hommes	61.9	58.6	53.8	48.9	44.2	39.8	35.6	31.7	27.8	24.0	20.5	17.2	14.1	11.5	9.2	7.2	5.7	4.3	3.1	2.4	1.8
Female - Femmes	72.4	69.0	64.1	59.3	54.4	49.7	45.0	40.5	35.9	31.5	27.1	22.9	18.9	15.3	11.9	8.9	6.5	4.5	3.0	2.2	1.7

21. Life expectancy at specified ages for each sex: latest available year, 1991 - 2010
Espérance de vie à un âge donné pour chaque sexe : dernière année disponible, 1991 - 2010 (continued - suite)

Continent, country or area and date / Continent, pays ou zone et date	0	5	10	15	20	25	30	35	40	45	50	55	60	65	70	75	80	85	90	95	100
ASIA - ASIE																					
Kuwait - Koweït																					
1992 - 1993																					
Male - Hommes	71.8	67.9	63.0	58.2	53.6	48.9	44.2	39.4	34.7	30.1	25.6	21.4	17.3	14.1	10.8	7.8	4.4	2.5	...	...	...
Female - Femmes	73.3	69.2	64.3	59.4	54.5	49.6	44.7	39.8	35.0	30.2	25.5	21.1	16.8	13.3	10.0	7.4	4.3	2.6	...	...	...
1990 - 1995																					
Male - Hommes	73.3	...	...	...	...	...	...	...	...	...	...	...	...	...	...	...	...	...	...	...	...
Female - Femmes	77.2	...	...	...	...	...	...	...	...	...	...	...	...	...	...	...	...	...	...	...	...
Kyrgyzstan - Kirghizstan																					
2009																					
Male - Hommes	65.2	62.3	57.4	52.5	47.7	43.0	38.5	34.2	30.0	26.0	22.1	18.6	15.3	12.3	9.9	7.7	6.3	5.1	3.8	2.4	1.4
Female - Femmes	73.2	70.1	65.2	60.3	55.4	50.6	45.9	41.2	36.5	32.0	27.5	23.2	19.2	15.4	12.1	9.0	6.8	5.0	3.7	2.7	0.8
Lao People's Democratic Republic - République démocratique populaire lao[19]																					
2005																					
Male - Hommes	55.0	...	...	...	...	...	...	...	...	...	...	...	...	...	...	...	...	...	...	...	...
Female - Femmes	63.0	...	...	...	...	...	...	...	...	...	...	...	...	...	...	...	...	...	...	...	...
Malaysia - Malaisie																					
2006																					
Male - Hommes	71.5	67.0	62.0	57.2	52.4	47.8	43.1	38.6	34.0	29.5	25.2	21.1	17.2	13.7	10.7	8.0	5.8	...			
Female - Femmes	76.2	71.6	66.7	61.8	56.9	52.0	47.1	42.3	37.5	32.8	28.2	23.8	19.6	15.6	12.1	9.0	6.6	...			
Maldives																					
2009																					
Male - Hommes	72.5	68.7	63.8	59.0	54.1	49.2	44.4	39.5	34.7	29.9	25.2	20.6	16.3	12.3	8.8	6.1	...				
Female - Femmes	74.2	70.2	65.3	60.4	55.5	50.6	45.6	40.8	35.8	31.0	26.3	21.6	17.1	12.9	9.1	6.0	...				
Mongolia - Mongolie																					
1998 - 2007																					
Male - Hommes	63.1	61.3	56.5	51.6	46.9	42.3	38.0	33.7	29.7	25.9	22.4	19.2	16.1	13.7	12.0	...					...
Female - Femmes	70.2	68.9	64.0	59.1	54.2	49.5	44.8	40.2	35.7	31.3	27.2	23.3	19.7	16.7	14.3	...					...
2009																					
Male - Hommes	64.3	...	...	...	...	...	...	...	...	...	...	...	...	...	...	...					...
Female - Femmes	71.8	...	...	...	...	...	...	...	...	...	...	...	...	...	...	...					...
Myanmar[20]																					
2008																					
Male - Hommes	64.3	61.0	56.9	51.5	46.9	42.4	38.2	34.4	30.9	27.4	24.0	20.7	17.4	14.1	10.9	8.0	5.9	3.9	...	...	...
Female - Femmes	68.3	65.0	60.4	55.6	51.0	46.5	42.2	38.0	33.9	29.8	25.8	21.9	18.1	14.3	10.9	7.8	5.3	3.4	...	...	...
Nepal - Népal																					
2008																					
Male - Hommes	63.6	...	...	...	...	...	...	...	...	...	...	...	...	...	...	...	...	...	...	...	...
Female - Femmes	64.5	...	...	...	...	...	...	...	...	...	...	...	...	...	...	...	...	...	...	...	...
Occupied Palestinian Territory - Territoire palestinien occupé																					
2001																					
Male - Hommes	70.5	67.5	62.7	57.8	53.1	48.4	43.6	38.9	34.2	29.6	25.2	21.1	17.2	13.8	10.7	8.1	6.1	...	...	...	...
Female - Femmes	73.6	70.3	65.5	60.5	55.7	50.9	46.1	41.3	36.6	32.0	27.5	23.2	19.0	15.2	11.7	8.8	6.4	...	...	...	...
2008																					
Male - Hommes	70.2	...	...	...	...	...	...	...	...	...	...	...	...	...	...	...	...	...	...	...	...
Female - Femmes	72.9	...	...	...	...	...	...	...	...	...	...	...	...	...	...	...	...	...	...	...	...
Oman																					
2008																					
Male - Hommes	72.2	68.1	63.2	58.3	53.6	48.8	44.1	39.3	34.6	29.9	25.2	20.9	16.8	13.2	10.1	7.8	7.2	...	...	...	...
Female - Femmes	75.7	71.5	66.6	61.7	56.7	51.8	46.9	42.0	37.2	32.4	27.7	23.3	19.3	15.8	12.6	10.3	9.3	...	...	...	...
Pakistan[21]																					
2007																					
Male - Hommes	63.6	65.3	60.7	55.9	51.3	46.7	42.2	37.7	33.3	29.0	25.0	21.3	18.1	15.2	12.7	10.8	9.2	7.3	...	...	...
Female - Femmes	67.6	68.6	64.1	59.5	54.9	50.3	45.7	41.1	36.5	32.1	27.7	23.5	19.6	16.2	13.4	10.9	8.6	6.1	...	...	...
Philippines																					
1991																					
Male - Hommes	63.1	62.8	58.2	53.5	48.9	44.5	40.1	35.6	31.2	27.0	22.9	19.1	15.5	12.3	9.5	7.1	5.1	...	...	...	...
Female - Femmes	66.7	65.7	61.1	56.3	51.7	47.2	42.7	38.2	33.8	29.4	25.2	21.2	17.3	13.7	10.6	7.9	5.6	...	...	...	...

Continent, country or area and date / Continent, pays ou zone et date	Age (in years) - Age (en années)																				
	0	5	10	15	20	25	30	35	40	45	50	55	60	65	70	75	80	85	90	95	100
ASIA - ASIE																					
Qatar 2008																					
Male - Hommes	77.9	73.7	68.8	63.9	59.1	54.3	49.4	44.6	39.8	35.0	30.3	25.6	21.2	17.0	13.3	9.9	7.1	...	...	...	...
Female - Femmes	78.1	73.9	68.9	64.0	59.1	54.1	49.2	44.3	39.3	34.5	29.6	24.9	20.5	16.6	13.2	10.0	7.8	...	...	...	...
Republic of Korea - République de Corée 2009																					
Male - Hommes	77.0	72.3	67.4	62.5	57.6	52.7	47.9	43.1	38.4	33.8	29.4	25.1	21.0	17.0	13.4	10.2	7.5	5.5	4.0	3.0	2.4
Female - Femmes	83.8	79.1	74.2	69.2	64.3	59.4	54.5	49.7	44.9	40.1	35.3	30.6	26.0	21.5	17.2	13.2	9.8	7.0	4.9	3.5	2.6
Singapore - Singapour[22] 2010																					
Male - Hommes	79.3	74.6	69.6	64.7	59.8	54.9	50.0	45.1	40.3	35.5	30.9	26.4	22.2	18.1	14.5	11.3	8.5	6.2	4.4	3.1	2.1
Female - Femmes	84.1	79.3	74.3	69.4	64.4	59.5	54.5	49.6	44.7	39.9	35.1	30.4	25.9	21.5	17.4	13.6	10.3	7.5	5.3	3.6	2.5
Tajikistan - Tadjikistan 2008																					
Male - Hommes	69.7	67.9	63.0	58.1	53.3	48.5	43.7	39.1	34.6	30.1	25.7	21.6	17.9	14.7	12.2	10.4	9.2	...	...	...	...
Female - Femmes	74.8	72.5	67.6	62.7	57.8	52.9	48.1	43.4	38.6	33.9	29.4	25.0	21.0	17.5	14.7	12.5	11.1	...	...	...	...
2009																					
Male - Hommes	70.5	...	...	...	...	...	...	...	...	...	...	...	...	...	...	...	...	...	...	...	...
Female - Femmes	75.3	...	...	...	...	...	...	...	...	...	...	...	...	...	...	...	...	...	...	...	...
Thailand - Thaïlande 2005 - 2006																					
Male - Hommes	69.9	...	...	...	...	...	...	...	...	...	...	...	...	...	...	...	...	...	...	...	...
Female - Femmes	77.6	...	...	...	...	...	...	...	...	...	...	...	...	...	...	...	...	...	...	...	...
Turkey - Turquie[23] 2009																					
Male - Hommes	71.5	...	...	...	...	...	...	...	...	...	...	...	...	...	...	...	...	...	...	...	...
Female - Femmes	76.1	...	...	...	...	...	...	...	...	...	...	...	...	...	...	...	...	...	...	...	...
United Arab Emirates - Émirats arabes unis 2006																					
Male - Hommes	76.7	72.5	67.6	62.7	57.9	53.1	48.3	43.5	38.7	33.9	29.3	24.8	20.7	16.9	13.8	11.3	10.2	...	...	...	...
Female - Femmes	78.8	74.5	69.5	64.6	59.7	54.8	49.8	44.9	40.0	35.2	30.4	25.8	21.6	18.0	15.4	14.0	14.5	...	...	...	...
Viet Nam 2008																					
Male - Hommes	70.6	67.7	62.9	58.0	53.3	48.6	43.8	39.1	34.5	30.0	25.8	21.8	18.2	15.0	12.3	10.0	8.3	...	...	...	...
Female - Femmes	76.0	72.1	67.2	62.3	57.4	52.5	47.7	42.8	38.1	33.5	29.0	24.6	20.6	16.8	13.6	11.0	8.9	...	...	...	...
2009																					
Male - Hommes	70.2	...	...	...	...	...	...	...	...	...	...	...	...	...	...	...	...	...	...	...	...
Female - Femmes	75.6	...	...	...	...	...	...	...	...	...	...	...	...	...	...	...	...	...	...	...	...
Yemen - Yémen 2004																					
Male - Hommes	60.2	...	...	...	...	...	...	...	...	...	...	...	...	...	...	...	...	...	...	...	...
Female - Femmes	62.0	...	...	...	...	...	...	...	...	...	...	...	...	...	...	...	...	...	...	...	...
EUROPE																					
Åland Islands - Îles d'Åland 2007																					
Male - Hommes	79.4	74.4	69.4	64.4	59.4	54.8	49.8	44.8	40.0	35.2	30.2	25.5	20.9	17.1	14.2	10.7	7.2	4.4	3.1	1.8	0.0
Female - Femmes	85.1	80.1	75.1	70.1	65.1	60.7	55.7	50.7	45.7	40.9	35.9	31.3	26.4	22.2	17.7	13.4	9.9	6.6	4.4	3.1	1.0
Albania - Albanie 2004																					
Male - Hommes	72.5	69.5	64.8	59.9	55.1	50.4	45.8	41.1	36.4	31.8	27.3	22.9	18.6	14.8	11.3	8.4	6.0	3.8	...	...	...
Female - Femmes	77.3	74.4	69.5	64.7	59.8	54.9	50.0	45.2	40.3	35.5	30.8	26.1	21.6	17.3	13.2	9.6	6.4	3.8	...	...	...
Austria - Autriche 2009																					
Male - Hommes	77.4	72.8	67.8	62.9	58.1	53.3	48.4	43.6	38.8	34.1	29.6	25.3	21.2	17.5	13.9	10.5	7.7	5.4	3.7	2.6	...
Female - Femmes	82.9	78.2	73.3	68.3	63.4	58.4	53.5	48.6	43.7	38.9	34.2	29.6	25.1	20.8	16.6	12.7	9.2	6.3	4.2	2.8	...
Belarus - Bélarus 2009																					
Male - Hommes	64.7	60.2	55.3	50.4	45.6	41.0	36.5	32.2	28.1	24.2	20.5	17.1	14.2	11.6	9.4	7.6	5.8	4.1	2.7	1.7	1.1
Female - Femmes	76.4	71.8	66.9	61.9	57.0	52.1	47.3	42.6	38.0	33.4	28.9	24.6	20.5	16.7	13.1	9.8	7.1	5.1	3.5	2.4	1.5

625

Continent, country or area and date / Continent, pays ou zone et date	Age (in years) - Age (en années)																				
	0	5	10	15	20	25	30	35	40	45	50	55	60	65	70	75	80	85	90	95	100
EUROPE																					
Belgium - Belgique																					
2006																					
Male - Hommes	77.0	71.4	66.5	61.5	56.7	51.9	47.1	42.4	37.7	33.1	28.6	24.3	20.3	16.5	12.9	9.7	7.1	5.0	3.4	2.5	...
Female - Femmes	82.7	77.0	72.1	67.1	62.2	57.3	52.4	47.5	42.6	37.9	33.2	28.7	24.3	20.1	16.0	12.1	8.8	6.1	4.1	2.8	...
Bosnia and Herzegovina - Bosnie-Herzégovine																					
2003																					
Male - Hommes	71.3	...	...	...	...	...	...	...	...	...	...	...	...	...	...	...	...	...	...	...	...
Female - Femmes	76.7	...	...	...	...	...	...	...	...	...	...	...	...	...	...	...	...	...	...	...	...
Bulgaria - Bulgarie																					
2007 - 2009																					
Male - Hommes	69.9	65.7	60.8	55.9	51.1	46.3	41.6	36.9	32.3	27.9	23.7	20.0	16.6	13.5	10.6	8.2	6.0	4.4	3.3	2.6	0.5
Female - Femmes	77.1	72.8	67.9	63.0	58.1	53.2	48.3	43.5	38.7	34.0	29.4	25.0	20.8	16.6	12.8	9.5	6.7	4.7	3.3	2.5	0.5
Czech Republic - République tchèque																					
2009																					
Male - Hommes	74.2	69.5	64.5	59.6	54.7	49.9	45.1	40.3	35.6	31.0	26.5	22.4	18.6	15.2	12.0	9.2	6.7	4.7	3.1	2.0	1.3
Female - Femmes	80.1	75.4	70.4	65.5	60.5	55.6	50.7	45.8	40.9	36.1	31.5	26.9	22.5	18.3	14.4	10.7	7.5	4.9	3.0	1.7	1.0
Denmark - Danemark[24]																					
2008 - 2009																					
Male - Hommes	76.5	71.9	66.9	61.9	57.1	52.3	47.4	42.6	37.9	33.2	28.7	24.5	20.4	16.6	13.0	9.9	7.2	5.1	3.4	2.6	2.4
Female - Femmes	80.8	76.1	71.1	66.2	61.2	56.3	51.4	46.5	41.6	36.9	32.2	27.7	23.4	19.3	15.4	11.9	8.8	6.3	4.3	2.9	2.1
Estonia - Estonie																					
2008																					
Male - Hommes	68.6	64.1	59.2	54.2	49.5	44.9	40.4	35.9	31.4	27.1	23.2	19.6	16.4	13.6	11.0	8.8	6.9	5.3	4.1	3.1	2.4
Female - Femmes	79.2	74.7	69.7	64.7	59.9	55.0	50.1	45.3	40.5	35.7	31.2	26.8	22.6	18.6	14.7	11.1	8.1	5.7	3.9	2.6	1.7
Faeroe Islands - Îles Féroé																					
2008																					
Male - Hommes	76.8	72.5	67.7	62.7	57.9	53.0	48.1	43.3	38.5	33.9	29.3	24.8	20.8	17.0	13.4	10.1	7.6	6.0	4.6	3.2	...
Female - Femmes	82.3	77.8	72.8	67.8	62.9	57.9	53.0	48.1	43.2	38.2	33.4	28.7	24.3	20.0	15.9	12.5	9.2	6.6	4.4	3.3	...
Finland - Finlande																					
2009																					
Male - Hommes	76.5	71.7	66.7	61.8	56.9	52.2	47.5	42.8	38.1	33.5	29.1	24.9	20.9	17.2	13.7	10.4	7.6	5.4	3.7	2.4	1.5
Female - Femmes	83.1	78.4	73.4	68.5	63.5	58.6	53.7	48.9	44.0	39.2	34.5	30.0	25.5	21.2	17.0	13.0	9.4	6.5	4.4	2.9	1.8
France																					
2006 - 2008																					
Male - Hommes	77.4	72.8	67.8	62.9	58.0	53.2	48.5	43.7	39.0	34.4	30.0	25.9	21.9	18.1	14.5	11.2	8.2	5.8	4.0	2.9	...
Female - Femmes	84.3	79.7	74.7	69.7	64.8	59.9	55.0	50.1	45.2	40.5	35.8	31.3	26.8	22.5	18.2	14.2	10.5	7.3	4.9	3.3	...
Germany - Allemagne																					
2005 - 2007																					
Male - Hommes	76.9	72.3	67.3	62.4	57.5	52.7	47.8	43.0	38.2	33.5	29.1	24.8	20.7	16.9	13.4	10.2	7.6	5.4	3.7	2.7	1.9
Female - Femmes	82.3	77.6	72.6	67.7	62.7	57.8	52.9	47.9	43.1	38.3	33.6	29.0	24.6	20.3	16.2	12.3	8.9	6.2	4.1	2.9	2.1
Gibraltar																					
2001																					
Male - Hommes	78.5	73.5	68.5	63.5	58.5	53.5	...	43.5	...	33.9	...	25.8	...	17.9	...	11.3	...	...	...	...	...
Female - Femmes	83.3	79.5	75.0	70.0	65.0	60.0	...	50.3	...	40.3	...	30.3	...	20.6	...	13.7	...	...	...	...	...
Greece - Grèce																					
2009																					
Male - Hommes	77.7	73.1	68.1	63.2	58.3	53.6	48.9	44.2	39.4	34.8	30.3	25.9	21.8	17.9	14.2	10.9	8.2	6.1	4.5	3.2	2.2
Female - Femmes	82.8	78.1	73.2	68.2	63.3	58.3	53.4	48.5	43.7	38.8	34.1	29.4	24.8	20.3	16.0	12.0	8.6	6.2	4.5	3.2	2.2
Hungary - Hongrie																					
2009																					
Male - Hommes	70.1	65.5	60.5	55.6	50.7	45.9	41.1	36.3	31.6	27.2	23.3	19.8	16.6	13.7	11.0	8.4	6.2	4.2	2.6	1.5	0.6
Female - Femmes	77.9	73.3	68.4	63.4	58.5	53.6	48.6	43.7	38.9	34.3	29.8	25.6	21.5	17.6	13.8	10.4	7.4	4.8	2.8	1.5	0.6
Iceland - Islande																					
2007 - 2008																					
Male - Hommes	79.6	74.9	69.9	65.0	60.1	55.4	50.5	45.7	40.8	36.1	31.4	26.8	22.4	18.2	14.2	10.9	7.9	5.5	3.9	2.8	1.5
Female - Femmes	81.3	76.6	71.6	66.7	61.7	56.9	52.0	47.1	42.2	37.5	32.7	28.1	23.6	19.4	15.4	11.9	8.8	6.1	4.3	3.0	1.5
Ireland - Irlande																					
2002																					
Male - Hommes	75.1	70.7	65.7	60.8	56.0	51.3	46.5	41.8	37.0	32.3	27.8	23.4	19.2	15.4	11.9	8.9	6.5	4.6	3.3	2.4	1.7
Female - Femmes	80.3	75.7	70.8	65.8	60.9	56.0	51.1	46.2	41.4	36.6	31.9	27.4	22.9	18.7	14.8	11.2	8.2	5.8	4.1	2.9	2.1

21. Life expectancy at specified ages for each sex: latest available year, 1991 - 2010
Espérance de vie à un âge donné pour chaque sexe : dernière année disponible, 1991 - 2010 (continued - suite)

Continent, country or area and date / Continent, pays ou zone et date	0	5	10	15	20	25	30	35	40	45	50	55	60	65	70	75	80	85	90	95	100
EUROPE																					
Isle of Man - Île de Man																					
1996																					
Male - Hommes	73.6	68.6	63.6	58.6	53.6	49.1	44.6	40.2	35.8	31.2	26.7	22.4	18.4	15.1	12.0	9.3	7.5	5.2	4.7	3.2	0.5
Female - Femmes	79.9	75.1	70.1	65.1	60.1	55.1	50.1	45.1	40.2	35.4	30.7	26.2	22.0	18.3	14.5	11.3	8.6	5.9	3.7	2.0	1.5
Italy - Italie																					
2007																					
Male - Hommes	78.7	74.0	69.1	64.1	59.2	54.4	49.6	44.8	40.0	35.3	30.7	26.2	21.9	17.9	14.1	10.7	7.9	5.6	3.8	3.0	2.0
Female - Femmes	84.0	79.4	74.4	69.4	64.5	59.5	54.6	49.7	44.8	40.0	35.2	30.5	26.0	21.6	17.3	13.3	9.8	6.8	4.6	3.2	2.2
Latvia - Lettonie																					
2009																					
Male - Hommes	68.3	63.9	59.1	54.2	49.3	44.6	40.1	35.6	31.2	27.0	23.0	19.3	16.1	13.3	10.7	8.4	6.4	4.9	3.5	2.8	...
Female - Femmes	78.1	73.8	68.8	63.9	59.0	54.1	49.2	44.4	39.6	35.0	30.5	26.2	22.0	18.1	14.3	10.8	7.8	5.4	3.7	2.7	...
Lithuania - Lituanie																					
2009																					
Male - Hommes	67.5	63.0	58.1	53.2	48.5	43.9	39.3	34.9	30.6	26.6	22.7	19.2	16.0	13.4	10.9	8.4	6.3	4.5	3.2	2.1	2.0
Female - Femmes	78.6	74.0	69.0	64.1	59.1	54.3	49.4	44.6	39.8	35.2	30.7	26.4	22.2	18.2	14.4	10.8	7.7	5.2	3.4	2.3	2.9
Luxembourg																					
2005 - 2007																					
Male - Hommes	77.6	72.9	67.9	63.0	58.0	53.3	48.5	43.7	39.0	34.3	29.8	25.4	21.3	17.6	14.1	10.9	8.1	5.7	3.7	0.4	...
Female - Femmes	82.7	78.0	73.0	68.1	63.1	58.2	53.4	48.5	43.6	38.9	34.2	29.6	25.2	20.9	16.9	13.1	9.7	6.8	4.5	2.2	...
Malta - Malte																					
2009																					
Male - Hommes	77.7	73.3	68.3	63.4	58.5	53.7	48.9	44.1	39.3	34.5	29.8	25.2	20.9	16.8	13.1	9.7	7.2	5.1	...	...	...
Female - Femmes	82.2	78.1	73.2	68.3	63.3	58.4	53.6	48.7	43.8	38.9	34.1	29.5	24.9	20.6	16.4	12.5	9.3	6.9	...	...	...
Netherlands - Pays-Bas																					
2009																					
Male - Hommes	78.5	73.8	68.8	63.9	59.0	54.1	49.2	44.4	39.5	34.8	30.1	25.6	21.4	17.3	13.6	10.3	7.5	5.3	3.6	2.6	...
Female - Femmes	82.7	77.8	72.8	67.9	62.9	58.0	53.1	48.2	43.3	38.5	33.8	29.3	24.9	20.6	16.5	12.7	9.2	6.4	4.3	2.9	...
Norway - Norvège[25]																					
2009																					
Male - Hommes	78.6	73.9	69.0	64.0	59.2	54.4	49.6	44.8	40.0	35.3	30.7	26.2	21.9	17.8	14.1	10.7	7.7	5.4	3.7	2.6	1.9
Female - Femmes	83.1	78.3	73.3	68.4	63.5	58.5	53.7	48.7	43.9	39.0	34.3	29.7	25.2	20.9	16.8	12.9	9.4	6.6	4.4	2.9	2.0
Poland - Pologne																					
2009																					
Male - Hommes	71.5	67.0	62.1	57.1	52.3	47.6	42.9	38.2	33.6	29.3	25.1	21.4	17.9	14.7	11.8	9.2	6.9	5.1	3.8	2.7	2.0
Female - Femmes	80.1	75.5	70.6	65.6	60.7	55.8	50.9	46.0	41.1	36.4	31.8	27.4	23.2	19.1	15.2	11.6	8.5	6.0	4.2	3.0	2.1
Portugal																					
2007 - 2009																					
Male - Hommes	75.8	71.1	66.2	61.2	56.4	51.6	46.8	42.0	37.4	32.9	28.5	24.3	20.2	16.4	12.7	9.4	6.4	3.9	2.4	1.5	1.0
Female - Femmes	81.8	77.1	72.2	67.2	62.3	57.4	52.5	47.6	42.7	38.0	33.3	28.7	24.1	19.7	15.4	11.4	7.9	4.9	3.0	1.8	1.1
Republic of Moldova - République de Moldova																					
2009																					
Male - Hommes	65.3	61.4	56.5	51.6	46.8	42.1	37.4	33.0	28.8	24.8	21.1	17.8	14.8	11.9	9.7	7.8	6.3	5.0	3.8	2.7	...
Female - Femmes	73.4	69.3	64.4	59.5	54.6	49.7	44.8	40.0	35.3	30.8	26.4	22.2	18.4	14.8	11.7	9.1	6.9	5.1	3.7	2.5	...
Romania - Roumanie																					
2007 - 2009																					
Male - Hommes	69.7	65.7	60.8	55.9	51.1	46.4	41.6	36.9	32.3	28.0	24.0	20.4	17.0	13.9	11.1	8.6	6.4	4.6	3.3	2.4	1.7
Female - Femmes	77.1	73.0	68.1	63.1	58.3	53.3	48.4	43.6	38.8	34.1	29.6	25.2	21.0	17.0	13.3	9.9	7.1	5.0	3.5	2.5	1.8
Russian Federation - Fédération de Russie																					
2009																					
Male - Hommes	62.8	58.5	53.6	48.7	44.0	39.5	35.4	31.5	27.7	23.9	20.4	17.3	14.4	12.0	9.6	7.7	6.2	5.0	3.8	3.3	...
Female - Femmes	74.7	70.3	65.4	60.5	55.7	50.9	46.2	41.6	37.1	32.7	28.3	24.1	20.1	16.4	12.8	9.6	7.0	5.0	3.4	2.5	...
San Marino - Saint-Marin																					
2000																					
Male - Hommes	78.0	73.6	68.6	63.7	59.1	54.4	49.6	44.7	39.9	35.0	30.4	25.9	21.5	17.3	13.6	10.6	7.7	5.5	3.8	2.5	...
Female - Femmes	84.6	80.1	75.2	70.2	65.2	60.2	55.3	50.4	45.5	40.7	35.9	31.1	26.4	22.0	17.7	13.5	9.6	6.7	4.6	2.5	...
Serbia - Serbie																					
2009																					
Male - Hommes	71.1	66.7	61.8	56.9	52.0	47.2	42.5	37.8	33.1	28.6	24.3	20.4	16.8	13.5	10.6	8.0	6.0	4.2	...	...	...
Female - Femmes	76.4	71.9	67.0	62.0	57.1	52.2	47.3	42.4	37.6	32.9	28.3	23.9	19.7	15.6	12.0	8.7	6.3	4.4	...	...	...

Espérance de vie à un âge donné pour chaque sexe : dernière année disponible, 1991 - 2010 (continued - suite)

Continent, country or area and date / Continent, pays ou zone et date	Age (in years) - Age (en années)																				
	0	5	10	15	20	25	30	35	40	45	50	55	60	65	70	75	80	85	90	95	100
EUROPE																					
Slovakia - Slovaquie 2009																					
Male - Hommes	71.3	66.9	61.9	57.0	52.1	47.3	42.6	37.8	33.1	28.7	24.4	20.6	17.0	13.9	10.9	8.3	6.1	4.3	2.9	1.9	0.7
Female - Femmes	78.7	74.2	69.3	64.3	59.4	54.5	49.5	44.6	44.6	35.0	30.4	26.0	21.7	17.6	13.6	10.1	7.1	4.6	2.8	1.6	0.7
Slovenia - Slovénie 2008																					
Male - Hommes	75.8	71.0	66.0	61.1	56.2	51.4	46.6	41.9	37.1	32.5	28.1	23.9	19.9	16.2	12.9	9.8	7.3	5.2	3.7	2.6	...
Female - Femmes	82.3	77.6	72.6	67.6	62.7	57.8	52.8	47.9	43.0	38.2	33.5	28.9	24.5	20.1	16.0	12.1	8.8	6.1	4.3	2.9	...
Spain - Espagne 2009																					
Male - Hommes	78.5	73.9	68.9	64.0	59.1	54.2	49.3	44.5	39.7	35.0	30.5	26.1	22.0	18.1	14.4	11.0	8.2	5.9	4.2	3.2	2.5
Female - Femmes	84.6	79.9	74.9	69.9	65.0	60.0	55.1	50.2	45.3	40.5	35.8	31.1	26.5	22.0	17.6	13.5	9.8	6.8	4.6	3.1	1.9
Sweden - Suède 2009																					
Male - Hommes	79.4	74.6	69.7	64.7	59.8	55.0	50.2	45.4	40.5	35.8	31.1	26.6	22.3	18.2	14.3	10.8	7.8	5.4	3.7	2.6	1.9
Female - Femmes	83.4	78.6	73.7	68.7	63.7	58.8	53.9	49.0	44.1	39.2	34.5	29.9	25.4	21.0	16.9	13.1	9.6	6.6	4.5	3.2	2.3
Switzerland - Suisse 2009																					
Male - Hommes	79.8	75.2	70.2	65.3	60.4	55.6	50.7	45.9	41.1	36.3	31.7	27.2	22.9	18.8	14.9	11.4	8.4	5.9	4.3	3.7	...
Female - Femmes	84.4	79.8	74.8	69.8	64.9	59.9	55.0	50.1	45.2	40.3	35.5	30.9	26.4	22.0	17.7	13.7	10.0	6.9	4.7	3.6	...
TFYR of Macedonia - L'ex-R. y. de Macédoine 2008																					
Male - Hommes	72.1	68.1	63.1	58.2	53.3	48.5	43.7	38.9	34.1	29.5	25.1	20.9	17.1	13.6	10.5	7.8	5.6	3.8	2.8	2.4	...
Female - Femmes	76.3	72.1	67.2	62.2	57.3	52.4	47.4	42.5	37.7	32.9	28.3	23.8	19.5	15.4	11.8	8.6	6.0	4.3	3.5	2.5	...
Ukraine 2007 - 2008																					
Male - Hommes	62.5	58.4	53.5	48.6	43.9	39.3	35.0	31.0	27.3	23.7	20.4	17.4	14.6	12.0	9.7	7.7	6.0	4.6	3.3	2.4	0.8
Female - Femmes	74.3	70.1	65.2	60.3	55.4	50.6	45.9	41.3	36.8	32.4	28.1	23.9	19.9	16.1	12.6	9.5	6.9	4.9	3.4	2.4	0.8
United Kingdom of Great Britain and Northern Ireland - Royaume-Uni de Grande-Bretagne et d'Irlande du Nord[26] 2006 - 2008																					
Male - Hommes	77.4	72.9	67.9	63.0	58.1	53.3	48.5	43.8	39.1	34.4	29.9	25.5	21.3	17.4	13.8	10.5	7.8	5.7	4.0	2.8	2.0
Female - Femmes	81.6	77.1	72.1	67.1	62.2	57.3	52.4	47.5	42.7	37.9	33.2	28.7	24.3	20.0	16.1	12.4	9.2	6.6	4.5	3.1	2.2
OCEANIA - OCÉANIE																					
American Samoa - Samoas américaines 2006																					
Male - Hommes	68.5	...	...	...	...	...	...	...	...	...	...	...	...	...	...	...	...	...	...	...	...
Female - Femmes	76.2	...	...	...	...	...	...	...	...	...	...	...	...	...	...	...	...	...	...	...	...
Australia - Australie 2007 - 2009																					
Male - Hommes	79.3	74.8	69.8	64.9	60.0	55.2	50.4	45.7	41.0	36.3	31.7	27.2	22.9	18.7	14.9	11.4	8.4	6.0	4.2	3.1	2.5
Female - Femmes	83.9	79.3	74.3	69.4	64.4	59.5	54.6	49.7	44.9	40.1	35.3	30.7	26.1	21.8	17.6	13.6	10.0	7.1	4.8	3.4	2.7
Cook Islands - Îles Cook[27] 2001																					
Male - Hommes	68.0	...	...	...	...	...	...	...	...	...	...	...	...	...	...	...	...	...	...	...	...
Female - Femmes	74.0	...	...	...	...	...	...	...	...	...	...	...	...	...	...	...	...	...	...	...	...
Fiji - Fidji 1996																					
Male - Hommes	64.5	...	...	...	...	42.4								10.7							...
Female - Femmes	68.7	...	...	...	...	46.4						...		13.0							...
2007																					
Male - Hommes	63.8	...	...	...	...	...	...	...	...	...	...	...	...	...	...	...	...	...	...	...	...
Female - Femmes	67.8	...	...	...	...	...	...	...	...	...	...	...	...	...	...	...	...	...	...	...	...

Continent, country or area and date / Continent, pays ou zone et date	0	5	10	15	20	25	30	35	40	45	50	55	60	65	70	75	80	85	90	95	100
OCEANIA - OCÉANIE																					
French Polynesia - Polynésie française																					
2008																					
Male - Hommes	73.0	68.9	63.9	59.0	54.2	49.8	45.2	40.5	35.7	31.2	26.7	22.5	18.2	14.5	11.4	9.0	6.5	4.2	...	...	...
Female - Femmes	78.2	73.8	68.9	63.9	59.0	54.2	49.3	44.4	39.6	34.9	30.4	26.0	22.0	17.8	14.0	10.4	7.6	5.1	...	...	...
Guam																					
2008																					
Male - Hommes	75.9	...	...	...	...	...	...	...	...	...	...	...	...	...	...	...	...	...	...	...	...
Female - Femmes	82.2	...	...	...	...	...	...	...	...	...	...	...	...	...	...	...	...	...	...	...	...
Kiribati																					
2005																					
Male - Hommes	58.9	58.2	53.6	48.9	44.4	40.0	35.6	31.3	27.1	23.1	19.4	16.0	13.0	10.4	8.3	6.6	5.3	4.2	...	...	...
Female - Femmes	63.1	62.6	57.9	53.1	48.6	44.1	39.7	35.4	31.2	27.1	23.2	19.5	16.1	13.1	10.4	8.1	6.2	4.7	...	...	...
Marshall Islands - Îles Marshall																					
2004																					
Male - Hommes	67.0	...	...	...	...	...	...	...	...	...	...	..:	...	...	...	...	...	...	...	...	...
Female - Femmes	70.6	...	...	...	...	...	...	...	...	...	...	...	...	...	...	...	...	...	...	...	...
Micronesia (Federated States of) - Micronésie (États fédérés de)																					
1991 - 1992																					
Male - Hommes	64.4	63.6	59.0	54.2	49.6	45.2	40.7	36.2	31.8	27.4	23.3	19.4	15.9	12.7	9.9	7.5	5.6	...	...	...	...
Female - Femmes	66.8	65.9	61.2	56.5	51.9	47.3	42.8	38.4	34.0	29.6	25.4	21.3	17.5	13.9	10.8	8.1	6.0	...	...	...	...
2000																					
Male - Hommes	66.5	...	...	...	...	...	...	...	...	...	...	...	...	...	...	...	...	...	...	...	...
Female - Femmes	67.5	...	...	...	...	...	...	...	...	...	...	...	...	...	...	...	...	...	...	...	...
Nauru																					
2006																					
Male - Hommes	55.2	...	...	...	...	...	...	...	...	...	...	...	...	...	...	...	...	...	...	...	...
Female - Femmes	57.1	...	...	...	...	...	...	...	...	...	...	...	...	...	...	...	...	...	...	...	...
New Caledonia - Nouvelle-Calédonie																					
2007																					
Male - Hommes	71.8	67.7	62.8	57.9	53.4	48.9	44.4	39.8	35.2	30.7	26.6	...	18.5	...	12.0	...	7.0	...	...	...	...
Female - Femmes	80.3	75.8	70.8	65.9	61.0	56.1	51.2	46.5	41.7	37.0	32.3	...	23.4	...	15.1	...	8.7	...	...	...	...
New Zealand - Nouvelle-Zélande																					
2007 - 2009																					
Male - Hommes	78.4	74.0	69.0	64.1	59.3	54.6	49.8	45.1	40.3	35.7	31.1	26.6	22.3	18.3	14.5	11.1	8.3	6.0	4.3	...	...
Female - Femmes	82.4	77.9	72.9	68.0	63.1	58.2	53.3	48.4	43.6	38.9	34.1	29.6	25.1	20.8	16.8	13.1	9.6	6.8	4.6	...	...
Niue - Nioué																					
2006																					
Male - Hommes	67.0	...	...	...	...	...	...	...	...	...	...	...	...	...	...	...	...	...	...	...	...
Female - Femmes	76.0	...	...	...	...	...	...	...	...	...	...	...	...	...	...	...	...	...	...	...	...
Northern Mariana Islands - Îles Mariannes septentrionales																					
2009																					
Male - Hommes	74.5	...	...	...	...	...	...	...	...	...	...	...	...	...	...	...	...	...	...	...	...
Female - Femmes	79.9	...	...	...	...	...	...	...	...	...	...	...	...	...	...	...	...	...	...	...	...
Palau - Palaos																					
2005																					
Male - Hommes	66.3	...	...	...	...	...	...	...	...	...	...	...	...	...	...	...	...	...	...	...	...
Female - Femmes	72.1	...	...	...	...	...	...	...	...	...	...	...	...	...	...	...	...	...	...	...	...
Papua New Guinea - Papouasie-Nouvelle-Guinée																					
2000																					
Male - Hommes	53.7	54.1	50.2	45.7	41.6	37.7	33.7	29.8	25.9	22.1	18.5	15.0	11.9	9.2	6.9	5.0	3.6	2.6	1.7	0.6	...
Female - Femmes	54.8	54.7	50.8	46.3	42.1	38.1	34.1	30.1	26.2	22.3	18.6	15.2	12.0	9.2	6.8	5.0	3.6	2.5	1.6	0.6	...
Samoa																					
2006																					
Male - Hommes	71.5	...	...	...	...	...	...	...	...	...	...	...	...	...	...	...	...	...	...	...	...
Female - Femmes	74.2	...	...	...	...	...	...	...	...	...	...	...	...	...	...	...	...	...	...	...	...

Continent, country or area and date / Continent, pays ou zone et date	Age (in years) - Age (en années)																				
	0	5	10	15	20	25	30	35	40	45	50	55	60	65	70	75	80	85	90	95	100
OCEANIA - OCÉANIE																					
Solomon Islands - Îles Salomon																					
1999																					
Male - Hommes	60.6	...	...	...	...	...	...	...	...	...	...	...	...	...	...	...	...	...	...	...	...
Female - Femmes	61.6	...	...	...	...	...	...	...	...	...	...	...	...	...	...	...	...	...	...	...	...
Tonga																					
2006																					
Male - Hommes	67.3	64.1	59.3	54.5	49.9	45.4	40.7	36.2	31.6	27.2	23.4	19.4	15.9	13.0	9.4	6.3	4.0	...	...	...	...
Female - Femmes	73.0	69.3	64.6	59.8	55.0	50.1	45.2	40.4	35.7	31.3	27.1	23.0	19.0	15.3	11.6	8.6	6.1	...	...	...	...
Tuvalu																					
1997 - 2002																					
Male - Hommes	61.7	59.5	54.8	50.0	45.2	40.6	35.9	32.1	28.0	24.1	20.0	17.1	13.7	10.8	9.0	6.9	5.4	...	...	...	...
Female - Femmes	65.1	62.6	57.7	53.7	50.0	45.3	40.9	36.6	32.2	28.1	23.8	20.3	16.9	13.2	10.6	7.9	6.4	...	...	...	...
Vanuatu																					
1999																					
Male - Hommes	65.6	...	...	...	...	...	...	...	...	...	...	...	...	...	...	...	...	...	...	...	...
Female - Femmes	69.0	...	...	...	...	...	...	...	...	...	...	...	...	...	...	...	...	...	...	...	...
Wallis and Futuna Islands - Îles Wallis et Futuna																					
2003																					
Male - Hommes	73.1	...	...	...	...	...	...	...	...	...	...	...	...	...	...	...	...	...	...	...	...
Female - Femmes	75.5	...	...	...	...	...	...	...	...	...	...	...	...	...	...	...	...	...	...	...	...

FOOTNOTES - NOTES

[1] Data refer to Algerian population only. - Les données ne concernent que la population algérienne.

[2] Based on the results of the population census. - D'après le résultats du recensement de la population.

[3] Based on the results of the Botswana Demographic Survey. - Données extraites de l'enquête démographique effectuée par le Botswana.

[4] Based on the results of the 2006 Population and Housing Census. - Données fondées sur les résultats du recensement de la population et de l'habitat de 2006.

[5] Based on population census of the same year. - Sur la base du recensement de population de la même année.

[6] Data refer to national projections. - Les données se réfèrent aux projections nationales.

[7] Excludes the islands of St. Brandon and Agalega. - Non compris les îles St. Brandon et Agalega.

[8] Data are based on a small number of deaths. - Les données sont basées sur un nombre limité de décès.

[9] Data refer to projections based on the 1992 population census. - Les données se réfèrent aux projections basées sur le recensement de la population de 1992.

[10] Excluding Indian jungle population. - Non compris les Indiens de la jungle.

[11] Data refer to projections based on the 2005 population census. - Les données se réfèrent aux projections basées sur le recensement de la population de 2005.

[12] Excluding nomadic Indian tribes. Data refer to national projections. - Non compris les tribus d'Indiens nomades. Les données se réfèrent aux projections nationales.

[13] Life expectancy in 2000 is calculated by the death data of 2000's Population Census, which modified by the mortality rates from the annual national sample surveys on population changes since 1990 . For statistical purposes, the data for China do not include those for the Hong Kong Special Administrative Region (Hong Kong SAR), Macao Special Administrative Region (Macao SAR) and Taiwan province of China. - L'espérance de vie en 2000 par est calculée en se fondant sur les données relatives aux décès issues du recensement de la population de 2000 modifiées par les taux de mortalité extraits des enquêtes nationales annuelles par sondage concernant l'évolution de la population depuis 1990. Pour la présentation des statistiques, les données pour la Chine ne comprennent pas la Région Administrative Spéciale de Hong Kong (Hong Kong RAS), la Région Administrative Spéciale de Macao (Macao RAS) et Taïwan province de Chine.

[14] Data refer to government controlled areas. - Les données se rapportent aux zones contrôlées par le Gouvernement.

[15] Including data for the Indian-held part of Jammu and Kashmir, the final status of which has not yet been determined. - Y compris les données pour la partie du Jammu et du Cachemire occupée par l'Inde dont le statut définitif n'a pas encore été déterminé.

[16] Including data for East Jerusalem and Israeli residents in certain other territories under occupation by Israeli military forces since June 1967. - Y compris les données pour Jérusalem-Est et les résidents israéliens dans certains autres territoires occupés depuis 1967 par les forces armées israéliennes.

[17] Data refer to Japanese nationals in Japan only. - Les données se raportent aux nationaux japonais au Japon seulement.

[18] Excluding data for Jordanian territory under occupation since June 1967 by Israeli military forces. Excluding foreigners, including registered Palestinian refugees. - Non compris les données pour le territoire jordanien occupé depuis juin 1967 par les forces armées israéliennes. Non compris les étrangers, mais y compris les réfugiés de Palestine enregistrés.

[19] Based on the results of the 2005 Population and Housing Census. - Données fondées sur les résultats du recensement de la population et de l'habitat de 2005.

[20] Data refer to urban areas only. - Données ne concernant que les zones urbaines.

[21] Based on the results of the Pakistan Demographic Survey. Excluding data for the Pakistan-held part of Jammu and Kashmir, the final status of which has not yet been determined. - Données extraites de l'enquête démographique effectuée par le Pakistan. Non compris les données concernant la partie du Jammu et Cachemire occupée par le Pakistan dont le statut définitif n'a pas été déterminé.

[22] Data refer to resident population only. - Pour la population résidante seulement.

[23] Data based on Address Based Population Registration System. - Les données sont basées sur le registre national de la population basé sur l'adresse.

[24] Excluding Faeroe Islands and Greenland shown separately, if available. - Non compris les Iles Féroé et le Groenland, qui font l'objet de rubriques distinctes, si disponible.

[25] Excluding Svalbard and Jan Mayen Islands shown separately, if available. - Non compris Svalbard et Jan Mayen qui font l'objet de rubriques distinctes, si disponible.

[26] Excluding Channel Islands (Guernsey and Jersey) and Isle of Man, shown separately, if available. - Non compris les îles Anglo-Normandes (Guernesey et Jersey) et l'île de Man, qui font l'objet de rubriques distinctes, si disponible.

[27] Excluding Niue, shown separately, which is part of Cook Islands, but because of remoteness is administered separately. - Non compris Nioué, qui fait l'objet

d'une rubrique distincte et qui fait partie des îles Cook, mais qui, en raison de son
éloignement, est administrée séparément.

Table 22

Table 22 presents number of marriages and crude marriage rates by urban/rural residence for every year with available data between 2006 and 2010.

Description of variables: Marriage is defined as the act, ceremony or process by which the legal relationship of husband and wife is constituted. The legality of the union may be established by civil, religious or other means as recognized by the laws of each country[1].

Marriage statistics in this table, therefore, include both first marriages and remarriages after divorce, widowhood or annulment. They do not, unless otherwise noted, include resumption of marriage ties after legal separation. These statistics refer to the number of marriages performed, and not to the number of persons marrying.

Statistics shown are obtained from civil registers of marriage. Exceptions, such as data from church registers, are identified in footnotes.

The urban/rural classification of marriages is that provided by each country or area; it is presumed to be based on the national census definitions of urban population which have been set forth at the end of the technical notes for table 6.

For certain countries, there is a discrepancy between the total number of marriages shown in this table and those shown in subsequent tables for the same year. Usually this discrepancy arises because the total number of marriages occurring in a given year is revised although the remaining tabulations are not.

Rate computation: Crude marriage rates are the annual number of marriages per 1 000 mid-year population. Rates by urban/rural residence are the annual number of marriages, in the appropriate urban or rural category, per 1 000 corresponding mid-year population. Rates presented in this table have been limited to those for countries or areas having at least a total of 30 marriages in a given year. These rates are calculated by the Statistics Division of the United Nations based on the appropriate reference population (for example: total population, nationals only etc.) if known and available. If the reference population is not known or unavailable the total population is used to calculate the rates. Therefore, if the population that is used to calculate the rates is different from the correct reference population, the rates presented might under- or overstate the true situation in a country or area.

Reliability of data: Each country or area has been asked to indicate the estimated completeness of the number of marriages recorded in its civil register. These national assessments are indicated by the quality codes "C" and "U" that appear in the first column of this table.

"C" indicates that the data are estimated to be virtually complete, that is, representing at least 90 per cent of the marriages occurring each year, while "U" indicates that data are estimated to be incomplete, that is, representing less than 90 per cent of the marriages occurring each year. The code "..." indicates that no information was provided regarding completeness.

Data from civil registers which are reported as incomplete or of unknown completeness (coded "U" or "...") are considered unreliable. They appear in italics in this table; rates are not computed for these data.

These quality codes apply only to data from civil registers. For more information about the quality of vital statistics data in general, see section 4.2 of the Technical Notes.

Limitations: Statistics on marriages are subject to the same qualifications that have been set forth for vital statistics in general and marriage statistics in particular as discussed in section 4 of the Technical Notes.

The fact that marriage is a legal event, unlike birth and death that are biological events, has implications for international comparability of data. Marriage has been defined, for statistical purposes, in terms of the laws of individual countries or areas. These laws vary throughout the world. In addition, comparability is further limited because some countries or areas compile statistics only for civil marriages although religious marriages may also be legally recognized; in other countries or areas, the only available records are church registers and, therefore, the statistics may not reflect marriages that are civil marriages only.

Because in many countries or areas marriage is a civil legal contract which, to establish its legality, must be celebrated before a civil officer, it follows that for these countries or areas registration would tend to be almost automatic at the time of, or immediately following, the marriage ceremony. This factor should be kept in mind when considering the reliability of data, described above. For this reason the practice of tabulating data by date of registration does not generally pose serious problems of comparability as it does in the case of birth and death statistics.

As indicators of family formation, the statistics on the number of marriages presented in this table are bound to be deficient to the extent that they do not include either customary unions, which are not registered even though they are considered legal and binding under customary law, or consensual unions (also known as extra-legal or de facto unions). In general, lower marriage rates over a period of years are an indication of higher incidence of customary or consensual unions.

In addition, rates are affected also by the quality and limitations of the population estimates that are used in their computation. The problems of under-enumeration or over-enumeration and, to some extent, the differences in definition of total population have been discussed in section 3 of the Technical Notes dealing with population data in general, and specific information pertaining to individual countries or areas is given in the footnotes to table 3.

Strict correspondence between the numerator of the rate and the denominator is not always obtained; for example, marriages among civilian and military segments of the population may be related to civilian population. The effect of this may be to increase the rates, but, in most cases, this effect is negligible.

It should be emphasized that crude marriage rates like crude birth, death and divorce rates, may be seriously affected by the age-sex-marital structure of the population to which they relate. Crude marriage rates do, however, provide a simple measure of the level and changes in marriage.

The comparability of data by urban/rural residence is affected by the national definitions of urban and rural used in tabulating these data. It is assumed, in the absence of specific information to the contrary, that the definitions of urban and rural used in connection with the national population census were also used in the compilation of the vital statistics for each country or area. However, it cannot be excluded that, for a given country or area, different definitions of urban and rural are used for the vital statistics data and the population census data respectively. When known, the definitions of urban in national population censuses are presented at the end of the technical notes for table 6. As discussed in detail in the notes, these definitions vary considerably from one country or area to another.

In addition to problems of comparability, marriage rates classified by urban/rural residence are also subject to certain special types of bias. If, when calculating marriage rates, different definitions of urban are used in connection with the vital events and the population data, and if this results in a net difference between the numerator and denominator of the rate in the population at risk, then the marriage rates would be biased. Urban/rural differentials in marriage rates may also be affected by whether the vital events have been tabulated in terms of place of occurrence or place of usual residence. This problem is discussed in more detail in section 4.1.4.1 of the Technical Notes.

Earlier data: Marriages and crude marriage rates have been shown in each issue of the *Demographic Yearbook*. For more information on specific topics, and years for which data are reported, readers should consult the Historical Index.

NOTES

[1] *Principles and Recommendations for a Vital Statistics System Revision 2,* Sales No. E. 01.XVII.10, United Nations, New York, 2001

Tableau 22

Le tableau 22 présente des données sur les mariages et les taux bruts de nuptialité selon le lieu de résidence (zone urbaine ou rurale) pour les années où l'information est disponible entre 2006 et 2010.

Description des variables : le mariage désigne l'acte, la cérémonie ou la procédure qui établit un rapport légal entre mari et femme. L'union peut être rendue légale par une procédure civile ou religieuse, ou par toute autre procédure, conformément à la législation du pays[1].

Les statistiques de la nuptialité présentées dans ce tableau comprennent donc les premiers mariages et les remariages faisant suite à un divorce, un veuvage ou une annulation. Toutefois, sauf indication contraire, elles ne comprennent pas les unions reconstituées après une séparation légale. Ces statistiques se rapportent au nombre de mariages célébrés, non au nombre de personnes qui se marient.

Les statistiques présentées reposent sur l'enregistrement des mariages par les services de l'état civil. Les exceptions (données provenant des registres des églises, par exemple) font l'objet d'une note à la fin du tableau.

La classification des mariages selon le lieu de résidence (zone urbaine ou rurale) est celle qui a été communiquée par chaque pays ou zone ; on part du principe qu'elle repose sur les définitions de la population urbaine utilisées pour les recensements nationaux telles qu'elles sont reproduites à la fin des notes techniques se rapportant au tableau 6.

Pour quelques pays il y a une discordance entre le nombre total de mariages présenté dans ce tableau et ceux présentés après pour la même année. Habituellement ces différences apparaissent lorsque le nombre total des mariages pour une certaine année a été révisé alors que les autres tabulations ne l'ont pas été.

Calcul des taux : les taux bruts de nuptialité représentent le nombre annuel de mariages pour 1 000 habitants au milieu de l'année. Les taux selon le lieu de résidence (zone urbaine ou rurale) représentent le nombre annuel de mariages, classés selon la catégorie urbaine ou rurale appropriée, pour 1 000 habitants au milieu de l'année. Les taux du tableau 21 ne se rapportent qu'aux pays ou zones où l'on a enregistré un total d'au moins 30 mariages pendant une année donnée. Ces taux sont calculés par la division de statistique des Nations Unies sur la base de la population de référence adéquate (par exemple : population totale, nationaux seulement, etc.) si connue et disponible. Si la population de référence n'est pas connue ou n'est pas disponible, la population totale est utilisée pour calculer les taux. Par conséquent, si la population utilisée pour calculer les taux est différente de la population de référence adéquate, les taux présentés sont susceptibles de sous ou sur estimer la situation réelle d'un pays ou d'un territoire.

Fiabilité des données : il a été demandé à chaque pays ou zone d'indiquer le degré estimatif de complétude des données sur les mariages figurant dans ses registres d'état civil. Ces évaluations nationales sont signalées par les codes de qualité "C" et "U" qui apparaissent dans la deuxième colonne du tableau.

La lettre "C" indique que les données sont jugées à peu près complètes, c'est-à-dire qu'elles représentent au moins 90 p. 100 des mariages survenus chaque année ; la lettre "U" signale que les données sont jugées incomplètes, c'est-à-dire qu'elles représentent moins de 90 p. 100 des mariages survenus chaque année. Le code "..." indique qu'aucun renseignement n'a été communiqué quant à la complétude des données.

Les données issues des registres de l'état civil qui sont déclarées incomplètes ou dont le degré de complétude n'est pas connu (code "U" ou "...") sont jugées douteuses. Elles apparaissent en italique dans le tableau et les taux correspondants n'ont pas été calculés.

Les codes de qualité ne s'appliquent qu'aux données provenant des registres de l'état civil. Pour plus de précisions sur la qualité des données reposant sur les statistiques de l'état civil en général, voir la section 4.2 des Notes techniques.

Insuffisance des données : les statistiques relatives aux mariages appellent les mêmes réserves que celles qui ont été formulées à propos des statistiques de l'état civil en général et des statistiques concernant la nuptialité en particulier (voir la section 4 des Notes techniques).

Le fait que le mariage soit un acte juridique, à la différence de la naissance et du décès, qui sont des faits biologiques, a des répercussions sur la comparabilité internationale des données. Aux fins de la statistique, le mariage est défini par la législation de chaque pays ou zone. Cette législation varie d'un pays à l'autre. La comparabilité est limitée en outre du fait que certains pays ou zones ne réunissent des statistiques que pour les mariages civils, bien que les mariages religieux y soient également reconnus par la loi ; dans d'autres, les seuls relevés disponibles sont les registres des églises et, en conséquence, les statistiques peuvent ne pas rendre compte des mariages exclusivement civils.

Étant donné que, dans de nombreux pays ou zones, le mariage est un contrat juridique civil qui, pour être légal, doit être conclu devant un officier d'état civil, il s'ensuit que dans ces pays ou zones l'enregistrement se fait à peu près systématiquement au moment de la cérémonie ou immédiatement après. Il faut tenir compte de cet élément lorsque l'on évalue la fiabilité des données, dont il est question plus haut. C'est pourquoi la pratique consistant à exploiter les données selon la date de l'enregistrement ne pose généralement pas les graves problèmes de comparabilité auxquels on se heurte dans le cas des statistiques concernant les naissances et les décès.

Les statistiques relatives au nombre des mariages présentées dans ce tableau donnent une idée forcément trompeuse de la formation des familles, dans la mesure où elles ne tiennent compte ni des mariages coutumiers, qui ne sont pas enregistrés bien qu'ils soient considérés comme légaux et créateurs d'obligations en vertu du droit coutumier, ni des unions consensuelles (appelées également unions non légalisées ou unions de fait). En général, une diminution du taux de nuptialité pendant un certain nombre d'années indique une augmentation des mariages coutumiers ou des unions consensuelles.

L'exactitude des taux dépend également de la qualité et des insuffisances des estimations de population qui sont utilisées pour leur calcul. Le problème des erreurs par excès ou par défaut commises lors du dénombrement et, dans une certaine mesure, le problème de l'hétérogénéité des définitions de la population totale ont été examinés à la section 3 des Notes techniques relative à la population en général ; des indications concernant les différents pays ou zones sont données en note à la fin du tableau 3.

Il n'a pas toujours été possible d'obtenir une correspondance rigoureuse entre le numérateur et le dénominateur pour le calcul des taux. Par exemple, les mariages parmi la population civile et les militaires sont parfois rapportés à la population civile. Cela peut avoir pour effet d'accroître les taux, mais, dans la plupart des cas, il est probable que la différence sera négligeable.

Il faut souligner que les taux bruts de nuptialité, de même que les taux bruts de natalité, de mortalité et de divortialité, peuvent varier sensiblement selon la structure par âge et par sexe de la population à laquelle ils se rapportent. Les taux bruts de nuptialité offrent néanmoins un moyen simple de mesurer la fréquence et l'évolution des mariages.

La comparabilité des données selon le lieu de résidence (zone urbaine ou rurale) peut être limitée par les définitions nationales des termes « urbain » et « rural » utilisées pour le classement de ces données. En l'absence d'indications contraires, on a supposé que les mêmes définitions avaient servi pour le recensement national de la population et pour l'établissement des statistiques de l'état civil pour chaque pays ou zone. Toutefois, il n'est pas exclu que, pour une zone ou un pays donné, des définitions différentes aient été retenues. Les définitions du terme « urbain » utilisées pour les recensements nationaux de population ont été présentées à la fin des notes techniques du tableau 6 lorsqu'elles étaient connues. Comme on l'a précisé dans les notes techniques relatives au tableau 6, ces définitions varient considérablement d'un pays ou d'une zone à l'autre.

Outre les problèmes de comparabilité, les taux de nuptialité classés selon le lieu de résidence (zone urbaine ou rurale) sont également sujets à des distorsions particulières. Si l'on utilise des définitions différentes du terme « urbain » pour classer les faits d'état civil et les données relatives à la population lors du calcul des taux et qu'il en résulte une différence nette entre le numérateur et le dénominateur pour le taux de la population exposée au risque, les taux de nuptialité s'en trouveront faussés. La différence entre ces taux pour les zones urbaines et rurales pourra aussi être faussée selon que les faits d'état civil auront été

classés d'après le lieu où ils se sont produits ou d'après le lieu de résidence habituel. Ce problème est examiné plus en détail à la section 4.1.4.1 des Notes techniques.

Données publiées antérieurement : les différentes éditions de l'*Annuaire démographique* regroupent des données sur le nombre des mariages. Pour plus de précisions concernant les années et les sujets pour lesquels des données ont été publiées, se reporter à l'index historique.

NOTE

[1] *Principes et recommandations pour un système de statistiques de l'état civil, deuxième révision*, numéro de vente : F.01.XVII.10, publication des Nations Unies, New York, 2003.

22. Marriages and crude marriage rates, by urban/rural residence: 2006 - 2010
Mariages et taux bruts de nuptialité, selon la résidence, urbaine/rurale : 2006 - 2010

Continent, country or area, and urban/rural residence / Continent, pays ou zone et résidence, urbaine/rurale	Code[a]	Number - Nombre					Rate - Taux				
		2006	2007	2008	2009	2010	2006	2007	2008	2009	2010
AFRICA - AFRIQUE											
Algeria - Algérie[1]											
Total	...	295 295	325 485	331 190	341 321	344 819	...	...	...	...	...
Botswana											
Total	+U	4 335	4 997	...	...	...	...	...	...	...	...
Egypt - Égypte[2]											
Total	+...	522 887	614 848	660 159	759 004	...	...	...	...	...	...
Urban - Urbaine	+...	168 323	204 910	216 120	282 598	...	...	...	...	...	...
Rural - Rurale	+...	354 564	409 938	444 039	476 406	...	...	...	...	...	...
Mauritius - Maurice[3]											
Total	+C	11 471	11 547	11 197	10 619	10 555	9.2	9.2	8.8	8.3	8.2
Urban - Urbaine	+C	3 468	3 483	3 440	3 372	...	6.6	6.6	6.5	6.3	...
Rural - Rurale	+C	8 003	8 064	7 757	7 247	...	11.0	11.0	10.5	9.8	...
Réunion											
Total	C	2 982	2 899	...	...	...	3.8	3.7	...	...	...
Saint Helena ex. dep. - Sainte-Hélène sans dép.											
Total	C	10	15	9	14	8	...	...	...	...	...
Seychelles[4]											
Total	+C	984	1 081	1 248	1 208	1 440	11.6	12.7	14.4	13.8	16.6
South Africa - Afrique du Sud											
Total	...	184 860	183 030	186 522	...	...	...	...	...	...	...
Tunisia - Tunisie											
Total	...	81 340	76 809	78 748	81 600	...	...	...	...	...	...
AMERICA, NORTH - AMÉRIQUE DU NORD											
Anguilla[5]											
Total	C	74	43	54	...	...	5.2	2.9	3.5	...	...
Antigua and Barbuda - Antigua-et-Barbuda											
Total	+C	1 950	1 863	...	...	...	23.1	21.7	...	...	...
Aruba[6]											
Total	C	546	531	*405	...	...	5.3	5.1	*3.8	...	...
Bahamas											
Total	C	2 599	2 021	1 969	...	...	7.9	6.1	5.8	...	...
Barbados - Barbade											
Total	+C	2 890	2 768	...	...	...	10.6	10.1	...	...	...
Bermuda - Bermudes											
Total	C	876	846	721	683	...	13.7	13.2	11.2	10.6	...
Canada[7]											
Total	C	149 792	*151 695	*150 423	...	...	4.6	*4.6	*4.5	...	...
Cayman Islands - Îles Caïmanes[8]											
Total	+C	529	482	487	544	...	10.2	8.9	8.7	10.3	...
Costa Rica[9]											
Total	C	26 575	26 010	25 034	23 920	*23 955	6.1	5.9	5.5	5.2	*5.3
Urban - Urbaine	C	14 964	13 868	12 918	12 628	*12 564	5.8	5.3	4.8	4.6	*4.5
Rural - Rurale	C	11 611	12 142	12 116	11 292	*11 391	6.5	6.7	6.5	5.9	*6.5
Cuba[10]											
Total	C	56 377	56 781	61 852	54 969	58 490	5.0	5.1	5.5	4.9	5.2
Urban - Urbaine	C	52 818	53 330	58 336	51 396	...	6.2	6.3	6.9	6.1	...
Rural - Rurale	C	3 559	3 451	3 516	3 573	...	1.3	1.3	1.3	1.3	...
Dominica - Dominique											
Total	+C	294	...	...	...	...	4.1	...	...	...	...
Dominican Republic - République dominicaine											
Total	+C	42 375	39 993	38 310	40 040	...	4.5	4.2	4.0	4.1	...
El Salvador											
Total[11]	...	24 500	28 675	27 714	...	...	...	...	...	...	...
Urban - Urbaine[12]	...	20 659	...	...	...	...	...	...	...	...	...
Rural - Rurale[12]	...	3 782	...	...	...	...	...	...	...	...	...
Guadeloupe											
Total	C	1 736	1 427	...	...	...	3.8	3.6	...	...	...
Guatemala											
Total	C	57 505	57 003	52 315	...	...	4.4	4.3	3.8	...	...

22. Marriages and crude marriage rates, by urban/rural residence: 2006 - 2010
Mariages et taux bruts de nuptialité, selon la résidence, urbaine/rurale : 2006 - 2010 (continued - suite)

Continent, country or area, and urban/rural residence Continent, pays ou zone et résidence, urbaine/rurale	Code[a]	Number - Nombre					Rate - Taux				
		2006	2007	2008	2009	2010	2006	2007	2008	2009	2010

AMERICA, NORTH - AMÉRIQUE DU NORD

Jamaica - Jamaïque											
Total	C	23 181	20 250	21 989	21 412	20 489	8.7	7.6	8.2	7.9	7.6
Martinique											
Total	C	1 477	1 341	...	...	...	3.7	3.4	...	...	...
Urban - Urbaine[13]	C	...	1 122	...	...	...	...	...	...	...	...
Rural - Rurale[13]	C	...	137	...	...	...	...	...	...	...	...
Mexico - Mexique											
Total	+C	586 978	595 209	589 352	...	...	5.6	5.6	5.5	...	...
Urban - Urbaine[14]	+C	445 475	450 665	443 959	...	...	5.5	5.5	5.4	...	...
Rural - Rurale[14]	+C	126 157	126 566	125 479	...	...	5.1	5.2	5.1	...	...
Netherlands Antilles - Antilles néerlandaises[15]											
Total	C	1 104	...	...	...	...	5.8	...	...	...	...
Nicaragua											
Total	+U	23 320	20 918	16 542	...	...	...	...	...	...	...
Panama											
Total	C	10 747	11 516	11 508	12 273[9]	...	3.3	3.4	3.4	3.6	...
Urban - Urbaine	C	9 033	9 584	9 490	9 689[9]	...	4.3	4.5	4.4	4.4	...
Rural - Rurale	C	1 714	1 932	2 018	2 584[9]	...	1.4	1.6	1.7	2.1	...
Puerto Rico - Porto Rico											
Total	C	23 185	21 613	18 620	...	...	5.9	5.5	4.7	...	...
Saint Vincent and the Grenadines - Saint-Vincent-et-les Grenadines											
Total	+C	524	576	588	573	...	5.2	5.8	5.9	...	...
Trinidad and Tobago - Trinité-et-Tobago											
Total	C	7 917	...	...	...	...	6.1	...	...	...	...
Turks and Caicos Islands - Îles Turques et Caïques											
Total	C	636	467	486	...	...	19.2	13.4	13.3	...	...
United States of America - États-Unis d'Amérique											
Total	C	2 193 000	2 197 000	2 157 000	2 077 000	...	7.3	7.3	7.1	6.8	...

AMERICA, SOUTH - AMÉRIQUE DU SUD

Argentina - Argentine											
Total	C	134 496	136 437	133 060	126 081	...	3.5	3.5	3.3	3.1	...
Bolivia (Plurinational State of) - Bolivie (État plurinational de)											
Total	U	35 608	*18 072	...	...	...	...	...	...	...	...
Brazil - Brésil[16]											
Total	U	889 828	916 006	959 901	935 116	...	...	...	...	...	...
Chile - Chili											
Total	+C	58 155	57 792	56 112	...	...	3.5	3.5	3.3	...	...
Urban - Urbaine[17]	+C	52 001	53 382	51 133	...	...	3.6	3.7	3.5	...	...
Rural - Rurale[17]	+C	6 154	4 410	4 979	...	...	2.8	2.0	2.3	...	...
Ecuador - Équateur[18]											
Total	U	74 036	76 154	76 354	76 892	...	...	...	...	...	...
French Guiana - Guyane française											
Total	C	629	667	...	...	...	3.1	3.1	...	...	...
Paraguay											
Total	U	19 476	19 726	18 832	...	...	...	...	...	...	...
Peru - Pérou											
Total	+C	89 162	90 883	94 971	87 561[19]	...	3.2	3.2	3.3	3.0	...
Suriname											
Total	C	2 144	2 161	...	...	...	4.3	4.2	...	...	...
Uruguay											
Total	C	12 415	12 771	12 180	...	...	3.7	3.8	3.7	...	...

22. Marriages and crude marriage rates, by urban/rural residence: 2006 - 2010
Mariages et taux bruts de nuptialité, selon la résidence, urbaine/rurale : 2006 - 2010 (continued - suite)

Continent, country or area, and urban/rural residence / Continent, pays ou zone et résidence, urbaine/rurale	Code[a]	Number - Nombre					Rate - Taux				
		2006	2007	2008	2009	2010	2006	2007	2008	2009	2010
AMERICA, SOUTH - AMÉRIQUE DU SUD											
Venezuela (Bolivarian Repubiic of) - Venezuela (République bolivarienne du)[20]											
Total	C	89 772	93 003	93 741	...	...	3.3	3.4	3.4	...	...
ASIA - ASIE											
Armenia - Arménie											
Total	+C	16 887	18 145	18 465	18 773	16 904	5.2	5.6	5.7	5.8	5.2
Urban - Urbaine	+C	11 139	12 058	12 198	12 441	...	5.4	5.8	5.9	6.0	...
Rural - Rurale	+C	5 748	6 087	6 267	6 332	...	5.0	5.3	5.4	5.4	...
Azerbaijan - Azerbaïdjan											
Total	+C	79 443	81 758	79 964	78 072	79 172	9.2	9.4	9.0	8.7	8.8
Urban - Urbaine	+C	39 345	41 814	40 996	40 708	...	8.6	8.9	8.6	8.4	...
Rural - Rurale	+C	40 098	39 944	38 968	37 364	...	10.0	9.9	9.6	9.1	...
Bahrain - Bahreïn											
Total	...	4 717	4 981	...	...	...	...	...	...	...	...
Brunei Darussalam - Brunéi Darussalam											
Total	...	2 095	2 176	2 391	...	...	...	...	...	...	...
China - Chine[21]											
Total	+C	9 450 000	9 914 000	...	...	...	7.2	7.5	...	...	...
China, Hong Kong SAR - Chine, Hong Kong RAS											
Total	C	50 328	47 453	47 331	51 175	...	7.3	6.9	6.8	7.3	...
China, Macao SAR - Chine, Macao RAS											
Total	+C	2 100	2 047	2 778	3 035	...	4.2	3.9	5.0	5.6	...
Cyprus - Chypre[22]											
Total	C	4 887	6 332	6 115	6 327	...	6.3	8.1	7.7	7.9	...
Georgia - Géorgie[9]											
Total	C	21 845	24 891	31 414	...	34 675	5.0	5.7	7.2	...	...
Urban - Urbaine	C	15 861	18 521	21 028	...	...	6.9	8.0	9.1	...	...
Rural - Rurale	C	5 984	6 370	10 386	...	...	2.9	3.1	5.0	...	...
Indonesia - Indonésie											
Total	U	1 904 153	1 944 569	2 101 057	...	...	...	...	...	...	...
Iran (Islamic Republic of) - Iran (République islamique d')[23]											
Total	+C	778 023	841 107	881 592	890 208	...	11.0	11.8	12.2	12.2	...
Urban - Urbaine	+C	556 658	602 309	633 179	629 893	...	...	12.3	12.8	12.5	...
Rural - Rurale	+C	221 365	238 798	248 413	260 315	...	...	10.7	11.0	11.4	...
Iraq											
Total	U	305 284	268 638	...	...	...	...	...	...	...	...
Israel - Israël[24]											
Total	C	44 685	46 448	50 038	...	...	6.3	6.5	6.8	...	...
Urban - Urbaine[25]	C	40 583	42 092	44 967	...	...	6.3	6.4	6.7	...	...
Rural - Rurale[25]	C	3 071	3 451	3 801	...	...	5.4	5.9	6.3	...	...
Japan - Japon[26]											
Total	+C	730 971	719 822	726 106	707 734	...	5.8	5.7	5.8	5.5	...
Urban - Urbaine	+C	666 236	659 390	666 651	650 746	...	...	...	...	...	...
Rural - Rurale	+C	64 735	60 432	59 455	56 988	...	...	...	...	...	...
Jordan - Jordanie[27]											
Total	+C	59 335	60 548	60 922	63 389	...	10.6	10.6	10.4	10.6	...
Kazakhstan											
Total	C	137 204	146 379	135 280	...	...	9.0	9.5	8.6	...	...
Urban - Urbaine	C	85 622	85 768	82 235	...	...	9.8	10.5	9.9	...	...
Rural - Rurale	C	51 582	60 611	53 045	...	...	7.9	8.3	7.2	...	...
Kuwait - Koweït											
Total	C	12 584	13 315	14 709	...	...	5.4	5.5	5.9	...	...
Kyrgyzstan - Kirghizstan											
Total	C	43 760	44 392	44 258	47 567	...	8.7	8.8	8.7	9.3	...
Urban - Urbaine	C	12 372	13 426	13 400	14 442	...	6.9	7.5	7.5	8.0	...
Rural - Rurale	C	31 388	30 966	30 858	33 125	...	9.7	9.5	9.4	10.0	...

22. Marriages and crude marriage rates, by urban/rural residence: 2006 - 2010
Mariages et taux bruts de nuptialité, selon la résidence, urbaine/rurale : 2006 - 2010 (continued - suite)

Continent, country or area, and urban/rural residence / Continent, pays ou zone et résidence, urbaine/rurale	Code[a]	Number - Nombre					Rate - Taux				
		2006	2007	2008	2009	2010	2006	2007	2008	2009	2010
ASIA - ASIE											
Lebanon - Liban											
Total	C	29 078	35 796	37 593	40 565	41 758	...	9.5	...	...	...
Maldives											
Total	...	5 556	...	...	...	...	...	...	...	...	...
Urban - Urbaine	...	2 514	...	...	...	...	...	...	...	...	...
Rural - Rurale	...	3 042	...	...	...	...	...	...	...	...	...
Mongolia - Mongolie											
Total	C	48 996[28]	40 965	32 982	34 071	...	19.0	15.7	12.4	12.5	...
Urban - Urbaine	C	31 529[28]	26 043	23 582	...	...	20.2	16.4	14.5	...	...
Rural - Rurale	C	17 467[28]	14 922	9 400	...	...	17.2	14.6	9.1	...	...
Occupied Palestinian Territory - Territoire palestinien occupé											
Total	C	28 233	32 685	33 774	...	...	7.8	8.8	8.8	...	...
Oman[29]											
Total	+U	...	...	...	25 608	...	...	...	...	...	...
Philippines											
Total	U	492 666	490 054	...	...	...	...	...	...	...	...
Qatar											
Total	C	3 019	3 206	3 235	3 153	2 901	2.9	2.6	2.2	1.9	1.7
Republic of Korea - République de Corée[30]											
Total	+C	330 634	343 559	327 715	309 759	...	6.8	7.0	6.6	6.2	...
Urban - Urbaine[31]	+C	261 377	274 592	262 357	248 050	...	6.6	6.9	6.5	6.2	...
Rural - Rurale[31]	+C	58 382	59 397	57 035	52 918	...	6.2	6.4	6.1	5.6	...
Saudi Arabia - Arabie saoudite[32]											
Total	...	115 549	130 451	...	...	...	...	...	...	...	...
Singapore - Singapour[33]											
Total	+C	23 706	23 966	24 596	26 081	24 363	5.4	5.2	5.1	5.2	4.8
Sri Lanka											
Total	+U	196 817	196 236	*198 578	*194 970	*200 985	...	...	...	...	...
Syrian Arab Republic - République arabe syrienne[34]											
Total	+U	205 557	237 592	...	...	...	...	...	...	...	...
Tajikistan - Tadjikistan											
Total	+C	57 278	97 713	106 388	100 678	...	8.2	13.7	14.6	...	...
Urban - Urbaine	+C	15 952	25 893	25 718	...	...	8.7	13.8	13.4	...	...
Rural - Rurale	+C	41 326	71 820	80 670	...	...	8.0	13.6	15.0	...	...
Turkey - Turquie[35]											
Total	C	636 121	638 311	641 973	591 742	572 677	9.2	9.1	9.0	8.2	7.9
United Arab Emirates - Émirats arabes unis[32]											
Total	...	13 190	12 987	15 041	...	...	...	...	...	...	...
Viet Nam											
Total	C	493 383	480 064	...	...	...	5.9	5.7	...	...	...
Urban - Urbaine	C	138 683	134 316	...	...	...	6.0	5.7	...	...	...
Rural - Rurale	C	354 700	345 748	...	...	...	5.9	5.7	...	...	...
EUROPE											
Åland Islands - Îles d'Åland											
Total	C	116	116	139	120	*140	4.3	4.3	5.1	4.3	*5.0
Urban - Urbaine	C	46	43	66	54	*49	4.3	4.0	6.0	4.9	*4.4
Rural - Rurale	C	70	73	73	66	*91	4.4	4.5	4.5	4.0	*5.4
Albania - Albanie											
Total	C	21 332	22 371	21 299	...	...	6.8	7.1	6.7	...	...
Andorra - Andorre											
Total	C	296	258	260	265	287	3.7	3.1	3.1	3.1	3.4
Austria - Autriche[36]											
Total	C	36 923	35 996	35 223	35 469	37 545	4.5	4.3	4.2	4.2	4.5
Belarus - Bélarus											
Total	C	78 979	90 444	77 201	78 800	76 978	8.1	9.3	8.0	8.2	8.1
Urban - Urbaine	C	64 965	74 894	64 281	65 149	...	9.2	10.6	9.0	9.1	...
Rural - Rurale	C	14 014	15 550	12 920	13 651	...	5.3	6.0	5.1	5.5	...

Continent, country or area, and urban/rural residence / Continent, pays ou zone et résidence, urbaine/rurale	Code[a]	Number - Nombre					Rate - Taux				
		2006	2007	2008	2009	2010	2006	2007	2008	2009	2010
EUROPE											
Belgium - Belgique[37]											
Total	C	44 813	45 561	45 613	43 303	*46 000	4.3	4.3	4.3	4.0	*4.2
Urban - Urbaine	C	44 231	44 944	45 040	42 673	...	4.3	4.3	...	...	...
Rural - Rurale	C	582	617	573	630	...	3.8	4.0	...	...	...
Bosnia and Herzegovina - Bosnie-Herzégovine											
Total	C	21 501	23 494	22 151	20 633	*19 731	5.6	6.1	5.8	5.4	*5.1
Bulgaria - Bulgarie[38]											
Total	C	32 773	29 640	27 722	25 923	24 286	4.3	3.9	3.6	3.4	3.2
Urban - Urbaine	C	26 159	23 456	21 844	20 592	...	4.8	4.3	4.0	3.8	...
Rural - Rurale	C	6 614	6 184	5 878	5 331	...	2.9	2.8	2.6	2.4	...
Croatia - Croatie											
Total	C	22 092	23 140	23 373	22 382	...	5.0	5.2	5.3	5.1	...
Urban - Urbaine	C	12 396	12 784	13 048	12 637	...	...	...	...	...	...
Rural - Rurale	C	9 696	10 356	10 325	9 745	...	...	...	...	...	...
Czech Republic - République tchèque											
Total	C	52 860	57 157	52 457	47 862	46 746	5.1	5.5	5.0	4.6	4.4
Urban - Urbaine	C	40 010	43 175	39 602	35 882	...	5.3	5.7	5.1	4.6	...
Rural - Rurale	C	12 850	13 982	12 855	11 980	...	4.8	5.1	4.7	4.3	...
Denmark - Danemark[39]											
Total	C	36 452	36 576	37 376	32 934	30 949	6.7	6.7	6.8	6.0	5.6
Estonia - Estonie											
Total	C	6 954	7 022	6 127	5 362	5 066	5.2	5.2	4.6	4.0	3.8
Urban - Urbaine[40]	C	4 893	4 811	4 218	3 693	...	5.3	5.2	4.5	4.0	...
Rural - Rurale[40]	C	1 810	1 958	1 687	1 456	...	4.4	4.8	4.1	3.6	...
Faeroe Islands - Îles Féroé											
Total	C	283	217	...	...	...	5.9	4.5	...	...	...
Urban - Urbaine	C	131	93	...	...	...	7.5	5.3	...	...	...
Rural - Rurale	C	152	124	...	...	...	4.9	4.0	...	...	...
Finland - Finlande[41]											
Total	C	28 236	29 497	31 014	29 716[42]	29 952	5.4	5.6	5.8	5.6	5.6
Urban - Urbaine	C	21 213	22 121	23 189	22 495[42]	...	6.0	6.2	6.4	6.2	...
Rural - Rurale	C	7 023	7 376	7 825	7 221[42]	...	4.1	4.3	4.6	4.3	...
France[43]											
Total	C	267 260	267 194	258 739	245 151	*243 000	4.3	4.3	4.2	3.9	*3.9
Urban - Urbaine[44]	C	196 863	196 151	190 122	181 876	...	...	...	...	...	...
Rural - Rurale[44]	C	63 937	65 407	63 935	58 391	...	...	...	...	...	...
Germany - Allemagne											
Total	C	373 681	368 922	376 998	378 439	*381 000	4.5	4.5	4.6	4.6	*4.7
Gibraltar[45]											
Total	+C	161	132	158	...	...	5.6	4.5	5.4	...	...
Greece - Grèce											
Total	C	57 802	61 377	53 500	59 212	...	5.2	5.5	4.8	5.2	...
Urban - Urbaine	C	40 536	43 010	37 500	41 719	...	...	...	...	...	...
Rural - Rurale	C	17 266	18 367	16 000	17 493	...	...	...	...	...	...
Hungary - Hongrie											
Total	C	44 528	40 842	40 105	36 730	*35 520	4.4	4.1	4.0	3.7	*3.6
Urban - Urbaine[46]	C	31 842	29 047	29 228	27 066	...	4.7	4.3	4.3	3.9	...
Rural - Rurale[46]	C	11 784	11 121	10 306	9 157	...	3.5	3.4	3.2	2.9	...
Iceland - Islande[6]											
Total	C	1 753	1 797	1 704	1 480	...	5.8	5.8	5.3	4.6	...
Urban - Urbaine	C	1 681	1 717	1 619	1 415	...	6.0	5.9	5.4	4.7	...
Rural - Rurale	C	72	80	85	65	...	3.2	3.6	4.0	3.2	...
Ireland - Irlande											
Total	+C	21 841	22 544	*22 243	*21 541	...	5.2	5.2	*5.0	*4.8	...
Italy - Italie											
Total	C	245 992	250 360	246 613	*230 859	*217 079	4.2	4.2	4.1	*3.8	*3.6
Jersey											
Total	+C	607	586	...	...	...	6.8	6.5	...	...	...
Latvia - Lettonie[9]											
Total	C	14 616	15 486	12 946	9 925	9 290	6.4	6.8	5.7	4.4	4.1
Urban - Urbaine	C	10 563	11 020	9 117	7 105	...	6.8	7.1	5.9	4.7	...
Rural - Rurale	C	4 053	4 466	3 829	2 820	...	5.5	6.1	5.3	3.9	...
Liechtenstein[9]											
Total	C	151	182	205	*154	*181	4.3	5.2	5.8	*4.3	*5.0

Continent, country or area, and urban/rural residence / Continent, pays ou zone et résidence, urbaine/rurale	Code[a]	Number - Nombre					Rate - Taux				
		2006	2007	2008	2009	2010	2006	2007	2008	2009	2010
EUROPE											
Lithuania - Lituanie											
Total	C	21 246	23 065	24 063	20 542	18 688	6.3	6.8	7.2	6.2	5.7
Urban - Urbaine	C	14 598	15 905	16 420	14 471	...	6.4	7.1	7.3	6.5	...
Rural - Rurale	C	6 648	7 160	7 643	6 071	...	5.9	6.4	6.9	5.5	...
Luxembourg											
Total	C	1 948[6]	1 969[6]	1 917[6]	1 739[47]	1 749[47]	4.1	4.1	3.9	3.5	3.5
Malta - Malte											
Total	C	2 536	2 479	2 482	2 353	2 596	6.2	6.1	6.0	5.7	6.2
Montenegro - Monténégro											
Total	C	3 462	4 005	3 445	3 829	3 690	5.5	6.4	5.5	6.1	5.8
Urban - Urbaine	C	...	...	2 708	3 517	...	...	...	6.8	8.8	...
Rural - Rurale	C	...	...	737	312	...	...	...	3.2	1.4	...
Netherlands - Pays-Bas[48]											
Total	C	72 369	72 485	75 438	73 477[50]	...	4.4	4.4	4.6	4.4	...
Urban - Urbaine[49]	C	41 783	42 532	44 679	43 475[50]	...	3.9	3.9	4.1	4.0	...
Rural - Rurale[49]	C	24 270	24 584	25 275	24 088[50]	...	4.4	4.4	4.5	4.3	...
Norway - Norvège[51]											
Total	C	21 721	23 471	25 125	24 299	23 577	4.7	5.0	5.3	5.0	4.8
Poland - Pologne											
Total	C	226 181	248 702	257 744	250 794	228 337	5.9	6.5	6.8	6.6	6.0
Urban - Urbaine	C	137 163	150 166	154 936	152 651	...	5.9	6.4	6.6	6.6	...
Rural - Rurale	C	89 018	98 536	102 808	98 143	...	6.0	6.7	6.9	6.6	...
Portugal											
Total	C	47 857	46 329	43 228	40 391[47]	*39 813[47]	4.5	4.4	4.1	3.8	*3.7
Republic of Moldova - République de Moldova											
Total	C	27 128	29 213	26 666	26 781	26 483	7.6	8.2	7.5	7.5	7.4
Urban - Urbaine	C	13 174	14 622	13 368	13 360	...	8.9	9.9	9.1	9.0	...
Rural - Rurale	C	13 954	14 591	13 298	13 421	...	6.6	6.9	6.3	6.4	...
Romania - Roumanie											
Total	C	146 637	189 240	149 439	134 275[47]	115 778[47]	6.8	8.8	6.9	6.3	5.4
Urban - Urbaine	C	96 605	104 445	96 963	86 363[47]	...	8.1	8.8	8.2	7.3	...
Rural - Rurale	C	50 032	84 795	52 476	47 912[47]	...	5.2	8.8	5.4	5.0	...
Russian Federation - Fédération de Russie[47]											
Total	C	1 113 562	1 262 500	1 179 007	1 199 446	1 215 066	7.8	8.9	8.3	8.5	8.5
San Marino - Saint-Marin[52]											
Total	C	216	216	202	...	...	6.9	6.8	6.2	...	...
Serbia - Serbie[53]											
Total	+C	39 756	41 083	38 285	36 853	35 815	5.4	5.6	5.2	5.0	4.8
Urban - Urbaine	+C	25 288	26 498	24 537	24 051	...	5.9	6.2	5.7	5.6	...
Rural - Rurale	+C	14 468	14 585	13 748	12 802	...	4.6	4.7	4.5	4.2	...
Slovakia - Slovaquie[9]											
Total	C	25 939	27 437	28 293	26 356	25 415	4.8	5.1	5.2	4.9	4.7
Urban - Urbaine	C	15 022	15 994	16 355	15 094	...	5.0	5.4	5.5	5.1	...
Rural - Rurale	C	10 917	11 443	11 938	11 262	...	4.5	4.7	4.9	4.6	...
Slovenia - Slovénie											
Total	C	6 368	6 373	6 703	6 542	*6 494	3.2	3.2	3.3	3.2	*3.2
Urban - Urbaine	C	3 357	3 203	3 460	3 337	...	3.5	3.2	3.4	3.3	...
Rural - Rurale	C	3 011	3 170	3 243	3 205	...	3.0	3.1	3.2	3.1	...
Spain - Espagne											
Total	C	207 766	204 772	194 022	174 062	*164 990	4.7	4.6	4.3	3.8	*3.6
Sweden - Suède											
Total	C	45 551	47 898	50 332	48 033[54]	50 730	5.0	5.2	5.5	5.2	5.4
Switzerland - Suisse[55]											
Total	C	39 817	40 330	41 534	41 918	*42 800	5.3	5.3	5.4	5.4	*5.5
Urban - Urbaine	C	30 658	30 947	31 883	32 119	...	5.6	5.6	5.7	5.6	...
Rural - Rurale	C	9 159	9 383	9 651	9 799	...	4.6	4.7	4.8	4.8	...
TFYR of Macedonia - L'ex-R. y. de Macédoine											
Total	C	14 908	15 490	14 695	14 923	*14 155	7.3	7.6	7.2	7.3	*6.9
Urban - Urbaine	C	7 848	8 347	7 696	8 067	...	...	...	...	...	...
Rural - Rurale	C	7 060	7 143	6 999	6 856	...	...	...	...	...	...
Ukraine											
Total	C	354 959	416 427	321 992	318 198	305 933	7.6	9.0	7.0	6.9	6.7
Urban - Urbaine	C	270 504	317 641	244 832	...	...	8.5	10.0	7.7	...	...
Rural - Rurale	C	84 455	98 786	77 160	...	...	5.6	6.7	5.3	...	...

22. Marriages and crude marriage rates, by urban/rural residence: 2006 - 2010
Mariages et taux bruts de nuptialité, selon la résidence, urbaine/rurale : 2006 - 2010 (continued - suite)

Continent, country or area, and urban/rural residence / Continent, pays ou zone et résidence, urbaine/rurale	Code[a] / Co-de[a]	Number - Nombre					Rate - Taux				
		2006	2007	2008	2009	2010	2006	2007	2008	2009	2010
OCEANIA - OCÉANIE											
American Samoa - Samoas américaines											
Total	C	171	...	...	...	...	2.6	...	...	...	...
Australia - Australie											
Total	+C	114 222	116 322	118 756	120 118	...	5.5	5.5	5.5	5.5	...
Cook Islands - Îles Cook[56]											
Total	+C	707	785	702	817	*846	29.8	37.4	31.8	35.7	*36.8
French Polynesia - Polynésie française											
Total	C	1 124	1 152	1 178	...	...	4.4	4.4	4.5	...	...
New Caledonia - Nouvelle-Calédonie											
Total	C	927	884	975	*932	...	3.9	3.6	4.0	*3.8	...
Urban - Urbaine	C	...	596	...	...	...	...	...	...	...	...
Rural - Rurale	C	...	288	...	...	...	...	...	...	...	...
New Zealand - Nouvelle-Zélande[9]											
Total	+C	21 423	21 494	21 948	21 628	20 900	5.1	5.1	5.1	5.0	4.8
Niue - Nioué											
Total	C	19	13	13	12	...	...	...	...	...	...
Norfolk Island - Île Norfolk[57]											
Total	+C	43	21	32	...	...	18.2	...	...	...	...
Samoa											
Total	U	*1 310*	*1 193*	*1 052*	*953*	...	...	...	...	...	...
Wallis and Futuna Islands - Îles Wallis et Futuna											
Total	C	...	...	53	...	...	...	...	3.9	...	...

FOOTNOTES - NOTES

Italics: data from civil registers which are incomplete or of unknown completeness. - Italiques : données incomplètes ou dont le degré d'exactitude n'est pas connu, provenant des registres de l'état civil.

* Provisional. - Données provisoires.

[a] 'Code' indicates the source of data, as follows:
C - Civil registration, estimated over 90% complete
U - Civil registration, estimated less than 90% complete
| - Other source, estimated reliable
+ - Data tabulated by date of registration rather than occurence
... - Information not available

Le 'Code' indique la source des données, comme suit :
C - Registres de l'état civil considérés complèts à 90 p. 100 au moins
U - Registres de l'état civil qui ne sont pas considérés complèts à 90 p. 100 au moins
| - Autre source, considérée pas douteuses
+ - Données exploitées selon la date de l'enregistrement et non la date de l'événement
... - Information pas disponible

[1] Data refer to Algerian population only. - Les données ne concernent que la population algérienne.
[2] Including marriages resumed after 'revocable divorce' (among Moslem population), which approximates legal separation. - Y compris les unions reconstituées après un 'divorce révocable' (parmi la population musulmane), qui est à peu près l'équivalent d'une séparation légale.
[3] Excludes the islands of St. Brandon and Agalega. - Non compris les îles St. Brandon et Agalega.
[4] Including visitors. - Visiteurs compris.
[5] Excluding visitors. - Les données non compris des visiteurs.
[6] Data refer to resident population only. - Pour la population résidante seulement.
[7] Since 2003, definition of marriage has been changed in some provinces and territories to include the legal union of two persons of the same sex. - Depuis 2003, la définition du mariage a changé dans certaines provinces et certains territoires afin d'englober les unions légales entre deux personnes du même sexe.
[8] Either bride or groom or both are residents. - Le marié, la mariée ou les deux sont des résidents.
[9] Marriages registered where the groom was resident. - Mariages enregistrés où le marié était un résident.
[10] Marriages registered by residence of bride. - Les mariages sont enregistrés selon le lieu de résidence de la mariée.
[11] Including marriages where bride/groom are non-residents. - Y compris les mariages pour lesquels le marié et la mariée sont des non-résidents.
[12] Data refer to the department where the event took place. - Les données font référence au département dans lequel l'événement est survenu.
[13] In urban/rural distribution, some data is not available which is the reason for the difference with the total. - Dans la répartition urbain/rural, certaines données ne sont pas disponible d'où la différence entre le total et la somme de urbain, rural.
[14] The difference between 'Total' and the sum of urban and rural is due to the unknown place of residence of bride/wife. Urban and rural distribution refers to the usual residence of the bride/wife. - La différence entre le total et la somme des chiffres urbains et ruraux s'explique par le lieu de résidence inconnu des maris. La répartition urbain/rural se réfère au domicile habituel de la jeune mariée/de l'épouse.
[15] Number of marriages of which at least one person was resident of the Netherlands Antilles (marital tourism is excluded). - Nombre de couples mariés dont l'un des membres au moins résidait aux Antilles néerlandaises (le tourisme conjugal n'est pas pris en compte).
[16] Excluding Indian jungle population. - Non compris les Indiens de la jungle.
[17] Urban and rural distribution refers to the usual residence of the groom/husband. - La répartition urbain/rural se réfère au domicile habituel du jeune marié/de l'époux.
[18] Excluding nomadic Indian tribes. - Non compris les tribus d'Indiens nomades.
[19] Based on National Registers of identification and civil status. - Chiffres fondés sur les registres nationaux d'identification et d'état civil.
[20] Residence established by place where marriage took place. - La résidence est déterminée par rapport au lieu où le mariage a été célébré.

[21] For statistical purposes, the data for China do not include those for the Hong Kong Special Administrative Region (Hong Kong SAR), Macao Special Administrative Region (Macao SAR) and Taiwan province of China. - Pour la présentation des statistiques, les données pour la Chine ne comprennent pas la Région Administrative Spéciale de Hong Kong (Hong Kong RAS), la Région Administrative Spéciale de Macao (Macao RAS) et Taïwan province de Chine.

[22] Data refer to government controlled areas. Data refer to resident population only. - Les données se rapportent aux zones contrôlées par le Gouvernement. Pour la population résidante seulement.

[23] Data refer to the Iranian Year which begins on 21 March and ends on 20 March of the following year. - Les données concernent l'année iranienne, qui commence le 21 mars et se termine le 20 mars de l'année suivante.

[24] Including data for East Jerusalem and Israeli residents in certain other territories under occupation by Israeli military forces since June 1967. - Y compris les données pour Jérusalem-Est et les résidents israéliens dans certains autres territoires occupés depuis 1967 par les forces armées israéliennes.

[25] The total number includes 'Unknown residence', but the categories urban and rural do not. Urban and rural distribution refers to the usual residence of the groom/husband. - Le nombre total inclue 'Résidence inconnue ', mais les catégories urbaine et rurale ne l'incluent pas. La répartition urbain/rural se réfère au domicile habituel du jeune marié/de l'époux.

[26] Data refer to Japanese nationals in Japan only. - Les données se raportent aux nationaux japonais au Japon seulement.

[27] Excluding data for Jordanian territory under occupation since June 1967 by Israeli military forces. Excluding foreigners, including registered Palestinian refugees. - Non compris les données pour le territoire jordanien occupé depuis juin 1967 par les forces armées israéliennes. Non compris les étrangers, mais y compris les réfugiés de Palestine enregistrés.

[28] Since 2006, the Government of Mongolia has started to implement " Newly married couple" programme that aims to promote marriage. - En 2006, le Gouvernement mongol a lancé le programme intitulé « jeunes mariés » qui vise à promouvoir le mariage.

[29] Data refer to registered events only. - Les données ne concernent que les événements enregistrés.

[30] Excluding alien armed forces, civilian aliens employed by armed forces, and foreign diplomatic personnel and their dependants. Data refer to residence of groom. - Non compris les militaires étrangers, les civils étrangers employés par les forces armées ni le personnel diplomatique étranger et les membres de leur famille les accompagnant. Les données correspondent à la résidence du marié.

[31] The total number includes 'Unknown residence', but the categories urban and rural do not. - Le nombre total inclue 'Résidence inconnue ', mais les catégories urbaine et rurale ne l'incluent pas.

[32] As published by the United Nations Economic and Social Commission for Western Asia. - Publié par la Commission économique et sociale des Nations Unies pour l'Asie occidentale.

[33] Excluding marriages previously officiated outside Singapore or under religious and customary rites. - Les figures excluent les mariages célébrés précédemment au dehors de Singapour ou sous les rites réligieuse ou accoutumés.

[34] Excluding nomad population. - Non compris les nomades.

[35] Data from MERNIS (Central Population Administrative System). - Données de MERNIS (Système central de données démographiques).

[36] Excluding aliens temporarily in the area. - Non compris les étrangers se trouvant temporairement dans le territoire.

[37] Including armed forces stationed outside the country, but excluding alien armed forces in the area unless marriage performed by local foreign authority. - Y compris les militaires nationaux hors du pays et les militaires étrangers en garnison sur le territoire, sauf si le mariage a été célébré pour l'autorité locale.

[38] Including nationals outside the country, but excluding foreigners in the country. - Y compris les nationaux à l'étranger, mais non compris les étrangers sur le territoire.

[39] Excluding Faeroe Islands and Greenland shown separately, if available. - Non compris les Iles Féroé et le Groenland, qui font l'objet de rubriques distinctes, si disponible.

[40] Urban and rural distribution of marriages and divorces is displayed by place of residence of groom/husband. The difference between 'Total' and the sum of urban and rural is due to the unknown place of residence of grooms/husbands and to grooms/husbands living outside country. - Les mariages et divorces sont classés par rapport à la résidence urbaine/rurale de l'époux. La somme des mariages et divorces par résidence urbaine/rurale est différente du 'total' car elle ne tient pas compte ni des résidences inconnues de l'époux ni des mariages et divorces d'époux vivant à l'étranger.

[41] Only marriages in which the bride was resident in Finland. - Seulement mariages où l'épouse réside en Finlande.

[42] Excluding Åland Islands. - Non compris les Îles d'Åland.

[43] Including armed forces stationed outside the country. - Y compris les militaires nationaux hors du pays.

[44] Data for urban and rural, excluding nationals outside the country. - Les données pour la résidence urbaine et rurale , non compris les nationaux hors du pays.

[45] Data refer to marriages where one or both partners are residents. - Les données se réfèrent aux mariages dont l'un des époux ou tous les deux sont des résidents.

[46] Total includes the data of foreigners, persons of unknown residence and homeless, but the categories urban and rural do not. - Total incluant les étrangers, les personnes de résidence inconnue et les sans-abri, ce qui n'est pas le cas pour les catégories urbaines et rurales.

[47] Marriages registered by place of occurrence of marriage. - Mariages enregistrés en fonction du lieu de l'événement.

[48] Marriages of couples of which at least one partner is recorded in a Dutch municipal register, irrespective of the country where the marriage was performed. Including same sex marriages. - Mariages où un des conjoints au moins est inscrit dans un registre municipal néerlandais, quel que soit le pays où le mariage a été contracté. Y compris les mariages entre personnes du même sexe.

[49] The difference between 'Total' and the sum of 'urban' and 'rural' is due to the cases of unknown place of residence or residence abroad. - La différence entre le 'Total' et la somme des données selon la résidence urbaine/rurale se rapporte à la situation ou on ignore la résidence ou si la résidence est à l'étranger.

[50] Including residents outside the country if listed in a Netherlands population register. Marriages registered by place of occurrence of marriage. - Y compris les résidents hors du pays, s'ils sont inscrits sur un registre de population néerlandais. Mariages enregistrés en fonction du lieu de l'événement.

[51] Excluding Svalbard and Jan Mayen Islands shown separately, if available. Only marriages in which the groom was resident in Norway. - Non compris Svalbard et Jan Mayen qui font l'objet de rubriques distinctes, si disponible. Seulement mariages où l'époux réside en Norvège.

[52] Includes civil and religious marriages as well as not specified. - Y compris les mariages civils, religieux ou non précisés.

[53] Excluding data for Kosovo and Metohia. - Sans les données pour le Kosovo et Metohia.

[54] Including same sex marriages. - Y compris les mariages entre personnes du même sexe.

[55] Data based on the residence of groom if he has permanent address in the country, otherwise, based on the residence of bride. If neither partner is a permanent resident, the marriage is not included in the official statistics. - Les données sont fondées sur la résidence du marié si celui-ci a une adresse permanente dans le pays, sinon elles sont fondées sur la résidence de la mariée. Si aucun des deux partenaires n'est un résident permanent, le mariage n'apparaît pas dans les statistiques officielles.

[56] A high percentage of marriages are non resident marriages, therefore the rates do not reflect the crude marriage rate of resident population. Excluding Niue, shown separately, which is part of Cook Islands, but because of remoteness is administered separately. - Un fort pourcentage sont des mariages entre partenaires qui ne sont pas résidents permanents, par conséquant les taux ne réfletent pas les taux bruts de nuptialité de la population résidante. Non compris Nioué, qui fait l'objet d'une rubrique distincte et qui fait partie des îles Cook, mais qui, en raison de son éloignement, est administrée séparément.

[57] Data cover the period from 1 July previous year to 30 June present year. - Pour la période allant du 1er juillet de l'année précédente au 30 juin de l'année en cours.

Table 23 and 23a

Table 23 presents the marriages cross-classified by age of groom and age of bride for the latest available year between 2000 and 2009. Table 23a presents the available data for year 2010.

Description of variables: Marriage is defined as the act, ceremony or process by which the legal relationship of husband and wife is constituted. The legality of the union may be established by civil, religious or other means as recognized by the laws of each country[1].

Marriage statistics in this table, therefore, include both first marriages and remarriages after divorce, widowhood or annulment. They do not, unless otherwise noted, include resumption of marriage ties after legal separation. These statistics refer to the number of marriages performed, and not to the number of persons marrying.

Age is defined as age at last birthday, that is, the difference between the date of birth and the date of the occurrence of the event, expressed in completed solar years. The age classification used for brides in this table is the following: under 15 years, 5-year age groups through 90-94, and 95 years and over, depending on the availability of data. Age classification for grooms is restricted to: under 15 years, 5-year age groups from 15 to 59, and 60 years and over.

In an effort to provide interpretation of these statistics, countries or areas providing data on marriages by age of groom and bride have been requested to specify "the minimum legal age at which marriage can take place with and without parental consent". This information is presented in the table 23-1 below.

Reliability of data: Data from civil registers of marriages that are reported as incomplete (less than 90 per cent completeness) or of unknown completeness are considered unreliable and are set in *italics* rather than in roman type. Table 23 and the technical notes for that table provide more detailed information on the completeness of marriage registration. For more information about the quality of vital statistics data in general, see section 4.2 of the Technical Notes.

Limitations: Statistics on marriages by age of groom and age of bride are subject to the same qualifications as have been set forth for vital statistics in general and marriage statistics in particular as discussed in Section 4 of the Technical Notes.

The fact that marriage is a legal event, unlike birth and death that are biological events, has implications for international comparability of data. Marriage has been defined, for statistical purposes, in terms of the laws of individual countries or areas. These laws vary throughout the world. In addition, comparability is further limited because some countries or areas compile statistics only for civil marriages although religious marriages may also be legally recognized; in other countries or areas, the only available records are church registers and, therefore, the statistics may not reflect marriages that are civil marriages only.

Because in many countries or areas marriage is a civil legal contract which, to establish its legality, must be celebrated before a civil officer, it follows that for these countries or areas registration would tend to be almost automatic at the time of, or immediately following, the marriage ceremony. This factor should be kept in mind when considering the reliability of data, described above. For this reason the practice of tabulating data by date of registration does not generally pose serious problems of comparability as it does in the case of birth and death statistics.

Because these statistics are classified according to age, they are subject to the limitations with respect to accuracy of age reporting similar to those already discussed in connection with Section 3.1.3 of the Technical Notes. It is probable that biases are less pronounced in marriage statistics, because information is obtained from the persons concerned and since marriage is a legal act, the participants are likely to give correct information. However, in some countries or areas, there appears to be a concentration of marriages at the legal minimum age for marriage and at the age at which valid marriage may be contracted without parental consent, indicating perhaps an overstatement in some cases to comply with the law.

Aside from the possibility of age misreporting, it should be noted that marriage patterns at younger ages, that is, for ages up to 24 years, are influenced to a large extent by laws regarding the minimum age for marriage.

Factors that may influence age reporting, particularly at older ages include an inclination to understate the age of the bride in order that it may be equal to or less than that of the groom.

The absence of data in the unknown age group does not necessarily indicate completely accurate reporting and tabulation of the age item. It is sometimes an indication that the unknowns have been eliminated by assigning ages to them before tabulation, or by proportionate distribution after tabulation.

Another age-reporting factor that must be kept in mind in using these data is the variation that may result from calculating age at marriage from year of birth rather than from day, month and year of birth. Information on this factor is given in footnotes when known.

Earlier data: Marriages by age of groom and age of bride have been shown for the latest available year in most issues of the *Demographic Yearbook*. Data cross-classified by age of groom and bride have been presented in previous issues featuring marriage and divorce statistics. For information on the specific topics and the years covered, readers should consult the Historical Index.

23-1 Minimum legal age at which marriage can take place

Country or area	With parental consent		Without parental consent	
	Groom	Bride	Groom	Bride
Africa				
Botswana	18	18	21	21
Burkina Faso[2]	18	15	20	17
Egypt	18	16	21	21
Ghana			18	18
Liberia	16	16	21	18
Libya[3]	18	18		
Malawi[4]			18	18
Mauritius	16	16	18	18
Morocco[4]			18	18
Namibia	18	18	21	21
Saint Helena ex. dep.	16	16	21	21
Senegal	Under 18	Under 18	18	18
Seychelles	16	16	18	18
Sierra Leone[4]			18	18
South Africa	18	15	21	21
Uganda[4, 5]			18	18
Zimbabwe	16	16	18	18
America, North				
Anguilla			18	18
Aruba	18	15	18	18
Bermuda[4]			18	18
Canada[6]	16	16	18	18
Cayman Islands	16	16	18	18
Costa Rica	15	15	18	18
Cuba	16	14	18	16
Dominican Republic	17	16	18	18
El Salvador	15	14	18	18
Greenland[7]	16	15	18	18

646

Country or area	With parental consent		Without parental consent	
	Groom	Bride	Groom	Bride
Jamaica	16	16	18	18
Mexico[8]	16	14	18	18
Montserrat[9]	16	16	18	18
Netherlands Antilles			18	18
Panama	16	14	18	18
Puerto Rico	18	16	21	21
Trinidad and Tobago[10]	Under 18	Under 18	18	18
America, South				
Brazil	16	16	18	18
Chile	16	16	18	18
Colombia	14	14	18	18
Ecuador	Under 18	Under 18	18	18
Suriname	17	15	21	21
Uruguay	14	12	18	18
Venezuela (Bolivarian Republic of)[4]			12	12
Asia				
Armenia			18	17
Azerbaijan	18	17		
Bahrain			15	
Cambodia			18	18
China, Hong Kong SAR	16	16	21	21
China, Macao SAR	16	16	18	18
Georgia	16	16	18	18
Indonesia			19	16
Iran	18	15		
Israel[4]			17	17
Japan	18	16	20	20
Kazakhstan	16	16	18	17
Kyrgyzstan	16	16	18	18
Malaysia[11]	18	16	18 and 21	16 and 21
Nepal	18	18	20	20
Occupied Palestinian Territory[12]		14.5	15.5	
Oman[4]			18	18
Philippines	18	18	21	21
Republic of Korea	18	18	20	20
Singapore[13]	Under 21	Under 21	21	21
Tajikistan	17	17	18	18
Turkey	16	16	18	18
Uzbekistan			17	17

Country or area	With parental consent		Without parental consent	
	Groom	Bride	Groom	Bride
Europe				
Åland Islands[4]			18	18
Albania	18	16		
Austria[14]	16	16	18	18
Belarus[15]			18	18
Belgium	Under 18	Under 18	18	18
Bosnia and Herzegovina			18	18
Bulgaria	16	16	18	18
Croatia	16	16	18	18
Czech Republic	16	16	18	18
Denmark	15	15	18	18
Estonia	15	15	18	18
Finland[16]			18	18
France[4]			18	18
Germany[17]	16	16	18	18
Gibraltar	16	16	18	18
Greece[18]			18	18
Hungary	16	16	18	18
Iceland[4]			18	18
Ireland[4, 19]			18	18
Isle of Man	16	16	18	18
Italy	16	16	18	18
Jersey	16	16	18	18
Latvia	16	16	18	18
Liechtenstein[14]			18	18
Lithuania[20]	15	15	18	18
Luxembourg			18	16
Malta			16	16
Montenegro	16	16	18	18
Netherlands	16	16	18	18
Norway	16	16	18	18
Poland[21]			18	18
Portugal	16	16	18	18
Republic of Moldova			18	16
Romania[4]			18	18
Russian Federation	16	16	18	18
Serbia	16	16	18	18
Slovakia[22]			16	16
Slovenia	15	15	18	18

Country or area	With parental consent		Without parental consent	
	Groom	Bride	Groom	Bride
Spain	14	14	18	18
Sweden [23]			18	18
Switzerland	16	16	18	18
TFYR of Macedonia	16	16	18	18
Ukraine	15	15	18	17
United Kingdom of Great Britain and Northern Ireland	16	16	18	18
Oceania				
Australia	16	16	18	18
Cook Islands	16	16	21	21
New Caledonia			18	18
New Zealand	16	16	18	18

NOTES

[1] *Principles and Recommendations for a Vital Statistics System Revision 2,* Sales No. 01.XVII.10, United Nations, New York, 2001.

[2] In addition, an age waiver may be granted by a civil court for a serious reason from 15 years for women and 18 years for men.

[3] According to the Islamic law, marriage requires parental consent. Consent of the bride herself, as well as the guardian's consent are fundamental in the marriage contract. Young men usually choose the consent of the parents. Minimum age at marriage is usually 18 years. According to the law, marriage is not restricted to individuals over the age of 18 years.

[4] The minimum legal age at which marriage can take place is the same respectively for bride and groom with or without parental consent.

[5] As reported by Uganda Bureau of Statistics, marriages with or without parental consent may occur much earlier than 18 years of age.

[6] Marriage is under provincial and territory legislations. Without parental consent, the minimum legal age at which marriage can take place is 18 years of age in all provinces and territories in Canada except in British Columbia, Newfoundland and Labrador, Nova Scotia, Nunavut, and Yukon where the minimum legal age is 19 years. With parental consent, the minimum legal age is 16 years in all provinces except in Northwest Territories, Nunavut, and Yukon. With parental consent, in Northwest Territories, and Yukon the minimum legal age is 15 years whereas in Nunavut, the minimum legal age is 18 years.

[7] To marry at age younger than 18 years, both parental and official consent are needed. Pregnancy is one of the very few reasons to get official consent.

[8] Each of the 31 Federal States and the Federal District has its own civil code for marriage. Exceptions to ages given in the table are as follows: without parental consent, the minimum legal age at which marriage can take place in Baja California and Tlaxcala is 16 years for males and 14 years for females whereas in Baja California Sur, it is 16 years for females. With parental consent, the minimum legal age for marriage is 16 years for both males and females in Aguascalientes, Campeche, Chiapas, Distrito Federal, Guerrero, Jalisco, Morelos, Puebla, Quintana Roo, Querétaro, San Luis Potosí, and Sonora. With parental consent, the minimum legal age for marriage is under 18 years for both males and females in Coahuila, Hidalgo, and Zacatecas. The Minimum legal age for marriage remains the same respectively for bride and groom with or without parental consent in Baja California, Baja California Sur and Tlaxcala.

[9] Consent can be given by a guardian or a person who has custody of the child wishing to marry. Also the Governor has discretion to permit persons as young as 15 years and 1 day old to marry, if he thinks that getting married is in the best interest of the persons who are intending to marry and the persons in this instance must have also received the necessary consent.

[10] With parental consent, age for marriage is 14 years for males and 12 years for females in a civil marriage; 16 years for males and 12 years for females in a Muslim marriage; 18 years for males and 14 years for females in a Hindu marriage; and 18 years for males and 16 for females in Orisa marriage.

[11] Without parental consent, it is 21 years of age for non-Muslim males and 18 years of age for Muslim males whereas it is 21 years of age for non-Muslim females and 16 years of age for Muslim females. For marriage with parental consent, approval of relevant authorities is required.

[12] The legal marriage age for females is 14 years, 6 months and 22 days. There must be parental consent (father or brother if the father is dead). The legal marriage age for males is 15 years, 6 months and 21 days. Parental consent is not required.

[13] Specified minimum legal marriage age refers to marriages contracted under the Women's Charter. For Muslim marriages under the Administration of Muslim Law Act, no marriage shall be solemnised when either party is below the age of 18 years. Notwithstanding that,

Muslim women below the age of 18 years who have attained the age of puberty may be married under the Administration of the Muslim Law Act.

[14] Persons less than 18 years old need a decision of the court.

[15] In compliance with the Marriage and Family Code of the Republic of Belarus, in the exclusive cases related to pregnancy, childbirth, and in case of acquiring by a juvenile of a full legal capacity under lawful age, the civil registration offices are in a position to reduce the marriage age of espousing persons, but not more than by 3 years. The marriage age is to be reduced by an application of espousing persons; the parental consent is not required.

[16] Persons less than 18 years old need the permission of the Ministry of Justice.

[17] Marriage at 16-17 years of age requires that the other spouse be an adult already betrothed (18 years) and an exemption from the requirement of majority by a competent family court.

[18] Under some conditions (e.g. pregnancy) the marriage can take place without age restrictions.

[19] An exemption on the minimum age can be granted by court order if granting of such an exemption is in the best interests of the parties to the intended marriage and good reasons for the application can be demonstrated.

[20] In addition to parental consent, persons less than 18 years old need judicial approval. In case of pregnancy, marriage can be allowed below 15 years of age.

[21] Females can marry at the age of 16 or 17 years with parental and court consent.

[22] A marriage cannot be entered into by a minor. The court may exceptionally and for important reasons approve of entrance into marriage by a minor older than sixteen years. Without this approval, the marriage is invalid and the court shall declare the invalidity even without a petition.

[23] With parental consent, no limit but authorities must approve; without parental consent, 18 years of age for Swedish citizens.

Tableau 23 et 23a

Le tableau 23 présente des statistiques concernant les mariages classés selon l'âge de l'époux et selon l'âge de l'épouse pour les années où les données sont disponibles entre 2000 et 2009. Le tableau 23a présente les données disponibles pour l'année 2010.

Description des variables : le mariage désigne l'acte, la cérémonie ou la procédure qui établit un rapport légal entre mari et femme. L'union peut être rendue légale par une procédure civile ou religieuse, ou par toute autre procédure, conformément à la législation du pays[1].

Les statistiques de la nuptialité présentées dans ce tableau comprennent donc les premiers mariages et les remariages faisant suite à un divorce, un veuvage ou une annulation. Toutefois, sauf indication contraire, elles ne comprennent pas les unions reconstituées après une séparation légale. Ces statistiques se rapportent au nombre de mariages célébrés, non au nombre de personnes qui se marient.

L'âge désigne l'âge au dernier anniversaire, c'est-à-dire la différence entre la date de naissance et la date de l'événement, exprimée en années solaires révolues. Le classement par âge pour l'épouse utilisé dans ce tableau comprend les groupes suivants : moins de 15 ans, groupes quinquennaux jusqu'à 90-94 ans, et 95 ans et plus, selon la disponibilité des données. Le classement par âge pour l'époux est : moins de 15 ans, groupes quinquennal de 15 jusqu' à 59 ans et 60 ans et plus.

Dans un effort de fournir l'interprétation de ces statistiques, les pays ou les zones fournissant des données sur les mariages par l'âge de l'épouse et de par l'âge de l'époux ont été demandés d'indiquer "l'âge légal minimum avec auquel le mariage peut avoir lieu avec et sans consentement parental". Cette information est présentée dans le tableau 23-1 ci-dessous.

Fiabilité des données : les données sur les mariages issues des registres de l'état civil qui sont déclarées incomplètes (degré de complétude inférieur à 90 p. 100) ou dont le degré de complétude n'est pas connu sont jugées douteuses et apparaissent en italique et non en caractères romains. Le tableau 23 et les notes techniques s'y rapportant présentent des renseignements plus détaillés sur le degré de complétude de l'enregistrement des mariages. Pour plus de précisions sur la qualité des données reposant sur les statistiques de l'état civil en général, voir la section 4.2 des notes techniques.

Insuffisance des données : les statistiques des mariages selon l'âge de l'époux et selon l'âge de l'épouse appellent les mêmes réserves que celles formulées à propos des statistiques de l'état civil en général et des statistiques de la nuptialité en particulier (voir la section 4 des Notes techniques).

Le fait que le mariage soit un acte juridique, à la différence de la naissance et du décès, qui sont des faits biologiques, a des répercussions sur la comparabilité internationale des données. Aux fins de la statistique, le mariage est défini par la législation de chaque pays ou zone. Cette législation varie d'un pays à l'autre. La comparabilité est limitée en outre du fait que certains pays et zones ne réunissent des statistiques que pour les mariages civils, bien que les mariages religieux y soient également reconnus par la loi ; dans d'autres, les seuls relevés disponibles sont les registres des églises et, en conséquence, les statistiques peuvent ne pas rendre compte des mariages exclusivement civils.

Le mariage étant, dans de nombreux pays ou zones, un contrat juridique civil qui, pour être légal, doit être conclu devant un officier d'état civil, il s'ensuit que, dans ces pays ou zones, l'enregistrement se fait à peu près systématiquement au moment de la cérémonie ou immédiatement après. Il faut tenir compte de cet élément lorsque l'on évalue la fiabilité des données, dont il est question plus haut. C'est pourquoi la pratique consistant à exploiter les données selon la date de l'enregistrement ne pose généralement pas les graves problèmes de comparabilité auxquels on se heurte dans le cas des statistiques des naissances et des décès.

Étant donné que ces statistiques sont classées selon l'âge, elles appellent les mêmes réserves concernant l'exactitude des déclarations d'âge que celles dont il a déjà été question à la section 3.1.3 des Notes techniques. Il est probable que les statistiques de la nuptialité sont moins faussées par ce genre d'erreur, car les renseignements sont donnés par les intéressés eux-mêmes, et, comme le mariage est un acte juridique, il y a toutes chances que leurs déclarations soient exactes. Toutefois, dans certains pays ou zones, il semble y avoir une concentration de mariages à l'âge minimal légal de nubilité ainsi qu'à l'âge auquel le mariage peut être valablement contracté sans le consentement des parents, ce qui peut indiquer que certains déclarants se vieillissent pour se conformer à la loi.

Outre la possibilité d'erreurs dans les déclarations d'âge, il convient de noter que la législation fixant l'âge minimal de nubilité influe notablement sur les caractéristiques de la nuptialité pour les premiers âges, c'est-à-dire jusqu'à 24 ans.

Parmi les facteurs pouvant exercer une influence sur les déclarations d'âge, en particulier celles qui sont faites par des personnes plus âgées, il faut citer la tendance à diminuer l'âge de l'épouse de façon qu'il soit égal ou inférieur à celui de l'époux.

Si aucun nombre ne figure dans la rangée réservée aux âges inconnus, cela ne signifie pas nécessairement que les déclarations d'âge et l'exploitation des données par âge aient été tout à fait exactes. C'est parfois une indication que l'on a attribué un âge aux personnes d'âge inconnu avant l'exploitation des données ou qu'elles ont été réparties proportionnellement entre les différents groupes après cette opération.

Il importe de ne pas oublier non plus, lorsque l'on utilisera ces données, que l'on calcule parfois l'âge des conjoints au moment du mariage sur la base de l'année de naissance seulement et non d'après la date exacte (jour, mois et année) de naissance. Des renseignements à ce sujet sont donnés en note chaque fois que possible.

Donnés publiées antérieurement : on trouve dans la plupart des éditions de l'*Annuaire démographique* des statistiques concernant les mariages selon l'âge de l'époux et selon l'âge de l'épouse qui ont été établies à partir des données les plus récentes dont on disposait à l'époque. Des données croisant l'âge des époux ont été présentées dans des éditions antérieurs, plus particulièrement consacrées aux statistiques de la nuptialité et de la divortialité. Pour plus de précisions concernant les années et les sujets pour lesquels des données ont été publiées, se reporter à l'index historique.

23-1 L'âge légal minimum avec auquel le mariage peut avoir lieu

Pays ou zone	Avec consentement parental		Sans consentement parental	
	Epoux	Epouse	Epoux	Epouse
Afrique				
Afrique du Sud	18	15	21	21
Botswana	18	18	21	21
Burkina Faso[2]	18	15	20	17
Egypte	18	16	21	21
Ghana			18	18
Libéria	16	16	21	18
Libye[3]	18	18		
Malawi[4]			18	18
Maurice	16	16	18	18
Maroc[4]			18	18
Namibie	18	18	21	21
Ouganda[4, 5]			18	18
Sainte-Hélène sans dép.	16	16	21	21
Sénégal	moins de 18	moins de 18	18	18
Seychelles	16	16	18	18
Sierra Leone[4]			18	18
Zimbabwe	16	16	18	18
Amérique du Nord				
Anguilla			18	18
Antilles néerlandaises			18	18

Pays ou zone	Avec consentement parental		Sans consentement parental	
	Epoux	Epouse	Epoux	Epouse
Aruba	18	15	18	18
Bermudes[4]			18	18
Canada[6]	16	16	18	18
Costa Rica	15	15	18	18
Cuba	16	14	18	16
El Salvador	15	14	18	18
Groenland[7]	16	15	18	18
Îles Caïmanes	16	16	18	18
Jamaïque	16	16	18	18
Mexique[8]	16	14	18	18
Montserrat[9]	16	16	18	18
Panama	16	14	18	18
Porto Rico	18	16	21	21
République dominicaine	17	16	18	18
Trinité-et-Tobago[10]	moins de 18	moins de 18	18	18
Amérique du Sud				
Brésil	16	16	18	18
Chili	16	16	18	18
Colombie	14	14	18	18
Equateur	moins de 18	moins de 18	18	18
Suriname	17	15	21	21
Uruguay	14	12	18	18
Venezuela (République bolivarienne du)[4]			12	12
Asie				
Arménie			18	17
Azerbaïdjan	18	17		
Bahreïn			15	
Cambodge			18	18
Chine, Hong Kong RAS	16	16	21	21
Chine, Macao RAS	16	16	18	18
Géorgie	16	16	18	18
Indonésie			19	16
Iran (République islamique d')	18	15		
Israël[4]			17	17
Japon	18	16	20	20
Kazakhstan	16	16	18	17
Kirghizistan	16	16	18	18
Malaisie[11]	18	16	18 et 21	16 et 21

653

Pays ou zone	Avec consentement parental		Sans consentement parental	
	Epoux	Epouse	Epoux	Epouse
Népal	18	18	20	20
Oman[4]			18	18
Ouzbékistan			17	17
Philippines	18	18	21	21
République de Corée	18	18	20	20
Singapour[12]	moins de 21	moins de 21	21	21
Tadjikistan	17	17	18	18
Territoire palestinien occupé[13]		14.5	15.5	
Turquie	16	16	18	18
Europe				
Albanie	18	16		
Allemagne[14]	16	16	18	18
Autriche[15]	16	16	18	18
Bélarus[16]			18	18
Belgique	moins de 18	moins de 18	18	18
Bosnie-Herzégovine			18	18
Bulgarie	16	16	18	18
Croatie	16	16	18	18
Danemark	15	15	18	18
Espagne	14	14	18	18
Estonie	15	15	18	18
Fédération de Russie	16	16	18	18
Finlande[17]			18	18
France[4]			18	18
Gibraltar	16	16	18	18
Grèce[18]			18	18
Hongrie	16	16	18	18
Île de Man	16	16	18	18
Îles d'Åland[4]			18	18
Irlande[4, 19]			18	18
Islande[4]			18	18
Italie	16	16	18	18
Jersey	16	16	18	18
L'ex-R. y. de Macédoine	16	16	18	18
Lettonie	16	16	18	18
Liechtenstein[15]			18	18

Pays ou zone	Avec consentement parental		Sans consentement parental	
	Epoux	Epouse	Epoux	Epouse
Lituanie[20]	15	15	18	18
Luxembourg			18	16
Malte			16	16
Monténégro	16	16	18	18
Norvège	16	16	18	18
Pays-Bas	16	16	18	18
Pologne[21]			18	18
Portugal	16	16	18	18
République de Moldova			18	16
République tchèque	16	16	18	18
Roumanie[4]			18	18
Royaume-Uni de Grande-Bretagne et d'Irlande du Nord	16	16	18	18
Serbie	16	16	18	18
Slovaque[22]			16	16
Slovénie	15	15	18	18
Suede[23]			18	18
Suisse	16	16	18	18
Ukraine	15	15	18	17
Océanie				
Australie	16	16	18	18
Îles Cook	16	16	21	21
Nouvelle-Calédonie			18	18
Nouvelle-Zélande	16	16	18	18

NOTES

[1] *Principes et recommandations pour un système de statistiques de l'état civil, deuxième révision,* numéro de vente F.01.XVII.10, publication des Nations Unies, New York, 2003.

[2] De plus, une dispense d'âge peut être accordée par un tribunal civil pour motif grave à partir de 15 ans pour les femmes et de 18 ans pour les hommes.

[3] Conformément à la loi islamique, le mariage requiert le consentement parental. Le consentement de la mariée, elle-même ainsi que le consentement du tuteur sont fondamentaux dans le contrat de mariage. Les jeunes hommes choisissent habituellement le consentement des parents. L'âge minimum du mariage est généralement 18 ans. Conformément à la loi, le mariage n'est pas limité aux individus âgés de plus de 18 ans.

[4] L'âge minimum légal du mariage est le même respectivement pour le marié et la mariée, avec ou sans le consentement parental.

[5] Tel que le signale l' "Uganda Bureau of Statistics", les mariages avec ou sans le consentement parental peuvent se produire beaucoup plus tôt que 18 ans.

[6] Le mariage est en vertu des législations provinciales et territoriales. Sans le consentement des parents, l'âge minimum légal du mariage est de 18 ans dans toutes les provinces et territoires du Canada sauf en Colombie-Britannique, Terre-Neuve-et-Labrador, la Nouvelle-Écosse, du Nunavut et du Yukon, où l'âge minimum légal est de 19 ans. Avec le consentement des parents, l'âge minimum légal est de

16 ans dans toutes les provinces sauf dans les Territoires du Nord-Ouest, Nunavut et Yukon. Avec le consentement des parents, dans les Territoires du Nord-Ouest et le Yukon l'âge minimum légal est de 15 ans alors que dans le Nunavut, l'âge minimum légal est de 18 ans.

[7] Pour se marier à un âge inférieur à 18 ans, les consentements à la fois des parents et des autorités sont nécessaires. La maternité est l'une des rares raisons permettant d'obtenir le consentement officiel des autorités.

[8] Chacun des 31 Etats fédéraux et du District fédéral a son propre code civil pour le mariage. Les exceptions aux âges figurant sur le tableau sont les suivantes : sans le consentement des parents, l'âge minimum légal du mariage en Basse-Californie et au Tlaxcala est de 16 ans pour les hommes et 14 ans pour les femmes alors que dans la Basse-Californie du Sud, il est de 16 ans pour les femmesfemelles. Avec le consentement des parents, l'âge minimum légal du mariage est de 16 ans pour les hommes et les femmes les femelles à Aguascalientes, Campeche, Chiapas, Distrito Federal, Guerrero, Jalisco, Morelos, Puebla, Quintana Roo, Querétaro, San Luis Potosí et Sonora. Avec le consentement des parents, l'âge minimum légal du mariage est en-dessous de 18 ans pour les hommes et femmes à Coahuila, Hidalgo, et Zacatecas. L'âge minimum légal du mariage reste le même, respectivement pour les mariés avec ou sans le consentement parental en Basse-Californie, Basse Californie du Sud et Tlaxcala.

[9] Le consentement peut être donné par un tuteur ou une personne qui a la garde de l'enfant qui souhaitent se marier. En outre, le gouverneur a la faculté de permettre aux personnes âgés d'au moins 15 ans et 1 jour de se marier, s'il pense que le mariage est dans le meilleur intérêt des personnes qui ont l'intention de s'unir et que les personnes concernées aient également reçu le consentement nécessaire.

[10] Avec l'âge du le consentement parental, l'âge minimum du mariage pour se marier est de 14 ans pour les hommes et de 12 ans pour les femmes pour un mariage civil ; de 16 ans pour les hommes et de 12 ans pour les femmes pour un mariage musulman ; de 18 ans pour les hommes et de 14 ans pour les femmes pour un mariage hindou, et de18 ans pour les hommes et de 16 pour les femmes pour un mariage orisa.

[11] Sans le consentement parental, il est de 21 ans pour les hommes non-musulmans et de 18 ans pour les hommes musulmans alors qu'il est de 21 ans pour les femmes non-musulmanes et il est de 16 ans pour les femmes musulmanes. Pour le mariage avec le consentement parental, l'accord des autorités compétentes est nécessaire.

[12] L'âge minimum légal du mariage spécifié correspond à des mariages contractés en vertu de la Charte des femmes. Pour les mariages musulmans sous l'administration de la « Loi sur le Droit Musulman », aucun mariage ne doit être célébré lorsque l'une des parties est en dessous de l'âge de 18 ans. Néanmoins, les femmes musulmanes en dessous de l'âge de 18 ans qui ont atteint l'âge de la puberté peuvent être mariées dans le cadre de l'administration de la « Loi sur le Droit Musulman ».

[13] L'âge légal du mariage pour les femmes est de 14 ans, 6 mois et 22 jours. Le consentement parental (du père ou du frère si le père est mort) est requis. L'âge légal du mariage pour les hommes est de 15 ans, 6 mois et 21 jours. Le consentement parental n'est pas nécessaire.

[14] Le mariage à 16-17 ans exige que l'autre conjoint soit un adulte déjà fiancée (18 ans) ainsi qu'une exemption de l'obligation de la majorité par un juge aux affaires familiales.

[15] Les personnes âgées de moins de 18 ans doivent obtenir l'autorisation de la justice.

[16] En conformité avec le Code du mariage et la famille de la République du Bélarus, dans les cas exclusifs liés à la maternité, l'accouchement et en cas d'acquisition par un mineur d'une pleine capacité juridique en vertu de l'âge légal, les bureaux d'état civil sont en mesure de de réduire l'âge du mariage des personnes souhaitant se marier, de 3 ans au plus. L'âge du mariage est abaissé suite à une demande des personnes se mariant, le consentement parental n'est pas nécessaire.

[17] Les personnes âgées de moins de 18 ans doivent obtenir l'autorisation du ministère de la justice.

[18] Dans certaines conditions (par exemple la grossesse), le mariage peut avoir lieu sans restriction d'âge.

[19] Une exemption sur l'âge minimum peut être accordée par ordonnance du tribunal si l'octroi d'une telle exemption est dans le meilleur intérêt des parties ayant l'intention de se marier et si la demande est appuyée par de bonnes raisons.

[20] En plus du consentement parental, les personnes de moins de 18 ans doivent obtenir l'autorisation du tribunall'approbation judiciaire. En cas de grossesse, le mariage peut être autorisé en dessous de 15 ans.

[21] Les femmes peuvent se marier à l'âge de 16 ou 17 ans avec l'autorisation des parents et du tribunal de la cour.

[22] Un mariage ne peut être conclu par un mineur. Le tribunal peut, exceptionnellement et pour des raisons importantes approuver l'entrée en mariage par un mineur de plus de seize ans. Sans cet accord, le mariage est invalide et le tribunal est en mesure de prononcer sa nullité, même sans une demande explicite.

[23] Avec le consentement des parents, aucune limite mais les autorités doivent approuver. Sans le consentement parental, l'âge minimum légal du mariage est de 18 ans pour les citoyens suédois.

23. Marriages by age of groom and by age of bride: latest available year, 2000 - 2009
Mariages selon l'âge de l'époux et selon l'âge de l'épouse : dernière année disponible, 2000 - 2009

Continent, pays ou zone, date, code et âge de l'épouse	Total	0-14	15-19	20-24	25-29	30-34	35-39	40-44	45-49	50-54	55-59	60+	Unknown Inconnu
AFRICA - AFRIQUE													
Botswana 2006 (+U)													
Total	4 335	-	-	50	639	1 299	968	582	369	211	106	111	...
0 - 14	-												
15 - 19	12	-	-	5	4	3	-	-	-	-	-	-	...
20 - 24	535	-	-	31	213	184	67	26	10	4	-	-	...
25 - 29	1 566	-	-	12	357	679	340	112	51	12	3	-	...
30 - 34	1 159	-	-	2	56	373	398	200	71	42	13	4	...
35 - 39	534	-	-	-	8	49	137	173	99	42	18	8	...
40 - 44	268	-	-	-	1	10	20	63	89	51	21	13	...
45 - 49	143					-	6	7	44	41	28	17	...
50 - 54	61					1	-	1	4	14	19	22	...
55 - 59	32					-	-	-	1	5	4	22	...
60 - 64	8											8	...
65 +	17											17	...
Egypt - Égypte[1] 2009 (+...)													
Total	759 004	...	12 653[i]	186 704	309 416	136 460	43 291	23 061	16 475	10 833	8 162	11 389	560
18 - 19	152 433	...	7 399[i]	61 750	63 151	16 704	2 301	535	294	136	61	95	7
20 - 24	371 516	...	4 337[i]	108 654	175 530	62 820	12 185	3 906	1 918	941	542	663	20
25 - 29	142 933	...	684[i]	13 239	62 101	40 364	13 845	5 784	3 159	1 612	1 058	1 079	8
30 - 34	46 607	...	154[i]	2 186	6 523	13 203	9 596	6 011	3 761	2 178	1 364	1 626	5
35 - 39	19 973	...	21[i]	388	1 227	2 279	3 867	3 942	3 106	1 902	1 492	1 747	2
40 - 44	11 546	...	21[i]	201	433	683	1 003	2 001	2 361	1 774	1 325	1 742	2
45 - 49	7 274	...	17[i]	140	226	253	347	659	1 448	1 445	1 191	1 548	-
50 - 54	3 339	...	9[i]	54	90	77	101	163	305	663	722	1 155	-
55 - 59	1 501	...	6[i]	27	49	35	30	40	89	124	313	788	-
60 - 64	717	...	1[i]	13	20	11	4	9	23	29	69	537	1
65 - 69	303	...	-[j]	11	13	8	5	2	4	22	15	223	-
70 - 74	92	...	-[j]	3	3	1	1	4	2	-	7	71	-
75 +	198	...	3[i]	26	27	10	5	3	2	5	3	114	-
Unknown - Inconnu	572	...	1[i]	12	23	12	1	2	3	2	-	1	515
Mauritius - Maurice[2] 2009 (+C)													
Total	10 619	-	160	1 378	3 520	2 418	1 187	751	489	328	192	196	-
0 - 14	59	-	1	6	20	14	8	5	1	2	-	2	-
15 - 19	1 266	-	115	500	477	136	29	5	1	1	1	1	-
20 - 24	2 931	-	37	664	1 481	599	104	30	8	6	1	1	-
25 - 29	2 922	-	6	160	1 261	987	334	107	48	11	5	3	-
30 - 34	1 500	-	1	30	221	539	405	200	62	29	9	4	-
35 - 39	723	-	-	6	39	105	229	193	91	40	12	8	-
40 - 44	522	-	-	3	14	25	56	145	139	83	37	20	-
45 - 49	339	-	-	4	4	8	16	50	97	89	47	24	-
50 - 54	199	-	-	1	2	1	5	13	30	50	52	45	-
55 - 59	91	-	-	-	-	1	-	2	9	11	22	46	-
60 - 64	40	-	-	-	1	1	-	-	3	5	6	24	-
65 - 69	13	-	-	-	-	-	-	-	-	1	-	12	-
70 - 74	5	-	-	-	-	-	-	1	-	-	-	4	-
75 +	2	-	-	-	-	-	-	-	-	-	-	2	-
Unknown - Inconnu	7	-	-	4	-	2	1	-	-	-	-	-	-
Réunion 2007[3] (C)													
Total	3 149	-	15	338	787	681	514	306	185	150	62	111	...
0 - 14	1	-	1	-	-	-	-	-	-	-	-	-	...
15 - 19	91	-	8	45	26	7	2	2	1	-	-	-	...
20 - 24	679	-	4	235	296	99	28	13	3	-	1	-	...
25 - 29	858	-	2	42	391	264	117	30	7	4	1	-	...
30 - 34	584	-	-	12	52	232	185	56	29	10	4	4	...
35 - 39	384	-	-	3	16	55	134	106	38	25	4	3	...
40 - 44	234	-	-	-	4	16	34	77	49	28	13	13	...
45 - 49	144	-	-	1	1	7	11	18	34	40	18	14	...
50 - 54	94	-	-	-	1	1	3	4	19	30	12	24	...
55 - 59	39	-	-	-	-	-	-	-	3	10	7	19	...
60 - 64	16	-	-	-	-	-	-	-	2	2	1	11	...
65 - 69	16	-	-	-	-	-	-	-	-	1	1	14	...

Continent, country or area, year, code and age of bride / Continent, pays ou zone, date, code et âge de l'épouse	Total	0-14	15-19	20-24	25-29	30-34	35-39	40-44	45-49	50-54	55-59	60+	Unknown Inconnu
AFRICA - AFRIQUE													
Réunion													
2007[3]													
70 - 74	7	-	-	-	-	-	-	-	-	-	-	7	...
75 +	2	-	-	-	-	-	-	-	-	-	-	2	...
Seychelles[4]													
2009 (+C)													
Total	1 203	-	4	78	248	289	203	180	92	61	48^s	...	...
0 - 14	-	-	-	-	-	-	-	-	-	-	-^s	...	...
15 - 19	18	-	1	11	5	1	-	-	-	-	-^s	...	...
20 - 24	136	-	2	44	58	20	6	3	2	1	-^s	...	...
25 - 29	349	-	1	16	130	113	54	22	8	3	2^s	...	...
30 - 34	299	-	-	6	35	122	68	42	16	7	3^s	...	...
35 - 39	189	-	-	1	14	22	59	56	25	8	4^s	...	...
40 - 44	108	-	-	-	5	8	13	37	23	14	8^s	...	...
45 - 49	65	-	-	-	1	3	3	17	15	16	10^s	...	...
50 - 54	23	-	-	-	-	-	-	1	3	8	11^s	...	...
55 +	16	-	-	-	-	-	2	-	4	10^s	...	...	
South Africa - Afrique du Sud													
2008 (...)													
Total	186 522	2	318	12 907	42 568	43 770	32 112	20 605	13 551	8 325	5 221	7 140	3
0 - 14	5	-	1	1	2	1	-	-	-	-	-	-	-
15 - 19	3 479	1	158	1 721	1 096	330	109	37	10	7	5	5	-
20 - 24	35 071	-	119	8 362	16 675	6 830	2 058	668	222	78	36	23	-
25 - 29	55 287	-	27	2 280	20 561	20 660	7 879	2 518	863	310	112	77	-
30 - 34	37 642	-	8	380	3 292	12 781	12 838	5 225	1 960	740	264	154	-
35 - 39	22 866	-	4	125	730	2 447	7 172	6 959	3 354	1 215	488	372	-
40 - 44	13 475	-	-	28	156	531	1 506	3 874	4 045	1 935	801	599	-
45 - 49	8 461	-	1	9	40	145	425	1 039	2 338	2 314	1 263	887	-
50 - 54	4 757	-	-	1	12	29	100	233	571	1 294	1 300	1 215	2
55 - 59	2 619	-	-	-	2	9	20	36	149	338	709	1 356	-
60 - 64	1 482	1	-	-	2	5	3	12	30	66	177	1 186	-
65 - 69	773	-	-	-	-	2	1	3	7	21	53	686	-
70 - 74	350	-	-	-	-	-	1	1	2	4	9	333	-
75 +	255	-	-	-	-	-	-	-	-	3	4	247	1
Unknown - Inconnu	-	-	-	-	-	-	-	-	-	-	-	-	-
Tunisia - Tunisie													
2007 (...)													
Total	76 809	...	200^e	5 130	20 482	26 252	13 140	5 056	2 038	1 888^n	...	1 716	907
15 - 19	6 114	...	...	...	...	...	...	...	...	...	...	...	...
20 - 24	23 270	...	...	...	...	...	...	...	...	...	...	...	...
25 - 29	25 494	...	...	...	...	...	...	...	...	...	...	...	...
30 - 34	11 582	...	...	...	...	...	...	...	...	...	...	...	...
35 - 39	4 694	...	...	...	...	...	...	...	...	...	...	...	...
40 - 44	2 497	...	...	...	...	...	...	...	...	...	...	...	...
45 - 49	1 247	...	...	...	...	...	...	...	...	...	...	...	...
50 +	792	...	...	...	...	...	...	...	...	...	...	...	...
Unknown - Inconnu	1 119	...	...	...	...	...	...	...	...	...	...	...	...
AMERICA, NORTH - AMÉRIQUE DU NORD													
Anguilla[5]													
2008 (C)													
Total	54	...	...	...	...	...	...	...	...	...	...	...	...
18 - 23	8	...	...	...	...	...	...	...	...	...	...	...	...
24 - 29	15	...	...	...	...	...	...	...	...	...	...	...	...
30 - 35	16	...	...	...	...	...	...	...	...	...	...	...	...
36 - 41	5	...	...	...	...	...	...	...	...	...	...	...	...
42 - 47	7	...	...	...	...	...	...	...	...	...	...	...	...
48 - 53	1	...	...	...	...	...	...	...	...	...	...	...	...
54	2	...	...	...	...	...	...	...	...	...	...	...	...
Aruba[3,6]													
2007 (C)													
Total	532	-	7	53	94	89	77	71	44	34	30	20	13
0 - 14	-	-	-	-	-	-	-	-	-	-	-	-	-
15 - 19	27	-	3	16	4	2	1	-	-	-	-	-	1

Continent, country or area, year, code and age of bride / Continent, pays ou zone, date, code et âge de l'épouse	Total	0-14	15-19	20-24	25-29	30-34	35-39	40-44	45-49	50-54	55-59	60+	Unknown Inconnu

Age of groom - âge de l'époux

AMERICA, NORTH - AMÉRIQUE DU NORD

Aruba[3,6]
2007

	Total	0-14	15-19	20-24	25-29	30-34	35-39	40-44	45-49	50-54	55-59	60+	Unknown Inconnu
20 - 24	71	-	3	17	29	12	7	2	-	-	1	-	-
25 - 29	93	-	-	7	39	27	9	6	1	1	1	-	2
30 - 34	97	-	-	5	15	25	28	12	6	2	-	-	4
35 - 39	63	-	-	3	1	12	12	15	8	5	4	2	1
40 - 44	55	-	-	-	1	6	8	19	10	6	1	4	-
45 - 49	45	-	-	-	-	1	5	10	8	7	7	3	4
50 - 54	21	-	-	-	-	-	1	2	4	3	7	4	-
55 - 59	17	-	-	-	-	-	-	-	3	1	9	3	1
60 - 64	4	-	-	-	-	-	-	-	-	2	-	2	-
65 +	2	-	-	-	-	-	-	-	-	-	-	2	-
Unknown - Inconnu	37	-	1	5	5	4	6	5	4	7	-	-	-

Bahamas
2008 (C)

	Total	0-14	15-19	20-24	25-29	30-34	35-39	40-44	45-49	50-54	55-59	60+	Unknown Inconnu
Total	1 969	-	17	212	493	405	305	189	149	88	53	52	6
0 - 14	-	-	-	-	-	-	-	-	-	-	-	-	-
15 - 19	66	-	11	30	20	4	-	-	1	-	-	-	-
20 - 24	399	-	2	129	164	65	22	10	3	3	-	-	1
25 - 29	486	-	3	35	212	134	65	23	8	3	2	1	-
30 - 34	384	-	-	13	60	139	95	44	22	5	4	1	1
35 - 39	264	-	-	1	29	39	83	49	36	16	9	2	-
40 - 44	160	-	-	2	4	18	24	39	40	20	7	6	-
45 - 49	103	-	1	1	3	4	9	20	26	23	14	2	-
50 - 54	54	-	-	-	-	1	5	3	10	14	9	12	-
55 - 59	21	-	-	-	-	-	1	1	2	3	7	7	-
60 +	24	-	-	-	-	1	-	-	-	-	1	21	1
Unknown - Inconnu	8	-	-	1	1	-	1	-	1	1	-	-	3

Bermuda - Bermudes
2009 (C)

	Total	0-14	15-19	20-24	25-29	30-34	35-39	40-44	45-49	50-54	55-59	60+	Unknown Inconnu
Total	683	-	1	25	136	135	120	84	63	65	20	34	-
0 - 14	-	-	-	-	-	-	-	-	-	-	-	-	-
15 - 19	5	-	1	3	1	-	-	-	-	-	-	-	-
20 - 24	46	-	-	15	19	8	1	3	-	-	-	-	-
25 - 29	171	-	-	7	79	51	22	9	1	1	1	-	-
30 - 34	156	-	-	-	24	60	53	15	2	2	-	-	-
35 - 39	104	-	-	-	10	11	29	23	22	5	2	2	-
40 - 44	68	-	-	-	2	5	10	23	16	6	2	4	-
45 - 49	63	-	-	-	-	-	3	9	14	27	6	4	-
50 - 54	37	-	-	-	1	-	2	2	5	18	5	4	-
55 - 59	15	-	-	-	-	-	-	-	3	4	2	6	-
60 - 64	12	-	-	-	-	-	-	-	-	1	1	10	-
65 - 69	5	-	-	-	-	-	-	-	-	1	1	3	-
70 - 74	-	-	-	-	-	-	-	-	-	-	-	-	-
75 +	1	-	-	-	-	-	-	-	-	-	-	1	-
Unknown - Inconnu	-	-	-	-	-	-	-	-	-	-	-	-	-

Canada
2002 (C)

	Total	0-14	15-19	20-24	25-29	30-34	35-39	40-44	45-49	50-54	55-59	60+	Unknown Inconnu
Total	146 738	...	919	19 421	43 355	30 788	18 266	11 497	7 711	5 667	3 686	5 347	81
15 - 19	3 504	...	544	2 047	644	189	45	24	6	1	1	1	2
20 - 24	31 526	...	324	13 344	13 341	3 313	815	241	82	37	6	5	16
25 - 29	45 377	...	39	3 381	23 768	12 896	3 740	1 064	302	103	41	15	19
30 - 34	25 579	...	9	489	4 529	10 739	6 334	2 367	730	253	80	36	13
35 - 39	14 675	...	2	112	814	2 775	4 970	3 387	1 608	660	225	115	7
40 - 44	9 526	...	-	37	189	644	1 683	2 864	2 190	1 180	506	229	4
45 - 49	6 827	...	1	6	55	170	515	1 169	1 892	1 620	885	512	2
50 - 54	4 349	...	-	4	9	50	122	298	691	1 292	1 027	854	2
55 - 59	2 372	...	-	-	1	7	31	61	167	405	669	1 029	2
60 - 64	1 254	...	-	-	-	-	3	13	32	86	183	934	3
65 - 69	807	...	-	-	-	-	2	5	5	23	52	719	1
70 - 74	481	...	-	-	-	2	2	1	2	5	3	465	1
75 +	431	...	-	-	-	-	-	-	3	2	7	419	-
Unknown - Inconnu	30	...	-	1	5	3	4	3	1	-	1	3	9

Costa Rica
2009 (C)

	Total	0-14	15-19	20-24	25-29	30-34	35-39	40-44	45-49	50-54	55-59	60+	Unknown Inconnu
Total	23 920	-	655	4 787	6 587	4 330	2 374	1 507	1 086	693	470	733	698
0 - 14	1	-	-	1	-	-	-	-	-	-	-	-	-

23. Marriages by age of groom and by age of bride: latest available year, 2000 - 2009
Mariages selon l'âge de l'époux et selon l'âge de l'épouse : dernière année disponible, 2000 - 2009 (continued - suite)

Continent, country or area, year, code and age of bride / Continent, pays ou zone, date, code et âge de l'épouse	Total	0-14	15-19	20-24	25-29	30-34	35-39	40-44	45-49	50-54	55-59	60+	Unknown Inconnu
AMERICA, NORTH - AMÉRIQUE DU NORD													
Costa Rica													
2009													
15 - 19	2 499	-	377	1 278	575	145	57	25	15	5	3	4	15
20 - 24	6 630	-	189	2 479	2 524	872	311	130	62	27	12	10	14
25 - 29	6 066	-	48	746	2 498	1 648	619	256	126	53	30	25	17
30 - 34	3 270	-	25	174	674	1 132	629	321	145	77	43	38	12
35 - 39	1 742	-	7	47	184	346	457	326	191	85	43	50	6
40 - 44	1 102	-	5	23	51	89	185	259	239	111	75	61	4
45 - 49	806	-	2	13	20	45	62	118	182	166	95	102	1
50 - 54	467	-	-	5	11	15	18	36	83	97	85	115	2
55 - 59	263	-	-	3	1	5	10	16	25	38	55	109	1
60 - 64	146	-	-	-	-	1	1	4	8	17	20	93	2
65 - 69	75	-	-	-	1	3	2	2	-	5	4	58	-
70 - 74	35	-	-	-	-	-	-	1	1	2	2	29	-
75 +	37	-	-	-	1	-	1	1	-	2	1	31	-
Unknown - Inconnu	781	-	2	18	47	29	22	12	9	8	2	8	624
Cuba													
2009 (C)													
Total	54 969	1	1 102	7 448	8 205	7 451	8 212	7 062	5 267	3 070	2 442	4 707	2
0 - 14	59	-	21	32	1	4	-	-	-	1	-	-	-
15 - 19	4 567	-	614	2 139	1 007	363	221	103	52	24	20	24	-
20 - 24	10 879	-	320	3 511	3 221	1 694	1 067	511	263	116	76	100	-
25 - 29	8 071	-	85	1 018	2 242	1 963	1 347	721	351	127	86	131	-
30 - 34	6 607	-	28	343	852	1 537	1 752	1 086	510	228	124	147	-
35 - 39	7 155	-	16	208	484	968	1 967	1 714	929	384	218	267	-
40 - 44	6 372	1	9	101	227	519	1 076	1 649	1 387	587	349	467	-
45 - 49	4 804	-	7	48	105	250	505	809	1 153	799	502	626	-
50 - 54	2 523	-	1	14	36	65	152	275	350	481	491	656	2
55 - 59	1 691	-	1	16	10	47	53	102	154	192	369	747	-
60 - 64	1 071	-	-	8	13	19	46	50	70	73	125	667	-
65 - 69	660	-	-	4	1	15	15	20	27	29	54	495	-
70 - 74	289	-	-	3	4	5	2	14	12	14	15	220	-
75 +	221	-	-	3	2	2	9	8	9	15	13	160	-
Unknown - Inconnu	-	-	-	-	-	-	-	-	-	-	-	-	-
Dominican Republic - République dominicaine													
2009 (+C)													
Total	40 040	...	448	4 962	9 113	7 339	5 481	4 103	2 858	2 057	1 373	1 967	339
0 - 14	9	...	2	4	1	1	-	-	-	-	-	1	-
15 - 19	2 337	...	209	1 000	667	229	109	58	34	12	6	13	-
20 - 24	8 635	...	149	2 416	3 249	1 471	615	330	189	92	50	66	8
25 - 29	9 634	...	56	959	3 498	2 578	1 227	593	341	186	100	87	9
30 - 34	6 717	...	15	336	1 058	1 955	1 631	821	408	228	120	130	15
35 - 39	4 406	...	8	134	345	649	1 119	1 012	535	294	161	143	6
40 - 44	3 139	...	2	60	159	267	467	738	673	382	179	208	4
45 - 49	2 038	...	2	19	57	97	165	333	430	442	264	225	4
50 - 54	1 280	...	2	11	25	44	75	131	153	279	256	303	1
55 - 59	721	...	2	2	8	10	37	54	52	84	153	318	1
60 - 64	351	...	-	2	2	5	5	11	20	28	45	230	3
65 - 69	182	...	-	2	4	-	4	3	4	10	22	133	-
70 - 74	70	...	-	-	-	1	-	-	2	2	5	59	1
75 +	52	...	-	1	4	1	1	1	3	4	-	37	-
Unknown - Inconnu	469	...	1	16	36	31	26	18	14	14	12	14	287
El Salvador[7]													
2007 (...)													
Total	28 675	-	1 202	6 562	7 366	4 763	2 897	1 812	1 296	878	669	1 211	19
0 - 14	45	-	13	19	6	3	1	-	3	-	-	-	-
15 - 19	3 807	-	643	1 815	804	321	128	44	17	17	11	4	3
20 - 24	7 946	-	408	3 293	2 656	962	368	130	69	32	13	12	3
25 - 29	6 646	-	91	1 045	2 780	1 613	612	251	121	77	25	27	4
30 - 34	3 927	-	27	272	770	1 297	803	391	182	88	44	50	3
35 - 39	2 218	-	9	67	215	375	653	427	225	106	55	85	1
40 - 44	1 545	-	1	24	86	132	218	389	337	153	96	109	-
45 - 49	980	-	1	9	28	37	72	124	239	200	140	130	-
50 - 54	624	-	1	4	9	12	27	38	73	147	143	170	-
55 - 59	369	-	3	3	2	4	5	11	20	34	99	188	-
60 - 64	233	-	1	-	-	1	6	6	1	15	27	176	-

Continent, country or area, year, code and age of bride / Continent, pays ou zone, date, code et âge de l'épouse	Age of groom - âge de l'époux											
	Total	0-14	15-19	20-24	25-29	30-34	35-39	40-44	45-49	50-54	55-59	60+	Unknown Inconnu
AMERICA, NORTH - AMÉRIQUE DU NORD													
El Salvador[7]													
2007													
65 +	298	-	1	3	-	2	1	1	8	7	16	259	-
Unknown - Inconnu	37	-	3	8	10	4	3	-	1	2	-	1	5
Grenada - Grenade													
2000 (+C)													
Total	616	...	2	44	132	149	112	70	50	18	14	24	1
15 - 19	18	...	2	8	4	3	1	-	-	-	-	-	-
20 - 24	89	...	-	23	43	15	7	-	1	-	-	-	-
25 - 29	163	...	-	10	60	58	21	10	3	1	-	-	-
30 - 34	122	...	-	2	18	52	33	14	3	-	-	-	-
35 - 39	93	...	-	-	5	13	33	26	14	1	-	1	-
40 - 44	58	...	-	-	2	7	12	15	11	6	4	1	-
45 - 49	38	...	-	1	-	1	3	3	13	8	4	5	-
50 - 54	13	...	-	-	-	-	1	2	3	2	3	2	-
55 - 59	9	...	-	-	-	-	1	-	1	-	3	4	-
60 - 64	8	...	-	-	-	-	-	-	1	-	-	7	-
65 +	4	...	-	-	-	-	-	-	-	-	-	4	-
Unknown - Inconnu	1	-	-	-	-	-	-	-	-	-	-	-	1
Guadeloupe													
2003 (C)													
Total	1 701	-	3	49	320	437	328	197	121	74	63	109	-
0 - 14	-	-	-	-	-	-	-	-	-	-	-	-	-
15 - 19	28	-	1	8	13	4	2	-	-	-	-	-	-
20 - 24	226	-	2	24	116	56	19	5	4	-	-	-	-
25 - 29	423	-	-	14	139	169	74	19	4	1	2	1	-
30 - 34	412	-	-	2	46	159	128	46	18	3	6	4	-
35 - 39	238	-	-	-	4	33	79	69	35	8	7	3	-
40 - 44	122	-	-	-	-	14	19	35	23	18	6	7	-
45 - 49	94	-	-	1	2	-	6	18	22	25	13	7	-
50 - 54	61	-	-	-	-	-	-	4	9	10	18	20	-
55 - 59	35	-	-	-	-	2	1	-	6	6	5	15	-
60 - 64	29	-	-	-	-	-	-	1	-	3	5	20	-
65 - 69	11	-	-	-	-	-	-	-	-	-	-	11	-
70 +	22	-	-	-	-	-	-	-	-	-	1	21	-
Guatemala													
2006 (C)													
Total	57 505	19	8 409	20 576	12 375	5 644	2 937	2 066	1 546	1 103	882	1 817	131
0 - 14	1 110	4	509	466	96	22	4	4	1	3	-	-	1
15 - 19	18 790	13	5 969	9 346	2 616	552	167	57	33	16	6	10	5
20 - 24	17 622	1	1 655	8 529	5 323	1 403	385	162	83	35	22	21	3
25 - 29	8 550	-	217	1 818	3 426	1 924	675	252	107	54	35	42	-
30 - 34	3 973	1	29	282	714	1 317	856	422	163	79	54	56	-
35 - 39	2 172	-	7	57	140	301	611	583	251	105	51	65	1
40 - 44	1 522	-	3	20	42	68	168	401	434	192	94	99	1
45 - 49	1 230	-	2	12	5	32	50	129	354	333	154	159	-
50 - 54	842	-	2	7	5	7	11	36	87	212	235	240	-
55 - 59	599	-	2	-	1	6	4	12	23	44	160	347	-
60 - 64	391	-	-	6	-	3	2	2	8	16	57	297	-
65 - 69	238	-	1	1	-	-	3	-	-	6	9	218	-
70 - 74	164	-	-	2	-	3	1	1	1	5	3	148	-
75 +	145	-	6	14	2	3	-	3	-	2	2	113	-
Unknown - Inconnu	157	-	7	16	5	3	-	2	1	1	-	2	120
Jamaica - Jamaïque													
2006 (C)													
Total	23 181	-	70	2 153	5 477	4 987	3 749	2 672	1 676	1 032	568	797	...
0 - 14	-	-	-	-	-	-	-	-	-	-	-	-	...
15 - 19	368	-	31	168	89	35	23	11	6	1	1	3	...
20 - 24	3 726	-	22	1 251	1 579	531	195	86	31	19	4	8	...
25 - 29	6 263	-	11	501	2 670	1 870	742	277	108	43	15	26	...
30 - 34	4 635	-	4	136	715	1 660	1 242	525	199	86	41	27	...
35 - 39	3 194	-	1	62	266	571	940	765	360	123	55	51	...
40 - 44	2 190	-	1	18	105	221	402	635	440	202	102	64	...
45 - 49	1 452	-	-	15	35	75	147	273	364	292	133	118	...
50 - 54	708	-	-	1	15	18	39	63	122	200	105	145	...
55 - 59	327	-	-	1	-	5	17	24	28	45	71	136	...
60 - 64	179	-	-	-	2	1	1	10	15	15	27	108	...

Continent, country or area, year, code and age of bride / Continent, pays ou zone, date, code et âge de l'épouse	Total	0-14	15-19	20-24	25-29	30-34	35-39	40-44	45-49	50-54	55-59	60+	Unknown Inconnu
AMERICA, NORTH - AMÉRIQUE DU NORD													
Jamaica - Jamaïque													
2006													
65 - 69	84	-	-	-	1	-	-	2	1	4	10	66	...
70 - 74	35	-	-	-	-	-	-	1	2	1	3	28	...
75 +	20	-	-	-	-	-	1	-	-	1	1	17	...
Martinique													
2007 (C)													
Total	1 341	-	19	128	297	284	185	155	117	63	32	61	...
0 - 14	-	-	-	-	-	-	-	-	-	-	-	-	...
15 - 19	55	-	11	35	8	1	-	-	-	-	-	-	...
20 - 24	217	-	4	63	108	25	13	4	-	-	-	-	...
25 - 29	273	-	3	20	123	99	16	7	1	4	-	-	...
30 - 34	243	-	1	4	38	97	65	24	11	2	1	-	...
35 - 39	173	-	-	4	12	42	54	49	9	3	-	-	...
40 - 44	146	-	-	1	3	11	26	47	45	10	3	-	...
45 - 49	84	-	-	1	3	6	6	19	29	14	5	1	...
50 - 54	53	-	-	-	2	3	3	3	15	11	10	6	...
55 - 59	31	-	-	-	-	-	1	-	7	12	3	8	...
60 - 64	24	-	-	-	-	-	-	1	-	4	8	11	...
65 - 69	12	-	-	-	-	-	-	1	-	2	-	9	...
70 - 74	16	-	-	-	-	-	-	1	-	1	2	12	...
75 +	14	-	-	-	-	-	-	-	-	-	-	14	...
Mexico - Mexique													
2008 (+C)													
Total	589 352	134	63 472	185 919	155 727	81 228	39 001	20 145	12 786	8 692	6 413	15 165	670
0 - 14	3 791	39	1 979	1 279	334	107	36	9	3	1	-	4	-
15 - 19	141 740	63	47 330	68 653	19 282	4 509	1 249	355	141	71	29	38	20
20 - 24	188 511	13	12 482	91 779	61 142	16 529	4 328	1 355	483	183	98	102	17
25 - 29	126 366	10	1 418	20 229	59 673	30 980	9 331	2 715	1 079	479	204	232	16
30 - 34	57 435	6	196	3 145	12 262	21 919	12 028	4 522	1 823	796	393	336	9
35 - 39	27 755	1	28	583	2 362	5 494	8 624	5 453	2 629	1 250	598	722	11
40 - 44	15 193	1	11	125	450	1 238	2 479	3 905	3 166	1 703	935	1 174	6
45 - 49	10 122	1	4	42	120	314	684	1 348	2 419	2 151	1 278	1 757	4
50 - 54	6 705	-	2	16	32	73	173	337	743	1 483	1 506	2 338	2
55 - 59	4 537	-	-	2	5	18	44	84	203	396	980	2 802	3
60 - 64	2 977	-	2	2	9	3	7	32	65	124	280	2 450	3
65 - 69	1 746	-	1	-	2	2	3	10	20	33	74	1 601	-
70 - 74	992	-	-	1	2	1	-	2	3	16	25	941	1
75 +	673	-	-	4	1	3	-	2	1	4	6	652	-
Unknown - Inconnu	809	-	19	59	51	38	15	16	8	2	7	16	578
Panama													
2009 (C)													
Total	12 273	-	115	1 572	2 889	2 435	1 579	1 844^m	...	884^n	...	788	167
0 - 14	9	-	-	5	2	1	1	-^{m}	...	-^{n}	...	-	-
15 - 19	595	-	70	306	147	37	17	10^m	...	3^n	...	-	5
20 - 24	2 429	-	32	884	930	329	116	63^m	...	7^n	...	3	65
25 - 29	3 182	-	10	277	1 291	1 018	360	156^m	...	26^n	...	8	36
30 - 34	2 070	-	1	73	352	753	513	292^m	...	69^n	...	15	2
35 - 39	1 268	-	2	19	101	182	370	449^m	...	99^n	...	44	2
40 - 49	1 519	-	-	5	19	74	157	731^m	...	356^n	...	175	2
50 - 59	680	-	-	-	3	5	10	73^m	...	296^n	...	293	-
60 - 69	225	-	-	-	-	-	-	3^m	...	23^n	...	199	-
70 +	56	-	-	-	-	-	-	1^m	...	4^n	...	51	-
Unknown - Inconnu	240	-	-	3	44	36	35	66^m	...	1^n	...	-	55
Puerto Rico - Porto Rico													
2008 (C)													
Total	18 620	-	734	3 690	4 638	2 960	1 933	1 287	999	732	1 646^s	...	1
0 - 14	27	-	14	12	1	-	-	-	-	-	-^{s}	...	-
15 - 19	1 820	-	535	947	249	61	19	9	-	-	-^{s}	...	-
20 - 24	4 360	-	154	2 074	1 516	404	140	41	18	10	2^s	...	1
25 - 29	4 484	-	27	512	2 194	1 120	413	133	50	17	18^s	...	-
30 - 34	2 589	-	4	113	515	929	587	262	106	42	31^s	...	-
35 - 39	1 649	-	-	20	111	313	513	348	188	85	71^s	...	-
40 - 44	1 136	-	-	6	38	86	175	266	251	149	165^s	...	-
45 - 49	945	-	-	5	10	32	61	160	259	193	225^s	...	-

Continent, country or area, year, code and age of bride / Continent, pays ou zone, date, code et âge de l'épouse	Total	0-14	15-19	20-24	25-29	30-34	35-39	40-44	45-49	50-54	55-59	60+	Unknown Inconnu
AMERICA, NORTH - AMÉRIQUE DU NORD													
Puerto Rico - Porto Rico													
2008													
50 - 54	626	-	-	1	2	8	22	50	92	151	300ˢ	...	-
55 +	984	-	-	-	2	7	3	18	35	85	834ˢ	...	-
Saint Lucia - Sainte-Lucie													
2003* (C)													
Total	489	-	1	31	114	103	95	61	34	18	9	23	...
0 - 14	-												...
15 - 19	8	-	-	6	2	-	-	-	-	-	-	-	...
20 - 24	84	-	1	17	41	17	7	1	-	-	-	-	...
25 - 29	128	-	-	8	41	47	23	4	3	1	-	1	...
30 - 34	102	-	-	-	23	30	30	11	5	2	1	-	...
35 - 39	71	-	-	-	4	6	26	22	8	5	-	-	...
40 - 44	41	-	-	-	2	1	7	16	10	2	2	1	...
45 - 49	23	-	-	-	1	-	2	3	7	5	2	3	...
50 - 54	13	-	-	-	-	2	-	3	1	2	1	4	...
55 - 59	8	-	-	-	-	-	-	-	-	1	1	6	...
60 - 64	4	-	-	-	-	-	-	-	-	-	1	3	...
65 +	7	-	-	-	-	-	-	1	-	-	1	5	...
Saint Vincent and the Grenadines - Saint-Vincent-et-les Grenadines													
2009 (+C)													
Total	573	...	...	...	...	...	...	...	...	...	...	...	...
0 - 14	-	...	...	...	...	...	...	...	...	...	...	...	...
15 - 19	3	...	...	...	...	...	...	...	...	...	...	...	...
20 - 24	48	...	...	...	...	...	...	...	...	...	...	...	...
25 - 29	134	...	...	...	...	...	...	...	...	...	...	...	...
30 - 34	120	...	...	...	...	...	...	...	...	...	...	...	...
35 - 39	84	...	...	...	...	...	...	...	...	...	...	...	...
40 - 44	59	...	...	...	...	...	...	...	...	...	...	...	...
45 - 49	48	...	...	...	...	...	...	...	...	...	...	...	...
50 - 54	28	...	...	...	...	...	...	...	...	...	...	...	...
55 - 59	16	...	...	...	...	...	...	...	...	...	...	...	...
60 - 64	15	...	...	...	...	...	...	...	...	...	...	...	...
65 +	8	...	...	...	...	...	...	...	...	...	...	...	...
Unknown - Inconnu	10	...	...	...	...	...	...	...	...	...	...	...	...
Trinidad and Tobago - Trinité-et-Tobago													
2005 (C)													
Total	8 144	-	122	1 350	2 247	1 591	927	703	458	297	180	269	...
0 - 14	3	-	1	-	1	1	-	-	-	-	-	-	...
15 - 19	623	-	72	300	178	50	14	7	1	-	-	1	...
20 - 24	2 285	-	39	794	907	355	120	43	16	7	2	2	...
25 - 29	2 127	-	9	197	911	629	234	89	36	12	7	3	...
30 - 34	1 177	-	-	38	186	376	288	179	62	21	11	16	...
35 - 39	716	-	-	15	45	125	189	187	90	36	16	13	...
40 - 44	503	-	1	4	15	45	61	130	131	58	32	26	...
45 - 49	330	-	-	-	2	8	10	49	90	80	39	52	...
50 - 54	188	-	-	2	1	2	6	10	24	59	44	40	...
55 - 59	92	-	-	-	-	-	1	6	5	19	15	46	...
60 - 64	56	-	-	-	-	-	3	3	2	5	10	33	...
65 +	43	-	-	-	-	-	1	-	1	-	4	37	...
Unknown - Inconnu	1	-	-	-	1	-	-	-	-	-	-	-	...
Turks and Caicos Islands - Îles Turques et Caïques													
2005 (C)													
Total	489	-	-	19	88	149	95	69	34	20	6	8	1
0 - 14	-												
15 - 19	3	-	-	1	1	1	-	-	-	-	-	-	-
20 - 24	40	-	-	12	18	8	1	1	-	-	-	-	-
25 - 29	120	-	-	4	45	48	14	5	2	1	-	1	-
30 - 34	142	-	-	2	19	69	31	13	5	3	-	-	-
35 - 39	103	-	-	-	5	18	37	28	9	5	1	-	-
40 - 44	37	-	-	-	-	1	9	15	7	2	1	2	-
45 - 49	31	-	-	-	-	4	3	5	7	7	4	1	-

Continent, country or area, year, code and age of bride / Continent, pays ou zone, date, code et âge de l'épouse	Total	0-14	15-19	20-24	25-29	30-34	35-39	40-44	45-49	50-54	55-59	60+	Unknown Inconnu
AMERICA, NORTH - AMÉRIQUE DU NORD													
Turks and Caicos Islands - Îles Turques et Caïques													
2005													
50 - 54	8	-	-	-	-	-	-	2	2	2	-	2	-
55 - 59	3	-	-	-	-	-	-	-	1	-	-	2	-
60 - 64	1	-	-	-	-	-	-	-	1	-	-	-	-
65 +	-	-	-	-	-	-	-	-	-	-	-	-	-
Unknown - Inconnu	1	-	-	-	-	-	-	-	-	-	-	-	1
2008 (C)													
Total	486	...	-	20	110	114	94	63	51	17	10	7	-
15 - 19	2	...	...	...	...	...	...	...	...	...	...	...	...
20 - 24	47	...	...	...	...	...	...	...	...	...	...	...	...
25 - 29	134	...	...	...	...	...	...	...	...	...	...	...	...
30 - 34	127	...	...	...	...	...	...	...	...	...	...	...	...
35 - 39	94	...	...	...	...	...	...	...	...	...	...	...	...
40 - 44	37	...	...	...	...	...	...	...	...	...	...	...	...
45 - 49	26	...	...	...	...	...	...	...	...	...	...	...	...
50 - 54	12	...	...	...	...	...	...	...	...	...	...	...	...
55 - 59	6	...	...	...	...	...	...	...	...	...	...	...	...
60 - 64	-	...	...	...	...	...	...	...	...	...	...	...	...
65 +	1	...	...	...	...	...	...	...	...	...	...	...	...
Unknown - Inconnu	-	...	...	...	...	...	...	...	...	...	...	...	...
AMERICA, SOUTH - AMÉRIQUE DU SUD													
Brazil - Brésil[8]													
2009 (U)													
Total	935 116	16	28 195	210 260	273 755	172 064	91 324	54 827	35 056	23 142	16 065	29 717	695
0 - 14	474	6	159	216	54	21	3	5	5	2	1	2	-
15 - 19	125 629	3	17 460	67 579	29 425	7 762	2 217	689	278	103	43	66	4
20 - 24	255 148	3	8 088	99 266	101 223	32 180	9 190	3 024	1 168	522	214	261	9
25 - 29	241 933	2	1 829	32 317	104 250	67 177	22 433	7 997	3 277	1 361	628	650	12
30 - 34	133 977	-	455	7 855	28 835	44 898	28 680	12 552	5 591	2 490	1 301	1 317	3
35 - 39	70 310	1	113	2 108	7 126	13 854	18 137	14 194	7 205	3 621	1 875	2 069	7
40 - 44	42 469	-	48	594	1 960	4 216	7 067	9 893	8 085	4 746	2 753	3 103	4
45 - 49	27 942	-	17	202	598	1 369	2 455	4 392	5 940	5 154	3 235	4 579	1
50 - 54	16 802	-	7	53	172	388	793	1 431	2 335	3 282	3 149	5 191	1
55 - 59	9 462	1	5	24	53	104	197	441	820	1 272	1 864	4 681	-
60 - 64	5 022	-	2	7	15	44	87	139	224	364	667	3 472	1
65 +	5 240	-	8	26	35	43	59	66	124	220	334	4 324	1
Unknown - Inconnu	708	-	4	13	9	8	6	4	4	5	1	2	652
Chile - Chili													
2008 (+C)													
Total	56 112	-	1 011	9 803	18 500	12 338	5 684	2 873	1 671	1 138	882	2 212	...
0 - 14	-	-	-	-	-	-	-	-	-	-	-	-	...
15 - 19	3 615	-	550	1 963	819	201	57	20	4	-	1	-	...
20 - 24	14 286	-	381	5 515	6 008	1 791	416	113	42	5	10	5	...
25 - 29	18 567	-	62	1 903	9 335	5 331	1 454	326	104	33	12	7	...
30 - 34	9 133	-	13	319	1 886	3 843	2 023	681	231	75	35	27	...
35 - 39	3 957	-	4	74	338	918	1 194	828	318	150	60	73	...
40 - 44	2 160	-	1	20	86	197	358	558	398	244	139	159	...
45 - 49	1 583	-	-	7	20	51	132	239	373	280	192	289	...
50 - 54	1 101	-	-	2	6	6	37	73	131	209	233	404	...
55 - 59	709	-	-	-	1	-	8	20	49	98	122	411	...
60 - 64	467	-	-	-	-	-	5	10	13	32	46	361	...
65 - 69	250	-	-	-	-	-	-	4	6	10	17	213	...
70 - 74	161	-	-	-	-	-	-	1	1	1	13	145	...
75 +	123	-	-	-	1	-	-	-	1	1	2	118	...
Unknown - Inconnu	-	-	-	-	-	-	-	-	-	-	-	-	...
Ecuador - Équateur[9]													
2009 (U)													
Total	76 892	24	6 021	22 232	20 172	11 704	6 276	3 660	2 328	1 525	1 019	1 737	194
0 - 14	647	7	284	250	77	20	8	1	-	-	-	-	-
15 - 19	15 546	12	4 093	7 923	2 474	661	245	71	39	10	4	6	8
20 - 24	23 978	5	1 395	10 687	7 981	2 565	799	322	128	43	17	17	19
25 - 29	16 781	-	179	2 546	7 235	4 368	1 553	502	223	96	31	34	14

23. Marriages by age of groom and by age of bride: latest available year, 2000 - 2009
Mariages selon l'âge de l'époux et selon l'âge de l'épouse : dernière année disponible, 2000 - 2009 (continued - suite)

Continent, country or area, year, code and age of bride / Continent, pays ou zone, date, code et âge de l'épouse	Total	\: Age of groom - âge de l'époux											Unknown Inconnu
		0-14	15-19	20-24	25-29	30-34	35-39	40-44	45-49	50-54	55-59	60+	
AMERICA, SOUTH - AMÉRIQUE DU SUD													
Ecuador - Équateur[9]													
2009													
30 - 34	8 376	-	37	563	1 717	2 886	1 855	765	307	141	58	44	3
35 - 39	4 335	-	12	135	436	806	1 168	916	463	201	97	96	5
40 - 44	2 698	-	10	56	141	231	422	712	565	278	130	150	3
45 - 49	1 811	-	1	19	48	103	151	246	426	400	225	191	1
50 - 54	1 050	-	4	11	8	20	40	74	125	251	249	267	1
55 - 59	574	-	-	2	5	13	15	26	37	68	143	265	-
60 - 64	347	-	-	-	2	2	2	9	9	19	49	255	-
65 - 69	204	-	-	-	-	1	2	-	-	9	9	182	1
70 +	252	-	-	3	7	2	3	2	1	6	5	221	2
Unknown - Inconnu	293	-	6	37	41	26	13	14	5	3	2	9	137
French Guiana - Guyane française													
2007 (C)													
Total	667	...	5	48	123	150	108	79	47	48	26	33	...
15 - 19	30	...	-	10	13	4	-	1	1	-	1	-	...
20 - 24	93	...	3	22	33	15	8	7	-	1	2	2	...
25 - 29	151	...	1	5	51	57	17	7	5	2	6	-	...
30 - 34	135	...	1	8	16	41	35	18	7	7	2	-	...
35 - 39	98	...	-	3	6	20	27	20	11	2	6	3	...
40 - 44	62	...	-	-	4	7	10	15	10	9	2	5	...
45 - 49	55	...	-	-	-	3	5	9	10	16	4	8	...
50 - 54	23	...	-	-	-	2	4	2	3	6	2	4	...
55 - 59	13	...	-	-	-	1	2	-	-	3	1	6	...
60 - 64	2	...	-	-	-	-	-	-	-	1	-	1	...
65 - 69	4	...	-	-	-	-	-	-	-	1	-	3	...
70 - 74	1	...	-	-	-	-	-	-	-	-	-	1	...
75 - 79	-	...	-	-	-	-	-	-	-	-	-	-	...
80 - 84	-	...	-	-	-	-	-	-	-	-	-	-	...
85 +	-	...	-	-	-	-	-	-	-	-	-	-	...
Paraguay													
2008 (U)													
Total	18 832	-	583	5 084	6 143	3 229	1 516	826	516	337	212	376	10
0 - 14	9	-	2	4	3	-	-	-	-	-	-	-	-
15 - 19	3 668	-	391	1 879	999	276	77	27	11	4	2	2	-
20 - 24	5 912	-	158	2 340	2 336	736	207	79	26	19	5	6	-
25 - 29	4 722	-	21	691	2 194	1 219	367	112	60	31	13	14	-
30 - 34	2 075	-	6	112	460	729	404	222	83	33	13	12	1
35 - 39	1 009	-	4	28	102	182	317	195	89	45	21	25	1
40 - 44	560	-	1	16	30	52	95	118	128	60	36	24	-
45 - 49	345	-	-	6	13	17	30	49	79	74	36	41	-
50 - 54	205	-	-	1	2	8	12	18	25	40	46	53	-
55 - 59	135	-	-	2	2	4	2	2	10	18	27	68	-
60 - 64	69	-	-	1	-	2	3	2	2	10	7	42	-
65 - 69	41	-	-	-	-	1	1	-	1	2	3	32	1
70 - 74	32	-	-	-	-	-	1	1	2	1	2	25	-
75 +	33	-	-	-	-	-	-	-	-	-	1	32	-
Unknown - Inconnu	17	-	-	4	2	3	-	1	-	-	-	-	7
Suriname													
2002 (C)													
Total	2 005	-	23	421	542	367	208	142	101	65	136[s]	...	...
0 - 14	6	...	...	...	...	...	...	...	...	...	...	...	...
15 - 19	382	...	...	...	...	...	...	...	...	...	...	...	...
20 - 24	596	...	...	...	...	...	...	...	...	...	...	...	...
25 - 29	333	...	...	...	...	...	...	...	...	...	...	...	...
30 - 34	233	...	...	...	...	...	...	...	...	...	...	...	...
35 - 39	187	...	...	...	...	...	...	...	...	...	...	...	...
40 - 44	113	...	...	...	...	...	...	...	...	...	...	...	...
45 - 49	72	...	...	...	...	...	...	...	...	...	...	...	...
50 - 54	36	...	...	...	...	...	...	...	...	...	...	...	...
55 +	47	...	...	...	...	...	...	...	...	...	...	...	...
Uruguay													
2002 (C)													
Total	14 073	...	453[e]	3 015	4 227	2 292	1 209	1 335[m]	...	1 542[r]	...	...	-
0 - 19	1 728	...	300[e]	978	342	78	15	9[m]	...	6[r]	...	...	-
20 - 24	3 618	...	111[e]	1 434	1 446	423	120	57[m]	...	27[r]	...	...	-

Continent, country or area, year, code and age of bride / Continent, pays ou zone, date, code et âge de l'épouse	Total	0-14	15-19	20-24	25-29	30-34	35-39	40-44	45-49	50-54	55-59	60+	Unknown Inconnu
AMERICA, SOUTH - AMÉRIQUE DU SUD													
Uruguay													
2002													
25 - 29	3 900	...	33e	468	1 890	930	366	177m	...	36r	...	...	-
30 - 34	1 890	...	3e	93	384	642	363	318m	...	87r	...	...	-
35 - 39	972	...	-e	33	111	141	234	309m	...	144r	...	...	-
40 - 49	1 011	...	6e	9	36	72	105	378m	...	405r	...	...	-
50 +	954	...	-e	-	18	6	6	87m	...	837r	...	...	-
Unknown - Inconnu	-	...	-e	-	-	-	-	-m	...	-r	...	...	-
Venezuela (Bolivarian Republic of) - Venezuela (République bolivarienne du)													
2007 (C)													
Total	93 003	19	3 803	21 810	27 776	16 657	9 160	5 199	3 216	2 171	1 275	1 917	...
0 - 14	562	-	180	230	85	43	8	4	1	1	3	7	...
15 - 19	12 806	5	2 411	6 445	2 650	828	285	105	32	17	8	20	...
20 - 24	27 006	3	898	10 802	10 070	3 341	1 159	427	164	64	19	59	...
25 - 29	25 124	2	222	3 355	11 264	6 316	2 478	856	360	141	69	61	...
30 - 34	12 459	2	43	676	2 732	4 310	2 516	1 195	508	270	95	112	...
35 - 39	6 429	2	23	194	676	1 255	1 792	1 208	663	343	150	123	...
40 - 44	3 618	-	7	60	175	371	615	919	718	394	189	170	...
45 - 49	2 180	1	4	24	67	115	206	337	496	458	241	231	...
50 - 54	1 263	1	4	7	24	35	67	107	178	309	266	265	...
55 - 59	728	1	3	3	6	15	19	32	66	121	168	294	...
60 - 64	378	1	2	1	1	8	3	7	21	36	47	251	...
60 +	828	2	8	14	27	28	15	9	30	53	67	575	...
65 - 69	218	-	2	2	2	7	8	2	6	15	17	157	...
70 - 74	91	-	1	-	5	2	-	-	2	2	3	76	...
75 - 79	73	1	-	2	7	5	3	-	-	-	-	55	...
80 - 84	43	-	-	6	8	4	1	-	-	-	-	24	...
85 +	25	-	3	3	4	2	-	-	1	-	-	12	...
ASIA - ASIE													
Armenia - Arménie													
2009 (+C)													
Total	18 773	...	153	4 608	7 796	3 482	1 313	560	325	208	132	196	...
15 - 19	2 010	...	122	928	825	124	11	-	-	-	-	-	...
20 - 24	9 521	...	28	3 366	4 655	1 278	170	19	2	3	-	-	...
25 - 29	4 516	...	2	282	2 151	1 474	478	95	27	7	-	-	...
30 - 34	1 467	...	-	26	130	539	455	215	76	17	9	-	...
35 - 39	528	...	-	4	20	47	165	154	92	32	10	4	...
40 - 44	238	...	-	2	8	13	22	52	72	42	16	11	...
45 - 49	161	...	1	-	2	4	6	14	39	53	20	22	...
50 - 54	153	...	-	-	4	3	4	8	8	45	47	34	...
55 - 59	101	...	-	-	-	-	1	2	4	5	25	64	...
60 +	78	...	-	-	1	-	1	1	5	4	5	61	...
Azerbaijan - Azerbaïdjan													
2009 (+C)													
Total	78 072	...	950	26 010	28 589	12 723	4 899	2 266	1 107	603	364	561	...
15 - 19	20 753	...	642	10 257	7 780	1 797	216	43	13	1	2	2	...
20 - 24	35 222	...	267	13 852	14 624	5 203	1 039	177	33	10	9	8	...
25 - 29	12 668	...	30	1 590	5 320	3 668	1 509	405	108	21	8	9	...
30 - 34	4 954	...	4	225	704	1 645	1 327	694	247	69	22	17	...
35 - 39	2 034	...	5	46	104	285	597	551	252	111	48	35	...
40 - 44	1 260	...	-	20	44	98	174	312	260	168	88	96	...
45 - 49	691	...	2	11	4	18	30	69	151	152	91	163	...
50 - 54	307	...	-	-	7	6	6	15	36	51	71	115	...
55 - 59	97	...	-	3	1	1	1	-	5	17	20	49	...
60 +	86	...	-	6	1	2	-	-	2	3	5	67	...
Bahrain - Bahreïn													
2007³ (...)													
Total	4 685	-	89	1 676	1 716	593	229	144	105	133r	...	...	...
0 - 14	18	-	4	10	2	2	-	-	-	-r	...	...	...
15 - 19	1 081	-	67	642	323	41	4	3	1	-r	...	...	...
20 - 24	2 202	-	15	952	968	182	45	20	12	8r	...	...	...

23. Marriages by age of groom and by age of bride: latest available year, 2000 - 2009
Mariages selon l'âge de l'époux et selon l'âge de l'épouse : dernière année disponible, 2000 - 2009 (continued - suite)

Continent, pays ou zone, date, code et âge de l'épouse	Total	0-14	15-19	20-24	25-29	30-34	35-39	40-44	45-49	50-54	55-59	60+	Unknown Inconnu
ASIA - ASIE													
Bahrain - Bahreïn													
2007[3]													
25 - 29	820	-	2	65	371	247	73	32	22	8[f]	...	...	...
30 - 34	301	-	-	5	44	89	64	45	24	30[c]	...	...	...
35 - 39	121	-	1	-	5	22	30	25	15	23[c]	...	...	...
40 - 44	80	-	-	2	1	6	10	13	20	28[f]	...	...	...
45 - 49	49	-	-	-	2	2	3	4	11	27[f]	...	...	...
50 +	13	-	-	-	-	2	-	2	-	9[f]	...	...	...
Brunei Darussalam - Brunéi Darussalam													
2008 (...)													
Total	2 391	-	68	527	870	534	177	73	53	40	23	26	-
0 - 14	6	...	...	...	...	...	...	...	...	...	...	...	...
15 - 19	205	...	...	...	...	...	...	...	...	...	...	...	...
20 - 24	701	...	...	...	...	...	...	...	...	...	...	...	...
25 - 29	954	...	...	...	...	...	...	...	...	...	...	...	...
30 - 34	403	...	...	...	...	...	...	...	...	...	...	...	...
35 - 39	66	...	...	...	...	...	...	...	...	...	...	...	...
40 - 44	37	...	...	...	...	...	...	...	...	...	...	...	...
45 - 49	15	...	...	...	...	...	...	...	...	...	...	...	...
50 - 54	3	...	...	...	...	...	...	...	...	...	...	...	...
55 - 59	1	...	...	...	...	...	...	...	...	...	...	...	...
60 - 64	-	...	...	...	...	...	...	...	...	...	...	...	...
65 - 69	-	...	...	...	...	...	...	...	...	...	...	...	...
70 - 74	-	...	...	...	...	...	...	...	...	...	...	...	...
75 +	-	...	...	...	...	...	...	...	...	...	...	...	...
Unknown - Inconnu	-	...	...	...	...	...	...	...	...	...	...	...	...
China, Hong Kong SAR - Chine, Hong Kong RAS													
2009 (C)													
Total	51 175	...	160[g]	3 689	12 789	13 565	7 778	4 462	3 244	2 279	1 316	1 893	...
16 - 19	735	...	83[g]	341	178	52	40	21	15	4	-	1	...
20 - 24	8 373	...	71[g]	2 572	2 961	1 266	774	341	220	106	38	24	...
25 - 29	18 372	...	5[g]	614	7 918	5 610	2 136	963	613	316	120	77	...
30 - 34	12 593	...	1[g]	97	1 440	5 626	2 696	1 205	699	438	211	180	...
35 - 39	5 890	...	-[g]	45	220	824	1 672	1 129	787	546	326	341	...
40 - 44	2 663	...	-[g]	14	52	141	338	561	523	405	233	396	...
45 - 49	1 398	...	-[g]	2	17	34	92	177	293	271	205	307	...
50 - 54	604	...	-[g]	3	1	6	19	52	70	145	109	199	...
55 - 59	287	...	-[g]	1	1	6	8	12	19	35	57	148	...
60 - 64	109	...	-[g]	-	1	-	3	1	3	13	14	74	...
65 - 69	58	...	-[g]	-	-	-	-	-	1	-	2	55	...
70 - 74	46	...	-[g]	-	-	-	-	-	1	-	1	44	...
75 +	47	...	-[g]	-	-	-	-	-	-	-	-	47	...
China, Macao SAR - Chine, Macao RAS													
2009 (+C)													
Total	3 035	-	18	608	1 023	697	286	157	98	68	39	41	...
0 - 14	-	-	-	-	-	-	-	-	-	-	-	-	...
15 - 19	66	-	5	40	17	3	1	-	-	-	-	-	...
20 - 24	993	-	12	445	353	125	36	14	5	3	-	-	...
25 - 29	1 166	-	1	109	575	313	94	42	13	11	7	1	...
30 - 34	444	-	-	10	62	212	83	33	25	12	5	2	...
35 - 39	195	-	-	4	9	30	62	41	26	8	8	7	...
40 - 44	72	-	-	-	5	8	9	17	12	9	6	6	...
45 - 49	58	-	-	-	1	4	1	7	16	14	8	7	...
50 - 54	20	-	-	-	1	2	-	3	1	9	2	2	...
55 - 59	11	-	-	-	-	-	-	-	-	1	2	8	...
60 - 64	4	-	-	-	-	-	-	-	-	1	1	2	...
65 - 69	1	-	-	-	-	-	-	-	-	-	-	1	...
70 +	5	-	-	-	-	-	-	-	-	-	-	5	...
Cyprus - Chypre													
2006[10,11] (C)													
Total	4 887	...	13	645	1 813	1 117	559	302	151	97	70	117	3
15 - 19	131	...	7	84	31	7	2	-	-	-	-	-	-
20 - 24	1 302	...	4	449	627	145	42	23	7	4	1	-	-

23. Marriages by age of groom and by age of bride: latest available year, 2000 - 2009
Mariages selon l'âge de l'époux et selon l'âge de l'épouse : dernière année disponible, 2000 - 2009 (continued - suite)

Continent, country or area, year, code and age of bride / Continent, pays ou zone, date, code et âge de l'épouse	Total	0-14	15-19	20-24	25-29	30-34	35-39	40-44	45-49	50-54	55-59	60+	Unknown Inconnu
ASIA - ASIE													
Cyprus - Chypre													
2006[10,11]													
25 - 29	1 931	...	-	83	985	573	178	71	21	10	7	3	-
30 - 34	838	...	2	21	134	319	214	93	29	15	4	7	-
35 - 39	313	...	-	5	24	50	91	60	42	16	7	18	-
40 - 44	155	...	-	3	10	14	23	36	23	18	14	14	-
45 - 49	107	...	-	-	2	6	9	17	24	15	13	21	-
50 - 54	54	...	-	-	-	3	-	1	3	15	14	18	-
55 - 59	31	...	-	-	-	-	-	1	2	4	8	16	-
60 - 64	13	...	-	-	-	-	-	-	-	-	1	12	-
65 - 69	6	...	-	-	-	-	-	-	-	-	1	5	-
70 - 74	2	...	-	-	-	-	-	-	-	-	-	2	-
75 - 79	1	...	-	-	-	-	-	-	-	-	-	1	-
80 +	-	...	-	-	-	-	-	-	-	-	-	-	-
Unknown - Inconnu	3	...	-	-	-	-	-	-	-	-	-	-	3
Georgia - Géorgie													
2008 (C)													
Total	31 414	...	1 168[9]	8 792	9 211	5 938	3 127	1 579	793	319	201	267	19
16 - 19	5 294	...	...	...	...	...	...	...	...	...	...	...	...
20 - 24	12 557	...	...	...	...	...	...	...	...	...	...	...	...
25 - 29	7 145	...	...	...	...	...	...	...	...	...	...	...	...
30 - 34	3 397	...	...	...	...	...	...	...	...	...	...	...	...
35 - 39	1 530	...	...	...	...	...	...	...	...	...	...	...	...
40 - 44	705	...	...	...	...	...	...	...	...	...	...	...	...
45 - 49	372	...	...	...	...	...	...	...	...	...	...	...	...
50 - 54	173	...	...	...	...	...	...	...	...	...	...	...	...
55 - 59	121	...	...	...	...	...	...	...	...	...	...	...	...
60 +	108	...	...	...	...	...	...	...	...	...	...	...	...
Unknown - Inconnu	12	...	...	...	...	...	...	...	...	...	...	...	...
Israel - Israël[12]													
2008 (C)													
Total	50 038	...	1 653	12 268	18 462	10 127	3 144	1 233	679	428	320	497	1 227
15 - 19	7 908	...	1 240	3 981	1 886	304	26	4	5	1	-	-	461
20 - 24	17 359	...	342	7 361	7 087	1 858	278	40	18	3	1	-	371
25 - 29	15 101	...	6	549	8 336	4 860	872	209	46	14	2	2	205
30 - 34	5 395	...	2	35	812	2 663	1 264	336	135	42	7	9	90
35 - 39	1 643	...	-	7	68	270	572	377	163	68	24	38	56
40 - 44	634	...	-	1	3	23	63	176	169	88	43	45	23
45 - 49	385	...	-	-	-	4	11	36	100	98	70	58	8
50 - 54	275	...	-	-	-	-	1	5	25	72	99	68	5
55 - 59	177	...	-	-	-	1	-	2	2	14	48	104	6
60 - 64	82	...	-	-	-	-	-	-	-	4	11	65	2
65 - 69	37	...	-	-	-	-	-	-	-	1	-	36	-
70 - 74	25	...	-	-	-	-	-	-	-	-	-	25	-
75 +	15	...	-	-	-	-	-	-	-	-	-	15	-
Unknown - Inconnu	1 002	...	63	334	270	144	57	48	16	23	15	32	-
Japan - Japon[13]													
2009 (+C)													
Total	592 179	-	5 787	71 152	197 170	152 836	85 413	35 871	17 180	9 745	7 318	9 706	1
0 - 14	-	-	-	-	-	-	-	-	-	-	-	-	-
15 - 19	12 664	-	4 256	5 396	1 761	731	276	96	62	37	30	19	-
20 - 24	106 927	-	1 361	48 433	37 060	12 740	4 590	1 431	651	341	201	119	-
25 - 29	228 297	-	127	14 168	128 555	60 163	17 730	4 535	1 616	690	421	292	-
30 - 34	137 029	-	34	2 472	25 044	63 722	31 960	8 836	2 865	1 142	576	378	-
35 - 39	64 147	-	7	575	4 102	13 374	25 785	12 586	4 450	1 704	935	629	-
40 - 44	21 096	-	1	93	549	1 769	4 216	6 771	4 081	1 869	977	770	-
45 - 49	9 062	-	-	12	77	282	711	1 303	2 651	1 968	1 179	879	-
50 - 54	5 178	-	1	3	15	45	115	261	634	1 512	1 418	1 173	1
55 - 59	3 509	-	-	-	5	9	21	44	132	364	1 160	1 774	-
60 - 64	2 267	-	-	-	1	1	6	8	33	92	338	1 788	-
65 - 69	1 166	-	-	-	1	-	1	-	5	24	66	1 069	-
70 - 74	518	-	-	-	-	-	1	-	-	2	15	500	-
75 +	319	-	-	-	-	-	1	-	-	-	2	316	-
Unknown - Inconnu	-	-	-	-	-	-	-	-	-	-	-	-	-

Continent, country or area, year, code and age of bride / Continent, pays ou zone, date, code et âge de l'épouse	Total	Age of groom - âge de l'époux											
		0-14	15-19	20-24	25-29	30-34	35-39	40-44	45-49	50-54	55-59	60+	Unknown Inconnu
ASIA - ASIE													
Jordan - Jordanie[14]													
2008 (+C)													
Total	60 922	...	...	...	...	...	...	...	...	...	...	...	
18 - 19	1 293	...	...	...	...	...	...	...	...	...	...	...	
20 - 24	16 310	...	...	...	...	...	...	...	...	...	...	...	
25 - 29	24 101	...	...	...	...	...	...	...	...	...	...	...	
30 - 34	10 944	...	...	...	...	...	...	...	...	...	...	...	
35 - 39	3 701	...	...	...	...	...	...	...	...	...	...	...	
40 - 44	1 704	...	...	...	...	...	...	...	...	...	...	...	
45 - 49	946	...	...	...	...	...	...	...	...	...	...	...	
50 - 54	569	...	...	...	...	...	...	...	...	...	...	...	
55 - 59	362	...	...	...	...	...	...	...	...	...	...	...	
60 - 64	394	...	...	...	...	...	...	...	...	...	...	...	
65 +	598	...	...	...	...	...	...	...	...	...	...	...	
Kazakhstan													
2008 (C)													
Total	135 280	120	3 870	50 022	44 135	18 895	8 267	4 159	2 485	1 427	851	1 048	1
0 - 14	1 691	39	409	982	225	30	4	1	1	-	-	-	-
15 - 19	17 070	53	2 113	10 510	3 670	618	78	17	7	1	2	1	-
20 - 24	68 159	27	1 242	34 207	25 518	5 809	1 047	217	68	16	7	-	1
25 - 29	26 297	1	90	3 755	12 348	7 129	2 144	588	168	50	16	8	-
30 - 34	11 205	-	13	459	1 969	4 251	2 790	1 100	422	133	49	19	-
35 - 39	5 092	-	1	81	325	873	1 743	1 222	541	195	61	50	-
40 - 44	2 363	-	2	21	55	151	362	732	609	243	120	68	-
45 - 49	1 545	-	-	4	19	29	81	231	480	405	167	129	-
50 - 54	880	-	-	1	5	4	15	43	137	293	221	161	-
55 - 59	498	-	-	2	-	1	3	6	42	72	162	210	-
60 +	480	-	-	-	1	-	-	2	10	19	46	402	-
Unknown - Inconnu	-	-	-	-	-	-	-	-	-	-	-	-	-
Kuwait - Koweït													
2008 (C)													
Total	14 709	...	596	4 517	3 921	1 835	1 114	724	457	283	162	190	910
0 - 14	306	...	87	148	43	6	5	2	1	2	-	-	12
15 - 19	3 092	...	367	1 753	580	80	36	10	8	6	4	8	240
20 - 24	5 433	...	113	2 243	1 897	510	123	59	24	12	8	7	437
25 - 29	2 752	...	15	226	1 013	695	344	177	86	35	18	10	133
30 - 34	1 310	...	8	43	201	362	313	168	99	36	24	25	31
35 - 39	757	...	-	20	68	82	189	164	99	66	28	30	11
40 - 44	410	...	-	5	24	32	63	91	82	48	28	25	12
45 - 49	206	...	-	2	9	18	17	36	38	41	20	23	2
50 - 54	115	...	1	-	3	4	5	10	16	26	23	24	3
55 - 59	26	...	-	-	-	1	-	-	2	6	4	12	1
60 +	29	...	-	-	-	-	-	1	-	1	2	24	1
Unknown - Inconnu	273	...	5	77	83	45	19	6	2	4	3	2	27
Kyrgyzstan - Kirghizstan													
2009 (C)													
Total	47 567	-	809	16 325	18 000	6 296	2 807	1 379	844	467	286	354	...
0 - 14	-	-	-	-	-	-	-	-	-	-	-	-	...
15 - 19	8 677	-	606	5 225	2 607	222	15	1	1	-	-	-	...
20 - 24	24 483	-	182	10 444	11 457	2 061	283	41	7	2	5	1	...
25 - 29	8 070	-	19	587	3 628	2 735	836	179	58	17	8	3	...
30 - 34	3 029	-	1	60	253	1 083	1 032	410	131	40	9	10	...
35 - 39	1 591	-	-	7	51	155	560	456	219	82	33	28	...
40 - 44	768	-	1	1	4	34	63	247	222	104	46	46	...
45 - 49	480	-	-	1	-	6	13	42	165	125	68	60	...
50 - 54	250	-	-	-	-	-	5	3	39	74	62	67	...
55 - 59	127	-	-	-	-	-	-	-	1	20	48	58	...
60 - 64	50	-	-	-	-	-	-	-	-	2	6	42	...
65 - 69	20	-	-	-	-	-	-	-	1	-	1	18	...
70 - 74	15	-	-	-	-	-	-	-	-	1	-	14	...
75 +	7	-	-	-	-	-	-	-	-	-	-	7	...
Mongolia - Mongolie													
2009 (C)													
Total	34 071	...	1 742[i]	15 582	10 852	4 219	1 057	369	147	103[r]	...	...	...
18 - 19	3 283	...	...	...	...	...	...	...	...	...	...	...	...
20 - 24	17 343	...	...	...	...	...	...	...	...	...	...	...	...
25 - 29	8 841	...	...	...	...	...	...	...	...	...	...	...	...

Continent, country or area, year, code and age of bride / Continent, pays ou zone, date, code et âge de l'épouse	Total	0-14	15-19	20-24	25-29	30-34	35-39	40-44	45-49	50-54	55-59	60+	Unknown Inconnu
ASIA - ASIE													
Mongolia - Mongolie													
2009													
30 - 34	3 187	...	...	...	...	...	...	...	...	...	...	...	...
35 - 39	1 003	...	...	...	...	...	...	...	...	...	...	...	...
40 - 44	274	...	...	...	...	...	...	...	...	...	...	...	...
45 - 49	95	...	...	...	...	...	...	...	...	...	...	...	...
50 +	45	...	...	...	...	...	...	...	...	...	...	...	...
Occupied Palestinian Territory - Territoire palestinien occupé													
2007 (C)													
Total	32 685	1	2 509	13 066	11 108	3 150	1 028	615	362	244	211	391	...
0 - 14	742	1	177	412	145	6	1	-	-	-	-	-	...
15 - 19	16 434	-	2 127	8 561	4 883	724	95	28	7	5	1	3	...
20 - 24	10 787	-	186	3 761	4 812	1 470	338	130	42	20	13	15	...
25 - 29	2 886	-	16	293	1 157	695	367	168	95	49	27	19	...
30 - 34	964	-	2	26	90	199	168	180	101	80	55	63	...
35 - 39	499	-	1	8	16	48	46	83	74	45	54	124	...
40 - 44	239	-	-	5	3	8	9	22	26	34	37	95	...
45 - 49	93	-	-	-	2	-	4	3	14	8	17	45	...
50 - 54	30	-	-	-	-	-	-	1	3	3	5	18	...
55 - 59	5	-	-	-	-	-	-	-	-	-	2	3	...
60 +	6	-	-	-	-	-	-	-	-	-	-	6	...
2008 (C)													
Total	33 774	-	2 553	13 279	11 693	3 293	1 093	622	400	246	191	404	...
0 - 14	724	...	...	...	...	...	...	...	...	...	...	...	...
15 - 19	16 744	...	...	...	...	...	...	...	...	...	...	...	...
20 - 24	11 359	...	...	...	...	...	...	...	...	...	...	...	...
25 - 29	3 077	...	...	...	...	...	...	...	...	...	...	...	...
30 - 34	972	...	...	...	...	...	...	...	...	...	...	...	...
35 - 39	502	...	...	...	...	...	...	...	...	...	...	...	...
40 - 44	251	...	...	...	...	...	...	...	...	...	...	...	...
45 - 49	103	...	...	...	...	...	...	...	...	...	...	...	...
50 - 54	27	...	...	...	...	...	...	...	...	...	...	...	...
55 - 59	10	...	...	...	...	...	...	...	...	...	...	...	...
60 - 64	3	...	...	...	...	...	...	...	...	...	...	...	...
65 +	2	...	...	...	...	...	...	...	...	...	...	...	...
Philippines													
2007 (U)													
Total	490 054	...	15 312ᵉ	144 422	169 845	80 840	35 320	17 335	10 279	16 599ʳ	...	...	102
0 - 19	69 052	...	8 734ᵉ	37 433	16 524	4 113	1 309	460	232	242ʳ	...	...	5
20 - 24	186 012	...	5 726ᵉ	82 967	68 408	18 887	5 458	2 047	1 072	1 428ʳ	...	...	19
25 - 29	136 584	...	700ᵉ	20 075	68 381	31 528	9 390	3 129	1 514	1 860ʳ	...	...	7
30 - 34	52 437	...	110ᵉ	2 936	12 993	19 841	9 766	3 605	1 492	1 687ʳ	...	...	7
35 - 39	22 507	...	27ᵉ	683	2 644	4 879	6 768	4 011	1 808	1 682ʳ	...	...	5
40 - 44	8 081	...	5ᵉ	138	434	794	1 300	2 120	1 683	1 605ʳ	...	...	2
45 - 49	5 985	...	3ᵉ	59	163	315	555	879	1 568	2 440ʳ	...	...	3
50 +	6 562	...	5ᵉ	48	77	126	172	337	534	5 262ʳ	...	...	1
Unknown - Inconnu	2 834	...	2ᵉ	83	221	357	602	747	376	393ʳ	...	...	53
Qatar													
2009 (C)													
Total	3 153	-	50	840	1 083	581	262	148	86	56	21	26	-
0 - 14	-	-	-	-	-	-	-	-	-	-	-	-	-
15 - 19	436	-	24	254	126	26	3	2	1	-	-	-	-
20 - 24	1 271	-	23	483	524	184	35	8	6	7	-	1	-
25 - 29	823	-	3	92	349	215	97	34	17	10	2	4	-
30 - 34	322	-	-	5	63	107	69	43	22	7	5	1	-
35 - 39	163	-	-	4	12	30	42	35	15	14	5	6	-
40 - 44	85	-	-	-	5	12	11	19	18	12	5	3	-
45 - 49	35	-	-	1	2	6	4	4	6	4	3	5	-
50 - 54	11	-	-	-	1	1	1	3	1	1	-	3	-
55 - 59	3	-	-	-	1	-	-	-	-	-	1	1	-
60 +	3	-	-	-	-	-	-	-	-	1	-	2	-
Unknown - Inconnu	1	-	-	1	-	-	-	-	-	-	-	-	-

23. Marriages by age of groom and by age of bride: latest available year, 2000 - 2009
Mariages selon l'âge de l'époux et selon l'âge de l'épouse : dernière année disponible, 2000 - 2009 (continued - suite)

Continent, country or area, year, code and age of bride / Continent, pays ou zone, date, code et âge de l'épouse	Total	0-14	15-19	20-24	25-29	30-34	35-39	40-44	45-49	50-54	55-59	60+	Unknown Inconnu
ASIA - ASIE													
Republic of Korea - République de Corée[15]													
2009 (+C)													
Total	309 759	-	622	9 158	97 852	106 285	45 112	19 456	13 336	8 459	4 651	4 702	126
0 - 14	-	-	-	-	-	-	-	-	-	-	-	-	-
15 - 19	5 297	-	465	785	674	842	1 545	794	155	33	4	-	-
20 - 24	30 673	-	141	5 836	13 800	5 591	2 920	1 649	561	134	33	8	-
25 - 29	144 037	-	9	2 236	73 966	56 356	8 686	1 771	693	253	53	14	-
30 - 34	70 496	-	6	256	8 630	39 369	17 804	2 931	953	376	115	56	-
35 - 39	24 997	-	1	37	666	3 574	11 484	5 972	2 092	785	256	130	-
40 - 44	13 567	-	-	6	83	465	2 139	4 639	3 930	1 528	520	257	-
45 - 49	10 561	-	-	1	27	72	458	1 393	3 845	3 023	1 163	579	-
50 - 54	5 905	-	-	1	6	14	65	267	974	1 992	1 628	958	-
55 - 59	2 317	-	-	-	-	2	11	35	104	284	733	1 148	-
60 - 64	1 062	-	-	-	-	-	-	4	25	44	134	855	-
65 - 69	458	-	-	-	-	-	-	1	1	3	11	442	-
70 - 74	185	-	-	-	-	-	-	-	2	2	-	181	-
75 +	78	-	-	-	-	-	-	-	1	2	1	74	-
Unknown - Inconnu	126	-	-	-	-	-	-	-	-	-	-	-	126
Singapore - Singapour[16]													
2009 (+C)													
Total	26 081	-	106	1 783	9 378	6 923	3 486	1 800	1 162	728	391	324	...
0 - 14	-	-	-	-	-	-	-	-	-	-	-	-	...
15 - 19	503	-	70	187	91	58	45	19	19	8	5	1	...
20 - 24	4 770	-	32	1 106	2 203	749	363	164	96	41	12	4	...
25 - 29	11 773	-	1	394	6 205	3 422	1 009	402	198	93	32	17	...
30 - 34	5 226	-	2	74	715	2 288	1 240	480	240	115	48	24	...
35 - 39	2 117	-	1	15	123	338	678	452	260	149	67	34	...
40 - 44	846	-	-	4	29	53	111	204	185	135	71	54	...
45 - 49	462	-	-	3	10	13	30	61	115	111	69	50	...
50 - 54	228	-	-	-	1	2	10	17	41	60	49	48	...
55 - 59	110	-	-	-	1	-	-	1	6	13	31	58	...
60 +	46	-	-	-	-	-	-	-	2	3	7	34	...
Sri Lanka													
2007 (+U)													
Total	196 236	-	4 874	50 475	77 223	37 758	13 636	5 693	3 065	1 585	988	939	...
0 - 14	20	-	7	7	5	1	-	-	-	-	-	-	...
15 - 19	35 127	-	3 814	19 794	10 010	1 301	168	27	6	3	1	3	...
20 - 24	73 649	-	899	26 759	35 730	8 980	1 043	174	44	12	4	4	...
25 - 29	55 088	-	135	3 335	29 096	18 013	3 732	560	160	29	16	12	...
30 - 34	17 764	-	15	432	1 881	8 373	5 319	1 316	310	74	29	15	...
35 - 39	7 468	-	3	123	400	864	2 930	2 070	815	185	47	31	...
40 - 44	3 529	-	-	10	74	184	350	1 307	1 008	389	157	50	...
45 - 49	1 852	-	-	8	14	31	74	194	600	536	278	117	...
50 - 54	958	-	1	5	8	8	18	39	98	299	294	188	...
55 - 59	471	-	-	1	5	2	2	6	17	43	138	257	...
60 - 64	193	-	-	1	-	1	-	-	6	13	21	151	...
65 - 69	71	-	-	-	-	-	-	-	1	1	1	68	...
70 - 74	31	-	-	-	-	-	-	-	-	1	2	28	...
75 +	15	-	-	-	-	-	-	-	-	-	-	15	...
Tajikistan - Tadjikistan													
2008 (+C)													
Total	106 388	-	4 041	49 478	33 148	11 459	4 669	1 636	767	376	227	480	107
0 - 14	-	-	-	-	-	-	-	-	-	-	-	-	-
15 - 19	36 345	-	3 246	24 427	8 052	525	55	9	5	-	-	-	26
20 - 24	47 229	-	739	23 934	18 674	3 216	514	99	4	6	1	1	41
25 - 29	14 636	-	51	1 021	6 011	5 629	1 506	333	5	34	18	14	14
30 - 34	5 023	-	1	40	343	1 923	1 903	582	25	88	38	77	3
35 - 39	1 653	-	-	-	34	151	632	425	97	122	63	126	3
40 - 44	637	-	-	-	1	5	44	162	223	60	44	97	1
45 - 49	374	-	-	-	-	-	3	23	196	49	40	62	1
50 - 54	218	-	-	-	-	-	1	3	143	14	12	45	-
55 - 59	101	-	-	-	-	-	-	-	64	3	6	28	-
60 - 64	18	-	-	-	-	-	-	-	5	-	4	9	-
65 - 69	10	-	-	-	-	-	-	-	-	-	-	10	-
70 - 74	10	-	-	-	-	-	-	-	-	-	-	10	-

23. Marriages by age of groom and by age of bride: latest available year, 2000 - 2000 2000
Mariages selon l'âge de l'époux et selon l'âge de l'épouse : dernière année disponible, 2000 - 2009 (continued - suite)

Continent, country or area, year, code and age of bride / Continent, pays ou zone, date, code et âge de l'épouse	Total	0-14	15-19	20-24	25-29	30-34	35-39	40-44	45-49	50-54	55-59	60+	Unknown Inconnu
ASIA - ASIE													
Tajikistan - Tadjikistan													
2008													
75 + ...	-	-	-	-	-	-	-	-	-	-	-	-	-
Unknown - Inconnu	134	-	4	56	33	10	11	-	-	-	1	1	18
Turkey - Turquie[17]													
2009 (C)													
Total............................	591 742	-	16 243	172 563	240 851	87 490	29 469	13 660	9 057	6 073	4 374	8 073	3 889
0 - 14	-	-	-	-	-	-	-	-	-	-	-	-	-
15 - 19	143 178	-	11 278	69 051	52 532	8 330	1 110	191	60	24	11	14	577
20 - 24	217 547	-	3 905	82 478	101 394	23 766	3 875	789	207	86	29	37	981
25 - 29	132 455	-	609	16 018	70 622	32 661	8 082	2 116	820	282	120	125	1 000
30 - 34	42 887	-	124	1 918	9 970	15 885	8 624	3 242	1 406	573	245	238	662
35 - 39	18 897	-	29	385	1 638	3 440	5 137	3 790	2 049	982	527	583	337
40 - 44	9 065	-	6	68	240	533	1 009	2 078	2 156	1 223	736	836	180
45 - 49	6 028	-	1	13	62	102	189	541	1 497	1 480	841	1 216	86
50 - 54	3 647	-	1	7	13	14	40	85	301	867	975	1 310	34
55 - 59	2 147	-	1	3	1	5	7	19	42	189	537	1 319	24
60 - 64	1 151	-	-	3	1	-	1	4	9	27	125	978	3
65 - 69	577	-	-	-	-	-	-	1	3	3	23	543	4
70 - 74	289	-	-	2	-	1	-	-	1	1	3	281	-
75 + ...	210	-	-	-	-	-	-	-	-	1	1	207	1
Unknown - Inconnu	13 664	-	289	2 617	4 378	2 753	1 395	804	506	335	201	386	-
Uzbekistan - Ouzbékistan													
2000 (C)													
Total............................	168 908	158c	8 625i	102 113	41 332	8 139	3 369	1 911	1 118	684	454	1 005	...
0 - 17	9 606	51c	1 711i	6 732	1 032	69	8	3	-	-	-	-	...
18 - 19	52 422	87c	5 600i	38 985	7 320	361	55	7	1	1	2	3	...
20 - 24	84 289	19c	1 280i	54 562	25 189	2 631	416	144	30	3	5	10	...
25 - 29	13 386	1c	33i	1 669	7 135	3 129	944	305	103	32	8	27	...
30 - 34	4 351	-c	1i	147	558	1 659	1 124	467	207	93	32	63	...
35 - 39	2 103	-c	-j	14	85	238	675	528	257	130	98	78	...
40 - 44	1 134	-c	-j	1	13	41	122	343	261	152	82	119	...
45 - 49	626	-c	-j	-	-	9	22	94	193	122	70	116	...
50 - 54	440	-c	-j	-	-	2	3	17	59	129	91	139	...
55 - 59	194	-c	-j	-	-	-	-	2	7	18	37	130	...
60 + ...	354	-c	-j	-	-	-	-	1	-	4	29	320	...
Unknown - Inconnu	3	-c	-j	3	-	-	-	-	-	-	-	-	...
EUROPE													
Åland Islands - Îles d'Åland													
2007 (C)													
Total............................	116	...	...	...	...	...	...	...	...	...	...	...	...
0 - 14	-	...	...	...	...	...	...	...	...	...	...	...	...
15 - 19	1	...	...	...	...	...	...	...	...	...	...	...	...
20 - 24	10	...	...	...	...	...	...	...	...	...	...	...	...
25 - 29	33	...	...	...	...	...	...	...	...	...	...	...	...
30 - 34	25	...	...	...	...	...	...	...	...	...	...	...	...
35 - 39	20	...	...	...	...	...	...	...	...	...	...	...	...
40 - 44	12	...	...	...	...	...	...	...	...	...	...	...	...
45 - 49	4	...	...	...	...	...	...	...	...	...	...	...	...
50 - 54	4	...	...	...	...	...	...	...	...	...	...	...	...
55 - 59	4	...	...	...	...	...	...	...	...	...	...	...	...
60 - 64	3	...	...	...	...	...	...	...	...	...	...	...	...
65 + ...	-	...	...	...	...	...	...	...	...	...	...	...	...
Unknown - Inconnu	-	...	...	...	...	...	...	...	...	...	...	...	...
Albania - Albanie													
2007 (C)													
Total............................	22 371	...	257e	4 716	10 147	4 648	1 540	509	272	282r	...	...	...
0 - 19	6 383	...	...	...	...	...	...	...	...	...	...	...	...
20 - 24	10 194	...	...	...	...	...	...	...	...	...	...	...	...
25 - 29	3 833	...	...	...	...	...	...	...	...	...	...	...	...
30 - 34	1 103	...	...	...	...	...	...	...	...	...	...	...	...
35 - 39	476	...	...	...	...	...	...	...	...	...	...	...	...
40 - 44	212	...	...	...	...	...	...	...	...	...	...	...	...

23. Marriages by age of groom and by age of bride: latest available year, 2000 - 2009
Mariages selon l'âge de l'époux et selon l'âge de l'épouse : dernière année disponible, 2000 - 2009 (continued - suite)

Continent, country or area, year, code and age of bride / Continent, pays ou zone, date, code et âge de l'épouse	Total	Age of groom - âge de l'époux											Unknown Inconnu
		0-14	15-19	20-24	25-29	30-34	35-39	40-44	45-49	50-54	55-59	60+	
EUROPE													
Albania - Albanie													
2007													
45 - 49	110	...	...	...	...	...	...	...	...	...	...	...	...
50 +	60	...	...	...	...	...	...	...	...	...	...	...	...
Austria - Autriche[18]													
2009 (C)													
Total	35 469	-	241	2 715	7 641	8 185	5 954	4 104	2 629	1 654	1 023	1 323	...
0 - 14	-	-	-	-	-	-	-	-	-	-	-	-	...
15 - 19	863	-	138	493	167	34	16	11	2	2	-	-	...
20 - 24	5 083	-	86	1 670	2 208	716	250	81	47	15	5	5	...
25 - 29	10 128	-	12	457	4 208	3 561	1 239	441	143	38	15	14	...
30 - 34	7 342	-	4	64	820	3 025	2 164	815	305	97	27	21	...
35 - 39	4 546	-	-	20	165	664	1 632	1 208	537	198	77	45	...
40 - 44	3 010	-	-	5	48	134	468	1 058	682	346	143	126	...
45 - 49	2 219	-	1	4	21	39	152	377	649	503	277	196	...
50 - 54	1 233	-	-	2	3	10	26	96	205	332	269	290	...
55 - 59	552	-	-	-	1	1	6	14	43	94	136	257	...
60 - 64	285	-	-	-	-	1	1	1	13	22	56	191	...
65 - 69	154	-	-	-	-	-	-	1	3	6	15	129	...
70 - 74	36	-	-	-	-	-	-	-	-	1	2	33	...
75 +	18	-	-	-	-	-	-	1	-	-	1	16	...
Belarus - Bélarus													
2009 (C)													
Total	78 800	65c	1 650i	27 149	24 131	10 058	5 425	3 404	2 700	1 858	1 085	1 275	...
0 - 17	915	26c	227i	535	112	12	2	-	1	-	-	-	...
18 - 19	6 532	29c	715i	4 253	1 307	172	40	10	2	1	2	1	...
20 - 24	34 045	9c	589i	18 083	12 214	2 373	549	150	52	16	7	3	...
25 - 29	18 008	1c	96i	3 594	8 300	3 912	1 361	460	202	51	21	10	...
30 - 34	7 614	-c	20i	537	1 693	2 502	1 674	726	308	106	33	15	...
35 - 39	4 283	-c	3i	113	394	795	1 251	941	502	187	68	29	...
40 - 44	2 393	-c	-i	24	87	211	381	693	611	254	92	40	...
45 - 49	2 057	-c	-i	7	20	70	136	310	691	539	187	97	...
50 - 54	1 423	-c	-i	3	3	7	25	91	258	528	320	188	...
55 - 59	769	-c	-i	-	1	2	5	18	60	139	265	279	...
60 +	761	-c	-i	-	-	2	1	5	13	37	90	613	...
Belgium - Belgique[19,20]													
2009 (C)													
Total	43 303	-	119	3 550	12 333	8 750	5 728	4 065	3 235	2 353	1 501	1 660	9
0 - 14	-	-	-	-	-	-	-	-	-	-	-	-	-
15 - 19	787	-	58	372	248	67	26	10	4	1	1	-	-
20 - 24	7 511	-	42	2 313	3 744	953	282	103	49	21	2	2	-
25 - 29	13 267	-	11	697	6 918	3 801	1 181	385	173	57	29	13	2
30 - 34	7 227	-	2	108	1 042	2 847	1 856	811	351	129	51	29	1
35 - 39	4 813	-	2	37	231	736	1 587	1 174	599	284	113	50	-
40 - 44	3 402	-	-	13	75	207	519	996	861	438	187	106	-
45 - 49	2 757	-	2	4	48	95	194	417	808	655	320	214	-
50 - 54	1 812	-	1	2	15	27	64	129	303	528	400	343	-
55 - 59	966	-	-	2	8	12	11	31	68	176	292	366	-
60 - 64	451	-	1	1	-	2	2	6	14	51	77	297	-
65 - 69	164	-	-	1	1	2	-	2	3	8	23	124	-
70 - 74	76	-	-	-	-	1	-	-	-	3	2	70	-
75 +	50	-	-	-	-	-	1	-	-	1	2	46	-
Unknown - Inconnu	20	-	-	-	3	-	5	1	2	1	2	-	6
Bosnia and Herzegovina - Bosnie-Herzégovine													
2009 (C)													
Total	20 633	-	250	4 755	7 594	4 083	1 659	862	528	302	207	382	11
0 - 14	-	-	-	-	-	-	-	-	-	-	-	-	-
15 - 19	2 711	-	160	1 591	780	146	25	7	2	-	-	-	-
20 - 24	7 357	-	81	2 642	3 479	930	156	44	15	3	1	4	2
25 - 29	5 927	-	7	463	2 942	1 879	479	109	25	8	7	4	4
30 - 34	2 267	-	2	33	330	954	596	226	92	18	8	5	3
35 - 39	950	-	-	15	38	140	311	262	118	46	9	11	-
40 - 44	521	-	-	-	10	21	70	164	146	60	25	24	1
45 - 49	363	-	-	2	2	7	13	32	104	96	43	64	-
50 - 54	224	-	-	1	2	-	4	11	17	54	58	77	-

23. Marriages by age of groom and by age of bride: latest available year, 2000 - 2009
Mariages selon l'âge de l'époux et selon l'âge de l'épouse : dernière année disponible, 2000 - 2009 (continued - suite)

Continent, country or area, year, code and age of bride / Continent, pays ou zone, date, code et âge de l'épouse	Total	0-14	15-19	20-24	25-29	30-34	35-39	40-44	45-49	50-54	55-59	60+	Unknown Inconnu
EUROPE													
Bosnia and Herzegovina - Bosnie-Herzégovine													
2009													
55 - 59	154	-	-	1	-	2	2	3	7	14	46	79	-
60 - 64	67	-	-	-	1	-	-	2	-	3	6	55	-
65 - 69	38	-	-	-	1	-	1	-	1	-	4	31	-
70 - 74	21	-	-	-	-	1	-	1	1	-	-	18	-
75 +	11	-	-	-	1	-	-	-	-	-	-	10	-
Unknown - Inconnu	22	-	-	7	8	3	2	1	-	-	-	-	1
Bulgaria - Bulgarie[21]													
2009 (C)													
Total	25 923	-	222	3 931	9 521	6 725	2 646	1 112	617	416	299	434	-
0 - 14	-	-	-	-	-	-	-	-	-	-	-	-	-
15 - 19	1 615	-	132	855	471	133	17	3	4	-	-	-	-
20 - 24	8 496	-	76	2 468	4 113	1 498	269	42	20	5	3	2	-
25 - 29	8 681	-	12	522	4 164	3 008	739	164	44	19	4	5	-
30 - 34	3 964	-	1	67	655	1 747	981	328	124	42	13	6	-
35 - 39	1 499	-	1	15	95	292	508	326	148	65	38	11	-
40 - 44	644	-	-	2	16	36	100	185	154	90	37	24	-
45 - 49	359	-	-	2	4	8	25	47	80	86	67	40	-
50 - 54	266	-	-	-	3	2	6	11	34	83	64	63	-
55 - 59	184	-	-	-	-	1	-	4	7	24	56	92	-
60 - 64	118	-	-	-	-	-	1	1	2	2	13	99	-
65 - 69	55	-	-	-	-	-	-	-	-	-	2	53	-
70 - 74	26	-	-	-	-	-	-	1	-	-	2	23	-
75 +	16	-	-	-	-	-	-	-	-	-	-	16	-
Unknown - Inconnu	-	-	-	-	-	-	-	-	-	-	-	-	-
Croatia - Croatie													
2009 (C)													
Total	22 382	-	184	3 441	8 664	5 692	2 033	922	489	305	208	442	2
0 - 14	-	-	-	-	-	-	-	-	-	-	-	-	-
15 - 19	1 276	-	113	703	359	85	11	2	1	-	-	2	-
20 - 24	6 450	-	64	2 114	3 095	949	172	43	8	4	-	-	1
25 - 29	8 496	-	5	557	4 413	2 717	601	140	41	13	4	4	1
30 - 34	3 518	-	1	54	700	1 648	740	266	82	20	2	5	-
35 - 39	1 212	-	1	9	80	254	410	266	122	45	16	9	-
40 - 44	507	-	-	2	12	28	79	161	113	57	24	31	-
45 - 49	311	-	-	1	3	7	16	36	81	69	57	41	-
50 - 54	243	-	-	-	-	-	2	6	30	69	51	85	-
55 - 59	154	-	-	1	-	-	1	2	6	19	39	86	-
60 - 64	96	-	-	-	-	-	-	-	2	7	12	75	-
65 - 69	59	-	-	-	-	-	-	-	2	1	-	56	-
70 - 74	33	-	-	-	-	-	-	-	1	-	1	31	-
75 +	19	-	-	-	-	-	-	-	-	-	2	17	-
Unknown - Inconnu	8	-	-	-	2	4	1	-	-	1	-	-	-
Czech Republic - République tchèque													
2009 (C)													
Total	47 862	-	112	3 405	13 977	14 376	6 220	3 147	2 157	1 693	1 284	1 491	-
0 - 14	-	-	-	-	-	-	-	-	-	-	-	-	-
15 - 19	674	-	61	294	195	85	26	11	2	-	-	-	-
20 - 24	8 226	-	35	2 011	3 880	1 689	429	105	47	15	10	5	-
25 - 29	17 788	-	10	830	7 826	6 668	1 741	437	184	56	25	11	-
30 - 34	10 505	-	4	202	1 755	4 785	2 315	862	342	145	60	35	-
35 - 39	3 958	-	1	43	245	883	1 233	832	416	173	86	46	-
40 - 44	2 174	-	-	16	57	192	323	589	479	302	123	93	-
45 - 49	1 716	-	1	7	14	61	117	230	459	431	257	139	-
50 - 54	1 290	-	-	1	3	12	28	60	162	390	355	279	-
55 - 59	870	-	-	-	-	1	6	17	52	144	266	384	-
60 - 64	397	-	-	-	1	-	2	4	9	30	77	274	-
65 - 69	163	-	-	-	1	-	-	-	3	4	17	138	-
70 - 74	69	-	-	-	-	-	-	-	-	3	6	60	-
75 +	32	-	-	1	-	-	-	-	2	-	2	27	-
Unknown - Inconnu	-	-	-	-	-	-	-	-	-	-	-	-	-

Continent, country or area, year, code and age of bride / Continent, pays ou zone, date, code et âge de l'épouse	Total	0-14	15-19	20-24	25-29	30-34	35-39	40-44	45-49	50-54	55-59	60+	Unknown Inconnu
EUROPE													
Denmark - Danemark[22]													
2009 (C)													
Total	32 934	-	30	1 253	6 010	8 536	5 653	3 668	2 473	1 791	1 253	1 693	574
0 - 14	-	-	-	-	-	-	-	-	-	-	-	-	-
15 - 19	186	-	14	100	43	8	4	1	-	-	-	-	16
20 - 24	2 845	-	11	840	1 218	470	99	34	16	3	2	-	152
25 - 29	8 086	-	3	210	3 530	3 075	768	219	82	30	15	8	146
30 - 34	8 036	-	-	34	890	3 917	2 165	627	207	66	24	14	92
35 - 39	4 456	-	1	10	112	686	1 850	1 116	417	124	57	24	59
40 - 44	2 842	-	-	2	27	120	471	1 048	688	289	93	63	41
45 - 49	1 961	-	-	1	6	26	83	367	650	496	205	100	27
50 - 54	1 493	-	-	-	5	5	19	89	235	515	359	246	20
55 - 59	873	-	-	-	1	1	-	13	46	118	300	386	8
60 - 64	554	-	-	-	1	-	-	3	7	42	93	401	7
65 - 69	254	-	-	-	-	1	-	-	2	8	23	215	5
70 - 74	120	-	-	-	-	-	-	-	-	3	5	111	1
75 +	60	-	-	-	-	-	-	-	-	-	1	59	-
Unknown - Inconnu	1 168	-	1	56	177	227	194	151	123	97	76	66	-
Estonia - Estonie													
2009 (C)													
Total	5 362	-	52	728	1 511	1 144	726	424	302	180	141	154	-
0 - 14	-	-	-	-	-	-	-	-	-	-	-	-	-
15 - 19	184	-	28	101	41	9	3	2	-	-	-	-	-
20 - 24	1 284	-	21	477	538	179	37	22	7	1	2	-	-
25 - 29	1 577	-	1	117	763	468	152	52	14	9	1	-	-
30 - 34	927	-	1	22	134	359	265	89	36	9	9	3	-
35 - 39	542	-	1	9	27	97	197	118	60	24	8	1	-
40 - 44	307	-	-	1	5	23	51	92	87	33	7	8	-
45 - 49	219	-	-	1	3	6	13	37	75	37	34	13	-
50 - 54	141	-	-	-	-	2	8	8	16	44	37	26	-
55 - 59	100	-	-	-	-	1	-	4	5	18	30	42	-
60 - 64	49	-	-	-	-	-	-	-	2	4	11	32	-
65 - 69	19	-	-	-	-	-	-	-	-	-	1	18	-
70 - 74	8	-	-	-	-	-	-	-	-	-	1	6	-
75 +	5	-	-	-	-	-	-	-	-	-	-	5	-
Unknown - Inconnu	-	-	-	-	-	-	-	-	-	-	-	-	-
Finland - Finlande[23,24]													
2009 (C)													
Total	29 716	-	274	2 830	7 699	6 814	3 701	2 767	2 325	1 343	925	1 038	-
0 - 14	-	-	-	-	-	-	-	-	-	-	-	-	-
15 - 19	714	-	177	408	92	26	6	3	1	-	1	-	-
20 - 24	4 479	-	78	1 782	1 988	462	107	40	14	5	3	-	-
25 - 29	8 925	-	12	510	4 571	2 867	660	219	58	16	7	5	-
30 - 34	5 837	-	2	83	827	2 751	1 415	523	181	39	11	5	-
35 - 39	2 991	-	2	22	135	538	1 039	780	336	102	28	9	-
40 - 44	2 173	-	2	13	51	121	336	761	598	205	60	26	-
45 - 49	2 161	-	1	6	23	32	109	338	868	452	219	113	-
50 - 54	1 067	-	-	4	5	12	22	80	205	343	256	140	-
55 - 59	698	-	-	2	5	3	5	19	54	133	233	244	-
60 - 64	423	-	-	-	2	2	2	2	9	38	87	281	-
65 - 69	163	-	-	-	-	-	-	2	-	7	15	139	-
70 - 74	54	-	-	-	-	-	-	-	1	2	3	48	-
75 +	31	-	-	-	-	-	-	-	-	1	2	28	-
Unknown - Inconnu	-	-	-	-	-	-	-	-	-	-	-	-	-
France[25]													
2009 (C)													
Total	245 151	-	257	14 558	64 485	57 056	36 936	23 230	16 287	12 687	8 903	10 752	-
0 - 14	1	-	-	1	-	-	-	-	-	-	-	-	-
15 - 19	2 055	-	102	952	680	220	64	21	7	4	3	2	-
20 - 24	32 105	-	110	9 793	15 944	4 415	1 215	357	147	70	29	25	-
25 - 29	76 786	-	28	3 148	39 898	24 357	6 559	1 797	579	237	84	99	-
30 - 34	48 174	-	11	445	6 308	21 938	12 787	4 205	1 522	566	255	137	-
35 - 39	30 200	-	3	134	1 157	4 604	11 709	7 397	2 968	1 338	545	345	-
40 - 44	19 807	-	1	38	318	1 073	3 343	6 353	4 712	2 334	1 016	619	-
45 - 49	13 884	-	1	28	103	334	929	2 161	4 043	3 461	1 665	1 159	-
50 - 54	10 365	-	-	10	38	78	249	688	1 667	3 190	2 583	1 862	-
55 - 59	6 266	-	-	5	13	24	54	196	501	1 126	1 919	2 428	-

Continent, country or area, year, code and age of bride / Continent, pays ou zone, date, code et âge de l'épouse	Total	0-14	15-19	20-24	25-29	30-34	35-39	40-44	45-49	50-54	55-59	60+	Unknown Inconnu
EUROPE													
France[25]													
2009													
60 - 64	3 313	-	1	3	2	3	16	42	118	303	627	2 198	-
65 - 69	1 175	-	-	-	1	4	5	11	17	38	132	967	-
70 - 74	566	-	-	-	3	1	1	1	3	14	28	515	-
75 +	454	-	-	1	20	5	5	1	3	6	17	396	-
Unknown - Inconnu	-	-	-	-	-	-	-	-	-	-	-	-	-
Germany - Allemagne													
2007 (C)													
Total	368 922	-	1 412	28 127	82 003	81 838	63 591	42 117	26 685	17 326	11 480	14 343	...
0 - 14	-	-	-	-	-	-	-	-	-	-	-	-	...
15 - 19	7 164	-	728	3 946	1 755	451	159	71	36	13	3	2	...
20 - 24	57 609	-	575	18 370	26 015	8 401	2 765	942	351	121	49	20	...
25 - 29	104 614	-	78	4 817	44 425	36 293	13 307	3 938	1 164	347	139	106	...
30 - 34	71 339	-	15	723	7 899	28 814	22 446	7 914	2 337	745	289	157	...
35 - 39	46 659	-	10	170	1 375	6 172	18 053	13 117	4 993	1 714	641	414	...
40 - 44	31 383	-	6	60	360	1 270	5 088	10 822	7 805	3 532	1 496	944	...
45 - 49	22 249	-	-	28	120	321	1 354	3 933	6 898	5 334	2 576	1 685	...
50 - 54	13 839	-	-	8	45	89	326	1 094	2 381	3 970	3 325	2 601	...
55 - 59	7 267	-	-	4	7	20	74	234	561	1 192	2 201	2 974	...
60 - 64	3 549	-	-	1	2	5	13	41	121	265	574	2 527	...
65 - 69	2 105	-	-	-	-	2	2	11	33	73	143	1 841	...
70 - 74	787	-	-	-	-	-	3	-	4	15	36	729	...
75 +	358	-	-	-	-	-	1	-	1	5	8	343	...
Greece - Grèce													
2009 (C)													
Total	59 212	5	277	2 939	15 094	20 356	10 517	4 656	2 118	1 301	732	1 217	...
0 - 14	37	3	23	7	3	1	-	-	-	-	-	-	...
15 - 19	1 293	2	179	550	378	126	42	14	1	1	-	-	...
20 - 24	8 366	-	54	1 599	3 775	2 100	613	158	40	14	8	5	...
25 - 29	22 082	-	10	623	8 518	8 956	2 964	716	186	66	26	17	...
30 - 34	16 341	-	9	113	2 073	7 652	4 361	1 461	421	153	65	33	...
35 - 39	5 931	-	2	28	270	1 257	2 044	1 368	598	230	90	44	...
40 - 44	2 410	-	-	15	51	201	383	694	515	324	115	112	...
45 - 49	1 243	-	-	4	18	39	87	186	240	296	175	198	...
50 - 54	757	-	-	-	7	16	16	48	92	159	147	272	...
55 - 59	412	-	-	-	-	6	4	8	18	44	82	250	...
60 - 64	203	-	-	-	1	-	3	3	5	11	20	160	...
65 - 69	88	-	-	-	-	2	-	-	2	2	3	79	...
70 - 74	29	-	-	-	-	-	-	-	-	1	1	27	...
75 +	20	-	-	-	-	-	-	-	-	-	-	20	...
Unknown - Inconnu	-	-	-	-	-	-	-	-	-	-	-	-	...
Hungary - Hongrie													
2009 (C)													
Total	36 730	-	299	2 548	10 366	11 677	4 930	2 263	1 312	1 155	940	1 240	-
0 - 14	-	-	-	-	-	-	-	-	-	-	-	-	-
15 - 19	1 076	-	225	501	221	90	25	9	1	-	4	-	-
20 - 24	6 127	-	58	1 328	2 894	1 419	319	70	19	11	6	3	-
25 - 29	13 002	-	12	537	5 588	5 154	1 257	295	86	48	11	14	-
30 - 34	8 588	-	4	138	1 399	4 082	1 938	649	211	102	41	24	-
35 - 39	3 147	-	-	35	209	723	1 029	640	276	120	78	37	-
40 - 44	1 603	-	-	6	41	152	269	432	312	225	103	63	-
45 - 49	1 013	-	-	2	10	46	68	117	240	271	163	96	-
50 - 54	884	-	-	-	4	8	16	37	116	244	261	198	-
55 - 59	723	-	-	1	-	3	8	13	42	104	210	342	-
60 - 64	331	-	-	-	-	-	-	1	7	22	46	255	-
65 - 69	157	-	-	-	-	-	1	-	1	6	13	136	-
70 - 74	59	-	-	-	-	-	-	-	-	1	3	54	-
75 +	20	-	-	-	-	-	-	-	-	1	1	18	-
Unknown - Inconnu	-	-	-	-	-	-	-	-	-	-	-	-	-
Iceland - Islande[6]													
2009 (C)													
Total	1 480	-	1	66	343	358	232	162	110	80	48	70	10
0 - 14	-	-	-	-	-	-	-	-	-	-	-	-	-
15 - 19	13	-	1	3	8	-	-	-	-	-	-	-	1
20 - 24	169	-	-	45	73	36	6	3	2	-	2	-	2
25 - 29	425	-	-	14	212	145	32	11	3	3	1	-	4

23. Marriages by age of groom and by age of bride: latest available year, 2000 - 2009
Mariages selon l'âge de l'époux et selon l'âge de l'épouse : dernière année disponible, 2000 - 2009 (continued - suite)

Continent, country or area, year, code and age of bride / Continent, pays ou zone, date, code et âge de l'épouse	Total	Age of groom - âge de l'époux											
		0-14	15-19	20-24	25-29	30-34	35-39	40-44	45-49	50-54	55-59	60+	Unknown Inconnu
EUROPE													
Iceland - Islande[6]													
2009													
30 - 34	332	-	-	3	41	149	87	34	10	5	1	1	1
35 - 39	194	-	-	1	6	23	84	56	13	4	2	3	2
40 - 44	108	-	-	-	-	-	18	40	34	13	3	-	-
45 - 49	81	-	-	-	1	2	4	9	33	20	8	4	-
50 - 54	69	-	-	-	1	-	-	5	14	26	13	10	-
55 - 59	31	-	-	-	-	-	-	-	-	5	14	12	-
60 - 64	20	-	-	-	-	-	-	-	-	2	1	17	-
65 - 69	13	-	-	-	-	-	-	-	-	-	2	11	-
70 - 74	6	-	-	-	-	-	-	-	-	-	-	6	-
75 +	6	-	-	-	-	-	-	-	-	-	-	6	-
Unknown - Inconnu	13	-	-	-	1	3	1	4	1	2	1	-	-
Ireland - Irlande													
2005 (+C)													
Total	21 355	-	116	1 025	6 475	7 903	3 145	1 289	598	358	209	232	5
0 - 14	-	-	-	-	-	-	-	-	-	-	-	-	-
15 - 19	246	-	78	103	43	13	6	2	-	-	-	1	-
20 - 24	2 052	-	31	551	981	372	83	21	9	2	1	1	-
25 - 29	8 481	-	3	293	4 165	3 155	679	138	33	8	5	1	1
30 - 34	6 733	-	3	58	1 093	3 681	1 391	361	98	32	9	3	4
35 - 39	2 208	-	1	14	150	585	785	438	151	64	14	6	-
40 - 44	780	-	-	5	21	67	154	242	145	81	39	26	-
45 - 49	404	-	-	1	13	21	36	68	111	82	44	28	-
50 - 54	223	-	-	-	5	1	8	15	43	65	40	46	-
55 - 59	120	-	-	-	-	1	1	2	6	19	40	51	-
60 - 64	58	-	-	-	-	1	-	-	1	5	17	34	-
65 - 69	21	-	-	-	-	-	-	1	1	-	-	19	-
70 - 74	9	-	-	-	-	-	-	-	-	-	-	9	-
75 - 79	5	-	-	-	-	-	-	-	-	-	-	5	-
80 - 84	-	-	-	-	-	-	-	-	-	-	-	1	-
85 - 89	1	-	-	-	-	-	-	-	-	-	-	-	-
90 - 94	1	-	-	-	-	-	-	-	-	-	-	1	-
95 +	-	-	-	-	-	-	-	-	-	-	-	-	-
Unknown - Inconnu	13	-	-	-	4	6	2	1	-	-	-	-	-
Isle of Man - Île de Man													
2005 (C)													
Total	404	-	6	42	72	87	63	51	26	22	17	18	...
0 - 14	-	...	...	...	...	...	...	...	...	...	...	...	...
15 - 19	5	...	...	...	...	...	...	...	...	...	...	...	...
20 - 24	65	...	...	...	...	...	...	...	...	...	...	...	...
25 - 29	98	...	...	...	...	...	...	...	...	...	...	...	...
30 - 34	79	...	...	...	...	...	...	...	...	...	...	...	...
35 - 39	61	...	...	...	...	...	...	...	...	...	...	...	...
40 - 44	40	...	...	...	...	...	...	...	...	...	...	...	...
45 - 49	26	...	...	...	...	...	...	...	...	...	...	...	...
50 - 54	16	...	...	...	...	...	...	...	...	...	...	...	...
55 - 59	5	...	...	...	...	...	...	...	...	...	...	...	...
60 - 64	7	...	...	...	...	...	...	...	...	...	...	...	...
65 - 69	1	...	...	...	...	...	...	...	...	...	...	...	...
70 - 74	-	...	...	...	...	...	...	...	...	...	...	...	...
75 - 79	1	...	...	...	...	...	...	...	...	...	...	...	...
Italy - Italie													
2008 (C)													
Total	246 613	-	621	12 274	58 388	82 333	45 665	20 659	10 276	6 013	4 209	6 175	-
0 - 14	-	-	-	-	-	-	-	-	-	-	-	-	-
15 - 19	4 271	-	341	2 233	1 221	351	83	29	4	5	2	2	-
20 - 24	31 867	-	204	6 979	16 106	6 344	1 598	391	137	50	33	25	-
25 - 29	81 326	-	49	2 279	31 906	34 787	9 300	2 033	581	189	105	97	-
30 - 34	69 050	-	13	505	7 397	33 422	19 765	5 463	1 553	523	227	182	-
35 - 39	30 884	-	6	151	1 230	6 167	11 908	7 027	2 618	988	458	331	-
40 - 44	13 819	-	4	78	311	924	2 412	4 308	2 946	1 483	713	640	-
45 - 49	7 070	-	1	31	129	205	462	1 129	1 768	1 446	935	964	-
50 - 54	4 122	-	3	9	54	77	86	227	512	933	1 000	1 221	-
55 - 59	2 221	-	-	4	17	33	27	38	121	309	545	1 127	-
60 - 64	1 072	-	-	2	11	17	12	7	24	73	149	777	-
65 - 69	537	-	-	1	4	4	9	1	10	11	35	462	-

Continent, country or area, year, code and age of bride — Continent, pays ou zone, date, code et âge de l'épouse	Total	Age of groom - âge de l'époux											Unknown Inconnu
		0-14	15-19	20-24	25-29	30-34	35-39	40-44	45-49	50-54	55-59	60+	

EUROPE

Italy - Italie
2008

70 - 74	213	-	-	1	1	2	2	2	-	1	4	200	-
75 +	161	-	-	1	1	-	1	4	2	2	3	147	-
Unknown - Inconnu	-	-	-	-	-	-	-	-	-	-	-	-	-

Latvia - Lettonie
2009 (C)

Total	9 925	-	60	1 570	3 135	1 850	1 139	673	518	329	232	419	-
0 - 14	-	-	-	-	-	-	-	-	-	-	-	-	-
15 - 19	312	-	31	188	73	10	5	4	1	-	-	-	-
20 - 24	2 634	-	25	1 024	1 147	309	93	23	8	3	1	1	-
25 - 29	3 003	-	2	290	1 518	788	276	81	32	6	5	5	-
30 - 34	1 498	-	2	51	306	544	340	161	64	19	6	5	-
35 - 39	870	-	-	13	64	145	273	192	116	46	12	9	-
40 - 44	517	-	-	-	18	44	116	129	119	58	17	16	-
45 - 49	372	-	-	4	6	7	30	57	104	80	52	32	-
50 - 54	295	-	-	-	2	3	3	20	60	80	61	66	-
55 - 59	167	-	-	-	1	-	3	5	10	27	51	70	-
60 - 64	116	-	-	-	-	-	-	1	4	7	20	84	-
65 - 69	72	-	-	-	-	-	-	-	-	3	4	65	-
70 - 74	50	-	-	-	-	-	-	-	-	-	3	47	-
75 +	19	-	-	-	-	-	-	-	-	-	-	19	-
Unknown - Inconnu	-	-	-	-	-	-	-	-	-	-	-	-	-

Liechtenstein
2009* (C)

Total	154	-	-	8	34	38	28	13	13	10	5	5	-

Lithuania - Lituanie
2009 (C)

Total	20 542	-	213	4 058	7 474	3 907	1 930	1 061	741	492	288	378	-
0 - 14	1	-	1	-	-	-	-	-	-	-	-	-	-
15 - 19	1 046	-	133	604	235	53	17	2	2	-	-	-	-
20 - 24	6 765	-	65	2 694	3 003	755	175	44	21	5	3	-	-
25 - 29	6 778	-	12	643	3 640	1 747	471	175	58	25	6	1	-
30 - 34	2 660	-	2	86	470	1 025	674	235	122	35	9	2	-
35 - 39	1 311	-	-	24	107	259	405	293	133	62	15	13	-
40 - 44	703	-	-	6	16	50	132	202	150	82	38	27	-
45 - 49	549	-	-	1	3	15	40	85	161	139	67	38	-
50 - 54	364	-	-	-	-	2	15	24	72	112	73	66	-
55 - 59	165	-	-	-	-	-	1	1	12	23	65	63	-
60 - 64	97	-	-	-	-	1	-	-	4	9	9	74	-
65 - 69	51	-	-	-	-	-	-	-	4	-	-	47	-
70 - 74	33	-	-	-	-	-	-	-	1	-	3	29	-
75 +	19	-	-	-	-	-	-	-	1	-	-	18	-
Unknown - Inconnu	-	-	-	-	-	-	-	-	-	-	-	-	-

Luxembourg
2009 (C)

Total	1 739	-	1	96	399	460	268	182	142	79	56	56	-
0 - 14	-	-	-	-	-	-	-	-	-	-	-	-	-
15 - 19	21	-	1	12	5	2	-	1	-	-	-	-	-
20 - 24	201	-	-	51	89	47	6	4	3	-	-	1	-
25 - 29	545	-	-	24	228	195	66	20	9	1	1	1	-
30 - 34	419	-	-	6	62	178	101	36	24	9	3	-	-
35 - 39	220	-	-	2	9	29	67	58	29	9	12	5	-
40 - 44	134	-	-	1	3	8	18	39	33	17	7	8	-
45 - 49	109	-	-	-	3	-	6	19	34	26	12	9	-
50 - 54	51	-	-	-	-	1	3	5	9	12	13	8	-
55 - 59	17	-	-	-	-	-	1	-	-	3	7	6	-
60 - 64	12	-	-	-	-	-	-	-	1	2	-	9	-
65 - 69	5	-	-	-	-	-	-	-	-	-	-	5	-
70 - 74	4	-	-	-	-	-	-	-	-	-	1	3	-
75 +	1	-	-	-	-	-	-	-	-	-	-	1	-
Unknown - Inconnu	-	-	-	-	-	-	-	-	-	-	-	-	-

Malta - Malte
2009 (C)

Total	2 353	-	3	203	956	637	265	93	63	53	33	45	2
0 - 14	-	-	-	-	-	-	-	-	-	-	-	-	-
15 - 19	41	-	1	18	15	7	-	-	-	-	-	-	-

678

Continent, country or area, year, code and age of bride / Continent, pays ou zone, date, code et âge de l'épouse	Total	0-14	15-19	20-24	25-29	30-34	35-39	40-44	45-49	50-54	55-59	60+	Unknown Inconnu
EUROPE													
Malta - Malte													
2009													
20 - 24	499	-	-	122	271	86	17	1	-	2	-	-	-
25 - 29	1 013	-	1	53	560	310	66	15	3	1	2	2	-
30 - 34	430	-	-	10	91	189	96	25	7	7	3	2	-
35 - 39	177	-	.	-	15	35	64	29	17	8	7	2	-
40 - 44	82	-	1	-	1	10	17	15	16	11	4	7	-
45 - 49	46	-	-	-	2	-	5	4	12	14	5	4	-
50 - 54	25	-	-	-	-	-	-	4	7	3	5	6	-
55 - 59	19	-	-	-	-	-	-	-	1	5	7	6	-
60 - 64	11	-	-	-	-	-	-	-	-	1	-	10	-
65 +	8	-	-	-	1	-	-	-	-	1	-	6	-
Unknown - Inconnu	2	-	-	-	-	-	-	-	-	-	-	-	2
Montenegro - Monténégro													
2009 (C)													
Total	3 829	...	26	619	1 371	876	425	232	131	66	31	52	...
15 - 19	376	...	15	172	131	41	11	4	1	-	-	1	...
20 - 24	1 268	...	9	358	600	217	53	22	6	2	1	-	...
25 - 29	1 243	...	1	75	549	406	151	47	12	1	1	-	...
30 - 34	517	...	-	8	81	176	135	79	33	5	-	-	...
35 - 39	203	...	-	3	8	32	60	47	33	16	2	2	...
40 - 44	96	...	-	2	1	2	15	25	31	10	7	3	...
45 - 49	55	...	1	1	-	1	-	7	12	15	7	11	...
50 - 54	34	...	-	-	1	1	-	1	1	15	6	9	...
55 - 59	22	...	-	-	-	-	-	-	2	1	5	14	...
60 - 64	8	...	-	-	-	-	-	-	-	1	2	5	...
65 - 69	7	...	-	-	-	-	-	-	-	-	-	7	...
70 - 74	-	...	-	-	-	-	-	-	-	-	-	-	...
75 +	-	...	-	-	-	-	-	-	-	-	-	-	...
Netherlands - Pays-Bas													
2009 (C)													
Total	72 119	...	85	4 976	16 276	17 802	11 712	7 321	4 939	3 443	2 300	3 265	...
15 - 19	687	...	47	385	178	49	17	8	3	-	-	-	...
20 - 24	11 006	...	32	3 710	5 283	1 374	408	120	56	14	5	4	...
25 - 29	20 820	...	4	735	8 958	7 932	2 233	615	211	87	26	19	...
30 - 34	15 428	...	2	108	1 548	6 998	4 516	1 456	522	162	66	50	...
35 - 39	8 770	...	-	24	239	1 136	3 385	2 481	947	347	118	93	...
40 - 44	5 477	...	-	10	47	232	843	1 888	1 455	646	211	145	...
45 - 49	3 879	...	-	3	13	54	239	575	1 193	1 035	482	285	...
50 - 54	2 754	...	-	1	7	19	57	136	436	884	707	507	...
55 - 59	1 553	...	-	-	-	6	10	35	83	213	501	705	...
60 - 64	962	...	-	-	2	2	3	5	26	42	146	736	...
65 - 69	489	...	-	-	1	-	-	2	7	12	32	435	...
70 - 74	170	...	-	-	-	-	1	-	-	1	3	165	...
75 +	124	...	-	-	-	-	-	-	-	-	3	121	...
Norway - Norvège[26]													
2009 (C)													
Total	24 299	-	58	1 515	5 001	5 642	4 328	2 781	1 801	1 317	896	960	...
0 - 14	-	-	-	-	-	-	-	-	-	-	-	-	...
15 - 19	401	-	31	181	110	36	27	8	5	2	1	-	...
20 - 24	3 372	-	20	1 034	1 436	508	202	94	40	17	9	12	...
25 - 29	6 782	-	4	262	2 843	2 315	833	285	130	61	28	21	...
30 - 34	5 355	-	1	29	518	2 255	1 557	581	239	98	49	28	...
35 - 39	3 391	-	1	7	79	454	1 297	897	360	169	70	57	...
40 - 44	2 016	-	1	2	10	59	330	663	518	258	97	78	...
45 - 49	1 294	-	-	-	5	12	66	205	381	356	173	96	...
50 - 54	810	-	-	-	-	2	14	43	97	260	240	154	...
55 - 59	480	-	-	-	-	1	2	5	23	79	177	193	...
60 - 64	245	-	-	-	-	-	-	-	6	16	42	181	...
65 - 69	99	-	-	-	-	-	-	-	1	-	6	92	...
70 - 74	37	-	-	-	-	-	-	-	1	1	4	31	...
75 +	17	-	-	-	-	-	-	-	-	-	-	17	...
Poland - Pologne													
2009 (C)													
Total	250 794	-	1 890	53 239	112 656	46 227	15 167	6 567	4 243	3 753	2 696	4 356	-
0 - 14	-	-	-	-	-	-	-	-	-	-	-	-	-
15 - 19	11 494	-	1 225	7 193	2 519	439	80	24	11	2	1	-	-

Continent, country or area, year, code and age of bride / Continent, pays ou zone, date, code et âge de l'épouse	Total	0-14	15-19	20-24	25-29	30-34	35-39	40-44	45-49	50-54	55-59	60+	Unknown Inconnu
EUROPE													
Poland - Pologne													
2009													
20 - 24	91 026	-	591	36 430	44 734	7 696	1 188	252	86	36	9	4	-
25 - 29	95 939	-	63	8 712	58 344	22 911	4 400	968	339	137	36	29	-
30 - 34	28 170	-	10	761	6 238	12 789	5 515	1 788	662	268	92	47	-
35 - 39	9 096	-	1	116	687	1 974	2 955	1 808	873	429	176	77	-
40 - 44	4 237	-	-	20	114	311	756	1 141	934	577	250	134	-
45 - 49	3 240	-	-	6	17	83	193	402	797	898	489	355	-
50 - 54	3 052	-	-	1	2	18	60	143	372	945	795	716	-
55 - 59	2 097	-	-	-	1	6	16	29	124	337	610	974	-
60 - 64	1 243	-	-	-	-	-	2	8	34	94	183	922	-
65 - 69	626	-	-	-	-	-	.1	3	7	19	34	562	-
70 - 74	379	-	-	-	-	-	1	-	1	7	17	353	-
75 +	195	-	-	-	-	-	-	1	3	4	4	183	-
Unknown - Inconnu	-	-	-	-	-	-	-	-	-	-	-	-	-
Portugal													
2009 (C)													
Total	40 391	-	297	4 891	13 741	10 245	4 307	2 159	1 501	1 036	774	1 438	2
0 - 14	-	-	-	-	-	-	-	-	-	-	-	-	-
15 - 19	1 430	-	149	855	295	103	17	7	3	1	-	-	-
20 - 24	7 988	-	110	2 778	3 726	1 017	237	71	26	11	6	6	-
25 - 29	14 423	-	27	974	7 601	4 401	988	260	100	36	20	14	2
30 - 34	8 097	-	10	215	1 723	3 652	1 588	542	228	80	36	23	-
35 - 39	3 398	-	-	55	296	825	1 009	615	326	154	72	46	-
40 - 44	1 831	-	1	10	66	185	317	421	384	215	109	123	-
45 - 49	1 210	-	-	3	24	47	111	170	285	253	163	154	-
50 - 54	855	-	-	1	7	11	30	55	108	200	178	265	-
55 - 59	517	-	-	-	2	1	8	12	33	60	123	278	-
60 - 64	316	-	-	-	-	2	1	5	4	16	49	239	-
65 - 69	160	-	-	-	-	-	-	1	4	5	11	139	-
70 - 74	101	-	-	-	-	-	-	-	-	3	5	93	-
75 +	63	-	-	-	-	-	1	-	-	2	2	58	-
Unknown - Inconnu	2	-	-	-	1	1	-	-	-	-	-	-	-
Republic of Moldova - République de Moldova[27]													
2009 (C)													
Total	20 396	-	473	9 203	7 825	2 188	453	146	55	28	11	14	...
0 - 14	-	-	-	-	-	-	-	-	-	-	-	-	...
15 - 19	3 462	-	267	2 264	804	115	8	2	1	1	-	-	...
20 - 24	11 889	-	193	6 123	4 627	820	93	26	5	2	-	-	...
25 - 29	3 993	-	12	749	2 145	881	164	25	11	5	1	-	...
30 - 34	760	-	-	54	215	319	127	38	3	3	1	-	...
35 - 39	193	-	1	10	31	43	56	38	10	4	-	-	...
40 - 44	42	-	-	2	2	8	3	12	9	5	1	-	...
45 - 49	24	-	-	1	1	2	2	5	10	3	-	-	...
50 - 54	9	-	-	-	-	-	-	-	4	1	2	2	...
55 - 59	10	-	-	-	-	-	-	-	2	3	2	3	...
60 - 64	5	-	-	-	-	-	-	-	-	-	4	1	...
65 - 69	3	-	-	-	-	-	-	-	-	1	-	2	...
70 - 74	4	-	-	-	-	-	-	-	-	-	-	4	...
75 +	2	-	-	-	-	-	-	-	-	-	-	2	...
Unknown - Inconnu	-	-	-	-	-	-	-	-	-	-	-	-	...
Romania - Roumanie													
2009 (C)													
Total	134 275	-	1 486	26 426	49 752	29 976	11 776	6 024	3 031	2 412	1 581	1 811	...
0 - 14	-	-	-	-	-	-	-	-	-	-	-	-	...
15 - 19	13 230	-	988	7 008	3 932	1 089	169	35	4	1	2	2	...
20 - 24	48 181	-	457	15 824	22 694	7 521	1 323	262	52	29	9	10	...
25 - 29	37 720	-	30	3 050	18 946	11 666	2 885	815	197	76	32	23	...
30 - 34	17 933	-	7	445	3 554	7 614	4 011	1 504	476	209	64	49	...
35 - 39	7 667	-	3	85	509	1 632	2 426	1 827	679	307	130	69	...
40 - 44	4 267	-	1	11	98	384	793	1 220	902	537	211	110	...
45 - 49	1 973	-	-	3	12	54	130	254	468	577	317	158	...
50 - 54	1 591	-	-	-	6	11	28	87	192	497	421	349	...
55 - 59	897	-	-	-	1	4	7	13	45	136	307	384	...
60 +	816	-	-	-	-	1	4	7	16	43	88	657	...

Continent, country or area, year, code and age of bride / Continent, pays ou zone, date, code et âge de l'épouse	Total	0-14	15-19	20-24	25-29	30-34	35-39	40-44	45-49	50-54	55-59	60+	Unknown Inconnu
EUROPE													
Russian Federation - Fédération de Russie													
2009 (C)													
Total	1199446	...	...	...	...	...	...	...	...	...	...	...	...
0 - 17	14 062	...	...	...	...	...	...	...	...	...	...	...	...
18 - 24	559 805	...	...	...	...	...	...	...	...	...	...	...	...
25 - 34	428 148	...	...	...	...	...	...	...	...	...	...	...	...
35 +	197 399	...	...	...	...	...	...	...	...	...	...	...	...
Unknown - Inconnu	32	...	...	...	...	...	...	...	...	...	...	...	...
San Marino - Saint-Marin[28]													
2004 (C)													
Total	207	-	-	9	56	59	30	14	7	3	8	4	17
0 - 14	-	-	-	-	-	-	-	-	-	-	-	-	-
15 - 19	-	-	-	-	-	-	-	-	-	-	-	-	-
20 - 24	16	-	-	4	4	1	-	2	-	-	1	-	4
25 - 29	63	-	-	1	28	20	4	-	1	-	1	-	8
30 - 34	37	-	-	-	3	13	13	4	-	-	-	-	4
35 - 39	11	-	-	-	-	2	2	2	1	-	2	1	1
40 - 44	5	-	-	-	-	1	-	2	-	-	2	-	-
45 - 49	4	-	-	-	-	-	1	1	-	1	1	-	-
50 - 54	2	-	-	-	-	-	-	-	-	1	-	-	-
55 - 59	1	-	-	-	-	-	-	-	-	1	-	-	-
60 +	-	-	-	-	-	-	-	-	-	-	-	-	-
Unknown - Inconnu	68	-	-	4	21	22	10	3	4	1	1	2	-
Serbia - Serbie[29]													
2009 (+C)													
Total	36 853	-	322	4 986	12 569	9 507	3 796	1 821	1 086	755	671	1 211	129
0 - 14	-	-	-	-	-	-	-	-	-	-	-	-	-
15 - 19	2 537	-	209	1 260	829	194	29	8	2	2	3	-	1
20 - 24	9 823	-	94	2 945	4 807	1 532	317	74	25	7	2	7	13
25 - 29	12 201	-	9	652	5 775	4 296	1 059	272	81	19	14	8	16
30 - 34	6 230	-	5	84	968	2 952	1 454	482	161	49	24	26	25
35 - 39	2 277	-	2	8	114	413	711	579	254	106	53	26	11
40 - 44	1 107	-	-	2	21	44	151	295	299	150	84	56	5
45 - 49	807	-	-	5	2	13	27	79	177	204	144	155	1
50 - 54	626	-	-	1	3	2	9	14	46	148	182	218	3
55 - 59	516	-	-	-	2	-	3	6	23	51	130	300	1
60 - 64	240	-	-	-	-	1	1	1	5	8	24	199	1
65 - 69	123	-	-	2	-	-	2	-	1	2	4	112	-
70 - 74	72	-	-	-	-	-	-	1	1	1	2	67	-
75 +	32	-	-	-	-	-	-	-	-	2	2	28	-
Unknown - Inconnu	262	-	3	27	48	60	33	10	11	6	3	9	52
Slovakia - Slovaquie													
2009 (C)													
Total	26 356	-	455	3 419	9 642	7 106	2 627	1 136	721	493	359	398	...
0 - 14	-	-	-	-	-	-	-	-	-	-	-	-	...
15 - 19	1 399	-	333	753	229	57	15	8	3	-	1	-	...
20 - 24	6 768	-	94	1 995	3 303	1 081	205	56	25	6	2	1	...
25 - 29	10 282	-	23	564	5 022	3 475	831	226	90	27	14	10	...
30 - 34	4 643	-	2	97	943	2 069	981	313	146	60	18	14	...
35 - 39	1 534	-	3	4	123	368	460	289	168	73	32	14	...
40 - 44	625	-	-	5	17	42	94	167	133	95	41	31	...
45 - 49	421	-	-	1	4	10	36	51	106	107	67	39	...
50 - 54	317	-	-	-	-	1	3	22	42	88	95	66	...
55 - 59	212	-	-	-	1	3	2	4	7	32	69	94	...
60 - 64	84	-	-	-	-	-	-	-	1	5	14	64	...
65 - 69	71	-	-	-	-	-	-	-	-	-	6	65	...
70 - 74	-	-	-	-	-	-	-	-	-	-	-	-	...
75 +	-	-	-	-	-	-	-	-	-	-	-	-	...
Slovenia - Slovénie													
2009 (C)													
Total	6 542	-	45	594	2 164	1 948	807	398	204	138	106	138	...
0 - 14	-	-	-	-	-	-	-	-	-	-	-	-	...
15 - 19	148	-	30	63	46	7	1	-	1	-	-	-	...
20 - 24	1 180	-	9	352	587	185	28	12	3	2	2	-	...
25 - 29	2 648	-	4	151	1 268	943	212	49	15	3	3	-	...
30 - 34	1 429	-	2	23	232	657	345	113	30	15	8	4	...

Continent, country or area, year, code and age of bride / Continent, pays ou zone, date, code et âge de l'épouse	Total	0-14	15-19	20-24	25-29	30-34	35-39	40-44	45-49	50-54	55-59	60+	Unknown Inconnu
EUROPE													
Slovenia - Slovénie													
2009													
35 - 39	528	-	-	3	20	125	178	124	47	18	7	6	...
40 - 44	241	-	-	-	8	26	31	77	49	29	12	9	...
45 - 49	155	-	-	2	2	4	8	14	34	39	34	18	...
50 - 54	93	-	-	-	-	1	4	8	14	23	22	21	...
55 - 59	60	-	-	-	1	-	-	-	9	6	14	30	...
60 - 64	31	-	-	-	-	-	-	-	-	3	3	25	...
65 - 69	13	-	-	-	-	-	-	-	2	-	-	11	...
70 - 74	12	-	-	-	-	-	-	-	-	-	1	11	...
75 +	4	-	-	-	-	-	-	1	-	-	-	3	...
Spain - Espagne													
2009 (C)													
Total	174 062	-	336	7 355	44 556	60 326	29 290	12 951	7 426	4 757	2 915	4 150	-
0 - 14	3	-	1	-	2	-	-	-	-	-	-	-	-
15 - 19	1 670	-	140	736	494	202	67	19	6	4	2	-	-
20 - 24	16 223	-	111	3 777	7 917	2 936	939	290	142	66	24	21	-
25 - 29	58 627	-	54	2 008	27 275	22 409	4 781	1 233	484	210	101	72	-
30 - 34	53 912	-	21	542	7 329	28 602	12 506	3 063	1 094	435	193	127	-
35 - 39	21 970	-	8	196	1 053	4 979	8 513	4 214	1 725	743	322	217	-
40 - 44	9 860	-	1	61	312	852	1 841	2 878	1 987	1 032	480	416	-
45 - 49	5 641	-	-	22	111	250	477	928	1 396	1 160	657	640	-
50 - 54	3 275	-	-	11	43	64	121	265	448	829	653	841	-
55 - 59	1 605	-	-	2	17	23	31	48	108	234	352	790	-
60 - 64	731	-	-	-	2	8	7	8	28	35	111	532	-
65 - 69	311	-	-	-	1	-	4	5	7	8	14	272	-
70 - 74	134	-	-	-	-	1	3	-	1	1	3	125	-
75 +	100	-	-	-	-	-	-	-	-	-	3	97	-
Unknown - Inconnu	-												-
Sweden - Suède													
2009 (C)													
Total	47 259	-	60	1 634	7 289	10 448	7 905	5 251	3 291	2 371	1 781	2 178	5 051
0 - 14	-	-	-	-	-	-	-	-	-	-	-	-	-
15 - 19	947	-	37	179	98	39	6	1	1	1	-	1	584
20 - 24	4 620	-	18	1 056	1 588	521	175	67	28	8	6	3	1 150
25 - 29	11 029	-	5	323	4 343	3 872	1 031	316	106	40	15	9	969
30 - 34	10 809	-	-	53	1 028	4 740	2 940	885	235	93	47	28	760
35 - 39	7 375	-	-	14	177	1 056	2 834	1 817	583	201	85	44	564
40 - 44	4 698	-	-	3	39	171	762	1 578	1 054	400	178	88	425
45 - 49	3 159	-	-	4	9	37	131	472	922	768	340	168	308
50 - 54	2 128	-	-	-	6	6	22	95	284	645	547	350	173
55 - 59	1 255	-	-	-	-	4	3	15	59	174	427	505	68
60 - 64	735	-	-	2	1	2	-	4	12	34	104	541	35
65 - 69	334	-	-	-	-	-	1	-	6	5	25	287	10
70 - 74	103	-	-	-	-	-	-	1	1	1	6	91	3
75 +	67	-	-	-	-	-	-	-	-	1	1	63	2
Switzerland - Suisse													
2009 (C)													
Total	41 918	-	104	2 957	8 640	11 108	7 544	4 325	2 660	1 815	1 208	1 557	...
0 - 14	-	-	-	-	-	-	-	-	-	-	-	-	...
15 - 19	657	-	49	385	158	33	19	6	3	2	2	-	...
20 - 24	5 607	-	42	1 860	2 315	858	308	120	64	22	10	8	...
25 - 29	11 649	-	10	494	4 516	4 172	1 568	508	206	91	52	32	...
30 - 34	11 081	-	3	133	1 228	4 748	3 061	1 144	453	174	81	56	...
35 - 39	5 590	-	-	45	249	960	1 947	1 321	574	276	130	88	...
40 - 44	3 002	-	-	20	85	220	455	849	652	383	190	148	...
45 - 49	1 934	-	-	14	50	59	136	267	478	419	267	244	...
50 - 54	1 262	-	-	5	28	32	37	79	157	323	287	314	...
55 - 59	619	-	-	1	8	18	8	25	45	101	133	280	...
60 - 64	285	-	-	-	3	6	3	4	16	18	47	188	...
65 - 69	126	-	-	-	-	2	1	1	8	4	6	104	...
70 - 74	68	-	-	-	-	-	1	1	2	1	3	60	...
75 +	38	-	-	-	-	-	-	-	2	1	-	35	...

23. Marriages by age of groom and by age of bride: latest available year, 2000 - 2009
Mariages selon l'âge de l'époux et selon l'âge de l'épouse : dernière année disponible, 2000 - 2009 (continued - suite)

Continent, country or area, year, code and age of bride / Continent, pays ou zone, date, code et âge de l'épouse	Total	0-14	15-19	20-24	25-29	30-34	35-39	40-44	45-49	50-54	55-59	60+	Unknown Inconnu
EUROPE													
TFYR of Macedonia - L'ex-R. y. de Macédoine													
2008 (C)													
Total	14 695	-	377	4 105	5 516	2 642	997	482	265	133	75	103	-
0 - 14	-	-	-	-	-	-	-	-	-	-	-	-	-
15 - 19	2 350	-	281	1 409	561	77	18	4	-	-	-	-	-
20 - 24	5 736	-	90	2 349	2 535	631	99	19	6	5	-	2	-
25 - 29	4 100	-	5	313	2 149	1 265	277	66	17	7	-	1	-
30 - 34	1 383	-	1	25	243	587	342	122	44	11	7	1	-
35 - 39	545	-	-	6	15	67	221	131	76	15	9	5	-
40 - 44	265	-	-	2	7	11	28	108	63	22	12	12	-
45 - 49	142	-	-	-	5	3	5	23	41	45	12	8	-
50 - 54	95	-	-	-	-	1	7	7	16	22	19	23	-
55 - 59	53	-	-	-	1	-	-	1	1	5	14	31	-
60 - 64	16	-	-	-	-	-	-	-	-	1	2	13	-
65 - 69	7	-	-	1	-	-	-	1	1	-	-	4	-
70 - 74	3	-	-	-	-	-	-	-	-	-	-	3	-
75 +	-	-	-	-	-	-	-	-	-	-	-	-	-
Unknown - Inconnu	-	-	-	-	-	-	-	-	-	-	-	-	-
Ukraine													
2008 (C)													
Total	321 992	5[a]	10 275[g]	113 361	90 631	40 985	21 786	13 012	10 583	7 641	5 424	8 289	...
0 - 15	327	-[a]	119[g]	153	47	8	-	-	-	-	-	-	...
16 - 19	49 023	5[a]	6 383[g]	31 190	9 723	1 406	225	56	25	6	2	2	...
20 - 24	133 695	-[a]	3 319[g]	68 098	46 640	11 578	2 817	791	280	117	33	22	...
25 - 29	62 741	-[a]	373[g]	11 749	26 490	15 103	5 836	2 035	744	273	93	45	...
30 - 34	28 413	-[a]	66[g]	1 752	6 009	9 058	6 457	2 949	1 371	490	176	85	...
35 - 39	15 124	-[a]	11[g]	320	1 360	2 835	4 370	3 205	1 874	731	291	127	...
40 - 44	9 207	-[a]	4[g]	63	281	715	1 452	2 434	2 407	1 171	441	239	...
45 - 49	8 309	-[a]	-[g]	29	64	242	494	1 156	2 636	2 143	950	595	...
50 - 54	5 990	-[a]	-[g]	5	8	32	100	304	933	1 955	1 617	1 036	...
55 - 59	4 176	-[a]	-[g]	2	7	6	28	68	264	602	1 438	1 761	...
60 +	4 987	-[a]	-[g]	-	2	2	7	14	49	153	383	4 377	...
United Kingdom of Great Britain and Northern Ireland - Royaume-Uni de Grande-Bretagne et d'Irlande du Nord[30]													
2002 (C)													
Total	293 021	...	2 023	28 666	74 858	72 592	44 189	25 558	15 910	11 891	8 055	9 279	-
0 - 14	-	-	-	-	-	-	-	-	-	-	-	-	-
15 - 19	7 505	-	1 100	3 628	1 771	687	191	77	31	9	7	4	-
20 - 24	51 478	-	659	16 996	21 406	8 351	2 659	909	283	128	54	33	-
25 - 29	82 892	-	167	5 757	37 256	26 710	8 790	2 792	826	351	154	89	-
30 - 34	62 279	-	57	1 525	10 717	26 222	14 924	5 598	1 960	794	335	147	-
35 - 39	35 978	-	27	519	2 725	7 698	11 770	7 452	3 328	1 483	622	354	-
40 - 44	21 019	-	9	169	709	2 178	4 131	5 582	4 120	2 436	1 102	583	-
45 - 49	13 232	-	3	51	205	547	1 245	2 231	3 469	2 927	1 688	866	-
50 - 54	8 955	-	1	13	45	154	366	698	1 439	2 565	2 151	1 523	-
55 - 59	4 903	-	-	5	14	36	90	182	350	925	1 408	1 893	-
60 - 64	2 366	-	-	-	8	7	13	22	91	210	406	1 609	-
65 - 69	1 251	-	-	1	2	-	8	9	10	48	97	1 076	-
70 - 74	662	-	-	1	-	2	2	5	2	12	20	618	-
75 - 79	328	-	-	-	-	-	-	1	-	1	9	317	-
80 - 84	128	-	-	1	-	-	-	-	1	1	1	124	-
85 - 89	44	-	-	-	-	-	-	-	-	1	-	43	-
90 - 94	1	-	-	-	-	-	-	-	-	-	1	-	-
Unknown - Inconnu	-	-	-	-	-	-	-	-	-	-	-	-	-
OCEANIA - OCÉANIE													
Australia - Australie[31]													
2009 (+C)													
Total	120 118	-	552	14 101	35 810	26 918	16 002	8 767	6 186	4 472	3 196	4 114	-
0 - 14	-	-	-	-	-	-	-	-	-	-	-	-	-

Mariages selon l'âge de l'époux et selon l'âge de l'épouse : dernière année disponible, 2000 - 2009 (continued - suite)

Continent, country or area, year, code and age of bride / Continent, pays ou zone, date, code et âge de l'épouse	Total	0-14	15-19	20-24	25-29	30-34	35-39	40-44	45-49	50-54	55-59	60+	Unknown Inconnu
OCEANIA - OCÉANIE													
Australia - Australie[31]													
2009													
15 - 19	2 134	-	295	1 174	481	118	34	15	-	3	-	4	-
20 - 24	23 325	-	205	9 701	9 784	2 468	726	225	121	49	20	17	-
25 - 29	40 136	-	39	2 686	20 974	11 417	3 438	949	345	138	83	60	-
30 - 34	23 188	-	-	373	3 724	10 182	5 790	1 846	736	294	145	90	-
35 - 39	12 399	-	-	108	690	2 197	4 455	2 748	1 318	504	212	152	-
40 - 44	6 611	-	-	34	117	411	1 127	1 972	1 556	790	367	228	-
45 - 49	5 111	-	-	18	31	96	328	751	1 478	1 302	663	444	-
50 - 54	3 319	-	-	-	-	18	76	219	478	1 036	863	616	-
55 - 59	1 883	-	-	-	-	-	18	37	103	277	611	826	-
60 - 64	1 032	-	-	-	-	-	-	-	40	59	178	742	-
65 - 69	504	-	-	-	-	-	-	-	-	15	43	439	-
70 - 74	292	-	-	-	-	-	-	-	-	-	-	279	-
75 +	184	-	-	-	-	-	-	-	-	-	-	181	-
Unknown - Inconnu	-	-	-	-	-	-	-	-	-	-	-	-	-
Fiji - Fidji													
2004 (+C)													
Total	7 076	-	125	2 060	2 429	1 113	522	334	217	125	74	77	...
0 - 14	-	...	...	...	...	...	...	...	...	...	...	...	...
15 - 19	1 176	...	...	...	...	...	...	...	...	...	...	...	...
20 - 24	2 990	...	...	...	...	...	...	...	...	...	...	...	...
25 - 29	1 438	...	...	...	...	...	...	...	...	...	...	...	...
30 - 34	656	...	...	...	...	...	...	...	...	...	...	...	...
35 - 39	367	...	...	...	...	...	...	...	...	...	...	...	...
40 - 44	204	...	...	...	...	...	...	...	...	...	...	...	...
45 - 49	128	...	...	...	...	...	...	...	...	...	...	...	...
50 - 54	62	...	...	...	...	...	...	...	...	...	...	...	...
55 - 59	35	...	...	...	...	...	...	...	...	...	...	...	...
60 - 64	13	...	...	...	...	...	...	...	...	...	...	...	...
65 +	7	...	...	...	...	...	...	...	...	...	...	...	...
Guam													
2003 (C)													
Total	1 334	...	41[e]	268	353	240	171	110	55	46	14	36	...
0 - 19	96	...	23[e]	49	18	3	-	3	-	-	-	-	...
20 - 24	334	...	14[e]	164	102	34	14	2	3	1	-	-	...
25 - 29	374	...	2[e]	36	180	104	24	15	6	4	1	2	...
30 - 34	230	...	1[e]	15	38	69	63	27	6	8	2	1	...
35 - 39	140	...	1[e]	4	12	26	48	32	11	4	1	1	...
40 - 44	74	...	-[e]	-	3	4	13	21	12	13	2	6	...
45 - 49	42	...	-[e]	-	-	-	7	10	10	8	4	3	...
50 - 54	23	...	-[e]	-	-	-	-	-	7	6	3	7	...
55 - 59	10	...	-[e]	-	-	-	-	-	-	2	-	8	...
60 - 69	8	...	-[e]	-	-	-	1	-	-	-	1	6	...
70 +	3	...	-[e]	-	-	-	1	-	-	-	-	2	...
New Caledonia - Nouvelle-Calédonie													
2007 (C)													
Total	884	...	...	45[f]	179	208	159	179[m]	...	71[n]	...	43	...
0 - 24	134	...	...	35[f]	52	31	5	7[m]	...	4[n]	...	-	...
25 - 29	222	...	...	8[f]	102	76	21	14[m]	...	1[n]	...	-	...
30 - 34	185	...	...	1[f]	18	79	56	22[m]	...	5[n]	...	4	...
35 - 39	132	...	...	1[f]	6	15	53	47[m]	...	8[n]	...	2	...
40 - 49	160	...	...	-[f]	1	7	24	82[m]	...	33[n]	...	13	...
50 - 59	38	...	...	-[f]	-	-	-	7[m]	...	17[n]	...	14	...
60 +	13	...	...	-[f]	-	-	-	-[m]	...	3[n]	...	10	...
New Zealand - Nouvelle-Zélande													
2009 (+C)													
Total	21 628	...	238	2 588	5 779	4 463	2 776	1 905	1 292	924	694	969	-
15 - 19	586	...	144	306	98	25	8	3	2	-	-	-	-
20 - 24	3 869	...	75	1 684	1 564	379	102	39	13	10	2	1	-
25 - 29	6 285	...	14	498	3 286	1 742	492	158	63	15	10	7	-
30 - 34	4 195	...	3	76	696	1 798	1 009	389	135	50	19	20	-
35 - 39	2 361	...	2	17	111	419	843	567	234	100	40	28	-
40 - 44	1 517	...	-	6	16	80	239	497	365	179	88	47	-

Continent, country or area, year, code and age of bride / Continent, pays ou zone, date, code et âge de l'épouse	Total	0-14	15-19	20-24	25-29	30-34	35-39	40-44	45-49	50-54	55-59	60+	Unknown Inconnu
OCEANIA - OCÉANIE													
New Zealand - Nouvelle-Zélande													
2009													
45 - 49	1 152	...	-	1	6	15	63	179	343	276	167	102	-
50 - 54	728	...	-	-	1	4	14	53	115	213	188	140	-
55 - 59	420	...	-	-	1	1	4	15	22	64	128	185	-
60 - 64	248	...	-	-	-	-	1	5	-	16	36	190	-
65 - 69	141	...	-	-	-	-	1	-	-	1	13	126	-
70 - 74	77	...	-	-	-	-	-	-	-	-	3	74	-
75 +	49	...	-	-	-	-	-	-	-	-	-	49	-
Unknown - Inconnu	-	...	-	-	-	-	-	-	-	-	-	-	-
Niue - Nioué													
2009 (C)													
Total	12	...	-	2	3	4	-	1	1	-	1	-	...
15 - 19	-	...	...	...	...	...	...	...	...	...	...	...	...
20 - 24	-	...	...	...	...	...	...	...	...	...	...	...	...
25 - 29	3	...	...	...	...	...	...	...	...	...	...	...	...
30 - 34	4	...	...	...	...	...	...	...	...	...	...	...	...
35 - 39	3	...	...	...	...	...	...	...	...	...	...	...	...
40 - 44	-	...	...	...	...	...	...	...	...	...	...	...	...
45 - 49	1	...	...	...	...	...	...	...	...	...	...	...	...
50 - 54	1	...	...	...	...	...	...	...	...	...	...	...	...
55 - 59	-	...	...	...	...	...	...	...	...	...	...	...	...
60 - 64	-	...	...	...	...	...	...	...	...	...	...	...	...
65 +	-	...	...	...	...	...	...	...	...	...	...	...	...
Samoa													
2001 (U)													
Total	821	...	10	149	223	165	116	60	40	25	9	20	4
15 - 19	71	...	...	...	...	...	...	...	...	...	...	...	...
20 - 24	285	...	...	...	...	...	...	...	...	...	...	...	...
25 - 29	177	...	...	...	...	...	...	...	...	...	...	...	...
30 - 34	114	...	...	...	...	...	...	...	...	...	...	...	...
35 - 39	83	...	...	...	...	...	...	...	...	...	...	...	...
40 - 44	39	...	...	...	...	...	...	...	...	...	...	...	...
45 - 49	23	...	...	...	...	...	...	...	...	...	...	...	...
50 - 54	12	...	...	...	...	...	...	...	...	...	...	...	...
55 - 59	11	...	...	...	...	...	...	...	...	...	...	...	...
60 - 64	1	...	...	...	...	...	...	...	...	...	...	...	...
65 - 69	2	...	...	...	...	...	...	...	...	...	...	...	...
70 - 74	-	...	...	...	...	...	...	...	...	...	...	...	...
75 +	-	...	...	...	...	...	...	...	...	...	...	...	...
Unknown - Inconnu	3	...	...	...	...	...	...	...	...	...	...	...	...
Tonga[32]													
2004* (+C)													
Total	677	-	34	237	203	83	59	27	14	20ʳ	...	...	-
0 - 14	-	...	...	...	...	...	...	...	...	...	...	...	...
15 - 19	107	...	...	...	...	...	...	...	...	...	...	...	...
20 - 24	262	...	...	...	...	...	...	...	...	...	...	...	...
25 - 29	161	...	...	...	...	...	...	...	...	...	...	...	...
30 - 34	76	...	...	...	...	...	...	...	...	...	...	...	...
35 - 39	44	...	...	...	...	...	...	...	...	...	...	...	...
40 - 44	17	...	...	...	...	...	...	...	...	...	...	...	...
45 - 49	6	...	...	...	...	...	...	...	...	...	...	...	...
50 +	4	...	...	...	...	...	...	...	...	...	...	...	...
Unknown - Inconnu	-	...	...	...	...	...	...	...	...	...	...	...	...
Wallis and Futuna Islands - Îles Wallis et Futuna													
2008 (C)													
Total	53	-	1	14	23	8	3	2	-	2	-	-	...
0 - 14	-	...	...	...	...	...	...	...	...	...	...	...	...
15 - 19	9	...	...	...	...	...	...	...	...	...	...	...	...
20 - 24	18	...	...	...	...	...	...	...	...	...	...	...	...
25 - 29	12	...	...	...	...	...	...	...	...	...	...	...	...
30 - 34	7	...	...	...	...	...	...	...	...	...	...	...	...
35 - 39	5	...	...	...	...	...	...	...	...	...	...	...	...
40 - 44	-	...	...	...	...	...	...	...	...	...	...	...	...
45 - 49	1	...	...	...	...	...	...	...	...	...	...	...	...

Continent, country or area, year, code and age of bride / Continent, pays ou zone, date, code et âge de l'épouse	Age of groom - âge de l'époux											
	Total	0-14	15-19	20-24	25-29	30-34	35-39	40-44	45-49	50-54	55-59	60+	Unknown Inconnu

OCEANIA - OCÉANIE

Wallis and Futuna Islands - Îles Wallis et Futuna
2008

	Total	0-14	15-19	20-24	25-29	30-34	35-39	40-44	45-49	50-54	55-59	60+	Unknown Inconnu
50 - 54	-	...	...	...	...	...	...	...	...	...	...	...	...
55 - 59	-	...	...	...	...	...	...	...	...	...	...	...	...
60 - 64	1	...	...	...	...	...	...	...	...	...	...	...	...
65 - 69	-	...	...	...	...	...	...	...	...	...	...	...	...
70 - 74	-	...	...	...	...	...	...	...	...	...	...	...	...
75 +	-	...	...	...	...	...	...	...	...	...	...	...	...

FOOTNOTES - NOTES

Italics: data from civil registers which are incomplete or of unknown completeness. - Italiques : données incomplètes ou dont le degré d'exactitude n'est pas connu, provenant des registres de l'état civil.

* Provisional. - Données provisoires.

'Code' indicates the source of data, as follows:
C - Civil registration, estimated over 90% complete
U - Civil registration, estimated less than 90% complete
| - Other source, estimated reliable
+ - Data tabulated by date of registration rather than occurence
... - Information not available

Le 'Code' indique la source des données, comme suit :
C - Registres de l'état civil considérés complèts à 90 p. 100 au moins
U - Registres de l'état civil qui ne sont pas considérés complèts à 90 p. 100 au moins
| - Autre source, considérée pas douteuses
+ - Données exploitées selon la date de l'enregistrement et non la date de l'événement
... - Information pas disponible

[a] Refers to 0-15 years of age. - Données se raportent au groupe d'âges 0-15.
[b] Refers to 0-16 years of age. - Données se raportent au groupe d'âges 0-16.
[c] Refers to 0-17 years of age. - Données se raportent au groupe d'âges 0-17.
[d] Refers to 0-18 years of age. - Données se raportent au groupe d'âges 0-18.
[e] Refers to 0-19 years of age. - Données se raportent au groupe d'âges 0-19.
[f] Refers to 0-24 years of age. - Données se raportent au groupe d'âges 0-24.
[g] Refers to 16-19 years of age. - Données se raportent au groupe d'âges 16-19.
[h] Refers to 17-19 years of age. - Données se raportent au groupe d'âges 17-19.
[i] Refers to 18-19 years of age. - Données se raportent au groupe d'âges 18-19.
[j] Refers to 19-24 years of age. - Données se raportent au groupe d'âges 19-24.
[k] Refers to 20-29 years of age. - Données se raportent au groupe d'âges 20-29.
[l] Refers to 30-39 years of age. - Données se raportent au groupe d'âges 30-39.
[m] Refers to 40-49 years of age. - Données se raportent au groupe d'âges 40-49.
[n] Refers to 50-59 years of age. - Données se raportent au groupe d'âges 50-59.
[o] Refers to 35+ years of age. - Données se raportent au groupe d'âges 35+.
[p] Refers to 40+ years of age. - Données se raportent au groupe d'âges 40+.
[q] Refers to 45+ years of age. - Données se raportent au groupe d'âges 45+.
[r] Refers to 50+ years of age. - Données se raportent au groupe d'âges 50+.
[s] Refers to 55+ years of age. - Données se raportent au groupe d'âges 55+.
[1] Including marriages resumed after 'revocable divorce' (among Moslem population), which approximates legal separation. - Y compris les unions reconstituées après un 'divorce révocable' (parmi la population musulmane), qui est à peu près l'équivalent d'une séparation légale.
[2] Excludes the islands of St. Brandon and Agalega. - Non compris les îles St. Brandon et Agalega.
[3] As reported by the country. Reasons for discrepancy with other tables not ascertained. - Données comme déclarées par le pays. On ne sait pas comment s'explique la divergence entre ces chiffres et les chiffres correspondants indiqués ailleurs.
[4] Including visitors. - Visiteurs compris.
[5] Excluding visitors. - Les données non compris des visiteurs.

[6] Data refer to resident population only. - Pour la population résidante seulement.
[7] Including marriages where bride/groom are non-residents. - Y compris les mariages pour lesquels le marié et la mariée sont des non-résidents.
[8] Excluding Indian jungle population. - Non compris les Indiens de la jungle.
[9] Excluding nomadic Indian tribes. - Non compris les tribus d'Indiens nomades.
[10] Data refer to marriages of residents only. - Chiffres se rapportent exclusivement aux mariages de résidents.
[11] Data refer to government controlled areas. - Les données se rapportent aux zones contrôlées par le Gouvernement.
[12] Including data for East Jerusalem and Israeli residents in certain other territories under occupation by Israeli military forces since June 1967. - Y compris les données pour Jérusalem-Est et les résidents israéliens dans certains autres territoires occupés depuis 1967 par les forces armées israéliennes.
[13] Data refer to Japanese nationals in Japan only; and to grooms and brides married for the first time whose marriages occurred in the same year. - Les données se raportent aux nationaux japonais au Japon seulement; et aux époux et épouses mariés pour la première fois, dont le mariage a été célébré et enregistré la même année.
[14] Excluding data for Jordanian territory under occupation since June 1967 by Israeli military forces. Excluding foreigners, including registered Palestinian refugees. - Non compris les données pour le territoire jordanien occupé depuis juin 1967 par les forces armées israéliennes. Non compris les étrangers, mais y compris les réfugiés de Palestine enregistrés.
[15] Excluding alien armed forces, civilian aliens employed by armed forces, and foreign diplomatic personnel and their dependants. - Non compris les militaires étrangers, les civils étrangers employés par les forces armées ni le personnel diplomatique étranger et les membres de leur famille les accompagnant.
[16] Excluding marriages previously officiated outside Singapore or under religious and customary rites. - Les figures excluent les mariages célébrés précédemment au dehors de Singapour ou sous les rites réligieuse ou accoutumés.
[17] Data from MERNIS (Central Population Administrative System). - Données de MERNIS (Système central de données démographiques).
[18] Excluding aliens temporarily in the area. - Non compris les étrangers se trouvant temporairement dans le territoire.
[19] Since 2003, marriage between persons of the same sex is authorized in Belgium, but the sex of spouses is not revealed. In this table, husband is used for first spouse, whereas wife is used for second spouse. - Depuis 2003, le mariage entre personnes de même sexe est autorisé en Belgique, mais le sexe des conjoints n'est pas indiqué. Dans ce tableau, la mention "mari" est utilisée pour le premier conjoint et la mention "femme" pour le second conjoint.
[20] Including armed forces stationed outside the country, but excluding alien armed forces in the area unless marriage performed by local foreign authority. - Y compris les militaires nationaux hors du pays et les militaires étrangers en garnison sur le territoire, sauf si le mariage a été célébré pour l'autorité locale.
[21] Including nationals outside the country, but excluding foreigners in the country. - Y compris les nationaux à l'étranger, mais non compris les étrangers sur le territoire.
[22] Excluding Faeroe Islands and Greenland shown separately, if available. - Non compris les Iles Féroé et le Groenland, qui font l'objet de rubriques distinctes, si disponible.
[23] Excluding Åland Islands. - Non compris les Îles d'Åland.
[24] Only marriages in which the bride was resident in Finland. - Seulement mariages où l'épouse réside en Finlande.
[25] Including armed forces stationed outside the country. - Y compris les militaires nationaux hors du pays.

[26] Excluding Svalbard and Jan Mayen Islands shown separately, if available. - Non compris Svalbard et Jan Mayen qui font l'objet de rubriques distinctes, si disponible.

[27] Data refer to first marriages only. - Données se rapportent aux premiers mariages seulement.

[28] Includes civil and religious marriages as well as not specified. - Y compris les mariages civils, religieux ou non précisés.

[29] Excluding data for Kosovo and Metohia. - Sans les données pour le Kosovo et Metohie.

[30] Excluding Channel Islands (Guernsey and Jersey) and Isle of Man, shown separately, if available. - Non compris les îles Anglo-Normandes (Guernesey et Jersey) et l'île de Man, qui font l'objet de rubriques distinctes, si disponible.

[31] Data for certain cells suppressed by national statistical office for confidentiality reasons. - Les données pour certaines cases ont été supprimées par le bureau national de statistiques pour des raisons de confidentialité.

[32] Data refer to the island of Tongatapu only. - Les données se réfèrent uniquement à l'île de Tongatapu.

Continent, country or area, year, code and age of bride / Continent, pays ou zone, date, code et âge de l'épouse	Total	Age of groom - âge de l'époux											
		0-14	15-19	20-24	25-29	30-34	35-39	40-44	45-49	50-54	55-59	60+	Unknown Inconnu

AMERICA, NORTH - AMÉRIQUE DU NORD

Costa Rica
2010* (C)

	Total	0-14	15-19	20-24	25-29	30-34	35-39	40-44	45-49	50-54	55-59	60+	Unknown Inconnu
Total	23 955	-	520	4 572	6 423	4 663	2 484	1 561	1 099	744	462	800	627
0 - 14	-	-	-	-	-	-	-	-	-	-	-	-	-
15 - 19	2 298	-	304	1 186	535	154	64	25	10	5	2	3	10
20 - 24	6 282	-	162	2 371	2 354	878	262	132	64	25	10	13	11
25 - 29	6 281	-	36	746	2 586	1 801	645	240	109	56	24	22	16
30 - 34	3 499	-	12	160	660	1 278	692	356	190	75	33	32	11
35 - 39	1 869	-	2	52	162	334	525	343	232	105	42	60	12
40 - 44	1 147	-	1	17	60	113	172	274	218	141	70	76	5
45 - 49	802	-	1	9	20	38	81	115	163	152	103	119	1
50 - 54	513	-	-	2	6	23	21	46	71	117	106	120	1
55 - 59	252	-	-	-	1	3	7	9	18	45	46	121	2
60 - 64	132	-	-	-	1	2	3	2	12	9	15	87	1
65 - 69	78	-	-	2	-	-	-	1	1	4	6	62	2
70 - 74	60	-	-	-	-	-	1	1	-	-	-	58	-
75 +	27	-	-	-	-	-	-	-	-	2	1	24	-
Unknown - Inconnu	715	-	2	27	38	39	11	17	11	8	4	3	555

FOOTNOTES - NOTES

* Provisional. - Données provisoires.

'Code' indicates the source of data, as follows:
C - Civil registration, estimated over 90% complete
U - Civil registration, estimated less than 90% complete
| - Other source, estimated reliable
+ - Data tabulated by date of registration rather than occurence.
... - Information not available

Le 'Code' indique la source des données, comme suit :
C - Registres de l'état civil considérés complets à 90 p. 100 au moins.
U - Registres de l'état civil qui ne sont pas considérés complets à 90 p. 100 au moins.
| - Autre source, considérée pas douteuses.
+ - Données exploitées selon la date de l'enregistrement et non la date de l'événement.
... - Information pas disponible.

Table 24

Table 24 presents number of divorces and crude divorce rates for as many years as possible between 2006 and 2010.

Description of variables: Divorce is defined as a final legal dissolution of a marriage, that is, that separation of husband and wife which confers on the parties the right to remarriage under civil, religious and/or other provisions, according to the laws of each country[1].

Unless otherwise noted, divorce statistics exclude legal separations that do not allow remarriage. These statistics refer to the number of divorces granted, and not to the number of persons divorcing.

Divorce statistics are obtained from court records and/or civil registers according to national practice. The actual compilation of these statistics may be the responsibility of the civil registrar, the national statistical office or other government offices.

The urban/rural classification of divorces is that provided by each country or area; it is presumed to be based on the national census definitions of urban population, which have been set forth at the end of the technical notes for table 6.

Rate computation: Crude divorce rates by urban/rural residence are the annual number of divorces per 1 000 mid-year population. Rates presented in this table have been limited to those countries or areas having at least a total of 30 divorces in a given year. These rates are calculated by the Statistics Division of the United Nations based on the appropriate reference population (for example: total population, nationals only etc.) if known and available. If the reference population is not known or unavailable the total population is used to calculate the rates. Therefore, if the population that is used to calculate the rates is different from the correct reference population, the rates presented might under- or overstate the true situation in a country or area.

Reliability of data: Each country or area has been asked to indicate the estimated completeness of the divorces recorded in its civil register. These national assessments are indicated by the quality codes "C" and "U" that appear in the first column of this table.

"C" indicates that the data are estimated to be virtually complete, that is, representing at least 90 per cent of the divorces that occur each year, while "U" indicates that data are estimated to be incomplete, that is, representing less than 90 per cent of the divorces occurring each year. The code "..." indicates that no information was provided regarding completeness.

Data from civil registers that are reported as incomplete or of unknown completeness (coded "U" or "...") are considered unreliable. They appear in *italics* in this table and the rates were not computed on data so coded. These quality codes apply only to data from civil registers. For more information about the quality of vital statistics data in general, see section 4.2 of the Technical Notes.

Limitations: Statistics on divorces are subject to the same qualifications as have been set forth for vital statistics in general and divorce statistics in particular as discussed in section 4 of the Technical Notes.

Divorce, like marriage, is a legal event, and this has implications for international comparability of data. Divorce has been defined, for statistical purposes, in terms of the laws of individual countries or areas. The laws pertaining to divorce vary considerably from one country or area to another. This variation in the legal provision for divorce also affects the incidence of divorce, which is relatively low in countries or areas where divorce decrees are difficult to obtain.

Since divorces are granted by courts and statistics on divorce refer to the actual divorce decree, effective as of the date of the decree, marked year-to-year fluctuations may reflect court delays and clearances rather than trends in the incidence of divorce. The comparability of divorce statistics may also be affected by tabulation procedures. In some countries or areas annulments and/or legal separations may be included. This practice is more common for countries or areas in which the number of divorces is small. Information on this practice is given in the footnotes when known.

The registration of a divorce in many countries or areas is the responsibility solely of the court or the authority which granted it. Since the registration recording such cases is part of the records of the court proceedings, divorces are likely to be registered soon after the decree is granted. For this reason the

practice of tabulating data by date of registration does not generally pose serious problems of comparability as it does in the case of birth and death statistics.

As noted briefly above, the incidence of divorce is affected by the relative ease or difficulty of obtaining a divorce according to the laws of individual countries or areas. The incidence of divorce is also affected by the ability of individuals to meet financial and other costs of the court procedures. Connected with this aspect is the influence of certain religious faiths on the incidence of divorce. For all these reasons, divorce statistics are not strictly comparable as measures of family dissolution by legal means. Furthermore, family dissolution by other than legal means, such as separation, is not measured in statistics for divorce.

For certain countries or areas there is or was no legal provision for divorce in the sense used here, and therefore no data for these countries or areas appear in this table.

In addition, it should be noted that rates are affected also by the quality and limitations of the population estimates that are used in their computation. The problems of under-enumeration or over-enumeration, and to some extent, the differences in definition of total population, have been discussed in section 3 of the Technical Notes dealing with population data in general, and specific information pertaining to individual countries or areas is given in the footnotes to table 3.

As will be seen from the footnotes, strict correspondence between the numerator of the rate and the denominator is not always obtained; for example, divorces among civilian plus military segments of the population may be related to civilian population only. The effect of this may be to increase the rates but, in most cases, the effect is negligible.

As mentioned above, data for some countries or areas may include annulments and/or legal separations. This practice affects the comparability of the crude divorce rates. For example, inclusion of annulments in the numerator of the rates produces a negligible effect on the rates, but inclusion of legal separations may have a measurable effect on the level.

It should be emphasized that crude divorce rates like crude birth, death and marriage rates may be seriously affected by age-sex structure of the populations to which they relate. Like crude marriage rates, they are also affected by the existing distribution of the population by marital status. Nevertheless, crude divorce rates provide a simple measure of the level and changes in divorces.

The comparability of data by urban/rural residence is affected by the national definitions of urban and rural used in tabulating these data. It is assumed, in the absence of specific information to the contrary, that the definitions of urban and rural used in connection with the national population census were also used in the compilation of the vital statistics for each country or area. However, it cannot be excluded that, for a given country or area, different definitions of urban and rural are used for the vital statistics data and the population census data respectively. When known, the definitions of urban in national population censuses are presented at the end of the technical notes for table 6. As discussed in detail in the notes, these definitions vary considerably from one country or area to another.

In addition to problems of comparability, divorce rates classified by urban/rural residence are also subject to certain special types of bias. If, when calculating divorce rates, different definitions of urban are used in connection with the vital events and the population data, and if this results in a net difference between the numerator and denominator of the rate in the population at risk, then the divorce rates would be biased. Urban/rural differentials in divorce rates may also be affected by whether the vital events have been tabulated in terms of place of occurrence or place of usual residence. This problem is discussed in more detail in section 4.1.4.1 of the Technical Notes.

Earlier data: Divorces have been shown in previous issues of the Demographic Yearbook. The earliest data, which were for 1935, appeared in the 1951 issue. For more information on specific topics and years for which data are reported, readers should consult the Historical Index.

NOTES

[1] For definition, please see section 4.1.1 of the Technical Notes.

Tableau 24

Le tableau 24 présente des statistiques concernant les divorces et les taux bruts de divortialité pour le plus grand nombre d'années possible entre 2006 et 2010.

Description des variables : le divorce est la dissolution légale et définitive des liens du mariage, c'est-à-dire la séparation de l'époux et de l'épouse qui confère aux parties le droit de se remarier civilement ou religieusement, ou selon toute autre procédure, conformément à la législation du pays[1].

Sauf indication contraire, les statistiques de la divortialité n'englobent pas les séparations légales qui excluent un remariage. Ces statistiques se rapportent aux jugements de divorce prononcés, non aux personnes divorcées.

Les statistiques de la divortialité proviennent, selon la pratique suivie par chaque pays, des actes des tribunaux et/ou des registres de l'état civil. L'officier d'état civil, les services nationaux de statistique ou d'autres services gouvernementaux peuvent être chargés d'établir ces statistiques.

La classification des divorces selon le lieu de résidence (zone urbaine ou rurale) est celle qui a été communiquée par chaque pays ou zone ; on part du principe qu'elle repose sur les définitions de la population urbaine utilisées pour les recensements nationaux, qui sont reproduites à la fin des notes techniques du tableau 6.

Calcul des taux : les taux bruts de divortialité selon le lieu de résidence (zone urbaine ou rurale) représentent le nombre annuel de divorces enregistrés pour 1 000 habitants au milieu de l'année. Les taux du tableau 23 ne se rapportent qu'aux pays ou zones où l'on a enregistré un total d'au moins 30 divorces pendant une année donnée. Ces taux sont calculés par la division de statistique des Nations Unies sur la base de la population de référence adéquate (par exemple : population totale, nationaux seulement, etc.) si connue et disponible. Si la population de référence n'est pas connue ou n'est pas disponible, la population totale est utilisée pour calculer les taux. Par conséquent, si la population utilisée pour calculer les taux est différente de la population de référence adéquate, les taux présentés sont susceptibles de sous ou sur estimer la situation réelle d'un pays ou d'un territoire.

Fiabilité des données : il a été demandé à chaque pays ou zone d'indiquer le degré estimatif de complétude des données sur les divorces figurant dans ses registres d'état civil. Ces évaluations nationales sont désignées par les codes de qualité "C" et "U" qui apparaissent dans la deuxième colonne du tableau.

La lettre "C" indique que les données sont jugées à peu près complètes, c'est-à-dire qu'elles représentent au moins 90 p. 100 des divorces survenus chaque année ; la lettre "U" signale que les données sont jugées incomplètes, c'est-à-dire qu'elles représentent moins de 90 p. 100 des divorces survenus chaque année. Le code "..." indique qu'aucun renseignement n'a été communiqué quant à la complétude des données.

Les données issues des registres de l'état civil qui sont déclarées incomplètes ou dont le degré de complétude n'est pas connu (code "U" ou "...") sont jugées douteuses. Elles apparaissent en italique dans le tableau et les taux correspondants n'ont pas été calculés. Les codes de qualité ne s'appliquent qu'aux données extraites des registres de l'état civil. Pour plus de précisions sur la qualité des données reposant sur les statistiques de l'état civil en général, voir la section 4.2 des notes techniques.

Insuffisance des données : les statistiques des divorces appellent les mêmes réserves que celles formulées à propos des statistiques de l'état civil en général et des statistiques de divortialité en particulier (voir la section 4 des notes techniques).

Le divorce est, comme le mariage, un acte juridique, et ce fait influe sur la comparabilité internationale des données. Aux fins de la statistique, le divorce est défini par la législation de chaque pays ou zone. La législation sur le divorce varie considérablement d'un pays ou d'une zone à l'autre, ce qui influe aussi sur la fréquence des divorces, laquelle est relativement faible dans les pays ou zones où le jugement de divorce est difficile à obtenir.

Du fait que les divorces sont prononcés par les tribunaux et que les statistiques de la divortialité se rapportent aux jugements de divorce proprement dits, qui prennent effet à la date où ces jugements sont rendus, il se peut que des fluctuations annuelles accusées traduisent le rythme plus ou moins rapide auquel les affaires sont jugées plutôt que l'évolution de la fréquence des divorces. Les méthodes d'exploitation des

données peuvent aussi influer sur la comparabilité des statistiques de la divortialité. Dans certains pays ou zones, ces statistiques peuvent comprendre les annulations et/ou les séparations légales. C'est notamment le cas dans les pays ou zones où les divorces sont peu nombreux. Lorsqu'ils sont connus, des renseignements à ce propos sont donnés en note à la fin du tableau.

Étant donné que dans de nombreux pays ou zones, le tribunal ou l'autorité qui a prononcé le divorce est seul habilité à enregistrer cet acte, et, comme l'acte d'enregistrement figure alors sur les registres du tribunal, l'enregistrement suit généralement de peu le jugement. C'est pourquoi la pratique consistant à exploiter les données selon la date de l'enregistrement ne pose généralement pas les graves problèmes de comparabilité auxquels on se heurte dans le cas des statistiques des naissances et des décès.

Comme on l'a brièvement mentionné ci-dessus, la fréquence des divorces est fonction notamment de la facilité relative avec laquelle la législation de chaque pays ou zone permet d'obtenir le divorce. Elle dépend également de la capacité des intéressés à supporter les frais de procédure. Il faut aussi citer l'influence de certaines religions sur la fréquence des divorces. Pour toutes ces raisons, les statistiques de divortialité ne sont pas rigoureusement comparables et ne permettent pas de mesurer exactement la fréquence des dissolutions légales des mariages. De plus, elles ne rendent pas compte des cas de dissolution extrajudiciaire du mariage, comme la séparation.

Dans certains pays ou zones, il n'existe ou il n'existait pas de législation sur le divorce selon l'acception retenue aux fins du tableau 23, si bien que l'on ne dispose pas de données les concernant.

De surcroît, il convient de noter que l'exactitude des taux dépend également de la qualité et des insuffisances des estimations de population qui sont utilisées pour leur calcul. Le problème des erreurs par excès ou par défaut commises lors du dénombrement et, dans une certaine mesure, le problème de l'hétérogénéité des définitions de la population totale ont été examinés à la section 3 des notes techniques, relative à la population en général ; des explications concernant les différents pays ou zones sont données en note à la fin du tableau 3.

Comme on le verra dans les notes, il n'a pas toujours été possible d'obtenir une correspondance rigoureuse entre le numérateur et le dénominateur pour le calcul des taux. Par exemple, les divorces parmi la population civile et les militaires sont parfois rapportés à la population civile seulement. Cela peut avoir pour effet d'accroître les taux, mais, dans la plupart des cas, il est probable que la différence sera négligeable.

Comme indiqué plus haut, les données concernant certains pays ou zones peuvent comprendre les annulations et/ou les séparations légales. Cette pratique influe sur la comparabilité des taux bruts de divortialité. Par exemple, l'inclusion des annulations dans le numérateur a une influence négligeable, mais l'inclusion des séparations légales peut avoir un effet appréciable.

Il faut souligner que les taux bruts de divortialité, de même que les taux bruts de natalité, de mortalité et de nuptialité, peuvent varier sensiblement selon la structure par âge et par sexe. Comme les taux bruts de nuptialité, ils peuvent également varier en raison de la répartition de la population selon l'état matrimonial. Les taux bruts de divortialité offrent néanmoins un moyen simple de mesurer la fréquence et l'évolution des divorces.

La comparabilité des données selon le lieu de résidence (zone urbaine ou rurale) peut être limitée par les définitions nationales des termes « urbain » et « rural » utilisées pour la mise en tableaux de ces données. En l'absence d'indications contraires, on a supposé que les mêmes définitions avaient servi pour le recensement national de la population et pour l'établissement des statistiques de l'état civil pour chaque pays ou zone. Toutefois, il n'est pas exclu que, pour une zone ou un pays donné, des définitions différentes aient été retenues. Les définitions du terme « urbain » utilisées pour les recensements nationaux de population ont été présentées à la fin des notes techniques du tableau 6 lorsqu'elles étaient connues. Comme on l'a précisé dans les notes techniques relatives au tableau 6, ces définitions varient considérablement d'un pays ou d'une zone à l'autre.

Outre les problèmes de comparabilité, les taux de divortialité classés selon le lieu de résidence (zone urbaine ou rurale) sont également sujets à des distorsions particulières. Si l'on utilise des définitions différentes du terme « urbain » pour classer les faits d'état civil et les données relatives à la population lors du calcul des taux et qu'il en résulte une différence nette entre le numérateur et le dénominateur pour le taux de la population exposée au risque, les taux de divortialité s'en trouveront faussés. La différence entre ces taux pour les zones urbaines et rurales pourra aussi être faussée selon que les faits d'état civil auront été

classés d'après le lieu de l'événement ou d'après le lieu de résidence habituel. Ce problème est examiné plus en détail à la section 4.1.4.1 des notes techniques.

Données publiées antérieurement : des statistiques concernant les divorces ont déjà été présentées dans des éditions antérieures de l'*Annuaire démographique*. Les plus anciennes, qui portaient sur 1935, ont été publiées dans l'édition de 1951. Pour plus de précisions concernant les années et les sujets pour lesquels des données ont été publiées, se reporter à l'index historique.

NOTE

[1] Pour la définition, voir la section 4.1.1 des Notes techniques.

24. Divorces and crude divorce rates by urban/rural residence: 2006 - 2010
Divorces et taux bruts de divortialité selon la résidence, urbaine/rurale : 2006 - 2010

Continent, country or area, and urban/rural residence / Continent, pays ou zone et résidence, urbaine/rurale	Co-de	Number - Nombre					Rate - Taux				
		2006	2007	2008	2009	2010	2006	2007	2008	2009	2010

AFRICA - AFRIQUE

Egypt - Égypte[1]											
Total	U	65 461	77 878	84 430	141 467	...	...	...	...	...	...
Urban - Urbaine	U	33 603	42 595	44 593	75 134	...	...	...	...	...	...
Rural - Rurale	U	31 858	35 283	39 837	66 333	...	...	...	...	...	...
Mauritius - Maurice[2]											
Total	+C	1 379	1 302	1 569	2 154	...	1.1	1.0	1.2	1.7	...
Réunion											
Total	C	1 553	...	...	...	...	2.0	...	...	...	...
Saint Helena ex. dep. - Sainte-Hélène sans dép.											
Total	C	4	10	6	5	...	...	...	...	...	...
Seychelles											
Total	+C	142	140	145	145	156	1.7	1.6	1.7	1.7	1.8
South Africa - Afrique du Sud											
Total	...	31 270	29 639	28 924	...	...	...	...	...	...	...
Tunisia - Tunisie											
Total	...	11 711	12 557	12 035	...	...	...	...	...	...	...

AMERICA, NORTH - AMÉRIQUE DU NORD

Anguilla											
Total	+C	19	12	...	...	...	...	...	...	...	...
Antigua and Barbuda - Antigua-et-Barbuda											
Total	+C	104	100	...	...	...	1.2	1.2	...	...	...
Aruba											
Total	C	529	417	*391	*410	*433	5.1	4.0	*3.7	*3.8	*4.0
Bahamas											
Total	C	296	*105	...	...	...	0.9	*0.3	...	...	...
Barbados - Barbade											
Total	+C	494	464	...	...	...	1.8	1.7	...	...	...
Bermuda - Bermudes											
Total	C	198	240	229	177	...	3.1	3.7	3.6	2.7	...
Cayman Islands - Îles Caïmanes											
Total	+C	158	162	196	*93	...	3.0	3.0	3.5	*1.8	...
Costa Rica											
Total	C	9 098	10 926	...	11 580	*11 556[3]	2.1	2.5	...	2.5	*2.5
Cuba											
Total	C	35 837	34 559	35 882	35 034	...	3.2	3.1	3.2	3.1	...
Urban - Urbaine	C	33 739	32 217	33 627	32 772	...	4.0	3.8	4.0	3.9	...
Rural - Rurale	C	2 098	2 342	2 255	2 262	...	0.8	0.8	0.8	0.8	...
Dominica - Dominique											
Total	+C	89	...	...	...	...	1.3	...	...	...	...
Dominican Republic - République dominicaine											
Total	+C	18 071	16 705	17 181	16 408	...	1.9	1.8	1.8	1.7	...
El Salvador											
Total	...	5 753	6 335	6 201	...	...	...	...	...	...	...
Urban - Urbaine[4]	...	5 369	5 940	...	...	...	...	...	...	...	...
Rural - Rurale[4]	...	207	198	...	...	...	...	...	...	...	...
Guatemala											
Total	C	1 917	2 128	2 834	...	...	0.1	0.2	0.2	...	...
Jamaica - Jamaïque											
Total	C	1 768	1 140[5]	1 654	1 853	2 371	0.7	0.4	0.6	0.7	0.9
Mexico - Mexique											
Total	+C	72 396	77 255	81 851	*84 302	...	0.7	0.7	0.8	*0.8	...
Urban - Urbaine[6]	+C	62 997	67 851	74 050	*76 193	...	0.8	0.8	0.9	*0.9	...
Rural - Rurale[6]	+C	3 458	3 238	3 765	*3 943	...	0.1	0.1	0.2	*0.2	...
Netherlands Antilles - Antilles néerlandaises											
Total	C	491	...	...	...	...	2.6	...	...	...	...
Nicaragua											
Total	+U	5 839	3 474	2 843	...	...	...	...	...	...	...

24. Divorces and crude divorce rates by urban/rural residence: 2006 - 2010
Divorces et taux bruts de divortialité selon la résidence, urbaine/rurale : 2006 - 2010 (continued - suite)

Continent, country or area, and urban/rural residence / Continent, pays ou zone et résidence, urbaine/rurale	Co-de	Number - Nombre					Rate - Taux				
		2006	2007	2008	2009	2010	2006	2007	2008	2009	2010
AMERICA, NORTH - AMÉRIQUE DU NORD											
Panama											
Total	C	2 866	2 893	2 997	3 469	...	0.9	0.9	0.9	1.0	...
Urban - Urbaine	C	...	...	2 656	2 926	...	...	...	1.2	1.3	...
Rural - Rurale	C	...	...	341	543	...	...	...	0.3	0.4	...
Puerto Rico - Porto Rico											
Total	C	14 826	14 182	14 849	...	...	3.8	3.6	3.8	...	...
Saint Vincent and the Grenadines - Saint-Vincent-et-les Grenadines											
Total	+C	128	78	...	...	...	1.3	0.8	...	...	...
Trinidad and Tobago - Trinité-et-Tobago											
Total	C	2 183	...	...	...	...	1.7	...	...	...	...
Turks and Caicos Islands - Îles Turques et Caïques											
Total	C	22[7]	27	8	...	...	...	...	...	...	...
AMERICA, SOUTH - AMÉRIQUE DU SUD											
Brazil - Brésil[8]											
Total	...	164 974	180 455	188 090	174 747	...	...	...	...	...	...
Chile - Chili											
Total	C	4 091[9]	2 416	2 013[10]	...	...	0.2	0.1	0.1	...	...
Ecuador - Équateur[11]											
Total	U	13 981	14 942	17 111	17 117	...	...	...	...	...	...
Peru - Pérou[12]											
Total	+C	2 825	...	...	...	...	0.1	...	...	...	...
Suriname[13]											
Total	C	663	645	...	...	...	1.3	1.3	...	...	...
Venezuela (Bolivarian Republic of) - Venezuela (République bolivarienne du)											
Total	...	24 841	28 823	29 044	...	...	...	...	...	...	...
ASIA - ASIE											
Armenia - Arménie											
Total	+C	2 797	2 931	3 031	2 829	...	0.9	0.9	0.9	0.9	...
Urban - Urbaine	+C	2 235	2 316	2 370	2 237	...	1.1	1.1	1.1	1.1	...
Rural - Rurale	+C	562	615	661	592	...	0.5	0.5	0.6	0.5	...
Azerbaijan - Azerbaïdjan											
Total	+C	7 817	8 340	7 933	7 784	9 061	0.9	1.0	0.9	0.9	1.0
Urban - Urbaine	+C	5 841	6 093	5 820	5 765	...	1.3	1.3	1.2	1.2	...
Rural - Rurale	+C	1 976	2 247	2 113	2 019	...	0.5	0.6	0.5	0.5	...
Bahrain - Bahreïn											
Total	...	1 141	1 198				...	...	...	...	...
Brunei Darussalam - Brunéi Darussalam											
Total	...	461	457	534	...	...	...	...	...	...	...
China - Chine[14]											
Total	+C	1 893 000	2 098 000	...	...	...	1.4	1.6	...	...	...
China, Hong Kong SAR - Chine, Hong Kong RAS											
Total	...	17 424	18 403	17 771	17 002	18 167	...	...	...	...	...
China, Macao SAR - Chine, Macao RAS											
Total	C	592	684	658	782	...	1.2	1.3	1.2	1.4	...
Cyprus - Chypre[15]											
Total	C	1 753	1 648	1 639	1 738	...	2.3	2.1	2.1	2.2	...
Urban - Urbaine[16]	C	1 424	1 256	1 256	...	...	...	...	...	...	...
Rural - Rurale[16]	C	268	329	304	...	...	...	...	...	...	...

24. Divorces and crude divorce rates by urban/rural residence: 2006 - 2010
Divorces et taux bruts de divortialité selon la résidence, urbaine/rurale : 2006 - 2010 (continued - suite)

Continent, country or area, and urban/rural residence / Continent, pays ou zone et résidence, urbaine/rurale	Co-de	Number - Nombre					Rate - Taux				
		2006	2007	2008	2009	2010	2006	2007	2008	2009	2010
ASIA - ASIE											
Georgia - Géorgie											
Total	C	2 060	2 325	3 189	...	4 726	0.5	0.5	0.7	...	...
Urban - Urbaine	C	1 987	2 239	2 665	...		0.9	1.0	1.2	...	...
Rural - Rurale	C	73	86	524	...	...	0.0	0.0	0.3	...	...
Indonesia - Indonésie											
Total	U	148 890	...	175 713	...		...	...	...	...	...
Iran (Islamic Republic of) - Iran (République islamique d')[17]											
Total	+C	94 040	99 852	110 510	125 747	...	1.3	1.4	1.5	1.7	...
Urban - Urbaine	+C	78 801	84 120	93 496	106 548	...	...	1.7	1.9	2.1	...
Rural - Rurale	+C	15 239	15 732	17 014	19 199	...	...	0.7	0.8	0.8	...
Israel - Israël[18]											
Total	C	13 439	13 105	13 488	...	...	1.9	1.8	1.8	...	...
Urban - Urbaine[16]	C	12 177	11 768	12 330	...	...	1.9	1.8	1.8	...	...
Rural - Rurale[16]	C	911	954	924	...	...	1.6	1.6	1.5	...	...
Japan - Japon[19]											
Total	+C	257 475	254 832	251 136	253 353	...	2.0	2.0	2.0	2.0	...
Urban - Urbaine	+C	232 234	231 106	228 233	230 655	...	...	...	...	...	...
Rural - Rurale	+C	25 241	23 726	22 903	22 698	...	...	...	...	...	...
Jordan - Jordanie[20]											
Total	+C	11 413	11 793	12 862	...		2.0	2.1	2.2		
Kazakhstan											
Total	C	35 834	36 107	35 852	...	...	2.3	2.3	2.3	...	...
Urban - Urbaine	C	29 533	28 011	27 475	...	...	3.4	3.4	3.3	...	...
Rural - Rurale	C	6 301	8 096	8 377	...	...	1.0	1.1	1.1	...	...
Kuwait - Koweït											
Total	C	4 239	4 945	4 907	...	...	1.8	2.1	2.0	...	...
Kyrgyzstan - Kirghizstan											
Total	C	6 870	7 371	7 419	7 381	...	1.4	1.5	1.5	1.4	...
Urban - Urbaine	C	3 947	4 113	4 144	4 044	...	2.2	2.3	2.3	2.2	...
Rural - Rurale	C	2 923	3 258	3 275	3 337	...	0.9	1.0	1.0	1.0	...
Lebanon - Liban											
Total	+C	4 388	5 859	5 389	5 957	5 897	...	1.6	...	...	...
Maldives											
Total	...	2 177	...	...	...		...	...	...	...	...
Urban - Urbaine	...	1 068	...	...	...		...	...	...	...	...
Rural - Rurale	...	1 109	...	...	...		...	...	...	...	...
Mongolia - Mongolie											
Total	C	1 448	1 757	1 901	...	...	0.6	0.7	0.7	...	...
Urban - Urbaine	C	1 310	1 590	1 745	...	...	0.8	1.0	1.1	...	...
Rural - Rurale	C	138	167	156	...	...	0.1	0.2	0.2	...	...
Occupied Palestinian Territory - Territoire palestinien occupé											
Total	C	3 756	4 043	4 399	...	...	1.0	1.1	1.1	...	...
Oman[21]											
Total	+U	...	...	...	2 675	...	...	...	...	...	...
Qatar											
Total	C	826	997	939	1 108	1 126	0.8	0.8	0.6	0.7	0.7
Republic of Korea - République de Corée[22]											
Total	+C	124 524	124 072	116 535	123 999	...	2.5	2.5	2.4	2.5	...
Urban - Urbaine[23]	+C	98 856	98 316	91 986	97 501	...	2.5	2.5	2.3	2.4	...
Rural - Rurale[23]	+C	22 576	22 429	20 934	22 818	...	2.4	2.4	2.2	2.4	...
Saudi Arabia - Arabie saoudite[24]											
Total	...	24 428	28 561	...	...		...	...	...	...	...
Singapore - Singapour											
Total	+C	6 679	6 827	6 852	7 033		1.5	1.5	1.4	1.4	...
Syrian Arab Republic - République arabe syrienne[25]											
Total	+U	19 984	19 506	...	...		...	...	...	...	...
Tajikistan - Tadjikistan											
Total	+C	3 018	4 752	5 178	5 593	...	0.4	0.7	0.7	...	...
Urban - Urbaine	+C	1 664	2 514	2 764	...	...	0.9	1.3	1.4	...	...
Rural - Rurale	+C	1 354	2 238	2 414	...	...	0.3	0.4	0.4	...	...

24. Divorces and crude divorce rates by urban/rural residence: 2006 - 2010
Divorces et taux bruts de divortialité selon la résidence, urbaine/rurale : 2006 - 2010 (continued - suite)

Continent, country or area, and urban/rural residence — Continent, pays ou zone et résidence, urbaine/rurale	Code — Co-de	Number - Nombre					Rate - Taux				
		2006	2007	2008	2009	2010	2006	2007	2008	2009	2010
ASIA - ASIE											
Turkey - Turquie[26]											
Total	C	93 489	94 219	99 663	114 162	116 369	1.3	1.3	1.4	1.6	1.6
United Arab Emirates - Émirats arabes unis[24]											
Total	...	2 491	2 783	3 855	...	...	...	...	...	...	...
Viet Nam											
Total	C	17 324	17 946	...	...	...	0.2	0.2	...	...	...
Urban - Urbaine	C	5 848	6 419	...	...	...	0.3	0.3	...	...	...
Rural - Rurale	C	11 476	11 527	...	...	...	0.2	0.2	...	...	...
EUROPE											
Åland Islands - Îles d'Åland											
Total	C	63	60	44	53	*52	2.3	2.2	1.6	1.9	*1.9
Urban - Urbaine	C	32	32	24	29	*25	3.0	2.9	...	...	...
Rural - Rurale	C	31	28	20	24	*27	1.9	...	...	...	...
Albania - Albanie											
Total	C	4 075	3 305	3 610	...	...	1.3	1.0	1.1		
Austria - Autriche[27]											
Total	C	20 336	20 516	19 701	18 806	17 474	2.5	2.5	2.4	2.2	2.1
Belarus - Bélarus											
Total	C	31 814	36 146	36 679	35 056	36 655	3.3	3.7	3.8	3.6	3.9
Urban - Urbaine	C	26 928	31 315	31 739	30 221	...	3.8	4.4	4.5	4.2	...
Rural - Rurale	C	4 886	4 831	4 940	4 835	...	1.8	1.9	1.9	1.9	...
Belgium - Belgique[28]											
Total	C	29 189	30 081	35 366	32 606	*33 000	2.8	2.8	3.3	3.0	*3.0
Urban - Urbaine	C	28 881	29 751	34 967	32 251	...	2.8	2.8	...	...	...
Rural - Rurale	C	308	330	399	355	...	2.0	2.2	...	...	...
Bosnia and Herzegovina - Bosnie-Herzégovine											
Total	C	1 659	1 826	1 369	1 402	*1 143	0.4	0.5	0.4	0.4	*0.3
Bulgaria - Bulgarie[29]											
Total	C	14 815	16 347[13]	14 104[13]	11 662[13]	11 012[13]	1.9	2.1	1.9	1.5	1.5
Urban - Urbaine	C	12 153	13 672[13]	11 515[13]	9 640[13]	...	2.2	2.5	2.1	1.8	...
Rural - Rurale	C	2 662	2 675[13]	2 589[13]	2 022[13]	...	1.2	1.2	1.2	0.9	...
Croatia - Croatie											
Total	C	4 651	4 785	5 025	5 076	5 058	1.0	1.1	1.1	1.1	1.1
Urban - Urbaine	C	3 371	3 375	3 492	3 476	...	...	...	...	...	...
Rural - Rurale	C	1 280	1 410	1 533	1 600	...	...	...	...	...	...
Czech Republic - Répùblique tchèque											
Total	C	31 415	31 129	31 300	29 133	30 783	3.1	3.0	3.0	2.8	2.9
Urban - Urbaine	C	25 214	24 627	24 574	22 147	...	3.3	3.2	3.2	2.9	...
Rural - Rurale	C	6 201	6 502	6 726	6 986	...	2.3	2.4	2.5	2.5	...
Denmark - Danemark[30]											
Total	C	14 343	14 066	14 695	14 940	14 460	2.6	2.6	2.7	2.7	2.6
Estonia - Estonie											
Total	C	3 811	3 809	3 501	3 189	2 989	2.8	2.8	2.6	2.4	2.2
Urban - Urbaine[31]	C	2 676	2 653	2 488	2 242	...	2.9	2.8	2.7	2.4	...
Rural - Rurale[31]	C	1 058	1 072	919	856	...	2.6	2.6	2.2	2.1	...
Faeroe Islands - Îles Féroé											
Total	C	69	64	...	...	...	1.4	1.3	...	...	...
Urban - Urbaine	C	24	31	...	...	...	...	1.8	...	...	...
Rural - Rurale	C	45	33	...	...	...	1.5	1.1	...	...	...
Finland - Finlande[13]											
Total	C	13 255[32]	13 224[32]	13 471[32]	13 474[33]	13 619	2.5	2.5	2.5	2.5	2.6
Urban - Urbaine	C	9 900[32]	9 836[32]	10 079[32]	10 100[33]	...	2.8	2.8	2.8	2.8	...
Rural - Rurale	C	3 355[32]	3 388[32]	3 392[32]	3 374[33]	...	2.0	2.0	2.0	2.0	...
France											
Total	C	135 910	131 316	129 379	...	...	2.2	2.1	2.1	...	...
Germany - Allemagne											
Total	C	190 928	187 072	191 948	185 817	185 817	2.3	2.3	2.3	2.3	2.3
Gibraltar											
Total	+C	121	96	78	...	...	4.2	3.3	2.7	...	...

Continent, country or area, and urban/rural residence — Continent, pays ou zone et résidence, urbaine/rurale	Co-de	Number - Nombre					Rate - Taux				
		2006	2007	2008	2009	2010	2006	2007	2008	2009	2010
EUROPE											
Greece - Grèce											
Total	C	13 218	12 994	13 163	...	...	1.2	1.2	1.2	...	...
Hungary - Hongrie[13]											
Total	C	24 869	25 160	25 155	23 820	*23 800	2.5	2.5	2.5	2.4	*2.4
Urban - Urbaine[34]	C	17 911	18 281	18 294	17 441	...	2.7	2.7	2.7	2.5	...
Rural - Rurale[34]	C	6 730	6 756	6 689	6 216	...	2.0	2.0	2.1	2.0	...
Iceland - Islande[35]											
Total	C	516	526	560	550	563	1.7	1.7	1.8	1.7	1.8
Urban - Urbaine	C	493	504	527	527	...	1.7	1.7	1.8	1.8	...
Rural - Rurale	C	23	22	33	23	...	...	...	1.5	...	...
Ireland - Irlande											
Total[36]	C	3 466	3 684	...	...	...	0.8	0.8	...	...	...
Total	+C	...	...	3 630	*3 341	3 113	...	...	0.8	*0.7	0.7
Italy - Italie											
Total	C	49 534	50 669	54 351	54 456	...	0.8	0.9	0.9	0.9	...
Latvia - Lettonie											
Total	C	7 249	7 403	6 214	5 099	4 930	3.2	3.3	2.7	2.3	2.2
Urban - Urbaine	C	5 545	5 535	4 582	3 813	...	3.6	3.6	3.0	2.5	...
Rural - Rurale	C	1 704	1 868	1 632	1 286	...	2.3	2.6	2.2	1.8	...
Liechtenstein											
Total	C	81	97	97	*101	*86	2.3	2.7	2.7	*2.8	*2.4
Lithuania - Lituanie											
Total	C	11 202	11 336	10 317	9 270	10 006	3.3	3.4	3.1	2.8	3.0
Urban - Urbaine	C	7 946	8 044	7 145	6 451	...	3.5	3.6	3.2	2.9	...
Rural - Rurale	C	3 256	3 292	3 172	2 819	...	2.9	2.9	2.9	2.6	...
Luxembourg											
Total	C	1 182	1 106	977	1 052	1 083	2.5	2.3	2.0	2.1	2.1
Montenegro - Monténégro											
Total	C	470	453	460	456	520	0.8	0.7	0.7	0.7	0.8
Urban - Urbaine	C	...	...	435	440	...	...	...	1.1	1.1	...
Rural - Rurale	C	...	...	25	16	...	...	...	...	...	...
Netherlands - Pays-Bas[37]											
Total	C	31 734	31 983	32 236	30 779[39]	...	1.9	2.0	2.0	1.9	...
Urban - Urbaine	C	22 019[38]	22 008[38]	22 607[38]	21 492[40]	...	2.0	2.0	2.1	2.0	...
Rural - Rurale	C	9 195[38]	9 457[38]	9 175[38]	8 802[40]	...	1.7	1.7	1.6	1.6	...
Norway - Norvège[41]											
Total	C	10 598	10 280	10 158	10 235	11 740	2.3	2.2	2.1	2.1	2.4
Poland - Pologne											
Total	C	71 912	66 586	65 475	65 345	61 300	1.9	1.7	1.7	1.7	1.6
Urban - Urbaine[42]	C	57 915	53 210	51 946	51 398	...	2.5	2.3	2.2	2.2	...
Rural - Rurale[42]	C	13 807	12 968	13 059	13 457	...	0.9	0.9	0.9	0.9	...
Portugal											
Total	C	23 935	25 411	26 394	26 464	...	2.3	2.4	2.5	2.5	...
Republic of Moldova - République de Moldova											
Total	C	12 594	13 923	12 601	11 884	11 504	3.5	3.9	3.5	3.3	3.2
Urban - Urbaine	C	9 652	11 003	10 749	10 300	...	6.5	7.4	7.3	7.0	...
Rural - Rurale	C	2 942	2 920	1 852	1 584	...	1.4	1.4	0.9	0.8	...
Romania - Roumanie											
Total	C	32 672	36 308	35 685	32 341	32 632	1.5	1.7	1.7	1.5	1.5
Urban - Urbaine	C	23 338	26 066	24 806	22 308	...	2.0	2.2	2.1	1.9	...
Rural - Rurale	C	9 334	10 242	10 879	10 033	...	1.0	1.1	1.1	1.0	...
Russian Federation - Fédération de Russie											
Total	C	640 837	685 910	703 412	699 430	639 321	4.5	4.8	5.0	4.9	4.5
Serbia - Serbie[43]											
Total	+C	8 204	8 622	8 502	8 505	6 644	1.1	1.2	1.2	1.2	0.9
Urban - Urbaine	+C	5 707	6 170	6 061	5 965	...	1.3	1.4	1.4	1.4	...
Rural - Rurale	+C	2 497	2 452	2 441	2 540	...	0.8	0.8	0.8	0.8	...
Slovakia - Slovaquie											
Total	C	12 716	12 174	12 675	12 671	12 015	2.4	2.3	2.3	2.3	2.2
Urban - Urbaine	C	8 926	8 378	8 637	8 311	...	3.0	2.8	2.9	2.8	...
Rural - Rurale	C	3 790	3 796	4 038	4 360	...	1.6	1.6	1.7	1.8	...
Slovenia - Slovénie											
Total	C	2 334	2 617	2 246	2 297	*2 393	1.2	1.3	1.1	1.1	*1.2
Urban - Urbaine	C	1 379	1 473	1 266	1 290	...	1.4	1.5	1.3	1.3	...
Rural - Rurale	C	955	1 144	980	1 007	...	1.0	1.1	1.0	1.0	...

24. Divorces and crude divorce rates by urban/rural residence: 2006 - 2010
Divorces et taux bruts de divortialité selon la résidence, urbaine/rurale : 2006 - 2010 (continued - suite)

Continent, country or area, and urban/rural residence Continent, pays ou zone et résidence, urbaine/rurale	Co-de	Number - Nombre					Rate - Taux				
		2006	2007	2008	2009	2010	2006	2007	2008	2009	2010
EUROPE											
Spain - Espagne											
Total	C	126 952	125 721	109 922	98 207	102 690	2.9	2.8	2.4	2.1	2.2
Sweden - Suède											
Total	C	20 295	20 669	21 377	22 211	23 593	2.2	2.3	2.3	2.4	2.5
Switzerland - Suisse											
Total	C	20 981	19 882	19 613	19 321	*21 500	2.8	2.6	2.6	2.5	*2.7
Urban - Urbaine[44]	C	16 469	15 578	15 279	15 063	...	3.0	2.8	2.7	2.6	...
Rural - Rurale[44]	C	4 512	4 304	4 334	4 258	...	2.3	2.1	2.1	2.1	...
TFYR of Macedonia - L'ex-R. y. de Macédoine											
Total	C	1 475	1 417	1 209	1 287	*1 720	0.7	0.7	0.6	0.6	*0.8
Urban - Urbaine	C	...	848	735	760	...	...	...	...	...	...
Rural - Rurale	C	...	569	474	527	...	...	...	...	...	...
Ukraine											
Total	C	179 123	178 364	166 845	145 439	126 068	3.8	3.8	3.6	3.2	2.7
Urban - Urbaine	C	138 993	138 630	128 909	...	...	4.4	4.4	4.1	...	...
Rural - Rurale	C	40 130	39 734	37 936	...	...	2.7	2.7	2.6	...	...
United Kingdom of Great Britain and Northern Ireland - Royaume-Uni de Grande-Bretagne et d'Irlande du Nord[45]											
Total	C	148 141	143 958	136 065	*126 500	...	2.4	2.4	2.2	*2.0	...
OCEANIA - OCÉANIE											
Australia - Australie											
Total	C	51 375	47 963	47 209	49 448	...	2.5	2.3	2.2	2.3	...
New Zealand - Nouvelle-Zélande											
Total	+C	10 065	9 650	9 713	8 737	...	2.4	2.3	2.3	2.0	...
Northern Mariana Islands - Îles Mariannes septentrionales[46]											
Total	U	*183*	*160*	...	...	...	...	...	...	...	...
Samoa											
Total	U	*32*	*35*	*10*	*48*	...	...	...	...	...	...

FOOTNOTES - NOTES

Italics: data from civil registers which are incomplete or of unknown completeness. - Italiques : données incomplètes ou dont le degré d'exactitude n'est pas connu, provenant des registres de l'état civil.

* Provisional. - Données provisoires.

'Code' indicates the source of data, as follows:
C - Civil registration, estimated over 90% complete
U - Civil registration, estimated less than 90% complete
| - Other source, estimated reliable
+ - Data tabulated by date of registration rather than occurence
... - Information not available

Le 'Code' indique la source des données, comme suit :
C - Registres de l'état civil considérés complèts à 90 p. 100 au moins
U - Registres de l'état civil qui ne sont pas considérés complèts à 90 p. 100 au moins
| - Autre source, considérée pas douteuses
+ - Données exploitées selon la date de l'enregistrement et non la date de l'événement
... - Information pas disponible

[1] Including 'revocable divorces' (among Moslem population), which approximate legal separations. - Y compris les 'divorces révocables' (parmi la population musulmane), qui sont plus au moins l'équivalent des séparations légales.
[2] Excludes the islands of St. Brandon and Agalega. - Non compris les îles St. Brandon et Agalega.
[3] Refers to registered divorces only. - Les données ne portent que sur les divorces enregistrés.
[4] Urban and rural distribution refers to the usual residence of the bride/wife. Unrevised data. - La répartition urbain/rural se réfère au domicile habituel de la jeune mariée/de l'épouse. Les données n'ont pas été révisées.
[5] Decrease in divorces is due to amendments made to Matrimonial Causes Rules in 2006, which resulted in a considerable backlog of divorce petitions. - La diminution du nombre de divorces s'explique par les modifications apportées au Règlement concernant les affaires matrimoniales en 2006, qui a provoqué un important retard dans le traitement des demandes de divorce.
[6] Urban and rural distribution refers to the usual residence of the bride/wife. The difference between 'Total' and the sum of urban and rural is due to the unknown place of residence of bride/wife. - La répartition urbain/rural se réfère au domicile habituel de la jeune mariée/de l'épouse. La différence entre le total et la somme des chiffres urbains et ruraux s'explique par le lieu de résidence inconnu des maris.
[7] Data include those that have been issued with divorce nisi only. - Jugements de divorce provisoire inclus.
[8] Excluding Indian jungle population. - Non compris les Indiens de la jungle.
[9] A new divorce law took effect from October 2005. - Une nouvelle loi sur le divorce est entrée en vigueur en octobre 2005.

Table 25

Table 25 presents the number of divorces according to the duration of marriage and the percentage distribution for the latest available year between 2001 and 2010.

Description of variables: Divorces are the final legal dissolutions of a marriage, which confer on the parties the right to remarry as defined by the laws of each country or area. Unless otherwise noted, divorce statistics exclude legal separations which do not allow remarriage. These statistics refer to the number of divorces granted, and not to the number of persons divorcing.

Duration of marriage is defined as the interval of time between the day, month and year of marriage and the day, month and year of divorce in completed years. It will be noted that this definition refers to the "legal" duration rather than the "effective" duration, it having been calculated until the day, month and year of the actual divorce decree rather than until the separation date or the date when the couple ceased to live as man and wife.

The duration of marriage classification used in this table to the extent possible, is the following: under one year, single years of duration through 9 years, 10-14 years, 15-19 years, 20 years and over and duration unknown, when appropriate.

Reliability of data: Data from civil registers of divorces which are reported as incomplete (less than 90 per cent completeness) or of unknown completeness are considered unreliable and are set in italics rather than in roman type. For more information about the quality of vital statistics data in general, see section 4.2 of the Technical Notes.

Limitations: Statistics on divorces by duration of marriage are subject to the same qualifications which have been set forth for vital statistics in general and divorce statistics in particular as discussed in Section 4 of the Technical Notes.

Earlier data: Divorces by duration by marriage, cross-classified by age of husband and by age of wife have been shown previously in issues of the Demographic Yearbook featuring marriage and divorce. For information on years covered, readers should consult the Historical Index.

Tableau 25

Le tableau 25 indique le nombre de divorces selon la durée du mariage et la répartition des pourcentages, pour la dernière année disponible entre 2001 et 2010.

Description des variables : le divorce est la dissolution définitive des liens du mariage qui confère aux parties le droit de se remarier, telle qu'elle est définie par la législation de chaque pays ou zone. Sauf indication contraire, les statistiques de la divortialité n'englobent pas les séparations légales qui excluent le remariage. Ces statistiques se rapportent aux jugements de divorce prononcés, non aux personnes divorcées.

La durée du mariage correspond à l'intervalle du temps qui s'est écoulé entre la date exacte (jour, mois et année) du mariage et la date exacte (jour, mois et année) du divorce exprimé en années révolues. On notera que cette définition est celle de la durée "légale" du mariage et non de sa durée "effective", puisque la durée est calculée jusqu'à la date (jour, mois et année) du jugement de divorce et non jusqu'à la date de la séparation ou la date à laquelle le couple a cessé de vivre comme mari et femme.

Le classement selon la durée du mariage utilisé dans ce tableau dans la mesure du possible comprend les catégories suivantes : moins d'un an, une catégorie par an jusqu'à 9 ans inclus, 10-14 ans, 15-19 ans, 20 ans et plus et, le cas échéant, une catégorie pour la durée du mariage inconnue.

Fiabilité des données : les données sur les divorces provenant des registres de l'état civil qui sont déclarées incomplètes (degré de complétude inférieur à 90 pour cent) ou dont le degré de complétude n'est pas connu, sont jugées douteuses et apparaissent en italique et non en caractères romains. Pour plus de précisions sur la qualité des données reposant sur les statistiques de l'état civil en general, voir la section 4.2 des Notes techniques.

Insuffisance des données : les statistiques des divorces selon la durée du mariage, appellent toutes les réserves qui ont été formulées à propos des statistiques de l'état civil en general et des statistiques des divorces en particulier (voir les explications figurant à la section 4 des Notes techniques).

Données publiées antérieurement : les statistiques des divorces selon la durée du mariage, classées selon l'âge de l'époux, d'une part, et selon l'âge de l'épouse, d'autre part, ont été présentées dans des éditions antérieures de l'Annuaire démographique qui avaient comme sujet spécial la nuptialité et la divortialité. Pour plus de précisions concernant les années pour lesquelles ces données ont été publiées, on se reportera à l'index historique.

25. Divorces and percentage distribution by duration of marriage, latest available year: 2001 - 2010
Divorces et répartition des pourcentages selon la durée du mariage, dernière année disponible: 2001 - 2010

Continent, country or area, year, code and duration of marriage (in years) / Continent, pays ou zone, année, code et durée du mariage (en années)	Number of divorces / Nombre de divorces	Per cent / Pour cent
AFRICA - AFRIQUE		
Egypt - Égypte		
2009 (U)		
Total	141 467	100.0
Less than 1 - Moins de 1	23 158	16.4
1	18 226	12.9
2	12 464	8.8
3	8 567	6.1
4	7 470	5.3
5	5 577	3.9
6	4 348	3.1
7	3 523	2.5
8	3 590	2.5
9	3 211	2.3
10 - 14	8 821	6.2
15 - 19	5 389	3.8
20 +	7 261	5.1
Not stated - Inconnu	29 862	21.1
Mauritius - Maurice[1]		
2009 (+C)		
Total	2 154	100.0
Less than 1 - Moins de 1	9	0.4
1	44	2.0
2	118	5.5
3	121	5.6
4	126	5.8
5	129	6.0
6	144	6.7
7	133	6.2
8	113	5.2
9	119	5.5
10 - 14	467	21.7
15 - 19	287	13.3
20 +	344	16.0
South Africa - Afrique du Sud		
2008 (...)		
Total	28 924	100.0
Less than 1 - Moins de 1	189	0.7
1	988	3.4
2	1 476	5.1
3	1 667	5.8
4	1 823	6.3
5	1 797	6.2
6	1 651	5.7
7	1 555	5.4
8	1 524	5.3
9	1 332	4.6
10 - 14	5 540	19.2
15 - 19	3 686	12.7
20 +	4 570	15.8
Not stated - Inconnu	1 126	3.9
AMERICA, NORTH - AMÉRIQUE DU NORD		
Aruba		
2007 (C)		
Total	417	100.0
Less than 1 - Moins de 1	-	0.0
1	12	2.9
2	30	7.2
3	15	3.6
4	18	4.3
5	42	10.1
6	26	6.2
7	13	3.1
8	12	2.9
9	25	6.0
AMERICA, NORTH - AMÉRIQUE DU NORD		
Aruba		
2007 (C)		
10 - 14	84	20.1
15 - 19	61	14.6
20 +	55	13.2
Not stated - Inconnu	24	5.8
Bermuda - Bermudes		
2009 (C)		
Total	177	100.0
Less than 1 - Moins de 1	-	0.0
1	3	1.7
2	5	2.8
3	18	10.2
4	14	7.9
5	9	5.1
6	4	2.3
7	13	7.3
8	9	5.1
9	11	6.2
10 - 14	47	26.6
15 - 19	26	14.7
20 +	18	10.2
Not stated - Inconnu	-	0.0
Canada		
2004 (C)		
Total	69 644	100.0
Less than 1 - Moins de 1	149	0.2
1	1 360	2.0
2	3 298	4.7
3	4 166	6.0
4	3 757	5.4
5	3 587	5.2
6	3 312	4.8
7	3 076	4.4
8	3 040	4.4
9	2 744	3.9
10 - 14	12 312	17.7
15 - 19	9 816	14.1
20 +	19 024	27.3
Not stated - Inconnu	3	0.0
Cuba		
2009 (C)		
Total	35 034	100.0
Less than 1 - Moins de 1	2 695	7.7
1	2 880	8.2
2 - 4	2 588	7.4
5 - 8	5 675	16.2
9	5 018	14.3
10 - 24	4 836	13.8
25 +	468	1.3
Not stated - Inconnu	468	1.3
El Salvador[2]		
2007 (...)		
Total	6 335	100.0
Less than 1 - Moins de 1	294	4.6
1	261	4.1
2	212	3.3
3	234	3.7
4	259	4.1
5	332	5.2
6	329	5.2
7	361	5.7
8	290	4.6
9	294	4.6
10 - 14	1 291	20.4
15 - 19	853	13.5
20 +	1 325	20.9
Not stated - Inconnu	-	0.0

Continent, country or area, year, code and duration of marriage (in years) / Continent, pays ou zone, année, code et durée du mariage (en années)	Number of divorces / Nombre de divorces	Per cent / Pour cent
AMERICA, NORTH - AMÉRIQUE DU NORD		
Jamaica - Jamaïque[3]		
2007 (C)		
Total	1 140	100.0
Less than 1 - Moins de 1	-	0.0
1	1	0.1
2	3	0.3
3	22	1.9
4	42	3.7
5	53	4.6
6	62	5.4
7	89	7.8
8	96	8.4
9	75	6.6
10 - 14	294	25.8
15 - 19	160	14.0
20 +	242	21.2
Mexico - Mexique[4]		
2009* (+C)		
Total	84 302	100.0
Less than 1 - Moins de 1	3 706	4.4
1	4 379	5.2
2	4 711	5.6
3	4 575	5.4
4	4 344	5.2
5	4 043	4.8
6	3 992	4.7
7	4 045	4.8
8	3 834	4.5
9	3 697	4.4
10 - 14	13 922	16.5
15 - 19	10 124	12.0
20 +	17 698	21.0
Not stated - Inconnu	1 232	1.5
Panama		
2009 (C)		
Total	3 469	100.0
Less than 5 - Moins de 5	797	23.0
5 - 9	676	19.5
10 - 14	604	17.4
15 - 19	447	12.9
20 +	945	27.2
Saint Lucia - Sainte-Lucie[5]		
2002 (C)		
Total	40	100.0
Less than 5 - Moins de 5	2	5.0
5	4	10.0
6	2	5.0
7	2	5.0
8	2	5.0
9	-	0.0
10 - 14	12	30.0
15 - 19	8	20.0
20 +	8	20.0
Not stated - Inconnu	-	0.0
Trinidad and Tobago - Trinité-et-Tobago		
2005 (C)		
Total	2 785	100.0
Less than 1 - Moins de 1	-	0.0
1	40	1.4
2	77	2.8
3	80	2.9
4	92	3.3
5	142	5.1
6	149	5.4
7	120	4.3
8	144	5.2
9	111	4.0

Continent, country or area, year, code and duration of marriage (in years) / Continent, pays ou zone, année, code et durée du mariage (en années)	Number of divorces / Nombre de divorces	Per cent / Pour cent
AMERICA, NORTH - AMÉRIQUE DU NORD		
Trinidad and Tobago - Trinité-et-Tobago		
2005 (C)		
10 - 14	572	20.5
15 - 19	417	15.0
20 +	838	30.1
Not stated - Inconnu	3	0.1
Turks and Caicos Islands - Îles Turques et Caïques		
2005 (C)		
Total	24	100.0
Less than 1 - Moins de 1	-	0.0
1	-	0.0
2	-	0.0
3	-	0.0
4	2	8.3
5	3	12.5
6	3	12.5
7	2	8.3
8	4	16.7
9	1	4.2
10 - 14	5	20.8
15 - 19	2	8.3
20 +	2	8.3
Not stated - Inconnu	-	0.0
AMERICA, SOUTH - AMÉRIQUE DU SUD		
Brazil - Brésil[6]		
2009 (...)		
Total	174 747	100.0
Less than 2 - Moins de 2	335	0.2
2	4 757	2.7
3	6 693	3.8
4	7 260	4.2
5	7 093	4.1
6	6 718	3.8
7	6 616	3.8
8	6 540	3.7
9	6 800	3.9
10 - 14	27 306	15.6
15 - 19	22 482	12.9
20 +	70 984	40.6
Not stated - Inconnu	1 163	0.7
Chile - Chili		
2007 (C)		
Total	2 416	100.0
Less than 1 - Moins de 1	57	2.4
1	67	2.8
2	118	4.9
3	85	3.5
4	69	2.9
5	65	2.7
6	84	3.5
7	82	3.4
8	66	2.7
9	67	2.8
10 - 14	377	15.6
15 - 19	320	13.2
20 +	653	27.0
Not stated - Inconnu	306	12.7
Ecuador - Équateur[7]		
2009 (U)		
Total	17 117	100.0
Less than 1 - Moins de 1	190	1.1
1	547	3.2
2	708	4.1

Continent, country or area, year, code and duration of marriage (in years) / Continent, pays ou zone, année, code et durée du mariage (en années)	Number of divorces / Nombre de divorces	Per cent / Pour cent
AMERICA, SOUTH - AMÉRIQUE DU SUD		
Ecuador - Équateur[7]		
2009 (U)		
3	790	4.6
4	714	4.2
5	724	4.2
6	730	4.3
7	768	4.5
8	757	4.4
9	790	4.6
10 - 14	3 260	19.0
15 - 19	2 503	14.6
20 +	4 636	27.1
Suriname[8]		
2005 (C)		
Total	724	100.0
Less than 1 - Moins de 1	17	2.3
1 - 3	73	10.1
4 - 6	119	16.4
7 - 9	113	15.6
10 - 12	99	13.7
13 - 15	63	8.7
16 - 18	62	8.6
19 - 21	54	7.5
22 - 24	34	4.7
25 +	90	12.4
Not stated - Inconnu	-	0.0
Uruguay		
2002 (+C)		
Total	6 761	100.0
Less than 1 - Moins de 1	48	0.7
1	113	1.7
2	198	2.9
3	252	3.7
4	284	4.2
5	331	4.9
6	354	5.2
7	360	5.3
8	316	4.7
9	284	4.2
10 - 14	1 265	18.7
15 - 19	1 006	14.9
20 +	1 950	28.8
Venezuela (Bolivarian Republic of) - Venezuela (République bolivarienne du)		
2008 (...)		
Total	29 044	100.0
Less than 1 - Moins de 1	54	0.2
1 - 4	1 992	6.9
5 - 9	7 527	25.9
10 - 14	6 757	23.3
15 - 19	5 530	19.0
20 +	7 062	24.3
Not stated - Inconnu	122	0.4
ASIA - ASIE		
Armenia - Arménie		
2009 (+C)		
Total	2 829	100.0
Less than 1 - Moins de 1	92	3.3
1	161	5.7
2	148	5.2
3	126	4.5
4	117	4.1
5 - 9	445	15.7
10 - 14	426	15.1
ASIA - ASIE		
Armenia - Arménie		
2009 (+C)		
15 - 19	514	18.2
20 +	800	28.3
Azerbaijan - Azerbaïdjan		
2009 (+C)		
Total	7 784	100.0
Less than 1 - Moins de 1	146	1.9
1	564	7.2
2	638	8.2
3	675	8.7
4	613	7.9
5	502	6.4
6	398	5.1
7	306	3.9
8	277	3.6
9	315	4.0
10 - 14	1 222	15.7
15 - 19	1 037	13.3
20 +	1 091	14.0
Bahrain - Bahreïn		
2006 (...)		
Total	1 141	100.0
Less than 1 - Moins de 1	233	20.4
1 - 2	247	21.6
3 - 4	120	10.5
5 - 6	89	7.8
7 - 9	73	6.4
10 - 14	82	7.2
15 - 19	44	3.9
20 +	59	5.2
Not stated - Inconnu	194	17.0
Brunei Darussalam - Brunéi Darussalam		
2008 (...)		
Total	534	100.0
Less than 1 - Moins de 1	7	1.3
1	18	3.4
2	30	5.6
3	35	6.6
4	43	8.1
5	53	9.9
6	32	6.0
7	43	8.1
8	32	6.0
9	30	5.6
10 - 14	92	17.2
15 - 19	52	9.7
20 +	67	12.5
Not stated - Inconnu	-	0.0
China, Macao SAR - Chine, Macao RAS		
2009 (C)		
Total	782	100.0
Less than 5 - Moins de 5	128	16.4
5 - 9	192	24.6
10 - 14	174	22.3
15 - 19	107	13.7
20 +	181	23.1
Cyprus - Chypre[9]		
2009 (C)		
Total	1 738	100.0
Less than 1 - Moins de 1	66	3.8
1	142	8.2
2	107	6.2
3	127	7.3
4	120	6.9
5	106	6.1
6	108	6.2
7	84	4.8

Continent, country or area, year, code and duration of marriage (in years) / Continent, pays ou zone, année, code et durée du mariage (en années)	Number of divorces / Nombre de divorces	Per cent / Pour cent
ASIA - ASIE		
Cyprus - Chypre[9]		
2009 (C)		
8	80	4.6
9	60	3.5
10 - 14	267	15.4
15 - 19	167	9.6
20 +	304	17.5
Georgia - Géorgie		
2008 (C)		
Total	3 189	100.0
Less than 1 - Moins de 1	105	3.3
1	152	4.8
2	129	4.0
3	124	3.9
4	116	3.6
5 - 9	588	18.4
10 - 14	613	19.2
15 - 19	539	16.9
20 +	641	20.1
Not stated - Inconnu	182	5.7
Israel - Israël[10]		
2008 (C)		
Total	13 488	100.0
Less than 1 - Moins de 1	380	2.8
1	815	6.0
2	741	5.5
3	698	5.2
4	659	4.9
5	555	4.1
6	528	3.9
7	497	3.7
8	468	3.5
9	441	3.3
10 - 14	1 790	13.3
15 - 19	1 195	8.9
20 +	2 650	19.6
Not stated - Inconnu	2 071	15.4
Japan - Japon[11]		
2009 (+C)		
Total	253 353	100.0
Less than 1 - Moins de 1	16 584	6.5
1	19 480	7.7
2	18 250	7.2
3	16 187	6.4
4	14 181	5.6
5 - 9	53 652	21.2
10 - 14	34 180	13.5
15 - 19	24 983	9.9
20 +	40 096	15.8
Not stated - Inconnu	15 760	6.2
Kazakhstan		
2008 (C)		
Total	35 852	100.0
Less than 1 - Moins de 1	1 647	4.6
1	2 482	6.9
2	2 690	7.5
3	2 516	7.0
4	2 373	6.6
5 - 9	7 939	22.1
10 - 14	5 756	16.1
15 - 19	4 717	13.2
20 +	5 730	16.0
Not stated - Inconnu	2	0.0
Kuwait - Koweït		
2008 (C)		
Total	4 907	100.0
Less than 1 - Moins de 1	1 383	28.2

Continent, country or area, year, code and duration of marriage (in years) / Continent, pays ou zone, année, code et durée du mariage (en années)	Number of divorces / Nombre de divorces	Per cent / Pour cent
ASIA - ASIE		
Kuwait - Koweït		
2008 (C)		
1	797	16.2
2	521	10.6
3	319	6.5
4	258	5.3
5 - 9	716	14.6
10 - 14	342	7.0
15 - 19	227	4.6
20 +	344	7.0
Kyrgyzstan - Kirghizstan		
2009 (C)		
Total	7 381	100.0
Less than 1 - Moins de 1	737	10.0
1	404	5.5
2	444	6.0
3	446	6.0
4	403	5.5
5	377	5.1
6	380	5.1
7	285	3.9
8	250	3.4
9	254	3.4
10 - 14	1 021	13.8
15 - 19	1 175	15.9
20 +	1 205	16.3
Mongolia - Mongolie		
2008 (C)		
Total	1 901	100.0
Less than 1 - Moins de 1	99	5.2
1 - 3	290	15.3
4 - 6	267	14.0
7 - 9	298	15.7
10 - 14	388	20.4
15 - 19	328	17.3
20 +	231	12.2
Occupied Palestinian Territory - Territoire palestinien occupé		
2007 (C)		
Total	4 043	100.0
Less than 1 - Moins de 1	1 792	44.3
1	660	16.3
2	320	7.9
3	228	5.6
4	139	3.4
5	107	2.6
6	104	2.6
7	82	2.0
8	50	1.2
9	62	1.5
10 - 14	191	4.7
15 - 19	139	3.4
20 +	169	4.2
Not stated - Inconnu	1	0.0
Qatar		
2009 (C)		
Total	1 108	100.0
Less than 1 - Moins de 1	43	3.9
1	78	7.0
2	106	9.6
3	96	8.7
4	60	5.4
5 - 9	172	15.5
10 - 14	105	9.5
15 - 19	51	4.6
20 +	61	5.5
Not stated - Inconnu	336[12]	30.3

25. Divorces and percentage distribution by duration of marriage, latest available year: 2001 - 2010
Divorces et répartition des pourcentages selon la durée du mariage, dernière année disponible: 2001 - 2010 (continued - suite)

Continent, country or area, year, code and duration of marriage (in years) / Continent, pays ou zone, année, code et durée du mariage (en années)	Number of divorces / Nombre de divorces	Per cent / Pour cent
ASIA - ASIE		
Republic of Korea - République de Corée[13]		
2009 (+C)		
Total	123 999	100.0
Less than 1 - Moins de 1	6 255	5.0
1	7 636	6.2
2	7 224	5.8
3	6 613	5.3
4	5 990	4.8
5	5 492	4.4
6	4 811	3.9
7	4 412	3.6
8	4 282	3.5
9	4 639	3.7
10 - 14	19 986	16.1
15 - 19	18 398	14.8
20 +	28 261	22.8
Not stated - Inconnu	-	0.0
Singapore - Singapour		
2009 (+C)		
Total	7 033	100.0
Less than 5 - Moins de 5	1 267	18.0
5 - 9	2 228	31.7
10 - 14	1 358	19.3
15 - 19	850	12.1
20 +	1 330	18.9
Tajikistan - Tadjikistan		
2008 (+C)		
Total	5 178	100.0
Less than 1 - Moins de 1	518	10.0
1	451	8.7
2	379	7.3
3	345	6.7
4	305	5.9
5	225	4.3
6	207	4.0
7	183	3.5
8	180	3.5
9	168	3.2
10 - 14	785	15.2
15 - 19	648	12.5
20 +	602	11.6
Not stated - Inconnu	217	4.2
Turkey - Turquie[14]		
2009 (C)		
Total	114 162	100.0
Less than 1 - Moins de 1	4 020	3.5
1	10 439	9.1
2	9 174	8.0
3	8 095	7.1
4	7 379	6.5
5	6 696	5.9
6	5 647	4.9
7	5 004	4.4
8	4 760	4.2
9	4 401	3.9
10 - 14	17 732	15.5
15 - 19	12 529	11.0
20 +	17 860	15.6
EUROPE		
Austria - Autriche[15]		
2009 (C)		
Total	18 806	100.0
Less than 1 - Moins de 1	364	1.9
1	873	4.6
EUROPE		
Austria - Autriche[15]		
2009 (C)		
2	1 093	5.8
3	1 390	7.4
4	1 259	6.7
5	1 166	6.2
6	909	4.8
7	791	4.2
8	742	3.9
9	721	3.8
10 - 14	2 967	15.8
15 - 19	2 406	12.8
20 +	4 125	21.9
Belarus - Bélarus		
2009 (C)		
Total	35 056	100.0
Less than 1 - Moins de 1	1 084	3.1
1	2 918	8.3
2	2 907	8.3
3	2 708	7.7
4	2 248	6.4
5 - 9	8 939	25.5
10 - 14	5 400	15.4
15 - 19	3 578	10.2
20 +	5 274	15.0
Belgium - Belgique[16]		
2009 (C)		
Total	32 606	100.0
Less than 1 - Moins de 1	131	0.4
1	748	2.3
2	1 725	5.3
3	1 939	5.9
4	1 959	6.0
5	1 773	5.4
6	1 524	4.7
7	1 310	4.0
8	1 306	4.0
9	1 297	4.0
10 - 14	5 050	15.5
15 - 19	4 769	14.6
20 +	9 075	27.8
Bosnia and Herzegovina - Bosnie-Herzégovine		
2009 (C)		
Total	1 402	100.0
Less than 1 - Moins de 1	83	5.9
1	138	9.8
2	113	8.1
3	97	6.9
4	86	6.1
5	84	6.0
6	84	6.0
7	44	3.1
8	63	4.5
9	45	3.2
10 - 14	189	13.5
15 - 19	107	7.6
20 +	269	19.2
Bulgaria - Bulgarie[17]		
2009 (C)		
Total	11 662	100.0
Less than 1 - Moins de 1	137	1.2
1	336	2.9
2	491	4.2
3	581	5.0
4	521	4.5
5	497	4.3

Continent, country or area, year, code and duration of marriage (in years) Continent, pays ou zone, année, code et durée du mariage (en années)	Number of divorces Nombre de divorces	Per cent Pour cent
EUROPE		
Bulgaria - Bulgarie[17]		
2009 (C)		
6	470	4.0
7	386	3.3
8	405	3.5
9	460	3.9
10 - 14	1 990	17.1
15 - 19	2 127	18.2
20 +	3 261	28.0
Croatia - Croatie		
2009 (C)		
Total	5 076	100.0
Less than 1 - Moins de 1	92	1.8
1	201	4.0
2	266	5.2
3	296	5.8
4	264	5.2
5	286	5.6
6	250	4.9
7	232	4.6
8	222	4.4
9	210	4.1
10 - 14	811	16.0
15 - 19	606	11.9
20 +	1 340	26.4
Czech Republic - République tchèque		
2009 (C)		
Total	29 133	100.0
Less than 1 - Moins de 1	302	1.0
1	1 205	4.1
2	1 449	5.0
3	1 380	4.7
4	1 365	4.7
5	1 206	4.1
6	1 216	4.2
7	1 228	4.2
8	1 148	3.9
9	1 066	3.7
10 - 14	4 723	16.2
15 - 19	4 887	16.8
20 +	7 615	26.1
Not stated - Inconnu	343	1.2
Denmark - Danemark[18]		
2009 (C)		
Total	14 940	100.0
Less than 1 - Moins de 1	172	1.2
1	629	4.2
2	896	6.0
3	955	6.4
4	926	6.2
5	879	5.9
6	801	5.4
7	835	5.6
8	806	5.4
9	773	5.2
10 - 14	2 794	18.7
15 - 19	1 976	13.2
20 +	2 498	16.7
Estonia - Estonie		
2009 (C)		
Total	3 189	100.0
Less than 1 - Moins de 1	83	2.6
1	202	6.3
2	256	8.0
3	236	7.4
4	186	5.8
5	179	5.6

Continent, country or area, year, code and duration of marriage (in years) Continent, pays ou zone, année, code et durée du mariage (en années)	Number of divorces Nombre de divorces	Per cent Pour cent
EUROPE		
Estonia - Estonie		
2009 (C)		
6	133	4.2
7	133	4.2
8	113	3.5
9	124	3.9
10 - 14	344	10.8
15 - 19	388	12.2
20 +	812	25.5
Finland - Finlande[8]		
2009 (C)		
Total	13 527	100.0
Less than 1 - Moins de 1	160	1.2
1	837	6.2
2	928	6.9
3	946	7.0
4	881	6.5
5	842	6.2
6	720	5.3
7	654	4.8
8	566	4.2
9	513	3.8
10 - 14	1 976	14.6
15 - 19	1 506	11.1
20 +	2 996	22.1
France		
2003 (C)		
Total	125 175	100.0
Less than 1 - Moins de 1	8	0.0
1	994	0.8
2	4 571	3.7
3	7 067	5.6
4	6 873	5.5
5	6 697	5.4
6	6 395	5.1
7	5 886	4.7
8	5 210	4.2
9	4 939	3.9
10 - 14	22 342	17.8
15 - 19	16 280	13.0
20 +	37 913	30.3
Germany - Allemagne		
2008 (C)		
Total	191 948	100.0
Less than 1 - Moins de 1	39	0.0
1	985	0.5
2	4 350	2.3
3	7 396	3.9
4	9 784	5.1
5	11 375	5.9
6	11 495	6.0
7	10 404	5.4
8	9 854	5.1
9	9 380	4.9
10 - 14	36 509	19.0
15 - 19	30 407	15.8
20 +	49 970	26.0
Greece - Grèce		
2005 (C)		
Total	13 494	100.0
Less than 1 - Moins de 1	2	0.0
1	38	0.3
2	724	5.4
3	739	5.5
4	688	5.1
5	624	4.6
6	802	5.9
7	669	5.0

Continent, country or area, year, code and duration of marriage (in years) Continent, pays ou zone, année, code et durée du mariage (en années)	Number of divorces Nombre de divorces	Per cent Pour cent	Continent, country or area, year, code and duration of marriage (in years) Continent, pays ou zone, année, code et durée du mariage (en années)	Number of divorces Nombre de divorces	Per cent Pour cent
EUROPE			**EUROPE**		
Greece - Grèce			**Latvia - Lettonie**		
2005 (C)			2009 (C)		
8	673	5.0	8	205	4.0
9	502	3.7	9	154	3.0
10 - 14	2 633	19.5	10 - 14	758	14.9
15 - 19	1 964	14.6	15 - 19	780	15.3
20 +	3 206	23.8	20 +	1 306	25.6
Not stated - Inconnu	230	1.7	**Liechtenstein**		
Hungary - Hongrie[8]			2007* (C)		
2009 (C)			Total	97	100.0
Total	23 820	100.0	Less than 1 - Moins de 1	-	0.0
Less than 1 - Moins de 1	267	1.1	1	5	5.2
1	814	3.4	2	9	9.3
2	1 058	4.4	3	7	7.2
3	1 130	4.7	4	2	2.1
4	1 120	4.7	5	9	9.3
5	1 133	4.8	6	5	5.2
6	1 082	4.5	7	6	6.2
7	1 018	4.3	8	7	7.2
8	1 030	4.3	9	4	4.1
9	1 019	4.3	10 - 14	10	10.3
10 - 14	4 035	16.9	15 - 19	13	13.4
15 - 19	3 813	16.0	20 +	20	20.6
20 +	6 301	26.5	**Lithuania - Lituanie**		
Iceland - Islande[2]			2009 (C)		
2009 (C)			Total	9 270	100.0
Total	550	100.0	Less than 1 - Moins de 1	125	1.3
Less than 1 - Moins de 1	10	1.8	1	438	4.7
1	24	4 4	2	553	6.0
2	37	6.7	3	574	6.2
3	34	6.2	4	509	5.5
4	26	4.7	5	434	4.7
5	38	6.9	6	342	3.7
6	33	6.0	7	304	3.3
7	25	4.5	8	296	3.2
8	34	6.2	9	333	3.6
9	33	6.0	10 - 14	1 494	16.1
10 - 14	68	12.4	15 - 19	1 583	17.1
15 - 19	57	10.4	20 +	2 285	24.6
20 +	128	23.3	**Luxembourg**		
Italy - Italie			2009 (C)		
2005 (C)			Total	1 052	100.0
Total	47 036	100.0	Less than 1 - Moins de 1	8	0.8
Less than 1 - Moins de 1	5	0.0	1	10	1.0
1	13	0.0	2	37	3.5
2	37	0.1	3	53	5.0
3	260	0.6	4	60	5.7
4	1 098	2.3	5	58	5.5
5	1 888	4.0	6	51	4.8
6	2 288	4.9	7	49	4.7
7	2 272	4.8	8	46	4.4
8	2 492	5.3	9	55	5.2
9	2 547	5.4	10 - 14	195	18.5
10 - 14	9 020	19.2	15 - 19	174	16.5
15 - 19	8 803	18.7	20 +	253	24.0
20 +	16 313	34.7	**Montenegro - Monténégro**		
Latvia - Lettonie			2009 (C)		
2009 (C)			Total	456	100.0
Total	5 099	100.0	Less than 1 - Moins de 1	11	2.4
Less than 1 - Moins de 1	21	0.4	1	38	8.3
1	107	2.1	2	48	10.5
2	297	5.8	3	42	9.2
3	380	7.5	4	39	8.6
4	344	6.7	5	32	7.0
5	274	5.4	6	19	4.2
6	250	4.9	7	16	3.5
7	223	4.4	8	16	3.5
			9	28	6.1

Continent, country or area, year, code and duration of marriage (in years) Continent, pays ou zone, année, code et durée du mariage (en années)	Number of divorces Nombre de divorces	Per cent Pour cent	Continent, country or area, year, code and duration of marriage (in years) Continent, pays ou zone, année, code et durée du mariage (en années)	Number of divorces Nombre de divorces	Per cent Pour cent
EUROPE			EUROPE		
Montenegro - Monténégro			Portugal		
2009 (C)			2007* (C)		
10 - 14	51	11.2	10 - 14	4 292	17.0
15 - 19	41	9.0	15 - 19	3 509	13.9
20 +	75	16.4	20 +	6 753	26.7
Netherlands - Pays-Bas[19]			Republic of Moldova - République de Moldova		
2009 (C)			2009 (C)		
Total	30 779	100.0	Total	11 884	100.0
Less than 1 - Moins de 1	327	1.1	Less than 1 - Moins de 1	424	3.6
1	1 028	3.3	1	801	6.7
2	1 297	4.2	2	915	7.7
3	1 406	4.6	3	823	6.9
4	1 468	4.8	4	715	6.0
5	1 523	4.9	5	662	5.6
6	1 586	5.2	6	536	4.5
7	1 433	4.7	7	452	3.8
8	1 428	4.6	8	432	3.6
9	1 371	4.5	9	396	3.3
10 - 14	5 243	17.0	10 - 14	1 771	14.9
15 - 19	4 702	15.3	15 - 19	1 643	13.8
20 +	7 967	25.9	20 +	2 314	19.5
Norway - Norvège[20]			Romania - Roumanie		
2009 (C)			2009 (C)		
Total	10 235	100.0	Total	32 341	100.0
Less than 1 - Moins de 1	21	0.2	Less than 1 - Moins de 1	651	2.0
1	200	2.0	1	1 754	5.4
2	434	4.2	2	2 254	7.0
3	513	5.0	3	2 111	6.5
4	583	5.7	4	1 876	5.8
5	681	6.7	5	1 832	5.7
6	707	6.9	6	1 502	4.6
7	647	6.3	7	1 400	4.3
8	521	5.1	8	1 344	4.2
9	529	5.2	9	1 262	3.9
10 - 14	1 787	17.5	10 - 14	5 354	16.6
15 - 19	1 173	11.5	15 - 19	4 478	13.8
20 +	2 257	22.1	20 +	6 523	20.2
Not stated - Inconnu	182	1.8	San Marino - Saint-Marin		
Poland - Pologne			2004 (+C)		
2009 (C)			Total	62	100.0
Total	65 345	100.0	Less than 1 - Moins de 1	1	1.6
Less than 1 - Moins de 1	601	0.9	1 - 3	14	22.6
1	2 198	3.4	4 - 6	8	12.9
2	3 034	4.6	7 - 9	8	12.9
3	3 257	5.0	10 - 19	18	29.0
4	2 999	4.6	20 +	13	21.0
5	2 962	4.5	Serbia - Serbie[21]		
6	2 803	4.3	2009 (+C)		
7	2 760	4.2	Total	8 505	100.0
8	2 786	4.3	Less than 1 - Moins de 1	344	4.0
9	2 835	4.3	1	529	6.2
10 - 14	11 207	17.2	2	530	6.2
15 - 19	9 920	15.2	3	481	5.7
20 +	17 983	27.5	4	449	5.3
Portugal			5	417	4.9
2007* (C)			6	431	5.1
Total	25 255	100.0	7	354	4.2
Less than 1 - Moins de 1	713	2.8	8	381	4.5
1	863	3.4	9	326	3.8
2	968	3.8	10 - 14	1 275	15.0
3	1 142	4.5	15 - 19	1 135	13.3
4	1 254	5.0	20 +	1 853	21.8
5	1 194	4.7	Slovakia - Slovaquie		
6	1 199	4.7	2009 (C)		
7	1 254	5.0	Total	12 671	100.0
8	1 126	4.5	Less than 1 - Moins de 1	82	0.6
9	988	3.9	1	319	2.5

25. Divorces and percentage distribution by duration of marriage, latest available year: 2001 - 2010
Divorces et répartition des pourcentages selon la durée du mariage, dernlère année disponible: 2001 - 2010 (continued - suite)

Continent, country or area, year, code and duration of marriage (in years) Continent, pays ou zone, année, code et durée du mariage (en années)	Number of divorces Nombre de divorces	Per cent Pour cent
EUROPE		
Slovakia - Slovaquie		
2009 (C)		
2	439	3.5
3	497	3.9
4	562	4.4
5	579	4.6
6	503	4.0
7	498	3.9
8	505	4.0
9	498	3.9
10 - 14	2 350	18.5
15 - 19	2 265	17.9
20 +	3 574	28.2
Slovenia - Slovénie		
2009 (C)		
Total	2 297	100.0
Less than 1 - Moins de 1	17	0.7
1	61	2.7
2	100	4.4
3	93	4.0
4	88	3.8
5	91	4.0
6	111	4.8
7	75	3.3
8	92	4.0
9	86	3.7
10 - 14	385	16.8
15 - 19	358	15.6
20 +	740	32.2
Spain - Espagne		
2009 (C)		
Total	98 207	100.0
Less than 1 - Moins de 1	991	1.0
1	2 872	2.9
2	4 001	4.1
3	4 566	4.6
4	4 461	4.5
5	4 739	4.8
6	4 332	4.4
7	4 046	4.1
8	4 056	4.1
9	4 118	4.2
10 - 14	16 425	16.7
15 - 19	14 469	14.7
20 +	29 131	29.7
Sweden - Suède		
2009 (C)		
Total	22 211	100.0
Less than 1 - Moins de 1	-	0.0
1	1 313	5.9
2	1 632	7.3
3	1 801	8.1
4	1 708	7.7
5	1 422	6.4
6	1 231	5.5
7	1 005	4.5
8	915	4.1
9	837	3.8
10 - 14	2 941	13.2
15 - 19	3 040	13.7
20 +	3 687	16.6
Not stated - Inconnu	679	3.1
Switzerland - Suisse		
2009 (C)		
Total	19 321	100.0
Less than 1 - Moins de 1	69	0.4
1	347	1.8
2	545	2.8

Continent, country or area, year, code and duration of marriage (in years) Continent, pays ou zone, année, code et durée du mariage (en années)	Number of divorces Nombre de divorces	Per cent Pour cent
EUROPE		
Switzerland - Suisse		
2009 (C)		
3	717	3.7
4	774	4.0
5	1 060	5.5
6	1 366	7.1
7	1 182	6.1
8	1 003	5.2
9	880	4.6
10 - 14	3 464	17.9
15 - 19	2 928	15.2
20 +	4 986	25.8
TFYR of Macedonia - L'ex-R. y. de Macédoine		
2009 (C)		
Total	1 287	100.0
Less than 1 - Moins de 1	68	5.3
1	156	12.1
2	132	10.3
3	98	7.6
4	89	6.9
5	93	7.2
6	69	5.4
7	49	3.8
8	47	3.7
9	43	3.3
10 - 14	148	11.5
15 - 19	130	10.1
20 +	165	12.8
Ukraine		
2008 (C)		
Total	166 845	100.0
Less than 1 - Moins de 1	6 366	3.8
1	11 187	6.7
2	12 577	7.5
3	10 638	6.4
4	11 083	6.6
5 - 9	39 200	23.5
10 - 14	26 910	16.1
15 - 19	19 973	12.0
20 +	28 911	17.3
United Kingdom of Great Britain and Northern Ireland - Royaume-Uni de Grande-Bretagne et d'Irlande du Nord[22]		
2003 (C)		
Total	166 735	100.0
Less than 1 - Moins de 1	55	0.0
1	3 352	2.0
2	7 211	4.3
3	8 723	5.2
4	9 440	5.7
5	9 562	5.7
6	9 313	5.6
7	8 821	5.3
8	8 292	5.0
9	7 570	4.5
10 - 14	32 564	19.5
15 - 19	23 119	13.9
20 +	38 713	23.2
Not stated - Inconnu	-	0.0

Continent, country or area, year, code and duration of marriage (in years)	Number of divorces	Per cent	Continent, country or area, year, code and duration of marriage (in years)	Number of divorces	Per cent
Continent, pays ou zone, année, code et durée du mariage (en années)	Nombre de divorces	Pour cent	Continent, pays ou zone, année, code et durée du mariage (en années)	Nombre de divorces	Pour cent
OCEANIA - OCÉANIE			OCEANIA - OCÉANIE		
Australia - Australie[23]			New Zealand - Nouvelle-Zélande		
2009 (C)			2009 (+C)		
Total	49 448	100.0	7	411	4.7
Less than 1 - Moins de 1	-	0.0	8	392	4.5
1	584	1.2	9	362	4.1
2	2 201	4.5	10 - 14	1 605	18.4
3	2 699	5.5	15 - 19	1 236	14.1
4	2 899	5.9	20 +	2 651	30.3
5	2 840	5.7	Northern Mariana Islands - Îles Mariannes		
6	2 607	5.3	septentrionales[25]		
7	2 225	4.5	2007 (U)		
8	2 143	4.3	Total	*160*	*100.0*
9	2 186	4.4	Less than 1 - Moins de 1	*2*	*1.3*
10 - 14	8 486	17.2	1	*3*	*1.9*
15 - 19	6 676	13.5	2	*5*	*3.1*
20 +	13 895	28.1	3	*9*	*5.6*
New Caledonia - Nouvelle-Calédonie[24]			4	*4*	*2.5*
2005 (C)			5	*14*	*8.8*
Total	341	100.0	6	*11*	*6.9*
Less than 1 - Moins de 1	1	0.3	7	*9*	*5.6*
1	6	1.8	8	*6*	*3.8*
2	6	1.8	9	*8*	*5.0*
3	12	3.5	10 - 14	*34*	*21.3*
4	16	4.7	15 - 19	*20*	*12.5*
5	17	5.0	20 +	*35*	*21.9*
6	23	6.7	Samoa		
7	21	6.2	2009 (U)		
8	18	5.3	Total	*48*	*100.0*
9	27	7.9	Less than 1 - Moins de 1	*-*	*0.0*
10 - 14	66	19.4	1	*-*	*0.0*
15 - 19	53	15.5	2	*-*	*0.0*
20 +	75	22.0	3	*2*	*4.2*
New Zealand - Nouvelle-Zélande			4	*-*	*0.0*
2009 (+C)			5	*1*	*2.1*
Total	8 737	100.0	6	*2*	*4.2*
Less than 1 - Moins de 1	-	0.0	7	*3*	*6.3*
1	-	0.0	8	*2*	*4.2*
2	207	2.4	9	*2*	*4.2*
3	337	3.9	10 - 14	*4*	*8.3*
4	454	5.2	15 - 19	*10*	*20.8*
5	570	6.5	20 +	*7*	*14.6*
6	512	5.9	Not stated - Inconnu	*15*	*31.3*

FOOTNOTES - NOTES

Italics: estimates which are less reliable. - Italiques: estimations moins sûres.

* Provisional. - Données provisoires.

'Code' indicates the source of data, as follows:
C - Civil registration, estimated over 90% complete
U - Civil registration, estimated less than 90% complete
| - Other source, estimated reliable
+ - Data tabulated by date of registration rather than occurence.
... - Information not available

Le 'Code' indique la source des données, comme suit:
C - Registres de l'état civil considérés complets à 90 p. 100 au moins.
U - Registres de l'état civil qui ne sont pas considérés complets à 90 p. 100 au moins.
| - Autre source, considérée pas douteuses.
+ - Données exploitées selon la date de l'enregistrement et non la date de l'événement.
... - Information non disponible.

[1] Excludes the islands of St. Brandon and Agalega. - Non compris les îles St. Brandon et Agalega.

[2] Data refer to resident population only. - Pour la population résidante seulement.

[3] Because of rounding, totals are not in all cases the sum of the parts. - Les chiffres étant arrondis, les totaux ne correspondent pas toujours rigoureusement à la somme des chiffres partiels.

[4] Duration of marriage is defined as the time from the day of celebration of the marriage till the day of filing of the divorce. - La durée du mariage est définie comme la période s'écoulant depuis le jour de la célébration de l'union jusqu'à la date de la demande de divorce.

[5] Unrevised data. - Les données n'ont pas été révisées.

[6] Excluding Indian jungle population. - Non compris les Indiens de la jungle.

[7] Excluding nomadic Indian tribes. - Non compris les tribus d'Indiens nomades.

[8] Including annulments. - Y compris les annulations.

[9] Data refer to government controlled areas. - Les données se rapportent aux zones contrôlées par le Gouvernement.

[10] Including data for East Jerusalem and Israeli residents in certain other territories under occupation by Israeli military forces since June 1967. - Y compris les données pour Jérusalem-Est et les résidents israéliens dans certains autres territoires occupés depuis 1967 par les forces armées israéliennes.

¹¹ Data refer to Japanese nationals in Japan only. - Les données se raportent aux nationaux japonais au Japon seulement.

¹² Data refer to before consummation. - Avant consommation.

¹³ Excluding alien armed forces, civilian aliens employed by armed forces, and foreign diplomatic personnel and their dependants. - Non compris les militaires étrangers, les civils étrangers employés par les forces armées ni le personnel diplomatique étranger et les membres de leur famille les accompagnant.

¹⁴ Data from MERNIS (Central Population Administrative System). - Données de MERNIS (Système central de données démographiques).

¹⁵ Excluding aliens temporarily in the area. - Non compris les étrangers se trouvant temporairement dans le territoire.

¹⁶ Including divorces among armed forces stationed outside the country and alien armed forces in the area. - Y compris les divorces de militaires nationaux hors du pays et les militaires étrangers en garnison sur le territoire.

¹⁷ Including annulments. Including nationals outside the country, but excluding foreigners in the country. - Y compris les annulations. Y compris les nationaux à l'étranger, mais non compris les étrangers sur le territoire.

¹⁸ Excluding Faeroe Islands and Greenland shown separately, if available. - Non compris les Iles Féroé et le Groenland, qui font l'objet de rubriques distinctes, si disponible.

¹⁹ Based on the general office for civil registration. Including same sex divorces. - D'après la direction générale du registre de l'etat civil. Y compris les divorces entre conjoints du même sexe.

²⁰ Excluding Svalbard and Jan Mayen Islands shown separately, if available. - Non compris Svalbard et Jan Mayen qui font l'objet de rubriques distinctes, si disponible.

²¹ Excluding data for Kosovo and Metohia. - Sans les données pour le Kosovo et Metohie.

²² Excluding Channel Islands (Guernsey and Jersey) and Isle of Man, shown separately, if available. - Non compris les îles Anglo-Normandes (Guernesey et Jersey) et l'île de Man, qui font l'objet de rubriques distinctes, si disponible.

²³ Data for certain cells suppressed by national statistical office for confidentiality reasons. - Les données pour certaines cases ont été supprimées par le bureau national de statistiques pour des raisons de confidentialité.

²⁴ Based on place of residence at marriage not at divorce. - Les divorces sont comptés en fonction du lieu de résidence au mariage, et non pas au divorce.

²⁵ Data refer to the islands of Saipan, Tinian and Rota only. - Les données se réfèrent uniquement aux îles de Saipan, Tinian et Rota.

Annexe I : Population au milieu de l'année, estimations des Nations Unies : 2001 - 2010

Continent and country or area Continent et pays ou zone	Population estimates (in thousands) - Estimations de population (en milliers)[1]									
	2001	2002	2003	2004	2005	2006	2007	2008	2009	2010
AFRICA - AFRIQUE										
Algeria - Algérie	30 982	31 442	31 913	32 396	32 888	33 392	33 907	34 428	34 950	35 468
Angola	14 388	14 890	15 420	15 957	16 489	17 010	17 525	18 038	18 555	19 082
Benin - Bénin	6 721	6 938	7 165	7 398	7 634	7 872	8 113	8 356	8 602	8 850
Botswana	1 784	1 808	1 830	1 852	1 876	1 901	1 928	1 955	1 982	2 007
Burkina Faso	12 648	13 015	13 396	13 790	14 198	14 622	15 061	15 515	15 984	16 469
Burundi	6 500	6 656	6 839	7 040	7 251	7 474	7 708	7 943	8 171	8 383
Cameroon - Cameroun	16 040	16 408	16 783	17 165	17 554	17 948	18 350	18 759	19 175	19 599
Cape Verde - Cap-Vert	445	453	460	467	473	478	483	487	492	496
Central African Republic - République centrafricaine	3 767	3 829	3 890	3 952	4 018	4 088	4 161	4 238	4 318	4 401
Chad - Tchad	8 518	8 831	9 154	9 475	9 786	10 084	10 372	10 654	10 937	11 227
Comoros - Comores	578	593	609	626	643	661	679	697	716	735
Congo	3 213	3 289	3 365	3 446	3 533	3 629	3 731	3 836	3 941	4 043
Côte d'Ivoire	16 893	17 181	17 456	17 732	18 021	18 326	18 647	18 987	19 350	19 738
Democratic Republic of the Congo - République démocratique du Congo	50 989	52 491	54 098	55 755	57 421	59 088	60 772	62 475	64 204	65 966
Djibouti	750	765	780	794	808	824	839	856	872	889
Egypt - Égypte	68 888	70 175	71 498	72 845	74 203	75 568	76 942	78 323	79 716	81 121
Equatorial Guinea - Guinée équatoriale	537	554	572	590	608	626	644	662	681	700
Eritrea - Érythrée	3 812	3 974	4 146	4 318	4 486	4 646	4 799	4 948	5 098	5 254
Ethiopia - Éthiopie	67 304	69 041	70 784	72 527	74 264	75 993	77 718	79 446	81 188	82 950
Gabon	1 263	1 291	1 317	1 344	1 371	1 397	1 424	1 450	1 478	1 505
Gambia - Gambie	1 336	1 376	1 418	1 460	1 504	1 547	1 591	1 636	1 682	1 728
Ghana	19 632	20 114	20 611	21 120	21 640	22 171	22 712	23 264	23 824	24 392
Guinea - Guinée	8 472	8 605	8 744	8 889	9 041	9 202	9 374	9 559	9 761	9 982
Guinea-Bissau - Guinée-Bissau	1 265	1 290	1 315	1 341	1 368	1 395	1 424	1 454	1 484	1 515
Kenya	32 076	32 928	33 805	34 702	35 615	36 541	37 485	38 455	39 462	40 513
Lesotho	1 989	2 010	2 029	2 047	2 066	2 086	2 106	2 127	2 149	2 171
Liberia - Libéria	2 939	2 996	3 037	3 093	3 183	3 314	3 477	3 658	3 836	3 994
Libya - Libye	5 331	5 434	5 541	5 653	5 770	5 894	6 023	6 150	6 263	6 355
Madagascar	15 846	16 339	16 842	17 358	17 886	18 427	18 980	19 546	20 124	20 714
Malawi	11 529	11 833	12 145	12 473	12 823	13 195	13 589	14 005	14 442	14 901
Mali	11 640	12 002	12 380	12 772	13 177	13 593	14 021	14 460	14 910	15 370
Mauritania - Mauritanie	2 720	2 800	2 882	2 965	3 047	3 130	3 213	3 295	3 378	3 460
Mauritius - Maurice[2]	1 208	1 221	1 234	1 246	1 257	1 267	1 276	1 284	1 292	1 299
Mayotte	154	159	164	169	175	180	186	192	198	204
Morocco - Maroc	29 129	29 454	29 770	30 082	30 392	30 702	31 011	31 321	31 635	31 951
Mozambique	18 691	19 200	19 721	20 246	20 770	21 291	21 811	22 333	22 859	23 391
Namibia - Namibie	1 936	1 973	2 008	2 043	2 080	2 119	2 159	2 200	2 242	2 283
Niger	11 308	11 706	12 118	12 547	12 994	13 460	13 946	14 450	14 972	15 512
Nigeria - Nigéria	126 705	129 832	133 067	136 399	139 823	143 339	146 951	150 666	154 488	158 423
Réunion	751	762	773	784	795	805	816	826	836	846
Rwanda	8 457	8 696	8 858	9 010	9 202	9 441	9 711	10 004	10 311	10 624
Sao Tome and Principe - Sao Tomé-et-Principe	143	146	148	150	153	155	157	160	163	165
Senegal - Sénégal	9 759	10 023	10 298	10 581	10 872	11 170	11 475	11 787	12 107	12 434
Seychelles	80	81	82	83	84	84	85	86	86	87
Sierra Leone	4 304	4 506	4 730	4 952	5 153	5 327	5 478	5 612	5 739	5 868
Somalia - Somalie	7 597	7 791	7 982	8 171	8 360	8 547	8 733	8 922	9 120	9 331
South Africa - Afrique du Sud	45 390	46 015	46 631	47 227	47 793	48 331	48 842	49 319	49 752	50 133
Sudan - Soudan	35 002	35 816	36 643	37 504	38 410	39 369	40 374	41 415	42 478	43 552
Swaziland	1 075	1 083	1 089	1 095	1 105	1 118	1 133	1 150	1 168	1 186
Togo	4 926	5 051	5 170	5 288	5 408	5 530	5 653	5 777	5 902	6 028
Tunisia - Tunisie	9 546	9 634	9 722	9 814	9 912	10 018	10 130	10 247	10 365	10 481
Uganda - Ouganda	24 984	25 794	26 642	27 522	28 431	29 370	30 340	31 339	32 368	33 425
United Republic of Tanzania - République Unie de Tanzanie	34 917	35 832	36 788	37 787	38 831	39 924	41 068	42 268	43 525	44 841
Western Sahara - Sahara occidental	337	362	389	416	440	462	480	497	513	531
Zambia - Zambie	10 450	10 693	10 938	11 192	11 462	11 750	12 055	12 380	12 724	13 089
Zimbabwe	12 575	12 608	12 613	12 598	12 571	12 530	12 481	12 452	12 474	12 571
AMERICA, NORTH - AMÉRIQUE DU NORD										
Anguilla	11	12	13	13	14	14	14	15	15	15
Antigua and Barbuda - Antigua-et-Barbuda	79	81	82	83	84	85	86	87	88	89
Aruba	92	95	97	99	101	103	104	106	107	107
Bahamas	302	306	310	315	319	324	329	334	338	343
Barbados - Barbade	268	269	269	270	271	271	272	272	273	273
Belize	257	263	269	275	281	287	293	299	305	312

714

Annex I: Annual mid-year population, United Nations estimates: 2001 - 2010
Annexe I : Population au milieu de l'année, estimations des Nations Unies : 2001 - 2010 (continued - suite)

Continent and country or area / Continent et pays ou zone	\multicolumn{10}{c}{Population estimates (in thousands) - Estimations de population (en milliers)[1]}									
	2001	2002	2003	2004	2005	2006	2007	2008	2009	2010
AMERICA, NORTH - AMÉRIQUE DU NORD										
Bermuda - Bermudes	63	63	64	64	64	64	65	65	65	65
British Virgin Islands - Îles Vierges britanniques	21	21	21	22	22	22	23	23	23	23
Canada	30 967	31 282	31 609	31 944	32 283	32 628	32 977	33 328	33 675	34 017
Cayman Islands - Îles Caïmanes	43	45	48	50	52	54	55	55	56	56
Costa Rica	4 003	4 083	4 160	4 236	4 309	4 382	4 453	4 522	4 591	4 659
Cuba	11 140	11 175	11 208	11 235	11 254	11 265	11 269	11 267	11 263	11 258
Dominica - Dominique	69	69	69	69	69	69	68	68	68	68
Dominican Republic - République dominicaine	8 726	8 861	8 995	9 130	9 264	9 398	9 532	9 665	9 797	9 927
El Salvador	5 966	5 988	6 009	6 029	6 051	6 074	6 101	6 130	6 160	6 193
Greenland - Groenland	56	57	57	57	57	57	57	57	57	57
Grenada - Grenade	102	102	102	102	103	103	103	104	104	104
Guadeloupe	431	435	439	442	446	449	452	455	458	461
Guatemala	11 513	11 800	12 099	12 405	12 717	13 035	13 359	13 691	14 034	14 389
Haiti - Haïti	8 792	8 935	9 075	9 213	9 347	9 479	9 608	9 736	9 864	9 993
Honduras	6 347	6 478	6 609	6 743	6 879	7 018	7 159	7 303	7 450	7 601
Jamaica - Jamaïque	2 604	2 626	2 646	2 665	2 682	2 696	2 709	2 720	2 731	2 741
Martinique	388	391	393	395	397	399	401	403	404	406
Mexico - Mexique	101 330	102 634	103 903	105 176	106 484	107 835	109 221	110 627	112 033	113 423
Montserrat	5	5	5	5	6	6	6	6	6	6
Netherlands Antilles - Antilles néerlandaises	180	180	182	184	186	189	192	195	198	201
Nicaragua	5 149	5 220	5 288	5 356	5 424	5 494	5 564	5 636	5 710	5 788
Panama	3 013	3 069	3 126	3 182	3 238	3 295	3 351	3 406	3 462	3 517
Puerto Rico - Porto Rico	3 817	3 813	3 803	3 792	3 782	3 773	3 765	3 759	3 754	3 749
Saint Kitts and Nevis - Saint-Kitts-et-Nevis	47	47	48	49	49	50	50	51	52	52
Saint Lucia - Sainte-Lucie	159	160	162	164	165	167	169	171	172	174
Saint Pierre and Miquelon - Saint Pierre-et-Miquelon	6	6	6	6	6	6	6	6	6	6
Saint Vincent and the Grenadines - Saint-Vincent-et-les Grenadines	108	108	108	109	109	109	109	109	109	109
Trinidad and Tobago - Trinité-et-Tobago	1 297	1 302	1 306	1 311	1 315	1 320	1 326	1 331	1 336	1 341
Turks and Caicos Islands - Îles Turques et Caïques	21	23	26	28	31	33	34	36	37	38
United States of America - États-Unis d'Amérique	285 545	288 467	291 291	294 063	296 820	299 564	302 285	304 989	307 687	310 384
United States Virgin Islands - Îles Vierges américaines	109	109	109	109	109	109	109	109	109	109
AMERICA, SOUTH - AMÉRIQUE DU SUD										
Argentina - Argentine	37 302	37 657	38 001	38 341	38 681	39 024	39 368	39 714	40 062	40 412
Bolivia (Plurinational State of) - Bolivie (État plurinational de)	8 477	8 647	8 816	8 983	9 147	9 307	9 463	9 618	9 773	9 930
Brazil - Brésil	176 877	179 289	181 633	183 873	185 987	187 958	189 798	191 543	193 247	194 946
Chile - Chili	15 604	15 784	15 960	16 132	16 302	16 469	16 633	16 796	16 956	17 114
Colombia - Colombie	40 423	41 078	41 732	42 386	43 041	43 697	44 352	45 006	45 654	46 295
Ecuador - Équateur	12 552	12 767	12 988	13 209	13 426	13 640	13 850	14 057	14 262	14 465
Falkland Islands (Malvinas) - Îles Falkland (Malvinas)	3	3	3	3	3	3	3	3	3	3
French Guiana - Guyane française	172	179	187	195	202	208	214	220	225	231
Guyana	735	738	741	744	746	748	750	752	753	754
Paraguay	5 454	5 565	5 676	5 787	5 898	6 009	6 119	6 230	6 342	6 455
Peru - Pérou	26 223	26 579	26 916	27 242	27 559	27 866	28 166	28 463	28 765	29 077
Suriname	473	480	487	493	499	505	510	515	520	525
Uruguay	3 325	3 325	3 323	3 321	3 323	3 327	3 336	3 346	3 357	3 369
Venezuela (Bolivarian Republic of) - Venezuela (République bolivarienne du)	24 811	25 273	25 736	26 200	26 664	27 129	27 593	28 057	28 520	28 980
ASIA - ASIE										
Afghanistan	23 677	24 640	25 679	26 693	27 615	28 421	29 146	29 840	30 578	31 412
Armenia - Arménie	3 066	3 061	3 061	3 063	3 066	3 070	3 074	3 079	3 085	3 092
Azerbaijan - Azerbaïdjan	8 191	8 280	8 377	8 480	8 588	8 702	8 821	8 944	9 067	9 188
Bahrain - Bahreïn	643	642	647	672	725	811	926	1 052	1 170	1 262
Bangladesh	131 945	134 266	136 515	138 633	140 588	142 354	143 957	145 478	147 030	148 692
Bhutan - Bhoutan	588	606	624	642	659	675	689	701	714	726
Brunei Darussalam - Brunéi Darussalam	334	342	349	356	363	370	378	385	392	399
Cambodia - Cambodge	12 654	12 845	13 024	13 194	13 358	13 516	13 670	13 823	13 978	14 138
China - Chine[3]	1 277 904	1 285 934	1 293 397	1 300 552	1 307 593	1 314 581	1 321 482	1 328 276	1 334 909	1 341 335
China, Hong Kong SAR - Chine, Hong Kong RAS	6 829	6 837	6 822	6 808	6 810	6 833	6 873	6 926	6 988	7 053
China, Macao SAR - Chine, Macao RAS	440	449	459	470	481	493	506	518	531	544
Cyprus - Chypre	961	980	998	1 016	1 033	1 048	1 063	1 077	1 090	1 104

Continent and country or area Continent et pays ou zone	Population estimates (in thousands) - Estimations de population (en milliers)[1]									
	2001	2002	2003	2004	2005	2006	2007	2008	2009	2010

ASIA - ASIE

	2001	2002	2003	2004	2005	2006	2007	2008	2009	2010
Democratic People's Republic of Korea - République populaire démocratique de Corée	23 083	23 265	23 437	23 597	23 746	23 882	24 009	24 126	24 238	24 346
Georgia - Géorgie	4 685	4 626	4 570	4 520	4 477	4 443	4 416	4 394	4 374	4 352
India - Inde	1 071 374	1 088 694	1 105 886	1 122 991	1 140 043	1 157 039	1 173 972	1 190 864	1 207 740	1 224 614
Indonesia - Indonésie	216 203	219 026	221 839	224 607	227 303	229 919	232 462	234 951	237 414	239 871
Iran (Islamic Republic of) - Iran (République islamique d')	66 314	67 213	68 062	68 893	69 732	70 582	71 435	72 289	73 137	73 974
Iraq	24 552	25 233	25 915	26 619	27 359	28 141	28 961	29 821	30 725	31 672
Israel - Israël	6 131	6 242	6 352	6 471	6 605	6 755	6 920	7 092	7 261	7 418
Japan - Japon	125 894	126 048	126 184	126 299	126 393	126 465	126 515	126 545	126 552	126 536
Jordan - Jordanie	4 910	4 998	5 097	5 210	5 342	5 495	5 667	5 849	6 026	6 187
Kazakhstan	14 898	14 902	14 959	15 053	15 172	15 312	15 476	15 655	15 841	16 026
Kuwait - Koweït	2 010	2 070	2 127	2 189	2 264	2 351	2 448	2 548	2 646	2 737
Kyrgyzstan - Kirghizstan	4 988	5 003	5 008	5 018	5 042	5 084	5 139	5 204	5 271	5 334
Lao People's Democratic Republic - République démocratique populaire lao	5 409	5 497	5 582	5 667	5 753	5 842	5 931	6 022	6 112	6 201
Lebanon - Liban	3 803	3 869	3 935	3 998	4 052	4 097	4 135	4 167	4 197	4 228
Malaysia - Malaisie	23 965	24 515	25 060	25 590	26 100	26 586	27 051	27 502	27 949	28 401
Maldives	278	282	287	291	295	299	304	308	312	316
Mongolia - Mongolie	2 435	2 459	2 485	2 514	2 547	2 584	2 625	2 667	2 712	2 756
Myanmar	45 324	45 609	45 844	46 070	46 321	46 605	46 916	47 250	47 601	47 963
Nepal - Népal	24 980	25 563	26 144	26 718	27 282	27 834	28 374	28 905	29 433	29 959
Occupied Palestinian Territory - Territoire palestinien occupé	3 285	3 356	3 419	3 483	3 556	3 638	3 728	3 827	3 931	4 039
Oman	2 279	2 303	2 336	2 378	2 430	2 491	2 561	2 637	2 712	2 782
Pakistan	147 558	150 407	153 140	155 860	158 645	161 513	164 446	167 442	170 494	173 593
Philippines	78 964	80 630	82 294	83 937	85 546	87 116	88 653	90 173	91 703	93 261
Qatar	608	624	654	715	821	978	1 178	1 396	1 598	1 759
Republic of Korea - République de Corée	46 211	46 421	46 625	46 831	47 044	47 268	47 499	47 734	47 964	48 184
Saudi Arabia - Arabie saoudite	20 682	21 463	22 334	23 214	24 041	24 799	25 504	26 167	26 809	27 448
Singapore - Singapour	3 981	4 032	4 086	4 160	4 266	4 410	4 585	4 772	4 946	5 086
Sri Lanka	18 922	19 134	19 370	19 611	19 843	20 062	20 272	20 474	20 669	20 860
Syrian Arab Republic - République arabe syrienne	16 455	16 963	17 490	18 005	18 484	18 921	19 321	19 694	20 054	20 411
Tajikistan - Tadjikistan	6 233	6 286	6 337	6 391	6 453	6 525	6 604	6 691	6 783	6 879
Thailand - Thaïlande	63 899	64 643	65 370	66 060	66 698	67 276	67 796	68 268	68 706	69 122
Timor-Leste	853	888	931	974	1 010	1 039	1 061	1 080	1 100	1 124
Turkey - Turquie	64 545	65 446	66 339	67 236	68 143	69 064	69 993	70 924	71 846	72 752
Turkmenistan - Turkménistan	4 552	4 600	4 648	4 697	4 748	4 802	4 859	4 918	4 980	5 042
United Arab Emirates - Émirats arabes unis	3 149	3 255	3 401	3 658	4 069	4 663	5 406	6 207	6 939	7 512
Uzbekistan - Ouzbékistan	25 043	25 275	25 489	25 708	25 947	26 214	26 504	26 812	27 128	27 445
Viet Nam	79 630	80 501	81 377	82 263	83 161	84 076	85 007	85 952	86 901	87 848
Yemen - Yémen	18 266	18 832	19 420	20 026	20 649	21 288	21 947	22 627	23 328	24 053

EUROPE

	2001	2002	2003	2004	2005	2006	2007	2008	2009	2010
Albania - Albanie	3 077	3 090	3 107	3 125	3 142	3 157	3 170	3 181	3 193	3 204
Andorra - Andorre	66	69	72	75	78	80	81	83	84	85
Austria - Autriche	8 038	8 083	8 134	8 186	8 232	8 273	8 310	8 342	8 370	8 394
Belarus - Bélarus	10 010	9 963	9 918	9 872	9 825	9 777	9 728	9 681	9 636	9 595
Belgium - Belgique	10 211	10 254	10 303	10 357	10 414	10 475	10 539	10 602	10 661	10 712
Bosnia and Herzegovina - Bosnie-Herzégovine	3 748	3 776	3 783	3 781	3 781	3 782	3 779	3 774	3 768	3 760
Bulgaria - Bulgarie	7 948	7 893	7 840	7 789	7 739	7 690	7 640	7 591	7 543	7 494
Croatia - Croatie	4 482	4 466	4 457	4 450	4 442	4 434	4 426	4 418	4 411	4 403
Czech Republic - République tchèque	10 226	10 210	10 199	10 202	10 221	10 259	10 314	10 377	10 440	10 493
Denmark - Danemark	5 356	5 371	5 384	5 400	5 419	5 443	5 469	5 497	5 525	5 550
Estonia - Estonie	1 363	1 357	1 352	1 348	1 346	1 344	1 343	1 342	1 342	1 341
Faeroe Islands - Îles Féroé	46	47	47	48	48	48	49	49	49	49
Finland - Finlande	5 185	5 197	5 211	5 226	5 244	5 266	5 290	5 316	5 342	5 365
France	59 391	59 775	60 184	60 597	60 997	61 378	61 745	62 098	62 445	62 787
Germany - Allemagne	82 384	82 432	82 484	82 524	82 541	82 536	82 516	82 475	82 405	82 302
Gibraltar	28	28	28	29	29	29	29	29	29	29
Greece - Grèce	11 032	11 073	11 111	11 147	11 183	11 219	11 256	11 292	11 327	11 359
Holy See - Saint-Siège	1	1	1	1	0	0	0	0	0	0
Hungary - Hongrie	10 185	10 159	10 135	10 110	10 087	10 064	10 043	10 022	10 002	9 984
Iceland - Islande	284	287	290	293	297	301	306	311	316	320
Ireland - Irlande	3 866	3 936	4 011	4 086	4 158	4 226	4 291	4 353	4 412	4 470
Isle of Man - Île de Man	78	78	79	79	80	81	81	82	82	83
Italy - Italie	57 199	57 499	57 864	58 264	58 671	59 082	59 495	59 891	60 249	60 551

Continent and country or area Continent et pays ou zone	Population estimates (in thousands) - Estimations de population (en milliers)[1]									
	2001	2002	2003	2004	2005	2006	2007	2008	2009	2010
EUROPE										
Latvia - Lettonie	2 367	2 350	2 334	2 319	2 306	2 293	2 282	2 271	2 261	2 252
Liechtenstein	33	34	34	34	35	35	35	36	36	36
Lithuania - Lituanie	3 480	3 462	3 447	3 432	3 416	3 398	3 379	3 360	3 341	3 324
Luxembourg	440	443	446	451	457	466	476	487	498	507
Malta - Malte	400	402	405	407	409	411	413	414	415	417
Monaco	35	35	35	35	35	35	35	35	35	35
Montenegro - Monténégro	630	629	628	627	627	627	628	629	630	631
Netherlands - Pays-Bas	15 953	16 046	16 138	16 225	16 305	16 378	16 443	16 503	16 559	16 613
Norway - Norvège	4 514	4 536	4 559	4 587	4 623	4 669	4 722	4 779	4 834	4 883
Poland - Pologne	38 267	38 230	38 198	38 175	38 165	38 170	38 190	38 218	38 249	38 277
Portugal	10 380	10 423	10 466	10 506	10 544	10 578	10 608	10 635	10 657	10 676
Republic of Moldova - République de Moldova	4 040	3 969	3 896	3 828	3 767	3 715	3 672	3 635	3 603	3 573
Romania - Roumanie	22 100	22 011	21 925	21 845	21 772	21 705	21 645	21 590	21 537	21 486
Russian Federation - Fédération de Russie	146 162	145 520	144 880	144 307	143 843	143 510	143 295	143 163	143 064	142 958
San Marino - Saint-Marin	28	28	29	30	30	31	31	31	31	32
Serbia - Serbie	10 077	10 013	9 950	9 895	9 856	9 836	9 833	9 841	9 851	9 856
Slovakia - Slovaquie	5 407	5 408	5 409	5 411	5 415	5 422	5 431	5 441	5 452	5 462
Slovenia - Slovénie	1 988	1 991	1 994	1 998	2 002	2 007	2 012	2 018	2 024	2 030
Spain - Espagne	40 767	41 365	42 040	42 732	43 395	44 018	44 604	45 146	45 638	46 077
Sweden - Suède	8 877	8 902	8 935	8 978	9 029	9 091	9 161	9 237	9 311	9 380
Switzerland - Suisse	7 208	7 255	7 307	7 361	7 415	7 468	7 522	7 573	7 621	7 664
TFYR of Macedonia - L'ex-R. y. de Macédoine	2 016	2 022	2 028	2 033	2 038	2 043	2 048	2 053	2 057	2 061
Ukraine	48 448	48 032	47 643	47 275	46 924	46 592	46 282	45 992	45 715	45 448
United Kingdom of Great Britain and Northern Ireland - Royaume-Uni de Grande-Bretagne et d'Irlande du Nord	59 097	59 340	59 604	59 892	60 203	60 538	60 896	61 270	61 652	62 036
OCEANIA - OCÉANIE										
American Samoa - Samoas américaines	59	60	61	62	63	64	65	66	67	68
Australia - Australie[4]	19 382	19 604	19 840	20 104	20 404	20 744	21 120	21 514	21 902	22 268
Cook Islands - Îles Cook	18	18	19	19	19	20	20	20	20	20
Fiji - Fidji	815	816	817	819	823	828	835	844	852	861
French Polynesia - Polynésie française	241	245	248	252	255	258	261	265	268	271
Guam	158	160	163	166	169	171	173	176	178	180
Kiribati	86	87	89	90	92	94	95	97	98	100
Marshall Islands - Îles Marshall	52	52	52	52	52	52	52	53	53	54
Micronesia (Federated States of) - Micronésie (États fédérés de)	107	108	108	109	109	110	110	110	111	111
Nauru	10	10	10	10	10	10	10	10	10	10
New Caledonia - Nouvelle-Calédonie	216	220	223	227	231	235	239	243	247	251
New Zealand - Nouvelle-Zélande	3 907	3 962	4 021	4 079	4 134	4 185	4 232	4 278	4 323	4 368
Niue - Nioué	2	2	2	2	2	2	2	2	2	1
Northern Mariana Islands - Îles Mariannes septentrionales	69	69	69	68	67	66	64	63	61	61
Palau - Palaos	19	20	20	20	20	20	20	20	20	20
Papua New Guinea - Papouasie-Nouvelle-Guinée	5 519	5 660	5 803	5 948	6 095	6 245	6 396	6 549	6 703	6 858
Samoa	178	178	179	180	180	181	181	182	182	183
Solomon Islands - Îles Salomon	420	432	444	457	470	483	496	510	524	538
Tokelau - Tokélaou	2	1	1	1	1	1	1	1	1	1
Tonga	98	99	100	100	101	102	102	103	104	104
Tuvalu	9	10	10	10	10	10	10	10	10	10
Vanuatu	190	195	200	206	211	217	222	228	234	240
Wallis and Futuna Islands - Îles Wallis et Futuna	15	14	14	14	14	14	14	14	14	14

SOURCE

United Nations, Department of Economic and Social Affairs, Population Division (2011). World Population Prospects: The 2010 Revision, DVD Edition – Extended Dataset (United Nations publication, Sales No. E.11.XIII.7). - Organisation des Nations Unies, Département des affaires économiques et sociales, Division de la population (2011). Perspectives de la population mondiale : La révision de 2010, Edition DVD - ensemble de données étendues (publication des Nations Unies, numéro de vente E.11.XIII.7).

FOOTNOTES - NOTES

[1] For 2001-2010 all data refer to annual interpolated estimates of mid-year population. - Les données pour 2001-2010 sont des estimations de population au milieu de l'année interpolées.

[2] Including Agalega, Rodrigues and Saint Brandon. - Y compris Agalega, Rodrigues et Saint Brandon.

[3] For statistical purposes, the data for China do not include Hong Kong and Macao Special Administrative Regions (SAR) of China. - A des fins statistiques, les données pour la Chine ne comprennent pas les Régions Administratives Spéciales (SAR) de Hong Kong et Macao.

[4] Including Christmas Island, Cocos (Keeling) Islands and Norfolk Island. - Y compris Christmas Island, Cocos (Keeling) Islands et Norfolk Island.

Annex II: Vital statistics summary, United Nations medium variant projections: 2005-2010
Annexe II: Aperçu des statistiques de l'état civil, variante moyenne, projections des Nations Unies : 2005-2010

Continent and country or area Continent et pays ou zone	Crude birth rate - Taux bruts de natalité[1]	Crude death rate - Taux bruts de mortalité[1]	Infant mortality rate - Décès d'enfants de moins d'un an[1]	Expectation of life at birth - Espérance de vie à la naissance[1]		Total fertility rate - Indice synthétique de fécondité[1]	Natural increase - Accroissement naturel[1]
				Male - Masculin	Female - Féminin		
AFRICA - AFRIQUE							
Algeria - Algérie...............................	20.8	4.9	25.0	70.9	73.7	2.38	15.9
Angola...	43.5	15.3	104.3	48.2	51.0	5.79	28.2
Benin - Bénin....................................	40.7	12.4	85.1	52.7	56.5	5.49	28.3
Botswana..	24.2	12.6	40.7	53.8	52.5	2.90	11.6
Burkina Faso.....................................	43.9	12.6	78.9	52.8	54.8	5.95	31.2
Burundi...	34.3	14.8	101.1	47.5	50.1	4.66	19.5
Cameroon - Cameroun.......................	37.2	15.0	94.1	49.0	50.9	4.67	22.2
Cape Verde - Cap-Vert.....................	21.9	5.2	20.6	69.4	77.4	2.60	16.7
Central African Republic - République centrafricaine.............	35.6	17.6	105.4	44.5	47.3	4.85	18.0
Chad - Tchad....................................	45.9	17.1	131.2	47.2	49.9	6.20	28.9
Comoros - Comores...........................	39.0	9.4	72.2	58.3	61.0	5.08	29.5
Congo...	36.0	11.7	72.4	54.9	57.2	4.64	24.3
Côte d'Ivoire.....................................	35.0	13.0	77.2	52.1	54.1	4.65	22.0
Democratic Republic of the Congo - République démocratique du Congo	44.9	17.2	115.8	45.9	48.9	6.07	27.8
Djibouti...	29.4	10.5	82.1	55.2	58.0	3.95	18.9
Egypt - Égypte..................................	23.9	5.2	25.9	70.5	74.3	2.85	18.7
Equatorial Guinea - Guinée équatoriale.........	37.3	15.1	102.5	48.9	51.5	5.36	22.2
Eritrea - Érythrée..............................	37.5	8.3	53.9	57.6	62.2	4.68	29.3
Ethiopia - Éthiopie............................	33.3	10.5	72.5	55.7	58.7	4.60	22.9
Gabon...	27.4	9.4	51.1	60.2	62.4	3.35	18.0
Gambia - Gambie...............................	39.3	9.8	73.8	56.3	58.5	5.10	29.5
Ghana...	32.6	8.3	49.6	61.8	63.6	4.34	24.4
Guinea - Guinée................................	39.9	13.9	93.2	50.9	54.0	5.45	26.1
Guinea-Bissau - Guinée-Bissau.........	39.3	17.5	118.7	45.3	48.2	5.27	21.9
Kenya..	38.0	11.3	64.7	54.0	55.9	4.80	26.7
Lesotho...	28.5	16.7	76.9	46.5	45.2	3.37	11.9
Liberia - Libéria................................	40.5	12.0	88.6	53.5	55.4	5.42	28.5
Libya - Libye.....................................	24.0	4.0	15.0	71.7	76.9	2.72	20.0
Madagascar.......................................	36.2	6.8	44.8	64.3	67.3	4.83	29.4
Malawi...	44.0	13.7	95.2	51.5	51.5	6.00	30.3
Mali...	47.6	15.5	101.4	48.9	51.0	6.46	32.1
Mauritania - Mauritanie.....................	34.8	10.1	77.3	55.9	59.2	4.71	24.8
Mauritius - Maurice[2]........................	13.4	6.8	12.8	69.5	76.2	1.67	6.6
Mayotte...	34.3	2.9	5.9	73.7	81.1	4.30	31.4
Morocco - Maroc...............................	20.2	5.8	34.1	69.0	73.4	2.38	14.3
Mozambique......................................	39.4	15.4	88.0	47.6	49.9	5.11	23.9
Namibia - Namibie.............................	27.4	8.6	37.8	60.4	61.6	3.40	18.8
Niger...	49.5	13.8	95.9	52.7	53.6	7.19	35.7
Nigeria - Nigéria...............................	40.4	15.1	96.1	49.5	51.0	5.61	25.3
Réunion..	18.2	5.7	5.9	73.7	81.1	2.40	12.5
Rwanda...	40.7	12.3	100.1	52.7	55.1	5.43	28.4
Sao Tome and Principe - Sao Tomé-et-Principe	32.4	8.2	51.7	62.5	65.1	3.85	24.2
Senegal - Sénégal............................	38.6	9.5	55.2	57.2	59.1	5.03	29.1
Sierra Leone.....................................	40.6	16.9	113.7	45.7	46.9	5.22	23.7
Somalia - Somalie.............................	44.2	15.5	106.7	48.7	51.8	6.40	28.7
South Africa - Afrique du Sud............	21.9	15.2	54.8	50.1	52.1	2.55	6.7
Sudan - Soudan................................	33.8	9.4	63.8	58.6	62.0	4.60	24.4
Swaziland..	30.1	14.9	75.9	47.6	47.0	3.57	15.2
Togo..	33.2	11.3	74.0	54.2	57.1	4.30	21.9
Tunisia - Tunisie................................	17.4	5.9	20.8	71.9	76.0	2.04	11.5
Uganda - Ouganda.............................	46.3	13.2	79.2	51.7	52.7	6.38	33.2
United Republic of Tanzania - République Unie de Tanzanie	41.6	11.5	64.5	54.6	56.2	5.58	30.2
Western Sahara - Sahara occidental	23.3	5.8	44.1	64.3	68.1	2.70	17.5
Zambia - Zambie	44.5	16.7	94.9	46.5	47.3	6.20	27.9
Zimbabwe..	29.4	15.1	59.3	47.5	45.4	3.47	14.3
AMERICA, NORTH - AMÉRIQUE DU NORD							
Aruba..	12.0	7.2	16.1	72.3	77.1	1.74	4.8
Bahamas	15.7	5.4	16.0	71.6	77.8	1.91	10.3
Barbados - Barbade	10.9	8.8	13.7	73.0	79.5	1.53	2.1
Belize..	25.2	3.9	17.2	73.9	76.8	2.94	21.4
Canada..	11.2	7.4	5.2	78.2	82.8	1.65	3.8
Costa Rica...	16.3	4.1	9.9	76.5	81.4	1.92	12.2
Cuba...	10.5	7.0	5.1	76.6	80.5	1.50	3.4

Continent and country or area Continent et pays ou zone	Crude birth rate - Taux bruts de natalité[1]	Crude death rate - Taux bruts de mortalité[1]	Infant mortality rate - Décès d'enfants de moins d'un an[1]	Expectation of life at birth - Espérance de vie à la naissance[1]		Total fertility rate - Indice synthétique de fécondité[1]	Natural increase - Accroissement naturel[1]
				Male - Masculin	Female - Féminin		
AMERICA, NORTH - AMÉRIQUE DU NORD							
Dominican Republic - République dominicaine......................	22.7	5.9	29.6	69.9	75.4	2.67	16.7
El Salvador	20.7	6.5	21.5	66.6	76.1	2.35	14.2
Grenada - Grenade	19.3	6.3	14.6	73.7	76.8	2.30	13.0
Guadeloupe..	14.8	6.7	7.0	75.7	82.9	2.14	8.1
Guatemala...	33.3	5.6	30.1	66.7	73.8	4.15	27.6
Haiti - Haïti	27.6	9.2	63.1	59.9	62.0	3.55	18.3
Honduras...	27.7	5.0	28.1	69.7	74.5	3.31	22.7
Jamaica - Jamaïque	19,1	7.4	24.4	69.6	75.0	2.40	11.8
Martinique..	12.7	7.5	7.6	76.7	83.2	1.91	5.2
Mexico - Mexique	20.6	4.7	16.7	73.7	78.6	2.41	15.9
Netherlands Antilles - Antilles néerlandaises	13.8	7.3	13.3	72.7	79.4	1.98	6.5
Nicaragua..	24.8	4.7	21.5	69.9	76.1	2.76	20.1
Panama...	20.8	5.0	18.2	73.0	78.2	2.56	15.8
Puerto Rico - Porto Rico...	13.6	7.7	7.6	74.7	82.7	1.83	6.0
Saint Lucia - Sainte-Lucie	18.1	6.4	13.1	71.4	76.6	2.05	11.8
Saint Vincent and the Grenadines - Saint-Vincent-et-les Grenadines	17.7	7.5	23.7	69.6	73.8	2.13	10.2
Trinidad and Tobago - Trinité-et-Tobago	14.9	8.0	26.6	65.8	72.9	1.64	6.9
United States of America - États-Unis d'Amérique................	14.0	8.3	6.8	75.4	80.5	2.07	5.7
United States Virgin Islands - Îles Vierges américaines........	13.0	6.9	10.6	75.9	82.0	2.05	6.0
AMERICA, SOUTH - AMÉRIQUE DU SUD							
Argentina - Argentine	17.5	7.7	13.4	71.5	79.1	2.25	9.8
Bolivia (Plurinational State of) - Bolivie (État plurinational de)	27.4	7.5	45.6	63.4	67.7	3.50	19.9
Brazil - Brésil	16.4	6.4	23.5	68.7	75.9	1.90	9.9
Chile - Chili...	14.7	5.3	7.2	75.5	81.7	1.90	9.4
Colombia - Colombie..	20.6	5.5	19.1	69.2	76.7	2.45	15.1
Ecuador - Équateur	21.6	5.0	21.1	72.1	78.1	2.58	16.6
French Guiana - Guyane française	25.0	3.6	14.0	72.6	79.9	3.27	21.4
Guyana..	18.8	5.9	41.7	65.5	71.9	2.33	12.9
Paraguay..	24.8	5.5	32.0	69.7	73.9	3.08	19.3
Peru - Pérou..	21.3	5.4	21.2	70.6	75.9	2.60	15.8
Suriname	19.1	7.3	21.6	66.4	73.1	2.42	11.9
Uruguay..	15.1	9.3	13.1	72.7	79.9	2.12	5.8
Venezuela (Bolivarian Republic of) - Venezuela (République bolivarienne du)..	21.4	5.1	17.0	70.8	76.8	2.55	16.4
ASIA - ASIE							
Afghanistan..	45.1	16.8	136.0	47.2	47.5	6.62	28.3
Armenia - Arménie	15.2	8.6	26.2	70.2	76.7	1.74	6.6
Azerbaijan - Azerbaïdjan	19.5	7.2	41.1	67.1	73.1	2.16	12.3
Bahrain - Bahreïn	20.7	2.8	7.2	74.0	75.4	2.63	18.0
Bangladesh..	21.5	6.3	49.0	67.4	68.3	2.38	15.2
Bhutan - Bhoutan	21.5	7.2	44.4	64.1	67.8	2.61	14.4
Brunei Darussalam - Brunéi Darussalam	20.1	3.1	4.8	75.3	80.0	2.11	17.0
Cambodia - Cambodge	23.3	8.3	62.4	60.2	62.6	2.80	15.1
China - Chine[3]	12.6	7.2	22.0	71.1	74.5	1.64	5.4
China, Hong Kong SAR - Chine, Hong Kong RAS..............	8.2	6.2	2.0	79.0	84.3	0.99	1.9
China, Macao SAR - Chine, Macao RAS	9.0	4.5	4.4	77.7	82.6	1.02	4.5
Cyprus - Chypre	11.9	6.8	4.6	76.8	81.1	1.51	5.0
Democratic People's Republic of Korea - République populaire démocratique de Corée	14.6	9.6	27.4	64.8	71.8	2.05	5.0
Georgia - Géorgie..	12.2	11.0	29.3	69.4	76.5	1.58	1.1
India - Inde	23.1	8.3	52.9	62.8	65.7	2.73	14.8
Indonesia - Indonésie	19.1	7.2	28.8	66.3	69.4	2.19	11.9
Iran (Islamic Republic of) - Iran (République islamique d').....	17.7	5.4	27.2	70.3	73.9	1.77	12.3
Iraq..	36.6	6.3	34.6	63.4	71.7	4.86	30.2
Israel - Israël...	21.1	5.7	3.8	78.4	82.9	2.91	15.4
Japan - Japon..	8.6	8.8	2.6	79.3	86.1	1.32	-0.2
Jordan - Jordanie	26.4	4.1	21.0	71.7	74.3	3.27	22.3
Kazakhstan...	21.4	10.6	27.0	60.2	71.5	2.54	10.9
Kuwait - Koweït	18.7	3.1	8.1	73.5	75.2	2.32	15.6

Continent and country or area / Continent et pays ou zone	Crude birth rate - Taux bruts de natalité[1]	Crude death rate - Taux bruts de mortalité[1]	Infant mortality rate - Décès d'enfants de moins d'un an[1]	Expectation of life at birth - Espérance de vie à la naissance[1]		Total fertility rate - Indice synthétique de fécondité[1]	Natural increase - Accroissement naturel[1]
				Male - Masculin	Female - Féminin		
ASIA - ASIE							
Kyrgyzstan - Kirghizstan	24.0	7.7	36.4	62.7	71.0	2.70	16.3
Lao People's Democratic Republic - République démocratique populaire lao	24.1	6.6	44.5	64.8	67.3	3.02	17.5
Lebanon - Liban	15.9	6.9	22.7	69.9	74.2	1.86	9.1
Malaysia - Malaisie	20.9	4.7	7.7	71.2	75.7	2.72	16.3
Maldives	17.2	3.7	9.8	74.6	76.5	1.90	13.5
Mongolia - Mongolie	23.4	6.5	36.0	63.4	71.5	2.50	16.9
Myanmar	17.9	8.9	55.0	62.1	65.0	2.08	9.1
Nepal - Népal	25.6	6.2	38.7	66.7	68.0	2.95	19.4
Occupied Palestinian Territory - Territoire palestinien occupé	33.8	3.6	22.2	70.6	73.8	4.65	30.2
Oman	19.1	3.7	9.4	70.9	74.8	2.52	15.3
Pakistan	28.1	7.7	70.9	63.8	65.4	3.65	20.4
Philippines	25.9	5.9	23.0	64.5	71.3	3.27	20.0
Qatar	14.1	1.6	8.8	78.1	77.3	2.40	12.5
Republic of Korea - République de Corée	10.0	5.1	4.8	76.5	83.3	1.29	4.9
Saudi Arabia - Arabie saoudite	22.1	3.8	18.5	72.2	74.4	3.03	18.3
Singapore - Singapour	8.9	4.6	1.9	78.5	82.7	1.25	4.2
Sri Lanka	19.0	6.5	12.4	71.2	77.4	2.36	12.5
Syrian Arab Republic - République arabe syrienne	23.9	3.5	15.0	73.9	76.9	3.10	20.4
Tajikistan - Tadjikistan	28.1	6.4	56.0	63.3	69.9	3.45	21.6
Thailand - Thaïlande	12.9	7.2	12.4	70.2	77.1	1.63	5.7
Timor-Leste	39.4	8.7	66.8	59.9	61.7	6.53	30.7
Turkey - Turquie	18.7	5.5	24.0	70.7	75.3	2.15	13.2
Turkmenistan - Turkménistan	22.0	7.7	50.5	60.6	68.9	2.50	14.2
United Arab Emirates - Émirats arabes unis	14.0	1.4	6.9	75.3	77.0	1.86	12.6
Uzbekistan - Ouzbékistan	21.7	6.6	48.7	64.3	70.7	2.46	15.1
Viet Nam	17.2	5.2	20.4	72.3	76.2	1.89	12.0
Yemen - Yémen	38.6	7.0	53.3	62.5	65.4	5.48	31.7
EUROPE							
Albania - Albanie	12.9	6.0	18.3	73.4	79.7	1.60	7.0
Austria - Autriche	9.1	9.1	4.0	77.4	82.9	1.38	0.0
Belarus - Bélarus	10.7	14.4	6.8	63.6	75.5	1.39	-3.7
Belgium - Belgique	11.5	9.7	3.8	77.0	82.5	1.79	1.9
Bosnia and Herzegovina - Bosnie-Herzégovine	8.9	9.5	13.4	72.4	77.7	1.18	-0.6
Bulgaria - Bulgarie	9.9	15.1	10.2	69.2	76.4	1.46	-5.1
Croatia - Croatie	9.5	11.7	6.0	72.5	79.5	1.42	-2.2
Czech Republic - République tchèque	10.7	10.1	3.2	73.8	80.2	1.41	0.6
Denmark - Danemark	11.8	10.3	4.0	76.0	80.5	1.85	1.5
Estonia - Estonie	11.7	12.4	4.7	68.4	79.2	1.64	-0.7
Finland - Finlande	11.2	9.4	2.8	75.9	82.8	1.84	1.8
France	12.8	8.6	3.5	77.5	84.3	1.97	4.2
Germany - Allemagne	8.4	10.3	3.7	77.2	82.4	1.36	-1.9
Greece - Grèce	10.4	10.0	4.6	77.0	82.0	1.46	0.4
Hungary - Hongrie	9.8	13.3	5.8	69.5	77.6	1.34	-3.6
Iceland - Islande	14.8	6.4	2.1	79.5	83.1	2.10	8.4
Ireland - Irlande	16.4	6.6	4.0	77.3	82.0	2.10	9.8
Italy - Italie	9.4	9.8	3.5	78.6	84.0	1.38	-0.4
Latvia - Lettonie	10.2	14.0	7.5	66.9	77.5	1.41	-3.8
Lithuania - Lituanie	10.1	13.4	6.5	65.5	77.2	1.41	-3.4
Luxembourg	11.4	8.1	2.3	76.7	82.0	1.62	3.2
Malta - Malte	9.3	8.2	5.8	76.3	81.2	1.33	1.1
Montenegro - Monténégro	12.6	10.3	8.7	71.6	76.5	1.69	2.3
Netherlands - Pays-Bas	11.3	8.2	4.4	78.1	82.2	1.75	3.1
Norway - Norvège	12.6	8.8	3.0	78.1	82.7	1.92	3.7
Poland - Pologne	10.2	9.9	6.1	71.2	79.9	1.32	0.3
Portugal	9.8	10.1	4.5	75.3	81.8	1.36	-0.3
Republic of Moldova - République de Moldova	12.3	13.5	15.5	64.4	72.1	1.50	-1.2
Romania - Roumanie	10.2	11.9	13.9	69.6	76.8	1.33	-1.7
Russian Federation - Fédération de Russie	11.4	14.2	11.3	61.6	74.0	1.44	-2.8
Serbia - Serbie	11.6	11.6	11.8	71.7	76.3	1.62	0.0
Slovakia - Slovaquie	10.1	9.8	6.3	70.7	78.7	1.27	0.4
Slovenia - Slovénie	9.8	9.3	3.5	75.0	82.0	1.39	0.6
Spain - Espagne	10.9	8.9	3.8	77.2	83.8	1.41	1.9
Sweden - Suède	11.9	10.1	2.6	78.8	82.9	1.90	1.8

Continent and country or area Continent et pays ou zone	Crude birth rate - Taux bruts de natalité[1]	Crude death rate - Taux bruts de mortalité[1]	Infant mortality rate - Décès d'enfants de moins d'un an[1]	Expectation of life at birth - Espérance de vie à la naissance[1]		Total fertility rate - Indice synthétique de fécondité[1]	Natural increase - Accroissement naturel[1]
				Male - Masculin	Female - Féminin		
EUROPE							
Switzerland - Suisse............................	9.9	8.2	3.7	79.3	84.1	1.46	1.8
TFYR of Macedonia - L'ex-R. y. de Macédoine......	11.1	9.1	14.7	72.1	76.3	1.46	2.0
Ukraine................................	10.4	16.7	12.9	61.8	73.5	1.39	-6.2
United Kingdom of Great Britain and Northern Ireland - Royaume-Uni de Grande-Bretagne et d'Irlande du Nord	12.2	9.5	4.9	77.4	81.7	1.83	2.7
OCEANIA - OCÉANIE							
Australia - Australie[4]................................	13.6	6.7	4.7	79.1	83.8	1.93	6.9
Fiji - Fidji................................	22.4	6.5	17.9	66.1	71.9	2.75	15.9
French Polynesia - Polynésie française	17.5	5.1	7.7	72.2	77.1	2.16	12.4
Guam................................	18.5	5.5	8.9	73.3	77.9	2.54	13.0
Micronesia (Federated States of) - Micronésie (États fédérés de)	25.5	6.2	34.9	67.6	69.1	3.62	19.3
New Caledonia - Nouvelle-Calédonie	17.2	6.1	4.8	72.3	78.7	2.19	11.1
New Zealand - Nouvelle-Zélande................	14.9	7.0	5.1	78.0	82.2	2.14	8.0
Papua New Guinea - Papouasie-Nouvelle-Guinée	31.5	7.9	50.1	59.5	63.7	4.10	23.6
Pitcairn	11.0	8.3	23.6	68.8	76.3	2.01	2.8
Samoa................................	25.9	5.5	22.4	68.6	74.9	3.99	20.5
Solomon Islands - Îles Salomon	33.3	6.2	42.9	65.1	67.8	4.40	27.1
Tonga................................	28.3	6.2	22.1	69.1	74.7	4.03	22.1
Vanuatu	30.4	5.1	28.7	68.2	72.1	4.00	25.3

SOURCE

United Nations, Department of Economic and Social Affairs, Population Division (2011). World Population Prospects: The 2010 Revision, DVD Edition – Extended Dataset (United Nations publication, Sales No. E.11.XIII.7). - Organisation des Nations Unies, Département des affaires économiques et sociales, Division de la population (2011). Perspectives de la population mondiale : La révision de 2010, Edition DVD - ensemble de données étendues (publication des Nations Unies, numéro de vente E.11.XIII.7).

FOOTNOTES - NOTES

[1] All data are mid-year medium variant projections. - Toutes ces données sont des projections de la population au milieu de l'année de variante moyenne.
[2] Including Agalega, Rodrigues and Saint Brandon. - Y compris Agalega, Rodrigues et Saint Brandon.
[3] For statistical purposes, the data for China do not include Hong Kong and Macao Special Administrative Regions (SAR) of China. - A des fins statistiques, les données pour la Chine ne comprennent pas les Régions Administratives Spéciales (SAR) de Hong Kong et Macao.
[4] Including Christmas Island, Cocos (Keeling) Islands and Norfolk Island. - Y compris Christmas Island, Cocos (Keeling) Islands et Norfolk Island.

Index
Historical index
(See notes at end of index)

Subject-matter	Year of issue	Time coverage	Subject-matter	Year of issue	Time coverage
urban/rural residence, below)				1981	1962-81
				1982-1985	Latest
- by birth order	1948	1936-47		1986	1967-86
	1949/50	1936-49		1987-1991	Latest
	1954	1936-53		1992	1983-92
	1955	Latest		1993-1999	Latest
	1959	1949-58		1999CD[iv]	1990-98
	1965	1955-64		2000-2010	Latest
	1969	1963-68			
	1975	1966-74	- by plurality	1965	Latest
	1981	1972-80		1969	Latest
	1986	1977-85		1975	Latest
	1999CD[iv]	1990-98		1981	1972-80
				1986	1977-85
- by birth weight	1975	Latest		1999CD[iv]	1990-98
	1981	1972-80			
	1986	1977-85	- by urban/rural residence	1965	Latest
	1999CD[iv]	1990-98		1967	Latest
				1968	1964-68
- by gestational	1975	Latest		1969	1964-68
	1981	1972-80		1970	1966-70
	1986	1977-85		1971	1967-71
	1999CD[iv]	1990-98		1972	1968-72
				1973	1969-73
- by legitimacy status	1959	1949-58		1974	1970-74
	1965	1955-64		1975	1956-75
	1969	1963-68		1976	1972-76
	1975	1966-74		1977	1973-77
	1981	1972-80		1978	1974-78
	1986	1977-85		1979	1975-79
	1999CD[iv]	1990-98		1980	1976-80
				1981	1962-81
- by month	2002	1980-02		1982	1978-82
				1983	1979-83
- by occupation of father	1965	Latest		1984	1980-84
	1969	Latest		1985	1981-85
				1986	1967-86
- by sex	1959	1949-58		1987	1983-87
	1965	1955-64		1988	1984-88
	1967-1968	Latest		1989	1985-89
	1969	1963-68		1990	1986-90
	1970-1974	Latest		1991	1987-91
	1975	1956-75		1992	1983-92
	1976-1980	Latest		1993	1989-93
				1994	1990-94
				1995	1991-95
				1996	1992-96
				1997	1993-97

Subject-matter	Year of issue	Time coverage	Subject-matter	Year of issue	Time coverage
	1998	1994-98		1999CD[iv]	1990-98
	1999	1995-99	- legitimate, by age of father	1959	1949-58
	1999CD[iv]	1980-99		1965	1955-64
	2000	1996-00		1969	1963-68
	2001	1997-01		1975	1966-74
	2002	1998-02		1981	1972-80
	2003	1999-03		1986	1977-85
	2004	2000-04	- legitimate, by age of mother	1954	1936-53
	2005	2001-05		1959	1949-58
	2006	2002-06		1965	1955-64
	2007	2003-07		1969	1963-68
	2008	2004-08		1975	1966-74
	2009-2010	2006-10		1981	1972-80
				1986	1977-85
- by urban/rural residence and age of mother	1965	Latest	- legitimate, by duration of marriage	1948	1936-47
	1969-1974	Latest		1949/50	1936-49
	1975	1966-74		1954	1936-53
	1976-1980	Latest		1959	1949-58
	1981	1972-80		1965	1955-64
	1982-1985	Latest		1969	1963-68
	1986	1977-85		1975	1966-74
	1987-1991	Latest		1981	1972-80
	1992	1983-92		1986	1977-85
	1993-1997	Latest		1999CD[iv]	1990-98
	1997HS[iii]	1948-96			
	1998-1999	Latest	Birth rates	1948	1932-47
	1999CD[iv]	1990-98		1949/50	1932-49
	2000-2006	Latest		1951	1905-30[v]
					1930-50
- illegitimate	1959	1949-58		1952	1920-34[v]
	1965	1955-64			1934-51
	1969	1963-68		1953	1920-39[v]
	1975	1966-74			1940-52
	1981	1972-80		1954	1920-39[v]
	1986	1977-85			1939-53
	1999CD[iv]	1990-98		1955	1920-34[v]
					1946-54
- legitimate	1948	1936-47		1956	1947-55
	1949/50	1936-49		1957	1948-56
	1954	1936-53		1958	1948-57
	1959	1949-58		1959	1920-54[v]
	1965	1955-64			1953-58
	1969	1963-68		1960	1950-59
	1975	1966-74		1961	1945-59[v]
	1981	1972-80			1952-61
	1986	1977-85			

Subject-matter	Year of issue	Time coverage	Subject-matter	Year of issue	Time coverage
	1962	1945-54[v]		2004	2000-04
		1952-62		2005	2001-05
	1963	1945-59[v]		2006	2002-06
		1954-63		2007	2003-07
	1964	1960-64		2008	2004-08
	1965	1920-64[v]		2009-2010	2006-10
		1950-65			
	1966	1950-64[v]			
		1957-66	- by age of father	1949/50	1942-49
	1967	1963-67		1954	1936-53
	1968	1964-68		1959	1949-58
	1969	1925-69[v]		1965	1955-64
		1954-69		1969	1963-68
	1970	1966-70		1975	1966-74
	1971	1967-71		1981	1972-80
	1972	1968-72		1986	1977-85
	1973	1969-73		1999CD[iv]	1990-98
	1974	1970-74		2007-2010	Latest
	1975	1956-75			
	1976	1972-76	- by age of mother	1948	1936-47
	1977	1973-77		1949/50	1936-49
	1978	1974-78		1951	1936-50
	1978HS[ii]	1948-78		1952	1936-50
	1979	1975-79		1953	1936-52
	1980	1976-80		1954	1936-53
	1981	1962-81		1955-1956	Latest
	1982	1978-82		1959	1949-58
	1983	1979-83		1965	1955-64
	1984	1980-84		1969	1963-68
	1985	1981-85		1975	1966-74
	1986	1967-86		1976-1978	Latest
	1987	1983-87		1978HS[ii]	1948-77
	1988	1984-88		1979-1980	Latest
	1989	1985-89		1981	1972-80
	1990	1986-90		1982-1985	Latest
	1991	1987-91		1986	1977-85
	1992	1983-92		1987-1991	Latest
	1993	1989-93		1992	1983-92
	1994	1990-94		1993-1997	Latest
	1995	1991-95		1997HS[iii]	1948-96
	1996	1992-96		1998-1999	Latest
	1997	1993-97		1999CD[iv]	1990-98
	1997HS[iii]	1948-97		2000-2010	Latest
	1998	1994-98			
	1999	1995-99	- by age of mother and birth order	1954	1948 and 1951
	1999CD[iv]	1985-99		1959	1949-58
	2000	1996-00		1965	1955-64
	2001	1997-01		1969	1963-68
	2002	1998-02			
	2003	1999-03			

Subject-matter	Year of issue	Time coverage	Subject-matter	Year of issue	Time coverage
	1997HS[iii]	1948-97		1952	1947-51 [vi]
	1998	1994-98		1953	Latest
	1999	1995-99		1954	1945-53
	2000	1996-00		1955-1956	Latest
	2001	1997-01		1957	1952-56
	2002	1998-02		1958-1960	Latest
	2003	1999-03		1961	1955-60
	2004	2000-04		1962-1965	Latest
	2005	2001-05		1966	1960-65
	2006	2002-06		1967-1973	Latest
	2007	2003-07		1974	1965-73
	2008	2004-08		1975-1979	Latest
				1980	1971-79
	2009-2010	2006-10		1981-1984	Latest
				1985	1976-84
- by age and sex	1948	1936-47		1986-1991	Latest
	1951	1936-50		1991PA[vii]	1960-90
	1955-1956	Latest		1992-1995	Latest
	1957	1948-56		1996	1987-95
	1958-1960	Latest		1997-2000	Latest
	1961	1955-60		2002	1995-02
	1962-1965	Latest		2004	1995-04
	1966	1961-65		2006	2002-06
	1967-1973	Latest		2008	2004-08
	1974	1965-73			
	1975-1979	Latest	- by cause, age and sex	1951	Latest
	1978HS[ii]	1948-77			
	1980	1971-79		1952	Latest
	1981-1984	Latest		1957	Latest
	1985	1976-84		1961	Latest
	1986-1991	Latest		1967	Latest
	1992	1983-92		1974	Latest
	1993-1995	Latest		1980	Latest
	1996	1987-95		1985	Latest
	1997	Latest		1991PA[vii]	1960-90
	1997HS[iii]	1948-96		1996	Latest
	1998-2010	Latest	- by cause, age and sex and urban/rural residence	1967	Latest
- by age and sex and urban/rural residence	1967-1973	Latest			
	1974	1965-73	- by cause and sex	1967	Latest
	1975-1979	Latest		1974	Latest
	1980	1971-79		1980	Latest
	1981-1984	Latest		1985	Latest
	1985	1976-84		1996	Latest
	1986-1991	Latest		2006	2002-06
	1992	1983-92		2008	2004-08
	1993-1995	Latest			
	1996	1987-95	- by marital status, age and sex	1958	Latest
	1997	Latest		1961	Latest
	1997HS[iii]	1948-96		1967	Latest
	1998-2006	Latest		1974	Latest
- by cause	1951	1947-50		1980	Latest

Index
Historical index

Subject-matter	Year of issue	Time coverage	Subject-matter	Year of issue	Time coverage
Divorce rates.....................	1952	1935-51		1981	1977-81
	1953	1936-52		1982	1963-82
	1954	1946-53		1983	1979-83
	1955	1946-54		1984	1980-84
	1956	1947-55		1985	1981-85
	1957	1948-56		1986	1982-86
	1958	1930-57		1987	1983-87
	1959	1949-58		1988	1984-88
	1960	1950-59		1989	1985-89
	1961	1952-61		1990	1971-90
	1962	1953-62		1991	1987-91
	1963	1954-63		1992	1988-92
	1964	1960-64		1993	1989-93
	1965	1961-65		1994	1990-94
	1966	1962-66		1995	1991-95
	1967	1963-67		1996	1992-96
	1968	1920-64[v]		1997	1993-97
		1953-68		1998	1994-98
	1969	1965-69		1999	1995-99
	1970	1966-70		2000	1996-00
	1971	1967-71		2001	1997-01
	1972	1968-72		2002	1998-02
	1973	1969-73		2003	1999-03
	1974	1970-74		2004	2000-04
	1975	1971-75		2005	2001-05
	1976	1957-76		2006	2002-06
	1977	1973-77		2007	2003-07
	1978	1974-78		2008	2004-08
	1979	1975-79		2009-2010	2006-10
	1980	1976-80			
	1969	1965-69	- by age of husband	1968	Latest
	1970	1966-70		1976	Latest
	1971	1967-71		1982	Latest
	1972	1968-72		1987	1975-86
	1973	1969-73		1990	Latest
	1974	1970-74			
	1975	1971-75	- by age of wife	1968	Latest
	1976	1957-76		1976	Latest
	1977	1973-77		1982	Latest
	1978	1974-78		1987	1975-86
	1979	1975-79		1990	Latest
	1980	1976-80			
	1969	1965-69	- for married couples	1953	1935-52
	1970	1966-70		1954	1935-53
	1971	1967-71		1958	1935-56
	1972	1968-72		1968	1935-67
	1973	1969-73		1976	1966-75
	1974	1970-74		1978HS[ii]	1948-77
	1975	1971-75		1982	1972-81
	1976	1957-76		1990	1980-89
	1977	1973-77			
	1978	1974-78	- by urban/rural residence	2002	1998-02
	1979	1975-79		2003	1999-03
	1980	1976-80			

Subject-matter	Year of issue	Time coverage	Subject-matter	Year of issue	Time coverage
	1952	1936-51		2001	1997-01
	1953	1936-52		2002	1998-02
	1954	1938-53		2003	1999-03
	1955	1946-54		2004	2000-04
	1956	1947-55		2005	2001-05
	1957	1948-56		2006	2002-06
	1958	1948-57		2007	2003-07
	1959	1949-58		2008	2004-08
	1960	1950-59		2009-2010	2006-10
	1961	1952-60			
	1962	1953-61	- by age of mother	1954	1936-53
	1963	1953-62		1959	1949-58
	1964	1959-63		1965	1955-64
	1965	1955-64		1969	1963-68
	1966	1947-65		1975	1966-74
	1967	1962-66		1981	1972-80
	1968	1963-67		1986	1977-85
	1969	1959-68	- by age of mother		
	1970	1965-69	and birth order	1954	Latest
	1971	1966-70		1959	1949-58
	1972	1967-71		1965	3-Latest
	1973	1968-72		1969	1963-68
	1974	1965-73		1975	1966-74
	1975	1966-74		1981	1972-80
	1976	1971-75		1986	1977-85
	1977	1972-76	- by period of		
	1978	1973-77	gestation	1957	1950-56
	1979	1974-78		1959	1949-58
	1980	1971-79		1961	1952-60
	1981	1972-80		1965	5-Latest
	1982	1977-81		1966	1956-65
	1983	1978-82		1967-1968	Latest
	1984	1979-83		1969	1963-68
	1985	1975-84		1974	1965-73
	1986	1977-85		1975	1966-74
	1987	1982-86		1980	1971-79
	1988	1983-87		1981	1972-80
	1989	1984-88		1985	1976-84
	1990	1985-89		1986	1977-85
	1991	1986-90		1996	1987-95
	1992	1987-91			
	1993	1988-92	- by sex	1961	1952-60
	1994	1989-93		1965	5 Latest
	1995	1990-94		1969	1963-68
	1996	1987-95		1975	1966-74
	1997	1992-96		1981	1972-80
	1998	1993-97		1986	1977-85
	1999	1994-98			
	1999CD[iv]	1990-98	- by urban/rural		
	2000	1995-99	residence	1971	1966-70
				1972	1967-71
				1973	1968-72
				1974	1965-73
				1975	1966-74
				1976	1971-75

Subject-matter	Year of issue	Time coverage	Subject-matter	Year of issue	Time coverage
	1977	1972-76	- legitimate	1959	1949-58
	1978	1973-77		1965	1955-64
	1979	1974-78		1969	1963-68
	1980	1971-79		1975	1966-74
	1981	1972-80		1981	1972-80
	1982	1977-81		1986	1977-85
	1983	1978-82	- legitimate by age		
	1984	1979-83	of mother	1959	1949-58
	1985	1975-84		1965	1955-64
	1986	1977-85		1969	1963-68
	1987	1982-86		1975	1966-74
	1988	1983-87		1981	1972-80
	1989	1984-88		1986	1977-85
	1990	1985-89		1996	1987-95
	1991	1986-90			
	1992	1987-91	**Foetal Death Ratios**		
	1993	1988-92	- by period of		
	1994	1989-93	gestation	1957	1950-56
	1995	1990-94		1959	1949-58
	1996	1987-95		1961	1952-60
	1997	1992-96		1965	5-Latest
	1998	1993-97		1966	1956-65
	1999	1994-98		1967-1968	Latest
	1999CD[iv]	1990-98		1969	1963-68
	2000	1995-99		1974	1965-73
	2001	1997-01		1975	1966-74
	2002	1998-02		1980	1971-79
	2003	1999-03		1981	1972-80
	2004	2000-04		1985	1976-84
	2005	2001-05		1986	1977-85
	2006	2002-06		1996	1987-95
	2007	2003-07		1999CD[iv]	1990-98
	2008	2004-08			
	2009-2010	2006-10	Foetal death ratios, late	1951	1935-50
				1952	1935-51
- illegitimate	1961	1952-60		1953	1936-52
	1965	5-Latest		1954	1938-53
	1969	1963-68		1955	1946-54
	1975	1966-74		1956	1947-55
	1981	1972-80		1957	1948-56
	1986	1977-85		1958	1948-57
				1959	1920-54[v]
- illegitimate,					1953-58
percent	1961	1952-60		1960	1950-59
	1965	5-Latest		1961	1945-49[v]
	1969	1963-68			1952-60
	1975	1966-74		1962	1945-54[v]
	1981	1972-80			1952-61
	1986	1977-85		1963	1945-59[v]
					1953-62
				1964	1959-63

Subject-matter	Year of issue	Time coverage
	1985	1975-84
	1986	1977-85
	1987	1982-86
	1988	1983-87
	1989	1984-88
	1990	1985-89
	1991	1986-90
	1992	1987-91
	1993	1988-92
	1994	1989-93
	1995	1990-94
	1996	1987-95
	1997	1992-96
	1998	1993-97
	1999	1994-98
	1999CD[iv]	1990-98
	2000	1995-99
	2001	1997-01
	2002	1998-02
	2003	1999-03
	2004	2000-04
	2005	2001-05
	2006	2002-06
	2007	2003-07
	2008	2004-08
	2009-2010	2006-10
- illegitimate	1961	1952-60
	1965	5-Latest
- legitimate	1959	1949-58
	1965	1955-64
	1969	1963-68
	1975	1966-74
	1981	1972-80
	1986	1977-85
- legitimate by age of mother	1959	1949-58
	1965	1955-64
	1969	1963-68
	1975	1966-74
	1981	1972-80
	1986	1977-85

G

Gestational age of foetal deaths (see: Foetal deaths)

Subject-matter	Year of issue	Time coverage
Gross reproduction rates (see: Reproduction rates)		

H

Homeless (see: Population)

Households

Subject-matter	Year of issue	Time coverage
- average size of	1962	1955-62
	1963	1955-63[vi]
	1968	Latest
	1971	1962-71
	1973	1965-73[vi]
	1976	Latest
	1982	Latest
	1987	1975-86
	1990	1980-89
- by age, sex of householder, size and urban/rural residence	1987	1975-86
- by family type and urban/rural residence	1987	1975-86
- by marital status of householder and urban/rural residence	1987	1975-86
	1995	1985-95
- by relationship to householder and urban/rural residence	1987	1975-86
	1995	1985-95
- by size	1955	1945-54
	1962	1955-62
	1963	1955-63[vi]
	1971	1962-71
	1973	1965-73[vi]
	1976	Latest
	1982	Latest
	1987	1975-86
	1990	1980-89
	1995	1985-95
- and number of persons 60 +	1991PA[vii]	Latest
- by urban/rural residence	1968	Latest
	1971	1962-71
	1973	1965-73[vi]
	1976	Latest
	1982	Latest

Index
Historical index

Subject-matter	Year of issue	Time coverage	Subject-matter	Year of issue	Time coverage
Infant deaths.....................	1948	1932-47		2001	1997-01
	1949/50	1934-49		2002	1998-02
	1951	1935-50		2003	1999-03
	1952	1936-51		2004	2000-04
	1953	1950-52		2005	2001-05
	1954	1946-53		2006	2002-06
	1955	1946-54		2007	2003-07
	1956	1947-55		2008	2004-08
	1957	1948-56			
	1958	1948-57		2009-2010	2006-10
	1959	1949-58			
	1960	1950-59	- by age and sex	1948	1936-47
	1961	1952-61		1951	1936-49
	1962	1953-62		1957	1948-56
	1963	1954-63		1961	1952-60
	1964	1960-64		1962-1965	Latest
	1965	1961-65		1966	1956-65
	1966	1947-66		1967-1973	Latest
	1967	1963-67		1974	1965-73
	1968	1964-68		1975-1979	Latest
	1969	1965-69		1980	1971-79
	1970	1966-70		1981-1984	Latest
	1971	1967-71		1985	1976-84
	1972	1968-72		1986-1991	Latest
	1973	1969-73		1992	1983-92
	1974	1965-74		1993-1995	Latest
	1975	1971-75		1996	1987-95
	1976	1972-76		1997-2004	Latest
	1977	1973-77		2005	1996-05
	1978	1974-78		2006-2010	Latest
	1978HS[ii]	1948-78			
	1979	1975-79	- by age and sex		
	1980	1971-80	and urban/rural		
	1981	1977-81	residence	1967-1973	Latest
	1982	1978-82		1974	1965-73
	1983	1979-83		1975-1979	Latest
	1984	1980-84		1980	1971-79
	1985	1976-85		1981-1984	Latest
	1986	1982-86		1985	1976-84
	1987	1983-87		1986-1991	Latest
	1988	1984-88		1992	1983-92
	1989	1985-89		1993-1995	Latest
	1990	1986-90		1996	1987-95
	1991	1987-91		1997-1999	Latest
	1992	1983-92			
	1993	1989-93	- by month	1967	1962-66
	1994	1990-94		1974	1965-73
	1995	1991-95		1980	1971-79
	1996	1987-96		1985	1976-84
	1997	1993-97			
	1997HS[iii]	1948-97	- by urban/rural		
	1998	1994-98	residence	1967	Latest
	1999	1995-99		1968	1964-68
	2000	1996-00		1969	1965-69
				1970	1966-70

Subject-matter	Year of issue	Time coverage		Subject-matter	Year of issue	Time coverage
	1981-1984	Latest			1966	2-Latest
	1985	2-Latest			1974	2-Latest
	1986-1991	Latest			1980	2-Latest
	1991PA[vii]	1950-90			1985	2-Latest
	1992-1995	Latest			1996	2-Latest
	1996	2-Latest			2008-2010	Latest
	1997	Latest				
	1997HS[iii]	1948-96		- survivors at		
	1998-2010	Latest		specified ages, by		
				sex	1948	1891-1945
- life expectancy					1951	1891-1950
at specified ages,					1952	1891-1951[vi]
by sex	1948	1891 -1945			1953	1891-1952
	1951	1891 -1950			1954	1891-1953[vi]
	1952	1891 -1951[vi]			1957	1900-56
	1953	1891 -1952			1961	1940-60
	1954	1891 -1953[vi]			1966	2-Latest
	1955-1956	Latest			1974	2-Latest
	1957	1900-56			1980	2-Latest
	1958-1960	Latest			1985	2-Latest
	1961	1940-60			1996	2-Latest
	1962-1964	Latest				
	1966	2-Latest		**Literacy (see: Population)**		
	1967	1900-66				
	1968-1973	Latest		**Localities (see: Population)**		
	1974	2-Latest				
	1975-1978	Latest		**M**		
	1978HS[ii]	1948-77				
	1979	Latest		**Major civil divisions (see: Population)**		
	1980	2-Latest				
	1981-1984	Latest		**Marriages**	1948	1932-47
	1985	2-Latest			1949/50	1934-49
	1986-1991	Latest			1951	1935-50
	1991PA[vii]	1950-90			1952	1936-51
	1992-1995	Latest			1953	1950-52
	1996	2-Latest			1954	1946-53
	1997	Latest			1955	1946-54
	1997HS[iii]	1948-96			1956	1947-55
	1998-2010	Latest			1957	1948-56
					1958	1940-57
- probabilities of dying at specified ages, by sex					1959	1949-58
	1948	1891-1945			1960	1950-59
	1951	1891-1950			1961	1952-61
	1952	1891-1951[vi]			1962	1953-62
	1953	1891-1952			1963	1954-63
	1954	1891-1953[vi]			1964	1960-64
	1957	1900-56			1965	1956-65
	1961	1940-60			1966	1962-66
					1967	1963-67
					1968	1949-68
					1969	1965-69
					1970	1966-70
					1971	1967-71

Subject-matter	Year of issue	Time coverage	Subject-matter	Year of issue	Time coverage
	1958	1930-57	- by age and sex	1948	1936-46
	1959	1949-58		1949/50	1936-49
	1960	1950-59		1953	1936-51
	1961	1952-61		1954	1936-52
	1962	1953-62		1958	1935-56
	1963	1954-63		1968	1955-67
	1964	1960-64		1976	1966-75
	1965	1956-65		1982	1972-81
	1966	1962-66		1987	1975-86
	1967	1963-67		1990	1980-89
	1968	1920-64ᵛ	- by sex among		
		1953-68	marriageable		
	1969	1965-69	population	1958	1935-56
	1970	1966-70		1968	1935-67
	1971	1967-71		1976	1966-75
	1972	1968-72		1982	1972-81
	1973	1969-73		1990	1980-89
	1974	1970-74	- by urban/rural		
	1975	1971-75	residence	1968	Latest
	1976	1957-76		1969	1965-69
	1977	1973-77		1970	1966-70
	1978	1974-78		1971	1967-71
	1979	1975-79		1972	1968-72
	1980	1976-80		1973	1969-73
	1981	1977-81		1974	1970-74
	1982	1963-82		1975	1971-75
	1983	1979-83		1976	1957-76
	1984	1980-84		1977	1973-77
	1985	1981-85		1978	1974-78
	1986	1982-86		1979	1975-79
	1987	1983-87		1980	1976-80
	1988	1984-88		1981	1977-81
	1989	1985-89		1982	1963-82
	1990	1971-90		1983	1979-83
	1991	1987-91		1984	1980-84
	1992	1988-92		1985	1981-85
	1993	1989-93		1986	1982-86
	1994	1990-94		1987	1983-87
	1995	1991-95		1988	1984-88
	1996	1992-96		1989	1985-89
	1997	1993-97		1990	1971-90
	1998	1994-98		1991	1987-91
	1999	1995-99		1992	1988-92
	2000	1996-00		1993	1989-93
	2001	1997-01		1994	1990-94
	2002	1998-02		1995	1991-95
	2003	1999-03		1996	1992-96
	2004	2000-04		1997	1993-97
	2005	2001-05		1998	1994-98
	2006	2002-06		1999	1995-99
	2007	2003-07		2000	1996-00
	2008	2004-08		2001	1997-01
	2009-2010	2006-10		2002	1998-02
				2003	1999-03

Index
Historical index
(See notes at end of index)

Subject-matter	Year of issue	Time coverage	Subject-matter	Year of issue	Time coverage
	2004	2000-04		2005	1995-04
	2005	2001-05		2006	1997-06
	2006	2002-06		2007	1997-06
	2007	2003-07		2008	1999-08
	2008	2004-08			
	2009-2010	2006-10	- by age	1951	Latest
				1952	Latest[vi]
Marriage rates, first				1957	Latest
-by detailed age of				1961	Latest
groom and bride	1982	1972-81		1967	Latest
	1990	1980-89		1974	Latest
				1980	Latest
Married population by age				1985	Latest
and sex (see: Population by					
marital status)			**Maternal mortality rates**	1951	1947-50
				1952	1947-51
Maternal death	1951	1947-50		1953	Latest
	1952	1947-51		1954	1945-53
	1953	Latest		1955-1956	Latest
	1954	1945-53		1957	1952-62
	1955-1956	Latest		1958-1960	Latest
	1957	1952-56		1961	1955-60
	1958-1960	Latest		1962-1965	Latest
	1961	1955-60		1966	1960-65
	1962-1965	Latest		1967-1973	Latest
	1966	1960-65		1974	1965-73
	1967-1973	Latest		1975	1966-74
	1974	1965-73		1976	1966-75
	1975-1979	Latest		1977	1967-76
	1980	1971-79		1978	1968-77
	1981	1972-80		1979	1969-78
	1982	1972-81		1980	1971-79
	1983	1973-82		1981	1972-80
	1984	1974-83		1982	1972-81
	1985	1975-84		1983	1973-82
	1986	1976-85		1984	1974-83
	1987	1977-86		1985	1975-84
	1988	1978-87		1986	1976-85
	1989	1979-88		1987	1977-86
	1990	1980-89		1988	1978-87
	1991	1981-90		1989	1979-88
	1992	1982-91		1990	1980-89
	1993	1983-92		1991	1981-90
	1994	1984-93		1992	1982-91
	1995	1985-94		1993	1983-92
	1996	1986-95		1994	1984-93
	1997	1987-96		1995	1985-94
	1998	1988-97		1996	1986-95
	1999	1989-98		1997	1987-96
	2000	1991-00		1998	1988-97
	2001	1991-00		1999	1989-98
	2002	1995-02		2000	1991-00
	2003	1995-02		2001	1991-00
	2004	1995-04		2002	1995-02

Subject-matter	Year of issue	Time coverage	Subject-matter	Year of issue	Time coverage
(see also: Households)				1970	1950-70
				1971	1962-71
	1962	1955-62		1973	1965-73[vi]
	1963	1955-63[vi]		1979	1970-79[vi]
	1968	Latest		1983	1974-83
	1971	1962-71		1988	1980-88[vi]
	1973	1965-73[vi]		1993	1985-93
	1976	Latest	20000 + inhabitants	1948	Latest
	1982	Latest		1952	Latest
	1987	1975-86		1955	1945-54
	1990	1980-89		1960	1920-61
	1995	1985-95		1962	1955-62
- by language and sex	1956	1945-55		1963	1955-63[vi]
	1963	1955-63		1970	1950-70
	1964	1955-64[vi]		1971	1962-71
	1971	1962-71		1973	1965-73[vi]
	1973	1965-73[vi]		1979	1970-79[vi]
	1979	1970-79[vi]		1983	1974-83
	1983	1974-83		1988	1980-88[vi]
	1988	1980-88[vi]		1993	1985-93
	1993	1985-93	- by locality size-classes and sex	1948	Latest
- by level of education, age and sex	1956	1945-55		1952	Latest
	1963	1955-63		1955	1945-54
	1964	1955-64[vi]		1962	1955-62
	1971	1962-71		1963	1955-63[vi]
	1973	1965-73[vi]		1971	1962-71
	1979	1970-79[vi]		1973	1965-73[vi]
	1983	1974-83		1979	1970-79[vi]
	1988	1980-88[vi]		1983	1974-83
	1993	1985-93		1988	1980-88[vi]
- by literacy, age and sex (see also: illiteracy, below)	1948	Latest		1993	1985-93
	1955	1945-54	- by major civil divisions	1952	Latest
	1963	1955-63		1955	1945-54
	1964	1955-64[vi]		1962	1955-62
	1971	1962-71		1963	1955-63[vi]
- by literacy, age and sex and urban/rural residence	1973	1965-73[vi]		1971	1962-71
	1979	1970-79[vi]		1973	1965-73[vi]
	1983	1974-83		1979	1970-79[vi]
	1988	1980-88[vi]		1983	1974-83
	1993	1985-93		1988	1980-88[vi]
- by localities of: 100000 + inhabitants	1948	Latest		1993	1985-93
	1952	Latest	- by marital status, age and sex (see also: married and single, below)	1948	Latest
	1955	1945-54		1940/50	1926-48
	1960	1920-61		1955	1945-54
	1962	1955-62		1958	1945-57
	1963	1955-63[vi]		1962	1955-62[vi]
				1963	1955-63[vi]
				1965	1955-65

Index
Historical index
(See notes at end of index)

Subject-matter	Year of issue	Time coverage
	1968	1955-67
	1971	1962-71
	1973	1965-73[vi]
	1976	1966-75
	1978HS[ii]	1948-77
	1982	1972-81
	1987	1975-86
	1990	1980-89
	1997HS[iii]	1948-96
- for persons 60+ and urban/rural	1991PA[vii]	Latest
percentage distribution	1948	Latest
- by religion and sex	1956	1945-55
	1963	1955-63
	1964	1955-64[vi]
	1971	1962-71
	1973	1965-73[vi]
	1979	1970-79[vi]
	1983	1974-83
	1988	1980-88[vi]
	1993	1985-93
- by school attendance, age and sex	1956	1945-55
	1963	1955-63
	1964	1955-64[vi]
	1971	1962-71
	1973	1965-73[vi]
	1979	1970-79
	1983	1974-83
	1988	1980-88[vi]
	1993	1985-93
- by sex: enumerated	1948-1952	Latest
	1953	1950-52
	1954-1959	Latest
	1960	1900-61
	1961	Latest
	1962	1900-62
	1963	1955-63
	1964	1955-64
	1965-1969	Latest
	1970	1950-70
	1971	1962-71
	1972	Latest
	1973	1965-73
	1974-1978	Latest
	1978HS[ii]	1948-78
	1979-1982	Latest
	1983	1974-83
	1984-1997	Latest

Subject-matter	Year of issue	Time coverage
	1997HS[iii]	1948-97
	1998-2010	Latest
estimated	1948-1949/5	1945and latest
	1951-1954	Latest
	1955-1959	Latest
	1960	1940-60
	1961-1969	Latest
	1970	1950-70
	1971	1962-71
	1972	Latest
	1973	1965-73
	1974-1997	Latest
	1997HS[iii]	1948-97
	1998-1999	Latest
	2000	1991-00
	2001	1992-01
	2002	1993-02
	2003	1994-03
	2004	1995-04
	2005	1996-05
	2006	1997-06
	2007	1998-07
	2008	1999-08
	2009-2010	2001-10
- by single years of age and sex	1955	1945-54
	1962	1955-62
	1963	1955-63[vi]
	1971	1962-71
	1973	1965-73[vi]
	1979	1970-79[vi]
	1983	1974-83
	1988	1980-88[vi]
	1993	1985-93
- cities (see: of cities, below)		
- civil division (see: by major civil divisions, above)		
- density (see: Density)		
- Disabled	1991PA[vii]	Latest
- economically active: by age and sex	1945	1945-54
	1956	1945-55
	1964	1955-64
	1972	1962-72

Subject-matter	Year of issue	Time coverage	Subject-matter	Year of issue	Time coverage
by age and sex and urban/rural residence				1995	1985-95
	1973	1965-73[vi]	by occupation, age and sex		
	1979	1970-79[vi]		1956	1945-55
	1984	1974-84		1964	1955-64
	1988	1980-88[vi]		1972	1962-72
	1994	1985-94	by occupation, age and sex and urban/rural residence		
by age and sex, per cent	1949/50	1930-48			
	1954	Latest			
	1955	1945-54		1973	1965-73[vi]
	1956	1945-55		1979	1970-79[vi]
	1964	1955-64		1984	1974-84
	1972	1962-72		1988	1980-88[vi]
by age and sex, per cent and urban/rural residence				1994	1985-94
			by occupation, status and sex		
	1973	1965-73[vi]		1956	1945-55
	1979	1970-79[vi]		1964	1955-64
	1984	1974-84		1972	1962-72
	1988	1980-88[vi]	by occupation, status and sex and urban/rural residence		
	1994	1985-94			
by industry, age and sex	1956	1945-55			
	1964	1955-64		1973	1965-73[vi]
	1972	1962-72		1979	1970-7vi[vi]
by industry, age, sex and urban/rural residence				1984	1974-84
				1988	1980-88[vi]
	1973	1965-74[vi]		1994	1985-94
	1979	1970-79[vi]	by sex	1948	Latest
	1984	1974-84		1949/50	1926-48
	1988	1980-88[vi]		1955	1945-54
	1994	1985-94		1956	1945-55
by industry, status and sex	1948	Latest		1960	1920-60
	1949/50	Latest		1963	1955-63
	1955	1945-54		1964	1955-64
	1964	1955-64		1970	1950-70
	1972	1962-72		1972	1962-72
by industry, status and sex and urban/rural residence				1973	1965-73[vi]
				1979	1970-79[vi]
	1973	1965-73[vi]		1984	1974-84
	1979	1970-79[vi]		1994	1985-94
	1984	1974-84	by status, age and sex		
	1988	1980-88[vi]		1956	1945-55
	1994	1985-94		1964	1955-64
by living arrangements, age, sex and urban/rural residence				1972	1962-72
			by status, age and sex and urban/rural residence		
	1987	1975-86		1973	1965-73[vi]

Subject-matter	Year of issue	Time coverage	Subject-matter	Year of issue	Time coverage
	1954	1930-53		1977	1970-77
	1955	1945-54		1978	1975-78
	1959	1949-58		1979	1975-79
	1963	1955-63		1980	1975-80
	1965	1955-65		1981	1975-81
	1968-1969	Latest		1982	1975-82
	1971	1962-71		1983	1980-83
	1973	1965-73[vi]		1984	1980-84
	1975	1965-74		1985	1980-85
	1978HS[ii]	1948-77		1986	1980-86
	1981	1972-80		1987	1980-87
	1986	1977-85		1988	1985-88
	1997HS[iii]	1948-96		1989	1985-89
in households by age, sex of householder, size and relationship to householder and urban/rural residence				1990	1985-90
				1991	1985-91
				1992	1985-92
				1993	1990-93
				1994	1990-94
				1995	1990-95
				1996	1990-96
				1997	1990-97
				1998	1993-98
	1987	1975-86		1999	1995-99
	1995	1991-95		2000	1995-00
institutional, by age, sex and urban/rural residence				2001	1995-01
				2002	1995-02
				2003	2000-03
				2004	2000-04
	1987	1875-86		2005	2000-05
	1995	1991-95		2006	2000-06
growth rates: average annual for countries or areas				2007	2005-07
				2008	2005-08
				2009-2010	2005-10
	1957	1953-56	average annual for the world, macro-regions (continents) and regions		
	1958	1953-57			
	1959	1953-58			
	1960	1953-59			
	1961	1953-60		1957	1950-56
	1962	1958-61		1958	1950-57
	1963	1958-62		1959	1950-58
	1964	1958-63		1960	1950-59
	1965	1958-64		1961	1950-60
	1966	1958-66		1962	1950-61
	1967	1963-67		1963	1958-62
	1968	1963-68			1960-62
	1969	1963-69		1964	1958-63
	1970	1963-70			1960-63
	1971	1963-71		1965	1958-64
	1972	1963-72			1960-64
	1973	1970-73		1966	1958-66
	1974	1970-74			1960-66
	1975	1970-75		1967	1960-67
	1976	1970-76			

Subject-matter	Year of issue	Time coverage
	1973	1965-73[vi]
	1979	1970-74[vi]
	1983	1974-83
	1988	1980-88[vi]
	1993	1985-93
	1987	1975-86
- living arrangements	1991PA[vii]	1950-90
	1995	1985-95
- localities (see: by localities, above)		
- major civil divisions (see: by major civil divisions, above)		
- married by age and sex (see also: by marital status, above): numbers and percent	1954	1926-52
	1960	1920-60
	1970	1950-70
- married female by percentage and duration of marriage	1968	Latest
- never married proportion by sex, selected ages	1976	1966-75
	1978HS[ii]	1948-77
	1982	1972-81
	1990	1980-89
- not economically active	1972	1962-72
- not economically active by urban/rural residence	1973	1965-73[vi]
	1979	1970-79[vi]
	1984	1974-84
	1988	1980-88[vi]
	1994	1985-94
- of cities: capital city	1952	Latest
	1955	1945-54
	1957	Latest
	1960	1939-61
	1962	1955-62
	1963	1955-63
	1964-1969	Latest
	1970	1950-70
	1971	1962-71
	1972	Latest
	1973	1965-73

Subject-matter	Year of issue	Time coverage
	1974-2010	Latest
of 100000 + inhabitants	1952	Latest
	1955	1945-54
	1957	Latest
	1960	1939-61
	1962	1955-62
	1963	1955-63
	1964-1969	Latest
	1970	1950-70
	1971	1962-71
	1972	Latest
	1973	1965-73
	1974-2010	Latest
- of continents (see: of macro regions, below)		
- of countries or areas (totals): enumerated	1948	1900-48
	1949/50	1900-50
	1951	1900-51
	1952	1850-1952
	1953	1850-1953
	1954	Latest
	1955	1850-1954
	1956-1961	Latest
	1962	1900-62
	1963	Latest
	1964	1955-64
	1965-1978	Latest
	1978HS[ii]	1948-78
	1979-1997	Latest
	1997HS[iii]	1948-97
	1998-2010	Latest
estimated	1948	1932-47
	1949/50	1932-49
	1951	1930-50
	1952	1920-51
	1953	1920-53
	1954	1920-54
	1955	1920-55
	1956	1920-56
	1957	1940-57
	1958	1939-58
	1959	1940-59
	1960	1920-60
	1961	1941-61
	1962	1942-62
	1963	1943-63
	1964	1955-64
	1965	1946-65

Index
Historical index
(See notes at end of index)

Subject-matter	Year of issue	Time coverage	Subject-matter	Year of issue	Time coverage
	1966	1947-66		1957	1920-56
	1967	1958-67		1958	1920-57
	1968	1959-68		1959	1920-58
	1969	1960-69		1960	1920-59
	1970	1950-70		1961	1920-60
	1971	1962-71		1962	1920-61
	1972	1963-72		1963	1930-62
	1973	1964-73		1964	1930-63
	1974	1965-74		1965	1930-65
	1975	1966-75		1966	1930-66
	1976	1967-76		1967	1930-67
	1977	1968-77		1968	1930-68
	1978	1969-78		1969	1930-69
	1978HS[ii]	1948-78		1970	1950-70
	1979	1970-79		1971	1950-71
	1980	1971-80		1972	1950-72
	1981	1972-81		1973	1950-73
	1982	1973-82		1974	1950-74
	1983	1974-83		1975	1950-75
	1984	1975-84		1976	1950-76
	1985	1976-85		1977	1950-77
	1986	1977-86		1978	1950-78
	1987	1978-87		1979	1950-79
	1988	1979-88		1980	1950-80
	1989	1980-89		1981	1950-81
	1990	1981-90		1982	1950-82
	1991	1982-91		1983	1950-83
	1992	1983-92		1984	1950-84
	1993	1984-93		1985	1950-85
	1994	1985-94		1986	1950-86
	1995	1986-95		1987	1950-87
	1996	1987-96		1988	1950-88
	1997	1988-97		1989	1950-89
	1997HS[iii]	1948-97		1990	1950-90
	1998	1989-98		1991	1950-91
	1999	1990-99		1992	1950-92
	2000	1991-00		1993	1950-93
	2001	1992-01		1994	1950-94
	2002	1993-02		1995	1950-95
	2003	1994-03		1996	1950-96
	2004	1995-04		1997	1950-97
	2005	1996-05		1998-1999	1950-00
	2006	1997-06		2000	1950-00
	2007	1998-07		2001	1950-01
	2008	1999-08		2002	1950-02
	2009-2010	2001-10		2003	1950-03
				2004	1950-04
- of major regions	1949/50	1920-49		2005	1950-05
	1951	1950		2006	1950-06
	1952	1920-51		2007	1950-07
	1953	1920-52		2008	1950-08
	1954	1920-53		2009-2010	1950-10
	1955	1920-54			
	1956	1920-55	- of regions	1949/50	1920-49

762

Index
Historical index
(See notes at end of index)

Subject-matter	Year of issue	Time coverage	Subject-matter	Year of issue	Time coverage
	1952	1920-51		2007	1950-07
	1953	1920-52		2008	1950-08
	1954	1920-53		2009-2010	1950-10
	1955	1920-54			
	1956	1920-55	- of the world	1949/50	1920-49
	1957	1920-56		1951	1950
	1958	1920-57		1952	1920-51
	1959	1920-58		1953	1920-52
	1960	1920-59		1954	1920-53
	1961	1920-60		1955	1920-54
	1962	1920-61		1956	1920-55
	1963	1930-62		1957	1920-56
	1964	1930-63		1958	1920-57
	1965	1930-65		1959	1920-58
	1966	1930-66		1960	1920-59
	1967	1930-67		1961	1920-60
	1968	1930-68		1962	1920-61
	1969	1930-69		1963	1930-62
	1970	1950-70		1964	1930-63
	1971	1950-71		1965	1930-65
	1972	1950-72		1966	1930-66
	1973	1950-73		1967	1930-67
	1974	1950-74		1968	1930-68
	1975	1950-75		1969	1930-69
	1976	1950-76		1970	1950-70
	1977	1950-77		1971	1950-71
	1978	1950-78		1972	1950-72
	1979	1950-79		1973	1950-73
	1980	1950-80		1974	1950-74
	1981	1950-81		1975	1950-75
	1982	1950-82		1976	1950-76
	1983	1950-83		1977	1950-77
	1984	1950-84		1978	1950-78
	1985	1950-85		1979	1950-79
	1986	1950-86		1980	1950-80
	1987	1950-87		1981	1950-81
	1988	1950-88		1982	1950-82
	1989	1950-89		1983	1950-83
	1990	1950-90		1984	1950-84
	1991	1950-91		1985	1950-85
	1992	1950-92		1986	1950-86
	1993	1950-93		1987	1950-87
	1994	1950-94		1988	1950-88
	1995	1950-95		1989	1950-89
	1996	1950-96		1990	1950-90
	1997	1950-97		1991	1950-91
	1998-1999	1950-00		1992	1950-92
	2000	1950-00		1993	1950-93
	2001	1950-01		1994	1950-94
	2002	1950-02		1995	1950-95
	2003	1950-03		1996	1950-96
	2004	1950-04		1997	1950-97
	2005	1950-05		1998-1999	1950-00
	2006	1950-06		2000	1950-00

Subject-matter	Year of issue	Time coverage	Subject-matter	Year of issue	Time coverage
	2001	1950-01		1999	1990-99
	2002	1950-02		2000	1991-00
	2003	1950-03		2001	1992-01
	2004	1950-04		2002	1993-02
	2005	1950-05		2003	1994-03
	2006	1950-06		2004	1995-04
	2007	1950-07		2005	1996-05
	2008	1950-08		2006	1997-06
	2009-2010	1950-10		2007	1998-07
				2008	1999-08
- rural residence (see: urban/rural residence, below)				2009-2010	2001-10
			by age and sex:		
- single, by age and sex (see also: by marital status, above):			enumerate	1963	1955-63
				1964	1955-64[vi]
numbers	1960	1920-60		1967	Latest
	1970	1950-70		1970	1950-70
percent	1949/50	1926-48		1971	1962-71
	1960	1920-60		1972	Latest
	1970	1950-70		1973	1965-73
				1974-1978	Latest
- urban/rural residence	1968	1964-68		1978HS[ii]	1948-77
	1969	1965-69		1979-1996	Latest
	1970	1950-70		1979-1997	Latest
	1971	1962-71		1997HS[iii]	1948-96
	1972	1968-72		1998-2010	Latest
	1973	1965-73			
	1974	1966-74	estimated	1963	Latest
	1975	1967-75		1967	Latest
	1976	1967-76		1970	1950-70
	1977	1968-77		1971-1997	Latest
	1978	1969-78		1997HS[iii]	1948-96
	1979	1970-79		1998-2010	Latest
	1980	1971-80			
	1981	1972-81	by country or area of birth and sex	1971	1962-71
	1982	1973-82		1973	1965-73[vi]
	1983	1974-83	by country or area of birth and sex and age	1977	Latest
	1984	1975-84			
	1985	1976-85			
	1986	1977-86	by citizenship and sex	1971	1962-71
	1987	1978-87		1973	1965-73[vi]
	1988	1979-88	by citizenship and sex and age	1977	Latest
	1989	1980-89		1983	1974-83
	1990	1981-90		1989	1980-88
	1991	1982-91			
	1992	1983-92	by ethnic composition and sex	1971	Latest
	1993	1984-93		1973	1965-73[vi]
	1994	1985-94			
	1995	1986-95			
	1996	1987-96			
	1997	1988-97			
	1998	1989-98			

Subject-matter	Year of issue	Time coverage	Subject-matter	Year of issue	Time coverage
	1979	1970-79[vi]	by school attendance, age and sex	1971	1962-71
	1983	1974-83		1973	1965-73[vi]
	1988	1980-88[vi]		1979	1970-79[vi]
	1993	1985-93		1983	1974-83
by households, number and size (see also: Households)	1968	Latest		1988	1980-88[vi]
	1971	1962-71		1993	1985-93
	1973	1965-73[vi]	by sex:		
	1976	Latest	numbers	1948	Latest
	1982	Latest		1952	1900-51
	1987	1975-86		1955	1945-54
	1990	1980-89		1960	1920-60
	1995	1985-95		1962	1955-62
by language and sex	1971	1962-71		1963	1955-63
				1964	1955-64[vi]
	1973	1965-73[vi]		1967	Latest
	1979	1970-79[vi]		1970	1950-70
	1983	1974-83		1971	1962-71
	1988	1980-88[vi]		1972	Latest
	1993	1985-93		1973	1965-73
by level of education, age and sex	1971	1962-71		1974	1966-74
	1973	1965-73[vi]		1975	1967-75
	1979	1970-79[vi]		1976	1967-76
	1983	1974-83		1977	1968-77
	1988	1980-88[vi]		1978	1969-78
	1993	1985-93		1979	1970-79
by literacy, age and sex	1971	1962-71		1980	1971-80
	1973	1965-73[vi]		1981	1972-81
	1979	1970-79[vi]		1982	1973-82
	1983	1974-83		1983	1974-83
	1988	1980-88[vi]		1984	1975-84
	1993	1985-93		1985	1976-85
by major civil divisions	1971	1962-71		1986	1977-86
	1973	1965-73[vi]		1987	1978-87
	1979	1970-79[vi]		1988	1979-88
	1983	1974-83		1989	1980-89
	1988	1980-88[vi]		1990	1981-90
	1993	1985-93		1991	1982-91
by marital status, age and sex	1971	1962-71		1992	1983-92
	1973	1965-73[vi]		1993	1984-93
by religion and sex	1971	1962-71		1994	1985-94
	1973	1965-73[vi]		1995	1986-95
	1979	1970-79[vi]		1996	1987-96
	1983	1974-83		1997	1988-97
	1988	1980-88[vi]		1998	1989-98
	1993	1985-93		1999	1990-99
				2000	1991-00
				2001	1992-01
				2002	1993-02
				2003	1994-03
				2004	1995-04
				2005	1996-05
				2006	1997-06

Subject-matter	Year of issue	Time coverage	Subject-matter	Year of issue	Time coverage
	2007	1998-07		1983	1974-83
	2008	1999-08		1993	1985-93
	2009-2010	2001-10	female: by number of children born alive and age		
percent	1948	Latest		1971	1962-71
	1952	1900-51		1973	1965-73[vi]
	1955	1945-54		1975	1965-74
	1960	1920-60		1978HS[ii]	1948-77
	1962	1955-62		1981	1972-80
	1970	1950-70		1986	1977-85
	1971	1962-71		1997HS[iii]	1948-96
	1973	1965-73	female: by number of children living and age	1971	1962-71
	1974	1966-74		1973	1965-73[vi]
	1975	1967-75		1975	1965-74
	1976	1967-76		1978HS[ii]	1948-77
	1977	1968-77		1981	1972-80
	1978	1969-78		1986	1977-85
	1979	1970-79		1997HS[iii]	1948-96
	1980	1971-80			
	1981	1972-81			
	1982	1973-82			
	1983	1974-83	Post-neo-natal deaths:		
	1984	1975-84	- by sex	1948	1936-47
	1985	1976-85		1951	1936-50
	1986	1977-86		1957	1948-56
	1987	1978-87		1961	1952-60
	1988	1979-88		1963-1965	Latest
	1989	1980-89		1966	1961-65
	1990	1981-90		1967	1962-66
	1991	1982-91		1968-1973	Latest
	1992	1983-92		1974	1965-73
	1993	1984-93		1975-1979	Latest
	1994	1985-94		1980	1971-79
	1995	1986-95		1981-1984	Latest
	1996	1987-96		1985	1976-84
	1997	1988-97		1986-1991	Latest
	1998	1989-98		1992	1983-92
	1999	1990-99		1993-1995	Latest
	2000	1991-00		1996	1987-95
	2001	1992-01		1997	Latest
	2002	1993-02		1997HS[ii]	1948-96
	2003	1994-03		1998-2010	Latest
	2004	1995-04			
	2005	1996-05			
	2006	1997-06	- by urban/rural residence	1971-1973	Latest
	2007	1998-07		1974	1965-73
	2008	1999-08		1975-1979	Latest
	2009-2010	2001-10		1980	1971-79
by single years of age and sex				1981-1984	Latest
	1971	1962-71		1985	1976-84
	1973	1965-73[vi]		1986-1991	Latest
	1979	1970-79[vi]		1992	1983-92

Subject-matter	Year of issue	Time coverage	Subject-matter	Year of issue	Time coverage
U			(see: Infant deaths)		
Urban/rural births (see: Births)			**Urban/rural population** (see: Population: urban/rural residence)		
Urban/rural deaths (see: Deaths)			**Urban/rural population by average size of households** (see: Households)		
Urban/rural infant deaths					

APPENDIX

Special text of each Demographic Yearbook:

Divorce:

'Uses of Marriage and Divorce Statistics', 1958.

Marriage:

'Uses of Marriage and Divorce Statistics', 1958.

Households:

'Concepts and definitions of households, householder and institutional population', 1987.

Migration:

'Statistics of International Migration', 1977.

Mortality:

'Recent Mortality Trends', 1951.
'Development of Statistics of Causes of Death', 1951.
'Factors in Declining Mortality', 1957.
'Notes on Methods of Evaluating the Reliability of Conventional Mortality Statistics', 1961.
'Recent Trends of Mortality', 1966.
'Mortality Trends among Elderly Persons', 1991PA[vii].

Natality:

'Graphic Presentation of Trends in Fertility', 1959.
'Recent Trends in Birth Rates', 1965.
'Recent Changes in World Fertility', 1969.

Population

'World Population Trends, 1920-1949', 1949/50.
'Urban Trends and Characteristics', 1952.
'Background to the1950 Censuses of Population', 1955.
'The World Demographic Situation', 1956.
'How Well Do We Know the Present Size and Trend of the World's Population?', 1960.
'Notes on Availability of National Population Census Data and Methods of Estimating their Reliability', 1962.
'Availability and Adequacy of Selected Data Obtained from Population Censuses Taken 1955-1963', 1963.
'Availability of Selected Population Census Statistics: 1955-1964', 1964.
'Statistical Concepts and Definitions of Urban and Rural Population', 1967.
'Statistical Concepts and Definitions of Household', 1968.
'How Well Do We Know the Present Size and Trend of the World's Population?', 1970.
'United Nations Recommendations on Topics to be Investigated in a Population Census
Compared with Country Practice in National Censuses taken 1965-1971', 1971.
'Statistical Definitions of Urban Population and their Use in Applied Demography', 1972.
'Dates of National Population and Housing Census carried out during the decade1965-1974', 1974.
'Dates of National Population and/or Housing Censuses taken or anticipated during the decade 1975-1984',
1979.
'Dates of National Population and/or Housing Censuses taken during the decade1965-1974 and
taken or anticipated during the decade 1975-1984', 1983.
'Dates of National Population and/or Housing Censuses taken during the decade1975-1984 and taken or
anticipated during the decade 1985-1994', 1988 and 1993.
'Statistics Concerning the Economically Active Population: An Overview', 1984.

'Disability', 1991PA[vii].
'Population Ageing', 1991PA[vii].
'Special Needs for the Study of Population Ageing and Elderly Persons', 1991PA[vii].

General Notes

This cumulative index covers the contents of each of the 61 issues of the Demographic Yearbook. 'Year of issue' stands for the particular issue in which the indicated subject-matter appears. Unless otherwise specified, 'Time coverage' designates the years for which annual statistics are shown in the Demographic Yearbook referred to in 'Year of issue' column. 'Latest' or '2-Latest' indicates that data are for latest available year(s) only.

---

[i] Only titles not available for preceding bibliography.

[ii] Historical Supplement to the 30th DYB published in a separate volume in year 1979.

[iii] Historical Supplement to the 49th DYB published in a separate volume (CD-ROM) in year 2000.

[iv] Supplement to the 51st DYB focusing on natality published in a separate volume (CD-ROM) in year 2002.

[v] Five-year average rates.

[vi] Only data not available for preceding issue.

[vii] Population ageing published in separate volume.

Index
Index historique (suite)
(Voir notes à la fin de l'index)

Index
Index historique (suite)
(Voir notes à la fin de l'index)

Index
Index historique (suite)
(Voir notes à la fin de l'index)

Index
Index historique (ouite)
(Voir notes à la fin de l'index)

Sujet	Année de l'édition	Période considérée	Sujet	Année de l'édition	Période considérée
		1930-50		2005	2001-05
	1952	1920-34 vi		2006	2002-06
		1934-51		2007	2003-07
	1953	1920-39 vi		2008	2004-08
		1940-52		2009-2010	2006-10
	1954	1920-39 vi			
		1946-53	-d'enfants de moins d'un an (voir: Mortalités infantile)		
	1955	1920-34 vi			
		1946-54	-estimatifs:		
	1956	1947-55	pour les continents	1949/50	1947
	1957	1930-56		1956-1977	Dernière
	1958	1948-57		1978-1979	1970-75
	1959	1949-58		1980-1983	1975-80
	1960	1950-59		1984-1986	1980-85
	1961	1945-59 vi		1987-1992	1985-90
		1952-61		1993-1997	1990-95
	1962	1945-54 vi		1998-2000	1995-00
		1952-62		2001-2005	2000-05
	1963	1945-59 vi		2006-2010	2005-10
		1954-63			
	1964	1960-64	pour les grandes régions (continentales)	1964-1977	Dernière
	1965	1961-65		1978-1979	1970-75
	1966	1920-64 vi		1980-1983	1975-80
		1951-66		1984-1986	1980-85
	1967	1963-67		1987-1992	1985-90
	1968	1964-68		1993-1997	1990-95
	1969	1965-69		1998-2000	1995-00
	1970	1966-70		2001-2005	2000-05
	1971	1967-71		2006-2010	2005-10
	1972	1968-72			
	1973	1969-73	pour les régions	1949/50	1947
	1974	1965-74		1956-1977	Dernière
	1975	1971-75		1978-1979	1970-75
	1976	1972-76		1980-1983	1975-80
	1977	1973-77		1984-1986	1980-85
	1978	1974-78		1987-1992	1985-90
	1978SR i	1948-78		1993-1997	1990-95
	1979	1975-79		1998-2000	1995-00
	1980	1971-80		2001-2005	2000-05
	1981	1977-81		2006-2010	2005-10
	1982	1978-82			
	1983	1979-83	pour l'ensemble du monde	1949/50	1947
	1984	1980-84		1956-1977	Dernière
	1985	1976-85		1978-1979	1970-75
	1986	1982-86		1980-1983	1975-80
	1987	1983-87		1984-1986	1980-85
	1988	1984-88		1987-1992	1985-90
	1989	1985-89		1993-1997	1990-95
	1990	1986-90		1998-2000	1995-00
	1991	1987-91		2001-2005	2000-05
	1992	1983-92		2006-2010	2005-10
	1993	1989-93			
	1994	1990-94	-selon l'âge et le sexe	1948	1935-47
	1995	1991-95		1949/50	1936-49
	1996	1987-96		1951	1936-50
	1997	1993-97		1952	1936-51
	1997SR ii	1948-97		1953	1940-52
	1998	1994-98		1954	1946-53
	1999	1995-99		1955-1956	Dernière
	2000	1996-00		1957	1948-56
	2001	1997-01			
	2002	1998-02			
	2003	1999-03			
	2004	2000-04			

Index
Index historique (suite)
(Voir notes à la fin de l'index)

Sujet	Année de l'édition	Période considérée
	1961	1952-60
	1966	1950-65
	1967	Dernière
	1972	Dernière
	1974	1965-73
	1975-1978	Dernière
	1978SR [i]	1948-77
	1979	Dernière
	1980	1971-79
	1981-1984	Dernière
	1985	1976-84
	1986-1991	Dernière
	1991 VP [v]	1950-90
	1992	1983-92
	1993-1995	Dernière
	1996	1987-95
	1997	Dernière
	1997SR [ii]	1948-96
	1998-2010	Dernière
-selon l'âge et le sexe et la résidence (urbaine/rurale)	1967	Dernière
	1972	Dernière
	1974	1965-73
	1975-1978	Dernière
	1979	Dernière
	1980	1971-79
	1981-1984	Dernière
	1985	1976-84
	1986-1991	Dernière
	1991 VP [v]	1950-90
	1992	1983-92
	1993-1995	Dernière
	1996	1987-95
	1997	Dernière
	1997SR [ii]	1948-96
	1998-2006	Dernière
-selon la cause	1951	1947-49
	1952	1947-51
	1953	1947-52
	1954	1945-53
	1955-1956	Dernière
	1957	1952-56
	1958-1960	Dernière
	1961	1955-60
	1962-1965	Dernière
	1966	1960-65
	1967-1973	Dernière
	1974	1965-73
	1975-1979	Dernière
	1980	1971-79 [vi]
	1981-1984	Dernière
	1985	1976-84
	1986-1995	Dernière
	1996	1987-95
	1997-2000	Dernière
	2002	1985-02
	2004	1995-04
	2006	2002-06
-selon la cause, l'âge et le sexe	1957	Dernière
	1961	Dernière
	1991 VP [v]	1960-90

Sujet	Année de l'édition	Période considérée
-selon la cause et le sexe	1967	Dernière
	1974	Dernière
	1980	Dernière
	1985	Dernière
	1991 VP [v]	1960-90
	1996	Dernière
	2006	2002-06
	2008	2004-08
-selon l'état matrimonial, l'âge et le sexe	1961	Dernière
	1967	Dernière
	1974	Dernière
	1980	Dernière
	1985	Dernière
	1996	Dernière
	2003	Dernière
-selon la profession, l'âge et le sexe	1957	Dernière
-selon la profession et l'âge (sexe masculin)	1961	Dernière
	1967	Dernière
-selon la résidence (urbaine/rurale)	1967	Dernière
	1968	1964-68
	1969	1965-69
	1970	1966-70
	1971	1967-71
	1972	1968-72
	1973	1969-73
	1974	1965-74
	1975	1971-75
	1976	1972-76
	1977	1973-77
	1978	1974-78
	1979	1975-79
	1980	1971-80
	1981	1977-81
	1982	1978-82
	1983	1979-83
	1984	1980-84
	1985	1976-85
	1986	1982-86
	1987	1983-87
	1988	1984-88
	1989	1985-89
	1990	1986-90
	1991	1987-91
	1992	1983-92
	1993	1989-93
	1994	1990-94
	1995	1991-95
	1996	1987-96
	1997	1993-97
	1998	1994-98
	1999	1995-99
	2000	1996-00
	2001	1997-01
	2002	1998-02
	2003	1999-03
	2004	2000-04
	2005	2001-05

Index
Index historique (suite)
(Voir notes à la fin de l'index)

Index
Index historique (suite)
(Voir notes à la fin de l'index)

Sujet	Année de l'édition	Période considérée	Sujet	Année de l'édition	Période considérée
	1972	1968-72		2007	Dernière
	1973	1969-73		2009-2010	Dernière
	1974	1970-74			
	1975	1971-75	-selon la durée du mariage, classés selon l'âge de l'épouse et selon l'âge de l'époux	1958	1946-57
	1976	1957-76		1968	Dernière
	1977	1973-77		1976	Dernière
	1978	1974-78		1982	Dernière
	1979	1975-79		1990	Dernière
	1980	1976-80			
	1981	1977-81	-selon le nombre d'enfants	1958	1948-57
	1982	1963-82		1968	1958-67
	1983	1979-83		1976	1966-75
	1984	1980-84		1982	1972-81
	1985	1981-85		2007	Dernière
	1986	1982-86	-selon la résidence (urbaine/rurale)	2002	1998-02
	1987	1983-87		2003	1999-03
	1988	1984-88		2004	2000-04
	1989	1985-89		2005	2001-05
	1990	1971-90		2006	2002-06
	1991	1987-91		2007	2003-07
	1992	1988-92		2008	2004-08
	1993	1989-93		2009-2010	2006-10
	1994	1990-94			
	1995	1991-95	**Divortialité, répartition des pourcentages**		
	1996	1992-96	- selon la durée du mariage	2007	Dernière
	1997	1993-97		2009-2010	Dernière
	1998	1994-98	- selon le nombre d'enfants	2007	Dernière
	1999	1995-99			
	2000	1996-00			
	2001	1997-01	**Divortialité, taux de**	1952	1935-51
	2002	1998-02		1953	1936-52
	2003	1999-03		1954	1946-53
	2004	2000-04		1955	1946-54
	2005	2001-05		1956	1947-55
	2006	2002-06		1957	1948-56
	2007	2003-07		1958	1930-57
	2008	2004-08		1959	1949-58
	2009-2010	2006-10		1960	1950-59
				1961	1952-61
-selon l'âge de l'épouse	1968	1958-67		1962	1953-62
	1976	1966-75		1963	1954-63
	1982	1972-81		1964	1960-64
	1987	1975-86		1965	1961-65
	1990	1980-89		1966	1962-66
				1967	1963-67
-selon l'âge de l'épouse, classés par âge de l'époux	1958	1946-57		1968	1920-64 [vi]
	1968	Dernière			1953-68
	1976	Dernière		1969	1965-69
	1982	Dernière		1970	1966-70
	1990	Dernière		1971	1967-71
				1972	1968-72
-selon l'âge de l'époux	1968	1958-67		1973	1969-73
	1976	1966-75		1974	1970-74
	1982	1972-81		1975	1971-75
	1987	1975-86		1976	1957-76
	1990	1980-89		1977	1973-77
-selon la durée du mariage	1958	1948-57			
	1968	1958-67			
	1976	1966-75			
	1982	1972-81			
	1990	1980-89			

Index
Index historique (suite)
(Voir notes à la fin de l'index)

Index
Index historique (suite)
(Voir notes à la fin de l'index)

Index
Index historique (suite)
(Voir notes à la fin de l'Index)

Index
Index historique (suite)
(Voir notes à la fin de l'index)

Index
Index historique (suite)
(Voir notes à la fin de l'index)

Index
Index historique (suite)
(Voir notes à la fin de l'index)

Index
Index historique (suite)
(Voir notes à la fin de l'index)

Index
Index historique (suite)
(Voir notes à la fin de l'index)

Sujet	Année de l'édition	Période considérée	Sujet	Année de l'édition	Période considérée
	1977	1973-77		1985·	1976-84
	1978	1974-78		1986-1991	Dernière
	1978SR [i]	1948-78		1992	1983-92
	1979	1975-79		1993-1995	Dernière
	1980	1971-80		1996	1987-95
	1981	1977-81		1997-1999	Dernière
	1982	1978-82			
	1983	1979-83	-selon la résidence	1967	Dernière
	1984	1980-84	(urbaine/rurale)	1968	1964-68
	1985	1976-85		1969	1965-69
	1986	1982-86		1970	1966-70
	1987	1983-87		1971	1967-71
	1988	1984-88		1972	1968-72
	1989	1985-89		1973	1969-73
	1990	1986-90		1974	1965-74
	1991	1987-91		1975	1971-75
	1992	1983-92		1976	1972-76
	1993	1989-93		1977	1973-77
	1994	1990-94		1978	1974-78
	1995	1991-95		1979	1975-79
	1996	1987-96		1980	1971-80
	1997	1993-97		1981	1977-81
	1997SR [ii]	1948-97		1982	1978-82
	1998	1994-98		1983	1979-83
	1999	1995-99		1984	1980-84
	2000	1996-00		1985	1976-85
	2001	1997-01		1986	1982-86
	2002	1998-02		1987	1983-87
	2003	1999-03		1988	1984-88
	2004	2000-04		1989	1985-89
	2005	2001-05		1990	1986-90
	2006	2002-06		1991	1987-91
	2007	2003-07		1992	1983-92
	2008	2004-08		1993	1989-93
	2009-2010	2006-10		1994	1990-94
				1995	1991-95
-selon l'âge et le sexe	1948	1936-47		1996	1987-96
	1951	1936-49		1997	1993-97
	1957	1948-56		1998	1994-98
	1961	1952-60		1999	1995-99
	1962-1965	Dernière		2000	1996-00
	1966	1956-65		2001	1997-01
	1967-1973	Dernière		2002	1998-02
	1974	1965-73		2003	1999-03
	1975-1979	Dernière		2004	2000-04
	1980	1971-79		2005	2001-05
	1981-1984	Dernière		2006	2002-06
	1985	1976-84		2007	2003-07
	1986-1991	Dernière		2008	2004-08
	1992	1983-92		2009-2010	2006-10
	1993-1995	Dernière			
	1996	1987-95	-selon le mois	1967	1962-66
	1997-2004	Dernière		1974	1965-73
	2005	1996-05		1980	1971-79
	2006-2010	Dernière		1985	1976-84
-selon l'âge et le sexe et la			**Mortalité infantile, taux de**	1948	1932-47
résidence (urbaine/rurale)	1968-1973	Dernière		1949/50	1932-49
	1974	1965-73		1951	1930-50
	1975-1979	Dernière		1952	1920-34 [vi]
	1980	1971-79			1934-51
	1981-1984	Dernière		1953	1920-39 [vi]
					1940-52

Index
Index historique (suite)
(Voir notes à la fin de l'index)

Index
Index historique (suite)
(Voir notes à la fin de l'index)

Index
Index historique (suite)
(Voir notes à la fin de l'index)

Index
Index historique (suite)
(Voir notes à la fin de l'index)

Index
Index historique (suite)
(Voir notes à la fin de l'index)

Index
Index historique (suite)
(Voir notes à la fin de l'index)

Index
Index historique (suite)
(Voir notes à la fin de l'index)

Index
Index historique (suite)
(Voir notes à la fin de l'index)

Index
Index historique (suite)
(Voir notes à la fin de l'index)

Index
Index historique (suite)
(Voir notes à la fin de l'index)

Sujet	Année de l'édition	Période considérée
-légitimes selon l'âge du père	1959	1949-58
	1965	Dernière
	1969	Dernière
	1975	Dernière
	1981	Dernière
	1986	Dernière
-légitimes selon la durée du mariage	1959	1950-57
	1965	Dernière
	1969	Dernière
	1975	Dernière
-selon l'âge de la mère	1948	1936-47
	1949/50	1936-49
	1951	1936-50
	1952	1936-50
	1953	1936-52
	1954	1936-53
	1955-1956	Dernière
	1959	1949-58
	1965	1955-64
	1969	1963-68
	1975	1966-74
	1976-1978	Dernière
	1978SR [i]	1948-77
	1979-1980	Dernière
	1981	1972-80
	1982-1985	Dernière
	1986	1977-85
	1987-1991	Dernière
	1992	1983-92
	1993-1997	Dernière
	1975SR [ii]	1948-96
	1998-1999	Dernière
	1999CD [vii]	1990-98
	2000-2010	Dernière
-selon l'âge de la mère et le rang de naissance	1954	1948 et 1951
	1959	1949-58
	1965	1955-64
	1969	1963-68
	1975	1966-74
	1981	1972-80
	1986	1977-85
	1999CD [vii]	1990-98
-selon l'âge de la mère et la résidence (urbaine/rurale) (voir: (urbaine/rurale), ci-dessous)		
-selon l'âge du père	1949/50	1942-49
	1954	1936-53
	1959	1949-58
	1965	1955-64
	1969	1963-68
	1975	1966-74
	1981	1972-80
	1986	1977-85
	1999CD [vii]	1990-98
	2007-2010	Dernière
-selon la durée du mariage (voir: légitimes selon la duré		

Sujet	Année de l'édition	Période considérée
du mariage)		
-selon le rang de naissance	1951	1936-49
	1952	1936-50
	1953	1936-52
	1954	1936-53
	1955	Dernière
	1959	1949-58
	1965	1955-64
	1969	1963-68
	1975	1966-74
	1981	1972-80
	1986	1977-85
	1999CD [vii]	1990-98
-selon la résidence(urbaine/rurale)	1965	Dernière
	1967	Dernière
	1968	1964-68
	1969	1964-68
	1970	1966-70
	1971	1967-71
	1972	1968-72
	1973	1969-73
	1974	1970-74
	1975	1956-75
	1976	1972-76
	1977	1973-77
	1978	1974-78
	1979	1975-79
	1980	1976-80
	1981	1962-81
	1982	1978-82
	1983	1979-83
	1984	1980-84
	1985	1981-85
	1986	1967-86
	1987	1983-87
	1988	1984-88
	1989	1985-89
	1990	1986-90
	1991	1987-91
	1992	1983-92
	1993	1989-93
	1994	1990-94
	1995	1991-95
	1996	1992-96
	1997	1993-97
	1998	1994-98
	1999	1995-99
	1999CD [vii]	1985-99
	2000	1996-00
	2001	1997-01
	2002	1998-02
	2003	1999-03
	2004	2000-04
	2005	2001-05
	2006	2002-06
	2007	2003-07
	2008	2004-08
	2009-2010	2006-10
-selon la résidence (urbaine/rurale) et l'âge de la mère	1965	Dernière

Index
Index historique (suite)
(Voir notes à la fin de l'index)

Sujet	Année de l'édition	Période considérée	Sujet	Année de l'édition	Période considérée
	1969	Dernière		1990	1971-90
	1975	1966-74		1991	1987-91
	1976-1980	Dernière		1992	1988-92
	1981	1972-80		1993	1989-93
	1982-1985	Dernière		1994	1990-94
	1986	1977-85		1995	1991-95
	1987-1991	Dernière		1996	1992-96
	1992	1983-92		1997	1993-97
	1993-1997	Dernière		1998	1994-98
	1997SR [ii]	1948-96		1999	1995-99
	1998-1999	Dernière		1972	1968-72
	1999CD [vii]	1990-98		1973	1969-73
	2000-2006	Dernière		1974	1970-74
				1975	1971-75
Nationalité (voir: Population)				1976	1957-76
				1977	1973-77
Nuptialité (voir: Mariages)				1978	1974-78
				1979	1975-79
Nuptialité, taux de	1948	1932-47		1980	1976-80
	1949/50	1932-49		1981	1977-81
	1951	1930-50		1982	1963-82
	1952	1920-34 [vi]		1983	1979-83
		1934-51		1984	1980-84
	1953	1920-39 [vi]		1985	1981-85
		1940-52		1986	1982-86
	1954	1920-39 [vi]		1987	1983-87
		1946-53		1988	1984-88
	1955	1920-34 [vi]		1989	1985-89
		1946-54		1990	1971-90
	1956	1947-55		1991	1987-91
	1957	1948-56		1992	1988-92
	1958	1930-57		1993	1989-93
	1959	1949-58		1994	1990-94
	1960	1950-59		1995	1991-95
	1961	1952-61		1996	1992-96
	1962	1953-62		1997	1993-97
	1963	1954-63		1998	1994-98
	1964	1960-64		1999	1995-99
	1965	1956-65		2000	1996-00
	1966	1962-66		2001	1997-01
	1967	1963-67		2002	1998-02
	1968	1920-646		2003	1999-03
		1953-68		2004	2000-04
	1969	1965-69		2005	2001-05
	1970	1966-70		2006	2002-06
	1971	1967-71		2007	2003-07
	1972	1968-72		2008	2004-08
	1973	1969-73		2009-2010	2006-10
	1974	1970-74			
	1975	1971-75	-selon l'âge et le sexe	1948	1936-46
	1976	1957-76		1949/50	1936-49
	1977	1973-77		1953	1936-51
	1978	1974-78		1954	1936-52
	1979	1975-79		1958	1935-56
	1980	1976-80		1968	1955-67
	1981	1977-81		1976	1966-75
	1982	1963-82		1982	1972-81
	1983	1979-83		1987	1975-86
	1984	1980-84		1990	1980-89
	1985	1981-85	-selon la résidence (urbaine/rurale)		
	1986	1982-86		1968	Dernière
	1987	1983-87		1969	1965-69
	1988	1984-88		1970	1966-70
	1989	1985-89			

Index
Index historique (suite)
(Voir notes à la fin de l'index)

Index
Index historique (suite)
(Voir notes à la fin de l'index)

Index
Index historique (suite)
(Voir notes à la fin de l'index)

Index
Index historique (suite)
(Voir notes à la fin de l'index)

Index
Index historique (suite)
(Voir notes à la fin de l'index)

Sujet	Année de l'édition	Période considérée	Sujet	Année de l'édition	Période considérée
estimée	1948	1932-47			
	1949/50	1932-49	-des principales divisions administratives	1952	Dernière
	1951	1930-50		1955	1945-54
	1952	1920-51		1962	1955-62
	1953	1920-53		1963	1955-63 [iii]
	1954	1920-54		1971	1962-71
	1955	1920-55		1973	1965-73 [iii]
	1956	1920-56		1979	1970-79 [iii]
	1957	1940-57		1983	1974-83
	1958	1939-58		1988	1980-88 [iii]
	1959	1940-59		1993	1985-93
	1960	1920-60			
	1961	1941-61			
	1962	1942-62	-des régions	1949/50	1920-49
	1963	1943-63		1952	1920-51
	1964	1955-64		1953	1920-52
	1965	1946-65		1954	1920-53
	1966	1947-66		1955	1920-54
	1967	1958-67		1956	1920-55
	1968	1959-68		1957	1920-56
	1969	1960-69		1958	1920-57
	1970	1950-70		1959	1920-58
	1971	1962-71		1960	1920-59
	1972	1963-72		1961	1920-60
	1973	1964-73		1962	1920-61
	1974	1965-74		1963	1930-62
	1975	1966-75		1964	1930-63
	1976	1967-76		1965	1930-65
	1977	1968-77		1966	1930-66
	1978	1969-78		1967	1930-67
	1978SR [i]	1948-78		1968	1930-68
	1979	1970-79		1969	1930-69
	1980	1971-80		1970	1950-70
	1981	1972-81		1971	1950-71
	1982	1973-82		1972	1950-72
	1983	1974-83		1973	1950-73
	1984	1975-84		1974	1950-74
	1985	1976-85		1975	1950-75
	1986	1977-86		1976	1950-76
	1987	1978-87		1977	1950-77
	1988	1979-88		1978	1950-78
	1989	1980-89		1979	1950-79
	1990	1981-90		1980	1950-80
	1991	1982-91		1981	1950-81
	1992	1983-92		1982	1950-82
	1993	1984-93		1983	1950-83
	1994	1985-94		1984	1950-84
	1995	1986-95		1985	1950-85
	1996	1987-96		1986	1950-86
	1997	1988-97		1987	1950-87
	1997SR [ii]	1948-97		1988	1950-88
	1998	1989-98		1989	1950-89
	1999	1990-99		1990	1950-90
	2000	1991-00		1991	1950-91
	2001	1992-01		1992	1950-92
	2002	1993-02		1993	1950-93
	2003	1994-03		1994	1950-94
	2004	1995-04		1995	1950-95
	2005	1996-05		1996	1950-96
	2006	1997-06		1997	1950-97
	2007	1998-07		1998-2000	1950-00
	2008	1999-08		2001	1950-01
	2009-2010	2001-10		2002	1950-02
				2003	1950-03

Index
Index historique (suite)
(Voir notes à la fin de l'index)

Index
Index historique (suite)
(Voir notes à la fin de l'index)

Index
Index historique (suite)
(Voir notes à la fin de l'index)

Index
Index historique (suite)
(Voir notes à la fin de l'index)

Sujet	Année de l'édition	Période considérée
	1971	1962-71
	1972	Dernière
	1973	1965-73
	1974-1978	Dernière
	1978SR [i]	1948-78
	1979-1982	Dernière
	1983	1974-83
	1984-1991	Dernière
	1991 VP [v]	1950-90
	1992-1997	Dernière
	1997SR [ii]	1948-97
	1998-2010	Dernière
estimée	1948-	
	1949/50	1945 et Dernière
	1951-1954	Dernière [iii]
	1955-1959	Dernière
	1960	1940-60
	1961-1969	Dernière
	1970	1950-70
	1971	1962-71
	1972	Dernière
	1973	1965-73
	1974-1997	Dernière
	1997SR [ii]	1948-97
	1998-2004	Dernière
	2005	1996-05
	2006	1997-06
	2007	1998-07
	2008	1999-08
	2009-2010	2001-2010
-urbaine/rurale (résidence)	1968	1964-68
	1969	1965-69
	1970	1950-70
	1971	1962-71
	1972	1968-72
	1973	1965-73
	1974	1966-74
	1975	1967-75
	1976	1967-76
	1977	1968-77
	1978	1969-78
	1979	1970-79
	1980	1971-80
	1981	1972-81
	1982	1973-82
	1983	1974-83
	1984	1975-84
	1985	1976-85
	1986	1977-86
	1987	1978-87
	1988	1979-88
	1989	1980-89
	1990	1981-90
	1991	1982-91
	1992	1983-92
	1993	1984-93
	1994	1985-94
	1995	1986-95
	1996	1987-96
	1997	1988-97

Sujet	Année de l'édition	Période considérée
	1998	1989-98
	1999	1990-99
	2000	1991-00
	2001	1992-01
	2002	1993-02
	2003	1994-03
	2004	1995-04
	2005	1996-05
	2006	1997-06
	2007	1998-07
	2008	1999-08
	2009-2010	2001-2010
féminine: selon le nombre total d'enfants nés vivants et l'âge	1971	1962-71
	1973	1965-73 [iii]
	1975	1965-74
	1978SR [i]	1948-77
	1981	1972-80
	1986	1977-85
	1997SR [ii]	1948-96
féminine: selon le nombre total d'enfants vivants et l'âge	1971	1962-71
	1973	1965-73 [iii]
	1975	1965-74
	1978SR [i]	1948-77
	1981	1972-80
	1986	1977-85
	1997SR [ii]	1948-96
fréquentant l'école selon l'âge et le sexe	1971	1962-71
	1973	1965-73 [iii]
	1979	1970-79 [iii]
	1983	1974-83
	1988	1980-88 [iii]
	1988	1980-88 [iii]
	1993	1985-93
par année d'âge et par sexe	1971	1962-71
	1973	1965-73 [iii]
	1979	1970-79 [iii]
	1983	1974-83
	1993	1985-93
selon la situation familiale selon l'âge et le sexe: dénombrée	1991 VP [v]	Dernière
	1963	1955-63
	1964	1955-64 [iii]
	1967	Dernière
	1970	1950-70
	1971	1962-71
	1972	Dernière
	1973	1965-73
	1974-78	Dernière
	1978SR [i]	1948-77
	1979-91	Dernière
	1991VP [v]	1950-90
	1992-97	Dernière
	1997SR [ii]	1948-97
	1998-2010	Dernière
selon l'âge et le sexe: estimée	1963	Dernière

Index
Index historique (suite)
(Voir notes à la fin de l'index)

Sujet	Année de l'édition	Période considérée
	1967	Dernière
	1970	1950-70
	1971-1997	Dernière
	1997SR [ii]	1948-97
	1998-2010	Dernière
selon l'alphabétisme, l'âge et le sexe	1971	1962-71
	1973	1965-73 [iii]
	1979	1970-79 [iii]
	1983	1974-83
	1988	1980-88 [iii]
	1993	1985-93
selon la composition ethnique et le sexe	1971	1962-71
	1973	1965-73 [iii]
	1979	1970-79 [iii]
	1983	1974-83
	1988	1980-88 [iii]
	1993	1985-93
	1971	1962-71
selon l'état matrimonial, l'âge et le sexe	1971	1962-71
	1973	1965-73 [iii]
selon la langue et le sexe	1971	1962-71
	1973	1965-73 [iii]
	1979	1970-79 [iii]
	1983	1974-83
	1988	1980-88 [iii]
	1993	1985-93
selon la nationalité juridique et le sexe	1971	1962-71
	1973	1965-73 [iii]
selon la nationalité juridique et le sexe et l'âge	1977	Dernière
	1983	1974-83
	1989	1980-88
selon le niveau d'instruction, l'âge et le sexe	1971	1962-71
	1973	1965-73 [iii]
	1979	1970-79 [iii]
	1983	1974-83
	1988	1980-88 [iii]
	1993	1985-93
selon le pays ou zone de naissance et le sexe	1971	1962-71
	1973	1965-73 [iii]
selon le pays ou zone de naissance et le sexe et l'âge	1977	Dernière
	1983	1974-83
	1989	1980-88
selon les principales divisions administratives	1971	1962-71
	1973	1965-73 [iii]
	1979	1970-79 [iii]
	1983	1974-83
	1988	1980-88 [iii]
	1993	1985-93
selon la religion et le sexe	1971	1962-71
	1973	1965-73 [iii]
	1979	1970-79 [iii]

Sujet	Année de l'édition	Période considérée
	1983	1974-83
	1988	1980-88 [iii]
	1993	1985-93
selon le sexe: nombres	1948	Dernière
	1952	1900-51
	1955	1945-54
	1960	1920-60
	1962	1955-62
	1963	1955-63
	1964	1955-64 [iii]
	1967	Dernière
	1970	1950-70
	1971	1962-71
	1972	Dernière
	1973	1965-73
	1974	1966-74
	1975	1967-75
	1976	1967-76
	1977	1968-77
	1978	1969-78
	1979	1970-79
	1980	1971-80
	1981	1972-81
	1982	1973-82
	1983	1974-83
	1984	1975-84
	1985	1976-85
	1986	1977-86
	1987	1978-87
	1988	1979-88
	1989	1980-89
	1990	1981-90
	1991	1982-91
	1992	1983-92
	1993	1984-93
	1994	1985-94
	1995	1986-95
	1996	1987-96
	1997	1988-97
	1998	1989-98
	1999	1990-99
	2000	1991-00
	2001	1992-01
	2002	1993-02
	2003	1994-03
	2004	1995-04
	2005	1996-05
	2006	1997-06
	2007	1998-07
	2008	1999-08
	2009-2010	2001-10
pourcentage	1948	Dernière
	1952	1900-51
	1955	1945-54
	1960	1920-60
	1962	1955-62
	1970	1950-70
	1971	1962-71
	1973	1965-73
	1974	1966-74
	1975	1967-75

Index
Index historique (suite)
(Voir notes à la fin de l'index)

Index
Index historique (suite)
(Voir notes à la fin de l'index)

Index
Index historique (suite)
(Voir notes à la fin de l'index)

APPENDICE

Texte spécial de chaque Annuaire démographique

Divorce:

"Application des statistiques de la nuptialité et de la divortialité", 1958.

Mariage:

"Application des statistiques de la nuptialité et de la divortialité", 1958.

Ménages:

"Concepts et définitions des ménages, du chef de ménage et de la population des collectivités", 1987.

Migration:

"'Statistiques des migrations internationales",1977.

Mortalité:

"Tendances récentes de la mortalité", 1951.
"Développement des statistiques des causes de décès",1951.
"Les facteurs du fléchissement de la mortalité",1957.
"Notes sur les méthodes d'évaluation de la fiabilité des statistiques classiques de la mortalité",1961.
"Mortalité: Tendances récentes",1966.
"Tendances de la mortalité chez les personnes âgées",1991VP [v].

Natalité:

"Présentation graphiques des tendances de la fécondité",1959.

"Taux de natalité: Tendances récentes",1965.

Population: ..

"Tendances démo-graphiques mondiales,1920-1949",1949/50.
"Mouvements d'urbanisation et ses caractéristiques",1952.
"Les recensements de population de 1950",1955.
"Situation démographique mondiale",1956.
"Ce que nous savons de l'état et de l'évolution de la population mondiale",1960.
"Notes sur les statistiques disponibles des recensements nationaux de population et méthodes d'évaluation de leur exactitude",1962.
"Disponibilité et qualité de certaines données statistiques fondées sur les recensements de population effectués entre 1955 et 1963",1963.
"Disponibilité de certaines statistiques fondées sur les recensements de population: 1955-1964",1964.

"Définitions et concepts statistiques de la population urbaine et de la population rurale",1967.
"Application des statistiques de la nuptialité et de la divortialité",1958.
"Ce que nous savons de l'état et de l'évolution de la population mondiale",1970.
"Recommandations de l'Organisation des Nations Unies quant aux sujets sur lesquels doit porter un recensement de population, en regard de la pratique adoptée par les différents pays dans les recensements nationaux effectués de 1965 à 1971",1971.
"Les définitions statistiques de la population urbaine et leurs usages en démographie appliquée",1972.

"Evolution récente de la fécondité dans le monde",1969.
"Dates des recensements nationaux de la population et de l'habitation effectués au cours de la décennie

Index
Index historique (suite)
(Voir notes à la fin de l'index)

1965-1974", 1974.

"Dates des recensements nationaux de la population et de l'habitation effectués ou prévus, au cours de la décennie 1975-1984",1979.

"Dates des recensements nationaux de la population et/ou de l'habitation effectués au cours de la décennie 1965-1974 et effectués ou prévus au cours de la décennie1975-1984",1983.

"Définitions et concepts statistiques du ménage",1968.

"Dates des recensements nationaux de la population et/ou de l'habitation effectués au cours de la décennie 1975-1984 et effectués ou prévus au cours de la décennie1985-1994", 1988, 1993.

"Statistiques concernant la population active: un aperçu",1984.

"'Etude du vieillissement et de la situation des personnes âgées: Besoins particuliers",1991VP [v].

"Les incapacités", 1991VP [v].

"Le vieillissement", 1991VP [v].

Notes générales

Cet index alphabétique donne la liste des sujets traités dans chacune de 61 éditions de l'Annuaire démographique. La colonne "Année de l'édition" indique l'édition spécifique dans laquelle le sujet a été traité. Sauf indication contraire, la colonne "Période considérée" désigne les années pour lesquelles les statistiques annuelles apparaissant dans l'Annuaire démographique sont indiquées sous la colonne "Année de l'édition". La rubrique "Dernière" ou " 2-Dernières" indique que les données représentent la ou les dernières années disponibles seulement.

---

[i] Le Supplément rétrospectif du 30ème Annuaire Démographique fait l'objet d'un tirage spécial publié en 1979.

[ii] Le Supplément rétrospectif du 49ème Annuaire Démographique fait l'objet d'un tirage spécial (CD-ROM) publié en 2000

[iii] Données non disponibles dans l'édition précédente seulement.

[iv] Titres non disponibles dans la bibliographie précédente seulement.

[v] Taux moyens pour 5 ans.

[vi] Vieillissement de la population.

[vii] Le Supplément du 51 Annuaire Démographique, ayant comme suject la natalité, fait l'objet d'un tirage spécial (CD-ROM) publié en 2002.